ENCYCLOPAEDIA JUDAICA

ENCYCLOPAEDIA JUDAICA

SECOND EDITION

VOLUME 13
LIF–MEK

FRED SKOLNIK, *Editor in Chief*
MICHAEL BERENBAUM, *Executive Editor*

MACMILLAN REFERENCE USA
An imprint of Thomson Gale, a part of The Thomson Corporation

IN ASSOCIATION WITH
KETER PUBLISHING HOUSE LTD., JERUSALEM

THOMSON
GALE

Detroit • New York • San Francisco • New Haven, Conn. • Waterville, Maine • London

THOMSON GALE

ENCYCLOPAEDIA JUDAICA, Second Edition

Fred Skolnik, *Editor in Chief*
Michael Berenbaum, *Executive Editor*
Shlomo S. (Yosh) Gafni, *Editorial Project Manager*
Rachel Gilon, *Editorial Project Planning and Control*

Thomson Gale
Gordon Macomber, *President*
Frank Menchaca, *Senior Vice President and Publisher*
Jay Flynn, *Publisher*
Hélène Potter, *Publishing Director*

Keter Publishing House
Yiphtach Dekel, *Chief Executive Officer*
Peter Tomkins, *Executive Project Director*

Complete staff listings appear in Volume 1

For more information, contact
Macmillan Reference USA
An imprint of Thomson Gale
27500 Drake Rd.
Farmington Hills, MI 48331-3535
Or you can visit our internet site at
http://www.gale.com

LIBRARY OF CONGRESS CATALOGING-IN-PUBLICATION DATA

Encyclopaedia Judaica / Fred Skolnik, editor-in-chief ; Michael Berenbaum, executive editor. -- 2nd ed.
v. cm.
Includes bibliographical references and index.
Contents: v.1. Aa-Alp.
ISBN 0-02-865928-7 (set hardcover : alk. paper) -- ISBN 0-02-865929-5 (vol. 1 hardcover : alk. paper) -- ISBN 0-02-865930-9 (vol. 2 hardcover : alk. paper) -- ISBN 0-02-865931-7 (vol. 3 hardcover : alk. paper) -- ISBN 0-02-865932-5 (vol. 4 hardcover : alk. paper) -- ISBN 0-02-865933-3 (vol. 5 hardcover : alk. paper) -- ISBN 0-02-865934-1 (vol. 6 hardcover : alk. paper) -- ISBN 0-02-865935-X (vol. 7 hardcover : alk. paper) -- ISBN 0-02-865936-8 (vol. 8 hardcover : alk. paper) -- ISBN 0-02-865937-6 (vol. 9 hardcover : alk. paper) -- ISBN 0-02-865938-4 (vol. 10 hardcover : alk. paper) -- ISBN 0-02-865939-2 (vol. 11 hardcover : alk. paper) -- ISBN 0-02-865940-6 (vol. 12 hardcover : alk. paper) -- ISBN 0-02-865941-4 (vol. 13 hardcover : alk. paper) -- ISBN 0-02-865942-2 (vol. 14 hardcover : alk. paper) -- ISBN 0-02-865943-0 (vol. 15: alk. paper) -- ISBN 0-02-865944-9 (vol. 16: alk. paper) -- ISBN 0-02-865945-7 (vol. 17: alk. paper) -- ISBN 0-02-865946-5 (vol. 18: alk. paper) -- ISBN 0-02-865947-3 (vol. 19: alk. paper) -- ISBN 0-02-865948-1 (vol. 20: alk. paper) -- ISBN 0-02-865949-X (vol. 21: alk. paper) -- ISBN 0-02-865950-3 (vol. 22: alk. paper)
1. Jews -- Encyclopedias. I. Skolnik, Fred. II. Berenbaum, Michael, 1945-
DS102.8.E496 2007
909'.04924 -- dc22

2006020426

ISBN-13:

978-0-02-865928-2 (set)
978-0-02-865929-9 (vol. 1)
978-0-02-865930-5 (vol. 2)
978-0-02-865931-2 (vol. 3)
978-0-02-865932-9 (vol. 4)
978-0-02-865933-6 (vol. 5)
978-0-02-865934-3 (vol. 6)
978-0-02-865935-0 (vol. 7)
978-0-02-865936-7 (vol. 8)
978-0-02-865937-4 (vol. 9)
978-0-02-865938-1 (vol. 10)
978-0-02-865939-8 (vol. 11)
978-0-02-865940-4 (vol. 12)
978-0-02-865941-1 (vol. 13)
978-0-02-865942-8 (vol. 14)
978-0-02-865943-5 (vol. 15)
978-0-02-865944-2 (vol. 16)
978-0-02-865945-9 (vol. 17)
978-0-02-865946-6 (vol. 18)
978-0-02-865947-3 (vol. 19)
978-0-02-865948-0 (vol. 20)
978-0-02-865949-7 (vol. 21)
978-0-02-865950-3 (vol. 22)

This title is also available as an e-book
ISBN-10: 0-02-866097-8
ISBN-13: 978-0-02-866097-4
Contact your Thomson Gale representative for ordering information.
Printed in the United States of America

10 9 8 7 6 5 4 3 2

TABLE OF CONTENTS

Initial letter "L" for Librum, *showing Haman being hanged, from the beginning of the Book of Esther in the* Moulins Bible, *a 12th-century Latin manuscript from France. Moulins, Bibliothèque Nationale, Ms. 1, fol. 284. Courtesy Bibliothèque Nationale, Paris.*

LIFE AND DEATH. In Jewish thought both life and death are part of the divine plan for the world.

Life

The opening chapter of Genesis states that all things are created by God. They are, therefore, all purposeful. They all have some value, as is clearly implicit in God's judgment on the created order: "God saw everything He had made, and behold, it was very good" (Gen. 1:31). But it is man who is at the apex of creation and the highest level in the order of value. All other things were created for his sake and constitute the theater of his operation and creative ingenuity.

Since life is the highest good, man is obliged to cherish it and preserve it. Every person is under mandate to marry and procreate in order to share in perpetuating the human species (Yev. 63b). He must preserve himself in a state of health. The Talmud includes many rules of hygiene and cautions against making one's home in a community where there is no competent physician (Sanh. 17b). Maimonides included a chapter on rules of health in his code *Mishneh Torah*, since "the preservation of the health of the body is one of the godly ways" (Yad 4). The rabbis ruled that the preservation of life supersedes the fulfillment of all commandments, except the prohibitions against murder, unchastity, and idolatry (Yoma 82a). One should be concerned as much with the preservation of others' lives as with one's own life. Rabbi Akiva regarded the commandment to love one's neighbor as oneself the most fundamental precept of the Torah (Sifra 19:18). Whoever sustains a single person, taught the rabbis, is as one who sustains the whole world, and whoever destroys a single person is as one who destroys the whole world; for every person bears the divine image, and every person was created unique and irreplaceable. Each one, therefore, has a right to say: "For my sake was the world created" (Sanh. 4:5). Indeed, man's obligations are not limited to his fellowmen. They extend to all existence. He must not wantonly and unnecessarily destroy any object in the world nor inflict pain on any living creature. In this spirit the 18th-century rabbi Ezekiel Judah *Landau forbade hunting (S. Wind, *Rav Yeḥezekel Landau* (1961), 54).

In stressing the sanctity of human life, the rabbis often

went beyond biblical precedent. For example, the Bible calls for capital *punishment for a wide variety of crimes, but the rabbis limited such punishment to conditions which in effect made the law inoperative. The Mishnah brands a court that imposes a sentence of capital punishment once in seven years, or according to another tradition, once in 70 years, a murderous court (Mak. 1:10).

Death

In view of the high value attached to man, death, which puts an end to man and his achievements, is the most baffling phenomenon. The account of Adam's sin (Gen. 2) is the biblical attempt to deal with the problem. Rabbinic literature contains a variety of views on the subject. Some rabbis regarded death as a punishment meted out to Adam and his descendants because of his sin in the Garden of Eden (Gen. R. 16:6), but others held that death was an appropriate termination for a finite creature and that it had been preordained at the time of creation (Gen. R. 30:8; Ex. R. 2:4). Death is the price paid for new birth, for the continued emergence of a new generation. Death must be deemed a good, noted Maimonides, since it is the means of "perpetuating existence and the continuity of individual beings through the emergence of one after the withdrawal of the other" (*Guide* 3:10).

Death was also robbed of its terror by the belief that after death individuals survive as incorporeal spirits (Ket. 103a; Ber. 18b). Related to this was the belief in retributive judgment. The righteous would be rewarded with eternal bliss in paradise and the wicked, punished in hell (see *Garden of Eden, *Gehinnom, and *Beatitude).

The final mitigation of the terror of death in rabbinic literature was the belief in the *resurrection of the dead and the world to come. At the end of the historical process God will create the dead anew reuniting body and soul, and then the resurrected dead will enjoy the bliss of the "world to come." The literalness of the belief in the resurrection appears to have been questioned by some rabbis. Thus, one view expressed in the Talmud states that in the world to come "there is no eating or drinking, no begetting children, no commerce, envy, hatred, or competition, but only this: that the righteous sit with crowns on their heads and delight in the splendor of God's presence" (Ber. 17a). The technical term for resurrection is *teḥiyyat ha-metim*, literally, "the revival of the dead." But there were Jewish philosophers, beginning with Philo, who interpreted this figuratively as referring to the immortality of the soul. Maimonides, especially, inveighed against the notion of a physical restoration as man's final state, and insisted that ultimate happiness consists of the incorporeal existence of men's intellect, attained by pursuing a life of virtue and wisdom.

To accentuate the rejection of a belief in physical resurrection, the Reform liturgy drops the praise of God as the *meḥayyeh ha-metim* ("He who revives the dead") from the *Amidah* and substitutes *note'a be-tokhenu ḥayyei olam* ("... who has implanted within us eternal life"). The Reconstructionist prayer book substitutes for *meḥayyeh ha-metim, zokher yeẓirav le-ḥayyim be-raḥamim* ("...who in love rememberest Thy creatures to life"). But many Jewish modernists use the traditional text, interpreting it, no doubt, as an allusion to the soul's *immortality.

BIBLIOGRAPHY: E. Fackenheim, in: *Commentary*, 39 (1965), 49–55.

[Ben Zion Bokser]

LIFE SCIENCES.

Introduction

Biology has become a vast subject which has increasingly merged with traditionally separate disciplines, particularly chemistry and physics. Indeed "life sciences" is now a more appropriate term than "biology." Furthermore the life sciences have provided the basis for most of the advances in medical science which stand up to objective scrutiny. In common with other sciences, the life sciences are an international enterprise and traditional schools of biological study based on personal opinion, ethnic approaches, or religious belief have become mainly obsolete. Indeed attempts to base investigations in the natural sciences on political or ethnic considerations have proved disastrous. Furthermore there is now little prospect that an individual scientist or even a small group of scientists will make an important scientific contribution in isolation. Thus a specifically Jewish interpretation of the life sciences is a matter of continuing historical and ethical interest but of limited relevance to scientific discovery in modern times. In contrast advances in medical science have made ethical issues a matter of central but not exclusive concern to Jews. Nevertheless it is equally mistaken to assume that religious belief has been entirely supplanted by a reductionist approach. Indeed it would be false to conclude that scientists universally explain all aspects of life including human consciousness solely in physico-chemical terms. This remains a live issue for many Jewish and non-Jewish scientists concerned with the life sciences which has scarcely been resolved by the continuing debate of physicists and cosmologists. Advances in genetics have illuminated many genealogical issues of specific Jewish interest such as the history of the kohanim and the nature of many inherited diseases encountered predominantly in Jews. This entry reviews areas of the life sciences to which Jews have made notable contributions since 1800 C.E. It alludes only briefly to related areas of crucial importance to these contributions which are considered in other entries.

The following account of the contributions of Jewish scientists in key fields is necessarily brief. Their achievements are described more fully in their separate biographical entries. Their achievements will be better understood by readers who have consulted general sources of scientific information in order to gain some understanding of the areas of scientific endeavor to which Jewish scientists have contributed.

Prelude to the Modern Era

Although research in the life sciences is in intellectual terms now entirely non-sectarian, it is nonetheless legitimate to consider the extent to which discoveries in the modern era were anticipated in traditional Jewish belief. Biological issues are raised in different contexts throughout the Bible. Genesis relates the divinely ordered hierarchy of species and much of Leviticus is concerned with classifying species as the basis for the dietary laws. In the Mishnah and the Talmud the tractates of the order *Zera'im* deal with agricultural laws and thereby consider many issues relating to animals and plants. These observations are not systematic or analytical in any modern sense. Indeed it is difficult to determine the extent to which they originate from Jewish sources or from the folklore of earlier or contemporary cultures. One of the earliest attempts to collate the then available knowledge of nature systematically was Maimonides' treatise on drug names whose efficacy is no less established than many similar drugs in contemporary complementary medicine. Long in advance of Darwin, there were challenges to the literal interpretation of Genesis that all living species were present at the creation. Indeed some authorities espoused views current in the Hellenistic and Roman world that living organisms can arise from inorganic substances through spontaneous generation. These seemingly fanciful notions have been given scientific respectability by modern debate about the origins of life on Earth and, even more speculatively, elsewhere in the universe.

Many Jewish beliefs on biological matters were based on direct observation especially at times when Jews lived predominantly in rural communities and engaged in agricultural pursuits. These observations were undoubtedly embellished by reports of miraculous deeds allegedly witnessed by travelers in an age of greater credulity. However, there is little reason to believe that there was any specific Jewish interpretation of the biological basis for the key events of birth, life, and death in humankind, the life cycle of other species, or of botanical events. The main rabbinical preoccupation was with the religious and ethical dimensions of human life. It is tempting to interpret textual passages in the Bible and other literary sources as evidence for early scientific insight anticipating modern discoveries. For example Jacob's manipulation of Laban's goat herds and sheep flocks is sometimes taken as astonishing insight into Mendelian principles of genetic selection (Gen. 30:32–43). Yet it is entirely possible that his experience had simply endowed him with exceptional powers of observation rather than modern analytical insight. Perhaps most importantly through the ages and often in common with other monotheistic faiths, Judaism's religious authorities have not attempted to interfere with man's attempts to understand the natural world through observation and the exercise of reason.

Life Sciences in the 19th Century

In the early 19th century Jews made many contributions which helped to lay the basis for rational investigation. In common with other scholars they were commonly polymaths with the freedom to roam intellectually because of the limited factual knowledge available in general and the constraints on academic activities. Even when antisemitism disrupted academic careers, re-location was relatively simple as individual speculation and observation were all important and laboratory technology was rudimentary. Robert *Remak was the first (c. 1840) to describe the major constituents of the embryo and also described salient anatomical features of the nervous system. Jacob *Henle made new observations on the structure of the kidney (c. 1830) and theorized that infectious agents existed which are too small to be discernible by conventional microscopes, a prediction fulfilled by the later discovery and characterization of viruses. Between 1850 and 1890 Ferdinand *Cohn improved microscope design and adapted this advance to study the developmental stages of plants, algae, and bacteria. Furthermore he was arguably the first naturalist to discern the association between bacterial infection and disease. In the latter half of the century Nathaneal Pringsheim made fundamental discoveries concerning plant morphology and physiology and founded the German Botanical Society. His contemporary Julius von *Sachs was also one of the first botanists to study and publish systematic studies of plant physiology. At this time Eduard *Strasburger further clarified the life history of plants. His findings have stood the test of time and led to his appointment to a chair in Jena at the age of 24, a remarkable achievement in the Germany of 1869 for a scientist of any religion. Not all the contributions of Jewish scientists of this era were so soundly based. Jacques *Loeb's work on parthenogenesis from the 1880s on was largely fanciful but still visionary in anticipating the momentous cloning techniques developed more than a century later.

Life Sciences in the Modern Era

By the beginning of the 20th century the challenges in the life sciences were at least more clearly defined. These are too numerous to list in full but the major problems were to understand the nature of heredity, the control of cell growth and differentiation, the biochemical processes which maintain the life of cells and organisms, and the processes which enable specialized systems such as the nervous system to operate. Human ability to manipulate these processes for medical or other purposes was so limited that ethical questions were almost entirely philosophical. At the beginning of the 21st century there are few controversies concerning the basic mechanisms operating in areas of former ignorance or the likely directions of future advances. The main challenge to investigators is how to order the vast amount of information generated by the greatly expanded scientific enterprise.

Complete mapping of the human genome has opened the still more complex field of proteomics which seeks to categorize and explain the actions and interactions of the huge range of proteins transcribed from the genome. This task would be impossible without the simultaneous advances in computing techniques and the mathematical handling of experimental data. This reality emphasizes the interdependence of all branches of the natural sciences.

A related challenge is the daunting range of ethical issues generated by advances in scientific techniques, particularly when applied to medicine and agriculture. The ethical difficulties are compounded by the social issues. A century ago, scientific progress was understood and debated by a privileged coterie of savants. Even politicians were largely indifferent unless the advance had military applications or was likely to increase national prestige. Today the practical application of most scientific advances is likely to provoke public debate and progress depends on a dialogue between scientists, politicians, and appropriately educated laymen.

THE MOLECULAR BASIS OF HEREDITY. Hermann *Muller's early appreciation of the importance of gene mutation in Darwinian selection emphasized that biologists long recognized the need to understand the mechanisms of genetic transmission. The elucidation of the structure of DNA was arguably the greatest achievement of 20th-century science. This discovery started the process of clarifying the molecular basis of genetics. It also established the central dogma that DNA determines the sequence of RNA, which in turn governs protein synthesis, even though exceptions to this rule were found later. Rosalind *Franklin's crystallographic picture of DNA, the Mona Lisa of scientific illustrations, was the key to Watson's insight that the DNA molecule is a helix. Her experiments were made possible by the application of X-ray crystallography to defining protein structure. Pioneers in this field included John *Bernal and Sir Max *Perutz. Perutz used this technique to

Bifurcation in crossbreeding the offspring of pure white sheep (A) with brown spotted sheep (b). The pure white gene is dominant over the spotted.

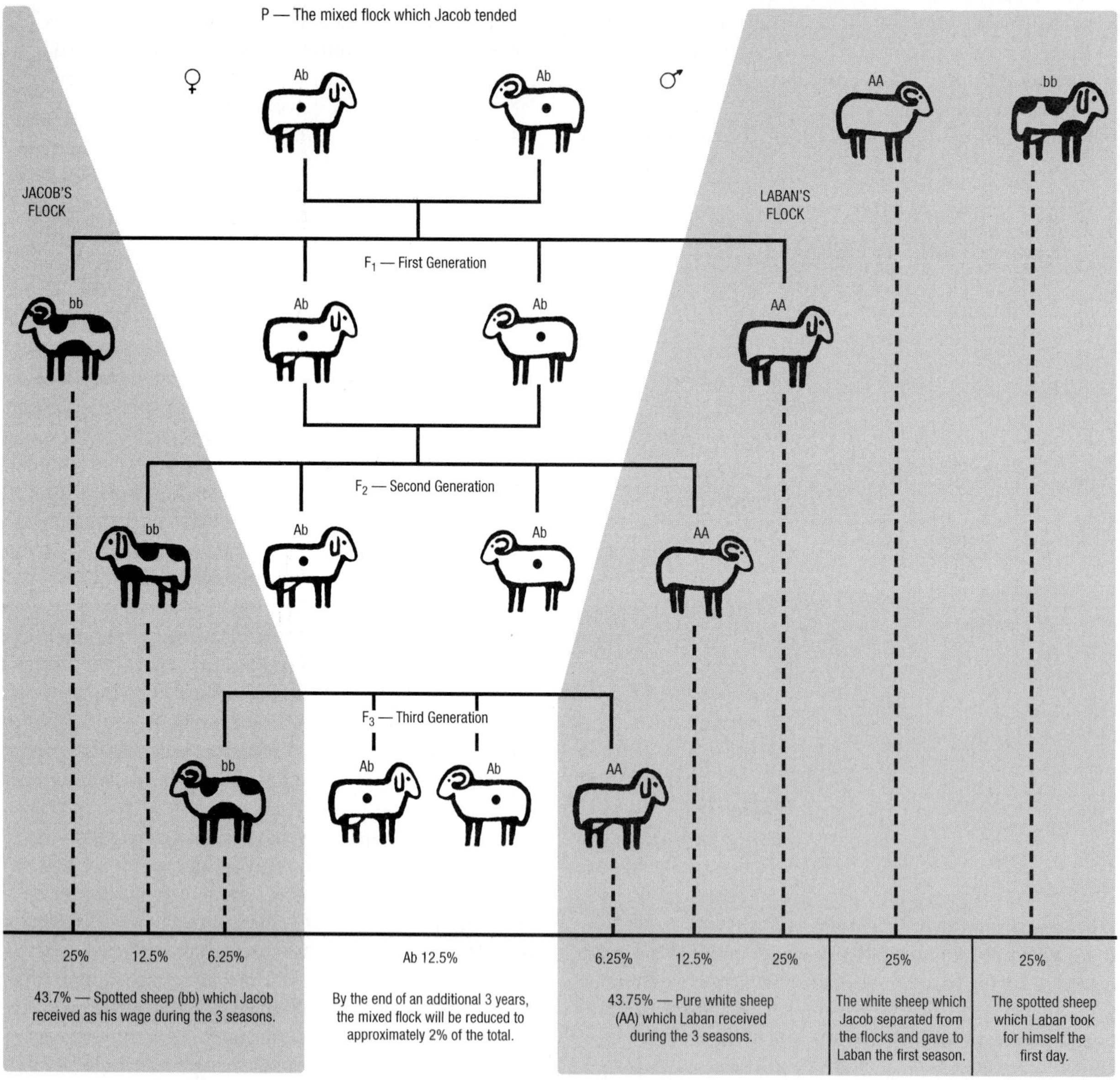

Jacob's crossbreeding of Laban's flock (Gen. 30). Chart by Jehuda Feliks, Jerusalem.

achieve the first biophysical description of a major molecule of biological importance, namely hemoglobin. Marshall *Nirenberg was one of the scientists who worked out the process by which the genetic information in DNA is transcribed by messenger RNA as the first step in protein synthesis. Once it was realized that the sequence of DNA bases is the genetic language it became necessary to devise methods for reading these sequences. One method was devised by Walter *Gilbert, who also showed that not all base sequences are utilized by the cell in protein synthesis even though these seemingly inactive "introns" later proved to have functional significance. Another important advance was Arthur *Kornberg's discovery of the first of the enzymes named DNA polymerases which regulate the copying of the DNA strand and hence the transmission of the cell's genetic information in newly synthesized DNA. Matthew *Meselson dissected the mechanisms by which DNA from different sequences recombine in the process of transferring genetic information. He also elucidated some of the ways in which DNA repairs mistakes liable to give rise to harmful mutations, a vital defense against the potentially disastrous effects of UV irradiation and other mutagenic agents. Another key development was the characterization of the enzymes which act on RNA transcribed from DNA to which Sidney *Altman made vital contributions. Indeed his work suggested the possibility that the earliest life forms on Earth may have been solely RNA dependent.

THE ORIGINS OF MOLECULAR BIOLOGY. Advances in genetics were accompanied by experiments in genetic manipulation using viruses called bacteriophages (phage) which infect bacteria. The interactions between phage and bacteria proved a vitally important model for understanding gene function and also the mechanisms which control gene activation and expression. Exploitation of this system marked the origins of what is now termed molecular biology. The findings in this model have proved broadly applicable to all other living species. Gunter *Stent, Salvador *Luria, Francois *Jacob, and Andre *Lwoff were members of the small and now legendary group of phage workers who transformed biology in a manner analogous to the revolution in physics initiated by quantum theory. They analyzed the interactions between phage and bacterial genes to formulate the general principles which determine the activation of some genes to initiate cellular events and other "repressor" genes which control activated genes. The manner in which repressor genes function was largely elucidated by Mark *Ptashne in an analogous experimental system. These insights into the manner in which genes operate were strengthened by Joshua *Lederberg's finding that bacteria exchange genes in a process termed recombination thereby altering the characteristics of the recipient bacteria. This work was extended by Stanley *Cohen's successful isolation and transfer of bacterial and mammalian genes, the technique of gene cloning now in universal use.

The isolation and study of defined DNA sequences was advanced by the discovery of enzymes by Daniel Nathans termed "restriction enzymes" which reproducibly cut DNA into manageable segments for analysis. Another vital step in the development of genetic manipulation was Sol Spiegelman's discovery that RNA sequences stick specifically to the DNA sequences from which the RNA was transcribed, a process termed hybridization. The ability to dissect and reconstruct genes was also greatly advanced by Paul *Berg's experiments with phage and also with mammalian cells infected by the virus SV40. He was also one of the first scientists to appreciate that a powerful method of discovering the function of a gene is to induce a deliberate mutation which will thereby cause the damaged DNA sequence to malfunction. Gene activation and repression is also an essential process in normal embryonic development. Chaim *Cedar discovered that chemical modification of DNA, a process known as methylation, is a key step in gene activation.

These advances in genetics were used by Sydney *Brenner to map the genetic control of the developing nervous system in the small worm C. elegans. These studies helped to establish the principle that the origin of human diseases can be investigated by detecting mutant genes and the abnormal proteins these genes encode. Robert *Horwitz's studies on the same species also highlighted the importance of genetically programmed cell death in normal development and function.

VIROLOGY. Elucidating the mechanisms of molecular genetics led to a greatly improved understanding of viral replication in cells and known viral infections. The new techniques also disclosed a viral cause for many diseases of previously unknown origin. Furthermore the longstanding suspicion that viruses may play a role in cancer and many chronic diseases is now open to rational investigation. Aaron Shatkin and Seymour S. *Cohen unraveled the sequential stages in viral infection of cells and Sir Aaron *Klug's work clarified the process assembly of new virus particles in infected cells. David *Baltimore and Howard *Temin found important exceptions to the previous dogma that all genetic information flows from DNA to RNA by showing that some RNA viruses transcribe DNA copies as the initial step in the production of new virus particles through the action of an enzyme called reverse transcriptase. Without this discovery the nature of AIDS and other retroviral infections could not have been rationally investigated. Although others had reported the induction of leukemia in mice with transmissible viruses many years before Charlotte Friend described similar findings in 1957, the interactions with cellular genes responsible for the disease were not elucidated before the work of Harry *Rubin in the 1960s and Harold *Varmus in the 1970s. Another achievement in virology was Baruch *Blumberg's discovery of hepatitis B virus which has proved not only of enormous clinical and epidemiological importance but has also given great insight into the genetic factors which determine the outcome of viral infections in different individuals. The history of research on "viral" infections continues to be unpredictable and a field where yesterday's heresy becomes a new orthodoxy. Stanley *Prusiner's work has established that infectious proteins called "prions" are devoid of nucleic acids yet are self-replicating and cause certain degenerative diseases of the nervous system.

CELL BIOLOGY. Cells have proved to be mini-organisms of great complexity and one can only discuss those fields of research on cell biology to which Jewish biologists have made especially significant contributions. Most tissues consist of self-renewing cells; their life cycles and the factors which regulate these cycles are of great basic interest and medical relevance. Marc Kirschner's work has helped to understand the signal pathways which induce cell division. The cell interior contains a complex network of channels and associated structures for the transport, processing, and degradation of proteins and other complex molecules imported into the cell or exported as the products of specialized cells. The findings of James Rothman and Randy Schekman have helped to clarify the structure and function of the most important of these cellular components. Another area of current basic and potential clinical interest is the identification and propagation of stem cells with full or limited potential to mature into specialized cells. Irving Weissman and Leo *Sachs were amongst the earliest workers to achieve success in this technically demanding field. It has also become apparent that cell division and maturation depend on the actions of growth factors produced by many cell types in a complex, inter-dependent manner. Nerve growth factor was the first such factor to be identified, by Rita *Levi-Montalcini, and Stanley Cohen. Cohen later discovered epidermal growth factor. These factors are now collectively termed "cytokines."

RECEPTORS, SIGNALS, AND PHARMACOLOGY. Cell membranes, their receptors, and the signals these receive largely govern the behavior of cells and organs. Martin *Rodbell and Alfred *Gillman greatly expanded our understanding of the receptor molecules which respond to external stimuli such as hormones and toxins and the signals these transmit to the cell in order to induce an appropriate response. Robert Lefkowitz and Ephraim *Katzir's scientific achievements center on the biophysical properties of membrane receptors. Especially noteworthy events in the development of pharmacology were Robert *Furchgott and Salvador Moncada's contributions to identifying nitrous oxide as a key molecule governing blood vessel flow and the similar role of prostacyclin discovered by Sir John Vane.

BIOCHEMICAL PATHWAYS. There is a consistent record of major contributions by Jewish scientists to characterizing the biochemical pathways which provide energy and govern other metabolic processes. This progress was greatly assisted by the introduction of isotopic methods for studying biochemical pathways by scientists who included Mildred *Cohn, David *Rittenberg, and Sidney Udenfriend. The crucial roles of oxidation and energy generation were appreciated early in the history of biochemistry and largely worked out by Otto *Warburg, extended by Fritz Lehmann's analysis of acetylation and further clarified by David Keilin. The related problem of energy creation in muscles was clarified by Otto *Meyerhof. The pathways for carbohydrate and urea metabolism and related intermediate pathways were characterized largely through the research of Philip Pacy *Cohen, Gerty *Cori, Hans Krebs, and Sarah Ratner. The steps in cholesterol synthesis were elucidated by Konrad *Bloch. The vital role of cholesterol receptors in controlling blood levels was established by Michael *Brown and Joseph *Goldstein.

Modern biochemistry has revealed a myriad biochemical processes other than the classical metabolic pathways. Edmond *Fischer and Sir Philip *Cohen have made key contributions to understanding protein phosphorylation, a complex process of fundamental importance for regulating a wide range of cell functions. The regulatory importance of the ubiquitin system has been shown by Aaron *Ciechanover and Avram *Hershko especially with respect to protein degradation. Carbon utilization is central to photosynthesis in plants and carbohydrate metabolism in mammals and was first methodically investigated by Melvin *Calvin. The precise structure of enzymes and other proteins as well as their amino acid sequence is crucial to their function, a problem largely resolved by the contributions of Christian *Anfinsen and William *Stein.

Two examples serve to illustrate specialized fields in the life sciences in which Jewish scientists have been especially prominent.

THE NERVOUS SYSTEM. Working out how each of the one hundred billion nerve cells in the brain communicates with one thousand other nerve cells is an enduring, largely unsolved challenge. The once controversial role of chemical neurotransmitters in communication between brain cells was firmly established by Julius *Axelrod's work on noradrenaline and Paul *Greengard's analysis of dopamine mediated signaling. The details of how peripheral nerves activate muscle fibers by releasing acetylcholine have been clarified by Sir Bernard *Katz. The part played by chemical neurotransmitters in transmission in the sympathetic and parasympathetic nervous system was also controversial until Otto *Loewi unequivocally demonstrated the role of acetylcholine and adrenaline. The basis of peripheral nerve function conduction was equally difficult to resolve before Joseph *Erlanger's detailed analysis of the electrical impulses involved in this process. The mechanisms of drug action on the brain are of practical importance, an area greatly illuminated by Hans Kosterlitz's studies in the field of natural opiate substances produced by the brain and the receptors on which these act. A still more formidable problem is to understand one of the brain's most distinctive functions, namely memory; Eric *Kandel's work showed that protein synthesis generated by nerve connections is involved in this process. The special senses pose different questions. Selig *Hecht and George *Wald have analyzed the molecular basis of the events in the retina which induce visual images after light exposure. Richard *Axel was one of the two scientists who showed that the recognition of the wide range of smells depends on receptors in the brain and not in the nose as one might have assumed. Another crucial issue is the role of genetic factors on brain function and susceptibility to neurological disease, an area of study largely founded by Seymour *Benzer.

THE IMMUNE SYSTEM. Simply stated, the central problem in immunology is to understand how the body rapidly generates molecules which combine specifically with the distinctive, mainly protein antigens expressed by infectious agents while avoiding autoimmune reactions with its own tissues. An early clear statement of the issues formed the basis of Ilya *Mechnikov's 1908 Nobel lecture. Michael *Heidelberger and Felix *Haurowitz were amongst the first scientists to analyze the antibody response in detail. This process culminated in the development by Cesar *Milstein and his colleagues of homogeneous monoclonal antibodies reactive with a single antigen. This advance has had momentous implications for the diagnosis and treatment of immunological and other diseases, for laboratory diagnosis and for biotechnology. The immune response to infections and indeed all foreign antigens is genetically controlled, a discovery largely based on the work of Baruj *Benacerraf, Michael *Sela, and Phil Leder. This control is largely determined by surface structures termed histocompatibility antigens in general and the HLA system in man which are expressed primarily by cells engaged in immune responses. Jack *Strominger contributed to the chemical and structural characterization of these antigens. The first recognition that certain human diseases result from autoimmunity came from the work of Noel Rose, Deborah Doniach, and Ivan Roitt. Among the greatest achievements of applied immunology is the virtual elimination of poliomyelitis with vaccines developed by Jonas *Salk and Albert *Sabin.

ORIGINS OF LIFE. Modern times have witnessed a loss of any inhibitions by Jewish scientists about discussing the origins of life on Earth. This has expanded into exobiology, the possibility that life exists elsewhere in the universe. Sol Spiegel and Leslie Orgel have proposed that self-replicating RNA was the primordial molecule in all life forms. Sidney Fox argued that amino acids, the building blocks of proteins, became self organized into replicating microspheres, an idea for which Stanley Miller has provided experimental support. A more general theory advanced by Stuart Kauffman is that randomly associating molecules in the correct chemical medium of the primitive Earth became autocatalytic and matured into living forms on a random basis. The subject has matured into a respectable topic for debate in scientific and religious circles.

Conclusions

The success of Jewish scientists in the life sciences as in other branches of science reflects a logical extension of traditional Jewish reverence for learning. However, this success has not been achieved by ignoring other aspects of Jewish learning and enterprise. An analysis of their careers shows that many have continued to support Jewish communal activities and even more have identified with Israel in general or have forged links with Israeli academic institutions. Indeed traditional scholarship and scientific discovery have been mutually supportive. "A scientific paper is a grave act to be undertaken with the utmost seriousness. To me it's holy writ and it should be an achievement that cannot be altered" (Joshua Lederberg, 1996).

[Michael Denman (2nd ed.)]

LIFSCHITZ, URI (1936–), Israeli painter. Lifschitz was born in kibbutz Givat ha-Sheloshah. His first paintings were lyrical abstractions, influenced by the Israeli painter Yossef *Zaritsky. His compositions are restless, with intense line and color. Since the late 1950s Lifschitz has become one of the leading representatives of the "New Figuration" in Israel art. He uses dramatic images as a direct and immediate reaction to social problems. In his large and expressive paintings of the 1960s, there is a mixture of abstract background and twisted figures drawn with black contours, and the artist himself is involved in the drama depicted on the canvas. There is a feeling of ironical criticism of the surrounding world, for example in his painting *In the Field* (1969), and the drawings *I am a chair* and *I don't know* (1969). In 1972, he held an exhibition in Tel Aviv, showing paintings and etchings made during 1971 in Spain. These reflect another artistic turning point in which he is inspired by Velasquez and Goya. In *After Velasquez* (1971) he uses a portrait made by the Spanish artist as an element in an abstract surrounding. Lifschitz has received many awards, including the Marc Chagall Fellowship in 1966.

[Judith Spitzer]

LIFSHITS, SHIYE-MORDKHE (1829–1878), pioneering Yiddish lexicographer, author, and a theoretician of the Yiddishist movement in the 19th century. With a solid intellectual background (he was a student of mathematics, physics, chemistry, languages) Lifshits propounded the idea of a secular Jewish culture on the basis of Yiddish. As a close friend of S.Y. *Abramovitsh (Mendele Mokher Sforim), it is thought that Lifshits was instrumental in convincing the "grandfather of modern Hebrew and Yiddish literature" to switch from Hebrew to Yiddish as a means of literary expression. A pioneer of the idea of Yiddish press, it is also assumed by some that under Lifshits' influence A. *Zederbaum began to publish the epoch-making Yiddish periodical *Kol Mevasser*, where Lifshits became a literary contributor on various topics.

Lifshits' lexicographic achievements are to a large extent unsurpassed in their quality and reliability, especially in depicting the South Eastern (Volhynian) Yiddish dialect. The manuscript of one of his dictionaries (Yiddish–German, German–Yiddish) unfortunately was lost. His excellent *Rusish-yidisher verter-bikh* went through four editions (1869–86). The Yiddish-Russian dictionary, *Yidish-rusisher verter-bikh*, was published in 1876.

A man of progressive ideas, Lifshits opened a tailor shop in the 1870s in Berdichev (where he died and was probably born) and shared the profits with the girls who worked there. He was deeply respected as a man of high ethical standards and admired even by his opponents. Although paralyzed in his later years, he continued his creative work to the very end.

BIBLIOGRAPHY: N. Shtif, in: *Di Yidishe Shprakh* (July–Oct. 1928); Rejzen, Leksikon, 2 (1930), 180–9; LNYL, 5 (1963), 210–5.

[Mordkhe Schaechter]

LIFSHITZ, DAVID (1907–1993), U.S. *rosh yeshivah* and rabbinical leader. Lifshitz was born in Minsk and studied under Simeon *Shkop in the Grodno yeshivah and at the Mir yeshivah. In 1935 he succeeded his father-in-law, Joseph Joselowitz, as rabbi of Suwalki where he soon established a yeshivah. Lifshitz became active in all communal affairs and assisted Ḥayyim Ozer *Grodzinski of Vilna in safeguarding the interests of Orthodoxy. After the deportation of the Jews of his community by the Nazis, Lifshitz succeeded in immigrating to the United States, where in 1942 he became a *rosh yeshivah* at Chicago's *Hebrew Theological College. In 1945 he was appointed to a similar position at *Yeshiva University. Lifshitz was active in guiding Orthodox Jewry in its relationship to the State of Israel and urged the religious parties to form a united religious front. He was a member of the presidium of the *Union of Orthodox Rabbis, the rabbinical advisory board to *Torah u-Masorah, and a director of Ezrat Torah, which aided rabbis and scholars throughout the world.

BIBLIOGRAPHY: O. Rand, *Toledot Anshei Shem* (1950), 76f.

LIFSHITZ, NEHAMAH (1927–), folk singer of Yiddish and Hebrew songs. Born in Kaunas (Kovno), Lithuania, where she started her schooling at the Hebrew high school, Nehamah Lifshitz was evacuated with her parents during World War II to Uzbekistan. After returning in 1946 to Soviet Lithuania, she studied at the Vilna conservatoire and in 1951 she gave her first concert. At an all-Soviet competition in 1958 she received the title of laureate of *estrada* (folk) artists. She traveled throughout the U.S.S.R., giving concerts of Yiddish (and some Hebrew) songs, drawing large crowds, including many young Jews. In 1959 and 1960 she visited France, Belgium, and Austria. In 1969 she was allowed by the Soviet authorities to immigrate to Israel where she was enthusiastically received as "the voice of the Jews of silence." On the occasion of her 70th birthday, Gila Flam and friends of the singer published in her honor an album including some of the recordings she made while in the Soviet Union.

[Binyamin Eliav]

LIFSON, SHNEIOR (1914–2001), Israeli biophysicist. He was born in Tel Aviv and was a member of kibbutz Nir David (1932–42), where he joined the Palmaḥ. He studied physics, mathematics, and chemistry at the Hebrew University of Jerusalem, receiving his Ph.D. (1954) followed by further studies in the U.S. and the Netherlands. He joined the Weizmann Institute as a research assistant (1949) and became professor (1961). He was chairman of its scientific council (1958–59 and 1961–63) and scientific director (1963–67). He was head of the department of chemical physics from 1963. Lifson's research concerned the fine details of protein structure and their functional significance. He was particularly involved in the biological implications of protein geometry and packing. Later in his career he was increasingly interested in the origins of life dependent on the transformation of inanimate to animate matter. He postulated that a changing environment acted on elementary "autocatalytic" matter to produce a self-sustaining process of replication, random variation, and natural selection. His publications attracted universal interest. He was awarded the Israel Prize for science (1969).

[Michael Denman (2nd ed.)]

LIGETI, GYÖRGY (1923–), composer and teacher. Ligeti's paternal great uncle, violinist Leopold Auer, was the teacher of Jascha *Heifetz and Mischa *Elman. Ligeti was born in Transylvania (then Hungary) and began his music studies at the conservatory of the provincial center of Kolozsvár (1941–43). In 1944 he was called up to the labor corps and only by chance was not sent to the death camps. In 1945–49 he was a student of composition at the Academy of Music in Budapest; among his teachers were Farkas, Veress, and Járdányi. From 1950 he became a teacher of harmony and counterpoint at the Academy. During those years he composed choral settings in folk style to meet the requirements of the Communist authorities while searching for his own style in pieces consigned to his desk drawer. In 1956, after the Soviet suppression of Hungary, Ligeti left for Austria, and in 1973 accepted a permanent position at the Musikhochschule in Hamburg, Germany, where he made his main home. The premiere of his *Atmosphères* for orchestra (1961) won him fame in avant-garde music circles. His unique technique of composition in this work, which he called "micropolyphony," was his highly individual transformation of the European Renaissance technique of multivoiced canons: Ligeti caused the polyphony to be unheard since the motives imitated were too short to distinguish them. His idea was to show the process of gradual change, to create a new type of musical phenomenon, called by him "continuous flow." "Micropolyphony" was also used in his *Requiem* (1965), *Lux aeterna* (1966), and *Lontano* (1967). In 1974–77 Ligeti composed his opera *Le Grand Macabre* (libretto based on Ghelderode's play), which was staged at many European theaters with great success. The opera is a stylistically varied work full of irony and satire. From the 1980s the composer became interested in various folk cultures, from his native Hungarian to Balkan, Caribbean, African, and Far Eastern. The rhythmic complexity and modal uniqueness of those cultures inspired the creation of the different musical language of his last three decades (*Etudes* for piano, from 1985, *Violin Concerto*, 1993, etc.). He received numerous honors, including the UNESCO International Music Council Music Prize and the Polar Music Prize of the Royal Swedish Academy.

BIBLIOGRAPHY: NG²; *György Ligeti in Conversation* (with Peter Várnai, Josef Häusler, and Claude Samuel, 1983); P. Griffiths,

György Ligeti (1983, 1996[2]); R. Steinitz, *György Ligeti: Music of the Imagination* (2003).

[Yulia Kreinin (2nd ed.)]

°LIGHTFOOT, JOHN (1602–1675), English Hebraist and Bible scholar. Lightfoot, a Puritan, was master of Catherine Hall, Cambridge, from 1650 and three years later he became vice-chancellor of Cambridge University. He began studying Hebrew after his ordination, but at first gave his attention to Bible research on scientific lines, publishing works such as *Harmonia, Chronica el Ordo Veteris Testamenti* (1647). However, he soon turned to rabbinic literature, a field in which he became the outstanding Christian authority of his time, showing a remarkable expertise in talmudic and midrashic scholarship. He published a *Descriptio Templi Hierosolymitani* (1650), on the Temple of Herod, and *Horae Hebraicae et Talmudicae* (1658–74), a study of the rabbinic sources of and background to the New Testament gospels. His first venture in Hebraica, published at the outset of his career, had been *Erubhin; or Miscellanies, Christian and Judaical, and others…* (London, 1629), and as a result of his unusual and objective investigation of rabbinic literature Lightfoot was accused of "rabbinism." He contributed to Bryan *Walton's *Biblia Sacra Polyglotta* (London Polyglot Bible; 1654–57), revising the Samaritan Pentateuch and specially preparing a geography of Palestine for the work. A Latin edition of his complete writings was later issued by his contemporary, Johann *Leusden, professor of Hebrew at Utrecht.

BIBLIOGRAPHY: D.M. Welter, *J. Lightfoot, the English Hebraist* (1878); DNB, 33 (1893), 229ff.

[Godfrey Edmond Silverman]

LIKKUT AẒAMOT (Heb. לִקּוּט עֲצָמוֹת; lit., "gathering of the bones"). In ancient Ereẓ Israel, the interment of the corpse did not take place immediately after death. First the body was left in the sepulchral chamber for some time until it was reduced to a mere skeleton, and afterward the bones were gathered together and then solemnly interred in the final resting place (TJ, MK 1:5; 80c–d; Sem. 12). This duty was generally performed one year after death by the children of the deceased and the laws of mourning were practiced on the day of the final interment (MK 8a; Sem. 12). Mourning was not continued the next day even if the gathering of the remains was only then completed. It was forbidden to deliver mournful eulogies on this occasion, and public condolences were not extended. However, the departed was praised and private condolences were conveyed (MK 8a; Sem. 12–13). The remains had to be reverently handled, and they could not, for example, be transported to their final resting place in a saddle bag (Ber. 18a). It was not considered respectful for the son to touch the remains of his parents directly with his bare hands (Sem. 12). Those engaged in the meritorious deed of *likkut aẓamot* were exempt from reading the **Shema*, and from all other positive commandments (Sem. 13). The gathering of the bones could not take place during the intermediate festival days since such an event would infringe upon the joy of the festival (MK 1:5). The laws pertaining to *likkut aẓamot* are also applicable in instances when *disinterment is permissible. However, when the coffin is still intact and is not opened during the disinterment procedure, the laws of mourning do not apply (TJ, Sanh. 6:11, 23d).

BIBLIOGRAPHY: S. Krauss, in: REJ, 97 (1934), 1–34; J.M. Tukacinsky, *Gesher ha-Ḥayyim*, 1 (1960[2]), 276–82; 2 (1960[2]), 183–91; J.J. (L.) Greenwald (Grunwald), *Kol Bo al Avelut*, 1 (1947), 223–49; 2 (1951), 75–94.

LIKUD ("Union"), Israeli political party that started off in 1973 as a list in the elections and a parliamentary group. Originally the Likud was made up of the *Ḥerut Movement, the *Israel Liberal Party – the two large components that remained its core until they finally merged into a single party in 1988 – and several small parties and groups: Ha-Merkaz ha-Ḥofshi, Ha-Reshima ha-Mamlakhtit, and part of the Movement for Greater Israel. Over the years the makeup of the Likud changed. Though Ariel *Sharon was the prime mover for the establishment of the Likud after he left active military service and joined the Liberal Party, from the outset it was headed by the leader of the Ḥerut movement, Menaḥem *Begin, and as of October 1983, by Yitzhak *Shamir. After the Likud turned into a party Binyamin *Netanyahu was elected chairman in 1993 followed by Ariel *Sharon in 1999.

Ideologically the Likud is right of center, with a socioeconomic policy that vacillates between Thatcherism and populism. In terms of Israel's defense doctrine and the war against terrorism the difference between the Likud and Labor is more in style and emphasis than in substance. In terms of the political process at first the Likud was unanimously opposed to any territorial compromise with regard to all the territories occupied by Israel in the course of the Six-Day War. However, in 1977 it was a government led by the Likud that returned the whole of the Sinai Peninsula, down to the last grain of sand in Taba, to Egypt. In the late 1980s the idea of a unilateral withdrawal from the Gaza Strip was also first sounded by MK Roni *Milo from within the Likud. When the Declaration of Principles signed with the PLO in 1993 was brought to the Knesset for approval several members of the Likud abstained, and in 1996, when the Likud returned to power, Prime Minister Netanyahu signed the Hebron memorandum and the Wye Plantation agreement, which were further steps in the realization of the Oslo Agreement. However, Netanyahu was much more blunt in his demand that the Palestinians disarm the terrorists and fulfill their obligation to amend the articles in the Palestine National Covenant advocating the destruction of Israel. The Likud's switch to political pragmatism was completed after the elections to the Sixteenth Knesset, when Prime Minister Sharon opted for a policy of disengagement from the Gaza Strip, and the dismantling of all the Jewish settlements there, and a few in northern Samaria. Nevertheless, this policy was strongly opposed by the Likud Conference, led by several old-time Likudniks such as Uzi Landau and David *Levy, and a group of extreme right-wingers that had joined the Likud toward the elections. Already in 1970, before he retired from the IDF and entered politics, Ariel Sharon supported the establishment of a Palestinian state – in Jordan. In 1978 Menaḥem Begin spoke of a solution of the Palestinian problem in the form of "autonomy." In general the Likud has been slower than Labor in accepting the concept of the establishment of a Palestinian state in most of the West Bank and Gaza Strip.

Though a secular party, the Likud has been more traditional and respectful of Jewish tradition than the Labor Party, and even though its leadership has not been less Ashkenazi than Labor's, it has been viewed as more hospitable to Sephardim. In terms of Jewish settlement in the territories occupied in 1967, such settlement began when Labor was still in power, but the settlement movement received much more governmental backing and support after the Likud came to power in 1977, with Ariel Sharon playing a major role in this respect in his various ministerial capacities.

Like the Labor Party, the Likud underwent a process of democratization from the end of the 1980s, but whereas in Labor the broad party membership was given most of the power to elect its representatives and leaders, in the Likud most of the power has remained in the hands of the Central Committee. This has weakened the traditional Likud leadership and strengthened extremist elements.

After receiving 39 seats in the elections for the Eighth Knesset in 1973, the Likud emerged as the largest parliamentary group after the elections to the Ninth Knesset in 1977 with 43 seats. In the 1981 elections it received 48 seats, in 1984 41 seats, in 1988 40 seats, in 1992 32 seats, in 1996 (together with *Tzomet and Gesher) 32 seats, in 1999 19 seats, and in 2003 38 seats. There was a Likud prime minister in the years 1977–84, 1986–92, 1996–99, and from 2001. From 1984 to 1990, from 2001 to 2002, and again in 2005 when the Likud formed a National Unity Government with Labor. However, in late 2005, Ariel Sharon broke away from the Likud to form the Kadimah Party (see *Israel, State of: Political Life and Parties) and consequently, in the 2006 elections, the Likud won just 12 seats with Binyamin Netanyahu again at the helm. The first time the Likud managed to get its candidate elected as president of the state was in 2003, when Moshe *Katzav ran against Shimon *Peres.

BIBLIOGRAPHY: A. Na'or, *Ketovet al Hakir: Le'an Movil ha-Likkud?* (1988); A. Ansky, *Mekhirat ha-Likkud* (2000); Y. Moskovitz, *Likkud beli Likkud: Ma'avakei Otẓma be-Mifleget ha-Likkud bein ha-Shanim 1974–2002* (2004).

LILIEN, EPHRAIM MOSES (1874–1925), Austrian illustrator and printmaker. Lilien was born in Drohobycz, Galicia. He studied art in Cracow for a short time, but lack of funds forced him to return home. He eventually earned enough as a sign painter to go to the Academy of Fine Arts in Vienna. In 1895 he worked in Munich as a cartoonist, where he obtained his first commission for the magazine *Jugend;* three years later he moved to Berlin, where he soon became known as a book illustrator. Lilien was the first artist to become involved in the Zionist movement. He took an active part in three consecutive Zionist Congresses and was a member of the *Democratic Fraction, which stressed the need to foster Jewish culture. In 1900 there was published *Juda,* a volume of ballads on Old Testament themes by a pro-Zionist German poet, Boerries Freiherr von Muenchhausen, illustrated by Lilien. This was followed by *Lieder des Ghetto* in which social adversity and the rejection of poor Jews were reflected. In 1902 he was one of the founders of the Berlin publishing house, *Juedischer Verlag, which he served not only as an illustrator but also as editor, manager, and publicity agent. Between 1908 and 1912 three volumes, of its planned ten, illustrated books of the Bible appeared. He collaborated closely with Theodor *Herzl; Lilien's photograph of the Zionist leader on the Rhine bridge, his Herzl portraits, and his decorations for the Golden Book of the Jewish National Fund became familiar to Zionists all over the world. In 1905 Lilien, along with Boris *Schatz and others, was a member of the committee formed to establish the *Bezalel School of Art in Jerusalem. He taught there for some months in the following year and revisited Palestine three times, on the last occasion as a lieutenant in the Austro-Hungarian army during World War I. In 1908 Lilien turned from book illustration to etching. Many of his etchings are views of Austria and Hungary, while others record his impressions of Palestine, Damascus, and Beirut. His drawings, executed mainly in India ink, show a crisp, elegant line and a strong contrast between black and white areas. Lilien combined biblical and traditional Jewish themes with the motifs and methods of Art Nouveau. His art expressed Jewish hopes and desires in the era of Zionism that looked beyond the exile.

BIBLIOGRAPHY: M.S. Levussove, *The New Art of an Ancient People: The Work of Ephraim Moses Lilien* (1906), includes plates; L. Brieger, *E.M. Lilien* (1922), includes bibliography. **ADD. BIBLIOGRAPHY:** O. Almog and G. Milchram (eds.), *E.M. Lilien. Jugendstil – Erotik – Zionismus,* Exh. cat. Juedischen Museums Wien (1998); M. and O. Bar-Am (ed. N. Feldman), *Painting with Light: the Photographic Aspect in the Work of E.M. Lilien* (1991); H. Finkelstein, *E.M. Lilien in the Middle East, Etchings (1908–25)* (1988); Galerie Michael Hasenclever, *E.M. Lilien. Unterwegs im alten Orient. Der Radierer und Lichtzeichner Ephraim Moses Lilien* (2004).

[Alfred Werner / Jihan Radjai-Ordoubadi (2nd ed.)]

LILIENBLUM, MOSES LEIB (1843–1910), Hebrew writer, critic, and political journalist. Born in Kedainiai, near Kovno, Lilienblum was one of the leaders of the Haskalah in its last period and a leader of Ḥibbat Zion.

His Life and Public Activity

His first teachers were his father, R. Ẓevi, a poor cooper, and his maternal grandfather, who was a teacher. Steeped in Talmud, Lilienblum established two yeshivot at the age of 22. At the same time, he began studying the Haskalah literature, secular subjects, and Russian and disseminated his views in public. In 1866 fanatic religious elements in Wilkomir, where he was then living, began to persecute him for his beliefs. Lilienblum retaliated in articles and an exchange of letters published in *Ha-Karmel* and *Ha-Meliẓ.* In 1868 he published his articles "*Orḥot ha-Talmud*" and "*Nosafot le-Orḥot ha-Talmud*" in *Ha-Meliẓ*, advocating reforms in religion and in society. Lilienblum stated that the Talmud contains progressive ideas modified to suit time and place, while the Shulḥan Arukh is rigid in tone and out of touch with life. He criticized the outstanding rabbis of his time through the pages of *Ha-Levanon* and *Kevod ha-Levanon*. In 1869 Lilienblum moved to Odessa, where he published his political satire, *Kehal Refa'im* (1870), in which he attacked many of his contemporaries, rabbis, writers, and editors, and called for the normalization of Jewish life through agricultural labor and the rational organization of work in industry, crafts, and commerce.

In 1871 Lilienblum began to edit the Yiddish journal, *Kol Mevasser*. In a series of articles he drew a grim picture of Jewish education in the *ḥeder* and in the yeshivot of the time. In articles written in 1871–73 he raised the problems of the emancipation of women, the mismanagement of Jewish community life, and religious and individual freedom. In his article "*Olam ha-Tohu*" (1873), a critique of Abraham *Mapu's book *Ayit Ẓavu'a*, he wrote of the need to reflect life as it really is, without romanticism, superstition, mysteries, or imagination, "a material view of life." In 1873–76 Lilienblum wrote his masterful autobiography *Ḥatte'ot Ne'urim*, in which he described his struggles and suffering and the development of his beliefs. In 1874–81 Socialism became the main subject of his writing. He published his article "*Mishnat Elisha ben Avuyah*" in Liebermann's *Ha-Emet*, urging the importance of labor in the life of the individual and the nation. He deliberately dated the article "The Day of Atonement, 1877." The year of the pogroms (1881) marks a radical shift in Lilienblum's career. He became a nationalist and a leader of the Ḥibbat Zion movement in Russia. He was one of the founders of the Odessa committee in 1883, and two years later was appointed its secretary and secretary of the Odessa *ḥevra kaddisha* ("burial society").

Lilienblum the Publicist

Lilienblum's career as a journalist had three stages: (a) 1866–70, the period of his struggle for religious reform. Lilienblum believed that the Jewish religion was stagnating and hindering the development of the nation. During this period Lilienblum advocated the introduction of the evolutionary principle into the field of religious practice. His main desire was to create close cooperation between Jews and their non-Jewish neighbors to be expressed in moderate reform of the more rigid religious precepts. (b) 1870–81, abandonment of the principle of religious evolution and the adoption of the demand for equal rights to be granted by the state as a prerequisite for the renaissance of Judaism in the spirit of the Haskalah. The Haskalah and progress are not a guarantee against antisemitism, and civil equality cannot be created only as a result of internal reforms in Judaism. (c) From 1881 until his death, the belief that the roots of antisemitism lie in the Aryan society's instinctive enmity toward the Semitic Jews. Legal equality is no guarantee of social equality. The aim of nationalist movements is either total assimilation of the Jews or their expulsion from their countries of residence. The source of the trials of the Jewish people lies in their constituting a nation within a nation. There is no basis for the hope that progress will bring about the end of antisemitism. The process of assimilation will not be implemented because of the firm stand of the Jewish people against the forces of disintegration, nor does it provide a solution to the problems of the Jewish people. Lilienblum concluded that it was necessary to concentrate the nation as one group in its own territory, and regarded Palestine as the suitable location, since there the nation would not constitute a foreign body; he opposed the creation of a Jewish haven in the U.S. His proposal was that land be purchased from the Turks and a quasi-governmental entity be established. It was not sufficient merely to establish settlements. In his view, the solution to the Jewish problem lay in the elimination of the Diaspora, and in the attainment of the status of an independent nation. The return to Zion could be implemented if the nation willed it. Lilienblum placed great hopes in the masses and in a certain stratum of the Jewish intelligentsia, whose task would be to arouse the desire for national independence. From 1889 onward he conducted a debate in the pages of *Ha-Meliẓ* and *Ha-Shaḥar*, with *Aḥad Ha-Am, *Ben-Avigdor, Zalman *Epstein, S.I. *Hurwitz, and *Dubnow, developing the ideology of the Ḥibbat Zion movement and practical Zionism. He grasped the dynamic and aggressive character of antisemitism, as did *Smolenskin, and foresaw the threat of total physical destruction of the Jewish people. Lilienblum rejected as artificial the autonomist approach, advocated by Dubnow, for the solution of the Jewish problem and regarded the theories of Aḥad Ha-Am and his disciples as making the existence of the Jewish people dependent on metaphysical speculations. He stressed that the Jewish people wanted to live for the sake of living and not for any purpose beyond life.

Lilienblum the Critic and Writer

In his literary criticism Lilienblum adopted the concepts of critical realism, bordering on nihilism, as advocated by Pisarev, Dobrolyubov, and Chernyshevski, even after having abandoned their political and social ideology. His literary and lyrical talent was small. *Kehal Refa'im*, his satirical work, is, in its way, an imitation of *Erter's satires, and the motifs are common ones in Haskalah literature. His only real contribution to literature is *Ḥatte'ot Ne'urim* (Vienna, 1876), his autobiography. Despite the sparsity of plastic description, the work is distinguished by its pathos and its insight into the inner emotional and moral conflict of the protagonist who struggles with social mores and the Jewish tradition.

Lilienblum wrote his literary criticism from the pragmatic viewpoint with the aim of educating the Jewish people to a true material view of life and freeing them from the useless life of the imagination. He admired only "real things." This anti-aesthetic pragmatic approach runs throughout his work and his critical articles. All art must be examined in the light of its usefulness to society. Lilienblum attached no importance to style and language as an integral part of artistic expression.

He was contemptuous of imagination. He dismissed most love poetry as lacking innovation, and regarded any deviation from rational logic to mysticism, such as the Kabbalah and Ḥasidism, as constituting a dangerous deviation from reality. He therefore rejected the Nietzschean revolt as expressed by Berdyczewski, his *Ha-Kera'im she-ba-Lev*, and the worship of hidden impulses. Lilienblum's philosophy is that "there is no aim in life except life itself."

His Books

Lilienblum prepared his own works for publication and they were published posthumously by J. Klausner in four volumes, *Kol Kitvei Lilienblum* (1910–13). *Derekh Teshuvah* (1899) and *Derekh La'avor Golim* (1899) were not included in this collection. Some of Lilienblum's letters were printed in *Hed ha-Zeman*, in *Ha-Olam*, in *Reshumot*, and in *Ketavim le-Toledot Ḥibbat Ẓiyyon*, edited by A.A. Druyanow in *Beḥinot* and in *Perakim*. His letters to J.L. Gordon were published in 1968, edited by S. Breiman, who also edited his autobiographical writings (3 vols., 1970). Lilienblum wrote a play in Yiddish entitled *Zerubbavel* (1887); he also edited the fifth volume of *Lu'aḥ Aḥi'asaf* (1897).

BIBLIOGRAPHY: J.S. Raisin, *The Haskalah Movement in Russia* (1913), index; Klausner, Sifrut, 4 (1953), 190–300; Breiman, in: *Shivat Ẓiyyon*, 1 (1950), 138–68; 2–3 (1953), 83–113; idem, introd. to *Ketavim Autobiografiyyim*, 1 (1970), 7–74 (incl. bibl.); A. Shaanan, *Ha-Sifrut ha-Ivrit ha-Ḥadashah li-Zerameha*, 2 (1962), 19–34; S. Streit, *Penei ha-Sifrut*, 1 (1938), 155–72; D. Ben-Nahum, *Be-Ma'aleh Dorot* (1962), 277–90; P. Lipovetzky (Ben Amram), *Ra'yon ha-Avodah ba-Sifrut ha-Ivrit* (1930), 54–68; S. Zemaḥ, *Eruvin* (1964), 37–50; Waxman, Literature, index; Spiegel, *Hebrew Reborn* (1962), 199–205.

[Shimon Oren]

LILIENTHAL, DAVID ELI (1899–1981), U.S. attorney, public official, and specialist in the development of natural resources. Lilienthal, who was born in Morton, Illinois, graduated from Harvard Law School in 1923 and was admitted to the Illinois bar that year. He practiced law in Chicago and was special counsel to that city in litigation concerning telephone rates until 1931. From 1926 to 1931, when he was appointed to the Wisconsin Public Service Commission, he also edited the journal *Public Utilities and Carriers Service*. In 1933 he was chosen by President Roosevelt to be director of the Tennessee Valley Authority. He held that post until 1941 when he was promoted to TVA chairman. In these capacities he defended TVA against attacks by Wendall L. Willkie and the power companies, resisted attempts to undermine the nonpolitical nature of appointments to the agency, and strove for decentralization of administration, voluntary cooperation of local communities, and planning in response to their needs.

In 1946 he left the TVA, as he was appointed by President Truman as the first chairman of the U.S. Atomic Energy Commission, which managed the peacetime use of nuclear power. His "Lilienthal Plan" called for an end to the nuclear arms race through international control of all atomic energy. He also publicly questioned the wisdom of America's decision to produce the hydrogen bomb. In the wake of controversy created by these views, Lilienthal returned to private life in 1950. In 1955 he formed the Development and Resources Corporation, a private venture in the designing and execution of development plans for underdeveloped countries. He served as a consultant on the utilization of human and natural resources to the governments of Colombia, Peru, Italy, Brazil, Iran, and Vietnam for various periods after 1955.

His books include *TVA: Democracy on the March* (1944), *This I Do Believe* (1949), *Big Business: A New Era* (1953), *Change, Hope, and the Bomb* (1963), *Management: A Humanist Art* (1967), *Atomic Energy, a New Start* (1980), and the seven-volume *Journals of David E. Lilienthal* (1964–83).

BIBLIOGRAPHY: J. Daniels, *Southerner Discovers the South* (1938), 46–97; Brooks, in: *New Yorker* (April 29, 1961), 45–90; P. Selznick, *TVA and the Grass Roots* (1949), which presents conclusions different from Lilienthal's own.

[Bernard Sternsher / Ruth Beloff (2nd ed.)]

LILIENTHAL, MAX (Menahem; 1815–1882), educator, author, and rabbi. Born in Munich, Bavaria, Lilienthal completed his studies at the university of his native town, and in 1839, on the recommendation of Ludwig Philippson, was appointed director of the Jewish school of Riga. He succeeded in this position, and also became known for the sermons which he delivered in German at the Riga synagogue (published as *Predigten in der Synagoge zu Riga*, 1841). He formed a friendship with the Russian minister of education S.S. *Uvarov, to whom he dedicated the above work.

In 1841, on the recommendation of Uvarov, the czarist government invited Lilienthal to draw up a project for the establishment of state schools for Jews providing a European-type education. Lilienthal set out upon his task by attempting to persuade the community leaders in the *Pale of Settlement to accept the project. His mission encountered opposition and mistrust among Jews there. Orthodox circles, and particularly the Ḥasidim, considered the project an attempt by the government to destroy traditional Jewish education, and possibly even to convert the Jews, while the *maskilim* also expressed misgivings. Lilienthal's meetings with the representatives of the Jews of Vilna, one of the main centers of Russian Jewry, ended in failure. His attempts to issue threats in the name of the government (it is not clear whether he was authorized to do so) aroused revulsion, while his strategy of contacting the representatives of the Orthodox and Ḥasidim and ignoring the *maskilim* alienated the latter from him. The publication of his proposals to invite teachers from Germany for the projected schools was a cause of further mistrust. In *Minsk Lilienthal found open hostility accompanied by personal abuse. His reaction, in 1842, was an appeal to Uvarov to enforce "educational reform" on the Jews through a series of laws. The minister of education refused to do so, but by means of a decree (June 22, 1842) he hinted to the Jews that the czar himself was in favor of the reform.

In order to sever the connection between the projected "reforms" and the personality of Lilienthal, Uvarov appointed a commission composed of Jewish personalities to study the proposals. Lilienthal was called upon to undertake an extensive journey through the Jewish centers to assess public opinion and guide it in the desired direction. Having learned from his previous experiences, Lilienthal on this occasion did not repeat his former suggestions, such as the employment of teachers from abroad and the imposition of a tax on the *melammedim (ḥeder* teachers), and succeeded in winning sympathy. However, his tactics in seeking an alliance with the Orthodox against the *maskilim* once more led to his failure. Lilienthal's appeal in *Maggid Yeshu'ah* (Vilna, 1842) brought a sharp retort from Mordecai Aaron *Guenzburg in the pamphlet *Maggid Emet* (Leipzig, 1843). The Commission for the Education of the Jews completed its task in 1843, and in 1844 a law for the establishment of state schools for the Jews was issued. In 1844, however, at the height of his success, Lilienthal had to leave Russia secretly. It appears that he had become convinced that the intentions of the czarist government were insincere and that it was scheming to exploit the network of schools as an instrument for eventual conversion to Christianity. The government's demand to exclude the study of Talmud from the curriculum marked the turning point in his outlook. Additionally, the law for the establishment of the schools was accompanied by other anti-Jewish laws in various spheres.

In 1845 Lilienthal immigrated to the United States, settling in New York City where he conducted a private boarding school for a few years. In 1849 he became rabbi of a short-lived union of the city's German congregations and directed their day schools. From 1855 until his death Lilienthal was rabbi of the important Bene Israel congregation of Cincinnati, which he led in the direction of moderate Reform. As a civic leader in his city on friendly terms with its Christian clergy, he was a member of its board of education (1860–69) and a trustee of the University of Cincinnati from 1872 until his death. He was perhaps the leading Jewish exponent in his day of the rigorous exclusion of all religious teaching from the public schools. Lilienthal actively cooperated with his fellow townsman Isaac Mayer *Wise in promoting Reform Judaism throughout the West, and was the publisher of *The Sabbath Visitor* from 1874, founder of the scholarly Rabbinical Literary Association, and taught at *Hebrew Union College from its opening in 1875. In 1857 he published *Freiheit, Fruehling und Liebe*, a collection of poems.

BIBLIOGRAPHY: D. Philipson, *Max Lilienthal, his Life and Writings* (1915); idem, *The Reform Movement in Judaism* (1931[2]), index; D. Kahana, in: *Ha-Shilo'aḥ*, 27 (1913), 314–22, 446–57, 546–56; J.S. Raisin, *The Haskalah Movement in Russia* (1915); P. Wengeroff, *Memoiren einer Grossmutter*, 1 (1908), 123–43; J. Shatzky, *Yidishe Bildungs-Politik in Poyln fun 1806 biz 1866* (1943), 71–80; H.B. Grinstein, in: HUCA, 18 (1943/44), 321–52; *The Sabbath Visitor* (April 14, 1882); *Der deutsche Pionier*, 14 (1882), 162–70, 211–6.

[*Encyclopaedia Hebraica*]

LILIENTHAL, OTTO (1848–1896), German inventor and aeronaut. Born in Anklam, Pomerania, Lilienthal and his brother, Gustav, studied the flight of birds and while still at school succeeded in constructing a glider. During the next few years the brothers built many gliders and executed a large number of flights. Lilienthal demonstrated the superiority of arched wings over flat-surfaced types, and brought gliding flight into a regular practice. He made over 2,000 flights, but finally while in flight his machine was upset by a sudden gust of wind, and he was killed near Rhinow. He wrote *Der Vogelflug als Grundlage der Fliegekunst* (1939[3]), and *Die Flugapparate* (1894). Lilienthal also made technical improvements in steam boilers, and designed children's building blocks. The Lilienthal brothers' Jewish origin has been disputed.

BIBLIOGRAPHY: G. Halle, *Otto Lilienthal* (1936), incl. bibl., 186–90; A. and G. Lilienthal, *Die Lilienthals* (1930); S. Kaznelson, *Juden im deutschen Kulturbereich* (1296[3]), 1053.

[*Encyclopaedia Hebraica*]

LILITH, a female demon assigned a central position in Jewish demonology. She appears briefly in the Sumerian Gilgamesh epic and is found in Babylonian demonology, which identifies similar male and female spirits – Lilu and Lilitu respectively – which are etymologically unrelated to the Hebrew word *laylah* ("night"). These *mazikim* ("harmful spirits") have various roles: one of them – the Ardat-Lilith – preys on males, while others imperil women in childbirth and their children. An example of the latter kind is Lamashtu, against whom incantation formulas have been preserved in Assyrian. Winged female demons who strangle children are known from a Hebrew or Canaanite inscription found at Arslan-Tash in northern Syria and dating from about the seventh or eighth century B.C.E. Whether or not Lilith is mentioned in this incantation, which adjures the stranglers not to enter the house, is a moot point, depending on the addition of a missing letter: "To her that flies in rooms of darkness – pass quickly, quickly, Lil[ith]." In Scripture there is only one reference to Lilith (Isa. 34:14), among the beasts of prey and the spirits that will lay waste the land on the day of vengeance. In sources dating from earlier centuries, traditions concerning the female demon who endangers women in childbirth and who assumes many guises and names are distinct from the explicit tradition on Lilith recorded in the Talmud. Whereas the Babylonian Lilu is mentioned as some kind of male demon with no defined function, Lilith appears as a female demon with a woman's face, long hair, and wings (Er. 100b; Nid. 24b). A man sleeping in a house alone may be seized by Lilith (Shab. 151b); while the demon Hormiz, or Ormuzd, is mentioned as one of her sons (BB 73b). There is no foundation to the later commentaries that identify Lilith with the demon Agrath, daughter of Mahalath, who goes abroad at night with 180,000 pernicious angels (Pes. 112b). Nevertheless, a female demon who is known by tens of thousands of names and moves about the world at night, visiting women in childbirth and endeavoring to strangle their newborn babies, is mentioned in the *Testament of Solomon*, a Greek work of about the third century. Although preserved in a Christian version, this work is certainly based on Judeo-Hellenistic magic. Here the female demon is called Obizoth, and it is related that one of the mystical names of the angel Raphael inscribed on an amulet prevents her from inflicting injury. Lilith is identified as a demon in the Dead Sea Scrolls (11QpsAp). The name Lilith was also inscribed on incantation bowls of Sassanian Babylonia. Although such bowls were not an exclusively Jewish phenomenon, some invoke rabbinic divorce formulas to exorcize demons.

Midrashic literature expands the legend that Adam, having parted from his wife after it had been ordained that they should die, begat demons from spirits that had attached themselves to him. It is said that "he was encountered by a Lilith named Piznai who, taken by his beauty, lay with him and bore male and female demons." The firstborn son of this demonic union was Agrimas (see the Midrash published in *Ha-Goren*, 9 (1914), 66–68; *Dvir*, 1 (1923), 138; and L. Ginzberg, *Legends of the Jews*, 5 (1925), 166). The offspring of this Lilith fill the world. A transmuted version of this legend appears in the *Alphabet of Ben Sira*, a Midrash of the geonic period, which sets out to explain the already widespread custom of writing amulets against Lilith. Here she is identified with the "first Eve," who was created from the earth at the same time as Adam, and who, unwilling to forgo her equality, disputed with him the manner of their intercourse. Pronouncing the Ineffable Name, she flew off into the air. On Adam's request, the Almighty sent after her the three angels Snwy, Snsnwy, and Smnglf; finding her in the Red Sea, the angels threatened that if she did not return, 100 of her sons would die every day. She refused, claiming that she was expressly created to harm newborn infants. However, she had to swear that whenever she saw the image of those angels in an amulet, she would lose her power over the infant. Here the legend concerning the wife of Adam who preceded the creation of Eve (Gen. 2) merges with the earlier legend of Lilith as a demon who kills infants and endangers women in childbirth. This later version of the myth has many parallels in Christian literature from Byzantine (which probably preceded it) and later periods. The female demon is known by different names, many of which reappear in the same or in slightly altered forms in the literature of practical Kabbalah (as, for example, the name Obizoth from the *Testament of Solomon*), and the place of the angels is taken by three saints – Sines, Sisinnios, and Synodoros. The legend also found its way into Arabic demonology, where Lilith is known as Karina, Tabi'a, or "the mother of the infants." The personification of Lilith as a strangler of babies is already clear in Jewish incantations, written in Babylonian Aramaic, which predate the *Alphabet of Ben Sira*. A late Midrash (*Ba-Midbar Rabbah*, end of ch. 16) also mentions her in this respect: "When Lilith finds no children born, she turns on her own" – a motif which relates her to the Babylonian Lamashtu.

From these ancient traditions, the image of Lilith was fixed in kabbalistic demonology. Here, too, she has two primary roles: the strangler of children (sometimes replaced in the Zohar by Naamah), and the seducer of men, from whose nocturnal emissions she bears an infinite number of demonic sons. In this latter role she appears at the head of a vast host, who share in her activities. Belief in her erotic powers led some Jewish communities to adopt the custom of sons not accompanying their dead father's body to the cemetery because they would be shamed by the hovering presence of their demon step-siblings, born of their father's seduction by Lilith. In the Zohar, as in other sources, she is known by such appellations as Lilith, the harlot, the wicked, the false, or the black. (The above-mentioned combination of motifs appears in the Zohar I, 14b, 54b; II, 96a, 111a; III, 19a, 76b.) She is generally numbered among the four mothers of the demons, the others being Agrat, Mahalath, and Naamah. Wholly new in the kabbalistic concept of Lilith is her appearance as the permanent partner of Samael, queen of the realm of the forces of evil (the *sitra ahra*). In that world (the world of the *kelippot*) she fulfills a function parallel to that of the *Shekhinah* ("Divine Presence") in the world of sanctity: just as the *Shekhinah* is the mother of the House of Israel, so Lilith is the mother of the unholy folk who constituted the "mixed multitude" (the *erev-rav*) and ruled over all that is impure. This conception is first found in the sources used by Isaac b. Jacob ha-Kohen, and later in *Ammud ha-Semali* by his disciple, Moses b. Solomon b. Simeon of Burgos. Both here, and later in the *Tikkunei Zohar*, there crystallizes the conception of various degrees of Lilith, internal and external. Likewise we find Lilith the older, the wife of Samael, and Lilith the younger, the wife of Asmodeus (see Tarbiz, 4 (1932/33), 72) in the writings of Isaac ha-Kohen and thereafter in the writings of most kabbalists. Some of these identify the two harlots who appeared in judgment before Solomon with Lilith and Naamah or Lilith and Agrat, an idea which is already hinted at in the Zohar and in contemporary writings (see Tarbiz, 19 (1947/48), 172–5).

Widespread, too, is the identification of Lilith with the Queen of Sheba – a notion with many ramifications in Jewish folklore. It originates in the *Targum* to Job 1:15 based on a Jewish and Arab myth that the Queen of Sheba was actually a jinn, half human and half demon. This view was known to Moses b. Shem Tov de Leon and is also mentioned in the Zohar. In *Livnat ba-Sappir* Joseph Angelino maintains that the riddles which the Queen of Sheba posed to Solomon are a repetition of the words of seduction which the first Lilith spoke to Adam. In Ashkenazi folklore, this figure coalesced with the popular image of Helen of Troy or the Frau Venus of German mythology. Until recent generations the Queen of Sheba was popularly pictured as a snatcher of children and a demonic witch. It is probable that there is a residue of the image of Lilith as Satan's partner in popular late medieval European notions of Satan's concubine, or wife in English folklore – "the Devil's Dame" – and of Satan's grandmother in German folklore. In the German drama on the female pope Jutta (Johanna), which was printed in 1565 though according to its publisher it was written in 1480, the grandmother's name is Lilith. Here she is depicted as a seductive dancer, a motif commonly found in Ashkenazi Jewish incantations involving the Queen of Sheba. In the writings of Hayyim Vital (*Sefer ha-Likkutim* (1913), 6b), Lilith sometimes appears to people in the form of a cat, goose, or other creature, and she holds sway not for eight days alone in the case of a male infant and 20 for a female (as recorded in the *Alphabet of Ben Sira*), but for 40 and 60 days respectively. In the Kabbalah, influenced by astrology, Lilith is related to the planet Saturn, and all those of a melancholy disposition – of a "black humor" – are her sons (Zohar, *Ra'aya Meheimna* III, 227b). From the 16th century it was commonly believed that if an infant laughed in his sleep it was an indication that Lilith was playing with him, and it was therefore advisable to tap him on the nose to avert the danger (H. Vital, *Sefer ha-Likkutim* (1913), 78c; *Emek ha-Melekh*, 130b).

It was very common to protect women who were giving birth from the power of Lilith by affixing amulets over the bed or on all four walls of the room. The earliest forms of these, in Aramaic, are included in Montgomery's collection (see bibl.). The first Hebrew version appears in the *Alphabet of Ben Sira*, which states that the amulet should contain not only the names of the three angels who prevail over Lilith, but also "their form, wings, hands, and legs." This version gained wide acceptance, and amulets of this type were even printed by the 18th century. According to *Shimmush Tehillim*, a book dating from the geonic period, amulets written for women who used to lose their children customarily included Psalm 126 (later replaced by Ps. 121) and the names of these three angels. In the Orient, also amulets representing Lilith herself "bound in chains" were current. Many amulets include the story of the prophet Elijah meeting Lilith on her way to the house of a woman in childbirth "to give her the sleep of death, to take her son and drink his blood, to suck the marrow of his bones and to eat his flesh" (in other versions: "to leave his flesh"). Elijah excommunicated her, whereupon she undertook not to harm women in childbirth whenever she saw or heard her names. This version is doubtless taken from a Christian Byzantine formula against the female demon Gyllo, who was exorcised by the three saints mentioned above. The transfer from the Greek to the Hebrew version is clearly seen in the formula of the 15th-century Hebrew incantation from Candia (see Crete), which was published by Cassuto (RSO, 15 (1935), 260), in which it is not Elijah but the archangel Michael who, coming from Sinai, encounters Lilith. Though the Greek names were progressively corrupted as time elapsed, by the 14th century new Greek names for "Lilith's entourage" appear in a manuscript of practical Kabbalah which includes material from a much earlier date (British Museum Add. Ms. 15299, fol. 84b). The story of Elijah and Lilith included in the second edition of David Lida's *Sod ha-Shem* (Berlin, 1710, p. 20a) is found in the majority of the later amulets against Lilith, one of her names being Striga – an enchantress, either woman or demon – or Astriga. In one of its mutations this name appears as the angel Astaribo, whom Elijah also encountered; in many incantations he takes the place of Lilith, a substitution found in a Yiddish version of the story dating from 1695. Also extant are versions of the incantation in which Lilith is replaced by the Evil Eye, the star Margalya, or the demon familiar in Jewish and Arab literature, Maimon the Black. In European belles lettres, the Lilith story in various versions has been a fruitful narrative theme.

[Gershom Scholem]

Lilith is identified as a demon in the Dead Sea Scrolls (11QpsAp). The name Lilith was also inscribed on incantation bowls of Sassanian Babylonia. Although such bowls were not an exclusively Jewish phenomenon, some invoke rabbinic divorce formulas to exorcise demons. Belief in her erotic powers led some Jewish communities to adopt the custom of sons not accompanying their dead father's body to the cemetery because they would be shamed by the hovering presence of their demon step-siblings, born of their father's seduction by Lilith.

Medieval Christian theology shows no explicit awareness of the Lilith of the *Alphabet of Ben Sira*, but its emphasis on female responsibility for the seduction and fall of Adam and Eve and the association of women with temptation and sin reflects a similar tradition. Christian literary texts allude to Lilith, usually in relation to Satan, but sometimes in relation to figures who are sexually miscast. For example, Lilith is the grandmother of the female pope described in a 15th-century German drama by Theodoricus Schernberg; she appears as Adam's first wife in poems and art by Dante Gabriel Rossetti; in Victor Hugo's *La Fin de Satan*; in a play by Achim von Arnim; and in Goethe's *Faust*.

In recent years, feminists have reconfigured the Lilith myth, claiming it reveals male anxiety about women who cannot be kept under patriarchal control. Lilith is admired as a woman who opposed Adam's attempts at hegemony over her, who had a firm will, and who possessed the power of secret knowledge to assert her autonomy. In feminist versions of the creation story, Lilith demands equality with Adam. Her expulsion from the Garden of Eden indicates not her evil, but the intolerance of male entities, Adam and God, who insist on defining and controlling women. Her independence and knowledge reveal not her demonic nature or sexual miscasting, but represent all women seeking liberation from the imposition of narrow gender roles. In a feminist Midrash, Judith Plaskow imagined Lilith returning to the Garden of Eden and forming a friendship with Eve, who now began to question her subservience to Adam. Plaskow's story concludes with God and Adam left in confusion, fearing "the day Eve and Lilith returned to the garden, bursting with possibilities, ready to rebuild it together."

Feminist reclamations of Lilith in the last quarter of the 20th century include the Lilith Fair, an annual summer women's music festival; *Lilith Magazine*, the first Jewish feminist periodical, founded in 1976; and a women's bookstore in Berlin named Lilith. Lilith is also the subject of art, poetry, and even new religious rituals designed to affirm women's strength and spirituality.

[Susannah Heschel (2nd ed.)]

BIBLIOGRAPHY: G. Scholem, in: KS, 10 (1934/35), 68–73; idem, in: *Tarbiz*, 19 (1947/48), 165–75; R. Margalioth, *Malakhei Elyon* (1945), 235–41; Y. Schachar, *Osef Feuchtwanger – Masoret-ve-Ommanut Yehudit* (1971); H. Von der Hardt, *Aenigmata Judaeorum religiosissima* (Helmstedt, 1705), 7–21; J.A. Eisenmenger, *Entdecktes Judentum*, 2

(1700), 413–21; J. Montgomery, *Aramaic Incantation Texts From Nippur* (1913); R. Dow and A. Freidus, in: *Bulletin of the Brooklyn Entomological Society*, 12 (1917), 1–12 (bibl. on Sammael and Lilith); I. Lévi, in: REJ, 67 (1914), 15–21; D. Myhrmann, *Die Labartu-Texte* (1902); Ch. McCown, *The Testament of Solomon* (1922); M. Gaster, *Studies and Texts*, 2 (1925–28), 1005–38, 1252–65; F. Perles, in: *Orientalistische Literaturzeitung*, 18 (1925), 179–80; I. Zoller, *Rivista di Antropologia*, 27 (1926); Ginzberg, Legends, 5 (1955), 87f.; H. Winkler, *Salomo und die Karina* (1931); J. Trachtenberg, *Jewish Magic and Superstition* (1939), 36f., 277f.; Th. Gaster, in: *Orientalia*, 12 (1942), 41–79; H. Torczyner (Tur-Sinai), in: *Journal of Near Eastern Studies*, 6 (1947), 18–29; M. Rudwin, *The Devil in Legend and Literature* (1931), 94–107; T. Schrire, *Hebrew Amulets* (1966); E. Yamauchi, *Mandaic Incantation Texts* (1967); A. Chastel, in: RHR, 119–20 (1939), 160–74; A.M. Killen, *Revue de littérature comparée*, 12 (1932), 277–311. **ADD. BIBLIOGRAPHY:** J. Dan, "Samael, Lilith, and the Concept of Evil," in: *Association for Jewish Studies Review*, 5 (1980), 17–40; R. Lesses, "Exe(o)rcising Power: Women as Sorceresses, Exorcists, and Demonesses in Babylonian Jewish Society of Late Antiquity," in: *Journal of the American Academy of Religion*, 69:2 (2001), 343–75; J. Plaskow and D. Berman, *The Coming of Lilith* (2005); E. Yassif, *Sippurei Ben Sira* (1984).

LILITH, non-profit independent U.S. Jewish feminist quarterly directed at a popular female audience. Founded in 1976 by a group of women led by Susan Weidman Schneider, *Lilith: The Independent Jewish Women's Magazine* has been concerned with fostering discussion of Jewish women's issues and with putting them on the agenda of the Jewish community. The magazine, to quote its editors, "charts Jewish women's lives with exuberance, rigor, affection, subversion and style." The magazine features award-winning investigative reports, new rituals and celebrations, contemporary and historical personal narratives, entertainment reviews, fiction and poetry, and art and photography.

BIBLIOGRAPHY: A.L. Lerner, "*Lilith*," in: P.E. Hyman and D.D. Moore (eds.), *Jewish Women in America*, vol. 1 (1997), 854–56.

LILLE, city in the département of the Nord, N. France. The Jewish community of Lille was formed in the 19th century. Beginning in 1872, Lille became the seat of a chief rabbinate. Its first chief rabbi was Benjamin Lippmann, formerly chief rabbi at Colmar, who had refused to remain in Alsace after it was annexed by Germany. According to the census of the Jewish population in occupied France carried out at the beginning of 1942, there were 1,259 Jews then living in Lille, only 247 of whom were born there. The Commissariat Générale aux Questions Juives (CGQJ) maintained an office in Lille. In reprisal for an underground raid the Germans executed five Jews in Lille in March–April 1942. Of the 461 French and foreign-born Jews who were deported from the region of the Nord, only 125 returned. Among those deported was Léon Berman, who was rabbi of Lille from 1936 to 1939 and who published a work titled *Histoire des Juifs de France*. He was arrested along with his wife and son in October 1943, interned at the camp of Drancy, and eventually transported to a death camp. In 1987 there were 2,800 Jews in Lille, which was the seat of the regional consistory. The Lille community maintained a number of institutions, including a synagogue erected in 1874, a number of small prayer halls, youth groups, a kosher butcher, and a community center. It also published a community bulletin.

BIBLIOGRAPHY: Z. Szajkowski, *Analytical Franco-Jewish Gazetteer 1939–1945* (1966), index; R. Berg, *Guide juif de France* (1971), 240–41.

[David Weinberg (2nd ed.)]

LIMA, ancient capital of the Peruvian viceroyalty and capital of *Peru; population more than 8,866,160 (2005). Ninety-eight percent of Peru's Jewish population of about 2,700 live in the city. The discovery of Peru and its enormous mining potential attracted a large number of *Conversos who disregarded the restrictions on the immigration of New Christians and arrived in the capital founded by Francisco Pizarro in 1535. Most of them arrived during the period of unification of the Spanish and Portuguese crowns (1580–1640), and were known as "Portuguese." On February 7, 1569, Philip II, king of Spain, decreed the royal document by which he ordered the establishment of the Inquisition in Lima that was to start the persecution of judaizers and descendants of Jews.

Until 1595, however, the number of victims was very small, and the Crypto-Jews could prosper especially in the import and export trade. The first auto-da-fé took place in Lima on December 17, 1595. Ten Judaizers were judged, four of them were released, and one, Francisco Rodríguez, was burned alive. On December 10, 1600, 14 judaizers were punished; on March 13, 1605, 16 judaizers; later the frequency and the numbers declined.

The general pardon for all the judaizers declared in 1601 attracted a considerable number of New Christians, most of whom were Crypto-Jews who had acquired an important position in the economic life of the Spanish colony. Therefore the sensational trials against judaizers were generally conducted against those who had accumulated a fortune, all their possessions being confiscated by the Holy Office after their condemnation. This was the case with Antonio Cordero, the local representative of a merchant from Sevilla, who was denounced by a local trader for having declined to sell on the Sabbath and having refused to eat pork. A secret investigation was conducted, accompanied by torture, which led to the great auto-da-fé of January 23, 1639 with 60 judaizers. The most famous among them was Francisco Maldonado de Silva, who remained in prison for 12 years, during which he maintained his loyalty to the Jewish faith and even converted two Catholic prisoners to Judaism. All the rest were members of what the Spanish authorities called "The Great Conspiracy" congregation of Crypto-Jews in Lima. The last victim of *La Complicidad Grande* was Manuel Enríquez, who was burned at the stake in 1664 together with the effigy of Murcia de Luna, who died at torture. This exemplary display of severity, together with the menace of total expulsion in 1646, from which they were able to free themselves through the payment of the fabulous sum of 200,000 ducats, curtailed the offense of judaizing for many years. According to unsubstantiated sources there were 6,000 Crypto-Jews in Peru.

The last victims of the accusations against judaizers were Ana de Castro, on December, 23, 1736, and Juan Antonio Pereira, on November 11, 1737. The last activities of the Inquisition in Lima were in 1806. At that time there were no remaining Crypto-Jews recognized as such. A very famous family of Crypto-Jews during the colonial period was that of "León Pinelo."

The León Pinelo Family

During the period of the Viceroyalty this family flourished, being gifted with exceptional intellectual qualities that were manifested in a variety of activities in Spain, Peru, and Mexico, whether in the legal profession, theology, or various branches of knowledge. The León Pinelo school in Lima is named after the brothers Juan, Antonio, and Diego, children of Captain Diego López de León and Catalina de Esperanza Pinelo, distant relatives of the Pinelli of Genoa.

Juan López, the grandfather of the brothers León Pinelo, was a Portuguese Jewish merchant who, together with his wife, was burned alive in Lisbon in 1595. The survivors of the family immigrated to Valladolid, where they remained while Diego, the father, moved to Buenos Aires in search of a better situation. When his position was stabilized thanks to his commercial activities, he managed to reunite the family in 1605.

Juan, the first son of Diego López de León, was born in Lisbon (Portugal). He studied in Chuquisaca (Bolivia). He moved to Lima with his father and brother Antonio. Juan distinguished himself as an orator in the court of Philip IV, and was named canon of the Cathedral of Puebla (New Spain), where he ended his life. The second son, Antonio de León Pinelo, was born in Valladolid in 1590. He studied in the Universidad de San Marcos (in Lima). He was mayor of the Oruro mines, and in 1621 he returned to Spain as the attorney of the city of Buenos Aires. In Madrid he established himself in the court, amazing everyone with his erudition. He was known as "the Oracle of America" for the vastness of his knowledge in matters concerning the Indies, particularly South America. He is credited with having established the basis, together with the judge Solórzano Pereira, of the famous collection of laws that was issued by the Spanish Crown for the government and administration of the colonies in the New World and printed in four volumes under the title *Recopilación de las Leyes de las India* (Collection of the Laws of the Indies). The idea of the collection of laws developed in Lima, when both León Pinelo and Solórzano Pereira cemented their friendship during a period when the former was endowed with a chair at the Universidad de San Marcos. Antonio de León Pinelo gained fame for being the first bibliographer to teach works published about America. He was a friend of Lope de Vega, Ruiz de Alarcón, and other well-known Spanish writers. His project on the History of Lima recounted the development of the capital of the Viceroyalty from the time of its foundation. In 1629 he was appointed *relator* in the Council of the Indies, a position that gave him access not only to the legislature promulgated for the colonies across the sea, but also enabled him to undertake the collection of the treaties on the administration of these territories. At the end of his life he was named chronicler of the Indies, in charge of writing the annals of the American past. He died in 1660.

Diego, the youngest brother, was born in Córdova del Tucumán. He started his university studies in Lima and finished them in Salamanca. Upon his return, he held chairs at the Universidad de San Marcos and was its rector between 1656 and 1658. In his judicial career he was general protector of the natives of Lima. He is especially remembered with respect to the apologetic treatise of the University of San Marcos (*Hypomnema Apologeticum Pro Regali Academia Limensi*, 1643), in which he defended the scientific hierarchy of the institute as well as the cultural achievements of the Peruvians, which he considered underevaluated by European scholars.

"León Pinelo" School in Lima

The history of the León Pinelo school began with the visit of Natán Bistritzky, who arrived in Peru in March 1945 on a mission of the Jewish National Fund. Bistritzky encouraged the leaders of the Jewish community, which at the time comprised only 2,500 persons, to create the Comité Pro-Colegio Hebreo with the objective of founding a Jewish day school in Peru. The community chose the name of "León Pinelo" for his historical ties with the Jewish and Peruvian people. The school was opened on May 1946 with 33 students. During its 50 years of existence, more than 1,600 students graduated from the school, with a high level of Jewish education. Most of the graduates continued their studies in universities in Peru, Israel, or the United States, and work as professionals in Peru or abroad.

BIBLIOGRAPHY: On the Colonial period see *Peru. L. Trahtemberg, *Antología de Judaísmo Contemporáneo*, vol. 1: "Antisemitismo" (1987); G. Lohmann Villena, *Antonio de León Pinelo, Gran Canciller de las Indias*. **WEBSITE:** www.lp.edu.pe.

[Leon Trahtemberg (2nd ed.)]

LIMA, MOSES BEN ISAAC JUDAH (1605?–1658), Lithuanian rabbi and halakhist. Lima studied at the yeshivah of Joshua *Falk in Cracow, where he became friendly with many who later were leaders of the generation. In 1637 he served as rabbi of Slonim and in 1650 was *av bet din* of Vilna, his colleagues being *Ephraim b. Jacob ha-Kohen and *Shabbetai Kohen, author of the *Siftei Kohen*. In 1655 he was appointed rabbi where he served until his death. One of his three sons, Raphael, published his father's work *Ḥelkat Meḥokek* (Cracow, 1670), a commentary on the Shulḥan Arukh, *Even ha-Ezer*, outstanding for its critical perceptiveness and profundity and acknowledged as one of the best halakhic works of the later generations. It was accepted as an authoritative work in its field, despite its difficult style, which at times makes a supercommentary necessary. The *Beit Shemuel* of *Samuel b. Uri Shraga Phoebus is devoted largely to a discussion of Lima's book. For the benefit of rabbis and *posekim* Lima and Samuel compiled *Kunteres ha-Agunot*, appended to chapter 17 of *Even ha-Ezer*, containing the essence of hundreds of books and responsa concerning the permission of *agunot* to remarry. Some later authorities expressed reservations as to whether it was permissible to base oneself on the work for practical decisions without reference to the sources. Of Lima's other works, there remain only a number of responsa in various collections.

BIBLIOGRAPHY: H.N. Maggid-Steinschneider, *Ir Vilna* (1900), 4f.; S.J. Fuenn, *Kiryah Ne'emanah* (1915²), 76–78; H. Tchernowitz, *Toledot ha-Posekim*, 3 (1948), 158–63; Szulwas, in: I. Halpern (ed.), *Beit Yisrael be-Polin*, 2 (1954), 21; Wilenski, in: *Sefunot*, 3–4 (1959–60), 541f.; Eidelberg, in: *Sinai*, 60 (1967/68), 188; Kahana, in: *Sinai*, 34 (1954), 311–24.

[Israel Moses Ta-Shma]

LIMAN, ARTHUR L. (1932–1997), U.S. lawyer. Born in New York City, Liman grew up in a suburb, Lawrence, L.I. He graduated magna cum laude from Harvard and then from Yale Law School, where he was first in his graduating class. Soon after he became an associate at Paul, Weiss, Rifkind, Wharton & Garrison, a firm with ties to the Democratic Party. Liman was considered a masterly legal strategist who represented both corporate tycoons and scalawags but made his public mark investigating pivotal events like the Iran-contra affair and the prison uprising in Attica, N.Y. Liman occupied the public stage in the summer of 1987 when he was chief counsel to the Senate committee investigating the Reagan administration's arms-for-hostage scheme known as the Iran-contra affair. On live television Liman jousted with Lieut. Col. Oliver L. North and other witnesses. The scandal centered on the sale of United States arms to Iran in the mid-1980s to obtain the release of American hostages in Lebanon. The sale, which involved diverting some of the profits to Nicaraguan contra insurgents, was done clandestinely and in violation of stated American policy. Liman was considered a master of cross-examination, a litigator with total recall of intricate details and supreme self-assurance. His blue-chip clients at Paul Weiss included Time-Warner, GAF, Weyerhaeuser, Pennzoil, Heinz, Continental Grain, CBS, and Calvin Klein. He also represented the fugitive financier Robert L. Vesco, Dennis B. Levine, a convicted Wall Street inside trader, and Michael R. *Milken, who admitted violating Federal securities law. Liman earlier was chief counsel to a New York State panel that spent a year investigating the inmate rebellion at Attica state prison, in which 43 inmates and guards were killed during four days of rioting and hostage-taking in September 1971. His commission issued a 470-page report that concluded that an assault by state troopers to recapture the prison, ordered by Gov. Nelson A. Rockefeller, was ill-considered and far too harsh, leading to needless loss of life. It was published in book form and was so well written that it was nominated for a National Book Award.

[Stewart Kampel (2nd ed.)]

LIMBURG, JOSEPH (1866–1940), Dutch politician. One of the founders of the Liberal Democratic Party, Limburg was a member of the second chamber of parliament (1905–17). The education act adopted in 1917 bears his name. He was a member of the Netherlands delegation to the League of Nations in 1920. In 1926 he was entrusted with the formation of a cabinet, but failed and left politics. He was a member of the Council of State until 1940, when, on the Netherlands' surrender to Germany, he committed suicide.

LIMERICK, seaport in southwestern Ireland. Jews began to settle there after the beginning of the Russian persecutions at the close of the 19th century. The attitude of the townspeople was hostile, and attacks on the Jews occurred in 1884. Nevertheless, immigration continued and a synagogue was established in 1889. The majority of the newcomers engaged in the drapery business; others in grocery and furnishing, trading partly on the "hire-purchase" system. In 1904, owing to the preaching of Father Creagh of the Redemptorist Order, an anti-Jewish riot broke out, followed by a boycott, and many Jews left. (The most complete account of the "Limerick pogrom," as it was sometimes called, may be found in Dermot Keogh's *Jews in Twentieth-Century Ireland* (1998), 26–53.) The community is now extinct.

BIBLIOGRAPHY: B. Shillman, *Short History of the Jews in Ireland* (1945), 136f.; C.H.L. Emanuel, *Century and a Half of Jewish History* (1910), 119, 160, 164; JC (Jan. 15, 1904). **ADD. BIBLIOGRAPHY:** L. Hyman, *The Jews of Ireland* (1972), index.

[Cecil Roth]

LIMITATION OF ACTIONS.

The Concept and its Substance

In the talmudic period, Jewish law generally did not recognize the principle that the right to bring an action could be affected by the passage of time (i.e., extinctive prescription); in the post-talmudic period, it came to be recognized as a principle that there was a limit to the claimant's right of instituting action on account of the passing of time, without extinction of the underlying right itself. In Jewish law, the principle of limitation of actions is grounded on the reasoning that delay in instituting action serves to cast doubt on the reliability of the claimant's evidence. Consequently, prescription serves to deprive the plaintiff of a remedial action only if the defendant denies the existence of the right forming the subject matter of the action, but not if he admits its existence.

In the Talmudic Period

In the Talmud, the principle of limitation of actions – apart from two exceptional cases – was wholly unrecognized: "a creditor may recover his debt at any time, even if it has not been mentioned" (Tosef., Ket. 12:3; cf. the version in TJ, Ket. 12:4, 35b and TB, Ket. 104a).

THE WIDOW'S CLAIM FOR HER KETUBBAH. One exception to the general rule is the claim of a widow for her **ketubbah*, which becomes prescribed under certain circumstances. In a dispute with R. Meir, the scholars held that "a widow, as long as she lives in her husband's house, may recover her *ketubbah* at any time; when, however, she lives in her father's house [and not with the heirs, and is therefore not inhibited from claiming her *ketubbah* from them], she may recover her *ketubbah* within 25 years only" (from the date of her husband's death; Ket. 12:4).

Thereafter, her right to recover the *ketubbah* is extinguished, on the assumption that she has waived it, taking into account the great delay in instituting action and the fact that the *ketubbah* "is not like a loan and therefore she has not suffered any loss" (Ket. 104a and Rashi ad loc.). R. Meir expressed the contrary opinion that, as long as she lives in her father's house, she may recover her *ketubbah* at any time, but as long as she lives in her husband's house, she may only recover her *ketubbah* within 25 years, for "25 years suffices for her to extend favors in exhaustion of her *ketubbah*" (as it may be assumed that during this period she made use of the assets of the estate to render favors (gifts) to her neighbors in an amount corresponding to the value of her *ketubbah*: Ket. 12: 4 and Rashi ad loc.). In the opinion of R. Ishmael, the period is three years only (Tosef., Ket. 12:3). The *halakhah* was determined according to the first view (Yad, Ishut, 16:21–24; Sh. Ar., EH 101:1–4). In talmudic times, this limitation of action in the case of a widow seeking to recover her *ketubbah* after the lapse of 25 years from the date of her husband's death already applied only where she was not in possession of the *ketubbah* deed; there was no limitation of action if she was in possession of such a deed at the time her claim was brought. Similarly, her right of action for recovery of the *ketubbah* remained intact even though she lived in her parents' home after her husband's death, provided that the attitude of the heirs toward her was particularly favorable ("delivering her maintenance to her on their shoulders"), on the presumption that the nature of this relationship had served to inhibit her from demanding her *ketubbah* from them (Ket. 12:4; 104b). On the widow's death, her heirs too could recover her *ketubbah* only within 25 years (Ket. 12:4), commencing, according to some of the *posekim*, from the date of their succeeding to her right, i.e., on her death (Tur and Sh. Ar., EH 101:1), and according to others, from the date that the cause of action arose, i.e., on the death of the husband (Rashi and Hananel, Shevu. 48a; *Beit ha-Beḥirah*, Ket. 104b).

THE WIDOW'S CLAIM FOR MAINTENANCE. Another exception to the general rule is to be found in a halakhic ruling from amoraic times stating that a delay of two years on the part of a poor widow – or three years on the part of a rich one – in claiming *maintenance from the estate of the deceased husband barred her from recovering maintenance for the period which had elapsed (Ket. 96a; TJ, Ket. 11:2, 34b has two or three months, respectively). The reasoning behind this quasi-limitation of action is likewise based on the assumption that the widow, by virtue of her delay, has waived her claim for maintenance (Rashi Ket. 96a; *Beit ha-Beḥirah ibid.*; Yad, Ishut, 18:26; Tur and Sh. Ar., EH 93:14). If, during the aforesaid period, the widow has borrowed for her maintenance or if she has been in possession of a *pledge, she cannot be presumed to have waived her claim for maintenance and it does not become prescribed (TJ, loc. cit.).

Roman Law

Roman law of that period also did not recognize the principle of limitation of actions, although there were the *actiones temporales*, which had to be brought within a fixed period, mostly within one year (the *annus utilis*). However, the reason for the limitation of those actions lay in the fact that they were founded on a right "granted" by the praetor, who limited in advance the period within which an action could be brought for enforcement. Consequently, once this period had elapsed, the remedial action, as well as the underlying right itself, became extinguished. In contradistinction to this, actions based on civil law (*actiones civiles*), as well as those praetorian rights in respect of which the praetor had not determined any fixed period for instituting action, were numbered among the *actiones perpetuae*, which could be brought at any time (save for a number of exceptions). It was only in 424 C.E., in a law of Honorius and Theodosius, that the principle of prescription was recognized in respect of all actions. The general period of prescription was fixed at 30 years and, in certain exceptional cases, at 40 years (R. Sohm, Institutionen (1949^7), 709–15).

In the Post-Talmudic Period

From the beginning of the 13th century, Jewish law began to give limited recognition to the principle of limitation of actions. While the principle was preserved that limitation of the right of action could not extinguish the underlying right itself, the doctrine evolved that delay in bringing an action served to cast doubt on the credibility of the evidence adduced in proof of the claim.

EFFECT OF DELAY ON CREDIBILITY OF CLAIMANT'S EVIDENCE. Thus, at the end of the 13th century, Asher b. Jehiel, dealing with a claim based on old deeds, expressed the fear that an unduly long silence might serve as a subterfuge to enable deceit to go unnoticed or to be forgotten; he accordingly demanded that a suit of this nature be thoroughly investigated if the defendant should plead that he paid the debt or should deny its very existence and, "if I assess as a strong probability (*umdenah de-mukhaḥ*) that the suit is a fraudulent one and unfounded, I say that no *dayyan* in Israel should grant relief in this suit, and this I write and sign for delivery into the hands of the defendant" (Resp. Rosh, 68:20; 85:10). However, this view was not generally accepted at once, and in the 14th century *Isaac b. Sheshet of Spain and North Africa gave his opinion that a plea by a defendant based on the plaintiff's long delay in bringing his action was "an idle plea, lacking in substance, and served neither to prove nor disprove the existence of the debt" (Resp. Ribash no. 404). In time, however, Asher b. Jehiel's view on the effect of delay in bringing an action came to be generally accepted, and even supplemented by various further details. In the 15th century, Joseph *Colon (of northern Italy) decided that overlong delay carried with it a suspicion of fraud, which obliged a careful investigation of the matter, even if it was written (in the deed) that the defendant would "raise no plea against the deed and took this upon himself on ban and oath" (Resp. Maharik no. 190; *Darkhei Moshe* ḤM 61, n. 5: *Rema* ḤM 61:9). The *halakhah* was decided accordingly by Joseph *Caro and Moses *Isserles (Sh. Ar., ḤM 98:1–2). In the 16th century Samuel di *Medina (of the Balkan countries and

Turkey) decided that where no reasonable justification could be found to account for the delay, the court should endeavor to effect a compromise between the parties (Resp. Maharashdam, ḤM 367), while Isaac *Adarbi, Medina's contemporary and compatriot, charged the court with compelling the parties to a compromise in a suit based on a long-delayed claim (*Divrei Rivot* no. 109). Until this time, i.e., the beginning of the 17th century, no fixed period of prescription had been determined and the court would investigate and determine each case on its merits.

FIXED PERIODS FOR LIMITATION OF ACTIONS. From the beginning of the 17th century, the need became increasingly felt for precise legal directions concerning the period within which a defendant could expect a particular action to be brought against him. Jewish law accordingly came to recognize the principle – by way of *takkanah* and custom (see **minhag*) – that the mere lapse of time sufficed to impugn the credibility of the evidence in support of the claim, without the need for any particular investigation by the court. Consequently, if the defendant denied the existence of the debt, he was absolved from liability when he delivered an oath as to the truth of his plea. At the same time the substantive principle, basic to prescription in Jewish law, that the lapse of time did not operate to extinguish the underlying right itself, was preserved, so that a debtor who did not deny the existence of the debt – and certainly one who admitted it – was obliged to make repayment notwithstanding prescription of the right of action. The period of prescription was determined in advance – generally three years and in certain cases six (*Pinkas ha-Medinah, Lita*, ed. by S. Dubnow (1925), *Takkanah* 205 of 1628; Benjamin Ze'ev Wolf, *Misgeret ha-Shulḥan*, 61, n. 16; Ẓevi Hirsch b. Azriel, *Ateret Ẓevi*, to Sh. Ar., *ibid.*; Jacob Lorbeerbaum, *Netivot ha-Mishpat, Mishpat ha-Kohanim*, n. 18). Once more, this new development with regard to the law of prescription was not immediately accepted by all the halakhic scholars. Thus Abraham *Ankawa (19th century, Morocco), in commenting on this development in Polish and Lithuanian Jewish centers, remarked that it was "a great innovation, and presumably a *takkanah* they enacted for themselves, although contrary to the law, for whatever reason they had at the time" (*Kerem Ḥamar* ḤM no. 33). So too, at the beginning of the 18th century, Jacob Reicher (Galicia) had decided in accordance with the principles laid down in the Shulḥan Arukh, in a matter concerning an old deed (*Shevut Ya'akov*, vol. 3, no. 182). His younger contemporary, Jonathan *Eybeschuetz expressed the opinion that "at this time much scrutiny is required to keep the court from giving effect [in the case of an old deed] to a fraudulent suit" (*Urim* ḤM 61, n. 18). In the course of time, however, this development came to be accepted as part of the law of prescription, and was even refined and supplemented by certain additional rules, namely: if the debt cannot be recovered from the debtor on account of his impoverishment, prescription is interrupted for the period of his impoverishment; prescription does not apply during the period in which either the plaintiff or defendant is a minor; prescription does not bar the institution of an action if the debtor has waived such a plea in writing, in clear and unequivocal terms, even after completion of the period of prescription (*Kesef ha-Kedoshim* 61:9).

In the State of Israel

A substantial number of the various provisions of the Prescription Law, 5718/1958 accord with the principles of prescription in Jewish law, including the principle that "prescription shall not per se void the right itself" (sec. 2). On the other hand, this law includes the provision that an admission by the defendant of the plaintiff's right shall only have the effect of nullifying the period of prescription already accrued if the admission is not "accompanied by a plea of prescription" (sec. 9). This provision is at variance with the Jewish law principle that the defendant – if he has admitted the existence of the plaintiff's right – is not entitled to void the claim by pleading that the period within which the action may be instituted has lapsed.

For prescription with regard to immovable property, see **Ḥazakah*.

[Menachem Elon]

In the Rabbinical Courts the question of the limitation of actions has also been raised in the context of "the law of the kingdom is law" (**Dina de-Malkhuta Dina*), viz., whether Rabbinical Courts must abide by existing state law or custom under which certain actions are limited, when this would negate the option of taking legal action.

Rabbi Ben-Zion Ouziel is of the opinion that Jewish Law only recognizes the principle of a passage of time limiting a right with regard to evidence, e.g., to disqualify a document, and only if other corroborative evidence impugned the authenticity or validity of the document, raising the possibility of a miscarriage of justice. Accordingly, he rejected unqualified compliance of Rabbinical Courts with state law in this context. In his opinion, limitation of actions cannot be regarded as a custom (and hence binding), because the binding nature of a custom is only applicable with regard to the accepted modes of acquisition, which the merchants have agreed to be bound by. By contrast, a promissory note in the hand of the creditor is proof of debt, and the argument that due to the custom of limitation the creditor has waived his claim supports the "robbery" of the debtor, and "robbery cannot be permitted on the basis of custom" (Mishpetei Ouziel, ḤM 28. 8)

In the Israeli Supreme Court the aforementioned position of Jewish Law on limitation of actions prompted the Supreme Court (Justice Menachem Elon), at the end of its decision in the *Boyer* case (CA 216/80 *Boyer v. Shikun Ovdim*, 38 (2) PD 561, 569) to make the following recommendation to a litigant who won his case exclusively on the basis of the claim of prescription (i.e., the passage of time invalidating the rival party's claim): "this is a classic case in which it is proper and desirable to go beyond the strict letter of the law (*lifnim mi-shurat ha-din*). For a detailed discussion of the matter, see *Law and Morality, and the Supreme Court decisions cited (ibid).

Moreover, the position taken by Jewish Law on limitation, which accepts the doubtful veracity of the evidence without negating the substance of the claim, was instrumental in establishing and confirming the position of the Israeli Supreme Court on this matter. It ruled that the laws of limitation should be interpreted so as to give priority to clarifying the truth rather than bestowing immunity on the litigants (CA 4114/96 *Hameiri v. Hachsharath Hayishuv*, PD 52(1) 857, Justice Tirkel).

BIBLIOGRAPHY: I.S. Zuri, *Mishpat ha-Talmud*, 7 (1921), 15f.; M, Elon, in: *Ha-Peraklit*, 14 (1957/58), 179–89, 243–79; idem, in: ILR, 4 (1969), 108–11; Z. Warhaftig, *Ha-Ḥazakah ba-Mishpat ha-Ivri* (1964), 263–85. **ADD. BIBLIOGRAPHY:** M. Elon, *Ha-Mishpat ha-Ivri*, (1988), 1:827; 3:1450f.; idem, *Jewish Law* (1994), 2:1013; 4:1724f.; E. Shochetman, *Sidrei ha-Din* (1988), 178.

LIMOGES, capital of the Haute-Vienne department, central France. A Jewish source, *Sefer Yeshu'at Elohim* (in A.M. Habermann, *Gezerot Ashkenaz ve-Ẓarefat* (1945), 11–15) contains an account of a semi-legendary anti-Jewish persecution in Limoges in 992 resulting from the activities of an apostate from Blois. The Christian writer Adhémar of Chabannes relates that in 1010 Bishop Alduin of Limoges gave the Jewish community the choice of expulsion or conversion. It is possible that both sources refer to the local manifestation of the general anti-Jewish persecutions which occurred around 1009 and which were followed by baptisms and expulsions. At any rate, whether or not the Jews were expelled from Limoges, the expulsion order was no longer in force from the middle of the 11th century; a certain Petrus Judaeus is mentioned in a local document between 1152 and 1173 and Gentianus Judaeus in 1081. Around the middle of the 11th century R. Joseph b. Samuel *Bonfils (Tov Elem) headed the Jewish community of Limoges and Anjou. The beginnings of the modern Jewish community in Limoges date from 1775. During World War II, Limoges became the largest center of refuge for Alsatian Jews; about 1,500 families and many institutions were transferred to the town. The present community, which was formed in 1949, grew to more than 650 by 1970 and possessed a synagogue and community center.

BIBLIOGRAPHY: Gross, Gal Jud (1897), 308–9; J. de Font-Reaulx (ed.), *Cartulaire du Chapître de St.-Etienne de Limoges* (1919), passim; *La Vie Juive*, 51 (1959), 15; B. Blumenkranz, *Juifs et Chrétiens…* (1960), index; Z. Szajkowski, *Analytical Franco – Jewish Gazetteer* (1966), 286; Roth, Dark Ages, index.

[Bernhard Blumenkranz]

LIMOUX, town in the department of Aude, *Languedoc, southern France. The existence of a Jewish community there is confirmed toward the end of the 13th century. Its privileges were withdrawn in 1292, as were also those of a number of other Jewish communities in Languedoc, but were restored in 1299. In 1302, the Jews of Limoux, again together with those of other localities in Languedoc, were freed by *Philip IV (the Fair), from liability to prosecution by inquisitors. At the beginning of the 14th century, some Jews from Limoux were living in Narbonne. A new community may have been constituted after 1315; this would be the one referred to in the *Shevet Yehudah* (ed. by A. Shochet, p. 149) under the name לשמאדש as having been massacred by the *Pastoureaux in 1320.

BIBLIOGRAPHY: G. Saige, *Les Juifs du Languedoc* (1881), 29, 33, 286; Gross, Gal Jud, 313–4; REJ, 2 (1881), 31; *ibid.*, 38 (1899), 106.

[Bernhard Blumenkranz]

LIMPIEZA DE SANGRE (Sp., "purity of blood"), an obsessive concern in Spain and Portugal from the 15th century, based on the mythical goal of a society in which all but the most humble functions would be exercised by "pure-blooded" Christians. In varying degrees this obsession afflicted Spain until well into the 19th century; blood purity was still a requirement for admission to the military academy until 1860, when it was legally abolished. In Portugal all legal distinctions between Old and *New Christians were officially removed in 1773. *Limpieza de sangre* continues to be a matter of concern on the island of Majorca, where Christians of Jewish ancestry are disdainfully referred to as **chuetas* and frequently suffer discrimination because of their "impure blood."

Although the pure-blood statutes established by the various communities of Spain in the 16th century adopted a routine formula directed against all Christians descended from Moors and heretics as well as Jews, the problem, both in its historical origins and in its later consequences, mainly concerned those of Jewish ancestry. The first such measure of which details are known, the so-called *Sentencia-Estatuto* adopted in Toledo in 1449 in the course of a popular uprising under the leadership of Pedro *Sarmiento against royal authority, was directed solely against the Toledan *Conversos. It prohibited them from testifying in legal proceedings and excluded them from all public office, especially notaryships which were most frequently in their hands, "under penalty of death and confiscation of all their goods."

This extraordinary measure against the Conversos or New Christians was a direct consequence of a series of anti-Jewish riots which swept through Spain in 1391. Protests against and denunciations of the *Sentencia-Estatuto* arose both among the affected converts as well as distinguished ecclesiastics of non-Jewish origin, including Pope Nicholas V. Nevertheless, the pure-blood statutes spread to such an extent that by 1500 most Spanish organizations, secular or religious, insisted on "blood purity" as a qualification for membership. The controversy concerning the legality and propriety of the *limpieza de sangre* discriminations continued until well into the 17th century, and Conversos were excluded from an increasing number of guilds, religious confraternities, most colleges, religious and military orders, and residence in certain towns. Churches and cathedrals reserved even their most humble benefices for Christians "without the stain of Jewish blood," leading one polemicist to observe that Jesus himself would have failed to qualify as a porter in Toledo Cathedral.

Spain's obsession with blood purity in the 16th and 17th centuries led to considerable social turmoil. A leading supporter of the *limpieza de sangre* statutes in the early 17th century was Juan Escobar del Corro in his *Tractatus.* His work suggests that the racial or ethnic grounds for the opposition to the Conversos cannot be canceled by religious and theological reasons. The *limpieza de sangre* was introduced when it was no longer possible to reject a descendant of Jews purely on religious grounds. As generations passed and the memory of the Jewish ancestry of Converso Spaniards faded, efforts were redoubled to unearth the traces of their long-forgotten "impure" forefathers. Communities vied with one another in the severity of their pure-blood statutes. The Old College of Saint Bartholomew of Salamanca, the source of Spain's most important leaders, took pride in refusing admittance to anyone even rumored to be of Jewish descent. Hearsay testimony and words spoken in anger to the effect that someone was a Jew, or a descendant of Jews, sufficed to disqualify a man, a kind of "civil death" understandably feared by Spaniards. As investigations into ancestries ranged even farther into the distant past, until "time immemorial" as some put it, even families considered Old Christian lived in constant fear lest some remote, forgotten "stain" be brought to light or a hostile rumormonger destroy their reputation.

Since no one could be absolutely certain of his blood purity "since time immemorial," *limpieza de sangre* ultimately became a qualification negotiated through bribed witnesses, shuffled genealogies, and falsified documents.

Américo Castro's attempt to demonstrate that the roots of the *limpieza de sangre* are to be found, not in the Christian-Iberian anti-Jewish feelings, but in much older sources, very distant from Spain, namely Jewish ones, has been rejected by scholars, such as B.Z. Netanyahu. Castro claims that the Jews introduced their racial beliefs into Spain, just as they introduced the Inquisition. Castro brings his evidence from ancient biblical sources, medieval rabbinic literature, and Spanish Jewish scholars, but is clearly unfounded and often based on mistaken views of the Jewish sources.

BIBLIOGRAPHY: J. Caro Baroja, *Los judíos en la España moderna y contemporánea*, 1 (1961), ch. 6; 2 pt. 4 (1961), chs. 2–7; A. Domínguez-Ortiz, *La clase social de los conversos en Castilla en la Edad Moderna* (1955); H.C. Lea, *A History of the Inquisition of Spain*, 1 (1906), ch. 3; A.A. Sicroff, *Les controverses des statuts de "puret de sang" en Espagne* (1960). **ADD. BIBLIOGRAPHY:** C. Carrete Parrondo, in: *Helmantica*, 26 (1975), 97–116; H. Méchoulan, in: REJ, 136 (1977), 125–37; M. Defourneaux, *Daily Life in Spain in the Golden Age* (1979), 28–45; B. Netanayahu, in: PAAJR, 46–47 (1979–80), 397–457; M. Orfali, in: *Actas de las Jornadas de estudios sefardíes* (1981), 245–50; F. Abad, in: *Actas de las Jornadas de estudios segfardíes* (1981), 239–44; H. Yerushalmi, *Assimilation and Racial Anti-Semitism: The Iberian and German Models* (1982); J. Fayard and M-C. Gerbert, in: *Histoire, économie et société*, 1 (1982), 51–75; E.M. Jarque Martínez, *Los procesos de limpieza de sangre en la Zaragoza de de la edad moderna*, (1983); Ch. Amiel, in: *Annales du* CESERE, 6 (1983), 27–45; A.A. Sicroff, *Los estatutos de limpieza de sangre; controversias entre los siglos* XV *y* XVII (1985) (trans. from French); P. Molas Ribalta, in: *Les sociétés fermées dans le monde ibérique (*XVI-XVIII*e s.); définitions et problématique* (1986), 63–80; H. Kamen, in: *Bulletin hispanique,* 88 (1986), 321–56; J. Edwards, in: *Proceedings of 9th World Congress of Jewish Studies* (1986), Division B, vol. 1, 143–50; idem, in: *Proceedings of the 10th World Congress of Jewish Studies* (1990), Division B, vol. 2, 159–66; J. Friedman, in: *Sixteenth Century Journal,* 18 (1987), 3–30; J.I. Gutiérrez Nieto, in: J.J. de Bustos Tovar and J.H. Silverman, *Homenaje a Américo Castro* (1987), 77–89; idem, in: *II Simposio sobre San Juan de la Cruz*, 33–60.

[Albert A. Sicroff / Yom Tov Assis (2nd ed.)]

LINCOLN, town in eastern England. The medieval Jewish community (first mentioned in 1159) was probably the second in importance in England after London. During the crusader riots which swept the country in March 1190, the Jews were attacked and took refuge under the protection of the sheriff. The citizens were subsequently fined for their unruly conduct. St. Hugh, the great bishop of Lincoln, protected the Jews, who later joined their fellow townsmen in mourning his death in 1200. The most prominent Anglo-Jewish financier of the time was *Aaron of Lincoln (c. 1123–86), whose operations extended over every part of the country but were especially important in Lincolnshire. R. Joseph of Lincoln is mentioned as a scholar (c. 1125–36). In the second half of the 13th century, the outstanding Lincoln Jews were Hagin (Ḥayyim), son of R. *Moses b. Yom Tov of London, who was *archpresbyter of English Jewry (1258–80), and his brother *Benedict of Lincoln (d. 1276?), identical with the tosafist R. Berachiah of Nicole, who has left some significant literary remains. The latter was absolved at the time of the ritual murder accusation in 1255 associated with the name of "Little" St. *Hugh of Lincoln when 91 Lincoln Jews were sent to London for trial and 18 executed. Notwithstanding this, the community continued to be important. In 1266, during the Barons' Wars, the "Disinherited Knights" attacked the Lincoln Jewry, sacked the synagogue, and burned the records registering debts. On the expulsion of Jews from England in 1290, assets were registered of 66 householders (not all still alive), and the property which fell into the king's hands exceeded £2,500, in addition to 30 houses. Specimens of medieval Jewish architecture, including a building which was probably the synagogue, may still be seen in the former Jewry (now Steep Hill). A small Jewish community existed again in Lincoln at the beginning of the 19th century. There was a small community of evacuees during World War II. At the outset of the 21st century, while no synagogues existed, a Lincolnshire Jewish community organization was maintained by the Progressive movement.

BIBLIOGRAPHY: J.W.F. Hill, *Medieval Lincoln* (1948), 217–38; Davis, in: *Archeological Journal*, 38 (1880), 178ff.; C. Roth, in: JHSET, 9 (1918–20), 28; idem, in: JJS, 1 (1948), 67–81; idem, *Medieval Lincoln Jewry and its Synagogue* (1934); Rosenau, in: *Archeological Journal*, 94 (1937), 51–56; JHSET, 1 (1893–94), 89–135; 3 (1896–98), 157–86; C.W. Foster (ed.), *Registrum Antiquissimum of the Cathedral Church of Lincoln*, especially vol. 7 (1931).

[Cecil Roth]

°**LINCOLN, ABRAHAM** (1809–1865), 16th president of the United States; first president to become officially involved in national questions of Jewish equality and anti-Jewish discrimination. Lincoln participated in two matters of Jewish historic significance. The first related to the appointment of Jewish chaplains for the army and for military hospitals. Legislation passed by the House of Representatives in July 1861 required that a chaplain be a "regularly ordained minister of some Christian denomination." Although a Jewish layman, Michael Allen did serve as chaplain; he resigned his commission after being accused of serving illegally. A campaign of public pressure was undertaken to change the law, and in December 1861 the Rev. Arnold Fishel of New York went to Washington, under the aegis of the Board of Delegates of American Israelites, to act as lobbyist and civilian chaplain. He secured an appointment with Lincoln who wrote him promising to use his best efforts "to have a new law broad enough to cover what is desired by you in behalf of the Israelites." New legislation was introduced in both the House and the Senate. By July 1862, a new law made it possible for rabbis to serve as military chaplains alongside Protestant ministers and Catholic priests, for the first time in history – a major step in the Americanization of the Jewish religion. Had Lincoln ignored Fishel's representations, or actively opposed them, it is unlikely that either house of Congress would have passed the legislation.

In December 1862, General Ulysses S. *Grant issued an order expelling all Jews from the area of his command, on the alleged grounds that Jews were engaging in illegal trade. This was brought to Lincoln's attention by a Jew from Paducah, Kentucky, Cesar Kaskel, in January 1863, and Lincoln, recognizing the injustice of the order, issued instructions for its immediate cancellation. General-in-Chief H.W. Halleck, in the second of a series of telegrams, explained to Grant that "as it in terms proscribed an entire religious class, some of whom are fighting in our ranks, the President deemed it necessary to revoke it." Lincoln, consenting to see another Jewish delegation after he saw Kaskel, assured the group, which included Rabbis Isaac M. *Wise and Max *Lilienthal, that "to condemn a class is, to say the least, to wrong the good with the bad. I do not like to hear a class or nationality condemned on account of a few sinners."

Lincoln was a close friend and political associate of Abraham *Jonas, a Jew from Quincy, Illinois, and their correspondence reveals a warm mutual appreciation and common political loyalties.

American Jews have felt especially attracted to Lincoln as the emancipator of the black slave, as a victim of violence, as a dreamer of peace, and as the spokesman of a way of life "with malice towards none, with charity for all," which matches the idealism of the prophets.

BIBLIOGRAPHY: B.W. Korn, *American Jewry and the Civil War* (1951); I. Markens, in: AJHSP, 17 (1909), 109–65; E. Hertz (ed.), *Abraham Lincoln, the Tribute of the Synagogue* (1927).

[Bertram Wallace Korn]

LINCOLN, TREBITSCH (1879–1943), adventurer and politician. The extraordinary career of Trebitsch Lincoln, born Ignacz Trebitsch in Budapest, the son of a Jewish merchant, has become well known through Bernard *Wasserstein's biography, *The Secret Life of Trebitsch Lincoln* (rev. ed. 1989). In his career, he worked as a Presbyterian, later Anglican conversionist minister to the Jews, and as an assistant to pioneering British social investigator Seebohm Rowntree. Then, remarkably, he was elected to the British Parliament as a Liberal from January to December 1910, immediately after changing his name to "Lincoln" and acquiring British citizenship. Defeated at the general election of December 1910, in quick succession he pursued a career as a failed company promoter in London and as a German spy during World War I, followed by a three-year stretch in a British prison for fraud. In 1920, even more remarkably, he served as press secretary to the right-wing militarist government of Wolfgang Kapp in Germany, where he met the then unknown Adolf *Hitler. From 1921 Lincoln lived in China, becoming a Buddhist priest under the name of Chao Kung. During World War II he worked for Japanese and, remarkably, German intelligence; it is believed, however, that he may have been murdered by the Gestapo in 1943. He wrote an *Autobiography of an Adventurer* in 1932. Some historians have seen his life as emblematic of the marginality of many Central European Jews of his time.

BIBLIOGRAPHY: ODNB online.

[William D. Rubinstein (2nd ed.)]

LINDAU, town in Bavaria, Germany. Jews are first mentioned in tax lists of 1242. The 13th-century town charter allowed Jews to trade in pledges on loans and the local Jewish *oath was short and humane. In 1344 the Jews offered to make loans at very advantageous terms (43⅓% interest instead of the 216⅔% demanded by Christians) if they were offered civic rights. Individual Jews were granted special civic status in 1385 and 1409. In 1348 *Charles IV granted the town the local Jewish tax; in that same year the community was destroyed during the *Black Death persecutions. However, they were again in residence by 1358. In 1430, 15 Jews, accused of the murder of a boy, were burned and the rest were expelled. In 1547 the city was granted the right to exclude the Jews, a privilege reaffirmed in 1559. Even during the 18th and early 19th centuries Jews were only allowed to stay for short periods on special permits. The group of Jews who settled in Lindau, seven in 1810, never numbered more than 30 and had fallen to only four in 1939. In 1967 two elderly Jews were still living in Lindau.

BIBLIOGRAPHY: Schweizer-Weitersheim, in: *Der Israelit* (Nov. 18, 1909), 2–5; Germ Jud, 1 (1963), 505; 2 (1968), 488–90; PK Bavaria.

LINDER, MAX (originally **Gabriel-Maximillien Leuvielle**; 1883–1925), French silent movie comedy star. Linder was born in Saint-Loubès to a family of vintners. His first film was *Première Sortie d'un Collegién* (1905); thereafter he turned out perhaps one film every week or so, to 1914. The character of the natty, slightly run-down, but highly-spirited Max achieved worldwide renown, inspiring Charlie Chaplin to develop a similar character early in his career. Linder fought in World

War I, permanently impairing his health and affecting his emotional stability. His last film was *Roi du Cirque* (1925). Few copies of his films have been saved.

LINDHEIM, IRMA LEVY (1886–1978), U.S. Zionist leader. She was born in New York City to a wealthy, assimilated family. She was educated in social work at Columbia University. During World War I she served as an ambulance driver, and in 1919 became president of the Seventh District of the Zionist Organization. She entered the Jewish Institute of Religion in 1922 and was accepted as a candidate for a rabbinical degree, while continuing her studies at Columbia under John Dewey. Irma Lindheim first visited Palestine in 1925 and incorporated her experiences into her book *Immortal Adventure* (1928). On her return to the U.S. she devoted herself to work with the Jewish National Fund. She became president of Hadassah (1926–28), and simultaneously was national vice president of the ZOA. Attracted by the Ḥalutz philosophy, Irma Lindheim joined the Labor Zionist group in 1930 and helped organize the League for Labor Palestine in 1932. In 1933 she decided to settle in Israel and moved to kibbutz Mishmar ha-Emek. She wrote many articles, and her autobiography, *Parallel Quest*, was published in 1962.

[Gladys Rosen]

LINDO, English family descended from ISAAC (LORENÇO RODRIGUES) LINDO (1638–1712), who was born in Badajoz. After being penanced in 1656 as a Judaizer by the Inquisition in the *Canary Islands, he settled about 1670 in London, where he became an elder of the synagogue and was a signatory of the **Ascamot* of 1694. He was one of the earliest "Jew Brokers" of the city (1697). His descendants continued in that capacity until the 19th century and the entire series of their brokers' medals is preserved. Other members of the family included MOSES (1712–1774) who immigrated in 1756 to South Carolina and became inspector general and surveyor of indigo, drugs, and dyes. He experimented scientifically with dyes and was responsible for some ambitious projects. ABRAHAM ALEXANDER, formerly of Jamaica, wrote pamphlets on the affairs of the island, and, in England, against the Reform movement. He delivered an address in the Sephardi Synagogue on the death of William IV in 1837. DAVID ABARBANEL (1772–1852), an active English communal worker, was at one time president of the elders of the Sephardi community. He was connected by marriage to the Disraeli family, and was the *mohel* of Benjamin *Disraeli. His daughter ABIGAIL (1803–1848) wrote *Hebrew and English and English and Hebrew Vocabulary, also Hebrew and English Dialogues* (1837; other eds. 1842, 1846) which displayed considerable learning as well as awareness of the potentialities of Hebrew as a spoken language. ELIAS ḤAYYIM (1783–1865) settled in London after a mercantile career in St. Thomas (West Indies) where he was president of the Jewish community. He published an English translation of *Manasseh Ben Israel's *Conciliador* (1842), *A History of the Jews of Spain and Portugal* (1848), and a *Jewish Calendar for Sixty-four Years* (1838) containing much historical information. Some of his unpublished translations of Jewish classics are in the library of Jews' College, London. The Lindos were closely related to many other Sephardi "cousinhood" families of note in Britain, including the *Mocattas and the *Montefiores.

BIBLIOGRAPHY: Roth, Mag Bibl, index; A.M. Hyamson, *Sephardim of England* (1951), index; B.A. Elzas, *Jews of South Carolina* (1903), 47–67; L. Wolf, *Jews in the Canary Islands* (1926), index; Abrahams, in: JHSEM, 3 (1937), 80–94; J.A.P.M. Andrade, *Record of the Jews in Jamaica* (1941), passim; C. Reznikoff and U.Z. Engelman, *Jews of Charleston* (1950), 23–34; C. Rabin, in *Leshonenu la-Am*, 137 (1963). **ADD. BIBLIOGRAPHY:** ODNB online; Katz, England, 375–76; J. Ranston, *The Lindo Legacy* (2000).

[Cecil Roth]

LINETZKY, ISAAC JOEL (1839–1915), Yiddish and Hebrew novelist, essayist, and translator. He was born into a ḥasidic family in Podolia, Ukraine, but in his youth rebelled against this milieu and became a spokesman of the Haskalah. Linetzky published his first Hebrew article in the journal *Ha-Meliẓ* in 1865 and his first Yiddish article in its Yiddish supplement, *Kol Mevaser*, in 1867. In the same weekly he published his novel *Dos Poylishe Yingl* ("The Polish Boy," 1869), criticizing Jewish life and satirizing Ḥasidim. His language was coarse, colorful, and grotesque. The novel appeared in 30 editions – the last in Kiev in 1939. A sequel appeared in 1888 in Shalom Aleichem's almanac, *Di Yidishe Folksbibliotek*, under the title *Der Vorem in Khreyn* ("The Worm in the Horseradish") and in book form as *Nit Toyt, nit Lebedik, oder dem Poylishn Yingls a Zun* ("Neither Dead nor Alive, or the Polish Boy's Son," 1898). Linetzky also published various collections under the title *Linetskis Ksovim* ("Linetzky's Writings," 1876), as well as pamphlets and brochures. Among these are *Der Beyzer Marshelik* ("The Angry Jester," satirical poems, 1879); *Amerika tsi Erets Yisroel* ("America or the Land of Israel," 1888); and *Di Kurtse Geografye fun Palestine* ("The Short Geography of Palestine," 1888). In the collections *Linetskis Ksovim* he formulated his positive approach to Yiddish, regarding the language not only as a vehicle for enlightenment, but as a medium of literary expression. Linetzky translated into Yiddish part of Heinrich Graetz's history of the Jews (1883–89), Lessing's *Nathan der Weise* (1884), and J.L. Gordon's *Koẓo shel Yod*. Though Linetzky's vogue faded with the rapid development of Yiddish literature and the emergence of great writers of the classical period, his major novel, *Dos Poylishe Yingl*, retains an enduring place in Yiddish literature.

BIBLIOGRAPHY: Rejzen, Leksikon, 2 (1927), 165–74; LNYL, 5 (1963), 163–8; S. Niger, *Dertseylers un Romanistn* (1946), 77ff.; R. Granovsky, *Linetzky un Zayn Dor* (1941); S. Liptzin, *Flowering of Yiddish Literature* (1963), 77–8. **ADD. BIBLIOGRAPHY:** D. Miron, *A Traveler Disguised* (1973).

[Elias Schulman]

LINGLE, LINDA (1953–), governor of Hawaii. Born Linda Cutter in St. Louis, Missouri, she moved with her family to southern California at the age of 12, attending public school in Van Nuys. She graduated from California State University at Northridge in 1975 and then relocated to Hawaii to join her father. In Honolulu, Lingle worked as public information officer for the Hawaii Teamsters and Hotel Workers Union. After moving to Moloka'i, she founded the *Moloka'i Free Press*, a community newspaper serving the island's 6,000 residents.

In 1980 Lingle began her political career with election to the Maui County Council, where she served two five-year terms, first as a representative of Moloka'i, then as a member-at-large. In 1990 she was elected mayor of Maui County. At 37, she was the youngest person to be elected mayor there; she was also the first woman and the only non-Maui-born person to have held the office. She served two terms as mayor, focusing on the growth of the tourism industry and the development of new jobs.

Lingle ran for governor of Hawaii in 1998, losing by less than one percent of the vote. She was nevertheless elected chair of the Republican Party in Hawaii; during her tenure the Republican Party gained seats in both houses of Hawaii's state legislature. In 2002 Lingle was again nominated as the Republican candidate for governor, running on a platform of "new beginnings" that emphasized reform. She was elected as Hawaii's first woman governor. With former Vermont governor Madeleine Kunin, she is one of only two Jewish women governors in U.S. history.

As governor, Lingle worked to promote tourism and economic growth and to balance the state budget. She cited increased access to health care as a priority, as well as the reduction of crime and substance abuse. Considered a rising star in the Republican Party, Lingle served as temporary convention chair for the 2004 Republican National Convention, fulfilling the role of permanent convention chair Dennis Hastert, Speaker of the House of Representatives, when Hastert was not on the dais.

In 2004 Lingle signed a Memorandum of Understanding between the state of Hawaii and the government of Israel, intended to promote cooperation for research and development in the fields of agriculture and aquaculture. She has continually claimed that her Jewish identity has given her a greater sensitivity to the diversity of religious and ethnic backgrounds of her constituents.

[Dorothy Bauhoff (2nd ed.)]

LINGUISTIC LITERATURE, HEBREW. This article is arranged according to the following outline:

INTRODUCTION

Foreword

The literature of linguistics arose against a background of both the literature of the *masorah and the exegetical literature of the Bible which is incorporated in the Talmuds and in the Midrashim. Breaking away from them, it came to constitute an independent branch of literature, with its own delimitations of subject matter, its own system, and phraseology.

The Beginning of Linguistic Literature

It is generally assumed that its formation was completed by the beginning of the tenth century C.E. at the latest. It is also commonly held that the works of *Saadiah Gaon – *Agron* (*Egron*), the first edition of which was written in 902, and *Kutub al-Lugha* – are the first two books of linguistics proper – the former dealing with lexicography and the latter with grammar.

The authors of the 12th century such as Abraham *Ibn Ezra (see for example the list of the "scholars of the language" in the introduction to his *Moznayim*), considered Saadiah Gaon to be the first grammarian; so too scholars of the 19th (such as Bacher) and 20th centuries (Skoss). The creation of this branch in Jewish literature was assisted at the beginning of the tenth century by a number of factors. First, the shaping of the form of the biblical text with regard to its letters, vocalization, cantillation, and masorah had been completed by the school of *Ben-Asher in Tiberias. From among the different vocalization systems which the Jews established in the third quarter of the first millennium C.E., the Tiberian system had already spread in the Diaspora and become established as the authoritative vocalization of the biblical text. This vocalized, cantillation-marked, masorah-bound text would serve the grammarian as a faithful source for the Hebrew language and he would describe the rules according to it. Secondly, at the beginning of the tenth century the cultural centers of the Jews were within the realm of influence of Arab culture and the contact between the two cultures was already quite close. Hence the intellectuals among the Jews already knew the linguistic teachings of the Arabs, which had developed as early as the eighth century. The Jewish grammarian was accordingly destined to describe the Hebrew language with the concepts and tools of that linguistic theory. Thirdly, it is possible that the emergence of *Karaism – for which the Bible was the sole source of Judaism and which therefore needed to carefully scrutinize the meanings of the words in it – stirred even the Rabbanite Jews to examine the Bible anew in a way which differed both from the masoretic literature and from the talmudic-midrashic literature.

Linguistic Literature and Its Background

It is rather astonishing that the initial emergence of the linguistic literature of the Jews had to be so late in time. There is, however, general agreement that in Semitic this kind of metalinguistic discourse could not have begun before the invention of the vowel points. As far as Hebrew is concerned this means that linguistic literature could not have begun until after the third quarter of the first millennium C.E. However, already in the literature of the talmudic period there are statements (and expressions) which were later adopted by grammarians in their treatises. Bacher (1895, 20–23) cites such statements from *Sefer Yeẓirah*, Berliner (1879), and others before him, e.g., Stern, *Mavo le-Korot ha-Lashon*, printed together with *Teshuvot Talmidei Menaḥem*, etc., 1870, o–x), Gross (on Menaḥem, 1872) and after him *Skoss (JQR, 1932/3, 1–12), gathered from talmudic and early midrashic literature expressions which seem to us grammatical statements. But these statements are outside the realm of linguistic literature, and as Goldziher (ZDMG, 1880, 375–384) already warned, care has to be taken not to attribute linguistic aims to statements whose aims were midrashic or mystic. As for the inventors of the *nikkudim*, it goes without saying that the act of providing the biblical text with vowel points itself presupposes a well-established phonological theory. But the generations which in the seventh and eighth centuries participated in this work did not leave us any explicit statement of their theory, as they were wholly concerned with its realization in providing the Bible text with vowel points, cantillation signs, and some other diacritical devices. Throughout the late eighth and ninth centuries, though, Jews produced a vast literature about the masorah. But this literature too stands outside the field of linguistics. Indeed, an essential difference separates the masoretic literature from the linguistic with regard to their respective aims, subjects, methods of investigation, and the phrasing of their discussions. The literature about the masorah always deals with the actual Bible text, i.e., with the written form and its actualization in reading. Its exclusive aim is to set (or preserve) a norm with regard to both the orthography of the Bible and its recitation. Its main activity is to enumerate certain types of actual occurrences (for example, homographs), to register them in classified lists, to provide them with mnemotechnical titles and to formulate rules concerning the occurrence of cantillation signs, vowels and letters. Abstractions used in these rules are the names of the types of cantillation signs, vowel signs, and letters, i.e., abstractions on the basis of the orthographic form. The masorah is an anonymous literary creation produced by many generations. Its statements are generally phrased in Aramaic (the mnemotechnical statements, for example) or in rhymed Hebrew prose (see *Masorah). Linguistic literature, on the other hand, is an investigation of the Hebrew language, of which the biblical text is a survival. Its aim is not to fix (or preserve) a norm for the orthography of the text or its recitation, but to describe the rules of the language, of which the text is a partial actualization. It does not enumerate the occurrences in the text, but imposes upon the Bible a grid (or system) of abstract linguistic units, classified and graded, and illustrates the operative abstractions by actual occurrences in the text. It then draws analogies from occurrences in the Bible to words which do not occur in it, whether found in the language or potential in it. It even makes assumptions, states principles, and comes to conclusions which are applicable to all languages including Hebrew, or specifically to Hebrew. During the ninth century there probably existed a vast literature which while *masoretic substantively* is already *grammatical adjectively*. Some remnants of this literature are known, especially through the efforts of scholars such as Allony. This type of literature did not disappear at the beginning of the tenth century but continued to exist, though not as prominently. To this type of masoretic (-grammatical) literature belongs also *Dikdukei ha-Te'amim* by Aaron Ben Asher (ed. Dotan, 1967), written about the same time as *Kutub al-Lugha* by Saadiah Gaon; but the two works are on the opposite sides of the border which separates masorah literature from linguistic literature. *Dikdukei ha-Te'amim* deals with cantillation signs, the vocalization of certain occurrences, and the ways of noting the *šewa'*. It contains sections taken from the literature written about the masorah which the author then endorses. Some hold that this compilation is a "new creation" (Dothan), while others believe that it was purposely done "uncritically" (Kurt Lewy). Everyone admits that it represents the end of the literature which aspired to fix a norm for the text. In *Kutub al-Lugha*, Saadiah Gaon opens his discussion with general suppositions (*muqaddamāt, maʿārif, qawāʾid*), some of which are universal in his opinion, while others are specific to Hebrew. On the basis of these suppositions he formulates rules of language (*qawānīn*). He does not count the occurrences but classifies and grades his abstractions and calculates their number. He does not even need the actual occurrences of the text, except as concrete illustrations of his abstractions. He even considers what is possible in the language and what is not (such as the precluded combinations of sounds). Aaron Ben Asher wrote in Hebrew in rhymed prose, while Saadiah, under the influence of Arabic linguistics, even borrowed its form of presentation. Thus Saadiah Gaon crossed the border which divides Masorah literature from linguistic literature. While Ben Asher, the last of the masoretes, was also among those who brought the literature about the Masorah to its zenith, Saadiah Gaon was the first grammarian among the Jews.

THE DEVELOPMENT OF LINGUISTIC LITERATURE

Foreword: A Well-Defined Unit

Until the beginning of the 16th century the authors of linguistic literature were almost exclusively Jewish. (Members of other religions, such as the Christians, who did produce works about Hebrew linguistics at the beginning of the 16th century did so only on the basis of the work of earlier or contemporary Jewish authors.) This literature, excepting the work of Samaritan grammarians, had two joint bases: the Masoretic Text of the Bible and the Arabic approach to grammar. Notwithstanding the differences of approach and opinion among the authors, it may be assumed that this literature consolidated into one linguistic school; and it is still the only one which the Jews have established in the investigation of the Hebrew language. Founded though it is on the two bases, it is worthwhile to consider this literature, whose course of development spans six centuries, as one well-defined and well-delimited unit in the history of the literature which deals with the scientific study of the Hebrew language.

The Four Periods

THE CRITERIA OF DIVISION. This unit can be divided into two parts, the border separating them being the middle of the 12th century, and two periods can be distinguished in each of the parts:

I. The time of the first attempts, which extends from the beginning of linguistic literature until the end of the tenth century.

II. The creative period, which reaches the middle of the 12th century;

III. The period of dissemination, ending in the first half of the 13th century;

IV. The period of the "standstill," which extends to the first half of the 16th century.

The first period is separated from the second by the publication of the works of Judah Ḥayyūj. An historical event separates the second from the third period: the tribulations of 1148 in Spain, followed by the migration of the Spanish scholars to the Christian lands. The third period is separated from the fourth by the appearance of the *Mikhlol* of David *Kimḥi. The fourth period ends with the first attempts of the Christian authors to write grammars for the Hebrew language – Johann *Reuchlin (1506), Sebastian *Muenster (1542) – in order to spread the knowledge of Hebrew among the Christians, and with *Mikneh Avram* (1523), the first systematic methodical attempt to apply Latin linguistics to the Hebrew language. A short survey of each period follows:

PERIOD I: THE FIRST ATTEMPTS. Throughout the tenth century C.E. works dealing with language were written (all in Arabic) in the East and in North Africa. In the second half of the century works were produced in Spain as well, but in Hebrew. It is in this period that the first attempts were made at exposition on the Hebrew language: the *Agron* of Saadiah Gaon is the first attempt at establishing a prototype of a dictionary for Hebrew, while *Kutub al-Lugha* is the first grammar of biblical Hebrew. In the second quarter of the century Judah *Ibn Quraysh wrote his *Risāla*, the first attempt at systematic comparison of biblical words, to Aramaic words, to Hebrew words from the Mishnah and Talmud, and to Arabic words. In *Kitāb al-Sabʿīn Lafẓa al-Mufrada* Saadiah Gaon had already tried to explain *hapax legomena* of the Bible according to their use in rabbinic literature. At about the same time *Dunash ibn Tamim also dealt with the close connection between Hebrew and Arabic in the area of vocabulary. Toward the middle of the century David b. Abraham *Alfāsi wrote the first comprehensive dictionary for Hebrew and biblical Aramaic, known in Arabic as *Jāmiʾ al-Alfāẓ*, and in Hebrew as *al-Agron*. In the third quarter of the century *Menaḥem ibn Saruq wrote his *Maḥberet*, the first comprehensive dictionary for biblical Hebrew and Aramaic to be written in Hebrew, and also the first linguistic work written in Spain. Controversy over the *Maḥberet* was then carried on in Hebrew until the end of the period and involved *Dunash b. Labrat, who wrote 180 criticisms of Menaḥem, the students of Menaḥem who replied to some of those criticisms, and a student of Dunash who in turn answered some of those objections. It is assumed that about the same time the "criticism" against Saadiah Gaon was written, allegedly by the same Dunash b. Labrat. However, neither the identity of the author of these "criticisms" nor the question of the language in which they were written has been clarified (see, however, Del Valle Rodriguez and others, section 6 below). Works of authors who wrote in Arabic (Saadiah Gaon, Ibn Quraysh, Ibn Tamim, Alfāsi) were widespread in the 11th century. Grammarians used them and quoted them whether they agreed with them or not, and in the East they served as a model for authors in the first half of the 11th century (*Abū al-Faraj, *Hai Gaon). However, in the middle of the 12th century, with the shift of the centers of Judaism from the Arab realm to the Christian lands, these works, not having been translated into Hebrew, were slowly forgotten in the Christian West, being remembered only from secondary sources, until ultimately they were completely lost. The surviving remnants were discovered only recently. The works written in Hebrew, however, understandably fared better. The *Maḥberet* of Menaḥem, for example, was found in many copies among the Jews of Italy and (northern) Franco-German Jewry and its influence continued until the end of the 12th century.

PERIOD II: THE CREATIVE PERIOD. In this period most of the works were written in Spain, and all in Arabic. The description of biblical Hebrew was completed in these works, in the areas of both grammar and the lexicon. About the year 1000 Ḥayyūj wrote his two works on the Hebrew verb – *Kitāb al-Af ʿāl Dhawāt Ḥurūf al-Līn* and *Kitāb al-Af ʿāl Dhawāt al-Mithlayn*; and thus a new period in the history of Hebrew linguistic literature was begun. In these works he applies the principle of the tri-radical root which had already been used in Arabic language theory since the eighth century. The first third of the century saw the controversy over these works of Ḥayyūj: by the second decade of the century Jonah *Ibn Janāḥ had written his *Kitāb al-Mustalḥaq*, in which he completed that which Ḥayyūj had "overlooked" and in a few instances even rejected the analysis of Ḥayyūj, suggesting his own solutions. *Samuel ha-Nagid wrote *Rasāʾil al-Rifāq*, in which he objected to some of the comments made by Jonah ibn Janāḥ in his *Kitāb al-Mustalḥaq*. At that, Jonah ibn Janāḥ replied to the *Rasāʾil al-Rifāq* in *Kitāb al-Tashwīr* and Samuel ha-Nagid replied in turn in his *Kitāb al-Ḥujja*. Jonah ibn Janāḥ replied in *Kitāb al-Taswiʾa* to other objections – reports of which had reached him in Saragossa – that the Nagid and his associates had voiced against *Kitāb al-Mustalḥaq*. A work entitled *Kitāb al-Istīfāʾ* was written in Saragossa, adding criticism of the works of Ḥayyūj which Ibn Janāḥ had not dealt with in *Kitāb al-Mustalḥaq*. Ibn Janāḥ replied to this work in *Risālat al-Tanbīh*. *Risālat al-Taqrīb wa al-Tashīl* is another work of Ibn Janāḥ, which explained difficult passages in the introductions of Ḥayyūj to his works. Even in the second half of the 13th century a late-developing echo of the dispute surrounding the works of Ḥayyūj was heard – in Meir b. David's *Hassagat ha-Hassagah*, in which he defends Ḥayyūj against the criticism of Ibn Janāḥ in *Kitāb al-Mustalḥaq*. It is reasonable to assume that this literature of "objections" and "replies" is the written expression of the many penetrating discussions which took place orally among intellectuals in Spain during the first half of the 11th century. In these disputes investigation of language was ever increasing in depth and refinement, and linguistic science became more and more consolidated. The study of the language never attained such fine and sharp distinctions as those in the controversy which developed around the works of Ḥayyūj in the generation of Ibn Janāḥ and Samuel ha-Nagid. In this controversy such fine issues were discussed as: the passive of *qal* in biblical Hebrew, the use of the term *infʿĪal* to indicate the transitive *nif ʿal* forms, and the use of the term *maṣdar* to denote the forms *qatol, qetol*, in Hebrew. In the 1040s, far from the noise of the dispute, Ibn Janāḥ and Samuel ha-Nagid settled down to summarize their teachings. Samuel wrote *Kitāb al-Istighnāʾ*, a dictionary of biblical Hebrew, which in many ways (such as its scope, arrangement of entries, wealth of references, and the precise mention of earlier authors) is perhaps the zenith of lexicography of the Hebrew language. It was lost, however, and only a few small remnants have survived. Ibn Janāḥ set down with the wisdom of age a complete description of biblical Hebrew in his work *Kitāb al-Tanqīḥ*, which consists of two parts: *Kitāb al-Lumaʿ* (grammar) and *Kitāb al-Uṣūl* (a dictionary). This two-part work, with the writings of Ḥayyūj and the shorter works of Ibn Janāḥ mentioned above, form the first complete description of biblical Hebrew, and no similar work – comparable in scope, depth, and precision – was written until modern times. This description constitutes the high point of linguistic thought in all the literature under discussion. In the second half of the 11th century certain Bible commentaries used the grammatical analyses and the dictionary definitions found in the works of Ḥayyūj, Ibn Janāḥ, and Samuel ha-Nagid. A series of monographs on defined linguistic issues was also written, in which their authors tried to go more profoundly into the teachings of their predecessors. Isaac *Ibn Yashush wrote *Kitāb al-Taṣārīf*, apparently on the subject of inflection, in the middle of the century, but it has been lost. In the third quarter of the century Moses b. Samuel *Gikatilla wrote *Kitāb al-Tadhkīr wa al-Taʾnīth*, a monograph concerning grammatical gender based on the statements of Ibn Janāḥ in *Kitāb al-Lumaʿ*, chapter 37 (38), and on various entries in *Kitāb al-Uṣūl*. At the end of the third quarter of the century Judah *Ibn Balʿam tried to give an exhaustive description of the particles of Hebrew in his *Kitāb Ḥurūf al-Maʿānī*; this subject had already intrigued Abū al-Faraj at the beginning of the century and Ibn Janāḥ in *Kitāb al-Uṣūl*. He also dealt with two topics which had not as yet been described systematically: denominative verbs in his *Kitāb al-Af ʿāl al-Mushtaqqa min al-Asmāʾ*, and homonyms in his *Kitāb al-Tajnīs*. In the last quarter of the century Isaac *Ibn Barūn wrote *Kitāb al-Muwāzana bayn al-Lugha al-ʿIbrāniyya wa al-Lugha al-ʿArabiyya* ("The Book of Comparison between the Hebrew and the Arabic Languages"); it is the most complete in-depth study of the relationship between Hebrew and Arabic until that time. In contrast to Ibn Quraysh, Ibn Tamim, Dunash b. Labrat and others who dealt with the comparison between Hebrew and Arabic in relation to vocabulary, Ibn Barūn also deals with grammar in the introduction to this work. It seems that introductions to linguistics were also written, such as *Sefer ha-Mafteʾaḥ* (?) of Levi *Ibn Altabban, composed in the third quarter of the century, and perhaps adaptations were made, such as *al-Kāmil* (?) of *Jacob b. Eleazar. Commentaries and criticism were written too, such as "pseudo-Ibn Yashush," which was probably an explanation of statements of Samuel ha-Nagid. There were also works written of which we have only heard and whose very names are unknown, such as the writing of *David ha-Dayyan ibn Hajjar, which apparently concerned the vowels. In the second quarter of the 12th century Moses *Ibn Ezra wrote in Arabic his *Kitāb al-Muḥāḍara wa al-Mudhākara*, the first Hebrew poetics. The authors of this period are the great creators of Hebrew linguistics. It is they who determined its scope, consolidated its system, and formulated its rules. It is they who fixed its terminology and phraseology: in part Aramaic-Hebrew, being drawn from the Masorah literature, and in part Arabic, being borrowed from Arabic linguistic literature.

PERIOD III: THE PERIOD OF DISSEMINATION. The tribulations of 1148 caused a sudden cessation of original contributions in Hebrew linguistics. The Jewish intellectuals of Spain who were exiled to Italy and to southern France brought with them the works which had been written in Spain and began to spread their contents among intellectuals in their new lands. The dissemination was accomplished in two ways: Hebrew adaptations and Hebrew translations. The Spanish exiles began to compose works in Hebrew which are nothing more than summaries of the ideas of Ḥayyūj, Ibn Janāḥ, Samuel ha-Nagid and other authors who had taught them. These adaptations include the grammatical works which Abraham ibn Ezra wrote during his wanderings in Italy and France between 1140 and 1160: *Moznayim* (Rome, 1140); a work defending Saadiah Gaon (title unknown); *Sefat Yeter (= Sefer Yesod Diqduq)* (Lucca, 1140–45); and *Ẓaḥot* (Mantua, 1145); *Sefer ha-Shem* and *Yesod Mispar* (both in Beziers before 1155), and *Safah Berurah* (apparently also in southern France). In 1161 Salomon ibn Parḥon wrote *Maḥberet he-Arukh* in Salerno, Italy, which is so faithful a representation of the works of Ḥayyūj and Ibn Janāḥ that it was once mistaken for a condensed translation of them. Joseph *Kimḥi wrote his *Sefer Zikkaron* in Narbonne. To conclude the survey of adaptations, the *Sefer ha-Makor* of Isaac ha-Levi may be mentioned. On the other hand, Spanish exiles began to translate into Hebrew the most important works that had been written in Spain. Moses ha-Kohen Gikatilla had already translated the two important works of Ḥayyūj by the third quarter of the 11th century, thus being the first to render grammatical works from Arabic into Hebrew. Abraham ibn Ezra translated the three works of Ḥayyūj again, apparently in Rome in 1140. Judah ibn *Tibbon completed his translation of *Kitāb al-Tanqīḥ* of Ibn Janāḥ in 1171 at Lunel, calling it *Sefer ha-Diqduq*: the first part of it, *Kitāb al-Lumaʿ*, under the title *Sefer ha-Riqmah*; and *Kitāb al-Uṣūl* under the name *Sefer ha-Shorashim*. From Judah ibn Tibbon we know of other attempts to translate *Kitāb al-Uṣūl*. At the end of the 12th century (or at any rate no later than the second quarter of the 13th century) Obadiah ha-Sefardi translated the *Kitāb al-Mustalḥaq* of Ibn Janāḥ, calling it *Sefer ha-Hassagah*. At Beziers in the mid-13th century, Solomon b. Joseph b. Job translated Ibn Janāḥ's *Kitāb al-Taswiʾa* ("The Book of Rebuke") under the incorrect title *Sefer ha-Hashvaʾah* ("The Book of Comparison"), and *Risālat al-Tanbīh*, which he called also *Sefer ha-Maʿaneh*. There is also an anonymous translation of the three monographs of Judah ibn Balʿam. Complete or almost complete copies of all these translations exist, except for those of Ben Job, of which only fragments are extant. In the last quarter of the 12th century Moses b. Joseph Kimḥi wrote *Mahalakh Shevilei ha-Daʿat*, for which he already used the works of Abraham ibn Ezra and even those of Joseph Kimḥi. David Kimḥi ended the work of adaption with his *Sefer Mikhlol*. This work is constructed in the same way as the *Kitāb al-Tanqīḥ* of Ibn Janāḥ. It also consists of two parts: grammar – *Mikhlol*, and lexicon – *Sefer ha-Shorashim*. For the content he drew upon the works of Ḥayyūj and Ibn Janāḥ, apparently in their Hebrew translations, and upon the works of adaptors who preceded him. In the *Mikhlol* the theoretical foundations, the methodological clarifications, the substantiations and explanations were reduced, and the mechanical, technical, paradigmatic side appended. The author gave prominence to the verb, devoting much space to it. This work of David Kimḥi, which did more than any other to spread the ideas of Ibn Janāḥ among the Hebrew-reading intellectuals, is the one which helped cause Ibn Janāḥ's own works to be forgotten. While the two parts of *Sefer Mikhlol* were printed many times (*Ḥeleq ha-ʾInyan [Sefer ha-Shorashim]* from 1480, and *Ḥeleq ha-Diqduq [Mikhlol]* from 1532–34), the works of Ibn Janāḥ himself were not published, even in their Hebrew translations, until the second half of the 19th century. At the end of the period under discussion Moses b. Isaac of London wrote *Sefer ha-Shoham*, the first linguistic work written by a Franco-German Jew upon the basis of the linguistic theory of the Spanish grammarians, as found in the writings of Abraham ibn Ezra, Parḥon, and Joseph Kimḥi, and in the translation of the works of Ḥayyūj and of *Kitāb al-Mustalḥaq*.

Although the works of adaptation and translation obviously made but a slight original contribution to linguistic thought, it would be difficult to exaggerate the importance of this literary activity. It was the translators and adaptors who saved Hebrew linguistics from oblivion and made it a permanent branch in the history of Jewish literature. They also translated into Hebrew the Arabic grammatical terms used in the works of Ḥayyūj and Ibn Janāḥ, and they fixed a mode of exposition for grammatical and lexicographical issues, that has existed until today in the study and teaching of the Hebrew language and in Hebrew biblical exegesis.

PERIOD IV: THE "STANDSTILL." During this period the West produced as much literature as during period III, yet from the aspect of quality there was almost a complete lack of progress. This period in the West bears the stamp of the almost exclusive influence of the works of period III, primarily that of the *Mikhlol* of David Kimḥi. Since the works of period II, which were written in Arabic, were forgotten, the *Mikhlol* became the authoritative formulation of Hebrew linguistics, the authoritative source for grammarians and lexicographers. The unshakable prestige of the *Mikhlol* was further strengthened by the widespread distribution of the Bible commentary of David Kimḥi. Some of the authors of period IV copy the statements of David Kimḥi in the most minute detail, while others take over most of his theories, though critically. No matter what, they were always dependent on his work. Most of the books of this period are partial adaptations of their sources and are of a practical nature, such as introductions to the study of Hebrew, and textbooks or learning aids to vocalizers of the biblical text. Despite the standstill of this period, however, sporadic attempts were made at widening the scope of linguistic literature. A chapter on the rules of poetic meter was regularly included in grammars and even complete works on poetics and rhetoric were written. A few dictionaries were written for types of post-biblical Hebrew, such as *al-Murshid al-Kāfī* by Tanḥum Yerushalmi, which was a dictionary of the *Mishneh Torah* of Maimonides, and *Tishbi* by Elijah (Baḥur) *Levita, which is a partial dictionary of talmudic and post-talmudic Hebrew. Elijah Levita also wrote a dictionary for the Aramaic of the Targumim of the Bible, entitled *Meturgeman*. The first dictionaries of synonyms were also written: *Ḥotam Tokhnit* of Abraham *Bedersi (second half of the 13th century) and *Ohel Mo'ed* of Solomon b. Abraham of Urbino (1480). In the second quarter of the 15th century Isaac b. Kalonymus wrote *Me'ir Nativ* (or *Ya'ir Nativ*) in Provence – the first concordance of biblical Hebrew. At the beginning of the 15th century Jehiel of Italy wrote *Makre Dardekei*, a Hebrew-Italian-Arabic dictionary, the first of its type. In the manner of Rashi, Abraham ibn Ezra, the Kimḥis, and others, several authors began to cite foreign loanwords from the vernaculars of the Jews and the languages of the Christian environment, in dictionaries, grammars, and commentaries. A small number of works written during this period are concerned with theoretical issues. First, the demand for basing linguistics upon logic began to make itself felt. In a way this was a rebellion against the mechanical nature of the *Mikhlol* and a return to the theoretical nature of *Kitāb al-Luma*ʿ. This tendency is already felt in the surviving portions of the work of Nethanel (b. al-Fayyūmī) of Yemen, of the 12th (?) century. It is prominent in *Ratukot Kesef* of Joseph ibn *Kaspi, who lived in Provence in the first third of the 14th century. It is most outstanding in *Ma'aseh Efod* of Profiat *Duran (1403), which also contains criticism of the *Mikhlol*. Theoretically there is a dialectical return in this work to Ibn Janāḥ, and this is one of the two most important contributions of this period to linguistics. Secondly, contact with Latin linguistics increased, i.e., as it was represented by such scholars as Donatus. Joseph Kimḥi was already influenced by this contact at the time when he mentioned the *grammatica* of Latin together with the *naḥw* (grammar) of Arabic. This influence is especially noticeable at the very end of the period. In 1523 Abraham de *Balmes in his *Mikneh Avram* tries to apply the ideas of Latin grammar to the description of the Hebrew language. Thus he devotes a chapter, the seventh, entitled *Harkavah* ("composition"), to the syntax of the Hebrew word. This work, together with *Ma'aseh Efod* of Profiat Duran, constitutes the most important contribution of the period, and actually begins a new chapter in the history of this literature. In 1506 Johann Reuchlin published *Rudimenta Linguae Hebraicae*. Based on David Kimḥi, it is the first Christian work for the instruction of Hebrew to Christians. In Basle in 1541, Sebastian Muenster wrote *Melekhet ha-Dikduk ha-Shalem*, which is based on the work of Elijah Levita. Thus it was that research into the Hebrew language ceased being exclusively Jewish and became part of European culture; with this too a new period in the history of Hebrew linguistic literature began.

The Motivating Factors for Writing on Linguistics

Around the end of the first millennium C.E. writing about linguistic issues was a new phenomenon in Jewish literature, considered by many important people as a vain, senseless activity. Therefore, in their introductions, the authors discuss the motivating factors which stimulated them to write their linguistic works. They seek to prove to their readers that it is incumbent upon Jews to take up the investigation of their language and their arguments include the following points: (1) language is the means for all discernment and linguistics is the means for all investigation and wisdom; (2) the fulfillment of the commandments depends upon the understanding of the written word, and in turn, the proper knowledge of the language is impossible without the aid of linguistics; (3) the Hebrew language is the most ancient tongue and the most perfect. When it was a living language it was incomparably rich and extensive, and had the Jews not been exiled from their land knowledge of it would now be complete. However, because of the exile it was forgotten for the most part and only a small part of it remained – i.e., the part contained in the 24 books of the Bible and another small segment contained in rabbinic literature. The Jews face the danger that their knowledge of their language will continue to be defective, or even forgotten altogether, because of their wanderings and the distance in time from the years when Hebrew was a living language. They are therefore obliged to preserve their cognition of the language in every way. In order to safeguard this knowledge the authors undertook to write their works. Consequently they had a twofold purpose. On the one hand they wanted to increase the knowledge of the language and thereby aid the understanding of the written word, and on the other hand they wanted to provide Hebrew writers with a suitable literary tool, and to prevent them from deviating from the rules of the exemplary language of the Bible. These two aims are already expressed by Saadiah Gaon, reappearing in a new guise in the authors who follow him. The actual motivation for producing a particular work, though, was sometimes polemical. The controversy which raged between Saadiah and the Karaites motivated him to write *al-Sab'īn Lafẓa al-Mufrada*. Later the frequent debates with the Christians stimulated the Jews to establish linguistic aids for themselves. Isaac b. Kalonymus wrote the first concordance to the Bible in the middle of the 15th century as an aid in refuting the proofs which Christians cited from Scripture. It is possible that this was also one of the motivations behind the writing of a Hebrew–Italian–Arabic dictionary at the beginning of the 15th century in Southern Italy. Controversies existed even among the grammarians themselves. The history of linguistic literature contains a succession of "criticisms," "replies," and "replies" to the replies, a characteristic case being the above-mentioned exchange involving Menaḥem and Dunash. About two hundred years afterwards Jacob *Tam wrote *Hakhra'ot* ("Decisions"), intending to decide between the *Maḥberet* of Menaḥem and the "objections" of Dunash. Joseph Kimḥi criticized the "Decisions" of Jacob Tam in his *Sefer ha-Galui*, and Benjamin, a student of Jacob Tam, replied to the criticism of Joseph Kimḥi. There is another work also attributed to Dunash, criticizing the linguistic works of Saadiah Gaon, but as yet there has been no satisfactory identification of the author. Abraham ibn Ezra wrote *Sefer ha-Haganah* (Pseudo-*Sefat Yeter*) to defend Saadiah Gaon against the "criticism" mentioned above. Mention has already been made of the controversy which raged about the works of Ḥayyūj, between Ibn Janāḥ and his group and Samuel ha-Nagid and his group. In 1517 Elisha b. Abraham wrote *Magen David* in Constantinople, defending David Kimḥi against the 60 "objections" which Profiat Duran had raised against his work.

Description of the Language

BIBLICAL HEBREW. From the motivating factors for this writing, it is easy to imagine that they dealt mainly with the language of the Bible. This language is considered complete and ideal: There is harmony and balance in its structure; it has been measured in the scales of justice and law; its rules are logical and its expressions clear. It is free of error and contradiction; everything in it can be explained and substantiated. Yet these characteristics are not obvious from the actual text, rather being hidden in it, so that it is the main task of grammar to reveal them after detailed investigation. Such investigation thus becomes the main object of the grammarian. This self-imposed limitation to biblical Hebrew is already noticeable in the *Agron* of Saadiah Gaon, where about 80% of the words explained are from the Bible. It is likewise clear from the *Kutub al-Lugha*, in which he discusses nothing but the grammar of Bible. This attitude prevailed among the authors who followed him, and lasted for centuries.

THE STATUS OF POST-BIBLICAL HEBREW. All types of post-biblical Hebrew, including mishnaic Hebrew, were marked as inferior and degenerate, for the fate of the language supposedly resembled that of the people. During the entire period under discussion not even one grammar on mishnaic Hebrew was written, nor any one work which described biblical Hebrew and mishnaic Hebrew as one. Still, mishnaic Hebrew was granted a special status; since the sages lived and worked at a time closer to the prophets, it was assumed that details of language remained in the Mishnah which were not included in the Bible. Therefore they used the Mishnah for their works, especially for understanding difficult words, such as *hapax legomena*. This comparison, mostly lexical, was already begun by Saadiah Gaon in *al-Sabʿin Lafẓa al-Mufrada*. Ibn Quraysh followed him in his *Risāla*, and all the others continued it. Ibn Janāḥ in *Kitāb al-Lumaʿ* compares biblical Hebrew to mishnaic 28 times, and in *Kitāb al-Uṣūl* 307 times. Needless to say, it never occurred to these grammarians to describe the Hebrew used in post-mishnaic texts, such as *piyyutim*. They neither listed its forms nor explained its words. They did not even deal with the Hebrew used in the writings of the Spanish poets who were their contemporaries. Only infrequently did they cite a verse of poetry and then it was not because they were interested in a practical description of its language, but rather to criticize or invalidate it, or to endorse it in accordance with usage found (whether frequently or rarely) in the Bible, or according to the virtually possible use of biblical language. There were some who were very severe in these roundabout judgments (such as Moses ibn Ezra and Abraham ibn Ezra), and others who were lenient (Ibn Janāḥ). The dichotomy between biblical and post-biblical Hebrew was absolute in the grammars and dictionaries. However, in works of poetics, illustrative examples were cited from both biblical and post-biblical poetry. Saadiah Gaon in *Agron* likewise cites the *paytanim* of Palestine for illustration, and Moses ibn Ezra quotes the poets of Spain in *Kitāb al-Muḥāḍara wa-l-Mudhākara*. Because of this dichotomy, as time passed special dictionaries were compiled for post-biblical varieties of Hebrew: Rav Hai Gaon composed towards the end of the first millennium his *Kitāb al-Ḥāwi*, an anagrammatic dictionary covering the Bible and the entire post-biblical Hebrew and Aramaic literature up to his time. *Nathan b. Jehiel wrote *Arukh*, a dictionary covering the Talmuds and the Midrashim, at the beginning of the 12th century, while in the middle of the 13th century, Tanḥum Yerushalmi wrote *Al-Murshid al-Kāfi* (mentioned above), an extensive work in Arabic for the Hebrew of the *Mishneh Torah* of Maimonides, which of course includes most of the vocabulary of mishnaic Hebrew. In 1541 Elijah Levita wrote *Tishbi*, which is, as mentioned above, a partial dictionary for the Hebrew of the Talmud and post-talmudic literature. Also extant are 15th- and 16th-century Yemenite dictionaries for Maimonides' *Mishneh Torah*, based also on his commentary to the Mishnah.

Comparison with Aramaic and Arabic

COMPARISON AS A MEANS TO A BETTER UNDERSTANDING OF HEBREW. From the very beginning of linguistic literature the authors compared Hebrew to Aramaic and Arabic, as a means to their main goal, the clarification of biblical Hebrew. Their explanation for this was as follows: Hebrew is the oldest of languages; in Genesis 11:1 it is called "one language and one speech," being "the language which Adam laid down." The three languages were "one language" at their source, and even after they separated from one another, Hebrew remained the "principal one," the others being "derivative" languages. In any event, because of the common origin and because of the geographical closeness of their first users, there is a high degree of affinity between them from borrowing, as well as from source. Although Arabic continued in all its richness and to a large extent so did Aramaic, Hebrew was for the most part forgotten. Hebrew linguistics was therefore likely to be aided by these two languages in solving difficult problems in the investigation of biblical language, such as the explanation of certain place-names in the Bible, *hapax legomena*, and rare forms. The resultant comparative linguistic studies chiefly involved vocabulary, and sometimes grammar as well. A similar explanation is already found early in linguistic literature, as for example, in the *Risāla* of Ibn Quraysh.

COMPARISON WITH ARAMAIC. Everyone agreed on the necessity for the comparison to Aramaic, Alfāsi and Menaḥem even including biblical Aramaic in their dictionaries. At the beginning of the 11th century Abū al-Faraj devoted the eighth chapter of his *al-Mushtamil* to the grammatical comparison between Hebrew and biblical Aramaic, while Ibn Janāḥ compares Hebrew to Aramaic ten times in *Kitāb al-Luma*ʿ and 266 times in *Kitāb al-Uṣūl*. Moses b. Isaac (middle of the 13th century) added a lexicon of biblical Aramaic to the third part of his *Sefer ha-Shoham*, and in 1531 Elijah Levita wrote *Meturgeman*, a dictionary for the Aramaic in the Targumim of the Bible.

COMPARISON WITH ARABIC. Comparison with Arabic was also instituted at the start of linguistic literature. Whereas the authors of the tenth century – Dunash ibn Tamim, Alfāsi, and Dunash b. Labrat – dealt with comparison in the area of vocabulary, Ibn Quraysh also used it somewhat for grammar. However, Menaḥem and his disciples were opposed to such comparisons. Dunash b. Labrat felt compelled to compile a list of 167 Hebrew words "whose solution is their meaning in Arabic," in order to prove to him the necessity of comparison with Arabic, and to "accuse" Menaḥem of having himself followed the system of such comparison when he used in his definitions the term כמשמעו ("as its sound") which was understood by Dunash "as its meaning in Arabic." Yet this opposition continued, so that Ibn Janāḥ, who compares Hebrew to Arabic 56 times in *Kitāb al-Luma*ʿ and 254 times in *Kitāb al-Uṣūl*, was obliged (in the introduction to the former work) to explain the nature of the comparison between the two languages in an apologetic tone. However, despite the opposition, the comparison between the two languages, which reached its peak in Ibn Barūn's *Kitāb al-Muwāzana bayn al-Lugha al-ʿIbrāniyya wal-Lugha al-ʿArabiyya*, became an important methodological tool in Hebrew linguistics. The topic of linguistic comparisons has been thoroughly studied by Maman (2004; see section 12 under Authors and Their Works below).

General Works

There are two main types of works in linguistic literature: the grammar and the dictionary. This division was already developed by Saadiah Gaon: *Agron* is the first attempt known to us of a prototype of a dictionary, while *Kutub al-Lugha* is the first grammar of which we know. Yet the clear delimitation of the areas of grammar and lexicography was a slow process, which ended only in the 1040s with the *Kitāb al-Tanqīḥ* of Ibn Janāḥ. Prior to *Kitāb al-Tanqīḥ* general linguistic works were usually written without any differentiation of categories whatever. One work of this type is that of Abū al-Faraj, the greatest Karaite grammarian, written at the beginning of the 11th century in Jerusalem. The author gave it the interesting title: *Kitāb al-Mushtamil ʿalā al-Uṣūl wa al-Fuṣūl fī al-Lugha al-ʿIbrāniyya* ("The Comprehensive Book of the Roots and Branches, i.e., of the General and Particular Principles, of the Hebrew Language"). It is mentioned by Ibn Janāḥ, who was his junior, as well as by Ibn Balʿam, Moses ibn Ezra, and Abraham ibn Ezra. It is quite an extensive work, its largest manuscript covering 579 pages, and is divided as follows: Part I is on the ten principles (*uṣūl*) which can be applied to any word whose form needs to be established; Part II, with 18 chapters, deals with infinitives; Part III deals with the letters of the alphabet and their division into basic letters (*jawhariyya*) and servile letters (*khawādim*); Part IV deals with particles; Part V, containing 16 chapters, is a potpourri of grammatical issues (such as gender, number, relation (*nisba*), conjunctive pronouns, the transitive and intransitive verb, and so on), lexicological matters (such as synonyms and homonyms), and other points; Part VI deals with the conjugation of the verb *h-l-kh*; Part VII is a lexicographical section, in which verbs of at least three radicals are arranged according to the anagram system; and Part VIII is a comparison of Hebrew and biblical Aramaic. The first general dictionaries (the *Al-Agron* of Alfāsi and *Maḥberet* of Menaḥem) are to some degree also comprehensive linguistic works, discussing grammatical issues both in introductions (and with Alfāsi also in prefaces to the sections) and within the entries themselves in the form of digressions. Both in the "criticisms" of Dunash and the "replies" of the pupils, grammatical issues are raised along with lexicographical matters. In his introduction to his "criticism" Dunash set out concisely and by chapter titles, a programmatic plan for the benefit of authors of *maḥbarot*. Among the "replies" of the pupils of Menaḥem one finds the "long objection," the first (polemical) discussion of the rules of meter for the poetry of Spain. Hence it is in Jonah ibn Janāḥ's *Kitāb al-Tanqīḥ* that grammar and lexicography are first delimited. In *Kitāb al-Luma*ʿ (grammar) the author refers to his dictionary 33 times and in *Kitāb al-Uṣūl* (dictionary) he refers 146 times to his grammar, thus clearly dividing the two main fields of linguistics.

Lexicography

THE ARRANGEMENT OF THE DICTIONARIES. The division of the letters of the alphabet into base letters and supplemental letters, first found in the writings of Saadiah Gaon, is used by the early authors in the arrangement of their dictionaries. In the first part of *Agron*, the words are listed in the alphabetical order of their first two base letters, but those words which are written with *sin* in the Bible are listed there under *samekh*. Saadiah Gaon is also inconsistent when the second letter is *waw* or *yod*, and does not bother at all about the alphabetical order of the letters which follow the second letter. It is in his writings too that we first find the combination of incompatible consonants, listed in the *Agron* under such entries as נל, לד, סז, and treated as "non-existent"; in the second part of the *Agron* the words are arranged in alphabetical order according to their final letters. These two arrangements were supposed to serve the purpose for which the *Agron* was written; the first was to supply the *paytanim* with a list of words for acrostics, while the second was for rhymes. No other Hebrew dictionary is known in which the entries are arranged alphabetically according to the final letter; in others the conventional arrangement by the initial letter predominates. This is the way the words are listed in the *Risāla* of Ibn Quraysh, and in the first general dictionaries: *Al-Agron* of Alfāsi and *Maḥberet* of Menaḥem: with *Kitāb al-Uṣūl* of Ibn Janāḥ this order became the regular one for arranging dictionaries. There were a few attempts to arrange the entries in the order of an anagram, as in the seventh chapter of *al-Mushtamil* of Abū al-Faraj, which deals only with tri-radical roots and quadri-radical roots derived from them. There the dictionary entries are divided into groups. The following are found in the extant remnant of the letter *ʿayin*: עבר, ערף, עמר, עשר, עפל, עצב. There are six permutations theoretically possible for every entry of three radicals (321; 231: 312: 132; 213; 123). From the six possible roots only those actually found in the Bible are listed. Under עבר (321) all other possible permutations of the roots are listed, namely: ערב (231), בער (312), ברע (132), רבע (213), רעב (123). The roots found in other entries are cited in this arrangement. The entries with the roots in the section involving the letter *ʿayin* are displayed in the table Entries with Roots Involving the Letter *ʿayin*.

Entries with Roots Involving the Letter *ʿayin*

The Entry	The Roots in the Entry				
(321)	(231	312	132	213	123)
עבר	ערב	בער	ברע	רבע	רעב
ערף	עפר	רעף	—	פער	פרע
עמר	ערם	מער	—	רעם	—
עשׂר	ערשׂ	שׂער	שׂרע	—	—
עפל	עלף	פעל	—	לעף	—
עצב	עבץ	—	צבע	—	בצע

The *Kitāb al-Ḥāwī* of Hai Gaon is likewise arranged in this manner (see bibliography in section 13 under Authors and Their Works below). Most of the dictionaries, however, as mentioned above, were arranged alphabetically according to the initial letter. Even the *al-Agron* of Alfāsi and the *Maḥberet* of Menaḥem were already organized this way, though they are not consistent in detail. Each consists of an introduction and twenty-two sections, corresponding to the initial letters of the entries. In *al-Agron* each section – except the sixth, which deals with *waw* – is divided into chapters following the order of the second letter of the entry. Although in theory each section should be divided into 22 chapters, actually this occurs for only three letters: *nun, yod*, and *sin*; for example, (1) נא (2) נב... (22) נת. The other sections are incomplete because Alfāsi does not include incompatible combinations as chapters. Each chapter opens with a list of the names of the entries to be discussed, with illustrative Bible passages, followed by the actual entries. In Menaḥem's work each of the 22 sections (each called a *maḥberet*) is divided into entries, which are listed at the beginning. In the printed version the uniliteral (one-letter) words of each *maḥberet* are given, at the beginning, the other entries following in the alphabetical order of their second letters. Entries of more than two letters are alphabetized according to their third letters, and so on. It is not known, though, if the *Maḥberet* of Menaḥem was originally arranged in this way (cf. Kaufmann ZDMG (1886)). *Kitāb al-Uṣūl* is the first dictionary in which alphabetical order is followed in careful detail. It is also divided into twenty-two sections (*maqālāt* – "essays") according to the initial letters of the entries. The order of the entries within the *maqāla* is as follows: At the beginning of the *maqāla* the entries whose first two letters are identical are listed; e.g., the fourth "essay," on the letter *dalet*, begins with the entry of double *dalet*, i.e., דד (Prov. 5:19), then the entries follow in alphabetical order – דאג, דאב and so on. So, too, each time the second letter of the entry changes within the *maqāla*, for example: *bet* and *dalet* (בד), *bet* and double *dalet* (בדד), *bet, dalet*, and *alef* (בדא) and so on. In the introduction to *Kitāb al-Uṣūl* Ibn Janāḥ also informs us that if the first two letters are identical (such as ככר, יין), he did not consider the second letter; thus יין is not found after יטב, but between ימר and ינה. The works of Ḥayyūj include a lexicon of the weak verbs arranged according to the *gezarot* (conjugations). All the weak verbs are listed as tri-radicals and arranged alphabetically according to the three letters. Moses b. Isaac used the same method in *Sefer ha-Shoham*, which consists of three parts: the third part, called *alfa beta*, is a dictionary in which all the words are listed according to morphological categories. First come the verbs, classified according to conjugations: sound, prima *yod*, prima *nun*, the hidden medial *waw*, final *he*, assimilated initial and final radical, geminate, and quadri-radical verbs. Within each conjugation the verbs are arranged alphabetically. The last part is a dictionary of nouns, which are likewise arranged according to the various patterns, and listed alphabetically according to their roots. It was only in the second half of the 13th century that Abraham b. Isaac Bedersi wrote *Ḥotam Tokhnit*, the first dictionary of synonyms for biblical Hebrew, including 360 groups of synonyms arranged alphabetically according to the words of the entry. Each group contains verbs, nouns, and particles. Bedersi's lexical and exegetical sources are: Parḥon, Ibn Ezra, Ibn Janāḥ, Ḥayyūj, Dunash and Menaḥem. He also mentions the first part of the *Moreh Nevukhim* of Maimonides. In 1480, Solomon b. Abraham of Urbino wrote the second dictionary of synonyms, *Ohel Moʿed*, in which he merely enumerates the synonyms in each entry and adds biblical references, only rarely adding the definition.

THE DICTIONARY ENTRY. In the early dictionaries (e.g., by Alfāsi and Menaḥem) there are entries of one, two, three letters, and so on. This is based on a differentiation between base and supplemental letters. The former are those which remain in all occurrences of the form, in all declensions of the words and in all the derivatives of a particular group of words. There are 14 single-letter entries in the work of Alfāsi, and 20 in that of Menaḥem, who lists them early in the text of the *maḥbarot* as individual entries, whereas Alfāsi enumerates them briefly in the general introduction and deals with them in detail in the introductions to the sections. In the *Maḥberet* about 20% of the entries are of two letters, and 65% are of three letters. There are no major differences between him and Alfāsi on this issue. The internal arrangement of the entries is still neither uniform nor permanent, while both authors enumerate the meanings of the words included in each entry. Menaḥem divides a third of all the entries into secondary semantic groups ("sections" or "issues"); 64% of all the two-letter entries contain two or more "sections," while of all the three-letter entries only 30% have two or more "sections." The high percentage of two-letter entries with several "sections" is to be explained by Menaḥem's concept of the dictionary entry, for he included in those two-letter entries words that have weak consonants, which, according to Ḥayyūj and Ibn Janāḥ, would come under different entries. After Ḥayyūj, Spanish lexicographers no longer maintained single-letter entries. Under two-letter entries they listed only particles, pronouns, and bi-radical nouns from which no verbs are derived. Hence, as the number of two-letter entries declined sharply, the number of three-letter entries increased, becoming the largest section of the dictionary. This pattern was finally fixed in *Kitāb al-Uṣūl*. In the East, scholars continued to list uniradical entries and used a great many bi-radical entries in the many condensations made from the *al-Agron* of Alfāsi. In the Christian countries the *Maḥberet* of Menaḥem was the only pattern for compiling dictionaries until the third quarter of the 12th century. Thus Nathan b. Jehiel wrote *Arukh* at the start of the 12th century according to the pattern of the *Maḥberet*; and Menaḥem b. Solomon wrote his *Even Boḥan* (1143) in the same way. Even in the first half of the 13th century a dictionary was written in Germany according to this pattern by a certain Samson. There is a finished system for the internal arrangement of a dictionary entry in *Kitāb al-Istighnā*ʾ of Samuel ha-Nagid, as may be seen from the two complete entries that we have (אמן, אמץ). The entry consists of three parts: The first includes the various meanings of the root in a systematic order, accompanied by examples. The second part gives explanations drawn from the literature of earlier exegetes and grammarians, some of them quoted by name. The third part gives a detailed inventory (the entry אמץ borders on a concordance list) of the grammatical forms derived from the root under discussion, beginning with the verb forms and followed by the nominal forms. Ibn Janāḥ discusses the internal arrangement of entries at the end of his introduction to *Kitāb al-Uṣūl*. In general, at the start of an entry he lists the meaning which he considers the main one and then gives its derivative forms in which this meaning is found. He defines the citations grammatically with the aid of terms derived from the root פעל. For the verb he notes conjugation, tense, and so on, and for the noun its pattern, status, gender, and number. After listing the other meanings, he draws attention to the degree of relation between the various meanings of the entry, for which he uses fixed terms. Not intending to make an exhaustive list of the forms, he offers a small selection of illustrations which are to suffice for the explanation of the meanings of the root and for an understanding of the forms derived from it. He does not, however, discuss grammatical issues extensively, but instead refers the reader to *Kitāb al-Luma*ʿ and to his other works. He is very brief with weak roots since he does not intend to repeat the statements of Ḥayyūj or those statements already made in his *Kitāb al-Mustalḥaq*, but he does treat in detail sound roots, particles, nouns from which no verbs are derived, nouns of size and weight, plants and animals. Thus in the work of Ibn Janāḥ a balance is created within the entry between the semantic definition of the root and the grammatical definition of the forms derived from it.

Grammatical Works

KUTUB AL-LUGHA BY SAADIAH GAON. The first grammar extant, though not in its entirety, is *Kutub al-Lugha* of Saadiah Gaon. Six of its 12 parts, containing 63 pages, have been published, and the content of a further four is known. The first part, devoted to the letters, apparently discussed their division according to the organs of speech (laryngeals, palatals, linguals, dentals, and labials), their division into the radical and servile letters, and the precluded combinations of letters (דט, קג, זש, זט, etc.). The second part, *al-Tafkhīm wa al-Ikhtiṣār* ("Augmentation and Contraction") deals with two topics. It opens with pairs of words each of which virtually shares one meaning, and compares the two in each case – e.g., אֲקוֹמֵם (Isa. 44:26), which is an expansion of אָקִים (Amos 9:11). This expansion is of a special type, the augmented word having two adjacent occurrences of the same letter, instead of the single occurrence in the contrasting form. Also surveyed are pairs of words in which there are, respectively, one and two adjacent occurrences of the same combination of letters, such as סַלְסְלֶהָ (Prov. 4:8), in contrast to סֹלּוּ (Isa. 57:14). Here, too, one word is an augmented form of the other. The second subject treated in this section is contraction. As forms in which contraction does not occur he mentions nouns in which the initial letter is ת, נ, מ, י, ו, ה, א (such as תנובה, נדר, מעשה, ישיבה, ולד, הלוך, אחיזה), while the forms which do show contraction are those derived from these basic forms, but lacking the initial letters (such as: אחז (Judg. 20:6), לך, ילד, ישב, יעשה, תדר, ינובון). Other pairs of words are listed there, such as שֵׁרִית (1 Chron. 12:39) in which there is contraction as opposed to שְׁאֵרִית in which there is no contraction. The third part, *al-Taṣrīf* ("Inflection"), begins with a tripartite division of the parts of speech – noun, verb, particle – and with their definitions as accepted in Arabic grammar. Inflection for Saadiah Gaon is the faculty of a word: to occur with the servile letters; to occur with the ten possessors; and to have "tense" apply to it. He classifies the parts of speech according to their capacity for inflection as defined above, and calculates the number of forms which can theoretically be fixed at each level of classification and for each part of speech. For example, for the verb he calculated that there are 48 forms of simple inflection (without objective pronominal suffixes) and another 368 forms of compound inflection (with the objective pronominal suffixes) – 416 forms in all. The section closes with a table of forms for the inflection of the verb, followed by examples of forms of the verb from the Bible. The fourth part, *al-Tašdīd wa al-Irkha* ("*Dageš* and *Rafeh*"), deals with the ability of the letters to occur with the *dageš* or without it, treating the subject according to the various forms of inflection. The fifth part, *al-Qawl fī al-Nagham* ("The Vowels"), begins with assumptions – in his opinion, universal – concerning the phonetic structure of the word, and deals with the articulation of the vowels, surveying those which can occur together in one word containing two vowels. Also discussed in this section are the changes which occur in the vowels of a word when the concepts of plural, construct state, tense, and pause apply to it. The sixth part, *al-Jazm* ("The *Šewa*ʾ"), deals with two types of *šewa*ʾ: *sākina* (quiescent) and *mutaḥarraka* (vocal), the different qualities of the latter being described. The seventh part is called *al-Aḥruf wa-* א, ע, ח, ה ("the non-laryngeals and the laryngeals"), while the eighth is called א, ע, ה, ח ("the laryngeals"). The two sections deal with two aspects of the same topic – the changes which are peculiar to the vocalization of the laryngeals, and the changes in vocalization which take place in the immediate context of laryngeals. He lists 50 changes in all. In the ninth part, *al-Zawāʾid wa al-Lawāḥiq* ("Added Consonants and Expletives"), Saadiah Gaon deals with other types of additions, which are not instances of *tafkhīm* ("augmentation") in principle; yet in fact this section contains matters already discussed in the second part of the work. The interchangeable letters are dealt with in the tenth part. The pattern which Saadiah Gaon set down for Hebrew grammar is characteristically pioneering work, but it was not accepted by his successors; his ideas were only in part repeated in the works of later grammarians; yet two of them became the foundation of Hebrew linguistics. His division of the letters into base and supplemental became the basic assumption for the arrangement of the first dictionaries, and his division of words into three types – noun, verb, particle – with his definitions of them, became the very foundation for all grammatical discussion of the word. In particular his statements about letters, vowels, the *šewa*ʾ, and the phonetic structure of the word were influential. However, the method by which he described the grammar of the word was too simplistic and too primitive. Most of the material which Saadiah Gaon collected in the second part as occurrences of augmentation was to be treated, beginning with Ḥayyūj, in chapters concerning the inflection of medial *waw* verbs, geminate verbs and quadriradicals. Most of the occurrences of contraction cited there are treated, beginning with Ḥayyūj, under the inflection of prima *ʾalef*, prima *yod*, and final *he* verbs. However, even in the grammar of the word the grammarians accepted some of his basic suppositions: for example, that when confronted by a great number of different occurrences in the text, the grammarian must differentiate and describe the relations between *uṣūl* (basic forms) and *furū*ʿ (secondary forms which he can represent as branching out from the first), and also describe the relations between the various basic forms. This differentiation is the starting point for all grammatical description. Ḥayyūj and Ibn Janāḥ applied it to all items of grammar.

WORKS OF ḤAYYUJ ON WEAK AND GEMINATIVE VERBS. Monographs written on decided grammatical subjects are the works of Ḥayyūj, above all his two works on weak and geminative verbs. In these works Ḥayyūj formulated the rule that every Hebrew verbal root consists of at least three letters. This is based upon the concept which Ḥayyūj had, following the Arab grammarians, concerning the phonetic structure of the word. According to this concept a word consists of letters which cannot be uttered except as accompanied by one of the vowels; a word cannot consist of one consonant, but must be always of two at least, the one which begins the word being always accompanied by a vowel (and hence a mobile letter), while the letter which closes it (a quiescent letter) is never accompanied by a vowel. Between the opening mobile consonant and the concluding quiescent consonant, a mobile letter or letters or even a quiescent consonant or consonants can occur. In any event, two quiescent consonants will not occur successively unless preceded by a mobile letter. (According to this concept, a word such as דָוִיד contains two quiescent letters, the *yod* and the second *dalet*, preceded by the mobile letter וִ.) This concept opened the way for the classification of the letters according to their mobility or quiescence, which Ḥayyūj formulated as follows. All letters of the alphabet can occur in mobile or quiescent form. However, with regard to quiescence there is a difference between (ה)א, ו, י, and all the other letters, which are "visible" when they are quiescent, that is, both written and pronounced. In contrast to them (ה)א, ו, י can at times be "hidden": though found in the structure of the word, they are not realized in its pronunciation and sometimes not even in its written form. Thus in the word קָאם (Hos. 10: 14), the *ʾalef* is quiescent, hidden in the pronunciation but visible in the writing; in the word קָם this *ʾalef* is equally quiescent, but hidden both in pronunciation and in writing. So too, a word such as וְאַתִּיקֶיהָא (Ezek. 41: 15) ends with a quiescent *ʾalef* hidden in pronunciation but visible in the writing, while the word אֵלֶיהָ ends with a quiescent *ʾalef* hidden both in pronunciation and writing. These two assumptions – that every root consists of at least three radicals and that the letters (ה)א, ו, י, are distinctive with regard to their quiescence – formed a descriptive framework for the discussion of the roots that include one of these four letters. These roots, like all those in the language, consist (according to the very definition of the concept "root") of three radicals. In the actual verb forms derived from these roots, one finds that these letters occur in mobile or in "visibly" quiescent form (as do all the other letters in the language). However, they sometimes occur as hidden quiescent letters or, more precisely, are hidden in the pronunciation but visible in the writing, as with the *yod* in בָּנִיתָ; and at times they occur hidden both in pronunciation and orthography, as does the initial *yod* of the root in the word תֵּשֵׁב. The grammarians who preceded Ḥayyūj, comparing a form such as יָשַׁב with a form like תֵּשֵׁב, and seeing that the *yod*, present in the first word, is missing from the second form, concluded that in these words, too, the *yod* is not a root letter, and accordingly fixed the root as a bi-radical: שב. Ḥayyūj, according to his suppositions, analyzed the case differently: The root always consists of at least three letters, in this case ישב. The absence of the *yod* in the form does not mean that it cannot be considered a root letter. It is simply missing from some of the actual forms derived from this root, and compensation needs to be made for its absence. This compensation he finds, for example, in "elongation" (*madd*), as in the case of the *ṣere* under the *taw* in תֵּשֵׁב. Ḥayyūj assumes, therefore, the existence of hypothetical tri-radical roots and a complete table of conjugations of basic forms (*aṣliyya*), in which there are no missing letters. He establishes the base forms by analogy with the parallel forms of the "sound" verbs which include the four letters under discussion:

שמר / תִּשְׁ־מֹר = ישב / X   X = תִּ־יְשֵׁב

These base forms either do not occur in the biblical text, or occur in it as exceptional forms from which one can neither draw analogies nor derive rules. Yet only in relation to these hypothetical base forms can one describe the actual forms. Ḥayyūj seeks to explain the difference between the actual form (תֵּשֵׁב) and the hypothetical form (תִּיְשֵׁב) which is adduced by analogy with the basic form (תִּפְעַל), by a certain number of devices, such as: (1) the deficiency and its compensation; (2) the substitution of one letter for another; (3) assimilation and the gemination which follows it. In the actual description concepts were created: the first, the medial, and the final radical of the root, respectively. Following the convention of the Arab grammarians, these concepts were denoted by reference to the three letters of the root פעל, as follows: the letter which occupies the position of the *pe*, the *ʿayin*, and the *lamed*. If all four of the weak letters occurred in all three positions of the root as hidden quiescents, Ḥayyūj would have to deal with 12 groups of roots. However, he considers that there are only four groups of verbs whose roots contain weak letters, namely:

1) the prima *ʾalef*
2) the prima *yod*
3) verbs with a medial weak radical
4) verbs whose final radical is weak.

These are in effect the four chapters of the first work of Ḥayyūj: *Kitāb al-Afʿāl Dhawāt Ḥurūf al-Līn*. Defective forms also occur for verbs whose roots contain identical second and third radicals; these are dealt with in the second work of Ḥayyūj: *Kitāb al-Afʿāl Dhawāt al-Mithlayn*. Having established a theoretical framework to deal with the derivation and conjugation of the weak verbs, Ḥayyūj goes on to explain why analogy does not apply to the verbs whose roots contain weak letters. He bases his explanation on the postulate that in Hebrew there is difficulty in pronouncing the א(ה), י, ו, quiescently and therefore these letters were "hidden," that is, not pronounced. He also included a dictionary of weak verbs, classified according to the groups mentioned above. For every root he listed the derivative verb forms, in each instance explaining the actual forms which, according to his suppositions, differed from the analogous base form.

THE KITĀB AL-LUMAʿ OF IBN JANĀḤ. The most profound and comprehensive grammar is *Kitāb al-Lumaʿ* by Ibn Janāḥ. According to the author this work constitutes a whole only together with the two above-mentioned works of Ḥayyūj, and with his own smaller works. For the subjects of the 45 (46) chapters, see *Ibn Janāḥ. It is possible to get some idea of the scope of the work by classifying its chapters according to the pattern of traditional grammar accepted today. The work begins with the division of parts of speech, with which his predecessors had already dealt, but he improves the definitions of Saadiah Gaon and their logical foundation. The different types of expressions are also classified in this chapter. Matters of pronunciation are considered in 13 chapters: a discussion of the letters, each one's place of articulation, and its position in the word, whether as base or supplemental letter. The meanings of the supplemental letters are given the most detailed discussion of this topic extant. Interchange of letters is also treated, as well as assimilation, the marking with a *dageš*, and the *mappiq he* of the third person feminine pronominal suffix. Vocalization, too, is discussed: interchange of vowels, the changes which occur in vocalization because of the laryngeals, the vocalization of the conjunctive *waw* (including *waw* conversive), and of the interrogative *he*. This concludes the issues of pronunciation. The grammar of the word – derivation and accidence – is treated in 13 chapters; the formation of the word, i.e., the derivation and the accidence of the verb and the noun, is treated in a unit which runs for five chapters. Pronominal suffixes, relation *(nisba)*, plural and dual forms, determination and indefiniteness, genders and numbers, are also discussed. The other chapters of the work deal with topics which are today included under syntax and rhetoric. Seven chapters are devoted to syntactical topics, including apposition, government of the verb, the construct case, and agreement in gender. Five chapters cover rhetoric: ellipsis, pleonasm, repetition, inverse order – forward or backward. Five of the six remaining chapters discuss classified groups of exceptional occurrences which the grammarian cannot include under any of the rules which he fixed or formulated. Therefore he uses an operative device called *taqdīr* (surmise), by means of which he expresses the intention of the written form, thus removing the exceptional character of the occurrences, so that they fall under one of the rules which he has established. Finally, in chapter 34 (35), he deals with all the linguistic means for expressing the question, that cannot be included in any of the accepted linguistic divisions. This attempt to present the subjects of the work according to the main topics of accepted grammatical thought does, indeed, give some idea of the scope of the grammatical study of Ibn Janāḥ, but it is likely to distort his division of the material and the methodological principles underlying it. Ibn Janāḥ did not divide grammar into the accepted sections of today, such as phonology, morphology, and syntax. We have seen that in chapter 34 (35) he deals with all the means (letter, particle, word) to express various types of questions. This is the way he treats other matters too, such as "compensation" (*badal*), which he treats in a unit of successive chapters: interchange of letters in chapter 6 (7), interchange of vowels in chapter 7 (8), and apposition in chapter 8 (9). From this point of view chapter 31 (32), dealing with changes in order, is interesting. It begins with a change in the order of the letters within a word (כשב–כבש), proceeds to deal with verbs in which the order of the weak letter changes (ייטיב–טוב ;יסופו–ספתה), and ends with a change in the order of the words, such as עַל הָרִים יַעַמְדוּ מָיִם (Ps. 104:6), which means (he claims) עַל מַיִם יַעַמְדוּ הָרִים.

THE GRAMMATICAL WORKS OF PERIOD III. The aim of the grammatical works written in period III (1150–1250) was to express in a concise Hebrew version the content of the works of Ḥayyūj and Ibn Janāḥ. Adaptations made in the West include the works of Abraham ibn Ezra, Parḥon, and the Kimḥis; and in the East, the works of Isaac ha-Levi b. Eleazar: *Sefat Yeter* and *Rikmah*. There are only meager innovations of principle in these works; rather, they attempt to consolidate a permanent framework for the discussion of grammatical issues. Hence they emphasize the mechanical and paradigmatic aspects of the grammar of the word.

Sefer Ẓaḥot by Abraham ibn Ezra. This tendency is already noticeable in *Sefer Ẓaḥot* of Abraham ibn Ezra (1145), whose contents are as follows: Chapter 1 deals with the vowels, the *šewa*ʾ, nominal patterns and poetic meter, which are based upon the vowels and the *šewa*ʾ. Chapter 2 deals at length with the letters: their names, forms, pronunciation, and use. There follow several chapters on parts of speech: the particles, the noun (including the numerals), and the verb. The author deals extensively with the bi-radical verbs and the conjugations *(binyanim)*. After a short digression in which he discusses words composed of two words or two forms, he deals with quadri-radical verbs. At the end of the work there is a short discussion of exceptional forms from the Bible. The main methodological innovation which Abraham ibn Ezra made in *Sefer Ẓaḥot* as compared with *Kitāb al-Lumaʿ* is the discussion of poetic meters; other authors followed in his footsteps, especially in period IV.

Sefer Zikkaron by Joseph Kimḥi. This work, divided in two parts, resembles *Sefer Ẓaḥot* in its scope. The order of the discussion in the first part is as follows: the letters according to their pronunciation and use, the formative letters at the beginnings and ends of words, the grammatical categories of the verb, the assimilated letters, the vowels, parts of speech, nominal patterns, and numerals. The second part begins with a discussion about fixing the root, proceeds with the regular verb according to its conjugations (*binyanim*), and comments upon special forms of *binyanim* and compound forms, the prima *yod*, quiescent verbs, verbs with assimilated prima *yod*, prima *nun*, verbs with medial *waw*, medial *yod* and final *he*, verbs with assimilated ends, and geminate verbs. The chapter concerning the vowels in *Sefer Zikkaron* (ed. Bacher (1888), 17–19) is most interesting. Joseph Kimḥi determines there that the number of vowels in Hebrew (in addition to the *šewa*ʾ) is ten: five long and five short. For each long vowel there is a corresponding short vowel: for *qameṣ gadol* (ָ) the *pattaḥ gadol* (ַ) is the corresponding short vowel; the correspondent for *ṣere* (ֵ) is *segol* or *pattah qatan* (ֶ); for *ḥolem* (וֹ, ֹ) the correspondent is *qameṣ ḥataf* (i.e., *qameṣ qatan* (ֳ)); the correspondent to *šuruq* with *waw* (וּ) is *šuruq* without *waw*, a vowel whose name is *qibbuṣ sefatayim* (ֻ); and the correspondent of *ḥireq* with *yod* (ִי) is *ḥireq* without *yod* (ִ). Joseph Kimḥi stated that "with regard to the manner of recitation" the long vowels are treated with "pause and delay" while for the short vowels "you should always be speedy in their reading." In spite of that the long vowels are not lengthened if the stress of the word is near them. That means that the *qameṣ* of -שָׁ is not lengthened except in the last of the following three examples: שָׁמַר, שָׁמַרְתָּ, וְשָׁמַרְתָּ. In any event, if a letter vocalized with a *šewa*ʾ follows the long vowel, then the long vowel is lengthened. Thus there would be a lengthening of the וֹ in the word שׁוֹמְרִים, but not in the word שׁוֹמֵר. The short vowels themselves are not short when they precede a mobile laryngeal, such as in the word יַעֲשֶׂה By this system there is no difference in pronunciation between שַׁאֲלוּ (the imperative) and שָׁאֲלוּ (the perfect). The scholars of the second half of the 19th century considered this theory to be an essential innovation in comparison with the theory of the seven kings (vowels) as found in the masorah literature and in that of the grammarians who preceded Joseph Kimḥi. Instead of the theory of the seven kings, which seemed to them to be basically a system of qualities only, the theory of Joseph Kimḥi appeared to be a system consisting of ten vowels which are distinguished from each other by five qualitative contrasts (*i, e, a, o, u*) and by a contrast in quantity (long:short). They also felt that besides deviating from that of the seven kings, the theory of Joseph Kimḥi is rather forced with regard to the Sephardi pronunciation in the Torah reading. Doubts have been expressed concerning this accepted idea; see Ben-David (*Leshonenu*, 1958). Popularized by Kimḥi's sons in their works, this vowel theory and division was accepted by most of the grammarians of period IV, and is found in Hebrew textbooks to this day.

Mahalakh Shevilei ha-Daʿat by Moses Kimḥi. An important step toward the consolidation of a firm systematic framework for the practical discussion of the grammar of the word was taken in *Mahalakh Shevilei ha-Daʿat* by Moses Kimḥi. This short work discusses mainly the definitions, the conjugation tables, citing a few examples. The order is as follows: 1. parts of speech, the grammatical categories of the verb, the letters, rules of the *dageš qal*, the stress, the vowels, and the *šewa*ʾ; 2. the types of nouns, the patterns and their declensions; 3. the conjugation of the verb according to the *binyanim*; the weak verbs: prima *nun*, prima *ʾalef*, prima *yod*, medial *waw*, final *ʾalef*, final *he*, geminate and quadri-radical verbs; verbal suffixes; other rules about pronominal suffixes. In the main part of the work – the formation of the verb – the paradigmatic system is especially prominent. The book gained wide distribution because of its practical nature, being used especially by Christians for the study of Hebrew. Elijah Levita added a commentary, Sebastian Muenster translated it into Latin, and it was printed many times.

Mikhlol by David Kimḥi. The climax of the attempts to systemize the discussion of the grammar of the word and to fix the study of the verb at its center is *Mikhlol* of David Kimḥi. The work begins with the division of the parts of speech, and correspondingly consists of three parts: *Sha'ar Dikduk ha-Pe'alim* ("The Chapter on Verbs," covering 66% of the work), *Sha'ar Dikduk ha-Shemot* ("The Chapter on Nouns" – 30% of the work) and the chapter dealing with particles, which covers only 4%. The subjects discussed include: 32 forms of conjugation of the basic verb stem, the *qal*; transitive and intransitive verbs; the formation of the *binyanim* and their meanings; conjugation tables of the verb in *qal* with the objective pronominal suffixes; a digression concerning the servile letters and their meanings, and an appendix on the omission of letters and other kinds of ellipsis; and the forms of conjugation of the other *binyanim*. Between the conjugations of the *binyanim* there are digressions concerning exceptional forms of conjugation. The weak verbs appear according to their forms and are listed alphabetically after the manner of Ḥayyūj: first verbs whose initial letters are assimilated (prima *yod*, prima *lamed*, prima *nun*), preceded by a discussion of assimilation. Then follow the weak verbs, preceded by a discussion of the special rules for the weak letters. The section on the verb concludes with the quadriliteral and quinqueliteral verbs. The section on the noun covers vocalization (vowels, *šewa'*), types of nouns, nominal patterns classified according to morphological groups: regular nouns; weak nouns. Under the regular noun are listed the simple patterns, followed by patterns with a suffix and those with a prefix. The declension of each nominal pattern is discussed. The weak patterns occur in the following order: initial defective; initial, medial, and final quiescent; both defective initial and quiescent final; final *'alef*; quiescent initial and final; geminate nouns: and quadriliteral and quinqueliteral nouns. The section dealing with the particles is arranged alphabetically.

MA'ASEH EFOD BY PROFIAT DURAN. Of all the works of the fourth period (from the middle of the 13th century until the beginning of the 16th century) the most important is *Ma'aseh Efod* by Profiat Duran, written in 1403. The volume comprises a long introduction (including interesting data for the study of the history of education among the Jews), 32 chapters, and a further chapter as a supplement. The first five chapters deal with the "causae" of the language in the terms of the accepted scheme of the Middle Ages following Aristotelian philosophy: chapter 1, the nature of language; chapter 2, its purpose; chapter 3, "the *cause efficiens*"; chapter 4, its divisions (the three parts of speech); chapter 5, its elements (the letters, vowels and cantillation signs). Three other introductory chapters follow: on the organs of speech and the production of sounds; on the fate of Hebrew after it was "the most perfect of languages"; here he maintains that about 2,000 roots remain, some 1,000 of them being used for deriving verbs; and on the science of language, which according to his definition includes grammar, rhetoric, and poetics. The actual work begins with chapter 9, which deals with the grammatical categories that apply to the noun. Chapter 10 treats the infinitive, chapters 11 and 12 cover the grammatical categories that apply to the verb, while chapter 14, interchange of letters and of vowels; chapter 15, the *binyanim* of the verb; chapter 16, the *qal*; chapter 17, *pi'el*; chapter 18, *hif'il*; chapter 19, *po'el* (intensive); chapter 20, *nif'al*; chapter 21, *hitpa'el*; chapter 22, those verbs "whose agents are not mentioned" (*pu'al, hof'al*); chapter 23, forms compounded from various *binyanim*, and quadri-radical verbs; chapter 24, nominal patterns; chapter 25, the fixing of the roots of verbs, nouns, and particles; chapter 26, the pronouns; chapters 27–29, exceptions (ellipsis, additions, change of order) which Ibn Janāḥ had already discussed in *Kitāb al-Luma'*; chapter 30, the particles; chapter 31, the letters בגדכפ"ת; chapter 32, the pronunciation of the written word, and hence important testimony concerning the Sephardi pronunciation in the reading of the Torah; chapter 33 (supplement) explains why Hebrew was called "the holy language." By virtue of its scope and its excessive fondness for theoretical discussion this work constitutes something of a revolt against the narrow pattern that David Kimḥi established in the *Mikhlol*, which until then had ruled supreme in linguistic literature. *Ma'aseh Efod* is on the one hand an attempt to return to the actual sources of linguistics (the works of Ibn Janāḥ and Ḥayyūj), and on the other hand it is an attempt to base Hebrew grammar on the late-medieval scholastic philosophy of the Christian West. The grammar of Profiat Duran and the dictionary *Ratukot Kesef* of Joseph ibn Kaspi, who preceded him, were destined to move linguistic literature out of the standstill and barren stereotyped ways which had prevailed under the influence of *Mikhlol* of David Kimḥi. Yet the influence of *Ma'aseh Efod* was limited; in the 15th century the empiricism of *Mikhlol* was re-established.

MIKNEH AVRAM BY ABRAHAM DE BALMES. At the very end of period IV, in 1523, *Mikneh Avram* was published. Chapter 1 offers a definition of Hebrew grammar, and classifies the elements of language into two types: the simple elements (the letters and vowels) and the compound (the syllables, words, and compound statements). Chapters 2 and 3 deal with the simple elements. Chapter 2 discusses the letters, their number, respective names, written forms and places of articulation, their classification both in relation to themselves and in relation to the words made from them (the base and the servile letters, compensation for letters, similarity and differences between letters, the combinations of the letters, i.e., possible and impossible combinations); chapter 3 deals with vocalization, the number of the vowels, their form and pronunciation, the rules of vocalization, and compensation for vowels. Chapters 4–6 deal with the grammar of the word. Chapter 4 begins with the classification of the parts of speech and deals with the grammar of the noun – the division of the nouns according to their meanings, and nominal patterns. Chapter 5 discusses verbs, their division into *binyanim*, their *gezarot*, and analysis. Chapter 6 deals with particles. Chapter 7, headed "*Compositio et Regimen*," is the first attempt in the history of linguistic literature to describe the syntax of Hebrew in the operative terms of syntax as shaped by Latin linguistics. Chapter 8 deals with pronunciation, penultimate and ultimate stress, and the *maqqaf*; and at the end there is an appendix by Kalonymus b. David on cantillation.

Through the arrangement of its discussions, this work constitutes the first attempt ever made – and not without success – to gather the grammatical teachings as they had crystallized in Hebrew linguistics under the influence of Arabic linguistics, side by side with the grammatical system which underlies the accepted description of Latin. It thus established a new tripartite pattern for the discussion of Hebrew grammar, comprising phonology, morphology, and syntax. In the chapter *Compositio et Regimen* de Balmes set up a new framework for the discussion of topics which had been scattered throughout previous works, such as the uses of the servile letter, pronouns agreement of gender and number, and government of the verb. On the other hand, he deals systematically with new topics, such as the combination of nouns with verbs, combination of nouns with other nouns, the agreement of noun (subject) and verb (predicate), and combination with the aid of particles. Through the talent of his pen De Balmes brought the system of concepts of syntax into Hebrew linguistics. By virtue of its originality and innovations, *Mikneh Avram* was the most important work in linguistic literature since *Kitāb al-Luma*ʿ. Since its structure deviates from the works discussed hitherto, this work opened up a new era in the history of this Hebrew literature.

THE STUDY OF LINGUISTIC LITERATURE

Fields of Activity

Research concerning linguistic literature has thus far concentrated upon three main activities: A. the publication of the works; B. discussion of the general course of development of this literature; C. discussion about the various authors, the course of their lives, their works, and their part in the development of Hebrew linguistics. A concise survey is given below.

Publication of the Works

This began soon after the invention of printing and has continued until today. Thus, for example, *Arukh* of Nathan b. Jehiel was one of the first Hebrew books published prior to 1480. Similarly, *Nofet Ẓufim* of Judah b. Jehiel, Messer Leon, was printed before 1480, in Mantua. *Sefer ha-Shorashim* of R. David Kimḥi was published in Rome before 1480 as well. In 1492 the book *Petaḥ Devarai*, whose authorship has not been established with certainty, was printed. In the first half of the 16th century this activity included not only the works of authors of that century (such as Elijah Levita, Abraham De Balmes and others), but also relatively old works: in 1508 *Mahalakh Shevilei ha-Da'at* of Moses Kimḥi was published, in 1511 *Kiẓẓur he-Arukh* appeared in Cracow and in the years 1532/1534 *Mikhlol* of David Kimḥi was issued in Constantinople. The activity of Elijah Levita throughout the entire first half of the 16th century is especially striking. Not only did he publish his own works and his commentaries to the writings of the Kimḥi brothers, but he also edited a collection of grammatical works which he published in 1546 under the title *Dikdukim*. Following his introduction, the volume includes these works: *Mahalakh Shevilei ha-Da'at* by Moses Kimḥi; *Petaḥ Devarai; Ẓaḥot* and *Moznayim* of Abraham ibn Ezra; *Sefer Harkavah* and *Pirkei Eliyahu* of Elijah Levita; and *Marpe Lashon* and *Darkhei No'am* of Moses b. Ḥabib. From then till the end of the 18th century virtually none of the early works were published, except those of the Kimḥi brothers and Abraham ibn Ezra; and when publication of the older works did resume the order in which they were issued was the opposite of that in which they were written: works produced in the 12th century were published before those of the tenth century and the Hebrew translations were published before their Arabic originals. Most of the works of Abraham ibn Ezra were published at the end of the 18th century and at the beginning of the 19th; *Maḥberet he-Arukh* of Parḥon was published in 1844, *Maḥberet* of Menaḥem in 1854, and the *Teshuvot* of Dunash and the "decisions" of Jacob b. Meir Tam were printed a year later. Until 1844 not even one Hebrew translation of a work written originally in Arabic appeared in print. In 1844 Leopold Dukes published Abraham ibn Ezra's translation of the works of Ḥayyūj, while the Arabic originals of Ḥayyūj were not printed until near the end of the century: *Kitāb al-Tanqīṭ* by Nutt (1870), his two main works by Jastrow (1897). In 1856 B. Goldberg published the *Sefer ha-Rikmah* of Ibn Janāḥ in the Hebrew translation of Judah ibn Tibbon, while the Arabic original *Kitāb al-Luma*ʿ was published by Derenbourg(-Bacher) only 30 years later (1886). Until the 1850s not one work was published in its entirety in its Arabic original. Munk published the introduction of Ibn Janāḥ to his *Kitāb al-Luma*ʿ *(Journal Asiatique*, 1850–51). In 1857 Bargés-Goldberg published the *Risāla* of Judah ibn Quraysh – the first manuscript of an Arabic-written treatise on Hebrew linguistics to be issued in its entirety. In the 1860s selections from the works of the Karaite authors were published (Pinsker, 1860) as well as *Ḥotam Tokhnit* of Bedersi, *Ma'aseh Efod* of Profiat Duran (both in 1865), the "objections" to Saadiah Gaon which are attributed to Dunash (Schroeter, 1866), the "objections" of the students of Menaḥem and those of the student of Dunash (Stern, 1870). All this activity, which extended from the end of the 18th century to the end of the 1860s, is to be considered, from the point of view of modern editorial technique, as initial attempts; the publications do not meet present-day editorial standards and most of the works need to be republished. In the last 30 years of the 19th century the actual sources of Hebrew linguistic literature were published; between 1870 and 1897 the works of

Ḥayyūj and Ibn Janāḥ were produced in their Arabic originals and with their Hebrew translations. The editions of Ḥayyūj are: Nutt (1870), Jastrow (1897). The works of Ibn Janāḥ were published by Neubauer (1873–75), Derenbourg (1880), Derenbourg-Bacher (1886); Bacher (1897); and from then until the present there has been a continuous attempt at improving the printed versions of these works; Bacher (ZDMG, 1884, 1888) published corrections for the Neubauer *Uṣūl* edition (1873–75), and then (JQR, 1899) his corrections for the Jastrow edition of the two main works of Ḥayyūj (1897); Kokowtzow (1911; see bibl.) published his corrections to the Derenbourg edition of the opuscules of Ibn Janāḥ (1880); Wilensky (1929–31, 550–63), published his corrections to the Derenbourg(-Bacher) edition of *Kitāb al-Lumaʿ* (1886); Razhabi (*Leshonenu*, 1966) listed variant readings to Neubauer (1875). Also published at the end of the 19th century were *Sefer Zikkaron* of Joseph Kimḥi (Bacher, 1888), remnants of *Kitāb al-Muwāzana* of Ibn Barūn (Kokowtzow, 1890–93), the anonymous work from Yemen (Neubauer, 1891), four chapters from *Kitāb al-Muḥāḍara wa al-Mudhākara* of Moses ibn Ezra (Kokowtzow, *Vostoĭniya Zametki*, 1895). In the 20th century there was a more intensive effort to publish the sources which were written in Arabic: Kokowtzow (1916) published remnants of the works of Samuel ha-Nagid, Ibn Gikatilla and Judah ibn Balʿam, additions to *Kitāb al-Muwāzana*, a remnant of the works of Nethanel al-Fayyumi (?) and also small selections from pseudo-Ibn Yashush. Skoss (1936–1945) published *Kitāb Jāmiʿ al-Alfaẓ* of David b. Abraham Alfāsī; he also published (JQR, 1942, 1952) large sections of *Kutub al-Lugha* by Saadiah Gaon. Klar (*Saadiah Gaon*, 1943) and Allony (*Sefer Goldziher*, 1958) published the original text of Saadiah's *Kitāb al-Sabaʿīn Lafẓa al-Mufrada*; Zislin (1962, 1965, see bibl.), published a selection from *al-Kāfi* by Abū al-Faraj Hārūn; and Allony (1969) issued the remnants of the *Agron* of Saadiah Gaon. The effort to publish works which were originally written in Hebrew has also continued: Levinger (1929) produced *Darkhei ha-Nikkud* of Moses b. Yom Tov; Ben-Menaḥem (1941) published eight pages missing from the missing version of *Safah Berurah* by Abraham ibn Ezra; Yalon (1945) published *Halikhot Sheva* of Almoli; Gumpertz (*Leshonenu*, 1958) published a chapter from *Ein ha-Kore* of Jekuthiel b. Isaac ha-Kohen; Yalon (1965) published *Shekel ha-Kodesh*; Allony (1966) issued *Derekh Laʿasot Ḥaruzim* of David b. Yom Tov ibn Bilia. Some of the works printed in the 19th century were reedited in the 20th: Wilensky (1924) republished a part of *Safah Berurah* by Abraham ibn Ezra; Klar (1946) again published the first part of *Sefer ha-Shoham* of Moses b. Isaac which Collins had already published (1882) and added a second part which had not been printed until then; Allony (1949) published a new selection from *Kitāb al-Taḍkīr wal-Taʾnith* of Moses ha-Kohen ibn Gikatilla together with the sections which Kokowtzow had printed (1916). Abramson (1963) published sections from the Arabic original of *Kitāb al-Tajnīs* of Ibn Balʿam together with the part published by Kokowtzow (1916). Allony (1964) published new selections from *Kitāb al-Tajnīs* and from *Ḥuruf al-Maʿāni* by the same author. The most important work published in the 20th century, however, after it had already appeared in print is *Sefer ha-Rikmah* of Ibn Janāḥ, which Wilensky reissued (1929–31); and a second edition of the work was printed in Jerusalem in 1964. Especially notable was the publication of a rich selection from the linguistic literature of Samaritan authors which Ben-Ḥayyim published (1957). Despite this extensive work of publication, knowledge of Hebrew linguistic literature is still defective. Some of the works have been completely lost and we only know of them from mention of their names; of others only quotations exist. Even the works of Ḥayyūj, Ibn Janāḥ, and Samuel ha-Nagid – have not reached us in complete form: the works of Samuel ha-Nagid were almost entirely lost, as was the *Kitāb al-Tashwīr* of Ibn Janāḥ; from the translations made by Solomon b. Joseph ibn Job of *Kitāb al-Taswīʾa* and *Risālat al-Tanbīh* only small parts remain. For further publications in the field up to 1984 see D. Téné, "The State of the Art in Hebrew Linguistic Literature," in *Meḥqarim be-Lashon* 8 (2001), 19–37 (in Hebrew). Latest research achievements are listed below, in the division "Authors and their Works," sections 1, 2, 5–9, 11–15, 22, 25, 26, 29, 30, 34, 36, 39, 45, 55, 58, 62, 63, 66, 67, 75, 85, 87, 92, 94.

General Development of Linguistic Literature

Abraham ibn Ezra gave the first survey of the authors who lived prior to the middle of the 12th century and of their works, in the introduction to his *Sefer Moznayim*. Some of the later authors followed in his footsteps – e.g., Parḥon, Joseph and David Kimḥi, Profiat Duran, and De Balmes. In modern times a few surveys of the general process of development of Hebrew linguistic literature have been written. Dukes (1844) reviewed what was known to him about a few of the authors mentioned by Abraham ibn Ezra – 14 in all: Saadiah Gaon, Dunash b. Tamim, Ibn Quraysh, Menaḥem, Dunash b. Labrat, Ḥayyūj, Hai Gaon, Isaac Gikatilla, Isaac b. Saul, Ibn Janāḥ, Solomon ibn Gabirol, Samuel ha-Nagid, Moses ibn Gikatilla, and Ibn Balʿam. Munk (*Journal Asiatique*, 1850–51) supplemented this review with many details, especially concerning the Karaite commentators who lived about the time of Saadiah Gaon. Neubauer (*Journal Asiatique*, 1861–63) reviewed the lexicographers of whom he knew from Saadiah Gaon until Saadiah ibn Danān (the end of the 15th century), but he refrained from discussing dictionaries for post-biblical Hebrew and the dictionaries of synonyms. From among the authors who lived after Abraham he discusses Isaac ha-Levi b. Eleazar, Al-Ḥarizi, Salomon b. Parḥon, Jacob b. Meir Tam, Jacob b. Eleazar, the Kimḥi family, David ha-Yevani, Joseph ibn Kaspi, and Saadiah ibn Danān. Lerner (*Ha-Shaḥar*, 1876) is more comprehensive: he reviews the authors and their works from the beginning of linguistic literature until Solomon Levinsohn at the beginning of the 19th century. The authors are arranged in chronological order. He lists all the Rabbanite writers known to him and he mentions incidentally the famous authors found among the Karaites and the Christians. But Rabbanite authors who wrote their works in Arabic are only incidentally mentioned.

These four surveys are outdated, though, and can no longer serve as reference surveys. Bacher (1892, see bibl.) served for a long time as the authoritative review of linguistic literature from its beginning until the 16th century. In his survey he included a bibliographical list up to the year 1890 and an index of names containing over 70 authors or translators. Bacher (ZDMG, 1895) is the first attempt to discuss in a historical-critical manner the grammatical issues found in the talmudic and midrashic literature, in *Sefer Yeẓirah*, in the masorah literature, and especially in the work of Aaron Ben Asher; he is equally the first to discuss similarly the main grammatical theories of the early authors from Saadiah Gaon to Ḥayyūj (but not including him). Rozenak (1898) reviews the authors and their works from Ḥayyūj to David Kimḥi, but does not add to Bacher (1892). Hirschfeld (1926; see bibl.) reviews grammatical literature and lexicographers (10th–16th centuries). He mentions the latest research achievements, especially by Kokowtzow (1916, see bibl.). Azar (1927, see bibl.) is a Hebrew translation of Bacher (ZDMG, 1895). The work of Yellin (1945, see bibl.) resembles Bacher's (ZDMG, 1895); the ideas of grammarians and lexicographers until Ḥayyūj (but not including him) are also reviewed there. Chomsky (JQR, 1944/45) examines the period ending with David Kimḥi with regard to its contribution to the history of linguistic literature. Meirowsky (1955) surveys the study of Hebrew from the beginning until the mid-20th century. For this period, the corresponding chapters add nothing beyond Hirschfeld.

[David Téné]

Monographs on Authors and their Works

Some of the authors were the subjects of monographs in which bio-bibliographical issues were discussed and sometimes even their efforts within the history of Hebrew linguistics were described. The following are the more important:

Saadiah as grammarian – Skoss (1955, see bibl.) and Dotan (1997; below section 1); *Saadiah* as lexicographer – Allony (1969, 15–139, see bibl.). *Alfāsi* – Skoss (1936). *Menaḥem* – Gross (1872), Del Valle (1981) and Sáenz-Badillos (1986). *Dunash* – Sáenz-Badillos (1980) and Del Valle (1981). *Ibn Nuḥ* – Khan (2000). *Ḥayyūj* – Drachmann (1885), Jastrow (1885), Kokowtzow (1916, Russian part, 1–73, see bibl.), Poznański (JQR, 1925/6), Goldenberg (1980), Watad (1994), Basil (1992), and Martinez Delgado (2004). *Abū-al-Faraj Hārūn* – Skoss (JQR, 1927, 11–27), Zislin (1960, 208–12, see bibl.), Khan et al. (2003). *Ibn Janāḥ* – Bacher (1885), Becker (1999) and Maman (2004). *Samuel ha-Nagid* – Kokowtzow (1916, Russian part, 74–194). *Moses Gikatilla* – Poznański (1895), Kokowtzow (1916, Russian part, 95–201). *Ibn Balʿam* – Fuchs (1893), Kokowtzow (1916, Russian part, 201–215), Abramson (1975). *Ibn Barūn* – Kokowtzow (1893), 1–158, see bibl.), idem (1916, Russian part, 216–33), Wechter (JOAS, 1941), idem (1964, see bibl.) and Becker (2005). *Judah Halevi's* statement about the Hebrew language (Kuzari, II, § 66–80) – Bacher (*Hebraica*, 1893) and R.C. Steiner, "*Meshekh ha-Tenu'ot be-'ivrit – Te'urim ve-Teoriot me-Hieronemos 'ad R. Yehudah ha-Levi le'Or ha-Polmos ha-Dati*," in *Meḥqarim be-Lashon*, 8 (2001), 203–8. *Rashi* as grammarian – Englander (HUCA, 1930, 1936, 1937–38, 1942–43); *Rashi as lexicographer* – I. Avineri, *Heikhal Rashi* (I 1980, II 1985). *Judah Hadassi* – Bacher (MGWJ, 1895). *Moses ibn Ezra*, his poetics – Schreiner (REJ, 1890). Diez-Macho (*Sefarad*, 1944–45, 1947–51). *Abraham ibn Ezra* as grammarian – Bacher (1882). *Parḥon* – Bacher (ZAW, 1890/91), Del Valle Rodriguez (1977a, 1977b, 2001), Sáenz-Badillos (2001); idem and Paton (2002). *Jacob Tam* – Englander (HUCA, 1940. *Joseph Kimḥi* – Blueth (MWJ, 1893), Eppenstein (MGWJ, 1896/97). *David Kimḥi* – Tauber (1867); his *Mikhlol* – Chomsky (1952). *Tanḥum* – Goldziher (1870), Bacher (1903) and Shay (1975). *Samson Nakdan* and the other *nakdanim* – Zunz (*Zur Geschichte und Literatur*, 1845, 109–18), Eldar (1979) and Ben Menachem (1987). *Profiat Duran* – Gronemann (1869). *Saadiah ibn Danān* – Blumgrund (1900); Jiménez Sánchez (1996) and Del Valle Rodriguez (2004). *Elijah Levita* – Levi (1881), Bacher (ZDMG, 1889), Weil (1963).

Miscellaneous Topics

Some of the works published in the past hundred years have tried to clarify problems of a literary historical nature, such as: Is Dunash b. Labrat the author of the "objections" against Saadiah which are attributed to him and were they originally written in Hebrew? Is Judah Ḥayyūj the same as Judah b. David, a student of Menaḥem? Who is the author of the additions in the translation made by Ibn Gikatilla of the works of Ḥayyūj and when were they added? Who is the author of *Shekel ha-Kodesh* – and so on. Only a small part of the works deals with actual aspects of linguistics, such as comparison of languages, vowel theories, terminology, etc.

AUTHORS AND THEIR WORKS

Excluded from the following list are those works which are part of the Masorah literature, those which belong to biblical exegesis, and others, such as the *Kuzari* of Judah Halevi or *Guide of the Perplexed* by Maimonides, which treat language matters among other issues. The authors have been arranged in chronological order as far as possible, within periods of 50 years. Titles created by contemporary editors are indicated by +. A short description of the work follows each title, together with the place and year of publication, and, as far as possible, the editor is noted as well. Critical editions are noted by "crit. ed." and regular editions by "ed."

900 C.E.

1. *SAADIAH GAON: *Sefer ha-Egron* or *Kitāb Uṣūl al-Shiʿr al-ʿIbrānī*. This is the first work on Hebrew lexicography and the first dealing with rules of Hebrew poetry. Two editions are known: the first written in 902 in Hebrew and the second, an expanded version, produced a few years later. A few remnants have survived, representing a fourth or fifth of the total. Crit. ed. N. Allony (Jerusalem, 1969); for a serious textual correction see A. Dotan, "*Qeta' Hadash mi-Sefer Egron*," in: *Leshonenu*, 45 (1981), 163–212.

Kitāb Faṣīḥ Lughat al-ʿIbrāniyyīn or *Kutub al-Lugha* ("Book of Elegance of the Language of the Hebrews," or:

"Books on the [Hebrew] Language"). Written in Arabic, it is the first book dealing with biblical grammar, and written in Hebrew. No complete copy is extant, but the surviving material was published: ed. Harkavy, in *Ha-Goren* (1906), 31–32; crit. ed. Skoss, in JQR (1942), 171–212; *ibid.* (1952), 283–317; crit. ed. A. Dotan, *Or Rishon be-Hokhmat ha-Lashon – Sefer Zahot Leshon ha-'Ivriyyim le-Rav Saadiah Gaon* (1997).

Kitāb al-Sabʿīn Lafẓa al-Mufrada. A brief lexicographical essay written in Arabic which treats some of the *hapax legomena* of the Bible, explained with the aid of rabbinic Hebrew. It has been published incompletely several times and most recently: crit. ed. N. Allony, *Sefer Goldziher* (Jerusalem, 1958), 1–48 (includes 96 *hapax legomena*). For new fragments see A. Dotan, "A New Fragment of Saadiah's *Sab'in Lafzah*," *Jewish Quarterly Review,* 80 (1989–1990), 1–14; I. Eldar, *Leshonenu,* 58 (1995), 215–34.

+ *Alfāẓ al-Mishna.* A small lexicological work which contains a list of difficult words from the Mishnah translated into Arabic. This list is arranged not alphabetically, but in the order of the tractates, chapters, and *mishnayot*. The surviving material (134 entries) was published: crit. ed. Allony, *Leshonenu* (1952–53), 167–78; (1954), 31–48; (1958), 147–72; but see Abramson, *Leshonenu,* 36 (1954), 49–50.

+ *Alfāẓ al-Talmūd* (?). A lexicological work of which no part is extant. Its very existence and identification are still in need of study.

In addition, there are many linguistic issues scattered throughout the commentary of Saadiah Gaon on *Sefer Yeẓirah* – ed. Lambert (1891); in his translation and commentary of the Bible, and in the various criticisms made against his works.

2. JUDAH *IBN QURAYSH: *Risāla.* A work which compares biblical Hebrew to Aramaic, mishnaic Hebrew, and Arabic; ed. Bargès-Goldberg (Paris, 1857); Hebrew translation under the title of *Iggeret* by Katz (1952); crit. ed. and Hebrew translation D. Becker (1964).

A comprehensive dictionary of biblical Hebrew, lost in its entirety, even its name being unknown (cf. Kokowtzow (1916, Russian part, p. 95, n. 2; Skoss (1936), p. LXII, n. 87 (cr. 41)); Y. Blau (*EJ*, s.v. Ibn Quraysh) holds, however, that this was not an independent work but rather the third part of the *Risāla.*

3. DUNASH *IBN TAMIM: A work comparing Hebrew to Arabic (and Aramaic) with regard to vocabulary; likewise lost, even as regards its name. Bacher, in ZDMG (1907), 700–04, published part of an anonymous work believing that it was part of this study.

4. DAVID B. ABRAHAM *ALFASI: *Kitāb Jāmiʿal-Alfaẓ* or *al-Agron.* The most comprehensive dictionary of biblical Hebrew and Aramaic of the tenth century, possibly written in Jerusalem between 930 and 950, and the most important dictionary by a Karaite. It was written in two versions, the shorter of which was published: crit. ed. Skoss (1936); idem (1945); while a chapter of the longer version was published by him in JQR (1932–33), 1–43. Other selections from the longer version, of moderate length, were published as a supplement to the abovementioned publication of the shorter version.

5. *MENAḤEM BEN SARUQ: *Maḥberet.* The first dictionary of biblical Hebrew and Aramaic written originally in Hebrew, and also the first dictionary produced in Spain; ed. Filipowski (London, 1854). For clarification of the text according to an old and reliable manuscript see Kaufmann, in ZDMG (1886), 367–409; crit. ed. A. Sáenz-Badillos, *Menaḥem Ben Saruq, Mahberet* (Granada, 1986); see also A. Maman, "Menaḥem ben Saruq's *Maḥberet* – The First Hebrew-Hebrew Dictionary," in: *Kernerman Dictionary News* 13 (2005), 5–10, and the bibliography listed.

6. *DUNASH B. LABRAT: Criticism of the *Maḥberet* of Menaḥem known by the name of "The Objections of Dunash to the *Maḥberet* of Menaḥem," written in Hebrew, contains 180 objections; ed. Filipowski (London, 1855); crit. reed. of introduction, Allony, *Beit Mikra* (1965), 45–63; crit. ed. A. Sáenz-Badillos, *Teshuvot de Dunash ben Labrat, Edicion critica y traduccion Española* (Granada, 1980).

(?) Criticism of the linguistic works of Saadiah Gaon, attributed to Dunash b. Labrat, and extant in a very Arabicized Hebrew. The problems of the authorship of the book and the language in which it was written have not yet been settled; ed. Schroeter (Breslau, 1866); see, however, C. Del Valle Rodriguez, *La Escuela Hebrea de Córdoba* (Madrid, 1981), 133–136, 624–633; Y. Oshri, "*R. Abraham ibn Ezra, Sefer ha-Hagana 'al Rav Saadiah Gaon*" (Ramat Gan: Bar-Ilan Univ., 1988), 7–9, 26–29; R. Chazon (Master's thesis, Tel Aviv Univ. 1995). According to Del Valle Rodriguez (ibid.), the title's original work was *Tiqqun haš-šegagot.*

7. STUDENTS OF MENAHEM: ISAAC *IBN KAPRON, ISAAC IBN *GIKATILLA, JUDAH B. DAVID (DA'UD): A criticism in Hebrew of Dunash b. Labrat (see section 6 above). It contains in all about 50 replies to the objections which he made against the *Maḥberet* of Menaḥem; ed. Stern (Vienna, 1870); crit. ed. S. Benavente Robles, *Teshubot de los discipulos de Menaḥem contra Dunash ben Labrat* (Granada, 1986). A "major criticism" in this work is directed against Dunash because he began the practice of writing Hebrew poems in the Arabic (quantitative) meter. This is the first known discussion in which Arabic and Hebrew are compared with regard to metrics. The "major criticism" has been printed several times.

8. YEHUDI B. SHESHET (OR: SHISHAT): A small work in which this author gave 41 replies to the objections of the students of Menaḥem (7.1.); ed. Stern (Vienna, 1870), together with 7.1; crit. ed. M.E. Varela Moreno, *Yehudi Ben Seshet, Teshubot de Yehudi Ben Seshet, Edition traduccion y comentario* (Granada, 1981).

9. *JOSEPH B. NOAH: Abū al-Faraj Hārūn ibn al-Faraj (see section 12) mentions a work of his by the name *(Kitāb) al-Dikduk*, part of which has been preserved (cf. Bacher, in REJ (1895), p. 251); crit. ed. G. Khan, *The Early Karaite Tradition of Hebrew Grammatical Thought Including a Critical Edition, Translation and Analysis of the Diqduq of 'Abū Yūsuf ibn Nūḥ on the Hagiographa* (Leiden, 2000).

10. ABU SAʿID *LEVI B. JAPHETH: This author condensed the long version of *al-Agron* of David b. Abraham Alfâsi (see

section 4). An incomplete manuscript and fragments are located in St. Petersburg, but have not been published (cf. Skoss (1936), cxxxv–cxxxvii).

1000 C.E.

11. JUDAH B. DAVID, known as *ḤAYYŪJ: *Kitāb al-Af'āl Dhawāt Ḥurūf al-Līn.* An essay on the grammar of the verb, dealing with verbs which have as a radical of their roots *'alef, waw,* or *yod* and as the third root letter *he.* The work, in Arabic, contains theoretical introductions and lexicons arranged alphabetically for the verbs with initial *'alef* or *yod,* medial *waw,* and final *he;* (crit.?) ed. Jastrow (Leiden, 1897).

Kitāb al-Af'āl Dhawāt al-Mithlayn. A work, also in Arabic, dealing with grammar of double radical verbs, with a theoretical introduction, followed by a lexicon of double radical verbs in alphabetical order; (crit.?) ed. Jastrow (Leiden, 1897), together with *Kitāb al-Af'āl Dhawāt Ḥurūf al-Līn.* The material of these two works has been the subject of several studies, among them G. Goldenberg, "*'Al ha-Shokhen he-Ḥalaq ve-ha-Shoresh ha-'Ivri,*" in: *Leshonenu,* 44 (1980), 281–92; A. Watad, *Mishnato ha-Leshonit shel R. Yehuda Ḥayyūj mibbe'ad le-Munnahav bi-Meqoram ha-'Aravi uv-Targumam ha-'Ivri* (1994); N. Basil, *The Grammatical Theory of Rabbi Judah Ḥayyūj* (in Hebrew; Ramat-Gan: Bar-Ilan Univ., 1992); J. Martínez Delgado, *El Libro de Ḥayyūý* (Granada, 2004).

Kitāb al-Tanqīṭ ("The Book of Vocalization"). Perhaps his first work, it deals with the vowels, both in relation to the letters used with them, and in relation to the accent, especially in *segholate* nouns. It is written in Arabic; ed. Nutt (London, 1870), together with Gikatilla's *Sefer Otiyyot Ha-No'aḥ ve-ha-Meshekh* and *Sefer Po'olei ha-Kefel* and Ibn Ezra's *Sefer ha-Nikkud.* A new fragment of the Arabic original has been published by I. Eldar, *Mehqarim be-Lashon,* 8 (2001), 141–81.

The fourth work of *Ḥayyūj* is a linguistic-grammatical exegesis to the eight books of the *Prophets.* Some fragments have been published by Allony, Abramson and Eldar. This material has been republished along with new fragments by N. Basil, *Kitāb al-Nutaf le-Rabbi Yehuda Ḥayyūj* (2001).

Concerning the translation of the works of Ḥayyūj into Hebrew see Moses ha-Kohen Gikatilla (section 21) and Abraham ibn Ezra (see section 36).

12. *ABU AL-FARAJ HĀRŪN IBN AL-FARAJ: *Kitāb al-Mushtamil 'alā al-uṣūl wa al-Fuṣūl fī al-Lugha al-'Ibrāniyya* ("The Comprehensive Book on the Roots and Branches of the Hebrew Language"). A comprehensive work on linguistics, the most important written by a Karaite grammarian. Its composition (in Arabic) broke off in 1026. It has been preserved in manuscripts in St. Petersburg, one of them containing 579 pages. This work has undergone condensations, which have in turn been condensed. Only brief selections have been published: Hirschfeld, *Arabic Chrestomathy in Hebrew Characters* (London, 1892), 54–60; Poznański, in REJ (1896), 24–39, 197–218; (1908), 42–69. Abū Al-Faraj's grammatical theory has been studied in several articles of M. Zislin, A. Maman, and N. Basil. For references see the bibliography in A. Maman, *Comparative Semitic Philology in the Middle-Ages: from Saadia Gaon to Ibn Barūn (10th–12th cent.)* (Leiden, 2004), 484–85.

Al-Kitāb al-Kāfī fī al-Lugha al-'Ibrāniyya ("The Adequate Book on the Hebrew Language"). A kind of compendium of *Kitāb al-Mushtamil* (see Abū al-Faraj, section 12). The complete Arabic manuscript located in St. Petersburg contains 400 pages. Fragments: crit. ed. Zislin, *Palestinskiy Sbornik* (7 (70), 1962), 478–84; idem, *Kratkiye Soobshcheniya,* 86 (1965), 164–77; crit. ed. G. Khan et al., *The Karaite Tradition of Hebrew Grammatical thought in its Classical form: A Critical Edition and English Translation of Al-Kitāb Al-Kāfī fi l-Luġa l-'Ibrāniyya by 'Abū al-Faraj Harūn ibn al-Faraj* (2003).

Al-Mukhtaṣar (*The Digest*), another compendium made out of *Al-Kitāb al-Kāfī.* See Khan, ibid. 1, p. xxx.

Kitāb al-'uqūd fī Tasārīf al-Lugha al-'Ibraniyya. Perhaps a further condensation of *Al-Kitāb al-Kāfī;* a selection has been published: ed. Hirschfeld, in JQR (1922–23), 1–7.

Hidāyat al-Qāri (*Guidance of the Reader):* see: I. Eldar, *The Study of the Art of Correct Reading as Reflected in the Medieval Treatise Hidāyat al-Qāri* (in Hebrew; Jerusalem 1994).

13. *HAI B. SHERIRA: *Kitāb al-Ḥāwi* ("The Collecting Book"). A Hebrew dictionary written in Arabic in which the roots are arranged according to the order of an anagram. Small selections from it have been published: ed. Harkavy, *Ḥadashim Gam Yeshanim,* 7 (1895–96), 3–5; idem, *Mi-Mizraḥ u-mi-Ma'arav,* 3 (1896), 94–96; S. Abramson, in: *Leshonenu,* 41 (1977), 108–116; A. Maman, *Tarbiz* (2000). Other parts, also from the Cairo *Genizah,* are in preparation for publication.

14. JONAH *IBN JANĀḤ: *Kitāb al-Mustalḥaq* (*Sefer ha-Hassagah;* "The Book of Criticism"). The express purpose of this book (finished in 1012) is to complete the two works of Ḥayyūj (*Kitāb al-Af'āl Dhawāt Ḥurūf al-Līn* and *Kitāb al-Af'āl Dhawāt al-Mithlayn*), though this completion is accompanied by critical additions. It was written in Arabic and translated into Hebrew by Obadiah ha-Sefardi (see section 46): (crit.?) ed. Derenbourg, *Opusculeṣet traités* (Paris, 1880); a critical edition of Obadiah ha-Sefardi's Hebrew version has been prepared by Téné and brought to press by A. Maman.

Kitāb al-Taswi'a (*Sefer ha-Tokhaḥat;* "The Book of Rebuke," or *Sefer ha-Hashva'ah*). A reply to the objections, which had reached Saragossa, made by Samuel ha-Nagid and his friends against *Kitāb al-Mustalḥaq* (see above). It was written in Arabic and translated into Hebrew by Solomon ibn Job (see section 58): (crit.?) ed. Derenbourg, *Opuscules et traités* (Paris, 1880).

Kitāb al-Tashwīr (Sefer ha-Hakhlamah; "The Book of Shaming"). A reply to the criticism which Samuel ha-Nagid had voiced against *Kitāb al-Mustalḥaq* in *Rasāil al-Rifāq* (see section 15). This work was written in Arabic, and it is not known whether it was translated into Hebrew: A selection appears in Derenbourg, *Opusculeṣet traités* (Paris, 1880); a new fragment was identified and published by M. Perez, in: *Kiriat Sefer,* 64 (1993), 1367–87; see also I. Eldar, in: *Mehqarim ba-Lashon ha-'Ivrit u-vi-Lshonot ha-Yehudim Muggashim li-Shlomo Morag* (1996), 41–61.

Risālat al-Tanbīh (trans. by Judah ibn Tibbon as *Sefer ha-He ʿarah*; "The Book of Admonition"). A reply to a work of criticism against *Kitāb al-Mustalḥaq* (see above) which was called *Kitāb al-Istīfā*ʾ ("The Book of Completion," "The Book of Detailed Treatment") and composed in Saragossa. *Risālat al-Tanbīh* was written in Arabic and translated into Hebrew by Solomon ibn Job (see section 58: (crit.?) ed. Derenbourg, *Opuscules et traités* (Paris, 1880).

Risālat al-Taqrīb wa al-Tashīl (*Iggeret ha-Keruv ve-ha-Yishur*; "The Epistle of Bringing Near and Making Easy"). A kind of explanation for beginners of difficult passages in the introductions of Ḥayyūj to his two works on verbs (*Kitāb al-Afʿāl Dhawāt Ḥurūf al-Līn* and *Kitāb al-Afʿāl Dhawāt al-Mithlayn*). A Hebrew translation of the Arabic original was made by Jacob b. Isaac Roman in the first half of the 17th century (cf. Bacher in his introduction to *Sefer ha-Shorashim* (1897), xxxii (see section 42 below)), but no copy of it has survived. The work was published as (crit.?) ed. Derenbourg, *Opusculeșet traités* (Paris, 1880).

Kitāb al-Tanqīh (*Sefer ha-Dikduk*; "The Book of Detailed Investigation"). The first complete description of biblical Hebrew, written in Arabic in the 1040s. No other work written by a Jew can be compared to it in scope and theoretical foundation. It consists of two parts:

Kitāb al-Lumaʿ (*Sefer ha-Rikmah*; "The Book of Colored Flowerbeds"), a grammar of biblical Hebrew: (crit.?) ed. Derenbourg (-Bacher; Paris, 1886).

Kitāb al-Uṣūl (*Sefer ha-Shorashim*; "Book of [Hebrew] Roots"). A dictionary of biblical Hebrew: (crit.?) ed. Neubauer (Oxford, 1873/5); beside the additions and corrections mentioned above, chap. "Publication of the Works," see also J. Blau, in: *Leshonenu*, 37 (1973), 232–33. The two parts of *Kitāb al-Tanqīh* were translated into Hebrew by Judah ibn Tibbon (cf. section 42, *Sefer ha-Rikmah* and *Sefer ha-Shorashim*). D. Becker, *Meqorot ʿArviyyim le-Diqduqo shel R. Jonah ibn Janāḥ* (Tel Aviv, 1999) and Maman (2004; above section 12) are among the latest research achievements on Ibn Janāḥ.

15. *SAMUEL HA-NAGID (B. NAGDELA): *Rasāʾil al-Rifāq* (*Iggerot ha-Ḥaverim* or *ha-Ḥaverut*; "Epistles of the Companions," or: "of Companionship"). A polemical work in Arabic against some of the comments which Ibn Janāḥ made in his *Kitāb al-Mustalḥaq* (see section 14) concerning the works of Ḥayyūj. Parts of it have been preserved in St. Petersburg, and one small selection was published: Derenbourg (Paris, 1880), LIX–LXVI (cf. section 14: *Risālat al-Taqrīb wa al-Tashīl*).

Kitāb at-Ḥujja ("Book of Evidence"). A polemical work in Arabic in reply to the *Kitāb al-Tashwīr* of Ibn Janāḥ (See section 14:*Kitāb al-Tashwīr*). No part of the book has survived, but it was mentioned by the Nagid himself and by Judah ibn Balʿam (see section 22).

*Kitāb al-Istighnā*ʾ ("Book of Amplitude"). A large dictionary of biblical Hebrew, in Arabic. Small parts which have been preserved in St. Petersburg have been published: crit. ed. Kokowtzow (Petrograd, 1916), 205–24. Large quotations from the book have been found in an anonymous commentary to Psalms and published by M. Perez, *Shenaton le-Ḥeqer ha-Miqra ve-Hamizraḥ ha-Qadum*, 12 (2000), 241–87. Z. Ukashy used Hanagid's poetic language usages to reconstruct some of his lost lexical definitions; see Ukashy's dissertation, "Hannagid's Dictionary based on his Poetry" (in Hebrew; Jerusalem, Heb. Univ., 1998).

16. SOLOMON IBN *GABIROL: *Anak* ("Necklace"). A didactical poem on Hebrew grammar, 98 verses out of the original 400 are known and have been published: Egers, *Zunz Jubelschrift* (1884) Hebrew part, 192–96; re-ed. Bialik-Rawnitzki, vol. 1 (Berlin, 1924), 173–80.

17. *ABRAHAM HA-BAVLI: A lexicographical work, only a part of which has been preserved and published: ed. Neubauer, *Journal Asiatique*, 2 (1863), 195–216.

18. *DAVID (HA-DAYYAN) IBN HAJJAR: Abraham ibn Ezra mentions him, saying that he produced a work known as *Sefer ha-Melakhim*, apparently on the vowels, but it has not been preserved. Moses ibn Ezra calls him Abū Suleimān ibn Muhāgīr (cf. Bacher on ibn Ezra (1882), 185; Neubauer (1963), 202).

1050 C.E.

19. *IBN YASHUSH, ISAAC: *Kitāb al-Taṣārīf* (*Sefer ha-Ẓerufim*; "Treatise on Conjugations"). Abraham ibn Ezra mentions it, but the work has not been preserved. The selections published by Derenbourg, *Opuscules* (1880), and Kokowtzow (1916) in fact belong to another work, which perhaps had the same name, but is of a later date (see section 24). Kokowtzow called the latter work "Pseudo-Ibn Yashush" (cf. Bacher on Ibn Ezra (1882), 186).

20. ELI B. ISRAEL: He made (in 1066?) a further condensation from the one made by Levi b. Japheth (see section 10) of the long version of *al-Agron* by Alfāsi (see section 4 above). It exists in manuscript (cf. Skoss (1936), CXXXVII–CXXXIX).

21. *MOSES HA-KOHEN *GIKATILLA: *Sefer Otiyyot Ha-Noʾaḥ ve-ha-Meshekh* ("Treatise on [Verbs Containing] Feeble Letters").

Sefer Poʿolei ha-Kefel ("Treatise of Verbs Containing Double Letters"). A Hebrew translation of the two works of Ḥayyūj on the weak verbs (*Kitāb al-Afʿāl Dhawāt Ḥurūf al-Līn* and *Kitāb al-Afʿāl Dhawāt al-Mithlayn*); one of the first translations from Arabic to Hebrew, and the first such translation of the works of a Jewish grammarian: ed. Nutt (London, 1870).

Kitab al-Tadhkīr wa al Taʾnith (*Sefer Zekharim u-Nekevot*; "Treatise on Masculine and Feminine Genders"). A monograph in Arabic concerning nouns in the Bible whose usage deviates from the accepted rule with regard to gender. Two selections have been published: crit. ed. Kokowtzow (Petrograd, 1916), 59–66; it was published with an additional selection (altogether about one tenth of the monograph) and a modern Hebrew translation: crit. ed. Allony, *Sinai* (1949), 34–67.

22. *JUDAH IBN BALʿAM: *Kitāb al-Tajnīs* ("The Book of Homonyms"). As far as we know this is the first monograph concerning homonyms. It was written in Arabic with the entries in an alphabetical-dictionary order, and some of the

surviving material (139 entries) has been published: crit. ed. Kokowtzow (Petrograd, 1916), 69–108; crit. re-ed. Abramson, *Sefer Yalon* (1963), 51–149; Allony, *Beit Mikra* (1964), 87–122.

Kitāb Ḥurūf al-Maʿanī (*Sefer Otiyyot ha-Inyanim*; "Book of Particles"). A lexicon of the particles of Hebrew, written in Arabic, selections of which have been published: crit. ed. Kokowtzow (Petrograd (1916), 109–32; Allony, *Beit Mikra* (1964), 87–122.

Kitāb al-Afʿāl-Mushtaqqa min al-Asmāʾ ("The Book of Verbs Derived from Nouns," Verba denominativa). A lexicon of verbs derived from nouns, written in Arabic, and published in part: crit. ed. Kokowtzow (Petrograd, 1916), 133–52.

An anonymous translation is extant of the three works of Ibn Balʿam, parts of which have been published at various places and several times. The translation of *Kitāb al-Afʿāl-Mushtaqqa min al-Asmāʾ* was published by: Polak, in *Ha-Karmel*, 3 (Vilna, 1862–63), 212, 229–230; Goldberg, in *Ḥayyei Olam* (1878–79), 53–61; Hirschensohn, *Hamisderonah* (Jerusalem, 1885), 21–23; 42–47. The translation of *Kitāb Ḥurūf al-Maʿanī* was published by Fuchs, *Haḥoker* (Paris, 1892/93), 113–28; 193–206; 340–2; *ibid.*, (Vienna, 1894), 73–83. It was later published by the editors of the above-mentioned Arabic original of the Ibn Balʿam works discussed here; the entire extant material from the philological books has been published by S. Abramson, *Shelosha Sefarim shel Rav Yehuda ben Balʿam* (1975).

23. LEV *IBN ALTABBAN: This author wrote a linguistic work which has been lost, even its contents remaining unknown. Abraham ibn Ezra and Elijah (Baḥur) Levita refer to it as *Sefer ha-Mafteʾaḥ*; cf. Pagis, in *Leshonenu* (1963–64).

24. ANONYMOUS (PSEUDO-IBN YASHUSH):

An anonymous work in Arabic which is a kind of long commentary on the linguistic work of Samuel ha-Nagid. It was believed to be the *Kitāb al Tasārīf* of Isaac Abū Ibrahim ibn Yashush but Ibn Yashush's work antedates it by a generation. Sections of the work were published by: Derenbourg, *Opuscules* (1880), XXXXI; Kokowtzow (1916, Russian part), in various places in the notes.

1100 C.E.

25. ANONYMOUS (Karaite)

An anonymous Karaite work in Hebrew entitled *Meʾor ʾAyin*, based on Abū Al-Faraj Harūn's grammatical theory (see section 12 above); crit. ed. M. Zislin (Moscow, 1990); review: A. Maman, in: *Leshonenu*, 58 (1995), 153–65.

26. ISAAC *IBN BARŪN: *Kitāb al-Muwāzana bayn al-Lugha al-ʾIbraniyya wa al-ʾArabiyya*. A monograph on the connection between Hebrew and Arabic, written in Arabic no earlier then 1080 and no later than 1128. It includes a short grammatical section and a long section on lexicography. About two-thirds of the monograph, which includes more than 600 dictionary entries, has been preserved, and published: crit. ed. Kokowtzow (Petrograd, 1890–93), 1–98; crit. ed. idem (1916), 153–72. A new Genizah fragment from this work has been discovered by A. Maman (see *Otzrot Lashon – The Hebrew Philology Manuscripts and Genizah Fragments in the Library of the Jewish Theological Seminary of America* (in press), entry MS 8713.1 MS R1978.1; cf. also "Dictionaries and Glossaries from the Collection of the Jewish Theological Seminary of America: Introductory Notes," in: *Leshonenu*, 65 (2003), 303–14, esp. n. 17). D. Becker, *Meqorot ʾArviyyim shel 'Sefer ha-Hashvaʾa bein ha-ʾIvrit veha-ʾAravit' le-Isaac ben Barun* (2005), discovered the sources used by Ibn Barūn for the Arabic part of his work. He has also been preparing the entire text of *Muwāzana* for a new critical edition.

27. *ALI IBN SULEIMAN:

He made a further condensation of the one made by Abū Saʿid Levi b. Japheth (10.1) of the long version of *al-Agron* of Alfāsi (4.1); preserved only in manuscript in St. Petersburg; cf. Skoss (1936), CXXXIX.

28. ABRAHAM IBN QAMNI'EL (OR: QANBIL):

According to Joseph Kimḥi he wrote a Hebrew grammar, which has been lost.

29. *JACOB B. ELEZAR: *Al-Kāmil (Sefer ha-Shalem*; "The Complete [Book]"). A work which apparently consisted of a grammar and a lexicon, referred to by David Kimḥi as *Sefer ha-Shalem*, and known in Arabic as *al-Kāmil*. Crit. ed. of the remnants of the work: N. Allony, *Yaʿaqov ben Elʿazar – Kitāb al-Kāmil* (1977) (cf. Bacher (1892), 110).

30. *NATAN B. JEHIEL OF ROME: *He-Arukh*. A comprehensive dictionary of the Talmuds, the Midrashim, and of early geonic literature, written in Rome at the beginning of the 12th century, and preserved in several copies. It has been published many times; the first edition appeared before 1480; crit. ed. H.Y. Kohut, *Arukh Completum* (1879–1892); see also: S. Abramson, *"le-Heqer he-Arukh,"* in: *Leshonenu*, 36 (1972), 122–49; 37 (1973), 26–42, 253–69; 38 (1974), 91–117.

31. ABU ISḤĀQ IBRĀHĪM B. FARAJ B. MARUTH: *Kitāb al Tawṭiʾa* (+*Sefer ha-Maslul*). A systematic work on the grammar of Samaritan Hebrew. According to Ben-Hayyim (1957), p. 30, it was written in the first half of the 12th century, and is one of the earliest works in the study of the language of the Samaritans. The author did not complete the work, but left only a small part lacking; crit. ed. Ben-Hayyim (Jerusalem, 1957), 3–127 (see especially 30–34).

32. MENAHEM B. SOLOMON: *Even Boḥan*. A comprehensive work for the study of Hebrew, including a grammar, a dictionary (the main part) and a section on exegesis. It was written in Rome in 1143; cf. Bacher, *Graetz-Jubelschrift* (Breslau, 1887), 94–115. Fragments: ed. Bacher (MHLW (*Oẓar ha-Sifrut*), 1896), 257–63; idem, *Ha-Goren*, 4 (1903), 38–58.

33. NETHANEL (B. AL-FAYYUMI?) OF YEMEN: A Hebrew (-Arabic?) grammar, written in Arabic, part of which has been published; ed. Kokowtzow (Petrograd, 1916), 173–89.

34. MOSES *IBN EZRA: *Kitāb al-muḥāḍara wa almudhākara*. The first work of poetics on Hebrew poetry, based on Arabic poetic theory: chapter 2 was published by Hirschfeld, *Arabic Chrestomathy* (1892), 61–63; the introduction and the first four chapters were issued by Kokowtzow (*Vostochniya Zametki*, 1895), 191–220. An early anonymous translation,

Eshkol ha-Kofer, is cited by A. Zacuto, in Yuḥasin (London (1857), p. 229). A free translation in modern Hebrew, entitled *Shirat Yisrael* (Berlin, 1924), was published by Halper; crit. ed. A.S. Halkin, *Moshe ben Ya'aqov ibn Ezra – Sefer ha-'Iyyunim veha-Diyyunim* (1975).

35. JUDAH HADASSI, THE KARAITE: *Eshkol ha-Kofer.* An encyclopedic work, in Hebrew, which includes an elaborate grammar based on Ḥayyūj and Ibn Janāḥ (begun in 1149): ed. Eupatoria (1836); inedited chapters ed. Bacher (JQR, 1896), 431–44.

36. ABRAHAM *IBN EZRA: *Sefer Moznayim* (or *Moznei Leshon ha-Kodesh*). An introduction to linguistics containing a survey of the grammarians who preceded him, a section on 59 grammatical terms and one on the conjugations of the verb; written in Rome in 1140; ed. Heidenheim (Offenbach, 1791; crit. ed. L.J. Paton, A. Sáenz-Badillos, *Abraham Ibn 'Ezra, Sefer Moznayim*, (Cordoba, 2002); J. Targarona Borras, "Conceptos gramaticales en el *Sefer Mo'znayim* de Abraham Ibn Ezra," *Abraham Ibn Ezra Y Su Teimpo* (Madrid, 1990), 345–52.

Sefer Otiyyot ha-No'aḥ.

Sefer Po'olei ha-Kefel.

Sefer ha-Nikkud.

Translations of the three works of Ḥayyūj (see section 11): ed. Dukes (Frankfurt on the Main, 1844). *Sefer ha-Nikkud* was reprinted by Nutt (London, 1870), together with Gikatilla's *Sefer Otiyyot Ha-No'aḥ ve-ha-Meshekh* and *Sefer Po'olei ha-Kefel*, and Ḥayyūj's *Kitāb al-Tanqīṭ*.

A work in defense of Saadiah Gaon directed against the criticism attributed to Dunash b. Labrat (see section 6) mistakenly called *Sefat Yeter* and published under that name (cf. Wilensky, KS, 3, 1926/7, 73–77); ed. Bisliches (1838); ed. Lippmann (Frankfurt on the Main, 1843); crit. ed. of a *genizah* fragment, Allony, *Leshonenu* (1944–45), 218–22; crit. ed. Y. Oshri, *R. Abraham ibn Ezra, Sefer ha-Hagana 'al Rav Saadiah Gaon* (Ramat Gan: Bar-Ilan Univ., 1988); A. Sáenz-Badillos, "La Obra de Abraham ibn Ezra sobre las Criticas Contra Se'adyah," *Abraham Ibn Ezra Y Su Tiempo* (Madrid, 1990), pp. 287–294.

Sefat Yeter. A comprehensive systematic grammar for beginners (Lucca, 1140–45). Bacher on Ibn Ezra (1882), 8–17, thought it *Sefer ha-Yesod* (or *Yesod Dikduk*), which, in his opinion, was not extant: but Wilensky, KS (1926/27), 73–77, proved that it was *Sefat Yeter.* The introduction was published: ed. Bacher on Ibn Ezra (1882), 148–9; crit. ed. N. Allony, *Yesod Diqduq hu Sefat Yeter me'et Rabbi Abraham ibn Ezra* (Jerusalem, 1984).

Sefer Ẓaḥot (*Ẓaḥot*). The main grammatical work of Abraham ibn Ezra, written in Mantua in 1145, which treats every grammatical topic; ed. Lippmann (Fuerth, 1827); crit. ed. C. Del Valle Rodriguez, *Sefer Saḥot de Abraham Ibn Ezra I Edicion critica y version castellana* (Salamanca, 1977); see also idem, *La obra gramatical de Abraham Ibn Ezra* (Madrid, 1977); L. Charlap, *Innovation and Tradition in Rabbi Abraham Ibn-Ezra's Grammar according to his Grammatical Writings and to his Bible Exegesis* (in Hebrew, 1995); C. Del Valle Rodriguez, "*Le-Ba'yat Hibburei ha-Diqduq shel Rabbi Abraham ibn Ezra*," in: *Mehqarim Be-Lashon*, 8 (2001), 253–281; A. Sáenz-Badillos, "*'al kamma 'amadot diqduqiyot shel R. Abraham ibn Ezra*," *ibid.*, 229–51.

1150 C.E.

Sefer ha-Shem (or *Sefer ha-Shem ha-Nikhbad*). Only in part a grammatical work. Of its eight chapters, the first three and the last two deal with personal names and adjectives; written in Béziers before 1155; ed. Lippmann (Fuerth, 1834).

Yesod Mispar. A short monograph about the numerals; written in Béziers before 1155; ed. Pinsker, in *Mavo el ha-Nikkud ha-Ashuri*, Vienna, 1863.

Safah Berurah. A grammar, apparently written in southern France; ed. Lippmann (Fuerth, 1839); crit. ed. Wilensky, *Devir*, II (Berlin, 1924), 274–302 (incomplete); Ben-Menaḥem, *Sinai* (1941), 43–53, crit. ed. of the 8 missing pages of the Lippmann (1839) edition.

Sefer ha-Yesod (or *Yesod Dikduk*). (See *Sefat Yeter*, above.)

37. SOLOMON IBN *PARHON: *Maḥberet he-Arukh.* A dictionary preceded by a grammar section, written in Hebrew (Salerno, 1161). It is almost a précis of *Sefer ha-Shorashim* by Ibn Janāḥ, with various additions taken from the works of Ḥayyūj, from *Kitāb al-Mustalḥaq*, and from *Sefer ha-Rikmah*; ed. Stern (Pressburg, 1844); inedited fragments: ed. Bacher, in ZAW (1891), 96ff. and in ZHB (1896), 59–61.

38. JACOB B. MEIR (RABBENU *TAM): A work known as *Hakhra'ot* in which he set out to decide between Menaḥem and Dunash; ed. Filipowski (London, 1855, with the objections of Dunash).

A didactic poem on cantillation signs and vocalization: ed. Halberstam, in *Jeschurun*, 5 (1865), Hebrew part, 123–31.

39. *SAMUEL BEN MEIR (RASBHAM): A grammatical work known as *Dayqut* is based on pre-Ḥayyūj grammatical theory, published by Yom-Tov Stein as "*Shiyurei Yom Tov, Diqduq me-Rabbenu Shemuel u-Perusho 'al ha-Torah 'al pi ha-Diqduq*," in: *Jahrbuch des Traditionstreuen Rabbinerverbandes in der Slovakei* (Tranava, 1923), i–vii, 33–67; crit. ed. R. Merdler, *Dayyaqut MeRabbenu Shemuel [Ben Meir (Rashbam)]* (Jerusalem 1999); Rashbam's grammatical theory has been studied in a dissertation by Merdler (Hebrew University, Jerusalem, 2004).

40. ISAAC HA-LEVI: According to Judah ibn Tibbon, Ha-Levi wrote a book called *Sefer ha-Makor.* The work has been lost.

41. ISAAC B. JUDAH (?) BARCELONI: According to Judah ibn Tibbon, he translated the first part of *Kitāb al-Uṣūl* of Ibn Janāḥ, but the translation is not extant.

42. JUDAH IBN *TIBBON: Completed the translation of *Kitāb al Tanqīḥ* of Ibn Janaḥ in 1171.

Sefer ha-Rikmah. Translation of the *Kitāb al-Luma'* of Ibn Janāḥ: ed. Goldberg (Frankfurt on the Main, 1856); French translation by Metzger, *Le livre des parterres fleuris* (1889); crit.

ed. Wilensky (Berlin, 1929–31), second ed. Wilensky-Téné, Jerusalem, 1964.

Sefer ha-Shorashim. Translation of the *Kitāb al-Uṣūl* of Ibn Janāḥ; crit. ed. Bacher (Berlin, 1894–97).

43. JOSEPH *KIMḤI: *Sefer Zikkaron* ("Book of Remembrance"). Together with the works of Abraham ibn Ezra, this is the first grammar written in Hebrew on the basis of the language study which had developed in Spain; interesting is his chapter on the division of the vowels into five long and five short ones; crit. ed. Bacher (Berlin, 1888).

Sefer ha-Galui. A reply to the "decisions" of Jacob b. Meir Tam (37.1); ed. Mathews (Berlin, 1887).

44. JOSEPH HACONSTANDINI: *Adat Devorim.* A work spanning the dividing line between masorah literature and linguistic literature (unpublished).

45. MOSES B. JOSEPH *KIMḤI: *Mahalakh Shevilei ha-Da'at.* A concise, schematic grammar based on the works of his father and Abraham ibn Ezra. Elijah (Baḥur) Levita published it in 1508, and it has been republished many times – according to Hirschfeld (1926), 82, thirteen (fourteen?) times during the 16th century alone; S. García-Jalón de la Lama y M. Veiga Díaz, *Repertorio de gramáticas hebreas impresas en Europa en el siglo XVI* (Salamanca 2000 = *Helmantica* 156), 615–18. Last edition Hamburg, 1785.

46. OBADIAH HA-SEFARDI: *Sefer ha-Hassagah.* Translation of the *Kitāb al-Mustalḥaq* of Ibn Janāḥ *Kitāb al-Tanqīṭ*, so named by the translator. See above subentry *Kitāb al-Mustalḥaq.*

1200 C.E.

47. DAVID B. JOSEPH *KIMḤI: *Sefer Mikhlol.* A complete description of biblical Hebrew consisting of two parts:

(a) *Mikhlol*, originally entitled *Ḥeleq ha-Diqduq.* The most widespread grammar of the Hebrew language. It has been printed many times: Constantinople, 1525, 1532–34, 1533; Venice, 1545, accompanied by the comments of Elijah Levita: Fuerth, 1793; and Lyck, 1864.

(b) *Sefer ha-Shorashim*, originally entitled *Ḥeleq ha-'Inyan.* Based on the most widespread dictionary of the Hebrew Language, *Kitāb al-Uṣūl* of Ibn Janāḥ in the translation of Judah ibn Tibbon (see section 42). It was printed in Rome before 1480 and in Naples in 1490 and has gone through several editions, the last two ones, Berlin 1838 and 1847, the latter with the comments of Elijah (Baḥur) Levita.

Et Sofer. A short work on vocalization and cantillation signs; ed. Goldberg (Lyck, 1864).

48. ANONYMOUS: Hebrew-French Glossary. Composed in the second quarter of the 13th century (1240–41?); crit. ed. Lambert-Brandin (Paris, 1905).

49. ANONYMOUS (DAVID?): A short work on grammar (second quarter of the 13th century). Poznański (1894) thought that the author had come from Greece and wrote the work in Prague. It begins with a division into three parts of speech and then briefly discusses the noun, verb, *milliyyot* (particles), and at the end vowels; ed. Poznański (Berlin, 1894).

50. ANONYMOUS: (+ *Ha-Meliẓ*). A Hebrew-Aramaic-Arabic dictionary on the vocabulary of the Samaritan Pentateuch. According to Ben-Ḥayyim (1957), 65–73, the work was composed in two stages. In the first stage it was a Hebrew-Aramaic dictionary written at the latest at the end of the 10th or the beginning of the 11th century. The Arabic was added at the second stage by another writer, probably between the second half of the 11th and the beginning of the 14th century. Crit. ed. Ben-Hayyim (Jerusalem, 1957), 439–616.

51. MOSES (AL-)ROTI: In *Darkhei ha-Nikkud* (see below) Moses b. Yom Tov mentions a grammarian of this name; see Wilensky, HUCA (1936), 647–9.

52. MOSES B. YOM TOV: *Darkhei ha-Nikkud ve-ha-Neginot* or *Sha'arei ha-Nikkud.* A work concerning vowels and cantillation signs; crit. ed. Lowinger, in: *Ha-Ẓofeh leḤokhmat Yisrael* (1929), 267–344.

53. ABU SA'ID B. ABU AL-HASAN B. ABU SA'ID: *Kitāb al-Qawanīn li Irshād al-Muta'llimīn.* A book on correct pronunciation in the reading of the Pentateuch, composed toward the middle of the 13th century; first ed. Noeldeke (1862); crit. ed. Ben-Hayyim (Jerusalem, 1957), 131–69; and see especially 34–39.

1250 C.E.

54. *MOSES (B. ISAAC) B. HA-NESI'AH: *Leshon Limmudim.* In the introduction to *Sefer ha-Shoham* (see below) the writer mentions that in his youth he wrote a grammatical work with this title.

Sefer ha-Shoham. The first grammatical work, based on the theory of Spanish grammarians, written by a Franco-German Jew; ed. Collins (London, 1882) – the first part; crit. ed. Klar (Jerusalem, 1946), the first and second parts (incomplete).

55. *TANḤUM YERUSHALMI: *al-Murshid al-Kāfī* ("The Adequate Guide"). A large dictionary written in Arabic for the Hebrew of the *Mishneh Torah* of Maimonides: ed. Toledano (Tel Aviv, 1961), part 1: letters א–כ. The letters ל–ש were edited by H. Shay as *"Al-Murshid al-Kāfī – ha-Madrikh ha-Maspiq le-Rabbi Tanhum be-Rabbi Yosef ha-Yerushalmi"* (dissertation, Heb. Univ. Jerusalem 1975). The letter *taw* was published: crit. ed. Shay, *Leshonenu* (1969), 196–207; 280–96. A crit. ed. of the entire dictionary has been prepared by Shay (in press).

56. JUDAH *AL-ḤARIZI: *Ha-Mavo li-Leshon ha-Kodesh.* According to Isaac ha-Levi b. Eleazar (55), Al-Ḥarizi composed a work of this name (cf. Neubauer (1863), p. 205).

57. ISAAC HA-LEVI B. ELEAZAR (?), ISAAC B. ELEAZAR HA-LEVI (?): *Sefat Yeter.* A yet unpublished condensed Hebrew translation of the two works of Ḥayyūj (11.1–2) and of *Kitāb al-Mustalḥaq* by Ibn Janāḥ (14.1). Poznański in: MGWJ (1895) 251–62, printed the introduction; cf. also Nutt (1870), x.

Ha-Rikmah. A collection of monographs on various grammatical and lexicographical issues which has remained unpublished.

58. SOLOMON B. JOSEPH IBN JOB: *Sefer ha-Hashva'ah*, Translation of *Kitāb al-Taswi'a* by Ibn Janāḥ under this in-

correct title (Béziers, 1264). Small parts have been preserved in manuscripts.

The manuscript has been described by M. Gaspar Remiro, "Los manuscritos de la Biblioteca Nacional," in: *Boletín de la Real Academia Española*, 6 (1919) 221–34, "Ms. 5460, fol. 1a-7b"; but several mistakes occurred in the description, which has been corrected by C. Del Valle Rodriguez, *Catálogo Descriptivo de los Manuscritos Hebreos de la Biblioteca Nacional* (Madrid, 1986), 35–40. The text has been published by J.M. Camacho Padilla, *Rabi Yona Ben Gannah. La segunda mitad del Sefer Hahaxua, version hebraica de su Kitab al-Taswiya por Salomon bar Yosef ben Ayyub* (Córdoba, 1929). See also C. Del Valle Rodriguez, *Historia de la Gramática Hebrea en España*, vol. 10, *La gramática hebrea de Ibn Danán en la versión árabe y hebrea*, (Madrid, 2004), 428.

Sefer ha-Ma'aneh. Translation of the *Risālat al-Tanbīh* of Ibn Janāḥ under this title.

59. ABRAHAM B. ISAAC *BEDERSI: *Ḥotam Tokhnit* ("The Seal of the Well-Built Edifice"). The first dictionary of synonyms in biblical Hebrew; ed. Polak (Amsterdam, 1865).

60. MEIR B. DAVID: *Hassagat ha-Hassagah*. A work in defense of Ḥayyūj against the criticism of Ibn Janāḥ in *Kitāb al-Mustalḥaq*; cf. *Ma'aseh Efod* (see section 78 below), pp. 116, 173.

61. SAMSON: A dictionary in which words are often translated into German.

62. SAMSON HA-NAKDAN: *Ḥibbur ha-Konim* or: *Shimshoni*. A work on vocalization ascribed by Ben-Yaakov to Samson (cf. Hirschfeld, 1926, N. 2); ed. Frensdorff (Hannover, 1865); I. Eldar, "*Mi-Kitvei Askolat ha-Diqduq ha-'Ashkenazit – ha-Shimshoni*," in: *Leshonenu*, 43 (1979), 100–11, 201–10; D. Ben Menachem, "*Hibbur ha-Qonim ha-Shimshoni by R. Shimshon ha-Naqdan (13th cent.)*" (Ph.D. thesis, U.S.A. 1987).

63. JEKUTHIEL B. ISAAC HA-KOHEN (or: ZALMAN NAKDAN OF PRAGUE);

Ein ha-Kore. A work on vocalization; a section of the introduction was published by Hirschfeld (1926, app. III) from Cod. Brit. Mus. Or. 853; and one chapter has been published, ed. Gumpertz, in *Leshonenu* (1958), 36–47, 137–46. The work has been studied by I. Eldar, *Leshonenu*, 40, 190–210; idem, *Masoret ha-Qeri'ah ha-qedam Ashkenzit*, I (1979), 191–96; idem, *Massorot*, 5–6, 10–16. A critical edition of the first part, *The Grammar*, has been published by R. Yarkoni, "*'Ein Hakore li-Yequti'el ha-Cohen*," 1–2 (dissertation, Tel Aviv Univ. 1985).

64. *MORDECAI B. HILLEL: Wrote two poems on vocalization; ed. Kohn, in MGWJ, 26 (1877), 167–71, 271–5.

65. *JOSEPH B. KALONYMUS:

Two poems on cantillation, one of which has been published, ed. Berliner (Berlin, 1886), under the name *Ta'amei Emet ba-Ḥaruzim*.

1300 C.E.

66. SOLOMON B. MEVORAKH: *Kitab al-Taysir. A Karaite Hebrew-Arabic dictionary based mainly on Ya'acov b. Eleazar's Kitab al-Kamil*, but on other sources too such as Alfāsi, Ḥayyūj and Ibn Janāḥ. The author is mentioned by the Karaite chronist Ibn Al-Hitti (G. Margoliouth, *JQR*, 9 (1897), 429–43). The dictionary is preserved in several manuscripts and has been prepared for publication by J. Martinez Delgado. See his article (in Hebrew) in *Studies in Hebrew Language and Literature – Madrid Congress – Brit Ivrit Olamit –Proceedings of the 13th Hebrew Scientific European Congress, University of Madrid, August 1998*, pp. 59–63.

67. BENJAMIN B. JUDAH OF ROME: *Hakdamah*. A small work which served as an introduction and supplement to grammars in use in Italy, published as the introduction to *Mahalakh Shevilei ha-Da'at* of Joseph Kimḥi (see section 45); cf. Bacher, in: REJ (1885), 123–44.

Mavo ha-Dikduk [or: *ha-Lashon*]. Ed. by W. Heidenheim, Roedelheim (1806) *cum Darkhei No'am*; crit. ed. and Spanish translation by A. Sáenz de Zaitegui Tejero, "Una revisión crítica de la gramática en el siglo xiv: La הקדמה de Benjamín de Roma," in: *Helmantica*, 154 (2000), 167–88.

68. *IMMANUEL B. SOLOMON OF ROME: *Even Boḥan*. 175 chapters in four parts, dealing with orthography, grammar, and other matters necessary for biblical exegesis, such as syncope, additions, and metathesis; cf. Bacher, MGWJ (1855), 251–75.

69. *JOSEPH IBN *KASPI: *Sharshot ha-Kesef* ("Garlands of Silver"). A dictionary which attempts to base its definitions on logical theory; ed. Last, London, 1906. Its theory has been studied by C. Aslanov, "De la lexicographie hébraïque à la sémantique générale: la pensée sémantique de Caspi d'après le Sefer Šaršot ha-Kesef," in: *Helmantica*, 154 (2000), 75–120.

Ratukot Kesef ("Chains of Silver"). A grammar.

A commentary to *Sefer ha-Rikmah* which has been lost.

70. *JOSEPH B. DAVID HA-YEVANI: *Menorat ha-Ma'or*. A dictionary with an introduction on grammatical issues: unpublished; excerpts: ed. Dukes, in: *Literturblatt des Orients*, 10 (1849), 705–9, 727–32, 745–7; 11 (1850), 173–6, 183–5, 215–8.

71. SOLOMON B. SAMUEL: *Sefer ha-Meliẓah* (or *Sefer Pitronei Millim*: "The Book of Translation"). A Hebrew (Aramaic)-Persian dictionary composed in 1339 in Turkestan, to serve Persian-speaking Jews versed in Hebrew with translations of Hebrew and Aramaic words from the Bible, the Talmud, and the Midrashim. Fragments: ed. Bacher, in *Jahresbericht der Landes-Rabbinerschule*. Budapest (1900), Hebrew part, 1–76.

72. SAR SHALOM: Solomon b. Abba Mari Yarḥi (see section 75) mentions a grammarian of this name.

73. DAVID B. YOM TOV IBN BILIA: *Derekh La'asot Ḥaruzim* (?). A short work on poetry written in Provence during the middle of the first half of the 14th century. The title, known only from one manuscript, was possibly given by one of the copyists. The first work which lists 18 types of meters in Spanish poetry; crit. ed. Allony, in *Kovez al Yad* (1966), 225–46.

74. SAMUEL BENVENISTE: Solomon b. Abba Mari Yarḥi (see section 75) and Profiat Duran (see section 78) mention a grammarian of this name.

75. SOLOMON B. ABBA MARI YARḤI: *Leshon Limmudim.* A grammar; small fragment, ed. Hirschfeld (1926), app. IV. A facsimile edition of the Parma MS 2776 of *Leshon Limmudim* along with an introduction by E. Goldenberg have been published (ed. B. Elizur, Jerusalem 1998) in honor of Z. Ben-Hayyim's ninetieth birthday.

76. ANONYMOUS, from Yemen: Unknown author of an untitled work in Arabic, which deals with the letters, vowels, and cantillation signs; ed. Neubauer (1891).

An expanded Hebrew translation of the work noted in the previous paragraph, including certain grammatical chapters in which a few chapters of *Kitāb al-Luma*ʿ of Ibn Janāḥ (14.6.1.) were adapted, apparently from the Arabic original; ed. Derenbourg, *Journal Asiatique* (1890).

77. ELEAZAR B. PHINEHAS B. JOSEPH: *Mukhtaṣar al-Tawtiʾa (Kiẓẓur ha-Maslul).* An abridged adaptation of *Kitāb al-Tawtiʾa (Sefer ha-Maslul)* of Abū Isḥāq Ibrāhim b. Faraj b. Mārūth (30.1) with additions by the adapter; crit. ed. Ben-Hayyim (1957), 170–221; see also 36–41.

1400 C.E.

78. ISAAC B. MOSES (ALSO PROFIAT *DURAN): *Maʿaseh Efod.* A grammar written in 1403 comprising a long introduction, 32 chapters, and a supplement. The most important work since the *Mikhlol* of David Kimḥi, it was an attempt to base linguistics on scholastic philosophy; (?) crit. ed. Friedlaender-Hakohen (Vienna, 1865).

79. JEHIEL (?): *Makre Dardekei.* A Hebrew-Italian-Arabic dictionary supplemented by the French and Provençal words used by Rashi and Kimḥi. The first of its type; ed. n. p. (1488).

80. JOSEPH B. JUDAH *ZARKO: *Rav Peʿalim.* A work dealing with the verb; Amsterdam (1730).

Baʿal Lashon. A dictionary.

81. ISAAC B. NATHAN KALONYMUS: *Me'ir Nativ* or *Ya'ir Nativ.* The first Hebrew concordance of the Bible, after the manner of the Latin concordance by the Franciscan Arlottus of 1290. The work was intended to assist in debates with Christians, with regard to the evidence they cited from the Bible. Written from 1437 to 1445; ed. Venice, 1533; re-ed. Basel, 1581.

1450 C.E.

82. DAVID B. SOLOM *IBN YAḤYA: *Leshon Limmudim.* A grammar, influenced by David Kimḥi and Profiat Duran, which, however, takes the liberty of criticizing them; ed. Constantinople (1506) together with *Shekel ha-Kodesh*; 2nd impression Constantinople, 1579.

83. MOSES BEN SHEM TOV *IBN ḤABIB: *Peraḥ Shoshan.* A grammar, quoted in *Darkhei Noʿam* and in *Mikneh Avram* of De Balmes (see section 93).

Marpe Lashon ("Healing of Speech"). A pamphlet concerning grammar; ed. Constantinople (beginning 16th century); re-ed. Elijah Levita (Venice, 1546) in *Dikdukim*; ed. Heidenheim (Roedelheim, 1806) *cum Darkhei Noʿam.*

Darkhei Noʿam ("Pleasant Ways"). Poetics based on Aristotle, and rules of meter; ed. Bomberg (1564); re-ed. Heidenheim (Roedelheim, 1806).

84. *JUDAH B. JEHIEL (MESSER LEON): *Livnat ha-Sappir.* A grammar of 122 chapters written in 1454, influenced by Profiat Duran (78).

Nofet Ẓufim. A long work on Hebrew rhetoric, based on Latin rhetoric as developed by Cicero and Quintilianus with regard to rules and terminology; ed. Mantua (1480); re-ed. Jellinek (Vienna, 1863).

The work *Petaḥ Devarai* is a grammar attributed to David Kimḥi or to David, the son of Judah b. Jehiel; ed. Naples (1492); ed. Elijah Levita (1546) in his *Dikdukim.*

85. *IBN DANAN, SAADIAH B. MAIMUN: *Al-Ḍarūri fi al-Lugha al-ʿIbrāniyya* comprising a dictionary, a grammar, and rules of meter in poetry. It was completed in 1473, and translated by the author into Hebrew. Fragments: ed. Bacher, in REJ, 41 (1901), 268–72; ed. Neubauer, in *Melekhet ha-Shir* (Frankfurt on the Main, 1865); M. Cohen, *Ha-Haqdamot ha-Diqduqiyot le-Sefer ha-Shorashim shel Rabbi Saadiah ben-Maimon ibn-Danan* (2000); crit. ed. C. Del Valle Rodriguez, *La gramática hebrea de Ibn Danán en la versión árabe y hebrea, Historia de la Gramática Hebrea en Espanña*, vol. 10 (Madrid, 2004).

Sefer ha-Shorashim. A Hebrew–Arabic dictionary, crit. ed. M. Jiménez Sánchez, *Seʿadyah ibn Danān, Sefer ha-Šorašim, Introducción, edición e indices* (Granada, 1996); reviewed by A. Maman, *Tarbiz*, 68 (1999), 287–301.

86. SOLOMON B. ABRAHAM OF URBINO:

Ohel Moʿed. A concise lexicon of synonyms; ed. Venice, 1548; ed. Willheimer (Vienna, 1881).

87. DAVID BEN YESHAʾ AL-ʾADANI: *Al-Jāmiʾ (ha-Meʾassef) (or Sharḥ al-Alfāẓ).* A Hebrew-Arabic dictionary, composed in Yemen between 1483 and 1486. Its entries are arranged according to the first letter (not according to their root) and based mainly on Maimonide's *Mishneh Torah* and his commentary to the Mishnah. A facsimile edition of one of the many extant manuscripts has been published (Jerusalem 1988), along with an introduction by Y. Tobi (pp. 175–187) and U. Melammed (pp. 188–189).

1500 C.E.

88. *REUCHLIN, JOHANN: *Rudimenta linguae hebraicae.* The first grammar written by a Christian to teach Hebrew to Christians. Written in 1506, it is attached to the *Mikhlol.*

89. ELISHA B. ABRAHAM B. MATTATHIAS: *Magen David* ("The Shield of David"). Written in 1517, in defense of David Kimḥi, against 50 criticisms of Profiat Duran (78) and five of David ibn Yaḥya in the latter's *Leshon Limmudim* (82); ed. Constantinople, 1517.

90. SAMUEL B. JACOB: *Reshit ha-Lekaḥ* ("The Beginning of Learning"). A grammar divided according to eight parts of speech, which are defined philosophically. It also discusses the

optative. Preserved in manuscript, it has not been printed (cf. Hirschfeld (1926), p. 98).

91. *ALMOLI, SOLOMON B. JACOB: *Halikhot Sheva*. A work about the rules of the *šewa*ʾ *na*ʿ and about nominal patterns. Written in Constantinople in 1520; crit. ed. Yalon (Jerusalem, 1945).

(?) *Shekel ha-Kodesh*. A work about poetics in 17 chapters, the first 14 with grammatical content. Printed in the Constantinople edition (1506) of *Leshon Limmudim* of David ibn Yaḥya (see section 82) as an anonymous work, and attributed by Allony and by Yalon, KS (1963–64), 105–8, to Almoli; crit. ed. Yalon (Jerusalem, 1965).

92. ELIJAH B. ASHER (*LEVITA, BAḤUR) AMSELIJAH B. ASHER (*LEVITA, *Baḥur*): A commentary on *Mahalakh Shevilei ha-Da'at* of Moses Kimḥi (45.1); Padua, 1504; ed. Pizaro, 1508; re-ed. Venice, 1546.

Baḥur. A work on the noun and the verb, supplemented by conjugation tables, written in Rome in 1517; ed. Rome, 1518; reprinted Isny, 1542 as *Dikduk Eliyahu ha-Levi*.

Pirkei Eliyahu. A supplement to *Baḥur*, partly rhymed. It deals with the letters and vowels, the number and gender of the noun, and the particles. Written in Rome in 1519; ed. Pisa, 1520; re-ed. Venice, 1546. In the latter edition a chapter on the classification of nouns was added.

Harkavah. A discussion of exceptional forms in the Bible, arranged alphabetically; written in Rome, 1517; ed. Rome, 1518; Venice, 1546. Study: A. Maman, "The Compound Words in the Eyes of Medieval Hebrew Philologists," *Yaakov Bentolila Jubilee Volume* (D. Sivan & P.I. Halevy-Kirtchuk, eds.), *Eshel Beer-Sheva*, 8 (2003), 277–95.

Meturgeman. A dictionary, for words in Aramaic Bible translations. Written in Rome between 1526 and 1531; ed. Isny, 1541.

Tuv Ta'am. A work on vocalization, the cantillation signs, and the masorah; written and ed. Venice, 1538.

Masoret ha-Masorah. The first systematic exposition and critical history of the masorah, and the first work to prove that the vocalization and cantillation signs are post-talmudic; written and ed. Venice, 1538.

Tishbi. A dictionary of 712 (=the arithmetical value of תשב"י) Hebrew entries in talmudic and post-talmudic language, written Venice-Isny (1540–41). This work contains many examples of the pronunciation and vocalization of talmudic and post-talmudic Hebrew words by German and Italian Jews; ed. Isny, 1541.

Nimmukin for *Sefer Mikhlol* (see section 47); ed. Venice, 1545.

Nimmukim for *Sefer ha-Shorashim* of David Kimḥi (see section 47); ed. Venice, 1547 (see A. Maman, *Otzrot Lashon* (section 26 above), introduction).

Sefer ha-Zikhronot. The first concordance of the masorah. Written in Rome, 1516–21, but unpublished; cf. Frensdorff, in: MGWJ (1863), 96–110.

93. ANONYMOUS YEMENITE AUTHOR: A dictionary of the *Mishneh Torah* of Maimonides, dealing only with the first two letters of the alphabet and based mainly on Tanḥum Yerushalmi (see section 55); frag. ed. Nathan (Berlin, 1905; inaugural dissertation).

94. ABRAHAM DE *BALMES: *Mikneh Avram*. A long grammatical work; the first systematic attempt to introduce a long chapter with a complete description of syntax into a Hebrew grammar, and the most original work since the time of *Kitāb al-Luma*ʿ of Ibn Janāḥ; ed. Venice, 1523, with Latin translation; the last chapter (144a–155b), on cantillation, was written by Kalonymus b. David. This work has been studied very little; see D. Téné, "Abraham De Balmes and his Grammar of Biblical Hebrew," in: *History of Linguistics* (1996), vol. 2: *From Classical to Contemporary Linguistics* edited by D. Cram, A. Linn, E. Nowak, (Amsterdam/Philadelphia, 1999), 249–68.

95. SEBASTIAN *MUENSTER: *Melekhet ha-Dikduk ha-Shalem*. A grammatical work, written in 1542, and attached to the works of Elijah Levita (92); ed. Basle, 1542.

[David Téné / Aharon Maman (2nd ed.)]

FROM THE 16TH CENTURY TO THE PRESENT

The Beginnings of Christian Hebrew Studies

The early 16th century is a turning-point in the history of Hebrew linguistics. There occurred then the sudden efflorescence of the knowledge of Hebrew as a part of Christian culture, which meant that Hebrew was no longer an esoteric subject, almost totally confined to Jews, and this eventually brought about a different kind of study of the language, carried on within a different context and intellectual atmosphere. The knowledge of Hebrew had not been entirely absent from the medieval Christian world; but such pockets as existed were entirely derived from Jewish philology and exegesis and contributed little or nothing to the progress of the subject in itself. There is no major name in Christian Hebrew studies between Jerome and Johann *Reuchlin. The sudden growth of Christian Hebrew studies in the early 16th century was part of the humanist impulse, which had revived the study of classical Latin and Greek, and which was animated with a zeal for the original ancient sources and their languages. The spread of printing had given new facilities for study, and the interest in the Bible, already stimulated by the new printed editions, was enormously increased by the Reformation controversies in the Church. There was an interest also in other Jewish sources, for example in the *Kabbalah, believed to be a source for philosophy and even for Christian doctrine, and also a stir of interest about the Talmud; Reuchlin was involved in bitter controversy because he opposed the burning of Jewish books as an obscurantist policy.

At first it was far from easy for non-Jews to find out much about Hebrew; the subject had been looked upon with some suspicion; informants were rare, and they might be suspected of seeking to proselytize. Some information came from Jews who embraced Christianity; conversely, some study among Christians was motivated by polemical aims. A freer atmosphere was found in northern Italy, and, soon after, in Germany. Even so, Conrad *Pellicanus, who anticipated Reuchlin with a small book about Hebrew (1503?), had to teach himself the language with only such limited aids as a brief section of the biblical text printed in Hebrew but in Latin characters. Early works such as his were little more than guides to the learning of the script. Nevertheless, the thirst for learning was very great, and substantial knowledge of Hebrew came to exist in the Christian world. Reuchlin's grammar, published with a dictionary in 1506, was very brief and simple; but by the end of his life his knowledge was considerable, and his immense reputation established Hebrew studies as a recognized subject in European education. He did much to ensure that chairs of Hebrew should be set up in the universities of northern Europe, and his pupils were available to occupy them. Within some decades a tradition had grown up and was accepted in some quarters, according to which Hebrew (and even Aramaic and Syriac) belonged along with Latin and Greek in the proper equipment of the cultivated man. In time, this more humanistic pursuit of Hebrew somewhat declined; Hebrew studies among Christians came to be carried on mainly as a part of theological study, and chairs were commonly occupied by men with theological training, interested primarily in biblical Hebrew; the humanistic cultivation of ancient languages concentrated on Latin and Greek.

The earliest Christian works on Hebrew were not only very rudimentary, but were also heavily dependent on Jewish tradition, and initially they were in no position to advance the subject beyond the state in which they had received it from the hands of their Jewish predecessors. Yet certain seeds of change were present from the beginning. Medieval Jewish grammars and lexicons had generally been in Arabic, or in Hebrew itself. Hebrew linguistic knowledge was now, however, set in a context which included the developed grammars of the classical languages, and works on Hebrew were written in Latin and, later, in various European languages such as German, French, and English. This involved an emphasis on methods of learning, since Christian students, unlike Jewish, generally had no antecedent native experience. More important, it raised questions of terminology: the Jewish tradition had evolved its own terms, or had relied upon the example of Arabic, a sister Semitic language; but could the terminology familiar to Europeans, and based mainly on Latin, also be applied to Hebrew? Certain of the terms which later became standard, such as "absolute state," go back to Reuchlin; what is now usually called the "construct state," on the other hand, was in earlier times called *status regiminis*, the "governing state." (See also *Hebraists, Christian.)

The person who did most, when the Christian study of Hebrew was established, to pass on to it a fuller heritage of knowledge from the older tradition of Jewish linguistics was Elijah Levita. Born in Germany, he lived most of his life in Italy, and mentally was well integrated with the humanist movement. He wrote several grammatical works, a commentary on the grammar of Moses *Kimḥi (1504), and his own *Sefer ha-Baḥur* and *Sefer ha-Harkavah* (1517). He was particularly noted for his studies in the masorah, the *Masoret ha-Masorah* (1538). The work of Levita was made available to a wider circle through the Latin translations of Sebastian *Muenster, professor at Basle from 1529, who was the most influential Christian Hebraist after Reuchlin. Through its clarity, Levita's work, as adapted, was well suited for teaching. The basis for Hebrew knowledge in the 16th century lay in the work of Moses and David *Kimḥi, and to some extent in that of Abraham ibn Ezra, as communicated through men like Levita and Muenster. Thus the main fund of knowledge, provided by medieval Jewish philology in its later and more clearly organized forms, was now directly accessible to Christian readers. The recent survey of Hebrew grammars printed in Europe during the 16th century (S. García-Jalón de la Lama y M. Veiga Díaz, *Repertorio de gramáticas hebreas impresas en Europa en el siglo XVI* (Salamanca 2000 = *Helmantica* 156)) enables us to understand and evaluate better the growth of Hebrew knowledge throughout Europe among Christian Hebraists (see also the bibliography included in this survey).

After Levita, however, no Jewish figure appeared for some time to become a recognized leader and authority on biblical studies, especially in the eyes of Christian scholars. Hebrew language studies were, in fact, making less distinguished progress within Judaism than had been the case in the Middle Ages. For this there were several reasons. The main intellectual effort within Judaism was now being directed toward talmudic studies. Catastrophes such as the expulsion from Spain had gravely dislocated Jewish academic life. The contact with Arabic grammar and the Arabic language, which had earlier been so suggestive and fruitful, was now very limited for the Jews of Europe. Finally, the work of discovery and clarification, with comparative reference to the cognate languages (Aramaic and Arabic), which had distinguished the medieval period, had probably gone as far as it could, and progress had already fallen off before 1500.

Correspondingly, the sense of heavy dependence on Jewish tradition which had marked the first Christian study of Hebrew began to pass. It is said of the dictionary of Johann *Forster of Wittenberg (1557) that it set aside the former reliance on rabbinic methods. Yet the dominance of Jewish traditional methods was still clear in the work of the two Johann *Buxtorfs, the elder and the younger. The masorah, a subject carefully studied by Levita, was a matter of extreme interest also to Buxtorf the elder, who wrote a masoretic commentary entitled *Tiberias* (1620). Buxtorf's own grammar far surpassed previous works in detail and exactitude. But the very existence of works that, even though written in heavy dependence on Jewish tradition, could be read and assimilated separately from it, made it possible for Western academic study of Hebrew in the universities to draw away from Jewish tradition.

Stirrings of Critical Attitudes

The Buxtorfs themselves illustrate how, by the early 17th century, Hebrew studies among Christians were marked less by the humanistic spirit and more by dogmatic theological considerations. Elijah Levita, following the Renaissance interest in detecting the late date of certain traditions, had averred that the vowel points were of late origin, and in 1624 the same argument was taken up by Ludwig Cappellus; but this was vigorously opposed by the Buxtorfs, to whom the argument seemed to threaten the Protestant orthodox view of biblical inspiration.

The question was, in fact, one of the first involving textual criticism, a movement which in the course of time substantially altered the direction of Hebrew language study. Medieval Jewish philology took the masoretic text as its basis, and the only ancient alternative text-form which was substantially used was the Aramaic Targum. Variants known in Hebrew, apart from special classes such as the *ketiv* and *keri*, were generally not of great importance for the meaning. Christian study, however, was familiar with older translations such as the Septuagint in Greek (originally a pre-Christian Jewish rendering) and the Latin Vulgate, which had been preserved in Christian tradition; to these was added the Syriac, a version in another Semitic dialect, preserved in Eastern Christianity and now once again made available for study in the West. The possibility was now suggested in principle that forms found in the Hebrew text might be the product of errors in written transmission, and that peculiar linguistic forms might therefore be explained through the decision to prefer a different text. Though there were certain precedents in earlier scholarship, both Jewish and Christian, and though hints of further progress appear, as in the 1620s with Cappellus, it was only in the later 18th century that textual criticism on something like its modern scale became established. The importance of textual criticism for linguistic study was that the grammar and lexicon did not have to accommodate every form transmitted by the textual tradition simply because it was in the text; some of the forms, which had been traditionally difficult for the linguistic scholar, might now be explained as the result of scribal errors. Though the full effect of this argument was not to be seen until much later, it gradually drove a wedge between the older linguistic study and the newer approach.

Throughout the entire period, grammars of Hebrew were published, some of which were very widely used. Most of them, however, were ephemeral, or local in their use, or merely one person's individual restatement of what was essentially the same grammatical doctrine; and the vast majority did nothing to advance the scientific study of Hebrew. Linguistic works written by Jews came in many cases, though not in all, to use the vernacular languages as the medium of instruction and exposition, rather than the Hebrew language itself. Works written in Holland often used Spanish and Portuguese for the needs of the Sephardi community; Italian was used in Italy. A grammar in Yiddish appeared in Prague in 1597. The first Hebrew grammar to be written by a Jew in Latin was that of Baruch *Spinoza, the greatest thinker ever to write a treatise on the Hebrew language. Latin had previously been used once or twice by Jews who had embraced Christianity, but Spinoza, who employed Latin in most of his works, was the first to use it for Hebrew grammar. His work, *Compendium grammatices linguae hebraeae*, is a brief, simple, and modest book, and it had no great effect on the progress of Hebrew linguistics. One sees at certain points the tendency to provide philosophical arguments to account for linguistic facts, a tendency which in Hebrew studies continued to have occasional effect up to the 20th century. Spinoza emphasized the noun as the pre-eminent word-class or part of speech in Hebrew; he seems to have considered the essential basis of verb forms to be the infinitive, i.e., a sort of noun form. He used unquestioningly such Latin terms as Nominative, Accusative, Mood, Case. Spinoza's effect on later developments was not, however, through the direct influence of his grammar, but through other aspects of his work. He took certain decisive steps toward a historical critical approach to the Bible, declaring it to be clear that the Pentateuch was written not by Moses but by someone who lived many centuries later. Among other significant Jewish grammatical writers of the 17th century mention may be made of Jedidiah Solomon b. Abraham *Norzi of Mantua, author of a detailed masoretic commentary completed in 1626 but published much later (1742–44) under the title *Minḥat Shai*; and, the most important of the writers of the century, Solomon b. Judah Loeb *Hanau.

During the 17th and 18th centuries the study of Hebrew linguistics, in spite of much accurate detailed knowledge, was somewhat hampered and confused by its entanglement with certain more general cultural problems. It was widely supposed that Hebrew was a language of divine origin, and even that it was the language of the Deity Himself; moreover, even as a human language, it was believed to have been the original tongue of humanity, from which others had been derived.

Meanwhile, however, a body of knowledge was being built up which was eventually to lead to a different understanding of the place of Hebrew in the world of language. Other Oriental languages were also being studied; chairs of Arabic existed at a number of universities, and the subject, first cultivated in connection with the missionary impulse directed toward Islam, and later fostered as an auxiliary to the study of Hebrew and the interpretation of the Bible, gradually became an independent academic field. The extensive Syriac literature, already mentioned, was also available. European exploration and curiosity about the Orient greatly extended the linguistic resources of scholarship; the grammar and lexicon of Ethiopic, a language close to Hebrew but formerly almost unknown, were learned. Samaritan texts were studied and printed. Remarkable typographical feats were performed in order to assemble all this material. Excellent polyglot Bibles were published; one of the most important, the London Polyglot of Bryan Walton (1657), contained (usually on the same page, for easy cross-reference) biblical texts in Hebrew along with the Samaritan Pentateuch and a number of Aramaic Targums, plus translations into Greek, Latin, Syriac, Ethiopic, Arabic, and Persian, with a Latin translation of each. To this Bible was added the *Lexicon Heptaglotton* of Edmund Castell (1669), which presented in a synoptic form the vocabularies of the

Semitic languages involved, along with a separate listing for Persian. Thus material was being assembled for a comparative philological approach more comprehensive and wide-ranging than that which had been possible for the medieval Jewish philologists, whose knowledge had been largely confined to the languages then in use among Jews and in their environment, principally Arabic and Aramaic, as well as Hebrew.

One of the main centers of this wider linguistic knowledge was Holland, and it was here that its effects upon the traditional conceptions about Hebrew were first and most strongly expressed. Albrecht *Schultens emphasized with revolutionary exaggeration the extent of the change brought about by the new knowledge. Far from accepting the traditional view that Arabic (like other languages) was a degenerate form of Hebrew, Schultens maintained that Hebrew was only one Semitic dialect, while the purest and clearest such dialect was Arabic. Numerous difficult passages in the Hebrew Bible could, he believed, be elucidated by appeal to an Arabic word which seemed similar and from which the true sense of the Hebrew could be deduced. But in spite of the high value accorded to Arabic by Schultens, his use of it was infelicitous and far from commendable even from the point of view of an Arabist. He nevertheless marked the beginning of an epoch which continued into the mid-20th century, in which one of the main forms of learned linguistic study was the use of cognate languages for the elucidation of difficulties in Hebrew. At this stage, however, the increasing knowledge of cognate languages was not yet organized in a form which made a breakthrough possible, principally because the method, though comparative, was as yet imperfectly historical in character. The impact of Arabic on Hebrew studies continued, and the comprehensiveness of classical Arabic (compared with the limited corpus of biblical Hebrew), along with the apparent primitivity of its forms (which could often appear to provide patterns logically earlier than those of Hebrew), made it increasingly important in the organization of linguistic works about Hebrew. A grammar following roughly the lines marked out by Schultens was written by Nicholas Wilhelm Schroeder (d. 1798) and widely used. A more substantial and permanent influence in approximately the same direction was exercised by Johann David *Michaelis, professor of Oriental languages and theology at Goettingen. The academic Hebraist was now expected to be an Orientalist; this meant not only knowledge of Arabic, but also an awareness of the new information brought by travelers from the East about customs, the physical surroundings of life, and now – in its first rudimentary form – archaeology. By this time the Christian Hebraist was less involved in traditional dogmatism, and was likely, on the contrary, to be something of a rationalist.

One who also contributed much to the appreciation of Hebrew in this period, though one could hardly call him a Hebraist in the technical sense, was the wide-ranging thinker Johann Gottfried *Herder. His essay, "The Origin of Language" (1772), attacks the view that language is a direct gift of God, claiming that it is a human product, though not one deliberately framed by man, but rather springing by necessity from man's inner nature. He admired what had grown naturally, and had an interest in what he considered to be primitive languages, in which, as he believed, the verb had had priority over the noun, numerous synonyms had existed, and bold metaphors had been used. The example he generally had in mind when he talked of primitive languages was Hebrew, which, by the time-scale then customary, seemed to go back almost to the beginning of human culture. Herder had a deep sense of the poetic and aesthetic power of Hebrew, and he wrote an influential book, *Vom Geist der hebraeischen Poesie* ("On the Spirit of Hebrew Poetry," 1782–83). He emphasized the verb as the characteristic and leading feature of the language and associated this with the dynamic forcefulness and energy of the literature. Some of these opinions have continued to be echoed up to the present day. Herder also made further moves toward a historical approach to the Bible, and emphasized its humanity. If Hebrew was brought down from the level of the divine, at the same time it was nevertheless accorded a place of high honor.

The Classical Historical Method

The great name in German Hebrew studies in the early 19th century is that of Heinrich Friedrich Wilhelm *Gesenius, professor at Halle, some of whose books, after numerous amendments and revisions, are still standard reference works. Particularly noteworthy are his lexicon, *Hebraeisches und chaldaeisches Handwoerterbuch* (17th German edition, 1915; new revision in preparation), which was used as the basis for the English dictionary of Francis Brown, Samuel Rolles *Driver and Charles A. Briggs (1907); and his two grammars, the more detailed *Lehrgebaeude der hebraeischen Sprache* (1817), and the briefer *Hebraeische Grammatik* (1813). Indeed, the latter, after successive new editions by Emil *Kautzsch and others, remains the standard reference grammar in many languages today (2nd English edition by Arthur Ernest Cowley, Oxford, 1910). He also wrote a history of the Hebrew language and worked on Samaritan and the Semitic languages in general. Modern readers, who may be impressed chiefly by the detail and the comprehensiveness of Genesius' approach, should know that in his own time his lectures were considered fascinating and drew students from far and wide. The strength of his work lies in its genius for detailed comprehensive empirical observation; his approach was sober and avoided speculation. Yet the empirical accuracy of Genesius' work does not conceal the fact that his conceptual terminology was often unsuited to the subject. He continually used the categories Nominative, Accusative, Genitive, which have formal representation in Latin and German, but not in Hebrew. He had nine declensions of the masculine noun. All forms of the noun are explained as if they were derived from the extant form of the masculine singular absolute. He wrote before the full unfolding of the comparative-historical linguistics of the 19th century, and his careful attention to Arabic or Syriac still does not produce a developmental framework; though historical in one sense, he had not yet made the systematic projections back into prehistory which were essential to the full comparative method. Thus he did not even diagnose that the ending *-am* as in *yomam* ("by day") is genetically connected with the Arabic case ending *-an*. He considered the consecutive *waw* to have been formed from the prefixing of the verb *hayah* ("to be"). Though later revisions of his work incorporated a more historical outlook, some of these defects persisted into modern revisions. For terminology, he still sometimes used the traditional Hebrew terms, but mostly employed Latin terms, though often aware that these might be misleading. He agreed with the older Jewish grammar in calling the two tenses, which later came to be called perfect and imperfect, by the names Past and Future, the idea of aspect not yet having been brought into consideration. The historical aspect of Genesius' work was better revealed within the biblical corpus itself; he was aware of the historical development of the language and distinguished the usage of different writers, as for example pre-exilic and post-exilic, prose and poetic. In the study of meanings in his lexicographical work he was both lucid in presentation and sober in his quest for valid analogies and his avoidance of speculative fancies.

The later editions of Genesius' works, and newer works produced in the following decades, had to take account of the great advances made in comparative philology. Hebrew had been elucidated through knowledge of the cognate Semitic languages as far back as the Middle Ages, long before the method was much applied outside the Semitic family. Yet it was work in the Indo-European langugages which in the early 19th century finally evolved a satisfactory comparative and historical method. This method included the projection or reconstruction of a common ancestor language, from which the extant languages were descended by statable changes. By application of the method to the Semitic family, proto-Semitic forms could be reconstructed; these, though not found in any historical document, could yet be deemed to have been the ancestral forms from which, by regular or fairly regular changes, the extant Hebrew (and, similarly, Arabic or Aramaic) forms had been evolved. Moreoever, reconstructions could also be done internally, by considering groups of phenomena within one language; for instance, the series *malki*, *malko* ("my king, his king") might suggest that the word "king" was *malk* at a prehistoric date, before it became *melekh* as in extant Hebrew texts. The method enabled a historical explanation to be given to phenomena which might otherwise be empirically registered but not accounted for; and it has remained of great importance, not least because there is no other way of penetrating the time before the earliest biblical texts. The effect of this method was that scholarly grammars eventually came to classify Hebrew forms not under the patterns which they assume in the masoretic text but under those patterns which they are taken to have had in the prehistoric stage; beginning with this prehistoric stage, the grammar undertakes to explain how the extant forms were derived. This is a thorough change in grammatical method, even if the empirical facts observed are the same. Beginning to appear in the late 19th century in grammars such as those of Justus *Olshausen (1861) and Bernhard Stade (1879), it reached monumental proportions only in the 20th century in the grammar of Hans *Bauer and Pontus Leander (1922) and the revisions of Gesenius by Gotthelf *Bergstraesser (1918).

This method also raised new questions, or old questions in new and more rigorous forms. The importance within it of the sound changes by which the reconstructed ancestor language alters into the extant dialect brought the question whether these changes followed an invariable rule or whether they might allow occasional exceptions. The matter was of great importance in lexicography, for a dictionary was expected to state some kind of etymology and give data of cognate forms in other Semitic languages, and the validity of these depended on the degree to which the normal sound correspondences must be insisted on and the degree to which similarities of meaning which seemed overwhelming might be expected to override them.

The new interest in linguistic discovery could also suggest new approaches to Hebrew. Knowledge of the Slavonic languages emphasized the category of aspect in verbs (nature of the action done, e.g., whether completed or not completed), and something similar was seen in Greek. The tenses of Hebrew had traditionally been regarded as past and future, both through the influence of Latin grammar and through the older Jewish view of the matter, but it was thought that something closer to the category of aspect might be more suitable, since the classification as past and future had long given much trouble. A number of important works in the 20th century were devoted to the attempt to define the verb system of Hebrew and to explain its evolution in relation to what is known of sister languages.

Modern Trends

The hundred years following Gesenius, then, were a period of more radical historical questioning about the development of the Hebrew language. The basic task was now seen no longer as that of classifying and registering the forms, but rather as that of piecing together a historical development, of which only certain portions were evident on the surface. This trend was further emphasized by certain other circumstances.

The first of these was the rise of historical criticism and its application to the sources of the biblical books. This made it possible to discern different linguistic strata in what had generally been taken in the past as unitary documents. Within the Pentateuch, for instance, the separation of chronologically different strata was accompanied by the identification of linguistic constants as characteristics of each. This process assisted in the identification and appreciation of various styles in the use of language and made possible a more fully historical understanding of Hebrew. The historical-critical separation of sources has never gone without opposition, and many applications of it have been questioned by competent linguists; nevertheless, the main principles of it seem to be sound and helpful, and the method has had great effect on the history of Hebrew linguistics. Modern grammars and dictionaries will often register phenomena as belonging to, or characteristic of, one or another of the recognized sources, such as the document J or P.

Second, the same period was one in which whole new languages were discovered, and these enriched knowledge of the linguistic environment of ancient Hebrew, while at the same time confirming the applicability of the comparative philological method and inviting its extension. Ancient Egyptian was deciphered early in the 19th century and, though not closely related to Hebrew, provided numerous points of contact, including among other things the means of correct identification of names and expressions of Egyptian origin in the Hebrew Bible, some of which had hitherto been explained as Hebrew and thereby confused our understanding of the latter. More immediate and important, *Akkadian, the language of the Assyrians and Babylonians, was discovered in the second half of the century and it turned out to have remarkably close relationships with Hebrew; its verb tense system, for instance, served to suggest new approaches to the verb system of Hebrew. The discovery of Akkadian, not least because of the ancient provenance of this language, did much to shift the balance of Semitic comparative philology away from excessive reliance on sources such as Arabic and Syriac, which were then known mainly from materials of later date. Extensive fresh discoveries of inscriptions in Canaanite, Phoenician, Moabite, Aramaic, Punic, South Arabian, and other dialects were made, and it became possible to a much greater extent than previously to see Hebrew as one of a group of dialects; and, since the inscriptions had been unchanged since the time of their origin, they formed a valuable resource for comparison with texts such as those of biblical Hebrew, which had been handed down by a copying process over many centuries. Archaeological researches produced archaic inscriptions even in Hebrew itself. It now became normal to consider that the task of the Hebraist was no longer to study Hebrew in and of itself, but to reconstruct the historical path by which it had developed in the midst of this group of related dialects, of which increasingly complex evidence kept coming to the fore. This movement was still further accelerated in the 1930s, when *Ugaritic, a language previously entirely unknown, was brought to light; it dated from the 14th century B.C.E. and had much in common with Hebrew.

Third, not only were other languages discovered, but great discoveries were made in the field of Hebrew itself. Particularly important was the study of biblical manuscripts with pointing different from the customary Tiberian system. These enabled a reconstruction to be made of Hebrew as it had been before the Tiberian pointing became authoritative. A number of scholars (particularly Paul *Kahle and Alexander Sperber) held that the masoretes had made certain innovations in the grammar of Hebrew and that it was now possible to penetrate accurately, with proof, back to a pre-masoretic state. For this purpose assistance was drawn from Hebrew words transcribed into Greek or Latin in early sources. Recourse was also had to the Samaritan tradition of Hebrew, both spoken and written, which had been investigated notably by Ze'ev *Ben-Hayyim, to provide another non-masoretic source. Further new texts were furnished by the Cairo **Genizah* since the end of the 19th century, including the recovered section of the Hebrew text of *Ben Sira, previously known almost solely in Greek. The culmination of this current of discovery was the appearance after World War II of the *Dead Sea Scrolls; these included Hebrew biblical texts many centuries older than those formerly known, as well as many new writings, previously quite unknown, which have greatly stimulated research into the state and history of Hebrew in the one or two centuries immediately before and after the beginning of the Common Era.

During the 19th century, along with changes in the social and educational position of the Jews, the currents of Jewish grammatical studies and of academic Hebrew studies, which had flowed somewhat apart, began to converge once again. The person who signalized this movement was Samuel David *Luzzatto. Though distinguished Jewish thinkers such as *Elijah Gaon of Vilna and Moses *Mendelssohn had written about the Hebrew language, their work had no great effect upon academic study. Luzzatto's work, on the other hand, stands in the full critical, historical, and reasoned light of the best academic method of his time.

In the 20th century the convergence of Jewish and non-Jewish Hebrew studies was facilitated by the fact that non-Jewish studies became once again more humanistic and less definitely attached to theology.

Jewish scholarship was particularly important in the field of post-biblical Hebrew, which had tended to be somewhat neglected by Christian scholarship, especially in the more modern period (the earlier epoch of Christian Hebrew studies had seen some profound rabbinic scholarship, as with John Lightfoot in England, 1602–75). The historical emphasis of the Wissenschaft des Judentums movement promoted exact and discriminating scholarship. A subject of much interest was the linguistic situation in Palestine at the time of the origin of Christianity and the interrelation of Hebrew and Aramaic; names of note in this discussion are Gustav *Dalman and Moses Hirsch *Segal; the latter provided the standard grammar of mishnaic Hebrew (1927). The main effort of Hebrew linguistics had always been directed toward the language of the Bible; but a historical perspective made it desirable to attempt the description also of other stages of Hebrew, and this task was given actuality by the revival of Hebrew as a spoken and written language from the time of the *Haskalah onward. The task of refashioning the language for modern needs involved considerable research into the resources of the past in order that these might be mobilized for the present; one outstanding monument of this effort is the *Thesaurus totius hebraitatis* (1908–59) initiated by Eliezer *Ben-Yehuda.

In the mid-20th century the main current of biblical linguistics continued to be concerned with the assimilation of the material known from comparative philological methods.

Notable scholars working in this field were Naphtali Herz Tur-Sinai in Israel, Sir Godfrey Rolles Driver in Oxford and William Foxwell *Albright in America. The emphasis on Ugaritic as a major source for the elucidation of Hebrew has been pushed to its extreme by Mitchell Dahood, but a more moderate position was taken by many other scholars, such as Umberto *Cassuto. New dictionaries, such as the third edition of Ludwig Koehler and Walter *Baumgartner's *Hebraeisches und Aramaeisches Lexikon* (1967), endeavor to incorporate the results of this approach. No full synthesis of comparative Semitics has appeared to supersede that of Carl Brockelmann (1908–13), nor has a full comparative etymological dictionary of the Semitic languages been published; nor, for comprehensive and purely empirical presentation, has the revised work of Gesenius been outdated.

Another form of study which achieved some importance in the 20th century has been the attempt (anticipated to some extent by Herder) to trace connections between the linguistic phenomena of Hebrew, e.g., the tense system, or the construct state, or the relation between root and meaning, and characteristic aspects of the thought of the ancient Israelites. The validity of this method, and the extent to which it can be pressed, have been a subject of some controversy.

From about the 1940s onward the seemingly assured dominance of comparative-historical study has begun to be challenged by the newer methods of descriptive linguistics, interested not only in the historical development of items but in the description of systems, and based on the study of living and spoken languages. Some of the workers who developed these newer linguistics were also in part Hebraists, such as Edward *Sapir, Zellig Sabbetai *Harris and Noam *Chomsky. The approach of descriptive linguistics found a ready application in the study of spoken Israeli Hebrew, as in Ḥayyim Rosen's *Ha-Ivrit Shellanu* and *A Textbook of Israeli Hebrew.* The interest in phonetics, which is part of the new descriptive approach, has had importance also for the historical linguistics of Hebrew, for it has been applied with profit to the detailed study of the speech habits of special Jewish communities such as the Yemenites, and this study influences in turn the understanding of the history of pronunciation and the systems of vocalization in ancient times, as has been shown by Shelomo Morag. It may be expected that the methods of descriptive linguistics will in the course of time exercise a wider influence on the study of Hebrew.

[James Barr]

BIBLIOGRAPHY: S. Pinsker, *Likkutei Kadmoniyyot* (1860); A. Jellinek (ed.), Judah ben Jehiel, *Nofet Ẓufim* (1863); L. Geiger, *Das Studium der hebraeischen Sprache in Deutschland vom Ende des XV. bis zur Mitte des XVI. Jahrhunderts* (1870); A. Berliner, *Beitraege zur hebraeischen Grammatik im Talmud und Midrasch* (1879); W. Bacher, *Abraham Ibn Esra als Grammatiker* (1882); idem, *Die grammatische Terminologie des Jehûdâ b. Dawid (Abū Zakarjâ Jahjâ ibn Dâud) Hajjûğ* (1882; = *Sitzungsberichte… Akademie der Wissenschaften*, vol. 100, no. 2, pp. 1103–54); idem, *Die hebraeisch-arabische Sprachvergleichung des Abulwalîad Merwân Ibn Ganâh* (1884; = *Sitzungsberichte…*, vol. 106, no. 1 pp. 11996); idem, *Die hebraeisch-neuhebraeische und hebraeischaramaeische Sprachvergleichung des Abulwalîad Merwân Ibn Ganâh* (1885; = *Sitzungsberichte…*, vol. 110, no 1, pp. 175–212); idem, *Leben und Werke des Abulwalîd Merwân Ibn Ganâh (R. Jonah) und die Quellen seiner Schrifterklaerung* (1885); idem, *Die hebraeische Sprachwissenschaft vom X. bis zum XVI. Jahrhundert* (1892; = J. Winter and A. Wuensche, *Die juedische Literatur*, vol. 2, pp. 121–235); idem, "*The Views of Jehuda Halevi Concerning the Hebrew Language*," in: *Hebraica*, 8 (1893), 136–49; idem, "*Die Anfaenge der hebraeischen Grammatik*," in: ZMDG, 49 (1895), 1–62, 335–92; idem, "*Jehuda Hanassi's Hermeneutik und Grammatik*," in: MGWJ, 40 (1896), 14–32, 68–84, 109–26; P. Haupt, "*The Names of Hebrew Vowels*," in: JAOS, 22 (1901/02), 1–17; C. Levias, "*The Names of Hebrew Vowels*," in: HUCA (1904), 138–46; S. Poznański, *Moses ben Samuel Hakohen Ibn Chiquitilla* (1895); S. Poznański, "*New Material on the History of Hebrew and Hebrew-Arabic Philology during the X–XII Centuries*," in: JQR, 16 (1925–26), 237–66; H. Hirschfeld, *Literary History of Hebrew Grammarians and Lexicographers, Accompanied by Unpublished Texts* (1926; Jews' College Publications, no. 9); H. Englander, "*Rashi's View of the Weak* ע״ע *and* פ״ן *Roots*," in: HUCA, 7 (1930), 399–437; idem, "*Grammatical Elements and Terminology in Rashi's Biblical Commentaries*," *ibid.*, 11 (1936), 367–89; idem, "*Rashi's Vowel Terminology*." pt. 2, *ibid.*, 12–13 (1937/38), 505–21; idem, "*Rabbenu Jacob ben Meir Tam as Grammarian*," *ibid.*, 15 (1940), 485–95; idem, "*A Commentary on Rashi's Grammatical Comments*," *ibid.*, 17 (1942/43), 427–98; D. Yellin, "*Hitabbekut Dunash ben Labrat*," in: *Sefer Zikkaron le-Asher Gulak veli-Shemuel Klein* (1942), 105–14; idem, "*Teshuvot Dunash ben Labrat*," in: *Leshonenu*, 11 (1942), 202–15; idem, *Toledot Hitpatteḥut ha-Dikduk ha-Ivri (Mi-Ymei ha-Masorah ve-Ad R. Yehudah Ḥayyūj)* (1945); N. Berggruen, "*Kelal He shel R. Eliyahu Baḥur – Perek be-Toledot ha-Dikduk*," in: *Leshonenu*, 16 (1949), 169–79; L. Prys, *Die grammatikalische Terminologie des Abraham Ibn Ezra* (1950); L. Kukenheim, *Contributions á l'historie de la grammaire grecque latine et hébraïque á l'époque de la Renaissance* (1951), pt. 3: "*La Grammaire hebraïque*," 88–129; I. Garbell, *Shitot Ḥalukkat ha-Tenu'ot ezel ha-Medakdekim ha-Ivryyim u-Mekoroteihen*, in: *Leshonenu*, 17 (1951), 76–80; W. Chomsky, *David Kimchi's Hebrew Grammar (Mikhol)* (1952); Z. Ben-Hayyim, "*He'arot le-Munnaḥei ha-Dikduk shel R(abbi) A(braham) (i)B(n) Ezra*," Rev. of L. Prys. Die gram. Termin. des Abraham Ibn Esra (1950), in: *Leshonenu*, 7 (1951), 241–47; idem, "*Torat ha-Tenu'ot le-Rav Sa'adyah Ga'on*," ibid., 18 (1952), 89–96; idem, "*Le-Inyan Kelalei ha-Sheva shel R. Yehudah Ḥayyūj*," ibid., 20 (1956), 135–8; S.L. Skoss, *Saadia Gaon the Earliest Hebrew Grammarian* (1955; = *Proceedings of the American Academy for Jewish Research*, 21 (1952), 75–100; 22 (1953), 65–90; 23 (1954), 59–73); A. Ben-David, "*Mekorot li-Fe'ulato shel Levi Altabban be-Meḥkar ha-Lashon*," in: *Leshonenu*, 22 (1958), 7–35, 110–36; G.E. Weil, *Elie Levita, humaniste et Massorete (1469–1549)* (1963); P. Wechter, *Ibn Barūn's Arabic Works on Hebrew Grammar and Lexicography* (1964); N. Allony, *Reshimat Munaḥim Kara'it me-ha-Me'ah haSheminit (Tokhnit Limmudim ve-Haskalah Kara'it Attikah)*, in: *Sefer Ha-Zikkaron le-Korngreen* (1964), 324–63; D. Pagis, "*Mekorot li-Fe'ulato shel Levi Altabban be-Meḥkar la-Lashon*," in: *Leshonenu*, 27–28 (1964), 49–57; H. Yalon, "*Mah Bein R. Shelomo Almoli le-R. Eliyahu Baḥur? (Kelal Yesodi bi-Netiyyot ha-Shem ve-ha-Po'al)*," ibid., 27–28 (1964), 225–9; H. Shay (ed.), "Letter Taw of Tanḥum Yerushalmi's Al-Murshid Al-Kafi," ibid., 33 (1969), 196–207, 280–96; N. Allony, "*Ali b. Judah ha-Nazir ve-Ḥibburo Yesodot ha-Lashon ha-Ivrit*," ibid., 34 (1970), 75–105, 187–209; M. Banit, "*Ḥeker ha-Glossarim ha-Mikra'im shel Yehudei Ẓarefat bi-Ymei ha-Beinayim, Shitah ve-Yissum*," in: *Divrei ha-Akademyah ha-Le'ummit ha-Yisre'elit le-Madda'im*, 2 (1969), 135–49; M.N. Zislin, "*K voprosu o znachenie gramaticheskogo sochineniya Abu-l-Faragā Kharuna 'Al-Kafi'*," in: *Problemy Vostokovedeniya*, 3 (1960),

208–12; idem (ed.), *"Glava iz gramaticheskogo sochineniya 'Al-Kafi' Abu-l-Fara,"* in: *Palestinsky Sbornik*, 70 (1962), 178–84; idem (ed.), *"Abu-l-Farag Kharun o spryazhenii yevreyskogo glagola,"* in: *Kratkie Soobshcheniya Instituta Narodov Azii*, 86 (1965), 164–77 (text: 170–1); P. Kokowtzow, *Kniga sravneniya yevreiskavo yazika j arabskim" Abu Ibragima (Isaaka) Ibn Barûna*, Heb. pt. (1890), Rus. pt. (1893); idem, *"Iz 'Knigi becgi i upominaniya' (Kitab Al-Mukhâdara va'l-Muzâkara) Moiceya Ibn Ezri,"* in: *Vostochniya Zametki* (1895), 191–220; idem, ed. of the first four chapters of Moses ibn Ezra's *Kitāb al-Muḥādara wa-al-Mudhākara* (1895); P. Kokowtzow, in: *Bulletin de l'Académie Impériale des Sciences de St. Petersbourg* (1911), 1219–36; idem, *Noviye materiali dlya kharakteristiki Yehudi Khayudja, Samuila Nagida i nekotorikh drugikh predstaviteley eyreiskoy filologicheskoy nauki v–x, xi i xii vieki*, Heb. pt. and Russ. pt. (1916); Azar (= A.S. Rabinovitz), *Nizzanei ha-Dikduk ha-Ivri* (1927). For additional bibliography, see "Authors and Their Works" above and the Bibliography in *Hebrew Language.

LINOWITZ, SOL MYRON (1913–2005), U.S. ambassador, lawyer, and business executive. Linowitz, who was born in Trenton, New Jersey, graduated from Cornell University Law School in 1938. He had a private law practice in New York and served as assistant general counsel to the Office of Price Administration (1942). From 1944 to 1946 he served in the U.S. Navy. After the war, Linowitz resumed his legal practice and began an association with Xerox Corporation. Linowitz eventually was appointed board chairman and head of Xerox International, Inc. Throughout his association with Xerox, he consistently tried to establish the image of the company as one dedicated to public service as well as profits. He served as chairman of the State Department's Advisory Committee on International Organizations, was a member of the Business Advisory Committee to the federal poverty program, and cofounded (with David Rockefeller) the International Executive Service Corps (IESC), a volunteer program that sends American executives to provide managerial and technical expertise to developing countries. Linowitz helped to establish Rochester's anti-poverty agency after the 1964 riots by blacks there. President Johnson appointed Linowitz the U.S. representative to the Organization of American States (OAS) and the Inter-American Committee of the Alliance for Progress (1966–69). Linowitz also served as a trustee of the American Jewish Committee. In 1977 he helped negotiate the transfer of the Panama Canal to Panama. Following the 1978 Camp David accords, he served as President Jimmy Carter's ambassador-at-large for Middle East peace negotiations (1979–81). In 1998, he was awarded the Presidential Medal of Freedom by President Bill Clinton. During his career, Linowitz also served as a director of Time Inc., Pan Am, and the Mutual Life Insurance Co. of New York; and was a partner and senior counsel with the international law firm of Coudert Brothers. Linowitz wrote *The Making of a Public Man, A Memoir* (1985) and *The Betrayed Profession: Lawyering in the 20th Century* (1994).

[Joachim O. Ronall / Ruth Beloff (2nd ed.)]

LINZ, capital of Upper Austria. Jewish moneylenders are recorded in Linz in 1304; a Jewish settlement in the growing market town is probably a century older. In 1335 a synagogue is mentioned; two Jews were baptized a year earlier. Jews were accused of desecrating the *Host in 1338. Although the community was not harmed during the *Black Death persecutions of 1348, a local persecution occurred in 1371. In 1396 Duke Albert IV permitted Jews to conduct only fiscal transactions with the burghers; the decree was renewed in 1412. The Jews were expelled from Linz in 1421, and in 1426 the synagogue was turned into a church. Jews were permitted to attend the biannual markets in the town in 1494, and Jewish horse dealers and feather and wool merchants, mainly from Moravia, continued to trade at the fairs until their entry was forbidden at the end of the 17th century. Only in 1783 were the markets officially declared open and in 1824 the Jews opened their own prayer room. A cemetery was consecrated in 1863, when the modern community was established. In 1869 there were 391 Jews (1.3% of the total population) and 533 in 1880. A new synagogue was opened in 1877 by Rabbi Adolf Kurrein (1876–82), publicist and author. His son, Rabbi Viktor Kurrein (1923–38), wrote the history of the community.

In 1923 there were 1,238 Jews in Linz, 671 in 1934 (0.6%), and in 1938, before the *Anschluss*, 650. On Nov. 10, 1938, the synagogue was burned down by the SS; the 65 remaining Jews were arrested and ordered to leave within three days for Vienna. The Nazis claimed that the Jews must leave the town because it was the capital of the province of Hitler's birth. Jewish shops were not looted because they had already been "Aryanized." Shortly after the end of the war, 2,400 Jewish refugees were housed in the nearby Bindermichen camp. A new community was reorganized, which numbered 238 in 1949 and 145 in 1961. In October 1957, an antisemitic demonstration was sparked off by a performance of *The Diary of Anne Frank*. Protests against a ban on *sheḥitah* were lodged in 1958. A new synagogue was consecrated in 1968.

BIBLIOGRAPHY: *Festschrift anlaesslich der Einweihung des neu erbauten Bethauses in Linz* (1968); V. Kurrein, *Die Juden in Linz* (1927); idem, in: *Menorah* (1927), 309–44; idem, in: JGGJČ, 2 (1930), 497–500; 4 (1932), 481–4; idem, in: *Juedisches Archiv*, 1:5–6 (1928), 3–7; Germ Jud, 2 (1968), 490–1; L. Moses, *Die Juden in Niederoesterreich* (1935), 185–6, no. 274, 279; H.H. Rosenkranz, *Reichskristallnacht – 9 November 1938 in Oesterreich* (1968), 51; PK Germanyah.

[Henry Wasserman]

LION. Called in the Talmud "the king of the beasts" (Ḥag. 13b), the lion has many Hebrew names: (אַרְיֵה *(aryeh)* or אֲרִי *(ari)*, and לָבִיא *(lavi)* fem. לְבִיאָה *(levi'ah)*, both of which are used for the lion in general, כְּפִיר *(kefir)*, usually a young lion, לַיִשׁ *(layish)*, mostly poetical, and according to some, "an old lion," שַׁחַל *(shaḥal)*, general name for the lion in poetry, though like שַׁחַץ *(shaḥaẓ)* perhaps the intention is any fierce animal, and גּוּר *(gur)* almost always meaning "a lion's whelp." The first five are all mentioned together by Eliphaz the Temanite (Job 4:10–11), on which Rashi comments that *ari* is the large lion, *shaḥal* the medium-sized one, and *kefir* the small lion, while the first six are cited in Sanhedrin 95a. (Note, however, that

Rashi in commenting on Ezekiel 19:5 says categorically that all references to *kefir* in the Bible refer to a grown mighty lion.) Similarly, Kimḥi breaks the different terms for lion into categories of size in his comment to Judges 14:5. More likely, though, the different terms with the exception of *gur*, "cub" (Nah. 2:13) are synonyms employed by the biblical poets. In fact, *lavi* (= Akkadian *lābu*), *shaḥal*, and *layish* (= Akkadian *nēšu*; l/n interchange) are attested only in poetry. In the Bible there are more than 150 references to the lion, many of them descriptive, metaphoric, and allegorical. To the lion were compared the tribes of Judah (Gen. 49:9) and Dan (Deut. 33:22); Balaam said of the Israelites: "Behold a people that riseth up as a lioness (*lavi*), and as a lion (*ari*) doth he lift himself up" (Num. 23:24); the mother of the kings of Judah was compared to a lioness and her sons to lion (*gureha*) cubs (Ezek. 19:2–3). David, of whom it was said that his "heart is as the heart of a lion" (II Sam. 17:10), declared in his lament over Saul and Jonathan that "they were swifter than eagles, they were stronger than lions" (*ibid.* 1:23). This combination of the lion, the king of the beasts, and the *eagle, the king of the birds (the biblical reference is to the *vulture), is very common in later Jewish art, particularly on the Holy Ark, and occurs in Ezekiel's vision of the lion, the ox, the eagle, and the cherub (Ezek. 1:10; 10:14). In Solomon's Temple there were carvings of "lions, oxen, and cherubim" (I Kings 7:29), while a lion with eagle's wings symbolized in the Book of Daniel (7:4) the kingdom of Babylonia. The lion is mentioned several times together with the bear as the most powerful beasts of prey (Lam. 3:10; Prov. 28:15; I Sam. 17:34; et al.). When a lion attacks its prey there is no escape from it, being mentioned in many parables, as when Amos (3:12) declares that a shepherd can rescue out of its jaws no more than "two legs, or a piece of an ear." Nor is a lion in the least frightened even when shepherds gather to chase it away (Isa. 31:4). An encounter between a man and a lion is usually fatal to the former (I Kings 13:24; 20:36), lions having killed new settlers in the cities of Samaria (II Kings 17:25), and having claimed victims, according to Jeremiah (5:6), in the land of Judah. Only in exceptional instances was a lion slain in such a clash, as when encountering a man of great personal courage such as Samson (Judg. 14:6), David (I Sam. 17:34), and Benaiah the son of Jehoiada (II Sam. 23:20). Among the Samaria ivories of the ninth century B.C.E. are two representations of lions (image in IDB 3, 137). From the eighth century is a seal inscribed, "property of Shema, servant of Jeroboam," with an engraving of a lion (Ahituv, 206).

From the Bible it is clear that lions did not permanently inhabit populated areas; their haunts were the mountains of Lebanon (Song 4:8), Bashan (Deut. 33:22), the thickets of the Jordan (Jer. 49:19), and the desert regions of the Negev (Isa. 30:6). From there they invaded populated areas, penetrating deeply and regularly, in particular at times of drought when wild animals, their usual prey, had decreased in number. Lions also multiplied when the country lay destroyed and derelict. In the neighborhood of Ereẓ Israel long- and short-maned lions were to be found. There are evidences that there were lions in the country in mishnaic and talmudic and even in crusader times (in the Negev). The last lions in the Middle East were destroyed in the 19th century.

[Jehuda Feliks / S. David Sperling (2nd ed.)]

In Folklore and Art

The lion figures prominently in folklore as a result of two main references to it in the Bible: the appellation of Judah as "a lion's whelp" (Gen. 49:9; Dan is also so called in Deut. 33:22, but the lion is always associated with Judah) and as one of the figures in the divine chariot of Ezekiel (Ezek. 1:10). A secondary motif is connected with the statement of Judah b. Tema (Avot 5:20) "Be as strong as a leopard, light as an eagle, fleet as a hart, and brave as a lion to perform the will of thy Father who is in heaven."

Based on the image of the Lion of Judah in Genesis, the name Aryeh ("lion") became a common Jewish personal name mostly in all combinations with Judah and with Leib (Loeb), its German or Yiddish translation, thus giving the composite names Judah Aryeh, Judah Leib, and Aryeh Leib. The Judah mentioned in the verse, however, is associated not only with the son of Jacob of that name, but with the tribe, and particularly with the House of David (cf. Rashi ad loc.), and as a result the Lion of Judah became one of the most common of Jewish symbols. It is also one of the appellatives of the king of Ethiopia, who according to Ethiopian tradition is descended from Solomon and the Queen of Sheba. The rampant Lion of Judah is a favorite embellishment of the synagogue ark, the mantle covering the scroll of the Torah, etc. The Lion of the Divine Chariot is one of the four figures of Ezekiel's *merkavah* (divine chariot) which consisted of a human being, a lion, an ox, and an eagle. Different opinions are expressed in the Talmud as to the permissibility of reproducing these figures, but the general consensus is that the only reproductions wholly forbidden are either the four together or the complete human form (see *Art). On the other hand, almost complete freedom was accorded in the reproduction of the lion, possibly both because of its national association as described above and because of the figures of lions upon the laver in Solomon's Temple (I Kings 7:29) and especially in the steps leading to his throne and on its sides (*ibid.* 10:20).

*Jacob b. Asher opens his *Tur Oraḥ Ḥayyim* with the above-quoted passage of Judah b. Tema, and the four animals mentioned in it have often been made the subject of paintings. The word lion is often employed figuratively in a laudatory sense, mostly referring to an outstanding scholar. Thus Joshua b. Hananiah refused to controvert the ruling of Eliezer b. Hyrcanus after the latter's death because "one does not answer a lion after its death" (Git. 83a). Ḥiyya is called "the lion of the brotherhood" (Shab. 111a); a scholar, the son of a scholar, is called "a lion, son of a lion," while one of no such distinguished parentage is called "the lion the son of a jackal" (BM 84b); and Simeon b. Lakish expressed his admiration for the learning of Kahana, who had come to Ereẓ Israel from Babylon, in the words "a lion has come up from Babylon" (BK 117a). In one instance, however, it is used in a pejorative sense. Proselytes to Judaism who convert for selfish personal motives are called, in contradistinction to *gerei ẓedek*, righteous proselytes, "the converts of lions" (e.g., Kid. 75b), the allusion being to the Samaritans who adopted the worship of YHWH only because of their fear of lions (II Kings 17:25–28).

[Louis Isaac Rabinowitz]

BIBLIOGRAPHY: Lewysohn, Zool, 68–70, no. 114; Y. Aharoni, *Zikhronot Zo'olog Ivri*, 2 (1946), 222; F.S. Bodenheimer, *Animal and Man in Bible Lands* (1960), passim. **ADD. BIBLIOGRAPHY:** W. McCullough and F. Bodenheimer, in: IDB 3, 136–37; S. Ahituv, *Handbook of Ancient Hebrew Inscriptions* (1992).

LION, LEON M. (1879–1947), British actor-manager. Born in London, Lion was well known particularly for his productions of Galsworthy. He acted in many West End plays and went into management in 1918. Four years later he launched a Galsworthy series, starting with *Justice* and including *Loyalties*, plays which he frequently revived and in which he acted. He presented two Galsworthy plays in Paris, 1928, and between 1918 and 1939 staged 70 productions. He was author or part-author of 20 plays, and also appeared in a number of British films during the 1930s.

LION OF WRATH (Heb. כְּפִיר הֶחָרוֹן, *kefir he-Ḥaron*), character mentioned in the Nahum and Hosea commentaries from Qumran Cave 4 (4QpNahum). In the comment on Nahum 2:12ff., where Nineveh is described as "the den of the lions… the feeding-place of the young lions (*kefirim*)," to which the lion brought home his prey – "he filled his caves with prey and his dens with torn flesh." These last words, says the Qumran commentator, refer to "the lion (*kefir*) of wrath, who smote with his mighty ones and the men of his counsel" and "took vengeance on the *Seekers after Smooth Things, in that he proceeded to hang them up alive [which was never done] in Israel before, for concerning one hung up alive on wood the Scripture says…" What the Scripture says is that he is an "affront to God" (Deut. 21:23). But the Scripture envisages the hanging of the body of an executed criminal on a tree until sunset; the commentator on Nahum has in mind something much more atrocious – hanging men up alive, or crucifying them. That such a thing "was never done in Israel before" implies that the perpetrator was an Israelite – not that he was a gentile ruler mistreating Israelites thus, like Nebuchadnezzar (Lam. 5:12) or Antiochus IV (Jos., Ant. 12:256). If he was an Israelite, the first Israelite ruler recorded to have crucified his enemies is Alexander Yannai, who in 88 B.C.E., having defeated his rebellious subjects who enlisted the aid of Demetrius III (Eukairos) against him, made an example of 800 of their leaders by crucifying them in Jerusalem (Jos., Wars 1:97; Ant. 13:380). This identification is supported by the commentator's reference in the same context to "[Deme-]trius, king of Javan, who sought to enter Jerusalem by the counsel of the Seekers after Smooth Things" – especially if the latter group should be identified with the Pharisees, whose sufferings at the hands of Yannai were long remembered in rabbinic tradition. Other identifications, however, have been suggested for the Lion of Wrath, ranging from Antiochus IV (preferred by H.H. Rowley) to John of Gischala (so C. Roth) and Simeon Bar Giora (so G.R. Driver).

BIBLIOGRAPHY: Allegro, in: JBL, 75 (1965), 89ff. (containing the editio princeps of 4Qp–Nahum); Rowley, in: PEFQS, 88 (1956), 107ff.; C. Roth, *Historical Background of the Dead Sea Scrolls* (1958), 40ff., 84; G.R. Driver, *Judaean Scrolls* (1965), 288ff.

[Frederick Fyvie Bruce]

LIOZNO (Pol. **Lozniany**), town in Vitebsk district, Belarus; under czarist rule it was included in the province (*gubernia*) of Mogilev. Jewish settlement in Liozno dates from the 18th century. The founder of Chabad Ḥasidism, R. *Shneur Zalman of Lyady, was born there in 1745. There were 82 Jewish poll-tax payers in the town in 1766. The community increased in the 19th century; in 1897 the community of Liozno numbered 1,665 (67.3% of the total population). In 1910 there were private Jewish schools for boys and girls. During the Soviet period the number of Jews dropped to 1,204 (46.3%) in 1926, and again to 711 (17.3%) in 1939. A Yiddish school functioned there. The Germans occupied Liozno on July 16, 1941. To the remaining 600 Jews were added refugees from Vitebsk, Minsk, Bobruisk, and Warsaw. On February 23, 1942, they were herded to the village of Adamenki and, over a period of three days, were murdered together with Jews from the environs, all together nearly 1,500 persons. No information is available on Jewish life in Liozno after World War II.

[Yehuda Slutsky / Shmuel Spector (2nd ed.)]

LIPCHITZ, JACQUES (**Chaim Jacob**; 1891–1973), U.S. sculptor. He was born in Druskieniki, Lithuania. He attended school in Bialystok and in 1909 went to Paris, where he adopted the name Jacques. There he studied and became a French citizen in 1925. In 1930 he had a large retrospective exhibition which gave him his international reputation. In 1940 the German advance compelled him to leave Paris and seek refuge in unoccupied France. In 1941 he went to the United States, and settled in Hastings-on-Hudson, New York.

Lipchitz was one of the foremost cubist sculptors – his first pure cubist sculpture is dated 1913. He was influenced by the painters Picasso and Braque, and by the visionary El Greco. He developed an interest in African wood carvings which he collected. During this early period, Lipchitz frequently worked in stone. These pieces, with their sharp edges, flat planes, and solid mass came very close to pure abstraction.

In the 1930s, Lipchitz abandoned cubism for a markedly baroque manner of expression. At the same time, he became interested in social and philosophical themes, as distinguished from the harlequins and dancers, bathers, and musicians he had fashioned in his youth. One of the most celebrated baroque pieces is based on the Prometheus myth. His first sketches, made about 1933, show Prometheus a triumphant figure, the guardian of the flame. The second Prometheus, slightly different in feeling, shows a warrior, still in the thick of battle and unsure of triumph. This was destroyed. Lipchitz recreated it in 1943–44 for the Brazilian government, to decorate the facade of a government building in Rio de Janeiro. The final version, made for the Philadelphia Museum of Art – the superman's battle with the vulture – was Lipchitz's own rendering of the myth, since no such battle is described in ancient literature.

Lipchitz often derived inspiration from his Jewish background. Beginning in the 1930s, he frequently turned to biblical episodes or themes taken from Jewish life and history to interpret tragic or joyous events. "Man is wrestling with the Angel," he said about his "Jacob Wrestling with the Angel": "It is a tremendous struggle, but he wins and is blessed." Similar sentiments are expressed in "David and Goliath," made under the impact of the Nazi destruction. "The Prayer" (an old man swinging a rooster in the **kapparot* ritual) is a grim reminder of the slaughter of Jews in Europe. "The Miracle" is inspired by the happy news of the creation of the Jewish state – an exultant figure with raised arms faces the Tablets of the Law, out of which grows the seven-branched candelabrum, the finials of which might be tiny flames, or young leaf buds of a tree.

Lipchitz's last work, *The Tree of Life*, a six-meter-high bronze, was unveiled posthumously on Sept. 21, 1978, outside the Hadassah Hospital on Mt. Scopus. The sculpture consists of the interwoven formalized expressionist figures of Noah, Abraham and Isaac at the *Akedah*, with the angel restraining the patriarch Moses in front of the Burning Bush, and rising from it a phoenix supporting the Two Tablets. Lipchitz referred to it as "the dynamics of our religion."

Lipchitz's work is represented in important museums, particularly in the United States and Israel. He left all his casts to the Israel Museum, Jerusalem.

BIBLIOGRAPHY: A.M. Hammacher, *Jacques Lipchitz, his Sculpture* (1961); I. Patai, *Encounters: The Life of Jacques Lipchitz* (1961); H.H. Aranson (ed.), *Jacques Lipchitz* (1970).

[Alfred Werner]

LIPINER, SIEGFRIED (1856–1911), Austrian poet and playwright. Born in Jaroslaw, Galicia, and raised in Tarnow, he moved to Vienna in 1871, devoting himself to literature and philosophy. Lipiner's first epic poem *Der entfesselte Prometheus* (1876) aroused much favorable comment. It was followed by the epic *Renatus* (1878), by a volume of lyrics entitled *Buch der Freude* (1880), and by a libretto, *Merlin* (1886), for which Karl *Goldmark wrote the music. The last work was staged by the Viennese Royal Opera in 1886. From 1881 until his death, Lipiner was librarian and archivist of the Austrian *Reichsrat*. Although he converted to Christianity in 1891 and avoided all reference to his Jewish descent, Lipiner was described by his admirer, Nietzsche, as a Polish Jew capable of imitating the various forms of European lyric fastidiously and "almost genuinely." His original poetry was much influenced by Schopenhauer, Wagner, and Nietzsche. He also published a German translation of Adam *Mickiewicz's *Pan Tadeusz*. Three of his plays were *Der neue Don Juan* (written in 1880, published in 1914), *Adam* (1913), and *Hippolytos* (1913). Lipiner's fame reached its peak while he was in his early twenties, but his verse later lost its popularity, though it often received mention in literary histories. He was a close friend of the composer Gustav *Mahler.

BIBLIOGRAPHY: H. von Hartungen, *Der Dichter Siegfried Lipiner*, dissert., Munich 1935 (1937). **ADD. BIBLIOGRAPHY:** H. Lengauer, "Siegfried Lipiner: Biographie im Zeichen des Prometheus," in: H. Zeman (ed.), *Die oesterreichische Literatur* (1989), 1227–1246; Q. Principe, "Il caso Lipiner e il caso Meyrink. La quadruplice radice dell'insufficienza," in: Q. Principe (ed.), *Ebrei e Mitteleuropa* (1994), 89–102; R. Mueller-Buck, "La salute del giovane Nietzsche," in: *Belfagor*, 59:4 (2004), 460–466.

[Sol Liptzin]

LIPKANY (Rom. **Lipcani**), small town in N. Moldova, in the region of Bessarabia. Jews appeared there in the middle of the 17th century. There were 82 Jewish families in Lipkany (out of a total of 203) in 1817, 4,410 persons (63% of the total population) in 1897, and 4,693 in 1930 (79.8% of the total). They were the chief exporters of farm products from Bessarabia to Austria and Germany. During the first half of the 19th century the *ẓaddik* Meir of Peremyshlyany lived in the town for several years. The writers Judah *Steinberg and Eliezer *Steinbarg were born there. In May 1936 the Cuza Fascist Party convened in Lipkany, but Jewish self-defense prevented attacks against Jews. In June 1940 the town was annexed to the Soviet Union, and included in the Moldavian S.S.R.

[Eliyahu Feldman / Shmuel Spector (2nd ed.)]

Holocaust Period

On June 22, 1941, the Germans bombed the town, and it was devastated. When the town was taken on July 8, 1941, by German-Romanian forces, they carried out a pogrom the same day in which many Jews were killed, and they robbed almost all houses. The survivors (about 4,000) were taken on July 18 to a forest near Vertyuzhany and from there were sent on a death march which took them to *Sekiryany, *Yedintsy, and *Khotin, and back to Yedintsy; the old, the sick, and the children, who were unable to withstand the pace, were shot on the journey. From Yedintsy, the survivors were deported to *Transnistria, where most of them died. Only a few dozen Jewish families from Lipkany were saved by the arrival of the Soviet army. Almost all the young Jews from the town who joined the Soviet army at the beginning of the war were either killed or returned as invalids. One Jew from Lipkany, Abram Schneider, was decorated as a "Hero of the Soviet Union." The few surviving families, who returned to Lipkany in 1944, left the town soon, immigrating to Palestine.

[Jean Ancel]

BIBLIOGRAPHY: M. Carp, *Cartea Neagrà*, 3 (1947), index; BJCE; Herz-Kahn, in: *Eynikeyt* (Oct. 2, 1945).

LIPKIN (Salanter), ISRAEL BEN ZE'EV WOLF (1810–1883), founder and spiritual father of the *Musar movement.

His father, author of the glosses *Ben Aryeh* on the Talmud and *rishonim*, served as rabbi in Goldingen, Latvia and Telz, Lithuania, and he was later appointed rabbi of Zhagare, where Israel was born. At the age of 12, Israel went to the yeshivah of Ẓevi Hirsch Broida in Salant, and his reputation there was such that his teacher referred to him as "the little *Alfasi"; other great contemporary scholars applied similar laudatory appellations to him. His chance meeting with R. Zundel of Salant – a great scholar and an unusually humble and modest man – had a decisive influence on him. Powerfully impressed by Zundel's personality, Israel attached himself to him, regarding him from then on as his principal teacher, and conducting himself according to Zundel's ethical principles. He refused to accept rabbinical office, even that of Brest-Litovsk – the major community in Lithuania.

During his whole life, Lipkin sought the best way in which to influence the community. Deciding to become a preacher or a *mashgi'aḥ* ("spiritual mentor") in a yeshivah, he accepted the position of head of a yeshivah in Vilna, where he was quickly renowned for his profound acumen. He soon resigned this post, however, and established his own yeshivah in Vilna. When his fame spread he began to preach sermons giving expression to the doctrine of *musar*, a moral movement based on the study of traditional ethical literature. These sermons attracted huge audiences. He proceeded to found groups for the study of *musar* on the lines of various ethical works. With the consolidation of these groups he established a special institution called a Bet Musar, in which he delivered his *musar* discourses and these became the pattern for similar discourses delivered in all the yeshivot which adopted the teaching of *musar*. These discourses were never recorded apart from several individual ones published by his pupil Shneur Zalman Hirschovitz in *Even Yisrael* (1883).

During the cholera epidemic which swept Vilna in 1848, Lipkin was in the forefront of all the most dangerous relief activities. He gave instructions that every kind of work was to be done on the Sabbath by Jews and was not to be relegated to non-Jews. On the Day of Atonement during the epidemic he ordered the congregation to partake of food, and set a personal example by mounting the pulpit and publicly eating. This dramatic action made a powerful impression both in contemporary and in later literature. His name was put forward to head the rabbinical seminary of Vilna, founded in 1848, but he refused to accept despite the attractive terms offered and the government pressure that was brought to bear upon him. As a result of this pressure he left Vilna and went to Kovno, where he founded a Musar yeshivah, which expanded greatly, attaining a roll of 150 students, many of whom were to become outstanding Lithuanian rabbis. His most important activity during this period was the improvement of the living conditions of the yeshivah students. He abolished the custom of the students being given daily hospitality in private homes, arranged suitable accommodation for them, and insisted that they be properly and neatly dressed. He also taught deportment and aesthetics. The period of study in his yeshivah was highly valued by the students, who saw themselves under "a new heaven and a new earth and an individual superior to all" (*Tenu'at ha-Musar*, p. 175). Lipkin obtained his livelihood from communal posts in Kovno. Opposition to his methods began during the period of his yeshivah in Kovno, and among his opponents were Joshua Hoeschel of Janow, Abraham Samuel of Rossiyeny, Mordecai Eliasberg of Bauska, and Isaiah of Salant.

In 1857, to the surprise of many, Lipkin moved to Germany – first to Halberstadt for medical attention and later to Koenigsberg, where he lectured to university students on Judaism. In 1860 he went to Memel near the German-Lithuanian border. There he published his periodical *Tevunah*, for the dissemination of Torah and *musar*, to which all the outstanding scholars of Lithuania and Galicia contributed; 12 numbers were published. In Memel he acquired German citizenship, adopted German dress, and even preached in German. He also mastered various secular subjects. He visited several German cities, including Tilsit, Berlin, Frankfurt, and Halberstadt. During this period he maintained contact with his pupils in Lithuania by correspondence. These letters constitute the main source for his system of *musar*. In 1877 he founded a **kolel* for young married students in Kovno; similar institutions were also set up in various towns. Lipkin's pupils began to establish large yeshivot in Volozhin, Kelme, Telz, and Slobodka, in which *musar* teaching was predominant. In 1880 he went to France in order to disseminate Judaism. Although he suffered greatly there because of his straitened circumstances, he did not cease his activity. He stayed in Paris two years and succeeded in strengthening its Jewish institutions. From Paris he returned to Koenigsberg where he died.

In general Lipkin was revolutionary in his ideas. He proposed the compilation of an Aramaic-Hebrew dictionary for the better understanding of the Talmud, the translation of the Talmud into Hebrew, its printing in one volume, its translation into European languages, its teaching in universities, and the provision of religious books in Russian. Lipkin was also active in the communal and political spheres. He left no large works. He published an article in the *Eẓ Peri* (1881) and a number of articles from *Tevunah* were later collected in a special work called *Imrei Binah* (1878). His well-known *Iggeret ha-Musar* ("ethical letter") was first published in Koenigsberg in 1858 and repeatedly republished. Twenty-two letters were collected by Isaac *Blaser, who published them under the title *Or Yisrael* (1900; English translation, 2004). A collection of his discourses recorded by pupils was published under the title *Even Yisrael* (1883); letters and collections appeared in various organs such as *Beit Yisrael, Ḥut ha-Meshullash*, etc. The letters of Lipkin, *Kitvei R. Israel Lipkin*, edited by M. Pacter, appeared in 1973. All these deal with his system of *musar* which spread throughout Lithuania and was adopted by all the yeshivot.

Lipkin was foremost an educator and ethicist, writing and teaching in response to the historical, social, and religious problems of his time. He was keenly aware of the changes going on all around him in the Jewish community, thus his teachings and writings must be seen as reflecting his social and educational activity.

The central issue that concerned him was the gap between an individual's professed beliefs and his actions. Searching for the causes of this phenomenon, Lipkin discovered that there was no direct relationship between a person's piety and his knowledge of Torah. Knowledge attained through the standard yeshivah curriculum did not necessarily produce moral behavior, but knowledge of divine retribution, knowing that no one escapes the consequences of his actions, does affect behavior. This insight, coupled with another one, formed the basis for Lipkin's *musar* campaign. The second insight relates to the difference between a person's appetites and desires and knowledge. Contrary to one's desires, which are innate in a person, knowledge is acquired. For this reason, attaining even the right knowledge is rarely enough to control one's appetites. To solve this problem, Lipkin developed behavioral mechanisms, i.e., the habitual repetition of emotional, cognitive, and behavioral stimuli, "to fortify the intellectual fear of God that the latter eventually achieves the level of distinct instinct capable of combating less worthy desires or even uprooting them totally" (Ross, *Immanuel*, 1983/84, 70). Later on in his career, Lipkin proposed a different solution based on improving character traits, thus changing one's personality. All of these teachings were Lipkin's means to achieve a particular end: an improvement in piety and religious observance.

Lipkin dealt with a number of philosophical issues peripherally in his sermons and writings. These included the paradox of divine knowledge and free will, miracles vs. natural law, the relative ability or inability of the human intellect to grasp objective truth in general or Torah in particular, and *emunat ḥakhamim* (blind faith in rabbinic dicta). This aspect of his teachings was developed by his students into "yeshivah ideology" (*ibid.*). Thus, Lipkin's disciples abandoned his *musar* methods and began to emphasize his philosophical ideas. Ironically, their *musar* technique became the identification with a set of proper ideas and opinions. Nevertheless, Lipkin had an enormous impact on yeshivah study. To this day, almost every yeshivah student spends a portion of his day studying Jewish philosophy and ethics.

Among Lipkin's sons were Yom Tov Lipman *Lipkin, a scientist with an international reputation; ARYEH LEIB HOROWITZ, author of the *Ḥayyei Aryeh* (1907) and rabbi of Choroszcz, Janow, and Brezhin; and ISAAC LIPKIN, rabbi of Janow, Korets, and Prosnitsa.

BIBLIOGRAPHY: S. Rosenfeld, *R. Yisrael Salanter* (Heb., 1911); L. Ginzberg, *Students Scholars and Saints* (1928), 145–94; K. Rosen, *Rabbi Israel Salanter and the Musar Movement* (1945); M.G. Glenn, *Israel Salanter* (1953); D. Katz, *Tenu'at ha-Musar*, 1 (1958^3), 137–38b; L. Jung (ed.), *Jewish Leaders*, 1 (1953), 197–211. **ADD. BIBLIOGRAPHY:** I. Salanter, *Ohr Yisrael: The Classical Writings of Rav Yisrael Salanter and His Disciples* (2004); I. Etkes, *Rabbi Israel Salanter and the Mussar Movement: Seeking the Torah of Truth* (1993); Z. Fendel, *The Ethical Personality: A Comprehensive Analysis of the Torah Approach to Ethics* (1986); H. Goldberg, *Israel Salanter, Text, Structure, Idea: The Ethics and Theology of an Early Psychologist of the Unconscious* (1982); idem, in: *Immanuel*, 17 (1983/84), 106–119; T. Ross, in: *ibid.*, 68–76; N. Ḥen, *Rabbi Yisrael Salanter: Mi-Toldotav, Ḥayyav u-Po'alo* (1988); M. Pachter, in: *Tarbiz* (1984), 621–50; idem, in: *The World of Rav Kook's Thought* (1991), 322–48; S. Wolbe, in: *Jewish Observer*, 17:6 (1984), 4–6; L. Geldwerth, in: *ibid.*, 9–17; H. Goldberg, in: *Tradition*, 22:3 (1986), 31–43; idem, in: *ibid.* 23:4 (1988), 14–46; L. Shalit, in: *Identity and Ethos: A Festschift for Sol Liptzin* (1986), 393–406.

[Itzhak Alfassi / David Derovan (2nd ed.)]

LIPKIN, YOM TOV LIPMAN (1845–1875), Russian mathematician, son of Israel Salanter (see Israel *Lipkin). In his early youth Lipkin demonstrated great interest and promise in the exact sciences, studying higher mathematics on his own. Leaving his family for Koenigsberg, he was admitted to the university there. After finishing at the Berlin Gewerbe-Akademie, he was accepted at the University in Jena, where he presented his dissertation, "Ueber die Raeumlichen Strophoiden," in 1870. Moving to St. Petersburg, he demonstrated his mechanical device for changing linear motion into circular motion, which he had previously written about in *Mélanges mathématiques de l'Academie Impériale à St. Petersbourg* (1870). His kinematic system was included in many Russian and foreign textbooks.

BIBLIOGRAPHY: Slonimski, in: *Vestnik russkikh yevreyev*, nos. 17, 19 (1871); *Ha-Ẓefirah*, 22 (1874); 22, 24 (1875).

LIPKIN-SHAHAK, AMNON (1944–), 15th chief of staff of the IDF (1995–98). Lipkin-Shahak was born in Tel Aviv. As a career officer he studied at the IDF Staff and Command College and the National Defense College. In the Six-Day War and Yom Kippur War he had commands in the paratroops. During his service he was twice awarded the Medal of Valor: in 1968 he commanded his troops under enemy fire and in 1973 in Lebanon he carried out his mission under enemy fire and with casualties. As deputy chief of staff he headed the Israeli military team to the negotiations with the Palestinians on the Gaza-Jericho Agreement. As chief of staff, he met with his Syrian counterpart to discuss security arrangements as part of the peace negotiations between the two countries. After his retirement from the IDF he joined the Center Party and was elected to the Knesset in 1999. As part of the coalition, he held the Ministry of Tourism and later of Transport. After the defeat of Ehud Barak in the 2001 election he resigned from the Knesset and became chairman of *Tahal.

[Shaked Gilboa (2nd ed.)]

LIPMAN, EUGENE JAY (1919–1993), U.S. Reform rabbi. Lipman was born in Pittsburgh, Pennsylvania. A traditionalist and a Zionist, Lipman would have attended the Jewish Theological Seminary but an interview with its chancellor who asked him only about the nature of his religious observance, and nothing more, alienated him. He went instead to the Hebrew Union College where he was ordained in 1943 and served for a year at Temple Beth-El in Fort Worth, Texas. As a chaplain in the U.S. Army (1944–46, 1950–51) he was instrumental in aiding the flight of Jews from Eastern Europe through Czechoslovakia. Together with such rabbis as Abraham Klausner and Herbert Freidman, Lipman provided enormous support for the seemingly clandestine escape of Jews – Holocaust survivors – into the American and British sectors. He worked with the Russians to transfer the last survivors in Theresienstadt to the U.S. occupation zone. He organized transports of survivors from Prague through Pilsen to Italy, en route to Palestine. He returned as a civilian as liaison officer for the U.S. Army and the Jewish Agency for Palestine, working with the Haganah (1947–48). His role of rescue and his work with the Haganah used to irritate right-wing critics of his more dovish views on Israel in the 1980s, who could not challenge his commitment or match his service. From 1951 to 1961 he was director of the Commission on Social Action and the Commission on Synagogue Activities of the Union of American Hebrew Congregations, where he was instrumental in the establishment of the Religious Action Center in Washington, D.C., the arm of the Reform movement in the heart of the American capital where it represents Liberal Judaism and liberalism in the political and social fights of the day. Because of his service in Europe, Rabbi Leo Baeck entrusted the young rabbi with a *Megillat Esther* that had been read in Theresienstadt. In return he demanded that the *megillah* be kept in proper order so that it could be read in the synagogue each year and that the story of this *megillah* – the story of Purim and of Theresienstadt – be told. Lipman complied. Years later when he wanted to make the *megillah* available for display at the United States Holocaust Memorial Museum, it was for 364 days a year: once a year it had to be returned to a synagogue where it would be read.

From 1961 he was rabbi of Temple Sinai, Washington, D.C., which had been the home of activist liberal rabbis. Lipman was active in every branch of Reform Judaism and also served as president of the Central Conference of American Rabbis and president of the Washington, D.C. Interfaith Conference, the first interfaith group in the United States which joined Jews, Protestants, Catholics, and Muslims. He took pleasure in mentoring young rabbis without regard to their movement or religious affiliation. He wrote *Justice and Judaism: The Work of Social Action* (1956) and coedited *A Tale of Ten Cities: The Triple Ghetto in American Religious Life* (1962). A classic scholar, he also edited and translated *The Mishnah: Oral Teachings of Judaism* (1975).

[Michael Berenbaum (2nd ed.)]

LIPMAN, JACOB GOODALE (1874–1939), U.S. soil chemist and bacteriologist. Lipman was born in Friedrichstadt, Latvia. His parents were expelled from Moscow in 1888, and went to the U.S. In 1898 he joined the New Jersey State Agricultural Experimental Station and was its director from 1911. In 1910 he became professor of soil fertility and bacteriology at Rutgers and from 1913 to 1939 was professor of agriculture. Among the books he wrote were *Bacteria in Relation to Country Life* (1908) and *A Laboratory Guide of Soil Bacteriology* (1911, with P.E. Brown). He edited several journals including *Soil Science* which he founded in 1916.

Lipman was director of the *Jewish Agricultural Society. In 1927 he was on the commission of experts surveying Palestine, and in 1929 he became a member of the Jewish Agency for Palestine.

BIBLIOGRAPHY: *Industrial and Engineering Chemistry*, 27 (1935), 103; *Soil Science*, 40 (1935); S.A. Waksman, *Jacob G. Lipman* (1966).

[Samuel Aaron Miller]

LIPMAN, LEVI (**Isaac Libman**; first half of 18th century), merchant of Courland and financial agent for the imperial Russian court. Lipman's name is found in documents from the reigns of Peter II (1727–30) and Anna (1730–40), occasionally with the addition of the titles *Ober-Hof-Kommissar* and *Kammeragent*, as a purveyor of various goods and precious stones to the imperial court. His name is sometimes mentioned as a *shtadlan* active on behalf of the Jews. He was a favorite of Prince Dmitri Golitsyn and later of Count Biron, the "strong man" at Czarina Anna's court. When Biron was appointed duke of Courland in 1737, he entrusted Lipman with all the financial affairs of the duchy. He pursued his commerce in St. Petersburg and maintained his relations with the imperial court even after the fall of Biron. As he was the sole Jewish figure at the court of St. Petersburg, his contemporaries exaggerated the extent of his influence. (One ambassador wrote of him: "Lipman is the actual ruler of Russia.") In fact, Lipman was merely one of the *Court Jews who were characteristic of that period in Europe.

BIBLIOGRAPHY: R.J. Wynderbar, *Geschichte der Juden in den Provinzen Liv-und Kurland* (1853), 23; Yu. Hessen, in: YE, 10, 224–5.

[Yehuda Slutsky]

LIPMAN, VIVIAN DAVID (1921–1990), British administrator and historian. Born in London, Lipman served in the British army during World War II before obtaining his doctorate at Oxford University. He entered the British Civil Service in 1947 and worked as an administrator on housing, local government, and urban planning. From 1972 to 1978, he served as director of ancient monuments and historic buildings, which included responsibility for archaeology and the royal palaces and parks. In addition to publications on administrative history, notably *Local Government Areas* (1949), and the British architectural heritage, he wrote extensively on Anglo-Jewish history, such as *Social History of the Jews in England* (1954), *A Century of Social Service* (1959), *The Jews of Medieval Norwich* (1965), and his edited collection, *Three Centuries of Anglo-Jewish History* (1961). Lipman's survey of modern Anglo-Jewry, *History of the Jews in Britain Since 1858* (1990), appeared posthumously. In his evolution as a historian, Lipman was influenced to a certain extent by the trend to see more antisemitism in British society than had been noted by previous historians, while providing a generally optimistic view. He served as president of the Jewish Historical Society of England and was an honorary research fellow of University College London and a fellow of the Society of Antiquaries. In collaboration with his wife, Sonia, he also wrote on contemporary social trends in Anglo-Jewry.

ADD. BIBLIOGRAPHY: I. Finestein, "Vivian David Lipman (1921–1990)," in: JHSET, 31 (1989–90), xv–xix; A. Rapoport-Albert, "Vivian Lipman: A Personal Tribute," in: *ibid.*, xx–xxii.

LIPMANN, FRITZ ALBERT (1899–1986), U.S. biochemist and Nobel Prize winner. Lipmann was born in Koenigsberg, Germany. From 1927 to 1931 he pursued research at the Kaiser Wilhelm Institute in Berlin and at Heidelberg. With the rise of the Nazi regime he left Germany and went to Denmark, working at the Biological Institute of the Carlsberg Foundation in Copenhagen from 1932 to 1939. He then immigrated to the United States and worked at Cornell University from 1939 to 1941, at the Massachusetts General Hospital from 1941 to 1947, and at the Harvard University Medical School, where he was professor of biological chemistry from 1949 to 1957. In 1957 he was appointed professor at the Rockefeller Institute for Medical Research in New York.

In 1953 Lipmann was awarded the Nobel Prize for medicine and physiology, which he shared with Hans *Krebs, for his discovery of coenzyme A and its importance for intermediary metabolism. This substance plays an important role in the "Krebs cycle" through which food is converted into carbon dioxide, water, and energy. Lipmann found that coenzyme A contains pantothenic acid, one of the vitamin B group. His hundreds of contributions to scientific journals include papers on metabolism, vitamin function, and cell structure.

BIBLIOGRAPHY: T.N. Levitan, *Laureates: Jewish Winners of the Nobel Prize* (1960), 173–5; *Chemical and Engineering News*, 26 (March 1948), 860.

[Samuel Aaron Miller]

LIPMANN, OTTO (1880–1933), German psychologist and expert in vocational guidance. Lipmann was one of the pioneers in Germany of psychological counseling for the selection of a profession. According to Lipmann, effective counseling came from a knowledge of the individual's characteristics and this determined the profession suitable for him. Lipmann suggested a method of examining the individual by means of tests and questionnaires, followed by an analysis of professions. Lipmann was the first psychologist to employ statistics in his work. He prepared several "psychograms" of professions such as telegraphist, typesetter, businessman, metal worker, academic worker, etc. Lipmann was the founder of the Institute for Applied Psychology in Berlin and editor (together with William Stern) of the *Zeitschrift fuer angewandte Psychologie*. His works include *Psychische Geschlechtsunterschiede* (2 vols., 1917, 1924²), *Wirschaftspsychologie und psychologische Berufsberatung* (1918, 1921²), *Die psychologische Analyse der hoeheren Berufe* (1920), and *Grundriss der Arbeitswissenschaft und Ergebnisse der arbeitswissenschaftlichen Statistik* (1926).

BIBLIOGRAPHY: *American Journal of Psychology*, 46 (1934), 152–4. **ADD. BIBLIOGRAPHY:** NDB, vol. 14 (1985), 645f.

[Haim Ormian]

LIPNIK NAD BECVOU (Czech. **Lipník nad Bečvou**; Ger. **Leipnik**), town in N.E. Moravia, Czech Republic. A synagogue is first mentioned there in 1540, though a Jewish settlement existed at least a century before. Most of Lipnik's Jews were engaged in textile production and in the import of livestock from Poland. In 1570 an economically injurious obligation to lend horses to the local gentry was abolished and the Jews' right of residence in perpetuity acknowledged in return for a payment. The community grew to 40 households in 1665. The rabbinate was founded in the late 16th century. Renowned rabbis included Moses Samson *Bacharach (1632–44), who composed a *seliḥah* on the sack of the town by Swedish troops in 1643, Isaac *Eulenburg (1652–57), and Isaiah b. Shabbetai Sheftel *Horowitz (1658–73). Under the rabbinates of Baruch *Fraenkel-Teomim (1802–28), Solomon *Quetsch (1832–54), and Moses *Bloch (1856–77), the yeshivah attracted pupils from all Europe. Rabbi F. Hillel (1892–1928) wrote the history of the community. In 1567 a third cemetery was opened (a fourth in 1883). The community was constituted as one of the political communities (see **Politische Gemeinde*) in 1850. Its population grew from 975 in 1794 to 1,259 in 1830, and 1,687 in 1857, but declined to 212 in 1921. In 1930 the community numbered 154 (2% of the total population). The community came to an end when its members were deported to the Nazi extermination camps in 1942. After World War II the congregation was renewed for a brief period. The synagogue equipment was sent to the Central Jewish Museum in Prague. The building was used from 1949 by the Hussite church. Lipnik was the birthplace of the industrialists David and Wilhelm *Gutmann, who established an institution for the poor in their mother's house in 1903.

BIBLIOGRAPHY: A. Springer, *Juedische Kulturbilder* (1904), 34–56; F. Hillel, *Die Rabbiner und die verdienstvollen Familien der Leipniker Gemeinde* (1928); idem, in: H. Gold (ed.), *Die Juden und Judengemeinden Maehrens* (1929), 301–6; A. Kohut, in: AZDJ, 78 (1914), 499–501. **ADD. BIBLIOGRAPHY:** J. Fiedler, *Jewish Sights of Bohemia and Moravia* (1991), 104–5.

LIPNO, town in Warsaw district. Jews are first mentioned in Lipno in 1677. In 1736 the community paid a poll tax of 150 zlotys. In 1808 there were 777 Jews (85% of the total population) in the town. Between 1824 and 1864 the authorities compelled the Jews to reside in a separate quarter. The Jewish population numbered 892 in 1827, increasing to 1,558 (40%) in 1857, and 2,079 (36%) in 1897. At that time more than 50% of the town's commerce was in Jewish hands. In 1921 there were 2,443 Jews (29%) in the town itself and 4,795 (5.2%) in the district. There were 102 Jewish industrial enterprises.

[*Encyclopaedia Judaica* (Germany)]

Holocaust Period

During World War II, Lipno belonged to Reichsgau Danzig-Westpreussen, included in the Reich by Hitler's decree of Oct. 26, 1939. Before the war, Lipno had about 1,300 Jews. When the war broke out many Jews fled to the east, mainly to the western towns of the General Government. The Warsaw ghetto in August 1940 had about 300 Jewish refugees from Lipno. By the end of December 1939, the town was declared *Judenrein.

[Danuta Dombrowska]

BIBLIOGRAPHY: Warsaw, Archiwum Akt Dawnych, *Akty Komisji rządowej do spraw wewnętrznych*, no. 107; E. Heller, *Żydowskie przedsiębiorstwa przemysłowe w Polsce…*, 1 (1922); B. Wasiutyński, *Ludność żydowska w Polsce…* (1930), 23; I. Schiper, *Dzieje handlu żydowskiego na ziemiach polskich* (1937), index.

LIPOVETS, town in Vinnitsa district, Ukraine. Jews appeared there in 1747 after the community was completely destroyed during the *Chmielnicki massacres (1648–49). Reestablished, it increased from 1,802 in 1847 to 4,135 (47.6% of the total population) in 1897. Two Jewish state schools existed there in the beginning of the 20th century. Jews numbered 3,605 (41.7%) in 1926, dropping to 1,353 (52.6% of the total) in 1939. During the Soviet period a Yiddish school operated there as did a Jewish local council in the 1920s. A few dozen Jewish families were occupied in farming. The Germans took Lipovets on July 24, 1941, and on September 12 they killed 163 Jews, and in October another 70. The rest were probably murdered in the beginning of 1942.

[Yehuda Slutsky / Shmuel Spector (2nd ed.)]

LIPPE (Lippe-Detmold), former state in N.W. Germany. Jews are first mentioned in 1345 when they were ordered by Bernard v to bring their cases before his ducal court and not the *Feme* or private courts, an order which promised them greater security. The capital, Detmold, became the leading community after Jews were permitted to settle there in 1500. In 1583, 12 Lippe families moved to Altona. During the late 17th and 18th centuries, *Court Jews, who generally controlled the tobacco monopoly, exercised broad executive power over the Jews of Lippe, filled the office of rabbi, and were court financiers as well. Though no dynasty of Court Jews established itself, Joseph Isaac was the most prominent and powerful. In 1732 complaints were lodged against the growing number of Jews. Family *names were imposed on the 175 Jewish families in the county (27 in Detmold) in 1810. Civil rights were granted in 1858 and 1879. Twelve communities were included in the regional union of communities. The number of Jews in Lippe declined from 1,024 in 1885 to 900 in 1904, 780 in 1913, and 607 (0.32% of the total population) in 1928. Until 1742 services were held in a rented prayer room; after that a barn was converted into a synagogue, and a new building was not erected until 1904. Lippe had no rabbi after 1879. After the Nazi rise to power (1933), the Jewish population came to an end through emigration, persecution, and deportation. After 1945 a small Jewish community was founded in Detmold, which was later united with the community in Herford. In 1989 the Herford-Detmold Jewish community numbered 23 and about 100 in 2005. About 90% of the members were immigrants from the former Soviet Union.

The tiny neighboring principality of Schaumburg-Lippe was notable for its dynasty of Court Jews founded by Isaak Heine, who received a letter of protection in 1682. In 1705/6 he and his cousin, Behrends *Leffmann, successfully averted an expulsion order. His family continued to serve the rulers of the principality for three generations; most distinguished of his descendants were the financier Salomon *Heine and the poet Heinrich *Heine.

BIBLIOGRAPHY: A. Feilchenfeld, in: MGWJ, 43 (1899), 273f.; FJW, 419–21; AVJW (May 28, 1965), 3; Germ Jud, 2 (1968), 492; H. Schnee, *Die Hoffinanz und der moderne Staat*, 3 (1955), 93–124; H.H. Hasselmeier, *Die Stellung der Juden in Schaumburg-Lippe von 1648 bis zur Emanzipation* (1967). **ADD. BIBLIOGRAPHY:** J. Ehrlinger, *Juedisches Leben in Westfalen und Lippe: Eine Bibliographie* (Warburger Schriften, volume 20; 1995); K. Pohlmann, *Juden in Lippe in Mittelalter und frueher Neuzeit. Zwischen Pogrom und Vertreibung. 1350 – 1614* (Panu derech, v. 13; 1995); D. von Faassen, "'Hier ist ein kleiner Ort und eine kleine Gegend' – Hofjuden in Lippe," in: R. Ries, J. Battenberg, J. Friedrich (eds.), *Hofjuden – Oekonomie und Interkulturalitaet. Die juedische Wirtschaftselite im 18. Jahrhundert* (Hamburger Beitraege zur Geschichte der deutschen Juden, vol. 25; 2002), 289–306.

[Larissa Daemmig (2nd ed.)]

LIPPE, KARPEL (1830–1915), early member of Ḥovevei Zion and the Zionist movement. Born in Stanislav, Galicia, Lippe became a physician in Jassy, Romania. From 1865 he published many articles as well as pamphlets and books on science, defense of the rights of Romanian Jews, apologetics on Judaism, the Jewish religion and its attitude toward Christianity, etc. He also composed poetry, which he would sometimes read at gatherings instead of delivering a speech. When a society to settle in Ereẓ Israel was established in Romania, Lippe became its chairman (1880). From that time he was active in the *Ḥibbat Zion movement, especially on behalf of the settlements of *Zikhron Ya'akov and *Rosh Pinnah, which were established by Romanian Jews. He was a participant at the conference of Ḥovevei Zion in Kattowitz (1884). When Theodor *Herzl's *Judenstaat* appeared, Lippe wrote an article in the Berlin monthly *Zion* (1896) in which he rejected the idea of a Jewish state. Instead, he counseled the Jews to settle in Ereẓ Israel as Turkish citizens and strive for autonomy similar to that of the Austrian Empire in Galicia. Lippe nonetheless joined the new Zionist movement, was elected to the First Zionist Congress in Basle, and, being its senior delegate, delivered the opening speech. He considered himself one of the three initiators of the Zionist idea, together with Leon *Pinsker and Isaac *Ruelf, and as such he published the book *Meine 25-jaehrige Zionistische Agitation* (1902). He was elected chairman of the Jassy Conference of Romanian Zionists (1903). In 1911, Lippe returned to Galicia and settled in Przemysl, but with the outbreak of World War I he fled to Vienna, where he died. Among his works are *Symptome der Anti-semitischen Geisteskrankheit* (1887) and *Zwei Vortraege ueber Unsterblichkeit und Spiritismus* (1907).

BIBLIOGRAPHY: I. Klausner, *Ḥibbat Ẓiyyon be-Rumanyah* (1958), index.

[Israel Klausner]

LIPPMANN, EDMUND OSKAR VON (1857–1940), German industrial chemist. He was born in Vienna and was director of sugar refineries in Duisburg (1881–86) and Halle (1890–1926). In 1926–32 he was honorary professor of chemical history in Halle. He wrote the standard books of his period on sugar, *Chemie der Zuckerarten* (1900^3), *Geschichte des Zuckers* (1890, 1900, 1929), and *Entwickelungen der deutschen Zuckerindustrie von 1850–1900* (1900). He was a leading historian of chemistry, writing *Entstehung und Ausbreitung der Alchemie* (1919, 1931), *Geschichte der Ruebe als Kulturpflanze* (1925), *Geschichte der Naturwissenschaften* (two volumes, 1923), *Geschichte des Wismuts zwischen 1400 und 1800* (1930), and others.

BIBLIOGRAPHY: J.C. Poggendorff, *Biographisch-literarisches Handwoerterbuch der exakten Naturwissenschaften*, 7a (1959), 111.

[Samuel Aaron Miller]

LIPPMANN, EDUARD (1842–1919), Austrian organic chemist. Born in Prague, Lippmann worked for a time with the French chemist, Charles Wurtz in Paris, and in 1868 became an instructor at the University of Vienna. In 1873 he went to teach at the Technische Hochschule at Brno, Moravia, but returned to Vienna in 1875 to become professor of chemistry at the university. In 1877 he was appointed professor of analytical chemistry at the Handelsakademie and from 1881 held the same position at the Technische Hochschule. Lippmann developed in 1886 what became the standard technique for determining carbon and hydrogen in organic compounds. Among the subjects dealt with in his numerous publications were benzyl alcohol, diethyltoluene, azobenzenes, anthracene, and alkaloids.

BIBLIOGRAPHY: J.C. Poggendorff, *Biographisch-literarisches Handwoerterbuch…*, 4 (1904), s.v.; 5 (1926), s.v.

[Samuel Aaron Miller]

LIPPMANN, GABRIEL (1845–1921), French physicist and Nobel Prize winner. Though born in Luxembourg, Lippmann spent most of his life in Paris. His association with the *Annales de chimie et de physique*, for which he prepared summaries of the articles written in German, enabled him to keep abreast of innovations in electricity. After working in Heidelberg and under the brilliant H.L.F. von Helmholtz in Berlin, Lippmann was appointed professor of probability and mathematical physics at the Sorbonne (1883–86). From 1886 he was professor of experimental science and director of the Sorbonne's research laboratories, a position which he held until his death. Lippmann was responsible for much basic work in classical physics. His early research at Heidelberg was concerned with the effects of electrical charges on surface tension leading to the development of the "capillary-electrometer." In 1879 he presented before the Académie des Sciences, to which he was elected seven years later, his work dealing with the effective mass of a charged body, in which he claimed that the moment of inertia in a charged body was higher than that of an uncharged body. This conclusion is of fundamental importance in the study of the electron. He also devised various scientific instruments: in astronomy his outstanding contributions were the development of the coelostat, an instrument for obtaining a stationary image of the sky, and the uranograph, an instrument for obtaining a map of the sky with lines of longitude at equal time-intervals. He achieved fame in 1891 through his production of color photographs based on the phenomenon of interference, although the three-color system proposed by J.C. Maxwell was preferred. Lippmann was nevertheless awarded the Nobel Prize for physics for the results of this research. His most important works were his *Cours de thermodynamique* (1886) and *Cours d'acoustique et d'optique* (1888). Lippmann was elected president of the Académie des Sciences in 1912.

BIBLIOGRAPHY: E. Lebon, *Savants du jour: Gabriel Lippmann* (1911), incl. bibl.; T. Levitan, *Laureates: Jewish Winners of the Nobel Prize* (1960), 56–58; N.H. de V. Heathcote, *Nobel Prize Winners in Physics, 1901–50* (1953), 65–69.

[Ariel Cohen]

LIPPMANN, WALTER (1889–1974), U.S. journalist, whose writing exerted influence on public policy. Born in New York, Lippmann was for several years an assistant to the philosopher George Santayana. In 1914 he began his journalistic career as founder and associate editor of *New Republic*, a journal of liberal opinion. He left at the outbreak of World War I to serve as an assistant to Newton D. Baker, secretary of war in the Wilson administration, and later helped prepare data for the Peace Conference at Versailles. Lippmann in 1921 joined the staff of the *New York World*, a crusading newspaper noted for its attacks on corruption, poverty, and injustice. He served as editor from 1929 until the paper ceased publication two years later. He then wrote a column on public affairs for the *New York Herald-Tribune*, which was syndicated to more than 250 papers in 25 countries and made him widely known and respected. He was awarded two Pulitzer Prizes, in 1958 and 1962. His political philosophy, as expressed in his newspaper writing and nearly 30 books, showed a gradual modification from socialism to liberalism to independent conservatism. His volumes include *Preface to Politics* (1913), *Public Opinion* (1922), *The Phantom Public* (1925), *Preface to Morals* (1929), *Good Society* (1937), *Cold War* (1947), *Essays in the Public Philosophy* (1955), and *Drift and Mastery* (1961).

BIBLIOGRAPHY: C. Rossiter and J. Lare (eds.), *Essential Lippmann* (1963); M. Childs and J. Reston (eds.), *Walter Lippmann and his Times* (1959); D.E. Weingast, *Walter Lippmann* (Eng., 1949).

[Irving Rosenthal]

LIPPOLD (d. 1573), Court Jew to Joachim II (1535–71), elector of Brandenburg. When in 1556 he was appointed "supervisor" of Brandenburg Jewry and collector of all monies paid by it to the court for ten years, the elector called him "our beloved, faithful Lippold." Nine years later he was elevated to the position of mintmaster, a post which involved clipping, devaluating, and reminting coins to the benefit of the elector. Lippold exploited Joachim's insatiable passion for women, alchemy, and money to attain a position of confidence and power. Ruthless and rapacious toward Jews and Christians alike, as private moneylender he charged an exorbitant interest rate (54%), borrowed large amounts with no intention of repaying them, and practiced embezzlement and extortion at will. Immediately after Joachim's death (Jan. 2, 1571) disorders broke out in Berlin and Lippold was arrested. At his trial his crimes, real and alleged, were revealed; he was also accused of sorcery and of poisoning the elector. On Jan. 28, 1573, he was executed and quartered, after refusing baptism and withdrawing his confession. The Jews were expelled from Brandenburg soon after.

BIBLIOGRAPHY: H. Schnee, *Die Hoffinanz und der moderne Staat*, 1 (1953), 38–47; A. Ackermann, *Muenzmeister Lippold…* (1910); G.A. Kohut, *Court Jew Lippold…* (1893); H. Rachel, *Berliner Wirtschaftsleben im Zeitalter des Fruehkapitalismus…* (1931). **ADD. BIBLIOGRAPHY:** K. Schulz, in: *Geschichte Berlins*, 1 (1987), 304–25.

LIPSCHITZ, JACOB HA-LEVI (1838–1921), Hebrew writer and opponent of the Haskalah. Born in Vilkomir (Ukmerge), Lithuania, Lipschitz was the secretary, assistant, and representative on public affairs for R. Isaac Elhanan *Spektor from 1870 to 1896. He was one of the organizers of the fact-finding mission on the 1881–82 pogroms and persecutions of Russian Jewry which sent reports to the Jewish centers of Western Europe. He wrote sharply-worded articles (usually anonymous) against the Haskalah and its leaders, gradually becoming the leading Orthodox journalist and Orthodoxy's spokesman in its polemics against the religious reforms proposed by the Hebrew writers M.L. *Lilienblum and J.L. *Gordon. He encouraged the publications of the religious press (e.g., *Ha-Levanon, Ha-Kerem, Ha-Peles, Ha-Modi'a*), to which he contributed regularly. He issued manifestos and lampoons against the Zionist movement from his office in Kovno ("the Black Office" to his opponents). His books include *Divrei Shalom ve-Emet* (1884), against the proposal to establish a rabbinical seminary in Russia, and a biography of Spektor (*Toledot Yiẓḥak*, 1897; also in Yid. as *Ge'on Yiẓḥak*, 1899). His Orthodox ideology is presented in *Sefer Maḥazikei ha-Dat* (1903). His *Zikhron Ya'akov* (3 pts., 1924–30), which he wrote during his World War I exile in the Ukraine, contains historical notes and personal memories. It was published after his death by his son Nathan Nata Lipschitz and is an important source for the history of the Jews in Russia during the 19th century.

BIBLIOGRAPHY: B. Dinur, *Be-Olam she-Shaka* (1958), 86–92; Kressel, Leksikon, 2 (1967), 282–3; Rejzen, Leksikon, 2 (1927), 178–9.

[Yehuda Slutsky]

LIPSCHITZ, RUDOLF OTTO SIGISMUND (1832–1903), German mathematician. Born in Koenigsberg, he later taught in the secondary schools of Koenigsberg and Elbing. In 1857 he was appointed a lecturer at the University of Bonn and later became rector. Lipschitz's work was greatly influenced by his teachers Peter Dirichlet (1805–1859) and G.F.B. Riemann. His contributions to mathematics and physical mathematics were mostly in the theory of numbers, the computation of variations, progressive series, and the theory of potential and analytic mechanics. With the French mathematician Augustin Louis Cauchy (1789–1857), he proved the theorem of prime importance in differential calculus and equations concerning the existing solutions to the equation $dy/dx = f(x,y)$.

[Ariel Cohen]

LIPSCHITZ (Lipschuetz), SOLOMON BEN MOSES (1675–1758), German *ḥazzan* and writer. Born in Fuerth, the son of a *ḥazzan*, Lipschitz practiced his profession as a *ḥazzan* in several communities, including Prague and Frankfurt, before settling in Metz in 1715. His book *Te'udat Shelomo* (Offenbach, 1718) combines instructions and moral precepts for the *ḥazzan* with the writer's personal reminiscences – both of them valuable historical evidence.

LIPSCHITZ, SOLOMON ZALMAN (1765–1839), Polish rabbi, first chief rabbi of Warsaw, known as "Ḥemdat Shelomo" after his works of that name. Lipschitz, who was of a wealthy family whose members included the kabbalist Solomon Zalman Auerbach (17th century), was born in Poznan. Until he was 40 years old he lived and studied there, and therefore was also known as Solomon Zalman Posner. In 1804, after he had lost his fortune and his father-in-law was unable to continue to support him, he became rabbi of Nasielsk, where he also founded an important yeshivah. Lipschitz was unable to bear the atmosphere of Nasielsk, which was becoming increasingly ḥasidic. In 1806 he received a call to be rabbi of his home town, but he refused in order to protect his children from the influence of the Haskalah, which had spread from Germany. In 1819 he was elected rabbi of Praga (a suburb of Warsaw) where there was a large Jewish population. With the development of the Warsaw *kehillah*, he was appointed rabbi of the community (1821). There, too, he founded an important yeshivah. Among its students were many who later became Polish rabbis. As chief rabbi of Warsaw, he led the opposition to the Haskalah movement, the assimilationists, and the rabbinical seminary established there, which became a stronghold of assimilation under the direction of Anton *Eisenbaum. During the Polish insurrection against the czarist regime in 1831, Lipschitz opposed Jews joining the city guard as they would have been obliged to shave off their beards. He was in halakhic correspondence with many contemporary rabbis, including R. Akiva Eger, Moses Lorbeerbaum, R. Jacob of Lissa (Leszno), R. Meir Weyl of Berlin, R. Abraham Tiktin, and R. Aryeh Leib Zinz, and many rabbis turned to him with their halakhic problems. His responsa and decisions are cited in the halakhic works of many Polish rabbis. When he died, a month of mourning was proclaimed. A special announcement issued by the community forbade women to wear jewelry during that month. Lipschitz is the author of three works, all entitled *Ḥemdat Shelomo*: responsa (Warsaw, 1836); novellae on various tractates of the Talmud (3 pts., 1851–92); and sermons (1890). Some of his original letters were saved from the Holocaust but have not been published.

BIBLIOGRAPHY: A.I. Bromberg, *Rishonei ha-Rabbanim be-Varsha* (1949), 9–79; J. Shatzky, *Geshikhte fun Yidn in Varshe*, 2 vols. (1947–48), index; D. Flinker, in: *Arim ve-Immahot be-Yisrael*, 3 (1948), 105–6; H. Seidman, in: *Velt Federatsie fun Poylishe Yidn. Amerikaner Ekzekutive Yorbukh*, 1 (1964), 242–7; Dubnow, Ḥasidut, 461f.

LIPSCHUETZ (Lipschutz, Lifschitz, Lifshyts, Lipszyc, Liebschuetz), widely dispersed Jewish family, which provided a large number of rabbis and scholars. The name is probably an indication of their origin and points to either Loebschuetz (Lubczyce; now Glubczyce) in Silesia, Liebschuetz in Thuringia, or to Liebeschitz in Bohemia. The derivation from the feminine name Liebscha is not acceptable. According to M. *Brann (see bibl.), the first well-known bearers of this name were the 16th-century R. MOSES BEN ISAAC LIPSCHUETZ of Brzesc-Kujawski and Gdansk (Danzig), and ISAAC LIPSCHUETZ of Poznan. In the first half of the 17th century members of this family included R. BENJAMIN BENUSH, rabbi in Brest-Litovsk, son-in-law of R. Saul *Wahl and perhaps the son of the aforementioned R. Moses; R. ISRAEL MORDECAI BEN ELIJAH, who was one of those who approved in 1609 the Prague edition of R. Eliezer b. Nathan's *Even ha-Ezer* (1610); R. ḤAYYIM BEN ISAAC, *ḥazzan* in Poznan, who published additions to a commentary on the *kinot* by the *ḥazzan* Asher b. Joseph (Lublin, 1617); R. MOSES BEN NOAH ISAAC in Poznan; and R. Gedaliah b. Solomon *Lipschuetz from Lublin. In the second half of the 17th century R. ELIJAH lived in Brest-Litovsk, R. MOSES BEN ENOCH in Burgpreppach. From Gedaliah Lipschuetz (see Israel b. Eliezer *Lipschuetz and his son Gedaliah), who lived in Ostrava at the beginning of the 17th century, descended an unbroken line of learned rabbis right to modern times. Among the last members of this learned family were the Mishnah commentator R. Israel b. Gedaliah *Lipschuetz and his son R. Baruch Isaac *Lipschuetz.

BIBLIOGRAPHY: Ẓ.H. Edelmann, *Gedullat Sha'ul* (1854), 24a; I.T. Eisenstadt and S. Wiener, *Da'at Kedoshim* (1897–98), 57, 83; D. Kaufmann, *Die letzte Vertreibung der Juden aus Wien…* (1889), 203; H.N. Maggid-Steinschneider, *Ir Vilna* (1900), 38–40; J.L. Feinstein, *Ir Tehillah* (1886), 23f., 154f., 202; S.Z. Kahana, *Anaf Eẓ Avot* (1903), 23; M.M. Biber, *Mazkeret li-Gedolei Ostraha* (1907), 62; I. de Terni, *Sefer ha-Makhri'a* (1897), introd.; A.J.L. Lipschuetz, *Avot Atarah le-Vanim* (1927), 46, 144; E. Kohan, *Kinat Soferim* (1892), 92a; J. Perles, *Geschichte der Juden in Posen* (1865), 49; A. Berliner, in: MGWJ, 50 (1906), 215–7; M. Brann, *ibid.*, 218f.; L. Lewin, in: JJLG, 5 (1907), 101ff.

[Samuel Abba Horodezky]

LIPSCHUETZ, BARUCH ISAAC BEN ISRAEL (1812–1877), rabbi and author. The son of Israel b. Gedaliah *Lipschuetz, Lipschuetz was born in Wronki where his father was rabbi. In 1833 he was appointed to succeed his father there, but had to relinquish the appointment because of Akiva *Eger's resolute opposition to a young unmarried man of 21 functioning as religious leader of a community. He subsequently became rabbi of Landsberg, where he served until 1853, when he was invited to Mecklenburg-Schwerin to succeed David *Einhorn, the reform rabbi, because the central government wished to strengthen the Orthodox section of the community. In 1858 he was compelled to resign because of his firmness in religious matters. Henceforth he accepted no other communal appointment, and lived first in Hamburg and then in Berlin, where he died. He was the author of *Ḥosen Shemu'el* (n.d., n.p.), an abstract of the Shulḥan Arukh *Even ha-Ezer* (incomplete), and *Torat Shemu'el* (1867), a devotional work. His *Beit Shemu'el* and *Shemesh u-Magen* remain in manuscript. He edited and republished his father's famous commentary on the Mishnah, *Tiferet Yisrael*, to which he made many editions. Some of his sermons were published in Ettlinger-Enoch's *Shomer Ẓiyyon ha-Ne'eman*.

BIBLIOGRAPHY: A. Walden, *Shem ha-Gedolim he-Ḥadash*, 1 (1864), 40b, no. 319; H.N. Maggid-Steinschneider, *Ir Vilna* (1900), 39; E. Duckesz, *Chachme AHW* (1908), 126 (Heb. section); Berliner, in: MGWJ, 50 (1906), 217.

[Samuel Abba Horodezky]

LIPSCHUETZ, ELIEZER MEIR (1879–1946), Hebraist, religious educator, and historical writer in Ereẓ Israel. Lipschuetz was born in Skole (Galicia). He was a businessman in Lemberg, but influenced by S. *Buber, he began studying medieval Jewish history and literature. Lipschuetz had early devoted himself to the revival of Hebrew, not only as a literary medium, but also and above all as a spoken language (in the Sephardi pronunciation). He attracted a circle of like-minded friends, such as Joseph Babad, A. *Barash, Ḥ. *Yalon, Mordecai Ben-Ezekiel, and, especially, S.Y. *Agnon. His wife, too, spoke Hebrew and his child was the first in Lvov to grow up with Hebrew as his mother tongue. In 1910 Lipschuetz began teaching Hebrew and Jewish history at the *Ezra teacher's seminary in Jerusalem. As the result of the Hebrew versus German conflict, he left to take up a post with the Hebrew Teachers Seminary. In 1917 he was expelled from Palestine by the Turks and found refuge in Berlin, where he continued studying and writing to Jewish scholars. In 1920 he returned to Palestine and the following year founded the Mizrachi Teachers' Seminary, which he headed until his death. Lipschuetz worked actively in the religious education department of the Zionist Organization and was one of the architects of the Mizrachi school network. He was also an active member of the Va'ad ha-Lashon, now the Academy of the Hebrew Language. In addition to Lipschuetz' *Raschi* (1912), a classic biography, he wrote a great number of essays on scholarly educational, literary, and linguistic subjects. Among these is one on S.Y. Agnon (1926), whose importance he was one of the first to recognize. A large part of his work was reissued in his collected writings, *Ketavim* (3 vols., 1947–57), but much remains in manuscript, including a voluminous correspondence.

BIBLIOGRAPHY: A.B. Posner, *E.M. Lipschuetz* (Heb., 1941); O. Wolfsberg (Aviad), *Deyokena'ot* (1962), 152–4; A.J. Brawer, *Zikhronot* (1966), 214–5, 441–6; Kressel, Leksikon, 2 (1967), s.v.

LIPSCHUETZ, GEDALIAH BEN SOLOMON ZALMAN (16th–17th century), Polish scholar, author, and Jerusalem emissary. Lipschuetz was a pupil of *Meir b. Gedaliah (the Maharam) of Lublin. In 1618 he emigrated from Poland to Ereẓ Israel. On the way he stayed in Prague where he obtained from the local scholars, Solomon Luntschitz and Isaiah ha-Levi *Horowitz (the Shelah), commendations for his work *Eẓ Shatul*, a commentary on the *Ikkarim* of Joseph *Albo. That same year he proceeded to Venice, where he published that work, and where he also proofread the collection of responsa of his teacher Meir, which were published that year, with the title *Manhir Eynei Ḥakhamim*. From there he continued to Ereẓ Israel and settled in Jerusalem. He was there in 1626 during the oppression of the Jews of Jerusalem at the hands of the tyrannical governor Muhammad ibn Farukh. When Farukh was dismissed the following year, and the heads of the Jerusalem community sent emissaries to the Diaspora to solicit aid in reconstructing the community, Lipschuetz was sent to the Balkans. At the beginning of the summer of 1629 he was in Belgrade, where he endorsed a halakhic responsum of Judah Lerma (see the latter's responsa *Peletat bat Yehudah*, no. 27, end).

BIBLIOGRAPHY: Frumkin-Rivlin, 2 (1928), 45f.; Ya'ari, Sheluḥei, 268.

[Abraham Yoffe]

LIPSCHUETZ, HILLEL ARYEH LEIB BEN ZE'EV DOV (1844–1907), Lithuanian rabbi and author. Lipschuetz studied under his father, who was rabbi of Srednik. In 1868 he became rabbi of Popelnya, then of Plunge, and later of the important town of Suvalki from 1880 to 1893, when he was elected rabbi of Lublin. He had a sound knowledge of many languages and an extensive general education. He is the author of *Beit Hillel*, novellae on the Shulḥan Arukh, *Ḥoshen Mishpat* (1890). A gifted writer, he contributed essays to the periodical *Ha-Levanon*, using the pseudonym Ha-Le'eh (from his initials), and translated into Hebrew the historical novel *Suess Oppenheimer* by Markus Lehmann (1873). His sons, Ezekiel, Eliezer, and Jacob also held rabbinical positions, Ezekiel being rabbi of Kalisz.

BIBLIOGRAPHY: S.B. Nissenbaum, *Le-Korot ha-Yehudim be-Lublin* (1900^2), 128; B. Eisenstadt, *Dor, Rabbanav ve-Soferav*, 4 (1902), 21.

[Itzhak Alfassi]

LIPSCHUETZ, ISRAEL BEN ELIEZER (d. 1782), German rabbi, studied under Ezekiel *Katzenellenbogen. In the responsa of his father titled *Heshiv R. Eliezer* (Nevewirth, 1649), there are included several items by the son, Israel, who is mentioned as being the rabbi of "Diez, Hadamar, and the environs." Later he served as rabbi in Cleves. In 1766–67 he came into prominence with regard to the cause célèbre known as the *Cleves *get*. Lipschuetz himself in 1770 published a collection of responsa supporting his standpoint under the title *Or Yisrael* (Cleves, 1770) in answer to the *Or ha-Yashar* published by *Aaron Simeon of Copenhagen in Amsterdam a year previously in support of the opposing side.

His son GEDALIAH (d. 1826) eked out a meager living serving as rabbi to various smaller Jewish communities in East Prussia, among them Obrzycko and Chodziez (now in Poland). In 1809 he came into conflict with the local authorities when he opposed an edict forbidding the settlement of conflicts by recourse to Jewish courts. Gedaliah was the author of *Ḥumrei Matnita* (Berlin, 1784) in six parts: comments on the Talmud and its main commentaries with special attention given to the tractates *Nazir* and *Nedarim*; an explanation of unusual words in the Talmud; novellae on *Asher b. Jehiel titled *Ateret Rosh*; notes on Isaac *Alfasi titled *Ma'aseh Ilpas; Minei Targimon*, comments on *Targum Onkelos* and Rashi's Pentateuch commentary; *Mirkevet ha-Mishnah*, comments on difficult passages in the Mishnah. In his approbation of this work the father mentions 17 works of his son as existing in manuscript form. Gedaliah also wrote *Regel Yesharah* (Dyhernfurth, 1777), containing a list of unusual words left unexplained by Rashi in his commentary on the Talmud, referring to other passages where an explanation is found; comments on the order *Nezikin* and the minor tractates of the Talmud; an excursus on talmudic weights and measures; and an elucidation of the geometrical matter in chapters three and five of the tractate *Kilayim*. The allegedly presumptuous tone of this work, combined with the conceit and contentious disposition of its author, led to its disparagement among the *maskilim* who coined the saying, "the author of the *Regel Yesharah* ("Straight Foot") is a twisted blockhead."

BIBLIOGRAPHY: Berliner, in: MGWJ, 50 (1906), 215–8; S.B. Freehof, *Responsa Literature* (1955), 158ff.; D. Kaufmann and M. Freudenthal, *Familie Gomperz* (1907), 74; Tal, in: *Sinai*, 24 (1948–49), 152–67.

[Jacob Haberman]

LIPSCHUTZ, ARYEH LEIB (d. c. 1849), talmudist and ḥasidic rabbi. He was born in Jaroslaw and was the pupil of Aryeh Leib b. Joseph ha-Kohen *Heller, author of *Keẓot ha-Ḥoshen*, and of Jacob Isaac Horowitz of Lublin. Aryeh was the son-in-law of Moses *Teitelbaum, rabbi of Ujhely, and himself served as rabbi in several Galician communities. His last post was at Brigal, where he died. He is the author of two books of novellae, *Ari she-ba-Ḥavurah* (1852), on *Ketubbot*, and *Ḥiddushei Aryeh de-Vei-Ilai* (1880), on *Kiddushin, Yoma, Menaḥot, Kinnim*, and *Niddah*. In addition he published a book of responsa *Aryeh de-Vei-Ilai* (1874) on the four parts of the Shulḥan Arukh.

BIBLIOGRAPHY: A. Walden, *Shem ha-Gedolim he-Ḥadash*, 1 (1965), 82.

LIPSCHUTZ, ELIEZER BEN SOLOMON (d. 1750), rabbi and talmudist. When he was over the age of 30, he became the rabbi of *Ostrowiecz (Poland). There he had many pupils, but he left for Germany where he wandered from post to post because of differences with his communities. Through the influence of his wife's uncle, Simeon Jolles, the leader of the community, he obtained a position in Cracow. There also he made enemies and after Jolles' death he left Cracow. Finally he secured a position at Neuwied where he remained until his death. He published *Heshiv R. Eliezer ve-Si'aḥ la-Sadeh* (Neuwied, 1749) in two volumes: (1) responsa with notes by his son Israel; and (2) (subtitled *Dammesek Eliezer*) novellae on *Yoreh De'ah* and *Ḥoshen Mishpat*. He carried on correspondence with noted authorities of the time. Another member of his family was R. Israel b. Gedaliah *Lipschutz, the author of *Tiferet Yisrael*.

BIBLIOGRAPHY: S. Chones, *Toledot ha-Posekim* (1910), 602; H.N. Dembitzer, *Kelilat Yofi*, 2 (1893), 133b.

LIPSCHUTZ, ISRAEL BEN GEDALIAH (1782–1860), German rabbinic scholar. Lipschutz served as rabbi in the towns of Wronki (1821), Dessau and Colmar (1826–37), and Danzig (1837–60). His fame rests upon his commentary to the Mishnah, entitled *Tiferet Yisrael*, one of the finest of its class. In this work, he explains the words of the Mishnah briefly, offers new interpretations to difficult passages, particularly in the orders of *Zera'im, Kodashim*, and *Tohorot*, and adds everywhere the halakhic ruling as decided on in the Shulḥan Arukh and its commentaries. To each of the orders of *Mo'ed, Kodashim*, and *Tohorot*, he prefaces general introductions comprising a methodic summation of all the principles of the order, after the manner of *Maimonides in his introduction to his commentary on the Mishnah. A considerable portion of the commentary is taken from that of his son, Baruch Isaac *Lipschutz, as well as from Akiva *Eger, *Elijah b. Solomon (the Gaon of Vilna), and others. *Tiferet Yisrael* became the most widespread Mishnah commentary and is regarded as an invaluable adjunct to that of Obadiah *Bertinoro. Lipschutz's commentary to *Zera'im, Zera Emunah*, and to *Tohorot, Ta'am ve-Da'at*, with a general preface entitled "*Yevakkesh Da'at*," was published in Hanover (1830). His commentary to *Nashim, Ḥosen Rav*, was published later (Danzig, 1843). Appended to it was *Avi Ezer*, a work by Lipschutz's father on the Shulḥan Arukh, *Even ha-Ezer*. The commentary to *Mo'ed, Davar be-Itto* (*ibid.*, 1844), included an introduction dealing with topics relevant to the Sabbath and intercalations. *Nezikin* was published in Danzig in 1845, along with a treatise on immortality and the resurrection. *Kodashim*, under the title *Ḥokhmat Elohim* (Koenigsberg, 1850), includes laws of the order entitled *Ḥomer ba-Kodesh* at the beginning, and diagrams of the Temple and altar at the end. The commentary was republished in its entirety (Berlin, 1862) with additions by Lipschutz's son Baruch Isaac. Lipschutz also composed an extensive commentary to the order *Tohorot, Ateret Tiferet* (Vilna, 1887–95), in which he separated the plain interpretation from the *pilpul*, calling the former "*Yakhin*" and the latter "*Bo'az*," and added a section giving the halakhic rulings, "*Hilkheta Gevirta*," at the end of each chapter. In later editions of the Mishnah *Tiferet Yisrael* was similarly divided. He also published a brief commentary to the Mishnah called *Zera Yisrael* (Vilna, 1852), and his ethical will was published in Koenigsberg in 1861. His son mentions that Lipschutz left in manuscript sermons, notes on the Talmud, on Maimonides and on the Shulḥan Arukh, and many responsa. He apparently also compiled *Rashei Avot*, a commentary on *Avot*, and *Megillat Setarim*.

BIBLIOGRAPHY: B.I. Lipschutz, in: *Ha-Maggid*, 4 (1860), 170–1; H.N. Maggid-Steinschneider, *Ir Vilna*, 1 (1900), 38–39; Brann, in: MGWJ, 50 (1906), 375; Ḥ. Albeck, *Mavo la-Mishnah* (1959), 253; Posner, in: *Shanah be-Shanah*, 4 (1963), 395–401.

[Abraham David]

LIPSCHUTZ, SHABBETAI BEN JACOB ISAAC (1845–1929), rabbi, kabbalist, and author. Lipschutz was born in Rohatyn, Galicia, and from 1907 served as a rabbi in Bereg-Ilosva (now Irshava, Sub-Carpathian Ruthenia, Ukraine). He wrote *Berit Avot* (also entitled *Sharvit ha-Zahav he-Ḥadash*), on the laws of circumcision (1898; with supplement, 1912); *Pidyon Nefesh* (also entitled *Sha'arei Pedut*), on the redemption of the firstborn (1899); *Segullot Yisrael* (also entitled *Sefer ha-Ḥayyim*) on healing by sympathetic treatment (1905); a second edition together with Sussman Sofer's *Even Segullah* (1908); notes on the *Shemirat ha-Nefesh* (1872) of Israel Mattathias Auerbach (1901); *Kol Todah*, a commentary on the Book of Esther (1884 and 1888); *Tiferet Ya'akov*, homilies on the Pentateuch (1912); *Sha'arei Raḥamim*, a commentary on Ephraim Zalman Margaliot's *Sha'arei Efrayim* (1932); and *Likkutei Shoshannim* (also entitled *Sefer ha-Eshel*), on various halakhic matters (1949). A number of his works have remained unpublished.

BIBLIOGRAPHY: S.N. Gottlieb, *Oholei Shem* (1912), 212; A. Stern, *Meliẓei Esh*, 3 (1962[2]), chapter *Adar*, 57b, no. 263.

[Samuel Abba Horodezky]

LIPSCHUTZ, SOLOMON BEN MORDECAI (d. 1736), Dutch rabbi. Born and educated in Lisse, Lipschutz was appointed rabbi of the Ashkenazi community in The Hague during the incumbency of David Nunes (c. 1700) as rabbi of the Sephardi community. About 1710 he was appointed rabbi of Rotterdam, remaining there until his death. His query in connection with the *eruv* of Rotterdam, based on the fact that the river could be regarded as its boundary, is published in Jacob *Poppers' responsa *Shav Ya'akov* (1702, pt. 1, no. 17). Having received conflicting rules from Ezekiel Katzenellenbogen and Jacob *Reischer, to whom he had first turned, he addressed himself to Jacob Poppers for a decision, and he appears to have written a book for which he obtained Poppers' approbation. The large Boompjes synagogue in Rotterdam was built while he was rabbi. After his death Solomon was succeeded as rabbi of Rotterdam by his son JUDAH (d. 1754) whom Jonathan Eybeschuetz called "a righteous and upright man who increased peace in the world and was pleasing to his brethren." Judah's son ABRAHAM (d. 1780) was also appointed a rabbi of Rotterdam, but his appointment stirred up a great controversy because two of the lay leaders were his relatives. The leaders of the community turned to Jonathan Eybeschuetz and David Berlin for a decision, and they decided in Abraham's favor.

BIBLIOGRAPHY: Ẓ.H. Horowitz, *Kitvei ha-Ge'onim* (1928), 21–25.

[Itzhak Alfassi]

LIPSET, SEYMOUR MARTIN (1922–), U.S. sociologist. Born in New York City, Lipset taught at Columbia University, the University of Toronto, and at Berkeley, California, before becoming professor in the department of social relations at Harvard University. He served as the Caroline S.G. Munro Professor of Political Science and Sociology at Stanford University (1975–90) and the George D. Markham Professor of Government and Sociology at Harvard (1965–75). He then became Hazel Professor of Public Policy at the Institute of Public Policy, George Mason University, and senior fellow at the Hoover Institute at Stanford University. He was also a senior scholar at the Progressive Policy Institute and the Woodrow Wilson Center for International Scholars.

Lipset is one of the foremost representatives of political sociology in the United States. He combines a "middle range" theoretical orientation with verification in research. In his major work, *Union Democracy* (with M.A. Trow and J.S. Coleman, 1956), he provides a negative proof for Roberto Michels' contention that large-scale organizational structures make bureaucratic procedures inevitable: this rule does not apply to the American Typographical Union, which Lipset investigated, because of its relatively small size and the high educational standards of its members.

Lipset was president of the American Professors for Peace in the Middle East; chair of the National B'nai B'rith Hillel Commission and the Faculty Advisory Cabinet of the United Jewish Appeal; and co-chair of the Executive Committee of the International Center for Peace in the Middle East. He is the only person to have been president of both the American Political Science Association (1979–80) and the American Sociological Association (1992–93). He was a director of the U.S. Institute of Peace and was a member of the Board of Foreign Scholarships, both presidential appointments. Lipset received the Leon Epstein Prize in Comparative Politics by the American Political Science Association; the Marshall Sklare Award for distinction in Jewish studies; and the Helen Dinnerman Prize by the World Association for Public Opinion Research.

Other important publications of Lipset's, apart from numerous scholarly papers, are *Agrarian Socialism* (1950, 1968^2), *Class, Status and Power* (edited with R. Bendix, 1953, 1966^2), *Social Mobility in Industrial Society* (with R. Bendix, 1959), *Political Man* (1960), *The First New Nation* (1963), *Berkeley Student Revolt* (1965), *The Left, the Jews and Israel* (1969), *The Politics of Unreason* (with E. Raab, 1973), *The Confidence Gap* (1983), *Continental Divide* (1990), *Jews and the New American Scene* (with E. Raab, 1995), *American Exceptionalism* (1997), and *It Didn't Happen Here* (with M. Gary, 2001). He edited *Sociology and History: Methods* (with R. Hofstadter, 1968).

[Werner J. Cahnman / Ruth Beloff (2nd ed.)]

LIPSHITZ, ISRAEL ("**Lippy**"; 1903–1980), South African sculptor. Born in Lithuania, Lipshitz was taken to South Africa in 1908, and, apart from a period of study in Paris, spent most of his life in Cape Town. He was regarded as a leader of the modern school in sculpture and, from 1950 to 1968, was associate professor at the Cape Town University's School of Fine Art. "Lippy" Lipshitz (as he was widely known) worked in a variety of media, e.g., marble, bronze, stone, and wood. He drew many of his subjects from nature and from the Bible including Lot's wife, Jacob wrestling with the angel, and a massive head of Moses, carved out of a fossilized tree trunk, acquired by the National Art Gallery in Salisbury, Rhodesia (now Harare, Zimbabwe). He died in Israel.

[Lewis Sowden and Louis Hotz]

LIPSKI, ABRAHAM (1911–), Belgian engineer. Born in Lodz to a Zionist family, Abraham Lipski settled in Belgium. A highly successful construction engineer, he specialized in techniques of "presolicitations" – a modern method in construction. In 1951 he won international renown with his invention of the "preflex" construction beam. In 1958 at the Brussels World Fair he acted as assistant general commissioner for the Israel pavilion. Among a vast variety of public and private constructions he erected are the Transport Pavilion at the 1958 Brussels Exhibition; wharf constructions at Ostend and Ghent; the Midi Tower in Brussels; the funicular railway in Haifa, the Carmelit; and the Shalom-Meyer Tower in Tel Aviv. He participated in the construction of the Lydda International Airport and the Tel Aviv bus station. Lipski devoted a great deal of time to Jewish affairs.

[Rose Bieber]

LIPSKY, LOUIS (1876–1963), U.S. Zionist leader, journalist, and author. Lipsky, who was born in Rochester, New York, and edited a weekly periodical *Shofar* there, was an active Zionist even before the opening of the First Zionist Congress (1897). In 1901 Lipsky founded *The Maccabean* (later *The New Palestine*) magazine in New York, the first English-language Zionist periodical in the U.S. Under Lipsky's editorship, the magazine often exercised a powerful influence on Zionist actions in the U.S. Lipsky also edited *The American Hebrew* (1900–14). Lipsky served first as secretary, then chairman of the executive committee of the Federation of American Zionists, which was replaced by the Zionist Organization of America (ZOA) in 1917. In the ensuing Brandeis-Weizmann rift over the financial support and control of Jewish Palestine, Lipsky backed Weizmann. Lipsky was ZOA president from 1922 to 1930, and then became president of the Eastern Life Insurance Company (1930–59).

Lipsky was a founder of the Keren Hayesod, the Jewish Agency, and the American and World Jewish congresses. In 1915 he had advocated the establishment of an American Jewish Congress, directly elected by American Jews, which would support the concept of a Jewish national home. In 1918 the first American Jewish Congress was elected. Lipsky subsequently served as its vice president and chairman of its governing council, and from 1934 to 1945 was deeply involved in the organization's attempts to call attention to the plight of European Jewry and to organize their rescue. A prolific author, Lipsky's three-volume *Selected Works* consisting of *Thirty Years of American Zionism, Stories of Jewish Life*, and *Shields of Honor*, a selection of his plays and short stories, was published in 1927. He also wrote *A Gallery of Zionist Profiles* (1956) and *Tales of the Yiddish Rialto* (1962).

His son ELEAZAR LIPSKY (1912–1993) was, for many years, head of the Jewish Telegraphic Agency in New York City. A second son, JOEL CARMICHAEL (1915–), wrote widely on subjects concerning Jewish history, the Middle East, and Russia. Among his books are *The Shaping of the Arabs* (1967), *A Short History of the Russian Revolution* (1964), *The Death of Jesus* (1962), *Birth of Christianity: Reality and Myth* (1992), *The Satanizing of the Jews* (1992), *Unriddling of Christian Origins* (1995), and *Russia: An Illustrated History* (1999).

BIBLIOGRAPHY: A. Friesel, *Ha-Tenu'ah ha-Ẓiyyonit be-Arẓot ha-Berit ba-Shanim 1897–1914* (1970); M.W. Weisgal, *Louis Lipsky* (Eng. 1964); S. Halperin, *The Political World of American Zionism* (1960), index; S.S. Wise, *Challenging Years* (1949), passim, index. **ADD. BIBLIOGRAPHY:** D. Lipstadt, *The Zionist Career of Louis Lipsky, 1900–1921* (1982).

[Moshe Gottlieb]

LIPSON, EPHRAIM (1888–1960), English economic historian. Born in Sheffield, and educated at Cambridge, Lipson was a reader in economic history at Oxford from 1921 to 1931. He was instrumental in founding the Economic History Society, and the *Economic History Review*, serving as editor until his resignation in 1934. His major works, some of which went through numerous editions, were *Economic History of England* (3 vols., 1915–31; 1959[12]); *Europe in the Nineteenth Century* (1916, rev. ed. 1962); *The History of the Woollen and Worsted Industries* (1921); *Europe 1914–1939* (1940[2]); *The Growth of English Society – A Short Economic History* (1949). In *A Planned Economy or Free Enterprise: The Lessons of History* (1944), he pleaded for a policy aiming "to preserve best in our present economic system, the spirit of enterprise, and fuse it with the team spirit, so that self-interest was held in check by the ideal of public service and devotion to the Commonweal." Lipson was left badly deformed by severe injuries in childhood; in adulthood, he was an extremely sensitive, solitary man. His failure, in 1931, to be appointed to the chair of economic history at Oxford (in part, it is said, because of unwise claims he made about himself in his application) left him permanently embittered. Lipson's view that the industrial revolution did not mark a sharp break in Britain's economic evolution was echoed by a number of more recent economic historians, and his contribution to the field seemed overdue for a reevaluation. His brother DANIEL LIPSON (1886–1963) was housemaster of the Jewish House at Cheltenham College, one of England's leading boarding schools. He served as mayor of Cheltenham from 1935 to 1937 and was Independent member of Parliament for Cheltenham from 1937 to 1950. He was an opponent of Zionism and frequently expressed his anti-Zionist views in parliamentary debates.

ADD. BIBLIOGRAPHY: ODNB online.

[Benjamin J. Klebaner / William D. Rubinstein (2nd ed.)]

LIPSON, MORDEKHAI (1885–1958), Hebrew writer and folklorist. Born in Bialystok, he was ordained as a rabbi in 1903. After teaching for several years, he immigrated to the United States in 1913. There he wrote for the Hebrew and Yiddish press and edited the Hebrew weekly *Ha-Ivri* (1916–21). He founded and edited the New York Hebrew daily *Hadoar* (1921–23), which was the only modern Hebrew daily to appear in the U.S. When the newspaper was taken over by the Histadrut Ivrit and turned into a weekly, Lipson served for a period as editor. He immigrated to Ereẓ Israel in 1930 and edited the religious daily *Ha-Ẓofeh* from its inception, in 1937, until 1944. For more than a generation he collected Jewish folklore which appeared in *Mi-Dor-Dor* (3 vols., 1928–29), *Anshei Middot* (5 vols., 1927–34), *Midrash Zuta* (1951), and *Emshol Lekha Mashal* (1956). He also translated many books from Hebrew to Yiddish and from Yiddish to Hebrew, including works by I.J. *Singer, I. Bashevis *Singer, and J. *Opatoshu.

[Getzel Kressel]

LIPSYTE, ROBERT MICHAEL (1938–), U.S. sports journalist, columnist, novelist, and scriptwriter. Born in the Bronx to Sidney and Fanny, both teachers, Lipsyte grew up in Rego Park, Queens, and attended Forest Hills High School, but a Ford Foundation program allowed him to skip his senior year and enroll at Columbia University. He graduated in 1957 at the age of 19, and landed a job as a copy boy in the sports department of the *New York Times*. Lipsyte worked at the *Times* for 14 years – with a timeout to receive a master's degree from the Columbia School of Journalism in 1959 – becoming a sports reporter at 21 and then a sports columnist for the paper in 1966. During that time he also co-authored *Nigger* (1964) with the controversial comic and activist Dick Gregory; *The Masculine Mystique* (1966); and published an edited collection of his columns, *Assignment: Sports* (1970). Lipsyte's first and best-known novel for young people, *The Contender* (1967), won a children's book award, and Lipsyte abandoned his journalism career in 1971 after 544 columns to concentrate on writing novels. Lipsyte also worked as a freelance writer, television scriptwriter, journalism professor (Fairleigh Dickenson and New York University), radio commentator (National Public Radio, 1976–82), and columnist for the *New York Post* (1977), was a television sports essayist for CBS *Sunday Morning* (1982) and stayed with that network until moving to NBC in 1986. After leaving NBC in 1988, he hosted *The Eleventh Hour* on PBS (1989), winning an Emmy Award in 1990 for On-Camera Achievement, and was author of a television documentary series about sports. Lipsyte returned to the *New York Times* to write a sports column in 1991. Among his 16 books are *SportsWorld: An American Dreamland* (1975), *Free to Be Muhammad Ali* (1978), *Jim Thorpe: Twentieth-Cen-*

tury Jock (1993), *Arnold Schwarzenegger: Hercules in America* (1993), *Michael Jordan: A Life above the Rim* (1994), *Joe Louis: A Champ for All America* (1994), *Idols of the Game: A Sporting History of the American Century*, with Peter Levine (1995), and *In the Country of Illness: Comfort and Advice for the Journey* (1995). In addition to the Emmy, Lipsyte's honors and awards include the E.P. Dutton Best Sports Stories Award, 1964, 1965, 1967, 1971, and 1976; Columbia's Meyer Berger Award for distinguished reporting, 1966 and 1996; Wel-Met Children's Book Award, 1967; *New York Times* outstanding children's book of the year citation, 1977; American Library Association best young adult book citation, 1977; and in 1992, he was a finalist for the Pulitzer Prize for commentary. In 2001, the American Library Association honored him with the Margaret A. Edwards Award for Lifetime Achievement. He is the subject of *Presenting Robert Lipsyte* (1995), by Michael Cart.

[Elli Wohlgelernter (2nd ed.)]

LIPTON, SEYMOUR (1903–1986), U.S. sculptor. Born in New York City, Lipton showed a predilection for art as a child. His parents, however, discouraged his ambitions and he received a D.D.S. degree from Columbia University in 1927. While practicing as a dentist, Lipton began carving stylized sculptures with Social Realist themes out of wood. He had a one-man show in 1938 and two years later started teaching sculpture at the New School for Social Research in New York (1940–65). By the mid-1940s Lipton was welding Surrealist-inspired forms out of lead, later using steel, and by 1955 Monel metal. Lipton worked in stages, conceptualizing a sculpture on paper, making a maquette, and then fabricating the metal sculpture.

The events of World War II influenced Lipton's subject matter, which evolved from specific representational themes to more timeless abstract comments on the human condition. Figuration seemed inadequate to describe the devastation of war, and in 1942 he began to work abstractly in metals. *Moby Dick #2* (1948, private collection), a bronze abstraction of Herman Melville's whale, appears fierce with spikes or possibly teeth projecting from rounded forms. Similar predatory imagery would recur at various times throughout Lipton's career. Around 1948 Lipton began exploring cage themes in works such as *Imprisoned Figure* (Museum of Modern Art, New York). Experiencing a sense of renewal with the war several years in the past, in the 1950s Lipton welded dynamic vertical or horizontal pieces exhibiting traces of organic life such as *Jungle Bloom* (1954, Yale University Art Gallery, New Haven), a bronze on steel sculpture from the "Bloom" series.

His sculptures decorate several buildings in the United States, including the Philharmonic Hall, Lincoln Center, New York; Temple Israel, Tulsa, Oklahoma; and Temple Beth-El, Gary, Indiana.

BIBLIOGRAPHY: A. Elsen, *Seymour Lipton* (1970); H. Rand, *Seymour Lipton: Aspects of Sculpture* (1979); L. Verderame, *An American Sculptor: Seymour Lipton* (1999).

[Samantha Baskind (2nd ed.)]

LIPTOVSKY MIKULAS (Slovak **Liptovsky Mikulás**; Hung. **Liptószentmiklós**), town in N. Slovakia, until 1998 Czechoslovak Republic, since 1993 Slovak Republic. Jews appeared for the first time in documentation related to Mikulas in the 17th century. The local legislation was emphatically anti-Jewish. Jewish merchants visited the region and developed business relations with the nobility. In 1720 Ephraim, a Jew from Holesov, negotiated Jewish settlement in Mikulas with Count Samuel Pongracz. The latter rented the Jews several of his houses in the main square, free of charge. In 1729 an independent community was founded. It purchased land for a cemetery, a synagogue, and space in the square for new houses. It founded a *bet midrash*, a *mikveh*, and a *ḥevra kaddisha*. In 1740, the congregation hired its first rabbi, who initiated a *talmud torah* and the expansion of the synagogue. His successor founded a yeshivah.

Intensely engaged in trade, the Jews exported wool, cheese, and leather. They also dealt in wood, noting the high quality of the forests. Wood and wood products have remained a characteristic part of the trade of Slovakian Jews.

Liptovsky Mikulas was divided into two parts: densely populated Vrbica, and the smaller Mikulas with a big concentration of Jews. In 1828 there were 801 Jews. In 1835, Izak Diner was elected president of the congregation, and in 1865 mayor of Mikulas. The first Jew in Hungary to be elected mayor of a city, he held the position until 1872.

The period of Rabbi Lob Kunitz established the basis for intellectual activity, for which Mikulas was named "the Jewish Athens."

The dispute between Reform and Orthodoxy started early in Mikulas. While the majority of the members chose the Reform path, the Orthodox established their own congregation in 1864. They selected their own rabbi and founded their own elementary school with emphasis on Jewish studies. The two congregations fused in 1875.

In 1848–49, the Spring of Nations affected Mikulas Jewry. Many local Jews considered themselves Magyar patriots and enlisted in the army. In 1880 the Jewish population numbered 1,115.

In May 1919 the National Federation of Jews in Slovakia convened in Mikulas. The Zionist movement was active, and it included the sports organization Maccabi, founded in 1921; Hashomer-Kadima, the Zionist scouting movement; and the youth movement Gordonia Maccabi ha-Ẓa'ir.

In 1939 Slovakia proclaimed independence, under the aegis of Nazi Germany. Although the new state immediately began to persecute the Jews, the Mikulas community did not feel particular pressure. The population behaved as it did in the past, until 1940 when the Aryanization – i.e., expropriation – of Jewish property began. Former neighbors turned hostile, deprived Jews of their property, income, and jobs, and pressed to evict them from their apartments. In 1942 the deportation of Jews to Poland began. About 885 Mikulas Jews were deported to Lublin and the Sobibor extermination camp. When deportations stopped temporarily in the fall of 1942, Slovak Jews, as well as some others, escaped and crossed Slovakia's border; Mikulas was among the small surviving communities that assisted the escapees. In the fall of 1944, when the Slovak anti-Nazi uprising began, several surviving Jews joined the forces, while others sought places to hide. The German army rounded up the surviving and hidden Jews; some were executed on the spot, others were deported to Poland.

About 20% of pre-war Jews managed to return to the town. In 1947 there were 394 Jews in Mikulas. Thirty-eight Jews participated in anti-Nazi resistance within Slovakia, in the Soviet Union, and in the west. In 1948–49, most of the Jews immigrated to Israel. The synagogue was turned into a warehouse, and the cemeteries were destroyed. In 1989 the synagogue underwent a thorough reconstruction, partially by young Jewish and Slovak volunteers. There was a plan to turn the synagogue into a memorial.

Simon Goldstein, a native of Mikulas and graduate of its schools, was the first Jewish lawyer in Hungary. Samuel *Fischer, another Mikulas native, founded the Fischer-Verlag publishing house in Berlin.

BIBLIOGRAPHY: E. Herzog, *A zsidók története Liptó-szt.-Miklóson* (1894); M. Lányi and H. Propperné Békefi, *Szlovenszkói zsidó hitközségek története* (1933), 179–224; Y.L. Bato, in: *Das neue Israel*, 21 (1968), 471–5; *Israelitische Annalen*, 3 (1841), 19–20; 181, 231–2; *Jews of Czechoslovakia*, 1 (1968), 72, 74, 77, 91; A. Schnitzer, *Juedische Kulturbilder* (1904); *Magyar Zsid Lexikon* (1929), 536, s.v. *Liptószentmiklós*; MHJ, 7 (1963), s.v. *Liptószentmiklós*. **ADD. BIBLIOGRAPHY:** E. Bàrkàny and L. Dojč, *Židovské náboženské obce na Slovensku*, (1991), 287–92.

[Yeshayahu Jelinek (2nd ed.)]

LIPTZIN, SOL (1901–1995), literary scholar and educator. Leaving his native Satanov, Russia, as a boy, Liptzin was raised in the U.S. He taught at City College, New York, where he became professor of German in 1948 and served as chairman of the department of Germanic and Slavonic languages (1943–58). His interest in the mutual interaction of 19th-century German and English literature finds reflection in works such as *Shelley in Germany* (1924), and *The English Legend of Heinrich Heine* (1954). He also wrote *Lyric Pioneers of Modern Germany* (1928), *Arthur Schnitzler* (1932), and *Richard Beer-Hofmann* (1936). Liptzin turned his attention to Yiddish literature in *Stories from Peretz* (1947), *Eliakum Zunser: Poet of His People* (1950), *The Flowering of Yiddish Literature* (1963), and *The Maturing of Yiddish Literature* (1970). His other works include *Germany's Stepchildren* (1945), on German-Jewish writers; and *The Jew in American Literature* (1966). Active in Jewish affairs, he was honorary president of the Jewish Book Council of America and editor of the *Jewish Book Annual* (1953–56). Liptzin was a visiting professor at Yeshiva University (1929–40) and, after settling in Israel in 1962, at Tel Aviv University (1962–63) and the Haifa Technion (1962–66). He was the *Encyclopaedia Judaica* departmental editor for German literature.

LIPZIN, KENI (Sachar, Kreine Sonia; 1856–1918), Yiddish actress. Born in Russia, she made her debut in Abraham Goldfaden's company. She joined Jacob P. *Adler's London company in 1884, and married the theater manager, V. Lipzin. Later she married Michael Mintz, publisher of the *Jewish Daily Herald*. Jacob Gordin wrote *Mirele Efros* and adapted Grillparzer's *Medea* for her. When a theater she ran faced bankruptcy, her husband committed suicide, but she continued to act and paid all her creditors. Jacob Gordin's controversial play *Khasye di Yesoyme*, about the miserable treatment of a poor relative by a rich family, was written in 1903 for Lipzin.

LISBON, capital of *Portugal.

The Middle Ages

Jews were apparently settled in Lisbon in the 12th century, at the time of the conquest of the territory from the Moors and the establishment of the kingdom of Portugal by Affonso I (1139–85). For a period of two centuries they appear to have lived in tranquility, sharing the lot of their coreligionists in the rest of the country. Many Jews were prominent in court circles as tax farmers, physicians, or astronomers; the *almoxarife* Dom Joseph ibn Yaḥya, descendant of a family founded by a Jew who accompanied the first king on his conquest of the country, constructed a magnificent synagogue at his own expense in 1260. The great *esnoga* of Lisbon was built by the *Arraby Mór* Dom Judah son of Guedalya in 1306–7, according to the foundation stone that was discovered after the earthquake of 1755. This was the synagogue where Isaac Abrabanel and his family prayed. The synagogue was situated in *Vila Nova,* which was previously known as *Judaria Grande*. When the religious and political organization of the communities of Portugal was revised by Affonso III (1248–79), Lisbon became the official seat of the **arraby mór*, or chief rabbi. The most important incumbent of this office was Dom Moses Navarro, physician to Pedro I (1357–67), who, with his wife, acquired a large landed property near Lisbon.

This initial period of prosperity came to an end in the reign of Ferdinand I (1367–83). When Lisbon was captured by the Castilian troops in 1373, the Jewish quarter was sacked and many Jews killed. After the king's death, the Jews were considered by the populace to be at the root of the rapacious policies of the queen dowager Leonora – notwithstanding the fact that she had deposed the Jewish collector of taxes at Lisbon, as well as Dom Judah, the former royal treasurer. A popular revolt led to the accession to the throne of the master of Aviz, the first of a new dynasty. The feeling in Lisbon against the Jews became extreme, and the people wished to take violent steps to discover the treasures left by the late instrument of royal greed. An anti-Jewish reaction followed in the political sphere. Nevertheless, the new king (known as John I) did his best to protect the Jews against actual violence, though they were henceforth excluded from the positions of trust they had formerly occupied and were forced to make disproportionate contributions to the gift exacted by the city for presentation to the new king. Toward the close of his life, the latter became a little more tolerant. There was a reaction, however, under his son, Duarte (1433–38), who attempted to enforce the complete separation of Jews and Christians. This led to a protest by the community of Lisbon, and as a consequence the severity of the recent decree was mitigated (1436).

Persecution and Expulsion

Popular feeling, nevertheless, continued to be antagonistic. In 1455, the Côrtes of Lisbon demanded restrictions against the Jews. The Portuguese sovereigns had not permitted the wave of rioting which swept through the Iberian Peninsula in 1391 to penetrate into their dominions. Nevertheless, as a result of some disorder in the fish market, there was a serious anti-Jewish outbreak in Lisbon toward the close of 1449 which led to many deaths, and another (in the course of which Isaac *Abrabanel's library was destroyed) in 1482. Owing to the tolerant if grasping policy of John II, a number of the exiles from Spain were allowed to enter Lisbon after the expulsion of 1492. Their crowded living conditions led to an outbreak of the plague and the city council had them driven beyond the walls. Royal influence, however, secured the exemption from this decree of Samuel Nayas, the procurator of the Castilian Jews, and Samuel Judah, a prominent physician.

When in 1496/97 the Jews were to be expelled from Portugal, Lisbon alone was assigned to them as a port of embarkation. Assembling there from every part of the country, they were herded in turn into a palace known as Os Estãos, generally used for the reception of foreign ambassadors; here the atrocities of forced conversion were perpetrated. Some were killed, including well-known rabbis, such as Rabbi Shimon Maimi, originally from Segovia, who was killed in 1497. Thus, the community of Lisbon, with all the others of Portugal, was driven to embrace a titular Christianity. In the period immediately before and after the general expulsion, however, some individuals managed to escape. They probably contributed a majority of the members to the "Portuguese" synagogues in various places in the Turkish Empire, such as Smyrna (*Izmir), while at *Salonika and elsewhere they established separate congregations which long remained known by the name of "the *kahal* of Lisbon" or "*kahal* Portugal."

Lisbon was the seat of the most tragic events in *Converso history during the course of the subsequent period. On Whitsunday, 1503, a quarrel in the Rua Nova (the former Jewish quarter) between some *New Christians and a riotous band of youths led to a popular uprising, which was suppressed only with difficulty. In 1506, on the night of April 7, a number of New Christians were surprised celebrating the Passover together. They were arrested, but released after only two days' imprisonment. On April 19 trouble began again, owing to the conduct of a Converso who scoffed at a miracle which was reported to have taken place in the Church of Santo Domingo. He was dragged out of the church and butchered, and a terrible massacre began – subsequently known as *A Matança dos Christãos Novos* ("The slaying of the New Christians"). The number of victims was reckoned at between two and four thousand, one of the most illustrious being João Rodriguez Mascarenhas, a wealthy tax farmer and reputedly the most hated man in Lisbon. Sailors from the Dutch, French, and German ships lying in the harbor landed to assist in the bloody work. The king, Manoel, sharply punished this outbreak, temporarily depriving Lisbon of its erstwhile title "Noble and Always Loyal," fining the town heavily, and executing a number of the ringleaders.

The Inquisition

The visit of David *Reuveni (c. 1525), and the open conversion to Judaism of Diogo Pires (subsequently known as Solomon *Molcho), created a great stir amongst the Lisbon Conversos. They were foremost in attempting to combat the introduction of the Inquisition into Portugal, but their efforts were in vain. Lisbon itself became the seat of a tribunal of the Holy Office and on Sept. 20, 1540, the initial Portuguese auto-da-fé took place in the capital – the first of a long series which continued over more than two centuries. Throughout this period, the Lisbon tribunal was the most active in the whole country. Inquisitional martyrs who perished there included Luis *Dias, "the Messiah of Setúbal," together with his adherents, the pseudo-prophet Master Gabriel, and the mystical poet Gonçalo Eannes Bandarra, an "Old Christian" (1542 etc.); Frei Diogo da Assumpçao (Aug. 3, 1603); António *Homem, the "*Praeceptor Infelix*," and others of his circle (May 5, 1624); Manuel Fernandes *Villareal, the statesman and poet (Dec. 1, 1652); Isaac de Castro *Tartas, with other Conversos captured in Brazil (Dec. 15, 1647); António Cabicho, with his clerk Manoel de Sandoval (Dec. 26, 1684); Miguel (Isaac) Henriques da Fonseca, with António de Aguiar (alias Aaron Cohen Faya), and Gaspar (Abraham) Lopez Pereira, all of whom were mourned by Amsterdam poets and preachers as martyrs (May 10, 1681).

At times during the Inquisition period, the New Christians as such suffered. Thus, for example, when in 1630 a theft occurred at the Church of Santa Engrácia at Lisbon, suspicion automatically fell on the New Christians. A youth named Simão Pires Solis was cruelly put to death; the streets of the capital were placarded with inflammatory notices; the preachers inveighed from the pulpits against the "Jews"; and 2,000 persons are said to have fled from Lisbon alone. Similarly, in 1671, when a common thief stole a consecrated pyx from the Church of Orivellas at Lisbon, suspicion again fell on the Conversos and an edict was actually issued banishing them from the country (but not put into effect). From the accession of the House of Bragança in 1640 the power of the Portuguese Inquisition had been restrained in some measure, and its suspension by Pope Clement X in 1674 gave the New Christians some respite, but it proved little less terrible than before on its resumption in 1681. After the outbreak of the War of the Spanish Succession (1701–14), there seems to have been a recrudescence of inquisitional power, and, in the subsequent period, it became customary to send to Lisbon for punishment all those persons found guilty by the other tribunals of the realm. An auto-da-fé held at Lisbon in 1705 was the occasion of the famous and savage sermon of the archbishop of Cranganur, which in turn provoked David *Nieto's scathing rejoinder. At the Lisbon auto-da-fé of Sept. 24, 1752, 30 men and 27 women were summoned – all but 12 for Judaizing. In addition to these, three persons were burned in effigy.

The Lisbon earthquake of 1755 allowed many Conversos, together with those incarcerated in the dungeons of the Inquisition, to escape, and prompted others to make their way to open communities overseas. After this, no further Judaizers suffered in the capital; the last victim of the Lisbon tribunal was Father Gabriel Malagrida – a Jesuit. The reforms of the Marquês de Pombal put an end to all juridical differences between Old Christians and New (1773), and the Conversos of Lisbon disappeared as a separate class, although there were many families who continued to preserve distinct traces of their Jewish origin.

The Renewed Community

The close association of Portugal with England, and the position of Lisbon as an intermediate port between Gibraltar and England, made it inevitable that a Jewish settlement would be established in the city as soon as Jews could land with safety. By the middle of the 18th century, some individuals had found their way there and began to practice Jewish rites privately, under the security of British protection. Most of them originated from Gibraltar, though there were some from North Africa and one or two families direct from England. In 1801, a small piece of ground was leased for use as a cemetery. The services rendered to the city by certain Jewish firms at the time of the famine of 1810 improved their status, and in 1813, under the auspices of a certain R. Abraham Dabella, a congregation was formally founded. The condition of the Jews in Lisbon at this period is unsympathetically portrayed by George Borrow, in his classical *The Bible in Spain* (1843); while Israel Solomon, an early inhabitant, gives an intimate glimpse in his memoirs (F.I. Schechter in AJHSP, 25 (1917), 72–73). A little later in the century, two other synagogues (one of which is still in existence) were founded. In 1868, the community received official recognition for the first time. It was, however, recognized as a Jewish "colony," not "community," and the new synagogue (Shaare Tikvah) constructed in 1902 was not allowed to bear any external signs of being a place of worship. Complete equality was attained only with the revolution of 1910. Until the outbreak of World War I, the vast majority of the community was Sephardim, mostly from Gibraltar and North Africa, and many of them still retained their British citizenship. Subsequently, however, there was a very large Ashkenazi influx from Eastern Europe. During World War II, about 45,000 refugees from Nazi persecution arrived in Portugal, and passed mainly through Lisbon, on their way to the free world. In Lisbon they were assisted by a relief committee headed by M. Bensabat *Amzalak and A.D. Esagny. The Jews of Lisbon numbered 400 in 1947, and 600 in 2005. In addition to the two synagogues, there was a cultural center and a home for the aged.

Scholars

In the Middle Ages, Lisbon did not play a very important part in Jewish scholarship. The most illustrious scholars associated with it are the *Ibn Yaḥya family. It was also the birthplace of Isaac Abrabanel, who did much of his literary work there, while Joseph *Vecinho, Abraham *Zacuto, and other notable scholars are associated with the city in the period after the expulsion from Spain. *Levi b. Ḥabib also passed his early years in Lisbon. Many of the most illustrious Conversos who attained distinction in the communities of Amsterdam or elsewhere were also natives of Lisbon – men like Moses Gideon Abudiente, Zacutus *Lusitanus (Abraham Zacuto), Paul de Pina (Reuel *Jesurun), Abraham Farrar, Duarte Nunes da Costa, Duarte da Silva, and perhaps *Manasseh Ben Israel. The outstanding figure in the modern community of Lisbon was Moses Bensabat Amzalak, who was important in public, economic, and intellectual life, as well as being a prolific writer on Jewish subjects.

Hebrew Printing

A Hebrew printing press was active in Lisbon from 1489 to at least 1492 (see *Incunabula) and was closely connected with that of *Híjar, Spain, from which it took over the excellent type, decorated borders, and initials. After 1491 a new type was used. The founder of the Lisbon press was the learned and wealthy Eliezer b. Jacob Toledano (in whose house it operated), assisted by his son Zacheo, Judah Leon Gedaliah, Joseph Khalfon, and Meir and David ibn *Yaḥya. Their first production was Naḥmanides' Pentateuch commentary (1489); in the same year Eleazar Altansi brought out David Abudraham's prayer book. Other works printed in Lisbon are Joshua b. Joseph of Tlemcen's *Halikhot Olam* (1490); the Pentateuch with Onkelos and Rashi in 1491 (text with the vowel and cantillation signs); Isaiah and Jeremiah with David Kimḥi's commentary (1492); Proverbs with David ibn Yaḥya's commentary *Kav ve-Naki* (1492); *Tur Oraḥ Ḥayyim* (also 1492?), and Maimonides' *Hilkhot Sheḥitah*. No other productions have been preserved apart from a fragment from a Day of Atonement *maḥzor*, which may have come from this press. On the expulsion from Portugal in 1497, the printers – taking their type, tools, and expertise with them – found refuge in *Constantinople, *Salonika, and *Fez where they continued to produce beautiful books.

BIBLIOGRAPHY: Roth, Marranos, index; J. Mendes dos Remédios, *Os judeus em Portugal*, 2 vols. (1895–1928), index; S. Schwarz, *Inscripções hebraicas em Portugal* (1923); M.B. Amzalak, *Tipographia hebraica em Portugal no século XV* (1922); M. Kayserling, *Geschichte der Juden in Portugal* (1867); J.L. d'Azevedo, *Históa dos Christãos Novos Portuguêses* (1921), index; King Manuel (of Portugal), *Early Portuguese Books: 1489–1600* (1929), 1, 23–43; J. Bloch, *Early Printing in Spain and Portugal* (1938), 32–35; B. Friedberg, *Toledot ha-Defus ha-Ivri be-Italyah* (1956^2), 102–4. **ADD. BIBLIOGRAPHY:** S. Schwarz, *A sinagoga de Alfama* (1953); H.B. Moreno, "O assalto à judiaria grande de Lisboa em dezembro de 1449," in: *Revista de ciências do honem*, 3 (1970), 207–53 (=reprinted in: idem, *Tenso~es sociais em Portugal na idade media* (1977), and in: idem, *Marginalidade e con-*

flitos sociais em Portugal nos séculos XIV *e* XV (1985), 89–132); Y.H. Yerushalmi, *The Lisbon Massacre of 1506 and the Royal Image in the "Shebet Yehudah"* (1976); T. Metzger, *Les manuscrits hébreux copiés et décorés à Lisbonne dan les dernières décennies du* XV*e siècle* (1977); A. de Vasconcelos Simão, in: *Armas e troféus*, 3, sér., 6 (1977), 216–35; A.M. Salgado, in: *Cultura, história e filosofia*, 5 (1986), 653–69; R. Faingold, in: *Zion*, 54 (1989), 118–24; E. Lipiner, *Two Portuguese Exiles in Castile* (1997), 148–58.

LISHANSKY, BATYA (1900–1992), Israeli sculptor. Born in the Ukraine, Lishansky immigrated in 1910 to Ereẓ Israel where she studied under Boris Schatz. Her work consisted mainly of small wood sculptures and later white marble cubist-like forms. From 1930 onward she produced a series of naturalist romantic profiles, and statues in stylized groups. Among her well-known works is a bust of her brother-in-law, I. *Ben-Zvi. She was awarded the Israel Prize in 1986 for sculpture.

LISHANSKY, YOSEF (1890–1917), member of the clandestine intelligence organization *Nili in Ereẓ Israel. Lishansky was born in the district of Kiev, Ukraine. He was orphaned, taken to Ereẓ Israel at the age of six, and raised by relatives living in Metullah. He joined the *Po'alei Zion Party, and for three years he worked as a watchman for *Ha-Shomer in Galilee, but was not accepted as a member of the organization. At the end of 1915 he joined Nili. In January 1917 he and Avshalom *Feinberg tried, on behalf of Nili, to cross the Sinai Desert to reach the British lines in Egypt. Feinberg was killed en route by Bedouins, but Lishansky, though wounded, reached Egypt. Upon his return to Ereẓ Israel, he joined Sarah *Aaronsohn in organizing the group's espionage work. When Nili was uncovered by the Turks, Lishansky sought refuge with former comrades in Ha-Shomer, who, however, decided that the safety and security of the Jewish population necessitated his death. Emissaries of Ha-Shomer set out to assassinate Lishansky, but succeeded only in wounding him, and he managed to escape. He tried to reach Egypt but was caught on the way and sentenced to death by the Turkish authorities in Damascus. He was hanged on Dec. 16, 1917, together with his Nili comrade Na'aman *Belkind, and was buried beside him at Rishon le-Ẓion.

BIBLIOGRAPHY: A. Engle, *Nili Spies* (1959), index; Dinur, Haganah, 1 (1954–56), 358–78, 409–11, 733–78; E. Livneh (ed.), *Nili, Toledoteha shel He'azah Medinit* (1961), index.

[Yehuda Slutsky]

LISITZKY, EPHRAIM E. (1885–1962), U.S. Hebrew poet and educator. Born in Minsk, he immigrated to the United States at the age of 15. In 1918, after peregrinations which took him to Boston, New York, Central Canada, Buffalo, and Milwaukee, he finally settled in New Orleans, where he spent the rest of his life. He became principal of the city's Hebrew School, one of the best in the United States.

Lisitzky was a prolific Hebrew poet. Though not marked by originality, he made lasting contributions to the thematic wealth of Hebrew literature. *Medurot Do'akhot* ("Dying Campfires," 1937), a story of two Indian tribes, is based on Indian legends and contains fine descriptions of the American landscape. It is written in the unrhymed trochaic tetrameter of *Hiawatha* and *Kalevala*. Out of black folktales and folk songs, sermons and spirituals, habits and customs, he composed *Be-Oholei Kush* ("In the Tents of Cush," 1953). In his narrative poem *Ki-Teko'a Shofar* (1922) he contrasts the spiritual aridity of the small town American Jew with the deep religiosity of Eastern European Jewry (*Shirim* (1928), 241–80). His dramatic poem *Naftulei Elohim* (1934), despite some happy phrases, must be considered a failure, overburdened with the poet's mythological inventions and with Jewish, Christian, Islamic, and Buddhist doctrine. Similarly unsuccessful is *Bi-Ymei Sho'ah u-Mesho'ah* (1960), which deals with the European Holocaust. Lisitzky's occasional articles on literature and educational matters in the Hebrew press were collected in his book, *Bi-Shevilei Ḥayyim ve-Sifrut* (1961). Lisitzky's reputation will ultimately rest on his moving autobiography *Elleh Toledot Adam* (1949; *In the Grip of Cross-Currents*, 1959), his book of black poems, and his Indian epic.

BIBLIOGRAPHY: A. Epstein, *Soferim Ivrim ba-Amerikah*, 1 (1952), 39–65; Waxman, Literature, 4 (1960²), 1063–65; Silberschlag, in: JBA, 21 (1963/64), 66–71. **ADD. BIBLIOGRAPHY:** M. Meirovitch, "*Li-Demuto ha-Ḥinukhit shel E. Lisitzky*," in: *Bi-Sdeh Ḥemed*, 32 (1972), 235-39; S. Katz, "To Be as Others: E.E. Lisitzky's Re-Presentations of Native Americans," in: *Hebrew Union College Annual*, 73 (2002), 249-97.

[Eisig Silberschlag]

LISMANN, HERMANN (1878–1943), German painter. Born in Munich, he studied in his native town and in Lausanne, and later went to Rome and to Paris (1904). Here he belonged to the group of artists that met regularly at the Café du Dôme. After serving in the German army in World War I he settled in Frankfurt, where many of his works were acquired by the local museum, and where for several years he taught aesthetics at the university. After the rise of Hitler he immigrated to France, residing in Tours. He was interned by the French at the outbreak of World War II as an enemy alien, but managed to escape to Montauban near Toulouse, in the unoccupied zone. However, in 1943 he was deported to his death in the extermination camp of Majdanek. His postimpressionist works, in the Staedelsches Museum at Frankfurt and in the museum of Wuppertal, were confiscated by the Nazis and disappeared. Nevertheless, a memorial exhibition held by the Frankfurt Kunstverein in 1959 was able to assemble 132 of his works.

[Alfred Werner]

LISPECTOR, CLARICE (1925–1977), Brazilian author. Born in the Ukraine, she arrived in Brazil as a child. She is considered the most important Brazilian woman writer of the century. Her narrative achieves unexpected and disturbing perspectives by focusing on the internal life of characters (especially women) who are always in conflict with social and psychological conventions. Among her novels and collections of short stories are *Perto do coração selvagem* (1944; *Near to the Wild Heart*, 1990); *Laços de família* (1960; *Family Ties*, 1972); *A maçã no escuro* (1961; *The Apple in the Dark*, 1967); *A paixão segundo G.H.* (1964; *The Passion According to G.H.*, 1988); *Água viva* (1973; *The Stream of Life*, 1989); *A hora da estrela* (1977; *The Hour of the Star*, 1992). She also wrote essays and stories for children. Though she identified herself as mainly Brazilian, criticism discusses the possible Jewish and biblical sources of her nonconformism, her belief in the power of words and her mystic overtones, and also her ironic attacks on the religious establishment. The name of the character Macabea (*A hora da estrela*), a socially deprived, powerless, and defeated young woman, seems deliberately chosen in contrast with tradition.

BIBLIOGRAPHY: H. Cixous, *Reading with Clarice Lispector* (1990); E. Fitz, *Clarice Lispector* (1985); R. DiAntonio and N. Glickman, *Tradition and Innovation: Reflections on Latin American Jewish Writing* (1993); L. Guerra Cunningham, *Splintering Darkness: Latin American Women Writers in Search of Themselves* (1990); N. Vieira, *Jewish Voices in Brazilian Literature* (1995). **WEBSITE:** N. Lindstrom, "Clarice Lispector's World of Cultural Allusions," <http://www.lanic.utexas.edu/ilas/brazctr/publications/papers/lindstrom/nlindstrom.html>.

[Florinda F. Goldberg (2nd ed.)]

LISSA, ZOFIA (1908–1980), musicologist. Born in Lvov, Zofia Lissa was cultural attaché at the Polish embassy in Moscow after World War II; she later joined the Polish Ministry of Art and Culture, and became professor of music at Warsaw University. Among her publications are *Zarys nauki o muzyce* ("The Outlines of Musical Science," 1934, 1952^3); *Uwagi o metodzie marksystowskiej w muzykologii* ("Remarks on the Marxist Method in Musicology," 1950); and *Historia muzyki rosyjskiej* ("History of Russian Music," 1955).

LISSAK, MOSHE (1928–), sociologist. Born in Tel Aviv, Lissak received his doctorate in sociology from the Hebrew University, where he became a professor of sociology in 1978. He did research and wrote on topics such as social and political history of the *yishuv*, society-army relations in Israel and in South East Asia, and on ethnic group relations in Israel. In 1992 he was awarded the Israel Prize for social sciences. Among his publication are *The Mass Immigration in the Fifties: The Failure of the Melting Pot Policy* (1978) and *Trouble in Utopia: The Overburdened Polity of Israel* (1989).

LISSAUER, ERNST (1882–1937), German poet and playwright. Born in Berlin, his earliest publications were two volumes of verse: *Der Acker* (1907) and *Der Strom* (1912). Lissauer is, however, remembered as the composer of the "Hymn of Hate" (*Hassgesang gegen England*, 1915), which German troops sang at the front during World War I. From 1924 he lived in Vienna and supported the German nationalists. He insisted that the Jews were not one people and that he, as a German Jew, had nothing in common with the Jews of Eastern Europe. Lissauer opposed Zionism and advocated complete assimilation. He wrote a number of plays including *Yorck* (1921), *Das Weib des Jephta* (1928), and *Luther und Thomas Muenzer* (1929).

BIBLIOGRAPHY: A. Schwadron, in: *Der Jude*, 1 (1916–17), 490–2; G.K. Brand, *Ernst Lissauer* (1923); D. Sadan, *Ha-Namer vi-Ydido ha-Menamnem* (1951), 124–5, 129–32, 188–91. **ADD. BIBLIOGRAPHY:** H. Schlösser, "Ernst Lissauer oder die Liebe zum Organischen. Ueber einen Berliner Dichter und sein 'Glueck in Oesterreich,'" in: B. Fetz and H. Schloesser (eds.), *Wien – Berlin* (2001), 32–44; R. Braendle, *Am wilden Zeitenpass. Motive und Themen im Werk des deutsch-juedischen Dichters Ernst Lissauer*, with an introduction by G. Stern (2002); E. Albanis, "German-Jewish Cultural Identity from 1900 to the Aftermath of the First World War. A Comparative Study of Moritz Goldstein, Julius Bab and Ernst Lissauer" (diss., Oxford, 2002).

[Sol Liptzin]

LISSER, JOSHUA FALK (d. 1807), rabbi and talmudist. Joshua studied under Moses Zerah *Eidlitz of Prague. As *dayyan* at Lissa he was involved in the decision to condemn and burn Naphtali Herz *Wessely's *Divrei Shalom ve-Emet*, which called on Jews to emancipate themselves. Lisser published *Binyan Yehoshu'ah* (Dyhernfurth, 1788), commentaries, including textual emendations, on the minor tractates *Avot de-Rabbi Nathan, Semaḥot, Derekh Ereẓ Zuta*. The commentary on *Avot de-Rabbi Nathan* was reprinted in 1858–64 in Zhitomir and in Romm's Vilna editions of the Talmud. Bearing in mind the spirit of opposition to critical scholarship at the time, Lisser apologized in the preface of his commentary for his suggested textual emendations. In defense of his work he pointed to the precedents of Solomon *Luria and Samuel *Edels, who had also suggested variant readings in their commentaries.

BIBLIOGRAPHY: L. Lewin, *Geschichte der Juden in Lissa* (1904), 271f.

LISSITZKY, EL (**Lazar**; 1890–1941), Russian painter. Born in Smolensk province, where his parents were hatters, he earned his living by giving drawing lessons. He was unable to enter the Academy of Art in St. Petersburg because the Jewish quota was filled. Instead he left for Germany, to study in Darmstadt. At the outbreak of World War I he returned to Russia. It was only after the 1917 Revolution that he could develop his original and versatile talent. When *Chagall was appointed director of the school of art at Vitebsk, Lissitzky joined him there as professor of architecture and graphic arts. In common with Chagall, he was deeply interested in Jewish folklore. Examples of this interest were his watercolor illustrations to the *Legend of Prague* by M. Broderzon, and his color lithograph illustrations to the *Ḥad Gadya*. These were distinguished by the bright, childlike colors of folk art. He also collaborated in the production of Jewish children's books, developing new ideas for typography and layout. Strongly influenced by Casimir Malevich, leader of the Russian cubists, Lissitzky was a major force in a related movement, constructivism. In this movement, which believed that the purpose of art was not necessarily to beautify, he tried to integrate his aesthetic concepts into Marxist theory. In 1919 he painted his first "prouns," a generic term he was to apply to his mature work, which is based on stereometric elements, fusing aspects of painting with architecture. In 1921 he was appointed professor at the Moscow Academy. However, angered by the government's hostility to the new trends, he joined the artists who left Russia for countries more receptive to radical aesthetic ideas. He lived and worked in Germany, France, Holland, and Switzerland, and at one time collaborated with Ilya Ehrenburg in the publication of a constructivist magazine. In 1925 the progressive museum director Alexander Dorner commissioned Lissitzky to install a special gallery for the showing of abstract art in the Landesmuseum at Hanover. The room was later destroyed by the Nazis. Lissitzky maintained his links with the Soviet regime, and in 1928 returned to Russia. The government, however, employed him only to design pavilions at a number of international exhibitions abroad, and also the restaurant at the Soviet section of the 1939 New World's Fair. He died of tuberculosis.

BIBLIOGRAPHY: S. Lissitzki-Kueppers, *El Lissitzky* (1968); Roth, Art, 800f.

[Alfred Werner]

LIST, EMANUEL (1888–1967), bass. Born in Vienna, List joined the Volksoper in Vienna in 1922, the Berlin State Opera from 1923 to 1933 and toured in Europe, the United States, and Australia. In 1938, forced to leave Germany, he settled in the United States. His deep bass made him suitable for Wagner villains; therefore he sang leading Wagnerian roles at the Metropolitan Opera, New York. He also became known as a singer of German lieder. Among his famous roles are Pogner (*Die Meistersinger*), Hunding (*Die Walküre*), King Mark, Ramfis (*Aida*), and Landgrave (*Tannhäuser*). List recorded several of his Wagner roles, including Hunding on Bruno Walter's famous 1935 recording of *Die Walküre*, Act 1.

BIBLIOGRAPHY: Grove online.

[Israela Stein (2nd ed.)]

LIST, GEORGE HAROLD (1912–), ethnomusicologist, composer, and educator. Born in Tucson, Arizona, List earned a diploma in flute, Juilliard School of Music (1933); B.S. and M.A., Teachers College, Columbia University (1941 and 1945); and his Ph.D., Indiana University (1954). After performing as a flutist and teaching music in several public schools, he joined the faculty of Indiana University in 1954 where he became active in the interdisciplinary fields of ethnomusicology and folklore. There, he was appointed associate professor of folklore, retiring as professor in 1976. He also served as director of the Archives of Traditional Music (1954–76), director of the Inter-American Program in Ethnomusicology (1966–76), and editor of *The Folklore and Folk Music Archivist* (1958–68).

From 1960 through 1970 he recorded and researched the traditional music of the Hopi Indians of Northern Arizona, the inhabitants of the Caribbean Littoral of Colombia, and the Indians of the Andes and the Amazon region of Ecuador. He received fellowships from the National Endowment for the Humanities, Indiana Historical Society, American Philosophical Society, and a Fulbright research award. His writings include *Music and Poetry in a Colombian Village* (1983); *Singing About It, Folksong in Southern Indiana* (1991); *Stability and Variation in Hopi Song* (1993) as well as numerous theoretical studies (see *Discourse…* in the Bibliography). Among his compositions are *Memoir and Scherzino* for flute and piano (1951); *Music For Children*, eight pieces (1952); symphonic satire *Marche O'Malley* (1947); and a string quartet (1951).

BIBLIOGRAPHY: Grove Music Online; James Hass, "Bibliography of G. List's Writings," in: Caroline et al. (eds.), *Discourse in Ethnomusiclogy Essays* (1978), 289–98.

[Israel J. Katz (2nd ed.)]

LISTOPAD, FRANTIŠEK (originally **Jiří Synek**; 1921–), Czech poet, author of fiction and essays. Born in Prague into an assimilated Jewish family, Listopad did not report for transport and from 1941 lived in the underground and took part in the resistance movement against the Nazis. After the war, he studied aesthetics and literature at Charles University in Prague and began to publish in many literary magazines. In 1947 he left for Paris; after 1948 he did not return to Czechoslovakia. In 1958 he moved to Portugal. His first collections of poems and a poem in prose "Little Loves" (1946) appeared in Czechoslovakia before 1947. Between 1947 and 1990, none of his work was allowed to be published in Czechoslovakia. Abroad, he issued collections of poems, such as *Freedom and Other Fruit* (1956) and *Black White, I Don't Know* (1973). After 1990 his collections of verses *Final rondi* (1992), *Far Near* (1993), and *Kyrie Eleison* (1998) appeared in Czechoslovakia and the Czech Republic. Human existence is the topic of Listopad's stories and lyrical prose, such as *The Vicious Dog without a Garden* (1996). The philosophical meditation of searching for one's place in life is the topic of many of his essays. Listopad writes and publishes in Portuguese as well, and his prose has appeared in other countries.

BIBLIOGRAPHY: J. Čulík, *Knihy za ohradou. Česká literatura v exilových nakladatelstvích* 1971–1989 (s.d.); P. Kubíková and P. Kotyk, *Čeští spisovatelé – Czech Writers* (1999); V. Menclová et al., *Slovník českých spisovatelů* (2000); *Slovník českých spisovatelů* (1982).

[Milos Pojar (2nd ed.)]

LIT, U.S. family, prominent in Philadelphia, Pennsylvania, in the 19th–20th centuries. The Philadelphia department store operation known as Lit Brothers was first established in 1891 as a dress and millinery shop by RACHEL P. LIT (1858–1919; later Wedell, still later Arnold), who was soon thereafter joined by her brothers Colonel SAMUEL D. LIT (1859–1929) and JACOB D. LIT (1872–1950). Samuel's only experience had been as an apprentice plumber and book salesman. However, he and Jacob brought tremendous energy and ambition to their task. The store expanded yearly, and by 1906 covered the entire city square on Market Street from Seventh to Eighth, where a new building was erected in 1907. Samuel served as a member of the Delaware River Bridge Commission and of the Board of City Trusts; he was also a member of the boards of Mikveh Israel Congregation and of the Jewish Hospital. Jacob was active in the leadership of the YMHA and was founder-president of the downtown Mt. Sinai Hospital (1900). In 1928 Lit's was purchased by City Stores, in which Albert M. *Greenfield was the controlling figure. After World War II, the business expanded into suburban areas of Pennsylvania and New Jersey, and in 1962 absorbed the four branches of Snellenburg's, thus becoming the largest department store chain in the Delaware Valley area. Rachel's daughter ETTA (d. 1953) was the wife of JULES E. MASTBAUM (1872–1926), motion picture exhibitor and executive who gave his magnificent collection of Rodin sculptures, drawings, and letters to the city, together with $1,000,000 for the erection of a museum to contain them, opened to the public as a landmark on the Benjamin Franklin Parkway in 1929. Another brother, JONKER LIT (1853–1919), had a daughter Juliet, who married J. DAVID STERN (1886–1971) the publisher of *Philadelphia Record* (1928–47), *Camden Courier-Post* (1919–47), and *The New York Post* (1933–39).

[Bertram Wallace Korn]

LITAUER, JAN JAKUB (1873–1949), Polish jurist. Litauer was professor of civil procedure at the University of Lodz (1945–47) and at the Polish Free College in Warsaw after 1949. He was a member of the committee for the codification of the law and one of the drafters of the Code of Civil Procedure. He was later a judge of the Supreme Court of Poland.

LITERATURE, JEWISH. Literature on Jewish themes and in languages regarded as Jewish has been written continuously for the past 3,000 years. What the term Jewish literature encompasses, however, demands definition, since Jews have lived in so many countries and have written in so many different languages and on such diverse themes. In this article it will be understood to include the following categories: (1) works written by Jews on Jewish themes in any language; (2) works of a literary character written by Jews in Hebrew or Yiddish or other recognized languages, whatever the theme; (3) literary works written by writers who were essentially Jewish writers, whatever the theme and whatever the language. This entry covers the subject up to the threshold of the modern period. The continuation will be found in other entries including *Hebrew Literature, Modern; *Yiddish Literature; *Ladino Literature.

This article is arranged according to the following outline:

EARLY BEGINNINGS TO THE MEDIEVAL PERIOD
BIBLICAL LITERATURE
APOCRYPHAL WORKS
APOCALYPTIC LITERATURE
HELLENISTIC LITERATURE
BIBLE TRANSLATIONS
- Greek
- Aramaic

EXEGESIS
PHILOSOPHY
HISTORY
HALAKHAH AND AGGADAH
- Halakhah
  - "MOTIVATED *HALAKHOT*"
  - MISHNAH
  - THE TOSEFTA ("ADDITIONS")
  - TALMUD
    - *Jerusalem Talmud*
    - *Babylonian Talmud*
- Aggadah
  - MIDRASHIM
    - *Midrash Rabbah*
    - *Tanḥuma-Yelammedenu*
    - *Pesikta*
    - *Other Homiletic Midrashim*
    - *Non-Homiletic Midrashim*

MEDIEVAL PERIOD (500–1750)
GRAMMAR AND LEXICOGRAPHY
BIBLE EXEGESIS
POETRY
RABBINIC LITERATURE (500–1250)
- Commentary
- Codes
- Responsa

RABBINIC LITERATURE (1250–1750)
- Commentary
- Codes
- Responsa
  - RESPONSA (1250–1500)
  - RESPONSA (1500–1750)

METHODOLOGY
- Philosophy and Theology
- Ethics
- Ethical Wills
- Philosophical Exegesis
- Mystical Literature
  - PRE-ZOHAR AND ZOHAR LITERATURE
- Prose Literature
  - HISTORY
  - GEOGRAPHY AND TRAVEL
  - BIOGRAPHIES AND AUTOBIOGRAPHIES
  - FICTION
  - TALES
  - SATIRE AND HUMOR
- Didactic Literature
- Polemical and Apologetic Literature
- Yiddish Literature
- Ladino Literature

EARLY BEGINNINGS TO THE MEDIEVAL PERIOD

BIBLICAL LITERATURE

The earliest, greatest, and most enduring Jewish literary works are the books of the Bible, known collectively in Hebrew as

Tanakh, made up of the initial letters of *Torah* ("Pentateuch"), *Nevi'im* ("Prophets"), and *Ketuvim* ("Hagiographa"). The Bible consists of either 25 or 39 books, depending on whether the 12 prophets are counted as one or 12 books and whether Samuel, Kings, and Chronicles are counted as one or two books each.

The Pentateuch comprises five volumes and offers an account of the creation of the world, the early history of mankind, the life and experience of the forefathers of the Jewish people, the experiences of Israel in Egypt, the Exodus, and the Jews' wanderings in the desert for 40 years under the leadership of Moses. Extended sections are devoted to laws governing individual and social behavior, to ethical principles, to theological statements, and to details of ritual for priest and layman. The underlying theme is that God has entered into a covenant with the patriarchs and subsequently, in a revelation at Mount Sinai, with the Jewish people as a whole. The covenant demands that the people of Israel worship God exclusively and abide by the law as set forth in the Torah; God, in turn, undertakes to make them "His own peculiar treasure" among the nations and to give them the Land of Canaan. The Jews thus became a choosing and a chosen people.

The *Nevi'im* are subdivided into two sections: Early Prophets and Later Prophets. The Early Prophets are historical works, portraying the experiences of Israel when entering Canaan (Book of Joshua), a period of turmoil and settlement (Judges), a period of consolidation under the kings (Samuel and Kings), and the period of division of the land into two kingdoms down to the destruction of the Northern Kingdom by the Assyrians and the Southern Kingdom by the Babylonians (Kings). These books are selective history and reflect a point of view and philosophy of history which seems to be that of the prophets. The Latter Prophets include the three large books of the major prophets: Isaiah, Jeremiah, and Ezekiel, and the 12 books of the minor prophets (so named because of the brevity of the books). The themes which unite the books are that the prophets present revelations from God whose substance is that Israel has strayed from true worship, has departed from proper ethical behavior, both individually and socially, and that it is called upon to repent its ways. The penalty for obduracy will be the destruction of the polity. The hope is, however, offered that "a saved remnant" of righteous people will have the opportunity to renew and continue the covenant with God. This prophetic preachment seems to have been a continuous element in Jewish life from the time of Moses (13th century B.C.E.) to the time of Malachi (450 B.C.E.) and seems to have been the concern and responsibility of "schools of prophets" or of a prophetic party.

The *Ketuvim* comprise works as diverse as the lyrics of the Psalms, the searching dramatic exploration of suffering of the Book of Job, the skepticism of Ecclesiastes, the love poetry of the Song of Songs, the laments attributed to Jeremiah, and such historical works or semihistorical works as the Chronicles, Ezra, Nehemiah, Esther, Ruth, and the foreshadowing of an apocalyptic literature in the Book of Daniel.

The books of the Bible were written over a period extending from the 11th century B.C.E. (upon the basis of traditions perhaps several centuries older) to the third century B.C.E. Although the canon was substantially closed by 250 B.C.E., an argument as to the propriety of including the Song of Songs and Ecclesiastes in the Bible was apparently not settled until about the year 90 C.E. The authorship of the various books of the Bible is rarely clear. The talmudic assumption is that all the books were written under the influence of "the holy spirit" which means that they are attributed to figures who were the recipients of divine revelation. Thus where no author is indicated, as in the Book of Judges, the Talmud ascribes it to the prophetic figure Samuel, more or less a contemporary, and in the case of the Book of Kings makes the assumption that it was the work of Jeremiah. The major books of the Bible, in terms of their significance for Jewish life, are the Five Books of Moses. The traditional view, which is used as an underlying assumption by the Talmud, and subsequently by Jewish law, is that they were a direct revelation from God to Moses and that every word, therefore, has chosen and special meaning. Biblical critical scholarship of the 19th and 20th centuries has assumed that the Pentateuch is the work of man and has proposed that its five books are an amalgam of several distinct and ancient versions which no longer exist and which are denominated as the J, E, and P documents. Presumably they were put together in one document by a redactor or a body of editors known as R sometime between the end of the seventh century B.C.E. and the middle of the fifth century B.C.E.

While the Bible is the only extant literature of the early centuries of Jewish existence, the Bible itself indicates that there were other works such as the "*Book of the Wars of the Lord" (Num. 21:14) and the "*Books of the Chronicles of the Kings of Judah and Israel" (II Chron. 25:26; 28:26; 32:32). It is also probable that there were works of "true prophets," writings of "false prophets," and a great many lyrical poems, like the Book of Psalms and the Song of Songs, which have not survived (see *Bible; *Pentateuch; the individual books of the Bible; *Allegory; *Poetry, Biblical; *Fable; *Parable).

APOCRYPHAL WORKS

From the third century B.C.E. the literary creativity manifested in the Bible continued undiminished in works called *Apocrypha (*Sefarim Ḥizonim*, meaning "excluded" or "hidden" works). These writings, usually of unknown authorship, included fictional and moralistic works (*Tobit); didactic books (*Ben Sira or Ecclesiasticus); disguised historical allegories (the Book of *Judith); historical works (the Books of the *Maccabees); and apologetic works (IV *Maccabees). Some of them, such as the Addition to Esther, were designed as supplements to the Bible to fill in apparent lacunae in that text. Some were imitations of biblical patterns, or conceived as continuations of biblical traditions, like Ben Sira which is in the vein of the books of Proverbs and Ecclesiastes, and the recently discovered Dead Sea *Thanksgiving Psalms Scroll which is in the tradition of the biblical psalter. Some were already early Midrashim, homiletic and moral extensions of biblical material, like the *Dead Sea Scrolls: the Genesis Apocryphon and the *Pesher Habakkuk which applies the prophetic statement of an earlier age to the Jewish-Roman confrontation of the first century B.C.E. and the first century C.E.

The extent of this literature is not known. The discovery of the Dead Sea Scrolls has made it clear that there were many works, perhaps sectarian books, which were not preserved as part of the literary and religious mainstream. Moreover, even the previously known works of the Apocrypha were excluded and hidden from Jewish literature, apparently in an attempt to prevent competition with the canon and to suppress dissident sectarian points of view. Consequently, most of them did not survive in their original language, whether Hebrew or Aramaic, but were preserved in Greek versions by Christians who invested them with semisanctity.

More striking than the literary quality of the works is the appearance of certain themes. The arguments about religious practices and philosophies and the emergence of new doctrines, such as immortality, resurrection, and Messianism are present in the Apocrypha. The confrontations of Jews with the Hellenistic world and the need to authenticate the Jewish tradition is reflected both in historical works and in apologetic books, like IV Maccabees and the Letter of *Aristeas. A nationalistic, revolutionary literature appears in the Dead Sea Scrolls, such as the War of the Children of Light against the Children of Darkness, and from the same source there are new indications of the stresses and strains within the Jewish community. It is a literature of dignity and beauty whose merit does not depend upon anything but its intrinsic quality (see *Apocrypha and Pseudepigrapha; *Dead Sea Scrolls; *Dead Sea Sect; *Hebrew Language of the Dead Sea Scrolls).

APOCALYPTIC LITERATURE

During the period of the Apocrypha (c. 200 B.C.E. to about the end of the first century C.E.) another body of literature, apocalyptic works, also developed. Like the Apocrypha, they were set aside by later Jewish authorities and were preserved in the Christian tradition surviving either in Greek or Ethiopic revisions. Features common to these works were a claim to be revealed books and to reveal the future, and their pseudepigraphy, purporting to be the writings of ancient heroic or saintly figures. Clearly reactions to political events of the time as well as to theological problems, their essential themes were eschatological – the question of evil and of suffering, the vision of the Messiah, Messianic times, the Day of Judgment, and the vision of a new world. IV *Esdras, a national Job, was probably written right after the destruction of the Temple. The author's solution to the tragedy of the Jewish people is to assert that while God's will is inscrutable, His love for Israel is abiding. After evil has run its course, there will be a 400-year Messianic period to be followed by the Day of Judgment, the resurrection, and the creation of a new world. Similarly, the Testament of the Twelve Patriarchs hesitates between a Messiah out of the tribe of Levi and one from the tribe of Judah and presumably represents a reaction, first positive then negative, to the rule of John *Hyrcanus, the Hasmonean ruler.

Another characteristic of the apocalyptic books is their tendency to employ elaborate allegories and embellish the biblical stories with much legendary material designed to fill the lacunae in the biblical text. Mainly Pharisaic (although the Book of *Jubilees differs in places, particularly in calendar dating, from authoritative doctrine), these works often depict the Messiah as a supernatural being, and much is made of angels. The Book of *Enoch in particular, with its view of the Messiah as "the son of man," its portrayal of fallen angels, and its vision of final judgment, foreshadowed much of Christian thinking.

Ten books are regarded as apocalyptic works, to which must be added some of the Dead Sea Scrolls, particularly the War of the Children of Light against the Children of Darkness, and the so-called *Zadokite fragments. It is probable that there were others as well and that they, and perhaps some of the known works, were of a sectarian character. The rabbinic attitude of the times led to their disappearance in their original languages of Hebrew and Aramaic. Some polemical works, however, such as the *Sibylline Oracles and the Assumption of *Moses were written in Greek in Alexandria, but have come down with many Christian interpolations. Thus the style of the apocalyptic books cannot really be gauged, but the sweep of imagination and the structure of several of them is of a very high order (see *Apocalypse; *Apocrypha and Pseudepigrapha; *Dead Sea Scrolls).

HELLENISTIC LITERATURE

While some books, written originally in Greek and probably the works of the Alexandrian community, have already been referred to as apocryphal or apocalyptic literature, a large body of writings was the product of the several million Jews who between the third century B.C.E. and the first century C.E. took up their residence outside Ereẓ Israel in lands dominated by Hellenistic culture. They produced a considerable and distinctive body of literature, much of which has been lost. The Bible was translated into Greek and upon these translations were written exegeses and interpretations, all of them designed to meet the needs of Jews in Hellenistic lands and to offer apologetics for the Jewish religion, which was under assault from within and from without. As an extension of these needs, Jewish philosophy developed with the aim of harmonizing Jewish and Hellenistic thought. At the same time, historical and belletristic works were composed both for the benefit of the Jewish population and for apologetic purposes. Thus a body of writings developed which was to be a prototype for an elaborate literature that would be produced whenever Judaism, in later centuries, came into contact with other dynamic civilizations. Simultaneously, in Palestine, a literature designed essentially for Jews free from the problems of acculturation and assimilation was being developed in Hebrew and Aramaic. Its objective was the explication of Judaism in religious, legal, and homiletic terms; it was also a prototype for the expansive Jewish literature of the ages (see *Hellenistic Jewish Literature, *Apologetics).

BIBLE TRANSLATIONS

Greek

Literary undertakings of Hellenistic Jewry started in the third century B.C.E. with the translation of the Bible into Greek (*Septuagint). According to the Letter of Aristeas, which purports to be the account of the emissary of the king of Egypt, Ptolemy II Philadelphus (285–246 B.C.E.), to Eliezer, the high priest, Ptolemy commanded that 70 translators be engaged to render the Bible into Greek. The facts seem to be that the Bible translation was undertaken by savants of Egyptian Jewry to meet the needs of the Jewish population. The Septuagint, as the first translation of the Bible, had a significant effect and was employed as a pattern for subsequent translations. The Greek style is not distinguished since it relied heavily on Hebrew constructions. It was not a literal translation, however, since it incorporated commentary in the text, consciously attempting to harmonize biblical and Greek thought and to include halakhic and aggadic ideas which were current in Palestinian commentary. Some interesting features of the text are its deletion of all anthropomorphic expressions and the provision of many readings of the text which are different from the standard masoretic version. Whether this was because the translators worked with different texts is not clear, but the variants have provided fruitful interpretations of difficult biblical passages and material for speculation on how the biblical text developed.

Two other translations into Greek were undertaken in subsequent centuries because Palestinian rabbis deemed the Septuagint not to be altogether authentic and because it had become subject to interpolations and manipulations by Christians. At the behest of R. Eliezer b. Hyrcanus and R. Akiva, *Aquila, a Greek-speaking native of Pontus and a proselyte, undertook a new translation at the beginning of the second century C.E. The result was a literal translation, incorporating many of the rabbinic interpretations. It was widely used and approved, but has disappeared, and only fragments are retained in the writings of *Origen (185–254 C.E.), one of the Church Fathers. The translation of Theodotion (about 200 C.E.), another proselyte, has also been lost, except for his version of the Book of Daniel. It was however integrated by the Church into a revised version of the Septuagint (see *Bible, Translations).

Aramaic

The translations of the Bible into Greek, undertaken in Alexandria, were paralleled in Palestine by translations (Targums) into Aramaic. Presumably, the same need for understanding the Hebrew text motivated the Aramaic translations, and in consequence, particularly in Babylonia, it became customary to read the Targum together with the original text. The standard Aramaic translation of the Pentateuch is Targum Onkelos which is printed in almost every edition of the Hebrew Bible. The Talmud ascribes it to a proselyte named Onkelos who worked under the direction of Joshua b. Hananiah and Eliezer b. Hyrcanus at Jabneh in the first third of the second century C.E. More probably, however, it was a standardization of translations which had continued for decades or even centuries. Like the Aquila translation, it gives a literal rendition of the text but adds halakhic interpretations and aggadic embellishments wherever they are deemed necessary to present the Bible in the best possible light. Anthropomorphisms are thus avoided and the biblical figure Rachel "takes" the teraphim rather than "steals" them (Gen. 31:19); the phrase "visiting the iniquity of the fathers upon the children" (Ex. 34:7) is rendered with the addition "when the children follow the sinful ways of their fathers." Another translation called the Targum Yerushalmi (the Palestinian Targum), known also as Pseudo-Jonathan (probably due to an early printer's error), is essentially a compilation of freely rendered passages of the Pentateuch rather than a translation. It bears the homilist stamp and is replete with midrashic, aggadic, and halakhic statements. From internal evidence it appears that it must have been finally redacted in the seventh century in Palestine, but that it contains layers of interpretations from centuries past.

The standard Aramaic translation of the Prophets, though ascribed by the Talmud to *Jonathan b. Uzziel, a pupil of Hillel, was probably an ordering of earlier material rather than the work of one man. It resembles the Onkelos in phrasing but makes more frequent use of aggadic material. It is particularly important for exegesis because it deviates frequently from the masoretic text and agrees with the Septuagint and with other sources which are unknown.

The translations of the third section of the Bible, the Hagiographa, are of uncertain origin and authorship and are incomplete. Except for the translation of Proverbs, which is quite literal, they make extensive use of the *aggadah*. The books of Daniel, Ezra, and Nehemiah, which were partly written in Aramaic, were not translated (see *Bible, Translations).

EXEGESIS

The great exegete of Hellenistic Jewry, *Philo of Alexandria (c. 30 B.C.E.–42 C.E.), sought to provide an interpretation of the Bible which would be acceptable in terms of Hellenistic thought. He wrote or began a commentary on the entire Pentateuch, but only parts of the commentary on Genesis and Exodus have survived (in an Armenian translation and a Latin translation). He also undertook an outline of Mosaic legislation which was supplemented by treatises on politics, on teaching virtue, and on the creation. A commentary on Genesis, his major exegetical work, consists of essays on various subjects such as the immutability of God and the value of sobriety. Philo's approach to the Bible was allegorical. Thus he interprets "Adam, where are thou?" as Adam being the symbol of wicked man who hides from the voice of Reason. *Ḥameẓ* is a symbol of passion and *matzah* of purity of soul. Despite his allegorical view, he insisted that the laws be obeyed literally and his interpretations show an awareness of the halakhic and aggadic interpretations which were current in Palestine (see *Bible, Exegesis).

PHILOSOPHY

Formal Jewish philosophy begins in the Hellenistic world as a result of the confrontation with another culture. Among the first philosophers is *Aristobulus (c. 150 B.C.E.) who sought to demonstrate the dependence of peripatetic philosophy upon Mosaic law. Philo, the major philosophic figure, exerted little direct influence upon Judaism, but much upon the history of philosophy and upon Christian thought. Concerned with the problem of the relation of a perfect God to an imperfect world, Philo proposed a series of intermediate causes, of which the main one is the Logos, described variously as the word of God, the supreme manifestation of divine activity, and as moral law. It is the chief medium through which God created the world. In Philo's philosophy there is in man, as in the universe, a dualism between the soul and the body, the spiritual which is good and the material which is evil. The greatest good for man is contemplation, but the basis of practical ethics is duty, induced by education and habit (see Jewish *Philosophy).

HISTORY

Between 200 B.C.E. and 100 C.E. a considerable body of Jewish historical works was written, but after this 300-year period Jewish historiography lapsed for almost two millennia, not to be taken up again until the 19th century. There are records and fragments of the work of *Demetrius, an Alexandrian (early third century B.C.E.), on the kings of Judah, and of *Eupolemus (middle of the second century B.C.E.), a Palestinian, on the same subject. The Letter of Aristeas is the source of the familiar story about the Septuagint, although it was probably written between 200–100 B.C.E. Philo also wrote history, describing contemporary events, and several poets apparently took events in Jewish history as themes, the most notable being *Ezekiel, whose drama *Exagoge* ("The Exodus") appeared about 250 B.C.E.

The most notable historian of the period was *Josephus whose major works, *The Wars of the Jews* (seven vols.), the *Antiquities of the Jews* (20 vols.), *The Life*, and *Against Apion*, were widely read and quoted throughout the ages. The books were at once a defense of the conduct of Josephus in the war against Rome (66–70 C.E.), a generally affirmative presentation of Judaism to the pagan world, and a defense of the doctrines of Judaism. One of the few Jewish sources for the postbiblical period, Josephus' works incorporate a great deal of aggadic material, but fail to give a sufficient view of the spiritual life of Jewry at the time. Essentially a political history, the material on the Great *Synagogue, the *soferim*, a group of scribes, and the nonpolitical talmudic sages is quite meager. His contemporary, *Justus of Tiberias, who wrote on the same themes, may have offered a different account, but his works were lost. The historical works of the period generally attempted to evolve a philosophy of Jewish history and through their apologetics show Judaism to be historically more significant and of a truer religious perception than the paganism which dominated the ancient world (see *Historiography).

HALAKHAH AND AGGADAH

The Bible, as the fundamental document of Judaism, became, in the course of time, the base of an inverted pyramid out of which a vast and varied literature developed that included law, theology, ethics, philosophy, poetry, and grammar. The most significant body of literature, extending over a period of 1,000 years (500 B.C.E.–500 C.E.), was a corpus of writing called **halakhah* and **aggadah*. Based on the Pentateuch, it was rooted in the tradition (set forth in the Mishnah, Avot 1:1) that Moses received not only a Written Law at Sinai but also an Oral Law which was transmitted to leading figures, including the prophets, of successive generations.

Save for stray references, there is no knowledge of the Oral Law during the First Temple period. Talmudic traditions, however, ascribe the beginning of great expansion in the Oral Law to Ezra (c. 450 B.C.E.), the *soferim*, and to the Great Synagogue. Employing the method of Midrash (from the root *darash*, to search out), they established the process of extending and detailing the law and set the pattern of finding biblical support for new practices and for some which had already become normative. Among their enactments were the public reading of the Torah with accompanying interpretation, the organization of the daily worship pattern, and the building of "fences" (cautionary rules and legislation) around the Torah.

A supreme court, the *Sanhedrin, headed by **zugot*, pairs of scholars, continued the work of the *soferim* from about 200 B.C.E. The last pair, *Hillel and *Shammai (fl. 20 B.C.E.–20 C.E.) were two of the greatest figures in the development of the law. During this 200-year period religiopolitical parties developed in Palestine whose differences were partially based on the interpretation and application of Jewish law. The major parties, the *Pharisees and the *Sadducees, alternated in ascendancy, but dominance in the religious legal field ultimately fell to the Pharisees, while the Sadducees became the major force in civil affairs. When the Jews lost their independence, the sphere of the Pharisees ultimately became primary and the talmudic record of the period reflects their dominance. Nonetheless, there were different strands of thought within the Pharisaic movement and the leading figures, Hillel and Shammai, represent different emphases which were perpetuated by their disciples. On the whole, the school of Hillel tended to be broader and more lenient in its interpretation of the law than the school of Shammai which was more literal in the application of biblical texts. The convention of the Talmud ultimately became that the ruling of the school of Hillel (presumably the majority) was accepted as law.

Hillel formalized the development of the *Oral Law by establishing seven rules of interpretation of the Torah which he and others employed as a measuring rod for the *halakhot* or laws which were being developed. The effect of the method and the authority of figures like Hillel became evident with the acceptance of the Hillelite ruling of *prosbul* which, in response to the economic needs of the time, enabled debtors and creditors to circumvent the explicit biblical law of the sabbatical year limitation on debts. His great disciple, *Johanan b. Zakkai, in the last decade of his life when the Temple was destroyed, initiated one of the great revolutions in Jewish history by transferring the seat of Jewish authority to Jabneh. He established there a Sanhedrin, which functioned like a senate, for Jews both inside and outside of Palestine. The need to define Jewish patterns anew led to a marked expansion of the Oral Law, which was accomplished by five generations of *tannaim*. Leading figures were Eliezer b. Hyrcanus and Joshua b. Hananiah in the first generation; their disciples Akiva and Ishmael; R. Akiva's disciples Meir, Judah, Simeon, and Yose b. Halafta. The major personality of the fifth generation was Judah ha-Nasi (135–219).

Simultaneously with the growth of the *halakhah*, another oral tradition, that of *aggadah* (from *hagged*, to impart instruction), was developed. A vast body of literature, it may be grouped under two major headings: legendary-historical material and ethicoreligious literature.

The legendary-historical material has ancient origins and comprises stories and chronicles in which the lives of biblical figures and biblical episodes are elaborated and accounts of national and personal trials, crises, and salvations are given. It often suggests a kernel of historical fact. Much of this material made its way into the Apocrypha and into the Targums. But, there were, in addition, special collections of the early talmudic period: the **Megillat Ta'anit*, organized around special days celebrated as minor feast days and special fast days; **Seder Olam* ("The Order of the World"), a chronicle of events in Jewish history from creation to the time of Alexander, which both records and interprets events and is ascribed to Yose b. Ḥalafta (middle of the second century).

The ethicoreligious *aggadah* concentrates on a philosophy of life and faith, with practical and metaphysical implications. Often cast in a semi-poetic form or in an aphoristic style, it includes fables and parables. Though some has been lost, much *aggadah* has been preserved in the Talmud and in the collections of Midrashim. Two of its finest works are *Pirkei *Avot* ("The Sayings of the Fathers"), a work of the Mishnah, and the **Avot de-Rabbi Natan* ("The Teachings of the Fathers According to the Collection of Rabbi Nathan"). Written in an aphoristic style, the works include much of the ethics and some of the theology of the talmudic sages. The *aggadah* generally employs the Bible as its frame of reference and represents the homiletic interpretations of preachers in the synagogue on Sabbath afternoons. They also resorted to **gematria* (using the numerical value of the letters for interpretation) and other devices. Since they were the works of preachers, they responded to events of the time, to the mood of people, and to the need to communicate faith and values. Stories, parables, and epigrams are therefore characteristic forms employed in the literature.

The oral tradition in *halakhah* and in *aggadah* became too complex as the decades went by and the difficult circumstances in Palestine, with periodic revolutions and the disruption of academies, finally made it imperative that the material be reduced to writing. This process essentially, though not entirely, concentrated on the halakhic material which represents the actual laws by which life was governed.

Halakhah

The compilation of the oral *halakhah* resulted in three bodies of works: "motivated *halakhot*," the Mishnah, and the Tosefta.

"MOTIVATED *HALAKHOT*." In "motivated *halakhot*" a rule of law was set forth together with the appropriate biblical verses and their interpretations. They include the **Mekhilta*, organized around the Book of Exodus and attributed to R. *Ishmael b. Elisha of the third generation of *tannaim*; the **Sifra*, a collection based on Leviticus attributed to R. Judah of the fourth generation; and the **Sifrei* material on the Books of Numbers and Deuteronomy, collected by R. Simeon of the same generation. In all probability these men were the original compilers and redactors, while the finished products were the work of later hands (see **Halakhah*).

MISHNAH. The greatest body of law, the Mishnah, is a compilation of "unmotivated *halakhot*," that is, material not related to a text. The work was begun in various academies, notably those of Akiva of the third generation, and of his disciple, Meir, in the second century C.E. Meir apparently developed a very complete work. The final redaction of the Mishnah however was by Judah ha-Nasi who was head of the court, the academy, and the Jewish civil government. He was a man of wide culture and organizing talent and while he based himself on the compilation of Meir, he studied in various academies and assembled different collections of *mishnayot* before he began his own work. In the Mishnah he redacted, which was the product of a collegium, the Oral Law was organized into six major orders (*sedarim*): (1) *Zera'im* ("seeds"), detailing agricultural laws and precepts connected with agriculture (e.g., *berakhot*, prayers, and blessings); (2) *Mo'ed* ("festival"), on the laws of holidays and the Sabbath; (3) *Nashim* ("women"), involving family law; (4) *Nezikin* ("damages"), including civil and criminal law, courts, and legal procedure; (5) *Kodashim* ("holy things"), dealing with sacrifices, the Temple service, and dietary laws; and (6) *Tohorot* ("purifications"), on ritual purity and impurity. The *sedarim* were divided into tractates (*massekhtot*) of related materials; a total of 66 tractates were compiled. These were subdivided into chapters (*perakim*) which were divided into sections (*mishnayot*).

The Mishnah was designed to organize a body of scattered material, to set forth a code for practice and for judgment, and to provide a code for study. It was intended to be all-inclusive in the sense that it dealt even with matters which were no longer observed, such as the laws of sacrifice. Simultaneously, however, it was exclusive in that it set an order of importance and left out thousands of *halakhot*. It was decisive in that it made rulings on matters which had been in dispute. But it was designed to promote development, as well, and therefore included minority opinions, and cited their proponents. While the Mishnah was essentially a legal document, it devoted a tractate (*Pirkei Avot*) to ethical statements and emphasized, in various tractates, certain dogmas, such as the unity of God, providence, reward and punishment in this world and the hereafter, freedom of will, the doctrine of the Messiah, and resurrection. Fundamental to its thinking was the notion that the Torah was revealed and every word of it was subject to interpretation; that the Oral Law was equally revealed and had been transmitted; that the Mishnah, which embodied it, therefore enjoyed authority; and that the sages had a right to interpret the law. The entire work, written in a direct and lucid Hebrew, was completed about 200 C.E. The Mishnah with later elaborations, the *Gemara*, represents hundreds of years of lawmaking and has been the decisive corpus of writings in Jewish life for almost two millennia (see *Mishnah).

THE TOSEFTA ("ADDITIONS"). This body of literature includes many of the *halakhot* omitted from the Mishnah, as well as elucidations of mishnaic statements and some *aggadah*. The work was begun by *Ḥiyya b. Abba and Oshaiah (Hoshaya) Rabbah, disciples of Judah ha-Nasi, but the final redaction probably took place about 500 C.E. (see *Tosefta).

TALMUD. The Mishnah had scarcely been completed when the process of expanding the Oral Law began. This activity resulted in a vast body of literature known as the *Gemara* (from the Aramaic *gamar*, to learn). The impetus came from the fact that the Mishnah was concise and, therefore, needed explanation; that there were thousands of *halakhot*, known as *beraitot* (*baraita*), which had not been included in either the Mishnah or the Tosefta and had to be reconciled with the Mishnah; and that new problems arose in daily living which demanded new solutions. These elements were particularly evident in Babylonia where the problem of maintaining Jewish law in the midst of a society governed by other laws was immediate. The classic formulation of R. *Samuel (Mar; 180–254), *dina de-malkhuta dina* ("the law of the land is law") so far as nonreligious matters are concerned, is an attempt at dealing with the question. There were, however, many other problems and the need to deal with them, as well as the conviction that the Jew's highest purpose was to study God's law, produced an extensive body of debates, decisions, obiter dicta, and historical material.

Two *Gemarot* were formulated: a shorter work developed in Palestine and known as the Jerusalem Talmud; and a longer body of writing, the product of the Babylonian community where perhaps a million Jews lived and which was studied throughout the ages. These *Gemarot* together with the Mishnah are collectively known as the Talmud.

There are *Gemarot* for 39 mishnaic tractates in the Jerusalem Talmud and for 37 tractates in the Babylonian Talmud. Presumably, there must have been *Gemarot* for all of the 66 tractates of the Mishnah but some of them may have been lost and others, such as the tractates dealing with *tohorot* (laws of purity and impurity) and *zera'im* (agricultural laws, tithes, and sabbatical year), may have been discarded as no longer pertinent to post-Temple days. The missing *Gemarot* are not necessarily the same in the two Talmuds. Thus the Babylonian Talmud has *Gemarot* for the order of *Kodashim* (dealing with the Temple cult), while those of the Jerusalem Talmud, mentioned by early authorities, were lost. The Jerusalem Talmud has *Gemarot* to the ten tractates of the order of *Zera'im*, whose laws were observed in Palestine in post-Temple days, and there is only one such *Gemara* (*Berakhot*) in the Babylonian Talmud.

The pattern of the text in both Talmuds is to record a Mishnah and to follow it with the *Gemara* discussion and debate. While the Mishnah bases itself upon the Bible, the *Gemara* bases itself upon the Mishnah as its authority, although in certain matters requiring clarification or in developing new *halakhot* it refers back to the Bible. The usual order of the text is to analyze the Mishnah and to broaden the debate by citing a *baraita* (an external *halakhah* not recorded in the Mishnah) which may then also be subject to analysis and to opposing statements. Connections are often loose because the oral tradition relied heavily upon memory. In consequence, while a series of unrelated statements of one man may be cited in full, probably only one of them is connected with the matter under discussion. This may expand into an explanation of the meaning of the other statements and their application which may prompt aggadic interpolations for several lines or pages. Then the halakhic theme is picked up once again, and usually, but not always, a halakhic decision is rendered. Both Talmuds contain much of *aggadah*: stories, philosophizing, proverbs, ethical maxims, historical information, medical and scientific observations, and practical advice for daily living. There is a certain amount of humor, considerable wit, and some sharp satirical comments. Approximately one third of the Babylonian Talmud and one sixth of the Palestinian Talmud are comprised of *aggadah*. The style of both Talmuds tends to be terse.

Jerusalem Talmud. The Jerusalem Talmud is the product of five generations of *amoraim* who conducted their studies at various academies. The major centers at first were Sepphoris, Galilee, the seat of the patriarchate, Judea, and later Tiberias, whither the patriarchate was transferred. Leading figures of the first generation were Ḥanina b. Ḥama, Yannai, Bar Kappara, Oshaiah Rabbah, and *Joshua b. Levi. *Johanan Nappaḥa and *Simeon b. Lakish were second generation notables in whose lifetime the academy at Tiberias became the major center, attracting students from Babylonia as well as from all over Palestine. This period represents the peak of creativity for the Jerusalem Talmud. The succeeding generations also produced men of note, among them Ammi, Assi, *Eleazar b. Pedat, Zeira, and *Abbahu (of Caesarea) who was the acknowledged leader of Palestinian Jewry. He was a diplomat and a formidable controversialist in polemics with Christians.

By the beginning of the fourth century, the condition of Jews in Palestine had begun to deteriorate due to heavy taxes, a worsening of the economic situation, more frequent persecutions, and the hegemony of Christianity which had now been established by a decree of Constantine. The situation was not propitious to learning or to the maintenance of the academies and many scholars immigrated to Babylonia. The decision was therefore made to reduce to writing the oral debates and decisions of the past five generations. The redaction seems to have been undertaken by Yose b. Bun and to have been completed about 365 C.E.

The Jerusalem Talmud is only about one eighth the size of the Babylonian Talmud and its intellectual, dialectical, and logical quality is inferior. Its explanations of the Mishnah tend to be direct and terse but at times seem cryptic. This was partly because subjects which called for debate in Babylonia were self-evident in Palestine where the terrain and the conditions were better known, and partly because of indifferent editing. Subjects are often juxtaposed without any connection between them; *halakhot* are neither introduced nor elaborated; and only parts of quotations are given. Clearly, the redaction was undertaken by a community under stress which was losing its grasp and authority to the extent that it abandoned the fixing of the calendar by witnesses and resorted to mathematical calculation.

Babylonian Talmud. The Babylonian Talmud was composed under more felicitous conditions. The community enjoyed size and stability, academies like Nehardea and Sura, later Pumbedita and Maḥoza, and an autonomous government under the leadership of the exilarch. The foundations of the Babylonian Talmud were laid by *Rav who had studied with Judah ha-Nasi, and by Samuel (Mar). Rav was a specialist in religious law, an aggadist, and a liturgist of note, while Samuel, the major authority in civil law at the time, was also famed as an astronomer and physician. Their disciples included Rav *Huna and Rav *Judah b. Ezekiel, who founded the academy at Pumbedita and developed the dialectical method which won for the sages of Pumbedita the reputation that they could cause "an elephant to go through the eye of a needle." Huna expanded the academy at Sura so that it had 800 students. Their successors, *Rabbah Nahamani and *Joseph b. Ḥiyya, developed their methods. Rabbah evolved the dialectical approach to a point where the subject matter of the Talmud increased to such an extent that in part it became independent of the Mishnah. Joseph excelled in accumulated knowledge, basing his teachings upon tradition, thus providing a rein to the exuberance of Rabbah. The fourth generation of scholars, in the first part of the fourth century, *Abbaye and *Rava, also expanded the subject matter and dialectical acuteness of talmudic study. The succeeding generations produced such notable figures as *Papa (b. Naḥman) and *Naḥman b. Isaac. It came to be clear, however, that the mass of material was too great for oral transmission and that systematization was needed. The redaction was undertaken by *Ashi (335–427), who became president of the academy of Sura at the age of 23, but a large group of scholars who met twice a year in Adar and in Elul, known as the *kallah* months, also engaged in the work, which lasted 30 years. At this time full academic sessions were held for the dispersed students who were often business and professional men and who otherwise pursued their studies at home. A tractate was edited at each session. After the edition was completed, all the tractates were revised, a process which apparently lasted another 30 years. Further editing and supplementation of the basic material was under the leadership of *Mar Bar Rav Ashi,*Meremar, and particularly *Ravina b. Huna who died in 499. In the following year (500) *Yose, his successor, declared the Talmud officially closed.

The Babylonian Talmud is much better edited than the Jerusalem Talmud. It was redacted over a period of 100 years, so that there was ample time for editing and revision. Logical connections are sought, quotations are complete, editorial explanations abound, and decisions on law are given. While the style is often verbose, the approach is subtle and highly dialectical. Material is analyzed minutely, hypotheses are offered and tested, and discussions are carried through. As in the Jerusalem Talmud, the language is Aramaic, but while the Palestinians employed the Western Aramaic dialect the Babylonians used Eastern Aramaic. In both there is an admixture of Hebrew, but the Babylonian text has a great deal more. The completed Talmud is more than a legal work; it reflects the Jewish view of God, man, and society; of theology and ethics; of Jewish values and of the way they were exemplified in daily life. While it is the work of many generations, it represents only the elite fraction of the population both in ability and in consideration for the people. The Talmud in its time elevated religious scholarship to the highest calling in Jewish life, and the long-term effects of this view have been evident ever since. For 15 centuries the Talmud has been the major concern of Jewish studies and the major guide to Jewish life. Judaism is far less the child of the Bible than that of the Talmud. If the Bible is the base of the Jewish structure, the Talmud is the house within which the Jews have dwelt (see *Talmud).

Aggadah

MIDRASHIM. The same concern for preservation which led to the compilation of the Oral Law caused the *aggadah* to be organized and committed to writing. While much of it was contained in the Talmud, it was widely scattered and not suitably arranged for reference. Both the scholar and the ordinary Jew had a need for works in which the interpretations of the Bible would be arranged according to books, chapters, and verses. The scholars required it to facilitate finding and comparing interpretations; the laymen needed it because the aggadic statements were major formulations of Jewish ethics, theology, and values, but at the same time were light reading and provided assurances and comfort in the dark hours which Jews, particularly those in Palestine, were experiencing.

The midrashic literature was compiled in places as diverse as Palestine, Babylonia, and Italy, approximately between the sixth and twelfth centuries, although much of the material is of an earlier date. Written largely in Aramaic, though some of the compilations have a considerable admixture of Hebrew, it consists largely of homilies preached by rabbis in synagogues on Sabbaths and festivals and at study classes. Unlike modern preachments, they involved not only the Pentateuch and the books of the Prophets, but the Hagiographa which was read in the synagogue on Saturday afternoons, the time when sermons were given. The Midrash does not contain complete sermons, but rather the core of ideas, insights, illustrations, and special interpretations upon which the sermon was based. The sermonic technique was to take a point of interest to the listener and to cast new light upon it or to relate it to other matters. The universal subjects of discourse were the Bible or Jewish observance and law. The sermon usually began by pointing out contradictions or similarities in widely scattered parts of the Bible or by raising a question of law, resolving it, and then proceeding to consider moral and religious aspects of the matter. Stories, poetic statements, parables, and epigrams were employed by gifted preachers (see *Aggadah, *Midrash).

Midrash Rabbah. The first major compilation was the **Midrash Rabbah* ("The Large Midrash"), so designated because of its length. It consists of Midrashim to each of the books of the Torah and to each of the five *megillot*. Internal evidence indicates that the earliest Midrash, **Genesis Rabbah*, dates from the sixth century and the latest, **Numbers Rabbah*, from the 12th. Most of them were composed in Palestine, although several seem to have been subjected to Babylonian re-editing. In many of the *Rabbah* Midrashim the homiletic commentary technique is used whereby a series of comments refer to a specific verse. **Leviticus Rabbah, Numbers Rabbah*, and **Deuteronomy Rabbah*, however, use the sermon method. They select a verse or two from the Torah reading of the Sabbath, adduce various comments, skip the rest of the verses, and proceed to verses derived from the next Sabbath reading. The triennial cycle, customary in Palestine, is the Torah order followed.

Tanḥuma-Yelammedenu. Another major midrashic compilation is the **Tanḥuma-Yelammedenu* cycle on the Pentateuch of which three versions are extant, either in part or whole. The original version was probably compiled in Palestine in the sixth century; the other two also seem to be products of Palestine but are probably late ninth-century. It is possible, however, that they may be from Babylonia and southern Italy. The *Tanḥuma* title is derived from Tanḥuma b. Abba, a noted Palestinian aggadist of the fourth century who is frequently quoted. The title *Yelammedenu* ("let our master teach us") refers to a formula frequently employed in the book which involved the raising and answering of a halakhic question after which the discussion branched off into *aggadah* and commentary.

Pesikta. The midrashic cycle *Pesikta* (*paska*, "to divide") has two versions: the **Pesikta de-Rav Kahana*, probably compiled in Palestine before the end of the seventh century, and the **Pesikta Rabbati*, which records the year 845 as the date of composition and in its use of Hebrew and of snatches of rhymed poetry gives evidence of having been influenced by the Palestinian Hebrew poetry school which began to flourish in the seventh century. The material consists of homilies on the Torah and prophetic readings for festivals and for special Sabbaths.

Other Homiletic Midrashim. In addition to these general compilations, there seem to have been in earlier times Midrashim on all the prophetic and hagiographic books, most of which have been lost. Extant are **Midrash Tehillim*, consisting of homilies; **Midrash Proverbs*, which is more in the nature of an aggadic commentary and is replete with parables, apothegms, and short homiletic interpretations; **Midrash Samuel*, a Midrash on Samuel I and II, a collection of sermons involving references to one or two verses. All three works are of 10th- or 11th-century origin and were probably compiled in southern Italy.

The characteristic patterns of all the midrashic cycles is their focus, either by way of commentary or sermon, on biblical verses and their reflection of the thinking and experiences of many generations. They are interrelated in a peculiar sense; they plagiarized from one another, sometimes even to the extent of bodily lifting passages. The *Tanḥuma* borrows from the *Pesikta de-Rav Kahana* and the *Pesikta Rabbati* from the *Tanḥuma*; the later books of the *Midrash Rabbah*, on Exodus, Numbers, and Deuteronomy, borrow heavily from the *Tanḥuma*. All of them derive a great deal of material from the scattered references in the Talmud (see *Homiletic Literature; *Preaching).

Non-Homiletic Midrashim. In addition to the homiletic Midrashim, there are midrashic works of another kind, e.g., the eighth-century Hebrew work **Pirkei de-Rabbi Eliezer*, in which biblical narratives serve to teach ethical and religious lessons on such themes as the Sabbath, reward and punishment, paradise and hell, and Messianic doctrine. It also discusses cosmogony, astronomy, and the calendar; abounds in legends and stories, many of them ancient and similar to stories in the Apocrypha; and is written in a poetic style. The resort to numbers as a form of organization is an interesting device and the use of numerical groups, especially of seven and ten, is common. It was probably written in Palestine. A book of a similar stamp, *Seder Eliyahu*, by Abba Elijah, a tenth-century Palestinian, is divided into two parts (*Rabbah*, large and *Zuta*, small) and includes a moral discourse on Torah, the love of Israel and of mankind, and the love of God. Written in Hebrew in a poetic style, it makes great use of stories and parables. Other midrashic compilations of the eighth, ninth, and tenth centuries, of undetermined authorship and provenance, are about Moses, Solomon, the Messiah, and paradise and hell. Later midrashic works rearranged traditional material and supplemented it. Such works were composed by *Moses ha-Darshan of Narbonne and Rabbi Tobiah of Germany, both of the 11th century. A more significant work, **Yalkut Shimoni*, by Simeon Karo (13th century), drew heavily on the Talmud and on many midrashic compilations. Karo organized a compendium of aggadic statements and commentaries on all the 25 books of the Bible.

In a sense midrashic literature has never ended since homily, commentary, and elaboration on biblical themes continue to be creative activities. Jewish and Christian traditions have drawn heavily on the midrashic literature whose roots are in deep antiquity. The Midrash lent color and variety to Jewish tradition; concentrated on ethical and theological problems; recorded and interpreted difficult episodes of Jewish history; and enriched Jewish culture. It was particularly sustaining to the average Jew, man and woman alike, who was not at home in halakhic literature. He drew his philosophy and his sense of worth and purpose from the stories, parables, proverbs, and intuitive insights in which midrashic literature abounded.

MEDIEVAL PERIOD (500–1750)

A characteristic feature of Jewish history is that while Jews lacked stability and experienced declining fortunes in one land, they prospered or were tolerated in another. In consequence, there was always one major center, and usually two or three, where Jewish literary creativity continued unabated. In the 1200-year period which constitutes the Jewish Middle Ages, Babylonia, North Africa, Spain and Provence, the Franco-German area, and Italy were the major centers. There were intermittent periods of significant literary activity in Palestine and, after the expulsion of the Jews from Spain, in the Eastern Levant, including Palestine, Turkey, and Egypt, which became centers for a century or two. From the 16th century onward Germany declined for about two centuries while the Slavic countries rose to a prominence both in literary productivity and in Jewish population which they retained until the 20th century.

On the whole, Jewish productivity was greatest and most varied in lands which were part of the mainstream of history, and declined as it began to bypass those countries. The most notable examples are Babylonia and Spain at the height of Arab culture and the most marked exceptions are Slavic countries where the general cultural level was low, but where Jewish literary productivity, concentrating almost exclusively on rabbinics, was high. One important factor which should be noted is that contact between Jewish communities was considerable and that what was produced in one land had an effect upon Jewish literature in other countries. There seems, in the earlier period, to have been two particular streams of influence – one flowing from Palestine into Italy and then into the Franco-German area, and the other stemming from Babylon, flowing through North Africa into Spain.

In the Middle Ages, as in antiquity, Jewish literature constituted several layers. As the Bible was the basis for the Mishnah and the Mishnah for the *Gemara*, the total tradition was the basis for the literary labors of the Middle Ages, much of which concentrated on the explication of the Bible and the Oral Law through grammar, exegesis, commentary, philosophy, mysticism, and liturgical and didactic poetry. Secular poetry, prose, and science were ornaments of the religious tradition which by the Middle Ages had become complex and stratified. Fundamental to the literature was a belief in the revealed Torah, God's providence, the chosenness of Israel, the coming of the Messiah, and the restoration to the Land of Israel. These ideas were examined, but never seriously disputed until the modern era. They reflected a national characteristic, manifested both in law and literature, which called for life to be lived and coped with, no matter what the circumstances, and which assumed that the details of living, according to the Torah, could be spelled out. In the same spirit, the many *kinot* ("lamentations") written during the Middle Ages were rarely overwhelmingly pessimistic and despairing.

The literature will be organized here into categories of writing. Obviously, there were interrelationships and effects which, however, cannot be noted; only highlights can be mentioned. Thus grammatical writing influenced Bible exegesis and poetry; rabbinics influenced Bible exegesis; and the impact frequently was all the greater because many of the writers were versatile, writing in many fields. Thousands of works have been lost and thousands more cannot be mentioned. The literary productivity of a small group, highly literate and dedicated to study, was phenomenal.

The question of language also deserves attention. Jews wrote in many languages, but mostly in Hebrew, Aramaic, and toward the end of the period, in Yiddish and Ladino. Much, however, was written in Arabic, and some in other languages. This multiplicity of languages points to another feature of Jewish literary activity which cannot be dealt with here. Since Jews were dispersed through many countries, were multilingual, and moved from land to land, they performed a major function as cultural intermediaries, translating from one language to another and making the riches of one culture available to the other. A third linguistic feature of significance is that the Hebrew language after the talmudic era, when it lapsed as a literary language, suddenly came to life in the early Middle Ages, notably in Palestine and Spain. Most of the great works during the entire 1200-year period were written in Hebrew.

GRAMMAR AND LEXICOGRAPHY

The formulation of rules of grammar prompted by a need to study and understand the Bible was basic to the revival of Hebrew as a literary language. The renewed interest in Bible study due to a controversy with the Karaites, who rejected the Oral Law and insisted that the Bible alone was authoritative, was sparked by the realization that the rabbinic position had to be defended. Such an examination inevitably led to the formulation of rules of language. It was further motivated by the fact that the correct reading of the Bible, in its vowels, accents, and *keri* (the way a word was read), as against *ketiv* (the way a word was written), was an oral tradition and needed to be set down, since Jews were dispersed in many lands. Finally, Arabic culture, which stressed poetry, and consequently grammar, had a major impact in those centers of Jewish life – Babylon, Palestine, and Spain – which came under Arab rule.

The first philological effort was the *masorah, a collective work of many generations. While its origins date back to Ezra, significant masoretic activity began in the sixth century, continuing to the tenth, and was concentrated in Palestine and Babylonia. The work resulted in a definition of vowels, accents, *ketiv*, and *keri*. It noted all exceptions in spelling and peculiarities of words and orthography. Through the use of accents, correct relationship of words and thought were achieved and the chant for biblical reading was fixed. In effect, the relating of words was itself a form of biblical commentary. Ultimately, all the masoretic works were compiled by Jacob b. Ḥayyim, an Italian scholar, and printed in the *Bomberg edition of the Bible (1525). The notes which were designed to clarify the text and to prevent further errors were of three kinds: the masorah *parva* ("small"), printed in the outer margin; the masorah *magna* ("large"), printed in the inner margin, or above, or below the text; and the masorah *finalis* at the end of the text, which also included an alphabetical list of word peculiarities. Since the masorah is a collective undertaking, few of the scholars who worked on it are known. However, the Tiberian school, where the major work was done, recorded the names of Pinḥas (eighth century) and Asher the elder (eighth century), the first of a family who for six generations labored on the masorah. Aaron *Ben-Asher (beginning of the tenth century) substantially brought the masoretic work to a close. Literary work on the masorah is found in Europe as late as the 12th century, and still later Elijah *Levita (1468–1549) published the *Masoret ha-Masoret*, in which he explained how to read and use the masoretic material.

The formal foundations of grammar and lexicography were laid in Babylon by *Saadiah b. Joseph Gaon (tenth century) in *Agron*, a dictionary, and in *Sefer ha-Lashon* ("Book of the Language"), a work on grammar. His most notable successors were *Menahem b. Jacob ibn Saruq of Spain whose Hebrew work *Maḥberet* ("Joined Words") is a dictionary of biblical language and a grammar. Judah *Ḥayyuj (end of the tenth century), writing in Arabic, established the principle of the bilateral Hebrew root and Jonah *Ibn Janaḥ almost completed the structure of Hebrew grammar in *Book of Critique* (in Arabic), in which he laid the groundwork of Hebrew syntax. A century later David *Kimḥi of Provence rearranged and expanded Ibn Janaḥ's study in his *Mikhlol* ("Compendium"), a grammar and dictionary of roots. In the 14th century Joseph ibn *Kaspi of Provence attempted a logical structuring of words and grammar, a venture which was repeated more elaborately by Isaac Profiat *Duran (15th century), who in *Ma'aseh Efod* ("The Work of the Ephod") combined logical structure with an elaborate philosophy of language. The last major grammatical authority of the Middle Ages was Elijah Levita, whose *Meturgeman* ("The Interpreter") is the first dictionary of the Targum (see *Hebrew Language).

BIBLE EXEGESIS

Simultaneously with literary creativity in grammar there was a development of biblical exegesis. The same scholars were often active in both fields. Four major methods of commentary were developed: *peshat* ("plain sense"), *derash* ("aggadic interpretation"), *remez* ("allegory and philosophy"), and *sod* ("mystical interpretation"). Here, too, the versatile Saadiah b. Joseph Gaon laid the foundations with his translation of the Bible and his commentaries in Arabic in a work most of which has been lost. The greatest figure of the era, *Rashi, wrote a phrase-by-phrase commentary on almost the entire Bible which was a harmonious blend of *peshat* and *derash*. His commentary was popular for many generations so that *Ḥummash* (Pentateuch) and Rashi became almost synonymous. His major rival, Abraham *Ibn Ezra (12th century) of Spain, a poet, grammarian, and scientist who was a master of grammar and Hebrew, chose the path of *peshat*. His commentary is lucid although occasionally he permitted himself veiled allusions to doubts he entertained about the text. He commented on the entire Bible but only the works on the Pentateuch, Isaiah, and some of the Hagiographa have survived. Preeminently an intellectual's commentator, Ibn Ezra was the subject of supercommentaries.

Another major commentator who is usually associated with the above-mentioned scholars is David Kimḥi, who emphasized *peshat*, but also resorted to aggadic and philosophic interpretations in his commentaries on the prophets, Psalms, Genesis, and the Books of Chronicles.

While the above are the best exponents of the *peshat* and *derash* methods, they based themselves on precursors. There were also contemporaries who pursued the same paths, and successors who adopted their methods. Thus, Rashi's grandson, R. *Samuel b. Meir, wrote extensive commentaries on the Bible in the *peshat* method. As mystical and philosophical tendencies were manifesting themselves in the Jewish world, the other two approaches (*sod* and *remez*) also began to be employed. *Sod* owed much to the rise of *Kabbalah, of which the *Zohar (itself a sort of commentary on the Torah) was the outstanding work of the period. Meanwhile the approach and spirit of *Maimonides' *Guide of the Perplexed*, which centered about the philosophic exposition of many biblical passages, gave impetus to *remez*. The major commentary in the mystical spirit was the work of *Naḥmanides (13th century), a major figure of Spanish Jewry. His commentary on the Pentateuch reflects the belief that the Torah is capable of yielding many meanings to the initiated, and he therefore offers multiple interpretations in the spirit of *halakhah*, *peshat*, and mysticism. His mysticism is, however, limited since he believed that mystic teachings in their full strength should be confined to an elect, and that the masses should be taught a Judaism based upon faith, piety, and reason. His younger contemporary, *Baḥya b. Asher, took the mystical approach further in his commentaries, and *Jacob b. Asher, the noted codifier, utilized the techniques of *gematria* (devising meanings from the numerical value of the words) and *notarikon* (employing initial or final letters of words to discern hidden meanings).

The outstanding exponent of the philosophical school was *Levi b. Gershom of Provence. Commenting on all the

Bible except the Latter Prophets, he attempted to find speculative truths in it, to ascertain the principles of ethics, and to supply reasoned interpretations of biblical precepts. His commentary enjoyed a high repute among Jewish intellectuals. To a lesser degree, the commentaries of Joseph b. Abba Mari Kaspi employed the same approach and enjoyed a similar reputation.

The last great commentator of the period was the statesman and financier, Don Isaac *Abrabanel of Spain. At home in both Christian and Jewish exegesis and in general literature, he brought all of these into play in his commentaries, which covered the entire Bible. In his approach he first posed a series of questions arising out of the text and then proceeded to resolve them through the use of philosophy, theology, history, and modified mysticism. Apart from his singular method, he is noted for devoting considerable attention to the problems of political philosophy and historical chronology (see *Bible, Exegesis).

POETRY

The Arabic influence and the renaissance of the Hebrew language also led to a remarkable flourishing of Hebrew poetry in the Middle Ages. An equally important factor was the structuring of the prayer book and the liturgy (at that time still fluid) which occurred during these centuries, when thousands of poems which became part of the liturgy were being composed. In this field there was continuity rather than innovation, since the composition of liturgy had persisted throughout the talmudic period. However, the writing of secular poetry – love songs, wine songs, didactic poetry, epigrams, and the like – represented a new development whose immediate origins may be traced to Arabic influence and whose remote roots may be found in the poetry of the Bible.

The characteristic forms of medieval Hebrew poetry are partly influenced by the Bible, but more by Arabic literature and, at the end of the period in Italy, by European forms like the sonnet and the tercet. Biblical poetry, based on parallelism, had occasionally used both the alphabetical form and rhyme. Medieval Hebrew poetry, while using some parallelism, employed the alphabetical form (forward or backward), the acrostic, rhyme, and meter as its characteristic elements. Rhyme, both in poetry and prose, was relatively easy due to the Hebrew suffixes; thus variant and more complicated forms developed. Palestinian and West European poetry tended to use the simple rhyme, while Babylonian and notably the Spanish poetry used the two- and three-syllable rhyme. Masters of the language, the Hebrew poets prided themselves on the ability to use the same word, with different meanings, for rhyming. Meter, introduced by *Dunash b. Labrat (tenth century) and current mainly in Spain, was essentially spondaic and iambic, but was employed in complicated forms so that 19 (or according to some 52) different meters developed. Trick poetry was also composed, often of surprisingly high quality, such as the "*Elef Alfin*" of Abraham *Bedersi in which each word of a 1,000-word poem begins with the letter *alef.*

The major types in medieval Hebrew poetry, secular verse and *piyyut*, ranging from doggerel to moving lyrics and to long, beautiful philosophical poems, were frequently composed by the same poets. The combination, however, was largely confined to Spain, Provence, and Italy. The Palestinian and Franco-German poets were essentially *paytanim* and their poetry was generally inferior in quality to that of their Iberian coreligionists. Both secular and religious poetry drew extensively on the same sources and employed biblical and aggadic phrases allusively in order to display technical mastery.

The liturgical poems composed in Palestine in the seventh and eighth centuries mark the beginnings of medieval Hebrew poetry. Some were anonymous, like "All the World Shall Come to Serve Thee" of the Day of Atonement service, but most of them can be attributed to three poets, *Yose b. Yose, *Yannai, and Eleazar *Kallir (ha-Kallir). Their compositions are standard prayers in the High Holy Days *maḥzor* and in the festival services. Yose is the author of the *Avodah* (a Temple service poem) recited on the Day of Atonement and Kallir wrote the *Geshem* ("Rain") prayer recited on Sukkot. The influence of Palestine was felt most notably in Italy (and from that country in the Franco-German area), which always followed of Palestinian developments and learning. In both areas there were families of *paytanim* who continued to compose *piyyutim, seliḥot* ("penitential verse"), and *kinot* in successive generations. Notable among them was the *Kalonymus family whose founder, *Meshullam, composed works in Italy and whose descendants moved to Germany at the end of the tenth century. In Germany Meshullam (c. 976), his son Kalonymus (c. 1000), the author of *U-Netanneh Tokef,* a prayer in the High Holy Days *maḥzor,* the latter's son, *Moses (c. 1020), and grandsons Kalonymus and Jekuthiel (c. 1050), were prolific in their writing of *piyyutim.* Other prominent poets in France and Germany were *Gershom b. Judah and *Ephraim of Bonn, the author of the *Hymn of Unity.* In later periods these countries produced hundreds of *paytanim.* Virtually every scholar tried his hand at this form of writing, including Solomon *Luria, Samuel *Edels, and Yom Tov Lipmann *Heller.

Spanish, Provençal, and later Italian poetry can claim many distinguished poets who wrote both religious and secular poems. They were men of varied accomplishments, very much at home in all the intellectual and social worlds of their time. The first major Hebrew poet of Spain, *Samuel ha-Nagid (11th century), vizier of Granada, a military commander and a talmudist, wrote extensively but his works have only recently become fully known. They include sacred poetry, reflections on war, love poems, wine songs, elegies, and three volumes of imitations of the books of Psalms, Proverbs, and Ecclesiastes. His younger contemporary, Solomon ibn *Gabirol, who died at an early age, is one of the outstanding figures of Hebrew poetry. Dexterous in the use of language and a master of every form of rhyme and meter, Gabirol wrote on all themes. His few surviving secular poems on nature, love, wine, and death are gems of their kind. His poetic genius found, however, full expression in his religious poetry and in several long philosophical poems of which *Keter Malkhut* ("The Royal Crown") is his most consummate work. The poem masterfully integrates the poet's great philosophical and scientific knowledge to create a lofty ode to God.

Moses *Ibn Ezra covered the gamut of secular and religious poetry. Author of more than 6,000 verses, he wrote about "wine and the delights of men," "the world and its vicissitudes," and "poems in praise of the creator." Many of his verses are reminiscent of Omar Khayyam, although Ibn Ezra's range, his delicacy of fancy, and use of imagery exceed the poetic quality of the Persian poet. His masterpiece, *Tarshish*, composed of 1210 verses, shows a great variety in language and themes. His religious poems are at once philosophical and deeply moving.

The peak of Spanish poetry is found in the harmonious verse of *Judah Halevi. Rejoicing in life, love, and friends and passionate in his quest of God, Halevi wrote of God and man with equal felicity. Love of Zion, expressed in several poems whose theme is "I am a harp for thy [Zion's] songs," also characterizes the work of Halevi. These poems, as well as his religious verse, have been incorporated into the liturgy.

Another great Spanish poet, Abraham Ibn Ezra, wrote on a wide variety of subjects. His secular poetry, while embracing conventional themes, displayed a mastery of style, form, and language, and a great capacity for wit and satire, turned as frequently against himself as against others. His religious poetry, however, is deeply fervent and moving, ranging from the lyrical to the philosophical. A restless traveler whose journeys took him to Babylonia and Persia, Ibn Ezra also roamed through the realms of the imagination. "The Letter of Hai ben Meliẓ" is an allegory in rhymed prose of a journey through three worlds.

The last major poet of Spain, Judah b. Solomon *Al-Ḥarizi, the author of *Taḥkemoni* ("Book of Wisdom"), wrote in *maqāma* form (rhymed prose) frequently interspersed with verse. The poems embraced devotional and love poetry, satire and narrative; some were riddles, others proverbs. The *Taḥkemoni*, consisting of 50 chapters, each devoted to a different subject and treated in a variety of forms, displays remarkable linguistic skill, manipulation of biblical phrases to serve unusual ends, wit, and great literary variety.

While poetry continued to be written in Spain for another two centuries, the golden age had passed. The poets of southern Spain, like Meshullam *da Piera, engaged largely in polemical verse as part of the *Maimonidean controversy; others, like Abraham b. Samuel *Ibn Ḥasdai and Shem Tov b. Joseph *Falaquera, wrote didactic poetry. In northern Spain, Solomon da *Piera (14th century) made his mark primarily as a religious poet, although he composed secular poetry as well. Solomon *Bonafed (15th century) wrote secular poetry. In one of his poems lamenting the decline of poetry, he incidentally left a record of Hebrew literature of the 14th and 15th centuries. In Provence medieval Jewish literature was distinguished by the Bedersis: Abraham (13th century) and Jedaiah (14th century), his son.

The major center of Jewish poetry from the 13th century onward was Italy, where *Immanuel of Rome wrote his *Maḥbarot*, following Al-Ḥarizi in the use of the *maqāma* form. Buoyant, gay, and sorrowing by turns, employing varied meters and diverse forms (including the sonnet), the *Maḥbarot* touches on widely different subjects and satirizes and parodies other poets. Two unusual features are that his love songs are highly erotic, and that the last of the 28 chapters is an imitation of Dante's *Divine Comedy*. Immanuel of Rome had no immediate successors of distinction; Moses *Rieti (15th century), however, modeled his *Heikhal* on Immanuel's imitation of Dante. After a period of decline, Italian poetry revived with Leone *Modena (mid-17th century) and notably with the brothers Jacob and Emmanuel *Frances (17th century). While Jacob wrote excellent caustic polemic poetry directed against the Shabbatean movement, his brother composed religious and secular verse in various styles, including a substantial number of epigrams. With Moses *Zacuto (17th century) Italian medieval poetry came to an end. Although he introduced poetic drama into Hebrew literature, Zacuto was a poet rather than a dramatist: *Yesod Olam* ("Foundations of the World") and *Tofteh Arukh* ("Hell Prepared"), his two dramas, resemble the medieval miracle play in form and development of plot.

A brief period in the composition of poetry in Palestine developed under the influence of the kabbalists. Israel *Najara wrote a substantial body of religious poetry. Employing Turkish, Arabic, Greek, and Italian forms and meters, Najara's themes were God, Israel, and the redemption. Many of his works are essentially love poems to God and a considerable number were incorporated into the liturgy, including the Sabbath table hymn *Yah Ribbon* (see *Poetry, Medieval; *Prayer).

RABBINIC LITERATURE (500–1250)

The most voluminous body of writings in the medieval period was the legal rabbinic literature consisting of commentaries, codes, and responsa. The number of writers probably runs into the thousands. Beginning with the *geonim* in Babylonia, the activity extended into every country, embracing the Slavic states, which became the major centers toward the end of the period. Due to its scope and quantity, this literature will be divided into two chronological sections: 500–1250 and 1250–1750.

Commentary

The first activity took place in Babylonia where in the ninth century the *gaon* *Ẓemaḥ composed an *arukh* ("A Prepared System") which was both a dictionary and a commentary on talmudic phrases and selected passages. Not long thereafter, Saadiah wrote brief commentaries (in Arabic), which have been lost, on several tractates. *Hai Gaon in his commentaries on large parts of the Talmud (not all are extant) explicated words and phrases and paraphrased passages in the Talmud. This pattern became the model for the commentaries of the

North African and Spanish schools which were in close contact with Babylonia.

In Babylonia, the talmudic tradition was kept alive in the very institutions where it had been nurtured and the need for commentary, therefore, was not great. However, in the newly developing centers, commentary was essential. Abraham *Ibn Daud associates the beginning of talmudic learning and academies outside Babylonia with four rabbis who set out from southern Italy, were captured, and ultimately dispersed to Cordova, Kairouan, and Alexandria. According to another tradition, at the end of the eighth or ninth century the Kalonymus family migrated to Mainz, in Germany, where an academy was founded. Whatever the case, by the tenth century talmudic learning was established in all these places.

From Babylonia, commentary activity passed first to Kairouan where R. *Hananel b. Ḥushi'el (11th century), employing the method of Hai, commented on several *sedarim* of the Talmud. He was however more elaborate in his paraphrase, often compared the discussion on the same subject in the two Talmuds, and gave a *pesak* ("decision") at the end of each discussion. His contemporary, *Nissim b. Jacob, pursued the same method in elucidating the Babylonian Talmud, but made more extensive comparisons with the Palestinian Talmud and tannaitic Midrashim. Other distinguished 11th-century figures were Spanish Jewish scholars. Isaac b. Jacob *Alfasi, the most eminent among them, had emigrated to Spain from Fez in 1088. His great work, *Halakhot*, a compendium of the Talmud, is a combination of code and commentary; it became a basic text for talmudic studies and was the subject of numerous supercommentaries. His immediate disciple, Joseph ha-Levi *Ibn Migash, also employed the method of paraphrase in his commentaries on many tractates.

A new method was introduced by *Maimonides of whose commentaries on three talmudic *sedarim* only fragments have survived, but whose commentary (in Arabic) on the Mishnah is complete. Maimonides applied logic and systematization to the Mishnah, analyzing the principles of Oral Law, classifying the *halakhot*, offering logical sequence for the order of the Mishnah, and providing a historical survey. He was concerned with aiding the ordinary student and in consequence was at pains to indicate the law in each case and to incorporate the relevant material from the *Gemara*.

In the Franco-German region, commentary was developing along different lines. At the academy of Mainz, headed by *Gershom b. Judah, hundreds of students engaged in the study of the Talmud. They took notes (*kunteresim*) on the lectures delivered, and the Commentary of Rabbi Gershom is in fact a collection of several generations of such *kunteresim* based on the teachings of R. Gershom b. Judah or his disciples. The academy developed the Franco-German system of running commentary on words and phrases, a method for the training of scholars, in contrast to the Spanish method which sought general principles under which particulars were organized and were designed as a resource for students who only learned periodically. The most notable representative of the Franco-German method is Rashi whose commentary on almost all tractates appears side by side with the text in every major edition of the Talmud. It reflects his capacity for lucidity, brevity, penetration to the heart of a matter, and is a notable example of pedagogy. Several commentators, members of Rashi's family, followed his method and rounded out his work. Among them were *Judah b. Nathan and Samuel b. Meir. Talmudic commentary in the Franco-German region however took a different turn in the commentaries known as the *tosafot* ("additions"). The tosafist undertook to restore the *Gemara* method: he raised questions about the text and resolved them, following the order of the *Gemara* page by page. The *tosafot*, a product of several generations, appear side by side with the text in all the standard editions. The major scholars who initiated the method and are quoted frequently were *Meir b. Samuel of Ramerupt and his three sons Samuel, *Isaac, and particularly Jacob (Rabbenu *Tam). The next generation produced the great luminary *Isaac b. Samuel of Dampierre who is quoted almost as frequently as Jacob b. Meir. Under the leadership of figures like *Samson b. Abraham of Sens, *Moses b. Jacob of Coucy, and *Meir b. Baruch of Rothenburg, tosafist activity flourished until the beginning of the 14th century.

Simultaneously with Franco-German scholarship there was considerable talmudic activity in Italy where *Nathan b. Jehiel of Rome (11th century) wrote the *Arukh*, a dictionary-encyclopedia of the Talmud which is the basis for all modern talmudic lexicography. Nathan explicated words and passages, quoted and cited authorities and comments which would otherwise have been lost, and in his explications and elucidations used comparative philology. Contemporaries and successors have imitated him and the tosafist school. A major figure of the next generation was *Isaiah b. Mali di Trani, the author of *Tosafot Rid*. In Provence, situated midway between the Spanish and Franco-German centers, academies also flourished and the methods of both northern and southern schools were employed. Zerahiah b. Isaac *Gerondi ha-Levi (12th century) in *Sefer ha-Ma'or* composed an analytical commentary on Alfasi which combined critical evaluations of earlier and contemporary commentaries with additions to Alfasi. *Abraham b. David of Posquières (12th century), the leader of the anti-Maimonides school, commented on several tractates of the Talmud and on the *Sifra*, and wrote a severe criticism on Maimonides' code.

Codes

The need for codes arose out of the demands of life: the Jewish community was dispersed and thus lacked readily available authority; the law had also become increasingly complex and required codification. The first responsa were written in Babylonia and were often intended for far-flung Diaspora communities. *She'iltot* by R. *Aḥa (Aḥai) Gaon of Shabḥa (eighth century) deals with the *mitzvot* as they are arranged in the Pentateuch and organizes the relevant talmudic material under those headings. It is assumed that the work, consisting of 171 discourses, originally dealt with the entire 613 commandments. Rabbi Aḥa initiated the method of codification in which decisions and sources are given. Another method is that of *Yehudai Gaon, head of the academy of Sura (757–61), in whose **Halakhot Pesukot* ("Halakhic Decisions") only decisions are handed down. The third major codification, the **Halakhot Gedolot* ("Large *Halakhot*"), ascribed by some to Simeon Kayyara (eighth century), compiled and organized under single headings the scattered material in the Talmud on given *mitzvot*. The order of the talmudic tractates is followed, except for the laws relevant to the Temple, which are omitted, with the author modeling himself on the *She'iltot* and quoting extensively from the Talmud. During the following century, *Amram b. Sheshna Gaon, adopting the method of Yehudai Gaon, wrote his *Seder* ("Ordering"), a code on the prayer book. Starting with general principles, Amram deduced subsidiary laws, which he subsequently divided into classes. Hai Gaon, the last *gaon* of Pumbedita, wrote a series of codes on civil law.

The great codes, however, were the products of other lands. Isaac b. Jacob Alfasi's *Halakhot*, partly commentary but mainly code, is an abridgment and paraphrase of the Talmud section by section which adheres to the main line of discussion of the Mishnah and comes to a conclusion about the law. Alfasi thus provides a basis for decisions, but fails, as the Talmud does, to achieve an orderly systematic discussion of all aspects of a subject. Such a systematization is the work of Maimonides in his *Mishneh Torah* ("The Second Law"). The code brings the entire body of Jewish law into an orderly and systematic arrangement, including laws which were omitted by Alfasi and his predecessors. It sets forth divergent opinions, decides between them, and renders clear decisions. Maimonides' work encompasses the Talmud, the *geonim*, and the works of other scholars. He bases himself upon the 613 precepts, but organizes them according to his own system: God and man, the life of the individual, laws relating to the Land of Israel, and laws relating to society. While the work was widely accepted and remains one of the monuments of Jewish literature, it also evoked opposition from those who feared it would supplant the study of the Talmud. It has one grave drawback, however, in that it fails to indicate the sources for the rulings, and it was this deficiency, plus the fact that new problems constantly arose, which led to the development of other codes (see *Maimonidean Controversy).

The Franco-German school followed different criteria and did not attempt to formulate an overall code of the scope and system of that of Maimonides, but many less comprehensive codes were written. *Isaac b. Abba Mari of Marseilles (12th century) in *Ittur Soferim* ("The Crowning of Scholars"), a code on civil law, marriage and divorce, and dietary laws, adopts the source method, including under each subject treated the relevant talmudic, geonic, and Alfasi discussions. *Ha-Terumah* ("The Heave-Offering") by *Baruch b. Isaac of Worms, dealing with dietary, Sabbath, and marriage laws, uses the code method; the work presents a selection of the best scholarship of his generation. More decisive was the **Maḥzor Vitry* of Simḥah of Vitry. Organized around the liturgy and the religious cycle, it cites prayers and laws and is a major work in the history of liturgy, as well as a significant source for geonic and midrashic texts which have otherwise disappeared.

An effort on a broader scale was made by *Eliezer b. Samuel of Metz in *Sefer Yere'im* where he attempted a complete code; he organized the material along the lines of Maimonides but cited sources verbatim. A code distinctively Franco-German in tone is that of *Eleazar b. Judah of Worms, *Roke'aḥ* ("A Compound of Spices"), which deals with the entire body of religious laws. The work, a pure code, without quoting sources, is at the same time a compendium of customs and practices which reflect the daily life of the period. Its pervading spirit, neither intellectual nor purely legal, is one of deep medieval piety which mirrors the effect of the Kabbalah in daily life (see *Codification of Law).

Responsa

Huge and varied, responsa literature is usually precisely what the name implies, responses to legal questions which were asked by individuals and communities. It is rarely an organized or systematic body of scholarship. Many responsa were written but many were undoubtedly lost and others have never been printed. Only a small amount of this vast body of writings is extant. The importance of the responsa is not only legal, but historical. They constitute source material for virtually every phase of Jewish life, since the responsa often involved comment upon community conditions.

The gaonate in Babylonia, the recognized authority for world Jewry for several centuries, produced a vast body of responsa of which only a few hundred have survived. On the whole they are very brief and direct. Many of them standardized synagogue practices and worship throughout the Jewish world. The famous responsum of Amram Gaon to a Spanish community was of this order. Other major writers of responsa were *Sherira Gaon and Hai Gaon. In North Africa, Alfasi left a considerable collection of responsa in Arabic as did his Spanish student, Joseph ibn Migash, and Maimonides, who wrote in Arabic as well as in Hebrew. *Mikhtav li-Yhudei Teiman* ("Letter to the Jews of Yemen") is a famous example of Maimonides' responsa. In France, Rabbi *Gershom b. Judah and Rashi wrote numerous responsa, which were not collected, but are referred to and quoted by others, as are the responsa of Kalonymus and Meshullam. By the 12th century, responsa had become lengthy essays written in Hebrew and incorporating an analysis of relevant material. They also began to be preserved by the authors themselves. There are collections of Jacob b. Meir Tam and of Solomon b. Abraham *Adret (13th century) of Spain, who wrote approximately 7,000 responsa. Meir of Rothenburg (13th century) of Germany, Jacob b. Moses *Moellin (14th–15th century), and Israel *Isserlein (beginning of 15th century) of Vienna also wrote extensively. Moellin insisted that responsa, as case law, were more important than the codes. In the 14th and 15th centuries Joseph *Colon, the great writer of responsa of Italy, *Isaac b. Sheshet, and his younger contemporary Simeon b. Ẓemaḥ *Duran of North Africa, greatly enriched responsa literature (see *Responsa).

RABBINIC LITERATURE (1250–1750)

The second half of the Jewish Middle Ages was marked by a heightening of persecution, an increased physical, social, and intellectual isolation of the Jews in most countries, and a consequent turning inward to peculiarly Jewish studies. It was characterized too by the rise to eminence of new Jewish centers, most notably those in Eastern Europe and the Turkish Empire, embracing Palestine. The production of rabbinic literature was vast, numbering thousands of works. Only a few of the major efforts can be considered here and they will be discussed chronologically rather than by country. This approach may be adopted the more readily since by the end of the 15th century Spanish Jewry had disappeared or been dispersed and German Jewry had declined in creativity.

Commentary

The significant commentators of the 13th century were Spanish Jews. Naḥmanides, a pupil of *Jonah b. Abraham Gerondi, adopted the French method and wrote extensive *novellae on three major orders of the Talmud, providing decisions as well as raising and resolving difficulties found in the Talmud. His disciple Solomon b. Abraham Adret wrote novellae to 16 tractates of the same three major orders of the Talmud, but was more analytical than his master and more given to straight commentary. He selects passages from virtually every page of the Talmud for his novellae. At the beginning of the 14th century *Asher b. Jehiel was the most eminent commentator. Originally from Germany, he became rabbi of Toledo in 1304 and enjoyed a reputation which brought students to his academy from all over Europe. Unconcerned with the sciences, opposed to philosophy, he concentrated his attention on the Talmud. His greatest achievement was a code, but he also wrote *tosafot* (glosses and remarks), which are characterized by simplicity and logic, to 17 tractates and commentaries to several tractates of the Talmud and to several orders of the Mishnah. Other scholars of the period were Meir b. Todros ha-Levi *Abulafia of Toledo whose *Yad Ramah* followed the old Spanish method of summary and comment, and Menahem b. Solomon *Meiri don Vidal of Provence, who wrote commentaries on all the tractates of the Talmud. Lucid and systematic in style, he adopted the approach of Maimonides. He introduced each section – whether tractate, chapter, or Mishnah – with a statement of its themes, and while his discussion centers on the Mishnah, he also gives the gist of the *Gemara* and the decision.

In the 14th century, Rabbi *Yom Tov b. Abraham Ishbili, a disciple of Solomon b. Abraham Adret, continued the novellae method, writing on the three major orders of the Talmud. His contemporary, *Nissim b. Reuben Gerondi, a major force in Spanish Jewry, not only wrote novellae on the same orders but composed one of the two major commentaries on Alfasi. His student Joseph *Ḥabiba completed the work on Alfasi and concentrated particularly on the classification of decisions, a practice which made him a favorite of later codifiers.

During the 15th century, a period of turmoil, significant scholarship declined but was again prominent in new centers in the 16th century. Obadiah of *Bertinoro, who had moved from Italy to Jerusalem, wrote his major exposition on the Mishnah, which is the standard commentary included in all editions. It discusses every order and does not only explain the words, but explicates entire passages, illuminating them with the discussions of the *Gemara*. Another commentator of the East, Bezalel *Ashkenazi of Egypt, in *Shitah Mekubbeẓet* excerpted and arranged the interpretations of a large number of commentators on difficult passages of the Talmud. He employed *tosafot*, Arabic commentaries, and commentators who were not well known and whose work would otherwise have been lost.

The 16th century also saw the rise of Poland as a major center of Jewish learning. The migration of German scholars to Poland initiated a period of activity which continued until the tragic end of Polish Jewry in the 20th century. In 1507 Jacob b. Joseph *Pollak, the most eminent of these scholars, headed the academy at Cracow where he continued his work for three decades. He developed the method of *ḥilluk* in the study of Talmud, i.e., division and analysis. It consisted of taking an apparently unified talmudic subject, dissecting it into its component parts, drawing shades of distinction, and building up a new subject out of the newly defined parts. Pollak, however, left no books. His younger contemporary, Solomon b. Jehiel *Luria, the first important talmudic commentator of Poland, wrote *Yam shel Shelomo* which is essentially a code and partly a commentary, on seven tractates of the Talmud, presented in a plain, non-pilpulistic style. A second work, *Ḥokhmat Shelomo*, consists of glosses and comments on the entire Talmud, on Rashi, and on *tosafot*. The great merit of the work is in its corrections of the texts, and it is considered so significant that the relevant comments are incorporated at the back of each talmudic tractate. The novellae of Meir b. Gedaliah *Lublin and Samuel Eliezer *Edels, two important scholars of the next generation, were essentially comments on Rashi and *tosafot* rather than on the *Gemara*. Those of Edels, more deeply penetrating, applied the tosafist method of posing challenges to the text in order to arrive at a new and more cogent answer.

Leading lights of the 17th century were Yom Tov Lipmann *Heller and Meir b. Jacob ha-Kohen *Schiff. Heller, in response to the need of Mishnah study groups, which had become common, and to what he felt were inadequacies in previous commentaries, composed a major commentary on the Mishnah, entitled *Tosafot Yom Tov* ("The Glosses of Yom Tov"). Basing himself upon Obadiah of Bertinoro's commentary, he expanded the material and introduced philosophic and ethical views. Schiff wrote extensive and very terse novellae on the entire Talmud with the intention of setting forth plain meaning, but only the comments on ten of the tractates remain, the others having been destroyed in a fire in 1711.

Penei Yehoshu'a, an 18th-century collection of novellae to most of the Talmud by Jacob Joshua *Falk, is distinguished by keen analysis and brilliance. The work has remained an accepted reference book for students of the Talmud. Ezekiel b. Judah *Landau (18th century), whose major reputation is that of a writer of responsa, and who was considered the leading rabbinic authority of his time, also wrote a highly pilpulistic collection of novellae, *Ẓelaḥ* (in Hebrew the initials of "Monument to a Living Soul").

Codes

Works of codification exceeded books of commentary during this period. The code of Maimonides, since it lacked sources and was a specifically Sephardi work, did not end the process of code making. Codes continued to be written among Franco-German and Spanish Jews, and at the end of the period, among Jews in Poland. The form followed the pattern of the previous era: a compendium, a digest of the talmudic discussion, arrangement according to the precepts of the Torah, arrangements according to the order in the Pentateuch, and compilation of groups of kindred laws. In the Franco-German region the first great code of the period was *Sefer Mitzvot Gadol* ("The Large Book of Precepts," also called *Semag*), by *Moses b. Jacob of Coucy (13th century). Basing himself on the 613 precepts, which he divided into affirmative and negative precepts, Moses distinguishes six categories of laws and in giving both the law and the sources, relies not only on the Talmud, but on later authorities as well. He does not limit himself to legal matters only, but discusses beliefs and ethics and cites Jewish philosophers. The Hebrew style is clear and excellent, and is similar to that of Maimonides. The *Semag* was inevitably followed by the *Semak* (*Sefer Mitzvot Katan*, "The Small Book of Precepts") by *Isaac b. Joseph of Corbeil (late 13th century). The book, designed for the scholarly layman rather than the scholar, classifies Jewish law into seven categories, but is much more sparing in the citation of sources than the *Semag*. Two other distinguished codes of the 13th century were *Or Zaru'a*, by Isaac b. Moses of Vienna, and *Mordekhai*, by *Mordecai b. Hillel ha-Kohen of Nuremberg. *Or Zaru'a*, a compendium rather than a code, cites sources copiously. It is intended for scholars, and is particularly useful because of its extensive resort to post-talmudic sources and decisions. *Mordekhai* is badly arranged and seems to be a source book for a code rather than the finished product. It comprehends, however, a great mass of material and cites many responsa on the subjects it treats. Both works were employed extensively by later codifiers as sources.

The 13th-century Italian school is represented by the *Shibbolei ha-Leket* of Zedekiah b. Abraham *Anav in which the author limits himself to the rituals and festivals. Employing the code method, he also presents a selection of material from other codes and responsa, including the opinions of Italian scholars. A digest of it, entitled *Tanya*, designed for popular use, was prepared by Jehiel b. Jekuthiel *Anav.

The great codes of the period were composed by Spanish Jews. They tend to be more systematic, less rigorous in decision, and less guided by custom than the Franco-German works. Among the 13th-century codes were some small works by Naḥmanides and the *Torat ha-Bayit* ("Household Laws"), by Solomon b. Abraham Adret, devoted to laws of the Jewish home. Adret, applying the same method, commented and interpreted extensively. He also wrote a résumé which appears in the margin of the book. Particularly noteworthy is the pedagogical work, *Sefer *ha-Ḥinnukh* ("Book of Education") attributed to Aaron ha-Levi of Barcelona which arranges the *mitzvot* according to the weekly portions of the Torah, discusses their origin, their ethical meaning, and their application. He does not quote sources, but indicates where they may be found. The book, written in excellent Hebrew, was and continues to be popular. The first major 13th-century code, *Piskei ha-Rosh*, the compendium of Asher b. Jehiel, a German-trained scholar who immigrated to Spain, bears the imprint of both the German and the Spanish schools. Its great value is that while it follows the Alfasi method of paraphrasing the Talmud section by section, it goes far beyond that. Alfasi relies on the Talmud, the *geonim*, and himself. Asher b. Jehiel brings to bear all the weight of preceding codes, commentaries, and responsa, with particular emphasis on the discussions of the Franco-German schools. Enjoying great authority, the decisions of the work are quoted in later codes and were used as a basis in *Sefer ha-Turim* (*Tur*) written by Jacob, Asher b. Jehiel's son. *Sefer ha-Turim* takes the rulings of Asher b. Jehiel as a basis for an entire code of Jewish law, excluding those which ceased to operate with the destruction of the Temple. The title refers to the four rows (*turim*) on the breastplate of the high priest. Jacob b. Asher consequently divided his code into four sections: (1) *Tur Oraḥ Ḥayyim* on daily religious conduct, the Sabbath, and the festivals; (2) *Tur Yoreh De'ah* on prohibited and permitted things, e.g., dietary laws, laws of purity, etc.; (3) *Tur Even ha-Ezer* on the laws of family relations; (4) *Tur Ḥoshen Mishpat* on civil law. The code provides decisions without sources and includes Franco-German and Spanish views. Clear in content, style, decision, and authority, it was accepted as the authoritative code by a large segment of Jewry for several centuries. The attempt by *Jeroham b. Meshullam of Provence, a pupil of Asher b. Jehiel, to codify *Piskei ha-Rosh* resulted in a pure code of all of Jewish law, except civil law, entitled *Toledot Adam ve-Ḥavvah*. The work was well regarded, but did not win general acceptance.

The work which finally became the decisive code of Jewry was that of Joseph b. Ephraim *Caro who was born in Spain and moved to Bulgaria, and ultimately to Safed. His great work, *Beit Yosef*, which Caro conceived of as a commentary to *Sefer ha-Turim*, was designed to include other opinions and to expand the source references in *Sefer ha-Turim*. It emerged, however, as an independent work which utilized the fourfold form of organization of *Sefer ha-Turim*, traced the development of laws, cited various opinions and the reasons for them, and finally concluded with Caro's decision. As a preparatory manual of study for the work, Caro composed the *Shulḥan Arukh which is arranged in the same way, but generally gives only one opinion and one decision and limits each paragraph to a specific point of law, a pattern which facilitates study and decision. In formulating decisions, Caro was guided by three earlier codes: Alfasi, Maimonides, and Asher b. Jehiel. His approach was to rely on any two opinions against the third. The code, essentially Sephardi in outlook, became the definitive code of Jewry and has remained so to the present day.

As it was written the Shulḥan Arukh was not acceptable to Franco-German and Polish (Ashkenazi) Jewry. Solomon Luria protested against it, and a way of meeting this protest was devised by Moses b. Israel *Isserles. Apart from other works, Isserles undertook an addition to the Shulḥan Arukh, *Mappat ha-Shulḥan*, in which he set forth the Ashkenazi view and, in cases of controversy, rendered decisions according to that outlook. In addition, he noted customs prevalent among Ashkenazi Jewry, raising many of them to the status of law. On the whole, he was more rigorous than Caro. But there are many instances where he is more lenient, notably in the case of *hefsed merubbeh*, instances involving a considerable loss. It was the Caro-Isserles Shulḥan Arukh which became the universal code.

While it was still struggling for universal acceptance, other codes were being formulated. The most important was *Levush* by Mordecai b. Abraham *Jaffe of Prague and Poland. He set out to create a code, midway between *Beit Yosef*, which he deemed too lengthy, and the Shulḥan Arukh, which he thought too brief. His method was to state a decision and to give the history of the law. His decisions frequently differed from those of Caro and Isserles. For a time, it appeared that this work might supplant the Shulḥan Arukh but in the end the Shulḥan Arukh prevailed, both because of the errors in *Levush* and because of the power of the combined authority of Caro and Isserles.

Although a definitive code had finally been produced, it proved, like all the others, to be imperfect both in itself and because new situations continued to arise for decision and codification. The result was that an entire field of commentaries on the various codes arose of which 186 commentaries on the Maimonidean code alone have survived, and there were doubtless many more. The first important commentary on the Maimonidean code, that of Shem Tov b. Abraham *Ibn Gaon (14th century) of Spain, entitled *Migdal Oz*, sought to classify Maimonides' way of reasoning in the code. Don *Vidal Yom Tov of Tolosa, Spain, defended the Maimonidean system in his *Maggid Mishneh* as did Caro in his *Kesef Mishneh*. *Sefer ha-Turim* was equally the subject of commentaries, the best known (apart from *Beit Yosef*) being *Darkhei Moshe* ("The Ways of Moses") by Isserles, which was essentially a polemic against Caro and was the foundation of his later glosses to the Shulḥan Arukh. The best commentaries on *Sefer ha-Turim* were those of Jacob Joshua Falk and *Bayit Ḥadash* by Joel *Sirkes. Falk added explanations, decisions, and sources to *Sefer ha-Turim*, while Sirkes sought to reestablish it as the decisive code in place of the Shulḥan Arukh.

The Shulḥan Arukh was also the subject of numerous commentaries which finally set the seal of authority upon it. David b. Samuel ha-Levi in *Turei Zahav* (abbr. as *TaZ* and meaning "Golden Rows") defended the rulings of the Shulḥan Arukh, quoted contrary opinions, and arrived at final decisions. *Siftei Kohen* (abbr. as *ShaKh* and meaning "The Lips of the Priest") was similarly motivated; it explained the sources of the code and attempted to harmonize the difference between Caro and Isserles. Characterized by intellectual brilliance and logical acumen, these works became the standard commentaries on the Shulḥan Arukh (see *Codification of Law).

Responsa

In the third major category of rabbinic literature of the period, responsa, there was remarkable productivity; the number of collections runs into several thousands, and thousands of others are still in manuscript. They were composed because life outstripped the codes and new problems arose which were either not properly dealt with in the codes or not included in them. Since the early Middle Ages every major rabbinic figure answered questions and the responsa, essentially essays in law, were collected either by himself or by others. These served as supplements to the codes and as bases for later codes.

Medieval responsa should be divided into two time periods: the 13th century to the end of the 15th, during which the rabbis responded to conditions in the Franco-German region and in Spain, and the 16th century through the 18th, when Jewish life was centered in the East, Germany, and Poland. Responsa reflect Jewish life of the times and thus differ greatly in content. The responsa from Spain and the East, where Jewish life was in greater contact with the surrounding world and enjoyed a larger measure of autonomy, testify to greater judicial authority, more severe punishments, better communal organization, and more cases dealing with moral behavior than other parts of the Jewish Diaspora. Spanish responsa also discussed questions of philosophy and theology, whereas the German-Polish questions centered mostly around law. The greater seclusion in Germany and Poland and the greater persecution are reflected in the frequent cases dealing with taxes, special levies, religious questions, cases of women whose husbands had disappeared (*agunot*), and the like (see *Responsa).

RESPONSA (1250–1500). The most important collections of Spanish responsa are those of Solomon b. Abraham Adret and Asher b. Jehiel. Adret's extant responsa number 3,000 of a possible original 7,000. Almost half of them deal with civil law and commercial affairs and thus reveal much about Jewish life in Spain. They reflect strong community organization, the power of leaders to fix prices, regulate promissory notes, and establish and prohibit study patterns. Philosophical and theological questions comprise another large section, including discussions on the relation between *mitzvot* and intention (*kavannah*). A third group deals with religious and family problems. Asher's 1,500 responsa are concerned essentially with *halakhah*. They indicate that Jews had and exercised the power of capital punishment, and that the community had great power to regulate economic, spiritual, and moral life. Two other collections of the period, those of Isaac b. Sheshet Perfet (14th century), a Spaniard who ultimately became rabbi of Algiers, and his successor Simeon b. Ẓemaḥ Duran, a mathematician and grammarian, reflect, apart from other matters, the turbulence of life in Spain at the end of the 14th century and the complicated problem of the Marranos. Duran also responded to many questions on mathematics and grammar.

The number of surviving collections of responsa from Germany (13th to 15th centuries) is not extensive but those that are extant are illuminating. Meir of Rothenburg wrote several thousand responsa on questions of lending with interest to gentiles, the duties and salaries of teachers, and the import and export business. Jacob Moellin left some 200 responsa on civil law and family life, and Jacob b. Judah *Weil, his disciple, deals extensively with community affairs. The responsa of Israel b. Pethahiah *Isserlein and Israel b. Ḥayyim *Bruna mirror the rigorous piety of medieval Germany, indicating the importance that customs assumed and their endorsement by the writers of responsa. During the same period Joseph Colon was writing responsa which reflect contemporaneous life in Italy. Among other things they point to the low scholarly level of the rabbinate in Italy, to the state of the medical profession among Jews, and to the fact that some physicians formed partnerships. The responsa of Judah b. Eliezer ha-Levi *Minz and Meir b. Isaac *Katzenellenbogen (16th century) broaden the picture of Italian Jewish life, indicating that the moral tone was rather lax in the upper stratum. The general tenor of the Italian responsa reflects, in contrast to Germany, a spirit of liberalism and a readiness to deal with problems arising out of the confrontation of Jews with the life of the general society.

RESPONSA (1500–1750). With the expulsion from Spain a large part of Spanish Jewry migrated to the East where an indigenous Jewish community had continued to exist. As a result intellectual activity greatly increased. Even before the exile, R. Elijah b. Abraham *Mizraḥi, a native of Constantinople and the chief rabbi of Turkey, had won a reputation as a major figure both in Jewish and secular learning. His responsa, reflecting Jewish life in Turkey, testify to the great autonomy enjoyed by the community. The rabbi was the recognized intermediary between the government and the community and the assessor of taxes for the Jews. Soon afterward David b. Solomon ibn Abi *Zimra, a native of Spain who had served as chief rabbi of Cairo for 40 years, became the leading Jewish authority in the East. His 3,000 responsa (of which 1,300 have been preserved) present a picture of life in Eastern lands. They indicate that polygamy was practiced, that the Jewish laws of emancipation regarding slaves were still in force, and that relations with Karaites were closer than they had been in earlier centuries, but had deteriorated since the time of Maimonides. Theological questions point to varied beliefs about dogma. Other important collections of the 15th and 16th centuries are those of Moses b. Isaac *Alashkar of Cairo, Jacob *Berab, *Levi b. Ḥabib, and Moses b. Joseph *Trani. The responsa of Trani have some particularly interesting comments about the role of Jews in the export trade and about a boycott organized by Turkish Jewish traders, at the instigation of Dona Gracia *Nasi, against the papal port of Ancona, Italy, as a reprisal against the pope for the burning at the stake of Marranos there (see *Responsa).

METHODOLOGY

A fourth area of rabbinic study, methodology, namely the rules of talmudic logic, the terms employed, and how decisions are made, which had scarcely been touched during the early Middle Ages, developed considerably in the 18th century. *Samson b. Isaac of Chinon (France) and *Jeshua b. Joseph ha-Levi of North Africa had dealt with the subject in the 14th and 15th centuries, respectively. The first major work on methodology, however, was *Yad Malakhi*, by *Malachi b. Jacob ha-Kohen (middle of the 18th century), which discusses 667 talmudic rules and terms, arranged in alphabetical order. Some sections are extended essays, such as the essay on the authenticity of halakhic statements which were transmitted by disciples in the name of their teachers. Another part of the book discusses the methods of the great codifiers. Isaac *Lampronti of Italy, in *Paḥad Yiẓḥak*, the second major work of the period, has arranged all the subjects and terms treated in talmudic and rabbinic literature in alphabetical order. Included also are talmudic sources and the views of codifiers and writers of responsa.

Philosophy and Theology

While there was less Jewish philosophical than exegetical, halakhic, and poetic writing in the Middle Ages, it was nonetheless substantial and of high quality. As in the Hellenistic period, medieval Jewish philosophy was born out of confrontation with other cultures. By the eighth century, Aristotle and Plato had been translated into Arabic, and Islam was trying to reconcile religion and reason through the philosophy of *Kalam* (meaning "word"). Judaism was also experiencing internal problems: the Karaites rejected the Talmud, and *Ḥiwi al-Balkhi (late ninth century) represented a school of thought which violently attacked the Bible. Jewish philosophy, primarily theological, sought to defend Jewish religion against philosophical attack, and to found the principles of belief on a speculative basis. Scholarly writings thus were directed toward metaphysics and related fields and to a philosophical interpretation of the Bible. These literary activities were undergirded by writings and translations in logic, psychology, and the sciences. Jews also made a significant contribution in these disciplines and other spheres as cultural intermediaries between the Islamic and Christian worlds.

The earliest Jewish medieval philosophers (9th to 11th centuries) wrote in Arabic. David ibn Marwān *al-Mukammis of Babylon in *Book of Twenty Tractates* advances proofs for the existence of God; Isaac b. Solomon *Israeli of Kairouan, in *Book of the Elements*, sought to defend the doctrine of creation against the theory of the eternity of matter. *Emmunot ve-De'ot* ("Doctrines and Beliefs"), by Saadiah Gaon, attempts to prove the compatibility of revelation, Torah, and reason. Saadiah posited ten basic principles, founding them on a theory of knowledge through which he established the existence and nature of God, the need for revelation, and the reasons for revealed doctrines and *mitzvot*. In his ethics he advocated the middle road between the contending forces in human nature. With regard to the Jewish people, he asserted that it was a people only by reason of the Torah. After Saadiah, Spain became the center of Jewish philosophy where the first philosopher of note was the brilliant young poet Solomon ibn Gabirol, whose major philosophical work *Mekor Ḥayyim* (originally Arabic, Latin *Fons Vitae*, 1150) had until the 19th century been ascribed to an Arab named "Avicebron." The book deviates from traditional medieval Jewish philosophy, being closer in tone to neoplatonism. It is a religious philosophical work concerned with personal salvation and with man's purpose and its thesis is that the human soul, which has been united with matter, seeks to return to its source through reason and contemplation. In this connection it discusses God, a theory of emanations, the world (composed of matter and form), and creation. *Mekor Ḥayyim*, which had a considerable effect in Christian circles, was rather less accepted among Jews, although Ibn Gabirol's thinking, often unattributed, was incorporated into Jewish mystical thought. About the same time, *Baḥya b. Joseph ibn Paquda, in *Ḥovot ha-Levavot* ("The Duties of the Heart"), primarily ethical in content, and in *Torat ha-Nefesh* ("The Doctrine of the Soul"), a philosophical work, advanced the theory of design as a proof of God's existence. He proposed the doctrine of negative attributes of God and developed a theory of emanations.

The first philosophical book in Hebrew is *Abraham b. Ḥiyya's *Hegyon ha-Nefesh ha-Aẓuvah* ("Meditation of the Sad Soul") where he sets forth the theory that the world was first created in potentiality and then actualized by the word. The microcosm doctrine was propounded by *Joseph b. Ẓaddik (in his *Olam Katan*, "the Microcosm"): man is a microcosm and can know the world by knowing himself. With Judah Halevi the emphasis in Jewish philosophy shifted. His *Kuzari* is a philosophy of Judaism which seeks to prove that the truths of revealed religion are superior to those of reason and that God is best understood through Jewish history. It is also a philosophy of history whose theme is that Israel is the heart of the nations, endowed with a prophetic capacity, and that the Torah is the expression of the Will of God. Within the framework of Jewish and human endeavors, he assigns a central role to the Land of Israel. Literarily, the *Sefer ha-Kuzari* is distinctive in Jewish philosophy since it is composed as a dialogue and is founded on a historical event (the conversion of the Khazars to Judaism). Abraham Ibn Ezra, however, reverting to the more conventional approach, proposes that God's Will flashing through the upper, middle, and lower worlds is the staying power for everything and that spirituality is resident in everything in the universe. Abraham ibn Daud (12th century) of Toledo also discusses familiar themes along Aristotelian lines, but pays great attention to the problem of free will and providence. Asserting that God knows man's options but not his choice, Ibn Daud discusses providence and suggests that there are gradations in providence which depend upon how earnestly a man strives for the knowledge of God.

The master work of Jewish philosophy, a synthesis of the Jewish philosophical process, is Moses Maimonides' *Guide of the Perplexed*, which was written in Arabic in 1190. Studied by Christians and Muslims, it had a deep effect on scholastic literature apart from its influence on all of Jewish thought. Maimonides, indicating that he is writing for those who know philosophy but are perplexed about contradictions between philosophy and religion, touches upon specific problems and often takes the biblical verse and expressions as his framework. Discussing anthropomorphism, he deals with proofs for the existence of God and with His attributes which, he asserts, can only be understood negatively. He rejects the doctrine of the eternity of matter as unproved and propounds the concept of *creatio ex nihilo*, in accordance with the Torah which he holds to be immutable. He contends that the Torah is designed to guide the body, the body politic, and the soul and to help a man endowed with sufficient contemplative capacity to achieve union with the active intellect in the universe and thus gain immortality. Other major themes in *Guide of the Perplexed* are Divine providence, which is presented as graduated according to man's capacity; evil, which is largely the work of man; and ethics, to which the Torah directs man.

The Maimonidean synthesis was almost immediately challenged in commentaries and in different systems as Jewish philosophy expanded its scope and embarked upon new ventures. Two main factors contributed to this development: (a) The major Arabic works in philosophy, translations and commentaries of the Greek philosophers, and original works of the Arabic philosophers, were translated into Hebrew along with the works of the Jewish philosophers. Thus *Plato, *Aristotle, *Al-Farabi, *Avicenna, *Al-Ghazali, and *Averroes became available to Hebrew readers in Christian Spain and Provence who did not know Arabic. Among the distinguished translators were Judah ibn *Tibbon (12th century), his son Samuel, and his son Moses. Other translators were Jacob b. Abba Mari *Anatoli (13th century), Jacob b. Machir Tibbon (13th century), and Kalonymus b. Kalonymus (14th century), all of Provence. In the same period the task of translating Latin philosophic works into Hebrew was also undertaken (see *Translators and Translations). (b) A Hebrew philosophic terminology was created. The way was now open to Jews, whose major literary language was Hebrew and whose audience read Hebrew, to engage in philosophical writing.

Once the basic philosophical language was developed and works were translated into Hebrew, several new spheres were open to Jewish philosophy, one of which was commentary. Some scholars wrote commentaries on Arabic and Greek philosophers, among them: Levi b. Gershom (14th century), on Averroes; *Moses b. Joshua of Narbonne on Averroes and

Al-Ghazali; and Joseph *Ibn Shem Tov and *Judah b. Jehiel Messer Leon on Aristotle. *Guide of the Perplexed* frequently served as the basis for commentaries which were often original works. The earliest commentary, *Moreh ha-Moreh* ("The Guide of the Guide"), by Shem Tov Falaquera, compiles extensive excerpts from Arabic and Jewish philosophers on subjects treated by Maimonides. *Maskiyyot Kesef* by Joseph *Kaspi represents the highly rationalistic Provençal school which set philosophic principles above tradition. Kaspi denies that *creatio ex nihilo* is a Jewish dogma and interprets the creation story, not literally, but in philosophical terms. Other commentaries, which are essentially explanatory and are usually printed with the text of *Guide of the Perplexed*, were those of Profiat Duran and Asher (Bonan) b. Abraham *Crescas.

Another field developed from the 13th century onward but treated only cursorily in the past is psychology. Averroes' restatement of Aristotle reflects the basic problem of psychology. For Averroes, the active intellect is not an integral part of the soul, but an immaterial substance, derived from the universal intellect, which unites with the soul during a man's life and returns to its source at death, without retaining any individuality. Thus the religious beliefs in personal immortality and reward and punishment came under attack. *Hillel b. Samuel of Verona, Italy, discusses these problems and related points in *Tagmulei ha-Nefesh* ("The Rewards of the Soul"). He attempts to establish that the intellect is not only part of the soul, but is the actual form of the soul which directs all its forces. It is at once eternal and yet retains its individuality so that it is subject to reward and punishment, which he conceives as elevation to a higher level of contemplation or awareness of degradation. In proving and pursuing his contentions, Hillel necessarily deals with the question of free will and God's foreknowledge which he resolves by asserting that necessity and possibility are inherent in the very nature of man and that God conceives every human action as a possibility. Approaching the same question from another point of view, Shem Tov Falaquera composed his *Sefer ha-Nefesh* ("The Book of the Soul") in the spirit that "knowledge of the soul leads to knowledge of God." Like Hillel, he concludes that the soul is immortal and individual and ultimately unites with the universal intellect. Through these works psychology became part of Jewish philosophical speculation, and it has been reflected in the mainstream of Jewish philosophy since the 13th century.

The first major philosophical figure after Maimonides was Levi b. Gershom, also a translator and Bible commentator, whose main work, *Milḥamot Adonai* ("The Battles of the Lord"), like Maimonides', is Aristotelian in outlook, but differs from his in that it gives precedence to philosophical conclusions over biblical teachings. He substitutes for *creatio ex nihilo* the notion that the world, created in time and by the will of God, was shaped out of chaos or formless matter. He further asserts that positive attributes apply both to God and to man, though in different degree. Levi b. Gershom deals with a wide variety of problems, including psychology and the immortality of the soul, freedom of will, divine providence, and cosmology. In general he follows the Aristotelian view of the world and the soul, as modified by Arab philosophers and by neoplatonists. He affirms the immortality of the individual soul in terms of his system, in which the sum total of a man's thoughts of God and the order of the universe constitute the immortal soul, whose reward, after death, consists not of new knowledge but of greater clarity about knowledge acquired during life. Providence, he contends, equally depends upon man's attainment and consists not in miracles but in prior awareness of potential difficulties. Man has individual freedom because God knows and predetermines the general order of events and of possibilities, but not which of the possibilities available to a man will be realized in a single life.

Aristotelianism runs its course with Levi b. Gershom; his major successor, Ḥasdai *Crescas of Barcelona, a man of great critical and innovative faculties, no longer blindly accepts either "the philosopher" or Maimonides but criticizes them both. His major work, *Or Adonai* ("Light of the Lord," completed 1410, published in Ferrara, 1555), designed as a section of a two-part work embracing both *halakhah* and philosophy, is essentially a work on dogmatics in which, after extended philosophic analysis, Crescas sets forth dogmas of the Jewish faith that differ, both in detail and in emphasis, from many of those of Maimonides. He is motivated partly by his emphasis on emotion and action in religion, rather than speculation, and partly by a desire to dispute certain Christian teachings. Attacking Maimonides' proof of the existence of God, which is based upon the Aristotelian doctrine that there cannot be infinite space or infinite causes, Crescas offers a novel proof that there is a being, God, who is the necessary cause of all existence. The existence of God is one of the basic roots that Crescas posits. In his theory of attributes, he asserts that the attributes of God are essential, positive, and infinite in number and extent. God is goodness, and he speaks of God's infinite happiness in His infinite love for His creatures. Crescas applies critical analysis and originality to the themes of free will, reward and punishment, immortality, and providence, all of which he affirms. His views were challenged by the talmudist and writer of responsa Simeon b. Ẓemaḥ Duran of Algeria, whose *Magen Avot* ("The Shield of the Fathers") defends the Maimonidean viewpoint. Essentially concerned with dogmatics, Duran uses the Mishnah *Sanhedrin* 10:1 ("All Israelites have a share in the world to come…") to classify Maimonides' 13 principles under three major headings: the existence of God, the divine origin of the Torah, and reward and punishment. His philosophical statement is basically a synthesis of Maimonides and Levi b. Gershom, though he is more conservative than either in asserting that Divine providence extends to all men regardless of intellectual capacity.

A contemporary of Duran, Joseph *Albo of Spain, evolved a philosophical system which borrowed largely from Maimonides and Crescas, but added new ideas to the field of dogmatics. Albo, reacting to the strong pressure of Christianity upon the Jewish population, sought to standardize the principles of Jewish religion, and to demonstrate that philosophy and religion go hand in hand. In *Ikkarim* ("Principles") he employs the same threefold classification of Jewish dogmas as Duran but takes the classification further. He defines God, revelation, and reward and punishment as universal characteristics of divine religion and distinguishes between a conventional religion rising out of social life and a divine religion which is revealed. He asserts that these three principles must be accepted on faith if necessary, although they can be buttressed by reason. What distinguishes an individual religion, however, is a series of secondary dogmas which must be justified by reason. Besides these, a Jew must accept another six doctrines which though obligatory are not principles: *creatio ex nihilo*, the *sui generis* nature of the prophecy of Moses, the immutability of the Torah, the capability of even one precept to perfect the human soul, resurrection, and the coming of the Messiah. The entire work is written in a lucid and popular style, and became a favorite Jewish work.

The last of the Spanish philosophers, Don Isaac Abrabanel, wrote a considerable number of philosophic works on specific topics. Widely read in Jewish, Arabic, and Christian philosophy, Abrabanel draws on his extensive and versatile knowledge to explicate and give a full view of the philosophical problems which he discusses. Following his exegetical method, Abrabanel in his philosophical works also poses a series of objections to a theory and then proceeds to answer them one by one. While he tends toward Maimonides' philosophical view, he is even more traditional in his concept of Providence, rejecting the idea that Providence depends on the intelligence of man. He also repudiates the rational theories of prophecy and miracles, regarding prophecy as a direct influence from God, not dependent on intellectual excellence. *Dialoghi di Amore* (1535), a philosophical work by his son, Judah *Abrabanel, which is written in Italian and in dialogue form, alludes profusely to classical mythology. Renaissance in tone, its theme is outside the conventional stream of Jewish philosophy and centers mainly on the concept of love of God and how it affects the soul, and the concept of the beautiful. Love is the principle which permeates and unites the universe, extending from God through all creation and back to Him. The influence of the treatise was greater in general thought than in Jewish life since it discusses only few distinctly Jewish themes.

The severe criticism of the rationalistic tendency in the development of philosophy throughout the 13th, 14th, and 15th centuries elicited defenses by scholars who also partly shared the view that rationalism had gone too far. They asserted that philosophy and religion were separate domains and that while philosophic truths were worthy of study and were proper guides, the Torah pointed to still higher truths and ways of life. The notable proponents of this view were the 15th-century Spanish thinkers Abraham *Bibago b. Shem Tov and Joseph ibn Shem Tov. The latter cautioned, however, that the basic principles of religion must agree with logical truth. In the interpretation of the Torah he distinguished between law, which he accepted, and opinion, which need not necessarily be accepted.

The last major philosophical figure of the Jewish Middle Ages was Baruch *Spinoza. Though the *Ethics* belongs to the sphere of general rather than Jewish philosophy, it was clearly influenced by Jewish thought, most notably by Crescas, from whom Spinoza borrowed much. Spinoza's pantheistic view, however, at odds with the Jewish philosophical approach, took him in different philosophical directions. Nevertheless *Tractatus-Theologicus-Politicus* is a distinctly Jewish work which examines the Old Testament critically and, in effect, initiates modern biblical criticism. Spinoza discusses exhaustively the election of Israel, prophecy, miracles, the dogmas of faith, the constitution of the Hebrew state, and the authority of the state in religious matters. His purpose was to defend freedom of thought against religious authority, thus establishing a distinction between religion and philosophical speculation. He contends that prophecy is characterized by imagination and not by speculation, and proceeds to work out the dogmas of universal religion, which very much resemble those of Crescas. Having distinguished between religion and philosophy, Spinoza proceeds to a discussion of the state, which he conceives as founded upon a social contract that protects the right of every man to freedom of thought. Since Spinoza is clearly fighting with the Jewish authorities and attempting to show that they are misrepresenting Judaism, the book is partly a polemic. A fundamental point developed in the work is that the scriptural laws were given for the Jewish body politic and lost their cogency, as did of course rabbinic law, after the destruction of the state. Even for the Jews only the moral laws remain binding. In this approach Spinoza foreshadows Reform Judaism (see *Philosophy).

Ethics

The distinction between philosophy and ethics in the Jewish Middle Ages was not very clear, since both fields centered on religious premises and Torah and the application of these to life. Accordingly, most of the philosophical works also discussed ethics, or at least were ethical in their implications. Nonetheless, there was a considerable corpus of writings whose purpose was distinctly ethical. Most of them were essentially pietistic or, like the *aggadah*, infused with the moral implications of biblical verses. Some of them, however, primarily works from Spain and Provence, presented formal ethical systems. Solomon ibn Gabirol's *Tikkun Middot ha-Nefesh* ("Improvement of the Moral Qualities"), written in Arabic, was the first noteworthy effort in this field. Predicated on psychological and physiological bases rather than religious premises, Gabirol's thesis conceives the soul as consisting of two parts: the higher, which strives for union with God, and the lower, the seat of the moral qualities of daily life. He proposed to teach the art of training and cultivating the soul. *Ḥovot ha-Levavot*, by Baḥya ibn Paquda, a more important and accepted work, has as its central thesis man's gratitude and relationship to God, which the author posits as the yardstick of moral behavior. After establishing a metaphysical foundation for his analysis in the first portal (section), Baḥya devotes nine portals to such virtues as sympathy, action for its own sake, meekness, and the harmonization of reason and passion. Altogether different in tone is **Sefer Ḥasidim* ("The Book of the Pious"), a 12th-century Franco-German work attributed to *Judah b. Samuel he-Ḥasid of Regensburg (c. 1200). Comprised of manuals on ethics and piety, it contains detailed instructions for daily living in the spirit of talmudic and aggadic literature. Its subjects range from worship to marital life, to treatment of servants, to table manners, and is abundantly illustrated with stories. Though marked by strong superstition, the work is imbued with a spirit of piety and ethical sensitivity. It enjoyed great popularity in its time and for many generations. An equally popular, though distinctly formal work, was the *Shemoneh Perakim* ("Eight Chapters") of Maimonides which constituted the introduction to his commentary on *Pirkei Avot*. Writing as though he were "a doctor of the soul," Maimonides suggests that there are good dispositions and bad ones, that man is a free agent and a *tabula rasa*, and that he can be educated to the good. He proposes "the middle way" as the norm of conduct.

By the 13th century, ethical literature began to proliferate, although formal, analytical systems were on the decline. Among the important books of the century were *Sha'arei Teshuvah* ("The Gates of Repentance") by *Jonah b. Abraham Gerondi and *Kad ha-Kemaḥ* by Baḥya b. Asher. Gerondi discusses the ways that arouse a man to repentance, the nature of repentance and forgiveness, and the obligatory precepts incumbent upon a Jew. He is particularly forceful in his demand for the observance of community enactments which, he says, are designed to strengthen the Jewish community and religion and thus to sanctify the name of God. Baḥya, like Jonah, writing from a religious point of view, arranges his subject matter alphabetically and discusses a wide variety of themes. Among his observations is the view that Jews are dispersed so that they may fulfill the mission of living like a model nation and spreading the knowledge of the One God and His Providence. Once the mission is fulfilled redemption will come.

**Sefer ha-Yashar*, an anonymous ethical work which was mistakenly attributed to Jacob b. Meir Tam and to Zerahiah ha-Yevani, is of the 14th century. The author saw the people of his time as being so engrossed in the pursuit of riches and pleasure that they needed to be redirected to the love of God and right conduct. Making an appeal both to reason and piety, he emphasizes, in the manner of Baḥya, the awe of God, the wonder of the world, and the need to imitate God and thus fulfill the purpose of creation and of perfecting man. Less theoretical, and more given to the practical exposition of behavior, are the 14th-century work *Menorat ha-Ma'or* ("Candelabrum of Light") by Israel b. Joseph *Al-Nakawa of Spain, which concentrates on the meaning and application of specific *mitzvot* like loving-kindness and the Sabbath, and the anonymous 15th-century treatise *Orḥat Ẓaddikim* ("The Way of the Righteous"), stemming from Germany, which examines the art of training the soul to seek the good.

The major work of the period, also called *Menorat ha-Ma'or*, by Isaac *Aboab of Toledo, enjoyed great popularity. In contrast to contemporary trends, Aboab stressed the importance of the *aggadah* whose teachings were concerned with the education of the soul. The author, as stated in his preface, wrote the book with the explicit purpose of giving instruction to all in practical ethics. He bases his work on three principles set forth in Psalm 34:15: "Depart from evil, and do good; seek peace and pursue it," which he divides into seven categories characterized as the seven *nerot* (lamps) that make up the "candelabrum of light." Avoiding evil involves neither desiring nor speaking evil; doing good demands the observance of the *mitzvot*, the study of the Torah, and repentance; pursuing peace calls for love and meekness. Fusing philosophical speculation and mysticism, the book is an exposition of the meaning and application of these seven qualities. The text is richly interwoven with allegories and parables drawn from the *aggadah* which serve as illustrations to the author's instruction. A spate of other books appeared in subsequent centuries. Among them were *Reshit Ḥokhmah* ("The Beginning of Wisdom") of Elijah b. Moses de *Vidas, written in a mystical spirit, and the many commentaries on *Pirkei Avot* which elaborated the ethical approach to life. Notable among the latter, in addition to the commentaries of Rashi, Maimonides, and Bertinoro, were those of Simeon Duran, Joseph b. Ḥayyim *Jabez, and Judah b. Samuel *Lerma.

A novel note in ethical works, heralding a new era, appeared about 1705 with *Kav ha-Yashar* ("The Measure of Righteousness") by Ẓevi Hirsch *Koidonover. Neither well ordered nor particularly distinguished, the work is important because it reflects the vigorous and mystical spirit of Polish Jewry, and was written both in Hebrew and in Yiddish (see *Ethical Literature).

Ethical Wills

A body of literature which had a great vogue during the entire Jewish Middle Ages, but most notably from the 11th century onward, is the corpus of documents known as "ethical wills." This literature had its precursors in the Bible, the Apocrypha, and the Talmud, but it became common only in the Middle Ages. Ethical wills were written in the form of the communication of a father's experience, insights, and mandates to his son and vary in length, some of them being as large as a small book. These works are important testimonies to the thinking and values of eminent men and reflect the life of different periods and places. One of the earliest extant wills, that of *Eliezer b. Isaac of Worms (11th century), examines the attitude of man to his fellow men, the fulfilling of *mitzvot*, the rules of hygiene, and the religious tone of life. Judah ibn Tibbon (12th century) in his "testament" urges the study of Torah and science, gives moral and scientific advice to his son, a physician, in the practice of medicine, and offers guidance on how to treat one's wife, children, and books. Writing from Palestine to his oldest son, Naḥman, Naḥmanides advises him on the practice of ethical virtues, especially emphasizing humility so that "every man should seem in thine eyes as one greater than thyself" in some respect. He enjoins his younger son, Solomon, who held a position in the king's court, not to be ensnared by glamour, but to cling to Jewish practice and study and to purity of conduct.

The testament of Asher b. Jehiel addressed to his children is a long work divided into 155 sections and written in an epigrammatic style, stressing honesty and humility, and the giving of charity. His two sons *Judah and *Jacob b. Asher also left testaments. Judah's will, divided into three parts, relates episodes of his life, urges his son to study, enjoins the virtues of truthfulness and humility, and discusses financial matters. In the third section he outlines a scheme for distribution of charity, which constitutes valuable historical data; reckons his salary for 23 years as rabbi of Toledo and directs that as a return his library be dedicated to the use of students. He also incorporates a family agreement to observe the practice of tithe and charity. Suffused with profound piety, the testament of Jacob b. Asher urges love of God to the point of being ready to undergo martyrdom, enjoins against consulting fortunetellers, and advocates the diligent study of Talmud and the avoidance of casuistry. *Sefer ha-Musar* ("The Book of Morality"), by Joseph Kaspi, a short systematic work on proper behavior written in the form of a will, attempts to enjoin a combination of belief, piety, and ethical behavior based on rational principles. Kaspi discusses the fundamental principles of Judaism which every Jew must apprehend by means of proof and logical reasoning. He, therefore, sets a curriculum of study including Bible, Talmud, mathematics, ethics, law, physics, and logic, culminating with the study of philosophy and theology from the age of 20 on. The work concludes with a defense of the study of philosophy.

The testaments of the 14th and subsequent centuries were written by laymen rather than scholars. Thus *Eliezer b. Samuel ha-Levi (14th century) of Mainz urges his children to live in large Jewish communities so that their offspring may receive a proper Jewish education, warns against card playing and dances, and enjoins the giving of charity and the conduct of household affairs in an orderly manner. Another layman, Solomon Isaac of Provence, is much concerned with study and advises his son always to have a volume of Talmud open so that he might be moved to study.

After the 16th century, testaments are clearly influenced by kabbalistic thought. The most important wills written during the following centuries are by Abraham, Jacob, and Sheftel Horowitz, in the 17th century, and Moses Ḥasid, Alexander Sueskind, Joel b. Abraham Shemariah of Vilna, *Israel b. Eliezer the Ba'al Shem Tov, and *Elijah b. Solomon Zalman, the Gaon of Vilna, in the 18th century. Ethical will literature did not end with the 18th century, but continued to be written down to our own day and to be circulated within families (see Ethical *Wills).

Philosophical Exegesis

The extensive literature which attempted to harmonize philosophy and religion led to interpretations of the Bible that were extreme, to allegorical explanations, and to commentaries which were basically homiletic. While the approaches of Levi b. Gershom and Isaac Abrabanel were systematic, the works of other scholars were either loosely organized or concentrated on limited themes. The 13th-century work *Yikkavu ha-Mayim*, by Samuel ibn Tibbon of Provence, is a major example of this type of literature. Starting with the question of creation and committed to proving the truth of the Bible, Ibn Tibbon, with much ingenious philosophical explanation and a moderate use of allegory, discusses angels, Divine providence, and creation. Provence produced a school which interpreted the Bible allegorically, but unfortunately the works have been lost. There is, however, some knowledge of their exegetical explanation: Abraham and Sarah represent form and matter while Isaac and Rebekah stand for the active and passive intellect. The most important work of philosophical exegesis, *Akedat Yiẓḥak* by Isaac b. Moses *Arama (15th century) of Spain, is a compilation of the author's sermons and philosophical discourses. Arama's avowed purpose is not only to explain words, a method which characterized most commentaries, but to elicit the full philosophical teachings of the Bible. In this, he claims to follow the approach of Christian preachers. Through his method, resembling that of Isaac Abrabanel – to pose a series of questions and to answer them – he discusses the soul, the symbolic meaning of paradise and the four rivers (Gen. 2:8–15), justice in the state, the Sabbath, and family life. The stories of the Bible are interpreted allegorically and the author refers extensively to Jewish literature and to general works on ethics, science, and politics to elucidate his arguments. *Akedat Yiẓḥak* was widely influential and served as a source for generations of preachers (see *Bible, Exegesis).

Mystical Literature

Throughout the Middle Ages, particularly the later medieval period, rationalist philosophy was supplemented by a great body of mystical literature. Its origins, found in the Apocrypha, the Talmud, and the *aggadah*, center around the theophany (*Ma'aseh Merkavah*) in the first chapter of Ezekiel (see *Merkabah Mysticism). Initially regarded as secret doctrine, it was transmitted orally from one generation of initiates to the next. The first mystical books, pseudepigraphically assigned to early *tannaim* such as R. Ishmael and R. Akiva, appear in the middle of the geonic period: *Alef-Bet de-Rabbi Akiva*, the *Heikhalot* texts, the *Ma'aseh Bereshit* literature, and the Book of Enoch. The first systematic mystical work, *Sefer *Yeẓirah*, was written in Hebrew by an unknown author (probably in Palestine between the second and sixth centuries). The great development of mystical literature began in the 13th century in the south of France and the north of Spain. By then the influence of mystical doctrines known as *Kabbalah ("tradition") had become apparent in exegetical and philosophical literature. One of the most influential personalities in its formative period was *Isaac the Blind (12th–13th century), the son of Abraham b. David of Posquières. There are, however, indications of direct influences from both Babylonia and Palestine, especially on the circles of *Ḥasidei Ashkenaz. The kabbalistic works of Eleazar b. Judah of Worms express the group's teachings in this sphere. They are also reflected in *Sefer Ḥasidim*.

PRE-ZOHAR AND ZOHAR LITERATURE. The literature of the "speculative Kabbalah" (*Kabbalah iyyunit*), which arose in Spain and Provence, is distinguished by originality of thought, aggadic style, and frequent pseudepigraphic ascriptions of the writings. In the nature of Midrashim, these works are written either in Hebrew or Aramaic or a combination of the two. The oldest kabbalistic text, the obscure *Sefer ha-*Bahir*, is attributed to a second-century *tanna*, but was probably edited in Provence in the 12th century. Other influential 12th-century works were the treatise *Massekhet Aẓilut* and the works of *Azriel of Gerona. Significant in the 13th century were the **Ma'arekhet ha-Elohut* and the central figure of ecstatic kabbalism, Abraham b. Samuel *Abulafia, whose main works were written at the same time as the *Zohar.

The latter, the most distinguished work of speculative, indeed theosophical, Kabbalah, the Zohar is written in Aramaic and attributed to Simeon b. Yoḥai of the second century; it is now taken to have been written by the Spanish kabbalist *Moses de Leon (13th century). During the succeeding two centuries the Zohar gave rise to an extensive mystical literature including the works of Menahem b. Benjamin *Recanati of Italy, Moses b. Isaac *Botarel, Shem Tov b. Joseph *Ibn Shem Tov, and Judah b. Jacob *Ḥayyat of Spain.

The next great flowering in kabbalistic speculation centered around Safed in the 16th century, and especially Moses b. Jacob *Cordovero, Isaac *Luria, and Ḥayyim b. Joseph *Vital. Luria's original and far-reaching conceptions, as presented by his disciples, reshaped kabbalistic thought and dominated it in subsequent centuries. Through Luria's essentially messianic doctrine, kabbalistic ideas acquired mass popularity.

The numerous kabbalistic works of the next two centuries, largely commentaries and compilations, though reflecting classical kabbalistic thinking and the Lurianic school, were original in thought. The most notable writers were Joseph Solomon *Delmedigo and Isaiah b. Abraham ha-Levi *Horowitz. The major work of the period, Isaiah Horowitz' *Shenei Luḥot ha-Berit*, a combination of code and kabbalistic commentary on the Pentateuch, profoundly influenced religious life in Eastern Europe and introduced practices and prayers whose sole source and authority was the Kabbalah. Later kabbalistic writing is reflected in the *Pitḥei Ḥokhmah* of Moses Ḥayyim *Luzzatto and especially in the practices and writings of *Ḥasidism. (For a full description see *Kabbalah. See also *Anthropomorphism, *Allegory, *Emanation, *Eschatology, *Immortality of the Soul, **Shekhinah*.)

Prose Literature

HISTORY. The dispersion of the Jews, a scarcity of reliable documents, and the fact that medieval scholars did not have a historical sense made the writing of Jewish history and geography difficult. The works of the period are often inaccurate and frequently credulous in their reliability on sources. Together with responsa, however, they provide sources for modern Jewish historical studies. Among the historical works of the early Middle Ages was the anonymous *Seder Olam Zuta*, a history of the Babylonian exilarchs from Zerubbabel down to the eighth century which emphasizes the Davidic line but ignores the most glorious exilarch of the seventh century, *Bustanai b. Ḥaninai. **Josippon* (tenth century), a widely read anonymous work, is a summary of Jewish history starting with Adam down to the destruction of the Temple. Relying primarily on Josephus, it also drew on non-Jewish sources and on Jewish legends. More factual contemporary accounts, emphasizing the history of the gaonate and the spiritual life of Babylonian Jewry, were provided by Saadiah Gaon (tenth century) and his contemporary *Nathan b. Isaac ha-Kohen who depict Babylonian life. An apparently authentic account of Jewry in southern Italy was provided by the family chronicle *Aḥima'aẓ* (1054; *Ahimaaz b. Paltiel) which testifies to the judicial autonomy enjoyed by Italian Jews and to the close relationship existing between southern Italy and Palestine over the centuries. The chronicles of Jews in France and Germany centering around the Crusades afford authentic and moving accounts of Jewish life in those areas; they include the works of Solomon b. Simeon and *Eliezer b. Nathan, both of Mainz (about 1140), and that of Ephraim of Bonn (after 1196). Abraham ibn Daud's *Sefer ha-Kabbalah* ("Book of Tradition"), a work of broader scope, includes a history of the political parties in the second commonwealth, the talmudic tradition, the geonic period, and Jewish intellectual life in Spain. Ibn Daud based himself on known sources and sources unknown today with the avowed intent of showing the superiority of the *Rabbanites over the *Karaites.

The historical works of the later Middle Ages are both far more numerous and more detailed than those of the earlier period. They also attempted to place Jewish history in the context of general history and were superior in orderly arrangement and, sometimes, in critical treatment of the material. They too, however, mixed fact and fancy and were parochial or tendentious in their themes and outlook. The works of the period included a considerable number of chronicles of communities, families, or specific events. Much of the writing, centering about the lives of Jewish heroes or about persecutions, was not history for its own sake, but served as a background to halakhic or aggadic works designed to show the continuity of Jewish tradition or to provide a history of scholarship. Social and economic histories were noticeably lacking. Among the chronicles of tradition were those of Menahem b. Solomon *Meiri of Provence (1287), whose work takes the history of Jewish tradition up to his own time and is a source of information on scholarship in Provence and in the Franco-German area. A century later Isaac de Lattes of Provence wrote *Sha'arei Ẓiyyon* which takes Menahem Meiri's work as a source. The work of Joseph b. Ẓaddik on the Spanish Jewish community provides full data about Spanish scholars up to 1487. *Abraham b. Solomon of Torrutiel in his *Book of Tradition* (1510) not only deals with scholarly accomplishment from the 12th century onward, but also describes the period of the expulsion from Spain. His eyewitness account of the expulsion is especially valuable as is his invective against the upper classes of Spanish Jewry and his accounts of the events after his exile. *Divrei Yosef* (1673), by Joseph b. Isaac *Sambari of Egypt, discusses the Jews of the East. Emphasizing the history and life of Egyptian Jewry, the author also lists scholars in other Eastern cities and persecutions in the area. The book contains a wealth of data, including legends, not found in other sources.

Another type of historical literature dealt with the frequent persecutions of the period. Two major works were *Shevet Yehudah*, by Solomon *Ibn Verga, written on the basis of the notes of his relative Judah, supplemented by the notes of his son Joseph; and *Emek ha-Bakha*, by *Joseph ha-Kohen (16th century) of Italy. While Ibn Verga's account of the persecutions is unsystematic and inaccurate, his eyewitness account of the Spanish expulsion, particularly the events following it, is both detailed and moving. He is particularly informative on the religious debates which took place in Spain in connection with which he relates the story of the three rings which Lessing also was to employ in his drama, *Nathan der Weise*. The material in *Emek ha-Bakha* is much better arranged and goes up to 1575; it is particularly informative about contemporary Italian Jewish life. The book is also noteworthy because of its account of Joseph *Nasi and his attempt to rebuild Tiberias.

The major histories of tradition during the period, written in the vein of Ibn Daud, are combinations of chronologies and biographies which gained importance because they threw light on creative activities in different countries at successively later periods. The first such history, *Sefer Yuḥasin* (1505), by Abraham b. Samuel *Zacuto, begins with the men of the Great Synagogue and takes history down to the author's own time. The work contains frequent and detailed citations and such interesting additional material as the diary of *Isaac b. Samuel of Acre about the authenticity of the Zohar. To place his writing in perspective, Zacuto devotes the last of his five sections to universal history. *Shalshelet ha-Kabbalah*, by Gedaliah b. David ibn Yaḥya (16th century) of Italy and Turkey, is an encyclopedic mélange of the history of Jewish tradition. It is a series of essays on aspects of Jewish history and on subjects ranging from embryology to the history of persecution. Confusing fact and fancy, the work was nonetheless popular because it marshaled a host of legends about major Jewish historical personalities and because of its eclectic character, which afforded room for many historical oddities. *Ẓemaḥ David*, by David b. Solomon *Gans (16th century), on the other hand, is dry, factual, and well organized. Discussing both historical events and figures, he is particularly informative about Polish and German Jewish history and provides chronological tables and citations of sources which are still of value today. An equally systematic approach characterized David *Conforte's *Kore ha-Dorot* (17th century), which is a history of Jewish scholars and scholarship from the period of the Talmud to the author's own day and is especially informative about the tosafists and Eastern scholarship of the 16th and 17th centuries. Its value as a reference source is enhanced by the fact that the author made considerable use of responsa. The primary value of *Seder ha-Dorot* by Jehiel Heilprin (17th–18th century) is also as a technical reference source, particularly in the field of bibliography. The work is also exceptionally detailed in its treatment of talmudic figures. Thus in his discussion on Judah b. Ilai, he lists almost 3,000 statements attributed to him. As in other books of the period, a critical approach to history is lacking, and thus while Heilprin adds to a knowledge of Jewish tradition, particularly in rabbinics, he mixes fact and legend uncritically in the biographies which are the warp and woof of the work.

Other noteworthy works dealing with literary history and bibliography of the period were those of Joseph Solomon *Delmedigo (17th century), Shabbetai b. Joseph *Bass (17th and 18th centuries), and Ḥayyim Joseph David *Azulai (18th century). In a letter in rhymed prose, *Iggeret Aḥuz*, Delmedigo reviewed medieval Jewish literary history, except for rabbinics. He discusses every field of literature and its principal figures. His style is epigrammatic and often mordantly witty, and he characterizes many of the personalities and books with a single phrase. Bass and Azulai did notable work in *bibliography; while Bass listed over 2,400 works in his *Siftei Yeshenim*, Azulai recorded 3,000 short biographies and bibliographical items. Almost all the historical works discussed above were also based on non-Jewish sources in an attempt to place Jewish history in historical perspective; they lacked, however, critical insight. The scholar who best combined general knowledge, a critical approach, and a historical sense with intensive Jewish knowledge was Azariah dei *Rossi (16th century) of Italy. In *Me'or Einayim* he used the short essay form to analyze critically some aspects of Jewish history, literature, and institutions. Dealing with the chronology of the Second Temple period, he disputes both the Talmud and his predecessors and arrives at a new chronology. In his analysis of the *aggadah* he questions the method of the rabbis in arriving at religious and ethical truths. Discussing science in the Talmud, he indicates errors in view and knowledge and lays down the principle that rabbinic authority applies only to the areas of law and tradition. It is the first work of critical history and initially engendered much controversy because it was considered radical in its views.

During the 16th century Jewish scholars were beginning to turn their attention also to general history, with illuminating side references to Jewish history. Thus while *Seder Eliyahu Zuta* (1523), by Elijah *Capsali of Crete, is essentially a work on the history of the Ottoman Empire, the author provides valuable data about the history of the Jews of Spain, Turkey, and Rhodes. Similarly, the history of the kings of France and the Ottoman Turks by Joseph ha-Kohen (16th century) contains much Jewish material, including an account of David Reuveni and Solomon Molcho (see *Historiography).

GEOGRAPHY AND TRAVEL. Current events, history, and legend fused in the literature of geography and travel of the 1,000-year period. A book which fired the Jewish imagination is the record of *Eldad ha-Dani who appeared in Kairouan in 890 with detailed accounts of independent Jewish kingdoms in East Africa, Arabia, Khazaria, and Persia, which he described as the *Ten Lost Tribes. Mingling fact and legend, he buttressed Jewish hopes and ego for many centuries. Equally bolstering was the correspondence between Ḥisdai ibn Shaprut (tenth century), a leader of Spanish Jewry, and *Joseph, king of the *Khazars, about the conversion of the latter's ancestor to Judaism. The king's answer, with a document from the Cairo *Genizah*, provides a fascinating picture of a bypath of Jewish history and Jewish proselytizing efforts.

The great Jewish travel book of the Middle Ages is *Benjamin of Tudela's account of his travels, depicting life in Southern Europe and in the East (1159–73). An eyewitness account of the life in many lands, which the author supplemented with data on Slavic lands, Persia, and India, he portrays a vital Jewish life in many communities and a record of such oddities of history as the black Jews of Malabar and the false messiah, David Alroy. The accounts of Benjamin's near contemporary *Pethahiah of Regensburg which record his travels in Slavic lands, Babylon, and Palestine between the years 1175 to 1185 are less detailed and more credulous. He confirms Benjamin's observations, adds data, and notes the presence of a great number of Karaites in the Crimea.

From the 13th century onward there is a considerable body of literature devoted to trips to Palestine and to a description of communities visited en route. While many are merely descriptions of religious sites and legends centering about holy people and places, others contain illuminating bits of information. Thus *Elleh ha-Massa'ot* by Jacob of Paris records the anomaly that he was sent to Palestine to raise money for a yeshivah in Paris. Meanwhile, he gives an account of Jewish life in Damascus and Baghdad. *Estori ha-Parḥi of Provence (14th century) has extensive topographical material on Palestine, and his contemporary, Isaac Ḥilo, provides an illuminating picture of Jewish life in Palestine. He notes that there are many scholars from France and Germany among the Jews of Haifa, that the Jews of Acre are quite rich, and that the Jews of Jaffa possess a fine library.

The varied character of Jewish life and the relatively rapid changes in it are mirrored in 15th- and 16th-century Jewish travel chronicles. Meshullam b. Menahem, an Italian, visiting Egypt in the 1480s, reports that the Cairo community has 850 Jewish families, several hundred Karaites, and 50 Samaritans, but he deprecates their way of life. Obadiah of Bertinoro, the commentator on the Mishnah, writing in the same decade, gives a detailed and affirmative description of these communities and also mentions that 50 former Marrano families settled in Cairo. On the other hand, while he is negative about the Jews of Sicily whom he describes as artisans, workers in the fields, and morally lax, he indicates that they are a tightly organized Jewish community enjoying great autonomy. Of Jerusalem, he reports that there are but 70 families, all of them poor and ignorant, which is a completely different account from that of Ḥilo of 150 years earlier. Later works include *Gelilot Ereẓ Yisrael* (1624), by Gershon b. Eliezer of Prague, a book replete with bizarre legends and wonder stories; several books by the Karaite *Samuel b. David (1642) of the Crimea who gives a glowing account of Karaite life in the East; Benjamin Yerushalmi (1786); and the itinerary of Simḥah b. Joseph of Poland who reports that the Constantinople Jewish community would annually charter a boat for pilgrimage to Palestine for the High Holy Days. The most fascinating travel book of all is that of David Reuveni (16th century), who appeared in Italy in 1523 claiming to be the brother of King Joseph, ruler of a small Jewish kingdom in the Arabian desert, and sent to negotiate with the pope about waging war against the Muslims. Describing his travels to Alexandria and thence to Italy, much of the book is devoted to his reception by Jews and gentiles in Europe, to his extended negotiations with the pope and the king of Portugal, and to his contacts with the Marranos in Portugal. Reuveni made a considerable impression upon Jews and gentiles, but he was ultimately arrested by the authorities and the book ends in *medias res* (see *Travelers and Explorers).

BIOGRAPHIES AND AUTOBIOGRAPHIES. Reuveni's work could also be classified in the memoir genre which began to appear in the 17th century. An early example of this kind, *Shivḥei ha-Ari*, composed by one of Luria's followers Solomon Shlumil of Dreznitz, is partly biographical, but primarily an account of the wonders performed by Isaac Luria. *Sefer Ḥezyonot*, by Luria's disciple, Ḥayyim Vital, is a similar mixture and centers about Vital himself, with some references to Luria.

There were, however, two autobiographies of distinction, one by Leone *Modena (16th–17th century) and the other by *Glueckel of Hameln (17th–18th century). Modena, who claimed 26 occupations, provides a fascinating account of his life, and, incidentally, of contemporary Italian Jewry. Writing in Hebrew, he indicates that he was instructed in Latin, in music, and in dancing. He wrote on many themes, served as rabbi, gambled unsuccessfully, engaged in polemics and in general, fit the picture of a Renaissance man. Glueckel's memoir is notable on several scores. It is one of the few works by a woman, was written in Yiddish, and presents a lively picture of the life of a well-to-do Jewish woman of the time and the community in which she lived. She tells of her childhood, the few years she studied in *ḥeder*, her marriage, her widowhood, the education of her children, business practices, study patterns, and religious observance among Jews. She avows a philosophy of faith in God's providence, displays a rich knowledge of Judaism garnered from reading and listening, and sets the study of Torah as primary. She relates that she sent her children to yeshivot and then gave them in marriage. Her book is a rich portrayal of contemporary German-Jewish life and values (see *Biographies and Autobiographies).

FICTION. As the field of Jewish literature broadened it came to comprehend belletristic prose which included tales, fables, and didactic works in which the ethical content is combined with satire, humor, proverbs, and apothegms for the sake of entertainment and aesthetic pleasure. While much of it was based on Arabic models, since the basic tales and proverbs tended to be universal, on which national or cultural forms were superimposed, there were also Jewish models taken from the Bible, the Apocrypha, and the *aggadah*. The bulk of these works, until the middle of the 14th century, were written in Spain and thereafter in Provence and Italy.

TALES. The earliest book of fables, *Sefer ha-Ma'asiyyot*, by Nissim b. Jacob b. Nissim ibn *Shahin of Kairouan, written in Arabic, was based largely on aggadic legends. The most notable early work, however, was the Hebrew book, *Sefer Sha'ashu'im*, by the physician Joseph *Ibn Zabara (12th century). A mélange of folktales, epigrams, and short passages of philosophy and science, the story centers around Zabara's encounter with a stranger who proves to be a devil. In their travels, they debate with one another, tell stories, and compete with one another in the telling of proverbs and epigrams. Characterized by wit, humor, and satire, the style resembles that of the **maqāma*; it is, however, not poetic in form.

Another major work, *Ben ha-Melekh ve-ha-Nazir*, by Abraham b. Samuel ha-Levi *Ibn Ḥasdai, is a Hebrew adaptation of an Arabic version (which has been lost) of an Indian tale based on the life of Buddha, whose theme is the vanity of the world and the value of the ascetic life. The Indian tale had already been adapted in many European languages. Ibn Ḥasdai's treatment of the material is original, and many of the parables and the content of the last 11 chapters, which reflect the moral and psychological teachings of 12th-century philosophy, appear in no other version. Written in rhymed prose, interspersed with poetry, abundantly ornamented by proverbs and poetry, the book is the story of a prince who through the instruction of a hermit is converted to an ascetic life.

Meshal ha-Kadmoni (1281), by Isaac ibn *Sahula, is another important work of the period. Based on aggadic stories but also including original tales, it is written in rhymed prose and embellished with puns and parodies based on biblical and aggadic expressions. The author indicates that his motive was to show Arabic-reading Jews that the Hebrew language was an equally suitable vehicle for entertainment. About the same time *Berechiah b. Natronai ha-Nakdan published his *Mishlei Shu'alim* ("Fox Fables"). Animal stories of this type were a familiar genre in medieval literature and much resemble Aesop's fables. The distinctive Hebraic character of Berechiah's version derives from the play of language. The animals converse in biblical Hebrew, interspersed with talmudic quotations, and readily resort to biblical puns and to parodies upon Jewish characters. A similar book which, however, was a direct translation from the Arabic, was the *Iggeret Ba'alei Ḥayyim*, by Kalonymus b. Kalonymus.

SATIRE AND HUMOR. The major medieval work of satire and humor, Al-Ḥarizi's *Taḥkemoni*, was the precursor of a considerable body of literature of lesser worth, one of which is *Sone Nashim* ("Hater of Women," 1298) by Judah ibn Shabbetai of Spain. Its obvious theme is elaborated with parodies on the Bible, on the liturgy, and on the marriage contract. A rejoinder, much inferior in quality, was written almost a century later by Jedaiah b. Abraham Bedersi (ha-Penini) under the title of *Ohev Nashim* ("Lover of Women").

The parodying of familiar literary forms, notably the Bible and the Talmud, centered about Purim which was an occasion for merrymaking and wine drinking. Of the large volume of literature written in this vein, the most representative are *Massekhet Purim* by the 14th-century *Kalonymus b. Kalonymus which parodies the talmudic style, and the rather more witty *Megillat Setarim*, by Levi b. Gershom, which celebrates wine and merrymaking. Similar works were composed in subsequent centuries, most of them centering about Purim, but a few parodying the Passover *Haggadah*. Kalonymus b. Kalonymus was also the author of the satirical and didactic work *Even Boḥan* in which he portrays the Jews of Provence and characterizes their formal religiosity as devoid of spirit. He attacks the doctors and holds the upper classes up for ridicule. Other parts of the book, however, are dedicated to the theme of the vanity of the world and are in the form of fine parables.

Didactic Literature

Mivḥar ha-Peninim, a book of proverbs culled from Arabic literature and intended to provide ethical instruction, attributed to Ibn Gabirol, is the precursor of a large body of ethical works, most of which were didactic, and of works in which ethical systems were formulated. What distinguished didactic from ethical works was essentially a form and a style which were light and popular rather than formal, since the intention of the author was to provide entertainment as well as instruction to his audience. *Milḥemet ha-Ḥokhmah ve-ha-Osher*, by Judah ibn Shabbetai, claims that both wisdom and wealth must be pursued. Its form is that of a dialogue between contending parties before a court and its style involves the use of puns and parody. *Ha-Mevakkesh* (1264), by Shem Tov b. Joseph ibn Falaquera, is a more serious work in which the author discusses various professions and crafts, reviews philosophy, ethical theory, and poetry and concludes with a discussion on religion, science, and philosophy. The book, he asserts, is designed to instruct people in proper conduct and is written in dialogue form, with the morals being brought home in short poems and proverbs. The conclusion is that a true understanding of religion depends upon a knowledge of science and philosophy.

Beḥinat Olam, written in the earlier part of the 14th century by Jedaiah Bedersi (ha-Penini), is altogether more solemn and is written in a poetic prose. Its themes are the pursuit of immortality and the cultivation of the soul toward that pursuit. Happiness, he asserts, resides in the observance of the Torah and in following the path of moderation in daily life.

Polemical and Apologetic Literature

From the 12th century onward, as a result of the confrontation of Judaism with Islam and Christianity, the literature of polemics and apologetics developed. Although having its roots in biblical and Hellenistic sources, this literature reached its zenith in the Middle Ages primarily in response to Christian attempts to proselytize Jews by force or persuasion, and to involve them in theological debates. The problem of confrontation was considerably less severe in Muslim countries where the central issues were usually biblical exegesis and articles of faith with which almost all medieval philosophers and theologians dealt, either in their major works or in separate treatises. In addition, within Judaism itself there was a tradition of polemical literature: between the Rabbanites and the Karaites, between philosophers and their critics, and between kabbalists and their opponents. Polemical efforts are, however, found as early as the ninth century in parts of David ibn Marwān *Al-Mukammis' larger works, in which he attacks both Christianity and Islam. He scores the former for undermining pure monotheism and the latter on the grounds that the style of the Koran does not prove divine origin. In the tenth century Saadiah Gaon took much the same line, questioning the validity of Christian and Muslim exegesis of the Bible and asserting the immutability of the Torah. Expressing his criticisms of the other faiths in the form of a debate with Christians and Muslims, Judah Halevi, in his *Sefer ha-Kuzari* (12th century), extensively elaborates the points of his Jewish polemical predecessors in accusing Christianity and Islam of retaining many elements of pagan idolatry. Maimonides, in his letter to the Jews of Yemen, defends Judaism and denies that there are biblical references presaging Muhammad.

The first polemical work as such, however, is *Sefer ha-Berit* by the 12th-century writer, Joseph *Kimḥi of Provence. Written in the form of a dialogue, the author presents a debate between a Jew and a Christian on such issues as the interpretations of biblical passages, original sin, the role of Jesus, and the traditional charges Christians had leveled against Jews, i.e., deicide and usury. Kimḥi's arguments were the same as those which had been commonly adduced by Jews, namely, that the doctrine of original sin contradicts the biblical view, that the Jews did not kill Jesus, and that Christian biblical exegesis is mistaken. In addition, Kimḥi asserts that the Jews had an elevated moral sense and a decent communal life.

The talmudic debate held in 1240 before the king in Paris is recorded in *Vikku'aḥ* by one of the disputants, Rabbi *Jehiel b. Joseph of Paris. The rabbi defends the Talmud against the charge that it contains anti-Christian statements by claiming that the passages in question refer to an earlier Jesus and not the Jesus of the New Testament. Jehiel further contends that irrational statements in the Talmud and Midrash belong to the *aggadah*, which need not be accepted. *Kol Nidrei* and the laws relating to gentiles are also explained.

Another important disputation records Naḥmanides' debate with Pablo *Christiani at Barcelona in 1263. The polemic deals primarily with such questions as to whether the Messiah has come, whether the Messiah is divine or human, and whether Judaism is a just and true religion. Naḥmanides, referring to the familiar biblical passages, asserts that "the suffering servant" implies the Jewish people; he attacks the doctrine of original sin and, in terms similar to those of Jehiel, describes the non-halakhic nature of the *aggadah*.

In the 14th century the increase of forced conversions and attacks on Judaism by apostates caused Solomon b. Abraham Adret to write a dialogue denouncing the dogmas of Islam and denying the divine origin of the Koran, while defending Jews from the charge of having eliminated references to Muhammad from the Bible. Vis-à-vis a Christian antagonist, Solomon repudiates the allegorical interpretations of the Bible, defends the immutability of the Torah, and explains certain talmudic passages.

More significant are Isaac Profiat Duran's two polemical works, the ironic letter *Al Tehi ka-Avotekha* ("Be not Like your Fathers"), and the lengthy *Kelimmat ha-Goyim* ("The Shame of the Gentiles"). The first is addressed to a Jew who, like Duran himself, was forcibly converted in 1391, and who reneged on an agreement with Duran to flee Spain and to abandon Christianity. Heavily satirical, the letter urges the friend not to be like his fathers who believed in the pure unity of God, but to accept the notion of corporal embodiment. In the same ironic manner of apparent advocacy, Duran attacks many Christian doctrines. He continues his criticism in a more detailed and systematic way in his second work where literary and historical methods rather than irony are employed to establish his views. Ḥasdai Crescas composed a no less powerful polemic, *Bittul Ikkarei ha-Noẓerim* ("Refutation of the Dogmas of Christianity"), which elicited Christian replies.

A major polemical work which evoked considerable controversy and many Christian retorts is the comprehensive *Sefer ha-Nizzaḥon* by Yom Tov Lippman *Muelhausen (15th century) of Prague. The book is both an attack on Christianity and a defense of Judaism and its dogmas. Lippman sharply refutes Christian interpretations of the Bible and the doctrines derived from them, and incidently provides many exegetical insights. His statement of Jewish dogmas is couched in philosophical terms. A contemporaneous work by Simeon b. Zemaḥ Duran, *Keshet u-Magen*, attacks both Islam and Christianity. In his criticism of Christianity, he makes the significant point that Paul's abrogation of the law was not intended for Jews, but only for gentiles in order to attract them to the new faith.

The debates of the 15th and the 16th centuries are more notable for their polemic nature than for any new insights. Thus contentiousness marked the debate, held at the invitation of the pope, at Tortosa, Spain, in which an apostate Jew argued with Joseph Albo, whose views are summarized in his *Ikkarim*, and with Don Vidal Benveniste, who headed a delegation of the leading Jewish scholars of Spain. Don Isaac Abrabanel dealt at length with Christian doctrines. In the latter part of the 16th century, Joseph *Nasi, Duke of Naxos, and his brother, David, who was the business agent of a cardinal of Crete, and Abraham ibn Migash, the physician of Sultan Suleiman, all wrote polemics against Christianity.

The 17th century saw the renewal of accusations against Jews by apostates and of proselytizing by Catholics and Protestants. These activities were condemned by Zalman Ẓevi Oppenhausen of Germany, Jacob of Venice, and Leone Modena. Public disputations were still being held as, for example, in Ferrara in 1617, which was recorded by an anonymous Jewish scholar in his book about the immutability of the Torah; and later in the century, Isaac Lupis participated in a debate in Marseilles. By the end of the century, however, the number of polemics against Christianity began to decrease. The only such production of note in the 18th century was Moses *Mendelssohn's famous letter to Johann Casper Lavater.

[Meyer Waxman and Mordecai Waxman]

Yiddish Literature

Following the large-scale migration of Jews to German-speaking territories in the course of the late first millennium C.E. and adoption and adaptation of the local language (a process that had already characterized Jewish migrations in antiquity, e.g., in the development of Judeo-Persian, Judeo-Greek, and Judeo-Aramaic), there gradually developed a new Jewish language – Yiddish – distinct from its various components (Romance, Germanic, and Semitic at this stage) that became the vernacular of the Jewish communities and ultimately also a literary language that complemented Hebrew literature over the course of a millennium of Ashkenazi cultural history. By the 17th century that literature spanned essentially the same broad range of genres as did, for instance, English, French, and German literatures of the period. As was also the case with those literatures, in early Yiddish there were a great many translations from other languages.

The earliest textual evidence of the existence of Yiddish is found in Rashi's commentaries on the Bible and Talmud, which include some three dozen Yiddish glosses, indicating the relevance of the language for Rashi (who studied in yeshivot in the Rhineland) and his students. The glossing tradition developed over the course of several centuries from such sparse beginnings to include comprehensive glosses of most biblical books, entered interlinearly, marginally, as separate lists in order of the words' occurrence, and ultimately as separate alphabetically ordered works. Among the important works of early Yiddish lexicography are Anshel b. Eliakim ha-Levi Ẓion's *Mirkeves Hamishno* ("The Second/Double Chariot," Cracow, 1534), a Hebrew-Yiddish biblical concordance and the first printed book substantially in Yiddish. Moses Sertels b. Issachar Halevi published a two-volume set of glossaries of the entire Bible: *Seyfer Lekaḥ Tov* ("Good Doctrine," Prague, 1604) and *Seyfer Beeyr Moushe* ("The Well of Moses," Prague, 1605). Not all glossaries focused on religious texts: both Nathan Nata b. Moses Hannover's *Sofo Bruro* (*Safah Berurah*; "Pure Speech," Prague, 1660) and Elijah Baḥur Levita (Elye Bokher)'s *Shmous Dvorim* (*Shemot Devarim*; "The Names of Things," Isny, 1542) are quadrilingual glossaries arranged thematically.

While glossaries aid readers with "difficult" words, the earliest biblical translations into Yiddish (15th-century manuscripts) were so very literal as to be comprehensible only when read alongside the Hebrew original. The first printed Yiddish translations of the Pentateuch and *haftarot* appeared in 1544: one by Michael Adam (Constance), the other by Paulus Aemilius (Augsburg), both slavishly literal. The next stage arrived in Judah Leib *Bresch's adaptation of those translations into a somewhat more idiomatic style, with an abridged version of Rashi's commentary (Cremona, 1560). Other books of the Bible followed in the ensuing decades, but they were all soon replaced by the *Tsenerene* (Hanau, 1622), probably the most read Yiddish book of all time and one of the most influential books in the history of Yiddish literature and indeed Ashkenazi culture. For four centuries it has been the Bible for Hebrew-less readers, male and female, and immediately became so popular that the Ashkenazi book market rejected the more idiomatic translations published in the ensuing decades (e.g., by Jekuthiel b. Isaac Blitz (Amsterdam, 1676–9) and Joseph b. Alexander Witzenhausen (Amsterdam, 1679)). Little is known of the book's author/translator, Jacob b. Isaac Ashkenazi of Janov. Probably written in the late 16th century, the earliest extant edition of 1622 was not the first edition; there have since been 210 further editions. The book is less a translation than a paraphrase with extensive incorporated commentary drawn from the learned Jewish tradition and rendered accessible to the broadest possible readership.

An innovative development in the literary treatment of biblical narrative was poetic adaptation with an admixture of midrashic material. Already in the earliest collection of Yiddish texts, the Cambridge *Genizah* codex of 1382 (from Cairo), half of the texts are related to this genre, especially the "Avrohom Ovinu" ("Abraham the Patriarch") and "Yousef Hatsadik" ("Joseph the Righteous"). The most famous examples of the genre are the *Mlokhim-bukh* ("The Book of Kings," Augsburg, 1543) and the **Shmuel-bukh* ("The Book of Samuel," Augsburg, 1544), whose authors demonstrate an intimate knowledge of both Jewish sacred and German heroic traditions; they share a four-line stanzaic form of two rhyming couplets (aabb). While the *Mlokhim-bukh* (2,262 stanzas) is the longest poem in early Yiddish, the *Shmuel-bukh* (1,792 stanzas), most likely composed in the late 15th century by Moushe Esrim Vearba, is one of the great narrative masterpieces of the tradition; it was sung to a melody that became famous and was used for many other Yiddish poems of the period.

The liturgy itself remained firmly in the linguistic realm of the sacred languages, Hebrew and Aramaic, and thus the Yiddish translations of the prayer book (complete by the 15th century) were not used in place of the standard prayers, but simply functioned to make them accessible to those who knew little Hebrew. Joseph b. Yakar's translation of the complete prayer book was the first to be printed (Ichenhausen, 1544). A number of important functions with respect to the liturgy were, however, fulfilled by Yiddish. Several texts from the Passover Haggadah, the hymn *"Addir Hu/Almekhtiger Got"*

("Almighty God"), "*Eḥad Mi Yode'a*" ("Who Knows One"), and "*Ḥad Gadya*" ("Song of the Kid"), all appeared in bilingual versions by the 15th century, and "*Ḥad Gadya*" may well have originally been composed in Yiddish and then translated into Aramaic. Significantly, this incorporation of Yiddish into the Passover liturgy takes place in a domestic, not a synagogal, ritual, where Hebrew retained its exclusive dominance. The most important realm of Yiddish in prayer was in *tkhines* (*teḥinnot*) and *slikhes* (*seliḥot*). *Tkhines* are generally rhymed *piyyutim* originating in the weekly fasts; the Yiddish form appeared early and came to dominate the genre. *Slikhes* are nonobligatory prayers for the forgiveness of sin, recited on all fast days and during the Days of Penitence. There were early collections of these prayers by both men and women; among the most famous composers were Toube Pan (17th-century Prague) and Sarah *Bas-Tovim (18th century).

Like liturgical texts, traditional legal textuals (*halakhah*) remained staunchly Hebrew-Aramaic. In rabbinical responses to legal issues posed by individual and community queries, however, Yiddish appears with some frequency, generally in the form of quoted testimony, which provides significant evidence of idiomatic speech at a time when literary texts mask such usage. Coterritorial civil jurisdiction often also leaves traces of Yiddish, especially in the genre designated *Urfehdebrief* or "Oath of Peace," sometimes required of released convicts to ensure that they not take action against their accuser or judge; some few such oaths required of Jews are bilingual, including a Yiddish text.

Among the most important and influential genres in early Ashkenaz were those designed to teach proper daily conduct according to locally defined usage (*minhagim*, books of custom) and proper morals (*muser*). The earliest extant Yiddish examples of custumals (ms. from 1503; printed book Venice, 1593), provided instructions for all aspects of conducting a proper Jewish life, e.g., how to *kasher* pots, how to conduct a circumcision, how to pray in the absence of a *minyan*. Manuals specifically for women, such as the *Seyder Noshim* (ms. 1504) and the rhymed *Mitsvous Hanoshim* ("Women's Laws," Venice, 1552), were quite popular. The earliest Yiddish example of *muser*, the *Seyfer Midous* ("The Book of Virtues," Isny, 1542), an adaptation of the anonymous Hebrew moralistic work, *Orḥot Ẓadikim* ("The Ways of the Righteous"), is dedicated to a woman, Morado of Ginzburg, identified as a doctor of medicine. Its discussions of vices and virtues are quite dense, abstract, and include little in the way of illustrative narratives, parables, and legends that later came to characterize this popular genre, as in the originally Yiddish composition *Der Brant Shpigl* ("The Burning Mirror," Cracow, 1602) by Moses Henochs Altshuler of Prague, who provided practical instruction in ritual hygiene, sexual matters, and rearing children. Rebecca *Tiktiner's *Meynekes Rivko* ("Nursemaid of Rebecca," Prague 1609) provided detailed instruction specifically for women. The very popular *Seyfer Lev Tov* ("Book of the Good Heart," Prague, 1620) by *Isaac b. Eliakim of Posen, almost immediately replaced the *Brant Shpigl*. Ẓevi-Hirsh Koydenover's *Seyfer Kav Hayosher* ("Book of the Correct Measure," Frankfurt am Main, 1705–6) offers rare insight into the spiritual crisis following the collapse of the messianic movement of Shaptse Tsvi/*Shabbetai Ẓevi, here expressed through a drive toward reinstitution of traditional practices now imbued with Lurianic Kabbalah. The *Seyfer Simkhas Hanefesh* ("Joy of the Soul," 2 vols., Frankfurt am Main, 1707; Fürth, 1727) provided the community with an abridged codification of Jewish law along with an annotated catalogue of the vices and virtues observed in Jewish communities; this is a prime example of the later form of the genre with its inclusion of poems and songs, including musical notation. Isaac Wetzlar's *Libs Briv* ("Love Letters," ms. 1749) combined the *muser* genre with a devotion to anti-elitist economic and educational reform that incidentally insists on equal education for girls.

One of the most remarkable of early Yiddish genres is the secular epic or romance. These adventure tales crisscrossed language and cultural boundaries so often in the course of the European Middle Ages that their precise origins are obscure. Even so, their obviously Christian character and orientation render them a curiosity in the early Yiddish canon. Already in the *Genizah* codex of 1382, however, the fragmentary *Dukus Horant* ("Duke Horant"), based on German material (although no German text on the subject is extant), narrates a typically adventurous bridal quest of a king. The *Vidvilt* or *Kenig Artis Houf* ("Vidvilt" / "King Arthur's Court," 15th–16th century) is an adaptation of a 13th-century Middle High German Arthurian romance (*Wigalois*) concerning Sir Gawain and his son Vidvilt. The centerpieces of the genre, however, are the typically medieval *Bovo d'Antona* (1507; printed Isny, 1541), composed by Elijah Levita (Elye Bokher) on the basis of a Tuscan romance, and the renaissance *Pariz un Viene* (Verona, 1594), adapted probably by one of Levita's students from another Italian romance. While Levita's rather conventional romance was perennially popular in countless further adaptations (as the **Bove-bukh*) over the course of several centuries, the consummately Italianate, humanistic *Pariz un Viene*, a Yiddish counterpart of its contemporaries, Ariosto's *Orlando furioso* or Shakespeare's tragedies, apparently enjoyed little popularity. The quasisecular nature of this genre as it developed in northern Italy was also reflected in some aspects of the corpus of early Yiddish lyric and fable (see below).

Insofar as narrative prose per se existed in early Ashkenaz, it was initially at least a Hebrew genre, and thus Yiddish examples were most often translations, e.g., the 15th-century *Ben Ha-Melekh ve-ha-Nazir* ("The Prince and Monk"), a reflex of the Buddha legend that had descended through a long line of adaptations from its Pahlavi original; the popular quasihistorical work, *Yousifen* (*Jossipon*, tr. Michael Adam, Zurich, 1546); or the Hebrew masterpiece of renaissance sensibility, the *Shevet Yehudah* ("Sceptre of Judah," Heb. 1554 (?), Yidd. tr. Cracow, 1591). It is not clear whether Yuspa Shamash's *Ma'asei Nisim* ("Miracle Tales") was written in Yiddish or in fact translated from a Hebrew original by his grandson Eliezer Liberman, who published it (Amsterdam, 1696). Despite the preponderance of translation in this genre, there are genuine masterpieces among the original Yiddish compositions as well. The *Maase Briyo veZimro* ("Tale of Briyo and Zimro," ms. 1585) is a tale of international intrigue, averted cultural extinction, the hero's journey to the Other World, and star-crossed young lovers. The centerpiece of the genre, the **Maase-bukh* ("Mayse-Book / Book of Tales," Basel, 1602), compiled and adapted from the Talmud, Midrash, and various folktale sources in the late 16th century, includes 255 tales, designed to be a vernacular *aggadah* that would teach the common people ethical principles by means of pious tales (in pointed opposition to other allegedly immoral collections then in circulation, such as the **Ki-bukh*; on which see below), as well as entertain. This book's popularity and profound and pervasive influence on later Yiddish literature was surpassed only by the *Tsenerene*. The magnificently anomalous book written by Glikl bas Leyb Pinkerle (*Glueckel of Hameln; untitled, composed 1691–1719; publ. 1898) is difficult to classify, since it combines attributes of the ethical instruction of *muser*, the pragmatic detail of *minhogim*, and the pious exempla of *mayse* collections, along with aspects of autobiography. Glikl provides unsurpassed insight into the mind, passions, spirituality, and daily cares of an intelligent and capable Jewish businesswoman of the period.

In addition to narrative texts, other Yiddish prose works abounded, e.g., instructional manuals in accounting and mathematics, geographical description, hygienic manuals, and the prolific genre of practical medicine (with an inevitable admixture of magical charms and potions). Perhaps most remarkably, in 1686–7, Yiddish added its own contribution to the century that witnessed the invention of European journalism: the *Dinstagishe/Fraytagishe Kurantn*, which appeared twice weekly in Amsterdam, reporting on political events from all over Europe, North Africa, and the Middle East, especially concerning the religious wars of Catholics and Protestants, Turkish incursions into the Balkans, weather catastrophes, and new inventions.

The origins of Jewish drama are obscure, but clearly connected with **Purimshpil* (Purim plays) as performed in private houses during that holiday. There are a few examples of early Purim poems, and Gumprekht of Szczebrzeszyn (resident in Venice) narrates the Esther story in suggestively dramatic form and provides the first usage of the word *purimshpil* (ms. 1555). In 1598, a satirical Yiddish poem indicates that a (non-extant) play called *Shpil fun Toyb Yeklayn*… ("Play about Deaf Jake") was performed at Tannhausen. An anonymous Yiddish adaptation of a German Jonah play survives from c. 1600, the function of which in Jewish culture is not clear. The earliest complete Purim play extant is an *"Akhashveyresh-shpil"* from 1697, which was, as were the other earliest extant examples, a bawdy poetic burlesque based on the biblical Esther story, in which the character of Mordecai was conceived as a clownish buffoon whose humor was often quite vulgar. Within a few decades, however, Purim plays had changed radically from folksy chamber plays to elaborate costumed and quite serious Baroque musical dramas with orchestral accompaniment that in one case at least is styled "like an opera." While branching out to include other subjects, such as Joseph and his brothers and David and Goliath, Yiddish drama was restricted to Purim plays until the advent of maskilic drama at the end of the 18th century.

An important genre of early Yiddish literature was the fable or moral tale, which appeared in a variety of forms. The earliest is a lion fable in the *Genizah* codex of 1382, where the aged tyrant is not healed by the other animals (as often is the tradition), but is the object of their vengeance. Anshel Levi's *Midrash le-Pirkey Ovous* ("Midrash on *Pirkei Avot*," ms. 1579), a recurringly popular subject of Yiddish translation and commentary in the period, also includes a humorous fable of a conceited king whose singing reminds one of the braying of an ass. *Berechiah ha-Nakdan's *Mishlei Shu'alim* ("Fox Fables," 12th century) was translated into Yiddish by Jacob Kopelman (Freiburg, 1583). Fables are also integral features of the infamous *Alfa-beta de Ben Sira* ("Alphabet of Ben Sira," 16th-century ms.). The most important collection is the *Ki-bukh* ("Book of Cows," Verona, 1595), which was castigated for its occasionally risqué morality in the prefaces of the *Maase-bukh* and Moses Wallich's *Seyfer Mesholim* ("Book of Fables," Frankfurt am Main, 1697, a barely adapted reprint of the *Ki-bukh*), both of which claimed to replace it with tales of moral rectitude.

While early Yiddish literature does not present a well-defined genre of lyric poetry, there are a number of culturally interesting examples of various lyric types. The earliest extant Yiddish poetic text is a blessing in couplet form found in the Worms *Maḥzor* (1272). As already noted, there are important Passover hymns and the rhymed penitential prayers; one might also note the Torah songs, some composed by women. There are also reflective philosophical poems such as "Das Mentsh Geglikhn" ("The Ages of Human Life Compared," 1554) or Isaac Wallich's *memento mori* poem "Vayl Ikh Itsundert an Mir Farshtey" ("For I Now Understand About Myself," c. 1700). Balancing such serious poems, whether religious or (quasi-) philosophical, however, there are also poems of playful philosophical disputation, e.g., Zalmen Soyfer's "Makhloukes Yain veHamayim" ("Debate between Wine and Water," 1516); biting Venetian satire, such as Elye Bokher's "HaMavdil Lid" ("Ha-Mavdil Song," 1514); "Eyn Sheyn Nay Lid fun Dray Vayber" ("A Fine New Song of Three Wives," c. 1650) in which three married women spend their evenings drinking in pubs, with only a belated and half-hearted moralistic conclusion; "Pumay" (ca. 1600), a drinking song of yeshivah students; and perhaps most surprisingly, a brief and hauntingly lyrical 14th-century love song written on the fly-leaf of a Rashi manuscript, "Vu Zol Ikh Hin?" ("Whither Shall I Go?").

Beyond the strictly lyrical genre, Yiddish poetry, like other European literatures of the period, also included historical narrative in poetic form, often with a specified melody, indicating that the compositions were commonly sung. These songs often commemorated recent events that affected the Jewish community, such as Elḥonon Hellen's *Megilas Vinẓ* ("The Vints Scroll"), on the *Fettmilch insurrection in Frankfurt am Main in 1614–16 (Amsterdam, 1648); the anonymous adaptation from German of a lament on the death of Emperor Ferdinand IV (?Prague, 1654); Joseph b. Eliezer Lipman Ashkenazi's *Kino al Gezeyrous haKehilous de'k"k Ukraine* ("Lament on the Destruction of the Ukrainian Communities," Prague, 1648), on the *Chmielnicki massacres; Jacob Tousk's (Taussig) *Eyn Sheyn Nay Lid fun Meshiekh* ("A Fine New Song about the Messiah," Amsterdam, 1666), the fervent expression of a pious believer's joy at Shabbetai Ẓevi's supposed fulfillment of messianic prophecy.

The cliché that Yiddish was no more than a "kitchen-language" and its literature in the early period no more than a primitive and embarrassing crutch for "pious women and ignorant men" (i.e., those who knew no Hebrew) has been so widespread over the course of the last half millennium that it has taken on mythic status, but like many myths, it lacks compelling evidence. While there is no doubt that much of early Yiddish devotional literature of the *muser* genre had a primarily female audience, a significant number of *muser* books directly addressed men. The obvious address of women is also the case, with some other qualifications, for the devotional prayers of the *tkhines* and *slikhes* types, and for the Yiddish *Pirkey Ovous*, and even that greatest bestseller of all time in early Yiddish, the *Tsenerene*, although its preface actually identifies men before women as its audience. But there were many genres of early Yiddish texts that were clearly *not* for women or unlettered men: biblical glosses and glossaries and biblical translations so literal that they are incomprehensible except when read in conjunction with the Hebrew text can only have been for the reader of the Hebrew text. The glosses in Rashi's texts indicate not only the existence of Yiddish at that early period, but also that it was one of the languages of Rashi's students, if not in fact one of the languages of his own teaching. Likewise not for women were the books that provide detailed practical information for traveling merchants on how to follow the commandments while on the road (e.g., Moses Cohen's *Derekh Moushe*, "The Path of Moses," Amsterdam, 1699), manuals detailing the method of Talmud study (ms. 1733), introductions to accounting (Arye Levi's *Seyfer Yedios Hakhezhbn*, "The Book of Computations," Amsterdam, 1699). Nor in fact are most of the other extant types of early Yiddish literature as outlined above inherently for women – in what sense is a poem about the Chmielnicki massacres, the *Ḥad Gadya*, or the Amsterdam newspaper, for instance, "women's" literature? One must also keep in mind that the audience of "pious women and ignorant men" identified in the prefaces of many early Yiddish texts in fact constituted the vast majority of the Ashkenazi population, only a tiny minority of which knew more Hebrew than was required for prayer (and of course even that Hebrew-literate minority also knew Yiddish). The functional audience for early Yiddish literature thus comprised the entirety of Yiddish-speaking Jewry, female and non-Hebrew-literate male, but also including in particular the most literate members of the culture, i.e., the educated men who, with few exceptions, wrote, edited, published, distributed, sold, and indeed also bought and read early Yiddish books.

[Jerold C. Frakes (2nd ed.)]

Ladino Literature

The beginning of Ladino literature may be traced to the 13th century with the translation of the Bible into Ladino. These translations, however, were in Latin script and it is only after the expulsion of the Jews from Spain that Ladino translations of the Bible were written in Hebrew script and the language acquired a distinctly Jewish character (see *Bible, Translations, Ladino). Another major literary activity in religious Ladino literature was the translation of exegetical and ethical works, moral handbooks, and prayer books. A number of original works were also produced such as *Almosnino's popular *Il Regimiento de la Vida* (Salonika, 1564), an ethical treatise which included a long dissertation on dreams. Most of Almosnino's works, however, were in Hebrew, although his compilation of data on Constantinople in Ladino, which Jacob *Cansino of Oran later published in Spanish under the title *Extremos y Grandezas de Constantinopla*, is a major work in Spanish Jewish literature and a significant historical source.

By the end of the 17th century poetry, mystical writings, biblical exegesis, history, and ethics were written in Ladino. **Me-Am Lo'ez*, the monumental ethical-religious work of Ladino literature, is an elaborate encyclopedic commentary on the entire Bible which in 1730 was initiated by Jacob *Culi who wrote the commentary on Genesis and a portion of Exodus. It is assumed that the subsequent commentaries are in part based on his manuscripts. The work, written in a popular style, was intended to make the Bible and Jewish learning readily understandable to the layman who no longer was able to use the Hebrew texts. Among original works of religious poetry in Ladino are *Proverbios morales* by Shem Tov (*Santob) de Carrion (14th century) and the *Poema de Yosef*, probably composed at the beginning of the 15th century, which is an adaptation of the story of Joseph and his brethren from the Midrash and *Sefer ha-Yashar*. The poem's strophic and metric form, influenced by the Hebrew *piyyut*, is also reminiscent of the *cuaderna via* literary structure which was developing at the time. Written also in Spanish in Arabic characters, the poem became an integral part of Spanish literature. The popular Ladino poem on the same subject, *Coplas de Yosef ha-Zaddik*, by Abraham de Toledo (1732), is known in two distinct versions: one written in Constantinople (1732) and the other in Belgrade (1861) which is based on the lost Salonika version (1755). The poem, consisting of 400 quatrains, was also sung on Purim. The *copla* genre which flourished in Ladino in the 19th century was mainly the poetic expression of minor works written for Purim (*Coplas de Purim*).

A distinctly secular mode of expression in Ladino literature is the *romancero* which formed part of the oral tradition of Jews in Spain. The Ladino *romancero* is largely a continuation and an adaptation of the Spanish *romancero* of the Middle Ages and the Renaissance. The original *romancero*, a traditional Spanish ballad widely popular in the 14th and 15th centuries, was often sung. There are also many original romances and songs in Ladino or later composition. The different types of *romanceros* found in Spanish literature (historical, tragic, humorous, amorous, satirical) were also found in Ladino, to which have been added three specifically Jewish types: wedding songs, religious hymns, and laments.

Other secular literature in Ladino are adaptations and translations of plays and novels, mainly from French literature. This led to the writing of original plays and novels, most of which, however, are of an inferior quality. There is a rich Ladino folk literature but most of it has neither been collected nor studied.

BIBLIOGRAPHY: Waxman, Literature: see bibliographies at end of each volume; Winter and Wuensche, *Die juedische Literatur* (1906); see also bibliographies for each relevant entry in the encyclopaedia. **ADD. BIBLIOGRAPHY:** YIDDISH LITERATURE: J.C. Frakes (ed.), *Early Yiddish Texts, 1100–1750* (2004); J. Baumgarten, *Introduction to Old Yiddish Literature* (2005).

LITHUANIA (Lithuanian **Lietuva**; Pol. **Litwa**; Rus. **Litva**; Heb. **Lita** ליטא or ליטה; Yid. **Lite** ליטע), southernmost of Baltic states of N.E. Europe; from 1940 Lithuanian S.S.R. (for early period, see *Poland-Lithuania). (See Map: Lithuanian Communities). For the list of alternative names for Jewish communities in Lithuania see Table 1: List of Alternative Names for Jewish Communities in Lithuania. With the partition of Poland at the close of the 18th century the territories of Lithuania passed to Russia. Subsequently, for more than 120 years, Lithuania ceased to exist as a political or administrative unit. It was divided up into six or seven provinces in which the history of the Jews was similar to that of the Jews throughout *Russia. Lithuanian Jewry nevertheless retained its specific character, and its influence on Russian Jewry – and on world Jewry in general – extended beyond the boundaries of historic Lithuania. Lithuanian Jewry was particularly oppressed during World War I. The attitude of the Russian military authorities toward the Jews was one of suspicion and hostility; rumors were spread that they were traitors, and the army therefore perpetrated pogroms against them. In the spring of 1915 expulsions of Jews from the provinces of *Suwalki, Kovno (*Kaunas), *Courland, and *Grodno began. During the fall of the same year, northern and western Lithuania were occupied by the German army. The population suffered from lack of food and unemployment. Limited aid arrived from the Jews of Germany and the United States and a ramified Jewish assistance organization was set up. A network of Hebrew and Yiddish schools, including secondary schools, was established. After the end of World War I, a considerable number of refugees returned to their former places of residence. Lithuanian Jewry was henceforward divided among three states: independent Lithuania, Belorussian S.S.R. (see *Belorussia), and Poland.

Character and Influence on the Diaspora

The notion of "Lithuanian" ("*Litvak*" in Yiddish) to be found in speech, folklore, and Jewish literature in all its languages applies to the Jewish community which developed within the boundaries of historic Lithuania, the region which formed part of the greater Polish kingdom during the 16th to 18th centuries. From the close of the 18th century until World War I this area came under the rule of czarist Russia and included the provinces of Kovno, *Vilna, Grodno, and northern Suwalki, which were essentially of Lithuanian-Polish character, and of *Vitebsk, *Minsk, and *Mogilev, which were Belorussian-Russian in character. A distinction is sometimes made between Lithuanian Jews in a restricted sense (from the provinces of Vilna, Kovno, and the northern parts of the provinces of Suwalki and Grodno) and the Belorussian Jews ("province of Russia"). At the close of the 19th century, about 1,500,000 Jews lived in this region; they constituted more than one-eighth of the total population. The Jews were mainly concentrated in the towns and villages, where in the main they were in the majority. There were more than 300 communities in Lithuania with more than 1,000 persons, including 12 large communities each numbering more than 20,000 persons: Vilna, Minsk, *Bialystok, Vitebsk, Dvinsk (*Daugavpils), *Brest-Litovsk, Kovno, Grodno, Mogilev, *Pinsk, *Bobruisk, and *Gomel; but even the smaller settlements with only some dozens of Jewish families had a vibrant and full Jewish life.

Both economic and historical factors were responsible for the unique character of Lithuanian Jewry. Lithuania was a poor country, and the mass of its inhabitants, consisting of Lithuanian and Belorussian peasants, formed a low social stratum whose national culture was undeveloped. The Jews who had contacts with them as contractors, merchants, shopkeepers, innkeepers, craftsmen, etc., regarded themselves as their superiors in every respect. Lithuanian Jewry was relatively less affected by the *Chmielnicki massacres that devastated the Jews of the Ukraine in 1648–49, and those perpetrated by the *Haidamacks during the 18th century. Even when the wave of pogroms swept Russia during the last decades of czarist rule, there were only isolated manifestations of anti-Jewish violence in Lithuania (Gomel, Bialystok). These circumstances gave the Lithuanian Jews a feeling of stability and security, as a result of which they developed no desire to adopt the language and culture of the surrounding peoples.

The Jews of Lithuania maintained their own way of life. They spoke a special dialect of Yiddish – Lithuanian Yiddish – which differed from the Yiddish spoken in Poland and Volhynia mainly in the pronunciation of the vowels (and in certain districts in the pronunciation of the שׁ (*shin*) as שׂ (*sin*) or ס (*samekh*). The world outlook and way of life of Lithuanian Jewry were based on the Written Law and the Oral Law. The Shulḥan Arukh and its commentaries guided them in their everyday life. Torah learning flourished among wide circles, and love of Torah and esteem for its study was widespread among the masses of Jews. The Jews who lived in the region bordering Lithuania, the "Poles" in the west and the "Volhyn-

Map showing Jewish communities in Independent Lithuania and in the Vilna region ceded to Lithuania in October 1939.

Table 1: List of Alternative Names for Jewish Communities in Lithuania

Lithuanian Name	Russian Name	Yiddish Name
Alytus	Olita	Alite
Anyksciai	Onikshtv	Aniksht
Balberiskis	Balkerishki	Balbirishok
Birzai	Birzhi	Birzh
Butrimonicai	Butymantsv	Butrimants
Darbenai	Dorbyany	Dorbian
Dusetoi	Dusjaty	Dusyat
Gargzdai	Gorzhdy	
Jonava	Janovo	Yanove
Joniskis	Yanishki	Yanishok
Jurbarkas	Jurbug	
Kaisiadorys	Koisedary	Kashedar
Kalvarija	Kalvariya	
Kaunas	Kovno	
Kedainiai	Keidany	Keidan
Kelme	Kelmy	Kelm
Klaipeda	Memel	
Krakiai	Kruki	Krok
Krakinava	Krakinovo	
Kretinga	Kretinga	Kretingen
Kudaros-Naumiestis	Vladslavov	
Kudirkos-Naumiestis	Novoe Mesto	Nayshtat
Kupiskis	Kupishki	Kupishok
Kursenai	Kurshany	Kurshan
Kybartai	Kibarty	Kibart
Lazdijai	Lozdzee	Lazdey
Linkuve	Linkovo	
Luoke	Lavkov	Luvkeve
Maletai	Maljaty	Malat
Marijampole	Mariampol	
Mazeikiai	Mazheiki	Mazheik
Merkine	Meretsch	
Nemaksciai	Nemokshty	Nemoksht
Obeliai	Abeli	Abel
Pandelis	Ponedeli	Ponedel
Panevezys	Ponevezh	
Pasvalys	Posvol	
Pilviskiai	Pilvishki	Pilvishok
Plunge	Plungyany	Plungyan
Prienai	Preny	Pren
Radviliskis	Radzivilishki	
Raguva	Rogov	Rogove

Table 1 (cont.)

Lithuanian Name	Russian Name	Yiddish Name
Raseiniai	Rossienyi	Rasseyn
Rietavas	Retovo	Riteve
Rokiskis	Takishki	Rakishok
Sakiai	Shaki	
Salakas	Soloki	Salok
Salantai	Salanty	Salant
Seda	Syady	Syad
Seduva	Shadov	Shadove
Seirijai	Seree	Serey
Siauliai	Shavli	Shavl
Silale	Shileli	Shilel
Simnas	Simno	
Sirvintos	Shervinty	Shirvint
Skaudvile	Skadvile	Shkudvil
Skuodas	Shkudy	Shkud
Sveksna	Shvekshni	
Taurage	Taurogen	Tavrig
Telsiai	Telschi	Telz
Trakai	Troki	
Ukmerge	Vilkomir	
Utena	Utsjany	Utyah
Uzpaliai	Uschpol	
Varniai	Vorni	Vorne
Veisijai	Veisee	
Vieksniai	Wekschni	Vekshne
Vilkaviskis	Volkovyshki	Vilkovishk
Vilkija	Viliki	
Virbalis	Verzhbolov	Virbaln
Zagare	Zhagory	Zhager
Zarasai	Novo Aleksandrovsk	Ezherene
Zasliai	Shosli	Zasle
Ziezmariai	Zhizhmory	Zemar
Zydikiai	Zhidiki	Zidik

ians" in the south, associated specific characteristics with the Lithuanian Jews: a certain emotional dryness, the superiority of the intellect over emotion, mental alertness, sharp-wittedness, and pungency. Their piety was also questioned (hence the popular derogatory appellation for the Lithuanian Jews, "*tseylem-kop*"). It was also a feature of Lithuanian Jewry that *Ḥasidism did not strike roots in northern Lithuania, while in the provinces of Belorussia it assumed a different nature and content – the Chabad trend – from the original Ḥasidism of Ukraine and Poland (see below). Lithuanian Jews were considered the "prototype" of the **Mitnaggedim*.

Spiritual Trends and Leaders

Until the 16th century the Jews of Lithuania were on the outer fringe of European Jewry. During the 16th and 17th centuries, they were influenced by Polish Jewry, and adopted its organizational methods (Lithuanian Council; see *Councils of the Lands), its educational system, and its mode of learning. The first prominent rabbis who were called upon to officiate in the large Lithuanian communities, such as Mordecai b. Abraham *Jaffe, author of the *Levushim*, and Joel *Sirkes, author of *Bayit Ḥadash* (the "Baḥ"), came from outside Lithuania. Solomon b. Jehiel *Luria (the Maharshal), who was of Lithuanian origin and promoted Torah learning there for a number of years, acquired most of his education and was mainly active beyond the borders of that country. It was only during the 17th century that leading Torah scholars emerged from the yeshivot of Lithuania. Among them were the commentators on the Shulḥan Arukh, *Shabbetai b. Meir ha-Kohen (the Shakh), and Moses b. Naphtali Hirsch *Rivkes, author of *Be'er ha-Golah*.

However, the personality which symbolized the supremacy of Torah learning within Lithuanian Jewry and determined its character for several generations was that of the Gaon of Vilna, *Elijah b. Solomon Zalman, who lived during the second half of the 18th century. He established his own method of study. Its main features were abstention from casuistic methods, close examination of the talmudic text and accuracy in its interpretation, a comprehensive knowledge of all the sources, and the study of grammar and the sciences which were essential for profound understanding of the teachings of the Torah.

R. Elijah appeared on the Lithuanian scene when winds of change were beginning to blow across that country. In the south, Ḥasidism blazed a trail, and the disciples of *Dov Baer the Maggid of Mezhirech arrived in *Shklov, Vitebsk, Vilna, and other communities, winning over a large following. From the West came the ideas of the *Haskalah; these at first were moderate in character and sought to adapt themselves to the old school (like the scholars of Shklov, R. Baruch b. Jacob *Schick, or Phinehas Elijah *Hurwitz, author of *Sefer ha-Berit*), but their revolutionary nature was rapidly revealed. R. Elijah's circle of disciples consolidated against these new forces; they regarded Torah study as a guarantee for the continued existence of the nation in its traditional form and converted religious learning into a popular movement, in which the great central yeshivot played a leading role. The first of these was the yeshivah established by Ḥayyim *Volozhiner in 1803 in the townlet of Volozhin. In its wake, both large and small yeshivot were founded in many towns and villages, as well as *kolelim* and *kibbuẓim* ("groups") for young men and *perushim* ("abstinents"), whose students prepared themselves for the rabbinate through self-instruction (the *kibbuẓ* of Eisiskes (Eishishok), near Vilna, was well known). During the 19th century, large yeshivot were established in *Mir, Telz (*Telsiai), *Slobodka (near Kovno), and other townlets. The personality of *Israel Meir ha-Kohen (the Ḥafeẓ Ḥayyim) left its imprint on his yeshivah in the little town of Radun, where Torah learning was combined with the study of *musar* (ethical literature). An attempt to adapt these studies to the spirit of the modern era was made by Isaac Jacob *Reines, a founder of the *Mizrachi organization, who in 1904 established a yeshivah in *Lida where secular studies were taught and modern Hebrew literature was studied.

During the middle of the 19th century, the *Musar movement emerged from within the ranks of Orthodox Jewry. Initiated by R. Israel (Salanter) *Lipkin, it endeavored to strengthen traditional Judaism against the dangers of the modern era by fostering the study of ethics. The "Musarniks" established several yeshivot (Keneset Yisrael in Slobodka; the yeshivah of *Novogrudok where an extremist, fanatical, and ascetic wing of the movement emerged). Their attempt to introduce this trend into other yeshivot gave rise to sharp polemics from their opponents, who feared that the study of *musar* would result in a neglect of Torah study.

The yeshivot of Lithuania attracted young men throughout Russia. They trained rabbis and religious communal workers for Jewish communities all over the world. Many who later abandoned traditional Judaism, including Ḥ.N. *Bialik and M.J. *Berdyczewski, were also educated in them. Over the last century, the rabbis of Lithuania became known throughout the Jewish world. They included Isaac Elhanan *Spektor of Kovno, Joseph Baer *Soloveichik of Brest, Joseph *Rozin and *Meir Simḥah ha-Kohen of Dvinsk, Ḥayyim Ozer *Grodzinski of Vilna, Jerohman Judah Leib *Perelmann ("Ha-Gadol mi-Minsk"), Isser Zalman *Meltzer of Slutsk, Abraham Isaiah *Karelitz (the Ḥazon Ish), and many others.

Ḥasidism did not spread through Lithuania to the same extent as in the other parts of Eastern Europe. Only one branch, Chabad Ḥasidism, struck roots in Belorussia. The descendants and disciples of its leader, *Shneur Zalman of Lyady, scattered in many towns and townlets and formed an energetic organization of Ḥasidism whose influence spread beyond the borders of Lithuania. Their headquarters were in the townlet of *Lubavich. This trend in Ḥasidism was of a scholarly, philosophical nature. It considered Torah study to be one of the fundamentals of Ḥasidism, to be combined with the study of ethical and ḥasidic works. At the close of the 19th century, the Chabad movement established its own network of yeshivot (*Tomekhei Temimim*). A more popular branch of Ḥasidism which developed in the region situated between Lithuania and Volhynia was centered around the *ẓaddikim* of the *Karlin-*Stolin dynasty.

An important cultural factor in Lithuania from the close of the 18th century was the Hebrew press. The first printing presses were founded in Shklov (1783) and Grodno (1788). During the 19th century Vilna became one of the world's leading centers for the printing of Hebrew books (of the *Romm family and other presses). It was here that the famous Vilna Talmud was printed, as well as a multitude of religious and ethical works, and Haskalah and popular literature in Hebrew and Yiddish.

Although Lithuania played an important role in the preservation of traditional Judaism, it also contributed largely to the movements which shook the Jewish world in recent generations and brought many changes in it. These were Haskalah, the Zionist movement, and the Jewish Socialist movement.

Haskalah

From neighboring Prussia Haskalah penetrated Lithuania, first to the small border towns and the cities of Vilna and Minsk, and from there to other localities. In Lithuania Haskalah assumed a particular character. The manifestations of national disavowal and *assimilation to other cultures which left their imprint on Haskalah in Western Europe, as well as in Poland and southern Russia, were absent in Lithuania. Circles of *maskilim* who adhered to their people and its language were formed. A Hebrew literature which spread Haskalah and its ideas developed. This literature was not confined to Jewish studies (Wissenschaft) but encompassed every aspect of life. Its exponents were poets such as Abraham Dov (Adam ha-Kohen) *Lebensohn, and J.L. *Gordon, novelists such as Abraham *Mapu and Perez *Smolenskin, publicists and critics such as A.U. *Kovner, A.J. *Paperna, M.L. *Lilienblum, and J.M. *Pines, scholars in Jewish studies (Joshua *Steinberg, E. *Zweifel), authors of popular works on general history and geography (M.A. *Guenzburg; K. *Schulman), and natural sciences (H.S. *Slonimski, Ẓevi *Rabinowitz, and S.J. *Abramovitsh, known as Mendele Mokher Seforim). The *maskilim* assisted the Russian government in its efforts to spread Russian culture among the Jews and cooperated with it in the establishment of a network of Jewish state schools, at the center of which stood the government rabbinical seminary of Vilna. They laid the foundations of both the Russian-Jewish literature (L. *Levanda) and modern Yiddish literature (I.M. *Dick, *Shomer (N.M. Shaikevich), J. *Dineson, and Mendele Mokher Seforim). They also paved the way for the *Ḥibbat Zion and Zionism on the hand and the Jewish Socialist movement on the other.

Hibbat Zion and Zionism

Lithuania was a fertile ground for the development of Ḥibbat Zion and Zionism. The Jews of Lithuania had been attached to Ereẓ Israel by powerful ties since the immigration there of the Ḥasidim and the disciples of the Gaon of Vilna from the end of the 18th century. Natives of Lithuania such as D. *Gordon, in the periodical *Ha-Maggid*, P. Smolenskin, in *Ha-Shaḥar*, J.M. Pines, and E. *Ben-Yehuda had already discussed Jewish nationalism and settlement in Ereẓ Israel in the 1870s. With the inception of Ḥibbat Zion, the movement spread to many towns and townlets, one of its centers being Bialystok, the residence of Samuel *Mohilewer, one of the leaders of the movement. Natives of Lithuania were among the most prominent propagators of the Ḥibbat Zion ideology throughout Russia and beyond (S.P. *Rabbinowitz, Hermann *Schapira, etc.). In 1902 the second convention of Russian Zionists was held in Minsk. This was the only Zionist convention to be held openly and attended by the public in the czarist period. From 1905 to 1912 the center of Russian Zionism was Vilna. The Zionists headed the movement for the revival of the Hebrew language and the establishment of modern Hebrew schools (*ḥeder metukkan*, "reformed *ḥeder*"). The first Diaspora institution for the training of Hebrew teachers was opened in 1908 in Grodno ("the Grodno courses"). The development of Hebrew literature in Lithuania and the activities of Hebrew authors and poets such as Z. *Shneour, Yaakov *Cahan, and I.D. *Berkowitz were closely connected with Zionism.

Jewish Socialist Movement

Lithuania was the cradle of the Jewish Socialist movement. It was characteristic that the Jews of Lithuania found it necessary to publish a Socialist literature, at first in Hebrew (A.S. *Liebermann and his colleagues) and later in Yiddish. The background to this was the existence of the many thousands of poor and oppressed Jewish workers and craftsmen who did not know Russian or Polish; the *maskilim* and Socialists were therefore compelled to address them in their own language. From the close of the 19th century, there rapidly developed an ideology in which revolutionary Socialism was allied to fragmentary and propitiatory nationalist formulae which in practice called for the fostering of a secular literature in Yiddish (Yiddishism) and Jewish cultural autonomy, centered on a secular community organization and Jewish schools giving instruction in the language of the masses (Ch. *Zhitlowsky). In order to mobilize the Jewish workers for revolutionary activities the *Bund was organized. The Bund rapidly extended its activities into Poland and Ukraine but its influence was essentially felt in Lithuania. Its emissaries gained adherents among the poverty-stricken Jews of the towns and townlets, and created a sense of self-confidence in the Jewish apprentices and workers and mobilized them into the service of the revolution. The Bund played a major role in the destruction of traditional Judaism and in opposition to Hebrew culture and Zionism.

The influence of Lithuanian Jewry on Russian and world Jewry gained in impetus from the middle of the 19th century. The Lithuanian yeshivot attracted students from every part of Russia, as well as from abroad. Religious and secular books from Vilna were sold throughout the Diaspora. Rabbis of Lithuanian origin served many of the world's communities and Lithuanian *melammedim* (teachers of elementary religious studies) were recognized as capable teachers in Poland and southern Russia.

One of the causes of the spread of Lithuanian influence was the dire poverty in the country, which led to a constant stream of emigration toward southern Russia and Poland and later to the countries of Western Europe and America. Wherever the Lithuanian Jews arrived, they brought with them their spiritual heritage and learning and thus contributed toward strengthening traditional Judaism and the forging of closer links among the Jewish people and its culture. They were also prominent among the Jewish populations of St. Petersburg and Moscow. Large numbers settled in Warsaw and Lodz. They streamed to America and formed a special concentration in South Africa. They also made an extensive contribution to the modern development of Ereẓ Israel.

Lithuanian Jewry was severely affected by World War I and the revolutions and border changes which ensued, bringing dissolution and economic and spiritual chaos. When the Jews were expelled from Kovno province, many communal leaders and activists there left for the interior of Russia, where they continued their activities. Once the regimes and their borders had consolidated, Lithuanian Jewry found itself divided among states: independent Lithuania, Belorussian S.S.R., and Poland.

In Belorussian S.S.R.

There were some 400,000 Jews living in Belorussian S.S.R. between the two world wars. The authorities adopted a policy of systematic repression of traditional Judaism, the Hebrew language and culture, and the Zionist movement, assisted in this by the *Yevsektsiya. During the 1920s, the elements remaining faithful to Judaism still carried on a difficult struggle and maintained clandestine yeshivot and *ḥadarim*, Zionist youth movements and *Heḥalutz organizations. The Jewish Communists endeavored to provide a substitute for Jewish culture. In Belorussia there even existed a trend among the Yevsektsiya which attempted to consolidate the national position of the Jews in this region by promoting Yiddish schools, Jewish publishing houses and newspapers, and the establishment of a higher institute for Jewish studies in Minsk which engaged in research on the history of the Jews in Lithuania, their dialect, and their popular culture. These experiments flickered out and were liquidated during the 1930s because the authorities did not support them and the Jewish masses were indifferent to them.

In Poland

After World War I the majority of the former Lithuanian Jews came within the boundaries of newly independent *Poland on the border strip extending from the north of Vilna to the Polesye marshes. They continued to develop independent cultural activities in every sphere. Yeshivot flourished in this region (among them, the great yeshivah of Mir with its hundreds of students, and those of Radun, *Slonim, *Lomza, *Kletsk, etc.). Hebrew schools, including secondary schools and excellent training colleges for teachers, founded by the *Tarbut organization were concentrated there. The network of Yiddish schools of the Central Yiddish School Organization (CYSHO) was also developed in this area, and in 1925 the Institute for Jewish Research (Yiddisher Visenshaftlicher Institut, *YIVO) was founded in Vilna. It became a world center for research into the Yiddish language and the history of the Jews and their culture in Eastern Europe. The Vilna theatrical company (*Di Vilner Trupe*) was established and a Yiddish press and literature flourished (the *Yung Vilner* group of poets included Chaim *Grade and A. *Suzkever). The Zionist and pioneer youth movements expanded in this region. When both independent and Polish Lithuania were annexed by Russia in 1939–40, the Jewish institutions were rapidly liquidated. The German invasion of June 1941 brought the physical annihilation of Lithuanian Jewry.

[Yehuda Slutsky]

In Independent Lithuania

About a year before the end of World War I, on Sept. 18–23, 1917, precisely two years after the capture of Vilna by the Germans, the Lithuanians were given permission by the German occupation force to hold a congress in Vilna to consider the future political fate of Lithuania. The congress put forward the demand for an independent Lithuanian state within its ethnographic boundaries with Vilna as the capital. The Vilna congress also elected a national council, Lietuvos Taryba, which on Feb. 16, 1918, proclaimed Lithuania an independent state. The Germans maintained their occupation of Lithuania until the end of 1918.

POPULATION. According to the census held on Sept. 17, 1923, the Jewish population numbered 153,743 (7.5% of the total), and was the largest national minority (see Table 2: Jewish Population of Lithuania – Sept. 17, 1923 Census). They formed just under one-third of the total population of the larger towns, 28.7% of the small-town population, and only 0.5% of the village inhabitants. In the following five towns the census showed the Jewish population to be: In *Memel (Klaipeda), which with its district belonged to Lithuania from 1923 to 1939 as an autonomous region, there were 2,470 Jews in 1929. Their number in the Memel region rose as a result of migration from other parts of Lithuania. At the beginning of 1939, shortly before the seizure of Memel by Germany, the territory had about 9,000 Jewish inhabitants. Statistics of 1937 show 157,527 Jews (75,538 males, 81,989 females; or 98% of the total) as having declared their nationality as Jewish, an indicator of the strength of Jewish consciousness among the Jews of Lithuania and the slight influence of assimilation.

Jews mainly spoke Yiddish among themselves, but a number of the professional intelligentsia used Russian. Although in time practically all Jews were able to speak Lithuanian, this did not become their regular spoken language.

ECONOMIC POSITION. The agrarian reforms which the Lithuanian constituent assembly adopted in 1922 also affected the few Jewish owners of farms of over 80 hectares in extent. The Lithuanian government, however, did little to satisfy the claims of Jews who had any rights to the ownership of land. The agrarian reforms only partly satisfied the land hunger of the poor peasants, and in addition to emigration abroad there was also a considerable migration from the rural districts to the towns. This general process of urbanization came into conflict with the long-established economy of the Jewish inhabitants of the town and *shtetl*. In this growing economic competition, the administration of the young Lithuanian republic actively took the part of the Lithuanians. To develop agrarian economy, the government assisted in the formation of cooperatives, which accumulated control of the entire export trade, including the trade in agricultural products. Thus many Jews were deprived of their livelihood.

Table 2. Jewish Population of Lithuania – Sept. 17, 1923 Census

	Jewish population	% total population
Kaunas (Kovno)	25,044	27.1%
Panevezys (Ponevezh)	6,845	35.6%
Siauliai (Shavli)	5,338	24.9%
Ukmerge (Vilkomir)	3,885	37.5%
Vilkaviskis (Volkovyshki)	3,206	44.1%

In 1923 there were 25,132 Jews engaged in trade and credit banking, 18,107 in industry and crafts, 4,996 in agriculture, 4,180 in the liberal professions, and 2,348 in transport. Jewish commerce was largely concentrated in small trade, while industry and crafts were mainly carried on in small factories or workshops.

During the early years of Lithuanian national independence the Jews had a predominant part in the export-import trade. However, shortly before World War II Jewish participation in the export trade amounted to only 20%, and in the import trade to 40%. In 1923 there were nearly 14,000 Jewish shops and 2,160 non-Jewish shops; in 1936 the respective numbers were approximately 12,000 and 10,200. The majority of Jewish shops were small-scale establishments. Jewish traders were unable to compete with the Lithuanian cooperatives, which enjoyed great privileges especially in the respect of taxation. They increased rapidly and, between 1919 and 1925, the number of such competitive enterprises ranged against Jewish trade doubled in number.

About one-third of the Jews earned their livelihood in crafts. There were Jews also in the professions, but their numbers continually decreased, and their places were taken by Lithuanians. At the beginning of 1931 there were 88 Jewish cooperative people's banks having more than 20,000 members and functioning in conjunction with an association of Jewish people's banks. The Jewish people's banks owned a portion of the working capital of the central bank for the support of Jewish cooperatives.

EMIGRATION. Both open and unofficial measures aiming at ousting Jews from their economic positions led many Jews to emigrate. Between 1928 and 1939, 13,898 Jews emigrated from Lithuania, of whom 4,860 (35%) went to South Africa; 3,541 (25.5%) to Palestine; 2,548 (18.3%) to Latin America; 1,499 (10.8%) to the United States; 648 (4.6%) to Canada; and 602 (5.8%) elsewhere. It is estimated that between 1923 and 1927 at least 6,000 to 7,000 Jews emigrated from Lithuania, and between 1919 and 1941, 9,241 Lithuanian Jews immigrated to Palestine (3.07% of all those who settled there in that period).

JEWISH AUTONOMY. In the early period of the republic, Lithuanian policy was concerned that Jewish influence in Lithuania and abroad, especially in the United States, should be exercised for the benefit of their country. In the first Lithuanian cabinet formed in Vilna, there were three Jews, J. Wygodsky (minister for Jewish affairs), Shimshon Rosenbaum (deputy foreign minister), and N. Rachmilewitz (deputy minister of commerce). At the end of 1918 the Germans evacuated Lithuania, and in January it was occupied by the Bolsheviks. The Lithuanian government then moved from Vilna to Kaunas (Kovno). Wygodsky remained in Vilna, which in 1920 was captured by the Poles under General L. Zeligowski, and the city and district of Vilna became a part of Poland. The other two members of the cabinet accompanied the government to Kaunas, and in 1919 Wygodsky was replaced as minister of

Jewish affairs by the Kaunas communal leader and Zionist Max *Soloveichik (Solieli).

On Aug. 5, 1919, the Lithuanian delegation to the Peace Conference at Versailles sent to the *Comité des Délégations Juives in Paris a letter in which the Lithuanian government guaranteed to the Jews of Lithuania the "right of national-cultural autonomy." This official declaration made possible the rise and development in Lithuania of institutions of Jewish national autonomy. As a result there arose a widespread system of legally recognized *communities (*kehillot*). On Jan. 5, 1920, the first communal conference was held in Kaunas with the participation of 141 delegates. A Jewish National Council was appointed and given the task, in conjunction with the Ministry of Jewish Affairs, of administering the Jewish autonomous institutions. Shimshon Rosenbaum was elected head of the Jewish National Council. The minister for Jewish affairs received directives from the National Council and was responsible to it. The National Council conducted widely ramified activity in all areas of Jewish life. During the early years of its existence it was much occupied with assistance to the Jewish war refugees who had returned from Russia, and also with helping immigrants. It obtained financial means from the American Jewish *Joint Distribution Committee and other Jewish aid organizations.

A statute concerning the communities was promulgated in March 1920 and recognized the community (*kehillah*) as a regular, obligatory, public, authorized institution, competent to impose taxes and issue regulations in order to meet the budgets for religious affairs, charity, social aid, educational institutions, and the like. The community was also responsible for the registration of Jewish births. The community administration, the community council, was elected on democratic principles. Every citizen whose documents showed him to be a Jew was automatically a member of the community. Only by conversion to another religion or on proof that his document was invalid, could anyone cease to be a member of the *kehillah*. The second communal congress, which opened in Kaunas on Feb. 14, 1922, was attended by 130 delegates representing all the Jewish communities in the towns and small towns in Lithuania. One of the focal problems of the congress was the question of the Jewish educational system, especially in respect of the school curriculum and the right of the pupils' parents to determine the ideological spirit of the school.

On the admission of Lithuania into the League of Nations, the Lithuanian government, in May 1922, signed a declaration that Lithuania would fulfill all obligations regarding her national minorities as formulated in the agreement concerning *minority rights in the newly established states. On Aug. 1, 1922, the Lithuanian Constituent Assembly accepted the constitution which assured national rights to the larger national minorities in the country. The years 1919 to 1922 were the golden age of Jewish national autonomy in Lithuania, when the political and citizenship rights of the Jews were recognized and confirmed. The end of 1922 and the start of 1923 saw the beginning of the erosion of Jewish autonomy. The reactionary clerical groups then standing at the helm of state launched a campaign, at first covertly and later openly, against Jewish autonomy and Jewish interests in general. There were many reasons for this new course taken by the Lithuanians with respect to their Jewish fellow citizens. Once the Lithuanian republic had found its feet, the Lithuanians no longer felt that they needed the help of Jews either at home or abroad. When the Constituent Assembly, in dealing with the draft constitution, removed the clauses relating to ministries for the affairs of the national minorities and the right of the minorities to use their mother tongue for public matters, the minister for Jewish affairs, M. Soloveichik, resigned from the cabinet. His portfolio was then held for a short time by Julius (Judah) *Brutzkus.

On Nov. 20, 1923, the Jewish National Assembly opened in Kaunas, consisting of delegates elected by the Jewish population by democratic proportional voting. The composition of the newly elected National Council was: General Zionists 11; *Mizrachi 10; *Ẓe'irei Zion (Hitaḥadut) 6; Zionist-Socialist 5; Craftsmen 4; *Po'alei Zion Left 2; *Folkspartei 2. The *Agudat Israel groups in general boycotted the elections. In dealing with the national budget for the year 1924, the Lithuanian parliament struck out the provisions for the Ministry of Jewish Affairs. In protest, Rosenbaum resigned from his portfolio in February 1924. The new cabinet, formed in April 1924, included no minister for Jewish affairs. The National Council continued in existence for a short time but when it met for a special session on Sept. 17, 1924, it was dispersed by the police, and subsequently ceased to exist. The democratically organized *kehillot* were also later dissolved. The government passed a new law for the *kehillot*, depriving them of their Jewish-national content. The Jews then boycotted the elections to these *kehillot* and they were not constituted. Later, as a result of the efforts of the Jewish parliamentary faction, two bodies were formed with limited functions: Ezra (for social aid) and Adass Yisroel (for religious needs). All that remained as remnants of autonomy were the Jewish people's banks and the Hebrew-Yiddish school system.

EDUCATION. The educational system set up in independent Lithuania was one of the most important achievements of the Jewish national autonomy. Teachers in the Jewish elementary schools who had teaching certificates approved by the ministry of education received their salaries from state funds in common with non-Jewish teachers in the general state schools. The running expenses of the schools were met by city government institutions. The three school systems comprised *Tarbut which was Zionist-orientated; "Yiddishist" schools for the Socialist trend; and Yavneh, the religious traditional schools. The language of instruction was Hebrew in the Tarbut schools, Yiddish in the Yiddishist schools, and Hebrew, and to some extent also Yiddish in the Yavneh schools. Each school system was supported by its own political-ideological groups. The Tarbut schools were in the front rank of Jewish schools in Lithuania. Because of the large number of its Hebrew schools of all grades, Lithuania acquired its reputation among Jews as the "second Ereẓ Israel." There were 46 Tarbut elementary schools in 1922, 72 in 1924, and 84 in 1932. The Agudat Israel and Mizrachi groups confined their interest to the Yavneh schools. There were also *ḥadarim, talmud torah* institutions, and *yeshivot. Apart from the celebrated yeshivot in Slobodka and in Telz there were large yeshivot also in *Panevezys (Ponovezh), *Kelme (Kelmy), and other communities. The Culture League (Kultur-Lige), founded in 1919, also had its schools, where at first the moderate Yiddishist elements were represented but later the Communists set the tone. These schools ignored Hebrew and introduced the phonetic spelling of Yiddish. The Culture League was closed down by the government in 1924, and some of its institutions (elementary schools, evening schools, and libraries) were abolished. Those that survived had no formal central management. However, an illegal organization of Yiddishist schools was maintained in Kaunas. In 1926 the Folkspartei created a Jewish educational association, and some of the Yiddishist schools were under its supervision.

The number of Hebrew and Yiddish elementary schools in Lithuania reached 108 in 1936, having 13,607 pupils and 329 teachers. There were in addition Hebrew and Yiddish kindergartens. In the school year 1935/36, there were 60 secondary schools, of which 28 were state schools and 32 private. Among the latter there were 14 Jewish secondary schools. Jewish pupils in the Jewish and non-Jewish secondary schools amounted to 18.9% of the total school attendance. There were also Hebrew and Yiddish presecondary schools which provided the first four grades of the secondary school course. The Jewish secondary and pre-secondary schools had to be largely maintained by the parents; the Ministry of Education reduced its subsidy to the Jewish educational institutions year by year. The medium of instruction in the Hebrew secondary schools was Hebrew in all eight grades. There were two secondary schools giving instruction in Yiddish, the Vilkomir (*Ukmerge) Reali school, and the Kaunas Commercial School.

Kaunas University in 1922 had a student body of 1,168, including "free auditors" or occasional students, among them 368 Jews (31.5%). In 1935 the student body (including occasionals) numbered 3,334, among them 591 Jews (16.4%). A **numerus clausus* was unofficially introduced in the medical faculty in the course of time, and in 1936 not a single Jewish medical student gained admittance. Because of the difficulties facing Jews trying to qualify in law, and the deterioration of prospects in the liberal professions generally, the proportion of Jewish students in the other faculties also fell sharply. Among the 411 professors, lecturers, and other members of the teaching staff of Kaunas University, there were no more than six Jews. The chair of Semitic studies was held by Ḥayyim Nachman *Shapira.

POLITICAL POSITION. During the democratic period of the independent Lithuanian republic (1919–26) there were four parliamentary elections. The constituent assembly (May 1920–November 1922) included six Jewish deputies, S. Rosenbaum, M. Soloveichik (both Zionists), N. Rachmilewitz, Rabbi A. Poppel (Aḥdut, i.e., *Agudat Israel), and N. Friedman and E. Finkelstein (both advocates and non-party democrats). N. Friedman was succeeded on his death by S. Landau. There was Jewish representation in parliamentary committees, and in the praesidium, and the Jews played their part in drawing up the basic citizenship laws of the young Lithuanian state. Their main task, however, was to safeguard the interests of the Jewish national minority. The Jewish parliamentary faction maintained close contact with the Jewish National Council.

On the basis of the election results for the first parliament (which sat from November 1922 to March 1923) the Jews were entitled to six seats, but because of a deliberately false interpretation of the election law, only three Jewish seats were recognized. The same happened with the Polish representation. The Jewish and Polish deputies, together with the other opposition members, thereupon expressed "no confidence" in the newly established government. The first parliament was accordingly dissolved. In the elections for the second parliament (which sat from May 1923 to May 1926), the Jews and other national minorities formed a nationalities bloc, and seven Jewish deputies were elected: M. Wolf, J. *Robinson, S. Rosenbaum, all Zionists; I. Brudny (Ẓe'irei-Zion, World Union), L. Garfunkel (d. 1976) (Ẓe'irei-Zion, Hitaḥadut), E. Finkelstein (Folkspartei), and Rabbi Joseph *Kahaneman. For various reasons there were subsequent changes in the Jewish representation. The last democratically elected parliament lasted in all just over half a year, and the coup d'etat of Dec. 17, 1926 put an end to democracy in Lithuania. Power then fell into the hands of the extremist nationalists (*Tautininkai*) who introduced an authoritarian regime. The parliament was dissolved in April 1927, and a temporary constitution was promulgated in May 1928, abolishing the most important democratic principles of the previous constitution.

The social and economic contrasts existing between the Lithuanians and Jews influenced their relationship and aggravated antisemitism. Economic antisemitism found its most conspicuous expression in the organization of Lithuanian traders and workers known as the Verslininkai ("skilled workers"). The organization was formed in 1930 and its slogan was "Lithuania for Lithuanians." Its attitude toward the Jews became increasingly aggressive, and although there were no pogroms in Lithuania as in Poland and Romania, antisemitic demonstrations occurred from time to time. The Jewish press played a great part in the struggle of the Jewish population for national political rights. Lithuanian Jewry, though small in number, published a number of newspapers and periodicals which helped to form Jewish public opinion both at home and abroad.

Soviet Rule in Lithuania, 1940–41

The U.S.S.R.-German Pact of Aug. 23, 1939, brought Soviet dominance to the Baltic area. On Oct. 10, 1939, the U.S.S.R. and Lithuania concluded an agreement in Moscow for "the transfer of Vilna and the Vilna province to the Lithuanian Republic and mutual assistance between the Soviet Union and Lithuania," which came into effect on the following day. With the incorporation of Vilna, the Jewish community of Lithuania grew by about 100,000. Previously the 160,000 Lithuanian Jews constituted 7% of the population, but with the annexed portions they totaled more than a quarter of a million, about 10% of the total population of the enlarged country. The number of Jewish refugees from Poland grew considerably (to 14,000–15,000) in the following months. About 10,000 stayed in Vilna and the rest in Kovno (Kaunas) and other places. About 5,000 refugees managed to emigrate from Lithuania. The Lithuanian Jews made every effort to assist refugees. On June 15, 1940, Soviet troops crossed the Lithuanian border and a "people's government" was established on June 17, which included two Jews, L. Kogan, minister of health, and H. Alperovitch, minister of commerce. On July 14, "elections" to the People's Sejm ("parliament") took place. Five Jews were among the deputies elected. On August 3 the Supreme Soviet acceded to the Sejm's "request" to become the 16th Soviet Republic. Shortly afterward, the provisional Lithuanian government was replaced by a soviet of people's commissars. All industrial and commercial enterprises, private capital, and larger dwelling houses were nationalized, and a new agrarian reform carried out. All social groups and organizations, general as well as Jewish, had to cease their activities, with the exception of those belonging to the Communists (who had been illegal until the Russian invasion), and the press (again excepting the Communist newspapers) was closed down. A wave of arrests swept over the country. At the same time a considerable number of Soviet officials entered Lithuania. Many of the former owners of the nationalized houses, firms, and factories were forced to settle in the provinces. The effect of the introduction of Soviet rule upon the Jewish population was particularly strong. The new Communist regime was in urgent need of experience and abilities possessed by the Jewish intelligentsia, so that Jews were given prominent positions in the economic, legal, and administrative apparatus. At the same time, although nationalization of all important branches of the economy applied equally to all citizens, irrespective of their ethnic origin, large segments of the Jewish population were affected with special harshness. A total of 986 industrial enterprises were nationalized, of which about 560 (57%) belonged to Jews; of 1,593 commercial firms nationalized, no less than 1,320 (83%) were owned by Jews. Jews were also strongly hit by the nationalization of houses and bank accounts.

The phase before the German attack on Lithuania was marked by deportations to Siberia. In the spring of 1941 the Soviet security services compiled lists of "counter-revolutionary elements" and submitted secret reports on those listed, which also included Jews in the following categories: leaders and journalists of various Zionist political groups; leaders of the Bund and Bundist journalists; leaders of Jewish military and "fascist" formations – e.g., of the Jewish veterans of Lithuania's war of independence, of the Jewish war veterans, of *Betar, the *Revisionists, and their affiliated bodies.

In mid-June 1941, one week before the German-Soviet war, many people, including Jews, were hastily deported as politically unreliable to Siberia and other parts of Soviet Asia. They were interned in forced labor camps and set to work in coal mines, wood cutting, and other heavy labor. Some of those deported were tried for "crimes" committed prior to the Soviet occupation. Although large numbers of Jews were also among the deportees, Lithuanian antisemites alleged that the deportations were the result of Jewish revenge on the local non-Jewish majority, carried out by "Jewish" security officers in charge of the deportations.

German Occupation, 1941–44

The entire country was occupied by the Germans within one week, so that only a handful of Jews managed to escape into the Soviet interior. Lithuania, called Generalbezirk Litauen, was included in the administrative province of the Reichs Kommissariat Ostland which also included the other Baltic republics, Estonia, Latvia, and also Belorussia. Hinrich Lohse was appointed Reich Commissar of Ostland, with headquarters in Riga. The Generalbezirk consisted of three districts: the Šiauliai (Shavli) district, the Kaunas (Kovno) district, and the Vilna district. Adrian von Renteln, the commissioner general for Lithuania, had his seat in Kaunas (called Kauen by the Nazis). The Germans also established a local administration, composed of pro-Hitler elements. Lithuanian "councilors general" (a sort of minister) were appointed, headed by Petras Kubiliūnas, a former general in the Lithuanian army.

On Aug. 13, 1941, Lohse issued secret "provisional regulations" to the general commissioners of Ostland specifying how to deal with Jews pending the application of the "final solution" of the "Jewish question" in Ostland. These orders applied to all the Jews in Ostland – former citizens of Germany, Czechoslovakia, Poland, the Baltic states, and other parts of the Soviet Union. There were special instructions for the treatment of foreign Jews and persons of mixed parentage. The commissioners general were required to register all the Jews under their regional jurisdiction and to issue compulsory orders to them to wear two yellow badges (one on the chest and one on the back). Jews were prohibited from moving from their house or place of residence without permission from the district or city commissioner; using the sidewalks; using public transportation; residing in spas; visiting parks and playgrounds, theaters, cinemas, libraries, museums, or schools; owning cars or radios. Ritual slaughter was also prohibited. Jewish doctors were permitted to treat only Jewish patients; pharmacies owned by Jews were turned over to Aryan pharmacists; Jews were not permitted to function as veterinarians, lawyers, notaries, bank officials, or commercial agents, nor could they deal in real estate or freight forwarding. All Jewish property was confiscated. Persons holding Jewish property had to report to the German administration which dealt with its confiscation. Only the bare necessities of furniture, clothing, and linen were left in Jewish possession, and an allowance of no more than 20 pfennig (about $0.05) per day per person was permitted to the Jews. Finally, the regulations provided for the concentration of the Jews in ghettos, where food and other necessities were supplied to them only insofar as no shortage resulted for supplying the general population. Inside the ghettos, the Jews were permitted "autonomy" in their affairs, subject to the supervision of the regional commissioner, and had their own *Ordnungsdienst* ("police force"). The ghettos were sealed off from the outside world and put under the guard of auxiliary police recruited from among the local population. Able-bodied Jews were put on forced labor, inside or outside the ghetto. Private persons or enterprises utilizing Jews in forced labor paid the regional commissioner directly. The commissars general were authorized to issue orders based on these regulations.

EINSATZGRUPPEN. The *Einsatzgruppen* (Action Units) played a major role in the destruction of the Jews in the occupied eastern territories, including Lithuania. *Einsatzgruppe A* was attached to the Northern German army and operated in the Baltic states and Leningrad area. Details of the murder of the Jews in Lithuania are contained in some of the 195 *Einsatzgruppen* reports regularly submitted to the *RSHA (Reichssicherheitshauptamt) in Berlin from the end of June 1941 to April 24, 1942. The following is an extract of these reports:

> ...a detachment of *Einsatzkommando* 3, assisted by a Lithuanian *Kommando*, has carried out actions in the following towns: Raseiniai, Rokiskis, Zarasai, Birzai, and Prienai. These executions bring the total number to date of persons liquidated by *Einsatzkommando* 3 (with the assistance of Lithuanian partisans), to 46,692... (Report No. 88, Sept. 19, 1941).

Important data on the extermination of Lithuanian Jewry is contained in a report by SS-Brigadefuehrer Stahlecker, commander of *Einsatzgruppe A*. The report, covering the activities of his group on the northern Russian front and in the occupied Baltic states, dates from the beginning of the war against Russia until Oct. 15, 1941. On June 23, 1941, *Einsatzgruppe A* joined the German forces on the northern Russian front. By June 25 Stahlecker, with a detachment of the *Einsatzgruppe*, reached Kovno, which was taken by the Germans the previous day. The following is an extract from his report:

> ...In the very first hours after the entry of German troops, local antisemitic forces were organized, despite the considerable difficulties involved, to carry out pogroms against the Jews. The security police received appropriate orders and were in fact prepared to solve the Jewish problem by all available means and with utmost severity. It seemed desirable, however, that at least in the beginning, the extraordinarily harsh means [to be employed] should not be recognized for what they were, for that would have caused concern even in German circles. On the surface the impression had to be created that it was the local population which had initiated the anti-Jewish measures as a spontaneous reaction to their oppression by the Jews for many years and to the Communist terror to which they had been exposed in the recent past.
>
> ...Partisan groups formed in Lithuania and established immediate contact with the German troops taking over the city. Unreliable elements among the partisans were weeded out, and an auxiliary unit of 300 men was formed under the command of Klimaitis, a Lithuanian journalist. As the pacification program progressed, this partisan group extended its activities from Kovno to other parts of Lithuania. The group very meticulously fulfilled its tasks, especially in the preparation and carrying out of large-scale liquidations.
>
> ...As the Baltic population had suffered from the Jews and the Communists during the Bolshevik occupation, it was to be expected that they would take their own measures against those of their [Jewish and Communist] enemies remaining in their midst. It was the task of the German security police to ensure the speedy completion of this goal. Furthermore, evidence had to be created in order to prove, at a later stage, that it was the local population which had squared their own accounts with the Jews and the Communists. The orders given by the German sources had to be concealed...
>
> In Lithuania the initiative was taken by the Lithuanian partisans. On the night of June 25–26, the partisans in Kovno, under the command of Klimaitis, staged a pogrom in which 1,500 Jews were killed. Several synagogues were burned down or otherwise destroyed and a Jewish neighborhood of 60 houses went up in flames. The next night, an additional 2,300 Jews were rendered harmless in the same manner. Kovno has served as a model for similar actions in other parts of Lithuania...
>
> ...Pogroms, however, could not provide a complete solution to the Jewish problem in Ostland. Large-scale executions have therefore been carried out all over the country, in which the local auxiliary police was also used; they cooperated without a hitch....
>
> ...Simultaneously with the executions ghettos had to be established. There were 30,000 Jews in Kovno. After the first pogroms and killings, a Jewish committee was formed, mainly to organize the transfer to the ghetto... In the establishment of the ghettos the security police were in charge of police matters, while the newly established ghetto administration [the Judenrat] was responsible for the provision of forced labor, food supplies, etc.

Appendix No. 8 of Stahlecker's report is contained in Table 3: Jews Killed in Lithuania, giving the number killed by *Einsatzgruppe A* in Lithuania (up to the end of October 1941).

Table 3. Number of Jews Killed by *Einsatzgruppe A* in Lithuania (Up to the End of Oct. 1941)

Place	Jews	Communists	Total
Kaunas (Kovno) (and vicinity)	31,914	80	31,994
Siauliai (and vicinity)	41,382	763	42,145
Vilna (and vicinity)	7,015	17	7,032
Grand Total	80,311	860	81,171

A map drawn up by *Einsatzgruppe A* to show the number of Jews killed in the Baltic states up to the end of December 1941, indicates that 136,421 Jews were murdered by that date in Lithuania (excluding Vilna), with 16,000 Jews remaining in the Kovno ghetto and 4,500 in the Šiauliai ghetto. A comparison of these figures with the Stahlecker report reveals that in this area alone, 56,110 Jews were killed in the last two months of 1941.

DESTRUCTION OF JEWISH COMMUNITIES IN THE PROVINCES. Most of the Jewish communities in the provinces were totally destroyed in the period from August to September 1941. Many communities were wiped out by sudden attack, not a single person surviving to tell the story of their martyrdom. The sparse material available conspicuously points to the active participation of Lithuanians from all walks of life, side by side with the Germans in the slaughter. Most of the Lithuanians who took part in the murder of Jews fled to Germany in the summer of 1944, when the Soviet army liberated Lithuania. After the war they were classified as Displaced Persons and were aided as Nazi victims.

At the first conference of liberated Lithuanian Jews in Germany, held in Munich in April 1947, a resolution was adopted on the "Guilt of the Lithuanian People in the Extermination of Lithuanian Jewry."

HELP FROM NON-JEWS. There were among the Lithuanians a few individuals who in the face of the Nazis extended a helping hand to the Jews, despite the mortal danger to which they thus exposed themselves. In Kovno, those who helped the Jews included E. Kutorgienė, P. Mažylis, the writer Sofija Čiurlionienė, the priest Paukštys, the nun Ona Brokaitytė, and the opera singer Kipras Petrauskas. In Vilna, Ona Simaitė was of the greatest help, while in Siauliai the daughter of the lawyer Venclauskas, the poet Jankus, the priest Lapis, and former mayor Saneckis were among those who distinguished themselves in aiding the Jews.

War Crimes Trials

On Dec. 20, 1944, the Soviet press published the "Declaration of the Special Government Commission Charged with the Inquiry into Crimes Committed by the German-Fascist Aggressors in the Lithuanian Soviet Socialist Republic." This lengthy document also includes a report on the mass murders committed at Ponary, near Vilna, and at the Ninth Fort near Kovno. In its final chapter the declaration lists a substantial number of Nazi war criminals responsible for the murders carried out in Lithuania during the German occupation. The list includes Von Renteln, commissioner general for Lithuania; Wysocki, chief of police in Lithuania; Fuchs, chief of the security police and the SD; Ditfurt, commandant of Vilna; Weiss, chief of the Vilna prisons; Kramer, city commissioner for Kovno; Lentzen, Kovno regional commissioner; Gewecke, Šiauliai regional commissioner; Buenger, Gestapo chief in Kovno; Goecke, commandant of the Kovno concentration camp (formed of remnants of the ghetto; in the fall of 1943 the Kovno ghetto was turned into a concentration camp). Lithuanians who collaborated with the occupying power are not listed at all.

In addition to the major Nazi war criminals who were tried by the International Military Tribunal in Nuremberg and the *Einsatzgruppen* commanders tried by the U.S. Military Court at Nuremberg (case no. 9), a number of Nazi criminals who had had a hand in the destruction of Lithuanian Jewry were tried by the U.S. Military Courts at Dachau and elsewhere. After the war, some trials also took place in Soviet Lithuania. On the whole, however, only a small number of the criminals were brought to account, as most of them succeeded in evading trial. Notable among the trials was the trial at Ulm, Germany (April 28–September 1958) against a group of *Einsatzgruppen* who in 1941 murdered 5,500 Jews in various places near the German border. The accused were sentenced to various terms of imprisonment.

Liberation

Lithuania was liberated by the Soviet army in the summer of 1944 (Vilna on July 13, Šiauliai on July 27, Kovno on August 1). The Jewish survivors consisted of several hundred Jewish partisan fighters, and a few families and children who had been hidden by gentiles. Jewish refugees who at the beginning of the war escaped to Soviet Asia also began to make their way back.

At the beginning of 1945, when Soviet troops liberated the Stutthof concentration camp, several hundred Jewish women from Lithuania were listed among the survivors, and when Dachau was liberated by the Americans, some Lithuanian Jewish men were found alive there. Both the women and the men had been deported from Lithuania in the summer of 1944, 80 of whom found their death in German concentration camps.

Some of the survivors returned to Lithuania, but the majority stayed in the *Displaced Persons (DP) camps established after the war in Germany, Austria, and Italy. Later, they were joined by other Lithuanian Jews who had escaped from Soviet Lithuania via the Jewish underground escape route (see *Beriḥah). When the DP camps were dissolved, the Lithuanian Jews settled in Israel, the United States, and other countries overseas together with other Jewish DPs.

After the War

The 1959 Soviet census report indicated the Jewish population of Lithuania at 24,672 (11,478 men and 13,194 women), constituting less than 1% of the total population (2,880,000). Of these, 16,354 Jews lived in Vilna, 4,792 in Kovno, and the rest in other urban areas. At the time the census was taken, 17,025 declared Yiddish as their native tongue (the highest percentage in all the areas where the census was taken), 6,912 Russian, 640 Lithuanian, and 95 specified other languages. In the academic year 1960/61 there were 413 Jewish students at institutions of higher learning (1.67% of the total Jewish population of Lithuania). Lithuania was one of the centers from which pressure came to establish a revival of Jewish cultural life after the war. The Soviet authorities eventually agreed to establish an amateur Yiddish theater group there.

For details on Jewish life in the postwar period see *Vilna, *Kaunas.

[Joseph Gar]

Later Developments

Lithuania seceded from the U.S.S.R. in August 1991. In 1979 the republic's Jewish population was recorded at 14,700 and in 1989 as 12,400. In 1988–89 the Jewish birthrate was 7.5 per 1,000 and mortality rate was 17.8 per 1,000.

In 1989, 780 Jews (743 of them from the capital Vilnius (Vilna)) emigrated. Immigration to Israel amounted to 2,962 (2,355 from Vilnius) in 1990 and to 1,103 in 1991.

There was no state antisemitism in Lithuania. In 1990 Emanuel Zingeris, an activist of the Lithuanian national front Sajudis and now co-chairman of the Jewish Culture Association of Lithuania, was elected as a deputy to the Supreme Soviet of Lithuania. The other co-chairman was Lithuanian-Jewish writer Grigorii Kanovich (who writes in Russian, but whose basic theme is Jewish life, particularly of the past, in his region). A Jewish museum has been opened in Vilnius and a monthly newspaper, *Litovskii Ierusalim* ("Jerusalem of Lithuania"), appears in Yiddish, Russian, Lithuanian, and English. September 23, the day the Vilna ghetto was destroyed, has been set aside to commemorate the mass murder of the Jews of Lithuania. A memorial complex, where annual public meetings are held, has been built at the site of mass executions at Ponary. A Jewish guide to Vilnius has been published. In November 1991 a Council of Jewish Communities of Lithuania was established. Due to the small number of Jews remaining in the country the majority of the numerous Jewish organizations registered in Lithuania have no more than a few members and scarcely function, and according to one local activist, "There are no Jews, there are just Jewish representatives."

On June 1, 1992, an air route was opened between Vilnius and Israel.

[Michael Beizer]

In March 1993, a presentation of the Judaica Center of the Vilnius University took place. The event was attended by Prof. Israel Gutman from the Hebrew University of Jerusalem, Prof. Yitzhak Warszawski from the Sorbonne, and Rabbi Rene Sirat from Paris.

There were three Jewish periodicals in Lithuania in 1993, all published in Vilnius, including "Jerusalem of Lithuania" which continued to appear; its editor was Grigorijus Smoliakovas.

The Holocaust memorial in Paneriai (Ponary) near Vilnius was vandalized in 1993. Jewish cemeteries were desecrated in Vilnius and Kaunas. A number of antisemitic articles appeared in the Lithuanian press. A common topic in such publications has been the theory of "dual Holocaust"; according to it, Jews are as equally responsible for the deportation of Lithuanians to Siberia in 1940–early 1941, as are Lithuanians for the massacre of Jews in 1941–43. Antisemitism, with accompanying vandalism, remained a constant factor in Lithuania into the 21st century.

By 1993 there were an estimated 6,000 Jews in Lithuania, with some 900 leaving for Israel in 1992–93. (See also *Latvia.) By the early 21st century just 3,500 remained. Efforts were being made to strengthen the Jewish community structure, with Chabad and other parties active.

[Daniel Romanowski (2nd ed.)]

BIBLIOGRAPHY: *Yahadut Lita*, 3 vols. (1959–71); J. Shatzky, *Kultur Geshikhte fun der Haskole in Lite* (1950); W.Z. Rabinowitsch, *Lithuanian Hasidism* (1970); D. Katz, *Tenu'at ha-Musar*, 5 vols. (1958–63[3]); S.K. Mirsky (ed.), *Mosedot Torah be-Eiropah be-Vinyanam u-ve-Ḥurbanam* (1956), 1–354; M.A. Szulwas, in: I. Halpern (ed.), *Beit Yisrael be-Polin*, 1 (1954), 13–35; A. Kariv, *Lita Mekhorati…* (1960), 7–16. INDEPENDENT LITHUANIA: *Lite*, 1 (1951), index; 2 (1965), index; J. Gar, in: *Algemeyne Entsiklopedye: Yidn*, 6 (1964), 330–41, 402; Kaunas, Centralinis Statistīkos Biuras, *Lietuvos Gyventojai* (1923); *Der Idisher Natsional Rat in Lite: Barikht vegn Zayn Tetikayt* (1922); *Barikht fun der Idisher Seym-Fraktsie fun Tsveytn Litivishn Seym 1923–26* (1926); *Farband fun di Idishe Folks-Baynk in Lite* (1929); *Di Idishe Handverker in Lite in Tsifern* (1936); B. Kagan, in: Z. Scharfstein (ed.), *Ha-Ḥinnukh ve-ha-Tarbut ha-Ivrit be-Eiropah bein Shetei Milḥamot ha-Olam* (1957); EJ, 10 (1934), 1022–290. REPUBLIC OF LITHUANIA: U. Schmelz and S. DellaPergola, in: AJYB (1995), 478; *Supplement to the Monthly Bulletin of Statistics*, 2 (1995); Y. Florsheim, in: *Jews in Eastern Europe*, 1:26 (1995), 25–33; M. Beizer and I. Klimenko, in: *Jews in Eastern Europe*, 1:24 (1995), 25–33; Institute of Jewish Affairs, *Antisemitism World Report 1994*, 142–43; Institute of Jewish Affairs, *Antisemitism World Report 1995*, 165–66; *Mezhdunarodnaia Evreiskaia* Gazeta (MEG), 1993. HOLOCAUST: IMT, *Trial of Major War Criminals*, 23 (1949), index; R. Hilberg, *Destruction of the European Jews* (1961), index; G. Reitlinger, *Final Solution* (1968), index; A. Dallin, *German Rule in Russia 1941–1945* (1957), 182–8; Embassy of the U.S.S.R., Washington, *Information Bulletin* (Feb. 1945); Werner, in: *The American Scholar*, 27 (1957/58), 169–78; N. Grinblat (Goren), in: *Tav Shin He* (1946), 557–79; E. Oshri, *She'elot u-Teshuvot mi-Ma'amakim* (1959), 221–300; idem, *Khurbn Lite* (1951); *Lite*, 1 (1951), vols. 1645–1840; M. Segalson et al. (comps.), *Vernichtung der Juden in Litauen: Talsachen aus den Jahren 1941–1945* (1959); *Anlageschrift* of the Ulm Trial (1958); *Sudebny protsess po delu o zlodeyaniyakh nemetskofashistskikh zakhvatchikov na territorii Latviyskoy, Litvoskoy i Estanskoy S.S.R.* (1946); J. Gar, in: *Algemeine Entsiklopedie: Yidn*, 6 (1964), 341–74, 402–3; idem, *Azoy is es geshen in Lite* (1965); M. Joffe (ed.), *Hitlerine okupacija Lietuvoye* (1961); S. Binkiene (ed.), *Ir be ginklo kariai* (1967); A.Z. Bar-On and D. Lewin, *Toledoteha shel Maḥteret* (1962).

LITIN, town in Vinnitsa district, Ukraine. In 1578 the king of Poland, Stephen Bathory, permitted the owner of the estate of Litin to establish a town on his land and to hold two annual fairs which "all the citizens of the land, Christians, Jews, and merchants from foreign countries," would be permitted to attend. In 1616 there were 88 houses in the town; 12 belonged to Jews. In 1765 there were 481 Jews; in 1847, 1,804; and in 1897, 3,874 (41% of the total population). Schools for Jewish boys and girls existed there in 1910. On May 14, 1919, a Ukrainian gang conducted pogroms in Litin and 180 Jews were killed and Jewish property looted. Other riots were in late May and July of that year. A Yiddish school operated in Litin from the early 1920s, and a Jewish woman headed the town council for many years. In 1926, 2,487 Jews lived in the town (30% of the total); by 1939 the number had dropped to 1,410 (27.8% of the total). The Germans occupied Litin on July 17, 1941. They executed 56 young Jews on August 20, and on December 19 they murdered 1,800 Jews. In a labor camp in town the Germans kept a couple of hundred skilled artisans who were killed off gradually in mid-1942, the last dozen being murdered that fall. About 1,000 Jews from Bukovina, who were deported there, were also murdered. All together 3,353 were killed according to Soviet sources.

BIBLIOGRAPHY: Ẓe'irei Ẓion Rusyah, *Naftulei Dor*, 2 (1955), 142.

[Yehuda Slutsky / Shmuel Spector (2nd ed.)]

LITINSKI, GENRIKH ILYICH (1901–1985), Russian composer and teacher. Born in the Ukraine, Litinski studied composition at the Moscow Conservatory with Glier and graduated in 1928. He taught there from 1928 to 1943, becoming a professor in 1933. In 1947 he joined the faculty of Gnesin Teachers Institute of Music, Moscow, and held a professorship at Kazan Conservatory from 1949 to 1964. Litinski organized musical activities in various Asiatic republics of the Soviet Union, and explored the folklore of the Yakut people in Siberia, which he utilized in his works. His compositions include operas, ballets, symphonies, 12-string quartets, and a string octet. Among his theoretical works are *Polifonicheskaya kompozitsia* ("Polyphonic Composition," Moscow, 1951), *Sovetskoe polifonicheskoe iskusstvo* ("Soviet Polyphonic Art"), Parts 1–3 (Moscow, 1952–54), *Zadachi po polifonii dlya kompozitorov* ("Polyphonic Exercises for the Composers"), Parts 1–3, (Moscow, 1965–67), and *Obrazovanie imitatsiy strogogo pis'ma* ("Forming of Imitations in Counterpoint," Moscow, 1971).

[Marina Rizarev (2nd ed.)]

LITMAN, SAMUEL (1910–), U.S. electrical engineer. Born in Boston, Litman was on the faculty at the University of South Carolina from 1940, and professor of electrical engineering from 1962. He wrote, with T.F. Ball, *Laboratory Experiments in Direct and Alternating Currents* (1940), and became an expert on information theory.

LITOMERICE (Czech. **Litoměřice**; Ger. **Leitmeritz**), town in N. Bohemia, Czech Republic. Jews are mentioned in the town's founding charter (1057) as salt merchants, thus making Litomerice the first town in Bohemia, after Prague, in which Jews are mentioned. There was a Jewish quarter in 1411. In 1514 the city council protected its "poor Jewish artisans" against financial demands of outside lords, and in 1529 the Bohemian royal authorities demanded that the town mayor provide proper protection for the Jews. Ferdinand I canceled a permit allowing free trade in wine in 1540, and in the following year, after a massacre, the Jews were expelled. The town was granted the privilege *de non tolerandis Judaeis* in 1546; the synagogue was turned into a hospital (a Hebrew inscription on the building was preserved). In 1584 Jews were permitted to attend fairs. Six Jewish families settled in Litomerice in 1851. In 1863 there were 100 Jews. The community was constituted in 1875 and a synagogue was dedicated in 1883. There were 616 Jews in 1921. Between the two world wars there was a training center for settlement in Ereẓ Israel at the Litomerice agricultural school. The Zionist politician Emil *Margulies lived in the town. In 1930 the community numbered 425 (2.3% of the total population), of whom 143 declared their nationality as Jewish. At the time of the Sudeten crisis (1938) nearly all of the community left the town, the few men who remained being deported to concentration camps.

During the war a branch of the Flossenburg concentration camp and a crematorium were set up in Litomerice. After World War II staff members of the Terezin (Theresienstadt) concentration camp and prison, German and Jewish, were tried in Litomerice. The records are deposited in the local court.

A Jewish community also existed in LOVOSICE (Lobositz) on the opposite bank of the Elbe. According to tradition the community was founded by the Jews who had been expelled from Litomerice in 1541. The first documentary evidence on the community is from 1704. There were 17 Jewish houses there in the 18th century. The *Hoenigsberg family lived in the town for some time. Lovosice Jews developed the business of shipping products to Germany on the Elbe, dealing in the production of chocolate. There were 201 persons in the community in 1930. At the time of the Sudeten crisis nearly all the community left the town. The few remaining males were sent to concentration camps.

BIBLIOGRAPHY: H. Ankert, in: H. Gold (ed.), *Die Juden und Judengemeinden Boehmens in Vergangenheit und Gegenwart* (1934), 363–9; Germ Jud, 1 (1963), 157; 2 (1968), 478. **ADD. BIBLIOGRAPHY:** J. Fiedler, *Jewish Sights of Bohemia and Moravia* (1991), 182–83.

[Jan Herman and Meir Lamed / Yeshayahu Jelinek (2nd ed.)]

LITTAUER, LUCIUS NATHAN (1859–1944), U.S. industrialist, congressman, and philanthropist. Littauer was born in Gloversville, New York, the son of an immigrant from Breslau, Prussia. Upon his graduation from Harvard College in 1878 Littauer entered his father's glove factory. He assumed directorship of the company in 1883, and under him it became the largest manufacturing enterprise of its kind in the country. An entrepreneur, he founded and participated in many other business enterprises, including public utilities, banking, textiles, and transportation.

Littauer became active in Republican politics and served in the U.S. House of Representatives from 1896 to 1907, representing predominantly non-Jewish upstate constituencies. An intimate friend and close political adviser of President Theodore Roosevelt, he was a leading member of the important House Appropriations Committee. From 1912 to 1914 he served as a member of the Board of Regents of the University of the City of New York. During the remainder of his life, Littauer devoted himself to the management of his widespread business interests, and, above all, to an increasing range of philanthropic activities. His initial gift in 1894 for the Nathan Littauer Hospital in Gloversville was followed by many substantial contributions for the building and support of numerous institutions in the area, including the Jewish Community Center. A statue of him was erected in Gloversville in 1929.

His donations helped social welfare, health, recreation, education, and the financial support of needy students aspiring to higher education. He contributed extensively to medical care and research, aiding medical schools and hospitals in New York City, Albany, Paris, and Breslau, where he endowed the Nathan Littauer Stiftung at its Jewish Hospital. At the New York University College of Medicine he endowed a professorship of psychiatry; he also gave a building to the National Hospital for Speech Disorders. In 1937 he made a large gift to the New School of Social Research, New York, for the support of its newly established University in Exile, where many distinguished refugee Jewish intellectuals and scholars found a haven to continue their teaching and research. An abiding interest in public affairs motivated his largest single gift: the erection and endowment at Harvard of the Littauer Center of Public Administration, and the establishment of the Graduate School of Public Administration. The Lucius N. Littauer Foundation, established in 1929, gives grants to a wide variety of causes, including the advancement of Jewish studies and Jewish learning.

Throughout his life, Littauer remained a faithful Jew in the Reform tradition. While in Congress, he advocated legislation to liberalize the immigration laws in order to help the victims of religious persecution in Eastern Europe. He firmly believed in the role of Jewish culture in U.S. intellectual life and supported the **Menorah Journal* and the Menorah movement. In 1925 Littauer endowed the Nathan Littauer professorship of Hebrew literature and philosophy at Harvard – the first of its kind in the U.S. – later augmented by other gifts to Harvard for publications, fellowships, and the acquisition of collections of rare Hebraica and Judaica. He contributed to the Central Conference of American Rabbis for scholarly studies. In 1938 he founded the Institute of Social and Religious Studies at the Jewish Theological Seminary of America. At New York University he initiated the endowment of a chair in Jewish and Hebrew studies. Littauer received a variety of awards and honors for his philanthropic and public activities.

BIBLIOGRAPHY: L. Littauer, *Louise Littauer, Her Book*, ed. by L.N. Littauer (1924); *The Letters of Theodore Roosevelt*, ed. by E.E. Morison, 2 (1951), 967; 7 (1954), 502; L. Einstein, *Roosevelt – His Mind in Action* (1930); J.A. Blanchard (ed.), *The H Book of Harvard Athletics…* (1923).

[Harry Starr]

LITTMAN, JOSEPH AARON (1898–1953), British property tycoon. One of the earliest and most successful of England's well-known property magnates, Joe Littman was born in Russia, lived in New York, and moved to London in the 1920s. He began purchasing properties in the 1930s, specializing in high street retailers in suburban London. Littman pioneered the so-called sale and leaseback agreement, under which a financial institution would buy a site and lease it back to him on very long (sometimes 999-year) leaseholds, he in turn subletting it to shops on short leases. Both he and the financial institution, usually a building society, thus benefited, meanwhile eliminating much of the red tape notorious in British real estate. Littman concentrated on already existing properties rather than on building new ones and, after 1945, moved heavily into blue chip retail investment in London's West End, especially Oxford Street. When Littman died of lung cancer at the age of 55, he left a fortune of £3.3 million, a fabulous sum given Britain's very high rates of taxation. Many other successful British property developers imitated his methods.

His son LOUIS (THOMAS SIDNEY) LITTMAN (1925–1987), a Cambridge-educated solicitor and farmer, was the founder of the well-known Littman Library of Jewish Civilization, which he began in 1965 in memory of his father. It has published many scholarly works and studies on Jewish history, religion, and culture.

BIBLIOGRAPHY: ODNB online; O. Marriott, *The Property Boom* (1967); L. Littman, "The Littman Library of Jewish Civilisation," in: JHSET, 29 (1982–86), 311–26.

[William D. Rubinstein (2nd ed.)]

LITTMAN, SOL (1920–), Canadian journalist and community activist. Littman was born in Toronto, Ontario, to East European immigrant parents. He earned a B.A. in sociology from the University of Toronto in 1946, an M.A. in sociology and anthropology from the University of Wisconsin in 1950, and a degree in social work from the University of Toronto in 1952. Littman had multiple careers. In 1955 he joined the staff of the Anti-Defamation League of B'nai B'rith (ADL) in the United States and for 13 years was involved in tracking right-wing and antisemitic groups and exposing discrimination in housing, employment, and social organizations. In 1968 Littman returned to Toronto to head ADL in Canada, later renamed the League for Human Rights. He spearheaded the organization's campaign against antisemitism and social discrimination.

In 1971 Littman turned to journalism, first as editor for two years of the *Canadian Jewish News* and writing a bi-weekly column on the arts for the *Toronto Star*. In 1973 he moved to the Canadian Broadcasting Corporation as a news documentary maker and in 1976 he joined the editorial staff of the *Toronto Star*, where he often wrote editorials on social issues. Taking early retirement to write, in 1982 he published *War Criminal on Trial*, the story of Helmut Rauca, the first Canadian deported from Canada to stand trial for war crimes. From 1985 to 1999 Littman was Canadian representative of the Simon Wiesenthal Center and pressured the Canadian government on the prosecution of Nazi war criminals who entered Canada after World War II. In large part through his efforts, in 1985 the government of Brian Mulroney established the Deschênes Commission of Inquiry on War Criminals in Canada.

In 2003 Littman published his second book, *Pure Soldiers or Sinister Legion*, about the Ukrainian Waffen-SS division, many of whose members were allowed to resettle in Canada after World War II.

[Harold Troper (2nd ed.)]

LITURGY.

Liturgy has conventionally been understood as the words that Jews recite in public worship. While written words are almost all that remains from earlier times, the study of liturgy today understands that the ways that these words are performed shapes their meanings profoundly. To the extent possible, then, the study of liturgical words must be combined with the study of all elements of their settings: of the gestures, postures, and intonations (musical or otherwise) accompanying them; of the physical setting where they are recited, usually the synagogue, and its ornamentation; of ritual objects accompanying them; and of the matrix of *halakhah*, custom, and theology that shapes their composition and recitation. Thus, liturgy in the Jerusalem Temple was primarily nonverbal, but filled with the ritual actions of sacrifice. Liturgy in synagogues has always been dominated by words, but not exclusively so. Liturgy in two synagogues might include very similar texts but look and sound entirely different, or express two very different sorts of spirituality. In addition, the synagogue is not the only locus of rabbinic liturgy; a prayer quorum can gather anywhere. Moreover, the individual, with or without the quorum, remains obligated to pray. Rituals based in the home, around meals, or formulated over a cup of wine (as in circumcision and marriage) are also integral elements of Jewish liturgy. (For studies that pursue some of these directions, see Ehrlich; Langer, *To Worship…*; Langer and Fine.)

BIBLICAL PERIOD

While the Jerusalem Temples stood, formal public worship of God occurred there, through the sacrifices and their accompanying rituals. Individuals also offered occasional *prayer, often freely composed as spontaneous reactions to personal events or experiences. The Hebrew Bible records the short prayers of Moses (Num. 12:13), Jethro (Ex. 18:10), and Hannah (I Sam. 1:11), and the extended prayer of Solomon at the inauguration of the First Temple (I Kings 8:15ff., 23ff.). The only formal prayers in the Bible are the confessions to be recited when bringing the first fruits (*Viddui Bikkurim*) and the tithe (*Viddui Ma'aser*; Deut. 26:5–15), and that of the high priest which had no prescribed formula (Lev. 16:21). Pious individuals may have prayed thrice daily (Dan. 6:11; cf. also Ps. 55:18), and some of the psalms may have served as texts for the levitical service twice a day in the First and Second Temples (I Chron. 23:30). There is no evidence, however, for communal prayer in the Temple. The Mishnah records a short liturgy for the priests on duty which comprised a benediction, the recitation of the **Shema* and the *Decalogue, three additional benedictions, and the *priestly blessing (Tam. 5:1). The laymen present for the sacrifices participated in the ritual by prostrating themselves (Tam. 7:3; cf. Ber. 11b) and at appropriate pauses, probably chanting such responses as "O give thanks unto the Lord, for He is good" (Ps. 136:1). This ceremony might have been one of the sources out of which rabbinic liturgy later developed.

The synagogue, the Greco-Roman association in its Judean form, the frequent fasts prescribed in times of drought for which a special liturgy was recorded in the Mishnah (Ta'an. 2:1–5; see *Fasting and Fast Days), and the *ma'amadot* institution (Ta'an. 2:7; 4:1–4) were elements of the world from which rabbinic liturgy emerged. The synagogue developed as a place for the regular ritual reading and exposition of Torah. Judean civic associations, perhaps known as *ḥavurot*, provided a forum for communal meals, ritual, and study. The *ma'amad* consisted of representatives of the people, some of whom were present at the sacrifices and the rest assembled at home, both conducting prayers four times a day – **Shaḥarit*, **Musaf*, **Minḥah*, and **Ne'ilat She'arim* (see **Ne'ilah*, **Mishmarot*, and **Ma'amadot*). The hours later fixed for the *Shaḥarit, Minḥah*, and **Arvit* prayers were in accordance with the times (of prayer of the members of the *ma'amadot* and thus) of the sacrifices as well as in accordance with the practices of pious individuals who fixed their prayer schedule according to the position of the sun (TJ, Ber. 4:1, 7b; Ber. 26b). The sectarian community at Qumran similarly gathered twice daily for formal prayers as well as communal meals. All these prayer gatherings correspond in timing to Temple sacrifices.

TALMUDIC PERIOD

Tannaitic texts record the basic outlines of rabbinic liturgy. Although *amoraim* attribute the composition of many of these prayers to the men of the *Great Synagogue (Ber. 33a), contemporary scholars debate how much, if any, of rabbinic liturgy predates the destruction of the Second Temple. The Mishnah also knows the obligation derived from the Pentateuch, to recite the **Shema* twice daily with its benedictions (three in the morning and four in the evening); the daily **Amidah*, known as *Tefillah*, comprising 18 benedictions (Ber. 4:3) on weekdays (but shortened on other days) and recited three times daily (four times on holidays); and the reading of *Torah on Sabbaths, Mondays, and Thursdays. Rabbinic meal rituals, with blessings before eating and an extended *Grace after Meals following, complete with invocations that reflect an association-like setting, also appear in the Mishnah (Ber. ch. 6–7).

The concept of *benedictions, i.e., *berakhot*, as the fundamental building block of prayer is already evident in Qumran literature and is presupposed by the rabbis, but with many variants. The *amoraim* demanded a single statutory formulation, *Barukh Attah Adonai* ("Blessed are You, Eternal"). In addition, the rabbis incorporated many Temple rituals, like the *priestly benediction, **shofar*, **lulav*, and **hallel* into appropriate points in their liturgies. (See the individual entries on all these prayers for their descriptions and histories.)

No rabbinic prayers were written down until much later. Contemporary scholars debate to what extent the rabbinic liturgical system achieved its form during the Second Temple period or under Rabban *Gamaliel in response to the destruction of the Temple. It is also unclear to what extent prayer texts were fixed or flexible within these accepted structures and how broadly rabbinic prayers were known among the Jews of the Land of Israel and even more so in the Diaspora. It is only around the fourth century that synagogue architecture in Israel begins regularly to reflect the physical orientation of rabbinic worship, especially the *Amidah*, towards Jerusalem. By that point, rabbinic prayer had become a function of the public synagogue, complete with a **sheli'ah ẓibbur* whose public recitation of the prayers enabled those incapable of praying properly on their own to fulfill their obligations to participate by listening and responding **amen*. There are ample indications that women attended the synagogue. However, there is no direct evidence for an architecturally separate women's section until the High Middle Ages.

At the very least, an accepted literary norm developed to the effect that the ideal language for prayer would be Hebrew (although other languages were acceptable for many prayers; Sot. 7:1, 32b–33a; Ber. 13a, etc.), and that this Hebrew would allude to but not duplicate biblical language. By the end of the talmudic period, general consensus existed as to the basic formulation of most prayers, though significant regional variations remained. Whether these variations arose as devolution from an original fixed composition or from gradual evolution towards this consensus is unclear. No manuscripts of Hebrew prayers exist from this period, and the few Greek manuscripts suggest only a vague adherence to rabbinic norms (Van der Horst, Langer, "Did… "). The Talmud preserves a few discussions of disputed prayer texts, and these decisions became normative in later generations as the Talmud itself became normative. However, the lack of early talmudic manuscripts also calls the historicity of many of these texts into question.

Around this core of statutory prayers, other elements seem to have emerged, probably in the amoraic period. These include the recitation of psalms and psalm-like passages, known as **pesukei de-zimra*, prior to the prayers themselves, in order to set an appropriate mood (Ber. 5:1), and the recitation of individual prayers after the *Amidah*. These latter prayers began as private supplications, including personal requests (known as *devarim*; Tos. to Ber. 3:10, also called *teḥinnah* or *taḥanunim*), but were gradually formalized (see **Taḥanun*). In contrast to the statutory prayers, both of these elements include extensive recitation of biblical texts as well as new compositions composed of concatenations of complete biblical verses. These elements took radically different forms in the Land of Israel and in Babylonia, as the findings of the Cairo **Genizah* attest (Fleischer, *Eretz-Israel…*), but their direct reliance on biblical language suggests that they had emerged before the *Karaites' insistence on purely biblical prayer became an issue.

Perhaps as early as the tannaitic period, traditions of **piyyut* (liturgical poetry) emerged in the Land of Israel as elaborations upon the statutory prayers (some simpler exemplars became part of this liturgy). By at least the late amoraic period, **ḥazzanim* produced and performed poetic versions of entire liturgical elements, especially on Sabbaths and holidays, replacing the statutory language with compositions relevant to the day and its Torah reading. This poetry was mostly in Hebrew, continuing the tradition of allusive references to biblical passages, and soon extending its content to include midrashic elements. *Piyyut* flourished mainly in the Land of Israel; Babylonian rabbis resisted its adoption until well into the geonic period. The universal triumph of the Babylonian rabbinic insistence on precise recitation of the statutory prayers, as well as on an annual cycle of Torah readings, left little room for the rich tradition of poetry from the west which had been written for a *triennial cycle; it remained unknown until the discovery of the Cairo *Genizah*.

GEONIC PERIOD

By early geonic times, two different rabbinic rites had already developed: the Palestinian and the Babylonian. We know little about the nature of Jewish prayer in the rest of the Diaspora, except where the correspondence of specific communities with the *geonim* has been preserved. In all cases, by the end of this period, their prayers largely conformed to Babylonian rabbinic norms. Contemporaneous Babylonian *responsa show great concern with universally establishing correct prayer texts according to their own customs and, concurrently, with the rejection of "deviant" customs which can often be identified as Palestinian or, later, Karaite. (Hoffman, *Canonization….*)

The old Palestinian rite, which flourished until the 12th century C.E. at least, became known in modern times only after the discovery of the Cairo *Genizah*. The first Palestinian liturgical texts were published by S. Schechter, in JQR, 10 (1898), 654–9. A bibliography of the numerous subsequent publications may be found in Y. Luger, *The Weekday Amidah …*; of particular importance is E. Fleischer, *Eretz-Israel….*

While there are considerable differences between the Palestinian usage and the other known rites, the discovered texts do not always show whether they were intended for private or public prayer. Among the characteristics peculiar to the Palestinian rite are the *triennial cycle of the Torah reading; the ending *Ẓur Yisrael ve-Go'alo* for the **ge'ullah* benediction after the *Shema* (morning and evening); different texts for several benedictions including the **Birkat ha-Torah*; a totally different recension of the 18 (not 19) benedictions of the *Amidah* in which the (otherwise also known) benedictions *Elohei David u-voneh Yerushalayim, she-Otekha be-yir'ah na'avod, ha-tov lekha lehodot, oseh ha-shalom* occur; an elaborate and complex ritual preceding the statutory prayers on the Sabbath that combines a version of *pesukei de-zimra* with a procession with the Torah and a recitation of the Ten Commandments (*tefillat ha-shir*); a special benediction before the *Shema, Asher kiddeshanu be-mitzevotav ve-ẓivvanu al mitzvat keri'at Shema*; and the addition of *Ya'aleh ve-Yavo* to the *Musaf Amidah*. Scattered elements of the Palestinian rite made their way into the various medieval European rites, especially those associated with the recitation of *piyyutim*. However, there is no discernable pattern of regular influence that suggests direct and sole dependence.

The old Babylonian rite is mainly known from geonic treatises and from Cairo *Genizah* fragments; the oldest treatise – which is also the oldest preserved complete prayer book – is the ninth-century *Seder R. Amram Gaon* of *Amram bar Sheshna (ed. by E.D. Goldschmidt, 1971), comprised of the texts of the prayers together with respective halakhic prescriptions. Both Amram and his near contemporary *Natronai b. Hilai in his responsum concerning the 100 benedictions (L. Ginzberg, *Geonica*, 2 (1909), 114 ff.) answered queries from Spanish Jews asking how to pray. This suggests the possibility that Jews in Spain were only then beginning to accept rabbinic liturgical requirements. The majority of medieval prayer books follow the organization of the *Seder Rav Amram Gaon*, including, frequently, its combination of prayer texts with the pertinent halakhic prescriptions. Unfortunately, its many copyists did not preserve Amram's original prayer texts, often substituting their own. Today's prayer books still follow his order of the prayers.

The *seder* was followed (a century later) by the *Siddur Rav* of *Saadiah (Gaon) b. Joseph with prescriptions in Arabic (ed. by I. Davidson, S. Assaf, and B.I. Joel (1941)) which, despite some influences of Palestinian usage, is a good example of geonic prayer books. However, Saadiah's organization was more suitable for study than for synagogue use, and it had no impact outside the Arabic-speaking world. Saadiah also includes significantly more *piyyutim*, including some of his own composition, indicating their increasing acceptance in Babylonia.

POST-GEONIC RITES

All the various medieval rites of Jewish liturgy developed from the Babylonian rite with varying influences from the Palestinian rite as well as what may be some remnants of local customs which are impossible to document. Although it is customary to divide the rites according to strict geographical boundaries, examination of the manuscript evidence suggests that this is useful mostly as a heuristic device, and actual local customs shaded one into the next, much as do linguistic dialects. Layered onto this were various halakhic and mystical concerns about precise language and performance of the prayers (including, especially, music) that further shaped the actual liturgical experience. Jewish mobility, voluntary and involuntary, also contributed to mixings of these rites. The rites evolved internally over time, especially but not exclusively around the edges of the statutory prayers.

Conventionally, scholars have constructed relationships among the rites mainly by the collections of *piyyutim* they adopted, dividing the rites into two groups: the Palestinian (comprising Italy, the Balkans, and the Franco-German countries) and the Babylonian (comprising the Spanish and Yemenite rites). However, this Eurocentric division ignores most of the rites driven out of existence after the expulsion of the Jews from Spain and presumes that all communities preserved their traditions of *piyyut* as carefully as did Ashkenaz. It also ignores the fact that the statutory prayers of all these rites are fundamentally Babylonian.

Until Iberian Jews began fleeing Spain, beginning in 1391 but especially after 1492, Jews who moved to a new area generally adopted the local custom, thus preserving the local and regional nature of Jewish rites. Mass immigration, however, created communities of Spanish Jews who considered their customs superior to those of the natives. With this, and in accord with kabbalistic teachings that one's prayers would only reach heaven if offered in the words appropriate to one's ancestral lineage, Jewish rites ceased to be regional. Printing of large numbers of identical prayer books also led to a loss of differentiations among local rites and the loss entirely of rites in which printers were not interested. As a result, the modern world is dominated by two rites: the Ashkenazi and the Sephardi (with identifiable subgroups), accompanied by a few surviving regional rites, most notably those of Italy and Yemen. None of these survive solely in their places of origin.

The most significant formative forces on the medieval rites were the continuing integration of Babylonian halakhic norms and the various schools of Jewish mystic thought. Liturgical *halakhah* continued to develop, as part of the larger processes of halakhic development, during this period. The parameters of correct prayer, as outlined in the *Seder Rav Amram Gaon*, *Halakhot Gedolot*, and *Massekhet Soferim* particularly received authoritative definition in the various medieval codes and related works. A significant number of these works, like the *Sefer Hamanhig* of *Abraham ben Nathan ha-Yarḥi (ed. Raphael, 1978), also contain valuable descriptions of actual regional practices in the course of their discussions of halakhic questions. The *Ḥasidei Ashkenaz were deeply interested in liturgy and in correctly reciting and understanding liturgical texts. Their traditions and commentaries, such as the *Perushei Siddur ha-Tefillah la-Roke'aḥ* of *Eleazar ben Judah of Worms (ed. Herschler, 1992), the *Siddur Rabbenu Shelomo / Siddur Ḥasidei Ashkenaz* (ed. Herschler, 1972), or the *piyyut* commentary, *Arugat ha-Bosem* of *Abraham ben Azriel (ed. E.E. Urbach, 1939–63), impacted subsequent understandings of the liturgy. Kabbalists were also interested in and concerned about liturgy, but most texts remain in manuscript. An exception is the 16th-century *Sefer Tola'at Ya'akov* of Meir ibn Gabbai (Jerusalem, 1967). (For some studies of the impact of Kabbalah on liturgy, see Hallamish.)

Description and identification of the medieval, pre-expulsion rites is still in its infancy. The work was begun by D. Goldschmidt in a series of articles describing individual manuscripts, collected posthumously in his *On Jewish Liturgy*. Since then, the addition of thousands of liturgical manuscripts to the collection of the Institute for Microfilmed Hebrew Manuscripts at the Jewish National and University Library in Jerusalem, the development of scholarly ability to manipulate data by computer, and advances in codicology have made detailed study of the medieval rites in their bewildering variety feasible and a desideratum. S. Reif provides an analytic summary in his *Judaism and Hebrew Prayer* (1993), Ch. 6, "Authorities, Rites, and Texts in the Middle Ages." In the meantime, the descriptions that follow present the salient features and editions of these rites as they have evolved over the past millennium.

Ashkenazi Rites

We begin, somewhat arbitrarily, with the Ashkenazi rites. These consist of three main subrites: of Northern France (Zorfat), of the Rhineland (Ashkenaz proper), and of the lands to the east of the Rhine (originally called the Canaanite rite, later the Polish rite). All are well established already in the earliest preserved manuscripts from the 12th and 13th centuries as well as in the literature of a slightly earlier time. The rite of Northern France largely ceased to exist with the persecutions and expulsions of the French Jews during the 14th century, but the other two persist today.

FRENCH RITE. The **Maḥzor Vitry*, composed by Rashi's student, R. Simḥah of Vitry, and presenting his teacher's lore, is one of the earliest exemplars of the Northern French rite. The edition published by S. Hurwitz (1923), based on a late manuscript with many interpolations from the 13th-14th centuries, has now been replaced by the critical edition of Aryeh Goldschmidt (2004). Goldschmidt argues that the *Siddur Rashi* (ed. S. Buber and J. Freimann (1910–11)) is really a version of this work. The 13th-century *Sefer ha-Maḥkim* and *Siddur Troyes* record that the French rite differs from the Ashkenazi rite only in certain additional *piyyutim*, a *kerovah* for the second day of Rosh Ha-Shanah, and some *ma'arivim*. However, manuscript evidence and the arguments of the Ḥasidei Ashkenaz suggest some more subtle differences in precise language, too.

Until the 1290 expulsion, English Jews also followed the ritual of Northern France. A complete *siddur* with a few *piyyutim* is contained in *Ez Ḥayyim* (printed in the edition of Sir Israel *Brodie, 1 (1962), 63–138), by R. Jacob Ḥazzan of London. Part of this rite also remained in use in three communities in Piedmont (northern Italy), Asti, Fossano, and Moncalvo (known as אפ״ם, AFM), until modern times. These communities had accepted the Ashkenazi rite upon their establishment in Italy, but on the High Holy Days continued to recite the *piyyutim* of the French *maḥzor* from handwritten copies. The community of Asti continued to hold High Holiday services in accordance with its ritual until about 1965. The *maḥzor* of these communities is described by D. Goldschmidt in *On Jewish Liturgy*, 80–121; and a list of the *piyyutim* is given by I. Markon, in: *Jewish Studies ... G.A. Kohut* (1935), Heb. pt., 89–101. The whole material of High Holidays *piyyutim* of the French *maḥzor* found in manuscript is included in the *Maḥzor la-Yamim ha-Nora'im*, ed. D. Goldschmidt, Jerusalem, 1970.

RHINELAND AND CANAANITE/POLISH RITES. The Rhineland, or pure, Ashkenazi rite, originally used by the German or German-speaking Jews, was the most widely followed and its *siddur* and *maḥzor* have been printed since the 16th century. Only fragments of the Palestinian texts (e.g., *Ẓur Yisrael* or the short *Emet ve-Yaẓẓiv* in connection with *piyyutim*) have been retained. The *maḥzor* contains *yoẓerot* for the special *Sabbaths and all festivals; *kerovot* for the Four *Parashiyyot*, *Shabbat ha-Gadol*, all the festivals, Purim (in some communities also for Ḥanukkah), and the Ninth of Av; and a large collection of *seliḥot* and *kinot*. Most of the *piyyutim* are by Palestinian or German authors. The rite is now followed in Germany (from the Elbe River westward, where post-Holocaust communities retain authentic rites), Switzerland, Holland, Belgium, northern France, and in a number of communities of Northern Italy.

From the earliest documented exemplars, a slightly different rite was common in communities to the east, known originally as Canaanites (an epithet for "slaves," i.e., the pagan Slavs). This branch eventually comprised the eastern part of Germany, Poland, Lithuania, Bohemia, Moravia, Hungary, the rest of Austria, all of Russia, Romania, and the rest of the Balkan countries, and later included also the Ashkenazi Jewish communities of Denmark, England, America, and Palestine. Differences between the two branches – the Western, called *Minhag Rainus* ("Rhine usage") in the Middle Ages; and the Eastern, called *Minhag Oystraikh* or *Minhag Peihem* ("Austrian or Bohemian usage"), today generally known as *Minhag Polin* – are hardly noticeable in the regular prayers; the main variances are in some special *piyyutim* and in the more elaborate opening to the Torah ritual. Different editions of *Minhag Ashkenaz* (Western) and *Minhag Polin* (Eastern) were published from the 16th century onward. The **selihot* point to local differences. Thirteen different rites have been printed (see the *Seder ha-Seliḥot* edition of D. Goldschmidt (1965), introd. 7).

A major contribution of the medieval Ashkenazi rites to the greater Jewish world was the development and regularization of memorial liturgies, ranging from the regular recitation of *Kaddish* during the year following a parent's death, to the annual recitation of *Kaddish* on the anniversary of a relative's death, to the recitation of **Yizkor* four times a year during the pilgrimage festivals and Yom Kippur. Many of these rituals developed in parallel to Christian interest in cults of the dead. They emerged in Ashkenaz in the aftermath of the destruction of Rhineland communities during the First and Second Crusades. Some Ashkenazi communities included a memorial element in most Sabbath services with the recitation of the prayer *"Av ha-Raḥamim,"* while others recited it only on the Sabbath preceding *Shavuot (the anniversary of the First Crusade) and the Sabbath preceding the Ninth of *Av. It is also in this context that *Aleinu* became part of the daily liturgy and not simply a part of the High Holy Day *Musaf* services.

Until the 18th century this rite was generally followed by all Ashkenazi Jews, but since the rise of Ḥasidism, the rite of Isaac Luria (*Nusaḥ ha-Ari*) was accepted in ḥasidic communities. Though retaining some of the Ashkenazi usage (e.g., the *taḥanunim*, the *Kedushah* for the *Shaḥarit* of Sabbath, Grace after Meals), *Nusaḥ ha-Ari* borrows significant elements from the Sephardi rite (see below) and is therefore popularly called *Nusaḥ Sefarad*. The *piyyutim* used by the ḥasidic communities are, however, according to the Ashkenazi (Polish) rite. Through the negligence of printers, the texts of this rite were badly emended and never really standardized. The special editions for the *Chabad Ḥasidim (after the revision of R. *Shneur Zalman of Lyady) are explicitly marked *Nusaḥ ha-Ari*.

Romanian (Romaniot) Rite

The Romanian (Greek) rite was followed by the Jewish communities of the Byzantine Empire. In use in Greece, the Balkans, and in European Turkey, at least until the end of the 16th century (manuscript evidence suggests that the *piyyutim*, at least, continued to be recited even later in some communities), it was superseded by the Sephardi rite. Four editions of *Maḥzor Romania* appeared in the 16th century, and many more of smaller prayer books (*siddurim*) of the rite. Distinctive features of the rite are *Hodu* before *Barukh she-Amar*; in the **Kaddish*, the addition *Ve-Yaẓmaḥ purkaneh vi-karev Meshiḥeh u-farek ameh be-raḥmateh*; several elaborations of the weekday *Amidah; Le-Dor va-Dor* for the third benediction of the *Amidah* (instead of *Attah Kadosh*); the short *Emet ve-Yaẓẓiv* on the Sabbath; *Keter* for the *Kedushah* in *Musaf. Maḥzor Romania* contains a large collection of *piyyutim* for *Shaharit* **petiḥah*, **reshut*, *Kaddish*, **Barekhu*, **yoẓer*, *ofan*, *zulat*, *mi-khamokha*; *Ma'arivim* for every festival (including the Day of Atonement); **kerovot* for fast days, Purim, the Day of Atonement, Rosh Ha-Shanah (in Mss. also for the other holidays and Ḥanukkah); and a large collection of **seliḥot* and **kinot*. Differences in the manuscripts and the printed editions show that the rite was edited in its final form at a comparatively late date. (For a description of this rite see: Zunz, Ritus, 79ff., and D. Goldschmidt, *On Jewish Prayer*, 122–52. For its *piyyut*, see L. Weinberger, *Jewish Hymnography: A Literary History* (1998), ch. 4–6, and his references to his publications of the *piyyut* texts.)

The ritual of the Jews of Corfu (their *maḥzor* was never printed) is almost identical with the Romaniot rite. The rite of the Jews of Kaffa (Feodosiya) and Karasubazar (Belogorsk) in the Crimea has, despite many elaborations of the texts, all the distinctions of the *Maḥzor Romania*. While their *siddur* was printed twice (last edition Kala, 1735), their *maḥzor* was never printed. I. Markon (in: *Festschrift ... A. Harkavy* (1908), 449–69) lists 315 *piyyutim* from their *maḥzor*.

Roman (Italian) Rite

The Roman (Italian) rite, also called *Minhag ha-Lo'azim*, is in use today in Rome, in the interior of Italy, in a few communities in Salonika and Constantinople, and also in the Italian synagogue in Jerusalem. Peculiar to this rite are *Le'eila Le'eila* in the usual *Kaddish; Keter* in all *Kedushot*; different wording to the *Amidah*; different *taḥanunim* (*ve-Hu Raḥum* is missing); a special piyyutic version of the *Arvit* for Friday evening (*Asher Killah Ma'asav*) and its *Amidah* (*U-me-Ahavatkha*); *kerovot* for the Day of Atonement and all the fast days, but not for Rosh Ha-Shanah and other festivals. A number of *piyyutim* had already been removed from the *maḥzor* before the invention of printing. Many manuscripts and editions of this rite continue the model of the *Seder Rav Amram Gaon* of interspersing prayers with halakhic instructions.

The first edition of this rite was that of Soncino, printed at Casal Maggiore, 1485–86. An introduction to this *maḥzor* was published by S.D. Luzzatto (1856), entitled *Mavo le-Maḥzor Benei Roma* (new edition, with supplement by D. Goldschmidt and a bibliography of the printed *maḥzor* and *siddur* by J.J. Cohen, Tel Aviv, 1966).

Sephardi (Spanish) Rites

Originally dominant in the Iberian Peninsula, the Sephardi rites spread, after the Jewish expulsion, to North Africa, Italy, the Balkans, and through all the countries of the east as far as India, superseding the fixed prayers of the local rites and often their traditions of *piyyut* as well. Former *Conversos brought the rite, in a slightly different form, to Holland, some communities in Germany (e.g., Altona, Vienna), England, and eventually North and South America.

In the process of the expulsion, almost all the local rites of the Iberian Peninsula lost their identities. The Catalonian and Aragonese rites were preserved only in Saloniki, where they were printed several times (first editions: Catalonian (Salonika, 1627), Aragonese (Salonika, 1629)) for the Catalonian and Aragonese Jews who settled there (D. Goldschmidt, *On Jewish Prayer*, 272–88). All surviving rites are versions of the Castilian rite.

The Sephardi rite differs from the Ashkenazi by putting *Hodu* before *Barukh she-Amar*; inserting *Ve-Yaẓmaḥ Purkaneh* in the *Kaddish*; introducing the *Kedushah* with *Nakdishakh* and *Keter;* different versions of the ninth benediction of the *Amidah* for summer and winter; minor differences in the general wording of the *Amidah*; and sometimes the formula *Le-Moshe Ẓivvita* (instead of *Tikkanta*) for the Sabbath *Musaf*. The collection of verses accompanying the movements of Torah from and to the ark are almost completely different. Although early Sephardi rites were rich in *piyyutim*, they had almost all been deleted or moved to the periphery of the service in Castile by the time of David ben Joseph *Abudarham (see his commentary to the Yom Kippur *piyyutim*, *Tashlum Abudarham*, ed. by L. Prins (1900)). From the 16th century, it became common to print this rite according to the kabbalistic traditions of the Ari. From the 18th century, most Sephardi communities removed *piyyut* entirely (Langer, *To Worship God Properly...*, 172–82).

NORTH AFRICAN RITES. There is very little evidence preserved for the original rites of the North African communities. Almost all manuscripts and printed editions reflect the rite of the Sephardi émigrés. An important exception is the *siddur* of Solomon b. Nathan of Sijilmassa (North Africa, 12th century; tr., ed. S. Haggai, 1995). E. Hazan, *Hebrew Poetry...* provides a comprehensive survey of the poetry characterizing these rites, before and after the arrival of the Sephardi refugees.

PROVENÇAL RITE. The Provençal rite (southern France) is nearly identical with the Sephardi rite, especially that of neighboring Catalonia, and was followed by the communities of Avignon, Carpentras, L'Isle sur la Sorgue, and Cavaillon until the 19th century. The text shows some additions due to the influence of the rite of northern France, e.g., the three *Kedushot* begin with *Nekaddesh*, *Na'ariẓakh*, *Keter*; in all the *Ami-*

dot, *Shalom Rav* is used instead of *Sim Shalom*. The *maḥzor* of Avignon was printed in Amsterdam (4 vols., 1765 ff.; a detailed description of it was given by Zunz, in *Allgemeine Zeitung des Judentums*, II (1838)–IV (1840)). The *maḥzor* of Carpentras, which abbreviated almost all the *piyyutim*, was printed in Amsterdam (1739–62, 4 vols.). The *maḥzorim* of L'Isle and Cavaillon, preserved only in manuscript, contain numerous *piyyutim* for festivals and Sabbaths, but only *kerovot* for the fast days, Rosh Ha-Shanah, the Day of Atonement, and the prayers of dew and rain. These *kerovot* were recited after the *Amidah* in accordance with the practice of the North African communities. A *siddur* with selected *piyyutim* for these communities was edited by M. Milhaud (*Rituel des Prières en Hébreu à l'Usage des Israélites de l'Ancien Comtat*, 2 vols., 1855).

Yemenite Rite

Minhag Teiman, the rite of the Jews of Yemen, follows the *Seder Tefillah* of Maimonides which is based on the *siddur* of Saadiah Gaon, but shows the influence of Sephardi elements (see L. Goldschmidt, in YMHS, 7 (1958), 188). A small number of *piyyutim* such as *Avodah, hoshanot*, and *seliḥot* are taken from the Sephardi prayer book. The Yemenite liturgy was first printed in Jerusalem (2 vols., 1894), entitled תכלאל, from which a handwritten (mimeographed) edition elaborated with many *piyyutim* was edited by J.S. Hobareh (1964 (תכלאל קדמונים)).

Eastern Rites

The Sephardi refugees imposed their rite on all the communities of the east, making the original rites there too difficult to retrieve and study. Among the best documented are the liturgy of the Persian Jews (published by Shlomoh Tal, *The Persian Jewish Prayer Book* (Heb., 1980)) and the rite of the Jews of Aleppo (*Maḥzor Aram-Zova*, printed in Venice, 1523–27), whose High Holy Days prayers, very similar to those of the Persian prayer book, were also influenced by the Romanian and Roman rites. There are a number of manuscripts extant that apparently hail from this general region, but we have no way of identifying their provenance at this time. All later prayer books conform to the Sephardi rites.

[Ernst Daniel Goldschmidt / Ruth Langer (2nd ed.)]

THE MODERN PERIOD

The economics of printing required mass production of single prayer books to meet the needs of multiple communities, meaning that local preferences for specific *piyyutim*, variants of individual words or phrases, and all the variety that accompanied a world in which prayer books were produced one at a time, were overridden. In addition, kabbalistic concerns led to many innovative additions and changes to the printed liturgies as well as a belief that only "correct" prayer was efficacious. Particularly in Poland, these changes combined with the prevalence of outright errors in the printed prayer books, inspired prominent rabbis, beginning in the 17th century, to establish the correct texts of the prayers. Important examples range from the 1617 *Siddur of R. Shabbetai Sofer of Przemysl* (ed. Yitzchok Satz (Baltimore, 1987)) commissioned by the Polish Jewish Council, to the labors of scholars like Wolf *Heidenheim (*Sefer Kerovot*, 9 vols., 1800–2) and Seligman *Baer (*Seder Avodat Yisrael*, 1868) in Germany, and Samuel David *Luzzatto (*Mahzor … ke-Minhag Benei Roma*, 1855–6) in Italy (Reif, *Judaism and Hebrew Prayer*, ch. 7–8). With the development of modern academic approaches to Jewish studies, the questions have shifted to those of retrieval of original and earlier forms of prayers and a recognition that "correctness" is not so easily defined. Moreover, the migrations of Jews caused by the Holocaust and the expulsions of Jews from Arab lands has created another leveling of regional rites as liturgical scholars have endeavored to create Israeli prayer books that might be used by all Israelis according to the major rites (like the *Siddur* and *Mahzor Rinat Yisrael*, ed. Sh. Tal).

Prayer book manuscripts, because of the labor and expensive materials involved, tended to be as concise as possible, rarely repeating prayers from one service to the next and frequently omitting all instructions on how to perform the liturgies. With the development of printing and more inexpensive book production, and increasing expectations that every worshiper would use a prayer book, the prayer book gradually became a more "user-friendly" text, repeating prayers at appropriate intervals and including instructions, frequently in the vernacular. The contemporary liturgical texts published by *ArtScroll and used widely in Orthodox congregations in the Diaspora represent the extreme expression of this phenomenon, giving instructions for every customary gesture. This represents a flattening of variety not only within the text itself, but also in its actual performance.

Another element that greatly shaped prayer books in the early centuries of printing was the introduction of kabbalistic elements. These included both instructions on how to recite and meditate on the prayers, corrections to existing prayer elements according to the customs of Isaac *Luria, and additional *kavvanot* (texts expressing the mystical intention of the prayer). Often, additional prayers were added to the printed prayer book intended for private recitation, both on a daily basis and also for specific occasions and personal needs.

In this context, collections of prayers specifically for women (in Yiddish, called **tkhines*) begin to appear in Ashkenaz and in Italy (in Hebrew). Some speculate that in Ashkenaz, they originated with the convention of having one woman lead prayers for the women's section, where women often could neither see nor hear the men. Although some of these prayers are clearly written by women, most are unattributed and many may have been written by men. Their language shows influences of Lurianic Kabbalah, suggesting that the printed texts themselves are early modern, but they may well have developed from earlier orally transmitted materials. If similar oral women's traditions existed in other communities, they were never written down. These prayers accompany the dramatic moments of synagogue liturgy, like the blowing of the *shofar* or the blessing of the New Month, but they also accompany moments in women's lives outside the synagogue, through both the life cycle and the annual cycle. The collections all provide prayers for the three *mitzvot* specially commanded for women: taking **hallah*, going to the **mikveh* after menstruation (**niddah*), and lighting *candles before the Sabbath and festivals (C. Weissler, *Voices of the Matriarchs ...*). In the 19th and 20th centuries, some of these Yiddish prayers were translated, not only into modern vernaculars but also to accord with modern sensibilities. The best known of these collections was Fanny Neuda's *Stunden der Andacht* (in English translation, *Hours of Devotion*). In recent years, many collections have been republished, sometimes in modern Hebrew versions.

19th Century Developments

While synagogue architecture and musical styles were consistently influenced by those of the surrounding cultures, pressures to conform liturgically became more intense and more deliberate as Jews approached emancipation in Western Europe. Acculturated Jews were very conscious of the fact that their liturgical modes were among the elements that marked them as different. If they desired to be considered as citizens of their countries of residence whose religion was Judaism, then the public statement of that Judaism needed to be one of which they could be proud. Reforms of the liturgy began as aesthetic reforms in the quality of musical production and in decorum. Improved decorum did not challenge halakhic norms but did lead to more formal seating patterns for prayers and more regular preaching, increasingly in the vernacular. Musical reforms, in contrast, led to halakhically problematic demands for inclusion in prayer of an *organ and mixed choir.

Reform liturgy had its first formal expression in the prayer book of the *Hamburg Temple, published in 1819. This prayer book, and those that followed it in Western Europe and eventually in the United States, not only provided translations of the prayers into the Western vernacular (itself not a new phenomenon) but considered these translations to be its primary prayer texts. Vernacular prayer itself pushed the reformers to create more radical liturgical changes. The act of translation created a confrontation with the theological statements of the received liturgy and with concepts that, once removed from their poetic Hebrew phraseology, became starkly troublesome when stated in a language that everyone understood well. Certain concepts, especially those driven by Kabbalah, but also prayers for the restoration of sacrifices, did not fit with the rationalist turn of the age and the reformers' sense of modernity; others, like prayers for the restoration of Zion, seemed inappropriate to Jews who considered their true homes to be their countries of residence; yet others were offensive to Jews' gentile neighbors. These concerns, combined with desires to shorten the service as well as leave room for a substantial sermon and enhanced music, led to radical changes in the prayers themselves. Reform prayer books, of which hundreds were produced, increasingly removed or revised theologically difficult passages and shortened the entire liturgy significantly. At its most extreme, in the late 19th and early 20th centuries, some prayer books retained only superficial similarities to the traditional liturgy, including only a few key sentences of Hebrew prayer and few hints of the service's traditional patterns. *Halakhah* was simply not a consideration and was often deliberately disregarded as appropriate only to another age. Reform synagogues and their services blended well with the Protestant liturgies of the Jews' neighbors, with vernacular prayers, short Scripture readings (with translation, or only in the vernacular for the **haftarah*, which was often declaimed, not chanted), extended sermons, and hymnals filled with vernacular songs designed for organ and choir (and not a cantor). Some of these hymns were adapted from Christian church music. As rabbis became liturgical officiants, like Christian clergy, congregants arrived on time, sat quietly in forward-facing pews, and left elevated by the awesome grandeur of the service. (See J.J. Petuchowski, *Prayerbook Reform in Europe: The Liturgy of European Liberal and Reform Judaism* (1968) and E.L. Friedland, "*Were Our Mouths Filled With Song*": *Studies in Liberal Jewish Liturgy* (1997).)

Such changes elicited objections and responses from the traditional world in Europe, especially in urban areas and in the west. On the one hand, Reform demands for decorum and for greater attention to the liturgy were deemed appropriate. In traditional synagogues, liturgical music was increased and enhanced, although performed by cantors with all-male choirs, and without instrumental music on Sabbaths and holidays. But traditional Jews understood the received prayers as halakhically mandated and immutable. Increasingly, they published prayer books with vernacular translations, intended to edify those less literate in Hebrew but not to serve as performed liturgical texts. As a result, these translations frequently lack literary finesse and are sometimes even incomprehensible. The greatest impact of Reform on the traditional liturgical world was a renewed questioning of the validity and necessity of the Ashkenazi traditions of *piyyut*. Many communities, over the course of the 19th century, ceased to recite most festival poetry, retaining only the *piyyut* of the High Holy Days and a few liturgical poems linked to the liturgical announcements of the prayers for rain and dew at Sukkot and Passover.

20th Century Developments

As they achieved a degree of maturity, the various West European and North American non-Orthodox movements sought to define themselves by creating standardized liturgies. How this process worked varied from country to country, depending on the organizational structures of the communities. In North America, liturgies tended to be standardized by each movement across the United States and Canada. In Germany, on the other hand, prayer books were largely produced for specific regional communities. Over the course of the 20th century, although movements never required adherence to their liturgies, these prayer books became elements of the movements' self-definition, reflecting the theology of the movement. Examples of such prayer book series from North America include the Reform movement's *Union Prayer Book* (published by the Central Conference of American Rabbis), with major editions in 1895, 1921 (revised), 1947 (newly revised), 1975 (the *New Union Prayer Book*, retitled *Gates of Prayer* for weekdays, Sabbaths, and holidays, *Gates of Repentance* (1978) for the High Holy Days), and with numerous versions for specific occasions and revisions. At the beginning of the 21st century, a new prayer book, *Mishkan Tefillah*, was in production. Publications of prayer books commissioned by the Conservative Movement's United Synagogue began with the 1927 *Festival Prayer Book*. Most Conservative congregations adopted the Sabbath and festival prayer book edited by Morris *Silverman (1946) and then those edited by Jules Harlow for the Rabbinical Assembly (*Mahzor*, 1972, *Siddur Sim Shalom*, 1985, both with subsequent revisions). The Reconstructionist Movement originally used the liturgies of Mordecai *Kaplan (*Siddur*, 1945, *High Holiday Prayer Book*, 1948), now replaced by the *Kol Haneshamah* series, edited by David Teutsch (1991–98 and ongoing). (See Caplan, *From Ideology to Liturgy*.) Similar series have been published by the Liberal and Reform movements in Great Britain. The Progressive and Masorati movements in Israel have also published their own liturgies in recent decades. All these movements also published corresponding *haggadot*, rabbi's manuals, and other home and life cycle liturgies, all of which have undergone continuing revisions over the years.

The differences among these series reflect these movements' differing understandings of the appropriate balance between innovation and tradition. While the Conservative prayer books increasingly include new materials, these are generally found on the periphery of the required prayers, and almost all changes to the central prayers have some historical precedent. The Reconstructionist prayers retain tradition except where such prayers contradict the movement's ideology. Hence, concepts like chosenness disappear entirely. The Reform prayer books reflect a growing acceptance of tradition and of Hebrew prayer, but never as a binding category; translations are often highly interpretative and reflect the concerns of the times.

Several elements characterize all these liturgies at the beginning of the 21st century, including those produced for the Orthodox world. Vernacular translations in the English-speaking world have moved from a deliberately archaic Elizabethan English to a contemporary form of the language, thus lessening the formality and "otherness" of the English prayers. Accompanying this is an increasing sensitivity to the layout of the prayer book and its visual dimension. Poetry is often printed as such. Typefaces and arrangements of type are designed to ease reading. Many encourage meditation on the prayers by generous "white space," others by providing rich commentary. Some of these commentaries are produced as study texts, not for active synagogue use. (See Harlow, *Or Hadash* on *Sim Shalom*; or Hoffman's series, *Minhag Ami, My People's Prayer Book*.)

By the 1970s and 1980s, all segments of Judaism had responded liturgically to the Holocaust and the existence of the State of Israel. The latter reality, particularly, transformed Reform traditions of rejection of a Jewish homeland and prayers for return to it. While Reform liturgies still exclude prayers for the restoration of the Temple and its sacrificial worship, references to Israel and its welfare now hold a valued place. Conservative and Reconstructionist liturgies never sidelined Israel, but they address sacrifices only as a past form of worship and do not pray for their restoration. Liturgies published in Israel, and many published elsewhere as well, including many Orthodox prayer books, incorporated the Israeli Chief Rabbinate's "Prayer for the Well-Being of the State of Israel," instead of or in addition to the traditional prayer for the government. Many also incorporate prayers for Israeli soldiers and liturgies for Israeli Independence Day and the anniversary of Jerusalem's reunification. The effect of a revitalized Jewish life in Israel on the non-Orthodox liturgies appears also in their selections of songs, in the increased use of Hebrew (especially in the Reform movement where it had almost disappeared), and in the melodies used for traditional prayers. Liturgical assimilation to the surrounding culture is now less evident, replaced by a conscious striving for authentic Jewish culture. The reintegration of ḥasidic or ḥasidic-like music, especially that influenced by Shlomo *Carlebach, speaks to a search for spiritually enriching worship across the spectrum of Jewish practices.

The effect of the Holocaust on Jewish liturgies, beyond its erasure of many local practices throughout Europe, has been less marked. Memorial prayers now regularly include prayers for the victims of Nazism; *kinot* (poetry of lamentation) on the Holocaust have been added to the Ninth of Av's liturgy. But consensus about an appropriate liturgical religious commemoration, as opposed to communal or secular observance of *Holocaust Remembrance Day, has yet to emerge.

The other major revolution to affect the liturgy in the second half of the 20th century, especially in non-Orthodox circles, was the feminist movement. Beginning in the 1970s, prayer book editors began to remove gendered references to the congregation of worshippers from the vernacular translations. By the 1980s and 1990s, gendered references to God also increasingly disappeared. This included not only a transformation of pronouns, but also the search for new names for God that would not have exclusively masculine referents. Although the process began with the vernacular prayers, this endeavor also extended to Hebrew names for God and to alternative blessing formulae that would better express feminist prayers. See, for example, M. *Falk's *The Book of Blessings: New Jewish Prayers for Daily Life, the Sabbath, and the New Moon Festival* (1996), which also includes exclusively women's voices in the nontraditional poetry of the services. While this prayer book has only superficial similarities to a traditional *siddur*, the ideals it embodies have affected subsequent non-Orthodox liturgical publications. All the American movements and their Israeli and European counterparts now include the matriarchs in the first blessing of the *Amidah* and other liturgical references to the ancestors (in the 1998 Conservative *Sim Shalom*, this is an option). Many include references to Miriam as well as Moses in the *Ge'ulah* benediction's allusions to the parting of the Red Sea. Women are present explicitly in these prayer books in a way unprecedented in Jewish history.

This transformation of the prayers grew from the transformation of women's roles in the synagogue itself. The non-Orthodox movements had abandoned the **meḥiẓah* and the prohibition on women's participation in choirs, but they had retained the traditional practice of reserving active leadership roles and honors for men. Egalitarianism achieved its first steps with the public celebration of bat mitzvah ceremonies during regular synagogue services. Regina *Jonas was privately ordained in 1935 in Germany, but she never took on liturgical roles. The most public role of modern liberal rabbis is precisely to lead services. Egalitarianism achieved its symbolic victory with the ordination of the first American woman rabbi by the Reform movement, Sally *Priesand, in 1972, followed by the Reconstructionist and Conservative movements and their counterparts in Europe and Israel. Ordination of women as cantors also followed in short order in these movements. Necessary to this process in the halakhically guided Conservative movement was a series of decisions by the Rabbinical Assembly that, at the discretion of individual congregations, women may be called to the Torah (1955), included in the **minyan* (1973), and lead public prayer (1974). Full participation by lay women in the community became increasingly common in the wake of these changes at the leadership levels. This includes greater women's participation on synagogue boards and other decision-making bodies.

In some corners of the Orthodox world, there have also been some subtle transformations in women's liturgical expression. Increased women's learning has led to increased female commitments to regular prayer and hence to an increased presence in the synagogue, which historically provided many more seats for men than for women. It is increasingly common for Orthodox women to recite **Kaddish* for deceased relatives. Some communities have begun women's *tefillah* groups, where women gather, in the synagogue or outside it, for regular prayer and often also Torah reading, but without prayers requiring a *minyan* of men. Some synagogues allow women to give sermons. In the early years of the 21st century, a new phenomenon has developed of synagogues that maintain separate seating but allow women to lead prayers not requiring a *minyan* and to read from and be called to the Torah.

[Ruth Langer (2nd ed.)]

BIBLIOGRAPHY: I. Elbogen, Gottesdienst, passim (Heb. trans. 1972, English trans. 1993); J. Heinemann, *Ha-Tefillah bi-Tekufat ha-Tanna'im ve-ha-Amora'im* (1962^2), passim (Eng. trans: *Prayer in the Talmud* (1977)); J.J. Petuchowski, *Prayerbook Reform in Europe* (1968). **ADD. BIBLIOGRAPHY:** E. Caplan, *From Ideology to Liturgy: Reconstructionist Worship and American Liberal Judaism* (2002); N.B. Cardin (ed., tr.), *Out of the Depths I Call to You: A Book of Prayers for the Married Jewish Woman* (1995); U. Ehrlich, *The Nonverbal Language of Prayer: A New Approach to Jewish Liturgy* (2004); E. Fleischer, "On the Beginnings of Obligatory Jewish Prayer," in: *Tarbiz*, 59 (1990), 397–441 (Heb.); idem, *Eretz-Israel Prayer and Prayer Rituals as Portrayed in the Geniza Documents* (Heb., 1988); E.L. Friedland, *"Were Our Mouths Filled With Song": Studies in Liberal Jewish Liturgy* (1997); D. Goldschmidt, *On Jewish Liturgy: Essays on Prayer and Religious Poetry* (1980); M. Hallamish, *Kabbalah: In Liturgy, Halakhah and Customs* (Heb., 2000); E. Hazan, *Hebrew Poetry in North Africa* (Heb., 1995); R. Langer and S. Fine (eds.), *Liturgy in the Life of the Synagogue* (2005); R. Langer, "Early Rabbinic Liturgy in Its Palestinian Milieu: Did Non-Rabbis Know the 'Amidah'?" in: D. Harrington, A.J. Avery-Peck, and J. Neusner (eds.), *When Judaism and Christianity Began*, 2 (2004), 423–39; idem, "Revisiting Early Rabbinic Liturgy: The Recent Contributions of Ezra Fleischer," in: *Prooftexts*, 19:2 (1999), 179–94 (see also 20:3 (2000)); idem, *To Worship God Properly: Tensions Between Liturgical Custom and Halakhah in Judaism* (1998); Y. Luger, *The Weekday Amidah in the Cairo Genizah* (Heb., 2001); M.A. Meyer, *Response to Modernity: A History of the Reform Movement in Judaism* (1988); S.C. Reif, *Judaism and Hebrew Prayer: New Perspectives on Jewish Liturgical History* (1993); P.W. van der Horst, "Neglected Greek Evidence for Early Jewish Liturgical Prayer," in: *Journal for the Study of Judaism* 29:3 (1998), 278–96; C. Weissler, *Voices of the Matriarchs: Listening to the Prayers of Early Modern Jewish Women* (1998); N. Wieder, *The Formation of Jewish Liturgy in the East and the West*, 2 vols. (Heb., 1998).

LITVAK, (Michael) ANATOLE (1902–1974), U.S. film producer and director. Born in Kiev, Litvak attended a Russian dramatic school until the age of 16, and then worked in Soviet film studios. After leaving the U.S.S.R. in 1924, he directed films in Europe and the United States in French, German, and English. His European films included *Dolly macht Karriere* (1930), *L'Equipage* (1935), and *Mayerling* (1936), a film that earned him international renown. In 1936 he was invited to work in Hollywood, where he began to make films for RKO and Warner Brothers. When the United States entered World War II, Litvak joined the U.S. Army, worked with director Frank Capra on the "Why We Fight" series, and was put in charge of the combat photography during the Normandy invasion.

Litvak's major American films, many of which he also produced, are *The Woman I Love* (1937), *Tovarich* (1937), *The Sisters* (1938), *Confessions of a Nazi Spy* (1939), *All This, and Heaven Too* (1940), *Blues in the Night* (1941), *The Snake Pit* (Oscar nomination for Best Picture and Best Director, 1949), *Sorry, Wrong Number* (1948), *Decision before Dawn* (Oscar nomination for Best Picture, 1951), *Act of Love* (1954), *The Deep Blue Sea* (1955), *Anastasia* (1956), *The Journey* (1958), *Goodbye Again* (1961), *Five Miles to Midnight* (1962), *The Night of the Generals* (1967), and *The Lady in the Car with Glasses and a Gun* (1970).

[Ruth Beloff (2nd ed.)]

LITVAKOV, MOSES (**Moyshe**; 1875–1937), Yiddish writer and editor. Litvakov was born in Cherkassy, Ukraine. At the age of 17 he abandoned talmudic studies for secular learning, attending the Sorbonne (1902–5). At first he drifted from *Aḥad Ha-Am Zionism to Socialist Zionism and wrote in Russian, Hebrew, and Yiddish on social and literary problems. After the revolution of 1905 he was a member of the central committee of the territorialist Socialist-Zionist (SS) Party, and edited its various periodicals in Vilna. Litvakov also published the pamphlet *Der Zionismus un di Ugande Frage* ("Zionism and the Uganda Question," 1905).

After 1917 he contributed to Yiddish journals in Kiev. In 1919 he joined the Communist Party, and in 1921 he assumed a leading role in Moscow's *Yevsektsiya and editorship of *Emes*, the central Soviet Yiddish daily. In its columns he demanded the uprooting of Jewish religious observances and national aspirations, attempting to place Yiddish literature at the service of the regime. Nevertheless, in his critical articles and as professor of Yiddish literature and Jewish history in the Jewish section of the Moscow Pedagogical Institute, he was often unable to avoid touching on the Jewish past. His essay collection, *In Umru* ("In Anxiety," vol. 1, 1918; vol. 2, 1926), dwelt on the cultural tradition which Jewish proletarian writers in the Soviet Union inherited from prerevolutionary writers, such as M. *Rosenfeld, A. *Reisen, *Sholem Aleichem, and I.L. *Peretz, insisting on the hegemony of the new Soviet Yiddish literature. Litvakov also published a booklet on the Yiddish Chamber Theater in Moscow (1924). With Esther *(Frumkin) he edited a Yiddish translation of Lenin's selected writings in eight volumes. In the ideological polemic among Yiddish writers, he was attacked for remnants of Jewish separatism and chauvinism, allegedly found in his essays. Outmaneuvering efforts to purge him through self-accusations in 1931–32, he continued editing *Emes* until the major purges of 1937, when he was arrested as an enemy of the people, brought to Minsk, and executed in December 1937.

BIBLIOGRAPHY: Rejzen, Leksikon, 2 (1927), 35–41; LNYL, 5 (1963), 90–4; Z. Schneour, *Bialik u-Venei Doro* (1958), 340–8; S. Bickel, *Shrayber fun Mayn Dor*, 1 (1958), 287–304. **ADD. BIBLIOGRAPHY:** M. Krutikov, in: G. Estraikh and M. Krutikov (eds.), *Yiddish and the Left* (2000), 226–41; G. Estraikh, in: *Jews in Eastern Europe*, 2 (2000), 25–55; D. Shneer, *Yiddish and the Creation of Soviet Jewish Culture* (2004).

[Sol Liptzin]

LITVIN, A. (pseudonym of **Shmuel Hurwitz**; 1862–1943), Yiddish journalist, poet, editor, and folklorist. Born in Minsk, he was self-educated. Believing in "redemption through physical labor," he tried to earn a living as street paver, carpenter, and typesetter, while contributing articles on miscellaneous subjects to Russian, Hebrew, and Yiddish periodicals. In 1901 he immigrated to the U.S., where he worked in a shoe factory and wrote for Yiddish journals. During the 1905 Revolution, he returned to Russia, edited the Vilna monthly *Lebn un Visnshaft* (1909–12), and published studies on *Shomer (1910) and I.M. *Dik (1911). Returning to New York in 1914, he wrote for radical and Labor Zionist organs, as well as for the dailies, the *Forverts* and *Morgn-Zhurnal.* During travels through the Polish, Lithuanian, and Galician Jewish communities (1905–14) he accumulated vast material on Yiddish folklore, folk characters, and half-forgotten villages, part of which he utilized in his main work *Yidishe Neshomes* ("Jewish Souls," 6 vols., 1916–17), a panorama of exotic, picturesque Jewish life in preceding generations. Selections from these volumes were translated into Hebrew by A. *Kariv and published in 1943. The greater part of Litvin's collection of Yiddish folk songs, folktales, and folk humor was deposited in the archives of *YIVO in New York and forms a rich source for scholarly research.

BIBLIOGRAPHY: Rejzen, Leksikon, 2 (1927), 142–6; LNYL, 5 (1963), 94–7; B.I. Bialostotsky, *In Kholem un Vor* (1956), 409–16; Kressel, Leksikon, 2 (1967), 263. **ADD. BIBLIOGRAPHY:** D. Charney, *Barg Aruf* (1935), 226–29; Sh. Levin, *Untererdishe Kemfer* (1946), 323–25; Tolush, *Yidishe Shrayber* (1955), 179–84.

[Sol Liptzin]

LITVINE, M. (pseudonym of **Mordkhe Boyarin**; 1906–1993), Yiddish essayist and translator. Born in Shavl (Siauliai), Lithuania, Litvine spent his early childhood in nearby Kovno (Kaunas). Following the expulsion of Jews from the border region, during World War I he lived in Slaviansk, where he attended a Russian secondary school. Modern literature, which he read in Russian and German as well as in Hebrew and Yiddish translation, was the focus of his interests. After returning to Kovno in 1921 he attended the local Jewish-Russian secondary school, after which he studied economics, philosophy, and art history at the university in Berlin, where he imbibed the city's rich cosmopolitan cultural life. He was also attracted to the hiking and camping activities of the German "Wandervogel" youth movement. In 1933 he returned home for compulsory service in the Lithuanian army, returning to Berlin in 1934. His anti-Nazi activities brought about his arrest and sentencing to 15 years' imprisonment (1935), but he was released in 1938 after the intervention of Lithuanian officials. After a short stay in Kovno he left for Paris in 1939 with a student visa. After the German invasion, he departed for the "Free Zone" to study at the University of Montpellier. In June 1942 he went into hiding in a small village and eventually joined a group of the French Resistance. After the war he settled in Paris. Because of his generous personality, fascinating lectures, and writings, he became over the decades one of the most esteemed and beloved intellectual figures of the Yiddish cultural scene in Paris and other Jewish centers. In 1944–58, he was on the staff of the Communist daily *Naye Presse*, writing mostly literary and theater criticism. In 1953–56 he edited the literary quarterly *Parizer Tsaytshrift*, where some of his translations and essays appeared. Beginning in the 1960s Litvine dedicated himself almost completely to literature, harmoniously combining extensive analysis of contemporary Yiddish poets with intense research about and practice of poetic translation. His brilliant analytical and synthetic intelligence, his vast erudition in various fields of literary aesthetics, as well as his literary talent and mastery of the Yiddish language are displayed in the outstanding quality of his published works. His most important essays, about I. *Manger, Ch. *Grade, A. *Sutzkever, and other major Yiddish poets, appeared in *Di Goldene Keyt* and other Yiddish publications. His most exceptional contribution to Yiddish literature is his *Frantseyzishe Poezye: Ibersetsungen un Komentarn* ("French Poetry: Translations and Comments," 2 vols., 1968, 1986). A collection of his translations from French, Russian, and German poetry, *Fun* *der Velt-Poezye* ("Poetry from the World," 2003), appeared posthumously.

BIBLIOGRAPHY: LNYL, 5 (1963), 97; B. Kagan, Leksikon (1986), 331–2; N. Gruss, in: *Di Goldene Keyt*, 65 (1981), 159–71; A. Shulman, in: *Yidishe Kultur* (May–June 1986), 44–7; V. Solomon, in: *Di Goldene Keyt*, 122 (1987), 73–83.

[Marc Miller]

LITVINOFF, EMANUEL (1915–), English poet. A Londoner by birth and upbringing, Litvinoff served in the army during World War II. Apart from his journalism (as editor of the periodical *Jews in Eastern Europe*), Litvinoff wrote poems, some of which were collected in two volumes, *The Untried Soldier* (1942) and *A Crown for Cain* (1948), and a novel, *The Lost Europeans* (1959). His work was largely concerned with the problems of the Diaspora Jew, mostly because he was influenced by the vigorous Jewish culture of London's East End and the antisemitism of the British Fascists in the thirties, and was deeply affected by the Holocaust and its aftermath. Litvinoff's most significant poem is, perhaps, "To T.S. Eliot," a protest against Eliot's occasionally sneering attitude toward Jews and a passionate self-identification of himself with the dead of Treblinka. In *The Lost Europeans*, Litvinoff describes the experience of a Jew in postwar Berlin, and in his second novel, *The Man Next Door* (1968), the workings of an antisemite's mind. In the late 1960s he resigned his position on the *Guardian* newspaper in protest at its anti-Israel stance. His later books include an autobiographical work, *Journey Through a Small Planet: Jewish Childhood in East London* (1997), and works of fiction. His brother, BARNET (1917–1996), journalist and Zionist worker, wrote a biography of David Ben-Gurion, *Ben Gurion of Israel* (1954); *Road to Jerusalem* (1965), on the development of the Zionist movement; *A Peculiar People* (1969), about contemporary Jewish communities; *The Burning Bush: Antisemitism and World History* (1988); and other works.

[Jon Silkin]

LITVINOV, MAXIM MAXIMOVICH (Wallach, Meir-Henokh Moiseevitch; 1867–1951), Russian revolutionary and Soviet diplomat. Born in Bialystok, Litvinov joined the illegal Social-Democratic Party in 1899 and was arrested and exiled. In 1902 he escaped to Switzerland and in 1903, after having joined the Bolshevik faction, he returned clandestinely to Russia and took part in the 1905 Revolution. He collaborated with Maxim Gorki on the newspaper *Novaya Zhizn* ("The New Life"). After the failure of the revolution he fled from Russia and lived in France and England. While in England he became closely associated with *Lenin and was instrumental in various underground operations of the Bolsheviks, including the smuggling of arms to the Caucasus. In London Litvinov married Ivy Low, niece of the English historian Sir Sidney *Low. Following the October Revolution in 1917 Litvinov was made Soviet diplomatic agent to Britain, but he was detained by the British government and exchanged for Bruce Lockhart, the British diplomatic agent in Soviet Russia. In 1921 he became deputy commissar for foreign affairs under Chicherin, and from 1930 until 1939 he was commissar of foreign affairs of the Soviet Union, concentrating in the field of Soviet diplomacy, particularly with the West. In 1919 he negotiated the first peace treaty of Soviet Russia (with Estonia), took part in the international conference in Genoa in 1922, which resulted in the Rapallo Treaty with Germany, and headed the Soviet delegation to the subsequent conference at The Hague and the disarmament conference in Geneva (1927). He was active in the USSR's joining of the League of Nations and represented it there in 1934–38. In 1933, at Franklin D. *Roosevelt's invitation, he personally conducted the negotiations for the establishment of American-Soviet diplomatic relations. In the period of Moscow's anti-Nazi policy (1934–39), Litvinov became the chief Soviet spokesman at the League of Nations where he demanded the establishment of a collective security system. However, in May 1939, when *Stalin decided to reverse his policy and to effect a rapprochement with Hitler at the expense of the West, Litvinov, being a Jew and known as a protagonist of a pro-Western orientation, was replaced by Stalin's closest collaborator, V.M. Molotov; in February 1941 he was even dropped from the party's central committee. Following the German invasion of the Soviet Union, in June 1941, Litvinov was appointed Soviet ambassador to the United States, where he remained until 1943. He was reappointed assistant commissar for foreign affairs for a short period in 1946, but retired soon afterwards. His publications include *The Bolshevik Revolution, its Rise and Meaning* (1918) and *Against Aggression, Speeches by Maxim Litvinov* (1939). Litvinov was never self-conscious about being a Jew. He became a lonely, forgotten figure in the last years of his life when Stalin's antisemitic campaign was in full swing.

BIBLIOGRAPHY: A.U. Pope, *Maxim Litvinoff* (Eng., 1943); G.A. Craig and F. Gilbert (eds.), *Diplomats 1919–1939* (1953), 344–77; D.G. Bishop, *Roosevelt-Litvinov Agreements: The American View* (1965); B.D. Wolfe, *Strange Communists I Have Known* (1965), 207–22; G.F. Kennan, *Russia and the West* (1960), index.

[Binyamin Eliav]

LITVINOVSKY, PINCHAS (1894–1985), Israeli painter. Born in Novo-Georgiyevsk, Russia, to a religious family of merchants, Litvinovsky studied art at the Academy of Art in Odessa on a scholarship. As a student he visited the Bezalel exhibition in Odessa and met Boris *Schatz, the founder of the Bezalel School of Arts and Crafts. Schatz persuaded the young, talented student to study art in Jerusalem at Bezalel. Litvinovsky stayed in Jerusalem for a brief period, then he traveled to Petrograd to study there at the local Academy of Art. In 1919 Litvinovsky and his wife, Liza, immigrated to Ereẓ Israel, mainly because of the pogroms brought on by the Bolshevik Revolution. After a short stay in Jerusalem, they moved to Bitanyah in Galilee, but Litvinovsky continued to work in Jerusalem. Litvinovsky participated in the famous exhibitions in the Tower of David in Jerusalem and in the Modern Artists' Exhibition at the Ohel Theater in Tel Aviv.

Though he spent most of his time in Jerusalem, he often traveled to Europe and United States. In 1980 he was awarded the Israel Prize.

Litvinovsky was among those artists who sought a unique Israeli style of painting. He was known for his portraits, though he did most of them to earn a living. In his other paintings he dealt with local types (*Selling Chickens*, 1920s, Israel Museum), animals, and landscapes. His style was almost abstract and was characterized by colorful intensity. It had a dual aspect, embracing on the one hand sensual-erotic paintings and, the other, hundreds of portraits of rabbis from the 19th century to his own time. The inability to decide between the earthly-instinctual and the spiritual-heavenly carried over into his style and was reflected in several ways, including the depiction of a complex relationship between man and beast.

Picasso, among others, inspired Litvinovsky. Bodies were roughly delineated but this did not prevent the display of typical signs and collage effects revealing such influences.

BIBLIOGRAPHY: Israel Museum, *Litvinovsky* (1990).

[Ronit Steinberg (2nd ed.)]

LITWACK, HARRY ("Chief"; 1907–1999), U.S. men's college basketball coach; member of Basketball Hall of Fame. Litwack was born in Galicia, Austria, to Jacob, a shoemaker, and Rachel, the sixth of seven children in a Yiddish-speaking family. Litwack's father immigrated to the U.S. in 1910, and saved up money to send for Litwack and his family two years later. After graduating from South Philadelphia High School in 1925, Litwack began a 48-year association with Temple University, beginning as an undergraduate when he played on the varsity and was captain and team MVP in 1927–28 and 1928–29. After graduating in 1930, Litwack began his coaching career at Gratz High School (1930–31), and then became head coach of the freshman team at Temple, leading them to a 181–32 record over the next 16 years, with no losing seasons. At the same time, Litwack was playing pro basketball with Eddie *Gottlieb's all-Jewish Philadelphia Sphas, from 1930 to 1936. Litwack also served during this time as assistant coach for the Temple varsity, which in 1938 won the inaugural National Invitational Tournament, the first-ever postseason college basketball tournament. Litwack was named Temple's head coach in 1947, and held the position until 1973, finishing with a record of 373–193 and only one losing season. He led the team to 13 postseason tournaments, winning the NIT in 1969, and coming in third in the NCAA tournament in 1956 and 1958. In 43 years coaching at Temple, Litwack was thrown out of a game by a referee only once. Litwack also served briefly as assistant coach for the Philadelphia Warriors (1948–51). He is credited with creating the box-and-one zone defense, which revolutionized the college game and made it necessary to develop new methods of coaching and playing, but Litwack maintained that he did not invent it; he just refined it. He was coach of the U.S. Maccabiah team in 1957, and was elected to the Basketball Hall of Fame in 1975.

[Elli Wohlgelernter (2nd ed.)]

LITWAK, A. (pseudonym of **Ḥayyim Yankel Helfand**; 1874–1932), popular publicist and propagandist of the *Bund. Born in Lithuania, he studied in yeshivot there. In 1894 he joined Social Democratic circles in Vilna, taking a leading part in the "Jargon Committees" for publishing and circulating popular educational and informational literature in Yiddish. Exiled to Siberia for revolutionary activities, on his return in 1904 he became active in the Bund in Vilna and Warsaw, and from 1910 a member of its central committee. A prolific and sharp-edged writer and lively speaker, Litwak was warmly attached to Jewish folk culture and way of life, and became known as the "*talmid ḥakham* of the Bund." He was a leader of the "hard" group in the Bund which stood out for preserving its independence from the Russian Social Democratic Party in 1906, and later criticized the doctrine of national neutralism put forward by Vladimir *Medem. For two years Litwak stayed in Vienna, and in 1915 went to the United States. Returning to revolutionary Russia in July 1917 he became a leader of the anti-Bolshevist faction in the Bund, and after its split, a leader of the "Social Democratic" Bund. After trying to settle down in Poland, where he moved in 1921, he proceeded to the United States (1926). There he was active in the *Jewish Socialist Farband, edited its organ *Veker*, and promoted secular education in Yiddish. He met with difficulties in his attempts to associate himself with the American Jewish Labor Movement.

BIBLIOGRAPHY: LNYL, 5 (1963), 83–90; B. Johnpoll, *The Politics of Futility* (1968), 134–5.

[Moshe Mishkinsky]

LIUZZI, family of Italian soldiers. GUIDO LIUZZI (1866–1941) was born at Reggio Emilia. He graduated from the Military Academy of Modena. He took part as a junior officer in the Italo-Turkish War of 1911–1912. At the beginning of World War I, in 1915, Liuzzi was a colonel on the General Staff. He was appointed brigadier general in 1917. Subsequently he was chief of the Service Corps of the Armies of the Grappa in 1918. After the war he directed the War Academy from 1919 until 1925. During World War I he was decorated with the Great Cross of the Order of Saints Maurizio and Lazzaro (Italy), and Croix de Guerre (France). In 1925–26 he commanded the Trento and Padova Divisions. Between 1928 and 1932 he commanded the First Army Corps at Udine. He left the army in 1932 and in 1934 he was elected president of the Jewish community of Turin. In 1938 he denounced the duplicity of both Mussolini and the king of Italy, who legislated the racial laws in 1938.

GIORGIO LIUZZI (1895–1983), son of Guido. He was born at Vercelli in 1895 and joined the Italian Army in 1915 at the beginning of World War I. In 1917, he was promoted to captain for exceptional merit. Giorgio Liuzzi was twice wounded during World War I, on Mount Zebio (June 10, 1917) and on the Bainsizza (Aug. 25, 1917). He was also decorated with the silver military medal (Middle Isonzo), and twice with the bronze medal on Mount Zebio and Piave Val Cordevole.

In 1938 Giorgio Liuzzi had the rank of colonel. In the same year, however, like all the other Jewish officers, he was dismissed from the army following Mussolini's racial laws. In 1943 he was arrested by the Germans and put in a concentration camp in the Marche. He escaped together with his brother Ferruccio and with his cousin Max Eckhart. In January 1944 Giorgio, together with his companions, arrived in Rome, where he put himself at the disposal of the underground CIL (Comitato Italiano di Liberazione) that directed the partisan war against the Nazis. When Rome was liberated by the Allies, Giorgio Liuzzi was reintegrated in the Italian Army, and soon thereafter he was appointed chief of staff of the "A" group of the General Staff of the Italian Army. In February 1945 he was appointed brigadier general with duties at Headquarters.

In 1948 Giorgio Liuzzi received the onerous task of reorganizing and commanding the Ariete Armored Division. In 1953 he was promoted to the rank of general, commander of Army Corps. From 1954 until 1959 he was the chief of staff of the Italian Army. General Liuzzi was a staunch supporter of Israel. As chief of staff he sold to Israel, in 1953 and in 1955, Spitfire and Mustang planes of the Italian Air Force, which were the mainstay of the IAF in the Sinai Campaign in 1956.

BIBLIOGRAPHY: G. Formiggini, *Stella d'Italia, Stella di David, Gli ebrei dal Risorgimento alla Resistenza*, Milano 1970, 52–53.

[Samuele Rocca (2nd ed.)]

LIUZZI, FERNANDO (1884–1940), musicologist and composer. Born in Senigallia, Liuzzi studied composition and conducting in Italy and Germany. He taught composition at the major Italian conservatories and musicology at the universities of Florence, Perugia, and Rome. Liuzzi composed several stage works, some modernized versions of medieval and Renaissance musical dramas, violin works, and songs. His research was in the fields of aesthetics and the history of Italian music, and his major work is *La lauda e i primordi della melodia italiana* ("The Lauda and the Origins of the Italian Melodic Style," 1935).

LIVERIGHT, HORACE BRISBIN (1886–1933), U.S. publisher and theatrical producer. Liveright was born in Osceola Mills, Pennsylvania. He worked briefly in Philadelphia in a broker's office and as a margin clerk, and then turned to selling bonds, which he did with great flair. In 1911 he established a paper-manufacturing company, and in 1917 he joined Charles Boni to form the publishing house Boni & Liveright. They published the Modern Library, which reproduced classics and near-classics, from 1918 to 1925, when it was sold to Bennett *Cerf, their editor. The Boni & Liveright list also included such political radicals as Max Eastman, Michael Gold, and John Reed. When Boni left the firm after a few years, Liveright added many U.S. authors to the list, including such luminaries of American letters as Theodore Dreiser, Sherwood Anderson, Ernest Hemingway, William Faulkner, Hart Crane, Eugene O'Neil, E.E. Cummings, Ezra Pound, T.S. Eliot (Boni & Liveright first published *The Waste Land* in 1922), Lewis Mumford, and Conrad Aiken, as well as famous European writers. Liveright sold these distinguished authors' works with flamboyant publicity and for about ten years the publishing company was a stupendous success. A leading opponent of pornography laws, he successfully set out to defeat a "clean books" bill before the New York State legislature which would have prohibited many publications (1924). As a theatrical producer and president of Stonelea Players, Liveright produced *Hamlet in Modern Clothes* (1925); a dramatization (1926) of Dreiser's *An American Tragedy* which was a big success; and *Dracula* (1927), among other plays. After the successful bustle of the 1920s, Liveright, who was maneuvered out of the publishing firm in 1930, spent his last three years in penury and isolation. Noel Coward's *The Scoundrel*, turned into a movie by Ben Hecht and Charles MacArthur in 1935, was partly based on Liveright's life and character.

BIBLIOGRAPHY: W. Gilmer, *Horace Liveright, Publisher of the Twenties* (1970); W.D. Frank, *Time Exposures* (1926), 111–7.

LIVERPOOL, seaport in N.W. England. It seems probable that Jews settled there before 1750, since in 1752 there was a "Synagogue Court" off Stanley Street and a Jewish place of worship, as the 1753 *Liverpool Memorandum Book* confirms. The site of this early synagogue and a picture of its facade have also been discovered in a map of Liverpool dated 1765. John Wesley refers to the excellent relations which the local Jews enjoyed with their Christian neighbors (*Journal*, entry of April 14, 1755). About 20 Jews are listed in the Liverpool Directory for 1790, some of whom bear names that inspired the unsubstantiated theory that the original community was Sephardi. They were mostly peddlers and traders catering to the seafaring population and included Benjamin Goetz (or Yates), a seal-engraver described as the "Jews' High Priest" (*ḥazzan?*).

The "Old" Hebrew Congregation was organized, or reorganized, at Turton Court in 1780. Its first cemetery was acquired nine years later and its Yiddish regulations drawn up in 1799. The first synagogue, built on a site in Seel Street donated by the Liverpool Corporation, was consecrated in 1808. The congregation's present handsome building on Princes Road was constructed in 1874. In the early 19th century the congregation's preacher was Tobias *Goodman, whose sermons are thought to have been the first delivered in English at a synagogue in the British Isles. Internal conflicts led to a secession in 1838, and to the subsequent establishment of a rival congregation at Hope Place. By about 1860, Liverpool's Jewish community, then numbering around 3,000, was second in size to London's. Toward the end of the 19th century, Russian and Polish refugees reached Liverpool on their way to America; a number remained to modify the character of Liverpool Jewry. A Levantine Sephardi community also existed between 1892 and 1914, and a small Liberal synagogue was established in 1928. A Liverpool and District Rabbinate was set up in 1904, its first two incumbents being Samuel Jacob *Rabinowitz, an early Zionist leader, and Isser Yehudah *Unterman, later chief rabbi of Israel. Other communal institutions include a pioneer Jewish welfare board (founded 1875), a philanthropic society (1811), a yeshivah (1915), and Hebrew-endowed schools (1840). During the first quarter of the 20th century British Jewry's first Hebrew day school flourished in Liverpool under the direction of Jacob Samuel *Fox. In 1971 there were in Liverpool nine congregations serving an estimated Jewish population of 7,500 (1% of the total). Some 700 Jewish children received their education at the King David schools.

Charles Mozley became the city's first Jewish mayor in 1863, and there were subsequently four other Jewish lord mayors. Important civic and other dignities were filled by the *Benas and *Cohen families and by Lord *Cohen of Birkenhead. Isaiah *Raffalovich and Izak *Goller were other prominent figures in latter-day communal history. The monthly *Liverpool Jewish Gazette* (1947–) mirrored the local scene, while the Zionist Central Council (1898) and the Merseyside Jewish Representative Council (1944) coordinated the community's activities. In the mid-1990s, the Jewish population numbered approximately 4,000. The 2001 British census recorded 2,698 declared Jews in Liverpool. At the outset of the 21st century, the city had four Orthodox and a Progressive synagogue, and a range of Jewish institutions.

BIBLIOGRAPHY: Roth, Mag Bibl, index; Lehman, Nova Bibl, index; L. Wolf, *History and Genealogy of the Jewish Families of Yates and Samuel of Liverpool* (1901); P. Ettinger, "*Hope Place*" in *Liverpool Jewry* (1930); C. Roth, *Rise of Provincial Jewry* (1950), 82; B.B. Benas, in: JHSET, 17 (1953), 23–37; Goodman, in: *In the Dispersion*, nos. 5–6 (1966), 52–67; G.E. Silverman, in: *Niv ha-Midrashiyyah* (Spring 1970), 74–81, English section.

LIVESTOCK, TRADE IN. The laws of ritual slaughter (**sheḥitah*) made it necessary for Jews to buy cattle for their own consumption. In Muslim countries the gentile population bought meat from Jewish butchers. In Christian countries many charters granted to the Jews contained articles regulating the slaughter of livestock by Jews as well as the right to sell meat to non-Jews. This was necessary because the surplus, ritually unclean, parts of animals had to be sold to the Christian populace, to the great resentment of the guild of Christian butchers. Churchmen also were indignant that Jews sold to Christians meat that they considered unfit to eat according to the law. Protests by butchers against the irregular sale of meat by Jews were common occurrences in most medieval cities, often resulting in limitations in Jewish trade which had been beneficial both to Jews and to most Christians. Trade in livestock became much more intensive following the expulsions of the 15th and 16th centuries, which had resulted in a considerable section of Central European Jewry adopting a rural mode of life. Henceforth their main occupations were as *peddlers, traders, brokers in agricultural products, and livestock traders. Many villages were composed largely of traders in cattle, goats, and horses. For example, in Eichstetten, Baden, four-fifths of the 68 Jewish families were livestock traders in the 19th century. In *Poland-Lithuania Jews traded in cattle on a larger scale. Herds of cattle, often numbering thousands of heads, were driven for sale to the west. In the *Arenda system the Jewish lessee would obtain both ritually clean and unclean animals. The problems arising from the maintenance and sale of the latter are dealt with in much of the halakhic literature of the 17th and 18th centuries.

Jewish participation in the livestock trade was a mainstay of the activity of military *contractors. Supplies from Poland-Lithuania helped boost this trade among German and Austrian Jews. Herds of draft oxen, cattle for meat, and horses for the cavalry were supplied by Samuel *Oppenheimer and Samson *Wertheimer of Vienna and many other *Court Jews. In Poland the *Nachmanovich family specialized in supplying large quantities of horses to the armies. The thousands of beasts necessary were amassed through a system of contractors and subcontractors, reaching down to the petty rural livestock trader. Isaac, son of Daniel *Itzig, became bankrupt in 1795 when he did not receive payment from *Cerfberr for delivering 8,835 out of 10,000 horses contracted for. The livestock trade was a predominantly Jewish occupation in Bohemia-Moravia, Hungary, and Eastern Europe. The familiar presence of the Jewish livestock trader made him a common figure in local folksong; a Westphalian example goes:

> Jew Itzig bought a cow
> and a calf as well;
> Itzig Jew didn't notice, the calf was *mo'beres*.

The use of a Hebrew word (*mo'beres-me'ubberet*, "pregnant") is typical, for the professional livestock traders' language in most of Europe was full of Hebrew and Yiddish expressions. The vocabulary of non-Jewish livestock traders in Holland after World War II consisted of about 90% corrupted Hebrew and Yiddish words. Jewish horse traders developed a secret trade dialect which non-Jewish horse traders first tried to understand and then eventually adopted for their own mercantile purposes.

Cattle was not only bought and sold but was also raised for meat and dairy products by Jews living in villages. The problem of the *firstborn animal was solved in *Hesse and neighboring regions in a unique manner: ritually pure calves and kids were sent to graze in the *Frankfurt on the Main cemetery and on their eventual death, of old age, were buried wrapped in a white sheet. These animals were butchered by Vincent *Fettmilch's mob and saved during the 1711 fire. This custom, mentioned by Ludwig *Boerne, was also followed in various communities in Eastern Europe.

In Switzerland, from which the Jews had been expelled in the 15th and 16th centuries and finally in 1622, Jewish livestock traders were nevertheless present throughout the country. Pacific Switzerland attracted the Jewish horse traders supplying the armies of neighboring states. The various cantons were forced to accept and encourage their presence, or to suffer stagnation in the livestock trade. Attempts were made to differentiate between the needed livestock buyers and unwanted traders and peddlers. The few Jewish communities that existed in Switzerland in the 18th and early 19th centuries subsisted primarily from livestock trading. In Endingen, of 144 heads of families, 48 were engaged in livestock trading and 5 were butchers. In relatively isolated Endigen and Lengnau a special horse traders' language persisted into the 20th century without passing through a process of de-Hebraization and Germanization.

When in 1689 the *Nuremberg council wanted to prohibit all trade between Jews and Christians, the Christian butchers protested and the council was forced to make an exception for the livestock trade. As against 1,590 transactions in cattle conducted by Jews between 1784 and 1800 in Winterborn (in the *Palatinate), only 82 were conducted by Christians. This predominance in rural markets had its anti-Jewish ramifications. Jewish livestock traders were frequently accused of trickery, primarily of *usury and exploitation, for the animals were generally bought and sold on credit. Accusations against Jewish livestock traders were particularly common in Alsace-Lorraine, Bavaria, Hesse, and Eastern Europe. Through channeling the resentment of the farmers in backward rural Hesse against Jewish livestock traders, Otto Boeckel was elected to the Reichstag. This type of antisemitic agitation was later adopted by the Nazis, particularly by the party's agricultural experts. Immediately after the Nazi seizure of power concerted steps were taken to break the Jews' dominant position in livestock markets, both on the local, regional, and national levels. Traditional markets were boycotted and special *judenfreie* ones were established, where farmers were urged to bring their livestock. Eventually, heavy pressure, both public and legal, had to be exerted in order to induce the farmers to sever their ties with Jewish traders. The campaign was intensified in the middle and late 1930s. On Jan. 26, 1937, only pure-blooded Germans were permitted to deal in livestock, and on Nov. 12, 1938, after the **Kristallnacht*, Jews were totally forbidden to attend markets and fairs.

Goats and cattle were raised on a small scale by many Jewish households; in the **shtetl* the owner of a few cows or goats supplied kosher milk and dairy products. Tales of such men were common in folklore and literature, the most famous being Tevyeh the milkman by *Shalom Aleichem.

BIBLIOGRAPHY: A. Kapp, *Die Dorfjuden in der Nordpfalz* (1968), 257ff.; U. Jeggle, *Judendoerfer in Wuerttemberg* (1969), index, s.v. *Viehhandel*; J. Picard, *The Marked One* (1956); F. Guggenheim-Grunberg, in: *The Field of Yiddish*, 1 (1954), 48–62; P.J. Diamant, in: *Zeitschrift fuer die Geschichte der Juden*, 1 (1964), 79–83; M. Shaḥaf, in: *Yeda Am*, 2 (1954), 42–46; B. Brilling, *ibid.*, 3 (1955), 15ff.; H. Bloom, *The Economic Activity of the Jews of Amsterdam* (1935), index, s.v. *Livestock*; H. Genschel, *Die Verdraengung der Juden aus der Wirtschaft im dritten Reich* (1966), index, s.v. *Viehhandel*; B. Rosenthal, in: MGWJ, 79 (1935), 443–50; M. Grunwald, *Samuel Oppenheimer und sein Kreis* (1913); Z. Szajikowski, *Franco-Judaica* (1962), index, s.v. *Horses, Cattle*; L. Davidsohn, *Beitraege ... Berliner Juden...* (1920), 52–56; G.L. Weisel, *Aus dem Neumarker Landestor* (1926), 105f; O. Donath, *Boehmische Dorfjuden* (1926); A. Weldler-Steinberg, *Geschichte der Juden in der Schweiz* (1966); A. Hertzberg, *The French Enlightenment and the Jews* (1968), index, s.v. *Horses, Cattle, Alsace*; S. Ettinger, in: *Zion*, 21 (1956), 107, 42; H.H. Ben-Sasson, *ibid.*, 183–206.

[Henry Wasserman]

LIVNAT, LIMOR (1950–), Israeli politician, Knesset member from the end of the Twelfth Knesset. Livnat was born in Haifa, to a mother who was a singer and a father who had been a member of Leḥi. She served in the IDF as an education and welfare sergeant, and then studied general literature at Tel Aviv University, where in 1972 she served as deputy chairman of the Students Association, being the first woman to serve in this post. While a student she became politically active in the Likud and in the Movement for Greater Israel. After leaving the university she worked in an advertising company, as a budget manager, and a toy distributor. In 1977 Livnat was elected chairperson of the Young Likud staff. In the elections to the Eleventh Knesset in 1984 she served as spokesperson of the Likud election staff. In 1989 she edited the magazines *Bein ha-Shurot* ("Between the Lines") and *Moked Ereẓ Yisrael* ("Focus on Ereẓ Israel") published by the Likud. From 1991 and until she entered the Knesset in April 1992 Livnat served as chairperson of the board of directors of the Construction Center.

Toward the end of the Twelfth Knesset she entered the Knesset for the Likud, replacing a Knesset member who resigned. In the Thirteenth Knesset she served as chairperson of the Committee for the Advancement of the Status of Women as well as of the Parliamentary Committee of Inquiry on the Murder of Women by their Spouses. In the primaries for the elections of a new Likud chairman in 1993 she supported Netanyahu and remained close to him until after he became prime minister. Livnat was head of the Likud information staff for the elections to the Fourteenth Knesset in 1996. After the Likud victory in these elections, she was appointed minister of communications, in which capacity she acted to open the communications branch to competition, working to open the market for international phone calls to competition and getting Israel to join the agreements of the World Trade Organization on communications issues. She also initiated the "Bezek Law," which enabled the publication of tenders for designated cable TV channels.

At the Likud Conference held in November 1997, Livnat led a move to remove Binyamin *Netanyahu from the party leadership. Following the Likud's defeat in the elections to the Fifteenth Knesset she supported Ariel *Sharon in the contest for the Likud leadership. In the Fifteenth Knesset she was a member of the Knesset Finance Committee, Education, Culture, and Sports Committee, and the Committee for the Advancement of the Status of Women. When Sharon was elected prime minister in 2001 Livnat was appointed minister of education, culture, and sport, retaining the position in the Sixteenth Knesset. As minister of education she has had to contend with a deepening crisis in the education system, which resulted in falling scholastic standards and growing violence by pupils. She tried to introduce a system under which all schools receiving government financial support, including schools from the *ḥaredi* independent system, must teach a certain core program. However, due to political circumstances, the *ḥaredi* schools were released from this requirement. In 2004 Livnat appointed the Dovrat Committee that proposed far-reaching reforms in the education system, including the cancelation of the middle schools, a five-day school week in return for a long school day, an increase in teachers' salaries hand in hand with longer teaching hours, and the laying off of close to 20,000 teachers. Livnat wholeheartedly supported these recommendations, which, after certain modifications, resulting from opposition by the various teachers' organizations, were partially implemented in the 2005–6 school year.

Livnat strongly objected to Sharon's Gaza disengagement plan but refrained from voting against it in the Knesset, and she did not resign from the government before it was implemented, as Netanyahu had done.

She is a member of the Women's Network and the management of Shorashim.

[Susan Hattis Rolef (2nd ed.)]

LIVNI, HILLEL (**Slavko Weiss**; 1906–1994), Zionist leader. Born and educated in Croatia, he lived in Zagreb, where he became a Jewish youth organizer and instructor. He was among the sponsors of a scouting group called Kibbutz ha-Zofim, with headquarters in Zagreb and chapters in several towns with Jewish populations. He also worked within the Federation of Jewish Youth Organizations, promoting the ḥalutzic (*aliyah* preparation) trend and was instrumental in the integration of Ha-Zofim into the Ha-Shomer ha-Ẓa'ir world movement. This movement was officially founded in Slavonski Brod in 1931, rapidly spreading across the country and becoming the largest body of organized Jewish youngsters in Yugoslavia. Livni was among the planners of seminars, summer camps, mountaineering units, and educational programs aiming at preparing future members of kibbutzim, having himself been among the founders of kibbutz Sha'ar ha-Amakim in the Haifa Bay area in the early 1930s. After his *aliyah* he was twice sent back to Yugoslavia as an emissary of his movement. In 1939, he participated as a delegate at the 21st Zionist Congress in Geneva.

In his kibbutz Livni performed various managerial duties. He also took part in the work of the Historical Commission of the Hitaḥdut (Association of Immigrants from Yugoslavia), assisting in research and editing.

As an ardent philatelist, he accumulated an impressive collection. Shortly before his death he sold it, thus enabling the erection of a memorial monument in his kibbutz for Holocaust victims who were relatives of members of Sha'ar ha-Amakim.

[Zvi Loker (2nd ed.)]

LIVNI, TZIPI (1958–), Israeli politician. Livni was born in Tel Aviv. Her father, Eitan Livni, was a member of Eẓel (*Irgun Ẓeva'i Le'ummi) and a member of the Knesset. A lieutenant in the IDF, she subsequently served in the Mossad and received a law degree from Bar-Ilan University, entering private practice and specializing in commercial and constitutional law before being elected to the Knesset in 1999 as a Likud MK. Previously she had served as director-general of the Government Companies Authority, overseeing the process of privatization. In the Knesset she was a member of the Constitution, Law and Justice Committee, and the Committee for the Advancement of the Status of Women. In 2001–2, she served as minister of regional cooperation, minister without portfolio, and minister of agriculture. In February 2003, she was appointed minister of immigrant absorption, also becoming minister of housing and construction. In December 2004 she was appointed minister of justice and, in January 2006, minister of foreign affairs by Acting Prime Minister Ehud *Olmert, after leaving the Likud with Ariel *Sharon when he founded the Kadimah Party. A staunch supporter of Sharon's political positions, including the withdrawal from the Gaza Strip in summer 2005, Livni proved to be a forthright and engaging spokesman for government policy, perceived by the public as a cut above the professional politician. The American press, too, was charmed by her during her visit to the U.S. in February 2006 for talks with Secretary of State Condoleezza Rice and an unscheduled meeting with President Bush, already billing her as the next Golda Meir.

LIVSHITS, BENEDIKT KONSTANTINOVICH (1886 [1887, New Style]–1939?), Russian poet. Born in Odessa, Livshits finished the Duc de Richelieu Gymnasium in 1905 and obtained a law degree from Kiev University in 1912. His early poetry (first published in *Antologiya sovremennoy poezii*, 1909) was inspired by classical antiquity and the French *poètes maudits* (especially Rimbaud, Corbière, and Laforgue). In 1910, Livshits began to contribute to *Apollon*, the influential St. Petersburg art journal; in 1911, he published his first book of verse, *Fleyta Marsiya* ("The Flute of Marsyas"). In 1912, under the influence of D. Burlyuk, Livshits left the *Apollon* group and joined the Futurist circle known as Hylaea, becoming one of its most prominent theoreticians. His poetry and manifestos appeared in the Futurist miscellanies *Sadok sudey* ("A Trap for Judges"), *Poshchechina obshchestvennomu vkusu* ("A Slap in the Face of Public Taste"), *Dokhlaya luna* ("The Croaked Moon"), etc. In 1914, Livshits published another collection of verse, *Volchye solntse* ("The Sun of the Wolves"). After Marinetti's visit to Russia, Livshits initiated an all-out attack against European Futurism. The French version of his manifesto "We and the West" was published by Apollinaire in *Mercure de France* (CVIII, Apr. 16, 1914). Hylaea began to disintegrate at about this time, however, and Livshits left the Futurist movement. His later poetics represent a refined synthesis of Hylaean Cubo-Futurism and *Mandelshtam's Acmeism. The poems of *Iz topi blat* ("Out of the Swamp," 1922) and *Patmos* (1926) are complex riddles, the solution of which demands great literary and historical erudition. In 1928, Livshits published a retrospective collection of his poetry, *Krotonskiy polden* ("The Crotonian Noon"). His memoir *Polutoraglazy strelets* ("The

One-and-a-Half-Eyed Archer," 1933) is outstanding both as a work of art and a historical document. Livshits also excelled as a translator, producing the most faithful and artistically satisfying Russian poetic translations of modern French verse (*Ot romantikov do surrealistov*, 1934). In 1938, he was arrested in connection with the so-called "translators' case" and died, according to official Soviet data, in May 1939.

As a rule, Livshits avoided Jewish themes in his poetry for fear of "cultural inbreeding": in a 1920 poem he spoke of the Jewish heritage in his blood as "the tender duty of the levirate," fulfilling which the "family-loving Hebrew possessed his brother's widow, mixing his blood with that of his brother" (cf. O. Mandelshtam's poem "Return to the Incestuous Bosom"). His other publications include *Gileya* (1931); *Frantsuzskiye liriki XIX–XX vv.* (1937); *U nochnogo okna* (1970). Some of his poems have been translated into English in V. Markov, ed., *Modern Russian Poetry: An Anthology* (1967; Eng. tr. by M. Sparks).

BIBLIOGRAPHY: V. Markov, *Russian Futurism: A History* (1968); *Manifesty i programmy russkikh futuristov* (1967).

[Omri Ronen]

°**LIVY** (**Titus Livius**; 59 B.C.E.–17 C.E.), Roman historian who mentioned Jews at least twice in his writings. He records that until the capture of the Temple in Jerusalem by Pompey (63 B.C.E.), the sanctuary had never been violated (Epitome, book 102). Livy's history is cited by Josephus (Ant., 14:68) as testimony to the heroic conduct of the priests, who even during the siege and capture of Jerusalem continued to offer the daily sacrifices.

ADD. BIBIOGRAPHY: M. Stern, *Greek and Latin Authors on Jews and Judaism*, vol. 1 (1974), 328–31.

[Jacob Petroff / Shimon Gibson (2nd ed.)]

LIWERANT SZCLAR, DANIEL (1945–), Mexican community leader and activist in international Jewish organizations. Born in Mexico City where he studied in the Tarbut Jewish school and in a national high school, he was an active member of the Hanoar Hatzioni youth movement. Liwerant continued his studies at the Hebrew University of Jerusalem, where he graduated in law.

Back in Mexico Liwerant's professional work was concentrated in the area of construction and real estate in which he founded and directed several companies. From the mid-1980s he served as vice president of the administrative council of Isal Investment Corporation which promoted investments in different areas of Israel's economy. From 1986 he was president of the board of Keren Fomento Atzmaut, México-Israel.

Liwerant focused his activities on the promotion of Diaspora-Israel relations. He presided over Keren Hayesod, Mexico (1990–94) and the World Board of Keren Hayesod (1997–2001). From 1995 he was an executive member of the board of trustees of Keren Hayesod, and of the board of governors and the Executive of the Jewish Agency. He was a member of the Joint Authority of Jewish-Zionist Education (1993–2003) and co-chairman of its Aliyah and Absorption Committee.

Liwerant was also active in Jewish education in Mexico, where he was a member of Reshut Hachinuch (Education Authority; 1993–97) and a member of the board of Universidad Hebraica (from 2000). He supported the Taglit-Birthright program in Mexico and was a member of its international consulting council.

Liwerant received many awards including an honorary doctorate from the Hebrew University of Jerusalem (1997). His wife, JUDIT BOKSER DE LIWERANT, is a recognized scholar in political science and a researcher of the Jewish community in Mexico. She is director of the Post-Graduate Program of the Universidad Nacional Autónoma de México UNAM and a member of the Mexican Academy of Science. She was also very active in the development and improvement of Jewish educational and cultural enterprises.

[Margalit Bejarano (2nd ed.)]

LIZARD (Heb. לְטָאָה), reptile included among the eight creeping things that are prohibited as food and whose dead body defiles anything with which it comes into contact (Lev. 11:30–39). Talmudic literature states that its tail moves convulsively when cut off (Oho. 1:6), that in intense heat it remains immovable, stirring only when water is poured over it (Pes. 88b). Both features are characteristic of various species of lizard, but the reference is apparently mainly to those belonging to the family Lacertidae, of which four genera (that include ten species) are to be found in Israel. Of the *Lacerta*, the most common are the brown lizard (*Lacerta laevis*) and the great green lizard (*Lacerta viridis*) which is the largest and most beautiful of this family, is commonly found in the mountainous regions, and feeds on insects. The dab lizard, which belongs to another family, is apparently to be identified with the צָב (*ẓav*), likewise included among the unclean creeping things (see *Tortoise).

BIBLIOGRAPHY: Lewysohn, Zool, 221f., no. 272; J. Feliks, *The Animal World of the Bible* (1962), 96; M. Dor, *Leksikon Zoʾologi* (1965), 177f. **ADD. BIBLIOGRAPHY:** Feliks, Ha-Ẓomeʾaḥ, 248.

[Jehuda Feliks]

LJUBLJANA (Ger. **Laibach**), capital of Slovenia; until 1918 in Krain, Austria. Individual Jews are mentioned in Ljubljana during the 12th century, and the repair of a synagogue is attested in 1217. A "Jewish Road" and a "Jewish Street" are remains of the former Jewish quarter. The Jews of Ljubljana were merchants, moneylenders, and artisans, and were allowed to own real estate. During the Middle Ages they were from time to time accused of child murder, well poisoning, etc. They were not expelled together with the rest of the Jews from Carinthia and Styria in 1496; in 1513, however, Emperor Maximilian gave in to the burghers' claims and forbade the Jews to engage in commerce, and in 1515 expelled them from Ljubljana. Under Leopold II in 1672 the whole of Krain was forbidden to Jews. Later Joseph II allowed them to visit the fairs.

During the Napoleonic Kingdom of Illyria, Abraham Heimann from Bavaria settled in Ljubljana with two relatives under protection of the French governor and opened an official money changer's office. When Ljubljana reverted to Austria in 1814, the emperor confirmed Heimann's right of residence, but he had to fight with the municipal authorities until the 1848 Revolution. After the *emancipation in 1867 Jews again settled in Ljubljana, and by 1910 there were 116 of them, but without an organized community. They were attached to the community of Graz in Austria until 1918, and after Slovenia became a part of the new Yugoslav kingdom, they were attached to the Zagreb community. Only one extended Jewish family remained there when the Germans took the town and handed it over to the Italians in 1941. A memorial to the Jewish victims of the Holocaust was erected after World War II. The Ljubljana community, founded after World War II, had 84 members in 1969. In the 1990s the renewed community took on the name "Judovska skupnost," availing itself of the services of a visiting rabbi from Trieste. Members used prayer books in the Slovenian language and even the *Haggadah* could be read in a Slovenian version.

BIBLIOGRAPHY: L. Šik, in: *Židov* (April 29, 1919); I. Vrhovec, in: *Jevrejski Glas* (May 20, 1938). **ADD. BIBLIOGRAPHY:** A. Vivian, "Iscripzioni masocritti ebraici di Ljubljana," in: *Egitto e Vicino Oriente*, 5 (1982), 93–140.

[Zvi Loker (2nd ed.)]

LLERENA, city in W. Spain, near the Andalusian border. Jews lived in Llerena throughout the 13th–15th centuries, up to the expulsion in 1492. In 1391, it was the only community that was attacked in the region of Extremadura. In 1474 the annual tax paid by the community amounted to 3,500 maravedis. It increased to 35,820 maravedis in 1491, probably because Jews recently expelled from Andalusia had settled in the city. A Jew of Llerena, Gabriel-Israel, served as interpreter to Ferdinand and Isabella during the war with Granada, and won the king's esteem. There were also Conversos living in Llerena. Toward the end of the 16th century a permanent tribunal of the Inquisition was established there which became one of the most active in Spain. David *Reuveni was imprisoned in the inquisitional dungeons in Llerena from 1532, and from 1631 onward a large group of fugitives from Badajoz was tried by the Llerena tribunal with tragic results. As late as 1652 six fugitive Judaizers were burned in effigy, at an auto-da-fé in Llerena, together with the bones of a woman who had died in prison.

BIBLIOGRAPHY: Baer, Spain, 317; Baer, Urkunden, 2 (1936), 233, 349, 398; H.C. Lea, *History of the Inquisition in Spain*, 1 (1906), 549–50; Suárez Fernández, Documentos, 36, 68, 81, 256, 257.

[Haim Beinart]

°**LLOYD GEORGE, DAVID (Earl Lloyd-George**; 1863–1945), British prime minister (1916–22) under whose government the *Balfour Declaration was approved. Lloyd George first came into contact with the Zionist movement in 1903, when the firm of solicitors for whom he worked prepared, at the request of Leopold *Greenberg, a draft connected with the *Uganda Scheme. After Britain's declaration of war on Turkey in November 1914, he told Herbert *Samuel that he "was very keen to see a Jewish State established in Palestine," so that when he first met Chaim *Weizmann in December 1914, he was already in a receptive mood toward Zionism. Lloyd George, the Welshman, was drawn toward Zionism both by his religious upbringing ("I was taught far more about the history of the Jews than about the history of my own people," he wrote) and by his belief that "it is the small nations that have been chosen for great things."

Although sentiment played no small part in Lloyd George's approach, on strictly rational grounds he was determined to make Palestine British, at a time when the Zionists regarded British administration of the country as vital to their aims. Before Sir Mark Sykes left for Egypt in April 1917 to become *Allenby's political adviser, Lloyd George impressed upon him three main points: (1) Palestine was to be under British rule; (2) no pledges should be given to the Arabs concerning Palestine; (3) nothing should be done to prejudice the Zionist aspirations with regard to Palestine. In the cabinet, Lloyd George enthusiastically supported the pro-Zionist Balfour Declaration, viewing it as a step toward the possible establishment of a Jewish state. A few days before the issue of the declaration, he told Weizmann: "I know that with the issue of this Declaration I shall please one group [i.e., the Zionists] and displease another [i.e., the assimilationists]. I have decided to please your group because you stand for a great idea." He also brought about ratification of the Balfour Declaration at the *San Remo Conference and its inclusion in the *Mandate for Palestine.

Lloyd George appointed Herbert Samuel as the first high commissioner for Palestine and fought vehemently against the Passfield White Paper of 1930 (see *White Papers). In his testimony before the Royal Commission for Palestine in 1937 he said: "… it was contemplated [in 1917] that when the time arrived for according representative institutions for Palestine, if the Jews had meanwhile responded to the opportunity afforded them and had become a definite majority of the inhabitants, then Palestine would thus become a Jewish commonwealth." He told the Royal Commission that halting Jewish immigration to Palestine would be "a fraud." He took the same firm stand against the anti-Zionist White Paper of 1939. An entire chapter on Palestine is included in his *Memoirs of the Peace Conference* (2 (1939), 721–74). Lloyd George's pro-Zionist, philo-semitic career was one of the high points of gentile pro-Zionism in Britain, occasioned by a unique conflation of political opportunity in the Middle East and the significant tradition of Protestant philo-semitism in England, as well as his own perceptions of the Jews as an oppressed small nation similar to his own people, the Welsh.

BIBLIOGRAPHY: L. Stein, *The Balfour Declaration* (1961), index; C. Weizmann, *Trial and Error* (1949), index; F. Owen, *Tempestuous Journey* (1954), index; R. Lloyd George, *Lloyd George* (1960), index; C. Sykes, *Crossroads to Israel* (1965), index. **ADD. BIBLIOG-**

RAPHY: ODNB online; A. Rose, *The Gentile Zionists: A Study in Anglo-Jewish Diplomacy, 1929–1939* (1973); W.D. Rubinstein and Hilary L. Rubinstein, *Philosemitism: Admiration and Support in the English-Speaking World for Jews, 1840–1939* (1999), 166–69; D. Vital, *Zionism: The Crucial Phase* (1987).

[Daniel Efron]

LOAN (Heb. הַלְוָאָה, *halva'ah*), a transaction in which a thing, usually money, is given by one person, called the *malveh* ("lender"), to another, called the *loveh* ("borrower"), for the latter's use and enjoyment, and in order that such thing or its equivalent be returned by the borrower at some later date. In halakhic literature the term *halva'ah* is often used to describe an obligation or debt (*ḥov*) in general – i.e., not necessarily one originating from a transaction of loan – and many of the *halakhot* applying to debt in the wide sense of this term apply to loan, and vice versa (see Gulak, Yesodei, 2 (1922), 5f.; see also *Obligation, Law of). In this article loan is treated in the restricted sense of the term defined above

Oral Loan (Milveh be-al Peh) and Loan in Writing (Milveh bi-Shetar)

A loan established orally is distinguished from one established in writing in two main respects: (1) in the former case the borrower's plea that he has repaid the loan is believed, whereas in the latter case such a plea by the borrower is not believed when the bond of indebtedness is in the lender's possession; (2) in the case of a loan in writing, the creditor has the right to levy on the debtor's *nekhasim meshu'badim* ("alienated and encumbered" assets, see *Lien; Obligation, Law of), a right not available to him in the case of an oral loan. The term *milveh be-al peh* is apparently a post-talmudic creation, although the distinction between the two forms of loan was recognized as early as tannaitic times (Gulak, loc. cit.; Herzog, Instit, 1 (1936), 352).

Mitzvah of Lending

The precept of lending to the poor of Israel is based on Exodus 22:24: "If thou lend money to any of my people that is poor by thee" (see Mekh., Mishpatim, s. 19), and is included in the enumeration of the *mitzvot* (*Sefer ha-Mitzvot*, Asayin no. 197; *Semag*, Asayin no. 93; *Sefer ha-Ḥinnukh* no. 66). Some scholars derived this precept from other biblical passages (*She'iltot* no. 114; *Semak* no. 248). The lender, if he apprehends that he may not be repaid, may make his loan conditional on the receipt of a *pledge from the borrower (Tos. to BM 82b; *Ahavat Ḥesed*, 1:13). The merit of fulfilling this precept was lavishly extolled by the scholars – even beyond the act of *charity (Shab. 63a). The duty was held to cover also a loan to a rich man in his hour of need (Sh. Ar., ḤM 97:1, *Sma* thereto, n. 1), but some scholars restricted its application to the case of a poor man only (*Even ha-Ezer*, Malveh ve-Loveh 1:1). In certain circumstances a person is prohibited from lending money to another. This is so if there are no witnesses to a loan (BM 75b), lest the borrower be tempted to deny his indebtedness or the lender forget that he gave the loan; it nevertheless became customary for a loan, even an oral one, to be given in the absence of witnesses, and the *aḥaronim* sought to explain the custom and reconcile it with the talmudic *halakhah* (*Pilpula Ḥarifta* to BM 75b; Resp. *Ben Yehudah*, 1:153). Similarly prohibited is a loan given to a poor man for the repayment of another debt, since – but for such loan – the creditor might come to his relief on account of his poverty (Tos. to Ḥag. 5a).

Nature of the Repayment Obligation

The nature of the borrower's obligation to repay the loan was a matter of dispute among the *amoraim*. R. Papa took the view that the duty of repayment was no more than a *mitzvah* – just as it was a *mitzvah* for the lender to give a loan – whereas R. Huna b. Joshua held that repayment was a legal duty (Ket. 86a; BB 174a; Nov. Ritba, Kid. 13b; Resp. Mabit, vol. 1, no. 51; *Semag*, Asayin 93). It seems that, alongside the legal duty, R. Huna recognized also the existence of a religious duty to repay the debt (Resp. Ribash 484; M. Elon (see bibl.), 20f. and n. 44, 45; for an opinion that the duty was a *mitzvah* only, see Nov. Ramban BB 173b). Some scholars held this *mitzvah* to be of Pentateuchal origin (Ritba, loc. cit.; Mabit, loc. cit., *Resp. Pitḥei Teshuvah*, ḤM 97, n. 4), while others interpreted R. Papa's statement as relating only to an oral loan (Rashbam BB 174a). A borrower who fails to repay the loan is described as *rasha* ("wicked"; Ps. 37:21; *Semag*, Asayin no. 93; see also *Contract; Obligation, Law of).

Halva'ah and She'elah

She'elah (loan for use and return) relates to "utensils" (*kelim*), and *halva'ah* (loan for consumption) to money or "produce" (*perot*). Utensils are things which are not counted by weight and measure, nor exchangeable one for the other; things which are counted and exchanged in this way are "produce" (Gulak, Yesodei, vol. 1, p. 95; vol. 2, pp. 20, 171). The *sho'el* (borrower for use and return) must return the subject matter of the loan in specie, whereas the *loveh* need not do so. Unless otherwise stipulated, a loan is for consumption, and the borrower will only be liable for payment of the equivalent in produce or other property (see also **Shomerim*).

Establishment of Loan

A loan transaction is concluded upon handing over of the money (or "produce") to the borrower. In post-talmudic times the opinion was advanced that a contract of loan might be established upon performance of a formal *kinyan* alone (see *Acquisition), without handing over of the money, and that thereupon the borrower would become obliged to repay the money (Tur, ḤM 39:19 and *Beit Yosef* ad loc.); however, this opinion was not accepted by scholars (*Beit Yosef* loc. cit.; ḤM 89:17). Once the money of the loan has been given to the borrower, the lender will no longer have any right to retract and demand its return, even if it is still intact in specie (*Baḥ*, ḤM 39:19; *Siftei Kohen*, ḤM 39, n. 49). Where the lender has undertaken to give a loan and the borrower has already written a deed on the former's instruction, some scholars hold that, as long as the money has not yet passed to the borrower, the lender remains free to retract from the loan (Resp. Rashba, vol. 1, no. 1054; Sh. Ar., ḤM 39:17), while others preclude him from so doing (*Sefer ha-Terumot* 48:1; *Maggid Mishneh*, Malveh, 23:5). In the case of an oral loan, the lender may withdraw at any time before handing over of the money (*Netivot ha-Mishpat*, Mishpat ha-Urim, 39, n. 17).

Repayment Date

WHEN SPECIFIED. If a specified date was stipulated between the parties, the lender may not reclaim the loan prior to that date (Mak. 3b; Yad, Malveh, 13:5). Some scholars maintain that the lender – even in circumstances where he has reason to fear the borrower's imminent departure abroad, or is aware that the latter may be squandering his assets and therefore become unable to repay the debt on the due date – is not entitled to anticipate the day of repayment (*Teshuvat ha-Ge'onim* no. 45; *Sefer ha-Terumot* 16:3; Tur, ḤM 73); other scholars invest the court with discretion in the matter and the power to order distraint of the property in the borrower's possession (Resp. Rif. no. 113; Resp. Rashba, vol. 1, no. 1111). It was held that the court might do this only if the borrower is squandering his assets, otherwise – even though his financial position may be steadily deteriorating for other reasons – the court will not have the power to intervene prior to the due date of repayment (*Yam shel Shelomo* BK 1:20; *Siftei Kohen* ḤM 73, no. 34, see also below; *Execution (Civil)).

WHEN UNSPECIFIED. A loan for an unspecified period is given for 30 days (Yad, Malveh 13:5), and may not be reclaimed within this period. If it is customary in a locality to retain a loan of unspecified duration for a longer or a shorter period, that custom is followed (Sh. Ar., ḤM 73:1, *Sma* and *Siftei Kohen* ad loc.). Some scholars expressed the opinion that in this matter even the gentile custom is followed (*Sma*, loc. cit.) – but others disputed this (*Siftei Kohen*, loc. cit., n. 1 and 39).

FURTHER DIFFERENCES. (1) In the case of a loan for a specified period, the borrower's plea that he has made repayment within the term of the loan is not believed, since "a person is not likely to make payment before the due date" (BB 5a), whereas in the case of a loan for an unspecified period the borrower's plea that he has paid within the 30 days as required is believed (Tos. to BB 5a). This distinction has been justified by the scholars on many grounds. Some hold that in the case of a specified repayment date, the borrower, for no particular reason, knows that he will have no money available until the due date, but not so in the case of an unspecified repayment date (Resp. Rosh, 76:3); others hold that when no date is specified, the borrower will feel ashamed if he should have money before the end of the 30 days and fail to make repayment – hence it is presumed that he will repay the loan, even within the said period, if he has the money (*Shitah Mekubbeẓet*, BB 5a); yet another view is that, in the case of an unspecified repayment date, the borrower is liable for repayment of the loan before expiry of the 30 days – save that he cannot be obliged by the court to make payment before then – hence he is likely to repay earlier if he has the money (*Devar Avraham*, vol. 1, no. 32). A minority opinion holds that, in the case of a loan for an unspecified period, the borrower is not likely to anticipate payment, and his plea to this effect is not to be believed (Nov. Ramban BB 40a).

(2) Apparently even those who adhere to the opinion that the property of a borrower – even when it is being squandered by him – cannot be distrained until due date of payment of the loan agree with all other scholars that, as regards a loan for an unspecified period, the court may distrain the property in the debtor's possession even before expiry of the 30 days (*Keneset ha-Gedolah*, ḤM 73; *Beit Yosef* 20b).

ANTICIPATION OF PAYMENT BY THE BORROWER. Since determination of the repayment date is for the borrower's benefit (Ran to Ket. 81a, s.v. *vegarsinan*), it is permissible for him to repay the loan before the due date, regardless of the lender's wishes (Ran, loc. cit.). He may not, however, anticipate payment without the lender's consent when there is a substantial apprehension of an imminent and official change in currency values (*Sefer ha-Terumot* 30:2; see also below).

Acceptance of Payment

Payment made to the lender against the latter's will is a valid payment; if the latter refuses to accept the money and the borrower throws it to him, he will be discharged (*Sefer ha-Terumot* 50:1; Tos. to Git. 75a). However, when the lender is prepared to accept payment, the borrower must make the payment into his hands and may not throw it to him (Git. 78b; Yad, Malveh 16:1). Payment to the lender's wife is held by some scholars to discharge the borrower, provided that she is accustomed to transacting her husband's business (see Husband and *Wife; Resp. Maharam of Rothenburg, ed. Prague, no. 225; *Rema*, ḤM120:2), but other scholars dispute that this is a valid discharge (*Yam shel Shelomoh* BK 9:39).

Place of Payment

The lender may claim repayment at any place, even in the wilderness (BK 118a; Sh. Ar., ḤM 74:1). Upon due date the borrower may oblige the lender to accept payment at any settled place (*yishuv*), even if this is not the place where the loan was transacted, nor the place of residence of the lender or borrower (*Sefer ha-Terumot*, 30:1; Sh. Ar., loc. cit.). If the loan was transacted in the wilderness, the borrower may oblige the lender to accept payment there (*Rema* ḤM 74:1).

Method and Means of Payment

A debt not yet due may be repaid little by little (BM 77b; *Mordekhai* BM no. 352; *Ittur*, vol. 1, pt. 2, s.v. *iska*); according to some scholars payment in this manner, although initially forbidden, is valid in retrospect (*Bedek ha-Bayit* ḤM 74; *Siftei Kohen* ḤM 74, n. 17). After due date the lender may, in the opinion of all scholars, refuse to accept payment in the said manner (*Mordekhai*, loc. cit.). The borrower must repay in money, and, if he has none, in land. The lender may refuse to accept the land and offer to wait until the borrower has money – even if this is after the due date (Resp. Rosh, 80:9; Sh. Ar., ḤM 74:6, 101:4). If the borrower has no money, the lender may not instruct him to sell his assets in order to receive money for them, but must either take the assets as payment or wait until the borrower has money (Tos. to BK 9a). If payment in money entails a loss for the borrower, he may repay the loan in land (Tos. Ket. 92a and Ran ad loc.). If the borrower has money, land, and chattels, and wishes to pay in money, while the lender asks for land or chattels, some scholars hold the law to favor the lender and others the borrower (*Sefer ha-Terumot* 4:2; see also *Execution (Civil)).

Fluctuation in Currency Values

In case of official withdrawal and replacement of the existing currency, the position is as follows: If the new currency is of the same kind, the borrower pays in the currency in circulation at the time of payment (BK 97). If, however, the withdrawn currency is circulating in another country on the same terms as it formerly did in the country of its withdrawal, the lender – if he has the means of reaching such a country and there is no particular difficulty in transferring the old currency – will be obliged to accept the withdrawn currency in payment (BK 97; Sh. Ar., ḤM 74:7). If as a result of a change in the value of the currency there is a reduction in the price index of the commodities ("produce"), the borrower pays in accordance with the new currency value and deducts for himself the excess (BK 97b, 98a); if the reduction in prices result from factors unconnected with a currency revaluation, the borrower pays in the stipulated currency, without any deduction (Sh. Ar., YD 165). The view that the rules stated with reference to a currency revaluation must also be extended, by analogy, to the case of a currency devaluation (*Aferet Zahar* no. 165) was accepted as *halakhah (Piskei ha-Rosh*, BK 9:12; *Ḥikrei Lev*, Mahadura Bafra, ḤM 9) in preference to a contrary opinion (*Piskei ha-Rosh*, loc. cit.; Resp. Rashba, vol. 3, no. 34).

In many Jewish communities *takkanot* were enacted which were aimed at reaching a compromise in disputes between parties relating to the manner of debt-payment in case of a change in currency values, and a decisive majority of the *posekim* inclined toward adjudging and compromising between the parties in terms of these *takkanot* (see Kahana, bibl.; **Takkanot ha-Kahal*).

Plea of Repayment (*Parati*; "I have repaid")

An oral loan is repayable without witnesses; a loan in writing, before witnesses. In a claim for repayment of an oral loan, the borrower's plea that he has already made repayment is believed (Sh. Ar., ḤM 70:1); such a plea is regarded as a general denial of the claim, and on taking a solemn *oath (*shevu'at hesset*) – the borrower is exempted (Sh. Ar., ḤM 70:1). Where there is a bond of indebtedness, the borrower's plea that he has made repayment is not believed, and the lender – on swearing an oath that he has not been repaid – proceeds to recover the debt (*ibid.*). (As regards the borrower's plea of payment prior to the due date, see above.) As a means of protecting the lender against such a possible plea of repayment, it became customary to stipulate, at the time of the loan, that credence be given to the lender upon his denial of a repayment plea by the borrower – such stipulation availing to dismiss the latter plea (Sh. Ar., ḤM 71:1). For the similar protection of the lender, the practice was adopted of stipulating at the time of the loan that it be repayable only before witnesses – the borrower's plea of repayment being thus deprived of credibility unless attested by witnesses (*ibid.*, 70:3). In the latter case it still remained possible for the borrower to plead that he had repaid the debt before witnesses A and B, who had since gone abroad, and – upon making a solemn oath – become exempted; to forestall this possibility the practice was adopted of stipulating, "You shall not repay me except before witnesses so and so, or before the court" – thus precluding the borrower from pleading that he made repayment before some other witnesses (*ibid.*, 70:4).

Multiple Loans

If a lender has given the same borrower two separate loans and the latter seeks to repay on account of one of them, the lender may appropriate the payment toward whichever loan he pleases, without any right on the borrower's part to protest or maintain that he intended otherwise (Tur., ḤM 83:2 and *Beit Yosef* ad loc.; *Sefer ha-Terumot* 20:2). This rule only applies when both loans have already fallen due for payment (*Sefer ha-Terumot*, loc. cit.); if one loan has fallen due but not the other, the payment is deemed to have been made on account of the former (Resp. Radbaz, 1252 (181)); if neither has fallen due, the law is apparently the same as for two loans already due (Radbaz, loc. cit.; *Keẓot ha-Ḥoshen* 83, n. 1).

Conversion into Loan of Other Contractual Obligation

At times the practice was adopted, for various reasons, of converting an obligation originating from a transaction other than loan into an obligation of loan. This practice is referred to as *zekifat ḥov be-milveh* and was adopted – for instance in the case of a purchaser indebted to the seller for the purchase price – because of the restricted number of pleas possible against a claim for a loan-debt as compared to a claim for a debt originating from the sale of goods (BM 77b; ḤM 190:10). *Zekifat ḥov* takes place in one of the following ways: (1) by the writing of a special bond of indebtedness for an already existing debt; (2) by the stipulation of a date for the repayment of an existing debt; and (3) by the gradual accumulation of a debt, for instance by purchase on credit from a shop. In this way the original obligation is largely – or even entirely – extinguished and converted into a new obligation. From the time of such *zekifah* the debt is an obligation of loan only, the new obligation retaining none of the legal characteristics of the old (Gulak, Yesodei, vol. 2, pp. 116–8).

Minor as Party to a Loan

By pentateuchal law, a minor has no legal capacity to lend. As long as the subject matter of such a loan is still intact (in specie), it must be returned by the borrower; hence in case of loss resulting from **ones* (force majeure) the borrower is exempt from liability, as the property is deemed to be in its owner's possession for purposes of loss arising from *ones*. The rabbis enacted that a loan given by a minor should be valid, the borrower being liable also for loss resulting from *ones* (Gulak, Yesodei, vol. 1, p. 40). A minor who has borrowed is exempt from returning the loan, even after reaching his majority. According to some scholars, a minor who has borrowed for his own maintenance can be recovered from even during his minority (Gulak, loc. cit.; see also Legal Capacity).

Measures to Prevent "Bolting the Door" to Borrowers

Hillel the Elder instituted a *Prosbul designed to overcome reluctance to lend to a borrower at the approach of the *shemittah* (sabbatical) year (Shev. 10:3; Rashi Git. 37a; see also **Takkanot*). Although according to pentateuchal law the need for *derishah* and *ḥakirah* (examination of witnesses) extends also to civil law (*dinei mamonot*) matters, the scholars enacted for the obviation of this procedure in the latter cases, so as not to bolt the door before borrowers (Sanh. 3a; see also *Practice and Procedure; *Witness). Despite an opinion upholding the need, by the pentateuchal law, for three expert judges in matters of *hoda'ot* ("acknowledgments") and loans, the scholars enacted for the competence of a court of three laymen, lest the door be bolted before borrowers, for fear that no expert judges may be found to enforce the law (*ibid.*; see also **Bet Din*). The scholars enacted that in certain circumstances the judges, if they erred, were not to be exempted from liability, in order not to discourage people from lending to others (*ibid.*). According to pentateuchal law, the creditor recovers the debt out of the *zibburit* ("worst land") of the debtor, but the scholars enacted that he might do so from the *beinonit* ("medium land"), for the reason mentioned above (Git. 50a; see also *Execution (Civil)). According to those who held that the doctrine of *shi'bud nekhasim* was non-pentateuchal, the scholars enacted for a lender on a bond to recover from the debtor's *nekhasim meshu'badim* ("encumbered and alienated property"; see *Lien; BB 175b).

[Shmuel Shilo]

The Community as a Debtor

The Responsa literature relates to the mode of conduct in cases where the community had taken a loan for its various affairs, and it has to settle the debt. Rabbi Shlomo b. Aderet (Rashba) was asked about a case in which community members were taxed in order to return the loan – whether taxation should be made according to the financial status of the community member at the time of taking the loan or according to the time of its discharge. Rashba ruled that legally this loan should be regarded as a loan taken by partners, and the burden of repayment is in the same proportion as when the loan was taken; therefore community members should be taxed according to their status at the time when the loan was taken. Nevertheless the community has the authority to enact that participation of each member should be made according to the time of repayment, because a loan taken by the community could be regarded differently from an ordinary loan – "they are unlike debtors who take the loan directly for themselves, but like debtors for the community chest." Nevertheless, Rashba negates the possibility of obliging recent citizens of the community, who were not members of the community when the loan had been taken, because it is like a retroactive obligation which is not equitable (Resp. Rashba, 1, no.777; 3, no.412; see **Takkanot ha-Kahal*). For the present discussion, see also *Legal Person.

[Menachem Elon (2nd ed.)]

BIBLIOGRAPHY: Gulak, Yesodei, 1 (1922), 145f.; 2 (1922), 33–35, 42f., 83–88, 105–9, 113–8, 170–2; 3 (1922), 102–6; 4 (1922), 85–90; idem, Oẓar, 205f., 208; J. Rappaport, in: *Zeitschrift fuer vergleichende Rechtswissenschaft*, 47 (1932/33), 256–378; Herzog, Instit, 1 (1936), 121–4, 219f., 359f.; 2 (1939), 57f., 186f., 215f.; J.S. Kahana, in: *Sinai*, 25 (1949), 129–48; ET, 1 (1951³), 263–6; 4 (1952), 110–4; 5 (1953), 92–132; 9 (1959), 215–40; M. Silberg, *Kakh Darko shel Talmud* (1961), 71–75; M. Elon, *Ḥerut ha-Perat…* (1964); idem, Mafte'aḥ, 48–57. **ADD. BIBLIOGRAPHY:** M. Elon, *Ha-Mishpat ha-Ivri* (1988), 1:104f., 120, 189f., 252, 264, 346, 418f., 476, 482f., 487f., 489, 498, 528, 531f., 533, 535, 569, 597, 600, 626, 636, 653f, 733, 775f, 813; 2:866, 983; 3:1443; idem, *Jewish Law* (1994), 1:117f, 135, 212f, 295, 309, 416; 2:510f, 580, 587f, 593f, 596, 607, 643, 646f, 649, 651, 699, 738, 743, 774, 788, 808f, 904, 953f, 996; 3:1058, 1187; 4:1716; M. Elon and B. Lifshitz, *Mafte'aḥ ha-She'elot ve-ha-Teshuvot shel Ḥakhmei Sefarad u-Ẓefon Afrikah* (legal digest) (1986), 89–103; B. Lifshitz and E. Shochetman, *Mafte'aḥ ha-She'elot ve-ha-Teshuvot shel Ḥakhmei Ashkenaz, Ẓarefat ve-Italyah* (legal digest) (1997), 61–67; I.Warhaftig, *Hitḥayyevut* (2001).

LOANZ, ELIJAH BEN MOSES (1564–1636), one of the outstanding kabbalists of Germany in the late 16th and early 17th centuries. Born in Frankfurt on the Main, he was a grandson of *Joseph Joselmann b. Gershom of Rosheim. His teachers included Akiva Frankfurter, Jacob Guenzberg of Friedberg, *Judah Loew b. Bezalel of Prague, and *Menahem Mendel b. Isaac of Cracow. Serving as rabbi in *Fulda, *Hanau, *Friedberg, and *Worms successively, he was also *rosh yeshivah*, preacher, and *ḥazzan* in Worms for a time. Because he was well known as a writer of kabbalistic amulets and incantations, early in his career he acquired the cognomen Elijah Ba'al Shem. Only one of his books, *Rinnat Dodim*, a kabbalistic commentary on the Song of Songs, was printed during his lifetime (Basle, 1600). Other published works include *Mikhlol Yofi*, a commentary on Ecclesiastes (Amsterdam, 1695). He was the author of occasional liturgical poetry and his secular poem, *Vikku'aḥ Yayin im ha-Mayim*, was translated into German. Among his works still in manuscript (Oxford Bodleian Library) are an incomplete commentary on Midrash *Genesis Rabbah; Ma'gelei Ẓedek*, a supercommentary on *Baḥya b. Asher's commentary on the Pentateuch; *Adderet Eliyahu*, a commentary on the Zohar; *Ẓafenat Pa'ne'aḥ* on *Tikkunei Zohar*; and a commentary on Baḥya ibn Pakuda's *Ḥovot ha-Levavot*. Some of his kabbalistic amulets and formulae are included in the collections *Toledot Adam* (Zolkiew, 1720) and *Mifalot Elohim (ibid.*, 1727). Loanz also prepared for press a number of halakhic works, notably *Darkhei Moshe* by Moses Isserles. He exchanged learned correspondence with the Christian Hebraist, Johannes *Buxtorf.

BIBLIOGRAPHY: M. Mannheimer, *Die Juden in Worms* (1842), 61; Landshuth, Ammudei, 16–17; L. Lewysohn, *Nafshot Ẓaddikim;*

Sechzig Epitaphien… (1855), 59; I. Tishby, in: *Sefer Asaf* (1953), 515–28; Neubauer, Cat. 1829–32; D. Kaufmann, *R. Jair Chajjim Bacharach* (1894), 33–34; A. Epstein, *Mishpaḥat Luria* (1901), 47ff.

[Theodore Friedman]

LOBATO (Cohen Lobato), Marrano family prominent in Amsterdam, Hamburg, and London. Of especial importance were the following: ABRAHAM COHEN LOBATO, Portuguese Marrano born in Lisbon where he was known as Diego Gomez Lobato. In 1599, when his kinsman, Paul de Pina (alias Reuel *Jesurun) set out for Rome with the intention of becoming a monk, Lobato wrote to Elijah Montalto at Leghorn, who dissuaded him from his plan. Lobato subsequently went with De Pina to Brazil. On their return to Europe, they both settled as professing Jews in Amsterdam. Abraham Cohen Lobato is not to be confused with another person of the same name (perhaps his grandson) who died in Hamburg in 1665. The name Rehuel (Reuel) remained common among his descendants. REHUEL COHEN LOBATO, probably his son, and father of Isaac Cohen, was cotranslator, with Moses *Belmonte, of *Avot*, published in Spanish in Amsterdam (1644). ISAAC COHEN LOBATO filled the role of "Mount Zion" in the original presentation of Reuel Jesurun's "Dialogue of the Seven Mountains" in 1624, and was one of the founders of the society Sha'arei Ẓedek in Amsterdam in 1678. REHUEL LOBATO (1797–1866), a Dutch mathematician, was author of scientific and statistical works.

BIBLIOGRAPHY: Roth, Marranos, index; M. Kayserling, *Sephardim an der unteren Elbe* (1859), 176; Kayserling, Bibl, 27, 64, 89; M. Grunwald, *Portugiesengraeber auf deutscher Erde* (1902), 115; M. De Barrios, *Casa de Jacob* (1685), 18, 24; H. Brugmans and A. Frank, *Geschiedenis der Joden in Nederland*, 1 (1940), 220, 264, 267.

[Cecil Roth]

LOCKER, BERL (1887–1972), Labor Zionist leader. Locker was born in Kriwiec, Galicia, and from 1902 he began to contribute to the Lemberg Labor Zionist newspaper, *Der Yidisher Arbeiter*, of which he later became editor. He organized the *Po'alei Zion party in the Austrian Empire before World War I. During the war Locker spent some time in the United States and from 1916 ran the world office of Po'alei Zion at The Hague. At the world conference of Po'alei Zion in Vienna (1920) he supported the split that brought about the separation of the pro-Communist wing and headed the World Union of Po'alei Zion ("right wing"). He was a member of the Zionist and Jewish Agency Executives in London from 1931 to 1936, when he settled in Palestine. Locker was a member of the *Histadrut Executive from 1936 to 1938, and from 1938 headed the political bureau of the Jewish Agency in London during the period of the struggle against the policy embodied in the White Paper of 1939 and for Jewish statehood. He tried to effect a rapprochement with the British government, particularly after the Labour Party took office in 1945.

From the establishment of the State of Israel (1948) until 1956, Locker served as chairman of the Jewish Agency Executive in Jerusalem. He was a member of the Third Knesset on the *Mapai list. Locker wrote many articles and pamphlets in Yiddish, German, Hebrew, and English. For the most part, he devoted himself to Zionist propaganda in England, and during the *yishuv's* struggle in Palestine he published the pamphlet, *A Stiff-Necked People – Palestine in Jewish History* (1946; the American edition is called *Covenant Everlasting*, 1947). A Hebrew translation and selections of his articles were published in *Be-Ḥevlei Kiyyum u-Tekumah* (1963). Among the various newspapers and publications of the Labor Zionists, he edited a selection of Ber *Borochov's work in Yiddish (1928). He also wrote *Mi-Kitov ad Yerushalayim* (1970).

BIBLIOGRAPHY: N.M. Gelber, *Toledot ha-Tenu'ah ha-Ẓiyyonit be-Galiẓyah* (1958), 771–3; Tidhar, 11 (1961), 3779.

LOCKER, MALKE (1887–1990), Yiddish poet and essayist. Born in Kuty, Galicia, into a well-to-do family, her education included, besides Yiddish, Hebrew, and Polish, several European languages. She married the Labor Zionist leader Berl *Locker, and because of her husband's activities lived in various countries. She was most attracted by romantic and symbolist poetry. She published lyrics in the Yiddish press from 1929 as well as in book form: *Velt un Mentsh* ("World and Person," 1931), *Du* ("You," 1932), *Shtet* ("Cities," 1942), *Di Velt is on a Hiter* ("The World is Without Guardian," 1947), and *Yerushalayim* (1967), as well as translations from Rainer Maria Rilke's works (1981), and biographies of Arthur Rimbaud (1950), Charles Baudelaire (1970), and Paul Verlaine (1976) which were translated into Hebrew and French, as was her book of Yiddish essays on German, English, and French romantic writers, *Romantiker* (1958).

BIBLIOGRAPHY: LNYL, 4 (1961), 463; M. Ravitch, *Mayn Leksikon*, 3 (1958), 219–20; C. Vigée, in: M. Locker, *Les Romantiques* (1964), 7–14 (introd.). **ADD. BIBLIOGRAPHY:** Y. Gotfarshteyn, in: *Di Goldene Keyt*, 34 (1959), 198–203.

[Sol Liptzin]

LOCKSPEISER, SIR BEN (1891–1990), British engineer and civil servant. The son of a London diamond merchant, Ben ("Benny" was his official given name) Lockspeiser was educated at Cambridge and served in World War I. Most of his career was spent as an aeronautical engineer at the Royal Aircraft Establishment at Farnborough, Hampshire, where he contributed significantly to the development of many technical innovations in aircraft design, especially wing de-icers. From 1939, he worked in the British government's Air Defence Department, becoming director-general in 1945 and, in 1946, chief scientist at the Ministry of Supply.

Lockspeiser was among the most influential scientific civil servants in modern British history and was in part responsible for producing the first electronic computers, for building the Jodrell Bank radio telescope, and for creating CERN (the European Council for Nuclear Research). He was knighted in 1946 and retired in 1956. Lockspeiser later served as head of the technical advisory board of the Israeli government.

BIBLIOGRAPHY: ODNB online.

[William D. Rubinstein (2nd ed.)]

LOCKSPEISER, EDWARD (1905–1973), musicologist and critic. Lockspeiser studied at the Royal College of Music and with Nadia Boulanger in Paris. After working as a composer and conductor, he began writing for the *Yorkshire Post* and the magazine, *Musical America.* In 1941, he joined the BBC, on whose music staff he remained until 1950. He was music editor for the *Encyclopedia Britannica* and wrote frequently for *The Listener, Music and Letters*, and *The Times Literary Supplement.* Lockspeiser was considered a leading authority on French music, especially Debussy: he wrote *Debussy* for the Master Musician series (1936; revised second edition, 1951), and later an aesthetic and psychological study in two volumes, *Debussy: His Life and Mind* (1962, 1965), his masterpiece. His other publications include *Berlioz* (1939), *Bizet* (1951), an adapted translation of *A New History of Music* by Henry Prunieres (4 vols., 1943), and *Music and Painting* (1972). In 1948, Lockspeiser was made an Officier d'Academie for services to French music.

LOCUST (Heb. אַרְבֶּה, *arbeh*), one of the four insects which, having "jointed legs above their feet, wherewith to leap upon the earth," are permitted as food (Lev. 11:21–22). The locust was one of the ten plagues of Egypt (Ex. 10:4–19). The reference is to the Sudanese locust, *Schistocerca gregaria*, a pest that reached Ereẓ Israel in large numbers every few years causing havoc to agriculture. The Bible and talmudic literature describe the plague of locusts as one of the worst visitations to come upon the country. Its gravity and extent varied from time to time, one of the severest plagues having taken place in the days of the prophet Joel who devoted most of his prophecy to it. His precise descriptions of the locusts' development, sweep, and damage were confirmed in the extremely serious plague of locusts that visited Ereẓ Israel in 1915 when the crops were entirely destroyed in most parts of the country.

During the plague the locust undergoes various metamorphoses from the larva to the fully-grown, the stages of its development being given in Joel (2:25) in the expressions אַרְבֶּה (*arbeh*), יֶלֶק (*yelek*), חָסִיל (*ḥasil*), and גָּזָם (*gazam*), the last of these being the fully grown male or female. After being fertilized, the female lays a cluster of eggs in a hole which it makes in the ground. From the eggs, dark wingless larvae, the size of tiny ants, are hatched, these being the *yelek*, a word apparently connected with לָקַק, "to lap," "lick up." Eating the tender vegetation of the field, the *yelek* grows rapidly, and since (as with all insects) its epidermis does not become bigger, it sheds it at various stages of its growth, during which it changes the color of its skin. The next stage, during which its skin is pink, is the *ḥasil*, which word, from the root חסל, refers to its total destruction of the vegetation of the field, for at this stage it consumes enormous quantities; hence *ḥasil* is used as a synonym for *arbeh*. Thus in Solomon's prayer at the dedication of the Temple he declared that during a plague of *arbeh ḥasil* people would come there to pray for its riddance (I Kings 8:37; cf. Ps. 78:46). It now casts its skin twice, grows short wings, and becomes the *gazam*. At this juncture, when no more vegetation is left in the field, it "cuts off" (this being the meaning of גָּזָם) and chews the bark of trees with its powerful jaws; as Joel (1:7) says: "he hath made it (the fig-tree) clean bare… the branches thereof are made white"; and Amos (4:9): it devours "your gardens and your vineyards and your fig-trees and your olive-trees." Finally, after casting a further epidermis, it becomes the fully grown, long-winged *arbeh*, the yellow-colored female which is fit to lay its eggs. This cycle of the locust's development extends from spring until June when the swarms of locusts return to their place of origin or are blown by the wind to the Mediterranean or Dead Sea (Joel 2:20).

Joel refers to the locust as "the northern one," which is seemingly strange since it comes from the south. But in contemporary times (especially in 1915) it was found that swarms of locusts reach Jerusalem from the north. The means of fighting an invading swarm of locusts were very limited. While attempts were made to drive them away by making a noise (Job 39:20), reliance was chiefly placed on the mercy of the Lord by praying and proclaiming a fast and a solemn assembly (Joel 2:15). In talmudic literature, locusts are included among the disasters for which the alarm of the ram's horn (*shofar*) was sounded and a public fast held (Ta'an. 3:5). A plague of locusts brought famine in its wake, sometimes even in the following years by reason of the damage done to fruit trees. Having no other source of food, the people collected the locusts, dried and preserved them as food. The Mishnah cites divergent views on whether the blessing "by whose word all things exist" is to be said when eating locusts (in the Mishnah גּוֹבָאי (*govai*), in the Bible גּוֹבָי (*govai*); Nah. 3:17), one view being that since it "is in the nature of a curse, no blessing is said over it" (Ber. 6:3). In ancient times however they were regarded as a frugal meal and especially associated with *asceticism, as when John the Baptist ate only "locusts and wild honey" (Matt. 3:4; Mark 1:6). Some Yemenite Jews still eat fried locusts. In recent years swarms of locusts have at times visited countries neighboring on Israel, frequently originating in Africa and the Arabian peninsula, but modern methods have succeeded in destroying them in time by spraying from the air or by poison on the ground.

BIBLIOGRAPHY: Lewysohn, Zool, 285ff., 370; Whiting, in: *National Geographic Magazine*, 28 (1915), 511–50; F.S. Bodenheimer, *Studien zur Epidemologie, Oekologie und Physiologie der afrikanischen Wanderheuschrecke* (1930). **ADD. BIBLIOGRAPHY:** Feliks, Ha-Ẓome'aḥ, 209.

[Jehuda Feliks]

LO-DEBAR (Heb. לְדְבָר, לוֹ דְבָר, לֹא דְבָר), city on the border of Gad in the northern part of Gilead (Josh. 13:26; Lidbir). Mephibosheth son of Jonathan lived there when Saul's family fled to Gilead after the disastrous battle at Mt. Gilboa (II Sam. 9:4ff.). Lo-Debar apparently fell into the hands of the Arameans during their wars with Israel and was recovered by Jeroboam (cf. Amos 6:13 where the name is translated as "a thing of nought"). The ancient name may be preserved in Umm al-Dabr in the eastern Jordan Valley 10 mi. (16 km.) south of the Sea of Galilee.

BIBLIOGRAPHY: Abel, Geog, 2 (1938), 304, 370; M. Noth, in: PJB, 37 (1941), 87; Press, Ereẓ, 3 (1956[2]), 517; EM, 4 (1962), 409–10.

[Michael Avi-Yonah]

LODÈVE, town in the department of Hérault, S. France. In 1092, Bernard III, bishop of Lodève, renewed the ancient canonical prohibition on mixed marriages. The Jewish community of Lodève, which a medieval document describes as having been flourishing and with many scholars (although no works from them have been preserved), appears to have dwindled away from the end of the 13th century; Jews originally from Lodève are subsequently found in Montpellier and later in Perpignan. During the 18th century, Jews from Avignon traded in Lodève. In June 1941, about 100 Jews were living there, according to the census of Jews carried out at that time. There is a Rue des Juifs in Lodève, and in the vicinity a grotto known as Pons des Jésiaous ("Well of the Jews").

BIBLIOGRAPHY: Gross, Gal Jud, 273ff.; REJ, 14 (1887), 73; 22 (1891), 265; 43 (1901), 295; G. Paris, *Histoire de Lodève* (1851), passim; Z. Szajkowski, *Analytical Franco-Jewish Gazetteer 1939–1945* (1966), 200.

[Bernhard Blumenkranz]

LODI, town in N. Italy, in the former duchy of Milan. Jewish moneylenders were possibly invited to Lodi in about 1420. In 1541 the Jews of Lodi and of other cities of the duchy obtained the protection of Pope *Paul III against the anti-Jewish preachings of the friars. Copies of the Talmud were burnt by order of the Inquisition in Lodi in 1559, and in 1597 other works were destroyed. The Jews were expelled from the duchy in 1597, and after the expulsion the Jews were allowed by the authorities to settle in the city only for a short period for professional reasons, with the exception of the Vitali family, bankers who resided permanently in Lodi until the end of the 18th century.

BIBLIOGRAPHY: Roth, Italy, index; Milano, Italy, index; Milano, Bibliotheca, index; Pavoncello, in: REJ, 119 (1961), 131–42; Joseph ben Joshua ha-Kohen, *Emek ha-Bakha* (1945[2]), passim; Dimitrowski, in: *Zion*, 20 (1955), 179–81; idem, in: *Talpioth*, 6 (1955), 708–22; Cremascoli, in: *Israel* (Jan. 24, Feb. 14, March 21, 1957); S. Simonshon, A *Documentary History of the Jews in Italy. The Duchy of Milan*, 4 vols. (1982–86).

[Federica Francesconi (2nd ed.)]

°LODS, ADOLPHE (1867–1948), French Protestant Bible scholar and historian. Lods was born in Courbevoie, near Paris. He served for a time as a pastor in Paris. After lecturing on Hebrew at the Faculté Théologique of Paris, in 1906 he began teaching Hebrew language and literature at the Sorbonne. He was elected to the Academie des Inscriptions in 1935. Lods published a study of Proverbs, *L'Ecclésiaste et la philosophie grecque* (1890); an edition of the book of Enoch from Greek fragments with variants from the Ethiopian text, translation, and notes, *Le livre d'Hénoch* (1892); and his major study, *La croyance à la vie future et le culte des morts dans l'antiquité Israelite* (2 vols., 1906). After the publication of *Jean Astruc et la critique biblique au 18ième siecle* (1924), Lods concentrated on more general studies, including *Israël, des origines au 8ième siecle* (1930; English trans. *Israel from the Beginning to the Middle of the Eighth Century* by S.H. Hooke, 1932) and its continuation *Des Prophètes a Jésus* (1935; English trans. of the first part, by S.H. Hooke, *Prophets and the Rise of Judaism*, 1937); *La religion d'Israël* (1939; Spanish trans. by A. Spivak, 1940); and *Histoire de la littérature hébraïque et juive* (to 135 C.E.; 1950). Lods published one of the earliest studies comparing Israelite prophecy with the related phenomenon in ancient *Mari in Syria of the second millennium B.C.E. He loved mountain climbing and was an accomplished watercolor painter.

BIBLIOGRAPHY: Bayet, in: *Comptes Rendus de l'Académie des Inscriptions et Belles Lettres* (1957), 315–27; H.F. Hahn, *The Old Testament in Modern Research* (1956), 166–9. **ADD. BIBLIOGRAPHY:** A. Lods, in: H. Rowley (ed.), *Studies in OT Prophecy Presented to T.H. Robinson* (1950), 103–10; J. Bullard, in: DBI, 2:86.

LODZ (Yid. **Lodskh**; Ger. **Litzmanstadt**), city in central Poland, center of the textile industry. In 1793 there were 11 Jews in Lodz; by 1809 (when the city was under Prussian rule) the number had risen to 98. A community was organized at that time and a wooden synagogue erected which was renovated in subsequent years. After 1820 (under Russian rule) Lodz became an important industrial center and consequently the Jewish population increased rapidly, until the community became the second largest in independent Poland. (See Table: Jewish Population in Lodz.)

Wishing to develop the textile industry in Lodz, the Russian government invited German weavers to settle on very favorable terms. To avert the possibility of Jewish competition, the Germans insisted that the same limitations on Jewish settlement as applied in *Zgierz should prevail in Lodz. According to these restrictions, Jews were not allowed to settle and acquire real property, nor were they allowed to sell liquor; only those who had previously kept inns were allowed to continue to do so without a special permit. However, the Jews were largely successful in preventing the Zgierz limitations from being applied. When the local authorities planned the town, they set aside the two streets near the market, Walburska and Nadrzeczna, for the Jews. In 1825 they declared that as from July 1, 1827, Jews would be permitted to acquire building sites, to build, and to live on the southern side of the Podrzeczna and Walburska streets and the market only. The only Jews allowed to settle outside this quarter were those

Jewish Population in Lodz

Year	General Population	Jewish Population	% Jews
1820	767	259	33.8
1823	799	288	36.0
1856	24,655	2,886	11.7
1897	310,302	98,676	31.8
1910	409,405	166,628	40.7
1921	452,623	156,155	34.5
1931	604,470	202,497	33.5

who established factories employing Jewish workers, wholesale merchants, members of the liberal professions who built houses, and two families who each possessed 20,000 zlotys. All Jews granted exceptional residence rights had to know Polish, French, or German, and their children over the age of seven had to attend general schools along with non-Jewish children. They were also forbidden to wear the traditional Jewish dress. For a time the authorities continued to harass even those Jews who fulfilled all these conditions. Anxious to eliminate competition from the growing number of Jewish weavers, the German textile workers pressed for the expulsion of the Jews. From 1832 Samuel Ezekiel Salzmann led the battle to extend the rights of Jewish settlement. As the number of Jews continued to grow he built many houses to alleviate the overcrowding and rising rents in the Jewish quarter.

In 1848 the czar abolished the limitations on Jewish settlement in Polish cities. By decrees of 1861 and 1862 the concept of a specific Jewish quarter in Lodz was finally abolished. Jews settled throughout the city, although many of them continued to be concentrated in the former Jewish quarter, the "Altstadt." A synagogue was erected on Wilki Street, outside the old quarter. Large numbers of Jewish craftsmen, peddlers, and factory workers were concentrated in the suburb of Balut (Baluty). This settlement began early in the 19th century, when Balut was still a separate village and Isaac Blauwatt and Isaac Birnzweig leased lands from its owner to sublet to Jews. Although no industrial enterprises were established in Balut itself, many Jewish weavers who worked for the large enterprises on a contractual basis lived there. Until 1916 Balut was officially a village outside the Lodz municipality, and hygienic conditions were consequently poor. Conditions remained the same when it was incorporated into the municipality. With rising unemployment and worsening conditions for handloom weavers, life in Balut steadily deteriorated in the interwar period.

Throughout the 19th century and up to 1939 Jews were active in much of the trade in Lodz, especially in supplying raw materials for the textile industry. Wholesale and retail traders, agents, and brokers formed over one third of the Jewish earners in Lodz. In the 20th century Jews entered industry on a considerable scale; by 1914, 175 factories (33.3% of the total) were owned by Jews; 150 of these were textile mills. Jews also owned 18,954 small workshops (27.7%); 18,476 of them textile enterprises. Of the 27,385 Jewish workers (32.9% of the labor force), 26,845 were employed in textile industries. Thus the majority of Jewish enterprise and workers was employed in the small workshops of the Jewish textile industry. Jewish mills produced mainly cotton although there were some woolen and linen mills. The most prominent industrialists were Poznański, Hayyim Jacob Wiślicki, Asher Cohen (Oskar Kohn), the brothers Ettingon, Jacob Kastenberg, and Tuvia Bialer.

Lodz was badly destroyed during World War I when the German residents collaborated with the German invaders. With the break-up of czarist Russia and the creation of independent Poland, the large Russian market was lost and consequently new markets were needed. The Polish government did not grant Jewish industry financial aid for reconstruction. In the early 1920s the anti-Jewish fiscal policies of Polish Finance Minister W. Grabski further hindered the recovery of Jewish industry. Those firms which managed to recover were again hit by the world crisis of 1929. During the 1930s, anti-Jewish economic policies were intensified throughout Poland. Jewish workers were squeezed out of industry, even the enterprises owned by Jews. Every growth in the scale of a plant or increasing mechanization meant that Jewish workers were likely to lose their jobs, both because Polish workers were opposed to their employment and because anti-Jewish government policy encouraged this opposition. Between the wars, ready-made tailoring in Lodz was almost entirely in Jewish hands. Jews were also engaged in building and related trades such as paving, making steps, and carpentry, working on a contractual basis. Polish anti-Jewish policy attempted to replace Jewish weavers by Polish craftsmen. In 1910 the First Union of Jewish Craftsmen was organized, also including large-scale Jewish industrialists, on the initiative of the Jewish Bank for Mutual Assistance. In 1912 it was renamed the Union of Industrialists. Craftsmen and middle-range industrialists joined its ranks. After World War I a union of craftsmen and industrialists was organized as was a union of Jewish merchants in 1925. Small tradesmen and retailers had their own unions. In 1926 a union of both Jewish and non-Jewish traders and retailers was formed; however, the non-Jews soon left it. The Jews formed their unions in collaboration with *Ort. The *Bund, the *Po'alei Zion, and the Polish Socialist Party (the *PPS) competed in organizing trade unions among the Jewish laborers in Lodz. In 1901, at a funeral of one of its members, the Bund held a demonstration in which 2,000 persons participated. During the revolution of 1905, the Bund was very active in Lodz. At the end of 1903, a Jewish section of the PPS was organized in the city on the initiative of the famous Polish leader Józef *Pilsudski. Jewish craftsmen in Lodz, as elsewhere in Poland, were faced in 1927 with a law which demanded examinations for craftsmen and a diploma awarded by a union of artisans.

Social Life and Culture

The official enactments against and intrusions into Jewish communal institutions from the 1820s (see *Russia, *Poland, *Community, **kazyonny ravvin*) had little effect in Lodz. The community maintained its *autonomy in difficult circumstances. With the official recognition of Jewish communal autonomy in independent Poland the first democratic elections for the community council of Lodz were held in 1924; seven of the members were Ḥasidim of *Aleksandrow, six Zionists and *Mizrachi, three Bund, 11 *Agudat Israel, one *Po'alei Agudat Israel, two representing the craftsmen, two left Po'alei Zion, one *Folkspartei, and one each from two Communist lists. The first chairman was the Zionist Dr. Uri Rosenblatt. In 1931 the authorities dissolved the community council and announced new elections. The results were: one Po'alei Agudat Israel, four

Zionists, 12 Agudat Israel, two Ḥasidim of Aleksandrow, one Folkspartei, one representing the small tradesmen, and one each of the four leftist lists. Leib Minzberg of Agudat Israel was elected chairman, a position he occupied until the Holocaust. The community maintained a kosher slaughterhouse, a **mikveh*, and a **talmud torah* for the poor, and collaborated with *TOZ and other charitable organizations. The most prominent was Gemilut Ḥasadim (Pol. Dobroczynnść), founded in 1899 by Jewish philanthropists such as Israel Poznański as a roof organization for many charitable societies. Rabbis of Lodz included Mendel Wolf ha-Kohen Jerozolimski (1825–32) and Ezekiel Nomberg (1832–56), a *Kotsk Ḥasid who was opposed by many in the community. (His great-grandson was the Yiddish writer Hirsch David *Nomberg.) With the growth of Jewish Lodz, the rabbinical seat gained in importance. After a heated election campaign, Moses Lipshitz, also a Kotsk Ḥasid, was chosen in 1857. He was followed by the famous Lithuanian rabbi, Elijah Ḥayyim Meisel (1873–1912), who enhanced the stature of the office by becoming the recognized leader of the Jews of Lodz. His successor was Eliezer Leib Treistman, a Gur Ḥasid, and former rabbi of Radom. After Treistman's death in 1920, because of disagreement between the parties, no other community rabbi was elected. Last of the Reform synagogue preachers and rabbis was Markus (Mordecai) *Braude, the founder of the Hebrew schools network (see below).

*B'nai B'rith established a lodge in Lodz in 1926 which supported the Ort vocational school, the orphanage, and various cultural institutions. A *bikkur ḥolim* organization was founded in 1881; in 1908 it was incorporated into the Dobroczynność. Between the two world wars, the convalescent home for sufferers from pulmonary diseases was particularly well known. There was also a *Linat ha-Ẓedek* society which visited Jewish patients in Lodz hospitals. In the course of time its activities were extended; between the two world wars it established a hospital for children and a *Linat ha-Ẓedek* pharmacy which was subsidized by the municipality of Lodz and the Jewish community. The synagogues organized societies for the relief of the sick and other charitable organizations, such as the Malbish Arumim which provided clothing for poor children. It subsequently undertook a variety of services: legal aid, the organization of cooperatives, and medical assistance. In the interwar period, there were soup kitchens for the needy which also distributed free meals to school children.

Jewish education in Lodz shared in the development and crises of the traditional Orthodox Jewish education system in modern times (and see **Ḥeder*, *Yeshivah). There were many yeshivot; some, e.g., Beth Israel of the Aleksandrow Ḥasidim and the Lithuanian-style Torat Ḥesed, were influential. The *talmud torah* founded by R. Elijah Ḥayyim Meisel in 1873 provided education for children of elementary school age. Some subjects were taught in Polish and some in Hebrew. A diversified network of educational institutions, from kindergarten to secondary school, existed in Lodz. A "reformed" *ḥeder* (known as the Jaroczyński School after the philanthropist of this name) was founded in 1890 and included secular subjects in its curriculum. The first Jewish gymnasium in Russia was established in Lodz by Markus (Mordecai) Braude in 1912. In accordance with the requirements of Russian law, it was named after a private person, Dr. D.B. Rabinovich. In it too some subjects were taught in Polish and some in Hebrew. Another secondary school was headed by Itzhak *Katzenelson, the noted Hebrew poet who perished in the Holocaust. In 1918 the first Yiddish school was established, named after B. Borochov. The Jaroczyński *talmud torah* was converted into a vocational school in 1921 and in 1927 it became a secondary vocational school for the study of mechanics, electricity, and weaving. A *Beth Jacob school for girls was founded in 1924.

Although Lodz was not a leading Jewish cultural center, there was considerable creativity in the city. The Hebrew authors and poets, Itzhak Katzenelson, David *Frischman, and Jacob *Cohen lived and worked in Lodz, as did the scholars J.N. *Simchoni, Philip *Friedman, Aryeh *Tartakower, and Ḥayyim Isaac *Bunin. Yiddish authors and poets included Isaiah Uger, the editor of the newspaper *Lodzher Togblat*, J.I. *Trunk, H.L. *Fox, and Ḥayyim Krol. Most famous of the many Jewish musicians were Chemjo *Vinaver, the conductor, and the composer I. Goldstein. Jewish drama companies were formed at the close of the 19th century, and from among these emerged the theater known as the "Great Theater," where the famous Yiddish actors, Julius Adler and Zaslavski, appeared. There were also well-known satirical theaters, directed by the Yiddish poet Moshe *Broderzon and actor Shimon *Dzigan.

Many Zionist societies were organized in Lodz soon after the First Zionist Congress of 1897, such as the Ohel Ya'akov, Ateret Zion, and Tikvat Zion, structured around synagogues. During World War I, Agudat Israel, whose main supporters were the Ḥasidim of Gur, engaged in numerous activities. The Zionist organizations were active in the propagation of the Hebrew language and Hebrew culture, initiated and organized by the historian J.N. Simchoni. The Hebrew cultural activities operated within the framework of the literary-musical society, Ha-Zamir, founded in 1899. It maintained a choir, a dramatic circle, and a library, and in 1915 formed a philharmonic orchestra. The D.B. Borochov Library was established by Po'alei Zion in 1914 and the Bund established the Grosser Library, named after the Bundist leader by the same name. Jewish newspapers included the Zionist *Lodzher Togblat* (1908), *Lodzher Morgnblat* (1912), *Lodzher Folksblat* (1915), *Nayer Folksblat* (1923), and other periodicals in Yiddish and Hebrew.

Until the Nazis began to disseminate antisemitic propaganda among the German minority in Lodz (from the mid-1930s) the antisemitic movement in the city followed the customary Polish pattern (see *Endecja, *Rozwój); from April 1933 there were many cases of murderous attacks on Jews. In May 1934 and in September 1935 Jews were wounded or killed in organized attacks. The antisemitic parties gained an overwhelming majority in the municipal elections of 1934 after conducting an election campaign on the platform of purging the town of Jews. Their rule was short-lived, for in the elections of 1936 the Polish and Jewish Socialist parties won a majority. Under different pretexts controllers and officials were introduced by the Polish authorities into the factories of Cohen, Ettingon, Poznański, and others. Rich Jews were arrested in 1938 and imprisoned in the camp of *Bereza-Kartuska. Guards were placed outside Jewish shops in order to prevent non-Jewish customers from entering them. In vain, the town's Socialist administration tried to prevent the growth of antisemitism and the accompanying agitation.

[Shimshon Leib Kirshenboim]

Holocaust Period

At the outbreak of World War II, Lodz had 233,000 Jews, about one-third of the city's population. As soon as the war broke out many Jewish inhabitants, including the social and cultural elite, the youth, and wealthier circles, left Lodz out of fear of persecution. Their exodus continued up to May 1940. They sought refuge in Warsaw and other towns in the General Government (see *Poland, Holocaust) and many escaped to the territories occupied by the U.S.S.R. The German army entered Lodz on Sept. 8, 1939. In October–November 1939 Lodz was annexed to the Reich as part of Warthegau (Wartheland), and given a German name, Litzmannstadt. The Jewish community council, now understaffed, reinstated its activities a few days after the capitulation (Sept. 12, 1939). The council mainly extended assistance, as it did formerly, to the ever-increasing number of impoverished Jews, to refugees from the vicinity, to the sick, and to victims of Nazi terror. In October 1939 the Germans disbanded the council and appointed its former vice chairman, Chaim Mordecai *Rumkowsky, as *Judenaeltester.* He formed an advisory but short-lived body, "Beirat," of 31 Jewish personalities. On Nov. 11, 1939, the Nazis deported the Beirat members to the nearby Radogoszcz camp (Radegast). After some time another purely formal body was set up, completely subordinate to *Gestapo orders and to the *Judenaeltester.* The brutal liquidation of the first Beirat was an indication of further acts of terror to come that November, when the Nazis burned down the great synagogue and publicly hanged two Poles and a Jew.

In December 1939 the Germans evicted many Jews living along the central streets of the town to settle *Volksdeutsche* in their place. On December 12–14 the authorities deported a few thousand Lodz Jews to the General Government, after which a mass "spontaneous" exodus of Jews occurred as a result of the fear of deportation. In January 1940 the Jews were segregated into the Old City and Baluty quarter, the area of the future ghetto, officially founded by a police order on Feb. 8, 1940. The ghetto (less than 2 sq. mi.; 4 sq. km.) generally lacked sewage disposal and its houses were fit for demolishing. To speed up confinement of the Jews into the ghetto, the Nazis organized a pogrom on March 1, 1940, known as "bloody Thursday," during which many Jews were murdered. Thousands of Jews were then driven into the ghetto without being permitted to take their property with them. On April 30, 1940, the ghetto was closed off. Its small area contained the 164,000 Jews still living in Lodz, for between Sept. 1, 1939, and May 1, 1940, 70,000 Jews had left the city. The ghetto was separated from the rest of the city by barbed wire, wooden fences, and a chain of "Schupo" (Schutzpolizei) outposts. The Jewish administrative body and the German ghetto council (Ghettoverwaltung) headed by Hans Biebow communicated with each other at the so-called Bałuty market, where some German and the central Jewish offices were located. The ghetto was crossed by two thoroughfares which did not, however, belong to the ghetto area. These streets divided the ghetto into three parts connected to one another by several gates (for traffic) and three bridges (for pedestrians). The isolation of the ghetto was strengthened by the fact that it was deliberately surrounded by a German population according to the "Germanization policy."

Up to October 1940 the local German authorities counted on the deportation of the ghetto inmates to "reserves" in the Lublin District or to Madagascar (see *Madagascar Plan). But German plans changed and the Lodz ghetto remained. The ghetto inhabitants were subjected to starvation, alleviated in part by the smuggling of foodstuffs (1940–41), but smuggling activities were vigorously combated by the ghetto branch office of the German Kriminalpolizei. The little food supplied by the authorities was rationed out on even lower standards than those applied in Nazi prisons. Apart from this a large quantity of the foodstuffs arrived in spoiled condition. In 1940 the majority of the ghetto population was left with no means of subsistence. Hunger demonstrations and riots resulted in the early fall. The economic situation of the inmates improved a little after some time, when a ghetto factory network was organized to produce goods, mainly for the Wehrmacht. In August 1942 there were 91 factories with 77,982 employees. Many of the workers earned too little to be able to buy even the inadequate food rations allotted to them, and working conditions were unbearable. Apart from starvation and exhaustion, the population underwent roundups for the forced labor camp at Warthegau. In 1940–44 the Germans sent 15,000 Jews from the ghetto to labor camps, but only very few ever returned, and they arrived back in a state of exhaustion. The branch office of the ghetto Kriminalpolizei carried out extensive robbery of the remaining Jewish possessions. It terrorized the ghetto inmates with house searches, requisition, and torture to uncover any hidden property. The extremely crowded living quarters, combined with bad hygienic conditions, starvation, and overwork, caused epidemics of dysentery, typhus, and typhoid fever, but mortality was due mostly to tuberculosis, the death rate for which was 26 times higher than it had been among Lodz Jews in 1936. The overall average death rate per month reached 7.23 per 1,000, whereas in 1938 it had been 0.91 per 1,000, i.e., the rate increased eightfold since prewar time.

In these appalling conditions, Rumkowsky tried to organize the life of the Jewish community. He created a widespread network of Jewish self-administration, which included departments that provided for the needs of the population as far as possible (the former Jewish social institutions having been liquidated by the Nazis), and other departments that fulfilled German orders, some sections performing both tasks. From 1940 to September 1942, the health department of the ghetto ran five to seven hospitals, five pharmacies, and several special infirmaries. The education department ran 45 primary religious and secular schools, two high schools, and one vocational school. The food supply department organized public kitchens in factories, offices, and schools. Apart from the general food control system (ration cards), an additional ration system was introduced for various categories of people (for those engaged in hard labor, excrement carriers, police and firemen, physicians, pharmacists, persons in leading positions, the sick, and confined women). The department for social welfare handed out regular small pittances for the unemployed and for those with meager income. There were two old age homes, a home for invalids, and a home for the chronically ill; however, conditions in these homes were extremely bad and the death rate very high. An orphanage and a children's camp were organized for 1,500 children as well as a morning camp for the summer period.

The agricultural department allotted small garden plots to the population. The factories, called Arbeitsressorte, exploited Jewish labor, but on the other hand gave the employees certain wages and additional food rations. The statistics department gathered – for the needs of the ghetto and the Germans – data on all branches of life in the ghetto. The archives department collected valuable documents and kept daily chronicles of ghetto life. (The majority of these documents found their way to the *Jewish Historical Institute in Warsaw.) The rabbinate oversaw the semi-legal religious life of the ghetto up to September 1942. On the other hand a department known as the Arbeitsamt (Arbeitseinsatz) supplied the Germans with Jewish manpower for the forced labor camps, and a special "purchasing department" bought Jewish property at the lowest prices and handed it over to the Ghettoverwaltung. These sales enabled the Jewish authorities to obtain the means for the purchase of foodstuffs for the ghetto (the Germans supplied food only in exchange for real goods, i.e., Jewish labor or Jewish property), and therefore the Jews found such sales were preferable to the outright requisitions made by the Kriminalpolizei. The Jewish police (Ordnungsdienst) administered order in the ghetto, but also took part in deportations and roundups of Jews for forced labor camps. A special police group (Sonderabteilung) under the orders of the Kriminalpolizei confiscated Jewish property. Its commander, David Gertler, and later M. Kligier, took orders from the Gestapo. A court and prison functioned. The latter was the collection point for those sent on forced labor or to extermination camps. Persons who returned from labor camps or who were held by the Gestapo were kept in the ghetto prison.

Several political and social groups (e.g., some Zionist organizations, WIZO, Bund, the communist "Trade Union Left," the organization of ex-combatants and invalids) held secret meetings, taught and provided self-education, organized demonstrations against the *Judenaeltester* Rumkowsky (1940) and strikes in factories, engaged in production sabotage, and listened in to the radio. Certain parties (Bund, Po'alei Zion), with Rumkowsky's approval, ran their own "kitchens" (1940–41) where they fed their members and held cultural gatherings. During the mass deportations these organizations engaged in saving their active members. The He-Ḥalutz ("pioneer") youth groups, in the spring of 1940, organized a *hakhsharah* (Zionist pioneer training program) on the outskirts of the ghetto (Marysin). The *hakhsharah* served different organizations and had 1,040 members, including non-Zionists such as members of the Bund and Agudah. Apart from farm work, the youth held cultural activities and provided self-education. In September 1940 several Zionist groups formed the Ḥazit Dor Benei Midbar, which continued its activities in the ghetto even after the liquidation of the *hakhsharah* in mid-1941.

The German authorities gave orders which imposed the sequence of events to come in Lodz ghetto. They allowed a period of relative autonomy (May 1940–September 1942) but ended it with a wave of mass deportations to the extermination camp at *Chelmno on the Ner. During January–April 1942 the Germans deported more than 44,000 Jews. In May 1942, 11,000 Jews originally from Prague, Vienna, Luxembourg, and various cities from the "Old Reich" were rounded up and deported for extermination. These Jews (20,000), mostly elderly and sick, had been taken in the fall of 1941 to Lodz ghetto, where they lingered on in terrible conditions, were crowded into unheated, mass quarters, and endured more severe hunger than the local population. By 1942, 5,000 among them died of typhus and starvation. After their deportation, the notorious *"Gehsperre" Aktion* was carried out to exterminate 16,000 Lodz Jews, including children up to ten years old, persons above 60, and the sick and emaciated. With this mass murder action, the population decreased from 162,681 in January 1942 to 89,446 on October 1, 1942, i.e., by nearly half. This decrease was in fact greater because 15,500 refugees from the liquidated provisional ghettos had been brought to Lodz ghetto in spring/summer 1942.

After the mass liquidation campaign the Germans transformed the ghetto de facto into a labor camp. There followed the reduction and liquidation of the Jewish administrative bodies which had served the needs of the population, e.g., health, food supply, welfare, education, and records departments, and the rabbinate. The orphanages, old-age homes, the majority of the hospitals, schools, and children's homes no longer existed. The number of factories increased to 119 (August 1943) and employed 90% of the population. Children from the age of eight worked in these factories. The Germans held control over all internal matters in the ghetto, such as food supply (additional rations), and they limited Rumkowsky's power to allow Kligier, chief of the Sonderabteilung, and Jakubowicz, chief of the Arbeitsressorte (factories), more sway.

Under these conditions the ghetto lingered on until its final liquidation in June–August 1944. By Sept. 1, 1944, the whole population, 76,701 (June 1, 1944 registration), was deported to *Auschwitz. By January 1945, only an Aufraeumungskommando (800 Jews) remained in the ghetto joined by some

Jews who were hiding in the area of the former ghetto. They were liberated when the Soviet army arrived on Jan. 19, 1945.

[Danuta Dombrowska]

Contemporary Period

When the Soviet army entered Lodz only 870 Jewish survivors were left in the city. Nevertheless, within the next two years Lodz became the largest reconstructed Jewish community in Poland. More than 50,000 Jews settled there by the end of 1946, of whom the overwhelming majority had survived the Holocaust period in the Soviet Union. A number of Jewish institutions began to function, including the Central Jewish Historical Commission, a Jewish theater, editorial staffs of a number of Jewish (Yiddish, Hebrew, and Polish-language) papers. Zionist organizations conducted intensive activity, with the support of the majority of Jews. A number of "kibbutzim" (homes for Jewish youth who prepared themselves for *aliyah*) were established. All these activities were stopped in 1950, when the Sovietization of Poland was completed. More than one-half of the city's Jewish population left Poland during 1946–50. After the second wave of *aliyah* to Israel during 1956–57, only a few thousand Jews remained. A club of the government-sponsored Jewish Cultural Society and a Jewish public school continued to function until 1968–69, when almost all remaining Jews left Poland. By the turn of the century only a few hundred Jews lived in Lodz.

[Stefan Krakowski]

BIBLIOGRAPHY: A.Z. Aescoly, *Kehillat Lodzh: Toledot Ir va-Em be-Yisrael* (1948); A. Alpern, *Żydzi w Łodzi: początki gminy żydowskiej, 1780–1822* (1928); idem, in: *"Haynt" Yubiley-Bukh* (1928), 106ff.; idem, in: *Rocznik Łódzki*, 1 (1928); F. (P.) Friedman, *ibid.*, 2 (1930), 319–65; idem, *Dzieje Żydów w Łodzi od początków osadnictwa Żydów do r. 1863* (1935), incl. bibl.; B. Weinryb, in: *YIVO Ekonomishe Shriftn*, 2 (1932), 34–55; idem, *Neueste Wirtschaftsgeschichte der Juden in Russland und Polen*, 1 (1938); A.W. Yasny, *Geshikhte fun der Yidisher Arbeter-Bavegung in Lodzh* (1937); M. Zer-Kavod, in: *Sinai*, 28 (1950/51), 241–78; A. Tenenbaum-Arazi, *Lodzh un Ire Yidn* (1956). HOLOCAUST PERIOD: A.W. Yasny, *Geshikhte fun Yidn in Lodzh in di Yorn fun der Daytsher Yidn-Oyszrotung*, 2 vols. (1960–66); *Lodzher Yizker-Bukh* (1943); J.I. Trunk, *Lodzher Geto* (1962); Y.L. Gersht, *Min ha-Meẓar: Zikhronot… be-Getto Lodzh…* (1949); S. Zelver-Urbach, *Mi-Ba'ad le-Ḥalon Beiti: Zikhronot mi-Getto Lodz* (1964); D. Dąbrowska (ed.), *Kronika getta Łodzkiego…*, 2 vols. (1965–66); *The Last Journey of the Jews of Lodz* (photo album, 1967). **ADD. BIBLIOGRAPHY:** J. Poznanski, *Pamietnik z getta lodzkiego* (1960); A. Ben Menahem and J. Rav (eds.), *Khronika shel Ghetto Lodz*, 4 vols. (1987); W. Pusia and S. Liszewski (eds.), *Dzieje Żydow w Łodzi 1820–1944* (1991).

LOEB, ISIDORE (1839–1892), French rabbi and scholar. Loeb, who was the son of a rabbi in Soultzmatt, Alsace, studied at the Ecole Rabbinique of Metz (which was later transferred to Paris). After tutoring in Bayonne and Paris, he became rabbi at Saint-Etienne (1865). In 1869 Loeb was appointed secretary of the *Alliance Israélite Universelle in Paris, a post he held until his death. As a result of his initiative, the Alliance increased its network of schools in Mediterranean countries and the Balkans and intervened in international conferences on behalf of oppressed Jewish minorities (cf. his *La situation des Israélites en Turquie, en Serbie et en Roumanie* (1877), and *Les Juifs de Russie* (1891)). The Alliance bulletins became, under his editorship, a main source of information to all those who were engaged in the fight for Jewish emancipation. Loeb founded and developed the library of the Alliance. From 1878 he taught Jewish history at the École Rabbinique. Loeb's scholarly work covered biblical and talmudic literature, medieval historiography, and the history of the Jews in France and Spain. His articles appeared in various journals including the short-lived *Revue Israélite*, which he edited from 1870 to 1872. He was also publication manager of the *Revue des Études Juives*, to which he contributed some 50 articles, and wrote for the *Grande Encyclopédie* (articles on Judaism from A to C). He prepared a French edition of the *maḥzor* (1869), and wrote mathematical works including *Tables du Calendrier* (1886). He also wrote *La Littérature des Pauvres dans la Bible* (REJ, 20 (1890); 21 (1890); 23 (1891); 24 (1892), which also appeared separately in 1892). Loeb contended that certain biblical books contain several passages (on whose dating scholars disagree), expressing the idealization of poverty and suffering. This Renan-inspired view has been discussed. A collection of his sermons was published in 1865.

BIBLIOGRAPHY: REJ, 24 (1892), 1–4; Z. Kahn, *ibid*, 161–83; J. Levi, *ibid.*, 184–224; M. Liber, *ibid.*, 105 (1940), 16–22; A. Neubauer, in: JQR, 5 (1892/93), 1–4.

[Georges Weill]

LOEB, JACQUES (1859–1924), U.S. physiological chemist. Born near Strasbourg, Alsace, into a family of Portuguese and Italian origin, Loeb studied medicine. He immigrated to the U.S. and became professor of physiology at the University of California (1902–10), and then head of the division of general physiology at the Rockefeller Institute for Medical Research in New York (1910–24). He founded and edited the *Journal of General Physiology* from 1918. A brilliant experimentalist, he was a pioneer in explaining vital processes on a basis of physical chemistry. Some of his special fields of work were the physiology of the brain, tropism, antagonistic salt action, the duration of life, and colloidal behavior. He wrote *The Organism as a Whole* (1916), *Regeneration from a Physico-chemical Viewpoint* (1924), and *Proteins and the Theory of Colloidal Behaviour* (1924^2).

BIBLIOGRAPHY: Osterhout, in: *Journal of General Physiology*, 8 (1925–28), ix–lix; Armstrong, in: *Journal of General Physiology*, 8 (1928), 653–70; Kobelt, in: *Journal of General Physiology*, 8 (1928), lxiii–xcii, bibl.

[Samuel Aaron Miller]

LOEB, JAMES (1867–1933), U.S. banker, philanthropist, and translator. Loeb, who was born in New York, joined his father's well-known banking firm of Kuhn, Loeb & Co. in 1888. He left the firm in 1901 and in 1912 established his residence in Murnau, Germany. The institutions which Loeb founded and endowed include the Institute of Musical Art in New York, later a part of the Juilliard Musical Foundation; the Deutsche Forschungsamstalt fuer Psychiatrie in Munich, for research into the various causes of mental disorders; and the famed Loeb Classical Library (1912), consisting of classic Greek and Latin works in the original, faced by English translations. Among the works which Loeb translated into English were Maurice Croiset's *Aristophanes et les partis a Athènes*; Phillippe Ernest Legrand's *Daos*; and Auguste Couat's study of Alexandrian poetry. He was also a competent cellist.

BIBLIOGRAPHY: *Festschrift fuer James Loeb...* (1930).

LOEB, LEO (1869–1959), pathologist and pioneer in cancer research. Loeb, who was born in Mayen, Germany, immigrated to the United States in 1900 and held a variety of academic and research posts until 1910, when he settled in St. Louis, Missouri. From 1915 to 1937 he was professor of pathology at St. Louis' Washington University. Loeb made significant contributions to cancer research. In a series of experiments on rats and mice, he and his co-workers found that the growth energy of cancer cells may be experimentally decreased and increased. They also showed that hormones may induce cancer in a mouse's mammary gland, vagina, and cervix. They studied growth and retardation factors influencing the thyroid gland. Loeb's papers included studies of blood coagulation and thrombosis, pathology of the circulatory organs, kidneys, and stomach, experimental cell fibrin tissue, old age, and the analysis of cell death. Leo Loeb was the brother of the physiologist and biologist Jacques *Loeb.

BIBLIOGRAPHY: S.R. Kagan, *Jewish Medicine* (1952), 229f.

[Suessmann Muntner]

LOEB, MORRIS (1863–1912), U.S. physical chemist and philanthropist; brother of James *Loeb. Loeb was born in Cincinnati, Ohio. In 1891 he became professor of chemistry at New York University, and was also attached to Clark University. In 1910 he resigned his chair to devote himself to research and his public activities. His main fields of research were on osmotic pressure, electrolysis, and the molecular weight of iodine. He was chairman of the New York section of the American Chemical Society and president of the Chemists' Club of New York City. His public and philanthropic work was carried out against the background of the intensive immigration of Jews into the United States at the time. He was director of the Jewish Agricultural and Industrial Aid Society and he created a Jewish Agricultural Experimental Station in New Jersey. He was president of the Hebrew Technical Institute, trustee of the Jewish Theological Seminary of America, and founder of the American Jewish Committee and of the Educational Alliance.

BIBLIOGRAPHY: T.W. Richards (ed.), *The Scientific Work of Morris Loeb* (1913); *Morris Loeb Memorial Volume* (1913); L.H. Baekeland, in: *Industrial and Engineering Chemistry*, 4 (1912), 784–5; C.L. Sulzberger, in: AJHSP, 22 (1914), 225–7.

[Samuel Aaron Miller]

LOEBEL, ISRAEL (late 18th century), preacher and *dayyan*, opponent of Ḥasidism. He was probably born in Slutsk, or at least lived there in his childhood, was preacher in Mogilev, and in 1787 was appointed permanent preacher and *dayyan* in Novogrudok. While he was still in Mogilev, his opposition to the Ḥasidim grew as a result of his brother's joining their ranks. When *Elijah b. Solomon, the Vilna Gaon, issued a proclamation against the Ḥasidim in 1797, Loebel obtained from R. Saadiah, an emissary and disciple of the Gaon, a letter of recommendation authorizing him to preach against the sect wherever possible, and approval for the publication of his books. He was likewise granted the approval of the **parnasim* of the Slutsk community, and at the gathering of the leaders of the Lithuanian communities at Zelva he was evidently authorized to travel throughout Poland and beyond, in order to disseminate anti-ḥasidic propaganda. His two booklets against Ḥasidism, *Sefer Vikku'aḥ* and *Kivrot ha-Ta'avah*, were printed in Warsaw in 1798; the latter is no longer extant. In his preachings in the communities of east Galicia, Loebel conducted anti-ḥasidic propaganda. According to his own testimony, Loebel was granted an audience with Emperor Francis II at Vienna in early 1799, as a result of which public meetings of Ḥasidim were prohibited in all the provinces of Poland which had then come under Austrian rule. There is, however, no historical evidence for this.

Sefer Vikku'aḥ describes a disputation between a Ḥasid and a *Mitnagged*. The author compared the Ḥasidim with heretical sects that had arisen within Judaism throughout its history. He denied the ḥasidic principle that considers prayer more important than Torah study and the ḥasidic emphasis on joy as a basic element in prayer; and objected to such ḥasidic customs as the acceptance of the Sephardi prayer rite and not observing the fixed times of prayer. He likewise attacked the ḥasidic leaders, claiming that they were ignoramuses whose every command was obeyed, who exploited the masses and enjoyed a rich life at their expense, and who deluded them with the belief that the *ẓaddik* atoned for their sins. *Sefer Vikku'aḥ* and its author became the target of attacks by the Ḥasidim, who prepared to reply with a pamphlet entitled *Mul Maggid Peti* ("Against the Foolish Preacher"), though it is not clear if this was in fact printed. They bought up practically the whole edition of *Sefer Vikku'aḥ* and tried to destroy it "by tearing up the book and trampling on it as on mud in the streets." In the 1820s the Hebrew writer Joseph *Perl made an unsuccessful attempt to reprint the book.

Loebel also wrote a booklet in German, *Glaubwuerdige Nachricht von einer neuen und zahlreichen Sekte unter den Juden, die sich Chassidim nennt...* (Frankfurt on the Oder, 1799). Though the original is not extant, it has been preserved in a reprint in the journal *Sulamith*, 2 (Dessau, 1807), 308–33. His homiletic works are *Ozer Yisrael* (Shklov, 1786), printed anonymously; *Takkanat ha-Mo'adim* (before 1787); *Iggera de-Hespeda* (possibly unpublished; the last two works are not extant); *Middot Ḥasidut*; and *Ta'avat Ẓaddikim* (both Warsaw, 1798); the latter, which is ambiguous in the original, includes a chapter against Ḥasidism. His *Even Boḥan* (Frankfurt on the Oder, 1799) is a polemic against the *maskilim*.

BIBLIOGRAPHY: M. Wilensky, *Ḥasidim u-Mitnaggedim* (1970); Dubnow, Ḥasidut, 278–86 and index; G. Scholem, in: *Zion*, 20 (1955), 153–62; I. Bacon, *ibid.*, 32 (1967), 116–22; H. Liberman, in: KS, 26 (1950), 106, 216; M. Mahler, *Ha-Ḥasidut ve-ha-Haskalah* (1961), index.

[Esther (Zweig) Liebes]

LOEBL, EUGEN (1907–1987), Czechoslovak economist and politician. Loebl was born in Holič, Slovakia, into a wealthy Jewish family. In 1934 he became a member of the Communist Party. In March 1939, when the Germans invaded Czechoslovakia, Loebl fled to England, where he served as economic consultant to Jan Masaryk, the foreign minister of the Czechoslovak government-in-exile. After World War II, he became a departmental head in the Ministry of Foreign Trade and a leading member of the Communist Party's economic council. In 1947 he headed the Czechoslovak mission to Moscow, which negotiated the first postwar political and economic agreement with the U.S.S.R., and in the following year, after the Communist seizure of power, became first deputy in the ministry of foreign trade. Loebl supported Czechoslovakia's acceptance of the American Marshall Aid Plan and also initiated the Czechoslovak-Israel transfer agreement. In November 1949 Loebl was arrested and put on trial together with Rudolf *Slansky. Under duress he confessed his guilt and in 1952 he was sentenced to life imprisonment. In 1963 he was rehabilitated and appointed director of the state bank in Bratislava. From 1965 onward, he campaigned for the implementation of economic reforms and the democratization of the Czechoslovak Communist regime. Following the Soviet invasion of Czechoslovakia in 1968, Loebl moved first to Israel, and from there overseas, trying his luck in Canada and the United States. In Canada he joined the World Slovak Congress, an organization of Slovak exiles, mostly former supporters of the wartime Slovak state. In this organization he was elected vice president. In the United States he worked as an economist. His writings include *Geistige Arbeit – die wahre Quelle des Reichtums* (1966), *Hinter den Kulissen des Slansky Prozesses* (1968), an account of the Slansky trial, and *Stalinism in Prague* (1969).

[Erich Kulka / Yeshayahu Jelinek (2nd ed.)]

LOEB-LEOPOLD CASE, U.S. murder case in 1924 which involved one of the most sensational crimes of the century. Richard Loeb (1905–1936), 18, a graduate of the University of Michigan, and Nathan Freudenthal Leopold (1904–1971), 19, a graduate of the University of Chicago, the well-educated scions of wealthy Chicago Jewish families, attempted, as they said at their trial, to perpetrate the perfect crime, when they kidnapped and killed a 14-year-old neighbor, Bobby Franks. After a thorough investigation and a highly publicized trial, in which the famous attorney Clarence Darrow represented the young men, they were sentenced to life imprisonment plus 99 years, the court recommending that they never be released. In jail the young men developed a correspondence school in which many subjects were taught to the inmates of 19 penitentiaries. In 1936 Loeb was murdered by an inmate. Leopold worked ceaselessly at his prison activities. Possessing a remarkably high IQ, he was a participant in the famous wartime malaria experiments and mastered 27 languages. His book, *Life Plus 99 Years* (1958), tells the story of his imprisonment. For a period of years there were unsuccessful efforts to release him. In 1957 Attorney Elmer Gertz took over the case and the parole board finally paroled Leopold in 1958 to Puerto Rico, where he worked at the Castaner General Hospital. Leopold earned a master's degree, taught at the University of Puerto Rico, and published a book on birds. The case was described by Meyer *Levin's novel *Compulsion* (1956; which Leopold characterized as unwarranted invasion of his privacy).

BIBLIOGRAPHY: M. McKernan, *Crime and Trial of Leopold and Loeb* (1925); C.S. Darrow, *Plea… in Defence of Richard Loeb and Nathan Leopold* (1924).

[Elmer Gertz]

LOESSER, FRANK (1910–1969), composer. Born in New York, Loesser wrote songs while at City College and then in the army during World War II, of which *Praise the Lord and Pass the Ammunition* became the best known. He settled in Hollywood and wrote music for films and musicals; the best known are *Hans Christian Andersen* (film, 1952), and the musicals *Guys and Dolls* (1950), *The Most Happy Fella* (1956), and *How to Succeed in Business Without Really Trying* (1961). He was three times the recipient of the New York Drama Critics Award for the best musical score. His brother, ARTHUR LOESSER (1894–1969), was a pianist and writer on music, and the author of *Men, Women and Pianos: A Social History* (1954).

LOEVENSTEIN, FEDOR (1901–1947), French painter. Born in Munich, of Czech parents, he settled in Paris in 1923. The bulk of his work was lost in 1940. Shortly before his death, his surviving work – fewer than 40 oils and watercolors –was exhibited at a Paris gallery. His work is characterized by strong intellectual discipline as well as great inventiveness. His idiom is abstract and his work has a dreamlike but firmly controlled quality.

LOEW, ELEAZAR (1758–1837), rabbi in Poland and Hungary. Loew was born in Wodzislav (Poland) and when only 17 years of age was appointed *dayyan* in his native city. At the age of 20 he was appointed rabbi of Pilica (Poland) and in 1800, on the recommendation of Mordecai *Banet, became rabbi of *Trest (Triesch). Subsequently he held positions as district rabbi of *Pilsen (1812–15), *rosh yeshivah* of Trest (1815–20), rabbi of Liptovsky Mikuláš, Slovakia (1821–30), and finally, from 1830 until his death rabbi of Santo (Abaujszanto), Hungary. Loew played a vigorous part in the fight against religious reform, and was an active opponent of Aaron *Chorin. Loew is best known mainly for his many scholarly works in all areas of *halakhah*, which are written with a rational approach, avoiding casuistry, and for his critical commentaries to early works.

Among his halakhic works are *Shemen Roke'aḥ*, 3 volumes of responsa (1788–1902), and under the same title novellae to the tractates *Berakhot, Pesaḥim, Beẓah* (Prague, 1812); *Torat Ḥesed*, on talmudic methodology (Vienna, 1800); *Sha'arei Ḥokhmah*, on various halakhic topics (Prague, 1807); *Zer Zahav*, annotations to *Hai Gaon's *Ha-Mikkaḥ ve-ha-Mimkar* (Vienna, 1800); *Sha'arei De'ah*, on the Shulḥan Arukh, *Yoreh De'ah*, pts. 1 and 2 (1821–28); and *Zikhron Aharon*, on *ḥazakah* ("legal presumption"; 1834). His homiletic works include *Sama de-Ḥayyei* (Warsaw, 1796), *Yavin Shemu'ah* (Prague, 1814), and *Minḥat Erev* (1911).

BIBLIOGRAPHY: Michael, Or, no. 484; L. Muenz, *Rabbi Eleasar, genannt Schemen Rokeach* (1895); A. Schnitzer, *Juedische Kulturbilder* (1904), 45f.; J.J.(L.) Greenwald (Grunwald), *Ha-Yehudim be-Ungarya* (1913), 45; I. Muenz, *Stammtafel des Rabbi Eleasar, genannt Schemen Rokeach* (1926); H. Gold (ed.), *Die Juden und Judengemeinden Maehrens in Vergangenheit und Gegenwart* (1929), 542f.; A. Klein, in: *Nachlath Z'vi*, 7 (1937), 139–47; M.M. Glueck (ed.), Eleazar Loew, *Zikhron Elazar* (1937), introd. 7–18; W.G. Plaut, *The Rise of Reform Judaism* (1963), 35f.

[*Encyclopaedia Hebraica*]

LOEW, IMMANUEL (1854–1944), Hungarian rabbi and scholar. Loew was the son of Leopold *Loew whom he succeeded in 1878 as rabbi of Szeged, Hungary, and whose collected works he published (5 vols., 1889–1900). He studied at the Hochschule fuer die Wissenschaft des Judentums in Berlin and at the Leipzig university. The new synagogue in Szeged, one of the most beautiful in the world, was built in 1903 according to Loew's plans (the architect was L. Baumhorn) and its stained-glass windows were made according to his designs. During the "white terror" and counterrevolution in Hungary (1920–21), Loew was imprisoned for 13 months on the allegation that he had made statements against Admiral Horthy. During his imprisonment he worked on his four-volume work, *Die Flora der Juden* (1924–34). From 1927 he represented the Neolog (non-Orthodox) communities in the upper chamber of the Hungarian parliament and also was a member of the Jewish Agency for Palestine. Soon after his 90th birthday, the Germans occupied Hungary and Loew was first sent to a brick factory in the local ghetto and then put on a deportation train. In Budapest, however, he was freed by Zionist workers. He died that year in Budapest.

Like his father, Loew was a great preacher in the Hungarian language, and several hundred of his sermons were published in four volumes between 1900 and 1939. On the occasion of his congregation's centenary he published (with Z. Kulinyi) the congregation's history (1885) and that of its *ḥevra kaddisha* (with S. Klein, 1887). In 1883 he published a prayer book (in Hungarian) for women, and rendered the Song of Songs and some psalms into the same language.

Loew's fame as a scholar rests above all on his pioneering work in the field of talmudic and rabbinic lexicography and in the study of *realia* (artifacts, such as a coin from talmudic times). He contributed to W. Gesenius' famous Bible dictionary (10th ed., 1886; 11th ed., 1890), and to K. Brockelmann's *Lexicon syriacum* (1895). Loew made critical annotations to S. Krauss' *Griechische und lateinische Lehnwoerter im Talmud, Midrash und Targum* (1899), and to the same author's supplement volume to Kohut's *Arukh ha-Shalem* (1937) and to his *Talmudische Archaeologie* (1910–12) which was dedicated to Loew and thus saved the author many etymological errors. There are also notes of his in J. Theodor-Ḥ. Albeck's edition of *Genesis Rabbah*, 3 pt. 2 (1965), 127–48ff. He also wrote on Jewish folklore. The special direction of Loew's scholarly interest in *realia* is already evident in his doctorate thesis *Aramaeische Pflanzennamen* (1879), and in his *Meleagros aus Gadara und die Flora Aramaea* (1883). Half a century later this line of research found its triumphant achievement in *Die Flora der Juden* (4 vols., 1924–34). Loew systematically uncovered the basis of flora terminology in the Hebrew and Aramaic of different periods and mastered the latest descriptive and terminological methods prevailing in this field of science. He familiarized himself with the literary sources for flora and made meticulous use of manuscript material. He clarified etymologies with the help of Semitic languages, especially Syriac. The result is a flood of light shed on biblical, talmudical, and rabbinical botanical terms; not only the past flora but also that of present-day Israel is brought to life. It was only natural that Loew should proceed to the realm of fauna and of minerals, and in both these fields he published a number of studies in various periodicals and other learned publications. The manuscript of a *Mineralien der Juden*, ready for publication, became a victim of the tragic events of 1944. Loew's other literary remains in these fields passed partly to the National and University Library of Jerusalem and partly to the *Landesrabbinerschule, Budapest. His essays on fauna and minerals were reissued in 1969 (*Fauna und Mineralien der Juden*) together with an introduction by Alexander Scheiber.

BIBLIOGRAPHY: E. Frenkel, in: *Festschrift I. Loew* (1934), 236–55 (a bibl.); idem, in: A. Scheiber (ed.), *Semitic Studies in Memory of I. Loew* (1947), 6–11 (bibl.); A. Scheiber, *ibid.*, 1–6 (Hung.), 357 (bibl.).

[Alexander Scheiber and Menahem Zevi Kaddari]

LOEW, LEOPOLD (**Lipót**; 1811–1875), Hungarian rabbi and scholar, the first Reform rabbi in Hungary. Loew, who was born in Czernahora, Moravia, was a descendant of *Judah Loew b. Bezalel. In his childhood Loew showed talent in music; he studied in Moravian yeshivot, translated Schiller into Hebrew, and also acquired a knowledge of Italian, French, Latin, and Greek. He was ordained as a rabbi by Solomon Judah *Rapoport, Aaron *Chorin, and Low *Schwab, later marrying Schwab's daughter. In 1840 Loew was elected rabbi of Nagykanizsa.

In 1844 he began to deliver his sermons in Hungarian. A strong advocate of Hungarian Jewish emancipation, he argued that the liberation of the Jews should not be made dependent upon abandonment or reform of their religion; in this he opposed the views of the great Hungarian liberator, Louis Kossuth. In 1846 Loew began serving as rabbi of Papa, where he was severely attacked by the Orthodox, who disapproved of his having studied at the Protestant High School and even produced false witnesses that Loew was not ritually observant. During the Hungarian revolution of 1848–49 he served as a chaplain in the army of the Hungarian revolutionaries, spurring them on with inflammatory speeches. Because of his patriotic stand, he was arrested in 1849 and served three months in jail.

From 1850 until his death Loew served as the rabbi of Szeged. Loew was in favor of Reform but insisted that reforms be instituted within the framework of the rabbinic tradition. His viewpoint made it possible for him to participate in the *rabbinical conferences in Breslau in 1845 and Leipzig in 1870. He also wrote a biography of Aaron Chorin, who had approached the cause of Reform in the same spirit. Though he did not participate in the Hungarian Jewish congress of 1868, which had been called to draw up the constitution of Hungarian Jewry and at which Hungarian Jewry was divided into two camps – Reform and Orthodox – he expressed his views on the issues in his *Die Juedischen Wirren in Ungarn* (1868). The medieval form of the Jewish oath was abolished in Hungary on the basis of a lecture he delivered at the Hungarian Academy of Sciences, *A zsidó eskű* (1868). He was first to suggest a Hungarian translation of the Bible for Jews, and published the Book of Joel in the translation of I. Bleuer (in *Magyar Zsinagoga*, 1, 1847). Loew served as the editor of the periodical *Ben-Chananja* from 1858 to 1867. He was the first to deal with the history of Hungarian Jewry; among his works are "Schicksale und Bestrebungen der Juden in Ungarn" and "Kalender und Jahrbuch fuer Israeliten" both in *Jahrbuch des deutschen Elementes in Ungarn* (1846/7) and *Zur neueren Geschichte der Juden in Ungarn* (1874). He contributed such pioneering works in the study of Jewish antiquities and folklore as *Ha-Mafte'aḥ* (1855), *Beitraege zur juedischen Alterthumskunde, I: Graphische Requisiten und Erzeugnisse bei den Juden* (2 vols., 1870–71), and *Lebensalter in der juedischen Literatur* (1875). His collected writings were edited by his son and successor, Immanuel *Loew, under the title *Gesammelte Schriften* (5 vols. 1889–1900).

BIBLIOGRAPHY: A. Hochmuth, *Leopold Loew als Theologe, Historiker und Publizist* (1871); W.N. Loew, *Leopold Loew: A Biography with a Translation of the … Tributes Paid to His Memory…* (1912); I. Loew and Zs. Kulinyi, *A szegedi zsidók* (1885), 172–240; I. Loew, *Gesammelte Schriften*, 5 (1900), 3–19 (bibl.); W. Bacher, in: *Magyar Izrael*, 4 (1911), 90–97; L. Venetianer, in: *Zsidó Plutarchos*, 1 (n.d.), 5–26.

[Alexander Scheiber]

LOEW, MARCUS (1870–1927), U.S. motion picture executive. Born in New York, Loew rose to a powerful position in the American film industry. He began his career in motion pictures by setting up penny arcades in New York City. Loew expanded these electric vaudeville machine parlors to other major U.S. cities and upped the penny ante equipment to nickelodeons, which showed films for five cents. He also began to purchase theaters and convert them into vaudeville-film houses. The idea of combining vaudeville with films proved so lucrative that in 1921 he opened the Loew's State Theater on Broadway with a seating capacity of 3,200. In 1919 he bought Metro Pictures, Inc., and in 1924 acquired Goldwyn Pictures. To eliminate the cost of renting films, Loew came up with the idea of producing films for use in his own theaters. With the appointment of Louis B. Mayer as vice president of the film company, the Metro-Goldwyn-Mayer (MGM) film studio was formed, with Loew's Inc. gaining controlling interest. By 1927 Loew had a chain of 144 deluxe theaters across the country, including several in Canada. At his death, Loew was president of Metro-Goldwyn-Mayer film studios of Hollywood and of Loew's Inc., one of the largest cinema chains in the United States.

BIBLIOGRAPHY: D. Naylor, *American Picture Palaces: The Architecture of Fantasy* (1981); B. Crowther, *The Lion's Share: The Story of an Entertainment Empire* (1957).

[Ruth Beloff (2nd ed.)]

LOEW, MORITZ (1841–1900), German astronomer. Born in Mako, Hungary, Loew joined the University Observatory at Leipzig. He was appointed head of the department in the Prussian Geodetic Institute of Berlin, and later professor. He wrote on the elements of planets and comets; studies on the theory of the transit instrument in the first vertical; and on astronomical-geodetical determinations of geographic positions.

[Arthur Beer]

LOEW-BEER, family of textile manufacturers in *Brno (Bruenn), Czechoslovakia. Three cousins, who originated from *Boskovice, began their career in the *textile industry as wool buyers for the Brno textile factories. In the 1840s various members of the family opened independent spinning-mills. One firm, founded by AARON and JACOB (d. 1866) in 1853, employed 1,200 workers. Another firm was set up by MOSES and later directed by MAX LOEW-BEER (1829–1887), who also established sugar refineries. The firm founded by SAMUEL (d. 1884) was later directed by IGNAZ LOEW-BEER. Other members of the family founded textile firms at the end of the 19th century. The whole family was active in Jewish and public life. A soup kitchen founded by JONAS LOEW-BEER for World War I refugees was taken over by the community in 1924. The various firms remained in existence until the German occupation in 1939.

BIBLIOGRAPHY: H. Heller, *Maehrens Maenner der Gegenwart*, 4 (1890), 102–3; *Jews of Czechoslovakia*, 1 (1968), 413.

[Meir Lamed]

LOEWE, FREDERICK (1904–1988), composer. Born in Vienna, Loewe studied piano with Busoni and d'Albert in Berlin and then began his career as a concert pianist. He went to the United States in 1924, where he soon began composing songs and musical comedies. Loewe's first Broadway shows were not very successful, but his fortunes changed when he met the librettist Alan Jay *Lerner in 1942. Together they wrote some of the most sophisticated theater music of the 20th century. Their first real hit was *Brigadoon* (1947), followed by *Paint Your Wagon* (1951), *My Fair Lady* (1956) based on Bernard Shaw's *Pygmalion,* and the film score for *Gigi* (1958), which won nine Academy Awards. Their final collaboration was the musical *Camelot* (1960). Loewe's music springs from the European operetta tradition, adapted to appeal to an American audience, and he accommodated his musical style to the characters and the location of the story of each play.

BIBLIOGRAPHY: Grove online; L. Gene, *Inventing Champagne: The Worlds of Lerner and Loewe* (1990).

[Naama Ramot (2nd ed.)]

LOEWE, FRITZ PHILIPP (1895–1974) meteorologist. Loewe was born in Berlin and studied law in Grenoble (1913) before World War I service in the German army for which he was awarded the Iron Cross, First Class. After the war he studied physics and geography and became fascinated by flight, meteorology, and mountaineering. He gained his Ph.D. in geography (1923) while working as a scientific assistant at the Potsdam Meteorological Observatory (1922–25). As first head of the Research Flight of the Prussian Meteorological Service based at the Lindenberg Observatory near Berlin (1925–29), he made some 500 flights to heights of 6,000 meters without supplementary oxygen for meteorological research. During this period he took part in the Meteor expedition to the Atlantic Ocean (1925) and studied cosmic radiation in the Swiss Alps. Loewe joined Alfred Wegener's first expedition to Greenland (1929) and the later expedition (1930–31) to "Eismitte" on the center of the Greenland icecap, the first party to spend the winter in this region. Loewe was one of the first scientists to measure the thickness of the ice using seismic waves created by explosions. However, his toes had to be amputated because of frostbite, and Wegener perished on the return journey. Loewe returned to Germany to recuperate but was interned by the Nazis in a concentration camp before he was allowed to leave for England. He joined the staff of the Scott Polar Institute in Cambridge as a research guest in polar meteorology (1934–37). Loewe was appointed reader at the University of Melbourne where he established and directed Australia's first meteorological department (1937–59), founded because of widespread concerns about aeronautical safety. He joined the French Antarctic expedition of Commandant Charcot to Port-Martin in Adélie Land (1951–52), where their hut was destroyed by fire during the winter. Loewe never retired and continued his research and teaching after he ceased to head the department in 1959. He regularly visited the Institute of Polar Studies (now the Byrd Polar Research Institute) in Columbus, Ohio, as Professorial Research Fellow. On behalf of UNESCO he set up a meteorology training school in Pakistan, where he also carried out Himalayan glaciology surveys. He published some 150 scientific papers in his field but the conservatism of the physics professors in Melbourne prevented Loewe from becoming a professor. He was a popular and distinguished teacher who trained the first generation of Australian meteorologists when weather forecasting became crucial for military purposes in World War II. In Australia he raised material and political support for Jewish victims of the Nazis. He died in Melbourne while still at work.

[Michael Denman (2nd ed.)]

LOEWE, HEINRICH (**Eliakim**; 1867–1950), one of the first Zionists in Germany, scholar in Jewish folklore, and librarian. Born in Wanzleben, Germany, into an assimilated family, Loewe was raised without a Jewish education and at the age of 13 began to study in a Protestant high school in Magdeburg. Afterward he studied at Berlin University and at the Hochschule fuer die Wissenschaft des Judentums in Berlin. Together with Shmarya *Levin, Yosef *Lurie, Naḥman *Syrkin, and Leo *Motzkin he established the Zionist group known as the Russian Jewish Scientific Society and was the only one among this group who was born in Germany. In 1892 Loewe founded Jung Israel, the first Zionist group in Germany. He was also among the founders of the Vereinigung Juedischer Studierender, which gave rise in 1914 to the *Kartell Juedischer Verbindungen, the roof organization for Zionist students in Germany. Loewe edited the *Juedische Volkszeitung* in Berlin from 1893 to 1894 and, from 1895 to 1896, the monthly *Zion*.

In 1895 Loewe visited Ereẓ Israel for the first time and became known to *Herzl even before the publication of *Der Judenstaat*. Two years later he returned to Ereẓ Israel with the intention of settling there, but he returned to Europe in August 1897 as a delegate from Ereẓ Israel to the First Zionist Congress. After the Congress he remained in Germany and established the Zionist Federation. From 1899 Loewe worked as a librarian in the University of Berlin. He quickly rose in professional status until he was appointed professor in 1915. From 1902 to 1908 he was the first editor of **Juedische Rundschau*, the central organ of the German Zionists. In 1905 he gave impetus to Joseph *Chasanowich's idea to establish a Jewish national library in Jerusalem by writing a memo to the Seventh Zionist Congress. His proposal was accepted unanimously. Throughout his career he worked for the library and was the moving spirit of the Verein der Freunde der Jerusalem-Bibliothek.

In 1933 Loewe settled in Palestine and assumed the post of librarian of the municipal library Sha'ar Zion in Tel Aviv. In 1948 he prepared a collection of his writings on Zionism formerly published in part under the pseudonym Heinrich Sachse as *Anti-semitismus und Zionismus* (1894) and *Zionistenkongress und Zionismus eine Gefahr?* (1897). He frequently published works in the field of Jewish folklore such as *Die Sprachen der Juden* (1911), *Die Juden in der katholischen Legende* (1912), *Schelme und Narren mit juedischen Kappen* (1920), and *Reste vom alten juedischen Volkshumor* (1922).

BIBLIOGRAPHY: J.L. Weinberg, *Aus der Fruehzeit des Zionismus: Heinrich Loewe* (1946).

[Jacob Rothschild]

LOEWE, HERBERT MARTIN JAMES (1882–1940), English Orientalist. Loewe was born in London, the grandson of

Louis *Loewe. After completing his studies at Cambridge, he lived for a time as a teacher in the Middle East and then held academic appointments in England. After his return from military service in India (1917–19), he became lecturer in rabbinic Hebrew at Oxford, and in 1931 he taught rabbinics at Cambridge and was lecturer in Hebrew at the University of London. For a generation, he was regarded in English academic circles as the representative of Jewish scholarship, in the same way as Israel *Abrahams had been regarded before him. His home in the two university cities was a focus of Jewish life. Within the Jewish community he represented informed and tolerant Orthodoxy, moving freely in liberal (Reform) Jewish circles and collaborating closely with C.G. Montefiore, the founder of Liberal Judaism in England. His works include *A Catalogue of the Aldis Wright* MSS. *in Trinity College, Cambridge* (1926), *"Render unto Caesar"* (1940), *Mediaeval Hebrew Minstrelsy* (1926), *Some Mediaeval Hebrew Poesy* (1927; on the **Zemirot*) and a volume of annotations to Abrahams' and Stokes' *Starrs and Jewish Charters in the British Museum*, 2 vols. (1930–32). He collaborated with C.G. Montefiore in *A Rabbinic Anthology* (1938, 1968^2), a widely used source book.

Herbert Loewe's elder son was RAPHAEL JAMES LOEWE (1919-), who wrote widely on Jewish subjects, in particular on the English Christian Hebraists of the Middle Ages. He was formerly Goldsmith Professor of Hebrew at University College, London.

BIBLIOGRAPHY: *The Times* (London, Oct. 12, 1940), 6; JC (Oct. 18, 1940), 5.

[Cecil Roth]

LOEWE, JOEL (**Bril**; 1762–1802), Hebrew writer, grammarian, and biblical exegete in the Moses *Mendelssohn circle in Berlin. Born in Berlin, Loewe studied under Isaac *Satanow and soon joined Mendelssohn's enlightenment movement. Together with Aharon *Wolfsohn, he edited **Ha-Me'assef* (1784–97), and was a frequent contributor to it. He signed his Hebrew works בריל (Ben R. Yehudah Leib Loewe). Mendelssohn helped him obtain a position as tutor in David *Friedlaender's household. In 1791, he was appointed principal of the Wilhelms-Schule in Breslau, serving in this capacity until his death.

Loewe's major contribution is his introduction and commentary to Mendelssohn's German translation of Psalms (1785–88), which includes a study on the structure and style of Hebrew poetry and on the history of ancient Jewish music. He wrote *Ammudei Lashon*, an attempt at a scientific grammar of biblical Hebrew of which only the first part was published (Berlin, 1794). He took an active part in Mendelssohn's Bible translation project, writing, in addition to his work on Psalms, commentaries to Ecclesiastes, Jonah, and with Wolfsohn, the Song of Songs. Loewe was the first Haskalah writer to publish original epigrams in the style of the Book of Proverbs, and was the first to translate the Passover *Haggadah* into German.

BIBLIOGRAPHY: P. Sandler, *Ha-Be'ur la-Torah shel Moshe Mendelssohn ve-Si'ato, Hithavvuto ve-Hashpa'ato* (1940), index; Fuenn, Keneset, 433f.; Lachower, Sifrut, 1 (1963^{12}), 79f., 146; Zeitlin, Bibliotheca, 215; Waxman, Literature, 3 (1960^2), 127.

LOEWE, LOUIS (**Ha-Levi, Eliezer**; 1809–1888), Orientalist. Loewe was born in Zuelz, Germany, and studied at the yeshivot of Lissa and Pressburg; later he specialized in Oriental languages at the universities of Vienna and Berlin. In 1833 he moved to London. At the suggestion of the scholarly Duke of Sussex (son of King George III) and of several leading French and English Orientalists, Loewe decided in 1837 to undertake an expedition to Egypt, in preparation for which he had mastered Egyptology and the Nubian and Ethiopic languages. On this journey he deciphered various inscriptions on the banks of the Nile, at Thebes, Alexandria, Cairo, and elsewhere.

From Egypt he proceeded to Palestine, but had the misfortune to arrive there during the revolt of the Druze; when he was in Safed they robbed him and destroyed 13 of his notebooks, already prepared for publication. He stayed in Shechem for a short time, studying Samaritan customs and literature. In Damascus he acquired a valuable collection of rare ancient coins. In Constantinople he studied the customs of the Karaite community and acquired many rare books and manuscripts of this sect. His impressions of his visit to Palestine were published in a series of letters in the German-Jewish weekly *Allgemeine Zeitung des Judenthums* for the year 1839 (in an abridged Hebrew translation by M.A. Guenzburg in his *Devir*, vol. 1, 1844).

From 1839, he accompanied Montefiore on all his journeys as his interpreter and secretary in Oriental languages, including Hebrew, and was Montefiore's devoted assistant in all his public activities. At the time of the Damascus Affair (1840) he accompanied Montefiore, Adolphe Crémieux, and Salomon Munk who went to Egypt and Turkey in an effort to intervene on behalf of the Jews. His command of Arabic enabled him to suggest a change in the wording of Muhammad Ali's firman, which resulted in the substitution of the term "honorable acquittal" for "pardon" (with its implication of guilt). Loewe accompanied Montefiore on visits to Russia in 1846 and 1872 and also on five trips to Palestine.

On his return to London in 1839 the Duke of Sussex offered him the post of director of the Oriental section of his extensive library, a position which he held for about 15 years. From 1856 to 1858 he was principal of *Jews' College in London. At Brighton in 1861 he established a school for Jewish boys, many of whom came from abroad. From 1869 to 1888 he was principal of Ohel Moshe vi-Yhudit, a theological seminary founded in 1869 by Moses Montefiore at Ramsgate. Loewe edited the *Diaries of Sir Moses and Lady Montefiore* (2 vols., 1890). His other works include *The Origin of the Egyptian Language* (1837); an English translation of and lengthy introduction to *Efes Damim* by I.B. Levinsohn (*No Blood*, 1841); an English translation of *Ha-Kuzari ha-Sheni o Matteh Dan* by David Nieto (1842); and *A Dictionary of the Circassian Language* (1854).

BIBLIOGRAPHY: J.H. Loewe, *A Descriptive Catalogue of a Portion of the Library of the Late Dr. Louis Loew* (1895), introduction; J. Kurrein, in: JJGL, 27 (1926), 148–61; I. Trywaks and E. Steinmann, *Sefer Me'ah Shanah* (1938), 97–121; A. Yaari, *Iggerot Ereẓ Yisrael* (1943), 379–408; *Enẓiklopedyah shel ha-Ẓiyyonut ha-Datit*, 3 (1965), 95–98. **ADD. BIBLIOGRAPHY:** ODNB online.

[Gedalyah Elkoshi]

LOEWE, LUDWIG (1837–1886) and **ISIDOR** (1848–1910), German industrialists. They were born in Heiligenstadt, Thuringia, sons of an indigent teacher. Ludwig Loewe founded in 1869 his first factory, L. Loewe & Co. Commanditgesellschaft, and became a wealthy machinery merchant in Berlin. In 1860 he was elected to the city council, in 1876 to the Prussian Landtag, and in 1878 to the Reichstag; he was first associated with the Fortschrittspartei and later with the Deutsch-Freisinnige Partei. In 1870 Ludwig visited the United States and studied modern American business and mass production methods. By introducing these into his sewing machine factory he set a pattern which led to a vast improvement in German industrial techniques. In 1872 he began to manufacture rifles for the German army and later exported them on a large scale.

Isidor Loewe joined his brother's firm in 1875 and became its general director in 1886. After Ludwig's death he effected a merger with the Mauser factory in order to fulfill orders for over a million rifles for Prussia and Turkey. In 1892 the antisemite Hermann *Ahlwardt wrote several scurrilous pamphlets on "Jew rifles" as a symbol of a "Jewish world conspiracy," accusing Loewe of being a traitor to Germany by using such poor materials that the rifles were a greater hazard to the user than to his enemy. Ahlwardt was charged with libel and sentenced to a term of imprisonment. Further mergers resulted in 1896 in the formation of the Deutsche Waffen- und Munitionsfabrik A.G., with the largest rifle factory in the world. In 1892, together with an American company, Isidor Loewe established a firm which built electric streetcars for German and Belgian cities. He also made automobiles and began to manufacture aircraft.

BIBLIOGRAPHY: K. Zielinziger, *Juden in der deutschen Wirtschaft* (1930); F. Wegeleben, *Die Rationalisierung im deutschen Werkzeugmaschinenbau* (1924). **ADD. BIBLIOGRAPHY:** NDB, 15 (1987), 77–78.

[Samuel Aaron Miller / Bjoern Siegel (2nd ed.)]

LOEWE, VICTOR (1871–1933), German historian and archivist. Born in Laurahuette, Silesia, Loewe became keeper of the State Archive at Breslau. Loewe's historical contributions include studies on German and Prussian administrative history of the 17th and 18th centuries. Much of his work was devoted to German historical bibliography, both national and regional. Among his numerous books are *Buecherkunde der deutschen Geschichte* (1903², 1913⁴); *Deutsche Geschichte* (1931); and *Das deutsche Archivwesen – Seine Geschichte und Organisation* (1921).

LOEWENSON, JEAN (Hans; Lavi, Yoḥanan; 1898–1966), Israel author and journalist. Born in Toruń, Poland, Loewenson was taken to Switzerland in 1907. After working as a newspaper correspondent in Paris and Geneva, he settled in Jerusalem in 1934. From 1936 he was correspondent for Havas, and then for Agence France-Presse until 1949. Later he worked for the French publications department of the Jewish Agency. Loewenson's literary quality shows best in his translations from German into French. His knowledge of Hebrew and of Jewish philosophy enabled him to produce outstanding versions of works by Martin *Buber and Gershom *Scholem. Loewenson's original poetical and philosophical prose works include *Variations sur le destin* (1944), *Femmes en Israël* (1950), *Virtualités* (1961), and *Pièces pour une armature* (1966).

BIBLIOGRAPHY: Gottgetreu, in: *Mitteilungsblatt* (Feb. 11, 1966); Catane, in: *Israelitisches Wochenblatt fuer die Schweiz* (April 1, 1966); idem, *Gazette de Lausanne* (April 5–6, 1966).

[Moshe Catane]

LOEWENSTAMM, 18th-century family of Dutch rabbis. ARYEH LOEB BEN SAUL LOEWENSTAMM (1690–1755) was born in Cracow, where his father SAUL had been rabbi; in 1707 Saul was appointed Ashkenazi rabbi of Amsterdam in succession to Moses Judah b. Kalonymus Kohen (known as Leib Ḥarif), but he died in Glogau on the way to take up his position. That same year Aryeh Loeb married Miriam, the oldest daughter of Ẓevi Hirsch Ashkenazi (the Ḥakham Ẓevi), then rabbi of Altona, Hamburg, and Wandsbeck. He accompanied his father-in-law to Amsterdam but later went to Poland, where he was appointed rabbi of Dukla and subsequently of Tarnopol (1720). This appointment was obtained by the intervention of the government, influenced by Loewenstamm's relatives, to have the incumbent deposed so that he could be appointed. As a result, his appointment was not received favorably by the community, and he himself was deposed shortly thereafter. He served as rabbi of Rzeszow (1724–28) and then of Glogau (1734–39), where he was involved in the dispute with regard to Moses Ḥayyim *Luzzatto, against whom he issued a ban in 1735, at the request of the rabbis of Venice. In 1740 he was appointed rabbi of Amsterdam, where he remained for the rest of his life.

Loewenstamm left no works. Some of his responsa, novellae, and notes, however, are to be found in the responsa of his father-in-law (no.76); in Mordecai of Dusseldorf's *Ma'amar Mordekhai* (Bruenn, 1790; nos. 62, 63); in David Meldola's *Divrei David* (Amsterdam, 1753; nos. 10, 53, 81); and in his son Saul's *Binyan Ari'el* (see below). In 1711 he published, together with Shemariah b. Jacob of Grodno, a second edition of the responsa of Moses Isserles, to which he added a *kunteres aḥaron*. He is also mentioned in the *takkanot* and minutes of the *Council of Four Lands. He took an active part in the Emden-Eybeschuetz controversy. Naturally siding with his brother-in-law, Jacob *Emden (the son of Ashkenazi), he was unsparing in his language against Eybeschuetz (see J. Emden, *Sefat Emet* (1876), 16).

Loewenstamm had two sons: one, known as Hirschel b. Aryeh Loeb *Levin, was rabbi of Berlin. The other, SAUL (1717–1790), born in Rzeszow, succeeded his father as rabbi of Amsterdam, having previously served as rabbi of Lakacz, Hungary, and Dubno, Lithuania. In Amsterdam he devoted himself to the yeshivah established by his father. Ḥ.J.D. Azulai, who met him in Amsterdam, refers to him in glowing terms. In 1754 he participated in the session of the Council of Four Lands in Jaroslaw. Saul Loewenstamm's most famous work is his *Binyan Ari'el* (Amsterdam, 1778), which is divided into three parts: on the Pentateuch, on the Five Scrolls, and comments on various talmudic passages. His glosses to tractate *Niddah* were published in the Amsterdam edition of the Talmud (1765). Saul was succeeded as rabbi of Amsterdam by his son JACOB MOSES (1747–1815), previously rabbi in Filehne (Poznania) and Cleves. When the "progressive" congregation Adat Yeshurun appointed as their rabbi Aaron Moses Isaac Graanboom, a proselyte whose father was also a proselyte, Loewenstamm debarred him from the rabbinate because of his association with Reform tendencies. Jacob's son, JEHIEL ARYEH LOEB (d. 1807) was appointed rabbi of Leeuwarden, and died in his father's lifetime.

BIBLIOGRAPHY: Michael, Or, no 535; A.L. Landshuth, *Toledot Anshei ha-Shem u-Fe'ulatam be-Adat Berlin* (1884), 72–75, 111, 118f.; Ḥ.N. Dembitzer, *Kelilat Yofi*, 1 (1888), 128a–136b; 2 (1893), 83a–b; S. Buber, *Anshei Shem* (1895), 37–40, 234; I.T. Eisenstadt and S. Wiener, *Da'at Kedoshim* (1897–98), 105f., 113, 121f.; J. Emden, *Megillat Sefer*, ed. by D. Kahana (1897), 65–69, 154; P. Pesis, *Ir Dubna ve-Rabbaneha* (1902), 22f.; H.Z. Margoles, *Dubna Rabbati* (1910), 14f.; J. Maarsen, in: HHY, 6 (1922), 15–19, 134–58; Z. Horowitz, *Kitvei ha-Ge'onim* (1928), 74–81, 115, 136; idem, *Le-Korot ha-Kehillot be-Polanyah* (1969), 138, 181–96; Halpern, Pinkas, index, s.v. *Aryeh Loeb b. Sha'ul*; idem, *Yehudim ve-Yahadut be-Mizraḥ Eiropah* (1969), 396f.; EG (1955), 31–34; *Rzeszów Jews Memorial Book* (1967), 43ff.

[Louis Isaac Rabinowitz]

LOEWENSTEIN, BERNHARD (1821–1889), rabbi, preacher, and pioneer of the Reform movement. Born in Mezhirech, western Poland, he was active in spreading *Haskalah and the ideas of the Reform movement. On the recommendation of Ludwig *Philippson, in 1845 he was appointed preacher and headmaster of a school in Liptó-Szent-Miklós, Hungary. In 1857 he became rabbi of the community of Bucovice in Moravia. His most important congregational work was done in Lemberg, where in 1862 he was officially elected rabbi and preacher of the community, and also served as teacher of religion at the high school and registrar of the community. His sermons attracted a large congregation, occasionally including even non-Jews. Loewenstein was involved in the opening of a new type of *talmud torah*, called Ohel Moshe, where Jewish and secular studies were taught. This was closed, however, after two years because of the opposition of the Orthodox. He was also active in the *Shomer Israel society which sought to disseminate culture among the mass of Jews in order to bring them closer to the culture of their surroundings. In addition to sermons, he published a collection of poems entitled *Juedische Klaenge* (Bruenn, 1862), translated into Hebrew by Judah Rohatiner. His son, Nathan *Loewenstein, was an assimilationist leader in Galicia.

BIBLIOGRAPHY: N. Samuely, *Rabbiner und Prediger Bernhard Loewenstein* (1889); Z. Karl, in: EG, 4 (1956), 439–40; J. Tenenbaum, *Galitsye Mayn Alte Heym* (1952), index.

[Moshe Landau]

LOEWENSTEIN, KARL (1891–1973), U.S. political scientist. Loewenstein practiced law in his native Munich and lectured at the university there from 1931 to 1933. He immigrated to the United States in 1934 and two years later became professor of jurisprudence and political science at Amherst College and in 1961 emeritus professor. In 1956 he was appointed professor of law at the University of Munich. During and after World War II, he served first as special assistant to the attorney general (1942–44) and then as legal adviser to the U.S. Military Government in Germany (1945–50). Lowenstein wrote extensively, in three languages, in the fields of public law and comparative government on European and American political systems. His earliest work, *Volk und Parlament nach der Staatsauffassung der franzoesischen Nationalversammlung von 1789* (1922) remains a standard work in the subject. His major work deals with U.S. constitutional law and practice, *Verfassungsrecht und Verfassungspraxis der Vereinigten Staaten* (1959). He also wrote a political science textbook *Political Power and the Governmental Process* (1957), *Hitler's Germany* (1939), *Brazil under Vargas* (1942), *Die Monarchie im modernen Staat* (1952), and many others, as well as numerous articles, some of which are collected in his book *Beitraege zur Staatsoziologie* (1961).

[Edwin Emanuel Gutmann]

LOEWENSTEIN, KURT (1902–1973), Zionist journalist and essayist. Born in Danzig, he studied law and economics at Breslau and Berlin universities and played a leading role in the German pre-Zionist youth movement Jung-Juedischer Wanderbund. Later he was closely associated with the Zionistische Vereinigung fuer Deutschland, serving as secretary for the Rhineland-Westphalia district; he contributed to *Die Juedische Rundschau* of Berlin, joining the editorial board in August 1933. In the following years he devoted much attention to youth education and vocational training of *ḥaluẓim*. He succeeded Robert Weltsch as the editor-in-chief of *Die Juedische Rundschau* before its final closure by the Nazi authorities in November 1938, but edited the only Jewish newspaper after 1938, *Juedisches Nachrichtenblatt*. In 1939, after a couple of journeys for the Palaestina-Amt 1935–36, Loewenstein settled in Ereẓ Israel, where he worked for various organizations of Jewish immigrants from Central Europe. In 1960, he became deputy editor-in-chief of *MB* (*Mitteilungsblatt*), the weekly of the organization of Jewish immigrants from Central Europe. Many of his articles were highly critical of official policy.

Loewenstein's analytical gifts also found expression in a number of major essays, some of which appeared in the *Bulletin of the Leo Baeck Institute*.

ADD. BIBLIOGRAPHY: *Biographisches Handbuch der deutschsprachigen Emigration nach 1933*, vol. 1 (1999), 456.

[Erich Gottgetreu]

LOEWENSTEIN, LEOPOLD (1843–1924), German rabbi and historian. Loewenstein, who was born in Gailingen, south Baden, studied at the University of Wuerzburg and with Ezriel *Hildesheimer in Eisenstadt. He served as district rabbi in Gailingen (1872–87) and then in Baden (1887–1924). He made important contributions to the study of German-Jewish history in his *Geschichte der Juden am Bodensee* (1879), *Geschichte der Juden in der Kurpfalz* (1895), *Geschichte der Juden von der babylonischen Gefan genschaft bis zur Gegenwart* (1904), *Familie Aboab* (1905), and *Zur Geschichte der Juden in Fuerth* (3 vols., 1909–13; repr. 1967), among other works. From 1899 to 1904 he edited the *Blaetter fuer juedische Geschichte und Literatur,* a monthly supplement to the Orthodox Jewish newspaper published in Mainz, *Der Israelit.*

BIBLIOGRAPHY: ZHB, 22 (1919), 71–76, bibl.; Wininger, Biog.

[Michael A. Meyer]

LOEWENSTEIN (Von Opoka), NATHAN (1859–1929), lawyer and political leader, born in Bucovice, Moravia. Loewenstein was the son of the preacher of Lemberg, Bernhard *Loewenstein. He became leader of the assimilationists of Galicia, and editor of the Polish nationalist-oriented weekly *Ojczyzna.* Between 1881 and 1886 he was a member of the community council, the municipality of Lemberg, and the Galician Sejm (parliament). From 1907 he was a deputy to the Austrian parliament as a member of the "Polish club." In 1906 he conducted an inquiry into the living conditions of the Jews of Galicia which served as the basis for his speech in the Galician Sejm (1907) on the gravity of the economic situation. During the parliamentary elections of 1911 there were bloody clashes in *Drogobych (Drohobycz) between his supporters and Zionist opponents over the question of his candidacy; the army intervened, and a number of Jews were killed. Loewenstein withdrew his candidacy, but after a few months he ran again and was reelected, retaining his seat until World War I. With the creation of independent Poland, he was automatically given a seat in the Polish Sejm, as deputy of the region where elections could not be held since there was a military and political struggle between the Poles and Ukrainians over the control of eastern Galicia. In the first Sejm he was prominent for his conservative approach as a landowner and an assimilationist, ignoring the Jewish deputies' campaign on behalf of the needy Jewish population. Having lost public support, he retired from political life after the elections of 1922. Loewenstein gained note at the *Steiger trial (1924–25) for his brilliant speeches in defense of the accused and his resolute struggle against the authorities, who introduced false evidence into their indictment. Loewenstein wrote a book on the Steiger affair, *O sprawe Steigera,* which was published in 1926.

BIBLIOGRAPHY: *Almanach Żydowski* (1937).

[Moshe Landau]

LOEWENSTEIN, RUDOLPH MAURICE (1898–1976), psychoanalyst and psychoanalytic theoretician. Loewenstein, who was born in Lodz, Poland, worked in Berlin from 1923 to 1925, and in Paris from 1925 until the outbreak of World War II, when he served with distinction in the French army. In France, in 1926, along with Marie Bonaparte and René Laforgue, he was one of the major founders of the Societé psychanalytique de Paris. As one of the SPP's main teachers, he trained some of the people who would later be regarded as the second generation of leading French psychologists, such as Daniel Lagache and Jacques Lacan.

Loewenstein settled in the United States in 1943. Together with Heinz *Hartmann and Ernst *Kris, Loewenstein staked out important aspects of psychoanalytic theory as propounded by *Freud, and developed them further, particularly in the field of ego psychology. In 1951 Loewenstein published, in French and English, *Christians and Jews: a Psychoanalytic Study.* In this he traced the historical and cultural roots of antisemitism. He viewed Christians and Jews as a mutually interdependent pair and suggested that the impossibly difficult ethic of the Christian religion may make the use of the Jew as a scapegoat a necessity for the Christian. Loewenstein collaborated with Princess Marie Bonaparte in translating some of Freud's works into French, and edited a series of psychoanalytic essays, *Drives, Affects and Behavior,* published in the princess's honor in 1953. He was an early co-editor of the annual *Psychoanalytic Study of the Child,* and served as president of both the New York Psychoanalytic Society and the American Psychoanalytic Association. *Practice and Precept in Psychoanalytic Technique: Selected Papers of Rudolph M. Loewenstein* was published in 1982.

BIBLIOGRAPHY: A. Grinstein, *Index of Psychoanalytic Writings* 3 (1958), s.v.

[Ruth Beloff (2nd ed.)]

LOEWENSTEIN-STRASHUNSKY, JOEL DAVID (1816–1850), *ḥazzan.* Born in Lemberg, he was the son of the *ḥazzan* of Vilna, Ẓevi Hirsch Loewenstein. At an early age, he became known for his fine voice and his mastery of the violin. After the death of his father in 1830, the 15-year-old lad succeeded him as *ḥazzan* and became known as "Der Vilner Balabesl" (the Little Householder of Vilna). After 1839 he began studying with the composer Moniuszko. In 1842, Loewenstein was invited to Warsaw where he gave recitals accompanied by a chorus and orchestra, which deeply impressed his audience comprised of the town's aristocratic and wealthy classes. The passage from the narrow ghetto world to a cosmopolitan atmosphere produced a mental shock on Loewenstein. Legend attributes it to a tragic infatuation with a Polish woman singer. He went into "voluntary exile" and for several years wandered through the communities of Central Europe, appearing in synagogues only on rare occasions. His life became the subject of legends and literary works including Mark Orenstein's *Der Vilner Balabesl* (Yid., 1908), and J.J. Wohl's *La-Menaẓẓe'aḥ bi-Neginot* (in *Aḥi'asaf,* 7 (1899), 177–97). Several of his prayer melodies have been preserved; *Ve-Havi'enu le-Shalom,* for example, was published by A. Nadel in *Ost und West* (5 (1905), 103–6).

BIBLIOGRAPHY: Sendrey, Music, 3533, 5678–84; Idelsohn, Music, 299–302; Ḥ.N. Steinschneider, in: *Talpiyyot* (1895), pt. 12, 8–13; E.B., in: *Ost und West*, 5 (1905), 102–8; Y. Appel, *Be-Tokh Reshit ha-Teḥiyyah* (1936), 565–77; M.S. Geshuri, in: *Ba-Mishor*, 1 (1940).

[*Hebrew Encyclopaedia*]

LOEWENTHAL, EDUARD (1836–1917), German political theorist. Born in Ernsbach, Prussia, Loewenthal advocated a new religion based on scientific truth and rejecting metaphysical concepts. He expounded his ideas in *System und Geschichte des Naturalismus* (1861, 1897[6]; *System and History of Nature*, 1882) which achieved considerable popularity. He founded the Cogitant religious society to propagate his views in 1865 and in 1869 formed the European Union, a pan-European society dedicated to the abolition of war. Following the outbreak of the Franco-Prussian War in 1870, Loewenthal was forced to leave Prussia but he returned in the following year to reorganize the European Union with a program of a world court and the compulsory arbitration of disputes. In 1874 he was forced to leave Prussia for a second time but continued to preach his pacifist philosophy abroad. He was nominated for the Nobel Peace Prize toward the end of his life but, to his chagrin, was not given the award.

BIBLIOGRAPHY: E. Loewenthal, *Mein Lebenswerk…* (1910); Wininger, Biog, 4 (1925) s.v., includes bibliography; EJ, s.v., includes bibliography.

LOEWENTHAL, JOHANN JAKOB (1810–1876), Hungarian chess master. Loewenthal found refuge in England after the abortive 1848 Hungarian revolution. He was recognized as a leading player as a result of his play in 1851 in a very strong London tournament won by Anderssen. He was successful in match play and wrote prolifically in the chess press.

LOEWENTHAL, ZDENKO (1914–), Yugoslav editor and historian of medicine. Born in Grabovac, Yugoslavia, Loewenthal directed the State Publishing House for Medical Literature, and from 1959 was lecturer in the History of Medicine at the Belgrade Medical Faculty. Loewenthal also headed the historical department of the Yugoslav Jewish Federation. He edited *Crimes of the Fascist Invaders Against the Yugoslav Jews* and *Jewish Almanac, 1954–1964*. He was the *Encyclopaedia Judaica* departmental editor for Balkan literature.

LOEWI, OTTO (1873–1961), pharmacologist and Nobel laureate in physiology and medicine. Loewi was born in Frankfurt on the Main but became a U.S. citizen in 1946. He graduated in medicine at the University of Strasbourg (then in Germany). After initial appointments in the universities of Marburg and Vienna he became professor of pharmacology at the University of Graz, Austria (1909–38). After the German invasion he was imprisoned, deprived of his possessions (including his Nobel Prize money), and allowed to leave. After working in Brussels and Oxford (1939–40), he was appointed research professor at New York University College of Medicine. Loewi's initial contributions concerned carbohydrate and nitrogen metabolism but his main research interest was in the sympathetic nervous system. He proved that nerve impulses in the parasympathetic nervous system are transmitted by acetylcholine and, with his collaborators, he established that nerve impulses in the sympathetic nervous system in general are mediated through chemical transmission. He was awarded the Nobel Prize (jointly with Sir Henry Dale) in 1936 for this work. His honors included foreign membership in the Royal Society (London). The Austrian government issued a stamp to commemorate the centenary of his birth.

[Michael Denman (2nd ed.)]

LOEWINGER, DAVID SAMUEL (1904–), Hungarian biblical and talmudic scholar and bibliographer. Loewinger was born in Debrecen, Hungary. While still a student he published with D. Friedmann the *Alphabet of Ben Sira* (1926) from a manuscript and *Darkhei ha-Nikkud ve-ha-Neginot* (1929, 1969[2]), ascribed to Moses ha-Nakdan. He also contributed the commentary on Habbakuk to A. Kahana's edition of the Bible (1930). From 1931 he lectured at the Budapest rabbinical seminary on Bible and Talmud and became its director in 1942. After World War II he was responsible for the reconstruction of the seminary and the resumption of its scholarly activities. In the prewar years Loewinger was one of the editors of *Ha-Soker* (1933–40) and **Magyar Zsidó Szemle* and also edited a number of jubilee volumes, e.g., on S. *Hevesi (*Emlékkony*, Hg. and Heb., 1934), E. Mahler (*Dissertationes in honorem Dr. E. Mahler*, 1937), M. Guttmann (*Jewish Studies in Memory of M. Guttmann*, 1946), and I. Goldziher (*I. Goldziher Memorial Volume* 1, 1948). In *Germánia prófétája* ("The Prophet of Germany," 1947) Loewinger attempted to trace Germany's Nazi antisemitic ideology to F. Nietzsche. With A. *Scheiber he published *Ginzei Kaufmann* (*Genizah Publications in Memory of D. Kaufmann*, 1949).

After immigrating to Israel in 1950, Loewinger became the scientific secretary and then director of the Institute of Microfilms of Hebrew Manuscripts at the National and University Library in Jerusalem. He was also associated with various projects relating to the Bible text. He specialized in the problems of Bible manuscripts, particularly of the famous Bible codex *Keter Aram Ẓova* ("Aleppo Codex"; in *Textus*, 1 (1960), 59–111). With others he prepared several manuscript catalogs, which were published by the Institute, including the catalog of the Hebrew manuscripts in the Vatican library (list of photocopies in the Institute, part 3: *Hebrew Manuscripts in the Vatican*, Jerusalem, 1968, Heb.). With B.D. Weinryb he published *Catalogue of the Hebrew Manuscripts in the Library of the Juedisch-Theologisches Seminar in Breslau* (1965).

LOEWINSON-LESSING, FRANZ YULYEVICH (1861–1939), Russian geologist, pioneer of magmatic petrology. Loewinson-Lessing occupied the chair of geology, petrology, and mineralogy first at the University of Dorpat (now Tartu), Estonia, and from 1902 until his retirement in 1930, at the Polytechnic Institute of St. Petersburg (Leningrad). In 1925 he was elected a member of the Soviet Academy of Sciences, where he was appointed director of the newly established Petrographical Institute. As early as 1897, in a paper presented to the international geological congress held in St. Petersburg, Loewinson-Lessing introduced a chemical classification of igneous rocks. This was followed by shorter papers on petrochemistry, in which he discussed the role of assimilation in the origin of magmatic rocks and applied the "phase rule" of physical chemistry to substantiate his synthetic-liquational theory of differentiation. In his later years he also dealt with the physical properties of rocks and the tectonic movements of igneous masses. The two books on petrography which he published in 1923, *Uspekhi petrografii v Rossii* ("Advances in Petrography in Russia") and *Voedeniye v geologiyu* ("Introduction to Geology"), became standard textbooks in the U.S.S.R.

BIBLIOGRAPHY: P.I. Lebedev, *Akademik P. Yu. Loewinson-Lessing kak teoretik petrografii* (1947); A.A. Zvorykin (ed.), *Biograficheskiy slovar deyateley yestestvoznaniya i tekhniki*, 1 (1958), 502–3.

[Leo Picard]

LOEWISOHN, SOLOMON (1789–1821), Hebrew writer. Born in Mor, Hungary, he received a Jewish education but at the same time studied secular subjects in a Capuchin monastery. With the aid of his relative Solomon Rosenthal, a wealthy scholar, he studied in Prague at a yeshivah and at the university. In 1811 and 1812 he published two grammatical studies that were collected and annotated by A.B. Lebensohn and J. Behak under the title *Meḥkerei Lashon* (1849). He wrote his first important poem, an elegy on the death of his friend Baruch *Jeiteles, in 1814.

In Prague Loewisohn eked out a meager living by giving private lessons. But the five years between 1815 and 1820 were the most productive and the most "affluent" years of his life. He became proofreader and counselor of Anton von *Schmid. After 1820, he became mentally ill. Insanity led to his untimely death. He published his chief work in 1816, *Meliẓat Yeshurun*, the first aesthetic interpretation of the Bible in the Hebrew language. It discusses in detail various poetic devices including allegory, irony, metaphor, and hyperbole. The work is prefaced by a remarkable hymn to beauty and poetry. Loewisohn allotted 27 pages of his book to an analysis of the Song of Songs which he regarded as a love song of King Solomon. Loewisohn also used non-biblical passages to illustrate figures of speech. In the chapter on apostrophe he quoted from the second part of *King Henry IV* (Act 3, Scene 1) – the first translation of Shakespeare into Hebrew. In 1819 he published *Meḥkerei Areẓ*, the first Hebrew geographical handbook for the biblical period. It utilized Josephus, Eusebius, Pliny, and Strabo. Translated into German two years after its publication, the book served as a handbook for generations of readers, developed a geographical terminology, and pioneered the way for utilization of rabbinic sources.

Loewisohn had also a keen interest in Jewish liturgy. He annotated and translated the *kinot* and also annotated the *Shir ha-Yiḥud* ("Hymn of Unity") and wrote a preface on the value of prayer for the *siddur* of Judah Leib *Ben Zeev (1816). Loewisohn also wrote in German and published several articles in the periodical *Sulamith*, and a history of the Jews, *Vorlesungen ueber die neuere Geschichte der Juden* ("Lectures on Recent Jewish History," 1820) which was praised by H. *Graetz.

BIBLIOGRAPHY: S. Klein, *Toledot Ḥakirat Ereẓ Yisrael ba-Sifrut ha-Ivrit ve-ha-Kelalit* (1937), 74–80; J. Fichmann, *Anshei-Besorah* (1938), 50–56; Ḥ.N. Schapira, *Toledot ha-Sifrut ha-Ivrit ha-Ḥadashah* (1939), 454–78; Schwartz, in: *Moznayim* (1963), 373–83; J.L. Landau, *Short Lectures on Hebrew Literature* (1938), index; Waxman, Literature, 3 (1960), 147–53. **ADD. BIBLIOGRAPHY:** T. Cohen, in: *Bikoret u-Farshanutt*, 6 (1974), 17–28.

[Eisig Silberschlag]

LOEWITH, KARL (1897–1973), German philosopher of Jewish origin. His teachers were E. *Husserl, M. *Geiger, and M. Heidegger in philosophy, and H. Spemann in biology. From 1928 he was privatdocent at Marburg University; from 1934 to 1936 a Rockefeller fellow at Rome; then professor at Sendai, Japan; from 1941 at the Hartford Theological Seminary; from 1949 at the New School for Social Research, New York; from 1952 at Heidelberg, Germany. Loewith's philosophy has its main non-contemporary sources in Hegel and in the development of thought after Hegel, which was one of the main subjects of his studies. His thinking shows the influence of Nietzsche and of Heidegger, whose existentialist-historicist ontology was later heavily criticized by Loewith. He tries to move back from modern thought with its anthropocentricism – through its Christian (biblical-Augustinian) origins – toward a predominantly Aristotelian horizon of thought: the horizon of a pure theory being knowledge for knowledge's sake – theory of nature (including human nature) and of the "cosmos" in its eternal being and becoming. Thus searching for the lost way of a really cosmological – and in Kantian language, "dogmatical" – philosophy, Loewith confronts the Greek *logos* of the cosmos with modern thinking in two papers presented in 1960 and 1964 to the Heidelberg Academy; and he further elaborates this search in his book on metaphysics from Descartes to Nietzsche, the last chapter of which deals with Spinoza's "Deus sive natura." Loewith's books include *Das Individuum in der Rolle des Mitmenschen* (1928); *Kierkegaard und Nietzsche* (1936); *Nietzsches Philosophie der ewigen Wiederkehr des Gleichen* (1935); *Jacob Burckhardt* (1956); *Von Hegel zu Nietzsche* (1941; *From Hegel to Nietzsche*, 1964); *Meaning in History* (1949), later published in German as *Weltgeschichte und Heilsgeschehen* (1953); *Heidegger, Denker in duerftiger Zeit* (1953); *Wissen, Glaube und Skepsis* (1956); *Gesammelte Abhandlungen zur Kritik der geschichtlichen Existenz* (1960); *Vortraege und Abhandlungen zur Kritik der christlichen Ueberlieferung* (1966); *Nature, History and Existentialism* (1966), a collection of Loewith's essays; *Gott, Mensch und Welt in der Metaphysik von Descartes bis zu Nietzsche* (1967); *"Philosophie der Vernunft und Religion der Offenbarung in H. Cohens Religionsphilosophie"* (*Sitzungsberichte der Heidelberger Akademie der Wissenschaften*, 1968).

BIBLIOGRAPHY: *Natur und Geschichte: Karl Loewith zum 70 Geburtstag* (1967).

[Otto Immanuel Spear]

LOEWY, EMANUEL (1857–1938), Austrian classical archaeologist. Loewy was born in Vienna and then traveled extensively in Greece and Asia Minor. In 1882 he took part in the excavations of a Lycian burial site, the "Heroon" of Gjölbaşi-Trysa, in which important Greek reliefs from the late fifth century B.C.E. were found. In 1887 he began his academic career as a lecturer in Vienna, becoming a professor in Rome in 1889. He returned to Vienna after World War I and was a professor of classical archaeology. His early writings on the history of ancient Greek artists were influenced by the philology-oriented Seminary in Vienna. His later activity was influenced by contemporary art historiographers of the Vienna School such as F. Wickhoff and A. Riegl; in place of philologico-antiquarian interpretation of ancient works of art, this school put form and style analysis, together with a reevalution of pre- and post-classical style periods. Loewy contributed essentially to the comprehension of the then underestimated archaic art of Greece with his *Naturwiedergabe* and *Typenwanderung*. Loewy considered the archaic style not as a preliminary to the classical period, but as an artistic creation, complete in itself. Apart from numerous scholarly works, Loewy reached a wide general public with his popular scientific works *Die Griechische Plastik* (2 vols., 1911, 1924[4]) and *Polygnot, ein Buch von griechischer Malerei* (2 vols., 1929). His works include *Inschriften griechischer Bildhauer* (1885); *Naturwiedergabe in der aelteren griechischen Kunst* (1900; Eng., 1907); *Typenwanderung* (Yearbook of the Austrian Archeological Institute, 12 (1909), 14 (1911)); and *Neuattische Kunst* (1922).

ADD. BIBLIOGRAPHY: NDB, 15 (1987), 114f.

[Penuel P. Kahane]

LOEWY, ISAAC (1793–1847), industrialist; founder of the town of Ujpest. Born in Nagy-Surány (now Surány), Hungary, Loewy studied at the yeshivah of Pressburg. He also learned his father's trade, that of tanner, and with his brothers Joachim and Bernát took over the family business in 1823. When in the early 1830s he tried to establish his workshop in Pest, the town council and guilds refused to admit him. At about that time some uncultivated lands to the north of the town were being parceled out for sale by the proprietor, Count István Károlyi; Loewy, his family, and his workmen settled on them. The terms of the sale stipulated that there would be no religious discrimination in the new settlement and that the traditional craft guilds would not be established there. By 1834 Loewy's new factory had started production, and the first residential building was erected in 1835. Several wealthy Jews of Pest followed Loewy, building rows of houses on the new settlement. In 1839 and 1840 a synagogue and school were built. In 1840 the settlement was officially declared a borough, with the name Ujpest ("New Pest"). This was mainly due to the efforts of Loewy, who was elected the first president of the town council of the new town. He also suggested the development of a port on the Danube at Ujpest. After his death a street in Ujpest was named after him.

BIBLIOGRAPHY: I. Reich, in: *Beth-El; Ehrentempel verdienter ungarischer Israeliten*, 1 (1868), 8–20; E. Ballagi, in: *Egyenlöség*, 41 (Dec. 16, 1922), 14; Gy. Ugró, *Ujpest* (1932), 19–21.

[Jeno Zsoldos]

LOEWY, JACOB EZEKIEL BEN JOSEPH (1814–1864), rabbi and author. Born in Hotzenplotz, Moravia, Loewy went at the age of nine to study with Baruch Te'omim Fraenkel in Leipnik. After Fraenkel's death in 1827, he studied at various yeshivot including those of Benjamin Wolf in Tepelstein and Jacob Meshullam *Ornstein in Lemberg; he spent one year in Berlin where his studies included secular learning. After his marriage he engaged in business, studying in his spare time. In 1846 he was appointed rabbi of Wadowice, his seat being in Oswiecim (Auschwitz). In 1854 he accepted the position of rabbi in Beuthen where he died. Among his works are *Tisporet Lulyanit* (1839) attacking the *Ma'amar ha-Tiglaḥat* (1835) of Isaac Samuel *Reggio who had permitted the cutting of the beard during the intermediate days of a festival; and *Bikkoret ha-Talmud* ("*Kritisch-talmudisches Lexicon*," vol. 1, Vienna, 1863). The latter purports to be a critical encyclopedia on the Oral Law and tradition, alphabetically arranged. The volume covers articles under the letter *alef.* In conformity with his conservative approach, Loewy attempted in his work to harmonize scientific criticism with tradition. In the article on marriage (pp. 155–65) he strongly attacks the extreme reform views of *Holdheim in his *Ma'amar ha-Ishut* and their qualified approval by Reggio. His halakhic work, *Shorshei Halakhah*, remains in manuscript. He also published a series of studies in *Ha-Maggid, Ha-Meliz*, and other periodicals.

BIBLIOGRAPHY: Fuenn, Keneset, 552.

LOEWY, MAURICE (1833–1907), astronomer. Loewy was born in Pressburg (Bratislava), where he trained in the local observatory. In 1861 Loewy was appointed assistant astronomer of the Paris observatory and astronomer in 1864. After the death of Amédée E.B. Mouchez in 1892, he was put in charge of the great international enterprise of the photographic "Carte du Ciel," and later became director of the observatory. He devised several new observational methods. His particular interest was the moon, and together with his collaborator, P.H. Puiseux, he produced a large photographic atlas, which has remained a masterpiece. He was a pioneer in astronomical photography, and the inventor of the "elbow" telescope. He received many honors including the Gold Medal of the Royal Astronomical Society in London.

BIBLIOGRAPHY: Royal Astronomical Society, *Monthly Notices*, 68 (1907–08), 249–52; (1942), 166–7, incl. list of major works.

[Arthur Beer]

LOGGEM, MANUEL VAN (1916–1998), Dutch author and critic. Van Loggem worked as a theater critic for several papers, as a psychotherapist, and as a graphologist. He is mainly known as the author of numerous dramas and television plays in which the characters are drawn with great psychological skill. His plays include the prizewinning *De Chinese fluitspeler* ("The Chinese Flutist," 1947) and *Jeugdproces* ("Youth Trial," 1962), which was translated into many languages. His plays for television include *Een zon op Hiroshima* ("A Sun over Hiroshima," 1962). Van Loggem also wrote novels and short stories, some of them on Jewish themes. Van Loggem's novel *Mozes, de wording van een volk* (1947) describes the genesis of the Jewish people. His short story "Deze plek komt me bekend voor," from the collection *Het tijdperk der zerken* ("The Age of Memorials," 1968) introduces the figure of the *Wandering Jew after Israel's capture of the Western Wall in Jerusalem in June 1967. His theoretical and critical prose includes *Oorsprong en noodzaak* ("Origin and Necessity," 1951), and *Inleiding tot het toneel* ("Introduction to the Theater," 1951). Van Loggem also wrote thrillers and science fiction.

[Gerda Alster-Thau / Hilde Pach (2nd ed.)]

LOGIC (Heb. חָכְמַת הַדִּבּוּר or מְלֶאכֶת הַהִגָּיוֹן), the study of the principles governing correct reasoning and demonstration. The term logic, according to Maimonides, is used in three senses: to refer to the rational faculty, the intelligible in the mind, and the verbal expression of this mental content. In its second sense, logic is also called inner speech, and in its third, outer speech. Since logic is concerned with verbal formulation as well as mental content, grammar often forms a part of logical writings. Shem Tov ibn *Falaquera, for example, prefaces his *Reshit Ḥokhmah* with an account of the origin of language, its nature, and its parts. As Maimonides had done in the introduction to the *Guide of the Perplexed*, Falaquera classifies terms into distinct terms, synonyms, and homonyms, a classification which was very important in the medieval philosophic exegesis of the Bible.

The two mental acts which are basic to logic are conception and judgment. The former is involved in the apprehension of the essence of things, the latter, in deciding whether propositions are true or false.

Maimonides does not consider logic a part of philosophy proper as the Stoics did, but follows the Peripatetics in viewing it as the instrument and auxiliary of all the other sciences.

Although some of the methods of biblical exegesis and legal interpretation (*middot*) employed by the rabbis of the talmudic period rest upon the rules of logic (see *Hermeneutics), it is doubtful that the rabbis had a formal knowledge of the subject. However, beginning with Saadiah, who refers to Aristotle's categories, proving that they are not applicable to God (*Emunot ve-De'ot*, 2:8), Jewish thinkers have been acquainted with the *Organon* – the title traditionally given to the body of Aristotle's logical treatises which formed the basis of logic – as propounded by the logicians of Islam. During the Islamic period, few works on logic were written by Jews. While Isaac *Israeli and Joseph ibn *Ẓaddik appear to have written works on logic, the first extant work on logic written by a Jew is Maimonides' *Maqāla fi-Ṣināʿat al-Manṭiq* (ed. by M. Turker (1961); Arabic text in Hebrew characters published by I. Efros in: PAAJR, 34 (1966), 9–42 (Hebrew section); translated by the same into English under the title *Maimonides' Treatise on Logic*, in: PAAJR, 8 (1937/38), 34–65). It was only when the setting of Jewish philosophy shifted to Christian countries and Arabic ceased to be the language of the Jews that logical works were translated into Hebrew and a greater number of Hebrew works on logic were written by Jews.

In the *Maqāla fi-Ṣināʿat al-Manṭiq* Maimonides offers concise exposition of the 175 most important logical, physical, metaphysical, and ethical terms used in the discussion of logical theory. The popularity of this treatise is attested by the fact that it was translated into Hebrew three times, under the title *Millot ha-Higgayon* or *Shemot ha-Higgayon*: once in a florid style by *Ahitub, a physician in Palermo in the 13th century; again, by Joseph ben Joshua ibn Vivas (of Lorca) in the 14th century; and by Moses b. Samuel ibn *Tibbon (all three translations appear in: PAAJR, 8 (1937/38), 23–129). This last translation was by far the most popular and has gone through many editions. Maimonides' work served not only as a handbook of logic, but, until comparatively recent times, also as an introduction to general philosophy. Of the commentaries written on it, those of Mordecai b. Eliezer *Comtino and Moses *Mendelssohn may be singled out.

While there is little information on the logical authorities used by the Jews up until the middle of the 12th century, it is known that by this time al-Fārābī was the acknowledged authority on logic. Maimonides, in a famous letter to Samuel ibn Tibbon, the Hebrew translator of his *Guide*, advises him to study logic only from the works of al-Fārābī, and, as M. Tucker has shown, Maimonides in his *Maqāla fi-Ṣināʿat al-Manṭiq* relied heavily on four works by al-Fārābī. During the first half of the 13th century, *Averroes too came to be regarded as an authority on logic, soon superseding al-Fārābī. Thus, Judah ben Samuel ibn *Abbas, in his *Ya'ir Nativ*, suggested that in order to learn the principles of logic, a student should read the works of al-Fārābī or Averroes.

While it appears that there were no translations into Hebrew of any of the books comprising the *Organon*, all the commentaries of al-Fārābī and Averroes were translated and annotated. Jacob b. Machir translated Averroes' *Epitome* of the *Organon*, and Jacob *Anatoli, Averroes' middle commentaries, which he completed in 1232. *Kalonymus b. Kalonymus and Moses b. Samuel ibn Tibbon were among some of the others who undertook to translate the logical writings of al-Fārābī and Averroes. Anatoli's translation of the middle commentaries was utilized by Joseph *Kaspi in his compendium of logic, entitled *Ẓeror ha-Kesef.*

The Jews were also familiar with the logical writings of Avicenna. Their knowledge of Avicenna's writings did not come from translations of Avicennian works, but rather through the logical portions of al-*Ghazālī's "Intentions of the Philosophers" (*Maqāṣid al-Falāsifa*). In addition to the Islamic tradition, a work by a Christian scholar, Peter of Spain's *Sum-*

mulae Logicales, was also popular, as the four or five Hebrew translations or extracts of it, which are still extant, testify.

These translations are of great importance because in many instances the original Arabic texts of the commentaries are no longer extant. Moreover, many of these texts were translated from the Hebrew into Latin by Jews who served as the intermediaries between the logicians of Islam and the scholastics. *Levi b. Gershom wrote supercommentaries on the middle commentaries and epitomes of Averroes, as well as an independent work on logic entitled *Ha-Hekkesh ha-Yashar* ("The Correct Syllogism"), which drew upon itself the attention of gentile scholars and was translated into Latin under the title *Liber Syllogismi Recti*. In the 15th century, *Judah b. Jehiel Messer Leon wrote a supercommentary on Averroes' middle commentaries which shows the influence of the scholastic Walter Burleigh.

BIBLIOGRAPHY: L. Jacobs, *Studies in Talmudic Logic and Methodology* (1961), 3–50; A. Hyman, in: *Actes du quatrième congrès international de philosophie médiévale* (1969), 99–110; I. Husik, *Judah Messer Leon's Commentary on the "Vetus Logica"* (1906); Steinschneider, Uebersetzungen, 43–168; Waxman, Literature, 1 (1960²), 319–20; 2 (1960²), 213.

[Jacob Haberman]

LOGOS, a Greek word meaning "speech," "organization," "rational order," "rational relationship," or "rational expression," common in Greek philosophical writings. As the word of God in all its manifestations, it appears in Jewish and Christian theological texts in Greek from the Hellenistic period. *Aristobulus of Paneas, Wisdom of *Solomon, and *Philo are the Jewish sources, and the Gospel of John, the earliest representative of the Christian ones. The later history of the term belongs to Christian theology, where, following John, logos is the Son, or the preexistent Messiah. Logos as an independent entity appeared in Jewish literature suddenly in the writings of Philo. Because of the connection between Philo's use of the term and the Johannine innovation, according to which logos is an intermediary between God and the world, scholars sought parallels elsewhere in Jewish writings, both for the word of God as a distinct concept and for its appearance as a divine intermediary. The *memra* ("word") of the Lord, one of the terms used to paraphrase the name of the Lord in the Targums, has been mistakenly viewed as such a parallel.

Greek Philosophy

Among early Greek philosophers Heraclitus (fifth century B.C.E.) considered logos as (1) the order in the universe, (2) the organizing force that originates and maintains that order, and (3) human apprehension and reasoned expression of it. All these things for him are one and the same, and are, it seems, to be identified with heat. Plato used the term primarily for logical discussion. However, in *Epinomis* (986c4), a dialogue probably not written by Plato himself, logos is identified with the intelligence that governs and imposes rational structure in the world; in the Sixth Letter (323d2f.), whose authenticity is also disputed, the son of the true god is identified as "the divine governor and origin of all things present and future," which may point to some notion of the logos as an intermediary between true reality and the world in Greek sources. In Stoic thought logos again has the threefold role of (1) being responsible for fashioning things, (2) accounting for the disposition of things (and so for the rational faculty in man), and (3) expressing reality in language.

Bible

The Word of God (*devar Adonai*) appears in the Bible as divine teaching, i.e., the medium of revelation and guidance (Gen. 15:1; I Sam. 3:21; Isa. 55:10–11; Ezek. and Zech. passim), the instrument of creation (Ps. 33:6; Gen. 1, though the technical term is not used), and the instrument that controls nature (Ps. 107:20; 147:18). This usage parallels in some ways the threefold, normative Greek philosophical identification of logos, except that the biblical emphasis is on moral, instead of natural, philosophy. The Word of the Lord is identified directly with Torah in Psalms 119 (*passim*), and the attributes of the Word or Torah (Ps. 89; 119) are ascribed to Wisdom in the first nine chapters of Proverbs. Indeed, Torah and Wisdom are identified in the apocryphal books Ben Sira (24:1–21, 22ff.) and Wisdom of Solomon (6:18ff.) in all the same aspects.

Jewish Hellenistic Literature

Aristobulus (fl. 160 B.C.E.) speaks of the voice of the Lord as the natural law, according to which the universe functions (Eusebius, *Praeparatio Evangelica*, 13:12). Thus, a rapprochement of the Jewish and Greek notions has occurred. In *Wisdom of Solomon* (7:17–21) also, Wisdom teaches natural philosophy to man. In the same work logos personifies divine Mercy (Wisdom 16:12), and slays the first-born of Egypt. In the *Haggadah* of Passover the Messenger (sometimes identified with logos by modern scholars), who was excluded from any role in the Exodus, may, if that passage is early and if it is a polemic against Wisdom of Solomon, point to an early popular hypostatization of logos; but the bulk of the evidence is opposed to such an early personification. The author of Wisdom of Solomon seems to distinguish between *sophia* ("wisdom") and logos, as two aspects of God's word, the former being human thoughts and actions in consonance with reality, and the latter, God's speech seen as a messenger, or angel. In addition, the former teaches natural philosophy, not logos.

Philo

Logos is central to Philo's thought. It is the chief power of God; it unites His strength and His goodness, and hence it is the rational term which connects opposites, another meaning of the Greek word. In this function, logos brings God to man and man to God. It is the representative of the Governor to His subjects; and its position is intermediate between created things and the uncreated (Her. 205). Logos is a copy (Gr. *eikon*) of God (I Spec. 81, etc.) through which the world was made (*ibid.*, III LA 96, etc.), and human intelligence is a copy of it (Her. 230, Fug. 68, Op. 69). Philo applies the term logos, or the holy logos, to Scripture itself, i.e., the Law (IV *Quaes-*

tiones et Solutiones in Genesin, 140; 1 Som. 229). It is not a person, according to Philo, nor is it an intermediary between God and man, although it is identified with the biblical angel of the Lord (Mig. 174, etc.). Rather, it is sometimes the same as wisdom (1 LA 65, etc.), because it is the most inclusive expression of the thoughts and ideas of God, which in turn are identified with the Law, or the Torah, with the pattern of all creation, and with the law that directs and maintains all things. Philo's identification of logos with Wisdom and Torah parallels the identification of Torah and Wisdom and the Word of God in rabbinic literature, and conforms to the roles assigned to each in Scripture and rabbinic sources.

Gospel of John

The prologue to the Gospel of John follows biblical and apocryphal sources in portraying the preexistent logos dwelling on earth; but the presentation of logos as an independent agent, and furthermore, as the preexistent messiah is a radical innovation. Apparently, Philo did not think of either notion (1 Som. 228f. is not evidence that such a belief existed earlier). Rabbinic and Christian Gnostic speculations, all of later date than John, do, however, understand logos as a second god. Some accounts of *Gnosticism, whose doctrine implies a logos-hypostasis, would even date gnostic sources before John. Among the rabbis a belief in a "second God," or divine intermediary, is represented in the heretical views of *Elisha b. Avuyah (cf. also *Metatron). His views seem related to speculations about Creation, in which the voice, or Word, of the Lord on the waters (Ps. 29:3 and Gen. 1) and at the revelation on Sinai (Ex. 20) are hypostatized. All this, however, is later than the use of the Greek word "logos" in Philo and in the fourth Gospel.

The *memra* of the Targums, whether it is used in an attempt to express the otherness of God, to avoid anthropomorphisms, or for some other reason, was not thought of as an intermediary between man and God, was certainly not personified in rabbinic thought, and was not identified with Torah regularly. In later rabbinic writing *ha-dibbur* ("the speech") is used to refer to God, but that phenomenon seems unrelated to the Jewish-Hellenistic logos.

BIBLIOGRAPHY: W. Kelber, *Die Logoslehre von Heraklit bis Origenes* (1958); H. Strack and P. Billerbeck, *Kommentar zum Neuen Testament aus Talmud und Midrasch*, 2 (1924), 353–5; H. Leisegang, in: Pauly-Wissowa, 25 (1926), 1047–81; H.A. Wolfson, *Philo*, 1 (Eng., 1947), 200–82.

[Daniel E. Gershenson]

LOḤAMEI HA-GETTA'OT (Heb. לוֹחֲמֵי הַגֶּטָּאוֹת; "The Ghetto Fighters"), kibbutz in the northern Coastal Plain of Israel, 3 mi. (5 km.) N. of Acre, affiliated with Ha-Kibbutz ha-Me'uḥad. Loḥamei ha-Getta'ot was founded in 1949 as one of the first villages to be erected in the framework of the comprehensive settlement scheme for Acre Plain and Western Galilee, by a group from Poland composed of survivors of the resistance against the Nazis in Polish and Lithuanian ghettos, among them Itzhak (Antek) *Zuckerman and Ziviah *Lubetkin. The kibbutz is located near an aqueduct built by Aḥmad Pasha al-Jazzār at the end of the 18th century to lead the *Kabri spring waters to Acre. Farming at Loḥamei ha-Getta'ot included dairy cattle in partnership with kibbutz *Ma'yan Barukh, poultry, avocado plantations, fishery, and field crops in partnership with the kibbutzim kibbutz *Adamit and kibbutz *Shomrat. The kibbutz ran a factory producing condensers and other electronic equipment and operated guest rooms and a restaurant. However, its main source of livelihood was the Tivall food company, which produced cholesterol-free products in partnership with the Osem company. The Ghetto Fighters' House in memory of Yitzḥak *Katznelson, the Holocaust Museum, and an educational center named after Janusz *Korczak are located in Loḥamei ha-Getta'ot. The kibbutz also published a research bulletin, *Yedi'ot*. At the close of the 1960s the population of Loḥamei ha-Getta'ot numbered 341, in the mid-1990s, it was approximately 530, while at the end of 2002 it declined somewhat to 480.

WEBSITE: hebrew.gfh.org.il/kibutz_lohamei_hagetaot.htm.

[Efraim Orni / Shaked Gilboa (2nd ed.)]

LOḤAMEI ḤERUT ISRAEL (**Leḥi**, or "**Stern Group**"), armed underground organization in Palestine founded by Avraham *Stern. In June 1940, after the *Irgun Ẓeva'i Le'ummi (IẒL) decided on a truce of underground armed activities during World War II, the Stern group broke away from IẒL. At first it called itself Irgun Ẓeva'i Le'ummi be-Israel and declared a continuation of war against the British, opposed the voluntary enlistment of Jews into the British army, and even attempted to contact representatives of the Axis. This attitude gained it the reputation of a "fifth column" in official circles, and the British Palestine police and secret service were mobilized against it. During January and February 1942 the clashes between members of the Stern group and the British military and civil authorities reached their peak, and the British forces reacted by arresting and killing leading Stern group members. On Feb. 12, 1942, Avraham Stern himself was caught in his hiding place and was killed on the spot by British police officers. Considerably weakened, the group was on the verge of complete disintegration when some of its detainees managed to escape from prison and regrouped their forces. They then gave themselves the new name of Loḥamei Ḥerut Israel. In early 1944 Leḥi resumed its operations under a triumvirate leadership (Yiẓḥak Shamir, Nathan *Yellin-Mor, and Israel Eldad-Scheib), continuing them with short interruptions until the end of the Mandate in 1948. Members of the group were ordered to be continually armed. Those who were caught admitted in court to being its members, refused to recognize the court's authority, and made political statements. In November 1944 two Leḥi members, Eliahu Ḥakim and Eliahu Bet-Ẓuri, assassinated Lord Moyne, British minister of state for the Middle East, in Cairo. They were caught, tried, and hanged in Cairo in March 1945. In July 1945 Leḥi and IẒL agreed to cooperate in their struggle against the British, and in November 1945 Leḥi joined the Haganah and IẒL in the Hebrew Resistance Movement (Heb. Tenu'at ha-Meri ha-Ivri), which existed for nine months. During and after this period, Leḥi carried out sabotage operations and armed attacks on military objectives and government installations (army camps, airfields, police stations, railway trains), while also attacking individual members of the British police and army and organizing expropriations to secure funds. Its clandestine radio station waged a continual propaganda campaign, and posters and declarations were distributed.

In April 1947 Leḥi began sabotage operations outside Palestine, mailing bombs to British statesmen. The Mandatory authorities reacted by making administrative arrests of anyone suspected of belonging to or helping Leḥi and by passing severe sentences on those caught in operations or even merely carrying arms. On March 17, 1947, Moshe Barazani was sentenced to death for having a hand grenade in his possession. Together with Meir Feinstein, a member of IẒL, Barazani blew himself up in the Jerusalem prison before the sentence could be carried out. The history of Leḥi was marked by frequent prison breaks and escapes from arrest in Palestine (Mazraʿa, Latrun, Jerusalem, Acre, Athlit) and from the countries of forced exile (Eritrea, Sudan, and Kenya). After the United Nations resolution on the partition of Palestine in November 1947, Leḥi participated in attacks on Arab regular and irregular forces, including the attack on the village of Deir Yāsīn near Jerusalem, which they captured together with IẒL (April 9, 1948).

On May 29, 1948, two weeks after the establishment of the State of Israel, members of Leḥi joined the Israel army. In Jerusalem, however, they continued to fight separately for a time. After the assassination of the UN mediator, Count Folke *Bernadotte, in Jerusalem on Sept. 17, 1948, an act which a group of Leḥi members were suspected of perpetrating, the Israel authorities enforced the final disbanding of Leḥi in Jerusalem. After its leading members were arrested and investigated for a short period, Leḥi ceased to exist. Its leaders took part in the elections to the First Knesset as the Fighters' List and Nathan Yellin-Mor was elected as representative. Memorial meetings in the memory of Avraham Stern are held annually by an association of Leḥi members.

BIBLIOGRAPHY: *Loḥamei Ḥerut Yisrael*, 2 vols. (1959); J. Banai (Mazal), *Ḥayyalim Almonim* (1958); G. Cohen, *Sippurah shel Loḥemet* (1962); I. Scheib (Eldad), *Ma'aser Rishon* (1950); D. Niv, *Ma'arkhot ha-Irgun ha-Ẓeva'i ha-Le'ummi*, 3 (1967); Y. Bauer, *Diplomacy and Resistance* (1970).

[David Niv]

°LOISY, ALFRED FIRMIN (1857–1940), French biblical commentator and theologian. Born in Ambrières (Haute-Marne), Loisy was ordained as a Catholic priest in 1879. He studied at the Institut Catholique de Paris, where he later lectured in Hebrew and exegesis. He was dismissed in 1893 on the order of the pope for the publication of his article "La Question biblique et l'inspiration des Ecritures," which took a view opposed to the traditional teaching of the Church. His special approach to biblical research and interpretation aroused the suspicion of the Catholic Church authorities, who also condemned his essay *La religion d'Israël* (1900; *The Religion of Israel*, 1910). In 1902 he published *L'Evangile et l'Eglise* (1902; *The Gospel and the Church*, 1903) which, though intended as a Catholic answer to the work of Adolph von Harnack, was unacceptable to the Church. The work was favorably received throughout Europe, but was placed on the Church Index of forbidden books. From 1901 onward he taught the history of the Christian religion at the Ecole des Hautes Etudes Pratiques. Loisy's polemics with the Church attracted considerable attention in Europe, especially after he was excommunicated in 1908. From 1909 to 1932 he was professor of Church history at the Collège de France.

Loisy is considered the leading exponent of biblical "modernism" and of the critical approach in the study of the New Testament and the problems of the Christian faith. He denied the supernatural inspiration of the Bible and based his research on a critical study of the sources and philological analysis. After World War I he became active in a new field of religious meditation, which paved the way for a progressive and humanistic sociology of religion. The majority of his works were banned by the papal orders of 1932 and 1938. Loisy founded and directed the bimonthly *Revue de l'enseignement biblique* until 1894, and from 1896 to 1922 edited the *Revue d'histoire et de littérature religieuse*. The most important of his works are *Histoire du Canon de l'Ancien Testament* (1890); *Les Evangiles synoptiques* (2 vols., 1907–08); *Les origines du Nouveau Testament* (1936; *The Origins of the New Testament*, 1950); and *Les mystères païens et le mystère chrétien* (1919, 1930[2]).

BIBLIOGRAPHY: M. Lepin, *Les Théories de M. Loisy: Exposé et Critique* (1909); N.Y. Lagrange, *A. Loisy et le Modernisme* (1932); Petre, in: *The Hilbert Journal*, 39 (1940), 5–14; F. Heiber, *Der Vater des Katholischen Modernismus: A. Loisy* (1947); A. Moutin, *La question biblique au XIX siècle* (1902); A. Détrez, *L'Abbé Loisy...* (1909), includes bibliography.

[Zevi Baras]

LOLLI, EUDE (1826–1904), Italian rabbi and university professor. Lolli was born in Gorizia. He was the son of Samuel Vita Lolli, and thus first cousin of Samuel David *Luzzatto (Shadal). He was educated at the lyceum of Gorizia. From 1845 to 1846 he attended the Rabbinical College of Padua, graduating in 1854. In 1865, upon the death of his cousin and mentor, Samuel David Luzzatto, he was appointed professor at the Rabbinical College of Padua, thus taking the chair of Shadal. Eude held the appointment until the institution was finally closed in 1871. In the last six years of its existence Lolli and Lelio Della Torre were the only teachers there. In 1869 he was elected chief rabbi of Padua, and in 1877 he became lecturer in, and in 1886 professor of, Hebrew and Chaldaic at the University of Padua. Lolli wrote the *Dizionario del Linguaggio Ebraico-Rabbinico* (Padua, 1869); *Prelezione ad un Corso di Lingua Ebraica e Caldaica* (1877); and *Corso di Grammatica della Lingua Ebraica* (1878). He also contributed a large section to S.D. Luzzatto's *La Sacra Bibbia Volgarizzata* (1872). Lolli was a supporter of Zionism, both cultural and political. However he stressed in his writings that Zionism was a solution only for those Jews who lived in countries where they were persecuted, and not for Jews living in Western Europe, such as Italy's Jewry.

DAVID LOLLI (1825–1884), brother of Eude, was an Italian physician and patriot. He was born in Gorizia; he studied medicine at Padua and Vienna. At the outbreak of the Italian war for liberation against Hapsburg Austria in 1848, he abandoned his studies and hastened to join the University of Padua's Artillery Battalion. Lolli took part in the unsuccessful attempt to hold Vicenza, and then joined the garrison guarding Venice against the Austrian army. When cholera broke out in the besieged city, Lolli was also stricken. On his recovery he returned to his native city, Gorizia, but subsequently established himself as a physician at Trieste. He continued to agitate for the independence of Italy and, consequently, often incurred great danger. Thus in 1859 he joined the Sardinian army that was fighting against the Austrians as an army doctor, although he was an Austrian subject.

Lolli wrote much on various medical subjects such as psychology and magnetism as well as on patriotic themes. He published the monographs *Sul Magnetismo Animale, Pubblicato Nell' Occasione di Conseguire la Laurea* (Padua, 1850); *Sulla Migliare, Due Parole di Occasione* (Trieste, 1857); *Sii Forte e Sarai Libero (Seneca): Sii Libero e Sarai Forte* (Milan, 1860, published anonymously for political reasons); *I Numi* (Milan, 1866), a symbolic story, published under the pseudonym "Aldo Apocalissio"; *Sul Cholera* (Trieste, 1866); and *L'Amore dal Lato Fisiologico, Filosofico, e Sociale* (Milan, 1883).

BIBLIOGRAPHY: EUDE LOLLI: M. Del Bianco Controzzi, *Il Collegio Rabbinico di Padova, Un' istituzione religiosa dell' ebraismo sulla via dell' Emancipazione*, Storia dell' Ebraismo in Italia, Studi e testi XVII (1995), 238–39, passim; A. Cavaglion, "Tendenze nazionali ed albori sionistici," in: G. Luzzatto Voghera and C. Vivanti (eds.), *Gli ebrei in Italia II, Storia d'Italia, Annali*, 11 (1997), 1300; M. Mortara, *Indice alfabetico dei rabbini e scrittori israeliti di cose giudaiche in Italia, con richiami bibliografici e note illustrative* (1886), 35; G. Tamani, "Gli studi ebraici a Padova nei secoli XVII–XX," in: *Quaderni per la storia dell' Università di Padova*, 9–10 (1976–77), 215–28, esp. 223. DAVID LOLLI: T. Haneman, "David Lolli," s.v., in: *The Jewish Encyclopedia*, 8 (1906), 152–53; S., Foà, *Gli ebrei nel Risorgimento italiano* (1978), 49.

[Samuele Rocca (2nd ed.)]

LOM, HERBERT (1917–), actor. Born in Prague, Lom was trained in London and made his first British picture in 1940, *Mein Kampf – My Crimes*. He became known for his earthy characterizations and made his first West End appearance in 1951 in *The Seventh Veil*. His most notable success was as the king in *The King and I* (1953). Lom had a long career as a Hollywood supporting actor, in such films as *War and Peace* (1956), *Spartacus* (1960), *El Cid* (1961), *The Lady Vanishes* (1979), *Ten Little Indians* (1989), and *The Pope Must Die* (1991). Probably his most famous role was as the long-suffering Superintendent Dreyfus in the *Pink Panther* films. He also starred in successful television series.

[Jonathan Licht]

LOMBARDY, region of N. *Italy; the political and physical borders, in which *Mantua also would be included, have not always coincided. References to Jews in Lombardy (*Milan) date to the fourth century; subsequently there is only slight evidence down to the very end of the 12th century, when Jews are found engaged in moneylending. In 1225 the Jews were expelled from *Pavia and *Cremona; in 1278 they began to be harassed by the conversionist sermons of the *Dominicans. Before the end of the 13th century, Jews of German origin arrived in Lombardy and engaged in moneylending, mainly settling in Cremona as the Jews were expelled from Milan in 1320. In the 14th century and during the first decades of the 15th, small communities were constituted in *Pavia, *Vicenza, and *Como. In general, however, the Jewish population in the region remained small. Although Jews were accorded favorable treatment by the Visconti and Sforza dukes of Milan, the populace in general remained hostile.

The Cremona community remained important in the 16th century; its talmudic academy and printing establishment were famous. Further groups of Jews were by now settled in *Alessandria and *Lodi. In 1452, Pope Nicholas V authorized Duke Francesco Sforza to maintain their existing privileges on condition that the restrictive ecclesiastical regulations were strictly enforced. However, the Jews were compelled to maintain loan banks in every town in Lombardy, even where they incurred losses, and to pay the government an exceptionally heavy annual tax. Even after the duchy of Milan passed under Spanish rule in 1535, the Jews there continued to have their residential permit renewed about every ten years, although they were not permitted to reside permanently in Milan itself. In 1565, Philip II of Spain decided to expel the Jews from the duchy. After lengthy negotiations in Madrid, permission was given for them to remain until 1597, when the 900 Jewish residents had to leave. Two families were allowed to remain in each of the three towns of Cremona, Lodi, and Alessandria. In the course of time, the Jews disappeared from the first two, but in Alessandria the Jewish population had increased to 230 by 1684. After Lombardy passed to Austria in 1713 a few Jews again settled in the region. Their number increased after 1800, and reached 500 by the middle of the 19th century, mainly concentrated in Milan.

After the incorporation of Lombardy in the Kingdom of Italy in 1859–61, and the commercial and industrial transformation of the region which followed, there was a considerable increase in the Jewish population. Former members of now disintegrating small Italian communities, as well as industrialists from Germany and Austria, settled in Lombardy. In the middle of the present century, there was Jewish immigration from Germany and after 1947 from Libya, Egypt, and Iraq. The Jewish population numbered 3,500 in 1901 (almost all living in Milan), and 11,000 in 1938, reduced during the Holocaust. Milan maintained a population of 6,500 into the 21st century.

BIBLIOGRAPHY: Roth, Italy, index; Milano, Italia, index, s.v. *Lombardia*; Milano, Bibliotheca, index; Rota, in: *Bollettino della società parese di storia patria*, 4 (1906), 349–82; Levi Minzi, in: *Israel* (Feb. 11, 1932); Scharf, in: RMI, 2 (1926/27), 33–49.

[Attilio Milano]

LOMBROSO, CESARE (1835–1909), Italian physician and criminologist. Born in Verona, Lombroso studied at Pavia, Padua, and Vienna. Lombroso took degrees in medicine and surgery in 1858. After his military service as a surgeon in the Italian army, he worked as a doctor at Pavia, Pesaro, and Regio Emilia. Lombroso then taught legal medicine and public hygiene at the Turin University. He was appointed professor of psychiatry in 1896, and in 1906, professor of criminal anthropology.

While at the University of Vienna he studied psychology and psychiatry, as well as the anatomy and physiology of the brain. For 30 years he advocated his revolutionary theories of criminology.

Lombroso begun his studies during his four years of army service. He made systematic measurements of physical differences among soldiers from various regions of Italy, including soldiers from the newly annexed territories of Southern Italy (formerly the Kingdom of Naples), and of differences between well-disciplined and aggressive or criminal soldiers.

Lombroso's theories were much influenced by French positivism and by Darwinian evolutionary theories. In his research on criminality Lombroso concluded that certain innate physical characteristics are connected with social behavior. His conception of the "born criminal" resulted from his observations, physical measurement, and comparisons of mentally ill and sane people, and of criminals and law-abiding citizens. All men, including the "born criminal," are born with certain faculties, both mental and physical, which decisively influence their behavior. Lombroso published his theory, asserting that the "true criminal" was atavistic, in his controversial *L'Uomo delinquente* ("The Criminal Man," 1876). It was in 1876 that Lombroso became professor of legal medicine and public hygiene at Turin University, which appointed him professor of psychiatry in 1896, and ten years later created a chair in criminal anthropology for him.

While Lombroso gradually came to admit the existence of acquired criminogenic factors, pathological or environmental, he continued to claim that the true criminal was a subspecies of man of an atavistic origin. In his later period he gave more attention to environmental factors as causes of crime, and developed an inclusive typology of the various forms of crime which recognized that a great deal of criminality is not organic or endogenous but a product of diverse exogenous and environmental factors. In the field of penology Lombroso supported such reformist ideas as the compensation of the victims of crime from the prison work of the malefactor. Despite his views on inherited delinquency he was against capital punishment, favoring the rehabilitation of the criminal by a "symbiosis" with his society, whereby the latter would make constructive use of the evildoer and his work potential.

Although the idea of the "born criminal" is no longer accepted, Lombroso remains an important figure in the history of the behavioral sciences. Scholars honor him as a pioneer, and even his critics credit him with shifting the emphasis in criminology from the crime itself to the criminal and his origins.

Lombroso's studies also covered other fields. Thus he wrote "The Man of Genius/The Gifted Man," published in 1888. In this work of scholarship Lombroso considered another type of deviant, the "genius."

A friend of Max *Nordau he had an interest in Zionism and espoused this doctrine in 1900. In 1894, he published a monograph on antisemitism in which he analyzed the manifestations of atavism in antisemites and their folly. Lombroso thus stressed the anthropological degeneration of the antisemite, as in the criminal.

Lombroso published a considerable number of books and articles of which only a few have been translated. His only important book translated into English is *Crime, Its Causes and Conditions* (1911).

BIBLIOGRAPHY: H. Mannheim, in: *Sociological Review*, 28 (1936), 31–49; Wolfgang, in H. Mannheim (ed.), *Pioneers in Criminology* (1960), 168–227; Vervaeck, in: *Archives de l'anthropologie criminelle*, 25 (1910), 561–83. **ADD. BIBLIOGRAPHY:** P.L. Bauma Bollone, *Cesare Lombroso, ovvero il principio dell' irresponsabilità* (1992); A. Cavaglion, "Tendenze nazionali ed albori sionistici," in: G. Luzzatto Voghera and C. Vivanti (eds.), *Gli ebrei in Italia 11, Storia d'Italia, Annali*, 11 (1997), 1313–16.

[Zvi Hermon and Ellen Friedman / Samuele Rocca (2nd ed.)]

LOMZA (Pol. **Łomża**; Rus. **Lomzha**; Yid. **Lomzhe**), Bialystok district. In 1556 the Jews were compelled to leave after the privilege *de non tolerandis Judaeis* was granted to the town, giving it the right to exclude Jews. They did not return there until after the Congress of Vienna (1815). Once their presence was authorized, the number of Jews increased, to 737 in 1826, 2,574 in 1852, 9,244 (54.8% of the total population) in 1897, and 11,088 in 1915 (including 1,500 refugees from the surrounding towns). Their numbers later declined to 9,131 (70.8%) in 1929, and 8,912 (56.7%) in 1931. During the 19th century they were integrated in the life of the country and took an active part in the Polish uprising of 1863. They played a major role in the economic life of Lomza, owned factories, and were the leading wholesalers in the grain and timber trades. Between the two world wars, Jews played an important part in the municipal administration. In the municipal elections of 1919, and again in 1926, they won half the seats. After this, however, as a result of the Polish policy of restricting Jewish influence in the town, the number of seats allocated to the Jews was limited. In 1921 there were 498 Jewish workshops in Lomza, 295 of them with salaried employees. During this period the Jews engaged in various crafts, but they were ousted from these by the antisemitic measures introduced by the Polish government. As a result of the economic crisis and the anti-Jewish *boycott imposed by the antisemitic trade unions and parties, the Jews were greatly impoverished, and many left Lomza. The community administration, which maintained social and educational institutions, was unstable after World War I. Following the elections to the community administration in 1939, interparty dissensions brought its activities to a complete standstill, and the government subsequently appointed an official commissioner to take charge of its affairs.

Educational institutions, such as the *talmudei torah* and the *ḥadarim*, had already been established in Lomza during the 19th century. In independent Poland, pressure was exerted on the Jews to send their children to the Polish government schools. A Jewish-Polish secondary school had already been established in 1916. The Great Yeshivah, founded in 1883 by R. Eliezer Szuliawicz, was transferred to Ereẓ Israel (Petaḥ Tikvah) in 1926, where it became known as Yeshivat Lomza. Jewish parties active in Lomza included *Agudat Israel, the *Bund, and the Zionist organizations. These published regular and occasional periodicals, including the *Lomzher Shtime, Lomzher Veker*, and *Lomzher Lebn* in Yiddish and others in Polish. The Great Bet Ha-Midrash was erected during the early 1840s and the Great Synagogue in 1880. The last rabbis of Lomza were Aaron Bakst and Moses Shatzkes.

[Shimshon Leib Kirshenboim]

Holocaust Period

On the outbreak of World War II there were about 11,000 Jews in Lomza. In September 1939 the Red Army entered the city. With the outbreak of the German-Soviet war, the Germans occupied the town on June 24, 1941, and established a ghetto on Aug. 12, 1941. On September 17 a large-scale *Aktion* took place and 3,000 Jews were killed. On Nov. 2, 1942, the deportations to *Zambrow camp began, and between Jan. 14 and Jan. 18, 1943 the inmates of Zambrow camp were deported to *Auschwitz. Thousands of Jews were brought out of the city and killed in the woods of Galczyn near Lomza. After the war, the Jewish community of Lomza was not reconstituted. Organizations of former residents of Lomza are active in Israel, France, Australia, and the United States.

BIBLIOGRAPHY: *Sefer Zikkaron le-Kehillat Lomza* (1952).

LONDON, capital of *England and seat of what has always been the largest Jewish community in the country.

Medieval Period

There is no reliable evidence for the presence of Jews in London until after the close of the Saxon period. After the Norman Conquest of 1066, a few Jews, attracted by the economic opportunities that now offered themselves, came over from the adjacent areas of the continent (in the first instance presumably from the duchy of Normandy, including *Rouen) and established themselves in London. The earliest recorded mention of the London community dates from the reign of William Rufus (1087–1100), who appears to have favored the Jews to some extent. In his reign, a religious *disputation took place at Westminster between the abbot and a Jew from Mainz who did business with the abbey. A Jewish quarter (*vicus Judaeorum*) is first mentioned in the *Terrier* of St. Paul's (c. 1128). In 1130 the Jews of London were accused of killing a sick man – possibly some sort of *blood libel – and were forced to pay the then enormous fine of £2,000. Intellectual life in the period was sufficiently flourishing to attract a visit from Abraham *Ibn Ezra, who wrote his *Iggeret ha-Shabbat* and his *Yesod Mora* in London in 1158. Until 1177 the relative importance of the community was so great that its cemetery served the whole of Anglo-Jewry.

During the reign of Henry II (1154–89), the community flourished and was augmented by fresh arrivals from abroad. The anti-Jewish riots which broke out at the coronation of Richard I (Sept. 3, 1189) began at Westminster and soon spread to London, where the Jewish quarter was set afire and 30 persons died – including the tosafist R. *Jacob of Orleans. The community soon recovered, however, and in 1194 contributed approximately one quarter to the levy raised by the Jews of the country toward the king's ransom. The reorganization which was then undertaken by the Ordinance of the Jewry confirmed London as the administrative center for the communities of the country. The first *archpresbyter of the Jews of England under the new system was Jacob of London. Anti-Jewish feeling again manifested itself in London during the reign of John (1199–1216) who rebuked the mayor on that account. The baronial opposition, both in his reign and in that of his son Henry III (1216–72), considered the Jews, not without justification, to be royal financial instruments and maltreated them accordingly. There was a baronial attack on London Jewry in 1215.

During the period of maladministration under Henry III, the Jews of London, with those of the rest of the country, were oppressed and mulcted of enormous sums. The climax came in 1244 when it was alleged that some gashes found on the body of a dead child constituted Hebrew characters and the Jews were accused of ritual murder. This resulted in a savage punitive levy on the Jews of the realm to the amount of 60,000 marks. On the outbreak of the Barons' War (1263–65), they suffered greatly at the hands of the insurgents under Simon de Montfort. During Easter week 1263, as the result of a trivial dispute between a Jew and a citizen concerning interest on a debt, the Jewry was sacked and several of its inhabitants killed. Later, on hearing a report that the Jews had manufactured Greek fire for the royal troops, Simon de Montfort returned to London and put the Jewry systematically to the sword. In 1266, another attack was made by the so-called "disinherited knights" on the remnants of the community, who sought refuge in the Tower of London.

The Jews of London profited from the period of pacification which followed the war. Edward I's *Statutum de Judaismo* of 1275, however, which prohibited Jewish moneylending, inevitably drove some into dishonest ways of making a living. In 1278 a number of London Jews were included in the 680 from all over the country who were imprisoned in the Tower of London on the charge of clipping the coinage. Nearly 300 are said to have been hanged (though this figure has been doubted). In the meantime, theological odium against the London Jews had been increasing. In 1232 Henry III confiscated their principal synagogue on the pretext that the chanting could be heard in a neighboring church. In the same year he founded the London *Domus Conversorum to encourage conversions. A further ritual murder accusation was followed by a civic order restricting the Jews henceforth to houses in the Jewry (1281). In 1283 the bishop of London ordered all the synagogues in his diocese to be closed, only one being subsequently reopened. Finally, in 1290, the Jews were expelled from England and the London community ceased to exist.

The number of Jews in London in the Middle Ages probably did not exceed 500, though contemporary Jewish writers speak of 2,000 households. The original Jewish quarter, which contained a number of strong stone houses, was situated in and near what is still known as the Old Jewry. In the 12th century, the Jews began to give up their houses here and to move a little distance westward, where the Church of St. Laurence Jewry commemorates their residence. The cemetery was in what is now known as Jewin Street and the surrounding area. Prominent medieval London scholars included Joseph b. Jacob, known as "Rubi Gotsce" (fl. 1130–60), the host of Abraham Ibn Ezra and the outstanding English Jew of his day, *Jacob b. Judah, of London (late 13th century), author of *Eẓ Ḥayyim*, R. Moses of London (d. 1268), grammarian and halakhist, and his son the illustrious *Elijah Menahem of London (d. 1284), who also enjoyed considerable repute as a physician.

Middle Period

The Domus Conversorum, established by Henry III in 1232, housed nearly 100 converts at the period of the expulsion, and never remained entirely empty in subsequent years. There was a constant, though slender, stream to London of poor foreign Jews who qualified for emoluments by the formal adoption of Christianity. In addition, a few isolated Jews visited London without being baptized: for example, the physicians Elias b. Sabbetai (Sabot) of Bologna, who came in 1410 with ten followers to attend Henry IV, and Master Samson de Mirabeau who attended the wife of Richard Whittington, mayor of London, in 1409. After the expulsions from Spain and Portugal, a few Marrano refugees settled in London. At the close of the reign of Henry VIII, the crypto-Jewish community comprised some 37 householders, and religious services were held in the house of one Alves Lopes to whom newly arrived fugitives would come for assistance and advice. In 1542, the group was disturbed in consequence of disclosures made during proceedings against Marrano fugitives on the continent. It was largely dispersed as a result of the Catholic reaction in the reign of Mary. Under Elizabeth, however, it attained again significant proportions. One of its leading members was Roderigo *Lopez, the queen's physician. When an envoy of Alvaro Mendes (Solomon *Abenaes), duke of Mytilene, was in London on an official mission in 1592, services were held at his house. Toward the end of the century, the importance of the secret community diminished, and in 1609 the Portuguese merchants living in London, who were suspected of Judaizing, were again expelled.

Resettlement Period

Nevertheless, when in 1632 the Marrano community of Rouen was temporarily broken up, some fugitives, the most important being Antonio Fernandez *Carvajal, found a home in London. Other Marrano settlers went directly from Spain and Portugal. Thus, when *Manasseh Ben Israel went to England in 1655, there was already established a secret community numbering several families. Though the Whitehall Conference convened by Oliver *Cromwell in December 1655 proved abortive, they were emboldened to begin organizing their religious life on a more formal basis. A petition was presented to Cromwell asking for protection (March 1656). A house was rented and adapted for use as a synagogue in the following December. A few months later, a piece of ground was acquired for use as a cemetery. After Cromwell's death various attempts were made to procure the suppression of the community. Charles II, however, intervened in its favor, and it henceforth enjoyed de facto recognition. The original synagogue, in Creechurch Lane, was enlarged and remodeled in 1674, and in 1701 a new place of worship in Bevis Marks – still one of the architectural monuments of the city – was erected.

As its spiritual leaders, the newly established community appointed a succession of foreign scholars. They were Jacob *Sasportas (1664–65), who fled because of the great plague of London, in which several members of his flock perished, Joshua da *Silva (1670–79), Jacob *Abendana (1681–85), Solomon *Aylion (1689–1701), and David *Nieto (1701–28). The congregation was continually reinforced by fresh Marrano refugees from Spain and Portugal. After the accession of William of Orange (1689), there was a considerable influx of Spanish and Portuguese Jews from Holland. The majority of the communal magnates at this time were brokers, importers, and wholesale merchants, with a sprinkling of physicians. In the course of the reorganization of the Royal Exchange in 1697, it was arranged to admit 12 Jews – the so-called "Jew brokers" who remained a feature of the City of London until the beginning of the 19th century. In order to secure the favor of the lord mayor, a purse containing 50 guineas was presented to him each year on a valuable piece of plate by the elders of the congregation.

Meanwhile, the original Sephardi settlers had been followed by Ashkenazim who arrived for the most part via Amsterdam or Hamburg. They organized their own congregation around 1690, and in 1696 a burial ground for their use was purchased by the wealthy Benjamin *Levy. The first rabbi of the congregation, Judah Loeb b. Ephraim Anschel ha-Kohen, subsequently of Rotterdam, left as a result of internal dissensions. His place was taken, first by R. Aaron b.

Moses the Scribe, of Dublin, and then by R. Uri Phoebus b. Naphtali Hirsch, known as Aaron *Hart. The latter's brother, Moses Hart, was the maecenas of the community. In 1722 he reconstructed the synagogue in Duke's Place. Further enlargement and reconstruction took place in 1766 and in 1790. In 1706 a secession had taken place in the Ashkenazi community, headed by Mordecai b. Moses of Hamburg, called Marcus Moses (a son-in-law of Glueckel von Hameln). This led to the organization of a rival body, which constructed its own synagogue (known as the Hambro' Synagogue) in 1726. The historic synagogal organization of the metropolis was completed in 1761, when another rival body, still called the New Synagogue, came into existence.

The primacy of the parent body (by now known as the Great Synagogue) was, however, generally recognized – not only by the other Ashkenazi communities in London, but also by those which had by now sprung up elsewhere in the country. R. Aaron Hart was followed in the rabbinate by R. Hirschell *Levin, known in England as Hart Lyon (1758–64), R. David Tevele *Schiff (1765–91), R. Moses Myers (who also officiated at the New Synagogue (1792–1802)), and R. Solomon *Hirschell, son of Hart Lyon (1802–42), who was the first formally recognized chief rabbi of the Ashkenazi communities of the whole of England. The Ashkenazim were by now the most numerous and influential element in the London Jewish population. The lower classes, however, mainly peddlers and dealers in old clothes, who were mostly recently arrived immigrants, were not greatly esteemed. P. Colquhoun, in his *Treatise on the Police of the Metropolis* (1800), asserted that they were responsible for a disproportionate amount of petty crime.

The 19th century was a period of expansion and reorganization. The first synagogue outside the City (later the Western Synagogue) had been organized in Westminster around 1761. The Borough Synagogue, on the south side of the river, owed its origin to a *minyan* begun about the middle of the 18th century. The board for *sheḥitah*, in which Sephardim and Ashkenazim cooperated, was organized through the advocacy of Baron Lyon de Symons in 1792–1804.

As early as 1760, the Sephardi community admitted representatives of the Ashkenazim to their committee of *deputados*, which was appointed from time to time to represent the community vis-à-vis the government. This ultimately developed into the *Board of Deputies of British Jews, on which, until 1838, only the London communities were represented. The old *talmud torah* of the Ashkenazi community, established in 1732 and placed on a broader basis in 1788, was reorganized in 1817 as the Jews' Free School, originally intended to meet the menace presented by the schools which were now being set up for Jewish children by Christian conversionists; this developed in due course into one of the largest schools in Europe. The struggle for Jewish *emancipation in England centered in London. In 1831 Jews were admitted to the freedom of the city, and hence to the privilege of carrying on retail trade, from which they had hitherto been barred. In 1835, David *Salomons was elected a sheriff of the city, the first Jew to attain that distinction. In 1847 he was the first Jewish alderman, and in 1855 the first Jewish lord mayor of London. From 1830 the City of London had shown sympathy with Parliamentary emancipation of the Jews, and its persistence in electing Baron Lionel de *Rothschild, notwithstanding the fact that he could not take his seat because of the form of the statutory oath, was in a large measure responsible for the admission of the Jews to Parliament in 1858.

The growing Anglicization of London Jewry hastened the reorganization of the community. A Reform congregation was established, nearer the fashionable centers of population in 1840. To meet this challenge, both the Sephardi and the Ashkenazi congregations established branch synagogues in the West End. Nathan Marcus *Adler, appointed in 1844, initiated a new period in the history of the Chief Rabbinate. Under his auspices, a modern theological seminary, *Jews' College, was founded in 1855, and a model charitable organization, the Board of Guardians for the Relief of the Jewish Poor, was established in 1859. In 1870 a union of the principal Ashkenazi congregations of the metropolis was formed under the title, the "*United Synagogue." Newer congregations in other parts of the metropolis later attached themselves to this organization, which is now perhaps the largest and the best organized of its kind in the world.

With the mass emigration from Russia which started after 1881, there was a great influx especially to London, and the population rose in the course of the next quarter of a century from some 47,000 to approximately 150,000, of whom about 100,000 lived in the East End. Thus, alongside the more or less "native" community, a new, essentially foreign, community grew up. A majority of the newcomers was absorbed by the tailoring, shoemaking, and cabinetmaking industries. Fresh charities were created to meet their requirements. A Yiddish press and an active trade union movement came into being. Numerous minor synagogues, with their related institutions, were created. In 1887 Sir Samuel Montagu (later Lord Swaythling) created the Federation of Synagogues to coordinate their religious activities. The strike of 10,000 Jewish tailors in London in 1889, lasting for six weeks, attracted great attention and ended the period of the unmitigated exploitation of the Jewish immigrants. The Royal Commission on Alien Immigration, as well as the various inquiries into slum life, dealt to a large extent with the conditions of the new Jewish life which had sprung up in the East End of London, and was arousing some antagonisms. The Aliens Act of 1905 stemmed the tide of immigration, though it continued in modified form until the outbreak of World War I in 1914. The Jew of the East End, as he became more well-to-do, tended to move away to the newer suburbs, particularly in the northeast (Stamford Hill) and northwest (Golders Green), where important congregations sprang up. The progress of the Reform movement, indeed, was comparatively slow, though the radical Liberal Jewish Synagogue, which grew out of the Jewish Religious Union (1902), was established in 1910.

The period between the two wars witnessed a considerable economic and geographical expansion of London Jewry, as it attained a greater degree of well-being, extended its interests, and hastened the movement from the traditional center of the East End into the northern suburbs. At the same time, there was some degree of organizational consolidation. The United Synagogue, in particular, extended its activities. A communal center for the major London Jewish institutions and a Jewish museum were established at Woburn House in the Bloomsbury area. The beginning of the persecutions in Germany in 1933 brought about a considerable influx of refugees who did a good deal to stimulate certain aspects of London Jewish life and to consolidate the organization of the extreme Orthodox wing.

Antisemitic movements were active during the 1930s, notably Sir Oswald Mosley's British Union of Fascists. The "Blackshirt" march through London's East End in October 1936 provoked massive disorders which led to the Public Order Act banning the political use of uniforms. The Mosleyites' march left a deep impression on the consciousness of London Jewry.

[Cecil Roth]

Postwar Period

DEMOGRAPHY. Between the two world wars, London Jewry experienced its first substantial population shift from the East End, a trend heightened during World War II, when, due to long periods of enemy bombing and extensive damage to the inner districts of London, Jews (together with the rest of the population) moved in large numbers to less vulnerable areas further from the center. With a rise in the standard of living in Britain, considerable urban renewal and suburban development took place.

During the 1950s and 1960s, Jews, who by this time had generally risen rapidly on the socioeconomic scale, settled in ever-increasing numbers in suburban areas, particularly in the north and northwest of London. It has been estimated that the East End, which at the beginning of the 20th century contained about 125,000 Jews and in 1929 still had some 85,000 Jews, was left with no more than 30,000 Jews within a few years after World War II. The northwest London area alone was said to have contained some 85,000 Jews by 1950. The vast majority of Jews always lived to the north of the Thames, and by the end of the 1960s they were spread along and below a suburban arc stretching from Wembley, Harrow, Stanmore, and Edgware in the west through Finchley and Palmers Green in the north to Ilford in the east. Below this arc were heavy concentrations of Jews in what may be termed "gilded ghettos," such as Golders Green, or semi-decaying "zones of transition," such as Stamford Hill, where newer non-Jewish immigrants settled in the 1960s in increasing numbers. The total Jewish population of Greater London in 1970 was estimated at 280,000. (For figures for the mid-1990s, see below.)

The pattern of settlement and the movement of London Jewry were of particular importance for their effect on Jewish identification. Evidence suggests that throughout the 20th century, the directions of the major shifts were strongly influenced by developments in transport facilities vis-à-vis the place of work, that is the industrial and commercial areas in the city. The fanning out of the transport system and the improvement in highways, however, made incursions into the traditional pattern of settlement symbolized by the Jewish district. Whereas some of the new suburbs were still thickly inhabited by Jews – Edgware with 10,000 Jews representing 40% of the local population was a case in point – in 1970 there were larger numbers of Jews living in a more scattered fashion away from Jewish districts and throughout the Home Counties in and around Greater London. Not only was the lack of proximity to Jewish centers and the negative effects of living in predominantly non-Jewish areas bound to affect the identification of such Jews, but the problem also arose of how to cater to this more fluid and spread-out Jewish population from the organizational point of view.

ORGANIZATIONS. Most observers of Anglo-Jewish life highlighted the fact that the community was over-organized, a situation that led to duplication, inefficiency, and waste. The organizational aspect of communal life came to the fore even more starkly in the case of London Jewry, first because it contained the headquarters of many organizations catering to Anglo-Jewry as a whole (e.g., Board of Deputies of British Jews, Anglo-Jewish Association, Association of Jewish Ex-Service Men, National Union of Hebrew Teachers, Jewish Initiation Society, Central British Fund for Jewish Relief, and so on), and secondly because the problems of organizational efficiency were greater in a large community, particularly one which had become more scattered. The latter point may best be illustrated by the fields of religious and educational organization. The closing of some synagogues in the older areas of London in the late 1960s, such as the branches of the United Synagogue in Dalston and Bayswater, was more than compensated by the construction of new synagogues in the many areas where Jews settled in the postwar period and more recent years. A proliferation of synagogues was further brought about by the fact that all the main synagogal bodies representing the various streams had their own building programs. Thus, most of the 200 synagogues in London belonged to the five major synagogal organizations. A somewhat similar situation obtained for day schools, which were in the hands of the London Board of Jewish Religious Education, the Zionist Federation, the Jewish Secondary Schools Movement, Yesodei Hatorah Schools, and the Lubavitch Foundation, plus a number of independent schools.

By contrast, there was greater efficiency and centralization in London in the sphere of welfare work. The London Jewish Welfare Board, which operated 19 homes for the aged and a host of other services for the needy, was the largest Jewish welfare institution in the country. London also had numerous societies concerned with the amelioration of physical and mental handicaps, e.g., the Jewish Blind Society, the

Jewish Deaf Association, schools for the mentally retarded and handicapped children, and Jewish hospitals. The various charitable institutions, friendly societies, and professional associations added further to the well-being of London Jews. The younger generation of the community was well provided for by the large number of youth clubs and societies, including some famous ones such as the Jewish Lads' Brigade (founded in 1895), the Brady Club (1896), and the Bernhard Baron Settlement (1914). The renewal and improvement of premises in the form of Jewish youth centers, however, progressed slowly. The large number of Jewish students in London, for instance, was provided by B'nai B'rith with a new and much enlarged Hillel House only in 1970. Finally, London Jewry had a whole array of Zionist organizations and a large number of bodies supporting Israel institutions (in 1970 there were 65 such organizations in London, most with branches in provincial communities).

CULTURE AND RELIGIOUS LIFE. The leading part played by London Jewry in English Jewish life was particularly apparent in the cultural sphere. The largest number of publications on Jewish themes – newspapers, magazines, journals, or books – emanated from London, which also had ten libraries and museums with Jewish collections open to the public. The permanent residence of the chief rabbi engaged by the United Synagogue, the largest synagogal body in the country with a membership of 40,000 and 80 synagogues, further added to London's leading position. These factors generally had the effect of centralizing the administration of communal affairs. Thus, the Chief Rabbinate and its *bet din* tended to administer the religious life of large sections of provincial Jewry through other *battei din* and rabbis. The two leading bodies dealing with religious education, the London Board of Jewish Education and the Central Council for Jewish Religious Education dealing with the provinces, both operated from London. The pattern was similar in the political and philanthropic spheres. However, after World War II, and particularly in the 1960s, there was a growing trend toward decentralization. For example, the second largest synagogal body, the Federation of Synagogues, with 17,000 members in some 50 branches, as well as the smaller religious groups, i.e., the Union of Orthodox Hebrew Congregations, the Reform and Liberal movements, and the Sephardim, set up independent *battei din*. Growing decentralization was also manifest in other fields, including Jewish education, despite efforts, mainly from the center, to maintain some overall organizational unity in the Jewish community of Britain.

London's position appeared even less formidable when a number of other important facts were taken into account. Although strict Orthodoxy made important strides there, particularly through the growing strength of the ḥasidic groups in the Stamford Hill area, the largest and most successful yeshivah was in the small provincial community of Gateshead in the northeast corner of England. As for Jewish day schools, Manchester undoubtedly took the leading position. However, when London Jewry was set in the proper perspective in relation to the rest of Britain's Jewish community, it became clear that it was a very strong force not only in that community but in world Jewry.

[Ernest Krausz]

Later Developments

Since the readmission of 1656 London has been the home of the largest Jewish community in Britain. In keeping with general demographic trends, the size and spread of London Jewry has changed since the 1970s. In terms of displacement London Jewry now constitutes "selected communities" as opposed to being a single entity. Greater London has expanded to include parts of Hertfordshire, Surrey, and Essex. Jewish migration within the capital has followed that expansion, in many instances crossing the green belt. There are now burgeoning communities in Radlett, Kingston, and Buckhurst Hill, districts which only 50 years ago had little or no Jewish presence. Within this area the largest concentration is located in the northwest London borough of Barnet. The second largest community is congregated to the east of London, in the borough of Redbridge. The Jewish community of Redbridge has access to London's only non-synagogue-based Jewish center.

Since 1970 London Jewry has expanded geographically but decreased numerically. The downward trend has been consistent since 1975, at which time the Jewish population numbered 221,000; by 1988 that figure had been reduced to 210,000, and by 2002 to 195,000. Overall the Jewish population of Britain fell from an all-time high of 420,000 in 1950 to 300,000 in 2002. The decline is attributable to a combination of factors: an excess of deaths over births, general social erosion as a result of increasing intermarriage, social and geographic movements away from community, and emigration.

During the 1990s London saw a continuation of the trend away from Jewish traditional central Orthodox synagogue membership toward both Progressive Judaism on the left and Ultra-Orthodox on the right. Mainstream Orthodoxy also lost members to the Masorti movement which was established in 1985 by Rabbi Louis Jacobs. There were six Masorti synagogues within the Greater London area.

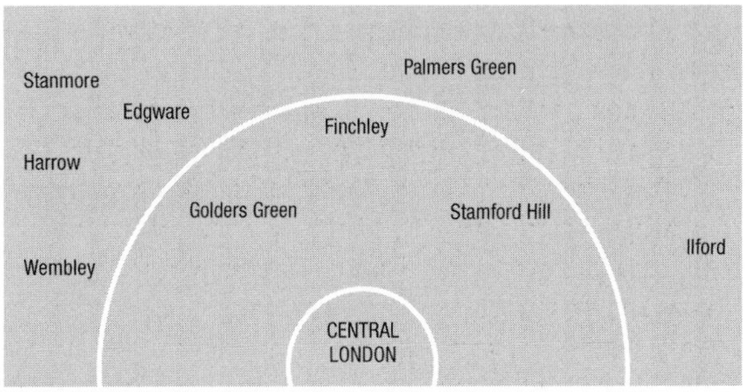

Map of London showing shift of Jewish population according to establishment of Hebrew congregations.

The London Jewish community is still served by a broad range of welfare organizations though recently there has been a movement toward rationalization following the amalgamation of the Jewish Blind Society and the Jewish Welfare Board, plus a number of other small societies, into Jewish Care. This organization provides daily for over 5,000 needy individuals and their families. Plans are also in the pipeline to merge the capital's two major Jewish child care institutions, Norwood and Ravenswood. London's expanding elderly community is provided for by a number of residential homes which offer both independent and full-care facilities. One of the largest is Nightingale House (Home for Aged Jews) in southwest London, which accommodates over 400 residents.

[Anne J. Kershen]

Hebrew Printing

Some Hebrew printing on wood blocks appeared in works printed in London from 1524, when a few isolated words and phrases figured in R. *Wakefield's *Oratio de utilitate... trium linguarum*. Movable Hebrew type was apparently first used in 1563 in W. Musculus' *Common Places of Christian Religion*, and consecutive Hebrew printing (a 14-line "sonnet") appeared in 1588 in a single-sheet broadside of poems in various languages by Theodore Beza celebrating the defeat of the Spanish Armada. In the 17th century a few books mainly or partly in Hebrew were published by Christian Hebraists, such as a Hebrew text of Psalms (1643), a vocalized text of *Avot* (1651), and Bryan *Walton's Polyglot Bible (1653–57). Communal controversies in the early 18th century produced the first Hebrew publications printed for (though not by) Jews, particularly the dispute that raged around haham David *Nieto's disputed Orthodoxy (1705) and a dispute concerning a divorce two years later (Aaron Hart's crudely produced *Urim ve-Tummim*, 1707). In 1714 – 15, some works by Moses Hagiz and Joseph *Ergas aimed against the Shabbateans appeared in London, presumably because of the unfavorable atmosphere in Amsterdam; and in the same year Nieto's classical *Matteh Dan* was brought out by Thomas Ilive's printing house in three editions – in Spanish alone, Spanish and Hebrew, and Hebrew alone. Thereafter there was a long hiatus in London Hebrew printing, though Ephraim *Luzzatto's poems *Elleh Benei ha-Ne'urim* appeared there in 1766 with a reprint in 1768. In 1770, printing by and for Jews at last began, possibly in consequence of the removal of some trade restriction. A consortium of Jewish printers from Amsterdam (who, however, failed after a few years) set up a printing house which produced ambitious editions of the Jewish liturgy (3 vols., 1770; other eds., 1771, 1785) and many other works. Simultaneously, A. *Alexander began his printing activity which was continued by his son Levi (mainly liturgical works) well into the 19th century. Other printers, Jewish and non-Jewish, appeared in the following years. In 1820 J. Wertheimer set up his Hebrew press, which was active for over a century, subsequently under the name of Williams, Lea, and Company. With the increase in the London Jewish population, especially after the emigration from Eastern Europe from the 1880s onward, Jewish printers and printing in London proliferated, though learned works were mainly produced at the presses of the universities of Oxford and Cambridge.

[Cecil Roth]

BIBLIOGRAPHY: Roth, Mag Bibl, index; idem, England, index; Lehmann, Nova Bibl, index; E.N. Adler, *[History of the Jews in] London* (1930); M. Gaster, *History of the Ancient Synagogue... Bevis Marks* (1901); C. Roth, *Federation of Synagogues* (1947); idem, *Great Synagogue, London, 1690–1940* (1950); A.B. Levy, *East End Story* (1951); A.M. Hyamson, *Sephardim of England* (1951); idem, *London Board for Shechita, 1804–1954* (1954); V.D. Lipman, *Social History of the Jews in England* (1954); idem, *Century of Social Service* (1959); idem, in: JHSET, 21 (1968), 78–103; idem, (ed.), *Three Centuries of Anglo-Jewish History* (1961); A. Barnett, *Western Synagogue through Two Centuries* (1961); idem, in: JHSET, 20 (1964), 1–50; S. Stein, *ibid.*, 63–82; A. Rubens, in: J.M. Shaftesley (ed.), *Remember the Days* (1966), 181–205; A. Ziderman, in: JJSO, 8 (1966), 240–64; E. Krausz, *ibid.*, 10 (1968), 83–100; 11 (1969), 75–95, 151–63; R. Apple, *Hampstead Synagogue* (1967); A.S. Diamond, in: JHSET, 21 (1968), 39–63; C. Bermant, *Troubled Eden* (1969); J. Gould and S. Esh (eds.), *Jewish Life in Modern Britain* (1964); C. Duschinsky, *Rabbinate of the Great Synagogue, London, from 1756–1842* (1921, 1971[2]).

LONDON, ARTUR (1915–1986), Czechoslovak statesman and Communist leader. He was born in Ostrava. In 1937 he went to Spain and joined the Communists within the International Brigade fighting in the Spanish Civil War. After the defeat of the Republican cause, London lived in France. Following the fall of France in 1940, he was arrested by the Nazis and deported to Buchenwald. London returned to France in 1945 where he represented the Czechoslovak information board. He was a prominent figure in the Czech Communist Party and following the Communist coup d'état of 1948 he was recalled to Prague to become a member of the central committee of the Communist Party. In the same year he became deputy minister of foreign affairs and as director of the ministry was responsible for the appointment of the diplomatic service. In 1951 London was arrested and charged with being a Zionist and a Trotskyite. He was one of the accused at the *Slansky Trial and in 1952 was sentenced to life imprisonment. He was released in 1955, however, and was later rehabilitated, becoming a member of the editorial staff of the monthly *Mezinárodní Politika*. In 1963 he left Czechoslovakia to join his family in France and in 1969 published his book *L'Aveu – Dans l'engrenage du procès de Prague* (ed. Gallimard), an account of the Slansky Trial, which was made into a film in 1970.

BIBLIOGRAPHY: P. Meyer et al., *Jews in the Soviet Satellites* (1953), index; *Procès des Dirigeants du Centre de Conspiration contre l'État dirigé par Rudolf Slansky* (1953), 200–20; E. Loebl, *Sentenced and Tried* (1969), 143–50; S. Orenstein, *Lefi Pekuddah mi-Moskvah* (1969), 165–74.

[Erich Kulka]

LONDON, FRITZ (1900–1954), German theoretical physicist. London was born in Breslau, and was at the University of Berlin until driven out by the Nazis. In 1927, together with

Walter Heitler of Zurich, he wrote a basic paper for physicists and chemists, on the homopolar chemical bond, interpreting valency in terms of electronic spin. This was followed by studies of activation energy, the tetravalency of carbon, and van der Waals forces. From 1933 to 1936 he worked in a laboratory in Oxford mainly on superconductivity at temperatures near absolute zero, and from then until 1939 he was director of research at the College de France in Paris. From 1939 he was professor at Duke University (Durham, North Carolina), first of theoretical chemistry, and finally of physical chemistry.

BIBLIOGRAPHY: *New York Times* (March 31, 1954), 27; *Nature*, 174 (July 10, 1954), 63.

[Samuel Aaron Miller]

LONDON (Burnstein, Burnsun), GEORGE (1920–1985), bass-baritone singer. Born in Montreal, London studied in Los Angeles where his first professional appearance, as Dr. Grenvil in *La Traviata,* was at the Hollywood Bowl (1941). Forced to support himself by performing light music and appearing in operetta, he began an international career with his debut at the Vienna State Opera in 1949. Thereafter he became world-renowned for his performances in operas by Wagner (at many Bayreuth seasons between 1951 and 1964) but his repertoire included also Don Giovanni, Gounod's Méphistophélès, the multiple villains in *Les contes d'Hoffmann*, the Dutchman, Scarpia, Mandryka (which he recorded impressively under *Solti), and the title role in Menotti's *Le dernier sauvage.* He was the first non-Russian to sing the title role in *Boris Godunov* at the Bolshoi, Moscow, in 1960; and he was awarded the title of *Kammersaenger* by the Austrian government in 1954. In later years (from 1968) he concentrated on opera house administration, and was appointed artistic administrator of the John F. Kennedy Center, Washington (1968), and general director of the Los Angeles Music Center Opera Association (1971). In his prime, London had few equals as a Wagnerian *Heldenbariton* of power and majesty.

ADD. BIBLIOGRAPHY: Grove online; T. Page: Obituary, *The New York Times* (March 26, 1985).

[Max Loppert / Israela Stein (2nd ed.)]

LONDON, JACOB BEN MOSES JUDAH (first half of 18th century), rabbi and scholar. Born in Wesel, Germany, Jacob was taken to London as a child, when his father was appointed cantor there. There are those, however, who maintain he was born in London. When his father died, Jacob settled in Frankfurt, where he attended the yeshivah of Samuel Schotten. After the fire in the Frankfurt Jewish quarter in 1711, London moved to Leszno, Poland, where he became cantor and director of the Jewish school. For several years he lived in Prague, holding the post of inspector of the Talmud Torah schools, but he returned to Leszno in 1728. For the next six years he was engaged in writing an allegorical work, *Histaʾarut Melekh ha-Negev im Melekh ha-Ẓafon* (Amsterdam, 1737), describing the struggle between the evil and the good inclination. He later traveled to Italy, where he published *Meginnei Shelomo* (Venice, 1741) by *Joshua Heschel b. Joseph of Cracow and *Shivah Einayim* (Leghorn, 1745), which consisted of halakhic writings by *Naḥmanides, Isaac *Alfasi, Isaac *Aboab, Judah de Leon, Isaac *Ibn Ghayyat, and Abraham Bulat. While on a journey to Piedmont, London was suspected of espionage on account of the Hebrew manuscripts that he had in his possession. In his introduction to *Meginnei Shelomo*, London mentions that he wrote a halakhic work entitled *Pegiʿat Yaʿakov*, which is no longer extant. He also wrote *Ez Ḥayyim*, a two-part work on moral precepts that was never published.

BIBLIOGRAPHY: Steinschneider, Cat Bod, 1230; Ghirondi-Neppi, 124; Landshuth, Ammudei, 108; Fuenn, Keneset, 553; Zunz, Lit Poesie, 450; Carmoly, in: *Revue Orientale*, 2 (1842), 334; L. Lewin, *Geschichte der Juden in Lissa* (1904), 289 ff.

[Samuel Abba Horodezky]

LONDON, MEYER (1871–1926), U.S. lawyer and Socialist leader. London was born in Gora Kalvaria, Poland, and followed his father to New York City in 1891. He was immediately drawn into radical politics, in large measure because of his father's involvement with anarchist and Socialist groups. Initially an adherent of the Socialist Labor Party, he joined the opposition to its leader, Daniel *De Leon, in 1897, and ultimately became a member of the Socialist Party of America.

London had a significant influence on the needle trades unions of New York City in their formative period prior to World War I. Admitted to the bar in 1898, he served as legal counsel for a multitude of unions and union members. London was intensely pragmatic in labor matters, and despite his Socialist ideology, he helped to formulate the Protocol of 1910, which attempted to establish collective bargaining and arbitration in the women's cloak trade. London resisted the argument of some Socialists that such agreements substituted mutuality of interest for class struggle. He favored unemployment insurance, the abolition of child labor, and other social-reform legislation designed to improve the conditions of life and labor for the worker.

In 1914, after repeated attempts at elective office, London won election to the House of Representatives as a Socialist from a largely immigrant Jewish district on the Lower East Side in New York City; he was reelected in 1916 and 1920. Although he was a moderate Socialist, he endured the full brunt of bitter anti-Socialist attacks.

As a congressman he was active and argued strongly for reform. He voted against restrictive immigration and the Fordney tariff and actively supported nationalization of the coal industry. One bill of his became law: an act protecting the employees of bankrupt firms.

Although he strongly opposed American entrance into World War I and fought efforts to curb the civil liberties of opponents of the war, London refused to resist all wartime activities without qualification. This position alienated him from many of his friends and associates in American radicalism. He also had little sympathy for Zionism, believing that the emancipation of the Jew had to be accomplished not through nationalism but by uplifting the working class. London died as the result of a car accident.

BIBLIOGRAPHY: H. Rogoff, *East Side Epic: Life and Work of Meyer London* (1930); A. Gorenstein, in: AJHSP, 50 (1961), 202–38; M. Epstein, *Profiles of Eleven* (1965), index.

[Irwin Yellowitz]

LONDON, SOLOMON ZALMAN BEN MOSES RAPHAEL (1661–1748), author, translator, and bookseller. London was born in Nowogrudok (Lithuania). Between 1709 and 1735 he published and sold books in Amsterdam, London, and Frankfurt on the Main. He is best known for *Kohelet Shelomo* (1722), a devotional handbook which included occasional and domestic prayers and benedictions together with ritual laws and instructions both in Hebrew and Yiddish. It became popular in Western Europe and was reprinted many times, including later editions in which the Yiddish was replaced by German (cf. the Ger. ed. of 1919 (?) and that by A. Sulzbach, 1908). *Kohelet Shelomo* also contains a Passover *Haggadah* with Leone de Modena's commentary *Ẓeli Esh*. This *Haggadah* also appeared separately (1733) and was reprinted several times. *Ḥinnukh Katan*, a small Hebrew-Yiddish vocabulary, was added to some of the editions. London's *Zokher ha-Berit* (1714), which followed the same lines, detailed the ceremonies and laws of circumcision and redemption of the firstborn, with Yiddish translation. He also published a *siddur*, according to the German-Polish rite, under the title *Tikkun Shelomo* (1712, 1733^2 often reprinted), with Yiddish text added; it included the *Tikkunei Shabbat* of Isaac Luria. London prepared a number of ethical and halakhic compendia by various authors, providing a Yiddish translation. These included such works as *Orḥot Ẓaddikim* (author unknown, 1735); Jonah Gerondi's (13th century) *Iggeret ha-Teshuvah* (1742); and Isaac b. Eliezer's (15th century) *Sefer ha-Gan* (1747).

LONG BEACH, U.S. city in California, located south of Los Angeles along the Pacific Coast (on the Los Angeles and Orange County border). The first Jewish family came to Long Beach in 1898 and since then the community has grown and prospered, reaching a population of 18,000 in 2001.

In 1898 Samuel Heller visited the city, liked its potential, and stayed to engage in real estate development. When the city introduced a municipal produce market in 1913, a number of Jewish produce men moved to Long Beach to operate stalls. By 1915 the population included 25 Jewish families. The first permanent Jewish organization was established after World War I with the chartering of B'nai B'rith Lodge 870 with 33 members. In 1922 the Community Building Association was established. It was dissolved in 1923 and reconstituted as a Reform congregation, Temple Israel, with Julius Liebert as its first full-time rabbi. In 1924 Temple Sinai (Conservative) was established with Lazar Friedland as its rabbi. Rabbis of Temple Israel included Harvey Franklin (1930), Elliot Grafman (1938), and Wolli Kaelter (1955). Temple Sinai had Jacob Friedman (1929), Shalom Ravetch (1935), and Sidney Guthman (1959). Jewish Welfare Fund campaigns began in 1929. In 1945 a Jewish Federation was established. A Jewish community center was organized in 1948; its first center building was dedicated in 1960. In 1952, with 6,300 Jews in the rapidly growing city, a second Conservative congregation was formed with Maurice Schwartz as rabbi, followed in 1962 by Rabbi Joseph Miller.

In 1960, when the first Jewish Community Center was dedicated, Long Beach was a quiet, conservative, small city and Orange County was a vast, fragrant orange grove. Today, Long Beach/West Orange County is an exciting 21st-century city with a World Trade Center, prominent hotels, and a revitalized downtown with a fine Cultural Arts Center and a convention center. International jazz concerts and local arts festivals have replaced the annual Iowa picnic and the Pike amusement park (Long Beach was once dubbed "Iowa by the sea"). Once rural, West Orange County now contains impressive suburban neighborhoods and pre-eminent commercial centers. At the edge of the Pacific Rim, Long Beach/West Orange County has become an exciting place to live and the changes have also affected the Jewish community. Increasing numbers of professionals and corporate executives with their families are moving there. At both ends of the age continuum the population is growing. Recognizing the need to meet the growing needs of the Jewish community, a campaign to build a new Jewish Community Campus was launched in the 1990s and on March 20, 1999, the Federation's Harry and Jeanette Weinberg Jewish Community Campus was dedicated. The over 80,000-square-foot Campus is home to the Barbara and Ray Alpert Jewish Community Center, Jewish Federation of Greater Long Beach & West Orange County, Jewish Family and Children's Service, Jewish Federation Foundation, and Hillel. The Hebrew Academy, also served by the Jewish Federation, is located in the Westminster/Huntington Beach area.

The Campus contains a beautiful Early Childhood Education Wing, gym, pool, state of the art health and fitness center, library, cafe, dance studio, auditorium, gift shop, art gallery, and meeting and office space that is available to the entire community.

The estimated Jewish population is approximately 20–25 thousand persons. They reside in the Greater Long Beach area (out of a total population of approximately 500,000), which includes the neighboring communities of Rossmor, Los Alamitos, Seal Beach, and Lakewood.

Jewish communal life in the Greater Long Beach area is thriving and consists of congregations of all denominations. Current congregations include P'nai Or (Renewal); Temple Israel, Temple Beth David, and Temple Ner Tamid (Reform); Temple Beth Shalom, Temple Beth Zion-Sinai, and Congregation Sholom of Leisure World (Conservative); Congregation Lubavitch, Chabad of Cypress, Ahavas Yisrael, and Shul by the Shore (Orthodox); and Adat Chaverim (Traditional). The synagogues and agencies have formed a Kehillah Leadership Council, under the auspices of Federation, and meet every other month to discuss common issues and work together to build a vibrant, cohesive Jewish community.

[Sharon Kenigsberg (2nd ed.)]

LONGO, SAADIAH (first half of 16th century), poet. Born in Turkey, Saadiah lived in Salonika, where he was a member of the Ḥakhmei ha-Shir ("scholars of poetry"), a group of poets supported by Gedaliah ibn Yaḥya, a wealthy Salonikan. In addition to his *Shivrei Luḥot* (Salonika, 1594), consisting of poems of elegy and lament, he composed poems of friendship and jest in the spirit of his age. He also wrote poems of "beliefs," a type of poem which commences in a serious vein and then goes on to deal with the self-evident; they are banal and lack originality. Poems of this kind were composed in a spirit of rivalry by the poets of the group, who disagreed on the method of composition and the use of poetic conventions. The poets sharply criticized each other's work, and their criticism sometimes degenerated into personal attack. Longo's disputant in these poems was Jacob Tarfon, a local contemporary.

BIBLIOGRAPHY: H. Brody, in: *Minḥah le-David* (1935), 205–20; A.M. Habermann, *Toledot ha-Piyyut ve-ha-Shirah* (1970), 232–4; EJ, s.v.

[Abraham Meir Habermann]

LONS-LE-SAUNIER, capital of the department of Jura, in *Franche-Comté, E. France. A *vicus Judeorum* ("Jewish quarter") is mentioned in Lons in 1220; the establishment of the community therefore preceded this date. The Rue des Juifs (later the Rue de la Comédie and Rue de la Balerne) is mentioned down to the 14th century. The Jews of Lons owned a cemetery, but there is no record of a synagogue. During the 14th century, Jews from Lons are found in numerous other localities of Franche-Comté. During World War II, a large number of Jews from Alsace and Lorraine who took refuge in Lons established a community numbering approximately 1,300 members. Lons also became the seat of a regional rabbinate. There was no organized community in Lons by the 1960s.

BIBLIOGRAPHY: B. Prost and S. Bougenot, *Cartulaire de Hugues de Chalon...* (1904), 496; L. Gauthier in: *Mémoires de la société d'émulation du Jura*, 3 (1914), passim; J. Brelot and G. Duhem, *Histoire de Lons-le-Saunier* (1957), 74; Z. Szajkowski, *Analytical Franco-Jewish Gazetteer* (1966), 208–9.

[Bernhard Blumenkranz]

LONZANO, ABRAHAM BEN RAPHAEL DE (late 17th–early 18th century), kabbalist and Hebrew grammarian. It seems that he was a descendant of the renowned kabbalist Menahem de *Lonzano. Abraham became well known through his *Kinyan Avraham* (Zolkiew, 1723) on Hebrew grammar, from which it appears that he came from Zakinthos (Zante), one of the Greek isles. Following the attacks of the local inhabitants against the Jews, many troubles befell him and he began to wander from country to country. He studied at the yeshivah Eẓ Ḥayyim in Amsterdam. At a later date, he appears to have been in Prague where he was persecuted by the scholars of the yeshivah because he criticized them sharply for studying Torah without a knowledge of the Hebrew language. He wrote a declaration against Neḥemiah Ḥiyya *Ḥayon in Genoa in 1715 (published in *Sefunot*; see bibliography). He was in Lemberg in about 1723. In one of his poems, which appeared in his book, he angrily attacked those who regard themselves as poets without having any knowledge of even the form and arrangement of a poem. He also wrote *Ḥamishah Kinyanim* (unpublished), a commentary to the *Sefer Yeẓirah*. He subsequently converted to Christianity in the Prussian town of Idstein and adopted the name Wilhelm Heinrich Neumann.

BIBLIOGRAPHY: Steinschneider, Handbuch, 85 no. 1201; J.F.A. de le Roi, *Die evangelische Christenheit und die Juden*, 1 (1884), 393; M. Friedman, in: *Sefunot*, 10 (1966), 602–6; Frumkin-Rivlin, 2 (1928), 156–7.

[Abraham David]

LONZANO, MENAHEM BEN JUDAH DE (1550–before 1624), linguist, poet, and kabbalist. Little is known about his life, but it is assumed that he was born in Constantinople. At the age of 25 he immigrated to *Jerusalem and later moved to *Safed. Forty years later, he went to *Turkey and to *Italy, and in 1618 he returned to Jerusalem.

Lonzano was best known for *Shetei Yadot* (Venice, 1618), which is divided into two sections (*Yad Ani* and *Yad ha-Melekh*). The first contains his original writings and the second the midrashic literature which he intended to edit. Each section is called *yad* ("hand") and has five *eẓba'ot* ("fingers"). *Yad Ani* includes the following: (1) *Or Torah* (also separately, Amsterdam, 1659), notes on the masorah ("text") of the Torah according to the weekly portions, comparing the printed Venice editions with important manuscripts which he knew. Because his work relates only to the Torah, it became second in importance to *Minḥat Shai*, by his contemporary Solomon *Norzi, which treats the entire Scripture. Despite this fact Lonzano's work was reprinted in many editions with additions and interpretations. (2) *Ma'arikh* (also separately, Leipzig, 1853), additions to the talmudic dictionary *He-Arukh* by *Nathan b. Jehiel of Rome. The work is based on his knowledge of Greek and Arabic and other languages (Turkish and Persian) used by his Jewish contemporaries. (3) *Avodat haMikdash* (also separately, Constantinople, 1572), prayers for the order of worship in the Temple, with additions according to "the wisdom of the Zohar." (4) *Derekh Ḥayyim* (also separately, Constantinople, 1573), moralistic poetry. (5) *Tovah Tokhaḥat*, a long moralistic poem. From *Yad ha-Melekh*, he only managed to publish the first section, *Aggedata de-Bereshit*, which was reprinted many times. He intended to conclude the publication of *Midrash Agur*, which had begun to appear in Safed in 1587, and also planned to publish other important Midrashim according to manuscripts which he himself discovered, but this material has been lost.

Lonzano's other works treat Lurianic Kabbalah and aroused bitter opposition: (1) *Omer Man*, a commentary on the *Idra Zuta* and the *Sifra de-Ẓeni'uta* (Vilna, 1883); (2) *Imrei Emet*, a critique of Luria's interpretation of *Sifra de-Ẓeni'uta* and repudiations of Ḥayyim *Vital. According to Lonzano, Luria wrote his commentary before he received divine inspiration and "if he could, he would have changed or hidden this work" (Ms. British Museum 9167). Other works planned by Lonzano were hidden and only parts of them were preserved in manuscripts or published posthumously. They include (1) a commentary on the Zohar (fragment, in manuscript); (2) comments on *Tikkunei Zohar* (Ms.); (3) *Haggahot le-Zohar Ḥadash* (Venice, 1643); (4) *Haggahot le-Talmud Yerushalmi* (Warsaw, 1737); (5) *Adi Zahav*, annotations on the book *Ha-Levushim* by Mordecai Jaffe; (6) comments on the prayer book (lost). Lonzano's originality caused him to suffer from the attacks of his opponents. In this matter his dispute with Gedaliah *Cordovero is of interest, but its background is still not clear. He was a thorough scholar. In search of manuscripts he made several trips abroad where he met with many scholars. As a poet, Lonzano was involved in a quarrel with Israel *Najara whom he criticized because of his use of erotic language and words such as "adulterers say to one another" (*Shetei Yadot*, 142) to describe the relationship between Israel and God.

BIBLIOGRAPHY: Frumkin-Rivlin, 1 (1928), 134–45; Davidson, Oẓar, index; G. Scholem, *Kitvei Yad be-Kabbalah* (1930), 115–6, 152, 156; M. Kasher, *Sarei ha-Elef* (1959), 16, 18; A. Yaari, *Ha-Defus ha-Ivri be-Kushta* (1967), 116; Rosanes, Togarmah, 2 (1938), 182–6; M. Wander, *Derekh ha-Ḥayyim* (1931), 1–29, introduction; I. Sonne, in: *Koveẓ al Yad*, 5 (1950), 197–204; S.H. Kook, *Iyyunim u-Meḥkarim*, 1 (1959), 241–5; R. Elitzur, in: KS, 42 (1967), 511.

[David Samuel Loewinger]

LOOKSTEIN, HASKEL (1932–), U.S. rabbi, educator, and activist. Lookstein served in rabbinical capacities at Congregation Kehilath Jeshurun in New York City immediately following his ordination from Yeshiva University in 1958. He served initially as an assistant under his father Rabbi Joseph H. *Lookstein. He was the third member of his family to lead this congregation, following his maternal great-grandfather Rabbi Moses S. *Margolies (the Ramaz) and his father. Commonly referred to as KJ, Congregation Kehilath Jeshurun grew under his leadership to a membership of over one thousand families.

In 1966, Lookstein also succeeded his father as the principal of Ramaz School, an Orthodox Jewish day school. Following the tradition established by his father and fostered by his own *rebbe*, Rabbi Joseph B. Solevitchik, Lookstein maintained Ramaz School as a leader in Jewish education, with a co-educational curriculum in which class offerings for over 1,100 young girls and boys were totally equal. In addition, under his leadership the Ramaz School sustained a student body that achieved the highest level of general education, combined and infused with both the education and the enthusiasm of a vibrant religious Zionist commitment. All of this Lookstein fostered while insisting that the students synthesize their studies and academic achievements with an unflinching commitment to *menschlichkeit*.

Lookstein was one of the most vigorous supporters and leaders of religious Zionism in America. He worked to encourage travel to Israel, Jewish education in Israel, *aliyah*, investment, and support for the Government of Israel – regardless of what the political leadership might be at any particular time.

Lookstein was one of the leading, early voices fighting and speaking out on behalf of the plight of Soviet Jewry. He traveled frequently to meet with Soviet *refuseniks* and encouraged his congregants and students to do so as well. He marched, demonstrated, was arrested, and spoke out on behalf of Russian Jews. By example and through persuasion, in this initiative as well as on behalf of Operation Moses, UJA, and Israel Bonds, Lookstein moved his community and the school to take a prominent role financially on behalf of the needs of the Jewish people.

Lookstein was a leading voice in the American Orthodox community to maintaining relations with all the other Jewish denominations. He was president of the Synagogue Council of America; served as vice president of the Beth Din of America and as a member of the board of directors of the JDC Board; and was a head of the national UJA Rabbinic Cabinet.

Lookstein graduated from Ramaz School, received his B.A. from Columbia College in 1953, his rabbinic ordination from Yeshiva University in 1958, and his Ph.D. in Modern Jewish History from Yeshiva in 1979. Lookstein was named the Joseph H. Lookstein Professor of Homiletics at Yeshiva University. His dissertation, "Were We Our Brothers' Keepers? The Public Response of American Jews to the Holocaust 1938–1944," appeared in 1985, and he published extensively in the U.S. and throughout the world.

[Gilbert N. Kahn (2nd ed.)]

LOOKSTEIN, JOSEPH HYMAN (1902–1979), U.S. rabbi and educator. Lookstein was born in Russia and immigrated to the United States as a child. In 1923 he became assistant rabbi to Rabbi Moses S. *Margolies (known as the "Ramaz") at Congregation Kehilath Jeshurun in New York City. In 1926 he married the Ramaz's granddaughter, and in 1936 he became the congregation's rabbi upon the passing of Rabbi Margolies. Lookstein would transform the pulpit into one of the most exciting and powerful voices in the entire American rabbinate.

Lookstein was ordained at the Rabbi Isaac Elchanan Theological Seminary in 1926. In 1929 he helped found the Hebrew Teachers Training School for girls and served as its principal for ten years; in 1937 Lookstein founded the Ramaz School on the Upper East Side of New York and in the heart of the state's German-American community in Yorkville. The school became part of a two-pronged force to challenge and to change Modern Orthodoxy. It was dedicated to educating young American children to be committed and knowledgeable Jews, while at the same time sustaining the finest in Western democratic values. Integrating a deep and abiding sense of Zionist spirit and identification with Palestine and then the State of Israel, Rabbi Lookstein presided as principal of Ramaz for over 30 years. The school has continued to be the premiere "modern" Orthodox Jewish day school in the world.

In 1958, Lookstein became acting president and chancellor of Israel's Bar-Ilan University. Lookstein had previously taught at Yeshiva University, where he had been a professor of sociology, homiletics, and practical rabbinics since 1931. While maintaining his fierce allegiance to Orthodoxy, Lookstein also maintained deep and sincere relationships with all the religious denominations and their leaders. Throughout his career, he translated this commitment into service and leadership on interdenominational committees and organizations. He kept the Ramaz School firmly in the Orthodox camp, but equally fiercely as a modern Orthodox institution where boys and girls studied together and had well-rounded activities, including mixed dancing.

He was chairman of the Jewish Welfare Board's Chaplaincy Commission (1954–57), president of the Rabbinical Council of America (1941–43), the New York Board of Rabbis, the Synagogue Council of America (1976), and the UJA Rabbinical Advisory Council (1978). Despite growing up as an Agudist, Lookstein was guided by Rabbi Margolies into actively supporting the Mizrachi movement. He served as Chairman of the Palestine Commission of the American Jewish Conference and as a consultant to the U.S. delegation to the 1945 San Francisco Conference. His philosophy of the integration of Judaism with the best of Western culture was expressed in the schools he founded and in his articles and books, which include *Judaism in Theory and Practice* (1931), *Sources of Courage* (1943), and *Faith and Destiny of Man* (1967). Lookstein served as rabbi with his son and successor, Rabbi Haskel *Lookstein, thus keeping the leadership of his flagship congregation within one family for more than a century.

[Louis Bernstein / Gilbert N. Kahn (2nd ed.)]

LOPES, English family whose assimilated descendants attained distinction in English life. MANASSEH LOPES (early 18th century), a prominent broker, made a fortune by speculation on false reports of Queen Anne's death. MANASSEH MASSEH (Massey) LOPES (1755–1831) was born in Jamaica, the son of the West Indian merchant MORDECHAI RODRIGUES LOPES (d. 1796). He converted to Christianity in 1802, becoming a member of parliament in that year, and was created a baronet in 1805. He was heavily fined and imprisoned in 1819 for corruption in a parliamentary election but was nevertheless later returned for Westbury. He resigned in 1829 in favor of Sir Robert Peel. Subsequently, he was recorder of Westbury. Lopes was among the earliest Jewish estate owners in England, spending over £100,000 on lands in Mairstow, Devon, and Plymouth. SIR RALPH LOPES (formerly Raphael Ralph Franco; 1788–1854), a descendant on the male side of the Leghorn *Franco family, succeeded his uncle, Manasseh Masseh Lopes, in the baronetcy. SIR LOPES MASSEY LOPES (1818–1908), eldest son of Ralph Lopes, was a civil lord of the Admiralty from 1874 to 1880 in Disraeli's government. Sir HENRY CHARLES LOPES (Baron Ludlow; 1828–1899), third son of Ralph Lopes, was a lord justice of the Court of Appeal 1885–1897. The head of the family held the title of Baron Roborough from 1938.

BIBLIOGRAPHY: J. Picciotto, *Sketches of Anglo-Jewish History* (1950³), 55, 209, 296–8, 407; A.M. Hyamson, *Sephardim of England* (1951), 201–4. **ADD. BIBLIOGRAPHY:** ODNB online.

[Cecil Roth]

LOPEZ, AARON (1731–1782), American merchant-shipper. Born in Portugal, Lopez went in 1752 to Newport, Rhode Island, where, renouncing his Marrano past, he remarried his wife Abigail in a Jewish ceremony, underwent circumcision, and in time became a leader of the Yeshuat Israel Congregation. Lopez' ties to the well-established *Gomez and Rivera families and the British America's economic boom during the French and Indian War assured him the credit he needed to expand his business beyond Rhode Island. Jacob Rodriguez *Rivera, whose daughter Sarah he married in 1763 after Abigail's death, often acted as his partner. Though a specialist in the whale oil and spermaceti candle industries, Lopez' business included livestock, groceries, lumber, rum, ships, and clothing. He was also among the few American Jews active in the slave trade. The credit he secured during the 1760s and 1770s from his English suppliers enabled Lopez to build an extensive transatlantic mercantile empire. Lopez had trading connections with the Caribbean, Western Europe, and West Africa and on the eve of the American Revolution, was Newport's leading merchant and her largest taxpayer. Lopez supported the rebel cause and withdrew from British-threatened Newport to Leicester in central Massachusetts. This diminished his business and he did not survive to recoup his losses. The Newporters, to whose prosperity he had contributed so signally before the Revolution, mourned him, wrote Stiles, with a "demonstration of universal sorrow."

BIBLIOGRAPHY: Bigelow, in: *New England Quarterly*, 4 (1931), 757–76; *Commerce of Rhode Island*, 2 vols. (1914–15); M. Gutstein, *Aaron Lopez and Judah Touro* (1939); J. Marcus, *Colonial American Jews*, 3 vols. (1970); S.F. Chyet, *Lopez of Newport* (1970).

[Stanley F. Chyet]

LOPEZ, ROBERT SABATINO (1910–1986), U.S. medieval historian, son of Sabatino *Lopez. Born in Genoa, Italy, Lopez began his teaching career at the teachers' colleges of Cagliari, Pavia, and Genoa, and at the University of Genoa. As the Fascist regime in Italy became more oppressive, Lopez migrated to the U.S. in 1939 and continued his studies. He was appointed professor at Yale University in 1955 and chairman of Medieval Studies (1963). Lopez was a prolific author and is particularly well known for several highly significant books and articles on various aspects of the economic history of the Middle Ages.

Among his books are *Studi sull'economia genovese nel medioevo* (1936), *Storia delle colonie genovesi* (1938), *Medieval Trade in the Mediterranean World* (with I.W. Raymond, 1955), *La prima crisi della banca di Genova* (1956), *The Birth of Europe* (1967), *The Three Ages of the Italian Renaissance* (1970),

Civilizations, Western and World (1975), *The Commercial Revolution of the Middle Ages, 950–1350* (1976), *The Medieval City* (with D. Herlihy, 1978), and *Byzantium and the World around It* (1978). He served on various Jewish committees concerned with Zionism and Israel.

[Howard L. Adelson / Ruth Beloff (2nd ed.)]

LOPEZ, RODERIGO (1525–1594), Portuguese Marrano physician. After graduating at Salamanca, he settled in London early in the reign of Queen Elizabeth. He became a member of the College of Physicians and was the first house physician at St. Bartholomew's Hospital. Subsequently, he was appointed physician to the earl of Leicester and in 1586 to Queen Elizabeth. He was connected by marriage with Alvaro Mendes (Solomon *Abenaes), duke of Mytilene, the adviser of the Turkish sultan. Lopez worked closely with the earl of Essex, the Queen's favorite, and participated in an intrigue to secure English intervention on behalf of Dom *Antonio, pretender to the throne of Portugal. Later, he broke with Dom Antonio and began to work for an understanding with Spain. The Spanish court secretly negotiated with him and offered a heavy bribe if he would murder the pretender. Early in 1594 he was arrested and accused of plotting to poison Elizabeth, was found guilty, and executed at Tyburn (June 7, 1594). There is little doubt that he was innocent, though his aims and methods were not above suspicion. The case attracted much attention, and it is generally believed that Lopez was the prototype of Shylock in *Shakespeare's *Merchant of Venice*.

BIBLIOGRAPHY: G. Harvey, *Lopez the Jew* (1920); Roth, England³, 140ff.; Hume, in: JHSET, 6 (1908–10), 32–55; Wolf, *ibid.*, 11 (1924–27), 1–34; Gwyer, *ibid.*, 16 (1945–51), 163–84; Kohler, in: AJHSP, 17 (1909), 9–25; DNB, s.v.

[Cecil Roth]

LOPEZ, SABATINO (1867–1951), Italian playwright, critic and novelist. Born in Leghorn, Lopez spent some years as a teacher before devoting himself to the theater and dramatic criticism. A playwright of Italy's realistic school, he wrote about 70 plays, including such successful comedies as *La buona figliola* (1909), *La nostra pelle* (1912), *Il brutto e le belle* (pub. 1913), *Parodi & C.* (1925), and *La Signora Rosa* (1928). Faithful to Italian theatrical tradition, Lopez was essentially an actor's writer, and his plays are full of scintillating dialogue. In the earlier ones, where the emphasis is on drama, he relied on French realistic fiction and Italian *verismo*; his mature works incline to satire and ironic, though superficial, criticism of late 19th-century bourgeois morals, the irony and comedy skillfully balanced by humane sentimentality. Lopez also wrote some plays in collaboration with other writers, a book of memoirs, *S'io rinascessi* (1950), and stories of stage life, *Le Loro Maest* (1920). Between 1911 and 1919 he directed the Italian writers' guild. Lopez took an active part in Jewish communal life and was for many years the chairman of the Zionist Organization in Milan. The historian Robert Sabatino *Lopez was his son. Another son was GUIDO LOPEZ (1924–), journalist and author. He was editor of the literary section of the weekly *Epoca* and wrote the novels *Il Campo* (1948) and *La prova del nove* (1953) and a popular guidebook to Milan, *Milano in mano* (1965). He also published several documents relating to his father's literary activity.

BIBLIOGRAPHY: L. Tonelli, *Sabatino Lopez* (It., 1920); S. D'Amico, *Il teatro italiano...* (1932), 184–7; B. Curato, *Sessant'anni di teatro in Italia* (1947), 156–61; I. Sanesi, *La Commedia*, 2 (1944), passim; G. Pullini, *Teatro italiano fra due secoli* (1958), passim; Ghilardi, in: *Il Dramma* (1967), nos. 371–2, 27–43; Levi, in: RMI, 34 (1968), 131–7; *Enciclopedia dello spettacolo*, 6 (1959), s.v. **ADD. BIBLIOGRAPHY:** McGraw-Hill, *Encyclopedia of World Drama*, 1972, 3, s.v.; G. Lopez, "Federico De Roberto e Sabatino Lopez cent'anni fa," in: *Belfagor* (1997), 52:3, 332–40.

[Giorgio Romano]

LOPEZ ROSA, Marrano family, members of which suffered at the hands of the Inquisition; possibly to be identified with the family of the same name who had a printing establishment in Lisbon in the middle of the 17th century. The following are noteworthy: MOSES (DUARTE) LOPEZ ROSA (second half of 17th century), a native of Beja, Portugal, Marrano physician and poet. In maturity he immigrated, first to Rome and then to Amsterdam, where he openly embraced Judaism. He became "arbiter" of the Academia de los Floridos, founded by the Baron de *Belmonte in 1685. A facile poet, he composed complimentary verses in honor of the English and Portuguese sovereigns and other prominent personalities. He is not to be confused with another DUARTE LOPEZ ROSA of Beja, likewise a physician, reconciled by the Inquisition in 1723. SIMON LOPEZ ROSA (alias Abraham Farrar, "the elder," first half of the 17th century), a Marrano physician, was an early warden of the Beth Jacob community in Amsterdam. In common with some of his contemporaries, he was critical of the authority of the rabbis; and it was in consequence of a dispute in the congregation, occasioned by an episode in which he figured, that the Beth Israel synagogue was established. Appeal was made to R. Joel *Sirkes of Brest-Litovsk, who recommended that he should be excommunicated; a similar case, in which his cousin Dr. David Farrar was implicated, led to an appeal to the rabbinate of Salonika and to Leone *Modena in Venice. Lopez Rosa was among the Marranos judaizing in Amsterdam who were denounced to the Lisbon Inquisition in 1617.

BIBLIOGRAPHY: M. Kayserling, *Geschichte der Juden in Portugal* (1867), 319; Kayserling, Bibl, 44, 95; idem, in: REJ, 44 (1901), 275f.; M.B. Amzalak, *Abraham Pharar: notícia biobibliográfica* (1927); C. Roth, *Life of Menasseh Ben Israel* (1933), ch. 7; idem, in: HUCA, 18 (1943/44), 221–4; Brugmans-Frank, 1 (1940), 678.

[Cecil Roth]

LOPIAN, ELIJAH (1876–1970), rabbi, educator, and exponent of *musar*. Born near Grajewo, Poland, Lopian studied at Lomza and at Kelme, where he came under the influence of Simḥah Zissel *Broida. Broida's doctrine of *musar*, which emphasized the need for constant soul-searching and moral scrutiny, left a deep impression on Lopian. In Kelme he founded a yeshivah which he headed until he received an invitation in 1926 to teach at the Etz Chaim Yeshivah in London. He served there both as *mashgi'aḥ* (moral tutor) and, for a short time, as principal, until his retirement in 1950. During his years in England, he was instrumental in training many English rabbis. Lopian immigrated to Israel at the age of 74, but even then spent the last 20 years of his life as *mashgi'aḥ* of the Keneset Ḥizkiyyahu Yeshivah at Kefar Ḥasidim. Although he never published any works, Lopian was renowned both as an orator of considerable power, and the greatest exponent of the old *musar* school. Of his nine sons three were heads of yeshivot: ḤAYYIM SHEM'UEL LOPIAN (1909–) at Sunderland, author of *Ravḥa de-Shemateta*; LIEB LOPIAN (1910–1979) at Gateshead; ELIEZER LOPIAN (1911–) at Torat Emet Yeshivah, London; as were two of his sons-in-law: Leib Gurwicz (1906–) at Gateshead, and Kalman Pinski at the Kamenitz yeshivah in Jerusalem.

[Alan Unterman]

LOPOLIANSKY, URI (1951–), first **ḥaredi* mayor of Jerusalem. Lopoliansky was born in Haifa. He served in the IDF as a medic, worked as a teacher, and studied public administration. In 1976 he established Yad Sarah – a nonprofit association that lends medical equipment to the disabled and ailing – and serves as its chairman. The association operates with 6,000 volunteers in 96 branches throughout Israel. For this project he won many prizes and awards, including the Israel Prize.

Lopoliansky was first elected as a member of the Jerusalem Municipal Council in 1989. He was deputy mayor of Jerusalem in 1993–2003 under Ehud *Olmert, and head of the Planning and Construction Department in the municipality. As deputy mayor he supported Olmert's policy of expanding the boundaries of the city eastwards, in order to maintain the demographic balance in favor of the Jewish population. After Olmert was reelected to the Knesset in January 2003 Lopoliansky became acting mayor, until the new municipal elections that were held in June. In this period he canceled the traditional reception held annually on Independence Day in front of the Tower of David Museum, which used to be attended by diplomats, Arab mukhtars, clergy, IDF officers, and citizens, though he attended other Independence Day celebrations. After being elected mayor of Jerusalem, beating the secular independent candidate Nir Barkat thanks to numerous secular votes that he received, he established a *ḥaredi*-right-wing coalition, even though he tried to bring Shinui and Meretz into his coalition but failed. He objected to opening the Temple Mount to prayer for Jews for halakhic reasons and supported surrounding Jerusalem with a barrier that will separate the city from the surrounding Arab areas, for security reasons. At the same time he favored improving the services given to the Arab inhabitants of the city. Lopoliansky walked a tightrope on issues to which he had objections in principle, such as meetings with Reform leaders, or the holding of gay processions in the city (Lopoliansky condemned the event, but did not prevent it). At the same time he went out of his way to discourage violent *ḥaredi* protests.

Lopoliansky was also a member of the national Council for Planning and Construction, and a member of the National Center for the Development of Holy Sites.

[Susan Hattis Rolef (2nd ed.)]

LORBEERBAUM, JACOB BEN JACOB MOSES OF LISSA (c. 1760–1832), Polish rabbi and halakhist. His father, the rabbi of Zborow, died before Lorbeerbaum was born and his relative, Joseph *Te'omim, brought him up. After his marriage he settled in Stanislav and engaged in business, but devoted most of his time to study. He frequently attended the lectures of Meshullam *Igra. When after a few years his business failed, he accepted the rabbinate of Monasterzyska where he founded a yeshivah. He was later appointed rabbi of Kalisz where he wrote most of his books and with exceptional humility published anonymously his work on parts of Shulḥan Arukh, *Yoreh De'ah: Ḥavvat Da'at*, a name by which he himself became known in scholarly circles when his authorship came to light. This work was accepted in the rabbinic world as a compendium of practical *halakhah*, and won him the reputation of an outstanding *posek*. In 1809 he was invited to become rabbi of Lissa, long a center of Torah in Poland. Lorbeerbaum enlarged the yeshivah, to which hundreds of students streamed, among them many who later became great scholars and pioneers of the Ḥibbat Zion movement such as Elijah *Gutmacher, Ẓevi Hirsch *Kalischer, and Shraga Feivel *Danziger. Many of Jacob's contemporaries turned to him with their problems. During his time the war between the reformers and the rabbis flared up, and Lorbeerbaum, together with Akiva *Eger and Moses *Sofer, unleashed a vehement attack against the *maskilim* and the reformers. In Lissa, however, as in other towns of Great Poland that came under Prussian rule after the partition of Poland, the influence of the Berlin reformers grew continually stronger. The schism between Lorbeerbaum and a large section of the community eventually became so great that in 1822 he decided to leave Lissa and return to Kalisz. There he devoted his time to study, rejecting all offers of rabbinic posts from large and ancient communities such as Lublin. In 1830 he quarreled with a powerful member of the community who denounced him to the government, compelling him to leave Kalisz. On the way to Budapest, where he had been invited to become *av bet din*, he passed through the regional town of Stryj and was persuaded to remain there.

The following of his works have been published: *Ḥavvat Da'at* (Lemberg, 1799); *Ma'aseh Nissim* (Zolkiew, 1801), on the Passover *Haggadah; Mekor Ḥayyim* (*ibid.*, 1807), novellae and expositions of the laws of Passover in the Shulḥan Arukh together with the glosses of *David b. Samuel ha-Levi and Abraham Abele *Gombiner on the *Oraḥ Ḥayyim* and novellae to tractate *Keritot*; *Netivot ha-Mishpat* (*ibid.*, 1809–16), on *Ḥoshen Mishpat*; *Torat Gittin* (Frankfurt on the Oder, 1813), the laws of divorce and novellae on tractate *Gittin*; *Beit Ya'akov* (Hrubieszow, 1823), expositions on *Even ha-Ezer*; *Kehillat Ya'akov* (1831), on *Even ha-Ezer* and some sections of *Oraḥ Ḥayyim*; *Derekh ha-Ḥayyim*, an anthology of liturgical laws for the whole year, first published with the prayer book (1828) and then separately (1860 or 1870); *Naḥalat Ya'akov* (1849), expositions of the Pentateuch; *Emet le-Ya'akov* (1865), expositions of talmudic *aggadot*; *Imrei Yosher*, commentaries on the five *megillot*, each published at a different place and time; his ethical will (1875); and *Millei de-Aggadeta* (1904), sermons and responsa.

BIBLIOGRAPHY: Z.Y. Michelsohn, *Toledot Ya'akov* (1913); L. Lewin, *Geschichte der Juden in Lissa* (1904), 168f., 204–22; Landau, in: HḤY, 6 (1922), 310–2; Fuenn, Keneset, 554f.; H. Tchernowitz, *Toledot ha-Posekim*, 3 (1947), 252–8; A.I. Bromberg, *Mi-Gedolei ha-Torah ve-ha-Ḥasidut*, 12 (1957); I. Lewin, in: *Sefer ha-Yovel ... A. Jung* (1962), 167–85 (Heb. part).

[Ephraim Kupfer]

LORGE, IRVING (1905–1961), U.S. educator. Born in New York, Lorge joined the Institute of Educational Research, Teachers College, Columbia University, as a research assistant in 1927, working closely with Professor Edward L. Thorndike. In 1946 he became professor of education and executive officer of the Institute of Psychological Research. Lorge pioneered in research in mental measurement and the capacity for human learning. His major work was on the nature of giftedness, the formulation of indexes of readability and of word frequency, the assessment of intellectual functioning of elderly adults, and the measurement of intelligence in young children. Some of the leading American psychologists and educators of the mid-20th century received their research training under him. During World War II, Lorge was special consultant to the secretary of war, the chief of the Corps of Engineers, and the Army Specialized Training Division. From 1944 to 1948 he was expert consultant to the adjutant general's office. His research for the armed forces brought radical changes in the service methods of teaching illiterates. Lorge's many publications include *The Lorge-Thorndike Intelligence Tests* (1954); *A Semantic Count of English Words* (1938); and in collaboration with J. Tuckman, *Retirement and the Industrial Worker: Prospect and Reality* (1953).

[Abraham J. Tannenbaum]

LORIA, ACHILLE (1857–1932), Italian economist and sociologist. Loria, a native of Mantua, was a professor at the universities of Siena, Padua, and Turin. He considered man's relationship to the amount of available free land to be a vital factor in the history of mankind, holding that the relative scarcity of free land condemned men to subjugation and exploitation by land owners. His deterministic economic theory of history reflects the influence of many 19th-century schools of thought, including those of Karl *Marx and Herbert Spencer. He seems also to have been influenced by the Irish land-reform debate.

Loria's voluminous writings include *Analisi della proprietà capitalista* (1889), *Verso la giustizia sociale* (1914–20), and *Ricordi di uno studente settuagenario* (1927). He was regarded by his contemporaries as one of the foremost scholars of his time, and his appointment to the Italian Senate in 1919 was only one of the many honors conferred on him. His stress on the importance of free land in the history of the United States had considerable influence on such economic interpreters of U.S. history as Charles Beard and Frederic Jackson Turner.

BIBLIOGRAPHY: L. Einaudi, in: *La Riforma Sociale*, 43 (1932), list of his works; idem, in: *Economic Journal*, 56 (1946), 147–50. **ADD. BIBLIOGRAPHY:** D'Orsi Angelo (ed.), *Achille Loria* (2000).

[Joachim O. Ronall]

LORJE, CHAIM (1821–1878), founder of the first society for the settlement of Ereẓ Israel (Kolonisations-Verein fuer Palaestina). Born in Frankfurt on the Oder, Lorje was an educator there and headed a children's boarding school. In 1864 he moved to Berlin where he lived until his death. He considered himself a descendant of the Safed kabbalist Isaac *Luria; he had a tendency toward mysticism throughout his life and this was probably the source of his initiative to establish the first society for the agricultural settlement of Ereẓ Israel in Frankfurt on the Oder (1860). Opposition from the old *yishuv* immediately arose against the scheme for they feared that Lorje's society would divert part of the *ḥalukkah* funds from abroad. On the other hand, the early harbingers of the Zionist idea, namely Z. *Kalischer, Y. *Alkalai, M. *Hess, David *Gordon, and others, joined Lorje. The society also published Kalischer's programmatic book *Derishat Ẓiyyon* (1862). At the close of the book is an appendix by Lorje on the society and its rules.

The center of the society was then moved to Berlin. At first it was successful and collected substantial funds; however, Lorje's egocentrism and aggressive tone toward his adversaries brought about the gradual weakening of the society until it ceased to exist in 1864. When other societies were established afterward, Lorje's group was honored as the direct and indirect inspiration for these societies and the Ḥibbat Zion movement in the West.

BIBLIOGRAPHY: Kressel, in: *Zion*, 7 (1942), 197–205.

[Getzel Kressel]

LORKI (i.e., of Lorca), **JOSHUA** (d. c. 1419), physician and writer who converted to Christianity and became an implacable enemy of Judaism. His father was Joseph Abenvives (or Ibn Vives) of Lorca, near Murcia in Spain. In his youth Lorki apparently studied in Alcañiz under Solomon ha-Levi (*Pablo de Santa María), and was greatly influenced by his teacher's conversion. Deeply impressed by the letter sent by Pablo to R. Joseph *Orabuena concerning the fulfillment of the messianic prophecies through Jesus, Lorki wrote to Pablo disclosing his own doubts in the Jewish faith and analyzing the causes of Pablo's conversion. Lorki nevertheless remained in the fold of Judaism until 1412, when he became converted under the influence of the Dominican preacher Vicente *Ferrer. On baptism, Lorki assumed the name Hieronymus de Sancta

Fide (or Gerónimo de Santa Fé). Immediately after his conversion, Lorki conceived the idea of convening a disputation with the leading Jews of Alcañiz. He submitted his proposal to the antipope *Benedict XIII, whose personal physician he became. Benedict recommended that the disputation should be held at *Tortosa, and that the foremost Jews of Aragon should take part in it. During the disputation Lorki treated his former coreligionists with contempt and threatened them with punishment by the Inquisition. The Jews referred to him as *"Megaddef"* ("The Blasphemer"), a combination of the initials of Maestre Gerónimo de [Santa] Fé. After the disputation, Lorki traveled widely, trying everywhere to win Jews to Christianity.

Probably when still a Jew, Lorki wrote a book in Arabic on plants and herbs and their therapeutic qualities at the request of Don Benveniste de la *Cavallería. It was translated into Hebrew by Don Vidal Joseph, son of Benveniste (*Gerem ha-Ma'alot*, Vienna Ms. 154). After his conversion, Lorki wrote two polemics against Judaism: *Contra perfidiam Judaeorum*, in which he cites aggadic passages allegedly attesting to the coming of Jesus, and *De Judaeis erroribus ex Talmuth* (Augsburg, c. 1468; Zurich, 1552; later Hamburg, n.d.; both in *Bibliotheca Maxima Veterum Patrum*, vol. 3, Frankfurt, 1602), under the name *Hebraeomastix*. Both works were written around the time of the Tortosa Disputation in 1413–14 and were used during the debates. Many days were spent in Tortosa arguing about the advent of the messiah, which is the topic of the first work. The second work deals with the Talmud, the main source of the Jews' errors.

One of Lorki's sons, PEDRO DE SANTA FÉ, was a favorite of Queen María, the wife of Alfonso V of *Aragon. Another descendant, FRANCISCO DE SANTA FÉ, filled various important public offices. At the end of 1485 Francisco was accused of being implicated in the murder of Pedro de *Arbues, the inquisitor of Saragossa, and arrested. He committed suicide in the prison of the Inquisition. His body was burned and its ashes thrown into the Ebro River.

BIBLIOGRAPHY: Baer, Spain, index, s.v. *Joshua Halorki*; Baer, Urkunden, 1 (1929), 809ff., 833ff.; L. Landau, *Das Apologetische Schreiben des Josua Lorki* (1906); A. Lukyn Williams, *Adversus Judaeos* (1935), 235ff.; A. Pacios López, *La Disputa de Tortosa*, 2 vols. (1957), index; J. Amador de los Ríos, *Historia Social... España y Portugal* (1960), 836ff. **ADD. BIBLIOGRAPHY:** M. Orfali, Jerónimo de Santa Fe's *El tratatado 'De iudaicis erroribus ex Talmut,' Introducción general, estudio y análisis de las fuentes* (1987); idem, in: *Annuario di studi ebraici*, 10 (1980–4), 157–78; idem, in: *Proceedings of the 10th World Congress of Jewish Studies* (1990), Division B, vol. 1, 109–15.

[Haim Beinart]

LORM, HIERONYMUS (pseudonym of **Heinrich Landesmann**; 1821–1902), Austrian poet and novelist. The son of a prosperous Moravian merchant, Lorm was born in Nikolsburg and raised in Vienna. He studied music until he lost his hearing at the age of 15. Shortly afterward his sight began to fail and he eventually became totally blind. Throughout the 1840s, Lorm wrote liberal lyrics and articles, using various pseudonyms in order to avoid political persecution. Moving first to Leipzig and then to Berlin, he became the literary correspondent of the influential periodical *Die Grenzboten*, but returned to Vienna in 1848. Here he befriended the young composer Anton *Rubinstein and the novelist Berthold *Auerbach. Auerbach, who married Hieronymus' sister, inspired the character of the young Jewish intellectual in *Gabriel Solmar*, Lorm's most popular novel, which originally appeared in 1855 as *Ein Zoegling des Jahres 1848*. *Gabriel Solmar* tells of a Jew's disillusionment with the panacea of general emancipation and of his return to his own people though not to religious Orthodoxy. It also deals with the political intrigues of the revolutionary period. Other novels of Jewish interest are *Am Kamin* (2 vols., 1857), *Todte Schuld* (1878), *Der Ehrliche Name: Aus den Memoiren einer Wiener Juedin* (1880), and *Ausserhalb der Gesellschaft* (1881). Since Lorm could communicate only by a touch system, he gradually reconciled himself to a life devoted solely to literary pursuits. He wrote several volumes of short stories, and some touching poems deeply influenced by Nicolaus Lenau's *Weltschmerz*. His last volume of poems, *Nachsommer*, appeared in 1896 and was filled with pessimism. The publication of his *Philosophisch-kritische Streifzuege* (1873) gained him an honorary doctorate from the University of Leipzig. From 1873 to 1892 Lorm lived in Dresden, where he worked as a journalist and published a dozen novels, the best known of which was *Die schoene Wienerin* (1886). He moved to Bruenn in 1892 and from then until his death devoted himself to philosophical writing, including his main work in this field, *Der grundlose Optimismus* (1894).

BIBLIOGRAPHY: K. Kreisler, *Hieronymus Lorms Schicksal und Werk* (1922); J. Straub, *Hieronymus Lorm* (Ger., 1960). **ADD. BIBLIOGRAPHY:** J. Vesely, *Marie von Ebner-Eschenbach und Hieronymus Lorm*, in: K.K. Polheim (ed.), *Marie von Ebner-Eschenbach* (1994), 81–96; idem, *Hieronymus Lorm und Adalbert Stifter*, in: I. Fialová-Fuerstová (ed.), *Maehrische deutschsprachige Literatur* (1999), 94–102.

[Sol Liptzin]

LORRAINE (Heb. לוֹתִיר), region in E. France, formerly Lotharingia. Although the region of Mainz-Speyer did not form part of Lotharingia, the Hebrew sources use *"Gedolei Lotar"* to denote not only *Gershom b. Judah, who was born either in Metz or Mainz, but also apparently his disciples in these two towns and the tosafists of Speyer as well as those of Metz, Toul, and Verdun. The Jews are only mentioned in the duchy proper from the time of Simon II (1176–1205), who is said to have expelled them. There is evidence for the presence of the Jews in *Trier from as early as the fourth century and in *Metz, *Toul, and Verdun in the Carolingian period. At the beginning of the 13th century, a group of Jews was driven out of Saint-Dié on the pretext that one of them had practiced sorcery. In 1286 Duke Ferri III (1251–1304) permitted a number of them to live in Lorraine (in exchange for a quitrent of pepper) and to acquire a cemetery in Laxon, near Nancy, to serve the whole of the duchy. In charters granted to towns in the duchy (e.g., Neufchâteau, Sierck) he stipulated the right to admit Jews. In

*Sarreguemines, Duke Raoul took three Jews under his protection in 1336, and acquired some land from another in Laneuve-ville-devant-Nancy, while many Jews who had been expelled from France settled in neighboring Barrois.

From that date the Jews seem to have disappeared from the duchy, probably as a result of the *Black Death, but Lorraine appears to have admitted some of the refugees from France at the end of the 14th century (according to Joseph ha-Kohen, *Emek ha-Bakha*, ed. Vienna (1852), 74). In about 1455 Duke John II (1453–70) sold to many Jewish families the right to reside in the market towns of *Nancy, Neufchâteau, Pont-à-Mousson, *Lunéville, Rosières-aux-Salines, and Sarreguemines. Duke René II (1473–1508), however, confiscated their belongings and expelled these families in 1477 as a way of "giving thanks to God" for his victory over Charles the Bold in the same year. In theory this expulsion decree remained in force until the 18th century, but from as early as the 16th century the duke, his officers, and his vassals turned a blind eye to the arrival of a few isolated individuals, as well as attracting the financier Maggino Gabrieli to Nancy in 1597 and authorizing a large group to reside in Saint-Hippolyte, on the Alsatian slope of the Vosges. Jews are also mentioned in various villages, especially of German-speaking northern Lorraine: first in Vaudrevange, Sierck, *Morhange, Vaudoncourt, and Faulquemont in about 1600; then in *Boulay, Dieuze, Frauenberg, Sarreguemines, and Puttelange under French rule (1633–97); and finally during the reign of Leopold I (1658–1705), to whom the territory was restored by the Treaty of Ryswick in 1697.

As he was in debt to the Jewish bankers of Metz, Leopold even authorized some of them, including Samuel *Lévy and Moses Alcan, to settle in Nancy, entrusting the former with the administration of his finances (1715). After Lévy's downfall Leopold turned against the Jews: his decree of August 1720 subjected the movements of foreign Jews to strict control and that of April 1721 expelled all those who had arrived in the duchy after 1680. A list of the 74 families authorized to remain was published. They were spread out in small groups (with the exception of 19 families in Boulay) in 24 localities, mostly in German-speaking Lorraine. All formed a single community with one officer, Moses Alcan of Nancy, and a central synagogue in Boulay. In 1733 their number was increased to 180 families and the officers, then three in number, were charged with raising an annual tax of 100,000 livres. The Jews of Lorraine were authorized to appoint a rabbi by Stanislaus I, duke of Lorraine and Bar (1736–66), but it was not until 1785 and 1788 that those of Lunéville and Nancy were able to open synagogues and cemeteries. Stanislaus interpreted liberally the restricted number of 180 families. A decree of 1753 shows that Jews had then settled in 28 new localities, including Lunéville, Etain, and Bar; those exceeding the official quota were granted special authorizations or, after the reunion of the territory with France (1766), were naturalized. In 1789 there were about 500 Jewish families in Lorraine, 90 of them in Nancy, where bankers, army purveyors, and merchants were able to develop the cloth trade and to establish industries; one member of the Cerfberr family even acquired the seigniory of Tomblaine. During the preparation of the Estates-General (1788–89) most of the memoranda of complaints ("*cahiers de doléances*") from *Alsace and Lorraine were bitterly anti-Jewish. From many villages of Lorraine came such suggestions as that the Jews should be forced to engage in manual labor, that usury should be forbidden, and even that the Jews should be totally expelled from France.

In 1789 Berr Isaac *Berr led a delegation of the Jews of Lorraine, Metz, and Alsace at the National Assembly and published two pamphlets calling for the emancipation of the Jews. After the dissolution of the single community of the Jews of Lorraine (1790) and the constitution of independent communities in Lunéville, Sarreguemines, Lixheim, etc., the two *consistories of Metz and Nancy, with 6,500 and 4,200 Jews respectively, included most of the Jews of Lorraine (1808). The number of rabbis increased and synagogues were also established in *Phalsbourg, Sarreguemines, Verdun, Epinal, and Toul. After 1871 many Jewish refugees from Alsace and Moselle settled in that part of Lorraine which remained French after the Franco-German War. The department of Vosges, which by then had 2,500 Jews, was incorporated in a new consistory formed in *Vesoul (subsequently transferred to Besançon). In the remainder of French Lorraine, the number of Jews rose to between 7,000 and 8,000 in 1900, 4,000 of whom lived in Nancy. In the part of Moselle annexed by Germany after 1871 there were 7,015 Jews in 1900 (in comparison with 8,571 in 1870). The Jews who remained in this department left many of the villages for Metz or the newly industrialized regions, where they were joined by immigrants from the rest of Germany and Eastern Europe. After Alsace-Lorraine had been ceded to France by the Treaty of Versailles (1919) more immigrants came to the region. The Jewish population of Lorraine was greatly reduced by assimilation and the massive deportations of World War II, especially in the south, although it was slightly augmented by the arrival of some 200 families from North Africa after 1962. In 1970 rabbinates were to be found in Metz, Nancy, and Sarreguemines only: other communities numbering more than 100 persons were in Thionville, Lunéville, Forbach, Epinal, Sarrebourg, and Saint-Avold.

BIBLIOGRAPHY: Germ Jud, 1 (1937), 160ff.; Gross, Gal Jud, 293–305; C. Pfister, *History of Nancy*, 1 (1902), 678–81; 3 (1908), 311–38; L. Vanson, in: *Revue juive de Lorraine*, 10 (1934); 11 (1935), passim; A. Hertzberg, *French Enlightenment and the Jews* (1968); Z. Szajkowski, *Economic Status of the Jews in Alsace, Metz and Lorraine* (1954); B. Blumenkranz, in: *Annales de l'Est* (1967), 199–215.

[Gilbert Cahen]

LORRE, PETER (**Laszlo Lowenstein**; 1904–1964), film actor. Born in Rozsahegy, Hungary, Lorre joined a German theatrical troupe at 17 and for a time worked with the German dramatist Bertolt Brecht. In 1931 his performance as the psychopathic killer in Fritz Lang's film *M* made him famous. Lorre, a thickset man who could look both amiable and sinister, went to London for Alfred Hitchcock's *The Man Who Knew Too Much* (1934) and then to Hollywood. Among his more than 80 films were *Crime and Punishment* (1935), *Mad Love* (1935), *Secret Agent* (1936), a series of eight *Mr. Moto* movies (1937–39), *The Maltese Falcon* (1941), *Casablanca* (1942), *Arsenic and Old Lace* (1944), *The Mask of Dimitrios* (1944), *Confidential Agent* (1945), *The Verdict* (1946), *Three Strangers* (1946), *My Favorite Brunette* (1947), *Casbah* (1948), *Die Verlorene* ("The Lost One," which he wrote and directed, 1951), *Beat the Devil* (1953), *20,000 Leagues under the Sea* (1954), *Silk Stockings* (1957), *The Big Circus* (1959), *The Raven* (1963), *The Comedy of Terrors* (1964), and *The Patsy* (1964).

With his distinctive accent and menacing voice, Lorre carved out a second career for himself as a radio actor, specializing in thrillers and mysteries.

BIBLIOGRAPHY: G. and S. Suehla, *Peter Lorre* (1999); S. Youngkin, *The Films of Peter Lorre* (1982); T. Sennett, *Masters of Menace: Greenstreet and Lorre* (1979).

[Ruth Beloff (2nd ed.)]

LORTEL, LUCILLE (1900–1999), U.S. theatrical producer. Born in New York, the daughter of Harry and Anna Wadler, she was tutored at home. She attended Adelphi College briefly and studied at the American Academy of Dramatic Arts. She took the name Lortel, an alliterative concoction, for the stage. She made her Broadway debut in 1925 in a bit part in the Theatre Guild production of George Bernard Shaw's *Caesar and Cleopatra*. She appeared in several plays over the years, but after her marriage in 1931 to Louis Schweitzer, a chemical engineer who made a fortune manufacturing cigarette paper, her acting career became sporadic. Instead, in 1947, she started the White Barn Theater, an experimental outpost free from commercial pressures, in Westport, Conn., on the family summer estate, and Lortel provided room and board for the actors. She built a permanent stage, brought in new and innovative troupes, established an apprentice school, and offered playwrights, actors, designers, composers, and directors a chance to spread their wings. Lortel mothered performers like Eva Marie Saint, Geoffrey Holder, and Zero Mostel, and presented plays by Samuel Beckett, Edward Albee, Eugene Ionesco, and Sean O'Casey. In 1955 her husband gave her a Manhattan theater, now known as the Lucille Lortel Theater, as a wedding anniversary gift. The first production at the house, then called the Theater de Lys, was Marc *Blitzstein's adaptation of Bertolt Brecht's and Kurt Weill's *Threepenny Opera*. It caused such a sensation that the production ran for seven years and put Off Broadway theater on the map. As an indication of her cutting-edge career, she brought Jean Genet to the attention of American audiences with a production of *The Balcony*, which she coproduced in 1960. She also oversaw the first American production of a play by Athol Fugard, the South African playwright. She earned the unofficial title Queen of Off Broadway by producing or coproducing some 500 plays. Several were moved to larger houses on Broadway. Lortel received virtually every theatrical award and honor. In addition, the first theater chair to be named for a woman bears her name, the Lucille Lortel Distinguished Professorial Chair in Theater at the City University of New York. She established the Lucille Lortel Fund for New Drama at Yale University to support the production of new plays at the Yale Repertory Theater and the Lucille Lortel Fellowship in Playwriting at Brown University. She also donated money for the annual Drama Circle awards and made sizable contributions to dance and music groups.

[Stewart Kampel (2nd ed.)]

LOS ANGELES, city in S. California with approximately 4,000,000 inhabitants occupying 469 square miles of territory; the third most populous city in the U.S. and the largest city in area in the world. Los Angeles County is the home of some 552,000 (2003) Jews, second only to New York City.

Beginnings

The origins of the city go back to the early Spanish colonization of California. Los Angeles was formally dedicated as a pueblo on Sept. 4, 1781, with 44 inhabitants. The town grew slowly to 1,100 inhabitants by 1840. A year later the first party of pioneers traveled overland to Los Angeles from the Middle West of the U.S. With them was Jacob Frankfort, the first Jewish resident of Los Angeles. The accession of California to the U.S. in 1850 as an aftermath of the Mexican War and the discovery of gold brought a surge of Jews from Western Europe and the Eastern U.S. to seek a quick fortune. The majority did not engage in gold mining but opened stores in the small towns and mining camps of northern California. The prosperity filtered down to the rancho country of southern California and to the small town of Los Angeles, which was its marketing and commercial center. A Los Angeles census of 1850 revealed a total of 1,610 inhabitants of which eight are recognizably Jewish: Morris Michaels, aged 19, Portland, Oregon; Abraham Jacobi, 25, Poland; Morris L. Goodman, 24, Germany; Philip Sichel, 28, Germany; Augustine Wasserman, 24, Germany; Felix Bachman, 28, Germany; Joseph Plumer, 24, Germany; and Jacob Frankfort, 40, Germany; all were unmarried and merchants, except for Frankfort who was a tailor. The Jewish population, in the wake of economic expansion, increased rapidly. Jews came from San Francisco and the East and directly from Germany and promptly set up businesses, or, procuring carts and wagons, began to trade with the prosperous Spanish rancheros. Jewish services probably began on the High Holidays in 1851 and were more formally established with the arrival of Joseph Newmark (1799–1881) in 1854. Rabbinically trained and traditionally oriented, he was the patriarch of the Jewish community until his death. Services were held in various rented and borrowed places until the first synagogue was built in 1873 at 273 N. Fort Street (now Broadway). The first visit of the artist S.N. Carvalho, in 1854, directly stimulated the founding of the Hebrew Benevolent Society of Los Angeles. Carvalho influenced his host, Samuel Labatt, to establish a philanthropic society and a Jewish cemetery. Thirty charter members elected S.K. Labatt as president; Charles Schachno, vice president; Jacob Elias, secretary and treasurer; and S. Lazard and H. Goldberg, trustees. This was the first social welfare organization in Los Angeles. A year later the society procured land from the City Council in Chavez Ravine for the Jewish cemetery, which served until 1900. In addition to furthering their economic interests and "the holy cause of benevolence," the Jewish merchants during these early years were also active in such civic affairs as the founding of the Masonic order, the first Library Association, the Odd Fellows order, the German Turnverein, and as elected members of the City Council and County Board of Supervisors. Jews participated freely in every facet of social and economic as well as communal life. From 1850 until 1880 one or two Jews continuously served as elected officials. In 1873 they took the initiative in organizing the first Chamber of Commerce. Jewish business, concentrating on wholesale and retail merchandising, was among the largest in town. In 1865 I.W. Hellman (1843–1920) ventured into the banking business to become ultimately the leading banker in Los Angeles and among the dominant financial powers in the state. By the 1890s I.W. Hellman and Henry Huntington became the two financial giants of southern California. In 1861 Beth El, a congregation of Polish Jews, was formed. It soon was replaced by the German Congregation B'nai B'rith, which invited the Orthodox Rabbi A.W. Edelman (1832–1907), a Hebrew school-teacher in San Francisco, to become its first rabbi. Congregation B'nai Brith's first officers were Joseph Newmark, president; Wolf Kalisher, vice president; M. Behrend, secretary; and Elias Levinthal, Isadore Cohen, and Louis Levy, trustees. It functioned as a traditional congregation until the middle 1880s, when it began moving to an unequivocal Reform position. Ephraim Schreiber of Denver became the rabbi from 1884 to 1889; Abraham Blum, 1889–95; M.G. Solomon, 1895; and Sigmund Hecht, 1900–19. The position of the Jewish community in Los Angeles was expressed by an editorial in the local *Daily News* in 1873, which summed up the prevailing attitude toward the Jewish population: "We commend them for their commercial integrity and their studied isolation from prevalent vices of gambling and inebriation. We commend them for their general business and personal probity… they are among our best citizens and the city suffers nothing in their hands…." The population of Los Angeles rose sharply during the 1880s with the arrival of the transcontinental railroad service and following a concerted program of promotion by the Chamber of Commerce. The population, only 11,000 in 1880, multiplied fivefold in a few years during a land boom of vast proportions. With the arrival of large numbers of Middle Westerners the easygoing, socially integrated society began to change. Jewish social life became more ingrown. Jews established separate social outlets including a Young Men's Hebrew Association for the young and the Concordia Club for the card-playing parents. Jews lost their places in the Blue Book, the local social register, which in 1890 listed 44 Jews, 22 in 1921, and in recent years, no discernible Jews.

Population Growth and Communal Development

At the beginning of the 20th century large numbers of East European Jews began to migrate to Los Angeles to begin in their turn the ascent to prestige, status, and security. Their movement to Los Angeles was aided by the Industrial Removal Office in New York, which sent them as part of a grand dispersal design. Approximately 2,000 Jews went to Los Angeles through this source of assistance, and subsequently brought their families. In 1900 the Los Angeles population was 102,000 and the Jews numbered 2,500. Twenty years later the Jews constituted 40,000 out of 576,000, and by 1930 the Jews numbered 70,000 out of 1,200,000. The rapid increase of population created for the first time recognizably Jewish neighborhoods. By 1920 the three major areas of Jewish concentration were Temple Street, Boyle Heights, and the Central Avenue district. The early Jewish community organizations, Congregation B'nai B'rith, B'nai B'rith Lodge No. 224, which had been established in 1874, the Ladies Hebrew Benevolent Society established in 1870, and the Hebrew Benevolent Society were by this time insufficient to meet the needs of a new era. The high percentage of Jews coming west for their health made the establishment of medical institutions the first order of communal business. In 1902 the private home of Kaspare Cohn was donated to become the Kaspare Cohn Hospital. A few years later, the hospital was forced to move outside the city when the treatment of tuberculosis, its main business, was declared illegal within the city limits. In 1911 the Jewish Consumptive Relief Association was established and began to build a sanitarium at Duarte for consumptives who came to seek relief; this evolved into today's City of Hope Medical Center. For the elderly people the Hebrew Sheltering Home was established, to become the Jewish Home for the Aged. In 1910 B'nai B'rith was the moving force for the establishment of the Hebrew Orphans Home, whose name ultimately became Vista Del Mar. In 1912 the Federation of Jewish Charities was established to unite all fundraising for Jewish institutions. The Kaspare Cohn Hospital gradually transformed itself into a general hospital. It gradually altered its character as a charity hospital and began to charge patients. In 1926 it moved to facilities on Fountain Street near Vermont Avenue, and was renamed the Cedars of Lebanon Hospital. The first meeting of the Federation of Jewish Charities was held in 1912 with Ben R. Meyer, the son-in-law of Kaspare Cohn, as president, and included Dr. David W. Edelman, son of Rabbi Edelman and the president of the Reform congregation; Louis M. Cole, son-in-law of I.W. Hellman; M.N. Newmark and Isaac Norton, members of pioneer families; and S.G. Marshutz of B'nai B'rith, the founder of the Orphans Home. They typified the local Jewish leadership, to whom philanthropy was central in Jewish community life. The first decade of the 20th century was marked by a transition from charity aid to social welfare. During World War I overseas needs began to assume a large role in the philanthropy of the Jewish community. In 1934 the United Jewish Community was organized alongside the United Jewish Welfare Fund and the United Community Committee, which was established to fight antisemitism. The new leaders were mostly lawyers and not men of inherited wealth. Men like Lester W. Roth, Harry A. Holzer, Benjamin J. Scheinman, and Mendel B. Silberberg succeeded the Newmarks and the Hellmans. In 1937 the United Jewish Community was incorporated as the Los Angeles Jewish Community Council, with the United Jewish Welfare Fund as its fund-raising arm. The United Community Council became the Community Relations Committee of the Jewish Community Council. The Federation of Jewish Charities continued as a separate entity until 1959, when a merger was effected between the Jewish Community Council with its pro-Israel interest and overseas concerns, and its orientation toward Jewish education, and the Federation of Jewish Welfare organizations typifying the earlier Jewish community, with its primary concern for local philanthropies. A few years later the Cedars of Lebanon Hospital and Sinai Hospital, which was established during the 1920s by the Eastern European community, also merged.

Religious Developments

In the early 1900s Congregation B'nai B'rith, which had served the entire community since 1861, was joined by the first Orthodox congregation, Beth Israel or the "Olive Street Schul." In 1906 Congregation Sinai, the first Conservative congregation, was organized, and built its first edifice three years later. Isadore Meyers was rabbi and his successors included Rudolph Farber, David Liknaitz, Moses Rosenthal, and Jacob Kohn. The congregation grew and moved in 1930 to an imposing edifice at 4th and New Hampshire streets. Two rabbis and two congregations towered over the religious life in Los Angeles Jewry until World War II. Wilshire Boulevard Temple was founded in 1860. It was classical Reform, with a magnificent structure erected in the 1920s on Wilshire Boulevard representing the affluence of its membership, including many of the movie colony. It was the "established" congregation of the Jewish community. Hushed worship, the garments of the minister, the mixed choir, the centrality of the sermon, and the absence of bar mitzvah, all marked the Reform temple. Its rabbi was Edgar F. Magnin (1890–1984). Under his influence membership rose from 300 to 2,000, to become reputedly the largest congregation in the United States. In 1930 Dr. Jacob Kohn (1881–1968) arrived at Congregation Sinai. He became renowned for his liberal forthrightness, philosophical depth, and Jewish scholarship. Rabbi Oser Zilberstein of the Breed Street Shul (1891–1973) was the preeminent Orthodox rabbi of his generation. At the end of World War II 150,000 Jews lived in Greater Los Angeles, an increase of 20,000 since the war began.

The major growth of the Jewish population in Los Angeles began after 1945 when thousands of war veterans and others moved West with their families. The city's population multiplied and the Jewish community grew apace. By 1948 the Jewish population was a quarter of a million, representing an increase of 2,000 people a month as Jews moved West in one of the great migrations in Jewish history. The Middle West was the major area of origin; perhaps 38% of the Jewry in Los Angeles in 1951 were from the Chicago area. In 1951 it was estimated that 330,000 Jews lived in Los Angeles. Dozens of suburban communities founded during this period were swiftly absorbed in the spreading Los Angeles metropolis. By 1965 the Jewish population of Los Angeles had reached half a million and the community had become one of the largest centers of Jewish population.

The vast increase in Jewish population resulted in a proliferation of congregations, synagogues, and religious functionaries. The national movement of the religious denominations "discovered" Los Angeles as the United Synagogue established its Pacific Southwest Region, the Union of American Hebrew Congregations established its Southern Pacific Region, and rabbis by the dozen wended their way West. By 1968 there were 150 congregations and even more rabbis in Los Angeles. The largest congregations were Wilshire Blvd. Temple, Temple Israel of Hollywood, Temple Emanuel, Temple Beth Hillel, and Temple Isaiah (Reform); Temple Beth Am, Valley Jewish Community Center, Sinai Temple, Hollywood Temple Beth El, and Valley Beth Sholom (Conservative); and Beth Jacob and Shaarei Tefillah (Orthodox).

All three branches of Judaism established schools of higher Jewish learning after 1945. The Jewish Theological Seminary established the University of Judaism, which in turn developed a Hebrew Teachers' College, a School of the Fine Arts, the Graduate School, and an extensive program of adult Jewish studies. Hebrew Union College similarly developed a branch in Los Angeles with a rabbinical preparatory school, cantors' training school, and a Sunday school teachers program.

Yeshiva University established a branch specializing in teacher training and adult education. All three institutions had extensive programs of public education and public lectures and exercised a maturing effect on the growing Los Angeles Jewish community. Brandeis Camp Institute, near the city, with a college camp, children's camp, and weekend cultural retreats exerted a cultural influence on the Jewish community; other summer camps were educational influences for children. The Bureau of Jewish Education did much to raise the level of teaching and encouraged and subsidized Hebrew secondary schools. By 1968 the Los Angeles Hebrew High School, the largest, had more than 500 students.

The community centers were organized under the Jewish Centers Association, founded in 1943. By 1968 there were the following neighborhood centers: The Olympic Jewish Center and the Valley Cities Jewish Center, the Los Feliz Jewish Center and the Bay Cities Jewish Center, the West Valley Jewish Center and the North Valley Jewish Center, all under professional direction. The directors of the Jewish Centers Association since the Second World War were Meyer E. Fichman, Bertram H. Gold, who later became the long-time head of the American Jewish Committee, and Charles Mesnick.

Los Angeles has been the capital of the movie industry. The development of films moved from New York to Los Angeles beginning in 1912. Film distributors or exhibitors like Marcus Loew, Adolph Zukor, William Fox, Carl Laemmle, Lewis Selznick, Samuel Goldfish (later Goldwyn), and Louis B. Mayer, many of whom had started in the clothing business, came to the suburb of Hollywood to make films. By 1925 the Hollywood movie colony was famous throughout the world. The advent of talking pictures was sparked by the Warner Brothers, Albert, Jack, Sam, and Harry, who produced *The Jazz Singer*, a film about a Jewish cantor's son who was reticent to uphold the tradition of his ancestors and wanted to be a singer. It starred Al Jolson, the son of a Washington, D.C., cantor who did not go into his father's profession. This ushered in a new era in the movies. In 1930 three of the eight major production companies were partly owned by Jews, and 53 of 85 production executives were Jewish. When television production established itself in Hollywood from 1950, Jews were again a considerable proportion of the writers and producers in the industry. The biggest Jewish business in town, however, was not entertainment but construction and financing. Many Jews were involved in one or another aspect of real estate, financing, and other elements of the building trade. They built some of the large suburban areas and tract cities such as Lakewood, La Mirada, Panorama City, and Santa Susanna.

Jews, too, were strongly represented in the research, electronic, aircraft, and educational institutions that dotted southern California. The University of California at Los Angeles, for instance, which reputedly had only one Jewish professor in the 1930s, had over 400 Jewish scholars on its faculty 30 years later. As elsewhere, Jews founded thriving practices in medicine, law, and accounting, and were heavily concentrated in furniture, food, sportswear, and retail merchandising. By 1968 Jewish mobility had brought an end to the formerly Jewish Boyle Heights, Adams Street, Temple Street, Wilshire District, and other areas of Jewish concentration. Jews settled in the western and newer sections of sprawling Los Angeles – Westwood, Santa Monica, and Beverly Hills. In the San Fernando Valley 100,000 Jews resided in communities from North Hollywood westward to the city limits. Other Jewish communities had been established in the San Gabriel Valley, while thousands moved to Orange County.

1970–2005

Swift currents of change that swept over the Jewish community during the 1970s and 1980s profoundly affected Jewish life in Los Angeles. In summary they were (1) the drastically reshaped demographics of a city which at a mind-boggling pace underwent an immigrant-driven transformation into America's first Third World city. This ethnic revolution had powerful Jewish consequences including the need for reexamination of Jewish self-identity; (2) profound internal religious changes, marked by significant movement toward increased adherence to historical traditions, alongside equally striking departures from traditional views and practices; (3) the assumption by the Los Angeles Jewish Federation of responsibilities and objectives commensurate with newly perceived qualitative needs of the world's second largest Jewish community (after New York).

THE DEMOGRAPHIC REVOLUTION IN LOS ANGELES. California in the 1980s grew by six million people, the biggest human surge in any state in U.S. history, with estimates of an additional million immigrants by the end of the century. One third of the new arrivals settled in Southern California, increasing its population to 14.5 million. Greater Los Angeles had abruptly become the largest metropolitan center in the country. It also had ceased to be a European outpost and was now a multi-racial world nation. Some 75% of the immigrants were Hispanic, Asian, and black. By the end of the 1980s, 51% of Los Angeles residents were Hispanic or nonwhite. Between 1980 and 1998, the Latino population of the United States doubled to 30 million, establishing Hispanics as the single largest minority community in the country. By 2003, 38 percent of L.A.'s population identified itself as Hispanic, resulting in portentous shifts in the city's political, economic, and cultural tectonics. The renaming of Brooklyn Avenue in the pre-war Jewish stronghold of Boyle Heights to Avenida Cesar Chavez in 1995 was one early indication of this demographic change. The election in 2005 of Antonio Villaraigosa, the city's first Hispanic mayor in over a century, signified a demographic sea change, although the vagaries of identity politics did not solely determine the outcome of this contest.

The city's Asian community, largely Chinese and Japanese, who in the 19th century had been viewed as ignorant, laboring class "coolies," had begun immigrating to the West Coast as colonizers of the Pacific Rim. Many were well educated, with massive investments in corporations and real estate. Others from Korea, Philippines, Vietnam, and dozens of other countries seemingly overnight established and built retail businesses, bought homes, and transformed neighborhoods. As examples, Monterey Park, a former Jewish enclave, became the Western world's first Chinese suburban city. Elite San Marino, which once staunchly restricted Jews, became 46% Asian. Congregation Judea in the midst of the Jewish Fairfax area was transformed in 1975 into a robust Korean Presbyterian church. California State University, Los Angeles, in 1989 had the following student profile: of 20,000 students, 30% were Latino, 11.5% Asian, 11.5% black, and 30% white. The vice president for academic affairs of the state college system announced that: "Cal State-L.A. is probably close in its student body representation to what any university campus in California, public or private, is going to look like in the early 21st century." These demographic estimates were inescapably destined to be among the powerful determinants of the character of Jewish life in the coming century.

THE JEWISH POPULATION OF LOS ANGELES. By 1989, Los Angeles Jewry was stable after a period of rapid growth. Another 90,000 Jews had settled in neighboring Orange County. The Greater Los Angeles Jewish community was now numerically larger than the Jewish population of any country other than the United States, Israel, and the Soviet Union. Some of the population increase represented the sunbelt-driven migration from the East and Middle West to Florida and the West Coast. A substantial portion of the new immigrants came from Israel (probably 50,000, although estimates ranged as high as 200,000. The Los Angeles Jewish Population Survey found that there were 14,170 Israeli-born Jews in L.A. but 52,400 who self-identified as Israeli, those who were born elsewhere but grew up in Israel). The Hebrew-speaking newcomers settled in the Fairfax area, a traditional gateway for Jewish immigrants boasting the city's largest population, in North Hollywood and, once they had established themselves financially, in Encino/Tarzana and the Conejo Valley, adjoining the western San Fernando Valley, with over 40,000 Jews, one of the fastest-growing communities in the country. This influx engendered anxiety within the established community, which at least initially regarded the "*yored*" (Hebrew pejorative for émigré, meaning one who descended, left Israel) presence as an embarrassing and unfortunate abnegation of Zionism. Unlike other Jewish immigrant populations, resident Israelis were "transnational": although they might well remain in the U.S. indefinitely, they thought of themselves as Israeli citizens fully intending to end their collective sojourn in the Land of Promise for a return to the Promised Land. This state of "living on one's suitcases" rendered their commitment to local Jewish continuity naturally suspect. Differences in language, style, comportment, and patterns of communal affiliation also contributed to estrangement. Relations improved shortly after the Gulf War, when Israeli Prime Minister Yitzhak Rabin, who had once denigrated the émigré community as the "fallout of weaklings," retracted his characterization and expressed gratitude to the Los Angeles Israeli community for its ongoing solidarity. American Jews, meanwhile, began to view immigrant Hebrew-speakers not so much as the spiritually fallen and psychologically ambivalent (if not thoroughly tormented by desertion-induced guilt), but as a valuable transfusion of Jewish authenticity and vitality. Jewish institutions, most notably the Jewish Federation Council, the city's Jewish community centers, and some synagogues, launched efforts to absorb Israeli families, some providing organizational venues in which they could express their cultural and linguistic proclivities. Increasingly, Israeli Angelinos themselves realized they were likely to remain for the long run, and would do well to address the problematics inherent in transmitting their national, linguistic, and cultural identity to children raised and acculturated in the U.S. Hebrew speaking, Israel-centered scouting movements, after-school programming, and adult cultural activities thrived as a result. In 1996, community-minded Israelis formed the Council of Israeli Organizations, an arm of a non-profit umbrella organization called the Promoting Israel Education and Culture Fund. Originally tasked with organizing the city's annual Israeli Independence Day Festival, which draws tens of thousands of Los Angeles-based Israelis, it reconstituted in 2001 as the Council of Israeli Community, with an agenda of fostering pro-Israeli rallies and more effective ties to the media and with other ethnic groups.

In 1991 2,900 Jews from the Soviet Union came to Los Angeles. By 1997, the numbers of Russian Jews arriving went to well below 1,000. Jews from the former Soviet Union were estimated at 24,500 according to the 1997 LAJPS, making this the third or fourth largest concentration after New York, San Francisco, and Chicago. Their presence in West Hollywood earned the neighborhood the nickname "Little Odessa." The Iranian Jewish presence is believed to number 18,000, the largest such concentration in the U.S. The Persian community, which has almost exclusively settled in the city's wealthy West Side and San Fernando Valley, is religiously, socially, and culturally distinct. Many have brought with them the skills of merchants. Others live in more humble circumstances, with trouble adjusting to their adopted country. Shops with Farsi and English signs dot the West Side. Their supermarkets and shops have the feel of Teheran. Eighty percent of the Iranian refugees coming to the U.S. resettled in L.A. and they transplanted to L.A. much of the leadership of the Tehrani Jewish community including the chief rabbi and Iranian Federation.

In addition, there are sizeable contingents from South Africa (the bulk of whom settled in Orange County and San Diego), Central Asia, South America, Australia, and Mexico. Like their Israeli counterparts, these immigrants have provided unique challenges to the Los Angeles Jewish community in matters of integration and acculturation. In contrast, a small but not insignificant community of Canadian Jews, most having arrived since the election of the separatist Parti Quebecois provincial government in 1976, many also highly trained professionals in pursuit of the material advantages offered by the American Dream, has blended into the existing community with such consummate ease as to render them nearly invisible.

Comprising half the Jews in California and perhaps as many as one in ten of the American Jewish population, Jewish Angelinos continue to enjoy pride of place in the finest sections of the city, including Beverly Hills, Bel Air, Westwood, the San Fernando Valley, Santa Monica, and Pacific Palisades. The Fairfax area continued to contain the largest single concentration of Jews in the city; Encino/Tarzana are a very close second. However, by 2005 the Fairfax area's Jewish ambience came under siege, in part due to the influx of other ethnicities and also because various Jewish storefronts found themselves having to move out due to exorbitant rents due to the development of a new shopping mall, The Grove, in the heart of the old Jewish neighborhood. In terms of Jewish ambience and vitality, the area has long been supplanted by Pico-Robertson and La Brea/Beverly – which is home to the more Orthodox community and has created the largest Jewish day school, Toras Emes, and numerous *kolelim* – some three miles to the southeast, which has emerged as the city's primary bastion of Orthodox Jewry. Synagogues, large and small, are found on Pico and Olympic Blvds. Elegant kosher restaurants and Judaica shops are also to be found along with fast food places, only distinguishable because of their *kashrut* certificate.

North Hollywood/Valley Village is a second Orthodox area, which also has many synagogues, restaurants, shops, etc.

Since the 1970s, Jewish Angelinos have played a major role in the political life of the community: the City Council,

Board of Supervisors, State Legislature, and the House of Congress. In addition the Jewish community could count on the non-Jewish congressmen and senators to vote with friendly sensitivity on matters of Jewish interest. They were conspicuous in the cultural, philanthropic, and economic life of the city. Indeed, they were the most cohesive, best-organized white body in the city with ties to the instruments of civic power.

These new realities contrasted sharply with the years from 1900 to 1960, when no Jew was elected to the City Council or the Board of Supervisors or to represent California in Sacramento or Washington. Nor were Jews considered worthy to be mentioned in the society pages of the *Los Angeles Times* or in the published social register. Their new status now meant that the organized Jewish community was, as a minority, enjoined to protect and advance its own interests but equally responsible, as a principal member of the white establishment, to seek the peace of the city, recognizing, to paraphrase Jeremiah, that only in its welfare, would they be at peace. This double identity was bound to create ambivalence and tension in the Jewish community in the years ahead. The Waxman-Berman machine, led by two veteran Jewish Congressmen Henry *Waxman and Howard *Berman, drew Jewish support for political campaigns. Zev Yaroslavsky made a seamless move from Jewish leadership to county commissioner. Three members of the City Council were Jewish in 2005 including an African American Jew by choice and the son of an Italian father and a Jewish mother. National leadership of AIPAC has come from Los Angeles including Edward Sanders in the 1970s; he later served as the Jewish liaison for President Jimmy Carter. Lawrence and Barbara Weinberg played a unique role from Los Angeles in the expansion of AIPAC and Barbara, known as Barbie, in the establishment of the Washington Institute for Near East Policy.

A major implication for the local Jewish community, which became crucial by the turn of the 21st century, was that Los Angeles had become a multi-racial metropolis with ethnic ties to every race and region in the world. The Jewish community, representing some 15 percent of L.A. voters, had thrust upon it a double identity. It had the obligation to assert itself and protect its rights. But in a situation without precedent, it came to be seen by many ethnic groups, including its former allies in the African-American community and by the newly assertive Latino bloc it had hitherto overlooked, as an integral representative of the white establishment. While Jews and Hispanics shared some communal interests, such as quality schools, safe neighborhoods, economic development, and civil equality, they have parted on various religious and educational issues, and have clashed in the political arenas. Characteristically, Jewish liberals have proved vulnerable to charges within some Latino quarters that they are integrally right-leaning whites unsympathetic to Latino aspirations. This vulnerability, the result of demographic pressures, a discernible shift by Jews to the political right and, especially in the aftermath of the 1992 Los Angeles riots, growing insularity and wariness, portends a decline in Jewish political power. Valley Jews tend to be middle class, ethnically diverse, somewhat conservative yet still supportive of public schools. Despite their predilection for progressive politics, West Side Jews remain staunch members of the city's power elites, and retreated from the public school system during the late 1970s, when school busing generated "White Flight." The defeat, in 2002, of efforts by the San Fernando Valley to secede from the Los Angeles municipality helped forestall the dramatic dissipation of Jewish clout.

The arrival of the Hispanic population, coupled with the withdrawal of Jewish stores and landlords from African-American neighborhoods, tended to dilute Black-Jewish tensions in the political arena.

The Religious Community

Judaism in Los Angeles was decisively shaped by a number of rabbis of varying denominations who were drawn westward by personal visions of what they might accomplish in a city largely unbeholden to Eastern power structures and patterns of organization. In a community capable of providing considerable human and physical resources if properly motivated, these rabbis created an opportunity to concentrate their energies as religious leaders along lines of personal interests and concerns. They became what might be termed rabbi-institution builders, rabbi-communal leaders, rabbi-social activists, rabbi-educators, and rabbi-visionaries. The following is a sampling of the impact on Judaism in Los Angeles by a few of the over 200 Los Angeles area rabbis.

RABBI-INSTITUTION BUILDERS. The Orthodox leaders in Los Angeles before World War II had such little faith in their own future that their leading synagogue was called "the modern synagogue," and their significant events were given enhanced status by the participation of a local Reform rabbi or his president. The resurgence of Orthodoxy in post-war Los Angeles was fueled by some determined rabbis, who were confident that American Jews, however acculturated, would be receptive to a return to authentic tradition if it were attractively clothed in American values, if it secured serious media attention, and if it could be identified as the natural heir to the Jewish heart.

The most significant of centrist Orthodox synagogues, the Beth Jacob Congregation, was led by Rabbi Simon Dolgin who arrived in 1938 and relocated Beth Jacob from West Adams to Beverly Hills in the 1950s. He also established the Hillel School and had a distinguished career before moving to Israel in the early 1970s. He was one of the very few rabbis who moved to Israel, neither at the beginning nor at the end but at the prime of his American career, where he became director general of the Ministry of Religion and a rabbi in Ramat Eshkol.

Rabbi Marvin Hier moved into Los Angeles from Vancouver in 1977, intending to establish a yeshivah, but ultimately founded the *Simon Wiesenthal Center, which became the Los Angeles community's first national and international Jewish organization. Rabbi Hier came to Los Angeles just as what Jonathan Woocher termed "the Judaism of sacred survival" was coming to the fore, when the remembrance of the Holocaust and the protection of the State of Israel were central to Jewish identity. Taking the name of the world famous Nazi hunter, but running the organization in almost complete independence from Simon Wiesenthal, Rabbi Hier propelled the Holocaust center onto the world stage to stake out an independent claim as an activist leader in the fight against antisemitism. In 1993, the center opened its landmark 160,000-sqare-foot Museum of Tolerance, a $50 million high-tech exploration of racism, prejudice, antisemitism, and genocide (including the Turkish decimation of the Armenians and that of vast segments of Cambodian people by their own government), and broke ground in 2004 on a no less controversial sister institution, slated to cost $200 million, in Jerusalem.

When Rabbi Hier came, lay leaders of the Rambam School approached him to take charge of the school. It reopened as Yeshiva University Los Angeles (YULA) and the school grew significantly. In 2002, Hier moved the YULA contingent that had shared the Wiesenthal Center's original building on Pico Boulevard into a new $12.6 million facility and a second school for girls on Robertson Blvd. Hier himself has been alternately criticized and credited for commandeering the bread-and-butter issues of longer-established organizations. There is little doubt, however, in his ability to interject himself as a key player on the world stage and in his cultivation of prominent state legislators (Governor Arnold Schwarzenegger once called the diminutive Hier "my hero"). He developed a broad based membership organization, mirroring the tactics used by political organizers so successfully, and he presents a self-confident, right-of-center American Orthodoxy. Taking seriously the organization's mission of tolerance, he has kept the Wiesenthal Center and its Museum of Tolerance open to all groups. For example, it hosted a 1997 exhibition on Jackie Robinson's integration of baseball. Much to the chagrin of Federation leadership, who have not fared well in the entertainment community, he has navigated Hollywood celebrity and mastered documentary film-making (the center has won several Academy Awards for Holocaust-related films produced by his in-house film unit). Hier is an unflagging Jewish juggernaut, feared, respected, and taken quite seriously. He is also a well-established spokesman on Jewish issues. Unlike many professionals who need clearance from lay leaders for statements and must achieve consensus, Hier operates with great freedom.

Hier was the first to establish a Los Angeles-based national organization that rivaled and soon outgrew in membership many long-established East Coast organizations. Instead of establishing himself as a West Coast branch of Yeshiva University and living in its shadows, Hier worked independently and over 15 years ago the school severed its ties with YU. The original hopes for a West Coast university-level campus did not materialize beyond the high schools for boys and girls and adult learning.

Los Angeles has two Holocaust Museums and a Memorial. In addition to the Simon Wiesenthal Center, the Los Angeles Holocaust Museum was established by the Federation and influential survivors as the Martyrs Memorial Museum, and after a 1994 earthquake forced the Federation to renovate its building, the Museum never returned. It has been independent since 2004. A Memorial of Six Pillars has been built in Pan Pacific Park adjacent to the Fairfax neighborhood. It is the site of the annual community Yom Hashoah observance. The Wiesenthal Center hosts its own. There are significant Holocaust education programs also at the Survivors of the Shoah Visual History Foundation, which in 2006 became part of the University of Southern California, at UCLA, and at the University of Judaism in addition to neighboring universities in Los Angeles suburbs such as Chapman University and Claremont-Mckenna College.

Rabbi Baruch Shlomo Cunin came to Los Angeles in the 1960s as the Rebbe's (Menachem Mendel *Schneersohn) emissary. His predecessor came in the 1950s, but did not last long. In subsequent years, Cunin became a major religious force in the state with an operating budget of $15 million from 50,000 contributors and was supported by a rabbinic staff of 106 impassioned young graduates of their yeshivah in Crown Heights, Brooklyn. He established and controlled an imposing and growing array of synagogues, day schools, adult Torah study centers, and social projects such as a shelter for the homeless, a counseling center for battered women, and two drug treatment centers financed substantially by federal grants. Woven into the program were public relations sorties, featuring Judaism in the streets such as *mitzvah* mobiles, and Hanukkah lighting celebrations in shopping malls and city halls. The annual climax was a hyperkinetic telethon in which movie and television personalities vied for the *mitzvah* of raising five million dollars a year for their particularist form of ḥasidic Judaism. The death of Schneersohn in June 1994 split the Chabad movement between those who believe he had been and continued (despite his manifest physical demise) to be the long-awaited Messiah, and those who preferred to avoid unambiguous pronouncements as to his exalted status. However problematic theologically (the Rebbe's cult of personality, which he did little to contain during his latter years, sometimes skirted the Christological), such speculation has done little to daunt Chabad's outward expansion. The organization continues to inject itself into some of the least hospitable communities imaginable, which in Southern California include such hedonistic fleshpots as Malibu, Pacific Palisades, and Santa Monica, Huntington Beach, Irvine, and Yorba Linda. There are now 79 Chabad centers statewide, and despite occasional setbacks and resistance, no lessening in zeal for achieving a ḥasidic version of Manifest Destiny. Indeed, Chabad's high birthrate and unceasing generation of successive waves of energized, inner-directed missionary cadres suggests that growth and expansion have become vital organizational imperatives, perhaps even linchpins of continued survival.

The official Jewish establishment, acutely conscious of the strategic necessity of maintaining the historic separation of church and state, was likewise periodically constrained to remain mute and resigned while Chabad aggressively broke down barriers between religion and the state in its public square religious practices, and while the Wiesenthal Center was prevailing on the California Legislature to contribute five million dollars to the Center's projected Museum of Tolerance. These rabbinical leaders, some of them affiliated with or coming out of the Ba'al Teshuvah movement, represented a new meld: totally Orthodox, totally American, rightward-leaning, willing to explore commonalities with similarly disposed Christian groups, technologically advanced, and with their work largely financed by non-Orthodox supporters.

Rabbi Nahum Braverman came to Los Angeles in the mid-1980s to establish a western outpost of *Aish Hatorah, a Jerusalem yeshivah located near the Western Wall and founded by an American rabbi, Noah Weinberg. In a few short years he created an outreach program of one-to-one Torah learning. He established a chain of study sessions in private offices and conference rooms and began the process of organizing Aish Hatorah synagogues. The students were prominent business and community leaders as well as film and TV industry celebrities. The program created a non-ḥasidic network of intellectual *Ba'alei teshuvah* (newly Orthodox), sympathetic to "authentic" Judaism and often prepared to support it, even though not necessarily embodying it in their lifestyles. Aish has proved especially popular among young singles, who attend Shabbat services, Shabbat dinners at the homes of local congregationalists, post-dinner lectures, and occasional "speed-dating" evenings.

Rabbi Daniel Lapin arrived from South Africa in 1977. Although only a young man he was already an engineer, physicist, airplane pilot, sailor, and Orthodox rabbi. Together with Michael *Medved, bestselling writer, movie critic on public TV and, subsequently, radio talk-show host, they took over a minuscule store front synagogue on the Venice beach, operated by and for a few remaining elderly Jews, and established the Pacific Jewish Center. It was an unusually strict Orthodox synagogue in which financial participation was voluntary, participation in Torah study compulsory, and outdoors adventuring a *mitzvah*. At first the members were overwhelmingly single; in time they married, moved into the neighborhood to be within walking distance of the synagogue, and so created a living and learning community, which former and disaffected members described as "cultlike." The congregation split in the early 1990s, ostensibly after a spat involving a decision to move the center's day school out of the area. Lapin subsequently left a truncated congregation to the administration of his brother, David, and to his longtime assistant, Rabbi Avi Pogrow. Lapin and Medved moved to the Seattle suburb of Mercer Island, where, as talk-show radio hosts, they established a small group dedicated to forging a pan-Jewish coalition with fundamentalist Christians, and to weaning American Jews from their Liberal affectations. Medved generated particular consternation within Jewish circles for his own impassioned defense of actor/director Mel Gibson, whose blockbuster film *The Passion of the Christ* was widely perceived as an antisemitic assault and reaffirmation of pre-Vatican II charges of deicide. In 2003, David Lapin left for Washington, D.C., leaving PJC to the ministrations of Ben Geiger, a graduate of an ultra-Orthodox rabbinical school in Baltimore and the center's first full-time rabbi. Lapin accepted support from many sources included the Orthodox Jewish Washington lobbyist Jack Abramov.

On March 1, 2005 (20 Adar 5765), 2,000 men gathered in the new Walt Disney Concert Hall to celebrate the *Siyyum ha-Shas*, the seven-year cycle of studying a page of the Talmud each day, every day, which enables the devout and the persistent to complete the entire Talmud. If one panned the crowd in Los Angeles, one would have seen physicians and lawyers, accountants, real-estate investors, jewelers and professional men, as well as Jews from all walks of life, a cross section of Jewish life in Los Angeles. Even a few of the men – very few – earned their living in the entertainment industry. Many had come to Los Angeles only in the past three decades and all were comfortable in calling Los Angeles their home. Many, but not all, were raised in Orthodox homes. Others were the results of the success of the various outreach programs in attracting Jews to turn toward tradition.

While one would not ordinarily associate Los Angeles with the ultra-Orthodox community, there are some 5,000 families who constitute that community. They live in different neighborhoods on the West Side of Los Angeles, Hancock Park with its large and sprawling houses, Fairfax, the traditional Jewish neighborhood, Pico-Robertson with its large Orthodox community, and even Beverly Hills and Westwood. They live in North Hollywood and the Valley. They have established large schools for every segment of the community. Yeshiva Rav Isaacson/Toras Emes Academy is the largest day school in Los Angeles with 1,100 students, directed by Rabbi Yakov Kraus for more than three decades. Or Eliyahu Academy is another significant school. The Yeshiva Gedolah, the high school, occupies a prominent former Seventh Days Adventist Church on Olympic Blvd. in Hancock Park. Students can continue in the Kolel of Los Angeles. The Cheder of Los Angeles is for ḥasidic students who can go on to the ḥasidic *kolel*. The Beis Yaakov School is a high school for some 375 girls. Rabbi Avraham Teichman heads Agudat Israel on the West Coast. Dr. Irving Lebovics, a prominent dentist, is the leading lay leader of the Agudah on the West Coast. Rabbi Gerson Bess is regarded as the most prominent of the halakhic authorities.

In the Valley, the most prominent Orthodox synagogue is Shaarei Zedek, led by Rabbi Aron Tendler, the son of Yeshiva University's Rabbi Moshe Tendler. Emek Hebrew Academy is the home of more than 700 students. Valley Torah Center, headed by Rabbi Avrohom Stulberger, serves some 300 students.

During the 1970s Reform rabbi Isaiah *Zeldin, who had come to Los Angeles to represent the Union of American Hebrew Congregations and subsequently became rabbi of Temple Emanuel in Beverly Hills, left his congregation and founded the Stephen S. Wise Temple in the sparsely settled Mulholland Drive area of western Los Angeles, which soon became the epicenter of the community strategically situated between the Valley and the West Side. In the course of 15 years, the congregation grew in numbers and in program to become one of America's largest, with a membership of 3,000 families, with an annual budget in excess of $11 million, and a physical plant of monumental proportions. Its campus on ten acres of land was *sui generis*: a total of 1,300 students in its school system, ranging from pre-school to an elementary day school through grade six, an all-day junior high school, and since 1992, an 18,000 square-foot, $33 million high school replete with an impressive library and resource center; its parenting center; its faculty with four rabbis at the helm assisted by a staff of 250 permanent personnel; and imposing facilities that included an immense special parking structure, Olympic swimming facilities, and a variety of specially designed and constructed recreational areas. The schools, which provide at least an hour of conversational Hebrew daily and are quite Israel-centered in terms of curriculum, have received Tel Aviv University's 2003 Constantiner Award for Jewish Education, the 1990 biannual Zalman Shazar Prize from the Jerusalem-based Shazar Center for Jewish History, and its director, the 1990 Milken Family Foundation's Jewish Educator's Award.

Conservative rabbi Harold *Schulweis moved to the Encino area of the San Fernando Valley from Oakland. With a rare combination of philosophical profundity and Jewish social engineering genius, he established a series of programs which stamped his congregation as a creative center of Jewish life: a havurah program in which the bulk of the members participated; a para-professional counseling center whose first lay counselors were volunteers from the board of directors who studied and trained for several years for this opportunity to serve; a para-rabbinic training program in which the synagogue leadership similarly learned to become rabbinic aides qualified to meet with members and teach them how to be Jews at home as well as in the synagogue; an outreach program which accepted the inevitability of an increasing proportion of interfaith marriages in our open society and chose to deal with it on the basis of inclusivity rather than a posture of exclusivity; and an assistant rabbi, engaged by the congregation after her ordination in 1990, who was herself a Jew by choice. Most of these and other innovative experiments were emulated nationwide. In 1994, Schulweis called on his congregation to accept Jewish homosexuals and lesbians as equal and accepted members of the community. Some years later, he bucked longstanding Jewish tradition by launching an effort aimed at urging Gentiles not necessarily involved with Jewish life-partners to consider conversion to Judaism. It was Jewish outreach to the unchurched. Most recently, he initiated Jewish World Watch, an effort to inspire Jews to emulate Righteous Gentiles by intervening on behalf of distressed or physically threatened populations abroad. The organization has been active in generating assistance on behalf of populations in the Sudan and Darfur. In 2004, the 80-year-old Schulweis stepped down as senior rabbi, turning his pulpit over graciously to longtime colleague and friend Rabbi Edward Feinstein.

RABBI-COMMUNITY BUILDERS. Some of the city's rabbis transcended their responsibilities to their synagogue by sharing their energies with the larger Jewish community. Rabbi Jacob *Pressman arrived in Los Angeles in 1946 to assist Rabbi Jacob Kohn at Sinai Temple. A few years later he left to join a small congregation, which grew to become Temple Beth Am, one of the large and influential Los Angeles synagogues. He helped establish Akiba Academy, one of the first day schools in the Los Angeles Conservative community and initiated Herzl School, the community's first non-Orthodox day school. At Beth Am, he created a K-8 day school that was named in his honor as the Rabbi Jacob Pressman Academy. Simultaneously he became a central figure in the building of Jewish institutions in the city. He was a key figure in the organization of the University of Judaism in 1947 and served as its volunteer founding registrar. He was one of the founders of Camp Ramah and the Los Angeles Hebrew High School, and helped start the Beverly Hills Maple Counseling Center as well as the forerunner of the Brandeis-Bardin Institute, in Simi Valley. He established the synagogue Israel Bond Appeal program and headed the synagogue division of Los Angeles Israel Bonds. He was chairman of the Los Angeles Board of Rabbis as well as of the Western States region of the Rabbinical Assembly. When Jews were threatening to leave the Mid-Wilshire neighborhood after the L.A. riots in the 1970s, Pressman went door-to-door to sign up 150 families and pledged that the synagogue would remain in the neighborhood if they would pledge to stay; as a result, the Carthay Circle and South Carthay neighborhood, once threatened, is now a thriving Jewish community composed of traditional Conservative Jews who walk to synagogue and walk their children to the Pressman Academy. At Beth Am, he permitted and enabled the creation of religious alternatives for more traditional Jews; the egalitarian Library Minyan is without a formal rabbi but is the religious home of many rabbis and scholars at the University of Judaism, Hebrew Union College, UCLA, USC, and UC Northridge as well as rabbinical students at UJ and HUC. One holiday morning there were more than 75 rabbis, spouses of rabbis, and children of rabbis in attendance, a rarity for Conservative synagogues. Beth Am is now a Synaplex, offering multiple services: meditative services, family services, a Neshama Minyan with the melodies of Shlomo *Carlebach on Friday evening, as well as a mainstream Conservative service. Ten of Pressman's students became rabbis, including his successor Rabbi Joel Rembaum. Well into his eighties, Pressman is a master preacher, talented musician, and raconteur.

In 1997, after a period of changing leadership Rabbi David Wolpe took over as Sinai's senior rabbi. He introduced a single service called Friday Night Live that brings single Jews to synagogue for an exciting musical service. A captivating speaker, he ignites his audience.

Rabbi Maurice Lamm replaced Rabbi Dolgin at Beth Jacob Congregation in 1971. Under Lamm, the congregation became more observant as Orthodoxy become more observant. His congregants, who once rode to the synagogue, began walking if possible. Upon his retirement, Rabbi Abner Weiss, from South Africa, became spiritual leader of the congregation. He was also the representative of moderate Orthodoxy in Los Angeles communal, religious, and educational circles. Rabbi Weiss also took pride in the "upstairs *minyan*" in which younger members were given an opportunity to take charge of their own Sabbath service as a popular alternative to the more staid and formal sanctuary service. A psychologist who incorporated Kabbalah into his practice, Weiss departed for England in 2002; since that time, Rabbi Steven Weil has served as senior rabbi of Beth Jacob. Young Israel of Century City, initially a "break away" from Beth Jacob, was, by 2005, a well-established congregation of 400 members led, since 1986, by Rabbi Elazar Muskin. A few blocks away from Beth Jacob and Young Israel, in the Pico-Robertson area, B'nai David Judea Congregation, headed by Rabbi Yosef Kanefsky as by Daniel Landes before him, championed a progressive Orthodoxy, including greater opportunity for women's involvement in synagogue rituals.

Rabbi Harvey Fields, longtime senior rabbi of the venerable Wilshire Temple, the first and still arguably the largest Jewish congregation in Los Angeles, led his congregation in new directions. He became chairman of the Middle East Commission of the Jewish Federation Council. A congregation which historically had rejected many traditions now settled into a life style which was comfortable with Hebrew instruction, bar mitzvah, bat mitzvah, and a *shofar*. Under Fields' stewardship, music became a fixture of services, and a full-time cantor began to lead services in 1999. Despite the move toward more traditional forms of observance, Fields maintained his focus on issues pertaining to social justice and interfaith dialogue. He was instrumental, for instance, in the creation of Hopenet, a network of religious institutions in the Mid-Wilshire corridor that feeds about 200 people every Sunday out of the temple, and provides affordable housing, clothing, and furnishings. Fields stepped down in June 2003, handing over the reins he held for 21 years to Rabbi Steven Leder.

Rabbi Laura Geller is the senior rabbi of one of Los Angeles' most prominent Reform congregations. Temple Emanuel has a day school and innovative religious services including a Sabbath morning service that attracts many HUC faculty members. By the size and the prestige of her congregation and by her own stature, she is the most prominent of the first generation of women rabbis in the United States.

RABBI-SOCIAL ACTIVISTS. A number of rabbis, mostly in the Reform movement, became leaders in movements dealing with peace, poverty, racial harmony, and AIDS. Rabbi Leonard Beerman established a congregation in the spirit and name of Leo Baeck, which over the years fostered an environment that made involvement in human concerns a normal congregational function. As one example among many, Rabbi Beerman led his congregation to join forces with the All Saints Episcopal Church in Pasadena to establish a professionally run Interfaith Center to Reverse the Arms Race. For years they supported and maintained a peace movement, which gave serious attention to the world's ultimate long-term threat. When world events signaled a suspension of the arms race, both congregations shifted their energies to establishing a shelter for the homeless in downtown Los Angeles. Beerman retired in 1986, leaving the congregation to Rabbi Sanford Ragins, who would serve as senior rabbi for 18 years while maintaining an academic career teaching history and homiletics at HUC-JIR and at Occidental College, in Eagle Rock. Ragins welcomed intermarried, interracial, and gay and lesbian families into the communal fold and championed the peace camp in Israel and labor and interfaith cooperation in the U.S. He served as chair for the Central Conference of American Rabbis' Committee on Ethics, which investigates allegations of wrongful behavior by Reform rabbis, and taught German divinity students in Germany about Judaism. Ragins helmed his congregation until 2002, when Rabbi Kenneth Chasen, a former TV music supervisor and soundtrack composer who became a rabbi in 1998, took over as senior rabbi. Chasen's task at the 650-family-strong temple was to nurture its traditional ties to broad, generally liberal causes, while also serving young, sometimes apolitical, families seeking innovative, home-centered synagogue life.

Rabbi Alfred *Wolf, a long time associate of Rabbi Magnin at Wilshire Temple, set himself to bridge the gulf between the faiths. In 1975 he knit together the Roman Catholic Archdiocese of Los Angeles with the Southern California Board of Rabbis and the American Jewish Committee. Together they established the Los Angeles Roman Catholic/Jewish Respect Life Committee which annually issued pastoral statements on subjects like "reflections on abortion and related issues," "caring for the dying person," "the single parent family," "nuclear reality," and "a covenant of care." He was one of the architects of the Southern California Interreligious Council for rabbis, ministers, and priests, which met regularly with Muslim, Buddhist, Sikh, and Bahai leaders. He also presided over the County Commission on Human Relations. When Pope John Paul II came to Los Angeles on a formal visit in 1989, Rabbi Wolf was chosen on behalf of the rabbinate to speak to him and he said, "we urge you, as we urge all our friends, to assist us in the continuing struggle against antisemitism – and in securing peace in Israel – including full diplomatic relations with the Vatican." Rabbi Wolf, upon retirement after 36 years of active service, became director of the newly established *Skirball Institute on American Values. He died in 2004 at 88.

Rabbi Gary Greenebaum of the American Jewish Committee took over the chairmanship of the Police Commission at a time when police actions were dividing the Los Angeles community and alienating its African-American citizens. He wisely walked the minefield with skill, determination, and integrity.

Rabbi Allen Freehling of University Synagogue was deeply immersed in social action issues. He received the Los Angeles social responsibility award from the Los Angeles Urban League, and the National Council of Christians and Jews honored him with the Humanitarian Responsibility Award. He was on the Los Angeles Commission to draft an ethics code for Los Angeles city government. He received the National Friendship Award by the parents and friends of lesbians and gays in 1989.When the AIDS epidemic began to spread, Rabbi Freehling became Los Angeles' heroic voice on behalf of Jewish religious action for AIDS victims. He was the citywide chairman of the Committee for AIDS, the founding chairperson of the County Commission on AIDS, and the founding chair of the AIDS Interfaith Council of Southern California. In 1998, Freehling led an interfaith pilgrimage to the Vatican to discuss Jewish history and antisemitism with Pope John Paul II. After the 9/11 attacks on the World Trade Center and other American targets, Freehling expended fresh energies reaching out to local Muslims and rejecting attempts to characterize them as monolithic apologists for terror. Freehling retired in 2003, after 30 years as senior rabbi, leaving his 900-family-strong congregation to Rabbi Morley Feinstein. Upon his departure, he announced his intent to engage in community building in the areas of human rights and civil liberties.

Los Angeles is also the home of several new age religious leaders and charismatic rabbis. Some are local figures with a local following and others are national and indeed international figures. Among the most prominent is Philip *Berg, who was influenced by an Israeli kabbalist by the name of Yehuda Brandwein. Rav Brandwein died in 1969. Beginning in Tel Aviv during the 1970s and expanding, after the Internet boom of the 1990s, to Los Angeles, Berg succeeded in popularizing Kabbalah and attracting media celebrities such as Madonna to his cause. Berg is at the helm of 50 centers claiming hundreds of thousands of paying adherents who help generate millions a year in revenue. The Kabbalah Centre directs its teachings to Jews and non-Jews alike. It has generated a "buzz" to borrow a term common in the entertainment community.

RABBI-EDUCATORS. In immediate post-World War II Los Angeles, there was no learning beyond bar mitzvah instruction and no employed Jewish scholars other than Dr. Samuel Dinin, who died in 2005 at the age of 103, then head of the Bureau of Jewish Education, and Rabbi Jacob Kohn (d. 1968) at Sinai Temple. Forty years later, the *University of Judaism was ensconced on 25 acres of land on Mulholland Drive, the Hebrew Union College was in the process of building a major cultural center in neighborly proximity, and Yeshiva University of Los Angeles (which is not affiliated with YU) was building a multi-story building on its site on Pico Boulevard. Additionally, UCLA and the state universities had developed serious programs of advanced Jewish studies as an integral part of their academic offerings, and a substantial community of Jewishly committed academics was helping to transform a Jewish desert into a possible oasis of Judaism. This came about largely through the efforts of rabbi-educators who put their lifetime learning and teaching experience to the task of building Jewish educational institutions.

The Union of American Hebrew Congregations (UAHC) in 1947 established in Los Angeles a college of Jewish studies to engage in teacher training and adult education. Five years later, the Cincinnati-based Hebrew Union College formed a degree-granting California school. Eventually, the school absorbed the UAHC College of Jewish Studies into a School of Education and Jewish Studies. In 1957, freshly ordained Rabbi Alfred Gottschalk was appointed dean of the school. He enrolled at the University of Southern California Graduate School of Religion to get a doctorate in Bible study. While there, he became good friends with the dean of the School of Religion. Their joint dream of the future bore fruit when in time an academic reciprocity agreement was negotiated whereby HUC would move to a major urban renewal site near USC, and the HUC students would receive a dual USC/HUC degree in selected graduate programs. HUC in turn would serve as the Jewish studies provider for the university. The campus was built and dedicated in 1971.

The Rabbinical School was the centerpiece of the program. Joining it was the nation's first School of Jewish Communal Service, headed by Gerald Bubis, who launched the academic training specific to Jewish communal workers. The Rhea Hirsch School of Education graduated educational administrators and teachers. The Skirball Museum was transferred from Cincinnati to Los Angeles expanding considerably the educational and cultural horizons of the school. It now increasingly regarded itself, except for its rabbinical department, as an institution for the entire Jewish community. When Gottschalk moved to Cincinnati to become fifth president of HUC, Uri D. Herscher became executive vice president of the Hebrew Union College-JIR world-wide and dean of the local school. He took the lead in conceptualizing and implementing a plan to build an imposing HUC Skirball Cultural Center and eventually established it as a separate, independent institution. David Ellenson, a long-time faculty member of the L.A. School, became the seventh president of HUC. In the 1990s, the school, began ordaining rabbis, who no longer went to Cincinnati or New York to complete their training.

By 1990, the concept, the new campus, and the funds were securely in hand. The renowned Israeli architect Moshe Safdie was commissioned to design a cultural center on an acquired choice Mulholland area site. When it opened later in the decade, Herscher left Hebrew Union College to head the Skirball Cultural Center, which established itself as an independent, thriving cultural center.

The fruitful relationship between HUC and USC reflected a growing, if unexpected rapprochement between the former WASP bastion and the Los Angeles Jewish community, which had long regarded the campus as a conservative Anglo-American redoubt inherently inhospitable to Jewish students and faculty. Although the university has often sought to downplay this aspect of its history, there was some merit in these perceptions, especially considered against the much warmer reception traditionally available across town at UCLA (sometimes disparaged as "Jew CLA").

An early president of the downtown Methodist campus, Joseph Widney, had in 1907 articulated a vision of Los Angeles (with USC at its forefront) as the world capital of Aryan supremacy. Rufus B. von Kleinsmid, USC's president from 1922 to 1946, and chancellor until his death in 1964, was widely rumored to have been a Nazi sympathizer. Various deans, including those of the medical and dental schools, alternately discriminated vigorously against Jewish enrollment (the Law and Medical schools were rumored to permit only one Jewish student a year during von Kleinsmid's tenure) or, in one episode involving the School of Dentistry in 1972, found themselves besieged by alumni charging pro-Jewish favoritism. In 1978, the university sparked another furor when it announced plans to accept a million dollars from Saudi Arabia for the King Faysal Chair of Islamic and Arab Studies (the plan, which entailed Saudi involvement in faculty appointments, was shelved after concerted protest from local Jewish organizations). In 1986, a campus fraternity was suspended for chanting anti-Jewish remarks outside the residency of a Jewish fraternity on Greek Row.

Today, however, some 11 percent of the student body (at 3,000 students, greater than every school in the California State University and University of California system, apart from UC Berkeley and Cal State Northridge) and a third of the faculty are Jewish. This is the result of ongoing, even unique, attempts by USC to escape its checkered past (and not incidentally, to attract Jewish financial support). By the turn of the 21st century, USC and HUC had jointly established the Casden Institute for the Study of the Jewish Role in American Life. This is reputedly the first academic research center on the West Coast to concentrate on contemporary issues in Jewish life, most notably the role that the American Jewish community has played in the development of the United States in general and the American West in particular. At the turn of the century, USC became the only university in the country, for instance, to hire a full-time Jewish student recruiter. At this juncture, the dean of religious life and the chairman of the board of trustees are Jewish. In October 2005, USC agreed to host Stephen Spielberg's Survivors of the Shoah Visual History Foundation, becoming the repository for 52,000 videotaped testimonies of Holocaust survivors and witnesses. Amassed since 1994, the archive is now the largest digital library in the world, containing testimonies from 56 countries in 32 languages and totaling 117,000 viewing hours. It is interesting to note that USC's vaunted film school did not accept the youthful Spielberg into its filmmaking program. The university subsequently awarded him an honorary doctorate and an appointment to its board of trustees.

UCLA remains the largest college campus in Los Angeles. It hosts about 4,000 students who identify themselves as Jewish. The largest Jewish group at UCLA is Hillel, which offers a range of student activity from Shabbat services to political advocacy and social action. Chabad has been active there for decades, and built one of its earliest local Chabad houses near the off-campus residencies in Westwood. In 2000, the university launched its UCLA Center for Jewish Studies, an initially modest program intended, eventually, to offer graduate degrees locally and doctorates throughout the University of California system. In 2005, the center joined the Autry National Center in a new research program to explore the Jewish place in the city's cultural mosaic. By 2007, the university expects to put an Israel studies program in place under the direction of UCLA political scientist Steven Spiegel, one of the field's eminent figures. The university has experienced considerable volatility between advocates and critics of Israel, and Jewish students there often feel they are on the front lines of confrontation with some Muslim and African-American students. Thanks largely to the efforts of long-time Hillel director Chaim Seidler-Feller, however, the campus has also seen the emergence of coalitions and joint programs involving moderate Jews, Muslims, and Arabs. The Jewish studies program, founded by noted Hebraist Arnold Band, thrives. There is a chair in Holocaust studies sponsored by the 1939 club. Its current incumbent is Saul Friedlaender who won the prestigious MacArthur Foundation's "genius award." Historian David Myers is among its faculty.

Jewish studies at California State University, Northridge (CSUN) enjoy a lengthy pedigree, dating back to 1969. In 2002, some 4,000 of the school's 31,000 students were estimated to be Jewish, and 400 students were registered in 14 different Jewish studies courses each semester. Jody Myers heads the program. In 2005, the Jewish Studies Interdisciplinary Program at CSUN offered 27 courses for students majoring or performing minors in Jewish studies. Jewish studies majors are also available at Cal State Long Beach.

The University of Judaism was founded in 1947 by the Jewish Theological Seminary in response to a visionary concept by Mordecai M. *Kaplan. He proposed to establish a Jewish institution with the academic rigor of a general university but devoted to specialized research, training, and education for Judaism defined as a civilization. It came into being just as Los Angeles was becoming a major center of Jewish life, second only to New York. At the same time, the Los Angeles Bureau of Jewish Education was prodding the seminary to provide them with a school that could qualify prospective teachers who would be needed for the city's growing Jewish school system. Additionally, the university planners saw the mission of the university as providing adult education, stimulating Jewish artistic expression, and offering continuing education to the young rabbis now flocking westward. JTS Vice Chancellor Simon Greenberg volunteered to act as founding director, and Samuel Dinin as founding dean on behalf of the Bureau. David Lieber came to the University of Judaism in 1956 as dean of students, and in 1962 became president. Early on he formulated educational and management principles that guided him through the decades of university growth: uncompromising academic excellence; partnership with scholars and laity in the running of the school; unswerving attachment to the principle of pluralism in recognizing the legitimate diversities in Judaism and in the faculty; the ultimate establishment of a liberal arts college that would integrate both Jewish and Western cultures in one school and in one curriculum. The university was radically reconstituted. A new campus was built in West Los Angeles, at the epicenter of L.A. Jewry, between the Valley and the West Side, that included residence halls for individuals and families that in time transformed the university from a commuting to a residential campus, from a local and Western institution to a national and international center. The school embarked upon a major program of expansion and diversification. The Hebrew teachers college was replaced by a master's program in Jewish education that qualified teachers to serve as administrators and educators; the courses for rabbis were replaced by a graduate school in Judaica for prospective rabbis who studied for two years at the UJ then spent a year in Israel and completed their training at the seminary in New York. A masters of business administration program was established under the direction of Dr. Judith Glass, whose purpose was to train future executives for Jewish and for not-for-profit secular institutions. Undergraduate students were grounded in both the Jewish and Western civilizations, with majors in a wide array of disciplines and qualified for graduate work in universities of their choice. The university's continuing education program grew to become the largest of its kind in the United States. Its annual catalogue of more than 50 pages described dozens of courses; an annual lecture series of six lectures held in five communities attracted a yearly audience of 25,000–40,000 persons; its elder hostel program was considered to be the most popular in the country. A vigorous arts program attested to the continuing concentration on the arts as being integral to Jewish education. Two new policy institutes were established in the late 1980s. The Wilstein Institute was an activist think tank that researched and recommended public policy on vital Jewish issues. In its first two years of existence, conferences on public policy were held in subjects relating to Jewish identity, crime and punishment, Soviet Jews in their homeland, and Jews and other ethnics in America. The Whizin Institute researched and experimented with new directions for the Jewish family, the synagogue, and the Jewish community. In the early 21st century, it added two small think tanks on Holocaust and contemporary Israeli studies.

By the 1990s, both the University of Judaism and the Hebrew Union College were thriving institutions with differing but also overlapping types of leadership and goals, which were beginning to establish modes of cooperation.

Robert *Wexler, a protégé of David Lieber, became president in 1992 and under his leadership he shaped UJ as a non-denominational institution serving all Jews, which increases its attraction to some, but diminishes the enthusiasm of stalwarts of the Conservative movement. A noteworthy recent example of this commitment was Yesod, an intensive two-year biblical and Jewish studies program established in partnership with ten local Conservative, Reform, and Reconstructionist synagogues. The university believes that charges against UJ for abandoning the Conservative movement are misplaced, and that apart from its rabbinical program and its involvement with Camp Ramah, it had always envisioned its mission as non-denominational. It also houses a *mikveh* used by non-Orthodox rabbis for conversion.

More than a half-century after its birth, the university has clearly set itself apart from the Jewish Theological Seminary of America (JTS) in New York City, the Conservative movement's preeminent entity for ordaining rabbis. In 1996 the University of Judaism received an endowment of more than $22 million dollars anonymously from a prominent Los Angeles Jewish family for the creation of its own rabbinical school, which is named the Ziegler School of rabbinic Studies. Instead of celebrating its creation and the expansion of opportunities for would-be Conservative rabbis, JTS Chancellor Ismar *Shorsch forced a confrontation, which he lost, and the Seminary and UJ parted ways. UJ ordainees are automatically accepted into the Rabbinical Assembly and they are competing successfully with Seminary graduates for the same jobs. JTS lost its monopoly on Conservative ordination. Ziegler students are perhaps less academically rigorous, especially when judged by the standards of Wissenschaft, but their spirituality is deepened and their training is wholesome and they are equipped to meet the religious needs of their congregants.

Created by Los Angeles-based rabbis in 2000, the Academy for Jewish Religion, California (AJR/CA) began with the intent of revitalizing Judaism. The Academy is non-denominational and deems itself pluralistic. In the fall of 2003, it enrolled 55 students. In 2005, it graduated five rabbis, two of them also cantors. Indeed, the academy hosts the only cantorial school west of the Hudson. The academy launched an innovative Jewish Chaplaincy Program to provide a vital and much-needed Jewish presence at hospitals, secular schools, police, fire and health departments, senior citizen centers, and other communal institutions.

Jewish Education

In many areas of Los Angeles, the Jewish community has opted out of the public school system. The result has been a boon to Jewish day school education. There are now 10,000 students enrolled in Jewish day schools. For many non-Orthodox the debate is not between public education and private education but between a Jewish day school education and private school. Nine synagogues – five Reform: Emanuel, Wilshire Blvd., Stephen Wise, Temple Israel of Hollywood, and Beth Hillel; and four Conservative: Valley Beth Shalom and Adat Ariel in the Valley, Sinai/Akiba and Pressman Academy on the West Side – have day schools that are affiliated with the congregations and such an affiliation is central to the future of the congregations. There are two liberal high schools, the Milken School and the New Jewish Community high school both established by Dr. Bruce Powell. Orthodox schools, large and small, proliferate, among the 37 Jewish day schools of Los Angeles. YULA has a high school for boys and one for girls. The girls' school became an independent school in Summer 2005, and it is expected that the boys' school will also become independent from Wiesenthal by summer 2006. Shalhevet is a progressive Orthodox high school modeled after the teachings of Harvard psychologist Lawrence Kohlberg, in which students participate in the governance of the school and, like Ramaz in New York, male and female students study together. It defines the liberal reaches of modern Orthodoxy. It was envisioned, established, and headed by Dr. Jerry Friedman who himself is a Harvard graduate and a prominent philanthropist.

The Jewish Federation Council

The Federation of Jewish Welfare Organizations was established in 1912 to serve as the disbursement, coordinating, and lobbying body for the 12 Jewish recipient agencies of the Los Angeles Community Chest. In addition the Federation took responsibility for raising modest sums for supplementary assistance. Under this arrangement only local Jewish needs were served. In 1929, responding to appeals from European and Palestine Jewry, and to local needs not supported by the Federation, a separate funding mechanism was established – the United Jewish Welfare Fund. Its first campaign year produced $93,000. By 1933, it became increasingly evident that there was need for a representative body that would be empowered to unite the Jewish community, including newer arrivals, around local concerns not addressed by the Federation or the Welfare Fund, such as Jewish education, youth organization, *kashrut* supervision, and newly formed synagogues. In response an umbrella body called the United Jewish Community was founded which in 1936 comprised 92 constituent organizations, congregations, and societies. In 1937, the United Jewish Community and the United Jewish Welfare Fund merged into a new body called the Jewish Community Council, which a few years later was given the authority to allocate the monies raised by the United Jewish Welfare Fund. There was a Federation and a Council. The Council became increasingly preeminent as it attracted the new leadership in the growing Jewish community, while the Federation remained the bastion of the traditional and largely German-Jewish émigré leadership; 156 of the 350 eligible Jewish organizations joined the Council. The new Jewish immigrants now arriving from the East Coast in increasing numbers tended to be politically liberal, equal-rights oriented, and devoted to Zionism and overseas needs. This contrasted strongly with the Federation of Jewish Welfare Organizations, which was conservative, local-needs oriented, and lukewarm to Zionism. The spectacular increase in fundraising from $2,750,000 in 1945 to $10 million in 1948, and from 33 to 58 thousand contributors, convinced the Federation leadership that their future was dismal, especially since Community Chest support, their major source of Jewish institutional income, was increasingly inadequate and increased public Jewish support was essential. The Federation and the Council negotiated for three years; the result was the Jewish Federation Council (JFC). In the decades ahead the Federation Council moved to become not only the spokesman but also the driving force behind Jewish community growth and development. It continued to expand its sense of community responsibility. Its goals originally were quantitative and defensive: raising more money from each contributor and from more contributors; dealing with emergencies that upset Jewish unity and harmony and so affect fundraising; and helping to maintain good relations in the community at large. In the wake of the Yom Kippur War, the Federation leadership began to consider the responsibilities of the Federation as potentially transcending practical needs. The Federation was already deeply involved in Jewish education. Its Bureau of Jewish Education guided, supported, subvented, and served as chief advocate for Jewish schools. Since its organization in 1937, it had striven to establish and raise standards, attract and increase financial support, and help to create a teaching profession. Under the initiative of Emil Jacoby, its director from 1983 to 1993, a number of programs were established which sought to raise the level and standards and effectiveness of Jewish education. However some thought more could be done to establish Federation responsibility for the welfare of Judaism as well as of Jews. Sensitive to the danger of crossing the line between religious autonomy and Federation responsibility, they suggested that the Los Angeles Federation formally accept responsibility for a community stake in what they termed "the quality of Jewish life." This was to be a revolutionary departure. Until now Jewish communities were divided into "organized" and "religious." Jewish organizational life mandated mutual independence between "church" and "state." In 1973 a Committee on Jewish Life was established by the JFC with the avowed goals of reducing tensions and adding to the potential cooperation between the communal and the congregational sectors of Jewish life. A year later the committee made its report and recommendations; as a result, in the fall of 1974, the Council of Jewish Life was established to implement the report. Its mandate at the time was to improve relationships between synagogues and the JFC; develop an outreach program to the unaffiliated including promotion of synagogue affiliation; and support of existing adult education programs. In succeeding years the Council of Jewish Life expanded its program, which aimed at "raising the quality of Jewish life." It established a number of commissions, which undertook projects with cultural, educational, and religious goals. It established a commission on synagogue affairs which organized synagogue councils in outlying areas, developed a task force on synagogue finance and administration, and circulated widely a letter written by the president of the JFC to welfare fund contributors describing the synagogue as "an indispensable link for the preservation and transmission of an authentic Jewish way of life" and urging affiliation with a synagogue. Nine hundred responses were received in response to this unprecedented appeal by a Jewish community organization, which openly committed itself to the synagogue as essential to the creative survival of Jewish life in America. Over the years the council established commissions that operated in areas considered significant. In

1988, they were adult Jewish education, the arts in Jewish life, the disabled, the Israelis, outreach to intermarried, outreach to singles, spirituality, synagogue funding. The Council, with funding from the Jewish Community Foundation, appropriated approximately $100,000 a year for support of synagogue proposals that were innovative. The grants were awarded by the committee on synagogue funding on a three-year basis. Grant requests by the end of the 1990s increasingly dealt with outreach concerns such as reaching the unaffiliated, the singles, the intermarried, and the disaffected. With the advent of the 21st century, however, the future of Jewish federations in general and L.A.'s in particular appeared to be both bleak and beyond the ability of commissioned studies and valiant slogans about the need for greater inclusion to easily reinvigorate. The bottom line is that its campaigns have not grown significantly while Jewish life has found other sources of Jewish support. The problem is not Jewish life in Los Angeles, which is thriving, but Jewish organizations formed in an earlier generation and enjoying less enthusiastic support from the younger generations.

In many respects, Los Angeles had become an innovative cauldron of new Jewish activity and organization entirely unbeholden to the East Coast, which in turn persisted in regarding itself as the sole arbiter of Jewish power in America and of national communal decision-making. It was this perceptual dichotomy, in fact, that resulted in several East-West spats that incensed the Los Angeles community. The first involved the Los Angeles regional chapter of the American Jewish Congress, which split from the national organization in 1999, reconstituting as the independent Progressive Jewish Alliance. Even more troubling was the impromptu dismissal, in 2002, of the Anti-Defamation League's regional director of 27 years' standing, David Lehrer, by the ADL's national director, Abraham Foxman. The latter's decision to terminate Lehrer without stated cause was taken as an affront to the entire community, not least of all by the ADL's regional board, which had achieved major strides in fundraising under Lehrer's stewardship, and resented being treated as a mere branch office. Lehrer was replaced by Amanda Susskind, a local attorney with a background in public policy.

Working against the community was the discovery that the Jewish population nationally was in decline. The Jewish population of Los Angeles has remained fairly constant from 1979 through today, despite significant immigration. The birthrate is extremely low. Affiliation rates, as in so many western communities, remain lower than those in the east. With intermarriage increasingly normative and the graying of the Jewish population proceeding farther apace than in many other ethnic communities, Jewish communal life and involvement inevitably became the purview of an increasingly smaller and self-limiting segment of the Jewish public. Secularization and assimilation occurred in parallel with fragmentation caused by a proliferation of new Jewish organizations and institutions; each determined to secure its share of an ever-diminishing pie. With Jews increasingly preferring to give to non-Jewish causes, federations became more dependent on a coterie of "big givers" for continued sustenance. In Los Angeles, attention to the needs and interests of this select, self-appointed, and sometimes self-serving few resulted not only in greater tensions between lay and professional leadership but in widespread malaise and alienation within the greater Jewish community.

Jewish Journalism Comes of Age in L.A.

The *Jewish Journal* is the flagship newspaper of the Los Angeles community. Prior to the *Jewish Journal's* appearance in 1986, Los Angeles had been served by three publications: the *Jewish Community Bulletin*, which had been the Federation's biweekly house organ, *Heritage*, a somewhat parochial, Israel-centered weekly established by Herb Brin in 1954, and the *B'nai B'rith Messenger*, aimed at the Orthodox community (the Israeli community, meanwhile, had its own Hebrew-language papers, notably *Israel Shelanu*, *Shalom L.A.*, and local supplements of the Israeli dailies *Yedioth Aharonoth* and *Maariv*). The *Jewish Journal* was the brainchild of a group of "Benefactors" who had long lamented the community's lack of a first-class Jewish paper. Armed with its forerunner's 75,000-strong subscription list and with an assertion of editorial independence, the paper initially exhibited scant awareness of the scope of Jewish life in Los Angeles. The paper made some headway broadening its coverage during the 1990s, most notably through the efforts of the late Marlene Adler Marks and the late David Margolis, writers with profound roots and sincere interest in hitherto ignored, misunderstood, or otherwise denigrated segments of the community. It also stepped up its Israel coverage. It was only with the appointment of local journalist Rob Eshman as editor, however, that the *Journal* was finally able to more fully and inclusively reflect L.A. Jewry's diverse, variegated, and sometimes contentious character. Like many Jewish newspapers, its critics contend that it plays it too safe.

The Rise and Fall and Rise of the JCCs

One of the earliest and most important points of entry into organized communal life in Los Angeles was the Jewish community center, the first of which, the Modern Hebrew School and Social Center, later renamed Soto-Michigan, came into being in Boyle Heights in 1924. A number of other centers followed, including one on West Adams, on Beverly-Fairfax, at City Terrace, and at Hollywood-Los Feliz. Initially underfunded and underused, these and subsequently created JCCs were placed under the aegis of a centralized organization, the Jewish Centers Association (JCA), in 1943. Subvented by the Los Angeles Jewish Federation Council, the JCA alternately bristled under the Federation's pecuniary oversight while holding tightly to the reins of individual centers that generated funds locally and often resented turning these resources and control over their own programming to the JCA. In 1952, the JCA flouted local opposition by closing the more ardently Zionist and overtly Jewish Menorah Center and merging it with the more intercultural Soto-Michigan Center. Declines in the Jewish population of the city's Eastside, and political pressure against Soto-Michigan's ostensibly radical leadership, resulted in its closure soon after, and that of the West Adams center as well.

As Jews moved into the city's western reaches and into the San Fernando Valley to the north, new Jewish community centers cropped up in their midst, ultimately resulting in a network of seven JCCs and a residential camp, three (Valley Cities, North Valley, and West Valley) in the San Fernando Valley alone. A joint JCA-Federation study conducted in the early 1970s resulted in the withdrawal of funding in 1976 for the Hollywood-Los Feliz JCC and for the Israel Levin Senior Adult Center (later the subject of "Number Our Days," the Academy Award-winning documentary based on the work of the late Barbara Myerhoff). Community protests outside Federation headquarters at 6505 Wilshire Boulevard resulted in their reinstatement.

The JCCs continued to muddle along, under-funded and undervalued, yet providing scarce services to segments of the community not quite established financially or sufficiently rooted in Jewish life to join synagogues, yet interested in childcare, programs for the elderly, scouting facilities for the children of Israelis, Jewish day camps, and other programs. Indeed, the Jewish pre-school program at Valley Cities JCC in Sherman Oaks developed under Bea Chankin Weisberg into one of the crown jewels of early childhood education in Los Angeles. During the 1990s, the JCCs spiraled downward. Their programs and membership dropped dramatically despite steep cuts in Federation funding, from 25 percent to 30 percent of their budgets to 13 percent. The North Valley JCC in Granada Hills, meanwhile, had its mettle severely tested in 1999, after a shooting spree by white supremacist Buford Furrow on the camp children that wounded several children and camp counselors and killed a mailman several miles away. The center lost little time resuming operations and regaining its footing and the community's confidence. Bailed out with Federation loans on several occasions, the parent organization, the Jewish Community Center of Los Angeles, finally collapsed, ostensibly due to mismanagement, in 2001. Several of the city's prized JCCs, valued more for their property than the services they provided, found themselves dragged onto the chopping block. The Bay Cities center in Santa Monica and the North Valley Center were ultimately sold, and the Conejo Valley Center closed up shop. The Westside and West Hills centers, both situated in extremely affluent neighborhoods, became independent. Their respective communities, meanwhile, rescued the centers in Silverlake and Sherman Oaks, at the last moment, although their continued existence is deemed tenuous. It is remarkable that in a city as affluent and as athletically and culturally oriented as Los Angeles, Jewish Community Centers are not thriving and came perilously close to extinction.

A Bounty of Innovative Institutions

Renowned (or notorious) as a capital of glitz and ostentation as well as of homelessness and hunger, in 1985, Los Angeles became home to an innovative response to the excess and overindulgence of some of its wealthier segments with the creation of Mazon. A non-profit, grassroots agency created in the aftermath of an Ethiopian famine, Mazon (Hebrew for "Sustenance") provides millions of dollars to over 300 hunger-relief agencies, including emergency food providers, food banks, multi-service organizations, and advocacy groups that seek long-term solutions to the hunger problem. Over $3 million are now culled annually from Jewish families and organizations as a self-imposed three percent tax on catered events. Founded by Leonard Fein, Mazon cites as inspiration the Torah's demands for justice and the rabbinic tradition of forbidding the commencement of life-cycle celebrations until the community's poor and hungry have been seated and fed. Since 1986, Mazon has provided more than $31 million to the hungry in the United States, in Israel, and in developing countries around the world.

Another noteworthy local innovation is *Beit T'Shuva* (Heb. "House of Repentance"), a recovery and reintegration center that seeks to integrate Jewish spirituality with the 12 steps of Alcoholics Anonymous and with traditional psychotherapy. With a campus in West Los Angeles, *Beit T'Shuva* provides therapeutic in- and outpatient accommodations to alcoholics, substance abusers, and discharged prisoners. *Beit T'Shuva* began as an outgrowth of a non-profit organization called the Jewish Committee for Personal Service (JCPS). That organization came into being in 1921 to provide social services to Jews in California mental hospitals and prisons. Forty years later, a donation from a JCPS client led to the establishment of the Gateways Hospital and Mental Health Center, which subsequently incorporated JCPS as one of its programs. Harriet Rossetto, who joined the staff of JCPS in 1984, discerned in an article by Dr. Abraham Twerski on Judaism and the Twelve Steps a possible antidote both to the recidivism of many of her patients and to the Jewish community's apparent lack of concern and support (many Jews erroneously believing that Jews as a rule did not suffer addictions). In 1987, with a grant from FEMA and a loan from the Jewish Community Foundation, Gateways Hospital bought an old house at 216 South Lake Street in Los Angeles and opened the doors of *Beit T'Shuva.* The original mission was to provide transitional living and reentry services to Jewish men being released from jails and prisons. The program has expanded its attentions in recent years to Jews struggling with addictive behaviors. A capital campaign raised five million dollars toward the purchase and renovation of a new facility, which opened in 1999. Two years later, *Beit T'Shuva* gained its independence from Gateways Hospital, becoming a constituent agency of the Los Angeles Jewish Federation. Its spiritual leader is himself a *Ba'al Teshuvah* and UJ ordainee Rabbi Mark Borowitz, who returned to tradition after his own incarceration.

Justice may be a Jewish imperative, but its pursuit in 21st-century America can be prohibitively expensive and beyond the grasp of most consumers, Jews and non-Jews alike. Enter *Bet Tzedek* (Heb. "House of Justice"), a five-day-a-week storefront community law office that dispenses free legal assistance to more than 10,000 Angelinos out of its Fairfax neighborhood headquarters, an office in North Hollywood, and 30 senior centers throughout the Greater Los Angeles region. With a staff of 55 and over 400 volunteers, the organization, founded in 1974, serves all eligibly needy residents of Los Angeles County, Jewish or otherwise. *Bet Tzedek* has been instrumental in fighting consumer fraud; in protecting employee rights; in assisting health-care providers and non-paid caregivers; in securing government benefits for eligible recipients; in combating slumlords and protecting tenants from unscrupulous landlords; in expanding elder law protection, and even in securing Holocaust reparations – they were the key organization to impact the way reparations are handled by the Claims Conference.

In 1982, Lowell and Michael Milken established the Milken Family Foundation. Active in education, medical research, and Jewish culture, the foundation has made noteworthy attempts to support and honor outstanding teachers locally and nationally, to foster school reform, and to generate enthusiasm for education as a lifelong process. The Milkens were also instrumental in founding the Milken Community High School, the crown jewel of the Stephen S. Wise Jewish school system.

In 2003, the foundation released the first of 90 projected compact disk recordings of Jewish music, under the aegis of the Milken Archives of American Jewish Music in New York City, established in 1990 to generate a $17 million compilation of over 600 pieces of Jewish music culled from over 350 years of American musical history. Of these, no less than 500 are new recordings of lost or never-preserved music, commissioned from orchestras, choirs, and soloists in 15 cities in the U.S. and Europe. These include Sephardic liturgies from the American Colonial period; recordings of complete Orthodox, Conservative, and Reform services; Klezmer-influenced concert works; ecstatic Hasidic music; Yiddish theater work with reconstructed orchestrations; and works commemorating or otherwise influenced by the Holocaust and the founding of the State of Israel. Distributed under the Noxos recording label, initial offerings included works by Kurt Weill, Mario Castelnuovo-Tedesco, David Krakauer, and Alberto Mizrahi, and orchestras led by such eminent conductors as Gerald Schwarz. The archive's artistic director is Neil W. Levin, of the Jewish Theological Seminary.

Jewish life – religious and secular, cultural and intellectual – thrives in Los Angeles, a city with intense affiliations and also a high rate of non-affiliation. The challenge of the early 21st century is how to preserve the intense core of Jewish life while attracting to that core those with but the most marginal of Jewish affiliations. It is not a problem unique to Los Angeles, but one acute in Los Angeles.

BIBLIOGRAPHY: M. Vorspan and L.P. Gartner, *History of the Jews of Los Angeles* (1970); H. Newmark, *Sixty Years in Southern California* (1930³); M.R. Newmark, in: *Historical Society of Southern California Quarterly*, 24 (1942), 77–97; 25 (1943), 5–65; 38 (1956), 167–84; S. Reichler, in: J. Meltz (ed.), *Mount Sinai Year Book* (1946); I. Soref, in: *Reconstructionist*, 18 (1952/53), 8–12; A. Laurie, "Social Adjustments of German Jewish Refugees in Los Angeles" (Thesis, University of Southern California, 1953); F. Massarik, *Report on the Jewish Population of Los Angeles* (1953); D. Bin Nun, *Religious and Other Cultural Factors Affecting the Assimilation of Jews in Los Angeles* (Thesis, University of Southern California, 1954); R. Glantz, *Jews of California from the Discovery of Gold until 1880* (1960); E. Lipman and A. Vorspan, *Tale of Ten Cities* (1962); J. Turner, in: AJHSP, 54 (1964/65), 123–64; N.B. Stern, *California Jewish History; a Descriptive Bibliography* (1967).

[Max Vorspan / Sheldon Teitelbaum (2nd ed.)]

LOSICE (Pol. **Łosice**; Rus. **Lositsy**; Yid. **Loshits**), town in Lublin province, E. Poland. Jews probably settled in Losice at the end of the 17th century. At the beginning of the 18th century the townsmen complained to the king about competition from Jewish craftsmen. A synagogue was erected in the 18th century against an annual payment of 200 zlotys. In 1765 there were 389 Jewish polltax payers in Losice and the vicinity. The community numbered 654 (42% of the total population) in 1827 and 917 (54%) in 1857. From then on its numbers increased considerably due to the horse markets in the town, in which large numbers of Jewish dealers took part. The Jewish population numbered 2,396 (71%) in 1897 and 2,708 (70%) in 1921. Before the outbreak of World War II there were about 2,900 Jews in Losice. The community was liquidated on Aug. 22, 1942, when the Jews were deported to *Treblinka camp.

BIBLIOGRAPHY: Halpern, Pinkas, index; B. Wasiutyński, *Ludność żydowska w Polsce w wiekach XIX i XX* (1930), 34; ICA, *Rapport pour l'année 1925*; M. Baliński and T. Lipiński, *Staro żytna Polska* (1845), IIIa; Yad Vashem Archives. **ADD. BIBLIOGRAPHY:** *Łshits, L'zekher an umgekumener Kehille* (1965).

[*Encyclopaedia Judaica* (Germany)]

LOSTICE (Czech **Loštice**; Ger. **Loschitz**), village in N.W. central Moravia, until 1992 Czechoslovak Republic and thereafter Czech Republic. Jewish settlement is first mentioned in Lostice in 1544. Another record, from 1630, mentions that there were 21 houses of Jewish ownership; only ten were inhabited after the Thirty Years' War (1650). A large number of Lostice Jews attended the Leipzig fairs in the 18th century. The community increased after the mid-17th century, when Jews were expelled from Ukraine and lower Austria. In Lostice there were 80 Jewish families (328 persons); 17 houses are recorded in 1727. In 1798 the number of families allotted to Lostice was 71 (see *Familiants Law). Before that time, Jewish houses had stood very close to the Catholic Church; but in 1727 the Jews were forced to move to other places, where they formed a ghetto. Their number declined sharply after the emancipation allowed the Jews freedom of movement. The number fell from 438 in 1848 to 284 in 1869, and to 115 in 1900.

In 1921 there were 2,708 Jews. In 1928 most of the Jewish quarter was destroyed by fire. In 1930, 55 Jews were left in the town. By 1938 six families remained. They were all deported during the Holocaust; 11 returned from the Nazi concentration camps. The synagogue was destroyed on November 11,

1938. The religious community was not revived after World War II.

The synagogue, probably from 1805, was used until the Nazi occupation; subsequently it was used as a storehouse. In 1966–80 it housed a municipal museum with an exhibition of the history of the Jewish community. Later, it served as an art and music school.

BIBLIOGRAPHY: Gold-Wachstein, in: H. Gold (ed.), *Die Juden und Judengemeinden Maehrens in Vergangenheit und Gegenwart* (1929), 318–20. **ADD. BIBLIOGRAPHY:** J. Fiedler, *Jewish Sights of Bohemia and Moravia* (1991), 107–8.

[Meir Lamed / Yeshayahu Jelinek (2nd ed.)]

LOST PROPERTY (Heb. *avedah u-meẓi'ah*; lit. "lost and found").

The Basis of the Law

Lost property, called *avedah*, is property which has passed out of its owner's possession and whose whereabouts are unknown to him. Both criteria must exist together for the property to be designated as an *avedah* (Rashi and Tos. to BM 30b, and see 31a). The Pentateuch enjoins that an *avedah* be returned to its rightful owner (Deut. 22:1–4). When the owner has clearly despaired of finding an *avedah* and of having it restored to his possession (see **Ye'ush*) his ownership in it ceases, and the finder is not obliged to return it but may retain it for himself (BM 21b). Even in the absence of the owner's *ye'ush*, the same consequence follows if there is no possibility of the *avedah* being restored to him (Tos. to BM 22b; Ran, Nov. Ḥul. 38b). The laws of *avedah u-meẓi'ah* comprise two categories:

(1) laws forming part of property law, namely the determination of what constitutes an *avedah* and the point at which ownership thereof ceases so as to enable the property to be acquired by the finder (*zekhiyyah*); and

(2) laws circumscribing the *mitzvah* of restoring the lost property, i.e., laws not appertaining to property law, since the finder who fails to return an *avedah* and who leaves it where it was found, transgresses the law but is not obliged to compensate the owner. However, the finder who takes an *avedah* and appropriates it for himself is considered a thief (BM 26b).

Avedah with Retention of Ownership

In accordance with the above definition, it may be noted that, for instance, an animal grazing on public land without the knowledge of the owner, and where it is not kept from getting lost, is considered an *avedah*, although not if it is grazing on a path when he is aware of its presence there (Ravad, in: Asheri BM 2:26). Similarly, a garment lying in a public thoroughfare is an *avedah*, but not one lying behind a fence (BM 31a). Nor would a vessel that is covered, even though found in a refuse heap, be deemed an *avedah* (BM 25b).

Restoration

The fact that an article has been lost does not in itself involve loss of ownership. Accordingly, a person who comes across property that appears to be lost is duty bound to take it into his custody and care until it can be restored to its owner. In certain circumstances, however, the finder is exempt from this duty. Thus a kohen is prohibited from entering a cemetery and therefore cannot be responsible for an *avedah* which he has seen there (BM 32a). Similarly a person is also exempt if he would not normally take the object, even if it were his own, such as an elderly person for whom such an action would be considered undignified (BM 30a). Furthermore, the finder of property which is of negligible value (i.e., less than a prutah; BM 27a), or a finder who would be involved in expense in restoring the property to its rightful owner (BM 30b), are also exempt. All other finders of lost property, however, must take charge thereof and seek out the owner, to whom it must be returned. Some scholars are of the opinion that the finder's degree of responsibility for an *avedah* – as long as it is in his care – must be the same as that of an unpaid bailee, while others equate the standard of care required to that of a paid bailee (BM 29a; see *Bailment). In the case of an animal, if the expense of its upkeep should prove to be too high to make its return to the owner worthwhile, the finder may sell the animal after a certain period, but has to account for the proceeds to the owner (BM 28b). Inanimate property may not be used by the finder except to prevent its deterioration (BM 29b).

When the owner's identity is unknown to the finder, he must bring the *avedah* to the notice of the public, i.e., by announcing it. If the claimant owner offers notable identification marks (*simanim*), the property is returned to him, but if he is suspected of being an impostor he must also produce evidence of his ownership (BM 28b). Before the destruction of the Temple, the announcement was made from a stone platform in Jerusalem, during the three festivals when the people were gathered there. In later times the announcement was made in the synagogues, and it was also enacted that, in places where the secular authorities expropriated all lost property, it would suffice if a finder made the matter known to his neighbors and acquaintances only (BM 28b). If no claimant responds to the announcement, the finder must retain the *avedah*, in trust for the owner, indefinitely (Sh. Ar., ḤM 267:15).

The *mitzvah* to restore lost articles to their owners is not limited to physical objects that are found, but it is extended to include the wider concept of preventing loss to one's fellow. Thus, if a man sees water flooding a neighbor's field and he is able to stop it, he has a duty to do so; or if he sees an animal destroying a vineyard he has a duty to drive it away (BM 31a). Furthermore, this wider concept even extends to the person of an individual, so that if anyone finds that another has lost his way, it is a *mitzvah* to set him right or to guide him as may be necessary (BK 81b).

Related to the *mitzvah* of returning an *avedah* is that of "loading and unloading" (*perikah u-te'inah*), which also involves saving one's neighbor from suffering losses. A person is required to come to the aid of a neighbor in the unloading and reloading of a heavily laden beast of burden (Ex. 23:5; Deut. 22:4; BM 32a–33a). In view of their common halakhic source, the laws of loading and unloading and of returning lost property are similar and interrelated (see Ḥ. Albeck, *Hashlamot* to *Mishnah*, BM 2:10).

Avedah with Loss of Ownership

When the owner despairs of having lost property restored to him, his ownership thereof ceases (see **Ye'ush*) and title to the property vests in the finder. *Ye'ush* may be inferred from speech or conduct, or may be assumed from the circumstances in which the lost property is found. For instance, an *avedah* which has no identification marks, or which is found in a public thoroughfare, or which appears to have been lost a long time before – factors which make it impossible for the property to be returned – are instances in which *ye'ush* would be inferred. Often it is doubtful whether under certain circumstances the owner is presumed to have despaired, and the sages disagree as to whether the finder has to restore the lost property or acquires ownership in it; e.g., where the lost property has identification marks but they are liable to be erased by being trodden upon, or when the property has marks which were not made intentionally, or whether the place in which the property was found can be an identification mark (BM 23a).

A second category of lost property which becomes ownerless, and may therefore be appropriated by the finder, is that of *avedah mi-da'at* ("intentional loss"), i.e., when it appears from the circumstances that the property has been intentionally abandoned or thrown away by its owner and that he no longer desires it, e.g., scattered fruit on a threshing floor, figs which have dropped from a tree alongside a road, open jars of wine or oil left in a public place (BM 21a,, 23b). Finally, lost property which can no longer be restored to its owner ceases to be owned by him and belongs to the finder, even if in the absence of the owner's *ye'ush*. Thus an *avedah* carried away by the river is lost to the owner and "to the whole world," even if the owner is unaware of his loss and even if he does not despair (Tos. to BM 22b). Some scholars nevertheless establish the owner's *ye'ush* in these circumstances, on which ground they justify the above rules (TJ, BM 2:1; 8b; Maim. Yad, *Gezelah va-Avedah*, 11:10). Similarly, geese and fowl which escaped from their owner and can no longer be restored to him belong to the finder (Ran on Rif Ḥul. ch. *Shillu'aḥ ha-Ken*, introd.).

In talmudic times it was already customary, as a matter of equitable law, to return certain classes of lost property, even if ownership thereof had already ceased, as in the case of an *avedah* dropped in a public thoroughfare (BM 24b). In post-talmudic times the communities of Europe adopted the practice of returning property carried away by a flood or similarly "lost to the world," either in terms of rabbinical enactments (**takkanot*) or in accordance with the principle of **dina de-malkhuta dina* (Mordecai, BM no. 257; Rema, ḤM 259:7; see also **Shomerim*).

The laws of the State of Israel require all lost property to be handed over to the police, but the finder may claim it for himself if after a certain period the owner is not found.

[Shalom Albeck]

The Commandment to Return Lost Property and the Law in the State of Israel

(a) Section 2 of the Restoration of Lost Property Law, 5733 – 1973 obligates a person who finds and takes any lost property to return it to its owner or to report the find to the police. However, the Law imposes no obligation to take the lost object ab initio. By contrast, Jewish Law imposes a religious-ethical obligation upon a person seeing a lost article or aware of its existence to take it, with the object of returning it to its rightful owner (Sh. Ar., ḤM 259:1). The obligation not to ignore a lost object led the Sages to develop precise definitions of the concept of lost property, so as to enable the finder of a lost object to ascertain when an obligation to return exists, when it is forbidden for him to take the object so that he will not be considered a thief or spoiler, and when he is entitled to take the object for himself.

(b) Both Jewish Law and Israeli Law recognize the finder's ability to acquire ownership of a lost object. However, the methods of acquisition in Israeli Law and in Jewish Law differ in a number of respects. Jewish Law recognizes the concept of "resignation" and rules that, if we may presume that the owner despaired of recovering his lost object before the finder took it, the finder is entitled to keep the object for himself (Sh. Ar., ḤM 259:3); however, if the lost object was taken before the owner reached this stage of resignation, the finder can never acquire it (Sh. Ar., *ibid.*). Israeli Law adopted the Jewish legal concept of "resignation" and even determined that the finder becomes the new owner of the object when "the owner shall be deemed to have given up the property" (section 4 of the Law). However, the Law also defines "resignation" as occurring only after four months have elapsed from the date of the find. Moreover, even in the case of property of negligible value, in which the Law recognizes the possibility of immediate resignation by the owner, the Law makes no distinction between whether the finder took the object before or after the owner abandoned hope of its return.

(c) A person who takes a lost object and fails to fulfill the obligations imposed on him by the Law is liable to the penalties prescribed in section 9 of the Law; if he retains the property for himself he commits theft (section 383(c) of the Israeli Penal Code, 5737 – 1977). Jewish Law also regards a person who keeps an object found by him, without returning it to its owner, as a thief.

(d) Conceptually speaking, the duty to return lost property is given extremely wide interpretation in Jewish Law and includes the obligation to prevent others from loss. Any act of deliverance is regarded as the restoration of something lost. It was thus that the Sages explained the verse: "and so shall you do with any lost object of your brother" (see BM 31a; Maim. Yad, *Gezelah va-Avedah* 11.20). Various concepts are mentioned in this regard, e.g. "lost property" (saving land from floods), "lost person" (saving a person's life and bodily integrity; see BK 81b), and even "lost spirit" (saving a person from transgressing; see *Minḥat Ḥinukh* 239:4). It is thus apparent that the duty of restoration applies to all types of property or interests of others which are endangered. By contrast, the Israeli legislator preferred the practical distinction between restoring a lost object and saving another person from loss – the latter including any activity for the preservation of another person's interest. The return of lost property is regulated by the Restoration of Lost Property Law (and the definition of lost property was thus limited to movable property, concerning which an act of restoration may be performed), while activities performed to preserve another person's interest are regulated by section 5 of the Unjust Enrichment Law, 5739 – 1979.

Case Law of the Israeli Supreme Court – Lost Property Found in Another Person's Domain

In the "Hendeles" judgment (CA 546/78 *Kupat Am Bank Ltd. v. Hendeles et al.*, PD 34(3) 57), the Israeli Supreme Court addressed the question of lost property found by one of the bank's customers on the floor of the bank's safe deposit room. The issue in these proceedings was whether this place, being open to the public, was considered "another person's domain" for purposes of section 3 of the Law, which states that "[a] person who finds lost property in another person's domain shall report the find to such other person and deliver up the property to him at his request" and adds that "[i]f the other person takes over the lost property, he shall be regarded as the finder."

Justice Barak sought to ascertain the primary purpose of the Law and reached the conclusion that the main purpose of the Law is to restore lost property to its rightful owner, and it therefore follows that the word "domain" should be construed in a manner that increases the chances of the original owner to retrieve his property. To this end, an examination needs to be made, on a case by case basis, as to whether this goal will be realized by leaving the object in the place it was found. If we reach the conclusion that it is better for the original owner if the object remains in the place where it is found, this consideration alone suffices to enable the place to come within the definition of "another person's domain," because by so doing the finder will become obligated to transfer the object to the owner of the "domain." To quote Justice Barak:

> It appears to me that in considering whether a lost article was found in another person's domain, there is no room to have recourse to the question of whether that other person is regarded in the eyes of the law as the holder of the lost property even prior to its discovery by the finder… This approach – who was the first holder – does not appear to be relevant to the main goals of the Restoration of Lost Property Law. If indeed the primary interest of the Law is the restoration of lost property to its rightful owner, and if in order to realize this interest… it is fitting for the lost property to be delivered to the owner of the place, the original finder is obligated to do so, whether he is the first holder of the property, or whether it is possible to regard – according to this or any other doctrine of the laws of possession – the owner of the place as the first holder.

Justice Barak notes two factors, on whose basis it may be decided whether the lost article should be left in its place:

> First, it is natural that the owner of the lost property will return to the place at which the object was lost. His reasonable expectation is that, if the object is found at that place, and if at that place there is a person whose connections to the place are such that he can be expected to guard it, he will be able to receive it there and will not need to search after the finder… Secondly, there is a high probability that the owner of the place where the lost property is found, by virtue of his links to the place, will guard the lost object for its owner to a greater extent than a random finder.

Since the bank is the "natural address" to which the owner of the lost property is liable to return when he recalls where the object was lost, the bank should be classified as a separate "domain" for the application of the provisions of section 3, and the finder is obligated to deliver to the bank the lost article that he found. If the owner of the lost object is not ascertained within four months, the owner of the "domain" – the bank – will take possession of the object, even if in terms of the laws of ownership, the original finder should become the owner.

Justice Elon, in the minority, disagreed with the opinion of his colleague and wrote: "Section 2 only applies in unusual cases – generally speaking, in the case of an article which is found in the thoroughfare of a city." By contrast, with respect to

> an article found in a place which is traversed freely by thousands and even tens of thousands of people, such as the main entrance hall of a bank, in department stores and in various types of supermarkets, on buses and other modes of transport, in government offices and public institutions etc. – the manner of restoration follows the provisions of section 3 of the Law. In this way, section 3 becomes the main provision of the Law (p. 72).

He repeats and summarizes his criticism against Justice Barak in the further hearing that took place in the case (FH 13/80, *Hendeles et al. v. Kupat Am Bank*, PD 35(2), 785) in the following language:

> According to his construction (that of Justice Barak), the provisions of section 3 form the main rule of the Law, whilst the provisions of section 2 are the exception. This conclusion, it seems to me, is at odds with the plain meaning of the Law, nor in my opinion does it conform with the object of the Law. It does not advance the Law's declared object of effecting and assuring the restoration of lost property to its owner, and the conclusion that follows, viz. that if the owner is not found after four months the property passes into the ownership of the bank and is not handed over to the immediate finder, fails to pass the test of reason and justice (p. 795).

According to Justice Elon:

> Since doubt has arisen over the correct interpretation of section 3 of the Law and the meaning of the phrase "another person's domain," and this doubt cannot be resolved by the terms and content of the Law itself, it is only right and proper to turn to the Jewish legal system to find in its provisions a way to solve the problem. This is certainly true when it is apparent that the Restoration of Lost Property Law of the Knesset and the Jewish Law relating to the restoration of lost property have a common central object – to restore lost property to its rightful owner.

In this light, Justice Elon presents the position of Jewish Law in relation to the case in question, viz. that a bank's safe deposit room, being a private domain that is open to the public, over which in practice the owners have no control, is not defined, for the purposes of the lost property laws, as "another person's domain," because it comes within the definition of a "courtyard that is not guarded," while only a "guarded courtyard" can effect an acquisition on a person's behalf.

The majority of the Court did not agree with the words of Justice Elon, and even in the further hearing the majority ruled in accordance with the opinion of Justice Barak. However, it is interesting to note that Justice Elon's critical words did not fall on deaf ears, because in a memorandum for the draft Civil Law (the codification of civil legislation in the State of Israel) which was disseminated in 2004, a proposal was made to amend section 3 and to add to it the following provision: "The Court is entitled to determine that the rights in a lost article shall be divided between the finder and the domain owner in equal shares, save where it deems it appropriate to determine a different proportion" (section 800(b) of the draft).

[Michael Wygoda (2nd ed.)]

BIBLIOGRAPHY: T. Lampronti, *Paḥad Yiẓḥak*, s.v. *Avedah*; Gulak, Yesodei, 1 (1922), 137ff.; 2 (1922), 190 n. 3; 3 (1922), 34, 40, 67f.; Herzog, Instit, 1 (1936), 299–317; ET, 1 (1951³), 11–15; 11 (1965), 53–100; H.E. Baker, *Legal System of Israel* (1968), 132–4. **ADD. BIBLIOGRAPHY:** *Encyclopedia Talmudit*, 11: 53–100 s.v. *"Hashavat Avedah"*; M. Elon, *Jewish Law* (1988), 281–282, 564–565, 1464–72, 1564–71; M. Wygoda, *Hashavat Avedah*, in: N. Rakover (ed.), *Ḥok le-Yisrael*, 4 (1991); Y.Y. Bloya, *Pitḥei Ḥoshen, Hilkhot Halva'ah va-Avedah* (1983).

LOT (Heb. לוֹט), son of Haran, grandson of Terah, and nephew of *Abraham (Gen. 11:27). Upon Haran's death in Ur, Terah took Lot with him when, with Abraham and Sarah, he left the city for the land of Canaan. After Terah's death in Haran (11:32), Abraham accepted Lot into the fold of his family in accordance with his patriarchal responsibility to the son of his deceased brother (12:4). Lot accompanied Abraham in his journeys from Haran to Canaan, from Canaan to Egypt, and from Egypt back to Canaan (12:5; 13:1). Abraham and Lot then passed through the Negev into the Benjamite hill country seeking pasture for their livestock which had multiplied in Egypt (12:16; 13:2). A personal quarrel then broke out between their respective shepherds, for "the land would not support them staying together" (13:6). In order to avoid strife, particularly between "kinsmen," Abraham suggested to Lot that they part company. He gave his nephew first choice of the land, whereupon Lot chose the fertile Jordan plain, and settled near Sodom (13:8–12). The biblical narrative tacitly contrasts Abraham's benevolence with Lot's self-interest, and points out that Lot chose to reside with the people of Sodom who "were very wicked sinners against the Lord" (13:13). Abraham continued to show concern for Lot even after their separation. When Lot and his property were captured by *Chedorlaomer and his allies, Abraham pursued them, rescued Lot, and brought him back safely to Sodom (14:1–16).

Parallels have been pointed out between Noah's position in the *Flood story and that of Lot in Sodom's destruction (19:1–29). In both cases, God's natural, destructive forces act against man because of his wickedness, and both narratives emphasize God's choice in saving the one worthy person of that generation. Lot's righteousness is not mentioned but his hospitality forms a clear contrast to the perversions and wickedness of the people of Sodom (19:2–10). Lot carried his hospitality so far in protecting his visitors, that when the Sodomites demanded to "become intimate" with them he offered his virgin daughters in their place (19:8). Lot is rescued from Sodom for the sake of Abraham (19:29), but his personal merit is implied in the contrast with his sons-in-law who frivolously disbelieved in the destruction of Sodom (19:14), and with his wife who, disobeying orders, looked back, only to become a pillar of salt (19:17, 26).

After the destruction of Sodom and Gomorrah, Lot, who had found protection in Zoar, took to the hills and lived in a cave with his two daughters (19:23, 30). Here, the girls, believing all other males to have become extinct, got their father drunk and without his knowledge committed incest with him (19:31–35). As a result, Lot's older daughter became the mother of *Moab and his younger daughter the mother of *Ben-Ammi (19:36–38). The name "sons of Lot" (Deut. 2:9, 19; Ps. 83:9) in biblical reference to Moab and Ammon is probably based on this etiological story.

It has been argued that the narrative of Lot and his daughters may be an indication of retributive punishment of Lot for offering his daughters to the Sodomites in place of his visitors. Just as he had allowed the claims of courtesy to transcend morality, so his daughters permitted their concern for the propagation of the species to outweigh the laws of incest. Yet, although offensive as Lot's offer may be to modern readers, the fact is that fathers had disposition over their daughters to the extent that they could even sell them into slavery (Ex. 21:7; according to rabbinic law a father could marry his daughter to a man who is disfigured and has boils; see Ket. 9b). In addition, the narrator does not condemn the actions of the women but informs us twice (Gen. 19:32, 34) that the daughters of Lot were motivated by the desire to preserve the human species, using the same phrase "to keep seed alive" that he uses for YHWH's words to Noah in Genesis 7:3 in the command to bring the animals onboard the ark. In other words, Lot's two daughters acted much in the manner of Tamar, who continued the family line by soliciting sexual intercourse from her father-in-law, which likewise violates the rules of incest (Lev. 18:15, 20:12), and which act is praised by the author of Ruth 4:12. (See also the rabbinic evaluation below.)

The present form of the Lot narrative leaves an unmistakable impression of Israelite ascendancy over Ammon and Moab: Haran, Lot's father and the grandfather of Ammon and Moab, was the youngest of Terah's sons, while Abraham was the oldest; Lot was continually in need of Abraham's protection and help; the incestuous union between Lot and his daughters disgraces their offspring, the Ammonites and Moabites.

The Dead Sea Scroll's Genesis Apocryphon (20–21), written in Aramaic, embroiders the scriptural narrative. According to this source, Lot not only accompanied Abraham to Egypt but also functioned there as spokesman to Pharaoh's agent. He acquired great possessions, obtained a wife, and built himself a house in Sodom.

In the *Aggadah*

The rabbis often represent Lot in an unfavorable light although in some sources he is praised for his virtues, the word *ẓaddik* of Genesis 18:23 being applied to him. When, however, he separated himself from Abraham, he at the same time separated himself from God (Gen. R. 41:5–7). He chose to settle in Sodom because of his lustful desires (*ibid.*). There he became a usurer (51:6). He was appointed head of the local tribunal (50:3), according to some, because he was the worst of all the five judges there (Tanḥ. B, Va-Yera 21). Although Lot owed his deliverance from Sodom to Abraham's intercession (Mid. Hag. to Gen. 13:11), it was also his reward for not having betrayed Abraham in Egypt when he said that Sarah was his sister (Gen. R. 51:6). A greater reward, however, is that the Messiah will be descended from him through Ruth the Moabite and Naamah the Ammonite (see Gen. R. 51:8 and Naz. 23b–24a). Lot had learned the virtue of hospitality from Abraham and invited the angels to his home although in Sodom this was punishable by death (PdRE 25). As a reward for this act, Israel was forbidden to wage war against his descendants (Yalkut 2 (1877), 782 on Is. 15). The whole night Lot pleaded in favor of Sodom (Lev. R. 23:9). Only the two unmarried daughters of Lot followed him when he left the city (Gen. R. 51:9). Lot is condemned for the negligence which caused him to sleep with his two daughters (Gen. 19:30–38). Although he was not aware of what he was doing he allowed himself to become intoxicated again after he had found out what had happened to him with his elder daughter. However, his daughters' intention was honorable (Hor. 10b).

ISLAM. Lūṭ (Lot) accompanied Abraham when he left Aram-Naharaim (Sura 29:25), but Muhammad has set aside an important place for him in his prophecies because he regards him to have been, like himself, a prophet sent to rebuke the wicked (22:43; 26:160; 37:133). The name of Sodom, however, is not mentioned in the Koran. It appears that the positive description of Lot in the Koran was influenced by Christian literature, because in the Jewish Midrashim there is no such appreciation. Muhammad's attitude toward the wife of Lot is negative (66:11). The later descriptions found in the works of Ṭabarī, Thaʿlabī, and al-Kisāʾī show an extensive familiarity with the events of Lot's life. They particularly deal at length with the description of the wickedness of Lot's wife, who reported the good deeds of her husband to the men of Sodom. The influence of the Jewish Midrash (Gen. R. 51:5) is obvious. Islamic legend, however, also influenced subsequent Jewish *aggadot*.

For Lot in the arts see *Sodom and Gomorrah.

[Haïm Z'ew Hirschberg]

BIBLIOGRAPHY: J. Skinner, *Genesis* (ICC, 1912), 251–67, 306–14; S.E. Loewenstamm, in: EM, 4 (1962), 447–9; N. Sarna, *Understanding Genesis* (1967), index; S.R. Driver, *The Book of Genesis* (1911), 151–5, 197–205; G. von Rad, *Das erste Buch Mose* (1952), 142–6, 184–92. IN THE AGGADAH: Ginzberg, Legends, index. IN ISLAM: Tabarī, *Taʾrīkh*, 1 (1357, A.H.), 205–16; Thaʿlabī, *Qiṣaṣ* (1356, A.H.), 86–90; Kisāʾī, *Qiṣaṣ* (1356, A.H.), 148–9; M. Gruenbaum, *Neue Beiträge zur semitischen Sagenkunde* (1893), 193ff.; H. Speyer, *Die biblischen Erzählungen im Qoran* (1931, repr. 1961), 157–8; J.W. Hirschberg, *Jüdische und christliche Lehren im vorund frühislamischen Arabien* (1939), 58, 122–4; Kuenstlinger, in: *Rocznik Orientalistyczny*, 9 (1930), 281–95 (Ger.); Heller, in: *Shorter Encyclopedia of Islam* (1953), s.v. **ADD. BIBLIOGRAPHY:** T. Alexander, in: JBL, 104 (1985), 289–300 (extensive bibl.); F. Spina, in: ABD, 4:372–74; "Lūṭ," in: EIS², 5 (1986), 832–33 (incl. bibl.).

LOTAN, GIORA (**Georg Lubinski**, 1902–1974), Israel social welfare expert. Born in Berlin, Lotan practiced as a lawyer. From 1933 to 1938 he headed the division of vocational training for youth and adults in the Organization of German Jewry, wrote many articles on social welfare in Germany, and was coeditor of a journal on social welfare. Immigrating to Ereẓ Israel in 1938, he succeeded Henrietta *Szold as director of the social welfare department of the *Va'ad Le'ummi. During World War II Lotan established and directed the Committee for the Welfare of the Families of Jewish Soldiers and carried out a similar assignment during the War of Independence. In 1948 he was a member of the Government of Israel Social Insurance planning committee. He was the first director general of the National Insurance Institute (1954–69). From 1959 to 1961 he also served as the director general of the Ministry of Social Welfare and later, director general of the Ministry of Labor. Lotan wrote many articles and published a study of social insurance in Israel (*National Insurance in Israel*, 1969).

[Jacob Neusner]

LOTHAR, ERNST (pseudonym of **Ernst Lothar Mueller**; 1890–1974), Austrian novelist, author, and stage director. Lothar was born in Bruenn and after studying law entered the Austrian civil service and became state attorney and counsellor at the Ministry of Trade. After World War I Lothar was the theater critic of the Viennese *Neue Freie Presse* and in 1935 he succeeded Max Reinhardt as director of Vienna's "Theater in der Josefstadt." He also staged a number of plays at the Salzburg festivals.

Although he converted to Catholicism and was at pains to sever all connections with Judaism and the Jewish community, Lothar was forced in 1938 to resign his post and leave Austria. He eventually immigrated to the U.S. and became professor of comparative literature at Colorado College. In 1946 he returned to Vienna as theater and music officer in the U.S. army of occupation. He later again became a stage director in Vienna. Lothar was a prolific and versatile writer. His works include the novels *Der Feldherr* (1918), *Der Hellseher* (1929; *The Clairvoyant*, 1931), and a trilogy entitled *Macht ueber alle Menschen* (1921–25). His most famous work in this genre, *Der Engel mit der Posaune* (1945, and frequently republished), was first published in English as *The Angel with the Trumpet* (1944); it deals with the problem of the Jewish wife in several generations of a non-Jewish family. *Unter anderer Sonne* (1961; first published in English as *Beneath Another Sun*, 1943) was an American best seller. Lothar's autobiography, *Das Wunder des Ueberlebens* (1960), deals largely with his years in exile.

BIBLIOGRAPHY: J.W. Nagl and J. Zeidler, *Deutsch-Oesterreichische Literaturgeschichte*, 4 (1937), 1377. **ADD. BIBLIOGRAPHY:** D.G. Daviau and J.B. Johns, "Ernst Lothar," in: J.M. Spalek and J.P. Strelka (eds.), *Deutschsprachige Exilliteratur seit 1933*, 2 (1989), 520–53; idem, "Ernst Lothar," in: J. Holzner (ed.), *Eine schwierige Heimkehr* (1991), 323–352; J.P. Strelka, "Ernst Lothar," in: I. Fialová-Fürstová (ed.), *Maehrische deutschsprachige Literatur* (1999), 202–214; idem, "Ernst Lothar," in: *Germanoslavica*, 7 (2000), 87–100; J. Thunecke, *"Bucina Angelica" oder was fuer ein Schmarren? Ernst Lothars "Der Engel mit der Posaune"* (1948); "Roman und Film – ein Vergleich," in: *Das Maerchen vom Glueck*, in: *Maske und Kothurn*, 46:1 (*Oesterreichischer Film in der Besatzungszeit*, 2001), 83–90; idem, "'Es gibt keinen Kompromiss mit dem Unrecht.' Ernst Lothars Exilroman 'Die Zeugin. Pariser Tagebuch einer Wienerin,'" in: A. Saint Sauveur-Henn (ed.), *Fluchtziel Paris* (2002), 288–297.

[Samuel L. Sumberg]

LOTHAR, RUDOLF (pseudonym of **Rudolf Spitzer**; 1865–1943), Austrian playwright and journalist. Lothar, a native of Budapest, became a contributor to the Viennese *Neue Freie Presse*. He wrote many dramas and comedies, some in verse. Erotic in content, they reveal clever psychological insight. The most popular were *Koenig Harlekin* (1900), *Casanovas Sohn* (1920), and *Der Werwolf* (1921). Lothar also wrote operas and the libretto for D'Albert's *Tiefland* (1904). His historical study, *Das Wiener Burgtheater*, was expanded in several editions from 1899 to 1934. His essays on drama, which include *Henrik Ibsen* (1902), and *Das deutsche Drama der Gegenwart* (1905), maintain the view that drama is applied psychology. Lothar's interest in recording techniques inspired *Die Sprechmaschine* (1924) and his work as editor of the *Jahrbuch fuer Phonotechnik und Phonokunst* (1925). A travel book, *Zwischen drei Welten* (1926), includes an account of his trip to Palestine and a study of Jewish culture.

BIBLIOGRAPHY: J.W. Nagl and J. Zeidler, *Deutsch-Oesterreichische Literaturgeschichte*, 4 (1937), 1448. **ADD. BIBLIOGRAPHY:** H.A. Strauss and W. Roeder (eds.), *International Biographical Dictionary of Central European Émigrés 1933–1945*, 2 (1983), 750; G. Ducrey, "La Collection Auguste Rondel et le répertoire germanique: Le Cas d'Arlequin-Roi de Rudolph Lothar (1902)," in: *Ateliers*, 18 (1998), 67–76; M. Rózsa, "Rudolph Lothar – Herausgeber und Theaterkritiker. Oesterreichisch-ungarische Kontakte in der Wiener Wochenschrift 'Die Wage' 1898–1907," in: *Biblos*, 49:1 (2000), 157–168; F.P. Kirsch, "Terra Baixa, Tiefland und das Oesterreichbild des Rudolf Lothar," in: M. Siguán and K. Wagner (eds. and intro.), *Transkulturelle Beziehungen: Spanien und Oesterreich im 19. und 20. Jahrhundert* (2004), 27–35.

[Samuel L. Sumberg]

LOTMAN, YURI MIKHAILOVICH (1922–), literary scholar and cultural anthropologist. Lotman was born in Petrograd into an assimilated Jewish family, and studied in the philological faculty of Leningrad University from 1939 to 1950, except for the years 1940–46 when he was in the Red Army, mainly at the front. From 1950 to 1954 Lotman worked at Tartu Teachers' Institute in Estonia, and from 1954 was at Tartu University where from 1960 to 1977 he was head of the Chair of Russian Literature. His main works are concerned with the history of Russian literature and social thought from the end of the 18th to the early 19th century, the theory of literature, cultural history, and semiotics. Basing himself on the work of the "formalist school," Lotman developed a methodology of analyzing the internal structure of poetic texts, applying quantitative methods of research to the semantics of verbal art. He developed ways of studying the links between the author, the structure, and addressees of artistic works, thus emerging as one of the first theoreticians of structuralism in literary study. His major works *Lektsii po struktural'nou poetike* ("Lectures on Structural Poetics," 1964); *Struktura khudozhestvennogo teksta* ("The Structure of the Artistic Text," 1970); *Analiz poeticheskogo teksta* ("Analysis of the Poetic Text," 1972); *Semiotika jino i problemy kinoestetiki* ("Semiotics of Cinema and Problems of Cinema Aesthetics," 1973, etc.) established principles of structural-semiotic research in the fields of literature and art. Many scholars, including Roman *Jakobson, took part in the Summer School for Modeling Systems which he organized in Tartu in 1964, 1966, 1968, and 1970. In 1964, Lotman inaugurated the publication of the series *Trudy po znakovym sistemam* ("Works on Signal Systems").

His sister, LIDIYA MIKHAYLOVNA LOTMAN (1917–), was also a literary scholar, who wrote on general problems of Russian literature of the 19th century. Her monograph *Realizm russkoy literatury 60–ª godov 19 v.* ("Realism of Russian Literature of the 60s of the 19th Century," 1974) is characterized by a complex elaboration of literary-historical and theoretical issues.

[Mark Kipnis / *The Shorter Jewish Encyclopaedia in Russian*]

LOTS.

Biblical Data

The Bible records the practice of casting lots as a means of arriving at decisions on a variety of problems. These may be grouped into two main categories: (a) the selection of one or more members from a group; (b) the division of goods among members of a group. To the first category belong the election of a king (1 Sam. 10:20, 21); the election of cult functionaries (1 Chron. 24–26); the selection of the "scapegoat" for the atonement ritual (Lev. 16:8–10); the selection of residents for Jerusalem (Neh. 11:1); the allocation of responsibility for supplying the wood for the altar (Neh. 10:35); the identification of a party guilty of some sacrilege (Josh. 7:10–26; 1 Sam. 14:41ff.; cf. Jonah 1:7); the assignment of a tribe as the first wave of troops in a military campaign (Judg. 20:18; cf. 20:9); the selection of a date for some future action (Esth. 3:7; 9:24; note the use of Akk. *pūru*, "lot," glossed by Heb. *goral*, "lot," and the survival of the former in the name of the festival Purim).

The second category involves the distribution of goods, usually booty (Isa. 17:14; Nah. 3:10; Ps. 22:19) or conquered territory. The latter instance accounts for most biblical references to the casting of lots. The division of one's land and its reapportionment to others by lot is cited as a divine punishment in Isaiah 34:17, Joel 4:3, and Obadiah 11. The apportionment of Canaanite territory by lot among the Israelites is related in Numbers 26:52–56; 33:54; 34:13; 36:2, and Joshua 14–19; 21:4–12 (the apportionment of levitical cities, cf. I Chron. 6:39ff.). Distribution of land by the casting of lots is paralleled in both ancient Mesopotamian legal documents and the customs of Palestinian Arabs. Although the Bible provides few details concerning the procedure adopted in the casting of lots, evidence can be supplied from several outside sources (see below; in Talmud and Midrash). It would seem that various objects might serve as lots, the most common ones being of wood and stone (cf. the element *GIŠ* "wood") in the Sumerian *GIŠ.ŠUB.BA* ("lot") and the determinative NA^4 ("stone") describing a lot. A die said to have been cast by the Assyrian official Jaḥali in 833 B.C.E. in the ceremonial selection of the annual eponym is in the form of an inscribed terra-cotta cube (see Hallo). For Hittite resort to the lots, see Kitz.

The technique of casting lots involved throwing lots to the ground and interpreting the results on the basis of a prearranged understanding. The element of "throwing" is also evident in the above-mentioned Sumerian term *GIŠ.ŠUB.BA*, "wood which is cast." So, too, the verbs regularly employed with "lot" in both Akkadian and Hebrew denote "to throw, cast down." In the *Iliad* (3:314ff.) there is preserved a rather detailed description of the procedure: the lots are placed in a helmet and shaken to the ground, the shaker averting his eyes by looking backward. The determination in such cases was based on whose lot fell to the ground first (cf., e.g., Josh. 21:10), each lot having been previously marked to identify its owner (cf. the inscribed names on the lot of the Assyrian eponym and the inscribed shards at Masada). This method is most appropriate in contests, and might be applied to any problem where a choice between participating parties or defined options was involved. In more complex cases, such as the division of land, the area is measured off and the options for partition decided upon (cf., e.g., Josh. 18:4–6), it being understood that specific parcels of land correspond to the lots thrown. It is in this way that words denoting "lot" come to denote that which is decided by the casting of a lot, e.g., a parcel of land, an assigned function, or, more generally, one's destiny.

The biblical notion that the divine will is reflected in the fall of the lots is most clearly expressed in Proverbs 16:33: "The lot is cast from (one's) bosom, but all of its decisions (derive) from the Lord." Divine guidance is also implied by the fact that the lots were cast "before the Lord" (Josh. 18:6; 19:51). Further, the sacral usage of the *Urim and Thummim would also seem to stress the role of lots as a divine means of communication (cf., e.g., I Sam. 14:41, 42). So, too, in Isaiah 34:17 it is the Deity who actually casts the lot determining the inherited portion. The same concept, identically expressed, is attested at Qumran (see the restoration of 1QS 4:26 in J. Licht's *Megillat ha-Serakhim* (1965), 105). In sharp contrast to this notion is the ancient Mesopotamian idea that the gods, as well as humans, are subject to the fall of the lots.

[Murray Lichtenstein]

In the Second Temple Period

The lot was extensively used during the Second Temple period, and particularly in the Temple itself in order to determine the allocation of duties among the priests. No biblical sanction, however, seems to have been sought for this practice, and, as the following passage shows, it was an arrangement of expediency arrived at through experience. "Originally whoever wished to clear the ashes from the altar did so. If they were many they used to run up the ramp and he that came first within four cubits secured the privilege… It once happened that both reached the decisive point simultaneously; and one of them pushed the other, and he fell and broke his leg. When the *bet din* saw that danger was involved they ordained that (the privilege of) clearing the altar should be done only by casting lots" (Yoma 2:1–2). The Mishnah goes on to detail the other three lots which were cast for the Temple service. The first covered 13 tasks connected with the sacrifice, from the actual slaughter of the animal to the bringing of the wine oblation, the second for offering the incense, and the third the carrying of the members of the sacrificial animal from the ramp to the altar (*ibid.* 3–4). The order to cast the lots was given by the overseer (*ibid.* 4; Tam. 1:2). The Talmud discusses whether or not the priests wore their sacred garments while casting the lots (Yoma 24b). According to the Tosefta (Ta'an. 2:1) the extension of the priestly watches (see **Mishmarot* and *Ma'amadot*) from the four which returned to Zion (Neh. 9:5; 11:10) to the 24 in the Second Temple was also decided by lot.

Whereas there is nothing in the Bible regarding the manner in which the lots were cast (see above) the Talmud gives details. The urn (Heb. *kalpei*; Gr. κάλπη) in which the lots were placed for choosing the scapegoat was originally of boxwood (*eshkero'a*), but Ben Gamala made one of gold (Yoma 3:9). The urn was shaken and the two lots were taken, one in each hand. If the one bearing the inscription "For the Lord" came up in the right hand, it was regarded as a good omen (4:1). The lot could be made of any material, e.g., olive wood, walnut wood, or boxwood (Yoma 37a). According to the Jerusalem Talmud (Yoma 4:1, 41b), they were made of black and white pebbles. The above, however, refers to the biblically ordained throwing of lots for the scapegoat. For other lotteries it would appear that pieces of paper, or shards, such as those found at Masada (see below), were used. They are referred to as *pitka'ot* (Gr. πιττάκιον).

The term "lot" at Qumran is used for both the heavenly lottery or allotment, which is already apportioned by God (e.g., 1QS 2:2), as well as the paraphernalia used for a lottery on earth for casting lots. At Qumran when the lot was cast under the supervision of a priest, its outcome was considered to be predetermined by divine appointment. CD 14:3–8 with 4Q279 5:2–6 indicates that the term "lot" was also used for each of the four categories of membership within the community: Priests,

Levites, Israelites, and Proselytes. Order within those categories was determined by pedigree, spirit, and casting lots. In this one's "lot" may be understood as one's divinely appointed station or position (e.g., 1QS 1:10; 2:23). The War Scroll (1QM) also utilizes the term for categories of angels. Similarly, but antithetically, the community's enemies were said to be of the "lot of Belial" (1QS 2:5; 1QM 1:5).

It is therefore not surprising that lots should be found during the excavations of Khirbet Qumran. Their form, however, differed from those found at Masada. The lots were smoothed balls of clay measuring 25 ± 5 mm in diameter with partially pierced holes arranged over the surface ranging in numerical value from 1 to 27. At least 59 lots were discovered at Qumran during the course of R. de Vaux's excavations. De Vaux recorded these according to item and locus number as "boulée piercée incompletes" and noted the size and number of holes on each. De Vaux, without understanding the actual use and significance of the items, chose to provide the simplest description of them (as he also did in the case of the sundial which he listed as "disque de calcaire" (KhQ909)). The PAM photographs of seven of these have been published in *The Dead Sea Scrolls on Microfiche.*

Josephus gives a number of historical incidents in which choice was made by lot. According to his own, suspect, account, he saved himself from death at Jotapata by arranging that the last ten leaders of the besieged city, of whom he was one, should cast lots, the second one to draw the lot putting to death the previous one, and so on, the last one left having to immolate himself. When he was left with the last other survivor, he persuaded him to abandon the plan (Wars, 3:387–91). A similar system was employed for the suicide of the last ten defenders of Masada. Ten were chosen by lot to be the executioners of the defenders, and then the ten drew lots among themselves to determine who should slay the remaining nine, the last then committing suicide (*ibid.*, 7:396ff.). A series of ostraca bearing the names of men found at Masada have been connected by Yadin with this episode. Josephus also states that the Zealots, during the last days of the Temple, in order to mock at the aristocratic families from whom the high priest was usually selected, elected *Phinehas b. Samuel by lot (*ibid.*, 4:155).

In the New Testament Zechariah (the father of John the Baptist) was chosen by lot (*kleros*) to offer the incense in the Temple (Luke 1:8–9). The disciples of Jesus determined who would replace Judas Iscariot by casting lots (Acts 1:26). The term is also used for "lot of the saints" (Acts 26:18; I Pet. 5:3) which may be applied to categories of angels (Col. 1:12). "Lot" can also mean "appointed position" in Acts 1:17 and 8:21. The term was also used in the Gospels for the casting of dice by Roman soldiers who competed for Jesus' garments (Matt. 27:35; Mark 15:24; Luke 23:34; John 19:24).

The *aggadah* extends the use of the lot to many instances of biblical history. The fact that although Eldad and Medad were "of them that were recorded" but they remained in the camp (Num. 11:26) is explained by stating that Moses chose the 70 elders mentioned in the context by placing 72 slips in an urn; on 70 of them the word "elder" was written, while two were blank, and six were selected from each tribe (Sanh. 17a). A similar lot was drawn to select the 22,000 firstborn (*ibid.*). The Midrash also adds that Jacob's sons drew lots to decide who was to bring the bloodstained coat of Joseph to Jacob (Gen. R. 84:8). Details are given of the manner in which the territory of Israel was divided among the tribes (BB 122a), and that brothers can divide by lot an estate bequeathed to them is laid down as the law (BB 106b).

[Louis Isaac Rabinowitz / Stephen Pfann (2nd ed.)]

Post-Talmudic Times

According to Jewish thought a decision arrived at by lot is not regarded as the result of blind choice. Only once is an objection taken to deciding matters by lot and, peculiarly enough, it has been included in the Shulḥan Arukh. The tosafists apparently had a reading to the *Sifrei Deuteronomy* 18:13: "From what do we learn that it is forbidden to enquire by casting lots? Since the Bible says Thou shalt be wholehearted with the Lord thy God" (see Tos. Shab. 156a). The statement does not occur in the present editions of the *Sifrei*, which give an entirely different deduction from this verse (in Pes. 113b the doctrine that "one should not enquire of the Chaldeans" is deduced from this verse, a reading which is supported by the context in which it occurs). Either the *tosafot* had a different reading, or, as appears probable, the deduction is based upon I Samuel 14:41, where the word *tammim* ("wholehearted" in Deut. 18:13) is taken to mean "lots" (see 14:42). Whatever the case may be, this statement has been incorporated in the Shulḥan Arukh (YD 179:1) in the laws against witchcraft. It is, however, an isolated statement; a tolerant and even positive view has been taken throughout the ages with regard to lotteries (but see *Gambling). A possible reflection of this is seen in the fact that although games of chance and gambling are not permitted in the State of Israel, the National Lottery is sponsored by the government and the proceeds of the weekly Mifal ha-Payis (*payis* is the talmudic word for lottery) are designated for hospitals and schools.

[Louis Isaac Rabinowitz]

BIBLIOGRAPHY: S. Bergheim, in: PEFQS (1894), 194; A. Bea, in: *Biblica*, 21 (1940), 198–9; (CAD I/J), 198–202, s.v. *isqu;* A.L. Oppenheim, *Ancient Mesopotamia* (1964), 99–100; Y. Yadin, *Masada* (1966), 201. **ADD. BIBLIOGRAPHY:** W. Hallo, in: BA, 46 (1983), 19–26, with illustrations of lots; W. Horowitz and V. Hurowitz, in: JANES, 21 (1992), 95–115; A. Kitz, in: JBL, 116 (1997), 401–10; A Berlin, *JPS Torah Commentary Esther* (2001), 38. SECOND TEMPLE PERIOD: S. Pfann, "The Essene Yearly Renewal Ceremony and the Baptism of Repentance," in: *Proceedings of the Provo Conference on the Dead Sea Scrolls, July 1996* (1998), 351–52; E. Tov with S. Pfann, *The Dead Sea Scrolls on Microfiche: A Comprehensive Facsimile Edition of the Texts from the Judean Desert*, (1995²). See PAM 40.236 (fiche 4), 42.682 (fiche 55), and 42.869 (fiche 59).

°**LOUIS**, name of 18 kings of France. Of particular importance in Jewish history are the following:

LOUIS I (the Pious; 778–840), king of Aquitaine (from the age of three), emperor of the West from 814. Of the Carolingian emperors, Louis was the best disposed toward the Jews. He retained several Jewish merchants at his court in the capacity of "merchants of the palace" who enjoyed extremely favorable privileges, part of which were no doubt also valid for all the Jews in the empire. These privileges guaranteed to their holders and their households (including near relatives, slaves, and servants) the widest liberty of movement, the right to acquire and sell property, and exemption from a variety of tolls and imposts affecting persons and goods in transit. Missionary activities by Christians among pagan slaves owned by these Jewish merchants were prohibited. They were authorized to employ Christians on condition that they were freed from work on Sundays and Christian holidays. Their real property and movable goods were safeguarded. In the judicial sphere, the holders of these privileges were exempted from "question" (torture) and trial by ordeal and could take the oath according to Jewish custom. These privileges later became the model for several privileges granted by local lords (such as Bishop *Ruediger to the Jews of Speyer) or by German emperors (*Henry IV to the Jews of Worms). However, the most serious consequences for the future legal status of the Jews, especially those of France and Germany, were contained in the provisions in Louis' privileges, which placed the Jews under the immediate jurisdiction of the emperor. These enabled him to benefit from the fines and indemnities imposed on persons who injured or killed one of these merchants, who were in the service of the palace or the imperial chamber and had been taken under the emperor's protection (*Mainbour*). Some scholars have concluded that this was the origin of the principle of "imperial servitude" of the Jews, the **servi camerae regis*.

That the greater part of the provisions in these privileges benefited not only the "merchants of the palace" but the whole of the Jewish population is evident from the efforts of *Agobard, bishop of Lyons, to have them repealed when the Jews of Lyons and other towns of his diocese took advantage of them. Louis had moreover appointed an imperial official, the *Magister Judaeorum*, who was responsible for the protection of the Jews. Toward 826–8 this position was held by a certain Evrard. Even before attacking the privileges held by the Jews, Agobard had already, in about 820, clashed with Louis over the Jews, when the bishop had attempted to baptize Jewish children in Lyons, Chalon, Mâcon, and Vienne. At the time, Louis accorded the Jews his full protection. His goodwill toward the Jews was not even weakened when his own deacon, *Bodo, fled to Muslim Spain and embraced Judaism. Texts erroneously attributed to Louis, in particular the "forged capitularies," include enactments less favorable to the Jews, as well as the formula for an oath to be taken in a humiliating manner; these are forgeries belonging to a later period.

LOUIS VI, king of France from 1108 to 1137. During his reign jurisdiction over the Jews (and their revenues) gradually passed from royal control to the hands of the Church. The Abbey of Saint-Denis, in 1112, obtained from the king judicial control over the Jews in the town. In 1119 Louis ceded half his income from the Jews of *Tours to the Abbey of Saint-Martin there; and in 1122 he granted five houses belonging to Jews to Abbot Suger of Saint-Denis.

LOUIS VII (called the Young), king of France from 1137 to 1180. In 1144, Louis banished from the kingdom those Jews who had been converted to Christianity and had later returned to Judaism. In 1146, Louis authorized the Jews to return to Sens, from where they had been expelled. During the preparations for the Second Crusade, of which Louis became one of the principal leaders, Peter the Venerable of Cluny wrote to the king advising him to confiscate the possessions of the Jews; however, Louis followed the more tolerant counsel of Bernard of Clairvaux, who suggested that only the interest on the debts that Crusaders owed to Jewish moneylenders should be canceled.

LOUIS VIII, king of France from 1223 to 1226. On Nov. 8, 1223, Louis published an edict on the Jews, which had strong fiscal motives. Even though only a number of barons signed this decree, it was declared to be equally binding upon those who had not. The edict, the first attempt by the monarchy to affirm its legislative power over all the baronies of the kingdom, ordained the suppression of all interest due on debts toward the Jews, and the repayment of these debts within three years, on the condition that they were registered. Nonregistered debts as well as those which had been pending for more than five years were to be considered as canceled. The king evidently received a quota of the debts collected in this way, which explains why the fiscal income from the Jews increased to a total of 8,682 livres in 1226. The seal which had served to authenticate debts toward the Jews was abolished. Furthermore, Jews were no longer allowed to move from one seigniory to another. This edict had extremely serious consequences for the future legal position of the Jews.

LOUIS IX, king of France from 1226 to 1270. In his attitude toward the Jews, Louis differed from his predecessors and successors solely in that he placed the interests of the Church before his personal concerns and those of the kingdom in general. This was especially evident in the material assistance he granted to converts: expenses on their behalf often exceeded the income derived from the Jews of France. On other occasions, when this income could not be used for this purpose because the king considered that it was defiled by the sin of usury, he tried to restore the money to the victims of usury or their heirs.

In all other respects Louis' attitude toward the Jews was characterized by implacable enmity, which endured throughout his long reign. As early as 1230, he issued the famous Ordinance of Melun which forbade the Jews to engage in any moneylending activities; at the same time, it was stipulated that no one was allowed to detain a Jew who was the property of another lord. However, Louis was compelled to bow to the economic pressures that rendered dependence on Jewish credit indispensable. In 1234 he seized one-third of the debts owed to the Jews and decreed that in the future they would be permitted to take pledges only in the presence of trustworthy witnesses. There is reason to believe that Louis took no measures to protect Jews persecuted by would-be crusaders in 1236 in several provinces (Anjou, Poitou, Mançois, Touraine, Berry). When in 1239 Pope Gregory IX requested the kings of France and Portugal to order the seizure of Jewish books for examination, Louis was the promptest and most zealous to comply; 24 cartloads of Jewish books were burned in 1242. The resolute and clear-sighted defense conducted by *Jehiel b. Joseph of Paris at the famous Paris *disputation in 1240 was to no avail, for the judgment was virtually predetermined. However, the king's outburst, reported by his biographer Jean de Joinville, that rather than discuss questions of faith with a Jew a layman should plunge his sword into him, was probably caused by his anger at the courageous arguments advanced by R. Jehiel (who was compelled to flee). When *Innocent IV, moved by the protests of the Jews that they could not teach the Bible without the Talmud, ordered it to be examined again, Odo (Eudes) of Chateaurous, chancellor of the University of Paris, opposed the pope and the condemnation stood. In December 1254 Louis threatened with expulsion any Jew who kept copies of the Talmud or other banned books; at the same time he forbade them to engage in any kind of moneylending and ordered them to earn a livelihood in manual toil or any other lawful trade. When he decreed in 1257 or 1258 that the profits of usury should be restored to its victims, the commissioners who carried out the task were authorized to sell the real properties of the Jews to raise the required sums of money. In 1268 Louis called for the arrest of all the Jews and the confiscation of their property in preparation for their eventual expulsion; however, this extreme measure remained in abeyance. A year later, under the influence of the apostate Pablo Christiani, the king ordered the Jews to wear a distinctive *badge and instructed his officers to assist the apostate in compelling Jews to listen to missionary sermons.

It is noteworthy that no Jewish historian mentions Louis on any occasion. Joseph ha-Kohen briefly describes his expulsion project of 1254 but without mentioning the king's name. A contemporary Christian author, Matthew of Paris, makes the most succinct comment on Louis' attitude to the Jews: "See how the king of France hates you and persecutes you."

LOUIS X (called Le Hutin: "The Quarreler"), king of France from 1314 to 1316. Soon after his accession, Louis paved the way for the return of the Jews expelled from the kingdom of France in 1306. On April 1, 1315, he suspended the collection of the debts owed to them which were still outstanding from the time of the expulsion. An ordinance was issued on May 17, 1315, regulating the jurisdiction of the Jews in the eventuality of their return to France, which he authorized on July 28, 1315. It permitted them to resettle in the localities where they had lived previously; ordered that their synagogues, cemeteries, and books, with the exception of the Talmud, should be restored to them; and prohibited them from moneylending against interest, allowing them only to take pledges. However, they were permitted to trade freely. The ordinance concluded with the king's guarantee to take the Jews under "his special protection and administration." In fact, in authorizing the return of the Jews, Louis was principally motivated by monetary interests. The duration of this right of residence was set for 12 years, with the possibility of prolongation and one year's notice of revocation. However, a new expulsion order was issued less than seven years later (1322) by Charles IV while the delay of one year's notice to enable the Jews to dispose of their possessions was not observed.

LOUIS XI, ruler of Dauphiné from 1440 (as Louis II), and king of France from 1461 to 1483. As dauphin, Louis tried to keep the Jews in his province and even to attract newcomers, offering them in 1449 advantageous privileges if they would settle in Crémieu. On several occasions he defended the Jews against the nobility of Dauphiné, confirming their privileges, and even granting them new ones in 1451, 1453, and 1455. However, after his accession to the throne of France, he imposed a heavy fine of 1,500 gold crowns on them in 1463, because "they had spoken ill of the king during his absence." Nevertheless, he reconfirmed the privileges of the Jews of Dauphiné in 1476, that is, 80 years after they had been banished from the kingdom.

LOUIS XII, king of France from 1498 to 1515. Louis ordered the final expulsion of the Jews from *Provence in 1501. In order to compensate for the loss to his revenues caused by the departure of the Jews from Provence, Louis introduced a tax in 1512 on the remaining Jews there, who had accepted baptism. Known as the "tax of the neophytes," it amounted to a total of 6,000 livres. Down to the 18th century, a number of noble Provençal families were held in discredit because they were reputedly descended from these "neophytes."

LOUIS XIII, king of France from 1610 to 1643 with his mother Marie de Medici as regent until he was declared of age in 1614. On April 23, 1615, Louis signed letters patent renewing the expulsion order "against not only Jews but also those who profess and practice Judaism." This order appears to have been directed especially against Marranos and possibly also against those Jews who had come to Paris with Concini (Maréchal d'Ancre), the young king's minister, and his wife, Leonora Galigai. The letters patent were recorded by the *parlement*, but as far as it is known they were not put into effect in any way. However, after the assassination of Concini at Louis' command, in 1617, Leonora Galigai was tried for sorcery and the charge of practicing Judaism was also brought against her. During Louis' reign, the Jews of *Comtat Venaissin could bring action against defendants living in the kingdom of France and even win their cases. When Louis visited Metz in 1632, he granted the Jews letters patent which declared their presence in the town a necessity.

[Bernhard Blumenkranz]

LOUIS XVI, king of France from 1774 to 1792. Among Louis' ministers were Turgot, Choiseul, and *Malesherbes, who were favorably inclined toward the Jews. On his order a census was taken of the Jews of *Alsace in 1784; letters patent concerning them were issued during the same year. Their delegate, Herz *Cerfberr, was received at Louis' court, although he had no official status, and notice was taken of his representations. The first important step toward improvement of the status of the Jews was the abolition of the body tax in 1784. Other projects to alleviate their situation were under study when the Revolution broke out.

[Renee Neher-Bernheim]

BIBLIOGRAPHY: LOUIS THE PIOUS: G. Kisch, *Forschungen zur Recht-und Sozialgeschichte der Juden in Deutschland waehrend des Mittelalters* (1955), 47–55; Baron, Social², 4 (1957), 48–49; B. Blumenkranz, *Juifs et Chrétiens dans le monde Occidental* (1960), index, s.v. *Louis le Pieux*. LOUIS VI: A. Luchaire, *Louis VI* (1890), 146; Suger, *Vie de Louis VI*, ed. by H. Waquet (1929), 265. LOUIS VII: H. Gross, in: REJ, 4–5 (1882), 171; W. Williams, *Saint Bernard of Clairvaux* (1935¹, 1953²), 267; Fr. Olivier-Martin, *Histoire du droit français* (1951), 119; R. Anchel, *Les Juifs de France* (1946), 100–2. LOUIS VIII: C. Petit-Dutaillis, *Etude sur Louis VIII* (1894), 414ff.; G.I. Langmuir, in: *Traditio*, 16 (1960), 215–21. LOUIS IX: L. Berman, *Histoire des Juifs de France* (1937), 95–105; Gross, Gal Jud, 503–5; Baron, Social², 10 (1965), 58ff.; S. Grayzel, *The Church and the Jews*... (1966²), index. LOUIS X: *Ordonnances des Roys de France*, 1 (1723), 554, 571f., 595ff. LOUIS XI: E. Pilot de Thorey, *Catalogue des actes du Dauphin Louis II*, 1 (1889), 261, 334, 392, 395, 452; 2 (1889), 237, 411. LOUIS XII: L. Brunschvicg, in: REJ, 33 (1896), 91; E. Camau, *La Provence à Travers les siècles*, 4 (1930), 348, 350; R. Anchel, op. cit., 136–8. LOUIS XIII: REJ, 12 (1886), 101 n. 4; R. Clément, *La condition des Juifs de Metz sous l'ancien régime* (1903), 33; R. Anchel, *Les Juifs de France* (1946), 128, 135, 147. LOUIS XVI: A. Hertzberg, *French Enlightenment and the Jews* (1968), index; R. Anchel, op. cit., index.

LOUIS, MORRIS (1912–1962), U.S. painter. Dubbed a post-painterly abstract artist and a Washington color painter, Morris Louis Bernstein, who changed his name in 1938, was born in Baltimore, Maryland. After studying at the Maryland Institute of Fine and Applied Arts in Baltimore (1929–32), he worked as a Works Progress Administration artist in Baltimore (1934) and then in New York City, where he lived from 1936 to 1940. He returned to Baltimore in the early 1940s and lived in Washington, D.C., from 1952 until his premature death. Early on he made allover compositions in the vein of Jackson Pollock's drip paintings and experimented with collage. His biomorphic *Charred Journal* paintings (1951) referred to the Nazi book burnings.

After seeing Helen *Frankenthaler's seminal painting *Mountains and Sea* (1952, National Gallery of Art, Washington, D.C.) in April 1953, Louis changed his working method. Influenced by Frankenthaler's thin veils of color staining the unprimed canvas, Louis began to saturate his paintings in three major series: *Veils* (1954, 1958–59), *Unfurleds* (1960–61), and *Stripes* (1961–62). Interwoven colors characterize *Veil* paintings such as *Blue Veil* (1958, Fogg Art Museum, Harvard University, Cambridge). To make these large works, Louis poured diluted paint down the angled canvas to create a wavelike effect of blended, layered color that covers nearly the entire surface of the work. In contrast to Pollock, Louis achieved a sense of painterliness without touching a paintbrush. *Unfurled* paintings such as *Beta Kappa* (1961, National Gallery of Art, Washington, D.C.) show colorful thin rivulets of paint running diagonally down and inward from the top corners of the canvas leaving large central portions of the painting white. Straight bands of color, varying in thickness and arranged horizontally or vertically across the white canvas, characterize the *Stripe* paintings. In all of these works Louis emphasized the flat ground, eschewing illusions of depth.

BIBLIOGRAPHY: M. Fried, *Morris Louis* (1970); M. Louis, *The Drawings of Morris Louis* (1979); D. Upright, *Morris Louis: The Complete Paintings, A Catalogue Raisonné* (1985); J. Elderfield, *Morris Louis* (1986).

[Samantha Baskind (2nd ed.)]

LOUIS-DREYFUS, JULIA (1961–), U.S. actress. Born in New York but raised in Washington, Louis-Dreyfus has roots in a prominent French banking and financial family. Her father is Gerard Louis-Dreyfus, an important French financier. Her grandfather, Pierre Louis-Dreyfus, fought for the French Resistance during World War II. Her cousin Robert Louis-Dreyfus was the owner of Adidas, the sports-equipment manufacturer, and of the French soccer club Olympique de Marseille. Julia Louis-Dreyfus studied theater at Northwestern University in Chicago and began her theatrical career there with the Practical Theater Company and the Second City Comedy troupe. After three years, 1982 to 1985, on the popular television series *Saturday Night Live* and appearances in a number of films, including *Hannah and Her Sisters* (1986) and *National Lampoon's Christmas Vacation* (1989), Louis-Dreyfus was cast as Elaine Benes, the ex-girlfriend and pal of Jerry *Seinfeld in the comedy series *Seinfeld* in 1989. The show proved to be the most popular series of the 1990s, and she won an Emmy Award as best supporting actress in a comedy series in 1996 for her role in *Seinfeld*. The series, famously about "nothing," but really about the everyday foibles of single people in New York City, also starred Jason *Alexander and Michael Richards. After the end of the series in 1998, Louis-Dreyfus starred in several other television situation comedies.

[Stewart Kampel (2nd ed.)]

LOUISIANA, south-central U.S. state at the mouth of the Mississippi River. In 2001 its population was estimated at 4,470,000 including about 15,000 Jews. The largest Jewish communities are Greater *New Orleans, which includes Metairie and the North Shore (13,000), Shreveport (1,100), and Baton Rouge, the state capital (1,200); there are also organized communities in Alexandria, Lafayette, Lake Charles, Monroe, and New Iberia. Jewish welfare federations function in New Orleans (1913), Alexandria (1938), Monroe (1938), and Shreveport (1941).There are approximately 18 congregations in the state; about 13 rabbis served these congregations. Many of the other congregations are served by student rabbis.

Early New Orleans

It has generally been assumed that the Louisiana Code Noir, or Black Code, promulgated in Paris in 1724 and excluding settlement by Jews and the practice of any religion other than Catholicism in the French colony of Louisiana, discouraged the immigration of Jews to the area.

Although there were transient Jews in the colony, the first recorded settler was Isaac Rodriguez Monsanto, a Dutch-born merchant who had taken his brothers and sisters to Curaçao before moving his headquarters to New Orleans in 1757. Between 1757 and 1769 Monsanto conducted successful business operations with settlers and merchants throughout Louisiana, the Illinois country, Atlantic and Caribbean ports, and Europe. In 1769, when Monsanto and his family and associates were expelled from New Orleans under the rigorous Spanish rule of Governor Alejandro O'Reilly, who invoked the first provision of the Code Noir for their expulsion, the Monsantos took refuge in British West Florida, but all gradually filtered back into Spanish Louisiana. The Monsantos, born Jewish, all participated in the rituals of the Protestant and Catholic churches without baptism.

Judah *Touro arrived in New Orleans from Boston in late 1801 or early 1802 and became, through diligence and his simple manner of living, a wealthy man. He was indifferent to Judaism until late in life, when he was persuaded by Gershom Kursheedt, the first truly religious Jew in the city, to build a synagogue for the second New Orleans congregation, Nefutzoth Yehudah, or Dispersed of Judah, organized in 1845. Other early settlers were equally unconcerned about the preservation of Jewish identity.

Of the approximately 15 Jews who were in New Orleans in January 1815, when the battle for the city between American forces, led by General Andrew Jackson, and the British took place, at least ten and possibly 11 had some part in the action. Touro suffered a near-fatal wound. Of these 15, seven remained bachelors, seven intermarried, and one, Manis Jacobs, married a Christian woman after his first (Jewish) wife died. It was Manis Jacobs who became the first president of Shaarei Chassed or Gates of Mercy (1827), the first congregation in Louisiana and indeed anywhere in the Mississippi Valley south of Cincinnati. This congregation, Sephardi at the outset, later became Ashkenazi as increasing numbers of Jews arrived in the town from the German-speaking lands. But Jewish religious life did not prosper in New Orleans. The wealthiest men did not support any of the three congregations in existence by 1850. (Gates of Prayer Congregation was established in the Lafayette suburb of New Orleans in January of that year.) Touro's building of a synagogue did not inspire others to do likewise. Intermarriage continued apace in New Orleans, perhaps more than in any major city in the United States.

German Jews at the port of New Orleans fanned out from that city into more rural areas and became peddlers and artisans. Significant numbers of Jews were country merchants and traders in small Louisiana towns before the Civil War. They established benevolent societies, cemeteries, or congregations in Alexandria (1854), Donaldsonville (1856), Baton Rouge (1858), and Monroe (1861). But the most significant Jewish institution in Louisiana was the Association for the Relief of Jewish Widows and Orphans of New Orleans (1854), one of the earliest agencies of its kind in the United States. Made necessary by frequent epidemics of yellow fever and cholera in the New Orleans area, this association was supported from its inception by assimilated Jews who demonstrated no other concern with their Jewish identity. The free-wheeling atmosphere of the state, dominated by New Orleans, encouraged the full participation and integration of Jews; there was then little anti-Jewish prejudice, which seems to have gained momentum only in the late 19th century. Among Louisiana's notable assimilated Jews were U.S. Senator Judah P. *Benjamin (1853–61); Henry M. Hyams, Benjamin's cousin, lieutenant governor of Louisiana in 1859; and Dr. Edwin Warren Moise, speaker of the Louisiana legislature at the same time and later state attorney general. It was apparently no accident that each of these men intermarried. In 1872, the first Rex, King of Carnival, was Louis J. Salomon, a great-grandson of Haym *Salomon, the well-known Revolutionary War patriot.

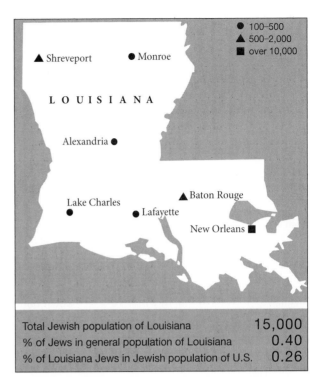

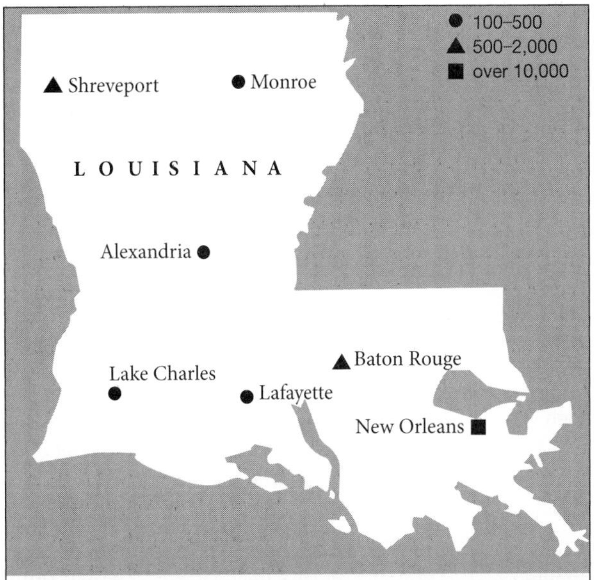

Total Jewish population of Louisiana	15,000
% of Jews in general population of Louisiana	0.40
% of Louisiana Jews in Jewish population of U.S.	0.26

Jewish communities in Louisiana. Population figures for 2001.

The Civil War and After

More than 200 Louisiana Jews are known by name to have served in the Confederate forces, but the true number is probably three times that large. Three of these men, S.M. Hymans, Edwin I. Kursheedt, and Leon R. Marks, achieved the rank of colonel. Benjamin Franklin Jonas, served as a private; he became the second Louisiana Jew to serve in the U.S. Senate

(1879–85). Dr. Joseph Bensadon, who was the first medical director of Touro Infirmary (1854), was a surgeon in the Confederate army from 1862 to 1865.

The distinctive leader of the Jews of New Orleans after the Civil War was Rabbi James K. *Gutheim, who before the war served as Reverend at Dispersed of Judah then moved to Gates of Mercy soon after the war's end. He encouraged the growing Reform movement within the congregation, but, when proposed reforms in the liturgy he recommended in 1868 caused an uproar, he accepted the position of Reader at Temple Emanu-el in New York City. He returned to New Orleans four years later in response to the creation of Temple Sinai, a new Reform congregation organized by his followers from Gates of Mercy.

Rabbi Isaac Leucht, who followed Gutheim to the pulpit at Shaarei Chassed, also became the rabbi when Gates of Mercy and Dispersed of Judah amalgamated in 1881. Leucht began calling the merged congregation Touro Synagogue, in memory of the philanthropist whose largesse assisted both congregations in their formative years. He assisted in relief work during the yellow fever epidemic of 1878, as well as in civic work; and he was a bridge to the gentile community, serving as president of the Red Cross Society and a member of the State Board of Education.

In 1882 the Hebrew Foreign Mission Society of New Orleans, in conjunction with the Hebrew Emigrant Aid Society, sponsored an agricultural colony of Russian Jews at Sicily Island in Catahoula Parish. But the project failed when the Mississippi River overflowed and flooded the entire area that year.

Jewish Life in the 19th and 20th Centuries

Beginning in the mid-19th century, Jewish merchants and traders organized communities throughout the state. The largest, except for New Orleans, was Shreveport, where a synagogue, Har El, was founded in 1859 and an Orthodox congregation was organized in 1892. One of the marks of the development of intolerance was a local ordinance (1873) prohibiting Jews from opening their stores on Sunday. Zionist, B'nai B'rith, and other communal organizations were formed, and in 1914 the Reform temple was dedicated. A Shreveport attorney, Sidney Herold, in 1915 successfully persuaded the State Court of Appeals to prohibit the reading of the Bible in public schools.

Baton Rouge, the state capital, had Jewish settlers in the early 19th century, but not until 1868 was their number sufficient to form the small congregation which became B'nai Israel in 1879. In Alexandria a Young Men's Hebrew Association was organized in 1882, and the city had Reform and Orthodox synagogues. Jewish communities appeared in Morgan City in 1875, in Opelousas in 1877, and in Lake Charles in 1895. In Bogalusa, an Orthodox congregation was organized in 1925. Communities also functioned in Plaquemine (1856–1932), St. Francisville (1877–1905), and Bastrop (1877–1923). Bastrop and other small communities are served by the United Jewish Charities of Northeast Louisiana, organized in 1938 in Monroe. From 1915 to 1933 Mendel Silber of New Orleans ministered to congregations in New Iberia, Morgan City, and Plaquemine.

In the 20th century movement from smaller to larger communities occurred among Louisiana Jews. Moreover, the total population of Louisiana Jewry declined somewhat after 1940, when there were about 16,000 Jews in the state. But despite the continuing small proportion of Jews in the state population, many Louisiana Jews have attained statewide or national prominence, including the 19th-century philanthropist Isidore *Newman; civic leader Julius Weis; Isaac Delgado, a charter member of the Louisiana Sugar Exchange who contributed to the art museum and Charity Hospital memorial building; the actress Adah Isaacs *Menken; U.S. congressman Adolph Meier (1891–1908); and state legislators George Joel Ginsberg (1928–32), who sought the impeachment of Governor Huey P. Long before the State Senate in 1929, and Norman Bauer, speaker of the House of Representatives in 1942. Henry A. Lazarus was a member of the state Supreme Court (1880) and Emile Godchaux (1909–18), Max Dinkelspiel (1919–24), and I.D. Moor served on the state Court of Appeals. Alexandria, Monroe, Crowley, Donaldsonville, and Morgan City have elected Jewish mayors, and many Jews have served as school board members and presidents. Jews have prospered financially in Louisiana, and the Jewish professional and managerial classes have grown significantly since 1940.

[Bertram Wallace Korn and Edward L. Greenstein]

In the wake of Hurricane Katrina in August 2005, the general population of Greater New Orleans has gone from approximately one million to about half that number. In Orleans Parish the population has fallen from 475,000 to less than 100,000. While most of the synagogues received some repairable damage, Congregation Beth Israel, the only congregation in the city that offered twice daily services before the hurricane, was inundated with ten feet of water. All of their Torahs were damaged and had to be buried. The members of the Jewish community have scattered to Houston, Dallas, Atlanta, Baton Rouge, Lafayette and points in between. When and whether they will return remains to be seen.

[Catherine Kahn and Irwin Lachoff (2nd ed.)]

BIBLIOGRAPHY: L. Shpall, *Jews in Louisiana* (1936); B. Kaplan, *Eternal Stranger* (1957), 39–43; B. Lemann, *Lemann Family of Louisiana* (1965); B. Korn, *Early Jews of New Orleans* (1969); Louisiana Historical Records Survey, *Inventory of Jewish Congregations and Organizations* (1941); A.P. Nasatir and L. Shpall, in: AJHSQ, 53:1 (1963), 3–43.

LOUISVILLE, the largest city in Kentucky and home to its oldest and largest Jewish community. Jews may have owned land in the Louisville area as early as the late 18th century and a few arrived at the beginning of the 19th, but the first Jewish institutions arose in the city only in the 1830s. An Israelite Benevolent Society was listed in the Louisville city directory in 1832 and regular worship services were established around 1838. Louisville's first Jewish congregation dates from 1842, when Adath Israel was chartered. Jews continued to arrive in the city over the next decade, primarily from the German states and from Posen, and in 1851 a second congregation was established, known first as the Polish House of Israel and soon after as Beth Israel. A third congregation, Brith Sholom, was organized in 1880. Among early Adath Israel spiritual leaders was Bernhard Henry Gotthelf (1819–1878), in 1862 appointed the second Jewish chaplain of the Union Army. Both Adath Israel and Brith Sholom were early adopters of Reform practices. Other organizations established by Louisville's 19th-century German-Jewish settlers included a lodge of B'nai B'rith, chartered in 1852, and the Standard Club (forerunner of the Standard Country Club), established in 1883. Louisville's Jewish population stood at about 2,500 in 1880.

Toward the end of the 19th century, the city's most prominent Jewish residents included clothiers Moses and Henry Levy (arrived in Louisville in 1861); dry goods magnate Henry Kaufman and his colleague Benjamin Straus (partners in 1883); attorney Aaron Kohn (1854–1916), Jefferson County prosecutor and a Louisville alderman in the 1880s; distiller and philanthropist Isaac W. Bernheim (1848–1945); and lawyer and scholar Lewis Dembitz (1833–1907), city tax attorney from 1884 to 1888 and the uncle of Louis D. Brandeis, himself a Louisville native whose ashes are interred beneath the portico of the University of Louisville law school that bears his name.

Around the turn of the 20th century, East European Jews began arriving in large numbers and they tended to cluster in a cohesive downtown neighborhood centered on Preston Street. As elsewhere in America, they engaged both in commercial activities and in wage labor in trades such as tailoring and cigarmaking. Five new congregations were established in Louisville between 1882 and 1905, at least four of them byproducts of the influx of East Europeans and Orthodox in outlook. These congregations were B'nai Jacob (1882), Beth Hamedrash Hagodol (1887), Anshei Sfard (1893), Adath Jeshurun (1894, the successor to Beth Israel), and Agudath Achim (1905). In 1902, Louisville's Orthodox congregations banded together to hire a "chief rabbi" and arrange for the supervision of *kashrut*, the maintenance of a *mikveh*, and the organization of a Talmud Torah Society.

Louisville's East Europeans established a number of ethnic and cultural organizations as well. As early as 1907 there were three Zionist circles in Louisville and a Yiddish Literary Society was established around World War I. A chapter of Hadassah was organized in 1919. Louisville's Jewish population was reported to be 12,500 in 1927 and 13,800 in 1937. In the period after World War II, the number of Jews in Louisville began to decline and the city's Jewish population, as well as its institutions, gradually migrated away from the downtown area, relocating mainly to the Highlands neighborhood at first, and then farther to the east as well. Louisville's Jewish population was reported as 8,500 in 1960 and 9,200 in 1984.

Already in the late 19th century, a number of Jewish service and welfare institutions were established in Louisville. These included a chapter of the National Council of Jewish Women, organized in 1893; a Young Men's Hebrew Association (the forerunner of the Louisville Jewish Community Center), incorporated in 1890; and a social service agency called Neighborhood House, founded in 1896. In 1903, Louisville's Jewish Hospital was established to provide facilities for Jewish doctors who were denied staff privileges elsewhere and to care for patients who might prefer treatment in a Jewish environment. By the end of the 20th century, Jewish Hospital was a world leader in both artificial heart and hand transplant surgery.

As the number of Jewish welfare institutions in Louisville increased, a Federation of Jewish Charities was created around 1908. This body became the Jewish Welfare Federation by 1918 and the Jewish Social Service Agency in 1951. In 1934, a second coordinating body was established: the Louisville Conference of Jewish Organizations. Intended primarily as a fundraising agency, over time the Conference developed into the community's principal coordinating and public relations body as well, adopting the name Jewish Community Federation of Louisville in 1971.

A sampling of prominent Louisville Jews of the 20th century includes bacteriologist Simon Flexner (1863–1946); juvenile justice and welfare advocate Bernard Flexner (1865–1945); medical education reformer Abraham Flexner (1866–1959); attorney Charles W. Morris (1892–1961), a civic and political activist and a founder of the Louisville Conference of Jewish Organizations; art historian Justus Bier (1899–1990) and musicologist Gerhard Herz (1911–2000), both of whom fled Nazi Germany and joined the University of Louisville faculty in the 1930s; businessman and humanitarian Arthur S. Kling (1896–81); community stalwart Lewis D. Cole (b. 1913), onetime chairman of the National Jewish Community Relations Advisory Council; Charles M. Leibson (1929–95), named a justice of the Kentucky Supreme Court in 1983; popular mayor Jerry Abramson (b. 1946), first elected in 1985; and community activist Marie Abrams (b. 1937), who became national chair of the Jewish Council for Public Affairs in 2004.

Among the more prominent rabbis who served in Louisville were Adolph Moses (1840–1902), an advocate of a radical form of Judaism he called "Yahvism"; Hyman G. Enelow (1877–1934), later rabbi of Temple Emanu-El in New York; Asher L. Zarchy (1863?–1932), chief rabbi of the Orthodox community from 1903 until 1932; the civic-minded Joseph Rauch (1880–1957), for whom the city's planetarium is named; Simcha Kling (1922–91), author of the text *Embracing Judaism*; and Herbert Waller (1914–1994), active in interfaith work.

At the turn of the 21st century, the communal institutions in Louisville included, aside from the Jewish Federation and Community Center, the Jewish Family and Vocational Service, created in 1978 as a successor to the Jewish Social Service Agency; Shalom Tower, providing subsidized housing for the elderly; the Four Courts Senior Center, a nursing home facility; the Louisville Vaad Hakashruth; the Eliahu Academy and Torah Academy day schools; and several supplementary education programs. Louisville's congregations at the turn of the century were Anshei Sfard (Orthodox), Adath Jeshurun

(Conservative), Keneseth Israel (Conservative, formed in 1926 by the merger of B'nai Jacob and Beth Hamedrash Hagodol), The Temple (Reform, created in 1976 by the merger of Adath Israel and Brith Sholom), and Temple Shalom (Reform, established in 1976). The Jewish population of the city at the turn of the century was approximately 8,700, with perhaps 10 percent being "new Americans" from the former Soviet Union.

BIBLIOGRAPHY: C. Ely, *Jewish Louisville: Portrait of a Community* (2003); L.S. Weissbach, *The Synagogues of Kentucky: Architecture and History* (1995); H. Landau, *Adath Louisville: The Story of a Jewish Community* (1981); I. Rosenwaike, "The First Jewish Settlers in Louisville," in: *The Filson Club History Quarterly*, 53 (January 1979), 37–53.

[Lee Shai Weissbach (2nd ed.)]

LOUNY (Ger. **Laun**), town in N.W. Bohemia, Czech Republic. Jews are first mentioned in Louny in 1254 – one year after it received its freedom as a town – as living on a Jewish street and having a synagogue and a cemetery. The city records for 1380–92 contained a special section for Jewish lawsuits. In 1505 there were 12 Jewish houses. A Jew, accused in 1541 of having acquired a monstrance, was burned and the community was expelled from the town. From 1655 only one Jewish family was protected by the town, but in 1680 a cemetery was established. The cemetery and the prayer room were used by Jews from the vicinity. At the end of the 18th century there were 43 "bad Jews" in Louny, i.e., Jews who did not have permission under the *Familiants Law to live there, and the first Jew to settle there in 1849 was forcibly returned to his former town by the crowd. Thereafter, Jews came to Louny, a synagogue was built, and in 1874 a German-language Jewish school was founded (given up in 1897); a new cemetery was built in 1875 (which still existed in 1970). Fifty-one Jewish families lived in Louny in 1880 and 567 persons in 1890. In 1893 the community adopted Czech as the official language. In 1902 there were 666 Jews in Louny and the 18 surrounding villages; and in 1930 there were 205 (1.8% of the total population). The community was deported to the Nazi death camps in 1942, and the synagogue's equipment was sent to the Central Jewish Museum, Prague. The community was briefly reestablished after World War II.

BIBLIOGRAPHY: K. Linhart, in: H. Gold (ed.), *Die Juden und Judengemeinden Boehmens in Vergangenheit und Gegenwart* (1934), 348–61; F. Štědry, *Dějiny města Loun* (1930); Abeles, in: *Juedisches Centralblatt*, 3 (1884), 115–6. **ADD. BIBLIOGRAPHY:** J. Fiedler, *Jewish Sights of Bohemia and Moravia* (1991), 108–9.

[Jan Herman]

LOURIE, ARTHUR (Vincent; 1892–1966), composer. Lourie was born in St. Petersburg, where he also studied and converted to Catholicism in his early 20s. He became head of the music department of the Commissariat for Public Instruction after the Revolution. In 1920 he settled in Paris and immigrated to the United States in 1941. His compositions include symphonies, operas, ballets, and choral works in the avant-garde idioms of their respective periods, the later ones turning to the re-creation of old forms. Lourie also wrote a biography of Serge *Koussevitzky (1931).

LOURIE, ARTHUR (1903–1978), Israeli diplomat. Born in Johannesburg, South Africa, Lourie practiced as a barrister-at-law and lectured in Roman-Dutch law at Witwatersrand University. He served as political secretary of the Jewish Agency in London from 1933 until 1948, working under Nahum *Sokolow and Chaim *Weizmann. He spent most of World War II in the United States, engaged in Zionist political work. In 1945 he was a member of the Jewish Agency delegation at the San Francisco UN Conference and, from 1946 to 1948, was director of the Jewish Agency UN Affairs Office in New York. From 1948 Lourie was a member of the Israel foreign service: from 1948 to 1953 he was Israel consul general in New York, from 1957 to 1959 he was ambassador to Canada, from 1960 to 1965 ambassador to the United Kingdom, and deputy director-general, Israel foreign ministry, 1965–72. A member of several Israel delegations to the UN General Assembly, he was head of the delegation in 1959.

[Benjamin Jaffe]

LOURIE, NORMAN VICTOR (1912–2003), U.S. social worker and government official. Born in New York, Lourie graduated from Cornell University in 1936. From 1937 to 1939 he was a research associate with the Russell Sage Foundation and from 1939 to 1943, an assistant director of the Bronx House and Madison House settlements in Manhattan. After serving in World War II as director of the social work section of the U.S. Army School for Military Neuropsychiatry, he became the director of the Hawthorne Cedar Knoll School for the correction of juvenile delinquents (1946–51). In 1951 he moved to Philadelphia to direct the work of the Association for Jewish Children and from 1955 onward was executive secretary of Pennsylvania's Department of Public Welfare. He took part in the White House Conferences on Children and Youth in 1950 and 1960 and was a member of the advisory council of the President's Committee on Juvenile Delinquency. He also taught in the graduate faculty of the School of Social Work at the University of Pennsylvania. Lourie was chairman of the editorial board of the *Journal of Jewish Communal Service* (1952–58) and *Child Welfare* (1962–64). He was president both of the National Association of Social Workers and the Academy of Certified Social Workers during 1961 to 1963, as well as of the American Orthopsychiatric Association, 1967. Active in community and professional affairs, Lourie assisted refugees from Vietnam. He served as senior policy adviser for the Institute for Economic Development (1980–82) and the National Immigration, Refugee and Citizenship Forum (1983–90), both in Washington, D.C.

LOUSE (Heb. כִּנִּים, כִּנָּם in plural. Talmud כִּנָּה, singular), insect; one of the ten plagues with which Egypt was smitten (Ex. 8:13–14; Ps. 105:31) was the plague of lice. The כֵּן in Isaiah (51.6): "They that dwell therein shall die *kemokhen*" may refer to the louse; i.e., "like a louse." The louse caused much suffering to people of all classes in former times. A distinction was made between the dark-colored head louse and the light-colored clothes louse (Pes. 112b), two strains of the *Pediculus hominis*, against which people sought to protect themselves by constantly changing and washing their clothes – although they were also compelled to search their garments to kill the lice (Tosef., Shab. 16:21, where the louse is called *ma'akholet*, i.e., the eater). Lice nits were regarded as the smallest of creatures, and hence the statement that "the Holy One blessed be He feeds the whole world, from the horned buffalo to the lice nits" (Av. Zar. 3b). Some maintained that "the louse does not multiply and increase" (Shab. 107b) but generates spontaneously.

BIBLIOGRAPHY: Lewysohn, Zool, 324–6; J. Feliks, *The Animal World of the Bible* (1962), 131.

[Jehuda Feliks]

LOVE.

In the Bible

In the Bible, "love" has, like the word "love" in most languages, many and various shades of meaning.

HEBREW WORDS FOR "LOVE." It is represented by Hebrew words which range from sensuous, and often evil, desire or passionate love between man and woman (II Sam. 13:4; Jer. 2:33), through family affection, up to theological conceptions of God's love for Israel, and of Israel's love for God. In most of the passages, "to accept, adopt, or recognize," could profitably be substituted for "to love," and "to reject, disown," or "repudiate," for "to hate." The root most commonly used is *ʾahav*. Another verb *riḥam* and the noun *raḥamim* point to the family feeling through their connection with *reḥem*, the mother's womb; they express the *compassion presupposing the suffering, distress, or weakness of the other party. The root *ḥafeẓ* means "wish for" or "delight in," but is also used, with a person as object, in the sense of "feel inclined." A similar meaning is attached to *raẓah*, "to be pleased with," and "accept." The root *ḥashaq* involves instead the sense of personal attachment. As for the verb *ḥanan* and the noun *ḥen*, both express the idea of concrete favor, rather than warm affection. Finally, the often-used word *ḥesed* means "loyalty," but sometimes designates the "real love" (Gen. 20:13; 47:29; I Sam. 20:8; II Sam. 9:1; Jer. 2:2; Ruth 2:20), which is evinced in acts of devotion and friendship, and is conditioned by the fact that there are two parties connected with each other by ties of family, tribe, nationality, treaty, covenant, etc.

LOVE AS A SPONTANEOUS RELATIONSHIP. The word "love" is first of all used to denote the father's or mother's love (Gen. 22:2; 25:28; 37:3; 44:20; Prov. 13:24; Ruth 4:15), the love between young people intending to marry (Gen. 29:18, 20; I Sam. 18:20), or between husband and wife (Gen. 24:67; 29:30, 32; Judg. 14:16; 16:15; I Sam. 1:5; Prov. 5:19; Eccles. 9:9; II Chron. 11:21). This use is largely attested in the Song of Songs, whose unique obvious theme is love between man and woman, celebrated in glowing colors and passionate words (e.g., 1:3, 4, 7; 2:5; 3:1, 2, 3, 4; 5:8). "Love" designates also the specifically sexual desire for a woman (II Sam. 13:1, 4, 15). The verb *ʾahev* denoted also affection and esteem. It is used in this sense for David and Jonathan, to express natural friendship (I Sam. 18:1, 3; 20:17; II Sam. 1:26; cf. I Sam. 16:21); for a servant, to denote his attachment to his master's family (Ex. 21:5); and for the people, to signify their enthusiastic sympathy for David (I Sam. 18:16, 22, 28). The participle *ʾohev* means "friend" at least 17 times out of the 62 occurring in the Bible. On the other hand, Isaac, for instance, is said to "love" game as Rebekah knew to prepare it (Gen. 27:4, 9, 14). The verb *ʾahev* seems to express there a preference, as in several other texts (Gen. 25:28; 37:3, 4; Deut. 21:15; I Sam. 1:5).

The rendering of *reʿa* in Leviticus 19:18 ("Love your *reʿa* as yourself"), and similar passages, by "neighbor" is hallowed by tradition; but "fellow citizen" would be more enlightening, since the reference here to one's fellow Israelite is obvious from its identification by parallelism with "kinsmen" (*benei ammekha*) in Leviticus 19:18 and the fact that an additional verse, verse 34, was needed in order to include the metic (*ger*, but see Love of Neighbor, below). Common sense tells that the "love" that these verses require the Israelite to extend to his fellow citizen and to the metic residing in Israel is consideration, or, as Jewish tradition realistically defines it, not treating them in a manner in which one would resent being treated (so the interpretation of Pseudo-Jonathan, Lev. 19:18, 34, in accordance with the famous saying attributed in Shab. 31a to Hillel but in Eusebius, *Praeparatio evangelica*, 8:7, 8, to Philo, and also to be found in Arist. 207; Tob. 4:15; Test. Patr., Iss. 5:2; Test. Patr., Dan 5:3).

THE RECIPROCAL LOVE OF GOD AND PEOPLE. In the Bible, the object of the divine love is generally the people of Israel. The two passages where Jerusalem is presented as the object of God's love (Ps. 78:68; 87:2) are only variants of that fundamental aspect. The relation of God to His people is conceived as a union marked by love on one side and demanding a corresponding love on the other. This reciprocal love of God and the people is expressed in categories of familial or social unity: father-son relationship, marriage analogy, or covenantal love.

The doctrine of God's love for Israel, and the imperative necessity of Israel's love for God are rarely found in the first four books of the Bible, but they constitute the basic principles of the Deuteronomic teaching. The Lord's love for Israel is there viewed as the result of His election, manifested in the covenant and sanctioned by it. This clearly appears in Deuteronomy 7:7–8, where the divine love for Israel is mentioned paralleling the oath sworn by God in the rite of the covenant-making, and is ultimately justified by God's free choice. His free and personal love to Israel is manifested above all in the deliverance from Egypt. This primal love of the Lord for Israel (Deut. 4:37; 7:13; 10:15; 23:6) is the basis for the obligation of Israel's love in return (Deut. 6:5; 7:9; 10:12; 11:1, 13, 22; 13:4; 19:9; 30:6, 16, 20). Love in Deuteronomy is therefore a love that

God can command: "You shall love the Lord your God with all your heart, and with all your soul, and with all your might" (Deut. 6:5; cf. 10:12; 11:1; 30:6). It is also a love intimately related to fear and reverence (Deut. 4:10; 5:29; 6:24; 8:6; 10:12; 14:23; 17:19; 31:13). Above all, it is a love which must be expressed in obedience to the requirements of the law. For to love God is to be loyal (*davaq*) to Him (Deut. 4:4; 10:20; 11:22; 13:5; 30:20), to walk in His ways (Deut. 10:12; 11:22; 19:9; 30:16), to keep His commandments (Deut. 10:13; 11:1, 22; 19:9), to fulfill them (Deut. 11:22; 19:9), to heed them or His voice (Deut. 11:13; 13:5), and to serve Him (Deut. 6:13; 10:12; 11:13; 13:5). It is, in brief, a love defined by and pledged in the covenant. If the people appear to be unworthy of the divine love because of its ingratitude or infidelity, the love will change into wrath.

W.L. Moran has established the relationship of this Deuteronomic concept of love with the ideology and the terminology of ancient Oriental treaties, from the 18th to the 7th centuries B.C.E., in which the term "love" is used to describe the loyalty and friendship joining independent and equal rulers (cf. I Kings 5:15), overlord and vassal, or king and subject. This use of the term "love" is no innovation of the author of Deuteronomy 6:5, which is generally considered the earliest reference to the love of God in Deuteronomy. Since Judges 5:31 belongs most likely to the original Song of Deborah and uses the expression "those who love Him," it is probable that the term "love" goes back to a very early period in the Israelite covenant tradition. The formula "those who love Me" appears also in the passage of Exodus 20:6 and Deuteronomy 5:10, which belongs to the Decalogue. The father-son relationship in Deuteronomy, which reflects the very ancient Israelite concept of Israel as the Lord's son (cf. Deut. 32:6, 10–11, 18–20), is also found in the body of the Book of Deuteronomy (Deut. 1:31; 8:5; 14:1). If there is tenderness in this relationship as seen in Deuteronomy 1:31; 32:10–11; Isaiah 63:16; Jeremiah 3:19; 31:9; and Hosea 11:1, the Lord is in Deuteronomy 8:5 the father who does not spare the rod, but this divine chastening is considered in Proverbs 3:11–12 as a sign of the divine love. Israel appears as a disobedient son also in Isaiah 1:2 and 30:9. He is disloyal even to the point of turning away from the Father to other gods (Deut. 32:18–20), just as a faithless vassal abandons his sovereign for another overlord. God intervenes then as one who is angry with his sons for their disloyalty (Deut. 32:19), and who is, therefore, ready to punish them (Isa. 30:1–5, 8–14). In Deuteronomy 14:1, the relationship between father and son as applied to God and Israel is a motive to obey a particular command. It is thus clearly akin to the covenantal love, which should exist between the suzerain and the vassal, called respectively father and son in the diplomatic terminology of the ancient Near East (cf. E. Lipinski, *Le poème royal du Psaume LXXXIX*, 1–5, 20–38 (1967), 57–66). Malachi 1:6 parallels the son with the servant, and expects reverence from each. Since covenantal love involves reverential fear, there may be here a later offshoot of the same tradition. It may reasonably be inferred, therefore, that the ancient Israelite concept of Israel as God's son is very close to the Deuteronomic conception of covenantal love between God and Israel, though it is also associated with the current imagery of father and son. It can be influenced too by the idea of divine Fatherhood, expressed in personal names of the type *ʾaviyyah* (Abijah), *ʾaviyyahu* (Abijahu), "the Lord is my Father." Occasionally, the affection of God for His people is also depicted as the love of a mother for her child (Isa. 49:15; cf. 66:13; Deut. 32:11).

The husband-wife metaphor of Hosea 2 recurs in the earliest poems of Jeremiah (Jer. 2–3; 31:2–6), who had most likely been influenced in his youth by the Hoseanic tradition. Ezekiel, too, knew the symbolism of the marriage (Ezek. 16; 23), which recurs again in Deutero-Isaiah as a means of describing Israel's restoration after the Exile: Zion was a deserted wife (Isa. 49:14; 54:6; cf. 60:15; 62:4), without children (Isa. 49:20; 51:18; 54:1), and reduced to captivity (Isa. 40:2; 52:2), because she has been repudiated by the Lord (Isa. 50:1); but the Lord had decided to take her back (Isa. 54:5–8). YHWH's wrath required the rejection of the people – the repudiation of the unfaithful wife. This was the historical turning point with which the prophets were confronted. Nevertheless, the people was the Lord's people, the chosen people, the object of God's love. What would become of the election and of the divine plan for Israel if the "repudiation" became definitive? A tension ensued between God's love and God's wrath. Even the end of Judah as an independent state did not mean the complete annihilation of the nation. The reason is that Israel is precious in the Lord's eyes, and is loved by the Lord. In Hosea 14:5 it is expressly said that God of His own free will and love will heal the faithlessness of His people. Ezekiel emphasizes that the Lord will restore Israel, but not because of her fidelity to the covenant (Ezek. 16:60–68); and Deutero-Isaiah (under the influence of Ezekiel, e.g., ch. 36) says that God blots out the transgressions of His people not because of their sacrifices, but "for His own sake," i.e., His sovereign love (Isa. 43:22–44:5).

A few texts affirm that God loves the righteous (Ps. 146:8; Prov. 15:9; cf. 3:12), and some psalmists refer to God's compassion (Ps. 25:6; 40:12; 51:3; 69:17; 119:77) for all His creatures (Ps. 145:9). Such texts are relatively rare: the Lord's love is almost exclusively love for Israel, the elect people. Even the prophets never say that the Lord "loves" other peoples, or that mankind is an object of His love; but God's actions in Israel's history are dictated by His love. The same is true of His punitive educative work as well as of His gracious gifts in the continued course of history. This is the main theme of the biblical theology of love, probably because the divine love is generally conceived as related to the covenant. The use of the word *ḥesed* reveals indeed that this term also belongs to the covenantal terminology.

The love for God is sometimes signified in an indirect way, without mentioning the divine name. Thus when Amos 5:15 exhorts the people to "love the good," he intends the justice demanded by the divine law (cf. Micah 6:8; Ps. 52:5), which is mentioned 11 times in Psalm 119 as an object of love (vs. 47, 48, 97, 113, 119, 127, 140, 159, 163, 165, 167). Of course, the author meant by law, the stipulations of the covenant. The love of wisdom (Prov. 8:17, 21; cf. 4:5–6; 7:4; 29:3; Eccles. 4:11–14) is also interpreted as love of the law (Wisd. 6:17–18; cf. 6:12; 7:10), but this theme probably has an Egyptian origin: the personified divine wisdom seems to be an Israelite adaptation of the Old Egyptian Maat, whose love was also highly recommended in texts celebrating this deified idea of truth and justice (cf. Ch. Kayatz, *Studien zu Proverbien 1–9* (1966), 98–102). The biblical passages mentioning the love for the Temple or Jerusalem (Isa. 66:10; Ps. 26:8; 122:9) express instead the desire for the divine familiarity, more vividly felt in the holy places.

[Edward Lipinski]

Post-Biblical

The Song of Songs has been called the world's greatest love poetry. In range of imagery, lyric quality, and personal insight, it has taught the true nature of love to much of mankind. While it was admitted to the Bible only after a struggle, and then, apparently, because it was seen as an allegory of the love of God for Israel, the manifest content of the poems could never be denied. Thus an intimate link was established in Jewish literature between human love and the love of God. Jewish mysticism made this a major motif in its esoteric teaching. Rabbinic literature likewise reveals its appreciation of love only tangentially but with the same deep feeling: "A man once said, 'When love was strong, we could have made our bed on a sword-blade; Now that our love has grown weak, a bed of 60 cubits is not large enough for us'" (Sanh. 7a).

It is not the love in itself, or the passion associated with it, or its sexual fulfillment which are valued in these writings, as much as the understanding and the generosity which love creates and sustains. Thus, understanding and generosity become the highest ideals for human relationships. Love between man and woman is almost always connected with marriage, which is either the goal of love or the motive which brings it into being. This ideal of love in marriage which leads to understanding and generosity, though influenced by the various cultural circumstances among which Jews found themselves, remained relatively stable over the centuries. Though the ideal of romantic, courtly love did penetrate the Jewish community in the 11th and 12th centuries, unrequited passion never became a major Jewish concern.

Following the Aristotelian denigration of the senses and passion, the Jewish philosophers, *Maimonides in particular, tended to denigrate sexual love, and to intellectualize the love of God.

They viewed the love of God as an essentially cognitive matter. Maimonides explains that "And thou shalt love the Lord thy God with all thy heart" means that "you should make His apprehension the end of all your actions" (*Guide of the Perplexed*, 1:39; see also 3:33; Yad., Teshuvah 10:3–4, 6).

Ḥasdai *Crescas, as part of his general attack on the Maimonidean system, rejected this intellectualization of man's fundamental relationship to God. In great measure this is due to Crescas' insistence that positive attributes may be postulated about God (see *God, Attributes of). Since he then connects will and goodness with God, it is obvious that the appropriate response to such a benevolent God is love (*Or Adonai*, 1:3, 3). This feeling becomes for Crescas the desired basis of man's service to God (*ibid.*, 2:6, 1–2).

Joseph *Albo's *Book of Principles* 3:35 treats human love of God and God's love for humanity in general, and for Israel in particular. God is worthy of human love because He is good, beneficent, and pleasant, the three criteria Aristotle posited for the object of love (*Nicomachean Ethics* 8:2; cf. Maimonides, *Commentary to Mishnah* Avot 1:6). God's love for people is analogous to a king's love of his subjects, a father's love of his children, and a husband's love of his wife. Albo also represents God's love for Israel as a "desire" (*ḥeshek*), which has not cause or reason (3:37).

The Renaissance philosopher Judah *Abrabanel (Leone Ebreo; Leo Hebraeus) devoted his book *Dialoghi di Amore* ("Dialogues of Love") to the theme of love, to the connection between love, passion, and reason, and to love as the principle moving the world and expressing the mutual relationship between God and his creatures.

The mystics, though they had an anti-corporeal, ascetic strain in their teaching, similar to the Aristotelian view of Maimonides, nevertheless, had a more emotional understanding of love, and, following the Song of Songs, could see in the sexual passion between man and wife the model of the reintegration of the presently fragmented divine unity (Zohar 1:49b–50a). In modern times, Jewish thinkers have tended to accept the general, gradual reaffirmation of the physical aspects of human existence as essentially healthy. In the 19th and early 20th century, before this change of attitude toward the physical aspects of love, most Jewish discussions of love remained under the influence of German idealistic philosophy.

The Neo-Kantian philosopher Hermann *Cohen emphasized the moral characteristic of love in Judaism: the love of the alien and of one's fellow Jew is a function of the feeling of compassion, and human love of God is defined as the love of the moral ideal. After World War I, the existentialist philosophy of Franz *Rosenzweig and Martin *Buber introduced a new concern for the whole person, and emphasized human relationships. For them, love becomes the very ground of one's being, the source of all meaning and the guide to all action.

Rosenzweig characterized divine revelation as an expression of love of man. Since revelation occurs in the present – creation being the past and redemption the future – the love of God is the embodiment of the human-divine encounter in every present moment. God being the source of love, He can also command man to love Him ("Love the Lord your God") as an expression of His love for man. Buber emphasized the necessary connection between love of one's fellow (*re'a*) and love of God, whom he calls "the eternal you (Thou)." Against Soren Kierkegaard, who felt the need to abandon his beloved fiancée in order to make room for love of God, Buber argued that only by love of the other person, the human "you"

("Thou"), can a person attain the love of God, the "eternal you" (Thou).

Love and Fear of God (Heb. 'אַהֲבַת ה'; יִרְאַת ה)

In his morning prayer the Jew asks God to "unify our hearts to love and fear Thy Name." This request indicates the recognition, prevalent in Judaism since a century or two before the destruction of the Second Temple, that the love and fear of God are the major motives for serving Him, and that there is some tension between them.

Both terms are widely used in the Bible, but the concept of fearing God appears much more frequently than that of loving Him. It is not clear, however, exactly what the biblical writers sought to convey about their faith by using a word for it which, when related to normal experience, regularly describes emotions of dread and fright (Josh. 10:2; Jer. 42:16). In many of its uses, the term loses all denotations of fear, and conveys a broad sense of one's religion, one's god, or one's pattern of worship (II Kings 17:28; Isa. 29:13). In some cases the term occurs in conjunction with the love of God, so that the two appear to have a similar content (Deut. 10:12). Some scholars have therefore argued that the terms are identical in meaning, but this interpretation seems unlikely in view of the heavy biblical emphasis on God's punishing sin and His utter transcendence of man. He is never described as simply loving man, though He does love Israel; rather the emphasis is on His mercy and benevolence, that is, though He is the master, He deals kindly. Hence, while the primitive denotations of fear have been sublimated in much biblical usage to a more intimate relationship with God, there is good reason to believe that the fear of God is a primary Hebrew response to God as the transcendent one, but it shades off into the love of God as the benevolent one. In both terms, however, the immediate connotation is action. Neither is used to commend an emotional state, worthy because of the feelings it arouses. Both are used as motivations for doing the will of God. They are means to observance.

By early rabbinic times, the emphasis on love had risen to parity with that on fear. Throughout talmudic times, the emphasis was increasingly placed on love as the most appropriate motive for the service of God. This is in accord with the rabbinic stress on carrying out the commandments for their own sake (*li-shemah*). The implication arises that, in doing them out of fear, it is reward and punishment which move the doer, which, to the rabbis, are extrinsic and inferior motives. They do not insist that doing the commandments for their own sake is the only acceptable way for Judaism, but rather accommodate themselves to human frailty by reasoning that from extrinsic motivation people will come to intrinsic motivation, which indicates their preference. Hence, though a number of rabbinic dicta make a distinction between the two motives, none of them prefers service from fear to service from love. The following are typical: "The reward of the lover is two portions; that of the fearer is one" (SER 28:140–1); "Act out of love, for the Torah makes a distinction between one who acts out of love and one who acts out of fear… In the former case his reward is doubled and redoubled" (Sif. Deut. 32).

A major addition to the meanings of loving God is the rabbis' association of martyrdom with the term. Love would naturally seem to imply a willingness to do anything for one's beloved. With R. Akiva as the model, the rabbis saw the will to give one's life for God and His teaching as the highest expression of love for Him (Ber. 61b; Sif. Deut. 32). The rabbis, however, considered martyrdom an end in itself, and placed severe restrictions on the conditions under which one had to give one's life for the love of God. This idea became a major part of the medieval Jew's sense of the right motive from which to serve God.

With the advent of Muslim-Jewish philosophy, with its rigorous, abstract evaluation of motives, a full-scale preference for the love of God over the fear of God began to pervade Jewish literature. For Maimonides, the rigorous philosophical estimate of all things led to a disparagement of the fear of God as a motive worthy of women and children alone (Maim., Yad, Teshuvah 10:1). Only the love of God, because it seeks nothing for itself, should be considered the motive which men ought to strive to achieve as the basis for their action. Yet Maimonides' Aristotelianism did not permit him to accept love in all its emotional connotations. What he carried over of love's normal meaning is its singleness of focus and its comprehensive relation to its object. In terms of man's inner state, however, since thinking was for Maimonides the most significant thing one can do, love was completely reinterpreted in terms of reason and cognition (*ibid.* 10:6). Even where Maimonides used the symbols of the love of God, his meaning always related to an intellectual activity which concentrates utterly on its object and seeks to carry that fixation into every other aspect of existence (Guide of the Perplexed, 3:51). Such intensive love of God is called "desire" (*ḥeshek*).

Isaac *Arama's treatise *Ḥazut Kashah* portrays the philosophers as attaining the rank of love of God resulting from admiration, but not the higher rank of *fear of God. On the other hand, the philosophers negated divine love of man, because in their view God does not relate in any way to individual humans. Baruch *Spinoza typifies such a philosophic position, emphasizing that God does not love individual people (Ethics 5:17). In Jewish mysticism, by contrast, though there are continual references to the fear and love of God, no clear-cut emphasis on one or the other becomes dominant in any of the major movements. The Zohar, for example, esteems both very highly. The concept of *devequt* calls on man to intimately associate his being with God and to be linked to Him in every activity of his life. This concept incorporates aspects of the traditional ideas of both the love and fear of God. It carries over the closeness of the former, yet maintains a sense of the distance and greatness of God.

Modern Jewish thinkers have avoided discussing the fear of God, since it seems too closely associated with the image of man as passive and abject. Wishing to ascribe to man an active role in his relationship with God, they have almost universally made the reciprocal love of God and man central to their teaching. Since this idea can easily be extended to the point where the distance between God and man is obliterated, as in various schools of humanism, some thinkers have begun to suggest that a concern for the fear of God is not incompatible with the dignity of man and is required by the transcendence of God.

Love of Neighbor

Leviticus 19:18 commands: "Love your neighbor (*re'akha*) as yourself: I am the Lord." The surrounding verses qualify this commandment. They prohibit unfair dealing and defrauding even of the defenseless, and forbid vengeance and the bearing of a grudge.

It is not clear whether the commandment to love one's neighbor applies to Jews only or to non-Jews as well. There is no substantial data from the Bible concerning the practice of the commandment. From the parallel term in the first part of the verse, *benei ammekha* ("children of your people"), it would seem that *re'akha* ("your neighbor") in the second part of the verse refers to specifically Jewish neighbors (see for example, Maim., Yad, De'ot 6:3), though the word *re'a* is used elsewhere in the Bible to refer to non-Jewish neighbors as well. The fact that the love of the resident stranger (*ger*) is enjoined in the same chapter in a separate verse (19:33–34) would seem to indicate further that "neighbor" in verse 18 refers specifically to Jews. It is clear that according to the interpretation of the rabbis of the talmudic period the commandment of loving one's neighbor does not refer to idolaters. Idolatry is, of course, the classic wickedness in Jewish eyes. While there is no commandment to hate idolaters, and while there are in rabbinic literature many stories about the positive relations between Jews and idolaters, the law places so many restrictions on association with idolaters and their goods that the commandment of neighborly love cannot easily be said to apply to them.

The rabbis had a clear appreciation of the significance of this commandment. Akiva called it the epitome of the Torah. Ben Azzai, in preferring the verse: "In the day that God created man, in the likeness of God made He him" is not denying Akiva's assertion of the importance of this commandment (Sifra 19:18). If anything, he is seeking a more inclusive verse, for "neighbor" might be understood literally or locally, but "creation in the image of God" excludes no human being. Similarly, both Hillel (Avot 1:12) and R. Meir (*ibid.* 6:1) enjoin that one should love all mankind ("creatures"). Concern for the non-Jew and his welfare is understood to be part of the Jewish goal of promoting peace among men, *mi-penei darkhei shalom* ("in the interest of peace"). From this commitment a whole range of moral responsibilities toward gentiles devolves upon Jews. Maimonides, in a typical ruling from the many in medieval writings, writes: "We bury the dead of heathens, comfort their mourners, and visit their sick, as this is the way of peace" (Yad, Avel 14:12).

In modern times, when the Jew's neighbor for the first time is widely understood as encompassing all humanity, the understanding of neighborly love by Jewish thinkers has been, correspondingly, universalized.

Moses *Mendelssohn argues that the commandment in Leviticus 19:18 cannot mean to love someone else as one loves oneself, which is impossible; moreover, had the Torah intended to command love of neighbor "as yourself," it would have said *ke-nafshekha*. The term *kamokha*, in his analysis, does not mean "as yourself" but "that which resembles you"; the commandment thus means "love your fellow, for he is like you, equal to you and resembling you, for he was also created in the image of God; he is human, like you. This includes all humans, since all of them were created in [God's] image" (*Be'ur* to Lev. 19:18; the commentary to Leviticus was prepared by H. Wessely, and was supervised and edited with bracketed additions by Mendelssohn).

Samson Raphael *Hirsch makes the love of all mankind a condition for being a true Israelite, and Hermann *Cohen considers it the necessary and unique concomitant of Jewish *monotheism. Cohen also follows Mendelssohn in interpreting the commandment as meaning love for the other who is like you: "The ethical self must be engaged in action. For this self, there exists no I without a Thou. *Re'akha* means "the other," the one who is like you. He is the Thou of the I. Selfhood is the result of an unending relation of I and Thou as well as its abiding ideal" ("Charakteristic der Ethik Maimunis" (1908), in: *Juedische Schriften* III, Eng. tr. in E. Jospe (ed.), *Reason and Hope: Selections from the Jewish Writings of Hermann Cohen* (1971), 218).

Leo *Baeck writes: "In Judaism neighbor is inseparable from man… there is no 'man' without 'fellowman,' no faith in God without faith in neighbor…" (*Essence of Judaism* (1936), 193).

[Eugene B. Borowitz / Raphael Jospe and Hannah Kasher (2nd ed.)]

BIBLIOGRAPHY: IN THE BIBLE: B.J. Bamberger, in: HUCA, 6 (1929), 39–53; D.W. Thomas, in: ZAW, 57 (1939), 57–64; E. Jacob, *Theology of the Old Testament* (1958), 108–13; W. Eichrodt, *Theology of the Old Testament*, 1 (1961), 250–8; 2 (1967), 290–301; W.L. Moran, in: CBQ, 25 (1963), 77–87; N.H. Snaith, *The Distinctive Ideas of the Old Testament* (1964³), 94–142; D.J. McCarthy, in: CBQ, 27 (1965), 144–7. ḤESED: A.R. Johnson, in: *Interpretationes ad Vetus Testamentum pertinentes Sigmundo Mowinckel septuagenario missae* (1955), 100–12; N. Glueck, *Ḥesed in the Bible* (1967). POST-BIBLICAL: N. Glatzer, *Franz Rosenzweig, His Life and Thought* (1961), xxiii–xxv; M. Buber, *Between Man and Man* (1948), 28–30, 51–58; M. Harris, in: JQR, 50 (1959/60), 13–44; idem, in: *Conservative Judaism*, 14 (1959/60), 29–39. LOVE AND FEAR OF GOD: A. Buechler, *Studies in Sin and Atonement in the Rabbinic Literature of the First Century* (1928), 119–75; Scholem, Mysticism, 233–5, and index, s.v. *Love of God*; G. Vajda, *L'Amour de Dieu dans la thélogie du moyen âge* (1957); F. Bamberger, in: HUCA, 6 (1929), 39–53. LOVE OF NEIGHBOR: S.R. Hirsch, *Horeb: A Philosophy of Jewish Laws and Observances* (1962), 52–54; H. Cohen, *Religion der Vernunft* (1929²), 144ff.; M. Buber, *I and Thou* (1937), passim. **ADD. BIBLIOGRAPHY:** S. Harvey, "Love," in: A.A. Cohen and P. Mendes-Flohr (ed.), *Contemporary Jewish Religious Thought* (1986), 557–63; Leone Ebreo, *The Philosophy of Love*, tr. F. Friedenberg-Seeley and J.H. Barnes (1937); W.Z. Harvey, "Albo on the Reasonlessness of True Love," in: *Iyyun*, 49 (2000), 83–86; H. Kreisel, "The Love and Fear of

God," in: idem, *Maimonides Political Thought* (1999), 225–66; E. Simon, "The Neighbor (*Re'a*) Whom We Shall Love," in: M. Fox (ed.), *Modern Jewish Ethics: Theory and Practice* (1975), 29–56.

LOVELL, LEOPOLD (1907–1976), South African politician who was the only white man in the first cabinet of independent Swaziland. Born of Russian immigrant parents, he practiced law in Benoni in the Transvaal. During the 1930s he organized resistance to the Greyshirt (pro-Hitler) movement, and had its gangs expelled from the town. Lovell represented Benoni (S. Transvaal) in the House of Assembly from 1949 until 1958 when the Labor Party ceased to be represented in Parliament, and was an outspoken opponent of the Nationalist Government's apartheid policies. He took up residence in Swaziland in 1961 and was admitted to the bar there. In 1967 he became a member of its Parliament and was appointed minister of finance, commerce, and industry.

[Lewis Sowden]

LOVESTONE, JAY (**Liebstein, Jacov**; 1897–1990), U.S. Communist Party leader; architect of U.S. organized labor's post-World War II anti-Communist foreign policy. Lovestone, who was born in Lithuania, was taken to the United States as a child and grew up on New York's Lower East Side.

Lovestone joined the Socialist Party as a youth and was active in that party's left wing. In response to the Bolshevik Revolution, Lovestone was a founder of the Communist Party of America in 1919, which merged with another faction in 1921 to form what became the Communist Party of the United States. He served as its executive secretary from 1927 to 1929. While American Communism's top bureaucrat, Lovestone outlined the notion of "American Exceptionalism," i.e., that the United States did not fit into the general Communist theory. However, he and his theory were reviled and ostracized after Stalin's Comintern declared a "third period" of capitalist crisis and revolutionary upsurge, which included the United States. Following the Stalinization of American Communism, Lovestone formed an opposition Communist Party (later the Independent Labor League) and during the Depression fought Communists in the auto workers' and ladies garment workers' unions. In 1944 Lovestone was chosen to head the Free Trade Union Committee. Thereafter, he guided the American Federation of Labor's anti-Communist foreign policy. He constructed a worldwide intelligence network which, throughout the Cold War era, worked closely with the CIA. When the AFL and CIO merged, Lovestone continued his anti-Communist activities within the merged labor movement's Department of International Affairs. In 1963 he became director of the AFL-CIO's International Affairs Department (IAD), which covertly channeled millions of dollars from the CIA to anti-Communist activities internationally, particularly in Latin America. During the 1960s he vigorously supported American military intervention in Cuba, the Dominican Republic, and Vietnam, and opposed the concepts and practitioners of neutralism and revolutionary nationalism. In 1974 he was expelled from the AFL-CIO when it came to light that he had been connected with the CIA.

BIBLIOGRAPHY: Lens, in: *The Nation* (July 5, 1965); Draper, *American Communism and Soviet Russia* (1960); L. Velie, *Labor U.S.A.* (1959). **ADD. BIBLIOGRAPHY:** T. Morgan, *A Covert Life: Jay Lovestone, Communist, Anti-Communist & Spymaster* (1999); R. Alexander, *The Right Opposition: The Lovestoneites and the International Communist Opposition of the 1930s* (1981).

[Kenneth Waltzer / Ruth Beloff (2nd ed.)]

LOVY, ISRAEL (**Lowy; Israel Glogauer**; 1773–1832), *ḥazzan* and composer. Born near Danzig, Lovy received his talmudic education in Glogau, where his father officiated as *ḥazzan*. From the age of 13 he acted as assistant *ḥazzan* in various communities of Moravia, Bohemia, Saxony, and Bavaria. In 1799 Lovy was employed in Fuerth, where he continued his education in European music. After temporary employment in Mainz, Strasbourg, and London, he went to Paris in 1818, and in 1822 he became the chief *ḥazzan* of the newly founded synagogue in the Rue Notre Dame de Nazareth. There he organized a four-voiced choir, for which he composed his *Chants religieux… pour les prières hébraïques* (1862). He had already appeared as a concert singer in Germany, and in Paris was urged to go on the stage, but refused. His tunes were popular among the German cantors, but his priority as a "reformist" passed to Solomon *Sulzer whose innovations had a wider influence. The "Polish airs" notated at the end of his *Chants* (149–57) are the first appearance in print of the "ḥazzanic-klezmeric" (folk) repertoire for weddings and other family rejoicings and an important relic of 18th-century traditions.

BIBLIOGRAPHY: E. Manuel, in: *Archives Israelites*, 11 (1850), 298–306, 344–52 (abbreviated version in the preface of Lovy's *Chants…*); Idelsohn, Music, 219, 226–9, 287; Sendrey, Music, 5687–88, 6260, 6707.

[Bathja Bayer]

LOW (**Loewe**), British family of Hungarian origin which became prominent in journalism and literature.

MAXIMILIAN LOEWE (1830–1900) was born in Hungary and joined the Nationalist party led by Louis Kossuth. After the failure of the 1848 revolution in Hungary, Loewe fled to England where he engaged in business. Within a short time he acquired a considerable fortune as a result of speculation but in 1878 lost it all. Loewe became interested in the Theist movement and helped to establish its church. He was a profound admirer of British culture and imbued his children with a love of English literature.

His son, SIR SIDNEY JAMES MARK LOW (1857–1932), became a lecturer at King's College, London. His bent was for literature but the state of the family finances compelled him to earn his living as a journalist which he successfully combined as literary editor of the *Standard* (1904). He edited, with F.S. Pulling, the *Dictionary of English History* in 1884 and 20 years later published his second and most important work, *The Governance of England* (1904). As a journalist, Low achieved a high reputation for his style and sense of history and was given access to the papers of eminent statesmen such as Lord Milner and Leopold S. *Amery. From 1888 to 1897 he achieved fame as editor of the *St. James Gazette*. During World War I, Low wrote a series of books on the British Empire in which he took a strict imperialist line with high propaganda value. He was knighted in 1918. An ardent patriot and confidant of leading statesmen, he was compelled to resign his official position as editor of the wireless service of the Ministry of Information in order to forestall a House of Commons question on his "Central European origin."

Maximilian's second son, SIR MAURICE LOW (1860–1929), was also a well-known journalist. He immigrated to the U.S. when the family fortunes waned and became Washington correspondent of the *Boston Globe* and subsequently of the London *Daily Chronicle* and *Morning Post*. He was considered one of the best correspondents in the United States and by his writing and lectures did much to arouse American public opinion to an awareness of the German menace and to improve the image of Britain. For these services, he was knighted in 1922. He wrote studies of the United States, of which the best known is *The American People* (2 vols., 1909–11), as well as books concerning World War I and a political novel.

Maximilian Loewe had six sons and five daughters. One daughter, Edith, who was a leader of *WIZO, married Montague David *Eder, psychologist and Zionist leader. Ivy, a daughter of Sir Sidney Low, married Maxim *Litvinov, the Soviet political leader.

BIBLIOGRAPHY: D. Chapman-Huston, *Memoir of Sir Sidney Low* (1936); *The Times* (June 18, 1929), 18 (obituary of Maurice Low). **ADD. BIBLIOGRAPHY:** ODNB online for Sir Sidney Low.

LOW, MINNIE (1867–1922), U.S. social service leader. Low was born in New York City and moved to Chicago with her family when she was 10 years old. Inspired by her friend, social reformer and Hull House Settlement director Jane Addams, Low helped found the Maxwell Street Settlement House in 1893. Low's work within Chicago's Jewish immigrant community earned her the reputation as the "Jane Addams of the Jews."

While organizing the Maxwell Street Settlement House, Low supported herself financially by working as secretary to Hannah Greenbaum *Solomon, the philanthropist and activist who founded the *National Council of Jewish Women. With Solomon's assistance, Low became executive director of the Seventh Ward Bureau (later known as the Bureau of Personal Service), a position that she held from 1897 until her death in 1922. The organization helped East European Jewish immigrants who settled in Chicago to secure housing, medical care, loans, and legal aid, and sponsored a workroom that compensated female workers with coal and secondhand clothes. A critic of institutions that dispensed alms, Low advocated a scientific approach to philanthropy that promoted self-sufficiency through a combination of work and loans.

The same year that Low began her affiliation with the Seventh Ward Bureau, she also helped to create the Woman's Loan Association. Administered exclusively by women, the Woman's Loan Association provided Jewish immigrants with interest-free loans primarily to start and maintain small businesses. Low also played a prominent role within other Chicago Jewish agencies: Central Bureau of Jewish Charities, Desertion Bureau, Helen Day Nursery, Home for Jewish Friendless, and Jewish Home Finding Society (an organization that helped widows with dependent children and placed children with adopted families).

Low's social work activity extended beyond the Jewish community. In 1899, for example, she joined a group of well-known Chicago social reformers including Hull House leaders Louise de Koven Bowen and Julia Lathrop, women's club activist Lucy Flower, and Judge Julian Mack to organize the Juvenile Court of Chicago, the nation's first separate juvenile court. Soon after the court's establishment, Low was hired as a probation officer. In addition, Low's reputation was not limited to Chicago. She achieved national recognition when her colleagues elected her president of the National Conference of Jewish Charities in 1914.

Limited finances and poor health plagued Low throughout her life. Never married, Low supported herself financially through employment as a salaried professional. Low left high school during the first year because of health problems and suffered from a prolonged illness before she died on May 28, 1922. At the memorial service, Addams delivered a eulogy that chronicled their friendship and honored Low's accomplishments.

BIBLIOGRAPHY: M.J. Deegan, "Minnie Low," in: R.L. Schultz and A. Hast (eds.), *Women Building Chicago, 1790–1990: A Biographical Dictionary* (2001); M. Low, "Chicago," in: C. Bernheimer (ed.), *The Russian Jew in the United States* (1905), 87–99; H. Meites, *History of the Jews of Chicago* (1924); Obituaries, *Chicago Tribune* (May 29, 1922) and *New York Times* (May 29, 1922); S. Tenenbaum, *A Credit to their Community: Jewish Loan Societies in the United States, 1880–1945* (1993); idem, "Minnie Low," in: P.E. Hyman and D.D. Moore (eds.), *Jewish Women in America: An Historical Encyclopedia*, (1997).

[Shelly Tenenbaum (2nd ed.)]

LOW (Lev), WILLIAM ZE'EV (1922–2004), Israeli physicist. Low was born in Vienna and studied in Canada and the U.S., receiving his doctorate from Columbia University in 1950. In the same year he immigrated to Israel, and was appointed professor of experimental physics at the Hebrew University in 1961. In 1960 he was elected president of the Physical Society of Israel. He has published nearly 200 papers in the field of solid state physics, laser physics, shockwaves, and microwaves, and is the author of *Paramagnetic Resonance in Solids* (1960). He was awarded the Israel Prize for exact sciences in 1962 and the Rothschild Prize for physical sciences in 1965.

A strictly observant Jew and profound talmudist, Low founded, and was first president of, the Institute of Science and Halakhah, the main purpose of which is to find scientific halakhic solutions to various problems connected with modern society and the Jewish religion, mainly in regard to observance of the Sabbath in an industrial society. The institute is also engaged in the collection of various rabbinical responsa connected with modern technological and agricultural problems. Low was also instrumental in establishing the Jerusalem College of Technology and was the first president and rector of this accredited college, whose purpose is to train yeshivah students as engineers for Israel industry, and thus bring them into direct contact with the economic and industrial life of the country. The staff consists of professors in the field of technology as well as yeshivah teachers. He has published two books of *responsa.

°LOWDERMILK, WALTER CLAY (1888–1974), U.S. land conservation and hydrology expert, friend of Zionism and Israel. Lowdermilk was born in North Carolina and studied at the universities of Arizona and California. After studying afforestation problems in Britain, he joined the afforestation department of the U.S. Department of Agriculture. Later, he studied soil erosion and conservation, being one of the first to base his conclusions on field experiments. In 1927, after five years as professor of afforestation at the University of Nanking, he founded a hydrological experimentation station in Southern California. His researches were the basis, in part, for U.S. soil conservation schemes in the 1930s, and from 1937 to 1947 he headed the research department of the U.S. Soil Conservation Service.

In 1939 Lowdermilk visited Ereẓ Israel, where he studied conditions and development prospects. He published his conclusion in *Palestine – Land of Promise* (1944), in which, contrary to the view upon which the Mandatory Government ostensibly based its White Paper restricting further Jewish immigration on the grounds that the economic absorption capacity of Ereẓ Israel was full, he showed that the country could support a population of three million. He warmly praised Zionist land settlement and agricultural development, and proposed a comprehensive plan for the development of the Jordan Valley along the lines of the U.S. Tennessee Valley Authority and the diversion of the river's sweet waters for irrigation for the benefit of Ereẓ Israel and the neighboring countries. After the establishment of Israel's independence, this scheme became the basis for the Israel National Water scheme. He also proposed the generation of electricity by the transmission of Mediterranean water through a tunnel to the Dead Sea. Lowdermilk visited Israel in the early 1950s and for three years served, on behalf of the UN Food and Agriculture Organization, as an advisor to the Ministry of Agriculture on the preparation of Israel's soil conservation and water schemes. In 1955 he returned to Israel on behalf of the U.S. government and helped to develop the Agricultural Engineering Department of the Technion in Haifa, which he headed for three years and which bears his name. His writings include *Jewish Colonization in Palestine* (1939) and "Assignment in Israel" in *The Land* (1960), pp. 168–83.

LOWE, ADOLPH (1893–1995), economist. Born in Stuttgart, Germany, Lowe was a civil servant in Germany's ministries of labor and economic affairs and in the central statistical office (1919–26). From 1926 to 1931 he was a professor of economics and sociology at the University of Kiel, where he became director of research at the Institute for World Economy. In 1931 he was appointed professor of economics at the University of Frankfurt. In 1933, with the advent of the Nazis, he went to England where, until 1940, he was a lecturer in economics and political science at the University of Manchester. He left England in 1940 because he was perceived as an enemy alien. He settled in New York City, where he began teaching at the New School for Social Research. From 1943 to 1951 he directed research at the Institute of World Affairs in New York City. General economic theory, economic development, and business fluctuations were his main professional interests. Lowe retired from teaching in 1963 but remained at the New School for Social Research in the capacity of lecturer. He returned to Germany in 1983, where he lived to the age of 102.

His major publications include *Economics and Sociology: A Plea for Cooperation in the Social Sciences* (1935), *The Price of Liberty* (1937), *The Classical Theory of Economic Growth* (1954), *Structural Analysis of Real Capital Formation* (1955), *On Economic Knowledge* (1965), *The Path of Economic Growth* (1976), and *Has Freedom a Future?* (1988).

[Joachim O. Ronall / Ruth Beloff (2nd ed.)]

LOWE, ELIAS AVERY (1879–1969), foremost 20th century authority on Latin paleography. Born in Lithuania, Lowe (originally Loew) came to New York at an early age and after studying at City College graduated from Cornell University. In 1902, aided by the philanthropist James Loeb, he went to Germany, where he received his doctorate in 1907 under the master paleographer Ludwig *Traube, writing on *Die ältesten Kalendarien aus Monte Cassino*. In *Studia Palaeographica* (1910) he established extremely sophisticated criteria for dating Beneventan and Visigothic minuscule manuscripts. His work *The Beneventan Script* (1914), a subject to which he returned with his two-volume *Scriptura Beneventana* (1929), was the first full-scale study of a particular Latin script. His work on the complex textual tradition of the rule of St. Benedict was an important supplement to that of Traube. In 1913 Lowe was appointed lecturer and in 1927 as reader in paleography at Oxford; but his most fruitful period was from 1936 on, when he was appointed professor at the Institute for Advanced Study at Princeton, retiring in 1946. There he was a close friend of Einstein. His master work was *Codices latini antiquiores*, a paleographical guide to all Latin manuscripts prior to the ninth century in 11 volumes (1934–66), arranged according to the country where the manuscripts are currently to be found and containing facsimiles of sample passages of each manuscript, with important notes on their date, origin and style. At the time of his death he was at work on a 12th volume, containing a supplement and a series of indices, as well as a companion to the work explaining how it was to be used. Jacob *Epstein, an early schoolmate, made a bust of Lowe, now in the Metropolitan Museum in New York.

[Louis Harry Feldman (2nd ed.)]

LOWENSTEIN, ALLARD KENNETH (1929–1980), U.S. political activist. Born in Newark, NJ, Lowenstein was raised in Westchester County, NY, and educated at the Horace Mann School, the University of North Carolina, Chapel Hill (B.A. 1949) and Yale Law School (LL.B. 1954). After graduating from UNC, Lowenstein became an aide to liberal North Carolina senator Frank P. Graham. Later he became president of the National Student Association (an organization substantially funded by the CIA unbeknownst to Lowenstein and other NSA leaders). He worked for Adlai Stevenson's presidential campaign in 1952. After the campaign he went to work for Eleanor Roosevelt at the United Nations.

After law school and two years in the U.S. Army, Lowenstein undertook a dangerous fact-finding trip to South Africa and South West Africa (now Namibia) to investigate apartheid, and wrote a book, *Brutal Mandate* (1962), about his findings. While practicing law in New York in 1960, he worked in the election campaign of liberal Democratic congressman William Fitts Ryan. In 1961 he began teaching at Stanford University, and became involved in student and civil rights activities. Fired for his activities at Stanford, he took a position at North Carolina State University at Raleigh, where he became a civil rights activist. A talented organizer, known as a kind of "pied piper" for idealistic students, Lowenstein soon became a strategist with movement leaders in the South, including Martin Luther King, Jr. He took a leading role in recruiting young white volunteers – many of whom were Jewish – for Freedom Summer, the campaign to register voters in Mississippi and other Southern states in 1964, on behalf of the Student Nonviolent Coordinating Committee (SNCC). But he fell out with the organizers over his attempts to control their activities and limit their ideas to those of traditional liberalism. At the 1964 Democratic Convention Lowenstein supported the compromise imposed by President Lyndon Baines Johnson over the struggle to seat an integrated delegation in place of the official white segregationist delegation from Mississippi.

In 1967 as opposition to the Vietnam War increased Lowenstein, from his teaching perch at City College of New York, began the Dump Johnson movement within the Democratic Party over the Vietnam War. He is credited with persuading Senator Eugene McCarthy to run against President Johnson in the party primaries in 1968, eventually causing Johnson to withdraw his candidacy. That year Lowenstein ran for, and won, a congressional seat from a largely Black and Jewish district centered in Long Beach. In Congress he was an outspoken voice against the Vietnam War and for draft reform.

He failed to win reelection in 1970, and also lost subsequent attempts in primaries to win election in other New York districts in 1972 and 1974. Various ḥasidic factions in Brooklyn opposed his election. In 1971 Lowenstein became the chairman of the liberal Americans for Democratic Action. In 1977 he was appointed by President Carter as the U.S. representative to the United Nations Commission on Human Rights. His later years were relatively quiet. However, in 1980 Lowenstein was shot to death in his law office in New York City by a mentally ill former associate from the civil rights movement. His funeral gathered many of those who had participated in his many causes.

[Drew Silver (2nd ed.)]

LOWENSTEIN, SOLOMON (1877–1942), U.S. social work executive and Reform rabbi. Lowenstein, who was born in Philadelphia, was ordained by Hebrew Union College in 1901. He was successively employed as superintendent of the United Jewish Charities in Cincinnati (1901–04); assistant manager of the United Jewish Charities in New York (1904); superintendent of the Hebrew Orphan Asylum (1905–18); deputy commissioner of the American Red Cross in Palestine (1918–19); and director of the Federation of Jewish Philanthropic Societies (1920–35). In 1935 he became the Federation's executive vice president and held this post until his death. During this period, coinciding with the depression of the 1930s, Jewish philanthropy greatly expanded and shifted and Lowenstein coordinated and systematized its operations. Lowenstein was president of the National Conference of Social Work (1938), and was also a trustee of both the American Jewish Committee and the American Jewish Joint Distribution Committee, and a vice president of the American Friends of the Hebrew University.

LOWENTHAL, MARVIN (1890–1969), U.S. Zionist writer. Born in Bradford, Pennsylvania, Lowenthal was sent by Louis *D. Brandeis to the West Coast to organize the Zionist movement there (1916–18). From 1924 to 1929 he traveled abroad as European editor of the *Menorah Journal*, and for part of this time also represented the American Jewish Congress. During these years he wrote extensively on literature, politics, and Zionism, evincing affection for the secular elements in Jewish culture. He became widely known in the United States through his essays and lectures, but his most enduring works are his travel and historical books. His craftsmanship and urbanity of style appear at their best in *The Jews of Germany* (1936; includes bibliography of his works). Lowenthal served on the Zionist Advisory Commission (1946–49) and was editor of *The American Zionist* (1952–54). His works include a book on Jews in Europe and North Africa, *A World Passed By* (1933); and he edited *Henrietta Szold: Life and Letters* (1942) and the one-volume precis of the *Diaries of Theodor Herzl* (1956). He translated and edited *Memoirs of Glueckel of Hameln* (1932) and a one-volume abridgment of Montaigne's *Autobiography* (1935).

BIBLIOGRAPHY: C. Madison, in: JBL, 28 (1970/71).

[Leo W. Schwarz]

LOWEY, NITA MELNIKOFF (1937–), U.S. congresswoman representing parts of Westchester and Rockland counties in the state of New York. Lowey, who was first elected to the House of Representatives in 1988, was the first woman and the first New Yorker to chair the Democratic Campaign Committee (2001–2002). The daughter of Beatrice and Jack Melnikoff,

Lowey was born in the Bronx, New York. She attended the Bronx High School of Science and Mount Holyoke College (B.A., 1959). She and her husband, attorney Stephen Lowey, had three children. They were active philanthropically in the New York City region Jewish community and were synagogue members.

In Congress Lowey was a member of the powerful House Appropriations Committee, and the ranking Democrat on the Foreign Operations, Export Financing, and Related Programs subcommittee. She was described as an extremely effective, committed, and influential legislator who "maneuvered skillfully through the appropriations process" so that she could successfully help New York. Lowey took a key position promoting a strong U.S./Israel relationship and was a leading advocate for the annual U.S. aid package for Israel. Additionally, she fought for and secured $50 million to help Israel resettle refugees from the former Soviet Union. Domestically, Lowey supported educational opportunity, school modernization, teacher development, and literacy programs, as well as support. On the Appropriations Committee she successfully pushed for increased federal investments in biomedical research on cancer, diabetes, and Alzheimer's disease and authored the first bill that mandated clear, concise food allergen labeling.

On the Select Committee on Homeland Security, Lowey advocated federalizing air and nuclear security and increasing port and rail security. She helped secure over $20 billion for the recovery of New York after the September 11, 2001, terrorist attacks and has supported a variety of anti-terror measures.

BIBLIOGRAPHY: A.J. Wall, "Lowey, Nita M.," in: Paula E. Hyman and D. Dash Moore (eds.), *Jewish Women in America: An Historical Encyclopedia*, 1(1997), 897.

[Judith Friedman Rosen (2nd ed.)]

LOWICZ (Pol. **Łowicz**), town in the province of Lodz, central Poland. The Jews began to settle there at the beginning of the 16th century. In 1516 they were expelled by Archbishop Jan Laski and established themselves in the surrounding towns. Until 1797 the presence of Jews in Lowicz was authorized only on market days and during fairs. At the regional church synod held in Lowicz in 1556 it was decided to inflict severe punishment on four Jews of *Sochaczew who had been accused of *Host desecration. At the close of the 16th and during the 17th centuries Jewish merchants played an important role in the Lowicz fairs. From the beginning of the 19th century the Jewish population of the town increased rapidly. The 60 Jews (2.5% of the population) who lived in Lowicz in 1808 earned their livelihood mainly as innkeepers and craftsmen. With the renewal of the Lowicz fairs in 1820 much of the trade in the town was in Jewish hands. In 1827 the Jewish community of Lowicz numbered 405 (11% of the population). In 1829 a wooden synagogue was erected; the local Jewish cemetery was founded in the early 1830s. In 1897 the construction of the Great Synagogue was completed. During the years 1828–62 the Jews were allowed to live only in the Jewish quarter. In the course of time Ḥasidism gained influence in the community. In 1863 some Lowicz Jews contributed funds to the Polish rebels and collaborated with them in smuggling arms.

The Jewish population increased from 1,161 in 1857 (21% of the population) to 3,552 in 1897 (35% of the total). Their principal sources of livelihood were shopkeeping, trade with the neighboring peasants and the soldiers of the local Russian military camp, and crafts. A considerable part of the Jewish poor was employed in the textile, stocking, and food manufacturing industries. Under the influence of the *Bund, Jewish workers and students participated in the revolutionary incidents which took place in Lowicz in 1905. From the beginning of the century Zionist groups were organized. At the end of 1914 there were Jewish victims and severe damage to property as a result of the battles which were fought in the town and its vicinity. In 1917 six Jewish delegates were elected to the municipal council, forming half of its membership. In 1921 there were 4,517 Jews (30% of the total population) in Lowicz. In the interwar period CYSHO (Central Yiddish School Organization) and Beth Jacob schools functioned. From 1935 to 1939 the weekly *Mazovsher Vokhenblat* was published in Lowicz. In 1931, 4,339 Jews (25% of the total population) lived in the town. In 1933 anti-Jewish riots occurred, which were repelled by the Jewish *self-defense.

[Arthur Cygielman]

Holocaust Period

On the outbreak of World War II there were about 4,500 Jews in Lowicz. The German army entered the town on Sept. 9, 1939. That day all Jewish males were ordered to assemble in the market place. They were imprisoned in the synagogue and tortured for two days. During 1940 about 3,500 Jews from the towns of Lodz province, which had been incorporated into the Third Reich, were forced to settle in Lowicz. In May 1940 a ghetto was established there. On June 17, 1941, a decree forbidding Jews to live in the town or country of Lowicz was issued. All the Jews were transferred to the *Warsaw ghetto and shared the plight of Warsaw Jewry. No Jewish community has been rebuilt in Lowicz.

[Stefan Krakowski]

BIBLIOGRAPHY: B. Wasiutyński, *Ludność żydowska w Polsce w wiekach XIX i XX* (1930), 20, 45, 70, 75; W. Tarczyński, *Łowicz, wiadomości historyczne* (1899); I. Schiper, *Dzieje handlu żydowskiego na ziemiach polskich* (1937), index; *Lowicz, A shtat in Mazovie* (1966). HOLOCAUST: T. Brustin-Bernstein, in: BŻIH, 1 (1952), 83–125.

LOWIE, ROBERT HARRY (1883–1957), U.S. anthropologist. Born in Vienna, Lowie was taken to the U.S. and educated in New York. He studied anthropology under Franz *Boas, and served two institutions, the American Museum of Natural History (1907–17) and the University of California at Berkeley (1917–50). He did field work among various American Indian tribes, especially the Crows. His early interest in comparative mythology led to his publishing several works, notably *Primitive Society* (1920) and *Primitive Religion* (1924). Lowie's contribution to anthropology was widely recognized and he edited the *American Journal of Anthropology*. During World War II he taught an "area" course on Germany and this experience, combined with ethnographical field trips, led to his publication of *The German People – a Social Portrait to 1914* (1945), and *Towards Understanding Germany* (1954), which assessed the impact of the war on the German personality. Though generally a follower of the Boas school, which insisted on the scientific method, Lowie contended that more importance ought to be allotted to the biological factor in accounting for differences among individuals as well as groups. He also resisted Freudian generalizations, and envisaged the possibility of applying correlation techniques to culture variables. In his ethnographical studies Lowie was concerned to illuminate the interaction between social organization, religion, and folklore. He has been considered by some the precursor of structural anthropology.

[Ephraim Fischoff]

LOWINSKY, EDWARD ELIAS (1908–1985), U.S. musicologist. Lowinsky was born in Stuttgart, Germany. In 1934, after the Nazi rise to power, he immigrated to the United States. He taught at the University of California at Berkeley and at the University of Chicago, where he initiated an entire generation of scholars, and in 1961 was appointed Ferdinand Schevill Distinguished Service Professor. His research in the music of the Renaissance represented a significant breakthrough; from 1964 to 1977 he was the general editor of the series Monuments of Renaissance Music. Lowinsky is considered one of the major figures of postwar musicology. His numerous publications include major critical editions and innovative historical and stylistic observations. Among his important publications are *Tonality and Atonality in Sixteenth Century Music* (1961), *The Medici Codex of 1518* (1968), *Cipriano da Rore's Venus Motet: Its Poetic and Pictorial Sources* (1986), and *Music in the Culture of Renaissance and Other Essays* (ed. Bonnie Blackburn, 1989).

BIBLIOGRAPHY: Grove online; MGG²; L. Finscher, "*Zu den Schriften Edward E. Lowinsky*," in: *Musikforschung* 15 (1962), 54–77.

[Jehoash Hirshberg and Amnon Shiloah (2nd ed.)]

LOWN, PHILIP W. (1890–1978), U.S. shoe manufacturer and philanthropist. Lown arrived in New York in 1907, later attending the University of Maine and obtaining a degree in chemical engineering (1918). Lown went into shoe manufacturing, eventually heading Lown Shoes Inc. (from 1933) and Penobscot Shoe Co. Settling in Lewiston, Maine, in 1935, he became active in civic and Jewish communal affairs, especially educational. Lown served as a longtime board member, vice president, and president of the American Association for Jewish Education from 1950 on, and was one of the leading philanthropists of Jewish education in the United States. He endowed a chair in Jewish philosophy at Brandeis University and founded the Lown School of Near Eastern and Judaic Studies. He was president of the Hebrew Teachers' College of Brookline, Massachusetts, from 1962 and vice president of the American Friends of the Hebrew University. He served as a national cabinet member of the UJA from 1950 and was treasurer of the Combined Jewish Philanthropies of Boston. A jubilee volume edited by Judah Pilch was published in his honor in 1967.

The Philip W. Lown School of Near Eastern and Judaic Studies, established at Brandeis University in 1953, is the center for teaching and research programs in the areas of Judaic studies, ancient Near Eastern studies, Islamic and modern Middle Eastern studies, and Jewish communal studies. The Hebrew College of Brookline has established the Philip W. Lown Medal for Distinguished Service to Jewish education and culture in the United States.

°LOWTH, ROBERT (1710–1787), Hebraist. Appointed professor of poetry at Oxford in 1741, Lowth devoted a series of 34 Latin lectures to the literary qualities of biblical poetry. Originally published as *Praelectiones de sacra poesi Hebraeorum* (Oxford, 1753), these were translated into English as *Lectures on the Sacred Poetry of the Hebrews* (London, 1787). Lowth was the first modern scholar to formulate the theory of parallelism as the metrical basis of biblical Hebrew poetry, a discovery which had been partially anticipated in the 16th century by Azariah de *Rossi, whom Lowth quoted. Renaissance scholars, relying on classical and contemporary verse forms, had tried unsuccessfully to scan poetic passages in the Bible as though they were classical hexameters, but Lowth showed that Hebrew poetry was fundamentally antiphonal, the latter part of each verse echoing the idea of the first by corroboration or contrast – "The mountains skipped like rams/the hills like children of the flock." His translation of the Book of Isaiah (1778) was also original in biblical translation, distinguishing between the prose and poetry of the original Hebrew. Lowth is notable for having stressed the sublimity of Old Testament literature and the vividness of its imagery in an era of prudery and circumlocution. He was bishop of Oxford 1766–67 and thereafter bishop of London.

BIBLIOGRAPHY: S.H. Monk, *The Sublime* (1935); M. Roston, *Prophet and Poet* (1965). **ADD. BIBLIOGRAPHY:** R. Marrs, in: DBI, 2, 89–90.

[Murray Roston]

LOWY, FRANK (1930–), Australian businessman. Born in Czechoslovakia, Lowy survived the Holocaust in Hungary before fighting for the Israeli army in the War of Independence. In 1952 he migrated to Sydney, Australia, where, with fellow Jewish migrant and long-time business partner John Saunders, he opened a delicatessen in a Sydney suburb. In 1959 Lowy and Saunders opened one of Australia's first suburban shopping centers, Westfield Plaza in Blacktown, Sydney. Westfield Holdings Ltd. grew into one of the most important retailers in Australia, developing a string of shopping centers around the country. By the 1990s Lowy had become one of the richest men in Australia, and in 2004 was credited with a fortune of $4.2 billion (about US $4 billion), ranked jointly as the second largest private fortune in that year's Australian "rich list." In 2001 he bought out nine shopping malls in the United States and also owned six shopping centers in Great Britain. Worth US $18 billion in 2004, the Westfield Group, as it was known, was the largest shopping center owner in the world. Lowy was also chairman of the Australian Soccer Association.

BIBLIOGRAPHY: BRW (*Business Review Weekly, Melbourne*) "Rich 200" (May 20–26, 2004), 114; R. Ostrow, *The New Boy Network: Taking Over Corporate Australia* (1987), 65–67; W.D. Rubinstein, Australia II, 361.

[William D. Rubinstein (2nd ed.)]

LOYTER, EFRAIM BARUKHOVICH (1889–1963), Russian theater director and teacher. Born in Berdichev, Loyter began his career in 1906 as a theater critic in Vilna newspapers. He also published Yiddish stories. He was close to the *Zionist-Socialist party. During World War I he was a representative in Central Russia of EKOPO, the Jewish Committee to Help War Victims. Together with L. Sobol, he edited the literary anthology *Yevreyskiy mir* ("Jewish World," Moscow, 1918).

Loyter was one of the heads and directors of the Jewish theatrical studio of the Kiev Culture League (Kiev-Moscow, 1919–24) where with a group of actors whom he had trained he staged plays by I.L. Peretz, Shalom Aleichem, Peretz Hirshbein, and others. He studied directing in Moscow with Y. Vakhtangov and C.Y. Meyerhold. In Baku in 1924–25 he headed the Workers' Theater and the Jewish theatrical studio. In 1925–28 he was director of the State Jewish Theater of the Ukraine where he staged *Purimspiel* and also *Vognye* ("In the Fire") by M. *Daniel and Loyter; *Two Kuni Lemels* by A. *Goldfaden, and other works. In 1929 in Moscow together with S. *Mikhoels he established a theatrical studio, teaching there (until 1935) and also at the Teaching-Theater Center (from 1933 to 1935). From 1935 to 1941 and 1945 to 1949 he was artistic director of the Odessa Jewish Theater where he staged, among other plays, Maxim Gorky's *Mother* (1938) and *Wandering Stars* (1940) by Shalom Aleichem. Loyter also directed plays in Russian and Ukrainian. During World War II, he was evacuated to Tashkent. During this time he staged plays in Uzbekistan (and was awarded the title of Honored Artist of the Uzbek SSR, in 1943) and Tadzhikistan. He wrote a book in Russian, *Slovo na stsene I estrade* ("Word on Stage and on the Boards," 1954), and an introduction to the anthology he compiled *Slovo na stsene* ("Word on Stage," 1958).

His brother NACHUM LOYTER (1891–1966) was also a theatrical director. In 1919 he studied at the theater studio of the Kiev Culture League and in 1922 graduated from the State Higher Directors' Workshop. From 1925 to 1929 he was the director of the Moscow Prolet-cult (Proletarian Culture) Theater. From 1930 he headed the State Jewish Theater of the Ukraine in Kharkov, from 1936, the Odessa Jewish Theater, and from 1937 the Kiev Jewish Theater. From 1940 to 1957 N. Loyter worked in the Y. Kolas Belorussian Theater, first in Vitebsk, then in evacuation in Uralsk. He was awarded the title of Honored Art Worker of the Belorussian SSR in 1945 and a Stalin Prize in 1946.

[Mark Kipnis / *The Shorter Jewish Encyclopaedia in Russian*]

LOZINSKI, SAMUEL (1874–1945), Russian historian. Born in Bobruisk, Belarus, he studied in the universities of Berlin, Paris, and St. Petersburg. In the years 1904–06 he was redactor of the foreign department of the newspaper *Kievskiye Otkliki* ("Kiev Echo"). Lozinski specialized in the history of Western Europe, writing studies on the modern history of France, Austria, Holland, and Belgium. He collaborated in editing and translating standard historical works into Russian, including E. Renan's *Histoire du peuple d'Israël* and H.C. Lea's *History of the Inquisition of Spain*. He also did research in Jewish history and edited the sections on Jewish culture in Europe and the history of the Jews in France and England in the Russian-Jewish encyclopedia (*Yevreyskaya Entsiklopediya*). Under the Soviet regime, Lozinski lectured in history at the universities of Leningrad, Minsk, Rostov, and other cities. During the 1920s he belonged to the small circle which was active in Jewish historical research under the conditions of the new regime. He edited a collection of documents, *Kazyonnye yevreyskiye uchilishcha* ("Jewish Governmental Schools," 1920), and co-edited the collections *Yevreyskaya Starina* and *Yevreyskaya Letopis*. To antisemitism he dedicated the work "The social roots of antisemitism in medieval and modern times" (1929). He also engaged in research on the history of the Church. His two works *Svyataya Inkvizitsiya* ("The Holy Inquisition," 1927) and *Istoriya Papstva* ("History of the Papacy," 1934) were published by the Academy of Sciences of the U.S.S.R.

BIBLIOGRAPHY: S. Lozinski, *Istoriya Papstva* (1961), preface; *Bobruisk* (Heb. and Yid., 1967), 521–2.

[Yehuda Slutsky]

LOZOVSKI (Dridzo), SOLOMON ABRAMOVICH (1878–1952), Soviet statesman and trade union leader. Born into a poor family in Danilovka, Yekaterinoslav province (today Dnepropetrovsk district, Ukraine), Lozovski went to work at the age of 11 and completed his studies on his own. He joined the Russian Social-Democratic Party in 1901 and in 1905 attached himself to the Bolshevik wing. Lozovski participated in the Revolution of 1905, and several times was arrested, but escaped. In 1909 he arrived in France where he was active in the socialist movement until 1917. Lozovski returned to Russia following the outbreak of the February Revolution and was immediately elected secretary of the Trade Union Council. His opposition to Lenin's policies during and after the October Revolution led to his expulsion from the party in March 1918 and until December 1919, when he rejoined the Bolsheviks, he was a leader of the Internationalist Social-Democrats. From 1920 on, he was appointed to a series of important posts, serving as head of the Communist Trade Union International (Profintern; 1921–37), director of the state publishing house (1937–39), deputy commissar of foreign affairs (1939–46), and deputy director and later director, of the Soviet Information Bureau. From 1939 to 1949 he was a member of the central committee of the Communist Party.

In his capacity as head of the Soviet Information Bureau, Lozovski was responsible for the work of the Jewish *Anti-Fascist Committee and was concerned with world Jewish affairs. It is believed that in 1944 he supported the plan to set up a Jewish autonomous settlement in the Crimea and that this led to his arrest in 1949, when the authorities began to liquidate Jewish culture in the Soviet Union. Lozovski was tried together with 24 other Jewish writers and intellectuals in July 1952, and was executed with them on August 12, 1952. He was posthumously rehabilitated in 1956.

BIBLIOGRAPHY: J.B. Salsberg, in: *Jewish Life* (Feb. 1957); I. Ehrenburg, *Memoirs 1921–1941* (1964), 498; vol. 2, p. 11, 120; H.E. Salisbury, *To Moscow and Beyond* (1960), 72; *Deyateli Sovetskogo Soyuza*, vol. 1, p. 333–7; *Bolshaya Sovetskaya Entsiklopediya*, 51 (1958²), 180; *Sovetskaya Litva* (March 30, 1963); *Sovetskaya Istoricheskaya Entsiklopediya*, 8 (1965), 760–1; *Voprosy istorii* KPSS, 10:7 (1966), 24.

[Benjamin Pinkus]

LOZOWICK, LOUIS (1892–1973), U.S. printmaker, painter, draftsman, and writer. Born Leib Lozowick in Russia, he changed his name to the more Anglicized Louis upon his arrival in America. At the age of nine he had lived with his brother in Kiev, where he attended secular school and took his first art classes at the Kiev Art School (1903–5). When his brother moved to the United States in 1906, Lozowick joined him in Newark, New Jersey.

After studying at the National Academy of Design in New York (1912–15) with the Jewish artist Leon Kroll and others, Lozowick went to Ohio State University, graduating Phi Beta Kappa in 1918. He served in the U.S. Army for a year before an extensive stay in Europe. Lozowick spent a year in Paris and then lived in Berlin for three years, befriending other Russian artists in Germany, including El *Lissitzky. With Lissitzky, Lozowick traveled to Moscow, where he became acquainted with Constructivist principles, gaining admiration for a machine aesthetic that highlighted the potential of the urban landscape. From 1919 to 1928 Lozowick made a series of canvases of ten American cities (e.g., *Minneapolis*, 1926–27, Hirshhorn Museum and Sculpture Garden, Washington, D.C.) rendered in a precisionist idiom. In 1923 Lozowick began making lithographs, often of the cities he had rendered in paint. He returned to America in 1924.

Lozowick worked on a series of pen and ink drawings of imagined technology called *Machine Ornaments* from 1922 to 1927. He incorporated three movable machine ornaments as the set design for the 1926 stage production of *Gas* in Chicago. The same year Lord and Taylor asked Lozowick to design the set for a fashion show and a window display. Again using the forms of his machine ornaments, Lozowick created larger-than-life Constructivist inspired architectonic backdrops.

He began to make drawings for the leftist periodical *New Masses* in the late 1920s. Around 1930 Lozowick admitted human figures into his art, often picturing laborers of the metropolis. His social imagery described injustices facing the workers as well as others; the lithograph *Lynching* (1936) was included in the 1936 American Artists' Congress print exhibition "America Today." Lozowick also worked as a New Deal artist (1934–37), designing two works for New York City's post office on 33rd street and several lithographs.

Later in life Lozowick moved away from Cubist-inspired industrial subjects. With a more supple line and sometimes increased color, Lozowick made increasingly realistic prints. Trips to Israel in 1954, 1964, and 1968 produced several images of the land. On a commission from the United Jewish Appeal, Lozowick executed a lithograph of a pious Jew in synagogue entitled *Lone Worshipper* (1966).

A prolific writer, Lozowick wrote *Modern Russian Art* (1925) and a monograph on William *Gropper; he contributed art criticism to several magazines, including *The Menorah Journal*. His autobiography, *Survivor from a Dead Age*, was published posthumously.

BIBLIOGRAPHY: J. Flint, *The Prints of Louis Lozowick: A Catalogue Raisonné (1982); L. Lozowick, Survivor from a Dead Age: The Memoirs of Louis Lozowick (1997).*

[Samantha Baskind (2nd ed.)]

LUBACZOW (Pol. **Łubaczów**), town in Rzeszow province, S.E. Poland. Jews are mentioned in Lubaczow as early as 1498. When confirming the municipal rights of the town in 1523, King Sigismund I granted a privilege according to which the Jews were forbidden to trade in the surrounding villages. In 1562 only two Jewish houses were mentioned in Lubaczow; there were three Jewish houses in the first half of the 17th century, but in 1662 there were no Jews at all, probably a result of the Swedish wars and the wars against the Cossacks (in 1655 the town was burned down by the Cossacks). In 1717 the Jews of Lubaczow paid 560 zlotys poll tax, 425 in 1719, and 500 in 1721; in addition they were to pay the king a yearly "kettle tax" of 1,200 zlotys, and for cattle slaughtering the shoulder blade duty (*łopatkowe*). In 1765 the community of Lubaczow together with the townlet of Potylicz and surrounding villages numbered 687 poll tax payers. In 1880 the community numbered 1,503 (34% of the total population), 1,911 in 1900, 2,171 in 1910, and 1,715 (32%) in 1921. At that time Lubaczow had 106 Jewish workshops, 33 of which had salaried workers.

Holocaust Period

Before the outbreak of World War II there were about 2,300 Jews in Lubaczow. The majority of them were deported in the autumn of 1942 to *Belzec death camp. The remaining Jews were exterminated on Jan. 6, 1943. After the war, the Jewish community of Lubaczow was not reconstituted.

BIBLIOGRAPHY: J. Kleczyński and F. Kluczycki, *Liczba głow żydowskich w Koronie z taryf 1765 r.* (1898); A. Prochaska, *Materyały archiwalne* (1899), no. 217; E. Heller (ed.), *Żydowskie przedsiębiorstwa przemysłowe w Polsce…*, 6 (1923); B. Wasiutyński, *Ludność żydowska w Polsce…* (1930), 114; Yad Vashem Archives.

[Raphael Mahler]

LUBARSKY, ABRAHAM ELIJAH (1856–1920), early member of Ḥovevei Zion (*Hibat Zion) in Russia. Born in Balta, Ukraine, Lubarsky was engaged in business. From 1893 he was agent for Wissotsky Tea in Odessa and traveled throughout the large communities in Russia, making connections with the prominent figures in Hebrew and Yiddish literature in the late 19th century. He was especially close with *Aḥad Ha-Am, whom he stimulated to write his famous first essay, *Lo Zeh ha-Derekh*. Lubarsky was one of the first members of the secret society *Benei Moshe and influenced K.Z. *Wissotsky to support the Hebrew monthly *Ha-Shiloʾaḥ*. He contributed to the Hebrew press throughout this period. In 1903 he immigrated to the United States, where he became the moving spirit of the Hebrew movement. Lubarsky was a founder there of the Histadrut Ivrit and its newspaper, *Ha-Toren*.

BIBLIOGRAPHY: P. Friedman, in: *Haaretz* (Oct. 21, 1920); Epstein, *ibid.* (Oct. 9, 1931); *Sefer ha-Congress* (1950^2), 374–5.

[Yehuda Slutsky]

LUBARTOW (Pol. **Lubartów**; Rus. **Lyubartov**), town in Lublin province, E. Poland. The poll tax paid by the Jewish community rose from 1,500 zlotys in 1717 to 2,400 zlotys in 1736. In 1765 there were 764 Jewish poll tax payers. The community also had jurisdiction over 217 Jews in the neighboring villages and 37 Jews in the townlet of Kamionka. Among the 218 heads of families were 14 contractors, 20 merchants, 34 tailors, 5 hatters, and 9 carters. The community maintained two synagogues and a *mikveh*; 164 houses were owned by Jews. In 1796 the owner of the town granted the Jews a privilege defining the status of the *kahal* and the Jewish craftsmen's guilds. Among the town's wealthiest Jews were the merchant family *Peretz and the chief contractor, Solomon Kosiowicz. In the first half of the 19th century the Jews were allowed to keep taverns only with the permission of the local overlord. The community numbered 2,074 (58% of the total population) in 1827; 1,820 (56%) in 1857; 2,623 (53%) in 1897; and 3,269 (54%) in 1921. In that year there were 176 Jewish workshops in the town, about half of them employing salaried workers.

Holocaust Period

About 3,500 Jews lived in Lubartow before World War II. In November 1939 over 2,500 Jews were ordered to leave the town and settle in Parczew and Ostrow. Most of them came back within a year. In May 1942 about 1,000 Jews from Slovakia were deported to Lubartow. On Oct. 11, 1942, Jews from Lubartow were deported to the Sobibor and Belzec death camps. Near Lubartow two Jewish partisan units were active for more than a year, under the command of Samuel Jegier and Mietek Gruber.

BIBLIOGRAPHY: Halpern, Pinkas, index; R. Mahler, *Yidn in Amolikn Poyln in Likht fun Tsifern* (1958), index; B. Wasiutyński, *Ludność żydowska w Polsce w Polsce w wiekach XIX i XX* (1930), 34, 62, 72; J. Bartyś, in: *Bleter far Geshikhte*, 8:3–4 (1955), 88–105; *Die juedischen industriellen Unternehmungen in Polen* (1921); *Khurbn Lubartow: A Matseyve…* (1947).

[*Encyclopaedia Judaica* (Germany)]

LUBAVICH (Lyubavichi), small town in Smolensk district, Russia; until 1917 it was in Mogilev province (gubernia), Belorussia. The Jewish population numbered 1,164 in 1847 and 1,660 (67.3% of the total) in 1897. Lubavich became the center of *Chabad Ḥasidism in Lithuania, Belorussia, and the eastern Ukraine after Dov Ber, the son of the founder of the *Chabad system, *Shneour Zalman of Lyady, moved from Lyady to Lubavich in 1813. His nephew and son-in-law Menahem Mendel (the "*Ẓemaḥ-Ẓedek*") extended the influence of the dynasty (see *Schneersohn). The Jews in the town mainly earned their livelihood from the flax trade, and in providing for the many Ḥasidim who visited their "rabbi" there. His grandson Shalom Baer established the yeshivah Tomekhei Temimim in 1897 in Lubavich. He left Lubavich in 1915, but the name of the town remained connected with the Chabad movement (the "Lubavich Ḥasidim"). After the 1917 Revolution the town's economy declined and the Jews suffered from persecution by the *Yevsektsiya. In 1926 there were only 967 Jews in Lubavich (50% of the total population). Of the 205 families living then, 43 were in engaged in agriculture, 80 in crafts, and 27 in trade, and the others unemployed. In 1939 the number of Jews dropped to a couple of hundred. The Germans entered the town on July 21 or 22, 1941, and a few days later a group of working Jews was executed. In November 1941 a ghetto was organized and refugees from Vitebsk and Rudnia were brought there. The ghetto's 483 inhabitants were soon murdered outside the town.

BIBLIOGRAPHY: Z. Har-Shefer, in: *He-Avar*, 2 (1954), 86–93; B. Dinur, *Be-Olam she-Shaka* (1958), 145–55; M. Fainsod, *Smolensk under Soviet Rule* (1958), 441–3.

[Yehuda Slutsky]

LUBETKIN, ZIVIA (1914–1978), founder of Jewish Fighting Organization (ZOB), fighter in the Warsaw Ghetto Uprising. Born in Beten, near Slonim, Zivia Lubetkin was a member of the Zionist labor youth movement Deror and a representative of *He-Ḥalutz on the National Jewish Council. She married Itzhak *Zuckerman (Cukierman). In the summer of 1939, she attended the Zionist Congress in Basle and returned to Poland in September. During the time of the German invasion she found herself in the Soviet zone of occupied Poland and made her way back to Warsaw, where she was part of the underground. After witnessing the deportations of the summer of 1942, when more than 265,000 Jews were shipped from Warsaw to Treblinka between July 23 and September 12 without resistance, she was one of the organizers of the Jewish Fighting Organization, the ZOB. She participated in the first armed resistance to the Germans in January 1943. At the time of the Warsaw Ghetto Uprising (April 1943), she was among the fighters in the central ghetto while her husband was one of the leaders of the revolt, operating on the Aryan side. On May 8, 1943, after the main bunker at Mila 18, which housed the command of the Jewish fighters' organization headed by Mordecai *Anilewicz, fell, Lubetkin escaped from the ghetto with the other surviving fighters through the sewage system. There had been no advanced planning for an escape route and the escape through the sewers was improvised by Simcha Rotem ("Kazik"). Upon arriving on the Aryan side the two clashed, as Lubetkin wanted to wait for other Jews hiding in the sewers and Kazik insisted that they leave rather than risk apprehension by the Germans. In August of the same year, she and her husband sent Isaac Schwarzbart, a member of the Polish National Council in London, a telegram that reported the results of the revolt in the ghetto, called for help, and included a warning to the Jews of Western Europe of the fate awaiting them after deportation to Poland. Zivia Lubetkin fought with the partisans and participated in the Polish revolt of October 1944, together with other survivors of the Warsaw uprising. After Poland was liberated from German occupation by the Soviet army in January 1945, Zivia Lubetkin settled in Palestine. She and her husband were among the founders of kibbutz *Loḥamei ha-Getta'ot, which built a memorial and museum to the ghetto fighters. They were active in the ghetto fighters' organization in Israel. As a member of the executive of *Kibbutz ha-Me'uḥad, she was appointed to the Executive of the *Jewish Agency (1966–68). In her testimony at the *Eichmann trial, she described the Warsaw Ghetto Uprising. A compilation of Lubetkin's extemporaneous speeches, *Days of Destruction and Revolt*, was published in 1979.

BIBLIOGRAPHY: Y. Cukierman and M. Basok (eds.), *Sefer Milḥamot ha-Getta'ot…* (1954), index; *Ha-Yo'eẓ ha-Mishpati la-Memshalah Neged Adolf Eichmann: Eduyyot*, 1 (1963), 242–61; N. Blumenthal and J. Kermisz, *Ha-Meri ve-ha-Mered be-Getto Varshah* (1965). **ADD. BIBLIOGRAPHY:** Z. Lubetkin, *In the Days of Destruction and Revolt* (1980); M. Sirkin, "The Passing of a Heroine," in: *Midstream* (October 1978).

[B. Mordechai Ansbacher / Michael Berenbaum (2nd ed.)]

LUBETZKY, JUDAH (1850–1910), French rabbi. Lubetzky was born in Russia. He went to Paris in 1880 and was appointed rabbi of the Eastern European Jews there the following year and a member of the Paris *bet din* in 1904. He published his edition of parts of the *Sefer ha-Hashlamah* of Meshullam b. Moses of Béziers from a manuscript in the Paris library of Baron *Guenzburg, together with his own commentary, entitled *Torat ha-Hashlamah*, and an introduction giving the biography of Meshullam and of other Provençal scholars (3 vols., 1885–1910). In 1896 he published *Bidkei Battim*, comprising: (1) notes and amendments to the *Sefer ha-Hashlamah* on tractates *Berakhot, Ta'anit, Yevamot*, and *Megillah*, with a biographical introduction on some Provençal rabbis; (2) Meshullam's criticism of Maimonides' laws of *Eruvin* and *Shevu'ot*, from a manuscript, with Lubetzky's own notes; (3) a critique of Mordecai Horowitz with regard to the *Cleves *get*.

Lubetzky became famous for the vigorous stand he took against the proposal to introduce a conditional clause into Jewish marriages in France, with the aim of making civil divorce effective in the dissolution of Jewish marriages. The proposal was first made in 1885 and again in 1893. By his articles in the Hebrew periodicals and by enlisting the opposition of the great rabbis of the time he was successful in having it rejected. In 1907 an assembly of French rabbis resolved to adopt the proposal. Lubetzky then collected the opinions of more than 400 eminent scholars and, supported by Baron Rothschild, succeeded in having the resolution rescinded. He prepared all the material relevant to the proposal for publication and sent it to Ḥayyim Ozer *Grodzinski. When the proposal was again raised, Grodzinski gave the material to Aaron D.A. Waronovski, who published it with the title, *Ein Tenai be-Nissu'in* (1930).

BIBLIOGRAPHY: Schapira, in: *Ha-Yehudi*, 14 (1910/11), nos. 35–36; *Der Israelit* (Sept. 29, 1910).

[Shlomoh Zalman Havlin]

LUBIN, ABRAHAM (1937–), *ḥazzan*. Lubin was born in London and immigrated to Israel in his youth. He sang in the Shirat Yisrael choir in Jerusalem with the cantor Zalman *Rivlin. In 1950 he returned to London and studied in Yeshivat Etz Haim and also furthered his studies in cantorial liturgy at Jews' College, and continued his musical studies, the culmination of which was his Doctor of Music degree *honoris causa* from the Jewish Theological Seminary. He settled in America in 1958 and from 1968 was cantor to the Rodfei Zedek congregation of Chicago. He was active in the Cantors' Assembly and also its president (1995–97), as well as an editor of the *Journal of Synagogue Music*. He published numerous articles and studies concerning the history of prayer and liturgy, including "The Influence of Jewish Music and Thought in Certain Works of Leonard *Bernstein." As a concert artist he was well versed in Hebrew, Israeli, and Yiddish songs and appeared in concert recitals throughout the United States, Europe, and Israel.

[Akiva Zimmerman / Raymond Goldstein (2nd ed.)]

LUBIN, ISADOR (1896–1978), U.S. economist. Born in Worcester, Massachusetts, Lubin received his Ph.D. in economics from the Brookings Institution (1926). He taught economics for a year at the University of Missouri (1917–18) and left to serve as statistician for the U.S. Food Administration, from which post he moved to the U.S. War Industries Board as a special expert. He returned to teaching in 1926, at the universities of Michigan and Missouri and Brookings Institute (1922–33). Subsequently, he served many public and semipublic institutions, including governmental agencies and the Allied Reparations Commission, the International Labor Organization, and the U.S. Mission to the United Nations.

In 1933 Lubin assumed the position of U.S. commissioner of the Bureau of Labor Statistics. He took part in drafting the National Industrial Recovery Act. He served as labor consultant on the Federal Emergency Administration of Public Works, advising on wages and projects (1933–39). A member of the President's Economic Security Committee (1934), he helped create the unemployment insurance section of the Social Security Act. He was also instrumental in getting the Fair Labor Standards Act passed in Congress in 1938. In 1940, President Franklin D. Roosevelt appointed Lubin deputy director of the labor division of the Office of Production Management. In 1941, he became FDR's economic assistant, in which capacity "his favorite economist" assembled and interpreted for the president the statistics on all war programs. From 1946 to 1951 Lubin was president and board chairman of the research organization Confidential Reports, Inc., and from 1950 chairman of the executive committee of the Franklin Delano Roosevelt Foundation.

Under President Truman, Lubin served as an assistant secretary of state for economic affairs (1949–1950) and advised on details of the Marshall Plan. From 1950 to 1953 he served as American minister to the United Nations Economic and Social Council. He subsequently served as New York State industrial commissioner under Governor Averell Harriman (1955–59).

In 1959–61 Lubin was professor of public affairs at Rutgers University. During the 1960s and 1970s he was a member of the board of directors of the New School for Social Research, consulted for the Twentieth Century Fund, and was consultant to the United Israel Appeal, Inc. (a U.S. body representing the Jewish Agency for Israel), in which capacity he paid frequent visits to Israel. He was also a member of the boards of the Weizmann Institute in Israel and Brandeis University.

Lubin's publications include *The British Coal Dilemma* (1927), *The British Attack on Unemployment* (with A.C.C. Hill, 1934), and *Our Stake in World Trade* (with F.D. Murden, 1954), all of which reflect his interests in labor economics, economic development, and trade policy.

[Joachim O. Ronall / Ruth Beloff (2nd ed.)]

LUBIN, SIMON JULIUS (1876–1936), U.S. economist, business executive, and public servant. Lubin, who was born in Sacramento, California, entered the Sacramento firm of Weinstock, Lubin & Company after his graduation from Harvard in 1903 and rose to become its president. Lubin drafted the California State Immigration and Housing Law and in 1913 Governor Hiram Johnson named him to head the California State Commission of Immigration and Housing. In that position he strove to improve conditions among migrant farm workers. In 1934 Lublin was appointed to a National Labor Board commission to settle agricultural strife in California's Imperial Valley. Lubin also was consultant to the California Emergency Relief Administration; founder (1926) and president of the Sacramento Region Citizens Council; and founder (1931) and president of the Pan-American Institute of Reciprocal Trade. Although a Republican, he vigorously supported much of the New Deal.

LUBITSCH, ERNST (1892–1947), film producer and director. Lubitsch was born in Berlin and gained early acting experience in Max *Reinhardt's troupe. From 1913 he played comic parts in the movies, creating the role of "Meyer" or "Moritz" (archetypical Jewish names in Germany), the butt of good-natured low comedy in a series of successful films. Lubitsch progressed from actor to director and from 1914 to 1917 made many slapstick comedies. Having been persuaded to make serious motion pictures, he produced several successful films which brought Pola Negri to the screen. In 1922 he moved to Los Angeles to direct *Rosita* with Mary Pickford. Many other successes followed, but Lubitsch really made his name with the advent of the "talkies," and especially with his film *The Love Parade* (1929), which starred Maurice Chevalier and Jeanette MacDonald. Lubitsch was a master of subtle humor which, when combined with fanciful situations, came to be regarded as the "Lubitsch touch." His pictures had a zany, implausible quality which appealed to millions of film-goers. His later successes included *The Smiling Lieutenant* (1931); *Trouble in Paradise* (1932); *The Merry Widow* (1934); and *Ninotchka* (1939), starring Greta Garbo.

BIBLIOGRAPHY: H.G. Weinberg, *The Lubitsch Touch* (1968), incl. bibl.; A. Sarris (ed.), *Interviews with Film Directors* (1967), 281–5; L. Jacobs, *The Rise of the American Film* (1939), index.

[Stewart Kampel]

LUBLIN, city in E. Poland, center of the district of the same name. In the 16th and 17th centuries Lublin was famous for its fairs (see Market Days and *Fairs). Annexed by Austria in 1795, it was incorporated in Russian Poland in 1815. From 1918 to 1939 it was in Poland and from 1939 to 1945 under German occupation; after World War II it was again in Poland.

Jews were first mentioned as transients in Lublin in 1316. The city denied Jews the right to settle there on the basis of its privilege *de non tolerandis Judaeis*. In 1336 King Casimir III permitted them to settle on land adjacent to the city, later known as Piaski Żydowskie ("Jewish sands"). Josko (Joseph) Sheinowicz, a rich tax-farmer for southeast Poland, built a house in Lublin in 1500. Later King Sigismund I permitted Jews to found a settlement in the vicinity of the castle, afterward known as Podzamcze. In the second half of the 16th century the community was given land for its institutions and for a cemetery. The Jews were allowed to set up movable stalls for shops but not to erect buildings. In 1602 there were 2,000 Jews in Lublin. The population figures did not change greatly until the second half of the 18th century; in 1787 there were 4,321 Jews in the city. Tension with the citizenry continued, largely centered around the right of the Jews to live within the city walls. Jews settled mainly in houses belonging to clergymen and feudal lords, who were outside the jurisdiction of the city council, paying them substantial sums for the privilege. They were very active at the Lublin fairs, engaged in local trade, and some were tailors, furriers, manufacturers of brushes, brewers, and bakers, despite the bitter opposition of the Christian merchants and artisans. The rivalry between the Christian and Jewish tailors ended in 1805 when a united guild was founded. In 1780 King Stanislaus II (Poniatowski) ordered the expulsion of the Jews from Lublin. As a result of the intervention of Jewish leaders the expulsion did not take place until 1795, when Lublin was annexed by Austria.

Tensions in the 16th to 18th centuries were aggravated whenever the Polish High Court convened in Lublin, especially when trying a *blood libel case. The court hearings were then followed by attacks on the Jews; some were murdered and their property stolen. If the High Court sentenced the accused Jew to death the execution usually took place on a Saturday in front of the Maharshal Shul synagogue, and elders of the *kehillah* and other Jews had to attend. An execution was often followed by an attack on the Jewish quarter. Like the whole of Jewry in Poland-Lithuania, Lublin Jews suffered greatly during the *Chmielnicki uprisings in 1648–49. Another period of hardship followed in the second half of the 18th century with the disintegration of the Polish state.

In spite of hardships, the fairs and yeshivah of Lublin became central in Jewish communal and cultural life in Poland (see *Councils of the Lands). The first known rabbi of Lublin was Jacob b. Joseph *Pollak; *Shalom Shakhna b. Joseph was nominated by the king of Poland in 1541 as rabbi for Lublin and district. Other rabbis were Solomon b. Jehiel *Luria, in office for 15 years; Mordecai b. Abraham *Jaffe; and Meir b. Gedaliah *Lublin, known in halakhic literature as Maharam of Lublin. Lublin communal institutions included a well-organized *ḥevra kaddisha* and a "preacher's house" which provided visiting preachers with food and lodging. The fortified Maharshal Shul, the most famous synagogue in Lublin, was built in 1567. It burned down in the great fire of 1655 but was later rebuilt.

In the 16th century Lublin had several well-known physicians. At the beginning of the century the king of Poland exempted one, Ezekiel, from various taxes in recognition of his services. Another famous physician of that century was Solomon Luria, author of a medical treatise. Physicians in Lublin in the 17th century were Samuel b. Mattathias, Moses Montalto, and Ḥayyim Felix Vitalis, who graduated from Padua in 1658 and served as physician to the Polish king. During the 19th century Lublin became an important commercial center through the exploitation of the economic opportunities created by the vast Russian markets. The Jews expanded their wholesale commerce and their industrial establishments. One of the largest cigarette factories was founded by a Jew in 1860 and employed about 100 workers; 95% of the tanning industry was owned by Jews. The increased number of Jewish workers became an important factor in Jewish social life: workers' unions were established in various trades, and the first groups of the *Bund emerged at this time. In 1806 there were 2,973 Jews in Lublin, increasing to 8,747 (56% of the total population) in 1857. In 1862, just before the annulment of the prohibition on Jewish residence within the city, they numbered 10,413; by 1897 they had increased to 23,586.

*Ḥasidism played a prominent role in Lublin, mainly through the influence of the local *ẓaddikim*, such as *Jacob Isaac ha-Ḥozeh ("the seer") of Lublin, and the Eiger dynasty from the middle of the 19th century. At the same time some of the community rabbis strongly opposed the Ḥasidim, particularly Azriel Horovitz (late 18th century) and Joshua Heshel Ashkenazi who was nominated in 1852. As the latter was rich and economically independent he led the struggle against Ḥasidism without any regard for the opinions of the *kehillah* members. In the 19th century traditional education in the *ḥeder* and yeshivah continued, although Lublin lost its communal and cultural prominence with the abolition of the Councils of the Lands and the predominance of Ḥasidism. From the second half of the 19th century, the first Jewish schools with instruction in Russian or Polish were founded. In 1897 the first Hebrew school was opened.

In independent Poland there were no substantial changes in the occupational structure of the Jewish community but the percentage of Jews in the population decreased. In 1921 there were 37,337 Jews in the city (34.7% of the population as opposed to 50.9% in 1897). The numbers remained steady; 38,937 in 1931 and 37,830 in 1939 (according to the German census). Many Jewish workers were engaged in the *leather industry; in 1939 the biggest leather factory in the city belonged to a Jew and half the employees were Jews. Consequently the trade union of Jewish leather workers had a membership of above 500. In Lublin, as in the whole of Poland, the Jews suffered from the hatred of the Poles and the anti-Jewish policies adopted by independent Poland between the two world wars. In the 1930s attacks on Lublin Jews were led by students of the Lublin Catholic University, whose rector was the author of antisemitic pamphlets. Antisemitic propaganda was the main topic of the leading Polish newspaper in the city, *Głos Lubelski* ("Voice of Lublin").

In spite of this Lublin Jews led an active social and cultural life between the wars. Trade unions were influenced by the Bund and the Left Po'alei Zion. In the middle-class sector the Orthodox *Agudat Israel and the *Folkspartei – both anti-Zionist – were influential. Branches of all the Zionist parties were active. The focus of local political interest until 1936, except in the Bund, was the community organization. In education the traditional *ḥeder* system was joined by *Beth Jacob schools for girls and by an Orthodox Zionist Yavneh school. The secular Zionist *Tarbut Hebrew school had its first graduates in 1933. Cultural activities included dramatic societies, libraries, orchestras, and a sports organization. A Jewish daily, *Lubliner Togblat*, was published. The most famous yeshivah of that period in Lublin was the Yeshivah Ḥakhmei Lublin, founded by Meir *Shapira, rabbi from 1925 to 1933. After the death of Shapira a court of three *dayyanim* functioned instead of a rabbi.

[Shimshon Leib Kirshenboim]

Hebrew Printing

The wandering printer Ḥayyim Schwarz (Shaḥor), his son, and son-in-law went to Lublin around 1547, where they began printing, with periodically renewed privileges (1550, 1559, 1578). Their first productions were liturgical items, notably the *maḥzor* of 1550. With the help of *Eliezer b. Isaac (Ashkenazi) of Prague they brought out a fine Pentateuch in 1557, and a (complete?) Talmud edition (1559–77), partly printed in nearby Konsha Wolowie when the plague broke out in Lublin in 1559. With a fresh outbreak of the plague in 1592, the printers moved temporarily to Bistrowitz. Kalonymus b. Mordecai *Jaffe, who had married Ḥayyim Schwarz's granddaughter and whose name appears in the Pentateuch mentioned above, took over when Eliezer b. Isaac and his son left for Constantinople around 1573. Kalonymus managed the printing house till his death in about 1603, and it was continued (with interruptions) under his descendants to the end of the century and possibly beyond. A fire destroyed the plant and most of the books in 1647, but printing was resumed soon after. A great variety of works – liturgical, homiletical, and rabbinical – were issued there, among them Mordecai Jaffe's *Levushim* (1591–?), a Mishnah (1594–96), the Talmud (1611–39), the first editions of Samuel Edels' *Novellae* (1617), and the Zohar (1623–24). Jacob Hirschenhorn and Moses Schneidermesser opened a Hebrew printing press in 1875 (from 1910 Hirschenhorn and Streisenberg); Feder and Setzer were active from 1894; and M. Schneidermesser in the 1920s.

Holocaust Period

At the beginning of 1941 the Jewish population of Lublin was about 45,000, including some 6,300 refugees. The city was captured by the Germans on Sept. 18, 1939. In the very first days of the occupation, Jews were forcibly evicted from their apartments, physically assaulted, and put on forced labor. Some Jews were taken as hostages, and all the men were ordered to report to Lipowa Square, where they were beaten.

For a while, the Nazis entertained the idea of turning the Lublin district into a Jewish reservation for the concentration of the Jews from the German-occupied parts of Poland and other areas incorporated into the Reich. At the end of 1939 some 5,000 refugees arrived in Lublin, and another 1,300 came in February 1940 (from Stettin). The group from Stettin did not remain in Lublin. In April 1940 the plan of a Jewish reservation was officially discarded; at a later stage, Lublin became one of the centers for the mass extermination of Jews. For a while, the city was the scene of the activities of Odilo *Globocnik, commander of the police and the S.D. and head of "*Aktion Reinhardt*" (see *Poland, Holocaust Period).

The existing Jewish community council remained in office until Jan. 25, 1940, when the Judenrat was appointed. The composition of the Judenrat did not differ greatly from the former community council; it consisted of 24 members, most of them prewar political figures, and was headed by Henryk Bekker, an engineer. The outstanding leader in the Judenrat however, was its deputy chairman, Mark Alten, who later became its chairman, when the Judenrat was reconstituted, on March 31, 1942, and restricted to 12 members. During the first period of its existence, the Judenrat did not confine itself to the execution of Nazi orders (such as the provision of forced labor) but initiated a number of projects designed to alleviate the harsh conditions. Public kitchens were established and provided meals for the local poor and the refugees; the ghetto was divided into a number of units for the purpose of sanitary supervision, each unit run by a doctor and several medical assistants. There were also two hospitals with a total of over 500 beds and a quarantine area in the Maharshal Shul with 300 beds. Hostels were established to house abandoned children, but the Judenrat did not succeed in reestablishing the Jewish school system, and the schooling that was available to the children was carried on as a clandestine operation.

In March 1941 the Nazis ordered a partial evacuation of the Jews in preparation for the official establishment of the ghetto. About 10,000 Jews were driven out to villages and towns in the area in the period March 10–April 30, 1941, and at the end of March the ghetto was created, with a population of about 34,000. On April 24, 1941, exit from the ghetto was restricted.

At the beginning of 1942, when the extermination campaign entered its decisive stage, the Jews of Lublin were among its first victims. Their deportation began on March 16, and in its course 30,000 Jews were despatched to the death camp at *Belzec or were murdered on the way. The rate of deportation was fixed at 1,500 per day, and attempts by the Jews to hide were of no avail. The remaining 4,000 Jews were taken to Majdan Tatarski, where they lived for a few more months under unbearable conditions. On Sept. 2, 1942, 2,000 Jews were murdered, as were another 1,800 at the end of October. Some 200 survivors were sent to the *Majdanek death camp. Some Jews, who were skilled craftsmen, were still employed in Lublin, but in May 1943 the workshops were liquidated and the Jewish workers sent to Majdanek. Another 300 were kept in the Lublin Fortress, where they were employed in a few remaining workshops until July 1944, when they too were put to death a few days before the Nazis evacuated the city.

Lublin was also the site of a prisoner of war camp for Jews who had served in the Polish army. The first prisoners arrived in February 1940. Those who came from the area of the General Government were set free, but some 3,000, whose homes were in the Soviet-occupied area or in the districts incorporated into the Reich, remained in detention. The Judenrat tried to extend help to the prisoners, and there was also a public committee which provided the inmates with forged documents in order to enable them to leave the camp. When the Germans stepped up the extermination campaign, there were some attempts to escape from the camp, to which the Germans responded by imposing collective punishment upon the prisoners. Nevertheless, there were continued efforts to obtain arms, and some prisoners succeeded in escaping to the nearby forests, where they joined the partisans; some of the escaped prisoners assumed senior command posts in the partisan units. On Nov. 3, 1943, the last group of prisoners was deported to Majdanek.

[Aharon Weiss]

Contemporary Period

On July 24, 1944 the Red Army liberated Lublin. The next day Polish regular army and guerilla units entered the city. A few thousand Jewish soldiers served in those units, and among the guerillas was a Jewish partisan company under Captain Jechiel Grynszpan. Until the liberation of Warsaw in January 1945, Lublin served as the temporary Polish capital. During that time some Jewish cultural and social institutions were established there, among others the Central Committee of Polish Jews. Several thousand Jews, most of whom survived the Holocaust in the Soviet Union, settled in Lublin, but the majority of them left during the years 1946–50 due to the antisemitic attitude of a great part of the Polish population. A club of the Jewish Cultural Society was still functioning in the city until 1968, when all remaining Lublin Jews left Poland.

[Stefan Krakowski]

BIBLIOGRAPHY: S.B. Nissenbaum, *Le-Korot ha-Yehudim be-Lublin* (1900); M. Balaban, *Di Yidn-Shtot Lublin* (1947); N. Shemen, *Lublin, Shtot fun Torah, Rabones un Khasides* (1951); S. Wojciechowski, in: *Bleter far Geshikhte*, 7 pt. 1 (1952), 124–7; B. Mandelsberg-Schildkraut, *Meḥkarim be-Toledot Yehudei Lublin* (1965); Friedberg, in: *Yerushalayim*, ed. by J. Kreppel, 1:3 (1900), 95–104. HEBREW PRINTING: Ḥ.D. Friedberg, *Le-Toledot ha-Defus ha-Ivri be-Lublin* (1900); idem, *Toledot ha-Defus ha-Ivri be-Polanyah* (1950²); idem, in: *Ha-Ẓofeh*, 10 (1926), 282–5; Steinschneider-Cassel, *Juedische Typographie* (1938), 36ff. HOLOCAUST PERIOD: N. Blumental, *Te'udot mi-Getto Lublin* (1967), Eng. summary; EG, 5 (1957), Lublin volume; *Dos Bukh fun Lublin* (1952), memorial book.

LUBLIN, MEIR BEN GEDALIAH (Maharam of Lublin; 1558–1616), Polish talmudist and halakhic authority. His acronym, **MaHaRaM**, stands for **M**orenu **Ha-R**av **M**eir, "Our teacher, Rabbi Meir." Meir was apparently born in Lublin. His principal teacher was his father-in-law, Isaac b. David ha-Kohen Shapiro, head of the yeshivah and *dayyan* of Cracow. Meir's eminence in learning was such that he became the head of the yeshivah at Lublin (1582–87) at the age of 24, and before he was 30, he was appointed *dayyan* and head of the yeshivah at Cracow (1587–95). He was rabbi in Lemberg from about 1595 until 1613, when he was appointed rabbi as well as head of the yeshivah at Lublin, where he died. Meir of Lublin was one of the greatest teachers of his generation. Wherever he settled, he established a yeshivah to which numerous pupils flocked from all parts of Poland and beyond. From all over Europe rabbis turned to him with halakhic questions or problems of communal concern, or for advice. He encouraged them by stressing his readiness "to reply to anyone putting a problem to me, for in this I find pleasure" (responsum no. 18).

In the introduction to his responsa, his son Gedaliah states that Meir wrote seven works, which he enumerates (see below). Only two, however, have been published. *Me'ir Einei Ḥakhamim* ("Illuminating the Eyes of the Wise") was published by his son Gedaliah (Venice, 1619). Regarded as a most important talmudic work and often republished, it was later printed in all editions of the Talmud. It is a commentary on most of the tractates of the Talmud and mainly centers around the statements of Rashi and the tosafists. In it Meir displays profound acumen, and although he treats the remarks of the tosafists with every respect as embodying the truth and not to be negated, he was nevertheless sometimes critical of them and emended various passages which he maintained had been wrongly inserted by copyists. His commentary, unlike the lengthy lectures he gave to his pupils, is distinguished by its brevity.

The other published work, *Manhir Einei Ḥakhamim* ("Enlightening the Eyes of the Wise"; *ibid.*, 1618), containing 140 responsa, throws light on the religious, economic, and political life of the Jews of Poland and of other countries (cf. Responsa 13, 15, 40, 56, 81, 86, 118, 128, 137, et al.). These responsa reflect his method, temperament, and qualities. Although he was influenced in his halakhic decisions by French, German, and Polish scholars, he displayed independence and was critical of his predecessors. Despite the importance of the Shulḥan Arukh as a supreme halakhic authority, Meir refrained from "building the basis of any ruling upon the implications of its words, since they were not derived from a single source, but were ... compiled from unconnected collections of sayings" (Responsa No. 11). On several questions, particularly in cases involving loss of money or livelihood, he adopted a lenient view (*ibid.* 50), and he showed concern for the status of women (*ibid.* 81) and for protecting the rights of widows and orphans (*ibid.* 109). Insistent that his decisions be accepted, he more than once declared that his opinion was "the clear truth" (*ibid.* 92, 111, et al.).

Although Meir, like his contemporaries, was given to casuistry in his responsa, a thread of clear thought and logic runs through all his statements. His responsa are one of the earliest sources for knowledge of the *Council of the Lands (*ibid.* 40, 125) to which he ascribed great importance and in whose meetings he participated on several occasions (*ibid.* 84, 88). Meir had hundreds of pupils, the most distinguished of them being Isaiah *Horowitz and *Joshua Heschel of Cracow. The five unpublished works mentioned in Gedaliah's introduction are *Ma'or ha-Gadol*, a commentary on the *Arba'ah Turim* of Jacob b. Asher; *Ma'or ha-Katan*, a commentary on *Sha'arei Dura; Ner Mitzvah*, on the *Sefer Mitzvot Gadol* (*Semag*) of Moses of Coucy; *Torah Or*, a commentary on the Pentateuch; and *Or Shivat ha-Yamim*. To this day, Meir's works are used to interpret the Talmud and are quoted in the application of the *halakhah*.

BIBLIOGRAPHY: S. Buber, *Anshei Shem* (1895), 132f.; J. Loewenstein, in: *Ha-Goren*, 1 (1898), 39–54; S.A. Horodezky, *ibid.*, 55–61; idem, *Le-Korot ha-Rabbanut* (1911), 175–82; idem, *Shelosh Me'ot Shanah Shel Yahadut Polin* (1946), 68–72; S.B. Nissenbaum, *Le-Korot ha-Yehudim be-Lublin* (1900), 31f.; Halpern, Pinkas, index; Z. Karl, in: *Arim ve-Immahot be-Yisrael*, 1 (1946), 312f.; C. Tchernowitz, *Toledot ha-Posekim*, 3 (1947), 120f.; I. Rivkind, in: *A. Marx Jubilee Volume* (1950), 427f.; N. Shemen, *Lublin* (Yid., 1951), 365ff.; I. Rosenthal, in: *Sinai*, 31 (1952), 311–38; B.Z. Katz, *Rabbanut, Ḥasidut, Haskalah*, 1 (1956), 65–69; Zinberg, Sifrut, 3 (1958), 190f.; J. Meisl, *Geschichte der Juden in Polen und Russland*, 1 (1921), 312f.; Waxman, Literature, 2 (1933), 117f., 187.

[Shlomo Eidelberg]

LUBLINSKI, SAMUEL (1868–1910), German playwright, literary historian, and philosopher of religion. Born in Johannisburg, East Prussia, Lublinski began work as an apprentice bookseller in Italy. He then started to write for various German journals and eventually devoted himself entirely to literature. His work took him to Berlin, Dresden, and finally to Weimar. Lublinski was at first influenced by Ibsen and the dominant naturalistic movement but he soon veered to the neoclassical theories and techniques of Paul Ernst. His plays on historical and mythological themes include *Der Imperator* (1901), *Hannibal* (1902), *Elisabeth und Essex* (1903), *Peter von Russland* (1906), and *Kaiser und Kanzler* (1910). He was best known, however, for his critical insight into literary trends and for his work as a philosopher of religion. Lublinski's views on naturalism and impressionism and his sociological approach to the study of literature appear clearly in *Literatur und Gesellschaft im neunzehnten Jahrhundert* (4 vols., 1899–1900), *Die Bilanz der Moderne* (1904), and *Der Ausgang der Moderne* (1909). His Jewish loyalties are evident in the essay *Juedische Charaktere bei Grillparzer, Hebbel, und Otto Ludwig* (1899), and in two somewhat unscientific religious works, *Die Entstehung des Judentums* (1902) and *Der urchristliche Erdkreis und sein Mythos* (2 vols., 1910). Lublinski was one of the earliest Zionists in Berlin.

BIBLIOGRAPHY: T. Lessing, *Philosophie als Tat* (1914), 343–52; A. Soergel, *Dichtung und Dichter der Zeit*, 2 (1925), 140–3. **ADD. BIBLIOGRAPHY:** P. Sprengel, "Urszene im Café Luipold – Theodor Lessings Satire auf Samuel Lublinski und die juedische Kontroverse um Assimilation und Zionismus," in: *Germanisch-Romanische Monatsschrift*, 42:3 (1992), 341–49; R. Heuer, "Zionister Traum und juedische Realität – Samuel Lublinskis Philosemitismus," in: R. Heuer et al. (ed.), *Antisemitismus – Zionismus – Antizionismus* (1997), 150–68; A. Woehrmann, *Das Programm der Neuklassik – Die Konzeption der modernen Tragoedie bei Paul Ernst Wilhelm von Scholz und Samuel Lublinski* (1979).

[Sol Liptzin]

LUBNY, a town in Poltava district, Ukraine. Jews settled in Lubny in the first half of the 17th century, under the auspices of the important Vixhnievietski family. Jews defended the town during the Pavliuk uprising (1637–38), and 200 of them were killed during the Chmielnicki massacres of 1648–49. The Jews appeared again in Lubny at the end of the 18th century. From 361 in 1847, their numbers increased to 3,006 (30% of the total population) in 1897. The writer Shalom Aleichem served there as state rabbi in 1880–82. In the 1881 riots some Jewish homes and stores were robbed. In the beginning of the 20th century there was a *talmud torah*, a library, and a bank. There was Zionist activity, and after the October 1917 revolution all members of the community council were Zionists. In the 1920s about 100 Jews worked in the tobacco factory, others worked in the flour mills, and 1,200 were artisans. A Yiddish elementary school existed in Lubny. In 1939 the Jewish population numbered 2,833 (10.5% of the total). The Germans occupied Lubny on September 13, 1941. On October 16, 1941, they gathered 4,500 Jews from Lubny and its environs, and murdered them outside of town. The remaining skilled laborers were killed in April–May 1942. The Jewish population numbered about 600 (2%) in 1959 and was estimated at about 250 in 1970. Although there was no organized Jewish religious life, once a year the Jews assembled at the mass grave of the Holocaust martyrs. Most Jews emigrated in the 1990s.

[Yehuda Slutsky / Shmuel Spector (2nd ed.)]

LUBOSHITZKI, AARON (1874–1942), Hebrew writer, poet, and educator. Born in Poland, he became a member of the Hebrew literary circle in Warsaw at the turn of the century. He served as headmaster of a Hebrew school and established Aviv, an educational publishing house. Later, he taught in Smolensk, Russia, again in Warsaw (where in 1922 he set up the Barkai publishing house), and then in Brest-Litovsk, Volkovysk, and Lodz. After Lodz fell to the Germans during World War II, he was sent to the Warsaw ghetto and was active in clandestine cultural activities until his death at the hands of the Nazis.

Luboshitzki began his literary career at the age of 15, and published articles and poems in most of the Hebrew journals of the time. His first volume of poetry, *Piẓei No'ar*, was published in 1894. Among his other works are *Pirkei Shirah* (originals and translations, 1897), *Yosele ha-Matmid* (1899), a story in verse, and *Viddui* (1899), poems with national themes. He wrote many children's poems, some of which were very popular, stories and plays for children and adults, and he translated poetry. His textbooks in Jewish history were widely used in Hebrew schools in Poland and elsewhere.

BIBLIOGRAPHY: Ofek, in: *Moznayim*, 17 (1963), 61–63; Kressel, Leksikon, 2 (1967), 174–5.

[Getzel Kressel]

LUBOSHUTZ, family of musicians. LEA LUBOSHUTZ (1887–1965), violinist, began her career as a concert violinist in Russia. She arrived in the United States in 1925 and gave violin recitals. She later became active mainly as a teacher and from 1927 was a faculty member of the Curtis Institute of Music, Philadelphia. Her son BORIS GOLDOVSKY (1908–2001) was a pianist, opera conductor, lecturer, and radio commentator in the United States. Her brother PIERRE LUBOSHUTZ (1891–1971) formed a piano duo with his wife Genia Nemenoff, and gave concerts in the United States and Europe. A sister of Lea and Pierre, Anna Luboshutz, was a cellist.

LUBRANIEC (Rus. **Lyubranets**; Yid. **Lubrentsk**), small town in Bydgoszcz province, central Poland. The Jewish community was founded in the first half of the 17th century. Jewish merchants of Lubraniec had commercial ties with Danzig and Leipzig. The Brest overlord granted Lubraniec Jews a privilege in 1780, permitting them to engage in commerce and crafts. The Jewish population numbered 241 in 1765. The stone synagogue was considered one of the oldest buildings in the town. The Jewish community numbered 475 (47% of the total population) in 1808; 1,148 (60%) in 1827; 987 (58%) in 1857; 816 (39%) in 1897; and 834 (38%) in 1921. Between the two world wars the town contained a children's home of the Central Yiddish School Organization (CYSHO; see *Education). Before the outbreak of World War II there were about 880 Jews in Lubraniec. The Jewish community was liquidated in the spring of 1942, when the Jews were deported to *Chelmno death camp.

BIBLIOGRAPHY: M. Freudenthal, *Die juedischen Besucher der Leipziger Messen in den Jahren 1675–1699* (1902), index; B. Wasiutyński, *Ludność żydowska w Polsce w XI–X i XX wiekach* (1930), 22; I. Schiper, *Dzieje handlu żydowskiego na ziemiach polskich* (1937), index.

[*Encyclopaedia Judaica* (Germany)]

LUCA, B. (originally **Luca Bernstein**; 1873–1931), Romanian poet and playwright. Luca was born in Ramnicul Sarat. He published verses in Jewish periodicals (*Hatikva; Lumea evree; Puntea de fildes*) beginning in 1913. Luca's first verse collection *Reflex de suflet* ("Reflection of a Soul," 1915) is a volume of elegies on the death of the author's child. Another volume, *Golgota* (1918), includes poems written during World War I describing the sufferings endured, in a realist form. Thanks to this volume, Luca came to be considered the first anti-war poet in Romanian literature between the wars. In 1919 he published a volume of anti-war sketches *Pacate* ("Sins"), and in 1922 another volume of poems *Versuri primitive* ("Primitive Verses"). In 1919 in Craiova, he edited and published the literary review *Zorile*. In 1919–22 he wrote a number of plays presented at the National Theater of Craiova, one of them called *Omul de prisos* ("The Superfluous Man"), and all published in a single volume (1922). Luca died in Bucharest.

BIBLIOGRAPHY: F. Aderca, in: Th. Loewenstein and N. Kitzler, *Israel in lume* (1939), 218; I. Bercovici, *Pirkei Romanyah* (1975), 36; A.B. Yoff, *Bi-Sedot Zarim* (1996), 188–89.

[Lucian-Zeev Herscovici (2nd ed.)]

°**LUCAN** (**Marcus Annaeus Lucanus**; 39–65 C.E.), Roman epic poet, the nephew of *Seneca the Younger. In his *Bellum Civile* (ii, 592–3) he, like Varro, *Tacitus, and others, describes the Jews as devoted to the rites of an unseen (or indefinite) God (*incertus deus*). Elsewhere, he mentions the military help sent by Idumeans to Pompey.

ADD. BIBIOGRAPHY: M. Stern, *Greek and Latin Authors on Jews and Judaism*, vol. 1 (1974), 438–40.

[Jacob Petroff / Shimon Gibson (2nd ed.)]

LUCCA, city in N. Italy. It was probably in the ninth century that the *Kalonymus family settled in Lucca and founded a talmudic academy there. In the year 917 members of the family moved to Mainz, thereby establishing talmudic studies in the Rhineland. In 1145 Abraham *Ibn Ezra wrote some of his works in Lucca. When *Benjamin of Tudela visited the city about 20 years later, he found some 40 Jewish families. Around 1431–32 Angelo di Gaio (= Mordecai b. Isaac) of Forlì opened a loanbank at Lucca; later the poet David b. Joab of Tivoli settled there. When the opinion of Savonarola was asked, he stated that while Jews should not be invited in order to lend at interest it was no sin if they did so once they came. As a result of the anti-Jewish preaching of *Bernardino da Feltre a *Monte di Pietà was founded in 1489 and the Jewish bankers were fined heavily. Since they did not pay, they were expelled. Around the middle of the 16th century a few Jews returned but after 1572 they were not allowed to stay for more than 15 days at a time. This restriction was set aside in individual cases from 1738. Since then, however, no more than a handful of Jews have lived in Lucca.

BIBLIOGRAPHY: Roth, Italy, index; Milano, Italia, index; Milano, Bibliotheca, s.v.; U. Cassuto, *Ebrei a Firenze nell' età del Rinascimento* (1918), index, s.v. *David di Dattilo da Tivoli* and *Lucca*; Roth, Dark Ages, index.

[Attilio Milano]

LUCCA, PAULINE (1841–1908), singer. Born in Vienna, she was the daughter of Koppelman Lucka, who had been baptized in 1834. In 1861 Giacomo *Meyerbeer recommended her for permanent engagement at the Berlin Opera, where she remained until 1872, also undertaking guest appearances. After 1872 she toured in the United States and from 1874 to 1889 was an honorary member of the Vienna opera. She created the role of Selina in Meyerbeer's *L'Africaine*, and was considered the best Carmen of her time. A *prima donna assoluta* in the grand tradition, she had a voice range of 2½ octaves.

LUCENA, town in Andalusia, in S. Spain, S. of Córdoba; important Jewish community in the 11th century. During the period of Muslim rule Lucena was famous as "the entirely Jewish city," and a tradition states that it was founded by Jews. Several prominent families, including that of the historian Abraham *Ibn Daud, claimed that their settlement in Lucena dated from the time of Nebuchadnezzar. Isaac *Abrabanel linked the derivation of the name of the town with the biblical town of Luz. Until the 12th century Lucena was a cultural center of Andalusian Jewry. In 853 Natronai Gaon wrote "that Alisana (Arabic for Lucena) was a Jewish place with no gentiles at all." In another responsum the *gaon* asked, "Is there a gentile who prohibits your activities? Why do you not establish an **eruv ḥaẓerot*?" (*Teshuvot Ge'onei Mizraḥ u-Ma'arav* (1888), para. 26). The 12th-century Arab geographer Idrīsī also commented on the Jewish character of Lucena and stated that while Muslims lived outside the city walls, Jews generally lived in the fortified part within the walls. Menahem b. Aaron ibn Zerah reports the same information at the end of the 14th century (*Ẓeidah la-Derekh* (Ferrara, 1554), 150). The Jews earned their living from olive groves, vineyards, agriculture, commerce, and crafts. Lucena was distinguished by its scholars. In the mid-ninth century *Amram Gaon sent his prayer book in response to a question by a scholar of Lucena. His contemporary Eleazar b. Samuel Ḥurga of Lucena received the titles *alluf* (*demin Ispania*) and *rosh kallah*, and became famous in the Babylonian academies (see A. Harkavy, *Teshuvot ha-Ge'onim*, Berlin, 1887, para. 386, p. 201, pp. 376–7). In the 11th century Isaac b. Judah *Ibn Ghayyat taught in the yeshivah of Lucena. He was succeeded by Isaac *Alfasi who was followed by Joseph *Ibn Migash. In 1066 the widow of *Joseph b. Samuel ha-Nagid and her son Azariah were among the refugees who came to Lucena in the wake of the anti-Jewish outburst in Granada (Abraham ibn Daud, *Sefer ha-Qabbalah – The Book of Tradition*, ed. G. Cohen (1967), 77). The last king of the Zirid dynasty, Abdallah, reported an uprising of the Jews of Lucena during his reign – at the time of the expedition against the Almoravides (c. 1090). At the turn of the century a contemporary of Ibn Migash, the *Almoravide ruler, Yusuf ibn Tāshfīn (1061–1106), demanded that the Jews convert to Islam. While the community was saved in exchange for a heavy bribe, many Jews of Lucena moved northward to Navarre and settled near Tudela. They called their settlement Lucena and continued to live in accordance with the customs and ordinances of their original community, Lucena. The grammarian Jonah ibn Janāḥ and the poets Moses and Abraham *Ibn Ezra, *Judah Halevi, and Joseph *Ibn Sahl were active in Lucena at some time during their lives. The 11th-century Hebrew poet Abu-ar-Rabia b. Baruch, known throughout Andalusia, lived in Lucena. In 1146 during the Almohad wars, the Jews were persecuted and many were forced to convert to Islam. The community, like many other Andalusian communities, totally disappeared. Lucena was conquered by Castile in 1240. The fate of its Jewish community during the riots of 1391 resembles that of the other Andalusian communities, total destruction. Many were killed, many were forcibly converted, some escaped.

BIBLIOGRAPHY: M. Maimonides, *Iggeret Teiman*, ed. by A.S. Halkin (1952), xxix, 100f.; Neuman, Spain, index; Ibn Daud, Tradition, index; Baer, Spain, index; Ashtor, Korot, 1 (1966²), 202f.; 2 (1966), 88–91; H. Schirmann, in: *Sefer Assaf* (1953), 496–514; E. Lévi-Provençal, in: *Al-Andalus*, 4 (1936), 113–6 (Fr.); Cantera Burgos, in: *Sefarad*, 13 (1953), 112–4; 19 (1959), 137–47; Cantera-Millás, Inscripciones, 168–70; Torres-Balbas, in: *Al-Andalus*, 19 (1954), 190. **ADD. BIBLIOGRAPHY:** A. Arjona Castro, in: *Lucena; nuevos estudios históricos* (1983), 65–88; J.L. Lacave, in: *Sefarad*, 47 (1987), 181–82; F. Díaz Esteban, in: J. Peláez del Rosal (ed.), *The Jews in Cordoba (x–xii Centuries)* (1987), 123–37; J. Peláez del Rosal (ed.), *Los judíos de y Lucena; historia, pensamiento y poesía* (1988).

[Haim Beinart]

LUCENEC (Slovak **Lučenec**; Hung. **Losonc**), town in S. Slovakia, until 1992 Czechoslovak Republic, since then Slovak Republic. The first appearance of Jews in the area was at the end of the 18th century. Under the patronage of Hungarian nobleman Szilassy, they settled in the Lucenec suburb of Tugar. The community was established in 1808 or 1814. The majority of the Jews lived on the Szilassy estate in Tuborg. Soon Jews could also be seen in Lucenec proper. In 1845, there were 45 Jewish families living in Tugar. In 1825 they established a *ḥevra kaddisha*, and in 1830 Rabbi Moses Hoegyes began to officiate. Since there was no synagogue, prayers were held in a private home. The first local Jews were rather poor and could hardly support a congregation. Moreover, the lives of the community members were constantly marred by frequent quarrels. Only a threat by local authorities to put the community under gentile supervision established some order. It was formally incorporated in 1852.

The proclamation of the Magyar Commonwealth in 1848 had rather unfortunate effects on the Jewish community. Fierce battles between the Magyars and the Imperial army in the Lucenec vicinity destroyed much property, including that of the Jews. Local Jews displayed marked Magyar patriotism, and when the Magyar army was defeated, the zealously patriotic Rabbi Hoegyes had to leave. This was followed by an extended search for a new rabbi. Also intense fighting between the Orthodox and the Reform had an impact on community life. After the Jewish Congress in 1868, the community chose a *Neolog path, while the Orthodox left this organization. A new round of quarrels started in the community. An Orthodox congregation gained formal recognition in 1930 by the Czechoslovak government.

In 1862 the congregation built the first synagogue, which was replaced in 1925 with an imposing new edifice. In 1878 a school was organized, with Magyar as the language of instruction. In 1885 a *mikveh* was built, and in 1890 a house for the rabbi. Both congregations became affluent. They kept separate cemeteries. The Orthodox had a *talmud torah* and a small yeshivah under Hillel Unsdoffer (1891–1944), an ardent Zionist. The Orthodox consecrated their synagogue in 1927. In 1937 a ḥasidic group following *nusaḥ sefarad* asked for formal recognition.

In 1840 no Jews were officially registered in Lucenec. In 1880 there were 1,193 registered Jews; in 1910 they numbered 2,135. The second Czechoslovak census (1930) recorded 2,278 Jews. In 1941 there were 2,103 Jews living in Lucenec.

The invasion of the Magyar Polshevics in the spring of 1919 caused disturbances, but there are no reports of anti-Jewish riots such as there were in many other parts of Slovakia.

During the war, Lucenec Jews participated in political activities. Some supported Magyar nationalist parties; only when these parties displayed open antisemitism did the Jews leave. Zionist organizations were active, and a large proportion of the local Jews identified itself as Jewish by nationality. The Jewish party clashed with Jewish Magyar assimilationists.

In November 1938 Lucenec, together with the rest of south Slovakia, was annexed by the Hungarian kingdom, and the anti-Jewish laws of that state were applied immediately to local Jewry. In 1941 Jewish men aged 18 to 45 were recruited for forced labor in the Hungarian army; many died in service. In March 1944, the German army occupied Hungary and immediately started to persecute the Jews, in cooperation with Magyar Fascists. At the beginning of June 1944, the Jews of Lucenec were ghettoized; on June 16 they were sent to Auschwitz, where most perished.

Some 80 Jews returned from the deportation; they organized a new community and reinstituted Jewish life. In 1945, the Joint Distribution Committee organized a kosher kitchen for the returned survivors. In 1947 there were 271 Jews in Lucenec. In 1948 the Neolog synagogue was reestablished. During 1948–1949, most of the Jews emigrated, a larger proportion to Israel. Nevertheless, Lucenec remained one of the few active congregations in Slovakia, and a *minyan* was kept until the Velvet Revolution of 1989. The cemetery was cleaned up and the Neolog synagogue rebuilt. In the 1990s there were 50 Jews. The local community was still active in 2005.

BIBLIOGRAPHY: *Magyar Zsidó Lexikon* (1929), s.v. *Losonc*; M. Lányi and H. Proppern Békefi, *A szlovenszkói zsidó hitközségek története* (1933), 229–34. **ADD. BIBLIOGRAPHY:** E. Bàrkàny and L. Dojč, *Židovské náboženské obce na Slovensku* (1991), 297–99.

[Meir Lamed / Yeshayahu Jelinek (2nd ed.)]

LUCERNE (Ger. **Luzern**), city in the canton of the same name, central Switzerland. Jews were first mentioned in Lucerne in 1252, when the terms of their protection were defined. During the 14th century, a fine was prescribed for anyone perpetrating a blood libel against the Jews without previously notifying the council. A regulation of 1310 deals with the sale of meat from animals slaughtered by Jews. The Jews, who were authorized to possess real estate, were principally engaged in moneylending. During the massacres following the *Black Death (1348–49) the community came to an end; the town was compelled to indemnify the duke of Austria for the losses he had thus incurred. In 1381, there were once more Jews living in Lucerne. A few Jewish physicians practiced there during the 15th and 16th centuries. In the mid-17th century, Jewish livestock merchants again appeared at the local markets. Some Jews, mainly from Alsace and *Endingen/Lengnau, visited markets in the canton Lucerne in the 18th and 19th centuries, though not without arousing a certain degree of opposition.

The local community was founded in 1866, but never developed to any considerable extent. In 1912, a synagogue was erected in the style of the Orthodox synagogue of Frankfurt/Friedberger Anlage. The leading family was the Erlangers, immigrating from South-Baden Gailingen. Abraham Erlanger became Orthodox and gave the community its special imprint already in the 1920s. In 1936 the oratory was devastated by Swiss Fascists. From 1958 there was a small Lithuanian-type *yeshivah ketanah* in Lucerne moving later to nearby Kriens. For some years a *Beth Jacob seminary for teaching Orthodox girls existed. The community became more Orthodox (*ḥaredi*) in the 1980s, so that some of its members left and joined communities in Zurich. In the Lucerne canton 399 persons declared themselves as Jewish in 2000; 200 were members of the community (2004).

BIBLIOGRAPHY: Schweizerischer Israelitischer Gemeindebund, *Festschrift zum 50-jaehrigen Bestehen* (1954); A. Weldler-Steinberg, *Geschichte der Juden in der Schweiz*, 2 vols. (1966/70), index. **ADD. BIBLIOGRAPHY:** *Germ Jud*, 2 (1968); *Germ. Jud*, 3:2 (1998), index, s.v. *Luzern*; R.U. Kaufmann, *Juden in Luzern* (1984); E. Hurwitz, *Bocksfuss, Schwanz und Hörner*, (1986, memoirs); R. Erlanger, *Stammbaum und Chronik der Familie Abraham Erlanger: ein Beitrag zur Geschichte der Juden in Luzern und Gailingen* (1998).

[Simon R. Schwarzfuchs / Uri Kaufmann (2nd ed.)]

°**LUCIAN OF SAMOSATA** (c. 120–c. 180), greatest Greek satirist, whose mother tongue was probably Aramaic. In a satiric essay, "Alexander the False Prophet" (13), Lucian tells how a charlatan Alexander of Abonoteichus (in Asia Minor) pronounced some meaningless words, which, he says, could be either Hebrew or Phoenician, thus dazzling his audience in his native city, who had not understood what he was saying except that he was somehow involved in the cult of the gods Apollo and Aselepius. In a mock-tragedy, *Podagra* (line 173), he speaks of a fool who allows himself to be taken in by the spells of a Jew.

[Louis Harry Feldman]

LUCKMAN, SIDNEY (**Sid**; 1916–1998), U.S. football quarterback, one of the pioneers who revolutionized the game in the 1940s as the first of the T-formation quarterbacks; member of the College and Pro Football halls of fame. Luckman was born in Brooklyn, N.Y., the child of German-Jewish immigrants, and grew up in Flatbush near Prospect Park, where he learned how to throw a football. After graduating as an All-City halfback from Erasmus Hall High School, Luckman played at Columbia University from 1936 to 1938, and was named AP All-America third team, Grantland Rice All-America honorable mention, and AP All-East first team in 1937. The next year he finished third in balloting for the Heisman Trophy. In 24 collegiate games, Luckman amassed 180 pass completions in 376 attempts (.479), for 2,413 yards passing and 20 touchdowns. Luckman then played quarterback, halfback, and defensive back in the NFL for the Chicago Bears from 1939 to 1950, leading the team to five Western Conference championships and four World Championships between 1940 and 1946. Luckman's greatness and importance to the game was his unparalleled understanding and grasp of the complex T-formation, which brought football into the modern age.

In the 1940 championship game, Luckman and the Bears beat the Washington Redskins 73–0 in one of the most lopsided scores in history. Luckman had his best season in 1943, when he threw a record 28 touchdowns in 10 games – a mark that stood until 1959 – and gained league MVP honors. On November 14 that season, Luckman had his greatest single game on "Sid Luckman Day" at the Polo Grounds against the New York Giants, when he threw a record seven touchdowns and a record 443 yards in the 56–7 trouncing, the first quarterback to surpass 400 yards in a game. In the 1943 title game he threw for 286 yards and five touchdowns in a 41–21 victory over the Redskins. He retired following the 1950 season, completing 904 of 1,744 passes (51.8 percent) for 14,686 yards (8.42 yards per pass) and 137 touchdowns in 128 career NFL games. He also punted 230 times for a 38.4-yard average, rushed for two touchdowns, and returned 14 interceptions for 293 yards and one touchdown. His TD pass percentage of 7.9 is the best ever, and his 8.42-yard-per-attempt mark is the second best. Luckman led the league in touchdown passes in 1943, 1945, and 1946, in yards per attempt in 1939, 1940, 1941, and 1943, and in passing yards in 1943, 1946, and 1947. He was named All-NFL five times (1940–44, 1947). Luckman was elected to the College Football Hall of Fame in 1960 and the Pro Football Hall of Fame in 1965. He wrote *Passing for Touchdowns* (1948) and *Luckman at Quarterback: Football as a Sport and a Career* (1949).

[Elli Wohlgelernter (2nd ed.)]

LUCUAS (early second century C.E.), Jewish "king" and leader of the Jewish rising in Cyrene (115–117 C.E.). The sources are divided as to the name of the Jewish leader; whereas Eusebius (Historia Eclesiastica 4:2) refers to the Jewish king Lucuas, Dip Cassius (68:32) calls him Andreas. It has been suggested, therefore, that the "king" had a double name: Λουκούας ὁ κάὶ

Ανδρέας. Mention of a Jewish "king" perhaps signifies the messianic overtones of the Jewish revolt in Egypt and Cyrene. One of the "Acts of the Alexandrine Martyrs" describes a dispute between a Greek and Jewish embassy before the Roman emperor Hadrian, and from its contents it is apparent that the subject under debate is connected with the Jewish revolt in Alexandria. A certain king of the stage and mime is mentioned as being brought forth by the Alexandrians to be mocked by the Roman prefect. Tcherikover, in analyzing the papyrus, points out that although it is possible that the "king" described is Lucuas, "he certainly would have been a prisoner in the hands of the Romans, and not of the Alexandrians" as is implied in the text. Furthermore, it is difficult to ascertain why Hadrian should be angry with the Alexandrians, if the object of their mockery was "the Jewish king" responsible for the uprising.

BIBLIOGRAPHY: Schuerer, Hist, 291f.; Tcherikover, Corpus, 1 (1957), 86, 89, 90 n. 83; 2 (1960), 87–99.

[Isaiah Gafni]

LUDO, ISAC IACOVITZ (1894–?), Romanian author, journalist, and translator. Ludo began his literary career in his native Jassy, but soon moved to Bucharest, where he contributed to the Jewish review *Lumea evree* and to leading Romanian periodicals. When the Jewish daily *Mântuirea* was founded in Bucharest in 1919, Ludo joined the staff and became one of its chief contributors. He also directed the Zionist daily *Şitri* and the periodical *Palestina ilustrată*, later editing the Jewish weekly *Adam*. A prominent figure in Romanian Jewish life, Ludo played a leading part in the fight against antisemitism, and in all his writings bitterly attacked both Jewish assimilationists and opponents of the Jews. He spent the two years before World War II in France.

Most of Ludo's works are concerned with Jewish problems. *Doi mari poeţi – Heinrich Heine ş A.C. Cuza* ("Two Great Poets – Heinrich Heine and A.C. Cuza," 1934), first published in *Adam*, mordantly satirizes the Romanian antisemitic leader Cuza, who fancied himself as a poet and claimed that the Jews were incapable of artistic creativity. In *Jurul unei obsesii* ("Around an Obsession," 1936), a lengthy analysis of Cuza's and the Nazis' anti-Jewish claims, he dealt incidentally with the scurrilous portrayal of Romanian Jews in Ionel Teodoreanu's popular novel *La Medeleni* (1926). Ludo also wrote several more books against the Nazis and Fascists, such as *Hitler salvează echilibrul istoric* ("Hitler Preserves the Balance of History"), *Nae lonescu apără pe Evrei impotriva jidanilor* ("Ionescu Defends the Hebrews against the Jews"), and *De la Rasputin la Hitler* ("From Rasputin to Hitler"). After World War II, he continued to write polemical works against the pre-Communist regime, the old political parties, and the defunct Romanian dynasty. He also published Romanian translations of Jewish classics, such as *An-Ski's *Dybbuk* (1927), *Zangwill's *King of the Schnorrers* (1934), and many short stories by *Shalom Aleichem.

BIBLIOGRAPHY: G. Călinescu, *Istoria Literaturii Romîne…* (1941), 712.

[Abraham Feller]

LUDOMIR, MAID OF (1806–1888?), popular title of **Hannah Rochel Werbermacher**, the only woman in the history of Ḥasidism to function as a rebbe or charismatic leader in her own right. Although unusual in her following, some of Werbermacher's activities had precedents in traditional Jewish female roles, including the *firzogern* or *zogerke* (prayer leader), *klogmuter* (professional mourner), and *vaybersher opshprecherke* (traditional healer). Born in the Volhynian town of Ludomir (Russian, Vladimir Volinski), Werbermacher exhibited extreme piety and a talent for learning as a child. At 12, Hannah Rochel experienced the traumatic death of her mother and one day fell into a coma at her mother's grave. After hopes for her recovery had been abandoned, the girl suddenly awoke and announced that the heavenly court had granted her a new and higher soul. From this point on, Hannah refused to marry and became known as the Maid of Ludomir (Yiddish, *Ludomirer Moid*); she began to wear a *tallit* and *tefillin* and to perform healings. The Maid's father, a wealthy merchant named Monesh, died when she was 19, leaving her a sufficiently large inheritance to support herself without a husband or community aid. She built her own *shtibl* (small prayer house) and held gatherings like a ḥasidic rebbe. In addition to teaching Torah and leading prayers in Ludomir, the Maid also traveled to other *shtetlakh* (towns), where she delivered homilies to groups of women. The Maid attracted a circle of followers, primarily women and working class men, known as the "Maid of Ludomir's Ḥasidim." She also attracted opponents, who accused her of being possessed by a dybbuk (malevolent spirit). Eventually, Mordechai of Chernobyl, the most powerful *ẓaddik* in the region, was asked to intervene. He convinced the Maid to marry; her new husband, however, awed by her holiness, could not consummate the marriage and the couple soon divorced. Subsequently, the Maid appears to have lost much of her influence in Ludomir and may have suffered a crisis of confidence. Around 1860, she immigrated to Eretz Israel, where she reestablished herself as a holy woman, first in the Old City of Jerusalem and then in Meah She'arim. Here, too, the Maid attracted a following of ḥasidic women and men, as well as Sephardi and possibly some Muslim Arab women, and led gatherings at the Western Wall, the Tomb of Rachel, and her own *besmedresh* (study house). After her death, her grave on the Mount of Olives became a site of devotion. While the original tombstone was apparently destroyed under Jordanian rule, in 2004 a new tombstone was erected on her possible gravesite and people began to pray at the location. Over the years, the Maid's story has been retold in plays, novels, stories, a play within a novel (Isaac *Bashevis Singer's *Shosha*), as well as several radio dramas starring Mollie *Picon.

BIBLIOGRAPHY: N. Deutsch, *The Maiden of Ludmir: A Jewish Holy Woman and Her World* (2003); A. Rapoport-Albert, "On Women in Hasidism: S.A. Horodesky and the Maid of Ludmir Tradition," in: A. Rapoport-Albert and S.J. Zipperstein (eds.), *Jewish History: Essays in Honour of Chimen Abramsky* (1988), 495–525.

[Nathaniel Deutsch (2nd ed.)]

LUDVIPOL, ABRAHAM (1865–1921), Hebrew journalist. Born in Novograd-Volynsk, he was active in the *Ḥibbat Zion movement in Odessa. In 1890 he sailed for Ereẓ Israel but was not permitted to land. After a sojourn in Alexandria he went to Paris, where he studied and began his career as a journalist, writing in Hebrew for *Ha-Meliẓ*, as well as in French and Yiddish for other papers. His reputation as a leading Hebrew journalist grew during the Dreyfus affair. When the daily **Ha-Ẓofeh* was founded in 1903 he was invited to take up the post of editor. In 1907 he settled in Ereẓ Israel to establish a Hebrew daily of Ḥovevei Zion, but the project fell through. He was active in public affairs in Tel Aviv, and when the daily **Haaretz* appeared at the end of World War I, he became a member of its editorial staff.

BIBLIOGRAPHY: J. Fichmann, *Be-Terem Aviv* (1959), 219–22; E.E. Friedman, *Sefer ha-Zikhronot* (1926), 283–8; Waxman, Literature, 4 (1960^2), 443; Kressel, Leksikon, 2 (1967), 177–8.

[Getzel Kressel]

LUDWIG (Cohn), EMIL (1881–1948), German biographer and author. The son of Hermann *Cohn, a famous ophthalmologist, Ludwig was born in Breslau. After 1907 he spent most of his life in Switzerland. He began his literary career as a playwright and novelist, but became internationally popular through his colorful biographies, which were translated into many languages. His vast output included *Goethe* (3 vols., 1920), *Napoleon* (1925), *Bismarck* (1921), *Wilhelm II* (1926), *Lincoln* (1930), *Michelangelo* (1930), *Hindenburg* (1935), *Cleopatra* (1937), *Roosevelt* (1938), *Simon Bolivar* (1939), and *Stalin* (1945). He also wrote shorter essays on Rembrandt, Beethoven, and Balzac, and character studies of three eminent German Jews, Sigmund *Freud, Ferdinand *Lassalle, and Walther *Rathenau. Like Lytton Strachey in England, Stefan Zweig in Germany, and André Maurois in France, Ludwig regarded a biography as a work of art. He did not pretend to compete with the scholars on whose research he based his presentation of historical figures and his personal views often cast doubt on the objective truth of his writing. Nevertheless, he always showed keen insight into the personalities of his subjects and into the historical and social conditions in which they lived, and his work was distinguished by a dynamic literary style. Among Ludwig's other books were one on Jesus, *Der Menschensohn* (1928), *Drei Diktatoren* (1939), and a study of the abdication of King Edward VIII (1939). He also wrote some geographical books, including *Der Nil* (1935, *The Nile*, 1936), and *Am Mittelmeer* (1923, *On Mediterranean Shores*, 1929). Ludwig was baptized in 1902, but 20 years later, after the assassination of Walter Rathenau, he publicly renounced Christianity. During his American exile he became one of the most decided enemies of the Third Reich, publishing several critical works, such as *How to Treat the Germans* (1943) and *The Moral Conquest of Germany* (1945).

BIBLIOGRAPHY: N. Hansen, *Der Fall Emil Ludwig* (1930). **ADD. BIBLIOGRAPHY:** C. Gradmann, *Historische Belletristik. Populäre historische Biographienin der Weimarer Republik* (1993); H.J. Perrey, "Der Fall Emil Ludwig. Ein Bericht über eine historiographische Kontroverse der ausgehenden Weimarer Republik," in: *Geschichte in Wissenschaft und Unterricht*, 43 (1992), 169–81; S.Ullrich, "Im Dienste der Weimarer Republik. Emil Ludwig als Historiker und Publizist," in: *Zeitschrift fuer Geschichtswissenschaft*, 49 (2001), 119–40.

[Sol Liptzin]

LUDWIG, REUBEN (1895–1926), Yiddish poet. Born in Lipowitz, Ukraine, Ludwig immigrated to New York in 1910. Suffering from tuberculosis, he moved in his twenties to the drier areas of the American Southwest, while making a meteoric appearance among the *In-Zikh group of Yiddish poets. His poems appeared in the major Yiddish periodicals, emphasizing the imminence of death, expressing sadness and hopelessness while longing for joy and glorious adventure. His *Gezamlte Lider* ("Collected Poems," 1927) include songs of the Rockies and of the American Southwest, then still undiscovered by Yiddish poets. He sympathized with and wrote about various minorities, including Indians, Mexicans, Chinese, and African-Americans.

BIBLIOGRAPHY: Rejzen, Leksikon, 2 (1927), 90ff.; LNYL, 5 (1963), 6ff. **ADD. BIBLIOGRAPHY:** Z. Weinper, *Yidishe Shriftshteler*, 1 (1953), 136–39; B.Y. Bialostotsky, *Kholem un Vor* (1956), 112–13; R.R. Wisse, *A Little Love in Big Manhattan* (1988).

[Sol Liptzin / Marc Miller (2nd ed.)]

LUDZA (Rus. **Lyutsin**), town in Latgale district, Latvia. A Jewish community probably existed in the 16th century and fled before Ivan the Terrible's soldiers in 1577. A substantial community appeared in the end of the 18th century, and in 1802 there were 582 Jews in the town and district. The Jewish population numbered 2,299 in 1847; 2,803 (54% of the total) in 1897; 2,050 (40.6%) in 1920; 1,634 (30.4%) in 1930; and 1,518 (27.4%) in 1935. In the second half of the 19th century Jews lived from trade in lumber, grain, flax, and other farm products. Sixty families went to southern Ukraine to settle there in the Jewish agricultural colonies. About 40% of the town's tailors were Jews. The community suffered greatly during and after World War I. The Jewish population also decreased because many Jews there moved to Riga, the capital of Latvia, and other larger population centers, or emigrated. Most of the Jews in Ludza were occupied as shopkeepers or artisans. Jews owned 191 of the 302 larger trade premises. A big fire in 1938 destroyed 95% of Jewish stores and houses. Most of the children studied in a Hebrew public school.

Ludza was famous for its rabbis and scholars. The best known were those of the Ẓioni family, and later the Don Yaḥya family, related by marriage. David Ẓioni officiated as rabbi from 1806 to 1808; he was succeeded by his son Naphtali (1808–56), who was followed by Aaron Zelig (1856–76), author of the responsa *Ẓioni* (1875). A prominent member of the Ẓioni family was Itzele Lutẓiner, author of *Olat Yiẓḥak* (1–2, 1885–97), who served as rabbi in *Rezekne. Eliezer b. Shabbetai Don Yaḥya, author of responsa on the Shulḥan Arukh, *Even Shetiyyah* (1893), was a disciple and son-in-law of

Aaron Zelig Ẓioni and his successor in the rabbinate of Ludza (1870–1926). Eliezer's son, Ben Zion, was the son-in-law of Isaac Ẓioni, and for 26 years officiated as rabbi in Vilaci; after the death of his father he succeeded him in the rabbinate in Ludza (1926–41). Ben Zion, who perished in the Holocaust, was the author of halakhic books and historical articles. Because of the high standard of Jewish learning the community was known as the "Jerusalem of Latvia."

Holocaust Period

Ludza was occupied by the Germans on July 3, 1941. A ghetto was founded on July 20, and murders, looting, rape, and forced labor began. On August 17, 1941, about 800 Jews were murdered at Lake Zorba outside of town. The few hundred that remained were killed in small actions, the last in May 1942. About 100 Jews returned after the war, but soon most of them left for Israel.

BIBLIOGRAPHY: *Yahadut Latvia* (1953), 286–300; M. Kaufmann, *Die Veruichtung der Juden Lettlands* (1947), 286–94.

[Shmuel Spector (2nd ed.)]

LUEBECK, Baltic port in Germany. An imperial city and capital of the Hanseatic League, Luebeck did not permit Jews to reside within its gates, although in the 17th century Jewish peddlers were common and their presence highly resented. In 1680 the city, in need of competent money changers, permitted two *Schutzjuden* to live there; in 1701 their number was restricted to one. Jewish peddlers, dealers in old clothes and secondhand goods, settled in the nearby village of Moisling, and in 1697 received permission to establish a recognized Jewish community. The attempts of the Luebeck authorities to restrict their activities met with little success. From 12 families in 1709 the settlement in Moisling had grown to 70 by the end of the century. In 1724 a rabbi was engaged and a cemetery opened; the community was under the jurisdiction of the Altona rabbinate. Although Moisling was annexed to Luebeck in 1806 the commercial and civil restrictions were not abolished until 1810, by the French occupation forces. A synagogue was dedicated in Luebeck itself in 1812. The downfall of Napoleon and the retreat of the French army threatened the Jews' newly acquired rights. C.A. Buchholz, a Luebeck lawyer, attempted to defend them at the Congress of Vienna (1815) but in vain. After a protracted legal battle, in 1824 they were forced to leave the city proper, returning to Moisling, where they built a new synagogue (1827) and opened a school (1837). Emancipation granted during the 1848 Revolution gave the Jews the right to settle in Luebeck, where a synagogue was opened in 1850; a new one was consecrated in 1880. The last five rabbis who served in Luebeck and Moisling were Ephraim Fischel Joel (1825–51), his son-in-law Alexander Adler (1850–69), his son-in-law Solomon Carlebach (1870–1919), who wrote a history of the Jewish community, succeeded by his son Joseph Carlebach (1920–22), and David A. Winter (1922–38). The Jewish population in the city rose from 522 in 1857 to 700 in 1913, but after the advent of the Nazis, declined to 250 in 1937. The last 85 Jews were deported to Riga in 1941–42. After the war a new community was established, which numbered 250 in 1948; by 1952 only 30 remained.

[Jacob Rothschild]

In 1960 the Juedische Gemeinschaft Holstein was founded as a federation of the few remaining Jews in the federal state of Schleswig-Holstein, including Luebeck. The number of members continued to decline, with the Gemeinschaft being dissolved in 1968 and the Jewish community of Hamburg taking responsibility for Jewish life in Luebeck. In 1994 and 1995 two arson attacks on the synagogue were carried out. In 2005 an independent Jewish community with more than 600 members was founded. Almost all the members were immigrants from the former Soviet Union.

[Larissa Daemmig (2nd ed.)]

ADD. BIBLIOGRAPHY: P. Guttkuhn, *Kleine deutsch-juedische Geschichte in Luebeck (Von den Anfaengen bis zur Gegenwart)* (2004); idem, *Die Geschichte der Juden in Moisling und Luebeck: Von den Anfaengen 1656 bis zur Emanzipation 1852* (Veroeffentlichungen zur Geschichte der Hansestadt Luebeck. Reihe B, volume 30; 1999).

°**LUEGER, KARL** (1844–1910), leader of the antisemitic *Christian Social Party in Austria. Born in Vienna into a lower middle-class family, he qualified as a lawyer. He began his political career with the left wing of the Progressive Party and was elected as its candidate to the city council in 1875. There he associated with Jewish members, among them Ignaz Mandl, a Jewish lawyer who remained his friend and political adviser even after Lueger had ousted him from the Democrats in 1889. In 1884 he sponsored the Democrats' electoral demand for "equality of all faiths." Elected to the parliament in 1885, he cooperated with the political antisemite Georg von *Schoenerer but denied being himself an antisemite. A year later he berated the Liberal majority in the city council for refusing to deliver a congratulatory address to Adolf *Fischhof on the occasion of his 70th birthday. In spite of this, Lueger made a violently antisemitic speech in 1887 in support of Schoenerer's bill against Jewish immigration from Russia and Romania. After allying himself with Karl von *Vogelsang, in 1893 he united the different Christian factions into the Christian Social Party, which he led until his death. Lueger was extremely popular with the lower middle classes, largely because of his folksy and vulgar speeches uniting popular economic and religious antisemitic prejudices. He succeeded in forging a party which channeled social discontent, depicting capitalism and Marxism alike as products of the Jewish mind and fusing these new themes with the centuries-old hatred of the Jews stemming from Church doctrine. In 1897 *Francis Joseph I confirmed Lueger as mayor of Vienna after he had refused to do so on three previous occasions. In this office, which he held until his death, he effected many social reforms. His administration pursued discriminatory practices against Jews, mainly through not employing them in the city services and limiting their numbers in high school and the university. Nevertheless he was in the habit of doing petty favors for poor Jews, even appearing in a synagogue wearing the mayoral chain. In his administration he employed, besides Mandl (who was baptized at the age of 72), the partly Jewish vice mayor Julius Porzer and the renegade Max Anton Loew. He accepted invitations to Jewish homes and is reported to have said: "*Wer ein Jude ist, bestimme ich*" ("It is up to me to decide who is a Jew"). A collection of Lueger's papers, translated and edited by R.S. Geehr, was titled after this notorious phrase: "*I Decide Who Is a Jew!*" (1982).

Lueger's antisemitism was opportunistic rather than racist, but he had a profound influence on the young Adolf Hitler in his formative years, and established on a firm footing the Viennese antisemitic tradition.

BIBLIOGRAPHY: P.G.J. Pulzer, *The Rise of Political Anti-semitism in Germany and Austria* (1964), index; D. van Arkel, *Anti-semitism in Austria* (1966), 67–80 and passim; O. Karbach, in: *Zeitschrift fuer die Geschichte der Juden*, 1 (1964), 1–8; 2–3 (1964), 103–16; 4 (1964), 169–78 – all passim; J.S. Bloch, *My Reminiscences* (1923), 227–58 and passim; J. Fraenkel (ed.), *The Jews of Austria* (1967), index; A. Fuchs, *Geistige Stroemungen in Oesterreich 1867–1918* (1949), index; W.A. Jenks, *Vienna and the Young Hitler* (1960), index; F. Heer, *Der Glaube des Adolf Hitler* (1968), index; idem, *Gottes erste Liebe* (1967), index; S. Mayer, *Wiener Juden* (1917), index; K. Skalnik, *Karl Lueger* (Ger., 1954); T. Heuss, in: ESS, 9 (1954^2), 629–30; H. Halborn, *A History of Modern Germany 1840–1945* (1969), 714. **ADD. BIBLIOGRAPHY:** J.W. Boyer, in: LBIYB, 26 (1981), 125–41; R.S. Wistrich, in: JJS, 45:3–4 (1983), 251–62; R.S. Geehr, *Karl Lueger: Mayor of Fin de Siècle Vienna* (1990).

LUENEBURG, city in Germany. The mention of a *Judenstrasse* in 1288 indicates that Jews were living there earlier. They maintained a synagogue and *mikveh* in the 14th century. The Jews dealt in moneylending and were under the protection of the dukes of Lueneburg. In 1350, during the *Black Death, the Jews were massacred, only a few managing to escape despite the feeble attempt of the duke to protect them. The houses of the Jews were subsequently sold by the duke to the very burghers who had participated in the massacre. By the late 14th century, Jews were again living in Lueneburg. Community life was repeatedly interrupted by expulsions in the 16th century (1510, 1553, and 1591). Jacob, son of Leffmann Behrends (the Hanover *Court Jew), was allowed to settle there in 1680; a number of **Schutzjuden* were subsequently permitted to reside there. The Jewish population increased slowly from 27 in 1811 to 145 in 1910. Between 1927 and 1930 the large synagogue, consecrated in 1894, was repeatedly desecrated and bombed by local antisemites and Nazis. By Oct. 1, 1936, only 36 Jews remained and on Oct. 30, 1938, final services were conducted in the synagogue which was then closed down. During World War II, 11 Jews were deported and lost their lives.

BIBLIOGRAPHY: Germ Jud, 2 (1968), 498–501.

LUFTSPRING, SAMMY (1915–2000), Canadian welterweight boxing champion, referee, and member of the Canadian Sports Hall of Fame. Luftspring was born in Toronto. He began his boxing career fighting for the Toronto Brunswick Talmud Torah School and throughout his career fought with a Star of David on his shorts. Considered a contender for the Olympic Gold Medal, Luftspring was selected to represent Canada at the Berlin Olympics in 1936. However, Luftspring, along with Norman "Baby" Yack, another Canadian Jewish boxer, opted to boycott the Nazi Olympics, and to compete instead in the alternative games, the Workers Olympics to be held in Barcelona. While on their way to the Barcelona competition, the two learned that the games had been canceled with the outbreak of the Spanish Civil War.

Turning to professional boxing in 1936, Luftspring won the Canadian welterweight championship in 1938 by defeating Frankie Genovese. He held that title for two years and in 1940 was third in line to fight the world welterweight champion Henry Armstrong. However, before Luftspring could fight Armstrong, his career was tragically cut short during a fight against Steve Belliose. Luftspring took a thumb to his left eye, and was forced to retire after he lost all his vision in the eye.

After his injury, Luftspring turned to refereeing. He refereed more than 2,000 boxing matches over the span of his career and made the *Guinness Book of World Records* in the 1970s for his accomplishments. In addition, in 1940 Luftspring and several partners successfully went into the nightclub business in Toronto. Luftspring published an autobiography in 1975, *Call me Sammy*.

[Avi Hyman and Brenda Cappe (2nd ed.)]

LUGANSK (1935–58, **Voroshilovgrad**), capital of the Lugansk district, Ukraine. The town was founded at the end of the 18th century and Jews started to settle there, numbering in 1897 1,505 (7.5% of the population). Three Jewish schools were opened in 1910. From 1908 to 1916 the position of **kazyonny ravvin* ("government-appointed rabbi") of Lugansk was held by the Hebrew writer J.B. Lerner. There he published two newspapers for Jewish children, one in Hebrew (*Peraḥim*) and another in Russian. During World War I many refugees arrived in Lugansk, and were aided by the community. In 1926 there were 7,132 Jews (c. 10%), increasing to 10,622 (5% of the total). In the 1920s many Jews were unemployed, mostly among the ex-bourgeoisie, but in the 1930s they began to work on the railroad and in industry. The city was occupied by the Germans on July 17, 1942. Most of the Jews were evacuated or fled. Of the remaining 1,038, the majority were murdered at Ivanitchev Yar on November 1, 1942, and January 21, 1943, together with Jews from other localities, all together 1,986 persons. There were 5,500 Jews (2.5%) in the city in 1959. Most remaining Jews emigrated in the 1990s.

[Yehuda Slutsky]

LUGO, small town in N. central Italy. The first record of a Jewish settlement in Lugo is a tombstone inscription of 1285. The rule of the House of Este (1437–1598) and the famous fairs of Lugo made the community prosperous. After Lugo came under direct papal rule in 1598, conditions deteriorated. In 1634, 606 Jews, some from neighboring towns, were confined in ghettos, located in the center of the city. In 1703 this number had been reduced to 54 families, among whom the *Finzi, the *Senigallia, and the *Del Vecchio were prominent. The Del Vecchio and later the *Fano families produced several eminent rabbis, more than would be expected from so small a community, though by 1797 it had grown to 648 members. They were mostly involved in market of textile, silver, and second-hand products. In 1796 the French authorities granted emancipation to the Jews, but during the reaction following the temporary withdrawal of the French troops the ghetto was plundered three times. In 1802 the Jews in the city numbered 470. When papal rule was restored in 1814, the old interdictions again came into force and became even harsher under Pope *Leo XII, with the result that several families left Lugo. In 1853, 396 Jews were there. Later they followed the drift to the larger cities. Twenty-six Jews were murdered in Lugo during the Holocaust period. In April 1945 the town was liberated by the Jewish Brigade. In 1969 there was only one Jewish family in Lugo.

BIBLIOGRAPHY: Milano, Bibliotheca, index; Roth, Italy, index; Servi, in: *Corriere Israelitico*, 6 (1867/68), 335–6; Volli, in: RMI, 23 (1957), 65–76; Sierra, *ibid.*, 24 (1958), 451–9. **ADD. BIBLIOGRAPHY:** A. Pirazzini, "Otto secoli di presenza ebraica a Lugo. Stato delle conoscenze e prospettive di indagine," in: *Studi Romagnoli*, 48 (1997), 81–90.

[Attilio Milano]

LUGOJ (Hung. **Lugos**), city in W. Romania (Transylvania), until 1918 in Hungary. Jews settled in Lugoj and its surroundings at the beginning of the 18th century. An organized community was founded between 1780 and 1790, and a *ḥevra kaddisha* in 1790. Some Sephardi Jews participated in the establishment of the community in the town alongside the Ashkenazim. Jews played an important role in the development of the extensive textile industry and the processing of natural silk there. The Jewish population numbered 550 in 1851, 1,303 in 1891, 1,878 in 1910, 1,774 in 1924 (8.9% of the total population), and 1,418 in 1930 (6% of the total). During World War I, 173 members of the community served in the Hungarian army. Simon Hevesi was the local rabbi between 1897 and 1905. With non-Jewish intellectuals, he organized popular educational institutions, the first of their kind in southern Hungary. An elementary school, founded in 1833, functioned until 1944. A large synagogue was erected in 1842. There were also some smaller synagogues. After the split within Hungarian Jewry in 1868 (see *Hungary), the community defined itself as neologist (see *Neology). A charitable organization of Jewish women functioned from 1875 and a *talmud torah* from 1903. After the 1919 unification of Transylvania with Romania, and because of the Romanian government's antisemitic policies, many Jews left the city. Zionist organizations were active in Lugoj, and from 1934 the Zionists were the dominant element in the community leadership. Between 1941 and 1942, the period of the Romanian Fascist regime, some of the Jewish men were conscripted for forced labor, and many Jews lost all their belongings. The Jewish population numbered 1,043 in 1942. A number of Jewish youngsters accused of Communist activities were deported to Transnistria by the Antonescu regime. After World War II the Jewish population increased, as Jewish refugees from the surrounding districts and northern Bukovina settled there (1,620 in 1947). The number of Jews declined from the 1950s through immigration to Israel. By 1970 only 220 were left.

BIBLIOGRAPHY: *Magyar Zsidó Lexikon* (1929), 546; O. Kálmán, in: *Magyar Zsidó Szemle*, 51 (1934), 79–106; PK Romanyah, 1 (1969), 316–8; T. Schwager, in: *Revista Cultului Mozaic*, 243 (Dec. 15, 1970).

[Yehouda Marton / Paul Schveiger (2nd ed.)]

LUIDOR, JOSEPH (d. 1921), Hebrew writer. Born in Galicia, Luidor settled in Ereẓ Israel as a youth, working as an agricultural laborer in various places, including Reḥovot and Ein-Ḥai (Kefar Malal). He was especially close to J.Ḥ. *Brenner, and, along with Brenner, was murdered by Arabs in 1921 in Jaffa. His body was never found. Luidor's stories, published in *Ha-Ẓefirah*, *Ha-Shilo'aḥ*, *Ha-Toren*, and *Ha-Po'el ha-Ẓa'ir*, were among the first writings to deal with the workers of the Second *Aliyah. He also wrote literary reviews. A collection of stories (*Sippurim*) was published in 1976, with an introduction by Dov Landau.

BIBLIOGRAPHY: Y. Yaari-Poleskin, *Ḥolemim ve-Loḥamim* (1946), 473ff. **ADD. BIBLIOGRAPHY:** E. Ben Ezer, *Beshulei Sippurav shel Y. Luidor*, in: *Moznayim*, 45 (1977), 119–127; G. Shaked, *Ha-Sipporet ha-Ivrit*, 2 (1983), 59–61; Y. Schwartz, "*Handasat ha-Adam ve-Izzuv ha-Merḥav ba-Tarbut ha-Ivrit ha-Ḥadashah*," in: *Mikan*, 1 (2000), 9–24; E. Ben Ezer, "*Or Ḥadash al Esther Raab ve-Yosef Luidor*," in: *Iton 77*, 255 (2001), 17–20.

[Getzel Kressel]

LUKA (Ger. **Luck**), small town in W. Bohemia, Czech Republic. According to tradition, Jews from Bavaria founded the town in the 11th century, and they are mentioned in local records for 1198. Luka Jews had to supply a chalice for King *Premysl Ottakar II (1253–78) when he visited the pope. A Jewish "place of worship" is mentioned in 1432. During the Thirty Years' War (1618–48) the community was almost decimated by the plague. Luka Jews, like those of Hroznetin (Lichtenstadt), did business in nearby *Carlsbad. The synagogue and community records were destroyed in a fire in 1842. In 1850, 1,150 Jews lived in Luka (80% of the total population). In the 19th century Feibel (Phillipp) Kohn was mayor of Luka for 28 years. Both an Orthodox rabbi and a Reform preacher served in the town. Even before the 1848 Revolution allowed them freedom of movement, Jews had begun to leave Luka; there were 446 in 1869, but by 1930 there was no *minyan*. On Nov. 10, 1938, the synagogue was burned down. Gravestones in the Jewish cemetery were sold by the Nazis to a stonemason.

BIBLIOGRAPHY: F. Ullmann, in: *Zeitschrift fuer die Geschichte der Juden*, 3 (1966), 117–23; H. Gold, *Die Juden und Judengemeinden Boehmens* (1934), 388–90.

LUKÁCS, GEORG (**György**; 1885–1971), Hungarian philosopher, literary critic, and socialist. Born in Budapest into a family of bankers, Lukács first attracted public attention through his collection of essays on art and philosophy entitled *Die Seele und die Formen* (1911) and he founded a new theater in Budapest for the production of modern plays. He left Judaism at this period. During World War I, Lukács championed the cause of the proletariat and joined the Communist Party in 1918. When the communist regime of Bela *Kun came to power in 1919 Lukács was made commissar for education. In this post he established a national council for culture to impose communist ideas on Hungarian literature and culture. After the collapse of the Kun regime Lukács fled to Vienna where he wrote *Geschichte und Klassenbewusstsein* (1923; *History and Class Consciousness*, 1971), a controversial volume of essays reinterpreting cultural values from a Marxist viewpoint which criticized Communism as it had developed in Russia. His biography, *Lenin* (1924), restored him to favor as an orthodox Marxist. In 1933, when Hitler came to power in Germany, Lukács fled to Russia where he edited several communist journals including *Internationale Literatur* and the Hungarian literary journal *Uj Hang* ("New Voice").

Lukács returned to Hungary after World War II and was elected a member of Parliament. He was made president of the Academy of Sciences and professor of aesthetics and cultural philosophy at the University of Budapest. His unorthodox views led to frequent clashes with the Hungarian Communist Party and after the abortive rising in 1956, he was forced to hide in the Yugoslav embassy. He was restored to favor in the following year and was the recipient of many tributes and honors on his 80th birthday in 1965.

A prolific writer, Lukács was well known for his Marxist interpretations of literature. He was much influenced, however, by the humanitarian concept of Socialism as preached by the Jewish socialist, Moses *Hess. His writings, especially his autobiography *Mein Weg zu Marx* (1933), reflected his opposition to the militant revolution of the orthodox Marxists and advocated humanitarian Socialism based on respect for the individual. His study of Hess, *Moses Hess und das Problem der idealistischen Dialektik*, was published in 1926.

BIBLIOGRAPHY: H. Althaus, *Georg Lukács* (1962); V. Zitta, *Georg Lukács' Marxism, Alienation, Dialectics, Revolution* (1964); F. Benseler (ed.), *Festschrift zum 80. Geburtstag von Georg Lukács* (1965); G. Lichtheim, *G. Lukács* (1971); G.H.R. Parkinson (ed.), *Georg Lukács: The Man, His Work and His Ideas* (1971).

[Sol Liptzin]

LUKAS, PAUL (1887–1971), U.S. actor, born in Budapest. After nine years at the Comedy Theater, Lukas went to the U.S. in 1927 and became prominent in films and plays. The high point of his career was his portrayal of Kurt Mueller, a German refugee, in *Watch on the Rhine*, on the Broadway stage in 1941 and on the screen in 1943. For his film performance, Lukas won a Best Actor Oscar, a Golden Globe, and a New York Film Critics Award. He also appeared on Broadway in *A Doll's House* (1937), *Call Me Madam* (1950), *Flight Into Egypt* (1952), and *The Wayward Saint* (1955).

His more than 90 films include *Little Women* (1933), *Dodsworth* (1936), *The Lady Vanishes* (1938), *Confessions of a Nazi Spy* (1939), *Address Unknown* (1944), *Deadline at Dawn* (1946), *Berlin Express* (1948), *20,000 Leagues under the Sea* (1954), *Four Horsemen of the Apocalypse* (1962), and *Lord Jim* (1965).

[Ruth Beloff (2nd ed.)]

LUKOW (Pol. **Łuków**; Rus. **Lukov**), town in the province of Lublin, E. Poland. By the 15th century there was considerable Jewish settlement in Lukow with a developed autonomous organization. A responsum (no. 59) of R. Meir b. Gedaliah *Lublin (1558–1616) mentions the synagogue of Lukow, which was destroyed by fire. Joel *Sirkes (the Baḥ) served as rabbi of the community at the end of the 16th or the beginning of the 17th century. At the time of the *Chmielnicki massacres (1648–49) the community suffered heavy material losses and the new synagogue was burned down. In 1659 the Jews of Lukow were granted a royal privilege which confirmed their former rights to live in the town, to acquire land and houses, and to engage in commerce and crafts; they were also authorized to erect a synagogue and maintain a cemetery. In 1727 a poll tax of 120 zlotys was imposed on the community. With the progress of economic activities in the town during the second half of the 18th century the Jewish population considerably increased. In the middle of the 18th century a dispute broke out between the communities of Lukow and Miedzyrzec Podlaski over the question of their authority over the small neighboring communities. According to the census of 1765, there were 543 Jews (137 families) there. During the 1780s the rabbi of the community was Samson Zelig b. Jacob Joseph ha-Levi, the author of *Teshu'ot Ḥen* (Dubno, 1797).

After the Congress of Vienna (1815), Lukow passed to Russia, being in Congress Poland. The Jewish population numbered 2,023 (c. 60% of the total population) in 1827, 2,114 (c. 68%) in 1857, and 4,799 (c. 55%) in 1897. In this period many of the Jews were Ḥasidim and followers of the *ẓaddikim* of Kotsk, Aleksandrow, Radzyn, and Gur. Between 1906 and 1920 the *ẓaddik* Hershele Morgensztern, the great-grandson of R. Menahem Mendel of *Kotsk, lived in Lukow. The Jewish population increased to 6,145 (49% of the total) by 1921; there were then 348 Jewish workshops in Lukow. Of the 24 members of the municipal council, ten were Jews (five being delegates of the *Bund). Between the two world wars the Jews of Lukow struggled against antisemitism, and an anti-Jewish economic boycott was organized. The last rabbi of the town (from 1937) was Aaron Note Freiberg, who perished with the members of his community in a death camp.

[Arthur Cygielman]

Holocaust Period

About 6,000 Jews lived in Lukow at the outbreak of World War II. In May 1942 over 2,000 Jews from Slovakia were deported to the town. In October 1942 they were sent, together with over 2,000 Jews from Lukow, to the *Treblinka death camp and exterminated. At the beginning of December 1942 a closed ghetto for the remaining Jews in Lukow was established. On May 2, 1943, the ghetto was liquidated by extermination of its inmates.

[Stefan Krakowski]

BIBLIOGRAPHY: Halpern, Pinkas, 17, 27, 109, 151, 480, 481, 511; B. Wasiutyński, *Ludność żydowska w Polsce w wieku xix i xx* (1930), 35; R. Mahler, *Yidn in Amolikn Poyln in Likht fun Tsifern* (1958), index; idem, in: YIVO *Historishe Shriftn*, 2 (1937), 644–5; T. Brustin-Bernstein, in: *Bleter far Geshikhte*, 3:1–2 (1950), 51–78, passim. **ADD. BIBLIOGRAPHY:** Sefer Lukow (1968), S. Zeminski, "Kartki dziennika nauczyciela w Lukowie z okresu okupacji hitlerowskiej," in: BŻIH, 27 (1958), 105–12.

LULAV (Heb. לוּלָב; "a shoot" or "a young branch of a tree"), a term applied in the Mishnah to all trees, e.g., "the *lulavim* of the terebinth, the pistachio, and the thorn" (Shev. 7:5) and to the vine (Or. 1:7). Its use, however, was particularly confined to the *palm branch, one of the components of the *Four Species (*Arba'ah Minim*; cf. Mish., Suk. 3 and 4). Its use in Jewish ritual is on the Feast of *Sukkot.

LUMBROSO, Italian-Tunisian family of scholars, diplomats, leaders, and rabbis of Castilian origin. JACOB and RAPHAEL, sons of DANIEL LUMBROSO, intervened on behalf of their community in 1686, after a heavy tax had been imposed upon it by the bey. They were the leaders of the *Gornim community (of Leghorn origin) in *Tunis.

ISAAC BEN JACOB (d. 1752) was one of the most brilliant representatives of Tunisian Jewry. He promoted talmudic studies and was largely responsible for the numerous rabbis of eminence who lived in 18th-century Tunis. During his period of office as chief rabbi, the split between the Tuansa (native Tunisian Jews) and Gornim occurred (1710). He attempted to find a compromise solution to the difficulties which arose between the two groups. For a long time he acted as the bey's tax collector; the bey also appointed him *qā'id* (= leader) of the Jews. Wealthy and generous, he gave his financial support to many students. His principal work, entitled *Zera' Yiẓḥak* ("Seed of Isaac," 1768), was published in Tunis after his death. It is a voluminous didactic commentary on several parts of the Talmud and also contains funeral eulogies delivered by the author, as well as some scholarly notes on several passages in the Bible. The second part of the book *Benei Joseph* by Joseph *Tanuji, consisting of notes on several tractates of the Talmud and seven responsa by Isaac Lumbroso, which were found by the editor after Lumbroso's *Zera' Yiẓḥak* had been printed, is also entitled *Zera' Yiẓḥak*. To this day, Isaac is widely renowned among Jews of Tunisian origin as having been a scholar and a mystic.

ISAAC VITA (1793–1871), who was born in Tunis, was known especially for his philanthropy. For several decades he was the undisputed leader of the Leghorn Jews in Tunis and president of the "Portuguese" congregation. He was also a *dayyan*.

His son ABRAM BEN ISAAC VITA (1813–1887), who was also born in Tunis, was appointed personal physician of the bey and minister of health in the Tunisian government. He established learned societies, and under the patronage of his sovereign he propagated Western culture in Tunisia. He was also a philanthropist. He wrote several authoritative scientific studies in the field of medicine. The king of Italy granted him the title of baron. His brother GIACOMO was one of the most prominent merchants of Marseilles, where until 1881 he was the exclusive representative of Tunisia for the whole of France, with the rank of consul general. DAVID (1817–1880), who was born in Tunis, was an important financier and diplomat. He played a prominent role in Tunisian politics. ACHILLE (1858–1914), who was born in Mahdia, was a shipowner in Gabès, where he represented Italy. He was known especially as a poet and author.

[David Corcos]

Abram's son, GIACOMO LUMBROSO (1844–1925), was a classical historian and archaeologist. Born in Tunis, he taught at the universities of Palermo, Pisa, and Rome, and was elected to the famous Accademia dei Lincei. A specialist in the hellenistic civilization of Egypt, he was widely recognized as an expert in the ancillary disciplines of papyrology and epigraphy. His major published works were *Recherches sur l'économie politique de l'Egypte sous les Lagides* (1870) and *L'Egitto al tempo dei Greci e dei Romani* (1882, 1895²). He also compiled a glossary in ten folio volumes, *Testi e commenti concernenti l'antica Alessandria*. After his death, publication of this work was begun under the auspices of the Italian journal *Aegyptus* (serie scientifica, vol. 4), but only a small part was printed (1934, 1936) before wartime priorities ended the project.

His son was ALBERTO EMMANUELE LUMBROSO (1872–1942), Italian historian, who was born in Turin, and like his father, turned from law to history. He specialized in the Napoleonic period, on which he wrote numerous articles and books. His first major work was a Napoleonic bibliography (1894–96) that was followed by a study of the continental system, *Napoleone I. e l'Inghilterra* (1897) and *Napoleone II* (2 vols., 1902–05). In 1903 he became director of the *Revue Napoléonienne* (published in Paris). In 1904, after the National Library in Turin suffered a disastrous fire, Lumbroso donated his personal library as the core of a new collection. In 1916–18 he was Italian military attaché to Greece. In his *Le origini economiche e diplomatiche della guerra mondiale* (2 vols., 1926–28), he argued that World War I represented a triumph of Anglo-Saxon imperialism. His *Bibliografia ragionata della guerra delle nazioni* was published in 1920.

[Frank D. Grande]

BIBLIOGRAPHY: D. Cazès, *Notes bibliographiques…* (1893), index; M. Eisenbeth, in: *Revue Africaine*, 96 (1952), 360–1; J. Ganiage, *ibid.*, 99 (1955), 153–73; Hirschberg, Afrikah, index.

LUMET, SIDNEY (1924–), U.S. theatrical and film director. Born in Philadelphia, Lumet, the son of actor Baruch Lumet and dancer Eugenia Wermus Lumet, was a child actor at the Yiddish Art Theater. He appeared on Broadway in 1937 and later directed off-Broadway shows. Between 1937 and 1948 he performed in such Broadway productions as *Dead End; The Eternal Road; Schoolhouse on the Lot; Morning Star; Journey to Jerusalem*; and *Seeds in the Wind*. In 1947 he founded an off-Broadway group of actors that consisted of former members of Lee Strasberg's Actors Studio, including Yul Brynner and Eli Wallach, who had become dissatisfied with Strasberg's concepts. On Broadway, Lumet directed *Night of the Auk* (1956); *Caligula* (1960); and *Nowhere to Go but Up* (1962).

Lumet joined the Columbia Broadcasting System in 1950 and gained a reputation as a director of live television dramas. He directed such TV series as *Studio One* (1948); *Danger* (1950); *Crime Photographer* (1951); and *You Are There* (1953), as well as the musical *Mr. Broadway* (1957); *All the King's Men* (1958); the miniseries *The Sacco-Vanzetti Story* (1960); and *Rashomon* and *The Iceman Cometh* (1960).

On the screen, the first film that Lumet directed was *Twelve Angry Men* (Oscar nomination for Best Director, 1957). In 1959 he directed Tennessee Williams' *The Fugitive Kind*, and in 1962 Eugene O'Neill's *Long Day's Journey into Night* and Arthur Miller's *A View from the Bridge*. His later movies, most of which were shot in New York City, include *Fail-Safe* (1964), *The Pawnbroker* (1965), *The Hill* (1965), *The Group* (1966), *Bye Bye Braverman* (1968), *Funny Girl* (1968), *The Appointment* (1970), *The Anderson Tapes* (1971), *Serpico* (1973), *Murder on the Orient Express* (1974), *Dog Day Afternoon* (Oscar nomination for Best Director, 1975), *Network* (Oscar nomination for Best Director, 1976), *Equus* (1977), *Prince of the City* (which he co-wrote; Oscar nomination for Best Screenplay, 1981), *Deathtrap* (1982), *The Verdict* (Oscar nomination for Best Director, 1982), *Family Business* (1989), *A Stranger among Us* (1992), *Guilty as Sin* (1993), *Night Falls on Manhattan* (which he also wrote, 1997), and *Gloria* (1999).

Among his numerous awards and nominations, Lumet was presented with a Lifetime Achievement Award by the Directors Guild of America in 1993; won the Joseph L. Mankiewicz Excellence in Filmmaking Award at the Director's View Film Festival in 2004; and received the Honorary Academy Award of Merit in 2005. Lumet's book, *Making Movies*, was published in 1995.

BIBLIOGRAPHY: J. Boyer, *Sidney Lumet* (1993); F. Cunningham, *Sidney Lumet: Film and Literary Vision* (1991, 2001²).

[Jonathan Licht / Ruth Beloff (2nd ed.)]

LUMINA ("The Light"), Jewish Social Democratic group in Romania in the 1890s. Its founders were M. *Wechsler, L. *Gelerter, L. Geller, M. Haimovitz – later well known in the "Arbeter Ring" (*Workmen's Circle) in the United States – and R. Schwartz. Lumina originated in *Jassy in 1893 as an opposition group to the leadership of the Romanian Social Democratic Party. It rejected the latter's tendency to closer cooperation with the liberal bourgeois party, which was the main factor in antisemitism in the country, and also demanded a clear stand on the "Jewish problem." The circle developed into a solely Jewish body which in 1895 emerged as an independent group. It published the periodical *Lumina* (1895–97) in Romanian and *Der Veker* ("Awakener") in Yiddish. Previously (December 12, 1887–January 29, 1888), another pioneer journal of Romanian Jewish socialism had been published under the same title, edited by Stefan Stanca. The society criticized the Social Democratic Party for contenting itself with a demand for general voting rights for all citizens while the Jews were still regarded as "aliens without rights." Lumina considered that one of its functions was to organize the Jewish workers for an independent struggle for political and civic rights, on the assumption that the "liberation of a nation is impossible if it is dormant and frozen." The society, which also had contact with Jewish Social Democrats in Russia, favored the principle of organizing special unions for workers of differing nationalities to function in cooperation. The Jassy group had connections with similar groups in other places in Moldavia (northern Romania). It sent a memorandum (in German) to the congress of the Socialist International in London in 1896, in which it set out its principles and requested a discussion of the problem of the Jews in Romania. The memorandum also explained that the Jewish proletariat and bourgeoisie, though in opposition from the class aspect, had a common interest in obtaining civil and political rights. Lumina had reservations on Zionism and religious attitudes, but *Veker* claimed that a man "who is unable to raise himself to love and sacrifice for his own people, can certainly not be such an idealist as to sacrifice himself for strangers."

BIBLIOGRAPHY: B. Liber, *A Doctor's Apprenticeship* (1957²), index; *Tazkir Aggudat Lumina la-Congress ha-Internazyonal be-London* (Heb. and Ger., 1969); J. Kissman, *Shtudiyes tsu der Geshikhte fun Rumenishe Yidn…* (1944), 63–86 (incl. Eng. summary). **ADD. BIBLIOGRAPHY:** C. Iancu, *Les Juifs en Roumanie 1866–1919* (1978), 244–49; A. Greenbaum, *The Periodical Publications of the Jewish Labor and Revolutionary Movements* (1998), 50–51.

[Moshe Mishkinsky]

LUNCZ, ABRAHAM MOSES (1854–1918), author, publisher, and editor of geographical works on Ereẓ Israel. Luncz emigrated in 1869 from Kovno, where he was born, to Jerusalem, and was accepted as a pupil in the Eẓ Ḥayyim yeshivah. The director, R. Moses Nehemiah Kahana, was in favor of secular education and the use of Hebrew as a spoken language. Because of this, Luncz was able to continue his secular studies and his reading of Haskalah books. The head of the Jerusalem *maskilim* at that time was Israel Dov *Frumkin; Luncz began to associate with him and took part in the founding of the Maskilim Circle and the Moses Montefiore Library (1873–74). In 1873 he began to write in Frumkin's *Ha-Ḥavaẓẓelet*, and like the latter, he criticized the methods of the **ḥalukkah* and its administrators. However, he did not always oppose the traditional community. When H. *Graetz attacked the Jerusalem community after his visit of 1873, during which he was insulted by religious fanatics, Luncz defended it in 1874 in his *Ivri Anokhi* ("I am a Hebrew"). After having already written several geographical articles, Luncz published in 1876 a guide to Jerusalem, *Netivot Ẓiyyon vi-Yrushalayim* ("Paths of Zion and Jerusalem"), the first work of this kind in Hebrew. From then until his death he worked tirelessly to perfect his geographical knowledge. In his search for books he visited the libraries of Christian institutions, a revolutionary step for a Jew in the Jerusalem of those days. In 1877 Luncz's sight began to fail. He went to Vienna and Paris to seek medical help, but it was of no avail; by 1879 he was blind. His misfortune did not deter him from his projects. In Vienna he contacted Perez *Smolenskin, in connection with the publication of his projected yearbook of Ereẓ Israel. The first volume appeared in Hebrew and English in 1882, after a second trip to Vienna, under the title *Jerusalem, Yearbook for the Diffusion of an Accurate Knowledge of Ancient and Modern Palestine*. Only 12 volumes appeared by the time of his death 36 years later. The first volume, of which both the Hebrew and the English part were written mostly by Luncz himself when he still had his sight, is the best. The second volume was printed in 1887 on Luncz's own press in Jerusalem. The articles of the second volume were written by some of the greatest scholars of Palestine and other countries. The material in the Hebrew section dealing with the history of the Jewish settlement is unique. Here again, Luncz was the main contributor. Volumes one and two appeared in Hebrew and English; three and four in Hebrew and German. In 1895 he began to publish the *Lu'aḥ Ereẓ Yisrael*, a literary almanac, which appeared yearly until 1915. Among the books which he published in improved editions with his own notes, the most important are *Kaftor va-Feraḥ* of R. *Estori ha-Parḥi; *Pe'at ha-Shulḥan* of R. Israel of *Shklov; and *Tevu'ot ha-Areẓ* of R. Yehoseph *Schwarz. In the three volumes of *Ha-Me'ammer* he published documentary material on Ereẓ Israel. A courageous experiment for a blind man was his publication of the Jerusalem Talmud according to a manuscript that he found in the Vatican Library. By the time of his death, he had reached the tractate *Shevi'it*. Luncz also wrote *Die juedischen Kolonien Palaestinas* (1902) and edited *Ha-Ikkar* ("The Peasant"), 1894–96. Besides these literary activities, he was an active member of the *Va'ad ha-Lashon ha-Ivrit ("Committee for the Hebrew Language") and in 1902, with two of his friends, he founded the Educational Center for the Blind.

BIBLIOGRAPHY: H. Luncz, in: *Yerushalayim*, 13 (1919), 329–50 (incl. list of works); Rivlin and Malachi, in: *Yerushalayim*, ed. by I. Press and E.L. Sukenik (1928), 1–16 (Heb. pt.); Rivlin, in: *Koveẓ Ma'amarim le-Divrei Yemei ha-Ittonut be-Ereẓ Yisrael*, 2 (1936), 66–81; I. Trywaks and E. Steinman (eds.), *Sefer Me'ah Shanah* (1938), 285–98; Malachi, in: *Talpioth*, 4 (1950), 759–69; idem, in: *Genazim*, 1 (1961), 276–89; BIES, 19 (1955), 1–28; H. Luncz-Bolotin, *Me'ir Netivot Yerushalayim* (1968); Kressel, in: *Netivot Ẓiyyon vi-Yerushalayim* (1970).

[Abraham J. Brawer]

LUNEL, town in Hérault department, S. France, home of a medieval Jewish community renowned for its scholars. According to local tradition, the town was founded by inhabitants of Jericho who arrived there after the conquest of their native city. Tourist brochures also claim that this community was outstanding for its medical studies and that its physicians carried out the first surgical operation in Europe. The nearby remains of the synagogue seem to have greater historical validity. The earliest historical evidence on the Jewish community of Lunel is recorded by *Benjamin of Tudela (1159). The community had probably been founded some time before, because by then it numbered at least 300 persons (or perhaps 300 families). Scant information on the Jewish community appears in non-Jewish sources. Toward the close of the 12th century, a Jew of Lunel, David ha-Kohen, son of Solomon, granted a loan to Agnète, wife of Guilhem VIII, lord of Montpellier. On the other hand, in 1293 the lord of Lunel sold part of the incomes from his barony to a Jew of Montpellier named Thauros. The existence of a cemetery is attested in documents dating from the end of the 13th century. On the eve of the expulsion in 1306, six Jews from Lunel were arrested and imprisoned in the Châtelet of Paris. The community must have been reconstituted after the return of the Jews to France in 1315 for, on Aug. 22, 1319, King Philip V the Tall ordered proceedings against the Jews of Lunel who, during Lent, had supposedly insulted the cross. A considerable amount is known about the Jewish scholars of Lunel. Benjamin of Tudela praised them for their erudition, piety, and generosity, not only toward the students who came to study at the yeshivah but also to every Jew in distress. *Meshullam b. Jacob was *rosh yeshivah* and a well-known halakhic authority. Of his five sons, the best known were Jacob, a commentator; *Aaron b. Meshullam of Lunel, impassioned defender of the philosophy of Maimonides; and *Asher b. Meshullam ha-Kohen of Lunel, a mystic and a brilliant talmudist. Meshullam b. Jacob's son-in-law, Moses b. Judah of Béziers, was living in Lunel at the time of Benjamin of Tudela's visit, as was Judah b. Saul ibn *Tibbon, who settled there after persecution forced him to leave Granada. Many scholars, such as Zerahiah b. Isaac ha-Levi *Gerondi and *Abraham b. David of Posquières, stayed in Lunel for varying periods of time. Others more intimately connected with the town included *Abraham b. Nathan ha-Yarḥi (second half of the 12th century); the talmudist *Jonathan b. David ha-Kohen of Lunel; Manoah, commentator on Maimonides' *Mishneh Torah*; and Abba Mari b. Moses, also known as *Astruc of Lunel, a halakhic authority and vigorous opponent of science and philosophy. His main supporters were Isaac b. Avigdor, Simeon b. Joseph of Lunel, and Meir b. Isaiah; and his staunchest adversary was Solomon b. Isaac of Lunel, referred to as Nasi, who lived in Montpellier. Meshullam b. Machir, also known as Don Bonet Crescas of Lunel (d. 1306), is the last scholar known to have been a native of the town. Throughout the 14th and 15th centuries, however, there were several scholars who bore the name "de Lunel" or "Ha-Yarḥi," especially in Provence. The name was later found among families in Comtat Venaissin and the author Armand *Lunel belonged to one of these.

BIBLIOGRAPHY: Gross, Gal Jud, 277–90; T. Millerot, *Histoire de la ville de Lunel* (n. d.), 87, 96f., 113; A.A. Rouet, *Etudes sur l'école* *juive de Lunel au Moyen Age* (1878); G. Scholem, *Ursprung und Anfaenge der Kabbala* (1962), index.

[Bernhard Blumenkranz]

LUNEL, ARMAND (1892–1977), French novelist. The descendant of an old Provençal Jewish family, Lunel was born in Aix-en-Provence. After studying law, he later taught philosophy in Monaco. Writing in his spare time, he made his name with his sensitive and imaginative portrayals of Provence and its colorful inhabitants, both Jews and non-Jews. Lunel's major works include *L'Imagerie du Cordier* (1924); *Nicolo-Peccavi, ou l'Affaire Dreyfus à Carpentras* (1926); *Noire et grise* (1930); *Le Balai de sorcière* (1935); *Jérusalem à Carpentras* (1937), a collection of short stories; *La Maison de la femme peinte* (1946); *Les Amandes d'Aix* (1949); and *La Belle à la fontaine* (1959).

Lunel wrote librettos for his childhood friend, the composer Darius *Milhaud, notably the text of *Esther de Carpentras* (1926), on which Milhaud later based his *opéra-bouffe, Barba Garibo* (1950), and the oratorio *David* (1954), which was performed for the 3,000th anniversary of Jerusalem. "Esther," inspired by an old Provençal Purim play, evokes the humor and drama of Jewish life in Carpentras during the Middle Ages. Lunel also initiated a series of books on the French provinces, to which he himself contributed *J'ai Vu Vivre La Provence* (1962). Lunel was awarded the Gobert History Prize of the French Academy for his *The Jews of Languedoc Provence* and *The French States of the Pope* (1975) and the 1976 French Grand Prix for Literature.

BIBLIOGRAPHY: A. Spire, *Quelques Juifs et demi-Juifs* (1928); *Guide Religieux de la France* (1967), 596.

[Moshe Catane]

LUNEL, JACOB DE (18th century), Provençal poet. In 1737 he was one of the scholars of Carpentras who approved the publication of the prayers for Rosh Ha-Shanah and the Day of Atonement according to the local rite. He revised and enlarged a Purim play by Mardochée Astruc written in Provençal, which he published in 1774 (new edition by E. Sabatier, 1877). Some of his liturgical poems appear in the *Seder ha-Kunteres (Maḥzor Avignon)*. He also composed a Hebrew ode on the occasion of Louis XV's escape from assassination in 1757; this poem was recited with musical accompaniment in the synagogue of Avignon.

BIBLIOGRAPHY: Zunz, Gesch, 467; idem, in: AZDJ, 3 (1839), 682 no. 47; Neubauer, Cat, 899 no. 2506; Lipschutz, in: REJ, 84 (1927); Davidson, Oẓar, 4 (1933), 414.

[Jefim (Hayyim) Schirmann]

LUNÉVILLE, town in the Meurthe-et-Moselle department, N.E. France. Several Jews were mentioned in Lunéville in 1470–72, just before the expulsion from the duchy of Lorraine. From 1702 Lunéville was the seat of the ducal court of Lorraine; Samuel Lévy took charge of the court's commercial interests in 1705. Two Jewish families were authorized to live in the town by an edict of 1753; there were 16 families residing there when the synagogue was constructed in 1785. A cemetery was not consecrated until 1791. The community numbered 315 persons in 1808 and 400 in 1855; from 1870 it was augmented by a number of manufacturers from Alsace. Among the Hebrew printing presses established in France in the latter part of the 18th century and early in the 19th was one belonging to Abraham Brisach, who produced in Lunéville a *maḥzor* with Judeo-German translation in 1797 and a *Likkutei Ẓevi* in 1798. A hospital, established in 1857, was in use until 1944. Alfred *Lévy, later chief rabbi of France and a native of Lunéville, was rabbi there from 1869 to 1880. During World War I the incumbent minister, S. Weill, and several other Jews were among the civilians slaughtered at Lunéville (1914); 18 other Jews from Lunéville fell in battle in this war and six in World War II. One hundred and ninety-four Jews (including the patients in the hospital and 65 refugees) were deported from Lunéville during the German occupation; only nine survived. In 1969 there were about 200 Jews in Lunéville, half of them from North Africa.

BIBLIOGRAPHY: H. Baumont, *Histoire de Lunéville* (1901), 210, 299–301, 559–61; P. Lang, in: *Revue Juive de Lorraine*, 11–14 (1935–38), passim; N. Gruss, in: REJ, 125 (1966), 90.

[Gilbert Cahen]

LUNGE, GEORG (1839–1923), German industrial chemist. Born in Breslau, Lunge started his own chemical factory in 1862. He went to England (1865) and worked in the coal tar and soda industries. He was a professor at the Zurich Polytechnicum (1876–1907) and wrote *Handbuch der Sodaindustrie* (2 vols., 1879); *Industrie der Steinkohlentheer-Destillation und Ammoniakwasser Bearbeitung* (2 vols., 1882); *Taschenbuch fuer die anorganisch-chemische Grossindustrie* (1908, 1921^6, with E. Berl); he edited (also with E. Berl) the *Chemisch-technische Untersuchungsmethoden* (4 vols., 1899; *Technical Methods of Chemical Analysis*, 6 vols., 1908, 1924^2); and *Technical Gas Analysis* (1914).

LUNIETZ (Ilintsky), GEDALIAH BEN ISSAC OF (d. 1785), ḥasidic preacher and *ẓaddik* in Ukraine, son of a *dayyan* in Polonnoye. An ardent preacher who stirred his listeners, Gedaliah was one of the sources of ḥasidic legend. His mentors in Ḥasidism were *Dov Baer the Maggid of Mezhirech and *Jacob Joseph of Polonnoye. Gedaliah was the most outstanding disciple of *Aryeh Leib of Polonnoye. He served as rabbi in Ostropol, Miropol, and Ilintsy. His *Teshu'ot Ḥen* (Berdichev, 1816) includes sermons, some of them on the importance and holiness of Ereẓ Israel, expressing a profound sense of the bitterness of exile and anticipation of redemption.

BIBLIOGRAPHY: L. Grossmann, *Kunteres Shem u-She'erit* (1943), 52.

LUNTS, LEV NATANOVICH (1901–1924), Russian playwright and literary theorist. Lunts was born into a well-educated St. Petersburg family which immigrated to Germany after the 1917 Revolution. He himself, however, remained in Russia for a time, suffered from malnutrition, and died in

Hamburg at the age of 23. Lunts was a founder and spokesman of the important young writers' group in Petrograd known as the Serapion Brothers and named after a hero in one of the novels of E.T.A. Hoffmann, the 18th-century German romantic. The group's aims were to free art from political pressures and to win tolerance for artistic dissent. In his articles Lunts argued that Russian literature was unduly tendentious and uniformly realistic, and recommended that it emulate Western models. His play *Vne zakona* ("Outside the Law," 1923) is set in Spain and its central theme is that power corrupts. It was translated into many languages and became part of the repertoire of several Western European theaters. The Soviet authorities saw in his plays criticism of the regime and forbade performing them in the Soviet theaters. Two of his stories, "V pustyne" ("In the Desert," 1922) and "Rodina" ("Homeland," 1923), deal with ancient Jewish historical events.

BIBLIOGRAPHY: M. Slonim, *Modern Russian Literature* (1953), 294–6; G. Struve, *Soviet Russian Literature – 1917–1950* (1951), 46–52, 61, 107.

[Yitzhak Maor]

LURIA (Lourie, Lurje, Loria, Lurja), well-known family traceable to the 14th century. The Luria family spread throughout Germany, Bohemia, Eastern Europe, Italy, and Oriental countries. The name perhaps derives from Loria, a small town near *Bassano in the Vicenza region of Italy, but this is by no means certain. All who bear this name did not necessarily belong to one family, and there is certainly no connection between this family and the Luria family (who were Levites) to which Isaac *Luria (the Ari) belonged. The main Luria family is descended from *Rashi and legend extends its descent to the *tanna* *Johanan ha-Sandelar. The source of the family history is the genealogical document compiled by Johanan b. Aaron Luria (see later) which *Joseph b. Gershom of Rosheim received from the author and incorporated in his *Sefer ha-Miknah*. Solomon b. Aaron b. Jehiel, Johanan's grandson, sent a copy to his relative, Solomon *Luria (Maharshal), who made an addition to the copy detailing his connection with Jehiel, brother of the author of the document. This copy is important for determining the link between the German and Polish branches. The document passed to Solomon Luria's descendants from generation to generation, each successive member adding his own name. One copy was published, after 300 years, in *Ha-Maggid* (vol. 1 (1857), 178) by Moses Eliezer *Beilinson, himself a member of the Luria family. This copy, which completed the German branch, was published in Solomon Luria's responsa (Fuerth, 1767; Lemberg, 1859).

The founder of the family was SOLOMON SPIRA (a son-in-law of Mattathias Treves; see *Treves family). It is related of his daughter MIRIAM (1350 – the second generation) that she taught *halakhah* from behind a curtain in the yeshivah. Nothing is known of Samson of Erfurt (third generation), Jehiel (fourth), and Nethanel (fourth) but their names, but Nethanel's son, AARON LURIA (1450), was known and honored as a rabbinical authority. He was one of the opponents of the convention of rabbis called by Seligman Oppenheim in Bingen in 1456 and his responsum on the subject was printed in the responsa of R. Moses *Mintz (no. 63) along with the views of other opponents. A number of the responsa (16, 19, 23, and 24) of Mintz and Israel *Bruna (nos. 259–61) are addressed to him. JOHANAN (late 15th–early 16th centuries), who compiled the genealogical table, was Aaron's son. He was given the right to establish a yeshivah in *Strasbourg or *Colmar. Losing all his wealth in the Burgundian wars of 1475, he passed the last years of his life in *Worms. He is the author of *Meshivat Nefesh*, a homiletical and kabbalistic commentary on the Pentateuch (Mss. Bodleian, nos. 257–8) with an appendix, *Teshuvat ha-Minim u-She'ar Inyanim*, which is a defense of Judaism against Christian criticism. His didactic ethical poem *Hadrakhah* has been published a number of times. His grandson SOLOMON (d. before 1583) compiled the second version of the Luria family tree for Solomon Luria. His only son, JOSHUA MOSES (d. 1591), who was responsible for the third version, served as rabbi in Worms. He is referred to in the customal of Worms (Mss. Breslau Seminary LXXXVII, 123) and in other works. His son AARON (d. 1613) was a *dayyan* in the *bet din* of Isaiah *Horowitz in Frankfurt. After him, unbroken knowledge of the German branch of the family ceases, but the family history does not come to an end then. Joseph of Rosheim was related to the head of the family, Solomon Spira, and his grandson, Elijah b. Moses *Loanz (1564–1636), was also the maternal grandson of Johanan Luria.

The name Luria is found in Prague until the end of the 16th century and still later, but the connection between this branch and the German one cannot be established. It is doubtful if the kabbalist Jehiel *Luria of Safed (late 16th–early 17th centuries) belonged to this family. Some identify him with Jehiel Ashkenazi *Luria, author of the *Heikhal ha-Shem* (Venice, 1601). The founder of the Russian-Polish branch was JEHIEL LURIA, brother of Johanan (above). Around 1470 he left Germany and died in Bassat, Lithuania, where he had apparently served as rabbi. His great-grandson was Solomon Luria (the Maharshal). JACOB MOSES BEN ABRAHAM HELIN ASHKENAZI, a grandson of the Maharshal, compiled a commentary, *Yedei Moshe*, on the *Midrash Rabbah* (Frankfurt on the Oder, 1705). SOLOMON LURIA (early 17th century), "the physician of Lublin," was a cousin of the Maharshal. Jehiel *Heilprin, author of *Seder ha-Dorot*, was the eighth generation from the Maharshal, and Abraham *Gombiner, author of *Magen Avraham*, the sixth generation. David b. Judah Judel *Luria (Radal) was the tenth generation. His nephew, David b. Jacob Aaron *Luria (1800–1873), devoted himself to improving Jewish education in Minsk.

In the 19th century, when the Jews of Russia were compelled to adopt surnames, many chose the name Luria without having any connection with the family. It is unclear what connection, if any, there is between bearers of the name Loria in Italy and the Luria family, and it is possible that the genealogical tree of this branch, transmitted by Z. *Margolioth in his *Ma'alot ha-Yuḥasin* (1900), 61–63, is a 17th-century forgery intended to connect the Italian family with the more renowned one.

In 2004, Neil Rosenstein published a complete Luria family genealogy. He traces the family back to the *tanna* Hillel, and from him back to King David. He presents numerous interlocking genealogical tables, many of which connect the Luria family to the leading rabbinic sages of the past 500 years.

BIBLIOGRAPHY: A. Epstein, *Mishpaḥat Luria, Shoshelet Yiḥusah…* (1901); JJLG, 5 (1907), 91ff.; A. Lourié, *Die Familie Lourié (Luria)* (1923); J. Cohen-Ẓedek, *Dor Yesharim* (1898). **ADD. BIBLIOGRAPHY:** N. Rosenstein, *The Lurie Legacy: The House of Davidic Royal Descent* (2004).

[Jacob Rothschild]

LURIA, ALEXANDER ROMANOVICH (1902–1977), Soviet psychologist. Luria was born in Kazan to a well-known physician. He graduated from the universities of Kazan (1921) and the 1st Medical Institute of Moscow (1937). In 1945 Luria was appointed professor in the department of psychology at the Moscow State University, a full member of the Academy of Pedagogical Sciences in 1947, and director of the Laboratory of Experimental Psychology and Restoration of Higher Cortical Functions, U.S.S.R. Academy of Medical Sciences, Moscow. He was one of the founders of neuropsychology. The most frequently translated Soviet psychologist, Luria was familiar to psychologists the world over having acted as the program chairman of the 18th International Congress of Psychology, held in Moscow in 1966. He had wide professional interests which included brain mechanisms of mental operations (neuropsychology), with special reference to disturbances associated with brain lesions, the role of speech in mental development and control of child behavior, and mental retardation. He was a prolific writer and his books include *Sovremennaya psikhologiya v yego osnovnykh napravleniyakh* ("Basic Trends in Modern Psychology," 1928); *Rech i intellekt derevenskogo, gorodskogo i besprizornogo rebyonka* ("Speech and Intellect of Country, City, and Homeless Children," 1930); *The Nature of Human Conflicts …* (1932); *Rech i razvitiye psikhicheskikh protsessov u rebyonka* (with F. Ya. Yudovich, 1956; *Speech and the Development of Mental Processes in the Child*, 1959); *The Mentally Retarded Child* (ed. and coauthor, 1961); *Higher Cortical Functions in Man* (1966); and *The Mind of a Mnemonist* (1968). Luria was a foreign member of the American National Academy and a member of many foreign research institutes in America and Europe.

[Josef Brozek]

LURIA, DAVID BEN JACOB AARON (1800–1873), educationalist; a pioneer of Haskalah in Russia. He was born in Minsk into a wealthy family. Influenced by the program of Max *Lilienthal, Luria concentrated on reform of the educational system of the community of Minsk. In 1843 he transferred the *talmud torah* of Minsk to new premises, provided its pupils with clothing, introduced European methods of study and order into the institution, engaged new teachers, and added secular studies and the Russian language to the traditional curriculum. The success of the institution encouraged the establishment in 1845 of a school for the children of "house owners" under the name of "Midrash Ezraḥim" ("School for Citizens") which was attended by about 100 children. At the end of 1846 the Russian authorities, who were about to open a government school for Jews of the town, closed Luria's educational institutions. He continued to spread the ideas of the Haskalah in Minsk, and his house was regarded by Orthodox circles as a "meeting place for heretics." He contributed to the periodicals *Ha-Maggid* and *Kokhavim* and published a collection of commentaries to verses of the Bible, and other essays, in the spirit of the Haskalah, *Omer ba-Sadeh* (Vilna, 1853).

BIBLIOGRAPHY: L. Levanda, in: *Yevreyskaya Biblioteka*, 3 (1873), 365–77; J.L. Levin, *Zikhronot ve-Hegyonot* (1968), 43–46; *Ha-Shaḥar*, 4 (1873), 569.

[Yehdua Slutsky]

LURIA, DAVID BEN JUDAH (1798–1855), Lithuanian rabbi and scholar. Luria was born in Bykhow, Mogilev region. He studied under Saul *Katzenellenbogen in Vilna, but in 1815 returned to his native town, where he remained for the rest of his life and where he founded a yeshivah. A false accusation that grew out of a family quarrel in Bykhow, supported by letters forged in his name attacking the czarist government, led to his imprisonment in the fortress of Schluesselburg, from which he was released when the forgeries came to light (1837/38). Luria was active in communal affairs and together with Isaac *Volozhyner met with Sir Moses *Montefiore when the latter visited Vilna in 1846 to investigate the condition of the Jews in Russia. Luria corresponded with I.B. *Levinsohn, encouraging the translation of his book, *Zerubavel*, as a useful weapon against the calumnious attacks on the Talmud by antisemites and the *maskilim*. In one of his responsa to the rabbis of Mantua, he vehemently attacked the reformists for their attempts to delete from the liturgy the prayers for the coming of the Messiah and the future redemption (Responsa, Ra-Dal (1898) 21c–d).

Luria was regarded as one of the Torah leaders of his generation, particularly after the death of his spiritual mentor, *Elijah b. Solomon (Gaon of Vilna). His literary works embrace almost all the books of the Oral Law. They are chiefly textual glosses, notes, source references, and expositions of the sayings of the talmudic scholars, reflecting extraordinary knowledge of Torah together with a feeling for scientific criticism and an understanding of the plain meaning reminiscent of the methods followed by the Gaon of Vilna.

Of his works the following are particularly worthy of note: his commentary to the Mishnah (Vilna, 1886–90); his notes to most of the Talmud, and his glosses to the *Midrash Rabbah*, which were published in the large Vilna (Romm) editions; his commentaries to the *Midrash Samuel Rabbati* (1852); to the *Pesikta Rabbati de Rav Kahana* (1893); to the *Pirkei de-Rabbi Eliezer* (1852) with an extensive and detailed introduction; *Kokhevei-Or* (1877), notes to *Sefer Yuḥasin* and to *Seder ha-Dorot; Kadmut Sefer ha-Zohar* (1856), notes to the Zohar, aimed at proving that its author was indeed Simeon b. Yoḥai; notes to the *She'iltot* of *Aḥai Gaon (1861); *Nefesh David* (appended to the *Yahal Or* (1882) of the Vilna Gaon), expositions of the Zohar and the *Zohar Ḥadash*; a commentary on the Book of Esther (1887); and several responsa (1898). Luria also arranged for the publication of several works of the Vilna Gaon, adding to them his own notes: *To'elet Eliyahu* (1856) on the *aggadot* to *Bava Kamma*, the glosses of the Gaon on the Jerusalem Talmud; order of *Zera'im*, and Luria's own glosses on the order *Mo'ed* (1858). He also wrote notes on *Aliyyot Eliyahu* (1882), Joshua H. *Lewin's book on the Gaon.

BIBLIOGRAPHY: S. Luria, in: D. Luria, *Kadmut Sefer ha-Zohar* (1887^{2}; repr. 1951), 2–16; I.B. Levinsohn, *Be'er Yizḥak* (1899), 163–5; Ḥ.N. Maggid-Steinschneider, *Ir Vilna* (1900), 157–9; S. Ginsburg, *Ketavim Historiyyim* (1944), 28–39.

LURIA, ISAAC BEN SOLOMON (1534–1572), kabbalist, referred to as Ha-Ari (האר״י; "the [sacred] lion"" from the initials of האלוהי רבי יצחק; *Ha-Elohi Rabbi Yizḥak*, "the divine Rabbi"). This cognomen was in use by the end of the 16th century, apparently at first in kabbalistic circles in Italy, but Luria's contemporaries in *Safed refer to him as R. Isaac Ashkenazi (הריא״ש), R. Isaac Ashkenazi Luria (הריא״ל), also as De Luria. His father, a member of the Ashkenazi family of Luria from Germany or Poland, emigrated to *Jerusalem and apparently there married into the Sephardi Frances family. As he died while Isaac was a child, his widow took the boy to *Egypt, where he was brought up in the home of her brother Mordecai Frances, a wealthy tax-farmer. Traditions concerning Luria's youth, his stay in Egypt, and his introduction to *Kabbalah are shrouded in legend, and the true facts are difficult to distinguish. Contradicting the widely accepted belief that he went to Egypt at the age of seven is his own testimony recalling a kabbalistic tradition which he learned in Jerusalem from a Polish kabbalist, Kalonymus (see *Sha'ar he-Pesukim*, para. *Be-Ha'alotekha*).

In Egypt, Luria studied under *David b. Solomon ibn Abi Zimra and his successor, Bezalel *Ashkenazi. Luria collaborated with the latter in writing halakhic works such as the *Shitah Mekubbeẓet* on tractate *Zevaḥim*, which according to Ḥayyim Joseph David *Azulai was burned in Izmir in 1735. Their annotations of some of Isaac *Alfasi's works were printed in *Tummat Yesharim* (Venice, 1622). M. Benayahu has conjectured that commentaries on passages in tractate *Ḥullin* and other talmudic tractates, extant in a manuscript written in Egypt not later than 1655 in the academy of a *ḥakham* named Mohariel, derive from notes made by pupils of Luria's yeshivah in Egypt. However, this is doubtful since the manuscript mentions *Sefer Pesakim*, a collection of halakhic decisions by the same author, and there is no evidence to indicate that Luria was the author of such a book, certainly not before he was 20 years old. It is certain, however, that Luria was familiar with rabbinical literature and was believed to be outstanding in the non-mystical study of the law. As well as religious study, he also engaged in commerce while in Egypt, as attested by documents in the Cairo **Genizah*. A document relating to his business in pepper dating from 1559 had been published by E.J. Worman (REJ, 57 (1909), 281–2), and a second, relating to grain, by S. Assaf (*Mekorot u-Meḥkarim* (1946), 204). Assaf connects this with Luria's sojourn in Safed, but there is no doubt that it was written in Egypt. The entire document is in Luria's handwriting, the only extant specimen to date. This material supports the evidence of Jedidiah Galante (in Leon Modena's *Sefer Ari Nohem*, ed. by S. Rosenthal; Leipzig, 1840) that, like many of the Safed scholars, Luria conducted business in the town; three days before his death he made up his accounts with his customers. Many of the scholars of Safed similarly engaged in business activities.

While still in Egypt, Luria began his esoteric studies and retired to a life of seclusion on the island Jazīrat al-Rawḍa on the Nile near Cairo. This island was owned by his uncle, who in the meantime had become his father-in-law. It is far from clear whether this retirement, which is reported to have lasted for seven years, took place in his youth at the beginning of the 1550s or when he was older. Legend antedates it considerably. In 1558, Luria endorsed a halakhic decision jointly with Bezalel Ashkenazi and Simeon Castellazzo. In his mystic study, he concentrated on the *Zohar and works of the earlier kabbalists, and, of the works of his contemporaries, made a particular study of Moses *Cordovero. According to evidence dating from the end of the 16th century, it was during this initial period of kabbalistic study that he wrote his single work, a commentary on the *Sifra di-Ẓeni'uta* ("Book of Concealment"), a short but important section of the Zohar (published in Vital's *Sha'ar Ma'amrei Rashbi*). The book gives no hint of the original kabbalistic system that Luria expounded at the end of his life and shows some influence of Cordovero. In Egypt he met Samuel ibn Fodeila, a kabbalist, to whom Luria wrote a lengthy letter on kabbalistic topics. Here he refers to his own book and asks him to examine it in his brother's house, evidently in Egypt. Luria may have made a pilgrimage to Meron before going to settle in Safed, since there are references to his presence at the *Lag ba-Omer festival in Meron. In 1569, or perhaps at the beginning of 1570, he settled in Safed with his family and studied Kabbalah with Cordovero for a short time. Some of his glosses on passages of the Zohar were evidently written while Cordovero was still alive and some after his death, since Luria refers to him both as "our teacher whose light may be prolonged" and "my late teacher." On the other hand, he had already begun to impart his original kabbalistic system to a number of disciples in Safed, among them distinguished scholars. After Cordovero's death at the end of 1570, Ḥayyim *Vital drew particularly close to Luria, becoming his principal and most celebrated disciple.

Luria may have gathered around him in Safed an academy whose members engaged in exoteric and esoteric studies. The names of some 30 of his disciples are known. Vital confirms (in the manuscript on practical Kabbalah, holograph in the Musajoff collection, Jerusalem) that a week before his preceptor died they had been studying the tractate *Yevamot*.

He also gives some information about Luria's system of study in the non-mystical parts of the law. Luria occasionally delivered homilies in the Ashkenazi synagogue in Safed, but generally refrained from religious teaching in public. On the other hand, he often took long walks with his closest disciples in the neighborhood of Safed pointing out to them the graves of saintly personages not hitherto known, which he discovered through his spiritual intuition and revelations. At this period, he had already become famous as a man who possessed the "holy spirit" or received the "revelations of Elijah." He taught his disciples orally, instructing them both in his original system of theoretical Kabbalah, and also in the way to communion with the souls of the righteous (*ẓaddikim*). This was accomplished by "unification" of the *Sefirot* and exercises in concentration on certain of the divine names and their combinations, and especially by means of *kavvanah*, i.e., mystical reflection or meditations in the act of prayer and the fulfillment of religious precepts. He himself wrote down little of his teaching, apart from an attempt to provide a detailed commentary on the first pages of the Zohar and glosses on isolated passages. These were collected from his autography by Vital and assembled in a special book, of which a number of handwritten copies are extant.

Luria acknowledges his inability to present his teachings in written form since the overflow of his ideas did not lend itself to systematization. Nor did he select the various subjects for study in his doctrine in a logical sequence but at random. He guarded the secret of his system and did not permit its propagation during his lifetime, therefore becoming celebrated at first mainly for his conduct and saintly qualities. Some who applied to study under him were rejected, including Moses *Alshekh. His relations with the scholars of Safed were friendly; a halakhic consultation addressed by him to Joseph *Caro appears in the responsa titled *Avkat Rokhel* (no. 136). Luria undoubtedly regarded himself as an innovator, preeminent among contemporary kabbalists. Certain allusions made to his disciples suggest that he believed himself to be "the Messiah, the son of Joseph," destined to die in the fulfillment of his mission. The period of his activity in Safed was brief, for he died in an epidemic on July 15, 1572. His grave in Safed was and remains a place of pilgrimage for successive generations.

Both in enthusiastic descriptions by his disciples and their pupils, written in the decade after his death, and in their careful preservation and collection of his teachings and faithful rendering of his personal traits, Luria's striking personality is attested. The relevant details are scattered in the writings of his disciples, particularly those of Vital. Some have been assembled in book form, such as the *Shulḥan Arukh shel R. Yiẓḥak Luria*, compiled from the writings of Jacob Ẓemaḥ and published a number of times (first in Poland, 1660–70), the *Orḥot Ẓaddikim*, on the precepts of Luria from the writings of Vital (vol. 2, Salonika, 1770), and in *Patora de Abba* (Jerusalem, 1905). In addition, a wealth of legend accumulated around his personality, with historical recollection and authentic fact being mingled with visionary pronouncements and anecdotes of other holy men. Such mythical elements already appear in works written 20 years after Luria's death, such as the *Sefer Ḥaredim* of Eliezer *Azikri, *Sefer Reshit Ḥokhmah* by Elijah de *Vidas, and the books of Abraham *Galante. The legend is crystallized in two important documents, whose sequence of publication is a matter of controversy. One is the collection of three letters written in Safed between 1602 and 1609 by Solomon (Shlomel) Dresnitz, an immigrant from Moravia, to his friend in Cracow. The letters were first published in 1629 in *Ta'alumot Ḥokhmah* by Joseph Solomon *Delmedigo, and circulated from the end of the 18th century under the title *Shivḥei ha-Ari* ("The Tributes of Ha-Ari"). The second document, *Toledot ha-Ari ("Biography of Ha-Ari"), appears in numerous manuscripts from the 17th century; one version is published under the title *Ma'asei Nissim* ("Miracles"), although inside it is called *Shivḥei ha-Ari*; it appeared at the beginning of *Sefer ha-Kavannot* (Constantinople, 1720). This version of the legend was generally regarded as the later one, based on the Safed letters. However, M. Benayahu has published a complete edition of this recension (1967) and argued that it served as the basis for the source of Dresnitz' letters. Benayahu considers that the book was compiled between 1590 and 1600 by one of the scholars of Safed, and its various recensions circulated widely in the Orient and Italy. This, the first kabbalistic hagiography, compounds fact and imagination in its biographical account of the life of the saintly man.

There is no doubt that the legend of the Ari was widespread and circulated earlier than the written sources treating his kabbalistic teaching. These compositions form an extensive literature. Although frequently described by kabbalists as *Kitvei ha-Ari*, "the writings of Luria," they are in fact the works of his disciples and their own disciples, edited and sometimes condensed. While most remained in manuscript, a few were published between 1572 and 1650. Moved by mystical inspiration, Luria expounded his ideas with many variants. His hearers seem to have noted down some of his teachings during his lifetime but mainly transmitted them from memory after his death, frequently superimposing their own interpretation. The conventicle of Luria's disciples included some important kabbalists who rated themselves highly and considered themselves faithful recorders of their master's doctrine. Personal friction and rivalry were not unknown. In the annals of the Kabbalah Ḥayyim Vital has won the laurels as Luria's chief disciple; the works of his associates and rivals have been passed over or erroneously attributed to Vital himself, in which case they acquired the reputation of authoritative sources of Luria's teachings. In fact, a number of variants of these are extant which, in the main, are not interdependent but represent independent traditions recorded by his disciples, including one which must be considered spurious. There are four such principal traditions:

(1) That of Moses *Jonah of Safed, crystallized in *Sefer Kanfei Yonah*. The complete authentic text is extant in numerous manuscripts, particularly in Ms. Sasson 993, copied by the

author himself in Constantinople in 1582. A defective edition was compiled by Menahem Azariah *Fano in Mantua (first printed in Korzec, 1786). This is an important source for the study of Lurianic Kabbalah, and as yet no satisfactory evaluation of it has been attempted. The author has omitted some of Luria's teachings, such as the doctrine of *ẓimẓum* ("withdrawal"), although, compared with Vital's rendering, his exposition of other teachings of Luria excels in clarity.

(2) That of *Joseph ibn Tabul who, after Luria's death, taught Lurianic Kabbalah to several pupils, among them Samson Bacchi, an Italian kabbalist. Ibn Tabul compiled a systematic exposition of Lurianic Kabbalah divided into *derushim* ("homilies"), with a number of supplements. The homilies are extant in manuscript and for a long time were attributed to Vital under the title *Derush Ḥefẓi-Bah* and were also published in his name (1921, at the beginning of *Simḥat Kohen* by Masʿūd ha-Kohen al-Ḥaddād). This text is most important for the version of the doctrine of *ẓimẓum* that it includes, parts of which were omitted by Vital.

(3) That of Ḥayyim Vital. In contrast to the comparatively limited scope of the preceding disciples, Vital rendered his preceptor's teachings in detail. He augments the words which he specifically quotes as Luria's or propounded according to what he heard, with numerous additions of his own. He also wrote his first versions immediately after Luria's death, although he confirms that certain expositions were only very briefly noted after he had heard them. Luria's teachings, in a book which he calls *Eẓ Ḥayyim* ("The Tree of Life"), were mainly written approximately between 1573 and 1576. However, he sometimes added a different version of the chapters, so that occasionally four variants on the same theme are found. The existence of these differing recensions has introduced considerable confusion into Vital's writings. The original sequence in *Eẓ Ḥayyim* falls into eight parts (called "Gates"): (a) all material in Luria's hand collected by Vital; (b) *Sha'ar ha-Derushim*, a systematic presentation of Luria's theosophical doctrine; (c) *Sha'ar ha-Pesukim*, explanations of biblical passages, arranged in a sequence that follows the Bible; (d) *Sha'ar ha-Gilgulim*, the mystical doctrine of metempsychosis, *gilgul*, and its source; (e) *Sha'ar ha-Kavannot*, on the mystical intentions and meditations required for prayer *(kavvanot ha-tefillah)*; (f) *Sha'ar ha-Mitzvot*, the reasons for the religious precepts; (g) the doctrine of amends for sins (*tikkunei avonot*); (h) instructions for mystical "unifications" (*yiḥudim*), which Luria transmitted to each disciple individually. This version of *Eẓ Ḥayyim* remains in manuscript. Using it, Ḥayyim Vital's son, Samuel *Vital, compiled eight further "gates" in which Luria's own literary heritage is distributed according to its contents. These are (a) *Sha'ar ha-Hakdamot*; (b) *Sha'ar Ma'amarei ashbi*; (c) *Sha'ar Ma'amarei Razal*; (d) *Sha'ar ha-Pesukim*; (e) *Sha'ar ha-Mitzvot*; (f) *Sha'ar ha-Kavannot*; (g) *Sha'ar Ru'aḥ ha-Kodesh*; (h) *Sha'ar ha-Gilgulim*. The first edition of this compilation, *Shemonah She'arim*, was published, without the title *Eẓ Ḥayyim*, in the above sequence in Jerusalem (1850–98; new ed. 1960–63). Many kabbalists, in particular among the Sephardim, recognized this version only as authoritative and rejected the rest of Luria's writings, including books which were assembled from Vital's own later recensions. Since "the eight gates" remained in the home of Vital and his son, and were only rarely copied by others before 1650, kabbalists wishing to study Lurianic Kabbalah used other recensions of Vital's books and eclectic anthologies of Lurianic kabbalism which circulated from 1586. Several of these, which were compiled in Safed itself, are extant (such as Schocken Ms. 97 of 1586 in Jerusalem), in the handwriting of Moses Jonah, and the manuscript of 1588 (Enelow collection 683, in the Jewish Theological Seminary, New York). Copies of Vital's writings that had remained in Jerusalem, where he stayed for several years in the 1590s, were also in circulation from the middle of the 17th century, and various collections have been compiled from them: *Sefer ha-Derushim, Sefer ha-Kavvanot*, and *Sefer ha-Likkutim*. It was not until the end of the 17th century that a comprehensive edition of Vital's writings relating to Luria's Kabbalah was made. This was compiled in Jerusalem by Meir *Poppers of Cracow with a few additions from Luria's other associates. Poppers divided his edition into *Derekh Eẓ Ḥayyim, Peri Eẓ Ḥayyim*, and *Nof Eẓ Ḥayyim*, which in fact includes all the subjects covered in the *Shemonah She'arim*. It was in this recension that Vital's writings became widely disseminated, especially in Europe, and became familiar long before the bulk of them were first published in Korzec in 1784. The printed book thereafter titled *Eẓ Ḥayyim* is actually the *Derekh Eẓ Ḥayyim* of Popper's recension. A number of books stemming from traditions compiled by Vital have been published in his name, such as *Mevo She'arim*, an introductory section (Korzec, 1784); *Oẓerot Ḥayyim* (*ibid.*, 1783); and *Arba Me'ot Shekel Kesef* (*ibid.*, 1804), part of which is indubitably a forgery.

(4) Superimposed on the tangled web of the three preceding traditions and their mutually interfused forms is a fourth deriving from the works of Israel *Sarug (Saruk), who propagated Lurianic Kabbalah in Italy and several other European countries after 1590. He is actually the author of *Sefer Limmudei Aẓilut* ("Doctrines on Emanation"), published in Vital's name (Munkacs, 1897), which contains an entirely different interpretation of the doctrine of *ẓimẓum* and the origin of divine emanation. Since Sarug was the first to spread this teaching in Italy, his version was accepted in wider circles, although there is no doubt that he added original speculations of his own to it. Sarug was not one of Luria's disciples in Safed but based his reconstruction on those works of Luria's principal disciples that reached him. He may have known Luria personally in Egypt, since there are grounds for assuming that he was born there, and his signature is appended to a kabbalistic manuscript written in Egypt in 1565 (British Museum, Almanzi 29) for Isaac Sarug (his father?). The innovations in his version in particular made a considerable impression, and for a long time it was the one accepted as authoritative, furnishing the basis for most of the earlier works on Lurianic Kabbalah; for example the *Ta'alumot Ḥokhmah* and *Novellot*

Ḥokhmah of Joseph Solomon Delmedigo (Basle, 1629–31), the *Emek ha-Melekh* of Naphtali *Bacharach (Amsterdam, 1648), and *Ma'ayan ha-Ḥokhmah (ibid.*, 1652) – which is in fact *Sefer Hatḥalot ha-Ḥokhmah*, a treatise originating in Sarug's circle. Lurianic Kabbalah, therefore, won adherents in the 17th century through the propagation of a version far removed from his original teaching. The inconsistencies in the different versions and the contradictions in Vital's own renderings gave rise to an exegetic literature which flourished particularly among the kabbalists in Italy, North Africa, and Turkey. Throughout these metamorphoses, however, the Lurianic system remained the crucial factor for the development of later Kabbalah. Apart from these variants, there are also a number of treatises and essays extant in manuscript, written by other disciples of Luria, such as Joseph *Arzin, Judah Mish'an, *Gedaliah ha-Levi, and Moses *Najara.

Before Luria's theoretical teachings became known, he won fame as a poet. A number of his liturgical hymns, only a few with mystical content, were published in the collection *Yefeh Nof* (Venice, 1575–80). Best known of his mystical poems are three hymns for Sabbath meals which have been included in most prayer books. Written in the language of the Zohar they describe, in kabbalistic symbolism, the meaning of the Sabbath and the special relationship between man and the world above on this day. Also published in Venice in 1595 were his *Tikkunei Teshuvah*, "penitence rituals" (titled *Marpe le-Nefesh*), and in 1620 his *Sefer ha-Kavvanot*, an anthology of mystical meditations on prayers and rules for behavior. There is a characteristic contradiction between Luria's theoretical Kabbalah, with its numerous bold innovations in theosophical doctrine and the concept of creation which changed the face of Kabbalah (see *ẓimẓum*; *Kabbalah), and his marked tendency to extreme conservatism when interpreting Jewish ritual customs and folkways. He upheld all the traditional usages, reading a mystical significance into them. He taught that each of the tribes of Israel could be regarded as having its own special entrance to heaven, which had resulted in differences in custom and liturgy, so that no particular usage could be considered superior to others. However, Luria did prefer the Sephardi liturgy, and the mystical meditations on prayer in which he instructed his disciples were based on Sephardi ritual. This was why only the Ashkenazi kabbalists and Ḥasidim accepted the Sephardi liturgy in prayer, as they adopted many of his other observances.

Luria himself attempted to clarify his position in relation to the Kabbalah of Moses Cordovero, and the question has occupied a number of other kabbalists. Answering inquiries on the difference between the two kabbalists, he replied that Cordovero treated of *olam ha-tohu*, "the world of confusion," while his own teaching dealt with *olam ha-tikkun*, "the world of restitution," – i.e., each was concerned with entirely different planes and states of being in the spiritual realm of emanation, and so Cordovero's province did not impinge on that of Luria. Most kabbalists refrained from attempting to mix or combine the two kabbalistic systems. Vital, too, who at first was Cordovero's disciple, wrote that he paved "the plain way [*derekh ha-peshat*] for beginners in his wisdom" while Luria traced the "inner, most important path" (stated in a dream in 1573 recorded in Vital's *Sefer ha-Ḥezyonot*). In reply to Vital's question (according to testimony in "*Sha'ar Ru'aḥ ha-Kodesh*") as to why he had penetrated more deeply into the mysteries than Cordovero, Luria said that this did not come about through reliance on divine revelation or similar phenomena but because "he took greater pains than the rest of his contemporaries."

The entire structure of Lurianic Kabbalah is permeated with messianic tension. The introduction of the eschatological element into his basic concept of Kabbalah fundamentally changed later thinking. This element is implicit in his doctrine of *Tikkun*, restitution or restoration of the inner and outer cosmos. In no small measure it prepared the ground for the messianic ferment of the Shabbatean movement (see Shabbetai *Ẓevi). The deeds of man are invested with mystical significance, not only because they are linked with the secret workings of creation, but also because they are integrated into a vast cosmological drama which is enacted in order to rectify the original blemish in the world and to restore everything to its proper place. It is not the role of the Messiah to accomplish the *redemption; the task of cosmological restitution is imposed on the entire Jewish people through strict observance of the precepts and prayer. When this spiritual restitution has been effected the Messiah's appearance is inevitable, for it signifies the consummation of the cosmic process. The primary concepts of Lurianic Kabbalah provide an explanation for the existence of evil and impurity in the world and relate at every stage to the Jewish national and messianic mission.

There is no justification for the theory, widely held by modern historians, that the principles Luria introduced are based on the traditions and ethical doctrine of the *Ḥasidei Ashkenaz. Nor should Lurianic Kabbalah be viewed as the epitome of "practical" Kabbalah in contrast to "theoretical," or speculative, Kabbalah. The theoretical and practical aspects are blended in every kabbalistic system, particularly in that practiced by the scholars of Safed. Luria's originality does not lie in his stress on the practical aspects of man's adhesion to his Creator, or on the performance of good deeds, but in his pioneer conception of the theoretical aspect of Kabbalah.

[Gershom Scholem]

The vast kabbalistic literature belonging to Lurianism has attracted the attention of many scholars over the last generation and their findings have contributed to substantial revisions of the scholarship on this kabbalistic school. Here only the main developments can be addressed. The first comprehensive surveys of the manuscripts were done by Avivi, Meroz, and Kallus, who offered different criteria for establishing the sequence of Luria's writings and their different versions, and the evolution of his thought. Detailed analyses of writings belonging to a major Lurianic school, that of R. Israel Sarug, are found in the studies of Meroz, who questioned the dominant view of the relationship between Luria and Sarug, claiming that the latter was an early – rather than a later – student of the former. Especially important are studies on material printed from other disciples of Luria such as ibn Tabul and Penzieri (see Meroz and Rubin). According to Meroz's analyses, the interactive situation involved in the relations between Luria and his disciples should be taken into consideration as a formative factor in the emergence of his teachings.

The scholarly understanding of the phenomenological structure of Lurianism has undergone substantial changes. The variety of tendencies found in the writings of the students is understood as not reflecting a unified position, which is sometimes found on the "esoteric" level. The concept of a significant change in Luria's thought, and divergences between his disciples, is dominant in more recent scholarship. Likewise, the importance of earlier concepts of Lurianic innovations, has been placed in relief, especially with regard to the concept of *Parẓufim*, *Ẓimẓum*, or *Adam Kadmon* (Huss, Idel, Liebes, Sack), and in more general terms the importance of the writings of Cordovero, who was Luria's teacher, emerges as substantial; the deep gap between the two assumed as axiomatic in earlier scholarship has been emphasized, especially in Sack. New elements in Luria's thought have been put in relief, attenuating the centrality of the axis of exile-redemption: the personality of Luria (Liebes), his visions of theurgy (Kallus), greater psychological understanding of Lurianic concepts (Liebes, Pachter), the revelationary aspects (Fine, Kallus), or his hermeneutics (Liebes, Maggid). Many of those developments were published in an important collection of articles on Lurianism edited by Rachel Elior and Yehuda Liebes, *Lurianic Kabbalah* (Heb., 1992) and in the major monograph on Luria by L. Fine.

The dissemination of Luria's writings in the decades following the death of his main followers has been discussed in Avivi, Gries, and Idel, whose findings qualified the former assumption of a wide acceptance of his views. The tension between Lurianism and Cordovero's in 17th-century thought, showing that the latter's thought did not disappear from the speculative horizons of important Kabbalists, has been analyzed by I. Tishby.

For a generation, through to 2005, a series of new editions of many of the major Lurianic treatises has been printed, as has previously unpublished material from manuscripts, and some material has been translated into English. Likewise, the impact of Luria's thought on European thought has been highlighted in studies of Allison Coudert. (See also *Vital.)

[Moshe Idel (2nd ed.)]

BIBLIOGRAPHY: Azulai, 1 (1852), s.v. *Yiẓḥak Luria*; D. Kahana (Kogan), *Toledot ha-Mekubbalim ha-Shabbeta'im ve-ha-Ḥasidim*, 1 (1913), 22–42; Kaufmann, in: *Yerushalayim* (A.M. Luncz ed.), 2 (1887), 144–7; S.A. Horodezky, *Torat ha-Kabbalah shel Rabbi Yiẓḥak Ashkenazi ve-Rabbi Ḥayyim Vital* (1947); idem, in: EJ, 10 (1934), 1198–1212; I. Tishby, *Torat ha-Ra ve-ha-Kelippah be-Kabbalat ha-Ari* (1942); Scholem, Mysticism, 244–86, 407–15; Scholem, Shabbetai Ẓevi, 1 (1957), 18–60; idem, *Kitvei Yad ba-Kabbalah* (1930), 103–6, 115–43; idem, in: *Zion*, 5 (1940), 133–60, 214–43; idem, in: KS, 19 (1953/54), 184–99; 26 (1860/61), 185–94; R. Margulies, *ibid.*, 17 (1951/52), 248, 423; M. Benayahu, *Sefer Toledot ha-Ari* (1967); idem, in: *Sefer ha-Yovel le-Ḥanokh Albeck* (1963), 71–80; idem, in: *Aresheth*, 3 (1961), 144–65; idem, in: *Sefunot*, 10 (1966), 213–98; D. Tamar, *Meḥkarim be-Toledot ha-Yehudim* (1969); P. Bloch, *Die Kabbala auf ihrem Hohepunkt und ihre Meister* (1905); S. Schechter, *Studies in Judaism*, 2nd series (1908), 202–306, 317–28; Rosanes, Togarmah, 2 (1938), 198–203. **ADD. BIBLIOGRAPHY:** J. Avivi, *Binyan Ariel, Introduction to the Homilies of R. Isaac Luria* (Heb., 1987), idem, "The Writings of Rabbi Isaac Luria in Italy before 1620," in: *Alei Sefer*, 11 (1984), 91–134 (Heb.); idem, "R. Ḥayyim Vital's Lurianic Writings," in: *Moriah*, 115/116 (1981), 79–91 (Heb.); M. Benayahu, "Rabbi Moshe Yonah, A Disciple of Luria and the First of Those Who Copied His Doctrine," in: *Studies in Memory of the Rishon le-Zion R. Yitzhak Nissim*, vol. 4 (1995), 7–74 (Heb.); idem, "*Shitrei Hikasherut she-le-Mekubbalei Ẓefat u-Miẓrayim*," in: *Assufot*, 9 (1995), 133–34 (Heb.); A.P. Coudert, *The Impact of the Kabbalah in the Seventeenth Century, The Life and Thought of Francis Mercury van Helmont (1614–1698)* (1999); idem, *Leibniz and the Kabbalah* (1995); A. David, "Halakhah and Commerce in the Biography of Isaac Luria," in: *Lurianic Kabbalah*, 287–97 (Heb.); L. Fine, *Physician of the Soul, Healer of the Cosmos, Isaac Luria and His Kabbalistic Fellowship* (2003), with an important bibliography; idem, "Maggidic Revelation in the Teachings of Isaac Luria," in: J. Reinharz and D. Swetschinski (eds.), *Mystics, Philosophers and Politicians – Essays in Jewish Intellectual History in Honor of Alexander Altmann*, (1982), 141–52; D. Gamlieli, "Stages of 'Becoming' in the Creation: Parallelism with Philosophical and Psychological Terminology," in: *Kabbalah*, 12 (2004), 233–320 (Heb.); Z. Gries, *Conduct Literature (Regimen Vitae), Its History and Place in the Life of the Beshtian Ḥasidism* (1989) (Heb); M. Hallamish, "Luria's Affinity to Ashkenazi Custom," in: *Daat*, 50–52 (2003), 243–54 (Heb.), idem, "Luria's Status as an Halakhic Authority," in: *Lurianic Kabbalah*, 259–86 (Heb.); B. Huss, "*Genizat ha-Or* in Simeon Lavi's *Ketem Paz* and the Lurianic Doctrine of *Ẓimẓum*," in *Lurianic Kabbalah*, 341–61 (Heb.); M. Idel, *Messianic Mystics* (2002), 154–182, idem, "On the Concept of *Ẓimẓum* in Kabbalah and Its Research," in: *Lurianic Kabbalah* (1992), 59–112 (Heb.); idem, "'One from a Town, Two from a Clan' – The Diffusion of Lurianic Kabbalah and Shabbateanism: A Re-examination," in: *Pe'amim*, 44 (1990), 5–30 (Heb.); English Version, *Jewish History*, 7:2 (1993), 79–104, idem, "The Image of Man Above the *Sefirot*: R. David ben Yehudah he-Ḥasid's Doctrine of the Supernal *Sefirot* (Ẓaḥẓaḥot) and Its Evolution," in: *Daat*, 4 (1980), 41–55 (Heb.); Y. Jacobson, "The Aspect of the 'Feminine' in the Lurianic Kabbalah," in: P. Schaefer and J. Dan (eds.), *Gershom Scholem's Major Trends in Jewish Mysticism, 50 Years After* (1993), 239–55; M. Kallus, "The Theurgy of Prayer and the Eschatology of the Lurianic Kabbalah" (doct. diss., Hebrew University, Jerusalem, 2002); idem, "Pneumatic Mystical Possession and the Eschatology of the Soul in Lurianic Kabbalah," in: M. Goldish (ed.), *Spirit Possession in Judaism* (2003), 159–85, 385–413; Y. Liebes, "Myth vs. Symbol in the Zohar and Lurianic Kabbalah," in L. Fine (ed.), *Essential Papers on Kabbalah* (1995), 212–42; idem, "The Songs for the Sabbath-Meals by R. Isaac Luria," in: *Molad*, 4 (1972), 540–55 (Heb.); idem, *Studies in the Zohar* (1993), 44–47, 60–63; idem, "'Two Young Roes of a Doe': The Secret Sermon of Isaac Luria before His Death," in: *Lurianic Kabbalah*, 113–70 (Heb.); S. Magid, "Conjugal Union, Mourning and Talmud Torah in R. Isaac Luria's *Tikkun Hazot*," in: *Daat*, 36 (1996), xvii–xlv; idem, "From Theosophy to Midrash; Lurianic Exegesis and the Garden of Eden," in: AJS *Review*, 22:1 (1997), 37–75; R. Meroz, "R. Israel Sarug, the Student of Luria? – A Reconsideration of the Question," in: *Daat*, 28 (1992), 41–50 (Heb.), idem,

"Faithful Transmission versus Innovation: Luria and His Disciples," in P. Schaefer and J. Dan (eds.), *Gershom Scholem's Major Trends in Jewish Mysticism, 50 Years After* (1993), 257–75; idem, "The School of Sarug, A New History," in: J. Hacker (ed.), *Shalem*, 7 (2001), 151–93 (Heb.); idem, "Two Early Lurianic Treatises," in: M. Oron and A. Goldreich (eds.), *Massu'ot, Studies in Kabbalistic Literature and Jewish Philosophy in Memory of Prof. Ephraim Gottlieb* (1994), 311–29 (Heb.); idem, "Selections from Ephraim Penzieri: Luria's Sermon in Jerusalem," in: *Lurianic Kabbalah*, 211–57 (Heb.); idem, "'*Zelem*' (Image) and Medicine in the Lurianic Teaching (according to the writing of R. Hayim Vital)," in: *Koroth*, 8:5/6 (1982), 170–77; M. Pachter, "Katnut ('Smallness') and Gadlut ('Greatness') in Lurianic Kabbalah," in: *Lurianic Kabbalah*, 171–210 (Heb.); idem, "The Image of Luria in the Eulogy of R. Samuel Uzeida," in: *Zion*, 37 (1972), 22–40 (Heb.); Z. Rubin, "The Zoharic Commentaries of Joseph ibn Tabul," in: *Lurianic Kabbalah*, 363–87 (Heb.); B. Sack, "Moshe Cordovero and Isaac Luria," in: *Lurianic Kabbalah*, 311–40 (Heb.); E. Starobinski-Safran, "Exode 3,14 dans l'interprétation de Rabbi Isaac Luria et chez quelques maîtres hassidiques," in: *Celui qui est* (1986), 205–16; D. Tamar, "The Image of Luria in the Eyes of Vital and Vital's Image in Luria's Eyes," in: *Sinai*, 108 (1991), 238–47 (Heb.); I. Tishby, *Studies in Kabbalah and Its Branches* (1982), 177–267 (Heb.); Evgeny A. Torchinov, "The Doctrine of the Origin of Evil in Lurianic and Sabbatean Kabbalah and in the 'Awakening of Faith' in Mahayana Buddhism," in: *Kabbalah*, 5 (2000), 183–98; E.R. Wolfson, "Divine Suffering and the Hermeneutics of Reading; Philosophical Reflections on Lurianic Mythology," in: R. Gibbs and E.R., Wolfson (eds.), *Suffering Religion* (2002), 101–62; N. Yosha, "Lurianic Kabbalah as a Metaphor in the Homilies of Abraham Miquel Cardozo," in: *Kabbalah*, vol. 8 (2003), 121–43 (Heb.).

LURIA, JEHIEL BEN ISRAEL ASHKENAZI (16th–17th century), kabbalist; scholar of *Safed and its emissary to Western Europe. It may be assumed that Luria was a relation of Isaac Ashkenazi *Luria (Ha-Ari). In 1599 he was in Worms and in 1601 in *Venice, apparently on his return journey to Ereẓ Israel. That year he published three works in Venice: *Heikhal ha-Shem* containing early Kabbalah fragments on the ten *Sefirot*, with an appendix of several sayings in the name of Isaac Luria and two *piyyutim* (the *Bar Yoḥai piyyut* and "an elegy on the desolation of the Temple to be said in the early morning vigil"); *Asis Rimmonim*, an abridgment of the *Pardes Rimmonim* of Moses Cordovero; and *Ḥaredim* of Eleazar *Azikri, the first edition from the manuscript. He returned to Ereẓ Israel from this mission and in 1604 was again sent out by the Safed community, on this occasion together with Solomon ibn Ẓur, to the countries of North Africa. Several letters about the mission are extant that were written from Safed to philanthropists in Algeria, and in these the conditions of the Jews of Safed at that time are described. A responsum by Luria on kabbalistic topics is cited by Abraham *Galante (in *Kol Bokhim* on Lam. 1:6).

BIBLIOGRAPHY: Yaari, Sheluḥei, 245–6, 248–9; S. Assaf, in: *Koveẓ Al Yad*, 13 (1940), 134–9; E. Loans, *Mikhlol Yofi* (a commentary on Ecclesiastes, 1695), ch. 14; Neubauer, Cat, no. 2578.

[Avraham Yaari]

LURIA, NOAH (**Lurye, Noyekh**; 1886–1960), Soviet Yiddish poet, essayist, editor, translator, and pedagogue. Born in Blashne, Belorussia, Luria joined the *Bund in 1905, was imprisoned in 1907–8, and joined the Russian army in 1917 after the February Revolution. From 1918 he was an official of the *Yidishe Kultur Lige* in Kiev and was active in reforming Jewish education there. He began to write in his early twenties, first in Hebrew and later in Yiddish, writing for children and translating European children's classics into Yiddish. From 1930 he mainly wrote realistic tales of Soviet Jewish life. His last Yiddish work to appear in his lifetime was a review in *Heymland*, 6 (July–August 1948), while a Russian translation of one of his works appeared in 1957. He died in Moscow, reportedly leaving behind many unpublished critical studies. His story "Oys Khaver" ("No Longer Friends") was reprinted in the first issue of *Sovetish Heymland* (1962).

BIBLIOGRAPHY: Ch. Shmeruk et al. (eds.), *Pirsumim Yehudiyyim bi-Verit ha-Mo'aẓot, 1917–1960* (1961); LNYL, 5 (1963), 33–5. **ADD. BIBLIOGRAPHY:** Rejzen, Leksikon, 2 (1929), 105–7; B. Orshansky, *Di Yidishe Literatur in Vaysrusland nokh der Revolutsye* (1931), 146–50.

[Leonard Prager]

LURIA, SALVADOR EDWARD (1912–1991), U.S. biologist and Nobel Prize winner. Born in Turin, Luria studied medicine at the university there working under Giuseppe *Levi, and from 1938 to 1940 did research at the Institute of Radium in Paris. After the fall of France in 1940, Luria immigrated to the U.S., where he taught at Columbia (1940–42), Indiana University (1943–50), and the University of Illinois (1950–59), before becoming a professor of microbiology at the Massachusetts Institute of Technology in 1959. In 1964 he was appointed professor of biology at MIT. He was an associate editor of the *Journal of Bacteriology* (1950–55), editor of *Virology* from 1955, and published *General Virology* (1953–67²). Luria was one of the pioneers of microbial genetics. In 1943, with Max Delbrueck, he showed that the appearance of bacteriophage-resistant strains of bacteria was the result of spontaneous mutations. The reasoning and design of this classic experiment became a model for subsequent research in vital and bacterial genetics. He dealt with lysogeny (the attachment of viral DNA to the bacterial chromosome), transduction (the transfer of genetic material from one bacterium to another by a virus), and the control of phage properties by the bacterial host. Luria's later experiments, employing novel techniques, extended the principles of genetics to viruses and bacteria and formed an essential part of the foundation of the new science of molecular biology. In 1969 Luria was a corecipient (with Max Delbrueck and Alfred Hershey) of the Nobel Prize for physiology and medicine.

[Mordecai L. Gabriel]

Luria's open stance as a member of the peace movement may explain his appearing on a federal blacklist of 48 scientists drawn up by the National Institutes of Health in 1969. A critic of both American involvement in Vietnam and the Israeli invasion of Lebanon, he was also an opponent of what he regarded as insufficient safeguards on nuclear power, and in 1976 he and other scientists called for an end to the building of new atomic power plants.

Luria founded the MIT Center for Cancer Research, and was director of the center from 1972 to 1985. In 1974 he won a National Book Award for *Life: The Unfinished Experiment*, a non-academic work. He officially retired from MIT in 1978, but remained active there. From 1984 he served as senior scientist for the biotechnology company, the Repligen Corporation.

[Rohan Saxena (2nd ed.)]

BIBLIOGRAPHY: *McGraw-Hill Modern Men of Science* (1966), s.v.

LURIA, SOLOMON BEN JEHIEL (1510?–1574), *posek* and talmudic commentator (known as **Rashal** or **Maharshal** = **M**orenu **ha-R**av **Sh**elomo **L**uria). Few biographical details are known of him. He was probably born in Poznan (Poland). His family was related to many of the important families of the time, including *Katzenellenbogen and *Minz of Padua. Luria was orphaned in his youth. He was educated by his maternal grandfather, Isaac Klober, a well-known scholar, and Luria took pride in the fact that he received most of his learning and traditions from him. Since his grandfather was his only teacher, Luria was primarily a self-taught scholar. This explains in part his sharp criticism of other sages and his unusual independence of thought. When 40 years old, he was appointed rabbi and *rosh yeshivah* of Ostrog. About 20 years later he moved to Brisk (Brest-Litovsk) where he may also have been rabbi before he went to Ostrog, and then to Lublin where he served as a *rosh yeshivah*, at first in the yeshivah founded by Shalom Shachna. However, after becoming involved in a quarrel with Israel, the son of Shalom, he left and in 1567 – with the permission of the government – founded his own yeshivah where he was able to teach in accordance with his own system. Although Luria raised many pupils who became rabbis in Poland and Lithuania during his own and the following generation, some left his yeshivah and went to R. Israel. Luria felt this desertion deeply and complained about it in harsh words. Among his outstanding pupils were Mordecai *Jaffe and Joshua *Falk.

Luria was unique for his time in the complete independence he showed in halakhic ruling and in the critical method which he employed. His *magnum opus* was the *Yam shel Shelomo*, a halakhic compendium that follows the order of the Talmud. For Luria, the Talmud was the ultimate source of Jewish law, which explains his decision to write his book as a halakhic commentary on the Talmud. At the same time, Luria felt that all the relevant sources should be used. Thus his legal decisions were based on a comparison of all the vast commentaries and halakhic material – both that compiled before and during his time – with the talmudic sources, showing remarkable profundity while strictly avoiding the *pilpul* and hairsplitting which then dominated the yeshivot of Poland, particularly that of Shalom Shachna. Luria valued Kabbalah to the point of quoting the Zohar and other kabbalistic works in his *Yam shel Shelomo*. However, he never used kabbalistic sources as the final arbiters of the law. Even though Luria meant his work to be of practical use, by tying his discussions to the order of the Talmud it became cumbersome to use. His rulings were accepted by most of his contemporary scholars with whom he was in correspondence and exchanged responsa. However, his extraordinary firmness – as well as his public accusations that many of the rabbis who were stringent in their rulings had their eye on monetary gain and "the benefit it brought them and their scribes" (responsum 21) – roused many opponents against him.

His criticism also included the quality of the printed text of the Talmud of which the first good and complete editions had been published in the preceding generation. His own personal glosses correcting the corrupt text were written into his personal edition of the Talmud. Despite the fact that these were made for his personal use, they were published, first as a separate work in 1581 and later in the margins of the printed Talmud texts. As a result, Luria had great impact on almost every page of the Babylonian Talmud, on its text, on Rashi's commentary, and on the Tosafot.

There is no doubt, as he himself states, that the method of *pilpul* was also used in Luria's yeshivah, but he distinguished between the oral teaching in the yeshivah which was designed to sharpen the minds of the pupils and that whose aim was purely to arrive at the truth, as well as between both these methods and the ability to posit the *halakhah*. His independence in his rulings was tempered with a great reverence for the school of Rashi and the tosafists and the early Franco-German authorities generally, and in particular for their traditions and customs, which he always accepted. In addition he relied heavily in *halakhah* on the decisions of Israel *Isserlein, the author of the *Terumat ha-Deshen* (Venice, 1519), even though he does not refrain at times from taking an independent line from him (responsum 39). Luria's works include an exceptionally wide range of literary sources, from commentaries and halakhic works, from the geonic period down to his own time, of which he had an extensive collection in his rich library – both of published works and manuscripts. In addition to his glosses and textual emendations of the Talmud, he also wrote on the liturgy, Maimonides' *Mishneh Torah*, the *Turim* (see *Jacob b. Asher), the *Semag* (see *Moses b. Jacob of Coucy), Rashi's biblical commentary, and other works. His interest encompassed many fields, including grammar and Kabbalah, to which he was greatly inclined, although he made very little use of it in his halakhic decisions. To philosophy and its study he was greatly opposed, and hard words on this subject passed between him and Moses *Isserles, his younger relative whom Luria held in high esteem despite the bitter dispute which arose between them toward the end of Isserles' life. Joseph *Caro's commentary to the *Turim*, *Beit Yosef*, was published at that time. Luria, though valuing the work for its own sake, was strongly opposed to the *halakhah* being decided in accordance with it since it was not primarily based upon the tosafists and the Franco-German scholars.

Luria seems to ignore the Shulḥan Arukh, although there is no doubt that he knew it.

Only some of Luria's works have been preserved, including the following:

(1) *Yam shel Shelomo* on the Talmud (on *Bava Kamma*; Prague, 1616–18; on *Ḥullin*; Cracow, 1633–35; etc.). It is not certain how comprehensive the original work was, only his comments to a few tractates having been preserved. The book is distinguished for its clarity and for its remarkably detailed, orderly, and erudite presentation of each topic. From it one can clearly follow the manner in which the *halakhah* with which he is dealing developed from the geonic period until his time;

(2) *Ḥokhmat Shelomo* (Cracow, 1582 or 1587), glosses on the text of the Talmud together with short comments. This work was published in most editions of the Talmud in a very abridged – and many times corrupt and meaningless – form, after many of his emendations had already been inserted into the actual text of the Talmud. Ironically, the corrupted text of his glosses was the result of further scribal and typographical error;

(3) *Ammudei Shelomo* (Basle, 1600), expositions of the *Semag*;

(4) *Yeri'ot Shelomo* (Prague, 1609), glosses and expositions of Rashi's Bible commentary and glosses to Elijah *Mizraḥi's supercommentary to it;

(5) *Ateret Shelomo* (Basle, 1599–1600), a commentary on the *Sha'arei Dura* (see *Dueren, Isaac Ben Meir);

(6) Responsa (Lublin, 1574–75). These responsa are exceptionally valuable for the insight they afford into the culture of the Jews of Poland and Lithuania in this period of their efflorescence, and the status and moral standard of the rabbinate of his time. Responsum 29 contains an early historical document on the chronology of the scholars of Germany from the time of *Gershom b. Judah, until the middle of the 14th century;

(7) Luria wrote a commentary to the Grace after Meals (Venice, 1603; Jerusalem, 1982);

(8) Luria also wrote a commentary to the Sabbath *Zemirot* (Lublin, 1596; Brooklyn, 1986) and expositions of scriptural verses;

(9) *Hanhagot Maharshal* (Brooklyn, 1986), Luria's personal customs, printed from manuscript.

His other works include a critique of Abraham Ibn Ezra's Pentateuch commentary; works on Kabbalah, including *Sefer Menorat ha-Zahav* (New York, 2002) and *Perush ha-Ilan* (in *Mesekhet Aẓilut*, Jerusalem, 2000); and other works.

BIBLIOGRAPHY: Assaf, in: *Sefer ha-Yovel… L. Ginzberg* (1946), 45–63 (Hebrew section); Graetz-Rabbinowitz, 7 (1899), 338–42; S.A. Horodezky, *Kerem Shelomo* (1897); idem, *Le-Korot ha-Rabbanut* (1911), 123–44; S. Hurwitz (ed.), *The Responsa of Solomon Luria* (1938); R.N. Rabinovitz, *Ma'amar al Hadpasat ha-Talmud* (1952²), 62f.; Raphael, in: *Sefer ha-Yovel… S. Federbush* (1961), 316–29; Shulvass, in: I. Halpern (ed.), *Beit Yisrael be-Polin*, 2 (1954), 16; *ibid.*, 239 n. 14; A. Siev, *Ha-Rama* (1957), 49–59; Sonne, in: KS, 8 (1931/32), 128f.; H. Tchernowitz, *Toledot ha-Posekim*, 3 (1947), 74–91. **ADD. BIBLIOGRAPHY:** M. Rafeld, "*Ha-Maharshal ve-ha-Yam shel Shelomo*" (Dissertation, 1990); idem, in: *Shenaton ha-Mishpat ha-Ivri*, 18–19 (1995), 427–37; Y. Ron, "*Bikkoret Nusaḥ ha-Talmud ha-Bavli shel Rabbi Shelomo Luria*" (Dissertation, 1989); idem, in: *Alei Sefer*, 15 (1990), 65–104; H.R. Rabinowitz, in: *Ha-Darom*, 44 (1977), 254–66.

[Israel Moses Ta-Shma / David Derovan (2nd ed.)]

LURIE, HARRY LAWRENCE (1892–1973), U.S. social worker. Lurie, who was born in Goldingen, Latvia, was taken to the U.S. in 1898. During 1913–14, Lurie was employed as a staff member by the Federation of Jewish Charities in Buffalo, New York. After service with the Detroit Department of Public Welfare (1915–22), he was subsequently employed as faculty member at the University of Michigan (1922–24); superintendent of the Chicago Jewish Social Service Bureau (1925–30); lecturer at the University of Chicago (1926–30) and the New York School of Social Work (1931); executive director of the Bureau of Jewish Social Research (1930–35); and executive director of the Council of Jewish Federations and Welfare Funds (1935–57). In the latter capacities, he was a leader in orienting Jewish social work toward the main currents of the American profession. He became editor of the *Encyclopedia of Social Work* in 1962 and wrote *A Heritage Affirmed* (1961), a history of the federation movement in American Jewish philanthropy.

LURIE, JOSEPH (1871–1937), Zionist leader and Hebrew educator. Born in Pumpenai, Lithuania, Lurie studied at the University of Berlin, where, together with Leo *Motzkin and Shemaryahu *Levin, he established the first Russian Jewish students' group (1889) and joined the *Benei Moshe association. Lurie was a delegate to the First *Zionist Congress. From 1899 to 1904 he edited the Zionist weekly *Der Yud* ("The Jew"), gathering around him the best of the Yiddish writers. He stressed the importance of the Yiddish language as a national heritage in a series of articles in the St. Petersburg daily *Der Fraynd*, the literary supplement of which he edited until 1906. In that year he was elected to the central committee of the Zionist Organization in Russia and became editor of the Zionist organ *Dos Yidishe Folk* ("The Jewish People") in Vilna. In 1907 he went to Ereẓ Israel, joining the staff of the Herzlia High School in Tel Aviv. Lurie was a key figure in the language controversy with the *Hilfsverein der deutschen Juden, which tried to introduce German as a language of instruction. During World War I he was banished by the Turkish authorities. From 1919 he headed the education department of the Zionist Organization, later of the Va'ad Le'ummi (National Council of the Jews in Palestine). An advocate of an understanding with the Arab national movement as vitally important to the Zionist movement, he was a member of *Berit Shalom in its early days. His book, *Ereẓ Yisrael* (1914), is a collection of his articles about life in Ereẓ Israel.

BIBLIOGRAPHY: D. Kimḥi (ed.), *Nefesh le-Doktor Yosef Lurie* (1938); I. Klausner, *Opoziẓyah le-Herzl* (1960), index; B. Dinur, *Benei Dori* (1965), 156–60; LNYL, 5 (1963), 27–29 (incl. bibl.).

[Yehuda Slutsky]

LURIE, RANAN RAYMOND (1932–), political cartoonist, editor, lecturer. A member of the renowned Luria family, Lurie was born in Port Said to a family that had been in Jerusalem for six generations. He was educated in Tel Aviv (Herzlia Hebrew Gymnasia) and in Jerusalem (art college) and served as a major (res.) in the IDF paratroops. He worked for Israeli newspapers until invited by *Life* magazine to come to the United States in 1968. There he worked as political cartoonist for *Life, Newsweek*, and *Time*, and his cartoons are syndicated in more than 1,000 publications in 102 countries with a total readership of 104 million. Ten books of his cartoons were published in five languages and he received many awards for his work. He contributed regularly to leading television shows and was editor in chief of *Cartoon News* magazine.

His son Rod was a radio talk show ("The Rod Lurie Show") host in Los Angeles and published *Once Upon a Time in Hollywood.*

LURIE, TED (1909–1974), Israel journalist. Born in New York, Lurie immigrated to Palestine in 1930 and joined the staff of the *Palestine Post* at its outset in 1931. He was news editor from 1937 to 1947 and was Jerusalem correspondent of the London *News Chronicle* (1944–46). From 1948 to 1950 he was acting editor of the *Palestine Post* (later the *Jerusalem Post*) and in 1955 was appointed editor and managing director.

LURIE, ZVI (1906–1968), *Mapam labor leader in Israel. Born in Lodz, Poland, Lurie went to Palestine in 1925 and worked as an agricultural laborer in *Petaḥ Tikvah. In 1925 he joined the *hakhsharah* group of Ha-Shomer ha-Ẓa'ir at Ein Gannim and settled with them at kibbutz Ein Shemer in 1927. From 1929 to 1931 he was an emissary for Ha-Shomer ha-Ẓa'ir in Poland, and from 1935 to 1937 he was secretary of the world leadership of Ha-Shomer ha-Ẓa'ir in Warsaw and editor of its weekly. In the following years he was active on all the central bodies of the movement in Palestine. From 1941 to 1948 Lurie served on the Va'ad Le'ummi and on its executive from 1946 to 1948 as director of the Information Department. In 1948 he joined the Provisional Council of the State of Israel and was a signatory of the Declaration of Independence. Lurie was on the *Jewish Agency Executive in New York from 1948 to 1955 and was a member of the Executive in Jerusalem and head of the Organization Department from 1956. A collection of his speeches entitled *Mi-Devarav* appeared in 1968.

BIBLIOGRAPHY: *Zvi Lurie, le-Zikhro* (1969).

[Benjamin Jaffe]

°LUSCHAN, FELIX VON (1854–1924), German archaeologist, ethnologist, explorer, and anthropologist. Von Luschan studied at the universities of Vienna and Paris and then joined the Berlin Museum fuer Voelkerkunde, of which he was the director from 1904 until his death. He undertook numerous expeditions to the Balkans, North and South Africa (especially Benin), and New Guinea and Anatolia. In 1881 he began anthropometric work in Lycia in western Asia and for three decades continued to assemble data on the physical evolution of man there. On the basis of his research and studies of the cephalic indices of a large number of Jews, Von Luschan came to the conclusion that the notion of a distinct Jewish race was fallacious. Early in his career he formulated a theory that the Jewish people was racially an amalgam of Semites, Hittites, and Aryan Amorites, a view he later recanted after it was espoused by antisemites like Houston Stewart *Chamberlain.

Von Luschan energetically combated all forms of racism and in his *Voelker, Rassen, Sprachen* (1922), particularly attacked antisemitism. Writing from the anthropological perspective, he rejected the notion of the biological inferiority of any given race and criticized the popular confusion of such distinct, autonomous entities as race, nationality, and culture.

BIBLIOGRAPHY: ESS, 9 (1933), 631. **ADD. BIBLIOGRAPHY:** L. Knoll, *Felix von Luschan – Ergaenzungen und Beitraege zu biographischen Daten eines Pioniers der Ethnologie* (2004); A. Zeller, *Felix von Luschan – Seine Bedeutung fuer die Beninforschung* (2004); M. Melk-Koch, "Zwei Oesterreicher nehmen Einfluss auf die Ethnologie in Deutschland – Felix von Luschan and Richard Thurnwald," in: B. Rupp-Eisenreich and J. Stagl (ed.), *L'anthropologie et l'Etat pluriculturel* (1995), 132–40.

[Ephraim Fischoff]

LUSTIG, ARNOST (1926–), Czech writer, screenwriter, and journalist. Born in Prague, Lustig was deported to the Theresienstadt concentration camp in 1942 and later to a number of others, including Auschwitz and Buchenwald. At the end of the war he managed to escape from the death train and reach Prague, where he later graduated from the School of Political and Social Sciences. Until 1968 he worked as a journalist at various periodicals (he was a war correspondent in Israel in 1948) and a screenwriter. During the brief period of liberalization in Czechoslovakia in 1967–68, Lustig was elected to the Central Committee of the Czechoslovak Writers' Union. After the Soviet invasion in August 1968, he left Czechoslovakia for Israel and Yugoslavia. He ultimately became a professor of the history of literature and film at the American University in Washington.

Lustig's work is based mainly on his tragic experiences in concentration camps and postwar life in his homeland. He made his literary debut with the collection of stories *Night and Hope* (1958) filmed as Z. Brynych's *A Transport from Paradise* (1962), and *Diamonds in the Night* (1958), filmed by J. Němec (1964) – both showing the life of young Jews in the Terezin ghetto. Other short story collections and novels appeared quickly one after the other, such as *The Street of Lost Brothers* (1959); *My Acquaintance Vili Feld* (1961); *First Destination Happiness* (1961); *Night and Day* (1962); *Dita Saxov* (1962, filmed by A. Moskalyk, 1967); *Thou Shalt Not Humiliate Anyone* (1963); *A Prayer for Catherine Horowitz* (1964), which won the Czech State Prize (1966) and was nominated for the American National Book Award (1973); *Waves in the River* (1964); *White Birches in the Autumn* (1966); *The Bitter Scent of Almonds* (1968); *The Lower* (1969), set against the

Arab-Israeli War of 1948; *A Street of the Lost Ones* (1973); and *From the Diary of Seventeen-Year-Old Perla S.* (1979). After the Velvet Revolution in Czechoslovakia and the establishment of the Czech Republic, he published *Darkness Casts No Shadow* (1991); *Colette: A Girl from Antwerp* (1992); *Tanga: A Girl from Hamburg* (1992); *House of the Returned Echo* (1994); and a number of short stories, such as "Friends"; "Chasm"; and "Fire on the Water."

Lustig wrote *Memories, 3 × 18* (2003) and many newspaper articles about the Czech political and cultural scene, including the problems of the Jewish community in the Czech Republic. Much of Lustig's fiction has been translated into several languages. In 2004 he was awarded the Vladislav Vančura Prize. From 2004 Lustig lived in Prague.

BIBLIOGRAPHY: Iltis, in: *Jewish Quarterly*, 13:2 (Summer 1965); J. Čulk, *Knihy za ohradou. Česk literatura v exilovch nakladatelstvch* 1971 – 1989 (s. d.); A. Haman, *Arnost Lustig* (1995); A. Mikulsek, *Literatura s hvězdou Davidovou*, vol. 1 (1998); *Slovník českch spisovatelů* (1982).

[Avigdor Dagan / Milos Pojar (2nd ed.)]

LUSTIG, MOSES (1906–1976), German journalist. Born in Tarnobrzeg, near Cracow, Lustig worked for the Polish press in Lodz from 1926. From 1933 to 1939 he co-edited a Polish weekly in Nowy-Sacz. After World War II he became the editor of the DP *Express* and was on the editorial board of *Ibergang* and other DP publications in Munich, Germany. In 1951 he founded the weekly *Muenchener Juedische Nachrichten* which he published until his death.

ADD. BIBLIOGRAPHY: *Der Journalist*, 11:2 (1961), 29.

LUSTIGER, JEAN-MARIE ARON (1926–), French cardinal. Born in Paris to a family of Jewish immigrants from Bendzin (Poland), during his childhood he converted to Roman Catholicism, being baptized on August 21, 1940, in Orléans. His parents were deported by the Nazis and his mother died in Auschwitz (his father survived). Ordained as a priest in 1954, he headed the Paroisse universitaire in Paris, a parish aimed at the student population, and from 1959 to 1969 the Centre Richelieu, which trained the chaplains working with students. In charge of a Parisian parish until 1969, he was then promoted by Pope John Paul II to bishop of Orléans and, in 1981, to archbishop of Paris, the highest position in the French Church, a position that he held until 2005. He was nominated a cardinal already in 1983 and was considered for many years to be a serious candidate for the papal succession. After his nomination as archbishop, he stated that he considered himself both a Jew and a Christian, a position that provoked controversy. With time, nevertheless, he was recognized as one of the outstanding promoters of better understanding and dialogue between the two religions, as when Jewish organizations opposed the establishment of a Carmelite convent at Auschwitz. In 1998, he received the Nostra Aetate Prize of the Sacred Heart University of Fairfield (Connecticut) together with former chief rabbi of France René Samuel Sirat. A member of the Académie française since 1995, he wrote numerous books, including an autobiography, *Le choix de Dieu* (1987).

[Philippe Boukara (2nd ed.)]

°**LUTHER, MARTIN** (1483–1546), German religious reformer. During the first period of his activity (approximately 1513–23), Luther often condemned the persecution of the Jews and recommended a more tolerant policy toward them, based on the spirit of true Christian brotherhood. Commenting on Psalm 22 (around 1519), he roundly condemned the "Passion preachers [who] do nothing else but exaggerate the Jews' misdeeds against Christ and thus embitter the hearts of the faithful against them." Speaking of the controversy between Johann *Reuchlin and Johann *Pfefferkorn, he strongly disapproved of the confiscation of the Talmud and rabbinic literature. Even in later times he referred to Reuchlin as his predecessor and teacher. Although declaring that it was impossible to expect the conversion of the whole Jewish people, he nevertheless nurtured the belief that, after listening to his teachings, many Jews would acknowledge the truth and accept Christianity.

Luther directly considered the Jewish question first in his pamphlet *Dass Jesus Christus ein geborener Jude sei* ("That Christ Was Born A Jew," 1523). Arguing that the Jews, who were from the same stock as the founder of Christianity, had been right in refusing to accept the "papal paganism" presented to them as Christianity, he added, "If I had been a Jew and had seen such fools and blockheads teach the Christian faith, I should rather have turned into a pig than become a Christian." Partly because of his polemics against the use of images in churches, he himself was branded a "half-Jew" (*semi-Judaeus*) by the church authorities. Perhaps encouraged by his conversion of one of the two Jews who had reportedly visited him at the Diet of Worms (1521), Luther had high hopes for the success of his mission among the Jews. Early missionary attempts had failed "not so much [because of] the Jews' obstinacy and wickedness, as rather [through] the absurd and asinine ignorance and the wicked and shameless life of the popes, priests, monks, and scholars." Pending their seeing the light, the Jews should be treated more considerately and given greater opportunities to gain a livelihood.

At first, Luther's disruptive impact on Roman Catholicism (which the Jews equated with the detested kingdom of *Edom) was welcomed by Jews as a break in the monolithic power of the Church. Others hoped that the turmoil arising in the Christian world through the spread of Lutheranism would lead to toleration of all forms of worship. Moreover they expressed the view that a partial reform of the Church was welcome since it led the Church away from its former evil. There were even some, like Abraham *Farissol, who regarded Luther as a Crypto-Jew, a reformer bent on upholding religious truth and justice, whose anti-idolatrous innovations were directed toward a return to Judaism. Some scholars, particularly of the Sephardi diaspora, such as Joseph ha-Kohen (1496-c. 1575), had strongly pro-Reformation sympathies.

However, although appreciating Luther's apparent kindliness toward them, the Jews resisted his message. Whether through irritation at their refusal to accept his truth or for some other reason, Luther grew increasingly hostile toward the Jews. In 1526 he complained of the Jews' stubbornness in clinging to their traditional interpretation of Scripture. His repeated attacks on usury began to assume an anti-Jewish bias and his successive *Table Talks* of the 1530s contain frequent complaints about "the stiffnecked Jews, ironhearted and stubborn as the devil." The increasing vehemence of his attacks is apparent in his "Letter Against the Sabbatarians," in which he harshly condemns that Protestant sect for adopting Jewish customs. Openly anti-Jewish and couched in Luther's characteristic style of extreme vituperation are two pamphlets written in 1542 and 1543, "On the Jews and Their Lies" and "On the Shem Hamephoras" ("The Ineffable Name"). Repeating the accusations and invective of medieval anti-Jewish polemics and making use of the works of the apostates Antonius *Margaritha and Bernhard Ziegler, he subjects the Jews to a torrent of vile abuse, calling them "venomous and virulent," "thieves and brigands," and "disgusting vermin." Although Luther poured out such violent language on the heads of all his enemies – princes, lawyers, bishops, and especially the pope – in the case of the Jews he also made practical suggestions, ranging from forced labor to outright banishment. As many of the Protestant rulers of the times relied on Luther's political advice, his attitude resulted in the expulsion of the Jews from Saxony in 1543 and the hostile *Judenordnung* of Landgrave Philip of Hesse in the same year. The tenor of his suggestions was equally virulent in his "Admonition against the Jews," a sermon preached in 1546, shortly before his death.

In Germany in particular, Luther's volte-face in his attitude toward the Jews caused bitter disappointment in Jewish circles. After his request to answer Luther's calumnies had been turned down by the authorities of Strasbourg in 1543, *Joseph (Joselman) b. Gershom of Rosheim expressed undisguised hostility to the Reformation, calling Luther "the unclean" (לא טהאר, a word play on his name). Among Reformation thinkers, a certain group (notably the Swiss Heinrich Bullinger and the Nuremberg preacher and Hebraist, Andreas *Osiander) criticized Luther's anti-Jewish stance.

Despite his fight against Judaism, Luther had a deep and abiding love for the Hebrew Bible. Although his Hebrew was weak and his Greek little better, his translation of the Bible into German was one of the most significant in literary history. He accepted the Hebrew language as the only one adequate for the expression of religious truth and sentiment. However, in his translation of and commentaries on the Bible he laid greater stress on intuition and revealed religion than on grammatical or linguistic questions. "I am not a Hebraist with respect to grammar [he said], nor do I wish to be one … I rather translate freely…. Accurate interpretation is a special gift of God." Although he often used, perhaps unwittingly, the interpretations of Rashi and recognized the importance of Moses and David *Kimḥi, on the whole he rejected rabbinic authorities, feeling that not only *Jerome but also *Nicholas de Lyre (on whom he relied heavily) were misled by them.

Inconsistency and violence characterized Luther's utterances in all fields, but perhaps in none with more disastrous consequences than in his statements on the Jews. Due to his vituperative anti-Jewish polemics, the Lutheran Church, unlike that which owed its foundation to John *Calvin, retained all the superstitious abhorrence of the Jews inherited from the medieval Catholic Church. Indeed Luther's attitude was worse, for he recognized no duty to protect the Jews. Throughout the subsequent centuries Luther's ferocious castigation of the Jews provided fuel for antisemites and the vicious force of that legacy was still evident in Nazi propaganda.

BIBLIOGRAPHY: H.H. Ben-Sasson, *Reformation in Contemporary Jewish Eyes* (1970); idem, in: HTR, 59 (1966), 385–9; Baron, Social 2, 13 (1969), 216ff., 421ff.; C. Cohen, in: JSOS, 25 (1963), 195–204; L.I. Newman, *Jewish Influence on Christian Reform Movements* (1925), 617–30; R. Lewin, *Luthers Stellung zu den Juden* (1911); S. Stern, *Josel of Rosheim* (1965), index; Mauser, *Kirche und Synagoge* (1953), 39–51, 88–105. **ADD. BIBLIOGRAPHY:** A.G. Dickens, *Martin Luther and the Reformation* (1967); H.G. Haile, *Luther: A Biography* (1981); J. Bodensieck (ed.), *The Encyclopaedia of the Lutheran Church*, 3 vols. (1965).

[Joseph Elijah Heller / B. Mordechai Ansbacher]

LUTOMIERSK, a suburb of Lodz, central Poland (formerly a town). Jews first settled in Lutomiersk, which had then an independent municipal status, at the end of the 17th century, and an organized community existed from the 18th century. In 1765, there were 404 Jews living in the town and 41 in eight surrounding villages. Lutomiersk belonged to the Sieradz and Wielun areas, where, according to decisions of the Sejmik (provincial parliament) of 1786, 1787, and 1788, Jews were forbidden to lease inns, taverns, and breweries. At the end of the 18th century four Jews founded a tannery; another Jew, Pinkus Israel, established a cloth factory in 1787, employing 20–30 workers. In 1796 this factory was commissioned by the Prussian government to supply cloth to the army in the province. The wooden synagogue, built in the 18th century by Hillel Benjamin of Lask, burned down during World War I (1915). The Jewish community numbered 657 (53% of the total population) in 1808 and 1,102 (51%) in 1827. Apart from shopkeeping, they were engaged mainly in weaving, tanning, tailoring, and carpentry. In 1857 their number had declined to 999 (46%) because many had moved to Lodz. They numbered 992 (38%) in 1897 and 775 (35%) in 1921 and 750 in 1939. A 1921 report of the *American Jewish Joint Distribution Committee mentioned 58 Jewish enterprises in Lutomiersk, 36 of which employed salaried workers.

[*Encyclopaedia Judaica* (Germany)]

Holocaust Period

When World War II broke out there were about 2,000 Jews living in Lutomiersk. The anti-Jewish terror began with the arrival of the Germans. Jews were kidnapped in the streets for hard and humiliating labor, their beards were cut off, and their property was requisitioned. Just before the occupation and within its first weeks, nearly 1,300 Jews escaped and by October 1939, only 750 Jews remained in Lutomiersk. In the summer of 1940 an open ghetto was created, but a year later it was closed off and no one could leave without a pass. Groups of Jews were daily led out of the ghetto for hard labor. At the end of 1941, the German authorities established a tailor shop for 20 Jewish tailors, which took many orders and provided the Jews with a small income. Lutomiersk ghetto was liquidated at the end of July 1942, when the surviving Jews were deported to the death camp in *Chelmno.

[Danuta Dombrowska]

BIBLIOGRAPHY: Warsaw, Archiwum Główne, Departymenta pogłównego żydowskiego: *Contribution to the Jewish Question*, no. 741; Warsaw, Archiwum Skarbowe, *Memoranda to the Finance Commission*, nos. 36 fol. 227, 38 fol. 103; I. Schiper, *Dzieje handlu zydowskiego na ziemiach polskich* (1937), 321, 324; B. Wasiutyński, *Ludność żydowska w Polsce...* (1930), 51; A. Breier, M. Eisler, and M. Grunwald, *Holzsynagogen in Polen* (1934), 28, 30, 35, 36, 39; E. Heller (ed.), *Żydowskie przedsiębiorstwa przmysłowe w Polsce...*, 2 (1923); R. Mahler, *Yidn in Amolikn Poyln in Likht fun Tsifern* (1958), index; D. Dabrowska, in: BŻIH, 13–14 (1955), 122–84, passim; Yad Vashem Archives, IM-837, IM-1209/4. **ADD. BIBLIOGRAPHY:** J. Goldberg, "Ludnosc zydowska w Lutomiersku w drugiej polowie XVIII wieku i jej walka z feudalnym uciskiem," in: BZIH (1956), nos. 15–16.

°LUTOSTANSKI, HIPPOLYTE (1835–1915), antisemitic agitator of Polish origin, born in Lithuania. Lutostanski was originally a Catholic priest but converted to the Greek Orthodox Church after he had been defrocked on charges of corruption. When Russian society became increasingly antisemitic at the end of the 1870s, he wrote several libelous books, including "The Problem of the Use of Christian Blood for Religious Purposes by Jewish Sects" (1876) and "The Talmud and the Jews" (1879). Scholars and public figures such as D. *Chwolson and Z. *Minor revealed his ignorance and distortions of fact. Lutostanski, who knew no Hebrew, drew the material for his books from the Christian anti-Jewish literature of Western Europe, and enjoyed the protection of prominent members of the court. In 1880 he was denounced as an impostor and forger by Alexander *Zederbaum, the editor of *Ha-Meliẓ*. Lutostanski sued Zederbaum but lost the case. From time to time he attempted to extort money from wealthy Jews by promising to put an end to his anti-Jewish activities, but in fact with the support of the authorities, he continued to bring out new editions of his books. These editions included new material mainly calculated to "prove" the responsibility of the Jews in general, and the Zionist Movement and the *Bund in particular, for the rise of the revolutionary movement in Russia.

BIBLIOGRAPHY: Z. Minor, *Rabbi Ippolit Litostanski* (Rus., 1879); N. Cohn, *Warrant for Genocide* (1967), 55–57.

[Yehuda Slutsky]

LUTSK (Pol. **Łuck**), capital of Volhynia district, Ukraine; until the end of the 18th century in Poland; under Russia until the end of World War I; between the two world wars again in Poland; and in 1939 annexed by the U.S.S.R., and included in the Ukrainian SSR. Nazi Germany occupied Lutsk in 1941, and after World War II it became again part of the Soviet Union. In the 13th century a community of *Karaites settled there while the Rabbanite Jews were probably included in the bill of privileges given by the Lithuanian prince Vitovt in 1388. The last are mentioned in 1409 and in the bill of 1432 given by King Vladislav the Jagelonian. They were expelled in 1495 together with the Jews of the Grand Duchy of Lithuania, and allowed to return in 1503. In the 15th and 16th centuries many of them leased custom revenues, other taxes, and estates. The importance of Lutsk as a political and economic center grew after the union of Poland and Lithuania in 1569, and Volhynia was included in the kingdom of Poland, and made the town capital of the district (vojevodstvo). The Jews benefited by this new situation, some being engaged in large-scale commerce, some leasing the customs revenue, breweries, and potash production plants, while others traded in forest and *agricultural products. Lutsk Jews participated in the fairs of Lithuania and Poland, and established their own craft guilds. In 1580 the king ordered that the municipal taxes collected from the Jews should not exceed their proportionate share in the general population. He also renewed their right to live in Lutsk, and allowed representatives of the Jewish community to attend the meetings of the city council when it debated the levying of the city taxes. During the *Chmielnicki massacres of 1648–49 both Rabbanites and Karaites suffered heavily, but the community was soon reconstructed. By royal order in 1649 and in 1664 the Jews of Lutsk were permitted to trade freely in shoes; it was again established that they should pay no more than a third of the municipal taxes, this being their proportion of the general population. In the 18th century Lutsk suffered from the *Haidamack uprising, and from a *blood libel in 1764.

The Lutsk community participated in the regional (*galil*) council of *Volhynia, as well as in the *Councils of the Lands. The city was a center of Torah study and had many yeshivot. Among its famous rabbis in the 17th and at the beginning of the 18th centuries were Moses b. Judah ha-Kohen (formerly of Cracow), Jacob Schor, the son of Ephraim Solomon *Schor, and Joel b. Isaac Halpern, known as the Great Rabbi Joel. Part of the fortress built by Prince Witold was rebuilt as a fortified synagogue, with the permission of King Sigismund III. From the gunmounts on the roof, Jews served as gunners during enemy attacks on the city, while underground tunnels led from the synagogue to other key buildings in the city. This building withstood the fires and enemy attacks of centuries. In 1765 there were 1,083 Jews in Lutsk, and under Russian rule during the 19th century the number of Jews in Lutsk was increased to 5,010 in 1847, and to 9,468 (out of a total of 15,804) in 1897, when the Jews were expelled from the rural communities following the czar's regulation of 1804. However, they lived under constant threat of expulsion, since Jews were prohibited from settling within 50 versts of the Russian border, and Lutsk was included in this category in 1844.

During World War I the Jews suffered both from the armies and from war devastation, as the city changed hands several times and was occupied by Russian and German troops. Under the rule of *Petlyura in 1918 many Jews were massacred, and when the Polish armies entered Lutsk they looted Jewish houses and organized anti-Jewish riots under the pretext that the Jews had helped their enemies. In the face of these assaults the Jews organized themselves in *self-defense. Between the two world wars the Lutsk community shared in the troubles and struggles of Polish Jewry, facing antisemitism and hostile economic and social legislation. For instance "Bata," the shoe factory opened in Lutsk with the assistance of the government, caused many Jewish shoe factories to close down.

The Jewish population grew in the 1920s. According to official figures, 14,860 Jews lived in Lutsk in 1921 (about 70% of the general population) whereas in 1931 they numbered 17,366 (48.5%). In 1937, however, they numbered only 15,880 (36.5%). The Jews took part in the civic life of the city and had their elected representatives in the city council. Between the world wars the Lutsk community led a rich religious and cultural life. Its last rabbi was Zalman *Sorotzkin. It had a hospital as well as several social and medical organizations, some of which were assisted by Lutsk *Landsmanshaften* in the U.S. A printing press attached to a Dominican monastery in Lutsk apparently produced some Hebrew books. Jewish schools were maintained by various organizations, among them the *Tarbut schools run by the Zionist organization and the Beth Jacob girls' school by the Agudat Israel.

[Shimshon Leib Kirshenboim]

Holocaust Period

By 1939 the Jewish population of Lutsk had increased to an estimated 20,000. Under Soviet occupation (1939–41) Jewish public life was repressed, Jewish organizations were disbanded, and private enterprises nationalized. Some Jewish businessmen were ordered to leave the town. In June 1940 the Soviet authorities uncovered the Zionist Gordonia underground and imprisoned its leaders. Many refugees who had fled to Lutsk from Nazi-occupied western Poland were deported to the Soviet interior. When the German-Soviet war broke out on June 22, 1941, many young Jews left together with the retreating Soviet forces. The town fell to the Germans on June 27, and a few days later some 300 Jews were murdered in retaliation for Ukrainian nationalist prisoners that had been killed, probably by the Soviet NKVD. On July 4, 3,000 Jews were put to death by the *Einsatzkommando 4a* in the nearby fortress (*zamek*) of Lubart. On October 19, 1941, a labor camp was established, and a ghetto was set up on December 11–12, 1941. The Jewish leaders made every effort to alleviate starvation and control epidemics. An orphanage, an old age home, and public kitchens were established in the ghetto, but the degree of suffering was hardly diminished. On March 15, 1942, a few hundred men were sent to Vinnitsa for the construction of the Fuehrer's HQ there. Only three survived by fleeing to Transnistria. In the spring of 1942 a group of young Jews attempted to escape from the ghetto to the forests, but most of them were caught and murdered by the Ukrainians. A few, however, managed to join the Soviet partisans and fought the Germans as part of the Kowpak units. One of the refugees of the Lutsk ghetto, Joel Szczerbato, became the commander of the seventh battalion of the partisans. Meanwhile the Germans carried out the large-scale *Aktion* in which the majority of the Lutsk ghetto was murdered (Aug. 20–23, 1942). About 17,500 Jews were led to the Polanka hill on the outskirts of the city and massacred. On September 1, 1942, some 2000, most who emerged from hiding, were murdered. The remaining 500 Jews, who were employed as artisans in the labor camp, were executed on Dec. 12, 1942. However, the Germans encountered armed opposition on the part of these Jews, who had fortified their building, armed themselves with a few guns and other weapons, and repeatedly repulsed German attacks. With German reinforcements the labor camp was taken, with some German losses. Among those who helped Jews was Vitold Fomenko, who supplied food to the ghetto and false identity cards to fugitives, found hiding places, and saved dozens of Jews. When the Soviets captured Lutsk on Feb. 2, 1944, only about 150 Jews came out from their hideouts or the nearby forests. No organized Jewish life was renewed in Lutsk. There are Lutsk societies in the United States and in Israel, *Sefer Lutsk* having been published in 1961 by the Israel Lutsk society. In the late 1960s there was a Jewish population of about 1,500, but there was no synagogue, the former old synagogue having been converted by the authorities into a movie theater. In the 1990s most Jews emigrated from Lutsk.

BIBLIOGRAPHY: *Sefer Lutsk* (Yid. and Heb., 1961); *Pinkas Hakehilot*, Poland, vol. 5; S. Spector, *Volhynia and Polesie* (1990).

[Aharon Weiss / Shmuel Spector (2nd ed.)]

°**LUTZ, CARL** (**Charles**; 1895–1975), Swiss diplomat who was responsible for saving Jewish lives in World War II. Lutz was made responsible for the interests of a number of countries who had severed relations with Hungary. He arrived in Budapest on January 2, 1942. As the representative of British interests, he came into contact with Moshe (Miklos) Krausz, the Jewish Agency immigration representative in Budapest. They developed a good relationship, working to maintain the modest flow of immigrants from Hungary to Palestine until the German occupation in March 1944.

Following the German occupation, Lutz gave Krausz and his team diplomatic protection in a Swiss office building. During the concentration and ensuing deportation of Hungarian Jewry – according to German documents 437,401 Jews were deported on 147 trains between May 15 and July 9, primarily to Birkenau, where a railroad spur was built directly into the camp to receive them – Krausz continued to try to foster emigration to Palestine and implored the Swiss and the Jewish Agency to influence the British to declare the holders of Palestine visas potential British citizens. At the height of the deportations, in late June 1944, the British agreed to Krausz's proposal. On July 7, the Hungarian regent, Miklos Horthy, declared that the deportations must cease. Soon after he also declared his willingness to allow 7,500 Jews to immigrate to Palestine, along with their families. This became known as the Horthy Offer, and it rendered Palestine visas even more valuable.

Working with Lutz, Krausz assembled a team, which was comprised mostly of Zionist youth movement members. From the Glass House on Vadasz Utca, a Swiss holding, they distributed Palestine visas along with *Schutzbriefe*, letters of protection in the name of Switzerland. Some 50,000 *Schutzbriefe* were disseminated. After October 15, 1944, when the fascist Arrow Cross leader Ferenc Szalasi was brought to power by the Nazis, Lutz and other neutral diplomats redoubled their efforts to protect Jews from deportation. In addition to safeguarding those Jews who held legitimate *Schutzbriefe*, they also tried to help the thousands who held counterfeit documents. They intervened with the Hungarian authorities, trying to stop the deportations altogether, and – until that was possible – to mitigate their effect.

In November, the Hungarian authorities declared that a ghetto must be established for those Jews without *Schutzbriefe*, while Jews holding legitimate papers would be housed under the auspices of their foreign protectors. Lutz and the other neutral diplomats did what they could to prevent the founding of the ghetto. Although they managed to have its establishment postponed, they could not avert its ultimate creation. Once it was set up, they did their best to care for the Jews' day-to-day needs, working with the Zionist youth underground. Lutz, along with other neutral diplomats, also procured homes for the Jews under his protection. Jews bearing false *Schutzbriefe* found their way in to these homes and Lutz did his best to protect them as well. Nonetheless, both he and Raoul *Wallenberg, a Swedish attaché, were forced to delineate between Jews with real documents and Jews with forged papers at the concentration point in Obuda. Lutz also tried to save the deportees, who were being marched from Obuda to the Austrian border by foot. He filled out unused Salvadorean visas in their names and managed to pluck Jews from the lines of the Death March. With the conquest of Pest by the Soviets in mid-January 1945, Lutz moved to Buda. There he protected Jews in a Swiss building until that side of the city was also taken in mid-February. Lutz's work in saving Jews was officially recognized by *Yad Vashem in 1965.

BIBLIOGRAPHY: Grossman, *Nur das Gewissen: Carl Lutz undseine Budapester Aktion; Geschichte und Portrait* (1986).

[Robert Rozett]

LUTZKY, A. (pseudonym of **Aaron Zucker**; 1894–1957), Yiddish poet. Born in Dimidovke (near Lutsk), Ukraine, he was privately educated and prepared for a career as a cantor. Before arriving in the U.S. in 1914, Lutzky had visited Warsaw and recited his poems to I.L. *Peretz, who was so delighted with them that he tried to retain him in Warsaw. Life was not easy for the young immigrant who worked as peddler, teacher, and violinist. When he published his first poems in 1917 in the *Yidishes Tageblat* and *Der Tog*, Abraham *Cahan, editor of the *Forverts*, recognized his talent, derived the pseudonym "Lutzky" for him from the name of his birthplace, lured him away from the rival dailies, and engaged him to write a weekly poem for the newspaper. A few months later, Lutzky was drafted into the U.S. army and fought at Verdun. When he returned, he astonished his readers with a strange, bizarre style. Special evenings, which increased his popularity, were arranged at which he acted out his new poems. Soon Herz Grossbard, Joseph *Buloff, and other famed actors discovered the dramatic quality of his work and spread his fame throughout the Yiddish world. Lutzky published his works in many periodicals, including *Fraye Arbeter Shtime, Tsukunft, Yidisher Kemfer*, and *Di Goldene Keyt*. Four books of lyrics appeared during his lifetime, of which the best known was *Breshis-In-mitn* ("Mid-Genesis," 1932), in which he philosophized on creation and destruction. A fifth volume, *Fun Aldos Guts* ("Of All Good Things," 1958), appeared posthumously and includes a bibliography. Some of Lutzky's lyrics were translated into Hebrew and into English. The pessimistic poet learned to transmute adversity into gay rhymes and images. His poems are playful parables, often devoid of any moralizing intent. They are theatrical narratives that animate the inanimate world through carefully chosen words and phrases. When Lutzky projected the drama of the waters that flow all over the world, or of pieces of paper that flutter about in the wind, or of beans that discourse before disintegrating in a seething pot, lifeless nature became poetically and dynamically alive.

BIBLIOGRAPHY: Rejzen, Leksikon, 2 (1927), 98–100; LNYL, 5 (1963), 20–4; S. Bickel, *Schrayber fun Mayn Dor* (1958), 58–63; B. Rivkin, *Yidishe Dikhter in Amerike* (1959), 172–90; J. Leftwich, *The Golden Peacock* (1961), 300–5. **ADD. BIBLIOGRAPHY:** A. Almi, *Mentshn un Ideyen* (1933), 222–40; Z. Weinper, *Yidishe Shriftshteler*, 1 (1933), 147–56; J. Glatstein, *In Tokh Genumen*, 1 (1956), 297–300; 2 (1960), 265–72; E. Fershleyser, *Af Shrayberishe Shlyakhn* (1958), 82–93.

[Shlomo Bickel / Marc Miller (2nd ed.)]

LUX, STEFAN (1888–1936), film producer. Born in Vienna, he was twice wounded during World War I as a volunteer in the Austrian army. He worked in his profession in Germany but immigrated to Prague in 1933 after *Hitler's advent to power. Alarmed by the world's indifference to Nazism's and Fascism's increasing influence, Lux decided to sacrifice his life to alert humanity. On July 3, 1936, he shot himself in the press gallery of the League of Nations Assembly Hall in Geneva, after leaving warning letters to Anthony Eden and other leaders.

BIBLIOGRAPHY: A. Hahn, *Vor den Augen der Welt! Warum starb Stefan Lux? Sein Leben – seine Tat – seine Briefe* (1936); Levani, in: *The Jewish Digest*, 12:2 (1966), 16–20.

[Yehuda Reshef]

LUXEMBOURG (Luxemburg), grand duchy, formerly a county, bordered by France, Germany, and Belgium. Jews were first noted in the city of Luxembourg, capital of the country, in 1276. In the early 14th century immigrants from the neighboring region of Trier formed several small Jewish settlements. During the *Black Death (1349) many of the Jews were massacred and the remainder expelled from the cities of Luxembourg and Echternach, notwithstanding the protection of Count Charles IV. They must have returned soon after, for in 1367 the existence of a *Porte des Juifs* ("Jews' Gate") is mentioned in the capital. The total expulsion of the Jews was decreed in 1391, but as early as 1405 some few individuals were once more living there. The homes of the Jews were destroyed and their possessions looted following an uprising in 1478. After that only two Jewish families remained, but by 1515 the number of families had grown to 15, residing in Luxembourg, Echternach, and Arlon, which was then still part of the county. The expulsion decreed in 1530 was fully implemented with the exception of some Marranos and a few traders at the fairs. Jews disappeared from Luxembourg until the Napoleonic period, when about 15 families from *Lorraine settled there. In 1808 the number of Jews was 75. Under Napoleonic legislation they were subject to the Trier consistory until the establishment of Luxembourg's own consistory in 1838. The first synagogue was built in 1823 and the first chief rabbi, Samuel *Hirsch, was appointed in 1843, serving until 1866. There were 87 Jewish families (369 persons) in the city of Luxembourg in 1880 and 63 families in the rest of the duchy. The growth of this population necessitated the construction of a new synagogue in Luxembourg in 1894, and another in Esch-sur-Alzette in 1899. The Jewish population, numbering 1,171 persons in 1927, increased considerably with the arrival of refugees from Germany; in 1935, 3,144 Jews were resident in the duchy.

[Simon R. Schwarzfuchs]

Holocaust Period

At the time of the invasion of Luxembourg on May 10, 1940, over 1,000 of the 4,000 Jews in the grand duchy (among them about 1,000 refugees) managed to flee to France. A new consistory was formed on the initiative of Rabbi Serebrenik, and in August 1940 the Nazis set up a civil administration under *Gauleiter* ("district head") Gustav Simon. After the German annexation, discriminatory racial laws operating throughout the Reich were extended to the grand duchy (Sept. 5, 1940), and 355 commercial enterprises were handed over to "Aryans." On Sept. 13, 1940 the *Gestapo announced that all the Jews would be deported on the following Day of Atonement if the consistory did not succeed in arranging their emigration prior to that date. Due to the consistory's efforts, particularly through a petition sent to *Himmler, this measure was postponed, but emigration remained the sole road to survival. Between Aug. 8, 1940 and May 26, 1941, when Rabbi Serebrenik was forced to leave in peril of his life, 700 Jews possessing more or less authentic visas fled overseas. In another operation, about 1,000 people were secretly evacuated to France in small groups. After these rescue operations the consistory became the Aeltestenrat der Juden and administered the remaining 850 Jews. Of these, 127 emigrated in January 1942 and the rest were deported; only 35 of the latter survived.

Contemporary Period

After World War II approximately 1,500 Jews returned to Luxembourg. Mostly merchants, they succeeded in renewing their business activities and, with financial assistance from the state, devoted themselves to reconstructing their community. The community's institutions were revived and a new synagogue built, the old one having been destroyed in 1943. Instrumental in these achievements was the consistory presided over by Edmond Marx, in cooperation with Rabbi Kratzenstein, who served the community from 1946 to 1948, and Rabbi Lehrmann (1949–59). In Esch-sur-Alzette a community of 40 families established itself with a new synagogue as its center. Maurice Levy was president of the consistory from 1961 to 1968 and was succeeded by Edmond Israël. From 1959 the chief rabbi was Emmanuel Bulz. In 1970, there were 1,200 Jews in Luxembourg. It was in the city of Luxembourg that the chancellor of the German Federal Republic, Konrad Adenauer, and Israel's foreign minister, Moshe *Sharett, signed on Sept. 10, 1952, the agreement on German reparations to Israel. There were around 600 Jews living in Luxembourg in the early 21st century. The community is dominated by Luxembourgers who returned after the Holocaust but there have been recent Jewish immigrants. The Consistoire appoints the chief rabbi.

[Emmanuel Bulz]

Relations with Israel

Luxembourg's relations with Israel have always been cordial. Luxembourg voted in the UN in Nov. 1947 in favor of the partition of Palestine and has maintained full diplomatic relations with Israel. Israel is represented in Luxembourg by her ambassador in Brussels, while Luxembourg's interests in Israel (as in most other countries) are represented politically by the Dutch embassy and economically by the Belgian embassy. Official visits of the foreign ministers of both countries were exchanged in 1969. Luxembourg, which plays a central role in the European Economic Community, wholeheartedly supported Israel's application for association with the Common Market. In 2005, as part of his visit to the Middle East, Jean Asselborn, president of the Council of the European Union and Luxembourg's minister for foreign affairs and immigration, visited Israel and affirmed the European Union's commitment to Israel as an important friend and partner.

BIBLIOGRAPHY: J. Stengers, *Les Juifs dans les Pays-Bas au moyen-âge* (1950); C. Lehrmann, *La communauté juive du Luxembourg dans le passé et dans le présent* (1953); H. Monneray, *La persécution des Juifs en France et dans les autres pays de l'Ouest* (1947), index; *Algemeyne Entsiklopedye*, 7 (1966), 217–20.

LUXEMBURG, ROSA (1871–1919), German economist and revolutionary. Born into a family of merchants in Zamosc, Poland, Rosa Luxemburg joined the Polish revolutionary movement as a schoolgirl in Warsaw. As a consequence of the threat of imprisonment she was forced to leave the country at the age of 18 and immigrated to Switzerland. There she studied political economy and history at the University of Zurich, worked in the underground Socialist movement of Polish emigrants, and met her longtime partner and lifetime comrade Leo Jogiches. In the early 1890s she helped to found the Social Democratic Party of Poland and Lithuania which cooperated for a time with the Marxist Russian Social Democratic movement. Migrating to Germany in 1898, she obtained German citizenship through a formal marriage with a printer. She became active among Polish workers and joined the editorial staff of the *Saechsische Arbeiter-Zeitung*, the *Leipziger Volkszeitung*, and later the *Vorwaerts*, and was a regular contributor to the *Neue Zeit*. Rosa Luxemburg was a leading figure in the revolutionary left wing of the German Socialist movement. As a correspondent of the *Vorwaerts* she participated in the revolution of 1905–06 in Warsaw, was imprisoned, but escaped and resumed her political activity in Germany, devoting a large part of her attention to the general strike as a revolutionary weapon. She was active in both the Polish and the German Labor movements and was a prominent figure in the Socialist International. She opposed World War I as an imperialist enterprise and spent a long period in prison as a consequence. In 1916, together with Franz Mehring, Karl Liebknecht, Leo Jogiches, and others she founded the "Spartakusgruppe," a revolutionary organization, which at the end of 1918 was transformed into the Spartakusbund and in the beginning of 1919 into the Communist Party of Germany (KPD). She was on friendly terms with Lenin but they disagreed on a number of issues. She was very critical of the Bolshevik reign of terror in the Soviet Union. With Karl Liebknecht she edited the Communist daily *Die Rote Fahne* from November 1918, and she was arrested with him in Berlin on January 15, 1919. They were brought to the Berlin Eden-Hotel, where both were tortured and murdered by army officers. Rosa Luxemburg's body was thrown into the Berlin Landwehrkanal and found only months later. On June 13, 1919, she was buried at the cemetery of Berlin-Friedrichsfelde, followed by a large funeral procession.

As an economist, Rosa Luxemburg is widely known for her theory of imperialism. She was convinced that in a pure capitalist society the inadequacy of the local market would lead to a search for markets in countries with more primitive methods of production. There would be a struggle for foreign markets, and imperialism would thus become the guiding principle of foreign policy. Although capitalism must automatically disappear with the exhaustion of external non-capitalist markets, it would collapse before reaching this limit, because expanding capitalism would produce profound social conflicts leading to a victorious proletarian revolution. She developed this theory in *Die Akkumulation des Kapitals* (1913). Of great interest are Rosa Luxemburg's views on nationalism. For her, Socialism and national self-determination were conflicting ideas. She opposed Poland's independence; her "fatherland" was the international working class, her aim the Socialist revolution. Although Rosa Luxemburg did not show any interest in Jewish matters or in a specifically Jewish labor movement, she was constantly attacked in antisemitic terms. Rosa Luxemburg's important publications include *Die industrielle Entwicklung Polens* (her doctoral thesis, 1898), *Sozialreform oder Revolution* (1899), *Massenstreik, Partei und Gewerkschaften* (1906), *Die russische Revolution* (ed. by Paul Levi, 1922, and by Ossip K. Flechtheim, 1963), *Einführung in die Nationalökonomie* (ed. by Paul Levi, 1925), and *Politische Schriften* (ed. by Ossip K. Flechtheim, 1966). Her *Gesammelte Werke* appeared in various editions from the 1920s on. Numerous collections of letters were published, among them *Briefe aus dem Gefaengnis* (1920), *Briefe an Karl und Luise Kautsky* (1923), *Briefe an Freunde* (ed. by B. Kautsky, 1950), *Briefe an Leon Jogiches* (1971), and *Gesammelte Briefe* (vol. 1–6, 1982–93).

BIBLIOGRAPHY: J.P. Nettl, *Rosa Luxemburg*, 2 vols. (Eng., 1966). **ADD. BIBLIOGRAPHY:** P. Froelich, *Rosa Luxemburg* (Eng., 1940); P. Peretz, in: *Juden und juedische Aspekte in der deutschen Arbeiterbewegung, 1848–1918* (1977); E. Silberner, in: *Jahrbuch des Instituts fuer Deutsche Geschichte*, 7 (1978), 299–337; O.K. Flechtheim, *Rosa Luxemburg zur Einführung* (1985); E. Ettinger, *Rosa Luxemburg* (Eng., 1986); R.S. Wistrich, in: A. Rapoport-Albert and S.J. Zipperstein (eds.), *Jewish History, Essays in Honour of Chimen Abramsky* (1988); K. von Soden (ed.), *Rosa Luxemburg* (1995); A. Laschitza, *Im Lebensrausch, trotz alledem. Rosa Luxemburg* (1996).

[Mirjam Triendl (2nd ed.)]

LUZ (Heb. לוּז), an old name for *Beth-El, first mentioned in the account of Jacob's dream there (Gen. 28:19). Beth-El is again called Luz in Genesis 35:6; in his blessing of Joseph's sons, Jacob refers to God's appearance at Luz, meaning Beth-El (Gen. 48:3). In the description of the borders of Ephraim, however, the two cities are treated as separate entities (Josh. 16:2); in the parallel account of Joshua 18:13, Luz is mentioned first, then the "side" (*katef*) of Luz, "the same is Beth-El." The man who delivered the city to the Israelites went into the land of the Hittites and built there another Luz (Judg. 1:26). According to later sources, Luz and Beth-El are the same city (Eusebius, Onom. 4:28ff.; 40:20; 120:8ff.; also Madaba Map). Eusebius locates Beth-El 12 mi. (c. 19 km.) north of Jerusalem on the left ("west") side of the road to Neapolis (Onom. 40:20). Some scholars have concluded from the biblical references that Luz remained the name of the city until the time of Jeroboam and that Beth-El was originally the name of the sanctuary to the east of it. A more probable view is that Luz was the ancient name of neighboring *Ai (Heb. *Ha-Ai*, "the ruin"); Beth-El, which was founded in the Middle Bronze Age, doubtless inherited the role and area of the prominent Early Bronze city only about 1 mi. (1½ km.) distant.

BIBLIOGRAPHY: Elliger, in: ZDPV, 53 (1930), 304; W.F. Albright, *The Vocalization of the Egyptian Syllabic Orthography* (1934), 9.

[Michael Avi-Yonah]

LUZ (Lozinsky), KADISH (1895–1972), Israeli politician and third speaker of the *Knesset, member of the Second to Sixth Knessets. Born in Bobruisk, Belorussia, Luz received traditional schooling. He studied economics and social sciences at the University of St. Petersburg, and science and agriculture at Odessa and Dorpat, Estonia. He was one of the founders of the *He-Ḥalutz movement. In 1916–17 he served in the Russian army and received the rank of officer at the outbreak of the Russian Revolution. He was one of the founders of the organization of Jewish soldiers in Russia, initiated by Joseph *Trumpeldor. In 1920 Luz settled in Palestine, where he worked on land reclamation at *Kiryat Anavim and *Be'er Toviyyah, and on road construction in the Jezreel Valley. In 1921 he joined kibbutz *Deganyah Bet. He was a member of the secretariat of the Central Control Committee of the *Histadrut in 1935–40, a member of the Tel Aviv Workers Council secretariat in 1941–42, and a member of the Ḥever ha-Kevuẓot secretariat in 1949–51. Later on he was a member of the secretariat of Iḥud ha-Kevuẓot ve-ha-Kibbutzim and a member of the Mapai Central Committee. Luz was a delegate to the Twentieth Zionist Congress in 1937 and of the Twenty-Second Congress in 1946. He was a member of the Haganah, and in the War of Independence fought in the Jordan Valley. Luz was elected to the Second Knesset on the Mapai list in 1951. He served as minister of agriculture in 1955–59. He was elected speaker of the Knesset in 1959, serving in this position for ten years. During this period the new Knesset building was built, and Luz presided over the festive opening in August 1966. He provided artist Marc Chagall with the quotes from the Old Testament on which he based most of the pictures that appear on the three tapestries he made for the Knesset State Hall. Luz's moderation and impartiality made him a popular figure with all the parliamentary groups in the House.

His writings include *Avnei Derekh* ("Milestones," 1962), a book of memoirs, *Eḥad mi-Sheneim-Asar* (1970), and numerous articles and booklets on labor problems and the kibbutz movement. In 1974 there appeared *Adam ve-Derekh: Devarim bi-Khtav u-Be'al Peh, Mi-Shelo ve-Alav*, containing items by and about him.

[Susan Hattis Rolef (2nd ed.)]

LUZKI (Lucki), ABRAHAM BEN JOSEPH SOLOMON (Aben Yashar) (1792–1855), Karaite scholar and poet in Crimea. He was born in *Lutsk (Luck) and moved as a child with his father Joseph Solomon b. Moses *Luzki in 1803 to Yevpatoriya, where the latter was *shofet*. He was subsequently sent to Constantinople, where he entered the service of a Karaite merchant Shabbatai Kvitzo for 13 years and married his daughter. Luzki devoted much time to the study of Talmud and rabbinic literature with Rabbanite teachers and acquired extensive knowledge of languages – Spanish, Greek, and Italian – before returning to Yevpatoriya. When in 1827 his father succeeded in obtaining exemption of the Karaites from military service, Luzki composed a poem in honor of Czar Nicholas I. In 1835 he was elected *ḥakham* of Yevpatoriya, but declined the office. In 1844 he founded a study house in Yevpatoriya and taught there until 1853. Some of his disciples, such as Yehuda Savuskan, Avraham Yefet, and Elijah *Kazaz, became well-known public figures of the Karaite communities in the Crimea. He died in the course of a visit in Ekaterinoslav.

His published works include *Iggeret Zug ve-Nifrad* (Yevpatoriya, 1833, reprint Ramleh, 1978), a decision concerning marriage law, mitigating former more severe Karaite rulings; liturgical poems, of which eight are included in the Karaite prayer book (Vienna ed. (1854), 168ff.); *Shoshannim Edut le-Yosef*, a collection of poems, lamentations, sermons, and obituaries (Ashdod, 2005); *Mishlei Musar*, a translation of fables into Karaite language (Yevpatoriya, n.d.) and a translation of Joseph *Ha-Efrati's drama, *Melukhat Sha'ul* ("The Reign of Saul") from Hebrew into Karaite language. There remain in the Inst. of Oriental Studies of St. Petersburg and in the National Russian Library a large number of MSS which comprises his correspondence, list of books, and MSS in his own library, comments on some treatises, and so on.

BIBLIOGRAPHY: E. Deinard, *Masa Krim* (1878), 72; Fuerst, Karaeertum, 3 (1869), 138; Mann, Texts, 2 (1935), 472 n. 10, 474 n. 11, 501.

[Jakob Naphtali Hertz Simchon]

LUZKI (Lutzki, Lucki), JOSEPH SOLOMON BEN MOSES (Yashar) (1770–1844), Karaite scholar and public figure, born at Kukizow near Lwow. He lived at Lutsk (Volhynia), had disciples there, and was a judge in the municipal council; he knew Russian and Polish well. In 1802 he moved to Yevpatoriya in the Crimea by invitation of the heads of the community to become *melammed* and *shofet*. He remained in these offices about 40 years and had many disciples. Luzki went with the Ḥakham Simḥah *Babovich to St. Petersburg where they succeeded in obtaining exemption for the Karaites from compulsory military service, imposed on the Jews in 1827. A detailed account of their journey and activities is given by Luzki in *Iggeret Teshu'at Yisrael* (Yevpatoriya, 1840; with a Tatar translation by the author's brother-in-law, Abraham *Firkovich). A thanksgiving prayer he composed on that occasion was subsequently recited by the Karaites every year on the anniversary. In 1831 Luzki visited Ereẓ Israel with his wife.

His works include *Sefer ha-Ḥinnukh le-Petaḥ Tikvah*, a didactic manual in two parts: (a) *Petaḥ ha-Tevah*, a primer and Hebrew prayers for children with Tatar translation; (b) *Zekher Rav*, by Benjamin *Mussafia, with Luzki's translation of the Hebrew words into the Tatar language (Constantinople, 1831); and *Tirat Kesef*, a comprehensive supercommentary on the *Sefer ha-Mivḥar* by the Karaite *Aaron b. Joseph (printed with *Sefer ha-Mivḥar*, Gozleve, 1835). Luzki is also the author of a calendar for the years 1859 to 1901 (printed posthumously, in Yevpatoriya, 1858), and of liturgical poems, prayers, and hymns, some of which were incorporated in the Karaite prayer book.

BIBLIOGRAPHY: A. Gottlober, *Biqoret le-toldot a-Karaim* (1865), 179; A. Firkovich, *Avnei Zikkaron* (1872), 4; S. Poznański, *Karaite Literary Opponents of Saadiah Gaon* (1908), 90; Mann, Texts, 2 (1935), s.v. *Jos. Sol. b. Moses Lucki*. **ADD. BIBLIOGRAPY:** Miller, Joseph Solomon Luzki, *Iggeret Teshu'at Yisrael* (1993).

[Isaak Dov Ber Markon]

LUZKI (Lucki), SIMḤAH ISAAC BEN MOSES (1716–1760), Karaite scholar and spiritual leader, known also as "the Karaite Rashi" and "Olam Ẓa'ir" (the latter meaning literally "microcosm" – acronym based on the *gematria* of his name). In the introduction to most of his works he mentioned that he was the son of Moses son of Simḥah, son of Joseph son of Yeshu'a (died in Derazhne in 1649 during the Chmielnicki revolt), son of Simḥah, son of Yeshu'a, son of Samuel, of a noble family. He was born in Lutsk and resided there until 1754, when he moved to Chufut-Qaleh by invitation of the rich patron Mordecai ben Berakhah, one of the heads of the local community, to become the head of the *bet midrash* after the demise of its head, Shmuel ben Josef *Kal'i. Luzki held that position until his death in Chufut-Qaleh.

Luzki copied many rare Karaite manuscripts and wrote about 24 books on various subjects. His treatises were devoted to such topics as Karaite *halakhah* (esp. laws of ritual slaughter, calendar) – *Akedat Yiẓḥak* (IOS A52, JNUL mic. 52308), *Sha'arei Ẓedek* (JTS mic. 9089, JNUL mic. 49546), etc.; history of the split (*ḥilluk*) between Rabbanism and Karaism; and exegesis of Karaite texts.

His book *Me'irat Einayyim* (1750; Ashdod, ed. Yosef Algamil, 2002) is a compilation of *halakhah*, exegesis, and historiography with a historical and bibliographical account of Karaism in its second part, *Ner Ẓaddikim*. His well-known treatise *Oraḥ Ẓaddikim* (1757) is an abridgment of *Ner Ẓaddikim* (*Oraḥ Ẓaddikim*, Vienna, 1830). It contains also important bibliographical material – a list of most of the Karaite books, the names of their authors and biographical details about some of them. Luzki introduces a traditional apologetic Karaite claim, that the split between Rabbanism and Karaism began during the First Temple period with the division of the Jewish state into two kingdoms. Some of Luzki's works were devoted to Kabbalah, philosophy, and theology. According to his own assertions, he was forced to study Kabbalah from books, because the Rabbanites refused to teach him (see *Livnat Sapir*, ed. Yosef Algamil, Ashdod (2002), 32–33). In his six treatises on Kabbalah (*Sefer Bereshit* (1746), *Olam Ẓa'ir* (1748), *Rekhev Elohim* (1750), *Kevod Melakhim* (1750), *Sefer ha-Tapu'aḥ* (1751) (Evr I, 707 [JNUL mic. 51379]), *Livnat Sapir* (1756); *Kevod Elohim* (1751; Algamil ed., Ramle, 2000)) Luzki explains main concepts of the Lurianic Kabbalah, such as *sefirot*, divine names, and Hebrew letters. There is no innovation in these works, except for the very attempt to make Kabbalah acceptable to the Karaites. Luzki knew about modern science, but rejected it as speculative (*Kevod Melakhim*, ed. Yosef Algamil, Ashdod, 2002). He also wrote an exegetical work, *Be'er Yiẓḥak* (1737); *Or ha-Ḥayyim* (Yevpatoriya, 1847), an extensive commentary on the philosophical work by Aaron b. *Elijah of Nicomedia, *Eẓ Ḥayyim*; *Torei Zahav im Nekuddot ha-Kesef*, a guide to the commandments of Jewish law (Algamil ed., 1978), and many other works.

Luzki also composed liturgical poems and a number of prayers. Some of them were included in the Karaite *siddur*. Most of his views and his philosophical theology were based on medieval science, which he combined with Lurianic Kabbalah.

Luzki acquired his knowledge from numerous Rabbanite sources, which he often quoted in his works (e.g., Maimonides, Rashi, Saadiah Gaon, Ibn Ezra, Naḥmanides, Joseph Albo, *Pirke de-Rabbi Eliezer*, Solomon ibn Gabirol, Judah Halevi, Ḥasdai Crescas, Profiat Duran, Yashar of Candia etc.). He continued the earlier Karaite trend of understanding most of Rabbanite literature as "the words of our forefathers." Luzki also cites such non-Jewish sources as Greek and Roman philosophers Plato, Aristotle, and Seneca; and such Arab thinkers as al-Ghazālī and al-Tabrizi.

BIBLIOGRAPHY: F. Astren, in: M. Polliak (ed.), *Karaite Judaism: A Guide to its History and Literary Sources* (2003), 55–64; D.J. Lasker, in: D. Shapira (ed.), *Eastern European Karaites in the Last Generations* (in press); D. Lasker, in: *Shefa Tal* (2004), 171–90 (Heb.); Mann, Texts, index, 1588.

LUZ OF THE SPINE, a bone which, according to the rabbis, is to be found at the base of the spine, an addition to the 18 vertebrae. Called the *luz she-ba-shidrah*, it is indestructible and is the source of the future resurrection of the body. According to the Midrash, R. Joshua b. Hananiah demonstrated it to the Emperor Hadrian, in answer to his questions as to how the resurrection would take place. "They put it in water and it did not dissolve, in fire and it was not consumed, on a mill and it was not ground. They placed it on an anvil and struck it with a hammer. The anvil cracked and the hammer split, but it remained whole" (Eccl. R. 12:5, no. 1; Lev. R. 18:1). It is apparently the statement that the *luz* is an addition to the 18 vertebrae which is the basis of the statement of the Talmud that the **Birkat ha-Minim*, the 19th blessing added to the original 18 of the daily **Amidah*, corresponds to the *luz* of the spine (Ber. 28b). On the other hand, the enumeration of the bones of the body in the Mishnah (Oho. 1:8) lists only the 18 vertebrae and does not mention the *luz*. There is no scientific basis for this legend. It may be connected with the statement that in the second city of *Luz (Judg. 1:26), which was still identified as existing in talmudic times as a place where the **tekhelet*, the blue dye for the ritual fringes (Num. 15:38), was manufactured, "the Angel of Death had no permission to pass through it, and when old men there become tired of life, they go outside the city to die." In *Genesis Rabbah* 69:8, the reading is, "they are carried out beyond the city walls to die." The belief in the indestructibility of the *luz* was linked with Ps. 34:21, which was translated, "He keeps all his bones; one of them cannot be broken." The Church Fathers Origen and Jerome also regarded it as a pointer to resurrection, and this was accepted by non-Jewish scholars in the Middle Ages, and they spoke of the "Jews' bone" (Judenknoechlein) and identified it with the last vertebra of the spinal column.

BIBLIOGRAPHY: Baer, S., Seder, 87n.; Kohut, Arukh, 5 (1926^2), 24–25, s.v. *Luz shel Shidrah*, and introd., lxii.

[Louis Isaac Rabinowitz]

LUZZATTI, LUIGI (1841–1927), Italian statesman and economist; the first Jew to become prime minister of Italy. Born in Venice, he graduated in law from the University of Padua. Luzzatti's devotion to economic and social studies arose from his desire to improve the condition of the poor. He began by founding a mutual aid society for the gondoliers of Venice which was opposed by the Austrian police and in 1863 he was expelled from Venice as a revolutionary. He went to Milan where he became professor of economics at the Instituto Tecnico and then professor of constitutional law at the University of Padua (1867). In 1869 Luzzatti became general secretary of the Ministry of Agriculture, Industry, and Commerce. He was elected to Parliament in 1871 and sat continuously for 50 years until 1921 when he was raised to the Senate. He was minister of the treasury on three occasions (1891–92, 1896–98, and 1904–06) and together with Sidney *Sonnino reduced the Italian treasury deficit and secured the conversion of the public debt, thus restoring Italy's finances. In 1909 Luzzatti became minister of agriculture and was prime minister (1910). His ministry introduced numerous reforms aimed at winning popular support, but his right-wing administration was defeated by a combination of Liberals and Socialists the following year. An outstanding orator and expert economist, Luzzatti founded the Banca Popolare in Milan and founded the first cooperative store in Italy. He also negotiated many of Italy's principal commercial treaties. During World War I, Luzzatti established the National Foundation for the sons of peasants fallen in the war and in 1922 presented a plan for international currency stabilization. Though religiously nonobservant, he retained his Jewish sympathies and acted on behalf of oppressed European Jews, intervening through diplomatic channels for the granting of civic rights to the Jews of Romania. Luzzatti supported Zionist enterprises in Palestine, particularly the agricultural settlements which he much admired. Luzzatti's writings were collected under the title *Opere di Luigi Luzzatti*, including *Grandi Italiani: grandi sacrifizi per la patria* (1924), and *Dio nella libertà: studi sulle relazioni tra lo Stato e la Chiesa* (1926; *God in Freedom*…, 1930), a collection of essays on religious liberty.

BIBLIOGRAPHY: F. Catalano, *Luigi Luzzatti: la figura e l'opera* (1965); Villari, in: H. Bolitho (ed.), *Twelve Jews* (1934), 123–52; L. Luzzatti, *God in Freedom* (1930), xvii–xxv (biography by D. Askowith). **ADD. BIBLIOGRAPHY:** F. Parrillo, (a cura di) *Attualita di Luigi Luzzatti* (1964); M. Berengo, "Luigi Luzzatti e la tradizione ebraica," in: *Luigi Luzzatti e il suo tempo* (1994), 527–41.

[Giorgio Romano]

LUZZATTO (sometimes **Luzzatti**), Italian family. The name is probably derived from Lausitz (Lat. Lusatia), from where according to tradition the family emigrated into Italy in the mid-15th century, settling in the Venetian territories. One of the seven Venetian synagogues bore the name "Scuola Luzzatto," and many members of the family are buried in the cemetery of the community on the Lido. Others lived in the towns and townships around Venice. The poet and kabbalist Moses Ḥayyim *Luzzatto derived from the Paduan branch of the family. In 1595 the two brothers ABRAHAM and BENEDETTO LUZZATTO, from Venice, settled in *San Daniele del Friuli. From this branch of the family were descended the brothers Ephraim *Luzzatto and Isaac *Luzzatto, both poets. Another descendant, MARCO (Mordecai b. Nathan; 1720–1799), was an author and translator. All of his works are in manuscript, and include a Hebrew-Italian dictionary. When the Venetian government introduced its policy of excluding the Jews from the smaller places under its rule in 1777, the San Daniele community became dispersed. The scholarly carpenter HEZEKIAH LUZZATTO settled in Trieste, where his son Samuel David *Luzzatto was born, the first historian of the family. His son PHILOXENUS (Filosseno; 1829–1854) was an Orientalist. He published many works, including studies on *Ḥisdai ibn Shaprut, the Beta Israel (Falashas), and Hebrew inscriptions. The most recent member was FEDERICO LUZZATTO (1900–1961) who, after a distinguished career in the Italian navy, settled as a farmer in Ereẓ Israel, and did valuable research on Italian Jewish history. Today members of the Luzzatto family, sometimes no longer professing Judaism, are to be found in most important Italian cities and scattered throughout the world.

BIBLIOGRAPHY: S.D. Luzzatto, *Autobiografia preceduta da alcune notizie storico-letterarie sulla famiglia Luzzatto*… (1882), 7–36; Roth, Italy, index; Milano, Italia, index; Milano, Bibliotheca, index; *Volume… Federico Luzzatto* (1962); F. Luzzatto, *Cronache storiche della Università degli ebrei di San Daniele del Friuli* (1964); Zoller, in: REJ, 94 (1933), 50–56; G. Bedarida, *Ebrei d'Italia* (1950), index.

[Umberto (Moses David) Cassuto]

LUZZATTO, EPHRAIM (**Angelo**; 1729–1792), Italian Hebrew poet and physician. Ephraim was born in San Daniele del Friuli, son of Raffael Luzzatto, scion of one of the earliest Jewish families who settled in San Daniele. Already his grandfather, Isacco, embraced the profession of physician. Ephraim studied medicine in Padua between 1742 and 1751. It seems that afterwards Ephraim practiced at Padua, Trieste, and Leghorn. Luzzatto's earliest record at the Bevis Marks Synagogue in London is for the year 1764, although it seems that he had arrived in England already in 1755. In 1779 Ephraim was appointed physician in London's Portuguese community hospital, Beth Holim. Luzzatto was well known in the medical world of 18th-century England. He appears in a very positive light in the memoirs of John Taylor, the oculist to George III. Like many of his contemporaries, Ephraim was known for his loose way of life. He frequented the gaming table as well as the theaters of Drury Lane. He had a quarrel with the actor Baddeley, whom, it seems, he cuckolded. In 1792 he left for a visit in Italy with his companion and lover Ann Davis. He died at Lausanne, and he was buried in the local burial ground.

Ephraim was also a poet. He collected his 55 poems, some of them written in Italy and some in England, *Elleh Benei ha-Ne'urim* ("These Are the Children of My Youth") in 1768 in London. The book was often republished, and influenced the poetry of M.J. *Lebensohn and J.L. *Gordon. The collection includes occasional poems, moralistic poetry, and some erotica. Most important, however, are his love sonnets which have, for the period, a remarkable lyrical quality. These displays a variety of moods: indulgent, satirical, and passionate. His poems reflect individual experience, and are thus an innovation and a precursor of the Hebrew lyric poetry of the Haskalah.

BIBLIOGRAPHY: Klausner, Sifrut, 1 (1952^2), 295–306; J. Fichmann, in: *Shirei Ephraim Luzzatto* (1942), v–xx (introd.); H. Schirmann, *ibid.*, 2 (1942/43); R.N. Salomon, in: JHSET, 9 (1922), 85–102; C. Roth, in: *Sefer Ḥayyim Schirmann* (1970), 367–70. **ADD. BIBLIOGRAPHY:** L. Bonifacio, "Varieta' di motivo nei sonetti di Ephraim Luzzatto," in: AFO, 28 (1989), 5–34; L. Bonifacio, "I sonetti di Ephraim Luzzatto nella poesia ebraico-italiana del settecento," in: *Italia*, 9 (1996), 97–113; S.G. Cusin and P.C. Ioly Zorattini, *Friuli Venezia Giulia, Itinerari ebraici, I luoghi, la storia, l'arte* (1998), 98; D. Mirsky, *The Life and Work of Ephraim Luzzatto* (1987); E. Morpurgo, "Samuel David Luzzatto e la sua famiglia," in: RMI, 39 (1973), 624–25.

[Elieser Kagan / Samuele Rocca (2nd ed.)]

LUZZATTO, GINO (1878–1964), Italian Socialist and economic historian. Born in Padua, Luzzatto graduated in philosophy and law and then lectured in economic history successively at the universities of Bari, Trieste, and Venice. He held a professorship from 1910 to 1953 except for the years 1938–45, when he was suspended because of Italy's antisemitic laws. Luzzatto supported the Socialist cause and was an indomitable opponent of Fascism. He was imprisoned by the authorities and on his release joined the underground resistance movement. During the period of antisemitic reaction in Italy his works were published under a pseudonym, Giuseppe Padovan, or with his name omitted. From 1946 to 1951 he was councilor and assessor of the municipality of Venice.

Luzzatto was active in Jewish affairs as vice president of the Venice Jewish community and president of the Italian *ORT. He also wrote several essays on the economic situation of Italian Jewish communities (e.g., *I banchieri ebrei in Urbino nell' età ducale*, 1903^2), as well as on the economy and the cooperative movement in Israel.

Luzzatto's writings extended over half a century. His main economic works include *Storia del commercio dall' antichità al Rinascimento* (1914); *Storia economica dell' età moderna e contemporanea* (2 vols., 1934, 1948), and *Studi di storia economica veneziana* (1954) and various volumes of *Storia Economica d'Italia* (1949–63).

BIBLIOGRAPHY: *Studi in onore di Gino Luzzatto*, 4 vols. (1950); *Nuova Rivista Storica*, 49 (1965).

[Giorgio Romano]

LUZZATTO, ISAAC (Isacco) (1730–1802), Italian poet and physician. Born in San Daniele del Friuli (Italy), Isaac, like his brother Ephraim *Luzzatto, graduated in medicine at Padua (1747). Upon the expulsion of the Jews from San Daniele, as from other rural localities in the Venetian Republic (September 1777), he alone was allowed to remain with his family and practice there. In the summer of 1779, Luzzatto traveled to Vienna and successfully petitioned Maria Theresa to authorize his fellow townsmen to continue living in the rural districts of Austria where they had established themselves. His *Toledot Yiẓḥak*, a collection of poetry, was published in 1944 by D.J. Eckert and M. Wilensky, with a biography and notes. It includes Hebrew poems, mostly sonnets, on religious and ethical themes, conundrums, and a parody of a mishnaic treatise satirizing the customs of his community (*Mishnayyot San Daniele*, or *Massekhet Derekh Ereẓ*). Luzzatto also translated into Hebrew *La Libertà a Nice*, by the Italian poet Metastasio, at the latter's request. Isaac Luzzatto's second wife, Tamar, was a sister of Hezekiah, father of Samuel David *Luzzatto.

BIBLIOGRAPHY: S.D. Luzzatto, *Autobiografia…* (1882), 22, 23; F. Luzzatto, *Cronache storiche della Università degli ebrei di San Daniele del Friuli* (1964), index. **ADD. BIBLIOGRAPHY:** P.C. Ioly Zorattini, in: *Gli ebrei a Gorizia e a Trieste* (1984), 113–16; idem, RMI (1999), 39, 65, 73; M. Del Bianco Cotrozzi, in: *Mondo Ebraico* (1991), 184, 196, 198, 210.

LUZZATTO, JACOB BEN ISAAC (16th century), rabbi and author. Luzzatto was born apparently in Safed where he spent his childhood. He later moved to Europe where he lived in Basle and probably also in Posen and Cracow. Luzzatto was the author of *Kaftor va-Feraḥ* or *Yashresh Ya'akov* (Basle, 1581; also called in another version *Kehillat Ya'akov*, Salonika, 1584), an attempt to defend talmudic *aggadot* attacked by the Christian censors as anti-Christian. Luzzatto explained the *aggadot* according to Rashi, the *tosafot*, Solomon b. Abraham Adret, and R. Nissim, citing also parallel readings in the Jerusalem Talmud, Midrashim, and kabbalistic works, giving them allegorical meanings. He was also probably the final corrector, after the censor, of the Basle Talmud (1578–81), since it contains some of his glosses. He edited (including a preface and index) the *Ta'amei ha-Mitzvot* (Basle, 1581) of Menahem Recanati and Solomon Molcho's *Sefer ha-Mefo'ar* (Cracow, 1570). A copy of the latter in Luzzatto's own handwriting is extant (Ms. Oxford, 1660). Luzzatto is identified with the Jacob b. Isaac Luzzat of Posen who corrected the *Toẓe'ot Ḥayyim* (Cracow, n.d.) of Elijah Vidas. He probably died in Ereẓ Israel, though some believe he died in Venice.

BIBLIOGRAPHY: S.D. Luzzatto, *Autobiografia…* (1882), 8–10; Brann, in: *Samuel David Luzzatto. Ein Gedenkbuch* (1900), 29, 31–33; Rosanes, Togarma, 3 (1938^2), 288; J. Perils, *Geschichte der Juden in Posen* (1865), 40.

[Umberto (Moses David) Cassuto]

LUZZATTO, MOSES ḤAYYIM (Heb. acronym **RaMḤaL**; 1707–1746), kabbalist, writer of ethical works, rhetorician, logician, and Hebrew poet; leader of a group of religious thinkers who were mainly interested in the problems of redemption and messianism and probably tried to use their mystical knowledge to hasten the era of redemption. Luzzatto was born in Padua, *Italy, into one of the most important, oldest, and most respectable families in Italian Jewry (see *Luzzatto family). Regarded as a genius from childhood, he knew Bible, Talmud, Midrash, halakhic literature, and classical languages and literature thoroughly. He also had an extensive knowledge of contemporary Italian culture. Luzzatto had a good scientific education, but his chief interest in Western culture was in literature. His main teachers were Isaac *Cantarini, who taught him poetry and secular sciences, and Isaiah Bassan, who taught him mainly *Kabbalah and became his friend and protector. Luzzatto's achievements, personality, and great knowledge of mysticism made him a leader of a group of young men in Padua, many of whom came there to study at the city's famous university and thus represented the more open and aware element among young Jews in Italy and in Eastern Europe. The group was formed originally for collective study, but eventually a more active line was adopted.

Probably the most important event in Luzzatto's personal life occurred in 1727. While he was immersed in kabbalistic speculations, he suddenly heard a divine voice, which he believed to be that of a **maggid* (i.e., a divine power inclined to reveal heavenly secrets to human beings). From that moment, the *Maggid* spoke to Luzzatto frequently and he noted these revelations, which comprised his kabbalistic writings for a few years. Most of them have not survived; only a few are known and have been published. Luzzatto used the *maggid's* revelations in his teachings to the members of the group around him, which by then had become a secret group dealing in messianic speculations and activity. One of the members of this group, Jekuthiel *Gordon, described in some letters the activities and character of the group. One of these letters fell into the hands of Moses *Ḥagiz, who believed it to be a description of a typical Shabbatean heretical group. Ḥagiz addressed the rabbis of *Venice, warning them of the danger he believed this activity signified, and the rabbis turned to Isaiah Bassan, Luzzatto's teacher, who tried to defend his beloved pupil. A vehement controversy followed, in which many of the leading rabbis of Italy took part, and numerous personal attacks were made on Luzzatto. It was believed that only a perfect scholar and kabbalist could receive a revelation from a *maggid*, and many thought that the young, unmarried Luzzatto did not measure up to that standard. According to a later testimony, a search was made at his home, and evidence of dealings in magic was uncovered. After a long struggle, Luzzatto yielded (1730) and agreed to give his kabbalistic writings to Bassan for safekeeping, to refrain from writing the *maggid*'s revelations (at least while out of the Holy Land), and from teaching Kabbalah.

This compromise did not resolve the conflict. In 1731 Luzzatto married. The continuing controversy in Italy forced him to leave for Amsterdam in 1735. While breaking his journey in Frankfurt, he asked for the protection of Jacob ha-Kohen. The latter, instead of helping him, used threats to make Luzzatto sign a statement denouncing the *maggid*'s revelations and his kabbalistic teachings as false (the rabbis of Venice had meanwhile announced that these writings should be burned). Luzzatto's writings were handed over to Jacob ha-Kohen, who probably burned some of them and hid the rest. Settling in Amsterdam, where he was left in peace, Luzzatto wrote on many subjects, but he did not openly teach Kabbalah. In 1743 he went to Ereẓ Israel, probably in order to escape from the prohibition on teaching Kabbalah. He lived a short time in Acre and died there, with his family, in a plague.

Luzzatto's Messianic Doctrine

When Luzzatto formulated his messianic doctrine, the circle around him began actively to seek messianic redemption. The first "code" of the group, which has survived (signed by the members in 1731), includes ten laws, dealing with the methods of study, the relationship between the members and Luzzatto, and a declaration of the group's aim: "That this study [or speculation] will not be regarded as a private *tikkun* of the members nor will it be atonement for personal sins, but its only *kavvanah* will be wholly dedicated to the *tikkun* of the holy *Shekhinah* and all of Israel." Seven members had signed this "code," including Jekuthiel Gordon. Other members joined later, among them Luzzatto's brother and Moses David *Valle, who became one of the group's leaders. He was the writer of the group, author of a voluminous commentary on the Bible, which is extant in a few manuscripts. The members of this group believed that the process of redemption had already begun, and that it was going to reach its culmination in a few years. Their saintly way of life and kabbalistic speculations were intended to facilitate this process. Moreover, they were sure that they, personally, had an important part to play in the process.

The writings of Moses David Valle seem to hint that Valle saw himself as the Messiah, son of David. Jekuthiel assumed the role of Serayah of the tribe of Dan, who was to be the commander of Israel's army in the messianic era. Other messianic roles were distributed among the other members. Luzzatto's own role becomes clear from a unique document preserved in his own handwriting – his commentary on his own *ketubbah*, which he wrote at the time of his marriage. This document proves that Luzzatto understood his marriage to signify a mystical event in the heavenly worlds, the union between Moses and Zipporah (which happened to be the name of his wife), who represent the elements of masculinity and femininity in the divine realm. The earthly marriage ceremony he understood as only a symbol of the redemption of the *Shekhinah* and her union with her divine husband. It is evident, therefore, that Luzzatto saw himself as a reincarnation of Moses, the man who rescued his people from the exile in Egypt and would redeem them from this last *galut* as well.

Luzzatto's opponents understood the messianic nature of his circle, and were afraid of the Shabbatean overtones which such activity might contain. The problem of whether Luzzatto's ideas and activities can be called "Shabbatean" or not is unsolved. Luzzatto himself admitted to being influenced by the writings of *Shabbetai Ẓevi's "prophet," *Nathan of Gaza. However, he maintained that the good element in them should be separated from the heretical context. In some of Luzzatto's kabbalistic ideas, elements of Shabbatean influence can be found, for he maintained that the Messiah must descend to the realm of Satan, the Shabbatean explanation for their Messiah's conversion. However, Luzzatto insisted that this should not involve the Messiah's earthly body; it should be a spiritual experience only, involving no sin. Luzzatto was also moderately inclined toward the Shabbatean idea that a sin might serve a holy purpose, but he always made radical changes in the Shabbatean ideas which avoided their heretical and antinomian nature.

His Treatises on Logic

A messianic figure, a man who conversed with the *maggid*, Luzzatto was also well versed in logic, an art traditionally seen as the high road to philosophy or its favored instrument (organon). Logic was for him the centerpiece, the indispensable tool to mold the spirit and to search for truth. While the forest grows wild, knowledge acquired through logic is like a "fair garden with well-defined alleys and well-drawn groves." Circa 1740, while residing in Amsterdam, Luzzatto penned two treatises, *Sefer ha-Higgayon* ("Treatise on Logic") and *Derekh Tevunot* ("The Way of Reason"). The first is a real primer on logic. Luzzatto does not specifically quote his sources and merely states that he found them in earlier works written in other languages than Hebrew. It seems that he knew very well the logical works of Aristotle, the *Millot ha-Higgayon* of Maimonides, and the corpus of medieval Hebrew logic (Joseph Kaspi, Gersonides, Moses Narboni). The influence of some Renaissance logicians, such as French Humanist Pierre de la Ramée (Petrus Ramus, 1515–1572), can also be perceived.

Following the Aristotelian formula, in his treatises Luzzatto deals successively with the three modes of reasoning: "Categories," or "Logical Terms," propositions, and syllogisms. He also postulates two methodological rules: order (*seder*) or gradation (*hadragah*), and distinction – *havḥanah*, both rules being complementary. Luzzatto uses a vocabulary very similar to that of Descartes in his Rules for the direction of the mind: whoever follows order can "keep himself on the straight path without straying" (Ways of Reasons, p. 4). The words "order" and "gradation" have the same meaning in his terminology. To respect order is to proceed gradually, while following the internal hierarchy of reality. Therefore, one must follow the gradation rule, which entails giving priority to general principles (*kelalim*), to species and kinds, to specific details (*peratim*), to individuals. To illustrate this rule, Luzzatto takes the classical example of the tree. Since, according to the logical order, principles come before details, the roots (*shorashim*) of the tree come before the branches (*anafim*). Instead of floundering amidst a flurry of details, instead of trying to embrace the infinite diversity of beings and things, the mind must strive to perceive the relatively small number of principles involved. The rule of distinction is the ability to seize what is specific to each being and to each thing, together with the link uniting each and every one of them. In order to differentiate properly, it is necessary to follow gradation, the hierarchical order, by discerning the place and the status of each of the elements of reality: whether it is a principle and a root or a detail and a branch.

Derekh Tevunot, the second work, is a handbook of talmudic logic in which Luzzatto reviews the reasoning processes used by the Sages. He sees logic as the one and only propaedeutic system to study Talmud, this "vast ocean set before us, whose arguments are mighty waves, whose laws roll forth rising to the heavens and plunging to the depths." Structurewise, *Derekh Tevunot* is identical to *Sefer ha-Higgayon*. Here again are the three parts of logic – categories, propositions, syllogisms – as well as the notions of gradation and distinction. What makes this work unique is the way Luzzatto uses these reasoning processes to unwind the tangle of talmudic discussions (*mahlokot*) and to identify clearly *halakhot* and other legal principles.

The fact that logic, which is a rational method, and Kabbalah are both at the heart of the work of Luzzatto has puzzled many commentators. By focusing only on the rather perfunctory contrast between rationalism and irrationalism, philosophy and mysticism, they often tend to see the link between the two domains as a mere product of proximity. A closer study of the texts helps to correct the conventional picture. It pinpoints many expressions of the close link between "the art of logic" and the "science of the Kabbalah." Luzzatto himself explicitly postulates that link by making logic the necessary preparation for accessing the "science of the divine." Furthermore, the logical rules of gradation and distinction play a central role in the Kabbalah as he sees it, and they are invested there with an ontological significance.

His Kabbalistic Writings

Commentators on Luzzatto's writings in the field of Kabbalah usually divide them in two groups: some are general works describing central kabbalistic ideas and emphasizing the importance of Kabbalah for attaining full religious life; the other writings convey his own original kabbalistic concepts. Most of the latter works were written under the influence of the *maggid*. In his correspondence, Luzzatto himself differentiates between two elements: the commentaries (*perushim*) in which he interprets the Zohar and the Lurianic Kabbalah, thereby perpetuating kabbalistic tradition; and the new writings (*ḥibburim ḥadashim*) in which he expounds his original vision of "divine unity" where he gives it a sense which is both ethical and historiosophical. In fact the elements of commentary and innovation are closely linked in the kabbalistic writings of Luzzatto. Luzzatto's outstanding kabbalistic work is *Kelaḥ* (= 138) *Pitḥei Ḥokhmah*, a systematic exposition of the Lurianic Kabbalah. There Luzzatto demonstrates the task which he has undertaken in the history of the Kabbalah: to reveal the internal meaning (*nimshal*) of the paradigms (*meshalim*) so numerous in the Lurianic writings, to which they tend to give an anthropomorphic coloring. Luzzatto often quotes from the works of Maimonides; in the same spirit he believes that it will be thus possible to get rid of the main cause of error concerning what is divine: materialization (*hagshamah*). Rejecting an interpretation which would accept the Lurianic descriptions literally (*ki-feshuto*) and in a materialistic sense, is for Luzzatto also part of the fight he is leading against Shabbateanism.

Kelaḥ Pitḥei Ḥokhmah is the perfect illustration of the close connection between logic and Kabbalah in the works of Luzzatto. The very structure of that treatise is built on the gradation rule. Each *petaḥ* – door or chapter – opens with a general principle (*kelal*), the details or particular aspects of which are then exposed. Before turning to commentary and explaining the themes which are unique to the Lurianic Kabbalah (such as *ẓimẓum*), Luzzatto innovates by exposing the principle on which his own kabbalistic doctrine is based: divine unity conceived both as the origin and the finality of creation. He uses the distinction rule to delineate with precision the object of Kabbalah, and details what he means by "divine" (Elohut). He thus refines a principle which was already present in the works of his predecessors, such as Menahem Azarya de Fano, while giving a completely novel interpretation of *ẓimẓum*, the act of contraction or withdrawal of the divine infinity (*Ein-Sof*) which preceded the emanation of *sefirot*. To the traditional division between divine essence and divine will Luzzatto adds a new distinction within the will, to stress two aspects: one, infinite (the *Ein-Sof*) and the other, finite (the *Sefirot*). Thus is the *ẓimẓum* assimilated to a movement tending to slant and orient the infinite aspect of the will toward its finite aspect, and hence toward the world and its creatures. This movement, which is achieved within the very core of divine will, is perceived by Luzzatto in an ethical sense, that is, as the wish to do good to another than the self (*hatavah*). A man of his time, Luzzatto takes this definition of *ẓimẓum* as a stepping stone for a whole new philosophy of history. He postulates that human history has a meaning beyond the seemingly disorderly course of events, and, in his view, it is moving according to divine direction (*hanhagah*) toward a finality which is no other but "doing good" (*hatavah*). He develops a true dialectic process according to which historical proceedings comprise two dimensions, the one being revealed and visible, corresponding to the factual events where evil is manifesting itself in all its power, and the other secret and invisible, consisting in the inescapable progress of mankind toward that ultimate end which is the "perfect good."

(Luzzatto's interpretation, by the way, was widely accepted, and even the early Ḥasidim adopted it.) The introduction to this work, also printed separately, *Derekh Eẓ ha-Ḥayyim*, explains the religious merits of kabbalistic study. This small work was widely read and accepted. Another work belonging to the same category is *Ḥoker u-Mekubbal* (*Maamar ha- Vikku'aḥ*), designed as a dialogue between a philosopher and a Lurianic kabbalist. In this work, Luzzatto answers, point by point, many criticisms against the Kabbalah which were current among the rationalists in Italy, and tries to prove that only Lurianic Kabbalah can give a satisfactory answer to Judaism's religious problems.

The most important of the writings influenced by the *maggid* was the *Zohar Tinyana*, which was written in Aramaic, the language of the original *Zohar. Most of the work is now lost; parts were printed as *Razin Genizin*, *Megillat Setarim*, and *Tikkunin Ḥadashim* (*Tikkunei Zohar* being one of the later parts of the original Zohar). Although Luzzatto used the Zohar's language and literary form, his main and almost sole idea expressed and studied in these works was the idea of the redemption. Luzzatto employed older kabbalistic ideas about the redemption but gave them a new form and new structure. Detailed study was devoted to the duties of the various messianic figures in the process of the redemption – the Messiah son of Joseph, Messiah son of David, and Moses. Luzzatto studied the function of the various heavenly *Sefirot* in this process, especially the third *Sefirah*, *Binah*, whose revelation and influence on this world would bring about the culmination of the redemption. Recently, a part of Luzzatto's diary describing the first revelations of the *maggid* was discovered, and the theological problems discussed there are the same as those in the other known parts of the *Zohar Tinyana*. Problems of the redemption and the history and adventures of the Messiah's soul are also dealt with in Luzzatto's short treatises, *Addir ba-Marom* and *Ma'amar ha-Ge'ullah*.

Luzzatto's Ethical Works

Long after his death, and after the controversy around him had subsided, Luzzatto became a saint in the eyes of most of Eastern European Jewry. This did not come about because of his kabbalistic writings, but because of his major works on ethics. His chief work in this field, and his best-known book, is *Mesillat Yesharim*, written in Amsterdam (English translation *Mesillat Yesharim: The Path of the Upright* by M.M. Kaplan with Hebrew text and introduction, 1936, 1964²), which uses as a framework the famous *baraita* of R. *Phinehas b. Jair (Sot. 9:15). Luzzatto instructs the reader in the path of ascent from the forsaking of sinful ways, through moral behavior, to the peak of prophecy and contact with the divine spirit. The popularity of the book resulted from its systematic exposition of every problem which might prevent the attainment of religious and ethical perfection. The author explains the importance and meaning of every step on the way, describes the means by which it can be made, and warns the reader of the dangers which might obstruct his way. Luzzatto wrote the book in a simple, rabbinic style, using some philosophical terms, but no kabbalistic element is evident, though detailed analysis reveals some underlying kabbalistic assumptions. This work was printed many times, translated into many languages, and alongside *Baḥya ibn Paquda's *Ḥovot ha-Levavot*, became the most influential ethical work in Judaism. In some yeshivot in Eastern Europe where the book was studied, pupils were expected to know it by heart.

In other ethical and theosophical works Luzzatto studied some basic theological questions, using philosophical language, although the underlying kabbalistic approach is apparent. In his *Derekh ha-Shem* and *Da'at Tevunot*, Luzzatto studied in detail the problems of the aim of creation, Adam's sin, the ways of divine justice, the relationship and mutual dependence between the just and the sinner, the next world and the world of the redemption, etc., alongside discussions of everyday problems of religious and ethical behavior – prayer, the Commandments, the ways to overcome evil desires, etc. All his works in this field were widely read and accepted, and contributed to his metamorphosis to sage and saint, instead of a controversial figure suspected of Shabbateanism.

Poetry and Letters

Luzzatto wrote numerous poetical works. Many of them were lost, and many are still in manuscript. A collection of his poems, published by S. Ginzburg (1945), includes mainly works written in honor or in memory of friends or for weddings. His talent is revealed through his rich and flowing imagery, and his use of the Hebrew language is masterly. These poems were written according to the ancient tradition of Hebrew poetry in Italy, which relied on the traditions of Hebrew poetry in both Muslim Spain and Renaissance Italy. Besides these, Luzzatto's published poems include a few religious pieces, all of which contain kabbalistic and messianic overtones; sometimes he added a mystical commentary to his own religious poems. He also wrote many prayers, and it seems that he wrote 150 religious poems in the form of the Psalms, but this work has not survived.

However, Luzzatto's most famous poetic works are his verse dramas. His first play, *Ma'aseh Shimshon,* was written before he was 20 years old to exemplify the rhetorical laws he propounded in his *Leshon Limmudim*, a treatise on rhetorics, in which he made use of his knowledge of classical and contemporary Italian literature. It seems that Luzzatto felt close to Samson, his tragic hero, possibly for messianic reasons, and that gave the play some poetic depth. His second and most important play, *Migdal Oz*, was written while he was still in Italy. It was composed in the form of contemporary Italian pastoral drama, but Luzzatto gave the plot such Jewish overtones that some critics think that the play is in fact a kabbalistic allegory. His third and last play, *La-Yesharim Tehillah*, written in Amsterdam, is one of Luzzatto's last works. The play is an allegory, which probably gives expression to the feelings of persecution he experienced at the time of controversy around him, and at the same time reflects his belief in the ultimate victory of the just. In *Migdal Oz* and *La-Yesharim Tehillah*, Luzzatto used commonplace love plots to give expression to poetic sentiments far beyond the conventional plots. Luzzatto's plays were accepted and admired by Hebrew writers and intellectuals in Italy and Western Europe, and many were influenced by them. Luzzatto's works, especially *Migdal Oz*, exercised a strong influence on Haskalah literature, especially its poetry and drama. These *maskilim*, who were inimical to the kabbalists, were so impressed by the plays that they forgot Luzzatto's kabbalistic writings and messianic aspirations and adopted him as if he were one of their own.

A vast amount of Luzzatto's personal writings was discovered and printed by S. Ginzburg. This collection includes many of Luzzatto's letters, as well as letters addressed to him, or concerning his activities and the controversy around him. The collection includes his personal revealing letters to his teacher and defender, Isaiah Bassan. Among other documents, this collection includes the texts of the regulations of Luzzatto's circle, texts of the accusations against him, etc. The details make possible a chronological reconstruction of Luzzatto's bibliography, though many of the works mentioned are unknown today.

Kinat ha-Shem Ẓeva'ot, a polemical work of a personal nature, was written in answer to the accusation that his theology and activities were Shabbatean in nature. A portion of this work was printed in Koenigsberg in 1862. Luzzatto clearly expresses his negative attitude toward Shabbatean heresy and antinomian practices, but he does not deny that there is truth in some Shabbatean kabbalistic ideas. However, he explains that these should be studied with care, to separate "the fruit from the husk."

Luzzatto's place in the history of Hebrew literature was the subject of a long argument, which still persists. Some scholars (e.g., *Lachover), seeing him as the first "modern" Hebrew writer, begin the history of Hebrew modern literature with the study of his dramatic poems. Others maintain that, as modern Hebrew literature was a revolutionary development that rebelled against the religious character of medieval literature, Luzzatto cannot be included among its creators, because of his strong ties with such past ideologies as Kabbalah and messianism. Yet others, however, see the development of modern Hebrew literature as an evolutionary process, which never broke completely from traditional ideas and concepts. These regard Luzzatto's works as a compromise between old and new, signifying the start of a new era in Hebrew literature.

It cannot be doubted that Luzzatto's works as a whole are a typical product of 18th-century culture: his Kabbalah was Lurianic Kabbalah, which was the accepted theology of the time; his strongest emotions were aroused by messianic problems, in common with most of the more aware thinkers of his age; a contemporary of Leibniz, he felt concerned by the problems of theodicy as well as of historiosophy; and he accepted the conventions of 18th-century Italian literature. However, Luzzatto's work is unique for at least three reasons. The first is the unique connection he achieved between such apparently foreign subject matters as rhetoric and logic on the one hand, and Kabbalah on the other hand. Through this encyclopedic aspect he takes his place among the great Italian thinkers of the Renaissance, from Pico de la Mirandola and Marsile Ficin to Johanan Alemano and Elijah del Medigo. The second is that, unlike previous Jewish-Italian thinkers, such as Leone *Modena or Azariah de *Rossi, Luzzatto did not doubt the fundamental Jewish beliefs, despite his close connections with Italian secular culture. He could be, at the same time, both a Jewish traditionalist and a writer of dramatic poems in the Italian manner. Thirdly, unlike any other writer of the 18th century, Luzzatto, though persecuted when alive, was accepted by the three main 19th-century Jewish movements, which were fighting bitterly among themselves: the Ḥasidim saw him as a saintly kabbalist and used some of his kabbalistic ideas; their opponents, the Mitnaggedim, regarded his ethical works as the clearest pointers toward a Jewish ethical, rabbinic way of life; and the Haskalah writers saw Luzzatto as a progenitor of their own movement, and his works as the beginning of Hebrew aesthetic writing. Every facet of Luzzatto's work, therefore, remained alive and creative in the divided and confused Jewish culture of the 19th century.

BIBLIOGRAPHY: A full bibliography of Luzzatto's printed works is to be found in: N. Ben-Menahem, *Kitvei Ramḥal* (1951); S. Ginzburg, *The Life and Works of M.H. Luzzatto* (1931); idem, R. *Moshe Ḥayyim Luzzatto u-Venei Doro* (1937); I. Almanzi, in: *Kerem Ḥemed*, 3 (1838), 112–69; J. Schirmann, *Gilyonot*, 21 (1947), 207–17; F. Lachover, *Al Gevul ha-Yashan ve-he-Ḥadash* (1951), 29–96; I. Tishby, *Netivei Emunah u-Minut* (1964), 169–203; idem, in: KS 45 (1970), 127–254, 300, 628; M. Benayahu, in: *Sefunot*, 5 (1961), 299–336; Waxman, Literature, 3 (19602), 90–107; Y. David, introd. to Moshe Ḥayyim Luzzatto, *Ma'aseh Shimshon* (1967), incl. bibl. **ADD. BIBLIOGRAPHY:** Y. David, *Moses Hayyim Luzzatto's Plays*, a comparative study (1972); *Migdal Oz*. Critical edition with introduction and commentary (1972); J. Hansel, *Le Philosophe et le cabaliste*, tr. from Hebrew and annotated (1991); idem, *Moïse Hayyim Luzzatto (1707–1746). Kabbale et philosophie* (2004); *Daat*, special issue on Luzzatto, no. 40, Winter 1998.

[Joseph Dan / Joelle Hansel (2nd ed.)]

LUZZATTO, SAMUEL DAVID (often referred to by the acronym of **SHaDaL** or **SHeDaL**; 1800–1865), Italian scholar, philosopher, Bible commentator, and translator. His father, Hezekiah, was an artisan at Trieste and a scholarly Jew who could claim descent from a long line of scholars (see *Luzzatto family). He wrote his first Hebrew poem at the age of nine. His mother died when he was 13 and his father's pecuniary status declined seriously making it necessary for the young Luzzatto to assist his father in his work. His own wife died after a long illness, and he eventually married her sister. He survived two of his children – one Philoxenus (or Filosseno), had been a young man of especially great promise. Samuel David's translation of the Ashkenazi prayer book into Italian appeared in 1821/22, and that of the Italian rite in 1829. He established a regular correspondence with the Jewish scholar, Isaac Samuel *Reggio, and through the efforts of the latter, Luzzatto was appointed professor of the newly established rabbinical college of Padua in 1829. There he spent the rest of his life teaching Bible, philology, philosophy, and Jewish history. His versatility and the scope of his learning are best seen in the mass of letters written to all the outstanding Jewish savants of the day – to *Geiger, *Zunz, *Rapoport, *Steinschneider, and others. Almost 700 of these letters were published and many run into several pages; some are in themselves dissertations. He wrote a Hebrew commentary on the Pentateuch (5 vols., with Italian translation, 1871–76; new ed. by P. Schlesinger, 1965) and the *Haftarot*, on the Book of Isaiah (together with a translation into Italian, 1845–97; new ed. by P. Schlesinger and completed by A.M. Hovev, 1970), on Jeremiah, Ezekiel, Proverbs, and Job and a long dissertation in Hebrew on Ecclesiastes (1876; repr. 1969). It is in this type of work that his attitude to Judaism is revealed. He was a traditionalist and had a great veneration for Rashi in particular. His antagonism toward Abraham Ibn Ezra is asserted boldly in his letters and Bible commentaries. He maintained that his own dislike for Ibn Ezra did not stem so much from the latter's departure from tradition as from his insincerity (see: Letters nos. 83, 242, 272, 275, and 543). Luzzatto had his grievances against Maimonides too, but in the case of the latter his language is more restrained. Luzzatto, as he himself wrote, divided seekers of truth into two groups – those who follow Rashi and Samuel b. Meir and those who are the disciples of Maimonides and Ibn Ezra (Letters nos. 272 and 275). His own commentary on the Pentateuch is not fundamentalist, and whereas he himself did not take the first chapters of Genesis literally, he criticizes those who treat them as an allegory (Letters no. 83). He believed them to be meant as model lessons from which we are to derive moral and ethical values. In his writings, he readily quotes the views of his pupils, mentioning their names when so doing. Although denying the Solomonic authorship of Ecclesiastes he upholds the unity of the Book of Isaiah. He maintained a firm belief in revelation and treated the text of the Torah with sacred regard although he occasionally allowed himself to depart from the traditional phrasing of the words as reflected in the Masorah and the Talmud. A natural corollary of his attitude to the classical authorities is Luzzatto's high regard for the Aramaic translation of Onkelos to which he devoted his *Ohev Ger* (the "Lover of the Proselyte," 1830), an allusion to the conversion of Onkelos to Judaism. He named his son Philoxenus (the Latin equivalent of *Ohev Ger*). He divided the work into two parts. The first demonstrates the method of Onkelos when the latter seems to depart from the literal translation of a text, especially when he wants to avoid anthropomorphisms. The second part of *Ohev Ger* deals with matters of text and is technical.

Luzzatto's philosophy may be compared with that of Judah Halevi. "I esteem Maimonides very greatly" he wrote (Letters no. 83), "but Moses the Lawgiver never dreamed of philosophy and the dreams of Aristotle." He lists his objections to the *Guide* of Maimonides and to some remarks in *Sefer ha-Madda* and to others in Maimonides' commentary on Mishnah *Sanhedrin* (ch. *Ḥelek*) and in the *Shemonah Perakim* (commentary on *Avot*). He was opposed to Maimonides' enumeration and formulation of the 13 principles of faith and his condemnation of those who did not subscribe to these (Letters no. 238). Luzzatto's attitude to Greek philosophy was negative and even hostile, and his negative views on Kabbalah are found in his *Vikku'aḥ al Ḥokhmat ha-Kabbalah* (1852). He blames rationalistic philosophy for having brought about – as a reaction – the flowering of Kabbalah and mysticism. As for the Zohar, he rejected the authorship of Simeon b. Yoḥai as did Jacob *Emden and Leone *Modena before him, and Luzzatto was apparently influenced by the latter's *Ari Nohem* (1840). Luzzatto's religious thinking does not rest at the rejection of "atticism" – Hellenism – as diametrically opposed to Judaism, and of a moral rationalism as represented in the Middle Ages by Maimonides and in modern times by Kant. For him the idolizing of "progress" and the utilitarianism which speaks from the craving for (outer but not inner) emancipation of modern Jewry were the very antithesis of free Jewish thinking and living. He had nothing but contempt for the rotten European civilization. In his theological writings, most of them published lectures such as *Teologia Morale israelitica* (1862; English translation by S. Morais in *Jewish Index*, 1872) and in his *Yesodei ha-Torah* (1880; repr. 1947; English translation by N.H. Rosenbloom, *Foundations of the Torah*, 1965) as well as in his letters, he develops his own positive system of Jewish theology and religious philosophy, based on the firm belief in revelation, tradition, and the election of Israel. These he wants to see protected from the prevailing winds of Christian-Protestant criticism and an evolutionary historical relativism. The Torah and the Commandments must not be rationalized and submitted to such relativism, nor can one separate morality from religion. They both flow from the same innate human quality of *ḥemlah* (empathy). The Jewish people is both the carrier and guarantor of this revealed, national religion which embodies its own universalism and humanitarianism. Hebrew language and literature, the main object of Luzzatto's scholarly work, help to foster and deepen Jewish spirit and loyalties. This romantic and nationalistic conception of Judaism embraces a sort of religious Zionism, while rejecting the "false holiness" of the idle *ḥalukkah* Jew. Luzzatto wants the youth of the *yishuv* to return to the soil and the soil of the Holy Land to its former productivity. This conception is apparent in his liturgical researches, in particular by his edition of the *Maḥzor Roma* which he provided with a comprehensive introduction (1856; new edition of the introduction by E.D. Goldschmidt, 1966).

Luzzatto also edited the medieval chronicle *Seder Tanna'im ve-Amora'im* (1839); and the prolegomena to an edition of *Joseph ha-Kohen's *Emek ha-Bakha* (1852), ostensibly by M. Letteris, are essentially Luzzatto's work. He also did pioneering work in his editions of Judah Halevi's poetry (*Betulat Bat Yehudah*, 1840; *Diwan Rabbi Judah Halevi*, 1, 1864) and his anthology of medieval Hebrew poetry (*Tal Orot*, 1881) and thus contributed greatly to the revival of interest in medieval Hebrew poetry. His own Hebrew poetry had great merit. The same intimate acquaintance with and fine feeling for the Hebrew language, the result of intensive biblical studies, helped Luzzatto with his linguistic and grammatical researches (see *Prolegomeni ad una grammatica ragionata della lingua ebraica* (1836; *Prolegomena to a Grammar of the Hebrew Language*, 1896); *Grammatica della lingua ebraica* (1853–69; Hebrew, 1901); *Elementi grammaticali del caldeo biblico*… (1865; *Grammar of the Biblical Chaldaic Language*…, 1876)). Of bibliographical importance are his *Opere del De Rossi* (1868^2) and *Yad Yosef* (1864), a catalog of the Almanzi collection. Luzzatto also published *Avnei Zikkaron*, on the Hebrew tombstone inscriptions of Toledo (1841), being the first to treat epitaphs as an important primary source for Jewish historical research. An autobiography of Luzzatto appeared in 1882 (Hebrew in *Ha-Maggid*, 1858–62; German, 1882), and memorial volumes in Italian (*Commemorazione*…, 1901) and in German (*Luzzatto-Gedenkbuch*, 1900). There are a number of collections of his articles such as *Beit ha-Oẓar* (3 vols., 1847, 1888, 1889) and *Peninei Shadal* (1888); but much of his scholarly work remains scattered over various periodicals, pamphlets, works of other authors, and much has never been published. An edition of all his Hebrew writings was begun in 1913 (*Ketavim Ivriyyim*) but was not completed.

BIBLIOGRAPHY: I. Luzzatto, *Catalogo ragionato con riferimenti agli altri suoi scritti e inediti* (1881); S. Baron, in: *Sefer Assaf* (1953), 40–63; N. Rosenbloom, *Luzzatto's Ethico-Psychological Interpretation of Judaism* (1965); S. Werses, in: *Me'assef le-Divrei Bikkoret ve-Hagut*, 5–6 (1965), 703–15; D. Rudavsky, in: *Tradition*, 7 (1965), no. 3, 21–44; *Samuel David Luzzatto 1800–1865. Exhibition on the Occasion of the 100th Anniversary of his Death*, arranged by B. Yaron, Catalog (Heb. and Eng., Jerusalem, 1966); RMI, 32 (1966), no. 9–10 (all articles dedicated to studies of Luzzatto); S. Morais, *Italian Hebrew Literature* (1926), 78–152.

[Alexander Tobias]

LUZZATTO, SIMONE BEN ISAAC SIMḤAH (1583–1663), Italian rabbi and author. He was born, probably in Venice, of a well-to-do family of German origin already established in the region for many generations. Luzzatto was ordained in 1606 and served as rabbi in Venice for 57 years. The affluent circumstances of his family made it unnecessary for him to waste his energies in miscellaneous work to supplement his livelihood, as was the case with his contemporary and associate Leon *Modena, after whose death in 1648 he became senior rabbi of the community. Unlike Modena he objected to the presence of gentiles at his sermons in the synagogue, though he had some non-Jewish pupils, including, for a month in 1646, the French mystic Charles de Valliquierville. Luzzatto was one of seven members of the *yeshivah kelalit* of Venice. He became head of this rabbinic council in 1648, after the death of Modena. Shortly after this, he became involved in a drawn-out dispute with the lay leaders of the community over the question of rabbinical ordination, on which he insisted in having a deciding voice. Among his responsa was one (no longer preserved) which permitted travel by gondola in Venice on the Sabbath. His work *Socrate ovvero dell'humano sapere*, dedicated to the Doge (1651), written in dialogue form with Socrates as the principle interlocutor, is an attempt to demonstrate that human reason is impotent unless assisted by revelation. There is nothing specifically Jewish about this work, which shows a considerable degree of competence in philosophy and in classical literature (though not in Greek), and is a remarkable exemplification of the degree of culture prevailing at this time in the Italian ghettos. His most important publication, however, was his work *Discorso circa il stato de gl' hebrei et in particolar dimoranti nell'inclita città di Venetia* (1638), in which he put forward reasoned arguments for the toleration of the Jews especially on economic grounds, given their role in international trade. He argued that they performed functions that could be achieved by no other element, while on the other hand, unlike foreign merchants, they were completely under the control of the government and would not transfer their profits outside the state. This was the first apologetic work of its type and the first in which economic arguments were brought forward systematically in order to advocate the toleration of the Jews, their retention of residential rights, and their unique commercial privileges. It is difficult to know if Luzzatto actually believed all of his arguments or just used them to defend the Jews of Venice and to strengthen his case. Of note is his refutation of Tacitus' view of the Jews. Indeed, since he devotes a major portion of the *Discorso* to his argument, it must be viewed as a rebuttal of contemporary political thought even more than a work of apologetics. Luzzatto emphasizes the decisive role of the Jewish community of Venice in the development of the city. A reply to the work was published by the Christian priest Melchior Palontritti under the title *Breve Risposta a Simone Luzzatto* (1642). A Hebrew translation was published in Jerusalem in 1950; and an English translation was prepared early in the 18th century by the English deist John *Toland (though not published), who used Luzzatto's arguments lavishly in his book of 1714 advocating the naturalization of the Jews. It is now known that the book was written at great speed when a dangerous crisis developed for the Venetian Jews owing to the discovery of large-scale commercial frauds in which some leading families were implicated.

Luzzatto also wrote an Italian treatise in which he vindicated the authority of tradition and of the Oral Law (now lost, but referred to by Samuel Aboab in his responsa, *Devar Shmuel* (1702), n. 152). He is said to have also written *Trattato delle opinioni o dogmi degli ebrei e dei riti loro principali* (Fuerst, Bibliotheca, 284) and, together with Leone de Modena, a work on the Karaites (Wolff, Bibliotheca, vol. 3, 347). He is also reputed to have had considerable competence as a mathematician. Luzzatto's pupil, the apostate Giulio Morosini, reports in his *Via della Fede* several instances of his liberal mind and outspokenness in matters of religion, shown for example when in 1649 he arbitrated a dispute between two former Marranos about the "seventy weeks" of Daniel. He is also said to have spoken contemptuously of the Kabbalah and to have disbelieved in the preservation of the Lost Ten Tribes. Christian contemporaries, misunderstanding his freedom of spirit, reported that he was prevented by force from embracing Christianity on his deathbed.

BIBLIOGRAPHY: S.D. Luzzatto, *Autobiografia*... (1882), 12–17, 33–36; Y.F. Baer, *Galut* (1947), 83–92; L. Blau, *Leo Modenas Briefe und Schriftstuecke* (1907), index; S. Luzzatto, *Ma'amar al Yehudei Venezyah* (1951), prefaces by Bachi and Szulwas; *In Memoria di A. Sacerdoti* (1936), 99–113; C. Roth, *Venice* (1930), 227–31; F. Secret, *Kabbalistes Chrétiens de la Renaissance* (1964), 328; Szulwas, in: HUCA, 22 (1949), 18–20 (Heb. pt.); Steinschneider, in: MGWJ, 43 (1899), 418f. **ADD. BIBLIOGRAPHY:** B. Ravid, *Economics and Toleration in Seventeenth Century Venice: The Background and Context of the Discorso of Simone Luzzatto* (1978); idem, in: *Mystics, Philosophers, and Politicians; Essays in Jewish Intellectual History in Honor of Alexander Altmann* (1982), 159–180; idem, in: *AJS Review*, 7/8 (1983), 301–51; B. Septimus, in: *Jewish Thought in the Seventeenth Century* (1987), 399–433; I. Barzilay, in: *Jewish Social Studies*, 31 (1969), 75–81; L. Roubey, in: *Journal of Reform Judaism*, 4 (1981), 57–63; A. Melamed, in: *Studies in Medieval Jewish History and Literature*, 2 (1984), 143–70; idem, in: *Gli Ebrei e Venezia, secoli XIV-XVIII; atti del Convegno internazionale... Venezia, giugno* (1983), 507–25; **WEBSITE:** http://www.helsinki.fi/hum/renvall/uses/sivut/s.htm.

[Cecil Roth / David Derovan (2nd ed.)]

LVOV (Pol. **Lwów**; Ger. **Lemberg**), main city of Lvov district, Ukraine.

The Early Settlements

It is thought that the first Jews in Lvov arrived from Byzantium and the southeast. After the conquest of the town by Casimir III of Poland (1340), they were joined by Jews from Germany and Bohemia who gave the settlement its Ashkenazi character. At the end of the 14th century, there were two communities in Lvov: the older and larger, the "Holy Congregation Outside of the Walls," founded in 1352; and the second, the "Holy Congregation Within the Walls," situated in the Jews' Street and first mentioned in 1387. Large fires occasionally swept both communities and they were only able to repair their quarters after controversies with the townspeople (this occurred in 1494, 1527, 1571, 1616, etc.). In 1550, 352 Jews lived inside the city walls in 29 houses, while 559 lived in 52 houses outside the town. In the vicinity of this suburban quarter, a *Karaite settlement existed until 1457.

The Jews of Lvov played an important role in trade between the Orient and the West, for which the town was an important transit center. They were equally well represented in the wholesale trade with the interior of the country. They also leased estates, operated brandy distilleries and breweries, acted as customs and tax agents, and loaned money to the nobility and the king. During the second half of the 16th century, the commercial agents of Don Joseph *Nasi were active in Lvov. However, the number of Jews who engaged in international trade and in large concerns was very limited and the majority earned their livelihood as shopkeepers, peddlers, and craftsmen. The rights of the Jews of Lvov were based on letters patent granted by the kings of Poland. They were in constant conflict with the townsmen over their rights to trade, especially in the retail branch, and to engage in crafts. Fortunately the royal decrees issued as a result of pressure from the townsmen were rarely absolute and the nobility often succeeded in having them amended. In 1493 King John Albert restricted the Jews to two branches of the wholesale trade: *textiles and *livestock. In 1503 and 1506 King Alexander Jagellon granted the Jews freedom to trade at the markets and fairs as well as the right to benefit from the reductions accorded to other citizens. King Sigismund I restricted Jewish trade (1521), then accorded unlimited trading rights (1527), and finally revoked the permit (in the same year). This uncertain state of affairs continued throughout the whole period. Temporary compromise agreements on the question of trading rights were concluded between the municipality and the Jews in 1581, 1592, and 1602. The renewal of these agreements and the determination of their exact contents were usually accompanied by protests from the townsmen. The Jewish craftsmen were also under constant pressure from Christian artisans.

The Community and its Institutions

The two congregations of Lvov maintained separate synagogues, *mikva'ot*, and charitable institutions. They shared the cemetery (first mentioned in 1411), and the Karaites were also buried there. From 1600 to 1606 there was a violent conflict between the Jews and the Jesuits over the synagogue which had been constructed (in late Gothic style, after the plan of an Italian architect) by the philanthropist Isaac b. Naḥman (founder of the famous *Nachmanovich family) in 1582. The Jesuits claimed that the land on which the synagogue was constructed was their property. The Jews were victorious and the synagogue, which was named the Taz (or "Di Gildene Roiz" after one of the daughters of the Nachmanovich family who died mysteriously), remained standing until the Holocaust. Lvov was the center of "Red Russia" (Galicia, i.e., Western Ukraine) and Podolia-Bratslav region, and its community leaders represented the whole region at the *Councils of the Lands. By the electoral system of the community, a limited number of the wealthy descendants of noble families were assured of long periods in office.

From 1684 to 1772

In the *Chmielnicki massacres of 1648–49 and the successive wars of the second half of the 17th and early 18th century, the Jews of Lvov, especially those who lived outside the town, suffered great losses in life and property. Their houses were at the mercy of the enemy and they were compelled to seek refuge within the town. Generally the Jews played an active part in the defense of the town. During Chmielnicki's siege in 1648 and the Russian siege of 1655, the attackers demanded that the Jews be delivered into their hands. Meeting with the refusal of the townsmen, they settled for a large ransom. During the whole of this period, the townsmen's struggle against the control of trades and crafts by the Jews continued. The latter's efforts to expand their quarter came under special attack. The Jewish quarter consisted of only 49 building lots and the houses built on them were too small to accommodate the established inhabitants and the refugees from many wars. All the efforts of the townsmen to confine the Jews to their quarter and to restrict their trade were in vain, for the nobles usually supported the Jews. At this time the Jews also opened shops in the center of town. During this period, war damages, ransom payments, the costs of court cases, the necessity to rebuild damaged houses, and the decline of Lvov in favor of other commercial centers brought about severe economic crises. In 1727 the community owed the municipality 438,410 zlotys, while in 1765 their debts to the noblemen, the clergy, and the religious orders amounted to 381,999 zlotys, and those to the municipality to 820,409 zlotys. Although direct and indirect communal taxes were raised the community was unable to become solvent. According to the census of 1764/65, 6,142 Jews lived in Lvov – over two-thirds of them outside the town walls – and only 57 of the 3,060 men were self-supporting.

When Shabbateanism began to spread in Poland, David Halevi (d. 1667), *av bet din* of the congregation outside the walls, sent his son and stepson to *Shabbetai Ẓevi; they returned his enthusiastic supporters. After Shabbetai Ẓevi's apostasy, his adherents in Lvov were excommunicated (1722). In 1754 Leib Krisse (Kriss), right-hand man of the pseudomessiah Jacob *Frank, came to Lvov to propagate the Frankist message. Frank himself arrived in the town in December of 1755, but he was compelled to leave. A disputation with the Frankists was held in 1759. The spokesman for the Jews was R. Ḥayyim Kohen Rapoport, *av bet din* of the town and region.

During the 18th century, the importance of the Lvov community declined and its authority was reduced. The limits of the provincial council's authority were also restricted after the annexation of Podolia to Turkey (1772). In Galicia itself, the expansion of the surrounding communities (Zholkva, Brody) further limited the authority of the Lvov community. At the meeting of the provincial council in 1720, it was declared that "we, the men of the province, have no further portion or inheritance in the holy congregation of Lvov and the rabbi who will be nominated by it." At the meeting of the council in Berezhany in 1740 the rabbinate of the province was divided into two regions and the *av bet din* of Lvov held office in only one of them. Conflicts within the community over the distribution of taxes, the election of rabbis, and other affairs resulted in the intervention of the secular authorities to a greater degree than in the past. Menahem Simḥah Emmanuel de Jonah (d. 1702), a member of a large family of physicians and himself court physician to King John III Sobieski, was highly influential during the second half of the 17th century. He was the "*nesi Ereẓ Israel*" (the chief treasurer of the funds for Ereẓ Israel collected in Poland), a *parnas* of the Councils of the Lands, and the holder of many public offices.

From 1772 to 1914

The Jewish population of Lvov rose from 18,302 in 1800 to 26,694 in 1869, and 57,000 (28% of the total population) in 1910. According to the 1820 census, 55% of the Jews engaged in commerce (the majority as shopkeepers and retail traders) and 24% in crafts. The 745 Jewish craftsmen included 249 tailors, 133 furriers, 51 bakers, and 34 goldsmiths. The Jews of Lvov controlled the wholesale trade between Russia and Vienna. Some were army purveyors, or wholesale dealers in tobacco, cereals, and salt; others owned flour mills; and Jews pioneered industry and banking in the town. Lvov Jewry suffered as a result of the economic crisis in Galicia during the 19th century. After 1772 the townsmen's struggle to restrict Jewish rights of residence and trade was supported by the Austrian authorities. From the beginning of the 19th century only the wealthy and educated merchants who had adopted the German way of life were authorized to live outside the Jewish quarter. In 1848 the Jews were allowed to participate in the elections to the municipal council, but their representation was limited to 15% and later to 20%. In spite of the religious equality granted in the Austrian Empire in 1849, the municipality continued to evict the Jews from the retail trade, and the Christian artisans' guilds struggled against Jewish artisans. The prohibition on acquiring real estate was abolished in 1860, and after the *Sejm of Galicia had revoked all discrimination against Jews the municipality of Lvov was compelled to annul those restrictions opposed to the Austrian constitution of 1867. Intensified antisemitic tendencies then prevalent among the Poles and Ukrainians of Lvov and the vicinity were partly caused by the assimilation of the upper strata of the Jews to the ruling German culture.

TRENDS WITHIN THE COMMUNITY. Ḥasidism made headway in Lvov at the end of the 18th century, and although no *ẓaddikim* settled there they occasionally visited the town. In 1792 and in 1798 there were open clashes between Ḥasidim and their opponents. During the 1820s, a ḥasidic *shtibl* was founded and in 1838 there were seven such prayer rooms. As the *Haskalah movement penetrated Lvov, an anonymous *ḥerem* was proclaimed in 1816 against a group of *maskilim* and especially against Solomon Judah *Rapoport, Benjamin Ẓevi Nutkis, and Judah Leib Pastor; it was only as a result of pressure from the authorities that it was rescinded by the *av bet din*, Jacob Meshullam Orenstein. During the 1830s a violent dispute broke out over the question of a change in the traditional Jewish dress. In 1844 a Reform Temple was opened and Abraham Kohen of Hohenems, Austria, was appointed as preacher. He was also made director of the German-Jewish school opened during the same year. The Orthodox were vigorously opposed to him and their opposition gained momentum after the authorities confirmed him as rabbi of the province in 1847. A year later he and his family were poisoned and Orthodox fanatics were accused of having committed the crime.

The assimilationist intelligentsia circles of Lvov identified themselves with German culture, and in 1868 the *Shomer Israel organization was formed, with its ideological organ, *Israelit*. The movement was opposed by the Doresh Shalom society, founded in 1878 and disbanded a short while later, and after it by the *Aguddat Aḥim (1883), which called for assimilation into Polish culture. Its organ was the *Ojczyzna* ("Fatherland"). Toward the end of the century, the move toward Polish assimilation gained in strength and the Jewish representatives from Lvov in the Austrian parliament joined the Polish camp. During the 1870s Orthodox circles organized themselves within the framework of the *Maḥzike Hadas, in which the Ḥasidim were predominant. Lvov was the home of Hertz *Homberg. Within the framework of his educational activities, four schools for boys, three for girls, and a teachers' seminary headed by Aaron Friedenthal were founded there. All were closed down with the liquidation of Homberg's educational network in Galicia in 1806. Jewish children, however, began to attend general schools. Legal restrictions against the attendance of Jews in secondary schools and universities were removed in 1846. There were then many Jews in the liberal professions, including distinguished lawyers and physicians. From the emancipation period, there were numerous cases of apostasy in Lvov. Between 1868 and 1907, 713 Jews abandoned their faith, while 86 Christians were converted to Judaism. In 1874 there were 69 registered *ḥadarim* in the city and the first "reformed *ḥeder*" (*ḥeder metukkan*), in which 381 pupils studied, was founded in 1885. An institute for religious studies opened in 1910.

During the Austrian period the two congregations in Lvov merged into a single community, which from the 1830s was led by moderate assimilationists. These included Immanuel *Blumenfeld, Meir Jerahmeel Mieses, and Emil *Byk. Rabbis who held office in this community were Joseph Saul Nathanson, Ẓevi Hirsch Orenstein, Isaac Aaron Ettinger (see *Ettinger Family), Isaac *Schmelkes, and Aryeh Leib Braude. The preachers at the temple were Dr. S.A. *Schwabacher, Dr. Y.B. Lewinstein, Dr. Ezekiel Caro (who in 1909 was confirmed as rabbi of the community together with R. Isaac Schmelkes), and Dr. S. Gutmann. During the late 19th and early 20th centuries, the power of the assimilationists declined and nationalist-Zionist influence began to be felt. The first Zionist societies, Mikra Kodesh and Zion, were formed in 1883 and 1888. They formed the nucleus of the all-Galician Zionist organization. Periodicals and newspapers were published: *Przyszlość*, *Wschód*, *Ha-Karmel*, *Der Veker*, and *Togblat*. Activists in the Zionist societies included Reuben Birer, Joseph Kobak, David Schreiber, Abraham and Jacob Kokas, and Adolph *Stand. The first moves were made toward a Jewish workers' movement and artisans' unions, while some joined the P.P.S., the Polish workers' movement; the representative of this group was Herman *Diamand.

From 1914 to 1939

With the outbreak of World War I, thousands of refugees arrived in Lvov from the regions bordering on Russia. The entry of the Russian army into the city in August 1914 was accompanied by robbery and looting, the closure of Jewish institutions, and the taking of hostages. With the return of the Austrians in June 1915, Jewish life was resumed, assistance to the refugees was organized, and the public institutions functioned once more. In November 1918, when the Poles and the Ukrainians fought for control of eastern Galicia, pogroms broke out in Lvov; 70 Jews lost their lives and many were wounded. It was then, when the German, Polish, and Ukrainian nationalistic cultures were in conflict, that the inherent risks of assimilation were made manifest to the Jews.

During the period of independent Poland (1918–39), the community of Lvov was the third largest in Poland and one of its most important centers. From 99,595 in 1910 the number of Jews increased to 109,500 (33% of the total population) in 1939. In the struggle between the Poles and the Ukrainians, each side accused the Jews of supporting the other. The rise of antisemitism and the severe economic situation were reflected in every sphere of Jewish life. The economic crisis was also illustrated by the reduction in community taxes: from 497,429 zlotys in 1929 to 310,481 zlotys in 1933. During this period, Lvov had three Jewish secondary schools with instruction in Polish; a Hebrew college for advanced studies in Judaism (founded in 1920), first directed by Moses *Schorr; a nationalist-religious school, Ma-Ta-T (Mi-Ẓiyyon Teẓe Torah); a vocational school; many *ḥadarim*; and a *talmud torah*. There were many Ashkenazi synagogues and ḥasidic prayer rooms. The newspapers *Chwila* ("The Moment"), *Lemberger Togblat*, and *Opinia* were published. The community was governed by assimilationists in coalition with the Orthodox, while for the greater part of this period the Zionists formed the opposition. In national politics, the Lvov members of the Polish parliament adopted a moderate line. They opposed the minorities bloc and were among the initiators of the *Ugoda (see also O. Thon and H. Rosmaryn), the agreement with the Polish government (1925). The Orthodox, especially the Ḥasidim of Belz, as well as the rich Jews, supported the government majority list.

[Avraham Rubinstein]

Hebrew Printing

After the first partition of Poland (1772), which brought Galicia under Austro-Hungarian rule, the government forced Jewish printers to transfer their presses from *Zolkiew (Zholkva) to the Galician capital of Lvov in order to facilitate their *censorship. The first to move were W. Letteris and H.D. Madpis, the latter producing Elijah Levita's *Pirkei Eliyahu* in 1783. The house of Madpis brought out a new edition of the Talmud (1859–68) and a seven-volume Shulḥan Arukh with standard commentaries (1858–61), still one of the best editions (a similar one was printed by J.L. Balaban and his son, who began printing in 1839). In 1785 J.S. Herz set up his press, which produced a good edition of Maimonides' *Mishneh Torah* (1805–11). Madpis' granddaughter, Judith Mann-Rozanes, also moved from Zolkiew, while her son, M.H. Grossmann, continued printing until 1858. About 20 other printers were active in Lvov in the century and a half before the outbreak of World War II, making the city one of the main centers for the production of Hebrew books, not only for Eastern Europe but for the Balkans as well.

Holocaust Period

In September 1939, at the beginning of World War II, Poland was partitioned between Germany and the U.S.S.R., and Lvov became part of Soviet Ukraine. The economy was nationalized; Jewish organizations, parties, and institutions were closed. Jewish schools turned into Yiddish ones with Soviet curriculum. A Jewish theater was opened at the initiative of actors from among the thousands of refugees who flocked to the city. But after the outbreak of the German-Soviet War, the Germans captured the city (July 1941); it then had a Jewish population of about 150,000, including thousands of refugees from the Nazi-occupied western part of Poland. The local Ukrainian population welcomed the German troops, while Stefan Bandera's units joined up with the invading forces and played a major role in stirring up hatred of the Jews and in murdering them. An incited mob attacked the Jews for three days. Thousands of Jews were put in jail, where they were tortured and murdered. During July several hundred Jewish public figures and youth were put to death; over 2,000 Jews were shot in "*Aktion* Petliura" (July 25–27). On July 15, the Jews were ordered to wear the yellow badge, and at the beginning of August a fine of 20,000,000 rubles ($4,000,000) was imposed upon them. Jewish property was confiscated and looted and in August the desecration and destruction of synagogues and Jewish cemeteries was carried out.

A Judenrat was appointed by the authorities, headed by Joseph Parnes, who was killed shortly afterward when he refused to supply the Nazis with a quota of men for forced labor. A similar fate was in store for two of his three successors; the last chairman of the Judenrat, Ebersohn, was executed together with the other members of the council in February 1943. Under German supervision, the Judenrat handled taxes, social welfare, and food and housing control. A Jewish police force came into being as a special department of the Judenrat; in the course of time it was manipulated by the Nazis to serve their own aims. On Aug. 1, 1941, Eastern Galicia was incorporated into the General Government, Poland, and all anti-Jewish restrictions that had been in force in western Poland for the past two years were now also applied to the Jews of Lvov (see *Holocaust, General Survey). Labor camps were set up in the city and vicinity, where many Jews were either murdered outright (especially young people) or died as a result of the inhuman conditions prevailing in the camps. In November 1941 the Jews of Lvov were all concentrated in a special quarter of the city and subjected to starvation.

In March 1942 about 15,000 Jews from Lvov were deported to *Belzec extermination camp. The big *Aktion*, however, took place from August 10 to 23, in which 40,000 Jews perished. Following the *Aktion* the S.S.-Gruppenfuehrer Fritz *Katzmann ordered the establishment of a ghetto, completely sealed off and surrounded by a barbed-wire fence. The overcrowding caused a series of epidemics which killed thousands of ghetto inmates. In further *Aktionen* (November 1942 and January 1943), another 15,000 Jews were murdered, some in Belzec and others in the Janowska Road camp. The rest of the ghetto inmates, some 20,000 people, were restricted to a portion of the ghetto designated as the Jewish camp and the Judenrat was liquidated. In the last *Aktion* (June 1943), which resulted in the death of most of the surviving Jews, the Jews offered armed resistance. In places where the Nazis encountered gunfire and hand grenades, they poured gasoline on the Jewish houses and set them in flames. The 7,000 Jews who survived the massacre were dispatched to the Janowska Road camp. Apart from a few Jews in labor camps, Lvov and the environs were made **judenrein*. A few hid in the "Aryan" part of the city.

JANOWSKA ROAD CAMP. The camp, a place of torture and murder, was set up on Janowska Road in October 1941. One part of the camp contained quarters for the SS men and camp police, and a prison barracks (the latter also served as a transit camp for deportees to Belzec extermination camp). The other part contained workshops which in the course of time developed into a special unit, the German Armament Works (DAW; see *SS, Enterprises in the East). Designed as a forced labor camp for Jews from Lvov and the area, Janowska in fact became an extermination camp. Tens of thousands of Jews from Eastern Galicia were brought there, some of whom were murdered on the spot and others sent on to Belzec. Prisoners were killed in many instances for the "entertainment" of the murderers. Yet in spite of the conditions, the Jews created cultural activities in the camp and prepared for armed resistance. The Germans, under the threat of possible resistance, liquidated the camp in a surprise *Aktion* on Nov. 20, 1943. Only a few individuals escaped. The special conditions prevailing in Lvov – a hostile Ukrainian population, the lack of forests in the area to provide shelter, and the absence of a local partisan movement – precluded the rise of organized Jewish resistance. However, a few sporadic and isolated attempts to resist were made. Some Jews fled to the remote forests, but in most instances the local peasants handed them over to the Nazis. Some instances of resistance have been recorded, e.g., during the liquidation of the ghetto and one in the Janowska Road camp. In one instance, a group of camp prisoners charged with the disposal and cremation of corpses attacked and killed several of the German guards. A few dozen prisoners then escaped, but most of them were caught and murdered.

When the Soviet forces entered in July 1944, a Jewish committee was established to help the survivors. Of the 3,400 Jewish survivors who registered with the committee by the end of 1944, only 820 were from Lvov ghetto itself. Most of the survivors settled in Israel, after wandering through Europe, while the rest emigrated to other countries overseas. Some of the ashes of the Lvov martyrs were taken to Israel and interred at the Naḥalat Yiẓḥak cemetery near Tel Aviv.

Contemporary Period

A monument to the memory of Jewish victims of the Nazis, with inscriptions in Hebrew, Yiddish, and Russian, was erected shortly after World War II. In the 1959 census 29,701 Jews were registered in the Lvov oblast (district), 5,011 of whom declared Yiddish to be their mother tongue. In the city, a center of Ukrainian nationalism, an anti-Jewish atmosphere prevailed in most spheres of life. In 1957 several Jewish students were arrested for "Zionist activities." Organized *maẓẓah* baking was prohibited in 1959, and in the same year pressure was brought to bear on the local *mohalim* to induce them to sign a declaration promising to abandon circumcision. In the Jewish cemetery only a small section was kept intact and used for burials. In 1962 several hundred Jews were arrested for "economic crimes." In that year several articles were published in the local Ukrainian newspaper, *Lvivska Pravda*, demanding the closure of the only remaining synagogue on the pretext that it served as a meeting place for "speculators" and other criminals. It was in fact closed toward the end of that year, and all synagogue officials were arrested and charged with "economic crimes." The community slaughterhouse was handed over to a local municipal organization. In 1965 local Jews addressed a petition to Prime Minister Kosygin asking to be given a place for worship. They were allotted a building site, but the financial burden of erecting a new synagogue was too great. In 1969 the militia broke into private *minyanim* and dispersed them by force. Most Jews emigrated in the 1990s.

[Emmanuel Brand]

BIBLIOGRAPHY: J. Caro, *Geschichte der Juden in Lemberg* (1894); S. Buber, *Anshei Shem* (1895, repr. 1968); Dubnow, Hist Russ, index, s.v. *Lemberg*; S. An-ski, *Ḥurban ha-Yahadut be-Polin u-Bukovina* (1929), 119–28, 183–203, and passim; *Lwów, Żydowska gmina wyznaniowa* (1928); M. Balaban, *Żydzi-lwowscy na przełomie 16 i 17 wieków* (1906); idem, in: *Studja lwowskie* (1932), 41–65; idem, *Geshikhte fun Lemberger Progresivn Templ* (1937); Neiwelt, in: *Pinkes Galitsye* 1925–45 (1945), 117–26 and passim; Yaari, in: KS, 17 (1939/40), 95–108; 21 (1945), 299–300; L. Chasanovich (ed.), *Les Pogromes anti-juifs en Pologne et en Galicie* (1919), 47–73; Karl, in: I.L. Fishman (ed.), *Arim ve-Immahot be-Yisrael*, 1 (1946), 290–344 (incl. bibl.); J. Tenenbaum, *Galitsye Mayn Alte Heym* (1952), index; Thon, in: *Pirkei Galiẓyah* (1957), 343–85; N.M. Gelber (ed.), EG, 1 (1956), incl. bibl.; idem, *Toledot ha-Tenu'ah ha-Ẓiyyonit be-Galiẓyah, 1875–1918* (1958), index; Ḥ.N. Dembitzer, *Kelilat Yofi* (1960), 1–156. PRINTING: Bałaban, in: *Soncino-Blaetter*, 3 (1929/30), 17–21; A. Yaari, in: KS, 17 (1939/40), 95ff.; 21 (1945), 299f.; Ḥ.D. Friedberg, in: EG 4 (1956), 539ff. HOLOCAUST: S. Szende, *The Promise Hitler Kept* (1945), 9–179; L. Weliczker-Wells, *Janowska Road* (1963); I. Lewin, *Aliti mi-Spezia* (1947); P. Schneck, in: *Davar* (Nov. 5, 1946); E. Brand, in: *Yedi'ot Yad Vashem*, 25–26 (1961), 17–18; EG, 4 (1956), 539–766; *Eduyyot*, 1 (1963), 195–216; *Forfaits hitlériens: Documents officiels* (1945), 201–32; M.M. Borwicz, *Uniwersytet zbirów* (1946); idem, *Literatura w obozie* (1946); J. Hescheles, *Oczyma dwunastoletniej dziewczyny* (1946); S. Gogołwska, *Szkoła okrucieństwa* (1964). **ADD. BIBLIOGRAPHY:** *Pinkas Hakehillot Poland* vol. 2, Eastern Galicia (1980).

LVOVICH, DAVID (known as **Davidovich**; 1882–1950), leader of the territorialist-Socialist movement and of *ORT. Born in southern Russia and brought up in an assimilationist environment, Lvovich first became acquainted with Jewish affairs and the Jewish workers' movement when he visited Minsk in 1903 and came into contact with the *Po'alei Zion. After he left Russia he maintained relations with the Ḥerut group founded by N. *Syrkin. In 1905 he visited Ereẓ Israel and on his return he abandoned general Zionism in favor of territorialism. After joining the *Zionist-Socialist Workers' Party (SS or ZS), he founded the SS League abroad and established student groups in Germany. A member of the party's committee in Odessa from late 1905, he was the leader of its *self-defense group during the October pogrom. At the SS convention in Leipzig (1906), he represented that trend which connected the future realization of territorialism with the unavoidable turn of the course of Jewish emigration from the towns toward agriculture and concentrated colonization. He later worked for an active policy in the organization and regulation of emigration. As the representative of the SS at the conventions of the Jewish Territorialist Organization (see *Territorialism) he was elected to the Angola Committee (Vienna, 1912). In 1907 he was the representative of the SS at the Socialist International Congress in Stuttgart. Lvovich tried to promote cooperation between SS, the *Jewish Socialist Workers' Party ("Sejmists"), and the Po'alei Zion. In 1917 he was elected to the Social-Revolutionary list by Jewish colonists of southern Ukraine as the only delegate of the *United Jewish Socialist Workers' Party at the constituent assembly. Turning his energies to working for ORT in Russia, he traveled abroad (1919) as its emissary, along with L. *Bramson, in order to establish the world ORT league (1921). Becoming a member of its executive council in 1937 he was elected vice president and in 1946 co-president. He published his memoirs in *Sotsialistisher Teritorializm* (1934), 79–89.

BIBLIOGRAPHY: ORT *khronik* (Yid., Oct. 1950); *Akhtsik Yor "ORT"* (1960), 119–41.

[Moshe Mishkinsky]

LWOFF, ANDRÉ MICHEL (1902–1994), French biologist and Nobel Prize winner. Born in the Allier department, France, Lwoff became head of the Microbial Physiology Laboratory of the Pasteur Institute in Paris in 1938. Lwoff's earlier work dealt with the morphology and biology of the ciliate protozoa, and particularly the problem of the genetic continuity of cell structures. His later research dealt with the biology of viruses, the genetics of bacteria, and the mechanisms by which viruses are replicated in the course of a viral infection. During World War II he was awarded the Medal of the Resistance for his work in the French underground. After the war Lwoff and his collaborators began a study of lysogeny. Lwoff demonstrated that in this condition the bacterial cell harbors a "prophage" which is harmless to the host cell and is transmitted genetically. It can be induced by external factors, such as ultraviolet light, to become virulent, causing destruction of the host cell and liberation of infectious virus particles. This discovery led to entirely new ideas as to the evolution and biological role of viruses. Lwoff was corecipient of the 1965 Nobel Prize for medicine and physiology. Among his books are *Problems of Morphogenesis in Ciliates* (1950) and *Biological Order* (1962). He was also editor of *Biochemistry and Physiology of Protozoa* (3 vols., 1951–64).

[Mordecai L. Gabriel]

LYADY, a town in Vitebsk district, Belarus; under Polish rule until 1772, when it was incorporated into Russia and was included in the Mogilev province. A Jewish settlement in Lyady is mentioned in documents of 1731. In 1766 there were 207 Jewish poll tax payers. During the 19th century, Lyady became a "Jewish" townlet, the Jews forming the majority of the population. There were 2,137 Jews registered with the community in 1847, and 3,763 (83.9% of the total population) in 1897. Lyady became known as the home of *Shneour Zalman, the founder of the Chabad movement, who lived there during the last 12 years of his life, and was referred to as the "Rabbi of Lyady." His son, Dov Baer, also lived there at first. In 1869 the great-grandson of Shneour Zalman, Shneour Ḥayyim Zalman, settled in Lyady. He and his sons maintained a ḥasidic "court" in the town. In 1926 there were 2,020 Jews (56% of the total population). In 1929 there was a Yiddish school and a kolkhoz, where 14 families worked. In 1939 the number of Jews in Lyady dropped to 897 (38% of the total). Lyady was the birthplace of Alexander Siskind *Rabinovitz (Azar) and Reuben *Brainin. The Germans occupied the town on July 18, 1941. In March 1942 some 2,000 Jews from the town and environs were assembled and murdered on April 2, 1942, outside Lyady.

BIBLIOGRAPHY: R. Brainin, *Fun mayn Lebens Bukh* (1946), 31–99; *Regesty i nadpisy*, 2 (1910), 301–02.

[Yehuda Slutsky]

LYAKHOVICHI (Pol. **Łachowicze**; Yid. לעכוויטש), city in Brest-Litovsk oblast, Belarus. Jews were living in Lyakhovichi by the first quarter of the 17th century. According to a decision of the Lithuanian Council of 1623 (see *Councils of the Lands), the community was subordinated to the *kahal* of *Pinsk. During the second half of the 18th century the city's annual fairs were an important meeting place for Jewish merchants. There were 729 Jewish poll tax payers in 1766; in 1847 the community numbered 1,071, increasing to 3,846 (76.6% of the total population) in 1897. A branch of the Karlin ḥasidic dynasty prevailed in the town. The chaos during World War I and the immediate postwar years caused a drop in the Jewish population and in 1921 it numbered only 1,656 (58.7%). A Tarbut school and a yeshivah with 50 pupils operated there.

[*Encyclopaedia Judaica* (Germany)]

Holocaust Period

On the eve of the German occupation (June 24, 1941) the community consisted of 6,000 Jews. The Germans entered town on June 26, and on June 28 a number of Jewish community leaders were murdered in the nearby forest, following which a pogrom broke out in which 82 Jews were killed (July 1). In fall 1941 the Jews were ordered to assemble in the marketplace, where a *Selektion* was made to separate the 1,500 able-bodied from the 2,000 "nonproductive." The latter were taken to a trench and murdered; some tried to escape but most of these were shot. The "productive" persons were interned in a ghetto. A group of young persons, led by Zalman Rabinowicz, Josef Peker, and Haim Abramowicz, organized resistance units. On June 10, 1942, a second *Aktion* was carried out in which 1,200 Jews were murdered. Some attempts at resistance were then made. When an *Aktion* to liquidate the entire ghetto was carried out the Germans met with armed resistance. Some ghetto inmates escaped to the forests and joined the partisans, among them Shmuel Mordkowski, who was an outstanding resistance fighter. The rest were killed on June 24, 1942. Fewer than ten Jews survived in Lyakhovichi. About 80 Jews from the town who had joined the Soviet army in 1941 also survived.

[Aharon Weiss]

BIBLIOGRAPHY: *Lachowicze, Sefer Zikkaron* (Heb. and Yid., 1949); Halpern, Pinkas, index; S. Dubnow (ed.), *Pinkas ha-Medinah* (1925), index; B. Wasiutyński, *Ludność żydowska w Polsce w wiekach XIX I XX* (1930), 84; I. Schiper (ed.), *Dzieje handlu żydowskiego na ziemiach polskich* (1937), index.

LYCK (Pol. **Elk**), town in Poland; before 1945 in E. Prussia. During the late 17th century Jewish tradesmen visited the market town and subsequently established a community which, in 1713, numbered 29 persons. Its *shoḥet*, Eliezer Lipmann Silbermann, founded the Hebrew weekly **Ha-Maggid* which was printed in Lyck from 1856 to 1891. The *Mekiẓei Nirdamim Society was also founded by Silbermann and, between 1864 and 1874, 15 of its publications were printed in Lyck. Among them was S.D. *Luzzatto's 1864 edition of *Judah Halevi's *Diwan*, S. *Buber's edition of the *Pesikta de Rav Kahana* (1868), and parts of I. *Lampronti's *Paḥad Yiẓḥak* (1864–74). In the second half of the 19th century many Hebrew books were printed in the town and smuggled across the border to Russian Jewry. The community of Lyck increased from 90 persons in 1845 to 250 (3.65% of the total population) in 1880, then declined to 137 in 1933 and 16 in 1939.

BIBLIOGRAPHY: Neufeld, in: AUJW (May 7, 1965), 6; PK Germanyah; *Du'aḥ shel Mekiẓei Nirdamim* (1935).

[Ze'ev Wilhem Falk]

LYDDA (Heb. לֹד, **Lod**), town in the coastal plain of Israel, 10 mi. (16 km.) S.E. of Tel Aviv-Jaffa. Lydda first appears in the Canaanite period (1465 B.C.E.) when it is mentioned in Thutmosis III's list of towns in Canaan. According to the Talmud (Meg. 1:3b–4a; TJ, Meg. 1:1), the city was fortified "in the days of Joshua the son of Nun," but according to the Bible, it was built by Shemed, a Benjamite (I Chron. 8:12). It appears with Ono and Hadid in the list of places resettled after the return from the Babylonian Exile (Ezra 2:33; Neh. 7:37), and it occurs with Ono and Ge-Harashim in the list of Benjamite settlements (Neh. 11:35).

In the Hellenistic period the town was outside the boundaries of Judea; it was detached from Samaria and given to Jonathan the Hasmonean by Demetrius II in 145 B.C.E. (I Macc. 11:34; Jos., Ant., 13:127), becoming a toparchy of Judea (Jos., Wars, 3:55). In Maccabean times it was a purely Jewish town; Julius Caesar restored the privileges of the Jews of Lydda (Jos., Ant., 14:208). In the Roman period it was counted as a village, although it was as populous as a city (Jos., Ant., 20:130). In 43 B.C.E. its inhabitants were sold into slavery by Cassius, the governor of Syria (Jos., Ant., 14:275). Quadratus, the Syrian governor in the time of Claudius, executed several Jews there; Cestius Gallus, the Roman proconsul of Syria, burned it on his way to Jerusalem in 66 C.E. It was within the command of John the Essene at the beginning of the First Jewish War (66–70); Vespasian occupied it in 68 C.E.

According to talmudic sources, Lydda was situated on the boundary of the Shephelah and the coastal plain, one day's journey from Jerusalem; other sources call the plain around it the Shephelah of Lydda (Ma'as. Sh. 5:2). The town flourished between the First and Second Jewish Wars. It had a large market; cattle were raised in the area; and textile, dyeing, and pottery industries were established. A Christian community existed there in the time of Peter (Acts 9:32–35). It was the seat of a Sanhedrin; famous talmudic scholars, such as R. Tarfon, R. Eliezer b. Hyrcanus, R. Akiva, Joshua b. Levi, Judah b. Pazi, Eleazar bar Kappara, and Ḥanina bar Ḥama taught there. Among its synagogues was one specially maintained by a community of Tarsians. After the war of Bar-Kokhba (132–135), Jews remained in Lydda, though its agricultural hinterland had been destroyed. The patriarch R. Judah I leased estates in its plain.

In 200, the emperor Septimius Severus established a Roman city at Lydda, calling it Colonia Lucia Septimia Severa Diospolis. Its territory consisted of the combined toparchies of Lydda and Thamna. The town remained partly Jewish. It took part in the revolt against the emperor Gallus in 351 and was punished when the revolt failed; according to one Midrash, out of ten measures of poverty in the world, Lydda had nine. The Samaritan element became more powerful in Byzantine times, although the town, part of Palaestina Prima, was predominantly Christian and had a bishop. Justinian built a church there. It was the legendary birthplace of St. George; hence its name Georgiopolis in late Byzantine and crusader sources. It was captured by the Muslim general ʿAmr ibn al-ʿĀṣ in 636 and until the foundation of Ramleh (c. 715) it served as headquarters of the province of Filasṭīn. In 1099 it was occupied by the crusaders and became a *seigneurie* with a vicomte in charge. The crusaders built a Church of St. George there, still partly preserved. In 1170, Benjamin of Tudela found only one Jewish family there. After Saladin's reconquest of the town in 1191, more Jews settled in it. In the 14th century, Estori ha-Parḥi found a Jewish community there. Under the Mamluks Lydda was the seat of an administrative district. The town seems not to have been inhabited by Jews during the early Ottoman period. Ancient remains in modern Lydda include a mound, a Jewish tomb, and a Greco-Samaritan inscription. A magnificent mosaic floor within a large villa was uncovered in recent archaeological work in the city; the floor has Nilotic scenes with sea creatures and boats.

[Michael Avi-Yonah]

Modern Period

In the 19th century a small Jewish community existed in Lydda, but the 1921 Arab riots compelled the last of its Jewish inhabitants to leave. Further attempts to reestablish the community during the British Mandate failed because of ensuing violence. The town, which numbered only a few hundred families at the beginning of the century, expanded quickly and in 1919 became an important railway junction. In 1944, Lydda numbered about 17,000 Arab inhabitants, one-fifth of them Christians and the rest Muslims.

During Israel's *War of Independence, Lydda was occupied by Israel forces in Operation Dani on July 10, 1949, and the great majority of its inhabitants abandoned the town. The first Jewish settlers went to Lydda at the end of 1948 when its population numbered 1,200, with 1,050 of them Arabs. In 1949 it received municipal council status. In 1955, in the spirit of a prototype plan made by architect Michael Bar, the Jewish settlers were housed in modern houses in the northern part of the city, and the Arab population was housed in the east. This separation has continued until today. The new parts of Lydda contrast with its ancient nucleus, which has preserved an Oriental character and retains its mosques and churches.

At the end of 1969 its population was 28,000, including 2,900 Muslims and Christian Arabs. In the mid-1990s, the population was approximately 49,500, with approximately 10,180 non-Jews. By the end of 2002 the population had risen to 66,500, including 18,000 non-Jews (26% of the city's population) and 15,000 new immigrants (mostly from the former Soviet Union and Ethiopia). The city's area is about 4 sq. mi. (10 sq. km.). The growth of the Arab population, together with the departure of the veteran Jewish population, has created racial tension in the city and a reputation as the drug capital of Israel. Income was well below the national average.

The nearby airport, Israel's international airport for passengers and freight, was originally built by the Mandatory government in 1936, with the Israel government greatly expanding its facilities. It serves as the home base for *El Al Israel Airlines. New passenger sections were completed in 1970. Now known as Ben-Gurion Airport, it has expanded still further with the construction and opening of the impressive Terminal 3 in 2005. Some 115,000 passengers passed through the airport in 1950, over a million in 1970, and five million in 2004. The airport served the town as an important source of employment, as did Israel Aircraft Industries.

[Shlomo Hasson / Shaked Gilboa (2nd ed.)]

BIBLIOGRAPHY: Press, Ereẓ, s.v.; EM, 4 (1962), 430–1 (incl. bibl.); S. Abramsky, *Ancient Towns in Israel* (1963); Benvenisti, *Crusaders in the Holy Land*, index. **ADD. BIBLIOGRAPHY:** J.J. Schwartz, *Lod (Lydda), Israel. From its Origins Through the Byzantine Period, 5600 B.C.E.–640 C.E.* (1991); Y. Tsafrir, L. Di Segni, and J. Green, *Tabula Imperii Romani. Iudaea – Palaestina. Maps and Gazetteer* (1994), 171; B.-Z. Rosenfeld, *Lod and Its Sages in the Period of the Mishnah and the Talmud* (1997).

LYDIA, LYDIANS (Heb. לוּד, לוּדִים, לודיים; Assyr. *Luddu*), people who, together with the Phrygians and other Anatolian peoples, infiltrated Anatolia after the decline of the *Hittite empire at the beginning of the 12th century B.C.E., and settled in the vicinity of the Maeander River (modern Buyuk Menderes) and the western part of the Anatolian heights. After their infiltration, the Lydian tribes assimilated within the local Hittite population and partly took on its language. It is significant to note that one of the kings of the first dynasty is called by the Hittite name Muršiliš (Gr. Myrsilus), a name which was common among the Hittite kings. This dynasty ended with a court uprising, when the head of the royal guard, Gyges, took over the rule. Gyges established the second Lydian dynasty, which ended with the reign of Croesus, when Lydia was conquered by the Persian king Cyrus. During the time of Gyges, relations were established between Lydia and the kingdom of Assyria, because Gyges sought the aid of the latter against the Cimmerians. An important part of this episode has been preserved in the Annals of Ashurbanipal, which records a request for aid by "Guggu king of Luddu (Lydia)" from the Assyrian king (Rassam Cylinder, 2:95). The name of Gyges, in its Hebrew form, *Gog, found its way into Ezekiel (38:2–3). He is referred to here as the head of two Anatolian peoples, Meshech and Tubal. It may thus be concluded that legends about Gyges were popular in both the classical world and the Assyrian empire. Gyges attempted to gain control of central Anatolia and its western coast. The Lydian capital was at this time already in *Sardis. The last Lydian king was Croesus, known throughout the Greek world for his legendary wealth; he was defeated by the Persian army in 547. This brought an end to the Lydian kingdom, which became a province of the Persian empire. The name of the area was preserved as Lydia until a later period, and appears in its biblical Hebrew form, Lud, in talmudic sources as well. The name appears in the Bible together with the names of the Anatolian peoples who were known in the ancient Near East in the eighth and seventh centuries. In Genesis 10:22, Lud is considered a son of Shem and listed together with Elam, Assyria, etc. This ethnic juxtaposition reflects the geographic relationship of the whole northeastern territory as well as an ethnic unity. The parallel list in I Chronicles 1:17 also includes Meshech, which emphasizes the geographic-ethnic orientation of the list. There is an interesting report in Jeremiah 46:9 which speaks of the army of Pharaoh Neco and which also mentions the Lydians as bowmen serving as auxiliaries of the Egyptian forces. Some scholars regard *Ludim* (Lydians) as a distortion of *Luvim* (Libyans), but it is more reasonable to assume that the verse refers to mercenary forces of Lydians who, like the Greeks, served in the Egyptian army.

[Aaron Kempinski]

Jews in Lydia

The beginning of Jewish settlement in Lydia is connected with the establishment of Jewish military settlements by Antiochus III. Josephus relates that during Antiochus' campaign in the East in 209–204 B.C.E. a revolt broke out in Lydia and Phrygia, and Antiochus decided to transfer 2,000 Jewish families from Mesopotamia to the rebellious regions. Each family received a plot of land upon which to build a house and for cultivation. They were to be exempt from taxation for ten years, and during the initial period their needs were to be provided for. They received special authority to live according to the customs of their ancestors. The authenticity of the document quoted by Josephus (Ant., 12:147ff.) is denied by some, but since Jews served as soldiers and dwelt in military settlements as early as in the Persian era, it can be regarded as genuine. These settlements became the nucleus of the Jewish settlement in Asia Minor generally and in Lydia in particular. Lydia remained in the possession of Antiochus until the battle of Magnesia in 190 B.C.E. when it was given by the Romans to Eumenes II king of Pergamum.

In 133 B.C.E. Attalus III bequeathed the kingdom to the Romans and an Asian province was created which included Lydia. Information about the Jews of Lydia derives chiefly from the Roman era. Many documents having reference to the Jews of Sardis have been preserved. From a resolution about the Jews by the citizens of Sardis it is clear that the Romans granted the Jews the right to live according to their customs and even to be judged by their own laws. The ancient synagogue of Sardis was discovered and excavated in the 1960s.

The sending of the half shekel to the Temple in Jerusalem was a source of friction between Jews and gentiles, who did not look favorably upon the export of the money from their city to a foreign country. The proconsul Gaius Norbanus Flaccus (in the time of Augustus, 27 B.C.E.–14 C.E.) wrote to the authorities of Sardis ordering them not to prevent the Jews from collecting the money and sending it to Jerusalem. There is extant from a still later period, the time of Trajan, an inscription from the city of Thyatira in Lydia (Frey, Corpus, 2 (1952), 16, no. 752). In this inscription the word *Sambatyon* occurs. Some consider it to be a Jewish inscription, while others regard it as being connected with "the God fearing ones" who were not regarded as full Jews. There is already reference to a "God fearing" woman from this city in an earlier period in Acts 16:14.

[Lea Roth]

BIBLIOGRAPHY: G. Radet, *La Lydie et le Monde Grec…* (1892); A. Goetze, *Kleinasien* (1957²), 206–9; A. Heubeck, *Lydiaka* (1959); G. Neumann, *Untersuchungen zum Weiterleben hethitischen und luwischen Sprachgutes* (1961); R.D. Barnett, in: CAH², vol. 2, ch. 30 (1967). JEWS IN LYDIA: A. Buechler, *Die Tobiaden und die Oniaden* (1899), 144ff.; Schuerer, Gesch, 3 (1909⁴), 12–15, 75; Juster, Juifs, 1 (1914), 190; Pauly-Wissowa, 26 (1927), 2197; Frey, Corpus, 2 (1952), 16–18, nos. 750, 751, 752; Schalit, in: JQR, 50 (1959/60), 289–318; V. Tcherikover, *Hellenistic Civilization and the Jews* (1959), 288.

LYON-CAEN, CHARLES LÉON (1843–1935), French jurist. The son of a tailor, Lyon-Caen spent some time on his father's business before studying law. His doctoral thesis, *Partages d'ascendants* (1867), earned him a considerable reputation as a jurist and he became professor of law at the Sorbonne in 1872, a post he held for nearly half a century. Lyon-Caen was an authority on commercial and international law and was the author of important works on both subjects. His *Precis de droit commercial* (2 vols., 1885) and *Traité de droit commercial* (8 vols., 1885), written with Louis Renault, became standard works, while his *Droit international privé maritime* (1883) was one of the first textbooks on maritime law as a separate branch of the law. His other works include *De la condition légale des sociétes étrangères en France* (1870). Lyon-Caen was elected to the Académie des sciences morales et politiques in 1884 and became its permanent secretary in 1893. He was active in Jewish affairs as president of L'œuvre des orphelins Israélites and the Comité d'aide aux émigrants juifs.

[Shulamith Catane]

LYONS, capital of the Rhône department, E. central France. According to a medieval Jewish legend one of the three boats loaded with Jewish captives taken during the siege of Jerusalem docked at Lyons. Herod Antipas, tetrarch of Galilee, was exiled to the city by Caligula in 39 C.E. Lyons seems to have had a Jewish population in both the first and the second centuries. Little more is known about Jews in Lyons until the beginning of the ninth century, however, when there was a large, prosperous, and powerful Jewish community in the city. The Jews owned slaves and also employed Christian laborers in their homes and in their commercial and agricultural enterprises. Relations between Jews and their Christian neighbors appear to have been amicable. Jewish vintners and butchers sold their merchandise to both Jews and Christians. Jews also served as purveyors to the imperial palace. Some Jews were employed in public service, especially as collectors of imposts and taxes. Their religious services also appear to have been attended by Christians, many of whom declared that they preferred the preaching of the Jews to that of the Catholic priests. Such opinions could only have been an extreme irritant to the bishop, *Agobard, who had hoped to convert the local Jews to Christianity. A first attempt around 820, targeting children, involved the use of a measure of force, and encountered determined resistance from parents and the vigorous intervention of the emperor, *Louis the Pious. Louis had to intervene on several other occasions against this troublesome bishop, at times dispatching his special envoys in charge of Jewish affairs, the *missi* or *magister Judaeorum*. *Amulo, Agobard's successor, mounted a campaign against the Jews of Lyons, but without success. In the Middle Ages the Jews lived in the Rue Juiverie at the foot of Fourvière hill. When they were expelled in 1250 they were living in the present Rue Ferrachat. For a century Jews only visited Lyons for short periods, but in the second half of the 14th century there was again a Jewish settlement in the city. They paid municipal taxes, and special officials were appointed with jurisdiction over them. As the city was not part of the Kingdom of France, the new community was not affected by the expulsion order of 1394. They were expelled some years later, however, probably in 1420; most of them moved to neighboring Trévoux. Beginning in the 16th century, Jews reappeared in Lyons sporadically as merchants at the fairs and probably also as correctors of Hebrew printing. A group of Jews arrived in Lyons in 1548 (perhaps from Spain and Portugal), but they too were forced to leave. Apparently Joseph *Nasi opened a bank there for some time, but it was closed down by Henri II. A community gradually reestablished itself in the 17th century, consisting mainly of families from Avignon as well as from Comtat Venaissin, Alsace, and Bordeaux. In 1775, the community officially requested permission to open a cemetery. At first they bought space in the vaults of the city hospital. Twenty years later they were able to purchase a cemetery at La Guillotière. Nevertheless, the number of Jews remained insignificant, and there was no synagogue or permanent prayer room.

[Bernhard Blumenkranz / David Weinberg (2nd ed.)]

The community was attached to the *Consistory of Marseilles in 1808. With the influx of Jews from Alsace and Lorraine, the community grew to number 300 in 1830, and 700 in 1840. The majority lived in very modest circumstances, inhabiting two poor quarters in the Rue Lanterne and Rue de la Barre. From 1838 a prosperous industrialist, Samuel Heyman de Ricqulès, was leader of the community. De Ricqulès initially endowed Jewish schools and charitable institutions with the intention of reforming them; after a few years, however, he encountered hostility from more traditional elements and was forced to retire. The number of Jews grew to 1,000 in 1848 and 1,200 in 1854. The community acquired the services of a salaried rabbi in 1850. In 1857 it formed its own consistory, which also included Saint-Étienne (116 Jews), Chalon-sur-Saône (125), Besançon (379), and Montbéliard (202). Among its presidents were Solomon *Reinach and Generals Levy and Worms. Solomon *Munk represented Lyons at the Central Consistory. In 1864 the Grande Synagogue was erected on the Quai Tilsitt. At the beginning of the 20th century, with the arrival of immigrants from the Mediterranean area, a Sephardi community was formed in the suburb of Saint-Fons. On the eve of World War II Lyons had 500–600 Jewish families.

[Moshe Catane / David Weinberg (2nd ed.)]

Holocaust and Postwar Periods

As a result of the Franco-German agreement (June 1940), Lyons became a "free" city. During much of World War II, it served as a refuge for Jewish organizations, particularly the offices of the Central Consistory, as well as philanthropic and Zionist bodies. Information, both official and unofficial, instructions to the Jewish communities in France, protests against anti-Jewish measures, and secret orders of the resistance all emanated from Lyons. Many Jewish leaders were arrested there. Lyons also hosted a center for Jewish studies for refugee intellectuals, to which Léon *Algazi notably contributed, and a reception center for Jewish physicians, on the initiative of *OSE. During the Occupation the city also provided sanctuary for large numbers of Jews. Probably its most important role was that of a major center of the Jewish resistance. Jewish resistance fighters generally operated in total isolation from other resistance organizations, with only occasional support and cooperation from Catholic and Protestant elements. Lyons was also the home of an active Catholic resistance effort, thanks to the pastoral letter which Cardinal Gerlier had read on September 6, 1942, in which he denounced the persecution of Jews. Led by the notorious Klaus *Barbie, local Nazi officials fought ruthlessly against members of the resistance and against Jews. The arrests, torture, and deportations reached a peak in August 1944, when prisoners from the "Jewish quarters" in the Monluc Fort prison were taken to Bron airfield to de-mine the area after the bombardment. After the war the remains of 109 individuals were uncovered.

After the war many Jewish refugees settled permanently in Lyons. Nevertheless, the community of approximately 7,000 was hardly any larger than in 1939. With the city's economic expansion and the influx of immigrants from North Africa in the 1950s and 1960s, the Jewish population had increased to over 20,000 in 1969. In 1961 the community inaugurated one of the first and foremost community centers in France. The various communal religious bodies – consistorial, Sephardi, and Orthodox – generally worked in close cooperation, and a new synagogue was inaugurated in 1966 in La Duchère, a new quarter of the city. A regional consistory was also founded in 1961. In 1987, there were said to be about 25,000 Jews living in Lyons. The community institutions include an ORT vocational school, two religious schools, and numerous kosher butchers and restaurants. There are more than 20 other communities in the vicinity. Two are especially notable. Villeurbanne, with a Jewish population of 1,900, has a synagogue that was built in 1965 with money from the Claims Conference and with the help of Aktion Suehnezeichen ("Repentance Society"), a group of young Germans seeking expiation for Nazi crimes. The community of Saint Fons-Vénissieux was originally founded in the interwar period by Jews from North Africa. Numbering about 1,000, a majority of whom are industrial workers, it maintains a synagogue and community center.

[Georges Levitte / David Weinberg (2nd ed.)]

BIBLIOGRAPHY: A. Lévy, *Notice sur les Israélites de Lyon* (1894); idem, in: *Univers Israélite*, 48–49 (1892/93–1893/94); T. Reinach, in: REJ, 50 (1905), lxxxi–cxi; S. Reinach, *ibid.*, 51 (1906), 245–50; B. Blumenkranz, *Juifs et Chrétiens dans le monde occidental* (1960), index; A. Coville, *Recherches sur l'histoire de Lyon* (1928), 538ff.; J. Kling, in: *Revue de Psychologie des peuples*, 13 (1958), 199ff.; E. Dreyfus and L. Marx, *Autour des Juifs de Lyon* (1958); F. Delpech, in: *Cahiers d'Histoire* (1959), 51ff.; H. Amoretti, *Lyon... 1940–1944* (1964), 142ff.; Z. Szajkowski, *Analytical Franco-Jewish Gazetteer* (1966), 252f.

LYONS, ALBERT MICHAEL NEIL (1880–1940), author, known as A. Neil Lyons. Born in Kimberley, South Africa, Lyons came to England as a child and was educated at Bedford Grammar School. From 1899 he was a journalist, chiefly for the *Topical Times.* He then became a prolific playwright. Lyons' best-known work, *London Pride* (1916), "a London play for London people," was written in collaboration with Gladys Unger. Other works by Lyons include *Kitchener Chaps* (1915); an anthology of short stories (1929); *Tom, Dick and Harriet* (1937), and a number of biographies.

ADD. BIBLIOGRAPHY: D. Griffiths (ed.), *Encyclopedia of the British Press, 1422–1992* (1992), 383.

LYONS, EUGENE (1898–1984), U.S. journalist and author. Born in Russia and educated in New York, Lyons spent seven years in Moscow after World War I as United Press correspondent. He expressed his disillusionment with the Soviet system in *Assignment in Utopia* (1937). He edited the magazines *American Mercury* and *Pageant*, and joined the staff of the *Reader's Digest* in 1946, becoming a senior editor in 1952. His books continued to reflect his anti-communist outlook: *Stalin, Czar of all the Russias* (1940), *The Red Decade* (1941), and *Our Secret Allies* (1953). He also wrote *Herbert Hoover, A Biography* (1964).

LYONS, ISRAEL (c. 1700–1770), English Hebraist. Lyons, who was born in Poland, settled in Cambridge (c. 1732), worked as a silversmith, and became an authorized teacher of Hebrew at the university. He contributed Hebrew verses to the volume of elegies (1738) on the funeral of Queen Caroline and published *The Scholar's Instructor, or Hebrew Grammar* (1735; many subsequent editions) and *Observations Relating to Various Parts of Scripture History* (1768). His son ISRAEL LYONS (1739–1775) was an astronomer, botanist, explorer, and mathematician. At the age of 19 he published *A Treatise on Fluxions* (1758), and *a Fasciculus Plantarum circa Cantabrigiam Nascentium* (1763). In 1773 he was appointed principal astronomer to the expedition of Captain Phipps to the North Pole. Lyons appears in a most flattering light in Maria Edgeworth's novel, *Harrington* (1817).

BIBLIOGRAPHY: H.P. Stokes, *Studies in Anglo-Jewish History* (1913), 224–6; C. Roth, *Rise of Provincial Jewry* (1950), 42–44; Roth, Mag Bib, index. **ADD. BIBLIOGRAPHY:** ODNB online.

[Cecil Roth]

LYONS, JACQUES JUDAH (1813–1877), *ḥazzan*, rabbi, and communal leader. Lyons was born in Surinam. He served as a *ḥazzan* of Congregation Neve Shalom in Paramaribo (1833–37). Immigrating to the United States, he served for two years as *ḥazzan* of Congregation Beth Shalom of Richmond, Virginia, and in 1839 began his ministry at the oldest Jewish congregation in the United States, the Spanish-Portuguese congregation Shearith Israel of New York City. Lyons, who was unyielding in his orthodoxy, served as superintendent of the Polonies Talmud Torah School attached to his congregation, as president of Hebra Hased va-Emet, the congregation's benevolent society, and as a director of the Sampson Simson Theological Fund, and was a founder of the Jews' Hospital. Lyons and Abraham *de Sola of Montreal prepared and published *A Jewish Calendar for Fifty Years* (1854), including an essay on the Jewish calendar system and historical data about Jewish communities in the United States, Canada, and the West Indies. From before 1861 to the end of his life, Lyons gathered data and sources on the history of the Jews of the U.S. Although he died before completing the work, this collection was donated to and calendared by the American Jewish Historical Society (see bibl.) and is a most significant source for students of early North American Jewish history.

Lyons is memorialized in the poem "Rosh Ha-Shanah, 5638" by his niece Emma *Lazarus.

BIBLIOGRAPHY: AJHSP, 21 (1913), xxiii–xxviii; 27 (1920), 144–9; D. and T. de Sola Pool, *An Old Faith in the New World: Portrait of Shearith Israel, 1654–1954* (1955), 178–82.

[Isidore S. Meyer]

LYONS, SIR JOSEPH (1848–1917), English caterer and founder of J. Lyons and Company. Lyons was born in London, educated in a Jewish school, and started his career as a watercolor painter, exhibiting at the Royal Institute. In 1887 he joined Alfred *Salmon, the brothers Montague, and Isidore *Gluckstein in founding the catering firm of J. Lyons and Company, of which he became the chairman. This concern began by catering at exhibitions, and in 1894 opened the first of many tea shops. It pioneered popular catering and developed into the largest catering establishment in Britain. Sir Joseph Lyons was deputy-lieutenant for the County of London. He was knighted in 1911. J. Lyons continued to be one of the best-known chains of cafeterias and tea shops in Britain for most of the 20th century.

BIBLIOGRAPHY: P.H. Emden, *Jews of Britain* (1943), 486–90. **ADD. BIBLIOGRAPHY:** ODNB online; DBB, 3, 888–89; S. Aris, *The Jews in Business* (1970), index.

LYONS, LEONARD (1906–1976), U.S. newspaper columnist. Born in New York, Lyons practiced as a lawyer while writing a column for the English-language section of the *Jewish Daily Forward*. In 1934 he started his popular column, "The Lyons Den," in the *New York Post*. For 40 years, Lyons churned out six columns a week, chronicling the activities of celebrities and important figures in all walks of life and all ranks up to the White House. His column was syndicated in more than 100 newspapers in the U.S. and abroad. His personal policy of focusing on the positive rather than the scandalous aspects of his subjects' lives endeared him to the many public figures he sought to interview. Blending his professional with his personal life, Lyons counted among his close friends such luminaries as Alfred Hitchcock, Ernest Hemingway, Ava Gardner, Marlene Dietrich, Orson Welles, Milton Berle, Sofia Loren, and Joe DiMaggio. His son Jeffrey Lyons was a well-known film and theater critic.

[Ruth Beloff (2nd ed.)]

LYOTARD, JEAN-FRANÇOIS (1924–1998), French postmodern and poststructuralist philosopher. Lyotard was a central figure in the theory debates in the last quarter of the 20th century. He combined political activities with an academic career. He was a socialist militant, although later he distanced himself from Marxism as a totalizing theory. He was active in the cause of Algerian liberation, and supported the student revolution of May 1968, when he was at the Philosophy Department at the University of Paris X, Nanterre. Lyotard held several university positions before becoming professor of philosophy at the University of Paris VIII, Vincennes. He was active in the Collège International de la Philosophie, with Jacques *Derrida, and also served as visiting professor in various American universities.

Work

Following his early interest in phenomenology (*La Phénoménologie*, 1954), Lyotard became critical towards his earlier work in *Discours, figure* (1971), preferring psychoanalysis to phenomenology. He also criticized Marxism and structuralism, including the psychoanalysis of Lacan, in the name of a "libidinal economy" (*Economie libidinale*, 1974). The publication of *Au juste* and *La Condition postmoderne*, both published in 1979, and foremost *Le Différend* (1984), represent further milestones in his thought.

La Condition postmoderne is the first philosophical essay in which the terms "postmodern" and "postmodernity" are keywords, expressing the idea of the incredibility of meta-narratives. For Lyotard, science does not justify itself; accordingly, it needs narratives, which in turn endow scientific knowledge with coherence and direction.

Lyotard was deeply suspicious of theories purporting to tell "the truth" about something. His thought had many political and social consequences. In characterizing society as "libidinal economy," Lyotard accentuated the role of desire in society. He described reality in terms of energy, feelings, and desires. There are different desires at work in political and social contexts. Lyotard advocated a "libidinal politics" in which a variety of desires would not be destroyed. Totalizing and terrorizing theories would not allow desires to flourish. He further maintained that there is a conflict between truth and justice. If one appeals to general truth in order to realize justice, this is unjust, since one excludes different desires and other views of truth. He argued that the "grand narratives," that present themselves as the comprehensive understanding of humankind and its history, had lost their credibility and failed. He challenged master narratives with the discourse of others and invited the reader to leave the grand narratives. Politics, contrary to what Plato and Aristotle thought, is not the science or art of the good; rather, politicians ought to choose the lesser evil, since other voices are always silenced by political decisions.

Libidinal philosophy thus renounces universal truth and the meta-narratives of science, work, freedom, universal fraternity and history, Marxism, and human emancipation, and uncovers what detached theories seek to keep at a distance. It was modernism's project to realize universality, yet this universality was often conceived as white and European or American. Lyotard did not believe in these narratives of progress and civilization, which culminate in Hegel's vision of history or in F. Fukuyma's ideas concerning the end of history. Lyotard thought that reality is made up of singular events that general theories cannot represent, and he opted for a society with a multiplicity of language games and codes of conduct.

In his work, Lyotard highlighted the role of the non-rational and showed how it differs from intelligible structure. In his critique of Lacan, for instance, he discloses how desire as a non-linguistic force is more than what is understood in the structuralist understanding of the unconscious as a symbolic system. In Lyotard's mind, Auschwitz counters Hegel's thesis that reality and rationality are reversible, in other words, that the deeper structure of reality is rational. Lyotard maintained that, in the Hegelian perspective, Auschwitz would be an accidental, irrational event that does not prevent history from becoming more and more rational. For Lyotard, the event of Auschwitz itself contradicts Hegel's thesis that reality conforms to a rational structure.

There is a clear influence of Emmanuel *Levinas in Lyotard's writings; for instance, both thinkers oppose totalization. But their philosophies are also very different, if only for the fact that Lyotard contrasts ethics and politics.

Lyotard and the "Jew"

Building upon Freud's thinking, Lyotard writes on the unforgettable that is always forgotten. He emphasizes the "forgotten" and defines real history as "anamnesis" (recollection). The "jew," which Lyotard wrote in lower case and between quotation marks, would represent the repressed, which is the object of psychoanalysis as *"la recherche du temps perdu"* (in search of lost time). The "jew," to whom Lyotard attributes a symbolic meaning, is the name that the West has given to its own unconscious anguish; the "jew" is linked to the disturbing Law and is not to be assimilated to others. Freud, Benjamin, Adorno, Arendt, and Celan would be great non-German Germans and non-Jewish Jews, stateless persons who, in their ethical life, detest geo-philosophy and are always linked to what brings a person out of the sameness, in contact with otherness. Lyotard developed a critical thinking concerning Martin Heidegger's ontology that lacks ethics. In his eyes, Freud belonged to those persons who knew that ethics is not linked to a place. On the background of Lyotard's thoughts of the crisis of the great ideals and of all unifying thinking, the "jews," who hold high the prohibition of making idols, are not to be distilled in a dubious all-encompassing, universal world history that does not distinguish between ideal and reality.

BIBLIOGRAPHY: A. Benjamin (ed.), *The Lyotard Reader* (1989); idem, *Judging Lyotard* (1992); G. Bennington, *Lyotard. Writing the Event* (1988); G. Gutting, *French Philosophy in the Twentieth Century* (2001), 318–31; W. James, *Lyotard: Towards a Postmodern Philosophy* (1998); idem, *Lyotard and the Political* (2000); V.E. Taylor and G. Lambert (eds.), *J.-F. Lyotard. Critical Evaluations in Cultural Theory*, 3 volumes (2005).

[Ephraim Meir (2nd ed.)]

°**LYSANIAS** (d. c. 36 B.C.E.), son of Ptolemy (son of Mennaeus), king of Chalcis in the region of the Lebanon. On the death of his father (c. 40 B.C.E.), Lysanias inherited the principality of Chalcis and continued to support the Hasmonean prince, Antigonus, in the latter's attempt to oust the house of Herod from Judea. To this end Lysanias induced the Parthian satrap of Syria, Barzapharnes, to restore Antigonus to his throne, offering the Parthian 1,000 talents and 500 women (cf. Jos., Wars 1:248; according to Jos., Ant. 14:331 the offer was made by Antigonus himself). The ensuing Parthian conquest of Judea (40 B.C.E.) was short-lived, and with the defeat of the Parthians Lysanias lost his kingdom, which was presented by Mark Antony to the Egyptian queen Cleopatra (37–36 B.C.E.). Lysanias was subsequently accused by Cleopatra of supporting the anti-Roman invasion, and was executed by order of Antony.

BIBLIOGRAPHY: Schuerer, Gesch, 4 (1911[4]), 75 (index), s.v.

[Isaiah Gafni]

°**LYSIAS** (d. 162 B.C.E.), Syrian general during the Hasmonean War. When in the spring of 165 B.C.E. Antiochus IV went on an expedition to the east he appointed Lysias ruler of the western sector of the Seleucid empire, from the Euphrates to the border of Egypt. Lysias was charged, among other things, with the care of the heir apparent and the crushing of the revolt of Judah Maccabee during the emperor's absence (I Macc. 3:31–37). Lysias accordingly sent an army under *Gorgias against Judah, but the defeat of Gorgias in the battle of Emmaus compelled him to march in person against Judea. According to I Maccabees (though some scholars cast doubt on the veracity of this account) fortune did not favor Lysias, and as a result of his failure the persecutions were abolished and a general amnesty proclaimed by Antiochus IV. On the death of Antiochus shortly afterward, Lysias became regent and de facto ruler of the empire, in the name of Antiochus V who was a minor. Judah's attempt to capture the *Acra compelled Lysias to come again to Judea, this time with a large army, and accompanied by the king. At the battle of Bet Zekharyah (163 B.C.E.) the Syrians gained the upper hand and Lysias besieged Judah and his followers who had fortified themselves within the Temple. He was, however, forced to raise the siege in order to fight against Philip, who had been appointed heir by Antiochus before his death. Lysias, whose influence with the young king was paramount, made peace with Judah and in addition to rescinding the edicts, restored the Temple to the Jews. The evidence in II Maccabees 11 completes the general picture and confirms Lysias' willingness to pacify the Jews not only by military means but also by rescinding the decrees and restoring religious freedom. When Demetrius I was appointed to the Syrian throne, Lysias was put to death.

BIBLIOGRAPHY: Schuerer, Hist., 31f., 36–39.

[Uriel Rappaport]

°LYSIMACHUS OF ALEXANDRIA (of uncertain date), author of several mythographical works and a book on Egypt. In addition to the scurrilous versions of the Exodus given by *Manetho and *Chaeremon, Josephus adds the account of Lysimachus, who, he says, "surpasses both in the incredibility of his fictions" (Apion, 1:304–20). According to Lysimachus' version, in the reign of Bocchoris (perhaps a corruption of *bekhor,* in allusion to the plague of the first-born during which the Jews left Egypt), king of Egypt, the Jews (see also *Tacitus, *Historiae*, 5:3), afflicted with leprosy and scurvy, took refuge in the temples. A dearth ensued throughout Egypt, and an oracle of Ammon informed the king that the failure of the crops could be averted only by purging the temples of impure persons, driving them out into the wilderness and drowning those afflicted with leprosy. After the lepers had been drowned, the others, numbering 110,600 were exposed in the desert to perish. A certain Moses, however, advised them to proceed until they reached inhabited country, instructing them to show goodwill to no man, to offer not the best but the worst advice, and to overthrow any temples which they found. When they came to the country now called Judea, they built a town called Hierosyla ("town of temple-robbers"). At a later date they altered the name to avoid reproach and called the city Hierosolyma. Josephus attempts to refute the account, not by offering other evidence, but by showing its intrinsic improbability.

BIBLIOGRAPHY: A. Gudeman, in: Pauly-Wissowa, 27 (1928), 32–39; Reinach, Textes, 117–20; Schuerer, Gesch, 3 (1909[4]), 535f.

[David Winston]

LYUBESHOV (Pol. **Lubieszów**; Yid. **Libeshey**), ḥasidic dynasty established in Lithuanian Polesie in the early 19th century, originating in Volhynia. Its founder, SHEMARIAH WEINGARTEN (d. 1846), was the son of Abraham Abba-Joseph of Soroca (Soroki) and son-in-law of the celebrated Volhynian *ẓaddik* David ha-Levi of Stepan. His leadership was acknowledged in Pinsk, *Kobrin, Lyubeshov, Janow, Telekhany, Motol, and Khomsk, among other places. Shemariah, who was also a scholar, was given a special right to the rabbinate in Kobrin and the surrounding villages, a unique case in the annals of Ḥasidism in Lithuania. The establishment of the dynasty helped to spread Ḥasidism in this part of Polesie. Shemariah's successor in Lyubeshov was his son JEHIEL MICHAEL, and later, his other son ABRAHAM ABBA (d. 1861), who served as rabbi of the nearby town of Janow and in Lyubeshov. At that time the influence of the Lyubeshov dynasty, especially in Kobrin, passed to the ḥasidic "court" of Kobrin. After Abraham Abba's death, his son ḤAYYIM ISAAC served as *ẓaddik* from 1861 to 1879, and his grandson JACOB LOEB from 1879 to 1922. In 1886 the second son of Ḥayyim Isaac, ABBA (d. c. 1924), served as *ẓaddik* in Janow, which caused a split among the Lyubeshov Ḥasidim. The successor of Jacob Loeb in Lyubeshov was his son ISAAC AARON, who lived in Pinsk and gathered around him the Lyubeshov Ḥasidim. Between the two world wars he visited his Ḥasidim in the U.S. He and his followers perished during the Holocaust.

It was characteristic of Lyubeshov Ḥasidim that their *ẓaddikim* served as rabbis of towns in Lithuania (Kobrin, Janow, and Lyubeshov). Essentially it was a branch of the Volhynian Ḥasidism. Their *ẓaddikim* left no written works. An important principle of Lyubeshov Ḥasidim was the holiness of the *ẓaddik*. They opposed fasting, emphasized the virtue of joy, and had their own melodies. They were concerned with settlement in Ereẓ Israel and during the 19th century set up a Lyubeshov **kolel* there.

BIBLIOGRAPHY: W.Z. Rabinowitsch, *Lithuanian Ḥasidism* (1970), index.

[Wolf Zeev Rabinowitsch]

LYUBOML (Pol. **Luboml**), city in Volhynia district, Ukraine. Jews are mentioned in documents in the years 1370–82. Under King Sigismund II Augustus in 1557 they obtained a privilege which freed them from any jurisdiction except that of the governor of the province, and guaranteed them the right of appeal to the king. In 1558 the community prohibited the Jews from buying houses and land within the city walls from gentiles, fearing that Jewish homes might be set on fire or the Jews expelled. King Michael Wiśniowiecki confirmed the privileges of Lyuboml Jewry in 1671. In the 1670s a synagogue in a fortress style was erected, to be part of city defense fortifications. The poll tax of 1721 amounted to 833 zlotys, but because of a fire which destroyed much Jewish property in 1729 it was reduced to 544 zlotys; 1,226 poll tax paying Jews then lived in Lyuboml and the settlements under the community's jurisdiction. In 1847, 2,130 Jews lived in the city, and by 1897 there were 3,297 (73% of the total population). In 1921 there were 3,141 Jews (94% of the total population), in 1931 3,807 (of 4,169 total population) in the city of Lyuboml. Most of the small traders and artisans were Jews, and they owned the flour mills, and the trade in farm productions. There were two Hebrew Tarbut schools, one Yavne religious school, and a small yeshivah.

[*Encyclopaedia Judaica* (Germany)]

Holocaust Period

Before the outbreak of World War II there were about 3,500 Jews in Lyuboml. The German army entered the town on Sept. 17, 1939, but according to the German-Soviet agreement, it withdrew after three days when the Red Army entered the town. The economy was nationalized, all Jewish organizations and institutions were closed, and one Yiddish school with a Soviet curriculum remained. The Germans occupied the town on June 25, 1941, and some of the 500 Jews who had been drafted into the Red Army were caught and executed. On July 22, 400 men were murdered, and on August 21 another 400 were killed, mostly women. On December 5, 1941, Jews were herded into a ghetto with a density of up to 20 persons per room. For a week from Oct. 1, 1942, the ghetto inmates were murdered – on the first day about 1,800 Jews were killed. There were groups who tried to escape, but only 30 succeeded in reaching the forests, and joined Soviet or Polish partisan units. After the war, the Jewish community of Lyuboml was not reconstituted.

BIBLIOGRAPHY: Halpern, Pinkas, index; B. Wasiutyński, *Ludność żydowska w Polsce…* (1930), 84; M. Balaban, in: *Yevreyskaya Starina*, 3 (1910), 189; *Yalkut Vohlin*, 16–17 (1953), 60–62. **ADD. BIBLIOGRAPHY:** S. Spektor (ed.), *Pinkas ha-Kehillot, Poland*, vol. 5, *Volhynia and Polesie* (1990).

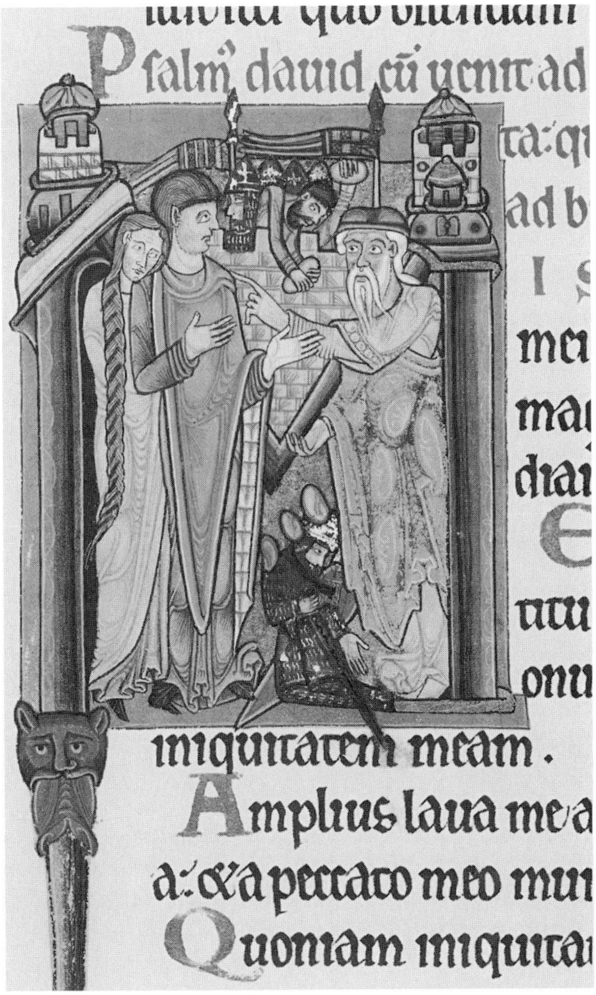

Initial letter for the word Misere mei, *"Have mercy upon me," at the beginning of Psalm 51 (Vulgate Ps. 50) from the 12th-century* Psalter of York. *Seen here are David, with Bath-Sheba behind him, being admonished by Nathan. Uriah the Hittite lies dead, stoned by an Ammonite. Copenhagen, Royal Library, Thott, 143, fol. 68r.*

MA-MEK

MAACAH (Heb. מַעֲכָה),

(1) one of David's wives, daughter of Talmai King of Geshur, mother of Absalom (II Sam. 3:3; I Chron. 3:2);

(2) one of Rehoboam's wives, daughter of *Absalom or Abisalom son of David, mother of Abijam or Abijah (I Kings 15:2; II Chron. 11:20, 22) and Asa (I Kings 15:11; II Chron. 15:16).

The references to the second Maacah pose certain problems, as a literal reading of all the passages related to her indicates that she is the daughter of Absalom, who, according to II Samuel 14:27, had only one daughter, Tamar. The above references also indicate that Maacah is the mother of Abijah. According to II Chronicles 13:2 (MT), Abijah's mother is Micaiah, daughter of Uriel. Finally the references show Maacah also to be the mother of Asa.

In order to resolve these contradictions, the Masoretic Text of II Chronicles 13:2 must be corrected in accordance with the Septuagint, which reads "Maacah daughter of Uriel." (Everywhere else in the Masoretic Text as well as in the Septuagint Abijah's mother is called Maacah daughter of Absalom.) With this correction the problems are more easily resolved. Maacah is then the granddaughter of Absalom, the daughter of Uriel and Tamar, the mother of Abijah, and the grandmother of Asa. Some of the original confusion results from the fact that the Bible often used the term "children" for "grandchildren" and even descendants who are generations removed (cf. Gen. 31:28; I Kings 15:11, et al.).

W. Rudolph (see bibl.) adopts the view of M. Noth (see bibl.) that II Chronicles 13:2 represents the original text of I Kings 15:2 which is now influenced by I Kings 15:10. Then Abijah would be the son of Rehoboam's wife Micaiah daughter of Uriel, and Asa the son of Abijah's wife Maacah, who would have been the literal daughter of an unknown Absalom, not the granddaughter of David's son Absalom. King Asa deposed Maacah from being queen mother because of an abominable image she had made for Asherah (I Kings 15:13). S. Yeivin maintains that Maacah is Abijah's mother, while Micaiah daughter of Uriel is Asa's mother, and that Asa is Rehoboam's son, and Abijah's half brother.

BIBLIOGRAPHY: S. Yeivin, in: BJPES, 10 (1943), 116–9; M. Noth, *Überlieferungsgeschichtliche Studien* (1943), 143; W. Rudolph, *Chronikbücher* (1955), 231–3; EM, 5 (1968), 193–4 (incl. bibl.). **ADD. BIBLIOGRAPHY:** S. Japhet, *I & II Chronicles* (1993), 670–72; M. Cogan, I *Kings* (AB; 2000), 392–93.

MA'AGAN MIKHA'EL (Heb. מַעֲגַן מִיכָאֵל; "Michael's Anchorage"), kibbutz on the seashore of Israel at the southern end of the Carmel Coast, affiliated with Ha-Kibbutz ha-Me'uḥad. Ma'agan Mikha'el was founded in 1949 by the first group of graduates of the Israel boy scout movement, who were later joined by immigrants from different countries. In 1969 Ma'agan Mikha'el had 665 inhabitants. By 2002 the number had increased to 1,290. Its economy was based on fruit plantations, crops, livestock, carp ponds, software, and an injection molding plant for plastic products. A nature reserve is located at Ma'agan Mikha'el, at the split mouth of the Tanninim ("crocodiles") River. The reserve, rich in water fowl, comprises the Yonim ("doves") islet in the sea and the former Kabāra swamps which were drained by the *Palestine Jewish Colonization Association (PICA), and hosts many migratory birds. Prehistoric finds were made in the nearby Kabāra caves. The name of the kibbutz commemorates Mikhael Pollak, a director of PICA.

WEBSITE: maaganm.kibbutz.org.il.

[Efraim Orni]

MA'ALEH ADUMIM (Heb. מַעֲלֵה אֲדֻמִּים), city located east of Jerusalem, on the Jericho road. Ma'aleh Adumim was founded in 1977 by Israelis and new immigrants. The city is located on land occupied by Israel during the Six-Day War, spreading over 20 sq. mi. (50 sq. km.). Various Israeli governments have avowed that Ma'aleh Adumim will remain part of Israel in any peace settlement. In 2002 the population of the city reached 26,500, growing at the high rate of 2.9% annually. The majority of the population works in nearby Jerusalem, while some are employed in the industrial area of the city.

[Shaked Gilboa (2nd ed.)]

MA'ALEH AKRABBIM (Heb. מַעֲלֵה עַקְרַבִּים; JPS, "ascent of Akrabbim"; "ascent of the scorpions"), locality mentioned several times in the Bible as being at the southern boundary of the Promised Land. According to Numbers 34:4, the border started "at the end of the Salt [Dead] Sea eastward" and turned south of Ma'aleh Akrabbim, continuing toward the "wilderness of Zin"; the account in Joshua 15:3 is similar. The border of the Amorites apparently ran from Ma'aleh Akrabbim, "from Sela, and upward" (Judg. 1:36). Abel identified it with Naqb al-Ṣafi to the west of the Arabah, while Mazar locates it to the east, on the road to Sela. The Akrabattine of I Maccabees 5:3 apparently refers to the district of Acraba to the north of Jerusalem.

Ma'aleh Akrabbim is now the name of a section of a road to Eilat that snakes down into the canyon of Naḥal Ẓin, about 2½ mi. (4 km.) west of the "Small Crater" (Makhtesh ha-Katan). Until the road to Eilat that passes through Ma'aleh ha-Aẓma'ut by Miẓpeh Ramon was built, all traffic to Eilat passed through Ma'aleh Akrabbim. The spot is an excellent lookout point over Naḥal Ẓin and the Arabah.

BIBLIOGRAPHY: Abel, Geog, 2 (1938), 46–47; W.J. Phythian-Adams, in: PEFQS, 65 (1933), 143ff.; EM, 5 (1968), 195f.

[Michael Avi-Yonah]

MA'ALEH HA-ḤAMISHAH (Heb. מַעֲלֵה הַחֲמִשָּׁה, "Ascent of the Five"), kibbutz in the Judean Hills, 8 mi. (13 km.) W. of Jerusalem, affiliated to Iḥud ha-Kevuẓot ve-ha-Kibbutzim, founded in 1938 as a *stockade and watchtower settlement by pioneers of the Gordonia youth movement from Lodz, Poland. In the weeks before setting up their village, the group, then living at nearby Kiryat Anavim, worked in reclaiming the site and planting forests. Arab terrorists killed five members of the group in an ambush. The name of the new kibbutz was chosen to commemorate them. In the Israeli *War of Independence (1948), it held out in its advanced position against the Arab Legion, which had taken possession of the nearby "Radar Camp." Until the *Six-Day War, the armistice border passed close by. On the evening of June 5, 1967, Israel forces launched an attack from the kibbutz on the Radar Camp, thereby opening the operations which eventually brought all of Jerusalem and Judea-Samaria under Israel control. The kibbutz economy was based on deciduous fruit orchards and vineyards, dairy cattle and poultry, on a sweets and confectionery factory, a large rest home, and a public swimming pool. Extensive forests were planted in the vicinity. Its population in 1968 was 290. By the mid-1990s, the population had expanded to approximately 480, but in by 2002 it had dropped to 347 inhabitants, with the economy based mainly on the rest home and other branches liquidated.

WEBSITE: www.inisrael.com/maale5/index.html

[E.O. / Shaked Gilboa (2nd ed.)]

MA'ALOT-TARSHĪḤĀ (Heb. מַעֲלוֹת־תַּרְשִׁיחָה; "Heights"), urban community in western Upper Galilee, 12 mi. (20 km.) E. of Nahariyyah, founded in 1957, to replace two *ma'barot* in the vicinity. In 1963 Ma'alot was united with the Arab village Tarshīḥā lying over 1 mile (2 km.) further west. Tarshīḥā was a center of western Galilee, and antiquities found in its vicinity date back to the Roman and Byzantine periods. In the Israeli *War of Independence, Tarshīḥā served as the headquarters of the Arab "Liberation Army" under Fawzi Kaukji until it was taken by Israel forces in Operation Ḥiram on Oct. 30, 1948. In 1965 a municipal council was set up in Ma'alot-Tarshīḥā. Although several industrial enterprises (textile, plastic, food, and building material) existed at Ma'alot in 1969, its economy was not yet firmly established due to the high percentage of welfare cases and the inadequacy of a local labor force. Tarshīḥā's economic situation was far better, as many of its inhabitants were employed as skilled laborers in the Nahariyyah and Haifa areas or maintained lucrative farmsteads. In 1969 the town had 4,750 inhabitants including 3,160 Jews in Ma'alot, the majority of whom originated from North African countries, and 1,590 Arabs at Tarshīḥā, some Muslim and some Christian. Ma'alot was the target of an early terrorist attack, in May 1974, when 21 schoolchildren were killed. In the mid-1990s, the population was approximately 12,800, rising to 20,650 in 2002, including 80% Jews, 9% Muslims, 10% Christians, and 1% Druzes. In 1996 Ma'alot-Tarshiḥa received city status. Its area is 2.7 sq. mi. (7 sq. km.). During the 1990s, the economic base of the city was expanded by the addition of 100 factories and workshops, but income remained well below the national average. From 1992 Ma'alot-Tarshiḥa has hosted the International Symposium for Stone Sculpturing.

WEBSITE: www.maltar.org.il.

[Efraim Orni / Shaked Gilboa (2nd ed.)]

MA'AMAD or **MAHAMAD**, council of elders in a Sephardi community or congregation in the West after the expulsion from Spain, corresponding to the *kahal (in the sense of the supreme community council) in Ashkenazi communities. Schooled by bitter memories of the crisis in Spain on the eve of the expulsion, the policy of the *ma'amad* tended to be conservative and authoritarian in the extreme. One of the characteristic features of *ma'amad* policy was that on completion of its term of office the *ma'amad* itself appointed its successors. A nominee was obliged to accept the assignment. Those who disobeyed the directives of the *ma'amad* were fined heavily, and in some cases were even excommunicated.

BIBLIOGRAPHY: Baron, Community, 2 (1942), 52.

[Natan Efrati]

MA'ANIT (Heb. מַעֲנִית; "Furrow"), kibbutz in central Israel, E. of Pardes Ḥannah, affiliated with Kibbutz Arẓi Ha-Shomer ha-Ẓa'ir. It was founded in 1942 by pioneers from Czechoslovakia. In the Israel *War of Independence (1948), the village, lying close to the Samarian Hills, was exposed to Arab attack. Ma'anit engaged in intensive farming (field crops, avocado plantations, citrus groves, and dairy cattle), and operated Galam, the country's leading fructose, glucose, and starch manufacturer for industrial and consumer use. In the mid-1990s, the population was approximately 550, dropping to 459 in 2002. Ma'anit lies near the site of ancient *Narbata where, in 66 C.E., Jews from Caesarea sought refuge when the war against Rome broke out (Jos., Wars, 2:5, 14). In its initial years, the kibbutz bore the name Narbata.

[Efraim Orni]

MA'ARAVOT (Heb. מַעֲרָבוֹת, also *ma'aravim*, sing. מַעֲרָבִית *ma'aravit*), an arrangement of *piyyutim* that embellish the *Ma'ariv* (*Arvit) prayers for festivals and special Sabbaths. The *piyyutim* are topical and conclude with an allusion to all the blessings recited before the *Amidah. Originally these *piyyutim* were used in place of the regular prayers, but in the course of time the regular prayers were reinstated and the *piyyutim* were offered at the end of each prayer just before its blessing. Except for the lengthy *piyyut* recited before *Mi Khamokha* ("Who is like Thee"), the *piyyutim* are brief. This lengthy *piyyut* is composed in the form of a single or double alphabetical acrostic with the name of the author appearing at the end. Some communities customarily added a *reshut* ("prelude") to the *Ma'ariv*. On the eve of Shavuot, *Tosefet Bikkur* ("Addition of First Fruit") or simply *Bikkur*, a *piyyut* whose subject is the bringing of the first fruits, is recited. The *ma'aravot* are in current usage in most Ashkenazi communities, but there are no *ma'aravot* in the Sephardi rite.

BIBLIOGRAPHY: Elbogen, Gottesdienst, 212; Idelsohn, Liturgy, 194, 330f.

[Abraham Meir Habermann]

MA'AREKHET HA-ELOHUT (Heb. מַעֲרֶכֶת הָאֱלֹהוּת; "The Order of God"), an anonymous systematic book of early Kabbalah literature. Moses Cordovero attributed it to Todros *Abulafia while Jacob Reifmann believed the author to be *Baḥya b. Asher. In the first edition, published in Ferrara in 1557, the book is attributed to *Perez the tosafist, but no author is named on the title page of the Mantua edition of 1558. The annotator remarks in his preface that "it is written that the author is the *Gaon* Perez the tosafist, but the truth is not known." There is no doubt whatsoever that the book cannot be ascribed to any of these writers. It was written at the end of the 13th or the beginning of the 14th century by a man who associated with the disciples of Solomon b. Abraham *Adret, in whose name and that of the kabbalist R. Isaac (probably Adret's colleague Isaac b. Todros), the author introduces some kabbalistic interpretations. There is reason to believe that he made use of *Keter Shem Tov* by Shem Tov (b. Abraham) ibn Gaon, which was written around that time.

Because of its systematic nature, *Ma'arekhet ha-Elohut* became one of the classical books of Kabbalah. The many commentaries on it, most of which were composed in Italy in the 15th and early 16th centuries, show the great interest it aroused. About ten commentaries were written, two of which were printed: the anonymous commentary which Judah *Ḥayyat called "*Paz*" (*Perush Zulati*, "commentary not by me"), and the commentary written by Judah Ḥayyat at the request of the elders of Mantua. The identity of the first commentator has not been established; recently it has become apparent that he was probably Reuben Ẓarefati, author of *Perush ha-Yeri'ah ha-Gedolah* and *Perush ha-Yeri'ah ha-Ketannah*. According to Judah Ḥayyat, and, as indicated by the many extant manuscripts, this commentary circulated widely in Italy during the late 15th century. "*Paz*" was printed in full in Ferrara and in a considerably abridged version in the Mantua edition (1558). The two commentaries are largely independent works and in their thematic discussions they go beyond the framework of a commentary. The systematic analysis of *Ma'arekhet ha-Elohut* by David Neumark (see bibl.) contributes very little to the understanding of the work, and Neumark's belief that it exerted a great influence on the Zohar is chronologically impossible and conceptually incorrect.

In general, the author's main aim was to remove, or at least weaken, the mythical elements which are basic in the Kabbalah and in certain rabbinic sayings. The author's theosophical tendency is not made apparent in the first two chapters, which are essentially theological and do not constitute a consistent theory. The author's purpose in the first chapter is to indicate that true faith is based on the concept of a personal God, the Creator of the world and its supervisor. God acts in the world and He can alter the laws of nature, as proven by the miracles related in the Bible. The second chapter, however, stresses the absolute unity of God, which is based on the denial of any corporeality, plurality, or change within Him. In God there is neither modification of thought nor of action. There is no change in Him and none in His deeds. The changes revealed by worldly events are caused by the actions of man. Man is a vessel which contains God's action, which is simple and undifferentiated but is received differently by different people, each one according to his merit.

The author's theosophical speculations first appear in the third chapter. The Divinity is here defined as the totality of the ten *Sefirot*, which constitute God's direction of the world. This aspect of God alone is expressed in the Bible and Talmud while the Divinity Itself, referred to as *Ein-Sof* ("infinity"), is hinted at only to initiates. *Ein-Sof*, the infinite, the hidden aspect of the Divine, is expressed neither through the order of nature nor in the laws of the Torah. The act of emanation itself, which is the emergence of the *Sefirot* from *Ein-Sof*, does not constitute an innovation or a change in the Divine: it is simply the revelation of what had been hitherto concealed. The author attempts to explain through reasoning and homily that both the legends of the rabbis on the modification in God's thought regarding the ways in which the world should be conducted and the description of the dynamic relations among the diverse *Sefirot* in Kabbalah literature are simply a projection of human experience upon Divinity. Because it is observable in human experience that man decides on the most desirable alternative by a process of choice and deliberation, he therefore ascribes to divine leadership an ideal synthesis of Justice and Mercy, as if it resulted from a similar process. In a similar manner, he expounds the aggadic legend concern ing the waning of the moon which the kabbalists related to an act occurring in the world of the *Sefirot*; other legends are also given a kabbalistic interpretation.

The chapter entitled "*Sha'ar ha-Harisah*" (about the nature of sin) is of particular interest. According to this, the sins related in the Bible as committed by individuals or generations are essentially sins of a mystical character. Though the sin was actually committed, its essential significance lies in the thought connected with it. In some instances the sin is brought about by an excess of meditation, while in others it results from the sinner's wish to disrupt the pattern of relationship of the *Sefirot*. Most of these themes had already appeared in earlier kabbalistic literature but here they are given a systematic description, and the book is also a systematic summary of most themes treated in early Kabbalah literature.

BIBLIOGRAPHY: D. Neumark, *Toledot ha-Filosofyah be-Yisrael*, 1 (1921), 192–206; G. Scholem, in: KS, 21 (1943/44), 284–95; Scholem, Mysticism, index; E. Gottlieb, *Ha-Kabbalah be-Khitvei Rabbenu Baḥya ben Asher* (1970), index; idem, in: *Sefer Zikkaron le-Binyamin De Vries* (1968), 295–304.

[Efraim Gottlieb]

MAARIV, Israeli daily newspaper published in Tel Aviv. *Maariv* was founded in February 1948 by journalists who had left **Yedioth Aharonoth* following disagreements with its proprietor. The group, led by Dr. Azriel *Carlebach, who became the editor of *Maariv*, included Aryeh *Dissenchik, Shmuel *Schnitzer, Shalom *Rosenfeld, and David Giladi; it sought to create a newspaper run as a journalistic cooperative. Sixty percent of the paper's equity and 50% of its voting shares were held by journalists. Requiring extra-journalistic financial backing, they turned to investor Oved Ben Ami. Although the cooperative-style journalistic management strengthened motivation through participation it created a cumbersome editorial decision-making process – which eventually contributed to *Maariv*'s losing its position as the country's largest selling newspaper to *Yedioth Aharonoth*. Originally the newspaper appeared in the late afternoon, but, like *Yedioth Aharonoth*, over the years it began appearing earlier in the day so that by the 1980s it had become a morning newspaper in all but name. The editorial board reflected a spectrum of political views, if mostly to the right. Until the 1980s, the newspaper was regarded as a mid-market newspaper, catering to a broad readership, with serious in-depth coverage of changing events, but without the intellectual stuffiness which characterized some of the morning daily press. After Carlebach died in 1956, he was replaced by Aryeh Dissenchik, whose wide connections in the political establishment brought the newspaper a slew of exclusive reports. But after Dissenchik's death in 1974, and his replacement by Shalom Rosenfeld, the paper's circulation declined, dropping still further when Shmuel Schnitzer, the paper's widely read columnist, succeeded Rosenfeld in turn. The paper's somewhat paternalistic and patriotic style failed to keep up with the country's changing political mood in the 1970s, and lacked appeal to younger people and the rising Sephardi class. In a vain attempt to halt the circulation decline, Iddo Dissenchik, son of Aryeh Dissenchik, was appointed editor in 1985. A graduate of the Columbia School of Journalism, Dissenchik had previously been a news editor on the paper and its foreign correspondent in the United States. He introduced a number of changes, including new supplements. But in order to inject further capital into the paper, 87% of its stock was sold to Robert *Maxwell, the British media mogul, who, in turn, appointed Dov *Yudkovsky, who since 1989 had represented Maxwell's Israeli interests, as editor. A $25 million full-color printing press was purchased. After Maxwell died in 1992 the newspaper was bought by arms dealer Yaacov *Nimrodi, who gave his son, Ofer, responsibility for the newspaper. At the time of Maxwell's death, the newspaper had accumulated debts of $40 million and its circulation was 90,000 daily and 200,000 on weekends as against *Yedioth Aharonoth*'s 295,000 daily and 350,000 on weekends. Dan *Margalit, *Maariv*'s op-ed editor, served briefly as editor, a post which Ofer Nimrodi himself filled from 1992 to 1995, when Yaacov Erez, the paper's veteran military correspondent, became editor. In the so-called wiretapping scandal Nimrodi was imprisoned for eight months in 1999 for wiretapping the phones of *Yedioth Aharonoth* publisher Arnon *Mozes and Dov Yudkovsky. Amnon Abramovitch, a *Maariv* investigative reporter, resigned from the newspaper after discovering that his telephone had also been tapped. In 2003 Amnon *Dankner, a *Maariv* columnist who had come to Nimrodi's defense in the wiretapping scandal, was appointed editor. Under Nimrodi, *Maariv* went downmarket in editorial content and layout, but while he succeeded in reducing the gap between *Maariv* and *Yedioth Aharonoth* – 23% of Israelis read *Maariv* daily and 28% on weekends according to a 2005 Teleseker survey – the gap remained. Nimrodi had additional media-related and other commercial interests. In 2004 the newspaper set up an Internet news site, NRG. The newspaper owned a number of magazines, including magazines for youth, and a publishing house, and had developed interests in the cellular phone industry.

BIBLIOGRAPHY: S. Rosenfeld, "The Carlebach Affair and the Establishment of *Maariv*," in: *Kesher*, 30 (Nov. 2001).

[Yoel Cohen (2nd ed.)]

MAARSEN, ISAAC (1893–1943), Dutch rabbi, chief rabbi of The Hague. Maarsen was born in Amsterdam, where he studied at the Amsterdam rabbinical seminary and at the university, graduating in classical philology. He was ordained as rabbi in 1918 and became teacher of Talmud in the high school department of the rabbinical seminary. In 1919 he was appointed a *dayyan* and member of the Amsterdam rabbinate. Five years later he was appointed chief rabbi of The Hague, then the second-largest community in Holland. He excelled chiefly as preacher and lecturer, and in his writings against Reform Judaism. He translated the tractate *Avot* and medieval and modern poetry from Hebrew into Dutch, and engaged in research on the history of the Dutch rabbinate. His reputation rests on his studies in the fields of rabbinical literature, which appeared in various Hebrew periodicals. His main works are *Tiferet le-Moshe* (1928), notes to Naḥmanides' commentary on the Pentateuch; *Parshandata* (1930–36), a critical edition of Rashi's commentary to the Prophets and Hagiographa, which he did not complete, only three parts appearing, on the Minor Prophets, Isaiah, and Psalms; and *Muḥlefet ha-Shitah* (1940), on the difference between Rashi's comments on the Bible and the same verses when quoted in the Talmud. He met his death in the Holocaust.

BIBLIOGRAPHY: *Elleh-Ezkerah*, 1 (1956), 304–8.

[Benjamin De-Vries]

MA'ARUFYA (Aram. מַעֲרוּפְיָא), medieval Hebrew concept signifying the tie between a Christian client and the Jew who was his permanent supplier, moneylender, or financial administrator. The *din ha-ma'arufya* ("law of *ma'arufya*") was never generally prevalent; where it applied it specified that the relationship between the Jewish merchant and his client was the exclusive prerogative of that Jew alone, which the *community (*kehillah*) protected by means of the **ḥerem* (ban). According to some scholars the term derives from the French while others consider that it comes from Arabic. Some scholars have drawn a distinction between the implications of *ma'arufya* and *ma'arifa*, considering that the first denotes a non-Jewish customer who maintains commercial relations with a certain Jew while the second denotes the exclusive right to trade with him. However, this view is untenable since both forms are used indiscriminately.

Ma'arufya was known in the communities of France and Germany in the tenth century. It is possible that this usage originated in the privileges granted to merchants by the municipal councils or lords of various European towns during the 10th and 11th centuries guaranteeing them trading monopolies. From the responsa of *Gershom b. Judah (Me'or ha-Golah), it appears that the *din ha-ma'arufya* was applied in almost every community. However, 11th-century sources indicate that by then the custom was not accepted everywhere: "there are places where the ma'arufya is enforced and there are places where it is not enforced" (Joseph Bonfils (Tuv Elem) in: *Haggahot Maimoniyyot* of Meir ha-Kohen, *Hilkhot Shekhenim*, 6:8). As Jewish business activities were narrowed down to *moneylending in Ashkenazi areas toward the end of the 12th century, *ma'arufya* lost much of its former importance. The *din ha-ma'arufya* is not explicitly recorded in the communities of Spain, although in them too the trend against competition is evident. The essence of *ma'arufya*, and often the term itself, was operative in the communities of Poland-Lithuania and Russia until the modern era. Because of the variety of occupations there, the scope of the concept was applied to give craftsmen and artisans exclusive rights over their customers. The regulations of the crafts' associations included articles intended to assure the established rights of artisans to their clients. If a craftsman had done work for the *ma'arufya* of another craftsman, he was obliged to remit all his profits to him without deducting his own expenses. These rights were bequeathed from father to son, and when there were no heirs the rights were transferred to the dead man's guild.

BIBLIOGRAPHY: I. Levitats, *Jewish Community in Russia* (1943), 235ff.; Sh. Eidelberg, in: HJ, 15 (1953), 59–66; Baron, Social^2, 4 (1957), 185; Dinur, Golah, 1 pt. 1 (1958^2), 382; 2 pt. 2 (1966^2), 250ff.; I. Agus, *Urban Civilization in Pre-Crusade Europe*, 2 vols. (1965), index.

MA'AS (Heb. מַעַשׂ; "Action" or "Deed"), moshav in central Israel, near *Petaḥ Tikvah, affiliated with Tenu'at ha-Moshavim, founded in 1934 in the framework of the Thousand Families Settlement Scheme by veteran agricultural workers. They gradually enlarged their holdings from auxiliary to full-fledged farms while earning their living as hired laborers in the Petaḥ Tikvah citrus groves (therefore calling their village, until the 1950s, Be-Hadragah, "Gradually"). Citrus groves constituted the prominent farm branch in Ma'as. In 1968 its population was 400. By the mid-1990s it had grown to approximately 645, maintaining its size with 667 inhabitants at the end of 2002.

[Efraim Orni]

MA'ASEH (Heb. מַעֲשֶׂה), a factual circumstance from which a halakhic rule or principle is derived; as such it constitutes one of the Jewish law sources. A legal principle originating from *ma'aseh* is formally distinguished from those originating from one of the other legal sources of Jewish law – such as Midrash (see *Interpretation), **takkanah*, **minhag*, and **sevara* (see **Mishpat Ivri*) – by the fact that in the latter cases the legal principle appears in selfstanding form, whereas in *ma'aseh* it is integrated with and bound to a particular set of concrete facts, from which it must be separated and abstracted if it is to be enunciated. As will be seen below, this formal distinction is also of substantive importance. The term *ma'aseh* is customarily used in tannaitic sources (Shab. 24:5; BB 10:8; Eduy. 2:3); in the Babylonian Talmud the equivalent term is *uvda* and in the Jerusalem Talmud sometimes *dilma* (see, e.g., TJ, Ber. 1:1, 2c; Pe'ah 3:9, 17d; et al.).

Substance of *Ma'aseh*

Ma'aseh constitutes a legal source in two ways: one is represented by the judgment given in a concrete "case" before the court or competent adjudicator (halakhic scholar) – as in other legal systems; the other, by the specific act or conduct of a competent halakhic scholar, not necessarily in his capacity as judge or *posek*. In either case *ma'aseh* serves as a source for the determination of a halakhic principle as regards both civil law (*dinei mamonot*) and ritual law (*dinei issur ve-hetter*).

Citation of a halakhic principle by way of *ma'aseh* does not in every case warrant the conclusion that such *ma'aseh* is necessarily the source from which the principle was evolved – since the principle may possibly have been in existence before and the halakhic scholar only having had applied it in such case. In this event, the *ma'aseh* is not constitutive but only declarative of the existence of the particular halakhic rule (see below). However, *ma'aseh* – even when only declarative – lends the particular halakhic principle a special validity, as *ma'aseh rav* ("an act is weightier," Shab. 21a) or *ma'aseh adif* ("an act is preferred," BB 83a), since a rule tested in the crucible of practical life is regarded by the scholars as having a different force from one for which there is no evidence of its practical application. Hence, once a particular halakhic principle has been followed in practice – even though its application is subject to dispute – it may no longer be varied, since "what has been done is no longer open to discussion" (RH 29b, concerning blowing of the *shofar* on Rosh Ha-Shanah when it falls on a Sabbath).

The particular force of a halakhic principle originating from *ma'aseh* is tied to the substantive principle underlying the entire halakhic system, namely that the Torah was entrusted to the authority (*al da'atan*) of the halakhic scholars (see *Authority, Rabbinical; **Mishpat Ivri*), it being presumed that the judicial decision and conduct in daily life of the competent halakhic scholar are the outcome of his penetration and correct understanding of the *halakhah*. The scholars were fully aware of the power attached to an act of deciding the law and for this reason exercised great care before doing so (Git. 19a, 37a, and Rashi thereto). In particular, the halakhic scholar is held to reveal, by his conduct, the active image of the *halakhah* and therefore "the service of the Torah is greater than the study of it" (Ber. 7b); one of the ways by virtue of which the Torah is acquired is "attendance on the sages" (Avot 6:6), since practical application of the Torah leads to appreciation of the living and active *halakhah*, its correctness and creative force. For this reason it was required of the halakhic scholars to act with much forethought in their day-to-day conduct of halakhic matters (Tosef., Dem. 5:24 concerning the discussion between R. Gamaliel and R. Akiva); R. Ishmael explained his particularly careful approach toward a certain rule concerning the *Keri'at Shema* in these words: "lest the pupils see and lay down *halakhah* for generations" (Ber. 11a; Tosef., Ber. 1:6).

In Jewish law, *ma'aseh* constitutes a legal source, not because it has the force of binding precedent which (as will be seen below, the Jewish legal system generally does not recognize as a principle), but because the scholars recognized it as a lawmaking source from which to derive halakhic principles becoming part of the general halakhic system. The fact that it remained permissible to dispute a halakhic principle derived from *ma'aseh* did not serve to deprive it of its substantive character as one of the legal sources of Jewish law – just as, for instance, Midrash remained such notwithstanding the fact that different and contradictory halakhic principles were often derived from it by the use of different methods of Bible exegesis.

An Act of Deciding the Law

The laws derived from *ma'aseh* form a very substantial part of the general system of Jewish law – the latter representing, in its nature and path of development, a classic example of a legal system founded on a series of legal acts or "cases," adding up to a comprehensive system of case law (see also *Codification of Law). This character was already stamped on the *halakhah* in the Torah, in which there are many laws enjoined in relation to a particular act or event, as, e.g., in the matter of the blasphemy of the Name (Lev. 24:10–23), the gathering of sticks on the Sabbath (Num. 15:32–36), the law of inheritance concerning the daughters of Zelophehad (Num. 27:1–11), and the law of the second Passover (Num. 9:1–8).

Talmudic sources are replete with *halakhot*, in all fields of the law, quoted in the form of an act of legal decision or in the form of an independent ruling which is, however, either preceded or followed by the facts of the relevant case. The case described does not always form the original source of the halakhic rule, but frequently, and in various ways, it is possible to prove that the rule was actually created as an outcome of the case. Sometimes this fact is expressly stated. Thus, with reference to the law that a bill of divorce must be prepared by the husband for delivery to his wife, the Mishnah states that it suffices if the bill be prepared by the wife provided that the husband procures the signature of witnesses to it since what matters is the signature and not the person by whom the bill is drawn up (Git. 2:5). This principle was learned from a case that occurred in a small village near Jerusalem, a case in which the scholars decided that it was only necessary for a bond of indebtedness to be signed, and not drawn up, by the witnesses (Eduy. 2:3). Similarly, the *amoraim* derived from earlier cases a number of halakhic principles concerning the laws of proselytization (Yev. 46b) and the laws of restoring a loss (*hashavat avedah*: cf. BM 25b with TJ, BM 2:4, 8c – the rule of Abba b. Zavda).

Sometimes derivation of a halakhic principle from the *ma'aseh* is not expressly acknowledged, but from the content it may be deduced that the principle was derived from the adjacent case description. Thus, according to ancient *halakhah*, suretyship for a loan undertaking was valid only if made prior to establishment of the principal debt, i.e., the creditor as it were agreeing to grant the loan on the strength of such suretyship. However, R. Ishmael, in a case that came before him, extended the scope of suretyship by holding it valid in certain circumstances, even if made after grant of the loan, i.e., if the person standing *surety signed after the signature by the witnesses of the deed of loan. Ben Nanas differed, maintaining that the suretyship had to precede grant of the loan. The new principle enunciated by R. Ishmael is earlier stated in the Mishnah, in the form of a selfstanding legal rule (BB 10:8; for further examples, see Ned. 8:5; BM 30a).

Conduct of a Halakhic Scholar

Talmudic sources also contain a great number of *halakhot*, in all fields of the law, stated in the form of a description of the conduct of a halakhic scholar and in like manner to the statement of acts of legal decision. Thus in one instance the Mishnah (Shab. 24:5) first quotes several *halakhot* concerning permissible labors on the Sabbath in the form of independent rules: "they may stop up a light-hole or measure a piece of stuff or a *mikveh*"; in continuation, it is stated that in the time of R. Zadok's father and in the time of Abba Saul b. Botnit there occurred a case in which such labors were done on the Sabbath and in conclusion it is stated that from such occurrence the permissibility of these labors on the Sabbath was learned. An analysis of the *halakhot* thus stated offers proof that even when the selfstanding halakhic ruling is stated in the Mishnah before the *ma'aseh*, it does not exclude the possibility that chronologically speaking the *ma'aseh* preceded such a ruling and that the former is the source of the latter – except that the compiler of the Mishnah saw fit to state first the ruling and then the *ma'aseh*. At times disputes concerning a tradition entertained by the halakhic scholars and relating to the conduct of a particular halakhic scholar led in turn to disputing opinions as regards the halakhic principle to be derived from the aforesaid conduct (see, e.g., Suk. 2:7 concerning the dispute between Bet Shammai and Bet Hillel, arising in connection with the *ma'aseh* of R. Johanan b. ha-Ḥorani).

Distinguishing *Ma'aseh*

Just as a halakhic principle acquires special force and significance from the fact that it has been applied in a practical case, so the latter fact entails the risk of possible error in the manner of deduction of the principle from the practical case. Hence, in deduction of the principle it is required that two important distinctions be made: first, the factual aspect of the case must be precisely distinguished from the legal aspect; secondly – and more difficult – the part that is not material and has no bearing on the halakhic conclusion must be distinguished from the material part which leads to the halakhic conclusion. This distinguishing process is sometimes directed toward a specific purpose, for instance toward restriction of the halakhic principle derived from a case when the need for it arises in a concrete matter for decision. In English law – which has the system of case law – the process of distinguishing is also greatly developed, and here too one of the main functions of the process is to distinguish between the *ratio decidendi* and mere *obiter dictum*. The distinguishing process has been of primary importance to the development of both legal systems.

The phrase commonly employed in the Mishnah for the act of distinguishing is *einah hi ha-middah*, "that is not the inference" (Pes. 1:6–7), and in the Talmud, "This was not stated explicitly but by implication" (BM 36a, et al.; see also BB 130b and Rashbam thereto, s.v. *halakhah adifah*), or "Tell me what actually transpired!" (BM 70a, et al.). The process of distinguishing is well illustrated in *Bava Meẓia* 36a. Rav is quoted as holding that a bailee who entrusted a bailment to another bailee is not liable – i.e., for any more than he would have been liable had he kept the bailment himself – since he entrusted it to a person having understanding (*ben da'at*); however, R. Johanan is recorded as holding the first bailee liable for all damage occasioned to the bailment while it is deposited with the second bailee, since the owner might say to the former that he entrusted the bailment to his personal care and did not wish it entrusted to another (see **Shomerim*). In the continuation of the discussion it is stated, "R. Ḥisda said: This was not stated by Rav explicitly but by implication," i.e., that Rav's rule was deduced by implication from a legal decision he gave in a practical case, but that the rule was deduced in error because no proper distinction had been made. The facts of the case decided by Rav were as follows: gardeners used to deposit their spades every day, on completion of their work, with an old woman; one day they deposited their spades with one of their members and the latter, wishing to join in some festivity, deposited them with the old woman, from whom they were stolen; when the other gardeners sought compensation from the bailee gardener for the loss of their spades, Rav held the latter exempt from liability. From his decision it had been erroneously concluded that the latter held in favor of exempting a first bailee from liability for damage occasioned to a bailment he had entrusted to a second bailee, for Rav had only exempted the first bailee in that particular case because of the fact that the gardeners had generally been accustomed to deposit their spades with the old woman, and were therefore precluded from saying that they wanted their spades entrusted to the gardener only. Generally, however, if the facts were different, a bailee would be liable if damage resulted to the bailment he entrusted to another, even in Rav's opinion. In this manner the Talmud records how the deduction of an erroneous legal conclusion from a particular case is illuminated by the process of distinguishing.

The Talmud (BB 130b) provides basic guidance on the manner of deriving a legal conclusion from a case without apprehension of error: "The *halakhah* may not be derived either from a theoretical conclusion or from a practical decision (without knowing the facts of the case) unless one has been told that the rule is to be taken as a rule for practical decisions; once a person has asked and been informed that a *halakhah* was to be taken as a guide for practical decisions (and therefore knows the facts), he may continue to give practical decisions accordingly" (see Rashbam, ad loc.). In the 13th century the approach to *ma'aseh* and the distinguishing process was expressed in these terms: "Not in vain were the many practical cases embracing various rules written into the Talmud, not so that the law concerning the relevant matter be applied in accordance with what is stated there, but so that the scholar, by having frequent reference to them, shall acquire the art of weighing his opinion and a sound approach in giving practical decisions" (Resp. Abraham b. Moses b. Maimon no. 97).

In Post-Talmudic Times

Ma'aseh, both as an act of legal decision and as the conduct of a halakhic scholar, continued to serve as an important legal source in post-talmudic times. The halakhic scholars of this period derived many legal conclusions from practical cases in talmudic literature. Thus Maimonides decided that a person engaged in study of the Torah shall stop studying and recite the *Keri'at Shema* whenever it is the time to do so; however, a person engaged in public matters shall not desist from such activity, even if meanwhile the time for *Keri'at Shema* passes (Yad, Keri'at Shema 2:5). Maimonides derived this *halakhah* from an account in the Tosefta stating that R. Akiva and R. Eleazar b. Azariah omitted to recite *Keri'at Shema* because they were preoccupied with public matters (Tosef., Ber. 1:4; see comment of Elijah Gaon to Sh. Ar., OH 70:4).

In like manner, *ma'asim* of the post-talmudic scholars, in the form of both practical decisions (see below) and conduct, served as a legal source for the deduction of *halakhot* by subsequent scholars. *Ma'asim* of the latter kind are frequently quoted in post-talmudic halakhic literature in the form of testimony by pupils to the conduct of their teachers in different matters of the *halakhah*. Special books of *halakhah* were even compiled in which a considerable part of the material was based on the author's observation of the conduct of his eminent teacher, for he had not only acquired the latter's teachings but also served him in daily life. An example of such a work is the *Sefer Tashbeẓ* of Simeon b. Ẓemah *Duran, a pupil of *Meir b. Baruch of Rothenburg, which deals mainly with the laws in the Shulḥan Arukh's *Oraḥ Ḥayyim* and *Yoreh De'ah*, and to some extent also with matters of family and civil law, largely quoted by the author as the manner in which he had seen his teacher conduct himself (see, e.g., sections 1, 7, 18–23, et al.).

The Responsa Literature

With the development in post-talmudic times of one of the main branches of the literary sources of Jewish law, namely the responsa literature, *ma'aseh* came to fulfill an important role as a lawmaking source. The responsa literature represents the case law of the Jewish legal system. A concrete problem that arose in daily life – whether in matters between individuals or in matters of man's relationship to the Almighty, in matters of civil or ritual law – was brought before the local *dayyan* or halakhic scholar, and they, whenever they experienced any doubt or difficulty in reaching a solution to the problem at hand, turned to the distinguished halakhic scholars of their generation. Certain matters, particularly disputes between the individual and the public or its representative bodies, came directly before the most prominent halakhic scholars. They deliberated all the factual and legal aspects of the case and submitted their findings and conclusion in a written responsum to the questioner. The *she'elah u-teshuvah* – question and response – accordingly represents a classic example of an act of legal decision, and answers to all the requirements set by the talmudic sages for recognition of *ma'aseh* as a legal source, since this procedure is a true application of "having asked and been informed that a *halakhah* is to be taken as a guide for practical decisions …" (above; BB 130b). This character of the responsa literature has served to lend the legal principle emerging from it a particular standing and force exceeding that of a principle derived from the commentaries and novellae and even, in the opinion of the majority of halakhic scholars, exceeding that of a principle derived from the books of *halakhot* and *pesakim* (see *Codification of Law) in cases of inconsistency between the two. Hence, "more is to be learned from the conclusions stated in the responsa than from those stated by the *posekim* [in the codes], since the latter did not write their conclusions in the course of deciding the law in a concrete instance" (Resp. Maharil no. 72). Similarly, "when *halakhah* is laid down in practice there is greater penetration to the heart of the matter than in the course of theoretical study; there is also greater divine guidance (*sayata di-shemaya*) in a practical case … for a conclusion that comes in answer to a practical case is preferable and more directed to the real truth than what is forthcoming from mere theoretical study" (*Meshiv Davar*, pt. 1, no. 24).

Jewish Law and Binding Precedent

Recognition in Jewish law of *ma'aseh* as a legal source from which may be derived the principles that emerge from it is unconnected with the question of whether any conclusion so derived has the force of binding precedent for the purpose of deciding the law in a similar case. In fact, as will be seen below, Jewish law does not recognize the principle of binding precedent.

PRECEDENT IN OTHER LEGAL SYSTEMS. The legal "case" occupies a very modest place in the source hierarchy of the Roman legal system; certainly the latter does not recognize at all the principle of binding precedent. Justinian expressly laid down that judgments be given according to laws and not precedents: "*non exemplis, sed legibus iudicandum est*" (C. 7. 45. 13; see J. Salmond, Jurisprudence (1966[12]), 141f.; C.K. Allen, *Law in the Making* (1964[7]), 342f.). Most continental legal systems, following that of Rome, exemplify the codificatory system of law, and in these the decisions of the courts represent no more than material of a theoretical and persuasive nature, without binding force (Salmond, *ibid.*). The position is different in English law: "The importance of judicial precedents has always been a distinguishing characteristic of English law. The great body of the common or unwritten law is almost entirely the product of decided cases, accumulated in an immense series of reports extending backward with scarcely a break to the reign of Edward I at the close of the 13th century... A judicial precedent speaks in England with authority; it is not merely evidence of the law but a source of it" (Salmond, p. 141). As regards the extent to which the courts are bound by precedent, Salmond goes on to say: "It is necessary to point out that the phrase 'the doctrine of precedent' has two meanings. In the first, which may be called the loose meaning, the phrase means merely that precedents are reported, may be cited, and will probably be followed by the courts. This was the doctrine that prevailed in England until the 19th century, and it is still the only sense in which a doctrine of precedent prevails on the continent. In the second, the strict meaning, the phrase means that precedents not only have great authority but must (in certain circumstances) be followed. This was the rule developed during the 19th century and completed in some respects during the 20th" (p. 142). The merits of this development toward the strict meaning of precedent have not remained unquestioned, and in recent times there has been increasing discussion of the correctness and efficacy of this approach (*ibid.*, p. 143 and see note, p. ix, concerning the extrajudicial statement made in the House of Lords in 1966, relaxing the rule of being bound to follow its own previous decisions "when it appears right to do so").

COMPARISON OF PRECEDENT IN ENGLISH AND IN JEWISH LAW. At their respective starting points the two legal systems have much in common in their approach to precedent but they diverge in their manner of development. In both "case" constitutes a source of law; both are, to a large extent, built up around case law, and have developed in consequence of concrete legal decisions in daily life; the basic material at the heart of most Jewish law codifications is likewise the product of legal principles derived from day-to-day legal decisions (see *Codification of Law), and from this point of view the main difference between the two legal systems is that the Jewish law equivalent of the "immense series of reports," namely the responsa literature, dates from the geonic period onward, i.e., from the middle of the eighth century and not, as in England, from the end of the 13th century (see **Mishpat Ivri*). On the other hand, Jewish law has not accepted the doctrine of precedent in the strict meaning of the term – as has English law, commencing from the 19th century – and the power of *ma'aseh* in Jewish law has been confined to that of precedent in the loose meaning of the term, as described by Salmond, "precedents are reported, may be cited, and will probably be followed by the courts." For two reasons, each of which will be dealt with below, Jewish law has been unable to adopt the doctrine of a binding precedent which imposes its inherent halakhic conclusion on the *dayyan* when deciding the matter before him: first, because of this legal system's conception of the substantive nature of a judgment given between the two parties to a suit; secondly, because of the method and approach of Jewish law toward deciding of the *halakhah* in general.

SUBSTANTIVE NATURE OF A JUDGMENT IN JEWISH LAW AND THE PROBLEM OF PRECEDENT. In Jewish law, the finality of a judgment is subject to many reservations, even in relation to the instant parties themselves. According to the original Jewish law, no judgment is absolute and final in the sense of *res judicata* in Roman law, except insofar as it accords with the true objective state of affairs as regards both the facts and the law. Hence, it always remained possible for a judgment given by the court on the available facts to be set aside, and for the matter to be heard afresh when either of the parties was able to produce new evidence. Since this possibility posed a serious obstacle to the due administration of justice and to orderly economic life, which demand an end to litigation, the practice was introduced of having the parties acknowledge – in court and prior to judgment – that they had no further evidence whatever to adduce, thereby annulling in advance the efficacy of any further evidence they might later wish to bring (see Sanh. 31a; Yad, Sanhedrin 7:6–8; Sh. Ar., ḤM 20). Similarly, the original law held that any judgment which transpires to be wrong in law – i.e., in case of error as regards decided and clear *halakhah* – is inherently invalid, although not so in case of an erroneous exercise of discretion. Here again the way was found to ensure the stability and finality of a judgment (Sanh. 33a; Yad, Sanhedrin 6:1; Sh. Ar., ḤM 25:1–3 and Rema thereto; see also Gulak, Yesodei, 4 (1922), 175–83, 201–3; and see *Practice and Procedure (Civil)).

A judgment in Jewish law accordingly has a dual nature: theoretically it is not final until the truth has been fully explored; in practice reservations were laid down – which would be accepted by the parties and normally would apply automatically – aimed at ensuring an end to litigation between the parties to a dispute and at acceptance of the judgment as decisive and as determining the respective rights of the parties.

The stated theoretical nature of a judgment, which applies even as regards determination of the law for the instant parties themselves, has necessarily entailed the conclusion that a judgment shall not have the force of a binding precedent in relation to a similar problem arising between different parties; hence "if another case comes before him even if it be a like case in all respects – he may deal with it as he sees fit, since the *dayyan* need only act according to what his own eyes see" (Nov. Ran to BB 130b; Nov. Ritba, BB *ibid.*).

METHODS AND APPROACH OF JEWISH LAW CONCERNING DECIDING OF THE HALAKHAH AND THE PROBLEM OF PRECEDENT. The doctrine of binding precedent also conflicts with the very method and approach of Jewish law concerning deciding the *halakhah* (see **Mishpat Ivri*; *Authority, Rabbinical; *Codification of Law). The fact of halakhic difference of opinion, as the latter developed in the course of time, is regarded as a phenomenon that is not only legitimate but also desirable and indicative of the vitality of the *halakhah* and of the possibility of different approaches, based on common general principles, in the search for solutions to new problems that arise. The decisive yardstick in a case of halakhic dispute, is the correctness of each opinion "in accordance only with the Talmud of R. Ashi" (i.e., the Babylonian Talmud: *Piskei ha-Rosh*, Sanh. 4:6) and based "with definite proof on the Talmud, as well as the Jerusalem Talmud and Tosefta, when there is no definite decision in the Talmud" (*Yam shel Shelomo*, introd. to BK). For this reason no codification of Jewish law was accepted which laid before the *dayyan* deciding the law one single, arbitrary, and final opinion on any given matter. For the same reason Jewish law accepted the doctrine of *hilkheta ke-Vatra'ei* ("the law is according to the later scholars"), which was designed to ensure freedom of decision for later scholars – albeit with due reference to and regard for the decisions of earlier scholars. The basic rule applicable is that the judgment of a person who has erred because he was unaware of the decisions of earlier scholars shall be of no force as soon as that person gains such knowledge and realizes his error; however, "if he does not find their statements correct and sustains his own view with evidence that is acceptable to his contemporaries – the authority of Jephthah in his generation was as that of Samuel in his, and there is only the judge that 'shall be in those days' – he may contradict their statements, since all matters which are not clarified in the Talmud of R. Ashi and Ravina may be questioned and restated by any person, and even the statements of the *geonim* may be differed from… just as the later *amoraim* differed from the earlier ones; on the contrary, we regard the statements of the later scholars to be more authoritative since the latter knew not only the legal thinking of their contemporaries but also that of the earlier scholars, and in deciding between the different views they reached the heart of a matter" (*Piskei ha-Rosh*, loc. cit.).

This conception of a flexible and dynamic legal order naturally left no room for the doctrine that especially a conclusion springing from a practical decision should impose itself on the judicial process. The court which is apprised of a matter has the task of referring to, and taking into proper consideration, all the available relevant laws and certainly the rules emerging from earlier practical decisions, particularly when the halakhic principle emerging from the practical decision has been accepted without exception in a series of legal decisions ("daily practical acts of decision," Ket. 68b; BB 173b; etc.). However, if after such study the judge should, in reasonable manner and in reliance on the halakhic system itself, come to a different legal conclusion from that reached by earlier scholars, he will have not only the right but also the duty to decide as he sees fit; such decision will take precedence over an earlier decision in a like matter, since the judge will also have known the legal thinking of earlier scholars and have decided as he did by going to the root of the matter.

Thus *ma'aseh* constitutes one of the significant lawmaking sources of the Jewish legal system, and every principle emerging from it becomes part of the accumulated body of laws comprising this system, in accordance with which the judge must decide. In standing and validity such principles are like any others deriving from the statements of *posekim* and halakhic scholars, and embraced by the common rule that the judge must consider every law on its substantive merits and decide, in the concrete case before him, according to his own knowledge and understanding deriving from due examination of all the relevant rules of Jewish law.

[Menachem Elon]

Ma'aseh and Precedent

PRECEDENT: THE RELATIONSHIP BETWEEN THE REGIONAL RABBINICAL COURTS AND THE RABBINICAL COURT OF APPEALS. Jewish law does not recognize the principle of a binding precedent obliging a *bet din* to rule in accordance with previous rulings. Today, after the establishment of the Rabbinical Court of Appeals (see *Appeal), this has ramifications for the compliance of the regional rabbinical courts with the rulings of the Rabbinical Court of Appeals, and specifically in cases in which the Rabbinical Court of Appeals rules that a case is to be returned for an additional hearing in the regional rabbinical court. In such cases, certain forums of the regional rabbinical courts accept the authority of Rabbinical Court of Appeals, to rehear the case and rule accordingly, whereas other regional rabbinical court forums refuse to accept the rulings of the Rabbinical Court of Appeals as binding upon them, believing that according to Jewish law, the regional rabbinical court is not required and may not rule other than in accordance with its own views, unless persuaded that it erred in its initial ruling. The practical solution in such cases of refusal is to have the matter transferred to a regional rabbinical court willing to rehear the case. In some cases the Supreme Court has intervened in cases in which the regional rabbinical court has refused to obey the instructions of the Rabbinical Court of Appeals, and has forced such compliance, or has nullified the regional court's ruling (see bibliography, Warhaftig, p. 131; see also *Appeal).

RABBINICAL COURT RULINGS AS A PRECEDENT IN A CIVIL COURT. According to Israeli law, civil courts adjudicating matters involving personal status are required to rule in accordance with Jewish law. (See *Mishpat Ivri: Jewish Law in the State of Israel.) The rule is that the High Court of Justice cannot sit as an appellate court on rabbinical court rulings and may not intervene in its rulings. The question of whether rulings of rabbinical courts should constitute binding precedents for the civil courts when questions already decided by the rabbinical courts arise in proceedings before the civil courts was decided in the *Yosef v. Yosef* case.

The *Yosef* case (CA 63/69, *Yosef v. Yosef*, 24 (1) PD 792) (hereinafter: "the decision") concerned a woman with independent income, who sued her husband for maintenance. While on a substantive level, the Supreme Court ruled in accordance with the ruling of the rabbinical courts, the court was divided over the question of whether it was bound by the rabbinical court's interpretation of the applicable Jewish law. The case concerned a woman earning income from her own work, who sued for maintenance from her husband. The Supreme Court ruled, in accordance with Jewish law and the decisions of the rabbinical courts, that her income should be deducted from the amount her husband owes her for her maintenance, and the husband must pay the balance between the wife's earnings and the amount of the maintenance payments, to the extent that the amount of maintenance is greater than the amount of the wife's earnings. (See *Husband and Wife".) Regarding the question of the civil court's subordination to the rulings of the rabbinical court, Justice Kister ruled that when a civil court is required to apply Jewish law, it must accept rabbinical court decisions as definitive of Jewish law. He explained:

> The reason why we must follow the decisions of the rabbinical courts in these matters is to be found in the laws of the Torah, which provide that one must obey the decisions of the halakhic authorities of each generation, "Jephtah in his generation can be equated to Samuel in his generation" (p. 805 of decision).

Justice Haim Cohn, in his minority opinion regarding the deduction of the wife's earnings from her maintenance payments, stated that the civil court is required to interpret Jewish law according to its own understanding, and is not bound by the interpretation given to it by the rabbinical courts:

> However, the rule regarding the authority of the judge "of that time" (Deut. 17:9) applies not only to rabbinical courts, but to every judge in Israel. The proof is that the three [judges] "of insubstantial quality (*kalei olam*)" – Jerubaal, Bedan and Jephtah, "are considered equal to the three most outstanding [judges] (*ḥamurei olam*)" – Moses and Aaron and Samuel. This teaches us that Jerubaal in his generation is equated to Moses in his generation, Bedan in his generation is equal to Aaron in his generation, Jephtah in his generation is equal to Samuel in his generation. This means that even if the most insignificant person is chosen as a community leader, he must be regarded as equal to the mightiest (p. 809 of decision).

Justice Cohn further argued that civil courts cannot accept the rulings of the rabbinical courts as either guiding or binding precedents, since these courts do not necessarily rule according to the laws of the State.

Justice Zvi Berinson wrote that while the civil courts are not bound to accept the rulings of the rabbinical courts, "it stands to reason that a secular court, in reaching a decision on an issue that has been definitively decided by a religious court, will give that determination greater weight, and will generally be guided by it" (p. 810, *ibid.*). According to recent court decisions, civil courts are competent and authorized to give their own interpretations of Jewish law in matters of personal status, and are not bound by prior rabbinical courts' rulings. Nevertheless, the High Court of Justice does not intervene in the content of a rabbinical court's rulings, and does not intervene in the rabbinical courts' interpretation of Jewish law. (See HCJ 5969/94 *Aknin v. Haifa Civil Court*, 50 (1) PD 370.)

[Menachem Elon (2nd ed.)]

BIBLIOGRAPHY: Epstein, Mishnah, 598–608; J.M. Guttmann, in: *Devir*, 1 (1922/23), 40–44; Ch. Tchernowitz, *Toledot ha-Halakhah*, 1 pt. 1 (1934), 189–96; A. Kaminka, *Meḥkarim ba-Mikra u-va-Talmud…* (1951), 1–41; A. Weiss, *Le-Ḥeker ha-Talmud* (1954), 111–67; Ḥ. Cohn, in: *Mishpat Ve-Khalkalah*, 3 (1956/57), 129–41; Ḥ. Albeck, *Mavo la-Mishnah* (1959), 92f.; E.Ẓ. Melamed, in: *Sinai*, 46 (1959/60), 152–65; B. de Vries, *Toledot ha-Halakhah ha-Talmudit* (1962), 169–78; M. Elon, in: ILR, 2 (1967), 548–50. **ADD. BIBLIOGRAPHY:** M. Elon, *Ha-Mishpat ha-Ivri* (1988), 1:205, 213, 238, 2381, 422ff., 426, 429ff., 437, 449, 492, 494, 524, 532, 608, 687, 768ff.; 2:894, 895, 1216ff.; 3:1499ff., 1503ff., 1521ff.; idem, *Jewish Law* (1994), 1:231, 239, 270, 271; 2:515–17f., 520, 523ff., 534, 549, 599, 602, 638, 648, 752, 848, 945ff.; 3:1089, 1090, 1457ff.; 4:1784ff., 1788ff., 1809ff.; idem, *Jewish Law Cases and Materials* (1999), 91–96; M. Elon and B. Lifshitz, *Mafte'aḥ ha-She'elot ve-ha-Teshuvot shel Ḥakhmei Sefarad u-Ẓefon Afrikah* (legal digest) (1986), 182–83; B. Lifshitz and E. Shochetman, *Mafte'aḥ ha-She'elot ve-ha-Teshuvot shel Ḥakhmei Ashkenaz, Ẓarefat ve-Italyah* (legal digest) (1997), 125; Z. Warhaftig, *"Ha-Takdim be-Mishpat ha-Ivri,"* in: *Shenaton ha-Mishpat ha-Ivri*, 6–7 (1979–80), 105; Y. Englard, *"Ma'amado shel ha-Din ha-Dati be-Mishpat ha-Yisraeli,"* in: *Mishpatim*, 2 (5730), 488, 531ff.; H.D. Halevi, *"Bet ha-Din le-Ir'urim,"* in: *Teḥumin*, 15 (5755), 187.

MA'ASEROT (Heb. מַעַשְׂרוֹת; "Tithes"), seventh tractate in the order *Zera'im*, in the Mishnah, Tosefta, and Jerusalem Talmud. It is sometimes referred to as *Ma'aser Rishon* ("First Tithe" – *genizah* fragments, Cambridge Ms., Tosefta Ms., and Maimonides' introduction to the Mishnah), but Albeck points out that this is a misnomer influenced by the name of the tractate following it, *Ma'aser Sheni* ("Second Tithe"). *Ma'aserot* deals chiefly with the precepts connected with the separation of the tithes to be given to the Levites from the produce of the land (see Num. 18:20–24), and the prohibition against making use of produce before the tithe has been separated.

The tractate contains five chapters. Chapter 1 defines the types of produce liable to tithing (1–4), the stage of growth at which they become liable, and when, after harvesting, untithed produce becomes forbidden. Chapter 2 gives circumstances in which casual eating of untithed produce is allowed, i.e., by the laborer. Chapter 3 continues with laws of tithe as they concern the laborer, and deals with the tithing of produce found on the road or in the field and the buildings or localities which render the produce brought there liable to tithe. Chapter 4 deals with the tithing of preserved fruits, liability for tithing arising through the onset of the Sabbath, chance eating from a vat of olives or a winepress, and the eating of insignificant parts of the produce. Chapter 5 deals with the liability for tithing of replanted produce, the selling of produce to those not trusted to tithe, and kinds of vegetables exempt from tithing.

The Tosefta has three chapters, supplementing the Mishnah with numerous accounts and decisions of the *tannaim*. Its editing appears to have been late, since it contains accounts (ch. 3) of Judah and Hillel, the sons of Rabban Gamaliel III. The order of the paragraphs does not correspond to that of the Mishnah, and there is no corresponding Tosefta to *mishnayot* 2:2, 6, 7; 4:4; and 5:6, 7. The Jerusalem Talmud covers about 14 columns of the Krotoszyn edition. It includes an interesting debate regarding the role of *aggadah* between Ze'eira and his colleague, who goes so far as to say that aggadic books are none other than "black magic" and attacks the aggadic method as being illogical (3:9, 51a). The Babylonian Talmud has no *Gemara* to *Ma'aserot*, as it has none on the whole of the order *Zera'im*, except for tractate *Berakhot*. This tractate was translated into English by H. *Danby, *The Mishnah* (1933), 66–73.

[David Joseph Bornstein]

MA'ASER SHENI (מעשר שני) "second tithe," name of a tractate in the Mishnah, Tosefta and Jerusalem Talmud, expounding on the biblical commandment (Dt. 14:22–27) to set aside a tenth of one's produce, to be consumed "before the Lord thy God, in the place which he shall choose to cause his name to dwell there"; i.e., in Jerusalem. The Torah states that, if it is inconvenient to transport the produce itself, then it may be exchanged for money with which foodstuffs may be purchased in Jerusalem. The rabbinic understanding was that this requirement would be superseded by the "poor tithe" that is separated instead on the third and sixth years of the sabbatical cycle according to Dt. 26:12–15. This interpretation is found in early sources like the Septuagint, though Jubilees (32:11) and Josephus (Ant. 4:8 [22]) state that the poor tithe is additional to the second tithe.

Much of the Mishnah tractate consists of specific definitions of the concepts mentioned in the Torah, such as: what items may or may not be purchased with the second tithe money; the legal procedures for the exchange; whether the sanctity of the tithe extends to containers and waste products; what qualifies as "eating"; under what circumstances may the coins be exchanged for other coins; defining the exact city limits of Jerusalem in which the second tithe food must be eaten; what counts as a coin for which the tithe may be redeemed.

The second tithe money may be spent on food, drink, and anointing oil for personal consumption, or for freewill *shelamim* offerings (which are eaten by the owner), but not on sacrifices for which the owners are otherwise obligated. The exchange of the original produce for cash was perceived by the rabbis as a "redemption" process in which the sanctity of the original items was transferred to the coin, and then to the foodstuffs that were purchased with it. Leviticus 27:31 requires that an additional fifth be added when redeeming a tithe. The *halakhah* understood this as a fifth of the total; i.e., one fourth of the original produce's value. The interpretations of this procedure were influenced by those for redemption of sacrifices (see Lev. 27:27, etc). The Mishnah discusses situations when the additional fifth need not be paid, and mentions some subterfuges for avoiding its payment.

According to the rabbinic interpretation, the designation that fruit (or grapes) in the fourth year after planting "shall be holy for giving praise unto the Lord" (Lev. 19:24) means that it must be consumed in Jerusalem, or exchanged for money under conditions similar to those prescribed for the second tithe. Because of the resemblance of the rules, the topic of fourth-year fruit is also dealt with in Chapter 5 of this tractate, though it probably belongs more appropriately to *Orlah*.

The Jerusalem Talmud (3:8, 50b) relates the story of Rabbi Joshua ben Korha's castigation of R. Eleazar ben Rabbi Simeon for assisting the Romans, in a shorter and more original version than that of the TB, BM 83b.

ADD. BIBLIOGRAPHY: Translation of Yerushalmi: H.W. Guggenheimer, *The Jerusalem Talmud: First Order: Zeraïm: Tractates Terumot and Ma'aserot: Edition, Translation, and Commentary* (2003); E.L. Ehrlich, *Studia Judaica*, (2002); S. Friedman, "*La-Aggadah ha-Historit ba-Talmud ha-Bavli*," in: S. Friedman (ed.), *Saul Lieberman Memorial Volume*, 335, 11 p. (1993).

[David Joseph Bornstein]

MAAYANI, AMI (1936–), Israeli composer and conductor. Born in Tel Aviv, Maayani studied composition with Paul *Ben-Haim at the Academy of Music in Jerusalem, and then graduated from the Faculty of Architecture at the Technion in Haifa. He wrote a monumental 1,000-page Hebrew monograph on Wagner. Maayani taught theory and composition at the Academy of Music, Tel Aviv University, and at the Rubin Academy of Music and Dance in Jerusalem. From 1993 until his retirement in 2003 he was head of the Academy in Tel Aviv. During this time he collaborated with architect Yoram Raz in designing the very successful auditorium for the Rubin Academy of Music in Tel Aviv. Mayani won the AKUM Prize (1974), the international competiton "Holocaust and Rebirth," and the IBA Prize for the 25th Anniversary of Israel.

Maayani's prolific output reflects his special penchant for idiomatic and brilliant instrumental writing. It includes concertos for harp (1960, 1966); concerto for violin (1987); concerto for cello (1967); *Qumran*, a symphonic metaphor (1971); three symphonies and other orchestral and chamber works; and *Yiddishe Lieder* for voice and orchestra (1973). Maayani's strong individualistic personality creates a unique synthesis of elements of Arabic music with traditional Western modality and harmony.

ADD. BIBLIOGRAPHY: L. Harbater-Silver, "Ami Maayani and the Yiddish Art Song (Part 2)," in: *Musica Judaica*, 9:1 (1986–87), 64; R. Fleisher, *Twenty Israeli Composers* (1997), 151–62.

[Uri (Erich) Toeplitz and Yohanan Boehm / Jehoash Hirshberg (2nd ed.)]

MAAZEL, LORIN (**Varencove**; 1930–), conductor, violinist, and composer. Born in France, Maazel studied violin and piano in Los Angeles and Pittsburgh, and conducting with Vladimir Bakaleinikoff. Between the ages of nine and 15, Maazel conducted many of the great American and Canadian orchestras. In 1945, he entered the University of Pittsburgh to study philosophy, languages, and mathematics. While a student, he was a violinist with the Pittsburgh Symphony Orchestra. Maazel made his European conducting debut in Italy in 1953. In 1960, his performance of Mahler was acclaimed for its scrupulous articulation and expressive power. The same year he was the first American and the youngest conductor ever to conduct at the Bayreuth festival. Soon after, he was being referred to as a "legend in his own time." Maazel conducted 5,000 opera and concert performances with over 150 leading orchestras around the world and held such prestigious posts as artistic director of the Deutsche Oper Berlin (1965–71), music director of the Berlin Radio Symphony Orchestra (1965–75), and music director of the Cleveland Orchestra (1972–82). He also conducted the Orchestre National de France, the Vienna Vienna Staatsoper, and the Pittsburgh Symphony. He was music director of the New York PO from the 2002–03 season. His latter-day operatic productions were at the Metropolitan Opera, Paris Opera, Royal Opera House (London), and La Scala (Milan), and he became involved in film opera productions. His discography encompasses over 300 recordings including the complete symphonies of Beethoven, Mahler, Rachmaninoff, Sibelius, and Tchaikovsky, and around 40 operas. Maazel gave benefit concerts for international organizations such as UNICEF and the International Red Cross. The governments of France, Germany, Italy, Portugal, and Sweden awarded him with their highest honors. He was named an honorary life member of the Israel Philharmonic in 1985 when he conducted their 40th anniversary concert. Among his publications are "Vom Herzen: Moge es wieder zu Herzen gehn" (in *Die 9 Symphonien Beethovens: Entstehung, Deutung, Wirkung*, 1994).

BIBLIOGRAPHY: Grove online; *Baker's Biographical Dictionary* (1997); I. Geleng. *Lorin Maazel: Monographie eines Musikers* (1971); L. Knessl. *Wiener Staatsoper: Die Direktion Lorin Maazel.* (1984).

[Naama Ramot / (2nd ed.)]

MA'BARAH (Heb. מַעְבָּרָה; plural **ma'barot**), transitional immigrants' camp or quarter in the early 1950s in Israel. At the end of 1949, 100,000 immigrants were living in camps, receiving accommodation, meals and services free, under demoralizing conditions. As the government and the *Jewish National Fund started large-scale development programs, and the newcomers began to earn their keep, the communal dining halls were closed down, and the inmates were enabled to make their own domestic arrangements. Camps which were not suitable for this system were closed down and new ones – *ma'barot* – set up, with a wooden, asbestos, or tin shack, or at least a tent, for each family, wherever there was a demand for labor, near the towns.

Although the *ma'barot* were a great improvement over the early camps, the primitive accommodation gave rise to serious social problems. They were gradually cleared by providing the newcomers with permanent housing and, from 1954, sending immigrants straight from the ship or plane to the villages or towns where they were to settle permanently.

BIBLIOGRAPHY: *Israel Government Year Book*, (1958), 356–7; Zionist Organization Executive, *Reports to Zionist Congress*, 24 (1956); 25 (1960).

[Misha Louvish]

MA'BAROT (Heb. מַעְבָּרוֹת; "Fords"), kibbutz in central Israel, near the Alexander River, affiliated with Kibbutz Arẓi ha-Shomer ha-Ẓa'ir. It was founded in 1933, as one of the first villages in the Ḥefer Plain by immigrants from Romania, Germany, Bulgaria, and Hungary, and later joined by others. Its economy was based on farming, such as field crops, citrus groves, orchards, fishery, and dairy cattle, and food enterprises – pet food, milk replacers for calves and lambs, and Materna milk substitutes and baby food. In the mid-1990s, the population was approximately 780, dropping to 734 in 2002.

WEBSITE: www.maabarot.org.il.

[Efraim Orni / Shaked Gilboa (2nd ed.)]

°MACALISTER, ROBERT ALEXANDER STEWART (1870–1951), Irish archaeologist. From 1899 to 1900 he participated with F.J. Bliss in the excavation of mounds in the Shephelah and in 1902–05 and 1907–09 directed the excavation of Gezer, publishing a three-volume report single-handedly in 1912. In 1925 he directed an excavation on the hill of Ophel in Jerusalem. In his later years, he was professor of Celtic archaeology at Dublin (1909–43). He was one of the pioneers of Palestinian archaeology, being the first to publish his finds in an exact manner and laying the foundations for comparative dating by ceramics and context dating. His works include *The Philistines* (1914) and *A Century of Excavation in Palestine* (1925).

[Michael Avi-Yonah]

°MACAULAY, THOMAS BABINGTON (**Lord Macaulay**; 1800–1859), English historian and politician. A member of a family which had been in the forefront of antislavery agitation, Macaulay was elected to parliament in 1830. His maiden speech in the House of Commons was in support of a bill for the removal of the political disabilities affecting Jews in England. In an article (subsequently translated into several languages) in the *Edinburgh Review* of January 1831, he argued the same cause, supporting it again in the House of Commons in 1833 and 1841. Macaulay argued that, "The points of difference between Christianity and Judaism have very much to do with a man's fitness to be a bishop or a rabbi. But they have no more to do with his fitness to be a magistrate, a legislator, or a minister of finance than with his fitness to be a cobbler." He also urged that it was inconsistent to deny formal political rights to Jews in a society where they had acquired the substance of political power. Rarely had the case for Jewish emancipation been presented with the literary force of Macaulay's essays and speeches; the support of one of England's leading men of letters had a significant effect on public opinion. They are still among the most cogent set of arguments made for religious toleration and liberalism. Macaulay's own relations with Jews, almost certainly very slight, remain to be examined in detail.

BIBLIOGRAPHY: T.B. Macaulay, *Essay and Speech on Jewish Disabilities*, ed. by I. Abrahams and S. Levy (1909); Roth, Mag Bibl, 55, 56, 60. **ADD. BIBLIOGRAPHY:** ODNB online.

[Sefton D. Temkin]

MACCABEANS, ORDER OF ANCIENT, a friendly benefit society in Britain whose members are Zionists. Founded in 1896 by Ephraim Ish-Kishor and registered under the Friendly Societies' Act, the Order of Ancient Maccabeans still exists. Its aims are those of all British friendly societies, namely, to assist members in distress, provide free medical aid, etc. Its special character is laid down in its rules concerning membership: all persons "of the Jewish faith who declare themselves adherents to the Zionist Movement" can become members. From its inception the order was a firm supporter of Zionism, contributed to its various funds, and became a champion of practical Zionist work in Ereẓ Israel. In 1914 a Maccabean Land Company was founded to enable its shareholders to acquire land in Ereẓ Israel. The organization of the order displays masonic features. A grand beacon and high degree council supervise its work; branches are called beacons, of which there are 25 (there once were beacons in Palestine as well); the principal officers are called grand commander, grand treasurer, and grand secretary. Members are called upon to obey the decisions of their order and are forbidden to inform nonmembers of the order's activities.

The revised statutes of the Zionist Organization passed by the Tenth Zionist Congress (1911) permitted the establishment of so-called *Sonderverbaende* (separate unions), in addition to the existing territorial organizations, on the condition that every *Sonderverband* numbered at least 3,000 shekel-buying members and that it professed special views on Zionist work. The Order of Ancient Maccabeans applied for this status, and though its claim was opposed by the English Zionist Federation, the order prevailed. In 1912 the Zionist Executive decided in favor of the order's status as *Sonderverband* on the condition that a Joint Zionist Council be formed, comprising representatives of both the order and the federation. In the 1930s, however, the order lost its special status. Prominent members of the order were Herbert *Bentwich, who served as grand commander; Chaim *Weizmann, who represented the order at Congresses; and Selig *Brodetsky, who served as grand commander. In 2004 its president was Sir Ian Gainsford. Its papers from the 1890s to 1964 are held at the Parkes Library, Southampton University.

[Israel Philipp]

MACCABEE, the additional name given to Judah, son of Mattathias, leader of the revolt against Syria (168 B.C.E.), later referred to as the "Maccabean Revolt." It was no accident that the revolt broke out at a rural location such as *Modi'in and not in Jerusalem itself. It began with the killing of a local who was willing to sacrifice to a pagan idol, and the action was taken by a zealous minor native priest, Mattathias (I Macc. 2:27; cf. 2:42) who subsequently called on those around him to follow the law and "maintain the covenant" and to fight the offensive edicts of Antiochus IV. The object was clearly to return to the religious autonomy Jews originally enjoyed, but the later successes of the revolt dictated otherwise. The name Maccabee is also applied loosely to other members of the family, as well as to the Hasmonean dynasty as a whole. For suggestions as to its derivation, see *Judah Maccabee and *Hasmoneans. The name is also given in Christian tradition to the seven children martyred by Antiochus Epiphanes when they refused to commit idolatry. Shrines to their memory and that of their mother Salome (in Jewish tradition Hannah) were established in many parts of the Christian world (see *Hannah and her Seven Sons).

BIBLIOGRAPHY: E.J. Bickerman, "The Maccabean Uprising: An Interpretation," in: J. Goldin (ed.), *The Jewish Expression* (1976), 66–86; F. Millar, "The Background to the Maccabean Revolution…," in: *Journal of Jewish Studies*, 29 (1978), 1–12; D. Mendels, *The Rise and Fall of Jewish Nationalism* (1992); D. Amit and H. Eshel, *The Days of the Hasmonean Dynasty* (1995).

[Shimon Gibson (2nd ed.)]

MACCABEES, FIRST BOOK OF (I Maccabees), a historical work extant in Greek, covering the period of 40 years from the accession of Antiochus Epiphanes (175 B.C.E.) to the death of Simeon the Hasmonean (135 B.C.E.). Its name in the Septuagint and in the writings of the Church Fathers (Eusebius and Clement) is Τα Μακκαβαϊκά, i.e., "Maccabean matters" or "the Book of the Maccabees." The original Hebrew name of the book is unknown. According to Origin it was "Sarbeth Sabaniel." Different hypotheses have been suggested to explain these words, which should perhaps read: סֵפֶר בֵּית סָרְבָנֵי אֵל (*Sefer Beit Sarevanei El*), the words *Sarevanei El* ("who strive for God") being a translation into contemporary (mishnaic) Hebrew of Jehoiarib, the name of the priestly order (see I Chron. 24:7; Neh. 12:6, 19) to which the Hasmonean family belonged. In support of this conjecture is the fact that in later times, after the glamor of the Hasmonean dynasty had become tarnished, the name Jehoiarib is found translated by the above word in its Aramaic form מסרבי (*mesarevei*; TJ, Ta'an. 4:8, 68d) though it is there used in a pejorative sense as "rebellious," "fractious."

I Maccabees is the main, and at times the only, historical source for the period. The book opens with the conquest of Alexander the Great, but immediately after this relates the activities of Antiochus Epiphanes and the Jewish Hellenizers (whom the author calls "the sons of Belial" – the reprobates) and summarily reviews the causes of the Hasmonean rebellion. From this point on it gives a more detailed account of the events of Mattathias' revolt, through the rededication of the Temple, down to the time when John *Hyrcanus, the eldest son of Simon the Hasmonean, was appointed ruler.

The many expressions in the Greek version which occur only in biblical Hebrew (e.g., from the hands of the gentiles: *mi-yad ha-goyim*; and his heart was raised: *va-yarom libbo*; before his face: *al panav*; and the matter found favor in their eyes: *va-yitav ha-davar be-eineihem*) clearly confirm the testimony of the Church Fathers that the original language of the book was Hebrew. The style was biblical Hebrew (including use of the *vav* conversive), and particularly that of the historical books of the Bible. Like Joshua and Judges, it begins with the *vav* conversive, but reflects the style of Ezra and Nehemiah in including historical documents and similar testimony. Like these biblical books, although it is written largely in prose, now and again it includes poetry, such as the Lamentation of Mattathias (2:7–13), prayers (3:18–22; 4:30–33; 7:41–42), and a hymn (14:8–15). Unlike II Maccabees it does not contain explanations of historical or personal psychological motivation, of the sort usually found in the works of the contemporary Greek historians.

The writer achieves a high degree of objectivity. He even refrains from censuring the *Hassideans who opposed the Hasmoneans, though it is clear where his sympathies lie since he regards the Hasmoneans as chosen by Providence "to give deliverance unto Israel" (5:62). The course of events described is not considered as diverging from the natural order, and supernatural intervention is almost entirely absent from the narrative, even though the basic assumption underlying the entire book is that Israel's success is a direct result of their faith and their steadfastness in their loyalty to the Torah and the keeping of the commandments. The author is very circumspect about mentioning God's name. In place of the Tetragrammation or the biblical *Elohim*, he either writes "Heaven" (3:18, 50, 60; 4:10, 40, et al.) or else uses a circumlocution to avoid the use of a proper name altogether (e.g., 2:21, 26; 3:22, 53; 4:10, et al.).

The book ranks high as an accurate historical source, and even the numbers it contains are not exaggerated. In spite of scholarly arguments to the contrary, the idiomatic constructions typical of this book incontrovertibly prove it to be the work of a single author. His name is unknown, but he almost certainly was an eyewitness to the events he describes (cf. 6:39). He avoids expressing outright partisanship, but the fact that he wrote at the beginning of John Hyrcanus' rule, when the latter was still a Pharisee, and lauds Mattathias' decision to permit defensive military action on the Sabbath – which was approved by the Pharisaic school (Jos., Ant. 12:276; 14:63; Tosef., Er. 4:6–7) – indicates that he was close to this circle.

The literary sources used by the author include both letters from official archives (such as those from the Seleucid kings and Roman officials to the Hasmoneans), and public documents (such as the people's declaration assigning the high priesthood and the chief executive position to Simeon), as well as other literary sources in Hebrew (among them the various poems). Thus it is that the author employs two different systems of dating: one for external affairs (where he starts the year in the fall, in the month of Tishri), and one for internal events (which he dates according to the calendar starting in the month of Nisan).

The original Hebrew version seems to have disappeared quite early. The Church included I Maccabees in its canon together with the rest of the Septuagint and this was ratified by the Catholic Church Council of Trent. After the Reformation, the Protestants removed it from their Bible and relegated it to the Apocrypha. A Hebrew translation was made in the 11th century (published by D. Chwolson).

BIBLIOGRAPHY: Charles, Apocrypha, 1 (1913), 59–124; O.F. Fritzsche, *Libri Apocryphi Veteris Testamenti Graece* (1871); A. Rahlf, *Septuaginta*, 1 (1935); H.B. Swete, *The Old Testament in Greek*, 3 (1894); W. Kappler, *Septuaginta, Vetus Testamentum Graecum*, 9 pt. 1 (1936); A. Geiger, *Urschrift und Uebersetzungen der Bibel* (Breslau, 1857); G. Rawlinson, in: H. Wace (ed.), *Apocrypha*, 2 (1888), 373ff.; B. Niese, *Kritik der beiden Makkabaeerbuecher* (1900); Schuerer, Gesch, 1 (1901[3]), 32–40; H. Ettelson, *The Integrity of I Maccabees* (1925); Y. Baer, in: *Zion*, 33 (1964), 101–24; F. Bickermann, *Der Gott der Makkabaeer* (1937); A. Kahana, *Ha-Sefarim ha-Ḥizoniyyim*, 2 (1937), 72–94; J. Heinemann, in: MGWJ, 82 (1938), 145–72; F.M. Abel, *Les Livres des Maccabées* (1949); P. Churgin, *Meḥkarim bi-Tekufat ha-Bayit ha-Sheni* (1949), 190–202; K.D. Schunck, *Die Quellen des I. und II. Makkabaeerbuches* (1954).

[Yehoshua M. Grintz]

MACCABEES, SECOND BOOK OF (II Maccabees), known in Greek as Τά Μακκαβαϊκά, that is, the narratives about (Judah called) the Maccabee. It was this title which gave the title to the other books of the *Apocrypha bearing the same name. It is an abridgment of a larger work of five books written by a *Jason of Cyrene who is otherwise unknown (see 2:23–28). Traces of the original division may be preserved in the similar conclusions in several chapters (3:40; 7:42; 10:9; 13:26; 15:37–39). Unlike I *Maccabees which was written in Hebrew, the original language of this book was Greek; and unlike the former, which begins with an account of the revolt of Mattathias and tells of the wars of his sons the *Hasmoneans up to the days of John Hyrcanus, this book deals solely with the deeds of *Judah Maccabee, and only until his victory over *Nicanor on 13 Adar II, 164 B.C.E. ("Nicanor Day"). However, the main account is prefaced by a lengthy introduction on the actions of the Hellenizers, Simeon of the priestly division of Minyamin (Bilgah), who wanted to be the *agoranomos* (the market overseer) in Jerusalem, and Jason the brother of the high priest Onias, and Menelaus the brother of Simeon, both of whom wanted to be high priests. Their acts of plunder and bribing the king caused the people to rise against them, but their contacts with kings led to the intervention of the Syrian king Antiochus IV Epiphanes and to the religious persecutions which were in fact the direct cause of the Maccabean revolt.

The events related subsequently are in general similar to those in I Maccabees, although the two books are independent of each other. However, chapters 8–12 present a different order: the death of Antiochus IV (10:1–9) and the arrival of Lysias at Beth-Zur (ch. 11) here precede the purification of the Temple. The epitomizer for some reason or other altered the original order (8:29, 34–36; 10:1–8; 8:30–33; 9:1–29; 10:9; he apparently thought that the letter in 11:22, in which Antiochus IV is regarded as having died, belonged to the same period as the other letters in that chapter which, however, preceded it by a year). If the original order is restored, however, the events accord with those in I Maccabees. In its extant form, II Maccabees begins with an addendum to the main body of the book, consisting of two letters sent at different times from Judea to Alexandria which request that the festival of Ḥanukkah be observed. The first was written, according to its date, in 124 B.C.E. (in the days of John Hyrcanus), while the second, undated one (which has all kinds of aggadic stories and is regarded as largely apocryphal) was written earlier, and is a letter from Judah (Maccabee) to Aristobulus, the tutor of King Ptolemy (Philometor, 180–145 B.C.E.)

The main part of the book commences with 2:19, at a time when Onias (III) was high priest, Seleucus ruled in Asia, and peace and tranquility reigned in Ereẓ Israel; however, the avarice of several high priests led to a complete reversal of the situation. Simeon of the priestly division of Minyamin (see above) informed the king's strategus in Syria and Phoenicia that there were vast treasures in the Temple. The king's mission to take the treasure failed (the envoy Heliodorus saw angels smiting him and fainted), and Jason and Menelaus (see above) then began to compete for the high priesthood. As a result of their rivalry and the base acts accompanying it in Jerusalem and Antioch (where Onias the high priest was killed), the people revolted, and Antiochus instituted religious persecutions against them. At first many suffered martyrdom. Then Judah Maccabee rose in revolt together with his men, defeating first the local governor, then the commanders Nicanor and Gorgias (8:8–29), and in the month of Xanthicus (Adar, March) 164 B.C.E. (11:1–15) triumphed over the commander in chief Lysias near Beth-Zur and purified the Temple (10:1–8). There follows a description of wars with various neighboring countries (8:30–33; 10:15–38; 12:2–9, 17–31), and an account of Antiochus IV's death (ch. 9: described here as a punishment from heaven) and his contrition (the author cites a letter from him to the Jews of Antioch (9:19) and interprets it as addressed to all the Jews). After this comes an account of the wars against Antiochus Eupator (13:1–27), the mission of the priest Alcimus, and Judah's victory over Nicanor (15:36).

In its literary form, as well as in its language, this book is entirely different from I Maccabees. Unlike the latter, which uses simple, matter-of-fact language, II Maccabees is written in the style of Greek historians: in ornate language, rich in idioms and poetic metaphors, and in expressions filled with pathos, drama, and rhetoric, stirring the reader. Also, as was usual with these historians, the book is full of various stories of miraculous events, of the intervention of heavenly creatures, directly (by angels) and indirectly (by signs in heaven and on earth presaging evil).

The purpose of the book is religious propaganda, the basic idea being that the sin of the nation is the cause of the divine punishment ("For it is not a light thing to do wickedly against the laws of God: but the time following shall declare these things"; 4:17). Yet the suffering that comes upon Israel is only to chasten the people (6:12–17), and is itself a sign of the divine providence – to warn them against sin. The aim of the introduction is to show that the sin of the priests lay in serving alien forces. In this book – for the first time – Judaism stands as an antipode to *Hellenism (2:21, 8:1, 14:38), and the Greeks are represented as barbarians, avid for plunder and pillage (4:8, 23, 32, 42; 5:16). In contrast, the strength of the Jews lies in the fulfillment of the practical *mitzvot* (the observance of the Sabbath – 6:11; 8:26; 12:38; the precaution against ritual uncleanness – 5:27), and outstanding examples of such acts of bravery are given. One is the story of the elderly Eleazar, who steadfastly refused to eat forbidden food despite all the torture inflicted on him; another is of the woman and her seven sons who suffered martyrdom for the sanctification of the Divine Name (6:18ff.; ch. 7 – see *Hannah and her Seven Sons). Much emphasis is also laid on the belief in the resurrection of the dead (7:14; 12:43). Although his views are very close to those of the Pharisees, it is impossible to tell whether the author, Jason, was one of them. He was apparently a contemporary of Judah Maccabee, as several incidents sound as if they emanate from an eyewitness.

BIBLIOGRAPHY: Charles, Apocrypha, 1 (1913), 125–54; C.L.W. Grimm, *Kurzgefasstes exegetisches Handbuch zu den Apocryphen des Alten Testaments*, 3 (1853); R. Laqueur, *Kritische Untersuchungen zum zweiten Makkabaeerbuch* (1904); idem, in: *Historische Zeitschrift*, 136 (1927), 229–52; W. Kolbe, *Beitraege zur syrischen und juedischen Geschichte* (1946); E. Bickerman, in: Pauly-Wissowa, 14 pt. 1 (1928), 779–97; idem, in: ZNW, 32 (1933), 233ff.; H. Bévenot, *Die beiden Makkabaeerbuecher* (1931); M. Hak, in: *Sinai*, 12 (1943), 92–99. For further bibliography, see *Maccabees, First Book of.

[Yehoshua M. Grintz]

MACCABEES, THIRD BOOK OF (III Maccabees), apocryphal book, included in the *Septuagint, probably dating from the first century B.C.E. It has nothing to do with the Maccabees, but relates a legend to explain why the Jews in Egypt have a Purim-like festival in the summer (the Egyptian date is given). It may have been grouped with the books of the Maccabees, because it, too, relates a persecution of Jews by a Hellenistic king and their miraculous rescue. In it, Ptolemy IV Philopator (221–204 B.C.E.), after his victory over Antiochus III at Rafa, visited neighboring temples. When he insisted upon entering the Temple of Jerusalem by force, the high priest's prayer brought down upon him the scourge of God. Returning to his capital, he took his anger out on the Alexandrian Jews. He ordered a census of the Jews, which was an infringement of their civil rights, and ordered that they be branded with the emblem of Dionysus. Those resisting initiation to Dionysus' mysteries were to be put to death, and those consenting were to be granted full citizenship. As most Alexandrian Jews remained loyal to their faith, the king ordered all the Jews of the country to be brought to Alexandria and put to death. Clerks attempted to register them but failed for shortage of writing material. Crowds of Jews were then concentrated in a hippodrome where they were to be trampled to death by intoxicated elephants. Their destruction was twice miraculously averted. On the third attempt two angels appeared and struck terror into the king, his army, and the elephants, the beasts turning about and falling upon the soldiers. In the end the king repented and prepared a banquet in honor of the rescued Jews. There are serious objections to the historicity of this story. The king's decree combines an infringement of civil rights that could apply only to Alexandrian Jews, with a census of the Jews of the whole country. Moreover, the only purpose of the census could be to institute a poll tax. However, this would become meaningless if the whole Jewish population were to be put to death; it is probably for this reason that the author had to find a device to stop it. The story of the elephants is told by Josephus (Apion, 2:53–55), but about another Ptolemy. The account of the two angels, as well as that of the king's intrusion into the Temple of Jerusalem, is derived from II Maccabees 3. The theme of the king who is instigated by his counselors to annihilate the Jews is from the Book of Esther. These and other details of the story can be put down as commonplaces of persecution literature. By prefacing his patchwork with a description, albeit irrelevant, of the battle of Rafa, taken from a reliable historian, the author manages to concoct an etiology for a festival, the original meaning of which had been forgotten. The book was written in Greek and its style is characterized by its many rare words and neologisms.

BIBLIOGRAPHY: Charles, Apocrypha, 1 (1913), 155–73; M. Hadas, *The Third and Fourth Books of Maccabees* (1953), includes bibliography. For further bibliography see Maccabees, First Book *of.

[Yehoshua Amir (Neumark)]

MACCABEES, FOURTH BOOK OF (IV Maccabees), apocryphal book, included in the Septuagint. It presumably dates from the first century C.E., and is erroneously ascribed by Christian tradition to *Josephus. It does not deal with the warriors of the Maccabean revolt, but with the story of the martyrs of the preceding religious persecution, as related in II Maccabees 6–7. It is of special interest as the only surviving major piece of Greek rhetoric in Jewish literature. IV Maccabees is a philosophical sermon on the theme "pious reason masters passion." This theme, stated at the outset, is frequently repeated in the course of the sermon. After an initial inquiry along the lines of standard Stoic doctrine into the nature of reason and the varieties of passion, the preacher offers historical examples of the ability of reason to control passion. He finally comes to examples provided by the "occasion of this day," the heroic death of the victims of Antiochus' persecution. After a short historical exposition, he describes old Eleazar and the mother (later known as *Hannah) with her seven sons, whom the king tries to force to eat ritually forbidden food. They refuse and each defends his refusal in a fervent speech in the face of cruel torture before being put to death. It seems that the details, as far as they are not drawn from II Maccabees, emanate from the author's own imagination. He spares no pains to excite the emotions of his audience, incorporating detailed descriptions of the torture instruments, delicate analysis of the mother's inner struggle, and great exclamations of admiration for the martyrs. This sermon is one of the outstanding specimens of the "Asianic" school of rhetoric, known for its linguistic excesses, neologisms, redundance of language, and overemphasis.

A most interesting feature is the interweaving of Greek philosophical and Jewish traditional motifs. Not only are moral conflicts and temptations illustrated by biblical stories but in line with the concept that the Torah is the "philosophy" of the Jews, biblical laws are presented as practical means of Stoic self-education and are thus classified according to the different cardinal virtues they help to develop. It passes unnoticed that in the course of this presentation the ideal of the Stoic sage is replaced by that of the God-fearing man, and that heroism is interpreted as the endurance of hardship. The martyr reaps all the glory. He is called an athlete and his ability to endure suffering is the apex of all the moral virtues. The author regards firmness in bearing pain as the victory of reason and as virtually destroying the tyrant's power. The principal religious motivation of the martyr is loyalty to God's law. Eleazar makes no distinction between greater and lesser commandments. Violation of either constitutes contempt for the Lawgiver. The martyrs are certain that God will reward their faithfulness after their death and that He will inflict eternal punishment on the godless king.

The sermon was obviously intended for delivery; otherwise, the mention of its "occasion" would be meaningless. However it may not have been a synagogue sermon, since, in Hellenistic (as in rabbinical) Judaism, such sermons seem always to have been based on a biblical verse. Perhaps it was a Ḥanukkah sermon, but in the absence of any known association of that festival with the martyrs, it may be more correct to think of it as intended for an assembly at their supposed tomb (at Antiochia?) on a traditional commemoration day.

No traces of IV Maccabees have been detected in later Jewish tradition, but Christianity adopted it, together with the "Maccabean Saints" (see *Hannah and her Seven Sons), to whom both the Eastern and the Western Church dedicated a Commemoration Day. Sermons delivered on that day, sometimes referring expressly to IV Maccabees, have been preserved from Gregory of Nazianzus, Augustine, and other Church Fathers. The heroism of the "Maccabees" left its mark on Christian martyr worship, although the Jewish source lacks the special note of longing for torments characteristic of Christian martyrology.

BIBLIOGRAPHY: Charles, Apocrypha, 2 (1913), 653–85; M. Hadas, *The Third and Fourth Books of Maccabees* (1953), including detailed bibliography. For further bibliography, see *Maccabees, First Book of. [Yehoshua Amir (Neumark)]

MACCABIAH, international games, recognized and approved by the International Olympic Committee, held every four years in Israel and open to athletes of the Jewish faith from all countries. The aim of the Maccabiah is to raise the standard of physical culture and sports among Jewish youth and to encourage and foster a sense of belonging to the Jewish people.

The idea of Jewish Olympics was conceived by one of the founders and veteran leaders of the Maccabi movement in Palestine, Joseph Yekutieli, who advocated it with zeal from 1921. After he had succeeded in persuading the mayor of Tel Aviv, Meir Dizengoff, to build the first sports stadium in the country, he brought his plan before the Maccabi World Congress at Ostrava, Czechoslovakia, in 1929 and it was enthusiastically approved. In 1932 the first Maccabiah was held in Tel Aviv, with contingents from 23 countries and 500 athletes.

A great number of the athletes and accompanying personnel remained in Palestine after the Maccabiah and thus the games became not only a tool for stimulating sports but also an important means for promoting Aliyah. The second Maccabiah in 1935 was even more of an "Aliyah Maccabiah," since most of the 1,700 sportsmen from 27 countries, and their escorts, remained in Palestine because of the antisemitism which was sweeping Europe following the Nazis' access to power in Germany. The third Maccabiah could not be held until 1950.

In 1953 the fourth Maccabiah was held. The Maccabi World Union congress which followed it adopted a resolution to build a Maccabiah village to house the visiting contingents. Since then the Maccabiah games have been held regularly every four years, the fifth in 1957, the sixth in 1961, the seventh in 1965, and the eighth in 1969, with an ever-increasing participation of athletes from over 30 countries. The main sports embraced by the Maccabiah are track and field events; gymnastics; swimming and water polo; boxing, wrestling, and fencing; tennis and table tennis; and soccer, basketball, and volleyball. The Maccabiah games contributed to Israeli sports and established themselves as an international Jewish events. Mark *Spitz, who won seven Olympic gold medals, participated in the Maccabiah along with many other world class athletes.

The Maccabi World Union Executive, which sponsors and organizes the Maccabiah games, appoints the International Maccabi Games Committee (IMGC). This generally includes the chairmen of the territorial Maccabi organizations. In countries where no organization exists, leading Jewish sportsmen and people connected with athletes are appointed to select and arrange the training of the various teams. Since the third Maccabiah, *Ha-Po'el Israel has taken an active part with its general secretary a member of the IMGC. The *Betar and *Eliẓur sports organizations also participate in the Maccabiah games.

The program for the Maccabiah games includes festive opening and closing ceremonies under the patronage of the president and the prime minister of the State of Israel, with contingents parading under their national flags.

In the 15th Maccabiah of 1997 a terrible tragedy clouded the games. During the opening ceremonies, a newly constructed bridge over the Yarkon River collapsed as the Australian contingent, numbering 731 members, was crossing it on the way to the stadium. Four of the athletes were killed immediately and 70 were injured. Many of the injuries became more serious because of the pollution of the river. The opening ceremonies continued while the rescue operation was under way, until Prime Minister Binyamin Netanyahu called a halt to the festivities. The event tarnished the image of the Maccabiah Games and damaged Israel-Australia relations, especially those with the Australian Jewish community.

In 2002 the 16th Maccabiah was held under the threat of terror attacks. The games were defined as a vehicle of identification of the Jewish people with the State of Israel, but fewer participated than in previous years.

BIBLIOGRAPHY: J. Yekutieli, *My Road to the First Maccabiah* (1969); Maccabiah, the 8th, *Maccabiah Omnibus* (1969).

[Menahem Savidor / Shaked Gilboa (2nd ed.)]

MACCABI WORLD UNION. The international Jewish sports organization which bears the name of *Judah Maccabee had its origin in the belief of young Eastern European Jews involved in the growing movement for a national home in Palestine at the end of the 19th century that one essential prerequisite was the improvement of the physique of ghetto youth. To this end, gymnastics clubs were founded in a number of Eastern and Central European countries. They were not immediately called Maccabi. The first club, opened in Constantinople, Turkey, in 1895, was called the Israel Gymnastics Club, while others were named after another hero, Bar Kokhba, or were known by the Hebrew names "Ha-Ko'aḥ" ("strength") or "Ha-Gibbor" ("strong man"). The Bar Kokhba club published a monthly journal *Juedische Turnzeitung*, later called *Der Makkabi*; it first appeared in 1900 and promoted athletics and national Jewish education. In 1897 the first of a series of Bulgarian clubs was opened in Plovdiv; a club was organized in Berlin in the following year and in Vienna in 1899. 1901 saw the establishment of a Polish club in Lemberg.

The concept of a nationalist sports movement received impetus in 1898 from a stirring address by the well-known Zionist leader, the physician Max *Nordau, at the second Zionist Congress in Basle, in which he proclaimed:

> Gymnastics and physical training are exceedingly important for us Jews, whose greatest defect has been and is a lack of discipline… nature has endowed us with the spiritual qualities required for athletic achievements of an extraordinary quality. All we lack is muscle, and that can be developed with the aid of physical exercise… The more Jews achieve in the various branches of sport, the greater will be their self-confidence and self-respect.

The truth of Nordau's contention was demonstrated in 1903 at the fourth Zionist Congress in Basle, where a group of 35 outstanding gymnasts from various European clubs staged an impressive display. It was at this Congress that the foundations were laid for the *Juedische Turnerschaft* – the Union of Jewish Gymnastics Clubs – which united all the existing sports clubs, beginning with a membership of some 1,500. It was headed first by Ernst Tuch and later by Theowald Sholom, both of them from Germany. During the first decade of the 20th century the movement spread to more countries on the European continent and to Palestine, where clubs were formed in Jaffa (1906) and Jerusalem (1911). The first real approach to Zionism came in 1912, when at a Maccabi conference in Berlin it was decided to organize group excursions to Palestine (1913 and 1914). By this time there were over 100 affiliated clubs in Europe, with a membership running into several thousands, and the movement had come to be accepted, unofficially, as part of the Young Zionist movement. World War I halted Maccabi activities, but with its close they were renewed everywhere in Europe. As the movement grew, so did the need for firmer integration and in 1921, at a convention in Carlsbad, Czechoslovakia, the Maccabi World Union was formed, and the first Maccabi World Union congress elected Dr. Heinrich Kuhn of Germany as its first president. With ten affiliated countries, the Maccabi World Union started its operations as an organic part of the Zionist movement. By the time of the second Maccabi congress a year later, under the presidency of Heinrich Lellever (1891–1947) of Germany, no less than 22 territorial organizations had affiliated, and the world membership had grown to nearly 100,000.

The first headquarters of the movement were in Vienna, but in 1927 they were moved to Brno, Czechoslovakia, and in 1929 to Berlin, where the movement flourished under the energetic leadership of Dr. Lellever. In 1929 the first international sports meeting was held in Prague; another was held in Antwerp, Belgium, the following year. These were forerunners of the world *Maccabiah games which were to be staged in Palestine from 1932 onward. In 1935 headquarters were transferred from Nazi Germany to London, where Selig *Brodetsky took over the presidency of the World Union, and the second Lord Melchett (*Mond) became honorary world president. In 1939 the world executive was divided into two sections, one operating in Britain and the other, under Lellever, in Palestine. By the time World War II broke out, the world membership was estimated at 200,000 with branches located in most countries of Europe and in Palestine, Turkey, Egypt, China, Australia, South America, and South Africa. It was in 1939 that a nucleus of refugees from Europe established Maccabi in the U.S.

During the war, the activities of the constituent branches of the World Union virtually ceased. Immediately following the war Maccabi leaders in England and Palestine revived the clubs still in existence and helped survivors of the Holocaust to get to Ereẓ Israel. In the countries that now came under Russian control, Jews were forbidden to engage in sports activities as Jews, although a Maccabi group did exist for a short period in the Russian zone of Berlin. In 1946 the first of the annual European Maccabi conferences was held in Basle. The decimation of Jewish communities by the Nazis and the prohibitions of the Iron Curtain countries reduced the number of young recruits to Maccabi in Europe, but new branches were springing up in North and South America, South Africa, and Australia. The birth of the State of Israel gave the movement a new focus and a new impetus, and from 1948 onward all the activities of Maccabi were oriented toward Israel, where the headquarters of the entire movement were established in Tel Aviv. By 1969, 38 countries were affiliated to the World Union, and the membership was estimated to be about 200,000. By the early 21st century the number of countries had grown to over 50 and membership to 400,000, organized in six confederations: Maccabi Israel, European Maccabi confederation, confederation Maccabi North America, confederation Maccabi Latin America (CLAM), Maccabi South Africa, and Maccabi Australia (APA). Seventy executive members elected by the confederations run the global organization.

[Menahem Savidor]

Israel

During World War II members of the Maccabi, formerly of the *Haganah, volunteered for the British army and established a Maccabi unit in 1941. In the same year the movement instituted what has become the tradition of the relay of runners carrying a lighted torch from Modi'in, the home of the Maccabees, to various parts of the country and, since the establishment of the State, to the presidential residence in Jerusalem. (In 1977 it reached the president of the United States.) Since the Six-Day War, Maccabi has organized marches "In the Footsteps of the Fighters" to such places as Mt. Sinai, the "Path of the 35" to Kefar Eẓyon, Masada, and the ascent of the Ḥermon.

Maccabi's soccer and basketball teams have dominated their sports in Israel. The Maccabi Tel Aviv soccer team has won 18 league championships and 22 state cups through the 2004/5 season, while the Maccabi Tel Aviv basketball team, in addition to winning 45 league championships and 35 state cups, has also won the European championship five times.

Maccabi has a junior organization "Young Maccabi" which was founded in 1929 and whose aims include training youth towards good citizenship and personal fulfillment in all branches of Israeli life and adherence to Jewish traditional values. (For Israel Maccabi until World War II, see *Sport in Israel before 1948.)

[Yehoshua Alouf]

BIBLIOGRAPHY: Maccabi, *Chairman's News Letter; Maccabi Bulletin; Maccabi World Review; Yedi'ot ha-Maccabi ha-Olami*; D. Rimon, *Ḥamishim Shenot ha-Maccabi ba-Olam 1894–1944* (1944). **WEBSITE:** www.maccabiworld.org.

MACCOBY, ḤAYYIM ZUNDEL (1858–1916), Zionist preacher, one of the first members of Ḥovevei Zion (see *Ḥibbat Zion) in England. Born near Kobrin, Poland, Maccoby decided to become a preacher when he discovered his oratorical talents, and he attracted many followers. In 1873 he was accepted as the preacher of Kamenets and from that time on was called "The Maggid from Kamenets." In 1875 he left Kamenets and was a preacher in several places until he became the first regular preacher of the Ḥibbat Zion movement, in 1883. In this office he traversed Russia, Lithuania, and Poland. About 300 societies for the settlement of Ereẓ Israel were founded because of his influence and in spite of the opposition of many rabbis. In 1890 he left Russia for England, where he also attracted large audiences to his sermons and was thus a pioneer of the Ḥibbat Zion movement in the country. Maccoby was one of the strongest opponents of *Herzl for religious reasons. In 1929 a collection of his sermons entitled *Ḥayyim* was published with a detailed biography.

BIBLIOGRAPHY: H.R. Rabinowitz, *Deyokena'ot shel Darshanim* (1967), 297–303; EZD, 3 (1965), 501–5; *Ha-Ma'or* (Sept. 1966–Dec. (1967); M. Temkin, in: *Jewish Review* (Feb. 3/Mar. 3, 1971).

[Getzel Kressel]

MACCOBY, HYAM (1924–2004), British scholar of ancient Judaism. Born in 1924 in Sunderland, the son of a mathematics tutor and the grandson of the Maggid of Kamenets (see *Maccoby, Ḥayyim Zundel), Poland, Hyam Maccoby was educated at Oxford. He became a schoolteacher and was then the librarian of Leo Baeck College, London. In 1998 he was made research professor at the Centre for Jewish Studies at Leeds University. Maccoby was widely known for his writings on Jesus, the founder of Christianity, and his milieu in Roman Judea. In such works as *Judea: Jesus and the Jewish Resistance* (1980), Maccoby argued that Jesus should be viewed as a liberal but Torah-observant Pharisee, who opposed the Romans but not other Jews. Maccoby also saw the origins of Christian antisemitism as beginning with the foundations of Christianity as a separate religion, a view he put forward in such works as *Judas Iscariot and the Myth of Jewish Evil* (1992) and in *Paul and Hellenism* (1991). Maccoby was widely known through his many appearances on television; he was frequently attacked by both Christians and Orthodox Jews.

[William D. Rubinstein (2nd ed.)]

°**MCDONALD, JAMES GROVER** (1886–1964), first U.S. ambassador to Israel. McDonald, who was born in Coldwater, Ohio, was assistant professor of history at the University of Indiana, before moving to New York. From 1919 to 1933 McDonald served as chairman of the Foreign Policy Association. During the 1920s he made numerous trips abroad for this organization becoming, in the process, a familiar figure at the League of Nations headquarters in Geneva. McDonald's interest in Zionism was sparked by his experiences as League of Nations high commissioner for refugees from Germany. He held this post from 1933 to 1935 when he resigned and issued a dramatic statement accusing the German government of planning a policy of race extermination and attacking League members for their indifference to the plight of the German refugees. In 1938 he was elected to head the newly created Presidential Advisory Committee on Political Refugees (PACPR), a quasi-official agency whose main task was to serve as a conduit for funneling the names of prominent refugees to be considered for special visitor's visas to the State Department. In September 1940 McDonald clashed with officials in the State Department who were imposing ever-stricter regulations to halt the influx of refugees. When the White House was finally called upon to mediate in the conflict, McDonald asked for and received Eleanor Roosevelt's support. However, despite her intercession, Roosevelt supported the State Department. In May 1943, seemingly affected by the lack of administration support for the refugee cause, McDonald rejected an opportunity to head the U.S. delegation to a refugee conference at Bermuda. During the next two years, he frequently advocated that Palestine be opened to immigration, "limited only by the absorption capacity of the area." In 1945 his efforts were partly rewarded when the Anglo-American Committee of Inquiry on Palestine, of which he was a member, recommended the admission of 100,000 displaced Jews. President Truman appointed McDonald U.S. special representative to Israel in 1948 and ambassador in 1949. McDonald served in this post until his retirement in 1951. He wrote *My Mission to Israel 1948–1951* (1953). After his retirement, McDonald devoted much time to Zionist-sponsored causes, especially the sale of Israel bonds.

BIBLIOGRAPHY: D.S. Wyman, *Paper Walls: America and the Refugee Crisis, 1938–1941* (1968); A.D. Morse, *While Six Million Died* (1968), passim.

[Henry L. Feingold]

MACEDONIA, region of southeastern Europe where Alexander the Great was born. As a result of the latter's conquests and subsequent Greek rule in Palestine, the Hebrew term "Javan" as it appears in the Bible was generally translated by the rabbis "Macedonia" (cf. Targum Pseudo-Jonathan to Gen. 10:2; Yoma 10a). Although the origins of a Jewish community in Macedonia are unknown, it is certain that such a colony existed toward the end of the Second Temple period. Philo, in the list of Jewish communities quoted from the correspondence of Agrippa I to Caligula, refers also to the Jews of Macedonia (The Embassy to Gaius, 281). Moreover, the fact that Paul and his followers made a number of journeys to Macedonia, and that their doctrines were readily accepted there, tends to substantiate the existence of a Jewish colony (cf. Acts 16:9; 18:5; 20:1; I Cor. 16:5; II Cor. 1:16; 2:13; 7:5). Josephus, in describing the Jewish community of Alexandria, claims that the Jewish residents there were granted the right to be called "Macedonians" (Wars 2:487–88; Ant. 12:8; Apion 2:35). However, papyrological research has shown that the phrase "Macedonian" eventually lost its original ethnic significance, and is in fact a designation of specific military status.

For later periods see also *Bulgaria; Byzantine *Empire; *Greece; *Yugoslavia.

BIBLIOGRAPHY: Schuerer, Gesch, 3 (1909⁴), 5; Juster, Juifs, I (1914), 187.

[Isaiah Gafni]

MACHABEY, ARMAND (1886–1966), French musicologist and composer. Born in Pont-de-Roide, France. Machabey studied classics and music in Paris with d'Indy and Pirro, concentrating on composition, but eventually devoted himself to musicology. His main contributions were made in the field of medieval musicology. He wrote his dissertation (1928) on the evolution of musical forms in the Middle Ages, for which he was awarded the Bernier Prize of the Académie des Beaux-Arts in 1930. His writings include monographs on Ravel, *Anton Bruckner* (1946), *Le Bel Canto* (1948) as well as *Traité de la critique musicale* (1946) and studies of notation such as *La Notation musicale* (1952). He also wrote about *Girolamo Frescobaldi* (1952) and *Guillaume de Machaut: la vie et l'oeuvre musicale* (2 vols., 1955), which are his best-known works. In 1957 he edited with Dufourcq and Raugel the *Larousse de la musique* encyclopedia. His compositions include chamber and solo instrument music such as six short preludes for piano, six pieces for violin and piano, and orchestral works.

ADD. BIBLIOGRAPHY: Grove online; F. Raugel, "Armand Machabey (1886–1966)," in: *Acta Musicologica*, 11 (1968).

[Israela Stein (2nd ed.)]

MACHADO, family name of Portuguese *Marranos. The best known is perhaps DAVID MENDEZ MACHADO (d. 1753), who left his native Lisbon in 1732 after he had aroused the suspicions of the *Inquisition that he practiced Judaism in secret. He arrived in Savannah, Georgia – by way of London – during 1733. Within that year he married Zipphorah Nuñez (c. 1714–1799), daughter of the former Portuguese court physician Samuel *Nuñez; Machado was then appointed *ḥazzan* at New York City's Spanish-Portuguese synagogue, Shearith Israel, serving from 1734 to 1753. His daughter, REBECCA (1746–1831), married Jonas *Phillips (1736–1803), the revolutionary war patriot. Among David Machado's descendants were Uriah Phillips *Levy and Mordecai Manuel *Noah. The record of freemen in New York City for 1739 lists an AARON MACHADO, probably the brother of the *ḥazzan*. The Machado family name appears also in the earliest records of the Mexican Inquisition: ANTONIO MACHADO and his daughter ISABEL were inculpated during the trial of Jorge de Almeida in 1600.

BIBLIOGRAPHY: Stern, Americans, index; D. de S. Pool, *Portraits Etched in Stone; Early Jewish Settlers, 1682–1831* (1952); Rosenbloom, Biogr Dict, 105; J.R. Marcus, *Early American Jewry*, 2 (1955), 59, 335.

MACHAERUS, Transjordanian frontier fortress erected by the Hasmonean king Alexander *Yannai (Jannaeus) in southern Perea, E. of the Jordan and adjacent to the border of Nabatean Arabia (Jos., Wars, 1:161; 3:46; 7:163–170). The place served as one of the depositories for his treasures (Jos., Ant., 13:417). It served as a base for Alexander and *Aristobulus in their resistance against the Romans. Pliny describes it as one of the strongest points in the region after Jerusalem (Pliny, *Historia Naturalis*, 5:16, 72) and Strabo lists the fortress among the Hasmonean strongholds (16:2, 40). Taken by Gabinius and destroyed, it was later rebuilt by Herod the Great. Machaerus was also the place where *John the Baptist was executed. According to Josephus (Ant., 18:116–117) John's activities in the lower Jordan River region so alarmed the Tetrarch *Herod Antipas (nicknamed the "fox": Luke 13:32), son of Herod the Great, that he had him executed. The story given in the gospels regarding the reason for John's execution is different, but in no way contradicts the reason given by Josephus. According to Mark (6:17–18; cf. Matt. 14:3–4; Luke 3:18–20) John spoke out publicly about the unlawfulness of the union between Herod and Herodias (in keeping with Lev. 18:6) which annoyed Herod considerably, but he was eventually beheaded owing to a request made by Salome on the occasion of Herod's birthday (Mark 6:14–29; Matt. 14:1–12). The place served as one of the stations for signaling the appearance of the new moon and the arrival of holidays (Tosef., RH 2:2). Herds, mainly of goats, were said to have been raised in the mountains of Machaerus (Tam. 3:8). In the Jewish War against the Romans the fortress was taken over by the Zealots (Jos., Wars, 2:485) and remained one of their strongholds even after the fall of Jerusalem (Jos., Wars, 4:555). In 72 C.E. the Roman legate Lucilius Bassus captured it after a short siege (Jos., Wars, 7:164ff.; which also includes a description of the site). Machaerus (Jabal al-Mishnaqa) is situated close to the present-day village of al-Mukāwir, 14 mi. (c. 22 km.) southwest of Madaba. The site was visited in the 19th century by J.L. Burckhardt, H. Tristram, and C.R. Conder. F.M. Abel made a survey of the site in 1909. In the 1920s a sculpted head identified by P. Ilton as the head of Salome was said to have been found in a cave 80 ft. north of Machaerus. Excavations were first made at the site by J. Vardaman in 1968, but the results were never published. In the early 1970s Strobel made a survey of the Roman siege-works around the site. Bassus' unfinished ramp is still visible on one side of the site. Father V. Corbo undertook major excavations at the site from the late 1970s. A few tombs from the first century C.E. were recently investigated at the site.

BIBLIOGRAPHY: F.M. Abel, *Une Croisière autour de la Mer Morte* (1911), 30–41. **ADD. BIBLIOGRAPHY:** F.M. Abel, "Mélange I, exploration de la vallée du Jourdain," in: *Revue Biblique*, 10 (1913), 218; J. Vardaman, "The Excavations of Machaerus" (manuscript in Hebrew University Library); A. Strobel, "Observations about the Roman Installations at Mukawer," in: ADAJ, 19 (1974), 101–27; idem, in: ZDPV, 90 (1974), 128–84; On V. Corbo's excavations: M. Picccirillo, "First Excavation Campaign at Qal'at el-Mishnaqa-Meqwer (Madaba)," in: ADAJ, 23 (1979), 177–83; V. Corbo, "La Fortrezza di Macheronte," in: LA, 27 (1978), 217–31; also S, Loffreda, in: ADAJ, 25 (1981), 85–94; V. Corbo, in: LA, 29 (1979), 315–26; D. Genequand, "Un hypogée hérodien à Machéronte (Jabal al-Mishnaqa, Jordanie)," in: C. Bottini, L. Di Segni, and L. Daniel Chrupcala (eds.), *One Land – Many Cultures* (2003), 327–39; and for a general summary about the site and the remains: S. Gibson, *The Cave of John the Baptist* (2004), 242–48.

[Michael Avi-Yonah / Shimon Gibson (2nd ed.)]

MACHAUT, DENIS DE (late 14th century), Parisian Jew who converted to Christianity. The provost of Paris decreed that his youngest child was to remain under the father's guardianship and receive a Christian upbringing, while the other three children were entrusted to Christian families. De Machaut was to be allowed to visit them but not his wife, who had remained Jewish. After a period of time determined by the provost, the children were to be interrogated on their intention to become Christians or not. A short while later, when Denis de Machaut disappeared, the Jews were accused of having seized him in order to attempt to bring him back to Judaism. Seven of the community's leaders were condemned to be burned at the stake. On April 6, 1394, parliament commuted the sentence to imprisonment until De Machaut was returned. The sentence was accompanied by repeated, severe corporal punishment, and the Paris community was also fined 10,000 livres. It has been claimed that this affair was a decisive factor in the expulsion decree against the Jews or France issued in 1394.

BIBLIOGRAPHY: L. Berman, *Histoire des Juifs de France* (1937), 206f.; R. Anchel, *Juifs* (1946), 117–9.

[Bernhard Blumenkranz]

MACHIR (Heb. מָכִיר), son of Manasseh and grandson of Joseph. Although Machir appears to have been an only son according to Numbers 26:29–34 (cf. Gen. 50:23), other traditions ascribe more sons to Manasseh (Josh. 17:2), and name Asriel as a brother (I Chron. 7:14). Machir's mother is said to have been an Aramean (*ibid.*). He married *Maacah who bore him Peresh and Sheresh (I Chron. 7:16). He also had a daughter (I Chron. 2:21). He is most frequently described as the father of Gilead (Num. 26:29; Josh. 17:1; I Chron. 2:21; 7:14). Machir is the eponym of one of the most important clans of the tribe of Manasseh, the special status of which is acknowledged in Genesis 50:23. In the Song of Deborah, Machir is mentioned along with Ephraim and Benjamin (Judg. 5:14) while Manasseh is missing, indicating that this powerful tribe is represented by Machir. Further, the Song distinguishes between this tribe and the Gilead who resides in Transjordan and who, along with the tribe of Reuben, did not participate in the war (Judg. 5:15, 17). However, the location of Machir west of the Jordan contradicts other sources which state that the Machirites captured the Gilead and the Bashan in Moses' time before the Israelites crossed the Jordan (Num. 32:39–40; Josh. 17:1). It is reasonable to suppose that at first the entire clan dwelt west of the Jordan. Later, a part of it crossed to the eastern side (cf. Josh. 13:31, "A part of the sons of Machir"). It was subsequent to this settlement that Machir became head of Gilead. According to Numbers 32:39–42, the clan settled in the northern Gilead from the Jabbok to the Yarmuk, while *Jair, son of Manasseh, and Nobah were located even farther north, in the Bashan (cf. Deut. 3:14). In contrast to this, Joshua 13:29–31 and 17:1–2 record that the Machirites settled both in the Gilead and in the Bashan, whereas Jair was situated in the land of Gilead (I Chron. 2:22). These contradictions may be reconciled by assuming that Jair was another branch of the larger clan of Machir or, in the course of time, became affiliated with it. Indeed, in I Chronicles 2:21 Jair is considered Machir's descendant. Further, Maacah's being Machir's wife (I Chron. 7:16) suggests that the Machirites settled north of the Yarmuk bordering the land of Maacah. The reference in I Chronicles 7:14 apparently hints at an ethnic assimilation of the families of Machir with the Aramean population north of the Yarmuk.

BIBLIOGRAPHY: A. Bergman, in: JAOS, 54 (1934), 169–77; idem, in: JPOS, 16 (1936), 224–54; J. Liver, in: EM, 4 (1962), 960–1.

[Bustanay Oded]

MACHIR BEN JUDAH (first half 11th century), younger brother of *Gershom b. Judah, "the Light of the Exile." Machir was the author of *Alef Bet de-Rabbi Makhir.* This work was in the possession of Rashi and the tosafists, who quote from it (Rashi, Gen. 43:11; Pes. 50a; Er. 22a; Tos. Nid. 7b s.v. *shammuti*, et al.), but it is now lost. It was the first talmudic dictionary to be compiled in Europe, not unlike the *Arukh* of *Nathan b. Jehiel of Rome. Its chief function was to connect words used in the Talmud with Scripture, to explain them, and to translate them into French. In consequence it also engaged in biblical exegesis. All the explanations in Machir's book were, evidently, given anonymously, no authorities being mentioned in it.

Machir had four sons: Nathan, Menahem, Nehemiah, and Yakar. These four collected the rulings, customs, and responsa of the great scholars of their locality. Menahem included all the material in a work which is referred to in the literature of the *rishonim as Ma'aseh ha-Makhiri* (Rabban – Eliezer b. *Nathan – Prague, 1610, 84c). Most of the material in his book, since lost, was included in the works of the *De-Vei Rashi* ("school of Rashi") and the whole book may have been used as the foundation for the *Ma'aseh ha-Ge'onim* (Berlin, 1909), certainly in respect of the information it affords about the customs of Speyer, Worms, and Mainz. The majority of the material in the *Ma'aseh ha-Ge'onim* is from these four brothers.

BIBLIOGRAPHY: A. Epstein, *Ma'aseh ha-Ge'onim* (1909), x–xiii (introd.).

[Israel Moses Ta-Shma]

MACHLUP, FRITZ (1902–1983), U.S. economist. Born in Wiener Neustadt, Austria, Machlup was a partner in a paper manufacturing enterprise in 1923. In 1929 he began lecturing at the Volkshochschule in Vienna. In 1933 he emigrated to the U.S. He was a research fellow at the Rockefeller Foundation in New York City, which he left in 1935 to become professor of economics at the University of Buffalo. In 1947 he was appointed professor of political economy at Johns Hopkins and in 1960 became professor of economics and international finance at Princeton University, serving at the same time as director of Princeton's international finance section (1960–71). During the 1960s, one of Machlup's principal interests was the expansion of international liquidity. In 1963, he formed an organization of academics, known as the Bellagio Group, to study the looming international monetary problems, develop an academic consensus, and offer practical solutions. Among the offices he held in academic organizations were the presidencies of the Southern Economic Association (1960); the American Association of University Professors (1962–64); the American Economic Association (1966); and the International Economic Association (1971–74). He also served as a consultant to the U.S. Treasury (1965–77).

He is regarded as one of the fathers of the concept of "the information society" and "the information economy." Although Machlup never won a Nobel Prize, the Nobel committee listed his name several times as a candidate

Machlup's many publications include *The Stock Market, Credit and Capital Formation* (1940); *The Political Economy of Monopoly* (1952); *The Economic Review of the Patent System* (1958); *The Production and Distribution of Knowledge in the United States* (1962); *International Payments, Debts, and Gold* (1964); *Education and Economic Growth* (1970); *Methodology of Economics and Other Social Sciences* (1978); the three-volume *Information through the Printed Word* (1978); and the first three volumes of the projected 10-volume series *Knowledge: Its Creation, Distribution, and Economic Significance* (1980, 1982, 1983).

ADD. BIBLIOGRAPHY: J. Dreyer (ed.), *Breadth and Depth in Economics: Fritz Machlup – the Man and His Ideas* (1978)

[Joachim O. Ronall / Ruth Beloff (2nd ed.)]

MACHPELAH, CAVE OF (Heb. מְעָרַת הַמַּכְפֵּלָה). The word "Machpelah," which in the Bible always appears with a definite article, is variously the name of a cave (Gen. 23:9, 19; 25:9); a field, "the cave which is in the field of Machpelah" (Gen. 49:30); and a place, "the field of Ephron, which was in Machpelah" (Gen. 23:17). The actual meaning of "Machpelah" is understood by all the early translations (Targum, Septuagint, et al.) as well as by the rabbis to mean "double" (from the Hebrew root *k-p-l*) and is interpreted in rabbinical literature as referring either to a double cave or to the "couples" buried in the cave. Machpelah is situated near Mamre, identified with Hebron (Gen. 23:19, 33:19). The Bible relates that Abraham, wishing to bury Sarah, purchased Machpelah from Ephron the Hittite for 400 silver shekels. Abraham himself, Isaac and Rebekah, Jacob and Leah were all later buried there. Jacob specifically commanded his sons not to bury him in Egypt but to lay him to rest with his fathers in the cave of Machpelah (Gen. 47:28–31; 49:30).

The site of the cave is today identified with Ḥaram el-Khalīl in modern Hebron. Surrounding the area, to a height of 39 ft. (12 m.), is a magnificent wall, distinguished by its decorative drafted-margin masonry, which are up to 23 ft. (7.5 m.) in length, and a very particular arrangement of pilasters. This wall is attributed to the time of Herod the Great and surrounding walls with pilasters also existed at the Temple Mount in Jerusalem and at Mamre (Ramat el-Khalil) (see Jacobson, Magen). Josephus, who describes the tombs of the patriarchs as "of really fine marble and exquisite workmanship" (Jos., Wars 4:532), does not, however, mention the surrounding wall (*temenos*). The first to prepare a plan of the structure was Ermete Pierotti between 1854 and 1861. A major study of the monument was later made by L.H. Vincent and E.J.H. Mackay following World War I in 1919. In 1968–69 excavations were conducted by Z. Yeivin along the southwestern side of the surrounding wall, bringing to light leveled rock surfaces, cupmarks, and a plastered installation. Interestingly, the monumental Herodian walls were very carefully adapted to the irregularities of the underlying surface of the rock, perhaps in an attempt to preserve the holiness of the hill.

The earliest source on the arrangement of the Patriarchal graves is in the Book of Jubilees (36:21) which states that "Leah is buried to the left of Sarah." According to the Jerusalem Talmud, the graves of the patriarchs are situated in the form used for the partaking of a meal; the most prominent reclining at the head, on the middle couch, the second above him and the third below him (TJ, Ta'an. 4:2). The two structures, which today mark the tombs of Abraham and Sarah, are indeed in the center of the compound area. The tombs of Jacob and Leah are at the northwestern end so that when facing the tombs from the southwest – the probable original entrance – the tomb of Leah is in fact to the left of Sarah's. The area inside the compound was evidently originally left roofless (a similar conclusion may be reached regarding the Mamre compound). The Byzantines built a church, later converted by the Muslims into a mosque, at the southeastern extremity, which left the two constructions marking Isaac and Rebekah's tombs inside, while those for Abraham and Sarah were outside, at the entrance. In the floor, inside the mosque, are two openings leading to the cave underneath. One of these, at the southeast wall, is covered by stone slabs fixed with iron hooks. The other, at the opposite wall, is open, as a Muslim custom requires the lowering of an oil lamp which is continually lit. The actual form of the cavern is uncertain but from the accounts of travelers it seems safe to conclude that there are at least two caves joined by a passage and possibly a third inner chamber. The entrance to the caves (apart from the two openings) is inaccessible today, though following the Six-Day War, Moshe *Dayan, who was serving as defense minister at that time, managed to gain access to a flight of steps leading to a narrow subterranean tunnel extending beneath the tomb of Isaac and leading to a chamber containing Moslem inscribed plaques. Rabbinic sources mention the burial of Adam and Eve in the Machpelah and the alternative biblical name for Hebron, Kiriath-Arba ("the town of the four"), is explained to refer to the four couples buried there. According to Josephus and apocryphal sources, the sons of Jacob were also buried in the Machpelah. A Muslim tradition maintains that Joseph was buried here, his tomb and the Mosque of Joseph being just outside the southwest exit of the compound. This tradition is probably due to a corruption of the Arabic name for Esau, whose head, according to aggadic sources, fell within the cave after he had been killed in a battle for the right of burial in the Machpelah (Sot. 13a; PdRE 39).

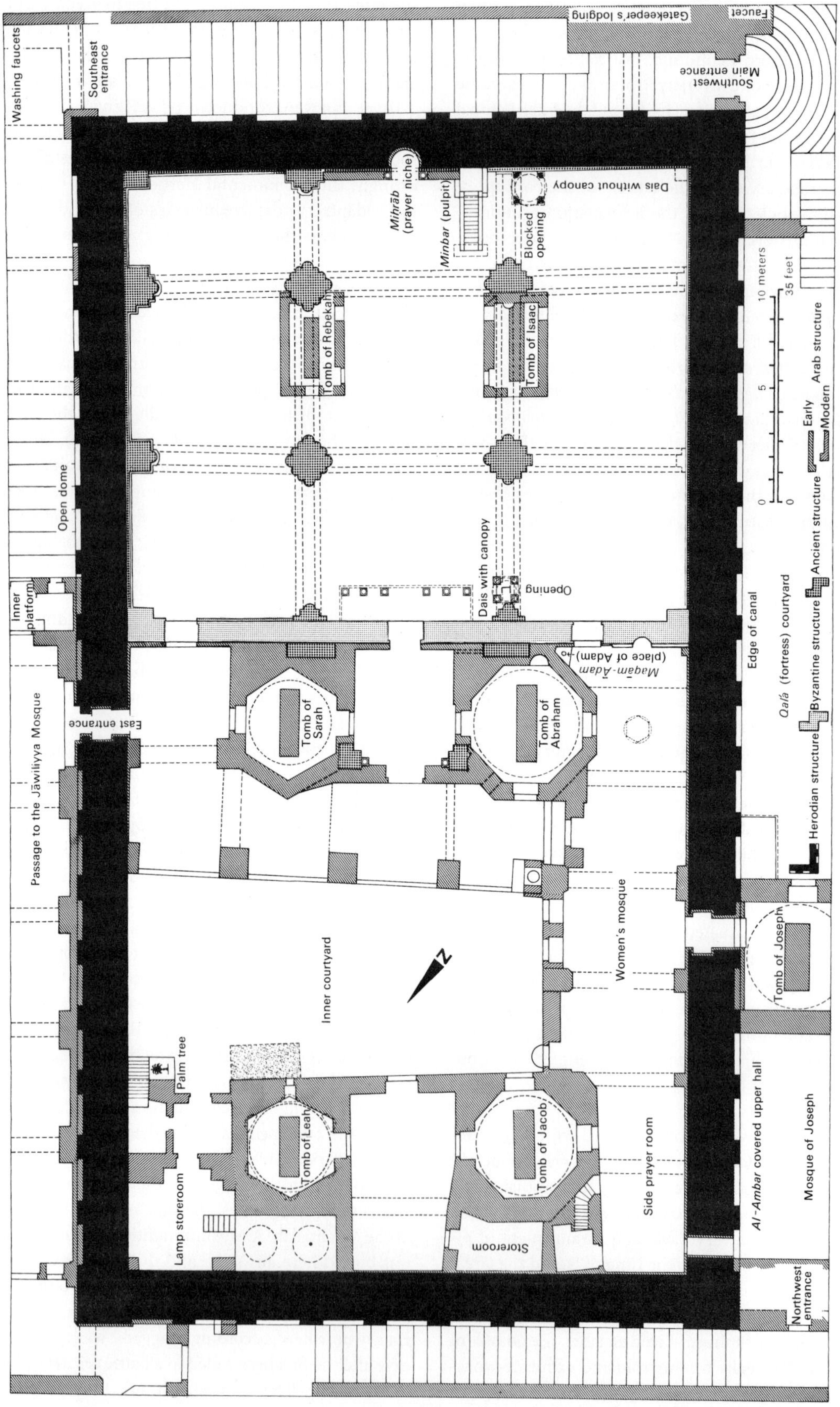

Plan of the mosque above the Cave of Machpelah. After L.H. Vincent et al., Hebron, Le Haram El Khalîl, Sépulture des Patriarches, *Paris, 1923.*

During the Byzantine period, the Jews were authorized to pray within the area. The Christians entered through one gate and the Jews through another, offering incense while doing so; when the Arabs conquered the country they handed over the supervision of the cave of Machpelah to the Jews, in recognition of their assistance. During the late 11th century, the official responsible for the area bore the title of "The Servant to the Fathers of the World." The Jews of Hebron were accustomed to pray daily in the cave of Machpelah for the welfare of the head of the Palestinian gaonate. Many Jews sought to be buried in the vicinity of the cave of Machpelah. It was then written of them that "their resting-place was with that of the Fathers of the World." *Benjamin of Tudela, the 12th-century traveler, relates that "many barrels, full of the remains of Jews, were brought there and they are still laid to rest there to this day." The Mamluk sultan Baybars prohibited the Jews and Christians from praying within the area (1267). Jews, however, were permitted to ascend five, later seven, steps on the side of the eastern wall and to insert petitions into a hole opposite the fourth step. This hole pierces the entire thickness of the wall, to a depth of 6 ft. 6 in. (2.25 m.). It is first mentioned in 1521, and it can almost certainly be assumed to have been made at the request of the Jews of Hebron, possibly on payment of a large sum, so that their supplications would fall into the cave situated under the floor of the area. The extremity of the hole is below the blocked opening in the mosque floor and leads to the cave.

Following the Six-Day War of 1967 the Machpelah became a popular center of pilgrimage, and Jews, after a period of 700 years, were once more able to visit the tombs of the patriarchs, and regular services were held there. Though strictly regulated, the use of the Machpelah by Jews and Muslims has made it one more bone of contention in a divided city. On Purim, February 25, 1994, Baruch Goldstein, Kiryat Arba's medical doctor, entered the Machpelah during Muslim prayers and opened fire with an automatic weapon, killing 29 and wounding 100.

BIBLIOGRAPHY: I.S. Horowitz, *Ereẓ Yisrael u-Shekhenoteha* (1923), 248–63; L.-H. Vincent and E.J.H. Mackay, *Hébron, Le Haram el-Khalīl, Sépulture des Patriarches* (1923); Braslavi, in: *Eretz Israel*, 5 (1958), 220–3; idem, in: *Beit Mikra*, 14 (1969), I, 50–56; Luria, *ibid.*, 13 (1968), iii, 10–11; M. Ha-Kohen, *Me'arat ha-Makhpelah ba-Mekorot u-va-Masorot* (1965); O. Avisar (ed.), *Sefer Ḥevron* (1970). **ADD. BIBLIOGRAPHY:** Z. Yeivin, "Note on the Makhpelah Cave (Hebron)," in: *Atiqot*, 7 (Hebrew Series, 1974), 58–60; Z. Yeivin, "The Cave of Machpelah," in: *Qadmoniot*, 9:36 (1976), 125–29; M. Dayan, "The Cave Beneath the Mosque," *ibid.*, 129–31; D.M. Jacobson, "Decorative Drafted-Margin Masonry in Jerusalem and Hebron and Its Relations," in: *Levant*, 32 (2000), 135–54; Y. Magen, "Mamre: A Cultic Site from the Reign of Herod," in: C. Bottini, L. Di Segni, and L. Daniel Chrupcala (eds.), *One Land – Many Cultures* (2003), 245–57.

[Joseph Braslavi (Braslavski) / Shimon Gibson (2nd ed)]

MACHT, DAVID I. (1882–1961), U.S. pharmacologist. Macht, who was born in Moscow, was educated in the U.S. He graduated from Johns Hopkins Medical School where he lectured in pharmacology from 1912 to 1932. From 1933 to 1941 he served as visiting professor of general physiology at Yeshiva College (see *Yeshiva University) and from 1944 onward was consultant and research pharmacologist at Sinai Hospital in Baltimore. Macht published over 900 scientific studies in his field and introduced a number of new methods of treatment of diseases. He discovered the curative qualities of benzyl alcohol as a substitute for cocaine; he found that morphine and codeine have a sedative or depressant effect on the respiratory center as opposed to other narcotic drugs that act as stimulants; he proved that a difference exists in the biological effects produced by Roentgen rays of varying wavelength and introduced a cure for pemphigus by application of "deep" X-rays; he made a special study of the thromboplastic properties of various medical agents, especially of antibiotics. He also did extensive research on the pharmacology of blood and spinal fluid of psychotic patients. An Orthodox Jew, Macht constantly attempted to show the harmonious relationship between religion and science. He studied medical descriptions appearing in the Bible and the Talmud and showed that many of the so-called "miracles" or "medical stupidities" were in reality accurate descriptions of either diseases or their treatments. (Some of these are listed in Friedenwald, *The Jews and Medicine*, 2 (1967²), index.)

BIBLIOGRAPHY: S.R. Kagan, *Jewish Medicine* (1952), 217–9; *New York Times* (Oct. 16, 1961), 29.

[Suessmann Muntner]

MACIAS, ENRICO (**Gaston Ghrenassia**; 1938–), French singer and entertainer. Born in Constantine, Algeria, Macias won popularity as a composer and singer of light songs, winning a reputation as the voice of the *pieds noirs* (French Algerians). In 1966 he sang before 120,000 people at the Dinamo Stadium in Moscow and performed in 40 other Soviet towns. He visited Israel in 1967 and sang for the troops and was then banned in Arab states. In 1968 he appeared in Carnegie Hall. In 1978, he was invited to Egypt by President Anwar Sadat and sang before 20,000 people at the foot of the pyramids. After Sadat's assassination he composed "Un berger vient de tomber" in his memory. His message of peace, brotherhood, and solidarity in songs like "Aimez-vous les uns les autres" brought him awards from the UN and engagements all around the world.

MACK, JULIAN WILLIAM (1866–1943), U.S. judge and Zionist leader. Mack, who was born in San Francisco, graduated from Harvard Law School in 1887, studied at the universities of Berlin and Leipzig, entered law practice in Chicago, and served as professor of law at Northwestern University (1895–1902) and the University of Chicago (1902–40). He was elected judge of the circuit court of Cook County, Illinois, in 1903, and was judge of the Chicago juvenile court (1904–07), and the U.S. commerce court (1911–13). In 1904 he became president of the National Conference of Social Workers. His interest in the welfare of children was recognized in his appointment as one of the chairmen of the White House conference on children in 1908. Mack was appointed to the U.S. circuit court of appeals in 1913 and presided over hundreds of civil and criminal cases until his retirement in 1941. As a judge in Chicago and subsequently, Mack fought for a progressive approach to the problem of juvenile delinquency. During World War I, he performed ably on several national assignments, including the establishment of standards for reasonable treatment of conscientious objectors. A member of the Harvard University Board of Overseers for 18 years, he was influential in blocking a proposal in 1922 for a *numerus clausus* for Jewish students.

Mack's interest in Jewish affairs was deep and abiding. In addition to active participation in social work and charitable endeavors, he was among the founders of the American Jewish Committee in 1906 and on its executive committee for 12 years. Influenced by *Brandeis, Mack became an ardent Zionist, served as president of the first American Jewish Congress in 1918, and first chairman of the *Comité des Délégations Juives at the Versailles Peace Conference in 1919. Mack was elected president of the *Zionist Organization of America in 1918, but resigned with Brandeis in a dispute over methods of developing Palestine. He continued his efforts, however, holding high posts in the Palestine Endowment Fund, World Jewish Congress, Jewish Agency for Palestine, United Palestine Appeal, and the Hebrew University. The Israel settlement Ramat ha-Shofet ("Judge's Hill") was so called in his memory. Mack's credo, "We ask no more for the Jew than we do for anyone else," expressed both his sense of justice and loyalty to his people. He wrote *Americanism and Zionism* (1918).

BIBLIOGRAPHY: Kallen, in: AJYB, 46 (1944–45), 35–46; *New York Times* (Sept. 6, 1943), 17:1; S.S. Wise, *As I See It* (1944), 178–83.

[Morton Rosenstock]

MACKLOWE, HARRY (1938–), U.S. real-estate developer. One of New York's best-known builders, Macklowe, the son of a garment executive from Westchester, dropped out of the University of Alabama, New York University, and the School of Visual Arts before throwing himself into the real-estate business in the 1960s. He moved quickly from broker to builder, developing a keen interest in architecture and modern art that were reflected in his sleek modernistic buildings and starkly white minimalist offices. Although he had been a prolific builder, Macklowe became well known in 1985 when his company tore down two single-room occupancy hotels in midtown Manhattan during the night without turning off the gas or obtaining permits. He was not criminally charged, but he paid New York City $2 million to settle a civil lawsuit, and one of his executives pled guilty to criminal misdemeanor charges. Years later he built the Macklowe Hotel on the site. But Macklowe, like many New York developers, lost a string of buildings, including the hotel, to lenders during the recession in the mid-1990s. When the New York real-estate market began heating up again in 1996, Macklowe found new financial partners and resurfaced. He converted a loft building into a luxury apartment house. He bought a tired-looking office building on Madison Avenue in 1996 for $45 million, a price that even his banker thought was too high. Macklowe renovated the building, installed more windows in the offices , and expanded the retail space on a valuable stretch of the avenue. It looked like a huge success until a section of the brick façade crashed to the street, closing traffic on Madison Avenue for weeks. In 2003 Macklowe bought the 50-story General Motors Building on Fifth Avenue in New York for $1.4 billion, then the most ever paid for a skyscraper in the United States.

[Stewart Kampel (2nd ed.)]

MACNIN (**Cohen ben Maknin**), Moroccan family of *Mogador which at the close of the 18th century was at first appointed "merchants of the sultan." MACʿŪD MACNIN (d. 1832) was sent to Europe in 1809 by Sultan Mulay Suleiman in order to acquire a large amount of military equipment for the defense of the Moroccan ports. In 1813 he arrived in London as minister plenipotentiary. From 1795 his brother MEIR (d. c. 1830) headed the important firm of Mogador, whose principal agencies were in Marseilles and London. From 1799 the latter agency was directed by his nephew Solomon Sebag, the father of the future Sir Joseph Sebag-Montefiore. From the beginning of his reign Mulay Abd al-Raḥmān (1822–59) granted Meir Macnin the exclusive right to export certain products and foodstuffs from *Tetuán and *Tangier and opened on his behalf the port of Tit to the maritime commerce of cereals. The port of Mazagan was put under his authority. From 1823 the sultan named him as his representative and envoy to the Christian courts, with the right of appointing consuls wherever he found the necessity. In 1826 he left on a special mission to London, and in 1828 he was appointed minister plenipotentiary.

BIBLIOGRAPHY: Hirschberg, Afrikah, 2 (1965), 369; Miège, Maroc, 2 (1961), 40–41, and passim.

[David Corcos]

MÂCON, capital of the department of Saône-et-Loire, E. France. The first *Church council of Mâcon (583) issued a series of decisions concerning the Jews. However, the first specific record of the presence of Jews in Mâcon dates from about 820, when *Agobard, archbishop of Lyons, began missionary activity among Jewish children at Mâcon who were sent to Arles for safety; he also arranged for the delivery of sermons condemning friendly relations between Christians and Jews. From 886 Jews are mentioned as owners of fields, and especially vineyards, on the outskirts of Mâcon and its surroundings, in at least 15 villages and places where they cultivated the land themselves. The Jewish quarter developed in Bourgneuf. The cemetery was situated not far from Pont Jeu, formerly known as Pont des Juifs. Several medieval Hebrew tombstones have been discovered, some of which are preserved in the Museum of Mâcon. Not far from the site of the cemetery, there was a house commonly known by the name Sabbat, a term sometimes employed in Burgundy for synagogue. In 1378, the municipality attempted to compulsorily segregate the 18 Jews still living in Mâcon in a separate quarter. They were expelled from the town in 1394. During the 17th and 18th centuries, Jews of Avignon visited Mâcon and its surroundings to trade. At the beginning of World War II, there were about 50 Jewish families living in Mâcon, but they were not organized into a community. The postwar community, consisting mainly of arrivals from North Africa, numbered 200 in 1969.

BIBLIOGRAPHY: Gross, Gal Jud, 339f.; B. Blumenkranz, *Juifs et chrétiens* (1960), index s.v. *Mâcon* and *Concile de Mâcon*; idem, in: *Bulletin philologique et historique 1959* (1960), 129–36; G. Jeanton, in: *Annales de l'Académie de Mâcon*, 20 (1917), 381ff.; idem, *Le Vieux Mâcon* (1934), 9ff., 81ff.; Loeb, in: REJ, 5 (1882), 104ff.; Z. Szajkowski, *Analytical Franco-Jewish Gazetteer 1939–1945* (1966), 255.

[Bernhard Blumenkranz]

°**MACROBIUS, AMBROSIUS** (c. 400), Roman grammarian. He credits *Augustus with a grim pun reflecting Jewish abstinence from swine flesh. On hearing that *Herod had ordered his own son to be killed, Augustus remarked: "I would rather be Herod's pig [Gr. *hus*] than his son [Gr. *huios*]" (*Saturnalia* 2:4, 11).

[Jacob Petroff]

MADABA, MEDEBA (Heb. מֵידְבָא), Moabite city, situated about 5½ mi. (9 km.) S. of Heshbon in the center of a fertile plain, the biblical Mishor, 2,550 ft. (785 m.) above sea level. The city was captured by the Israelites from the Amorite king Sihon and was allocated to the tribe of Reuben (Num. 21:30; Josh. 13:9, 16). Near Madaba, David defeated the Aramean allies of Ammon (I Chron. 19:7; cf. II Sam. 10). Israel lost its hold on the city when the monarchy was divided. Omri recaptured it, but the Moabite king Mesha restored it to Moab. In Mesha's inscription (the "Moabite Stele"), King Omri is referred to as having taken "possession of all the land of [the] Me(ha)deba" (see also II Kings 3:4–5). In c. 160 B.C.E. persons from Madaba were accused of killing John, brother of Judas Maccabaeus (I Macc. 9:35–42; Jos., Ant., 3.1.2). Subsequently Jonathan and Simon retaliated. It was finally conquered by John Hyrcanus I and remained in Hasmonean control down to the time of Alexander *Yannai (Jannaeus). Hyrcanus II ceded it to the Nabateans, handing it over to Aretas III in return for his help against his brother Aristobulus II (Jos., Ant., 14.1.4). Two funerary inscriptions are known mentioning the Beni ʿAmirat family from the time of the Nabatean hegemony in the region. In 106 C.E. it was incorporated into the Roman province of Arabia (*Provincia Arabia*). The town was mentioned by various writers including Eusebius (128:20), Ptolemy (Geog. 5.16.4), Hierocles (Syn. 720–21), George of Cyprus (No. 1062), and Stephen of Byzantium (Eth. 449:6). A number of inscriptions are known, one mentioning the city council (bolkeuta) of Madaba, and two others the names of Roman centurions from the Third Cirenian Legions stationed at Madaba. An imperial inscription relates that an important building was erected in 219/20 C.E. next to the city gate. Jews lived there in Mishnaic times (Mik. 7:1), but they were probably a minority. It was a flourishing Christian city in Byzantine times, with the town expanding considerably, serving as a bishropic from the mid-fifth century. It had numerous churches, most of which were paved with mosaics, dating mainly from the sixth to eighth centuries. The best known of these is the northern church with a mosaic pavement designed as a map of the Holy Land (see below). According to an Arab historian (947 C.E.), al-Masʿudi, Madaba was ruled by the Ghassanids in the sixth century. An inscription found within a large cistern credits the emperor Justinian with building activities at Madaba. A pictorial representation of the city of Madaba appears in one of the panels of a mosaic uncovered in the Church of St. Stephen at Umm Rasas dating to the early Abbasid period. Few descriptions of Madaba are known from the Abbasid through to Ottoman periods. In the early 21st century Madaba was a flourishing town in Jordan with Christian and Muslim inhabitants.

The first explorers to describe the ancient ruins of Madaba were U. Seetzen in 1806, followed by J. Burkhardt in 1812, members of the American Palestine Exploration Society in 1872, C.R. Conder in 1881, and G. Schumacher, P.M. Séjourné, and F.J. Bliss in the 1890s.

The Madaba Mosaic Map

In 1884 the mosaic map was discovered during the erection of a new Greek Orthodox church, but it was only in 1896, when part of it had already been ruined, that it finally came to the attention of scholars, with the announcement made in 1897. The mosaic was restored and recorded in color by a German expedition in 1965–66. The map was laid in the transept of a Byzantine period church and originally measured 72 ft. (22 m.) × 23 ft. (7 m.). It represented the biblical Holy Land and neighboring regions, from Byblos (Gebal) in the north to No-Ammon (Thebes in Egypt) in the south. The map was oriented toward the east, with the Mediterranean Sea at the bottom. The scale is uneven, largest for the more important areas (central Judea – 1:15,000; Jerusalem – 1:1,650). In general, it follows the *Onomasticon* of Eusebius; it was based on a Roman road map, with the addition of vignettes representing the principal cities. The Greek texts give biblical and contemporary names, sometimes with a historical note or verse from the Septuagint. Important places and tribal areas are marked in red. The extant part of the map covers an area from Neapolis (Nablus) to Egypt. The most valuable section is the detailed plan of Jerusalem, showing two colonnaded streets, the Tower of David, many churches and monasteries, including the Church of the Holy Sepulcher and that on Mount Zion, baths, and perhaps even the Western Wall. Most of the other cities indicated on the map are fragmentary. It notes many names in the Negev which are not recorded elsewhere. A few natural features are indicated on the map, as well as boats in the Dead Sea, animals in the deserts, and ferries across the Jordan. In some details, the Madaba map shows clear evidence of the influence of Jewish lore, as in the location of the mountains Ebal and Gerizim near Jericho (although a second Tur Gerizim is placed in its true position near Nablus). The mosaic is dated by consensus of opinion to the mid-sixth century C.E., but a few scholars (notably Bahat) would like to date it much later to the second half of the seventh century C.E.

BIBLIOGRAPHY: Abel, Geog, 2 (1938), 381–2; Aharoni, Land, index; P. Palmer and H. Guthe, *Die Mosaikkarte von Madeba* (1906); A. Jacoby, *Das geographische Mosaik von Madaba* (1905); O'Callaghan, in: DBI, 5 (1957), s.v.; M. Avi-Yonah, *The Madaba Mosaic Map* (1954); Donner, in: ZDPV, 83 (1967), 1ff.; U. Lux, in: ZDPV, 84 (1968), 106–42. **ADD. BIBLIOGRAPHY:** H. Donner, *The Mosaic Map of Madaba* (1992); D. Bahat, "A New Suggestion for the Dating of the Madaba Mosaic," in: G. Barkay and E. Schiller (eds.), *Eretz-Israel in the Madaba Map* (1996), 74–75; P.M. Bikai and T.A. Dailey (eds.), *Madaba: Cultural Heritage* (1996); M. Piccirillo and E. Alliata (eds.), *The Madaba Map Centenary 1897–1997. Travelling Through the Byzantine-Umayyad Period*, Proceedings of the International Conference, Amman, 1997 (1998).

[Michael Avi-Yonah / Shimon Gibson (2nd ed.)]

MADAGASCAR, island off Africa. Legends and theories about alleged Jewish descent of and influence on inhabitants of Madagascar are current and widespread, but the resemblance of certain customs is probably a consequence of contact with Islam through trade activities in the late Middle Ages. Various theories and suppositions regarding affinities to the ancient Hebrews were published by a French Lazarist missionary, Joseph Briant, in a booklet entitled *L'hébreu à Madagascar.*

Madagascar never had a sizable Jewish population. A few score of Jewish families settled in Tananarive during the French colonial period, but no community was created.

Relations with Israel

The State of Israel was among the very first (and still few) countries to establish an embassy in the newly proclaimed Malagasy Republic (1960), and, over the years, Presidents Tsiranana and Ben-Zvi exchanged visits and Israel Prime Minister Eshkol and Foreign Minister Golda Meir also visited Madagascar. Israel activities in Madagascar include the construction of the first luxury hotel, and agricultural experts have helped to produce citrus and improve poultry breeding and corn production. In addition, about 200 people from the Malagasy Republic have undergone technical training in Israel. Relations between the two countries were close, although the intimate relationship between France and Madagascar cast a shadow over the picture after the 1967 change in French policy toward the Arab-Israel conflict. Following the Yom Kippur War, Madagascar broke off diplomatic relations with Israel, but ties were resumed in 1993.

[Zvi Loker]

MADAGASCAR PLAN, proposal for Jewish settlement devised by the Nazi regime in the 1930s. Like most of the Nazis' schemes to solve the "Jewish question," the Madagascar Plan had already been conceived by others. In 1885 the German antisemitic nationalist Paul de *Lagarde had advocated deporting the Jews of Poland, Russia, Romania, and Austria in preparation for German colonization of the East. He preferred the French island colony of Madagascar on the east coast of Africa over Palestine. In 1926 and 1927, both Poland and Japan investigated Madagascar and proposed the island as a possible solution to their overpopulation problem; both dismissed the idea as not feasible. In 1937, a new Polish commission was sent to Madagascar to determine if Jews could be induced to settle there. Leon Alter, the director of *HICEM in Warsaw, and Salmon Dyk, an agricultural engineer from Tel Aviv, took part in the mission. The assessments of the commission's director Major M. Lepecki and of Alter differed widely, but it was obvious to all that the area was generally inhospitable to Europeans and that there was a serious danger of potential settlers contracting endemic tropical diseases. This point was emphasized by the French governor-general of the island Marcel Olivier in his statements and writings opposing the proposal. Yet the proposal refused to die. On December 9, 1938, French Foreign Minister Georges Bonnet informed German Foreign Minister Joachim *Ribbentrop that, in order to rid France of 10,000 Jewish refugees, it would be necessary to ship them elsewhere. According to Ribbentrop, the French were seriously considering sending them to Madagascar.

The island of Madagascar was also discussed within the Nazi regime, which generally considered mass emigration to be the "Final Solution" to the "Jewish problem." On March 5, 1938, the SS officer in charge of forced Jewish emigration, Adolf *Eichmann, was commissioned to assemble material to provide the chief of the Security Police (SIPO) Reinhardt *Heydrich with "a foreign policy solution as it had been negotiated between Poland and France," i.e., the Madagascar Plan. Temporarily shelved in the wake of the war, the project was again taken up after the fall of France in the summer of 1940. Eichmann prepared a detailed official report on the island and its "colonization" possibilities based on information gathered from the French Colonial Office. He added an evacuation plan calling for 4,000,000 Jews to be shipped to Madagascar over a period of four years. Eichmann also advocated the creation of a "police reserve" as a giant ghetto ("*Gross-Getto*"). The plan was to be financed by a special bank managing confiscated Jewish property and by contributions exacted from world Jewry. The idea was also analyzed by Martin Luther's department in the German Foreign Office, which served as a liaison with the SS. The plan leaked out and was published in Italy in July. The *American Jewish Committee was alarmed enough to commission Eugene Hevesi to write a special report, which was eventually published in May 1941, that sought to demonstrate that Jews, as Europeans, could not survive the conditions on the island. By that time, of course, the Nazis were already preparing a completely different "*Final Solution." In August 1940, the Third Reich officially endorsed the Madagascar Plan. The 20-page proposal presented a detailed plan which no longer depended upon the consent of defeated France. The operation, whose code word was "*Endloesung*," was repeatedly discussed throughout 1940 and 1941. By the fall of 1941, the extermination program was already well underway. On February 10, 1942, only a few weeks after the *Wannsee Conference, the Madagascar Plan was officially shelved and replaced in public policy statements by the program of "evacuation to the East."

BIBLIOGRAPHY: G. Reitlinger, *Final Solution* (1968[2]), 23, 49, 79–82; J. Robinson, *And the Crooked Shall be Made Straight* (1965), index; E. Hevesi, in: *Contemporary Jewish Record*, 4 (1941) 381–94.

[Leni Yahil]

MADISON, capital of Wisconsin since 1837. Madison's Jewish presence dates back to roughly 1850, when a merchant named Aaron Boskowitz clerked in a store. By 1863, about 40 Jewish households, mostly storekeepers from Bohemia and West Prussia, had established a synagogue, a burial society, and a women's auxiliary. Through the 1870s, most of the original members died, stopped practicing Judaism, or moved away. The synagogue dissolved altogether in 1922. From 1880 to 1910, a small Jewish community existed in the nearby city of Monroe, Wisconsin. Its members were merchants from Poland and Austria who had ties to wholesale houses in Chicago. Several of Monroe's Jews came to Madison, notably Solomon Levitan, who had run a store in nearby New Glarus. A Progressive, Levitan served seven terms as Wisconsin state treasurer during the 1920s and 1930s.

Madison's present Jewish institutions trace their roots to Jews who arrived in the Madison area in the 1890s from Minsk, via Milwaukee. Like Jewish immigrants elsewhere, they tended to work in the junk and grocery businesses. In 1904, they built an Orthodox synagogue whose members went on to found Madison's present-day Conservative and Reform congregations. Elias Tobenkin, who came from the shtetl of Kapule, Minsk, in 1899, wrote about Madison in his novels *Witte Arrives* (1914) and *God of Might* (1925).

Rachel Szold Jastrow, sister of Henrietta *Szold, founded Madison's chapter of Hadassah. Jewish men in Madison tended to affiliate with cliquish lodges, but Hadassah brought together women from all strata of Madison's Jewish community.

What distinguished Madison from other small Jewish communities was the presence of the University of Wisconsin. Jews had been students there since the early 1860s, and Joseph Jastrow, a psychologist and the first Jewish faculty member, was hired in 1888. In 1911, philosopher Horace Kallen began a chapter of the Menorah Society, an early Jewish student organization. Antisemitism in many university departments prevented many Jews, such as Ludwig *Lewisohn, Lionel *Trilling, and Milton *Friedman, from obtaining tenure-track professorships. However, economist Selig *Perlman, kinesthesiologist Blanche Trilling, pharmacologist Arthur Solomon Loevenhart, among others, held tenured positions at Wisconsin before World War II. In addition to the Menorah Society, some Jewish students at Wisconsin joined Avukah, a student Zionist society, a Reform student congregation, and Jewish fraternities and sororities. The Hillel Foundation, established in 1924, served as a clearinghouse for Jewish activities on campus. Scholars fleeing the Holocaust settled at Wisconsin. Some, like pharmacist George Urdang, escaped before the war; others, like historian George Mosse and poet Felix Pollak, came to Wisconsin afterwards. During the late 1940s and 1950s, departments across the university ended their prejudice against hiring Jewish faculty.

During World War II, the Madison Jewish Welfare Fund organized USO events at Truax Air Force Base, and many Jews who served there returned to Madison after the war. As antisemitism faded, Jewish families began to move to new subdivisions across the city. Increased access to graduate and professional schools, combined with the consolidation of traditional Jewish businesses, prompted more Jews to seek work in education, government, and the professions.

Although members of the state legislature hinted that "out-of-state radicals" were responsible for campus protests, vaguely antisemitic statements like these made little difference to most Madison Jews. Some student-movement leaders, such as future Madison mayor Paul Soglin, had Jewish roots, but many were gentile Wisconsinites.

Totaling roughly 6,000 people in the early 2000s, Madison's Jewish community has continued to thrive since the 1970s. Observant Jews attend local Reform, Reconstructionist, Conservative, and Lubavitch congregations, plus the Hillel synagogue on campus. The Madison Jewish Community Council and Jewish Social Services support local and international Jewish initiatives. Immigrants from Canada, South Africa, Israel, and the former Soviet Union continue to settle in Madison, often as professors, doctors, and other professionals.

[Jonathan Pollack (2nd ed.)]

°**MADISON, JAMES** (1750–1836), fourth president of the United States. The son of a prominent Episcopalian family, Madison graduated from the College of New Jersey in 1771. Because he was then considering a career in the ministry, he spent an additional year studying theology and Hebrew. Throughout his political career, he contended that complete religious liberty was essential for a harmonious society and that religious institutions established by the state engendered "ignorance and corruption." During the Virginia constitutional convention in 1776, he opposed a provision for full religious "toleration," proposing instead that the law declare "the full and free exercise of it [religion] according to the dictates of conscience." In 1784 he successfully led the opposition to a resolution in the Virginia House of Delegates for a tax in "support of the Christian religion, or of some Christian church" and warned that "Instead of holding forth an asylum to the persecuted, it is itself a signal of persecution." As president he vetoed two bills in 1811 which would have granted legal prerogatives to certain churches.

While serving as a congressman from 1780 to 1783, Madison borrowed money from the Jewish broker Haym *Salomon, whom he later referred to gratefully in a letter. Writing to Mordecai M. *Noah in 1818, he expressed delight at the blessings conferred upon Jews by religious liberty in America, while in 1820 he wrote to Jacob *De La Motta that while being little known, "the history of the Jews must be forever interesting."

During his presidency he appointed several Jews to government posts, including John *Hays as collector for the Indian Territory in 1814, Mordecai Noah as consul general at Tunis in 1813, and Joel *Hart as consul at Leith, Scotland, in 1817.

BIBLIOGRAPHY: G. Hunt, *The Life of James Madison* (1902), 8–12, 77–86; S.K. Padover (ed.), *The Complete Madison* (1953), 298–312; Kohler, in: AJHSP, 11 (1903), 60–65.

[Edward L. Greenstein]

MAḌMŪN BEN JAPHETH BEN BUNDĀR (d. 1151), son of the first **nagid* of the Jews of South *Yemen. Maḍmūn continued in his father's position as the "official of the merchants" in *Aden, representing the merchants who traded with India, and in this capacity was also the leader of the Jews and the *nagid* of the communities of South Yemen. Dozens of letters have been preserved in the **Genizah* which were written to or by him, as well as court actions connected with his name and poems in his honor. More details are known about him than about any other *nagid* of Yemen from the 11th to the beginning of the 14th centuries. He was in charge of the port of Aden and supervised the customs payments. He formulated the agreements about prices of merchandise and his house served as a post office for the Jewish merchants, as well as a warehouse for merchandise. He owned ships which sailed from Aden to Ceylon. Among his wide-ranging activities, he jointly owned a ship with a vizier in Yemen. In a court action he is named "the confidant of rulers whether on the sea or in the desert," which means that he was held in esteem by the Muslim rulers and drew up agreements with tribal leaders and the leaders of pirates in order to assure free navigation on the sea routes between Egypt and India. In the above-mentioned court action it is stated that he was "appointed on behalf of the *rashei galuyyot* ["exilarchs"] and the *rashei yeshivot* ["academy heads"]." It is not clear whether the reference here is to the exilarch in Babylon or to a person representing the exilarch who lived in Yemen; there is an hypothesis that the reference is to the *bet din* in *San'a. *Rashei yeshivot* refers to the Palestinian academy in Egypt.

Maḍmūn maintained close contact with the *gaon* Maẓli'aḥ b. Solomon ha-Kohen, who was active in 1127–39 as head of the Palestinian academy which moved to Egypt as a result of the conquest of Palestine by the Crusaders. Maḍmūn sent the *gaon* questions on *halakhah*, together with expensive gifts which were also given to the scholars of his academy. He ordered that the name of the *gaon* be mentioned in the *reshut* prayer after the name of the exilarch. His attachment to the Palestinian academy aroused the opposition of the supporters of Babylonia. In documents he is called "the *nagid* of God's people, the minister of ministers, head of the communities." The Tunisian merchant Abraham b. Peraḥyah b. Yiju writes of him in his eulogy: "with seven names given by the exilarch," among which are mentioned, *alluf, nagid*, and friend of the academy. When he died, his eldest son, Ḥalfon, who is also called *nagid*, continued in his father's position in economic and public life.

BIBLIOGRAPHY: J. Mann, in: HUCA, 3 (1926), 301–3; E. Strauss, in: *Zion*, 4 (1939), 217–31; S.D. Goitein, in: *Sinai*, 33 (1953), 225–37; idem, in: *Sefer ha-Yovel… M.M. Kaplan* (1953), 45, 51–53; idem, in: *Tarbiz*, 31 (1962), 357–70; idem, *Bo'i Teiman* (1967), 15–25; idem, in: JQR, NS, 53 (1962), 97; E. Subar, *ibid.*, 49 (1958/59), 301–9.

[Eliezer Bashan (Sternberg)]

MADON (Heb. מָדוֹן), Canaanite city in the north of Ereẓ Israel whose king was defeated by Joshua in the battle at the waters of Merom (Josh. 11:1; 12:19). It is usually identified with the tell at Qarn Ḥiṭṭīn (Horns of *Hittin), a peak about 4 mi. (7 km.) west of Tiberias. Remains of walls, including one of cyclopean masonry, and potsherds from the Canaanite and Israelite periods were found on this tell. The identification is based on the similarity between the names Madon and Khirbat Madīn, situated south of Qarn Ḥiṭṭīn, which Arabic tradition connects with Moses' father-in-law Jethro, the priest of Midian, whose grave is venerated nearby. Some scholars, however, question the form of the name Madon, which is the sole basis for the identification. No town with this name is known from any other source; the Septuagint calls it Marron and identifies it with the city Merom near the site of the battle (in LXX: *Hydor Marron*, "waters of Merom"). *Merom is known from various sources as an important city in Upper Galilee and Madon may be a corrupt form of its name.

BIBLIOGRAPHY: Abel, Geog, 2 (1938), 372f.; J. Garstang, *Joshua, Judges* (1931), 102, 187ff.; Aharoni, Land, index; idem, *Hitnaḥalut Shivtei Yisrael ba-Galil ha-Elyon* (1957), 91f.

[Yohanan Aharoni]

MADRAS (today **Chennai**), city in S. India. Formerly known as Fort St. George, Madras was the first territorial acquisition of the English East India Company in 1639. In the last decades of the 17th century its diamond trade attracted Anglo-Portuguese Jewish merchants, who were allowed by the Company to establish a merchant colony which continued until the end of the 18th century. In the Madras corporation, established in 1688, the "Hebrew merchants" were represented by Jewish aldermen. Among the Jewish merchants prominent in the early days were Bartholomew *Rodrigues, Domingo do Porto, Alvaro da *Fonseca, Jacques *Paiva, Francis Marques, Isaac do Porto, Joseph d'Almanza, and Isaac Sardo *Abendana. In the 18th century many Ashkenazi Jews from London participated in the profitable trade, including Marcus *Moses and his family, Ephraim Isaac, the *Franks, and later the Portuguese family De *Castro and Salomon *Franco. The Jewish merchants in Madras were integrated into the English society and were on good social terms with several of the governors.

The fluctuating nature of the merchant colony apparently prevented the organization of a Jewish community and the only communal institution seems to have been a cemetery. Some tombstones still remain, but they have been transferred to a new municipal site in Madras called the "People's Park," the entrance of which bears a tablet inscribed in Hebrew *Beit ha-Ḥayyim*. Only 20 Jews were living in Madras in 1968. Unlike those of *Cochin, *Bombay, and *Calcutta, the Jews in

Madras did not create any literary works. It was only due to the Christian mission that some Hebrew books were published there in the 19th century. A noteworthy Jewish literary event there was the publication of the *Travels from Jerusalem…* of *David d'Beth Hillel in 1832. In the early 21st century the Jewish community of Chennai consisted mainly of expatriates.

BIBLIOGRAPHY: Fischel, in: *Journal of the Economic and Social History of the Orient*, 3 (1960), 78–107, 175–95 (incl. bibl.); Roth, Mag Bibl, 106; H.D. Love, *Vestiges of Old Madras*, 4 vols. (1913); A. Yaari, *Ha-Defus ha-Ivri be-Arẓot ha-Mizraḥ*, 2 (1940), 98–99.

[Walter Joseph Fischel]

MADRID (**Magerit**), capital of Spain. Mentioned as a Moorish stronghold, it was a tiny town in the Middle Ages. A small Jewish community existed there in the 11th century. Most of the Jews there were apparently merchants during the Muslim period. Nearby was located the small town of Alluden, whose name is derived from the Arabic *al-Yahūdiyīn* ("the Jews"). Madrid was captured from the Muslims by Alfonso VI in 1083.

[Haïm Z'ew Hirschberg]

The Community's Status

The community began to flourish during the 13th century, the Jewish quarter being located on the present Calle de la Fé ("Street of the Faith"). The synagogue, which was destroyed during the persecutions of 1391 (see below), was situated next to the Church of San Lorenzo. In 1293 a copy of the resolutions passed by the Cortes in Valladolid was sent to Madrid, in which Sancho IV ratified a series of restrictions concerning the Jews. They were barred from holding official positions, the rate of usury they were permitted to charge was defined, and they were prohibited from acquiring real estate from Christians or from selling them properties already acquired, among other limitations. In 1307, when Ferdinand IV confirmed these prohibitions at the Cortes in Valladolid, a copy of them was passed to Madrid. They were endorsed by Alfonso XI in 1329. A directive from the time of *Asher b. Jehiel (early 14th century) permitting action to be taken against an *informer who had harmed the community is extant (Asher b. Jehiel, Responsa, Constantinople (1517), ch. 17, no. 6).

The Jews of Madrid owned goods and real estate in the town and its environs. In 1385 John I acceded to the request of the Cortes and delivered a copy of its resolutions to Madrid. He then imposed a series of restrictions concerning the relations between Jews and Christians, prohibiting Jews from holding official positions, canceling debts owed them by Christians for 15 months, and abrogating the right to acquire stolen goods, among other regulations.

Persecutions and Expulsion

The persecutions of 1391 were disastrous for the Madrid community. Most of its members were massacred, some adopted Christianity, and community life came to an end. The municipal authorities, in a report sent to the Crown, complained of the *pueblo menudo* ("little people") who continued the rioting and pillaging for a whole year. Several of the rioters were arrested and tried, but many escaped justice. Apparently the community was later reestablished, although it was greatly impoverished.

During the early 1460s, *Alfonso de Espina preached in Madrid against the *Conversos. It was there that he turned to *Alfonso de Oropesa, the head of the Order of St. Jerome, to enlist his support in eradicating judaizing tendencies among them. In 1478 the municipal council complained that the Jews and the Moors there were not wearing a distinctive sign (*badge). The Crown answered the complaint on November 12 and ordered that the offenders should be punished in the prescribed manner. On February 2, Ferdinand and Isabella renewed the restriction issued by John II in 1447 which prohibited the Jews of Madrid from trading in foodstuffs and medicaments and from practicing as surgeons.

No details are known as to how the community fared after the decree of expulsion of the Jews from Spain was issued in March 1492. However, on Oct. 7, 1492, Ferdinand and Isabella ordered an investigation into reports of attacks on local Jews by various persons who had promised to assist them in reaching the frontiers in order to go to the kingdoms of Fez and Tlemcen. On Nov. 8, Fernando Nuñez Coronel (Abraham *Seneor) and Luis de Alcalá were authorized to collect the debts still owing to Jews.

In Madrid there were two Jewish quarters. One existed until 1481, the other was established that year. In the 15th century Jews lived in various parts of the town, in the area of Puerta del Sol and in the neighborhood of Santiago. The Jewish quarter until 1481 was near Puerta de Valnadú, in today's Isabell II square.

The Conversos

Several Conversos of Madrid were tried by the Inquisition. They were at first tried in Toledo; however, in 1561 when Madrid became the capital of the kingdom during the reign of Philip II, the supreme tribunal of the kingdom was established there and subsequently numerous *autos-da-fé were held in the city. During the 17th century, many Portuguese Conversos were tried there and one of the large autos-da-fé in this period has been painted by Rizzi de Guevara. During the 1630s, Jacob *Cansino negotiated with the Conde-Duque de Olivares concerning the possible return of the Jews to Madrid, after the example of the Jewish community in Rome. However, the talks had no results because of opposition from the Inquisition. Throughout this period, Madrid was the principal center of the activities of the Portuguese Conversos, several of whom were connected with the court, while others developed diversified business enterprises and maintained relations with the Converso centers outside the Iberian Peninsula.

The Reestablished Community

Jewish settlement in Madrid was gradually renewed from 1869, with the conferment of the constitution and the arrival of Jews from North Africa, who were joined by Jewish immigrants from Europe. However, it was only during the 1920s that a community was organized. During World War I, Madrid gave asylum to a number of refugees, and Max *Nordau and A.S. *Yahuda, who lectured there in Semitic philology, lived there during this period. Among the first Jews to settle in Madrid was the Bauer family, whose members played an important part in the organization and development of the community. The law of 1924 which granted citizenship to individuals of Spanish descent encouraged the further development of the community, and in the early 1930s there was an addition of refugees from Nazi Germany. During the Spanish Civil War, the community underwent much suffering and most of its members dispersed.

In 1941, the Arias Montano Institute for Jewish Studies was founded and a department of Jewish studies headed by Professor Francisco Cantera-Burgos was organized within the University of Madrid. It was later headed by Professor F. Perez Castro. Madrid also gave asylum to war refugees, who were supported by the American Jewish *Joint Distribution Committee. After the war, the community began reorganization. A synagogue was founded in Calle del Cardinal Cisneros. In 1958, a Jewish center with a synagogue was opened. In 1959, while the representative of the World Sephardi Federation, Yair Behar Passy, was visiting Madrid, an exhibition of Jewish culture in Spain was held at the National Library of Madrid. An Institute for Jewish, Sephardi, and Near Eastern Studies was founded jointly by the Higher Council for Scientific Research and the World Sephardi Federation in 1961. (In 1968 the institute amalgamated with the Arias Montano Institute.) Within the framework of the institute, the first symposium on Spanish Jewry was held in Madrid in 1964. Leaders of the Madrid community in the late 1960s included A. Bauer, H. Cohen, L. Blitz, and M. Mazin (the president of the community). In that year the community numbered over 3,000, a level it maintained into the 21st century. It served as a center for Jewish students from abroad coming to study in Madrid. Jewish immigrants from North Africa constitute the majority of the Jews. In 1968 the community inaugurated its new communal center and synagogue. Dr. B. Garzon was appointed first rabbi of the community, which had a recognized school and a Jewish scout movement. The Sephardi Federation of Spain in Madrid coordinates the activities of all the Jewish communities in Spain.

In Madrid there are several institutions that have great importance from the Jewish historical point of view. In the Archivo Histórico Nacional, the Biblioteca Nacional, and the Academia de la Historia there are numerous documents related to the Jews. In the Biblioteca we find the Bible of Ferrara and kept in the Casa de Alba is the famous Bible translated by Moses Arragel into Castilian. In El Escorial, near Madrid, are valuable Hebrew manuscripts in the library of the monastery. The Institute Arias Montano, dedicated to research in Jewish and Sephardic studies, publishes the journal *Sefarad* devoted to the these topics.

[Haim Beinart / Yom Tov Assis (2nd ed.)]

BIBLIOGRAPHY: Baer, Spain, 2 (1966), index; Baer, Urkunden, 2 (1929), index; Fita, in: *Boletín de la Academia de la Historia, Madrid*, 8 (1885), 439–66; F. Cantera, *Sinagogas españolas* (1955), 241–2; R.T. Davies, *Spain in Decline* (1957), 76–77; AJYB, 63 (1962), 318–22; J. Gomez Iglesias (ed.), *El Fuero de Madrid* (1963); Suárez Fernández, Documentos, index; Ashtor, Korot, 2 (1966), 145; H. Beinart, *Ha-Yishuv ha-Yehudi he-Ḥadash bi-Sefarad* (1969). **ADD. BIBLIOGRAPHY:** J.A. Cabezas, *Madrid y sus judíos* (1987); J. Blázquez Miguel, *Madrid: judíos, herejes y brujas. El Tribunal de Corte (1650–1820)* (1990).

MADURO, RICARDO (1946–), president of Honduras. Maduro is a member of a prominent Jewish family of Portuguese origin that can be traced from Portugal to Amsterdam and then to Curaçao and Panama. His father, Osmond Levy Maduro of Panama, settled in Tegulcigalpa, the capital of Honduras. Ricardo Maduro studied economy at Stanford University and became a successful businessman. As a supporter of democracy he became active in the Nationalist Party of Honduras. After losing his son to kidnappers, he also worked for measures to ensure law and order. After he was accused of being a Panamian, and therefore ineligible to run for president, the High Election Tribunal declared him a Honduran citizen; he was elected president on Jan. 27, 2002.

[Mordechai Arbell (2nd ed.)]

°MAES, ANDREAS (Masius; 1515?–1573), Flemish Hebraist and Orientalist. A lawyer and a diplomat, Maes spent much of his life in Italy, where he met Guillaume Postel, under whom he studied Arabic and with whom he thereafter maintained an interesting correspondence. In Venice, Maes joined the humanist circle of Daniel Bomberg and was in touch with the pioneer grammarian Elijah Levita. Maes contributed to the Antwerp polyglot Bible (1568–72), in which he published an edition of the Targums and the first printed grammar and lexicon of Syriac. His Hebrew-Greek edition of Joshua, *Josuae imperatoris historia*… (Antwerp, 1574), which appeared posthumously, aroused controversy because of its independence in regard to the masoretic text. This work lists the rabbinic and kabbalistic manuscripts in Maes' library, which must have been one of the major collections of Judaica in the Renaissance. Maes was apparently a member of the heretical Flemish sect ("The Family of Charity") led by Postel, Arias Montano, and the printer Christophe Plantin. Maes opposed the papal condemnation of the Talmud and the burning of rabbinic books at Rome in 1559.

BIBLIOGRAPHY: J. Perles, *Beitraege zur Geschichte der hebraeischen und aramaeischen Studien* (1884), index; M. Lossen (ed), *Briefe von Andreas Masius und seinen Freunden, 1538 bis 1573* (1886); U. Cassuto, *I Manoscritti Palatini Ebraici della Biblioteca Apostolica Vaticana* (1935), 48, 65f.; C. Roth, *The Jews in the Renaissance* (1959), 149; B. Rekers, *Benito Arias Montano* (Dutch, 1961), index; F. Secret, in: *Bibliothèque d'Humanisme et Renaissance*, 23 (1961), 524–40; idem, *Les Kabbalistes Chrétiens de la Renaissance* (1964), 54–56.

[Godfrey Edmond Silverman]

MAESTRO, YAAKOV (Jacko; 1927–), Greek Holocaust prisoner. Maestro was born in Salonika. In 1943, at age 15, he arrived at Auschwitz in the first deportation from Salonika. In Salonika, he had learned German from his father, who was a tourist guide, and had done odd jobs during the German occupation of Salonika as a shoeshine boy and porter, coming into contact with German and Italian soldiers. Upon arriving in Auschwitz, camp commander Schwartz, who had replaced Rudolph Hess, noticed that he was a German speaker. He became a translator and was in charge of work assignments for 16,000 prisoners in Auschwitz. He worked under the political prisoner Yeze Pozinski during the morning hours in the *Fuhrerbarrack* in the office of the *Arbeitsdienst*. The two prisoners coordinated the work schedule according to demand and registered the details of the prisoners on card files in the *Kartei* Department. Maestro could ease conditions for prisoners by not sending them to difficult work groups. He could also arrange for them to remain in the barracks to avoid hard labor. He helped many Jews, possibly hundreds, to survive. He concerned himself with the needs and fate of the Greek Jewish prisoners and passed notes between separated family members in the camp complex. He also supplied additional food, and in order to manipulate the work schedule he often bribed the Nazi commanders with money, food, cigarettes, or vodka, which he acquired on the black market in the camp or from political prisoners, or from civilian workers, who could buy him various items on the outside in exchange for payment. He also bribed Nazi guards and commanders to save prisoners from punishment and helped keep *musselmen* from being sent to death.

On three occasions his sister Esther (whose married name was Sidikario after the Holocaust) saved a total of 181 girls from Bloc 25 in Birkenau who were destined for gassing, sneaking them out through the windows to an adjacent shack.

After the war Maestro immigrated to Israel and ran a car repair garage.

[Yitzchak Kerem (2nd ed.)]

MAFTIR (Heb. מַפְטִיר; "one who concludes"), name given to the three or more concluding verses of the weekly Sabbath *sidrah* ("Torah portion") as well as to the final verses of the portions read on festivals and public *fast days. The person who is called up to the reading from the Torah of these passages and who then recites the *haftarah from the Prophets is also called *maftir.*

MAGDALA (Migdal), a city on Lake Gennesaret (the Sea of Galilee) in Galilee, about 7 km. north of Tiberias. It is overlooked by a high escarpment near the Wadi Hamam (the Valley of the Robbers). "*Migdal*" is an Aramaic word meaning "tower" or "fortress." The Greeks called the village Taricheia, a word meaning "pickling," because of Magdala's fish salting industry, one of the mainstays of its economy. The other important element of its economy was its boat-building.

Magdala was first excavated in 1971–74 by Corbo and Loffreda, who found what they misidentified as a mini-synagogue (actually a stepped fountain house or *nymphaeum*), a water reservoir, and some mosaic floors. One of the mosaics, now on display at Capernaum, depicts an ancient boat with both sails and oars. Situated west of Capernaum (Jos., Life, 59, 72), Magdala was walled on the land side and contained a stadium. Even in antiquity, Magdala was well known, and among its prominent citizens were Jannaeus son of Levi and Dassion, friends of Agrippa II (Jos., Life, 131; Wars, 2:597).

When three Roman legions under the control of Vespasian laid siege to the city of Tiberias in 67 C.E., the city opened its gates, and Josephus and his forces surrendered. The city was attacked by the Roman army, which advanced from Sennabris to Tiberias and then to Magdala (Jos., Wars, 3:462–505, 532–542). Since Tiberias – along with Tarichaea-Magdala, Bethsaida-Julias, and its 14 villages – had been given to Herod Agrippa II by the emperor Nero prior to the war, and since Josephus and the inhabitants of the city openly surrendered to Vespasian and his forces, the Romans permitted Tiberias to remain under Jewish rule until 100 C.E. (Jos., Wars, 3:445–61).

After the destruction of the Jewish Temple in Jerusalem, Magdala became the seat of one of the 24 priestly divisions and as the city grew there were several Roman style villas built, with baths and mosaics, and the cardo (the main street) was paved. Magdala is mentioned directly only once in the New Testament (Matthew 15:39), where it is recorded that Jesus visited the area by boat. However, it is referred to as Magadan, not Magdala. The area of Magdala is also associated in the New Testament with the name Dalmanutha, as seen in Mark 8:10. All other references to the city are indirect ones (Mark 16:9; Luke 8:2).

It was said to be the hometown of Mary the Magdalene (Matt. 27:56; Mark 15:40). In Talmudic sources it appears as Migdal Nunaiya, a center for fishing and the preserving industry (Pes. 46a). R. Isaac and R. Judah were two of the *amoraim* living in Magdala. Resh Lakish sought refuge there against the wrath of the patriarch Judah II. After the destruction of the Temple, the priests of the family of Ezekiel settled there.

BIBLIOGRAPHY: R. Arav and J.J. Rousseau, *Jesus and His World* (1996); D. Baly, *The Geography of the Bible* (1974), 164; R. Bauckham, *Gospel Women* (2002), 143; L.F. DeVries, *Cities of the Biblical World* (1997), 327–28; L.I. Levine, *The Ancient Synagogue. The First Thousand Years* (2000), 67; C. Meyers, C.T. Craven, and R.S. Kraemer (eds.), *Women in Scripture* (2000); E. Netzer, "Did the Water Installation in Magdala Serve as a Synagogue?" in: A. Kasher, A. Oppenheimer, and U. Uriel Rappaport (eds.), *Synagogues in Antiquity* (Heb., 1988).

[Lidia Domenica Matassa (2nd ed.)]

MAGDEBURG, city in Germany. The Jewish community of Magdeburg is one of the oldest in Germany. As early as 965 there were Jews living in the town, and they were placed under the jurisdiction of the archbishop by Otto the Great. They traded in the "clothing-court" (*Kleiderhof*), in the merchants' quarter, and conducted their trade even beyond the Oder River. Their quarter, the *Judendorf*, was situated in the south of the city, in the archbishop's domain. The Jews took part in the funeral procession of Archbishop Walthard von Magdeburg in 1012. The cemetery dates from the 13th century – the oldest gravestone bears the date 1268 – later enlarged in 1312 and 1383. In 1213 the soldiers of Otto IV destroyed the *Judendorf*, and four years later the Jews moved to nearby Sudenburg, where numerous other Jews already lived. Demanding jurisdiction over the Jews in 1260, the canons of the cathedral laid claim to the fines they paid in silver, while those paid in gold were to remain the property of the archbishop. Prominent in the city were R. Hezekiah b. Jacob, who corresponded with R. Isaac Or Zaru'a (*Issac ben Moses of Vienna), and R. *Ḥayyim b. Paltiel, rabbi in Magdeburg in 1291, who was in correspondence with R. Meir of Rothenburg. The Jews were persecuted in 1302 and again during the *Black Death disturbances of 1349, despite the attempts of the archbishop and the city authorities to protect them. They were attacked again in 1357 and 1384 when another epidemic broke out. Archbishop Dietrich employed a Jewish court banker between 1361 and 1367. In 1410 Archbishop Guenther issued a letter of protection (*Schutzbrief*) for a period of six years, at a cost to the community of 40 silver marks. During the 15th century the community maintained a flourishing yeshivah. In 1493 the Jews of Magdeburg were expelled; the synagogue was converted into a chapel and the cemetery destroyed.

When the great elector, Frederick William, readmitted Jews to *Prussia (1671), *Schutzjuden* settled once more in Magdeburg. From 1703 they were to be found in Sudenburg, from 1715 in the newer part of town (the *Neustadt*), and from 1729 in the *Altstadt*. A religious school was founded by the modern community in 1834 and a *ḥevra kaddisha* in 1839. Rabbis of the community included Ludwig *Philippson, editor of **Allgemeine Zeitung des Judentums*; Moritz *Guedemann, and Moritz Spanier, both of whom wrote a history of the community. Eduard *Lasker and Otto *Landsberg were repeatedly elected to parliament from Magdeburg. The prosperous community, which included 45 doctors (who founded their own club in 1903), had about 20 social, cultural, and charitable organizations in 1933. The number of Jews increased steadily from 330 in 1817 to 559 in 1840; 1,000 in 1859; 1,815 in 1885; 1,843 in 1910; and around 3,200 in 1928, then dropped to 2,361 (0.6% of the total population) in 1933. The synagogue, built in 1851 and enlarged to seat 900 in 1897, was burned down on November 10, 1938. The men were interned in *Buchenwald. By May 17, 1939, only 679 Jews remained in the town, and the majority were transported to concentration camps. On July 1, 1944, there were still 185 Jews living in Magdeburg, mainly partners of mixed marriages, who managed to survive the war. After the war, some Jews returned to Magdeburg. In 1962 the Jewish community numbered 79 and diminished to 49 in 1969. It declined even more during the 1970s and 1980s, dwindling to 35 in 1989. But in 2005 it rose to 635 members due to the immigration of Jews from the former Soviet Union. Magdeburg is the seat of the Association of Jewish communities in the State of Saxony-Anhalt, which was founded in 1994.

BIBLIOGRAPHY: M. Guedemann, in: MGWJ, 14 (1865), 241–56, 281–96, 321–35, 361–70; M. Spanier, *Geschichte der Juden in Magdeburg* (1928); idem, in: ZGJD, 5 (1892), 273, 392–5; Vogelstein-Rieger, 1 (1895), 315; D. Kaufmann and M. Freudenthal, *Die Familie Gomperz* (1907), 236–42; MGADJ, 1 (1909), 110; 3 (1911/12), 164; S. Neufeld, *Die Juden im Thueringisch-Saechsischen Gebiet…*, pt. 2 (1927), 8, 14–16, 168–70; Germ Jud, 1 (1963), 163–70; 2 (1968), 505–10; FJW (1932); PKG; E. Forchheimer, in: *Geschichtsblaetter fuer Stadt und Land Magdeburg*, 46 (1911), 119–78, 328–40; O. Simon, in: *AJR Information*, 15 (Nov. 1960): S. Stern, *Der preussische Staat und die Juden*, 1 (1962), Akten, no. 135–9, 371–410a; 2 (1962), Akten, no. 496–571. **ADD. BIBLIOGRAPHY:** C. Seibert, "Magdeburg," in: J. Dick, *Wegweiser durch das juedische Sachsen-Anhalt*, vol. 3 (1998), 23–36; K. Kaergling, (ed.), *Juedisches Kult- und Kulturgut. Spuren zur Geschichte der Juden in Magdeburg* (1992); G. Kuntze, *Unter aufgehobenen Rechten* (1992); A. Maimon, M. Breuer, Y. Guggenheim (eds.), *Germania Judaica*, vol. 3 (1987), 772–83.

[Louis Lewin / Larissa Daemmig (2nd ed.)]

MAGDEBURG LAW, term applied to the constitutional and commercial urban law which developed in *Magdeburg in the Middle Ages and became a pattern for new city constitutions in Central and Eastern Europe. The Magdeburg law was adopted by most cities in central, eastern, and northern Germany, Bohemia, and Moravia. Magdeburg, the mother town of the constitutions, possessed a supreme court, to which appeals and queries were addressed, including litigation between Christians and Jews. These cases were treated fairly, without discrimination and with no accompanying degrading oaths. In the 14th century the charters of many towns in Galicia were copies of this law, as were those of Lublin (1317), Sandomierz (1356), Lemberg (Lvov; 1356), Vilna (1387), Brest (1370), and Grodno (1391); in the following century it was extended to several towns in southern Poland, among them Lutsk (1432) and Minsk (1496), and in the 16th century to the towns of Pinsk (1511), Kovel (1518), Tarnopol (1550), Mogilev (1578), Vitebsk (1582), and others. Originally, the privileges enshrined in the law were granted only to German craftsmen and merchants, Jews and all other non-German town dwellers being excluded. However, in the charter granting the law to the city of Lemberg (June 17, 1365), the Jews, Armenians, and other nationals were free to decide whether they wished to avail themselves of it or whether they preferred to abide by their own laws and remain subject to the jurisdiction of their elders, under the chairmanship of the local bailiff. Later the law was granted to all the townspeople, including Jews (as in Kiev and Podolia). One of the paragraphs of the Magdeburg law which was of importance for the Jews provided that no Jew could be forced to stand warranty for objects he had bought or received as a pawn, i.e., to reveal from whom he had bought or received them. The Jews were therefore not responsible for receiving stolen property.

BIBLIOGRAPHY: Kisch, Germany, 62–70, index; idem, *Jewry Law in Medieval Germany* (1949), index; I. Bershadski, *Litovskie Yevrei* (1888), 221, 234, 241–3.

MAGEN DAVID (Heb. מָגֵן דָּוִד; "shield of David"), the hexagram or six-pointed star formed by two equilateral triangles which have the same center and are placed in opposite directions.

From as early as the Bronze Age it was used – possibly as an ornament and possibly as a magical sign – in many civilizations and in regions as far apart as Mesopotamia and Britain. Iron Age examples are known from India and from the Iberian peninsula prior to the Roman conquest. Occasionally it appears on Jewish artefacts, such as lamps and seals, but without having any special and recognizable significance. The oldest undisputed example is on a seal from the seventh century B.C.E. found in Sidon and belonging to one Joshua b. Asayahu. In the Second Temple period, the hexagram was often used by Jews and non-Jews alike alongside the pentagram (the five-pointed star), and in the synagogue of Capernaum (second or third century C.E.) it is found side by side with the pentagram and the swastika on a frieze. There is no reason to assume that it was used for any purposes other than decorative. Theories interpreting it as a planetary sign of Saturn and connecting it with the holy stone in the pre-Davidic sanctuary in Jerusalem (Hildegard Lewy, in *Archiv Orientální*, vol. 18, 1950, 330–65) are purely speculative. Neither in the magical papyri nor in the oldest sources of Jewish *magic does the hexagram appear, but it began to figure as a magical sign from the early Middle Ages. Among Jewish emblems from Hellenistic times (discussed in E. Goodenough, *Jewish Symbols in the Greco-Roman Period*), both hexagram and pentagram are missing.

The ornamental use of the hexagram continued in the Middle Ages, especially in Muslim and Christian countries. The kings of Navarre used it on their seals (10th and 11th centuries) and (like the pentagram) it was frequently employed on notarial signs in Spain, France, Denmark, and Germany, by Christian and Jewish notaries alike. Sometimes drawn with slightly curved lines, it appears in early Byzantine and many medieval European churches, as, for example, on a stone from an early church in Tiberias (preserved in the Municipal Museum) and on the entrance to the Cathedrals of Burgos, Valencia, and Lerida. Examples are also found on objects used in the church, sometimes in a slanted position; as on the marble bishop's throne (c. 1266) in the Cathedral of Anagni. Probably in imitation of church usage – and certainly not as a specifically Jewish symbol – the hexagram is found on some synagogues from the later Middle Ages, for example, in Hamelin (Germany, c. 1280) and Budweis (Bohemia, probably 14th century). In Arab sources the hexagram, along with other geometrical ornaments, was widely used under the designation "seal of Solomon," a term which was also taken over by many Jewish groups. This name connects the hexagram with early Christian, possibly Judeo-Christian magic, such as the Greek magical work *The Testament of Solomon*. It is not clear in which period the hexagram was engraved on the seal or ring of Solomon, mentioned in the Talmud (Git. 68a–b) as a sign of his dominion over the demons, instead of the name of God, which originally appeared. However, this happened in Christian circles where Byzantine amulets of the sixth century already use the "seal of Solomon" as the name of the hexagram. In many medieval Hebrew manuscripts elaborate designs of the hexagram are to be found, without its being given any name. The origin of this use can be clearly traced to Bible manuscripts from Muslim countries (a specimen is shown in Gunzburg and Stassoff, *L'ornement hèbraïque* (1905), pl. 8, 15). From the 13th century onward it is found in Hebrew Bible manuscripts from Germany and Spain. Sometimes parts of the masorah are written in the form of a hexagram; sometimes it is simply used, in a more or less elaborate form, as an ornament. Richly adorned specimens from manuscripts in Oxford and Paris have been reproduced by C. Roth, *Sefarad*, 12, 1952, p. 356, pl. II, and in the catalog of the exhibition "Synagoga," Recklinghausen, 1960, pl. B. 4.

In Arabic magic the "seal of Solomon" was widely used, but at first its use in Jewish circles was restricted to relatively rare cases. Even then, the hexagram and pentagram were easily interchangeable and the name was applied to both figures. As a talisman, it was common in many of the magical versions of the *mezuzah* which were widespread between the tenth and 14th centuries. Frequently, the magical additions to the traditional text of the *mezuzah* contained samples of the hexagram, sometimes as many as 12. In magical Hebrew manuscripts of the later Middle Ages, the hexagram was used for certain amulets, among which one for putting out fires attained great popularity (see Heinrich Loewe, *Juedischer Feuersegen*, 1930).

The notion of a "shield of David" with magical powers was originally unconnected with the sign. It is difficult to say whether the notion arose in Islam, where the Koran sees David as the first to make protective arms, or from inner traditions of Jewish magic. From earlier times there is only one instance connecting the hexagram with the name David on a sixth-century tombstone from Taranto, southern Italy. There seems to have been some special reason for putting the hexagram before the name of the deceased. The oldest text mentioning a shield of David is contained in an explanation of a magical "alphabet of the angel *Metatron" which stems from the geonic period and was current among the *Ḥasidei Ashkenaz of the 12th century. But here it was the holy Name of 72 names which was said to have been engraved on this protective shield, together with the name MKBY, which the tradition of the magicians connected with Judah Maccabee. In cognate sources this tradition was much embellished. The name of the angel Taftafiyyah, one of the names of Metatron, was added to the 72 holy names, and indeed an amulet in the form of a hexagram with this one name became one of the most widespread protective charms in many medieval and later manuscripts. (From c. 1500 onward the name *Shaddai* was often substituted for the purely magical one.) This must have provided the transition to the use of the term *"magen David"* for the sign. What caused the substitution of the figure instead of the "great name of 72 names" is not clear, but in the 16th century instructions can still be found stating that the shield of David should not be drawn in simple lines but must be composed of certain holy names and their combinations, after the pattern of those biblical manuscripts where the lines were composed of the text of the masorah. The oldest known witness to the usage of the term is the kabbalistic *Sefer ha-Gevul*, written by a grandson of Naḥmanides in the early 14th century. The hexagram occurs there twice, both times called "*magen David*" and containing the same magical name as in the aforementioned amulet, demonstrating its direct connection with the magical tradition. According to other traditions, mentioned in Isaac Arama's *Akedat Yiẓḥak*, the emblem of David's shield was not the image known by this name today, but Psalm 67 in the shape of the *menorah*. This became a widespread custom and the "*menorah* Psalm" was considered a talisman of great power. A booklet from the 16th century says: "King David used to bear this psalm inscribed, pictured, and engraved on his shield, in the shape of the *menorah*, when he went forth to battle, and he would meditate on its mystery and conquer."

Between 1300 and 1700 the two terms, shield of David and seal of Solomon, are used indiscriminately, predominantly in magical texts, but slowly the former gained ascendancy. It was also used, from 1492, as a printers' sign, especially in books printed in Prague in the first half of the 16th century and in the books printed by the Foa family in Italy and Holland, who incorporated it in their coat of arms. Several Italian Jewish families followed their example between 1660 and 1770. All these usages had as yet no general Jewish connotation. The official use of the shield of David can be traced to Prague, from where it spread in the 17th and 18th centuries through Moravia and Austria and later to southern Germany and Holland. In 1354, Charles IV granted the Prague community the privilege of bearing its own flag – later called in documents "King David's flag" – on which the hexagram was depicted. It therefore became an official emblem, probably chosen because of its significance as a symbol of the days of old when King David, as it were, wore it on his shield. This explains its wide use in Prague, in synagogues, on the official seal of the community, on printed books, and on other objects. Here it was always called *magen David*. Its use on the tombstone (1613) of David Gans, the astronomer and historian, was still exceptional, obviously in reference to the title of his last work *Magen David*. Except for one tombstone in Bordeaux (c. 1726), no other example of its being used on tombstones is known before the end of the 18th century. A curious parallel to the development in Prague is the one case of a representation of the Synagogue as an allegorical figure, holding a flag bearing the *magen David* in a 14th-century Catalan manuscript of the *Breviar d'amor* by Matfre d'Ermengaud (Ms. of Yates Thompson 31 in the British Museum).

The symbol early moved to other communities. Its use in Budweis has been mentioned above, and the Vienna community used it on its seal in 1655. In the following year it is found on a stone marking the boundary between the Jewish and the Christian quarters of Vienna (according to P. Diamant) or between the Jewish quarter and the Carmelite monastery (according to Max Grunwald). Apparently it was an officially recognized symbol. When the Viennese Jews were expelled in 1670 they took the symbol to many of their new habitats, especially in Moravia, but also to the Ashkenazi community of Amsterdam, where it was used from 1671, first on a medallion permitting entrance to the graveyard. Later it became part of the community's seal. Curiously enough, its migration eastward was much slower. It never occurs on official seals, but here and there during the 17th and 18th centuries it appears as an ornament on objects for use in synagogues and on wood carvings over the Torah shrine (first in Volpa, near Grodno, 1643).

The use of the hexagram as an alchemical symbol denoting the harmony between the antagonistic elements of water and fire became current in the later 17th century, but this had no influence in Jewish circles. Many alchemists, too, began calling it the shield of David (traceable since 1724). But another symbolism sprang up in kabbalistic circles, where the "shield of David" became the "shield of the son of David," the Messiah. Whether this usage was current in Orthodox circles too is not certain, though not impossible. The two kabbalists who testify to it, Isaiah the son of Joel Ba'al Shem (Jacob Emden, *Torat ha-Kena'ot*, p. 128) and Abraham Ḥayyim Kohen from Nikolsburg, combine the two interpretations. But there is no doubt that this messianic interpretation of the sign was current among the followers of *Shabbetai Ẓevi. The famous amulets given by Jonathan *Eybeschuetz in Metz and Hamburg, which have no convincing interpretation other than a Shabbatean one, have throughout a shield of David designated as "seal of MBD" (Messiah b. David), "seal of the God of Israel," etc. The shield of David was transformed into a secret symbol of the Shabbatean vision of redemption, although this interpretation remained an esoteric one, not to be published.

The prime motive behind the wide diffusion of the sign in the 19th century was the desire to imitate Christianity. The Jews looked for a striking and simple sign which would "symbolize" Judaism in the same way as the cross symbolizes Christianity. This led to the ascendancy of the *magen David* in official use, on ritual objects and in many other ways. From central and Western Europe it made its way to Eastern Europe and to Oriental Jewry. Almost every synagogue bore it; innumerable communities, and private and charitable organizations stamped it on their seals and letterheads. Whereas during the 18th century its use on ritual objects was still very restricted – a good specimen is a plate for *mazzot* (1770), reproduced on the title page of *Monumenta Judaica*, catalog of a Jewish exposition in Cologne, 1963 – it now became most popular. By 1799 it had already appeared as a specific Jewish sign in a satirical antisemitic engraving (A. Rubens, *Jewish Iconography*, no. 1611); in 1822 it was used on the Rothschild family coat of arms when they were raised to the nobility by the Austrian emperor; and from 1840 Heinrich Heine signed his correspondence from Paris in the *Augsburger Allgemeine Zeitung* with a *magen David* instead of his name, a remarkable indication of his Jewish identification in spite of his conversion. From such general use it was taken over by the Zionist movement. The very first issue of *Die Welt*, Herzl's Zionist journal, bore it as its emblem. The *magen David* became the symbol of new hopes and a new future for the Jewish people, and Franz Rosenzweig also interpreted it in *Der Stern der Erloesung* (1921) as summing up his philosophical ideas about the meaning of Judaism and the relationships between God, men, and the world. When the Nazis used it as a badge of shame which was to accompany millions on their way to death it took on a new dimension of depth, uniting suffering and hope. While the State of Israel, in its search for Jewish authenticity, chose as its emblem the *menorah*, a much older Jewish symbol, the *magen David* was maintained on the national (formerly Zionist) flag, and is widely used in Jewish life.

BIBLIOGRAPHY: G. Scholem, in: *The Messianic Idea in Judaism and Other Essays* (1971); J. Leite de Vasconcellos, *Signum Salomonis* (Portuguese, 1918); Mayer, Art, index s.v. *Magen David*; M. Avi-Yonah, in: *Quarterly of the Department of Antiquities in Palestine*, vol. 14, pp. 64–65, pl. 23; P. Diamont, in: *Reshumot*, 5 (1953), 93–103; I. Feivelson, in: *Ha-Levanon, Me'assef Sifruti* (Warsaw, 1912), 53–56; Goodenough, Symbols, 7 (1958), 198–200; J.L. Gordon, *Iggerot J.L. Gordon*, 2 (1894), 36–37; M. Grunwald, in: HJ, 9 (1947), 178–88; J.M. Millás Vallicrosa, in: *Sefarad*, 17 (1957), 375–8; T. Nussenblatt, in: *YIVO-Bleter*, 13 (1938), 460–76, no. 583–4; P. Perdrizet, in: *Revue des Etudes Grecques*, 16 (1903), 42–61; E. Peterson, *Heis Theos* (Goettingen, 1926), 121; J. Reifman, in: *Ha-Shaḥar*, 2 (1872), 435–7; C. Roth, in: *Scritti in Memoria di Leone Carpi* (1967), 165–84; A. Scheiber in: *Israelitisches Wochenblatt fuer die Schweiz*, 66, no. 3 (Jan. 21, 1966), 33–35; B. Vajda, in: *Mitteilungen zur juedischen Volkskunde* (1918), 33–42; Wolf, Bibliotheca, 3 (1727), 997, 1214.

[Gershom Scholem]

MAGEN DAVID ADOM (MDA, Hebrew "Red Shield of David"), Israel's emergency medical first aid society (equivalent to the Red Cross). Magen David Adom was founded in 1930 and was recognized by the government of Israel and by the Knesset (MDA Knesset Law 1950/1970). It operates several major services: first aid, ambulance, and mobile intensive-care services; national blood bank services, including a fractionation institute for plasma by-products; and first aid instruction. The MDA institutions include the MDA executive committee, the MDA council, and the MDA conference. The conference is held every four years and deals with organizational activity and future goals. The council consists of 45 members and the executive committee consists of 12 members; both institutions are made up of MDA members and public representatives named by various government bodies.

Magen David Adom operates in 11 geographical areas, running 95 first aid stations, with some 700 ambulances deployed in these stations and in ambulance posts in kibbutzim and settlements. In addition, there are operational at first aid stations – on alert and in reserve – some 50 mobile intensive-care units, 22 mobile disaster units, and 18 blood mobiles. MDA employed 1,500 workers in 2006, while its volunteer force numbered more than 5,000 in 1991 and 10,000 in 2006. MDA National Blood Service is responsible for the collection, processing, examination, and distribution of blood units to hospitals all over Israel. The services include the national donor operation, the central blood bank, and the plasma processing institution, which were located inside Tel Hashomer hospital and employed 200 workers in 2005. The services collect about 280,000 blood units each year.

In time of war, Magen David Adom is part of Israel Civil Defense, more precisely, of the IDF Home Front Command, and operates in close cooperation with the IDF Medical Corps.

MDA's budget for 1995 came to $33 million, covered by income from ambulance services, blood services, first aid and first aid equipment sales, and other internal sources as well as a government subsidy.

Its equipment and development budget for 1995 totaled some $7 million. This sum, raised for MDA by its Friends societies in 15 countries, is earmarked for special development projects and purchase of lifesaving vehicles, medical equipment, etc. MDA Friends societies are active in Argentina, Australia, Belgium, Canada, France, Germany, Great Britain, Italy, The Netherlands, South Africa, Sweden, Switzerland, the United States, Uruguay, and Venezuela.

Following worldwide efforts – supported by prominent statesmen in many countries – to have Magen David Adom in Israel admitted into the International Federation of Red Cross and Red Crescent Societies, this finally occurred in 2006.

Notwithstanding the delay, over the years MDA continued to cooperate with the International Red Cross and offer assistance to other countries afflicted by natural and other disasters.

Special relations on a bilateral basis are conducted by the MDA with the American Red Cross, German Red Cross, The Netherlands Red Cross, Czech Red Cross, and Hungarian Red Cross.

In 1978 the American Red Cross issued a directive to all its national chapters to display the flag of MDA at all functions and meetings at which other emblems of National Red Cross and National Red Crescent Societies are displayed.

WEBSITE: www.mdais.org.

MAGGID (Heb. מַגִּיד; pl. *maggidim*), literally "one who relates" (cf. II Sam. 15:13). The term, however, has two special connotations in later Hebrew: a) a popular – and often itinerant – preacher, and b) an angel or supermundane spirit which conveys teachings to scholars worthy of such communication in mysterious ways.

The *Maggid* as Preacher

Itinerant preachers appear in Jewish history long before the emergence of the specific term. Descriptions of the life and social standing of some *tannaim* and *amoraim* depict them as leading the lives of itinerant preachers. During the geonic period, however, there is no record of them and it is not until the 11th century that one finds mention of them. Tales about some of the *Ḥasidei Ashkenaz show them as begging itinerant preachers. The tradition of the itinerant *maggid* developed during the late Middle Ages. The 14th-century anonymous author of the *Sefer ha-Kaneh* and *Ha-Peli'ah* sets much of his bitter social and moral criticism in the context of his experiences while wandering and preaching in various communities. In the second half of the 16th century *Ephraim Solomon b. Aaron Luntschitz was a typical, if much respected and influential, itinerant *maggid*. He relates that "in my later years, yielding to the importunities of prominent men, I preached in Lublin, especially during the great fairs, where Jewish leaders as well as large masses of the people gathered. There I used to express myself quite freely covering the shortcomings of the rabbis as well as of the laity, undeterred by any consideration or fear. This boldness, naturally enough, created for me numerous enemies who heaped slander upon my name and otherwise persecuted me… Of course, I could well have avoided all this wrath and uproar had I been willing to be more restrained in my utterances, or were I more chary of my personal honor. But I had long resolved to put the honor of God above my own" (*Ammudei Shesh* (Prague, 1617), introduction). In this, as in many other passages, Luntschitz shows his strength of character and the troubles that beset a courageous itinerant preacher, attuned to the mood and spiritual needs of his public but fearless in criticizing them. Use of the parable (*mashal*) is already much in evidence in his writings, which also show a conscious effort to stimulate his public and impress them through a show of wit and learning. All these traits were common from the 18th century on when the name *maggid* came into regular use to denote both an itinerant and non-itinerant preacher. There are records of salaried *maggidim* appointed by the community. Some historians have ascribed a considerable part in the social and religious upheavals of the end of the 17th and during the 18th centuries to the influence of itinerant *maggidim*, who, they consider, functioned as a kind of "non-establishment intelligentsia," having much of the learning and influence of the regular scholars but largely without their connections in the upper strata of Jewish society. They have thus attributed the rise and early success of *Ḥasidism to the influence of such *maggidim*, pointing out that several of the early ḥasidic leaders were called *maggid* or the synonym for *maggid, mokhi'aḥ* ("morals preacher"), such as *Dov Baer of Mezhirech or *Jacob Joseph of Polonnoye. Others, however, note that even the most radical of the 18th-century *maggidim*, *Berechiah (Berakh) b. Eliakim Getzel the Younger, considered himself, despite his outspoken social criticism, to be allied by the nature of his office to that of the communal rabbi. They show also that much of the anti-ḥasidic propaganda was conducted by *maggidim*, chief among them being Jacob *Kranz "the Maggid of Dubno," an admiring pupil of *Elijah b. Solomon Zalman, the Gaon of Vilna, who expressly followed the advice of the Gaon on the method of preaching. Kranz, who was celebrated for his parables, exemplifies the type of *maggidim* who were associated with the **Mitnagged* leadership in Lithuanian Jewry. Lithuania and the *Mitnagged* culture remained throughout the 19th and into the 20th centuries the field of activity of the *maggidim*. Sometimes the office of *maggid* was combined with that of *dayyan*, hence the modern titles, mostly in Eastern Europe, of *maggid meisharim u-moreh ẓedek* (the *maggid* of uprightness (cf. Is. 45: 19) and teacher of righteousness, the latter being a synonym for a *dayyan*). Sometimes the *maggid* was appointed to a town, with the official title of *maggid de-mata*, in Yiddish *Shtotmagid*. Vilna had a *Shtotmagid*, usually a respected and outstanding scholar, until recent times. Men like Ezekiel b. Isaac ha-Levi *Landau, the *Shtotmagid* of Vilna; the great itinerant *maggid* *Moses Isaac Darshan, the "Kelmer Maggid"; or the *maggid* suspected of Haskalah leanings, Ẓevi Hirsch b. Ze'ev Wolf *Dainow, the "Slutzker Maggid," continued a tradition of preaching expressly intended for the masses, which contained much social criticism but also provided social guidance. Their preaching was also characterized by the mournful sing-song intonation of their delivery (see also *Musar movement). Their direct successors were the "Zionist *maggidim*" like Z. *Maccoby the "Kamenitzer Maggid," and Ẓevi Hirsch *Masliansky. Many of the *meshullaḥim* (**Sheluḥei Ereẓ Israel*) for the yeshivot and Ereẓ Israel actually filled the function of *maggidim*. Wherever *Mitnagged* communities were established in other countries, *maggidim* accompanied the immigrants. In modern Ereẓ Israel, Ben Zion Yadler and Benzion *Alfes were in the tradition of the great *maggidim*. A few *maggidim* are still active in the State of Israel and the United States (see also **Darshan*; *Preaching).

[Haim Hillel Ben-Sasson]

In Kabbalah

The angel or heavenly force called the *maggid* passes secrets to a kabbalist, when he is asleep or awake, speaks words from his mouth, or dictates to him when he is writing. This revelation is one of the outstanding phenomena in Kabbalah in the 16th to 18th centuries. Throughout the history of Kabbalah, kabbalists relied on heavenly inspirations, the revelations of Elijah, *Metatron, and other angels, or even on heavenly forces such as the Holy Spirit, in addition to questions in dreams and magical means of communication with heavenly forces. An early stage of this phenomenon may be seen in the questioning in dreams practiced before the formation of the Kabbalah, and even regarding the problems of Kabbalah, e.g., by Jacob of Marvège (Provence), author of *She'elot u-Teshuvot min ha-Shamayim* (commentary by R. Margulies, Lvov, 1929). The *maggid* of the 16th to 18th centuries is simply another version of the previous occurrence, though at times the phenomenon seems, in particular cases, to have personal psychological roots.

The image of the *maggid* who reveals heavenly secrets was apparently first crystallized in the circle of Joseph *Taitaẓak, who lived at the time of the Spanish expulsion and whose circle included many of the great kabbalists and preachers of Safed. The revelations of Taitaẓak (or those attributed to him) were written prior to the expulsion and were presented as coming from God Himself. In the Safed literature, the main expositions of the essence of the *maggid* are found in the writings of Moses *Cordovero and Ḥayyim *Vital. In this circle the most outstanding phenomenon was the appearance of the *maggid* of Joseph *Caro. Recording the words of the *maggid*, Caro wrote *Sefer ha-Maggid*, of which only a fragment has survived, called by the printers *Maggid Meisharim*. The major statements of Caro's *maggid* were sermons interpreting the secrets of the Kabbalah and biblical commentary, but many of his pronouncements have a personal and practical meaning. The *maggid* guided Caro in his wanderings in Turkey and directed him to immigrate to Ereẓ Israel. He stimulated Caro to write his halakhic works and to behave morally, promising him achievements in *halakhah* and in his personal life, toward attaining his great dream – martyrdom, like Solomon *Molcho. Caro's *maggid* was the *Shekhinah* ("Divine Presence"), the tenth *Sefirah* in the kabbalistic system, which took on the form of the Mishnah, the Oral Law. To bring about the appearance of the *maggid*, Caro would study *mishnayot*. The *maggid* spoke to him while he was awake, often just as he awoke. Scholars have not reached a conclusion concerning the psychological nature of this revelation, but it is clear that it did not affect the relation of Caro's personality to reality; it was one aspect of his personality which neither contradicted nor harmed the whole.

The Shabbatean movement gave great impetus to appearances of *maggidim* and many revealed secrets to the Shabbateans. The revelations of a *maggid* to Isaac Ẓurgeon, an associate of *Shabbetai Ẓevi in Adrianople in 1668 who confirmed the latter as Messiah and defended his apostasy, have been published (R. Schatz, in: *Sefunot*, 12). There also exists particularly detailed information on the appearance of a *maggid* in the house of study of Abraham *Rovigo, leader of a Shabbatean circle in Modena, Italy, from 1675 to 1691. The first *maggid* to appear in his house of study was that of Baer Perlhefter whose revelation had a great impact on him. Many letters of Meir Rofe who directs his questions to the *maggid*, and their answers, are in existence. The central question discussed in the revelations concerns the reason for Shabbetai Ẓevi's death and a prediction of his return in a year's time. Apparently, a *maggid* was later revealed to Rovigo himself. The most detailed revelations in this house of study have been transmitted by Mordecai Ashkenazi, a pupil of Rovigo's from Zolkiew who was neither a scholar of Torah nor of esoteric matters but who astounded Rovigo with his Shabbatean revelation. Ashkenazi's notebook and other documents relating the revelations of his *maggid* have survived. This *maggid* always revealed himself in a dream; at first only his voice was heard and afterward his form was seen. Scholem has suggested that this was a projection of the image of Rovigo, Ashkenazi's teacher. His revelations include Shabbatean theories, and together with them private advice, mostly on routine matters and on Ashkenazi's education and studies. Apparently they even included criticism of the former *maggid*, that of Baer Perlhefter, based on suspicions of Perlhefter's sins toward the end of his life, whose nature is not clear. Ashkenazi's *maggid* – like Caro's – encouraged his master and teacher to immigrate to Ereẓ Israel and gave him practical advice on ways of realizing this aim, whose background was Shabbatean messianism.

A lengthy and stormy dispute was caused by a *maggid* who revealed himself to Moses Ḥayyim *Luzzatto in Italy in 1727. The *maggid* dictated to Luzzatto, in the language of the Zohar, *Razin Genizin*, *Tikkunim Ḥadashim*, and other works, which were meant to become a second Zohar (*Zohar Tinyana*). The *maggidim* of Ashkenazi and Caro also spoke the language of the Targum, i.e., Aramaic. The record of the first revelation of Luzzatto's *maggid*, who appeared on Wednesday, Rosh Ḥodesh (the New Moon of) Sivan 1727, still exists. This *maggid* was a voice without an image who spoke to the recipient while he was awake and not in a dream, and alone. This angered Moses *Ḥagiz and others, because they thought that the young Luzzatto was not worthy of such a heavenly revelation and also because they suspected the Shabbatean character of the revelations.

The nature of the phenomenon apparently must be examined in the general context of kabbalistic mysticism, which consistently seeks heavenly confirmation for the secrets revealed to the kabbalist. At different times, various forms were given to these confirmations – some by pseudepigraphy and some by a divine revelation. In general, it appears that there was no fraudulent basis to these revelations, that their source lay in the kabbalist's complete conviction of the hidden heavenly truth in the secrets revealed to him, and that his testimony that he heard them from a divine source is honest. In addition, it seems that the *maggid* is also connected with the parapsychological phenomenon of the materialization of part of the kabbalist's soul which, acquiring an independent form, disassociates itself from the rest of his person and, confronting him objectively as it were, speaks to him.

[Joseph Dan]

BIBLIOGRAPHY: Baron, Community, index; I. Bettan, *Studies in Jewish Preaching* (1939), 273–315; B.Z. Dinur, *Be-Mifneh ha-Dorot* (1955), 97–100, 133–6; J. Katz, *Massoret u-Mashber* (1958), index; H.H. Ben-Sasson, *Hagut ve-Hanhagah* (1959), 34–54, 254–6; idem, in: *Zion*, 31 (1966), 68–69, 200–3. IN KABBALAH: G. Scholem, *Ḥalomotav shel ha-Shabbetai, R. Mordecai Ashkenazi* (1938); R.J.Z. Werblowsky, in: *Tarbiẓ*, 27 (1958), 310–21; idem, *Joseph Karo, Lawyer and Mystic* (1962); M. Benayahu, in: *Sefunot*, 5 (1961), 299–336; I. Tishby, *Netivei Emunah u-Minut* (1964), 81–107; G. Scholem, in: *Sefunot*, 11 (1970), 67–112. **ADD. BIBLIOGRAPHY:** Z. Schechter, in: *Meḥkarim be-Toledot Am Yisrael ve-Ereẓ Yisrael* (1980), 219–30.

MAGGID, DAVID (1862–1942?), scholar and writer. Maggid was born in Vilna, son of Hillel Noah *Maggid-Steinschneider. As secretary to S.J. *Fuenn, he assisted him in writing *Ha-Oẓar* ("The Treasury," 1884–1903) and *Keneset Yisrael* ("Assembly of Israel," 1886–90), a biographical dictionary of Jewish authors and scholars. Later, in St. Petersburg, he taught Jewish religion in government secondary schools. The author of numerous articles on Jewish history and art, he was also a contributor to the *Yevreyskaya Entsiklopediya*. His research encompassed Jewish music of antiquity and the Middle Ages as well as the folklore of the Jews of Crimea. In 1919 he succeeded A.A. *Harkavy as librarian of the Jewish and Oriental department of the National Library of Petrograd. In 1921 he was appointed professor of art history at the Russian Institute in Petrograd and in 1925 became professor of Hebrew at the university. He continued to publish articles and works outside the Soviet Union. Notable are his reminiscences of his father and the first *maskilim* of Vilna, published in *Fun Noenten Ovar* (1937). Other works include *Toledot M. Antokolski* ("The Life of M. Antokolski," 1897), *Rabbi Mordekhai Aharon Guenzburg* (1897), and the completion of his father's work *Toledot Mishpeḥot Guenzburg* ("The History of the Guenzburg Families," 1899).

BIBLIOGRAPHY: Rejzen, Leksikon, 2 (1927), 356–9; LNYL, 4 (1963), 535–7.

[Yehuda Slutsky]

MAGGID-STEINSCHNEIDER, HILLEL NOAH (1829–1903), Hebrew scholar and writer. Maggid-Steinschneider, born in Vilna, owed the first part of his name to his grandfather Phinehas, who was *Maggid* in Vilna, and the second part to his profession, stonemasonry (*Steinschneider*). He also was a bookdealer. As a stonemason he often composed tombstone inscriptions, which led to an interest in and research about the lives of well-known Vilna families and personalities, particularly those buried in the old and new cemeteries of the town. He published *Ir Vilna* (part 1 only, 1900), a biographical work containing hundreds of biographies of famous Vilna personalities. Maggid also assisted S.J. *Fuenn in collecting material for his history of Vilna Jewry, *Kiryah Ne'emanah* (1860), and also prepared its second edition with numerous additions and a biography of the author (1915). He wrote a history of the *Guenzburg family completed by his son (*Toledot Mishpeḥot Guenzburg*, 1899) and a biography of David Oppenheim (in Y. ben Ḥayyim Mezah (ed.), *Gan Peraḥim*, 1882); with his father-in-law J. Gordon he composed a Thousand Year Calendar, *Lu'aḥ al Elef Shanim* (1854).

Maggid contributed numerous biographical and genealogical articles to Hebrew periodicals, such as *Ha-Shaḥar*, *Ha-Karmel*, and *Ha-Maggid*. He was put in charge of the *Straschun and S.J. Fuenn libraries when they were given to the Vilna community. Maggid's biographical and bibliographical research, much of which remained unpublished, was of importance, though like other works of the transitory period from old to modern scholarship, his writings lacked organization and literary form.

BIBLIOGRAPHY: Kressel, Leksikon, 2 (1967), 314ff.; Rejzen, Leksikon, 2 (1927), 356ff.; H.N. Maggid, *El ha-Kore* (1900), 7–10, introd.; D. Maggid, in: *Fun Noentn Over*, 1 (1937), 3–12; *Budushchnost*, 4 (1903), 248–52.

[Yehuda Slutsky]

MAGHAR, AL-, Druze village in northern Israel, 10 mi. (16 km.) N.W. of Tiberias. One of the major Druze centers, the village had 5,750 inhabitants in 1969, of whom a minority were Christian and Muslim Arabs. Its economy was based on hill farming and on local workshops. By the end of 2002 Maghar's population had tripled its size to 17,900 (57% Druzes, 23% Christians and 20% Muslims). The village has municipal council status and extends over an area of 9 sq. mi. (23 sq. km.). In 2000, income there was about half the national average. The place is possibly identical with Ma'ariyyah or Me'arot where a priestly family lived in talmudic times (*Baraita of the Twenty-Four Mishmarot*).

[Efraim Orni / Shaked Gilboa (2nd ed.)

MAGHREBI-MA'ARAVI, name of Jewish personalities and congregations originating from North Africa. The Arab geographers designate North Africa and Spain as Maghreb, the West. The name Maghreb-Ma'arav ("West"), Maghrebi-Ma'aravi ("the Westerner"), occurs in geonic literature and later. It continues to be applied to North African congregations and their rites. The Maghrebis speak different Arabic dialects, which, in addition to special rites and patterns of life, distinguishes their language from other, Eastern Judeo-Arabic dialects and their customs from other congregations.

BIBLIOGRAPHY: Hirschberg, Afrikah, 1 (1965), 59, 344; idem, in: *Bar Ilan*, 4/5 (1967), 475–79. **ADD. BIBLIOGRAPHY:** EIS², 5 (1986), 1183ff., s.v. al-Maghrib.

[Haïm Z'ew Hirschberg]

MAGIC.

Early Magic

Broadly defined, magic is a system of non-canonical ritual practices aiming at changing reality. In early Jewish magic this system was based on the use of powerful verbal performative formulae – incantations – whose oral or written expression was realized in the framework of a ceremony. The purpose of the magical act was generally to compel metaphysical entities such as demons, angels, stars and celestial bodies, holy names, and even God Himself, to bring about for the user the reality he desired. Early Jewish magical literature is evidenced in magical writings and objects from the Land of Israel, Babylonia, and North Africa, dating from the third century until the 12th (prior to the development of the Kabbalah and the change it effected in Jewish magic in the direction of practical Kabbalah). This literature enables us to trace the verbal elements of the adjuration as a magical text, such as the employment of the verbal root, šbʿ, addressing the metaphysical forces in the first person singular, the utilization of expressions of urgency, and threats towards them, indicating the client mentioned in the magical object by his first name and the name of his mother, and more. On this basis we can establish that as more of these textual characteristics are found in any given Jewish text, its magical tendency increases. From here we can also define all the Jewish magical cultural products. Texts that include adjurations, such as books of guidance for sorcery, are magic texts in a broader sense, and those that express beliefs and customs commonly found in texts of both these categories are magic texts in the broadest sense; objects upon which adjuration texts are found such as sheets of paper, leather, cloth or metal, or clay bowls are magic objects (amulets, magic bowls), and in the wider circle are included objects that serve as a means of ritual power in the context of the outlook expressed in the magical literature; ceremonies where adjuration texts are written or uttered, or where use is made of magical objects, are considered as ceremonies of magical character. This manner of definition of magic allows a flexible relationship between it and the other components of Jewish culture, and in particular the religion. Instead of an a priori culture-dependent dictionary distinction that strives to distinguish between what is magic and what is not viewed as such, one finds a dynamic system of phenomena characterized as possessing a greater or lesser magical essence, but not necessarily related to their place in the overall socio-cultural system of ritual power. Relinquishing the apposition of magic to religion in the phenomenological dimension allows us to divert the distinction between them to the social plane where the non-canonical position of magic finds expression. Texts, magical objects, and ceremonies generally do not have a routine place in the Jewish canonical system of practice for attaining ritual power. At the same time it is not impossible that portions of the latter, such as the biblical examination of the suspected adulteress, the recitation of the **Shema* before going to sleep, and the **mezuzah*, be defined as possessing a magical character. In this manner the cultural products of early Judaism itself testify to the gap between the official and explicit perception (in the Bible and the Mishnah) that prohibits sorcery and considers it as a capital sin and its firm place in the day-to-day lives of the people. Recognition of the existence of this gap is naturally related to the recognition of the distance between the inner-cultural definition of magic as an illegitimate form of ritual activity by its very essence, and its external, academic definition, based on sociological notions of religion, that views it as the non-canonical, marginal, and in most cases prohibited part of the overall activity aimed at attaining ritual power (which also includes a legitimate-canonical side, i.e., religion), repressed by the ruling religious center of society as concerns its struggle over power and control.

The sources documenting early Jewish magic may be divided into two kinds: primary sources, those originating in magical culture itself, and secondary sources, those found in texts that are not, in essence, magical. Primary sources from the biblical era are rare. Noteworthy among them are silver amulets from the end of the seventh century B.C.E., found in a burial network in the Hinnom valley in Jerusalem, and upon which the priestly blessing is inscribed. In the Bible itself, sorcery and divination are prohibited and those who dealt in them were persecuted. It would appear, however, that this prohibition, closely tied in the Bible to the religious-ethical uniqueness of the people of Israel and its distinctiveness from the surrounding nations, well testifies to the perpetuation of these ritual practices that priestly and prophetic circles aspired to marginalize in favor of those that they themselves offered and to which they attributed canonical status. Nevertheless, at least in one outstanding case, that of the ordeal for examination of the suspected adulteress (Num. 5:11–31), one suspects the acquisition of a magical practice (which underwent an intercultural, priestly, oicotypification) by the religious establishment. The result bears testimony to the belief in the performative power of curses among both that priestly establishment and the people as a whole. Metaphysical beings central to magical practice such as angels, Satan, and demons are indeed mentioned in the biblical literature, however in a way that is unconnected to the overall system of typical magical beliefs and practices in which they were to function later. First and foremost, they are not introduced as being under any kind of vigorous human manipulation. In the only case where Satan is mentioned as being expelled by words that may reflect an exorcistic formula, it is by God Himself, and from His presence (Zech. 3:2). Human power to manipulate concrete reality is admitted in the bible in both the hands of foreign sorcerers, such as the Egyptians, or Balaam, and God's prophets. In any case, it is always subservient to God's will and force. Even the marvels manifested time and again by God's prophets are not performed on account of their own power. Being men of the one and only omnipotent God, their miracles are viewed mainly as a didactic performance of what He Himself executes.

The apocryphal literature in general, and particularly the writings of the Dead Sea sect, increased immeasurably the angelological and demonological deliberations and well reflect the metaphysical expansion of society within Judaism in this period. The figure of Satan (also called Belial or Mastema) has evolved into the head of an army of evil spirits and the lord of the demons. The origin of these demons, imageless and highly harmful spiritual beings, was perceived as the product of the impure hybrid coupling of rebellious angels with the daughters of Adam (a tradition alluded to in Genesis 6:1–4, and expanded in I Enoch and in the Book of Jubilees). At that time, it is told, sorcery was brought down to the world and given to women. Alongside it the Book of Remedies was delivered to Noah, according to God's command, for protection against the wicked demons that had attacked his children. The Qumran scrolls reveal to us a well-developed demonological perception. Qumranic Psalm fragments testify to apotropaic ritual practices against demons. The works of Josephus and the New Testament reflect a similar reality in the first century C.E. Demons were perceived as the cause of both corporal and mental disorders and their removal through rituals that featured magical objects, roots, and verbal formulae was a common method of healing. Comparing the depictions of exorcism and healing performed by Jesus according to the New Testament with the Greek magical papyri reveals his place as a Jewish magician within the intercultural tradition of Late Antiquity as well as his uniqueness within that tradition (both in terms of his actions of healing and exorcising, and in utilizing them as a means of his religious mission). According to the testimony of the Gospels, Jesus was accused by his Jewish opponents of using the power of Beelzebub, the prince of the demons. In other words, he was accused of being a sorcerer, i.e., possessing considerable supernatural power, but that this power was derived from an impure source and was therefore illegitimate.

His followers naturally saw him as a holy man who was performing miracles through divine power.

The apocryphal literature and the Dead Sea sect literature also demonstrate the considerable angelological expansion of social reality; only here human magical power vis-à-vis the angels is not yet reflected. Their assistance to men is judged a gesture of good will, a divine mission, or preordained reality, but not the result of their compulsion to act in this way through human efforts. This notion appears in full force in the primary sources of early Jewish magic: amulets and incantation bowls that were geared primarily for protection, healing, and success and which document actual magical activity for the clients mentioned in them by name, and magical recipes collected in compositions and books of recipes. The magical recipe literature presents to us the notion that magic is a part of normal life. It is hard to imagine an area of life for which no magical assistance is offered in this literature. The amulets and magic bowls connect this theoretical literature to the actual day-to-day lives of the Jews of Late Antiquity.

Ancient Jewish magical praxis was based on a system of beliefs that concerned the connection between physical and metaphysical reality and the manner by which language is capable of connecting between them for human profit. Social reality was expanded to include metaphysical beings that were divided into four categories: (a) God; (b) celestial beings such as angels, stars and planets, divine names, etc.; (c) various demons and evil spirits (including personifications of harmful sorcery); (d) the dead. The correct use of an adjuration (mostly by a suitable person within a well-defined ceremony) was viewed as being able to subordinate any one of the above to obey the adjurer's will. Generally the adjurations were aimed at activating the celestial beings, principally angels or demons. The magical use of God or the dead is rarely documented. Magical compositions such as the Book of Mysteries (*Sefer ha-Razim*) or the Sword of Moses (*Ḥarba de-Moshe*) reveal to us a highly developed angelological perception. The names of the angels, their order and relative powers are placed at the disposal of whosoever wishes to manipulate them. Divine aid, in the form of a command that God sent to his angels, is what allows man to take power over them through the use of incantations and divine names and to manipulate them at will. Magical practice is therefore portrayed in these works as a part of the Jewish monotheistic belief and not as anomalous to it. Alongside this angelology a rich demonology is also revealed in the magical literature. Demons were perceived as responsible for every misfortune in human life and in particular when it affected the body. Protection from them and their removal from the moment they penetrated someone's life space was a central purpose of Jewish magical activity. However, the magical literature testifies to the use of magical means for dealing with many other matters. These include the relations between people such as marriage and sexual relations, success in litigation, control over one's fellow being, injuring someone, protection from injury, victory in battle, and so on. They appear to be further used in such daily cares as improving the products of labor and agricultural produce, fishing, trade, and even minor objectives such as kindling an oven in winter or the expulsion of crickets or mice from the house. Besides all this, another area of great importance was served by magic: knowledge. Angels, demons, and the dead functioned in the Jewish magic culture as agents of almost limitless knowledge that could be adjured to reveal to man whatever he desired to know. Summoning angels for this purpose was associated on occasion with the practice of the dream request. Thus, while divination is not identical to magic, there is much evidence of Jewish magical divination practices based on utilizing adjurations as well as other magical means.

As noted, the basis of early Jewish sorcery was in the use of adjurations. These verbal formulae, which were defined with precision and adapted individually for their specific objectives, were mostly uttered or written in a ceremonial framework. The ritual state of all the participants in the ceremony was also well defined and almost always entailed the purity (in halakhic terms) of the performer. The conditions of the performance of the ceremony and its verbal, material, and behavioral components varied with each case. On more than one occasion they were borrowed from Hellenistic magic. Professional terms loaned from the Hellenistic magical jargon testify, too, to the intercultural relationship in this field, the other expression of which was the penetration by indubitably Jewish elements into Hellenistic magical practice. It is not easy to chart with precision the elements of the magic ceremony. However, beyond the variety of means one central mechanism, which constitutes a system, stands out: the sympathetic mechanism. In early Jewish magic it is usual to find attempts to bring about a reality by means of juxtaposing it to another based on the principle: "Just as A, so B." The depiction of one reality (A) may be done simply and freely, or it may be through similitude (for example, "Just as the sky is suppressed before God and the Earth is suppressed before people… so may the inhabitants of this town be suppressed and broken and fallen before Yose son of Zenobia"). Often, serving this purpose are biblical verses whose meaning, or words appearing in them, are relevant for the desired effect (for example, "Noah found favor with the Lord" (Gen. 6:8) is quoted for attaining "grace and favor"; "I will not bring upon you any of the diseases that I brought upon the Egyptians" (Ex. 15:26) is quoted for healing). The choice of magic materials necessary for the sorcery may also reflect this aim (for example, a round bowl would serve for protection from all sides, a heart of a young lion for attaining courage). Often, the ceremony includes the preparation of a magical object, that is, an object which has adjuration texts on it. This will serve the client over a length of time. Amulets were worn on the body or were buried in the house or even in the synagogue. Incantation bowls were buried in the corners of rooms or below the threshold, dwelling places of demons against whom the bowls were intended. Occasionally the verbal adjuration was sunken into a piece of food or a liquid that the client would have to swallow or to rub over his body. In this way the magical quality of the words passed into the client's body and strengthened him from within.

The secondary magical sources, the rabbinic literature, and early Jewish mystical works demonstrate that the magic outlook was not confined to the more boorish classes of society. The early Jewish mystical literature testifies to the central place of performative ritual power in two areas: (a) as a means to overcome the hostile angels in the course of a mystical journey to God's Throne of Honor; (b) as a social advantage in the possession of the mystic in this world following his return from his heavenly journey. The magical matter is so pronounced in the early Jewish mystical literature that some of the scholars judge this aspect (and not the experiences of the ascent to the higher realm and the sight of God) as the kernel unifying all the writings that constitute this literature. Rabbinic literature, too, indicates the place of the magical and demonological outlook, and the accompanying practices, in the social-religious elite. Three approaches are reflected in it alongside each other (as is typical of this polyphonic literature), and all are founded on the very recognition of the efficacy of sorcery: (a) an official halakhic position that associates sorcery with the "Ways of the Amorite," meaning the gentile customs prohibited for Jews on account of the Jews' distinctiveness from them, prohibits it in every way, and punishes those who dabble in it by stoning (while distinguishing the real acts of magic from acts of deception that are not judged as the sin of sorcery); (b) a pragmatic approach that permits the use of those magic objects and verbal means (that are not, of course, denoted as such) whose benefit has been proven (primarily for medicinal purposes), permits the study of sorcery (as opposed to its operation), and even requires of those taking a seat in the Sanhedrin to be "masters of sorcery"; (c) a narrative approach that uses, in the manner of the talmudic homiletic story, magical motifs for didactic purposes. Here a dual tendency is noticeable whereby on the one hand the ritual-magical powers of the sages themselves (which naturally are not identified with sorcery but rather with holiness based on a life of Torah and observance of the divine commandments) are extolled, while on the other hand accusations are leveled at the "other," primarily women and heretics, for acts of sorcery. This labeling is intended to mark out these "others" as dangerous people who act with illegitimate power, and to marginalize them, placing them far from the desirable-legitimate focus of power, that of the sages themselves, who are both the narrators and the heroes of the narratives. The climax of this dual tendency is found in the stories that describe struggles between sages and sorcerers or sorceresses, which, as is to be expected, end in the sages' victory, and in this way exemplify their worthy socio-religious model. It would appear therefore that the contradiction between the halakhic and narrative approaches toward magic is not to be resolved through distinguishing between the "rabbis' genuine viewpoint," which was negative and deprecatory by virtue of their religious beliefs and the laws deriving from them, on the one hand, and their "lip service" to the beliefs of the ignorant masses (which originated in the penetration of foreign influences), through lack of choice, and for didactic purposes, on the other hand, as was done in the past, but by recognizing the aspirations of the rabbis for a social monopoly over ritual power. The rabbinic demonological stories are to be understood in a similar way. They, too, should be seen as a narrative shaping of motifs that rest upon popular beliefs in both their own circles as well as amongst the masses, with a didactic objective. More than the stories are concerned with demonic reality in itself, they are about the relations between this reality and that of the sages, and more specifically the relative superiority of the sages and their disciples over all that affects the ways of the demons. This includes protection from them and control over them by the power of their holiness, their legal authority, and ritual-magical means. Thus, the demonological stories join the magical and mystical ones in revealing a ramified system of beliefs and ritual practices relating to angels, demons, and sorcery in the Jewish culture of Late Antiquity. Primary magical evidence completes the picture by tying the literary testimony to day-to-day experience and exposing the actual praxis of ancient Jewish magic.

[Yuval Harari (2nd ed.)]

In Medieval Hebrew Literature

TERMINOLOGY. The terms "magic" (*kishuf*), "magician" (*mekhashef*), and "witch" (*mekhashefah*) are relatively rare in medieval Hebrew literature, especially when compared with the frequency with which magic practices are mentioned. The underlying reason is undoubtedly the explicit biblical prohibition against the practice of magic (repeatedly dwelt upon in medieval Hebrew literature) and the Bible's abhorrence of magicians and soothsayers. There is, therefore, no favorable allusion to magic practices in medieval literature, and they are rarely dealt with in a purely informative manner, although the numerous texts of the *Genizah* dealing with this topic allow us to understand in how many ways magic was present in Jewish life during the Middle Ages. Such terms as *kishuf*, *mekhashef*, and *mekhashefah* were descriptive of the wicked, sinners, and non-Jews. Magic was discussed in medieval Hebrew literature, but surreptitiously, under the guise of different names, such as *segullot* ("remedies" or "charms"), *kame'ot* ("amulets"), *refu'ot* ("cures"), *goralot* ("destinies" or "fortunes"), *simanim* ("signs" or "omens"), and *refafot* ("bodily itches as a portent"). The medieval writer thus was able to circumvent the term "magic" and eschew a direct confrontation with the biblical prohibition. In fact, the practice of magic was very popular and widespread among medieval Jews, and the number of texts including magical elements is very striking.

SOURCES AND DISSEMINATION. Literature on magic is universal in its character, its methods, and its structure. Each society, each language, and every period contributed toward magic literature, enriching it or modifying it in the light of the particular characteristics of the society, the culture, and the times. The main themes and methods in magic were, however, transmitted from country to country, from language to language throughout the ages without any basic changes being wrought. In the Middle Ages, Jewish magic literature differs very little from the magic literature of other nations. Magical practices were very widespread during the Middle Ages not only in Jewish communities but also among Muslims and Christians. Textbooks of magic circulated in the three cultures, although theoretical considerations were less frequent. Hebrew works on magic quote extensively from non-Jewish magic literature, citing especially sources that medieval scholarship attributed to ancient Greek authors. The basic terminology and methods found in Hebrew works are similar to those dominant in non-Jewish works. In some Hebrew works a term may be used which was originally Hebrew but is applied in such a way as to show that it was copied from a non-Hebrew work; its Hebrew origin had apparently been unknown to the Hebrew writer, for example, the term *Elo'i Sabaot* derived from the Hebrew *Elohei Zeva'ot*. Angelology and magic formulas in Hebrew, Greek, and Latin of the Hellenistic period were basic to the development of medieval magic literature. Since this period led to the fusion of Hebrew and non-Hebrew formulas, the process continued throughout the Middle Ages when terms and formulas from Arabic, German, French, Slavic, and other languages were added to medieval Hebrew magic literature. To date there is no serious study on the sources on which medieval Hebrew magic works drew. The various influences have neither been defined nor classified and no clear distinction can therefore be made between the following sources: the Assyrian and Babylonian (which apparently also influenced the Talmud), the Hellenistic (Jewish-Hellenistic and Greek), the ancient Egyptian and their later adaptations during the syncretistic periods of the Roman Empire, the original Arabic and their fusion with the Persian and Indian, and the European which were intermingled with Arabic and other sources. Principally, however, there is as yet no way to distinguish in every case between traditional Hebrew magic, derived from the biblical and talmudic periods, and the magic elements which reached Jewish writers from foreign sources. An example is a Greek and Arabic traditional connection between Saturn and magic; in Jewish medieval thought both magic and Saturn, who is in charge of the Jewish people, are also connected with the Sabbath day (Idel). We know today that Jewish magic in the Middle Ages was strongly influenced by two Arabic treatises, al-Kindi's *De radiis* and al-Majariti's *Picatrix*, which were translated into Latin and Hebrew, but their actual degree of influence has not been sufficiently studied. Until such studies are made, only impressions and generalizations can serve as basis for any assumption as to the nature of medieval Hebrew magic works.

Though there are no detailed studies on hand, there is no doubt that Jewish medieval magic drew on all the above-mentioned sources. Some medieval Hebrew works correspond very closely to non-Jewish magic writings. Others, for example a number of 18th-century collections of Hebrew magic formulas, differ little from magic formulas which survived from the geonic period. Collections which originated in North Africa are very similar to works on magic by Jews in Germany. There is thus no essential difference in the basic magic formulas and the attitude toward magic between the various nations, countries, and periods. The same fusion of ancient and medieval sources is to be found in each of these works, all of which contain Arab, European, and authentic Jewish elements.

THE CHARACTER OF HEBREW MAGIC LITERATURE. The character of Hebrew magic literature was influenced not only by the biblical prohibition on witchcraft but by the nature of this literature. Works on magic neither use nor are identified by terms denoting magic, but were written under the guise of concepts which neither reveal their special character nor their contents. There are hundreds of collections on magic, in print and in manuscripts, appearing under such names as *simanim*, *refafot*, *refu'ot*, *goralot*, and *segullot*. These works are usually not devoted only to one branch of magic or popular superstition, but to a variety of practices such as dream interpretation, popular medicine, and amulets. Unfortunately, the complete typology of magic literature has not yet been seriously studied.

Many of these works are anonymous; in others the name of the editor or compiler appears in the introduction. (The term "author" is not applicable to such works, which are nothing but collections drawn from various sources.) Rarely is there anything known of them from other sources; most of them were obscure writers who did not engage in scholarly activities. This may be the underlying reason for the low level of the language and literary merit of most of these works. Some of the writings on magic are attributed to ancient sages and scholars; thus, for example, works which are partly devoted to the interpretation of dreams are often ascribed to the biblical figures Daniel or Joseph; works on *goralot* ("destinies" or "fortunes") are attributed to the wise *Ahithophel the Gilonite, etc. Babylonian *geonim* and early scholars, from Saadiah b. Joseph Gaon to Naḥmanides, have had works on magic ascribed to them. Though widely disseminated, works on magic were mostly not written within the framework of medieval and early modern scholarly Hebrew literature. In any case, the corpus of Jewish magic, including complete books and fragments, is very large. Some of the better known works that discuss magic are Maimonides' *Guide of the Perplexed* and *Mishneh Torah*, including sorcery and magic among the forbidden practices; the commentaries on the Pentateuch by Naḥmanides (13th century); the responsa of Solomon ben *Adret and the sermons of Nissim *Gerondi in the 14th century; *Nishmat Ḥayyim* by *Manasseh Ben Israel, in which the author devotes a long chapter to the description of magical practices; *Derekh ha-Shem* by Moses Ḥayyim *Luzzatto, has a section on magic; and *Shalshelet ha-Kabbalah*, an important historical work in which the author, Gedaliah b. Joseph *Ibn Yaḥya, a Renaissance scholar, also discusses magic.

The literature of the *Ḥasidei Ashkenaz, probably more than any other medieval corpus of Hebrew scholarly writings, is a source on medieval magic (12th and 13 centuries), especially

Sefer Ḥasidim and the esoteric works of *Judah b. Samuel ha-Ḥasid of Regensburg and of his disciples, of which *Ḥokhmat ha-Nefesh*, a work on psychology by *Eleazar b. Judah of Worms, is a prime example. The concern of the Ashkenazi Ḥasidim with magic practices and phenomena has its roots in some of their theological ideas.

MAGIC AND MEDIEVAL DISCIPLINES. Medieval man, as reflected in the literature on magic, did not clearly differentiate between magic and other branches of knowledge, especially between medicine, astrology, and magic. There were very different kinds of magic, some of them of a high cultural level, and other more popular types. Cultural magic was considered a branch of medieval science, at the same level as medicine or astrology. Many times, this magic was a kind of alternative medicine. Most of the collections dealing mainly with magic do not distinguish between the treatment of an ailment according to the accepted norms of popular medicine, such as the application of heat, herbs, and certain foods, and magic means, calling for the help of angels and demons to heal the patient. This failure of distinction was not only due to the lack of a scientific framework but to the desire to lend authority and legitimacy to magic formulas when combined with medical practice. These works also do not clearly distinguish between astrology and magic. Works on *goralot* ("destinies" or "fortunes") include astrological calculations which portend the fate of a man according to the constellations at his birth, and determine his character traits and religious, economic, and social status. The same works also contain magic instructions on how to use the auguries of the constellations for other purposes and how to change a man's fate through incantations and amulets, etc.

Most of the magic in the extant collections is devoted to *simanim* which derives from the fact that the Talmud, contrary to its injunction against the practice of magic, allows the practice of "signs." This literature describes various events, feelings, or even the itching of various parts of the human body (*refafot*), which are indicative of an oncoming event. Incantations are often chanted and charms used in an attempt either to nullify an ominous portent or to enhance a benign prophecy. To this category also belongs the literature of "dream interpretation" which describes in detail various occurrences within dreams thought to reveal the future to the dreamer. Sometimes advice is tendered in the use of magical means to prevent the bad dreams from being realized. Compilations of popular medical literature, such as *The Book of Women's Love* (perhaps 13th century), contained many magic (mainly love magic) elements and formulas; most of these practices, reflected in the written materials or transmitted in oral form, were current during the Middle Ages. Their main goal was to manipulate sexuality, intervening in human relationships. Some of these formulas are taken from the tradition of the "practical Kabbalah."

The *segullah* is basic to all magic formulas and is the main magic means used by the person himself. Knowledge of many charms is the professional distinction of the expert magician. The central element in the *segullah* is a name or a series of names which is considered holy. The common appellation of a magician in Eastern Europe in the 17th and 18th centuries as *Ba'al Shem* or *Ba'al Shem Tov* ("owner of the Holy Name" or "owner of the Holy Good Name") is rooted in this practice. The name used is most frequently that of an angel, or, sometimes, one of the many names of God. Sometimes even the name of a demon is resorted to which would seem to make this form of magic "black magic." The demon invoked in such charms is, however, thought to be a "bad angel" (*malakh ḥabbalah*) who should be addressed when the magician intends to harm someone, kill an enemy, cause damage, find the whereabouts of a thief and make him return his loot, etc. Some of the names in the *segullah* are common biblical or talmudic-midrashic names, mostly polysyllabic so as to awe the hearer and to seem as strange as possible. Many of the names were culled from *Heikhalot* and Merkabah writings, the Hebrew mystical literature of the talmudic and geonic period from which the major part of Hebrew medieval angelology is derived; sometimes even from non-Hebrew sources; others were created anagrammatically according to a definite system, either from other known names or from biblical verses.

The name, which is the essence of the *segullah*, is supplemented with various elements which differ from book to book and even from page to page in the same work. The *segullah*, or the petition for magical intercession (of a supernatural power), must be written in a clear form or enunciated clearly and loudly. Sometimes the time at which the deed should occur (a certain hour of the day or night or a certain day of the month) is also given; an astrological element was thus added to the magical charm. Certain substantive elements are also added, such as bits of flesh, bone, or skin from various animals (or even the human body), or certain herbs or plants. In the classic cases of sympathetic magic sometimes the performer of the act of magic, when he directs an incantation against a certain person, draws a picture of the latter or writes his name, or even molds his likeness in clay. These means were especially resorted to in the case of a thief. The suffering inflicted by sympathetic magic on the thief caused him to reveal the cache of the stolen goods and give them back. Through these means demons could also be compelled to serve man, when an incantation with the name of the culprit proved ineffective.

The *segullah* is used both as a direct magic act to attain a certain aim and as an auxiliary to medical aid, to reveal a man's fate, to appease or prompt the auguries of a "sign," or to interpret a dream. An amulet, for instance, is usually nothing more than a *segullah* written in a certain form, so that a person could carry it with him always. Such a charm is usually protective, invoking the heavenly powers to safeguard the wearer against any harm.

The contents of works on *segullot* are arranged according to their purposes. A title states the function of the charm after which there is a description of the charm including the holy names and the other necessary elements. Another type of *segullot* literature, sometimes called *shimmushim* ("uses"), is arranged according to the holy names indicating the purpose and uses to which each name can be put. Thus, for instance, *Sefer ha-Ḥeshek* lists 70 names of the archangel *Metatron, after each of which the author gives the use that it can be put to and what magical purpose can best be served by using one particular appellation of this angel. The holy divine names, composed either of 42 letters or 72 letters, which are comprised of units of three or six letters, serve many magic purposes; each name can be the means of achieving a specific magic goal. Treatises on the magic use of the Psalms (*Sefer Shimmush Tehillim*) and on the properties of the members of animals were very common in Jewish houses. Some form of magic was even practiced by rabbis who did not see them as opposed to Judaism (Barkai). "*Shimmushei Tehillim*" ("The Uses of the Psalms"), a body of magic writings, describes the magic power inherent in certain verses and chapters in the Psalms and in some other Scriptures. The Bible was also used for the purpose of "sign" magic, i.e., prophecies. A person practicing this magic would open the Bible, put his finger at random on a certain verse and the content of this verse would reveal the attitude of the Divine Powers to the question or request of the person inquiring.

RELATIONSHIP BETWEEN MYSTIC AND MAGIC LITERATURES. Scholars believe that the extent of the influence of magic on Jewish mysticism has not yet been sufficiently studied. Historical circumstances rather than literary or conceptual affinities have created an impression, especially in modern times, that there is a similarity or even identity between mystic literature and magic in Jewish life and thought. One expression of this view is the term "*kabbalah ma'asit*" ("practical tradition"), which is magic, and "*kabbalah iyyunit*" ("theoretical tradition"), which is mysticism. "Kabbalah" in this context means nothing more than tradition and does not denote any special mystical system. Nineteenth-century scholars of Jewish studies who were fiercely opposed to *Ḥasidism, which is one derivation of the Kabbalah proper (the mystical ideology), saw Ḥasidism and Kabbalah as representing medieval superstition, and did not try to differentiate between mystical thought and magic practice, which to them seemed to derive from the same source. Their ideas were accepted even by some 20th-century scholars.

Still, there is some connection between the development of magic literature and mystical literature. In talmudic times there undoubtedly existed a unique magic literature to which such works as *Sefer ha-Razim*, published in a scholarly edition (by M. Margalioth, 1966; there is an English translation by M.A. Morgan, 1983), clearly testify. The book is an example of early Jewish magic which did not have any mystic tendency, and which is influenced mainly by non-Hebrew sources.

If the magic elements are not very dominant in this kind of rabbinic literature, the writings of the *Heikhalot* and the Merkabah have a strong magical component. Included are works of a clear magical character, e.g., *Hakkarat Panim ve-Sidrei Sirtutim*, a work on chiromancy. Even major works of this literature, such as *Sefer Heikhalot Rabbati*, include some material concerning prophecies, signs, and even incantations. According to the conceptual view of *Heikhalot* and Merkabah literature, when the angels revealed heavenly mysteries (revelations which constitute the body of this literature) to the talmudic sages they also made esoteric magic disclosures in which they described the divine worlds and eschatological secrets. These texts of early Jewish mysticism include many adjurations of magical character asking the angels to come down and reveal to man the mysteries of heaven and earth, including the complete knowledge of the Torah, and sometimes alluding to the necessary rituals for the heavenly journey of the mystic. The means of achieving the goals of this mysticism is magic; the authors of this literature "attempted to integrate magic into Judaism" (Schaefer). The magical view of the Hebrew language, combining letters for forming divine names, is one of the bases of this form of Jewish mysticism. Medieval scholars, the Ḥasidei Ashkenaz, and the kabbalists who resorted to *Heikhalot* and Merkabah literature in their esoteric and mystical speculations also accepted the magic tradition that it embraced and sometimes even practiced it.

Magic is relatively little treated in theoretical Kabbalah writings, especially in works which concentrated on matters concerning the structure of the divine worlds, the *Sefirot*, and the developments within the divine realm (themes central to kabbalistic literature). Many kabbalists, from those in the Gerona circle (13th century) on, did not practice magic at all. The doctrines of medicine and astrology are undoubtedly nearer to that of magic than the doctrines of Jewish mysticism. A detailed examination of magic literature clearly shows that most of those who practiced magic, or the authors of works on magic, did not know anything about mysticism in general, or Kabbalah in particular. It is therefore very unlikely that kabbalistic symbolism of the holy *Sefirot*, or the kabbalistic concept of evil, would appear in magic charms. When the Zohar became part of the holy literature and widely known, it was used for magic purposes, but no more than the Book of Psalms. The use that both works were put to does not reflect their original content. Supernatural knowledge and powers were, however, attributed to many kabbalists. Even Isaac the Blind, one of the earliest kabbalists who lived in Provence, was described as having the power to distinguish between a new soul, which appeared for the first time in the world, and an old soul, which had been reincarnated. This tradition of magic and supernatural hagiography of prominent kabbalists developed continually up to the times of Isaac *Luria and *Israel Ba'al Shem Tov. The writings of Moshe *Cordovero (16th century), the kabbalist of Safed, are also full of magical views, since he adopted a type of Kabbalah very close to astral magic.

Based on a tradition preserved in a talmudic text on the creation of an artificial man, unable to speak, and using techniques found in the *Sefer Yeẓirah* (combination of letters), medieval kabbalists and ḥasidic circles developed the idea of the *golem*, which was from the very beginning replete with magic content. There were different modalities of this idea in Franco-Ashkenazi and Sephardic centers, going from the purely material being to the fully spiritual one. Zoharic and Lurianic kabbalists were not interested in the topic, while ecstatic kabbalists and Cordovero paid attention to it. In particular, the Ashkenazi texts dealing with the *golem* were basically magical, as shown by Idel.

Magic in Kabbalah literature is touched upon in discussion of earthly or demonological matters, but even in this literature it was cautiously treated and circumscribed. Few magic elements are found in the Zohar, and in the writings of other early kabbalists there are even less. The case of the ecstatic Kabbalah, the school of Abraham *Abulafia, is very different: for him, magical techniques like the combination of letters can be a help in attaining the personal mystical experience that endows the mystic with magical powers.

Later magic literature and kabbalistic doctrine were also seldom fused. Ḥayyim *Vital describes some magic practices in his autobiographical work *Sefer ha-Ḥezyonot* ("Book of Visions"), which, however, he does not relate to the special kabbalistic doctrine of his teacher, Isaac Luria. In his theological works, magic is a marginal theme. Though he accepted magic, it did not impinge on his innermost spiritual beliefs expressed in the kabbalistic myth which he set down in many books. The same applies to the writings of many other kabbalists.

The Ḥasidei Ashkenaz discussed magic in their works at length and also had some magic works attributed to them. The relationship they established between esoteric theology and magic speculation was rooted in a peculiar theological development. The Ashkenazi ḥasidic theology is based on the concept that God, far away from the natural world and the laws that govern it, is revealed, according to these laws, within the world of man in specific, well-defined phenomena which confirm to man His existence. Such phenomena, miraculous in character, including magic, witchcraft, and demonology, defy the laws of nature and reveal the power of the hidden Godhead. The Ḥasidei Ashkenaz consequently tried to collect in their writings as many descriptions of such phenomena as possible which they analyzed and on which they commented in the light of their own esoteric doctrine. The inference, however, cannot be drawn that they dealt in practical magic more or less than other scholars of that period. The implication is merely that they were theologically interested in such matters more than others, and therefore included them in their literature.

The Ḥasidei Ashkenaz thus became famous as scholars possessed of magic knowledge, and many legends revolved around them, such as the story about a competition in magic between *Samuel b. Kalonymus he-Ḥasid, and three non-Jewish magicians; the story about the ability of Eleazar b. Judah of Worms to get very quickly from place to place (*kefiẓat ha-derekh*) by the power of a magical formula; the tale of Judah b. Samuel he-Ḥasid who overpowered an evil magician; and many others. How far the legends woven about scholars were removed from the actual lives of these scholars may be seen by the fact that Abraham *Ibn Ezra, the Spanish Jewish philosopher and commentator, became the hero of many magic stories (probably because of his astrological works).

Some 19th-century scholars described modern Ḥasidism, founded by Israel Ba'al Shem Tov, as a prime example of magic and superstition. While many leaders of the ḥasidic movement believed in magic and practiced it, especially in giving amulets (the Ba'al Shem Tov himself dealt in magic and probably made his living as a popular healer and magician), ḥasidic theoretical literature, the vast homiletic literature which describes its ideology, is devoid of all magic elements. Ḥasidic tales might contain elements of the use of magic or of overcoming magic deeds performed by evil non-Jews, but ḥasidic doctrines eschewed magic elements even more than the kabbalistic literature which the Ḥasidim had inherited and developed. The difference between the "practical tradition" of Ḥasidism, which practiced magic, and the "ideological (theoretical) tradition" of the movement is probably more pronounced in modern Ḥasidism than in any other mystic movement.

MEDIEVAL JEWISH MAGICIANS. The terms *mekhashef* ("magician") and *mekhashefah* ("witch") in medieval literature designate two very different categories. A *mekhashef* is a person possessed of secret knowledge in magic which he uses for his own profit or to help others. He is considered a professional and is paid for his services. While in medieval Hebrew literature there are few records of a Jew being described as a *mekhashef*, in the early modern period the usage is much more frequent but under the name *Ba'al Shem (i.e., "owner of the Holy Name").

Mekhashef designates a certain psycho-pathological state, often connected with cannibalism. The term alludes to women and men who wander in forests, singly or in groups, or sometimes live in a community and kidnap babies or even grown-ups in order to eat them or suck their blood. While the term *mekhashefah* frequently recurs in medieval Hebrew literature, the actual phenomenon it represents seems to have been rare. In the 12th and 13th centuries in Central Europe these vampires were called *"shtria"* for the female (from the Latin *strix*, *striga*) and werewolf for the male. Such vampires do not necessarily possess any supernatural powers or secret knowledge. In *Sefer *Ḥasidim*, a 13th-century ethical work, there is a description of a baby born with teeth and a tail. The rabbi of the community advised that these be cut, so that when he grew up he would not eat people. This seems to testify to a case where a child was considered to have been born a werewolf, and could be cured naturally. No supernatural elements seem to be involved either in the birth of the werewolf or the proposed cure. A community where women ate children is also described in *Sefer Ḥasidim*. When threatened that if they continued their practice their teeth would be ground on the stones of the well, they stopped. The story is told as a clinical fact (which it probably was) and there seems to be neither any supernatural nor religious connotation or implication. On the other hand, in other stories from 13th-century Central Europe such creatures are immortal. They never die naturally but are killed in a prescribed manner. In one case, a witch was offered divine forgiveness if she were to reveal the secret of how she might be killed. Thus the person who committed the sin of cannibalism could religiously be saved. The phenomenon, apparently pathological in nature, was, in some cases, explained supernaturally – as if such cases were already dead, and therefore could not be killed. The *mekhashefah* does not belong to magic in the strict sense but designates a species of abominable creatures who form a category in themselves to which should be added the beliefs associated with them such as the belief in the "mare," a woman who strangles men in their sleep (hence the word "nightmare"). Other unnatural creatures who do not fit into either of the above categories should be classed somewhere between demons and magicians, or demons and witches. The term *mekhashefah* and the literature that evolved around it had relatively little influence on the development of medieval Jewish culture; the term *mekhashef*, however, is much more prominent.

In the 17th and 18th centuries in Eastern Europe the position of magicians ("*ba'alei Shem*") began to emerge on the Jewish social scene. The *ba'alei Shem* practiced magic and popular medicine, used amulets, drove away demons, and prophesied. Owing to the power inherent in the names they knew to use, they could discover thieves, retrieve lost articles, purify houses from evil spirits, etc. From the historical point of view, however, these magicians were of special significance in that many of them disseminated Shabbatean ideas throughout Eastern Europe; magicians were also instrumental in the development of the ḥasidic movement.

MAGIC IN MEDIEVAL JEWISH SOCIETY. In the opinion of some scholars, a negative attitude in respect to magic has relegated the study of magic, and its role in medieval Jewish society, to the margins of Jewish studies. The existing materials, in particular the fragments of the *Genizah*, have not yet been adequately studied, and we still lack today good monographs on medieval Jewish magic and divination. For that reason, it is not easy to attain an accurate picture of the social role of magic during these centuries. Jewish intellectuals did not consider magic either as an ideological or social challenge which had to be dealt with. But the texts of the *Genizah* show that magic was familiar at both the elite and popular levels of culture (Wasserstrom). The belief in the power of magic was apparently universal in Jewish society, both in the East and in the West, from the beginning of the Middle Ages up to early modern times. Opposition to magic was voiced by but a few which, when expressed in writing, formed a minor element within their work. While Maimonides, like some other Jewish philosophers, rejected magic and the use of amulets, he was not deeply concerned with it and only devoted a few passages to the problem in *Guide of the Perplexed*, much less, for instance, than to his argument with astrology on which he wrote a special treatise. Among others who repudiated magic were Saadiah Gaon (who rejected it in the same way as astrology) and Hai Gaon; they too, however, did not stress the question in their writings. As a consequence belief in magic hardly ever called forth any defenders in Hebrew literature. In the great 13th-century controversy the rabbis of France in their criticism also denounced Maimonides for his opposition to magic; it was, however, a very minor point. Menahem Ẓiyyoni's short treatise on the defense of magic and the belief in demons, *Ẓefunei Ẓiyyoni* (in Ms.), is written from a kabbalistic point of view as were similar treatises by other kabbalists.

The practice of magic (which is quite different from a belief in magic) was also not a major problem in Judaism, though magic as such was condemned outright because of the biblical prohibition and it therefore was practiced under the guise of different names. The practice of "signs," "charms," amulets, astrology, and popular medicine was never a subject of serious scholarly discussion. Magic was employed without deep discussion in many areas of life: for influencing people's feelings and opinions, for healing all kinds of illness, for incantations, for mystical trance-inducement, for apotropaic charms, and even for finding hidden treasures. Some halakhists tried to accept the situation, distinguishing between magical practices that were directly forbidden and other practices that could be seen as not properly magic and were allowed. It was not strange that some magical practices, connected first of all with popular medicine or with human relations, or even with mystical traditions, were explained as something natural, and as such were not forbidden. Other kinds of magical practices, performed with the intention of influencing astral forces, or related to black magic, were usually prohibited. Owing to the biblical prohibition on magic the most vulgar and "black" forms of magic did not become common in Judaism and such practices as necromancy were very rare. While some books on magic contain formulas for killing an enemy by magic means, for love potions, etc., there is no evidence that these were practiced. These formulas were probably copied from non-Jewish sources. Sorcery was many times identified with black magic, and while some jurists did not see in it any real danger, others saw it in the context of demons or destructive angels and considered it forbidden as contrary to God's will.

As a result the practice of some kinds of magic was not a legitimate and commonly accepted profession in medieval Jewish society and the religious convictions of a man who practiced magic were suspect. Formulas were thus written down since there was no oral transmission within a special class of practitioners of magic. Many Jews, especially in the East, usually consulted non-Jewish magicians rather than Jewish magicians.

The Christian injunctions against magic and witchcraft and the fierce persecutions against those who practiced magic, which started around the end of the 15th century, affected in a particular way many *Conversos, but also old Christian families that had to face similar charges. Jews and Conversos were accused of ritual crimes and were persecuted by the Inquisition, as in the case of "the holy child of La Guardia" at the end of the 15th century which was considered a case of black magic. This kind of attitude does not have parallel in Judaism. There are few examples in Judaism of Jews persecuting Jews because of magic practices. In those rare cases where there is evidence of such persecutions, the accusation served as a camouflage for more fundamental reasons. Thus the accusations of the rabbis of Venice against Moses Ḥayyim Luzzatto for dealing in magic were a guise for their suspicion that he had Shabbatean tendencies. In those Jewish communities where Christian anti-witchcraft persecutions had an influence, such as Italy, the relationship between Jews and non-Jews was closer than elsewhere.

The only social sphere of Jewish life in which magic practice attained legitimacy was in the formulas of the *ḥerem* ("excommunication"). Many *ḥerem* texts have incantations with a clear magic undertone.

The un-transcendental purposes of most magical practices were probably one of the reasons why magic played such a minor role in cultivated medieval Jewish literature. There are few records of major significance in which magic featured, such as *Joseph della Reina's attempt to hasten the redemption through magic means. Magic literature centers around such minor matters as toothaches and lost articles, and some attempt at prophecy of private persons' destiny. It thus did not always relate to the major historical and ideological problems of medieval Jewish society. The private character of the practice rendered it unimportant in the eyes of both its supporters and opponents so that it never became a major issue of dispute.

In spite of the relatively small influence that magic had on medieval Jewish thought, some scholars consider that the widespread use of magical practices among Jews made the members of other communities see magic as a Jewish specialization. This can in no way justify the fact that Jewish magic became a cause for antisemitism and hatred toward the Jews in the Middle Ages. The belief that every Jew was an evil magician, possessed of supernatural evil powers, was very widespread among certain popular groups of Christians in the Middle Ages and early modern times. In some uncultivated ambiances Jews were believed to be the people of Satan and they thus possessed supernatural secrets. This concept was one of the major sources of persecutions and blood libels throughout that period. Jewish reality in the Middle Ages hardly gave any substance to such accusations or to such an impression of the Jewish people. The basis for it was Christian theology, which in ecclesiastical circles described the Jews as deicides, therefore Satanic, and therefore possessors of magic.

[Joseph Dan / Angel Saenz-Badillos (2nd ed.)]

BIBLIOGRAPHY: BIBLE: H. Zimmern, *Beiträge zur Kenntnis der babylonischen Religion* (1901), 91–95, and passim; A. Erman, *A Handbook of Egyptian Religion* (1907), 148–64; R.C. Thompson, *Semitic Magic* (1908); F. Cumont, *Oriental Religions in Roman Paganism* (1911), 138; J. Pedersen, *Der Eid bei den Semiten* (1914), 1–2; A. Jirku, in: ZAW, 37 (1917–18), 109–25; W.O. Oesterley, *Immortality and the Unseen World* (1921), 125–36; S. Mowinckel, *Psalmenstudien* (1921²); Pedersen, Israel, 1–2 (1926), 430ff.; N. Nicolsky, *Spuren magischer Formeln in den Psalmen* (1927); A.S. Cook, *The Religion of Ancient Palestine in the Light of Archaeology* (1930), 66–86, 200–1, 213; A. Falkenstein, *Die Haupttypen der sumerischen Beschwörung* (1931); H. Birkeland, *Die Feinde des Individuums in der israelitischen Psalmenliteratur* (1933); G. Meier, *Die assyrische Beschwörungssammlung Maqlû* (1937); A. Guillaume, *Prophecy and Divination* (1938), 26, 34, 233ff., 387–90; idem, in: JRAS, 2 (1942), 111–31; C.H. Gordon, in: AFO, 12 (1937–39), 115–17; Kaufmann, Y., Toledot, 1 (1937), passim; S.H. Hook, *The Origins of Early Semitic Ritual* (1938); W.F. Albright, in: BASOR, 76 (1939), 5–11; 150 (1958), 36; Th. H. Gaster, in: *Orientalia*, 11 (1942), 41–79, 186–8; H. Torczyner (Tur-Sinai), in: JNES, 6 (1947), 18–29; H. Tur-Sinai, *Ha-Lashon ve-ha-Sefer*, 1 (1954²), 53–65; M.D. Cassuto, *Ha-Elah Anat* (1950), 66–67, 80; J. Wilson, *The Culture of Ancient Egypt* (1951), 117–8, 142–3; A. Falkenstein and W. von Soden, *Sumerische und akkadische Hymnen und Gebete* (1953), 23–24, 214–7, 295–354; R. Malinowsky, *Magic, Science and Religion* (1954), 17–87; J. Liver, in: *Eretz-Israel*, 3 (1954), 99ff.; E. Reiner, in: JNES, 15 (1956), 129–49; A. Goetze, *Kleinasien* (1957²), 151–61; J. Gray, in: VTS, 5 (1957), 11, 36, 42, 147; Pritchard, Texts, 326–8, 346–58, 383–91; R.O. Gurney, in: *Iraq*, 22 (1960), 221–7; P. Artzi, in: EM, 4 (1962), 348–65. MEDIEVAL HEBREW LITERATURE: J. Trachtenberg, *Jewish Magic and Superstition* (1939, incl. bibl.); S. Lieberman, in: *Tarbiz*, 27 (1958), 183–9; Y. Dan, *ibid.*, 32 (1963), 359–69; idem, *Torat ha-Sod shel Ḥasidut Ashkenaz* (1968), 184–202; N. Golb, in: *American Philosophical Society Year Book* (1965); H.J. Zimmels, *Magicians, Theologians and Doctors* (1952). **ADD. BIBLIOGRAPHY:** M. Held, in: *ErIsr*, 16 (1982), 76–85; (S).D. Sperling, in: A. Green (ed.), *Jewish Spirituality from the Bible through the Middle Ages* (1986), 5–31; T. Abusch, *Babylonian Witchcraft Literature: Case Studies* (1987); J. Neusner et al. (eds.), *Religion, Science, and Magic* (1992); L. Grabbe, *Priests, Diviners, Sages: A Socio-Historical Study of Religious Specialists in Ancient Israel* (1995); J. Tigay, *JPS Torah Commentary Deuteronomy* (1996), 172–75; N. Spronk, in: W. Watson and N. Wyatt (eds.), *Handbook of Ugaritic Studies* (1999), 270–96; R. Schmidt, *Magie im Alten Testament* (2004); *Sefer ha-Razim*, ed. Margaliot (1966); *Sepher ha-Razim, The Book of the Mysteries*, trans. M.A. Morgan (1983); J. Caro Baroja, *Inquisición, brujería y criptojudaísmo* (1970); S. Shaked, in: *Pe'amim*, 15 (1983), 15–26; idem, in *Jewish Studies Quarterly*, 2 (1995), 197–219; idem, in: *Judaism and Islam* (2000), 97–109; R. Barkai, *Mada, Magyah u-Mitologyah bi-Ymei ha-Beinayim* (1987); idem, in: *La Càbala* (1989), 17–57; idem, in: *Judíos entre árabes y cristianos* (2000), 73–85; P. Schaefer, *Hekhalot-Studien* (1988); idem, in: *Journal of Jewish Studies*, 41:1 (1990), 75–91; idem, in: *Gershom Scholem's "Major Trends in Jewish Mysticism," 50 Years After* (1993), 59–78; D. Schwartz, in: *Proceedings of the American Academy of Jewish Research*, 57 (1990/91), Heb. sect. 17–47; I.J. Yuval, in: *Judentum im deutschen Sprachraum* (1991), 173–189; M. Idel, *Golem: Jewish Magical and Mystical Traditions on the Artificial Anthropoid* (1990); idem: *Hasidism: between Ecstasy and Magic* (c. 1995); idem, in: *Mada'ei ha-Yahadut*, 36 (1996), 25–40; idem, in: *Envisioning Magic* (1997), 195–214; idem, and A. Grafton, eds., *Der Magus: seine Ursprünge und seine Geschichte in verschiedenen Kulturen* (2001); L. Schiffman and M.D. Swartz, *Hebrew and Aramaic Incantation Texts from the Cairo Genizah: Selected Texts from Taylor-Schechter Box K1* (1992); S. Wasserstrom, in: *Genizah Research after Ninety Years* (1992), 160–66; R.P. Hsia, in: *From Witness to Witchcraft* (1996), 419–33; A. Ackerman, in: *Kabbalah*, 1 (1996), 73–80; M.J. Geller, in: *Journal of Jewish Studies*, 49:2 (1998), 334–40; L. Girón Negrón, in: *Miscelánea de Estudios Árabes y Hebraicos*, 48:2 (1999), 133–62; S. Klein-Braslavi, in: *Encuentros & desencuentros* (2000), 105–129; J. Seidel, in: *Spirit Possession in Judaism* (2003), 73–95; H. Ben-Shammai, in: *Aleph*, 4 (2004), 11–87; C. Caballero-Navas, *The Book of Women's Love* (2004); G. Bohak, in: *Ginzei Qedem*, 1 (2005), 9–29. TEXTS AND TEXTUAL

STUDIES: G. Barkai, "The Priestly Benediction on the Ketef Hinnom Plaques," in: *Cathedra*, 52 (1989), 37–76 (Heb.); Y. Harari, *The Sword of Moses: A New Edition and Study* (Heb., 1997); M. Margalioth, *Sepher Ha-Razim: A Newly Recovered Book of Magic from the Talmudic Period* (Heb., 1966); J.A. Montgomery, *Aramaic Incantation Texts from Nippur* (1913); J. Naveh and S. Shaked, *Amulets and Magic Bowls, Aramaic Incantations of Late Antiquity* (1987); idem, *Magic Spells and Formulae, Aramaic Incantations of Late Antiquity* (1993); P. Schaefer and S. Shaked, *Magische Texte aus der Kairoer Geniza*, Bände 1–3 (1994–99); L.H. Schiffman and M.D. Swartz, *Hebrew and Aramaic Incantation Texts from the Cairo Genizah* (1992); G. Scholem, "Havdalah de-Rabbi Aqiba: A Source of the Jewish Magical Tradition from the Geonic Period," in: *Tarbiz*, 50 (1980/1) (Heb.); J.B. Segal, *Catalogue of the Aramaic and Mandaic Incantation Bowls in the British Museum* (2000); A. Yardeni, "Remarks on the Priestly Blessing on Two Ancient Amulets from Jerusalem," in: *Vetus Testamentum*, 41 (1991), 176–85. STUDIES: Y. Avishur, "'Ways of the Amorites': The Canaanite-Babylonian Background and the Literary Structure," Ch. Rabin et al. (eds.), in: *Studies in the Bible and the Hebrew Language Offered to Meir Wallenstein* (1979), 17–47 (Heb.); M. Bar Ilan, "Exorcism by Rabbis: Talmudic Sages and Magic," in: *Da'at*, 34 (1995), 17–31 (Heb.); idem, "Between Magic and Religion: Sympathetic Magic in the World of the Sages of the Mishnah and Talmud," in: *Review of Rabbinic Judaism*, 5:3 (2002), 383–99; L. Blau, *Das altjuedische Zauberwesen* (1898); B. Bokser, "Wonder-Working and the Rabbinic Tradition: The Case of Hanina Ben Dosa," in: *Journal for the Study of Judaism*, 16 (1985), 42–92; S. Fishbane, "'Most Women Engage in Sorcery': An Analysis of Sorceresses in the Babylonian Talmud," in: *Jewish History*, 7, 27–42; I. Gruenwald, "*Ha-Ketav, ha-Mikhtav ve-ha-Shem ha-Meforash – Magiah, Ruḥaniyyut u-Mistikah*," in: M. Oron and A. Goldreich (eds.), *Massu'ot: Studies in Kabbalistic Literature and Jewish Philosophy in Memory of Prof. E. Gottlieb* (1994), 75–98 (Heb.); M. Haran, "The Priestly Blessing on Silver Plaques: The Significance of the Discovery at Ketef Hinnom," in: *Cathedra*, 52 (1989), 77–89; Y. Harari, "'If You Wish to Kill a Person': Harmful Magic and Protection from It in Early Jewish Magic," in: *Jewish Studies*, 37 (1997), 111–42 (Heb.); idem, "Love Charms in Early Jewish Magic," in: *Kabbalah*, 5 (2000), 247–64 (Heb.); idem, "Power and Money: Economic Aspects of the Use of Magic by Jews in Ancient Times and the Early Middle Ages," in: *Pe'amim*, 85 (2000), 14–42 (Heb.); idem, "What is a Magical Text?: Methodological Reflections Aimed at Redefining Early Jewish Magic," in: M.J. Geller and S. Shaked, *Officina Magica* (forthcoming); J.M. Hull, *Hellenistic Magic and the Synoptic Tradition* (1974); E.C.D. Hunter, "Who Are the Demons? Iconography of Incantation Bowls," in: *Studi Epigrafici e Linguistici sul vicino Oriente antico*, 15 (1998), 95–115; A. Jeffers, *Magic and Divination in Ancient Palestine and Syria* (1996); A. Lange, "The Essene Position on Magic and Divination," in: M. Bernstein, F.G. Martínez, J. Kampen (eds.), *Legal Texts and Legal Issues: Proceedings of the Second Meeting of the International Organization for Qumran Studies* (1997), 377–435; D. Levene, "Curse or Blessing, What's in the Magic Bowls?" in: *Parke Institute Pamphlet*, 2 (University of Southampton, 2002); R.M. Lesses, *Ritual Practices to Gain Power: Angels Incantations, and Revelation in Early Jewish Mysticism* (1998); idem, "Exe(o)rcising Power: Women as Sorceresses, Exorcists, and Demonesses in Babylonian Jewish Society of Late Antiquity," in: *Journal of the American Academy of Religion*, 69 (2001), 343–75; J. Naveh, *On Sherd and Papyrus* (1992), 145–76; J. Neusner, "Rabbi and Magus in Third-Century Sasanian Babylonia," in: *History of Religions*, 6 (1966/7), 169–78; B.Z. Rosenfeld, "R. Simeon B. Yohai – Wonder Worker and Magician Scholar, *Sadiq* and *Hasid*," in: REJ, 158 (1999), 349–84; P. Schaefer, "Jewish Magic Literature in Late Antiquity and the Early Middle Ages," in: *Journal of Jewish Studies*, 41 (1990), 75–91; idem, "Merkavah Mysticism and Magic," in: P. Schaefer and J. Dan (eds.), *Gershom Scholem's "Major Trends in Jewish Mysticism," 50 Years After* (1993), 59–83; idem, "Magic and Religion in Ancient Judaism," in: P. Schaefer and H.G. Kippenberg, *Envisioning Magic* (1997), 19–43; J. Seidel, "Charming Criminals: Classification of Magic in the Babylonian Talmud," in: M. Meyer and P. Mirecki (eds.), *Ancient Magic and Ritual Power* (1995), 145–66; S. Shaked, "Bagdana, King of the Demons, and Other Iranian Terms in Babylonian Aramaic Magic," in: *Acta Iranica*, 24 (1985), 511–25; idem, "'Peace Be Upon You, Exalted Angels': On Hekhalot, Liturgy and Incantation Bowls," in: *Jewish Studies Quarterly*, 2 (1995), 197–219; idem, "Popular Religion in Sasanian Babylonia," in: *Jerusalem Studies in Arabic and Islam*, 21 (1997), 103–17; idem, "Jews, Christians, and Pagans in the Aramaic Incantation Bowls of the Sasanian Period," in: A. Destro and M. Pesce (eds.), *Religions and Cultures* (First International Conference of Mediterraneum) (2002), 61–89; M. Smith, *Jesus the Magician* (1981); M. Swartz, "Magical Piety in Ancient and Medieval Judaism," in: M. Meyer and P. Mirecki (eds.), *Ancient Magic and Ritual Power* (1995), 167–83; idem, *Scholastic Magic: Ritual and Revelation in Early Jewish Mysticism* (1996); J. Trachtenberg, *Jewish Magic and Superstition* (1970); G.T. Twelftree, *Jesus the Exorcist* (1993); G. Veltri, *Magie und Halakha: Ansätze zu einem empirischen Wissenschatbegriff im spätantiken und frühmittelalterlichen Judentum* (1997); idem, "The Meal of the Spirits, the Three Parcae and Lilith: Apotropaic Strategies for Coping with Birth Anxieties and Child Mortality," in: *Henoch*, 23 (2001), 343–59; E.E. Urbach, *The Sages: Their Concepts and Beliefs*, tr. I. Abrahams (1975), 97–134; E.R. Wolfson, "Phantasmagoria: The Image of the Image in Jewish Magic from Late Antiquity to the Early Middle Ages," in: *Review of Rabbinic Judaism*, 4 (2001), 78–120; E. Yassif, *The Hebrew Folktale: History, Genre, Meaning*, tr. J.S. Teitelbaum (1999), 144–66.

MAGIDOR, MENACHEM (1946–), president of the Hebrew University of Jerusalem. Magidor was born in Petaḥ Tikvah, Israel. He received his academic education at the Hebrew University of Jerusalem, getting his B.Sc. in mathematics and physics in 1965, a M.Sc. in mathematics in 1967, and a Ph.D. in mathematics in 1972. In 1968 he joined the department of mathematics at the Hebrew University. From 1975 to 1977 he was a lecturer in the department of mathematics of Ben-Gurion University and in 1976–78 he was head of the computer science program there. In 1978 he returned to the Hebrew University, where he became professor in 1982. In 1987–89 he was chairman of the Institute of Mathematics and Computer Science and in 1988–89 he was member of the executive committee of the board of governors of the university. In 1992 Magidor was named dean of the faculty of sciences, a position he held until 1996. From 1997 he was the president of the Hebrew University. Magidor was a member of professional and academic associations in the field of mathematics. He served as editor of several academic journals and book series and published some 50 articles.

[Shaked Gilboa (2nd ed.)]

MAGIDOV, JACOB (1869–1943), Yiddish writer and editor. Born in Odessa, he received both a traditional and a secular education. Immigrating to the United States in 1886, he worked in a shirt factory and studied law at night, passing the bar examination in 1904 and for a time practicing law. Active in the Jewish labor movement from his arrival, he played an important role in 1888 in the founding of the United Hebrew Trades, an important institution devoted to organizing Jewish workers into unions. He was also active in the Socialist Labor Party. Magidov began his career as a writer and editor in the Jewish socialist press in 1894. He wrote for *Di Arbeter Tsaytung* on American politics and became city editor of the *Dos Abend Blat* at the end of the 1890s. After writing for the *Forverts* for a short time he joined *Der Morgn-Zhurnal* in 1901 and remained associated with it for the rest of his life. His book *Der Shpigl fun der Ist Side* ("The Mirror of the East Side," 1923) contains valuable insights into Jewish personalities of his generation. Magidov was one of the many immigrant intellectuals who felt it their duty to bridge the gap between the Yiddish-speaking masses and their new environment. Especially as the city editor of *Der Morgn-Zhurnal*, he served them as an interpreter of events in the new homeland.

BIBLIOGRAPHY: LNYL, 5 (1963), 389ff.

[Henry J. Tobias]

MAGINO, MEIR (late 16th century), Venetian inventor. In 1587 Pope Sixtus V invited him to introduce into the Papal States his process of extracting silk thread from the cocoon twice a year. Concerning this new process, Magino published an Italian work entitled *Dialoghi di M. Magino Gabrielli Hebreo venetiano sopra l'utili sue invenzioni circa la seta* (Venice, 1588); this elegantly printed book contains numerous illustrations, among them a portrait of the author, and a Hebrew poem written by him with an Italian translation by S. Tellarino. A second patent secured for Magino the rights to a new process for polishing mirrors and colored cut glass with a special kind of oil. He was also granted the exclusive right to produce special wine bottles, which are still in use in Roman wineshops. One of his children, GABRIEL induced Ferdinand I of Tuscany to issue the famous appeal to Jews to come and settle in Leghorn (1593). He was promised the office of consul general of the Jews in Pisa and Leghorn, but the appointment did not materialize.

BIBLIOGRAPHY: Roth, *Jews in the Renaissance* (1959), 238f.; A. Milano, *Ghetto di Roma* (1964), 81f.

[Attilio Milano]

MAGNES, JUDAH LEON (1877–1948), U.S. rabbi and communal leader. He was chancellor and first president of the Hebrew University of Jerusalem. Magnes was born in San Francisco, California, to parents who emigrated from Poland and Germany in 1863. He attended the Hebrew Union College, where he was ordained as a Reform rabbi in 1900. Magnes spent the years 1900–03 studying in Berlin and Heidelberg. During his years in Germany he traveled widely in Eastern Europe and was profoundly moved by the intensive Jewish life he found. It strengthened his earlier sympathetic feeling toward Zionism and brought him to the commitment to make Zionism and service to his people his mission in life.

On his return from Germany he became rabbi of Temple Israel in Brooklyn (1904–05) and afterward the assistant rabbi of Temple Emanu-El in New York (1906–10). At the same time he served as the secretary of the American Zionist Federation (1905–08) and later became the president of the Kehillah of New York *City from its founding in 1908 until its demise in 1922; he left for Palestine in the same year. Founded to advance and coordinate Jewish life in New York City, the Kehillah dealt vigorously with such internal problems as religious life and Jewish education; in the latter area its Bureau of Jewish Education, directed by Samson *Benderly, pioneered in the centralization and modernization of Jewish education in the U.S. The Kehillah was active and effective in labor arbitration and helped to repress crime in the immigrant Jewish areas in cooperation with the city's police department. It provided a nexus for cooperation between "uptown" and "downtown" Jews and a forum for Jewish public opinion. Magnes was the Kehillah's moving spirit and most competent leader, spokesman, peacemaker, fund raiser, and philosopher, and thus a leading figure in the metropolis. In 1905 he participated in the Zionist Congress at Basle as a member of the U.S. delegation. It was there that he came face to face with the leaders of Russian Jewry and through them he reached a greater understanding of East European Jewry. Back in New York (after his first visit in Palestine) he headed the greatest Jewish demonstration against the Kishinev pogroms and established the Self-Defense Association which collected funds for the purchase of arms to be smuggled to the Jewish *self-defense bodies in Russia. In 1904 he joined Solomon *Schechter's inner circle and moved toward religious traditionalism. In Zionism he became a disciple and follower of Aḥad *Ha-Am, whom Magnes called "The Harmonious Jew." After the Kishinev pogroms he helped Cyrus *Sulzberger and Louis *Marshall in establishing the American Jewish *Committee. In 1908 he married Beatrice Lowenstein, the sister-in-law of Louis Marshall, and this brought him closer to the leading Jewish circles. At the same time he strengthened his ties with the East European Jews.

Magnes' shift toward religious traditionalism brought him to break with Temple Emanu-El. His unfulfilled demands for religious changes led him to resign in 1910. From 1911 to 1912 he was rabbi of B'nai Jeshurun, a leading Conservative congregation, after which he left congregational work altogether to devote himself to Jewish public service. However, Magnes' opposition to U.S. entry into World War I in 1917 out of pacifist convictions, and his activity in the peace movement during the war, undermined his leadership of a Jewish community firmly committed to the war and concerned over possible imputations of disloyalty. His brilliant U.S. Jewish communal career actually ended in 1917. In 1922 Magnes emigrated with his family to Palestine, where he continued his activities in establishing the Hebrew *University of which he was the chancellor (1925–35) and first president (1935–48) until his death. He was active in raising funds for the university, in securing the donation of several personal libraries, and in developing several of its major divisions, especially the Institute for Jewish Studies which was inaugurated in 1924, even before the official opening of the Hebrew University in 1925. The Hebrew University honored him first by publishing *Sefer Magnes* in 1938 and later by naming one of the Chairs of Bible and the press of the University after him, as well as by granting him and Chaim Weizmann the first honorary degrees of the university. With the beginning of World War II, in spite of his pacifistic outlook on life, he called for war against Nazi Germany, serving as chairman of the Supply Board Scientific Advisory Committee of the War. He also helped his life-long friend Henrietta *Szold in her Youth Aliyah work and became the chairman of an Emergency Council of Hadassah in Palestine, as well as the chairman of the Middle East Advisory Council of the *American Jewish Joint Distribution Committee which he had helped found in World War I. During World War II he helped Jews who escaped to Turkey from Nazi-occupied countries, became responsible for the direction of relief work amongst the Jews throughout the Orient. Out of his pacifist convictions and the belief that the Jews are not like all nations, he sought an accord with the Palestinian Arabs and entered the political arena with the conviction that Jewish-Arab accord is of the greatest importance not only for the peaceful building of the country but also for the Jewish spirit. He started his political agitation immediately after the 1929 disturbances (see Israel, State of: Historical *Survey), stating, "One of the greatest cultural duties of the Jewish people is the attempt to enter the promised land, not by means of conquest as Joshua, but through peaceful and cultural means, through hard work, sacrifices, love and with a decision not to do anything which cannot be justified before the world conscience" (Opening Speech of the Hebrew University Academic Year 1929/30). Magnes renewed his activities after the riots in 1936 and opposed the Royal Commission's suggestion for the partitioning of Palestine, always believing in the policy of establishing Palestine as a binational state and feeling that it was his personal mission to bring the Arabs and Jews together (see Berit *Shalom; Palestine Partition and Partition *Plans; *Palestine, Inquiry Commissions on). With this belief he carried on his political activities until his death in New York in 1948 while on a visit there. He was later reinterred in Jerusalem. A Judah L. Magnes Memorial Museum was set up in Oakland, California, in 1961, and later moved to Berkeley. Magnes' writings and speeches were collected in *War-Time Addresses 1917–1921* (1923), *Addresses by the Chancellor of the Hebrew University* (1936), and in *The Perplexity of the Times* (1946).

BIBLIOGRAPHY: N. Bentwich, *For Zion's Sake – A Biography of Judah L. Magnes* (1954); A. Goren, *New York Jews and the Quest for Community: The Kehillah Experiment 1908–1922* (1970); S.L. Hattis, *The Bi-National Idea in Palestine During Mandatory Times* (1970), 64–71, 169–72, 258–71 and index; L. Roth, in: *Jewish Education*, 20 (1949); S.H. Bergman, *Faith and Reason* (1961); Z. Szajkowski, in: *Conservative Judaism*, 22 no. 3 (1968); H. Parzen, in: JSOS, 29 (1967), 203–33; 32 (1970), 187–213.

[Lloyd P. Gartner / Daniel Efron]

MAGNES MUSEUM, JUDAH L. Located in Berkeley, in a century-old mansion about a mile from the University of California, the Magnes Museum contains the third largest collection of Judaica in the United States. The Museum was founded in 1962 in Oakland by the New York-born Jewish educator Seymour Fromer, with editor and writer Rebecca Camhi Fromer as co-founder, and moved to its current location four years later. It is named in honor of Judah L. Magnes, who was born in San Francisco in 1877 and raised in Oakland, the first native Californian to receive rabbinical ordination. Magnes was the founder and first president of the Hebrew University of Jerusalem and his friend and colleague Martin Buber became honorary chair of the museum soon after its inception.

During Seymour Fromer's 36-year tenure as museum director, and following his retirement in 1998, the museum has collected, preserved, and made available artistic, historical, and literary material reflecting Jewish life and culture throughout history. In 1968, the Siegfried Strauss Collection was acquired as the core of the museum's ceremonial art holdings, which have expanded to include one of the world's largest collections of Hanukah menorahs and Torah binders, costumes, and other textiles. The museum also rescued artifacts from endangered Jewish communities such as Czechoslovakia, Morocco, Egypt, and India.

Over the decades the museum has acquired thousands of prints, drawings, portfolios, and posters of Jewish interest including works by Hermann Struck, Ben Shahn, and Marc Chagall. It holds the works of painters such as Max Liebermann, Daniel Moritz Oppenheim, Toby Rosenthal, Lazar Krestin, Lesser Ury, Muriel Minkowski, Isadore Kaufman, and Raphael Soyer; and sculptors such as Elbert Weinberg and Harold Parris. In 1974, the museum won accreditation by the American Association of Museums, the first U.S. Jewish museum to receive such recognition, and three years later was a founding member of the Council of American Jewish Museums.

The museum is also a repository for historical documents of Jews in the American West. Its Western Jewish History Center, initiated in 1967 and directed for more than three decades by San Francisco State University Professor Moses Rischin, was the first regional Jewish history center in the U.S. It contains a comprehensive archival research library, including letters and diaries, organization reports and minutes, portraits and photographs, marriage and death certificates, and Anglo-Jewish newspapers published since 1857. In addition, the Western Jewish History Center has published more than a dozen books on Northern California Jewry: bibliographies, narrative histories, and personal memoirs. Through its Commission for the Preservation of Pioneer Jewish Cemeteries and Landmarks, the Museum has restored, and continues to maintain, seven Jewish Gold Rush cemeteries in the California Mother Lode in the foothills of the Sierra Mountains.

The Museum sponsored the Jewish-American Hall of Fame, which has minted medals annually in recognition of Jews who have made significant contributions to American life. Annual poetry, video, and photography competitions were established to showcase the work of contemporary artists and filmmakers. The Museum's Harry and Dorothy Blumenthal Rare Book and Manuscript Library has a significant collection of illuminated *ketukbot*, manuscripts, and printed materials relating to Jewish customs and ceremonies, and to Jews in India and the Karaites.

From its inception, the Magnes has made Holocaust studies one of its leading priorities and was one of the first museums to have a gallery devoted to the artifacts and art of the Shoah. In the mid-1960s, under the guidance of leading Oakland Rabbi Harold Schulweis, it established the Institute for the Righteous Acts, a center documenting and analyzing the altruistic behavior of rescuers of Jews during the Nazi Era. The museum has published numerous survivor memoirs and has emphasized the post-liberation period, with a publication and exhibit on the detention camp in Cypress, and several works on the Displaced Persons camps.

Drawing on its own collections and loans from the U.S., Europe, and Israel, the Magnes has maintained a regular schedule of art, history, and ethnographic exhibits on Jewish life and culture. The Jacques and Esther Reutlinger Gallery was built in 1981 to accommodate changing exhibits and associated educational programs.

Especially in the 1970s and 1980s, the museum was one of the key catalysts of a Jewish cultural renaissance in the Bay Area as Fromer nurtured many young Jewish scholars and artists. He provided studio and exhibition space for the revival of illuminated Ketubot, led by David Moss; he assisted Deborah Kaufman in founding and developing the first Jewish Film Festival; he commissioned the California Jewish historian Ava Kahn to create educational materials for schools; he provided the impetus to Fred Rosenbaum who founded the adult school Lehrhaus Judaica and wrote several books on local Jewish history published by the museum.

In 2002, a younger Jewish museum in San Francisco emphasizing contemporary art merged with the Magnes. But disagreements about the direction of the merged institution resulted in a de-coupling in about a year. The Magnes looks forward to erecting a new center in the growing arts district of downtown Berkeley.

BIBLIOGRAPHY: R. Rafael, *Western Jewish History Center: A Guide to Archival Collections* (1987); F. Helzel, *The Print and Drawing Collection of the Judah L. Magnes Museum* (1984); S. Morris, *A Traveler's Guide to Pioneer Jewish Cemeteries of the California Gold Rush* (1996); R. Eis, *Twenty-five Years Judah L Magnes Museum* (1977); R. Eis, *Hanukkah Lamps of the Judah L. Magnes Museum* (1977); F. Helzel and E. Battat, *Witness to History: The Jewish Poster, 1770–1985* (1987).

[Fred S. Rosenbaum (2nd ed.)]

MAGNIN, EDGAR FOGEL (1890–1984), U.S. Reform rabbi and communal leader. Magnin was born in San Francisco to a well-known mercantile family. He was ordained at Hebrew Union College (1914). After a year as rabbi in Stockton, California (1914), Magnin led Congregation B'nai B'rith, called from 1929 onward the Wilshire Boulevard Temple in Los Angeles, which grew under his leadership from 400 families to 2,000 to become one of the largest and most influential congregations in the country. During his tenure, the landmark building on Wilshire Boulevard that still serves as the home of his congregation was built and opened. His service to the congregation coincided with the dramatic expansion of Los Angeles Jewry in size and in influence. Outspoken, colorful, forceful, Rabbi Magnin was for many decades the unofficial voice and representative of the Los Angeles Jewish community in a variety of religious, governmental, social, educational, and cultural organizations and institutions and the leading voice of West Coast Reform Judaism. He was an early pioneer in Christian Jewish dialogue. During World War II he represented the Jewish Welfare Board and traveled to combat zones under the auspices of the National Conference of Christians and Jews. Within the Jewish community he was a leader in the Los Angeles Jewish Community Council, Cedars-Sinai Hospital, University Religious Conference, Los Angeles Hillel Council, Hebrew Union College-Jewish Institute of Religion, and B'nai B'rith, among many others. Rabbi Magnin was a lecturer in history at the University of Southern California (1934–55) and at the California School of Hebrew Union College. The graduate school at HUC in Los Angeles is named the Edgar F. Magnin School of Graduate Studies. Deeply involved in political life, he delivered a prayer at the first inauguration of Richard M. Nixon in 1969. Author of *How to Lead a Richer and Fuller Life* (1951), he was columnist for the *Los Angeles Herald Examiner* and the Anglo-Jewish weekly *Heritage*. The street in front of the temple is name Edgar F. Magnin Square.

[Max Vorspan]

MAGNIN, MARY ANN COHEN (1849–1943), founder of I. Magnin and Company, a fashionable department store catering to an exclusive clientele in the western United States. An extraordinary businesswoman known for her fashion sense and insistence on quality, Magnin, the daughter of a rabbi, was born in Scheveningen, Holland, and emigrated to London with her family. In 1865 she married Isaac Magnin, a Dutch-born gilder and carver in the Great Synagogue of London. The couple had eight children, seven of whom were born in London. In the mid-1870s, in the wake of the California gold rush, the family journeyed around Cape Horn to San Francisco, where Isaac hoped to locate gilding work. Magnin, who had learned fine sewing and lace-trimming from her mother, began making baby clothes, lingerie, and bridal trousseaux to supplement the family's income. She opened a small store in Oakland, before moving her business to San Francisco, soon hiring seamstresses to keep up with orders. Renamed I. Magnin in 1877, the store relocated to the city's prime commercial district. Despite its name, Isaac Magnin, who died in 1907, was not involved in its management. As Magnin brought her sons into the business, merchandise selection expanded with fine women's wear from New York and Europe. Beyond the main San Francisco store, others were built across the western United States, including Los Angeles, Seattle, Oakland, Santa Barbara, and other fashionable locales. All stores were designed by respected architects and the buildings became instant landmarks. When her store was destroyed by fire following the 1906 earthquake, Magnin retrieved her merchandise from the spared Customs House and continued to sell garments from her undamaged home, hiring carriages to bring customers to her makeshift store. In this way, she clothed the new needy and made a substantial profit. Dubbed "Queen Victoria" by her family because of her regal demeanor, Magnin lived into her mid-nineties, daily inspecting the main San Francisco store until her death.

BIBLIOGRAPHY: Magnin Family collection, Western Jewish History Center of the Judah Magnes Museum, Berkeley, California; C. Magnin and C. Robins. *Call Me Cyril* (1981); H. and F. Rochlin, "Jews on the Western Frontier: An Overview," pt. 2, in: *Arizona Highways* (Sept. 1985).

[Ava F. Kahn (2nd ed.)]

MAGNUS, English family. SIR PHILIP MAGNUS (1842–1933) was an educator and politican. Born in London, he was a minister of the West London Synagogue of British Jews (Reform) from 1866 to 1880, and lectured in applied mathematics at University College, London. In 1880 Magnus was appointed organizing secretary and director of the newly established City and Guilds of London Institute. He served on the Royal Commission whose report led to the Technical Education Act of 1884. Magnus was responsible for inclusion of a faculty of engineering at the reconstructed London University in 1889. From 1906 to 1922, he was the university's member of parliament, the first Jew to be elected for a university seat. He was knighted in 1886 and created a baronet in 1917. Magnus played a leading part in Anglo-Jewish affairs, as chairman of the council of the West London Synagogue and as a vice president of the *Board of Deputies of British Jews and the *Anglo-Jewish Association. He was violently opposed to Zionism and was one of the founders of the anti-Zionist League of British Jews. Sir Philip's wife KATIE MAGNUS (1844–1924) was a writer. The daughter of the Portsmouth goldsmith and communal figure Emanuel Emanuel, she published traditional and historical tales for young readers and her often reprinted *Outlines of Jewish History* (1886) was an especially successful evocation of the past. Her *Jewish Portraits* (1888) included studies of *Judah Halevi, *Heine, and Moses *Mendelssohn. Sir Philip and Lady Magnus' son, LAURIE MAGNUS (1872–1933), began his writing career mainly with studies of English poetry. In 1902 he wrote *Aspects of the Jewish Question*, which revealed him to be an anti-Zionist like his father. Four years later, in *Religio Laici Judaici* ("The Faith of a Jewish Layman"), he again propounded the view that Judaism was a religion and not a nationality. For 14 years, from its inception in 1917 to its suspension, he edited the anti-Zionist *Jewish Guardian*. He was active in Jewish communal life as a warden of the West London Reform Synagogue, a member of the council of Jews' College, London, and president of the Union of Jewish Literary Societies. His most important books were *Dictionary of European Literature* (1926) and *The Jews in the Christian Era and their Contribution to its Civilization* (1929). He was also a director of Routledge, the publishers. He married Dora (c. 1882–1972), the daughter of Sir Isidore *Spielmann. As Laurie Magnus shortly predeceased his father, the baronetcy devolved directly upon his son SIR PHILIP MONTEFIORE MAGNUS (1906–1988). Educated at Westminster school and Oxford, he was originally a civil servant before becoming a full-time writer. He was the author of a number of successful and highly regarded biographies: *Edmund Burke* (1939), *Sir Walter Raleigh* (1952), *Gladstone* (1954), *Kitchener* (1958), and *King Edward VII* (1964). He severed his connections with Judaism, and in 1951 formally added his wife's family name to his own, becoming Sir Philip Magnus-Allcroft. His best-selling biography of Gladstone is credited with restoring the reputation of the Victorians after its decline following World War I.

BIBLIOGRAPHY: F. Foden, *Philip Magnus, Victorian Educational Pioneer* (1970). **ADD. BIBLIOGRAPHY:** ODNB online; R. Sebag-Montefiore, "A Quest for a Grandfather: Sir Philip Magnus, 1st Bt., Victorian Educationalist," in: JHSET, 34 (1994–96), 141–59.

[Vivian David Lipman / William D. Rubinstein (2nd ed.)]

MAGNUS, EDUARD (1799–1872), German painter. Born in Berlin, Magnus studied medicine, philosophy, and architecture and traveled in France, Italy, Spain, and England before turning to painting. Magnus was a member of the generation of painters who effected the changes of art in Berlin in the 1830s and 1840. Magnus' work reflects the transition in German art of the period from Biedermeier to Realism. Beginning as a Nazarene (see Philipp *Veit), he developed a romantic neoclassicism influenced by the French painter Ingres, and finally a realistic style. He had a good reputation as a portrait painter. His paintings differ from other portraits in the posture of his figures and in their natural facial expression, as seen in the 1845 portrait of Felix Mendelssohn Bartholdy (private collection). Among his other subjects were the singer Jenny Lind, the sculptor Thorwaldsen, and members of the Prussian royal family. Magnus also left some paintings recording his travels. He perceived the talent of the young artist Adolf Menzel and encouraged him by buying his paintings. He was baptized as a child.

BIBLIOGRAPHY: Wininger, Biog; M. Bryan, *Bryan's Dictionary of Painters and Engravers* (1904); Roth, Art, 546; L. Gläser, *Eduard Magnus. Ein Beitrag zur Berliner Bildnismalerei des 19. Jahrhunderts* (1961).

[Jihan Radjai-Ordoubadi (2nd ed.)]

MAGNUS, HEINRICH GUSTAV (1802–1870), German chemist and physicist. Magnus, who was born in Berlin into a wealthy family, left Judaism. He began teaching at the University of Berlin in 1831. From 1845 to 1869 he was professor of physics and technology at Berlin, and in 1861 became rector of the university. His numerous discoveries include the first platinum-ammonia complex, Magnus' green salt

$(Pt(NH_3)_4)Pt\text{-}Cl_4$) and the "Magnus Effect." The latter referred originally to projectiles which, subjected to rapid rotation, are turned aside from their original direction by forces which act upon them crosswise. It has important aerodynamic applications.

BIBLIOGRAPHY: Huntress, in: *Proceedings of the American Academy of Arts and Science*, 81 (1952), 70f.

[Samuel Aaron Miller]

MAGNUS, MARCUS (also known as **Mordecai ben Manlin Dessau, Raubach,** and **Weisel**; d. 1736), court agent of the Prussian crown prince, later King Frederick William I. In his struggle for power in the *Berlin community, his great rival was Jost *Liebmann and later Liebmann's widow, Esther. In 1709 he became head of the community and in 1720 the spokesman for provincial Jewry before the Prussian authorities. After a protracted quarrel, in which both sides appealed to the king, Magnus persuaded the community to erect one public synagogue instead of the private ones maintained by Liebmann and the Veit and Riess families (1712/14). In 1722 he was appointed salaried permanent chief elder of the Berlin community together with Moses Levi *Gomperz, a position he held until his death.

BIBLIOGRAPHY: L. Geiger, *Geschichte der Juden in Berlin*, 1 (1871), 19, 21; H. Schnee, *Die Hoffinanz und der moderne Staat…*, 1 (1953), 68, 110–1; L. Stern, *Der preussische Staat und die Juden*, 1 (1962), index; 2 (1962); S. Stern, *The Court Jew* (1950), 181, 185.

[Meir Lamed]

MAGNUS, PAUL WILHELM (1844–1914), German botanist. His father, Meyer Magnus, was a member of the Berlin City Council. Under the influence of the botanist Paul *Ascherson, the young Magnus abandoned the thought of a medical career and turned to the study of botany. After obtaining his degree, Magnus was invited by the Ministry of Agriculture to participate in scientific surveys of the North and Baltic Seas. His studies of specimens brought back from these expeditions led to important contributions on the growth patterns of algae as well as to pioneering investigations of the chytrids, an obscure and still poorly understood group of fungi. Magnus joined the faculty of the University of Berlin in 1875 and was promoted to the rank of *Professor Extraordinarius* in 1880. In 1911 the honorary title of *Geheimer Regierungsrat* was conferred upon him. His most important work was concerned with the systematics and life histories of a number of parasitic fungi.

BIBLIOGRAPHY: G. Lindav, in: *Berichte der deutschen botanischen Gesellschaft*, 32 (1914), 32–63.

[Mordecai L. Gabriel]

MAGNUS, RUDOLPH (1873–1927), German physiologist and pharmacologist. Magnus, who was born in Brunswick, became one of the foremost co-workers of the famous physiologist Sir Charles Sherrington in Oxford. He investigated the mechanisms governing the posture and balance of the body and discovered its center of reflexes in the brainstem up to the midbrain. He became lecturer in pharmacology at Heidelberg until his appointment at Utrecht (1908), where he founded the first pharmacological institute in Holland. Magnus studied the pharmacology and physiology of the intestines, and worked on digitalis. In 1924 he collected the works of his institute in *Koerperhaltung; Koerperstellung, Gleichgewicht und Bewegung bei Saeugern*, with A. de Klein (1930); and *Lane Lectures on Experimental Pharmacology and Medicine* (1930). Other works are *Vom Urtier zum Menschen* (1908) and *Wilhelm Boelsche* (1909).

BIBLIOGRAPHY: S.R. Kagan, *Jewish Medicine* (1952), 215–6; I. Fischer, *Biographisches Lexicon*, s.v.

[Nathan Koren]

MAGNUS, SOLOMON WOLFF (1910–1992), Zambian lawyer and politician. Born in Russia, Magnus was taken to England as a child. He was educated at University College, London, and at Gray's Inn. Magnus practiced at the bar, and later served in British intelligence during World War II. He went to Zambia (Northern Rhodesia) in 1959 and in 1962 was elected to the Legislative Assembly. In 1968 he was made a High Court judge, serving until 1971. From the 1970s he again lived in England and was commissioner of the Foreign Compensation Commission from 1977 to 1983. He was active in Jewish affairs both in England and in Zambia, where he headed the Jewish community. Magnus was a prolific legal writer, especially on housing and tenant law, and was the author or co-author of many standard legal textbooks.

MAGYAR ZSIDÓ SZEMLE ("Hungarian Jewish Review"), Hungarian Jewish monthly journal which was established in 1884 and appeared until 1948 in a total of 65 volumes. During the first decade each volume of *Magyar Zsidó Szemle* contained more than 600 pages, but the number was subsequently reduced; in the period of crisis following the two world wars only individual issues were published annually. The aims of the journal were: to serve as a platform for Hungarian Jewry; to deal in Hungarian with Jewish scholarly subjects; to publish sources of the history of Hungarian Jewry; to discuss problems of religious education; and to review works on Judaica and Jewish history published outside Hungary. The editorial board was headed by professors and directors of the Budapest rabbinical seminary: W. *Bacher (1884–90), L. *Blau (1891–1930), and D.S. *Loewinger (1931–48). The first associate editors did not belong to the seminary (J. Bánóczi, 1884–90; F. Mezey, 1891–95), but the subsequent ones were professors and lecturers at that institute: *M.Guttmann, H. Guttman, S. *Hevesi, F. Hevesi, D. Friedmann, J. Hahn, A. *Scheiber, and M. Weiss.

Attempts were made to transfer some of the many and varied subjects covered by the journal to periodicals devoted to special topics: *Yavneh*, which dealt with problems of religious education (1928–30, vols. 1–3), and *Moriah*, in which sermons were published (1930, vol. 1). Of the appendices to the journal, the most important is the Hebrew supplement

Ha-Ẓofeh me-Ereẓ Hagar which appeared from 1911 onward. Among its contributors were distinguished Judaic scholars in the world. Until the outbreak of World War I its first four volumes appeared as a supplement to *Magyar Zsidó Szemle*. Subsequently from 1921 to 1930 it was published separately as a quarterly, under the title of *Ha-Ẓofeh le-Ḥokhmat Yisrael*.

During this decade the circle of its scholarly contributors widened still further and the journal became a focal point of scholarship of prime importance in the Jewish world. After *Ha-Ẓofeh* ceased publication, its role was continued by *Ha-Soker*, which appeared between 1933 and 1940 (i–vi) under the editorship of D.S. Loewenger, with J.M. Guttman, F. Hevesi, and D. Friedmann as associate editors. Between the two world wars a change also took place in the contents of *Magyar Zsidó Szemle*, in which there began to appear articles not only in Hungarian but also in other European languages, as well as in Hebrew. The authors of these articles were Hungarian Jewish scholars, as well as Jewish and non-Jewish scholars from Hungary and other countries.

BIBLIOGRAPHY: S. Eden, in: S. Federbush (ed.), *Ḥokhmat Yisrael be-Ma'arav Eiropah*, 1 (1958), 554–9; S. Weingarten, *ibid.*, 2 (1963), 380–402.

[David Samuel Loewinger]

MAḤAL, abbreviation of *Mitnaddevei Ḥuẓ la-Areẓ* (Foreign Volunteers), the term used for volunteers from abroad, mainly Jews, who enlisted in the Israel Defense Forces (IDF) and participated in the *War of Independence, 1948/49. In practice the Maḥal section of the IDF Manpower Branch handled volunteers who were citizens or residents of countries outside Eastern and Central Europe. No reliable statistics are available, but it was officially estimated that Maḥal comprised about 5,000 volunteers. Of these, about 1,500 were from U.S.A. and Canada, about 500 from South Africa, and about 1,000 from Great Britain. The small Jewish community of Finland contributed the largest proportion of volunteers, a total of only 30, but 2% of its strength.

The first groups of volunteers were organized after the UN General Assembly recommended the partition of Palestine in November 1947. In some instances, the initiative was spontaneous and local. This was the case in Canada, where two Jewish ex-servicemen issued a call for volunteers for Israel. The same was true in Scandinavia. In South Africa, the movement was organized after the arrival of two representatives of the *Jewish Agency who contacted the South African Jewish servicemen's association. By the beginning of 1948, volunteer organizations were at work in most Jewish communities in the Western world. In many countries the activities were under cover: the official destination of the volunteers was France. A small number of volunteers, mainly with military skills urgently needed by the *Haganah, were smuggled into the country before the State of Israel was proclaimed. The majority of the volunteers were channeled through training camps in France and Italy, organized by the Haganah European Command (with headquarters in Paris) and staffed by instructors from Palestine. Most were World War II veterans, and some had been officers. Transport facilities across the Mediterranean were difficult to arrange.

On arrival, the Maḥal volunteers were absorbed in IDF units according to the need for reinforcements, not fighting in separate formations. They thus fought on all fronts. Their contribution was not in numbers but in quality and experience, most necessary in a new army whose fighting tradition was that of an underground movement. Maḥal's major contribution was to the air force, which was organized, commanded, and to a large degree, staffed by overseas volunteers and by foreign air force veterans on special contract. Maḥal volunteers also played an important part in staffing the army medical corps. Individual volunteers also made important contributions to the engineers' corps, the signal corps, the armored units, and the artillery. Approximately 150 Maḥal volunteers were killed in action, the majority from U.S.A. and Canada. About 300 remained in Israel or returned later to settle there, but the majority came, fought, and returned to their countries of origin.

[Herbert Pundik]

MAHALALEL BEN SHABBETAI HALLELYAH (d. after 1675), rabbi, kabbalist and Hebrew poet. Born at the beginning of the 17th century in Civitanova, Mahalalel suffered many hardships in his youth in Italy as a result of which he seems to have been compelled to wander to various places. Before 1660, he was appointed rabbi of Ancona. He was known primarily for his collection of poems and *piyyutim, Hallelyah*, recited in synagogues on Sabbaths and festivals. This collection also included prayers which were kabbalistic in spirit. Mahalalel and his community were ardent believers in *Shabbetai Ẓevi even after his apostasy in 1666. Two completely different versions of his hymn to Shabbetai Ẓevi and his prophet, *Nathan of Gaza, appear in *Hallelyah*, one version, apparently, composed before and the other after the apostasy. Some of the poems from this collection were published by S. Bernstein (see bibliography). From those of Mahalalel's letters which were also included in this collection and published in part by Bernstein, it seems that he had close ties with the great contemporary scholars in Italy. The following works by him remain in manuscript: *Kodesh Hillulim*, a commentary on the Pentateuch, and *Hallel Gamur*. Sixty-eight halakhic rulings, his responsa, are included in manuscripts (Mantua, Municipal Library, Ms. 88; Ferrara, Talmud Torah, Ms. 20/1).

BIBLIOGRAPHY: S. Bernstein, in: *Mizraḥ u-Ma'arav*, 3 (1929), 200–2; idem, in: HUCA, 7 (1930), 497–536; idem: *Mi-Shirei Yisrael be-Italyah* (1939), 66–73, 154–6; M. Wilensky, in: *Sinai*, 25 (1949), 66; G. Scholem, *Shabbetai Ẓevi*, 2 (1957), 404f.; idem, in: *Sefer ha-Yovel Z. Wolfson* (1965), 225–41.

[Abraham David]

MAHALLA AL-KUBRA, town in Lower Egypt, halfway between *Alexandria and *Damietta. There was a flourishing Jewish community in Mahalla al-Kubra under the *Fatimids. Yosef ha-Yerushalmi, who stayed in Mahalla al-Kubra for a short time, sent a letter to this community at the end of the 11th century. The community in Mahalla al-Kubra is noted in the Ebiatar Gaon scroll from the second half of the 11th century. *Benjamin of Tudela, the 12th-century traveler, relates that he found 500 Jews living there (E.N. Adler (ed.), *Jewish Travellers* (1930), 74). According to a list of contributions to ransom Jewish prisoners, the sum donated by the Mahalla community in the middle of the 12th century was the largest of the Delta communities (Mann, Egypt, 2 (1922), 290). Many documents written in Mahalla during the 12th and early 13th centuries have been found in the Cairo **Genizah*. The Jews of Mahalla were engaged in handicrafts and commerce, such as the silk trade. According to a marriage *takkanah*, in 1187, R. Peraḥyah b. Joseph was *dayyan* in Mahalla. The community developed after the great fire in Fustat in 1168. Rabbi Ḥayim ben Hananel ben Abraham al-Amshafti settled there after the fire. He was a famous physician and served also in the Fatimid court. Joseph *Sambari, the 17th-century Egyptian chronicler, mentions the *Sefer Torah* in the synagogue of Mahalla, which was read only on the New Moon and on which people took the oath (Neubauer, Chronicles, 1 (1887), 119). A document from the year 1726 reports that the local Jews were ruled by the Jewish leaders of the Cairo community. A document from 1772 notes the *gabbai* of the synagogue was the leader of the community. The *shoḥet* Isaac ben Solomon Cohen Yadi'a Karmon was also a *melammed*, *sofer*, and cantor. In 1729 the leader of the community was the Spanish Rabbi Abraham Zadik. In this century the Spanish congregation was wealthier than the Must'arab congregation. Abraham Zadik was a merchant. He obtained a ruling from the Muslim court of law allowing for the restoration of the synagogue in Mahalla. In the 19th century the community sent part of its income to the community of Cairo. In 1896 the community paid money to the representative of the Vizier Ahmad, according to local tradition to pay for the use of their synagogue. According to popular tradition, the tomb of R. Ḥayyim ibn al-Amshatī is situated under the synagogue and pilgrimages (Arabic *ziyāra*) were held there every year on the first day of Iyyar. According to Jacob *Saphir (*Even Sappir*, 1 (1866), 21b), in the middle of the 19th century there were 20 Jewish families in the town. As was the case with other Egyptian Jewish communities, Mahalla's Jewish population increased considerably at the end of the 19th century, and by 1897 there were 200 Jews there. When the Zionist movement spread in the beginning of the 20th century, the Jews of Mahalla established a Zionist association. In 1901 the rabbis of Cairo declared their new *kiddushin* regulation in Mahalla al-Kubra. The Jewish population fell to 91 by 1927, and further declined to ten families by 1937. In 1932 Israel Ben-Ze'ev visited the place and found there an old cemetery from the time of Maimonides. For many generations this cemetery was the cemetery of the Delta Jews. In the Jewish ghetto he found a few old buildings and a synagogue. In the beginning of the 20th century the ghetto was closed at night.

BIBLIOGRAPHY: J. Blau (ed.), *Teshuvot ha-Rambam*, 1 (1957), 177–8, no. 105; 2 (1960), 624–5 no. 348; Mann, Egypt, index; Worman, in: JQR, 18 (1905/06), 10; Assaf, in: *Sefer Klausner* (1937), 232–4; idem, in: *Tarbiz*, (1937/38), 34; idem, in: *Melilah*, 3–4 (1950), 224–9; Ashtor, in: JJS, 18 (1967) pp. 38ff.; Ashtor, Toledot, 1 (1944), 251; 2 (1951), index; 3 (1970), index; Goitein, in: *Tarbiz*, 20 (1948/49), 201–2; 32 (1962/63) 192–4. **ADD. BIBLIOGRAPHY:** I. Ben-Ze'ev, in: *Sefunot*, 9 (1965), 266–70; J.M. Landau, *Jews in Nineteenth-Century Egypt* (1969), 42–45, 179; N. Golb, in: *Journal of Near Eastern Studies*, 33 (1974), 132; S.D. Goitein, *Ha-Yishuv be-Ereẓ Yisrael be-Reshit ha-Islam ...* (1980), 51, 84, 316–18, 340, 342; A. David, in: J.M. Landau (ed.), *Toledot ha-Yehudim be-Miẓrayim ba-Tekufah ha-Otmanit* (1988), 19–21; L. Bornstein-Makovetsky, in: J M. Landau (ed.), *ibid.*, 143.

[Eliyahu Ashtor / Leah Bornstein-Makovetsky (2nd ed.)]

MAHANAIM (Heb. מַחֲנַיִם), locality east of the Jordan which was named by Jacob before he crossed the Jabbok on his way to *Penuel; according to the etiological version in Genesis 32:3, he named it "God's camp" after he saw the angels of God there. It was on the border between the territories of the half-tribe of Manasseh and of the tribe of Gad (Josh. 13:26, 30); it also appears as a levitical city in Gad (Josh. 21:38; I Chron. 6:65). After the disastrous battle of Mt. Gilboa, Abner son of Ner, captain of Saul's army, took Ish-Bosheth, Saul's son, to Mahanaim and established it as the capital of the dynasty of Saul (II Sam. 2:8); from Mahanaim he started out on his ill-fated expedition to Gibeon and to it he later returned (2:12, 29). It was also chosen by David as his capital during Absalom's rebellion; here he received supplies from Barzillai and other Gileadites (17:24, 27), set out for battle with the rebels, and received the news of Absalom's death. It appears for the last time in the Bible as the capital of Solomon's seventh district with Ahinadab the son of Iddo as its governor (I Kings 4:14). In Shishak's list of conquered towns, it occurs as one of the cities captured during his campaign in the fifth year of Rehoboam. All sources point to its location in the vicinity of the Jabbok in central Gilead, but its exact identification is disputed. The earliest identification of the place with Khirbat al-Makhna 2.5 mi. (4 km.) north of Aijalon, following Estori ha-Parḥi (13th century), has been discarded by modern scholars. Dalman was the first to point to the twin site of Tulūl al-Dhahab on the Jabbok; Glueck, however, would look there for Penuel. Aharoni suggests that the western mound of Tulūl al-Dhahab is Mahanaim and that the eastern mound is Penuel. De Vaux and Noth suggest Tell al-Ḥajaj, uphill and to the south of the Jabbok.

BIBLIOGRAPHY: Glueck, in: AASOR, 18/19 (1939), 232–5; EM, s.v. (incl. bibl.); Aharoni, Land, index.

[Michael Avi-Yonah]

MAḤANAYIM (Heb. מַחֲנַיִם; "Two Camps," allusion to Gen. 32:3 and other verses, although biblical *Mahanaim was in Transjordan), kibbutz in northern Israel in the Ḥuleh Valley, affiliated with Ha-Kibbutz ha-Me'uḥad. First founded as a moshavah for Orthodox Jews in 1898, but soon abandoned. In 1902, the *Jewish Colonization Association (ICA) settled a small group there whose economy was to be based on tobacco cultivation. The attempt failed, as did another plan to settle Jews from the Caucasus on the site to raise beef cattle. A further attempt was made in 1918, when a laborers' group set out to establish a moshav there. Finally, in 1939, the present kibbutz was established, when the Jewish institutions stepped up settlement on the land as a reply to the British *White Paper (1939). In 1970 Maḥanayim's economy was based on intensive farming. At the outset of the 21st century its economy included a few farming branches and industry based on Diuk Technology, a leading manufacturer of building profiles and metal components for solar heaters. In addition, Mahanayim had guest rooms and an interest in a nearby tourist site. Also nearby was the Maḥanayim airfield, servicing the northeastern part of the country. In the mid-1990s, the kibbutz population was approximately 440, declining to 361 in 2002.

[Efraim Orni / Shaked Gilboa (2nd ed.)]

MAHER SHALAL HASH BAZ (Heb. מַהֵר שָׁלָל חָשׁ בַּז), traditional vocalization of the name which, according to Isaiah 8:3–4, *Isaiah was commanded by the Lord to give to the son who was born to him during the Aramean Ephraimite war against Judah (734/3–732 B.C.E.), with the explanation that "before the lad is able to call 'father!' and 'mother!' the wealth of Damascus and the spoils of Samaria shall be carried off before the king of Assyria." Since the four words express twice the idea of speed and booty, it is easy to understand how the name can signify that, but the traditional vocalization leaves the parallelism imperfect; for according to it the words mean literally "Hurry, spoil! Booty has rushed." It therefore seems probable that either the vocalization of the third word is to be corrected to *ḥush*, in which case the name will mean, literally, "Hurry, spoil! Rush, booty!" or the vocalization of the first word is to be corrected to *mihar*, yielding the literal sense, "Spoil has hurried, booty has rushed." Such prophetic namings as portents of the future notoriously not only portend the future but help to bring it about, exactly like other prophetic acts that symbolize what they predict (see *Prophecy). Accordingly, the writing involving the four words in 8:1–2 is also intended at once to portend and to effectuate the early plundering of Damascus and Samaria by the Assyrians; on some problems of detail, see Isaiah A, Panel 3, Field A.

[Harold Louis Ginsberg]

MAHLER, ARTHUR (1871–1916), classical archaeologist and Zionist parliamentarian. Born in Prague, from 1902 Mahler was a professor of classical archaeology at the German University in Prague. He joined the Zionist Movement at the beginning of the 20th century, and in the elections of 1907 he was elected, together with A. Stand and H. Gabel, to the Austrian parliament on a pro-Zionist ticket. Together they established the Jewish Club headed by B. Straucher, which was the first of its kind in parliamentary history. Because of the Austrian government's intrigues and the influence of Jewish assimilationists, however, the pro-Zionist list lost the 1911 elections. Mahler then left Prague and settled in Vienna.

[Getzel Kressel]

MAHLER, EDUARD (1857–1945), Hungarian Orientalist, mathematician, and astronomer. Mahler was born in Cziffer, Hungary. In 1882 he became assistant to the astronomer Theodor Oppolzer at the Vienna Observatory and, in 1885, assistant at the Institute of Weights and Measures. The same year he published his *Astronomische Untersuchungen ueber die in der Bibel erwaehnte aegyptische Finsterniss* and *Astronomische Untersuchung ueber die in hebraeischen Schriften erwaehnten Finsternisse*. ("Astronomical Researches on the Egyptian Darkness Account in the Bible" and "Astronomical Research on the Accounts of Darkness in the Hebrew Scriptures"). He had already written some important mathematical studies, particularly on the theory of surfaces, but his interest turned more and more to astronomy and chronology of the ancient Orient, as is evident in his *Biblische Chronologie und Zeitrechnung der Hebraeer*, "Biblical Chronology and the Hebrews' Time-Reckoning" (1887) and his translation of and commentary on Maimonides, *Kiddush ha-Ḥodesh* (1889). In 1896 Mahler went to Budapest as assistant at the Institute of Trigonometry. Two years later he became assistant keeper in the department of archaeology of the Hungarian National Museum and also began lecturing on Oriental history and languages at Budapest University; in 1914 he was appointed professor there. In 1912 he became director of the newly founded Egyptological Institute and, in 1922, director of the Oriental Institute. Mahler explored the date of the Exodus and tried to demonstrate that the biblical data relating the Exodus are accurate in *Der Pharao des Exodus*, "The Pharaoh of the Exodus" (1896), and in various articles. He wrote the "Bibel-Babel" controversy, on the *Elephantine documents, and on calendar reform. Further chronological studies culminated in his classic *Handbuch der juedischen Chronologie* (1916, repr. 1967), in which he established the systems of the different Jewish calendars and chronologies in the light of ancient Near Eastern and medieval reckonings. He also provided comparative tables which make possible the conversion of a date in one system to the corresponding date in another system, especially the Christian calendar. Mahler later took up the problem of the Easter date and that of Jesus' death. He was associated with the excavations of an old Roman settlement at Dunapentele, where evidence for the earliest presence of Jews in Hungary was discovered.

BIBLIOGRAPHY: *Jubilee Volume… E. Mahler* (1937), incl. bibl.

MAHLER, GUSTAV (1860–1911), composer and conductor. Born in Kalischt, Bohemia, Mahler began his career as a conductor of operettas in Bad Hall. He rose through positions in Ljubljana, Olomouc, Kassel, Prague, Leipzig, Budapest, and Hamburg and progressed to become, in 1897, the director of the Vienna Court Opera. (He had to convert to Catholicism to secure this position and was baptized in the spring of 1897.) His tenure in Vienna brought the opera to a level of artistic achievement previously unknown there. However, he resigned in 1907 because of hostile intrigues. His remaining winters were spent in New York where he conducted the Metropolitan Opera and the New York Philharmonic. He died in Vienna.

Mahler, although one of the most popular symphonic composers today, was overshadowed as a composer in his lifetime by his successes as a conductor. His attempts to compose opera were abortive despite his genius as opera director. His libretto *Ruebezahl* survives, without music, and unpublished. Though no opera by Mahler exists, his sense of musical drama is evident in his ten symphonies and his "symphony in songs," *Das Lied von der Erde*. Four of the symphonies contain substantial vocal sections; in fact, the Eighth is a gigantic choral work. Mahler did not live to complete his Tenth Symphony; however, Deryck Cooke's "performing version" has been widely accepted as an authentic presentation. Mahler's songs, often written to folk texts, show deep understanding of the voice. Many themes from the songs were reworked in the symphonies. The most important song cycles are *Lieder eines fahrenden Gesellen* (1884) and *Kindertotenlieder* (1900–02).

BIBLIOGRAPHY: MGG; Grove, Dict; Riemann-Gurlitt; Baker, Biog Dict; O. Klemperer, *Minor Recollections* (1964), 9–41; A.M. Mahler, *Gustav Mahler, Memories and Letters* (1968); B. Walter, *Gustav Mahler* (1970); D. Mitchell, *Gustav Mahler: The Early Years* (1958); D. Newlin, *Bruckner-Mahler-Schoenberg* (1947, rev. ed. 1971).

[Dika Newlin]

MAHLER, MARGARET (Schoenberger; 1897–1985), child psychiatrist and psychoanalyst. Born in Sopron, Hungary, in the early 1930s she directed in Vienna the first psychoanalytically oriented child guidance clinic. In 1938 she settled in New York and in 1941 was appointed associate in psychiatry at Columbia University College of Physicians and Surgeons. In 1955 she was appointed clinical professor of psychiatry at the Albert Einstein College of Medicine. She was a training analyst at the New York Psychoanalytic Institute and in 1957 became the director of research of Masters Children's Center, where parallel studies of psychotic and normal children and their mothers are conducted. A comprehensive summary of Mahler's work of the 1940s appeared in the *Psychoanalytic Study of the Child*, vols. 3–4, 1948. Two main concepts associated with her name are the symbiotic infantile psychosis and the separation-individuation process of normal development during the first three years of life. In her book *On Human Symbiosis*, vol. 1 (1968), Mahler describes the core of infantile psychosis as "faulty or absent individuation" resulting from a deficiency in the child's intrapsychic utilization of the mothering partner during the symbiotic phase.

In 1970 the Margaret S. Mahler Psychiatric Research Foundation was established in Wynnewood, Pennsylvania. Its objective is to increase understanding of children's psychological and emotional development, particularly in the separation-individuation process, and to transmit that information to parents, therapists, and childcare providers.

Other books by Mahler include *The Psychological Birth of the Human Infant* (1975) and *The Memoirs of Margaret S. Mahler* (with P. Stepansky, 1988).

BIBLIOGRAPHY: A. Grinstein, *Index of Psychoanalytic Writings*, 3 (1958), 1295–97, and 7 (1964), 3687–88. **ADD. BIBLIOGRAPHY:** S. Kramer and S. Akhtar (eds.), *Mahler and Kohut* (1994); J. McDevitt et al., *Separation-Individuation: Essays in Honor of Margaret Mahler* (1971).

[Miriam Ben-Aaron / Ruth Beloff (2nd ed.)]

MAHLER, RAPHAEL (1899–1977), historian. Mahler, who was born in Nowy Sącz, eastern Galicia, Poland, studied at the rabbinical seminary and the University of Vienna until 1922. He served as a teacher of general and Jewish history in Jewish secondary schools in Poland. In 1937 he immigrated to the United States and was a teacher in various educational institutions in New York. He was a member from his youth of the left Po'alei Zion party and was connected with *YIVO in its research studies and administration, both in Poland and in the U.S. In 1950 he went to Israel, where he lectured on the history of Israel at Tel Aviv University and in 1961 was appointed professor there. He wrote many studies on the history of the Jews in Yiddish, Polish, German, English, and, after going to Israel, chiefly in Hebrew. Among his works are the following: *Di Yidn in Amolikn Poyln* (New York, 1946, in the publication *Di Yidn by Poyln*); *Ha-Kara'im* (1946), on the Karaites; *Yidn in Amolikn Poyln in Likht fun Tsifern* (Warsaw, 1958); *Yehudei Polin bein Shetei ha-Milḥamot* ("Jews in Poland Between the Two World Wars," 1968). Among his articles is "*Torat Borochov ve-Shitato be-Yameinu Anu*" (in: *Ba-Derekh*, 1965). His major work, *Divrei Yemei Yisrael; Dorot Aḥaronim* ("History of the Jewish People in Modern Times"), has been published only in part: first part (on 1789–1815) in 4 vols. (1956–62), and the first volume (1970) of part two (on 1815–48). In his introduction to the work Mahler explains his theory of Jewish history in accordance with historical materialism, his division of Jewish history in the modern period in conformity with social and economic evolution, and the class war and changes of governments during these years. His scientific work is based upon an abundance of sources and a rich bibliography. In 1977 he was awarded the Israel Prize for contributions to the study of Jewish history.

BIBLIOGRAPHY: Kressel, Leksikon, 2 (1967), 319; LYNL, 5 (1963), 393–7.

MAHLON AND CHILION (Heb. מַחְלוֹן and כִּלְיוֹן), the two sons of Elimelech and Naomi (Ruth 1:2ff.; 4:9–10). They were Ephrathites of Bethlehem who migrated to Moab, together with their parents, during a drought in the time of the Judges. After their father's death, the two brothers married Moabite women, Chilion marrying Orpah, and Mahlon, *Ruth. Both died childless. Their names have been taken to mean "sickness" and "destruction" and have been explained as symbolic of their untimely death. But Mahlon could be connected with *maḥol*, "dance," and Chilion with a word meaning "completion."

In the Aggadah

Mahlon and Chilion are identified with Joash and Saraph of I Chronicles 4:22, the different names indicating their characteristics and destiny. Joash was so called because he lost hope (from the root יאשׁ, "to give up hope") of the messianic era; Saraph because he was condemned to be burned (from the root שׂרף, "to burn"); Mahlon, because he committed acts of profanation (from the root חלל, "to profane"); and Chilion because he was condemned by God to destruction (כלה "to destroy"; BB 91b). They sinned in leaving Erez Israel (BB 91a), and in that they neither proselytized their wives nor ensured that they performed ritual immersion (Ruth R. 2:9). Before they died, they were rendered penniless (Ruth R.2:10).

BIBLIOGRAPHY: Noth, Personennamen, 54, 249; Ginzberg, Legends, 4 (1925), 31; 6 (1925), 189; Y. Ḥasida, *Ishei ha-Tanakh* (1964), 258–9.

MAH NISHTANNAH (Heb. מַה נִּשְׁתַּנָּה; "What is different?"), first words of the four questions asked at the Passover *seder* service. The questions come at the beginning of the recital of the *Haggadah and are usually asked by the youngest participant. The first sentence reads: "Why is this night different from all other nights?"

According to the Ashkenazi rite, the questions come in the following order: (1) Why on this night is only *mazzah* ("unleavened bread") eaten? (2) Why are bitter herbs consumed? (3) Why are herbs dipped twice (in salt water and in *ḥaroset*) during the *seder* meal? (4) Why do we sit reclined at the *seder* table? The text of the answers "We were slaves unto Pharaoh in Egypt…," follows the set of four questions. The reply is usually made by the father, or the person conducting the *seder*.

The *Mah Nishtannah* dates back to mishnaic times (Pes. 10:4) and originated in contemporaneous dining customs (manners and sequence) at festive meals. The questions were made part of the *seder* celebration as an introduction and reminder to the father to fulfill the biblical injunction: "And thou shalt tell thy son in that day, saying: it is because of that which the Lord did for me when I came forth out of Egypt" (Ex. 13:8; see also Ex. 13:14, 15). The Mishnah enumerates four questions to be asked during the *seder* (Pes. 10:4); the third, "Why do we eat only roasted meat [of the paschal sacrifice]?" was omitted after the Destruction of the Temple and the consequent cessation of sacrifices, and for it was substituted another question which is not mentioned in the Mishnah (Why do we recline?). The Sephardi ritual retained the geonic order of the four questions: (1) dipping, (2) unleavened bread, (3) bitter herbs, (4) reclining.

In the geonic literature (and as late as *Rashi and *Maimonides, Yad, *Ḥamez u-Mazzah*, 8:2) the *Mah Nishtannah* was probably recited by the person conducting the *seder* and not asked by the children. Where there is no child present at the *seder* table, the questions should be asked by the housewife, and if only men participate, they must ask each other, even if they are learned scholars (Pes. 116a). The *Mah Nishtannah* questions form part of the *Haggadah* ritual of all trends and segments in Judaism, including Reform.

BIBLIOGRAPHY: E.D. Goldschmidt; *Haggadah shel Pesaḥ* (1960), 10–13; J. Levy, *A Guide to Passover* (1958), 27, 31.

MAḤOZA, town on the River Tigris (Ber. 59b), on the bank of the Nahar Malka (Fluvius Regum), one of the canals connecting the Euphrates with the Tigris. Maḥoza was a suburb of Be-Ardashir, situated on the left bank of the Tigris, and of the town of Ctesiphon, situated on its right bank (Er. 57b). Ctesiphon, established by Seleucus Nicator, the founder of the Seleucid dynasty about 300 B.C.E., was destroyed by the Roman commander Avidus Cassius in 165 C.E. On its ruins Ardashir I (226–240 C.E.) erected a new city after his name, the Be-Ardashir mentioned occasionally in the Talmud. Both cities served as the capital. Maḥoza's importance derived also from the fact that it was situated on a central trading route through which caravans passed, as well as considerable merchandise which passed on the rivers. The Jews of Maḥoza took a very active part in the commercial life, both within the town (BB 29b) and beyond it (Git. 6a). The merchants were very successful. They ate well (Shab. 109a), drank much wine (Ta'an. 26a), and were hedonists (RH 17a). Of the women of Maḥoza it is related that they were lazy (Shab. 32b) and wore many ornaments (BK 119a). Among the Jews of Maḥoza were also successful farmers. Some of them possessed fields and orchards, irrigating their fields from the waters of the Tigris (Ber. 59b; Ket. 67a). They reared cattle (Er. 26a; BB 36a, Rashbam ad loc.) and also traded in grain (Git. 73a). A Jewish settlement in Seleucus and Ctesiphon during the first century C.E. is mentioned by Josephus (Ant., 18:310 ff.).

Maḥoza is mentioned for the first time as a center of study after the destruction of the academy of *Nehardea in 259 (*Iggeret R. Sherira Gaon*, ed. by B.M. Lewin (1921), 82). Maḥoza attained the height of its fame after the death of *Abbaye in 338 when the academy of Pumbedita together with its scholars moved to Maḥoza, where Rava, who headed the academy for 14 years from 338–352, dwelt (*ibid.*, 88 f.). During this period Maḥoza had a considerable Jewish population. They constituted the majority of its inhabitants and Abbaye was surprised that there was no **mezuzah* on the city gate (Yoma 11a). It also contained many proselytes (Kid. 73a). Because of Maḥoza's proximity to Be-Ardashir, Rava had close relations with the government (see *Shapur II). When the emperor Julian invaded Babylon in 363, Maḥoza was destroyed. However, on his death and the withdrawal of the Romans, it was rebuilt. Maḥoza declined as a Jewish settlement in the second half of the fifth century as a result of the uprising of the Nestorian Christians.

BIBLIOGRAPHY: Neubauer, Géogr, 356 f.; A. Berliner, in: *Jahres-Bericht des Rabbiner-Seminars zu Berlin* (1882–83), 39–43; J. Obermeyer, *Die Landschaft Babylonien* (1929), 161–78. **ADD. BIBLIOGRAPHY:** B. Eshel, *Jewish Settlements in Babylonia during Talmudic Times* (1979), 141–44.

[Moshe Beer]

MAH TOVU (Heb. מַה טֹּבוּ; "How goodly"), the opening words of a prayer recited by Ashkenazi Jews upon entering the synagogue. The initial words are a quotation from Numbers 24:5. The remainder of the prayer consists of Psalms 5:8; 26:8; 69:14; and 95:6 (with Ps. 95:6 modified from the plural to the singular form). The Talmud interprets the "tents" and "dwellings" of Numbers 24:5 to refer to synagogues and schools (Sanh. 105b), and the "time of grace" mentioned in Psalms 69:14, to mean the time of public worship (Ber. 8a). At one time, the rabbis apparently intended to include Balaam's blessing of the children of Israel (Num. 22–24) in the recitation of *Shema; however, they decided that it was too lengthy for the congregation (Ber. 12b).

Sephardi Jews recite Psalms 5:8 on entering the synagogue, and Psalms 5:9 on leaving.

See *Liturgy; **Shaharit*.

BIBLIOGRAPHY: Elbogen, Gottesdienst, 87, 526; Idelsohn, Liturgy, 73f.; E. Levy, *Yesodot ha-Tefillah* (1952^2), 76, 131.

MAḤZIKE HADAS (Mahazikei ha-Dat), organization in Galicia and Bukovina, representing the first attempt of the Orthodox to unite for political action in order to foster its beliefs in the sphere of Jewish social life. The organization was initiated by a meeting of the larger Jewish communities which was convened by *Shomer Israel in Lvov (Lemberg), in 1878, in connection with their opposition to the founding of a rabbinical seminary and to the organizational changes in the communities. The Maḥzike Hadas society was founded primarily to ward off the dangers that lay in such new plans. It was headed by Simon *Sofer (Schreiber) of Cracow (son of the Ḥatam Sofer) and Joshua Rokeaḥ, the rabbi of *Belz. The founding convention took place on March 13, 1879. There the statutes of the new organization were determined and the bimonthly *Maḥzikei ha-Dat* which appeared in both Hebrew and in Yiddish and which was directed against the publication *Izraelita was founded. The organization came out with a special list of candidates for the elections of the Austrian parliament of 1879. Of the four candidates it put forward only one, Simon Sofer, was elected, Sofer joined the "Polish club" in opposition to the Jewish assimilationist representatives. In 1882 the organization convened a large conference which was attended by 200 rabbis and 800 representatives of communities. The purpose of the conference was to protect the religious character of the communities from the reform tendencies of the progressives. The conference passed a resolution that only Jews observing the precepts of the Shulḥan Arukh were to be granted full voting rights for communal elections. The death of Simon Schreiber in 1883 temporarily weakened the movement, but in 1908 the rabbi of Belz renewed its vigor by publishing a proclamation *Kol Maḥazikei ha-Dat* which denounced any attempt to introduce a progressive spirit into the communities according to the patterns of Western Europe or, under the influence of Zionism and socialism, to inject into them a secular national content. The rabbi of Belz also denounced the efforts of the Vienna community to set up a central union for Austria. After World War I, when Poland became independent, a section of the Orthodox community, under the influence of the rabbi of Belz, organized an independent political party, calling itself Maḥzike Hadas. The party was founded at a convention which was attended by representatives from 100 communities and which took place in Grodek Jagiellonski (Gorodok), on Dec. 22, 1931. Its influence was chiefly felt throughout Galicia as a rival to *Agudat Israel.

BIBLIOGRAPHY: N.M. Gelber (ed.), in: EG, 4 (1953), 310ff.; M. Busak, in: A. Bauminger et al. (eds.), *Sefer Kraka* (1959), 103–7; Z. Fischer-Schein (Zohar), *Be-Sod Yesharim ve-Edah* (1969), 125; I. Schiper (ed.), *Zydzi w Polsce odrodzonej*, 1 (1932), 410; 2 (1933), 258.

[Avraham Rubinstein]

MAḤZOR (Heb. מַחְזוֹר, *maḥazor*; "cycle"), festival prayer book. The word is similar to the term *Maḥzarta* of the Syrian Church, which means a breviary, and was originally applied to the poetical insertions to be recited in prayers throughout the yearly cycle. In Ashkenazi usage, it came to refer distinctly to the festival prayer book, as distinct from the *siddur* (the daily prayer book). The term is also used by Sephardi Jews.

Mahzorim, Illuminated

Illuminated *maḥzorim* flourished in the Ashkenazi world throughout the 13th and 14th centuries, mainly in southwest Germany, in the Rhine valley, making their appearance soon after an authoritative "cycle" of prayers emerged. In the 15th century the fashion moved to northern Italy, where many Ashkenazim had settled, and influenced Italian Jewish illumination. While the Ashkenazi *siddur* contained the daily and personal prayers, both for home and synagogue, the *maḥzor* contains the synagogal communal prayers for the festivals and the seven special Sabbaths of the Jewish year. In the Italian rite, the term *maḥzor* embraced both the daily and festival prayers. Primarily intended for the use of the *ḥazzan*, the German *maḥzorim* are usually large – written in clear, bold letters – and contain a large selection of *piyyutim* ("liturgical poems") for each festival, offering the cantor a variety of choice. A large number of German *maḥzorim* are illuminated with initial-word panels and with illustrations of a ritual and textual nature. These *maḥzorim* were executed over a period of some 100 years, from the mid-13th to the mid-14th century.

The earliest surviving illustrated *maḥzor* manuscript of the 13th century is the two-volume codex of the Michael Collection in the Bodleian Library (Mss. Mich. 617 and Mich. 627), written in 1258 by Judah b. Samuel, called Seltman. Though it is not extensively illustrated it is important, since it proves that illuminated *maḥzorim* existed prior to this date. It was probably illuminated by a gentile, since the first initial-word panel was painted upside down, as though it was a Latin manuscript. However, despite this, the manuscript contains motifs which became traditional in later *maḥzorim* and which could not have been invented by gentiles. The finest examples of *maḥzorim* from the south of Germany are the first volume of the *Worms Maḥzor* of 1272 (see below); the *Laud Maḥzor* of about 1290 (Bodleian Library, Ms. Laud Or. 321); the *Leipzig Maḥzor* of about 1300 (see below); the *Dou-*

ble Maḥzor in Dresden (Saechsische Landesbibliothek, Ms. A 46a) and Breslau (State and University Library Cod. Or. I. 1); the *Tripartite Maḥzor* of about 1320 (Budapest, Hungarian Academy of Sciences, Ms. A. 384, British Museum, Add. Ms. 22413, and Bodleian Library, Ms. Mich. 619), and the *Darmstadt Maḥzor* of 1340 (Hessische Lands-und Hochschulbibliothek, Cod. Or. 13).

These *maḥzorim* illustrate both the development of style in southern Germany and the use of a special Jewish *iconography. An example of such development in both style and in motif is found in the distortion of human figures. In all manuscripts before 1300, the use of animal-headed people is consistent; in the *Leipzig Maḥzor*, people have birds' beaks instead of a nose and mouth; but the artists of the later *Tripartite Maḥzor* did not understand the reason for such distortions, and painted all the male figures with ordinary human heads and all the females with animal heads.

Southern German *maḥzorim* have a very wide range of text illustrations. Most of them begin with the prayers for the four special Sabbaths before Passover, continuing with Passover, the Feast of Weeks, the New Year, the Day of Atonement, and the Feast of Tabernacles. Four of the *megillot* ("scrolls") are also usually included in the *maḥzor* – sometimes placed together, at other times appended to the particular celebrations with which they were associated. The Book of Esther was usually written separately on a scroll, to be read at the festival of Purim.

Most German *maḥzorim* have illustrations of the signs of the zodiac for each of the verses of a *piyyut* in the prayer for dew recited on the first day of Passover (*Leipzig Maḥzor*, vol. 1, fol. 133; *Worms Maḥzor*, vol. 1, fol. 95v.; Ms. Mich. fols. 49–51). The signs of the zodiac are depicted in small medallions in the margin. In the *Worms* and the *Tripartite* manuscripts, the labors of the months are depicted in medallions next to the signs of the zodiac. Some specifically Jewish elements have developed in the zodiac illustrations, such as a bucket instead of Aquarius; in some cases a draw well is depicted instead of a mere bucket, and in some *maḥzorim* a kid is shown next to the well to illustrate both Capricorn and Aquarius, which are referred to in one verse of this *piyyut*. In one *maḥzor* (Bodleian Library, Ms. Opp. 161, fol. 84), 11 signs of the zodiac are depicted in one large roundel divided into 12 sections, similar to the arrangements of the signs of the zodiac in floor mosaics of early synagogues (e.g., Bet Alfa). This example may be an indication of a traditional way of depicting the astronomical zodiac *circulus*, which survived into the Middle Ages.

The illustration for the Feast of Weeks traditionally depicts Moses receiving the Tablets of the Law and giving them to the Israelites, who are standing at the foot of Mount Sinai (e.g., *Leipzig Maḥzor*, vol. 1, fol. 130v.; British Museum, Ms. Add. 22413, fol. 3v.; *Worms Maḥzor*, vol. 1, fol. 151). In the *Land Maḥzor* (fol. 127v.) the giving of the Law is combined with an illustration of Moses sprinkling the blood of the Covenant over the Israelites. In the *Leipzig Maḥzor* (vol. 1, fol. 130) the Israelites are standing as though within the mountain, illustrating the Midrash which states that God erected a mountain over the Israelites until they agreed to accept the Torah.

The second volume of an Ashkenazi *maḥzor* normally starts with the prayers for Rosh Ha-Shanah, illustrated by the sacrifice of Isaac, with the ram caught in a thicket by his horns. The sounding of the ram's horn (*shofar*) on New Year's day is a commemoration of God's covenant with Abraham at the time of the sacrifice (e.g., *Leipzig Maḥzor*, vol. 2, fols. 26v., 66; Bodleian Library, Ms. Laud Or. 321, fol. 184, and Ms. Reg. 1, fol. 207v.; *Double Maḥzor*, Breslau, fol. 46v.). In some *maḥzorim*, a horned and claw-footed devil is depicted next to a *shofar* blower, who sometimes supports his right foot on a three-legged stool in order to ward off the earthly influence of evil. This is in accordance with the common superstition that a three-point object keeps evil spirits away (e.g., Budapest, Ms. A. 388, vol. 2, fol. 12v.; Paris, Bibliothèque de l'Alliance Israélite Universelle). Openings of prayers from the Day of Atonement are usually illustrated by initial words and by parts of prayers written within full-page arches resembling doors, an allusion to the Gates of Mercy, now opened to accept the individual prayers of every Jew (e.g., *Leipzig Maḥzor*, vol. 2; Berlin, Preussischer Kulturbesitz, Ms. Or. Fol. 388, fol. 69; *Worms Maḥzor*, vol. 2; *Double Maḥzor*, Breslau, fol. 89).

The prayers for the Feast of Tabernacles are sometimes illustrated by a man holding the fruits of the Holy Land: the *lulav* ("palm branch"), the *etrog* ("citrus fruit"), *Hadas* ("myrtle"), and *aravah* ("willow").

Some *maḥzorim* are merely decorated and contain no illustrations at all. An example is the *Nuremberg Maḥzor* of 1331, which for six centuries was owned by the municipality of Nuremberg and is now in the Schocken Library in Jerusalem (Ms. 24100). Its large initial-word panel for the first day of Passover is decorated with foliage scrolls, grotesques, and an architectural top. In the 15th century, the illumination of large-sized *maḥzorim* was no longer fashionable. The smaller-sized illuminated prayer book which became more common continued to be called a *maḥzor*. One such example is the *Maḥzor of Rabbi Friedman of Ruzhin*. This mid-15th century eastern German prayer book was probably intended for use in the synagogue and at home by a wealthy member of the Jewish community. Though the system of illustration remained Ashkenazi, the decoration shows the influence of Italian motifs, evident in the marginal miniatures, initial-word panels, and human busts emerging from flowers. An example of the fusion of the two traditions is the *Schocken Italian Maḥzor* of 1441 (Ms. 13873), which is a large volume, written and decorated in Roman style, of the Roman rite, but with illustrations following the Ashkenazi tradition.

Most of the 15th-century Italian *maḥzorim* are personal rather than synagogal prayer books, stressing the daily prayers, and containing a *Haggadah* which was recited at home. They are therefore small, handy to carry to and from the synagogue, with the prayers arranged for the individual, starting with the daily and Sabbath prayers and the Festival ones. These illuminated small *maḥzorim* were not usually extensively illustrated;

besides the decorated openings of prayers, they contained fairly simple marginal pen drawings. Good early examples are those related to famous families of northern and central Italy. Such are *maḥzorim* executed at the order of Daniel b. Samuel ha-Rofe b. Daniel ha-Dayyan, one at Bertinoro in 1390 (Bodleian Library, Ms. Can. Or. 81) and another at Forli in 1393 (British Museum, Add. Ms. 26968). In these works, as in others done for the same patron, the tinted drawings are of Lombard style. A *maḥzor* from Pisa of 1397 ordered by another well-known patron, Jehiel b. Mattathias of the Beit-El family (Sassoon Ms. 1028), is in the same style. Some of the text illustrations in these *maḥzorim* resemble those of the traditional Ashkenazi ones: a horn-blower for the New Year; a *sukkah* for Tabernacles; the balance for Sabbath *Shekalim*; a crescent and star for Sabbath *Ha-Ḥodesh*; and more detailed illustrations for the Passover *Haggadah*.

The same system of illustration was also used by the Ashkenazi scribe and illuminator Joel b. *Simeon. Of the three *maḥzorim* executed in his workshop in the third quarter of the 15th century, the last was probably made for a woman, since it contains several marginal pen drawings of a ritual nature in which a lady called Maraviglia is the main character. Closely related to the Florentine style of Joel b. Simeon are some more elegant *maḥzorim* which have pen and colored decorations on almost every page. Such is the *Rothschild Maḥzor* of 1492 from Florence (Jewish Theological Seminary in New York, Ms. 03225), which was illuminated in three different styles and techniques, with elaborate illuminated opening pages, illustrations to each section, and tinted decorations on each page. Moses receiving the Tablets of the Law illustrating the opening to the mishnaic tractate *Avot* (fol. 139) is an example of the second kind. Other *maḥzorim* with a similar system of illustration are fairly common, though some are richer than others.

The *maḥzor* in the *Rothschild Miscellany*, Ms. 24, Israel Museum, Ms. 180/51, which has sumptuous Ferrarese illuminations from about 1470, consists of textual illustrations for each festival and prayers for special occasions. In fact, it contains a wealth of material illustrating almost every custom of daily life in a rich Jewish Renaissance household. No other manuscript equals the richness and scope of the illumination of this miscellany, though only a portion of its 473 leaves is a *maḥzor*. The *Pesaro Maḥzor* of 1480 (Sassoon Ms. 23), containing almost as many pages as the *Rothschild Miscellany*, consists only of a prayer book of Roman rite. Its borders are very richly decorated by a Ferrarese artist, but there are fewer text illustrations, mostly within a wreath in the lower part of the border.

Two of the outstanding Ashkenazi *Maḥzorim* are described in detail below.

The Leipzig Mahzor

(Leipzig, University Library, Ms. v. 1102) is the most sumptuous of the south German illuminated *maḥzorim* and has the most extensive array of text illustrations. Almost all the special Sabbaths, feasts, and festivals are illustrated. The first volume was written by Menahem, who decorated his name (fols. 113, 137) in the same way as Menahem the scribe who copied the *Birds' Head Haggadah* (see Illuminated *Haggadot). The second volume was copied by a scribe called Isaac. The two volumes were wrongly bound with additions and corrections in later dates. The giant manuscript was probably intended initially for a *ḥazzan* of a very rich community on the Upper Rhine. The first volume of the *Leipig Maḥzor* opens with a frontispiece representing Samson rending the lion, possibly an allusion to the phrase "Grow strong like a lion to fulfill the will of your Maker," sometimes referring to the *ḥazzan* (vol. 1, fol. 19). At the end of the short introductory prayers, there is a miniature depicting the *ḥazzan* standing covered with his *tallit* ("prayer shawl") in front of a marble pulpit, on which a large open book rests. This probably represents the first volume of the Leipzig manuscript. The second volume is shown in the hands of a young man wearing a Jewish hat, who is standing behind the *ḥazzan* accompanied by a bearded Jew (vol. 1, fol. 27). A man holding a scale is a common illustration for the Sabbath of *Parashat Shekalim*, referring to the payment of the annual half-shekel for the Temple sacrifices (Ex. 30:11–16).

Most illustrations in the *Leipzig Maḥzor* are common to other south German *maḥzorim*, such as the tall tree from which Haman and his ten sons are hanging (vol. 1. fol. 51v.), illustrating a *piyyut* for Purim; a red heifer illustrates *Parashat Parah* (1, 53v); the sun and moon illustrate *Parashat ha-Ḥodesh* (1, 59); a betrothed couple sitting on a bench illustrates a *piyyut* for the "Great Sabbath" before Passover, alluding to the Torah as the bride of the people of Israel (1, 64). The Egyptians pursuing the Israelites illustrate the Passover Eve prayer (1, 72v.–73), the signs of the zodiac the prayer for dew recited on the first day of Passover (1, 85–87), and Moses receiving the tablets of the Law illustrating Shavuot (1, 130v.). An additional illustration (1, v. 131) depicts the contemporary custom of initiating children into the study of the Torah. The child is brought to his teacher's lap to lick the honey-covered alphabet tablet in order to sweeten his introduction to the study of the Torah, while the other children, in celebration of his initiation, receive eggs and cakes. The first volume ends with the *kinot* ("dirges") for the Ninth of Av, which are hardly ever illustrated. As is common in Ashkenazi *maḥzorim*, the second volume begins with the prayers for Rosh Ha-Shanah, with illustrations of the *akedah and the ram caught in a thicket. The opening prayers for the Day of Atonement are illustrated with the customary arches resembling doors, alluding to the Gates of Mercy (2, fols. 74v., 85, 164v.), but one of the arches has in the lower margin the additional midrashic illustration of Abraham being saved from the fire of the Chaldeans because of his belief. The feast of Sukkot is illustrated by a man holding the prescribed "four species," and in the lower margin the legendary beasts, the leviathan and behemoth are fighting, an event which is supposed to take place before the end of time. The style of the *Leipzig Maḥzor* is related to south German illumination around 1300. A fascimile of 68 illuminated pages from the *Leipzig Maḥzor*, with an introductory volume, was published in 1964.

The Worms Mahzor

(Jerusalem, Jewish National and University Library, Ms. Heb. 4781/I–II) consists of two unrelated volumes, which were kept together in the Worms Synagogue from 1578. The fact that the page size, text area, and style of script are different in each volume, and that Ecclesiastes is repeated in both, indicates that they were executed independently. Only the first volume is dated, through a colophon (fol. 34v) stating that it was completed on Jan. 1, 1272, written by Simḥah b. Judah for his uncle R. Baruch b. Isaac. Another entry mentions the scribe, his father Judah of Nuremberg, and Shemaiah the Frenchman, who may have been the artist. Neither volume was intended for the Worms community, since they both contain *piyyutim* and prayers which are not included in the Worms rite while one *piyyut* was common in the rite of Mainz. The first volume of the *Worms Maḥzor* is one of the earliest dated illuminated *maḥzorim* from southern Germany. Associated with the colored initial-word panels are many text illustrations for the special Sabbaths, Passover, and Shavuot. The illustration for *Parashat Shekalim* depicts a man holding a balance, weighing the half-shekels for the payment in the Temple (fol. 39v.) Although the illumination of the *Worms Maḥzor* is somewhat crude, it resembles south German Latin illumination of the second half of the 13th century. Another link with the south German Jewish school of illumination is the style of the animals, birds, and distorted heads of human figures. The second volume contains a very few decorations of a somewhat later south German style.

[Bezalel Narkiss]

BIBLIOGRAPHY: M. Steinschneider, *Jewish Literature* (1857, 1965), 165ff.; Idelsohn, Liturgy, xiiif. ILLUMINATED MAḤZORIM: Mayer, Art, 1792 (J. Mueller); 1496 (J. Leveen); 2246 (S. Rothschild); 2846, 2876 (R. Wischnitzer-Bernstein); 857 (E.D. Goldschmidt); 2239, 2240 (E. Roth); 2969 (J. Gutmann); 1222A (B. Narkiss); 2232 (C. Roth); 58 (Z. Ameisenowa); 2933 (B. Ziemlich); 393 (N. Bruell, p. 115–8); 2074 (Recklinghausen); 730 (Frankfurt); 523 (Monumenta Judaica); J. Gutmann, in: *Art Journal*, 27 (1967/68), 172; B. Narkiss, in: *Haaretz* (May 15, 1957); idem, *Hebrew Illuminated Manuscripts* (1969), 30–33, 37–39, pls. 26, 27, 33, 34, 35, 44, 49, 52, 53, 56; idem, in: *Papers of the Fourth World Congress of Jewish Studies*, 2 (1968), 129–33; idem, *Hebrew Illuminated Manuscripts from Jerusalem Collections*, The Israel Museum, Exhibition Catalog no. 40 (1967), nos. 5, 10; M. Beit Arié, in: *Leshonenu*, 29 (1965), 27–46, 80–102; Margoliouth, Cat, 2 (1899), 285–8, no. 662; A. Wurfel, *Historische Nachrichten von der Judengemeinde Nuernberg* (Nuremberg, 1755), 97–105; D.S. Sassoon, *Ohel David*, 1 (1932), 289–93; Neubauer, Cat, no. 2373; I. Levi, in: REJ, 89 (1930), 281–92.

MAḤZOR VITRY, halakhic-liturgical composition by Simḥah b. Samuel of Vitry, a small town in the department of Marne, France. Simḥah was an outstanding pupil, or even a colleague, of Rashi and apparently died during his teacher's lifetime (i.e., before 1105 – see Gross, Gallia Judaica, 196). His son Samuel married Rashi's granddaughter and he was the grandfather of the famous tosafist, Isaac of *Dampierre (Urbach, Tosafot, 115). Like his colleague Shemaiah, Rashi's secretary, he occupied himself with the arrangement of his master's halakhic rulings, and later authorities sometimes confused their names. There is however no basis for the assumption of some scholars that there existed two works, one by Shemaiah and one by Simḥah, both entitled *Maḥzor Vitry* (Urbach, *ibid.*, 33). *Maḥzor Vitry* belongs to the group of works from the school of Rashi (e.g., the *Pardes, Sefer ha-Orah, Siddur Rashi*) which are based upon Rashi's rulings and usages, but which are expanded with additions from other authorities, sometimes even discussing and criticising their views, in order to defend those of Rashi. *Maḥzor Vitry* is in the form of a halakhic-liturgical work, the purpose of which was to give the halakhic rulings of the liturgy for the whole circle (*maḥzor*) of the year, weekdays, Sabbaths, and festivals, and connect them with the accepted formula of the prayers. The fact that it also includes laws of Sabbath, *eruv, marriage, and ritual slaughter makes it wider in scope than the *siddurim* of *Amram and Saadiah *Gaon, which were also sent to various communities at their request. The *Maḥzor Vitry*, referred to by 13th-century authorities, such as the *Sefer Mitzvot Gadol* of Moses b. Jacob of *Coucy (Positive Commandments 27) and the *Or Zaru'a* (part 1, p. 55) of Isaac b. Moses of *Vienna exist in various versions which differ considerably from one another both in scope and arrangement. Apparently it gained instant acceptance and it was enlarged, as was the custom of that time, by successive additions. There does not yet exist a critical edition based on all available manuscripts. The published edition (by S. Hurwitz, 1889, 1923²) is from the London manuscript (Margolioth, Cat, no. 655) containing many additions, some indicated by the letter ת, most of them apparently from Isaac b. Durbal, a contemporary of Jacob Tam, but also including later responsa and extracts from the *Sefer ha-Terumah* of Baruch b. Isaac. It reflects the state of the work in the 13th and 14th centuries. The Oxford manuscript (Bodleian Library, Ms. Opp. 59) omits most of these additions in those fragments preserved in two manuscripts. On the other hand, they contain compilations which have no connection with the *maḥzor*. A more original text occurs in the Reggio manuscript (now in the library of the Jewish Theological Seminary of America) which has as yet not been examined because of its poor state of preservation, and the Parma manuscript (B. Pal. 2574).

Contents and Form

The halakhic portion of the *Maḥzor Vitry* precedes the liturgical formulae, and includes commentaries to the prayers taken from the *aggadah*. The Reggio manuscript includes the following topics: weekday prayers (with their relevant laws), the night prayer, the order of prayers for the Sabbath and its conclusion, the New Moon, the Sanctification of the Moon, Ḥanukkah, Purim, Passover *Haggadah*, and the Aramaic translation of the reading for the 7th day of Passover (Ex. 13:17–15:26) and the laws of Shavuot with a similar Aramaic translation. (Both these Aramaic translations are much enlarged and are to be found in many medieval *maḥzorim*.)

There follow *Avot* with a commentary, *Hilkhot Derek Ereẓ, Pirkei Ben Azzai*, a commentary on the *Kaddish* and on the Ten Commandments, the order of service for the Ninth Av, the laws of fasts and mourning, Rosh Ha-Shanah, the Day of Atonement, Sukkot and the *Hoshanot with a commentary, the order of service for Simḥat Torah, the order of service for marriage and circumcision, and the laws of *sheḥitah and *terefot. In the enlarged text in the London manuscript there have been added the laws of *Niddah, Ẓiẓit, Tefillin, Mezuzah, Sefer Torah*, the complete text of tractate *Soferim*, tractate *Kallah* and the laws of divorce, and *ḥaliẓah. In addition there are many *piyyutim* and *aggadot*. The main sources of *Maḥzor Vitry* are the decisions and customs of Rashi. Simḥah apparently based himself on the *Siddur Rashi* with whose text the *maḥzor* is often identical (see Buber, *Siddur Rashi*, introd. p. 54) but it excludes all the texts of the prayers. In the halakhic portion the sources, in addition to the Talmud, are the geonic literature, especially the Halakhot *Gedolot and Halakhot *Pesukot, and the *siddur* of Amram Gaon, which is often quoted verbatim, without giving the source. The talmudic quotations often differ from those in the existing text. *Maḥzor Vitry* is an important source for the historical study of *halakhah* and liturgy, particularly according to the French tradition. The *piyyutim* in the *maḥzor* differ in the various manuscripts, making it difficult to determine which were current during the period when the *Maḥzor Vitry* was composed. The text of these *piyyutim* which were apparently collected at a later period and appended to the London manuscript have been published separately under the title "*Kunteres ha-Piyyutim*" by H. Brody (Berlin, 1894).

BIBLIOGRAPHY: S. Hurwitz and A. Berliner, *Mafte'aḥ u-Mavo le-Maḥzor Vitry*, in: S. Hurwitz (ed.), *Maḥzor Vitry le-rabbenu Simḥah*, (1923^2); S. Buber (ed.), *Siddur Rashi* (1906), introd. liv-lv; Urbach, Tosafot, 33; Gross, Gal Jud, 196.

[Ernst Daniel Goldschmidt]

MAIER, JOSEPH (1911–2002), U.S. sociologist. Born in Leipzig, Germany, the son of a rabbi, Maier studied in Germany and in the U.S. He received his M.A. (1934) and his Ph.D. (1939) from Columbia University. After the War, Maier did voluntary service in Germany and participated in the Nuremberg Trials, becoming chief of the analysis section of the Interrogation Division. In 1947 he was appointed professor of sociology at Rutgers University and became chairman of the department until his retirement in 1980. Maier was a specialist in the sociology of religion and became widely known as the author of a weekly column in the New York German-language Jewish newspaper *Aufbau* dealing with the application of halakhic wisdom to contemporary social problems.

With Werner Cahnman, Maier established the organization for the Preservation of Jewish Cultural Monuments in Europe, later called the Rashi Association (1978). From 1980 on, he served as its president, helping to establish such projects as the Institute of Judaic Studies at the University of Munich.

Among Maier's published works are *On Hegel's Critique of Kant* (1939) and *Sociology* (with J. Rumney, 1953). With J. Marcus and Z. Tarr he edited *German Jewry: Its History and Sociology: Selected Essays by Werner J. Cahnman* (1989).

BIBLIOGRAPHY: J. Marcus (ed.), *Surviving the 20th Century* (1999).

[Werner J. Cahnman / Ruth Beloff (2nd ed.)]

MAILER, NORMAN (1923–), U.S. novelist and essayist. Born in New Jersey, Mailer grew up in New York City and attended Harvard College. His two years with the U.S. Army in the Pacific theater during World War II provided him with the background for his bestselling novel *The Naked and the Dead* (1948), whose violent dialogue and often lyric prose that evoked the fears and passions of men at war made him an overnight literary celebrity. *Barbary Shore* (1951) was a semi-surrealistic political novel set in a Brooklyn rooming house and *The Deer Park* (1955) a novel about Hollywood; in both of these books, which he himself called "existential," he revealed his growing fascination with the individual who intellectually, physically, or morally feels compelled to drive himself to extremes beyond the norms of human conduct in order to experience his own individuality. Mailer's increasing impatience with the novel as a medium for expressing his extraordinarily fertile if undisciplined mind and his ability to yoke together ideas of the most varied political, psychological, and philosophical nature led him in the 1950s to turn more and more to the essay, of which he published several collections: *Advertisements for Myself* (1959), *The Presidential Papers* (1963), and *Cannibals and Christians* (1966). *Why Are We in Vietnam?* (1967) represented an experiment to deal in symbolic fictional terms with a burning political issue of the day. In 1968, Mailer wrote *Armies in the Night*, an eyewitness account of an anti-Vietnam demonstration held in front of the Pentagon in Washington whose melange of reportage, social and political speculation, and personal confession, written in a wildly exuberant prose, established his reputation by general critical consensus as the most brilliant virtuoso stylist in the United States. A second documentary, *Miami and the Siege of Chicago* (1968), about the Republican and Democratic nominating conventions of 1968, was again a masterpiece of its kind.

Mailer's interest in radical politics took him from Socialism to anarchism to a generalized hostility toward the regimentation and mechanization of modern life that he labeled "radical conservatism." Always partial to publicity, he sought to popularize his ideas by running in the New York mayoralty campaign of 1969.

A Fire on the Moon (1970) was about the implications of the U.S. space program. In 1971, Mailer's *The Prisoner of Sex* was published, drawing the ire of the feminist movement. In 1980 Mailer was awarded the Pulitzer Prize in fiction for *Executioner's Song*, which offered a detailed account through an ensemble of characters of the life and execution of Gary Gilmore, a convicted murderer. *Ancient Evenings* (1983), a novel, is set in the Egypt of the 13th to the 12th century B.C.E.

His look at the CIA, *Harlot's Ghost*, appeared in 1991, and his study of Lee Harvey Oswald, *Oswald's Tale*, was published in 1995. *The Time of Our Time* (1998) is a massive sampling of Mailer's work. His *The Spooky Art: Some Thoughts on Writing* (2003) is a gathering of his thoughts about writers, his own work, and the writing life.

Evaluations of Mailer often return to his fascination with violence and sexuality. Mailer's reading of violence in "The White Negro" (found in *Advertisements for Myself*) is a good example. Mailer argued that the Negro could survive his perilous American existence by accepting the desires of the body, living sensuously within the present moment. This creation of the self through action leads to the existential recognition of the self, in part, as body. The existentialist "must be able to feel oneself ... to know one's desires, one's rages, one's anguish ..." Jazz, for Mailer, the endowment of "orgasm," became one of the commanding achievements of the African-American, and spoke to, and of, "instantaneous existential states to which some whites could respond." The hipster's consecration of the present, his living his hatreds, his seeking the end of cultural and political repression through a life outside bourgeois mores, would be shaped in the future by the African-American's winning equality, a "potential superiority" that was feared, providing the background for domestic politics. Mailer's essay cemented into a mosaic the Holocaust, the concentration camp, African-American humiliation, endurance, and self-resurgence. Its affirmative violence coupled with sexuality provides a clue to some of Mailer's other work, most notably "The Time of Her Time" (found in *Advertisements for Myself*), *An American Dream* (1965), and possibly his life (he stabbed his second wife, Adele, in 1960).

His place in American literature is large, though his place in American-Jewish writing is problematic. (In her "Toward a New Yiddish" (*Judaism*, Summer 1970) Cynthia *Ozick believed that he would become a minor, if not forgotten writer because he did not write within the liturgical and moral richness of Jewish tradition.) On the one hand, his sharp indictments of the alliance among American politics, commercialism, and violence are insightful and enduring. His choice of characters and their novelistic development concentrate one version of American culture within the psychological and social existence of his subjects (whether fictional or actual; whether individuals or actual events). On the other hand, his influence on the American-Jewish novelist is, perhaps, that of craft. He is at ease in developing a realism in both its narrow and extreme senses – a focus on the empirical furniture of experience as well as a concentration on American myths and cultural directives informing the way we perceive, and act upon, the world.

ADD. BIBLIOGRAPHY: H. Bloom (ed.), *Norman Mailer* (1986); M. Dearborn, *Mailer: A Biography* (1999); P. Manso (ed.), *Mailer: His Life and Times* (1985).

[Hillel Halkin / Lewis Fried (2nd ed.)]

MAIMI, SIMON (d. 1497), a rabbi from Segovia, in Castile, who found refuge in Portugal. Maimi was martyred when *Manuel I, king of Portugal, tried to force him to accept Christianity, thinking that if the chief rabbi set the example all the Jews could soon be baptized. The attempt to convert Portuguese Jewry occurred during the spring of 1497, following the promulgation of the edict of expulsion on Dec. 4, 1496. Maimi and about eight leading personalities – including his son-in-law, and probably Abraham b. Jacob *Saba, Abraham b. Samuel *Zacuto, and Isaac b. Joseph *Caro – were thrown into a dungeon and buried up to their necks. The group refused to yield, and when the wall was torn down a few days later Maimi was dead. His body was stealthily taken by several Marranos who, at the risk of their lives, succeeded in burying him in the Jewish cemetery near Lisbon.

BIBLIOGRAPHY: Roth, Marranos, 60; N. Slouschz, *Ha-Anusim be-Portugal* (1932), 9, 63.

MAIMON (Fishman), ADA (1893–1973). Israeli labor leader, member of the First and Second Knessets. Born in Marculesti, Bessarabia, Maimon was the sister of Judah Leib *Maimon, who was a member of the United Religious Front in the first Knesset. Ada Maimon received a traditional and general Hebrew education. In her youth she joined a movement that was connected to Ha-Po'el ha-Ẓa'ir. She settled in Ereẓ Israel in 1912, and worked as a teacher in Petaḥ Tikvah, Reḥovot, Nes Ẓiyyonah, and Ben Shemen. In 1914 she was sent to open a Hebrew girls school in Safed. In 1913–20 Maimon was a member of the Ha-Po'el ha-Ẓa'ir Central Committee, and was a delegate to the Prague conference in 1920 at which the Hitaḥadut – the union between Ha-Po'el ha-Ẓa'ir and Ẓe'irei Ẓiyyon – was established. She participated in the founding conference of the *Histadrut in 1920, and was elected to its Executive Committee. She was one of the founders of the Women's Workers Council (*Mo'eẓet ha-Po'alot) and its secretary in 1921–30. In 1930 she founded the Ayanot Agricultural School near Nes Ẓiyyonah, and headed it for many years. In 1946–47 Maimon headed the Immigration Department of the Histadrut, and in this capacity visited displaced persons camps in Germany and British detention camps in Cyprus. In 1949 she was elected to the First Knesset on the Mapai list. In the First and Second Knesset she was a member of the Constitution, Law and Justice Committee, and actively participated in initiating and passing legislation concerning the status of women. Unlike most other women labor leaders, she was also a member of the Executive of World *WIZO.

Ada Maimon wrote *Tenu'at ha-Po'alot be-Erez Yisrael* (1929), *Ha-Ḥaluẓah be-Erez-Yisrael* (1930), *Ayanot, Mi-Meshek Po'alot le-Veit Sefer Ḥakla'i Tikhon* (1946), *Ḥamishim Shenot Tenu'at ha-Po'alot, 1904–54* (1955), and *Le-Orekh ha-Derekh: Mivḥar Devarim ve-Iggerot* (1973).

[Susan Hattis Rolef (2nd ed.)]

MAIMON (Fishman), JUDAH LEIB (1875–1962), rabbi and leader of religious Zionism. Born in Marculeşti, Bessarabia, Maimon studied in Lithuanian yeshivot and, after being ordained, served as a preacher (*Maggid meisharim*) in Marculesti and in 1905–13 as rabbi in Ungeni. In 1900 he met Rabbi Isaac Jacob *Reines, founder of *Mizrachi, and afterward took an active part in the founding conference of Mizrachi, which was held in Vilna, and in its first world conference in Pressburg (Bratislava). Beginning with the Second Zionist Congress, he participated in all the subsequent Congresses and was for many years a member of the Zionist General Council. From 1935 he served as Mizrachi's representative on the Zionist Executive, was vice chairman of the Executive, and headed the Department for Artisans and Retail Business as well as the Department of Religious Affairs.

Maimon settled in Ereẓ Israel in 1913 and was among the founders of the educational network of Mizrachi there. At the outbreak of World War I he was imprisoned and expelled by the Turkish authorities. He went to the United States, where he was active in the effort to strengthen Mizrachi and published hundreds of articles in the press. He returned on the first ship to reach the shores of Palestine after the war and met Rabbi *Kook, with whom he became very friendly. Together they established the chief rabbinate of Palestine, and Maimon formulated the rabbinate's constitution and organized its founding ceremony. In 1936 he established the Mosad ha-Rav Kook, which published hundreds of books. His private library contained over 40,000 volumes, among them many very rare books, first editions, incunabula, and the only extant copies of many important manuscripts.

Although he maintained his adherence to the organized framework of the *yishuv*, Maimon often expressed his sympathy with the secessionist organizations, Irgun Ẓeva'i Le'ummi (IẒL) and Loḥamei Ḥerut Israel (Leḥi), and gave evidence on behalf of IẒL prisoners. He proclaimed the right of every Jew to bear arms in his own defense and in the defense of Jewish rights in Ereẓ Israel. When the Haganah began actively to suppress IẒL (1944–45), Maimon expressed his opposition to these activities. On "Black Saturday" (June 1946) he was interned as acting chairman of the Jewish Agency Executive. His imprisonment aroused a great furor, since the British had compelled him by force to desecrate the Sabbath, and after great pressure he was released by special order of the high commissioner.

In the first years after the establishment of the State of Israel, Maimon advocated the institution of a Sanhedrin as a supreme religious authority, but this attempt aroused opposition in many religious circles. He was appointed minister of religions and minister in charge of war casualties both in the provisional government and in the first elected one; and was a member of the First Knesset. He later relinquished his political activities and devoted himself entirely to literary work.

Maimon was a prolific author. His first work was *Ha-Noten ba-Yam Derekh* (1903). His second work *Ḥadar Horati*, a collection of articles on *halakhah*, Maimonides, and *aggadah*, was published ten years later. He also published other articles and biblical investigations. In 1907 he began to publish the talmudic-literary journal, *Ha-Yonah*, which was banned by censorship, however, and its publication discontinued. In 1921 Maimon founded the Mizrachi weekly, *Ha-Tor*, whose publication was continued for 15 years. He later founded and edited the monthly *Sinai*, of which he issued 50 volumes. His major work, *Sarei ha-Me'ah* (6 vols., 1942–47), describes the greatest Jewish scholars of the last century. His other writings include *Le-Ma'an Ẓiyyon Lo Eḥesheh* (2 vols., 1954–55), *Middei Ḥodesh be-Ḥodsho* (8 vols., 1955–62), *Ḥaggim u-Mo'adim* (1950^3), *Ha-Ẓiyyonut ha-Datit ve-Hitpatteḥutah* (1937), *Rabbi Moshe ben Maimon* (1959), *Toledot ha-Gra* (1954), and an edition of Judah b. Kalonymus' *Yiḥusei Tanna'im ve-Amora'im* (1942).

BIBLIOGRAPHY: G. Bat-Yehudah, *Elleh Toledot Rabbi J.L. Maimon* (1964); EẒD, 3 (1965), 422–94 (incl. comprehensive bibl.).

[Itzhak Goldshlag]

MAIMON, SOLOMON (1753–1800), philosopher. Maimon was born in Sukoviburg, Poland (now Belarus). He was a child prodigy in the study of rabbinical literature. Married at the age of 11 and a father at 14, Maimon supported his family by working as a tutor in neighboring towns. In his spare time he studied Jewish philosophy and Kabbalah; he adopted the name "Maimon" in honor of Maimonides. His attempt to demonstrate that the Kabbalah is based on philosophy caused the Ḥasidim with whom he associated to regard him as a heretic. He turned to the study of secular subjects and left his home and family to study in Berlin. In about 1777, after many hardships, he arrived at the gates of Berlin but was refused entry by officials of the Jewish community. After six months as a mendicant he arrived in Posen (Poznan), where he was received and aided by the rabbi, Ẓvi Hirsch b. Abraham. He taught for two years in Posen, but, finding the religious atmosphere of the community stifling, he made another trip to Berlin; this time he was able to enter the city.

In Berlin he became a member of Moses *Mendelssohn's circle, but was abandoned by Mendelssohn a few years later because of the dissolute life he led. Forced to leave Berlin, he moved first to Hamburg and then to Amsterdam. In Hamburg he beseeched a Lutheran pastor to convert him to Christianity, yet he confessed his disbelief in Christian doctrines. The pastor retorted that Maimon was too much a philosopher to be a Christian. Thereafter, between 1783 and 1786, with the help of some benefactors, he was able to study at the gymnasium of Altona. Still poverty-stricken, he moved from Altona to Berlin, then to Breslau, and in 1787 back to Berlin. There he studied Kantian philosophy and under its influence wrote his first work in German, *Versuch ueber die Transzendentalphilosophie* (1790). He sent a manuscript of the book to Marcus *Herz, who sent it to Immanuel *Kant. Kant remarked in a letter to Herz (May 26, 1789) that it was clear to him from a cursory study of the book that its value was very great, and that nobody understood his philosophy as well as Maimon (E. Cassirer (ed.), *Immanuel Kants Werke*, 9 (1918), 415). Kant's letter determined Maimon's future. He found a publisher for his book and scholarly journals accepted his articles for publication. From 1790 to 1795 Maimon was supported by a benefactor, Count Adolf Kalkreuth, at whose residences near Berlin and Freistadt, Silesia, he lived. When Maimon died, he was buried outside the Jewish cemetery as a heretic.

Other Works

In 1791 Maimon published a philosophical lexicon, containing a series of essays on the principal points of philosophy (new edition 1970). In 1793 he published his *Streifereien im Gebiete der Philosophie*, followed by three works on the history of philosophy: *Ueber die Progresse der Philosophie* (1793); *Versuch einer neuen Logik* (1794; 1812^2), in which he attempted to expound a system of logic; and *Die Kategorien des Aristoteles* (1794, 1798^2). In 1797 his work *Kritische Untersuchungen ueber den menschlichen Geist* was published.

Maimon also wrote the following works in Hebrew, but only the first was published: *Givat ha-Moreh* (1791; ed. by S.H. Bergman and N. Rotenstreich, 1966), a commentary on the first part of Maimonides' *Guide of the Perplexed; Ta'alumot Ḥokhmah*, on mathematical physics; and *Ḥeshek Shelomo*, which was divided into four parts, namely "*Ma'aseh Nissim*," on the 12 sermons of Nissim b. Reuben Gerondi, "*Eved Avraham*," on Ibn Ezra's commentary on the Pentateuch and Psalms, "*Ma'aseh Livnat ha-Sappir*," which are reflections, and "*Ma'aseh Ḥoshev*," on algebra. Maimon's autobiography (*Solomon Maimons Lebengeschichte, von ihm selbst geschrieben*), his only book to win wide acclaim, was published in Berlin in 1793 (Eng. trans. by M. Hadas (1947) and S.H. Bergmann (ed.; 1954); Heb. trans. (1942). It is an important source for the study of Judaism and Ḥasidism in Eastern Europe in that period. The 12th chapter describes Mendelssohn and his thought.

Philosophy

To account for the origin of knowledge and its objectivity, the German philosopher Kant had posited the "thing-in-itself" as something existing outside the mind but unknowable in itself. Maimon's main contribution was to give a new direction to Kant's discussion of it. Maimon agreed with Kant that the cognition process must have a cause and that this cause must also guarantee the objectivity of the knowledge. But he differed from Kant by holding that this cause exists in the mind, not outside it. Invoking Kant's distinction between sensibility and understanding, Maimon affirmed that the concepts of understanding arise from perceptions of sensibility, which he appears to assume are the same for everyone, and which therefore guarantee their objectivity. Maimon maintained further that sensibility is a kind of understanding, but more limited and imperfect than understanding itself.

The "thing-in-itself" had another meaning for Maimon, namely, as the final goal toward which all cognition tends. Our knowledge is always fragmentary, but as it increases it approaches an ideal knowledge. This may be illustrated by a polygon, which approaches a circle as sides are added, but does not reach it.

INFINITE INTELLECT. While Maimon rejected Kant's extramental "thing-in-itself" as the cause of knowledge and the guarantor of its objectivity, he still had to answer Kant's question of how knowledge is related to a world outside the mind. In his words, "To find a passage from the external world to the mental world is more important than to find a way to East India, no matter what statesmen may say." Maimon bridged this gap by assuming that our sensibility is only an imperfect expression of intellectual reality which underlies the world. Hence the objects of the outside world presented to sensibility are concepts and their relations. But since concepts and their relations must inhere in some intellect, Maimon posits an infinite intellect. Our intellect is derived from this infinite intellect. As finite creatures we can only comprehend a small portion of this rational structure of the world.

The assumption of an infinite intellect permits Maimon to bridge the gap between the intra-mental and extral-mental worlds. But the infinite intellect, in turn, does not receive concepts from objects lying outside of it; rather, it creates objects from within itself. There is no distinction between the form of knowledge and its content. Maimon summarized his position: "We posit... an infinite intellect... which creates out of itself all possible kinds of relations of things. Our intellect is the very same intellect, but in a more limited degree."

LAW OF DETERMINABILITY. Maimon had to face the further problem of how to describe the mode of thinking of the infinite intellect, that is, how the concepts cohere to create the structure of the rational world. To answer that question Maimon formulated the "law of determinability" ("*Satz der Bestimmbarkeit*"). One account of this complex notion was based on Kant's distinction between analytic and synthetic judgments. Analytic judgments, whose form is "A is A," are tautological and they do not produce knowledge; synthetic judgments, whose form is "A is B," produce certain knowledge. Maimon criticizes Kant's notion that synthetic judgments are certain, since in his view subject and predicate in these judgments are foreign to one another. Against Kant's two kinds of judgments, Maimon posited a third – the "law of determinability" – according to which there exists a judgment which is both analytic and synthetic. Using the proposition "the color is blue," Maimon states that the subject (the color) can exist without the predicate (blue), and, hence, the relation between subject and predicate is synthetic; on the other hand, the predicate (blue) cannot exist alone but only in connection with the subject and, hence, it is analytic. Maimon had hoped that through this law he could open new possibilities for metaphysics, but he was too careful a philosopher to attempt to build this speculative structure himself.

MAIMON'S SKEPTICISM. Despite the rationalist structure of his idealist philosophy, Maimon exhibited a skeptical streak. While he claimed that the hypothesis of an infinite intellect and the discovery of the law of determinability provide the possibility of viewing the world as a rational structure, he never claimed that one could know with certainty that this rational structure in fact exists in the world. The kind of doubts raised by skeptical philosophers such as David Hume remained. Philosophy can only show that it is possible to construct a rational structure for the world, but it cannot show that this rational structure exists in fact. Hence, one can only philosophize "conditionally."

Maimon's philosophy strongly influenced the philosopher Johann Fichte and, through Fichte, German idealist philosophy. During the 19th century, Maimon was neglected; as a result of the efforts of the historian of philosophy J.E. Erdmann (in his *History of Philosophy* (1892^3), index), however, interest in Maimon has been revived in the 20th century. In recent years several basic books dealing with his system have appeared. A new photostatic edition of his collected works began to appear in 1965.

BIBLIOGRAPHY: N.J. Jacobs, in: KS, 41 (1965/66), 245–62 (bibl. of his writings and writings about him); S.H. Bergman, *The Philosophy of Solomon Maimon* (1967). **ADD. BIBLIOGRAPHY:** G. Freudenthal, *Salomon Maimon: Rational Dogmatist, Empirical Sceptic* (2003).

[Samuel Hugo Bergman]

MAIMON, YA'ACOV (1902–1977), Israel government stenographer. In 1976 Maimon was awarded the Israel Prize for services in immigrant absorption. Born in Russia, Maimon immigrated in 1922. With the influx of immigrants to Israel after the establishment of the state he devoted himself, in a voluntary capacity, to the absorption of immigrants and organized hundreds of volunteers who followed his example. Maimon served as the official stenographer of the government and invented the system of Hebrew stenography.

MAIMON BEN JOSEPH (d. 1165/1170), Spanish rabbi and *dayyan*; father of *Maimonides. Maimon studied in Lucena under Joseph *Ibn Migash, and transmitted his teachings, both oral and in writing, to his son, who utilized them as the basis for his own halakhic works. Maimon was a *dayyan* of Cordoba for many years, until he and his family were compelled to leave, in consequence of the edict of forced conversion issued by the *Almohads after their conquest of the city about 1149. For about ten years he wandered through Spain and probably also Provence. About 1160 he immigrated with his family to Fez, Morocco, where it was easier for forced converts to preserve their Judaism. In Fez he forbade the people to follow the false messiah, Moses Dari, who was popular there at the time. In 1165 he proceeded to Ereẓ Israel, where he died, possibly in the following year. According to one tradition, his grave is in Tiberias. Some scholars think, however, that he went to Egypt with his son and died there.

Maimon was one of the most outstanding and influential scholars of his generation and the first of his distinguished family of whom a written work is known. His *Iggeret ha-Neḥamah*, written in his second year in Fez (published in the original Arabic by M. Simons, see bibliography; and in a scholarly Hebrew translation by B. Klar, 1945), was designed to comfort and guide the forced converts of Islam in their effort to preserve their Judaism. "We who are in exile can be compared to a man who is drowning. The water has reached our nostrils but we still grasp hold of something … and as the water threatens to engulf us, behold, a rope consisting of God's precepts and His Torah dangles from heaven to earth. Whoever seizes hold of it still has hope of living … and surely he who holds on even only with the tips of his fingers has more hope than he who lets go completely."

Maimon's fundamental premise – later adopted by his son Maimonides and accepted as law among Jews in Islamic countries – is that Islam, in that it is free from personification of the Deity, is not to be regarded as idolatry. In keeping with this view, he opposed martyrdom to avoid conversion to Islam. Unlike other scholars, who left the people without hope, Maimon asserts that those who perform the precepts in secret will be rewarded, laying particular stress on the value of reciting the *Amidah three times daily, even in its abridged form, and even in Arabic. He also places great emphasis upon the importance of belief in the divinity of the mission of Moses, to whose virtues the work is largely devoted, comparing such belief to belief in God Himself. This principle, later embodied by Maimonides in his 13 principles, was designed to nullify belief in the divine mission of Mohammed, for which reason Maimon also stresses that Daniel was the last of the prophets. Maimon's work reflects the spirit of despair that had seized the Jews of the countries during the time of the Almohads, and it fortified his readers that the tyrannical rule would not continue for long, as had been promised by the prophets. Maimon also wrote commentaries to the Talmud, from which his son quotes abundantly; a book on the laws of prayer and the festivals, from which only isolated quotations have been preserved (Simon b. Zemaḥ Duran,*Tashbeẓ*, 1, no. 2); responsa, a number of which have been published by A.H. Freimann (see bibl.); a commentary on the Torah; a work on the laws of ritual purity; and, apparently, an exposition of an Arabic astronomical book. With the exception of the responsa, all his works were written in Arabic.

BIBLIOGRAPHY: Marmorstein, in: *Sefer ha-Rambam shel ha-Tarbiz* (1935), 182–4 (= *Tarbiz*, 6 (1934/35), 426–8); Freimann, *ibid.*, 164–76 (= *Tarbiz*, 6 (1934/35), 408–20; idem, in: *Alummah*, 1 (1936), 9–13; J.L. Fishman, in: Maimon b. Joseph, *Iggeret ha-Neḥamah*, tr. by B. Klar (1945), introd.; Halkin, in: *Joshua Starr Memorial Volume* (1953), 102–3; Hirschberg, Afrikah, 1 (1965), 100f., 122–4, 263; Simons, in: JQR, 2 (1890), 62–66, 335–69; J.M. Toledano, *Sarid u-Falit*, 1 (1960), 7–8.

[Israel Moses Ta-Shma]

MAIMONIDEAN CONTROVERSY, a vast complex of disputed cultural, religious, and social problems, focusing around several central themes. Some of the elements of this controversy considerably antedate *Maimonides (1135–1204); and of the questions brought into sharp relief by his ideas and writings, some have remained topical in many Jewish circles. Vast fields of human experience and thought are encompassed by it: reason and philosophy in their relation to faith and tradition; what components are permitted and what prohibited in the education of a man following the Torah; the proper understanding of *anthropomorphism as expressed in the Bible and Talmud; central theological concepts such as the *resurrection of the body; and the very form of Maimonides' *Mishneh Torah* and its attitude toward talmudic discussion. The question of hierarchical leadership versus intellectual, personal leadership was one of the early causes of this controversy. In the Middle Ages the controversy had four climaxes: (1) during the last years of Maimonides' life, following the publication of his Mishneh Torah in 1180 until his death in 1204; (2) around 1230–35, involving David *Kimḥi, *Solomon b. Abraham of Montpellier, *Naḥmanides and others, and centering in *Provence; (3) the years 1288–90 in the Near East, involving Solomon Petit and Rabbi Isaac of Acre; (4) around 1300–06, involving Abba Mari b. Moses *Astruc, Solomon b. Abraham *Adret, *Asher b. Jehiel, *Jedaiah b. Abraham Bedersi (ha-Penini, and Menahem b. Solomon *Meiri, and centering in Christian Spain and Provence. In between these moments when the conflict flared up anew and reached climaxes as a result of specific circumstances and the personalities involved, tensions and disputes continued among proponents and opponents of philosophy and Maimonides.

Although it is convenient to frame the four climaxes of the controversy as distinct historical stages, recent research has led to a reappraisal, in light of which these climaxes cannot be characterized as separate stages in a homogeneous process. It is certainly true that there were some essential differences among the stages. For example: in the fourth and final stage Maimonides himself no longer was the subject of the controversy, and even the conservative party accepted his positions, whereas in the early stages his *Guide of the Perplexed* and *Book of Knowledge* (the first section of the *Mishneh Torah*, containing philosophical material) were the main target; in the early stages the opposition was to philosophy per se, whereas in the latter stages the opposition was to unrestricted access to and teaching of philosophy, not a total rejection of it. Historians of the controversy over Maimonides and philosophy have tended to focus on extreme positions in each period, which lend themselves to simple characterization. On the other hand, the evidence increasingly supports the view that many Jewish intellectuals did not fall into either extreme camp – that of excessive rationalist allegorization or that of opposition in principle to all "foreign wisdom." Many of the rationalist camp were strictly observant in their personal life and maintained the supremacy of the authority of the Torah, such as Judah b. Samuel ibn Abbas and Kalonymos, who were confirmed rationalists but rejected extreme philosophical positions. At the same time, among the conservative halakhic authorities were those who did not object in principle to the study of philosophy (to the contrary, they themselves had philosophical educations) but only to premature exposure of the youth to philosophy and to extreme rationalist allegorization, especially in public sermons in the synagogue. Abba Mari *Astruc ha-Yarḥi, for example, who played a major role in promoting the limited Barcelona ban on philosophy in the fourth and final climax of the controversy (1305), wrote a philosophical work, *Sefer ha-Yare'aḥ*, which in many respects is rationalist in outlook.

The crisis of Spanish Jewry in the 15th century accentuated the main educational and social themes of the old controversy. In Renaissance Italy and in the diversified and flourishing Jewish center of Poland-Lithuania the old quarrel again became topical, though in a milder form. With the enlightenment (*Haskalah) of the 18th century the "Maimonidean side" of the controversy was given a new, greatly secularized, and radical expression by Moses *Mendelssohn and his followers – an expression that could scarely have been imagined by the former protagonists. In German *neo-Orthodoxy, the "Maimonidean side" – particularly in its striving for a synthesis of Jewish faith and "general culture," as well as in certain of its social tendencies – found a new, conservative expression. In Yemen in the 19th century and well into the 20th, there was a distinct "Maimonidean camp" and a struggle against it (see Kafaḥ).

In the last two decades of the 20th century and the first years of the 21st century, Maimonides again became the focus of a controversy in ultra-Orthodoxy, as a result of the emphasis placed by Rabbi Menaḥem Mendel *Schneersohn of Chabad-Lubavitch Ḥasidism on the study of the *Mishneh Torah*. The non-ḥasidic leadership, in particular of the Lithuanian type of yeshivah, vehemently rejected placing Maimonides at the center of the curriculum in place of such classic codes as Joseph Caro's *Shulḥan Arukh*.

The First Clash: During Maimonides' Lifetime

Through the charisma of his personality and the trend of his thought and leadership Maimonides himself initiated this. An exile from Muslim Spain, he met in the Near East the hierarchical traditions of the exilarchate and the *geonim*. Maimonides was willing and ready to respect the *exilarch as scion of the royal house of David and as the proper authority, from the halakhic point of view, to appoint and ordain judges.

His mind and heart vehemently opposed the claims of the *geonim*. He criticized sharply the way they:

> fixed for themselves monetary demands from individuals and communities and caused people to think, in utter foolishness, that it is obligatory and proper that they should help sages and scholars and people studying Torah … all this is wrong. There is not a single word, either in the Torah or in the sayings of the [talmudic] sages, to lend credence to it … for as we look into the sayings of the talmudic sages, we do not find that they ask people for money, nor did they collect money for the honorable and cherished academies (commentary to Avot 4:5).

This attempt to undermine the economic and social foundations of the leadership of the Babylonian *geonim* went hand in hand with Maimonides' opposition to their program of studies and his contempt for their very office. The *Gaon* at Baghdad at this time was *Samuel b. Ali, a strong and authoritarian personality. In an ironic "apology" for Samuel b. Ali's attacks on the *Mishneh Torah*, Maimonides explains to one of his pupils:

> Why, my son, should you take offense that a man whom people accustom from his youth to believe that there is none like him

> in his generation; when age, high office, aristocratic descent, the lack of people of discernment in this town, and his relationship with individuals, all have combined to produce this execrable consequence that each and every individual hangs expectantly on each word pronounced from the academy in anticipation of an honorific title from there… – why do you wonder that he has acquired such [evil] traits? How, my son, could you imagine that he should love truth enough to acknowledge his weakness?… This is a thing that a man like him will never do, as it was not done by better men who preceded him (letter to Joseph b. Judah in: D.H. Baneth (ed.), *Iggerot ha-Rambam* (1946), 54f.).

The gaonate is represented as corrupt, and typical academy study as being of questionable value. Concerning Zechariah, the son-in-law of the *Gaon*, Maimonides writes:

> He is a very foolish man. He studies very hard at this talmudic discussion and its commentaries, and thinks that he is the greatest of his generation, having already attained the peak of perfection. My esteemed son knows that my appreciation of the greatest of the sages of Israel is such that I evaluate their worth according to their own criteria. They themselves have defined 'the argumentations [*havayot*] of *Abbaye and *Rava [as] a small matter.' If this is a small matter, why should I pay attention to an old man who is really miserable, an ignoramus in every respect? To my eyes he is like a newborn baby; one has to defend him, according to the measure of his [Zechariah's] foolishness (*ibid.*, 56ff.; the bulk of this passage has been erased in most manuscripts).

This vehement revolt against the authority of the *geonim* came at a time when Samuel b. Ali was attempting to minimize the authority of the exilarch on the grounds that what the people needed then was no more than the leadership of the *geonim* and the guidance of their study in the academy. Small wonder that such a revolt aroused reciprocal anger, coming, as it did, in defense of Maimonides' *Mishneh Torah* which claimed expressly (in the introduction) to supersede the Talmud in popular usage, replacing its deliberations – the very core and substance of the life of academies and *geonim* – by his systematic code. The claim of the intellectual to replace an aristocratic hierarchy seemed to be combined with an attempt to impose Greek systematic modes of codification in place of the traditional many-voiced flow of talmudic discussion. It is hardly suprising that Samuel b. Ali, Zechariah, and *Daniel b. Saadiah ha-Bavli all sought and found halakhic flaws in this code. Some of their arguments have philosophical and theological overtones, but these were to come to the forefront only in the second stage of the controversy. In the main, in this phase, it was Maimonides' creativity which was found provocative, as well as his attitude to Talmud study and to the leadership of established institutions, all of which were being defended against him.

The First Stage in Europe

In this first flare-up, the controversy was thus not over philosophy as such, or over Maimonides' philosophy in particular, since his *Guide of the Perplexed* was translated into Hebrew only at the very end of his life. The criticism was leveled primarily against his *Mishneh Torah* and his attitude toward resurrection. The criticism of the *Mishneh Torah* focused on Maimonides' methodology, the fact that he did not cite sources for his decisions, and his claim that the study of his Code would replace the study of Talmud: "A person should study the written Torah first, and then read this [book], and thereby know the entire oral Torah, so that he will not need to read any other book in between them." The criticism also reflected divergent local traditions and custom (*minhag*). Maimonides' great Ashkenazi critic, R. *Abraham b. David of Posquières (Ravad), in his critical gloss (*hasagah*) to the Introduction to the *Mishneh Torah*, asserted that Maimonides "has abandoned the method of all the authors who preceded him, because they brought proofs for their words, and cited their sources … But this way, I do not know why I should disregard my tradition and my proof for the sake of this author's book." Ravad also attacked Maimonides on theoretical issues. Maimonides had categorized as a heretic (*min*) anyone who affirms that there is one God but that God has a body (Yad, Teshuvah 3:7). In his *hasagah* to this passage, Ravad protested: "Why did he call such a person a heretic, when some who were greater and better than he followed this opinion, according to what they found in the Bible and even more, according to what they found in *aggadot* which corrupt opinions?" What is significant here is not that Ravad defended corporealist beliefs – he also rejected the corporealism of "*aggadot* which corrupt opinions" – but that he attacked the legitimacy of Maimonides' categorization of such corrupt opinions as heresy.

As for the criticism of Maimonides' regarding the traditional belief in bodily resurrection, because of his consistent emphasis on an intellectualist understanding of the world to come (*olam ha-ba*) in terms of the survival only of the actual intellect in proportion to its attainment of knowledge, Ravad wrote (on Yad, Teshuvah 8:2): "The words of this man seem close to one who says that there is no bodily resurrection of the dead, but only of the soul." Others were equally critical of Maimonides' apparent denial of resurrection.

Ramah (R. Meir b. Todros ha-Levi *Abulafia), who was active in the first two climaxes of the controversy, was in many respects a sincere admirer of Maimonides. In the first period he was shocked at the implication that Maimonides did not affirm the resurrection of the body as a halakhic principle. In an angry letter sent to the scholars of *Lunel he not only sought to prove by copious quotations the dogmatic truth of bodily resurrection, but also added passionately that if there is no such resurrection, "to what end did the bodies stand watch for their God, did they go in darkness for the sake of their God? If the bodies are not resurrected, where is their hope and where are they to look for it?" (*Kitāb al-Rasīl'* (1871), 14). Abulafia also attacked Maimonides on other halakhic points. It was only after he saw Maimonides' *Treatise on Resurrection* that he became satisfied that Maimonides, in fact, affirmed the traditional belief. While some of his correspondents agreed with his earlier criticism, others tried to convince him that he had misunderstood the purport of Maimonides' teaching on resurrection, and this latter view was accepted wholeheartedly by the *nasi* Sheshet b. Isaac of Saragossa, who in a very radical sense gave expression to Maimonides' rationalism and philosophic synthesis. Writing about 1200, he attacked sharply and derisively what he regarded as the simplicism and materialism of Abulafia's view (A. Marx, in: JQR, 25, (1934/35), 406–28). To speak about bodily resurrection is "to bring down our saintly fathers from the highest level – the status of the angels who enjoy divine glory and live forever – to the status of man, through their returning to the impure body which cannot exist except through food and drink, and must end in dust and worms ... but the life of wisdom is greater than foolishness, as light is greater than darkness. These notions seem to me like the words of one confused" (*ibid.*, 418). The only correct conception of resurrection, he thought, is the one also accepted by the pagan philosophers. Resurrection means the eternal life of the soul of the sage-philosopher. "If the soul – while still in the body – was yearning for its Creator, subordinating its passion to its reason, [then] when it leaves the body, [it] will attain the highest status, for which it yearned while still in the body; and over it God will emanate of His spirit. This, in the view of the sages, is the resurrection of the dead and the reward of the just at the end of days" (*ibid.*, 421ff.). All pronouncements in the Bible and the Talmud about bodily resurrection are only for the simple men who constitute the majority of mankind and who understand only material rewards, and the same holds true for the Muslim paradise (*ibid.*, 424).

> I ask this fool who maintains that the souls will return to the dead corpses and that they are destined to return to the soil of Israel. Into which body will the soul return? If it is to the body from which it has departed, [then this will] already have returned to its elements thousands of years earlier; [it is now] earth, dust, and worms. Where it has been buried, a house has been built, a vineyard planted, or some other plants have taken root and you cannot find the earth or the dust or the worms into which the body has turned. If, however, this soul is to return to another body, which God will create, then it is another man who will be created in his own time, and has not been dead; how, then can you say that he is being resurrected and that God rewards him, as he has not as yet achieved anything? (*ibid.*, 426).

Sheshet records opposition to the *Mishneh Torah* by reporting the opinion of one of the judges who quarreled with him and refused to judge according to Maimonides: "As he does not adduce proofs from the sayings of the talmudic sages for his decisions, who is going to follow his opinion? It is far better to study Talmud. We will have nothing to do with his books and his writings." In Sheshet's view this opposition stems from the fact that until the *Mishneh Torah* the whole matter of legal decision was so confused that the vast majority of Jews, being ignorant of the Talmud, had to obey their judges, whereas now people had before them a clear and open code and were not dependent on judges alone (*ibid.*, 427).

Maimonides was aware of the criticism leveled against him, and responded to it by his *Treatise on Resurrection* (*Maqalah fi Teḥiyat ha-Metim*, 1190–91). Maimonides' defense of resurrection in that work was accepted at face value by such early critics as Ramah (Rabbi Meir b. Todros ha-Levi Abulafia), who then retracted his criticism. Ravad's critical glosses were incorporated into standard editions of the *Mishneh Torah*. So the first climax in the Maimonidean controversy subsided with Maimonides death in 1204, but the criticism of the *Mishneh Torah* was preserved for later generations together with the Code itself.

The Second Climax: 1230–1235 in Europe

What led to periodic controversies over Maimonides and philosophy? In the first period, as we have seen, it was Maimonides' enormous status which led towards the end of his life to the rapid availability in Hebrew of his works in Europe, including his *Guide of the Perplexed*, outside his own immediate sphere of influence. It was this almost immediate availability of his philosophical views in areas previously unexposed to philosophical culture which in turn aroused resistance. In the second period, external circumstances contributed to the flare-up of the controversy. Furthermore, whereas Maimonides himself was the subject of controversy in the first period, he was merely the catalyst for a much broader and fundamental controversy in the second period, when philosophy itself came under sharp attack. In addition, whereas Maimonides, however much his views were criticized in the earlier period, was personally highly regarded, in the later period the philosophers themselves were attacked and subject to suspicion.

Maimonides' works reached Christian Europe, chiefly in the southwest – Spain and Provence – entering a cultural and social climate very different from the one in which they had been created in the Arabic-Islamic culture of Egypt. As we have seen, Maimonides' authority in the *Mishneh Torah* had been criticized halakhically by Ravad and *Moses ha-Kohen, among others. The Christian Reconquest was proceeding apace in the Iberian peninsula. Mystical tendencies and visionary approaches began to find explicit and strong expression in the developing *Kabbalah of Provence and Spain. Jews everywhere were suffering from the impact of the *Crusades, with martyrdom (**Kiddush ha-Shem*) in their wake. Maimonides' grand attempt at a synthesis between the Jewish faith and Greek-Arabic Aristotelian philosophy was received with enthusiasm in some circles, mainly of the upper strata of Jewish society, and with horror and dismay in others, imbued with mysticism and dreading the effects of Greek thought on Jewish beliefs. The old and continuously smoldering issue of "Athens versus Jerusalem" conceived in the Talmud as the problem of "Greek wisdom" – *ḥokhmah yevanit* (BK 82b–83a; Meg. 9a–b), now burst into flames. Essentially the problem is one of the possible synthesis or the absolute antithesis between monotheistic revealed faith and intellectually formulated philosophy. Both faith, based on revelation, and philosophy, based on human reason, were understood to fundamentally contradict each other's methodology and undermine each other's authority. The rational method of inquiry, which in classical and medieval times was equated with science (the distinction between philosophy and the natural sciences being a modern phenomenon), is an open system. It can lead to any conclusion, and the conclusion is justified and necessitated by the integrity of the method of inquiry itself, which can be replicated by others; furthermore, it is universal, transcending national, cultural, or religious differences. Faith, which differs from scientific knowledge precisely in that it involves an affirmation of truth without conclusive and demonstrative proof, basically is a closed system which reverses the process of inquiry: one begins with the conclusion, which is given as a revealed fact, which one can then subject after the fact to rational analysis and explication, but which cannot itself be rejected or denied. Faith, moreover, begins with revelation occurring within a particular national, cultural, linguistic, or religious context, and its authority is thus conventional, even if it claims to be ultimately universal in its significance and application.

This problem is common to Judaism, Christianity, and Islam. In the view of H.A. Wolfson, all of Western religious philosophy, whether in Hebrew, Latin, or Arabic "garb," is essentially the same regarding the problematical relationship between revelation and reason. In Wolfson's scheme, *Philo was the first "synthetic" philosopher, and the greatest figure in the history of Western philosophy after Plato and Aristotle, because he attempted to synthesize biblical revelation (which did not know philosophy) and philosophy (which was pagan and did not know revelation), and all subsequent philosophy in the Middle Ages was "Philonic" in structure, until Spinoza destroyed that structure and made possible modern philosophy by freeing philosophy from revelation (Wolfson, *Philo: Foundations of Religious Philosophy in Judaism, Christianity and Islam* (1947)).

In all three traditions, therefore, tensions exist between rationalistic religious belief, inclining in the main toward synthesis, and mystic belief, which is largely opposed to it.

The problem was not new in Judaism. In Islamic countries in the tenth century it was in the main decided in favor of rationalism and synthesis. Maimonides was not the only one in the 12th century who expressly sought a synthesis between Greek philosophy and Judaism; a philosophic approach was attempted by Abraham *Ibn Daud (see, e.g., his *Sefer ha-Emunah ha-Ramah* (1852), 2, 58), and he was preceded by a rationalist tradition of synthesis going back to *Saadiah Gaon and *Samuel b. Hophni who denied the historical veracity of the incident of Samuel and the Witch of Endor.

Yet in Maimonides' time radical changes were taking place in Jewish communities in Europe. The influence of the Christian environment became more pervasive. Increasingly, Christianity was involved in similar problems, as the conflict between Peter *Abelard and *Bernard of Clairvaux clearly shows. After the Crusaders captured Constantinople in 1204 (the year of Maimonides' death), the Greek works of Aristotle became directly accessible to Western Christians, who no longer had to rely on Latin translations of the Greek texts made (often by Jews) from Arabic or from Hebrew versions based on Arabic translations from the Greek. The growing universities increasingly challenged the monasteries as centers of learning. While the traditional doctrines of the Church were being confronted by secular learning, Christian Orthodoxy was also challenged in the 12th and 13th centuries by "heresies," especially that of Cathari and the related heresy of the rationalist Albigensians, who had begun in the 11th century to interpret Scripture allegorically and who denied the literal interpretation of the miraculous events of Jesus' life and death that was central to Catholic dogma. Such "heresy" spread especially among the upper classes. The Church moved against both threats in the first decades of the 13th century. Against the threat of secular philosophy, the Church issued repeated bans on the study of Aristotle and commentaries on his works. Pope Innocent III launched the Albigensian Crusade, to eliminate the heresy (which he regarded as instigated by educated Jews). In 1231 the bans on Aristotle were renewed by Pope Gregory IX, who established the permanent Inquisition under the Dominicans, with the aim of completely eradicating Albigensianism. There were, in fact, certain parallels between the Christian Albigensian "heresy" and the Jewish philosophers of the day, at least in the eyes of their respective opponents, who accused them of indiscriminate allegorization of Scripture and of antinomian laxity in moral or ritual behavior. The stormy winds of anti-rationalism in the Christian environment were a contributing factor in the exacerbation of long existing, if usually dormant, tensions within the Jewish community.

Social upheavals in Jewish society during the 12th and 13th centuries also added communal tension to the spiritual strife. When Maimonides was still young, and most of his work as yet unwritten, *Judah Halevi warned: "Turn aside from mines and pitfalls. Let not Greek wisdom tempt you, for it bears flowers only and no fruit.… Listen to the confused words of her sages built on the void.… Why should I search for bypaths, and complicated ones at that, and leave the main road?" (from his poem beginning *"Devarekha be-Mor Over Rekuḥim"*).

Maimonides' prestige and the external pressures thus combined in a volatile mixture for Jews in Europe. Despite common admiration for Maimonides and his all-embracing devotion to Torah and the Jewish faith, there was in reality no common language between the two radical positions. Gradually the opponents of Maimonides began to attack his very conception of a synthesis between Greek philosophy and Jewish faith.

Solomon b. Abraham of Montpellier, together with David b. Saul and *Jonah b. Abraham Gerondi (a relative of *Nahmanides) agitated against philosophy, and in 1232 succeeded in persuading the rabbis of northern France to issue a total ban on the study of philosophy, including Maimonides' *Guide of the Perplexed* and *Book of Knowledge* (the first section, containing philosophical material, of the *Mishneh Torah*). The traditionalists' arguments against philosophy were based on three oft-repeated claims (recurring in the later stages of the controversy as well), which were consistently denied by the philosophers: (1) *Theological* – The philosophers were depicted as denying miracles, as regarding prophecy as a purely natural phenomenon, as undermining the authority of the Torah, and as rejecting traditional eschatology; (2) *Exigetical* – The traditionalists charged the philosophers with engaging in indiscriminate allegorization of Scripture and of denying the historicity of various biblical persons and events; (3) *Practical* – The philosophers were suspected of laxity in observance of the commandments.

The controversy of the 1230s also involved exchanges of letters, many between the philosopher and biblical exegete Radak (David *Kimḥi) and the physician and courtier, Judah *Ibn Alfakhar. Remarkably, the letters from both sides of the controversy were preserved in a collection *Iggerot Kena'ot*, "Letters of Zealotry" (published in *Kovez̧ Teshuvot ha-Rambam*, Leipzig, 1859). When Kimḥi traveled about the communities of Provence to rally the supporters of Maimonides, he was greatly surprised to be answered by Judah ibn Alfakhar with a bitter attack on Maimonides' very attempt to rationalize and explain away miracles and wondrous tales. Ibn Alfakhar was against half acceptance; logical proofs were not so important, "for each true proof needs great checking, since sometimes it may include misleading elements of that false wisdom called sophistry in Greek, and when a proof is joined to this it misleads even sages." Maimonides' "erroneous" intention was to explain matters according to the laws of philosophy and nature "so as to put the Torah and Greek wisdom together, to make out of them one whole." He imagined that the one would live with the other like two loving twin deers. In reality this has resulted in sorrow and dissension, for they cannot live together on the earth and be like two sisters, for the Hebrew women are not like the Egyptian ones. To this our Torah says: 'No, my son is the living one, and yours is the dead' (I Kings 3:22) and her rival angers her. I want peace; if I start to talk to them, they go to war" (letter to Kimḥi, *Iggerot Qena'ot*, 2a). Thus, through radical rationalistic argumentation, this physician and courtier in Spain rejects the synthesis of the physician and courtier in Egypt and the logical compromise it involves. As suggested by S. Harvey (1987), the dispute of the 1230s between Kimḥi and Alfakhar may well have served as the model for the book "The Epistle of the Debate" by Shem Tov ibn *Falaquera, who was a participant in the next, third climax of the controversy.

The demand for logical consistency was also answered from the Maimonidean camp. Increasingly they inclined toward extreme allegoristic explanations of talmudic and even biblical expressions and tales. Their opponents accused them of even inclining to explain away as no more than symbols certain practical commandments, which need be fulfilled only by simple men, but not by educated people. The rationalists denied this. Social overtones became stronger. The anti-Maimonideans berated their upper-class opponents for their hedonistic, luxurious, and sinful way of life. The Maimonideans countered by accusing their adversaries with anarchy, harshness, ignorance, simplicity of mind, and of being under Christian influence.

The anti-Maimonidean camp turned to the great sages of northern France. Never having been acquainted with Aristotelian philosophy, they never felt the need for synthesis with it; therefore, they unhesitatingly pronounced a *ḥerem* on Maimonides' philosophical works. Some report that they excommunicated even parts of his halakhic code. In Provence and Spain the anti-Maimonidean camp was led by Solomon b. Abraham of Montpellier, *Jonah b. Abraham Gerondi, the poet Meshullam *da Piera, and above all Naḥmanides. The position of Naḥmanides is remarkable for its simultaneous flexibility in expression and rigidity of mental attitude. Seeing that the extreme anti-Maimonidean stance taken by the rabbis of northern France and by Solomon of Montpellier had no chance of finding support among the leading circles of Jewish society in Provence and Spain, he therefore advised the anti-Maimonidean camp to adopt a moderate stand in order to achieve at least what was possible. Writing to the north French rabbis (printed in: MGWJ, 9 (1860), 184–95) he expresses his devotion and admiration, but he humbly submits that they "are nourished in the bosom of [true] faith, planted in the courts of tradition," and therefore had to understand Maimonides in his peculiar cultural and social circumstances. The situation he describes is actually that of Spanish and Provençal Jewish upper society in the early 13th century:

> They have filled their belly with the foolishness of the Greeks ... they ... make fun ... of the trusting souls.... They did not enter profoundly into the ways of our Torah; the ways of alien children suffice for them. But for the words of [Maimonides], but for the fact that they live out of the mouth of his works ... they would have slipped almost entirely.

It is not only a matter of false spiritual pride and alien culture; it is also a case born of social necessity:

> God save and guard us, my teachers, from such a fate. Look about and see: is there a pain like our pain? For the sons have been exiled from their fathers' tables; they have defiled themselves with the food of gentiles and the wine of their feasts. They have mixed with them and become used to their deeds ... courtiers have been permitted to study Greek wisdom, to become acquainted with medicine, to learn mathematics and geometry, other knowledge and tricks, so that they make a living in royal courts and palaces.

This intrinsically hostile description of the life of the upper classes of Jewish society in Provence and Spain is given in order to put Maimonides in the light of a great talmudic sage who – argues Naḥmanides – would certainly and gladly have written and lived as the northern French rabbis did. Alas, it was not granted him: "Did he trouble himself for your sake, you geniuses of the Talmud? He saw himself compelled and constrained to structure a work which would offer refuge from the Greek philosophers.... Have you ever listened to their words, have you ever been misled by their proofs?" He goes on to explain that extremism would bring about an irreparable split. It is far better to educate gradually this misled society and bring it back to the right way of northern France, by partial prohibitions only. The region most afflicted is Provence; Spain he considers to be in far better order.

Naḥmanides was merely temporizing in his writings to the northern French rabbis. His true temper and the temper of the entire anti-Maimonidean camp is revealed in his commentary on the Torah, which is basically a mystical work against Maimonides and Abraham *Ibn Ezra. The very concept of a system of laws of nature ordained by God in His wisdom to be admired by man through his reason, as expressed by Maimonides (see, e.g., *Mishneh Torah, Sefer ha-Madda*), he and his colleagues believe to be sheer heresy. The workings of nature are to be conceived of only and always as "hidden miracles." God performs extraordinary *miracles in order that we should understand the miraculous nature of all existence and life:

> Through the great and famous miracles man recognizes the hidden foundation of the entire Torah. For no man has a share in the Torah of Moses until we believe that all our matters and accidents are miracles, the product neither of nature nor of the way of the world, whether for the multitude or for the individual; but if a man fulfills the commandments his reward will bring him success, if he transgresses them his punishment will strike him – all by divine decree (Comm. to Ex. 13:16).

Though their tactics might thus vary, dogmatics were radical and clearly defined on both sides. *Ḥerem* was hurled against counter-*ḥerem*, as the authority of northern France was met by the authority of local scholars and communal leaders in Provence and Spain. Emissaries of both camps traveled about, rallying their supporters. A profusion of letters and counter-letters, sermons and counter-sermons, commentaries and counter-commentaries poured out. The weapons in the campaign were polemics, original and translations, and the Ibn *Tibbon and *Anatoli families made their name in both. In the work of men like Jonah Gerondi the struggle against Maimonides was merged with a general reforming spirit in morals and community leadership. This battle was ended by a terrible shock when Maimonides' books were burned by the *Dominicans in 1232. Proponents and opponents of Maimonides and philosophy alike interpreted this calamity as a punishment for the opposition. Accordingly, Jonah Gerondi relented in his views and many adherents of the anti-Maimonidean camp followed suit.

The controversy returned to the Muslim countries in the East. Maimonides' son, *Abraham b. Moses b. Maimon, was outraged at what had happened in the West. He attacked "many overseas [scholars who are] mistaken. They cling to the literalistic sense of biblical verses, Midrashim, and *aggadot*. This pains our heart; at the sight of this our eyes have darkened, and our fathers are dumbfounded: How could such an impurity, so like the impurity of idol worship, come to be in Israel? They worship idols, deny God's teaching, and worship other gods beside Him." Flinging these accusations against Maimonides' opponents in Europe, Abraham holds that through their exegetical explanations they are guilty of pagan-like anthropomorphism (*Milḥamot ha-Shem*, ed by R. Margalioth (1953), 52). He compares their faith to that of the Christians (*ibid.*, 55). Continuing his father's line of thought, he attacks the European antirationalistic scholars for their exclusive devotion to talmudic studies only, while neglecting the philosophical and philological foundations of the faith (*ibid.*, 49). They are among "those that walk in the darkness of their understanding and in the paucity of their wisdom" (*ibid.*, 50). He expressly prefers Islamic surroundings and influence – conducive to a rationalistic-monotheistic faith – to a Christian environment, which influences men in the direction of antirationalism and anthropomorphism (*ibid.*, 51). Abraham restates the basic rationalistic principle of faith and exegesis:

> Know ye God's people and His heritage, that God differentiated men from animals and beasts through the reason, wisdom, and understanding which He granted them. He also differentiated Israel from the gentiles through the Torah He gave them and the precepts He commanded them. Hence reason preceded Torah, both in creation of the world, and in each and every one living in it. Reason has been given to a man since the six days of creation; Torah was given to man 4,448 years after creation. Should someone say to you, 'But the sages have explained that the Torah was created two thousand years before the world,' you should reply that this Midrash needs many commentaries to justify it. It is impossible to take it in its simple sense.... Reason was implanted in each and every one of the seed of Israel before his knowledge of Torah. Know and understand that it is because the child's reason is not yet ripe, that God did not oblige him to fulfill commandments (*ibid.*, 57–58). In Abraham's view, corporealist beliefs, rather than philosophy, constituted the true denial of the Torah.

While this blast was going forth from the East, extremists from the West caused the desecration of Maimonides' tomb at Tiberias, which shocked not only the Maimonidean camp but also the majority of the anti-Maimonideans. When in the early 1240s the Disputation of Paris and the burning of the Talmud added shock to shock, public quarrels among Jews were set aside for several decades, and the second climax of the controversy came to an end.

It remains a much disputed point whether the Dominicans set fire to Maimonides' writings on their own initiative, scenting heresy wherever they could find it, or whether their action resulted from a denunciation by Jews, as contemporary Maimonideans believed. Neither the social nor the cultural motivating forces of the controversy disappeared with the cessation of polemics. The rise of kabbalistic circles and literature (see *Zohar) on the one hand, and the continuing philosophical activity and way of life of the upper and "professional" circles of Jewish society on the other implied a continuation and an intensification of the struggle between rationalists and anti-rationalists.

The Third Climax: A Renewed Outbreak of the Controversy in 1288–1290

Whereas the controversy of the 1230s took place largely in southern France, within a Christian environment, most of the controversy towards the end of the 13th century took place in the Near East. Solomon Petit, a mystic and anti-rationalist, had first agitated against Maimonides in northern France and Germany, where he was supported in his attempts to ban the study of the *Guide* and the *Book of Knowledge*. In 1288, Petit immigrated to Acre, where he taught Kabbalah; many of his students had been students of Naḥmanides after his emigration to Israel. In Acre, Petit continued to agitate against Maimonides and to urge the burning of his books, especially the *Guide*. But he met with consistent failure, and was himself banned no less than four times. Petit had fundamentally miscalculated: he was now living in the Land of Israel, which came under the jurisdiction of the *nagid* (governor) of Egyptian Jewry, David b. Abraham b. Maimonides. In the Arabic environment of the Near East, the Jews were long accustomed and exposed to philosophical culture, unlike the Jews of Christian Europe who had originally supported Petit.

Petit was also opposed in the west. The last known work of Shem Tov ibn Falaquera, *Mikhtav al Devar ha-Moreh* ("Letter Concerning the Guide") defended Maimonides against the attacks of Petit and others. In his "Letter," Falaquera mocks Maimonides' opponents in a poem: "I wonder about those who differ with Moses [i.e., Maimonides] / How they don't remember the punishment of Korah. / He is a true teacher, and his word / Is like fire; their word is like ice." Playing on Petit's name, Falaquera calls him a *peti* (fool). Falaquera argued that Maimonides was compelled to write the *Guide* because of widespread corporealist beliefs among the Jews, even among the great rabbis. But such people, wrong as they are, were not the perplexed for whom Maimonides had written his *Guide*. No wonder that Maimonides had been misunderstood – after all, even the Torah had been misunderstood. The masses of Jews in the Torah had rebelled against God and Moses; no wonder that they rebel against the Moses of today. The opponents of philosophy, Falaquera suggested, glorified in their ignorance of science and philosophy, and had to rely on faulty and misleading Hebrew translations of the *Guide* because they were ignorant of Arabic.

The Fourth and Final Climax: 1300–1306

When the controversy flared up again for the fourth and final time at the end of the 13th and beginning of the 14th century, the immediate catalyst was the extreme allegorical exegesis of certain rationalists. In the century since Maimonides' death, philosophy and science had become deeply entrenched in Jewish culture. Therefore, whereas in the 1230s the traditionalists sought a total ban on the study of philosophy, in the fourth and final climax of the controversy the traditionalists also accepted the validity of philosophy and science. They did not seek to ban totally the study of philosophy, but only to limit it, especially among the youth who lacked the intellectual and spiritual maturity to deal with its challenges to tradition. What they rejected was the philosopher's extreme allegorization of Scripture and alleged denial of creation and miracles, which they saw as basic to the affirmation of the Torah. The traditionalists also objected to the rationalists' use of astral magic for medical purposes; they saw such magic not as scientific but as forbidden *avodah zarah* (idolatry). In particular, the controversy focused on the content of Jewish education and the question of the possibility or impossibility of synthesis between "Greek wisdom" and the Torah of Moses. Abba Mari Astruc ha-Yarḥi of Lunel turned to Rashba (Rabbi Solomon b. Abraham *Adret) in Barcelona for guidance on the rationalists' allegorical interpretations, which he saw as heretical. Despite Astruc's strong partisan views, he preserved a collection of the exchange of letters from both sides in his *Minḥat Kena'ot*, "The Offering of Jealousy" (cf. Num. 5:15) (ed. M. Bisliches, Pressburg, 1838; reprinted Jerusalem, 1968; new and superior ed., H. Dimitrovsky, *Teshuvot ha-Rashba*, Jerusalem, 1990, 2 vols.). Astruc charged the philosophers with treating historical figures and events in the Bible purely symbolically, at the expense of their historicity; with regarding Plato and Aristotle, rather than the Torah, as the criteria of truth; with rejecting miracles and divine revelation; and with being personally lax in observance of Jewish law.

Although these charges, especially those of interpreting biblical figures purely symbolically and laxity in observance, were consistently denied by the rationalists, such as Menahem b. Solomon Meiri and Jedaiah b. Abraham Bedershi ha-Penini, they were on some level accurate. For example, Jacob b. Abba Mari Anatoli (1194–1296), the son-in-law of Samuel ibn Tibbon, in his book *Malmad ha-Talmidim*, had interpreted the patriarchs and matriarchs allegorically, rather than historically. Abraham and Sarah symbolized form and matter; Lot and his wife symbolized the intellect and the body; Isaac symbolized the active soul, and his wife Rebecca the intelligent soul; Leah symbolized the perceptive soul, and her sons the five senses; Leah's daughter Dinah represented sensations induced by imagination; Joseph symbolized practical reason, while Benjamin symbolized theoretical reason. He also interpreted the seven-branched *menorah* (candelabrum) as representing the seven planets, the twelve tribes as symbolizing the constellations, and the Urim and Thummim of the high priest as representing the astrolabe.

The traditionalists feared that such views could only lead to laxity in observance. If the Torah is true only on a symbolic level, the commandments might also be interpreted purely symbolically, at the expense of their actual observance, which is based on the literal text. Nevertheless, their attacks on individual rationalists like Levi b. Abraham b. Ḥayyim of Villefranche (who seems to have been the immediate catalyst of the outburst), were unwarranted, since these rationalists, as they themselves insisted in their own defense, did not in fact go beyond Maimonides' views or give up strict observance of the law, despite their radical allegorization.

Toward the end of the 13th century, a fierce dispute broke out in Provence between traditionalists and rationalists. While the main bone of contention was ostensibly radical rationalist allegorical exegesis of the Bible, the dispute actually flared up over the rationalist practice of healing with astral magic. Astral magic was included in the curriculum of medical studies in the universities. Paradoxically, it was thus the rationalist camp which employed astral magic in healing, and it was their use of such magic which the traditionalists, led by Abba Mari of Lunel, rejected as idolatrous *avodah zarah* and as prohibited by the *halakhah*.

Abba Mari tried to drag R. Solomon b. Adret (Rashba) into the argument, but failed. Rashba noted that he himself, before the anti-philosophical controversy had arisen, had unhesitatingly permitted the fashioning of effigies for medical purposes, and even while the controversy was still raging refused to issue an absolute prohibition of the medical use of astral magic. As against Maimonides' approach, denying the reality of sorcery, Rashba pointed out that both the Babylonian and Jerusalem Talmuds contain an abundance of magical material which violates no religious precept. Moreover, Rashba accused the opponents of sorcery of denying the possibility of miracles. To support his acceptance of the possibility that spirituality might descend upon amulets, he wrote:

> And I say that it was the kindness of the Supreme Being at the start of Creation to create in his world things that would ensure the health of the created beings, that if the existents happen to fall ill or for any other reason deviate from their natural perfection, these [things] are ready to restore them to their realm or to make them healthy. And He placed these forces in the essence of things found in nature, as may be attained by study, such as medications and aids known to scholars of medicine, or in nature based on properties but not attainable by study. And it is not impossible that such a power should also be in speech, as in the case of amulets and similar things (*Minḥat Kena'ot*, in Rashba, *Responsa*, ed. H.Z. Dimitrovsky, p. 302).

The possibility that stellar forces could be used to heal the sick was provided for in advance by God. Whether such practices were permissible or not depended, according to Rashba, on the magician's innermost intention: it was his awareness that God was the primary cause of recovery that legitimized the astral-magical practice. Thus, Abba Mari was unable to persuade Rashba to join him in condemnation of astral magic.

Through the 14th century, the dispute became increasingly acrimonious; at least four positions can be distinguished with regard to the status of astral magic:

(a) False and forbidden: The moderate rationalists rejected astral magic of any kind and therefore also considered it halakhically prohibited. They thus accepted Maimonides' firm negation of any reality of astral magic and his prohibition of its practices. These thinkers, then, took up Maimonides' approach in content, style, and language (Menaḥem ha-Meiri, David ha-Kokhavi). Some rationalists chose almost to ignore the issue, probably because they attached no reality whatever to astral magic (Joseph ibn Kaspi).

(b) Dubious and forbidden: This was the view of the traditionalists, who consistently battled the radical rationalists and in fact defined the latter group, inter alia, in terms of their employment of astral magic for medical purposes (Abba Mari, Jacob b. Solomon ha-Zarfati). They, too, prohibited the practice absolutely, as did the moderate rationalists, although they did not entirely deny the possible reality of astral magic. Their most characteristic trait was the connection they perceived between the practice of astral magic and the magician's affinity for philosophy: in their view, a rationalist philosophy was bound to lead to the practice of astral magic.

(c) False in respect of its reality but psychologically effective, and forbidden: Some circles denied that astral magic could actually bring down stellar forces, but believed that there was some psychological benefit in the practice. Nevertheless, they, too, prohibited its use from the standpoint of Halakhah (Gersonides, Jedaiah ha-Penini of Béziers). In a sense, this might be considered an intermediate position, though it is closer to that of the moderate rationalists and its proponents were essentially a subgroup of the latter.

(d) Real and permitted: Certain thinkers believed in the absolute reality of astral magic (Nissim of Marseilles, Frat Maimon) and even considered it halakhically legitimate (Levi b. Abraham). For such thinkers, astral magic was a theological principle that could be used in interpreting various biblical passages.

All these issues provided the background for Rashba's ultimate decision to support a limited ban.

After much hesitation, and spurred on by the influence of Asher b. Jehiel, Rashba and the Barcelona community issued a *ḥerem* on July 26, 1305, against "any member of the community who, being under the age of 25 years, shall study the works of the Greeks on natural science or metaphysics, whether in the original language or in translation."

Works by Jewish philosophers were excepted, as was the study of medicine. The ban was intended to prevent young men from being influenced by Greek philosophy to turn away "from the Torah of Israel which is above these sciences. How can any man dare to judge between human wisdom based on analogy, proof, and thought, and the wisdom of God, between whom and us there is no relation nor similarity? Will man, who is embodied in a vessel of clay, judge … God his creator to say, God forbid, what is possible and what he cannot do? Truly this, sometimes leads to utter heresy" (Resp. Rashba pt. 1, no. 415). A ban was also pronounced against all who "say about Abraham and Sarah that in reality they symbolize matter and form; that the 12 tribes of Israel are [an allegory] for the 12 planets … [and] that the Urim and Thummim are to be understood as the astrolabe instrument.… Some of them say that everything in the Torah, from *Bereshit* to the giving of the law, is entirely allegorical" (*ibid.*, no. 416).

The condemnation of extreme allegory did not arouse opposition, but the prohibition on the study of "Greek wisdom" until the age of 25 was sharply opposed on grounds of principle, though to Rashba and his group this formula was certainly in many respects a compromise. Among the many communities and individual sages in Provence and Spain who opposed the ban, the great talmudic scholar Menahem b. Solomon Meiri was one of the most eloquent voices. In his counter-*ḥerem* (printed in excerpts in *Jubelschrift… L. Zunz* (1884), Heb. pt. 153–72) he reminded Adret of the failure of the early 13th-century attacks against Maimonides. Rejecting insinuations that the study of philosophy causes heresy, he pointed to many talmudic scholars who were students of philosophy. Meiri stressed that sciences such as mathematics were necessary for the understanding of many passages in the Talmud. He regarded the prohibition against certain types of study as self-defeating: "Each individual [nature] will search for what suits him according to his natural inclination." This trait of human intellect and nature, he maintains, will even cause the second generation of the excommunicating community to seek ways out of this prohibition. Meiri was well aware that there was a more radical wing among the rationalists, which he opposed (see his commentary to Psalms, ed. by J. Cohn (1936), e.g., ch. 36, p. 78f., and many passages in his commentary to Proverbs and to Mishnah Avot).

Finally, Jedaiah b. Abraham Bedersi (ha-Penini) wrote Adret a "letter of apology" (*Ketav Hitnaẓẓelut*) – actually a sharp attack against the anti-rationalists – basing himself on the spiritual greatness of Provençal Jews and praising rationalism and philosophy. He daringly proclaims:

> My rabbis, please look into the mighty pattern of the benefits of philosophy to all of us, even to those who despise it. For it is extremely well-known that in ancient times anthropomorphism was widespread, one may say almost in the entire Diaspora of Israel … but in every generation there arose *geonim* and sages – in Spain, in Babylonia and in the cities of Andalusia – who, thanks to their familiarity with the Arabic language, had the great opportunity to smell the perfume of the sciences, some much, some a little, for they are translated into this language. It is thanks to this that they began to elaborate and clarify many of their opinions on the Torah, above all as to the unity of God and the abolition of anthropomorphism, especially by the philosophical proofs taken from scientific works.

He goes on to list this rationalistic literature, from the days of Saadiah Gaon onward (Resp. Rashba pt. 1., no. 418). This long epistle concludes:

> Relinquish your *ḥerem* for the heart of this people will not turn away from philosophy and its books as long as there is breath in their frame and soul in their bodies, especially as together with it [i.e., with devotion to philosophy], they are true to Torah and commandments. Even if they had heard it from the mouth of Joshua bin Nun they would never have accepted it, for they intend to do battle for the honor of the great teacher [i.e., Maimonides] and his works; and for the holiness of his teaching they will sacrifice fortune, family, and soul as long as there is a breath in their bodies. And thus they will teach and command their children in generations to come (*ibid.*).

On this sharp though inconclusive note, the great controversy of the early 14th century petered out. In any event, the expulsion of the Jews from France by King Philip IV on July 22, 1306, almost exactly one year after the Barcelona ban was issued, overshadowed the internal Jewish controversy. The greater external threat totally eclipsed a potential internal threat from philosophy. Like its predecessors, the Barcelona ban, as limited as it was in comparison to earlier bans, also proved ineffective and unenforceable, and to that extent, the rationalists had the last word in the controversy.

Aftermath of the Controversy

The tension between rationalists and antirationalists never abated throughout the Middle Ages. Among the beleaguered Jews of 15th-century Christian Spain, Maimonidean rationalism was seen by many as the root cause of the misfortunes and the reason for *apostasy. On the other hand, a man like Abraham *Bibago, throughout his *Derekh Emunah*, defended rationalism, not only as being justified but as the very essence of Judaism. Proudly calling himself "a pupil of Maimonides," he believed that the Jewish people is the bearer of reason – weak in this world as reason is weak against the unreasonable passions. Generalizing the traditional rationalistic view, he stated:

> The reasonable creature having reason has to study the sciences; and being a believer, he will study Torah and acquire faith and its roots and dogmas. The first study will be a kind of carrier and vessel to bear the second study. In the same way that life is an assumption and carrier by which humanity and speech are carried, so through the form of reason – by whose accomplishment one studies and acquires the sciences – Torah study will be assumed and carried. Thus faith will be complete and without doubt, and the one attitude [faith], will not conflict with the other [philosophy]. Therefore did the sage say, 'Reason and faith are two lights.' To solve all doubts we must explain that 'Greek wisdom' cannot be the above-mentioned wisdom of reason belonging to man insofar as he is a man. Hence it is a human wisdom and not a Greek one. The wisdom called [by talmudic sages] 'Greek wisdom,' must be something peculiar to the Greeks and not to another nation (see above, pt. 2, ch. 3, 46a).

That views like this were acceptable also among 16th-century Ashkenazi Jewry is proved by the fact that the *Sefer ha-Miknah* by *Joseph b. Gershom of Rosheim is in reality a kind of synopsis of Bibago's *Derekh Emunah*. In Renaissance Italy Jehiel b. Samuel of *Pisa wrote a detailed treatise (*Minḥat Kena'ot*) against rationalism, while the life and works of many of his contemporaries and countrymen constituted a clear espousal of it. In Poland-Lithuania in the 16th–17th centuries the tension between Maimonideans and anti-Maimonideans likewise continued, as evidenced, for example, by the dispute between Moses *Isserles and Solomon b. Jehiel *Luria (see Moses Isserles, Resp., nos. 687; and see also his *Torat ha-Olah*).

The problems of the synthesis between Judaism and other cultures, of the proper content of Jewish education, and of the right way to God – through reason or through mystic union – has remained, though formulations and expressions have changed considerably. The old hierarchical basis of Jewish leadership, wholeheartedly hated by Maimonides, has disappeared, but the leadership of the individual scholar, even after Maimonides, retained many hierarchical and sacral elements (see **Semikhah*). The *Mishneh Torah* did not supersede the Talmud, and Maimonides' aristocratic opposition to monetary support for Torah study failed completely. So strong was his personality, however, that most of his opponents made great efforts to say that they opposed not Maimonides himself but some element of his teaching or, better still, some misguided interpretation or citation of his work. The Maimonidean controversy is both very specifically at the heart of Jewish culture and, at the same time, part or a set of problems central to Judaism, Islam, and Christianity alike.

BIBLIOGRAPHY: D.J. Silver, *Maimonidean Criticism and the Maimonidean Controversy, 1180–1240* (1965), bibl., 199–210; S.Z. Halberstam, in: *Jeschurun* (Kobak), 8 pt. 1–2 (1871), Heb. pt. 17–56; pt. 3–4 (1895), Heb. pt. 89–100; J. Sarachek, *Faith and Reason: the Conflict over the Rationalism of Maimonides* (1935); H.H. Ben-Sasson, in: *Ha-Ishiyyut ve-Dorah* (1963), 93–106; idem, *Toledot Am Yisrael*, 2 (1969), 155–8, 216–23, 303–6; I. Twersky, *Rabad of Posquières* (1962); idem, in: *Journal of World History*, 11 (1968), 185–207; A.S. Halkin, in: *Perakim*, 1 (1968), 35–55; Baer, Spain, index; Schatzmueller, in: *Zion*, 34 (1969), 126–44; idem, in: *Meḥkarim le-Zekher Ẓevi Avneri* (1970), 129–40; Dinur, Golah. **ADD. BIBLIOGRAPHY:** D. Schwartz, "Changing Fronts toward Science in the Medieval Debates over Philosophy," in: *Journal of Jewish Thought and Philosophy*, 7 (1997), 61–82; G. Freudenthal, "Les Sciences dans les communautéa juives médiévales de Provence: leur appropriation, leur role," in: REJ, 152 (1993), 29–136; idem, "Science in the Medieval Jewish Culture of Southern France," in: *History of Science*, 33 (1995), 23–58; D. Schwartz, "*Meharsim, Talmudiyyim* and *Anshei Ha-Hokhma* – Judah Ben Samuel Ibn 'Abbas's Views and Preaching," in: *Tarbiz*, 52 (1993), 585–615; "The Debate over the Maimonidean Theory of Providence in Thirteenth-Century Jewish Philosophy," in: *Jewish Studies Quarterly*, 2 (1995), 185–96; *Faith and Reason: Debates in Medieval Jewish Philosophy* (Heb., 2001); J. Shatzmiller, "In Search of the Book of Figures: Medicine and Astrology in Montpellier at the Turn of the Fourteenth Century," in: *AJS Review* 7:8 (182/183), 383-407; I. Twersky, "Beginnings of *Mishneh Torah* Criticism," in: A. Altmann (ed.), *Jewish Medieval and Renaissance Studies* (1967), 95–118; R. Jospe, "Faith and Reason: The Controversy Over Philosophy in Jewish History," in: I. Kajon (ed.), *La Storia Della Filosofia Ebraica* (*Archivio di Filosofia*, 61 (1993)), 99–135; B. Septimus, *Hispano-Jewish Culture in Transition: The Career and Controversies of Ramah* (1982); S. Harvey, *Falaquera's Epistle of the Debate: An Introduction to Jewish Philosophy* (1987).

[Haim Hillel Ben-Sasson / Raphael Jospe and Dov Schwartz (2nd ed.)]

MAIMONIDES, MOSES (**Moses ben Maimon**; known in rabbinical literature as "**Rambam**"; from the acronym **R**abbi **M**oses **B**en **M**aimon; 1135–1204), rabbinic authority, codifier, philosopher, and royal physician.

BIOGRAPHY

The most illustrious figure in Judaism in the post-talmudic era, and one of the greatest of all time, Maimonides was born in Cordoba, Spain, to his father *Maimon, *dayyan* of Cordoba and himself a renowned scholar and pupil of Joseph *ibn Migash. He continues his genealogy, "the son of the learned Joseph, son of Isaac the *dayyan*, son of Joseph the *dayyan*, son of Obadiah the *dayyan*, son of the rabbi Solomon, son of Obadiah" (end of commentary to Mishnah); traditions extend the genealogy to R. Judah ha-Nasi. Posterity even recorded the day and hour and even minute of his birth, "On the eve of Passover (the 14th of Nisan) which was a Sabbath, an hour and a third after midday, in the year 4895 (1135) of the Creation" (*Sefer Yuḥasin*). Maimonides' grandson David gives the same day and year without the hour (at the beginning of his commentary to tractate *Rosh Ha-Shanah*).

As a result of the fall of Cordoba to the *Almohads in May or June, 1148, when Moses had just reached his 13th birthday, and the consequent religious persecution, Maimon was obliged to leave Cordoba with his family and all trace of them is lost for the next eight or nine years, which they spent wandering from place to place in Spain (and possibly Provence) until in 1160 they settled in Fez. Yet it was during those years of wandering, which Maimonides himself describes as a period "while my mind was troubled, and amid divinely ordained exiles, on journeys by land and tossed on the tempests of the sea" (end of commentary to Mishnah) that he laid the strong foundations of his vast and varied learning and even began his literary work. Not only did he begin the draft of the *Sirāj*, his important commentary on the Mishnah, in 1158, but in that same year, at the request of a friend, he wrote a short treatise on the Jewish calendar (*Ma'amar ha-Ibbur*) and one on logic (*Millot Higgayon*) and had completed writing notes for a commentary on a number of tractates of the Babylonian Talmud, and a work whose aim was to extract the *halakhah* from the Jerusalem Talmud (see below Maimonides as halakhist). According to Muslim authorities the family became formally converted to Islam somewhere in the period between 1150 and 1160. But Saadiah ibn Danan (Z. Edelmann (ed.), *Ḥemdah Genuzah* (1856), 16a) relates that the Muslims maintain the same about many Jewish scholars, among them Dunash ibn Tamim, Ḥasdai b. Ḥasdai, and others. In any case in the year 1160 Maimon and his sons, Moses and David, and a daughter, were in Fez. In his old age 'Abd al-Mu'min, the Almohad ruler, somewhat changed his attitude to the Jews, becoming more moderate toward those who were living in the central, Moroccan, part of his realm. It was probably on account of this that in 1159 or early in 1160 Maimon deemed it worthwhile to emigrate with his family to Morocco and settle in Fez. Living in Fez at that time was R. Judah ha-Kohen ibn Susan, whose fame for learning and piety had spread to Spain, and Maimonides, then 25, studied under him. Many Jews had outwardly adopted Islam and their consciences were troubling them, and this prompted Maimon to write his *Iggeret ha-Neḥamah* ("Letter of Consolation") assuring them that he who says his prayers even in their shortest form and who does good works remains a Jew (*Ḥemdah Genuzah*, pp. LXXIV–LXXXII). Meantime his son worked at his commentary on the Mishnah and also continued his general studies, particularly medicine; in his medical works he frequently refers to the knowledge and experience he gained among the Muslims in North Africa (see Maimonides as physician). Here also he wrote his *Iggeret ha-Shemad* ("Letter on Forced Conversion") also called *Iggeret Kiddush ha-Shem* ("Letter of the Sanctification of the Divine Name"). These letters of father and son, as well as Maimonides' utterances after leaving Morocco, do not point to outrages and bloody persecutions. Although Maimonides in the opening lines of the *Iggeret ha-Shemad* most strongly deprecates the condemnation of the forced converts by "the self-styled sage who has never experienced what so many Jewish communities experienced in the way of persecution," his conclusion is that a Jew must leave the country where he is forced to transgress the divine law: "He should not remain in the realm of that king; he should sit in his house until he emigrates…" And once more, with greater insistence: "He should on no account remain in a place of forced conversion; whoever remains in such a place desecrates the Divine Name and is nearly as bad as a willful sinner; as for those who beguile themselves, saying that they will remain until the Messiah comes to the Maghreb and leads them to Jerusalem, I do not know how he is to cleanse them of the stigma of conversion" (*Iggeret ha-Shemad*, in: Z. Edelmann (ed.), *Ḥemdah Genuzah*, 11b–12a).

Maimon and his sons acted in accordance with this advice, as certainly did many others. Maimonides' departure from the country of the Almohads is commonly assumed to have taken place in 1165; according to Saadiah ibn Danan (*Seder ha-Dorot*, in: *Ḥemdah Genuzah*, 30b.), it was promoted by the martyrdom of Judah ibn Susan, who had been called upon to forsake his religion and had preferred death to apostasy. R. Maimon and his family escaped from Fez, and a month later they landed at Acre. The day of his departure as well as that on which the ship was saved from a tempest were instituted as a family fast enjoined on his descendants, and that of his arrival in Ereẓ Israel as a festival (E. Azikri (Azcari), *Sefer Ḥaredim*; Maim. Comm. to *Rosh Ha-Shanah*, ed. Brill, end).

The family remained in Acre for some five months, striking up an intimate friendship there with the *dayyan* Japheth b. Ali. Together with him they made a tour of the Holy Land, visiting Jerusalem where Maimonides states, "I entered the [site of the] Great and Holy House and prayed there on Thursday the 6th day of Marḥeshvan." Three days later they paid a visit to the Cave of Machpelah in Hebron for the same purpose. Maimonides also appointed both these days as family festivals. The family then left Ereẓ Israel and sailed for Egypt. After a short stay at Alexandria they moved to Cairo and took up residence in Fostat, the Old City of Cairo.

Maimon died at this time either in Ereẓ Israel or in Egypt. It has been suggested that the reason for the choice of Alexandria was the existence at that time "outside the town" of "the academy of Aristotle, the teacher of Alexander" to which "people from the whole world came in order to study the wisdom of Aristotle the philosopher" mentioned by Benjamin of Tudela (ed. by M.N. Adler (1907), 75). It is not certain what prompted the move to Cairo. That Maimonides' influence was decisive in virtually destroying the hitherto dominating influence of the Karaites who were more numerous and wealthy than the Rabbanites in Cairo is beyond doubt (see below) and in the 17th century Jacob Farajī, a *dayyan* in Egypt, states that it was this challenge which impelled Maimonides to move to Cairo (see Azulai, letter M150).

For eight years Maimonides lived a life free from care. Supported by his brother David who dealt in precious stones, he was able to devote himself entirely to preparing his works for publication and to his onerous but honorary work as both religious and lay leader of the community. His *Sirāj*, the commentary to the Mishnah, was completed in 1168. The following year he suffered a crushing blow. His brother David drowned in the Indian Ocean while on a business trip, leaving a wife and two children, and with him were lost not only the family fortune but moneys belonging to others. Maimonides took the blow badly. For a full year he lay almost prostrate, and then he had to seek a means of livelihood. Rejecting the thought of earning a livelihood from Torah (see his commentary on *Avot* 5:4, and especially his letter to Joseph ibn Sham'un in 1191, "It is better for you to earn a drachma as a weaver, or tailor, or carpenter than to be dependent on the license of the exilarch [to accept a paid position as a rabbi]"; F. Kobler (ed.), *Letters of Jews Through the Ages*, 1 (1952), 207) and he decided to make the medical profession his livelihood.

Fame in his calling did not come to him at once. It was only after 1185 when he was appointed one of the physicians to al-Faḍil, who had been appointed vizier by Saladin and was virtual ruler of Egypt after Saladin's departure from that country in 1174, that his fame began to spread. It gave rise to a legend that Richard the Lionhearted "the King of the Franks in Ascalon" sought his services as his private physician. About 1177 he was recognized as the official head of the Fostat community. Ibn Danan says of him, "Rabbenu Moshe [b. Maimon] became very great in wisdom, learning, and rank." In the so-called *Megillat Zuta* he is called "the light of east and west and unique master and marvel of the generation."

These were the most fruitful and busy years of his life. His first wife had died young and in Egypt he remarried, taking as his wife the sister of Ibn Almali, one of the royal secretaries, who himself married Maimonides' only sister. To them was born their only son Abraham to whose education he lovingly devoted himself, and an added solace was his enthusiastic disciple Joseph ibn Sham'un (not Ibn Aknin, as often stated), whom he loved as a son, and for whom he wrote, and sent chapter by chapter, his *Guide of the Perplexed*. It was during those years, busy as he was with the heavy burden of his practice and occupied with the affairs of the community, writing his extensive correspondence to every part of the Jewish world (apart from the Franco-German area), that he wrote the two monumental works upon which his fame chiefly rests, the *Mishneh Torah* (compiled 1180) and the *Guide* (1190; according to Z. Diesendruck, in: HUCA, 12–13 (1937–38), 461–97, in 1185), as well as his *Iggeret Teiman* and his *Ma'amar Teḥiyyat ha-Metim*.

The following passage in the letter to the translator of the *Guide*, Samuel b. Judah ibn *Tibbon, in which he describes his multifarious cares and duties, with the aim of dissuading Ibn Tibbon from coming to visit him, has often been quoted:

> I dwell at Miṣr [Fostat] and the sultan resides at al-Qāhira [Cairo]; these two places are two Sabbath days' journey distant from each other. My duties to the sultan are very heavy. I am obliged to visit him every day, early in the morning; and when he or any of his children, or any of the inmates of his harem, are indisposed, I dare not quit al-Qāhira, but must stay during

> the greater part of the day in the palace. It also frequently happens that one or two royal officers fall sick, and I must attend to their healing. Hence, as a rule, I repair to al-Qāhira very early in the day, and even if nothing unusual happens, I do not return to Miṣr until the afternoon. Then I am almost dying with hunger … I find the antechambers filled with people, both Jews and gentiles, nobles and common people, judges and bailiffs, friends and foes – a mixed multitude who await the time of my return.
>
> I dismount from my animal, wash my hands, go forth to my patients, and entreat them to bear with me while I partake of some slight refreshment, the only meal I take in the twenty-four hours. Then I go forth to attend to my patients, and write prescriptions and directions for their various ailments. Patients go in and out until nightfall, and sometimes even, I solemnly assure you, until two hours or more in the night. I converse with and prescribe for them while lying down from sheer fatigue; and when night falls, I am so exhausted that I can scarcely speak.
>
> In consequence of this, no Israelite can have any private interview with me, except on the Sabbath. On that day the whole congregation, or at least the majority of the members, come to me after the morning service, when I instruct them as to their proceedings during the whole week; we study together a little until noon, when they depart. Some of them return, and read with me after the afternoon service until evening prayers. In this manner I spend that day.

The two major works will be described below, but something must be said of the two letters. The Arab ruler in Yemen, who, unlike the sultans in Egypt who were Sunnites, belonged to the sectarian Shiʿites, instituted a religious persecution, giving the Jews the choice of conversion to Islam or death. Not only did many succumb, but there arose among those Jews a pseudo-Messiah, or a forerunner of the Messiah who, seeing in these events the darkness before the dawn, preached the imminent advent of the Messianic Age. In despair the Jews of Yemen turned to Maimonides, who probably in 1172 answered their request with the *Iggeret Teiman* (*al-Risāla al-Yamaniyya*). It was addressed to R. *Jacob b. Nethanel al-Fayyumi, with a request that copies be sent to every community in Yemen. Deliberately couched in simple terms, "that men, women, and children could read it easily," he pointed out that the subtle attack of Christianity and Islam which preached a new revelation was more dangerous than the sword and than the attractions of Hellenism. As for the pseudo-Messiah, he was unbalanced and he was to be rejected. These trials were sent to prove the Jews.

The effect of the letter was tremendous. In gratitude for the message of hope, combined with the fact that Maimonides also used his influence at court to obtain a lessening of the heavy burden of taxation on the Jews of Yemen, the Jews of Yemen introduced into the **Kaddish* a prayer for "the life of our teacher Moses b. Maimon" (Letter of Naḥmanides to the rabbis of France, in: *Kitvei Ramban*, ed. by C.B. Chavel (1963), 341).

This remarkable tribute, usually reserved for the exilarch, has an indirect connection with the third of his public (as distinct from his private) letters, the *Ma'amar Teḥiyyat ha-Metim* ("On Resurrection"; 1191). Maimonides wrote the letter with the greatest reluctance. It was the direct result of his *Mishneh Torah* and constituted his reply to the accusation leveled against him that in this work he denied, or did not mention, the doctrine of personal resurrection which was a fundamental principle of faith among the Jews of his time. An objective study of his work does lend a certain basis to the allegation. It is true, as he indignantly protests, that he included this doctrine as the last of his famous Thirteen Principles of Judaism, but in his *Mishneh Torah* the undoubted emphasis is on the immortality of the soul and not on individual bodily resurrection. That the allegation was not based upon mere malice or envy of his work is sufficiently proved by the fact that anxious queries were addressed to him from the countries in which he was most fervently admired, Yemen and Provence, and Maimonides answered them. Abraham b. David of Posquières wrote: "The words of this man seem to me to be very near to him who says there is no resurrection of the body, but only of the soul. By my life, this is not the view of the sages" (Comm. to Yad, Teshuvah 8:2). Some Jews from Yemen however, unsatisfied, wrote to *Samuel b. Ali the powerful and learned *Gaon* in Baghdad who sent a reply, which although couched in terms of respect to Maimonides, vigorously denounced his views. It would appear that the vehemence of this reply was connected with Samuel's desire to assert his authority as *gaon* over Egypt, which he thought was being usurped by Maimonides. On the other hand, Maimonides held the exilarch Samuel (of Josiah b. Zakkai's line), the successor of the exilarch Daniel b. Ḥisdai, in higher esteem than the *gaon* Samuel b. Ali. Thus the relations between Maimonides and the *gaon* remained strained, although there was never open hostility. Joseph ibn Sham'un, in Baghdad, who had also queried Maimonides' views on resurrection, sent a copy of Samuel's reply to Maimonides and with great reluctance Maimonides felt himself compelled to write his *Ma'amar Teḥiyyat ha-Metim* in which he asserted and confirmed his belief in the doctrine.

Maimonides was active as head of the community. He took vigorous steps to deal with the Karaites, and as a result brought about the supremacy of the Rabbanites in Cairo. On the one hand he emphatically maintained that they were to be regarded as Jews, with all the attendant privileges. They might be visited, their dead buried, and their children circumcised, their wine permitted; they were however not to be included in a religious quorum (Resp. ed. Blau, 449). Only when they flouted rabbinic Judaism was a barrier to be maintained. One was particularly to avoid visiting them on their festivals which did not coincide with the dates fixed by the rabbinic calendar. One of the inroads which they had caused in orthodox observance was with regard to ritual immersion for the **niddah*. Their view that an ordinary bath was sufficient had been widely adopted among the Rabbanites. Maimonides succeeded in restoring rabbinic practice in this matter, but generally his policy toward the Karaites was more lenient in his later years, and was continued by his son Abraham. (For an exhaustive treatment of this subject see C. Tchernowitz, *Toledot ha-Posekim* (1946), 197–208.)

Maimonides made various changes in liturgical custom, the most radical of which was the abolition of the repetition of the **Amidah* in the interests of decorum. With the completion of the *Guide*, Maimonides' literary work, apart from his extensive correspondence, came to an end. In failing health he nevertheless continued his work as head of the Jewish community and as court physician. (It is doubtful whether he actually held the appointment of *nagid* as is usually stated; see M.D. Rabinowitz, Introduction to *Ma'amar Teḥiyyat ha-Metim* in *Iggerot ha-Rambam*, 220–7.)

It was during this period however that he engaged in his correspondence with the scholars of Provence in general and with Jonathan of Lunel in particular. In some instances the border line between responsum and letter is not clearly defined (e.g., his letter to Obadiah the Proselyte, see below), but, as Kobler comments, the letters of Maimonides mark an epoch in letter writing. He is the first Jewish letter writer whose correspondence has been largely preserved. Vigorous and essentially personal, his letters found their way to the mind and heart of his correspondents, and he varied his style to suit them. But above all they reveal his whole personality, which is different from what might be expected from his *Mishneh Torah* and the *Guide*. The picture of an almost austere and aloof intellectual above human passions and emotions derived from there is completely dispelled.

Maimonides died on December 13, 1204. There were almost universal expressions of grief. Public mourning was ordained in all parts of the Jewish world. In Fostat mourning was ordained for three days and in Jerusalem a public fast and the Scriptural readings instituted concluded with the verse "the glory is departed from Israel, for the Ark of the Lord is taken" (I Sam. 4:22). His remains were taken to Tiberias for burial, and his grave is still an object of pilgrimage.

Influence

The influence of Maimonides on the future development of Judaism is incalculable. No spiritual leader of the Jewish people in the post-talmudic period has exercised such an influence both in his own and subsequent generations. Despite the vehement opposition which greeted his philosophical views the breach was healed (see *Maimonidean Controversy). It is significant that when Solomon *Luria strongly criticized Moses Isserles for his devotion to Greek philosophy, Isserles answered that his sole source was Maimonides' *Guide*, thus giving it the cachet of acceptability (Resp. Isserles 7). It was probably due to his unrivaled eminence as talmudist and codifier that many of his views were finally accepted. They were very radical at the time. To give but one example, the now universally accepted doctrine of the incorporeality of God was by no means accepted as fundamental before him and was probably an advanced view held by a small group of thinkers and philosophers. Even Abraham b. David of Posquières protested the statement of Maimonides that anyone who maintains the corporeality of God is a sectarian: "Why does he call him a sectarian? Many greater and better than he accepted this idea [of the corporeality of God] basing themselves on Scripture" (Yad, Teshuvah 3:7). C. Tchernowitz (*Toledot ha-Posekim*, 1 (1946), 193) goes so far as to maintain that were it not for Maimonides Judaism would have broken up into different sects and beliefs, and that it was his great achievement to unite the various currents, halakhic and philosophic.

Maimonides is regarded as the supreme rationalist, and the title given by Aḥad Ha-Am to his essay on him, "*Shilton ha-Sekhel*" ("The Rule of Reason"; in: *Ha-Shilo'aḥ*, 15 (1905), 291–319) included in his collected works, *Al Parashat Derakhim* (1921), has become almost standard in referring to him, and so long as one confines oneself to his three great works, the commentary on the Mishnah, the *Mishneh Torah*, and the *Guide*, a case can be made out for this view.

In the *Mishneh Torah*, Maimonides rigidly confines himself to a codification of Jewish law, refraining almost entirely from allowing his personal views to obtrude. Where he does advance his own view to which he can find no talmudic authority, he is careful, as he explicitly states in a letter to Jonathan of Lunel, to introduce it with the words "it appears to me" (cf. Yad, Sanhedrin 4:11). From his knowledge of medicine he was aware that certain disabilities in animals which in the time of the Talmud were regarded as fatal were susceptible to cure, while some which were not so regarded were in fact fatal, yet he lays it down that the talmudic view must be applied (Sheḥitah 10:12 and 13). Among the few exceptions the most striking is his outburst against belief in witchcraft and enchantment. After faithfully giving in their minutest details the talmudic description of, and laws concerning, these practices, he adds: "All these and similar matters are lies and falsehood… it is not fitting for Jews, who are intelligent and wise, to be attracted by them or believe that they are effective… whosoever believes in them, and that they are true, only that the Bible has forbidden them, belongs to the category of fools and ignoramuses and is in the class of immature women and children" (*Avodat Kokhavim* 11:16). In his work on the calendar included in the *Mishneh Torah* (*Hilkhot Kiddush ha-Ḥodesh*) he maintains vigorously that one should have recourse to works written by non-Jewish astronomers (11:1–6). At the end of *Hilkhot Temurah*, he defends the search after reasons for the biblical commandments (4:13).

In the *Guide* he allows himself more freedom, but the main difference between the two works lies in their different purpose and aim. The *Mishneh Torah* was written for the believing Jew untroubled by the apparent contradictions between revealed law and current philosophy, and its aim was to tell him how he should conduct himself in his desire to live according to the law. The *Guide*, as its name conveys, was designed for those whose faith had been weakened by these doctrines and its aim was to tell him why he should adhere to traditional Judaism. This helps to explain the contradictions between the two.

In both works one sees only the unemotional man of intellect. It is in his letters that Maimonides emerges as the warm human being, his heart open to the suffering of his people, and expressing and responding to both affection and hostility. It comes almost as a shock to read in his letter to Japheth b. Ali, when he informs him of the death of his brother David, that he remonstrates with him for not sending a letter of condolence to him on the death of his father which took place 11 years earlier though he had received innumerable such messages from all over the Jewish world, repeating the complaint twice. The letter was written eight years after his brother's death, yet he writes, "I still mourn, and there is no comfort.... Whenever I come across his handwriting or one of his books, my heart goes faint within me, and my grief reawakens" and in that letter he continues that he will never forget those days which he passed in Ereẓ Israel with his correspondent (Kobler 192–3). The personal human element is equally to the fore in the above-quoted letter to Samuel ibn Tibbon, while his letter-responsum to Obadiah the Proselyte reveals Maimonides' spirit to the full. It was surely only to his intimate disciple that he could open his heart and declare, "when I see no other way of teaching a well-established truth except by pleasing one intelligent man and displeasing ten thousand fools, I choose to address myself to the one man and take no notice whatsoever of the condemnation of the multitude" (Introduction to the *Guide*). On the other hand Maimonides is almost virulent in his opposition to songs and music: "song and music are all forbidden, even if unaccompanied by words ... there is no difference between listening to songs, or string music, or melodies without words; everything which conduces to the rejoicing of the soul and emotion is forbidden." It is immaterial whether they are in Arabic or in Hebrew. "A person who listens to foolish songs with musical accompaniment is guilty of three transgressions, listening to folly, listening to song, and listening to instrumental music. If the songs are sung with accompaniment of drinking, there is a fourth transgression, if the singer is a woman there is a fifth." The references in the geonic sources to singing are only to liturgical hymns (Resp. ed. Blau, 224. cf. 269; Guide 3:8; Yad, Ta'anit, 5:14). Despite this last permission he was opposed to the insertion of *piyyutim* in the prayers (180, 207, 254, 260, 261). If the ignorant insist on them and their ways prevail, they should be said before the *Shema*, the beginning of the essential service (207).

No praise can be too high for the outer form of his works, both in language and logical method. The *Mishneh Torah* was the only work which he wrote in Hebrew, and the language is superb, clear, and succinct. He regretted that he did not prepare Hebrew versions of his other works. In answer to Joseph b. Gabir's request written in 1191 that he translate the work into Arabic, not only does he state that it would thereby lose its specific character, but that he would have liked to translate his works written in Arabic into Hebrew (Kobler 199); and when the rabbis of Lunel asked him to translate the *Guide* into Hebrew, he stated that he wished he were young enough to do so (*ibid.*, 216).

The *Mishneh Torah* is a model of logical sequence and studied method, each chapter and each paragraph coming in natural sequence to its preceding one. More impressive is the fact that in his earliest work one can so clearly discern the seeds of the later, so that it can confidently be stated that his whole subsequent system and ideas were already formulated in his mind when he wrote it. The *Shemonah Perakim* which form the introduction to his commentary on *Avot* is almost a draft of the first portion of *Sefer Madda*, the first book of the *Mishneh Torah*. When attacked on his views on resurrection he pointed out that he had included it in the Thirteen Principles which he evolved in his commentary to the tenth chapter of *Sanhedrin*. The radical view found in the very last chapter of the *Mishneh Torah* that the messianic age is nothing more than the attainment of political independence in Israel is stated in detail in that same excursus, and his original view on the possibility of the reestablishment of the Sanhedrin, which he carefully puts forward as his own ("it appears to me") and which he qualifies by the statement "but the matter must be weighed up" (Sanhedrin 4:11), is already expressed in his commentary on the Mishnah (Sanh. 1:1).

[Louis Isaac Rabinowitz]

AS HALAKHIST

Maimonides' halakhic activity began during his youth with his commentary to some tractates of the Talmud (introduction to commentary to the Mishnah). Only fragments on several tractates have survived (see S. Asaf, in: *Sinai*, 6 (1940), 103–32, on *Shabbat*; M. Kamelhar (1956) on *Yoma*): the commentary to *Rosh Ha-Shanah*, published in its entirety (by J. Brill, 1865; Y.A. Kamelhar, 1906), is of doubtful authenticity (see M.J.L. Sachs, *Ḥiddushei ha-Ra-MBa-M la-Talmud* (1963), introd. 13–23). His *Hilkhot ha-Yerushalmi* ("Laws of the Palestinian Talmud"), alluded to in his commentary to the Mishnah (Tamid 5:1), is not extant; the authenticity of the fragments published by Saul Lieberman (1947) has been challenged (Benedikt in: KS, 27 (1950–51), 329–49). It is interesting to note, in view of the fact that his famous code, the *Mishneh Torah*, embraces the whole of Jewish law, both practical and theoretical, that in both these works he confined himself to the practical *halakhah*, his commentary on the Talmud being confined to the orders **Mo'ed*, **Nashim*, and *Nezikin and the tractate **Ḥullin*, which deals with dietary laws.

Commentary to the Mishnah

It is through his commentary to the Mishnah that one can begin to review Maimonides as a halakhist. In his commentary, Maimonides sets out to explain to the general reader the meaning of the Mishnah, without having recourse to the involved and lengthy discussions in the *Gemara*, the language of which was more difficult than the Mishnah itself (*Mishneh Torah*, introd.). Out of the mishnaic and other tannaitic texts and corresponding passages in the *Gemara*, often widely scattered throughout the Talmud, Maimonides evolves the underlying principles of the subjects discussed, which a particular

Mishnah, chapter, or entire tractate presupposed. In some cases he interprets the Mishnah differently from the *Gemara* (cf. in Sanh. 1:1). It has been asserted that even during his early work as a commentator, Maimonides was at the same time a codifier, a role which he later successfully developed in the *Sefer ha-Mitzvot* and the *Mishneh Torah* (M. Guttmann, in: J. Guttmann et al. (eds.), *Moses ben Maimon*, 2 (1914), 306–30; idem, in: HUCA, 2 (1925), 229–68). Following his explanatory glosses to the mishnaic passage, Maimonides gave the halakhic decision in each Mishnah based on his reading of the discussion in the *Gemara*.

Of special significance are the lengthy introductions he included in his commentary. The general introduction which heads his commentary to the order of *Zera'im* is in reality an introduction to and history of the Oral Law from Moses until his own days. The introduction to *Avot*, known as the *Shemonah Perakim* ("Eight Chapters") is a philosophical and ethical treatise in which its author harmonized Aristotle's ethics with rabbinical teachings. In the introduction to Mishnah *Sanhedrin* (10:1), which begins with the words "All Israel has a portion in the world to come," Maimonides dealt at length with the fundamental doctrines of Judaism which are formulated in the Thirteen *Articles of Faith. Especially extensive and exhaustive is the introduction to the difficult order *Tohorot*, in which Maimonides systematizes all that had been said in talmudic literature on the subject of ritual purity and impurity. The standard Hebrew translation, the work of a number of hands, is a poor rendering of the Arabic original. A new and more faithful translation was made by Y. Kafaḥ, *Mishnah im Perush ha-Rambam* … (1963–68).

The Responsa of Maimonides

The publication of the critical editions of the responsa of Maimonides (ed. by A. Freimann, 1934; J. Blau, 1957–61) affords a better opportunity to appraise his role in the communal life of the Jews of Egypt and neighboring countries. The responsa, which were in the language of the questioner, whether Hebrew or Arabic, number 464; some of them soon found their way into halakhic literature. Although not all responsa bear the date of composition, it has been ascertained that Maimonides' responsa extend from about 1167, a short time after his arrival in Egypt, until a little before his death. The questioners include prominent scholars like R. Anatoli and R. Meshullam, *dayyanim* in Alexandria; *Jonathan ha-Kohen of Lunel; Joseph b. Gabir; Nissim of Damascus; and Samuel b. Ali, *Gaon* of Baghdad. From these responsa one learns of the growing tension between the *gaon* of Baghdad and Maimonides in connection with traveling on the high seas on the Sabbath, prohibited by Samuel b. Ali but permitted by Maimonides (ed. Blau, no. 308–9). Some of the responsa to Jonathan of Lunel, who was a disciple of *Abraham b. David of Posquières, are in essence rejoinders to the latter's criticisms, for his questions coincide with the language and style of these criticisms (ed. Freimann, introd. xliv = ed. Blau, 3 (1961), 43).

The bitter experience of his youth failed to nurture in Maimonides rabid anti-Muslim feelings, and he consistently declined to classify Muslims as idolators. Even the ritual practices connected with the Ka'ba stone in Mecca did not in his opinion deny Islam its purely monotheistic nature (ed. Freimann, no. 369 = ed. Blau, no. 448; see S. Baron, in: PAAJR, 6 (1935), 83f.). In reply to an inquiry by Saadiah b. Berakhot about the authenticity of the gnostic work, *Shi'ur Komah*, Maimonides writes: "Heaven forfend that such work originated from the sages; it is undoubtedly the work of one of the Greek preachers … and it would be a divine act to suppress this book and to eradicate its subject matter" (ed. Freimann, no. 373 = ed. Blau, no. 117; see Scholem, Mysticism (1946²), 63ff.). Of special interest is his responsum to Obadiah the Proselyte (ed. Freimann, no. 42 = ed. Blau, no. 293), who inquired if he was permitted to say in the blessings and prayers, "Our God and God of our Fathers," "Thou who has chosen us," "Thou who has worked miracles to our fathers," and similar expressions. Maimonides' responsum, apart from its halakhic merit, is a unique human document displaying grave concern for the feelings of this lonely proselyte who was so unsure of himself. Obadiah was advised that he was to recite all those prayers in the same way as one born a Jew, that he must not consider himself inferior to the rest of the Jews. The major part of this responsum has been translated into English by F. Kobler (see also S.B. Freehof, *Treasury of Responsa* (1962), 28–34). These responsa, although confined to halakhic decisions, nevertheless display Maimonides' views on matters of doctrine and fundamentals of Judaism.

Sefer ha-Mitzvot ("Book of the Commandments")

Maimonides found all previous attempts at enumerating the traditional 613 *commandments unsatisfactory. He therefore composed the *Sefer ha-Mitzvot* in which he gave his own enumeration of the 248 positive and the 365 negative commandments. As an introduction to this work, he laid down 14 principles which guided him in the identification and enumeration of the commandments. He severely criticized the work of his predecessors, such as the enumeration of the *Halakhot Gedolot and of R. Ḥefeẓ, as well as those *paytanim* like Solomon ibn Gabirol, who composed the *Azharot*, religious hymns based on enumeration of the commandments.

Maimonides' sharp criticism of the *Halakhot Gedolot* evoked a defense of the latter by Naḥmanides, a staunch apologist "for the ancients," who in his *Hassagot* strongly criticized Maimonides, accusing him of inconsistencies. He was also challenged by Daniel ha-Bavli, a disciple of Samuel b. Ali, the anti-Maimonist. His criticisms took the form of questions which he sent to Abraham, the son of Maimonides, who replied to them. The *Sefer ha-Mitzvot*, however, was generally accepted, and a whole body of literature was produced in defense of it, apart from the general works on the 613 commandments according to Maimonides' classification and enumeration (see A. Jellinek, *Kunteres Taryag*, 1878).

The *Sefer ha-Mitzvot*, originally written in Arabic, was translated several times into Hebrew. The version by Abraham ibn Ḥasdai is no longer extant, while the translation by Moses ibn Tibbon, in its critical edition by H. Heller, is accepted as the standard text (1946).

The Mishneh Torah ("Repetition of the Law")

The *Sefer ha-Mitzvot* was not an end in itself but an introduction to the *Mishneh Torah* (Responsa, ed. Freimann, no. 368 = ed. Blau, no. 447), on which Maimonides labored for ten successive years. The purpose of the work is explained by Maimonides:

> In our days, many vicissitudes prevail, and all feel the pressure of hard times. The wisest of our wise men has disappeared; the understanding of our prudent men is hidden. Hence, the commentaries of the *geonim* and their compilations of laws and responsa, which they took care to make clear, have in our times become hard to understand, so that only a few individuals fully comprehend them. Needless to add that such is the case in regard to Talmud itself, both Babylonian and Jerusalem, and the *Sifra, Sifrei*, and Tosefta, all of which require, for their comprehension, a broad mind, a wise soul, and considerable study. Then one might learn from them the correct way to determine what is forbidden and permitted, as well as other rules of the Torah. On these grounds, I, Moses the son of Maimon the Sephardi bestirred myself, and relying on the help of God, blessed be He, intently studied all these works, with the view of putting together the results obtained from them … all in plain language and terse style, so that thus the entire Oral Law might become systematically known to all without citing difficulties and solutions of differences of view … but consisting of statements, clear and convincing, that have appeared from the time of Moses to the present, so that all rules shall be accessible to young and old … (introduction to *Mishneh Torah*).

Maimonides then set for himself the task of classifying by subject matter the entire talmudic and post-talmudic halakhic literature in a systematic manner never before attempted in the history of Judaism. The *Mishneh Torah* was divided into 14 books, each representing a distinct category of the Jewish legal system. (In Hebrew 14 is *yad* and hence the alternative name of the work *Yad ha-Ḥazakah*, i.e., "the strong hand.")

Even though the *Guide of the Perplexed* was written after the completion of the *Mishneh Torah*, Maimonides succeeded in incorporating many of its philosophic and scientific aspects into this purely halakhic work. Philosophy and science were handmaidens to theology. Hence Book 1 contains a complete system of metaphysics, Book 3 the astronomical calculations for reckoning the calendar, and Book 14 a discussion of the doctrine of the Messiah and a refutation of Christianity, Islam, and their founders. These digressions, which technically speaking are not halakhic in essence but rather ethical and philosophic, occur frequently in the halakhic writings of Maimonides.

Unlike the commentary to the Mishnah and *Sefer ha-Mitzvot* which were written in Arabic, the *Mishneh Torah* was written in a beautiful and lucid Hebrew, the like of which had not been known in halakhic literature since Judah ha-Nasi composed the Mishnah. The *Mishneh Torah* influenced the language of later codes, including the Shulḥan Arukh (see J. Dienstag, in: *Sinai*, 59 (1966), 54–75).

OPPOSITION TO THE CODE. The entire structure, form, and arrangement of the *Mishneh Torah* was a cultural and historical phenomenon unprecedented in Jewish dogmatic jurisprudence (see *Codification of Law) which both awed and shocked the scholarly world for centuries (see *Maimonidean Controversy). The architectural beauty of its structure, its logical arrangement, and ready-reference nature were the main targets for criticism, for it was feared that students would turn away from the study of the Talmud and commentaries, the source and wellspring of dynamic halakhic creativity. The severest criticism came from Abraham b. David of Posquières, an older contemporary of Maimonides, who probably equaled him in talmudic scholarship. The most serious of his charges was that Maimonides neglected to cite the sources and authorities from which his decisions were derived:

> He [Maimonides] intended to improve but did not improve, for he forsook the way of all authors who preceded him. They always adduced proof for their statements, citing the proper authority; this was very useful, for sometimes the judge would be inclined to forbid or permit something and his proof was based on some other authority. Had he known there was a greater authority who interpreted the law differently, he might have retracted… hence I do not know why I should reverse my tradition or corroborative views because of the compendium of this author. If the one who differs from me is greater than I, fine; and if I am greater than he, why should I annul my opinion…? Moreover, there are matters on which the *geonim* disagree and the author has selected the opinion of one…. Why should I rely on his choice…. It can only be one that an overbearing spirit is in him (Abraham b. David's *Hassagot* to introduction of *Mishneh Torah*).

These charges were not motivated by personal animosity, as claimed by some scholars of the Haskalah period, for on many occasions Abraham b. David traces certain sources of laws in the Code or comments upon it. At other times he is overwhelmed by this compendium (see I. Twersky, in: *Sefer ha-Yovel … Ẓevi Wolfson* (1965), 169–86). Abraham b. David's objections were shared by lesser-known scholars (I. Twersky, in: A. Altmann (ed.), *Biblical and other Studies* (1963), 161–82), who added their own criticism. During the 19th century, opposition to the *Mishneh Torah* was still a subject of controversy between S.D. Luzzatto, N. Krochmal, and others (J. Dienstag, in: Bitzaron, 55 (1967), 34–37).

In a series of letters Maimonides replied to his criticism that his intention in writing the *Mishneh Torah* was not to discourage talmudic studies, including the *halakhot* of Alfasi. On the contrary, he had lectured to his pupils on these subjects (A. Lichtenberg (ed.), *Kovez̦ Teshuvot ha-Rambam* (1859), pt. 1, no. 140 p. 25, b–c). He regretted the omission of his sources and hoped to include them in a supplement (*ibid.*). Maimonides never realized this hope. However, practically every commentary on the *Mishneh Torah* attempted to trace its sources. If his aim in compiling the Code was "so that no other work should be needed for ascertaining any of the laws of Israel," the more than 300 commentaries and novellae which have been written on it – and their number is growing – is an ironic phenomenon that could not have been anticipated by Maimonides. The *Mishneh Torah* did not become the definitive code its venerated creator had hoped. Actually, it surpassed his hopes, for it became the major source of halakhic creativity and talmudic research equaled only by the Talmud itself.

Maimonides the Halakhist in Modern Jewish Scholarship

Finally, it is interesting to note that no other halakhic authority has been the subject of so much modern Jewish scholarship as Maimonides. The tendentious, albeit subtle, anti-halakhic orientation of many of the exponents of the Wissenschaft school and the scholars of the Haskalah (including the leaders of Reform Judaism) has dampened, if not outright discouraged, intensive research in *halakhah* per se. Some of those who did engage in this discipline, such as A. Geiger, N. Bruell, J.H. Schorr, and others, were motivated by their anti-traditional bias and sought to undermine its authority and advance the cause of modernism and reform. The preoccupation of modern Jewish scholarship with Maimonides as halakhist is out of proportion to its interest in rabbinic literature and the stream of systematic studies on the subject has continued unabated.

[Jacob I. Dienstag]

PHILOSOPHY

Maimonides was, by general agreement, the most significant Jewish philosopher of the Middle Ages, and his *Guide of the Perplexed* is the most important philosophic work produced by a Jew. The Arabic original *Dalālat al-Ḥā'irîn* was completed about 1200 and shortly thereafter was twice translated into Hebrew as *Moreh Nevukhim*. The first translation, a literal one, was made by Samuel ibn Tibbon with Maimonides' advice and was completed in 1204. The second, a freer translation, was made by the poet Judah *al-Ḥarizi a little later. In its Hebrew translations, the *Guide* determined the course of Jewish philosophy from the early 13th century on, and almost every philosophic work for the remainder of the Middle Ages cited, commented on, or criticized Maimonides' views.

While the *Guide* contained the major statement of Maimonides' position, his philosophic and theological views appeared in a variety of other writings, among which the most important are the three lengthy essays in his commentary to the Mishnah (see above), first book of the *Mishneh Torah, Sefer ha-Madda* which is devoted to God and His attributes, angelic beings, the structure of the universe, prophecy, ethics, repentance, free will and providence, and the afterlife, and the last section of the work, *Mishneh Torah, Hilkhot Melakhim* which includes a discussion on the Messiah and the messianic age.

Influences on Maimonides

In his philosophic views Maimonides was an Aristotelian (see *Aristotle), whose philosophy also contained some neoplatonic elements, and it was he who put medieval Jewish philosophy on a firm Aristotelian basis. But in line with contemporary Aristotelianism his political philosophy was Platonic. In his works he quotes his authorities sparingly (see "*Shemonah Perakim*," introduction, end), but in a letter to his translator Samuel ibn Tibbon (A. Marx, in: JQR, 25 (1934–35), 374–81) he indicated his philosophic preferences explicitly. In this letter he advises Ibn Tibbon to study the works of Aristotle with the help of the Hellenistic commentators *Alexander of Aphrodisias and *Themistius and of Maimonides' contemporary *Averroes. It appears, however, that Averroes' commentaries reached Maimonides too late to have any influence on his *Guide*. He recommends highly the works of the Muslim al-*Fārābī, particularly those on logic, and he speaks of the writings of the Muslim *Avempace (Ibn Bāja) with approval. The works of *Avicenna (Ibn Sīnā) in Maimonides' view are also worthy of study, but they are inferior to those of al-Fārābī. Of Jewish philosophers he mentions only Isaac *Israeli, of whose views he disapproves, and Joseph ibn *Ẓaddik, whom he praises for his learning, though he states that he knew only the man, not his work. He also mentions some other philosophers of whose views he disapproves. Al-Fārābī, Avempace, and Averroes interpreted Aristotle rationalistically, and it appears that Maimonides preferred their interpretations to the more theologically oriented one of Avicenna, though he relied on Avicenna for some of his views.

(For a full discussion of sources, see S. Pines, *Guide of the Perplexed* (1963), translator's introduction lvii–cxxxiv.)

Maimonides considered himself in the tradition of the Aristotelians, adapting and developing their teachings in accord with his own views; but he differed from them in the works he produced. While the Muslims had composed commentaries on Aristotle's works, summaries of his views, and independent philosophic treatises, Maimonides produced no purely philosophic work of his own, the early *Treatise on Logic* excepted. He held that the extant philosophic literature was adequate for all needs (Guide 2, introd., proposition 25, and ch. 2), and he devoted himself to specific issues, particularly those bearing on the interrelation of philosophy and religion.

Distinction between Intellectual Elite and Masses

Fundamental to Maimonides' approach is a division of mankind into two groups: an intellectual elite, who, using reason, can understand by means of demonstrative arguments, and the masses (including those scholars who study only religious law), who, using imagination, understand by means of persuasive arguments. In the light of this distinction Maimonides' works may be divided into two kinds: *Guide of the Perplexed*, addressed primarily to an intellectual elite, and his other writings, addressed to the masses.

This distinction had one further consequence for Maimonides. Maimonides identified *ma'aseh bereshit* (the account of the creation) and *ma'aseh merkavah* (the account of the divine chariot of Ezekiel) with physics and metaphysics respectively. According to the Mishnah, however (Ḥag. 2:1) one may not teach the former to two persons, nor the latter even to one, unless he is wise and able to understand by himself. Maimonides codifies this as *halakhah* (Yad, Yesodei ha-Torah, 2:12; 4:10–13) and in his commentary to the Mishnah gives as the reason for the prohibition the current philosophical opinion that the teaching of abstract matters to someone who cannot grasp them may lead to unbelief.

This prohibition against the public teaching of *ma'aseh merkavah* and *ma'aseh bereshit* posed a problem. How could he write the *Guide*, a book devoted to these esoteric topics, when putting something in writing is equivalent to teaching it in public? Maimonides solved this problem by making use of certain literary devices. First, Maimonides addressed the book to his disciple, Joseph ben Judah ibn Sham'un, who after studying with him left for Baghdad. Hence, the *Guide* in its formal aspect is a personal communication to one student. Moreover Maimonides, in a dedicatory letter at the beginning of the *Guide*, relates Joseph's intellectual history, showing that he had acquired some philosophic wisdom and that he was able to reason for himself. Hence, Joseph had fulfilled the conditions necessary for studying the esoteric disciplines.

But Maimonides was well aware that persons other than Joseph would read his work. Hence, he had to make use of other devices. Invoking modes of esoteric writing also current among Islamic philosophers, Maimonides wrote his work in an enigmatic style. Discussing the same topic in different passages, he would make contradictory statements about it. He describes this method in the introduction to the *Guide*, where he speaks of seven types of contradictions which appear in literary works, stating explicitly that he will make use of two of them. It is left to the perceptive reader to discover Maimonides' true views on a given issue.

The enigmatic nature of the *Guide* imposed great difficulties on medieval and modern commentators, and two schools of interpretation arose. Some, such as Julius Guttmann, while aware of Maimonides' method, consider him a philosopher who attempted to harmonize the teachings of religion with those of philosophy. Others, such as Leo Strauss, considered Maimonides a philosopher, whose views were in agreement with those of the rationalistic Aristotelians, and who expressed religious opinions largely as a concession to the understanding of the masses. For example, Maimonides, according to the first interpretation, believed that the world was created, while according to the second, his true view was that the world is eternal.

With all these distinctions in mind one may proceed to an exposition of Maimonides' philosophy based largely on the *Guide*.

Purpose of the Guide

Maimonides wrote his work for someone who was firm in his religious beliefs and practices, but, having studied philosophy, was perplexed by the literal meaning of biblical anthropomorphic and anthropopathic terms. To this person Maimonides showed that these difficult terms have a spiritual meaning besides their literal one, and that it is the spiritual meaning that applies to God. Maimonides also undertook in the *Guide* the explanation of obscure biblical parables. Thus, the *Guide* is devoted to the philosophic interpretation of Scripture, or, to use Maimonides' terms, to the "science of the Law in its true sense" or to the "secrets of the Law" (Guide, introd.).

God

Maimonides' first philosophical topic is God. In line with his exegetical program he begins by explaining troublesome biblical terms, devoting the major portion of the first 49 chapters of the first part of the *Guide* to this task. Representative of his exegesis are his comments on the term "image of God" (*ẓelem Elohim*), found in the opening section of Genesis. Some have argued, Maimonides states, that since man was created in the image of God, it follows that God, like man, must have a body. He answers the objection by showing that the term *ẓelem* refers always to a spiritual quality, an essence. Hence, the "image of God" in man is man's essence, that is his reason but not physical likeness (Guide 1:1).

DIVINE ATTRIBUTES. Maimonides then takes up the question of God's attributes (Guide 1:50–60). The Bible describes God by many attributes, but it also states that God is one. If He is one in the sense of being simple, how can a multiplicity of attributes be ascribed to Him? Medieval philosophers held that attributes applied to substances are of two kinds: essential and accidental. Essential attributes are those that are closely connected with the essence, such as existence or life; accidental attributes are those that are independent of the essence and that may be changed without affecting the essence, such as anger or mercifulness. Medieval logicians generally agreed that accidental attributes introduce a multiplicity into that which they describe, while they disagreed concerning essential attributes. Some, such as Maimonides' contemporary Averroes, held that essential attributes are implicitly contained in the essence and, hence, do not introduce multiplicity; others held that they provide new information and, hence, produce multiplicity. Avicenna was an exponent of the latter view, holding that essential attributes, particularly existence, are superadded to the essence. Maimonides accepted Avicenna's position on this point. Maimonides came to the conclusion that accidental attributes applied to God must be interpreted as attributes of action, that is, if it is said that God is merciful, it means that God acts mercifully; and essential attributes must be interpreted as negations (or more precisely, negations of privations), that is, if God is said to be existing, it means that he is not nonexistent.

(See also *God, Attributes of).

EXISTENCE, UNITY, AND INCORPOREALITY OF GOD. Prior to Maimonides, Islamic and Jewish *Kalām philosophers had offered arguments for the existence, unity, and incorporeality of God and for the creation of the world. Maimonides summarized the teachings of the Kalām philosophers in order to refute them (Guide 1:71–76). In the case of the existence, unity, and incorporeality of God, Maimonides held that these are legitimate philosophic issues, but that the Kalām philosophers, relying on categories of the imagination rather than reason, had not solved them correctly. In the case of creation he held that to demonstrate the creation or eternity of the world lies outside the competence of the human mind.

Maimonides prefaces his own proofs for the existence, unity, and incorporeality of God with 25 metaphysical and physical propositions, which he considers to have been demonstrated in the philosophic literature of his days. To these he adds a 26th proposition, namely, that the world is eternal. However, it appears that this proposition does not reflect Maimonides' own belief concerning the origin of the world (see below), but serves, rather, a methodological function. It can be seen readily, Maimonides implies, that if it is assumed that the world is eternal, the existence of God can still be demonstrated (Guide 2, introd.).

EXISTENCE. To demonstrate the existence of God, Maimonides makes use of four proofs current in his day: from motion, from the composition of elements (also a kind of argument from motion), from necessity and contingency, and from potentiality and actuality (causality). The common structure of all of them is that they begin with some observed characteristic of the world, invoke the principle that an infinite regress is impossible, and conclude that a first principle must exist. For example, Maimonides begins his first proof, that from motion, by noting that in the sublunar world things constantly move and change. These sublunar motions, in turn, are caused by celestial motions which come to an end with the motion of the uppermost celestial sphere. The motion of that sphere is caused by a mover that is not moved by another mover. This mover, called the Prime Mover, is the last member in the chain of causes producing motion. Maimonides uses the following example as an illustration. Suppose a draft of air comes through a hole, and a stick is used to push a stone in the hole to close it. Now the stone is pushed into the hole by the stick, the stick is moved by the hand, and the hand is moved by the sinews, muscles, etc., of the human body. But one must also consider the draft of air, which was the reason for the motion of the stone in the first place. The motion of the air is caused by the motion of the lowest celestial sphere, and the motion of that sphere, by the successive motions of other spheres. The chain of things moved and moving comes to an end with the last of the celestial spheres. This sphere is set in motion by a principle which, while it produces motion, is itself not moved. This is the Prime Mover, which for Maimonides is identical with God.

Maimonides then turned to the nature of the Prime Mover. Four possibilities exist: Either the Prime Mover exists apart from the sphere, and then either corporeally or incorporeally; or it exists within the sphere, and then either as distributed throughout it or as indivisible. It can be shown that the Prime Mover does not exist within the sphere, which rules out the last two possibilities, nor apart from it as a body, which rules out the third. Hence, it exists apart from the sphere and must be incorporeal. Maimonides shows, further, that there cannot be two incorporeal movers. Thus, it has been established that the Prime Mover exists, is incorporeal, and is one.

Maimonides' proof from necessity and contingency rests on the observation that things in the world are contingent, and that they are ultimately produced by a being that is necessary through itself. This proof was first formulated by Avicenna and was rejected by Averroes (Guide 2:1; for a more popular discussion of Maimonides' conception of God, and his attributes, see Yad, Yesodei ha-Torah, 1–2).

Creation

Maimonides next turned to the incorporeal intelligences of the celestial spheres which he identifies with the angels (Guide 2:2–12), and then to creation of the world (Guide 2:13–26). On the last subject he begins by enumerating three theories of the origin of the world: that of the Torah, that the world was created by God out of nothing; that of Plato and others, according to which God created the world out of preexistent matter; and that of Aristotle, according to which the world is eternal. A major portion of the discussion is devoted to showing that Aristotle's and his followers' proofs of the eternity of the world are not really proofs. From an analysis of Aristotelian texts Maimonides attempted to show that Aristotle himself did not consider his arguments as conclusive demonstrations but only as showing that eternity is more plausible than creation. Maimonides' own position is that one can offer plausible arguments for the creation of the world as well as for its eternity. From this it follows that a conclusive demonstration of the creation or the eternity of the world lies beyond human reason; the human mind can only offer likely, technically known as dialectical, arguments for either alternative. However, an examination of these arguments reveals that those for creation are more likely than those for eternity, and on this basis Maimonides accepts the doctrine of creation *ex nihilo* as his own. An additional reason is that Scripture also teaches creation. Maimonides' intellectual daring is apparent in his statement (ch. 25) that had the eternity of the world been demonstrated philosophically, he would not have hesitated to interpret the Bible accordingly, just as he did not hesitate to interpret anthropomorphic terms in the Bible allegorically. He also states that the principle of creation is the most important one after that of God's unity, since it explains the possibility of miracles and similar occurrences. It should be noted, however, that some interpreters understand Maimonides' esoteric teaching as propounding the eternity of the world.

If the world was created, will it come to an end at some future time? He answers in the negative and adds that the future indestructibility of the world is also taught in the Bible (Guide 2:27–29). Maimonides concludes this phase of the discussion with an explanation of the creation chapters at the beginning of Genesis and a discussion of the Sabbath, which in part is also a reminder of the creation.

Prophecy

In the introduction to the *Guide* Maimonides incidentally discussed the nature of the prophetic experience, likening it to intellectual illumination. In the present section (Guide 2:32–48) he is interested in the psychology of prophecy and its political function. He begins by listing three possible theories of how prophecy is acquired: that of the unsophisticated believer, who holds that God arbitrarily selects someone for prophecy; that of the philosophers, according to which prophecy occurs when man's natural faculties, particularly his intellect, reach a high level of development; and that of Scripture, which specifies the same development of natural faculties but adds dependence on God, Who can prevent someone from prophesying, if He so desires. According to this last view, God's role in prophecy is negative, rather than positive.

Maimonides defined prophecy as an emanation from God, which, through the intermediacy of the Active Intellect, flows first upon man's intellectual faculty and then upon his imagination. While a well-developed imagination is of little significance for the illuminative experience of the prophet, it is central to his political function. In line with the views of the Islamic Aristotelians, particularly al-Fārābī, Maimonides conceives of the prophet as a statesman who brings law to his people and admonishes them to observe it. This conception of the prophet-statesman is based on Plato's notion, found in the *Republic*, of the philosopher-king who establishes and administers the ideal state. For Maimonides the primary function of prophets other than Moses is to admonish people to adhere to the Law of Moses; this requires that the prophets use the kind of imaginative language and parables that appeal to the imagination of the masses. Maimonides characterizes three personality types: philosopher, who uses only his intellect, the ordinary statesman, who uses only his imagination, and the prophet, who uses both.

Though he discusses the phenomenon of prophecy extensively, Maimonides mentions Moses, the chief of the prophets, only in passing in the *Guide*. However, in his halakhic writings he singles out Moses for special discussion. Moses, he states, differed so much from other prophets that he and they had virtually only the name "prophet" in common. Moses' prophecy is distinguished from that of the other prophets in four ways: other prophets received their prophecy in a dream or vision, Moses received his while awake; other prophets received their prophecy in allegorical form, Moses received his directly; other prophets were filled with fear when they received prophecy, Moses was not; other prophets received prophecy intermittently, Moses received it when he wished (*Hakdamah le-Ferek Ḥelek*, Principle 7; Yad, Yesodei ha-Torah, 7:6; cf. Guide 2:35). Moses also differed from other prophets and legislators in that he conveyed a perfect law, that is, one that addressed itself not only to man's moral perfection but also to his intellectual perfection by requiring the affirmation of certain beliefs.

Nature of Evil

Maimonides begins the third part of the Guide (introd. ch. 1–7) with a philosophic interpretation of the divine chariot (*merkavah*); this exposition brings to a close that part of the *Guide* that deals with speculative matters, that is, physical and metaphysical topics (Guide 3:7–end). Next he turns to practical philosophy, discussing evil and providence first.

Maimonides accepts the neoplatonic doctrine that evil is not an independent principle but rather the privation, or absence, of good. Like the Neoplatonists and other monists he had to accept this position, for to posit an independent principle of evil was to deny the uniqueness and omnipotence of God. There are three kinds of evil: natural evils, such as floods and earthquakes, which man cannot control, social evils, such as wars, and personal evils, the various human vices, both of which man can control. Natural evils are infrequent, and, hence, the majority of evil in the world, which is caused by man, can be remedied by proper training. Maimonides also argues against those who hold that the world is essentially evil, stating that if one looks at the world at large, rather than at one's own pains and misfortunes, one finds that the world as a whole is good, not evil (Guide 3:8–12).

Divine Providence

Maimonides discusses divine omniscience and then turns to the related question of divine providence. He distinguishes between general providence, which refers to general laws regulating nature, and individual providence, which refers to God's providential concern for individual men. He lists four theories of providence that he rejects: the theory of Epicurus (see *Epicureanism), which states that everything that happens in the world is the result of chance; that of Aristotle (really that of the commentator Alexander of Aphrodisias), which states that there is only general, not individual, providence; that of the Islamic Asharites (see *Kalām), which states that the divine will rules everything – this is equivalent to individual providence extended to include all beings, animate and inanimate; and that of the Muʿtazilites (see *Kalām), which states that there is individual providence extending even to animals but not to inanimate objects. Last, Maimonides discusses the attitude toward providence of the adherents of the Torah. They all accept man's free will and God's justice. To these principles some more recent scholars (Maimonides had in mind the *geonim*, most likely Saadiah) have added the principle of *yissurin shel ahavah* ("afflictions of love"), which explains that God may cause suffering to a righteous person in order to reward him in the hereafter. Maimonides rejected it, however, stating that only an unjust God would act in this manner, and asserted that every pain and affliction is a punishment for a prior sin. Finally, Maimonides gave his own position: there is individual providence, and it is determined by the degree of development of the individual's intellect. The more developed a man's intellect, the more subject he is to divine providence (Guide 3:16–21). Maimonides used this theory of providence in his interpretation of the Book of Job, in which the characters of that book represent the various attitudes toward providence discussed above (Guide 3:22–23).

Nature of Man and Moral Virtue

Maimonides' final undertaking in the *Guide* is his explanation of the Law of Moses and its precepts. But this account is based on his philosophy of man, which he summarizes only in his "*Shemonah Perakim*." From this summary it is clear that Maimonides' philosophy of man was one current among Muslim Aristotelians. Man is composed of a body and a soul, the soul, particularly the intellect, being the form of the body. The soul, which is unitary, contains five basic faculties: nutritive, sensory, imaginative, appetitive, and rational. Of these faculties, the appetitive and rational are important for the good life and for happiness on earth and in the hereafter. Man attains happiness through the exercise of moral virtues to control his appetites and by developing his intellectual powers. In Maimonides' discussion of morality he follows Aristotle in holding that virtuous action consists of following the mean, but he holds that all should go to the extreme to avoid pride and anger (Yad, Deot, 2:3). While in his halakhic writings Maimonides embraced a morality of the mean, in the *Guide* he advocates a more ascetic life, and he particularly recommends curbing the sexual drive. As in Aristotelian thought, the moral virtues serve only a preliminary function, the final goal being the acquisition of intellectual virtues.

(For another discussion of Maimonides' moral philosophy, see Yad, Deot.)

Law of Moses

In the *Guide* 3:26–49 Maimonides discusses the reasons of the commandments. Maimonides considers a distinction made by Muʿtazilite philosophers, *Saadiah among them. These philosophers had divided divine law into two categories: rational commandments, such as the prohibitions against murder and theft, which the human mind can discover without revelation; and revealed commandments, such as prayer and the observance of holidays, which are neutral from the point of view of reason and can be known only through revelation. Maimonides understands this position as implying that the revelational commandments come from God's will rather than His reason. Against this view, Maimonides argues that all divine commandments are the product of God's wisdom, though he adds that some are easily intelligible (*mishpatim*), and others intelligible only with difficulty (*ḥukkim*). However, Maimonides adds that particular commandments have no rational principle behind them and are commandments only because God willed them.

Maimonides postulates two purposes of the Law: the well-being of the soul (intellect) and the well-being of the body, by which he means man's moral well-being. The former is acquired through true beliefs; the latter, through political and personal morality. The beliefs which a man must accept are graded according to his intellectual ability. There are also true beliefs, such as the existence of God, His unity, and His incorporeality, which everyone must accept regardless of intellectual ability; and there are beliefs, such as that God gets angry at those who disobey Him, which have primarily a political function and are considered necessary beliefs. Ordinary men will accept the Law only if they are promised rewards or threatened with punishment, and it is the function of the necessary beliefs to provide such motivation. They are unnecessary for the philosopher, who obeys the Law because it is the right thing to do regardless of consequences.

Although reasons for general moral laws can readily be found, it is more difficult to explain the numerous ritual laws found in the Bible. Maimonides explains many of them as reactions to pagan practices, and he makes use of his extensive familiarity with such books as the *Nabatean Agriculture*, which describe such practices (see *Commandments, Reasons for). Thus, for example, he explains the biblical prohibition against wearing garments made of wool and linen combined as a reaction to a pagan practice requiring priests to wear such garments. Maimonides also considers certain commandments as concessions to historical situations, such as those dealing with sacrifice. Worship without animal sacrifices is preferred, but it would have been unrealistic to require the Israelites leaving Egypt to give up sacrifices altogether. Hence the Bible commanded sacrifices, restricting, however, the times and places for them and permitting only priests to offer them. We should not infer from this, however, that Maimonides believed in a progressive development of Jewish law; in fact, he codifies all of rabbinic law in his *Mishneh Torah*. The *Guide* concludes with a supplementary section on the perfect worship of God and man's perfection.

Eschatology

Eschatology is barely mentioned in the *Guide*, although Maimonides developed it fully in other works. Following traditional Jewish teachings, he deals with the Messiah and messianic times, the resurrection of the dead, and *olam ha-ba* ("the world to come"). He proceeds characteristically by stripping these occurrences of supernatural qualities as much as possible. The Messiah is an earthly king, descended from the house of David. He will bring the Jews back to their country, but his major accomplishment will be to bring peace and tranquility to the world, thereby facilitating full observance of God's commandments. The Messiah will die of old age and be succeeded by his son, the latter, by his son, and so on. No cataclysmic events will take place during messianic times, but the world will continue in its established natural order. Maimonides calculated the year of the coming of the Messiah ("*Epistle to Yemen*"), although he generally opposed speculations of this kind (*Hakdamah le-Ferek Ḥelek*, principle 12; Yad, Melakhim, 12:2 – uncensored edition).

During messianic times the dead will be resurrected with body and soul reunited though later the human person will die again. (For his affirmation of this doctrine in reply to criticism that he rejected it, see above.) Undoubtedly, the central notion of Maimonides' eschatology is his account of *olam ha-ba*. In his view the intellect, but not the body, has an afterlife, and in that afterlife the intellect is engaged in the contemplation of God. Generally, he speaks of incorporeal intelligences (plural), implying that immortality is individual, but there are passages which suggest that immortality is collective, that is, in the world to come there exists only one intellect for all mankind (*Hakdamah le-Ferek Ḥelek*; Yad, Teshuvah, 8–10, Guide 1:41; *Treatise on Resurrection*).

Basic Principles of Judaism

Maimonides' intellectualism is reflected in the formulation of 13 principles that in his view every member of the Jewish community is bound to accept (see *Articles of Faith). Did he intend these principles as a means of developing the intellects of the masses, thus enabling them to share in *olam ha-ba*, or as a political expedient, that is, to make the masses aware of intellectual issues so that philosophers can live safely in their midst? Proponents of both views are found among Maimonides' interpreters (see A. Hyman, in: A. Altmann (ed.), *Jewish Medieval and Renaissance Studies* (1967), 119–44).

Influence

Maimonides' *Guide*, as has been noted, profoundly influenced the subsequent course of medieval Jewish philosophy. Among the extensive literature that arose were numerous full and partial commentaries on the *Guide*, most of them still unpublished. However, four of these have been printed and they appear many times with the Hebrew text of the *Guide*. They are those of Profiat *Duran (Efodi), Shem Tov ben Joseph *Ibn Shem Tov, Asher *Crescas, and Isaac *Abrabanel. In addition, the following commentaries have appeared in print: *Moreh ha-Moreh* by Shem Tov ibn *Falaquera, which also contains corrections of Ibn Tibbon's Hebrew translation based on the Arabic original (edited by M.L. Bisseliches, 1837); Yair Shiffman has published a critical edition of Shem Tov Ibn Falaquera's commentary *Moreh ha-Moreh* (Jerusalem, 2001); and a commentary by *Moses Narboni (all three reprinted in *Sheloshah Kadmonei Mefareshei ha-Moreh*, 1961). Samuel ibn Tibbon composed a philosophic glossary on the *Guide* entitled *Perush me-ha-Millot ha-Zarot asher be-Ma'amarei ha-Rav*, which has also been printed many times. One aspect of the commentary literature is the attempt to reconcile Maimonides' views with the divergent ones of his contemporary Averroes. Of commentaries and notes that have appeared on the *Guide* in more recent times are those of Solomon Maimon's *Givat ha-Moreh* (edited by Samuel Hugo Bergman and N. Rotenstreich, 1966), the notes in S. Munk's French translation of the *Guide*, and the Hebrew commentary in Ibn Shmuel's edition.

In addition to its significance for medieval Jewish philosophy, the *Guide* also had a formative influence on modern Jewish thought. Maimonides provided a first acquaintance with philosophic speculation for a number of philosophers of the Enlightenment period and served as a bridge for the study of more modern philosophy. Moses *Mendelssohn is a case in point. In addition, Maimonides became a symbol for their own philosophic endeavors; he had attempted to introduce the spirit of rationalism into Jewish teachings during medieval times, just as they tried to do in their own time. Among modern thinkers influenced in some way by Maimonides are, in addition to Mendelssohn and Solomon Maimon (c. 1752–1800), Nahman *Krochmal, Samuel David *Luzatto (who opposed Maimonides' rationalism), S.L. *Steinheim, Hermann *Cohen, and *Aḥad *Ha-Am.

Maimonides exercised an extensive influence on Christian scholastic thought. Among these scholastics are *Alexander of Hales, *William of Auvergne, *Albertus Magnus, Thomas *Aquinas, Meister *Eckhart, and *Duns Scotus. These scholastics generally quote Maimonides by name, but sometimes they cite his views anonymously. Giles of Rome composed a treatise entitled *Errores philosophorum* about 1270 (edited by J. Koch, with an English translation by J.O. Riedl, 1944), the 12th chapter of which is devoted to a refutation of Maimonides' views. (For Maimonides' influence on scholastic philosophy, see B. Geyer, *Die patristische und scholastische Philosophie* (1928), index; E. Gilson, *History of Christian Philosophy in the Middle Ages* (1955), index; Görge Hasselhoff, *Dicit Rabbi Moyses, Studien zum Bild Moses von Moses Maimonides im lateinischen Westen vom 13. bis zum 15. Jahrhundert* (Würzburg, 2004) Kaufmann, Schriften, 2 (1910), 152–89; Jacob Guttmann, in: *Moses ben Maimon*, J. Braun et al. (editors), 1 (1908), 135–230; and see also other studies by Jacob Guttman, Issachar Joel, and Isaac Husik.)

In early modern times Maimonides influenced the secular philosophers Baruch *Spinoza (see H.A. Wolfson, *The Philosophy of Spinoza* (1954), index) and Gottfried Wilhelm Leibnitz.

[Arthur Hyman]

AS PHYSICIAN

Maimonides was probably first taught medicine by his father, but, as stated above, during the seven years which his family spent in Fez, Maimonides probably had the opportunity to pursue his medical studies and mingle with well-known physicians. In his "Treatise on Asthma" he describes discussions with the Jewish physician Abu Yūsuf b. Mu'allim and with Muhammad, son of the famous Avenzoar, and others. From his commentary on drugs it may also be concluded that he received his basic medical education in Morocco. He refers to "our physicians in the West" and to Morocco and Spain. Most of the names of drugs are given there not only in Arabic but also in Berber and Spanish. The only authors quoted by name are Spanish-Moroccan physicians (Ibn Juljul, Ibn Wāfid, Ibn Samajūn), who lived one to two centuries before him, and his older contemporary al-Ghāfiqī. Maimonides was certainly very familiar with Arabic translations of the writings of Greek physicians as well as with the writings of the older Arab physicians, for he himself condensed some of them.

That Maimonides was highly regarded as a physician among the Muslims is evident from the statements of the historians Ibn al-Qifṭī (c. 1248) and Ibn Abi Uṣaybiʿa (c. 1270) as well as of the physician ʿAbd-al-Laṭīf of Baghdad, who visited Maimonides when he was in Cairo in 1201. A song of praise which was written by a grateful patient, Saʿīd b. Ṣanā' al-Mulk, has been preserved by Ibn Abi Uṣaybiʿa:

> Galen's art heals only the body
> But Abu-Amran's [Maimonides'] the body and the soul.
> His knowledge made him the physician of the century.
> He could heal with his wisdom the sickness of ignorance.
> If the moon would submit to his art,
> He would free her of the spots at the time of full moon,
> Would deliver her of her periodic defects,
> And at the time of her conjunction save her from waning.
> (Translation taken from B.L. Gordon, *Medieval and Renaissance Medicine* (1959), 235.)

Moreover, from certain statements made by Ibn Abi Uṣaybiʿa, it is clear to us that Maimonides also lectured on medicine and taught disciples such as his own son Abraham, as well as Joseph b. Judah ibn Shamʿun, and Rashīd al-Dīn.

Maimonides classified medicine into three divisions: preventive medicine; healing of the sick; and care of the convalescent, including invalids and the aged. His medical teachings, based on the then prevailing humoral pathology as taught by Hippocrates and Galen, are of a strictly rational character. He disapproved strongly of the use of charms, incantations, and amulets in treating the sick, and was outspoken against any blind belief in authority. He encouraged his disciples to observe and reason critically and insisted on experiment and research. In his "Treatise of Asthma" Maimonides stresses that the physician is important not only during sickness but also when the body is healthy. Unlike any other craftsman, the physician must use art, logic, and intuition. Maimonides also added that the physician must be able to take a comprehensive view of the patient and his circumstances in order to make a diagnosis of both his general condition and of diseases of individual organs.

Except for part of his Galen compendium, all of Maimonides' medical writings, most of which were apparently written in Arabic in Cairo during 1190–1204, have been preserved. The majority of these works were translated into Hebrew and Latin and helped to spread his fame in the West.

(1) *Al-Mukhtaṣarāt* is a compendium of the works of Galen for teaching purposes, of which only three, in Arabic, have been preserved.

(2) A commentary by him on the *Aphorisms* of Hippocrates, which had been translated into Arabic by the ninth-century translator Ḥunayn ibn Isḥāq, in general follows Galen's commentary; it has been only partially preserved in two defective Arabic manuscripts.

(3) *Fuṣūl Mūsā* ("The Aphorisms of Moses") is possibly the most famous and most widely quoted of all Maimonides' medical writings. It was translated into Hebrew under the title *Pirkei Moshe*, in the 13th century. In this work Maimonides included a large number of medical aphorisms and sundry information, mostly from Galen's own writings or his commentaries on Hippocrates, but also from Arab authors. On speaking of the relation between the right-hand part of the heart and the lungs (1:55), Maimonides seems to have touched on the lesser circulation, without, however, venturing further afield. The passages in 1:19 as well as 8:57 and 62 strongly indicate that he was speaking of arterioles connecting the arteries and the veins.

(4) *Sarḥ asmā' al-ʿuqqār* is a commentary on drugs, the manuscript of which was found in Istanbul in 1932. It consists of 56 pages of 17 lines each. In the introduction Maimonides deals with the necessity of identifying drugs by their popular names. He then lists, in alphabetical order, about 350 remedies, mainly derived from plants. The Arabic names are often followed by Greek and Persian terms as well as colloquial Spanish, Moroccan, Egyptian, and Berber names. The so-called "Prayer of a Physician" was not written by Maimonides but was added later.

(5) *Fī al-Bawāsīr* is a work on hemorrhoids and was written for a young aristocrat.

(6) *Fī al-Jimāʿa*, a treatise on sexual intercourse, was written for the sultan Omar son of Nur al-Dīn.

(7) *Maqāla Fī al-Rabw* ("Treatise on Asthma") was written in 1190. Maimonides regards bronchial asthma as largely due to nervousness, and believes that some people thus inclined react strongly to certain irritants. Correct diet and spiritual treatment, he says, have a beneficial effect on the asthmatic.

(8) *Kilāb al-Sumūm wa al-Mutaḥarriz min al-Adwiya al-Qitāla* ("On Poisons and Their Antidotes"), a very famous manuscript, includes a classic description of the various symptoms of poisoning and is of value even today. Maimonides is the first to distinguish between the various types of snake venoms and suggests the establishment of collections of antidotes in state pharmacies. For snakebites he advises cautery, local tourniquets, rest, and general treatment against shock.

(9) *Fī Tadbir al-Ṣiḥḥa* ("Guide to Good Health"), a treatise on hygiene, is one of the most popular of Maimonides' works. It was written in 1198 for the Egyptian sultan Afḍal Nūr al-Dīn Ali, who suffered from attacks of depression accompanied by physical symptoms. Maimonides teaches that physical convalescence is dependent on psychological well-being and rest. He stresses the necessity of hygienic conditions in the care of the body, physical exercise, and proper breathing, work, family, sexual life, and diet, and suggests that music, poetry, paintings, and walks in pleasant surroundings all have a part to play toward a happy person and the maintenance of good health.

(10) *Maqāla Fī Bayān al-Aʿrāḍ* ("Explanation of Coincidences") was also written for the sultan Afḍal Nūr al-Dīn Ali, who requested an explanation of the causes of his continued depression. It is a short treatise on the subject, in 22 chapters.

In the formation of his opinions on man's spiritual wellbeing, Maimonides' scientific and psychological experiences are closely interwoven with his religious principles. Physical and biological rules are integrated with moral and ethical principles in his world of values. To integrate oneself consciously into the natural biological laws of the world represented for

Maimonides the fulfillment of the idea of walking in the paths of science and wisdom and achieving true knowledge and perfect bliss.

[Suessmann Muntner]

AS ASTRONOMER

Maimonides did not compose a systematic treatise on astronomy, but his competence in the subject is well illustrated by a number of passages in the *Moreh Nevukhim* (*Guide of the Perplexed*) and by his treatise on the calendar, *The Sanctification of the New Moon* (*Kiddush Rosh Ḥodesh* in *Mishneh Torah*). In the *Guide* there are references to technical aspects of Ptolemaic astronomy, and it is revealed that Maimonides' disciple Joseph ibn Sham'un had studied Ptolemy's *Almagest* under him. Maimonides states that he was acquainted with the son of Jābir ibn Aflaḥ of Seville (d. c. 1150), the author of a well-known astronomical text which takes exception to some Ptolemaic principles. He also refers to a lost work of Ibn Bāja (d. 1139), concerning the principles of astronomy, that he had obviously read with care. According to Maimonides, the physical difficulties of eccentric and epicyclic spheres need not concern the astronomer, whose task is merely to propose a theory in which the motions of the planets and the stars are uniform and circular, and conform to observation. In the *Sanctification*, Maimonides describes the calendric rules that were used in the time of the Sanhedrin, the rules of the fixed calendar that apply to this day, and the astronomical determination of the beginning of the month. The third section again shows Maimonides to be competent in the technical aspects of Ptolemaic astronomy, although he made no original contribution to the subject. In 1194 Maimonides wrote a letter addressed to the rabbis of southern France strongly denouncing *astrology as a pseudoscience opposed to the true science of astronomy, an opinion rarely expressed by Jewish scholars in the Middle Ages. In this letter Maimonides stated that astrology was the first secular subject he studied, and that he had read everything available in Arabic on the discipline.

[Bernard R. Goldstein]

TRANSLATIONS

Among Maimonides' halakhic works, Y. Kafaḥ published a new Hebrew translation of the *Sefer ha-Mitzvot* (1958) from the original Arabic, on which C.B. Chavel based his English version, *The Commandments: Sefer ha-Mitzvoth of Maimonides*, 2 vols. (1967). An English translation of the entire *Mishneh Torah,* almost all of whose volumes have appeared as of 2005, is being published in the Yale Judaica Series (begun 1949). An edition with an English translation of the first two books of *Mishneh Torah,* based on the Bodleian (Oxford) codex, was published by Moses Hyamson in 1962.

The Arabic original of the *Guide* was edited, with a French translation, by S. Munk (*Le guide des égarés*, 3 vols. (1856–66); ed. by I. Joel, based on Munk's text, 1931). Samuel ibn Tibbon's Hebrew translation was first printed in Rome before 1480, and again in Venice, 1551, Sabionetta, 1553, and frequently thereafter. Yehudah Even-Shemuel (Kaufmann) edited part of this text with introductions and a commentary in three volumes (1935–59). Yehudah Even-Shemuel (Kaufman) also published a full edition of the Samuel ibn Tibbon translation, but without commentary, in 2000. Y. Kafah published the Judaeo-Arabic original with a modern Hebrew translation in three volumes in 1972. Michael Schwarz published a modern Hebrew translation from the Arabic with a modern Hebrew commentary and bibliography in two volumes in 2002. The translation of Judah al-Ḥarizi was edited, with notes, by L. Schlossberg in three parts (1851–79; 19123). Both versions were translated into Latin: that of Ibn Tibbon by J. Buxtorf (Basel, 1629) and Al-Ḥarizi's edited by A. Justinianus (Paris, 1520). The *Guide* was translated into English by M. Friedlaender, 3 volumes (1885; 1904^2; repr. 1956), and by S. Pines (1963), with introductions by L. Strauss, and the translator C. Rabin published an abridged translation with an introduction by J. Guttmann (1952). German translations were undertaken in the 19th century (R. Fuerstenthal, pt. 1, 1839; M. Stern, pt. 2, 1864; S. Scheyer, pt. 3, 1838), all based on the Hebrew version of Ibn Tibbon. There is also a modern Hebrew translation from the Arabic by A. Siman and E. Mani, and versions in Italian, Spanish, and Hungarian.

I. Efros published an English translation of Maimonides' *Treatise on Logic* (in: PAAJR, 8, 1938), together with part of the Arabic original and three Hebrew versions. He also published a revised edition of the full Arabic text (in Hebrew alphabet) based on the edition of M. Tuerker (in: PAAJR, 34 (1966), 155ff.). J. Gorfinkle translated the *Shemonah Perakim* into English under the title *The Eight Chapters of Maimonides on Ethics* (1966). The *Iggeret Teiman* was translated by Boaz Cohen, *Moses Maimonides' Epistle to Yemen* (1952), edited by A.S. Halkin. Translations by Abraham Halkin and discussion by David Hartman of *The Epistle on Martyrdom, The Epistle to Yemen,* and *The Essay on Resurrection* are found in *Crisis and Leadership: The Epistles of Maimonides* (1985). S. Muntner edited versions of many of Maimonides' medical works: *Perush le-Firkei Abukrat* ("Commentary on the Aphorisms of Hippocrates" (1961), with an Eng. introd. (*Pirkei Moshe bi-Refu'ah* ("Maimonides' Medical Aphorisms" (1959), with Eng. introd.); *Sefer ha-Kaẓẓeret* (1940; *Treatise on Asthma*, 1963); *Sammei ha-Mavet* (1942; *Treatise on Poisons and Their Antidotes*, 1966); and *Hanhagat ha-Beri'ut* ("Guide to Good Health" (1957); *Regimen Sanitasis*, Ger., 1966). Volume I of *The Medical Aphorisms of Moses Maimonides* (ed. F. Rosner and S. Muntner) appeared in 1970. Selected letters of Maimonides are to be found in English translation in F. Kobler (ed.) *Letters of Jews Through the Ages*, 1 (1952), 178–219 (see also introduction, lx–lxi).

BIBLIOGRAPHY: It is recommended that for an ongoing bibliography of writings about Maimonides, the reader consult *Reshimat Ma'amarim be-Madda'ei ha-Yahadut (Index to Articles on Jewish Studies),* a journal that lists articles in European languages and Hebrew on an ongoing basis. This bibliographic journal is now available on the internet at http://jnul.ac.il/rambi. GENERAL: D. Yellin and I. Abrahams, *Maimonides* (1903; repr. 1936); J. Guttmann et al. (eds.), *Moses ben Maimon, sein Leben, seine Werke und sein Einfluss*, 2 vols. (1908–14); Graetz-Rabbinowitz, 4 (1916), 326–406, 459 n. 2, and appendix by A.E. Harkavy, 51–59; A. Cohen, *Teachings of Maimonides* (1927; repr. 1968); I. Epstein (ed.), *Moses Maimonides* (1935); B. Dinur, *Rabbenu Moshe ben Maimon* (1935); S. Baron (ed.), *Essays on Maimonides* (1941); A.S. Halkin, in: *Joshua Starr Memorial Volume* (1953), 101–10 (Heb.); M.D. Rabinowitz (ed.), *Iggerot ha-Rambam* (1960), introductions to the three letters; J.L. Maimon, *Rabbi Moshe ben Maimon* (1960); Hirschberg, Afrikah, 1 (1965), index; A. Neubauer, in: JQR, 8 (1896), 541–61. **ADD. BIBLIOGRAPHY:** H.A. Davidson, *Moses Maimonides: The Man and His Works* (2005); ALLEGED CONVERSION: On the question of his alleged conversion: those who maintain it are A. Geiger (*Nachgelassene Schriften*, 3 (1876), 42), S. Munk (*Notice sur Joseph ben-Iehouda* (1842), and in: AI, 12 (1851), 319 ff.), and Graetz. The allegation is examined and opposed by M. Friedlaender (*Guide for the Perplexed* (19042), xviii), D.S. Margoliouth (JQR, 13 (1901), 539–41), and S.P. Rabbinowitz (Graetz-Rabbinowitz, 4 (1916), 332, 462). See also J.L. Maimon, op. cit., 235–50; D. Corcos, in: *Zion*, 32 (1967), 138–60. As HALAKHIST: I. Epstein (ed.), op. cit., 59–82; I. Herzog, *ibid.*, 137–53; A. Marmorstein, *ibid.*, 157–74; Levey, in: CCARY, 45 (1935), 368–96; C. Tchernowitz, *Toledot ha-Posekim*, 1 (1946), 193–307; J. Levinger, *Darkhei ha-Maḥashavah ha-Hilkhatit shel ha-Rambam* (1965); A. Zuroff, *Responsa of Maimonides* (Diss., Yeshiva University, 1966); M. Havazelet, *Ha-Rambam ve-ha-Ge'onim* (1967); J.T. Dienstag, in: *Talpioth*, 9 (1968); idem, *Ein ha-Mitzvot* (1968). AS PHILOSOPHER AND SCIENTIST: Guttmann, Philosophies, 152–82 and index; Husik, Philosophy, 236–311 and index; D. Rosin, *Die Ethik Maimonides* (1876); I. Efros, *Philosophical Terms in the Moreh Nebukim* (1924); L. Roth, *Spinoza, Descartes, and Maimonides* (1929); J. Sarachek, *Faith and Reason: the Conflict over the Rationalism of Maimonides* (1935); F. Bamberger, *Das System des Maimonides* (1935); L. Strauss, *Philosophie und Gesetz* (1935); idem, in: MGWJ, 81 (1937), 93–105; idem, in: Baron (ed.), op. cit., 37–91 (repr. in: L. Strauss, *Persecution and the Art of Writing* (1952), 38–94); idem, in: PAAJR, 22 (1953), 115–30; G. Vajda, *Introduction à la pensee juive du moyen âge* (1947), 129–51; J. Becker, *Mishnato ha-Filosofit shel ha-Rambam* (1956); L.V. Berman, *Ibn Bājjah ve-ha-Rambam: Perek be-Toledot ha-Filosofyah ha-Medinit* (1959); H.A. Wolfson, in: JQR, 1 (1911/12), 297–339; 25 (1934/35), 441–67; 26 (1935/36), 369–77; 32 (1941/42), 345–70; 33 (1942/43), 40–82; idem, in: *Essays… Linda R. Miller* (1938), 201–34; idem, in: PAAJR, 11 (1941), 105–63; idem, in: *Louis Ginzberg Jubilee Volume* (1945), 411–46; idem, in: *Mordecai M. Kaplan Jubilee Volume* (1953), 515–30; Z. Diesendruck, in: *Jewish Studies… Israel Abrahams* (1927), 74–134 (Ger.); idem, in: HUCA, 5 (1928), 415–534 (Get.); S. Rawidowicz, in: I. Epstein (ed.), *Moses Maimonides* (1935), 177–88; E. Rosenthal, *ibid.*, 191–206; I. Heinemann, in: MGWJ, 79 (1935), 102–48; A. Altmann, *ibid.*, 80 (1936), 305–30; idem, in: BJRL, 35 (1953), 294–315; A.J. Heschel, in: *Sefer ha-Yovel… Levi Ginzberg* (1945), 159–88; A. Hyman, in: *La filosofia della natura nel medioevo* (1966), 209–18; S. Pines, in: *Encyclopedia of Philosophy*, 5 (1967), 129–34; A.J. Reines, *Maimonides and Abrabanel on Prophecy* (1970). **ADD. BIBLIOGRAPHY:** (General Works): C. Sirat, *A History of Jewish Philosophy in the Middle Ages* (1985), 157–203; D.H. Frank, "Maimonides and Medieval Jewish Aristotelianism," in: D.H. Frank and O. Leaman (eds.), *The Cambridge Companion to Medieval Jewish Philosophy* (2003), 136–56; H. Kreisel, "Moses Maimonides," in: D.H. Frank and O. Leaman (eds.), *History of Jewish Philosophy* (1997), 245–80; T. Langerman, "Maimonides and the Sciences," in: *The Cambridge Companion to Medieval Jewish Philosophy* (2003), 157–75; O. Leaman, *Moses Maimonides* (1990); B. Ben-Shammai, "*Esrim ve-Ḥamesh Shenot Meḥkar ha-Rambam: Bibliographia 1965–1990*," in: *Maimonidean Studies*, 2 (1991), 17–42; J. Buijs (ed.), *Maimonides: A Collection of Critical Essays* (1988); A. Hyman (ed.), *Maimonidean Studies* (1990–ongoing); J.L. Kraemer (ed.), *Perspectives on Maimonides: Philosophical and Historical Studies* (1991); J.L. Kraemer, "The Life of Maimonides," in: L. Fine (ed.), *Judaism in Practice* (2001),413–28; H. Levine and R.S. Cohen (eds.), *Maimonides and the Sciences* (2000); David R. Lachterman, "Maimonidean Studies 1950–86: A Bibliography," in: *Maimonidean Studies*, 1 (1990), 197–216; T. Lévy and R. Rashed, *Maimonide, philosophe et savant (1138–1204)* (2004); C.H. Manekin, *On Maimonides* (2005); E. Ormsby (ed.), *Moses Maimonides and His Times* (1989); S. Pines and Y. Yovel (eds.), *Maimonides and Philosophy* (1986); I. Robinson, L. Kaplan, and J. Bauer (eds.), *The Thought of Moses Maimonides: Philosophical and Legal Studies* (1990); F. Rosner and S. Kottek (eds.), *Moses Maimonides, Physician, Scientist and Philosopher* (1993); I. Twersky (ed.), *A Maimonides Reader* (1972); I. Twersky, *Studies in Maimonides* (1990). AS PHYSICIAN: W.M. Feldman, in: I. Epstein (ed.), *Moses Maimonides* (1935), 107–34; F. Rosner, in: *Bulletin of the History of Medicine*, 43 (1969); S. Muntner, in: *Ha-Refu'ah* (1954); idem, in: *Korot*, 3 (1964), 7–8; W. Steinberg and S. Muntner, in: *American Journal of Obstetrics and Gynaecology*, 91 no. 3 (1965); I. Jakobovits, *Jewish Medical Ethics* (1959); F. Rosner and S. Muntner, *The Medical Aphorisms of Maimonides*, 1 (1970). AS ASTRONOMER: A. Marx, in: HUCA, R. Lerner and M. Mahdi (eds.), *Medieval Political Philosophy* (1963), 227–36. HIS VIEWS ON MUSIC: H.G. Farmer, *Maimonides on Listening to Music* (1941); E. Werner and I. Sonne, in: HUCA, 16 (1941), 281–3, 313–5; B. Cohen, *Law and Tradition in Judaism* (1959), 167–81. **ADD. BIBLIOGRAPHY:** ESSAYS AND BOOKS ON SPECIAL TOPICS: A. Altmann, "Maimonides on the Intellect and the Scope of Metaphysics," in: *Von der mittelalterlichen zur modernen Aufklärung* (1987), 60–129; idem, "Maimonides' Four Perfections," in: *Essays in Jewish Intellectual History*, 65–76; E. Benor, *Worship of the Heart: A Study in Maimonides' Philosophy of Religion* (1995); K.P. Bland, "Moses and the Law according to Moses," in: J. Reinharz and D. Swetschinski (eds.), *Mystics, Philosophers, and Politicians: Essays in Jewish Intellectual History in Honor of Alexander Altmann* (1982), 49–66; H.A. Davidson, "Maimonides' Secret Position on Creation," in: I. Twersky (ed.), *Studies in Medieval Jewish History and Literature*, vol. 1 (1979), 16–40; M. Fox, *Interpreting Maimonides: Studies in Methodology, Metaphysics, and Moral Philosophy* (1990); M.A. Friedman, *Maimonides, the Yemenite Messiah, and Apostasy* (Heb., 2002); A. Funkenstein, *Maimonides: Nature, History, and Messianic Beliefs* (1997); A.L. Gluck, "Maimonides' Arguments for Creation 'ex nihilo' in the 'Guide of the Perplexed'," in: *Medieval Philosophy and Theology* 7:2 (1998), 221–53; S.D. Goitein, "Moses Maimonides, Man of Action: A Revision of the Master's Biography in the Light of the Geniza Documents," in: G. Nahon and Charles Touati (eds.), *Hommage á George Vajda* (1980), 155–67; L.E. Goodman, "Maimonides' Philosophy of Law," in: *Jewish Law Annual*, 1 (1978), 72–107; J. Guttmann, "Philosophie der Religion oder Philosophie des Gesetzes?," in: *Proceedings of the Israel Academy of Sciences and Humanities*, 5 (1971–76), 147–73 (also published as a separate pamphlet and in a Hebrew version); D. Hartman, *Maimonides: Torah and Philosophic Quest* (1976); A. Ivry, "Maimonides on Possibility," in: J. Reinharz and D. Swetschinski (eds.), *Mystics, Philosophers, and Politician: Essays in Jewish Intellectual History in Honor of Alexander Altmann* (1982), 67–84; idem, "Ismaili Theology and Maimonides' Philosophy," in: D. Frank (ed.), *The Jews of Medieval Islam* (1995), 271–99; idem, "The Logical and Scientific Premises of Maimonides' Thought," in: A. Ivry, E.R. Wolfson, and A. Arkush (eds.), *Perspectives on Jewish Thought and Mysticism* (1998), 63–97; L. Kaplan, "Maimonides on the

Miraculous Element in Prophecy," in: *Harvard Theological Review*, 70 (1977), 233–56; J. Kraemer, "On Maimonides' Messianic Posture," in: I. Twersky (ed.), *Studies in Medieval Jewish History and Literature*, vol. 2 (1984), 109–42; H. Kreisel, "The Practical Intellect in the Philosophy of Maimonides," in: HUCA, 59 (1989), 189–215; idem, *Maimonides' Political Thought: Studies in Ethics, Law, and the Human Ideal* (1999); D. Lobel, "'Silence Is Praise to You' Maimonides on Negative Theology, Looseness of Expression, and Negative Theology," in: *American Catholic Philosophical Quarterly*, 76 (2002), 25–49; *Maimonide-Délivrance et Fidélité* (1987); S. Pines, "The Limitations of Human Knowledge according to al-Farabi, Ibn Bajja and Maimonides," in: I. Twersky (ed.), *Studies in Medieval Jewish History and Literature*, vol. 1 (1979), 82–109; N.M. Samuelson, "Maimonides' Doctrine of Creation," in: *Harvard Theological Review*, 84:3 (1991), 249–71; D. Schwartz, "Avicenna and Maimonides on Immortality," in: *Medieval and Modern Perspectives on Muslim-Jewish Relations* (1995), 185–97; S. Schwarzschild, "Moral Radicalism and 'Midlingness' in the Ethics of Maimonides," in: *Studies in Medieval Culture*, 9 (1977), 65–94; S. Stroumsa, *"Ẓave'im shel Haran ve-Ẓave'im eẓel ha-Rambam al Hitpatteḥut ha-Dat lefi ha-Rambam,"* in: *Sefunot*, 3 [23], 277–95; C. Touati, "Les deux théories de Maimonide sur la Providence," in: S. Stein and R. Loewe (eds.), *Studies in Jewish Religious and Intellectual History* (1979), 331–43; G. Vajda, " La pensée religieuse de Moise Maimonide: unité ou dualité," in: *Cahiers de civilization médiévale*, 9 (1966), 29–49; R.L. Weiss, *Maimonides' Ethics: The Encounter of Philosophic and Religious Morality* (1991).

MAIMUNA, celebration held by all Maghrebi Jews and many Eastern communities at the end of the last day of Passover which, according to tradition, is the anniversary of the death of *Maimonides' father *Maimon b. Joseph who lived for a time in Fez. In every home, tables are set with food and drinks having a symbolic significance, varying according to local custom. These include fresh pitchers of sweet milk, garlands of leaves and flowers, branches of fig trees, and ears of wheat. Usually a live fish (a symbol of fertility) is placed on the table, swimming in a bowl. The menu includes lettuce leaves dipped in honey, buttermilk, and pancakes spread with butter and honey. There is a "lucky dip," a bowl of flour in which golden objects are placed. In some places a plate of flour is set on the table with five eggs and five beans and dates set in it. In Oran, vessels of silver and gold are included in the table decoration. On this night people eat only dairy foods and wafers made of fried dough resembling pancakes, known as *muflita*. No meat is to be consumed. The Jews visit each other, taking gifts of food. On the day following the holiday, the actual day of Maimuna, people go out to the fields, cemeteries, or the beaches and organize large social gatherings. In modern Israel Jews of Moroccan extraction celebrate the day after Passover with communal outings and picnics, and a central gathering is held in Jerusalem. The exact meaning of the word Maimuna is unknown. A suggestion that it is connected with the name of Maimun, the king of the jinns, has been questioned by scholars. In an article in *Tarbiz* (41,2, Jan–March 1972), Y. Einhorn quotes new sources to support his contention that the name Maimuna is, in fact linked with the king of the jinns.

BIBLIOGRAPHY: H.Z. Hirschberg, *Me-Ereẓ Mevo ha-Shemesh* (1957), 77.

[Reuben Kashani]

MAINE, northernmost New England state, had an estimated Jewish population of 9,300 out of a total of 1,277,000 (0.7%) in 2001. More than 7,000 lived in the southern part of the State (in Portland, the largest city, Biddeford, Saco, Brunswick, and Bath). Other substantial communities were Bangor, approximately 1000; Lewiston-Auburn, approximately 500; Rockland approximately 200; Waterville, approximately 200; Augusta, approximately 200; and 200 in other parts of Maine in such communities as Calais, Gardner, Caribou, Rumford Falls, Old Town, Old Orchard Beach and Bar Harbor. A large Jewish summer population added considerably to this number but was difficult to estimate.

There were five congregations in Portland, including a Chabad center, three in Bangor, two in Augusta, and one each in Old Orchard, Biddeford, Augusta, Rockland and Bath.

The Jewish Community Alliance of Southern Maine, located in Portland, and the Bangor Jewish Community Council are the two representative Jewish organizations in the State. The Cedars Nursing Home, the successor to the Jewish Home for the Aged in Portland, is the only such Jewish facility in Maine. Both Portland and Bangor maintained Jewish funeral chapels and Portland also maintained a Jewish Day School. There were Hillel Foundation groups at the University of Southern Maine, University of Maine in Orono and at the private Bates, Bowdoin and Colby Colleges. In addition, the history of Jewish life in Maine was maintained through the Judaica Collection at the Sampson Center for Diversity on the Portland campus of the University of Southern Maine and through the Documenting Old Portland Jewry project.

A Jewish Film Festival has been an annual event in Portland since 1999. Camp Modin, located in Belgrade and founded in 1922, is among America's oldest overnight camps and New England's oldest Jewish camp.

Susman Abrams (1743–1830), a native of Hamburg, Germany, was the first known Jewish resident of Maine. He came to the state in the post-Revolutionary period and lived in Waldborough, Thomaston, and finally in Union where he operated a tannery. Abrams married a Christian woman but did not himself convert to Christianity.

Maine had relatively few German or Sephardic Jewish residents. The Campanal and Decoster families, with Sephardic roots, have been prominent in Maine for several decades and Joseph M. Papo, who was the executive director of the Portland Jewish Federation in 1947–48, wrote the well-regarded book *Sephardim in Twentieth Century America: In Search of Unity* (1987).

German Jews were among the earliest Jewish residents of the state and began to settle in Bangor by 1829. Bangor developed numerous Jewish institutions and a Jewish cemetery was created in Waterville in 1830.

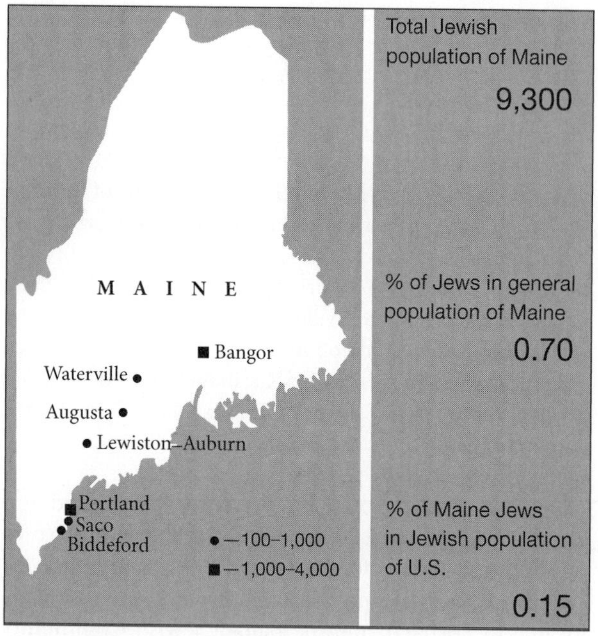

Jewish communities in Maine. Population figures for 2001.

These Jews, many of them originating in the Boston area, came to Maine as peddlers, walking the roads of the huge state and going from farm house to farm house to sell their wares. Haiman Philip Spitz was the first modern Jewish settler in the Bangor area and helped found, along with five other Jewish families, Congregation Ahawas Achim, which was officially formed in 1849, although the Rev. Isaac Leeser's *Occident and American Jewish Advocate* mentions the formation of a Bangor congregation in November 1847. Because of economic difficulties, the synagogue and most of the German Jews who founded it, disappeared by 1856. A second group of German Jews, who came to Bangor in the 1860s and 1870s, intermarried itself out of existence within a few years. Yet, Captain A. Goldman, most likely a member of one of the Bangor Jewish families, was the only known Maine Jew to give his life in the cause of the Union during the Civil War as a member of Maine's 17th regiment.

The first German Jew known to have settled in Portland was William M. Shine, who was born in Kempen, Prussia, in 1852 and arrived in Portland in 1867. By the 1870s, there were several German Jewish families in the Portland area. The first East European Jews began to arrive in Portland in 1866 and were peddlers like the German Jews who came to Maine a few decades before them. In 1875, the Portland Lodge of B'nai B'rith purchased a site in Cape Elizabeth. The site became the first Jewish cemetery in Portland, the Smith Street Cemetery, located in what later became a part of South Portland.

But there was little organization in the Jewish community of the time, that is until 1886 when Portland celebrated its centenary on July 4. Although only a handful of Jewish families lived in the community, as Bernard Aaronson designated to speak for the small Jewish community of the time observed, "We number sixty families, and over the majority portion being of the middle or poorer class, yet content with their lot…."

That contentment was reflected in a sense of pious synagogue worship, a piety that earned Portland Jewry the nickname of the "Jerusalem of the North."

The first synagogue in Portland, Congregation Beth Judah, was founded in 1883, although informal *minyanim* were held a number of years earlier in private homes. In 1885, Reverend Israel Levine became Portland's first rabbi. A number of other synagogues were founded in the years after 1883. Congregation Shaarey Tphiloh, founded in 1904, is most likely the oldest extant synagogue in Maine, celebrating its centennial in 2004. One of the earliest Chassidic rabbis to settle in America, Rabbi Gershon Ackerman, a Brezner Chasid (from the Russian Polish town of Berezno), came to Portland in 1909 and lived in the city until 1928.

The Jews of Maine were fortunate in not having to endure a large amount of anti-Jewish sentiment. That was reserved for Maine's Catholic population, especially its French Catholic community. Know-Nothing activists in the 1840s burned down Catholic churches and tarred and feathered Catholic priests.

In the 1920s, the Ku Klux Klan of Maine, part of a rejuvenated national KKK movement, marched through the streets of several Maine communities, but aimed most of their animosity again at Maine's Catholics rather than the much smaller and less visible Jewish or African American communities.

But Maine's Jews were not immune from social restrictions. Many resorts, country clubs, and private social organizations still restricted Jews by formal or informal means. Finally, in the late 1960s, a number of non-Jewish politicians, including Maine's governor, Kenneth Curtis, decided to end, once and for all, these discriminatory practices. It was a non-Jew, Charles W. Allen (1912–2003), the father of Maine Congressman Tom Allen, a Portland lawyer and member of the Portland City Council, who led the struggle to force private clubs in Maine to open their memberships to Jews and African Americans.

Among the most important Maine Jewish family names, among others, are those of Stern, Bernstein, Povich, Berliawsky, Lown, Wolman, Lipman, Goldsmith, Marcus, Cohen, Cutler, Escovitz, Glickman, Unobskey and Alfond. They, and many other families, have contributed to the success and continuity of Jewish life in Maine.

Other Maine Jews have established their imprint on the national scene as well. Hiram Abrams (1878–1926) was a cofounder of Paramount Pictures Corporation and founded the United Artists Corporation. Shirley *Povich (1905–1997), born in Bar Harbor, was one of the best-known and beloved sports writers in American journalism who wrote for the *Washington Post*. Albert Abrahamson, born in Portland in 1905, was a professor of economics at Bowdoin College and held various positions in government including that of assistant director of the War Refugee Board, created in 1944 and the only American governmental institution that sought to rescue European Jews from the Holocaust.

Louise *Nevelson (1899–1988) was born in Russia but came to America in 1904 and settled with her family in Rockland, Maine. She became one of the most famous American sculptors. Dahlov Ipcar (born in 1917) is the daughter of another famous American Jewish sculptor, William *Zorach. She came to Maine in 1936 and settled in Georgetown. She is a renowned painter, illustrator, and soft sculptor. Linda *Lavin (born 1937) is a movie, television, and Broadway actress. William S. *Cohen (born 1940), the son of a Jewish delicatessen owner in Bangor, was elected to the United States Congress from Maine in 1972 and to the United States Senate in 1984. He was appointed the U.S. Secretary of Defense in 1997. Cohen's mother was not Jewish and when the rabbi insisted on conversion before his bar mitzvah, Cohen was angered and left Judaism.

BIBLIOGRAPHY: B. Band, *Portland Jewry: Its Growth and Development* (1955); M. Cohen, "Jerusalem of the North. An Analysis of Religious Modernization in Portland, Maine's Jewish Community, 1860–1950" (Honors thesis, Brown University, 2000); J.S. Goldstein, *Crossing Lines. Histories of Jews and Gentiles in Three Communities* (1992); J.M. Lipez, "A Time to Build Up and a Time to Break Down: The Jewish Secular Institutions of Portland, Maine" (Honors thesis, Amherst College, 2002).

[Abraham J. Peck (2nd ed.)]

MAINTENANCE (Heb. מְזוֹנוֹת, *mezonot*), generally speaking, the supply of all the necessaries of the party entitled thereto, i.e., not only food, but also matters such as medical expenses, raiment, lodging, etc. (Sh. Ar., EH 73:7; see *Husband and Wife). When, however, the maintenance obligation is based on a personal undertaking (see below) and not on the operation of law, it will not cover raiment and perhaps not even medical expenses, unless the contrary is indicated by the terms of the undertaking (Sh. Ar., EH 114:12; *Rema*, ḤM 60:3; *Siftei Kohen* thereto n. 14). The liability of maintenance exists generally by virtue of law, but in the absence of any legal duty it may also be based on a voluntary undertaking (e.g., by the husband toward his wife's daughter by a previous marriage). Even though it is normally for an unfixed amount, such an undertaking will be binding and be governed by the general law of obligations (Sh. Ar., ḤM 60:2, contrary to the opinion of Yad, Meḥirah 11:6; see also *Contract; *Obligations, Law of).

The liability of maintenance by virtue of law is imposed on (1) a husband toward his wife; (2) a father toward his small children; and (3) the heirs of the deceased toward his widow. A divorced wife is not entitled to maintenance from her former husband (Sh. Ar., EH 82:6; see *Divorce), nor, generally speaking, a betrothed woman from the bridegroom (Sh. Ar., EH 55:4 and *Rema* thereto). Only maintenance between husband and wife, as a liability by virtue of law, will be discussed below (see also *Widow; *Parent and Child).

Scope of the Maintenance Obligation

The husband's duty to maintain his wife is one of the duties imposed on him by virtue of his marriage as *obligatio ex lege* (Yad, Ishut 12:2; Sh. Ar., EH 69:2). He has to provide her with at least the minimal needs for her sustenance in accordance with local custom and social standards (Yad, Ishut 12:10; Sh. Ar., EH 70:3). In addition and subject to the aforesaid, the wife's right to maintenance is governed by the rule that she "goes up with him but does not go down with him" (Ket. 61a; Tur, EH 70), i.e., the wife, regardless of the standard of living she enjoyed prior to the marriage, is entitled to a standard of living which matches that of her husband and to be maintained in accordance with his means and social standing. At the same time, she is not obliged to suffer having her standard of living reduced to one below that which she enjoyed prior to her marriage, at any rate not as compared with the standard of living customary in her paternal home with regard to family members backed by means similar to those available to her husband, even if he should choose a lower standard of living than he can afford (Yad, Ishut 12:11; Sh. Ar., EH 70:1, 3 and *Ḥelkat Meḥokek* thereto n. 1). In addition to providing for all the domestic needs of the common household and as part of his duty of maintenance in its wider sense, the husband must give his wife a weekly cash amount for her personal expenses, again in accordance with their standard of living and social custom (Sh. Ar., EH 70:3; *Ḥelkat Meḥokek* thereto n. 7). In return for this obligation, the husband is entitled to his wife's "surplus handiwork," i.e., to her earnings from work done beyond the call of her legal duty toward him (*Ma'aseh Yadeha*). The said obligation being imposed on the husband as part of his duty to maintain his wife, she may, of her own choice, waive her right to the weekly allowance in order to retain for herself such surplus earnings, just as she may waive her maintenance in order to acquire for herself the proceeds of her handiwork (*Ḥelkat Meḥokek* loc. cit.). The unspent balance of the money given the wife for her maintenance belongs to her husband, since he is only required to give her an amount sufficient for her needs (Ket. 65b; Yad, Ishut 12:13; *Pitḥei Teshuvah*, EH 70 n. 1). However, if such balance results from the wife's spending less than she requires for her own needs, it belongs to herself; she need not invest the amount of it and if she should do so, the fruits of such investment would belong to her alone (see *Dowry). Another opinion is that money given by the husband for his wife's maintenance always remains his own, except insofar as she actually expends it on the household or on her own maintenance, and therefore any balance, even if saved, belongs to him (see *Rema*, EH 70:3; *Pitḥei Teshuvah*, EH 70 n. 1; PDR 2:229 and 289).

The wife's right to be maintained in the manner described above is independent of the fact that she may be able to maintain herself out of her own property and the fact that her husband may be in financial difficulties. She will accordingly not be obliged to sell her property or to use fruits thereof, to which her husband has no right, in order to facilitate his fulfillment of his obligation to maintain her, since he has undertaken the obligation on the marriage and it is also expressed in the *ketubbah* deed in the phrase, "I shall work and support you" (see below, Sh. Ar., loc. cit. *Pitḥei Teshuvah*, EH 70 n. 2; PDR 1:97, 101f.).

Separated Parties

In general, the husband is only obliged to maintain his wife as long as she lives with him or, at any rate, if he is not responsible for the fact that they are separated (*Rema*, EH 70:12). Hence in the case of separation of the parties, it is necessary to establish which of them has left the common home.

WHEN THE HUSBAND LEAVES THE HOME. In principle the wife's right is not affected: "She was given to live and not to suffer pain" (Ket. 61a) and the husband remains responsible for her maintenance (*Mordekhai*, Ket. no. 273). To frustrate her claim, the husband must prove a lawful reason for his absence and refusal to maintain her, e.g., her responsibility for a quarrel justifying his departure (*Rema*, EH 70:12). However, even in circumstances where the husband is responsible for maintaining his wife despite their separation, it will nevertheless be presumed that he has left her with sufficient means to support herself for a reasonable period during his absence and therefore, in general, she will not be awarded maintenance during the first three months following his departure (Ket. 107a; Sh. Ar., EH 70:5). For the wife to succeed in a claim brought within this period, she must prove that her husband has left her without any means at all, or will have to rebut the above assumption in some other manner, e.g., by proving that her husband left the home as a result of a quarrel or with the intention of returning after a short interval but for some reason failed to do so (*Rema*, EH 70:12; *Beit Shemu'el* 70 n. 11; *Ḥut ha-Meshullash*, 1:6, 4).

The husband is not entitled to demand that his wife should work and support herself out of her earnings during his absence unless she has expressly or by implication consented to do this (Yad, Ishut 12:20; *Maggid Mishneh* thereto; Sh. Ar., EH 70:9; *Ḥelkat Meḥokek* 70 n. 33). This is so regardless of whether or not she has been accustomed to working prior to his departure and handing over her earnings to her husband, according to law. The court will not of its own initiative investigate the matter of the wife's earnings from her own handiwork, but will take this into account only if it emerges out of the wife's own arguments. However, if after his return the husband can prove that the wife has been working and earning during his absence, he will not be obliged to repay a loan his wife has taken for her maintenance (see below), to the extent that he proves that she was able to support herself from such earnings during his absence. In this event he will similarly be entitled to demand that she refund to him all amounts she has recovered out of his property for the purposes of her maintenance (Yad, Ishut 12:16; Sh. Ar., EH 70:5).

When the wife is entitled to maintenance but her husband leaves her without sufficient means and she does not maintain herself out of her own earnings, she has the right to borrow for her maintenance and to hold her husband liable for the repayment of such a loan (Ket. 107b; Yad, Ishut 12:19; Sh. Ar., EH 70:8). This is not the case if prior to his departure she was supporting herself by her own efforts and remained silent when he publicly disavowed responsibility for debts she might contract, thus seeming to have consented to this (*Rema*, EH 70:12; *Beit Shemu'el* 70 n. 32). The husband's duty to repay such a loan is toward his wife only and he is not directly liable to the creditor. If, however, the wife has no property of her own, or if for any other reason the creditor might have difficulty in recovering from the wife, he may claim repayment of the loan from the husband directly, in terms of the **Shi'buda de-Rabbi Nathan* (permitting the creditor to recover the debt directly from a third party who owes money to the principal debtor if the creditor has no other means of recovering from the latter (Yad, Ishut 12:19; *Rema*, EH 70:8)).

If the wife has sold some of her own property to support herself, she will be entitled to recover from her husband the equivalent of the amount realized, provided that the facts do not demonstrate any waiver of this right on her part, such as an express declaration to this effect made by her before witnesses at the time of the sale, or if at that time there was a suit for divorce pending between the parties. If proof to this effect is forthcoming, the wife will not be entitled to recover anything from her husband since it is presumed that as long as the marriage tie is in existence, she will not do anything which might bring about its complete severance and will therefore also be prepared to waive her pecuniary rights against her husband (*Rema*, EH 70:8; *Beit Shemu'el* 70 n. 29; PDR 2:289, 291f.). Whenever the wife is not entitled to a refund of the amounts she has expended, during the period of her husband's absence, the earnings from her handiwork will be loans to her (*Rema*, EH 70:8).

Third parties who of their own accord assist the wife in respect of her maintenance are not entitled to be refunded for their expenditure – neither from the wife since she has not borrowed from them, nor from her husband since he has not instructed them to do so – but they are in the position of one who "has put his money on the horns of a deer" (*Rema*, EH 70:8; see also *Unjust Enrichment). If the wife can prove that the assistance was given her in the form of a loan, the question of repayment will be governed by the aforesaid ordinary rules concerning a loan for purposes of the wife's maintenance, even if the assistance was given by her own parents (*Mordekhai*, Ket. no. 273).

WHEN THE WIFE LEAVES THE HOME. In principle the husband is not obliged to maintain his wife unless she lives with him (see above). Hence the mere fact of her leaving him, or her refusal to return to him after she has left him lawfully, provides the husband with a *prima facie* defense against her claim for maintenance, since by living apart from him she precludes herself from carrying out her marital duties, on due fulfillment of which her right to maintenance is dependent. Therefore, to succeed in a claim for maintenance in these circumstances, the wife must discharge the onus of proving facts justifying her absence from the marital home (*Rema*, EH 70:12; *Beit Shemu'el* 70 n. 34; PDR 6:33, 52f.). These may arise either from the husband's bad conduct toward her – e.g., his responsibility for a quarrel justifying in law her refusal to continue living with him together in the marital home (*Beit Yosef*, EH 70, end; Sh. Ar., EH 70:12) – or from other circumstances which are independent of the husband's blameworthy conduct toward her, such as his refusal to comply with her justified demand to move to another dwelling or to live away from her husband's relatives who cause her distress (see *Husband and Wife). In general it may be said that any reason sufficient to oblige the husband to grant his wife a divorce will entitle her to claim maintenance from him even though she may have left the home, since the fact that the husband is obliged to grant her a divorce means that he must acquiesce in their living apart; therefore her refusal to live with him entails no breach of her duties toward him. Moreover, by unlawfully withholding a divorce from his wife the husband prevents her from marrying someone else who could maintain her, and there is a rule that a husband who, contrary to law, prevents his wife from marrying another man renders himself liable to maintain her until he grants her a divorce (PDR 1:74, 77–80). If the wife leaves the home on account of a quarrel she has unjustifiably caused, and generally when she has no justifiable reason for living apart from her husband, she will not be entitled to maintenance from him.

For other cases in which the wife forfeits her right to maintenance, see *Husband and Wife (s.v. *moredet*); *Divorce.

Claim for Maintenance Cannot Be Assigned or Set Off

The husband is not entitled to set off against her claim for maintenance any pecuniary claim he may have against his wife, such as one arising from her sale, contrary to law, of her husband's property for purposes of her maintenance during his absence. His duty to maintain his wife means to provide her with the necessities of life with him, i.e., entails responsibility for her daily needs with regard to food, raiment, lodging, etc. This affords the wife a right against which pecuniary debts cannot be set off, since those two differ in their legal nature and her daily needs cannot be satisfied by a reduction of the debt she owes him (PDR 1:333, 338; 2:97, 99). If, however, the wife's claim is based on a right whose legal nature is purely pecuniary, e.g., her claim for repayment of a loan she has taken for her maintenance, there will be no bar to the husband setting off against such claim any other pecuniary claim he may have against her, if, for instance, she is indebted to him for a loan she obtained from him for the purpose of supporting her relatives – he may also set off such pecuniary claim against her claim with regard to payment of her *ketubbah* at the time of their divorce (see PDR 1 loc. cit.). The same reason that entitles the wife to receive actual payment of her maintenance prevents her from assigning this right to others (*Beit Shemu'el* 93 n. 18).

Arrear Maintenance

If the wife, although entitled to maintenance, does not bring an action for it in the court, she will be unable to claim maintenance for any period preceding the date of bringing her suit, since it will be presumed that she preferred to suffer rather than unfold her troubles before the court and her silence will therefore be interpreted as a waiver of her right for such a period (Yad, Ishut 12:22; Sh. Ar., EH 70:11). This presumption may be rebutted by evidence showing that she insisted on her rights, e.g., that she demanded her maintenance from her husband and refrained from instituting action only because of his promise to comply without recourse to the court (*Rema*, EH 80:18; *Beit Shemu'el* 80 n. 27); institution of action has the same effect for any period thereafter even if a considerable amount of time elapses before judgment is given (*Rema* 70:5; *Beit Shemu'el* 70 n. 12; see also *Limitation of Actions).

Non-payment of Maintenance: Consequences

On the husband's failure to maintain his wife in the manner to which she is entitled, the court – at her instance – will order him to do so, whether he refuses payment although he has the means to meet it or whether he lacks the means because he does not work although he is able to work and earn this amount. In other words, the husband will be ordered to pay maintenance in accordance with his potential working and earning abilities, and not necessarily his actual earnings, for he has undertaken in the *ketubbah* to work and to maintain his wife (*Rema*, EH 70:3; *Ḥelkat Meḥokek* 70 n. 12). If he has sufficient for his own needs only for a single day, he must still share this with his wife since he is liable to maintain her "with himself" (*Rema*, EH 70:3). On the other hand, as he has to maintain her "with him" only, i.e., to no greater extent than he is able in respect of himself, he will be exempt from maintaining her if he cannot afford it because he is in a position of utter poverty and unable to work and earn for reasons beyond his control (*Pitḥei Teshuvah*, EH 70 n. 2; *Perishah*, ḤM 97 n. 41). For the same reason, inability to pay maintenance is excused on grounds of the husband's need to repay regular debts, these taking preference over the former (*ibid.*). If the wife should not wish to content herself with a claim for maintenance, she may possibly be entitled to demand a divorce.

In the State of Israel

Maintenance for the wife is a matter of personal status within the meaning of article 51 of the Palestine Order in Council, 1922, and is therefore governed by Jewish law (sec. 51 thereof) even when claimed in a civil court by virtue of section 4, Rabbinical Courts Jurisdiction (Marriage and Divorce) Law, 5713 – 1953. So far as a Jewish wife is concerned, the above position was left unchanged by the Family Law Amendment Maintenance Law, 5719 – 1959, which expressly provides that the question of her maintenance shall be governed solely by Jewish law (sec. 2; see Supr. PD 15 (1961), 1056, 1058). If the husband refuses to comply with a judgment of the court for the payment of maintenance, he may be imprisoned for a period not exceeding 21 days for every unpaid installment (Executive Law 5727 – 1967, sec. 70ff.); see also Imprisonment for *Debt.

[Ben-Zion (Benno) Schereschewsky]

Maintenance (*Mezonot*) in the State of Israel

Maintenance payments in Israel are determined in accordance with Jewish law, as stipulated in Section 2 of the Family Law (Maintenance) Amendment Law, 5719 – 1959. In this respect, the position described above remained unchanged. This update will deal with a number of issues in which new arrangements were established in Israeli law, in both the rabbinical courts and the general courts.

MAINTENANCE UNDER THE LAW OF MEUKEVET MEḤAMATO (A WOMAN PREVENTED FROM REMARRYING OWING TO HER HUSBAND'S REFUSAL TO GIVE HER A GET). In Jewish law – and in Israeli law, too, which applies Jewish law – the husband's obligation to pay maintenance derives from the fact of the marriage and the husband's undertaking in the *ketubbah* to provide for his wife – an obligation that terminates upon divorce. Accordingly, where the husband is obligated to grant a divorce – and refuses – the question arises as to how this refusal affects his maintenance obligation. Under Jewish law, even if the couple do not live together, the husband remains liable for maintenance, because his refusal to grant his wife a *get* prevents her from marrying someone else, thereby denying her maintenance from a potential husband. Furthermore, in such circumstances a different set of rules applies. By law, the husband owns the wife's handiwork (*ma'aseh yadeha*) – the fruits of his wife's labor – and practically, such fruits (e.g., income) are deducted from her maintenance. But when the maintenance obligation is imposed by reason of the husband's refusal to give a *get*, the latter is not entitled to deduct her income. The explanation is that the husband's ownership of his wife's handiwork against his obligation to support his wife derives from the consideration of ill-feeling (*eivah*). In other words – it was instituted in the interests of domestic peace (*shelom bayit*) between the spouses (see *Husband and Wife). However, when the husband refuses to grant a *get* to the wife, there is no justification for entitling him to her earnings, because there is no longer an interest in fostering domestic harmony, but rather in terminating the marriage with a *get*. The Israeli Supreme Court thus ruled that a maintenance award based on the wife's inability to marry because of her husband is only applicable after the rabbinical court has ruled on divorce, in one of the following manners: forcing or obligating the husband to grant a *get*, as well as the more "moderate" case in which the court orders the parties to divorce. This principle was established by the Rabbinical Court of Appeals (*dayyanim* A. Goldschmidt, S. Yisraeli, J. Kapah; Appeal 205/5733, PDR 10, 294), and was adopted in a ruling of the Supreme Court (comments of President, M. Shamgar, CA 792/82, *Nuni v. Nuni*, 40 (3) PD 744, following Justice M. Elon, HC 644/79 *Gutman v. the Rabbinical Court*, 34 (1) PD 443, and the comments of Judge Y. Cahn in HC 661/77 *Haber v. the Rabbinical Court*, 32 (3) PD 324).

PROCEDURES. In 1975, a chapter dealing with maintenance was added to the Civil Procedure Regulations – Chapter 23 (3) of the Civil Procedure Regulations, 5723 – 1963. Its central innovation was the requirement that every statement of claim or defense dealing with maintenance be supported by an affidavit. In addition, a detailed specification had to be submitted as an appendix to any claim or defense, detailing the complete assets and income of each party (including documentation, such as wage slips for an entire year), as well as the sums that, in that party's opinion, would meet the maintenance needs of the (rival) parties. Under these regulations, the District Court (which had jurisdiction over maintenance cases at that time) conducted an initial enquiry based on the material submitted, fixing temporary maintenance accordingly, without having to conduct a separate proceeding. These regulations also established sanctions for failure to comply with the regulations, by not attaching substantiating documentation, concealing particulars, or otherwise contravening the regulations. The sanctions ranged from orders to comply with the regulations, to the possibility of accepting the other party's claims (see, e.g., the ruling of the Jerusalem District Court, AM 470/03 *Anon. v. Anon.*; AM 789/05 *AD v. AY*).

The Civil Procedure Regulations 5744 – 1984 incorporated the same maintenance provisions in Chapter 21 (Regulations 259–266). In 1995 the Family Courts Law (see Family Courts Law, 5755 – 1995) was adopted and the powers of civil instances to adjudicate maintenance cases were transferred to the Family Court. Maintenance suits are now governed by the civil procedure regulations applying to all claims adjudicated in the Family Courts (Part 3.1 of the Civil Procedure Regulations, 5744 – 1984; Regulation 258A –258GG).

Apparently, the enactment of procedure related regulations in the general court system, including with respect to the Family Court, led to the enactment of the new regulations governing rabbinical courts procedure (1993). Regulation 33 of these regulations determined that a maintenance claim must be submitted together with the form indicated in Regulation 211, and the defendant is instructed to follow suit when submitting his statement of defense. Pursuant to Regulation 211, special forms were prepared for maintenance claims in the rabbinical courts, in which, as part of the specification of data, the husband is required to declare the sums of maintenance paid prior to submission of the claim together with particulars of his income and property. A number of rulings have determined that failure to attach the specification of data form, or to properly complete it, may be taken into account when assessing the sincerity of the "inclusion" of a maintenance claim in a divorce suit in the rabbinical courts (see FF (Tel Aviv) 16981/96 *Dahan v. Dahan*; on the inclusion of maintenance with a divorce case, see **Bet Din Rabbani* – Rabbinical Court in Israel).

ENFORCEMENT OF MAINTENANCE PAYMENT. The State of Israel enforced court maintenance awards by means of the Execution Office, pursuant to the provisions of the Execution Law, 5727 – 1967. This mechanism likewise enforces maintenance awards of rabbinical courts (see under *Rabbinical Court; *Execution, Civil).

Maintenance differs, in principle, from any other monetary ruling. In a regular civil file, the court is only required to consider the question of whether the defendant is liable or not; the defendant's financial capacity to pay the sum of the claim does not affect his liability. On the other hand, liability for maintenance, in principle, is based on the financial capacity and situation of the liable party, and the sum of maintenance is fixed in accordance with a number of parameters, inter alia, the liable parties' financial ability to pay a particular sum of monthly maintenance (after he has borne his own expenses). This distinction affects the discretion exercised by the head of the Execution Office in determining how a debt is paid. Regarding a regular debt, the head of the Execution Office may, and is often compelled to, consider the debtor's financial situation, in view of which he determines whether he should pay the debt in one payment or in installments. Regarding a maintenance ruling, the head of the Execution Office does not have such discretion and must implement the court's ruling literally, inasmuch as the judicial forum that ruled on maintenance (a rabbinical court or the family court) has already considered this data and the sum of the maintenance ruling was determined on the basis of that data.

Another difference between collection of a financial debt as distinct from a maintenance debt relates to the use of imprisonment. The Execution Law and Supreme Court rulings restricted the cases in which imprisonment can be imposed against a person who fails to discharge his civil debt (see the detailed ruling of Deputy President Judge M. Elon in HC 5304/92, *Perach v. the Minister of Justice*, 47 (4) PD 715; see in detail: *Execution, Civil). In contrast, Section 74 of the Execution Law determines that regarding a maintenance debt, the head of the Execution Office may, at the request of the person entitled to maintenance, issue an arrest warrant against the debtor, even without investigating his financial ability (one of the minimal terms required for imprisonment with respect to a civil debt). The Supreme Court emphasized the difference between collection of a maintenance debt and collection of a regular civil debt: the maintenance award is fixed by a judicial instance [after having consideration for the liable party's financial situation]; the dependency of the persons entitled to the maintenance on the maintenance payments for their sustenance; the fact that a maintenance ruling is not final and the debtor may apply to a rabbinical court or the family court to alter the amount of the maintenance if there has been a change of circumstances justifying its alteration (p. 731 of the *Perach* decision).

In addition, a special social welfare law was enacted in Israel enabling receipt of maintenance payments through the National Insurance Institute (The Maintenance (Assurance of Payment) Law, 5732 – 1972). According to this law, a person with a maintenance ruling in his favor (such as a spouse or child) may present a copy of the judgment to the National Insurance Institute and the latter will pay the maintenance sum on a monthly basis (subject to a statutory ceiling; see Section 4 of the law). The National Insurance Institute acts on behalf of the person entitled to maintenance, and concurrently initiates execution proceedings against the maintenance debtor. In this way, those entitled to maintenance receive the monthly payment with dignity and without tension or pressure in the event of the maintenance debtor's failure to pay. This law is particularly effective when the maintenance debtor changes addresses and cannot be traced or absconds abroad. The difference between the sum awarded as maintenance by the Court (either Rabbinical or Family Court) and the sum actually paid by the National Insurance Institute, may be collected by the entitled party by opening a file in the Execution Office (see Section 10 of the law; AM 789/05 *AD v. AY*).

[Moshe Drori (2nd ed.)]

BIBLIOGRAPHY: Gulak, Yesodei, 1 (1922), 37; 2 (1922), 68–70; 3 (1922), 37–39; Gulak, Oẓar, 149–58; ET, 1 (1951^{3}), 324f.; 4 (1952), 80–83, 91f.; 6 (1954), 656; Regional Rabbinical Court, Tel Aviv, Judgment, in: *Ha-Torah ve-ha-Medinah*, 9–10 (1957/59), 185–99; B. Cohen, in: PAAJR, 20 (1951), 135–234; republished in his: *Jewish and Roman Law*, 1 (1966), 179–278; addenda: *ibid.*, 2 (1966), 775–7; B. Schereschewsky, *Dinei Mishpaḥah* (1993^{4}), 106–33; Elon, Mafte'aḥ, 122f.; idem, *Ḥakikah Datit…* (1968), 44–46, 60–62; H. Baker, *Legal System of Israel* (1968), index. **ADD. BIBLIOGRAPHY:** M. Elon, *Ha-Mishpat ha-Ivri* (1998), 1:111, 129, 188, 468f., 518, 638, 653; 3:1337, 1392f., 1417, 1476, 1479, 1499f., 1596; idem, *Jewish Law* (1994), 1:125, 145, 211; 2:571f., 631, 791, 808; 3:1597; 4:1660f., 1687, 1756, 1760, 1784f., 1904; M. Drori, "*Sidrei Din Ḥadashim bi-Teviot le-Mezonot*," in: *Ha-Praklit*, 31 (1977), 317–40.

MAINZ (**Mayence**; Heb. מענץ, מגנץ, מגנצא), city on the Rhine in Germany.

The Medieval Settlements

Mainz is one of the oldest Jewish communities in Germany. It is presumed that Jews came to the city as merchants in the Roman era and may even have founded a settlement there. The date of the first medieval community is uncertain. A church council in Mainz declared in 906 that a man who killed a Jew out of malice must make amends like any other murderer, and presumably there were some Jews in the city at the time. The *Kalonymus family of Lucca is believed to have moved to Mainz in 917, but the date is not completely reliable. Evidence of the existence of a Jewish community is indisputable only from the middle of the tenth century. Archbishop Frederick (937–54) threatened the Jews with forcible conversion or expulsion. They were in fact expelled by Emperor Henry II in 1012 after a priest had converted to Judaism. Soon after, however (according to Jewish sources only a month), they were allowed to return and continued to play a lively part in the trade of the city, which was a commercial center on the Rhine and Main rivers. An organized community was in existence in the late tenth century (when *Gershom b. Judah was teaching in Mainz; his son apostatized in 1012), although land for a cemetery was not acquired until the time of the expulsion (gravestones dating from the 11th–14th centuries, discovered in 1922 in the fortified inner city, came from this cemetery). Many Jews left the city in 1084 after they had been accused of causing a fire in which their quarter was also damaged; settling in *Speyer, they founded the community there.

At the beginning of the First *Crusade (1096) the Mainz

parnas, Kalonymus b. Meshullam, obtained an order from Emperor Henry *IV protecting the Jews, but nonetheless, and in spite of an armed and spirited resistance, on May 27 more than 1,000 died – some at the hands of the crusaders and many by suicide as an act of *kiddush ha-Shem*. Kalonymus escaped with a group to Ruedesheim but committed suicide the next morning during an attack led by Count Emicho. The synagogue (first mentioned in 1093) and Jewish quarter were burned down on May 29. Twelfth-century Jews immortalized the Mainz martyrdom as an example of supreme **akedah*. The community slowly recuperated in the following years after Henry IV had permitted those forcibly converted to return to Judaism, decreeing that the Jews were also to enjoy the "king's peace" (*Landfrieden*). During the Second Crusade (1146–47) it suffered several casualties (see also *Bernard of Clairvaux). During the Third Crusade (1189–92) the Jews of Mainz were unharmed because of the resolute protection of Frederick I Barbarossa; large numbers temporarily went into hiding in Munzanberg (near *Friedberg). In 1259 Mainz Jews were ordered to wear the Jewish *badge. In 1281 and 1283 numerous Jews fell victim to the blood *libel; the synagogue was also burnt in these years. As a result of these repeated persecutions some Jews of Mainz, along with those of other German cities, wished, in 1285, to immigrate to Ereẓ Israel under the leadership of *Meir b. Baruch of Rothenburg; others escaped the boundaries of the empire. During the *Black Death (1349) almost the whole community perished; some of them in a battle against the mob, and the majority (6,000 persons) in the flames of their burning synagogue and quarter, set on fire by their own hands in *kiddush ha-Shem*.

In the next decade (following the charter of the German Empire known as the Golden Bull of 1356) Jews again began to settle in Mainz. The community did not attain its former standing, even though a considerable number of Jews settled (in 1385 they presented the council with 3,000 gulden "out of gratitude" for its protection during the anti-Jewish disturbances that had broken out in various places). With the gradual transfer, in the later Middle Ages, of *Judenschutz* ("guardianship over the Jews") to the cities, their financial obligations grew heavier. The Jewry taxes, granted to the city in 1295 and renewed in 1366, became henceforth ever more burdensome. In 1438 Mainz Jews left the city after a dispute with the council (they may in fact have been expelled); the synagogue and cemetery were confiscated and the tombstones utilized for building. In 1445 they were readmitted, only to be expelled in 1462; permitted to return in 1473, they were finally forced to leave the city ten years later. The synagogue was converted into a chapel.

The Community in the Middle Ages

Until the second half of the 12th century, the Jews conducted lively mercantile activities and from a very early date attended the *Cologne fairs. Discoveries in the area of the oldest Jewish settlement in Mainz provide evidence of commercial connections with Greece and Italy. From this period onward *moneylending became of increased importance in Mainz, as in all German communities. Records of the 12th, and especially of the 13th century, often reveal that churches and monasteries owed money to Jews. In 1213 Pope *Innocent III released all Christians in the Mainz province who were about to set out on a Crusade from paying interest on debts to Jews. Mainz Jewry also suffered when Emperor *Wenceslaus annulled debts owed to Jews (1390).

Until the Black Death, Jews were allowed to possess land in the city and were recognized as owners of houses. Mainz Jews were probably permitted to reside outside the Jewish quarter, for the protective wall, customary in other cities, was missing. A *Judengasse* is mentioned in 1218, and at the end of the century 54 Jewish houses are recorded. The Jewish community was led by a so-called *Judenbischof*, nominated by the archbishop, and by not less than four elders (Vorsteher) who together constituted the Judenrat ("Jews' council") from 1286 until the end of the 14th century. The supreme non-Jewish juridical authority was the archbishop (from 1209). A yeshivah was founded in the tenth century by the Kalonymides and became central under R. Gershom b. *Judah and his pupils and contemporaries, Judah ha-Kohen, Jacob b. *Yakar, Isaac ha-Levi, and Isaac b. *Judah. Gershom's *takkanot ("regulations"), which were applicable to the Rhenish cities, were acknowledged by all the other German communities and even by other European ones, thereby achieving the force of law, a fact which enhanced the reputation of Mainz. The chronicle of Solomon b. *Samson recounting the *kiddush ha-Shem* of 1096 regards Mainz as the main, most ancient, and most famous Jewish community on the Rhine; he praises its learning and pious way of life (see A.M. Habermann (ed.), *Sefer Gezerot Ashkenaz ve-Ẓarefat*).

From the early 12th century on, *Speyer, *Worms, and *Mainz (in Jewish sources named שו"ם (*shum*), an abbreviation made up of the first letter of their names) were recognized as the leading Jewish communities in Germany. Synodal assemblies were held in Mainz (1150, 1223, 1250), in which primarily representatives of the three leading communities took part; their resolutions, the *takkanot Shum*, were acknowledged by the rest of the communities of Germany. The Mainz rabbi, Jacob b. Moses *Moellin (1356–1427; known as Maharil), promulgated *takkanot* (chiefly concerned with ritual matters) aimed at the German and primarily the Rhenish communities. His collection of **minhagim* (compiled by his pupil Zalman of St. Goar), which rely mainly on Mainz traditions, are connected with all German and some non-German communities and were used to a large extent in the Shulḥan Arukh, *Oraḥ Ḥayyim*. Outstanding among the many notable scholars and personalities in medieval Mainz are, in addition to those already mentioned, Nathan b. *Machir b. Judah (c. 1100); *Eliezer b. Nathan (c. 1150); *Meshullam b. Kalonymus (c. 1150); *Judah b. Kalonymus b. Moses (c. 1175); and Baruch b. Samuel (1200).

Resettlement and the Modern Community

In the early modern era only a few Jews lived in Mainz. In

1513 the archbishop designated Weisenau, near Mainz, as the seat of the rabbinate for the diocese of Mainz, presumably because few resided in the city itself. These few were expelled in 1579, but a new community was reconstituted in 1583, reinforced by emigration from *Frankfurt (1614), Worms (1615), and *Hanau. A rabbi was subsequently engaged and a synagogue built (1639; see also *Landesjudenschaft*). During the French occupation (1644–48), the Jews suffered and were subsequently subjected to ever-harsher restrictions. The permitted number of Jewish families was limited to 20, and later 10 (1671); they were allowed to inhabit one special street only (ghetto).

Influenced by the **Toleranzpatent* (1784) of **Joseph II*, the archbishop-elector improved the legal position of the Jews and allowed them to open their own schools and attend general ones. After the revolutionary French occupation of Mainz (1792), the **Leibzoll* ("body tax") was abolished and on September 12 the gates of the ghetto were torn down. Until the end of the occupation (1814) the Jews of Mainz were French citizens (they sent delegates to the *Sanhedrin in Paris). The Napoleonic edict of May 17, 1808, remained in force until 1848. After the German war of liberation (1813–15), Mainz passed to *Hesse-Darmstadt. Full civil rights, promised in June 1816, were not granted.

In the mid-19th century, the community split when R. Joseph *Aub introduced ritual reforms in the newly built synagogue (1853). The Orthodox founded the Israelitische Religionsgesellschaft, with its own synagogue, and engaged Marcus *Lehmann as rabbi; he founded a Jewish school (a high school with instruction in foreign languages) in 1859. Until the Prussian law of 1876 regulating secession from religious communities, the Orthodox remained within the community and seceded only later. In modern times, too, a number of scholars originated from Mainz, notably Michael *Creizenach; Isaac *Bernays; Joseph *Derenburg; and Ludwig *Bamberger. Among the former communal institutions were the Israelite Home for the Sick and Disabled, the Jewish Sistership Organization for the Care of Jewish Antiquities, and the *talmud torah*. The Israelitische Religionsgesellschaft possessed a school (eight classes and 68 pupils), a library, and supplied religious instruction to 30 children. The communal budget totaled 220,000 marks in 1931. Twelve communities from the surrounding district were administered by the Mainz rabbinate. In the 19th century the Jewish population of Mainz increased, but its percentage of the general population remained steady: 1,620 Jews in 1828 (5.3% of the total population); 2,665 in 1861 (5.8%); 2,998 in 1871 (5.8%). From then on, both numbers and ratio declined, to 3,104 (3.7%) in 1900; 2,738 (2.5%) in 1925; and 2,730 (1.8%) in 1933.

Holocaust and Contemporary Periods

On November 9/10, 1938, the main synagogue (including the museum and library) was looted and burnt down. The Orthodox and Polish synagogues suffered similar treatment. On May 17, 1939, only 1,452 Jews remained, 70% of whom were 40 years or over. A steady flow of emigrants was partly balanced by an influx of refugees from the countryside. In March and September 1942 the majority of the community was deported to Poland and *Theresienstadt. On February 10, 1943, the final liquidation of the community, which had been moved to the hospital, took place. After the war, a new community was organized, which numbered 80 persons in 1948 and 122 in 1970 (with an average age of 53). In 1989 the Jewish community numbered 140, and about 1,000 in 2005. The increase is explained by the immigration of Jews from the former Soviet Union. In 2005 a second (liberal) Jewish congregation was founded with about 70 members. It is a member of the Union of Progressive Jews in Germany. The congregation wished to use the restored synagogue in Mainz-Weisenau, which was inaugurated in 1996, as a cultural and educational center on Jewish history and tradition for the citizens of Mainz. It also planned to build a new synagogue.

BIBLIOGRAPHY: Aronius, Regesten; K.A. Schaab, *Diplomatische Geschichte der Juden in Mainz* (1855); M. Wiener, *Regesten* (1862); Germ Jud, 1 (1963), 174–223; 2 (1968), 512–21; Salfeld, Martyrol, index; idem, *Bilder aus der Vergangenheit der juedischen Gemeinde in Mainz* (1903); idem, in: *Festschrift... A. Berliner* (1903); idem, in: *Festschrift... Hermann Cohen* (1912), 347–76; idem, in: *Festschrift... Martin Philippson* (1916), 135–67; E. Carlebach, *Die rechtlichen und sozialen Verhaeltnisse der juedischen Gemeinden Speyer, Worms und Mainz* (1901); L. Rothschild, *Die Judengemeinden zu Mainz, Speyer und Worms von 1349–1438* (1904); Finkelstein, Middle Ages, index, s.v. *Mayence*; S. Levi, *Beitraege zur Geschichte der aeltesten juedischen Grabsteine in Mainz* (1926); idem, in: *Menorah* (Vienna-Frankfurt), 5 (1927), 705–16; idem, in: ZGJD, 5 (1934), 187ff.; idem et al. (eds.), *Magenza* (1927); *Mitteilungsblatt des Landesverbandes der israelitischen Religionsgemeinden Hessens*, 5, no. 3 (1930), 9–10; 6, no. 1 (1931), 7; no. 12, 1; 7, no. 1 (1932), 4; J.S. Mencel, *Beitraege zur Geschichte der Juden in Mainz im XV. Jahrhundert* (1933); A.M. Habermann (ed.), *Gezerot Ashkenaz ve-Ẓarefat* (1946); Baron, Social², 4 (1957), 65–75; E.L. Rapp, in: *Jahrbuch der Vereinigung "Freunde der Universitaet Mainz"* (1958; 1959; 1962); K. Schilling (ed.), *Monumenta Judaica*, 2 (1963), index; A.M. Klein (ed.), *Tagebuch einer juedischen Gemeinde 1941–43* (1968). **ADD. BIBLIOGRAPHY:** E. Rapp, *Chronik der Mainzer Juden: Die Mainzer Grabdenkmalstaette* (1977); F. Schuetz (ed.), *Juden in Mainz* (1979³); R. Doerrlamm, *Magenza. Die Geschichte des juedischen Mainz* (1995); F. Schuetz, "Die Geschichte des Mainzer Judenviertels," in: M. Matheus (ed.), *Juden in Deutschland* (Mainzer Vortraege, vol. 1) (1995), 33–60; M. Drobner, *Zur Entwicklung der Mainzer Juedischen Gemeinde im Kontext gesamtgesellschaftlicher Prozesse des 19. Jahrhunderts* (Europaeische Hochschulschriften, Reihe 19, Volkskunde, Ethnologie, vol. 52) (2000). **WEBSITE:** www.jgmainz.de.

[Bernard Dov Sucher Weinryb / Larissa Daemmig (2nd ed.)]

MAIORESCU (MAYER), GEORGE TOMA (1928–), Romanian poet and author. In *Ochii Danielei* ("Daniela's Eyes", 1963) the poem *"Amintiri ins-xîngerate"* ("Bloodstained Memories") is a nightmare evocation of his father's death in a Nazi labor camp. This versatile writer's other works include accounts of a journey to South America, a collection of love poems, and *Dialog cu secolul şi cu oamenii sąi* ("A Dialogue with Our Century and Its People", 1967). He has been translated into more than 20 languages.

MAIROVICH, ZVI (1909–1974), Israeli painter. Born in Poland, he immigrated to Palestine in 1935, settling in Haifa. In 1947–48 he was a founder member of the *New Horizons* group. Mairovich arrived at abstractionism quite late. In his expressive compositions, there is always a portrait, a landscape, or a still life. He formed a link between abstract-lyrical painters, and Israel expressionists.

MAISEL, ELIJAH ḤAYYIM (1821–1912), Polish talmudist and rabbinic leader. Maisel studied at Volozhin and at the age of 20 was appointed rabbi of Gorodok. After serving for two years, he resigned the office, devoting the next ten years to study. After serving as rabbi in a number of small communities, he was appointed to the important rabbinate of Lomza, and then in 1874 to the even more important one of Lodz. He was an erudite scholar, with a great understanding of and sympathy for humanity. Though a *Mitnagged*, he was loved by the people of Lodz, most of whom were Ḥasidim. He was a firm and fearless leader, taking an active part in all the community's philanthropic and religious institutions, to assist which he devoted most of his income. When they lacked money, he would borrow and himself guarantee the repayment. If the wealthy members of the community refused to meet these debts, he changed his post, making it a condition that the new town paid his charitable debts in his old community. On one occasion the community of Bialystok offered to pay his debts in Lodz. However, not wishing to lose him, the community of Lodz immediately paid the debts. He kept open house and none who came for help was turned away empty-handed. Though lenient to others in personal religious matters, he strove with all his energies to prevent the breakdown of public religious life. He once stood on the Sabbath at the entrance of a Jewish shop until its owner promised to keep it closed in future.

BIBLIOGRAPHY: O. Feuchtwanger, *Righteous Lives* (1965), 12–15.

[Mordechai Hacohen]

MAISELS, ISRAEL AARON (1905–1994), South African lawyer and communal leader. Born and educated in Johannesburg, Maisels was admitted to the bar in 1930. During World War II he served in the South African Air Force with the rank of major. In 1948 he became king's counsel and was leader of the Johannesburg, as well as the South African, Bar for several years. He successfully defended Nelson Mandela and 90 other people of all races in the "Treason Trial" which ended in 1961. He was appointed a judge of the High Court of Southern Rhodesia, retiring in 1963, and later acted as a part-time judge of appeal for Botswana, Lesotho, and Swaziland. He served as arbitrator in disputes of public concern. Maisels was at various times president of the South African Jewish Board of Deputies, the South African Zionist Federation, and the United Hebrew Congregation in Johannesburg.

[Louis Hotz]

MAISELS, MOSES ḤAYYIM (**Misha**; 1901–1984), Hebrew writer. Born in Warsaw, Maisels, as a member of the staff of the Hebrew papers *Ha-Yom* and *Ha-Ẓefirah* in his native city, contributed numerous articles on contemporary and literary problems. In 1930 he emigrated to the United States where, from 1932, he was a member of the staff of *Hadoar* and, after the death of M. *Ribalow, its editor. In 1959 he emigrated to Israel where he became one of the editors of Mosad Bialik, the scholarly publishing house of the Jewish Agency for Israel. His major work, *Maḥashavah ve-Emet* (1939), is a two-volume essay: the first deals with philosophy in the past and its implications for the present; the second, with Judaism in the context of general philosophy. An abridged edition appeared under the pseudonym of M.Ḥ. Amishai (1961) and an English translation and condensation was published by A. Regelson under the name *Thought and Truth, a Critique of Philosophy* (1956). Among Maisels' translations are Upton Sinclair's *Oil*, published under the pseudonym of M. Avishai (1929); M. Balaban's Polish studies on the history of the Jews (1930–33), and on the Frankist movement (1934–35); and Louis M. Epstein's *The Jewish Marriage Contract* (1954). Maisels' passion for anonymity led him to publish under numerous pseudonyms.

BIBLIOGRAPHY: Kressel, Leksikon, 2 (1967), 343.

[Eisig Silberschlag]

MAISEL-SHOḤAT, HANNAH (1890–1972), Israeli pioneer and educator, wife of Eliezer *Shoḥat. Hannah Maisel was born in Grodno, Belorussia, and studied education, agronomy, and science in Russia, Switzerland, and France. Active in the Po'alei Zion movement in Russia, she settled in Ereẓ Israel in 1909, and in 1911 founded the first women's agricultural farm in Kinneret on the shores of Lake Tiberias, with 14 pupils (among them the poetess *Raḥel (Bluwstein)). In 1919, she established the first "Labor Kitchen" in Tel Aviv, and later the WIZO School for Home Economics. In 1920, she was elected to the first executive of WIZO, and in the following year she and her husband were among the founders of the first moshav, *Nahalal. From the very first years of her *aliyah* Hannah Maisel-Shoḥat realized the importance of training the young women who had come on *aliyah* in agriculture and home economics, and her initiative, vision, and activity in this sphere constitute an important chapter in the history of the development of agriculture and education in Israel. In 1929 she founded the WIZO Agricultural High School in Nahalal and was its principal from its foundation until 1960. As a leader of the *Mo'eẓet ha-Po'alot (Council of Women Workers) she was one of the organizers of the first conference of the Labor Movement in Ereẓ Israel.

BIBLIOGRAPHY: Tidhar, 15, 4745–46.

[Benjamin Jaffe (2nd ed.)]

MAIUMAS, a popular licentious feast connected with water festivals undertaken in various places (13 according to Lev. R. 5:3, et al.); four localities were named after it (see below). Information about the Maiumas festivals is provided by Melalus from Antioch in Syria. He relates that the festival in honor of Dionysus and Aphrodite was held every three years, lasted 30 days, and was celebrated with night-time stage performances. An imperial edict issued by the Emperor Commodus, who renewed the Olympic Games, included ceremonies from which income was to be channeled to the Maiumas rituals. According to Livia an attempt to prohibit the festivities – apparently by Julian the Apostate – was not a success.

(1) Maiumas near Gaza served as the port of that city. It is first mentioned in the Zeno Papyri (259 B.C.E.; Cairo Papyrus 59.006). In the fourth century it became a Christian city called Constantia Neapolis, and was consequently freed from dependence upon the pagan city of Gaza. It is identified with al-Mīnā, 2½ mi. (4 km.) from Gaza, on the Mediterranean coast. A synagogue with a mosaic pavement representing King David as Orpheus and dated to 508/9 C.E. was excavated there in 1967.

(2) A Maiumas located on the coast near Ashkelon is mentioned by Antoninus Placentinus. It is perhaps to be identified with Khirbat al-Ashraf at the entrance to the Shikma Valley (Wadi Sikrayr).

(3) Khirbat Miyāmās has been identified with Shuni, east of Caesarea, on the road linking Binyamina and Zikhron Ya'akov, identified as the village of Kfar Shumi (or Shami) from the third century C.E. mentioned in the Jerusalem Talmud (Ḥallah 58, 73). The site was probably referred to by the Bordeaux Pilgrim in 332 C.E.: "At the third mile from there [Caesarea] there is Mount Sina and there is a spring in which, should a woman bathe, she will fall pregnant." Since 1986 excavations have been conducted at the site by E. Shenhav on behalf of the Jewish National Fund. The Roman theater was uncovered and it consists of an orchestra, seating arrangements, vaults, and a pool, all of which together form an oval complex, containing stepped pools with mosaic floors, fountains, and a hostel apparently used by pilgrims. Storerooms and residential quarters were also exposed, as well as a large public building that may have served as a shrine during the water festivals performed at the site. Some of these festivities would have taken place within the semi-circular pool on the other side of the theater. This pool had a mosaic floor with built-in recesses for flags and was marked with lines and lanes. It is assumed that these denoted the directions of the water games and the positions taken by the players. Two inscriptions were exposed on the floor of the pool, one of which was complete and could be read as follows: "In the time of Flavius Marcianus son of Antipatris the most honorable consul the work of quarrying the mountain from the foundation was completed." The person mentioned may have been the governor of Caesarea in the fourth century C.E. Clearly the water games at the site continued during the early part of the Byzantine period.

(4) Betomarsea in the vicinity of Charachmoba (al-Karak) is called Maiumas on the Madaba Map and was connected in ancient sources to the Baal-Peor of Numbers 25:3–9.

BIBLIOGRAPHY: Strabo, *Geographia*, 16:2, 21; Ptolemaeus, 5:15, 5; Jerome, *Vita Hilarionis*, 3; Eusebius, *Vita Constantini*, 4:38; G.A. Smith, *Historical Geography of the Holy Land* (1896^4), 190; Avi-Yonah, in: BIES, 30 (1966), 221–3; idem, *Madaba Mosaic Map* (1954), no. 14; A. Ovadyah, *Qadmoniot*, 1 (1968), 124–7, pls. 3–4.

[Michael Avi-Yonah / Shimon Gibson (2nd ed.)]

MAJD AL-KURŪM. Arab village in northern Israel, 10 mi. (16 km.) E. of Acre. In the Israel War of *Independence, the village capitulated to Israel forces (Oct. 30, 1948). In 1964 Majd al-Kurūm received municipal council status. It has an area of 3.5 sq. mi. (9 sq. km.) and had a 1969 population of 3,690, most of whom were Sunnite Muslims. The village economy was based on hill farming, with olive groves, deciduous fruit tree orchards, and vegetables and local workshops, stone and marble quarries, and factories, particularly for food processing. By the end of 2002 the population of Majd al-Kurūm had tripled to 11,400 inhabitants, with income less than half the national average. Its site is assumed to be identical with the talmudic Bet Kerem ("House of Vineyards"), known for its fertile soil and rich water resources (Nid. 2:7; Tosef., Nid. 3:11).

[Efraim Orni]

MAJDAL AL-SHAMS, Druze village in the N. Golan, at the foot of Mt. Hermon. Under Israeli military administration after the *Six-Day War (1967), Majdal al-Shams was the largest of all Druze villages in the region. In 1968 it had 3,500 inhabitants whose social and economic services were greatly improved after 1967. Profits from its rich fruit orchards increased and new sources of income were created in tourism, construction of new roads (e.g., the one leading from the village to the top of Mt. Hermon), etc. In 1982 Majdal al-Shams received municipal council status. The village is spread over 4.5 sq. mi. (12 sq. km.) and reached a population of 8,240 in 2002. Income was about a third of the national average. Majdal al-Shams maintained friendly contact with the Israeli administration and close contact with the Druze community in Israel, while maintaining its contacts with the Druze community across the border in Syria.

MAJDANEK (Maidanek), concentration and death camp on the southeastern outskirts of *Lublin, Poland, in the Generalgouvernment, German-occupied Poland. It was also called Lublin-Majdanek and Majdan Tatarski, after the suburb of Lublin in which it was situated. Originally set up on July 21, 1941, for Soviet prisoners of war, it was soon turned into a camp for Jews and Poles with a maximum capacity for 35,000 inmates. Majdanek covered 667 acres; situated on the Lublin-Zamosc-Chelm Highway, it was ringed by two layers of barbed wire and guarded by 19 watchtowers, each 26.5 feet high. It contained 227 buildings, gas chambers, two gallows, and a small crematorium. The camp was divided into six sections which in 1943 contained a women's camp; a field hospital for Russian collaborators attached to the German army; a men's camp for Polish political prisoners as well as Jews from Warsaw and Bialystok; a men's camp for Soviet prisoners of war, civilian hostages, and political prisoners; a men's hospital camp; and a section for further expansion.

As with Auschwitz, but unlike the other major killing centers of Sobibor, Belzec, Treblinka, and Chelmno, Majdanek was also a slave labor and prisoner camp. Also, unlike the other major killing centers, which were used almost exclusively for the murder of Jews, Majdanek's prisoners were more diverse; many died from its primitive conditions, perhaps more than died in its gas chambers

The camp commandants were the SS officers Karl Otto Koch (September 1941–July 1942), Max Koegel (August–October 1942), Hermann Florstedt (October 1942–September 1943), Martin Weiss (September 1943–May 1944), and Arthur Liebenschel (May until liberation on July 24, 1944).

The first transport, consisting of 5,000 Soviet prisoners of war, arrived in the autumn of 1941. They died of starvation and exposure. The camp population was mixed: Soviet prisoners of war, Polish farmers, Ukrainians, Byelorussians and, of course, Jews. The first groups of Jews arrived from Slovakia and the Protectorate of Bohemia and Moravia (15,000) and then Poland (36,500). Early in 1943, 6,000 Dutch and Greek Jews arrived, followed by 74,800 Polish Jews, mostly from *Warsaw, *Bialystok, and Lublin. Altogether 130,000 Jews were sent to Majdanek in 1942–43.

Until the spring of 1942 prisoners were usually shot in a nearby forest, but from October 1942 until the end of 1943, Majdanek had three gas chambers located in one building, which used both carbon monoxide and, like Auschwitz, Zyklon B gas to kill prisoners.

Jewish prisoners who were not killed immediately were employed in various work projects in the camp or in the Lublin area. If further workers were needed in 1942, some trains en route to Belzec were stopped and Jews able to work were removed before the train resumed its journey toward the death camp.

In May 1943 some 18,000 Jews from the Warsaw Ghetto were sent to Majdanek following the Ghetto Uprising and some ghetto factories were transferred there. They were not to stay long. In the summer of 1943, 10,000 able-bodied Jews were transferred from Majdanek for work in "Hasag" camp and Auschwitz.

Toward the end of 1943 a strong partisan movement developed in the Lublin district. Uprisings had taken place in Vilna and Bialystok, and even in the death camps of Sobibor (August) and Treblinka, unnerving the Germans. In retaliation, they carried out a massacre (euphemistically named the "Harvest Festival") of 42,000 Jews, some of whom had been brought from the nearby work camps. This "action" included the machinegunning of 18,000 Jews in a single day (November 3, 1943) in front of the ditches that the victims were made to dig to serve as their own graves.

Between 170,000 and 235,000 persons died or were killed at Majdanek. Most died because of the harsh conditions, starvation and disease, torture, forced labor, and despair. The number of victims of Majdanek's gas chambers is unknown.

When the camp was liberated by the advancing Soviet armies (July 24, 1944), only a few hundred prisoners of various nationalities were still alive. In their hasty evacuation, the Germans could not destroy the camp entirely and thus a clear remnant of the camps, barracks, gas chamber, and crematoria remained. The liberation of Majdanek was covered widely. Western correspondents had entered the death camp and written stories about it. H.W. Lawrence, a correspondent for the *New York Times*, wrote: "I have just seen the most terrible place on earth." These revelations were not given the credence they deserved.

Press coverage was intense. Roman Karman, a well-known Soviet correspondent, filed this report on August 21, 1944:

> In the course of my travels into liberated territory I have never seen a more abominable sight than Majdanek near Lublin, Hitler's notorious *Vernichtungslager*, where more than half a million European men, women, and children were massacred … This is not a concentration camp; it is a gigantic murder plant.
>
> Save for the 1,000 living corpses the Red Army found alive when it entered, no inmate escaped alive. Yet full trains daily brought thousands from all parts of Europe to be coldly, brutally massacred.
>
> In the center of the camp stands a huge stone building with a factory chimney – the world's biggest crematorium … The gas chambers contained some 250 people at a time. They were closely packed … so that after they suffocated they remained standing … It is difficult to believe it myself but human eyes cannot deceive me…

In the postwar years the Polish authorities established a museum and research institute at Majdanek. Poland established an impressive memorial at Majdanek and made significant efforts to preserve the remaining buildings, which are used to portray what happened there. More than 500,000 shoes taken from prisoners filled one of the barracks.

In July 1944 the Polish-Soviet Investigation Commission began to look into the crimes of Majdanek; it published a report in September; 6 of the 1,300 people who had served at Majdanek were tried in November 1944, 4 of them were hanged. Between 1946 and 1948, 96 additional men were tried and between 1975 and 1980 16 former staff members, 6 of them women, were tried in West Germany.

BIBLIOGRAPHY: E. Gryn and Z. Murawska, *Majdanek Concentration Camp* (1966); IMT, *Trial of the Major War Criminals*, 23 (1949), index; A. Werth, *Russia at War 1941–1945* (1964), 889–99, and index; G. Reitlinger, *Final Solution* (1968[2]), index; Z. Lukaszkiewicz, in: *Biuletyn Głównej Komisji Badania Zbrodni Hitlerowskich w Polsce*, 4 (1948), 63–105; T. Berenstein and A. Rutkowski, in: BŻIH, no. 58 (1966), 3–57; *Zeszyty Majdanka*, 3 vols. (1965–69) with Eng. sum. **ADD. BIBLIOGRAPHY:** G.Z. Murawska, *Majdanek* (1984).

[Danuta Dombrowska / Michael Berenbaum (2nd ed.)]

MAJOR, ERVIN (1901–1967), musicologist and composer. Born in Budapest, the son of Julius *Major, he studied composition with Zoltan Kodaly and Leo *Weiner at the Budapest Academy of Music (1917–21) and philosophy at the Budapest Scientific University (1920–24). In 1930 he received his doctorate for a dissertation on the relationship of popular Hungarian music to folk music. From 1926 to 1928 he was the editor of *Zenei Szemle* and later became a member of the editorial board of the periodicals *Muzsika* (1929–30) and *Magyar muzsika* (1935–36). He was also a librarian and lecturer of composition, music theory, and history at the Budapest Conservatory and at the Budapest Academy of Music. In 1951 he became a member of the musicological committee of the Hungarian Academy of Sciences. He was one of the founders of Hungarian historical musicology, specializing in the 18th and 19th centuries and in the tracing of Hungarian influence in the works of classical composers. He also contributed a number of central articles to the *Zenei lexikon* ("Music lexicon"; edited by B. *Szabolcsi and A. Tóth, 3 vols. 1930, 1965[2]) and established successful methods of research, using public and private archives, periodicals, and collected editions of music. His compositions include chamber, piano, organ and choral works, and arrangements of old Hungarian melodies.

ADD. BIBLIOGRAPHY: Grove online.

[Israela Stein (2nd ed.)]

MAJOR, JULIUS (**Gyula Jacob**; 1858–1925), composer, conductor, pianist, and teacher. Born in Kassa (Kosice), Major studied with Liszt, Volkmann, and Erkel. He wrote symphonies, concertos, lieder, and operas, many of which demonstrate a felicitous synthesis of the Hungarian national idiom and Western European forms. His teaching activities included founding and directing the State Music Teachers' College and the Hungarian Women's Choral Association.

MAJORCA (Sp. **Mallorca**), largest and most important of the Balearic Isles. It is difficult to determine when Jews first arrived in Majorca, but it may be assumed that the settlement was ancient because of the island's location at the crossroads of the maritime trade routes and its proximity to the coasts of both North Africa and the Iberian Peninsula. The presence of Jews on the nearby island of *Minorca during the fifth century implies their presence on Majorca also, and several lead tablets (attributed to the fourth–fifth centuries) bearing the name of Samuel b. Ḥagi (or Ḥaggai) have recently been found. Practically nothing is known of the history of the island from the sixth to the eighth centuries – and even less of the history of the Jews there during that period. It appears that the Jewish settlement was destroyed when the Byzantine general Belisarius overcame the Vandals and took Majorca (534 C.E.). Similarly, few details are available on the period of the Muslim conquest. When the *Almohads attacked southern Spain (12th century), refugees from Andalusia arrived in Majorca and it may be assumed that there were some Jews among them. The earliest evidence for the presence of Jews on the island during the Muslim period is from 1135, when Ramón Berenguer III, count of Barcelona, took some Jews of Majorca under his protection.

The Beginning of Aragonese Rule

When James I of Aragon conquered Palma de Mallorca (1229–32), there were several Jews in his retinue, noteworthy being Bahye and Solomon Alconstantini, from Saragossa, whose knowledge of Arabic was greatly appreciated and when the distribution of properties took place after the conquest they were among the beneficiaries, notably Samuel *Benveniste, *alfaquim* of Count Nuño Sánchez of Roussillon. Properties were also granted to Jews who settled in other parts of the island: Inca, Petra, and Montiori. In Palma (then named Majorca, like the island itself), a residential area was set aside for the Jewish settlers in the fortress of Almudaina which was later known as "the fortress of the Jews." With the consolidation of Christian rule, Jews arrived from Marseilles and other towns of Provence-Languedoc, from North Africa, and even from Alexandria in Egypt. The king, who controlled settlement on the island, undertook to protect the permanent residential area of the Jews in the same way as other places. The Jews, however, rapidly left the fortress of Almudaina, settling in the vicinity, a move which later led to disputes. Besides the communities mentioned above, there were others in Felanitx, Sineu, Alcudia, Sóller, and Pollensa. James I also gave letters of protection to Jewish settlers from North Africa, among whom was Solomon b. Amar of Sijilmassa (1247).

From the start the Jewish settlers integrated into the economy of the island; they owned Muslim, Turkish, and Tatar slaves, whom they were accustomed to convert to Judaism, although the civil authorities and the church issued a series of decrees designed to prevent this. The papal Inquisition was very active against Jewish merchants. Between 1276 and 1343, except for the years 1285–1298, the Kingdom of Majorca that included the Balearic islands and the counties of Roussillon and Ceradagne was independent. The independent kings of Majorca pursued more or less the same policy towards the Jews that was adopted in the Crown of Aragon. Under Sancho I (1311–24) the synagogue in the city of Majorca was converted into the church of Santa Fe. With the conquest of Majorca in 1343 by Pedro IV of Aragon, a period of great achievements began for the Jews of the island. From that year on, they developed ramified commercial activity. They engaged in the international maritime trade and became renowned for their skill in crafts such as gold- and silversmithery and shoemaking. In 1250 James I confirmed the rights of the Jewish settlers, granting them further privileges in conformity with his Jewish policy in the kingdom of Aragon. The problem of interest rates was one of the most severe in the relations between Jews and Christians on the island. Many royal ordinances dealt with the subject: restrictive decrees were issued; rates which had been fixed were cancelled; and occasionally the Jews were obliged to return the interest. In other matters, James I authorized the Jews of Majorca to address their complaints directly to himself and assured them of his protection. In 1254, he assessed their property, along with that of the Jews of Minorca and Ibiza, and constituted them as an independent taxation group. The community of Barcelona nevertheless continued to influence the island communities in their administrative affairs, as well as in all other aspects of communal life. In 1269 the Jews of Palma were granted an important privilege authorizing them to purchase houses, vineyards, and any other property in and around the town and to live in the houses which they had acquired or rented. Toward the close of the 13th century, the Jews in Palma lived in the area between Temple and Calatrava streets and this quarter became the focus of Jewish life in the town until the destruction of the community.

During the early 1270s, James I authorized the Jews to trade on a credit system with the Christians in textiles, cereals, oil, linen, saffron, and other goods. The Jews of Majorca were already fairly prosperous during this period. About 1271 the community of Palma paid an annual tax of 5,000 sólidos. During the same year, together with those communities of Catalonia, *Perpignan, and *Montpellier, it granted the king the sum of 25,000 sólidos toward the expenses of his campaign in Leon. He nevertheless forbade Jews to live side by side with Christians (1273), although he authorized them to purchase new houses. James I also renewed the permit for a separate *sheḥitah* on the island. During this period, the preacher Raimon Lull, who wielded considerable power on Majorca, was active there, conducting religious disputations with the Jews with the aim of bringing them over to Christianity.

From the Time of Alfonso III (1285–95) until the Rule of Pedro IV (1343)

James I divided the kingdom of Aragon in his will, setting up the independent kingdom of Majorca under his second son James II (of Majorca). Reigning from 1276, James II confirmed the privileges which had been granted by his father. In 1285 his nephew Alfonso III seized the island from him, ruling it until 1295. Alfonso confirmed a series of privileges and decrees issued by James I and further exempted the Jews from various taxes. The Jews of Majorca granted the king a special allowance of 10,000 sólidos for his own use, and Alfonso authorized them to appeal to him against legal decisions taken by his officials, provided that the town's interests were not prejudiced by these appeals (1286). During that year, he also borrowed 20,000 sólidos from the trustees of the community. A year later, the Jews of Majorca had to assist the king with a special contribution of 30,000 sólidos. At the same time, Alfonso showed concern for the regular payments of the debts owed to them by Christians, although he occasionally granted to the latter a remission of debts for a given period. Continuing to make yearly demands for support from the Jewish community in addition to the annual tax, in 1290 he imposed a payment of 37,000 sólidos in reparation for the offense of taking excessive interest; he also collected 12,000 sólidos for the right of establishing a "Jewish street," surrounding it with a wall, and installing gates at the points of entry.

James II returned to the island in 1295, reigning there until his death in 1311, when he was followed by his son Sancho I. The situation of the Jews further deteriorated until the island was reconquered by Pedro IV (1343). From the earliest days of the independent kingdom, they were compelled to pay tithes whenever they acquired land and houses from Christians. Anti-Jewish riots broke out in 1305, and in 1309 the first *blood libel occurred on the island when several Jews were accused of the murder of a Christian child. Riots ensued; the king ordered the attackers of the Jews to be punished and the activity of Christians within the Jewish quarter to be restricted. During the same year, similar riots broke out in Inca and many Jews were killed. Nevertheless the island admitted several Jewish settlers who had been expelled from France (1306). Among these was R. Aaron ha-Kohen who studied under R. Shem Tov Falcón in Majorca and later wrote his *Orḥot Ḥayyim* there. The king even sent an emissary to reassure the Jews of their security, and this assurance was reiterated by his son, Sancho I, in 1311. When several Christians from Germany arrived in Majorca in 1314 the community of Palma accepted them as proselytes (even though they had previously been rejected by the communities of *Lérida and *Gerona), thereby arousing considerable ill feeling on the island. Under the influence of Majorca's bishop, Sancho ordered the confiscation of the synagogue of Palma, which was converted into a church, and imposed a heavy fine on the community. A year later he ordered the confiscation of the property of the Jews of Palma, but left them with enough for subsistence. After the fine was paid, Sancho was again willing to take the Jews under his protection. During the same year, a long series of regulations dealing with Jewish matters was issued. The regulations concerned community administration, taxes on foodstuffs and wine, and commerce. It was prohibited to try Jews on their festivals; any Jew who expressed his desire to convert while imprisoned was to be confronted with two other Jews, before whom he had to declare that his conversion was of his own free will; if he reconsidered his decision, he would be authorized to remain a Jew. It was also stated that the Inquisition's investigations against Jews would not take place without the consent of the king; the trustees of the community would be authorized to seize those who disregarded communal regulations and imprison them; a Jew from abroad who came to trade in Majorca would be authorized to carry on to Minorca with his goods without having to pay any additional taxes. A year later, Sancho allowed the Jews of Majorca to import goods and property acquired in Moorish countries even though he was at war with them. He also authorized the erection of a new synagogue to serve as a house of prayer and *bet midrash* but stipulated that it be less splendid then the former building. In 1331 James III, Sancho's nephew, ordered the viceroy on the island to assist the Jews in the erection of the synagogue in spite of the opposition of Pope John XXII.

After the death of Sancho in 1325, the regent Philip, who ruled in the name of James III, confirmed the existing privileges of the Jews on the island and granted them civic rights. Treating them with tolerance, he stopped the legal action against several Jewish merchants accused of smuggling goods to North Africa (after the merchants had promised to pay him a considerable sum) and in 1327 he prohibited the forced conversion of Jews and their pagan slaves. During the reign of James III (1327–43) a poll tax was imposed on the Jews of Majorca. When the Palma community refrained from paying this in 1332, the king imposed a fine on it; after some time, he reduced the fine for several families. In 1337 he granted the trustees of the Majorca community the right to punish those guilty of religious or moral offenses, but they were forbidden to expel them or to administer corporal punishment. In spite of the restriction in the rights of the Jews of Majorca to try cases of criminal law, the *dayyanim* strictly adhered to Jewish law and the customs of Spanish Jewry.

The Organization and Administration of the Majorca Communities

Details of the organization of the Palma community have come down from the close of the 13th century. In its communal and religious life Majorcan Jewry was very much influenced by the Catalan Jewish communities. The rabbis of Majorca were in close contact with those of Barcelona. In its administration, too, the community followed in the footsteps of the community in Barcelona. In 1296 the community was authorized to elect three *muqaddimūn* or trustees; the right of jurisdiction over the Jews was at first in the hands of the communal leaders, who were even authorized to expel any Jew for disreputable conduct. Throughout the period of the independent kingdom, the community was generally headed by six trustees and an executive council of eight "good men," though this council does not seem to have functioned regularly. In 1327, when the regent Philip allowed four of the trustees to dismiss a fifth who had been appointed by Sancho I, he recognized the exclusive right of the Jews of Palma to elect their own officers without any outside intervention, even from the king himself. When Pedro IV conquered Majorca in 1343, he confirmed the existing arrangements. When in 1348 the trustees wished to coopt one of the "small taxpayers" on to the committee distributing charity funds, one of the "large" taxpayers complained to Pedro IV who supported him, declaring that it was preferable that charity be distributed by those who had contributed it. In the inter-communal organization for the entire Crown of Aragon that met in 1354 it was felt that Majorca was important enough to be represented on the board. In 1356 Pedro confirmed a communal regulation excluding physicians and brokers from serving as trustees. At that time, the governor of the island appointed a "Council of Thirty" which functioned until 1374, when the king ordered that the former communal leaders were to be responsible for its administration. Members of the council were to be elected by the community itself, and assisted by members appointed on the recommendation of the wealthier taxpayers. Several regulations on the assessment of the communal taxes, which indicate an attempt to create a reasonably objective assessment system, were confirmed by Pedro in 1378. Under the influence of R. Jonah *Desmaestre, Pedro issued in 1383 a series of instructions on the organization of communal life: the right to judge criminal law was restored to the community; the right of individuals to draw up testaments was not to be infringed upon; Jews were not to be compelled to hold disputations with apostates; no Jew of Majorca would be exempted from communal taxes, nor would any extraordinary tax be imposed upon him; no Jew might claim office in the community nor would he be exempted from public office if such was imposed upon him. Confirming these regulations John I granted the trustees of Palma the additional right of trying criminal law cases with the assistance of five rabbis, either according to Jewish law or Roman law. The community of Majorca benefited from these regulations until its destruction in 1391. When the Jewish settlement on the island was renewed, it appears that these regulations were again applied until it ceased to exist.

From the Reign of Pedro IV (1343–87) Until the End of the Jewish Settlement

After Pedro IV conquered the Balearic Isles (1343), the situation of the Jews of Majorca improved. The king's retinue included the physician Maestre Eleazar ibn Ardut of Huesca and Ḥasdai Crescas, the grandfather of R. Ḥasdai *Crescas. Immediately after the conquest, Pedro exempted the Jews of Majorca from the taxes imposed upon them by James III and canceled the bonds for the payment of the poll tax. He reconfirmed the privileges which had been granted by James II, Alfonso III, and the regent Philip, and ordered that those Jews who had left the island and newcomers also be given favorable opportunities to settle there. One of the supporters of James III was an alchemist named Menahem who was brought to trial in 1345; later he entered the service of Pedro as alchemist, physician, and astrologer. In 1346, Pedro decreed that a separate quarter be built for the Jews in Inca, in order to prevent both undue familiarity and quarrels between Jews and Christians. However, it appears that this separation did not apply in practice. The island communities suffered extensively at the time of the *Black Death and during the plagues which also broke out in the 1370s and 1380s. Rioting occurred as an aftermath of the plagues, and in 1374 the Christians called for the expulsion of the Jews from the island, but both the king and the infante John endeavored to restore order.

At the end of the 1340s, the Jewish physician and scholar Judah *Mosconi (Leo Grech) left Greece to settle in Majorca. From then until the close of the century, a school of Jewish astronomers and cartographers developed on the island. Among them were Abraham *Cresques (d. 1387), who was made a *magister mapa mundorum et buxolarum*, and his son Judah. Both were also granted by royal decree the privilege of appointing all the ritual slaughterers on the island. In 1359 R. Isaac *Nifoci, an astronomer, was chosen as the companion of the king of Aragon (in 1390 he joined the rabbis of the island). In the 14th century Majorca became a center of Torah learning. *Aharon ha-Kohen of Lunel wrote his *Orḥot Ḥayyim* there. At the end of the 1360s, R. *Isaac b. Sheshet corresponded with R. Solomon Zarfati, the talmudist, who was invited to come to Majorca by Jucef Faquim. R. Vidal Ephraim Gerondi, astrologer to the infante John and Solomon Ẓarfati's rabbinical rival, died a martyr's death in 1391. During the 1380s, R. Jonah Desmaestre did much to strengthen religious observance on the island and acted as *rosh yeshivah* in Palma (Simeon b. Ẓemaḥ *Duran was his son-in-law). Together with R. Ḥasdai Crescas, he undertook the reconstruction of the communities which had been destroyed during the persecutions of 1391. The physician Maestre Aaron Abdal-Ḥagg was also well-known; in spite of the prohibition of 1356, he was appointed as trustee of the community of Palma. In 1381 Pedro IV appointed Solomon b. Abraham Benallell as *mustaçaf* ("town market supervisor") over the Jews of Majorca in appreciation of his services, also leasing him the right to manufacture soap on the island. Granting him a "rabbinical" position in Palma, he authorized him to appoint a ritual slaughterer or to slaughter for the requirements of the community.

During the second half of the 14th century, the island communities developed to the point of gaining the regard of the communities of Aragon, and in 1354 Majorca was invited to send a delegate to the supreme council of the communities of Aragon. In all this period, the Jews of Majorca carried on an intensive local trade and supplied goods from North Africa to the Spanish mainland. Others continued to engage in agriculture and crafts, but small craftsmen and owners of small plots of land were compelled to sell their land in times of difficulty; in an effort to help them Simeon b. Ẓemaḥ Duran (Resp. 1, no. 51) attempted to modify the Jewish *usury laws so that they would be able to take loans. During the 14th century, the Jews of the island still owned slaves and the problems connected with their possession which had arisen during the 13th century persisted. Essentially the prominence of the leading Jewish merchants was based on their maritime trade in the Mediterranean, with Alexandria, Sicily, Sardinia, and other places. It was these merchants who imported grain to the island in times of famine and scarcity, although they were not shipowners; there was even a series of privileges which declared that Christian shipowners must not refuse cargoes loaded on their ships by Jews. Eminent among these merchants was Don Jucef Faquim (Joseph Ḥakim) whose family had arrived on the island in 1332. In 1365 he argued before the king that he should be exempted from taxes because his property consisted of goods scattered over many countries and these possessions were insecure; the king ordered the trustees to appoint two merchants to assess his payments. In 1370 Jucef Faquim supplied grain to the army, which was quartered on Sardinia. When the Jews of Majorca complained to Pedro IV in 1351 about sailors who took some of their number into captivity and removed them elsewhere if they were not redeemed in time, he ordered that the captives be set free against the payment of a ransom of 30 livres of silver. During this period Majorca Jews also engaged in moneylending and frequent governmental measures attempted to reduce the interest rates.

The form of the Jewish *oath in force in Majorca, established by Pedro in 1352, required them to swear on a text containing the Ten Commandments only, without the addition of the reproof sections. In 1359 the king renewed the privilege which stipulated that Majorca Jews could not be tortured without explicit royal approval. In the same year, he authorized the Jews of North Africa to enter and to leave the island, against a payment of one-eighth of the price of goods which they bought or sold on the island. After the inhabitants of the town of Inca had attacked the Jews in 1373, many left the island. After several conversions had taken place, the Jews of Majorca complained to the king, who in 1373 ordered the bishop of Majorca to pay heed to the ancient decree concerning the conversion regulations (see above). In 1376 the Jews of Porreras were set upon by the local population. However, the following year Pedro intervened in favor of the Jews, ordering them to present their claims in person before the mercantile court (*consulado del mar*). During this period the king continued to impose compulsory loans on the Jewish communities (especially in 1380 and 1383).

The 1391 Persecutions

When news of the anti-Jewish riots sweeping Spain in 1391 reached Majorca, the leaders of the Jews appealed to Francisco Sa Garriga, viceroy of John I, to find a way of preventing the outbreak of similar riots on the island. It was decided to cordon off the Jewish quarter and allow no weapons inside. As soon as they heard reports of the riots in Valencia, Jews began to leave the island and those who lived in the villages moved to the towns, into the fortified Jewish quarters. In Palma the riots broke out on July 10; youths bearing crucifixes infiltrated the Jewish quarter. Although the gates were closed the mob broke them down and massacred scores of Jews. The next day the authorities made attempts to mitigate the storm, but on August 2 the riots broke out again. The community of Inca was completely wiped out, as were those of Sóller, Sineu, and Alcudia. Several leaders of the riots were captured, but the mob set them free; villagers traveled to the towns in order to share in the pillage. Many Jews died as martyrs, notably R. Vidal Ephraim Gerondi, and several distinguished personalities accepted baptism; among these were R. Isaac Nifoci, who later atoned for his act by emigrating to Ereẓ Israel, and Judah Cresques, who became a prominent courtier. A list of 111 heads of families who were converted is still extant; they were given the names of their baptismal godfathers (several of the converts were named after the viceroy, Francisco Sa Garriga). In spite of the governor's prohibition on leaving the island, many Jews fled to North Africa, among them Simeon b. Ẓemaḥ Duran, who settled in Algiers and held rabbinical office there. Majorcan Jewish settlers in North Africa speak of a Jewish community of more than 1,000 families in Majorca, prior to the massacres. The figure seems exaggerated but indicates the prestige and splendor the community had in Jewish eyes. In September 1391 the peasants demanded that the surviving Jews be baptized or put to death; in rejecting this demand the authorities explained that Christianity sought to achieve conversion through free will and not by force. However, the peasants renewed their demands a month later, and it appears that there were numerous converts at that time.

At the beginning of 1392, the authorities took steps to normalize the situation. The populace was ordered to hand back plundered property; surviving Jews and forced converts were required to provide within ten days a written list of the debts owing to them; the forced converts were called upon to appear before the viceroy and declare whether they desired to continue to live in the Jewish quarter or rent houses to Jews who had been left homeless; and the inhabitants were ordered to return the doors which they had removed from Jewish houses. The bailiff of Palma, one of the leaders of the riot, was executed in January 1392. Fearing that the island's peasants might rebel, the crown granted an amnesty to the rioters and canceled debts to Jews contracted over the previous ten years. Despite the governor's decree forbidding the forced converts to leave the island, many fled to North Africa and returned to Judaism; among them were members of the Najjār family. In January 1393, the governor prohibited further assaults on Jews; anyone molesting them would be hanged if he was of the lower class and flogged if he belonged to the nobility. Nevertheless, a new amnesty was granted to the rioters. As early as 1393, there are instances of the authorities prosecuting forced converts who had returned to Judaism.

In an attempt to reestablish the Jewish communities of the island, in 1394 the authorities invited 150 families from Portugal to settle there, and they arrived in 1395. At the same time the crown granted a writ of protection and exemption from special taxes to all Jews who had fled to North Africa and other places and wished to return to Majorca. However, their resettlement was doomed to failure. In 1413, Vicente *Ferrer visited the island and induced several members of the community to accept baptism. Seeking to undermine the position of the Jews of Majorca, Ferdinand I issued in 1413 a series of restrictions resembling the 1412 decrees of Valladolid with an additional provision prohibiting the emigration of forced converts to North Africa. There was a slight alleviation in the situation during the reign of Alfonso V, who included the Jews of Majorca in his favorable decree of 1419 which ordered that copies of the Talmud be returned to the Jews; that the system of Jewish jurisdiction be set in order; that their synagogue be restored; and that they be exempted from forced attendance at sermons. A *blood libel was perpetrated in Majorca in 1432, and in 1435 the community ceased to exist: 200 persons were converted and the remainder fled to join their coreligionists in North Africa.

The Fate of the Conversos of Majorca

The papal Inquisition was already active in Majorca during the 13th century, but it was only from the beginning of the 15th that its activities really made themselves felt. In 1407 a *Converso who had twice returned to Judaism was condemned to be burnt at the stake, and in 1410 Benedict XIII ordered that measures be taken against the Conversos of Majorca. Antonio Murta, the inquisitor of the Balearic Islands from 1420 to 1436, was responsible for the conversion of many Jews in 1435. The Spanish *Inquisition began to operate in Majorca in 1488. From the start, many Conversos were brought back to the Church. Until the close of the 15th century, 346 trials were held and 257 persons were handed over to the secular arm for the death penalty. During the 16th century, especially after 1520, the tribunal's activities decreased, but they were resumed with renewed ferocity in 1675 and 1677. In 1675, a large group of Conversos from Majorca, referred to by the Inquisition as "Portuguese," was brought to trial. Martyrs included Alonso López; others were sentenced in absentia and burned in effigy. Among those sentenced in 1677 were Pedro Onofri Cortes and Raphael Valis, who were prominent members of the Converso community. The tribunal's activities reached their peak in 1691, when 86 Conversos (including 46 women) were sentenced and another 39 reconciled with the church. From then on its activities appear to have waned. By 1771 the Inquisition had sent a total of 594 Conversos to the stake and reconciled a further 460 with the church. During the 18th century, tribunal officials occasionally arrested Jewish travelers on the Balearic Isles on the suspicion that they were Conversos. In 1718 Jacob Cardozo Nuñez of Bayonne, and Samuel Nahon and his relative Solomon Nahon of Tetuán were arrested. Cardozo was imprisoned until 1721.

Conversos in Majorca were given the name of **chuetas*, a name which persisted into the mid-20th century. They continued to live in separate quarters and all social and public advancement were denied to them. They formed a closed society in which the overwhelming majority secretly observed Jewish rites, for which they were often brought to trial. It was not until the end of the 18th century that the government attempted to alleviate their condition and in 1782 the Conversos were permitted to settle in any part of the town or the island; at the same time it became an offense to molest them by word or deed. After the French conquest of the island, the Inquisition was abolished in 1808 and the Conversos were granted further concessions. However, when Ferdinand IV returned to power (1814) the Inquisition was reintroduced and its final abolition barely improved the lot of the Conversos. In 1856 riots broke out against them once more when several prominent members of the community sought to join the exclusive *Circulo Balear* club. There was a renewed debate on the place of the *chuetas* within the island's society toward the close of the 19th century with the publication of the work of the priest José Tarongi in 1877, condemning their social ostracism and explicitly blaming the clergy for this. Also influential was the work of Vicente Blasco Ibañez, *Los muertos mandan* (1916). Jews began to take an interest in their condition. During the Republican regime in Spain (1931), a work by Garao, *La Fe Triunfante*, was republished. Written a century before it sought to stress the Jewishness of the *chuetas* as grounds for their total rejection.

[Haim Beinart]

The Jewish Quarter

The Jewish quarter of Majorca was famous for its size and prosperity. It was only at the beginning of the 14th century that the locality known as the *call* came into being. It was then that the Jews were compelled to live in a separate district. Beforehand, many of the Jews had resided in the place called *Almudaina*. The new Jewish quarter was in the district of the Temple and Calatrava. The medieval Jewish quarter included the streets known today as C. del Sol, C. Montesión, C. Montserrat, C. Calatrava and all the streets connecting between them. In Majorca there were at least four synagogues, including the Mayor and the Menor or Nueva. The two famous *rimmonim* found in the cathedral are of Sicilian origin and were bought for the cathedral in 1493. In the Archivo del Reino de Mallorca there are two beautiful ketubbot.

[Yom Tov Assis (2nd ed.)]

Contemporary Period

A small Jewish community – the first since 1435 – was established in 1971 in Palma de Mallorca, the capital of the island. This was the result mainly of the efforts of Mr. Alec Kesselman, then the supervisor of the *kasher* section of a hotel in Palma. In reply to his application the Spanish minister of justice gave approval to the establishment of the Communidad Israelita de Palma de Mallorca on July 8, 1971. In addition to services held at a hotel there were weekly services in the Palacio de Congresos, Palma. The *kasher* section of the hotel was closed, however, in 1978. The community numbered around 300 people (although some estimates were higher): most were silver- and goldsmiths and a few were small merchants. Some were successful businessmen and a few even left for Spain, where they managed to find a place in Spanish society. In the early 2000s the community maintained a synagogue.

BIBLIOGRAPHY: B. Braunstein, *Chuetas of Majorca* (1936); A.L. Isaacs, *Jews of Majorca* (1936), incl. bibl.; Baer, Spain, index; Baer, Urkunden, 1 (1929), index; M. Kayserling, *Juden in Navarra…* (1861), 153–89; J. Amador de Los Rios, *Historia política… de los Judíos en España…*, 3 (1876), 638ff.; J. Rullan, *Historia de Sóller*, 2 vols. (1875–76); H.C. Lea, *A History of the Inquisition of Spain*, 3 vols. (1906), index; F. Fita, in: *Boletín de la Real Academia de la historia*, 36 (1900 = *La España hebrea*, 1889–98); J.M. Millás Vallicrosa and J. Busquets Mulets, in: *Sefarad*, 4 (1944), 275–86; A. Pons, *ibid.*, 15 (1955), 69–87; J.M. Millás Vallicrosa, *ibid.*, 18 (1958), 3–9; 21 (1961), 65–66; J. Goñi, *ibid.*, 22 (1962), 105f.; F.L. Lacave, *ibid.*, 23 (1963), 375–6; L. Torres Balbás, *Al Andalus*, 19 (1954), 194; Cantera-Millás, Inscripciones, 319–21, 389–91, 393–4; A. Pons, in: *Hispania*, 78 (1960), 3–54; 79 (1960), 163–266; 80 (1960), 368–540 (incl. bibl.) [republished as *Los judíos del Reino de Mallorca durante los siglos XIII y XIV* (1984) 2 vols]; R. Patai, in: *Midstream*, 8 (1962), 59–68; J.N. Hillgarth and B. Narkis, in: REJ, 120 (1961), 297–320; M. Fortoza, *Els descendents dels jueus conversos de Mallorca* (1966). **ADD. BIBLIOGRAPHY:** F. Riera i Montserrat, in: BSAL, 34 (1973–75), 377–403; K. Moore, *Those of the Street: The Catholic-Jews of Mallorca* (1976); G. Llompart, in: *Fontes Rerum Balearum*, 2 (1978), 181–99; idem, in: BSAL, 38 (1981), 261–78; idem and J. Riera i Sans, in: *Fontes Rerum Balearum*, 3 (1979–80), 141–92; R. Soto Company, in: BSAL, 36 (1978), 145–84; J. Mas i Vives, in: BSAL, 37 (1979), 378–409; J. Bestard, in: *L'Avenc*, 42 (Oct. 1981), 19–21; P. de Montaner, in: BSAL, 40 (1984), 255–71; G. Corte's Corte's, *Historia de los judiíos mallorqines y de sus decendientes cristianos* (1985), 2 vols.; A.S. Selke, *The Conversos of Majorca: Life and Death in a Crypto-Jewish Community in XVIIth Century Spain* (1986); M.A. Lozano Galán, in: *Miscelánea de Estudios Árabes y Hebráicos*, 34:2 (1985), 93–108; idem, in: *ibid.*, 35:2 (1986), 53–80; E. Laub, and J.F. Laub, *El mito triunfante* (1987); J. Riera i Sans and R. Rosselló Vaquer, in *Calls*, 3 (1988–89), 83–101; J.N. Hillgarth and J. Rosselló Lliteras (ed.), *The "Liber comunis curiae" of the Diocese of Majorca (1364–1374)* (1989); J.N. Hillgarth, in: A. Mirsky (ed.), *Exile and Diaspora* (1991) 125–30; D. Abulafia, *A Mediterranean Emporium, The Catalan Kingdom of Majorca* (1994); E. Pérez i Pons, *Fonts per a l'estudi de la comunitat jueva de Mallorca, Regesta i bibliografia* (2005) [= Catalonia Hebraica VI].

MAJORITY RULE, deciding a matter according to the majority opinion. In the field of the *halakhah* this rule is applied in three principal instances:

(a) determination of the binding law according to (the view of) the majority of halakhic scholars;

(b) adjudication of dispute by the majority decision of the courts' judges; and

(c) imposition by majority decision of the community, or its representatives, of a communal enactment (see **Takkanot ha-Kahal*), binding on all members of the community. The basis for the majority rule is to be found in the exegesis of the scriptural phrase, *aḥarei rabbim le-hattot* (to "follow a multitude…" Ex. 23:2).

In Deciding the *Halakhah*

In the Talmud the phrase *aḥarei rabbim le-hattot* was converted into a decisory canon: "where there is a controversy between an individual and the many, the *halakhah* follows the many" (Ber. 9a). The sages of the Talmud explained the existence of this rule as a practical necessity, for if the Torah had been given in the form of an exhaustive codex, "the world could not have existed" (TJ, Sanh. 4:2, 22a; cf. Mid. Ps. 82:3). The halakhic opinion that has prevailed is that the law is decided in accordance with the view expressed by a majority of the scholars, and this is so even if in a particular matter a heavenly voice (see **Bat-Kol*) should declare that the law is according to the minority opinion (BM 59a).

The individual may continue to express his opinion that the majority has erred, but may not instruct in practice according to the minority opinion; if he actually instructs others to follow the minority opinion, he becomes (when there is a Sanhedrin) a **zaken mamre* (i.e., a "rebellious scholar"; Maim., Yad, Mamrim, 3:5–6). If a majority of scholars should arrive at the same conclusion but each for a different reason, some scholars hold this to be a majority opinion which is binding while other scholars hold the contrary view (*Maggid Mishneh*, Ishut 7:12; Maharik, resp. nos. 41, 52, 94, 102).

Some of the *geonim* and *rishonim* took the view that a minority opinion is to be preferred above a majority opinion of scholars of lesser wisdom. This question first arose in a responsum of Hai Gaon concerning a court decision on the concrete matter in issue, and not as concerns deciding of the *halakhah* in general (*Ge'onim Kadmoniyyim*, resp. no. 144; Ramban nov. Sanh. 23a; *Sefer ha-Ḥinnukh*, no. 67). Some of the scholars op-

Heinrich Bunting, German, 1546–1606. *The Whole World in a Clover Leaf.* Woodcut, 1581.

Gift of Tamar and Teddy Kollek, Jerusalem. The Israel Museum, Jerusalem. Photo: Z. Radovan, Jerusalem.

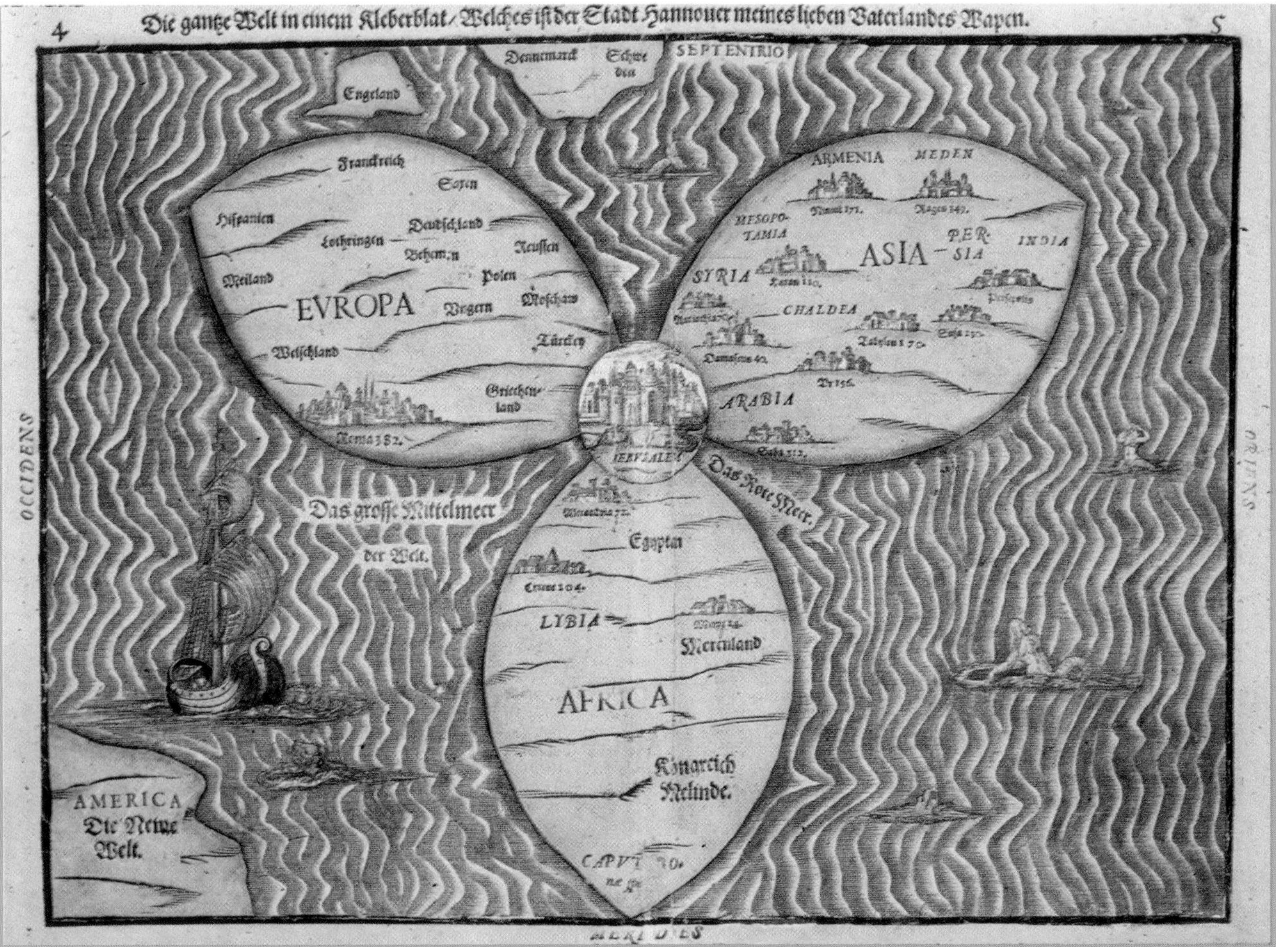

The history of the mapping of the Holy Land epitomizes the history of cartography. Evincing the longest unbroken sequence of mapping in the world, the Holy Land has been the focus of intense interest for countless generations of cartographers under its various names–Canaan, The Promised Land, Palestine, or Terra Sancta. Two principal cartographic traditions dominate this fascinating history: the religious, based on the Bible and its exegeses; and the classical, based on Ptolemy's work, which laid the foundations for modern cartography.

HOLY LAND IN MAPS

Frans Hogenberg, Flemish, 1535–1590. Map of Jerusalem, the Holy City. Hand-colored etching, 330 x 418mm. From Georg Braun and Frans Hogenberg, *Civitates Orbis Terrarum*, Cologne, 1575. *Gift of Karl and Li Handler, Vienna. Collection, The Israel Museum, Jerusalem. Photo © Israel Museum, Jerusalem/Ilan Sztulman.*

Mizrach (East)—Ornamental plaque to be hung on an eastern wall in one's house, orienting people toward Jerusalem. Illustrated with a map of the Land of Israel and the holy cities and sites. Colored lithograph on paper, Jerusalem, 1914. *Collection of Isaac Einhorn, Tel Aviv.*

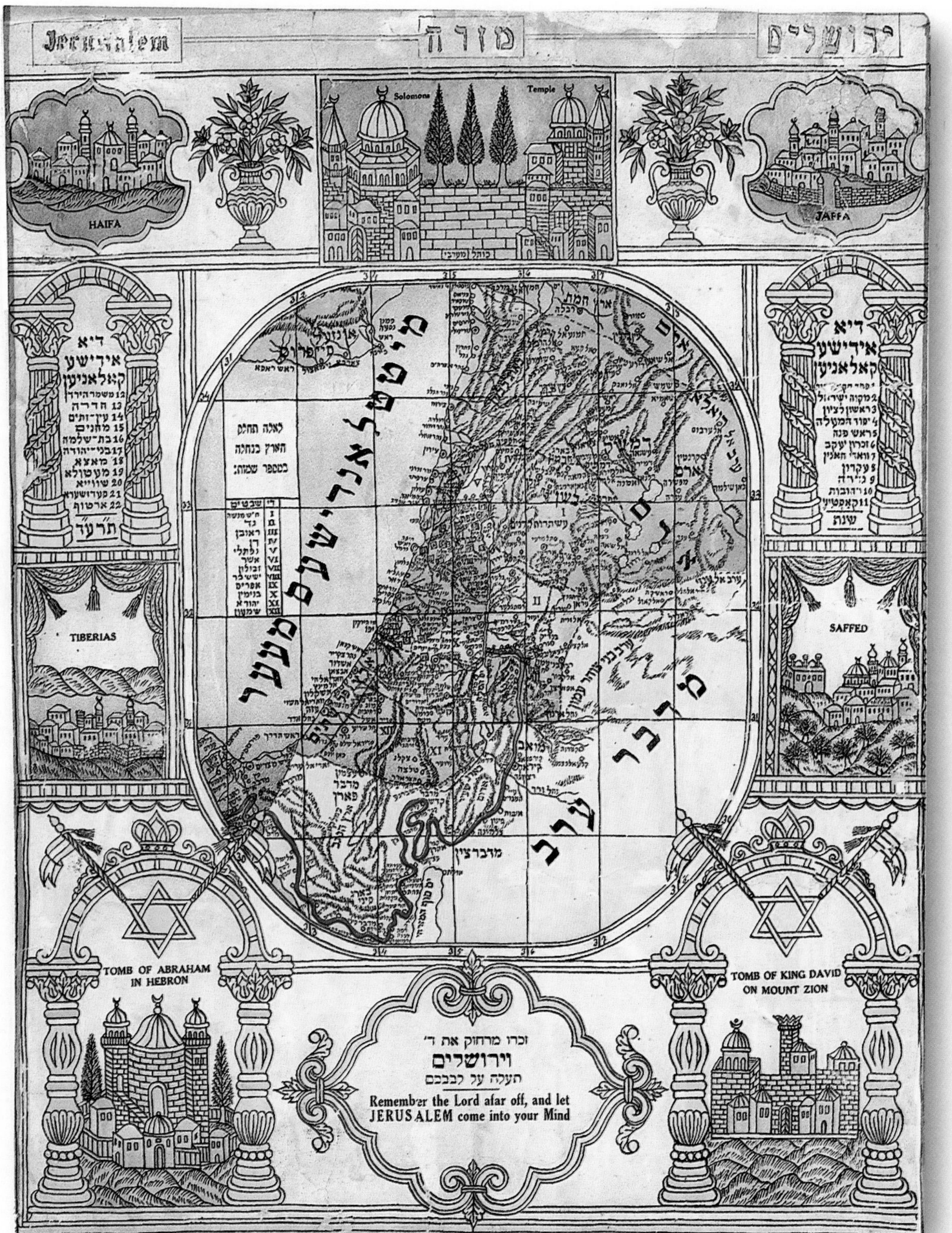

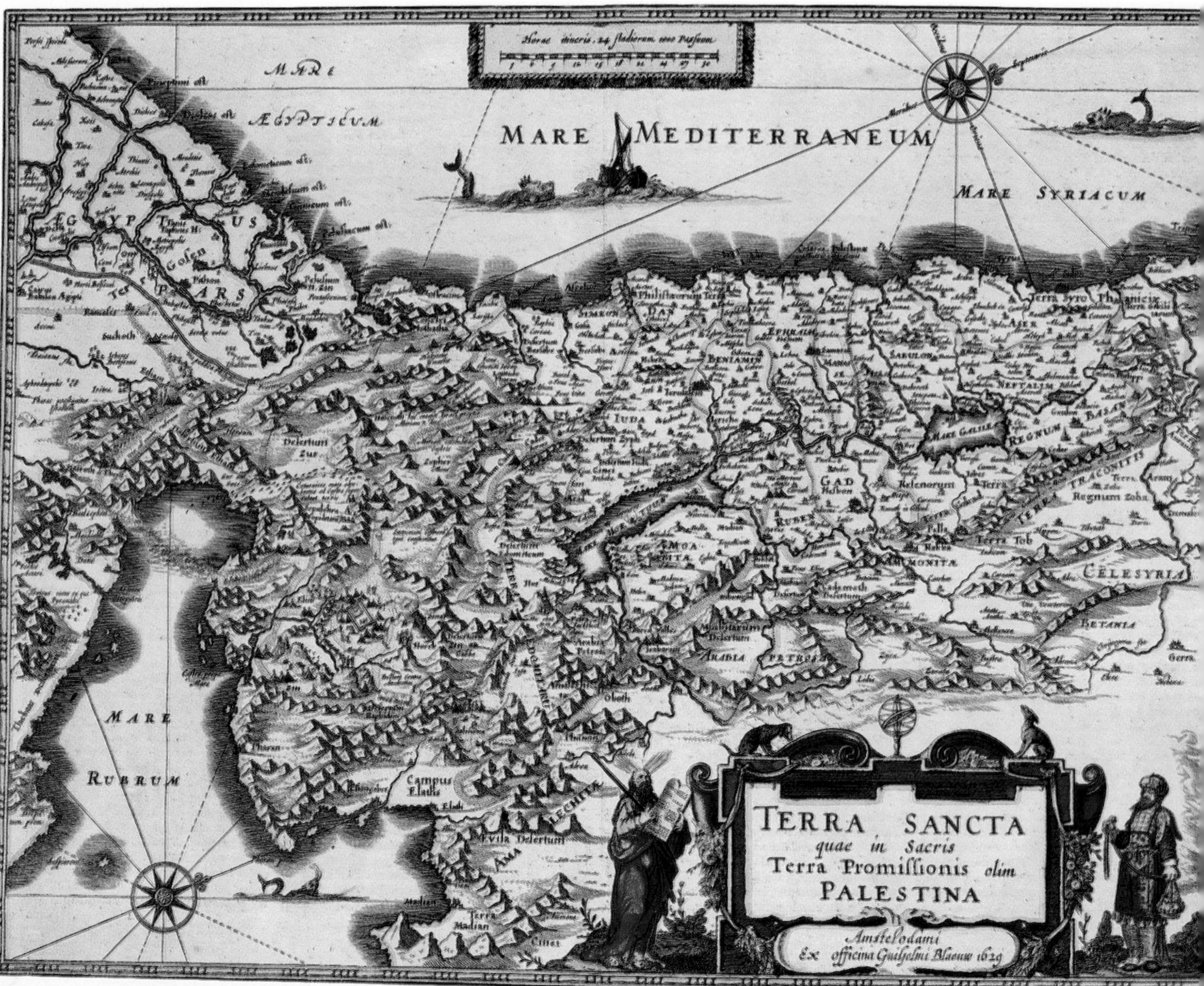

ABOVE: Willem Janszoon Blaeu, Dutch, 1571–1638. *Terra Sancta quae in Sacris Terra Promissionis olim Palestina* (The Holy Land known in the Scriptures as the Promised Land, former Palestine), after Jodocus Hondius Jr., Dutch, after Laicstain-Schrott, Hand-colored engraving, 1629, 386 x 503 mm. From *Le theatre du monde ou nouvel atlas*, 1640. *Gift of Karl and Li Handler, Vienna. Collection, The Israel Museum, Jerusalem. Photo © The Israel Museum, Jerusalem/Ilan Sztulman.*

(opposite page) TOP: Abraham Bar Jacob, German, 17th century. Map of the Holy Land: The route of the Exodus. Hand colored engraving by Moses Wiesel, 262 x 480mm. From *Haggadah shel Pessah* (Passover Haggadah), Amsterdam, 1695. *Gift of Dr. Silberstein, Geneva. Collection, The Israel Museum, Jerusalem. Photo © Israel Museum/Ilan Sztulman.*

(opposite page) BOTTOM: Anonymous artist. Drawing of the Madaba mosaic map, c. 1900, a mosaic depiction of the Holy Land set in the floor of a Byzantine church in the Jordanian town of Madaba. Ink, gouache, and watercolor on paper, 90 x 137.5 cm. *Gift of Prof. Harold A. Layer, San Francisco, through American Friends of the Israel Museum. Collection, The Israel Museum, Jerusalem. Photo © The Israel Museum, Jerusalem, by Avshalom Avital.*

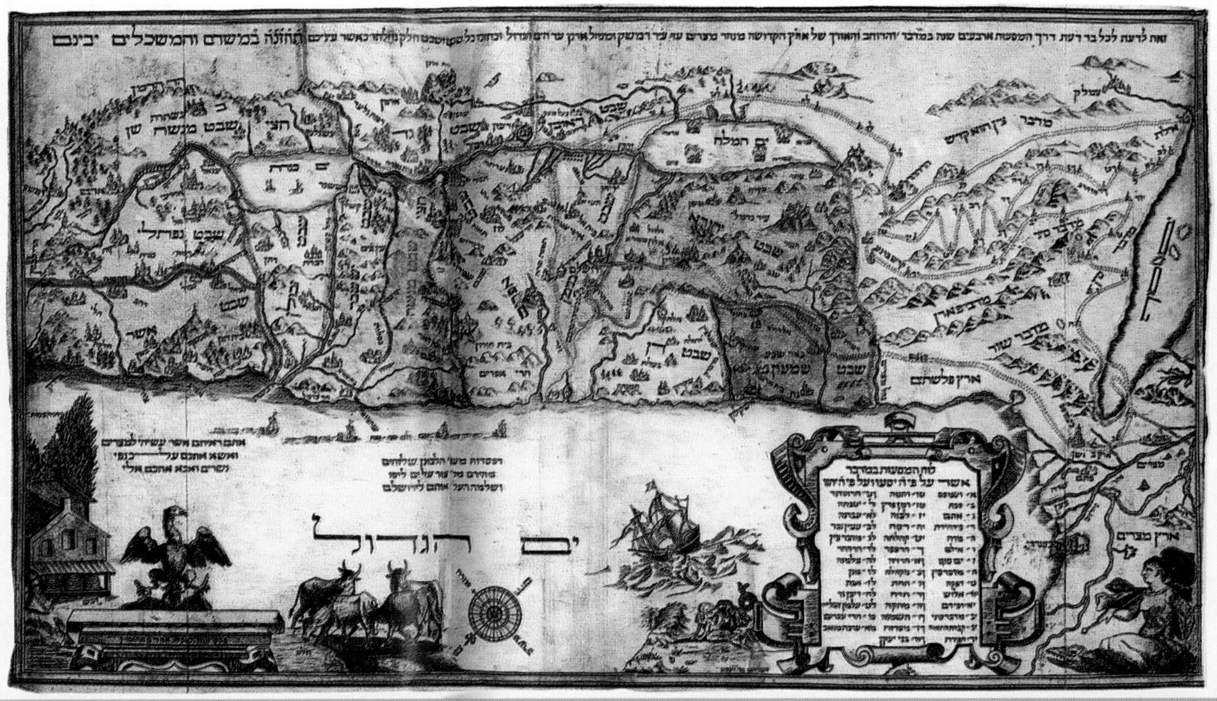
ים הגדול

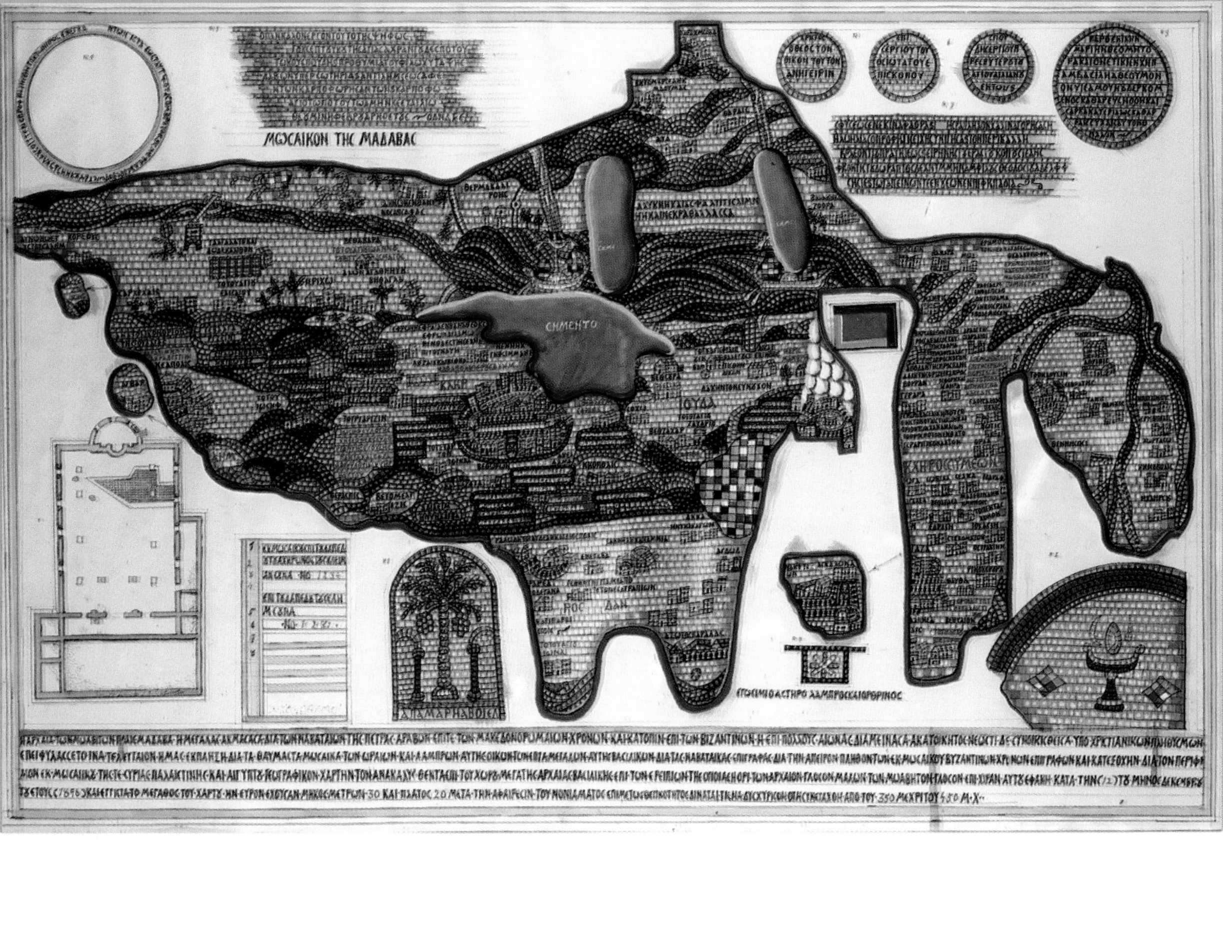
ΜΩΣΑΙΚΟΝ ΤΗΣ ΜΑΔΑΒΑΣ

Petrus Plancius, Flemish, 1552–1622. Geography of the Exodus, adaptation by D.R.M. Mathes. Hand-colored engraving, c. 1600, from a Dutch Bible. *Collection of Isaac Einhorn, Tel Aviv.*

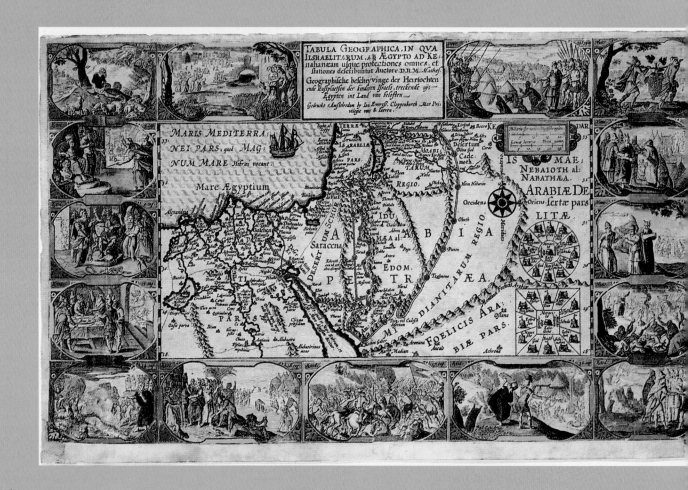

Crusader's map of Jerusalem, including the Sacred Sites and the Temple of Solomon. From Robert the Monk's *Historia Iherosolimitana* (History of the First Crusade), ca. 1099. © *Gianni Dagli Orti/Corbis.*

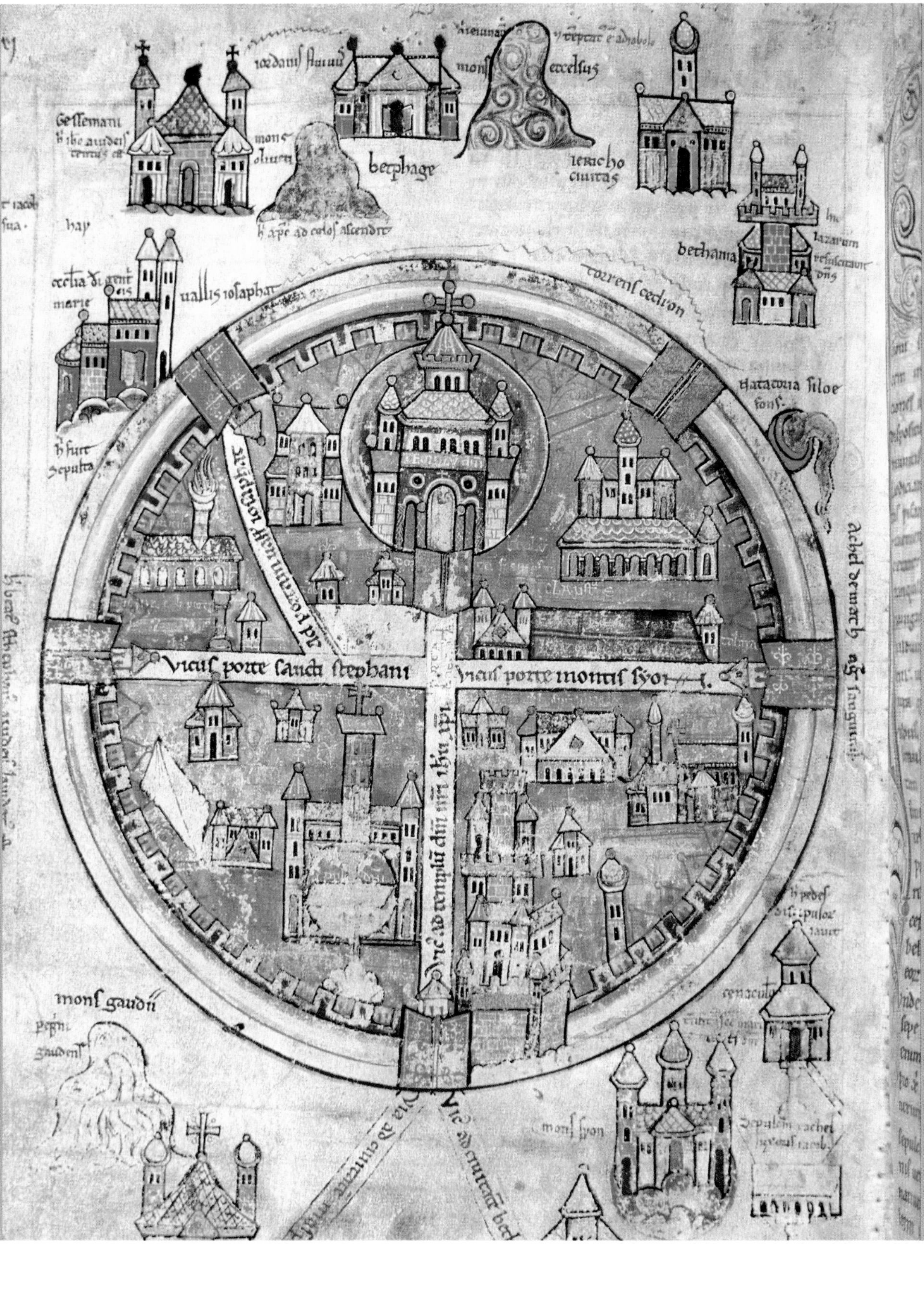

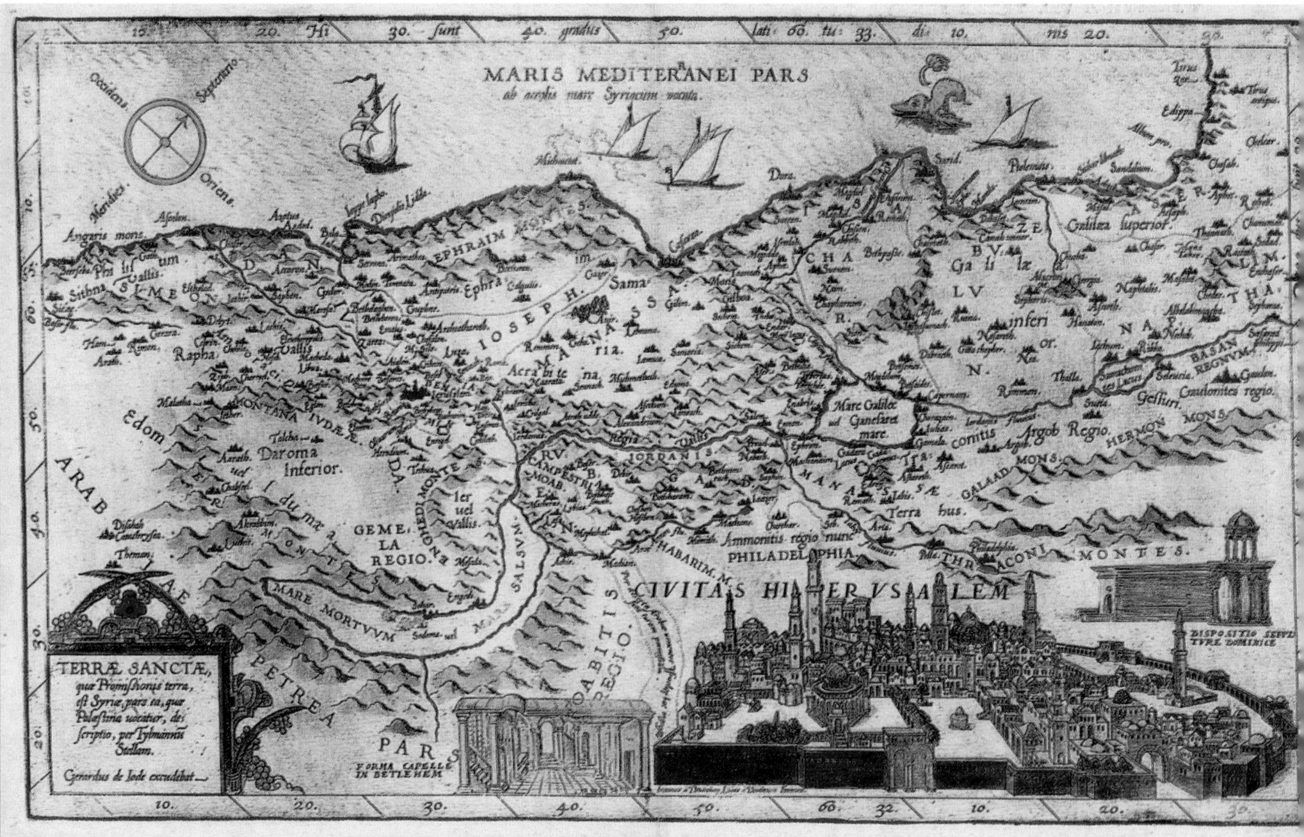

Gerard de Jode, Flemish, 1509–1591, after Tilemannus Stella, German, 1525–1589. *Terrae Sanctae, quae Promissionis terra. . .* (Description of the Holy Land, or the Promised Land. . .). Hand-colored etching by Johannes and Lucas Doetechum, 1578, 307 x 513mm. From Gerard de Jode, *Speculam orbis terrae*, edited by the author's son, Cornelis de Jode, Antwerp, 1593. *Collection, The Israel Museum, Jerusalem. Photo © Israel Museum, Jerusalem/Ilan Sztulman.*

Christian van Adrichom, Dutch, 1533–1585. *Situs Terrae Promissionis SS Bibliorum intelligentiam exacte aperiens* (The disposition of the Promised Land precisely clarifies biblical writings). Hand colored engraving, c. 1585, 354 x 1010 mm. From Christian van Adrichom, *Theatrum Terrae Sanctae et Biblicarum Historiarum*, Cologne, Officina Birkmanica, 1590. *Gift of Adam Mekler in honor of Ariel Gabriella Mekler. Collection, The Israel Museum, Jerusalem. Photo © Israel Museum, Jerusalem/Ilan Sztulman.*

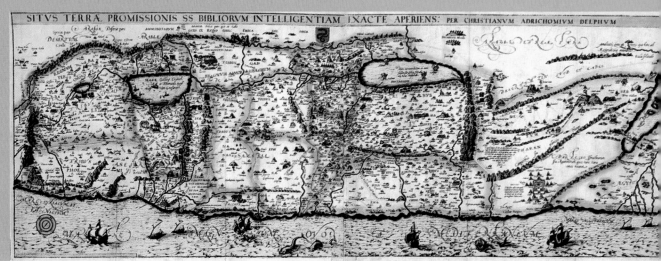

posed this opinion, holding that the law is always as decided by the majority (*Haggahot Asheri*, Av. Zar. 1:3; *Siftei Kohen*, supplementary note to YD 242), while other scholars laid down that whenever the minority opinion is qualitatively superior to the majority opinion, the position is as if opinions are divided equally and either may be followed (Ramban nov. Sanh. 23a; Ritba, RH 14b). In the Shulḥan Arukh, the most authoritative code of Jewish law, determination of the *halakhah* is generally made by application of the majority rule, the author (Joseph Caro) having adopted for himself the principle that the binding *halakhah* was to accord with the opinion held in common by any two of three great halakhists preceding him, namely Alfasi, Maimonides, and Asher b. Jehiel – or with the majority opinion selected on a different basis if a particular matter had not been dealt with by the three above-mentioned scholars. See *Codification of Law.

Decision by the Court

Within its plain meaning and read within its context, the above-mentioned scriptural passage (Ex. 23:2) has reference to a judgment of the court. The sages of the Talmud derived therefrom an additional interpretation relating to the field of criminal law – in which there is need for a specific majority, i.e., of two at least: "Thou shalt not follow after the many to do evil – I conclude that I must be with them to do well. Then why is it written [to follow] after the many to change judgment? [It means that] thy verdict of condemnation shall not be like thy verdict of acquittal, for thy verdict of acquittal is reached by the decision of a majority of one, but thy verdict of condemnation must be reached by the decision of a majority of two" (Sanh. 1:6 and cf. Mekh., Kaspa 20). Some scholars explain the need for a specific majority in matters of the criminal law on the basis that in matters of the civil law no judgment solely condemns or solely absolves, since any suit involves two litigants and what is to the one's benefit is to the other's detriment; whereas in criminal law matters the judgment is condemnatory, i.e., to the detriment of the accused (Tos. to Sanh. 3b).

A majority is only required in the event that a judicial decision has to be made in a concrete case before the court, whereas in deciding the *halakhah* in the criminal law field – outside the context of instant litigation – a simple majority of one suffices as it does in all other cases (Resp. Radbaz, *Li-Leshonot ha-Rambam*, no. 1690).

The *amoraim* question how a judgment in a civil law matter, arrived at by majority decision, should be worded. It was decided, in accordance with the opinion of R. Eleazar, that the judgment must be written in the name of the court without mention being made of the names of the judges favoring one view or the other (Sanh. 30a; Maim., Yad, Sanh. 22:8); similarly, that a judgment given by a majority decision must be signed also by the judge dissenting therefrom (TJ, Sanh. 3:10; *Avkat Rokhel*, no. 19; Mabit, vol. 2, pt. 1, resp. no. 173; ḤM 19 – *Urim*, n. 4). Hai Gaon's opinion (see above) that a preponderance of wisdom should be preferred above numerical majority, also with reference to court decisions, and even that the opinion of one individual may prevail against that of the many, remained generally unaccepted in later generations. Even those who favored wisdom above a numerical majority as the basis for deciding the *halakhah*, agreed that the majority opinion was to be preferred as the basis for a judgment by the court in the concrete matter before it (*Sefer ha-Ḥinnukh*, no. 67; Ramban nov. Sanh. 23a).

Communal Decisions and Enactments

The view that has prevailed in Jewish law is that communal resolutions and enactments are passed by a decision of the majority and bind the minority (see Elon, in bibl., 11 n. 34).

This general view was dissented from by Rabbenu Jacob *Tam, who held that only after an enactment had been passed by the whole community might the majority lay down fines for transgression thereof, and that the minority could not be compelled by the community to comply with a decision of the majority to which it had been opposed (*Mordekhai*, BK 179 and BB 480). The doctrine of *aḥarei rabbim le-hattot* has been relied upon by the scholars in support of the right to pass a communal enactment by majority decision (Rosh, resp. no. 6:5).

According to some of the scholars, the ordinances of a guild or an association – as distinguished from communal enactments – must be passed with the consent of all members in order to be binding (Ramban, nov. BB 9a; *Nimmukei Yosef*, BB 9a; *Leḥem Rav*, no. 216).

In the case of a judicial tribunal, it was laid down that a majority decision is not binding unless all the judges have participated in the proceedings and the judgment is that of the majority of the full complement (Sanh. 5:5). Some scholars deduced therefrom that also a communal enactment passed by majority decision is not binding unless the minority has participated in the proceedings (Rashba, vol. 2, resp. no. 104; Maharik, resp. no. 180; Maharit, vol. 1, resp. no. 58). Since this ruling, if followed, might enable the minority to impose its will on the majority by absenting itself from the discussions of the community, it came to be laid down in the course of time that the decision of the majority shall be binding despite the minority's nonparticipation in the discussions leading thereto. The scholars supported the conclusion either on the basis of a presumption that the absentee minority impliedly agrees to accept the decision of the majority which exerts itself to participate (*Mishpat Shalom*, no. 231; *ibid.*, *Kunteres Tikkun Olam*, "vav"), or on the basis that the minority impliedly delegates authority to the majority (*Ḥatam Sofer*, ḤM, resp. no. 116); custom too is relied upon by some scholars in support of the majority rule of those participating in the proceedings in communal legislation (Mabit, vol. 1, resp. no. 264). If the community has delegated authority to its representatives, the latter decide by majority decision, but only if the minority too is present (*Penei Moshe*, vol. 2, resp. no. 110; *Birkei Yosef*, ḤM 13:7).

[Shmuel Shilo]

Halakhic Decision-Making and the Importance of Minority Opinions

The determination of practical *halakhah* by the majority does not contradict the concept of freedom of expression nor detract from the importance of any view, even if that view is a lone view.

Early Jewish law, as reflected in the sources, is characterized by its anonymity and its uniformity. Prior to the era of *Hillel and *Shammai, halakhic disputes were rare, since any problem which arose was resolved by the Sanhedrin, which enjoyed complete judicial authority (Sanh. 88b; Tosefta, Sanh. 7:1). From the generation after Hillel and Shammai – i.e., the beginning of the first century – and until the end of that century, following the destruction of the Second Temple and a concomitant decline in the status of the Sanhedrin, the halakhic world split into two schools of thought – the School of Hillel and the School of Shammai (see *Bet Hillel and Bet Shammai). Each school practiced the law in accordance with its own beliefs, while differences even extended to legal questions with fundamental and basic ramifications:

> When the disciples of Shammai and Hillel, who had insufficiently studied, increased in number, disputes multiplied in Israel and the Torah became as two Torot (*ibid.*).

Practically speaking, this period of pluralistic halakhic rulings could not continue for long, as it led to the possibility that families belonging to one school of thought could not marry into the other, thereby dividing the nation into two separate endogamous groups. At the beginning of the second century, when the center of Jewish law moved from Jerusalem to Yavneh, with Rabban Simeon ben Gamaliel II as its head, the original uniformity in practical application that had previously existed in the *halakhah* was restored.

In deciding between the opinions of the School of Hillel and the School of Shammai, the Sages ruled that "both are the words of the living God, but the law is in accordance with the School of Hillel" (TJ, Ber. 1d).

It was this trend toward deciding between opposing views that led to the early stages in the process of redaction of various legal collections which later constituted the basis for the redaction of the Mishnah. Nevertheless, during the process of redaction of the Mishnah, the divergent views and disputes among the various *tannaim* were preserved and recorded. One reason for this is stated explicitly in the Mishnah itself (Eduyyot 1:5), namely: that should a later court of law see fit to rule in accordance with the individual opinion, it would be at liberty to do so. In the words of the Tosefta: "Rabbi Judah says: Why is the minority view recorded [in the Mishnah] alongside the majority view.... So that a [later] court that agrees with the minority view can rely on" (Tosefta, Eduyyot 1:4).

Rabbi *Samson of Sens (France, Palestine; 12th and 13th centuries) interprets the aforementioned sources as follows:

> Even though the individual opinion was not accepted in the first instance, and the majority disagreed with the individual, a later generation may arise, the majority of whom might agree to the opinion of the individual, and then the matter will be decided in accordance with their opinion. All of the Torah was transmitted to Moses in this fashion: there are considerations to purify and considerations to render impure. (Moses) was told: How long will we have to clarify every situation? He said to them: "The rule is according to the majority; however, both opinions are the words of the living God."

According to this interpretation, there is no such thing as an absolute and unequivocal ruling. In every case there are multiple considerations. While the final ruling in halakhic decision-making is indeed determined by the majority, a different majority at another period in time might arrive at a different conclusion. In the Supreme Court of the State of Israel, this justification for citing minority opinions has been presented – on the basis of the sources cited above – as an explanation for the crucial need to present minority opinions in fundamental court rulings (FH 13/80 *Hendeles v. Bank Kuppat Ha'am* 35 (2) PD 785, p. 796; HC 669/85 *Kahane v. Knesset Speaker*, 40 (4) PD 393, 404–420 per Justice Menachem Elon).

An additional explanation, that is both connected to and founded on the previous one, is the pluralistic nature of the *halakhah* – not in terms of practical actions, but in terms of opinions. The *halakhah* accepts uniformity in halakhic decision-making as an operative necessity. On the theoretical plane, however, it considers each and every opinion as important, and it sees the importance of presenting the full spectrum of halakhic views. A sage who disputes the opinion of his fellows – even after the Sanhedrin has ruled against his opinion – may continue to adhere to his opinion, so long as he does not rule accordingly for others. Such a sage will not be considered to be a "rebellious elder" (Mishnah, Sanhedrin 11:2).

This position, which sees the multiplicity of opinions and the importance of transmitting all of those opinions to the learning community as a value, may be found in the words of halakhic authorities of later eras.

Rabbi Ḥayyim ben Bezalel Ashkenazi states that, if a halakhic authority were to rule in accordance with a particular opinion on one day, and in accordance with a different opinion on the next day – "this would not be evidence of any change or deficiency which would cause us to say that the Torah has become, God forbid, as two Torahs; on the contrary – such is the way of the Torah, and both are the words of the living God" (*Vikku'aḥ Mayim Ḥayyim* (Introduction), par. 7; Poland, 16th century).

Rabbi Solomon Ephraim of Lonshitz (*Keli Yakar*, on Deut. 17:2) applies the same statement to the legal decision of a judge in a case adjudicated before him. In his opinion, in every case there are considerations in either direction, and there is no absolute ruling of pure or impure, permitted or prohibited. That is why, when a court of law rules, we must always rely on its rulings; the court has ruled in accordance with the intellectual discretion of the majority of its members, a fact that endows their opinion with obligatory validity. This, however, does not detract from the essential truth of the opposing opinion, in and of itself. Rabbi Jehiel Michal Epstein (*Arukh ha-Shulḥan*, ḤM, Introduction; beginning of 20th century) sees the diversity of opinions as the glory of the Torah. He compares it to a choir made up of many voices:

> For those who truly understand, all of the disputes of the *tannaim* and *amoraim*, the *geonim* and the *posekim* are truly the words of living God, and each of them have validity in the *halakhah*. In truth, that is the glory of our holy and pure Torah. All of the Torah is called "song," and the glory of a song is when the voices are different from each other. That is the essence of its beauty.

These words regarding the phenomenon of multiple opinions as an integral part of the world of the *halakhah*, have been cited and discussed at length in the rulings of the Supreme Court of the State of Israel by Justice Menachem Elon, in the Neiman case, in the Shakdiel case, and in the Kestenbaum case. In all of these cases he relied on those sources in order to establish the legitimacy of different and divergent opinions in the realm of *halakhah*, in the spectrum of political opinions in the State of Israel, and in the field of public administration in the State of Israel (EA 2/84 *Neiman v. Chairman, Central Elections Committee*, 39 (2) PD 225, 292–296; HC 153/87 *Shakdiel v. Minister of Religious Affairs*, 42 (2) PD 221, 263–264; CA 294/91; CA 294/91 *Burial Society v. Kestenbaum*, 46 (2) PD 464, 505–506).

[Menachem Elon (2nd ed.)]

BIBLIOGRAPHY: A.H. Freimann, in: *Yavneh*, 2 (1947/48), 1–6; I.A. Agus, in: *Talpioth*, 5 (1950), 176–95; 6 (1953), 305–20; B. Reicher, in: *Sinai*, 33 (1953), 174–7, 244–6, 383f.; A.I. Zaslanski, *ibid.*, 36 (1954/55), 451–4; I.A. Agus, in: JQR, 45 (1954/55), 120–9; ET, 9 (1959), 241–339; B. Lipkin, in: *Ha-Torah ve-ha-Medinah*, 2 (1960), 41–54; S. Federbusch, in: *Mazkeret… T.H. Herzog* (1962), 575–81; M. Elon, in: *Meḥkarei Mishpat le-Zekher A. Rosenthal* (1964), 1–54; M.P. Golding, in: JSOS, 28 (1966), 67–78; A.J. Blau, in: *Torah she-be-al Peh*, 10 (1968), 128–34. **ADD. BIBLIOGRAPHY:** M. Elon, *Ha-Mishpat ha-Ivri* (1988), 1:227f., 320, 397, 443–44, 552, 562, 583f., 718f., 813, 820; 2:870–78, 947f., 1007, 1016, 1018, 1094f., 1212; 3:1465, 1553f.; idem, *Jewish Law* (1994), 1:256, 383; 2:485, 541f., 672, 683, 886f., 996, 1004; 3:1061–1072, 1147f., 1218, 1228, 1230, 1317, 1452; 4:1740, 1845f.; idem, *Jewish Law (Cases and Materials)* (1999), 493–522, 524–33; A. Grossman, "Majority and Minority in the Teachings of 11th-Century Ashkenazic Sages" (Heb.), in: *Proceedings of the Sixth World Congress of Jewish Studies, Section B* (1973), 135–140; J. Kaplan, "Majority and Minority in the Decisions of Medieval Jewish Communities" (Heb.), in: *Shenaton ha-Mishpat ha-Ivri* (1997), 213–280.

MAKAI (Fischer), EMIL (1870–1901), Hungarian poet and playwright. Born in Mako, Makai was the son of Rabbi Enoch Fischer. In 1884 he entered the Budapest rabbinical seminary, but during his years there he spent much of his time writing. Finally, in 1893, after much heart searching and with the encouragement of the great Jewish poet József *Kiss, he decided to give up his rabbinical studies and devote himself entirely to writing.

Makai began the first, exclusively Jewish phase of his literary career with a collection of lyric verse, *Vallásos énekek* ("Religious Hymns," 1888). This was followed by a biblical drama, *Absalon* (1891), and *Zsidó költők* ("Jewish Poets," 1892), translations from the works of leading Hebrew writers in medieval Spain. These had an epoch-making effect on Hungarian literature, and established Makai's reputation as a poet. In 1893, his paraphrase of the Song of Songs (*Énekek éneke*) was published. Unlike almost all his contemporaries, Makai was an "urban poet," a type virtually unknown in Hungarian literature.

In his second, "worldly" phase of creative writing, Makai wrote primarily about love, notably in the collection *Margit* (1895). His plays include the three-act verse comedy *Tudós professzor Hatvani* ("The Learned Professor Hatvani," 1900), depicting the life of a humorous Faustian character. From 1892 Makai translated more than 100 operettas which, by reason of his masterly metrical technique, established the style of the Hungarian operetta. They included Abraham *Golfaden's *Sulamit* and *Bar Kochba*, the former a major success on the Hungarian stage. A two-volume selection of Makai's writings was published in 1904.

BIBLIOGRAPHY: *Magyar Zsidó Lexikon* (1929), s.v.; *Magyar Irodalmi Lexikon*, 2 (1965), 178; F. Ványi (ed.), *Magyar Irodalmi Lexikon* (1926), s.v.; N. Várkonyi, *A modern magyar irodalóm 1880–1920* (1928), index; K. Sebestyén, *Makai Emil* (Hung., 1923); *Makai Emil munkái* (1904), introd. by G. Molnár; *Révai nagy lexikona*, 13 (1915), s.v.; Mezey, in: IMIT (1912), 158–69.

[Paul Blau]

MAKAROV, town in Kiev district, Ukraine. Jews were first mentioned in 1721, and in 1765, 217 Jews were counted there as paying poll tax. Jews were occupied in leasing and trade in alcoholic beverages. The Jewish community had grown to 848 in 1847. During the 1840s, R. Nahum *Twersky, the grandson of Menahem Nahum the Maggid of *Chernobyl, established his court in Makarov and the town became a center of Ḥasidism. The number of Jews had risen to 3,953 (c. 75% of the total population) in 1897. From the second half of the 19th century there existed within the town boundaries a Jewish farm colony with 32 families, but it was destroyed during the Civil War. Most of the shops were in Jewish hands. On July 6, 1919, a band of peasants invaded the town and looted it for eight days, also killing a few Jews. On August 15–18 the Matveenko band killed 20 Jews and looted and burned down 20 shops. When this was followed in September of the same year by a pogrom which claimed over 100 victims, perpetrated by the soldiers of *Denikin's army, the Jewish population left for *Kiev and other towns in the vicinity. Only 152 Jews remained in Makarov in 1923. Some returned and in 1926 there were 585 (out of a total population of 2,943). In the 1930s many left for bigger cities, and in 1939 there were 269 Jews (out of a total of 3,368). Makarov was occupied by the Germans on July 10, 1941, and after a while 100 Jews were executed. The others hid but were found and 149 Jews were taken to Kiev and murdered, probably in Babi Yar. In 1970 the Jewish population was estimated at about 150 (30 families). The synagogue was unused, having been closed down by the authorities.

[Yehuda Slutsky / Shmuel Spector (2nd ed.)]

MAKHSHIRIN (Heb. מַכְשִׁירִין), eighth tractate in the order *Tohorot*, in the Mishnah and Tosefta. The word *makhshirin*, the causative *hiphil* form of *kasher* ("to be fit"), means "those things which render fit," but it is here used in a technical sense. In accordance with Leviticus 11:34, 37–8, that food can become liable to ritual impurity only if it has been moistened by water, *makhshirin* is employed to refer to all liquids which have this quality. For the same reason, the tractate is sometimes called *Mashkim* ("Liquids"). It is laid down on the basis of verse 38 that there must be some intention or desire on the part of the owner that the food be so moistened, and the tractate deals primarily with these two points – the liquids which render food liable to ritual impurity and the intention of having the food moistened. Every possible cause of foods becoming moist is detailed – from rain, ordure, damp walls, absorption of water in the food's vicinity, dripping through a leak in the roof, bilge water, steam caused by rain dripping on hot iron, the juice of grapes, etc. The tractate concludes (6:4–8) with a discussion of liquids other than water which render produce susceptible to impurity. Epstein has pointed to various layers which can be detected in *Makhshirin*. According to him 1:3 belongs to the Mishnah of R. Joshua; 1:4 to that of Akiva; 5:2 and 6:2 to Meir; and 6:3 to Judah b. Ilai, Akiva's disciple. He maintains that Joshua's ascription of Mishnah 6:4 (Ter. 11:2) to "the sages" is evidence that it is an early one. Mishnah 6:8 is interesting in that, although *mishnayot* and *beraitot* usually contain only the discussions of colleagues, this Mishnah also gives disciples' questions and Akiva's reply (cf. Epstein, Tanna'im, 88). The standard text of *mishnah* 5:1 deals with a drunken man who pushes someone into the water. S. Lieberman has shown that the text is corrupt. The correct reading should be "if he pushed him in order to injure him" (*leshovero*, לשוברו not *leshokhero*, לשכרו), and is one of several mishnaic references to the prevalent custom of dangerous water sports, of which the rabbis strongly disapproved. In the Tosefta there are some passages of historical interest. One tells of the overruling by the rabbis of Joshua b. Peraḥyah's ruling declaring all Alexandrian wheat (a major source of supply) unclean (3:4) and the alterations made by the farmers of Sepphoris in their methods of harvesting in order to remove the suspicion of defilement from their produce (3:5–6). *Genizah* fragments of the tractate have been found and their alternate readings throw light on several passages (JJLG, 18 (1927), 28ff.). Neusner (1980) devoted a study to the form-critical analysis of the Mishnah, using *Makhshirin* as his primary focus. The Mishnah of this tractate was translated into English by H. Danby (1933), while J. Neusner published a translation of both the Mishnah (1991) and the Tosefta (2002).

BIBLIOGRAPHY: S. Lieberman, in: *Sinai*, 4 (1939), 57–58; idem, *Tosefet Rishonim*, vol. 4 (1939); Epstein, Tanna'im, passim; idem, *The Gaonic Commentary on the Order Toharot* (Hebr.) (1982); Ḥ. Albeck, *Shishah Sidrei Mishnah*, 6 (1959), 411–3, 512–6. **ADD. BIBLIOGRAPHY:** J. Neusner, *A History of the Mishnaic Laws of Purities* (1974–77), vol. 17; idem, *Form Analysis and Exegesis: A Fresh Approach to the Interpretation of the Mishnah* (1980); idem, *From Mishnah to Scripture* (1984), 89–92; idem, *The Philosophical Mishnah*, 2 (1989), 251–56; idem, *Purity in Rabbinic Judaism* (1994), 97–102.

MAKKABIM-RE'UT (Heb. מַכַּבִּים־רֵעוּת), urban community in central Israel, midway between Tel Aviv and Jerusalem. It received municipal council status in 1990. In 2002 its population was 10,700, occupying an area of 1.4 sq. mi. (3.5 sq. km.). In 2003 its municipality was united with that of the nearby city of *Modi'in.

[Shaked Gilboa (2nd ed.)]

MAKKEDAH (Heb. מַקֵּדָה), Canaanite city in the Shephelah which marked the farthest limit of the Israelite pursuit of the five kings who united to punish Gibeon but were defeated at Aijalon (Josh. 10). The kings fled to a cave at Makkedah where they were captured and executed by hanging in the Israelite camp. The city was afterward conquered and destroyed and, accordingly, the king of Makkedah is mentioned in the list of defeated Canaanite cities (Josh. 12:16). In the topographical description of Judah, it is located, with Lachish, in the southern Shephelah (Josh. 15:41). Eusebius places the city 8 mi. (c. 13 km.) to the east of Eleutheropolis (Bet Guvrin; Onom. 126:22ff.). The identification of the ancient site is uncertain.

BIBLIOGRAPHY: Abel, Geog, 2 (1938), 378; Aharoni, in: *Atlas Yisrael* (1956), Map IX: 4c; J. Garstang, *Joshua-Judges* (1931), 394; Aharoni, Land, index.

[Michael Avi-Yonah]

MAKKOT (Heb. מַכּוֹת; "Flagellation"), fifth tractate in the order *Nezikin*, in the Mishnah, Tosefta, and Babylonian and Jerusalem Talmuds. The tractate deals with three separate topics and is a continuation of the preceding tractate *Sanhedrin*, as it also deals with judicial punishments administered by the courts. The first chapter discusses the laws of plotting witnesses ("*zomemim*"; Deut. 19:16–20), the kind of testimony that constitutes such plotting, when such witnesses are punishable by the sentence they intended the court to impose upon the accused, and when their punishment is merely flogging. Chapter 2 contains an exhaustive treatment of circumstances under which the inadvertent murderer is banished to a city of refuge (Num. 35:6f.; Deut. 19:2f.), those liable and those exempt from banishment, the character of the cities of refuge and the protection they afford, and the connection between the death of the high priest and the return of the manslayer to his hometown (Num. 35:25). Chapter 3 gives a list of offenses for which the penalty is flogging; discusses whether flogging is incidental to offenses punishable by death, and describes in detail the imposition of the penalty. The tractate ends with an aggadic passage on the value to Israel of the commandments and a summation of the principles which inspire them. An interesting *mishnah* (1:10) deals with capital punishment: "R. Eliezer b. Azariah says: A Sanhedrin that effects a capital punishment once in 70 years is branded a destructive tribunal. R. Tarfon and R. Akiva say: Were we members of the Sanhedrin, no person would ever be put to death. [Thereupon] Rabban

Simeon b. Gamaliel remarked: If so, they [these rabbis] would multiply shedders of blood in Israel."

The Tosefta consists of five chapters (ch. 2 is found only in the Erfurt manuscript published by Zuckermandel). Chapter 1 of the Tosefta parallels chapter 1 of the Mishnah; chapter 2, Mishnah 2:1–4; chapter 3, the remainder of chapter 2; while chapters 4 and 5 correspond to chapter 3. De Vries maintains that the Mishnah and Tosefta in this case both derive from an earlier compilation which the Tosefta follows closely, but from which the Mishnah deviated considerably. In his opinion the Mishnah was originally divided into five chapters – as is the Tosefta – and that it was later abridged into three chapters. The Babylonian Talmud has *Gemara* on all three chapters, but the Jerusalem Talmud only on the first two. In addition, the Babylonian Talmud on *Makkot* is much richer in aggadic material. It concludes with the moving story of a group of rabbis who were shocked to see a jackal emerging from the recess of the Holy of Holies. All with the exception of Akiva, burst into tears, while he laughed. He explained his joy with the observation that with this calamity the worst prophecy about the Jews had been fulfilled, and one could now anticipate that the comforting prophecy of Zechariah, "There shall yet old men and old women sit in the broad places of Jerusalem" (Zech. 8:4), would likewise be fulfilled.

Although the printed editions of the Jerusalem Talmud have no *Gemara* to the third chapter, Lieberman has shown that such a *Gemara* existed, but since the topics with which it dealt were discussed in the *Gemara* to Mishnayot in other places, the copyists omitted these duplicated discussions from the third chapter of the tractate. In fact, the early authorities quote references from the Jerusalem Talmud to *Makkot* which do not occur elsewhere in the existing text. A fragment from the Jerusalem Talmud belonging to chapter 2 of *Makkot* and found in the Cairo *Genizah* has been published by S. Wieder. Published translations of the Mishnah include one in Latin, with extracts from the *Gemara*, by J. Coccejus (Amsterdam, 1629), one in German by H.L. Strack (1910), and one in English by Danby (1933). The Babylonian Talmud was also translated into English by H.M. Lazarus in the Soncino edition (1935). Although the imposition of the penalties discussed in *Makkot* was not practiced directly in the Diaspora, yet because of its importance for the theoretical discussion of criminal law it is much discussed and frequently referred to in rabbinic literature.

BIBLIOGRAPHY: Ḥ. Albeck, *Shishah Sidrei Mishnah, Seder Nezikin* (1959), 211–8, 461–7; Epstein, Tanna'im, 417; B. De Vries, in: *Tarbiz*, 26 (1956/57), 255–61 (= *Meḥkarim be-Sifrut ha-Talmud* (1968), 102ff.); S. Klein, in: *Kovez ha-Ḥevrah ha-Ivrit la-Ḥakirat Erez Yisrael ve-Attikoteha*, 3 (1935), 81–107; S. Lieberman, *Hilkhot ha-Yerushalmi le-Rabbenu Moshe b. Maimon* (1947), 67f.; S. Wieder, in: *Tarbiz*, 17 (1947), 129–37.

[David Joseph Bornstein]

MAKLEFF, family of Ereẓ Israel pioneers.

ARYEH LEIB MAKLEFF (1876–1929) was born in the Grodno district of Russian Poland and settled in Ereẓ Israel in 1891. At the age of 18 he moved from Jerusalem to Petaḥ Tikvah and worked on his brother's land. Eventually he settled in Moẓa and put many years of labor into the vineyard planted by his father-in-law Yehiel Chemerinski, one of the founders of the Maḥaneh Yehudah quarter in Jerusalem. As an agricultural expert he was instrumental in choosing the land for Ḥuldah before the Jewish National Fund purchased it. For 25 years his home was the center of the settlement of Moẓa. During the riots of 1929, the sheikh of the nearby Arab village, Qālūnya, promised him that Moẓa would not be attacked. Nonetheless, the settlement was stormed by its Arab neighbors, and Makleff was killed along with his wife, BATYAH ḤAYYAH (b. in Jerusalem, 1877); his son, AVRAHAM (b. 1907); and his daughters MINNAH (b. 1905) and RIVKAH (b. 1910).

MORDECHAI MAKLEFF (1920–1978), Aryeh Leib's youngest son, survived the slaughter of his family by taking shelter in a neighbor's home and grew up to become chief of staff of the Israel Defense Forces. Born in Jerusalem, he received a religious education and graduated from the Reali school in Haifa in 1938. He joined the Special Night Squads led by Orde Wingate against Arab terrorists. In 1940 he joined the British army and was sent to officers' school. He saw action in World War II with the *Jewish Brigade in Italy. In 1948 he was the commanding officer of the Haganah unit that captured Haifa and represented the Haganah in its negotiations with the Arabs of the city. He then took part in the battle for Mishmar ha-Yarden and the lightning operation to capture eastern Galilee. He headed the Israel delegation to the armistice talks with Lebanon and Syria. In 1949 Makleff became assistant chief of staff under Yigael *Yadin, and in 1952 he received the appointment of chief of staff, a post which he held for a period of one year. In 1958 he became managing director of the Dead Sea Works, and ten years later was appointed director of the Citrus Marketing Board of Israel.

MAKO (Hung. **Makó**), town in S. Hungary. Jews were first authorized to settle in Mako in 1740. In 1748 they founded a *ḥevra kaddisha* in the town, and the community was probably organized at that time. A Jewish school was also opened. The first synagogue was erected in 1814, and the magnificent great synagogue was built in 1914. After 1868 the community was split into two factions and in 1870 the Orthodox built a synagogue. There were 158 Jews in Mako in 1773, earning their livelihood mainly from trade, especially in onions which grew abundantly in the surroundings. There were also Jewish craftsmen. From 154 in 1824 the Jewish population increased to 1,200 by 1858. The Jews numbered 1,928 in 1918, 2,380 in 1920, and 1,125 in 1941. The first rabbi of the town was Jacob Selig (1773). Others were Solomon *Ullman (1826–1863), who maintained a yeshivah, and Enoch Fischer (1864–1896), the father of the poet Emil *Makai. The last rabbis were the historian A. *Kecskeméti (1898–1944) and M. Vorhand (Orthodox). The renowned journalist and publisher Joseph *Pulitzer was born in this town. After the German invasion (March 19, 1944) a ghetto was set up for the 3,000 Jews of Mako and the surrounding area. All were transferred to Szeged at the end of June and deported to *Auschwitz, with some going to Austria; only around 600 returned to reestablish a community in 1949. The synagogue was demolished in the late 1960s. In 1970 there were 98 Jews in Mako.

BIBLIOGRAPHY: Á. Kecskeméti, *A csanádmegyei zsidók története* (1929); A. Scheiber, in: MHJ, 12 (1969), 5–18.

[Alexander Scheiber]

MAKOW MAZOWIECKI (Pol. **Maków Mazowiecki**; Rus. **Makov**), town in Warszawa province (before 1795 Mazovia province), Poland. An organized Jewish community is traceable to the second half of the 16th century. At the end of the 17th century a Jew, Nachman ben Nathan, was executed as a result of a blood libel. King Augustus III (1733–63) confirmed the rights of the Jewish community. According to the 1765 census, 1,258 poll tax payers, of whom 827 lived in neighboring villages, were under the jurisdiction of the Makow *kahal*. Of the 113 Jewish families (431 persons) living in Makow, 54 owned their houses; 21 families earned their livelihood as craftsmen (tailors, carpenters, tinsmiths). The Jewish population numbered 2,007 (72% of the total population) in 1808; 4,090 (90%) in 1827; 4,100 in 1856; and 4,400 in 1897. Of rabbis in Makow in the 18th century the following are known by name: Moses ben Gershon, Abraham Abish and David ben Zion Jehezkel (d. 1815), *dayyan* and *Maggid*, who was a central figure in the historical controversy between Ḥasidim and *Mitnaggedim*. Of the 19th century rabbis mention should be made of Arye Leib Zunz, Eliezer Hakohen Lipschutz, and Judah Leib Graubard. Nathan Chilinowicz founded a yeshivah at the end of the 19th century which existed until 1939.

Holocaust Period

At the outbreak of World War II, there were about 3,500 Jews in Makow Mazowiecki. Shortly after the German invasion of Poland, another 500 Jews settled there. At the end of 1940 several hundred young Jewish men were deported to the nearby forced-labor camp in Gasiewo. In September 1941 the ghetto was established. On Nov. 5, 1942, the Germans concentrated Jews still living in the smaller places of Makow county in the ghetto. A few days later (Nov. 14–18, 1942) the first deportation to the *Treblinka death camp took place, and over 500 Makow Jews were exterminated there. On Dec. 8–12, 1942, all the remaining Jews (over 4,000) were deported to Treblinka and exterminated there. No Jewish community was reconstituted in Makow Mazowiecki.

BIBLIOGRAPHY: R. Mahler, *Yidn in Amolikn Poyln in Likht fun Tsifern* (1958), index; B. Wasiutyński, *Ludnosć Zydowska w Polsce w wiekach XIX i XX* (1930), 18, 25, 48, 70, 75, 78, 184; A. Eisenbach et al. (eds.), *Żydzi a powstanie styczniowe, materiały i dokumenty* (1963), index; *Sefer Zikkaron li-Kehillat Makov Mazovyetsk* (Yid. and Heb., 1969).

[Stefan Krakowski]

MAKUYA. The word "Makuya" is the Japanese translation of the Hebrew phrase Ohel Moed אהל מועד, the meeting place between God and man, the dwelling place of God's Shekhinah (Ex. 29:42–43), and has been adopted by an indigenous Japanese group of Bible believers, strongly identified with the cause of Israel and believing that the Japanese people have historical connections with ancient Israel through the dispersion of the Lost Tribes. Makuya was founded in May 1948 by a charismatic leader, Abraham Ikuro Teshima (1910–73), who was then a successful businessman and ardent Christian believer. He emphasized the importance of the personal encounter with the Spirit of God and the return to the dynamic faith of the original Gospel of early Hebraic Christianity, as opposed to the dogmatic, institutionalized, European-dominated churches. He tried to revive the devastated spiritual condition of postwar Japan by proclaiming the words of the living God (Amos 8:11). He said, "The Bible is the light to all peoples and the biblical faith perfects all religions. Even today the God of Israel is living and vividly intervenes in the human society with his abundant goodness and mercy." His followers believed that he was divinely endowed with spiritual power and prophetic vision, and attributed to him many miraculous deeds by his prayers. A commentator on the Bible and prolific writer, Teshima maintained that deeper understanding of the Jewish faith, its people and history, is essential to the full comprehension of the Bible. Makuya now counts some 50,000, mainly in Japan but also in the United States, Brazil, Mexico, Greece, Israel, and other Asian countries. Their religious life is somewhat akin to the early ḥasidic movement with characteristics of *hitlahavut* (exuberant joy) and total commitment to God. The religious thinkings of Rabbi A.I. *Kook, Martin *Buber, and Abraham *Heschel are among the cherished elements of their belief. Their fervent love of the Bible and firm attachment to Zion brings hundreds of Makuya pilgrims annually to Israel. Over 250 Makuya students have been sent to Israeli kibbutzim to work together with the people of the Bible, and to study Hebrew and the biblical background. Some of them continue their academic studies in universities. They have published their first Hebrew-Japanese dictionary. The Makuya see in the establishment of the State of Israel – founded at the same time as their movement, as they stress – and the unification of Jerusalem a fulfillment of biblical prophecies. Israel is the experimental nursery of God and Jerusalem the capital of His universal kingdom; Divine history of redemption unfolds around the city of Zion. Whenever the Makuya get together they sing secular and religious Hebrew songs, many of them the songs of modern Israel. They adopt Hebrew names, observe the Sabbath, and keep a form of *kashrut*. They light candles on Friday evening, break *ḥallah,* and read from the *siddur.* Their view of the world is informed by a profound admiration for Israel and the Jewish people. Their love for Israel often finds practical expression: a Makuya volunteer was wounded in the 1967 Six-Day War and in the wake of the Israeli victory a Makuya "pilgrimage" marched through Jerusalem carrying a banner proclaiming "Congratulations on the Greater Jerusalem." In the fall of 1973, in the aftermath of the Yom Kippur War and the Arab oil boycott, Teshima and thousands of his followers staged a massive pro-Israel demonstration in downtown

Tokyo. And in 1975, when the United Nations condemned Zionism as a form of racism and racial discrimination, they sent a petition of protest containing 37,000 signatures to the UN General Secretary. Makuya show great hospitality to visiting Israelis and Jews, and it is possible to find Makuya Hebrew speakers in most important Japanese towns. To some extent their admiration for Jews derives from the Christian part of their ideology. But, in addition, it springs from the national nature of Judaism – the idea that Judaism is the religion of the Jewish people – and from Zionism. The Makuya are intensely nationalistic and, in some ways, are looking towards the redemption of the Japanese nation which will be modeled upon the redemption of Israel.

ADD. BIBLIOGRAPHY: T. Parfitt, *The Lost Tribes of Israel: the History of a Myth* (2004); idem, *The Thirteenth Gate* (1987).

[Akira Jindo / Tudor Parfitt (2nd ed.)]

MALACH, LEIB (pseudonym of **Leib Salzman**; 1894–1936), Yiddish poet and dramatist. Born in Zwolen, Poland, he had a traditional education, lived in Warsaw in 1907–22, and worked at various trades until his literary talent was discovered by the novelist H.D. *Nomberg. From 1922 until his death in Paris, he lived in a number of countries, his longest stay being in Argentina. He began his literary career with songs and ballads, later turning to prose and drama. His travel sketches were widely read, and his drama *Ibergus* ("Overflow," 1926) about white slave traffic helped in the struggle against this social evil in Buenos Aires. His novel *Don Domingo's Kraytsveg* ("Don Domingo's Crusade," 1930) is an epic of adventurous and idealistic Jewish life in Latin America.

BIBLIOGRAPHY: Rejzen, Leksikon, 2 (1927), 431–4; LNYL, 6 (1965), 4–8; M. Ravitch, *Mayn Leksikon* (1945), 135–7; *L. Malach Bukh* (1949); *Bleter tsum Ondenk fun L. Malach* (1936), incl. bibl. **ADD. BIBLIOGRAPHY:** G.G. Branover (ed.), *Rossiĭskaia evreĭskaia entsiklopediia*, 2 (1995), 232.

[Melech Ravitch]

MALACHI, BOOK OF, the last (12th) book of the section of the Bible called *Minor Prophets. In the Qumran fragment 4QXIIa, however, Malachi seems to be followed by Jonah. It contains "The pronouncement of the word of the Lord to Israel by Malachi" (Mal. 1:1). The Hebrew word (Heb. מַלְאָכִי) (*mal'akhi*) means "My messenger." According to A. von Bulmerincq, the word could be a shortened form of מַלְאָכִיָּה (*mal'akhiyyah*, "messenger of the Lord"). However, since this name is not found elsewhere in the Bible, the Septuagint, in which it appears as *mal'akho* ("by the hand of His messenger"), is probably right in not regarding it as a personal name. The Targum follows the masoretic text, but adds a note to the effect that "My messenger" is *Ezra: "by the hand of My messenger whose name is called Ezra the scribe." The same tradition is mentioned and accepted by Jerome. Had Ezra been the author of the book, however, it is unlikely that his authorship would have been thus concealed. In fact, the occurrence of the word in the title is naturally explained as derived from Malachi 3:1: "Behold, I send My messenger" (cf. Mal. 2:7). It is noteworthy that whereas the activity of Haggai and Zechariah is noted in Ezra 5:1; 6:14, no mention is made of Malachi, a further indication that the book, should be regarded as anonymous, the title having been added by the compiler who had given similar editorial titles to the anonymous oracles beginning with *Zechariah 9:1 and 12:1. The reason behind the separation of the Book of Malachi from the preceding Book of Zechariah is that the "Malachian" chapters constitute a characteristic unit, different from Deutero- and Trito-Zechariah (Zech. 9–11; 12–14). The separation also provides a twelfth prophetic book, corresponding to the traditional twelve tribes of Israel.

The contents of the Book of Malachi fall into six clearly marked sections introduced by a statement of the Lord or of the prophet, which is then challenged by the people or the priests, and defended by the Lord Himself in words of reproach and doom. The Lord's love for Israel, in contrast with His treatment of Edom, is emphasized at the outset (Mal. 1:2–5). The second speech reproaches the priests for their neglect of the sacrificial cult (1:6–2:9): their attitude should express a proper regard for the ritual of the Lord's worship, yet any offering, however imperfect, has been thought good enough for His altar. In this, as no doubt in other matters, the priests show themselves unworthy of their forefather Levi, by misleading "the many" into sin with their lax rulings. Let the priests, therefore, take warning, and return to their ancient ideals. This section seems to have been subsequently expanded by the insertion of 1:11–14. The aspect of God as their common father should inspire correct relations between Jew and Jew, and not such conduct as repudiating Jewish wives for the sake of marrying non-Jewish women (2:10–16). In its present form, this speech reproaches the Jews for contracting mixed marriages. The view of Ch.C. Torrey (JBL, 17 (1898), 1–15) and F.F. Hvidberg (*Weeping and Laughter in the Old Testament* (1962)) that a reproach for the adoration of foreign gods is actually meant has little to commend it. A problem, however, arises from the secondary character of 2:11b–13a, or 11–12. Several modern scholars have challenged the genuineness of this passage for literary reasons and consider it a later addition. Without these verses, 2:10–16 contains no reference to mixed marriages, but rather attacks the abuse of divorce by Jews, exhorting them to remain loyal to the wives of their youth (cf. Prov. 5:15–20). If the sacredness and religious value of marriage are implied, the reproach indicates that men were divorcing wives casually and callously. It is also possible to read the section as an attack on divorcing Jewish women for the purpose of marrying gentile women, who are described as (2:11) "daughter of a foreign god" (see below). Such a union is opposed by "the One" (2:15) who desires "divine seed" (Hebrew *zera elohim*), elsewhere called "holy seed," (Hebrew *zera kodesh*; Ezra 9:2), i.e., children who are not products of sexual intermingling with gentiles. The connection between loyalty to a Jewish wife and to God was facilitated by the characterization of marriage as *berit*, "covenant," a notion first attested in Ezekiel 16:8.

The prevalence of wrongdoing had provoked skepticism about divine justice. The fourth section asserts against these doubts that the Lord is the God of judgment and will restore the rights of the people; His messenger is already at hand to purge indifferentism from worship and immorality from conduct (Mal. 2:17–3:5). A. von Bulmerincq's assumption that Ezra is the "messenger" of 3:1 is unlikely, because the conception here is rather that of a heavenly being. According to the next section, the people's neglect in paying tithes and other sacred dues has been punished with drought, locusts, and failure of crops; however, the punctilious payment of the withheld tithes will be rewarded with abundance (3:6–12). This fifth section thus enforces the duty of giving tithes. The last section promises the despondent pious Jews vindication for themselves and punishment for the ungodly ones on the Day of Judgment (3:13–21). Religion may seem useless, warns the author, but the Lord remembers His own, and will soon distinguish them openly from the irreligious. The book closes with an appeal to observe the Law that the Lord gave to Moses at Horeb, and with the announcement that the prophet Elijah will come before the threatened judgment (3:22–24). The appeal to the "Law of Moses" is part of the redactional process of Scripture in which Torah is declared superior to the Prophets and Hagiographa. Thus, Joshua 1, which opens the Prophets, emphasizes the book of Torah. Malachi, which ends the Prophets, closes with Torah, and Psalm 1, which opens the Hagiographa opens with Torah. These concluding words are likewise an addition, namely a later interpretation of 3:1, saying that the anonymous "messenger" is Elijah. Nonetheless, the addition shares with the body of the book its deuteronomic orientation: the book evidently regards the entire tribe of Levi as priestly, the closing appeal names Horeb instead of Sinai as the mount of revelation. These facts favor an early rather than a late post-Exilic date. Other features bear this out.

Like Haggai and Zechariah 1–8, the Book of Malachi is an expression of the changed outlook of prophecy in post-Exilic times. The topics noted above clearly relate the book to the post-Exilic period, when the Temple had been rebuilt (1:10; 3:1, 10), the province of Judea was ruled by a representative of the Persian government (1:8), and there had been time enough for the loss of earlier religious enthusiasm. The three main abuses attacked in the text are the degeneracy of the priesthood (1:6–2:9), intermarriage with foreign women (2:11), and the people's remissness in the payment of tithes (3:8). These abuses, especially the second and the third, are mentioned prominently in the Book of *Ezra and Nehemiah, and are those which both reformers strenuously set themselves to correct (Ezra 9:2; 10:3, 16–44; Neh. 10:31, 33–40; 13:10–14, 23–29). The independent character of Malachi's attack against divorcing Jewish wives in order to marry foreign women (Mal. 2:10–16) suggests a date of composition prior to that of the work of Ezra (Ezra 9:2; 10:3, 16–44). This earlier date is made still more likely if the reproach against mixed marriages in Malachi 2:11b is a later insertion, one which precisely reflects the preoccupations of the time of Ezra and Nehemiah. The time of Ezra's activity, unfortunately, is uncertain. Following A. van Hoonacker and S. Mowinckel, above all, many scholars have assumed that Ezra was not active under Artaxerxes I (in 458 B.C.E.), but under Artaxerxes II (in 398 B.C.E.; cf. Ezra 7:8). The problems of mixed marriages and unpaid tithes, however, existed also in the time of Nehemiah (Neh. 10:31, 33–40; 13:10–14, 23–29), i.e., between 445 and about 424, the year Artaxerxes I died (cf. Neh. 2:1; 13:6). The insertion of Malachi 2:11b–13a may thus date from that period, and it may reasonably be inferred, therefore, that the original Book of Malachi dates prior to the age of Nehemiah and Ezra. In fact, most modern scholars agree that the prophet prepares the way for the work of those reformers.

There is no evidence of sufficient strength to substantiate a later date. The assumptions of H. Winckler (*Altorientalische Forschungen*, 2 (1898), 531ff.) and O. Holtzmann (ARW, 29 (1931), 1–21), who date the book to the first half of the second century B.C.E., are highly speculative and, at the present state of knowledge, inadmissible. The opinion of A. von Bulmerincq, who identifies the "messenger" of Malachi 3:1 as Ezra, becomes still more doubtful if Nehemiah is considered to have preceded Ezra. The period of Nehemiah's absence at the Persian court in approximately 430 B.C.E. (Neh. 13:6) has been proposed as the time of composition by S.R. Driver (*An Introduction to the Literature of the Old Testament* (1897^6), 357) and A. Gelin (*Introduction à la Bible*, 1 (1957), 572), but an earlier date is the most likely. One of the chief duties of the priest was still the proclamation of the Oral Law (Mal. 2:6–9), and not as yet the solemn reading of the Written Law, as in Nehemiah 8–10. In fact, the prophet seems to be influenced by earlier deuteronomistic theories concerning the priests; at the same time, it is doubtful whether he knew the Priestly Code regulations on tithes found in Numbers 18:20–32, where the tithe is designated in its entirety for the maintenance of the levites (whereas, according to deuteronomic legislation (Deut. 14:22–29; 26:12–15), the levites only took part of the tithe). It appears that the Priestly Code, in its present form, is not presupposed by the Book of Malachi.

An earlier date for the composition of Malachi is also suggested by the allusion to the destruction of Edom in Malachi 1:3–4. The Arab invasion of this Transjordanian kingdom cannot be dated with precision, but Edom was apparently entirely taken over by Arab tribes toward the end of the sixth century B.C.E. Since the remaining Edomites still expected a restoration of their ruined country (1:4), approximately 500 B.C.E. is a more probable date for the composition of the Book of Malachi than the first half of the fifth century. A.C. Welch even thought that the book dated from the age of the prophet Haggai (520 B.C.E.). The bad harvests and locust plagues alluded to in 3:11 would then reflect the same situation as in Haggai 1:6, 9–11; 2:16–17. However, the existence of the Temple as implied by Malachi indicates a somewhat later date. All things considered, it may reasonably be assumed that the book dates from approximately 500 B.C.E.

The work reflects the various currents of thought and modes of life in the Jerusalem of about 500 B.C.E., affording an interesting and valuable glimpse of the post-Exilic community in the period between the age of Haggai and Zechariah on the one hand, and the time of Nehemiah and Ezra on the other. The situation in Judea was one of depression and discontent. The expectations which earlier prophets had aroused had not been fulfilled. The return from Babylon had brought with it none of the ideal glories promised by Deutero-Isaiah. The completion of the Second Temple (515 B.C.E.) had been followed by disillusionment over the anticipated prosperity announced by Haggai in 520 B.C.E., by consequent indifference to worship, skepticism as to divine justice, and moral laxity. In view of these conditions, the message of Malachi is to reassert the true relation of the people to their God, and to recall the nation to religious and moral earnestness, especially in regard to questions of ritual and marriage. Yet the author is no formalist. Ritual observances are of value in his eyes only as expressions of spiritual service; for example, he supposes that God does not accept offerings presented by disloyal husbands (2:13b–14). Moral and social offenses are fiercely condemned by the prophet (3:5), and from the concept of the brotherhood of all Jews under one Father (2:10), he deduces the duties which they have toward each other, and the wrongfulness of the selfish practice of divorce prevalent in his day (2:14–16).

The Book of Malachi is a significant landmark in the religious history of Israel. Despite its emphasis on the observance of ritual, it shows genuine prophetic spirit. Its denunciation of those who divorced their Jewish wives to marry "the daughter of a strange god" reflects the prophetic ideal of a permanent covenant between God and His people, which had been represented as a marital relation since the days of *Hosea. The denunciation also involves a protest against the influences of foreign marriages, the prohibition of which was to be made effective, at least in Yehud, by the reforms of Nehemiah and Ezra. The influence of the closing words of the book (3:22–24) on later messianic expectation is apparent in the Jewish post-biblical literature (Ecclus. 48:10; Suk. 52b; Mid. Ps. to 42:1; Targ., Lam. 4:22; Targ. Yer., Deut. 30:4) and in the New Testament (Matt. 17:3, 4, 10–13; 27:47, 49; Mark 9:4–5, 11–13; 15:35–36; Luke 9:30, 33; John 1:21, 25). In the New Testament the end of Malachi serves as a proof text to identify John the Baptist with Elijah.

[Edward Lipinski / S. David Sperling (2nd ed.)]

In the Aggadah

The author of Malachi was considered the last of the prophets, along with Haggai and Zechariah. Upon their death, the spirit of prophecy departed from Israel (Yoma 9b). Malachi was identified with Ezra by R. Joshua b. Korḥa and with Mordecai by R. Naḥman. The sages, however, declared that Malachi was his proper name (Meg. 15a). Targum Jonathan to the words "by Malachi" (1:1) added the gloss "who is known by the name of Ezra the scribe." R. Joshua validated this viewpoint by explaining the references in Malachi to the "daughter of a strange god" (2:11) as identical with the "foreign women" described by Ezra (10:2; Meg. 15a). Malachi was a member of the Great Synagogue, and traditions were later reported in his name (cf. RH 19b).

BIBLIOGRAPHY: W. Nowack, *Die kleinen Propheten* (1922³); S.R. Driver, *The Minor Prophets: Nahum, Habakkuk, Zephaniah, Haggai, Zechariah, Malachi* (1906); G.L. Robinson, *The Twelve Minor Prophets* (1953); A. Gelin, in: *La Sainte Bible… de l'Ecole Biblique de Jérusalem* (1960³); W.L. Sperry, in: *The Interpreter's Bible*, 6 (1956); D.R. Jones, *Haggai, Zechariah and Malachi. Introduction and Commentary* (1962); E.G. Kraeling, *Commentary on the Prophets*, 2 (1966). SPECIAL STUDIES: K. Budde, in: ZAW, 26 (1906), 1–18; O. Holtzmann, in: ARW, 29 (1931), 1–21; A.C. Welch, *Post-Exilic Judaism* (1935), 113–25; A. Pautrel, in: DBI suppl., 5 (1957), 739–46; H.J. Boecker, in: ZAW, 78 (1966), 78–80; L. Kruse-Blinkenberg, in: *Studia Theologica*, 20 (1966), 95–119; 21 (1967), 62–82; Kaufmann, Y., Toledot, 4 (1967⁵), 366–77; M. Margalit, in: Kahana (ed.), *Sefer Terei Asar* (1930), 193–212. **ADD. BIBLIOGRAPY:** R. Smith, *Micah-Malachi* (Word; 1984), 296–342; B. Jones, *Book of the Twelve* (1998); A. Hill, in: ABD, 4:478–85; idem, *Malachi* (AB; 1998), incl. bibli.; ibid, 95–129, incl. illus.; S.D. Sperling, *The Original Torah* (1998), 61–74; J. O'Brien, in: DBI, 3:110–13.

MALACHI, ELIEZER RAPHAEL (1895–1980), U.S. Hebrew scholar and bibliographer. Born in Jerusalem, Malachi emigrated to the United States at the age of 17. A conscientious and diligent scholar, he began his literary career with original and translated stories, but in early life switched to scholarship. Though he wrote prolifically, he published only two books of essays: *Massot u-Reshimot* (1937), on contemporary and past writers, and *Ẓilelei ha-Dorot* (1940), on historical occurrences.

His first publication, as a boy of 15, was an essay on Hebrew newspapers, which appeared in Luncz's *Luaḥ Ereẓ Yisrael* (1910). In 1913 he became a contributor to the newly established monthly *Hatoren*, where he exhibited his expertise as a bibliographer in his pioneering historical survey of the American Hebrew press, which he traced from its beginnings in the 1870s. Subsequently, the monthly published his bibliography of the writings of Mendele Mokher Sforim (Sholem Yankev *Abramovitsh), which remains a model to this day. His succeeding work embraced Diaspora Hebrew periodicals, the Yiddish press, Hebrew poetry in America, Hebrew literature, historical essays, and individual bibliographies of Hebrew scholars and writers. His bibliographies of scholars include A.M. Luncz, J.N. Simhoni, S.A. Horodetsky, S. Krauss, N. Slouschz, S. Dubnow, A. Elmaleh, J. Schatzky, and S. Tchernowitz, the last of which also appeared separately as *Peri Etz Ḥayyim* (1946). His bibliographies of writers include such Haskalah figures as J.L. Gordon and Mendele Mokher Seforim and such late Hebrew writers as Bialik, Tschernichowsky, Shneur, Sokolow, Peretz, H. Zeitlin and Kabak, while his bibliographies of Hebrew writers in America – containing much information in a generally neglected field – include S.B. Maximon, N. Touroff, B.N. Silkiner, Ẓ. Scharfstein, S. Halkin, M. Ribalow, and H. Bavli. The latter was reprinted separately (*Zekher le-Hillel*, 1962). Malachi also published *Iggerot David Frischmann* (1927), a book of David Frischmann's letters, and *Iggerot Soferim* (1932), miscellaneous letters of other writers, with notes and introductions. In addition, he edited a book on the State of Israel and its history, *Yisrael* (1950). In 1955, Malachi's *Treasury of Hebrew Lexicography* appeared as an appendix to the American edition of Mandelkorn's *Concordance to the Bible*, in which Malachi provided detailed descriptions of all the biblical concordances and dictionaries that had been published in Hebrew and other languages. Some of his other work includes his bibliography of "Hebrew Educational Literature in America" (1944) and "History of the Hebrew Movement in America" (1974).

Regarded by many as the greatest Hebrew bibliographer of recent times, he was, in quantity alone, the most productive Hebrew bibliographer, having written thousands of articles. Malachi wrote mainly in Hebrew, but his body of work includes much material in Yiddish as well.

After Malachi's death, his papers – containing his collection of letters and documents – were transferred to the archive of the Ben-Zvi Institute in Jerusalem.

BIBLIOGRAPHY: Shunami, Bibl, 925–6.

[Eisig Silberschlag / Ruth Beloff (2nd ed.)]

MALACHI BEN JACOB HA-KOHEN (d. 1785–1790), Italian scholar. Little is known of his life. He was the pupil of Abraham Ḥayyim Raphael Rodrigues and of the kabbalist R. Joseph *Ergas, whom he succeeded as rabbi of Leghorn after the latter's death in 1730. He arranged Ergas' work *Divrei Yosef* for publication (Leghorn, 1742). He also drew up an order of service *Shivḥei Todah* ("Praises of Thanksgiving"; Leghorn, 1744), for the 22nd day of Shevat, an annual fast day proclaimed to commemorate the rescue of the Leghorn community from the earthquake of 1742. He lived to an old age, dying in Tripoli, where he had apparently served as an emissary for Ereẓ Israel. Malachi is best known through his work *Yad Malakhi* (*ibid*., 1767), which deals with the methodology of the Talmud and the codifiers. Part 1 contains principles of the Talmud in alphabetical order; Part 2, principles of the codifiers in chronological order; and Part 3, principles of various laws in alphabetical order. His novellae and responsa are found in the works of contemporary scholars. A manuscript of his responsa, *Teshuvot Yad Malakhi*, was published by E. *Gruenhut in *Ha-Me'assef*, 5 (1900). Malachi was also a liturgical poet. He composed *Sefer Shirei Zimrah*, which includes poems and dirges, part of which was published by S. Bernstein (*Mizraḥ u-Ma'arav*, 3 (1929), 245–61). His poem written on the occasion of the inauguration of the synagogue in Leghorn in 1742 was also published in Piperno's *Kol Ugav* (Leghorn, 1846).

BIBLIOGRAPHY: Landshuth, Ammudei, 173–6; S. Bernstein, *Mi-Shirei Yisrael be-Italyah* (1939), 81–86; N. Slouschz, *Massa'i be-Ereẓ Luv* (1937), 246; J. Schirmann, *Mivḥar ha-Shirah ha-Ivrit be-Italyah* (1934), 399–400; A. Toaff and A. Lattes, *Gli Studi ebraici a Livorno* (1909), 25ff.

[Abraham David]

MÁLAGA, port in Andalusia, S. Spain. A Phoenician-Punic necropolis has been discovered there. In the Muslim period, the Jewish quarter was located in the eastern part of the city: the cemetery was on the slopes of Gibralfaro. In 863, at the time of the heresy of the bishop of Málaga, Hostegesis, he was alleged to have attached Jews from Málaga to the regional clerical councils as specialists in the principles of Christianity. Málaga served as a refuge for *Samuel ha-Nagid and other Jews who reached there in 1013 after the Berbers captured Córdoba. Solomon ibn *Gabirol was born in Málaga (c. 1021). In the mid-11th century the Jews numbered 200 out of a population of approximately 20,000.

When Málaga was captured by Ferdinand and Isabella in 1487 there were 100 Jewish families living there, and another group of 55 Jews were living in nearby Vélez-Málaga. All these were taken captive. The Jews of the kingdom had to pay 10 million maravedis for their ransom. Abraham *Seneor and Meir of Segovia traveled through Andalusia to raise the money, and Solomon *Ibn Verga was also active.

The Catholic Monarchs had already ordered in 1490 that Málaga should be settled by Christians. The Jews and Moors, excepting certain Moors named in the royal edict, were ordered to leave Málaga within 15 days. Sixty-two exiles whose names were stated left Málaga, most of them persons in poor circumstances. Judah b. Jacob *Ḥayyat in his introduction to *Ma'arekhet ha-Elohut* records how on leaving Portugal in 1493 his ship was seized by Basque pirates and brought to Málaga, where local clergy attempted to convert the captives. The community of Málaga was revived in the early 1960s by Jews from North Africa. It has a community center and is affiliated to the organization of Jewish communities in Spain.

BIBLIOGRAPHY: Baer, Spain, 2 (1966), index; Baer, Urkunden, 1 (1929), index; Ashtor, Korot, 1 (1960), 29, 63–64; idem, in: *Zion*, 28 (1963), 52–53; J. Millás Vallicrosa, in: *Sefarad*, 1 (1941), 316; A. Garcia y Bellido, *ibid*., 2 (1942), 25f., 52, 83, 90, 286f.; L. Torres Balba, in: *Al Andalus*, 19 (1954), 197; J. Wiseman, *Roman Spain* (1956), 200; Suárez Fernández, Documentos, index; M.A. Ladero Quesada, in: *Hispania*, 27 (1967), 76–83 (Sp.). **ADD. BIBLIOGRAPHY:** C. Carrete Parrondo, in: *Actas del I Congreso de Historia de Andalucía* (1978), vol. 1, *Andalucía medieval*, 321–27; Y. Kaplan, in: *Actas del I Congreso de Historia de Andalucía* (1978), vol. 2, *Andalucía moderna*, 109–16; M.F. García Casar, in: *Helmantica*, 33 (1982), 157–62; M.I. Pérez de Colosía Rodríguez, *Auto inquisitorial de 1672: el criptojudísmo en Málaga* (1984).

[Haim Beinart]

MALAKH, ḤAYYIM BEN SOLOMON (between 1650 and 1660–1716 or 1717), leader of the Shabbatean sect. Malakh was born in Kalish. Nothing is known about his early career, but he became a highly respected rabbinic scholar, kabbalist, and preacher. He was soon attracted by the Shabbatean movement and became closely associated with the Shabbatean prophet Heshel *Ẓoref in Vilna. In 1690 he went to Italy, probably on a mission on behalf of the movement, staying there several months with Abraham *Rovigo and Benjamin *Cohen, the heads of the Italian Shabbateans. They studied the writings of Isaac *Luria and *Nathan of Gaza, and Ḥayyim Malakh received their secret traditions concerning Shabbetai Ẓevi. From 1692 to 1694 he was back in Poland, active as a Shabbatean missionary among rabbinic circles. One of his students (about 1693) was the famous talmudist Mordecai Suskind Rotenburg, rabbi of Lublin. During this period he attracted the attention of R. Ẓevi *Ashkenazi, the father of Jacob *Emden, who became Malakh's bitter foe. Possibly because of a ban due to his heretical activity or possibly because of his own doubts concerning the Shabbatean theology, he went to Turkey. He stayed for two to three years with Samuel *Primo in Adrianople, becoming his fervent follower and receiving the traditions and secrets of the circle of Shabbetai Ẓevi's personal pupils. He went to Bursa (Turkey) where some outstanding Shabbateans lived, and toward the end of his stay, had a vision which caused him to return to Poland and join another Shabbatean leader, *Judah he-Ḥasid. He arrived in Zolkiew, late in 1696, and stayed for some time, finding many influential followers. From Zolkiew he sent a letter to his Italian masters informing them that he was leaving their camp since he had found the authentic spring of Shabbatean teaching in Turkey. It is quite possible that he went back to Turkey in 1697 where he seems to have met Abraham *Cardozo in Adrianople. Malakh took Primo's side in the discussions with Cardozo whose speculative dissertations he refused to read. It is not clear whether at this time or later he came into contact with the young leader of the most radical wing of the *Doenmeh sect in Salonika, Baruchiah Russo (Osman Baba), several of whose sayings were quoted by Malakh to one of his pupils (in a Shabbatean notebook, probably written in Damascus, now in Columbia University Library).

After his return he became one of the founders of the new "Association of the Ḥasidim" which advocated an immigration of ascetic scholars to Jerusalem to await the imminent coming of the Messiah. Privately this Messiah was understood to be Shabbetai Ẓevi whose return in 1706, forty years after his apostasy, had been predicted by Malakh. Apparently during these years, Malakh acquired the surname Malakh, "the angel." He became generally known by this title from the late 1690s on: whether this was because of his gifts as a preacher or because of his asceticism is unknown. Certainly he was considered the chief kabbalist of the group. In connection with the "ḥasidic" propaganda which attracted many secret Shabbateans in Poland, Germany, and the Hapsburg Empire, he spent some time in Germany and Moravia, where, at the end of 1698, he attended a council of the Shabbatean leaders of the Ḥasidim in Nikolsburg (Mikulov), an eyewitness report of which has survived. He also went to Vienna and announced that he would discuss the Shabbatean belief and teachings with any duly initiated kabbalist. Abraham *Broda, the rabbi of Prague, sent his pupils, Moses Ḥasid and Jonah Landsofer, but the dispute, which lasted two weeks, ended inconclusively. Malakh then went to Ereẓ Israel where, after the sudden death of Judah he-Ḥasid in October 1700, one faction of the Ḥasidim chose him as its leader. What exactly happened in the Shabbatean circle in Jerusalem is unknown or blurred by biased and half-legendary reports. At any rate, internal dissensions between moderate and radical Shabbateans contributed to the break-up of the group, but the precise date of Malakh's expulsion from Ereẓ Israel is unknown. It is probable that he went to Constantinople and again to Salonika, meeting with Baruchiah. Since that meeting Malakh acquired the reputation of being an emissary of the antinomian wing of Shabbateanism. This led to his prolonged persecution by the rabbinical authorities. A circular letter of the Constantinople rabbis, written in 1710, denounced him vehemently. He returned to Poland where he founded the radical sect in Podolia from which the Frankist movement sprang (see Jacob *Frank), but he also served as an emissary for some Ashkenazi groups in Ereẓ Israel. As such he is mentioned in the records of the community of *Tiktin (Tykocin) in 1708. In public he denied any Shabbatean connections, preferring to divulge his doctrine in private. Forced to leave Poland, he wandered through Germany and Holland. In 1715 he was in Amsterdam where a letter from Abraham Broda, then rabbi of Frankfurt, urging Malakh's immediate expulsion arrived soon after his departure. He died shortly after his return to Poland in 1716 or 1717. He was generally considered an expert in Kabbalah and a persuasive spokesman for the Shabbatean movement after it was forced to go underground. None of his writings has survived.

BIBLIOGRAPHY: J. Emden, *Torat ha-Kena'ot* (1871), 50, 70–71; D. Kahane, *Toledot ha-Mekubbalim, ha-Shabbeta'im ve-ha-Ḥasidim*, 2 (1913), 175–80; C. Bernheimer, in: JQR, 18 (1927/28), 125; G. Scholem, in: *Zion*, 6 (1941), 123–4; 11 (1946), 168–74; idem, in: RHR, 143 (1953), 209–20; M. Benayahu, in: *Sefer Ḥida* (1957), 73–74; idem, in: *Sefunot*, 3–4 (1960), 136–8; idem, in: *Eretz-Israel*, 10 (1971).

[Gershom Scholem]

MALAMAT, ABRAHAM (1922–). Israeli Bible scholar. Born in Vienna, Malamat settled in Palestine in 1935 and received his doctorate from the Hebrew University of Jerusalem in 1951 for a thesis on the history of the Arameans written under B. *Mazar. He then spent two years at the Oriental Institute of the University of Chicago studying under the Sumerologist T. Jacobsen and the Assyriologist B. *Landsberger.

Many of his writings are concerned with the relationship between the history of ancient Mesopotamia to Ancient Egypt and the Bible. He has made a major contribution through his discoveries of the relation of the ancient *Mari documents to the study of the Bible. His record and study of Mari in the third and second pre-Christian millennia contributed to our understanding of the historical background of ancient Israel. Malamat argued that much of biblical historical narrative had "telescoped" events of long periods of time.

In 1954 he was appointed lecturer in Biblical and Ancient Jewish History at the Hebrew University of Jerusalem and professor in 1964. He taught there until his retirement in 1991. Malamat taught widely around the world and trained many students. He has served as editor of the Hebrew bulletin of the Israel Exploration Society and is a member of the board and scientific council of the Israel Society for Military

History, the international editorial board of the *Zeitschrift fuer die alttestamentlische Wissenschaft*, and the *Journal for the Study of the Old Testament.*

Malamat has published over 250 papers in Hebrew, English, and German. His Hebrew works include: *Israel in Bible Times – Historical Essays* (1983–1984); *Jeremiah, Chap. One – The Prophetic* Call (1954), and *The Arameans in Aram Naharayim* (1952). A full bibliography through 1993 is available in his jubilee volume published as *ErIsr*, 24 (1993). After his retirement Malamat was a fellow at the Dinur Center for Research in Jewish History at the Hebrew University. His later publications can be found on the website of the center.

ADD. BIBLIOGRAPY: G. Galil, in: DBI, 2:113–14.

[Elaine Hoter / S. David Sperling (2nd ed.)]

MALAMUD, BERNARD (1914–1986), U.S. novelist. Born in New York City, Malamud began to teach in 1939, went west to Oregon State College (an experience used in his third novel, *A New Life*, 1961), and later taught at Harvard. Malamud was elected president of the American PEN Club for 1980. One of the most significant of the younger generation of mid-20th century American writers, Malamud was profoundly influenced by realistic novelists such as Dostoievski. His first novel, *The Natural* (1952), about the rise and fall of a baseball hero, was a brilliant tour de force, displaying a characteristic mixture of realistic detail, vernacular language, and free-ranging symbolism and fantasy. Malamud found his true voice, however, with his second novel, *The Assistant* (1957), and a collection of short stories, *The Magic Barrel* (1958). With magnificent virtuosity and integrity, he (like Saul *Bellow) used a dialect of American English mixed with Yiddish, and succeeded in transferring to the American scene the intense moral concern, the comic yet pathetic irony, and the traditional situations of East European Jewish culture. Within the narrower Jewish world, he wrote with special love about the idealistic *shlimmazel*, the obscure and the lonely and the suffering, as in the title story of *Idiots First* (1963); this is also the case with Morris Bober, the grocer protagonist of *The Assistant*. Another recurring theme is the relations between Jews and gentiles: the New York Italian assistant falls in love with Bober's daughter and finally becomes a Jew; stories set in Italy deal with love between Jewish men and gentile women; and "Angel Levine" and "Black is My Favorite Color" are concerned with Jews and blacks. Malamud was deeply conscious of the role of the Jew as a symbol of the human tragedy. All his concerns were fused, and grew in scope and significance, in *The Fixer* (1966), which won the National Book Award and the Pulitzer Prize in 1967 and was made into a motion picture. Yakov Bok, a Russian-Jewish handyman falsely accused of ritual murder, is based on Mendel *Beilis, victim of the notorious Kiev Blood Libel of 1913. An obscure little man in flight from his heritage, Bok is thrust into a situation requiring unusual courage. The stages by which he comes to a full understanding of his responsibility, and develops the strength of will to face his ordeal, are powerfully described. Malamud said of this novel: "The drama is as applicable to the American people as it is to the Russian." *Pictures of Fidelman* (1969), subtitled "An Exhibition," uses three previously collected stories, and adds three more, about the picaresque misadventures of an American-Jewish artist in Italy. In Rome, Milan, Florence, and Venice, Arthur Fidelman seeks both "perfection of the life" and "of the work"; in each city, he works at a different art or problem, and lives with a different woman. At the end, "Prometheus Fidelman" has learned his limitations: back in the U.S., "he worked as a craftsman in glass and loved men and women." In "Pictures of the Artist," a "Jewish refugee from Israel" named Susskind is imagined preaching a sort of parody of the Sermon on the Mount. *The Tenants* (1971), a novel of clashing aspirations and dislikes dramatized by a Jewish and an African-American writer, also represents the struggle of writers appropriating subjects and histories that exhaust their sense of the human. In *Dubin's Lives* (1979), arguably one of Malamud's finest works, Dubin, a biographer whose life is lived largely in books, is forced to confront the disruptive yet life-giving nature of passion. In *God's Grace* (1982), Malamud dramatizes the Jewish dialogue with a God of awe and the understanding we have of our own finitude. Allegorical, as well as dystopian, it deals with resignation to, as well as acceptance of, freedom within limitation. Its humor is that of the pathos of human existence, driven by power and its vanities. *The People and Uncollected Stories*, composed in the main of an unfinished novel about a Jew living with an Indian tribe, was published in 1989. *Conversations with Bernard Malamud*, edited by Lawrence Lasher appeared in 1991. Malamud's *The Complete Stories* edited by Robert Giroux was published in 1997.

Malamud's contribution to American-Jewish literature remains large. (He appears as the novelist E.L. Lonoff in Philip Roth's *The Ghost Writer*, 1979). Yet his achievement also seals an epoch in which the Jew was portrayed as helpless, and forced to justify his existence. Suffering, in much of Malamud's work, marked American-Jewish life. It also was the human condition. Malamud's Jewish characters are often victimized by their sense of self. They are also often diminished by their environment, by capitalism, and by political and social malevolence. His protagonists escape a constricting life at the cost of a deeper remorse: the abandonment of their authentic selves.

A new American-Jewish literary type, one willfully accepting conditions of success and ease in America, gains its strength against the background and achievement of Malamud's art.

ADD. BIBLIOGRAPHY: E. Abramson, *Bernard Malamud Revisited* (1993); E. Avery, *Rebels and Victims: The Fiction of Richard Wright and Bernard Malamud* (1979); H. Bloom (ed.), *Bernard Malamud* (1986.)

[Sholom Jacob Kahn / Lewis Fried (2nd ed.)]

MALAVSKY, SAMUEL (1894–1983), **ḥazzan*. Born in Smela, near Kiev, Ukraine, Malavsky sang as a *meshorer* (see *Music) with various *ḥazzanim*. He went to the U.S. in 1914 and auditioned for Josef *Rosenblatt, thus beginning a lifelong association. Malavsky sang duets with Rosenblatt in concerts and on recordings as well as officiating as *ḥazzan* in many leading congregations. In 1947 he formed the Malavsky family choir, "Singers of Israel," with his two sons and four daughters. They achieved great international popularity through their appearances in synagogues, concerts, and on recordings. Malavsky created a unique style for his family choir by introducing a strongly marked beat and syncopation into traditional Eastern European *ḥazzanut*.

MALAYSIA, federation of states in S.E. Asia formerly under British protection. A few Jews settled in Penang, of whom the first was Ezekiel Menassah from Baghdad, in 1895. Although remaining the only Jew in the whole area for nearly 30 years he continued Jewish observances, kept a *kasher* household and welcomed visiting coreligionists. Other Jews arrived there after World War I, mostly poor peddlers. During World War II the community was evacuated to *Singapore, subsequently occupied by the Japanese. Of the Jews who settled in Penang after the war, some 20 families remained by 1963. Only three families lived there in 1969.

BIBLIOGRAPHY: I. Cohen, *Journal of a Jewish Traveller* (1925), 207–8.

MALBEN (Heb. initials מוֹסְדוֹת לְטִפּוּל בְּעוֹלִים נֶחֱשָׁלִים, *Mosedot le-Tippul be-Olim Neḥshalim* – "Institutions for the Care of Handicapped Immigrants"), agency of the *American Jewish Joint Distribution Committee (JDC) for the care of aged, infirm, and handicapped immigrants in Israel. Its funds are derived mainly from the *United Jewish Appeal. The mass immigration after Israel declared its independence included thousands of old people – often the last survivors of families destroyed by the Nazis; victims of tuberculosis acquired in the concentration camps or Middle East ghettos; and others physically or emotionally incapacitated by poverty, wartime suffering, or Nazi persecution. In 1949, Malben was founded by the JDC to relieve the Israel government of the burden of caring for these immigrants. It constructed a network of about a hundred institutions, converting army barracks and whatever buildings were available into old-age homes, hospitals, TB sanitariums, sheltered workshops, and rehabilitation centers.

Once emergency needs were under control, Malben began to consolidate its programs of direct care, while cooperating with other agencies to create more municipal and regional facilities for the aged and handicapped, and to develop indirect services which would enable elderly people to live on their own as long as possible. These measures include cash relief, constructive loans to help the aged and handicapped to earn a living, employment assistance, home medical care and housekeeping services, and the establishment of "Golden Age" clubs to provide elderly people with facilities for social and community life. Malben also cooperates with the government, the Jewish Agency, and the municipalities in the fields of mental health, chronic illness, and the care of physically and mentally handicapped children and adults among the settled population. Between 1949 and 1968, Malben-JDC helped some 250,000 immigrants – every fifth newcomer and one in ten of the population – at a total cost of $164 million. It maintained a hospital for chronic invalids, 12 old-age homes and villages with 3,000 beds, and extramural services for some 48,000 persons. By the end of 1975 all the homes, hospitals, and other programs initiated by Malben had been handed over to the government and local authorities.

BIBLIOGRAPHY: American Jewish Joint Distribution Committee, *Doors to Life* (1968).

[Misha Louvish]

MALBIM, MEIR LOEB BEN JEHIEL MICHAEL WEISSER (1809–1879), rabbi, preacher, and biblical exegete. The name Malbim is an acronym formed from Meir Loeb ben Jehiel Michael. Born in Volochisk (Volhynia), Malbim was a child when his father died. He studied in his native town until the age of 13, with Moses Leib Horowitz, among others. He married at the age of 14, but after a short time divorced his wife. He went to Warsaw, where he became widely known as the "*illui* from Volhynia." From there he went to Leczyca, where he married the daughter of the local rabbi Ḥayyim Auerbach, who maintained him, and he was thus able to devote himself to literary work. In 1834 he traveled to Western Europe to obtain commendations from contemporary rabbis for his *Arẓot ha-Ḥayyim* (1837), visiting, among other places, Pressburg, Amsterdam, and Breslau. In 1839, on the recommendation of Solomon Zalman Tiktin of Breslau, he was appointed head of the rabbinic court of Wreschen (district of Posen). From there he went to Kempen in 1840, where he remained for 18 years, and was therefore sometimes referred to as "The Kempener." While in Kempen he was invited to the rabbinate of Satoraljaujhely in Hungary but refused the offer. He finally agreed to accept the call of the Bucharest community, and in the summer of 1858 he was officially inducted as chief rabbi of Romania.

In Bucharest, Malbim set new *kashrut* standards, imposed restrictions on the kosher butchers, constructed a new *eruv*, personally supervised the educational institutions in town and began to attract large crowds to his sermons. All of these activities, combined with his insistence that his congregants become more observant, resulted in friction between Malbim and the enlightened intellectuals in the Jewish community, who were actually wealthy, foreign nationals. When Malbim objected to the building of a new modern synagogue, the Choral Temple, because it would include an organ and choir like the Reform synagogues in Western Europe, his opponents complained to the authorities, claiming falsely that Malbim was preaching against Christianity. In 1860, he published the first volume of his commentary on the Pentateuch – on Leviticus. In the introduction he wrote a scathing attack against Reform Judaism. His son, Aaron, passed away in 1862. This personal tragedy had a severe effect on Malbim. At the same time, his rapidly deteriorating relations with the enlightened members of his community made his position precarious. Because of Malbim's uncompromising stand against Reform, disputes broke out between him and the communal leaders of the town, leading to his imprisonment. On Friday, March 18, 1864, Malbim was arrested and jailed. He was freed only on the intervention of Sir Moses *Montefiore and on condition that he leave Romania and not return. Upon release, he was placed in a boat sailing down the Danube River. He was put ashore at the Bulgarian border town of Ruschuk. M. Rosen has published various documents which disclose the false accusations and calumnies Malbim's Jewish-assimilationist enemies wrote against him to the Romanian government. They accused him of disloyalty and of impeding social assimilation between Jews and non-Jews by insisting on adherence to the dietary laws, and said, "this rabbi by his conduct and prohibitions wishes to impede our progress." As a result of this the prime minister of Romania issued a proclamation against the "ignorant and insolent" rabbi for his effrontery in "publishing libelous letters against those eating meat from any butcher shop and he has preached against the idea of progress and freedom." In consequence the minister refused to grant rights to the Jews of Bucharest, on the grounds that the rabbi of the community was "the sworn enemy of progress" (from the official newspaper *Moniturul* March 6, 1864). Determined to refute the false accusations made against him, Malbim went to Constantinople to lodge a complaint against the Romanian government, which was then under Turkish domination. Following the rejection of his appeal and his failure to obtain the help of the Alliance Israélite Universelle (in transmitting a memorandum written in 1864 in Paris in which Malbim, with the help of Adolphe Crémieux, addressed himself to the Romanian ruler, stressing his patriotism), he was compelled to leave Romania (1864). During his wanderings in the following years he suffered persecution and calumny. He served as rabbi intermittently in Leczyca, Kherson (1869–70), Lunshitz (1870–71), and Mogilev (1872–75), and wherever he went he was persecuted by the assimilationists, the *maskilim*, and the Ḥasidim. The *maskilim* accused him of being an extremist and a rebel against the enlightenment. He was invited to Mainz, and on his way stopped at Koenigsberg, where he remained for about four years (1875–79). In 1879 he received an invitation from Kremenchug, Poltava oblast, to serve as its rabbi, but died in Kiev on his way there.

Malbim's fame and his immense popularity rest upon his commentary on the Bible, which was widely esteemed. His first published commentary was on the Book of Esther (1845), followed by one on Isaiah (1849). In 1860 his commentary *Ha-Torah ve-ha-Mitzvah* on the Sifra was published in Bucharest. His commentary on the Song of Songs, *Shirei ha-Nefesh*, was published first in Krotoszyn and then in Bucharest in 1860. The remaining commentaries to the books of the Bible were completed and issued during the years 1867–76. His commentary encompasses all of the books of the Bible except Lamentations and Ecclesiastes. Malbim's commentary on the Bible was motivated by his opposition to the Reform movement, which in his view could potentially undermine the very foundation of Judaism. He began with Leviticus and the Sifra because the Reformers attacked the very idea of sacrifice and the halakhic Midrash on Leviticus as lacking any *peshat*. He wished to combat these Reform ideas in particular and in general to strengthen the position of Orthodox Judaism in the spheres of exegesis, knowledge of Hebrew, and the exposition of the Bible according to its plain meaning, and thereby counteract and weaken the Reformers in precisely those three spheres in which they had made appreciable achievements. In his long introduction to the commentary *Ha-Torah ve-ha-Mitzvah* (1860) on the Book of Leviticus and the Sifra, Malbim refers to the Reform Synod at Brunswick in 1844, calling it a gathering of "rabbis and preachers as well as readers who butcher their communities." Because of these Reformers' negative approach, Malbim decided that "it was time to act for the Lord, and to fortify the wall around the Law, Written and Oral … so that violators could not assail and desecrate it." From that time he began to compose commentaries on the Bible with the aim of proving "that the Oral Law is the law given from heaven, and that all its words are necessary and implicit in the plain meaning of the verse and in the profundity of the language, and that the interpretation is only the plain meaning based upon accurate, linguistic rules."

His commentary to the Bible is based upon three fixed principles: In the text of the Torah and the figurative language of the prophets there are no repetitions of mere synonyms; consequently every word in a sentence is essential to the meaning in accord with the rules of the language despite the fact that they seem to be mere synonymous repetitions. Every statement conveys a sublime thought: all the metaphors are of importance and replete with wisdom for they are the words of the living God (introduction to Isaiah). In Malbim's opinion the sages had "important principles and fixed rules for the grammatical forms and the foundations of the language and of logic," according to which they understood all the words of the revelation transmitted at Sinai. He arranged these rules and principles in a special work, *Ayyelet ha-Shaḥar*, which he prefaced to his commentary on the Sifra. In it he noted 613 paragraphs (248 on linguistic usage and 365 in explanation of the verbs and synonyms) that are the foundations of tradition and the Oral Law. He stresses the superiority of the literal interpretation and complains that the commentators after David Kimḥi – except for Isaac Abrabanel – were exponents of homiletical exegesis "and no one exerted himself to breathe life into the verses by the literal method" (end of his introduction to Joshua). In his commentary on the Pentateuch, Malbim treated the narrative portions differently from the legal sections. His *peshat* commentary to the narrative portion is accompanied by questions which are the opening gambit to his exegesis. The commentary on the legal sections focuses more on the halakhic Midrash, explaining its connection to the straightforward meaning of the biblical text. Overall, his Pentateuchal commentary is accompanied by *Torah Or*, essays on the *aggadah* combined with Kabbalah and philosophy;

Remazim, hints of broader issues on the Tabernacle sections in Exodus; and *Ner Mitzvah*, which answers questions by other commentaries on the Midrash. While his commentary on the Pentateuch is meant more for scholars, the commentary on the rest of the Bible is aimed at a broader audience.

It should be noted that at the end of his commentary to Daniel, Malbim devotes himself to the calculation of the date of the redemption, which was to have been in the period 1913–1928: "We are writing these words in 1868 and according to our calculation the time of the redemption will be removed a further 60 years… for the rise of a scion of the house of David, the building of the Temple, and all the promises of the prophets will be fulfilled at the same time, and their luster will shine forth from the year 1913 to the year 1928, when the Temple will already have been established."

The following of his talmudic works are noteworthy: *Arẓot ha-Ḥayyim*, contains novellae and expositions on Shulḥan Arukh, *Oraḥ Ḥayyim* (Part 1, on chapters 1–24, 1837; Part 2, on chapters 25–31, 1861), with the novellae of his son-in-law Elijah Joel Heilprin. The work, in three parts, comprises novellae on the responsa of Moses Isserles with source references and a pilpulistic exposition of the Shulḥan Arukh. Malbim provides a synthesis of *halakhah* and natural science on the one hand, as well as *halakhah* and Kabbalah on the other hand. *Yalkut Shelomo* (1938; 1966^2) was a collection of his novellae on the tractates of the Talmud, published (1966^2) after editing by Solomon Drillich, who also prepared and arranged a new edition of *Ha-Torah ve-ha-Mitzvah*, on the Pentateuch, with the title *Sefer ha-Torah ve-ha-Mitzvah ve-ha-Ḥinnukh*, in three parts (1967). *Alim li-Terufah* (1904) is a small work consisting of an exposition of the fourth chapter of *Hilkhot De'ot* in Maimonides' *Mishneh Torah. Arẓot ha-Shalom* (1838) contains nine sermons which reveal the profundity of his homiletical ideas. Characteristic of this work is the fact that the sermons are based upon biblical verses only and do not rely upon rabbinic dicta. Each sermon encompasses a specific subject and is preceded by a poetic introduction. This method was regarded by some as an innovation in sermonic literature. His oral sermons were distinguished by verbal precision and strict logic. His *Ereẓ Ḥemdah* (Warsaw 1882) contains sermons on the Pentateuch and expositions of *aggadot*. His works on language, poetry, and logic include: *Ya'ir Or* (1892), on synonymous nouns and verbs, containing 662 synonymous nouns; selections from his commentaries on synonyms found in the *Likkutei Shoshannim* (1875), and *Ha-Karmel* (1900) and arranged by J. Greenbaum; *Yesodei Ḥokhmat ha-Higgayon* (1900), a textbook on logic in 20 chapters comprising a survey on the principles of logic; *Mashal u-Meliẓah*, first published by Jehiel Brill (1867) – an allegorical play in four acts that was a visionary poem on the vice of hypocrisy. His autobiography was published in serial form in *Ha-Levanon* (vol. 2, 1865). Throughout his works Malbim quotes ideas from both Jewish and non-Jewish philosophers, including Aristotle and Kant. However, it is very difficult to know if his knowledge of their works was firsthand or secondhand from other sources.

A number of Malbim's works were translated into English. His commentary to Esther appears in two different editions: *Tournabout: The Malbim on Megillas Esther* (Southfield, Michigan, 1990), and *The Malbim Esther* (Southfield, Michigan, 1998). *Malbim on Mishley* is an abridged version published in Jerusalem (1982). *The Malbim Haggadah* appeared in 1993. E. Parkoff published *Fine Lines: A Study of the Torah's Outlook on Human Suffering Based on Malbim's Commentary on Iyov* (1994).

After his death, the Bucharest Jewish community built a Bet Midrash honoring Malbim. It became the center for Orthodox Jewish life in Bucharest until 1980 when it was destroyed by the Communist regime of Nikolai Ceacescu.

BIBLIOGRAPHY: C.H. Brawermann, in: *Keneset Yisrael*, 3 (1888), 207–12; J. Meisl, in: *Jeschurun*, 12 (1925), 112–26; J. Mark, *Gedolim fun unzer Tsayt* (1927), 147–52; idem, *Bi-Meḥiẓatam shel Gedolei ha-Dor* (1957), 129–33; A. Guenzler, in: *Oẓar ha-Ḥayyim*, 6 (1930), 35–37; A.A. Hartstein, *ibid.*, 150f.; H.H. Tscharnotschepki, *ibid.*, 10 (1934), 21–23, 38f.; S.D. Posener, *Eshed ha-Nahar* (1932), 130–42; S.J. Glicksberg, *Ha-Derashah be-Yisrael* (1940), 402–7; E. Herbert, in: *Journal of Jewish Bibliography*, 2 (1940), 112–5; D. Druck, *Di Meforshim fun der Torah*, 3 (1941), 164–80; M.D. Ḥaklai, in: *Talpioth*, 4 (1949/50), 364–70; A. Schischa, *ibid.*, 6 (1953), 498–505; H.R. Rabinowitz, *Deyokna'ot shel Darshanim* (1967), 336–8; M. Rosen, in: *Hagut Ivrit be-Eiropah* (1969), 376–410; J.J. Cohen, in: KS, 44 (1969), 152f. **ADD. BIBLIOGRAPHY:** M. Margaliot, "*Megamot ve-Kavei Yesod ha-Me'afyenim et ha-Sifrut ha-Ivrit ha-Ḥaredit-Mitnagdit be-Eiropa be-Me'ah ha-18 ve-ha-19*" (dissertation, 1993); Z.S. Schechter, "*Mishnato shel ha-Malbim*" (dissertation, 1983); idem., in: *Iyyun u-Meḥkar be-Hakhsharat Morim*, 6 (1999), 259–76; E. Tuito, in: *Deot*, 48 (1980), 193–98; N. Mazuz, in: *Mikhlol*, 22 (2001), 19–28; N.H. Rosenbloom, in: HUCA, 57 (1986), 39–86; idem., *Ha-Malbim – Parshanut Filosofiyah Mada u-Mistorin be-Khitvei ha-Rav Me'ir Leibush Malbim* (1986); Y. Geller, in: *Sinai*, 79 (1976), 82–93; idem., in: PAAJR, 52 (1985), 1–41; idem, *Ha-Malbim Ma'avako ba-Haskalah u-ve-Reformah be-Bukharest (1858–1864)* (2000); idem, in: *Asufot*, 14 (2002), 357–75; idem, in: *Studia et Acta Historiae Iudaeorum Romaniae*, 7 (2002) 176–82; Z. Tabori, in: *Or ha-Mizraḥ*, 19 (1970), 83–88; T. Horvitz, in: *Sha'anan*, 8 (2002), 73–80; D.M. Rosen, in: *Hagut Ivrit be-Eiropa* (1969), 376–410; A. Frisch, in: *Maḥanayim*, 4 (1992), 370–79; E.Z. Melamed, in: *Sedeh Ilan: Sefer Zikaron le-Aryeh Ilan* (1968), 71–82; M.M. Yasher, *Ha-Gaon Malbim – Ḥayav Mishnato Ma'avakav u-Mifalav* (1976); S. Faber, in: *Jewish Book Annual*, 36 (1978–79), 79–87.

[Yehoshua Horowitz/ David Derovan (2nd ed.)]

MALCA (ben, ibn Malkah), Jewish-Moroccan family name, known from the early 14th century through the kabbalist NISSIM IBN MALCA, the author of *Ẓenif Melukhah*. His son was the philosopher, Judah ben Nissim ibn *Malkah. He was strongly influenced by neoplatonic doctrines and wrote several works of which only one has been published, *Uns al-Gharīb*. This was completed in 1365 probably in Fez. Lengthy extracts from it were translated into French and published by G. Vajda (see bibl.).

JACOB BEN JOSEPH BEN MALCA (d. 1771) was a rabbinical authority in Morocco. At first, he was *dayyan* in Fez, together with Judah *Benatar and Jacob *Abensur. Of a quarrelsome disposition, he was often in conflict with his colleagues, who nevertheless respected his profound erudition in the fields of rabbinical law and casuistry. During the famine which struck Fez in 1738 he moved to Tetuan, where he was appointed *av bet din*. He left a large number of decisions on various religious subjects, some of which have been published in the works of various Moroccan authors.

KHALIFA BEN MALCA (d. c. 1750) was a member of a wealthy family of Safi. He studied in Fez with Judah Benatar and Samuel *Sarfaty and later continued his studies in his native town with Joseph Bueno de *Mesquita, where Abraham ibn Musa and Jacob Abensur were his fellow students. Having lost his fortune, he settled in Agadir, where he represented Moses Guedalla of Amsterdam. He married Deborah, the daughter of the wealthy scholar Isaac *Mendes. In 1728 a plague claimed many victims, among them his wife and one of his daughters. In 1737 he lost large sums of money when the community was plundered and its synagogue set on fire. He then traveled to Holland and London. He wrote a commentary on the *siddur* entitled *Kav ve-Naki*, and also wrote commentaries to the Shulḥan Arukh, which he entitled *Rakh va-Tov*. He was particularly remembered for his piety, and both Jews and Muslims regarded him as a saint. Up to the 1960s regular pilgrimages were still made to his tomb in Agadir.

BIBLIOGRAPHY: Azulai, 66, 81; I. Bloch, in: REJ, 14 (1887), 114–6; J.M. Toledano, *Ner ha-Ma'arav* (1911), 41, 143–4; J. Ben-Naim, *Malkhei Rabbanan* (1931), 64a, 80a; G. Vajda, *Judah ben Nissim Ibn Malka* (Fr., 1954).

[David Corcos]

MALCHI, ESPERANZA (d. 1600), *kiera who served Safiye, favorite consort of Sultan Murad III (1574–95) and mother of Sultan Mehmed III (1595–1603).

Both Esperanza and her contemporary Esther *Handali served in a period known as "The Women Sultanate," when the strong ladies of the harem were involved in a variety of internal and external intrigues and became very influential in the Ottoman court. Besides being the main supplier of jewels and other luxury items to the harem, Esperanza was Safiye's most trustworthy contact with the outside world. She influenced important nominations, mediated in diplomatic conflicts, supplied diplomatic intelligence, and communicated with foreign envoys on Safiye's behalf. In a letter in Italian, dated November 16, 1599, addressed to Queen Elizabeth I of England, Malchi described herself as "a Hebrew by law and nation." She mentions a previous gift that was presented to her mistress, the Queen Mother, by the English ambassador, and lists the gifts which are being delivered to Queen Elizabeth through the ambassador who is soon to depart to England. In return she requests the Queen of England to send "distilled waters of every description for the face and odoriferous oils for the hands […] clothes of silk or wool, articles of fancy suited for so high a Queen as my Mistress." The "articles for ladies" should be delivered discreetly through Esperanza's hands only (Kobler, *Letters*, 393–94).

As a reward for her longtime services, Esperanza and her sons received various profitable concessions, among them the control of customs in Istanbul. Her great wealth and special privileges, as well as her undisguised influence on the Sultan's mother and her interference in state matters gained her many enemies. On April 1, 1600, she was publicly stabbed to death by rebellious soldiers and her eldest son was killed the next day. Esperanza's second son converted to Islam in order to save his life and a third son managed to escape. The family's enormous fortune and estates were confiscated.

BIBLIOGRAPHY: F. Kobler, *Letters of Jews through the Ages*, 2 (1953), 391–92; M. Rozen, *A History of the Jewish Community in Istanbul: The Formative Years (1453–1566)* (2002), 205–7.

[Ruth Lamdan (2nd ed.)]

MALDONADO DE SILVA, FRANCISCO (1592–1639), Marrano martyr in Peru. Son of the physician Diego Nuñez de Silva (d. 1616) who was reconciled by the Inquisition in 1605, Francisco was born in Tucuman (now Argentina) and studied at the University of San Marcos in Lima, Peru. He was reared as a devout Catholic, and educated as a physician. His reading of the anti-Jewish *Scrutinium Scripturarum* by the apostate Pablo de *Santa Maria (Solomon ha-Levi) led him to pose questions to his father on the relative merits of Judaism and Christianity. His father acknowledged that he was still a Jew at heart, and guided his son in studying Judaism. Maldonado was persuaded to become a secret Jew. After his father's death he moved to Chile, where he married and in 1619 was appointed surgeon of the hospital in Santiago. He continued practicing Judaism, but was denounced to the Inquisition in 1627 by his two sisters, whom he had sought to convert. Despite continued efforts by the Inquisition to shake his faith, including 14 attempts by theologians to better him in religious debates, he held fast to Judaism. After each hearing he signed his testimony "Eli Nazareno, unworthy servant of the God of Israel, alias Silva." He circumcised himself with a pocketknife and scissors and resorted to long and agonizing fasts. Though suffering from numerous ailments, he used an improvised rope made from corn husks to lower himself into other cells, where he found some Judaizers whom he fortified in their faith, also converting Catholics to Judaism. Using scraps of paper and a pen made from a chicken bone, he wrote several tracts in support of his beliefs. He was burned at the stake in Lima at the conclusion of the auto-da-fé of 1639. News of his death made a profound impact on writers like Isaac *Cardozo and Daniel Levi (Miguel) de *Barrios, although the latter confuses him with Tomás Treviño de *Sobremonte.

BIBLIOGRAPHY: B.Lewin, *Mártires y conquistadores judíos en la América Hispana* (1954), 177–207; idem, *El Santo Oficio en América* (1950), 142–52, 182; Roth, Marranos³, index s.v. *Silva*; H.C. Lea, *Inquisition in the Spanish Dependencies… Peru…* (1908), index.

[Martin A. Cohen]

°MALESHERBES, CHRETIEN GUILLAUME DE LAMOIGNON DE (1721–1794), liberal French statesman. As minister of the Maison du Roi in 1787, he was responsible with Turgot for the decree granting civic status to "non-Catholics," thus opening the way for effective action by the Jews on their own behalf. Malesherbes' main reason for wanting improved treatment of the Jews was his belief that it would lead to their conversion; he was opposed to the organized Jewish community, considering it as a state within a state. Jewish individuals were not free to convert, said Malesherbes, because they were so closely tied to the whole community. He therefore proposed that Jews be enabled to use public legal registers for their personal status, thus weakening their ties with Jewry. In spring 1788 Malesherbes set up an informal committee to study the question, coopting as advisers men well-disposed toward the Jews, including Pierre Louis *Roederer. Eight Jewish leaders were summoned to the committee, among them *Cerfberr for Alsace, Berr Isaac *Berr for Lorraine, Abraham *Furtado and D. Gradis for Bordeaux. The purpose of the committee was to conduct a preliminary inquiry on a new system for regulating the condition of French Jewry, and to prepare a memorandum. However, meetings were few and the differences between the two delegations, the "Portuguese" and the "German," were so marked that they could not reach agreement. The "Portuguese" memorandum in answer to Malesherbes' questionnaire on the current state of Judaism was later to influence the one presented by Napoleon's representatives to the *Assembly of Jewish Notables and the French *Sanhedrin. In July 1788 the delegates returned home, without having come to any decision. Malesherbes remained a staunch royalist and was later guillotined.

BIBLIOGRAPHY: Szajkowski, in: *Zion*, 18 (1953), 31–79; idem, in: PAAJR, 25 (1956), 119–35; idem, in: JQR, 49 (1958), 63–75; A. Hertzberg, *The French Enlightenment and the Jews* (1968), 323–6; P. Grosclaude, *Malesherbes – témoin et interprète de son temps* (1961), 631–49.

[Simon R. Schwarzfuchs]

MALEV, WILLIAM S. (1898–1973), U.S. Conservative rabbi. Malev was born in Homel, Russia, and immigrated to the United States in 1908. He received his B.A. from the City College of New York in 1919; as a student at the Teachers Institute, and president of the Jewish Teachers Association (1921–22), he was persuaded by Mordecai *Kaplan to enter the rabbinate and was ordained at the *Jewish Theological Seminary in 1925. Over the next 20 years, Malev developed three thriving synagogue centers in the New York metropolitan area: the Concourse Center of Israel (Bronx, 1925–27); Kingsbridge Heights Jewish Center (Bronx, 1927–28); and the Jamaica Jewish Center (Jamaica, 1928–46). In 1946, he moved to Houston, Texas, where he built Congregation Beth Yeshurun into the state's leading Conservative synagogue and was instrumental in establishing the first day school in the Southwest United States. He was president of the Texas Kallah of Rabbis and a force on behalf of Zionism as the foremost regional orator for the *Zionist Organization of America. As president of the Houston Ministerial Association, and a weekly columnist for the *Houston Post*, Malev was a principal civic leader in interfaith and interracial affairs. He also lectured at the University of Houston. Primarily a shaper of Conservative Judaism in the Southwest, his major role in the framework of the national movement was as chairman of the *Rabbinical Assembly's Committee on College Youth (1945–46), established to build bridges between RA members and the next generation of American Jewish leaders.

BIBLIOGRAPHY: P.S. Nadell, *Conservative Judaism in America: A Biographical Dictionary and Sourcebook* (1988).

[Bezalel Gordon (2nd ed.)]

MALIK AL-RAMLĪ (of Ramleh in Ereẓ Israel; mid-ninth century), founder of the sect of Ramlites or Malikites. Like some other sectarians, Malik taught that Shavuot must fall only on a Sunday, that the fat tail of the sheep comes under the heading of forbidden fat, and that marriage to a niece is incestuous. Within a century or so the Ramlites vanished, probably having been absorbed into the larger sect of *Karaites.

BIBLIOGRAPHY: Nemoy, in: HUCA, 7 (1930), 330, 389; idem, *Karaite Anthology* (1952), 53, 335; Mann, Texts, 2 (1935), 6, 11, 65 n. 117; Z. Ankori, *Karaites in Byzantium* (1959), 276n., 371n.

[Leon Nemoy]

MALINES (Mechelen), transit camp established by the Nazis in Belgium, between its two largest Jewish communities, Antwerp and Brussels, in October 1941 to concentrate Jews before transporting them to Eastern Europe. An infrastructure was already in place and a railway line led directly to the camp, which became an antechamber to death. The camp was surrounded by local inhabitants. The first group of Belgium Jews was arrested on July 22 and taken to Breendonck and then to Malines. The first transport from Mechelen was on August 4, 1942, and arrived in *Auschwitz on August 6. According to a list in the Mechelen archive, between August 4, 1942 and July 1944 there were 28 transports to the east with more than 25,257 Jews; some gypsies were transported in 1943 and 1944. All the inmates of the camp had to wear identification badges. The badges differed for the Jews in the camp. The various known symbols were: *T* = *Transport-Juden* (Jews who would be sent to the east), *Z* = citizens of the Allied countries or neutral countries, *E* = *Entscheidungsfalle*, borderline cases, whose identity required further investigation, *G* = *Gefaehrliche Juden* (dangerous Jews to be sent to punishment camps elsewhere). Jews who were married to non-Jews were sent to Drancy in German-occupied France. Members of the Committee for Jewish Defense (CDJ) which was in contact with the Belgian resistance movement, and the Catholic fighters' organization, penetrated into Mechelen a number of times in order to warn the inmates and try to liberate them. The organized Jewish community sent in packages. The camp was finally liberated by the Allies in September 1944; a few hundred Jews had managed to survive.

See *Belgium, Holocaust.

BIBLIOGRAPHY: J. Robinson, *And the Crooked Shall Be Made Straight* (1965); Belgium, Ministère de Justice. Commission des crimes de guerre, *Les Crimes de guerre, commis sous l'occupation de la Belgique 1940–1945. Persécution antisémitique en Belgique* (1947); *Belgium. Nuremberg document UK-76* (undated); *Nuremberg Trials Documents: Case 11, NG5219*; International Tracing Service, Arolsen, Germany, *Vorlaeufiges Verzeichnis der Haftstaetten unter dem Reichsfuehrer-SS 1933–1945* (1969). **ADD. BIBLIOGRAPHY:** S. Klarsfeld and M. Steinberg, *Memorial de la deportation des juifs de Belgique* (1980); Steinberg, M. Malines Antishambre de las mort," in: *Regards* 128 (March 1979).

[B. Mordechai Ansbacher / Michael Berenbaum (2nd ed.)]

MALINO, JEROME (1911–2002), U.S. Reform rabbi. Malino was born in New York City, earning his B.A. from City College in 1931. He was ordained at the Jewish Institute of Religion (later merged with Hebrew Union College, (HUC-JIR)) in 1935 and was awarded an honorary D.H.L. from Alfred University in 1958, as well as an honorary D.D. from HUC-JIR in 1960. After ordination, he became rabbi of the United Jewish Center in Danbury, Conn., a position he held for his entire career. In 1981, he was named rabbi emeritus and joined the faculty of HUC-JIR as adjunct lecturer in Homiletics; he had previously taught at Western Connecticut State University and been a member of the Commission for Higher Education for the state of Connecticut. For more than 40 years, he served as a chaplain at the federal correctional institution in Danbury (1940–83).

Malino was a leader of the *Central Conference of American Rabbis on both regional and national levels. He served as president of the New England Region of the CCAR (1961–63) and was the long-time chairman of its admissions committee (1964–73). A consistently outspoken proponent of rabbinic ordination for women, he was elected vice president of the CCAR in 1977 and president in 1979. Following his two-year term of office, he chaired the Committee on Rabbinical Growth. He was also a member of the Alumni Overseers of the HUC-JIR, which honored him by establishing the Jerome Malino Award, bestowed on the best first-year student at JIR.

Malino, a member of the National Executive Committee of the Jewish Peace Fellowship, was a pacifist and supporter of conscientious objectors to military service, even during World War II – a controversial position for a rabbi at the height of the battle against Hitler. Moreover, his advocacy of non-violence extended to the theater of the Israeli-Palestinian conflict. Malino also served as president of the Institute of Religion in an age of science, delivered scholarly papers at its conferences, and contributed numerous articles to professional and religious journals. In 1988 Malino received the Rabbi Israel and Libby Mowshowitz Award from the New York Board of Rabbis.

BIBLIOGRAPHY: Kerry M. Olitzky, Lance J. Sussman, and Malcolm H. Stern, *Reform Judaism in America: A Biographical Dictionary and Sourcebook* (1993).

[Bezalel Gordon (2nd ed.)]

MALINOWSKI, JOSEPH BEN MORDECAI (**Troki**; d. after 1625), Karaite scholar. Joseph was the pupil of Isaac b. Abraham *Troki, and was the leading Karaite scholar in Poland-Lithuania after his teacher's demise in 1594. Malinovski completed Isaac's *Ḥizzuk Emunah* after Isaac's death. According to his correspondence (Mann, Texts, 1196–8), in 1624 he was a spiritual leader of Troki. As such he endeavored to organize the communal affairs of the Birzhe Karaite community. He established a number of ritual customs for Polish-Lithuanian communities, which were published in *Karaite Siddur* I (Vilna 1890), 456–64. Some of them were close to Rabbanite practice. In 1624 he moved to Lutsk, evidently to become a spiritual leader of the community.

He had extensive knowledge of both Karaite and rabbinic scholarship. He wrote a book *Sefer Minhagim* (IOS A 208, JNUL mic. 52984), concerning prayer, reading the Torah, etc. *Manasseh Ben Israel's press printed his composition *Ha-Elef Lekha* (Amsterdam, 1643), a long mystical liturgical poem. Simhah Isaak *Luzki wrote his commentary *Kevod Elohim* on it and they were published together (*Kevod Elohim*,Y. Algamil ed., Ramla 2000). His *Kizzur Inyan Sheḥitah* on the ritual slaughter of animals was printed together with Mordecai b. Nissan's *Dod Mordekhai* (Vienna, 1830). Joseph died in Lutsk. He composed several liturgical poems, some of which had been included in the Karaite *Siddur.*

BIBLIOGRAPHY: A. Gottlover, *Biqoret le-toldot a-Karaim* (1865), 178–9; Mann, *Texts*, 2 (1935), index, 1557.

[Leon Nemoy]

MALKAH, JUDAH BEN NISSIM IBN (fl. c. 1260), philosopher, probably living in Morocco. Three of his works written in Judeo-Arabic have been preserved. (1) *Uns al-Gharīb* ("Familiarity with the Unfamiliar"), consisting of the author's own views and of a commentary on the *Sefer Yeẓirah*, preceded by a long introduction. One extract was published by H. Hirschfeld, *An Arabic Chrestomathy in Hebrew Characters* (1892), 19–31; an anonymous Hebrew abridgement was published by G. Vajda (1974); (2) a commentary on the *Pirkei de Rabbi Eliezer*; published by P. Fenton (*Sefunot* 21 (1993), 115–65); (3) *Tafsīr al-Ṣalawāt*, a commentary on the liturgy (fragment). Besides these, Judah refers to a work which he wrote on astrology, which probably bore the title *Kitāb al-Miftāḥ* ("The Key Book").

The doctrine of Judah b. Nissim rests on two fundamental theses: the unknowability of God and universal astral determinism. From the first thesis flows a metaphysics of emanation having at its apex the prime intellect, to which the functions of the first cause, and consequently those of the God of religion, have been transferred. From the second thesis flows a view of the world according to which even revealed religions are completely determined by astral influences. In the light of this, the superiority of Judaism is that it is best adapted to the demands of astral determination. The only ones who can penetrate this mystery, however, are the philosophers who are adept in the allegorical exegesis of religious texts, whereas the masses are obligated to observe the letter of the law. Judah's philosophy is in many ways similar to the Neoplatonic speculations adopted by the Islamic Ismmāʿīliyya in constructing their theology, but no precise historical connection can be established between them. His views on astral determinism are not alien to the Jewish thought of the Middle Ages (particularly that of Abraham *Ibn Ezra and certain Averroists), but they are brought to conclusions which no one else had perhaps dared to formulate with such boldness. On the other hand, the deductions which Judah drew from the unknowability of God are similar to the Kabbalah. In fact, the author was familiar with the Kabbalah and referred to it; although, besides the *Sefer Yeẓirah*, he cites only the *Bahir* and the *Razi'el*. It has been possible to establish that he availed himself of the kabbalists of *Gerona (*Azriel, Jacob b. Sheshet *Gerondi, and *Naḥmanides), and even of the Zohar. Nevertheless, he did not consider the teachings of the Kabbalah superior to those of philosophy, but rather identified the Kabbalah with philosophy. More precisely, he regarded the Kabbalah as a particular symbolic expression of God's unknowability and of astral determinism. It appears that Judah had some influence on subsequent Jewish thought, especially on Samuel *Ibn Motot and Joseph b. Abraham *Ibn Waqar.

BIBLIOGRAPHY: S. Munk, *Les Manuscrits Hébreux de l'Oratoire* (1911), 15–17; Steinschneider, Uebersetzungen, 405–6; J.M. Toledano, *Ner ha-Ma'arav* (1911), 41; G. Sarton, *Introduction to the History of Science*, 3 pt. 2 (1947), 1444; G. Vajda, *Juda ben Nissim Ibn Malka, philosophe juif marocain* (1954); idem, in: *Homenaje a Millas-Vallicrosa*, 2 (1956), 483–500; idem, in: REJ, 15 (1956), 25–71; 16 (1957), 89–92. **ADD. BIBLIOGRAPHY:** M. Idel, in: *Pe'amim*, 43 (1990), 4–15.

[Georges Vajda]

MALKHI, EZRA BEN RAPHAEL MORDECAI (d. 1768), Safed talmudist and emissary. Ezra was the son of a well-known physician and scholar in Jerusalem, who had emigrated from Italy. His brother, Moses, became head of the Safed community and he was a brother-in-law of *Hezekiah da Silva and Moses *Ḥagiz. In 1749–50 Ezra went to Turkey and the Balkans as an emissary of Safed. While in Salonika he published his *Malkhi ba-Kodesh* (Salonika, 1749), laws for the night of Passover, and a commentary on the *Haggadah*, together with some halakhic novellae. He appended a note apologizing for the many errors in the work because he could not stay in the town during the printing, but was again in Salonika in 1750 when he had halakhic discussions with Joseph Samuel Modigliano. Owing to the bad economic situation in Safed, Ezra did not return there on the completion of his mission, and was appointed rabbi of Rhodes, where he remained for the rest of his life. In 1752 his signature appears on the *takkanot* of the community. His other books are *Shemen ha-Ma'or* (Salonika, 1755), on the novellae of *Zerahiah ha-Levi and *Naḥmanides on *Bava Meẓia; Ein Mishpat* (Constantinople, 1770), responsa, many of which were written during his mission, published by his disciple Raphael Jacob de Mayo; and *Einat Mayim* (Salonika, 1811), exposition and novellae on various tractates of the Talmud.

BIBLIOGRAPHY: Yaari, Sheluḥei, 438–40, 884.

[Avraham Yaari]

MALKHI, MOSES (b. Ezra?; mid-18th century), emissary of Safed, Malkhi had the distinction of being the first emissary of Ereẓ Israel to visit the New World. He was in New York in the summer of 1759 for four and a half months, and it is assumed that he remained there at the request of the members of the Sephardi community "Shearith Israel" who had no rabbi, in order to arrange their religious affairs. In the account book of that community it states that they gave the emissary 18 pounds sterling for 18 week's accommodation and for provisions and traveling expenses to Newport, Rhode Island, which was then the wealthiest Jewish community in America. There he met the Christian theologian Ezra *Stiles who was greatly interested in the emissary from Ereẓ Israel. Stiles relates that Malkhi was born and brought up in Safed, and he sent a letter in Latin through him to one of the heads of the Greek Church in Ereẓ Israel requesting exact information on the geography of the country and its inhabitants which he needed for his research on the *Ten Tribes. This Malkhi must be distinguished from his namesake, Moses (b. Raphael Mordecai *Malkhi). He may have been the son of Ezra *Malkhi.

BIBLIOGRAPHY: Yaari, Sheluḥei, 446; D. de Sola Pool, in: *Brandeis Avukah Annual* (1932), 356–7; G.A. Kohut, *Ezra Stiles and the Jews* (1902).

[Avraham Yaari]

MALKHI, MOSES BEN RAPHAEL MORDECAI (d. 1747), head of the Safed community in the first half of the 18th century. Moses was a brother of Ezra *Malkhi. He was head of the Jewish community of Safed for many years, and as such his signature appears first on the letters of appointment of various Safed emissaries. Malkhi was one of the intermediaries between Sheikh Ẓāhir al-Omar and Ḥayyim Abulafia for the renewal of the Jewish community in Tiberias in 1740. He died in Acre and was buried in Kafr-Yasīf. In the letter of the community of Safed reestablishing the Jewish community of Kafr-Yasīf written in Elul of that year, the tomb of "the distinguished rabbi Moses Malkhi of blessed memory" and that of Moses Ḥayyim Luzzato, who died that year in the plague in Acre and was buried in Kafr-Yasīf, are listed together with those of *tannaim* and *amoraim*. It may be conjectured that Malkhi also died in that plague during a visit to Acre in connection with the affairs of the Safed community.

BIBLIOGRAPHY: Yaari, Sheluḥei, 431, 432, 437, 438, 501, 850.

[Avraham Yaari]

MALKHUYYOT (Heb. מַלְכֻיּוֹת; verses describing God's "sovereignty"), name of the first part of the central section of the *Musaf prayer for *Rosh Ha-Shanah. It consists of 10 verses, four from the Pentateuch, three from Psalms, and three from the Prophets; all of them proclaim God as King and anticipate the realization of His kingdom on earth. According to the Talmud (RH 32a), the number ten symbolized the ten praises sung by David (Ps. 150), or the Ten Commandments, or the "ten sayings" by which God created the world (cf. Avot 5:1). The *Malkhuyyot* prayer and two similar sections, *Zikhronot and

*Shofarot, form the *Teki'ata de-Vei Rav.* At the end of each section during the Reader's repetition (and in some rites during the congregation's silent reading), the *shofar* is sounded. The recital of *Malkhuyyot-Zikhronot-Shofarot* verses dates back to mishnaic times (cf. RH 4:5, 6) and was, most probably, part of the prayer service in the Temple. The Talmud, however, does not specify which verses had to be chosen for this purpose (RH 32a–b). The present selection and order of the verses are ascribed to the Babylonian scholar *Rav (175–247 C.E.), as are the introductory and concluding passages.

BIBLIOGRAPHY: Elbogen, Gottesdienst, 141–4; Idelsohn, Liturgy, 213–4.

MALKIEL, THERESA SERBER (1874–1949), U.S. labor and women's rights activist and socialist. Malkiel was born in Bar, Russia, in what is today western Ukraine. The daughter of a well-to-do Jewish family that immigrated to New York City in 1891, she was well educated and literate in German and Russian. Supporting herself with work in the garment industry, she was a member of the Russian Workingmen's Club and later a founder of the Infant Cloakmakers Union, serving as its president. She was active in various labor organizations in New York in the 1890s, including the Socialist Labor Party (SLP) and its Socialist Trade and Labor Alliance. In 1901, tired of the factionalism of the SLP, she joined the Socialist Party of America, which became her activist home for the next two decades.

Theresa married fellow socialist (and lawyer) Leon Malkiel in 1900; their daughter was born in 1903. Theresa Malkiel gave up wage work after the family moved to Yonkers, north of New York City, but remained committed to working women and socialist politics. She took a particularly active role as an advocate for women within the Socialist Party and in 1909 was elected to the Women's National Committee (WNC), the body that oversaw the Women's Department within the party. On the WNC, she became an advocate for the establishment of International Women's Day as an annual holiday to commemorate women and promote female suffrage. With her husband, she was a founder of the socialist newspaper the *New York Call.*

Malkiel also became a member of the Women's Trade Union League, a strong advocate of female suffrage, and an indefatigable campaigner for women's rights, within the Socialist Party and in the wider society. She was a strong supporter of the great Shirtwaist Strike in New York City in 1909–10, gave speeches at several major rallies, reported on the strike in the *New York Call*, and wrote a fictional account that appeared shortly after the strike's conclusion, *The Diary of a Shirtwaist Striker* (1910). In 1914 Malkiel led the Socialist Suffrage Campaign in New York, organizing meetings, writing pamphlets, and publishing a regular column in the *Jewish Daily Forward.* Two years later, Malkiel joined a national suffrage tour sponsored by the Socialist Party. The success of female suffrage with the passage of the Nineteenth Amendment led Malkiel to run an unsuccessful campaign for the New York State Assembly as a Socialist candidate. For the remainder of her life she was active in adult education, founding the Brooklyn Adult Students Association. In 1932 she organized a summer camp for the education and naturalization of immigrant women at which she worked until her death.

BIBLIOGRAPHY: F. Basch, Introduction to *The Diary of a Shirtwaist Striker* (1990); S.M. Miller, "From Sweatshop Worker to Labor Leader: Theresa Malkiel, a Case Study," in: *American Jewish History,* 68 (1977), 189–205; E. Taitz, "Malkiel, Theresa Serber," in: P.E. Hyman and D. Dash Moore (eds.), *Jewish Women in America,* 2 (1997), 885–86.

[Thomas Dublin (2nd ed.)]

MALKIEL, YAKOV (1914–1998), U.S. philologist. Born in Kiev, Russia, educated in Berlin, Malkiel immigrated to the United States in 1940. From 1942 he was a faculty member at the University of California (Berkeley) and later professor of linguistics and Romance philology. In 1947 he became founder and editor-in-chief of the journal *Romance Philology.* He was president of the Linguistic Society of America in 1965. He was author of numerous articles and monographs dealing with historical linguistics, Hispanic lexicology, and the theory of etymology and lexicography, and he constantly attempted to mediate between general linguistics and Romance philology.

Among his works are *Studies in the Reconstruction of Hispano-Latin Word Families* (1954), *Essays on Linguistic Themes* (1968), *Yakov Malkiel: A Tentative Autobibliography* (1988), and *Etymology* (1993). He edited *Directions for Historical Linguistics: A Symposium* (1968), with Winfred P. Lehmann.

[Jonas C. Greenfield / Ruth Beloff (2nd ed.)]

MALLER, JULIUS BERNARD (1901–1959), U.S. educationist and sociologist. Born in Vobolniki, Lithuania, Maller went to the U.S. in 1921. Having received both a secular and religious higher education, Maller's professional life was divided between teaching posts at Howard University, Washington, D.C., and Yeshiva University (1949–59). He was also active in Jewish organizations. Maller devised (1929) the "Guess Who" technique, a sociometric test for use with children. His personality tests, known as the "Maller Personality Sketches" (1936) and the "Maller Character Sketches" consisted of cards with descriptions of personality or character traits, to be sorted into groups. He demonstrated that intelligence test scores at the fifth grade level were closely related to socioeconomic levels. A close relationship was shown between delinquency, density of population, and economic level. His chapter on personality tests in *Personality and the Behavior Disorders* (1944) was adopted as a standard treatment. Later he became a consultant to various government agencies in addition to his interests in Jewish education, his work with Jewish service organizations and his teaching activities. His most important publications were: *Cooperation and competition: an experimental study of motivation* (1929); *Studies in the nature of character:* volume 2; *Studies in service and self-control* (with Hartshorne and May, 1929); and *Testing the Knowledge of Jewish History*

(1932). He was also a frequent contributor to Jewish educational periodicals.

[Menachem M. Brayer]

MALLOW, plant of the genus *Malva*. Six species are found in Israel, the most common, found in almost every part of the country, being the *Malva nicaensis, Malva silvestris*, and *Malva parviflora*. During the siege of Jerusalem in 1948 the citizens of Jerusalem picked them and prepared from them a variety of dishes. The mallow is popularly known by its Arabic name *khubeiza* which means "small loaf," because its edible seeds are flat and round like Arab bread (*pittah*). Job characterizes "the juice of *ḥallamut*" ("mallow") as insipid, so that even in his distress "my soul refuses to touch them; they are as the sickness of my flesh" (Job 6:6). Despite this, the name *ḥallamut* or *ḥelmit* in the Mishnah appears to be connected with *ḥalam* meaning "healthy." It may be, however, the same as *laḥmit*, through transposition of letters, which has the same connotation as its Arabic name "small bread." The Mishnah refers to *ḥelmit* as a vegetable (Kil. 1:8) and the *Arukh* of Nathan b. Jehiel identifies it with *Malva* (mallow). The leaves of some mallows are sensitive to light, and Rashi in his commentary on the vegetable *adani* (Shab. 35b) notes: "It is a vegetable called *malva* whose leaves turn to the sun. In the morning they incline eastward, at midday they are upright, and in the evening they incline westward." The identification of the *ḥallamut* of the Bible with mallow is not certain, and it has been identified with many other plants. The JPS renders *ḥallamut* as "mallow" (AV: "white of egg"), while the AV renders *malu'aḥ* in Job 30:4 as "mallow" (JPS correctly as "saltwort"; see *Orach).

BIBLIOGRAPHY: Loew, Flora, 1 (1928), 292–4; N.H. Tur-Sinai, *Sefer Iyyov*, 1 (1941), 85f.; H.N. and A.L. Moldenke, *Plants of the Bible* (1952), 53f.; J. Feliks, *Olam ha-Ẓome'aḥ ha-Mikra'i* (1968^2), 188–90. **ADD. BIBLIOGRAPHY:** Feliks, Ha-Tzome'aḥ, 63.

[Jehuda Feliks]

MALMÖ, port in S. Sweden. The Jewish community, the third largest in Sweden, was founded by Polish Jews in 1871, when it numbered 250. In 1900 the congregation appointed its first rabbi, Dr Josef Wohlstein, and in 1903 the first synagogue was built. Most of Malmö's original Jews came from Germany and during the first two decades of the 20th century, many Jewish immigrants arrived from Poland, Russia, the Ukraine, and the Baltic countries. Many of these new arrivals settled in the nearby town of Lund, creating a separate but related Jewish community there. The closing stages of World War II saw the large-scale rescue of Danish Jews from German-occupied Denmark to Sweden by sea and at the end of the war, many thousands of survivors of Nazi concentration camps were brought to Sweden via Malmö. Many of these survivors, however, were in such poor health that they died on reaching Swedish soil, which explains the large number of Jewish "refugee graves" in Malmö. A monument to commemorate the victims of the Holocaust was later created at the cemetery by Willy Gordon, a well-known Swedish-Jewish artist. Over the decades the community grew considerably, reaching a peak of around 1,700 in the late 1960s but subsequently declining to a 2004 figure of 1,200 despite the influx of immigrants from the former Soviet bloc, in particular from Russia, the Ukraine, Estonia, and even Kirgistan.

Haquinus Stridzberg's *Kohen Gadol sive Pontifex-Maximus Ebraeorum* was printed in Malmö in 1689.

BIBLIOGRAPHY: H. Valentin, *Judarna i Sverige* (1964); L. Herz, in: JJSO, 11 (Dec. 1969), 165–73; I. Lomfors, in: S. Scharfstein, *Judisk historia från renässansen till 2000-talet* (2002). **WEBSITE:** http://www.ijk-s.se/jfm/jfmintro.htm.

[Ilya Meyer (2nd ed.)]

MÁLNAI, BÉLA (1878–1941), Hungarian architect. After a period in which his work leaned towards Secessionism, he returned to historicizing neo-styles. His main work was the Czech-Hungarian Industrial Bank.

[Eva Kondor (2nd ed.)]

MALOVANY, JOSEPH (1941–). Born in Tel Aviv, Malovany served as cantor at Tel Aviv's Bilu synagogue, cantor of the Israeli army, and then from 1963 to 1968 *ḥazzan* of the Yeoville synagogue, Johannesburg, and from 1968 to 1973 of the Edgeware Synagogue, London. In 1973 he was appointed chief cantor to the Ateret Ẓevi Congregation of Fifth Avenue, New York. Malovany held music diplomas from the Tel Aviv Academy of Music and Great Britain's Royal Academy and Trinity College of Music. He was also honorary president of the Cantorial Council of America and past chairman of the board of the American Society of Jewish Music. He held the academic positions of distinguished professor of liturgical music at Yeshiva University and dean of the JDC Moscow Academy of Jewish Music. Malovany possessed a brilliant spinto tenor voice and was a much sought-after artist with orchestras and choirs worldwide. He was the possessor of an extensive discography of cantorial and contemporary Jewish music. On January 26, 2004, he received the honor of being knighted as Commander of the Legion of Honor by the president of Poland in appreciation of his musical contribution to the international and Polish communities. He was the first Jewish cantor to receive this award from Poland.

[Akiva Zimmerman / Raymond Goldstein (2nd ed.)]

MALSIN, LANE BRYANT (1879–1951), U.S. fashion innovator and entrepreneur. A gifted seamstress, Lena Himmelstein immigrated alone to New York from Lithuania at 16. Not quite 20, she married Russian immigrant jeweler David Bryant, who died a few months after their son, Raphael, was born in 1900. Bryant supported herself and her son by sewing lingerie and other apparel from her apartment; in 1904 she applied for a bank loan to open a shop. From then on her name became Lane Bryant, either because a bank officer misspelled her name on a business account application or she signed her name incorrectly on that application and was too embarrassed to correct the mistake. Bryant pioneered a special line of maternity clothing which became increasingly popular. After her 1909 marriage to Albert Malsin, who became her business partner, the couple started the first mail order catalog for maternity ware. By 1917 mail order revenues netted more than a million dollars and by 1950 their sales made them the sixth largest mail order retailer in the U.S. Lane Bryant's other major innovation was ready-made clothes for stout-figured women, and this clothing line was also a great success. Bryant opened the first of many branch retail stores in Chicago in 1915. When her husband died in 1923, Lane Bryant, Inc. was grossing $5,000,000 a year.

Lane Bryant was committed to good customer service and employee benefits, offering her workers decent wages, profit sharing, group life insurance plans, and medical expenses. When the company went public she provided one-fourth of the stock for employee investment. An exemplar of corporate philanthropy, Bryant teamed up with the American Red Cross and provided any Lane Bryant customer with a wardrobe to replace clothing destroyed in a disaster; she was also a supporter of the Hebrew Immigrant Aid Society, New York Federation of Jewish Philanthropies, and other charities. She was survived by three sons, who continued to be involved with the business after her death, a daughter, and 12 grandchildren.

[Sara Alpern (2nd ed.)]

MALTA, Mediterranean island. That Jews were present there in Roman times is attested by the discovery of a catacomb with the symbol of the **menorah*. There must have been a community under Arab rule (870–1090) and in 1240 there were 25 Jewish families there and eight in the neighboring island of Gozo. During the Middle Ages the two islands were part of the Kingdom of Sicily, and a great deal is known of their history from materials preserved in the Sicilian archives. The communities came to an end with the expulsion of the Jews from Sicily in 1492. From 1530 to 1798 the islands were ruled by the Knights of St. John, who in the course of their forays against the Muslims captured and brought back to Malta large numbers of Jewish prisoners. The Societies for Redeeming the *Captives (Ḥevrot Pidyon Shevuyim) in Venice and elsewhere were mainly engaged in raising funds for ransoming the Jewish prisoners in Malta, where the Venetian society kept a permanent Christian agent. Under the latter's auspices, the Jewish slaves were able to maintain a synagogue for worship, and there was also a cemetery. A regular community, mainly deriving from North Africa, began to develop during the last days of the rule of the Knights and under British rule (from 1800). In 1804 the *blood libel raised against the handful of Jews was firmly suppressed by the English poet S.T. Coleridge, then colonial secretary on the island. The community remained small, numbering 16 families in 1968 and 60 Jews in the mid-1990s. A synagogue was opened in Valetta in 1984.

[Cecil Roth]

Relations with Israel

Israel established friendly relations and cooperation with Malta even before the latter achieved independence in 1964. In the late 1950s the leader of the Maltese Labor Party, Dom Mintoff, tried to mediate between Israel and Egypt, albeit unsuccessfully. In 1966 an Israel embassy was established with a resident chargé d'affaires, while Israel's ambassador in Rome also serves as nonresident ambassador to Malta. Israel experts assisted in the development of dairy, poultry, and afforestation projects. Trade with Malta has been modest.

BIBLIOGRAPHY: C. Roth, *The Jews of Malta* (1931; = offprint from JHSET, 12 (1928–31), 187–251); S. Assaf, *Be-Oholei Ya'akov* (1943), 107–15; Roth, Mag Bibl, 113; idem, *Personalities and Events* (1961), 112–35.

MALTER, HENRY (1864–1925), rabbi and scholar of medieval Jewish philosophy. Malter was born in the village of Bonze, Galicia. His father was his teacher and provided him with the fundamentals of a rabbinic education. Hardly past childhood, Malter became interested in secular knowledge, having somehow obtained access to *Ha-Maggid*, a Hebrew periodical with a Haskalah viewpoint. At the age of 16 in search of broader knowledge he journeyed to Lyck and from there to Berlin. While earning his living by teaching Hebrew, he prepared himself for entering the university and at the same time continued his Jewish education at the Veitel-Heine-Ephraimsche Lehranstalt. There he attracted the attention, and became the favorite pupil, of Moritz *Steinschneider, who encouraged his interest in medieval Jewish bibliography and whose book in that field, *Juedische Literatur* (1850), Malter translated into Hebrew as *Sifrut Yisrael* (1897). With his work on the influence of the 11th-century Muslim philosopher Al-Ghazzali on Jewish thought, *Die Abhandlung des Abu Hamid al-Gazzali* (1894), Malter earned a doctorate in philosophy from the University of Heidelberg. In 1898 he received a rabbinical diploma from the Lehranstalt fuer die Wissenschaft des Judentums. The newly founded library of the Berlin Jewish community then invited him to become its librarian. He held this post for a year. Malter went to the United States in 1900 at the invitation of Hebrew Union College in Cincinnati to teach medieval Jewish philosophy. He also taught Bible and rabbinic law and literature, and at the same time served as rabbi at the Shearith Israel congregation in Cincinnati. However, he disagreed with the theological attitudes of American Reform Judaism and was, therefore, in conflict with Kaufmann *Kohler, then president of Hebrew Union College; consequently, he left the college in 1907. Thereafter, in New York he collaborated with J.D. Eisenstein on the Hebrew encyclopedia *Oẓar Yisrael*, contributing articles on Jewish literature, among others. With the opening of Dropsie College in 1909, Malter assumed the chair of talmudic literature which he occupied to the end of his life. He was a stimulating teacher in Talmud and particularly in medieval philosophy and ethics. Painstaking in his scholarship, Malter published a number of important essays in the *Jewish Quarterly Review* and elsewhere. His chief published work is *Saadia Gaon, His Life and Works* (1921). The study is based on a meticulous review of every fragment, including *genizah* material, by and about the head of the Sura academy in the tenth century. It is a model of a biography of a scholar by a scholar: it deals with *Saadiah's eventful life, analyzes his works, and in a bibliographical section shows his influence by citing the numerous references to him in the course of the centuries. Two other books, both published posthumously, deal with the talmudic treatise *Ta'anit: Treatise Ta'anit of the Babylonian Talmud* (1928), critically edited on the basis of manuscripts and old editions, and *Massekhet Ta'anit min Talmud Bavli* (1930), a critical edition of the text with notes and explanations on the basis of 24 manuscripts. With Alexander *Marx, Malter edited the *Gesammelte Schriften* of Moritz Steinschneider, of which only the first volume appeared (1925).

BIBLIOGRAPHY: A. Marx, *Essays in Jewish Biography* (1947), 255–64; D. Druck, in: *Der Amerikaner,* 20 (April 28, 1922), 4; (May 5, 1922), 6; A. Marx, in: AJYB, 28 (1926), 261–72, also in: A. Marx, *Studies in Jewish History and Booklore* (1944), 409–17.

[Solomon Grayzel]

MALTIN, LEONARD (1950–), U.S. film critic-historian. Maltin was born in New York to lawyer and immigration judge Aaron I. Maltin and singer Jacqueline Martin (née Gould). As a 15-year-old high school student in Teaneck, N.J., Maltin took over as the editor of the film magazine *Film Fan Monthly.* Circulation of the magazine increased dramatically under the young film aficionado, and at age 18 he was contracted to produce the annual paperback reference guide *TV Movies*, now released under the title *Leonard Matlin's Movie and Video Guide.* Maltin graduated from New York University in 1972 with a bachelor's degree in journalism. He joined the faculty at New School for Social Research in 1973, leaving the magazine in 1975. He joined the television entertainment magazine show *Entertainment Tonight* as a correspondent in 1982. He also hosted a daily radio feature on home videos, broadcast in Los Angeles on news station KNX. In 1995 and 1996, he served as president of the Los Angeles Film Critics Association. Maltin served as host, consultant, and writer for a variety of cable television programs and film retrospectives; as an adjunct professor at the University of Southern California's School of Cinema and Television from 1998; and adviser to the National Film Preservation Board from 1997. Other books by Maltin include *The Disney Films* (2000[4]), *Leonard Maltin's Family Film Guide* (1999), *The Great American Broadcast: A Celebration of Radio's Golden Age* (1997), *Leonard Maltin's Movie Encyclopedia* (1995), *The Little Rascals: The Life and Times of Our Gang* (1992), *Of Mice and Magic: A History of American Animated Cartoons* (1987), *Selected Short Subjects* (1983), *The Great Movie Comedians* (1978) and *The Art of the Cinematographer* (1978).

[Adam Wills (2nd ed.)]

MALTZ, ALBERT (1908–1985), U.S. playwright and novelist. Maltz, who was born in Brooklyn, wrote his first play in 1931 in collaboration with George Sklar. Entitled *Merry-Go-Round*, it was an exposé of corrupt Tammany politics in New York City. Maltz became associated with the left-wing Theater Union for which he wrote an antiwar drama, *Peace on Earth* (with George Sklar, 1934), and *Black Pit* (1935). From the late 1930s he began writing novels, notably *The Happiest Man on Earth* (1938); *The Underground Stream* (1940); *The Cross and the Arrow* (1944), which was made into a motion picture; and *The Journey of Simon McKeever* (1949). He also published essays and the scenarios for films including *This Gun for Hire* (1942), *Destination, Tokyo* (1943), and *Naked City* (1948). In 1947, during the HUAC investigation of the motion picture industry, Maltz refused to "name names" and was indicted with several other Hollywood writers. He spent nine months in prison. After his release in 1951 he settled in Mexico. A later novel was *A Long Day in a Short Life* (1957). His *Afternoon in the Jungle: The Selected Short Stories of Albert Maltz* was published in 1970.

ADD. BIBLIOGRAPHY: J. Salzman, *Albert Maltz* (1978)

[Milton Henry Hindus]

MALVANO, GIACOMO (1841–1922), Italian diplomat. Born in Turin, he was secretary general of the foreign ministry from 1876 to 1885. Malvano was minister to Tokyo from 1887 to 1889 when he resumed the post of secretary general of the foreign office, which he held until 1907. Malvano was a senator from 1896 and later was appointed to the Council of State, eventually becoming its president. He was also president of the Italian Geographic Society for many years.

An opponent of Zionism, Malvano refused to assist Theodor Herzl on his visit to Rome (Jan. 26, 1904) on the ground that he was only "a modest civil servant." Herzl ironically refers to him, "He is a clerk in the wholesale firm of 'Italy, Inc.'"

[Giorgio Romano]

MALZBERG, BENJAMIN (1893–1975), U.S. psychiatric statistician and epidemiologist. Malzberg was born in New York City and from 1923 to 1928 served as statistician to the Department of Welfare of New York State. After serving on the Committee on State Hospital Problems, he moved to the New York State Department of Mental Hygiene in 1940, becoming the director of its statistical bureau in 1944, and its consultant in 1956. Malzberg performed numerous studies of a statistical and epidemiological nature. Among his early researches were "Mortality among Patients with Mental Disease" (1934); "Hereditary and Environmental Factors in Dementia Praecox and Manic-Depressive Psychoses" (with associates, 1938); "Social and Biological Aspects of Mental Disease" (1946). *Migration and Mental Disease* appeared in 1956, as did his important study *Mental Disease among Jews in New York State* (1960). *Mental Disease among Jews in Canada* appeared in 1963 and *Ethnic Variations in Mental Disease in New York State* in 1966. His studies also covered the mental health of African-Americans and alcoholic psychoses. In his studies of mental illness among Jews, Malzberg demonstrated a higher incidence of psychotic depression among Jews than among white non-Jews (as measured by hospital admissions). His research confirmed the general knowledge that the incidence of alcoholism was very low among Jews.

[Louis Miller]

MAMET, DAVID (1947–), U.S. playwright. Born in Chicago, Mamet received a B.A. from Goddard College in 1969 and taught playwriting there for a brief period. He started his theatrical career as an actor and director before his own plays were ever produced. He began writing for the stage in 1971 with *The Duck Variations.* In 1973, Mamet founded, along with three friends, his own theater company in Chicago (St. Nicholas) and remained its artistic director through 1975.

A primary theme running throughout his work is the question of whether moral people can exist in an excessively immoral world. The environment he depicts is often devoid of any emotion and spirituality, and morality, if it exists, is on the decline. The strong male characters for which Mamet is known find it difficult to survive let alone thrive in such a world. In fact, the characters that do thrive are typically devoid of morality as well. His dialogue is often a stylized, almost poetic, version of the streetwise speech found in noir films and novels.

Mamet's plays include *Sexual Perversity in Chicago* (1973), *Reunion* (1973), *Squirrels* (1974), *American Buffalo* (1976), *A Life in the Theater* (1976), *The Water Engine* (1976), *The Woods* (1977), *Lone Canoe* (1978), *Prairie du Chien* (1978), *Lakeboat* (1980), *Donny March* (1981), *Edmond* (1982), *The Disappearance of the Jews* (1983), *Glengarry Glen Ross* (1984), and *Speed the Plow* (1988), which received the Tony Award for Best Play of the Year, *Oleanna* (1993), *The Cryptogram* (1995), and *The Old Neighborhood: Three Plays* (1998).

Mamet received the New York Drama Critics Circle Award for *American Buffalo* (1977) and *Glengarry Glen Ross* (1984), for which he was also the recipient of the Pulitzer Prize for drama. The play depicts desperate salesmen and the extreme measures, from ethically questionable to positively illegal, to which they resort to sell undesirable units of real estate. Mamet has also written screenplays, among them *The Postman Always Rings Twice* (1979), *The Verdict* (1980), for which he received an Academy Award nomination for Best Screenplay Adaptation, *The Untouchables* (1987), *House of Games* (1987, also directed), *Things Change* (1988, also directed), *Glengarry Glen Ross* (1992, an adaptation of his play), *Hoffa* (1992), *The Spanish Prisoner* (1997, also directed), *Wag the Dog* (1997, adapted from Larry Beinhart's novel *American Hero*), *State and Main* (2000, also directed), and *The Heist* (2001, also directed).

The prolific author has also written novels, including *The Old Religion: A Novel* (1997), *Bar Mitzvah* (1999), and *Wilson: A Consideration of the Sources* (2001); children's books including *Passover* (1995) and *The Duck and the Goat* (1996); and nonfiction including *Writing in Restaurants* (1987), *Some Freaks* (1989), *The Cabin: Reminiscence and Diversions* (1992), and *Three Uses for a Knife: On the Nature and Purpose of Drama* (1998).

ADD. BIBLIOGRAPHY: C. Bigsby (ed.), *The Cambridge Companion to David Mamet* (2004); L. Kane, *Weasels and Wisemen: Ethics and Ethnicity in the Work of David Mamet* (1999).

[Jonathan Licht / Robert L. DelBane (2nd ed.)]

MAMISTABOLOB, ABRAHAM, Georgian poet, born in the village of Staliniri, formerly Tskhinvali. A collection of his poems published in 1957 includes two poems based on Jewish themes, "Wedding in the Jewish Quarter" and "The Family."

[Mordkhai Neishtat]

MAMLUKS (lit. slaves), a military class which ruled *Egypt from 1250 to 1517 and *Syria (including *Palestine) from 1260 to 1516. Under the Mamluk sultans in Egypt and Syria, local Jews often suffered at the hands of government officials and Muslim zealots, although at times the sultan and his representatives were also a restraining influence on fanatical mobs or leaders. The Mamluks were one of the most important dynasties in the history of medieval *Islam, gaining fame for stopping the *Mongol advance into Syria and for eradicating the Crusader presence in Palestine and elsewhere along the Syrian coast. They were great patrons of culture, and many buildings with the distinctive building style of the period are scattered throughout Israel, especially Jerusalem. Scholars divide the Mamluk era into almost two equal sub-periods: the Baḥrī period (1250–1382), when the dominant group was mainly composed of Qipchaq Turks; and, the Circassian period (1382–1517) when Mamluks from the northern Caucasus region were predominant, although Turks continued to play an important role. The latter period is often still mistakenly called the Burjī period. Most Mamluk sultans were themselves Mamluks of slave origin, although some were the sons of sultans.

Military slavery, primarily of pagan Turks brought as youngsters from the Eurasian Steppe, had existed in the heart of the Muslim world since the ninth century. Later referred to as Mamluks (pl. *mamālik*), these soldiers of slave origin – particularly those who became officers – played an important role in the military and political life of many Muslim states. Turks were particularly favored since they combined hardiness, horsemanship, and archery which they had begun to learn in their Central Asian milieu. These nascent skills were reinforced by years of training in military schools in which the young Mamluks were enrolled after their conversion to Islam. Generally the sons of Mamluks were excluded from this military formation: Muslim rulers had learned that the sons of Mamuks had neither the hardiness nor loyalty of their fathers and therefore there was a continual import of young Mamluks to the centers of the Muslim world. In other words, the Mamluk system was a one-generational, continually replicating military elite. On the whole, Mamluks fought in organized units of mounted archers, and were generally loyal to their patrons, be they sultans or senior officers, although there were some notable exceptions.

Mamluks were certainly important in the armies of the *Ayyubid sultans and princes, and, since the time of the dynasty's founder Saladin (d. 1193), played a key role in the war against the Crusaders. In 1250, they overthrew their masters in Egypt; ten years later, in the aftermath of their victory over the Mongols at Ayn Jalut in northern Palestine, they gained control of all of Syria up to the Euphrates River, and embarked on a 60-year war against the Mongols, whom they successfully kept at bay. The Sultan Baybars I (1260–77) was the real architect of Mamluk power, expanding and strengthening the army, reforming the judicial system and generally bringing stability to the subjects of the state, in spite of his many wars against the Mongols and Crusaders. The latter culminated in the conquest of Acre in 1291. The Mamluk Sultanate was a relatively centralized state, governed from *Cairo, although most of the military activities were in Syria. Although the Mamluk regime became increasingly oppressive and rapacious over the decades, it was never seriously threatened by internal opposition. There were, however, many cases of urban disorder and riots, often over food shortages or other economic matters. The position of the *dhimmīs ("protected people," i.e. Christians and Jews) was also a source of occasional disorder and dissatisfaction, not the least because of the many Christians (and some Jews) still employed in various government offices, some of them holding relatively high positions. Without a doubt, the Mamluk period saw an increase in anti-*dhimmī* feeling and the consequent decline of the position of these peoples. This appears to be a result of several factors: the militant rhetoric of the Mamluks themselves, engaged in holy war (*jihād*) for decades; the culmination of almost two centuries of war against the Crusaders; the apparent perception that the local Christians, while Arabic speakers, were secretly sympathetic to the enemies of the state, be they Crusaders or Mongols; the declining economic situation, which began to be felt from the mid-14th century onward, particularly after the outbreak of the Black Plague in the region in 1349; and perhaps the competition over government jobs in which members of the Muslim learned class had a particular interest. It should be noted that the lion's share of anti-*dhimmī* feelings were directed at the Christians of Egypt and Syria, a much larger group than the Jews and better represented in the government bureaucracy. The impression gained is that the acts and activities against the Jews were often side effects of steps taken against their Christian "colleagues." It appears that, during the Mamluk period, there was a long-term islamization process among the Sultanate's Christian population (certainly among the Copts of Egypt). It is difficult to gauge the exact long-term impact of the Mamluk period on the size of the Jewish community, but there was some demographic decline caused by conversions and perhaps emigration, although apparently not to the same degree as among the Christians.

The paucity of the Cairo **Genizah* documents from the Mamluk period indicates the great change in Egyptian Jewry; whereas these archives of Cairo Jewry contain many documents from the 11th and 12th centuries, there are relatively few preserved from the subsequent period. Perhaps rather than indicating only the decline of the Jewish community in Old Cairo, it may reflect the weakening of Egypt's participation in the Mediterranean trade, which was the economic basis of this particular Jewish community. In any event, the numerous Arab chronicles and other sources for the Mamluk period contain much information on the Jews. From these and various Jewish sources we can reconstruct a picture of the main developments of the Jewish community in the main provinces of the Mamluk Sultanate. The difficulties experienced by the Jews were not only with the Muslim majority and authorities, but were also related to tensions within the community and "the depressed condition of community life" (M.R. Cohen). On the whole, we can say that during the Baḥrī period there was a series of acute outbreaks of anti-*dhimmī* activity and measures, which also affected the Jewish population of the Sultanate. In the Circassian period, the anti-*dhimmī* (and therefore anti-Jewish) measures were generally less sweeping, but the Jews (and the Christians) suffered from both chronic and temporary harassments. The terms of the so-called Covenant of *Omar are mentioned time and again during the period as the model which the *dhimmīs* were expected to follow, indicating perhaps that, between the anti-*dhimmī* measures enacted and mentioned in the sources, the non-Muslims lived under easier conditions. On the other hand, the repeated acts took their toll.

When Damascus was reconquered from the Mongols in 1260, there were riots against the local Christians, which spilled over to the Jews; the latter were soon curtailed when it was remembered that the Jews had not cooperated with the Mongols. Five years later the Christians in Cairo were accused of arson. Thereupon Sultan Baybars I (1260–77), who had just returned from Syria and the conquest of Caesarea and Arsuf from the Crusaders, assembled many Christians and Jews and ordered that they be burned alive, but released them on condition that they pay a heavy tribute in annual installments. These were, however, sporadic measures, which show how Jews could be caught up in what was originally a mainly anti-Christian activity. One act directed only against Jews was in *Damascus in 1271. There the Sufi shaykh Khidr, a Rasputin-like figure who was the favorite of the sultan, attacked and expropriated the largest synagogue. However, this figure was known for his attacks on Christians too. It was mainly later that more concerted and widespread actions against the *dhimmīs* were taken, including the frequent dismissal of non-Muslim officials. One Arab chronicler, al-ʿAynī, notes that, already under Sultan Qalāwūn (1279–90), "the *dhimmīs* had been in a state of extreme humiliation and degradation." Arab chroniclers sometimes mention only measures taken against Christians, but they state explicitly that Jews suffered during the dismissal of the officials in 1293 under Sultan al-Malik al-Ashraf Khalīl (1290–93), which followed riots that broke out in Cairo in the aftermath of supposed overweening behavior by Christians. In 1301 the hatred of non-Muslims burst into severe persecution; riots occurred in several towns in Egypt and many Christians and Jews were compelled to adopt Islam, including all the Jews of Bilbeis, in Lower Egypt, according to the Jewish-Egyptian chronicler of the Ottoman period, Joseph b. Isaac *Sambari. All churches and synagogues in Cairo were closed; in Alexandria, houses of non-Muslims which were higher than those of their Muslim neighbors were destroyed. These were unprecedented acts. Furthermore, the government decreed that henceforth Christians must wear blue turbans; Samaritans, red; and Jews, yellow. The willingness of the Mamluk authorities in this case to countenance the anti-*dhimmī* disorders and to enact stringent sumptuary laws may have been strengthened by the embarrassing defeat at the hands of the Mongols in Syria at the end of 1299, so that this became a way of diverting attention and demonstrating to the population the Mamluk commitment to Islam. In 1309, however, under Byzantine pressure, several churches and a synagogue were reopened, so there were occasional rays of light in this difficult period. There were again riots against Christians in Egypt, in which Jews are not mentioned, except in so far as some Christians borrowed their clothes to escape the wrath of the mob. In 1354 there was another general persecution of the non-Muslims in Egypt. There were riots during which Christians and Jews were attacked in the streets, with the rioters "throwing them into bonfires if they refused to pronounce the *shahādatayn* [the Muslim profession of faith]" (D.P. Little). Jewish and Coptic leaders were forced to listen to a list of the sumptuary measures which theoretically had already been in force. Non-Muslim government officials were dismissed, even those who embraced Islam. This particular set of measures seems to have had some impact on the conversion of Copts to Islam; whether it affected the Jews in the same way is unclear.

The anti-*dhimmī* atmosphere was not only a result of riots or repeated enactments of sumptuary laws. The early Mamluk period saw the appearance of several anti-*dhimmī* polemical works, such as that by al-Ghāzī b. al-Wāsiṭī, as well as the *fatwas* (responsa) and essays by the famous, but uncompromising, scholar Ibn Taymiyya. In addition, sometime in the first century or so of Mamluk rule, a humiliating oath which Jews had to take when appearing in Muslim courts was reintroduced after a hiatus of some 500 years (the text of the oath, from al-Umarī's *Tarif*, is found in Stillman, *Jews of Arab Lands*, 267–68).

In the second half of the 14th century restrictive laws and various vexations followed. Non-Muslim officials were dismissed in Damascus in 1356 and in 1363. At that time Jews and Christians were forbidden to ride horses and mules. They were allowed to ride donkeys only, using packsaddles and mounted so that both feet were on one side of the animal. In public baths they had to distinguish themselves by wearing little bells around the neck, and women had to wear one black and one white shoe. In 1365 Muslim zealots in Damascus searched Jewish and Christian homes for wine and poured the wine they found into the streets and rivers. Restrictive laws were again enforced; Jewish and Christian women were forbidden to frequent the public baths. Although the frequency of these ordinances proves that the discriminatory laws were not systematically kept, it is evident that their periodic enactment humiliated Jews and Christians whose communities were sizably weakened and diminished by the end of the rule of the Baḥrī Mamluks in 1382.

The image of the non-Muslim communities in the chronicles from the reign of the Circassian Mamluks (1381–1517) is somewhat different. With the end of the crusaders' principalities, the non-Muslims were no longer accused of conspiring with the enemies of the sultan; hence, general persecutions of non-Muslims in Egypt and Syria were to a degree lessened. Nevertheless, the actions of the second Mamluk dynasty were in some ways even worse than its predecessor. The frustration of the population increased and the sultans were thus often inclined to enforce the restrictive laws on the *dhimmīs* or extort heavy contributions from them. Under Sultan al-Malik al-Mu'ayyad Shaykh (1412–19), the authorities harassed the Jews and Christians in Egypt for drinking wine. In 1417 non-Muslims were ordered to dress simply in order that they not resemble Muslim judges. Furthermore, they were forbidden to ride swift asses. Two years later non-Muslim officials were again dismissed from government posts. Al-Malik al-Ashraf Barsbāy (1422–38) readily complied with the suggestions of Muslim zealots. Immediately after his accession he dismissed non-Muslim officials, and in 1426 he again demanded distinctive signs, ordering Jews and Christians to reduce the size of their turbans and put iron rings around their necks when going to public baths. Periodically, he sent officials to search the non-Muslim quarters of Cairo for wine. In 1442, during the reign of Sultan Jaqmaq (1438–53), the dais (referred to as a *minbar* in Arabic) of a synagogue in Cairo was destroyed when it was thought that it contained anti-Muslim blasphemies, and several other Jewish institutions as well as Christian buildings were also in danger of being damaged or ruined. This same sultan prohibited in 1448 non-Muslim physicians from treating Muslims, and in 1450 reinforced the regulations regarding their dress. In 1463 Sultan Khushqadam (1461–67) solemnly reinforced all the restrictive laws imposed on non-Muslims, with the exception of those which forbade them to be physicians and money changers. The last Mamluk sultans did not introduce new restrictions, but periodically imposed heavy tribute. Arab historians report that Qa'itbāy (1468–96) did this in 1488 and 1491 and that similar contributions were extorted from the Jews in 1500 and 1501. Yet, there was another side to late Mamluk attitudes towards the *dhimmīs* which should not be ignored, namely the occasional protection of the non-Muslims against the actions of intolerant Muslim religious figures or the mob. Thus, in 1473–75, the Mamluk authorities, eventually under the direct orders of the sultan, prevented the Muslim population of *Jerusalem from expropriating a synagogue, although an enraged mob had destroyed it; the Jews were permitted to restore it. This episode shows that legalistic niceties were often enforced, and, even at a time of general anti-*dhimmī* feelings and measures, non-Muslims "could not be abused with impunity" (D.P. Little).

The decline of the Jews' situation in the Mamluk state in the second half of the 15th century, economically and demographically, is pointed out by the traveler Felix Fabri, as it is likewise vividly depicted in the letters of Obadiah of *Bertinoro and his anonymous pupil, an Italian Jew who settled in Jerusalem at the end of the 15th century. In the capitals of Egypt and Syria there were still large communities, but in the other towns they had dwindled to small groups. Everywhere they were subject to legal discrimination and had to pay special taxes, e.g., on drinking wine. Their letters also stressed the general lawlessness and anarchy from which the Jews suffered (which was, however, not only the fate of the Jews, but also that of the Christians, and often the population at large). The authors of these travelogues, however, were not aware of the great change that Egyptian and Syrian Jewry had undergone under the impact of Mamluk rule. The flourishing Jewish middle class, once the mainstay of the Jewish communities, had greatly declined under the Mamluks (probably part of the general economic decline of the Sultanate, and not a result of an anti-Jewish policy) and most Jews had become poor. Social discrimination and the hostility of the upper classes caused many of the Jewish physicians and other well-situated Jews to adopt Islam. A relatively great number of biographies of these apostates appear in the writings of Arab historians of this period. On the other hand, the Mamluk sultans allowed the Jews to retain their judicial autonomy in cases of civil law, and until the end of their rule recognized the **nagid* as head of all the Jewish communities in Egypt, Palestine, and Syria. The *negidim*, who had deputies in Jerusalem and Damascus, represented the Jews, *Karaites, and Samaritans to the government. Until the end of the reign of the Baḥrī Mamluks, the post was held by the descendants of *Maimonides. The last was David II. In the 15th century the post was filled by Jewish court physicians. The Mamluk sultans apparently did not interfere with Jewish settlement in Egypt and Syria after the expulsion from Spain in 1492. The economic decline and the overall brutalization of life in the Sultanate in the 15th century (and perhaps before) weakened the community and contributed to a worsening of relations within it, as seen by the *Genizah* document from 1442 published by M.R. Cohen in 1984. In general, in spite of the deterioration of the community, one can still state with a great deal of certitude that the legal conditions of the Jews in the Mamluk Sultanate were still superior to those of their fellow Jews in most of contemporary Europe. The economic, social, and demographic condition of the Jewish communities of Syria and Egypt was to improve discernibly under the *Ottomans, who ended Mamluk rule and gained control over these countries in 1516 and 1517, respectively.

BIBLIOGRAPHY: Ashtor, Toledot; Baron, Social, vol. 17 (1980²), 154–228. **ADD. BIBLIOGRAPHY:** C.E. Bosworth, "Christian and Jewish Religious Dignitaries in Mamlûk Egypt and Syria: Qalqashandī's Information on Their Hierarchy, Titulature, and Appointment," in: *International Journal of Middle East Studies*, 3 (1972), 59–74, 199–216; idem, "'The Protected Peoples' (Christians and Jews) in Medieval Egypt and Syria," in: *Bulletin of the John Rylands University Library*. 62 (1979), 11–36; M.R. Cohen, "Jews in the Mamluk Environment: The Crisis of 1442 (A Geniza Study)," in: *Bulletin of the School of Oriental and African Studies*, 47 (1984), 425–48; P.M. Holt, *The Age of the Crusades: The Near East from the Eleventh Century to 1517* (1986); R. Irwin, *The Middle East in the Middle Ages: The Early Mamluk Sultanate, 1250–1382* (1986); D.P. Little, "Communal Strife in Late Mamluk Jerusalem," in: *Islamic Law and Society*, 6 (1999), 69–96; idem, "Ḥaram Documents Related to the Jews of Late Fourteenth Century Jerusalem," in: *Journal of Semitic Studies*, 30 (1985), 227–64; idem, "Religion under the Mamluks," in: *The Muslim World*, 73 (1983), 165–81; D.S. Richards, "Dhimmi Problems in Fifteenth-Century Cairo: Reconsideration of a Court Document," in: *Studies in Muslim-Jewish Relations*, 1 (1993), 127–63; N.A. Stillman, *Jews of the Arab Lands: A History and Source Book* (1979), 67–73, 264–77; idem, "The Non-Muslim Communities: The Jewish Community," in: C.F. Petry (ed.), *The Cambridge History of Egypt*, vol. 1 (1998), 208–10; R. Amitai, "The Mamluk Institution: 1000 Years of Military Slavery in the Islamic World," in: P. Morgan and C. Brown (eds.), *Arming Slaves* (2005).

[Eliyahu Ashtor / Reuven Amitai (2nd ed.)]

MAMPSIS, city in the Negev. According to Eusebius it was situated between Hebron and Elath, one day's march from Thamara (Onom. 8:8). The Madaba Map shows it between Beersheba and Thamara and calls it Maps. Ptolemy also refers to it as Maps. It appears in the episcopal lists of Palaestina tertia. Mampsis is identified with Kurnub where excavations were conducted by A. Negev from 1966. The town, which is surrounded by a wall, consists of three hillocks. On the western side of the town are the remains of a palace including a guard room, audience hall, records room, and stairs leading to an upper story with balconies; nearby is a tower with office rooms. A complex of residential buildings extending over 1,900 sq. yds. (1,600 sq. m.) on the eastern hill included stables with mangers. Some of the rooms were decorated with frescoes; a hoard of 10,400 Roman tetradrachms was discovered there. Mampsis was apparently settled in about 50 C.E. and continued into Byzantine times; its ruins include two churches. A Nabatean and a Roman military cemetery were found nearby. The remains of several dams were found in the vicinity. New excavations conducted at the site in the 1990s revealed additional Nabatean-Roman remains, including buildings, pottery, and middens.

BIBLIOGRAPHY: C.L. Woolley and T.E. Lawrence, *The Wilderness of Zin* (1915), 121ff.; Kirk, in: PEFQS, 70 (1938), 218ff.; A. Reifenberg, *Milḥemet ha-Mizra ve-ha-Yeshimon* (1950), 62, 130; Applebaum, in: BIES, 30 (1956), 224ff.; Negev, in: IEJ, 16 (1966), 145ff.; 17 (1967), 48ff.; idem, in: *Zeitschrift fuer Kunstgeschichte und Archeologie*, 7 (1967), 67–86. **ADD. BIBLIOGRAPHY:** T. Erickson-Gini, "Recent Advances in the Research of the Nabatean and Roman Negev," in R. Rosenthal-Heginbottom (ed.), *The Nabateans in the Negev* (2003).

[Michael Avi-Yonah / Shimon Gibson (2nd ed.)]

MAMRAM (or **Mamran**; ממר״ם, ממר״מ, ממרנ״י, ממר״א and at times abbreviated to מ״מ), a form of promissory note distinguished by its brevity. In Hebrew sources it is mentioned for the first time during the 12th century in the *tosafot* of *Elhanan

b. Isaac of Dampierre to the tractate *Avodah Zarah*. There is evidence of its use in Poland from the 14th century at least, but it was only during the 16th century that it became the distinctive promissory note used by Jewish merchants in their internal trade. There are various opinions on the etymological origin of this term, the most important being: a derivation from the Hebrew word המיר (*hemir*, "to change"); a contracted form of the Latin *in memoriam*; and a derivation from the word *membrana*, which in medieval Latin signified a scrap of parchment. The signature of the debtor appeared on one side of the document, while, on the other, in the same place as the signature, the sum owed and the date of payment were recorded. According to the regulations of the community councils, the document had equal validity with the ordinary handwritten promissory note even though the lengthy traditional formula was absent. Since the name of the creditor was not mentioned in the *mamram*, it was payable to the person who presented it to the debtor. As a result, the *mamram* was purchased by one person from another by simple transfer without any written documentation. The brevity of the *mamram* and the possibility of its easy transfer gave it a great advantage over the ordinary bill, encouraging its popularity. It was most common in Poland, especially during the 16th century, and the trading of *mamramim* became a frequent occurrence.

Another kind of *mamram* frequently employed in Poland during the 16th century was the blank *mamram* (in Polish *membran goły*). Its principal feature was that neither the amount of the debt nor the date of payment were mentioned. The signature of the creditor appeared on one side and the other side was blank. It is evident that a document of this kind could only exist in a society where the honesty of the debtor was taken for granted. The blank *mamram* came to satisfy the demands of the commerce practiced by the Jews of Poland during that period and it was particularly suited for use at the large fairs then held in the country. The merchant did not bring large sums of cash to the fairs because of the many dangers attendant on his journey and many deals were concluded at the fairs on short notice. Thus the merchant was in need of credit during that time and the *mamram* document satisfied his requirements. Through its use merchants could borrow unlimited sums, which in turn permitted the orderly development of business. The *mamramim* thus fulfilled the functions later provided by banks. The blank *mamram* was also different in that it was signed not by the debtor but by the person providing the credit. When in need of funds, the debtor sold it and thus received the amount he required. Because the halakhic basis of the blank *mamram* was highly dubious, some eminent rabbis objected to it and invalidated it and its use. Most authorities sanctioned it, however, because "it has already become the custom in these lands to collect by it according to the regulations of the countries." It was still in use among Polish Jews in the first half of the 19th century.

BIBLIOGRAPHY: P. Bloch, in: *Festschrift… A. Berliner* (1903), 50ff.; A. Gulak, *Yesodei ha-Mishpat ha-Ivri*, 2 (1923), 142ff.; idem, *Oẓar ha-Shetarot* (1925), 214ff.; S. Dubnow, *Pinkas ha-Medinah* (1925), index; Halpern, Pinkas, index; idem, *Takkanot Medinat Mehrin* (1952), index; S. Lipschutz, *Ḥemdat Shelomo, Ḥoshen Mishpat* (1969); M. Breger, *Zur Handelsgeschichte der Juden in Polen im 17. Jahrhundert* (1932), 45ff.; J. Katz, *Tradition and Crisis* (1961), 70ff.

MAMRE (Heb. מַמְרֵא), oak grove near *Hebron which was one of the favorite dwelling places of Abraham (Abram; Gen. 13:18); it is also the name of one of the clans of Hebron which was an ally of Abraham (14:13, 24). At Mamre, Abraham learned of the captivity of Lot and received the three angels (14:13; 18:1). It is described in Genesis 23:17 as having Machpelah "before" it; elsewhere, it is identified with Hebron (23:19; 35:27). In the time of Josephus, a tree some distance north of Hebron was assumed to be the "terebinth" of Abraham (Ant., 1:186; Wars, 4:533). In the Mishnah (Ma'as. 5:2), the site appears as Elath, one day's journey from Jerusalem, and in the Talmud (TJ, Av. Zar. 1:4, 38d) and the Midrash (Gen. R. 47:10) as Butnah (Butnan), the site of a famous trade fair where Hadrian sold the captives of the Bar Kokhba War into slavery. Later Christian sources refer to the site as a place of prayer; Constantine built a church there (which is shown on the Madaba Map). Jews, Christians, and pagans worshiped together there until the Arab conquest. The site is now identified with Rāmat al-Khalīl, 2 mi. (3.2 km.) north of Hebron. E.A. Mader, excavating there in 1926–28, cleared a Herodian enclosure wall, some blocks of which measure 14 × 4 ft. (4.3 × 1.2 m.). At its southwest corner was a well into which pilgrims threw gifts and money. In the eastern part of the enclosure, Constantine built a basilica measuring 60 × 50 ft. (19 × 16 m.), with a double narthex, a nave, and two aisles. Pottery from the ninth and eighth centuries B.C.E. indicates that the site was inhabited under the kings of Judah.

BIBLIOGRAPHY: E.H. Mader, *Mamre*, 2 vols. (1957); D. Winton Thomas (ed.), *Archaeology and Old Testament Study* (1967), index.

[Michael Avi-Yonah]

MAMZER (Heb. מַמְזֵר), usually translated as "bastard."

Definition

"If she cannot contract a legally valid marriage to this man, but can contract a legally valid marriage to others, her offspring [from the former] is a *mamzer*. Such is the case when a man has sexual relations with any of the *ervot* ["forbidden"; see *Incest] in the Torah" (Kid. 3:12; cf. Yev. 4:13). Thus, a *mamzer* is the issue of a couple whose sexual relationship is forbidden according to the Torah and punishable by **karet* or death. Because of this a marriage between them is void (Sh. Ar., EH 4:13), and thus, for example, the issue of a union between brother and sister or between a man and a woman validly married to another at the time is a *mamzer* (see *Adultery; Yev. 45b; Maim., Yad, Issurei Bi'ah 15:1; Tur and *Beit Yosef*, EH 4; Sh. Ar., EH 4:13). On the other hand, in Jewish law – unlike in other systems of law – the mere fact that a child is born (or conceived) out of lawful wedlock does not make him a *mamzer* and he is not an illegitimate child, i.e., one whose status or rights are impaired. The parents of the *mamzer* are indeed unmarried – either in fact or since they are so considered in law because of an absolute legal bar to a marriage between them – but unlike a man and a woman who, from the legal point of view, can marry each other but do not want to, the parents of the *mamzer*, owing to the said legal bar, cannot marry each other even if they want to. If one parent is non-Jewish this fact alone does not make the child a *mamzer* (see *Marriage; Yev. 45b; Maim., Yad, Issurei Bi'ah 15:3; Tur, EH 4; Sh. Ar., EH 4:19).

Consequences of the State of *Mamzerut*

These are twofold and relate to marriage and to personal status.

(1) Marriage. The Bible lays down: "A *mamzer* shall not enter the congregation of the Lord" (Deut. 23:3), i.e., a marriage between a *mamzer* (male or female) and a legitimate Jew or Jewess is prohibited. If such a marriage is nevertheless contracted, it is legally valid but must be dissolved by divorce (see *Marriage, Prohibited). A marriage between two *mamzerim* is permitted (Yev. 45b; Kid. 69a; 74a; Maim., Yad., Issurei Bi'ah 15:33; Sh. Ar., EH 4:24) and so also is a marriage between a *mamzer* and a proselyte (Yev. 79b; Kid. 67a and *Rashi* thereto; 72b–73a; Maim., Yad, Issurei Bi'ah 15:7; Sh. Ar., EH 4:22).

(2) Personal status. The offspring of a *mamzer* (whether male or female) and a legitimate Jew or Jewess are also *mamzerim*, since "*mamzerim*… are forbidden and forbidden for all time, whether they are males or females" (Yev. 8:3) and the rule is that in the case of a prohibited union the offspring follows the status of the "defective" parent (Kid. 3:12; see **Yuḥasin*). On the other hand, as the offspring of a union between a Jew and a gentile takes the status of the mother, a child born of a *mamzer* and a gentile mother will be gentile and not a *mamzer*; thus after proper conversion to Judaism, he will acquire the status of a legitimate proselyte and the fact that his father was a *mamzer* will be wholly irrelevant (Kid. 67a, *Rashi*; Maim., Yad, Issurei Bi'ah 15:3; Tur and *Beit Yosef*, EH 4; Sh. Ar., EH 4:20).

Except with regard to marriage, as stated above, the personal status of a *mamzer* does not prejudice him in any way. His rights of inheritance are equal to those of any other heir (Yev. 22b; Maim., Yad, Naḥalot 1:7; Sh. Ar., ḤM 276:6). His birth releases his father's wife from the obligation of *levirate marriage and *ḥalizah*. The *mamzer* is eligible to hold any public office, the highest (i.e., that of a king), for he remains "thy brother" and "from among thy brethren shalt thou set a king over thee" (Deut. 17:15; Tos. to Yev. 45b). Furthermore, according to the Mishnah, "a *mamzer* who is a scholar [*talmid ḥakham*] takes precedence over a high priest who is an ignoramus [*am ha-arez*]" (Hor. 3:8).

***Asufi* ("a Foundling")**

Sometimes a doubt may arise whether a child is legitimate or not and therefore he has the status of "doubtful" *mamzer*. One such case is that of a foundling, i.e., a child found abandoned in a public place when the identity of neither parent is known; in this case it is unknown whether the parents are legitimate or *mamzerim* (Kid. 4:12; Maim., Issurei Bi'ah 15:13; Tur, EH 4; Sh. Ar., EH 4:31). If such a child is found in or near a place inhabited by both Jews and gentiles, so that it is impossible to know even if he is of wholly Jewish parentage or not, he is considered both a "doubtful" *mamzer* and a "doubtful" gentile, so that if he later marries a Jewess and then afterward she wants to marry another man, she will require a divorce because of this latter doubt (Ket. 15b; Maim., *ibid.* 15:25; Tur, EH 4; Sh. Ar., EH 4:33). If, however, such a child is found in or near an exclusively Jewish place, he is assumed to be of wholly Jewish parentage; but as the identity and hence the status of such parents (whether *mamzer* or legitimate) is unknown, he is considered a "doubtful" *mamzer* (Kid. 74a; Maim., Issurei Bi'ah 15:21; Sh. Ar., EH 4:31–36). Thus, he cannot marry either a legitimate Jewess (because he may be a *mamzer*) or a female *mamzer* (because he may in fact be legitimate). However, the suspicion of *mamzerut* only attaches to him if the circumstances in which he was found were such as to cast doubt on the status of legitimacy of his parents; for instance if it was clear that they did not care for his survival. If there is any indication at all that he was abandoned out of necessity, such as hunger or in time of war, or if there are some signs of minimal concern for his welfare and future, such as his being circumcised, clothed, or abandoned in a place (like a synagogue) where he is likely to be comparatively safe from danger or any other place where people are more likely to find and take care of him, then it is assumed that his parents are of unimpeachable status and so is he. Therefore no suspicion of *mamzerut* will be attached to him (Kid. 73b; Maim. Yad, Issurei Bi'ah 15:31; Tur, EH 4; Sh. Ar., EH 4:31).

***Shetuki* (lit. "Undisclosed")**

The other case where the status of "doubtful" *mamzer* may arise is that of a child known to be born of an unmarried Jewish mother who either refuses to disclose the identity of the father or claims not to know it (Kid. 69a; Maim., Yad, Issurei Bi'ah 15:12). Since the father's status is unknown, the child is likely to be considered a "doubtful" *mamzer* (Kid. 74a; Maim., *ibid.; Arukh ha-Shulḥan*, EH 4:47). However, if the majority of the inhabitants of the district and of those who habitually visit there are Jews of unimpeachable status, it will be presumed that the father was also of such unimpeachable status and therefore no suspicion of *mamzerut* will be cast on the child (Tur, *Beit Yosef*, Bah EH 6 (at the end); Sh. Ar., EH 6:17–18; *Beit Shemu'el* 6, n. 31; but cf. Maim., Issurei Bi'ah 18:13–15; *Arukh ha-Shulḥan*, EH 4:34). The mother can always avert the suspicion of *mamzerut* being cast on her child by declaring that the father was a legitimate Jew or a gentile. In the latter case the child takes its status from the mother (i.e., he is a Jew; Kid. 74a; Maim., Yad, Issurei Bi'ah 15:12, 14; Sh. Ar., EH 4:26; *Arukh ha-Shulḥan*, EH 4:30, 31, 56).

Karaites

Halakhic problems concerning a "doubtful" *mamzer* have arisen in connection with the *Karaites because, while their form of *kiddushin* (*kiddushei-kesef* or *kiddushei bi'ah*) may be valid according to Jewish law (see *Marriage) their method of divorce does not accord with the *halakhah*, as their *get* (bill of divorce) is not in the form prescribed by the sages. Accordingly, a Karaite woman divorced by such a *get* is not properly divorced and remains a married woman (*eshet ish*) so that any child she bears to another man whom she marries on the strength of such a *get* is a *mamzer*. Since it is impossible to determine who, throughout the generations, remarried on the strength of such invalid divorce, Jewish law casts the suspicion of "doubtful" *mamzer* on all members of that community (*Beit Yosef*, EH 4 – end; *Darkhei Moshe*, EH 4, n. 14; Rema, EH 4:37; *Turei Zahav*, EH 4, n. 24; *Ba'er Heitev*, EH 4, n. 49). Some *posekim*, however, did permit marriages between Karaites and Rabbanite Jews on varying halakhic grounds and such marriages were particularly prevalent in the 11th and 12th centuries. Especially noteworthy is the permission to contract such a marriage granted by David b. Solomon ibn Abi Zimra who based his decision on the grounds that the *kiddushin* of the Karaites are also invalid according to *halakhah*, as they are deemed to have taken place without witnesses, the witnesses of the *kiddushin* being disqualified according to *halakhah* (Resp. Radbaz, nos. 73 and 796). Thus, according to him, no stigma of *mamzerut* is to be attached to a child of a woman who married, was divorced, and then married another man, all in accordance with Karaite rites only, since – in Jewish law – she is regarded as never having been married at all. On the strength of this argument and for some additional reasons arising out of the specific circumstances of the case, in 1966 a rabbinical court in the State of Israel permitted the marriage of a non-Karaite Jewess to a Karaite man by whom she had become pregnant (see also *Oẓar ha-Posekim*, EH 4, n. 175).

[Ben-Zion (Benno) Schereschewsky]

Rabbinic Efforts to Avoid Declaring *Mamzer* Status

The *mamzer* rule is intended to deter adults from violating the severe prohibitions against proscribed sexual relationships. The result, that the offspring of such illicit behavior bear the punishment of their parents' act, seems to contradict a major principle of Jewish law which punishes only the sinner (see *Punishment). The Midrash expounds on this problem (Lev. R. 32, ed. Margolis, 32:8), in its comments on the verse, "I further observed all the oppression that goes on under the sun: lo, the tears of the oppressed, and there is none to comfort them; their oppressors have power – and there is none to comfort them" (Eccl. 4:1).

The Midrash elucidates the verse as follows: "'I further observed all the oppression' – *Hanina*, the tailor, relates this verse to *mamzerim*: 'I further observed all the oppression' – These are the *mamzerim*. 'Lo, the tears of the oppressed' – [of] their mothers. [Other versions: their fathers.] They transgressed, and we banish these unfortunates? This person's father engaged in illicit sexual relations, but this person – what has he done? Of what relevance is it to him? 'There is none to comfort them,' but 'their oppressors have power' – this is the Great Sanhedrin of Israel that comes upon them with the power of the Torah and banishes them in the name of [the verse], 'no *mamzer* shall be admitted into the congregation of the Lord' (Deut. 23:3). 'There is none to comfort them' – the Holy One, blessed be He, said: I must comfort them, for in this world there is a defect in them, but in the world to come… [they are] of pure gold."

This Divine comfort in the world to come does nothing to alleviate the *mamzer*'s present condition. Thus, to reduce this injustice, the Sages developed a series of rules and presumptions so that even when there is only a remote possibility that a person is not a *mamzer*, they could legitimate him and avoid the stigma of *mamzerut* with its dire implications. Thus, a married woman, even if "it is rumored that she has been unfaithful to her husband, and everyone's tongue is wagging about her – her children are not suspected of being *mamzerim*." The explanation is the legal presumption that "most of her [the married woman's] acts of intercourse are with her husband" (Sot. 27a; Yad, Issurei Bi'ah 15:20; Sh. Ar, EH 4:15).

The Sages established an additional presumption, that a fetus could spend up to 12 months in the uterus, to enable the attribution of a child's paternity to its mother's husband. Thus, if a wife has cohabited with her husband at any time within the 12-month period prior to her child's birth, paternity is ascribed to him (Yev. 80b; Yad, *ibid.*, 15:19; Sh. Ar., EH 4:14).

Even when the mother explicitly declares that she was impregnated by someone other than her husband, her declaration is inadmissible (Sh. Ar., EH 4:29). Admittedly, in relation to a father's declaration that he is not the father of a child, the rule according to most authorities is that his declaration is valid. This claim is called "*yakir*" – based on the verb in Deut. 21:17, "He shall acknowledge [*yakir*] the first-born, the son of the hated, by giving him a double portion," i.e., the father recognizes that son as his firstborn. However, R. Simeon Kayyara of the geonic period in his *Halakhot Gedolot* limits the father's authority to grant "recognition" to determination of birthright, so that in any other case, a father's testimony rendering his son a *mamzer* is invalid: "Even if his wife is most licentious, most acts of intercourse are ascribed to the husband" (end of section 29, Hilkhot Arayot).

In addition, the Mishnah cites a tradition that "Eliyahu will not come [in the future] to declare the pure, impure – nor to declare the impure, pure; nor to distance those who are near or to draw near those who were distanced, but only to distance those drawn near by force and to draw near those distanced by force" (Eduyyot 8:7). R. Obadiah of Bertinoro interprets the citation as meaning that Eliyahu will only distance those who are publicly known to be tainted but were forcibly intermingled among the Jewish People, "but where there is a tainted individual in a particular family, but this is not publicly known, owing to the family having intermingled [into the Jewish community], Eliyahu will let it remain so and let the family retain its presumption of legitimacy." This was the basis for the Rema's ruling (Sh. Ar., EH 2:5) that if a person learns that one of the progenitors of a particular family is tainted by *mamzerut*, he may not reveal this, "but rather he should allow the presumption of their legitimacy to remain intact, for all the families that have become assimilated into Israel are legitimate in the future."

TISSUE TYPING AND THE ESTABLISHMENT OF PATERNITY. The Talmud (BB 58a) records a case where a man learns that nine of his children are *mamzerim* and only one is his real child. Before his death, the man bequeathed his property to his real child, but he did not know who the real child was. When the case was brought before R. Bena'ah, he ordered a test to determine which son, according to his characteristics, was the legitimate heir. *Sefer Ḥasidim* (section 232) discusses a method, considered scientific by the standards of the time for determining paternity. Rabbi Samuel Strashun (*Haggahot ha-Rashash*) comments on the talmudic source that R. Bena'ah refrained from employing the "scientific" test mentioned in *Sefer Ḥasidim* because by doing so he would have revealed that the other sons were *mamzerim*.

With the development of scientific means for identifying family relations by genetic testing of tissues, these principles have become more significant. Rabbinical courts have considered the validity of a scientific test that produces results that contradict juridical presumptions of Jewish law, such as the one mentioned above, that "most acts of intercourse are attributed to the husband." Rabbi Shlomo Dikhovsky (File 866/41 PDR 13, 51) rules that one must accept tissue typing intended to establish paternity for purposes of ruling on child support payments (see *Maintenance), but for establishing *mamzerut* one may disqualify reliance on tissue typing because it is not infallible (p. 60). The Rabbinical Court of Appeals has ruled in a number of cases that even for determining maintenance payments, tissue typing to establish paternity may not be used as an absolute criterion, and there is also a need for supporting evidence.

This question was brought before the Israeli Supreme Court (CA 548/78, *Sharon v. Levi*, 35 (1) PD 736 per Justice Menahem Elon), that ruled that in Israeli courts tissue typing for establishing paternity should be admitted as evidence. The court emphasized, though, "that tissue-typing would not, in every case, establish paternity." Moreover, in certain instances the court may decide not to make use of this test, when the test is liable to label a minor as "tainted," e.g., when a married woman claims that while she was married she became pregnant by someone other than her husband, and that the person by whom she became pregnant is the father of her child. If true, this statement of the married woman would result in the minor being stigmatized as a *mamzer*. In this or in similar cases involving the establishment of status, "proof provided by tissue typing is insufficient to establish paternity" (p. 748 of decision). Thus, in such cases, paternity shall be established based on the juridical presumption assumption that "most acts of intercourse are ascribed to the husband." This ruling is based on Jewish law's sensitivity to a person being stigmatized and branded by *mamzer* status and the halakhic principles of making various legal presumptions to avoid such stigmatization. Further on its ruling, the court cites some of the Jewish law sources cited above upon which it based its ruling.

In another ruling (CA 1354/92, *Attorney General v. Anon.*, PD 48(1) 711, per Justice Menahem Elon), based on these considerations, the court ruled that even when both parents give their consent to tissue typing for establishing the parenthood of a minor, such a test should not be conducted if there is risk involving the minor's best interests, inter alia raising doubts about his legitimacy, and these interests supersede the interest in investigating the truth.

The court added (pp. 739–40) that although the rabbinical courts have no reason to suspect that such testing would determine an individual's status as a *mamzer*, since only rabbinical courts have the authority to declare someone a *mamzer*, there are two reasons for discouraging such testing.

First, acceptance of such findings in a civil court might socially brand the minor, sufficient reason for prohibiting the testing. Secondly, there is no certainty that the rabbinical court will not change its stance and decide to recognize such results as sufficient to supersede the juridical presumptions assumptions cited above: "Since no one can assure us that if indeed the test is performed and if it indicates that the mother's husband is not the father of the minor, a rabbinic court would not consider the results and rule accordingly. As we have seen, the *halakhah* relies on various presumptions assumptions and fictions to preclude the tainting of a child as a *mamzer*, by reason of his married mother having been impregnated by someone other than her husband. But as we noted, according to *halakhah* as well, when it is clear that the child cannot be the offspring of the mother's husband, such as a case in which it has been proved that for 12 months there were no relations between the husband and wife, even the *halakhah*, for lack of alternative, declares the offspring a *mamzer*. Thus, several rabbinical courts have ruled against relying on tissue typing for proving paternity" (p. 740).

[Menahem Elon (2nd ed.)]

BIBLIOGRAPHY: ET, 1 (1951³), 202; 2 (1949), 71–74; *Ha-Ma'or*, 12 (1961), issue 9, p. 28 (English numbering of the same: 11 (1961), issue 7); S.M. Pasmaneck, in: HUCA, 37 (1966), 121–45; B. Schereschewsky, *Dinei Mishpaḥah* (4th ed., 1993), 352–66; M. Elon, *Ḥakikah Datit…* (1968), 178–81. **ADD. BIBLIOGRAPHY:** M. Elon, *Ha-Mishpat ha-Ivri* (1988), 1:297, 303, 352, 432, 463, 519, 543, 636, 670, 814; 2:873; 3:1405, 1464; idem, *Jewish Law* (1994), 1:352, 353, 361, 424; 2:527, 565, 631, 660, 788, 828, 997; 3:1065; 4:1674, 1739; idem, *Jewish Law (Cases and Materials)* (1999), 353–61, 549–55; idem, *Ma'mad ha-Ishah* (2005), 306, 338, 342; M. Elon and B. Lifshitz, *Mafte'aḥ ha-She'elot ve-ha-Teshuvot shel Ḥakhmei Sefarad u-Ẓefon Afrikah* (legal digest), 1 (1986), 167; B. Lifshitz and E. Shochetman, *Mafte'aḥ ha-She'elot ve-ha-Teshuvot shel Ḥakhmei Ashkenaz, Ẓarefat ve-Italyah* (legal digest) (1977), 108–9; D. Frimer, *"Kevi'at Avhut al yedei Bedikat Dam be-Mishpat ha-Ivri u-ve-Mishpat ha-Yisra'eli,"* in: *Shenaton ha-Mishpat ha-Ivri*, 5 (1978), 219; A. Steinberg, *Enẓiklopediyah Hilkhatit Refu'it*, 1 (1994), 1–6; D. Helek, *Hokhaḥat Abahut* (1987).

MAN, THE NATURE OF.

IN THE BIBLE

Names of Man

The idea of man is expressed in the Bible by a number of words that reflect various aspects of his nature. The following are the most important.

ʾADAM: collective, "men, human beings," also (in prose, with the article) "mankind," *Homo sapiens*, in distinction to other creatures (Gen. 6:7), or to God (Isa. 2:17). It is occasionally used of individuals (Neh. 2:10); etymologically it may be compared with Arabic *anạm*, "creatures," "mankind." The plural is *bene ʾadam*.

ISH: "husband," "male," "individual" (Gen. 2:23–24; 13:16; 41:33; Hos. 2:18 [16]); very often used in collective sense (Josh. 9:6). In certain passages it has the meaning of "servant" or "soldier" (I Sam. 23:3, 12; cf. the expression *ʾish ha-ʾElohim*, "man of God"). The antithesis in Psalms 49:3[2] between *bene ʾadam* and *bene ʾish* apparently contrasts "men of low degree" with "men of high degree." Its etymology is uncertain. The plural *ʾanashim* is evidently from the same root as *ʾenosh*.

ʾENOSH: mostly a collective denoting the human race. Occasionally it is used of individuals (Isa. 56:2; Jer. 20:10). In antithesis to God it connotes frail, mortal man (Isa. 51:7, 12; Ps. 90:3; Job. 28:4). The word is probably related to the Arabic *anisa*, Ugaritic *ans* ("to be friendly, social"), Aramaic *enash*, and Arabic *ʾinsām* (pl. *ʾunās*, coll. *nās*). Other cognates show that it cannot be related to Arabic *anutha*, "to be weak."

GEVER: the adult male being in contrast to women and children (Ex. 10:11; Josh. 7:14). In poetry it often has a more general sense. The stem means "to be strong, mighty."

METIM: used only in plural, "males," "men," "people" (Gen. 34:30; Deut. 2:34; 4:27). In Isaiah 3:25 it may mean "warriors." The singular occurs in Ugaritic and other cognate languages and is possibly to be seen in names like Methushael and Methuselah.

According to this terminology, man is conceived as both strong and weak, as a member of the human race and of the family unit, and as an individual.

Psychological Terms

Further insight into the nature of man is furnished by certain psychological terms that describe different aspects of the human personality. *Nefesh* can denote the essence of any living creature (Gen. 2:7); it may even be equated with the blood (Gen. 9:4; cf. Lev. 17:11). It signifies the "individual," "ego," "person" (Gen. 46:26; I Sam. 1:26; Job 16:4), and hence even "body" (Ex. 21:23). *Ruʾaḥ* "spirit," is sometimes synonymous with *nefesh* (Gen. 6:17), but is also distinguished from the latter. It represents power and energy (Ex. 35:21; Isa. 31:3) that comes to man from without; it provides the impulse to higher life and finds expression in special skill (Ex. 28:3), might, or leadership (Judg. 3:10; Isa. 11:2). *Neshamah*, "breath," is not only the vitalizing element breathed into man by God (Gen. 2:7), but the divine spirit and lamp – the soul – within him (Prov. 20:27). In contrast to these spiritual aspects of man, *basar* signifies his physical nature, the living body (Gen. 2:23, 24), and, as such, it symbolizes human frailty (Isa. 40:6).

The Bible also regards certain organs as the seat of given psychological attributes. *Lev*, the "heart," is the center of thought (Ps. 45: 2[1]), conscience (I Sam. 24:6[5]; Job 27:6), and emotion (love: Deut. 6:5; anger: Deut. 19:6; joy: Isa. 30:29; hatred: Lev. 19:17; courage: Jer. 48:41, and the like). By synecdoche, the heart represents the whole inner life of man (Gen. 6:5; Ps. 51:10; Ezek. 36:26; Prov. 4:23). *Kelayot*, the "kidneys" (in artificial "biblical" English "veins"), are likewise the source of emotion and conscience, and in conjunction with "heart" describe the fundamental character of man (Jer. 12:2; Ps. 7:10; 16:7; 26:2). *Meʿayim*, "bowels," are the seat of overpowering feelings (Isa. 16:11; 63:15; Lam. 1:20); modern versions sensibly substitute "heart" for "kidneys" or "bowels" in such contexts. *Kaved*, "liver," also means "being" (Lam. 2:11; cf. *Heart). *Raḥamim* – from *reḥem*, "womb" – means "compassion" (Deut. 13:18). *Yad*, "hand," is often used in a conative sense, indicating "power" (Deut. 2:7, 24; 32:36). Other shades of psychological significance are expressed by other parts of the body, e.g., face, eyes, ears, head, and so forth.

This extensive nomenclature points to the complexity of the human personality, but is not exhaustive. The complete picture of man's nature as envisaged by the Bible can only be seen in the full context of scriptural evidence.

Man's Origin

The key is to be found in the story of man's origin (Gen. 1:27; 2:7). He is not a descendant of the gods (as in certain pagan mythologies); the term child(ren) used with reference to man in relation to God (Deut. 14:1; Ps. 2:7) has in Scripture a metaphorical connotation. Nor is man the product (as some philosophical systems hold) of the blind forces of nature. He is the artifact of God, fashioned purposefully out of two diverse elements: his body is of the earth, but it is animated by the divine breath of life (Gen. 2:7). Yet man is not a dichotomy of body and soul (a view characteristic of Orphism and Platonism), and certainly not a trichotomy (I Thes. 5:23). His is a multifaceted unitary being – *nefesh ḥayyah*, "a living person" (Gen. 2:7). Of particular significance is the concept that all human beings, irrespective of ethnic and cultural differences, stem from two common ancestors, Adam and Eve. Humanity, despite its diversification, is essentially a single family, and men remain brothers even in the face of hate and murder (Gen. 4:9–10). To this inherent Brother-hood and equality of all, even slaves (unlike the Greek view) were no exception (Job 31:13, 15). Furthermore, the world was divinely planned to be one of creaturely peace, harmony, and understanding; man, as well as other living beings, was not to destroy his fellow creatures even for food (Gen. 1:29–30; 2:19). The permission granted to Noah to eat flesh was a sad concession to a world that had lost its original idealism (Gen. 9:3). Monogamy is clearly viewed in the creation story as the proper state of marriage. Women play a pivotal role in numerous biblical stories, and there are women prophetesses, like Deborah and Huldah.

The Image of God

However, the Bible does not merely stress the creatureliness of man. It depicts him as the peak of creation. He climaxes the ascending course of the six days' work of the Beginning. He is formed by special resolve (Gen. 1:26) and in a unique manner (Gen. 2:7), and attracts to himself three of the six occurrences of the stem *bara'* ("to create") in the creation story. However, his crowning glory is contained in the statement that he was made in the divine "image" and "likeness" (for a suggested distinction between the two words see I. Epstein, in bibl., 224), which endows him with unique worth. Man alone among the creatures is capable of sustained thought, creativity, and awareness of God; the light of God is immanent in his spirit (Prov. 20:27). Hence he is given dominion (the "image" is the symbol of the Deity's presence) over the earth (Gen. 1:26, 28) and is privileged to commune with God and enjoy His fellowship (Gen. 2–3). In the language of later rabbinic literature, he became a "partner" of the Creator (Gen. R. ed. H. Albeck (1940), 73; cf. Shab. 10a). The dualism of man's status and significance within the unified framework of his psychophysical being is given unmatched expression by the Psalmist: "What is man that Thou art mindful of him… Yet Thou hast made him little less than the angels" (literally, "God-like beings"; 8:4–5).

Free Will

There is still another aspect of the divine image reflected in man, which plays a crucial role in the profound parable of the Garden of Eden. In a supreme act of self-limitation the Absolute God gave man freedom of moral choice. He could will to do right or wrong, to obey or disobey his Maker. It was heaven's greatest gift to man: he was not to be an automaton. However, the immediate consequences were calamitous. Man rebelled against the Creator; he introduced disharmony into the universal harmony. Sin was born and in turn begot suffering and death. History had begun. Israel was the first people to evince a sense of the historic.

While the Bible is unequivocal in its assertion of the reality of human responsibility for evil (Eccles. 7:29) and in condemning sin trenchantly as estrangement from and treason against God (this is the meaning of the story of Eden), it is no less emphatic in its affirmation of God's grace (Ps. 103:13–16) and readiness to forgive (Num. 14:20; Jer. 33:8). Sin is never final. It is punished, or rather punishes itself. However, retribution is part of the divine redemptive process. It helps man to seek atonement, which the divine love never fails to vouchsafe (Ezek. 33:11).

The road of redemption, however, is hard and long. Outside the Garden of Eden man's iniquity reaches new depths. Brotherhood as well as "sonship" are destroyed. Cain's example was widely imitated (Gen. 6:11). It almost seemed that the making of man was a divine error (Gen. 5–6), which only the Flood could expunge. At this point, however, a new providential principle manifests itself – the elective factor. The family of Noah is chosen from a doomed generation to be saved and to save the world. Later Abraham is elected to be a source of blessing to all mankind (Gen. 12:3). Israel, the seed of Abraham, were chosen to be "a kingdom of priests and holy nation" (Ex. 19:6). Though themselves far from perfect (Deut. 9:5), they were destined to become a light to the world (Isa. 60:3), illuminating the way of ethical and spiritual truth. To this end God made a covenant with Israel at Sinai (Deut. 5:2), which found detailed expression in the Torah. Religious and secular precepts are inextricably intermingled in the Law, for human life is a unity and must be dedicated to God's will in all its diversified aspects. God is served in the righteousness of human relationships – in love between man and man, which reflects God's image – as well as in divine worship. When the "image" is wronged, religious service becomes an abomination (Isa. 1:13–17). The path toward God is further delineated and interpreted by the Prophets, and even by figures (like Abraham, and Job, and some of Psalmists) who question God's moral government of the world. Revelation – the word of God understood in its broadest sense – is the great antidote to sin, leading man to repentance and regeneration. The relevance of this biblical teaching is not confined to Israel. In a deep sense, the Bible tells the story of Everyman in all generations. Even when Israel is the focal point of the Bible's concern, the universal concept of mankind is never ignored (Amos 9:7; Isa. 19:24–25). Israel's significance derives from its relationship to all humanity, whose significance, in turn, flows from man's relation to God. History is thus seen as the moral and spiritual drama of the human species.

The Afterlife

The beginning of that drama, with its hope and tragedy, was enacted in Eden. Inevitably the question arises: Where will the denouement take place? Has human life a divinely designed goal? Later Jewish theology, elaborated in apocryphal and rabbinic literature, answers these questions (solving at the same time the problem of theodicy) on the individual level, by postulating the belief in the afterlife. There the disembodied soul is judged, the wicked are condemned, and the righteous are rewarded with eternal bliss. This doctrine is unknown to Scripture. There is an unmistakable finality about the biblical conception of death (Ps. 146:4; Job 7:9; Isa. 38:18). The Bible is primarily concerned with the world; it seeks heaven upon earth in the form of the kingdom of God (Zech. 14:1), and continued life in descendants rather than in personal immortality (II Sam. 7:12). Nevertheless death does not mark the complete extinction of existence. The dead continue to live a shadowy, ghostlike existence in Sheol, a region of darkness and silence deep within the recesses of the earth. Yet the dead are not without consciousness (I Sam. 28: 15ff.; Isa. 14:9ff.), nor beyond God's judgment (Ps. 139:8). Two holy men escaped death altogether: Enoch (Gen. 5:24) and Elijah (II Kings 2:11). In Job there is a yearning for continued life after death (14:13ff.; 19:26); in certain psalms the definite hope is expressed that death will not end the human fellowship with God (49:16; 73:24ff.). Whether resurrection is envisaged in Isa. 26:19ff. is a matter of exegesis, but it is certainly envisaged in Daniel 12:2. The preexistence of the soul is first taught in the Apocrypha (Wisd. 8:19ff.), but Jeremiah was "a thought of God" (B. Duhm) before ever he was formed in the womb (Jer. 1:5). Thus the Bible lacks a definite theology of the afterlife, and belief in resurrection is still vague and inchoate. Yet Scripture contains undoubted intimations of immortality, on which future epochs built their religious doctrines.

The End of Days

The true goal of history, however, is to be sought in "the end of days." It will be the age of regeneration, when the work of creation will be completed in accordance with God's original plan. Man and God, and man and man, will be reconciled. The treason man perpetrated in the Garden of Eden will be transmuted into universal voluntary obedience to God's will, and the crime of Cain will be atoned for in a state of international peace and brotherhood (Isa. 2:2–4; Micah 4:1–5). The immature knowledge man acquired from the forbidden fruit will give way to a higher wisdom. For inherently knowledge is good (Prov. 8); it is man's unwise use of it that vitiates it (Eccl. 1:18). A new earth and a new heaven will issue from the new heart and spirit of man (Isa. 65:17; Ezek. 36:26), and human communion with God will be restored (Joel 3:1–2). The Garden of Eden will, as it were, become worldwide, and the pristine glory of the reflected image of God in man will be renewed. The end of days is undated. It is an elusive horizon; yet its advent remains a prophetic certitude.

[Israel Abrahams]

IN RABBINIC THOUGHT

The Physical Nature of Man

The process of human gestation, and especially the preservation of the embryo, prompted the sages to the observation that these were evidence of both God's skill and solicitude in the fashioning of man (Ber. 10a; Nid. 31a; Lev. R. 14:3, 4; 15:2, 3; 34:3). The fact that every hair of man's head is fed through a separate root is cited as further evidence (BB 16a). Man receives five parts of his body from each of his parents, and ten parts from God. From his father, he receives bones, veins, nails, brain, and the white of the eye; from his mother, skin, flesh, blood, hair, and the pupil of the eye. To his formation, God contributes breath, soul, light of countenance, sight, hearing, speech, touch, sense, insight, and understanding. Hence, the rabbinic saying that there are three partners in man – his father and mother and God (Kid. 30b; Nid. 31a; TJ, Kil. 8:3, 31c; Eccl. R. 5:10, 2). A late Midrash (Mss. *Midrash ha-Ḥefeẓ*) describes the human body as possessing ten orifices, including the navel. The marvel is, the Midrash continues, that when the child is in the embryonic state, the navel is open and the other orifices are closed but, when it issues from the womb, the navel is closed and the other orifices are opened.

In the totality of his physical structure, man constitutes a microcosm (see *Microcosm and Macrocosm). An elaborate parallel, covering 30 items, is drawn between the various components of the human body and similar features in the physical world (ARN[1]:31). A hardly less complex parallel is found to exist between the organs of the human body and the structure and vessels of the Tabernacle (Mid. Tadshe, Beit ha-Midrash, Jellinek, vol. 3, 175f.; cf. the New Testament denomination of the human body as a tabernacle, II Cor. 5:1, 4; II Pet. 1:13, 14). A simpler summation of man's physical being is deciphered in the word *adam* ("man") as being an acronym (**notarikon*) for "dust" (*efer*), "blood" (*dam*) and "gall" (*marah*; Sot. 5a). They give a remarkably accurate enumeration of the 248 organs of the human body (Oho. 1:8). It may be fairly said that the rabbinic reflection on the complex mechanism of man's physical structure served as occasion for admiring reverence for the skill and wisdom with which God created him. Indeed, its unknown aspects suggested the argument that if man does not know his own body, he certainly cannot fathom God's acts (San. 39a). But for all its marvelous mechanism, it is destined, save for the soul, to return to the earth from which it originally came. Only one tiny bone remains indestructible and, in the time of resurrection, will serve as the nucleus out of which the body will be restored (Gen. R. 28:3; Eccl. R. 12:5; see **Luz of the Spine*).

Nowhere in rabbinic literature is there any denigration of the human body so characteristic of contemporary Platonic, Stoic, and Gnostic thought. On the contrary, since even the body is conceived as having been created in the image of God, man is duty bound to honor it by maintaining it in a state of cleanliness. No less an authority than *Hillel termed such action a religious duty (Lev. R. 34:3).

Character

Since Genesis describes Adam as having been both created in God's image (1:27) and formed out of the dust of the earth (2:7), the sages declare that man possesses both heavenly and earthly qualities. In four respects, he is said to resemble the animals and the angels respectively. Like the angels, he possesses the power of speech, intelligence, upright posture, and glance of the eye. In his physical aspects, he resembles the animals (Gen. R. 12:8; 14:3). Indeed, God created man because he was not completely satisfied with either the angels or the animals. The former failed to satisfy him because they lacked the evil inclination. The animals, on the other hand, lacked the good inclination. God therefore created man, who possesses both a good and evil inclination and is confronted with the need to exercise free will. This is the origin of the ambivalent character of man. If he pursues evil, he is likened to an animal; if he chooses the good, he is likened to an angel (Gen. R. 14:3, 4). The contradictory nature of man is highlighted by the legend describing the sharp difference of opinion evoked by God's taking counsel with the angels as to whether or not man should be created. The angels that favored his creation contended that man would be affectionate and a doer of justice. Those who opposed his creation claimed that he would be quarrelsome and riddled with falsehood (Gen. R. 8:3–9; in the qualities of lovingkindness, righteousness, peace, and truth are hypostatized).

Man's moral ambivalence derives from the two inclinations within him: the good inclination (*yeẓer tov*) and the evil inclination (*yeẓer ra*) (see Inclination, *Good and Evil). The fact of human individuality exhibits God's power, for although all men are cast from the same mold since all are descendants of Adam, no two men are alike (Sanh. 4:5). Their physical differences are to be noted in their voice, taste, and appearance (ARN[1] 4).

In their attitude toward possessions, men fall into four distinct categories, ranging from the average to the wicked and the saint (Avot 5:10). It is assumed, as a legal principle, that all men become excited when their property is at stake (Shab. 117b, 153a). This concept is further reflected in the dictum that every artisan is hostile toward his fellow craftsmen (Gen. R. 19:6). It is assumed further, as a matter of legal principle, that in money matters no man is likely to regard himself as culpable (Ket. 105b). The rabbis look askance at him who has an excess of material things. They conclude that such a situation can only produce deplorable moral consequences (Tosef., Sot. 3:6; Ber. 32a; Sanh. 108a; Gen. R. 26:5; 28:6). Indeed, when a man is poor, he can be relied upon to have trust in God. Riches incline him to trust in his money and thus displace his piety (Tanḥ. Naso 28). For all the rabbinic recognition of the powerful influence of the economic motive on human conduct, a certain basic honesty is assumed as characteristic of all men. Hence, the assumption is made that a man makes no legal monetary claim unless there is some substance to it (Shevu. 40b), and that a man is not brazen as to deny outright the existence of his debt in the presence of his creditor (BM 3a). A man's basic character is recognizable by his drinking (how he behaves when under the influence of liquor), by his rectitude in financial transactions (Rashi's interpretation) and by his anger (to what extent he is able to control his temper). To this generalization, some add, also by his laughter (his good humor; Eruv. 65b).

Man and Woman

The difference in the origin of man and woman described in Genesis served the sages as points d'appui for their observations on the contrast between the character and psychology of man and woman. The latter, having been fashioned from a more durable substance (man's rib-bone) than man (dust of the earth), can more readily withstand disagreeable circumstances and possesses greater inurement to pain (Tanḥ. Toledot 8). A woman, moreover, is blessed with greater native intelligence (instinct?; Nid. 45b). Whose intelligence matures sooner is a matter of opinion (*ibid.*). A man is more hospitable towards guests and more generous than a woman (Sif. Num. Shlaḥ 100). An aggrieved man is more readily reconcilable than a woman (Nid. 31b). Peculiarly characteristic of woman is her proclivity to tears (BM 59a) and an inordinate curiosity (Toh. 7:9). At the time of her creation, God, anticipating woman's faults, sought to obviate them. He knew that she would be arrogant, wanton-eyed, an eavesdropper, a tattler, a meddler, and a gadabout. Hence, he fashioned her from a chaste part of man's body that is free of these faults (Gen. R. 18:2; 45:5).

Destiny

The phenomena experienced in the theophany afforded the prophet Elijah (I Kings 19:11–12) are interpreted as symbolic of the four worlds through which man must pass. The wind symbolizes the evanescent quality of the life of this world. The earthquake represents the day of death, since on it man quakes and trembles. Fire is the symbol of man's judgment in Gehenna. The "still small voice" is the Last Judgment (Tanḥ. Pekudei 3). A more elaborate articulation of the worlds (i.e., stages) through which man passes in this life describes seven distinct phases. Each phase is marked by its own characteristics, few of which are flattering (*ibid.*). All of life is clouded over by uncertainty, for a man goes on his way and knows not whether good or evil awaits him (Tan. Toledot 12). A trace of a tragic view of human destiny is to be discerned in a few rabbinic statements. Throughout his lifetime, man is caught in the impossible dilemma of either obeying his Creator (*yoẓer*) or his evil inclination (*yeẓer*). Whatever he chooses, he finds himself perpetually at odds with the other (Ber. 61a–b). Though man enters and leaves the world surrounded by love, both his entrance and exit are marked by sighing and weeping (Eccl. R. 5). The vanity of human ambition is expressed in the observation that man comes into the world with his fists clenched, as if to say, "I will grasp the whole world"; he leaves with palms outstretched, as if to say, "See what I am carrying away" (*ibid.*). Wherever man dies, there the earth will accept him, for the first man was created by God from dust gathered from the four corners of the earth (San. 38a–b; Tan. Pekude 3). Whether it were better for man to have been born or not to have been born is the subject of a prolonged controversy between the schools of Shammai and Hillel. The debate terminates with the decision that it would have been better for man never to have been born. But once having entered the world, "let him scrutinize his deeds" (Er. 13b). The pessimistic conclusion is unique and has no parallel in rabbinic literature. (Talmudic commentators have sought to temper it by interpretation. See Maharsha to Mak. 23b, and Urbach, in bibliography, pp. 224–6.)

Significance

Rabbinic thought considers all creation as having been called into being for the sake of man (Gen. R. 8:3–9); he is the only creature formed directly by the hand of God (Alphabet of R. Akiva 59); he was created last because he was to have dominion over all (Gen. R. 19:6). One man is worth the whole of creation (ARN1 31). R. Akiva is moved to exclaim: "Beloved is man who was created in the image (of God); still greater was the love in that it was made known to him that he was created in the image of God" (Avot 3:15). Man's likeness to God, a doctrine meant to emphasize the singular position of man in the world, is a common doctrine in rabbinic Judaism and occurs in a wide variety of contexts. (However, one meets the occasional notion that man was created in the image of the angels and not in that of God; (Gen. R. 14:3; 21:5). (See Ginzberg, op. cit. in bibliography, vol. 5, p. 65, note 6 for a proposed explanation of this extraordinary view.) Man's superiority over the angels is to be found in his superior wisdom (Num. R. 19:3) and in his possession of free will (Gen. R. 21:5). In poetic fashion, man is termed God's candle in the world (Tan. B. Gen. 28).

[Theodore Friedman]

BIBLIOGRAPHY: I. Epstein, *The Faith of Judaism* (1954); Kaufmann Y., Toledot; U. Cassuto, *From Adam to Noah* (1961); N.W. Porteous, in: IDB, 3 (1962), s.v. (incl. bibl.); R. Gordis, *The Book of God and Man* (1965). IN RABBINIC THOUGHT: S. Schechter, *Some Aspects of Rabbinic Theology* (1923), ch. 15; W. Hirsch, *Rabbinic Psychology* (1947); G.F. Moore, *Judaism in the First Centuries of the Christian Era*, 3 vols. (1927–40), index, s.v. *Man*; Ginzberg, Legends, index, s.v. *Man*; E. Urbach, *Ḥazal* (1969), 190–226; H. Malter, in: JQR, 2 (1911/12), 453f.

MANĀKHAH, city in *Yemen amid the high mountains of Ḥarāz (2200 m), 90 km S.W. of *Sanʿa, on the way to *Ḥudaydah. Manākhah was a prominent commercial center and Jews from the surrounding villages would gather together on the weekly market day there, when the local Jews would also abandon their workshops and engage in trading. The Jewish community of Manākhah, one of the largest in Yemen, actually started to gain importance and size in the 1850s through Jews who had fled from *Sanʿa owing to the worsening political situation, which explains the fact that the way of life in Manākhah was the same as in Sanʿa. In the last generation it numbered 600 Jews. It was also the richest Jewish community in Yemen, excluding *Aden. Many of the Jews were businessmen, in import and export; some of them monopolized the coffee trade and even owned land. Nevertheless, they were careful to maintain an external appearance of abject poverty, and their poor houses had the appearance of prisons. In this way the local Jews could maintain good relations with the Muslims. Others were craftsmen: gold- and silversmiths, ironsmiths, carpenters, and tanners. The Jews lived in their separate walled-off neighborhood and had three synagogues. There was a local three-judge *bet din*, serving as a spiritual center for the Jewish population of nearby and far-off towns and villages, such as Muḍmār, Jirwāḥ, and Hawzān. The authority of the temporal leader (*ʿāqil*), appointed and paid by the Muslim government, was usually stronger than that of the chief rabbi. Some of the local Jewish families took part in the smuggling of Jewish orphans from Sanʿa to the Holy Land.

BIBLIOGRAPHY: J. Saphir, *Even Sappir* (1886), 70; K. Rathjens and H. Wissmann, *Landeskundliche Ergebnisse* (1934), 67–73; Y. Tobi, "The Jewish Community in Yemen," in: Y. Tobi, *Moreshet Yehudei Teiman* (1977), 69–72.

[Yosef Tobi (2nd ed.)]

MANARAH (Heb. מְנָרָה; derived from the Ar. al-Manara; for a time the Hebrew name Ramim, "heights," was used), kibbutz near the Israel-Lebanese border on the Naphtali Ridge of Upper Galilee, affiliated with Ha-Kibbutz ha-Me'uḥad. Its founding in 1943 by pioneers from Germany and Israel-born youth was a bold enterprise. The settlers had to climb a 5 mi. (8 km.), steep footpath to reach the site – 2,990 ft. (920 m.) above sea level – and withstand isolation in a place where the winter is snowy and stormy, and where no water sources are present in summer. In the Israel *War of Independence (1948), the settlers held out under enemy siege. In violation of the cease-fire arrangements the surrounding positions were occupied by irregular Arab forces commanded by Fawzī al-Qāuqjī (October 1948). The area and all of Galilee were liberated by Israel's Operation Ḥiram. In the first years after 1948 the water problem was solved when a pumping installation was built to bring water from the Einan Springs in the Ḥuleh Valley 2600 ft. (800 m.) below. A highway was paved and the kibbutz, in addition to its hill farming (mainly deciduous fruit), received fields and carp ponds in the valley. Manarah also had a metal factory for electricity grids and control panels, an amplifier rental service, guest rooms, and a big, modern chicken run. In 2002 its population was 248. The crusader castle ruins of Hūnīn (Chasteau Neuf) are located nearby.

WEBSITE: www.manara.co.il.

[Efraim Orni]

MANASSEH (Heb. מְנַשֶּׁה), elder son of *Joseph and the name of one of the 12 tribes of Israel. Manasseh was born to Joseph in Egypt by *Asenath, daughter of Poti-Phera (Gen. 41:50–51). The name is said to be symbolic of Joseph's turn of fortune. Manasseh is distinguished by several traditional historical peculiarities. Whereas ten of the tribes (or 11 if Levi is included) are conceived as immediate sons of Jacob, Manasseh and *Ephraim are presented as the sons of Joseph and, thus, as the grandsons of Jacob. This feature of the tradition is in part a device to retain the number 12 as normative for the tribal roster. There are in fact two basic versions of the tribal roster:

(1) the enumeration which counts Joseph as one tribe and includes Levi and

(2) the enumeration which subdivides Joseph into Ephraim and Manasseh and omits Levi. It is commonly believed that the former is the older reckoning dating to the time when Joseph was still a single tribal entity and when Levi was as yet a secular tribe. The second is assumed to stem from a later period when Joseph broke into two segments and Levi became a priestly tribe and was dropped from the tribal roster. However, it may also be argued that the tribal league of 12 members did not become the normative until David made the old tribes into administrative subdistricts of his kingdom, in which case the version including Ephraim and Manasseh was older. Once the kingdom divided after Solomon's reign, the 12-fold tribal roster became a sacral tradition and Levi had to be included for religious reasons. To retain the number 12, Ephraim and Manasseh were coalesced under the heading

Joseph. This bracketing of Ephraim and Manasseh as Joseph within the 12-tribe roster points, however, to an older affinity between the two tribes reflected in some texts (e.g., Gen. 41:50–52; 48:8–22; Deut. 33:13–17; Josh. 17: 14–18). Ephraim and Manasseh were geographically contiguous, occupying the fertile mountains and small plains extending northward from Bethel to the plain of Jezreel in the region later to be known as Samaria. Manasseh lay to the north of Ephraim. The relationship between the two tribes is portrayed in the Bible as ethnic; they migrated into the central highlands as one people who later divided under the decentralizing pressure of settlement in rather different geographical-agricultural and cultural-political zones. It is, however, conjectured by some scholars that they were ethnically distinct and had entered the land separately, but were closely linked in a common religious conversion. The decision on this point depends largely on whether Ephraim and Manasseh are seen as Exodus tribes or are regarded as early converts to the religion brought to them by Levi or other tribes. The rivalry and struggle for priority between Manasseh and Ephraim is strongly attested to in the traditions. In most tribal lists Ephraim is named first, which reflects its political predominance as epitomized in the leadership of Ephraimites (e.g., Joshua and Jeroboam I). By contrast, some lists name Manasseh first (Num. 26:28–37), which accords with the genealogical claim that Manasseh was the firstborn of Joseph (Gen. 41:50–52). This discrepancy between Ephraim's genealogical subordination and its historical dominance has been harmonized by inserting an etiology that accounts for the greater blessing which Jacob gave to Ephraim (Gen. 48:17–20). That Manasseh is sometimes represented as having priority probably points to its larger territory and population, to the prominence of the Manassite city of Shechem, and to the tribe's political leadership under Gideon.

Yet another traditional historical peculiarity of Manasseh is its stylization as a "half-tribe" in the central highlands west of Jordan and as a "half-tribe" in the highlands east of Jordan. It appears that colonists from the Manassite holdings in the Samarian highlands crossed the Jordan eastward and settled on the slopes of the Gilead Mountains from the Jabbok River northward to the Sea of Galilee. Since the biblical account of the conquest tradition pictured all Israel as entering the Land of Canaan from the east as a unit, the presence of Israelites in Transjordan is explained by an initial occupation of Transjordan by two and a half tribes: Reuben, Gad, and the half-tribe of Manasseh (Num. 32). There are scholars, however, who believe that all these Transjordan settlements were the result of movements from the western highlands eastward across the Jordan. Historically, the Transjordan settlement was relatively light and always tenuous prior to the monarchy; even under the monarchy it was precarious except when a strong king secured the frontiers against the Arameans, Ammonites, and Moabites. The colonization of Transjordan by Manassites was matched by Ephraimite colonization in the same region (Judg. 12:4; II Sam. 18:6), and it is strongly suspected that Reuben and Gad were either offshoots of more established tribes in

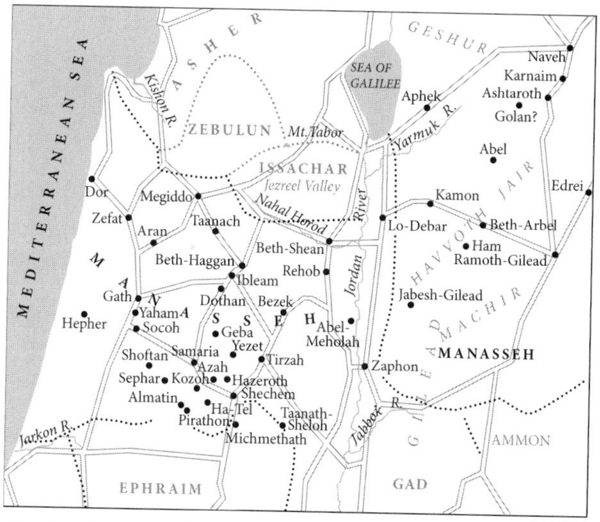

Territory of the tribe of Manasseh. After Y. Aharoni in Lexicon Biblicum, *Dvir Co. Ltd, Tel Aviv, 1965.*

the western highlands or transplants of reduced or decimated tribes originally located in cis-Jordan. That Manasseh alone was credited with territory on both sides of the Jordan is probably an index of its greater success in colonization.

Another name for Manasseh was Machir (Judg. 5:14). Machir elsewhere is credited as a major clan within Manasseh, the latter's "firstborn" and "the father of Gilead" (Gen. 50:23; Josh. 17:1). If Machir was the original name of the tribe, Manasseh would have been introduced once colonization had extended the group holdings and the need was felt for a more inclusive term. The adoption of the term Manasseh would probably also have been a function of the desire to relate the tribe more closely to Ephraim, the two being regarded as "sons of Joseph."

Manasseh's territorial holdings as described in Joshua 17 and in Judges 1:27–28 appear in an account of the tribal allotments at the time of the Conquest, which some exegetes regard as an incomplete and mutilated sketch of the tribal administrative subdistricts of David's kingdom. The boundary of Manasseh with Ephraim to the south is given with some precision. The borders with Issachar and Asher to the north have been obscured as a result of redaction of the sources. Similar uncertainty exists in delimiting the Transjordan holdings of Manasseh in relation to Gad. It is doubtful whether, before the time of David, Manasseh settled the coastal plain on the west, the Carmel highlands on the northwest, the plain of Jezreel to the north, or the plain of Beth-Shean on the northeast. In Transjordan, Manassite colonization, it is supposed, hardly penetrated beyond the crest of the Gilead Mountain Range and perhaps some distance up the Jabbok Valley. The major settlements in west Manasseh, prior to the expansion under David, were Shechem, Dothan, Tirzah, Thebez, Arumah, Ophrah, Bezek, and Arubboth. In east Manasseh the major towns were Jabesh-Gilead and Abel-Meholah. The settlements of Succoth, Penuel, Zarethan, and Zaphon, located in or around the Jabbok Valley and its juncture with the Jordan, may also have been Manassite, although some of them are attributed to Gad. Among the clans of Manasseh (Josh. 17:2–3) are Canaanite cities, such as Shechem, some of which probably remained non-Israelite down to David's time, even though surrounded by Israelites. The approximate position of several of the clans in the west Jordan highlands can be plotted on the basis of their occurrence as place names in the Samaria Ostraca (Albiezer, [A]sriel, Helek, Hoglah, Noah, Shechem, Shemida).

[Norman K. Gottwald]

In the Aggadah

Manasseh emerges in the *aggadah* as his father's right-hand man. He was sent by Joseph to spy on his brothers after they entered Egypt (Tanḥ. B., Gen. 202). He is identified as the interpreter between Joseph and his brothers (Gen. 42:23) when his father feigned ignorance of Hebrew (Gen. R. 91:8), and it was he who overcame Simeon despite his martial prowess and cast him into prison (Tanḥ, Va-Yiggash, 4). As the steward of his father's house, Manasseh also prepared the repast for Joseph's brothers (Tar. Pseudo-Jon. Gen. 43:16), and was later sent to search the sacks for the silver cup (Tanḥ. B., Gen. 197). On the flag of the tribe of Manasseh was embroidered a wild ox, an allusion to Deuteronomy 33:17, which refers to Gideon (Judg. 6:11), a descendant of Manasseh (Num. R. 2:7).

For the relationship between Ephraim and Manasseh see *Ephraim in the *Aggadah.*

BIBLIOGRAPHY: EM, 5 (1968), 45–51 (incl. bibl.); M. Noth, in: PJB, 37 (1941), 50–101; idem, in: ZAW, 60 (1944), 11–57; J. Simons, in: PEQ, 79 (1947), 27–39; idem, in: *Orientalia Neerlandica* (1948), 190–215; M. Naor, *Ha-Mikra ve-ha-Areẓ*, 1 (1952), 145–6; 2 (1954), 63–68; E. Danelius, in: PEQ, 89 (1957), 55–67; 90 (1958), 32–43; E. Jenni, in: ZDPV, 74 (1958), 35–40; W. Phythian-Adams, in: PEQ, 61 (1929), 228–41; IDB, 3 (1962), 252–4; 4 (1962), 705; Aharoni, Land, index; Z. Kallai, *Naḥalot Shivtei Yisrael* (1967), 142–51, 248–54, 259, 375ff. IN THE AGGADAH: Ginzberg, Legends, index.

MANASSEH (Heb. מְנַשֶּׁה; perhaps "one who causes [an earlier deceased, child] to be forgotten"), king of Judah (698–643 B.C.E.), son of *Hezekiah. Manasseh ascended the throne at the age of 12 and reigned for 55 years (II Kings 21:1). In those years Assyrian power reached its pinnacle; Manasseh's reign coincided with more than half of Sennacherib's (705–681 B.C.E.), all of Esarhaddon's (680–669), and most of Ashurbanipal's (668–627). During most of Manasseh's reign, Judah was a submissive dependent of Assyria. Manasseh is mentioned, together with 22 kings of Syria, Palestine, and Cyprus, in one of Esarhaddon's inscriptions relating that he imposed forced labor upon them, making them convey timber and stones for the construction of his palace in Nineveh (Pritchard, Texts, 291). Most of these kings, including Manasseh, are also mentioned in one of Ashurbanipal's inscriptions which recounts that their armies accompanied him to Egypt in his campaign against *Tirhakah (687; Pritchard, Texts, 294). Several scholars hold that part of Manasseh's army remained in Egypt as a garrison, and that they were the first inhabitants of the Jewish settlement in *Elephantine. Further evidence of Judah's subordination to Assyria is found in a fragment of an inscription from the period between Sargon and Esarhaddon, which lists the tribute of Judah after that of Ammon and Moab, the amount of the former being smaller than that of the latter. This probably relates to the period after *Sennacherib's campaign in Judah, when the country was impoverished.

The Book of Kings does not mention any political events during Manasseh's reign, but in Chronicles it is stated that, because he did what was displeasing to the Lord, the Lord caused the Assyrian officers to oppose him and put him in chains, transporting him to Babylon, where he submitted to God's will and was returned to Jerusalem and his throne (II Chron. 33:10–13). To the degree that there is any historical validity to the story, the imprisonment was probably brought about by an attempted revolt against Assyria, and not by foreign religious practices, which would be a sign of submission to Assyria. The tradition that he was transported to Babylon appears strange, unless the Assyrian king happened to be there in response to a Babylonian revolt. It is likely that Manasseh was involved in the revolts which broke out against Assyria at the time of Shamash-shumukîn's revolt in Babylon against his brother Ashurbanipal (668–631). Further evidence of Manasseh's efforts to overthrow Assyrian domination may be seen in the fortification of Jerusalem and his appointing of officers over all the walled cities in Judah (II Chron. 33:14), although these events may refer to a later period. The account of Manasseh's return from imprisonment to the throne is given credence by the policy of Ashurbanipal, who, having exiled rebellious Egyptian princes to Assyria, came to favor Neco (671–663), the father of Psammetichus I, and returned him to Egypt as vassal ruler.

Manasseh abolished the religious reforms of his father Hezekiah and introduced alien rites into the Temple (II Kings 21:3). It has been argued that this course was forced upon him by the Assyrian overlords. Ashurbanipal imposed religious duties upon several Chaldean states in southern Mesopotamia after crushing their attempted revolt. (However, his actions in defeated territories need not be conclusive evidence concerning his policies in lands ruled by his vassals. (For a nuanced discussion, see Cogan 1993). It is significant, though, that none of the negative cultic activities attributed to Manasseh is Assyrian. Instead it appears that whereas Hezekiah had been an adherent of the "Yahweh-alone" party (Smith), Manasseh supported the majority position that ignoring other gods with a long history of worship in Israel was perilous. Indeed, the severe territorial losses suffered by Hezekiah could have been attributed to his excessive zeal for monolatry, just as the fall of Judah in 586 was attributed to Josiah's reforms by the exiled Judahites in Jeremiah 44 (Cogan). The abolition of Hezekiah's reforms was therefore part of the internal struggle in Judah between those who had supported a policy of acceptance of the ancient native cults and perhaps some newer Syro-Palestinian ones dating from the time of Ahaz, and the devout circles around the prophets. It was a ruthless struggle, and

Manasseh is described as having shed "very much innocent blood …" (II Kings 21:16). According to II Chronicles 33:12ff., Manasseh fully repented upon his return from Babylon, but this does not agree with II Kings 21:16, which relates that he died without repenting. It appears unlikely that the destruction of Jerusalem would have been so emphatically attributed to the sins of Manasseh had he completely repented as described in Chronicles.

[Jacob Liver / S. David Sperling (2nd ed.)]

In the Aggadah

Manasseh's mother was the daughter of the prophet Isaiah, and married King Hezekiah after his miraculous recovery (Ber. 10a). Manasseh and his brother Rab-Shakeh soon showed their total dissimilarity from their parents. Once, when Hezekiah was carrying his two sons on his shoulders to the schoolhouse, he overheard their conversation. One said, "Our father's bald head might do well for frying fish." The other rejoined, "It would be good for offering sacrifices to idols." Enraged by these words, Hezekiah threw his sons to the ground. Rab-Shakeh was killed by the fall, but Manasseh escaped unhurt (Dik. Sof., Ber. 10a). His name is derived from נשה (*nashah*; "he forgot"), in that he forgot his God and indulged in idolatry, murder, and other abominable acts (Sanh. 102b). After his father's death, Manasseh began to worship idols. He destroyed the altar and set up an idol with four faces, copied from the four figures on the divine throne of Ezekiel, so that from whatever direction a man entered the Temple he saw a face of the idol (Sanh. 103b). Manasseh also made another idolatrous image so heavy that it required 1,000 men to carry it. New bearers were employed daily because the king had each group executed at the end of the day's work (*ibid.*). He expunged the name of God from the Scriptures (*ibid.*) and delivered public lectures whose sole purpose was to ridicule the Torah (Sanh. 99b). He also committed incest by violating his sister (Sanh. 103b).

Manasseh sat in judgment on his own grandfather, Isaiah, and condemned him to death. The indictment against him was that his prophecies contradicted the teachings of Moses. Isaiah refused to defend himself, knowing that his efforts would be of no avail and preferring that his grandson act out of ignorance rather than from wickedness. He fled for safety and when he pronounced the Ineffable Name a cedar tree swallowed him up. Manasseh ordered that the tree be sawn in two, causing the prophet's death (Yev. 49b). Manasseh was carried off to Babylon in the 22nd year of his reign (SOR 24) and there placed in a heated oven. In his torture, he prayed in vain to the idols he had formerly worshiped, and at last besought the God of his fathers. The angels pleaded with the Almighty not to accept his penance. The plea was not accepted, God saying, "If I do not accept him I will be closing the door of repentance in the face of all repentant sinners." Immediately a wind arose and carried Manasseh back to Jerusalem (TJ, Sanh. 10:2, 28c).

Manasseh is included among those who have no share in the world to come. Despite his restoration to Jerusalem, the rabbis felt that he had forfeited eternal life because of his previous sins. R. Judah, however, held that he was also restored to his portion in paradise (Sanh. 10:2). Manasseh possessed a profound knowledge of the Torah and could interpret Leviticus in 55 different ways (Sanh. 103b). He justified his actions by pointing to the corrupt behavior of his times. R. Ashi once announced a lecture about him, saying, "Tomorrow, I shall speak about our colleague, Manasseh." That night, the king appeared to Ashi in a dream and asked him a ritual question which Ashi could not answer. Manasseh then revealed the solution to him. Amazed by the king's scholarship, R. Ashi asked why one so erudite had worshiped idols. Manasseh answered, "Had you lived at my time, you would have caught hold of the hem of my garment and sped after me" (Sanh. 102b).

BIBLIOGRAPHY: Bright, Hist, 271–99; Nielsen, in: *Fourth World Congress of Jewish Studies*, 1 (1967), 103–6; EM, 5 (1968), 41–45 (incl. bibl.); Ginzberg, Legends, 4 (1947⁴), 277–81; 6 (1946), 370–6. **ADD. BIBLIOGRAPY:** M. Smith, *Palestinian Parties and Politics that Shaped the Old Testament* (1971); M. Cogan, *Imperialism and Religion* (1974); M. Cogan and H. Tadmor, *II Kings* (AB; 1988), 264–73; idem, in: JBL 112 (1993), 403–14; H. Spieckermann, *Juda unter Assur in der Sargonidenzeit* (1982); C. Evans, in: ABD IV, 496–99; S. Japhet, *I & II Chronicles* (1993), 999–1014.

MANASSEH, PRAYER OF, brief penitential psalm incorporated among the books of the *Apocrypha. According to II Chronicles 33:11ff. Manasseh, king of Judah, repented his sins when he was taken to Babylonia in fetters (cf. also II Baruch 64:8). Shortly before the beginning of the Christian Era, an unknown author drew up a prayer appropriate for the occasion. Its style is comparatively simple and clear, concise and expressive, breathing throughout a spirit of deep and genuine religious piety. Its contents may be summarized as follows: O, God whose might and mercy are immeasurable (verses 3–7a), Thou hast promised forgiveness not for the righteous but for sinners (verses 7b–8). I have committed many iniquities and am now weighed down with sin. Therefore I confess my transgressions, and implore forgiveness (verses 11–13). Thou wilt save me in Thy mercy, and I will praise thee continually. For all the host of heaven sings thy praise, and thine is the glory for ever. Amen (verses 14–25). It is disputed whether the prayer was composed in Hebrew, Aramaic, or Greek. The theology and literary style of the prayer appear to be more in accord with the teachings of Palestinian than of Hellenistic Judaism. The two main ideas that permeate the prayer are the infinite mercy of God, and the efficacy of true repentance.

The position of this ancient prayer in biblical texts varies considerably. Its first appearance in literary history is in the *Didascalia Apostolorum*. In several Greek manuscripts (including codex B, 5th century C.E.) it is included among the 14 odes appended to the Psalter. In medieval manuscripts of the Vulgate it often follows II Chronicles. Several Syriac, Armenian, Ethiopic, and Old Slavonic manuscripts have the prayer, some at the close of the Psalter, some at the end of II Chronicles. Among printed Bibles its position varies. In editions of the Vulgate printed before the Council of Trent, the prayer stands after II Chronicles; in official printings of the Vulgate after the Council, it is placed in an appendix after the New Testament. In Luther's German Bible it stands at the close of the Apocrypha. Among English versions it usually stands among the Apocrypha before I Maccabees, although in the Geneva Bible (1560), widely used by the Puritans, it is included among the canonical books, following II Chronicles. The Roman Catholic Douai Bible of 1609–10 places it in an appendix after II Maccabees.

BIBLIOGRAPHY: Schuerer, Gesch, 3 (1909[4]), 458–60; Ryle, in: Charles, Apocrypha, 1 (1913), 612–24; R.H. Pfeiffer, *History of New Testament Times* (1949), 457–60; B.M. Metzger, *Introduction to the Apocrypha* (1957), 123–8.

[Bruce M. Metzger]

MANASSEH (Menasseh) BEN ISRAEL (1604–1657), Amsterdam scholar, printer and diplomat. Manasseh, who was born a Marrano in Lisbon or La Rochelle, was baptized as Manoel Dias Soeiro. According to an unreliable document of the Portuguese Inquisition, he was born on the island of Madeira. His father, Gaspar Rodrigues Nuñez (a nail-seller), escaped from Lisbon after appearing as a penitent in an *auto-da-fé and settled in 1613/14 in Amsterdam, where he took the name Joseph b. Israel and called his two sons Ephraim and Manasseh respectively and his daughter Esther. His mother, Antonia Soeira took the name Rachel. Manasseh made prodigious progress in his education. He became a member of the Ḥevrah for Talmud Torah at the age of 12, began to frequent the yeshivot when he was 14, made his first public oration in Portuguese when he was 15, and at 17 wrote his first book, *Safah Berurah*, a grammatical work (unpublished and known from two manuscripts). He succeeded R. Isaac *Uzziel as preacher to the Neveh Shalom congregation in 1622. In 1623 he married Rachel Abarbanel. They had three children, Gracia (Hannah), Joseph, and Samuel. His extraordinarily extensive knowledge in the theological rather than the talmudic sphere and his linguistic abilities made him a forerunner of the Jewish scholars of the 19th century who attempted to present Judaism in a sympathetic manner acceptable to the Christian world. He founded the earliest Jewish Hebrew printing press in Amsterdam (1626), where he continued to publish works in Hebrew, Yiddish, Latin, Spanish, Portuguese (and some in Dutch or English) for the remainder of his life. The first book of his press, a Hebrew Sephardi prayerbook, appeared on January 1, 1627 (13 Teveth 5387). It was financed by Ephraim Bueno and Abraham Sarphati and corrected by Isaac Aboab da Fonseca. Today it is known in only very few copies. *Penei Rabbah*, his index to the Midrashim, appeared in 1628. In 1628–29 he published Joseph Solomon Delmedigo's *Sefer Elim* and *Mayan Gannim* on religious, metaphysical and scientific matters with mathematical illustrations. Some chapters were prohibited by the Portuguese *parnasim*. He issued a number of Hebrew and Spanish biblical texts (from 1627 to 1654), Sephardi and Ashkenazi prayerbooks in Hebrew, Spanish, and Yiddish (from 1630 to 1650) and several Hebrew editions of the *Mishnah* (1631–32; 1643–44; 1646). The first part of his *Conciliador* (1632, in Spanish; 1633 in a Latin translation by Dionysius Vossius), reconciling apparently discordant biblical passages, gained him a great reputation in Christian circles (the remaining three parts appeared in Spanish only, 1641–51). This was followed by a series of works also largely directed to non-Jews: *De Creatione* (1635, Latin only); *De Termino Vitae* (1634, Latin only); *De Resurrectione Mortuorum* (1636); and *De Fragilitate Humana* (1642). Beside other minor works, he produced *Thesouro dos Dinim*, a code of Jewish law for returned Marranos (1645–47); *Piedra Gloriosa*, with (in a few copies) containing four etches by Rembrandt (1655); and *Nishmat Ḥayyim* (1651) on the nature of the soul. The Manasseh b. Israel press, which was not always in his own hands, published about 80 titles. For these works, as well as his synagogue sermons (at which gentile scholars and notables were often present), he was regarded in the world of scholarship as the leading representative of Hebrew learning. In May 1642 he was honored to deliver an official address of welcome to Queen Henrietta Maria of England, her daughter Mary, and their hosts Stadtholder Frederick Henry and his son William (II) in the Portuguese synagogue at the Houtgracht. Manasseh published his address in the same year in Portuguese (*Gratulaçaõ*), Latin, and Dutch. He had close personal relationships with luminaries such as Gerardus Joannis Vossius and especially with his son Isaac, Hugo *Grotius, Petrus Serrarius, Caspar Barlaeus, Claudius Salmasius, Paul Felgenhauer, Samuel Bochart and many more. He boasted to have written more than 200 letters to all his friends and relations, which he intended to publish separately. This never happened. Very few of these letters have survived as autographs, of which the Amsterdam University Library possesses six. Though continuing to serve the Amsterdam community in various capacities, he was never its official chief rabbi. In 1640, when he intervened in a quarrel between the synagogue authorities and his brother-in-law, Jonas Abrabanel, he was put under the ban. Despite his publishing activities, his income was never adequate, and in 1640 he planned to immigrate to *Brazil. When after the Puritan revolution the return of the Jews to England was proposed, Manasseh took a prominent share in the negotiations. In 1650 he dedicated the Latin edition of his work, *The Hope of Israel*, describing the reported discovery of the *Ten Lost Tribes in South America, to the English parliament in an effort to solicit their goodwill. At the same time, he entered into discussions with various Englishmen by correspondence and in person, on the possibility of permitting the return of the Jews; this, in his view, had messianic implications, because it would complete the dispersion of the Jews to *Keẓeh ha-Areẓ* ("the end of the earth"), the medieval Hebrew term for Angle-Terre (cf. Deut. 28:64). Because of political circumstances and his own health, Manasseh did not avail himself of an opportunity to go to England in 1652, though his friend Manuel Martinez (David Dormido *Abrabanel) and his son Samuel Soeiro conducted some negotiations on his behalf. Eventually however, he went there in 1655, and submitted his petition to *Cromwell for the recall of the Jews. Although this was not formally granted, assent was given to a subsequent petition which merely asked for permission to establish a synagogue and acquire a cemetery. This arrangement eventually proved providential, since it placed no conditions on the return of the Jews. During his stay in England, Manasseh wrote *Vindiciae Judaeorum* (1656) to defend the Jews against the attacks which were then being made on them. He was bitterly disappointed at the apparent frustration of his hopes, although Cromwell showed his personal sympathy by granting him a pension of £100 a year. He returned to Holland in the autumn of 1657, but died at Middelburg shortly after his arrival. He was buried at the Portuguese cemetery Beth Haim at Ouderkek on the Amstel, where his tomb (restored by British Jews in 1960) can still be visited. The historical facts about Manasseh b. Israel in R. Menasse's novel *Die Vertreibung aus der Hölle* (2001) are unreliable. His portrait was engraved by Salom Italia (1642). Whether a portrait etching by Rembrandt of 1636 (Bartsch 269) represents Manasseh is doubtful, and painted portraits of Manasseh by Rembrandt or by Ferdinand Bol are not known.

BIBLIOGRAPHY: C. Roth, *A Life of Menasseh ben Israel, Rabbi, Printer and Diplomat* (1934; repr. 1975); L. Wolf, *Menasseh ben Israel's Mission to Oliver Cromwell* (1901); A. Yaari, *Mi-Beit Defuso shel Menasheh ben Yisrael* (1947); H. van de Waal. "Rembrandts Radierungen zur Piedra Gloriosa des Menasseh ben Israel," in: *Imprimatur*, 12 (1954–55), 52–61; L. Fuks and R.G. Fuks-Mansfeld, "Menasseh ben Israel as a Bookseller in the Light of New Data," in: *Quaerendo* 11 (1981), 34–45; idem, *Hebrew typography in the Northern Netherlands 1585–1815*, vol. 1 (1984), 99–135; H.P. Salomon, "The Portuguese background of Menasseh ben Israel's Parents as Revealed through the Inquisitorial Archives at Lisbon," in: *Studia Rosenthaliana*, 17 (1983), 105–46; Menasseh ben Israel, *The Hope of Israel. The English Translation by Moses Wall, 1652*. Ed., with introd. and notes by H. Méchoulan and G. Nahon (1987); Y. Kaplan, H. Méchoulan, R.H. Popkin (eds.), *Menasseh ben Israel and his world* (1989); A.K. Offenberg, "Menasseh ben Israel's Visit to Christina of Sweden at Antwerp, 1654," in: *Lias* 16 (1989), 265–74; J.H. Coppenhagen, *Menasseh ben Israel. A bibliography* (1990), with over 2,000 titles.

[Cecil Roth / A.K. Offenberg (2nd ed.)]

MANASSEH BEN (Porat) JOSEPH OF ILYA (1767–1831), one of the forerunners of the *Haskalah in Lithuania and Russia. He was born in Smorgon, Lithuania, and was renowned as a child for his remarkable memory and intellectual precocity. He received a talmudic education in the home of his father, who was a *dayyan*. In 1784 he married and went to live in the house of his father-in-law, a wealthy merchant in Ilya. Manasseh was among the disciples and intimates of *Elijah b. Solomon Zalman, the Gaon of Vilna, and became friendly with Joseph Mazal from Viasyn, who owned an excellent Hebrew library including scientific and research works. Gradually he reached theoretical and practical conclusions tending toward increasing rationalism and called for some change in *halakhah*. In his works, his attitude to Talmud study is based on these conceptions. In several places, for example, he challenged the Talmud and Rashi's understanding of certain pronouncements of the Mishnah. He regarded natural sciences with respect and was critical of the Kabbalah. Demanding the abrogation of halakhic commands that were not an integral part of the basic, early law and that people could not carry out in actual life, he advocated the principle of alteration and leniency in *halakhah*, according to changing trends. He likewise called for a changed and orderly curriculum of traditional studies (see also *Judah Loew b. Bezalel): first the Bible, Mishnah, and *Gemara* and, for talented youth, secular studies as well.

Manasseh has been credited with the invention of several agricultural machines which the unsophisticated environment rejected. Raising the problem of the poor in Jewish society, he called for justice for them, as "the overwhelming majority of these people lack their basic needs, are hungry and thirsty, have no garment against the cold, and their spirit is faint within them." Social responsibility and service for society he regarded as a duty, even at the cost of personal advantage. He attacked the custom of *kest*, by which a newly married couple was supported for several years by the wife's parents, since he was in favor of productivization. Regarding trade as "robbery," he called for "proper leadership" to enable the Jewish masses to earn their livelihood through crafts. From time to time he suggested that the leading rabbis confer to deliberate on the problems of a "general improvement" of Jewish conditions and culture. Manasseh was persecuted. A rabbinical convention deliberated his excommunication and he was prevented from going to Berlin. He therefore completed his studies in the Polish and German languages at home and read antiquated scientific works in those languages, thus gaining a sketchy knowledge in this field. To make a living, he later worked as a private teacher in various places in Russia and Galicia. It was then that he became acquainted with Nachman *Krochmal and other Galician *maskilim*.

Manasseh was a prolific writer, but it was not easy for him to publish his writings, because none of them was issued with approbation of the rabbis. His *Pesher Davar* (Vilna, 1807) was burnt by many rabbis. When he attempted to publish his principal work, *Alfei Menasheh*, in Volhynia, the printer burned the manuscript and the copies that had already been printed as soon as he became aware of the content of the work; when it was printed in Vilna (1822), the author was required to omit a paragraph which alluded to reforms in *halakhah*. His *Binat Mikra* (Grodno, 1818), written in the form of unsystematic novellae, deals with the cantillation marks of the Bible as factors in syntax and meaning. In his pamphlet *Sama de-Ḥayyei* (Yid. trans. *Lebn-Mittel*), he sought to present his views to the people at large and to outline "proper and useful behavior for life in this world." Though he had intended to publish additional pamphlets, no more appeared, possibly because of the opposition of the rabbis and community leaders. After *Sama de-Ḥayyei*, Manasseh published anonymously the pamphlet *Shekel ha-Kodesh*, in which he apologized to those who considered him "a nonconformist in several matters," and suggested that his opponents "choose several men who would be willing to clarify their opinions with me."

Manasseh visited *ḥadarim* and encouraged young men to study mathematics and sciences. In 1827 the Jews of his native town elected him as their rabbi, but he resigned after a year, refusing to be involved in the cruelty of the *Cantonist mobilization. He died in a cholera epidemic. Most of his literary remains were destroyed in the fire which broke out in Ilya in 1884, but some extracts appeared in the second volume of *Alfei Menasheh* (1904), published by his grandson Isaac Spalter, head of a yeshivah in Smorgon. Circles of pupils and admirers cherished his memory, and using this tradition, M. *Plungian, one of the first Lithuanian *maskilim*, wrote his biography of Manasseh, *Ben-Porat* (Vilna, 1858). *Maskilim of the 19th century (M. *Lilienblum, R.A. *Braudes, and others) used Manasseh's opinions against rabbis of the old school.

BIBLIOGRAPHY: S.I. Stanislawski, in: *Ha-Shiloah*, 18 (1908), 274–7; S. Rosenfeld, in: *Ha-Tekufah*, 2 (1918), 250–88; Z. Rejzen, *Fun Mendelsohn Biz Mendele* (1923), 183–260; Zinberg, Sifrut 6 (1960), 153–61; Klausner, Sifrut, 3 (1953), 25–32; B. Katz, *Rabbanut, Ḥasidut, Haskalah*, 2 (1958) 187–203; R. Mahler, *Divrei Yemei Yisrael ba-Dorot ha-Aḥaronim*, 4 (1956), 63–68.

[Yehuda Slutsky]

MANCHESTER, city in northern England. Its Jewish community, the second largest in Britain, dates from about 1780, the first synagogue being founded by two brothers, Lemon and Jacob Nathan, formerly of Liverpool. A cemetery was acquired in 1794 and the first local charity was the Manchester Jewish Philanthropic Society (1804) which provided winter relief for poor resident Jews. After a temporary schism in the congregation in 1840, a more serious split followed during the rabbinate of S. *Schiller-Szinessy and led to the establishment of a Reform synagogue in 1856. Two years later, the original community moved to its new synagogue ("the Great") on Cheetham Hill still in use in the 1970s. The early settlers and community leaders came mainly from Liverpool and included a tailor, a pencutter, and an optician. Nathan Meyer *Rothschild's first residence in England was in Manchester, from where he exported cotton goods from 1798 to 1805. The second half of the 19th century brought to the city substantial merchants from Central Europe, some political refugees from the 1848 liberal risings in Europe, Romanian Jews fleeing from the 1869 persecutions, and in the 1870s young men escaping service in the Russian army. In 1871, small groups arrived from North Africa and the Levant, areas connected with the Manchester cotton industry, forming the nucleus of the flourishing 20th-century Sephardi congregations of south Manchester. The most significant influx, however, resulted from the great Russo-Polish immigration of 1881–1914. The Jews of Manchester spread northward, settling in the adjacent city of Salford and in the suburban districts of Prestwich and Whitefield. In the 20th century, the south Manchester Jews spread into the suburban areas of Cheshire.

Some of the earlier immigrants became waterproof-garment manufacturers, an industry developed by Jews which flourished until it was superseded by the technologically superior "rainproof," in the manufacture of which Jews were not prominent. The Russo-Polish immigrants followed the usual immigrant trades of tailoring and capmaking. There were also large numbers of jewelry travelers, hawkers, and street-traders. Communal institutions proliferated. The first Jewish school was founded in 1842, and by 1904, 2,300 pupils were being educated in Jewish schools. A Board of Guardians on the London pattern was founded in 1867. Many small *ḥevrot* were opened by immigrants. A weekly journal, the *Jewish Telegraph*, is published there. In the 20th century, Manchester had its own *bet din* and *sheḥitah* board and a Jewish hospital. The representative body, the Council of Manchester and Salford Jews, had 68 synagogues and organizations affiliated to it. At its peak around 1910, Manchester's Jewish population was estimated at 35,000. It probably remained at just under this figure until about the 1970s, when a decline was obvious.

As Manchester was the home of Chaim *Weizmann from 1904 to 1916, the city became the training ground of some of the outstanding British Zionists, personalities prominent also in British life: Lord Simon *Marks, Harry *Sacher, Leon *Simon, *Rebecca and Israel *Sieff. In civic life, too, Jews played an increasingly important role. Nathan and Sarah *Laski were followed by a large number of Jewish lord mayors of both Manchester and Salford. Several Jews were Labor members of parliament for Manchester constituencies, especially after 1945, including Leslie and Harold *Lever and Frank Allaun. The novelist Louis *Golding lived in Manchester and set several of his novels in the city. Even in the very recent past Manchester produced a number of communal leaders with a power base separate from London Jewry, such as Sir Sidney *Hamburger.

In the mid-1990s, the Jewish population numbered approximately 27,000. According to the 2001 British census, the first to include an optional religious question, Manchester's Jewish population totaled 21,733. It still contained more communal institutions than any British city apart from London. The community was headed by a Jewish Representative Council of Greater Manchester and Region. There were about 32 synagogues, all but three of which were Orthodox. The Orthodox community, which included a highly visible Strictly Orthodox community, maintained a local Council of Synagogues, a *Beth Din*, and a range of institutions. Remarkably, Manchester also had no fewer than 16 Jewish day schools, ranging from Strictly Orthodox to Liberal. There was also a well-presented Manchester Jewish Museum on Cheetham Hill Road. The history of the community down to recent times has been fairly well chronicled by historians such as Bill *Williams.

BIBLIOGRAPHY: C. Roth, *Rise of Provincial Jewry* (1950), 83–84; JYB; V.D. Lipman, *Social History of the Jews in England, 1850–1950* (1954), index; L.P. Gartner, *The Jewish Immigrant in England, 1870–1894* (1960), index; Ch. Weizmann, *Trial and Error* (1949), index. **ADD. BIBLIOGRAPHY:** B. Williams, *The Making of Manchester Jewry, 1740–1875* (1976); idem., *Manchester Jewry: A Pictorial History* (1988). M. Dobkin, *Tales of Manchester Jewry and Manchester Jewry in the Thirties* (1986); M. Levine, *Cheetham to Cordova: A Manchester Man of the Thirties* (1984); R. Liedtke, *Jewish Welfare in Ham-*

burg and Manchester, c. 1850–1914 (1998); Z.Y. Wise, *A Brief History of the Jewish Community in Prestwich, Whitefield and Bury* (2003).

[Vivian David Lipman / William D. Rubinstein (2nd ed.)]

MANCHURIA, N.E. region of China, adjacent to the Soviet Union. After the Russian Revolution of 1917 many refugees sought shelter in Manchuria, including some 5,000 Jews. Most of them gravitated to *Harbin, but small groups settled in Dairen, Mukden, and other cities. Those Jews who were not employed by the Chinese Eastern Railway worked as educators, physicians, or merchants. The Japanese occupied Manchuria (1931–45); as Axis partners during World War II they accepted the antisemitic policy of their Nazi ally and their treatment of the Jews was oppressive. After the Japanese defeat in 1945, civil war broke out in Manchuria between the Chinese Nationalists and the Communists. Those Russian Jews who did not succeed in escaping before the Communist takeover eventually returned to the Soviet Union.

BIBLIOGRAPHY: H. Dicker, *Wanderers and Settlers in the Far East* (1962), 17–60.

[Rudolf Loewenthal]

MANCROFT, family of British politicians. ARTHUR MICHAEL SAMUEL, first BARON MANCROFT (1872–1942), English politician and philanthropist. Born into a wealthy family long-settled in the Mancroft district of Norwich, Arthur Samuel became head of one of the family shoe manufacturing concerns but retired in 1912 to devote himself to public affairs. He contributed large sums and devoted service to various causes in Norwich, including the Castle Museum and Picture Gallery, and was lord mayor of Norwich from 1912 to 1913. During World War I he worked at the War Office and later at the Ministry of Supply where he dealt with arms contracts. Samuel was elected to Parliament as a Conservative from 1918, and became parliamentary secretary to the Board of Trade and minister for the Department of Overseas Trade. From 1927 to 1929 he was financial secretary to the Treasury. In 1932 he was made a baronet and in 1937 was raised to the peerage as Baron Mancroft. His writings include the biography *Piranesi* (1910), *The Herring: Its Effect on the History of Britain* (1918), *The Mancroft Essays* (all written under the name Arthur Michael Samuel), and numerous articles on economic and financial matters. While not active in communal affairs, Lord Mancroft occasionally defended Jewish interests in and out of Parliament.

Lord Mancroft was succeeded by his son, STORMONT MANCROFT, the second baron Mancroft (1914–1987). He was undersecretary to the Home Office from 1954 to 1957, when he became parliamentary secretary to the Ministry of Defense. He entered the cabinet as minister without portfolio, but resigned in the following year. In 1964 Stormont Mancroft was the central figure in a controversy which broke out when he was appointed chairman of the Board of the Norwich Union Insurance company, with which his family had long been associated. Although he had never shown any Jewish or Zionist interests, he was removed from the post as a concession to Arab pressure.

[Vivian David Lipman]

MANDATE FOR PALESTINE. The mandate system was established after World War I by the Treaty of Versailles for the administration of the former overseas possessions of Germany and parts of the Turkish Empire. Its purpose was to implement the principles of Article 22 of the Covenant of the League of Nations, which said in paragraph 4:

> Certain communities formerly belonging to the Turkish Empire have reached a stage of development where their existence as independent nations can be provisionally recognized, subject to the rendering of administrative advice and assistance by a Mandatory until such time as they are able to stand alone. The wishes of these communities must be a principal consideration in the selection of the Mandatory.

Class A of the mandates included former Turkish provinces constituted as Palestine, Iraq, and Syria. The first two were assigned to the administration of Great Britain and the third to France. The mandates for Iraq and Syria ended in 1932 and 1936, respectively, their main purpose having been to prepare the countries to be able "to stand alone." The mandate for Palestine differed from the other "A" mandates in that its primary purpose was the establishment of a national home for the Jewish people, as stated in its preamble, paragraph 3, "putting into effect the declaration originally made on November 2, 1917 [the *Balfour Declaration] by the Government of His Britannic Majesty, and adopted by the other Allied Powers …" Moreover, the reason for the establishment of a national home for the Jewish people in Palestine is related to the recognition of "the historical connection of the Jewish people with Palestine and to the grounds for reconstituting their national home in that country" (para. 3). Great importance was attached to the wording of this paragraph, as it made it clear that Palestine was not just a country in which a national home should be built, but was taken as the historic land of the Jews. Therefore the national home is to be reconstituted, and not just constituted, there (see *White Papers).

The second article of the mandate makes it the responsibility of the mandatory power, i.e., Great Britain, to place "the country under such political, administrative, and economic conditions as will secure the establishment of the Jewish national home, as laid down in the preamble." To this is added the aim of "the development of self-governing institutions," an intentionally vague phrase that implied the gradual preparation of Palestine for self-rule as a process parallel to the establishment of the Jewish national home (particularly when compared with the Mandate for Iraq (Mesopotamia)). The fulfillment of the main purpose of the Palestine mandate was to be assured by establishing "an appropriate Jewish Agency for the purpose of advising and cooperating with the Administration of Palestine," by facilitating Jewish immigration into Palestine, encouraging close settlement by Jews on the land (art. 6), and "facilitating the acquisition of Palestinian citizenship by Jews" (art. 7). The Zionist Organization was recognized as such an agency until the establishment of the *Jewish Agency in 1929 (art. 4).

The Hebrew language was recognized as one of the three official languages of the country (art. 22). The Mandate was also to safeguard the "civil and religious rights of all the inhabitants of Palestine, irrespective of race and religion" (introd. and art. 2) and to set up the judicial system so that it assured the rights of all and respected the "personal status of various peoples and communities" and that religious interests (in particular waqfs) be "fully guaranteed" (art. 9). Also many other articles dealt with religious autonomy for the various religions strongly emphasizing this as one of the important functions of the mandate (see arts. 13, 14, 15, 23). Each community was allowed to maintain its own schools in its own language (art. 15); and no modification of the mandate was possible without the consent of the League of Nations (art. 27). According to Article 25 of the mandate, "In the territories lying between the Jordan and the eastern boundary of Palestine as ultimately determined, the Mandatory shall be entitled, with the consent of the Council of the League of Nations, to postpone or withhold application of this mandate as he may consider inapplicable," and by virtue of this saving clause, Transjordan was severed from the territory destined to include the Jewish national home (see *White Papers).

The mandate for Palestine was given to Great Britain at *San Remo on April 25, 1920, and a civil administration (which superseded the British Military Administration), headed by Sir Herbert *Samuel, was effected on July 1, 1920. The mandate itself was ratified by the Council of the League of Nations on June 24, 1922. A special American-British Palestine Mandate Convention was ratified in March 1925, as the United States was not a member of the League of Nations. In this convention the United States agreed to the terms of the mandate and Great Britain agreed that no modification in these terms would be possible without the assent of the United States (art. 7); thus any modification in the mandate needed the assent of both the League of Nations and the United States. The mandate terminated with the establishment of the State of Israel on May 14, 1948.

BIBLIOGRAPHY: League of Nations, *Mandate for Palestine* (1922); reproduced in W. Laqueur (ed.), *The Israel-Arab Reader* (1969), 34–61; U.S. Department of State, *Mandate for Palestine* (1927, 1931^{2}); Ch. Weizmann, *Trial and Error* (1949), 347–64 and index; N. Bentwich, *The Mandates System* (1930); B. Joseph, *British Rule in Palestine* (1948).

[Daniel Efron]

MANDEL, ARNOLD (1913–1987), French author and journalist. Of Polish immigrant parentage, Mandel was born in Strasbourg. A libertarian radical until World War II, Mandel rediscovered his Jewish identity as a soldier in North Africa in 1940, and then in occupied France. He fled to Switzerland, where he was interned until 1944, after which he fought in the Maquis. From 1945, Mandel was one of the chief spokesmen for French Jewry. Under the influence of Samson Raphael *Hirsch and of ḥasidic mysticism, he returned to neo-Orthodoxy. His knowledge of Yiddish and of Jewish lore made him one of the few able interpreters of Yiddish literature in France. A prolific writer, Mandel defined the originality and distinctiveness of Jews – particularly French Jews – in the modern world. His works deal mainly with his search for identity in a gentile world, and with his intellectual and spiritual quest for a Judaism both modern and Orthodox. They include *L'Homme-Enfant* (1946); *Chair à Destin* (1948); *Les Temps incertains* (1950); *Les Vaisseaux brûlés* (1957); *Le petit livre de la sagesse populaire juive* (1963); *La Voie du Hassidisme* (1963); and *Les Cent Portes* (1968). Mandel contributed to most Franco-Jewish periodicals, particularly *La Terre retrouvée, Evidences,* and *L'Arche.*

[Pierre Aubery]

MANDEL, ELI (1922–1990), Canadian author. Mandel is among the most challenging writer-critics to gain prominence as part of the explosion of Canadian literary activity in the 1960s. Born in Estevan, Saskatchewan, he served in the Canadian armed forces during World War II. His first book, *Trio,* appeared in 1954, just after he completed his Ph.D. in literature at the University of Toronto. This division of labor, between working poet and active scholar and teacher, was a pattern he maintained throughout his career. In the middle 1950s Mandel taught at the College militaire royal de Saint-Jean; from 1957 until 1967 he was at the University of Alberta. He spent the remainder of his career at York University.

Mandel's published work, which reflects his varied interests and talents, includes poetry collections, volumes of personal and critical essays, as well as a number of important poetry and critical anthologies that both reflected their times and influenced the course of Canadian literary studies. The bulk of Mandel's anthologizing work took place in the early 1970s, when the Canadian literary scene was undergoing impressive growth and change, alongside the rise of a new cultural nationalism. In his published criticism, Mandel addressed a wide area of Canadian intellectual trends, from the influence of Northrop Frye to the linguistic and political implications of postmodernism. He also contributed to discussions related to regionalism and the role of ethnic writing.

Jewish themes appear intermittently in Mandel's work, but they are not central as they are in the writings of Leonard *Cohen, Irving *Layton, and A.M. *Klein. Most interesting are a 1984 essay entitled "Auschwitz and Poetry," in which Mandel explores his own efforts to address the Holocaust in his art, as well as a remarkable text called *Out of Place* (1977), which explores Mandel's family history in the Jewish prairie farming colony of Hirsch in southern Saskatchewan. In *Out of Place* Mandel juxtaposes the particularity of Jewish prairie life with questions of Canadian history, memory, and landscape, making use of a poetic method that is spare and lightly ironic. The outcome, like much of Mandel's work, is a surprisingly original view of Canadian cultural life.

Mandel's awards include the Governor General's Award in 1967 for his collection *An Idiot Joy*.

BIBLIOGRAPHY: E. Mandel. *The Other Harmony: The Collected Poetry of Eli Mandel*, eds. A. Stubbs and J. Chapman (2000); N. Ravvin, "Eli Mandel's Family Architecture: Building a House of Words on the Prairies," in: R. Menkis and N. Ravvin (eds.), *The Canadian Jewish Studies Reader* (2004): 266–82; A. Stubbs, *Myth, Origins, Magic: A Study of Form in Eli Mandel's Writing* (1993).

[Norman Ravvin (2nd ed.)]

MANDEL, GEORGES (**Louis** (not Jeroboam as represented by antisemites) **Rothchild**; 1885–1944), French statesman, born in Chatou, near Paris. Mandel became a close associate of Georges Clemenceau in 1903, after joining Clemenceau's staff at *L'Aurore*, a radical daily newspaper which campaigned for the rehabilitation of Alfred *Dreyfus. When Clemenceau became prime minister in 1906, he appointed Mandel head of his office (*chef de cabinet*), a position Mandel held until 1909, and again from 1917 to 1919 in Clemenceau's war cabinet. At the peak of World War I Mandel was put in charge of the trials dealing with treason and defeatism. In 1920 he was elected a deputy and after 1935 he was appointed minister a number of times. As cabinet minister he urged France's speedy rearmament to meet the threat of German National Socialism and in 1936 he opposed Germany's remilitarization of the Rhineland. As minister of the interior in Paul Reynaud's government (from May 1940 to the fall of France), Mandel ordered the arrest of numerous suspected Nazi sympathizers and also interned Jewish refugees from Germany and Austria. After the retreat of French troops, he opposed Pétain's and *Laval's policy of capitulation and collaboration. Pétain had Mandel arrested in Bordeaux, but upon his release he went to Morocco to organize the renewal of combat. Arrested a second time, Mandel was taken to prison in France and assassinated by the Vichy militia in 1944. Mandel did not participate in Jewish community life.

BIBLIOGRAPHY: G. Wormser, *Georges Mandel, l'homme politique* (1967); P. Coblentz, *Georges Mandel* (1946); J.M. Sherwood, *Georges Mandel and the Third Republic* (1971).

[Lucien Lazare]

MANDEL, MARVIN (1920–), U.S. politician. Mandel, born in Baltimore, Maryland, the son of East European immigrants, was raised in an Orthodox, Yiddish-speaking home. After graduation from Johns Hopkins and the University of Maryland (1942) and service in the army during World War II, Mandel practiced law in Baltimore until his election to the lower house of the Maryland legislature in 1951. In 1963 he was chosen speaker of the Maryland House of Delegates, and also served as chairman of the Maryland State Democratic Committee. As speaker, he was credited with helping push through the legislature tax reform, a fair housing law, and the repeal of the state anti-miscegenation law. When Spiro T. Agnew, Maryland's Republican governor, was elected vice president of the United States in 1968, Mandel was elected governor (Democrat) by legislature vote. Reelected twice (in 1970 and 1974), he served as governor until 1979. He also served as chair of the Comprehensive Health Planning Agency (1969); the Governor's Executive Council (1969–79); the Board of Public Works (1969–79); and the Maryland Council on the Environment (1970–79). In addition, Mandel was a member of such entities as the State House Trust (1969); the Hall of Records Commission (1969–70); the Maryland Highway Safety Coordinating Committee (1969–79); the Maryland Education Council (1969–79); and the Southern Regional Education Board (1969–79).

In 1977 Mandel was found guilty of mail fraud, racketeering, and bribery, for which he served 19 months in prison. He was pardoned by President Ronald Reagan; in 1989 the Supreme Court overturned his conviction.

Among his honors and awards, Mandel received the House of Delegates Thomas Kennedy Award in 2002. From 2003 he served as chair of the Governor's Commission on the Structure and Efficiency of State Government and a member of the Board of Regents for the University System of Maryland. A former state commander of the Jewish War Veterans, Mandel was active in Jewish communal affairs.

ADD. BIBLIOGRAPHY: J. Bradford, *Thimbleriggers: The Law vs Governor Marvin Mandel* (1984).

[Bernard Postal / Ruth Beloff (2nd ed.)]

MANDEL, SHELOMOH (1909–1981), *ḥazzan. Mandel was born in Nowy Zanz, Galicia. He studied *ḥazzanut*, the specific melodies and musical style of the solo cantorial singer, under Moshe Steinberg and Moshe *Koussevitzky in Vilna and music at the Warsaw Conservatory. After serving as *ḥazzan* in Warsaw and Cracow he was appointed to the Berea synagogue in Johannesburg in 1934, remaining there until he immigrated to Israel in 1974. Of a ḥasidic background, he incorporated ḥasidic melody into the traditional melodies. Among his records is one of the whole Passover Haggadah. He taught *ḥazzanut.*

[Akiva Zimmerman (2nd ed.)]

MANDELBAUM, BERNARD (1922–2001), U.S. rabbi, educator, community leader, administrator. Mandelbaum spent the better part of his professional life as one of the most important figures in the Conservative movement in the 20th century. He was born in Brooklyn, New York, received a B.A. degree from Columbia University in 1942, and was ordained at the Jewish Theological Seminary (1946), obtaining there a Doctor of Hebrew Letters degree in 1953.

Following his ordination, Mandelbaum spent 27 years at the seminary serving, inter alia, as professor of homiletics, instructor of Midrash, registrar and dean of students at its Rabbinical School, director of the seminary's department of religion and psychiatry, World Brotherhood, American Student Center in Jerusalem and Schocken Institute for Jewish Research, and program editor of *The Eternal Light*, an NBC television show. Mandelbaum, ultimately, became provost and, in

1966, in anticipation of the retirement of Louis *Finkelstein as chancellor, was elected to serve as president of the seminary, seemingly anointed as Finkelstein's successor.

While already in the mid-1950s there were stirrings within the Conservative movement to reform the prayer book and introduce a full measure of egalitarianism at worship services, 1966 became a fateful year for the seminary as it searched for a replacement of Finkelstein as chancellor. Two factions among the conservative leadership arose, one which supported Mandelbaum for the chancellorship, not only because of his intellectual credentials, proven leadership and dedicated service to the seminary, but because he was fully committed to preserving the traditional roots of Conservative Judaism. The stronger faction aspired to bring to the seminary a worthy leader who would be more amenable to the changes they sought, such as the ordination of women, through a more liberal interpretation of the *halakhah*. When Dr. Gerson D. *Cohen was selected over Mandelbaum as chancellor, the stage was set for an accelerated ideological shift in Conservatism.

Mandelbaum became president emeritus of the seminary in 1973, and accepted leadership roles, thereafter, in the American-Israel Cultural Foundation, serving as its president (1973–77) and then as executive vice president of the Synagogue Council of America and director of its Institute for Jewish Policy Planning and Research.

Among his published works are *Assignment in Israel* (1960); *Pesikta De Rav Kahana: A Critical Edition* (1962); *The Maturing of the Conservative Movement* (1968); *To Live With Meaning* (1973); *Add Life To Your Years* (1974); *Art and Judaism: Conversation Between Yaakov Agam and Bernard Mandelbaum* (1981); and *From the Sermons of Milton Steinberg*, 2 volumes (1954–63).

BIBLIOGRAPHY: Pamela Nadell, *Conservative Judaism in America* (1988).

[Stanley M. Wagner (2nd ed.)]

MANDELBAUM, DAVID GOODMAN (1911–1987), U.S. anthropologist. Born in Chicago, he studied at Northwestern and Yale Universities. Mandelbaum joined the faculty of the University of Minnesota and from 1943 to 1946 served in the U.S. Army in India and Burma. In 1946 he moved to the University of California at Berkeley, becoming professor and serving as a director of educational resources in anthropological projects (1959–62). His major interests were the ethnology of Southeast and South Asia, anthropological theory, and applied anthropology. He was one of the first cultural anthropologists to undertake ethnographic research in Burma. In addition to his extensive fieldwork in southern India, he worked with the Plains Cree and Chippewa Indians in the U.S.

BIBLIOGRAPHY: His works include *The Plains Cree* (1940), *Soldier Groups and Negro Soldiers* (1952), *Change and Continuity in Jewish Life* (1955), and *Society in India* (1970). He edited *Culture, Language, and Personality* (1956) and *Resources for the Teaching of Anthropology* (1963). **ADD. BIBLIOGRAPHY:** P. Hockings, *Dimensions of Social Life: Essays in Honor of David G. Mandelbaum* (1987).

[Ephraim Fischoff / Ruth Beloff (2nd ed.)]

MANDELBERG, AVIGDOR (**Victor**; 1870–1944), physician; delegate to the Second Russian Duma. Born in Berdichev, Mandelberg graduated from the faculty of medicine of the University of Kiev (1893) and settled in St. Petersburg, where he took a part in the organization of workers' circles and their intellectual activities. He was exiled for his activities to Irkutsk, eastern Siberia, in 1899 for four years, and while there, he joined the Social Democratic Labor Party, playing an active role in its organization in Siberia. Upon his release he attended his party's second congress as a delegate of the Siberian alliance and joined the Menshevik faction. He then returned to Siberia, took part in the revolutionary activities of 1905, and was elected to the Second Duma (1907), avoiding any collaboration with the three other Jewish delegates, who had joined the Kadet faction (the Russian Liberals). After the dismissal of the Second Duma and the arrest of the Social Democrats, he escaped abroad. He lived in Italy and returned to Russia with the outbreak of the revolution of 1917. When the Bolsheviks came to power, Mandelberg left for Siberia, emigrating to Palestine in 1920. He was chief physician of Kuppat Ḥolim of the *Histadrut and one of the founders of the League against Tuberculosis. In 1941 he helped found the League for Friendship with the Soviet Union (v League) and was a member of its central committee. Among his works should be mentioned: *Iz perezhitogo* ("Experiences," 1910) and *Me-Ḥayyai* (1942).

BIBLIOGRAPHY: Ha-Ligah li-Ydidut Yisrael-S.S.S.R., *Dr. Avigdor Mandelberg, Dappim le-Zikhro* (1946).

[Yehuda Slutsky]

MANDELBROT, BENOIT (1924–), U.S. mathematician, scientist, and educator. Born in Warsaw, Poland, the nephew of the expert in mathematical analysis Szolem Mandelbrojt, Mandelbrot moved to France with his family in 1936. The need to avoid detection during the German occupation of France in World War II greatly disturbed his education, but he gained admission to the Ecole Polytechnique – one of France's leading science schools – after the occupation ended in 1944. After graduating in 1947, he gained an M.Sc. in aeronautics at the California Institute of Technology. It was in the doctoral thesis he presented for his 1952 Ph.D. at the University of Paris that Mandelbrot first used scaling, a concept that refers to the manner in which the fine details of patterns replicate those patterns' large-scale irregularities. This was to become the unifying theme of his work. He was J. von Neumann's postdoctoral fellow at the Institute of Advanced Study in Princeton when he realized that the *Hausdorff-*Besicovitch fractal dimension is not an esoteric notion of mathematics but can be used to measure roughness numerically. Mandelbrot's interdisciplinary bent led him to join IBM and apply his theories successfully to both the problem of random noise on telephone circuits and that of fluctuations in stock-market prices. In the latter case, he was able to offer a highly effective statistical method for predicting such fluctuations' riskiness over a range of time scales. Over time, his theory of fractals was found to be applicable to a very wide variety of phenomena, from turbulence to the dispersion of blood vessels through the body. Increasingly, it came to be recognized that fractality reveals an important and hitherto unrecognized characteristic of nature and natural development as a whole. The theory exerts a profound influence upon modern scientific theory, helping to provide descriptions of anything from the behavior of the human heart under stress to the shapes of mountains and clouds or the pattern of water seepage into the soil, in addition to forming a key tool in modern chaos theories. Mandelbrot synthesized these view in his book *The Fractal Geometry of Nature* (1982). The Mandelbrot set that Mandelbrot discovered and that is named in his honor is called the most complex orderly object in mathematics. Many of its properties are understandable even to young students but have not yet been proven rigorously. Early on, Mandelbrot's eclectic and wide-ranging approach meant that he was often regarded with suspicion by a scientific establishment that valued compartmentalization and specialization in a single field, but the undoubted value of his discoveries have led to wide recognition of his importance. He has been IBM Fellow and Sterling Professor of Mathematical Sciences at Yale, has held many visiting positions, and received many awards.

[Rohan Saxena / Gali Rotstein (2nd ed.)

MANDELKERN, SOLOMON (1846–1902), Russian lexicographer, Hebrew poet, and translator. Mandelkern was born in Mlynow and in his youth was among the Ḥasidim of Menahem Mendel of Kotzk. However, he soon came under the influence of Haskalah. At the age of 19 he divorced his very pious wife and went to study at the newly founded rabbinical seminaries of Vilna and Zhitomir. He also studied Semitic languages at the University of St. Petersburg. From 1873 to 1880 Mandelkern served as assistant to the government-appointed rabbi at Odessa, being one of the first to preach in Russian. During this period he studied law at the university and compiled a history of Russia, *Divrei Yemei Rusyah* (3 vols., 1875), on behalf of the "*Society for the Promotion of Culture among the Jews of Russia." Because of his personal animosity toward the editor of the periodical *Ha-Meliẓ*, Alexander *Zederbaum, Mandelkern submitted a false report of a *blood libel in Bessarabia for publication in it. When this was discovered, the periodical was forced to suspend publication, and Mandelkern, to leave Russia. He studied at Jena and afterward settled in Leipzig, where he devoted himself to research. An early supporter of Ḥibbat Zion and Herzl's Zionism, he attended the first Zionist Congress in Basle in 1897. Mandelkern's great contribution to Jewish scholarship is his monumental Bible concordance *Heikhal ha-Kodesh* (1896, 1959[8]; abridged edition, *Tavnit Heikhal*, 1897), the fruit of 20 years of scholarly labor. This concordance was a great improvement on its predecessors and was the first to follow the Jewish arrangement of the Hebrew Bible. In later editions of the work by F. Margolin and M. Goshen-Gottstein (1967[7]) and H.M. Brecher and A. Avrunin (1955, with an English introduction by A.M. Freedman and Hebrew bibliographical essay on concordances by A.R. Malachi) many of its imperfections were corrected. Mandelkern had also begun to work on a Talmud and Midrash concordance, which, however, remained fragmentary and has not been published. Mandelkern's output as a writer, poet, and translator of poetry was equally considerable. They include an early ode to Czar Alexander II, *Teshu'at Melekh Rav* (1866), on his escape from an attempted assassination; a love poem *Bat Sheva* (1866), which earned him praise from Adam ha-Kohen (1896[2]); aphorisms, *Ḥiẓẓim Shenunim* (1864); and an anthology *Shirei Sefat Ever* (3 vols., 1882–1901), which contained apart from his own poetry translations of great poets from various languages. He also translated Byron's *Hebrew Melodies* into Hebrew as *Shirei Yeshurun* (1890); Mapu's *Ahavat Ẓiyyon* into German, *Thamar* (1885; 1897[2], without mentioning the author), and *Ashmat Shomeron* as *Suende Samarias* (1890); and into Russian *Bogdan Chmielnicki* (1878) and Lessing's *Fables* (1885). Mandelkern expended great mental and physical efforts producing his works and soliciting buyers for his concordance, even traveling to the U.S. in 1899, and late in his life suffered mental illness. He also became increasingly interested in the theory and practice of spiritualism.

BIBLIOGRAPHY: Klausner, Sifrut, 5 (1956[2]), 243ff., incl. bibl.; S. Verba, in: *Hadoar*, 32 (1953), 524–5; G. Bader, *ibid.*, 829; R. Malachi, *ibid.*, 35 (1956), 93ff., 115; Y.H. Zagorodski, in: *Sefer ha-Shanah*, 4 (1903), 291–300.

MANDELSHTAM, LEONID ISAAKOVICH (1879–1944), Soviet physicist. Mandelshtam was born in Odessa and entered the New Russian (Novorossiyskiy) University in Odessa in 1897. He was expelled one year later for taking part in student protests and completed his education at the University of Strasbourg. He returned to Russia in 1914; in 1918 he was appointed professor at the Odessa Technical Institute. In 1925 he became professor of physics at Moscow University. Mandelshtam's main scientific works were in the fields of optics, theory of oscillations, and radiophysics. In his work *Ob opticheski odnorodnykh i mutnykh sredakh* ("On optically isotropic and cloudy media," 1907) he disproved J.W. Rayleigh's theory about molecular dispersion of light and showed that the medium must be anisotropic to be able to disperse light. He made several important contributions to the nonlinear theory of oscillations, and together with N.D. Papaleksi invented a new method of creating electrical oscillations. In radiophysics Mandelshtam solved several problems of propagation of radio waves over the surface of the earth. He also proposed the idea of exact distance measurements with the help of radio waves and together with Papaleski built radiointerferometric distance measuring devices. He also wrote papers about statistical and quantum physics and relativity theory, the philosophical basis of which has been criticized lately by the scientific community. From 1931 to 1936 Mandelshtam served as coeditor with Abram Fyodorovitch *Joffe of *Khimicheskiy Zhurnal*, the journal of the Russian Physico-Chemical Society, Leningrad.

Mandelshtam was awarded the Stalin Prize in 1942 for his work on nonlinear oscillations and propagation of radio waves. In 1945 the Academy of Sciences established two prizes in his name for the best work in physics and radio-physics.

BIBLIOGRAPHY: I.V. Kuznetsov (ed.), *Lyudi russkoy nauki*, 1 (1948), 260–71; A.A. Semyonov, in: *Voprosy filosofii*, 3 (1953), 199–206; N.D. Papaleski, in: *Uspekhi fizicheskikh nauk*, 27 no. 2 (1945).

[Gerald E. Tauber]

MANDELSHTAM, NADEZHDA YAKOVLEVNA (1899–1980), Russian writer and philologist. Mandelshtam was born in Saratov, to a lawyer father who was the son of a *cantonist and turned to Russian Orthodoxy, and a Jewish mother who was a physician. She herself was baptized as a child. She was educated in Kiev, where she studied art in the studio of the painter A. Ekster and worked as an assistant stage designer. In 1919, she met the poet O.E. *Mandelshtam, whom she married in 1921. She assisted her husband in his translation work, herself translating from English. After his exile and death, she preserved his manuscripts and helped to prepare them for publication. In 1956, she was awarded the degree of Candidate of Philological Sciences for her dissertation *Function of the Accusative in Anglo-Saxon Poetic Monuments.* Mandelshtam achieved considerable literary fame in the West following publication of her remarkable memoirs, *Hope against Hope* (1970). Her second book of memoirs, *Vtoraya Kniga* (1972), was translated into English as *Hope Abandoned* (1974). After her death her friends collected her poems, commentaries, and other materials into a third book of memoirs, published in Paris in 1987. Mrs. Mandelshtam lived in Moscow. She was buried at services conducted by the Russian Orthodox Church, with which she identified all her life.

MANDELSHTAM, OSIP EMILYEVICH (1891–1938?), Russian poet. Mandelshtam was born in Warsaw but as a child moved with his parents to St. Petersburg, where his father, a scion of an obscure Kurland branch of the well-known Mandelshtam rabbinic family, was a leather merchant and taught himself German and Russian, becoming a student of Schiller, Goethe, and Koerner. His mother, Flora Osipovna née Verblovsky, was born and educated in Vilna, belonging to an enlightened and assimilated Jewish family related to the Wengeroffs. A piano teacher and of discriminating literary taste, she passed on to her son her love for music and Russian literature.

Mandelshtam grew up in St. Petersburg. In 1907 he finished the Tenishev School, one of the best and most modern and liberal private institutions in Russia. His teacher for Russian literature was Vladimir Gippius, a pioneer of the Russian Symbolist movement. Between 1907 and 1910 he traveled in France, Germany, Italy, and Switzerland, spending one term at the Sorbonne and two at Heidelberg, where he studied Old French. Forced to interrupt his education abroad owing to financial difficulties, he converted to Lutheranism in order to be able to enter the University of St. Petersburg.

During these years Mandelshtam attended the poetic circle (*Proacademia*) of the learned Symbolist poet Vyacheslav Ivanov. His earliest poems, enclosed with his letters to Ivanov, were recently found in the latter's archives in Russia and published in the West. In these poems, as well as in the pieces selected for his literary debut in 1910 (in the pages of *Appolon*, a trend-setting journal of art and letters), young Mandelshtam emerges as a thoughtful preserver of the European Symbolist heritage and a courageous seeker of new means of poetic expression, combining Verlaine's *musique* with a conscious and creative stock-taking of the 19th-century Russian poetic vocabulary (especially that of Pushkin and Tyutchev), which receives a new and unexpected meaning in the framework of his complex symbolism.

In 1911 Mandelshtam joined the Guild of Poets (*Tsekh poetov*). Its founder N.S. Gumilev, whom Mandelshtam had earlier met in Paris, became his closest friend and literary associate, as did another member of the Guild, Anna Akhmatova. By 1912 Mandelshtam's Symbolist apprenticeship was over. Gumilev proclaimed a new poetic trend, Acmeism, demanding a "more stable balance of forces" in poetic texts and a "more accurate definition of the subject-object relationship" than the mystically inclined Russian Symbolists could provide. To these demands Mandelshtam added, in his programmatic essay "*Utro akmeizma*" ("The Morning of Acmeism"; written c. 1913 but published only in 1919), the requirement that "the conscious meaning of the word, Logos," be redefined in formal aesthetic terms and granted "equal rights" with such constructive elements of poetry as rhythm, sound texture, etc. Employing the already existing cultural codes to effect shifts of meaning, Acmeism, after some initial crises, developed into a major trend in modern Russian poetry and a powerful rival of Futurism, which sought to emancipate the poetic language from everyday meanings by purely linguistic means. In Mandelshtam's own poetry the semantic potentialities with which the poetic word is endowed through the history of its use in other poetic contexts are activated by means of elliptic riddle-like quotations that force the reader to turn to their sources in order to find a frame of reference (the so called "subtext") in terms of which an Acmeist text has to be decoded.

The essential features of this method are already evident in the compact and erudite poems of Mandelshtam's first collection, *Kamen* ("The Stone," 1913; 2nd and 3rd eds., greatly enlarged, 1916 and 1923); the title of the book represents an etymologically justified anagram of the Greek work *akme* ("sharp point," "summit,") from which Acmeism derived its name. During World War I, Mandelshtam published, in addition to *Kamen*, several remarkable literary and historical essays ("Chaadayev," "François Villon," "On the Interlocutor," etc.). The revolution of 1917 found Mandelstam in St. Petersburg. His attitude toward the Bolshevik takeover, as reflected in his poetry, gradually changed from initial revulsion ("When the October favorite of fate prepared for us/A yoke of violence and malice …") to manly acceptance of whatever "the vast, clumsy, squeaking turn of the rudder" might bring. In the spring of

1919 Mandelshtam moved to Kiev, where he met his future wife, Nadezhda Yakovlevna Khazina (see previous entry). After the arrival of the White Army, which brought in its wake a terrible pogrom, Mandelshtam moved to the Crimea, where he was jailed by General Wrangel's counterintelligence, but was freed shortly after through the intervention of a friendly White colonel. He left the Crimea for Tiflis, and was promptly jailed again as a Red spy, this time by the Menshevik secessionist government of Georgia. In the fall of 1920 Mandelshtam returned to Soviet Russia in the company of I. *Ehrenburg. Later, despite the execution of Gumilev on conspiracy charges, followed by a political drive against Acmeism, Mandelshtam and Akhmatova staunchly refused to emigrate. In 1922–23 Mandelshtam's second collection of poetry appeared first in Berlin (under the title *Tristia*, given in Mandelshtam's absence by M. Kuzmin), then in Moscow (*Vtoraya kniga*, "The Second Book"). Three longer poems composed by him in 1923, "The Horseshoe Finder," "The Slate Ode," and "1 January 1924," marked a turning point in Mandelshtam's art. Their artistic and intellectual complexity and tragic power remain unsurpassed in modern poetry.

After 1923 Mandelshtam's name disappeared from the lists of contributors to literary periodicals, and during the rest of the decade he was effectively silenced as a poet and confined himself almost entirely to prose (the publication of his collected poetry in 1928 was brought about by the personal intervention of N.I. Bukharin). A collection of autobiographical essays, *Shym vremeni* ("The Noise of Time," 1925), described by Prince Svyatopolk-Mirsky (D.S. Mirsky) as "one of the most significant books of our time," was followed by the long story "*Egipetskaya marka*" ("The Egyptian Stamp," 1928), and, in 1930, by "*Chetvertaya proza*" ("Fourth Prose"), which could not be printed in the U.S.S.R. During these years Mandelshtam was forced to make a living as a translator and in 1928 became the victim of a vicious campaign, in the course of which he was accused of "plagiarism" by A. Gornfeld, a minor literary critic (these events are described in "Fourth Prose").

In 1930, following a trip to Armenia (see *Puteshestviye v Armeniyu*. 1933), Mandelshtam resumed writing poetry, some of which he succeeded in publishing. However, in May 1934 he was arrested for having written an epigram on Stalin and sentenced to three years' exile in Cherdyn in the Urals. There Mandelshtam attempted to commit suicide as he developed hallucinations and other symptoms of mental disorder following interrogation and torture at the Lubyanka prison. An intercession by Bukharin, the last one, resulted in his transfer to a less severe place of exile, Voronezh, where, in 1935–37, he wrote his last book of poetry (known as *The Voronezh Notebooks*).

In 1937 Mandelshtam was allowed to return to Moscow. Arrested again on May 1, 1938, he was sentenced without trial to five years' hard labor and, according to unverifiable reports, died of inanition either in the Vtoraya Rechka transit camp near Vladivostok on December 27, 1938 (the "official" date of his death), or early in 1940 in a labor camp on the Kolymar River.

A major part of Mandelshtam's unpublished work was saved by the heroic efforts of his widow. Some of the Voronezh poems appeared after his "rehabilitation" in Soviet literary journals, and his *Razgovor o Dante* ("Talking about Dante"), edited by L. Pinsky and A. Morozov, was published in Moscow in 1967. However, the edition of his collected poetry, announced on three occasions by the series "Biblioteka poeta," never materialized.

In the U.S., the collected works of Mandelshtam were published by G. Struve (*Sobraniye sochineniy*, 1955; *Sobr. soch.*, 1–3, 1965–71, 2 editions).

During the 1960s intensive studies of Mandelshtam's work gained momentum in various scholarly centers, e.g., Cambridge, Mass. (R. Jakobson and K. Taranovsky, and their students), Moscow (V.V. Ivanov and his colleagues), Tartu (members of the Summer School on Secondary Modeling Systems), Uppsala (N.A. Nilsson), etc.

Jewish Themes in His Art

Unlike another modern Russian poet of Jewish origin, B. *Pasternak, Mandelshtam never renounced his spiritual Jewish identity. However, his attitude toward the world of Judaism was marked by the tragic ambivalence that no great Jewish writer working in European literature could ever escape. His autobiographical essays, *Shum vremeni*, contain a painfully frank description of an assimilated Jewish childhood in a great center of European culture, with its vulgar official brand of Judaism, ostensible pride in Jewish history, and deep day-to-day shame. He never learned Hebrew but appreciated "the admirable equilibrium of its vowels and consonants in the clearly enunciated words, which imparted an invincible power to the chants." Of the Yiddish language, he wrote with tenderness: "… that melodious, always surprised and disappointed, interrogative speech with sharp pitches on half-stressed syllables."

In his earliest poems Mandelshtam spoke of himself as "a rustling reed growing out of an evil and muddy pool to breathe forbidden life" and then sinking back into "the cold and boggy abode," "the beloved ooze" (1910). In 1915, the same image appeared in his poem about Christ (never included in his collections): "He reigned and drooped, as a lily, into the native pool, and the depth, in which stems sink, celebrated its law." In the poem about his mother's funeral (1916), Mandelshtam contrasted the "terrible yellow sun" illuminating the Jewish temple with the black sun of Apocalyptic Christianity rising at the gates of Jerusalem (the black and yellow colors of the *tallit* are associated in his poetic vocabulary with Judaism). Religious critics made much of Mandelshtam's so-called Christianity as reflected in a number of his poems and essays. In point of fact, however, Mandelshtam turned with equal enthusiasm to Chaadayev's Catholic universalism, Kautzky's Marxism, Florensky's Orthodoxy, Greek mythology, neoplatonic mysticism, medieval nominalism, the heresy of the Russian "Name-Praising" sect, and the evolutionary theories of Goethe and Darwin in his search for an "integral world view" and an "internal sense of rightness" without which he found writing poetry unthinkable. In *Tristia*, Mandelshtam actually wrote: "I drink the cold mountain air of Christianity"; but this opposition between the "water" of Judaism and the "air" of Christianity was canceled in 1923 by a belated admission: "Air can be as dark as water … Air is mixed as thickly as earth …" ("The Horseshoe Finder").

Mandelshtam's realization that the Jewish predicament cannot be escaped by turning to alien cultures and religions was expressed with greatest force in his 1920 poem addressed to Leah, the exegetic symbol of creative life. Here he predicts the eventual return of his muse to the bosom of Judaism, a reunion that he describes as "incestuous":

> Return to the incestuous bosom, whence, Leah, you have come, because you have preferred the yellow dusk to the sun of Ilion.
>
> Go! Nobody shall touch you. Let the incestuous daughter drop her head on her father's breast.
>
> Yet a fatal change must be accomplished in you: you shall be Leah, not Helen. You have been so named not because
>
> It is harder for royal blood than for any other blood to course in veins. No! You shall fall in love with a Jew, disappear in him – and so be it.

Ten years later, in "Fourth Prose," Mandelshtam wrote with a conviction born out of hard-earned experience: "I insist that writerdom, as it has developed in Europe, and above all in Russia, is incompatible with the honorable title of Jew, of which I am proud. My blood, burdened with the inheritance of sheep breeders, patriarchs, and kings, rebels against the thieving gypsyishness of the writing tribe."

The motif of the prodigal son's return to the faith and the land of his fathers found its final culmination in the "Canzona" (1931): "I shall leave the land of the Hyperboreans to fill with vision the outcome of my fate. I shall say 'selah' to the head of the Jews for his raspberry-colored caress."

Some of Mandelshtam's writings have appeared in translation: *The Prose of Osip Mandelstam*, transl., with a critical essay, by C. Brown (1967); "Talking About Dante," *Books Abroad*, Special Issue: A Homage to Dante (1965), 25–47; "Fourth Prose," transl. by C. Brown, in *Russia's Other Writers* (1970), 130–45; *Gedichte* (transl. by Paul Celan, 1959).

BIBLIOGRAPHY: N. Nilsson, in: *Scande-Slavica*, 9 (1963); B. Bukhshtab, in: *Russian Literature Triquarterly*, 1 (1971), 263–82; K. Taranovsky, in: *Calif. Slavic Studies*, 6 (1971), 43–48; *Slavic Forum* (1975); V. Terras, in: SEEJ, 10 (1966), 251–67; O. Ronen, in: *Studies Presented to R. Jakobson…* (1968), 252–64; essays by S. Broyde, D. Segal, Yu. Levin. L. Foster, et al., in: *Slavic Poetics: Essays Dedicated to K. Taranovsky* (1975); N. Mandelstam, *Hope against Hope* (1970); J. Harris (ed.), *The Complete Critical Prose and Letters of Osip Mandelshtam* (1978).

[Omri Ronen (2nd ed.)]

MANDELSON, PETER (1953–), British politician. One of the best-known and most controversial of recent British politicians, Peter Mandelson was the son of a Jewish father; his mother was the daughter of Herbert Morrison (Baron Morrison of Lambeth), Britain's deputy prime minister and then foreign secretary under Clement Attlee from 1945 to 1951. Mandelson was educated at Oxford and worked as a television producer; he was elected to Parliament in 1992, holding his seat until he resigned in 2004. "Mandy," as he is widely known, became campaign manager (and chief "spin doctor") of Tony Blair, the center-left politician who became leader of the Labour Party in 1994 and was elected prime minister with a huge majority in 1997. Some within the Labour Party resented Mandelson's enormous influence. From 1997 he served as Blair's minister without portfolio, responsible for building London's Millenium Dome for 2000, and then entered the cabinet in 1998 as secretary of state for trade and industry. Later in the same year, he was forced to resign over an allegedly improper loan he had received. He returned to the cabinet in 1999 as secretary of state for Northern Ireland, but in 2001 was again forced to resign over an alleged impropriety regarding a businessman seeking British citizenship. In 2004 Blair appointed Mandelson Britain's European commissioner responsible for trade.

[William D. Rubinstein (2nd ed.)]

MANDELSTAMM, BENJAMIN (1805–1886), Hebrew author. Born in Zagare, the older brother of Leon *Mandelstamm, he received both a traditional and a secular education. In the 1840s, he moved to Vilna and became one of the extremists in Haskalah circles. In a memorandum which he presented to Max *Lilienthal when the latter visited Vilna in 1842 during his survey of the condition of Russian Jewry, Mandelstamm accused Russian Jewry of six faults which were responsible for their backwardness: (1) Russian Jews do not speak the Russian language, but rather some confused tongue; (2) they dress quaintly; (3) they do not participate sufficiently in the arts; (4) nor in the crafts; (5) they have no factories; and (6) they are neither farmers nor herdsmen.

The only solution recognized by Mandelstamm was harsh governmental intervention "forbidding the printing of the Talmud, completely removing from circulation books on the Kabbalah and Ḥasidism, dissolving the *ḥeder* thus removing the teachers (*melammedim*) who devour the children, and educating the children of Israel in Russian." When the enlightened community of Vilna established its own synagogue (*Tohorat ha-Kodesh*), Mandelstamm criticized it sharply for not daring to reform its liturgy and religious customs. In 1877 his writings and memoranda were published in Vienna under the title *Ḥazon Binyamin ben Yosef mi-Ma'aleh ha-Shekedim* (*Ḥazon la-Mo'ed*) with an introduction by Pereẓ *Smolenskin, a collection of great importance for the history of the Russian Haskalah during the 1840s. Mandelstamm also published a collection of aphorisms entitled *Mishlei Binyamin* (in *Ha-Asif*, 1885 and 1886).

BIBLIOGRAPHY: Kressel, Leksikon, 2 (1967), 403–4; Zinberg, Sifrut, 6 (1960), 209–12, 214–6.

[Yehuda Slutsky]

MANDELSTAMM, LEON (**Aryeh Loeb**; 1819–1889), writer and adherent of the *Haskalah in Russia. Born in Zagare (Lithuania), Mandelstamm had a thorough religious and general education. In 1840 he became the first Jew to enroll at a Russian university (Moscow) and in 1844 graduated in Oriental languages from the University of St. Petersburg. His research concerned the history of political regimes in ancient Israel. During his student years, he produced a book of poetry in Russian (1840). In 1846, after further studies at German universities, Mandelstamm was appointed in charge of Jewish affairs in the Ministry of Education in succession to M. *Lilienthal. He was mainly concerned with establishing a network of government schools for Jews, and supervising the Jewish *ḥeder* and *talmud torah* schools. For this purpose he traveled extensively throughout the *Pale of Settlement and prepared textbooks; these were published by means of funds raised through the *candle tax, and even private Jewish teachers were required to buy them. The books, which contained texts accompanied by German translations, included selections from the Mishnah, an anthology of Maimonides' writings, the Bible along with the *Biur* of Moses *Mendelssohn and his pupils, and the *Kevod Melekh* of R. Jehiel *Heller, which stressed the Jew's religious duty to respect secular kings and rulers. Mandelstamm was dismissed in 1857 as a result of attacks by his opponents among the *maskilim* and wealthier Jews of St. Petersburg who accused him of wasting funds and engaging in activities for his own profit. During his period in office, Mandelstamm corresponded with and met Haskalah leaders and prominent Hebrew writers, often arranging for them to be given posts. After losing his job, he lived for many years in Germany where he engaged in trade and in contracting. He wrote for both the Jewish and general press, and published, in German, several collections of studies in Bible and Talmud. The translation of the Pentateuch into Russian which Mandelstamm had produced in Germany was forbidden in Russia because of the general prohibition on scriptural works which were not approved by the Church. In 1872, however, permission was given to import and reprint his work there, provided that the translation was accompanied by the original Hebrew version. Toward the end of his life Mandelstamm returned to St. Petersburg where he died forgotten and in poverty.

BIBLIOGRAPHY: *Ha-Meliẓ*, no. 198 (Sep. 5, 1889), M.P. (Kantor), *ibid.*; no. 199 (Sep. 6, 1889), *ibid.*, no. 201 (Sep. 8, 1889); S. Ginzburg, *Amolike Peterburg* (1944), 74–87; M. Margulis, *Voprosy yevreyskoi zhizni* (1889), 71–147; Ginsburg, in: *Perezhitoye*, 1 (1908), 1–50; L.S. Dawidowicz, *The Golden Tradition* (1967), 154–60.

[Yehuda Slutsky]

MANDELSTAMM, MAX EMMANUEL (1839–1912), ophthalmologist and leading member of the Zionist and Territorialist movements in Russia. Mandelstamm was born in Zagare, Lithuania. His father Ezekiel Mandelstamm, the brother of Leon *Mandelstamm and Benjamin *Mandelstamm, was an educated merchant who wrote a biblical lexicon entitled *The Book of Names* (1862). Mandelstamm was among the first Russian Jews to study in a Russian high school, but he received his main education at the German University of Dorpat (Estonia). After he completed his medical studies at Kharkov University, he continued his studies in ophthalmology in Berlin. Upon his return to Russia he opened a clinic in Kiev and became well known as an expert ophthalmologist throughout southern Russia. Mandelstamm also served as a lecturer in ophthalmology at Kiev University, but he left the university when his candidacy as an associate professor was not approved.

The pogroms in southern Russia at the beginning of the 1880s moved Mandelstamm into the field of Jewish public activities. He was the head of the Committee to Support Victims of Pogroms. At the conference of representatives of Jewish communities in St. Petersburg in 1881, he was the only one to support emigration from Russia as a radical solution to the problems the Jews faced there. From that time, emigration from Russia became the basis for his outlook on public affairs. In 1883 he participated along with L. *Pinsker, M.L. *Lilienblum, and H. Shapira in a meeting in Odessa at which the foundations of the *Ḥibbat Zion movement in Russia were laid. His wide-ranged organizational work then began and came to an end only after sharp opposition from the authorities.

Mandelstamm joined the Zionist Organization at the First Zionist Congress and from then on was one of *Herzl's most devoted associates and one of the most faithful political Zionists among the Russians. Herzl depicted him in *Altneuland* as the first president of the Jewish state – "an ophthalmologist from Russia, Dr. Eichenstam." He was elected to the Zionist Actions Committee and at the Second Zionist Congress was appointed deputy of the Kiev district. At the Sixth Zionist Congress, Mandelstamm was among the enthusiastic supporters of the *Uganda Scheme and fought for its acceptance even at the *Kharkov Conference. He organized the supporters of the plan to meet the challenge of the Russian Zionists. After the Seventh Zionist Congress he joined I. *Zangwill and participated in the founding conference of the Jewish Territorial Organization (JTA). The pogroms that accompanied the first Russian Revolution (1905–06) strengthened his conviction that it was imperative to organize the flight of the Jews from Russia through Territorialism. He headed the emigration office established by the Territorialists in Kiev that concerned itself basically with organizing the emigration of Jews destined for *Galveston, Texas (under the Galveston Plan) with the aim of creating a Jewish Territorialist center in the southern United States.

BIBLIOGRAPHY: D.A. Friedman, in: *Ha-Refu'ah*, 18, no. 4 (1940); Y. Slutsky, in: *He-Avar*, 4 (1956), 56–76; 5 (1957), 44–68; Th. Herzl, *Complete Diaries* (1960), index; I. Klausner, *Be-Hitorer Am* (1962), index; idem, *Mi-Kattowitz ad Basel* (1965), index.

[Yehuda Slutsky]

MANDL, SAADIA (1931–), architect. Born in Novi Sad, Yugoslavia, he arrived in Palestine in 1938. He studied at École des Beaux Arts, Paris, and at the Archeology School,

London, spending his internship period in Rome, Paris, and Stockholm.

In 1960 he opened an independent office in Haifa; during 1968/9 he resided in Jerusalem, where he held the position of dean of the Bezalel Art School. In later years he worked from Tel Aviv / (Old) Jaffa, which he helped to reconstruct. For his achievements he was awarded the Rokach Prize. He was chief architect of the Caesarea Development Corporation and from 1965 served as chairman of the Council for the Preservation of the Architectural Heritage. For his projects in Jerusalem, he received the Uri Rozen Prize, together with Yaari and Fraenkel, and the Sandberg Prize, together with Eli Gross, "for the renewal of the Neveh Sha'anan quarter."

Mandl was considered one of the outstanding modern architects of Israel.

[Zvi Loker (2nd ed.)]

MANDRAKE (Heb. דּוּדָאִים (*dūdā'īm*)), *Mandragora officianarum*, a plant of the nightshade family native to the Mediterranean region and related to the deadly *Atropa belladonna*. The mandrake is best known for its large, brown roots that can extend several feet into the ground and branch off into thick, bizarre shapes, even crudely resembling the human form. Since antiquity, the mandrake has been credited with aphrodisiac and fertility-producing powers as well as the ability to induce sleep, relieve pain, or serve as a purgative; it is one of the most frequently mentioned plants in folklore, preserved in literature from the Mediterranean basin from antiquity to the modern era.

The earliest reference may be in Ugaritic literature of the 14th century B.C.E., where the term is found in relation to the goddess of love and war, Anat, whose brother Baal sends her a message concerning peace, love, and "passion" (*ddym*). Mandrakes appear twice in the Bible, in contexts suggesting that the plant had properties conducive to sex and conception. Perhaps in a word-play with *d(w)d*, "love," it is mentioned in the Song of Songs (7:14) as having an odor that would arouse the lovers' passion. The well-known story of Rachel and the mandrakes in Genesis 30:14–17 indicates that this plant was believed to aid conception, for the barren Rachel gives her sister and co-wife Leah a night with their husband Jacob in exchange for mandrakes procured by Leah's son Reuben. The text reports that Rachel subsequently became pregnant when God heeded her. Her use of mandrakes provides an example of the magico-medical means for dealing with problems inherent in the reproductive process, part of women's religious culture in ancient Israel as in most traditional societies. That Rachel resorts to the ancient equivalent of a fertility drug is not at all contradictory to the overarching notion that divine providence is involved in overcoming barrenness; prayer along with actions we would consider magic were understood as complementary ways for women to become pregnant.

Post-biblical lore and legends refer less to mandrake's aphrodisiac qualities and more to its other medicinal properties. Digging for mandrake roots was thought to be dangerous, with the animal pulling out the roots meeting a vicarious death for its master (Jos. Wars, 7:183ff.), a risk also found in other ancient writers, such as Theophrastus and Pliny. The Talmud's prohibition against reciting biblical verses while uprooting mandrakes (TJ Shab. 6:2, 8b), may allude to their supposedly lethal quality. Maimonides (*Guide*, 3:29) mentions that superstitious people are "deluded" about them.

BIBLIOGRAPHY: Loew, *Flora*, 3 (1924), 363–8; H.N. and A.L. Moldenke, *Plants of the Bible*, no. 132 (1952), 137–9. **ADD. BIBLIOGRAPHY:** M.H. Pope, *Song of Songs* (1977), 600, 647–50; C.B. Randolph, "The Mandragora of the Ancients in Folklore and Medicine," in: PAAAS, 12 (1924), 487–537; M. Zohary, *Plants of the Bible* (1982), 188–89.

[Jehuda Feliks / Carol Meyers (2nd ed.)]

MANÉ-KATZ (originally **Emanuel Katz**; 1894–1962), French painter. Mané-Katz was born in Kremenchug, Ukraine. In 1913 he went to study in Paris. He returned to Russia during World War I, working and exhibiting in Petrograd. After the October Revolution of 1917 he returned to Kremenchug, where he taught art. As the city was the scene of continued fighting during the Civil War, there was little chance for him to work and in 1921 he migrated to Paris. He painted assiduously, and a decade later won a Gold Medal at the Paris World's Fair for his painting "The Wailing Wall." In 1939, Mané-Katz was mobilized and on the fall of France was imprisoned briefly by the Germans. He managed to get to the United States, but returned to Paris after the war. Mané-Katz was an eminent Jewish representative of the School of *Paris. His output was prodigious. He painted so fervently and with so little concern for detail that he seems to be carried away by his own exuberance. His color is sometimes blatant, but rarely coarse. His smaller works, particularly those of the 1920s, show an intensity of expression and a baroque ecstasy. The subject matter of his early works is exclusively Jewish – ḥasidic rabbis, talmudic students, fiddlers and beggars of the Pale of Settlement with meager bony faces and deep-set eyes, the same haggard figures placed against an almost barren background. He later painted the sights of Paris, orchestras, bullfights, the scenery of the Riviera, portraits, and numerous flower pieces, usually with a childlike delight in raw colors. He made several sculptures. He died in Israel and left his collection, including many fine specimens of Jewish ritual art, to the city of Haifa.

BIBLIOGRAPHY: M. Ragon, *Mané-Katz* (Fr. and Eng., 1961); A. Werner, *Mané-Katz* (Eng., 1960); J. Aimot, *Mané-Katz* (Fr., 1933).

[Alfred Werner]

MANESSIER DE VESOUL (**Menssier de Vezou**; d. 1375), "*procureur-général*" and "*commissaire*" of the Jews of Langue-d'Oyl (central and northern France) during the reign of *Charles V (1364–80). He was a member of the family of Héliot de Vesoul, a banker of that town during the early 14th century, and in 1349 he himself was expelled from Vesoul. It was Manessier who, in 1359, negotiated with Charles, duke of Normandy (subsequently King Charles V) for the return of the

Jews to France and then acted as the financial intermediary between the Jews of northern France and the monarchy – to his own personal profit as well. In 1374 he secured a further ten-year extension of the Jewish right of residence in France. When the Jews were once more obliged to wear a distinctive *badge, he and all his family were exempted. It is not certain whether it was this Manessier or a namesake who was involved in a lawsuit in 1365. After his death (between June 28 and October 1375), his children, his eldest son in particular, succeeded to his functions and privileges (which included complete exemption from the payment of taxes). When his son Joseph was converted to Christianity in 1382, he recovered the family properties, which had previously been seized. Nothing is known of the family after this.

BIBLIOGRAPHY: L. Lazard, in: *Annuaire des Archives Israélites de France*, 7 (1890/91), 52–56; R. Anchel, *Juifs de France* (1946), 115f.

[Bernhard Blumenkranz]

°**MANETHO** (third century B.C.E.), Greco-Egyptian historian. Manetho, native of Sebennytos, *Egypt, served as priest in Heliopolis. Thoroughly versed in Egyptian lore, he was also associated with the religious policy of the Ptolemaic dynasty, in particular with the introduction of the cult of Serapis. Manetho was the first Egyptian to give an account of the history of his country in Greek. A number of fragments from this work are preserved in *Contra Apionem* of *Josephus, who apparently did not draw from Manetho's work at first hand, but from extracts in Hellenistic Jewish historians. The fragments fall into two categories, the first of which describes the origin of the rule of the *Hyksos in Egypt (Jos., Apion 1:73ff.). Manetho (in accordance with later Egyptian accounts) writes that the Hyksos were a nation of alien conquerors who set fire to Egyptian towns, razed the temples of the gods, and treated the natives with cruelty. After their expulsion from Egypt, the Hyksos crossed the desert on their way to Syria, and in "the country called Judea" built a town, which they named Jerusalem. Although Manetho does not mention the Jews by name, he is clearly referring to them. Josephus himself distinguishes between the first group of fragments of Manetho's writings and the second (*ibid.*, 1:228ff.), "where he had recourse to fables and current reports." In this second group of fragments it is stated that the Egyptian king Amenophis wished to be granted a vision of the gods and on the advice of his namesake, Amenophis son of Paapis, decided to purge the country of lepers and other polluted persons. He collected 80,000 people and sent them to work in the quarries east of the Nile. Afterward, acceding to their request, he assigned them Avaris, the ancient capital of the Hyksos, for settlement. Here they appointed as their leader one Osarsiph, a former priest of Heliopolis. Osarsiph decreed that his people should neither worship the gods nor abstain from the flesh of animals reverenced by the Egyptians, and cultivate close connections only with members of their own confederacy. Similarly, he sent representatives to the inhabitants of Jerusalem, who had been expelled from Egypt. Osarsiph's people defeated the Egyptians in a concerted effort, their behavior to the inhabitants being far worse than that of the Hyksos in their day. Here Manetho identifies Osarsiph with Moses.

Some historians completely deny the authenticity of Manetho's entire Osarsiph story, while some object only to his identification of Moses with Osarsiph. However, there are no convincing reasons for doubting the intended identification. The Osarsiph story throughout has much in common with such Egyptian tales as the "Prophecy of the Lamb" or the "Potter's Oracle," which could easily be fused with anti-Jewish elements. The biblical account of the Exodus challenged the Egyptians to provide a suitable answer, and anti-Jewish feelings were common in Egypt even before its conquest by the Greeks. It is therefore unnecessary to postdate Manetho's account to the later Ptolemaic period. The descriptions of the historian *Hecataeus show how easily the story of the Exodus was assimilated into the tale of the expulsion of the strangers because of calamities visited on the Egyptians. Nor was Manetho necessarily the first to combine the story of the lepers with Moses and the Jews. A synthesis, similar though not completely identical, is encountered in subsequent writers. Nevertheless, Manetho may undoubtedly be considered a central figure in the emergence of the anti-Jewish polemical writings of Alexandrian-Greek literature.

BIBLIOGRAPHY: V. Tcherikover, *Hellenistic Civilization and the Jews* (1959), 361–4; Schuerer, Gesch, 3 (1909^4), 529–31; A. von Gutschmid, *Kleine Schriften*, 4 (1893), 419ff.; E. Meyer, *Aegyptische Chronologie* (1904), 71ff.; Meyer Gesch, 2 pt. 1 (1928), 420–6; F. Staehelin, *Anti-semitismus des Altertums* (1905), 9ff.; W. Helck, *Untersuchungen zu Manetho und den aegyptischen Koenigslisten* (1956), 38ff.

[Menahem Stern]

°**MANETTI, GIANNOZZO** (1396–1459), Hebraist and humanist. Manetti acquired a wide knowledge of Hebrew language and literature and was even taught to speak Hebrew by a Jewish teacher (later baptized) who lived with him. Manetti took lessons also from a Florentine Jew named Immanuel (probably the loan-banker Manuelo of San Miniato), giving him instruction in philosophy in exchange. Many of the Hebrew manuscripts in the Vatican library were originally in Manetti's possession. He made a Latin translation of the Psalms, which he defended against its critics in a five-volume work. In 1447 Sigismondo Malatesta of Rimini organized a religious *disputation at his court between Manetti and Jewish scholars.

BIBLIOGRAPHY: U. Cassuto, *Ebrei a Firenze nell' età del Rinascimento* (1918), 275–7; C. Roth, *Jews in the Renaissance* (1959), 103, 139–40, index; Vespasiano da Bisticci, *Vite di uomini illustri*, ed. by L. Frati, 2 (1893), 33–200 (abbr. Eng. tr. by W.G. and E. Waters, *Vespasiano Memoirs* (1926), 372–95); W. Zorn, *Gianożzo Manetti, seine Stellung in der Renaissance* (Endingen, 1939).

[Umberto (Moses David) Cassuto]

MANEVICH, LEV YEFIMOVICH (**Izrailovich**: pseud. **Eten** (**Etienne**), 1898–1945), Soviet intelligence agent. Between 1910 and 1917 Manevich lived and studied in Geneva. In 1918 he volunteered for service in the Red Army and joined the Communist Party. From 1918 to 1920 he was the commissar of an armored train, the commander of a special unit. He graduated from the Higher School for Staff Service of the Command Staff (1921) and the Military Academy (1924). He served in the Intelligence Directorate of the Red Army (GRU – Glavnoye Razvedovatelnoye Upravlenie) from 1935 with the rank of colonel. From the mid-1920s until 1936 he carried out intelligence activities, mainly in Austria, Germany, Italy, and Spain. In 1936 he was arrested by Italian counterintelligence and sentenced to 12 years imprisonment. However, even in prison he continued to collect and transmit valuable information. In 1943 he was handed over to the Nazis and imprisoned in the concentration camps of Mauthausen and Melk and Ebenze. Although severely ill, he exhibited great willpower and courage by participating in the anti-fascist underground. In May 1945 he was liberated by the American army but died later that year. In 1965 he was posthumously awarded the honor of Hero of the Soviet Union.

[*The Shorter Jewish Encyclopaedia in Russian* (2nd ed.)]

MANGER, ITZIK (1901–1969), Yiddish poet, dramatist, novelist. Born in Czernowitz, his first poem was published in 1921 in the Romanian Yiddish journal *Kultur,* and his first book of poems was *Shtern Oyfn Dakh* ("Stars on the Roof," 1929), where he combined folksong and bardic simplicity with sophisticated stanzaic structures and technical skill. The poems express delight in the entire universe and find beauty and value even in suffering and sorrow. In 1929 Manger moved to Warsaw, where he published more mature poems in *Lamtern in Vint* ("Lantern in the Wind," 1933). In his *Khumesh Lider* ("Bible Poems," 1935), patriarchal figures are portrayed as Eastern Europe *shtetl* Jews. Thus when Abraham welcomes the three angels, he is the pious Reb Avrom, in a silk skullcap and smoking a pipe; in speaking to Sarah, colloquial Yiddish expressions naturally spice his conversation. Manger's *Megile-Lider* ("Scroll Songs," 1936) recast the traditional Purim play as dramatic lyrics. He added new incidents and characters to the biblical narrative, such as the rivalry between the tailor's apprentice Fastrigosse and King Ahasuerus for the love of Esther. These ironic and sentimental lyrics were enthusiastically received when staged as a musical in Israel in 1967 and again in the United States (in English, 1968; music by Dov Seltzer). Manger also adapted *A.Goldfaden's plays for a post-Goldfaden generation; most successfully *Di Kishefmakhern* ("The Witch") and *Dray Hotsmakhs* ("Three Hotsmakhs,"1936, 1937). He paid tribute to Goldfaden, Eliakum Zunser, Berl Broder, and other predecessors with imaginative essays in *Noente Geshtaltn* ("Intimate Portraits," 1938, 1961; also in *Shriftn in Proze* "Writings in Prose," 1980). His most piquant tale is the imaginative novel, *Dos Bukh fun Gan-Eydn* (1939; English tr. by L. Wolf, *The Book of Paradise*, 1965), in which Shmuel-Abba, formerly an angel and now a newborn, relates his prenatal adventures in Paradise. The story is a satire on the imagined Eden and the harsh realities of Jewish life and human foibles.

Manger was most productive in Warsaw, where he also published *Felker Zingen* ("People Sing,"1936), *Demerung in Shpigl* ("Twilight in the Mirror," 1937), *Far Yugnt* ("For the Young," 1937), *Velvl Zbarzher Shraybt Briv tsu Malkele der Sheyner* ("Velvl Zbarzher Writes Letters to Malkele the Beautiful," 1937). He left Warsaw in 1938 for Paris. After unsuccessful attempts to reach Palestine and the United States, he escaped to London where he published *Volkns ibern dakh* ("Clouds over the Roof," 1942), *Hotsmakh Shpil* ("Hotsmakh Play," 1947), and *Der Shnayder-gezeln Notte Manger Zingt* ("The Tailor-Apprentice Notte Manger Sings," 1948). In 1951 he moved to New York, where his volume of selected poems *Lid un Balade* ("Poems and Ballads") was published in 1952, and then in 1967, to Israel. His poems were translated into Hebrew, the principal European languages (English in S. Betsky, *Onions and Cucumbers and Plums* (1958), and in J. Leftwich, *The Golden Peacock* (1961)), and were included in the UNESCO anthology of world poetry in 1961. His short story "The Adventures of Hershl Summerwind" is in I. Howe and E. Greenberg, *Treasury of Yiddish Stories* (1965), 438–46. New translations of his work continued to be published.

BIBLIOGRAPHY: E.H. Jeshurin, biblio. in *Noente Geshtaltn* (1961); LNYL, 5 (1963), 435–43; M. Ravitch, *Mayn Leksikon* (1945), 125–7; N. Meisel, *Forgeyer un Mittseitler* (1946), 394–407; S. Bickel, *Shrayber fun Mayn Dor* (1958), 133–44; J. Glatstein, *In Tokh Genumen* (1956), 306–14; S. Liptzin, *Maturing of Yiddish Literature* (1970), 232–8; Y. Mark, in: JBA, 28 (1970/71). **ADD. BIBLIOGRAPHY:** Ch. Kazdan, *Itsik Manger* (1968); idem, *Di Letste Tkufe in Itsik Mangers Lebn un Shafung* (1973); Y. Panner, *Shtrikhn tsum Portret fun Itsik Manger* (1976); Y. Hoffer, *Itsik Manger* (1979); D.G. Roskies and L. Woolf (eds), *The World According to Itzik: Selected Poetry and Prose* (2002); A. Shpiglblat, *Bloe Vinklen: Itsik Manger – Lebn, Lid un Balade* (2002).

[Sol Liptzin / Helen Beer (2nd ed.)]

MANHEIM, BILHAH (1929–), Israeli sociologist specializing in the sociology of work and considered one of the leading scholars in the field. At the Industrial Engineering Faculty of the Technion she taught many executives how to manage human resources. Manheim was born in Germany and immigrated to Israel with her family in 1936. She received her B.Sc. from the University of Kansas in 1951. In 1953 she completed her M.A. and in 1957 her Ph.D. from the University of Illinois. From 1957 she taught sociology at the Technion and from 1959 to 1969 she lectured at Haifa University. In 1980 she became a professor at the Technion. From 1981 until her retirement in 1997 she directed the Yigal Allon Chair for Human Sciences in Work. During these years she was visiting professor at universities in the U.S. and Australia. She was also a member of several academic societies and associations as well as public bodies. She published many articles and a number of books, such as *The Influence of Reference Groups and Membership Groups on the Self-Image* (1957) and *The Human Fac-*

tor in Work (co-author, 1965). In 2003 she was awarded the Israel Prize in sociology.

[Shaked Gilboa (2nd ed.)]

MANI (**Mana II**; fourth century C.E.), Palestinian *amora*. His teachers were firstly his father *Jonah,R. Yose (TJ, Ter. 8:9, 46a; Sanh. 3:6, 21a), and then R. Judah III (TJ, Pes. 6:1, 33a; Beẓah 1:1, 60a); he also referred to Hezekiah as his teacher (TJ, Ber. 3:5, 6d, et al.). He visited Caesarea where he attended lectures by R. Isaac b. Eliashib (Ta'an. 23b) and other scholars of that town (e.g., Oshaya b. Shemi, Zerikah, etc). In his early years he lived in Tiberias, but later R. Ḥanina (or Hananiah), the head of the academy in Sepphoris, retired in his favor (TJ, Pes. 6:1, 33a) and he remained there until his death (Eccl. R. 11:3). He held halakhic discussions with Zeira II (Mak. 22a). Z. Frankel dates his death in 399 C.E. (the view of I. Halevy that it was before 355 is untenable). It is not known whether he outlived R. Judah III (the statement in Weiss, Dor, vol. 3, p. 102 is due to a mistranslation of a passage in TJ, Ber. 3:1, 6a: "When R. Judah's sister died, Mani did not attend her funeral"). He appears to have been strict and uncompromising in his halakhic rulings, and he expressed his strong doubts as to the correctness of the permission granted by his father and R. Yose for bread to be baked on the Sabbath for the army of Ursicinus (c. 353 C.E.; TJ, Sanh. 3:5, 21b), despite that fact, in a case of extreme emergency he permitted the bakers of Sepphoris to sell their bread in the market on the Sabbath for the army of Proclus (*ibid.*; see Lieberman, in: JQR, 36 (1946), 352–3). He also refused to agree that agricultural activity take place during the sabbatical year in a place called Yabluna on the grounds that it was not in Ereẓ Israel proper. On one occasion he strongly disapproved of his teacher, Judah, making appointments for money (TJ, Bik. 3:3, 65d). Most of his teachings are in *halakhah*, but the few in *aggadah* are of great interest. He explained Saul's reluctance to exterminate the Amalekites, including their children and cattle, on the grounds that they were innocent according to the Torah (Yoma 22b). He also taught that reciting the *Shema* at its proper time was greater than studying the Torah (Ber. 10b). Mani was apparently not altogether easy to get on with. Not only was he not on good terms with the patriarch and his household, who distressed him so much that he had to pray for relief, but in his domestic life he was also unhappy (Ta'an. 23b).

In addition to R. Mani, there was an earlier *amora* called Mana and it is not always certain which is meant. In Ecclesiastes Rabbah 5:4–5 both are found.

BIBLIOGRAPHY: Weiss, Dor, 3 (1904[4]), 102–3; Halevy, Dorot, 2 (1923), 373–84; Hyman, Toledot, s.v.; Epstein, Mishnah, 399–404; Ḥ. Albeck, *Mavo la-Talmudim* (1969), 398.

[Harry Freedman]

MANI, family in Iraq and Ereẓ Israel. According to family tradition, the family is of Davidic origin and its name is an acrostic of *Mi-Geza Neẓer Yishai*.

ELIJAH BEN SULEIMAN (1818–1899), one of the best-known Iraqi rabbis, was born in Baghdad, where he studied at the Beit Zilka rabbinical academy and was one of the outstanding pupils of R. Abdallah *Somekh. In 1856 he settled in Ereẓ Israel, first in Jerusalem, but two years later he moved to Hebron. He played a prominent role in the development of the Jewish community there. In 1865 he was appointed chief rabbi of Hebron and retained this post until his death. By nature an unassuming and generous man, he was outspoken and adamant in matters of religious observance. He made several journeys on behalf of the Hebron community: to India in 1873; Egypt, 1872 and 1878; and Baghdad 1880. In 1879–80 a fierce argument broke out between R. Elijah and two prominent members of the community, Mercado Romano and R. Raḥamim Joseph Franco, which split the community into two factions. In the end R. Elijah's views prevailed. R. Elijah wrote several books dealing with traditional and mystical Jewish studies. Of these, the following were published: *Zikhronot Eliyahu*, a collection of religious precepts, arranged in alphabetical order, of which two parts appeared (Jerusalem, 1936, 1938); and *Karnot Ẓaddik* (Baghdad, 1867). Many of his responsa were published in the Jerusalem *Me'assef* and in the writings of contemporary rabbinic scholars.

[Abraham Ben-Yaacob]

SULEIMAN MENAHEM (1850–1924), Elijah's eldest son, was appointed *rosh av bet din* in Hebron when his father died. After the death of Ḥayyim Hezekiah *Medini, he was elected chief rabbi of Hebron. ISRAEL (1887–1966), the son of SHALOM EZEKIEL, Elijah's second son, studied law in Paris. During the British Mandate he was appointed magistrate (1927) and district judge in Jaffa (1932). In 1936 he became the first Jewish judge in the newly established Tel Aviv district court. ISAAC MALCHIEL (1860–1933), Elijah's fourth son, became a district judge in Hebron. He was an enthusiastic supporter of *Herzl. In 1901 he moved to Jerusalem to practice law. From 1926 to 1929 he was district judge in Jaffa. His sons-in-law were Daniel *Auster and Giulio *Racach. ELIJAH MOSES (1907–), great-grandson of Elijah, during the Mandatory regime served as a lecturer in the Jerusalem law school. In 1948 he was appointed judge in the district court of Jerusalem, and from 1962 he served as a justice of the Supreme Court of Israel. His brother ABRAHAM (1922–) was professor of physics at the Hebrew University of Jerusalem. MAZAL (Mathilda) *MOSSERI was the daughter of Isaac Malchiel.

BIBLIOGRAPHY: M. Mani, *Rabbi Eliyahu Mani* (1936); A. Ben-Yacov, in: *Ḥemdat Yisrael ... le-Zekher Rabbi Ḥ. Ḥ. Medini* (1946), 89–97; O. Avisar (ed.), *Sefer Ḥevron* (1970), 100–7, 132–4, 153–4.

MANI, EZRA (1913–2005), Israeli lexicographer. Born in Bagdad, Iraq, where he received his elementary education in Jewish schools and in the Ahiever youth movement, whose goal was to spread the Hebrew book, he immigrated to Israel in 1934, taught Arabic, enlisted in the IDF in 1948, and served in the Intelligence Department of the IDF, in which he was a colonel. Though he did not receive any academic training, he is the author of *The Mani Dictionary* on Arabic military terms and of their Hebrew equivalents, including 10,000 entries based on Arabic documents, military reviews, TV, films, and colloquial Arabic from several Arab countries. This dictionary aids Intelligence operations and to date only exists in a computerized on-line internal IDF edition. His work is considered highly original by international standards. Mani received the Israel Prize in 1976 for services to Arabic linguistics and was the first military officer to have won this prize.

MANICHAEISM, a system of religious beliefs and doctrines named after Mani or Manes (c. 215–275), who lived and taught in Persia. In his youth he seems to have associated with Jewish-Christian (Elchasaite) sectarians. Manes was put to death for his heretical doctrines, but his teachings spread from the Middle East to Rome and to North Africa where they had numerous adherents in the fourth century. Manichaean documents have also been found in Chinese Turkestan. A curious mixture of diverse gnostic, Persian-Zoroastrian, and other dualistic doctrines (see *Dualism), Manichaeism preached a severe asceticism, including vegetarianism, and survived in small and often clandestine sects into the Middle Ages.

Several heretical movements in medieval Christianity are thought to have been influenced, directly or indirectly, by Manichaean sects. Manichaean doctrines seem to have been very influential also during the first centuries of Islam, as witnessed by the anti-dualistic polemics of orthodox apologists and theologians. Dualistic attacks on traditional teachings appear in the ninth and tenth centuries and had to be countered by a polemic reminiscent in some ways of the early rabbinic polemic against gnostic dualism (*shetei rashuyyot*). Saadiah argues against dualism both in his *Book of Beliefs and Opinions* and in his polemical tract against Ḥiwi al-Balkhi. The dualism, however, which he attacked was not just of the Zoroastrian type but seems to have been indebted to contemporary Manichaeism.

BIBLIOGRAPHY: G. Widengren, *Mani and Manichaeism* (1965); J. Darmesteter, in: REJ, 28 (1889), 1–15; H. Puech, *Le Manichéisme* (1949).

[R.J. Zwi Werblowsky]

MANI LEIB (pseudonym of **Mani Leib Brahinsky**; 1883–1953), Yiddish poet. Born in Nizhyn (Chernigov district, Ukraine), Mani Leib arrived in the U.S. in 1905 after having participated in the Russian revolutionary movement. He immediately began publishing poems in New York's leading Yiddish periodicals and in the anthologies of the American Yiddish literary movement Di Yunge, which had impressionistic, art-for-art's-sake poetic principles that Leib helped to establish and followed faithfully. Largely eschewing social concerns, he crafted formally unified poems that affirmed a belief in the ability of art to compensate for human suffering. His "sound poems" drew renewed attention to the Yiddish language through their skillful use of alliteration and repetition. His most prolific year was 1918 when 11 of his collections appeared. His ballads and tales were incorporated into the Yiddish school curriculum and formed the basis of his widespread popularity. In 1925 he was coeditor, with Zishe *Landau and Reuben *Iceland, of *Inzel* ("Island"), one of the principal anthologies of Di Yunge. His reputation continued to grow after his death, when several volumes were published: *Lider un Baladn* ("Songs and Ballads," 2 vols. 1955); *Sonetn* ("Sonnets," 1961); the former volume was reprinted in 1963 with parallel Hebrew translations by Shimshon Meltzer, and an introduction by Itzik *Manger, who was in many respects a kindred spirit. The second volume of *Lider un Baladn* contains a short autobiographical sketch as well as an extensive bibliography. Mani Leib's lifelong relationship with the poet Rochelle Weprinsky is documented in *Briv: 1918–1953* ("Letters: 1918–53," 1980).

BIBLIOGRAPHY: Rejzen, Leksikon, 2 (1927), 306–10; LNYL, 5 (1963), 450–7; J. Glatstein, *In Tokh Genumen* (1956), 113–21; S.D. Singer, *Dikhter un Prozaiker* (1959), 5–54; A. Tabachnik, *Dikhter un Dikhtung* (1965), 140–69. **ADD. BIBLIOGRAPHY:** H. Bass, *Mani Leib: Monografye* (1978); R. Wisse, *A Little Love in Big Manhattan* (1988).

[Sol Liptzin / Alisa Braun (2nd ed.)]

MANILOW, BARRY (**Barry Alan Pincus**; 1943–), U.S. singer, producer, and songwriter. Born in New York, Manilow graduated from Eastern District High School in Brooklyn, after which he attended the Juilliard School of Music. Manilow entered the music business writing commercial jingles, such as "I'm stuck on Band-Aids." He became rich singing the popular "You Deserve a Break Today" (1973) commercial for the McDonald's hamburger empire. Soon after, Manilow became Bette Midler's record producer and then turned performer himself. His first record, *Mandy* (1974), went straight to number one on the charts and sold four million singles. Manilow then adapted a Chopin sonata and turned it into the hit song "Magic" (1975). Subsequently he recorded a long succession of top-selling singles (not all of which he wrote), such as "It's a Miracle" (1975), "I Write the Songs" (1976), "This One's for You" (1976), "Weekend in New England" (1976), "Looks Like We Made It" (1977), "Copacabana" (1978), "Can't Smile without You" (1978), "Even Now" (1978), "Ready to Take a Chance Again" (1978), "What a Friend You Turned Out to Be" (1983), and "Sometimes When We Touch" (1997). Rated the number one adult contemporary artist of all time, Manilow had an unprecedented run of 25 consecutive Top 40 hits in the 1970s and 1980s. In 1978, five of his albums were on the charts at the same time, a record that has been equaled only by Frank Sinatra and Johnny Mathis.

Among his innumerable honors and awards, Manilow won a Grammy ("Copacabana," 1978); an Emmy (*The Barry Manilow Special*, 1977); and a Tony (*Barry Manilow on Broadway*, 1977); and he was nominated for an Academy Award (Best Song: "Ready to Take a Chance Again" in *Foul Play*, 1978). In 2002 he was inducted into the Songwriters Hall of Fame in New York.

In 1994 his two-act musical *Barry Manilow's Copacabana – The Musical* premiered in the U.K. His next theatrical project, *Harmony*, was a musical based on the true story of the Comedian Harmonists, a talented group of male singers (three of whom were Jewish) who performed in Nazi Germany until 1934.

With more than 30 albums to his credit and reportedly having made his last grand tour, Manilow signed a long-term contract with the Las Vegas Hilton theater, performing *Barry Manilow: Music and Passion*.

Manilow wrote the autobiographical *Sweet Life: Adventures on the Way to Paradise* in 1987.

BIBLIOGRAPHY: P. Butler, *Barry Manilow: A Biography* (2001); M. Strunk, *The Whole World Sings: The Fans behind Barry Manilow* (1999); A. Clarke, *The Magic of Barry Manilow* (1981); T. Jasper, *Barry Manilow* (1981).

[Jonathan Licht / Ruth Beloff (2nd ed.)]

°**MANIN, DANIELE** (1804–1857), Italian patriot. Manin's father belonged to the Jewish Medina family who had been converted to Christianity. In 1848 he became president of the revived Venetian Republic and was ultimately appointed "dictator." The revolutionary government which he headed distinguished itself by its moderation and financial profits. His cabinet included two Jews: Leon Pincherle as minister of agriculture and Isaac Pesaro Maurogonato as minister of commerce. After leading fruitlessly the heroic resistance of the city in the long siege by the Austrians, he went into exile in Paris, where he died.

BIBLIOGRAPHY: G.M. Trevelyan, *Manin and the Venetian Revolution* (1923); C. Roth, *Venice* (1930), 364–6; Milano, Italia, 363; A. Ottolenghi, in: RMI, 5 (1930/31), 25–35. **ADD. BIBLIOGRAPHY:** P. Galletto, *La vita di Daniele Manin e l'epopea veneziana del 1848–49* (1999); E. Padova, *Daniele Manin lo chiamava il 'mago': saggi* (1999); E. Capuzzo, "Gli ebrei e la rivoluzione di Venezia, *1848–49*," in: *Costituenti e Costituzioni* (2002), 427–42.

[Giorgio Romano]

MANISCHEWITZ, HIRSCH (1891–1943), U.S. Orthodox rabbi, business executive, and philanthropist. Manischewitz, who was born in Cincinatti, Ohio, was educated in Palestine at several yeshivot during 1901–14. While there he helped organize charitable organizations, and, upon his return to Cincinnati in 1914, he continued his philanthropic activities, serving as president of the Orthodox Jewish Orphan's Home. With his brothers he helped maintain the Rabbi Ber Manischewitz Yeshivah of Jerusalem from 1914 until 1943. Moving to New York in 1931, Manischewitz served from that time until his death as an officer of the family B. Manischewitz Baking Co. and helped to build it up into one of the largest manufacturers of Jewish food products in the United States. He was the U.S. representative of over 30 Palestinian and European institutions and organizations of Jewish higher learning. He also served as vice president of the Mizrachi Organization of America, and executive board member of Yeshiva College and of the Orthodox Jewish Congregations of America and Canada.

MANISSA, identical with the ancient Magnesia, today the chief town of the Turkish province bearing the same name, N.E. of *Izmir. A Jewish community probably existed in Manissa from the first century C.E., but there is no extant information on it. During the Byzantine period, there was a congregation in the town and a synagogue, Eẓ ha-Ḥayyim. After the Ottoman conquest of Istanbul, according to the Surgun system, the Sultan Mehmet II transferred the Jews of Manissa to Istanbul and the Jewish community of Manissa ceased to exist. After 1492, however, groups of Jews expelled from Spain arrived in Manissa; they founded two congregations and two synagogues, Lorca and Toledo. Later, as a result of a dispute which broke out in the town, a third congregation, Shalom, was established. At the end of the 15th century, there were more than 100 Jewish families in the town. Rabbi Eliahu Mizrachi writes in a responsum dated after 1504: "But in our case, while in the town of Magnesia people from these places stay there only occasionally, the Sephardim came and settled by themselves without any strangers among them." In the 16th century there was a yeshivah in Manissa, and in the second half of that century the physician and scholar Rabbi Shem Tov Melamed lived and wrote there and in Üsküb. A document from the year 1530/31 notes 88 Jewish families and 33 Jewish bachelors in the city. In 1543 a regulation was passed by the Toledo and Lorca congregations in which they forbade the establishment of a new congregation for a period of 20 years. In the 16th century there existed in the community a society for the ransoming of captives and a *ḥevra kaddisha* society, a cemetery, and other charity institutions. In 1575, according to a Turkish document, there were 117 Jewish households and 10 bachelors in the city.

In the 17th century there were three synagogues in Manissa before the large-scale emigration from the city. The Jews of Manissa suffered from the attacks of the Cellali gangs at the beginning of the century. These bands attacked Manissa in 1632 and plundered the Jewish community, and most of the Jews lost their property. With the rising importance of Izmir, and as a result of a plague which broke out in the town in 1617, many families left for Izmir. During this period the local rabbi was R. Aaron *Lapapa. Many Jews followed *Shabbetai Ẓevi's movement in 1665–66. During the 17th–19th centuries there existed in Manissa an Ashkenazi congregation and a Sephardi one. Three Jewish cemeteries and some tombstones from the 17th century have survived, the oldest of which is dated 1646. In 1671 the community was very poor and could not pay taxes to the government, because most of the Jews had left the city. In 1702 the traveler Tourenfort found in Manissa three synagogues, and another traveler, Pococke, wrote in 1733 that most of the merchandise in the city was concentrated in the hands of the Jews. The old charity institutions existed throughout the *Ottoman period and for halakhic questions the Jews of Manissa turned frequently to the rabbis of Izmir. In 1692 the Hebron emissary Rabbi Nissim Rozilio visited the community. In the responsa literature of the 16th and 17th centuries many regulations and *minhagim* of the community are recorded. Many old *minhagim* and traditions are mentioned in the 19th century by Rabbi Ḥayyim Falaji of Izmir. A known rabbi in the community in the 18th century was Raphael Abraham Mazliah (d. 1784).

At the beginning of the 19th century, the synagogues were renovated and a plot of land was consecrated for a new cemetery. In 1837, 200 Jews died of the plague. In 1838 the Jewish community numbered about 1,200, and in 1873 about 3,000. The main families of the community in the 19th century were Alazraki, Algranati, Gomel, Danon, Mazliah, Franco, Cohen, Levy, Ben-Djoya, Polity, Ninio, Nahom, Shikar, Shochet, Gargir, Lere'ah, Pessoah, Ashkenazi, Azar, Shalom, Buenavida, Israel, Dayan, Saban, Simsolou, Cherkerdji, Conforte, Misriel, Tobi, Beja, Mendes, Janon, Gagin, Sereno, Armaltes, Gayero, Faradji, Cheres, Mizrahi, Gourdji, and Uziel. There were blood libels against the Jews in the town in 1883 and 1893. In 1892 the first school for boys was founded, and in 1896 this was followed by a school for girls. Both were administered by the *Alliance Israélite Universelle. Rabbi Baruch Kalomity (d. 1825) was active in Manissa and Izmir. The rabbis of the community in the second half of the 19th century and at the beginning of the 20th were Abraham Mazliah (d. 1861); Moshe Mazliah, the author of the halakhic book *Em ha-Banim* (died in Jerusalem); David Gomel (d. 1904); and Ḥayyim Mazliah (d. 1906). The last *ḥakham bashi*, Rabbi Ḥayyim Nahum, was born in Manissa. At the end of the 19th century many local Jews immigrated to America, Egypt, South Africa, and other places. At the beginning of the 20th century the Jewish community numbered about 2,000, out of a total population of some 40,000. During this period two additional synagogues were built. The president of the community in 1908–18 was Bechor Abraham Gomel. After the conquest of the region by the Greeks in 1919, the Jews continued to support the Turks. They did not fly the Greek flag on their institutions and did not attend the Congress (August 1922) which demanded autonomy for Izmir and its surroundings. When the Greeks retreated in 1922, a great fire broke out in the town, as a result of which a number of Jewish institutions, including the yeshivah, were destroyed. In the late 1930s the community numbered only 30 families. The principal occupations of the Jews were commerce – the export of agricultural products (fruit, tobacco, and raisins) and the import of manufactured goods – and crafts – tailoring, shoemaking, money changing; there were also some farm owners. A few Jews served as physicians in the government hospitals, as judges, and as translators in the foreign consulates of the town. In the mid-20th century many families immigrated to the U.S., South Africa, Egypt, and Israel. By 1970 no Jews were living in Manissa. In a work by the Turkish writer Nazim Hikmet, written in 1936, there appears a historical character, a Jew who had converted to a heretical sect for which he gave his life. This Jew was Samuel, who was known by the name of Torlak Kemal of Manissa.

BIBLIOGRAPHY: Rosanes, Togarmah, 1 (1930^2), 172–3; 5 (1937–38), 57–58; A. Galanté, *Histoire des Juifs d'Anatolie*, 2 (1939), 70–100. **ADD. BIBLIOGRAPHY:** A. Galanté, in: ISIS, 4, 30–60, 304, 329, 330; 6:135, 259, 260; G. Scholem, *Sabbatai Sevi* (1973), index; L. Bornstein, in: *Mi-Mizraḥ u-mi-Ma'arav* (1974), 94; M. Benayahu, *Ha-Yeḥasim bein Yehudei Yavan li-Yehudei Italyah* (1980), 137. E. Bashan, *Sheviyah u-Pedut* (1980), 99–100, 199–200; M.A. Epstein, *The Ottoman Jewish Communities and Their Role in the Fifteenth and Sixteenth Centuries* (1980), 245; Y. Barnai, in: *Pe'amim*, 12 (1982), 49–54; A. Levy, in: A. Levy (ed.), *The Jews of the Ottoman Empire* (1994), 114–20; N. Gürsel, in: A. Levy, *The Jews of the Ottoman Empire* (1994), 648–54; J. McCarthy, in: A. Levy (ed.), ibid., 380; F.M. Emecen, *Unutulmuş bir Cemaat, Manisa Yahudileri* (1997); idem, *XVI. Asirda Manisa Kazasi* (1989), 50, 53, 62–65, 79, 81, 86, 298; A. Rodrigue, *Ḥinukh, Ḥevrah ve-Historiyah, Kol Yisrael Ḥaverim ve-Yehudei ha-Yam ha-Tikhon, 1860–1929* (1991), 39, 169; J. Hacker, in: A. Rodrigue (ed.), *Ottoman and Turkish Jewry, Community and Leadership* (1992), 34, 63.

[Abraham Haim / Leah Bornstein-Makovetsky (2nd ed.)]

MANITOBA, midcontinent province of Canada, bordering on North Dakota and Minnesota to the south, Ontario to the east, and Saskatchewan to the west. In 1877 the first known Jewish residents of Manitoba were Reuben Goldstein, a peddler, and Edmond Coblentz, a clerk, one of three brothers from Alsace-Lorraine. The 1881 Canadian census listed 33 Jews in Manitoba, 21 of them in Winnipeg. Among those outside Winnipeg were Dr. Hiram Vineberg, originally from Montreal and medical health officer in Portage la Prairie, and Harry Wexelbaum, a hotel operator in West Lynne.

In the spring of 1882, Manitoba's Jewish population expanded more than tenfold with the arrival of 350 refugees fleeing czarist pogroms and promised "free" homesteads. Land had previously been assigned for Mennonites, Icelanders, Scottish, and French settlers but no land was allotted for the Jews in spite of a request by Alexander Galt, Canadian high commissioner in London. Most of the new arrivals were housed in Winnipeg immigration sheds while earlier Jewish residents started an immigrant aid committee and raised $360 for immediate needs. But the newcomers did not wait for charity; men soon found work hauling lumber, women took domestic jobs, and by mid-June, 150 Jewish men were employed laying track across the prairies for the Canadian Pacific Railway. Others took to peddling and trading. The arrival of these Russian Jews was not favorably received in the Winnipeg media. The *Manitoba Free Press* commented: "… they are not likely to be of any great value to the country."

It took two years until land was found for the Jews, 300 miles west, at Moosomin, beyond the Manitoba border. By this time just 27 families were still willing to go on the land. This settlement, dubbed "New Jerusalem," was declared a failure after several years, but some of the failed farmers returned to Winnipeg to launch successful business enterprises and to help found synagogues and schools.

In 1887, land was first assigned to Jewish farm settlers within Manitoba, at Niverville, 30 miles southeast of Winnipeg, and after the turn of the century in Bender Hamlet and Camper, 70 miles north of Winnipeg. Closer to Winnipeg several Jewish farmers set up dairy farms. At one time there were reported to be Jewish merchant and farm families living in 118 Manitoba towns and villages outside Winnipeg. However, in 1961 Jews were reported living in just three – Portage la Prairie, 111; Brandon, 101; and Flin Flon, 60. In 2004, descendants of Jews who live in one farming town, Winkler, organized a memorial event and dedicated a plaque to the memory of 15 Winkler Jewish pioneer families who lived there between 1890 and 1914. Among Winkler-born Jews was Israel Nitikman, a judge of the Manitoba Court of Queen's Bench, and Ernest Sirluck, president of the University of Manitoba in 1970–76. As in Winkler, most Jews in smaller communities eventually moved on, especially to Winnipeg

The total number of Jews in Manitoba, including Winnipeg, grew from 31 in 1881, to 791 in 1891 and to 1,514 in 1901. By 1911 the number ballooned more than sevenfold to 10,741, then by more than half again to 16,669 in 1921. The population of Jews in Manitoba eventually reached 19,341 in 1931 and remained steady until 1971 when population numbers began a decline to 15,215 in 2001. The vast majority of these Jews lived in Winnipeg, the center of Manitoba Jewish life.

Jewish religious services in Manitoba were first held on Yom Kippur in 1879, in a private Winnipeg home. Regular Sabbath services began after the arrival of the Russian Jews in 1882. Some Jewish laborers celebrated Rosh Ha-Shanah that year in a tent at a railway station 40 miles from Winnipeg; they raised $100 among themselves to order a *Sefer Torah* and a *shofar* from New York. Synagogues also were established in Brandon in 1906, Portage la Prairie in 1908 and, meeting the needs of summer vacationers, in Winnipeg Beach in 1951. The first two synagogues have long been closed; the latter opens every summer. In the past, several smaller Jewish communities, including Winkler, also had synagogues or at least organized High Holiday services.

With the vast majority of Manitoba Jews congregated in Winnipeg, arguably the greatest area of Jewish impact in Manitoba was in politics – federal, provincial, and municipal. As early as 1882, Harry Wexelbaum served as a municipal councilor in West Lynne, before that community merged with the neighboring town of Emerson. Later Samuel Rosner served as mayor of Plum Coulee. In Flin Flon in Northern Manitoba, with only 60 Jews in a population of 10,200 residents during the 1960s and 1970s, Jack Freedman served as mayor for more than 10 years. Harry Trager was mayor of the neighboring town of The Pas, which could not muster a *minyan* among its 5,031 population.

Serious political activity took place in Winnipeg, where Jews often sparred politically with one another. In 1904, Moses Finkelstein of the Conservative Party was the first Winnipeg Jew elected to the city council, where Jews served continuously for most of the 20th century. In 1910, S. Hart Green (Liberal) was elected to the Manitoba Legislature, the first Jew to sit in a Canadian provincial assembly. In 1912, Alter Skaleter (Conservative) was elected to the city council, serving for five years, and was succeeded by Labour candidate Abraham A. Heaps. Heaps was a leader in Winnipeg's 1919 General Strike, and was arrested with other strike leaders. In 1926 he was elected Labour Member of Parliament from the heavily Jewish Winnipeg North riding and served until 1941. Max Steinkopf, a lawyer and leader in the YMHA and B'nai B'rith, was elected to the School Board in 1916. He supported the anti-strike Committee of 1000, which was formed in response to the 1919 General Strike. In 1920, Steinkopf was defeated by Labour candidate Rosa Alcin. In 1927 and again in 1932, William Tobias (Conservative) was elected to the Manitoba legislature. Marcus Hyman (Labour) was elected and, of special note, sponsored the first group libel law adopted in Canada. In 1959 Maitland Steinkopf became the first Jewish cabinet minster in Manitoba under Conservative Premier Duff Roblin; he declined to run again in 1966 but continued to serve the province in his capacity as chair of the Manitoba Centennial Corporation until his death in 1970.

Three prominent left-leaning politicians, Morris A. Gray, David Orlikow, and Saul M. Cherniack, began political careers as Winnipeg School Board representatives before moving to the city council and then to the Legislature. In 1962 Orlikow was elected to the House of Commons, and in 1969 Cherniack became one of three Jewish cabinet ministers in Manitoba's first New Democratic Party government, along with Saul A. Miller, who had been mayor of suburban West Kildonan, and Sidney Green. In the early 1970s, Sidney J. Spivak served as leader of the opposition Progressive Conservative Party, and Israel H. Asper sat in the Legislature briefly as leader of the Liberal Party before going on to become a media mogul and philanthropist. In 1986 Mira Spivak was appointed a Progressive Conservative senator from Manitoba; from 2004 she sat as an independent. In 2000 Anita Neville (née Schwartz), former School Board member, was elected to Parliament as a Liberal and re-elected in 2004. Also in 2004 Israeli-born Sam Katz, an entrepreneur and entertainment and sports promoter, was elected as the first Jewish mayor of Winnipeg.

[Abraham Arnold (2nd ed.)]

MANKIEWICZ, HERMAN JACOB (1897–1953), U.S. journalist, playwright, and screenwriter. Mankiewicz was born in New York City. In 1905, the family moved to Wilkes-Barre, Pennsylvania, where his father was an editor for a German-language newspaper and his mother worked as a dressmaker. In 1917, Mankiewicz graduated from Columbia with honors, having written a humor column for the *Spectator*. He worked as managing editor for the *American Jewish Chronicle* until 1918, when he enlisted as an Army flying cadet, but joined the Marines and served as a private first class. After the war he spent several years in Europe, collecting stories about the Red Cross for the organization's press office and as a correspondent for a variety of publications. Upon Mankiewicz's return to New York, he worked for the *New York World*, and in 1923 he joined the drama department of the *New York Times*. Along with Dorothy *Parker and Ben *Hecht he became a member of the Algonquin Round Table. In 1925, he was hired as the first drama critic for the *New Yorker*, a position he held for one year. Soon after, Paramount Publix Studios extended an invitation to him to join the first wave of screenwriters heading west. By 1933, he was working for Metro-Goldwyn-Mayer, having written or collaborated on a variety of films, including *Dinner at Eight* (1933) and the Marx Brothers' *Monkey Business* (1931) and *Horse Feathers* (1932). By 1939, his penchant for gambling led to his dismissal from the studio. Orson Welles hired Mankiewicz to adapt Mercury Theater dramatizations. It was during this time that Mankiewicz developed and wrote *Citizen Kane* (1941). Although the film earned him an Oscar for best original screenplay and restored his reputation in Hollywood, it was seen as a betrayal by his friends William Randolph Hearst and Marion Davies. By the end of the 1940s his health was declining and he became a recluse by the 1950s. Mankiewicz died of uremic poisoning in Los Angeles.

[Adam Wills (2nd ed.)]

MANKIEWICZ, JOSEPH LEO (1909–1993), U.S. film writer, producer, and director. Born in Wilkes-Barre, Pennsylvania, Mankiewicz worked on scripts for Paramount, MGM, and Fox. He received Academy Awards for *A Letter to Three Wives* (Best Director and Best Screenplay, 1949) and *All About Eve* (Best Director and Best Screenplay, 1950).

His early screenwriting credits include *Skippy* (Oscar nomination for Best Adaptation, 1931), *Million Dollar Legs* (1932), *Manhattan Melodrama* (1934), *Our Daily Bread* (1934), *Forsaking All Others* (1934), and *I Live My Life* (1935).

Mankiewicz produced such films as *Fury* (1936), *The Shopworn Angel* (1938), *The Philadelphia Story* (Best Picture Oscar, 1940), *The Feminine Touch* (1941), *Woman of the Year* (1942), and *The Keys of the Kingdom* (and screenplay, 1948). In 1952 he formed Figaro, Inc., and produced, wrote, and directed *The Barefoot Contessa* (Oscar nomination for Best Screenplay, 1954) and *The Quiet American* (1958). Films he directed include *Dragonwyck* (and screenplay, 1946), *Somewhere in the Night* (and screenplay, 1946), *The Ghost and Mrs. Muir* (1947), *No Way Out* (Oscar nomination for Best Screenplay, 1950), *People Will Talk* (and screenplay, 1951), *5 Fingers* (Oscar nomination for Best Director, 1952), *Julius Caesar* (1953), *Guys and Dolls* (and screenplay, 1955), *Suddenly Last Summer* (1959), *Cleopatra* (and screenplay, 1963), *The Honey Pot* (and screenplay, 1967), *There Was a Crooked Man* (1970), and *Sleuth* (Oscar nomination for Best Director, 1972).

Mankiewicz's films are characterized by their intelligence, sophistication, and witty dialogue, and a number of them demonstrate his masterful use of the flashback.

His brother HERMAN (1897–1953) was a screenwriter and producer. His son Tom is a writer and director and his son Christopher is a producer.

[Jonathan Licht / Ruth Beloff (2nd ed.)]

MANKOWITZ, WOLF (1924–1998), English novelist and playwright. Mankowitz was born and raised in London's East End. He studied English at Cambridge, then, like his father, became an antique dealer, revealing his expertise in *Wedgwood* (1953), *The Portland Vase* (1952), and *A Concise Encyclopedia of English Pottery and Porcelain* (1957) with R.G. Haggar. He turned increasingly to literature and wrote a number of books inspired by his childhood recollections of the East End. These include *A Kid for Two Farthings* (1953), the title of which was suggested by the Passover allegorical ditty **Ḥad Gadya; Make Me An Offer* (1952); *The Boychick* (1954); and *The Mendelman Fire* (1957). In his early writing, Mankowitz's Jewishness was somewhat muted, revealing itself merely in a preference for Jewish characters. His typical mingling of humor and pathos comes out strongly in the play, *The Bespoke Overcoat* (1955), a Jewish reworking of a Russian tale by Gogol. Like several of his other stories, this was made into a motion picture. Mankowitz was primarily a humorist with a talent for elaborating anecdotes, but he gradually developed a more astringent tone in his writing, e.g., *Expresso Bongo* (1960), a satire on the world of "pop" music, and in his satirical novel about film-makers, *Cockatrice* (1963). He later devoted himself to screen-writing and to publicity work in support of the Ḥasidic sect of Lubavitch. Mankowitz was the author or co-author of a number of well-known screenplays, including *The Day the Earth Caught Fire* (1961), *Casino Royale* (1967), and *The Hireling* (1973).

BIBLIOGRAPHY: S.J. Goldsmith, *Twenty 20th Century Jews* (1962), 69–75; JC (March 22, 1968).

MANN, ABBY (1927–), U.S. screenwriter. Born Abraham Goodman in Philadelphia, Pennsylvania, the son of a Russian Jewish immigrant jeweler, Mann grew up in a working-class area of East Pittsburgh, a largely Catholic area, and attended Temple University and New York University. Mann wrote dramas for such 1950s television programs as *Playhouse 90* and *Studio One*, and is considered a leader in the genre of the made-for-television movie; social justice issues are Mann's main inspiration. He received an Academy Award for his screenplay for *Judgment at Nuremberg* (1961), based on the postwar trial of Nazi judges. Reuniting with *Nuremberg*'s director, Stanley *Kramer, Mann wrote *A Child Is Waiting* (1963), about special-needs children, and then adapted the Katherine Anne Porter novel *Ship of Fools* (1965). Mann took Emmys for *The Marcus-Nelson Murders* (1973), the pilot for the series *Kojak*, as well as for *Murderers Among Us: The Simon Wiesenthal Story* (1989) and *Indictment: The McMartin Case* (cowritten with his wife, Myra Mann, in 1995). In 1975, Mann developed *Medical Story*, a short-lived series that cast a light on the medical world. Ten years after the assassination of Martin Luther King, Jr., Mann explored whether there was a conspiracy to kill the civil-rights leader in the miniseries *King* (1978). In 1985, he wrote *The Atlanta Child Murders*, a case that focused on Wayne Williams, a black man accused of killing young boys after procuring them for his gay father.

[Adam Wills (2nd ed.)]

MANN, ABRAHAM AARON OF POSNAN (mid-17th century), Hebrew writer. Mann, who was a *ḥazzan* in Poznan, wrote a short work, *Urim ve-Tummim* (Amsterdam, 1653), dealing with such matters as the proper way to fulfill the ethical commandments, repentance, and the way to achieve the state of *devekut* and the love of God. Instructions are also given regarding correct social behavior, in accordance with Jewish ethics, based directly on talmudic and midrashic ideas. The work is divided into short paragraphs (each beginning with a different letter of the alphabet), arranged in a *notarikon* system forming the author's name several times. The work likewise includes a short ethical poem, also arranged in a *notarikon* system, and, at the end, several brief sermons.

BIBLIOGRAPHY: Steinschneider, Cat Bod, 4274; Benjacob, Oẓar, 30, no. 596.

[Joseph Dan]

MANN, DANIEL (**Daniel Chugerman**; 1912–1991), U.S. director. Mann was born in New York and began his career in entertainment as a musician in resorts. He served in the army in World War II, was trained at Neighborhood Playhouse in New York, began directing television productions, and was later a director for theater and for movie adaptations of the same plays, including *Come Back, Little Sheba* (1950; 1952), and *The Rose Tattoo* (1951; 1955). On Broadway, he also directed *Paint Your Wagon* (1952), *The Immoralist* (1954), and *A Loss of Roses* (1959).

Mann directed such films as *I'll Cry Tomorrow* (1955), *The Teahouse of the August Moon* (1956), *The Last Angry Man* (1959), *Butterfield 8* (1960), *Ada* (1961), *Five Finger Exercise* (1962), *Who's Been Sleeping in My Bed?* (1963), *Our Man Flint* (1965), *Judith* (1966), *For Love of Ivy* (1967), *Willard* (1971), *A Dream of Kings* (1971), *Maurie* (1973), *The Revengers* (1973), *Lost in the Stars* (1974), *Interval* (1974), *Journey into Fear* (1975), and *Matilda* (1978).

On the small screen, Mann's directorial credits include the miniseries *How the West Was Won* (1977) and the TV movies *Another Part of the Forest* (1972), *Playing for Time* (1980), *The Day the Loving Stopped* (1981), and *The Man Who Broke 1,000 Chains* (1981).

[Jonathan Licht / Ruth Beloff (2nd ed.)]

MANN, DELBERT (1920–), U.S. director. Born in Lawrence, Kansas, Mann served in the U.S. Air Force during World War II and entered the theater as stage manager and then director for repertory and summer playhouse productions. From 1949 to 1955 he directed a number of television dramas, including Playhouse 90 and Omnibus productions, and in 1955 directed the movie *Marty*, from his television adaptation of Paddy Chayevsky's drama. It earned him an Academy Award for Best Director. Mann also directed the movies *Bachelor Party* (1957), *Separate Tables* (1958), *Desire under the Elms* (1958), *Middle of the Night* (1959), *Dark at the Top of the Stairs* (1960), *The Outsider* (1961), *Lover Come Back* (1961), *That Touch of Mink* (1962), *Dear Heart* (1964), *A Gathering of Eagles* (1964), *Quick Before It Melts!* (1965), *Kidnapped* (1971), *The Pink Jungle* (1968), *Birch Interval* (1977), and *Bronte* (1983). In 1968 he began working outside the United States, directing movies premiered on television and then shown in movie theaters, including *Heidi* (1969), *David Copperfield* (1970), *Jane Eyre* (1971), and *All Quiet on the Western Front* (1979), for which he was nominated for an Emmy.

Mann's TV films include *All the Way Home* (1981), *The Member of the Wedding* (1982), *The Last Days of Patton* (1986), and *Incident in a Small Town* (1994). He also wrote *Looking Back … At Live Television and Other Matters* (1998).

Mann served as president of the Directors Guild of America (1967–71). In 2002 the DGA awarded him an Honorary Life Member Award.

[Ruth Beloff (2nd ed.)]

MANN, FREDERIC RAND (**Maniyevich**; 1903–1987), U.S. public figure. Mann, who was born in Gomel, Russia, was taken to the U.S. at the age of two. A successful businessman, he had a varied public career. He was appointed a member of the U.S. Mint Assay Commission in 1943, served as director of commerce and city representative of Philadelphia, and as a Pennsylvania commissioner of the Delaware River Port Authority. President Johnson appointed Mann the first U.S. ambassador to Barbados (1967) and U.S. special representative to the Caribbean islands of Antigua, Dominica, Grenada, St. Lucia, and St. Kitts-Nevis (1968). Active in Jewish affairs, Mann was vice president of the American Committee for the Weizmann Institute of Science, a founder of the Israel Philharmonic Orchestra, which is housed in the Mann Auditorium in Tel Aviv bearing his name, and treasurer of Dropsie College in Philadelphia.

The Mann Center for the Performing Arts in Philadelphia, built in 1976, also bears its benefactor's name. One of the largest outdoor amphitheaters in the United States, it seats 4,000 under cover and an additional 10,000 in the open air.

MANN, HERBIE (**Herbert Solomon**; 1930–2003). U.S. jazz flautist. When Mann began his career as a flute player in the early 1950s, he was essentially the only flautist playing jazz. A product of the Manhattan School of Music, he sought models in the world of Latin music, where the flute was a much more common sound. As Mann said in interviews, "When [accordionist] Mat Matthews gave me an opportunity to record jazz on flute [in 1952], there was no tradition of straightahead jazz on the flute…. When Symphony Sid [Torin], the DJ in New York suggested I add conga drums, … the audience understood where the flute was. It was jazz, but it was Latin jazz." The Latin-jazz fusion would prove to be merely the first of many hyphenate jazz styles Mann would explore. He would register bestselling records playing jazz-funk, jazz-rock, disco-inflected jazz, Brazilian jazz, and jazz-reggae. After he was diagnosed with inoperable cancer in 1998, he even went back to his own musical roots, playing East European Jewish-influenced material. Mann's enormous commercial success was a mixed blessing; jazz purists frequently dismissed his records and playing for their ease, bordering on glibness. Regardless of the merits of his own playing, he established the flute as a jazz instrument.

BIBLIOGRAPHY: J. Bradley, "Herbie Mann Knows No Limits," in: *Denver Post* (Jan. 17, 1998); I. Carr, "Herbie Mann," in: *Jazz: The Rough Guide* (1995); D. Hodges, Daniel, "Herbie Mann," in: *Contemporary Musicians,* Vol. 16 (1996); J. Newsom, "Herbie Mann's New Groove," in: *The Port Folio* (July 9, 2002).

[George Robinson (2nd ed.)]

MANN, JACOB (1888–1940), scholar of the **Genizah* period and of the Jews under the *Fatimids, and particularly of the *Genizah* fragments. The son of a *shoḥet* from Przemysl, Galicia, where he received a traditional Orthodox education, Mann went to London in 1908 where he pursued his secular studies. At the same time he pursued rabbinic studies at Jews' College and qualified for the ministry in 1914. Soon after, he began publishing learned papers, including his excellent series, "The Responsa of the Babylonian Geonim as a Source of Jewish History" (in JQR, 7 (1916/17); 11 (1920/21)). The field in which he was later to distinguish himself as a great scholar was *Genizah* research. Mann for the first time undertook to collect and explain all the documents from the period preceding the Crusades to the fall of the Fatimids. His book, *The Jews in Egypt and in Palestine under the Fatimid Caliphs* (2 vols., 1920–22; reprinted with introd. by S.D. Goitein, 1970), was a masterpiece *sui generis.* By establishing the dates of a great number of the largely undated *Genizah* documents, Mann provided the chronological framework for the history of the Jews in the Near East. He revealed the great role played by the *Jerusalem gaonate in the period before the Crusades and shed new light on the various forces within the Jewish communities then living in the lands ruled by the Fatimids. Although Mann neglected the Arabic documents, abstained avowedly from drawing general conclusions, and was mainly interested in the communal history of the Jews, his work is of lasting value as a great collection of hitherto unknown sources, which he ably deciphered and annotated. After the first volume of the above-mentioned book appeared, Mann went to the United States, first as lecturer at Hebrew College in Baltimore and a year later as professor at Hebrew Union College in Cincinnati. There he taught Jewish history and Talmud and continued his research. His second major work, *Texts and Studies in Jewish History and Literature* (2 vols., 1931–35, repr. 1970), contains various documents concerning European Jewry and Geonica and texts elucidating the history of the *Karaites in the Near East and in Eastern Europe. In the last years of his life Mann embarked on the study of one of the most difficult branches of Hebrew literature, the Midrashim. In his work, *The Bible as read and preached in the Old Synagogue; a study in the cycles of the reading from Torah and Prophets, as well as from Psalms and in the structure of the Midrashic homilies,* he tried to establish the dependence of the Midrashim from the chapters of the Torah and from the *haftarot* which were read on the Sabbath on cycles of three and one-half years respectively. The first volume of the book was published in 1940. Material left by Mann for the second volume was prepared for publication by Isaiah Sonne; after the latter's death the work was continued by Victor Reichert; it appeared in 1966.

BIBLIOGRAPHY: R. Mahler, in: *Yivo Bleter,* 16 (1940), 170–81, incl. bibl.; 17 (1941), 92.

[Eliyahu Ashtor]

MANN, MENDEL (**Mendl Man**; 1916–1975), Yiddish novelist and painter. Mann was born in Płonsk, Poland. When his art education in Warsaw was interrupted by the Nazi invasion, he fled eastwards and enlisted in the Red Army, in which he witnessed the siege of Moscow and the occupation of Berlin. After the war he settled in Łodz and published a volume of verse, *Di Shtilkayt Mont* ("Silence Calls," 1945). Following the Kielce pogrom, he moved to Regensburg in 1946, where he edited a Yiddish DP newspaper. He immigrated to Israel in 1948, where he published *Oyfgevakhte Erd* ("Awakened Earth," 1953), a collection of stories reflecting the lives of Jewish refugees living in a former Palestinian village. From 1949 he was a co-editor of *Di Goldene Keyt.* The novel, *In a Farvorloztn Dorf* ("In an Abandoned Village," 1954), is based on the life of Zionist emigrants to Palestine from Jewish villages in the vicinity of Płonsk. His most outstanding work is a trilogy of novels reflecting his wartime experiences. The constituent volumes are *Bay di Toyern fun Moskve* (1956; *At the Gates of Moscow,* 1963), *Bay der Vaysl* ("At the Vistula," 1958), and *Dos Faln fun Berlin* ("The Fall of Berlin," 1960). The action deals with fighting on the Eastern Front seen through the eyes of Jews serving in the Red Army (whose contribution is minimized to indulge Stalin's prejudice), the reactions of the Russian and Ukrainian population as the Nazis approach Moscow, the instinctive patriotism of ordinary Soviet soldiers and their aspirations for greater freedom after the war. The Nazi leaders are portrayed as histrionic charlatans. Further important prose works are *Nakht iber Glushino* ("Night over Glushino," 1957), *Di Gas fun Bliendike Mandlen* ("The Street of Almond Blossoms," 1958), a collection of stories set in Palestine, *Al Naharoys Poyln* ("By the Rivers of Poland," 1962), and a further volume of stories, *Der Shvartser Demb* ("The Black Oak," 1969). In 1961 Mann moved to Paris and became the editor of *Undzer Vort.* He built up a significant art collection and became a friend of Marc Chagall. In 1963 he edited the Yiddish section of *Sefer Plonsk ve-ha-Sevivah,* the Płonsk memorial volume. There were exhibitions of his paintings in the 1930s in Warsaw and in 1967 in Paris. His works have been extensively translated into French and German.

BIBLIOGRAPHY: LNYL, 5 (1963), 431–14; J. Glatstein, *Mit Mayne Fartog Bikher* (1963), 427–32; S. Bikl, *Shrayber fun Mayn Dor,* 2 (1965), 408–19. **ADD. BIBLIOGRAPHY:** C.A. Madison, *Yiddish Literature: Its Scope and Major Writers* (1968), 516–17; G. Sapozhnikov, *Der Goyrl fun Yidn Tsvishn di Umes-Hooylem: An Analitisher Araynblik in der "Milkhome-Trilogye" fun Mendl Man* (1976).

[Josef Schawinski / Hugh Denman (2nd ed.)]

MANN, THEODORE R. (1928–), U.S. attorney and communal leader. Mann was born in Czechoslovakia, and came to the U.S. with his parents in 1929. After studying at various yeshivot in New York, he graduated from Pennsylvania State University and Temple University's School of Law. He was the editor of Temple University's *Temple Law Quarterly*. He clerked in the U.S. 3rd Circuit Court of Appeals and then taught at the University of Pennsylvania Law School.

For 31 years he was a senior partner at the law firm of Mann, Ungar, Spector & Labovitz, concentrating on securities fraud litigation, anti-trust litigation, and other complex commercial issues. Mann played a leading role in several major civil rights and church-state separation cases. He successfully argued cases involving the admissions policy of Girard College and challenges to Bible reading in the public schools. He also argued before the U.S. Supreme Court in *Lemon v. Sloan*, a case challenging public aid to parochial schools, and in several Sunday "blue law" cases. Mann joined the WolfBlock law firm, serving as Of Counsel in the Business Litigation Practice Group in the company's Philadelphia office.

Long active in Jewish communal affairs, he served as president of the Jewish Community Relations Council of Greater Philadelphia and of the Greater Philadelphia Council of the American Jewish Congress and as national vice president of the Congress. He was also chairman of the Jewish Council for Public Affairs and the Israel Task Force of the National Jewish Community Relations Advisory Council. Mann succeeded Rabbi Alexander M. Schindler as president of the Conference of Presidents of Major American Jewish Organizations, holding office until 1980. He also held official positions with the National Conference on Soviet Jewry, the American Jewish Congress, and the Executive Committee of the Israel Policy Forum. He was the founding chairman of Project Nishma and of Mazon: A Jewish Response to Hunger. In 2000, the Jewish Council for Public Affairs presented Mann with the Albert Chernin Award for his "exemplary voluntary service to the field of Jewish community relations and the leading role he has taken in defending the First Amendment and religious freedoms for all Americans."

[Ruth Beloff (2nd ed.)]

°**MANN, THOMAS** (1875–1955), German novelist and the leader of Germany's anti-Nazi intellectuals. Mann married Katia Pringsheim (1883–1980), whose parents were both of Jewish background: Alfred Pringsheim (1850–1941), professor of mathematics at Munich University, and Hedwig Dohm (1855–1942), the daughter of the famous feminist and author Hedwig Dohm (born Hedwig Schlesinger, 1831–1919), who had married in Berlin in 1853 the political and satirical publicist Ernst Dohm (formerly Elias Levy, 1819–1883), editor-in-chief of the satirical periodical *Kladderadatsch*.

It was the Berlin Jewish publisher, Samuel *Fischer, who launched Thomas Mann on his literary career. He introduced Jewish characters in many of his masterpieces, such as *Koenigliche Hoheit* (1909, *Royal Highness*, 1916), *Der Zauberberg* (1924; *The Magic Mountain*, 1927), and *Doktor Faustus* (1947; Eng., 1949). He withdrew his short story "Blood of the Walsungs" (Waelsungenblut, 1905), the original conclusion of which could be considered antisemitic, from publication after protests of his father-in-law and published it only as a private printing and with a different ending in 1921. Before the rise of Hitler he rarely wrote on Jewish matters, but his 1907 essay "Solving the Jewish Question" stood in the tradition of emancipation ideology by advocating mixed marriage and conversion. When Jacob *Wassermann, in 1921, voiced his despair at the prevalence of antisemitism in Germany, Mann answered his fellow-novelist that Germany was the country least suited for the growth of this evil. But from 1922 Mann warned of the Nazi danger. He called Munich as early as 1923 "the town of Hitler" and fought actively against the danger ("Kampf um Muenchen als Kulturzentrum," 1926; "Deutsche Ansprache. Ein Appell an die Vernunft," Berlin, 1930). When Hitler came to power, Mann, unlike his brother Heinrich (1871–1950) and his children, at first remained silent about the Nazi regime, hoping that it would not last too long. To wait things out he chose voluntary exile in southern France and Switzerland. In January 1936 he broke his silence on the persecution of German Jews in a leading article in the *Neue Zuercher Zeitung*. While disclaiming the appellation "philo-Semite," Mann expressed his repugnance for German antisemitism as the product of a racial myth designed for the rabble, and urged Jews not to despair: having survived many storms in the past, they would outlive this new oppression too. As a Czechoslovak citizen from November 1936, the Nazis deprived him of German citizenship in December, because of his "solidarity with Jewish associates." In response to the stripping of his title of Dr. h.c. of the University of Bonn, Mann warned in his published reply already in January 1937 of the coming war. During the early Nazi years he was at work on his prose epic *Joseph und seine Brueder* (4 vols., 1933–42, *Joseph and his Brothers*, 1934–45), the most profound treatment of this biblical theme in literature. He went to the United States in September 1938, teaching as an honorary professor at Princeton University, and moved to California in 1941. From the beginning of World War II he broadcast from America through BBC London 55 speeches to German listeners ("Deutsche Hoerer!"). In 1942, when news of the extermination of the Jews reached him, Mann broadcast the information, hoping it would reach German listeners. In 1943 he called attention to the "maniacal resolution" of the Nazis to exterminate the Jews totally. He begged the United States not to cling bureaucratically to its immigration laws while millions of Jews were being massacred, but to prove by a modification of those laws that the war was indeed being waged for humanity and human dignity. He lived in California until 1952, when he moved to Switzerland. His public views on the Jewish question from the years 1936–48 were published in 1966 (*Sieben Manifeste zur juedischen Frage*, ed. by W.A. Berendsohn).

His eldest child, ERIKA MANN (1905–1969), trained as an actress, directed *Die Pfeffermuehle*, an anti-Nazi cabaret, from January 1933. She went into exile in February 1933 and was in the U.S. from 1936, became a war correspondent, and eventually settled in Switzerland. Her works include *Zehn Millionen Kinder. Die Erziehung deutscher Jugend im Dritten Reich* (1938) and *Das letzte Jahr* (1956), a biography of her father. She was an outspoken critic of post-World War II German democracy. Her brother, KLAUS MANN (1906–1949), an anti-Nazi writer and journalist, published two journals (*Die Sammlung*, 1933–35; *Decision*, 1941–42) and resumed his career in the U.S. Army as a propagandist. He wrote various novels and an autobiography, *The Turning Point* (1944; German ed., 1952). He and his sister also published *Escape to Life* (1939), about the talented victims of Hitlerism. Klaus Mann committed suicide in Cannes.

BIBLIOGRAPHY: A. Eloesser, *Thomas Mann, sein Leben und sein Werk* (1925); K. Hamburger, *Thomas Manns Roman "Joseph und seine Brueder"* (1945). **ADD. BIBLIOGRAPHY:** H. Jendreiek, *Thomas Mann. Der demokratische Roman* (1977); S.D. Dowden (ed.), *A Companion to Thomas Mann's Magic Mountain* (1999), 141–57; D. Prater, *Thomas Mann, A Life* (1995) H. Kurzke, *Thomas Mann. Das Leben als Kunstwerk* (1999; *Life as a Work of Art*, tr. Leslie Willson, 2002); M. Dierks and R. Wimmer (ed.), *Thomas Mann und das Judentum. Die Vortraege des Berliner Kolloquiums der Deutschen Thomas-Mann-Gesellschaft* (2004).

[Sol Liptzin / Dirk Heisserer (2nd ed.)]

MANNA (Heb. מָן), referred to as "bread from heaven" (Ex. 16:4; cf. Ps. 105:40). Manna is described in Exodus as coming down in the wilderness of Sinai within the area of the Israelites' encampment every morning except on Sabbaths in the form of "a fine, scale-like thing, fine as the hoarfrost on the ground." The Israelites collected "an *Omer* a head," which they ate within 24 hours, for if left until the next morning it bred worms and rotted. When the sun shone on the ground the manna melted. The double portion collected on the sixth day, however, did not rot and sufficed also for the Sabbath when no manna fell. In form "it was like coriander seed, but white; and the taste of it was like wafers made with honey." For 40 consecutive years the Israelites ate the manna, "until they came to the land of Canaan" (Ex. 16:26–36).

Some, drawing an analogy between the manna and the quails, which also miraculously descended to the children of Israel, contend that, like the latter, the manna was a phenomenon of nature which sometimes occurs in the wilderness of Sinai. Something similar is stated by Josephus (Ant. 3:26ff.): "And to this very day all that region is watered by a rain like to that which then the Deity sent down for men's sustenance." As early as from the time of St. Anthony (c. 250–355 C.E.), Christian pilgrims tell of a tradition, current among the monks of the monastery of St. Catherine in Sinai, that the biblical manna comes from the secretion of insects on the branches of tamarisk trees, which to this day grow in the wadis of the southern Sinai mountains. Bodenheimer has suggested a similar explanation of the origin of the manna. Two genera of coccidae parasitize on tamarisk trees of the species *Tamarix mannifera*. On those growing in the Arabah Valley, in the lowlands of the southern Negev, and in Sinai, there are large numbers of the coccus *Najacoccus serpentinus minon*, which is covered with a pocket in the form of an elongated tube in which it lays its eggs. Another coccus, the *Tradutina mannipara*, lays its eggs in a cone-like pocket. These two coccidae extract the sap, rich in carbohydrates, of the branches of the tamarisk, the excess carbohydrates which their bodies cannot absorb being secreted in the form of drops of transparent liquid that congeal into white globules, composed chemically of glucose, fructose, and a very small quantity of pectin. The globules melt in the heat of the sun. A large proportion of these globules of "manna" is eaten by ants, which collect them in their nests. In years of plentiful rain, the Sinai Bedouin, who also call the globules *man*, gather as much as 600 kilograms (about 1,300 lbs.) of them, which they use as a substitute for honey.

Although there is some resemblance between this "manna" and that described in the Pentateuch, and despite the importance of the early tradition supporting that identification, it is very doubtful whether this is the manna of the Bible, lacking as it does several features of the biblical food. There is the additional fact that the nutritional value of the "manna" produced by the cocci of the tamarisk is very slight, since it contains no proteins at all, whereas the Pentateuch speaks of the manna as "bread" and as a basic food. And finally, the quantity of this "manna" is not enough to feed a tribe or even a family, let alone a nation wandering in the wilderness. Some identify the biblical manna with the *Lecanora esculenta*, a species of lichen, large quantities of which are sometimes borne by winds to the central Asian steppes and to the heights of the Atlas Mountains. This species, however, has thus far not been found in the Arabian Peninsula or in the neighborhood of Israel.

[Jehuda Feliks]

In the Aggadah

Manna was one of the ten objects created in the twilight on the eve of the Sabbath of Creation (Avot 5:6). It was ground by the angels in heaven (Tanḥ. B., Ex. 67), where manna is constantly being prepared for the future use of the pious (Ḥag. 12b). Manna deserved its name, "bread of the angels" (lit. "bread of the mighty" לֶחֶם אַבִּירִים, Ps. 78:25) because those who ate it became equal to the angels in strength. Furthermore, like angels, they had no need of relieving themselves since the manna was entirely dissolved in their bodies (Tanḥ. B., Ex. 67), and it was not until they sinned by complaining about the taste of the manna that they once again had to relieve themselves like ordinary mortals (Yoma 75b). Each day sufficient manna to sustain the Jewish people for 2,000 years fell (Tanḥ. B., Ex. 66), and this spared the Israelites the need of carrying it during their wanderings, and thus also enabled them to enjoy it while it was still hot. Receiving a new supply every day constantly made them turn their hearts to God for their daily bread (Yoma 76a).

Before the manna fell, a north wind swept the surface of the desert, which the rain then washed clean; dew next descended and was congealed into a solid substance by the wind so that it would serve as a table for the manna which next fell from heaven; it was then covered by another layer of dew which protected it from vermin and insects (Mekh., Va-Yassa, 4). The manna fell directly in front of the homes of the righteous, but the average person had to go out and gather it, and the wicked had to go far from the camp to attain their share (Yoma 75a). At the fourth hour of the day when the manna melted, it formed a river from which the righteous will drink in the hereafter. The heathens also attempted to drink out of these streams, but the manna that tasted so delicious to the Israelites had a bitter taste in their mouths. They could enjoy it only indirectly, by catching and eating animals that drank the melted manna; even in this form it was so delicious that the heathens cried, "Happy is the people that is thus favored" (Tanḥ. B., Ex. 67). There was no need to cook or bake the manna. It contained the flavor of every conceivable dish. One had only to desire a specific food, and the manna assumed its taste (Yoma 75a). To the child it tasted like milk, to the adolescent like bread, to the old like honey, and to the sick like barley steeped in oil and honey (*ibid.*). The manna exhaled a fragrant odor, and served the women as perfume and cosmetics. Together with manna, precious stones and pearls also fell down from heaven to the Israelites (Yoma 75a).

The amount of manna gathered by each family was found to correspond to the number of its members. This rendered the manna useful in solving many difficult problems. For instance, when two people came before Moses, one accusing the other of having stolen his slave and the other claiming to have bought the slave, Moses deferred his decision to the following morning, when the quantity of manna in their respective houses revealed to whom the slave truly belonged (Yoma 75a). When, many centuries later, the prophet Jeremiah exhorted his contemporaries to study the Torah, they responded by saying, "How shall we maintain ourselves?" The prophet then brought forth the vessel with manna which had been placed in the Temple, and exclaimed: "O generation, see ye the word of the Lord; see what it was that served your fathers as food when they applied themselves to the study of the Torah. You, too, will be supported by God in the same way if you will devote yourselves to the study of the Torah" (Mekh., Va-Yassa, 6). When the destruction of the Temple was imminent, the vessel with manna was concealed along with the Ark and the sacred oil. In the messianic period, the prophet Elijah will restore all those hidden objects (*ibid.*).

BIBLIOGRAPHY: F.S. Bodenheimer, *Ha-Ḥai be-Arẓot ha-Mikra*, 2 (1956), 297–302; F.S. Bodenheimer and O. Theodor, *Ergebnisse der Sinai-Expedition 1927* (1929); Kaiser, in: ZDPV, 53 (1930), 63–75; Ginzberg, Legends, index; B.J. Malina, *Palestinian Manna Tradition* (1968).

MANNE, MORDECAI ẒEVI (1859–1886), Hebrew lyric poet and artist. Born near Vilna, he was sent at the age of 13 to study at yeshivot in Minsk. After his talent for painting was discovered he went to Vilna and enrolled at its school of art. He taught himself Russian and general studies, and wrote his first poems, lyrical studies of nature. In 1880 he was accepted as a student at the Academy of Arts in St. Petersburg. On the recommendation of A. *Zederbaum, Manne's studies were subsidized by A. Kaufman, a wealthy communal leader, and he served as his Hebrew secretary. He contributed poems and articles to *Ha-Meliẓ* and *Ha-Ẓefirah* under the pen name Ha-Meẓayyer ("the painter"; also Heb. acronym of – **M**ordecai **Z**evi**y**e**l**id **R**adoshkewitz). In 1884 he went to Warsaw and contributed to Nahum *Sokolow's *Ha-Asif* and S.P. *Rabbinowitz' *Keneset Yisrael*, designing the covers of both anthologies. A victim of tuberculosis, his health deteriorated after 1884. At the end of his life he wrote a popular poem, *Masat Nafshi*, wherein he expressed his longing for Palestine. Only some of his poems and articles were published during his lifetime; his collected works appeared after his death, edited by his friend A.L. Schoenhaus (1897).

Manne's poetry displays an individual lyricism, and he is at his best in descriptions of nature, in which his talents as writer and painter fuse. His poems are clearly influenced by the classical Russian and German poetry which he translated extensively. In his critical articles he wrote that "the poem and the poetic phrase have no purpose outside themselves, they are in themselves a purpose." Manne dreamed of "artists who loved their people and their religion," and who would devote themselves to depicting the beauty, the sacred values, and the history of Israel. A list of his works translated into English appears in Goell, Bibliography, p. 34.

BIBLIOGRAPHY: *Kol Kitvei Manne* (1897), preface by Schoenhaus; J. Klausner, *Yoẓerim u-Vonim*, 1 (1944), 258–72; H. Toren, in: *Moznayim*, 22 (1946), 18–26, 97, 101, 156–63, incl. bibl.; Waxman, Literature, 4 (1960²), 207–10. **ADD. BIBLIOGRAPHY:** A. Holtzman, "*M.Z. Manne, Ha-Meshorer ke-Ẓayyar*," in: *Mahut* 11 (1994), 68–93; idem, "*Temurot be-Ma'amadah shel ha-Omanut ha-Plastit be-Maḥshevet ha-Sifrut ha-Ivrit*," in: *Tarbiẓ*, 63, 4 (1994), 557–596.

[Yehuda Slutsky]

MANNE, SHELLY (**Sheldon**; 1920–1984), U.S. jazz drummer, club owner. Manne's father and two uncles were drummers so he had percussion in his blood. Although New York-born, he is most strongly associated with the "West Coast school" of post-WWII jazz and spent most of his career in Los Angeles and its environs. He got his first professional experience on transatlantic cruise ships, then played for Raymond Scott and Les Brown. But the big breakthrough for Manne came when he was hired as Stan Kenton's drummer in 1946. He enjoyed two successful stints with Kenton, proving that a swift, sure drummer could make even the Kenton behemoth swing. In between he played with Woody Herman and small groups headed by Charlie Ventura and Herman alumnus Bill Harris. After leaving Kenton for good in 1952, he relocated to the West Coast, where he was much in demand for studio work. But he continued playing live jazz whenever possible, fronting his own band, Shelly Manne and His Men. From 1960 to 1974 he was owner of and frequent performer at his own Los Angeles club, Shelly's Manne-Hole. After the club folded, he co-founded the LA 4 combo, which would last until his death 10 years later. Manne was a highly intelligent player, modest but self-assured. He stated his own rules for drummers in a 1955 piece in *Down Beat*: "I'm not in favor of the bombastic approach to drumming. A display of technique leaves me cold if a good line, good sound, and sensitivity are ignored."

BIBLIOGRAPHY: J. Ephland, "Shelly Manne," *Down Beat Magazine* archives, at: www.downbeat.com; "Manne, Shelly," MusicWeb Encyclopaedia of Popular Music, at: www.musicweb.uk.net; P. Priestley, "Shelly Manne," in: *Jazz: The Rough Guide* (1995); "Shelly Manne Offers His Concept of Jazz Drums," *Down Beat Magazine* archives, at: www.downbeat.com.

[George Robinson (2nd ed.)]

MANNES, family of musicians. DAVID MANNES (1866–1959), U.S. violinist and conductor, was interested in civic betterment. In 1912 he founded the Music School Settlement for Colored People, New York. In 1916 he founded the David Mannes School of Music, with a faculty of eminent musicians. He published an autobiography, *Music is My Faith* (1938). He married CLARA DAMROSCH MANNES (1869–1948), a pianist and the daughter of conductor Leopold *Damrosch. His son, LEOPOLD *MANNES (1899–1964), a pianist and teacher and inventor, succeeded his father as director of the Mannes School.

MANNES, LEOPOLD (1899–1964), U.S. pianist and co-inventor with Leopold *Godowsky of the Kodachrome color process. He was born in New York, the son of David Mannes, the violinist and conductor of the New York Symphony Orchestra. He studied musical composition in Rome and was an accomplished pianist. He worked with Godowsky and together they found a successful method of producing color film. They experimented in the Eastman Kodak Laboratories in Rochester, New York. In 1939 Mannes left Rochester and joined his father as codirector of the Mannes School of Music. In 1953 he reorganized it as Mannes College of Music of which he was president.

MANNHEIM, city in Baden, Germany. Jews first settled in Mannheim (which was founded in 1606) around 1652, and the first rabbi, Naphtali Herz, served from 1657 to 1671. The community was granted a highly favorable charter in 1660. A cemetery was acquired a year later (in use until 1839), and a synagogue and *mikveh* were built in 1664. In 1663 there were 15 Jewish families in the town, two of them Portuguese, founders of a Portuguese community that later maintained its own schoolteacher and enjoyed particular privileges. In 1674 the *ḥevra kaddisha* (*Kippe*) was established. By 1680 there were 78 Jewish families in Mannheim; in 1689 they aided the burghers in the defense of the city against the French; on its destruction, they took refuge in the communities of *Heidelberg and *Frankfurt. Eighty-four families had returned to the city by 1691 when a new charter was issued. Modeled on the first one, it included the Portuguese, fixed the number of tolerated families at 86 (increased to 150 in 1698), established an interest rate of 5%, and abolished the yellow *badge. The charter of 1717 (also including the Portuguese) raised the number of tolerated families to 200 and permitted an interest rate of 10%. The favorable position of the Jews there is expressed in a contemporary reference to Mannheim as "New Jerusalem." There were many local followers of *Shabbetai Ẓevi in the community, vigorously opposed by its rabbi, Samuel Helmann (1726–51). In 1708 the synagogue and *ḥeder* (*Klaus*), donated by Lemle Moses Rheinganum, was consecrated and later endowed with 100,000 gulden (it remained in use until 1940). Soon after, it was enlarged considerably. An unsuccessful attempt was made when the Jewish charter was renewed in 1765 to establish a separate Jewish quarter. Political emancipation came in 1807, followed by full civil rights in 1862. The main synagogue was consecrated in 1855. A public elementary school was in existence between 1821 and 1870. The number of families increased from 225 in 1761 to 247 in 1771, and the number of Jews in Mannheim rose from 940 in 1801, to 4,249 in 1885; 6,402 in 1913; and 6,400 (2.3% of the total population) in 1933. The community issued a monthly bulletin (1922–38) and maintained a *Lehrhaus* (school for adults) between 1922 and 1938, as well as numerous charitable, cultural, and social organizations. Jews were active in the social, cultural, and political life of the city.

The interior of the synagogue was demolished on April 1, 1933. By 1938 only 3,000 Jews remained. On November 10, 1938, the main synagogue was burnt, and the community was forced to transfer the remains of 3,586 bodies interred in the old cemetery to the public one. On October 22, 1940, some 2,000 Jews were deported to the concentration camp of *Gurs, and the remainder to Auschwitz a year later. After World War II, Jews returned to Mannheim; they numbered 68 in 1945; 386 in 1970; and 338 in 1977. A new synagogue was opened in 1957. In 1987 a new community center with a synagogue was consecrated. The Jewish community numbered 400 in 1989 and more than 500 in 2005.

BIBLIOGRAPHY: F. Hundsnurscher and G. Taddey, *Die juedischen Gemeinden in Baden* (1968), 186–96; I. Unna, in: JJLG, 17 (1926), 133–46; idem, in ZGJD, 1 (1929), 322–8; 3 (1931), 277–8; B. Rosenthal, *Heimatgeschichte der badischen Juden* (1927), 110, 129, 330f.; idem, in: ZGJD, 5 (1934), 192–9; 7 (1937), 98–102; idem, in: *C.V. Kalender* (1930), 13–18; H. Eppstein-Strauss, in: *Juedische Wohlfahrtspflege und Sozialpolitik*, 1 (1930), 465–72. **ADD. BIBLIOGRAPHY:** K. Watzinger, *Geschichte der Juden in Mannheim 1650 – 1945. Mit 52 Biographien* (Veroeffentlichungen des Stadtarchivs Mainz, vol. 12) (1987²); V. Keller, *Juedisches Leben in Mannheim* (1995); B. Becker and F. Teutsch, *Spuren und Staionen juedischen Lebens in Mannheim. Quellen des Stadtarchivs Mannheim* (Arbeitsmaterialien aus dem Stadtarchiv Mannheim, vol. 4) (2000); T. Bayer, *Minderheit im staedtischen Raum: Sozialgeschichte der Juden in Mannheim waehrend der 1. Haelfte des 19. Jahrhunderts* (Quellen und Darstellungen zur Mannheimer Stadtgeschichte, vol. 6) (2001). **WEBSITES:** www.alemannia-judaica.de; www.jgm-net.de.

[Louis Lewin / Larissa Daemmig (2nd ed.)]

MANNHEIM, HERMANN (1889–1974), lawyer and criminologist, pioneer of the teaching of criminology in Britain. Born in Russia of German parents, Mannheim was educated in Germany. He combined his work as a judge in the Berlin criminal and appeals court with that of a professor of criminal law at Berlin University. When in 1933 his career in Germany came to an end, he had already achieved a position of both judicial and academic eminence. In 1934 Mannheim settled in England where he continued his studies in the sociological and psychological problems connected with crime and punishment and introduced the systematic teaching of criminology into British universities. His courses at the London School of Economics, where the post of reader in criminology was created for him in 1946, were attended by social scientists, lawyers, psychologists, and psychiatrists from all over the world. In those years Mannheim already wrote some of his influential books, among them: *The Dilemma of Penal Reform* (1939), *War and Crime* (1941), and *Criminal Justice and Social Reconstruction* (1946, 2nd ed. 1949, 3rd ed. 1967). He took a leading part in the establishment and the development of almost every important scientific and public activity aiming at the study of crime, the understanding of the offender, and the peno-correctional treatment of delinquents and criminals. For several years he served as president of the scientific committee of the International Criminological Society. He was co-founder and coeditor of the *British Journal of Criminology* (1950–66) and of the International Library of Criminology. The London Institute for the Study and Treatment of Delinquency and the Howard League for Penal Reform were among the causes to which he dedicated his life. In 1955 he published (together with L.T. Wilkins) his *Prediction Methods in Relation to Borstal Training*, the first examination in Britain of the efficacy of penal methods. The Home Office adopted its findings in the administration of the Borstal and prison services. His textbook, *Comparative Criminology* (2 vols., 1965), is the definitive statement on the study of crime in the United States, Britain, and Continental Europe, dealing with the causes of crime, the sociological, psychological, and physical factors involved, and also critically analyzing the various methods used in criminological research. He edited *Pioneers in Criminology*, which has become one of the basic readings for the student of criminology in the Anglo-Saxon world.

BIBLIOGRAPHY: T. Grygier et al. (eds.), *Essays in Honour of Hermann Mannheim* (1965), includes a full bibliography. **ADD. BIBLIOGRAPHY:** ODNB online.

[Zvi Hermon]

MANNHEIM, KARL (1893–1947), sociologist. Born in Budapest, Mannheim was a student of Max Weber in Heidelberg. He was professor of sociology in Frankfurt in 1930, emigrating in 1933 to London, where he taught at the London School of Economics until his death.

Combining influences coming from Marx, Dilthey, and Max Weber, Mannheim became – together with the philosopher Max Scholer – the initiator of the sociology of knowledge. This branch of sociology is based on the conviction that cognition is not a purely intellectual act but formed by vital relations that are non-theoretical in character and largely defined by the position of the actor in the social structure. Cognition is based on volition and volition, in turn, on the antecedents and concrete circumstances of a person's life. Mannheim denied that this view was leading to sociological relativism or to a disparagement of the spirit; rather, in his opinion, the mind was to be set free by the recognition of the nonrational roots of a consciousness.

After his emigration, Mannheim's interest turned largely toward the problem which was posed by the rise of Nazism, namely, how democracy in a period of mass movements could be prevented from sliding into totalitarian dictatorship. Mannheim's thesis was that *laissez-faire* liberalism, through loosening all societal bonds, would carry with it the danger of totalitarianism and that a fighting democracy would have to "plan for freedom"; the intention ought to be to guarantee the values of personality by means of social regulation. He even went so far as to suggest the cooperation of sociology and theology to that end. Mannheim's early work, *Ideologie und Utopie* (1929; Eng. trans., 1936), opposes "utopian" thinking, carried by the discontented and emphasizing change, to "ideological" thinking which is essentially conservative in nature. Still earlier appeared *Die Strukturanalyse der Erkenntnistheorie* ("The Structural Analysis of Knowledge"; 1922), "Das Problem einer Soziologie des Wissens" (in: *Archiv fuer Sozialwissenschaft und Sozialpolitik*, 53 (1925), 577–652). and "Das Konservative Denken" (in: *Archiv fuer Sozialwissenschaft und Sozialpolitik*, 57 (1927), 68–142; 470–95). The major works of Mannheim's second period are *Man and Society in an Age of Reconstruction* (1940) and *Diagnosis of Our Time* (1943). Three posthumous publications were: *Freedom, Power and Democratic Planning* (1950), *Essays on Sociology and Social Psychology* (1953), and *Systematic Sociology* (1958). Mannheim was the founder of the International Library of Sociology and Social Reconstruction, which published many well-known monographs. He had an important unofficial influence on some aspects of British government policy such as the 1944 Education Act. Mannheim contracted pneumonia and died at the age of only 53.

BIBLIOGRAPHY: J.J.P. Maquet, *Sociology of Knowledge… a Critical Analysis of the Systems of Karl Mannheim and Pitirim A. Sorokin* (1951); D. Kettler, *Marxismus und Kultur: Mannheim und Lukacs in den ungarischen Revolutionen [1918/19]* (1967); E. Manheim, in: *The American Journal of Sociology*, 52 (1947), 471–4 (includes list of his publications); A. Salomon, in: *Social Research*, (1947), 350–64. **ADD. BIBLIOGRAPHY:** ODNB online; C. Loader, *The Intellectual Development of Karl Mannheim* (1985); G. Werner Remming, *The Sociology of Karl Mannheim* (1975); H.E.S. Woldring, *Karl Mannheim: The Development of His Thought* (1986).

[Werner J. Cahnman]

MANNHEIM, LUCIE (1899–1976), actress. Born near Berlin, she became a leading actress at the Volksbuehne, Berlin and from 1924 to 1930 appeared at the Staatstheater, Berlin where one of her roles was Nora in Ibsen's *A Doll's House*. After the Nazis came to power, she settled in England where she appeared on the London stage, repeating her success as Nora. After World War II she frequently appeared in Germany. She also appeared in a number of British films, including Alfred Hitchcock's *The 39 Steps* (1935).

MANNHEIMER, ISAAC NOAH (1793–1865), Vienna preacher and creator of a moderate, compromise Reform ritual. Born in Copenhagen, he was the son of a Hungarian *ḥazzan*. He received his general education at the local secular school and studied Hebrew literature and Talmud with R. Gedaliah Moses, the liberal pedagogue of Copenhagen. While attending the university of Copenhagen he continued with his talmudic studies. When in 1816 the Danish government issued regulations for Jewish religious instruction, he was appointed head teacher of religion (*Hauptkatechet*) and entrusted with the task of examining his students and preparing them for confirmation. The first confirmation took place with considerable fervor on May 9, 1817, with the accompaniment of organ music and in the presence of high state and university officials. He held services every Wednesday evening for adherents of Reform *Judaism that were characterized by the total elimination of the Hebrew language and the use of music by Christian composers. Mannheimer preached in the Danish language, much to the dismay of the traditional majority of the community who lodged an official protest with the government. In 1821 he went to Berlin to conduct services in the Reform synagogue, then to Vienna, and back to Copenhagen. He finally left Copenhagen to preach in 1823 in Hamburg and then went to Leipzig. At the suggestion of Lazar *Biedermann, he was asked in 1824 to officiate at the new Seitenstetten Synagogue in Vienna. Since Jews in Vienna were not permitted to constitute a community at that time, he was officially known as headmaster of the religious school. Mannheimer became one of the leading preachers of the 19th century, attracting all segments of the Jewish population; he adhered to an inspirational rather than didactic concept of preaching. His sermons, in which the *aggadah* was translated into modern terms, remained classical in form and content, yet they were the least rule bound and formalistic of contemporary sermons. Moreover, he was not reluctant to acknowledge his debt to Christian masters of the art of preaching. In his mature years in Vienna he rejected radical Reform and adopted a middle course in his service, eliminating some traditions without destroying their essence. He insisted on Hebrew as the language of worship, retained the prayers of Zion and Jerusalem, did not incorporate organ music into the service, and vigorously defended circumcision as a ritual of fundamental importance. In creating a form of worship known as "worship according to Mannheimer" (or "the Viennese rite") he prevented a split in the community, and became a pioneer in this type of service in the communities of Austria, Hungary, and Bohemia. His service was also imitated in some German communities.

Despite his moderate Reform tendencies, Mannheimer was strongly attacked by the *Orthodox community. He helped to foster reforms in religious education, retaining Hebrew as an important element and introduced birth, marriage, and death registers into the community. He also helped to found a number of charitable and cultural organizations and fought for the rights of the Jews in general society; with great persistence he sought to gain legal recognition of the Viennese community. Together with 24 Austrian rabbis he achieved the abolishment of the oath more *judaico, although his own modified form was not fully accepted. In 1842 he successfully defeated the proposal of Professor Rosas to limit the number of Jewish medical students.

During the revolution in 1848 Mannheimer delivered an eloquent eulogy on two of its Jewish victims who were buried together with Christian victims in a Christian cemetery (March 17). On March 31, 1848 he published a "Declaration on the Jewish Problem" and submitted an effective draft law to the political commission. In the same year the city of Brody elected him to the Reichstag, where, in cooperation with A. *Fischhof and the rabbi D.B. *Meisels, he succeeded in obtaining the removal of the "Jews' tax." Nevertheless, he warned the Jewish community against pleading on its own behalf. Jewish emancipation, he said, might be discussed, but only after it had been broached by the non-Jews. In the Reichstag he made a striking plea for abolishing the death penalty. The Vienna community, whose subservient attitude to the government he criticized, tried to restrict his liberal activity, in part out of concern that his outspokenness might embroil them with the increasingly reactionary forces in the government. They even sought to censor his utterances in the Reichstag. Reluctantly Mannheimer eventually withdrew from political life.

Mannheimer's most important literary work is the exemplary German translation of the prayer book and the festival prayers (Vienna, 1840, later in a number of editions). Of his sermons there have been published *Pradikender holdne ved det mosaiske Troessamfunds Andagts övelser i Modersmaalet i Sommerhalbaaret 1819* (Copenhagen, 1819), and *Gottesdienstliche Vortraege ueber die Wochenabschnitte des Jahres* (vol. 1, on Genesis and Exodus, 1834); *Gottesdienstliche Vortraege gehalten im Monat Tishri 5594* (1834). A posthumous edition of additional sermons was published by B. Hammerschlag (1876). Some of his sermons on Genesis and Exodus were translated in Hebrew by E. Kuttner and published under the title *Mei No'aḥ* (1865). Of importance, too, are his *Gutachten fuer das Gebetbuch des Hamburger Tempels* (1841), and *Gutachten gegen die Reformpartei in Frankfurt a. M. in Angelegenheit der Beschneidungsfrage* (1843).

BIBLIOGRAPHY: G. Wolf, *Isak Noa Mannheimer* (1863); idem, *Geschichte der Kultusgemeinde in Wien* (1861), 43–54; M. Rosenmann, *Isak Noa Mannheimer…* (1915^2); idem, in: AZDJ, 86 (1922), 30f.; M. Bisstritz (ed.), *Mannheimer-Album* (1864); MGWJ, 61 (1917), correspondence with L. Zunz; L.A. Frankel, *Zur Geschichte der Juden in Wien* (1853), 66f.; L. Geiger, in: AZDJ, 59 (1895), 271–3; M. Grunwald, *Vienna* (1936), index; A. Altmann, *Studies in 19th Century Jewish Intellectual History* (1964), index; S. Baron, in: PAAJR, 20 (1951), 1–17; G. Weil, in: JJS, 8 (1957), 91–101.

[Bernard Suler]

MANNHEIMER, THEODOR (1833–1900), Swedish banker. Mannheimer is regarded, together with A.O. Wallenberg, a non-Jew, as the founder of modern Swedish banking. Born in Copenhagen, he settled in Göteborg, Sweden in 1855 and began his business career in the grain trade. He turned to banking later and by 1864 had become managing director of the newly founded Skandinaviska Kreditaktiebolaget (Scandinavian Joint Stock Credit Company, now known as the Skandinaviska Enskilda Banken, or SEB), the first of its kind in Sweden. Under Mannheimer's leadership Skandinaviska Banken soon became Sweden's most important financial institution, chiefly concerned with placing securities for industry and transport. Mannheimer was also deeply involved in railway and mining enterprises. From 1870 to 1876 and from 1881 to 1894 he was a member of the Göteborg municipal council.

BIBLIOGRAPHY: *Svenska män och kvinnor*, 6 (1949).

[Hugo Mauritz Valentin]

MANOAH OF NARBONNE (end of 13th and first half of 14th century), Provençal scholar. No biographical details are known of him. Even the name of his father is uncertain (see Hurvitz in bibl.). Some (Geiger, according to Isaac b. Sheshet, resp. no. 85, and Samuel b. Meshullam Gerondi, *Ohel Mo'ed* pt. 1, Jerusalem 1886 ed., 88b) are of the opinion that his father's name was Simeon; others (Zunz, Gross, and the New York-Schulsinger publishers of Maimonides' Yad) without giving reasons state that it was Jacob. A third view is that there were two scholars named Manoah – one, the subject of this article, whose patronymic is unknown, and a second, the son of Simeon, mentioned in the above responsa, who was the author of *Hilkhot Terefot*. Manoah's teachers were Meir b. Simeon ha-Me'ili and Reuben b. Ḥayyim. Internal evidence suggests that he was active in Narbonne (ch. 12 of *Hilkhot Tefillah*: "the custom of this town, Narbonne" quoted in the *Shem ha-Gedolim* of Azulai).

Of his works in the sphere of rabbinical literature, that on Maimonides' *Mishneh Torah* on the laws of leavened and unleavened bread, *shofar*, the Day of Atonement, *sukkah*, and *lulav* has been published (Constantinople, 1718; with the commentary of Simeon Sidon, 1879). An additional portion on the laws of the reading of the *Shema*, prayer, and the priestly and other blessings is extant in manuscript (Moscow-Guenzburg no. 123). This may be the manuscript seen by Ḥ.J.D. Azulai (*Shem ha-Gedolim*, 1 (1852), 126 no. 46). An excerpt from this section was published by Hurvitz in *Talpioth*, 9 (1965). This work is much quoted by Joseph Caro in his *Beit Yosef* and *Kesef Mishneh*.

BIBLIOGRAPHY: A. Geiger, *Kevuẓat Ma'amarim*, ed. by S.A. Poznański (1910), 254; S.M. Chones, *Toledot ha-Posekim* (1910), 348; Hurvitz, in: *Talpioth*, 9 (1965), 136–76, 490–3.

[Shlomoh Zalman Havlin]

MANOR, EHUD (1941–2005), Israeli songwriter. Manor was born in Binyaminah. He began writing songs in the late 1960s, and immediately became very popular and productive, often collaborating with song composer Nurit *Hirsh as in "*Ba-Shanah ha-Ba'ah*" (1970). In the 1970s and 1980s Manor wrote songs for many musicians with a personal style, including Matti Caspi ("*Brit Olam*," 1976); Ḥanan Yovel ("*Dor*," 1984). and Boaz Sharabi ("*Halevay*," 1986). He made many contributions to song festivals such as "*Abanibi*" (1978), winner of the Eurovision song contest. He also produced Hebrew versions of various foreign songs, such as the Brazilian "*Eretz Tropit Yafah*" (1978). In later years, Manor continued to work with artists of the older generation, but also with younger ones and even adopted the Mediterranean style, as in "*Hayiti be-Gan Eden*" (1999). He also translated many musicals, including *Hair* (1971) and *Chicago* (2004) as well as the plays *L'Ecole des femmes* (1987); and *Twelfth Night* (1989). Over the years, Manor edited and presented numerous productions as well as radio and television programs, especially those featuring popular songs (Israeli and foreign). Although a large part of Manor's output consists of light songs, his most famous ones achieve deep resonance on a national level, like "*Ein li Eretz Aḥeret*" (1984), and several are highly personal, like "*Aḥi ha-Tza'ir Yehudah*" (1969) and "*Yemei Binyaminah*" (1974). In 1998, Manor was awarded the Israel Prize for lifetime achievement in the field of Hebrew song. His song collections and writings include *50 Hits by Ehud Manor and Nurit Hirsh* (1969), *Mi Ra'ah et Beni – Children's Songs* (1989), *Ein li Eretz Aḥeret – Shirim ke-Biografiah* (2003), and with Zippora Shapira *Children's Rhymed Dictionary* (2001).

BIBLIOGRAPHY: Y. Rotem, "Ehud Manor" (www.mooma.com).

[Yossi Goldenberg (2nd ed.)]

MANOSQUE, town in the department of Basses-Alpes, S.E. France. Jews are mentioned in Manosque from 1240. In 1261 the community was already sufficiently numerous to maintain two butcher's stores. Before the *Black Death in 1348, there were about 30 Jewish families in Manosque. The Jews owned at least one synagogue and cemetery. They lived in their own street, the Carriera Judaica, on the site of the present Rue Bon-Repos. When an epidemic broke out in 1364, the services of a Jewish physician were still called for. However, from 1370 on there were frequent anti-Jewish disturbances, the most violent in 1455 and 1495. In 1498 the town expelled its Jews.

BIBLIOGRAPHY: Gross, Gal Jud, 361f.; E. Baratier, *Démographie provençale…* (1961), 70; C. Arnaud, *Histoire d'une famille provençale* (1888), 450f.; D. Arnaud, *Etudes historiques sur… Manosque*, 1 (1847), 51ff.

[Bernhard Blumenkranz]

MANS, LE (Heb. מנש), capital of the department of Sarthe, in western France. A Jew, Vaslinus, is mentioned as a moneylender there between 1104 and 1115. In 1138, the Jews of Le Mans were attacked by local inhabitants. They lived in the quarter formed by Rues Marchande, Saint-Jacques, Falotiers or de Merdereau, Barillerie, Ponts-Neufs and de la Juiverie, and owned a synagogue and a cemetery (in the parish of Sainte-Croix), which was also used by other Jews in the vicinity. They probably also had their own market and a hospital. Another attack upon Jews may have occurred around 1200, since several Jewish converts are found in Le Mans in 1207, and in 1216,

Berengaria, the widow of Richard the Lion-Hearted, Lady of Le Mans, disposed of the so-called "school of the *Juiverie*," i.e., the synagogue. Records show the existence of a Jewish quarter during the second half of the 13th century, the Jews of Le Mans then being under the jurisdiction of the bishop. Reference to Jewish scholars of Le Mans is found in rabbinical literature from the end of the ninth century, the most celebrated being *Avun the Great (tenth century) and Elijah b. Menahem ha-Zaken (11th century). The Jews were expelled from Le Mans in 1289 at the same time as the Jews of Maine and Anjou. During World War II many of the Jews in Le Mans were deported. A new community was formed after the war, many of its members coming from North Africa. It numbered 400 in 1969. A stained-glass window dating from the 12th century depicting the allegorical defeated Synagogue can be seen in the Cathedral of Le Mans.

BIBLIOGRAPHY: B. Blumenkranz, in: *Mélanges ... R. Crozet*, 2 (1966), 1154; Z. Szajkowski, *Analytical Franco-Jewish Gazetteer* (1966), 256; Gross, Gal Jud, 392–3.

[Bernhard Blumenkranz / David Weinberg (2nd ed.)]

MANSFELD, ALFRED (1912–2004), architect. Born in Russia, he went to Paris in 1933 and in 1935 to Ereẓ Israel and worked from 1936 as an independent architect, mainly in Haifa. He designed and built several housing schemes in Haifa (including Ramat Hadar), and also various public buildings, including the Institute for Jewish Studies of the Hebrew University in Jerusalem (Mount Scopus) and the Hydraulic Institute of the Technion (with M. Weinraub). In 1963, his design for the international airport at Lydda was awarded first prize. He designed and built (in partnership with Dora Gad, interior decorator), the Israel Museum in Jerusalem (1959–65). From 1949, he lectured at the Faculty of Architecture of the Technion, and from 1954 to 1956 he was dean of the faculty. In 1966 he received the Israel Prize.

BIBLIOGRAPHY: R. Pedio, *Profilo dell'architetto Alfred Mansfeld* (It., 1965), with Eng. preface.

[Abraham Erlik]

MANSO, LEO (1914–1993), U.S. painter and educator. Manso trained at the National Academy of Design, New York City, from 1930 to 1934, the Educational Alliance, and the New School for Social Research. He taught at Cooper Union, Columbia University from 1950 to 1955, and New York University. Working as a book illustrator early in his career, Manso took the position of art director at World Publishing in New York, and in 1943, worked for Simon & Schuster illustrating book covers. He made his summer studio and home in Provincetown, Mass., in 1947 and assisted in the organization of Gallery 256, the period's first regional artists' cooperative. Manso's early work reflects the influence of Abstract Expressionism: he exhibited with the American Abstract Artists, whose members included Josef Albers and Ben Nicholson. Describing himself as an "Abstract Impressionist," Manso's light-suffused art of this period testifies to his study of the Impressionists, especially Claude Monet, as well as such painters as J.M.W. Turner and Sung artists. Manso stated that his work possessed two themes: a concern with landscape and an endeavor to find a visual equivalence for certain philosophical ideals. His work developed from landscapes with rapid, thick, expressive brushwork in an Abstract Expressionist vein, such as *Bay/Dusk* (1954) and *Grey Sun* (1957) to more serene images composed of related planes of tone. Manso's collages, such as *Tanka III* (1968) are small and intimate, owing a debt to the artist's study of quattracento Italian artists and to the collages of his friend and contemporary Robert Motherwell. To study the expressive qualities of color, Manso studied Persian miniatures, Romanesque and Etruscan art, and such modern artists as Paul Klee and Pierre Bonnard. Manso traveled widely: to Mexico in 1945, where he met the artists Jose Clemente Orozco and Rufino Tamayo, to Maine the following year, to Haiti in 1958, to India, Nepal, and Africa in the early 1970s, to Italy in 1975, and again to Rome in 1980 and 1981. In 1979–80, he was artist-in-residence at the Accademia Americao, Prix-de-Rome. Manso experimented with the use of simple geometric forms, making circular supports, as in his *Vista I (Valley of Katmandu)* (1974), or contained large triangles within the rectangular format of the canvas or paper. The title of a 1984 collage, *Firenze*, refers explicitly to the artist's beloved Italy. The composition features tones of russet, ocher, and lavender in overlapping planes of delicate texture further enunciated by the inclusion of a handwritten letter and envelope dated 1846. Manso counted among his friends the artists Milton Avery, Jacques Lipschitz, and Kurt Seligmann. Manso participated in many group and solo shows since 1946: in New York City; Rome; Provincetown, Massachusetts; Washington, D.C.; the San Francisco Museum; and the Museum of Modern Art, among other venues. His work is owned by private collectors and by many museums, including the Museum of Modern Art, New York, the Museum of Fine Arts, Boston, the Whitney Museum, the Hirschhorn Museum, and the Glicenstein Museum, Safed, Israel.

BIBLIOGRAPHY: *Leo Manso: A Retrospective of Four Decades 1952–1992*, Oct. 4–Oct. 23, 1992, Art Students League of New York (1992); *Leo Manso, Assemblage: Feb. 8–Mar. 5, 1966*, Rose Fried Gallery (1966).

[Nancy Buchwald (2nd ed.)]

°**MANṢŪR** (**Al**; full name: **al-Mansur Ibn Abi ʿAmir**; in Christian sources, **Almanzor**; d. 1002), chamberlain (Ar. *ḥājib*) of Caliph Hishām II (976–1013) of Spain. Al-Manṣūr in effect ruled *Umayyad Spain as virtual dictator and in 996 assumed royal titles. His reign marked the climax of the Umayyad political, economic, cultural, and military supremacy in Spain. A religious fanatic, al-Manṣūr embarked on a lengthy and successful campaign against the Christians in northern Spain (against Catalonia in 985), in which he ruthlessly destroyed Christian holy places. He, however, did not harm the Christian and Jewish communities in his domain. The responsa of R. Ḥanokh of Cordoba attest to the conversions of Jews to Islam under al-Manṣūr, who intensified and increased Muslim preaching and other religious activities. Spain was extremely prosperous during his reign and Jewish immigration therefore increased. The Jews came mainly from North Africa (present Morocco and Algeria), together with many *Berbers, whom al-Manṣūr employed in his military campaigns. The military security and economic stability contributed to an efflorescence of Jewish culture, *halakhah*, poetry, etc. (see *Spain). The 12th-century historian Abraham *Ibn Daud recalls "King" al-Manṣūr's appointment of Jacob *Ibn Jau, a wealthy and opportunistic silk merchant, to the position of *nasi* in charge of all Jewish communities in his domain. Al-Manṣūr empowered Ibn Jau to collect taxes from whomever he desired. He had Ibn Jau imprisoned one year later for not collecting enough money from the Jews. Al-Manṣūr's son ʿAbd al-Malik al-Muẓaffir succeeded him, thus founding the Amirid dynasty.

BIBLIOGRAPHY: E. Levi-Provençal, *Histoire de l'Espagne Musulmane*, 2 (1950), 196–272; Ashtor, Korot, 1 (1966²), 244–8; ibn Daud, *Sefer ha-Qabbalah – the Book of Tradition*, ed. and tr. by G.D. Cohen (1967), 69.

MANSURA (**El Mansura**; **al-Mansura; Al-Mansurah**), town in Lower Egypt, on the right bank of the eastern arm of the Nile. Founded during the 13th century, Mansura has become an important center for the cotton commerce in modern times. There was a Jewish community from the 16th century. In 1583 and 1597 there were Jewish written deeds in Mansura. Around 1560 the physician Eleazar Scandari received the position of *sarraf* (banker) of *Mahalla al-Kubra and Mansura. The Jewish population grew under *Ottoman rule and by the 17th century there was an organized community led by the rabbis Elijah Shushi (Shoshi) and Shabbetai ha-Kohen. During the middle of the 19th century, Jacob *Saphir found 40 families in the town, most of whom had come from *Cairo and *Damietta. During the second half of the 19th century, when blood libels were brought against Jews in various Egyptian towns, the Jews of Mansura were also accused. In 1877 during Passover, the Jews were accused of having slaughtered a Muslim child in order to use his blood for the baking of *mazzot*. In the mid-19th century 40 Jewish families lived there. At the end of the century, the number of Jews was about 500 and continued to increase at the beginning of the 20th century. In 1901 the *Cairo rabbis declared the new *kiddushin* regulation in Mansura and other cities. A well-organized community was set up in 1918 and educational and charitable institutions were established. An *Alliance Israélite Universelle school was inaugurated in 1903. In 1917 the Jewish community reached 586 people, its number continuing to increase. A Zionist association was also founded in the town. After World War I there was a decrease in the population. In 1927 there were still 563 Jews there, but a few years later there were only 150 to 200 Jews left, and by 1971 the community no longer existed.

BIBLIOGRAPHY: J. Saphir, *Even Sappir* (1866), 8a; J.M. Landau, *Jews in Nineteenth-Century Egypt* (1969), 38–40. L. Bornstein-Makovetsky, in: J.M. Landau (ed.), *Toledot ha-Yehudim be-Mizraim ba-Tekufah ha-Otmanit* (1988), 143, 150, 160; S. Della Pergola, in: ibid., 42; E. Bashan, in: ibid., 95. A. David, in: ibid., 16.

[Eliyahu Ashtor and Jacob M. Landau / Leah Bornstein-Makovetsky (2nd ed.)]

MANSURAH, SAADIAH BEN JUDAH (19th century), Yemenite scholar living in *San'a. He was author of *Sefer ha-Maḥashavah*, which appeared under the title *Sefer ha-Galut ve-ha-Ge'ullah* (1955), which consists of seven sections written in rhymed prose. Like the *Sefer ha-Musar* of R. Zechariah al-Ḍāhri, it describes the hardships endured by the community of San'a in his time. The principal hero is Eitan ha-Ezraḥi (i.e., Abraham the Patriarch) and the narrator Ḥazmak (i.e., Saadiah, after the "*Atbash" method of interchanging Hebrew letters) is the poet himself. The narrator tells the founder of the nation of the misfortunes of Yemenite Jewry, and the latter in turn relates the servitude of Israel in the Egyptian exile. He deals with the exiles into which Israel was sent, with the return to Zion and the redemption of the people. The last section consists of eulogies of the rabbis of *Yemen and the author himself. Mansurah also wrote poems and prayers, the subject of which is exile and redemption, as well as an introduction to Yemenite poetry. In the field of *halakhah*, he wrote *Sha'ar ha-Moda'it* on the laws of *sheḥitah* and *terefot*.

BIBLIOGRAPHY: S. Mansurah, *Sefer ha-Galut ve-ha-Ge'ullah* (1955), introd.

[Yehuda Ratzaby]

MANSURAH, SHALOM BEN JUDAH (d. c. 1885), Yemenite scholar. A member of one of the distinguished families of *San'a, Mansurah was the brother of the poet Saadiah *Mansurah. In addition to his knowledge of the Torah, he also engaged in popular and natural medicine and was renowned as a practical kabbalist. In 1854 he was appointed leader of the Jews of San'a. Three of his works on Torah and *halakhah* (in manuscript) are known. In addition to his own writings, he corrected many works of others. His notes in the margins of books, both published and in manuscript (especially those of R. Yiḥya Ṣalaḥ), are numerous.

BIBLIOGRAPHY: A. Koraḥ, *Sa'arat Teiman* (1954), 45.

[Yehuda Ratzaby]

MANTINO, JACOB BEN SAMUEL (d. 1549), physician and translator. Mantino was apparently of Spanish origin but he spent most of his life in Italy. After graduating in medicine at Padua in 1521, he developed a flourishing practice in Bologna, Verona, and Venice, especially among the upper classes. At the same time he became known for his translations from Hebrew into Latin of philosophical works, mainly those of Averroës and Avicenna. In the stormy debate on the annulment of the marriage between Henry VIII of England and Catherine of Aragon he opposed Henry's supporters, thus earning the gratitude of Pope Clement VII, and at his request Mantino was appointed lecturer in medicine in Bologna in

1529. In 1533 the pope invited him to Rome where, unlike his protector, Mantino took a strong stand against the messianic claims of Solomon *Molcho. In 1534 Pope Paul III appointed him his personal physician and in 1539–41 professor of practical medicine at the Sapienza in Rome. In 1544 he returned to Venice. Five years later he left for Damascus as personal physician of the Venetian ambassador. He died soon after his arrival there.

BIBLIOGRAPHY: Kaufmann, in: REJ, 27 (1893), 30–60, 207–38; Milano, Italia, 242, 625, 631; idem, *Ghetto di Roma* (1964), 60, 68f.; C. Roth, *Jews in the Renaissance* (1959), index; Ravà, in: *Vessillo Israelitico*, 51 (1903), 310–3; Muenster, in: RMI, 20 (1954), 310–21.

[Attilio Milano]

MANTUA, city and province in N. Italy, an important Jewish center in late medieval and modern times.

History

The first record of a Jewish settlement in Mantua dates from 1145, when Abraham *Ibn Ezra lived there for a while. A small Jewish community existed during the heyday of the city-republic. Sometime after the Gonzaga had become lords of Mantua, Jewish bankers were invited to start operations in the capital and province. Subsequently the Jewish population increased, reaching 3,000 by 1600. The merchant and artisan population soon outnumbered the bankers. Some 50 Jewish settlements of varying size flourished in the province, the major ones being *Bozzolo, *Sabbioneta, Luzzara, Guastalla, Viadana, Revere, Sermide, and Ostiano. The Jews were protected by a series of privileges granted them by popes, emperors, and the Gonzaga rulers. A Christian loan bank (**monte di pietà*) was established in Mantua in 1486 to compete with Jewish banking, but initially at least had little success. Anti-Jewish riots took place at Mantua in the 15th century, fostered by the Church and aided and abetted by the business competitors of the Jews. There was also an isolated case of *blood libel in 1478. At the end of the 15th century the regulation imposing the Jewish *badge was introduced in Mantua. Rioting in 1495, after Duke Francesco Gonzaga's indecisive encounter with the French forces at Fornovo, resulted in the confiscation of the house of the leading Jewish banker in the city, Daniel *Norsa, and the erection of the Church of the Madonna della Vittoria on the site. David *Reuveni visited Mantua in 1530, but failed to obtain the support of either the ruler or the Jews. Two years later Solomon *Molcho was burned at the stake there.

The Counter-Reformation began to affect the Jews of Mantua adversely in the last quarter of the 16th century. Restrictive measures and anti-Jewish propaganda culminated in riots and murder. The worst outrage occurred in 1602, when seven Jews were hanged on a charge of blasphemy at the instigation of a Franciscan rabble-rouser. Some ten years later the Jews of Mantua were confined to a ghetto. The worst disaster in their history befell Mantuan Jewry in 1629–30, when they were despoiled of their possessions during the sack of the city by the German troops and then banished. A moving account of the disaster and of the return of the survivors is the contemporary *Ha-Galut ve-ha-Pedut* ("Exile and Deliverance") by Abraham Massarani (Venice, 1634). The events of 1630 decimated the Jewish community which never quite recovered its former importance. In 1708 the duchy of Mantua came under Austrian rule. In the last quarter of the 18th century Mantua became the chief center in the struggle for Jewish civil rights in Austrian Lombardy. On the Jewish side were ranged R. Jacob *Saraval of Mantua and Benedetto *Frizzi of Ostiano who had to contend with the lawyer G.B. Benedetti of Ferrara and G.B.G. d'Arco, a political economist. During the 18th century the Jewish population increased: In 1707, 1,723 Jews lived in Mantua and in 1764, 2,114. In 1754 the guild of silversmiths threatened the Jewish ghetto and the Jews were maltreated for a month in spite of the defense of ducal troops. When in 1797 the French revolutionary army captured Mantua the ghetto was abolished, its gates were torn down, and the ghetto square was renamed Piazza della Concordia. After its recapture by the Austrians in 1799, however, several Jewish "revolutionaries" were banished from Mantua, among them Issachar Ḥayyim Carpi of Revere, who described the events in his *Toledot Yiẓḥak* (1892). The French again ruled Mantua from 1801 to 1814 and R. Abraham Vita *Cologna of Mantua was among the foremost personalities in the Napoleonic *Sanhedrin. During the last period of Austrian rule in Mantua (1814–66) there occurred yet another blood libel (1824), and in 1842 anti-Jewish riots took place. A number of Jews from Mantua began to immigrate to Milan from the end of the 18th century mainly because of greater professional and socio-cultural activities.

The Jews of Mantua, like their coreligionists elsewhere in Italy, took an active part in the Italian Risorgimento. Among them were Giuseppe *Finzi of Rivarolo, one of the "martyrs of Belfiore," and the writer Tullo *Massarani. When Mantua was incorporated in the Kingdom of Italy (1866) the last restrictions affecting the Jews were removed. At that time the Jewish population reached 2,795, its highest figure since 1603. Subsequently migration and assimilation reduced the community. In 1931 the community numbered only 669 Jews, mainly because of immigration to Milan and other Italian cities and also because of assimilation. The anti-Jewish measures of the Fascist regime (see *Italy) seriously affected the Jews of Mantua, coming to a climax under the German domination in 1943–45. A concentration camp was set up in Mantua. From the province of Mantua 44 Jews were deported to the death camps, and over 50 Mantuan Jews perished. Only some of the survivors returned to Mantua after the war. By 2000 fewer than 100 Jews lived in Mantua, but in spite of the number they maintained one of the former synagogues with services. Thanks to the active and economic support of the Mantua municipality and funds from the Italian State Ministry of Culture the Jews carried out cultural activities and were able to maintain their rich archive and library, inventoried and in part deposited at the City Hall Library of Mantua.

Cultural Life

During its heyday in the 16th and 17th centuries the community of Mantua made important contributions to the development of Jewish communal institutions in Italy. The assembly of all taxpayers elected a "large" council, which in turn elected a "small" or executive council of seven to ten members. Alongside these, several smaller executive committees functioned. The chief officers were two *massari* (ממונים). Communal regulations, especially those pertaining to taxation, were published in Hebrew at regular intervals, as were also sumptuary laws for the restriction of ostentation in clothing and festivities. The synagogues of Mantua included the Great Synagogue of the Italian rite, and several smaller synagogues of the Ashkenazi and Italian rites. The community maintained a public school system and welfare institutions, including medical services for the poor. The rabbinical court had extensive powers until the grant of Jewish emancipation. Its procedure was laid down in the *Shuda de-Dayyanei* ("Judges' Verdict") of 1677–78.

Mantua was an important Jewish cultural center during the Renaissance in Italy. Prominent scholars in the 15th century included Judah Messer *Leon, rabbi, physician, and philosopher; R. Joseph *Colon, the greatest rabbinical authority in Italy; Mordecai *Finzi, mathematician, astronomer, doctor, and banker; and Baruch de Peschiera, scholar and merchant. Abraham *Conat, a physician and talmudist, founded at Mantua about 1475 one of the first Hebrew printing presses; the first dated work issued was the *Tur Oraḥ Ḥayyim* (1476). His wife, Estellina, assisted him as a printer. Other Hebrew printers active at Mantua included Samuel Latif (1513–15), Joseph b. Jacob Shalit and Meir Sofer, both of Padua, Jacob ha-Kohen of Gazzuolo (1556–76), Samuel Norsa and his sons Isaac and Solomon (16th century); the Perugia and d'Italia families (17th and 18th centuries). The Hebrew press in Mantua was the second largest in Italy after Venice. Sixteenth-century scholars included Azariah de' *Rossi, author of *Me'or Einayim*; the versatile Abraham Yagel *Gallico; R. Azriel *Diena of Sabbioneta; the preacher Judah *Moscato; several members of the *Norsa (Norzi) family including Jedidiah Solomon Norsa, author of *Minḥat Shai*; the Provençal brothers *Moses, *David, and Judah, rabbis and scholars; Abraham Colorni, engineer and inventor; members of the *Finzi, *Cases, *Fano, *Rieti, and Sullam families; the *Portaleone family, physicians for three centuries; and Judah Leone b. Isaac *Sommo, playwright, poet, and author of the famous "Dialogues on the Theater." Mantua was the most important center of Jewish participation in the Renaissance theater. The community provided its own theater company, which put on comedies and other plays for court performances throughout the 16th and early 17th centuries. The Jews of Mantua were also active in music and the dance. The greatest Jewish composer in Mantua and the first composer of modern Jewish music was Salamone de' *Rossi, whose sister "Madama Europa" acted on the Mantuan stage. Other Jewish musicians, dancers, and actors at Mantua included Abramo Dall' *Arpa and his nephew Abramino; Isaac Massarani; Angelo de' Rossi; and Simone Basilea. In the 17th and 18th centuries there lived at Mantua the Basilea family of rabbis and scholars, including Solomon Aviad Sar-Shalom *Basilea; Judah Briel, rabbi and polemicist; Moses *Zacuto, mystic and poet; Samson Cohen Modon, rabbi and poet; Jacob Saraval, rabbi, polemicist, traveler, and preacher; the brothers Jacob and Immanuel *Frances, poets; the Cases family, rabbis, physicians, and scholars; and Samuel *Romanelli, poet and playwright. Outstanding modern Jewish personalities include Marco *Mortara, rabbi and bibliophile; Tullo Massarani, writer; and Vittore *Colorni, jurist and historian.

BIBLIOGRAPHY: S. Simonsohn, *Toledot ha-Yehudim be-Dukkasut Mantovah*, 2 vols. (1962–64); Milano, Bibliotheca, index, s.v. *Mantova*; Milano, Italia, index, s.v. *Mantova*; M. Mortara, *Indice Alfabetico dei Rabbini…* (1886), passim; Roth, Italy, index; idem, *Jews in the Renaissance* (1959), index; D.W. Amram, *Makers of Hebrew Books in Italy* (1909), 30ff., 323ff.; M. Steinschneider and D. Cassel, *Juedische Typographie* (1938), 14, 23, 26ff.; H.D. Friedberg, *Toledot ha-Defus ha-Ivri be-Italyah* (1956²), 15ff. **ADD. BIBLIOGRAPHY:** P. Bernardini, *La sfida dell'uguaglianza. Gli ebrei a Mantova nell'età della rivoluzione francese* (1997).

[Shlomo Simonsohn / Federica Francesconi (2nd ed.)]

°**MANUEL I** (1469–1521), king of Portugal 1495–1521. He was termed Manuel the Great because of the achievements of his reign: Vasco da Gama's discovery of the sea passage to India via the Cape of Good Hope (1498) and the acquisition of Brazil (1500). For the Jewish citizens, however, Manuel's reign brought an end to their life in Portugal. Initially Manuel was well disposed to Jews. He retained the esteemed Abraham b. Samuel *Zacuto as his astronomer, and removed the Jewish disabilities imposed by his predecessor John II. But in 1496 the king entered a politically motivated marriage with Princess Isabella of Spain, daughter of *Ferdinand and Isabella, who made their consent conditional to Manuel's ridding Portugal of the Jews. On Dec. 4, 1496, an edict was passed ordering every Jew to leave Portugal before November 1497, on penalty of death. Manuel assured the Jews of every assistance in travel and free departure with their belongings. As the mass emigration got under way, Manuel realized that the loss of his Jewish citizenry would have dire economic results for Portugal. To stem the departures, he ordered all Jews desiring to emigrate to come to Lisbon, supposedly for embarkation. When some 20,000 had convened in Lisbon, Manuel herded them together for forced conversion. On May 30, 1497, he decreed that the Conversos would be free from the Church's discipline for 20 years. When the king learned soon after that the Conversos were emigrating in large numbers, he quickly withdrew their liberty to dispose of property and emigrate. When some 4,000 of the *New Christians were massacred by a Lisbon mob in 1506, Manuel responded by executing the Dominican friars who had incited the riot, and restored all previous rights and immunities to the New Christians, only to reverse his decision in the year of his death.

BIBLIOGRAPHY: Graetz, Hist, 4 (1894, repr. 1949), 372–81, 485–8; Roth, Marranos, 55–66, 86, 196; M. Kayserling, *Geschichte der Juden in Portugal* (1867), 120–56, 334; J. Mendes dos Remedios,

Os Judeus em Portugal (1895), 275–342; S. Usque, *Consolation for the Tribulations of Israel*, tr. by M.A. Cohen (1965), 5–7, 202–5.

MANUEL, FRANK EDWARD (1910–2003), U.S. historian. Manuel was born in Boston. He was professor of history at Brandeis from 1949 to 1965 and at New York University, and then again at Brandeis from 1977 to 1986. Upon his retirement from Brandeis, he was named professor emeritus. Manuel's chief field of specialization was the history of ideas. Regarded as one of the most respected scholars of European intellectual history of the last century, Manuel was well known for his study of utopias of the 18th and 19th centuries. He also wrote about modern history, Christian-Jewish intellectual relations, psychohistory, and eminent thinkers such as Isaac Newton and Karl Marx. His book *Realities of American-Palestine Relations* (1949) was an important contribution to the understanding of American policies in Palestine from 1832. His *Utopian Thought in the Western World* (1979), which he co-authored with his wife, Fritzie P. Manuel, won the American Book Award in History, the Melcher Award, and Phi Beta Kappa's Ralph Waldo Emerson Award.

Manuel's other publications include *The Age of Reason* (1951), *The 18th Century Confronts the Gods* (1959), *The Prophets of Paris* (1962), *Shapes of Philosophical History* (1965), *A Portrait of Isaac Newton* (1968), *The Changing of the Gods* (1983), *The Broken Staff: Judaism through Christian Eyes* (1992), and *A Requiem for Karl Marx* (1995).

BIBLIOGRAPHY: R. Bienvenu, *In the Presence of the Past: Essays in Honor of Frank E. Manuel* (1991)

[Ruth Beloff (2nd ed.)]

°MANUEL I COMNENUS, Byzantine emperor (1143–1180). He added humiliating procedures to the standard *oath *more judaico* requiring that the Jew spit on his circumcision. But he also continued to permit the Jews to use the older and less offensive formula of the oath. Manuel confirmed Jewish access to ordinary courts, giving them recourse to the protection of imperial law, thus abolishing the practice of having Jews summarily tried by a minor local official. Manuel had a Jewish physician who may have influenced him to moderate his position toward the Jews. The economic and cultural life of Byzantine Jewry during Manuel's reign is described by Benjamin of Tudela.

BIBLIOGRAPHY: M.N. Adler (ed.), *Itinerary of Benjamin of Tudela* (1907), 10–14; J. Starr, *Jews in the Byzantine Empire 641–1204* (1939), 221–3, and index; Baron, Social², 4 (1962), 194f.; Patlagean, in: REJ, 124 (1965), 138–51.

[Andrew Sharf]

MANUSCRIPTS, HEBREW, term which includes religious and secular books, as well as letters and documents written on papyrus, parchment, hides, and paper in Hebrew characters, sometimes using them for the writing of languages other than Hebrew, e.g., Aramaic, Yiddish, Ladino, etc. Hebrew manuscripts have been preserved in archives and public and private libraries. It has been estimated that there are about 60,000 manuscripts (codices) and about 200,000 fragments, most of which have come from the Cairo *Genizah* (and a certain number from the Judean Desert).

500 B.C.E.–500 C.E.

Documents and letters, some with accurate dates, have been preserved from the period of 500 B.C.E. to 500 C.E. The most important of them are a collection of *papyri from Yeb (*Elephantine) and Assuan in Egypt (494–407 B.C.E.); papyri from Edfu, also in Egypt, are thought to belong to the third century B.C.E., as are parts of the Book of Jeremiah and fragments of II Samuel among the *Dead Sea Scrolls. The other scrolls from the Judean Desert are regarded as dating from the second century B.C.E. to the Bar-Kokhba War (132–135), including some written or dictated by him (see bibl. nos. 1–5).

500–1500

No material is available which can be proven with any certainty as belonging to the first centuries of this period. The oldest manuscripts of the period date from the end of the ninth century. Information has been published on a biblical manuscript in St. Petersburg dated to 846. On the other hand, some of the fragments found in the Cairo *Genizah* belong, without doubt, to the beginning of this period and possibly even to the end of the previous one. The development of Hebrew paleography should make it possible to determine with greater accuracy the dates of these most valuable fragments.

BIBLE AND BIBLE EXEGESIS. The oldest dated biblical manuscripts are: Prophets as vocalized by Moses b. Asher, which was found in the Karaite synagogue of Cairo and written in Tiberias in 895; Latter Prophets, with Babylonian punctuation, in the Saltykov-Shchedrin Library in Leningrad (No. 3), now the Russian National Library, was copied in 916; and a Pentateuch which was copied by Solomon b. Buya'a (who also prepared, according to a note at its end, the so-called *Keter Aram Ẓova*, later vocalized by Aaron b. Asher) in 929 and vocalized by his brother Ephraim b. Buya'a (it appears that both were active in Tiberias). This particular *Keter Aram Ẓova* (*keter*, "crown" being an appellation for a Bible codex; *Aram Ẓova*, "Aleppo") is at the Ben-Zvi Institute, Jerusalem (see bibl. nos. 5–7). There are biblical manuscripts in the Saltykov-Shchedrin Library and others, which, according to their *colophons, were written during the tenth century, but doubts have been raised as to the reliability of these colophons. Finally, there is the Bible manuscript (St. Petersburg B 19A) which was written in 1009 in Egypt. The text is complete and the date appears to be authentic.

MISHNAH, TOSEFTA, TALMUD, AND HALAKHIC MIDRASHIM. The oldest dated manuscripts of the Mishnah are: Paris Manuscripts 328/9, the complete text with Maimonides' commentary and written and vocalized by Joab b. Jehiel, the "Physician of Beth-El," from the province of Cesena (Italy), between 1399 and 1401. Individual orders (*sedorim*), written and vocalized (in part) from 1168 (*Zera'im, Nezikin, Kodashim*), are in Oxford (nos. 393, 404), and *Mo'ed* of the same set is in the Sassoon Library (no. 72). Not dated but definitely early works are: Kaufmann Number 50 (facsimile edited by G. Baer, 1929) and Parma Number 138. The oldest Tosefta manuscripts are Erfurt Number 159, which was thought to have been written in 1150, and Vienna Number 46. The oldest dated halakhic Midrashim are Sifra of 1073 (Vatican Library, no. 31) and Sifra of 1291 (Oxford, no. 151), which also includes the *Mekhilta*. The only manuscript of the Jerusalem Talmud, which was written in 1299 by Jehiel b. Jekuthiel b. Benjamin, the Physician, is at Leyden. There is also only one complete extant manuscript of the Babylonian Talmud (Munich, Bayerische Staatsbibliothek, Cod. Heb. 95). It was written "on the twelfth of the month of Kislev, in the year 103 of the sixth millennium" (1342) by Solomon b. Samson, probably in France (facsimile edited by H. Strack, 1912). At the end of this manuscript several minor tractates are added. Individual tractates from 1176 and after have been preserved in the Library of Florence, as well as a manuscript from 1184 in the Hamburg Library and in the Jewish Theological Seminary Library (Av. Zar., 1290).

AGGADIC MIDRASHIM. Among the extant manuscripts of aggadic Midrashim are *Genesis Rabbah* and *Leviticus Rabbah* from 1291 (*Bibliothèque Nationale* of Paris, no. 149). There is a manuscript from the same year of the *Pesikta de-Rav Kahana* in the Bodleian. The Parma Library possesses a manuscript from 1270 (no. 1240) which contains *Song of Songs Rabbah*, *Lamentations Rabbah*, *Tanḥuma*, *Pesikta Rabbati*, *Midrash Proverbs*, and others.

MISCELLANEA. Thousands of medieval manuscripts in the fields of philosophy and Kabbalah are extant; these are as numerous as those in medicine, astronomy, astrology, geography, and other natural sciences. A considerable number of these manuscripts are translations from Greek, Arabic, and other languages spoken and written in the countries of the Diaspora. Polemics, poetry, philology (grammar, dictionaries, *masorah*), history, sectarian literature, *halakhah* (responsa, novellae, codes, ritual compendiums), ethics, and homiletics are well represented, as is liturgy (*siddurim* and *maḥzorim*). Due to their constant use many tens of thousands of them were stored away in *genizot* after being worn and damaged. Occasionally autographs were also preserved, i.e., either manuscripts from the hand of the author, such as Maimonides' Mishnah commentary and miscellaneous writings (ed. S.D. Sassoon, 1966), or confirmations of the correctness of the copy as the one added by Maimonides to a copy of his code: "Corrected from my [original] copy, I, Moses, son of Maimon of blessed memory" (Oxford Ms. 577).

1500–1970

Manuscripts of this last period are also extant; some of them were published, some not. A considerable number of the manuscripts of this period were written in countries where there were no Hebrew presses (e.g., the Yemen). They were either contemporary works or those of earlier periods, but some were copied from printed works which had reached them from Western countries and are therefore of no original value. Manuscripts written by the authors themselves are of special importance because of their corrections. They make it possible to reconstruct the original text and compare it with other copies, either handwritten or printed editions. Early authorities, who wrote in the early years after the appearance of printing, made use of manuscripts of classic books and commentaries. In later centuries this practice naturally waned.

Owners and Other Lists

At the beginning and the end of manuscripts it was customary to note the name of the owner, with a formula such as "a man should always sign his name in his book lest a man from the street come and say it is mine." Owners, who usually were scholars, often added notes of their own to the text. At times, the names of several generations of a single family appear in these lists, and well-known names in Jewish literature and history are found among the owners, e.g., a manuscript of Maimonides' *Guide* (1472, Parma 660) belonged successively to David, Abraham, and Moses Provençal (father, son, and grandson).

Modern manuscript catalogs generally register these notes and lists in detail. The same pages were also used to commemorate family and general events, and documents which are sometimes of great historical value were also copied on them, although they may have no connection with the contents of the manuscript. Among this material are lists of books describing whole or parts of private collections. Such lists shed light on the cultural standards of various periods and environments. The prices of the manuscripts which are mentioned in them are of particular interest (see *Book trade).

Collection of the Material

The Institute for the Photography of Hebrew Manuscripts was founded in 1950 by the Israel Government (Ministry of Education and Culture) in order to enable a comparative processing and registration of all possible material. In 1962 the institute was placed under the authority of the Hebrew University and became affiliated with the National and University Library. During its 20 years of activity the Institute has photographed – mainly in the form of microfilms – approximately half of the collections of manuscripts and fragments scattered throughout the libraries of the world. The most important works which had not been previously published in the form of facsimiles were enlarged by the Institute, as were all the fragments which reached it. Some of the material has been listed in the publications of the Institute (bibl. nos. 24–27). The Jewish Theological Seminary of America houses the Louis Ginzberg Microfilm Collection, which aims at the microfilming of important Hebrew manuscripts from all over the world. The list below cites all libraries containing over 100 Hebrew or Samaritan manuscripts. The numbers of the manuscripts and fragments are given in parenthesis, and the names of the authors of the catalogs and the year of their publication are given after the colon. The numbers of the manuscripts given here are not always identical with those which are classified in the catalogs, as additions were acquired after their publication.

AUSTRIA. VIENNA: *Nationalbibliothek* (216; 308 fragments): A.Z. Schwarz (1925); *Bibliothek der Isr. Kultusgemeinde* (215): A.Z. Schwarz-Oesterreich (1932; 40 Mss. transferred to the Jewish Historical Institute, Warsaw).

DENMARK. COPENHAGEN: *The Royal Library* (244): N. Allony-E. Kupfer (1964).

ENGLAND. CAMBRIDGE: *Trinity College Library* (160): H. Loewe (1926); *University Library* (1,000; 100,000 fragments): S. Schiller-Szinessy (1876); *Westminster College Library* (3,000 fragments). LEEDS: *University Library* (371): C. Roth (Alexander Marx Jubilee Volume; 1950). LETCHWORTH: *D.S. Sassoon Collection* (1,220): D.S. Sassoon (1932). LONDON: *Bet Din and Bet Ha-Midrash* (161): A. Neubauer (1886); *British Museum* (includes the first part of the Gaster Collection, 2,467; 10,000 fragments): G. Margoliouth (1899–1935); *Jews College Library* (Montefiore Collection: 580); H. Hirschfeld, in: JQR (1902–03). MANCHESTER: *John Rylands Library* (second part of the Gaster Collection: 750; 10,000 fragments): E. Robertson (only the Samaritan Mss.; 1938–62). OXFORD: *Bodleian Library* (2,650; 10,000 fragments): A. Neubauer-A.E. Cowley (1886–1906).

FRANCE. PARIS: *Bibliothèque de l'Alliance Universelle* (338; 4,000 fragments): M. Schwab, in: REJ (1904, 1912); B. Chapira, in: REJ (1904); *Bibliothèque Nationale* (1459); H. Zotenberg (1886); *Ecole Rabbinique de France* (172): M. Abraham, in: REJ (1924–25). STRASBOURG: *Bibliothèque Nationale et Universitaire* (176; 292 fragments): S. Landauer (1881).

GERMANY. BERLIN: *Preussische Staatsbibliothek* (510): M. Steinschneider (1878–97); N. Allony-D.S. Loewinger (1957). FRANKFURT: *Stadt-und Universitätsbibliothek* (400; 10,000 fragments): R.N.N. Rabbinowitz (1888); N. Allony-D.S. Loewinger (1957; including the Merzbacher Collection; 10,000 *Genizah* fragments lost during World War II). HAMBURG: *Stadtbibliothek* 476); M. Steinschneider (1878; including the Levy Collection). MUNICH: *Bayerische Staatsbibliothek* (476): M. Steinschneider (1895); E. Roth (1966).

HUNGARY. BUDAPEST: *Hungarian Academy of Sciences* (Kaufmann Collection: 595; 600 fragments): M. Weisz (1906); D.S. Loewinger-A. Scheiber (1947); *Library of the Jewish Theological Seminary* (315; 400 fragments): D.S. Loewinger (1940).

ITALY. FLORENCE: *Biblioteca Mediceo Laurenziana* (187): A.M. Biscioni (1757). LEGHORN: *Talmud Torah* (134): C. Bernheimer (1915). A part transferred to the Jewish National and University Library in Jerusalem. MANTUA: *Comunità Israelitica* (167): M. Mortara (1878). MILAN: *Biblioteca Ambrosiana* (183): C. Bernheimer (1933). N. Allony-E. Kupfer (*Aresheth*; 1960). PARMA: *Biblioteca Palatina* (1,552): G.B. De-Rossi (1803); P. Perreau (1880). ROME: *Biblioteca Casanatense* (230): G. Sacerdote (1897). *Biblioteca Apostolica Vaticana* (see Vatican, below). TURIN: *Biblioteca Nazionale* (247): B. Peyron (1880). (A great part destroyed by fire in 1904.)

ISRAEL. JERUSALEM: *National and University Library* (6,000): G. Scholem (1930); B. Joel (1934). N. Ben-Menahem (120); *Hechal Shlomo* (150): J.L. Bialer (1966–69); *Mosad ha-Rav Kook* (1,000): N. Ben-Menahem in: *Aresheth*, 1 (1959), 396–413; *Ben-Zvi Institute* (1,100); *Schocken Library* (400). RAMAT GAN: *Bar Ilan University Library* (Margulies Collection: 750). TEL AVIV: *Bialik House* (200).

NETHERLANDS. AMSTERDAM; *Portugeesch Israelitisch Seminarium Etz Haim – Livraria D. Montezinos* (160): N. Allony-E. Kupfer (1964); *Universiteitsbibliotheek* (Rosenthaliana; 305); M. Roest (1875); N. Allony-E. Kupfer (1964). LEIDEN: *Bibliotheek der Universiteit* (118): M. Steinschneider (1858).

POLAND. WARSAW: *Jewish Historical Institute* (1,500): E. Kupfer-S. Strelcyn (Przegląd Orientalisticzny; 1954–55). WROCLAW (formerly Breslau): *Jewish Theological Seminary of Breslau* (405): D.S. Loewinger-B. Weinryb, 1965 (partly transferred to the Jewish Historical Institute in Warsaw).

SWITZERLAND. ZURICH: *Zentralbibliothek* (238): L.C. Wohlberg (1932); N. Allony-E. Kupfer (1964).

U.S.A. CINCINNATI: *Hebrew Union College Library* (1,500). LOS ANGELES: *University Library* (Rosenberg Collection from Ancona; the third part of the Gaster Collection, etc., 400). NEW HAVEN: *Yale University Library* (300): L. Nemoy (Journal of Jewish Bibliography; 1938–39). NEW YORK: *Columbia University* (1,000); *Jewish Theological Seminary of America* (10,000; 25,000 fragments): E.N. Adler (1921); *JTS Registers* (1902ff.); *Jewish Institute of Religion – Hebrew Union College* (200); *Jewish Teachers Seminary Library* (120); *R.H. Lehmann Collection* (400); *The New York University, Jewish Culture Foundation Library* (114); *Yeshiva University* (1,000); YIVO *Institute for Jewish Research Library* (1,200). PHILADELPHIA: *Dropsie College for Hebrew and Cognate Learning* (256; 500 fragments): B. Halpern (1924). SAN FRANCISCO: *California State Library* (Sutro Collection, 167): W.M. Brinner (1966).

RUSSIA. ST. PETERBURG: *M.S. Saltykov-Shchedrin State Library* (now *Russian National Library*) (1,962; 15,000 fragments; including the Firkovich Collections): A. Harkavy-H.L. Strack (1875); A.I. Katsch (1957/58; 1970). *Asiatic Museum* (2,347). Moscow: *Lenin State Library* (now *Russian State Library*) (Ginzburg Collection, 2,000).

VATICAN. VATICAN: *Biblioteca Apostolica Vaticana* (801): U. Cassuto (1956); N. Allony-D.S. Loewinger (1968).

[David Samuel Loewinger / Ephraim Kupfer]

Judaica and Hebraica Manuscripts in Russia

BACKGROUND. Dr. A.I. Katsh first visited the Soviet Union, Poland, and Hungary in 1956, when he arranged for the microfilming of several thousand manuscripts and rare documents of Judaica and Hebraica in various collections in those countries. It was the first, and so far the only, such undertaking by a Western scholar. In subsequent journeys behind the Iron Curtain in 1958, 1959, 1960, 1969, and 1976, he augmented this collection, which was then housed at the *Dropsie College, Philadelphia.

In this article Prof. Katsh gives an account of the five major collections of Judaica that are to be found in Leningrad and Moscow as the situation was prior to the dissolution of the Soviet Union. Today the Russian collections are accessible to scholars.

INTRODUCTION. Shortly after the Russian Revolution, the majority of the private collections of rare manuscripts on Judaica and Hebraica, which had been gathered over the centuries by Jewish scholars, disappeared. The only collections which remained were those in the possession of the Czarist government.

These collections constitute a bibliographer's paradise. They consist of a number of individual archives which include those of Israel *Zinberg, Daniel *Chwolson, Abraham Baer *Gottlober, David *Maggid and Shalom *Aleichem.

There is also valuable Hebraica material in the Academy of Tbilisi, the capital of Georgia; in the government library of Yerevan, the capital of Armenia; in Kiev, Vilna and the synagogues of Moscow and St. Petersburg.

Apart from those, however, the Russian collections consist of five major collections: the Baron David Guenzburg Collection, the Friedland Collection, the Two Firkovitch Collections, and the Antonin Genizah Collection.

THE GUENZBURG LIBRARY. The *Guenzburg Library was founded by Joseph Yozel Guenzburg (1812–78) and added to by his son Horace (1833–1909) and his grandsons David (1857–1910) and Alfred (1865–1930).

David Guenzburg was a brilliant scholar and an outstanding Orientalist who was reputed to have a knowledge of 34 languages. He founded the famous Guenzburg Academy in St. Petersburg. He was, however, also actively involved in all matters affecting the Jewish community.

In collaboration with Vladimir Stassoff, David published *L'Ornement Hebraïque*, a collection of artistic reproductions from the ancient Hebrew manuscripts in the St. Petersburg collection. In assembling their library the Guenzburgs had the help and advice of such experts as Adolf *Neubauer, who was the custodian of the Oriental Department of the Bodleian Library, and the scholar Raphael Nathan Nata *Rabbinovicz, the author of *Dikduke Soferim*.

In 1865, while the collection was in France, the renowned bibliographer Senior *Sachs was appointed its custodian. Ten years later he began work on a catalog to be called *Reshimat Sefarim Kitve-Yad be-Oẓar ha-Sefarim Shel Guenzburg* (list of manuscripts in the Guenzburg Library). The planned catalog was designed in such elaborate detail that it took 48 pages to describe the first two manuscripts. Realizing that this approach was impractical, Sachs then prepared a brief handwritten list of 831 items for the use of the family. This was apparently completed in 1887, when the Guenzburgs moved the collection from Paris to St. Petersburg, and it is now housed in the Russian State Library in Moscow. (Sachs himself, pensioned by the family, remained in Paris until his death on Nov. 18, 1892.)

A second handlist of items 832 to 1,908 was later prepared and catalogued, probably by a later scholar, by book size rather than by subject matter. Copies of these two handlist volumes are extremely rare. A Russian translation of the first 831 titles is now available in the Russian State Library. The actual number of titles may be as high as 5,000, because most of the codices list several items. However, not all the manuscripts listed in the handwritten catalogs are extant, since some were lost during the moving of the volumes from one place to another.

The manuscripts in the Guenzburg collection deal with a great variety of subjects, including Bible, Mishnah, Talmud, Responsa, Midrash, Kabbalah, philosophy, medicine, astronomy and mathematics. The biblical literature consists of 40 texts, 30 translations and 180 commentaries. Among the latter are Rashi, Ibn Ezra, Kimḥi, Naḥmanides, Levi b. Gershom and Jacob ben Asher.

The section dealing with Mishnah, Talmud and Halakhah is rich in quality and quantity (350 items) and also contains a number of works of the Gaonic period. The Responsa material includes the names of Rabbenu Gershom, Alfasi, Rashi, the Tosafists, Maimonides, David ha-Nagid, Abraham B. David, Naḥmanides, Solomon ben Adret (Rashba), Meier of Rothenberg, and Asher b. Yeḥiel. Hebrew poetry, secular and religious, is represented by Judah Halevi, Solomon ibn Gabirol, Abraham ibn Ezra, Judah Al-Ḥarizi and Immanuel of Rome. Some of the prayerbook manuscripts are illuminated in beautiful colors.

The collection includes a vast literature on the Shabbetai Ẓevi movement, works by Aristotle, as well as philosophical treatises in Hebrew (or Judeo-Arabic) by Averroes, Maimonides, Al-Ghazālī, Isaac Israeli, Jacob Anatoli, Crescas and others. Some of these works are no longer extant in the languages in which they were originally written. The Guenzburg collection includes important works on astronomy and mathematics and about 40 volumes on medicine. In addition, there are works by 19th-century Hebrew authors and scholars which are now of great value, since most of the unpublished manuscripts of the leading Jewish scholars of the 19th century were destroyed in the Holocaust. Of special interest are works by the biblical scholar Wolf Heidenheim (d. 1832), by his disciple S. Baer (d. 1897), and by the first Hebrew novelist, Abraham Mapu.

FRIEDLAND COLLECTION. The Friedland collection, housed in the Oriental Institute of the Academy of Science in St. Petersburg, contains unique manuscripts on the Bible: biblical commentaries in Judeo-Arabic, Persian, Turkish and other Middle Eastern languages; lexicography; ethics; astronomy; theology; philosophy; music; and historical material such as travel narratives, documents, archives and records of Jewish communities in Middle Eastern countries. There is a great deal of Karaitic literature. One of the rare Bibles, consisting only of the Later Prophets, bears the date 847 C.E.

A manuscript catalog begun by the late Yonah Y. Ginzburg was completed several years ago by A.M. Gasov-Ginzberg. The Oriental Institute in St. Petersburg, formerly under the direction of K.B. Starkova, has prepared an eight-volume catalog describing in detail the entire manuscript collection.

This catalog lists the following: 339 items dealing with Bible, commentaries and lexicography; 291 items dealing with philosophy, ethics, mysticism and theology; 332 items dealing with mathematics, physics, astronomy, medicine and music; 215 items dealing with Karaitic and liturgical works; 149 items of material on the Golden Age of Spain and literature of the Middle Ages, such as responsa, letters, records and documents.

The circumstances under which the Friedland collection was assembled, and its subsequent presentation to the Imperial Institute of St. Petersburg, is of more than passing interest and merits that it be given in some detail, especially in view of the fact that it explains the contents of this invaluable library.

Moses Aryeh Leib Friedland (1826–99) was a prominent Jewish leader in Czarist Russia and corresponded with all the leading rabbis of Russia in his endeavors to ease the economic and political plight of the Jews of the country during the era of the "Cantonists," when Jews were confined to the *Pale of Settlement and professions and trades were closed to them. Moreover, following the Congress of *Vienna (1814–15) some two million Jews were added from the Duchy of Warsaw or the Kingdom of Poland and draconic steps were taken by the authorities to uproot them from their settlements and change their way of life.

Into this oppressive and tyrannical atmosphere was tossed the complicated and stormy question of the *Haskalah*, the "enlightenment" movement which, according to its proponents, was to secure new standing for the Jews as a people, by means of an orderly and suitable process of integration into the life of the state. Against this background one can appreciate Friedland's leap into the battle occupying his people, which was one of the factors contributing towards the acquisition of his huge library.

Friedland did not belong to the same upper social class as the Guenzburgs. Starting from humble beginnings he traveled through the vast Russian steppes under the most trying conditions and in face of real danger, and he learned at first hand the joy of succeeding by dint of one's own labor. He felt the need to broaden the curriculum of education among Jews in Russia, by introducing into the *yeshivah* curriculum secular subjects and the Russian language. Convinced that this was the only way to salvation for the Jewish masses in Russia, Friedland ardently espoused the cause of the Haskalah and engaged in a voluminous correspondence with the great rabbis of the time in an attempt to persuade them to modernize their curriculum. Friedland's brother, Meir, was connected by marriage to Dr. Azriel *Hildesheimer. Friedland saw in his brother the ideal combination of religious and secular learning he strived for. Wherever he traveled in Russia he recorded accurate statistics concerning the size of the Jewish population, its communal institutions and his reason for demanding enlightenment and accepting the government's regulations, for under the circumstances that prevailed it was no longer possible to conceal from the authorities what was happening in Jewish communal life. All this had a direct bearing on the content of his library. Among his manuscripts is the *Kol Negidim* in four volumes, which is a veritable treasure house of information on the Jewish community of Russia during the 19th century. It consists of hundreds of letters, correspondence with the leading rabbis of his time dealing with their history and the many problems facing them. Included are the following references:

(1) The leaders of Russian Jewry at the time of Poliakoff, Guenzburg and others.

(2) Friedland's suggestion to include the teaching of the Russian language in Yeshivat Mir similar to the program in Yeshivat Volozhin.

(3) The rabbinical authorities – their attitudes to the introduction of secular education into the *yeshivot*.

(4) The Petersburg Congress of leading rabbis.

(5) The condition of Russian Jewry in Siberia, the Ukraine and elsewhere.

(6) The government requirement that every rabbi study the Russian language for six years.

(7) The controversy over deleting liturgical poems (*piyyutim*) and *kinot* in the prayers.

(8) The plan of Rabbi Isaac Jacob *Reines to establish a special *yeshivah* at Lida.

(9) The controversy between Rabbi Jacob Lifshitz and the leaders of the enlightenment movement.

In addition to these Friedland set himself the task of gleaning the treasures of Jewish learning in order to disseminate through them a knowledge of this heritage. He amassed a large collection of books, some of them extremely rare, at his own expense. These books were not limited to any one field or subject. His library was quantitatively large and qualitatively valuable, which was considered unique in the sphere of private libraries. Included also was a complete collection of the books of the Talmud, both early and late; books of rabbinical decisions (*poskim*); books of research and responsa in *halakhah*; books of meditation and thought; and numerous volumes of "enlightenment" books. Among the manuscripts in this collection are copies of Maimonides' *Guide to the Perplexed*, with numerous variants, two translations of the Koran in Hebrew by Jacob b. Israel Halevi, works by Tanḥum b. Joseph ha-Yerushalmi, Isaac b. Judah ibn Ghayyat, Judah Halevi, Solomon ibn Gabirol and Judah Al-Ḥarizi.

In the foreword to *Kehillat Moshe*, St. Petersburg 1896, S. Wiener wrote: "Moshe [Aryeh Leib Friedland], in addition to his good deeds for the general welfare of his people, and for the welfare of the individual in his support of several thousand families who bless his name, as the best known and most famous throughout the dispersion, this man also managed to build an everlasting sanctuary for the works of Jewish scholars. In this he has been eminently successful for he has collected in his home more than 14,000 of the finest works and has placed them as eternal witness for permanent safekeeping forever for all generations to come, in a building of the Asiatic Museum of the Imperial Academy of Science in St. Petersburg where, together with the museum's collection, the number of volumes listed will exceed 24,000." In my archives there is a personal letter written by S. Wiener to a friend of his, a learned scholar in Warsaw, on 12 Tevet 1891, in St. Petersburg, in which he says: "The number of books being published in the holy tongue [Hebrew] is about 10,000, and there are about 400 handwritten manuscripts. There is no treasure that compares with this except in Oxford and in London; this one is third in quantity and value." Friedland's library included "the collection which the learned grammarian Ber Bamfi of Minsk gathered throughout his life (he died on 28 Adar 1888). He spent a vast fortune on locating and building up a library of new and old and even rare volumes in all the subjects of Jewish learning and literature, the like of which has never before been seen in our city" (Naphtali Maskileison, *Alon Bachut, Ha-Meliẓ*, 1888, No. 53).

Friedland's library also contained the collection of books of Elieser Lipman Rabinowich who died in Ḥeshvan 1887 (see *Ha-Meliẓ*, No. 147). It contained also the choicest volumes collected by the prominent man of wealth, Shmaryahu Zuckerman of Mogilev (died in 1879), among which is the *Mekhilta* with the commentary on *Zeh Yenaḥameinu*, which the Gaon of Vilna studied and revised with his own hand (Wiener's foreword to *Kehillat Moshe*). Likewise included in Friedland's library were "about 2,000 volumes from the superb and valuable collection assembled throughout his life by the excellent bibliographer Joseph Mazal of Wiazin" (*ibid.*) as well as priceless volumes from various collections acquired for Friedland in Europe and other places. Friedland prized his library and was fully cognizant of its importance and value. In the initial stage he attended to his collection himself, but in the course of time – as it expanded and became more ramified – he engaged people specifically to catalog and classify the works according to subjects and to supervise and direct the progressive completion of the collection by acquiring every rare and priceless volume available in order to render his library complete.

In 1880 there appeared in *Ha-Meliẓ* an announcement which aroused consternation throughout the Jewish community. It declared that Friedland had decided to transfer his invaluable library to the Imperial Institute in St. Petersburg. It created a storm of controversy; it was considered by some as a betrayal of the Jewish people, especially since access to the institute was forbidden to Jews. Only one rabbi in Russia, Rabbi David ben Samuel *Friedmann of Karlin, at that time an active member of the *Hibbat Zion movement, while expressing his concern and sorrow at this step, tried to reason him out of it and proposed to Friedland that he transfer his library to Jerusalem. In a deeply moving letter he praised him for the labor and expense invested in this collection. The fact, however, that it would be housed in an institution closed to the Jews would result in "these volumes and the wisdom of their authors remaining locked up in darkness… Therefore, my advice to you is to establish a Jewish library in Jerusalem, the holy city, under the supervision of its rabbis, both Sephardi and Ashkenazi." He went into meticulous detail relevant to the implementation of his proposal: the binding of books, cataloging, means of keeping it up to date, budget requirements, librarians.

Rabbi Friedman's letter aroused a responsive chord in Friedland's heart. He regretted, however, that the suggestion had come too late; had it come earlier he would have accepted it.

In point of fact, Friedland was aware of the probable fate of his library, insofar as its use for Jews was concerned, if he gave it to St. Petersburg, since the authorities had closed the Jewish library in Warsaw and the Strashun Library in Vilna, and he sent 1,500 volumes of his library to the Great *Bet Hamidrash* of Dinaburg. To his consternation and dismay, however, he discovered that they had not even been taken out of their containers and he went to the expense of putting up shelves and appointing a librarian. But when the authorities refused to pay the wages of the librarian, he finally decided to give it to the St. Petersburg Institute. It was open daily and its "personnel consisted of people who regard Jewish learning very highly." Moreover, the authorities added to it some 3,000 duplicate copies of works already in their possession and undertook to appoint a special official in charge. The famous Russian Orientalist, Paul K. Kokovtsov, undertook the responsibility for its care and maintenance. Friedland consoled himself with the hope that circumstances would change. He believed that, housed within the Asiatic Museum, his library was destined to be used extensively. Many would study the volumes and contemplate their contents and would, through them, develop a familiarity with and esteem for the people which had produced men of such spirit and wisdom. The transfer of the library to the governmental institute was therefore, in Friedland's eyes – under the circumstances which then ruled the life of the Jews of Russia – a form of the most superior kind of "intercession" because as he saw it: "We shall find favor in the eyes of the government, for the benefit of our people, just as our Father Jacob placed the entire camp before him, when he went to face Esau, to ensure his safe journey."

Thus did the Friedland Library find its home in St. Petersburg.

THE FIRKOVITCH AND ANTONIN COLLECTIONS. The Firkovitch and Antonin collections are housed in the Russian State Library in St. Petersburg and contain principally *genizah* material.

The Firkovitch Collections. A native of the Crimea, Abraham *Firkovitch (1786–1874) was imbued with the notion that the Karaites of Babylonia were descended from the Ten Lost Tribes who had settled in the Crimea in the 6th century B.C.E. In his quest for documentary proof, he traveled throughout the Caucasus and the Middle East, exploring the *genizot* of ancient Jewish communities, and eventually assembled the most extensive collection of Hebrew, Samaritan and Karaitic manuscripts in the world, which was acquired in 1859 by the Imperial Library of St. Petersburg.

Some noted authorities, who checked the collection, accused him of tampering with dates on the manuscripts in order to prove his "theory" about the Karaites. Yet even his most severe critics admit that the manuscripts are extremely rare. Thus A. Harkavy and H.L. Strack wrote in 1875: "Though we, in the interest of science, deplore the numerous falsifications mentioned in our catalog, we gladly admit that A. Firkovitch, by the successful results of his tireless zeal for collecting manuscripts, assured himself everlasting recognition in the fields of Bible studies, Karaitic, and rabbinic literature." A considerable portion of the Firkovitch I collection consists of copies and molds of inscriptions found on old Jewish tombstones, mostly assembled by him while in the Crimea. These inscriptions are, in some cases, the only evidence we possess of the existence of Jewish settlements in early Crimean history. In the main, this collection consists of extremely valuable Hebrew, Karaitic and Judeo-Arabic manuscripts originating in Palestine, Egypt, Syria, and the Crimean Peninsula. When Firkovitch visited these places, the manuscripts there were still plentiful and he was able to make a choice selection. He kept the material in his possession for a good many years, studying and classifying it. He gradually compiled a handwritten catalog, which he attached to the memo when he offered to sell the collection to the Russian government in 1856. Firkovitch's catalog contains 830 items, in addition to several hundred letters and documents.

The biblical manuscripts of this first Firkovitch collection, catalogued by Harkavy and Strack, consist of five Torah scrolls written on leather, 41 scrolls written on parchment, 76 manuscripts in codex form, and 23 manuscripts containing text and translation in Aramaic, Arabic, Persian, and Tatar.

Of particular importance in the Firkovitch collection is the section dealing with disputations between the Karaites and Rabbinites.

Included are a manuscript of the *Ḥizzuk Emunah* by the Karaite scholar Yiẓḥak b. Abraham, and by Moses b. Ezra, dealing with the history of Hebrew poets of the Middle Ages, containing material not found elsewhere, and the archives of Judah al-Ḥarizi.

A large number of the manuscripts deal with poets who lived in Palestine, Egypt, and Syria.

In addition to the first Firkovitch collection, another small collection of important Hebrew manuscripts came into the possession of the Imperial Library in St. Petersburg around the year 1863. This was the collection of the Society for History and Antiquity in Odessa. Since it contained manuscripts originally belonging to Firkovitch, the authorities of the library demanded that it be added to the Firkovitch collection. Harkavy-Strack included in their catalog of the Odessa collection 35 Torah scrolls and 20 in codéx form.

This important acquisition of unique manuscripts immediately placed Russia in a favorable position for Hebrew manuscript study, especially in biblical research. The announcement of this collection and the first reports of its contents aroused great excitement among biblical scholars and manuscript collectors. According to Firkovitch's description, and supported by Prof. Daniel Chwolson, there were in this collection 13 Bibles belonging to the period from the 5th to the 9th centuries and 15 Bibles of the 10th century. In his memorandum to the Russian government, Chwolson stated: "In the future, no edition of biblical text should be considered without consulting these important early manuscripts."

The Firkovitch Collection II was acquired by the Russian Imperial Library in 1876. For a long time little was known of its contents, nor was the exact origin of its material certain. Although Firkovitch himself did not provide this kind of information, there is no doubt that the greater part of it came from the *genizot* of the old synagogues in the Crimea. A substantial number of the fragments appears to have come from the Cairo *genizah* in Egypt. A detailed description of the contents of the Firkovitch II collection was given by the late Prof. P. Kahle, who examined the material while on a visit to Leningrad. According to Kahle it includes: 1,582 items of biblical fragments with *masorah* written on parchment; 725 items of biblical material written on paper; 159 items of scrolls of the Bible on leather or parchment; over 6,000 Hebrew and Judeo-Arabic fragments; and 344 non-biblical manuscripts. The material in the Firkovitch collections and the other Hebraica collections in Russia undoubtedly comprise the largest biblical manuscript collection in the world.

The Antonin Collection. The Antonin *genizah* collection was acquired by the Russian Archimandrite, Antonin Kapustin, who lived in Jerusalem from 1865 until his death in 1894. When he learned about the discovery of the Cairo *genizah* he was among the first to be on the scene and was able to acquire a choice selection of material. Upon his death, this material went to the Government Library at St. Petersburg. The Antonin collection occupies an outstanding place, not so much for its quantity as for its quality. The fragments deal with the Bible, biblical translations in Aramaic and Judeo-Arabic, Karaite polemics, historical documents, *Kabbalah*, liturgy, medicine, theology, philosophy and *Ketubot*. They are written in Hebrew, Arabic, Judeo-Arabic, and Samaritan. The late Prof. S. Assaf in his book *Gaonic Responsa* (1929) lamented the fact that the Antonin material in Russia was not accessible to scholars, nor was a catalog available. As a result of many visits to the U.S.S.R. this author was able in 1963 to prepare and publish the only catalog of the entire Antonin material.

According to my classification, the Antonin *genizah* collection of 1,189 items represents 36 subjects ranging from biblical texts to *Zohar*, including such rare items as the Bible in Samaritan, Ibn Ezra's commentary on the Bible, and medical notes in Arabic. The proportions of these various subjects is interesting. Half the collection consists of biblical literature; liturgical material comes next with one-sixth; Talmud, Midrash, *Halakhah*, with one-seventh. This uneven proportion is due to the fact that the sacred books were in wide use among the people. Each household possessed a Bible and one or more prayerbooks. Each scholar had a Talmud and some midrashic and *halakhic* books, whereas the other non-sacred books were confined to special individuals only. The reason that so much non-religious material was found in the Cairo *genizah* at all is that the synagogue at Fostat-Cairo was also used for the offices of the rabbinical courts, where they kept the community archives. Later all this became part of the general *genizah*. Furthermore, the placing of discarded material in the *genizah* was not officially controlled; individuals merely sent their unwanted old books and papers to the *genizah*. No one examined the contents before they were stored away. Thus among the *genizah* contents are private papers, business letters and accounts, and a great number of documents in Arabic script. Prof. Harkavy, in evaluating the Antonin *genizah*, noted: "... the Hebrew and Arabic fragments ... have the same origin as the material of the second Firkovitch collection, namely, from the *genizot* of Egypt. They complement each other to a great degree. Together they add great honor and glory to the Royal Public Library."

[Abraham I. Katsh]

BIBLIOGRAPHY: S. Sachs, *Catalogue or the Guenzburg Collection*, 2 volumes. A.I. Katsh, *The Friedland Library in the Leningrad Oriental Institute*, NYU 1963. Y.Y. Ginzberg, *Hebrew Manuscript Collection at the Oriental Institute of the Academy of Sciences* (Report in Russian, 1936). A.A. Harkavy and H.L. Strack, *Catalog der Hebraischen Bibelhandschriften der Kaiserlichen Orientlich Bibliothek in St. Petersburg*, 1875. H.L. Strack, *A. Firkovitch und seine Entdeckungen*, Leipzig, 1868. K.B. Starkova, "Forty Years of Semitic Studies in the U.S.S.R.," *Publication of the Oriental Institute of Academy of Sciences*, XXV, 1960, pp. 263–77 (Russian). K.B. Starkova, "The Firkovitch Manuscript Collection in the Saltykov-Shchedrin Government Library" (Russian), *Publication of the Academy of Science*, Institute of Oriental Studies, Moscow, 1974, pp. 165–92. A.I. Katsh, *Catalogue of Microfilms of the U.S.S.R. Hebraica Collection*, Part I, 1957; Part II, 1968, NY. *The Antonin Genizah in the Saltykov-Shchedrin Library in Leningrad*, NYU, 1963, *Yigal Hazon*, Jerusalem, 1964 (from a 13th-century Barcelona manuscript in Moscow). *Midrash David Hanagid*, Jerusalem, Genesis (1964), Exodus (1968), Lamentations (1969), from Judeo-Arabic manuscripts in the U.S.S.R. Hebrew Collection, Jerusalem. *Ginze Mishna*, Jerusalem (1970). *Ginze Talmud Babli*, Jerusalem, 1975. *Ginze Talmud Babli*, Vol. II, Jerusalem, 1978. "S. Baer's Unpublished Targum Onkelos," in *Text and Studies in Honor of A.A. Neuman*, Philadelphia, 1962. JUDAICA AND HEBRAICA IN THE U.S.S.R.: C. Burchard, *Bibliographie zu den Handschriften vom Toten Meer* (1959, 1965); E. Sachau, *Aramaeischer Papyrus und Ostraka* (1911); N. Avigad, in: *Scripta Hierosolymitana*, 4 (1958), 56–87; idem, *Ha-Paleografyah shel Megillot Yam ha-Melaḥ...* (1963), 107–34; G.R. Driver, *Aramaic Documents of the Fifth Century* (1954); I. Ben-Zvi et al., *Meḥkarim be-Keter Aram Ẓova* (1960); I. Yevin, *Keter Aram Ẓova...* (1969); L. Zunz, in: ZHB, 18 (1915), 58–64, 101–19; A. Freimann, *ibid.*, 11 (1907), 86–96; 14 (1910), 105–12; idem, in: *Alexander Marx Jubilee Volume* (1950), 231–342 (Eng. sect.); S. Poznański, in: ZHB, 19 (1916), 79–122; C. Bernheimer, *Paleografia Ebraica* (1924); S.A. Birnbaum, *Hebrew Scripts* (1954–57; 1 vol. of plates; Part 1 not publ.); C. Sirat and M.Beit-Arié, *Manuscripts médiévaux en caractères hébraiques...* (1969); *Reshimat Kitvei-Yad...* (1960), includes *"Kitvei-Yad... Faksimiliyyot"*: 54–69; S. Shaked, *A Tentative Bibliography of Geniza Documents* (1964); S. Loewinger and A. Scheiber, (eds.) in: *Geniza Publications in Memory of D. Kaufmann* (1949), xiii–xv; A. Scheiber, *Héber kodexmaradványok...* (1969); *Die hebraeischen Uebersetzungen des Mittelalters und die Juden als Dolmetscher* (1893); Shunami, Bibl. (for the literature on and from M. Steinschneider); M. Steinschneider, *Vorlesungen ueber die Kunde hebraeischer Handschriften* (1897; Hebrew edition by A.M. Habermann, in: *Aresheth*, 4 (1966), 53–165; separate ed., 1965); A. Freimann, *Union Catalog of Hebrew Manuscripts and their Location*, 2 (1964); N. Allony and D.S. Loewinger, *List of Photographed Manuscripts, Austria-Germany* (1957); N. Allony and A. Kupfer, *List... Belgium, Denmark, Holland, Spain, and Switzerland* (1964); N. Allony and D.S. Loewinger, *List... Vatican Library* (1968); D.S. Loewinger and E. Kupfer, *List... Parma Library* (in preparation); D.S. Loewinger, *Sekirah al Pe'ullot ha-Makhon...* (1965); idem, in: *Haaretz* (Sept. 21, 1969); M. Beit-Arié, in: KS, 43 (1967/68), 411–28; 45 (1969/70), 435–46.

MA'ON (Heb. מָעוֹן, biblical Maon).

(1) City in Judah, the dwelling place of Nabal (I Sam. 25:2, 3); there was also a desert of the same name (I Sam. 23:25). Maon belonged to the seventh district of Judah (Josh. 15:55). In talmudic sources it is called Maon of Judah to distinguish it from Bet Maon near Tiberias (Mekh. Yitro 1). The place is identified with Tell Maʿīn, about 4 mi. (7 km.) S.E. of Yaṭṭa.

(2) The Maonites, a tribe, oppressed Israel along with the Zidonians and the Amalekites (Judg. 10:12). This tribe may be identical with the Meunim whose tents were destroyed by the Simeonites (I Chron. 4:41) and were later defeated by Uzziah, king of Judah (II Chron. 26:7). The area in which this tribe was located is in dispute.

(3) Site southwest of Gaza, called Menois in Roman times. It was the westernmost point of the Palestinian limes (Codex Theodosius 7:4, 30; *Notitia Dignitatum in partibus Orientis* 34:19, 2). The place is shown on the Madaba Map (mid-sixth century). Eusebius mistakenly identified it with the Madmannah of Joshua 15:31 (Onom. 130:7). It is now identified with Ḥorvat Ma'on (Khirbat al-Maʿin) near Nirim, southeast of Gaza. A kibbutz called Ma'on was established near the site in 1949. Remains of mosaic pavements and other debris show that the area contained an extensive settlement from the fourth century C.E. onward. The most interesting building is a synagogue which was excavated in 1957–58. It is oriented toward the northeast and consists of a hall, 14.8 × 11.8 m., with two rows of four columns forming the nave and two aisles. In the vicinity was a ritual bath (*mikveh*). The stone-paved aisles and narthex form a sort of ambulatory around the mosaic-paved nave. The design of the mosaic shows a vine trellis issuing from an amphora flanked by peacocks; the trellis forms medallions within which pairs of various animals are represented. The section of the pavement nearest to the apse has symbolic designs: two palm trees with doves at their bases and above them a *menorah* with two *etrogim*, a *shofar*, and a *lulav*, flanked by two lions. The Aramaic inscription mentions the congregation as a whole and three individual donors of a gold *dinar* each. The pavement, which dates to the early sixth century, has an interesting parallel in a church pavement found at nearby Shellal. They were both, according to Avi-Yonah, made in the same workshop in Gaza (see recently Ovadiah on this matter).

BIBLIOGRAPHY: (1) Beyer, in: ZDPV, 54 (1931), 228; Noth, in: PJB, 30 (1934), 35. (2) EM, s.v. (includes bibliography). (3) Alt, in: PJB, 26 (1930), 33; Abel, Geog, 2 (1938), 180; Avi-Yonah, Geog, index; idem, *Madaba Mosaic Map* (1954), 74; Levi et al., in: BRF, 3 (1960), 1–40. **ADD. BIBLIOGRAPHY:** S. Levy et al., "The Ancient Synagogue of

Ma'on (Nirim)," in: *Bulletin III* of the Rabinovitz Fund for the Exploration of Ancient Synagogues, Hebrew University (1960); S.J. Saller, *Second Revised Catalogue of the Ancient Synagogues of the Holy Land* (1972), 61–62; Z. Ilan, *Ancient Synagogues in Israel* (1991), 283–85; A. Ovadiah, "The Mosaic Workshop of Gaza in Christian Antiquity," in: D. Urman and P.V.M. Flesher (eds.), *Ancient Synagogues. Historical Analysis and Archaeological Discovery* (1995), 367–72.

[Michael Avi-Yonah / Shimon Gibson (2nd ed.)]

MAOR, GALIA (1943–), president and CEO of Bank Leumi. Maor received an M.B.A. from the Hebrew University of Jerusalem and began her banking career at the Bank of Israel in 1963. She filled a long series of positions from assistant to the manager of open markets to adviser to the director general. From 1982 to 1987 she served as the supervisor of banks. During her time in that position, the banks' manipulation of their own share prices was revealed in a major scandal. She retired from the Bank of Israel in 1989 and worked for two years as a consultant for the Somech-Haikin accounting firm. In 1991 she joined Bank Leumi, first as deputy CEO and from 1995 as CEO. Maor is considered a top-flight manager who led Bank Leumi to numerous successes, positioning it second after Bank Hapoalim in the hierarchy of Israeli banks. In 2004 she was ranked 36th in Forbes' list of the world's most successful women.

BIBLIOGRAPHY: "Galia Maor, CEO of Bank Leumi," at: www.ynet.co.il (Apr. 4, 2004).

[Shaked Gilboa (2nd ed.)]

MA'OR KATAN (Lucerna, Lutzerner, Luzerner), family of physicians in Vienna and Prague in the 17th century, who intermarried with the *Fraenkel-Teomim family. The family is well known mainly because of their internal correspondence from 1619, preserved in the Viennese imperial archives. The first of the family, MOSES BEN LOEB (d. 1605), was elected in 1570 and 1573 as physician of the Frankfurt community. He presented a certificate by the *bet din* of Mantua that he belonged to the Freistaedtl family there. His son, JUDAH LEIB (Leva, Leo Lucerna Hebraeus Aulicus; d. 1635), was physician and at the same time rabbi in Vienna. He built himself a synagogue in his house, and left unpublished books. His grandson, Menahem Mendel *Auerbach, describes him in his *Atteret Zekenim* (1702), para. 572. Another son, AARON, was employed by the Prague Jewish community in 1619 as physician, attending Christians as well. Through his mother and his wife he was related to Yom Tov Lipmann *Heller, who in his *Ma'adanei Melekh* on *Ḥullin* 66b acknowledges information supplied by Aaron. Besides attaining the degree of doctor of medicine he was also a doctor of physics and philosophy from the university at Padua, and was the only Jewish physician fully recognized by the Vienna medical faculty.

BIBLIOGRAPHY: B. Wachstein, *Die Inschriften des alten Judenfriedhofes in Wien*, 1 (1912), index; A. Landau-B. Wachstein, *Juedische Privatbriefe aus dem Jahr 1619* (1911), index; G. Kisch, in: JGGJČ, 6 (1934), 15; I. Kracauer, *Geschichte der Juden in Frankfurt a. M. (1150–1824)*, 2 (1927), 260; M. Grunwald, *Vienna* (1936), index.

[Meir Lamed]

MA'OZ ḤAYYIM (Heb. מָעוֹז חַיִּים), kibbutz in central Israel, in the Beth-Shean Valley near the Jordan River, affiliated to Ha-Kibbutz ha-Me'uḥad. It was founded in 1937 during the 1936–39 Arab riots, as the first *stockade and watchtower village east of Beth-Shean, by four groups, three of whom set out a few months later to establish further kibbutz outposts: *Kefar Ruppin, *Mesillot, and *Neveh Eitan. Most of the founders of Ma'oz Ḥayyim were Israel-born. In the Israel *War of Independence (1948), the kibbutz held an advanced defense position; it again suffered repeated shelling in the period after the *Six-Day War (1967). The kibbutz economy was based on field crops, fruit orchards, carp ponds, dairy cattle, and a factory for packaging materials. Nearby, the Ma'oz Bridge (known in Arabic as Jisr e-Shaikh Husain) spans the Jordan, over what is assumedly the ford used by the Midianites in their flight from Gideon's army; by Pompey in 63 B.C.E.; by the Arab-Muslim army in 635 C.E.; and by Saladin in 1187 when he invaded the country. Today the bridge serves a transit point between Israel and Jordan. The name, "Ḥayyim's Stronghold," commemorates Ḥayyim *Sturman, a Ha-Shomer veteran killed by Arabs on a land-purchasing mission in the Beth-Shean Valley. In 2002 the population of Ma'oz Ḥayyim was 596.

[Efram Orni / Shaked Gilboa (2nd ed.)]

MA'OZ ẒUR (Heb. מָעוֹז צוּר (יְשׁוּעָתִי); "O Fortress, Rock (of My Salvation)", see: Isa. 17:10), initial words and title of a hymn sung, in the Ashkenazi ritual, in the synagogue and at home after the kindling of the *Ḥanukkah lights. The song originated in Germany probably in the 13th century (Zunz. Lit Poesie, 580); the author is an otherwise unknown poet by the name of Mordecai as shown by the acrostic of the first five stanzas. Some scholars indentify him with Mordecai b. Isaac, the author of the Sabbath table hymn *Mah Yafit*. The original *Ma'oz Ẓur* consists of six stanzas, the first expressing Israel's messianic hopes for the reestablishment of the ancient Temple worship. The following three stanzas praise God for the deliverance of Israel from the Egyptian bondage, from the Babylonian exile, and from *Haman's plot. The fifth stanza summarizes the miracle of Ḥanukkah, and the last one is a plea for the speedy redemption of Israel. The reference in it to *Admon* – as a synonym for Edom – has been understood to refer to the German Emperor Frederic Barbarossa (1121–90 C.E.). This last verse is now omitted and does not figure in most *siddur* editions, though its acrostic חזק (*ḥazak*, "strong"), seems to show that it is part of the original composition. Another six verses have been added to *Ma'oz Ẓur* in the course of time by various authors, the first, so it is claimed, by Moses *Isserles. The theme of these additions, too, is a plaint against persecution by Edom and Ishmael (Christians and Arabs), and a prayer for divine vengeance and redemption. An English version of this hymn, called *Rock of Ages*, was written by M. *Jastrow and G. *Gottheil. It differs slightly from the original Hebrew text, with its strong plea for vengeance. Some editions of British prayer books (J.H. Hertz, 1963, p. 950) changed the Hebrew text itself. In Conservative and Reform synagogues the English version is sung in addition to or instead of *Ma'oz Ẓur.*

Musical Rendition

The most commonly sung melody of *Ma'oz Ẓur* is of West European Ashkenazi origin and may be dated from around the early 15th century. E. *Birnbaum and A.Z. *Idelsohn, on the basis of the similarity of isolated motives, related it to a group of early Protestant chorales and a German soldiers' song. There is a much closer correspondence in the entire melodic line to the church melody *Patrem omnipotentem* which appears in several Bohemian-Silesian manuscripts, the earliest of which is dated 1474. The earliest notation attesting to the use of the melody for *Ma'oz Ẓur* so far located is found in the manuscript of Judah Elias of Hanover (1744) as a "melodic reminder" in settings of *Hodu* for Ḥanukkah. The first printed version appears in Isaac *Nathan's *Hebrew Melodies* (1815) set to Byron's "On Jordan's Banks." None of the standard sources of the 19th and early 20th centuries has the repetition of the last sentence of the stanza, which is a recent and inept "improvement." In Ashkenazi usage, from the beginning of the month of Kislev onward and during the week of Ḥanukkah, various prayers are also sung to the *Ma'oz Ẓur* melody or feature its motives. Other melodies also exist, but their distribution is limited. The melody of the Tedesco (German-Italian) Jews was first notated by the gentile composer Benedetto Marcello in his *Estro poetico-armonico* (Venice, 1724, 1803²). It is still sung in Italy, and sometimes also in Israel and the United States. However, the standard West European Ashkenazi melody has become the dominant and representative one, in spite of objections to its "non-Jewish" character.

Sources

STANDARD MELODY: Idelsohn, Melodien, 6 (1932), pt. 1no. 53; pt. 2 no. 43, both "*Hodu* for Ḥanukkah " from cantors' manuals of the end of the 18th century; Idelsohn, Melodien, 8 (1933), no. 311. Judah Elias of Hanover, Ms. dated 1744, two *Hodu* for Ḥanukkah published by A. Nadel: one, no foliation indicated, in *Der Orden Bne Briss* (Sept.–Oct. 1935), 95; another *Hodu* no. 215, in *Musica Hebraica*, 1–2 (1938), 28, 69. The Ms. is lost; John Braham and Isaac Nathan, *A Selection of Hebrew Melodies… by Lord Byron* (London, 1815), 31–36 ("On Jordan's Banks"); Ms. formerly in the possession of the Lieben family of Prague, dated 1820 or 1826, lost, 2 copies made in 1920, one in Jewish Museum, Prague (no no. given), one in JNUL, Jacob Michael Collection of Jewish Music, Ms. no. JMA 4705. fol. 16a. Published by H. Avenary in *Taẓlil*, 7 (1967), 127; A. Baer, *Baal T'fillah* (1883²), no. 188; E. Birnbaum, *Chanuca Melodie "Maos Zur" fuer Pianoforte bearbeitet* (1889), textless; M. Wodak, *Hamnazeach* (1898), no. 94. GERMAN-ITALIAN: Benedetto Marcello, *Estro poetico-armonico* (Venice, 1724–26, 1803²), tom. III, xii–xiv, setting for 1 voice and 2 instruments, prefaced on p. xii by notation of the synagogal tune. Published in Idelsohn, Melodien, 6 (1932), appendix, no. 2 (p. 231), and elsewhere. GERMAN: Elhanan Kirchhan (Kirchhain), *Simḥat ha-Nefesh* (Fuerth, 1726/27), fol. 6b, textless, but with superscription in Judeo-German "Sing the song with devotion on the eight Ḥanukkah days" and fits the meter and rhythm of *Ma'oz Ẓur.* Published a) Facsimile ed., 1926, b) Idelsohn, Melodien, 6 (1932), appendix, no. 7 (p. 233). SILESIAN-POLISH: (based on *Eli Ẓiyyon*). Idelsohn, Melodien, 9 (1932), no. 413, after E. Kirschner, in *Mitteilungen zur juedischen Volkskunde*, 16 (1905), 113. MORAVIA: Ms. Lieben (1820 or 1826; see above) fol. 16b. HASIDIC: attributed to R. Mordecai "The *ḥazzan* of Saslaw" pupil of the Ba'al Shem Tov, fl. c. 1770, in M.S. Geshuri *Ha-Niggun ve-ha-Rikkud ba-Ḥasidut*, 1 (1956), 270. ḤASIDIC-GUR: L. Levi (see bibl.), music supplement p. 12. ITALY-GORIZIA: L. Levi (see bibl.), loc. cit.

[Bathja Bayer]

BIBLIOGRAPHY: Landshuth, Ammudei, 202; Abrahams, Companion, ccv-vi; Davidson, Oẓar, 3 (1930), 159 no. 1955; J.T. Levinski, *Sefer ha-Mo'adim*, 5 (1954), 180f.; A. Carlebach, in: *Shanah be-Shanah 5730* (1969), 270–4; Hertz, Prayer, 275; *Union Prayer Book*, 1 (1924), 354; *Sabbath and Festival Prayer Book* (1946), 365. MUSICAL RENDITION: L. Levi, in: *Sefer ha-Mo'adim*, 5 (1954), 182–5; D. Kaufmann, in: *He-Assif*, 2 (1885), 298; Zunz, Lit Poesie, 422, 429; H. Avenary, in: *Taẓlil*, 7 (1967), 125–8; Idelsohn, Melodien, 9 (1932), xii; idem, in: HUCA, 11 (1936), 569–91; E. Werner, in: MGWJ, 81 (1937), 393–416.

MAPAI (Hebrew acronym for **Mifleget Po'alei Ereẓ Yisrael**), a social-democratic workers party that existed in 1930–68. The party was founded in 1930 through a union between *Aḥdut ha-Avodah and *Ha-Po'el ha-Ẓa'ir as "a Zionist Socialist party faithful to the ideal of national redemption and the ideal of socialism in the homeland." Among its founders were Berl *Katznelson, David *Ben-Gurion, Yitzhak *Ben-Zvi, and Yosef *Sprinzak. Mapai soon became the dominant party in the labor movement, and in the *yishuv* as a whole. It obtained 27 out of 71 seats in Asefat ha-Nivḥarim (the Elected Assembly of the *yishuv*) in 1931, and 165 out of 201 at the 1933 *Histadrut convention. At the 18th Zionist Congress in 1933, the labor delegation was the largest, numbering 138 out of 318 delegates, and four Mapai members – David Ben-Gurion, Eliezer *Kaplan, Moshe Shertok (*Sharett), and Berl *Locker – were elected to the ten-member Jewish Agency Executive, which Ben-Gurion chaired from 1935 to 1948. Mapai's approach to socialism was pragmatic rather than Marxist. Its aim was not so much the accrual of power by labor as a gradual advance, in Ben-Gurion's phrase, *mi-ma'amad le-am* ("from class to people"). It regarded labor as the central force in the nation, responsible for the achievement of national aims, and called for the unification of all the labor parties. Its main political rivals were the *General Zionists and the right-wing *Revisionists on the one hand, and the left-wing *Ha-Shomer ha-Ẓa'ir on the other, and it established an historical alliance with the religious *Mizrachi and *Ha-Po'el ha-Mizrachi and, later on, with the more moderate General Zionists. It was the leading member in the World Union (Ha-Iḥud ha-Olami) of *Po'alei Zion, and was a member of the Second (Socialist) International.

The party was divided over the Peel Commission's partition plan of 1937, but finally decided to accept the principle of partition. Later, it opted for the establishment of a Jewish

Commonwealth in Palestine after the War – a position that was approved by the *Biltmore Conference in 1942. Mapai called for participation by Jewish military units in the British army to fight the Nazis in World War II, combined with opposition to the restrictions of the 1939 White Paper on Jewish immigration and land settlement. It advocated self-defense through the *Haganah under the authority of the Jewish national institutions (Jewish Agency and Va'ad Le'ummi), and the use of physical resistance and even armed force to combat British measures against clandestine immigration, while opposing terrorist reprisals against individual Arabs and all-out rebellion against the Mandatory government.

A leftist group in Mapai, Si'ah Bet ("Faction B"), criticized the reformist tendencies of the majority, who held all the key positions. The struggle came to a head in 1942, when the Mapai convention prohibited factions within the party. As a result, Si'ah Bet broke away in 1944, supported by over half of the Kibbutz ha-Me'uḥad, and formed the Tenu'ah le-Aḥdut ha-Avodah. Despite the split, Mapai retained its absolute majority in the Histadrut, though reduced from 69.3% in 1942 to 53.8% in 1944. It remained the strongest party in Asefat ha-Nivḥarim (63 delegates out of 171 in 1944), and retained a dominant position in the Jewish Agency Executive.

During the preparations for the establishment of the State, Mapai was allotted ten seats out of 37 in the National Council and four out of 13 in the National Administration, which became the Provisional State Council (legislature), and the Provisional Government respectively when the State of Israel was proclaimed. It won 46 out of 120 seats at the elections to the First Knesset in 1949, 45 in the elections to the Second Knesset in 1951, 40 in the elections to the Third Knesset in 1955, 47 in the elections to the Fourth Knesset in 1959, and 42 in the elections to the Fifth Knesset in 1961. It ran together with Aḥdut ha-Avodah–Poa'lei Zion in the elections to the Sixth Knesset in 1965 in the Alignment list, which won 45 seats. Mapai, and later the Alignment, had the support of two to five members of associated Arab minority lists.

It was the dominant force in all the Israeli governments until 1968, holding, among others, the portfolios of Prime Minister, Defense, Foreign Affairs, Finance, Education, Agriculture, and Police. In the Jewish Agency, it held the chairmanship of the Executive and headed most of the central departments. In the Histadrut it maintained its absolute majority until 1965 and its representatives held leading positions in all its organs. Mapai nominees headed most of the local authorities. There was a Mapai mayor in Jerusalem in 1955–65, in Tel Aviv from 1959 to 1968, and in Haifa from 1951 to 1968.

Mapai was badly shaken by the *Lavon Affair that began as the *Esek Bish* in 1954. The affair finally led to a split in the party in 1965 when Ben-Gurion and a group of followers that included Moshe *Dayan and Shimon *Peres, broke away from Mapai and established a new party by the name of *Rafi. A year after the Six-Day War Mapai, Aḥdut ha-Avodah–Po'alei Zion, and Rafi became a single party called the *Israel Labor Party. In the institutions of the new party Mapai received 57% of the seats, while the other two received 21.5% each.

BIBLIOGRAPHY: P.Y. Medding, *Mapai in Israeli Political Organization and Government in a New Society* (1972); Y. Shapiro, *The Formative Years of the Israel Labour Party: The Organization of Power, 1919–1930* (1975); Y. Goldstein, *Mifleget Po'alei Ereẓ Yisra'el* (1975); idem, *Ba-Derekh le-Hegemonya: Mapai – Hitgabbeshut Mediniyyutah* (1980); A. Zimmerman, *Ha-Vikku'ah betokh Mapai al Ra'ayon ha-Medinah ba-Shanim 1929–1946* (1979).

[Misha Louvish / Susan Hattis Rolef (2nd ed.)]

MAPAM (Hebrew acronym for **Mifleget ha-Po'alim ha-Me'uḥedet** – The United Workers' Party), an Israeli Zionist-Socialist party, founded in 1948, when Ha-Shomer ha-Ẓa'ir merged with *Aḥdut ha-Aavodah–Po'alei Zion.

In its early days Mapam advocated radical socialist positions, based on class struggle and links with international socialism, but at the same time it also called for the concentration of the majority of the Jewish people in Ereẓ Israel. Its declared aims were the achievement of socialism in Israel through the democratic hegemony of the labor movement; the establishment of publicly owned enterprises; communal land settlement in the form of kibbutzim; state ownership of the land; cooperation with private capital while condemning all forms of profiteering and "parasitism"; a planned economy to ensure full employment, and the attainment of an egalitarian society.

In 1951 it was the main force behind the violent seamen's strike in the ZIM shipping company, which was viewed by many as an attempted revolt against the *Mapai establishment.

In the early period Mapam also advocated a pro-Soviet policy. Nevertheless, during the 1952 *Slansky Trial in Prague, at which the Zionists were accused of espionage and subversion in the Communist countries, a prominent Mapam member, Mordechai Oren, was arrested and received a 15-year prison sentence. Despite the antisemitic flavor of the trial in Prague, and the Jewish doctors' trial in Moscow, the pro-Soviet group within Mapam advocated that the party support the position of the Soviet Union. In 1954, a small pro-Soviet group within Mapam, led by Moshe *Sneh, broke away from the party, and joined the Israel Communist Party (MAKI). In the same year Aḥdut ha-Avodah–Po'alei Zion decided to break away from Mapam as well and reestablish an independent party. The background to this decision was criticism of the pro-Soviet line and Mapam's decision to accept Arab members into its ranks. Mapam advocated cooperation with the Arab working class and the belief that Israel could achieve peace with its neighbors by integrating into the Middle East. Mapam continued to run as an independent list until 1969, and then in the elections to the Seventh to the Eleventh Knessets ran within the framework of the Alignment together with the *Israel Labor Party.

Mapam was not a member of the government until after the elections to the Third Knesset in 1955, but then was a member of all the Mapai and Labor Party-led governments until 1977. Both of Mapam's historic leaders, Me'ir *Ya'ari and Ya'akov *Ḥazan, supported its entering the Alignment with the Labor Party, which greatly dampened what remained of the party's radical zeal. This trend strengthened after the elderly leaders retired from membership in the Knesset in 1974, after the elections to the Eighth Knesset. In 1974 Mapam Minister of Health Victor *Shem-Tov proposed, together with Aharon *Yariv of the Labor Party, a formula for the holding of negotiations with Palestinians, who would recognize Israel's right to exist, be willing to live in peace with Israel, and refrain from performing acts of terror. However, the Yariv–Shem-Tov formula was not accepted at the time by the Government, though almost 20 years later it constituted the basis for Israel's willingness to sign the Declaration of Principles with the PLO.

Following the elections to the Eleventh Knesset in 1984, when the Labor Party decided to enter a National Unity Government with the Likud, based on parity and a rotation in the premiership, Mapam decided to leave the Alignment, but only after the coalition agreement had been signed. Mapam ran independently in the elections to the Twelfth Knesset, and then joined with the Civil Rights Movement, and *Shinui in establishing *Meretz, in which it constituted the socialist component. In February 1997 the three components of Meretz joined into a single party, and Mapam ceased to exist as a separate party. Meretz was a member of the government formed by Yitzhak *Rabin in 1992, in which Mapam's Ya'ir *Tsaban served as minister of immigration absorption. Though Tsaban exerted little influence on the Government's policies in the sphere of economics and the peace process, he was active in the spheres of religion and state and social issues. In the years 1994–97 Ḥayyim Oron of Mapam was treasurer of the Histadrut, after running in the 1994 Histadrut elections on Haim *Ramon's Ḥayyim Ḥadashim ba-Histadrut list.

Traditionally the party's power came from the Kibbutz ha-Arẓi kibbutz movement, on the one hand, and organized urban groups, on the other. Until the 1980s it was the first group that was dominant. Later on the latter gained the upper hand. Mapam's gradual loss of strength was a function of the general deterioration of the Left in Israel.

Mapam's secretary generals since its foundation were Me'ir Ya'ari, 1948–71; Me'ir Talmi, 1973–79; Victor Shem-Tov, 1979–85; Eleazar Granot, 1985–97.

Its Knesset representation was as follows: First Knesset – 19; Second Knesset – 15; Third Knesset to Fifth Knesset – 9; Sixth Knesset – 10; Seventh Knesset – 9; Eighth to Eleventh Knesset within the Alignment: Eighth Knesset – 8, Ninth Knesset – 4; Tenth Knesset – 7; Eleventh Knesset – 6; Twelfth Knesset – 3; Thirteenth to Fourteenth Knesset within Meretz: Thirteenth Knesset – 4; Fourteenth Knesset – 3.

Until 2005 Mapam published a daily newspaper, **Al ha-Mishmar*, which closed down for financial reasons, as well as a weekly in Arabic, *Al Marsad*.

BIBLIOGRAPHY: Y. Amitai, *Aḥvat Ammim be-Mivḥan: Mapam 1945–48, Emdot be-Sugyat Arviyei Ereẓ Yisrael* (1988); S. Paz, *Bein Ideologya le-Pragmatism: Tefisoteiha ve-Emdoteiha ha-Mediniyyot ve-ha-Bitḥoniyyot shel Mapam ba-Shanim 1948–54* (1993); V. Shem-Tov, *Mifleget ha-Po'alim ha-Me'uḥedet – Sof ha-Derekh* (1994).

[Susan Hattis Rolef (2nd ed.)]

MAP MAKERS. The first reference to a map is found in Ezekiel 4:1. The prophet is bidden to outline on an unburned brick, a plan of a city under siege, such as is found on Babylonian monuments. Nearer to real map making is a rudimentary map of the borders of Ereẓ Israel which Maimonides attached to one of his responsa (ed. Freimann, no. 346, 311).

The earliest examples of real maps known to have been designed by Jews belong to the so-called portolano maps, which are charts of the coastlines of the oceans, mostly of the Mediterranean, designed for the use of navigators. Portolanos are first mentioned in connection with reports on the second Crusade of Louis IX, king of France, in Tunisia in 1270. They were drawn with surprising precision and distances are also remarkably accurate. These maps, whose origin is still somewhat of a mystery, may preserve an ancient Greek and Byzantine tradition of sea charts, with Jews serving, as in other branches of science, as intermediaries between antiquity and the Middle Ages. Jews on the Spanish island of Majorca, as well as from Alexandria and Safed, have signed their names as makers of portolanos.

The 14th and 15th Centuries

Abraham *Cresques, cartographer and maker of portolanos, worked at Palma in Majorca, then part of the kingdom of Aragon. As the "master of maps and compasses" to the king of Aragon, he is said to have produced in 1376–77, together with his son, the six large leaves of the "Catalan Atlas," which were presented by his sovereign to Charles VI of France. His son Judah, also a geographer and cartographer, was forcibly baptized in 1391 and christened Jaime (or Jacome) Ribes de Majorca; he became director of the nautical observatory at Sagres. Another Jewish cartographer of Majorca – who is conjectured to have belonged to Abraham Crescas' family – was Ḥayyim ibn Rich. He, too, was converted at the time of the persecutions in 1391, adopting the name Juan de Vallsecha. He was probably the father of the Gabriel de Vallsecha who made another famous *mappa mundi* in 1439 – now one of the treasures of the Institute of Catalan Studies in Barcelona; it belonged to Amerigo Vespucci – in which the meridian of the Azores is used for the first time in the history of cartography. Another Majorcan cartographer of Jewish birth was Mecia de Viladestes, a map of whose (dated 1413) is preserved in the Bibliothèque Nationale in Paris.

Other Jewish Map Makers

Judah Abenzara (or ibn Zara) is known as the maker of three portolano maps (Alexandria, 1497, in the Vatican College Library, Cincinnati; and the third with his signature followed by the words "Safed in Galilee, October 1505"). Gerard de Jode (de Judeis; 1509–1591), a maker of maps and publisher in Antwerp, was apparently of Jewish origin. A not very successful competitor of Abraham Ortelius, he published single maps and atlases. His work was based on sound geographical knowledge and was executed with elegance and technical perfection. His son Cornelius de Judeis (1558–1600) was his partner and successor. Abraham b. Jacob was an engraver at the end of the 18th century in Amsterdam. He engraved the map of Palestine in the Passover *Haggadah* which was printed by Moses Wesel in Amsterdam in 1696. It was the first map with Hebrew lettering. Aaron b. Ḥayyim of Grodno's map of Palestine appeared in his *Moreh Derekh* (Grodno, 1839²), which was printed by Meir Isaac Bajarski. Ḥayyim Solomon Pinia of Safed made a pictorial map of the Holy Land, which was edited by Joshua Alter b. Moses b. Phinehas Feinkind of Turek and lithographed by S. Litmanowitz in Turek (near Kalisz, Poland) in 1875; the text is in Hebrew. Another edition with a supplementary German text is lithographed on fabric.

BIBLIOGRAPHY: E.G. Ravenstein, in: EB, 17 (1911¹¹), 633–53; G. Hoelscher, *Drei Erdkarten…* (1949); H.M.Z. Meyer, in: M. Avi-Yonah et al., *Jerusalem: the Saga of the Holy City* (1954), 59–76 (incl. bibl.); C. Roth, *Jewish Contribution to Civilization* (1956³), 59–61; G. Grosjean and R. Kinauer, *Kartenkunst und Kartentechnik* (1970), 29ff.

[Herrmann M.Z. Meyer]

MAPS OF EREẒ ISRAEL. Graphic descriptions of Ereẓ Israel relating to its topography and history and based on factual data, are not only extremely valuable sources for the reconstruction of the physiographic and anthropogenic conditions prevailing there at the time they were drawn, but are also nearly always far more important as documents which give evidence on contemporary developments of cartography in general. In this respect the cartographic representation of Ereẓ Israel differs fundamentally from that of any other country. The main reason for that was its unique status and its special significance for believers in the three monotheistic religions which had such a decisive influence upon the culture and history of the Occident. Consequently Ereẓ Israel became a main – at times almost a sole – object of cartography for several countries. There are innumerable maps depicting the "Holy Land," and they date back to the very dawn of cartography. Another important aspect is that there is no major break in the cartographic representation of Ereẓ Israel over more than a millennium and a half; thus the subsequent depictions of the country reflect the general developments of cartography and at times are even the principal reason for it. This resulted from the fact that the "Holy Land" was treated as a very special, even unique, geographical-historical and even cosmological object, involving specific problems as to adequate cartographic expression and therefore necessitating techniques and means that were not applied at all, or applied only partially and usually much later in maps dealing with other countries.

Ereẓ Israel in Ancient Cartography

Only four map-like documents dating back to classical times are known at present. Of these only one has been preserved in the original (Madaba Map mosaic), while the three others exist in medieval copies only.

MADABA MOSAIC. This mosaic, partly destroyed when a church floor in Madaba was unearthed, is a typical pictorial map whose subject is the biblical countries, i.e., besides the land of Israel – to which it is mainly devoted – it depicts parts of Lower Egypt, Sinai, and southern Syria. For further details see *Madaba Map. It became one of the most important and reliable sources for the reconstruction in particular of the anthropogenic landscape of Ereẓ Israel in the Byzantine period.

THE PTOLEMAEUS MAPS. In the maps which are ascribed to Claudius Ptolemaeus, a second-century Alexandrian cartographer, and which are drawn presumably to illustrate his treatise Γεωγραφικὴ ὑφήγησις (preserved only in medieval copies), Ereẓ Israel is represented in the map entitled "The fourth part of Asia." Its scale is very small; nevertheless, it is of great value since it contains much information pertinent to Ereẓ Israel in the period of the Antonine dynasty. From the cartographic point of view its greatest importance lies in the fact that (as will be detailed below) it changed thoroughly all the fundamental long-held clichés concerning the representation of the Holy Land, and introduced northern orientation and an exact scale by the use of the longitude and latitude grid.

THE PEUTINGER TABLE (TABULA PEUTINGERIANA). The Peutinger Table seems to have been one of the very common road maps in use in the Roman Empire. The original table seems to have been drawn in the third century, and the extant copy probably dates from the 13th century. It is exceedingly long in proportion to its width (682 × 33 cm.), and its main subject, to which all other details are subordinated, is a communications network of the contemporary Roman Empire, specifically emphasizing its stations and the distances between them. Originally drawn in one piece, it was apparently cut into a series of sections of equal size later on. Ereẓ Israel is depicted on it in the lower portions of the sections IX and X. It is assumed that the copy does not differ appreciably from the original; the most pronounced variances are, significantly, several "Christian" additions localizing, illustrating, and explaining sights and events of Christian-biblical interest and thus mainly found in the portion depicting Ereẓ Israel and the adjacent regions. It has been assumed, therefore, that this preserved map was copied in order to serve as a guide to pilgrims traveling to Ereẓ Israel and Rome. The map is not drawn to any scale, and the location of the provinces represented on it is dictated merely by the space provided by the elongated shape of the map which led to extreme distortions in their outlines and situation.

THE "SAINT JEROME MAPS." There are two maps known as the Saint Jerome Maps, both of these copies drawn in the third century. They are included in a manuscript in St. Jerome's *De hebraicis quaestionibus et interpretationibus nominum Veteris et Novi Testamenti*, and their contents provide evidence that the originals were produced at the time of the Church Fathers, but not necessarily by Jerome himself. Both are rather crude black-ink sketches very generalized in style and content, and were thus important as precursors of a great number of maps drawn by monks in the medieval period. One of the drawings depicts the Roman Empire according to its division into provinces, emphasizing the places of special interest to Christians. As a portion of this map is missing, only the northern part of Ereẓ Israel appears on it: the Mt. Hermon area and the sources of the Jordan (designated here as "Jor" and "Dan" – a toponymic deduction from the name of the river that prevailed throughout the Middle Ages). The second sketch contains both the whole of Ereẓ Israel and the adjacent countries, Egypt, Syria, and Mesopotamia. Some of the most characteristic features of almost all the "scholastic" medieval maps are also present here: Ereẓ Israel occupies the central part of the drawing and is represented out of all proportion to the surrounding countries, which appear as small unimportant appendages. Similarly, only places and topographical features of biblical interest appear on this map sketch.

In the Middle Ages

Although in general, cartography in the Middle Ages was of a low standard, cartography of Ereẓ Israel reached a peak in this period, both in quantity and quality. For several centuries, Ereẓ Israel was the sole, or at least the most important and prominent, subject of map making. Two kinds of maps existed in the Middle Ages:

a) World maps (*mappae mundi*), almost all of which were of an abstract nature, and were largely the work of monks. Their purpose was to explain and illustrate contemporary ecclesiastical views of cosmography and geography, which, rather than being based on a knowledge of reality, were based on the Scriptures, as interpreted by the Church Fathers and the scholastics, as well as by the writings of ancient polyhistors such as Pliny, Pomponius Hella, and Solinus. Not only was the content of these world maps decisively influenced by the Bible, even their shape (a circle or rectangle) was a result of dogmatic interpretations of certain biblical passages. The world maps are "oriented," i.e., their top denoted the East, the presumed site of Paradise (which is shown on many of these maps as a geographical actuality). In all the maps, Ereẓ Israel occupies a prominent place, in many instances as much as a sixth of the entire space (as for example in the famous "Anglo-Saxon" map). In some of the maps, which are so abstract in conception and drawing as to represent mere cartograms, Ereẓ Israel takes up so much space that the other countries tend to appear as insignificant background only. The description of Ereẓ Israel on these maps consists entirely of biblical topography, with an addition of explanations and traditional identifications of places. Furthermore, from the beginning of the Crusades up to the 16th century, Jerusalem, believed to be the "navel of the world," was placed at the very center of all world maps. This of course, dictated the whole framework, structure, and composition of the map, fulfilling the role played in present maps by the reference location of the poles and the equator. The proportionally great detail of the historio-geographical and physiogeographic facts in which traditional particulars of Ereẓ Israel were depicted or verbally denoted on the maps (such as Mt. Gilboa, Mt. Tabor, various springs, caves, trees, holy places, etc.), however, made it necessary to invent new forms for expressing such details, and this seems to have had a lasting effect upon the development of symbols and signs used in maps in the following centuries. Among medieval maps there were many sketchlike maps of Jerusalem that were generalized and geometrical and served as guides to pilgrims and Crusaders.

b) The portolano maps, which appeared in the late Middle Ages, were used mostly for purposes of navigation and were probably derived from charts developed as early as the Byzantine period. Many Jewish cartographers were involved in the production of this kind of map, in particular those of the Catalan school, centered in Majorca. The most renowned representatives of this school were Abraham and Judah (Jaime) Cresques; the latter drew the Catalan Atlas, the most beautiful and advanced project of the portolano cartography. Although on these maps Ereẓ Israel no longer occupies a disproportionate amount of space, it continues to exhibit many specific aspects, both as to content and cartographic execution. Since these maps were sea charts aimed at serving navigation, they concentrated primarily on the delineation of coastlines and the location of ports, and show hardly any details of the interior, except perhaps for a flag (banner?) signifying the political control of the country. An exception is made in the case of Ereẓ Israel, for which the relevant portion of the map shows great inland detail, such as the Jordan and its lakes, holy places, and important churches and monasteries. The Red Sea is shown in red or crimson (whereas other bodies of water are shown in blue or light green); a white strip marks the site where the Israelites are presumed to have crossed the Red Sea. It has become increasingly certain that the portolano maps served as the basis of the few regional maps made in the Middle Ages (at least the few that have been preserved). All of these maps (with one exception, which also contains Britain; see the Matthew Paris map, below) have Ereẓ Israel as their subject. Considering the period in which they were made, these are exceptional maps: (1) They are the outcome of either direct observation or factual and critically adapted information. (2) Their contents are of a topical nature, describing Ereẓ Israel during and after the time of the Crusader Kingdom of Jerusalem, though they also contain many details based on biblical tradition – so important for every Christian pilgrim in the Middle Ages but not corresponding to the reality of the country and in contrast to the factual content of the map. (3) They generally serve a practical purpose, i.e., as guides for armies or pilgrims. (4) Some of the maps and techniques exhibit specific features that denote marked progress in cartography and were used in the maps of other countries only much later.

The outstanding medieval maps of Ereẓ Israel that have been preserved are the following: (1) A large map (2,080 sq. cm.), preserved at Florence, that is extraordinary not only with regard to its delineation of the coast, which corresponds closely to reality as is the rule with portolano maps, but also as to its wealth of detail. The details, however, are of a much lower standard; for example, the markings of locations – which is a major subject of all medieval maps – are out of proportion to the areal extension of the map. The map is oriented to the East, in contrast to the portolanos, thus reflecting the prevailing influence of the *mappae mundi* and their affinities. (2) A sketch map of Ereẓ Israel at Oxford, whose portolano origin is evidenced by its orientation to the North. It contains a great number of topical details, including some based on observation, such as a unique description of the road leading from the coast to Jerusalem. (3) Another map kept at Florence, outstanding in the quality of its illustrations and colors, but inferior in content to the two maps mentioned above. Because of its highly heraldic and ornamental designs and its wonderful coloring, it represents one of the most pronounced examples of the artistry employed in the late Middle Ages. (4) A map drawn by Matthew Paris of England (1250 C.E.), outstanding for its unique description of the road system and its allusions to caravan traffic between Ereẓ Israel and Syria. Some places, especially Acre, the most important Crusader fortress, are depicted in great detail in a separate small vignette. Paris was also the author of an illustrated road guide (England to the Holy Land) which is unique in cartography. The map has the form of a long strip and signifies with miniature designs the stops along the route between the two countries; the stops were usually churches or monasteries that pilgrims customarily visited, and even the roads leading from one stop to the next are indicated by two parallel lines. (5) Medieval cartographic presentation of the Holy Land reached its climax in a series of maps and sketches attached to a memoir by the Venetian Marino Sanuto, appealing for a renewal of crusading (*liber secretorum fidelium crucis*). The map appendage consists of a map of Ereẓ Israel, a rather stereotyped *mappa mundi*, a map of the Near Eastern countries, and a detailed, extremely accurate sketch of Acre, and a far more conventional one of Jerusalem. It is now established that at least the maps of Israel and of the Near East were drawn by Pietro Vesconte, a noted portolano cartographer. The map of Ereẓ Israel is an astounding piece of work, anticipating various future cartographical developments by several centuries. It is not only relatively exact in scale – a characteristic common to most portolanos as far as the coasts are concerned – but also exhibits a grid of longitudinal and latitudinal lines equally spaced throughout at the distance of 1 "leuca" (approx. 2,500 meters). The location of the towns and villages, at least those existing at the time, is rather exact, as are the sites of most topographic features represented in the map. Another extraordinary feature is the wealth of information (besides the usual indication of biblical sites, the areas assumedly occupied by the tribes of Israel, and pertinent remarks and explanations derived from the Bible) on the contemporary situation, based, as were the above-mentioned features of the map, on the author's personal observation and/or intensive study of the memoir. Because of its relative accuracy and abundance of detail, the map served as a pattern for other maps during the Renaissance period; however, its grid was generally replaced by the Ptolemaic latitude and longitude grid. (6) A map drawn by William Wey in the 15th century. It is a typical medieval depiction of Ereẓ Israel, in which all the elements of medieval presentation of this country are incorporated and superbly executed, in particular the pictorial embellishments and the coloring (illumination).

Ereẓ Israel in Arab Cartography of the Middle Ages

In general, medieval Arab maps were more exact, more detailed, and more comprehensive than European maps, but in technique they were far more uniform and stereotyped, employing outlines and symbols of a strictly geometric nature. In Arab maps, Ereẓ Israel did not occupy the most prominent place. The best and most comprehensive Arab map of Ereẓ Israel was made by Idrissi, whose cartographic works represent a mixture of Moslem and Western European style and content.

In Modern Times

The cartographical representation of Ereẓ Israel underwent some fundamental changes in modern times: 1. As a result of constantly growing geographical knowledge (gained from the works and maps of Ptolemaeus) and the extensive discoveries of whole continents, accompanied by the development of the sciences, in particular those dealing with the earth – its astronomical position, movements, and surface nature, Jerusalem could no longer be regarded as the "navel of the world" and ceased to be used as the center of world maps. 2. The mathematical and astronomical fixing of locations – by means of lines of longitude and latitude – based upon the method used by Ptolemaeus and arrived at by exact measurements, made it possible to establish the proper outlines of the countries and their relative size. Each map was now based on a distance scale and it was no longer possible to exaggerate the size of Ereẓ Israel in comparison with the other countries of the world. 3. However, whereas the maps of other countries usually contained only details of a contemporary nature, maps of Ereẓ Israel retained their historical character. The main purpose of these maps was to describe the topographical and geographical background of the events described in the Bible and the Gospels, and they ignored the actual landscape of the country, and in particular, the anthropogenic features (villages, roads, etc.). For this reason, a contemporary map of Ereẓ Israel (*tabula moderna*) was usually attached to the Ptolemaeus maps, made to a much larger scale, orientated to the East, and containing many traditional topographical designations. Most of these maps were based on that of Sanuto. Nevertheless, for a variety of reasons, maps of Ereẓ Israel retained their special importance in the early modern period: (1) For various historical and religious reasons (the Reformation, Bible translations), the invention of printing made maps of Ereẓ Israel the most popular and most widely distributed maps; they were also the first to be produced in print. (2) The competition resulting from the wide demand for maps of Ereẓ Israel that provided the location of sites mentioned in the

Bible, caused these maps to become generally the most splendid and beautiful ones produced in this period; this applies particularly to the signs and symbols used on the maps, the decoration of the margins, and the cartouche, i.e., the part of the map separated by an ornamental enclosure containing the title of the map, its author, the scales, sources, and so on. The historical content, that seemed to illustrate the background of the Bible and Gospels with the little contemporary geographical detailing that was available during the Renaissance period, made it possible to experiment with the maps and even led to innovations as regards scales, symbols, shading, coloring (illumination), etc. Thus the first indication of magnetic variation was made on a map of Ereẓ Israel.

EREẒ ISRAEL IN THE ERA OF ATLASES. The magnificent atlases produced during and after the Renaissance, in Western and Central Europe, usually contained at least two maps of Ereẓ Israel, which were the works of different cartographers and were scarcely compatible with each other. One of the maps forms an integral part of each atlas and is usually based on Ptolemaeus; it is oriented to the North, contains some slight changes in the delineation of the coast and some additional relief features and hydrographic details, and a wealth of place-names mentioned in the Scriptures, in the works of Josephus and so on. Thus, in essence, the map depicts Ereẓ Israel as it is shown in "The fourth part of Asia" by Ptolemaeus. There are numerous instances, however, in which the Ereẓ Israel map in the atlas is oriented to the East and is much closer in content and nature to the Sanuto map, with the important addition of the use of the astronomic longitude and latitude grid derived from Ptolemaeus. The second map of Ereẓ Israel (and sometimes even a third, produced by yet another cartographer) is found among the numerous addenda (*additamentum*) that were attached to the atlases in this period. Important Ereẓ Israel maps in this period were produced by Ortelius, Mercator, Tilemanus Sigenensis, Laicstein, Blaeu, Janszon, Homann, Sanson, Seutter, de Lille, Bonne, and d'Anville. The maps made by the last three cartographers mentioned (who represent the French school) were superior to others in the precision of their content and may be regarded as the most advanced maps prior to those of the 19th century. There were also maps of Ereẓ Israel that were attached to the numerous cosmographies published in this period (of which that by Sebastian *Muenster was the most widely distributed). Even more important, as a source for the maps appearing in the atlases, were the various works on Ereẓ Israel, which contained maps made to a large scale. Among these, mention should be made of the works of Jacob Ziegler, Adrian Adrichomius (1590), and last and most important, Hadrianus Relandus' *Palaestina ex monumentis veteribus illustrata*, which contains a number of detailed and relatively precise maps, especially one showing the relief and the consequent physiographic division of the country in the coastal plain, the mountains, the Valley of the Jordan, and the Transjordan plateaus. Only a single map of Israel, made in 1483 by Bernard Breitenbach, is based entirely on the author's personal observation and describes the country as he saw it. Combining both the medieval and modern cartographic style, the map enjoyed great popularity.

In the 18th and 19th Centuries

The first mapping of Ereẓ Israel based partly on topographical survey was made in connection with Napoleon's campaign in Egypt and Ereẓ Israel. The main result of this was a series of 47 maps of Egypt, Sinai, and Ereẓ Israel, named the Jacotin maps after their author (1810). Six of the maps depict parts of Ereẓ Israel, especially those parts through which the army passed on its invasion of the country. The scale is 1:100,000, and the maps show precise details of the areas where measurements were taken by means of the trigonometric methods that had developed in Europe by this time (based on the theodolite and the principle of triangulation). Thus, even the representation of relief on these maps was relatively exact and adequate. Relative differences in height and the diverse gradients of the slopes are shown by hachuring (i.e., expressing the gradient of the slope by discontinuous, proportionally dimensioned lines extending down from the summit to the base of the slope; the steeper the slope the shorter but thicker the hachure line and vice versa), and in general, the rest of the details shown on the maps, i.e., symbols and so on, are of a high standard. Some of the place-names are given in Arabic script, in addition to Latinized transcription. For a period of about 50 years these were the maps used in the exploration of the country.

Toward the end of the 18th century and in the first half of the 19th century, Ereẓ Israel became the subject of numerous exploratory voyages and expeditions, as though it was still "unknown territory." Although the emphasis was on the archaeological and historical aspects of the country, much attention was also paid to its natural conditions including its physiography. In particular, interest was centered on the Jordan Valley and the Dead Sea, because they formed the lowest depression on earth. The works produced by such itinerant scholars and explorers as Seetzen, Burckhardt, Buckingham, and Robinson generally included sketch maps of some areas and sites, and an overall map of the country. Outstanding among these maps is the one attached to Robinson's work, drawn by Kiepert, the well-known German cartographer. An American naval expedition, led by Lynch, executed a map survey of the Jordan River and the Dead Sea. All these works were summarized in *Erdkunde von Asien* ("Geography of Asia"), the famous work by Ritter, which also contains a comprehensive list of all known maps of Ereẓ Israel, from ancient times up to the 19th century. A companion to Ritter's work, the atlas by Zimmermann, contains detailed maps of Ereẓ Israel, to the scale of 1:333,333. All the maps listed above were used as an important source for the study of the landscape of Ereẓ Israel in the first half of the 18th century. The final work of this period of individual research and mapping was the map of Van de Velde (scale 1:315,000), one of the most beautiful maps of Ereẓ Israel of this time.

In the second half of the 19th century, the existing maps were felt to be insufficient to meet the requirements of the growing interest in the country, especially for archaeological purposes. The Palestine Exploration Fund (PEF) was established in Britain to carry out a systematic survey of Ereẓ Israel "from Dan to Beer Sheba." The work of the fund was preceded by a survey of the coastline and the adjoining hinterland, ordered by the British Admiralty (1858–62). They established not only the exact outline of the coastline but also a fixed number of points that were of great help in the survey that followed. An early project undertaken by the Fund was a survey of the Sinai Peninsula, aimed at establishing the route of the Exodus and the location of Mt. Sinai. The maps of Jebel Katerina (the presumed location of Mount Sinai) and Jebel Serbal, whose relief is expressed by form lines, are among the finest maps of the entire area. The first undertaking of the Fund in Ereẓ Israel proper was a survey of Jerusalem and its surroundings (1864), carried out with a precision hitherto not applied in the Near East. In the resulting maps the relief was presented by the hachuring method. In 1871 an expedition of the Fund, led by Conder and later on by Kitchener, embarked upon the main mapping project. The survey encompassed the entire country, from the Qasimiye River up to south of the Dead Sea, and resulted in a set of 26 sheets, made to the scale of 1:63,360 (inch to mile), as on the British topographical maps, and based on a precise triangulation (two base-lines), leveling (Acre–Sea of Galilee, Jaffa–Dead Sea), and altimetric measurements. The relief is represented by means of shading and tinting. In many instances the height is also given in figures; rivers and springs are shown in blue; the various kinds of vegetational cover are indicated by accordant symbols, as are also anthropogenic features. The maps are particularly accurate in the location of the many existing ruins of ancient places of settlement; much effort was also devoted to establishing the names of places and their proper transliteration. The Fund published its *Memoirs*, and they serve to this day as an important geographical and historical source.

"The Survey of Western Palestine" was followed by efforts to carry out a similar survey of Transjordan, which, however, failed for a variety of reasons. Only the Deutscher Palaestina Verein eventually carried out a survey of Gilead, executed to the same scale as the maps of PEF. The maps of the PEF and, to some extent, the German maps too, served as a basis for Ereẓ Israel maps that were produced up to the conquest of Palestine by the British. Among later maps based on those of the PEF, the most important was the Bartholemew map, in which the relief is expressed by contour lines and the subsequent altitude zones are also indicated by varying coloring. In World War I the existing maps were adapted to military requirements, with the help of aerial photography. The maps employed by the British army were made to a scale of 1:40,000, those of the German army to 1:50,000. Shortly before World War I a survey of the Sinai Peninsula was carried out by Newcombe, to a scale of 1:125,000; this included the Negev and the relief was represented by contour and form lines. Shortly after its establishment, the Mandatory government embarked upon a new survey of the country, using up-to-date methods. Two series of maps were printed, one a topo-cadastral set, made to a scale of 1:20,000, and the other a topographical set made to a scale of 1:100,000. This survey was also restricted to the area of Ereẓ Israel extending from the northern political boundary to somewhat south of Beersheba, and consisted of 16 sheets. In these maps the relief was presented by contour lines with a vertical interval of 25 meters. Agricultural areas appear in green and the hydrographic network in blue. The mapping was executed with comprehensive triangulation and fieldwork. Other maps produced by the Mandatory government were maps of the major cities and villages (scale 1:10,000) and a geographical map of the country (1:250,000). During the Mandatory period, efforts were also made to produce a Hebrew map of the country (Press, Brawer, Lief). These were necessarily adaptations of 19th-century maps and those issued by the government Survey Department but they made important contributions to the proper identification of localities, and the use of historical place-names and Hebrew transliteration. With the establishment of the state, "Survey of Israel" became one of its basic governmental institutions in view of the country's ever-expanding exigencies, in particular those connected with economic-demographic planning. These were met by extensive triangulation, leveling which also resulted in a dense altimetric network, new additions (Hebrew) of totally revised and updated map series 1:20,000 and 1:100,000, largely improved not only by the above-mentioned measurements but also by the thorough use of photogrammetric techniques. The 100,000 series is continuously supplemented by a far more comprehensive one at a scale of 1:50,000. The Israel Atlas (Heb. 1956–64) and its English edition (1970) – the latest additions to the series of "National Atlases" – summarize both the history and the development of the cartographic representation of the country and its present state in all the fields given to cartographic expression. In the early 21st century, the Survey of Israel was responsible for producing new maps in various fields, such as historical maps, topographical maps, regional maps, general maps, satellite maps, etc. The recent maps were produced with new techniques such as GIS (Geographical Information Systems) and satellites. The Survey of Israel was also in charge of the updating of the Israel Atlas.

BIBLIOGRAPHY: L. Bagrow, *History of Cartography* (rev. and enlarged by R.A. Skelton, 1964; orig. Ger., 1951), index, s.v. *Palestine*; R. Roehricht, *Bibliotheca Geographica Palestinae* (enlarged and ed. by D. Amiran, Jerusalem, 1963[2], Ger.); H.M.Z. Meyer, *The Holy Land in Ancient Maps* (Jerusalem, 1965[3]); Z. Vilnay, *The Holy Land in Old Prints and Maps* (1965[2]); *Old Maps of the Land of Israel*. Exhibition, Maritime Museum, Haifa. Cafalog by H.M.Z. Meyer (1963); M. Avi-Yonah, *The Madaba Mosaic Map* (1954); K. Miller, *Weltkarte des Castorius, genannt die Peutinger'sche Tafel* (1888); B. von Breydenbach, *Die Reise ins Heilige Land … 1485* (with the repr. of Reuwich's woodcut map, 1961); Z. Vilnay, *The Hebrew Maps of the Holy Land* (Jerusalem, 1968[2]); *The World Encompassed. An Exhibition of the History of Maps*, Catalog, Baltimore, Md. (1952); R.A. Skelton, *Decorative Printed Maps of the 15th to 18th Centuries* (1952); C.R. Beazley, *The Dawn of Modern*

Geography, 3 vols. (1897–1906, repr. 1949); J.E. Bailey, *Palestine Geography in the Seventeenth Century*, 4 (1872); I. Schattner, *The Maps of Palestine and their History* (Jerusalem, 1951); Y. Karmon, in: IEJ, 10 (1960), 155–73; C.R. Conder, *Tent Work in Palestine* (1878); *Atlas of Israel* (Amsterdam, 1970). **WEBSITE:** www.mapi.gov.il.

[Isaac Schattner]

MAPU, ABRAHAM (1808–1867), creator of the modern Hebrew novel. One of the principal exponents of the Haskalah movement in Eastern Europe, he is best known for his first and most successful novel *Ahavat Ẓiyyon* ("The Love of Zion," Vilna, 1853), which represents a turning point in the development of modern Hebrew literature. The son of an indigent and scholarly teacher, Mapu was born in Slobodka, a poverty-stricken suburb of Kovno, where he early acquired a reputation as a brilliant student, and, having mastered much of the talmudic learning of the day, he was considered fit for independent study at the age of 12. Following his marriage at 17, Mapu continued his studies in the home of his wealthy father-in-law in Kovno. After a brief flirtation with Ḥasidism, he resumed an interest in Kabbalah and mysticism, previously fostered by his father. This occasioned a period of close contact with Elijah *Ragoler. The chance finding of a copy of the Psalms with a Latin translation in Ragoler's home aroused his interest and he taught himself Latin, virtually an unknown study among pious Jews in Eastern Europe. Eventually he acquired a fair proficiency in French, German, and Russian, in spite of the prevailing hostility in Orthodox Jewish circles to the learning of languages. These studies plus an interest in such equally neglected subjects as Bible, Hebrew grammar, and modern literature laid the foundations of his subsequent achievements.

Throughout his life Mapu struggled to maintain his family. He became a teacher of young children and was invited in 1832 to tutor the children of a wealthy merchant in the nearby town of Georgenberg. While separated from his family for two or three years, he was drawn to the Haskalah movement, and, on his return to Kovno, he began to disseminate its doctrines among the local youth. In 1837 Mapu moved his family to Rossyieny, where he taught for about seven years. In spite of his economic hardship, Mapu found the cultural atmosphere of Rossyieny attractive. There his friendship with Senior *Sachs engendered a profound interest in the history of ancient Israel. In an attempt to improve his finances Mapu returned to Kovno in 1844. His wife died in 1846, and the following year he moved to Vilna to tutor the son of the wealthy but unlettered Judah Opatov. Despite Vilna's reputation as a great center of Haskalah, Mapu found the city no more congenial than the house of his harsh employer. On learning of Mapu's appointment to teach at a government school in Kovno in 1848, Opatov assaulted him physically. Mapu, deeply humiliated, fled the house. He avenged the insult by modeling the character of the boorish upstart, Ga'al, in his novel *Ayit Ẓavu'a* ("The Hypocrite") on his former employer. From the Hebrew writers of Vilna, however, Mapu acquired the taste for Romanticism which permeates his novels.

As the new post proved permanent, Mapu settled in Kovno and remarried in 1851. For about ten years domestic happiness and improved financial circumstances coincided with his most fruitful literary period. His growing reputation was enhanced in 1857 by the personal congratulations of the Russian minister of public institutions, Norov, a singular honor which induced Mapu to include a poem in Norov's honor in the introduction to his lost novel *Ḥozei Ḥezyonot* ("The Visionaries"). But from 1860 his health began to fail beneath the burdens of overwork and persecution by the pious opponents of Haskalah who managed to influence the censors to delay or even forbid his publications. His meager resources were further undermined by his second wife's long illness, from which she died in 1863. His later years were relieved only by a short visit to St. Petersburg in 1861, where his first acquaintance with opera appealed to his romantic imagination. The loneliness of his last years was aggravated by a disease of his fingers, which made every line he wrote an agony.

Although Mapu was 45 when *Ahavat Ẓiyyon* was published he seems to have labored on the novel, despite its modest length, for more than 20 years. While the plot may well have been originally modeled on the allegorical dramas of M. Ḥ. *Luzzatto, the influence of Senior Sachs directed Mapu's attention toward the Bible, so that the first Hebrew novel also became the world's first novel in a biblical setting. *Ahavat Ẓiyyon* won immediate acclaim, and its continued popularity is attested by at least 16 editions, as well as translations into many languages including English, French, German, Russian, Arabic, Judeo-Arabic, Judeo-Persian, Ladino, and Yiddish. The more liberal spirit prevailing in Russia during the early reign of Alexander II prompted Mapu to choose a contemporary setting for his second novel *Ayit Ẓavu'a*. Of the five parts comprising this long and rambling novel, the first was published in Vilna in 1858, the second in 1861, and the third in 1864. A second edition containing all five parts appeared posthumously in Warsaw in 1869. About ten editions show its popularity. Mapu had been simultaneously composing a third novel, *Ḥozei Ḥezyonot*, depicting the period of the pseudo-Messiah, *Shabbetai Ẓevi. Reputed to have been in ten complete parts, the work was sent to the censor in 1858, together with the first two parts of *Ayit Ẓavu'a*. Whereas the publication of the latter was subject only to irritating delays, the campaign of the fanatical opponents of Haskalah persuaded the censor to forbid publication of *Ḥozei Ḥezyonot* altogether. The manuscript disappeared, and only a seven-chapter fragment remains. Mapu never completely recovered from this loss. To avoid the persecution of his opponents, he reverted to a biblical background for his fourth and last novel, *Ashmat Shomron* ("The Guilt of Samaria," Vilna, first part, 1865; second part, 1866). Again, this achieved some ten editions.

Apart from his novels, Mapu published several books designed to improve the clumsy educational methods of his day. Two of his textbooks, *Ḥanokh la-Na'ar* and *Der Hausfranzose*, appeared in Vilna in 1859. The former outlines the author's method for teaching elementary Hebrew, while the latter comprises a primary textbook for the study of French. Written in German but with Hebrew characters, it constitutes an interesting example of the attempts made by the exponents of Haskalah to broaden the cultural interests of the Jewish community. A third textbook, *Amon Pedagog* (Koenigsberg, 1867), again deals with the teaching of Hebrew. But even within the framework of a textbook, his creative talent emerges in the form of a story, later published separately by J. Klausner under the title *Beit-Ḥanan* (Jerusalem, 1920), which is unfolded section by section to illustrate the rules to be explained. *Amon Pedagog* served as a standard textbook until the end of the century, and went through five editions.

Mapu's creativity contains both strongly imitative and highly original features. The influence of the Bible is naturally most conspicuous in the setting, style, and language of the two historical novels, *Ahavat Ẓiyyon* and *Ashmat Shomron*, which depict life in ancient Israel in the days of Isaiah. In lesser measure it also extends to *Ayit Ẓavu'a* which portrays contemporary Jewish life, mainly in his native Lithuania. Aspects of his novels were derived from other sources, principally Hebrew and French writers. His limited inventiveness is demonstrated by his frequent borrowing of dramatic devices and by the many repetitions and similarities which occur in his stories.

Of the Hebrew writers who influenced Mapu, M.Ḥ. Luzzatto's example may be discerned in the plots, dramatic devices and symbolic names, as well as in the didactic and ethical ideas, and the interest in nature. From N.H. *Wessely, whom he held in almost equal esteem, Mapu derived less specific but no less important elements, such as the linguistic narrative possibilities inherent in the Bible. Moreover, the social and educational reforms advocated in Wessely's series of open letters *Divrei Shalom ve-Emet* found an enthusiastic echo in Mapu's novels, especially *Ayit Ẓavu'a*. Among Hebrew prose writers, the Galician exponents of Haskalah, J. *Perl and I. *Erter exerted considerable influence on Mapu. From their satires on the shortcomings of society, he learned how to use melodrama and farfetched incidents. The letters and dreams which Perl and Erter frequently introduce as convenient media for their satirical purposes are a characteristic feature of Mapu's novels. Many of his characters embody their demands for radical changes in outlook and occupation in Jewish society.

Mapu's novels also owe a considerable debt to the French romantic novelists, the elder Dumas and Eugène Suë. Like Dumas, Mapu turned his attention to the national past, infusing an historical situation with heroism and romantic love, and introducing historical personages side by side with his own creations. From Dumas, Mapu learned the art of creating atmosphere and of clothing his plots in a romantic historical mantle while the influence of Eugène Suë is particularly noticeable in Mapu's novel of contemporary life. But whereas the violence and intrigue encountered in Suë's *Mystères de Paris* are perfectly in keeping with its background of the Paris underworld, the attempt in *Ayit Ẓavu'a* to superimpose such elements on a backcloth of Jewish society in Eastern Europe, which was characterized by sobriety, timidity, and a rigid control of the passionate emotions, is primarily responsible for the incongruity of the setting and the plot.

The original and creative element in Mapu's writings does not lie in the external forms of his novels. The structure, dramatic techniques, and characterizations and stereotypes personifying vice and virtue, all lean heavily on previous writers, and all display grave weaknesses and limitations. For Mapu's own generation, however, the plots, particularly of the historical novels, were the most attractive and fascinating aspect of his work, both because this literary medium was unknown in Hebrew literature and because the adventure and excitement provided so striking a contrast to the colorless lives of most of his readers. The vivid descriptions of heroism and action, the free expression of emotion, and above all the colorful scenes of a people living unrestricted in its own land inflamed the imagination of a life-starved generation. His success in arousing imagination and emotion and his ability to transfuse a somewhat dry and intellectual literature with the feelings of heroism and romantic love constitute the most striking elements of his achievement. By fostering pride in the national past and focusing attention on the land of Israel, Mapu provided an emotional stimulus for generations of young readers. Indeed, the contribution of his novels to the rise of the Jewish national movement from which Zionism later emerged must be regarded as an important factor in modern Jewish history.

Mapu's use of language was equally remarkable. The restricted vocabulary of biblical Hebrew and its limited dialogue seriously curtail its suitability for the modern novel. The narrative power of the biblical story stems, moreover, from its tantalizing brevity and its ruthless pruning of extraneous detail. The Bible story relates a series of events in sequence of time, with little analysis or speculation. It presents a skeleton narrative, leaving the reader to supply the flesh and blood. But the novel demands techniques of a different kind. It is expansive and has to supply those very elements and details which the Bible is so careful to omit. Yet Mapu adopted a medium for expansion whose main strength lies in strict omission, knowingly risking the constant comparison of his own creation with the lofty grandeur of the original. Mapu attempted to solve the problem of language by using his material to the full. The entire Bible became a source for his invention. His style constitutes a fusion of elements of the prose and the poetry of the Bible. Appropriating and refashioning at will, he molded the material to suit his purpose, while retaining much of its original spirit. In spite of the frequent introduction of entire phrases and complete images, he avoided the danger of producing a jumbled patchwork of biblical snippets. So smoothly do they merge with the texture of his own style that the result is neither an imitation nor a parody of the Hebrew Bible. This sensitivity to language is one of the most attractive features of his novels. But Mapu was well aware that he had stretched his material to the limit. In *Ayit Ẓavu'a* he deliberately introduced post-biblical elements, and himself protested that biblical Hebrew was not an adequate vehicle of expression for the modern novel. His writing may be regarded as the consummation of the neobiblical style advocated by the exponents of Haskalah. No major Hebrew novelist attempted to emulate his achievements.

Although aesthetically the least satisfying, it was *Ayit Ẓavu'a* with its emphasis on social and educational reform that exerted the most influence on subsequent Hebrew writers. The realistic elements of Mapu's social novel may be traced in the words of many writers, including P. *Smolenskin, J.L. *Gordon, R.A. *Braudes, M.D. *Brandstaedter, and S.J. *Abramovitsh (Mendele Mokher Sforim), all of whom furthered the positivist and social aspects of his work. Indeed, the realistic novel depicting the problems of contemporary society has continued to occupy a dominant position in Hebrew literature.

For the Hebrew reader, Mapu's first novel, *Ahavat Ẓiyyon*, was uniquely influential. It opened the prospect of a free and independent life to a people hopelessly fettered by political, social, and economic restrictions. Its significance lies in the fresh possibilities of art and life which it revealed, and in the new awareness it promoted. As the first Hebrew novel, it represents the first expression of a people's longing for a fuller and better life. The English translations of *Ahavat Ẓiyyon were published under various titles: *Amnon, Prince and Peasant*, tr. by F. Jaffe (1887); *In the Days of Isaiah*, tr. by A.M. Schapiro (1902; the same translation was published later under the title *The Shepherd Prince* in 1922 and 1930); *The Sorrows of Noma*, tr. by J. Marymont (1919). His letters were published by B. Dinur under the title *Mikhtevei Avraham Mapu* (1971). Following the 1928 edition of Mapu's works in five volumes, further editions were published in 1945 and 1953.

BIBLIOGRAPHY: D. Patterson, *Abraham Mapu* (Eng., 1964); Waxman, Literature, 3 (1960²), 267–78; Klausner, Sifrut, 3 (1950³), 269–360 (incl. bibl.). **ADD. BIBLIOGRAPHY:** J. Fichman, *Avraham Mapu* (1920); Y. Karmiel, "*Ha-Ẓiyyur bi-Lshono shel Mapu*," in: *Leshonenu*, 34 (1970), 306–308; S. Haramati, *Mapu ha-Moreh le-Ivrit* (1972); G. Alkoshi, "*Mikhtevei A. Mapu*," in: *Ha-Sifrut*, 4 (1973), 376–395; J. Even-Cohen, *Avraham Mapu* (1973); D. Miron, *Bein Ḥazon la-Emet* (1979); Y. Rabi, in: *Al ha-Mishmar* (November 2, 1979); S. Werses, "*Zeman u-Merḥav ba-Roman Ayit Ẓavu'a*," in: *Te'udah*, 5 (1986), 67–84; D. Patterson, "Epistolary Elements in the Novels of A. Mapu," in: *A Phoenix in Fetters* (1988), 21–33; S. Werses, *Ha-Tirgumim le-Yidish shel Ahavat Ẓiyyon* (1989); T. Cohen, *Ẓevu'im vi-Ysharim, Elilot ve-Lilyot: A. Mapu* (1991); R. Oren, "Relativity of Time in the Story '*Ahavat Zion*,'" in: *Acta Academica*, 24:4 (1992), 85–99; S. Haramati, *Benei Aliyah Manḥilei Lashon Bekhirim ba-Dorot ha-Aḥaronim* (1993); V. Dohrn, "Abraham Mapus 'Zionsliebe,' die Geburt einer neuen Zionsidee in Osteuropa," in: *Der Traum von Israel* (1998), 108–139; Y. Schwartz, "'*Handasat ha-Adam' ve-Izzuv ha-Merḥav ba-Tarbut ha-Ivrit ha-Ḥadashah*," in: *Mikan*, 1 (2000), 9–24.

[David Patterson]

MAQĀM, and its regional equivalents – *maqom, mugham, dastgah* and *tbā'* – designate characteristic modal scales that are identified by a multitude of individual names like *rast, buzurk, segah, dil bayāt*, etc. In a broader sense the *maqām* concept is also associated with a series of compositional principles, including the use of melodic types that are characterized by tonal material and motifs as well as a series of conventions prevalent in major centers of the world of Islam, from India to North Africa. In its most sophisticated form the concept of *maqām* and its principles are applied to many compound and cyclic vocal and instrumental compositions with contrasting parts that include various levels of improvisation. This is for instance the case of the *shashmaqom* in Uzbekistan and Tajikistan, the *Azarbaidjani maqām*, the Persian *radif*, the Turkish *fasil*, the Egyptian *wasla*, the *Irāqī maqām* and the North African *nuba* and *tbā'*. The modal scale includes a complex of rules. It is conceived as combination of several small groups of notes, whether of the same intervallic structure or not, called genera (*ajnās*, s. *jins*). As a result of this characteristic, many combinations can be created theoretically, but only a limited number have been admitted or commonly accepted and are known by their individual names. Part of the modal scale is linked to a definite pitch, and a group of notes transposed is considered to be a different entity and consequently may receive a new name. In brief, the tonal material and the structural rules are put at the disposal of the musician who in playing and singing invents new variants, improvises, and adds musical ornamentations. In addition to this, ethical and cosmological speculations are linked to the concrete application of the *maqāmāt* in diverse circumstances. Aleppan Jews are very fond of this linkage.

It has been proposed, with weighty arguments, that the puzzling designations found in the headings of many *Psalms ("upon the *sheminit*," "upon *yonat-elem-reḥokim*," etc.) may not be names of instruments, scales, or prototype melodies, but of *maqām*-like melodic schemes; and such are probably also the superscripts and subscripts of the song texts found in Assyrian and Babylonian cuneiform documents.

The Near Eastern Jewish communities use the local *maqāmāt* for the creation and classification of many of their liturgical and paraliturgical melodies. Even the cantillation of the masoretic accents is submitted to a "maqamic correlation," and is obviously affected by it in its melodic content. The following selection of "maqamic correlations" is based mainly on the research of A.Z. *Idelsohn; *maqām Sīgah* can be correlated with the Pentateuch, Ruth, Ecclesiastes, Esther, and the *Amidah* for the High Holy days; *maqām Bayāt* with the prophetic books and Lamentations; *maqām 'Ajam* (Persian name: *Naurūz*, "The New Year's Day"), associated with exaltation, magnificence, and actual or symbolic wedding functions and ceremonies, with Simḥat Torah, Shavuot, the seventh day of Passover, and *Shabbat Shirah; maqām Nawa* with Sabbath Eve (cf. **Lekhah Dodi*) and Sabbath morning; and *maqām Ṣabā* with circumcisions and prayers on Sabbaths on which the weekly portion of the Bible mentions circumcision.

In several Near Eastern communities the prayer of each Sabbath and festival has its own appropriate governing *maqām*. The Aleppan **bakkashot* singing is entirely governed by a sophisticated maqamic organization, and between the single or grouped *bakkashot* there is a *petiḥah* (opening – a vocal improvisation), a verse or a psalm serving as a melodic vehicle for modulation from one *maqām* to the other. This attains its zenith in the performance of the sabbatical psalm (Ps. 92) wherein each verse is sung on a different *maqām*. Such modulations are also made in the solemn recitation of the Ten Commandments, the *ḥazzan* displaying his virtuosity by skillfully passing through the maximum number of *maqāmāt*. The Moroccan *bakkashot* are organized into a series of *piyyutim* corresponding to the number of Sabbaths between Succot and Passover, each having its appropriate *tbāʿ*.

All the above are unwritten conventions. The written indication of the *maqām* is found in all manuscript and printed collections of *piyyutim* produced in the Near East since the time of Israel *Najara, who was apparently the first to compose and organize his *piyyutim* according to this system. In his *Zemirot Yisrael* the poems are divided by *maqāmāt*, in the following order: *Ḥusseini, Rast, Dūgah, Sīgah, Nawa, Busilik* (a Turkish *maqām*), *Ḥusseini, Naurūz-ʿAjam, Uzāl*, and *Iraq*. The practice has continued to this day, and even recent songs have been fitted into the system, so that in the collection *Shirei Yisrael be-Ereẓ ha-Kedem* of the Adrianople community (Constantinople, 1922) the anthem *Ha-Tikvah can be found in *maqām Nihawand*.

BIBLIOGRAPHY: Idelsohn, Melodien, 4 (1923), 53–112; A.Z. Idelsohn, in: *Sammelbaende der Internationalen Musikgesellschaft*, 15 (1913–14), 1–63; idem, in: MGWJ, 57 (1913), 314ff.; J. Chailley, in: *Acta Musicologia*, 28 (1956), 137–63; H. Farmer, in: *New Oxford History of Music*, 1 (1957), 447–50.

[Bathja Bayer / Amnon Shiloah (2nd ed.)]

MAQĀMA (pl. *maqāmāt*), a narrative in rhymed prose, a collection of short independent stories interlaced with short metrical poems. The *maqāma* originated in about the tenth century C.E. with the Arab poet Ibn al-Fātiḥ Aḥmad ibn Ḥusaynī (Al-Hamdhānī) and reached its peak with al-Ḥarīrī of Bosra (c. 1054–1112). It was imitated in different languages (Persian, Hebrew, Syriac) and times. Derived from the Arabic word *maqām* ("place"; cf. Hebrew *makom), maqāma* refers to the public place where people gathered to listen to rhetoric; it has been translated also as "assemblies" or "sessions," alluding to the meetings themselves. In Hebrew the accepted name for this genre is *maḥberet* (pl. *maḥbarot*). In all the languages in which it was written it meant a relatively later variation in respect to the conventions of poetry that usually preceded this genre in prose. In later times it was considered no less valuable, and even more difficult, than poetry, involving its own style, content, and peculiarities. The *maqāma* was a very imaginative art of writing, full of extravagant, mannered rhetoric with a large amount of humor, and its stories included realistic or caricatured characters that could never have been introduced in a poem. It was also less formal and conventional than poetry, more realistic, like many other cultural manifestations of medieval society. However, the literary study of these compositions, and of Hebrew rhymed prose in general, has been, in the words of D. Pagis, "sorely neglected."

The classical *maqāma* was created when a narrator described the particular behavior of a talented and quick-witted hero, skillful at mockery and jest, who appeared at the "place," in the middle of the "assembly," flaunting his erudition, particularly in language and literature, and delighting listeners (and ultimately readers) with humorous remarks and stories. At the "place" he frequently encountered an acquaintance of similar abilities or the narrator himself. The two, pretending not to know each other, would engage in an amusing conversation which culminated in the mutual recognition of their friendship.

Hebrew classical *maqāma* has a rather fixed structure, with different episodes or adventures of the protagonist told by the literary narrator. A narrative frame, creating a background and describing the scene, and a more or less conventional conclusion, encloses the details of the different episodes. The language used is pure biblical Hebrew, constituted many times by a mosaic of biblical quotations (*shibbuẓ*) that receive a completely new meaning.

Shortly after they were introduced as spoken expressions, *maqāmāt* were put into writing. In the course of time other humorous stories and pieces in rhymed prose began to be called *maqāmāt* even though they did not contain the typical gay talk of the classical *maqāma*. Scholars today, however, have very different attitudes in respect to the use of the name "*maqāma*" for all kinds of narrative texts in rhymed prose. It is true that even the Arabic *maqāma* changed notably with different times and places: for instance, in al-Andalus artistic storytelling created new forms, including long narratives with single plots. In Hebrew literature from the 12th to 15th centuries there are narratives that do not have all the characteristics of the classic Arabic *maqāma*, and it is disputed among researchers whether we should use the same name for this kind of composition, or if they have to be classified as *maqāma*-like narratives, as many literary historians prefer today.

The author of the first known Hebrew *maqāma* is Solomon ibn Zakbel (*Ibn Sahl) who lived in Muslim Spain during the first half of the 12th century. Later authors of Hebrew works in this genre are Joseph *Ibn Zabara, who wrote *Sefer ha-Shaʿashuʿim* and *Judah ibn Shabbetai, who wrote *Minḥat Yehudah Sone ha-Nashim*. However, the greatest writer of the Hebrew *maqāma* is Judah *Al-Ḥarizi. After translating into Hebrew, under the title *Maḥbarot Ittiʾel*, the *maqāmāt* of Al-Ḥarīrī (adapting their content and language to his audience), he wrote in Hebrew the *Taḥkemoni*, which contains 50 *maqāmāt*. Al-Ḥarizi said that he composed this book to prove that it was possible to use Arabic literary forms in Hebrew. Al-Ḥarizi greatly influenced such later Hebrew poets as Abraham ibn Ḥasdai, Jacob b. Eleazar, and Immanuel of Rome. Particularly worthy of mention is Isaac ibn *Sahula whose *Meshal ha-Kadmoni* (compiled in 1281), based on Jewish themes, was written in conscious contrast to the Arabic *maqāmā*. Following some Arabic models, from the 13th century a special type of *maqāmāt* also appears in Hebrew: the symbolic or allegoric one, represented, for instance, by the "Scroll of the Fawns" by Eliyahu ha-Kohen (ed. by Z. Malachi, 1986), continued in some narratives of Mattathias (15th century) or Tanhum Yerushalmi (Orient, 16th century).

The Hebrew style of the *maqāma*, especially of those written in later periods, has occasionally appealed to contemporary authors, the best example being Bialik's *Alluf Baẓlut ve-Alluf Shum* ("Lord Onion and Lord Garlic").

BIBLIOGRAPHY: C. Brockelmann, in: EI, 3 (1936), 174–7; H.A.R. Gibb, *Arabic Literature* (1963), 100–2, 123–5; I. Perez (ed.), *Maḥbarot Itti'el* (1951), 13–17; I. Goldziher, *Kiẓẓur Toledot ha-Sifrut ha-Aravit* (1952), 81f.; A.M. Habermann, *Toledot ha-Piyyut ve-ha-Shirah* (1970), 194–6, 201–7; N. Gubrin in: *Me'assef le-Divrei Sifrut, Bikkoret ve-Hagut*, 8–9 (1968), 394–417. **ADD. BIBLIOGRAPHY:** Y. Ratzaby, *Yalkut ha-Maqama ha-Ivrit, Sippurim be-Ḥaruzim* (1974); F. De la Granja, *Maqāmas y risālas andaluzas* (1976); D. Pagis, in: *Scripta Hierosolymitana*, 27 (1978), 79–98; C. del Valle (tr.), *Las asambleas de los sabios: (Taḥkĕmoní)* (c. 1988); Z. Malachi, in: *Maḥanayim*, 1 (1991), 176–79; idem, in: *Aharon Mirsky Jubilee Volume: Essays on Jewish Culture* (1986), 317–41; idem, in: R. Nettler (ed.) *Medieval and Modern Perspectives on Muslim-Jewish Relations* (1995), 127–58;J. Dishon, in: *The Heritage of the Jews of Spain* (1994), 65–75; Y. Yahalom, in: *Israel Levin Jubilee Volume*, 1 (1994), 135–54; M. Huss, in: *Tarbiz*, 65 (1996), 19–79; idem, *Meliẓat Efer ve-Dinah le-Don Vidal Benbenesht: Pirkei Iyyun u-Mahadurah Bikortit* (2002); J. Hämeen-Anttila, in: *Asiatische Studien/Études Asiatiques*, 51 (1997), 577–99; Schirmann-Fleischer, *The History of Hebrew Poetry in Christian Spain and Southern France* (Hebrew; 1997), 93ff.); R. Drory, in: *The Literature of Al-Andalus* (2000), 190–210; D.S. Segal (tr.), *Judah ben Solomon al-Harizi, The Book of Taḥkemoni: Jewish Tales from Medieval Spain* (2001); N. Katsumata, in: *Middle Eastern Literatures*, 5:2 (2002), 117–37; R. Loewe (ed.), Isaac Ibn Sahula, *Meshal Haqadmoni: Fables from the Distant Past: A Parallel Hebrew-English Text* (2004).

[Abraham Meir Habermann / Angel Sáenz-Badillos (2nd ed.)]

MAQUEDA, small town in Castile, central Spain, on the territory of the Order of *Calatrava. Because of the resemblance to the biblical name of Makkedah (Josh. 10: 10, 28, etc.), some Jewish commentators (cf. Isaac *Abrabanel's commentary to Kings) asserted that the Spanish city had been founded by Jews from Makkedah who had been exiled by Nebuchadnezzar. Conversely, Moses *Arragel tried to demonstrate to the head of the Order of Calatrava that Makkedah in Ereẓ Israel had been founded by the king of Maqueda in Spain. The beginning of Jewish settlement in Maqueda probably coincided with the transfer of the region to the ownership of the Order of Calatrava in 1177.

In 1238, Ferdinand III ordered the community to make the Church an annual payment of 30 denarii symbolizing the amount of money received by Judas Iscariot. In 1290 the community paid an annual tax of 11,162 maravedis. During the reign of Ferdinand IV (1295–1312), the tax was reduced from 8,000 to 5,000 maravedis to dissuade the Jews from leaving Maqueda. Alfonso XI confirmed this reduction in 1316, but the amount of tax for services collected from the Jews there remained unchanged. The Jews earned their livelihood from the same occupations as the other inhabitants of the region, including agriculture.

During the persecutions of 1391 its two synagogues were sacked. In 1415, the antipope *Benedict XIII answered an appeal sent by the apostate rabbi of the community, who had been maintained from the vineyards and fields which it owned and was left without means of subsistence. Benedict authorized him to take possession of the synagogue appurtenances and property.

By the beginning of the 15th century, the community had been reestablished, and in 1430 Moses Arragel completed there the translation of the Bible into Spanish commissioned by Don Luis de Guzman, head of the Order of Calatrava. The role played in 1464–65 by R. Maymaran, rabbi of Maqueda, in persuading Conversos to return to Judaism, emerges from the trial of Ḥayyim Fichel by the Inquisition held at *Huesca in 1489. The community still paid 50,000 maravedis in taxes in 1491. The status of the community may be gauged from the fact that a meeting of representatives of the communities of Castile was convened there in the fall of 1484, when important decisions concerning the practice of usury by the Jews in the kingdom were passed. After the decree of expulsion of 1492 was issued, Ferdinand ordered that inquiries should be made among the Jews of Maqueda to discover whether they were ready to adopt Christianity. The king ordered that watch should be kept over the synagogue until its future was decided and that a register should be made of Jewish property, of the debts owed to Jews, and those they owed to others. In the folklore of the Sephardim, stories were preserved about simple-minded Jews of Maqueda of the same type as those recounted about the Jews of *Chelm.

BIBLIOGRAPHY: Baer, Urkunden, index; Beinart, in: *Tarbiz*, 26 (1956/57), 78; idem, in: *Estudios*, 3 (1962), 7–10; F. Cantera, *Sinagogas españolas* (1955), 243–4; Suárez Fernández, Documentos, index; C.O. Nordström, *Duke of Alba's Castillian Bible* (1967), 12, 16, 20, 32, 234. **ADD. BIBLIOGRAPHY:** H. Beinart, in: *Zion*, 56 (1991), 239–53.

[Haim Beinart]

MAR (**Aram.** מָר; lit. "lord"), a term of respect and endearment used in addressing an important person. Daniel addressed the king as *mari* ("my lord"; Dan. 4:16). The rabbis related that King *Jehoshaphat rose from his throne upon seeing a scholar, embraced him, and exclaimed, "My master, my master; my teacher, my teacher" (Ket. 103b; Mak. 24a). In Babylonia *mar* was used as a deferential and respectful form of address. A son reporting his father's teachings was urged to say, "thus said my father, my master" (Kid. 31b). When *Rav acted as interpreter for Shila, the latter asked him to cease, proclaiming Rav his "master" upon perceiving his greatness (Yoma 20b). Abbaye referred to his uncle and teacher, Rabbah b. Nahamani, simply as *Mar*, without adding any name (Pes. 101a). Tavyomi's colleagues always called him *Mar* and he is therefore always referred to in the Talmud as "*Mar bar Rav Ashi" (Kid. 31b). *Mar* finally became a title preceding the name, and it became customary in Babylonia to call scholars *mar* and not *rav*. This was particularly so in the case of the two famous contemporaries of Rav, Mar *Samuel and Mar *Ukba, as well as Mar *Zutra. When a passage already quoted in the Talmud is quoted again for the purpose of further elucidation, it is introduced with the words "*Mar* said," which in the context merely means "It has been stated above" (e.g., Bet. 2a).

In modern Hebrew *Mar* is used as a term of address like the English "Mister."

BIBLIOGRAPHY: Hyman, Toledot, 897ff.; J. Schechter, *Oẓar ha-Talmud* (1963), 244.

MAR BAR RAV ASHI (d.c. 468), Babylonian *amora*. Mar was the son of *Ashi. According to one passage he signed his name in a letter "Tavyomi" (BB 12b), Mar apparently being a title of honor. He is extensively quoted in the Babylonian Talmud. He possessed great authority, and according to a tradition found in Rashi (to Ḥul. 76b) the *halakhah* follows him except in two cases. He studied under his father, who headed the famous academy of Mata Meḥasya, near Sura. On the death of Ashi, Mar stayed on under his successor Maremar (Ber. 45b). His companions were Ravina (the younger, Ber. 36a), Judah b. Maremar, and Aḥa of Difti (Ber. 45b). In 455 he became head of the academy after competing for the post with *Aḥa. The *aggadah* describes his appointment as an example of prophecy having been given to fools. Mar was standing in the manor of Maḥoza when he heard a lunatic exclaim: "The man to be elected head of the academy of Mata Meḥasya signs himself Tavyomi." He quickly went to Mata Meḥasya and arrived in time to sway the voting in his favor (BB 12b). The *aggadah* also relates that Mar had great knowledge of the ways of demons and great power over them (Ḥul. 105b). Sherira Gaon in his letter reports that in the time of Mar, King Yezdegerd III, who was hostile to the Jews, was swallowed by a dragon while he was in his bed (ed. by B.M. Lewin (1921), 95). Mar had a brother Sama and a sister, and a dispute between them over the bequest of their father was arbitrated by Ravina (Ket. 69a). He was a wealthy man (Git. 7a). He was succeeded by Rabbah Tosfa'a.

BIBLIOGRAPHY: Bacher, Trad, index; Hyman, Toledot, 897–9; Ḥ. Albeck, *Mavo la-Talmudim* (1969), 445f. **ADD. BIBLIOGRAPHY:** A. Cohen, "Mar Bar Rav Ashi and his Literary Contribution" (Hebrew) (Ph.D. Dissertation, Yeshiva University (1980)).

[David Joseph Bornstein]

MAR BAR RAVINA (מר בריה דרבינא), a fourth-century Babylonian *amora*, famous for his saintly character. In his youth, he was carefully tended by his mother, who provided him with clean garments every day, so that he could study in comfort (Er. 65a). Although well-to-do, he lived austerely, fasting by day except on Pentecost, Purim, and the eve of the Day of Atonement (Pes. 68b). At his wedding, a note of seriousness was struck by Rav Hamnuna Zuta who, when asked to sing for the guests, chanted to them, "Alas for us that we are to die" (Ber. 31a). An even sadder note was injected at his son's wedding when Mar, seeing that the company was in a merry mood, deliberately broke a precious cup to dampen their spirit (Ber. 30b–31a). This is probably the origin of the custom of breaking a cup at a Jewish wedding ceremony. He held that even gentiles who observed the seven Noachide laws did not thereby earn any heavenly reward (Av. Zar. 2b–3a). He also had an extremely low opinion of Balaam – the arch-prophet of the gentile world – whom he charged with bestiality (Sanh. 105a) and singled out as the only major sinner against whom biblical passages could be expounded so as to discredit him (Sanh. 106b). Mar bar Ravina had a reputation as a pious, God-fearing man (Ber. 39b; Shab. 61a), who regarded the profanation of God's name as the most heinous sin (Kid. 40a). He was also credited with miraculous escapes from grave perils (Ber. 54a). Characteristic of his piety was his prayer which is still recited at the conclusion of the Eighteen Benedictions: "O my God, keep my tongue from evil and my lips from speaking guile. And to them that curse me may my soul be silent; yea, let my soul be as the dust to all. Open my heart in thy law, and let my soul pursue thy commandments …" (Ber. 17a).

BIBLIOGRAPHY: Hyman, Toledot, 900f.; Ḥ. Albeck, *Mavo la-Talmudim* (1969), 368.

[Moses Aberbach]

MARBURG, city in Hesse, Germany. A document dated May 13, 1317 – the first to mention Jews in Marburg – indicates that they then had an organized community and a synagogue, and lived in a special quarter. The community was annihilated during the *Black Death persecutions (1348/49), but Jews were living in the town once more by 1364. In the middle of the 15th century they were apparently expelled from Marburg; the synagogue was demolished in 1452 and the cemetery passed into non-Jewish hands. The Jewish population eventually returned, only to be driven out again by a decree of 1523. However, in 1532 Duke Philip abolished the decree and permitted the Jews to reside there for a six-year period. In subsequent years the number of Marburg Jews remained low: six families in 1744 and eight in 1776. Jews from outside the town were permitted to remain there only during the annual fairs. The number of Jews increased during the course of the 19th century, reaching 512 (2.5% of the total population) in 1905. From 1823 Marburg was the seat of the district community organization and later of the district rabbinate. The community maintained a synagogue (built in 1897), a school, a convalescent home, and a number of other institutions. Hermann *Cohen, professor at the local university, founded the Marburg school of Neo-Kantianism. In 1933 there were about 325 Jews in Marburg. On November 10, 1938, the synagogue was burned down. By May 17, 1939, only 143 Jews remained; ten survived the war, while the rest left or were deported in 1941–42. About 300 Jews lived in Marburg between 1945 and 1948; but by 1959 only 50 remained, and by 1961 the number had shrunk to 15. In 1989 a new community center was inaugurated. The building was provided by the municipality of Marburg. The Jewish community numbered 30 in 1989 and about 350 in 2005. Most of the members are immigrants from the former Soviet Union. Since the community center was too small to accommodate the increased membership, a new one was opened in 2004. This building, too, was provided by the municipality of Marburg.

BIBLIOGRAPHY: L. Munk, *Zur Erinnerung an die Einweihung der neuen Synagoge in Marburg* (1897); FJW (1932–33), 191–4; Germ Jud, 2 (1968), 522–3; M. Hirschhorn, in: *Juedische Wohlfahrtspflege und Sozialpolitik*, 3 (1932), 342ff.; 6 (1937), 29ff. **ADD. BIBLIOGRAPHY:** G. Rehme and K Haase, … mit Rumpf und Stumpf ausrotten… *Zur Geschichte der Juden in Marburg und Umgebung nach 1933* (Marburger Stadtschriften zur Geschichte und Kultur, vol. 6) (1982); A. Maimon, M. Breuer, Y. Guggenheim (eds.), *Germania Judaica* vol. 3. 1350–1514 (1987), 832–46; A. Erdmann, *Die Marburger Juden. Ihre Geschichte von den Anfaengen bis zur Gegenwart. Dargestellt anhand der staatlichen Quellen unter besonderer Beruecksichtigung des 19. Jahrhunderts* (1987); B. Haendler-Lachmann and T. Werther, *Vergessene Geschaefte – verlorene Geschichte. Juedisches Wirtschaftsleben in Marburg und seine Vernichtung im Nationalsozialismus* (1992); E. Dettmering (ed.), *Zur Geschichte der Synagoge und der juedischen Gemeinde in Marburg* (Marburger Stadtschriften zur Geschichte und Kultur, vol. 39) (1992). **WEBSITE:** www.jg-marburg.de.

[Larissa Daemmig (2nd ed.)]

MARCEAU, MARCEL (1923–), French mime. Marceau was born in Strasbourg, the son of a butcher who was executed by the Nazis during World War II. Marceau worked for the French underground, helping Jewish children to cross the border into Switzerland. In 1944, he entered Charles Dullin's School of Dramatic Art and studied with Etienne Decroux (1898–1991). He made his début as *Harlequin* in Jean-Louis Barrault's production of *Baptiste* in 1947. That same year he formed his own company and created his famous character "Bip," a flour-faced clown always in conflict with the physical world. He wrote *The Story of Bip*, which was published in 1976, and celebrated Bip's 50th anniversary in 1997. Marceau, who is the best-known exponent of modern mime, toured either as a solo artist or with a small company in many parts of the world. In his U.S. tours in 1955–56 and 2000 he also made many television appearances. His silent eloquence and unique synthesis of corporeal mime with 19th century pantomime captured the public's imagination wherever he appeared. Most of Marceau's programs consisted of small sketches featuring "Bip," but in 1951 he created an extended drama, *The Overcoat*, based on the novel by Gogol. He also made a number of films. In 1971 he collaborated with the Hamburg Ballet on a version of *Candide*. Marceau described mime as "the art of expressing feelings by attitudes and not a means of expressing words through gestures." In 1998, French President Jacques Chirac named Marceau a Grand Officer of the Order of Merit. He was elected a member of the Academies of Fine Arts in Berlin and Munich, the Academie of Beaux Arts in France, and the Institut de France.

ADD. BIBLIOGRAPHY: Y. Karsh, *Portraits of Greatness* (1959), 124; B. Martin, *Marcel Marceau: Master of Mime* (1979).

[Selma Jeanne Cohen / Amnon Shiloah (2nd ed.)]

MARCK, SIEGFRIED (1889–1957), German philosopher. Marck, who was born in Breslau, became a professor there in 1924. After the Nazis came to power, he taught at Dijon, France, and from 1940 in Chicago. Marck's thought derives from the Marburg neo-Kantians. He compared the fundamental concepts of Kant, Hegel, and Marx in his *Kant und Hegel* (1917) and *Hegelianismus und Marxismus* (1922). He applied *Cassirer's and *Kelsen's concepts in his *Substanzund Funktionsbegriff in der Rechtsphilosophie* (1925). His main work, *Die Dialektik in der Philosophie der Gegenwart* (2 vols., 1929–31), develops his own "critical dialectic." Marck also wrote *Der Neuhumanismus als politische Philosophie* (1938), and *Grosse Menschen unserer Zeit* (1954).

BIBLIOGRAPHY: *National Cyclopaedia of American Biography*, 43 (1961), 257–8.

[Richard H. Popkin]

MARCKWALD, WILLY (1864–1950), German organic chemist. Marckwald was born in Jakobskirch, Silesia, and was professor at Berlin University from 1899. He was also director of the chemistry department of the university's physico-chemical institute. In 1910 he was appointed a privy councillor and was president of the German Chemical Society from 1928 to 1931. When the Nazis rose to power, he escaped to Brazil. Marckwald's scientific papers dealt with the physical properties of organic compounds, stereochemistry, and radioactivity. He was the first to isolate the element polonium in pitchblende, which helped toward the discovery of radium. He observed changes caused by light in the color of certain compounds, and called this phenomenon "phototropy."

Marckwald wrote *Ueber die Beziehungen zwischen dem Siedepunkte und der Zusammensetzung chemischer Verbindungen* (1888), *Die Benzoltheorie* (1898), and *Radium in Biologie und Heilkunde* (1911–12).

[Samuel Aaron Miller]

MARCOSSON, ISAAC (1876–1961), U.S. journalist and author. Born in Louisville, Kentucky, Marcosson worked on *World's Work, Saturday Evening Post*, and *Munsey's Magazine*. Specializing in finance, he wrote several books on business and commerce. He was in St. Petersburg during the Russian Revolution and recorded his observations in *Rebirth of Russia* (1917). He also wrote *Adventures in Interviewing* (1920), *The Turbulent Years* (1938), and an autobiographical work, *Before I Forget: A Pilgrimage to the Past* (1959).

MARCOUSSIS (originally **Marcous**), **LOUIS** (1883–1941), French painter. Marcoussis was born in Warsaw. As a student at the Academy of Fine Arts in Cracow he was one of the avant-garde Young Poland group which was strongly inclined to French culture. In 1903 he moved to Paris to study. When his father was no longer able to support him, he lived by contributing frivolous drawings to *La Vie Parisienne* and *L'Assiette au Beurre*. Marcoussis visited the United States in 1934 and his engravings were shown in New York and Chicago. When the Germans occupied Paris in 1940 Marcoussis and his wife happened to be staying in a village in central France where he was able to live in safety until his death the following year. Marcoussis is listed generally among the cubists. Yet in his early still lifes, the element of fantasy is stronger than the purely analytical one. He was an excellent print-maker, who made illustrations for books by Gérard de Nerval, Guillaume Apollinaire, and Tristan Tzara. In his portraits, he abandoned cubism for a tight classical style.

BIBLIOGRAPHY: J. Lafranchis (ed.), *Marcoussis* (Fr., 1961).

[Alfred Werner]

MARCULEŞTI, Jewish agricultural colony in Bessarabia. It was founded in 1837 on an area of 549 hectares leased from a private owner by 239 settlers from Podolia. In 1888 the land was acquired by the settlers, but because of the *May Laws of 1882 it was registered under the name of a Christian property owner. According to the census of 1897 there were 1,336 Jewish inhabitants. However, the survey conducted by the *Jewish Colonization Association in 1899 records 292 families (1,534 individuals), of whom 123 were landowners (with an average of 4.5 hectares to a family). After the railway to Odessa was laid, and a station was built close to Marculesti, an impetus was given to trading mainly in farm products. The settlement gradually lost its agricultural character, and turned into a typical Jewish town. Under the agrarian reform in Romania in 1922, 105 Jews in Marculesti received plots of land. In 1901 a school was opened which was directed by the writer Shelomo *Hillels. Of the 541 members registered in the local loan fund in 1925, 195 were farmers. In 1930 the Jewish population numbered 2,319 (87.4% of the total). *Tarbut elementary and high schools functioned there during the 1930s. The colony was destroyed when the Germans and Romanians invaded Bessarabia in July 1941, after its incorporation within the Soviet Union. On the 8th of that month, about 1,000 Jews living there were murdered. In September–November 1941 a transit camp was established in Marculesti for Bessarabian Jews who were deported to *Transnistria. Ada *Maimon and Rabbi Y.L. *Maimon (Fishman), who served as the rabbi of the colony from 1900 to 1905, were born in Marculesti.

[Eliyahu Feldman]

MARCUS, AARON (1843–1916), scholar, writer on Kabbalah and Ḥasidism. Marcus was born and educated in Hamburg, studied at the yeshivah of Boskovice (Moravia) but also acquired a wider philosophical education. In 1861 he left for Cracow where he joined the Ḥasidim. Between 1862 and 1866 he made several long visits to the ḥasidic rabbi of Radomsk, Solomon Rabinowicz. He later maintained close relations with many ḥasidic leaders in Poland and Galicia. A major part of his literary work (mainly in German but with a small amount in Hebrew) was devoted to the defense of Ḥasidism and an explanation of ḥasidic doctrines and Kabbalah. His work testifies to great erudition, but has proved unacceptable by the current standards of modern critical scholarship. In his work he defended traditional Judaism against modern Bible criticism and scientific materialism. At the same time, he tried to find confirmation for new insights in philosophy and science in Jewish religious literature, particularly in the writings of Ḥayyim b. Moses *Attar, M.Ḥ. *Luzzatto, and Ḥabad Ḥasidism. Marcus was one of the few Orthodox Jews in Germany who totally adopted Ḥasidism in theory and practice. He published: *Hartmanns inductive Philosophie des Unbewussten im Chassidismus* (2 pts., 1889–90); *Der Chassidismus* (under the pseudonym Verus, 1901, 1927[3]); *Barsilai, Sprache als Schrift der Psyche* (1905); an edition of Jacob of Marvège's responsa *She'elot u-Teshuvot min ha-Shamayim* with a commentary *Keset ha-Sofer*, 1895, 1957[2]); *Keset ha-Sofer* (Bible annotations, largely in Ms., 1912); and *Juedische Chronologie* (vol. 1, posthumously, 1935). From 1898 to 1899 Marcus edited *Krakauer Juedische Zeitung*, a paper he published as a vehicle for his ideas. He became an enthusiastic supporter of Theodor Herzl and his *Judenstaat* (see his *Theodor Herzls Judenstaat…*, 1897; second ed. 1919 with a eulogy of Marcus), thus becoming one of the pioneers of religious Zionism, though later he turned toward the anti-Zionist Agudat Israel.

BIBLIOGRAPHY: Moeller, in: *Jeschurun* (ed. Wohlgemuth), 4 (1917), 154–60; T. Herzl, *Diaries*, ed. by R. Patai, 1 (1960), 347; H. Schwab, *Chachme Ashkenaz* (Eng., 1964), 94 (incl. bibl.); M. Marcus, *A. Marcus, die Lebensgeschichte eines Chossid* (1966); G. Scholem, in: *Beḥinot*, 7 (1954), 3–8.

[*Encyclopaedia Judaica* (Germany)]

MARCUS, BERNARD (1929–), U.S. entrepreneur, philanthropist. Born to Russian immigrant parents, Marcus grew up in a tenement in Newark, N.J., wanting to be a doctor. After high school, he could not afford medical training. Instead, he worked his way through Rutgers University and earned a degree in pharmacy. After college he worked at a drugstore and a cosmetics company. By the late 1970s he had worked his way up to chairman of Handy Dan, a home-improvement chain in California. He and one of his colleagues there, Arthur M. *Blank, were fired in 1978 over disagreements about the chain's future. Marcus and Blank decided to go into the home-improvement business themselves. After surveying four cities, they settled on Atlanta, Ga., as their home base, believing that it had the right market and real estate conditions to test their theory that consumers would flock to big stores offering a broad selection of home-improvement products, low prices, and friendly, knowledgeable service. In 1979 they opened three Home Depot stores. In their first year, on $7 million in sales, they lost $1 million. But they persevered and in 1981 they went public. By the early years of the 21st century, Home Depot had more than 1,500 stores in the United States, Canada, Puerto Rico, and Mexico, becoming the world's largest home-improvement retailer. With a familial structure, embracing all employees with stock options and other incentives, plus a harsh sense of competition, Home Depot helped drive Handy Dan, the Blank-Marcus nemesis, out of business. Becoming the do-it-yourself giant, providing everything from screws to electrical wiring to appliances and lawn supplies, Home Depot had more than 150,000 employees and more than $30 billion in sales. Although Marcus, the older of the founders, was chairman for more than 20 years, he and Blank saw eye to eye on almost everything. Marcus was a hands-on visionary, but he also was known for sparring with investment bankers and for telling jokes at company dinners.

Marcus and Blank became philanthropic leaders in Atlanta. While Blank gave to the Atlanta Symphony Orchestra, youth projects, and many Jewish organizations, Marcus devoted more than 20 years to the City of Hope, a cancer research center. He is also a major supporter of the nation's largest rehabilitation hospital for spinal care patients, the Shepherd Spinal Center, and a new wing of that hospital was named in honor of his wife, Billi. The Marcus Developmental Resource Center provides services and information to disabled individuals and their families. Marcus spent several years in the early years of the 21st century designing and building a $200 million aquarium, known as the Georgia Aquarium. It will have 100,000 fish, including giant groupers, octopuses, and two white beluga whales. The star attraction will be two whale sharks, the world's biggest fish, which can exceed 40 feet in length.

Marcus has given significant sums to Jewish causes. A Jewish community center in Atlanta is named for him and he was one of the founders of the U.S. Holocaust Museum. In 2000, Marcus and the governor of Georgia led a delegation to major Israeli cities to try to persuade Israeli technology companies to make Georgia their home. Marcus was international chairman of the Israel Democracy Institute, an independent political research organization in Jerusalem, and often visited Israel for both business and pleasure. He attends a philanthropic roundtable of the major American Jewish philanthropists that includes Edgar and Charles Bronfman, Michael Steinhardt, and Leslie Wexner among others.

[Stewart Kampel (2nd ed.)]

MARCUS, DAVID DANIEL (1902–1948), U.S. soldier, commander of the Jerusalem front in the Israel *War of Independence. Marcus was born on New York City's Lower East Side. In 1920 he entered the West Point Military Academy, graduating in 1924. He also studied law, and, when he left the army in 1927, was employed in the U.S. Attorney General's Office. In 1934 Mayor Fiorello La Guardia invited him to join the New York City Department of Correction, and in 1940 he was sworn in as a commissioner of correction. After the outbreak of World War II in Europe he rejoined the army with the rank of lieutenant colonel as divisional judge advocate and divisional headquarters' commander. In 1943 he was called to the Civil Affairs Division of the War Department and attended the meetings of the "Big Five." On D-Day he volunteered to participate in the airborne assault, parachuting into Normandy despite his lack of previous training. In 1945 he was on the staff of General Lucius D. Clay's military government in Germany. Recalled to Washington, he was appointed head of the War Crimes Branch. In 1947 he retired from the army with the rank of colonel and returned to legal practice, after being awarded a number of major U.S. and British decorations.

At the request of the *Jewish Agency and the *Haganah, he went to Palestine at the end of January 1948, serving as David *Ben-Gurion's military adviser under the *nom de guerre* of Mickey Stone. He immediately perceived the special spirit and conditions of the new Israel army which was emerging from the underground. After a brief visit to the United States, he returned to Israel in May 1948 and on May 28, 1948, was appointed commander of the Jerusalem front. Marcus was the first officer to receive the new rank of *alluf* (Major General). Before dawn on June 11, he went outside the perimeter fence of his headquarters in Abu Ghosh and was accidentally killed by a sentry. His body was transferred with military honors to the United States and buried at West Point. A village in Judea, Mishmar David, is named after him.

BIBLIOGRAPHY: N. Lorch, *The Edge of the Sword* (1961), index; I. Berkman, *Cast a Giant Shadow* (1962; movie, 1965).

[Jehuda Wallach]

MARCUS, ERNST (1856–1928), German jurist and philosopher. Marcus studied law and was a judge. As a philosopher, he was a Kantian who opposed the new interpretations offered by H. *Cohen and L. *Nelson. For Marcus the "thing-in-itself" remained central, deducible from reason. He developed a theory of the *a priori* "organism" which the "I" constructs. He wrote many works on Kant including *Kants Revolutionsprinzip* (1902); *Das Erkenntnisproblem* (1905), *Die Beweisfuehrung in der Kritik der reinen Vernunft* (1914), and *Kants Weltgebaeude* (1917). He also wrote *Theorie einer natuerlichen Magie* (1924). Using Kant's theory, Marcus criticized Einstein in his *Kritik des Aufbaus der speziellen Relativitaetstheorie* (1926) and in *Die Zeit-und Raumlehre Kants* (1927).

BIBLIOGRAPHY: S. Friedlaender, *Der Philosoph Ernst Marcus als Nachfolger Kants* (1930); idem, *Kant gegen Einstein* (1932).

[Richard H. Popkin]

MARCUS, FRANK (1928–1996), German-born playwright. Marcus emigrated to Britain in 1939. Originally an actor, Marcus had his own first play produced in 1950. His later works include *The Formation Dancers* (1964), *Cleo* (1965), and *The Killing of Sister George* (1965), a drama about lesbianism that was made into a successful motion picture.

MARCUS, JACOB RADER (1896–1995), U.S. rabbi and historian. Marcus was the first trained historian of the Jewish people born in America and the first to devote himself to the scholarly study of America's Jews. Through the American Jewish Archives, which he founded in 1947, and through the many books that he published during his long life, he defined, propagated, and professionalized the field of American Jewish history, achieving renown as its founding father and dean. At the time of his death, he was also the oldest and most beloved member of the Reform rabbinate and the senior faculty member at Hebrew Union College-Jewish Institute of Religion (Cincinnati), where he had taught for some three-quarters of a century.

Born in New Haven, Penn., at the age of 15 Marcus came to Cincinnati's Hebrew Union College where he pursued rabbinical studies and simultaneously attended high school and then the University of Cincinnati where he specialized in Jewish history. Following service in World War I, he was ordained in 1920. He went on to obtain his Ph.D. in 1925 at the University of Berlin in general history. In Berlin, he was profoundly influenced by the historian Simon Dubnow and by the techniques of Fritz Baer.

During his time abroad, Marcus also visited Palestine. He then returned to Hebrew Union College, where he taught successfully for the next 70 years. Legions of students credited him for helping to sustain them through rabbinical school, and many of these same students turned to him again later, as rabbis, for help with their congregations or their personal problems. His students reciprocated, electing him president of the Central Conference of American Rabbis in 1949 and lifetime honorary president of the Conference in 1978.

Marcus's most important early publications consisted of a monograph on Israel *Jacobson (1928), and a popular, derivative history of German Jewry (1934). In 1938, he published a volume of carefully edited documents titled *The Jew in the Medieval World*. In 1947, he published his last significant scholarly study of German Jewry, *Communal Sick-Care in the German Ghetto*.

In the 1940s, Marcus shifted his attention to American Jewish history. During the next half-century, he worked systematically to establish American Jewish history as a scholarly discipline. He founded both the American Jewish Archives (1947) and the American Jewish Periodical Center (1956) on the campus of Hebrew Union College (Cincinnati). He served as president and later honorary president of the American Jewish Historical Society. He collected and published thousands of pages of edited primary sources. He created reference tools and a semi-annual scholarly journal, *American Jewish Archives* (1948–). He also authored *Early American Jewry* (2 vols, 1951–53), *Memoirs of American Jews* (3 vols., 1955), *The Colonial American Jew 1492–1776* (3 vols, 1970), *United States Jewry 1776–1985* (4 vols., 1989–1993), and *The Jew in the American World: A Source Book* (1996). To ensure that his work continued, he left his entire fortune in trust for the American Jewish Archives, renamed the Jacob Rader Marcus Center of the American Jewish Archives in his memory.

BIBLIOGRAPHY: S.F. Chyet, "Jacob Rader Marcus--A Biographical Sketch," in: *Essays in American Jewish History to Commemorate the Tenth Anniversary of the Founding of the American Jewish Archives under the Direction of Jacob Rader Marcus* (1958), 1–22; R.M. Falk, *Bright Eminence: The Life and Thought of Jacob Rader Marcus* (1994); G.P. Zola (ed.), *The Dynamics of American Jewish History: Jacob Rader Marcus's Essays on American Jewry* (2004), which includes a full bibliography of his writings.

[Jonathan D. Sarna (2nd ed.)]

MARCUS, JOSEPH (1897–1977), Hebrew scholar. Born in Derevno, Russia (Vilna province), Marcus was taken to the United States in 1910. He was ordained by the Jewish Theological Seminary in 1924. After briefly holding several rabbinical positions, he assisted Israel *Davidson in the preparation of the latter's *Oẓar* ("Thesaurus of Medieval Hebrew Poetry"); later he assisted *Bialik and *Rawnitzki in preparing their editions of the poems of Ibn *Gabirol and Moses *Ibn Ezra, copying for them poems from the Seminary's *genizah* collection. In the course of this work (1929), Marcus discovered a leaf from a hitherto unknown Hebrew manuscript of *Ben Sira (Ecclesiasticus). After holding positions in various Jewish libraries, followed by a brief return to the rabbinate, Marcus became librarian and instructor in medieval Hebrew literature at the Hebrew Teachers College of Boston in 1946. In 1963 he settled in Israel, where he became librarian at the Mosad ha-Rav Kook in Jerusalem.

Marcus' works include *A Fifth Manuscript of Ben Sira* (1931); *Ginzei Shirah u-Fiyyut* ("Liturgical and Secular Poetry of the Foremost Medieval Poets," 1933); *Studies in the Chronicle of Ahimaaz* (1934); *Iggerot Bialik* (1935); *Yoẓerot le-Arba Parashiyyot* (1965); and studies on the poetry of Isaac *Ibn Ghayyat.

[Raymond P. Scheindlin]

MARCUS, RALPH (1900–1956), U.S. scholar of Hellenistic Judaism. Born in San Francisco the son of the talmudic scholar Moses Marcus, Marcus was educated at Columbia, where he wrote his doctoral dissertation on *Law in the Apocrypha* (1927), and at Harvard where he studied with Harry A. Wolfson (1925–27). He taught at the Jewish Institute of Religion, at Columbia (1927–43), and at the University of Chicago (1947–56).

Marcus is best known for editing, translating, and annotating four volumes of Josephus and two of Philo in the Loeb Classical Library series. His notes show an unusual wealth of lexical and historical knowledge, and his translations are accurate and lucid. His invaluable appendixes on select points in Josephus are careful, critical monographs. His bibliographies in these volumes and in separate works (PAAJR, 16 (1946/47), 97–181; *Jewish Studies in Memory of G.A. Kohut* (1935), 463–91) show his mastery of the literature and his critical acumen. He successfully undertook the extraordinarily difficult task of translating Philo's *Quaestiones et Solutiones* from the Armenian and restored the Greek in numerous places.

Marcus' lexicon to Josephus, continuing the work of Thackeray, reached the letter *epsilon*. His 62 articles excel in etymologies, grammatical and lexical points, and in utilizing his vast knowledge of the various languages of the classical and Jewish worlds. Marcus intended to write a history of the Jews during the Second Temple period, and many of his most fertile ideas for future work in the field are found in his "The Future of Intertestamental Studies" (in: H.R. Willoughby's *The Study of the Bible* (1947), 190–208). Marcus also wrote semipopular articles on Hellenistic Judaism for L. Finkelstein's *The Jews* and L.W. Schwarz's *Great Ages and Ideas of the Jewish People* as well as for the *Encyclopaedia Britannica*. In the controversy between H.A. Wolfson and E.R. Goodenough on Philo, Marcus strongly supported Wolfson's contention that Philo closely parallels Pharisaic Judaism (*Review of Religion*, 13 (1949), 368–81). Toward the end of his life Marcus became much involved in the controversies surrounding the Dead Sea Scrolls. He connected the Qumran Covenanters with the Essenes and discerned in them a strong gnosticizing flavor.

BIBLIOGRAPHY: G.E. von Grunebaum, in: JNES, 16 (1957), 143–4; BRE, 3 (1958), 44–46, a list of his works.

[Louis Harry Feldman]

MARCUS, RUDOLPH ARTHUR (1923–), chemist and Nobel Prize winner. Marcus was born in Montreal, Canada, and educated there at McGill University. He taught at the Polytechnical Institute of Brooklyn, N.Y., 1951–64, at the University of Illinois, 1964–1978, and at the California Institute of Technology, where he became the Arthur Amos Noyes Professor of Chemistry in 1978.

Marcus was awarded the Nobel Prize in chemistry in 1992 for his mathematical analysis of the cause and effect of electrons jumping from one molecule to another, ideas which he developed from 1956 to 1965. When electrons in molecules in a solution jump from one molecule to another, the structure of both molecules changes. The occurrence of this change temporarily increases the energy of the molecular system, resulting in a "driving force" for electron transfer. It was only in the 1980s that Marcus' theories were finally confirmed by experiments. His work has been useful in understanding many complicated chemical reactions, among them photosynthesis. Marcus is also well known for his theory of unimolecular reactions in chemistry, the RRKM theory, which more than 50 years after its development is still the standard theory in the field. It treats the fragmentation of high-energy molecules, as in the atmosphere and in combustion. His research also ranges from the strange fluorescent behavior of nanoparticles to the anomalous isotopic composition of the ozone in the stratosphere and of the earliest solids in the solar system.

MARCUS, RUTH BARCAN (1921–), U.S. logician and philosopher who played a key role in many of the philosophical debates of the second half of the 20th century. Born and educated in New York City, Ruth Barcan received her B.A. in mathematics and philosophy from New York University in 1941. After her marriage to Jules Alexander Marcus, she earned her Ph.D. in philosophy from Yale in 1946. While raising her four children, she held various postdoctoral fellowships and visiting positions, including a Guggenheim Fellowship (1953–54). In 1957, she became an assistant professor at Roosevelt University in Chicago; two years later she was promoted to associate professor. From 1964 to 1970, she served as professor of philosophy and department chair at the newly established University of Illinois at Chicago, building up her department to attain national recognition. After three years as professor at Northwestern University (1970–73), she returned to Yale in 1973 and remained there as Reuben Post Halleck Professor until her retirement in 1992. Thereafter, she continued as a senior research scholar at Yale and as distinguished visiting professor at the University of California at Irvine.

Widely recognized as a leading figure in the field of philosophical logic, Barkan was well known for her contributions to modal logic, especially the Barkan formula, as well as her work on the philosophy of logic and language, epistemology, and ethics. She published numerous articles and essays over a period of 50 years, many of which appeared in the highly regarded collection of her works, entitled *Modalities* (1993). She received many prestigious awards and fellowships, including fellow of National Science Foundation (1963–64); the Center for Advanced Study, University of Illinois (1968–68); the Center for Advanced Study in the Behavioral Sciences at Stanford (1979); Wolfson College, Oxford (1985–86); Clare Hall, Cambridge (1988); and the National Humanities Center (1992–93), as well as the Medal of the College de France (1986). The University of Illinois awarded her an honorary doctorate of humane letters in 1995. Marcus was actively involved in many professional organizations, serving as president of the Association for Symbolic Logic (1983–1986) and vice president of the Institut International de Philosophie (1989–92), as well as chair of the National Board of Officers of the American Philosophical Association (1977–83).

BIBLIOGRAPHY: P.E. Hyman and D. Dash Moore (ed.).*Jewish Women in America*, 2 (1997), 889–90; W. Sinnott-Armstrong (ed.), *Modality, Morality, and Belief: Essays in Honor of Ruth Barcan Marcus* (1995).

[Harriet Pass Freidenreich (2nd ed.)]

MARCUS, SIEGFRIED (1831–1898), German inventor, born in Malchin. Marcus joined the Berlin engineering firm of Siemens und Halske in 1848 and worked on the establishment of telegraphic communication between Berlin and Magdeburg. In 1852 he settled in Vienna, where from 1860 he had his own laboratory. In 1864 he patented a petrol-driven automobile. A car he built in 1875 was preserved in the Vienna Industrial Museum. His patents included an electric lamp (1877), telegraphic relays, a microphone, a loudspeaker, electric fuses for submarine mines, and other devices which were developed by others in later years.

BIBLIOGRAPHY: *Zeitschrift der Oesterreicher Ingenieure und Architekten* (1928), 262; Skowronnek, in: *Umschau*, 35 (1931), 743f.; Postal, in: *American Hebrew*, 129 (1931), 405, 416.

[Samuel Aaron Miller]

MARCUS, STANLEY (1905–2002), U.S. retailer. Marcus was two years old when his family founded Neiman Marcus, but it was his merchandising talent that made the store an internationally known symbol of quality, service, luxury, and exclusivity. Born in Dallas, Texas, he was the eldest of four sons. A high school graduate at 16, Marcus entered Amherst College in Massachusetts. When a fraternity refused to admit him after learning he was a Jew, he transferred to Harvard College and joined a Jewish fraternity. He earned a B.A. from Harvard in 1925 and attended Harvard Business School for a year. He wanted to go into the book business, but his family persuaded him to join the family store, which had been founded in 1907 by Marcus's father, Herbert; his uncle, Abraham Lincoln Neiman; and his aunt, Carrie Marcus Neiman. Marcus did so in 1926 as secretary-treasurer and a director. In 1927 he created the first weekly fashion shows to be staged in an American department store. When business slumped during the Great Depression, he reached out to the middle-income market as well as Neiman Marcus's more affluent customers, declaring, "We want to sell the millionaire, his young daughter – and his secretary." He was appointed executive vice president in 1935 and was among the first retailers outside New York to advertise regularly in national fashion magazines. In 1938, he launched the Neiman Marcus Awards that are given annually to fashion luminaries. The following year, Neiman Marcus mailed its first holiday catalog, a promotion that became a well-publicized annual event, attracting international attention with such sumptuous offerings as Chinese junks, "his and her" airplanes, and a Black Angus steer, either "on the hoof" or as steaks. Marcus also initiated a series of annual "fortnights," two-week extravaganzas that featured the products of a specific country or region, a promotion widely copied by other retailers. In 1950, when his father, Herbert, died, Marcus succeeded him as president. In 1969, he helped engineer the sale of the company to Broadway-Hale Stores, a merchandising conglomerate, and a major expansion program was soon under way. In 1973, he became chairman and chief executive officer and was succeeded as president by his son, Richard. Marcus became chairman emeritus in 1975 and established his own consulting company. He was inducted into the Advertising Hall of Fame in 2000, only the second retailer to be so honored. Marcus wrote two popular books about his experiences at Neiman Marcus, *Minding the Store* (1974) and *Quest for the Best* (1978). Feisty and forthright, he was an outspoken liberal in generally conservative Dallas. In 1963, following the assassination there of U.S. President John F. Kennedy, he took out full-page newspaper ads called "What's Right With Dallas" that asked residents to respect "differing points of view" and to reject "the spirit of absolutism for which our community has suffered." From the mid-1980s until 1999, he wrote a weekly column in the *Dallas Morning News*, sounding off on everything from fashion to civil rights to the image of his native city.

His family's business, which had eventually become part of Harcourt General, was spun off in 1999 as the Neiman Marcus Group, a discrete entity that included Bergdorf Goodman and NM Direct. By 2005, the original Neiman Marcus store in downtown Dallas had evolved into 35 units throughout the U.S. with annual sales that had grown from $20.6 million when Marcus became president to more than $3.5 billion.

BIBLIOGRAPHY: *Dallas Morning News* (Jan. 23, 2002); *New York Times* (Jan. 23, 2002); *Women's Wear Daily* (Oct. 15, 2002).

[Mort Sheinman (2nd ed.)]

°**MARCUS AURELIUS ANTONINUS** (121–180 C.E.), Roman emperor, 161–180 C.E., adopted son and successor of Antoninus Pius; the ideal philosopher-king as envisaged by political thought of the period. Ironically enough, the years of his reign were spent in war defending the borders of the Roman Empire. In 164–5 C.E., Aurelius' general Avidius Cassius captured Seleucia and the Parthian capital Ctesiphon, bringing the Mesopotamian Jews temporarily under Roman rule. When Cassius later proclaimed himself emperor in Syria, the Jews are supposed to have supported him, as a result of which Aurelius "crushed them by means of his preses and legates" (Marcellinus, 23:3). Aurelius held a highly unfavorable opinion of the Jews of Palestine. After passing through the country on his way to Egypt, where he was harassed by their importunities and turbulence, he exclaimed "I find these people [the Jews] to be worse than the Marcomanni, the Quadi, and the Sarmatae!" (*ibid.*, 22:5). There may be an allusion to Marcus Aurelius in the *Sybilline Oracles (5:51). Possibly some characteristics of this philosopher-emperor find expression in the portrayal of the *Antoninus found in the Talmud.

BIBLIOGRAPHY: H.D. Sedgwick, *Marcus Aurelius* (1922), 216–7, 226–7; S. Krauss, *Antoninus und Rabbi* (1910).

[Uriel Rappaport]

MARCUSE, HERBERT (1898–1979), philosopher and social theorist. Born in Berlin, Marcuse studied in Berlin and Freiburg, where he was influenced by Heidegger. In World War I he served in the German army and, as a delegate from his unit, participated in the abortive German revolution of 1918–19. In his works, elements of Schillerian aesthetics, existentialist ontology, and utopian political thought are combined with a modified Marxist outlook and a modified Hegelian (dialectical) method to produce what Marcuse calls "Critical Theory": a critical, "negating" analysis of prevailing social, political, and cultural institutions and theories.

A member of the Frankfurt Institut fuer Sozialforschung, Marcuse left Germany in 1933, moving with the Institute to Geneva, then (1934) to New York. His first important work, "Neue Quellen zur Grundlegung des historischen Materialismus" (in *Die Gesellschaft*, vol. 9, 1932), an interpretation of the then newly discovered "Economic and Philosophical Manuscripts" of Karl Marx, established him as a pioneer in the exploration of "Marxist Humanism." He contributed to the Institute's *Studien ueber Autoritaet und Familie* (1936) and wrote a number of critical essays for its journal, notably "Der Kampf gegen den Liberalismus in der totalitaeren Staatsauffassung" (in *Zeitschrift fuer Sozialforschung*, vol. 3, 1934), in which Fascist-Nazi ideology is shown to be the ideology of capitalism in its monopolistic phase, and thus not so much antagonistic to, as an outgrowth of, liberalism – the ideology of capitalism in its (earlier) competitive phase.

After serving in the OSS and the State Department (1941–50), Marcuse was a fellow, successively, of the Russian research centers at Columbia and at Harvard. His first full-fledged academic appointment was in 1954, as professor of politics and philosophy at Brandeis University. He left there in 1965 to become professor of philosophy at the University of California, San Diego.

In *Reason and Revolution; Hegel and the Rise of Social Theory* (1941, 1954^2), Marcuse contrasted the negative (critical) social theory stemming from Hegel with the positive (positivistic) social theory founded by Comte. Marcuse next undertook a number of critical studies: of Freud's pessimistic theory that civilized society is necessarily repressive (*Eros and Civilization*, 1955); of Russia's Stalinized Marxism (*Soviet Marxism*, 1958); and of the repressive nature of a successful capitalist society (*One-Dimensional Man*, 1964.) Such a society, Marcuse argues, can satisfy material wants and employ industrial skills while it suppresses genuinely human needs and faculties and reduces man to a single, conformist dimension in order to maintain the established order and to secure the production of a surplus for the benefit of the ruling elements.

In later years Marcuse became something of a hero and an authority to many members of the *New Left. His essay on "Repressive Tolerance" (in H. Marcuse et al., *Critique of Pure Tolerance*, 1965), in which he argues that only progressive (i.e., radical) values and movements ought to be tolerated, while toleration should be denied to repressive (i.e., rightist) values and movements, was influential among young radicals.

Marcuse's critique of a capitalist system which satisfies – and tolerates – only those needs that it itself generates (precisely because it can satisfy them to its profit) while it perpetuates domination and exploitation is resumed in *An Essay on Liberation* (1969). He also wrote *Studies in Critical Philosophy* (1973) and *The Aesthetic Dimension* (1978).

BIBLIOGRAPHY: A. Macintyre, *Herbert Marcuse: An Exposition and a Polemic* (1971); G. Kateb, in: *Community* (Jan. 1970), 48–63. **ADD. BIBLIOGRAPHY:** R. Wolin, *Heidegger's Children* (2003); B. Katz, *Herbert Marcuse and the Art of Liberation* (1982); M. Schoolman, *The Imaginary Witness* (1980); P. Robinson, *The Freudian Left* (1969).

[Heinz Lubacz]

MARCUSE, LUDWIG (1894–1971), German essayist. Born in Berlin, Marcuse began his career as a drama critic and as the biographer of Buechner (1922) and Strindberg (1924). During his last years in Germany, he also published perceptive biographies of *Boerne (1929) and *Heine (1932). The implicit parallels between Heine's age and his own are prominent in the latter. In 1933 he emigrated to France, visited the Soviet Union, and escaped to the U.S. in 1939. In 1945 he became professor of German literature and philosophy at the University of Southern California. After 1949 he visited Germany several times and resettled there in 1962. He was increasingly drawn to the history of ideas: significant works in this field are his *Pessimismus, ein Stadium der Reife* (1953) and *Amerikanisches Philosophieren* (1959). These are stylized, luminous histories of ideas, written for the literate layman. In his autobiographical *Mein zwanzigstes Jahrhundert* (1960) he records a vast array of intellectual experiences, and presents a kaleidoscope of personalities in Germany, France, the U.S., and Israel.

ADD. BIBLIOGRAPHY: D. Lamping, "Der Aussenseiter und seine 'arme Freiheit' – Ueber Ludwig Marcuse," in: M. Braun et al. (eds.), *Hinauf und Zurueck in die herzhelle Zukunft – Deutsch-Juedische Literatur im 20. Jahrhundert* (2000), 267–79; D. Lamping, *Ludwig Marcuse – Werk und Wirkung* (1987); K.U. Fischer, *Ludwig Marcuses schriftstellerische Tätigkeit im franzoesischen Exil 1933–39* (1976); K.H. Hense, *Glueck und Skepsis – Ludwig Marcuses Philosophie des Humanismus* (2000).

[Harold von Hofe]

MARCUSE, MOSES (late 18th century), physician and Yiddish writer who grew up in Germany. In his book *Sefer Refu'ot* ("Book of Medicines," 1790) he claims to have studied medicine at the University of Koenigsberg, but his name does not appear in the University's matriculation lists. In 1774 he went to Poland and practiced medicine in several communities. The declared aim of *Sefer Refu'ot* was to transmit elementary knowledge of hygiene in Yiddish to those to whom no doctor was available. The book appears to have gone into a second edition, but only three copies have survived, and it has become a bibliographical rarity. Large extracts from it were published by Noah Prylucki (*Zamlbikher*, 2 (1917), 1–55). Marcuse goes beyond purely medical information; as an early pioneer of enlightenment among Eastern European Jews, he calls for a change of occupations among Jews and for a different type of education. The book is important for Jewish cultural history since it records customs, living habits, and economic conditions among the Jewish masses, familiar to him as a practicing physician.

BIBLIOGRAPHY: Rejzen, Leksikon, 2 (1927), 345–7; LNYL, 5 (1963), 519ff.; Z. Rejzen, *Fun Mendelssohn biz Mendele* (1923), 83–104; Zinberg, Sifrut, 5 (1959), 98–108.

MARCZALI, HENRIK (1856–1940), Hungarian historian. Marczali was born in Marcali, where his father, Mihály Morgenstern, was rabbi. At the University of Budapest he gained distinction as a lecturer and historical scholar, but because he refused to renounce Judaism, he was denied a full professorship until 1895. Marczali was the first Jew to obtain a chair at Budapest University. He was elected to the Hungarian Academy of Sciences in 1893, but was dismissed from his post in 1924. A historian of the positivist school and a pioneer of source criticism in Hungary, Marczali wrote many works, notably the three-volume *Magyarország története II, József korában* (1885–88; *Hungary in the Eighteenth Century*, 1910); *A magyar történet kútföinek kézikönyve* ("Handbook of the Sources of Hungarian History," 1901); and *Az 1790/1-diki országgyülés* ("The Sessions of the Diet During the Years 1790–91," 1907). Internationally recognized as one of Hungary's outstanding historians, Marczali also edited volumes 2–4 of the *Monumenta Hungariae Judaica* (1937–38).

BIBLIOGRAPHY: G. Szekfű and Z. Tóth, in: IMIT, 65 (1943), 125–37; *Magyar Irodalmi Lexikon*, 2 (1965), 186, includes bibliography; E. Léderer, in: *Századok*, 96 (1962), 440–69.

[Alexander Scheiber]

MARDIN, town in Southeast Turkey; population (2004), 71,100. A Jewish community existed in Mardin from the Middle Ages to the 20th century. In 1291 Abinadab b. Saadiah Halevi of Mardin copied *Maimonides' *Moreh Nevukhim* (*Guide of the Perplexed*) in Arabic. During the middle of the 14th century, a Jew of Mardin named Najīb al-Dawla Abraham b. Yeshu'ah held a government position (Neubauer, Cat, nos. 180, 1249). At the beginning of the 19th century the number of Jews was small, but an ancient synagogue and holy places, such as the so-called Cave of the Prophet Elijah, were preserved. In 1827 the traveler *David D'Beth Hillel found in the town "about six locally born, poor Jewish families with a small synagogue." *Benjamin II relates that in 1848 there were 50 Jewish families, most of whom worked on the land. They spoke Hebrew and their leader was the *nasi* Mu'allim Moses. The number of families remained unchanged during the second half of the century, but the community was dispersed during the 20th century.

BIBLIOGRAPHY: A. Ben-Jacob, *Kehillot Yehudei Kurdistan* (1961), 139. **ADD. BIBLIOGRAPHY:** EIS², 6 (1991), 539–42.

[Abraham Ben-Yaacob]

MARDUK (Heb. מְרֹדָךְ, Jer. 50:2), patron deity of the city of Babylon. Although known as a minor god as early as the third millennium, Marduk became an important local deity at the time of the advent of the First Babylonian Dynasty as can be seen mainly from the literary introduction of the *Hammurapi Stele and other documents. However, he was elevated to the rank of the chief deity and national god of Babylon only during the Middle Babylonian period and especially during the reign of Nebuchadnezzar I (c. 1100 B.C.E.; post-Kassite period) and not, as is commonly assumed, during the reign of Hammurapi (1848–1806 B.C.E.). This can be ascertained from the diffusion during the Old and Middle Babylonian periods of the name Marduk as a component of personal names or as a titular deity in legal and other procedures. Apart from its appearance in Jeremiah 50:2, the name Marduk is found in the Bible in personal names such as *Evil-Merodach and *Merodach-Baladan. In Jeremiah 50:2, the name of Marduk is paralleled by the word *bel* (Heb. בֵּל), a transliteration of the Akkadian attribute of Marduk, *bēlum*, "lord" (Sumerian EN), which he inherited in the second millennium from Enlil, the "former" most powerful god of the Mesopotamian pantheon. (According to the Old Babylonian conception expressed in the introduction to the Hammurapi Code, he received at this time only the *illilūtu*, the governorship of the people, which had formerly rested on Enlil.) The origin of Marduk's name is unknown but there are some suggested etymologies, the most accepted being from Sumerian (A) MAR. UTU (K), "the young bull [or calf] of Samaš [Utu] the Sungod." This explanation was well known in the Babylonian tradition. (For "the 50 names of Marduk" see below.) Another etymology, put forward by Th. Jacobsen, is "the son of the storm" (or "maker of storm"?), Marud(d)uk, which brings the form of his name closer to the Aramaic-Hebrew transliteration. Abusch understands the name to reflect original Sumerian *amar.uda.ak*, meaning "Calf of the Storm," because Marduk was never a solar deity.

Marduk's rise to the status of national god was slow but exceptionally comprehensive. It is very possible that, apart from being an historical process, his elevation was deeply influenced by his connection – not entirely proven – with Enki (Ea), the benevolent god of wisdom, incantations, and the sweet waters of the deep (Sum. ABZU, Akk. *apsû*), from Eridu, the most ancient holy city of Sumer.

This connection with Enki was maintained in the theology and practice of the cult of Marduk, e.g., in his identification with Asalluhi, the son of Enki, active in healing or exorcistic incantations, and in the naming of his temple in Babylon *Esagila* ("the house of the [high] raised head") after that of Enki in Eridu. Thus Marduk emerges as a national and popular god of the "second [younger] generation," who exercises influence in every walk of life as the healer and saviour of the Babylonians. In this capacity he appears in incantations, prayers, hymns, philosophical poems (e.g., *Ludlul bēl nēmeqi*, "Let me praise the God of wisdom," a variant of which was known also in Ugarit, see *Job), and epics such as the *Erra Epic*, where the "disappearance" of Marduk because of displeasure wreaks havoc in the world and brings about the temporary rule of Erra, the god of destruction.

Marduk is the hero of *Enūma eliš* ("When above ..."), the Babylonian creation myth. In this myth the Son of the Storm is appointed by the gods to lead the fight against Tiāmat (Heb תְּהוֹם, "Ocean") who has planned to destroy them. In the struggle between these two personified natural elements, Marduk gains the upper hand. At the end of the didactic-cultic epic the assembly of gods praises Marduk with 50 name-exegeses and builds the *Esagila* in his honor.

Enūma eliš was read aloud in front of Marduk's statue during the *akītu* (New Year; see Klein), Babylonia's most important festival. In these ceremonies the statues of Marduk and his son Nab – (Heb. נְבוֹ) were carried from Marduk's temple in Babylon to the house of the *akītu* festival outside the city walls. The elaborate ritual of this festival, known chiefly from a late (Seleucid) edition, greatly influenced many theories about supposed parallel developments in the Israelite cult (see *Psalms, *Kingship).

The cult and theology of Marduk began its expansion during the renewed expansion of Babylonian culture beyond Babylon in the Middle Babylonian-Assyrian period. Marduk was accepted into the Assyrian royal pantheon after Aššur and other important gods. The Babylonian elaboration of the theology of Marduk, which expressed itself also in speculative identification and the absorption of the functions of other gods into that of Marduk (this was not exclusive to Marduk), as well as the identification of Marduk with the Babylonian national entity, had momentous consequences in that in the course of time Marduk became identified as a symbol of Babylonian resistance to Assyria. The conception of Marduk decisively influenced the cult of Aššur who was also elevated to a parallel or even higher position. Thus, for example, in the Assyrian version of *Enūma eliš*, Aššur takes the place of Marduk. The tension between the two nations resulted in a most decisive dislike of Marduk in the middle of the first millennium. After the "experiments" of *Tiglath-Pileser III and *Sargon, who were kings of Babylon in every respect, came *Sennacherib who during most of his reign was uniformly anti-Babylonian and "anti-Marduk," and who expressed this by destroying Babylon and *Esagila*. The emblems and statues of Marduk went into "captivity" many times. The return of the statue of Marduk, which was always connected with Babylonian resurrection, was interpreted as a theological change of destiny and as a punishment inflicted by Marduk on Babylon's enemies, as in the case of Sennacherib. Thus, this antagonism became a major issue in the entire destiny of the Ancient Near East in the middle of the first millennium. A very striking example of this antagonism is found in an Assyrian satirical, quasi-theological composition (correctly reinterpreted by W. von Soden) which, far from being an "apotheosis" of the "dead and resurrected Marduk" (as was suggested earlier), is a "mock trial" of Marduk ending probably with his "execution," as a god who – from the point of view of the Assyrians and other peoples – caused much enmity and treachery (see below). This trial is a "logical" continuation of that of the god Kingu and of his execution in *Enūma eliš*, where Marduk was the judge.

In the time of the final Assyrian period (Esarhaddon, Ašhurbanipal) and the Neo-Babylonian Dynasty, from Nabopolossar on, and again in the Early Persian period (Cyrus), Marduk was the chief god of Babylon. Because they opposed the oppressive measures of Nabonidus, the last Neo-Babylonian king, the priests of Marduk were those who made possible the peaceful occupation of Babylon by Cyrus (539; see also *Babylon; *Mesopotamia).

Marduk in the West and in the Bible

Marduk is first mentioned in the West (Syria-Palestine) in Akkadian documents from Ugarit (Middle Babylonian period around 1350; see: *Ugaritica*, 5 (1968), 792) where, as mentioned, one version of the philosophical treatise *Ludlul bēl nēmeqi* was known. Also there is an incantation letter against *nambul* ("The Wrong"; "The Bad") directing him to appear before Marduk. The first appearance of Marduk in Palestine occurs in the same period and takes the form of the personal name of Šulum-Marduk in the *el-Amarna letters (EA). According to EA 256:20, as interpreted by Albright (in BASOR, 89 (1943), 12ff.), the royal house at ʿAštartu (the contemporary king being A-ia-ab (= Job)) was called "The House of Šulum-Marduk." (Another reading for "house" is advocated by Moran, 309, but the name Šulum-Marduk remains.) Marduk was known also among the Hittites, and Middle Babylonian cylinder seals dedicated to him have been found at Thebes, Greece. In the first millennium Marduk's name appears in Assyrian and Aramean treaties from Sefire that were concluded with King Matiʾilu of Arpad (COS II, 213). In the Bible, apart from Marduk (see above), Bel (his appellative attribute) together with his son Nab – (see above) is mentioned in Isaiah 46:1 and Jeremiah 51:44. In both these prophecies divine judgment (not the judgment of a "rival" as in the case of Aššur) is pronounced against a symbolic polytheistic entity within the framework of a particular stage in history. The historical placement of these verses is difficult. Nevertheless, the announcement of biblical-prophetic judgment is consistent with the attitude of the other antagonists to Marduk and Babylon, described above.

BIBLIOGRAPHY: S.A. Pallis, *The Babylonian Akîtu Festival* (1926); W.F. Albright, in: BASOR, 89 (1943), 12; E. Dhorme, *Les Religions de Babylonie et d'Assyrie* (1949), 139–50; F.M. Th. Boehl, *Opera Minora* (1953), 282–312; W. von Soden, in: ZA, 51 (1955), 130–66; 53 (1957), 229–34; Pritchard, Texts, 60–72, 331–4; H. Schmoekel, in: *Revue d'assyrologie et d'archéologie orientale*, 53 (1959), 183ff.; H. Tadmor, in: *Eretz-Israel*, 5 (1959), 150–63; W.G. Lambert, in: W.S. McCullough (ed.), *The Seed of Wisdom* (1964), 3–13; B. Meissner, *Die Keilschrift*, ed. by K. Oberhuber (1967), 153–4; Th. Jacobsen, in: JAOS, 88 (1968), 104–8; P. Artzi, in: EM, 5 (1968), 442–5. **ADD. BIBLIOGRAPY:** W. Moran, *The Amarna Letters* (1992); J. Klein, in: ABD, 1:138–40; L. Handy, in: ABD, 4:522–23; T. Abusch, in: DDD, 543–49.

[Pinḥas Artzi and Raphael Kutscher]

MAREK, PESACH (**Piotr**; 1862–1920), historian of Russian Jews and Yiddish folklorist. After completing his law studies at the University of Moscow, Marek was among the founders of the Benei Zion society of the Moscow Zionists in 1884. Among his studies published in the journal **Voskhod* were articles on Jewish printing in Russia (1888), on the history of Moscow's Jews (1893, 1895, 1896), and on the Jewish Community Council of Belorussia (1903). His most important contribution was *Di Yidishe Folkslider in Rusland* ("Yiddish Folk Songs in Russia," 1901), which he compiled with Saul *Ginsburg. This volume laid the foundation for later studies in the field. Marek's sketches for a history of Jewish education in Russia, published in 1909, embraced the period from 1844 to 1873 and dealt with both traditional and secular systems of education. Marek also wrote for Russian-Jewish historical periodicals and was a contributor to the Russian Jewish encyclopedia. Due to the famine he moved to Volsk, Saratov district, and there he finalized his two works "The History of Religious Struggle" in two volumes, and "The History of the Jewish Intelligentsia in Russia."

BIBLIOGRAPHY: Rejzen, Leksikon, 2 (1927), 338–42; LNYL, 5 (1963), 504–5.

[Yehuda Slutsky]

MARESHAH (Heb. מָרֵשָׁה, Marissa), city in Judah connected with the families of Shelah and Caleb (I Chron. 2:42; 4:21). It was in the fourth district of the territory of the tribe of Judah (Josh. 15:44). Mareshah was one of the cities fortified by Rehoboam (II Chron. 11:8–9). It was the home town of the prophet Eliezer the son of Dodavahu (II Chron. 20:37) and possibly also of the prophet Micah (Micah 1:1; Jer. 26:18). In Persian or Hellenistic times, a Sidonian colony settled there and it served as an administrative center (Zeno Pap.

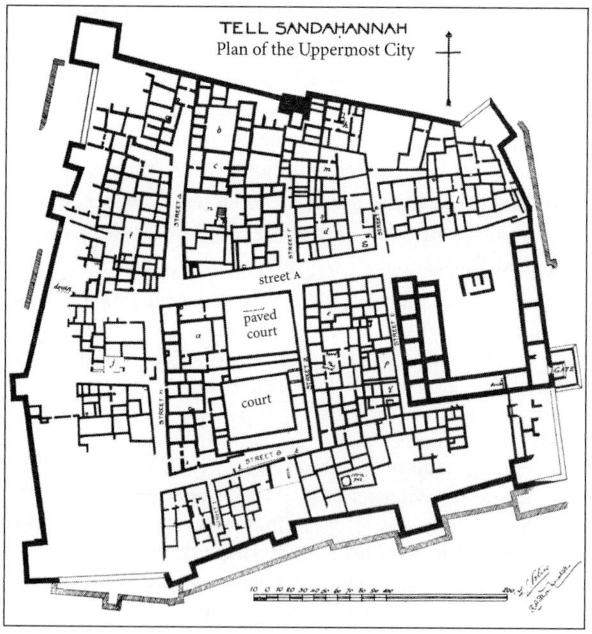

Plan of the Hellenistic city of Mareshah, dating from the second century B.C.E. *From F. J. Bliss and R. A. S. Macalister,* Excavations in Palestine, *London, 1902.*

59006, 59015, 59537). Its population, however, was mostly Edomite, and as such, Mareshah served as a base for the Seleucid armies at war with Judah Maccabee, who ravaged its territory (I Macc. 5:66; II Macc. 12:35). John Hyrcanus conquered it with the rest of Idumea and it remained in Hasmonean possession until Pompey. In 40 B.C.E., shortly after its "liberation" by Pompey, the Parthians completely destroyed it (Jos., Ant., 12:353; 14:75, 364; Wars, 1:269). After the destruction of the city, Bet *Guvrin became the center of the region. Robinson identified it with Tell Ṣandaḥanna, south of Bet Guvrin. Bliss and Macalister, excavating there in 1900, uncovered the Hellenistic stratum, which contained a city wall nearly square in plan (measurements, at its widest points: 520 ft. (156 m.) wide from east to west; 500 ft. (150 m.) wide from north to south). Inside, the town was laid out in the so-called Hippodamic plan, with streets intersecting at right angles. This plan was slightly distorted at a later stage of the town's existence. In the eastern part of the town were a marketplace and a temple. Ptolemaic inscriptions, pottery, and execration texts on limestone tablets were the main finds. In 1902, Hellenistic tombs with paintings and inscriptions were found near Mareshah. The principal tomb is decorated with representations of real and mythological animals; the inscriptions are of one Apollophanes, head of the Sidonians at Mareshah, and his family. The tomb was used from the second to the first century B.C.E. and the inscriptions indicate a gradual assimilation of the Sidonians into the Idumean and Jewish populations there. Other tombs of similar character were found in 1925 and 1962.

[Michael Avi-Yonah]

Later Excavations

Excavations undertaken in the 1980s and 1990s by the Israel Antiquities Authority under A. Kloner's direction uncovered many underground installations quarried in the limestone bedrock (oil presses, columbaria, tombs, and a sanctuary) connected to villas of the Lower City surrounding the tel (acropolis). The exploration of the largest (northwestern) tower of the Hellenistic fortification of the acropolis showed that it was inserted inside the glacis of the Persian period fortification, which, itself, modified the Iron Age II wall (of the eighth century B.C.E.). Its construction is dated to the turn of the third–second century, at the time of the Seleucid conquest of the area over the Ptolemies. An outer wall (*proteichisma*) surrounded the bottom of the tel, and an insula of the Lower City, attached to its face, consisted of a network of shops, with some craft installations, and dwellings above them. The Lower City was probably built under Antiochus IV (according to the so-called Hippodamic plan), but limited activities took place there already in the Iron Age, Persian, and Early Hellenistic periods. The rich finds comprised local and imported wares, among which the amphoras are evidence for the relation of the Levant with the main production centers of wine, oil, and probably fish products of all the Mediterranean, especially in the second half of the second century B.C.E. (Asia Minor, the Aegean, the Black Sea, Italy, and North Africa). Many ostraca were also found, including the copy of a wedding contract between Idumean families, written in Aramaic. The chronological distribution of the coins and the Rhodian amphora stamps provides a refinement of the historical events. The consequences of the destruction by Judah Maccabee lasted until the second half of the second century B.C.E., when a significant revival of the activities is evidenced by the discovery of an inscribed standard of measures, *in situ* inside a shop, made under the responsibility of two agoranomes in 143/2 B.C.E. The war of the Seleucid brothers Antiochus VIII and Antiochus IX initiated the decline of the city, the wealth of which was based on trade and agricultural production (oil and cereals), and in connection with the nearby port of Ascalon. The entrances of some of the houses were sealed, evidence for abandonment at the time of the conquest by John Hyrcanus, who did not destroy the city. The conquest took place probably in two stages: the first right after 113/2 B.C.E. – as evidenced by a funerary inscription and a hidden hoard of silver coins from Ascalon, both dating to that same year – and then around 108/7 B.C.E. – as evidenced by the last series of many inscribed lead weights, endorsed by the agoranome of that same year. This latter stage was most likely followed by the conversion of the inhabitants who remained in Idumea. The reduced occupation under the Hasmoneans seems evidenced by the two *mikva'ot* uncovered on the acropolis by Bliss and Macalister. The re-foundation by Gabinius in 57–55 B.C.E. was marked by the mint of coins under his name in Mareshah. However, no material evidence dates to the period of the Parthian destruction, in 40 B.C.E. Maresha appears to have been an Idumean city administered according to the Greek tradition (*polis*). This is strengthened by the recent discovery of a fragment of a civic inscription on stone, the first of its kind in the whole Southern Levant.

[Gerald Finkielsztejn (2nd ed.)]

BIBLIOGRAPHY: F.J. Bliss and R.A.S. Macalister, *Excavations in Palestine* (1902), 52ff; 204ff.; J.P. Peters and H. Thiersch, *Painted Tombs in the Necropolis of Marissa* (1905); F.M. Abel, RB, 34 (1925), 267–75; E. Oren, *Archaeology*, 18 (1965), 218–24. **ADD. BIBLIOGRAPHY:** G. Finkielsztejn, *Bulletin of the Anglo Israel Archaeological Society*, 16 (1998), 33–63; A. Kloner (ed.), *Maresha Excavations Final Report 1. Subterranean Complexes 21, 44, 70. IAA Reports*, 17 (2003), especially 157–62.

MARGALIOT (Margulies), MORDECAI (1909–1968), scholar of midrashic and geonic literature. Margaliot was born in Warsaw and immigrated to Palestine as a child; he studied at the Mizrachi Teachers' Seminary in Jerusalem and he was one of the first graduates of the Hebrew University. He taught rabbinical literature at the Hebrew University 1950–57, and from 1958 midrashic and geonic literature at the Jewish Theological Seminary in New York.

In 1938 he published a scholarly edition of *Ha-Ḥillukim she-Bein Anshei Mizraḥ u-Venei Ereẓ Yisrael* ("Differences in Religious Customs Between Babylonian and Palestinian Jewries"), a small compilation, which in his view was written in Palestine about the year 700 C.E. This was followed in 1942 by an edition of *Halakhot Keẓuvot* ascribed to *Yehudai Gaon, which, according to Margaliot, was composed in southern Italy in the middle of the ninth century.

He also edited *Midrash ha-Gadol* on Genesis (1947) and Exodus (1956); *Hilkhot ha-Nagid* (1962), on Samuel ha-Nagid as halakhist, and *Sefer ha-*Razim* (1966), a treatise on magic from the talmudic period, which he reconstructed from fragments found in various libraries. This work provided new, important insights into Jewish magic and mysticism. His major work was a critical edition of *Midrash Va-Yikra Rabbah*, 5 vols. (1953–60), which is considered to be a model of critical editing of a midrashic text. Margaliot also contributed to scholarly publications and was the editor of two popular biographical dictionaries, one on the sages of the Talmud and the *geonim*, *Enẓiklopedyah le-Ḥakhmei ha-Talmud ve-ha-Ge'onim*, 2 vols. (1946), and the other of later rabbinical scholars, *Enẓiklopedyah le-Toledot Gedolei Yisrael*, 4 vols. (1946–50).

Margaliot's wife Rachel wrote *Eḥad Hayah Yeshayahu* (1954, 1956²), a defense of the unity of the Book of Isaiah.

BIBLIOGRAPHY: Tidhar, 4 (1950), 1720–21; 17 (1968), 5247; Kressel, Leksikon, 2 (1967), 419–20.

[Tovia Preschel]

MARGALIOT, REUBEN (1889–1971), rabbinic scholar and author. Born in Lemberg (Lvov), Margaliot qualified as a rabbi, but remained in business, eventually as a bookseller. Having been active in the Mizrachi movement in Lvov, he settled in Israel in 1935, becoming librarian of the Rambam Library in Tel Aviv. He devoted several studies to ḥasidic lore such as *Or ha-Me'ir* and *Marganita de-R. Meir* (1926, 1964); and *Hillula de-Ẓaddikaya* (1929, 1961). At a later stage he turned to Kabbalah, producing a monumental annotated edition of the Zohar (1964⁴), of the *Tikkunei Zohar* (1948), of M.Ḥ. Luzzatto's *Zohar Ḥadash* (1953), and of the early kabbalistic work *Sefer ha-Bahir* (1951). He also wrote *Sha'arei Zohar* (1956), a comparative study of the Zohar's system. Margaliot also wrote on the *Emden-*Eybeschuetz controversy and received a reply from G. Scholem (1941).

Earlier he had also published sermons and homiletical material and annotations to Ḥayyim b. Moses *Attar's pentateuchal commentary *Ner la-Ma'or* (1932, 1959). He wrote biographies of S. Edels (1912); of Ḥayyim b. Moses Attar (1925); of Maimonides' son Abraham (1930), whose *Milḥamot Adonai* he published in 1953; as well as *Le-Toledot Anshei Shem bi-Lvov* (1950), on the scholars of his native city. On Talmud and *halakhah* Margaliot wrote among others *Margaliyyot ha-Yam* (novellae on tractate *Sanhedrin*, 1958) and *Nefesh Ḥayyah* on the Shulḥan Arukh *Oraḥ Ḥayyim* (1954²). Of special interest is a study of the halakhic aspects of a political resettlement of Ereẓ Israel (*Kavvei Or*, 1921) written under the impact of the Balfour Declaration. Among halakhic studies in a more modern vein and idiom are his *Yesod ha-Mishnah va-Arikhatah* ("Foundations of the Mishnah and Its Redaction," 1956⁴); and *Meḥkarim be-Darkhei ha-Talmud* ("Studies in Talmudic Methodology," 1967). Also of importance are his editions of medieval texts, particularly his annotated *Sefer Ḥasidim*, attributed to Judah b. Samuel (12th century), first published in 1924 and republished many times since. Margaliot also prepared an edition of the responsa of the tosafist *Jacob of Marvège (*She'elot u-Teshuvot min ha-Shamayim*, 1957³); of the disputations of Naḥmanides with Pablo Christiani in Barcelona in 1263 (with a biography of Naḥmanides, 1929); and of Jehiel of Paris of 1240 (1928, 1944). He received the Israel Prize in 1957 for his research on Kabbalah and Ḥasidism.

BIBLIOGRAPHY: Kressel, Leksikon, 2 (1967), 421–3.

MARGALIT, DAN (1938–), Israeli journalist. Margalit graduated from the Hebrew University of Jerusalem and entered journalism in 1960 working at *Ha-Olam ha-Zeh*, a satirical political news magazine put out by Uri *Avneri, and then at *La-Ishah*, the women's magazine. In 1964 he joined *Haaretz* covering political and parliamentary affairs, first as a Knesset reporter covering parliamentary committees and later as a political columnist. In 1977, as the paper's Washington correspondent, he disclosed that Leah Rabin had an illegal foreign bank account, the disclosure of which resulted in the fall of the Rabin government and elections which brought the Likud to power for the first time. Well connected to the country's political leaders, in the 1980s Margalit began a parallel career as host of Education Television's *New Evening* daily interview program on current affairs, and in the 1990s as host of *Po-Politika* (later *Politika* on Israel's Channel 2), a round-table talk show in front of a live audience on topical issues. The program, while earning high ratings, often got out of hand as participants tried to outshout one another. An endearing but probing style made Margalit a popular and controversial interviewer. In 2004, following differences with the Channel 2 management, he moved to Channel 10 to present a similar program, *Politika-Plus*. In 2001 he left *Haaretz* for *Maariv* as op-ed editor and political columnist, after having served briefly in 1992 as *Maariv*'s editor following its purchase by Ofer *Nimrodi.

[Yoel Cohen (2nd ed.)]

MARGALIT, MEIR (1906–1974), actor. Born in Ostroleka, Poland, Margalit immigrated to Ereẓ Israel in 1921 and worked as a laborer in the *Gedud ha-Avodah. He began to appear on the stage as an amateur in his school days and was a member of the drama circle of the Gedud formed by Manya Arnon. He joined the Ohel studio established by the Cultural Committee and became one of its first members when it became the *Ohel theater. In his long acting career he played leading roles. He received the Israel Prize for arts in 1964.

MARGARETEN, REGINA (1862–1959), pioneer in the American kosher food industry. Born in Miskolc, Hungary, Margareten came to the United States with her husband, father, mother, and four brothers in 1884. Out of the small bakery the family opened on the Lower East Side of Manhattan came Horowitz Brothers & Margareten, which continues to manufacture matzot, noodles, and other kosher products. Regina Margareten took over management of the business after her father's death in 1885 and achieved further authority after her husband's death in 1924. As of her 95th birthday she continued her daily work as treasurer and a director of the company located in Long Island City, Queens. Her 1957 birthday celebration included some 400 family members from all over the world, including children, grandchildren, great-grandchildren, and great-great-grandchildren. A philanthropist, Margareten was active in over 100 institutions. She was president of Daughters of Zion for over 50 years. Upon her death in 1959 the faculty, the Board of Directors, and students of Yeshiva Torah Vodaath and Mesivta called her "a noble woman whose long lifetime of good deeds provided a model for all Jewry" (*New York Times*, Jan. 19, 1959).

[Sara Alpern (2nd ed.)]

MARGARITA (Margalita), ANTON (b. c. 1490), apostate and anti-Jewish writer. Although the son of a rabbi, Samuel son of Jacob *Margolioth of Regensburg, while he was still a Jew, denounced the Regensburg community to the authorities. He converted to Catholicism in 1522, and later became a Protestant. He was a lecturer in Hebrew at Augsburg, Meissen Zell, Leipzig, and from 1537 until his death, at Vienna University. In his first anti-Jewish book, *Der Gantz Juedisch Glaub...* (first published in Augsburg, 1530), Margarita modeled himself on similar writings by the apostates Johannes *Pfefferkorn and Victor von *Carben. In an attempt to ridicule the religious precepts of the Jews, their customs, and their habits, he accused them of lacking charity, of reviling Christianity (in the *Aleinu prayer), and finally of treason. The large number of Jewish prayers in his own translation included in the book reveal his ignorance of Jewish writings (as noted by Johann *Wagenseil in his Latin translation of tractate *Sotah* (Altdorf, 1674), 1105) and his scanty knowledge of Hebrew. The book formed the basis of a religious disputation between *Joseph (Joselmann) b. Gershom of Rosheim and Margarita held at the Diet of Augsburg of 1530 at the instance of Emperor *Charles v. When Joseph of Rosheim succeeded in proving that the apostate's allegations were unfounded, Margarita was imprisoned and later banished from Augsburg. However, his book was reprinted many times (Frankfurt, 1544, 1561, 1689; Leipzig, 1705, 1713) and was widely read. It particularly influenced Martin *Luther, who quoted it many times in his *Von den Juden und ihren Luegen*. Margarita was also the author of *Dar Muschiach Schon Khomen* (1534).

BIBLIOGRAPHY: Wolf, Bibliotheca, 1 (1715), 202–4; 3 (1727), 129–30; 4 (1733), 789; G. Wolf, *Studien zur Jubelfeier der Wiener Universitaet* (1865), 28–29; L. Geiger, in: ZGJD, 2 (1888), 324–5; H. Breslau, *ibid.*, 5 (1892), 310–2; A. Fuerst, *Christen und Juden* (1892), 191; J. Mieses, *Die aelteste gedruckte deutsche Uebersetzung des juedischen Gebetbuches... und ihr Autor Anton Margalita* (1916); Graetz, Hist, 4 (1949), 551; Baron, Social², 13, 223ff.; Josef Ish Rosheim, *Sefer ha-Minḥah* (1920), introd., 25ff.

[Bernard Suler]

MARGET, ARTHUR W. (1899–1962), U.S. economist. Born in Chelsea, Massachusetts, after serving with the U.S. army during World War I he taught at Harvard and at the University of Minnesota. In World War II he again joined the armed forces and rose to the rank of lieutenant colonel. After the war he was chief of the finance and economic division of the United States element of the Allied Commission for Austria and during 1947–48 was chief of the United States finance division in Paris. In 1950 he joined the Board of Governors of the Federal Reserve System in Washington and became the director of its international finance division. In 1961 he resigned and went to Guatemala as regional adviser to the State Department's Agency for International Development. His major publication is *The Theory of Prices*, 2 vols. (1938–42).

[Joachim O. Ronall]

MARGHITA (Hung. **Margitta**, also **Margita**; referred to by the Jews as מארגארעטען (**Margaretten**)), town in Transylvania, W. Romania. Until the end of World War I and between 1940 and 1945 it formed part of Hungary. Jews began to settle there during the 18th century. A geographical-historical description of Hungary which was published in 1799 mentions Jewish inhabitants among the Hungarians and Romanians. The first Jewish settlers appear to have come from the neighboring village Petra. A community headed by a rabbi has probably existed by the close of the 18th century. The synagogue was erected in 1862. In 1885 the community also became a center for the Jews of the surrounding region. The Jewish population numbered 944 (18% of the total population) in 1900 and 1,623 (26.7%) in 1930.

From its inception the community was an Orthodox one. The influence of Ḥasidism was felt, particularly between the two world wars. The rabbis of the community included R. Joshua Aaron Ẓevi Weinberger, author of the *Mahariaẓ* responsa (first half of the 19th century); his descendants succeeded him in the rabbinical office until the liquidation of the community. For a short period, from 1850, R. Hillel *Lichtenstein was rabbi of the town. The students of the community's yeshivah included some who came from far away, and their numbers occasionally rose to 350. The last rabbi, who perished in the Holocaust, was R. Mordecai Azriel Weinberger; he was also the last head of the yeshivah. A Jewish press functioned in Marghita between the two world wars.

After 1940, when the city was returned to Horthiite Hungary, the Hungarian-speaking local Jews discovered that the official and public attitude towards them had changed, and that Hungarian antisemitism was no better than its Romanian variant, which they had experienced during the interwar period.

At the time of the Holocaust, in the summer of 1944, the local Jews were taken to the district capital of *Oradea-Mare and deported from there to Auschwitz. After the war some Jews returned to the town, numbering about 500 in 1947. Their numbers gradually decreased through emigration to Israel and other countries, so that they were finally reduced to 10 families in 1970 (out of a total population of 12,000), and their number continued to drop, mostly through immigration to Israel and old age.

[Yehouda Marton / Paul Schveiger (2nd ed.)]

MARGO, BORIS (1902–1995), U.S. painter, graphic artist, and educator. Margo taught art at many leading American universities. Born in Wolotschisk, Ukraine, Margo studied at the Polytechnik of Art in Odessa, the Workshop for the Art of the Future (Futemas) in Moscow, and the Analytical School of Art in Leningrad. His wife was the painter and printmaker Jan Gelb. After receiving a degree from the Polytechnik, he worked as a muralist in Montreal and then moved to New York City in 1930. There, he studied and then taught at the Roerich Museum, founded by Russian Nicolas Roerich. For a time, he was artist Arshile Gorky's assistant. In 1943, he attained American citizenship, and worked in New York City and Provincetown, Massachusetts. Early in his career, Margo developed a method of printmaking called *cellocut*, a technique in which celluloid dissolved in acetone is poured onto any smooth support, including brass, aluminum, cardboard, and copper; when solidified the plastic can be worked in various ways, such as scraping and gouging with etching and woodcut tools. Margo often combined cellocut with painting and monoprinting. The titles of an exhibition of his cellocuts at the Brooklyn Museum in 1947 suggested an involvement with science and human achievement: *Yellow Dawn* (1944), *Genetic Field* (1946), and *Radar Outpost* (1947). Like Max Ernst, he applied decalcomania in painting, for example in his work *Enchanted Beach* (1938). In this process, paint on one surface is pressed and transferred to another surface, creating variously shaped and textured patches of pigment. This Surrealist imagery of *Enchanted Beach* depicts a ravaged, apocalyptic landscape, perhaps a reference to the bombed and war-torn landscapes of Germany and England; the composition is strewn with architectural ruins in and around which emerge ill-defined biomorphic shapes in earth-toned colors. However, the reference to magic and water reveals a hope for renewal even in the face of human suffering and devastation. *Enchanted Beach* shares stylistic features with the Surrealist works of Yves Tanguy, Max Ernst, Salvador Dali, Joan Miro, and Arshile Gorky, among others. In the 1950s, Margo's work often featured a thin vertical or horizontal line which possesses both an atmospheric and spiritual quality. Margo founded galleries in Orlando, Florida, and Provincetown, Mass. He received his first solo show at the Artists Gallery, New York, in 1939. Since then, Margo's work has been exhibited in a number of solo and group shows, at the Brooklyn Museum, Betty Parsons Gallery, the Museum of Modern Art, and the Whitney Museum, among other venues. In 1946, he received the Mildred Boericke Purchase Prize, First Award for cellocut print, Philadelphia Print Club. The Brooklyn Museum awarded him a Purchase Print Award in 1947, 1953, 1955, 1960, and 1964. In 1988, he was a recipient of a Pollock-Krasner Foundation Grant. His work is owned by many American museums, including the Museum of Modern Art, the Whitney Museum, the Art Institute of Chicago, and the National Museum of American Art, Washington, D.C.

BIBLIOGRAPHY: *Boris Margo: A Catalogue of His Graphic Work, 1937–1947*, Oct. 9, 1947–Nov. 16, 1947, Brooklyn Museum (1947); M. Herskovic (ed.), *New York School Abstract Expressionists: Artists Choice by Artists: A Complete Documentation of the New York Painting and Sculpture Annuals, 1951–1957* (2000); L. Schmeckebie, *Boris Margo: Graphic Work, 1932–1968, from the Collection of Syracuse University*, with a catalog raisonné by J. Gelb and A. Schmeckebier (1968).

[Nancy Buchwald (2nd ed.)]

MARGOLIES, ISAAC BEN ELIJAH (1842–1887), Polish rabbi and author. Born in Kalvarija, S.W. Lithuania, the son of a rabbi, Margolies devoted himself in his early youth solely to talmudic studies. After his marriage in 1862 to the daughter of a prominent member of the community of Merech in Vilna province, he took up residence there and began to take a keen interest in the Haskalah. This interest aroused the hostility of anti-Haskalah zealots, which, together with reverses in his father-in-law's business, compelled him to seek employment elsewhere. After spending some 15 years as a teacher, particularly in the house of Ezekiel Jaffe in Kovno, Margolies was appointed rabbi of Druskinnikai in Grodno province. There too he was persecuted by the opponents of the Haskalah, and two years later he accepted the invitation of the congregation of Anshei Kalvarija in New York, where he became renowned as a public lecturer and teacher. Margolies is the author of two works, *Ma'oz ha-Talmud* (1869) and *Ma'oz ha-Yam* (1871), in which he uses his outstanding talmudic knowledge to defend the Talmud against its critics. He is also the author of *Sippurei Yeshurun* (1877), an anthology of aggadic and talmudic literature written in a pleasant and easily readable Hebrew. Margolies contributed to the Hebrew periodicals *Ha-Maggid, Ha-Shaḥar, Ha-Meliẓ,* and *Ha-Ẓefrah.*

BIBLIOGRAPHY: *Ha-Asif,* 4 (1887), 72–74 (first pagination); *American Hebrew,* 32 no. 1 (Aug. 12, 1887), 8.

[Anthony Lincoln Lavine]

MARGOLIES, MOSES ZEVULUN (1851–1936), U.S. Orthodox Rabbi. Rabbi Margolies was born in the small Lithuanian city of Meretz, not far from Kovna and Slobodka. On his father's side, he was the grandson of Rabbi Abraham Margolies, chief of the *bet din* of Telshe, and of Rabbi Wolf Altschul, chief of the *bet din* of Lutzan who traced his lineage to Rashi. On his mother's side, he was the grandson of Reb Eliyahu Kroszer, the brother-in-law of the Vilna Gaon. Ordained by his uncle and by Rabbi Yom Tov Lippman Halpern, the rabbi of Bialystok in the year 1876. He served as rabbi of Sloboda for 12 years. In 1889 he was invited to assume the chief rabbinate of Boston. In 1906 he was called to the rabbinate of Congregation Kehilath Jeshurun in New York, a post which he held until his death. His primary occupation was study. The Talmud was always open on the dining room table. He began study at five in the morning and he would make a *siyyum* on the completion of the whole Talmud every year on the yahrzeit of his mother. It meant that he covered seven pages of the Talmud every day. Rabbi Margolies introduced the system which supervised the distribution of kosher meat in New York City. He served as president of the Union of Orthodox Rabbis of the United States and Canada. He founded the New York Kehillah and the Central Relief Committee (later absorbed by the American Jewish Joint Distribution Committee). An early Zionist, Rabbi Margolies was a member of the Mizrachi Organization of America. He also served as president of the Rabbi Isaac Elchanan Yeshiva (which ultimately became Yeshiva University) for several years, presiding over the ordination of a generation of Orthodox rabbis.

Gifted with a sharp and crisp wit, he used it not to entertain people but to drive home a point and to help solve a problem. He was consulted by people of all religious persuasions on both personal matters and communal issues. On one occasion, he was consulted by the impresario Meyer Weisgal who had scheduled a performance of "The Romance of a People" at the Polo Grounds in New York on a Saturday night in late August which coincided with the first *seliḥot* (penitential service). The performance was to start 8:00 in the evening which, at that season of year, would involve violating the Sabbath. Weisgal wanted the rabbi to grant absolution for the Sabbath violation. "Mr. Weisgal," the rabbi responded, "You came to the wrong Moses; I would have to refer you to the original Moses. He was the one who gave us the Sabbath." A wise and witty observation ended the inquiry.

Rabbi Margolies' natural inclination in deciding questions of Jewish law was toward leniency and tolerance. He had the scholarly erudition which enabled him to back up his decisions with abundant halakhic sources. His openness to all brought him into contact with many of the lay and rabbinic leaders of the wider Jewish community. He once shared a platform at a Zionist meeting with Rabbi Stephen S. Wise who was delivering an address. Wise turned to the rabbi and then to the audience and said "Look what Zionism can do. It can bring to the same platform a goy like me and a sage like Rabbi Margolies."

His last public appearance just months before his death was at a Madison Square Garden rally against Hitler's Nuremberg laws. He had to be carried on to the stage. His hands trembled, but his voice never wavered, as he read his message. When he finished, 20,000 people rose to their feet in reverence and appreciation. He was known to many as the RaMaZ (an acronym for Rabbi Moses Zevulun). The Ramaz School in New York was established one year after his passing in 1937 by his grandson, Rabbi Joseph H. *Lookstein and Congregation Kehilath Jeshurun. It was named for him as an everlasting memorial to a giant of scholarship and leadership in the Jewish community.

[Haskel Lookstein (2nd ed.)]

MARGOLIN, ANNA (pseudonym of **Rosa Lebensboym**; 1887–1952), Yiddish poet and journalist. Born into a maskilic family in Brest-Litovsk, Belorussia, Margolin studied in the Odessa Jewish gymnasium. She came to the United States for the first time in 1906 and, working as a secretary for the philosopher Dr. Chaim *Zhitlowsky, began to publish in the Yiddish press. Subsequently, as secretary for the Yiddish anarchist newspaper *Di Fraye Arbeter Shtime*, she published short stories under the pseudonym Khava Gros. She lived in London, Paris, and Warsaw (1910–11). After she married the writer Moyshe Stanvski, the couple immigrated to Palestine, but the marriage was short-lived, and, after she bore a son, she left her husband, returning first to Warsaw, and then, in 1914, to New York. As a writer and editor for the Yiddish newspaper *Der Tog*, Margolin wrote a weekly column, "In der Froyen-Velt" ("In the World of Women") under her own name, as well as articles under the pseudonym Clara Levin. In 1919 she married the Yiddish poet Reuben *Iceland. She began to write poems under the pseudonym Anna Margolin in 1921, which she published in the prominent Yiddish papers and literary journals of the day in New York, Warsaw, and other Yiddish centers. She published a single volume of her own poems, *Lider* ("Poems," 1929) and edited an anthology, *Dos Yidishe Lid in Amerike* ("The Yiddish Poem in America," 1923). Her poems received the warmest acclaim from her contemporary Yiddish critics. Both then and now, Margolin has been perceived as the quintessential modernist woman poet. Poems in English translation appeared in: Leftwich, *The Golden Peacock*; I. Howe and E. Greenberg (eds.), *A Treasury of Yiddish Poetry* (1969); I. Howe et al. (eds.), *Penguin Book of Modern Yiddish Verse*

(1987); M. Kay et al. (eds.), *The Tribe of Dina: A Jewish Women's Anthology* (1989); A. Kramer (ed.), *A Century of Yiddish Poetry* (1989); R. Whitman (ed.), *An Anthology of Modern Yiddish Poetry: Bilingual Edition* (1995); J. Chametzky et al. (eds.), *Jewish American Literature: A Norton Anthology* (2001).

BIBLIOGRAPHY: Rejzen, Leksikon, 2 (1927), 209–12; LNYL, 5 (1963), 478–80; A. Novershtern, in: Anna Margolin, *Lider* (1991), v–lviii; S. Swartz, in: P. Hyman and D.D. Moore (eds.), *Jewish Women in America: An Historical Encyclopedia*, 2 (1997), 891–2; A. Norich, in: *ibid.*, 1526–9; K. Hellerstein, in: *Prooftexts*, 20 (2000), 191–205.

[Kathryn Hellerstein (2nd ed.)]

MARGOLIN, ARNOLD (1877–1956), Ukrainian lawyer. Born in Kiev, the son of a rich sugar manufacturer, Margolin was well-known for his role in pogrom trials, and especially in the *Beilis case. He was disbarred for his stand against the czarist court authorities but his rights were restored after the revolution. After M. *Mandelstamm's death in 1912, Margolin became, together with Dr. I. Jochelman, the leader of the Territorialist Organization in Russia (see *Territorialism). In 1918 he was appointed associate justice of the highest Ukrainian court, and later deputy minister of foreign affairs in the Ukrainian government. Although he resigned in March 1919 after the *Proskurov pogrom, he nevertheless defended the *Petlyura government, considering that the pogroms were perpetrated only by the Black Hundreds (see *Union of Russian People) and other agitators. In 1919 he became the diplomatic representative of the Ukrainian government in England, and in 1922 he left London for the United States, where he was a journalist and lecturer. He was admitted to the bar association of Massachusetts in 1929 and to that of Washington, D.C., in 1936. Margolin wrote several books, among them *Ukraina i politika antanty* ("Ukraine and the Policy of Entente," 1922), *The Jews of Eastern Europe* (1926), and *From a Political Diary* (1946).

BIBLIOGRAPHY: E. Tcherikower, *Di Ukrainer Pogromen in Yor 1919* (1965), 186–9; J. Frumkin (ed.), *Russian Jewry* (1966), 164, 199.

MARGOLIN, ELIEZER (1874–1944), one of the commanders of the *Jewish Legion during World War I. Born in Belgorod, Russia, Margolin settled in Ereẓ Israel with his family in 1892 and lived in Reḥovot. He was outstanding in agricultural labor and in affairs of self-defense. With the death of his parents and the difficult economic situation in the country, he went to Australia in 1900 and worked in agriculture and trade there. During World War I he joined the Australian army. He was noted for his heroism on the Gallipoli front (1915–16) and became acquainted with Vladimir *Jabotinsky and the volunteers of the Zion Mule Corps from Ereẓ Israel. He was transferred to the French front under the command of General *Monash and achieved the rank of lieutenant colonel. Jabotinsky met with him in London and offered him the command of the Second Battalion of the Jewish Regiment, which consisted mostly of Jewish volunteers that had arrived from the U.S. and Canada, the 49th Royal Fusiliers (among its members were Izhak *Ben-Zvi and David *Ben-Gurion). Margolin accepted the offer and, with the agreement of the military authorities, arrived in Palestine in the summer of 1918 as commander of the battalion. He also cultivated friendly relations with the Ereẓ Israel volunteers of the third battalion of the Jewish Legion, disregarding the norms of military hierarchy. His battalion broke through the Turkish front on the Jordan River and captured the Transjordanian town of Salt, of which he was made military governor.

In December 1919, when the Legion was officially given its Jewish name, First Judeans, with the seven-branched *menorah* as its symbol, Margolin became its commander. Margolin constantly struggled against the hostile attitude toward the Legion of the British military command and military authorities in Palestine. But his sense of order could not be gainsaid; he never revealed his deep relationship to the *yishuv* and the first nucleus of its self-defense network to the outside world. With the riots that broke out in Palestine in the spring of 1920, the armed legionnaires were dispersed, with Margolin's knowledge, throughout the Arab villages, an act that prevented further bloodshed. Margolin argued with his superior officers for his right to command the Legion in this manner, an attitude that was not usually accepted in military circles.

With the gradual dismantling of the Legion, the British Military High Command decided to establish the Palestine Defense Force, composed of a Jewish and an Arab unit. Margolin was destined to be the commander of the Jewish unit (March 1921). Riots again broke out in Jerusalem and Tel Aviv-Jaffa (spring of 1921), and on May 1 Joseph *Brenner and his friends were killed. Jewish legionnaires, including discharged ones, took arms out from the military camp in Sarafand without Margolin's knowledge and used them to stop the riots. Margolin arrived in Tel Aviv on May 2, mobilized both in-service and discharged soldiers, and provided them with arms from the military stores. This act served as a pretext to abandon the plan of the Palestine Defense Force and finally disband the Legion. Margolin resigned from the army, rather than face a court martial, returned to Australia, and went into business. Throughout his life he longed to return to Ereẓ Israel. In 1950 his remains were transferred to Israel and reinterred in Reḥovot. A childhood friend from Reḥovot, the Hebrew author Moshe *Smilansky, described Eliezer Margolin in one of his stories, named after the Arab and Bedouin nickname for him, "Ḥawaja Nazar."

BIBLIOGRAPHY: Tidhar, 5 (1952), 2324–25; M. Smilansky, *Mishpaḥat ha-Adamah*, 3 (1951), 167–76; B. Dinur (ed.), *Sefer Toledot ha-Haganah*, 1–2 (1954–63), index; Ever Hadani, *Am be-Milḥamto* (1953³), 178–81; E. Gilner, *War and Hope: A History of the Jewish Legion* (1969), index.

[Getzel Kressel]

MARGOLIN, JULIJ (1900–1971), Israeli publicist, writing in Hebrew and Russian. Born in Pinsk (Belorussia), the son of a physician, Margolin spent his youth there and in the Ukraine. After World War I, he studied philosophy in Berlin. In 1936 he settled in Tel Aviv with his family and worked as a writer and journalist. However, when on a private visit to Poland in the summer of 1939, he was arrested by the advancing Russians after the outbreak of World War II and sentenced to five years in labor camps for alleged infringement of passport regulations. Margolin wrote three works in the labor camps: *The Theory of the Lie, The Doctrine of Hate*, and *On Liberty*, but they were discovered during a search of his effects before his release and were destroyed.

After his return to Ereẓ Israel in 1947, Margolin wrote a factual account of his horrifying experiences; this was one of the most detailed reports published until then on conditions in Soviet labor camps. The book first appeared in a French translation under the title *La Condition Inhumaine*, and later in New York in the Russian original, and in 1968 in a German edition.

In Israel, Margolin worked for various periodicals. He founded an Israel Association of Former Prisoners of Soviet Labor Camps and during his last years he was involved in various activities in support of Jewish emigration from Soviet Russia. He also wrote *A Tale of Millenia: A Condensed History of the Jewish People*, which appeared posthumously with a foreword by Michael Zand.

BIBLIOGRAPHY: E. Gottgetreu, in: *Allgemeine Juedische Wochenzeitung* (Feb. 12, 1972); H. Reichmann, *To the Memory of a Friend* (Russian, 1971).

[Erich Gottgetreu (2nd ed.)]

MARGOLIN, MOSES (1862–?), Zionist writer. After completing his studies at the University of St. Petersburg, Margolin was appointed secretary of the editorial board of the Russian *Entsiklopedicheskiy Slovar* ("Encyclopedic Dictionary") of Brockhaus-Efron and of several other Russian encyclopedias. He was active in Jewish public life, in the *Society for the Promotion of Culture among the Jews of Russia, the *Jewish Colonization Association, and other organizations. In 1904 he was one of the editors of the Russian-language Zionist newspaper, *Yevreyskaya Zhizn*. In his studies in Jewish history Margolin attempted to demonstrate the legitimacy of the historic development of the Jewish people. He deals with this in *Osnovye techeniya v istorii yevreyskago naroda* ("Basic Trends in the History of the Jewish People," 1900, 1917[2]) and in *Yevreyskaya zemlya* ("A Jewish Land," 1918). Under the Soviet regime Margolin belonged to the small group of Jewish intellectuals who attempted to continue their research work in Jewish history; he contributed until 1930 to the publications which these circles published. No information about his subsequent fate is known.

[Yehuda Slutsky]

MARGOLIOT, MOSES BEN SIMEON (d. 1781), Lithuanian rabbi and commentator on the Jerusalem Talmud. Margoliot was born in Kedziniai, near Kovno, Lithuania. His pupils included *Elijah of Vilna, then a boy of seven. Margoliot served as rabbi in several communities in the Samogitia region of Lithuania.

His main claim to fame rests on his important commentary on the Jerusalem Talmud, to all intents and purposes the first of its kind. His commentary is divided into two parts: *Penei Moshe*, an explanation of the text; and *Mareh ha-Panim* which gives the parallel passages in the Babylonian Talmud, and attempts to explain the differences between the two with regard to both text and content. Only part of his commentary, to the order *Nashim* (Amsterdam, 1754), and to the order *Nezikin* and the tractate *Niddah* (Leghorn, 1770), was printed with the text in his lifetime. His commentaries to the remaining tractates were published after his death (to *Berakhot*, Leghorn, 1785?) and the full commentary was not published until 80 years after his death, together with the text of the Talmud (Zhitomir, 1860–67). It has become the standard commentary on the Jerusalem Talmud and has been printed in almost every edition, affording ample evidence of Margoliot's vast erudition in Talmud and rabbinic literature as a whole. He paid careful attention to problems of the text, and had at his disposal many early manuscripts. He was the first to realize the vital importance of the Tosefta for an understanding of the Jerusalem Talmud, and he had an ancient manuscript of it which was superior to the printed text of his day both in completeness and accuracy. Margoliot also endeavored to acquire the knowledge of the natural sciences requisite for a proper understanding of the Jerusalem Talmud. In 1779, when he was nearly 70 years of age, his name is found among the students enrolled in the botanical department of the University of Frankfurt on the Oder. His interest in botany was undoubtedly due to his desire better to understand the agricultural laws in Ereẓ Israel found in the order of *Zera'im* in the Jerusalem Talmud, but to which there is no *Gemara* in the Babylonian.

Margoliot's commentary is one of the two standard commentaries on the Jerusalem Talmud, of much greater importance than that of David *Fraenkel, and has become indispensable to the student. From his introduction to the commentary, it is clear that he wandered from country to country. For several years he served as a rabbi in Amsterdam, during which time his commentary to the order *Nashim* was printed. He was in London for some time before 1754, and was in Leghorn when his commentary to the order *Nezikin* was published there. The statement by Joshua Heschel *Lewin in his book *Aliyyot Eliyahu*, 28 that Margoliot traveled to Vilna after the publication of his commentary to *Nashim*, and there met R. Elijah of Vilna, must be regarded with reservation, because the latter never saw his commentary. In his commentary, Margoliot mentioned two of his works: *Be'er Mayim Ḥayyim*, a commentary to the tractates *Shabbat* and *Eruvin*, and *Penei ha-Menorah*, on the Pentateuch. He died in Brody, Galicia.

BIBLIOGRAPHY: Gelber, in: JJLG, 13 (1920), 132; Lewin, *ibid.*, 15 (1923), 92–94; L. Ginzberg (Ginzburg), *Perushim ve-Ḥiddushim ba-Yerushalmi*, 1 (1941), 55–58 (Eng. introd.).

[Abraham David]

MARGOLIOTH (**Margoliouth**, **Margulies**, **Margolies**, and various other spellings), family that traditionally traces its descent from *Rashi. The name derives from *margalit* (מרגלית), Hebrew for "pearl." The earliest identifiable member of the family was Jacob of Regensburg (see Jacob *Margolioth). Jacob's son Samuel may be identical with SAMUEL MARGOLIOTH, nominated elder of Great Poland and Masovian Jewry in 1527 by Sigismund I. Samuel's son was Anton *Margarita, the apostate anti-Jewish writer. Another son, MOSES (1540?–1616), was rabbi at Cracow and head of the yeshivah there. NAPHTALI MARGOLIOTH (b. 1562) embraced Christianity in 1603, as Julius Conrad Otto. He became professor of Hebrew at Altdorf and later returned to Judaism. Samuel's grandson MENDEL (d. 1652), rabbi at *Przemysl, had eight sons, all distinguished talmudists. The most outstanding member of this line, which was widely dispersed throughout Eastern Europe, was EPHRAIM ZALMAN *MARGOLIOTH. There was a MOSES MARGULIES among the first inhabitants of the Vienna ghetto, founded in 1620. His son, MORDECAI (Marx Schlesinger), was leader of the Vienna community at the time of the 1670 expulsion. Some members of the family settled permanently in Eisenstadt. Those who later returned to Vienna called themselves Margulies-Jaffe and registered themselves as "Schlesinger."

BIBLIOGRAPHY: J. Mieses, *Die aelteste gedruckte deutsche Uebersetzung des juedischen Gebetbuches aus dem Jahre 1530…* (1916); B. Wachstein, *Die Grabschriften des alten Judenfriedhofs in Eisenstadt* (1922); L. Loewenstein, *Geschichte der Juden in der Kurpfalz* (1895), 93.

MARGOLIOTH, EPHRAIM ZALMAN BEN MENAHEM MANNES (1760–1828), rabbi and author. Ephraim studied under his uncle, Alexander Margolioth, rabbi of Satanov, Isaac of Ostrow, author of *Berit Kehunnat Olam*, and Ezekiel *Landau. In his youth he was rabbi of Ohanov, but later left the rabbinate, according to some reports declining an offer of the rabbinate of Frankfurt. Ephraim settled in Brody and went into business, in which he was highly successful. He owned commercial establishments in Vienna and it was said of him: "From the time of the minister Saul *Wahl there has not been Torah and wealth such as belong to Margolioth." He spent most of his time in study, leaving the conduct of his business to his partner Simeon Dishze. He also studied esoteric works with a group of kabbalists at Brody, and had a sound knowledge of history. Margolioth wrote many books and exchanged responsa with the greatest rabbis of his time, with some of whom he maintained close relations. He was involved in the controversy caused by Joshua Heshel *Ẓoref's book *Ha-Ẓoref* and established the fact that it had strong leanings toward Shabbateanism. He also contended with the communal leaders of Brody over the leniency extended to the wealthy *parnasim* under the prevailing system of communal taxation and demanded their full participation in community expenditure.

Margolioth gave his approbation to a great number of books, including many by ḥasidic rabbis. His own works, which appeared in many editions, and many of his halakhic decisions have been accepted.

His works include *Beit Efrayim*, part 1 entitled *Peri Tevu'ah*, with commentary *Rosh Efrayim* (Lemberg, 1809); part 2 Shulḥan Arukh, *Yoreh De'ah* (*ibid.*, 1810); responsa *Beit Efrayim* (*ibid.*, 1818); and another collection of responsa *Beit Efrayim* (Brody, 1866); *Shem Efrayim*, on Rashi's commentary to the Pentateuch and *haftarot* (Ostrow, 1826); *Zera Efrayim* on the *Pesikta Rabbati* (Lemberg, 1853); *Yad Efrayim*, on Shulḥan Arukh, *Oraḥ Ḥayyim* (in Dubno ed. of Shulḥan Arukh, *Oraḥ Ḥayyim*, 1820). He also wrote *Ma'alot ha-Yuḥasin*, a genealogical book on the families Landau, Margolioth, etc. (Lemberg, 1900). R. Ẓevi Hirsch *Chajes of Zolkiew was among his pupils.

BIBLIOGRAPHY: J.A. Kamelhar, *Dor De'ah*, 2 (1928), 145–9; Rubinstein, in: *Hadorom*, 4 (1958), 3–13; Rabinowitz, in: *Zion*, 6 (1941), 80–84; *Arim ve-Immahot be-Yisrael*, 6 (1955), 65–66.

[Itzhak Alfassi]

MARGOLIOTH, JACOB (d. between 1499 and 1512), rabbi of Regensburg (Ratisbon), originally from *Worms. In 1497 he corresponded with Johannes *Reuchlin on kabbalistic literature. Margolioth was considered a halakhic authority by his contemporaries and praised by them. His son SAMUEL, father of the apostate Anton *Margarita, succeeded him as rabbi of Regensburg until the expulsion in 1519; he subsequently moved to Posen (Poznan), where he served as *av bet din* of Great Poland until after 1537. Another of Jacob's sons, ISAAC EIZIK (d. 1525), was a member of the *bet din* of R. Jacob *Pollak of Prague. Jacob's *Seder Gittin ve-Ḥaliẓah* has been preserved in two copies, one made by his son Isaac (Bodl. Ms. 2010/3) and the other by his son SHALOM SHAKHNA under the title *Yam she-Asah Shelomo* (Bodl. Ms. 803). Part of his work was printed at the end of *Tur Even ha-Ezer* (Berlin, 1702). A privilege of Frederick III dated 1487 mentions a second JACOB MARGOLIOTH (d. before 1492), of Nuremberg. A halakhic declaration by him is noted in the responsa of R. Judah *Minz (no. 13), on the legality of a declaration of refusal (*me'un*) to marry. R. Elijah *Capsali named Jacob Margolioth as one of the supporters of R. Moses *Capsali in his bitter controversy (1475–80) with R. Joseph *Colon (*Likkutim Shonim*, 1869, p. 16), but it is unclear to which of the two he was referring.

BIBLIOGRAPHY: M. Wiener, in: MGWJ, 12 (1868), 345–51; S. Wiener, *Pesak ha-Ḥerem shel ha-Rav Ya'akov Pollak* (1897), 67–68; Graetz-Rabinowitz, 6 (1898), 436–7; A. Freimann, in: *Festschrift… M. Philippson* (1916), 89–90; J. Mieses, *Die aelteste gedruckte deutsche Uebersetzung des juedischen Gebetbuches aus dem Jahre 1530* (1916), 12–26; A. Marx, *Studies in Jewish History and Booklore* (1944), 123, no. 66; R. Straus, *Urkunden und Aktenstuecke zur Geschichte der Juden in Regensburg* (1960), no. 672.

[Abraham David]

MARGOLIOTH, JUDAH LOEB (1747–1811), rabbi and preacher, one of the precursors of the Haskalah in Eastern Europe. Margolioth, who was born in Zborov, Galicia, served as rabbi in various East European communities and from 1805 in Frankfurt on the Oder. He was familiar with medieval and contemporary Hebrew scientific literature as well as with contemporary Haskalah literature. In his books of sermons, he emphasized social justice and criticized the rich. He opposed Ḥasidism but also objected to the study of philosophy which he regarded as undermining faith. Thus he criticized *Mendelssohn for advocating freedom of ideas in Judaism in his book, *Jerusalem*, but advocated the study of Hebrew grammar, the sciences, and mathematics. He wrote *Or Olam al Ḥokhmat ha-Teva* ("Light of the World – On Science," Frankfurt on the Oder, 1777). The main point of the book is the classification of the "wisdoms" into science, mathematics, physics, and metaphysics; and the art of leading men: politics, economics, and ethics. The book was well received and was enthusiastically praised by Russian and Polish rabbis. His other works include interpretations of the Torah, responsa, sermons, and linguistic studies. Margolioth's books give expression to the mood of Eastern European Jews in the early days of the Haskalah, and demonstrate the initial willingness among certain Orthodox elements to accept social reforms and even secular studies, but their disillusionment when they witnessed the radical results of Enlightenment.

BIBLIOGRAPHY: Zinberg, Sifrut, 3 (1957), 290–1, 314–7; 5 (1959), 137–40; Kressel, Leksikon, 2 (1967), 419; Klausner, Sifrut, 1 (1952), 85–86; B. Dinur, *Be-Mifneh ha-Dorot* (1955), 264–5; R. Mahler, *History of the Jewish People in Modern Times*, 4 pt. 1 (1956), 40–44.

[Yehuda Slutsky]

MARGOLIOUTH, DAVID SAMUEL (1858–1940), classical scholar and Orientalist. Born in London the eldest son of the convert missionary Ezekiel Margoliouth, Margoliouth was educated at Winchester and at New College, Oxford, where he gained two first class degrees and won the probably unprecedented total of 11 university prizes; later he was a fellow of New College (1881–89). In 1889 he was appointed professor of Arabic at Oxford University (apparently without knowing Arabic, although he quickly mastered the language), holding the position until his retirement in 1937. In 1899 he was ordained and in 1913 he became moderator in Oriental languages at London University, where he also delivered the Hibbert lectures. Margoliouth was honored by many learned societies; in 1915 he was elected as a member of the British Academy, and from 1934 to 1937 he was president of the Royal Asiatic Society. Margoliouth was an outstanding scholar in the fields of Islamic history and literature and was an important editor of medieval Arabic texts. Among his extensive writings the following are of particular Jewish interest: *A Commentary on the Book of Daniel by Jephet ibn Ali…* (edited and translated, 1889); *The Place of Ecclesiasticus in Semitic Literature* (1890); *The Origin of the "Hebrew Original" of Ecclesiasticus* (1899); and *Relations Between Arabs and Israelites Prior to the Rise of Islam* (Schweich lectures 1921, published 1924). He also edited Whiston's English translation of Josephus (1906).

ADD. BIBLIOGRAPHY: ODNB online.

MARGOLIOUTH, MEIR OF OSTRAHA (**Ostrog**; d. 1790), ḥasidic rabbi in Poland; a disciple of *Israel b. Eliezer the Ba'al Shem Tov. He was descended from a celebrated rabbinical family. From a very early age he and his elder brother became devoted and loved disciples of the Ba'al Shem Tov. R. Meir, who gained a reputation as one of the greatest scholars of his age, served as rabbi in Jaslo and later in Horodenka (Gorodenka); in 1755 he was appointed rabbi in the Lvov region and in 1777 was appointed *rabbi Ostraha*, a title officially confirmed by the King of Poland, Stanislas II Augustus, which established his authority over all the rabbis of the district. He wrote works on *halakhah* and Kabbalah, and also long didactic poems. His great prestige helped to promote Ḥasidism, which at that time gave it important support. He had five sons, all of whom became noted rabbis and scholars. His works are *Meir Netivim* (Polonnoye, 1791–92); *Sod Yakhin u-Vo'az* (Ostrog, 1794); *Derekh ha-Tov ve-ha-Yashar* (Polonnoye, 1795); and *Kotnot Or* (Berdichev, 1816).

BIBLIOGRAPHY: M. Biber, *Mazkeret li-Gedolei Ostraha* (1907), 198–209, 270–3; S. Buber, *Anshei Shem* (1895), 137–49, 202.

[Adin Steinsaltz]

MARGOLIOUTH (Margalita), MOSES (1818–1881), English priest. Margoliouth, who was Jewish by birth, was born in Suwalki, Poland. In his youth he studied in yeshivot, and in 1837 he left Poland for Liverpool, where, under the influence of Jewish converts to Christianity, he himself became a Christian in 1838. After his studies at Trinity College, Dublin (1840–44), he served as curate in Liverpool (1844). From 1877 until his death he served as vicar in Little Linford in Buckinghamshire. Among his works are *The Fundamental Principles of Modern Judaism Investigated* (1843 with Margoliouth's autobiography); *The History of the Jews of Great Britain* (1857); and *A Pilgrimage to the Land of My Fathers* (1858), a travelogue of Palestine. He was probably, but not certainly, a relative of the father of David Samuel *Margoliouth, whose close friend he was.

His nephew, GEORGE MARGOLIOUTH (1853–1952), like his uncle Moses Margoliouth, converted to Christianity and became an ordained priest of the Church (1881). Margoliouth excelled in biblical and Oriental studies and was in charge of the Hebrew, Syriac, and Ethiopic manuscripts of the British Museum from 1891 to 1914. His works included *The Liturgy of the Nile* (Palestine Syriac Text, Translation and Vocabulary; 1896); *The Palestine Syriac Version of the Holy Scriptures* (London, 1897); and the *Catalogue of the Hebrew and Samaritan Manuscripts in the British Museum* (3 vols.; 1909–15), which has served scholars as a key bibliographical guide to this most important collection.

ADD. BIBLIOGRAPHY: ODNB online; Katz, England, 379–80; P. Jones, *Moses: A Short Account of the Life of Reverend Moses Margoliouth* (1999).

[Alexander Tobias]

MARGOLIS, GAVRIEL ZEV (1847–1935), rabbi of and leading figure in the rejectionist wing of American Orthodoxy. Born in Vilna, he studied with Rabbi Joshua of Vilna, the uncle of the Ḥafeẓ Ḥayyim. He continued with Rabbi Jacob Beirat before entering the yeshivah of Volozhin. He was ordained in 1869 and then worked with Rav Eizele Charif to publish a commentary on the Jerusalem Talmud, titled *Noam Yerushalmi*. He went on to become head of the Rabbinical Court in Dobrova and after two years moved to Yahnovka. He then returned to Grodno where he was the leading halakhic authority, succeeding his father-in-law Rabbi Nahum Kaplan. He combined the life of a scholar and communal leader. He was one of the rare rabbis to embrace Ḥovevei Zion and was a delegate to the Second Zionist Congress in Basel. When secular leadership dominated the Zionist movement, Rabbi Margolis became alienated.

After the pogroms of 1903 he fiercely opposed the Jews who had embraced the revolutionary movement and received death threats. He wanted to declare them no longer members of the Jewish community; a harsh but more moderate proposal passed the gathering of rabbis in Cracow. Political conditions were such that he welcomed and accepted an offer from Boston and arrived in the United States in 1907. Four years later, he moved to New York as rabbi of Adath Israel, a Lower East Side congregation, a position he held for almost a quarter of a century. He arrived in the United States after having served for almost 40 years as a European rabbi and was not about to accommodate himself to the American situation too easily.

He opposed Orthodox participation in the Kehillah and would not cooperate with the Agudat Harabbonim regarding *kashrut*; he thus established a separate movement Kenneset Harabbonim and attracted some significant colleagues to the fledgling organization.

He initially supported RIETS and welcomed its creation. He was one of the speakers at its opening in 1915, but as it embraced secular learning and sought to become a college and not only a yeshivah, his support turned to opposition. Moshe Sherman said: "The major thrust of his efforts to transplant the European world of Jewish piety and observance to the United States proved to be difficult" – at least in his generation when Americanization was the primary interest of immigrants and especially of their children.

He published *Shem Olam* (1905); *Torat Gavriel*, 5 volumes (1910, 1925, 1926); *Agudat Ezov* (1924); *Ginzei Margoliot Shir ha-Shirim ve-Rut* (1921); and *Ginzei Margoliot Kohelet ve-Eikhah* (1925).

BIBLIOGRAPHY: J. Hoffman, "The American Rabbinic Career of Rabbi Gavriel Zev Margolis" (M.A. Thesis, 1992); M.D. Sherman, *Orthodox Judaism in America: A Biographical Dictionary and Sourcebook* (1996).

[Michael Berenbaum (2nd ed.)]

MARGOLIS, MAX LEOPOLD (1886–1932), U.S. biblical and Semitic scholar. Born in Russia, Margolis received a thorough training in Bible and Talmud as well as in modern sciences and languages in his native country and in Berlin. In 1889 he went to the United States. His first field of specialization was the text-criticism of the Talmud to which his dissertation was devoted. His earliest work reveals meticulous attention to detail, thorough mastery of the subject, rigorous application of the inductive method, and brilliance and solidity in the conclusions. At the end of his fellowship year at Columbia University, Margolis was invited by Hebrew Union College in Cincinnati to serve as assistant professor of Hebrew and biblical exegesis. During his incumbency he published his *Elementary Textbook of Hebrew Accidence* (1893), a succinct and original contribution to Hebrew grammar and phonetics, as well as several works dealing with Reform Jewish theology. In 1897 he went to the University of California at Berkeley to teach Semitic languages and in 1905 returned to Hebrew Union College as professor of biblical exegesis. He resigned from Hebrew Union College in 1910, after he and other faculty members differed with the College president regarding educational philosophy and Zionism – Margolis was a strong Zionist. He went to Europe to complete his work on his pioneering and still classic *Manual of the Aramaic Language of the Babylonian Talmud*, which appeared both in English and in German (1910). The Jewish Publication Society chose Margolis to be secretary of the Board of Editors and editor-in-chief of their new translation of the Bible into English. To this major task he devoted himself until 1917. After the translation appeared, his mimeographed *Notes on the New Translation of the Holy Scriptures* (1921), which served as the basis of the work, appeared in a tome of 646 pages for private circulation. When Dropsie College was opened in Philadelphia, Margolis became professor of biblical philology, a position he occupied from 1909 until his death. Two brief popular works *The Story of Bible Translations* (1917) and *The Hebrew Scriptures in the Making* (1922) were never expanded into full-length scholarly treatments because his energies were increasingly absorbed by his vision of a truly critical edition of the Septuagint. Choosing the Book of Joshua, he collated all the existing Greek manuscripts and by dint of minute and brilliant analysis established the principal recensions of the Septuagint, which he called Palestinian, Egyptian, Syrian, Constantinopolitan, and Mixed. On the basis of these he then recreated what he regarded as the original septuagintal text. While some scholars have differed with his underlying theory as to the nature of the Greek translation, *The Book of Joshua in Greek* (1931) is considered a work of brilliant scholarship. In the area of septuagintal studies, he also published scores of technical papers. In the field of biblical exegesis he published a brief but valuable English commentary on Micah, *Holy Scriptures with Commentary: Micah* (1908), and Hebrew commentaries on Zephaniah and Malachi in the Kahana Bible Commentary Series (1930). The book by which he is perhaps most widely known is a one-volume *A History of the Jewish People* (1927, 1962^2) written in collaboration with Alexander Marx. Within the confines of a single volume the multitude of details of nearly 40 centuries of Jewish history were compressed with conciseness, clarity, and completeness. Moreover, the entire work is informed by a broad philosophic grasp of the subject, a rare balance and objectivity of treatment, and a warm love for the Jewish people and its heritage.

BIBLIOGRAPHY: R. Gordis (ed.), *Max Leopold Margolis: Scholar and Teacher* (1952), includes an annotated bibliography of Margolis' writings.

[Robert Gordis]

MARGOLIS-KALVARYSKI, HAIM (1868–1947), pioneer and administrator of Jewish settlement in Ereẓ Israel. Born in the province of Suwalki (then Russian Poland) where his parents were landowners, Margolis-Kalvaryski was active from his youth in the *Ḥibbat Zion movement. After studying agriculture in Montpellier, France, he went in 1895 to Ereẓ Israel and became the secretary of *Benei Moshe in Jaffa. He taught at the *Mikveh Israel Agricultural School and later worked at *Mishmar ha-Yarden on behalf of Baron Edmond de *Rothschild's administration. In 1900 he became administrator of the settlements that the *Jewish Colonization Association (ICA) founded in Lower Galilee. Margolis-Kalvaryski established a training farm for the settlers at Sejera and brought over Russian peasant families who had converted to Judaism. Between 1901 and 1905, Margolis-Kalvaryski founded the settlements Sejera (*Ilaniyah), *Yavne'el, *Kefar Tavor, Beit Gan, and *Menaḥemiyyah. In 1906 he was appointed manager of the settlements in Upper Galilee.

In 1913 he and Nahum *Sokolow met Arab leaders in Damascus to try to reach an understanding between them and the Zionist Movement. During World War I he defended the settlers imprisoned and persecuted by the Turks and helped establish collective settlements including *Ayyelet ha-Shaḥar, *Tel Ḥai, *Maḥanaim, and *Kefar Giladi. In 1920 Margolis-Kalvaryski negotiated with the short-lived Arab government in Damascus and attempted to save the settlements in Upper Galilee from attacks through negotiations with local Arab leaders. He became manager of the ICA setttlements in northern Palestine, a member of the Palestine Government Advisory Council, and a member of the Va'ad Le'ummi (until 1929). Between 1923 and 1927 he was head of the Arab Bureau of the Zionist Executive and between 1929 and 1931 headed the joint bureau for Arab affairs of the *Jewish Agency Executive and the Va'ad Le'ummi.

Margolis-Kalvaryski saw Ereẓ Israel as a common homeland for Jews and Arabs belonging to a Middle East federation. He was a founder of *Berit Shalom and similar groups which sought to reach agreement with the Arabs. In his later years he opposed official Zionist policy, which, in his opinion, was not sufficiently active in this direction. He wrote on Arab-Jewish relations in *She'ifoteinu*, 2, 3 (1931–33) and in *Be'ayot ha-Zeman* (1948). The moshav Margaliyyot in Upper Galilee is named after him.

BIBLIOGRAPHY: *Be'ayot ha-Zeman*, no. 27 (1947); A. Ever-Hadani, *Ha-Hityashevut ba-Galil ha-Taḥton* (1955), 18–162; M. Smilansky, *Mishpaḥat ha-Adamah*, 3 (1954), 176–84.

[Yehuda Slutsky]

MARGOSHES, SAMUEL (1887–1968), Yiddish journalist, editor, and Zionist leader. Born in Galicia, he early joined the Zionist movement, and immigrated to the United States in 1905. From the Jewish Theological Seminary he received his rabbinical degree in 1910 and later a doctorate in Hebrew literature. From Columbia University he received his doctorate in philosophy. After engaging in various communal, educational, and relief activities before, during, and after World War I, he began his long association with the New York Yiddish daily *The Day* in 1922. He served as editor (1926–42), English columnist, and commentator on Jewish events.

Margoshes espoused the causes both of Zionism and of Diaspora Jewry. For him the survival and growth of the Jewish people everywhere were of prime importance. The strengthening of the State of Israel, while a necessary means to achieve this objective, was for him not an end in itself. Hence, he emphasized the need for Yiddish as well as Hebrew, and the building of an American center of Judaism as well as the Israel center, both interdependent and influencing each other's development, economically, politically, and spiritually. As vice president of the Zionist Organization of America, he participated in World Zionist congresses and served on the Zionist General Council for many years.

BIBLIOGRAPHY: Rejzen, Leksikon, 2 (1927), 326–8; LNYL, 5 (1963), 487–90; S. Kahan, *Meksikaner Viderklangen* (1951), 176–9.

[Sol Liptzin]

MARGOULIES, BERTA (O'Hare; 1907–1996), U.S. sculptor. Margoulies was born in Lubitz, Poland. The artist's early life was marked by frequent emigration: to Belgium shortly before its invasion by Germany in World War I, to Holland, and then to England. She went to the U.S. in 1921, graduating from Hunter College in 1927. In 1928, she received a fellowship from the Gardner Foundation in Boston, which enabled her to travel to Paris for two years of study at the Académie Julien and Académie Calorossi; she also studied at the École des Beaux-Arts for a brief period. In 1931, she returned to New York City; she supported herself as a social worker while opening an art studio and taking classes at the Art Students League. The New Deal offered Margoulies many opportunities to further her career: she completed a head of Andrew Jackson for the Works Progress Administration and received a commission from the Treasury Section of Fine Arts for *Postman, 1691–1775* (1936), an historically accurate aluminum statue for the Washington, D.C., Post Office Building. Margoulies' and sculptor Concetta Scaravaglione's *Railway Mail* form part of ten aluminum figures positioned in the entrance lobby to the building. In addition, Margoulies sculpted *Woman and Deer* for the 1939 New York World's Fair garden court. With funds provided by the U.S. Treasury Department, Margoulies completed a painted plaster relief entitled *Stillman Foote Acquires Homestead of John Harrington* for the Canton, Ohio, Post Office in 1939. The following year, the artist fashioned *Tomato Sculpture*, a wall-mounted terracotta sculpture commissioned for the Monticello, Arkansas, Post Office. In the composition, male and female figures work side by side to cultivate and harvest tomatoes, a crop associated with Monticello. Margoulies' sculptures, some fashioned of beaten lead and bronze, often depicted human figures. Her simplification, stylization, and exaggeration of sculpted anatomy indicates her work's affinity with expressionism, especially that of Ernst Barlach, Kathe Kollwitz, Paula Mondersohn-Becker, and Jacques Lipschitz, among other artists. The gently smiling face of the sculpture *Walnut Boy* (1947) suggests early Greek sculpture, while the features of *Young Girl* (1936), especially her long nose and mask-like eyes, calls to mind Modigliani paintings of seated figures or Karl Schmidt-Rottloff's *Male Head* (1917). Many of her pieces possess overtly social and political themes, such as the bronze sculpture *Mine Disaster* (1942), a loosely pyramidal shaped grouping of figures awaiting news about the fate of fathers, husbands, and brothers. She also completed many pieces with Jewish themes and motifs: *Blessing Candles, Wailing Wall,* and *Promised Land,* the latter depicting a figure reminiscent of Moses with arms upraised. Margoulies won an Avery Award from the Architectural League in 1937, another award from the Society of Arts and Letters in 1944, and a fellowship from the Guggenheim Foundation in 1946. She lived in New Jersey and Massachusetts. Margoulies' work has been collected by the Des Moines Art Center, Whitney Museum of American Art, the Neuberger Museum, State University of New York, and Salisbury University, Maryland, among other places.

BIBLIOGRAPHY: J. Heller and N.G. Heller, *North American Woman Artists of the Twentieth Century: A Biographical Dictionary* (1995); C.S. Rubenstein, *American Women Sculptors: A History of Women Working in Three Dimensions* (1990).

[Nancy Buchwald (2nd ed.)]

MARGULES, MAX (1856–1920), Austrian meteorologist. Born in Brody, Margules lectured in Vienna on mathematics and physics from 1880 to 1882. His refusal to convert to Christianity blocked his academic advancement and he left the university to become secretary of the Central Institute of Meteorology in Vienna. He held this post for 24 years. In 1906, still refusing to convert and disappointed with his lack of academic success under the Austro-Hungarian academic system, he retired on early pension. He left the field of meteorological research, set up a chemical laboratory in his home, and concentrated on independent research. The post-World War I inflation rendered his small pension insufficient to live on, and he died from malnutrition.

Margules' first group of writings dealt with the changes of barometric pressure and their diurnal double fluctuations due to inner oscillations and waves in the free atmosphere of the earth. The second group of writings dealt with the effect of hot and cold air masses on climate. In the 1890s, he organized a network of closely spaced stations in a 60-kilometer circumference around Vienna, fitted with thermo-barographs. He showed the progress of the cold and hot waves of pressure and storms, and was able to arrive at an understanding of the phenomenon. In 1901 he showed that the kinetic energy in storms would have to be much greater in order to be produced by the pressure gradient. His conclusion later replaced the accepted theory on the generation of winds. Margules published his most important work on the energy of storms in 1903 (in *Jahrbuch der Zentralanstalt fuer Metereologie und Geodynamik*). Here he replaced "the energy of the storm" with the "potential energy of distribution of masses on the vertical plane" known as the Margules equation. This introduced a three-dimensional distribution of energy in place of the previously accepted two-dimensional distribution. He stressed that the study of air masses in their space expansion led to an understanding of their movements and proved the impossibility of understanding the problem according to methods of surface barometers only.

BIBLIOGRAPHY: J.C. Poggendorff, *Biographisch-literarisches Handwoerterbuch*, 3 (1898); 4 (1904); 5 (1926); Wininger, Biog, s.v. *Margulies, Max*, includes bibliography.

[Dov Ashbel]

MARGULIES, EMIL (1877–1943), lawyer and Zionist leader. Born in Sosnowiec, Poland, Margulies became an ardent Zionist as a young man and, after his settlement in Bohemia, had a great share in the development of Zionism there and in the west Austrian district. At the Tenth Zionist Congress (1911), he submitted a new statute for the Zionist Movement. Throughout his life he was a "political" Zionist, and in 1923 he was co-founder of the Radical Zionist Fraction (Democratic Zionists), fighting against the enlargement of the *Jewish Agency by non-Zionists. Parallel to his Zionist activities, Margulies was one of the principal founders of the Czechoslovak "Jewish Party," of which he became president for a time. He also actively participated in the work on international minority problems and was a Jewish representative to the Congress of National Minorities. Margulies attained world renown through his action in the *Bernheim Petition. In 1939 he settled in Palestine, where, together with some colleagues, he opened an office for legal advice.

BIBLIOGRAPHY: M. Faerber, *Dr. Emil Margulies* (Ger., 1949); Tidhar, 4 (1950), 1680–81.

[Oskar K. Rabinowicz]

MARGULIES, SAMUEL HIRSCH (1858–1922), rabbi and scholar. Margulies was born at Brzezan in Galicia; he was a descendant of Rabbi Ephraim Zalman Margolioth. *Margulies laid the foundations of his talmudic-rabbinical knowledge at home. In 1878 he entered the university and the Jewish Theological Seminary at Breslau. In 1883 he took a degree in Semitic Languages at the University of Leipzig. He served from 1885 to 1887 as rabbi of the Congregation Newe Shalom in Hamburg; from 1887 until 1890 he was the rabbi of the congregation at Weilburg, in Hesse-Nassau.

When in 1889 the Jewish community of Florence advertised in Jewish newspapers in Italy, France, and Germany that the position of chief rabbi was vacant, Margulies answered the call and he was appointed chief rabbi of Florence. Margulies' dealings with the Jewish community of Florence were not too easy at the beginning. The community looked with a suspicious eye at the foreign rabbi with distinctive Zionist ideas. Nevertheless, his personal charm as well as his teaching abilities soon established him as the undisputed spiritual leader of Florence's Jewish community.

When in 1899 the *Collegio Rabbinico Italiano was transferred to Florence, Margulies became its head, and thus trained several generations of Italian Jewish spiritual leaders. Altogether he did much to revive Jewish life and consciousness in Italy and to foster contacts between Italian and other European Jewries. He founded *Rivista Israelitica* in 1904, the learned journal of his seminary (1904–15), and was one of the initiators of the weekly *Settimane Israelitica* (later named *Israel*). Margulies also established several charitable institutions in Florence.

Margulies published several essays in Berliner's *Magazin* and in the *Monatsschrift*; he wrote *Saadja Alfajûmi's Arabische Psalmen-Uebersetzung*, published at Breslau in 1884, an edition of Saadiah's Arabic translation of the Psalms from a Munich manuscript with German translation and commentary; From his German period there are also *Zwei Pesach-Predigten*, published at Frankfurt-on-the-Main in 1888, and *Dichter und Patriot*, on the life and work of D. Levi, published at Treves in 1896. His later writings include "Schwertlied Ezechiels" (also in Hebrew, in *Scripta Universitatis... Hierosolymitanarum...*, 1 (1923)); articles in his own (*Rivista Israelitica*) and other periodicals; and volumes of sermons, among them *Discorsi Sacri* (1891, repr. 1956). An autobiographical note appeared in his *Discorsi e Scritti vari* (1923).

Margulies was a leading advocate of the 1920 "Jewish Commune" experiment in Florence, which caused disagreements between Zionists and non-Zionists Jews. Margulies died on Purim day, 1922, while he was talking to the children of the Jewish School.

BIBLIOGRAPHY: D. Disegni, in: L. Jung (ed.), *Guardians of Our Heritage* (1958), 447ff.; J.M. Pacifici, in: L. Jung (ed.), *Men of the Spirit* (1964), 645ff. **ADD. BIBLIOGRAPHY:** G. Celata, "Cinquanta anni dalla scomparsa di S.H. Margulies," in: RMI, 38:4 (1972), 195–221; L. Viterbo, "La nomina del Rabbino Margulies," in: RMI, 60 (1993), 67–89.

[Umberto (Moses David) Cassuto / Samuele Rocca (2nd ed.)]

MARGUL-SPERBER, ALFRED (1898–1967), German author, translator, journalist. Margul-Sperber grew up in a German assimilated family in Bukovina. After World War I, during which his family fled to Vienna, Margul-Sperber went to Paris and New York (1920–24). Returning to Bukovina, he started to work as journalist for the *Czernowitzer Morgenblatt*, soon becoming an important figure in the literary circles of Czernowitz and Vienna. In 1934 he published *Gleichnisse der Landschaft*, the first of 14 volumes of poetry which made him widely known not only for his description of the (symbolic) landscape of Bukovina, but also, especially later, as a political writer, with such poems as "Der Neger Jessy Owens U.S.A. er laeuft den olympischen Weltrekord, Fackellaeufer" (1936) and "Gespraech mit einem Kind. Aus Hitlerdeutschland 1936" (1941), in which he criticized racism and Nazism. In 1940 Margul-Sperber fled from Soviet troops to Bucharest. As a leftist intellectual he was highly regarded after 1945 in Romania, writing in the style of social realism. Poems like "Auf den Namen eines Vernichtungslagers" (ca. 1959), "Aus dunkelsten Tagen, Der Tod Mosis," and "Nach einer chassidischen Sage and Das Ostermahl" (1941) reflect the Holocaust. At the same time, Margul-Sperber was a promoter of young German Jews writing in German like Rose *Auslaender and Paul *Celan, whom he influenced in his early work.

BIBLIOGRAPHY: A. Kittner, in: Alfred Margul-Sperber, *Geheimnis und Verzicht* (1975), 589–614; B. Rosenthal, in: *Bulletin des Leo Baeck Instituts*, 68 (1984), 41–58; P. Motzan, in: A. Schwob (ed.), *Die deutsche Literaturgeschichte Ostmittel- und Suedosteuropas von der Mitte des 19. Jahrhunderts bis heute* (1992), 119–36; S.P. Scheichl, in: *Suedostdeutsche Vierteljahresblaetter* 47 (1998), 219–26.

[Andreas Kilcher (2nd ed.)]

MARḤAB AL-YAHŪDĪ IBN AL-ḤĀRITH (d. 629), warrior of Arabia, renowned for his courage. His family is said to have been of Ḥimyarite origin and several other members gained fame as warriors. They were mentioned by many Muslim historians, and were noted for their outstanding courage. Marḥab's two brothers, al-Ḥārith and Yāsir, distinguished themselves in the *Khaybar war against *Muhammad. Zaynab, a woman famous in Islam, who attempted to poison Muhammad to avenge the death of her husband, father and uncle in that war, was also a member of the family. Arab sources refer to him as Marḥab al-Yahūdī (Marḥab the Jew), omitting mention of his father's name. The references to the woman Zaynab are somewhat confused. One source states that al-Ḥārith was "Zaynab's father and Marḥab's brother" (al-Maqrīzī, 1:314). The same source, however, refers to Zaynab as "Zaynab the Jewess, al-Ḥārith's daughter, and Marḥab's sister." Marḥab and his brother, Yāsir, both composed poetry in the *rajaz* meter. Arab historians and biographers of Muhammad state that Marḥab died in a duel during one of the battles at Khaybar. The story, as preserved by the ninth-century historians al-Wāqidī and Ibn Hishām, states that, during the siege by Muslim forces of one of the Khaybar fortresses, Marḥab threw a heavy millstone over the walls of the fort, killing Maḥmūd ibn Maslama. His cousin Ali ibn Abu Ṭālib promptly challenged Marḥab's brother to a duel and killed him. Marḥab, singing an *urjūza* (poem in *rajaz* meter), then came to avenge his brother's blood and met Maḥmūd ibn Maslama's brother, Muhammad ibn Maslama. In the duel Marḥab's sword stuck in his adversary's shield and Mūhammad then struck Marḥab a mortal blow. Marḥab's second brother, Yāsir, was also killed in a duel, while Zaynab's husband fell in battle. The distraught Zaynab, having lost her husband and her brothers, attempted to poison Muhammad in revenge, but he was saved by his foresight. There are conflicting traditions as to whether Muhammad had Zaynab killed, or released her after her conversion to Islam.

BIBLIOGRAPHY: A.P. Coussin de Perceval, *Essai sur l'histoire des Arabes...*, 3 (Paris, 1847), 195–8; Graetz, Hist, 3 (1894), 82–84; Ibn Hishām, Abd el-Malik, *Kitāb Sīrat Rasūl Allah, Das Leben Muhammeds*, ed. by F. Wuestenfeld (1859), 670–1; Ibn Saad, *Kitāb al-Ṭabaqāt al-Kabīr... Biographien Muhammed's...*, ed. by J. Horovitz,

2 pt. 1 (1909), 80–81; al-Wāqidī, *The Kitāb al-Maghāzī*, ed. Marsden Jones, 2 (London, 1966), 645, 653–4; al-Maqrīzī, Ahmad ibn Ali, *Imtā*ʿ *al-Asmā*ʿ, ed. Mahmud M. Shākir, 1 (Cairo, 1941), 187, 311–16, 321–2; al-Diyārbakrī, Hussein ibn Muhammad, *Taʾrīkh al-Khamīs…*, (Cairo, 1283 H. (1866 C.E.)), II, 50–3; al-Ḥalabī Ali ibn Burhān al-Dīn, *Insān al-*ʿ*Uyūn*, 3 (1320 AH, 1902 C.E.), 43–46; H.Z. Hirschberg, *Yisrael ba-*ʿ*Arav* (1946), 55, 148, 251.

[Shmuel Moreh]

MARḤESHVAN (Heb. מַרְחֶשְׁוָן), the post-Exilic name of the eighth month of the Jewish year, frequently shortened to Ḥeshvan (Heb. חֶשְׁוָן). Its pre-Exilic name is Bul (I Kings 6:38). The name occurs in the *Antiquities* of Josephus, **Megillat Taʿanit,* and later branches of rabbinic literature, but nowhere in the Bible. It is believed to be etymologically connected with *Arahsammu*, the Assyrian for "eighth month." The zodiacal sign of this month is *Scorpio.* Like *Kislev, it consists of 29 or 30 days in either common or leap years (see *Calendar). The 1st of Marḥeshvan never falls on Sunday, Tuesday, or Friday. In the 20th century, Marḥeshvan, in its earliest occurrence, extended from October 6th to November 4th (3rd), and, in its latest, from November 4th to December 3rd (2nd). Historic days in Marḥeshvan comprise: (1) 6th of Marḥeshvan, the marking of the blinding of King Zedekiah at the command of Nebuchadnezzar (II Kings 25:7), once observed as a fast (Meg. Taʿan. 13); (2) 7th of Marḥeshvan, the commencement in Ereẓ Israel of the Prayer for *Rain, inserted in the ninth benediction of the **Amidah* prayer (Taʿan. 1:3); (3) 17th of Marḥeshvan, the commencement of the Flood (Gen. 7:11), and of a series of fasts by pious individuals in their intercession for rain in years of drought (Taʿan. 1:4); (4, 5, 6) 23rd, 25th, and 27th of Marḥeshvan, formerly commemorative of the respective victories of the Hasmoneans and Pharisees over the Greeks, Samaritans, and Sadducees (Meg. Taʿan. 8).

[Ephraim Jehudah Wiesenberg]

MARI, one of the principal centers of Mesopotamia during the third and early second millennia B.C.E. The archaeological and epigraphical discoveries there are of prime significance for the history of Mesopotamia and Upper Syria. The Akkadian-language documents from Mari date from the Old Babylonian period and are thus centuries earlier than those of the Hebrew Bible. However, the residents of Mari were western Semites, ultimately related to the Israelites and Arameans who first surface in the late second millennium but who are best known from the first. In consequence, although there is no demonstrable direct connection with the history of ancient Israel as was once thought (see * Genesis and *Patriarchs), there are numerous linguistic, cultural, and social data from Mari that aid us in the study of ancient Israel and the Bible. Mari (sometimes *Maʾeri* in the cuneiform sources) was located at Tell Ḥarīrī, at present some 1.5 mi. (2.5 km.) west of the Euphrates, near Abu Kemal, around 15 mi. (25 km.) north of the modern Syrian-Iraqi border. It was in an optimal position for contacts with the West and its location on the river artery, yet immediately adjacent to the desert, was decisive in the shaping of its fortune and character.

A. Excavations and Discoveries

The French excavations at Mari were instituted in 1933 under the direction of A. Parrot and exploration continued as regularly as the international situation allowed. The archaeological evidence indicates that Mari was founded in the fourth millennium B.C.E. at the very beginning of the Early Dynastic period (ED I), reaching a cultural-artistic peak during the first half of the third millennium B.C.E. Dating to this period (known as "Early Dynastic II–III," or "pre-Sargonic") are a ziggurat and several sanctuaries: including a temple where the earliest list of the Mari pantheon was discovered, temples to Shamash, Ninḫursag, and Ishtar, and the pair of temples of Ishtarat and Ninni-Zaza. In the latter three, there came to light many inscribed statues of local kings (such as Lamgi-Mari, Iku-Shamagan, and Iblul-Il), lesser royalty, and courtiers. Although Sumerian culture was predominant, the character of the cultic installations, the appearance of bearded figures in art, and especially the occurrence of particular divine and private names are all clearly indicative of a basic Semitic element from earliest times, with Semitic rule there centuries before the rise of Akkad.

Since 1964, the excavations have revealed two superimposed palaces from pre-Sargonic times, most impressive in themselves, including a royal chapel with an earthen altar (cf. Ex. 20:24), the sacred tradition of which was preserved even in the Old Babylonian palace built there some 700 years later (see below). Within the palace complex, a jar came to light containing a "treasure" including a lapis lazuli bead with a votive inscription mentioning Mesannepada, founder of the First Dynasty at Ur. This indicates a close contact between Mari and Ur at an early date, as do other finds from Mari, such as shell inlays essentially identical with those of the "Ur Standard" (war panel). The pre-Sargonic palace was destroyed either by Eannatum of Lagash (mid-25th century B.C.E.) or, rather, by Lugal-zaggesi of Uruk (mid-24th century B.C.E.).

After Sargon's conquest, in the second half of the 24th century B.C.E., Mari became a vassal city within the empire of Akkad; among the epigraphic evidence from this period are the names of two daughters of Naram-Sin, king of Akkad. In the final two centuries of the third millennium B.C.E., Mari was a sort of loose dependency of Third-Dynasty Ur, flourishing anew under (local) governors who bore the title *šakkanakku* (eight of whom are known by name). Indeed, a ruler of Mari is known to have given his daughter in marriage to a son of Ur-Namma, king of Ur.

The pre-eminence of Mari throughout the third millennium B.C.E. is well reflected in epigraphic sources: in the Sumerian King List it appears as the seat of the tenth postdiluvian dynasty; in the inscriptions of Eannatum mention is made of the penetration and repulse of forces from Mari as far south as Lagash; and it also appears in the inscriptions of Sargon and Naram-Sin of Akkad. At the close of the third mil-

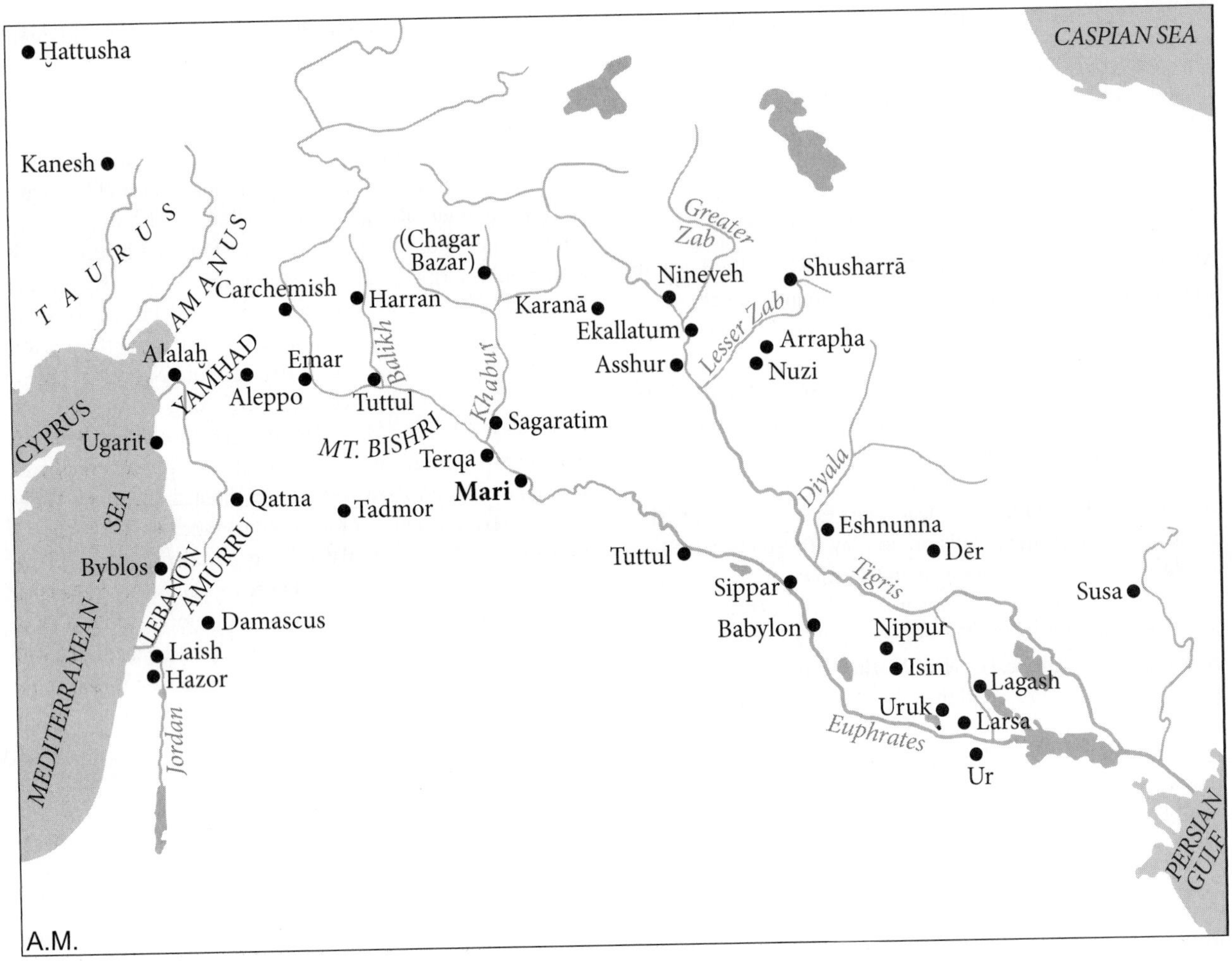

The Near East in the Mari Age.

lennium B.C.E., Ishbi-Irra, "a man of Mari," founded the Isin Dynasty and facilitated the collapse of the empire of Third-Dynasty Ur. After an obscure period of two centuries (from which several economic texts and 32 inscribed liver models are known), Mari reached its final period of glory in the 18th century under West Semitic rule. This latter was quashed by Hammurapi, king of Babylon, and Mari never regained its former position.

In the 13th century, Tukulti-Ninurta I conquered the meager settlement there and stationed a garrison in the city for a short time. The uppermost layer on the site dates to the Seleucid-Roman period.

In the second half of the second millennium B.C.E., Mari was still sufficiently important to be mentioned in the *Nuzi documents (horses and chariots were sent there), in recently found texts at *Ugarit ("Ishtar of Mari" in an alphabetic text, and in an epithet of another deity in a Hurrian text), and in the Egyptian geographical lists of Thutmosis III and probably also of Ramses III. The land of Mari appears in the neo-Assyrian geographical treatise describing Sargon's Akkadian empire (on the basis of which W.F. Albright identified Mari with Tell Ḥarīrī, long before the start of excavations there). Finally, Mari is mentioned in a Greek itinerary, in the (Aramaic) form *Merrhan*.

THE OLD BABYLONIAN PALACE AND ROYAL ARCHIVES. The main discoveries at Mari are from the period of its domination by the West Semitic dynasties, in the last quarter of the 19th century and the first half of the 18th century B.C.E. (according to the middle chronology; or 64 years later according to the low chronology). Several temples of this period were built over corresponding sanctuaries of pre-Sargonic times – the temples of Ishtar, Ninḫursag, and Shamash; a temple of Dagan, also known as the "lions' temple" (from bronze lions found flanking its entrance), was founded by the late third millennium B.C.E. This latter deity, the biblical *Dagon, held a prime position in the West Semitic pantheon, and at Mari bore the titles "King of the Land" and "Lord of all the Great Gods."

The outstanding architectural discovery from this period, however, is the royal palace – a structure of unparalleled magnificence and widespread fame in its time. This residence, enlarged successively by each of the West Semitic rulers at Mari, reached its zenith under Zimri-Lim, with an area of about eight acres and including over 300 chambers, corridors, and courts. Besides the private quarters for the royal family and entourage, there are administrative offices, a scribal school, quarters for visiting dignitaries, a royal chapel, a throne room, and a reception chamber. Service areas included guard quarters, workshops, and storerooms. Special elegance was provided in several halls and courts by multicolored frescoes depicting chiefly ritual and mythological scenes, including an investiture of a king (Zimri-Lim?) in the presence of several deities. This ceremony takes place in an idealized garden, its trees guarded by "cherubim" and symbolically watered by four streams flowing from a single source – all reminiscent of the biblical Paradise story. Many of the figures in these murals are depicted as typical West Semites.

The discovery of greatest impact on historical and biblical research comprises the more than 20,000 cuneiform tablets from the several archives in the palace (there was no library), written in the Babylonian language (see below). The original discovery has been supplemented since 1979 by fragments of a few thousand documents discovered by Margueron's excavations. The earliest publication of the documents was begun by the Assyriologists G. Dossin (dean of the Mari epigraphers), M. Birot, J. Bottéro, Mme. M.L. Burke, A. Finet, J.R. Kupper, and the late G. Boyer and Ch.F. Jean, mostly in the series *Archives royales de Mari* (ARM). In the early years, the texts appeared in two parallel series, not necessarily at the same time: one containing cuneiform copies, and the other with transliterations, French translations, brief notes, and some form of commentary or glossary. Thanks to computer printing technology, the more recent publications often include hand copies and high-quality photographs alongside texts. The texts published so far (through ARM 29 (2005)) have shed much light on the administrative, economic, cultural, and political facets mainly of Upper Mesopotamia and Upper Syria in the 18th century B.C.E. – regions previously known only vaguely.

The archives were found to be distinguished according to subject. The political-diplomatic archives include correspondence between the king of Mari and his agents, both at the palace and abroad, as well as with foreign potentates. They provide the earliest insight into the complexities of "suzerain-vassal" relationships, diplomatic protocol, and the fluctuating alliances and plots rampant in the Ancient Near East. A noteworthy class of letters is the unusually extensive women's correspondence published, in ARM, 10, revealing the prominent role of women in activities of the realm. The outstanding case is that of Shibtu, Zimri-Lim's queen (chief wife), who enjoyed the king's utter confidence, representing his interests during his absence from the city and exercising considerable influence in her own right.

The majority of documents are economic or administrative in nature, dealing with the maintenance of the palace, official trade abroad, lists of goods, and rosters of persons in royal employ (such as a list of nearly 1,000 captives [?] from the Harran-Nahor region engaged in the manufacture of clothing for the palace). Of a unique category are the some 1,300 tablets containing lists of daily provisions for the palace, often summarized by month. Though dealing only with "vegetarian" foodstuffs and beverages, they shed light on Solomon's "provisions for one day" and possibly also his monthly quantities (cf. I Kings 4:22–23, 27 [5:2–3, 7]; cf. also Neh. 5:17–18). The royal table at Mari, known to have entertained hundreds of guests on occasion, was served by spacious kitchens – in one of which were found numerous molds for preparing fancy cakes some bearing animal and goddess motifs (cf. Jer. 44:19).

Dozens of legal tablets were also found, mostly contracts concerning transactions and loans of silver or grain (ARM, 8), revealing that the palace served as a sort of exchange. Of exceptional interest is an adoption contract which ensured the "primogeniture" of the "eldest" (i.e., first adopted) son, stipulating that he receive a double portion of the inheritance; this is in full accord with biblical law (cf. Deut. 21:15–17).

The very few literary and religious compositions found at Mari include a lengthy Ishtar ritual in Babylonian, as well as six texts in Hurrian. That Hurrian was used occasionally in diplomatic correspondence is known from the only other tablet at Mari in that language, a letter written to Zimri-Lim.

B. Mari under West Semitic Rule

The origins of the West Semitic, or "Amorite," dynasties are shrouded in darkness, though there are clues pointing to North Syria for the local line at Mari. Thus, the theophoric name element-*Lim* (perhaps derived from the word for "folk," "people"; cf. Ugaritic *l'im* and Heb. *Le'om*) is found at both Aleppo, in the dynastic name Yarim-Lim, and Mari, in the royal names Yagid-Lim, Yaḫdun-Lim, and Zimri-Lim. It is also present in the name of Yashi-Lim, ruler of Tuttul (probably the one at the mouth of the Balikh River), and Ibbit-Lim, ruler of Ebla (probably Tell Mardikh), both several generations earlier than the above. Furthermore, the title "king of Mari, Tuttul, and the land of Ḫana" was borne by both Yaḫdun-Lim (Disc Inscription) and Zimri-Lim (cf. a fragmentary inscription from Terqa, between Tuttul and Mari). And, indeed, the site of ancestor worship for both the local and the "Assyrian" dynasties at Mari lay at Terqa, around 44 mi. (70 km.) to the northwest, at the mouth of the Khabur River. Hence, the immediate origin of the West Semitic rulers at Mari would appear to be in the Terqa region.

THE REIGN OF YAHDUN-LIM. The historical figure of Yaggid-Lim, founder of the local dynasty at Mari, is vague, and none of his records have been found, though there is a seal of one Qišti-Iliba who calls himself servant of Yaggid-Lim (*RIME* 4: E.4.6.7). Nor have many tablets from the reign of his son, Yaḫdun-Lim, been published, though in 1965 an archive of some 300 of his economic texts came to light. It is known, however, that Yaḫdun-Lim was able to stabilize his kingdom, establishing his dominance over the entire Middle Euphrates region, as is evident from the dozen known year-formulas and especially the two extant royal inscriptions from his reign (*RIME* E4.6.8; E4.6.8.1).

The shorter inscription (the "Disc Inscription") relates that Yaḫdun-Lim fortified Mari and Terqa, founded a fortress on the desert fringe (naming it after himself – Dur-Yaḫdun-Lim), and laid out an extensive irrigation system (boasting that "I did away with the water bucket in my land"). The other text, the Foundation Inscription of the Shamash temple, is a splendid literary composition relating his campaign to the Mediterranean coast and the "Cedar and Boxwood Mountain," where he obtained several types of choice wood, "and made known his might." However, this was probably only a passing episode and not a lasting conquest. Thirty-five economic texts published in 1970 are dated by two year-formulas for one Sumu-Yamam, an obscure character who ruled at Mari either before or after Yaḫdun-Lim. Also elusive is his kinship – whether to the local dynasty or otherwise – for the few other references to him, such as in a "letter to a god" (ARM, 1, 3), are inconclusive. This same letter also reveals the assassination of Yaḫdun-Lim (or Sumu-Yamam) in a court conspiracy, much to the benefit of Shamshi-Adad, scion of a rival West Semitic dynasty, who established himself in Assyria, swiftly gaining control over large portions of Mesopotamia.

THE ASSYRIAN INTERREGNUM. Yaḫdun-Lim's removal facilitated a take-over by Shamshi-Adad, who installed his son, Yasmaḫ-Adad, as viceroy at Mari. Under his father's tutelage, Yasmaḫ-Adad reorganized the local administration, cultivated ties with neighboring lands, and secured his flank against marauding nomads. Though his brother Ishme-Dagan, upon succeeding to the throne of Assyria, promised to maintain the protective policy of their father, Yasmaḫ-Adad was left adrift only three or four years later, when he was defeated by Eshnunna, a West Semitic kingdom beyond the Tigris. Altogether, Assyrian control of Mari lasted some 20 years.

THE KINGDOM OF ZIMRI-LIM. Thus, the stage was set for the advent of Zimri-Lim, the son of Yaḫdun-Lim, who in the interim had lived in exile under the wing of Yarim-Lim, king of Yamḫad (capital, Aleppo). Yarim-Lim, who had become Zimri-Lim's father-in-law, was most instrumental in restoring him to the throne of Mari. Thirty-two year-formulas are known for Zimri-Lim's reign – though many of them may have been alternate designations for the same year, for (chronologically) he cannot have ruled for so long a period. Zimri-Lim's reign, during the tumultous interval between Assyria's decline and the rise of the empire of Hammurapi, marks Mari at its apogee. It is this period which is best represented by the archives found at Mari which provide a thorough insight into the organization of the kingdom. Interestingly, several of Zimri-Lim's letters have been found in the royal archives at Tell el-Rimah (between the Upper Khabur and the Tigris), probably to be identified with the city of Karana, mentioned in the Mari correspondence. Mari had become a principal political force in Mesopotamia, alongside Babylon, Larsa, Eshnunna, Qatna, and Yamḫad (as is known from a contemporary political report). Relying heavily on his diplomatic cunning, Zimri-Lim developed an elaborate intelligence system – within his sphere of influence and beyond it. Frequent alliances, as with Yamḫad and Babylon, were designed to meet the danger of the moment – e.g., now against Eshnunna, then against Elam. His military endeavors were directed mainly against the hostile tribal federation of the Yaminites (the previously subdued Ḫanean tribes were already in his service; for both, see below). This political situation crystallized hand in hand with the development of economic ties branching out as far as the island of Dilmun (in the Persian Gulf), Elam (in the east), Arrapḫa and Shusharra (in southern Kurdistan), Cappadocia (in the north), Phoenicia and Palestine (in the west), and even Kaptara (Crete, in the Mediterranean). Indeed, tolls from caravan and riverine trade were one of Zimri-Lim's principal sources of income. This golden age at Mari came to an abrupt end, however, when Hammurapi turned on his former ally and conquered the city in his 32nd year, during the consolidation of his empire (in 1759 B.C.E. – middle chronology; or 1695 B.C.E. – low chronology). Two years later he ordered the razing of the city to the ground.

MARI AND THE WEST. Mari was bound closely with the lands to the west – Syria, and even northern Palestine – in economy, politics, culture, religion, and ethnic background. Already noted were the ties between the local dynasty at Mari and that of the kingdom of Yamḫad; Zimri-Lim's queen, Shibtu, was from Aleppo and he appears to have held land there, which was either a patrimony or received as a dowry. Similarly, the rival Assyrian dynasty at Mari secured political ties in the west through the marriage of Yasmaḫ-Adad to a princess from Qatna, Yamḫad's southern adversary. Another form of contact with the west is the already-mentioned campaign by Yaḫdun-

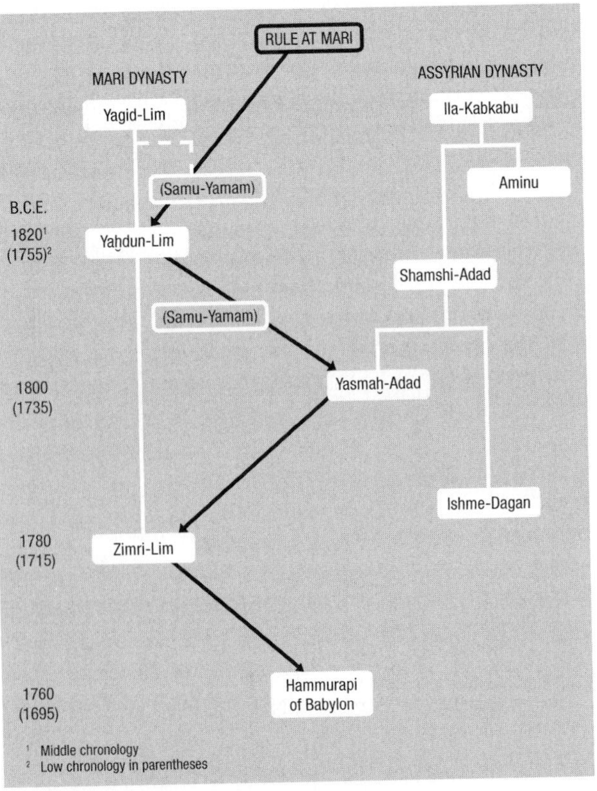

Lim and the later expedition by Shamshi-Adad to the Levant. Zimri-Lim is also known to have visited various places in the west: Yamḫad, where he had presented a statue to "Adad the great god of Aleppo," and Ugarit, where he was accompanied by a select bodyguard (*ṣabum beḫru*; see below).

The region farther southwest is only sparingly mentioned in the Mari archives, but references are found to Byblos on the Phoenician coast and the land of Amurru in southern Syria (the Apum of the Mari texts is most probably only that in the Khabur region, and not the one around Damascus, known from the contemporary Egyptian Execration Texts and various later sources). In northern Palestine, Hazor is noted several times in the Mari archives as the destination of diplomatic and economic emissaries. In one instance, emissaries passing through Mari are on their way to Yamḫad, Qatna, and Hazor, and a fourth place whose name is broken (the traces in ARM, 6, 23:23 may perhaps be restored to read "Megiddo," rather than "Egypt" as is sometimes proposed, which surprisingly does not appear in the Mari archives). In an economic document, Aleppo, Qatna, and Ugarit are listed, alongside Hazor ("Ibni-Adad, king of Hazor") and Laish ("Waritaldu at Laish," the later Dan north of Hazor), as destinations of large consignments of tin, a commodity of major importance among the exports to the west (it being alloyed with copper to produce bronze). On the other side of the ledger, Mari imported from the west horses and fine woods (from the Qatna region), various precious vessels of Syrian and "Cretan" style, Cypriot copper, fabrics, and garments (especially from Aleppo and Byblos), and large quantities of foodstuffs, such as honey, wine, and olive oil.

C. Mari and the Bible

The Mari documents bear indirectly upon Israelite history geographically; the "patriarchal homeland" (Aram-Naharaim, so called at a later date) lay within Mari's horizons; ethnic-linguistically, the Hebrews were of the same West Semitic (or Amorite) stock as that strongly manifest at Mari (see above); and sociologically, for the descriptions of tribalism comprise the most extensive insight into the nomadic and settled phases of the Israelite tribes.

1. PATRIARCHAL HOMELAND. The cities of Harran and Nahor (cuneiform *Naḫūr*), in the Upper Balikh Valley – which figure in the Bible as ancestral habitats of the Patriarchs – are well documented as important dependencies controlled by governors from Mari (one of whom, Itur-asdu at Nahor, is the subject of ARM, 14). Both cities were foci of tribal foment: at the temple of Sin in Harran, a treaty between the "kings" of Zalmaqum and the Yaminites was sworn against Mari; while at Nahor reinforcements had often to be called in to quell local uprisings inflamed by the *Habiru. Alongside the West Semitic peoples in this region was a considerable Hurrian element (note the typically Hurrian name of King Adalshenni, who at one time gained control over Nahor), which may well have left an imprint upon the initial ethnic and cultural composition of the Hebrews. The picture revealed in the Mari archives, of far-reaching tribal migrations (such as those of Yaminite groups) and caravan conditions between the Euphrates region and Syria-Northern Palestine, provides an analogy for the biblical narratives of the patriarchal wanderings between Aram-Naharaim and Canaan.

2. ETHNO-LINGUISTIC AFFINITIES – THE WEST SEMITIC IDIOM. Evidence for the West Semitic (or *Amorite) origin of the majority of the people figuring in the Mari documents is revealed in the onomasticon (name-stock) and specific linguistic features of the Mari dialect. Many of the hundreds of proper names known from the Mari texts are paralleled in the Bible, especially in the patriarchal narratives and the Exodus-Conquest cycle, which demonstrate a strong archaizing tendency. At Mari, where Yahweh was unknown, these names occur often with (other) theophoric (god-bearing) components; e.g., Jacob and Ishmael – i.e., *ḥaqba-ḫammu/-aḫim/* etc. and *Yasmaḫ-El/-Adad/-Baʿal/* etc. The names of the Israelite tribes of *Levi and *Benjamin also seem to have their parallels. Thus, the tribal designation at Mari, *DUMU.MEŠ-yamin(a)*, "Yaminites," bears the same connotation as Benjamin – "son(s) of the South," i.e., southerners, and it is preferable to render the logogram for "sons" as West Semitic *bini-yamina* a form conveniently homophonic with the Hebrew *Binyamin*. The West Semitic imprint on the standard Old Babylonian (OB) dialect of the Akkadian language in use at Mari is evident to a certain extent in phonology, morphology, syntax, and, especially, vocabulary. The lack of terms in OB for certain specific features in the society and way of life of the population of the Mari region necessitated the frequent adoption of West Semitic expressions in the shape of either Akkadian words employed in new, West Semitic connotations or out-and-out loanwords from the West Semitic – words well represented in biblical Hebrew (often in exalted language, as also at Mari). Besides the linguistic yield, a comparative study of the West Semitic loanwords at Mari and their Hebrew cognates may broadly illuminate the nature of the societies involved. Thus, a list of such lexical items would include the following:

Geographical terms – *ḫamqum* = Hebrew *ʿemeq*, "valley"; *k/qaṣum* = Hebrew *qaẓeh*, "(desert) frontier"; *ḥen* (as a place-name) = Hebrew *ʿayin*, "spring"; points of the compass – *aqdamātum* = Hebrew *qedem*, "east"; *aḫarātum* = Hebrew *aḥar, aḥor*, "west"; north and south were preserved in the tribal names *DUMU.MEŠ-simʾal* = Hebrew *semol*, and *DUMU.MEŠ-yamina* = Hebrew *yamin*; fauna – *ḫa(ya)rum* =Hebrew *ʿayir*, "donkey foal"; *hazzum* = Hebrew *ʿez*, "goat"; *ḫiglum* = Hebrew *ʿegel*, "calf" (referring to a zoomorphic vessel at Mari); flora – *suḫrum* = Hebrew *seʿorah*, "barley"; *ḫimrum* = Hebrew *ḥemer*, "a fermented drink"; military terms – *be(ḫ)rum* = Hebrew *baḥur*, "(select) trooper"; *bazaḫātum*, "military outpost" (cf. Heb. root *bẓʿ*); *sag/qbum*, "guard" (later Heb. *zaqif?*); note perhaps *madārum* = later Hebrew *mador (?)*, "dwelling place"; *mas/škabum* = Hebrew *mishkav*, "a lodging"; probably *sablum* = Hebrew *sevel*, "corvée"; and *yagâtum* = Hebrew *yagon*, "sorrow."

A series of West Semitic terms is also found for tribal organization and institutions (see below, Nos. 3 and 4), which were quite foreign to contemporary Mesopotamia and therefore found no adequate means of expression in the pure Babylonian lexicon; cf., e.g., the set of terms for various tribal units: *gāyum* = Hebrew goy; *ḥibrum* = Hebrew *ḥever*; and perhaps *ummatum* = Hebrew *u'ummah*. West Semitic verbs unknown in standard Babylonian Akkadian but with cognates in biblical Hebrew include the following: *ḥakûm*, "to wait"; *ḥalûm*, "to be ill"; *ḥarāšum*, "to be silent"; *naḥālum*, "to inherit, apportion"; *naqāmum*, "to avenge" (only in personal names); *qatālum*, "to kill"; *šapāṭum*, "to judge, govern" (and see below).

3. PATRIARCHAL TRIBAL SOCIETY. The Mari archives provide the most abundant and fruitful source material concerning West Semitic tribes of any Ancient Near Eastern source – shedding invaluable light on Israelite tribal society, its structure and organization, as well as its institutions. The wide range of the tribes mentioned at Mari – from fully nomadic to fully sedentary – and their confrontation with the indigenous population, bear directly upon an understanding of the gradual process of the Israelite settlement in Canaan and their ensuing relationship with its inhabitants. The most revealing material at Mari concerns the broad tribal federations of the Ḫaneans and Yaminites. The former were concentrated principally along the Middle Euphrates and comprised an appreciable segment of the general population (and of the army) of Mari. Indeed, the Middle Euphrates region became known as the "land of Ḫana," and "Ḫana" was applied also to a type of soldier and a kind of wool. The name, which was basically gentilic, also came to denote in general the generic concept of a (semi-) nomad; it seems to be in this sense that Zimri-Lim was called "king of the Ḫaneans," in parallel to "king of the Akkadians" – which together reflect the two main population strata, seminomadic and indigenous sedentary (see below). The Yaminites were in general less settled and posed the greater threat in this period, both to the rest of the population and to the authorities. In their subtribes (Ubrabu, Amnanu, Yaḫruru, Yariḫu, and the affiliated Rabbeans), they were dispersed over a wide arc from the city of Sippar (and even as far south as Uruk) and the eastern banks of the Tigris around to the Khabur and the Balikh valleys up to the Euphrates bend, where their main concentration lay. In the west, they had crossed the Euphrates toward Mount Bisir (Jabal Bishri) and encroached upon the land of Amurru in southern Syria. Little mention is made in the Mari archives of the DUMU.MEŠ-*sim'al*, the "sons of the north," who roamed the "upper country" in the Harran region, or of the Sutu, the fully nomadic tribe which appears more often in subsequent history. This latter ranged in the Syrian steppe and the Bishri mountains, raiding the adjacent oasis of *Tadmor (spelled *Tadmer* at Mari) on at least one occasion. The Mari archives are surprisingly silent on the "Amorites" as a definite tribal entity (though one reference is made to a *gāyu Amurum* as a sub-clan of the Ḫaneans); in general, the designation (both spelled phonetically and in the logogram MAR.TU) is restricted to the land of Amurru, far to the west, or to the military titles "great-of-Amurru" and "scribe-of-Amurru" (the latter only at Mari).

Patterns of Settlement. The tribal society depicted in the Mari archives is essentially dimorphic, i.e., it encompasses both nomadic and urban modes, with their inherent distinctions and interactions, social as well as economic. Tribal groups would sometimes undergo a gradual process of sedentation, splitting into partly settled and partly nomadic factions (cf. ARM 8, 11), or leading a life of transhumance – in the steppe or desert in the grazing season and in urban bases during the "off" months.

Depending on the stage of sedentation, the Ḫaneans and Yaminites dwelt in towns and hamlets (both designated at Mari as *ālāni*, literally, "cities"; the term *kaprum*, "village," is rare in this context) and engaged in urban-agricultural pursuits (as well as herding), or in temporary encampments (*nawūm*) and engaged in purely pastoral pursuits. At Mari, the standard Babylonian word *nawūm*, "desert, uncultivated field," or even "a savage," took on the West Semitic connotation of a pastoral abode, precisely the connotation of the Hebrew *naweh* (primarily in poetic usage in the Bible). An illustration of this dual mode of life, is found in the distinctions *Ḫana ša nawīm*, loosely, "steppe Ḫaneans," and *ḫibrum ša nawīm*, the nomadic faction of a partly settled clan (in this case, of Yaminites).

Another type of settlement originating among nomadic and seminomadic populations was the *ḥaṣārum* (pl. *haṣirātum*), which, rather than an enclosure for sheep or cattle (as usually assumed), denotes a dwelling place, as does the cognate Hebrew term *ḥaẓerim*, referring to settlements of the Ishmaelites, the Avvites, and the "sons of Kedar" (Gen. 25:16; Deut. 2:23; and Isa. 42:11 (cf. Jer. 49:33), respectively).

Tribal Leadership. The Mari archives indicate that tribal leadership was in the hands of family heads (cf. the biblical *bet-'av*, "family," the basic unit of the patriarchal tribal organization), called *abū bītim*, "father of the household" (pl. at Mari *abūt bītim*, a West Semitic form, equivalent to Heb. *'avot*). The actual tribal rulers were elevated from among these family heads, leading to the use of the term *abū bītim* for certain officials, and occasionally *abū* served as a synonym for "tribal chiefs," e.g., *abū ḥana* and *abū Idamaraṣ*. As in pre-monarchical Israel, the council of the "elders" (*šībūti*) appears in the Mari documents as a central institution, deciding on matters of war and peace, functioning in treaty making, and representing the tribe before the authorities.

A capital role in the tribal organization, unknown outside the Mari texts, is that of *sugāgum/suqāqum* (meaning unknown), whose function is somewhat vague. He may have been a sort of mukhtar, chief of a tribal unit or village appointed (or at least approved) by the Mari authorities from among the local leadership; this office (*sugāgūtum*) was sometimes purchased with money or sheep.

At the head of the tribal hierarchy stood the "kings" (Akk. *šarru*, p. *šarrāni*), who usually appear in the Mari texts as wartime leaders – again suggesting a special West Semitic connotation (in this case, military), much like the Hebrew *sar*. Thus, Yaḥdun-Lim's royal inscriptions record that he defeated "seven kings, fathers (*abū*) of Ḫana" and, on another occasion, "three Yaminite kings." This plurality of "kings" must be understood as referring to subtribal rulers that collectively comprised the tribal leadership; such a structure is also found among the Midianites (Num. 31:8; Judg. 8:12), the early Arameans (I Sam. 14:47), and perhaps the Edomites (Gen. 36:31ff.).

4. TRIBAL TRADITIONS – FUNCTIONAL AND RELIGIOUS. The convergence of the West Semitic tribes at Mari with urban Mesopotamia involved a dual process of friction and strife alongside symbiosis and mutual adaptation; this interaction between a tribal heritage and an established civilization was characteristic also of the settlement of Israelite tribes in Canaan. In Mari, this was especially evident at the court, where despite the process of assimilation of Sumero-Akkadian civilization, much of tribal tradition was still preserved. The advice of the palace prefect to Zimri-Lim on a point of protocol may thus be interpreted: "[If] you are the king of the Ḫaneans, you are, moreover, a 'king of the Akkadians.' [My lord] should not ride horses [i.e., in tribal fashion]. May my lord drive in a wagon and mules [i.e., in a "civilized" manner], and may he [thus] honor his royalty" (ARM, 6, 76:20–25). This same distinction is found, too, at the early Israelite court, though there the mule was ridden (II Sam. 13:29; 18:9; I Kings 1:33) and the horse yoked to the chariot (I Sam. 8:11; II Sam. 15:1; I Kings 1:5).

Tribal heritage from the nomadic phase did persist in spite of the curbs of sedentation and acquiescence to royal administration of Mari. Tribal customs and institutions, legal, military, and political procedures, and ritual or religious practices all find expression in the Mari texts. These traditions, largely unknown outside Mari, serve to illuminate early Israelite practices. Here are some of the major points.

Making a Covenant. In the largely illiterate society of the tribe, treaties were concluded not by means of documents but solely by symbolic acts – in the cases recorded in the Mari texts, by the ritual of "killing an ass-foal" (note the purely West Semitic expression applied here – *ḥa(ya)rum qatālum*). (Another symbolic expression in this context is *napištam lapātum*, "to touch the throat.") In one case, a possible ploy was made to introduce other animals into the ritual: in a report on a peace treaty made between the Ḫaneans and the land of Idamaraṣ, a Mari official in the Harran region tells his king that "they brought to me a whelp and a goat, but I obeyed my lord and did not give (permission for the use of) a whelp and a goat. I caused 'the foal, the young of a she-ass' (cf. Gen. 49:11; Zech. 9:9) to be slaughtered" (ARM, 2, 37:6–12). The Bible mentions a parallel ceremony, involving the cutting in two of young animals (cf. the covenant between God and Abraham – Gen. 15:9–10; and one with the leaders of Judah during the Babylonian siege of Jerusalem – Jer. 34:18–19). In all these ceremonies, the common denominator is the ritual sacrifice of young and tender animals.

Census. The Mari authorities used to take periodic censuses of the tribes, both nomadic and settled. This activity was denoted by the terms *ubbubum* (D-stem of *ebēbum*), "to cleanse," and its derivative *tēbibtum* (literally, "cleansing," "purification"), and is most likely West Semitic in origin. The purpose of the census seems to have been military conscription, taxation, and land distribution, although at least originally it was accompanied by a ritual of purification, similar to that associated with the census of the Israelites in the wilderness (which involved a tax, the payment of which was regarded as a ritual expiation, Heb. *kippurim*; cf. Ex. 30:11–16). Some scholars, however, view the *tēbibtum* as a purely administrative procedure to clear persons or property of legal or financial claims (as would be indicated by the fact that it is carried out by secular, not religious, officials).

Patrimony. The Mari legal documents employ, inter alia, the West Semitic term *naḥālum*, "to inherit or apportion," in referring to land transfers effected within a quasi-familial inheritance framework and not in the normal sales procedures. This type of transaction was inherently a part of the patriarchal tribal system, in which land ownership was not on an individual basis but was a patrimony (*niḥlatum* at Mari = Heb. *naḥalah*). The patrimony could not, theoretically, be transferred other than by inheritance, and, therefore, various means were contrived to circumvent this rule. The Israelites upheld a similar custom, where the patrimony was considered an inalienable possession, "the Israelites must remain bound each to the ancestral portion of his tribe" (Num. 36:7; cf. Lev. 25:13, 25–28; I Kings 21:1ff.; Ezek. 46:16–18).

The "Judge." The Mari documents employ several derivatives of the West Semitic root *špṭ* (verb: *šapāṭum*; participle: *šāpiṭum*; abstract nouns: *šipṭum* and *šapiṭūtum*), which may serve to elucidate the biblical cognates *shafoṭ*, *shofeṭ*, and *mishpaṭ*, usually translated as "judge" (verb and noun) and "norm or law," respectively. However, neither in the Mari documents nor in the Bible is the primary connotation of these terms judicial (for which the Akkadian employs *dayānu*); rather, they connote the much broader concept of governorship and rule. Thus, the *šāpiṭum* and his counterpart in the Book of Judges, the *shofeṭ*, were actually prominent tribesmen who had acquired an authority far exceeding that of a mere "justice" (and cf. the later Punic *suffetes*). The expression *šipṭam nadānum/šakānum*, met with in the Mari documents, corresponds to the bibical *sim mishpaṭ*, "lay down a ruling" (by a duly authorized person) employed in connection with the authoritative acts of a Moses, a Joshua, and a David (cf. Ex. 15:25; Josh. 24:25; I Sam. 30:25).

The Ban. A peculiar expression at Mari, *asakkam akālum* (lit. "to eat the *asakku*"), refers to the infringement of a taboo or the profaning of something revered, and may be a loan translation of some West Semitic concept paralleling that of the biblical ban (*ḥerem). The *asakku* of a particular deity, and/or king, is frequently invoked in penalty clauses of contracts, in oaths, and in royal decrees as the sacrosanct and inviolable element. The closest parallel between Mari and the biblical practice is in the imposition of the ban on spoils of war (cf., e.g., the Achan incident, Josh. 7). However, whereas the biblical ban functioned on a purely religious plane (whatever was banned was exclusively God's), the taboo at Mari was applicable also on a human level, and its infringement there, though theoretically still considered a capital offense, was expiated by payment of a simple fine.

God of the Father. Among the central religious concepts of the Hebrew Patriarchs is the "God of the/my/your/his father," i.e., a personal, innominate deity, revered by subsequent offspring (cf. Gen. 28:13; 31:5, 29, 42, 53; 32:10; 49:25; Ex. 3:6, 15; 15:2, etc.). A direct parallel occurs in one Mari text, where the king of Qatna swears "by the name of the god of my father" (ARM, 5, 20:16; and cf. Gen. 31:53), and in another where Hammurapi (undoubtedly Yarim-Lim's successor as king of Aleppo) is appealed to "by the name of (the god) Adad, Lord of A[leppo] and the god of [your] father" (ARM, 10, 156:10–11). It is significant for the biblical comparison that both instances are in the west, as are all other references to such a deity outside Mari – in the slightly older Assyrian tablets from Cappadocia, the later texts from Ugarit (in Akkadian, Ugaritic, and Hurrian), and, again at Qatna, in temple inventories and in an Amarna letter sent from there.

[Abraham Malamat]

Prophetic Revelation. One phenomenon at Mari that has drawn the attention of biblicists is that of apostolic prophecy, in which individuals, male and female, deliver messages, often unsolicited, in the name of a god. Before the discovery of Mari the Hebrew phenomenon of apostolic prophecy had tended to be viewed in isolation, and often treated as a unique phenomenon.

At Mari we can distinguish between the intuitive manticism of the apostolic prophet, and the mechanical manticism of the diviner who examines the entrails of animals, primarily sheep livers, for divine messages and decisions. His learned arts are considered authoritative, as shown by the fact that he is regularly called upon to authenticate the message of the prophet, often an ecstatic. The Mari prophets are often professionals, but sometimes ordinary people. The professionals are (1) *āpilu* (masculine) *āpiltu* (feminine), "answerer," attested once as *aplû*, "the one answered"; (2) *muhhû* (masc.)/*muhhûtu* (fem.), "ecstatic"; (3) *assinnu*, a cultic functionary of a goddess, possibly a eunuch; (4) *qammatum*, etymology uncertain, perhaps referring to a distinctive hair style; (5) *na/ābû* (see *Emar), the least attested but closest etymologically to *nabi*, the most common biblical word for "prophet." Derived from the verb *nabû*, "call," this is either a passive participle, "the one called," or an active participle, "the caller." It is noteworthy that in our extant texts the *muhhûm* prophesies in the name of two gods in whose name the *āpilum* does not prophesy: Itur-Mer, the chief god of Mari, and the goddess Anunitum.

All the male and female divinities in whose name prophecies are delivered are high gods. Some of the goddesses, Belet-Ekallim; Anunitum, and Diritum, are manifestations of Ishtar, worshipped in Mari and its surroundings. Dagan is the god to whom the most prophecies (16) are attributed, followed by Hadad (7). Among the goddesses the most frequent is Anunitum.

In most instances the prophets spoke their words in those temples to which they were connected. This suggests that these prophets routinely prophesied in their temples, and that only a small number of their prophecies have reached us. In addition, it is likely that most of the prophecies directed to the king were uttered publicly in the royal palace and did not require reduction to writing, in contrast to those prophecies communicated from afar by royal officials, and accordingly, preserved for posterity. Only the activity of the *muhhûm* is attested outside Mari; at Andarig, Babylon, and Yamhad (Aleppo). Sometimes the prophets specify that they are god's messenger by use of the verb *šapāru*, "send," the semantic parallel of *šālaḥ*, regularly said of the Hebrew prophets and by them. In one case a prophet describes his mission by the verb *šūhuzu*, "instruct," indicating that he was instructed to deliver his message.

The Mari letters provide important descriptions of the circumstances in which prophecies were delivered. The writers describe the prophet's arrival, his standing up in order to deliver the prophecy and the like, as well as the verb used by the prophet to describe the message. What follows are some specific examples describing the delivery of the message arranged by prophetic category.

āpilum: He is described variously as speaking, as coming and speaking, standing up and speaking, and standing and shouting at length at the gate. Sometimes he comes to the palace gate and writes his message to the king; or he dictates his prophecy to a reliable scribe. Finally, he may come and claim that the god has sent a message to the king through him.

muhhûm: The method of delivery agrees in some respects with that of the *āpilum* but differs in others. Of the *muhhû* it is said simply that he delivers his message, or, he comes and delivers his message, or, he comes and speaks emotionally and forcefully. He calls out repeatedly. It must be noted that his activity is never described by the verb *namhû*, "to act crazed," "to become ecstatic," which demonstrates that the verb is never used of a professional ecstatic, but only of an *assinnum* or any ordinary man or woman overcome by ecstasy (see below). Prophecy described as being "given" (*têrtam nadānum*) is uttered by the *mahhû* and the *assinnum*, but never by the *āpilu*.

Ordinary people: A woman speaks her message; a married woman comes and says that Dagan sent her. Someone's daughter or serving girl becomes ecstatic (*namhû*) and speaks. An unidentified man becomes ecstatic and speaks.

Virtually all the prophecies that have reached us were uttered either in Mari when Zimri-Lim was away, or were uttered elsewhere in the kingdom when Zimri-Lim was at Mari. We may assume that ordinarily when the prophet spoke directly to the king his words were not committed to writing, and accordingly, are not preserved. At the same time it should be noted that all of the royal officers, commanders, and priests were obligated to provide the king with all information relevant to the welfare of the kingdom that reached him. Some of these functionaries were bound by oath to convey that information orally or in writing. Apparently, this is why they felt the need to convey the prophetic messages to the king. Some examples follow of the writers of the prophetic letters and the prophets involved:

1) *āpilum*: The writers of the letters hear a prophecy and relate it to the king, or send it in writing to the king. At times the *āpilum* himself sends his words in writing to the king either directly or through an intermediary. He may also write to the queen, who delivers the message in writing to the king.

2) *muhhûm*; In contrast to the *āpilum*, the *muhhûm* never writes the king, but he may speak to the king directly. In most cases someone who has heard his words writes them down and sends them to the king. The queen writes to the king about a prophecy that she has heard personally, or she relates that someone who heard the prophecy of the *muhhû* has written her about it. There are instances in which a priest or a governor hears a prophecy in a temple and writes it down and sends it to Bahdi-Lim, governor of Mari who rewrites it and sends it to Zimri-Lim.

3) *qammatum*: The *qammatu* comes to the (female) letter-writer who writes the king.

4) *assinnu*: Someone who heard his words writes the king, or, he comes to the queen and she writes the king.

5) The category of prophecy has not survived: Someone hears a prophecy and writes the king, as required by his position. Sometimes the prophet speaks to Queen Shibtum and she writes to Zimri-Lim. Finally, a female prophet turns to Itur-Asdu, a prefect of Zimri-Lim at Nahur who sends her words to Zimri-Lim.

There are instances in which a god speaks from the throat of the prophet in the first person:

1) *āpilum*: One formula describes how the *āpilum* quotes the words of the god: Thus (says) the *āpilum* of Shamash: Thus (says) Shamash; or: Abiya the *āpilum* of Addad, Lord of Halab (Aleppo), came to me and thus he said to me: Thus (says) Adad. In contrast, sometimes the *āpilu* speaks through the throat of the prophet: The *aplû* / *āpilu* of Dagan of Tutul stood up and said thus: "I shall gather you … I shall hand you over." This is true as well of the prophecies of Adad, Lord of Kalassu, and Adad, Lord of Halab. In both cases they speak from the throat of the *āpilu*.

Thus far, the Mari texts have not yet produced an Amos or a Hosea. Nonetheless, one finds the same kind of prophetic call for social justice known from the Bible. Letter A.1968 (Roberts, 166–69) reports that Abiya the *āpilum* of Halab sent to Zimri-Lim reminding him the king that it was the god who restored him to his ancestral throne and had given the king the weapons with which the god had fought the sea(!) It was the god who anointed Zimri-Lim so that none might stand in his way. The god then commands the king, "When someone who has a lawsuit calls to you saying, 'I have been wronged,' stand up and judge his lawsuit" (Akkadian: *dīnšu din*). Similarly, in A.1121+ A.2731 (Roberts, 172–77), an *āpilu* sends to the king: "When an oppressed man or woman calls out to you, 'render their judgment'" (Akkadian: *dīnšunu din*).

The very manifestation at Mari of intuitive divination – revealing a consciousness of prophetic mission among West Semitic tribes in a period predating Israelite prophecy by centuries – places the history and investigation of Near Eastern prophecy in general, and both earlier and later biblical prophecy in particular, in an entirely new perspective (see also *Prophets and Prophecy).

BIBLIOGRAPHY: GENERAL SURVEYS: A. Parrot (ed.), *Studia Mariana* (1950), includes bibliography; idem, *Mari* (1953); Ch.-F. Jean, *Six campagnes de fouilles à Mari* 1933–1939 (1952); A. Malamat, in: EM, 4 (1962), 559–79; G.E. Mendenhall, in: *Biblical Archaeologist Reader*, 2 (1964), 3–20; J.R. Kupper (ed.), *La civilisation de Mari* (XVe *recontre assyriologique internationale* = RAI, 15, 1967); A. Petitjean and J. Coppens, in: *Bibliotheca Ephemeridum Theologicarum Lovaniensum*, 24 (1969), 3–13 (incl. bibl.). ON A: ARCHAEOLOGICAL REPORTS: A. Parrot, *Mission Archéologique de Mari*: vol. 1, *Le temple d'Ishtar* (1956); vol. 2, pt. 1, *Le palais – architecture* (1958); vol. 2, pt. 2, *Le palais – peintures murales* (1958); vol. 2, pt. 3, *Le palais – documents et monuments* (1959); vol. 3, *Les temples d'Ishtarat et de Ninni-Zaza* (1967); vol. 4, *Le trésor d'Ur* (1968); idem, in: *Syria*, 46 (1969), 191–208 (17th campaign); 47 (1970), 225–43 (18th campaign). OTHERS: W.F. Albright, in JAOS, 45 (1925), 225–6; 46 (1926), 220–30; M. Rutten, in: *Revue d'assyriologie et d'archéologie orientale*, 35 (1938), 36–52; I.J. Gelb, *ibid.*, 50 (1956), 1–10; M. Civil, *ibid.*, 56 (1962), 213; G. Dossin, *ibid.*, 61 (1967), 97–104; D.O. Edzard, in RAI, 15 (1967), 51–71; P. Carlmeyer, *ibid.*, 161–9; J.R. Kupper, in: JCS, 21 (1967), 123–5; A. Moortgat, in: *Baghdader Mitteilungen*, 3 (1964), 68–74; 4 (1968), 221–31; M.C. Astour, in: JAOS, 88 (1968), 738; idem, in: *Ugarit Forschungen*, 2 (1970), 2; E. Sollberger, in: *Revue d'assyriologie et d'archéologie orientale*, 63 (1969), 169–70; A. Caquot, in: *Syria*, 46 (1969), 246–7. OLD BABYLONIAN ARCHIVES: *Archives royales de Mari*: vol. 1, G. Dossin, *Correspondance de Šamši-Addu* (1950); vol. 2, Ch.-F. Jean, *Lettres diverses* (1950); vol. 3, J.R. Kupper, *Correspondance de Kibri-Dagan* (1950); vol. 4, G. Dossin, *Correspondance de Šamsi-Addu* (1951); vol. 5, G. Dossin, *Correspondance de Iasmaḫ-Addu* (1952); vol. 6, J.R. Kupper, *Correspondance de Baḫdi-Lim* (1954); vol. 7, J. Bottéro, *Textes economiques et administratifs* (1957); vol. 8, G. Boyer, *Textes juridiques* (1958); vol. 9, M. Birot, *Textes administratifs de la salle 5 du palais* (1960); vol. 10, G. Dossin, *La correspondance féminine* (1967; cuneiform only); vol. 11, M. Lurton Burke, *Textes administratifs de la salle III du palais* (1963); vol. 12, M. Birot, *Textes administratifs de la salle 5 du palais* (1964); vol. 13, G. Dossin, et al., *Textes divers* (1964); vol. 15, J. Bottéro and A. Finet, *Répertoire analytique des tomes I a V* (1954); G. Dossin, in: *Syria*, 19 (1938), 105–26; 20 (1939), 97–113; idem, in: *Revue d'assyriologie et d'archéologie orientale*, 35 (1938), 1–13; W. von Soden, in: *Die Welt des Orients*, 1 (1947–52), 187–204; F. Thureau-Dangin, in:

Revue d'assyriologie et d'archéologie orientale, 36 (1939), 1–28; G. Goossens, *ibid.*, 46 (1952), 137–54; E. Laroche, *ibid.*, 51 (1957), 104–6; I. Mendelsohn, in: BASOR, 156 (1959), 38–40; A.L. Oppenheim, *Letters from Mesopotamia* (1967), 96–110; A. Malamat, in: *Qadmoniot*, 1 (1968), 80–87; P. Artzi and A. Malamat, in: *Orientalia*, 40 (1971), 75–89. ON B: G. Dossin, in: *Syria*, 32 (1955), 1–28; idem, in: *Revue d'assyriologie et d'archéologie orientale*, 64 (1970), 17ff., 97ff.; W.F. Leemans, *ibid.*, 49 (1955), 201–4; idem, *Foreign Trade in the Old Babylonian Period* (1960), 176–81; B. Landsberger, in: JCS, 8 (1954), 35–36; J.M. Munn-Rankin, in: *Iraq*, 18 (1956), 68–110; J.R. Kupper, *Les nomades en Mésopotamie au temps des rois de Mari* (1957); H. Lewy, in: *Die Welt des Orients*, 2 (1959), 438–53; idem, in: RAI, 15 (1967), 14–28; I.J. Gelb, in: JCS, 15 (1961), 27–47; A. Goetze, in: JSS, 4 (1959), 142–7; D.O. Edzard, in: *Fischer Weltgeschichte*, 2 (1965), 165–91; K.A. Kitchen, *Ancient Orient and the Old Testament* (1966), index; W. Roellig, in: RAI, 15 (1967), 97–102; J.J. Finkelstein, in: JCS, 20 (1966), 95–118; A. Malamat, in JAOS, 88 (1968), 87–97; W.F. Albright, *Yahwe and the Gods of Canaan* (1968), index, s.v. *Mari*; J.M. Sasson, *The Military Establishments at Mari* (1969). ON THE WEST: F.M. Tocci, *La Siria nell'età di Mari* (1960); G. Dossin, in: *Bulletin de l'Académie royale de Belgique (classe des lettres)*, 38 (1952), 224–39; 40 (1954), 417–25; J.R. Kupper, in: CAH^2, vol. 2, ch. 1 (1963); A. Malamat, in: *Eretz-Israel*, 5 (1958), 67–73; idem, in: JBL, 79 (1960), 12–19; idem, in: *Studies in Honor of B. Landsberger* (1965), 365–73; idem, in: J.A. Sanders (ed.), *Essays in Honor of N. Glueck* (1970), 164–77; idem, in: IEJ, 21 (1971); B. Mazar, in: IEJ, 18 (1968), 65–97. ON C 1–3: G. Dossin, in: *Mélanges Dussaud*, 2 (1939), 981–96; idem, in: *Revue d'assyriologie et d'archéologie orientale*, 52 (1958), 60–62; 62 (1968), 75–76; M. Noth, in: *A. Alt Festschrift* (1953), 127–52; idem, *Urspruenge des alten Israel im Lichte neuer Quellen* (1961); A. Finet, *L'accadien des lettres de Mari* (1956); idem, in: *Syria*, 41 (1964), 117–42; idem, in: *Revue d'assyriologie et d'archéologie orientale*, 60 (1966), 17–28; W.L. Moran, in: *Orientalia*, 26 (1957), 339–45; D.O. Edzard, in: ZA, 19 (1959), 168–73; H. Klengel, in: *Orientalia*, 29 (1960), 357–75; idem, in: *Archiv Orientální*, 30 (1962), 585–96; idem, in: *Das Verhaeltnis von Bodenbauern und Viehzuechtern in historischer Sicht* (1968), 75–81; P. Fronzaroli, in: *Archivio Glottologico Italiano*, 45 (1960), 37–60, 127–49; J.C.L. Gibson, in: *Glasgow University Oriental Society Transactions*, 18 (1959–60), 15–29; idem, in: JSS, 7 (1962), 44–62; P. Artzi, in: *Oz le-David (Ben-Gurion)* (1964), 71–85; H.B. Huffmon, *Amorite Personal Names in the Mari Texts* (1965); G. Buccellati, *The Amorites of the Ur III Period* (1966); A. Malamat, in: JAOS, 82 (1962), 143–50; idem, in: RAI, 15 (1967), 129–38; W. von Soden, in: *Die Welt des Orients*, 3 (1966), 177–87; Lambert, Klima, Cazelles, Rowton, in: RAI, 15 (1967); M. Weippert, *Die Landnahme der Israel. Staemme* (1967), 102–23; J. Klima, in: *Das Verhaeltnis von Bodenbauern…* (1968), 83–89; L.R. Bailey, in: JBL, 87 (1968), 434–8. ON C4: G. Dossin, *Studies in Old Testament Prophecy (Th. H. Robinson Volume)* (1950), 103–10; W. von Soden, in: *Die Welt des Orients*, 1 (1947–52), 397–403; M. Noth, in: BJRL, 32 (1950), 194–206; idem, in: *Annuaire de l'Institut de Philologie et d'Histoire Orientales et Slaves*, 13 (1955), 433–44; idem, in: JSS, 1 (1956), 322–33; G. Wallis, in: ZAW, 64 (1952), 57–61; G.E. Mendenhall, in: BASOR, 133 (1954), 26–30; M. Held, *ibid.*, 200 (1970), 32–40; E.A. Speiser, *ibid.*, 149 (1958), 17–25; idem, in: JBL, 79 (1960), 157–63; A. Malamat, in: *Eretz-Israel*, 4 (1956), 74–84; 5 (1958), 67–73; idem, in VTS, 15 (1966), 207–27; idem, in: *Biblical Essays, Proceedings of the 9th Meeting, Die Ou Testamentiese Werkgemeenskap in Suid-Afrika* (1966), 40–49; W. Richter, in: ZAW, 77 (1965), 40–72; R. de Vaux, in: *Ugaritica*, 6 (1969), 501–17; C. Westermann, *Forschung am Alten Testament* (1964), 171–88; F. Ellermeier, *Prophetie in Mari und Israel* (1968); H.B. Huffmon, in: BA, 31 (1968), 102–24; J.G. Heintz, in: VTS, 17 (1969), 112–38; W.L. Moran, in: *Biblica*, 50 (1969), 15–55; idem, in: Pritchard, Texts^3, 623–31; J.F. Ross, in: HTR, 63 (1970), 1–28. **ADD. BIBLIOGRAPHY:** A. Malamat, *Mari and the Early Israelite Experience* (1984); idem, *Mari and the Bible* (1998); Ö. Tunca (ed.), *De la Babylonie à la Syrie, en passant par Mari Mélanges…Kupper* (1990); M. Anbar, *Les tribus ammurite de Mari* (1991); idem, in: A. Rainey (ed.), *Kinattūtu ša dārâti* (1993), 1–5; J.C. Margueron, in: ABD, 4: 525–29; J.M. Durand, ibid., 529–36; B. Keck, ibid., 536–38, bibl.; P. Villard, in: CANE, 2:873–83; J.C. Margueron (on art and architecture at Mari), ibid., 885–89; idem, *Mari, métropole de l'Euphrate au IIIe et au début du IIe millénaire av,* J.C. (2004); J.M. Durand, *Documents épistolaires du Palais de Mari I, Littératures anciennes du Proche-Orient* (= LAPO) 16 (1997); idem, *Documents épistolaires du Palais de Mari II, Littératures anciennes du Proche*-Orient (= LAPO) 17 (1998); idem, in: *Amurru*, 3 (2004), 111–97; A. Kuhrt, *The Ancient Near East c. 3000–330 BC* (1995), 95–108; J. Roberts, in: idem, *The Bible and the Ancient Near East* (Mari prophetic texts in transliteration and translation) (2002), 157–253; W. Heimpel, *Letters to the King of Mari* (2003); D. Charpin and N. Ziegler, *Mari et le Proche-Orient à l'époque amorrite. Essai d'histoire politique* (Mémoires de N.A.B.U. 6, Florilegium marianum V; 2003); D. Charpin, in: P. Attinger, W. Salaberger, and M. Wäfler (eds.), *Mesopotamien: Die altbabylonische Zeit, Annäherungen*, 4 (OBO 160/4; 2004), 132–330, 453–76.

MARIAMNE (Mariamme).

MARIAMNE I (60?–29 B.C.E.) was the daughter of *Alexander the son of Aristobulus, the granddaughter of John Hyrcanus, and the second wife of *Herod. Herod's aim in contracting this marriage was to establish his standing with the royal house. Herod was only betrothed to her, but not yet married, when in 40 B.C.E. he was forced to flee to Idumea from Antigonus, who was supported by the Parthians, and he had placed Mariamne together with the other women of the royal household in the fortress of Masada for safety. When Herod's sovereignty over Judea was ratified by the Roman senate on the recommendation of Mark Antony, he went in 37 B.C.E. to Samaria to marry Mariamne while his army was still besieging Jerusalem. Herod's love for Mariamne was unbounded, but it was met by hatred of him on her part, because Herod had put to death practically all the members of her family. Aware of Herod's feelings for her, she was bold enough to speak harshly to him, which others feared to do. In addition to this, however, her anger was directed against the rise of the new dynasty which had replaced her own – the *Hasmonean – and this caused her to act disdainfully toward the members of the royal Idumean family, particularly to Herod's mother and his sister Salome. As a result these two harbored a grudge against her and were malevolently provocative toward her, fabricating such libels about her as that she had sent her portrait to Antony in Egypt.

When Herod went to visit Antony he entrusted his wife to Joseph, the husband of Salome, ordering him to put Mariamne to death should Antony sentence him to death. Joseph informed Mariamne of this with the intention of showing her how great was the love Herod bore her. When Herod returned from his journey he discovered from Mariamne that Joseph had revealed this secret order to her. According to one account in Josephus, it was then that in his rage Herod ordered both Joseph and Mariamne to be put to death. A parallel account, however, is given by Josephus in the section dealing with Herod's journey to Octavius at Rhodes after the battle near Actium. The first story belongs to the period before 31 B.C.E., while the second is later. It seems that both stories were true, but that the execution of Mariamne took place in 29 B.C.E., and that on the previous occasion Herod did not go so far as to murder his wife. Mariamne bore Herod three sons and two daughters. One of the sons died in his youth. The other two, Alexander and Aristobulus, were executed on the order of their father in 7 B.C.E.

MARIAMNE II (d. circa 20 B.C.E.), the daughter of Simeon b. Boethus the high priest, was the third wife of Herod. She belonged to a priestly family from Alexandria. Her son, also named Herod, was designated to succeed to the throne after Antipater. It was because of this that although Mariamne II knew of Antipater's intentions to kill his father, she held her peace. As a result, when the plot of Antipater was discovered, Herod erased from his will the name of his son Herod II as his heir and sent Mariamne away.

BIBLIOGRAPHY: Jos., Wars; Jos., Ant.; A. Schalit, *Koenig Herodes* (1969), index; Klausner, Bayit Sheni, 3 (1950^2), 261, 268; 4 (1950^2), 14–18, 153f. (Mariamne I); 4 (1950^2), 42, 153 (Mariamne II); A.H.M. Jones, *Herods of Judea* (1938), index.

[Abraham Lebanon]

MARIANOS (sixth century), artist who – together with his son Ḥanina – designed the pictorial mosaic floor of the Bet Alfa (Ḥefẓi-Bah) synagogue near Beth-Shean. Their names also appear in an ornamental mosaic floor adjoining a synagogue at Beth-Shean. They are known only through these two mosaics. The inscription in Greek at Bet Alfa reads: "May the craftsmen who carried out this work, Marianos and his son Ḥanina, be held in remembrance." Below this inscription, a partially destroyed Aramaic legend dates the mosaic to the reign of the Byzantine emperor Justin (I), viz., 518–527 C.E. It is clear that, as local Galilean artists, they worked in the standard Greco-Oriental manner of the time, combining Eastern frontality, patterning, and lack of modeling and perspective, with Western costumes, composition, and mosaic technique. The similarity of their work to mosaics in other sixth-century synagogues of the Palestinian littoral indicates that they followed standard patterns. The style of their work appears to reflect rug designs. In the Bet Alfa mosaic the motifs of the border designs and of two of the three panels, that of the zodiac and of the holy symbols, are paralleled elsewhere (e.g., the sixth-century synagogue of Tiberias). The third panel located just inside the entrance to the prayer room depicts the sacrifice of Isaac, combining an artistic and symbolic complexity that belies the direct, seemingly naive manner in which the mosaic is worked. (See *Bet Alfa.)

BIBLIOGRAPHY: B. Goldman, *Sacred Portal* (1966); E.L. Sukenik, *Ancient Synagogue of Beth Alpha* (1932); N. Tsori, in: *Israel Exploration Journal*, 13 (1963), 148–9.

[Bernard Goldman]

°**MARIA THERESA** (1717–1780), empress of Austria from 1740, the first female heir to the Hapsburg throne as a result of the "Pragmatic Sanction" (1713). She continued the hostile policy of *Charles VI, her father, against the Jews. Her passionate hatred, nurtured from childhood, culminated in the expulsion of *Prague Jewry (1744), which she revoked in 1748 after international intervention on behalf of the Jews. She declared in 1777 that she knew "no worse plague for the state than this nation, because of its deceitfulness, its usury," and noted that the Jews "bring the state more harm than good." She granted audiences to Jews from behind a partition. In spite of this, she profited from the services of such individuals as Diego d'*Aguilar, Israel von *Hoenigsberg, and Wolf Wertheimer. Pursuing a mercantilist policy on the advice of Joseph von Sonnenfels she granted special privileges to Jews, allowing them to establish factories with the condition that gentile labor be employed. She forbade the baptism of Jewish children against the will of their parents, and in 1754 issued the *General Polizey Ordnung* ("statute") for Moravian Jewry based on the long-standing *Shai Takkanot*. In 1742 she confirmed the judicial autonomy of Lombardian Jewry (reconfirmed in 1752 and 1764), and in 1744 refrained from carrying out her intention of expelling the Jews from *Naples. In 1753 she permitted the reestablishment of a prayer room at *Usov (Maehrisch-Aussee) and in 1762 reconfirmed the privileges of Mantuan bankers. The unified toleration tax introduced in 1749 in Hungary was called "*malke-geld*" ("queen money"); it was fear for the loss of the revenue from this tax that induced the empress to prohibit the spread of blood libels in 1764. Despite her concern for ensuring the revenues of the kingdom, her hatred of the Jews found frequent expression. In 1746 she ordered the expulsion of Jews from Buda (Ofen; see *Budapest) and *Timisoara, and in 1774 she expelled the Jewish community from *Hodonin (Goeding), her private domain. In 1752 she had a census taken of the Jews living in Vienna, checked personally on them every three months lest their number multiply illegally, and in 1764 issued a new statute for Lower Austria. Her reign was characterized by the attempt to modernize and centralize the country. As a result of the annexation of the former Polish territories Galicia (1772) and Bukovina (1775), the Hapsburg monarchy became the country with the largest population of Jews.

BIBLIOGRAPHY: M. Grunwald, *Vienna* (1936), 139–44; R. Pick, *Empress Maria Theresa* (1966), index s.v. *Jews*; H. Tietze, *Juden Wiens* (1935), 98–110; B. Mevorakh, in: *Zion*, 28 (1963), 125–64 (bibliography about Prague expulsion: 125–7 in remarks 1–5); idem, in: *Meḥkarim … le-Zekher Ẓevi Avneri* (1970), 188–232; H. Gold, *Juden und Judengemeinden Maehrens* (1929), 220, 338; S. Simonsohn, *Toledot ha-Yehudim be-Dukkasut Mantovah* (1963), index; R. Kestenberg-Gladstein, *Neuere … Boehmens*, 1 (1969), index; C. Schieber, in: *Zeitschrift fuer die Geschichte der Juden*, 1 (1964), 55–58, 153–7; A. Newman, in: JHSET, 22 (1970), 30–37. **ADD. BIBLIOGRAPHY:** I. Cerman, "Maria Theresa in the Mirror of the Mock Jewish Chronicles," in: *Judaica Bohemiae*, 38 (2003), 5–47; S. Plaggenborg, "Maria Theresa und die boehmischen Juden," in: *Bohemia*, 39:1 (1998), 1–16; G. Radichevich, "Das oesterreichische Judentum im Zeitalter der Aufklärung," in: F. Potoschnig et al. (eds.), *Semitismus und Antisemitismus in Oesterreich* (1988),

103–16; E. Dillmann, *Maria Theresa* (2000); F. Herre, *Maria Theresia* (2004); K. Schmal, *Die Pietas Maria Theresias im Spannungsfeld zwischen Barock und Aufklärung* (2001).

[Meir Lamed / Bjoern Siegel (2nd ed.)]

MARI BEN ISSUR (first half of the fourth century), Babylonian *amora*. Mari's father was a non-Jew who became converted to Judaism after his son was conceived and was henceforth known as Issur the Proselyte (BB 149a). According to Rashi (Bet. 16a, BM 73b) his mother was Rachel, the daughter of Samuel (Mar or Samuel Yarḥina'ah) who had been taken captive (Ket. 23a); Mari is therefore identical with the Mari b. Rachel and the "Mari, the son of Samuel's daughter" who are often mentioned in the Babylonian Talmud, and he was called after his mother because of his non-Jewish paternity. This view is upheld by Samuel b. Meir (Rashbam to BB 149a) but is contested by the *tosafot* (ad loc.) since according to the Talmud the daughters of Samuel were ransomed from captivity in Ereẓ Israel and married Simeon b. Abba, one after the other, all dying shortly after the marriage (Ket. 23a; TJ, Ket. 2:6, 26c). Moreover there is a chronological difficulty in identifying the daughter of Samuel, who died in 256, with the mother of Mari, who died in the second half of the fourth century. Issur, after his conversion to Judaism, became friendly with R. Safra (BM 31b) and particularly with Rava and under their influence Mari attended the *bet midrash* and devoted himself to study. Issur left Mari 12,000 *zuz* which he deposited with Rava (BB 149a). Mari had two sons: Mar Zutra and Adda Saba, contemporaries of Ashi (Kid. 65b).

BIBLIOGRAPHY: Hyman, Toledot, 903–5; Ḥ. Albeck, *Mavo la-Talmudim* (1969), 369.

[David Joseph Bornstein]

MARIBOR (Ger. **Marburg**), town in Štajersko (Steiermark) province of Slovenia. Jews lived there from the Middle Ages, arriving from the north, mostly from the Rhineland area. They were moneylenders and artisans, known only by their first names, such as Meyer, Isaac, or Mosch (Moses). Among the moneylenders was an Abraham ben Jacob, and Rabbi ben Petaḥya Isserlein as well as his grandchildren are on record in the 14th century.

Jews lived in a ghetto from 1277; they had to wear a yellow badge. Rabbi Isserlein, locally mentioned as Israel Marburg, worked in Maribor some time in the 1430s. The Jewish physicians, Hayyim and Michael, are noted in documents. To arbitrate disputes between Jews and Christians, a special court was established, consisting of eight judges, four of them Jewish, presided over by a Christian. Later, however, a one-man office, called *Judenrichter* (Judge of the Jews), came into existence.

In 1465 the Jewish quarter was surrounded by a wall, parts of which still exist, called "Židovski stolp" (Jew's tower). It formed part of the city's fortifications. By the edict of Emperor Maximilian I of March 1496 all Jews were expelled. They migrated to Burgenland in the north or westward to Trieste and Istria, some even wandering to Poland. In 1501 the synagogue was converted into the Church of All Saints. Only in the second half of the 19th century were Jews re-admitted to Maribor. They were linked at first to the Graz community (Austria), later to that of Varaždin (Croatia). In the early 1930s about a hundred Jews were noted.

No Jews now live in Maribor. The synagogue was preserved and renovated and is used as a cultural center.

BIBLIOGRAPHY: A. Rosenberg, *Geschichte der Juden in Steiermark* (1914); H. Schulsinger, in: *Jevrejski Almanah, Vršac, 5690* (1929/30); M. Detoni, in: *Jevrejski Almanah 1957–58*, pp. 72–74 (with illustrations).

[Zvi Loker (2nd ed.)]

MARIENBAD (Czech. **Mariánské Lázně**), town in W. Bohemia, Czech Republic. The first Jew settled in Marienbad in 1820; prior to this time Jews only went to Marienbad during the health cure season. The Jewish community grew, as did the town, during the 19th century, drawing its settlers mainly from the Drmouly (Duerrmaul; see *Chodová Planá) and *Lázně Kynžvart (Koenigswart) communities. Many foreigners also settled there. Instrumental in the development of Marienbad was the professor and balneologist Samuel Basch, whose statue was removed by the Nazis, and reerected in 1970. On the initiative of Prague notables a Jewish hospice with a prayer room was built in 1861, with the help of gifts from Jewish visitors. Another balneologist, Heinrich Enoch *Kisch, also lived in Marienbad, contributing greatly to its development. He was the head of the Jewish hospice and a street was named for him. In 1875 a congregation was constituted and in 1884 a synagogue was dedicated. Marienbad was very popular among Russian Jewry at the end of the 19th century. According to the municipal election statute (in force until 1918), no Jew could be elected to the municipal council. The community numbered 405 in 1930 (3.3% of the total population). In 1937 the great assembly (*Keneset ha-Gedolah*) of *Agudat Israel was held in Marienbad. The World Council of Agudat Israel was held there in 1947. At the time of the Sudeten crisis (1938) most of the community left the town; those who remained were arrested by the Nazis. The synagogue was burned down and its site is now a park. In 1945 a community was refounded. It was made up mostly of Jews from Carpatho-Russia who had opted to live in Czechoslovakia rather then in their country of birth. Some were demobilized soldiers of the Czechoslovak army in the Soviet Union. It numbered 196 in 1949. For a period of time there was a yeshivah for survivors of the Nazi persecutions in the town. In 1970 Marienbad was a center of Jewish life in Czechoslovakia as its Jewish old-age home (with a prayer room and a *kasher* restaurant) had about 100 residents from all over the country. The old age home and prayer room were closed in 1972.

BIBLIOGRAPHY: J. Steiner, in: H. Gold (ed.), *Juden und Judengemeinden Boehmens…* (1934), 396–7; J.C. Pick, in: *Jews of Czechoslovakia*, 1 (1968), 378; R. Iltis (ed.), *Die aussaeen unter Traenen…* (1959), 23; *Věstnik židovských náboženských obce v Praze*, 16 no. 6 (1954), 47; Yad Vashem BJCE. **ADD. BIBLIOGRAPHY:** J. Fiedler, *Jewish Sights of Bohemia and Moravia* (1991), 111–12.

[Meir Lamed]

MARIJAMPOLE (Rus. **Mariampol**), city in S. Lithuania. In 1856 there were 2,853 Jews in Marijampole; in 1897 there were 3,268 (c. 49% of the total population); and on the eve of World War I, 5,000. Many of them were admitted to Russian boys' and girls' secondary schools. In addition to the traditional *ḥadarim*, a "reformed *ḥeder*," where Hebrew was the language of instruction, was established. During World War I the Jews were expelled and a number were imprisoned for allegedly collaborating with the enemy. In 1923 there were 2,545 Jews (21% of the total). The majority of them earned their livelihood from trading in agricultural produce and small industry. There were also some landowners and smallholders. The Jews of Marijampole engaged in extensive nationalist political and cultural activities. They established welfare and cultural institutions of a high standard, including the first Hebrew secondary school in Lithuania (1919). There was also a farm which provided training for *ḥalutzim* in the vicinity of the city. When the Germans occupied the city in 1941, the Jews were concentrated in a local ghetto together with other Jews from the surrounding area. Over 7,000 of them were massacred at the beginning of September 1941.

BIBLIOGRAPHY: *Lite*, 1 (1951), 1563–67, 1839–42.

[Dov Levin]

MARIL, HERMAN (1908–1986), U.S. painter. Born in Baltimore, Maryland, Maril painted seascapes and landscapes, often of the Cape Cod area. He studied at the Maryland Institute of Fine Arts, participated in federal works projects during the Depression, and painted during his World War II military service. He taught painting, drawing, and watercolor at the University of Maryland until his death, while exhibiting in galleries in New York, Washington, D.C., and Baltimore. He created lyrical works in oil, watercolor, and ink which referenced landscape, seascape, and sports subjects with various levels of modernist abstraction. Maril's careful, balanced compositions are characterized by rich, even sensuous color, large, simplified shapes and forms, and a flattened picture plane. The artist worked in the American Scene style in the 1930s but soon developed a personal idiom which incorporated the tenets of modernism: spare, broad swathes of color, emphasis on facture, flattened forms, and a purging of details. While working in the 1950s Maril never adopted an Abstract Expressionist style, but continued to develop his robust, individualized vision, indebted to the socially attuned work of such artists as Raphael Soyer, Ben Shahn, and Lyonel Feininger. His subjects range from Matisse-inspired goldfish in a bowl, to farmyards and skyscrapers. While working in New York in the 1930s, he met a number of other artists, including Soyer, Marsden Hartley, Mark Rothko, and Chaim Gross. In 1935, the art critic Olin Dows characterized Maril's abstract art as possessed of a personal style, despite his indebtedness to Picasso, Braque, and Mondrian, among other artists of the first quarter of the 20th century. While living in Cape Cod and Baltimore, Maril traveled to California, Mexico, Italy, and Spain. His acquaintance with Duncan Phillips, founder of the Phillips Collection in Washington, D.C., boosted the artist's success and visibility, garnering him exhibitions, WPA projects, including a post office mural in Scranton, Penn., and notice by Eleanor Roosevelt, who hung one of his paintings in the White House. With another nod to Matisse, Maril's work between the 1950s and his death prominently feature open windows and doors, which interweave exterior and interior on the surface of the work. The Phillips Collection owns 13 of Maril's works. Maryland University College in Adelphi, Md., has exhibited a permanent retrospective of Maril's work since 1986. Over 60 museums in the United States and Europe own examples of Maril's work, including the Baltimore Museum, the Cleveland Museum, the Corcoran Gallery, the National Museum of American Art, the San Francisco Museum, the Whitney Museum, and the Walters Art Museum.

BIBLIOGRAPHY: W. Hauptman (ed.), *Herman Maril: University of Maryland Art Department Gallery, College Park, Maryland, February 17–March 17, 1977* (1977); *Herman Maril (1908–1986): Paintings and Works on Paper from the 1920s and 1930s: April 29 through June 4, 1999* (1999); H.E.Wooden, *The Neglected Generation of American Realist Painters, 1930–1948: Wichita Art Museum, Wichita, Kansas, May 2 thru June 14, 1981* (1981).

[Nancy Buchwald (2nd ed.)]

MARINI, SHABBETHAI ḤAYYIM (**Vita**; c. 1690–1748), rabbi, poet, and physician. Born in Padua, Marini studied there under Isaac Ḥayyim Cohen de *Cantarini, whom he succeeded in the rabbinate of the town. Marini was renowned for his sermons which fascinated not only members of the Jewish community but many educated Christians as well. He was also held in high esteem as a physician.

Marini's main work is a Hebrew translation of the first three books of Ovid's *Metamorphoses*, based on the Italian paraphrase by Giovanni Andrea dell' Anguillara. Originally Marini planned a joint translation with Isaiah *Bassano. Marini, however, completed the translation alone, and it is not certain whether Bassano's 100 octaves are included in Marini's 850. The translation, entitled *"Shirei ha-Ḥalifot le-Oved*," was to have been published in Mantua, but Marini died when only one sheet had been printed. The original manuscript of the translation is in the municipal library in Mantua (Ms. 77 Comunità Israelitica). Others are: Parma, de Rossi, Ms. 1110 Budapest, Kaufmann Ms. 547; British Museum, Ms. Add, 26916, Vienna, Ms. 91. A longer excerpt of the translation was published in S.D. Luzzatto's letters.

Marini also wrote numerous poems for special occasions, including an elegy on the death of his teacher Cantarini and a wedding poem which could be read either as Italian or as Hebrew. The Mantua and the Vienna manuscripts of the Ovid translation contain 34 of Marini's poems (mostly sonnets), and a fragment of his poetic paraphrase of *Pirkei Avot. Isaiah Romanin wrote an elegy on Marini's death (Oxford, Bodleian Library, Ms. Mich. 439, fol. 376).

BIBLIOGRAPHY: G.B. De' Rossi, *Dizionario Storico degli Autori Ebrei*, 2 (Parma, 1802), s.v. 39f.; Fuerst, in: *Literaturblatt des Orients*,

1 (1840), 124; Ghirondi-Neppi, 342–4; S.D. Luzzatto, *Iggerot Shadal*, 3 (1882), 394f., 404, 416, 419; Steinschneider, in: *Vessillo Israelitico*, 27 (1879), 3ff.; 28 (1880), 149; Schirmann, Italyah, 389–94.

[Jefim (Hayyim) Schirmann]

MARINOFF, JACOB (1869–1964), Yiddish poet, editor, and publisher. Born in Russia, he received a traditional *kheyder* education. He immigrated to England, then the U.S. and lived briefly in Denver, where he worked with *Yehoash and Dr. Chaim Spivak to found the Jewish Tuberculosis Sanitorium. From 1895 he contributed poems to Yiddish periodicals. In 1909 he and Joseph *Tunkel cofounded *Der Groyser Kundes*, a journal of political and social satire, internationally important also as a watchdog of the Yiddish press and of Jewish institutions. Among the contributors to the weekly were *Sholem Aleichem, Yehoash, A. *Reisen, M.L. *Halpern, and M. *Nadir, as well as cartoonists Z. Maud, S. Raskin, and L. Israel (Lola). Marinoff wrote three volumes of verse: *Shpil un Kamf* ("Play and Struggle," 1938), *Mir Veln Zayn* ("We Want to Be," 1944) and *Shtark un munter* ("Strong and Hearty,"1947) and coedited a collection, *Humor un Satire* ("Humor and Satire," 1912, from *Der Groyser Kundes*).

BIBLIOGRAPHY: Reyzen, Leksikon, 3 (1927), 333–7; LNYL, 5 (1963), 500–2; N.B. Minkoff, *Pionern fun Yidisher Poezie in Amerike*, 3 (1956), 169–218.

[Sol Liptzin / Edward Portnoy (2nd ed.)]

°**MARITAIN, JACQUES** (1882–1973) and **RAÏSSA** (1883–1960), French writers who took a positive stand on the Jewish issue during the Nazi era. Raïssa Oumansoff, a Russian Jew, was taken to Paris as a child, and there in 1904 she married Jacques Maritain, a Protestant by birth and a former disciple of Henri *Bergson, who became one of the foremost protagonists of neo-Thomism. Having lost touch with their respective religions, the Maritains became Catholics in 1905. These experiences were sensitively narrated by Raïssa Maritain in *Les grandes amitiés* (1941; *We Have Been Friends Together*, 1942). The conversion, which pained and scandalized their families, paradoxically induced the young couple to meditate on the Jewish destiny. Raïssa's poems, essays, and diary reveal a very pure, mystical approach, the source of which she described: "My maternal grandfather was a Ḥasid, and my father's father was a great ascetic sage. This is my inheritance." Through Raïssa, Jacques Maritain learned that "inspiration and spiritual sources of life come from the people chosen by God." When the times demanded that he speak up for the Jews, the philosopher became the man of action. From the moment the Nazi persecutions began, Maritain spoke out and he continued to champion the Jews while an exile in the U.S. during World War II, as French ambassador to the Vatican after 1945, and following the establishment of the State of Israel. Jacques Maritain's many articles and statements on the subject (1926–61) were collected by the author in a single volume, *Le Mystère d'Israël* (1965).

BIBLIOGRAPHY: J. Maritain (ed.), *Journal de Raïssa* (1963); D.A. and I.J. Gallagher, *The Achievement of Jacques and Raïssa Maritain: a Bibliography, 1906–61* (1962).

[Brother Marcel-Jacques Dubois O.P.]

MARITIME LAW. The Talmud discusses many laws concerning shipping, and sea and river journeys – such as the sale of ships, instances of shipwreck salvage and rescue, rules of passage at sea, lading and charter agreements, and also various details of the laws of the Sabbath and ritual purity applicable to ships. Such laws do not, however, serve to create a distinct branch of maritime law proper, since they are interwoven into the wider principles of the laws of *contract and *damages (contrary to the view expressed by J. Dauvillier, in *Revue Internationale des Droits de l'Antiquité*, 6 (1959), 33–63). Although in this field special shipping customs, if any, are followed, this is no more than an application of the general principle of contract law relating to local or trade customs (Rashba, Resp., vol. 2, no. 268).

With regard to the sale of ships, as with other sales, reference is made to accessories which are customarily sold with the ship and others which are considered as being independent and must therefore be purchased separately (BB 5:1). It is also stated that it was the practice of shipowners to receive not only the hire for the ship but also payment for its loss if shipwrecked (BM 70a). On arrangements for sea traffic it is stated: "Where two boats sailing on a river meet; if both attempt to pass simultaneously, they will sink; whereas if one makes way for the other, both can pass [without mishap]. Likewise if two camels met each other while on the ascent of Beth-Horon [which is a narrow pass; see Josh. 10:10 and 11]... if one is laden and the other unladen, the latter should give way to the former; if one is nearer [to its destination] than the other, the former should give way to the latter. If both are equally near or far, make a compromise between them, and the one [to go through] must compensate the other" (Tosef. BK 2:10; Sanh. 32b). If a person hires a ship for carriage of cargo and it sinks in mid-journey, he must pay for half the journey; if, however, he hires a specific ship for shipping a specific cargo, he loses the hire if he has already paid for it but is not obliged to pay if he has not already done so (BM 79b and Tos.). In a case where a man hired boatmen to deliver goods, stipulating that they guarantee against any accident (see **Ones*) occurring on the way, and the river dried up during the journey, it was held that the boatmen had not guaranteed against this possibility since such an accident was not foreseeable (Git. 73a).

Various *halakhot* were decided with regard to shipwrecks. Thus when a boat is in danger of sinking and part of the cargo is thrown overboard to lighten the vessel, the resulting loss is not apportioned equally amongst the cargo owners, nor is it calculated according to the value of the goods of each owner, but the loss is apportioned according to the weight of the cargo of each owner – provided that this does not conflict with local maritime customs (BK 116b). In one instance a donkey being transported threatened to sink the boat and was thrown overboard, whereupon it was decided that no compensation was payable to its owner, since the deed was justified on the grounds of self-defense, the donkey being considered as pursuing with intent to kill (BK 117b). An interesting *halakhah* concerning maritime insurance is related: "The sailors can stipulate that whoever loses a ship shall get another one, but if the boat was lost due to his own negligence or if he sailed to a place to which boats would not normally sail, he would not be provided with another boat." The same rule applies also to carriers on land (Tosef. BM 11:26; BK 116b).

In the post-talmudic period many responsa dealt with trade customs (see e.g., Rashba, Resp., vol. 2, no. 268), some of them marine customs. Solomon b. Abraham *Adret (Rashba), who lived in Barcelona, where the well-known collection of marine customs *Consulat de Mar* was compiled, records the custom of depositing goods with a merchant traveling by sea for the latter to trade therein at the risk of the depositor – leaving the sailor exempt from liability for accident (his resp. vol. 2, no. 325; vol. 1, no. 930 and cf. no. 924). Also mentioned is the custom of paying the full wages, even if the journey for which the employee was hired was not completed due to accident overtaking the employer (Rashba, Resp., vol. 6, no. 224).

In the State of Israel maritime law is based on Israeli legislation, conforming with the law of the maritime nations in those matters and also with Ottoman-French laws and English law.

BIBLIOGRAPHY: Krauss, Tal Arch, 2 (1911), 338–49; Herzog, Instit, 2 (1939), 252–4, 268–70. **ADD. BIBLIOGRAPHY:** M. Elon, *Ha-Mishpat ha-Ivri* (1988), 1:452, 560, 752; idem, *Jewish Law* (1994), 2:552, 681, 927.

[Shalom Albeck]

MARIX, ADOLPH (1848–1919), U.S. naval officer. Born in Germany he was taken to the United States by his father, Henry Marix, who was an official translator to the U.S. Treasury. Adolph Marix was appointed to the U.S. Naval Academy at Annapolis and in 1872 joined the judge advocate-general's department. He commanded a number of ships between 1894 and 1898 including the U.S.S. *Maine* until shortly before its mysterious sinking in the Bay of Havana. Marix was appointed judge advocate in the court of enquiry into the sinking, and his findings led to the U.S. declaration of war on Spain. Subsequently, he was president of the navy board which experimented in the use of submarines and in 1908 was promoted to rear admiral, the first Jew to attain that rank.

MARK, BERNARD (**Berl**; 1908–1966), scholar and historian. Born in Lomza, Mark studied law at Warsaw University. Prior to World War II, he published articles in Polish and Yiddish on literary history and edited left-wing periodicals. Between 1932 and 1939, he published a two-volume work in Yiddish entitled *Geshikhte fun di Sotsiale Bavegungen in Poyln* ("The History of Social Movements in Poland," 1938–39). During World War II, he lived in the Soviet Union, where he was active on the Jewish *Anti-Fascist Committee, and in the Związek Patriotów Polskich ("Polish Patriots' Union"). In Moscow he published his first work on Jewish anti-Nazi uprisings in Poland. Upon returning to Poland (1946), he published a series of essays and collections of documents on Holocaust subjects. In 1949, Mark was appointed director of the *Jewish Historical Institute in Warsaw, and editor of its *Bulletin* and *Bleter far Geshikhte*. In 1954 he was appointed an associate professor. Mark visited Israel in 1957 and lectured at the Second World Congress of Jewish Studies. He strengthened the ties between the Jewish Historical Institute and research institutions in Israel, e.g., *Yad Vashem and the Central Archives for the History of the Jewish People (Jerusalem). His main works are *The Extermination and the Resistance of the Polish Jews During the Period 1939–1944* (1955); *Dokumenten un Materialen vegn Oyfshtand in Varshever Geto* (1953); *Der Oyfshtand in Varshever Geto* (1963), translated into Polish, German, and Dutch; *Di Yidishe Tragedye in der Poylisher Literatur* (1950); *Di Umgekumene Shrayber fun di Getos un Lagern un Zeyere Verk* (1954); *Der Oyfshtand in Byalistoker Geto* (1953^2); and *Di Geshikhte fun Yidn in Poyln* (1957). **ADD. BIBLIOGRAPHY:** A. Grabski, *Dzialalnosc komunistow wsrod Zydow w Polsce, 1944–1949* (2004), index.

[Nathan Eck]

MARK, JULIUS (1898–2002), U.S. Reform rabbi. Mark was born in Cincinnati, where he earned his B.A. from the University of Cincinnati in 1921 and was ordained at Hebrew Union College in 1922. He served as rabbi of Temple Beth El in South Bend, Ind. (1922–26), and the Vine Street Temple in Nashville, Tenn. (1926–48) before becoming rabbi of New York City's Temple Emanu-El. Under Mark's leadership, Emanu-El more than doubled in size (to 3,200 families) and grew to become the largest Jewish congregation in the world. During World War II, he joined the U.S. Navy and served for several years as Jewish chaplain to the Pacific Fleet, rising to the rank of lieutenant commander on the staff of Fleet Admiral Chester W. Nimitz. Returning to civilian life, he served on the executive committee of the United States Commission for UNESCO; as a life trustee of the Federation of Jewish Philanthropies; on the boards of the National Conference of Christian and Jews and the Anti-Defamation League; as honorary vice chairman of the Lighthouse for the Blind; and as honorary president of the American Jewish Encyclopedia Society. He also joined with the clergy of neighboring churches to work for social justice in New York City.

In the service of Reform Judaism, Mark was a member of the governing board of the World Union for Progressive Judaism, a member of the Executive Board of the *Central Conference of American Rabbis, and chairman of the CCAR-UAHC Commission on Justice and Peace. He also served two terms as president of the *Synagogue Council of America. For his many contributions, he received the Human Relations Award of the Methodist Church (1963); the Gold Medallion for Courageous Leadership of the National Conference of Christian and Jews (1966); Clergyman of the Year Award from Religious Heritage of America (1969); and repeated recognition from the State of Israel Bonds Organization (1967, 1968, 1970). Five colleges and universities awarded him honorary doctorates in law, divinity, humanities, sacred theology, and humane letters. Among the books Mark wrote was *Reaching For the Moon* (1959). Rabbi Ronald B. Sobel and Sidney Wallach edited a collection of papers entitled *Justice, Justice Shalt Thou Pursue* on the occasion of Mark's 75th birthday, as an expression of gratitude of the Jewish Conciliation Board with whose services and leadership Mark has long been identified.

[Bezalel Gordon (2nd ed.)]

MARK, MARY ELLEN (1940–), U.S. photographer. After growing up in suburban Philadelphia, Mark earned a bachelor's degree in painting and art history but decided she was not good enough to be a painter. She then earned a master's in photojournalism at the University of Pennsylvania, having chosen photography almost at random, she said, and falling in love with the camera the moment she held one in her hand. "From the very first night, that was it," she said. "I became obsessed by it. I knew immediately it would be my life's work. I knew I had a chance of being good at it." The camera proved her ticket to independence.

After traveling around Europe, Mark sought work in the late 1960s shooting film stills for Hollywood productions. It led to her first large-scale project. While shooting at the Oregon State Mental Hospital in 1973 for *One Flew Over the Cuckoo's Nest*, she befriended the hospital's director and was permitted to spend time living with and shooting the women of the institute's maximum security Ward 81 in 1976. This series of photographs is sentimental and disturbing at the same time, and fulfilled Mark's goal to portray the lives of "people who haven't had the best breaks in society." The book *Ward 81* was published in 1979. "For years I'd planned to go live in a mental hospital," she said. "I wanted to see if I could feel something of what it was like to be set aside from society." At her own expense, she lived in the state's only locked ward for women. "I think I was interested because my father had several nervous breakdowns and was hospitalized several times," she said.

With a special affinity for working with women, she turned her attention to the brothels of Bombay, India, in 1978. She encountered violent resistance from some of her would-be subjects, but she befriended a few, leading to a series of color photographs published as *Falkland Road: Prostitutes of Bombay* in 1981. She said the book "was meant almost as a metaphor for entrapment, for how difficult it is to be a woman." She did a series on Mother Teresa of Calcutta for *Life* magazine, published as *Photographs of Mother Teresa's Missions of Charity in Calcutta* in 1985 as well as a series depicting street children in Seattle who turn to prostitution and drugs as a means of getting by. That work led to the film *Streetwise*, directed and photographed by her husband, Martin Bell; it was nominated for an Academy Award. It was in Seattle, in 1983, that she befriended a 12-year-old, Erin Blackwell ("Tiny"), a child prostitute whom she photographed over the years as Tiny had five children with five different fathers. She first photographed the Damm family of Los Angeles, a husband, wife, and two children, in 1987, after they had been thrown out of a shelter and were living in their car. In one picture, the mother and father sprawl in the front seat of the car as the children peer anxiously out the back window. In 1994, with two more children and the parents seriously into drugs, the family was again Mark's subject, squatting in squalor but still a family, at a rundown ranch in Llano, California. In October 2003 she published *Twins*, featuring 20 × 24 Polaroid prints of twins.

Mark published 14 books and won many awards, including the second Cornell Capa Award of the International Center of Photography, and her images have been shown worldwide.

[Stewart Kampel (2nd ed.)]

MARK, YUDEL (1897–1975), Yiddish educator, philologist, and author. Born in Palanga, Lithuania, Mark became active in Jewish politics while studying at Petrograd University (1915–18). In Libava (Liepaja), Latvia, he organized the local branch of the Yidishe *Folkspartei, later becoming the secretary-general of the Jewish National Council in Lithuania (1923), and secretary and vice president of the Folkspartei in the same country. From 1930 to 1934 he was the editor of the daily *Folksblat*. Mark was the founder (1920) and principal of the Yiddish Real-Gimnazye of Vilkomir (Ukmerge), the first of its kind in Lithuania, and between 1927 and 1930, taught Yiddish at various schools and seminaries. After settling in the U.S. in 1936, Mark continued his activity in the field of Yiddish education. He settled in Israel (Jerusalem) in 1970.

Mark's first literary publication appeared in the Kovno (Kaunas) daily *Nayes* (1921), and he subsequently contributed extensively to a wide range of Yiddish political, literary, and educational publications, such as *Eynheytlekhe Folkshul* (1922). In addition he edited various Yiddish periodicals, His books include a Yiddish school grammar, *Shul-Gramatik* (1922), various textbooks on Yiddish language teaching, Yiddish literature, Jewish history (*Der Yidishe Poyps*, c. 1947; *Dovid ha-Reuveni un Shloyme Molkho*, 1941), biography, as well as children's books in Yiddish. Among his translations into Yiddish are works of Thomas Mann and Erich Maria Remarque. He also edited various books, notably the *Groyser Verterbukh fun der Yidisher Shprakh* (2 vols., 1961) jointly with Judah A. *Joffe; further volumes were in preparation (1971).

Among Mark's attainments as a linguist are his numerous studies on Yiddish grammar and style, on the Hebrew-Aramaic component in the Yiddish language, and his stylistic analyses of the Yiddish authors. He was also the editor of the *YIVO's *Yidishe Shprakh* (1941–68).

BIBLIOGRAPHY: Rejzen, Leksikon, 2 (1927), 342–4; LNYL, 5 (1963), 510–4.

[Mordkhe Schaechter]

MARKAH (Heb. מרקה; fl. second half of fourth century C.E.), well known and venerated Samaritan poet who wrote in Aramaic. The great esteem in which he is held by Samaritan tradition is shown by his epithet "Founder of Wisdom" in the Samaritan chronicle *Tolidah* or "Fountain of Wisdom" (Yanbūʿ al-Ḥikma) in that of *Abu al-Fat and by the legend that the name Markah (מרקה) was bestowed upon him because it has the same numerical value as the name Moses (משה), which no other human being is allowed to bear. Actually, Markah is an Aramaized form of the Latin name Marcus. According to the Samaritan chronicles, he was the son of the liturgical poet Amram Darah whose byname, Tūta, is explained as a development of the Latin name Titus.

Like his father, Markah wrote liturgical poems, part of which belong to the earliest portions of the Samaritan common prayer book, the *Defter* (see *Samaritan Language and Literature). His style is more elaborate than that of his father, and none of his poems is composed in the style of "Verses of Durran" (see *Amram Darah). The verses of his poems are arranged in an alphabetic acrostic and the number of lines in each verse is nearly always equal. Once his name is contained in the acrostic of the first four verses of a poem. Through his terse and polished style, he succeeds in conveying the fiery religious feelings of his soul. That is why many of his expressions became fixed figures of speech used by later Samaritan poets.

The work that established Markah's fame and gained him the epithet "Founder of Wisdom" is his great midrashic composition *Meimar* or *Tevat Markah*, a compendium of exegetical and theological teachings. It is divided into six books, the main subjects of which are the wonders revealed to Israel from Moses' call to Israel's victory at the Red Sea; a commentary on Exodus 15; a commentary on Deuteronomy 27:9–26; the commission of Joshua and instructions to various classes of the people, whereby priests are witnesses to Israel and to themselves; a commentary on Deuteronomy 32; Moses' death; speculations about the 22 letters of the alphabet. There are many thoughts and figures of speech shared by this work with Markah's poems. All extant manuscripts, the earliest dating from the 14th century, contain recognizable later additions.

BIBLIOGRAPHY: Z. Ben-Ḥayyim, *Ivrit va-Aramit Nosaḥ Shomron*, 3 pt. 2 (1967), 15–16, 133–262; J.A. Montgomery, *The Samaritans* (1907), 294–5; A.E. Cowley, *Samaritan Liturgy*, 2 (1909), xx–xxi and index; J. Macdonald, *Memar Merqah*, 2 vols. (1963), incl. bibl.; J. Bowman, *Transcript of the Original Text of the Samaritan Chronicle Tolidah* (1955), 16b; Abū'l-Fath ibn Abi'l-Ḥassan al-Sāmirī, *Annales Samaritani…*, ed. E. Vilmar (1865).

[Ayala Loewenstamm]

MARKEL, LESTER (1894–1977), U.S. journalist who was responsible for changing the nature of the Sunday newspaper. Born in New York City and trained at Columbia University's School of Journalism, Markel was from 1923 to 1964 Sunday editor of the *New York Times*. It was he who conceived the idea of separate Sunday sections, which would bring the reader the news in greater depth than was possible in daily papers. He was personally responsible for the *Times Magazine*, the "Book Review," and the "Arts and Leisure" section. In 1935 he instituted the "News of the Week in Review," a report in perspective of the week's events, which won Markel and the *New York Times* a Pulitzer Prize. Markel wrote and lectured widely. In 1951, he founded the International Press Institute to foster the free flow of information and freedom of the press in general. In 1964, he became associate editor of the *New York Times* and head of its department of public affairs. He also started a television series in which he and others discussed the news in depth.

[Stewart Kampel]

MARKEL-MOSESSOHN, MIRIAM (1839–1920), Hebraist, translator, and journalist, who exercised a profound influence on the *maskilim* of her day, particularly Judah Leib *Gordon (1831–1892) who dedicated to her "Koẓo shel Yod" (The Tip of the Yod), his 1876 poem satirizing the treatment of women in traditional Jewish society. Born in Volkovyshki (Vilkaviskis), Lithuania, to Ḥayyah and Shimon Wierzbolowki, an affluent merchant, Markel-Mosessohn underwent rigorous training in Hebrew language and literature from an early age with the assistance of private tutors and also received a thorough grounding in secular subjects, including German and French.

Miriam married Anshel Markel-Mosessohn (1844–1903) when she was 24 and the groom 19. The couple, whose 40-year marriage was childless, shared a love for Hebrew and was committed to its revival. Anshel supported his wife's literary efforts, granting her freedom and financial backing to travel to pursue the publication of her work. Markel-Mosessohn corresponded briefly with Abraham *Mapu and maintained a 20-year professional and personal correspondence with Gordon, although the two never met. With Gordon's support, the first volume of Markel-Mosessohn's Hebrew rendition of the German history book *Die Juden und die Kreuzfahrer unter Richard Lowenherz* by Eugen Rispart appeared in 1869 as *Ha-Yehudim be-Angliyah*. The second volume of the translation was not published until 1895, apparently because of Markel-Mosessohn's poor health and financial problems. In 1887 she briefly became the Viennese correspondent for *Ha-Meliẓ*, the newspaper Gordon edited; however, after publishing only four articles, she abruptly renounced authorship, claiming "my desire and my ability are not one and the same."

Markel-Mosessohn succeeded in entering the rarefied, male world of Hebrew letters during the very period in which the language was being revived, but the strict pronouncement and observance of gender differentiations by the leaders of the **Haskalah*, distinctions which Markel-Mosessohn herself accepted, precluded her from obtaining the status of *maskil*. Copies of Markel-Mosessohn's letters to Judah Leib Gordon and other literary papers are housed at the Jewish National and University Library Archive, Hebrew University of Jerusalem.

BIBLIOGRAPHY: C.B. Balin, *To Reveal Our Hearts: Jewish Women Writers in Tsarist Russia* (2000), 13–50; A. Yaari (ed.), *Ẓeror Iggerot Yalag el Miriam Markel-Mosessohn* (1936); B.-Z. Dinur (ed.), *Mikhtavei Avraham Mapu* (1970), 160, 164, 183–84.

[Carole B. Balin (2nd ed.)]

MARKET DAYS AND FAIRS. The nomadic nature of early medieval trade and the wide-ranging contacts of Jewish merchants throughout the period made Jewish traders early and eager participants in market days and fairs, in spite of the religious and social problems attendant on such participation, especially in Christian countries. As merchants were prominent in European Jewish leadership and *autonomy, fairs were suitable meeting places for deliberating Jewish affairs. Around 825 Archbishop *Agobard complained that the day on which the *Lyons weekly market was held had been changed from Saturday to suit Jewish traders. In the following three centuries there are many references in both Hebrew and Christian sources to Jews attending fairs, particularly in cities of the Rhineland such as Cologne and *Treves. *Gershom b. Judah mentions a fair at a sea or river port during which the assembled merchants from various communities enacted an ordinance. *Champagne and *Provence, believed to be where the fairs began, had many Jewish communities, whose members in all probability participated in them. Jewish attendance at markets and fairs decreased after the era of the *Crusades when moneylending and pawnbroking became the major source of Jewish livelihood in northwestern and central Europe. In other areas, where the trade in goods formed an important Jewish occupation, their attendance continued.

The 16th century, in Eastern and subsequently in central Europe, witnessed the creation of economic and social patterns adapted to the attendance of large numbers of Jews of various fairs and markets. In *Poland-Lithuania it was expressly forbidden to fix the dates of fairs and markets on the Sabbath or Jewish holidays. The Jews' commercial rights at fairs and markets were the only ones not challenged by competing Christian merchants. When persecutions in 1539–40 resulted in Lithuanian Jews ceasing to travel to fairs, the nobility appealed to the king to suppress the persecutions at once. One of the most important fairs was the "Gromnice" (February 2), when many Jewish merchants and heads of communities convened at *Lublin; much trade was done and debts and taxes were gathered. Others fairs took place in *Brody, *Gniezno, *Gdansk (Danzig), *Torun, *Lvov, and *Cracow, and there were innumerable lesser ones as well. As the fairs bore the names of their patron Christian saints, these became common usage and were inscribed on official and business documents. The distinctive creation of Polish Jewry, the *Councils of the Lands, was an outgrowth of a *bet din* which officiated at the Lublin fairs. Meetings of the councils took place there regularly, twice a year, during the 16-day spring and summer fairs; sometimes they were held during the *Jaroslaw fairs in the fall. The Lithuanian Council also convened during fairs, and common sessions took place at *Leczna. One of the tasks of the Councils was regulating the nomination of a *parnas and *dayyan for the duration of the fair. As both positions carried wide powers, they had to be judiciously distributed among the contending lands. In Poland-Lithuania the social aspects of the fair were as significant as the economic and communal leadership ones. N.N. *Hannover described a mid-17th-century fair: "the head of the yeshivah journeyed with all his pupils to the fair on market day … and at each fair there were hundreds of heads of yeshivot, thousands of pupils, and tens of thousands of youths and Jewish merchants.… And whoever had an eligible son or daughter went to the fair and arranged a match, for everyone could find one to his liking. And at every fair hundreds of matches were made, and sometimes thousands; and the children of Israel, men and women, wore kingly vestments at the fair" (*Yeven Meẓulah*, 1966, 86f.). Meir b. Gedaliah (Maharam) of *Lublin (1558–1616) described another aspect of Jewish life at the fairs: "It is a regular custom that at every fair a place is determined as a synagogue for daily prayer, and every Sabbath scholars and yeshivah students and leaders of the land and people congregate there and read the Torah" (Responsa, 84).

Jews had been expelled from Breslau in 1455, but they were never absent from the fairs. In 1537 the municipal council opposed an attempt by Ferdinand I to levy a special poll tax on Jewish visitors to the fairs. A century later, at the request of the textile guilds and the imperial authorities and despite the opposition of the local merchants, Jews were permitted to be in the town a few days before and after the fairs. In 1697 the authorities divided the Jews into five categories whose duration of stay depended on the scope of their economic transactions.

Jews attended the fairs as a corporation of merchants based on their communities or countries of origin. These corporations were also responsible for nominating their officials: a *parnas ha-yarid*, in charge of keeping order and representing the fair corporations; a *dayyan ha-yarid*, who held regular judicial authority and was empowered by the chief rabbi of the land (first mentioned in 1698); supervisor of ritual law; and *shames* (*shammash*), the distinctive Breslau functionary, who was permitted to remain between the fairs and guarantee the continuity of business transactions. First mentioned in 1673, he was elected by his *Judenschaft*, authorized by the Councils of the Lands, recognized by the Breslau municipal council, sworn in, and allowed to wear a sword. In 1696 there were ten *shamosim* at the fair, one each for the four Polish lands and one for Bohemia, *Moravia, *Glogau, *Posen, *Leczno, and *Zuelz. The number of Jewish visitors at a fair in 1685 was 332, and they practically monopolized Polish trade, particularly in textiles, silks, spices, tobacco, and above all in furs.

Jewish attendance at fairs within the Austrian Empire was encouraged by Emperor *Maximilian I, who in 1494 permitted Jews to attend markets in the imperial cities from which they had been expelled on payment of three florins *Mautgeld* ("body tax"; see *Leibzoll). This right, confirmed by his successors in return for extraordinary taxation, became the legal cornerstone of Jewish economic activity. *Joseph II eventually abolished the *Leibzoll* and declared all markets open to Jews (1782/83). In practice, however, many restrictions remained in force until 1848. At *Brno, for example, the Jews were allowed to enter through only one gate (*Judentor*) at fixed hours, were restricted to one market, and forced to lodge in one inn, the

Neue Welt in the Krona suburb. They struggled for many years for the right to erect stalls. Complaints by Christian merchants against underselling and inferior wares were continuously raised, and peddlers (called *pinkerljuden*) were particularly harassed at the Brno fairs. The Council of Moravia regulated the supervision of dietary laws at the fairs, distributed stalls before the fairs commenced, and prohibited the Jews from being at the fair on the day before it opened. There was a tendency to establish Jewish communities near locations of major and minor markets and fairs.

There were a great many fairs in central Europe. Many Jewish calendars recorded dates of fairs, which Jews attended as peddlers who both bought and sold wares, as merchants buying goods wholesale for retailing, and sometimes as popular performers like jugglers. Registers of the special scales for weighing feathers at the *Linz markets of 1594 and 1603 show that there were 131 Jewish traders in feathers and only 12 Christian dealers. Other important commodities were leather, skins, old clothes, and new clothes and textiles imported from Bohemia. In 1714 Bohemian "*Federjuden*" had to have special permission to attend because of the plague. About 300 Jews dealing in similar articles attended the *Krems fairs annually; in 1701 the Moravian Jews boycotted it because a Jew had been arrested as a thief.

The records of Zurzach fairs in Switzerland mention the *Judengeleit* (*Leibzoll*), a tax of between 7 and 19 batzen according to age and wealth which was a considerable source of income. The number of Jews attending grew from about 150 in the mid-18th century to about 200 at its close; most foreign Jews were from Gailingen, *Hohenems, and communities in *Baden, *Alsace, and Swabia, which were composed primarily of peddlers and merchants. More than three-quarters of the households of the nearby communities of Endingen and *Lengnau attended these fairs. Although Jews were not tolerated throughout most of Switzerland, they were allowed and encouraged to attend the fairs, particularly the *livestock merchants. In France in 1741, the controller-general of finances wrote a circular letter to all provincial governors asking them about the commercial activities of the Jews. Unanimously they replied that Jews should not be excluded from the fairs and markets because they helped keep down prices. The monopolistic guilds were forcing up prices, while the outside merchants, who came for the duration of the fair, forced them down. An endemic source of strife and litigation between Jews and local merchants and the authorities was the constant attempt to sell outside the market, or not on market days, or on the way to or back from markets, or to remain in the area after the fair was over. In Italy Jews were to be found at the major fairs and often participated in the festive processions which inaugurated them. The community of *Mantua bought and erected stalls at the fairgrounds for its members; there was an unsuccessful attempt to prohibit their use in 1740. A Jewish community had the right to tax Jewish merchants attending the fairs for the use of communal amenities. In 1720 the Jewish communities of the duchy of Parma tried, without success, to tax Jewish merchants attending the Parma city fairs (where there was no community). A long dispute (1748–51) between the community of *Verona, which had attempted to exact a business tax from foreign visitors at the fairs, and the communities of Mantua, *Ferrara, and *Modena ended with rabbinical authorities in Italy and Germany deciding against Verona's action.

European rulers were aware of the economic benefits resulting from Jewish participation in fairs. Joachim II, elector of *Brandenburg, expelled the Jews in 1510 but subsequently allowed them to attend fairs. After the 1573 expulsion from Brandenburg, Posen Jews regularly received permission to attend the *Frankfurt on the Oder fairs. Elector Frederick William (1640–88) encouraged Polish Jews to attend fairs in his realm long before he admitted 50 Jewish families from Austria to settle and trade freely throughout his lands (1671). Though Jews were rigorously excluded from *Saxony, the internationally important *Leipzig fairs needed Jews to participate in large numbers. Between 1675 and 1764, 82,000 Jews attended the biannual *Leipzig markets; their number fluctuated according to political and economic factors, but grew steadily from about 400 a year in the mid-17th century to twice that amount by the end of the century and continued to grow; they generally constituted about one-fifth of the total attendance. Their number increased from an average of 1,073 in the 1780s to 3,370 in the 1800s and 6,444 in the 1830s, when they formed around one-quarter of the participants. Between 1675 and 1764 the majority of Jewish participants came from Central Europe, though the number of East European Jews was increasing slowly, eventually amounting to one-third of the total Jewish attendance in the early 19th century. The attendance lists of the fairs offer a true mirror of 18th-century Jewish society. Members of the leading families attended (see *Bacharach, *Fraenkel, *Gomperz, *Ephraim, Itzig families, and Samuel *Oppenheimer, David *Oppenheim, and Samson *Wertheimer). *Glueckel of Hameln recorded her husband's transactions at fairs with Jost *Liebmann, the Court Jew. The leading *Court Jews of the day, Alexander David, Behrend *Lehmann, and Leffmann *Behrends, were also present. Jewish visitors to Leipzig congregated in the Bruehl, which became in effect a Jewish quarter for the duration of the fairs. The *Landrabbiner* of *Anhalt had rabbinical jurisdiction there and those who died at the fair were buried in Dessau. At Leipzig Jews bought wares worth about half a million thalers annually between 1773 and 1775, primarily textiles. Officially they sold wares worth one-fifth of that amount, but the sales figure was not the true one, for the "sales tax" (*Wagegold*) was 1% of all sales; it was not until 1813 that it was reduced to 0.5%, the same as the Christian tax. In addition the city exacted a high entrance fee. "*Volljuden*," who did not enjoy special privileges and protection and were the majority, paid six thalers each and three for a wife or servant. Jewelers paid eight thalers and cooks (*Judenkoch*) ten thalers and 12 groschen.

In the *Pale of Settlement and Austrian Galicia the market square and the regular market days became the center of the *shtetl* and the heart of its economy. To a large extent the economic and social life in these townships was regulated by buying from peasants and selling to them on the fixed market day in the appointed place; taverns were therefore erected around the market square. Jewish emigrants carried over this type of market (with some changes) into large cities in Western Europe; an example is the Petticoat Lane Market in London.

BIBLIOGRAPHY: R. Mahler, *Toledot ha-Yehudim be-Polin* (1946), index, s.v. *Yarid*; M. Breger, *Zur Handelsgeschichte der Juden in Polen im 17. Jahrhundert* (1932), 15ff.; B.D. Weinryb, *Neueste Wirtschaftsgeschichte der Juden in Russland und Polen* (1934), index, s.v. *Messe*; S. Dubnow, *Pinkas ha-Medinah* (1925), index, s.v. *Yarid*; Halpern, Pinkas, s.v. *Yarid*; D. Evron, *Pinkas ha-Kesherim shel Kehillat Pozna* (1967), index, s.v. *Yarid*; S. Simonsohn, *Toledot ha-Yehudim be-Dukkasut Mantovah* (1964), index, s.v. *Yarid*; I. Halpern, *Takkanot Medinat Mehrin* (1952), index, s.v. *Yarid*; H. Gold (ed.), *Die Juden und Judengemeinden Maehrens* (1929), 144ff.; F. Guggenheim-Gruenberg, *Die Juden auf der Zurzacher Messe im 18. Jahrhundert* (1957); A. Hertzberg, *The French Enlightenment and the Jews* (1968), index, s.v. *Fairs*; Z. Szajkowski, *Franco-Judaica* (1962), index, s.v. *Markets*; A.F. Pribram, *Urkunden und Akten zur Geschichte der Juden in Wien* (1918), index, s.v. *Markt, Jahrmarkt*; L. Moses, *Die Juden in Niederoesterreich* (1935), 91–94; idem, in: A. Engel (ed.), *Gedenkbuch ... Kuratoriums* (1936), 90–101; V. Kurrein, *Die Juden in Linz* (1927), 26–38; idem, in: JGGJČ, 4 (1932), 481–4; A. Weldler-Steinberg and F. Guggenheim-Gruenberg, *Geschichte der Juden in der Schweiz* (1966), 21–86; B.B. Brilling, *Geschichte der Juden in Breslau von 1454 bis 1702* (1960); R. Markgraf, *Zur Geschichte der Juden auf den Messen in Leipzig* (1894); M. Freudenthal, *Leipziger Messgaeste* (1928); W. Harmelin, in: YLBL, 9 (1964), 239–66.

[Henry Wasserman]

MARKISH, PERETZ (1895–1952), Soviet Yiddish poet, novelist, and playwright. Born in Volhynia, Markish received a traditional Jewish education and prepared for entrance to a university. He began writing Russian poetry at age 15 and Yiddish poetry in 1918–19, when he published in the Kiev journals *Eygns* and *Baginen*, whose contributing writers and editors broke with past models of artistic representation to craft a new revolutionary Jewish culture. Markish stood out among other Yiddish poets, like David *Hofstein and Leib *Kvitko, for his creative admixture of German expressionism and Russian futurism. His first book of poetry, *Shveln* ("Thresholds," 1919), made his reputation as *the* poet of the new generation. He moved briefly to Moscow before leaving for Warsaw in late 1921, where he helped found the Yiddish modernist movement through his participation in the literary group, *Khalyastre* ("The Gang"), and by co-founding *Literarishe Bleter*. His poem "Hunger" appeared in the second edition of the Moscow *Shtrom*, and in 1922 he published *Di Kupe* ("The Heap"), an epic poem that commemorated the 1921 pogroms that swept the Ukraine. In 1926, he returned to Moscow, where he became one of the most prolific writers of Soviet Jewish letters, publishing in the Kiev journal *Royte Velt* and the Minsk journal *Shtern*. Markish's career reflected a general shift away from modernism and poetry to socialist realism and prose, as demonstrated in his first novel, *Dor oys, dor ayn* ("Generations," 1929), which describes the tension between modernity and tradition in a Jewish family during the Revolution. Markish quickly rose to a position of power in the Union of Soviet Writers (established 1932), and during the Great Purges of 1936–38 he denounced defendants at one of the trials in a poem whose publication showed Markish to be firmly established within the Soviet system. During World War II, he wrote the play *Kol Nidre*, and in 1942 joined the leadership of the Jewish *Anti-Fascist Committee (JAFC), which served as the center of Jewish cultural life during and after the war. Markish's last major work, the 1948 epic poem *Milkhome* ("War"), chronicles a wide spectrum of wartime experiences, focusing particularly on the plight of the Jews. In January 1949, during the antisemitic anti-cosmopolitan campaign, several major cultural figures who worked in Yiddish, Markish included, were arrested. In 1952, he and several others were convicted of anti-Soviet activities, spying, and bourgeois nationalism and were shot. Rehabilitated after Stalin's death, Markish's poems were again published in 1957 (in Russian translation only). His novel of Polish-Jewish heroism during World War II, *Trit fun Doyres* ("The Footsteps of Generations," 1966), was published posthumously in Soviet Russia; ironically, the novel is replete with praise for the regime and political system.

BIBLIOGRAPHY: Sh. Niger, *Yidishe Shrayber in Sovet Rusland* (1958), 229–61; LNYL, 5 (1963), 523–8; J. Glatstein, *In Tokh Genumen* (1947), 31–9; Ch. Shmeruk (ed.), *A Shpigl Oyf a Shteyn* (1987^2), 373–512, 751–6; no. 3934; M. Altshuler (ed.), *Briv fun Yidishe Sovetishe Shraybers* (1980); Ch. Kronfeld, *On the Margins of Modernism* (1996); D. Shneer, *Yiddish and the Creation of Soviet Jewish Culture* (2004); S. Wolitz, in: *Yiddish* 6 (1987), 56–67.

[David Shneer (2nd ed.)]

MARKON, ISAAC DOV BER (1875–1949), Russian scholar and librarian. Markon was born in Rybinsk on the Volga and studied at the St. Petersburg University under D. *Chwolson and at the *Hildesheimer Rabbinical Seminary and the University of Berlin. He was librarian at the Imperial Public Library in St. Petersburg (1901–17), instructor at the Higher Courses of Oriental Studies (1908–11), instructor and later professor of Jewish studies at the university in St. Petersburg (1917–20), and professor at the Belorussian University at Minsk (1922–24). He also served for a time on the scholars' advisory committee for the Czarist Ministry of Education. For four years he was an editor of the Russian Jewish encyclopedia *Yevreyskaya Entsiklopediya* and planned the publication of a new encyclopedia, *Oẓar ha-Yahadut*, of which a prospectus appeared in 1914. He founded and edited the quarterly *Ha-Kedem* (with A. Sarzowski) which appeared from 1907 to 1909 in Hebrew and German. Markon left Russia for Berlin in 1926 where he joined the editorial staff of the *Encyclopaedia Judaica* and the *Eshkol Enẓiklopedyah Yisre'elit*, in charge of the departments of *Karaism and bibliography. For a time he also lectured at the Rabbinical Seminary. In 1928 Markon was appointed librarian of the Hamburg Jewish community. As he was a Jewish Soviet citizen, he was expelled from Germany in 1938. He went first to Holland and in 1940 escaped to England, where he joined Montefiore College at Ramsgate.

Markon's first step in Jewish scholarship was his prize-winning comparison of Christian canonical with talmudic and Karaite marriage law (Russ., 1901). In the same field are his *Mekorot le-Korot Dinei Nashim* (about laws relating to women) 1, pt. 1 (1908) and various editions of Karaite works. Markon also published a study of the Slavonic glosses in the *Or Zaru'a* by Isaac b. Moses of Vienna (1906). With D. Guenzburg he edited the *Festschrift… A. Harkavy* (1908). Autobiographical reminiscences by Markon appeared in *Meẓudah* (2 (1944), 187ff.; 3 (1945), 341ff.; 4–6 (1948), 474ff.) as well as in some of his letters in G. Kressel (ed.) *Genazim* (1 (1961), 244ff.).

BIBLIOGRAPHY: Kressel, Leksikon, 2 (1967), 429.

MARKOVA, ALICIA (1910–2004), British-born prima ballerina who joined Diaghilev's Les Ballets Russe in 1925 when she was just 15 years old. She was one of the famous "Baby Ballerinas" of the company. Her real name was Alice Lillian Marks, a name which, for Diaghilev, was not Russian or at least not French enough to appear in his company's programs. So without being asked, she was named Markova. Many years and famous roles later, she became – by order of Queen Elizabeth – Dame Alicia.

Markova created many of the central roles in the ballets of Balanchine, Ashton, and other contemporary choreographers. In 1931 she was back in her native London and joined the first professional ballet company in the U.K., the Ballet Rambert, founded and directed by another daughter of a Jewish family, one more dancer whose name was changed by Diaghilev because Miriam Rambam-Ramberg sounded too Jewish and not Russian enough and thus became Marie *Rambert. With this company Markova danced for many years as well as with the Vic-Wells Ballet, which later became The Royal Ballet.

Markova danced the leading roles in the classics as well as in new, contemporary works, such as Ashton's *Façade*, Tudor's *Lysistrata*, and De Valois' *The Rake's Progress*. She was the prima ballerina of the London Festival Ballet in the 1950s. She stopped dancing in 1962 and in the years 1963–69 Markova was the ballet director for the New York Metropolitan Opera Ballet.

BIBLIOGRAPHY: IED, vol. 4, 267–71.

[Giora Manor (2nd ed.)]

MARKOVITS, RODION (**Jakabs**, 1888–1948), author and journalist. Following capture by the Russians during World War I, Markovits later became a political commissar in the International Brigade fighting with the Red Army after the October Revolution. His *Szibériai garnizon* (1927; *Siberian Garrison*, 1929) enjoyed worldwide success in translation. Two later works were *Aranyvonat* ("The Golden Train," 1929) and *Reb Áncsli és más avasi zsidókról szóló széphistóriák* ("Reb Anschel and Other Jewish Stories," 1940).

MARKOWITZ, HARRY M. (1927–), economist and Nobel Prize winner. Born in Chicago, Markowitz received his higher education, B.A. through Ph.D. (1954), at the University of Chicago. He was on the research staff of the Rand Corporation and technical director of Consolidated Analysis Centers, both in Santa Monica, California. After serving as a professor at UCLA (1968–69), he moved to New York where he was president of the Arbitrage Management Company (1969–72), worked as a private consultant (1972–74), and was a member of the research staff of T.J. Watson Research Center of IBM (1974–83). From 1982 he was been the Speiser Professor of Finance at Baruch College of City University of New York. From 1990 he was research director at Diawa Securities Trust.

In 1990 he shared the Nobel Prize in economics with William Sharpe of Stanford University and Merton Miller of the University of Chicago "for their pioneering work in the theory of financial economics." For Markowitz, the Nobel award was in honor of his theory, first defined in the 1950s, of "portfolio choices," which showed that investors would do best if they built up a diversified investment portfolio. His theory sought to prove that a portfolio that mixes assets in order to minimize risk and maximize return could be practical. His techniques for measuring risk associated with various assets, and his techniques for mixing assets, became standard investment methods. His work on portfolio theory paved the way for financial microanalysis to become an accepted area of research in economic analysis.

Markowitz also developed Simscript, a computer language that is used to write economic-analysis programs.

Books by Markowitz include *Portfolio Selection: Efficient Diversification of Investment* (1959), *Mean-Variance Analysis in Portfolio Choice and Capital Investments* (1987), and *The Theory and Practice of Investment Management Workshop* (with F. Fabozzi and L. Kostovetsky, 2004).

[Ruth Beloff (2nd ed.)]

MARKS, HARRY HANANEL (1855–1916), British journalist and politician. Born in London, Marks was a son of David Woolf Marks (1811–1909), a prominent Reform rabbi. He took up journalism in the U.S. and worked five years on the *New York World* and *Daily Mining News*. Returning to England in 1883, he established and edited *Financial News* and wrote a book, *Small Change, or Lights and Shades of New York* (1882). In 1889–98 he was a member of London County Council and was elected a Conservative member of Parliament in 1895–1900 and 1904–09. Marks was a bitter anti-Zionist. In 1879, however, he wrote a satirical work denouncing antisemitism, *Down With the Jews! A Meeting of the Society for Suppressing the Jewish Race.*

ADD. BIBLIOGRAPHY: ODNB online; D. Porter, "Trusted Guide for the Investing Public: Harry Marks and the *Financial News*, 1884–1916," in: *Business History*, 28 (1986), 1–17; DBB, 4, 133–35.

MARKS, HAYMAN (1772–1825), early U.S. merchant and Mason. Marks, whose place of birth is unknown, was among the early Jewish settlers of Richmond, Virginia. Mention of him is found in several documents involving litigation. A well-known citizen of Richmond, he was one of the signers of a petition to the Virginia legislature asking for the incorporation of a bank there. Marks later moved to Philadelphia, where he became active in Congregation Mikveh Israel, ultimately becoming its president (1815–18). Marks was known to be a member of the Masonic fraternities of both Richmond and Philadelphia. His wife was Grace Judah, of the New York *Judah family.

MARKS, MARCUS M. (1858–1934), U.S. clothing manufacturer, civic official, and philanthropist. Marks was born in Schenectady, N.Y., and joined his father's clothing manufacturing firm, M. Marks and Son, which he later headed (1890–1913). From 1913 to 1917 Marks served as Manhattan borough president under the reforming mayor John P. Mitchel, establishing open public markets, welfare work, and joint trial boards for civil service employees. He was active in a variety of public causes. He was president of the National Daylight Association in 1917. As president of the National Association of Clothiers, he promoted the idea of cooperation among merchants, particularly in labor relations. As a member of Theodore Roosevelt's Nobel Prize Committee on Industrial Peace, Marks mediated many labor disputes. He was a founder and leader of several peace groups, of the Educational Alliance, of the Hospital Saturday and Sunday Association, and of the Tuberculosis Preventorium for children. An advocate of university exchange study between the U.S. and Europe, he served as chairman of the selection committee of the Institute of International Education.

MARKS, SAMUEL (1845–1920), South African industrialist and financier. Marks, who was born in Neustadt-Sugrind, Lithuania, emigrated to the Cape in 1868. With the Lewis brothers, he founded the firm of Lewis and Marks, which eventually controlled large industrial and mining undertakings in the Transvaal. The partners began as traveling traders ("tochers"). When diamonds were discovered they moved to Kimberley, where they opened the first general store in a prefabricated wooden building brought from the Cape by wagon. Lewis and Marks established themselves in the Transvaal in the 1880s, first on the Barberton gold workings and later on the Rand and in Pretoria. Marks, who was popularly known as Sammy, was noted for his salty humor and his fondness for biblical quotations. He understood the Boer outlook, particularly that of his friend President Kruger. He assisted the Transvaal government financially, obtained industrial concessions, and acquired land on the Vaal River on which he founded the town of Vereeniging. He developed rich coal deposits in the area, established fruit farms, and planted extensive forests. He also started the manufacture of bricks, glass, and leather goods and pioneered the steel industry. In 1897 Marks accompanied a deputation to Kruger asking, with indifferent results, for the repeal of laws which placed disabilities upon Jews in common with other non-Protestants and *uitlanders* ("foreigners"). In the conflict between the Boers and the British he commanded the respect of leaders on both sides and was a mediator in the negotiations which ended the South African War in 1902. He served as a senator in the first Union Parliament in 1910. Marks donated £10,000 for the statue of President Kruger which now stands in the center of Pretoria. In 1896 he helped endow the first chair in Hebrew studies at the South African College, later the University of Cape Town, and in 1905 founded a Hebrew school in Pretoria.

BIBLIOGRAPHY: L. Herrman, *History of the Jews in South Africa* (1935); P.H. Emden, *Randlords* (1935), index; G. Saron and L. Hotz (eds.), *Jews in South Africa* (1955). **ADD. BIBLIOGRAPHY:** G. Wheatcroft, *The Randlords* (1985), index.

MARKS, SIMON, BARON (1888–1964), British businessman, philanthropist, and Zionist. Born in Leeds, Simon Marks was the son of Michael Marks, who emigrated in 1882 from Russia to the U.K. where he began as a peddler. In 1884 he opened a market stall in Leeds and later a number of Penny Bazaars in the Midlands. They grew into the great multiple-store chain of Marks & Spencer Ltd. Simon Marks was elected chairman of the board in 1917 and from then on, until he died at his office desk, steered the firm to phenomenal commercial and financial success. His close business associate was Israel Moses (later Lord) *Sieff; they had married each other's sisters. The high quality of their goods and business probity set a tradition in British retail merchandising. Indeed it was said that they were largely responsible for a quiet revolution in British life by raising living standards through making high quality goods available at popular prices. "Marks and Sparks" remains probably the best-known and most famous of all British high street retail chains, although its founding families largely severed their direct connection with the firm in the 1980s.

From their mid-20s Marks and Sieff were loyal and devoted supporters of Chaim *Weizmann in his Zionist activities originally in Manchester and later in London, and were joined by other members of their families. In 1919 Marks went as secretary of the Zionist delegation to the Versailles Peace Conference. Later he became chairman of the Keren Hayesod Committee, vice president of the Zionist Federation and in 1950 was elected a member of the Zionist Exceutive. He was president of the Joint Palestine Appeal at his death. Marks participated with Weizmann and the Zionist leadership in political negotiations with successive British governments and in other Zionist efforts until the State of Israel was established. He and Lord Sieff were leading contributors to the Daniel Sieff Research Institute (1934) and later in the Weizmann Institute of Science (1949) both at Reḥovot, Israel. Their personal and family trust benefactions to public causes in Britain and Israel totaled tens of millions of pounds over six decades. The Marks and Sieff families were reputed to have been the greatest donors to Zionist causes in the Diaspora.

Marks rendered distinguished public service in the period between and during both world wars. He helped to found the Air Defense Cadet Corps in Britain in 1938 and headed wartime production coordination in the London and southeast England area. He was also an adviser to the Ministry of Petroleum Warfare and one of the first directors of British Overseas Airways. In 1944 he received a knighthood and 1961 was created a baron.

BIBLIOGRAPHY: G. Rees, *St. Michael, A History of Marks and Spencer* (1969); I. Sieff, *The Memoirs of Israel Sieff* (1970). **ADD. BIBLIOGRAPHY:** ODNB online; DBB, 4, 138–146; M. Sieff, *Don't Ask the Price* (1986).

[Julian Louis Meltzer (2nd ed.)]

MARKSON, AARON DAVID (1882–1932), Hebrew author and educator. Born in Lithuania, Markson went to the United States in 1904, and taught Hebrew in New York and other cities. He contributed essays and stories to Hebrew periodicals, edited a miscellany *Mi-Keren Zavit* (1921), and translated Mark Twain's *The Prince and the Pauper* (1923). His writings were posthumously collected in *Kitvei A.D. Markson* (1938), which also contains autobiographical material, a brief memoir by his daughter, and evaluations of his work by several authors.

BIBLIOGRAPHY: Waxman, Literature, 4 (1960^2), 1080; Kressel, Leksikon, 2 (1967), 430.

[Eisig Silberschlag]

MARKUS, LUDWIG (1798–1843), historian. Born and educated in Dessau, Germany, he studied medicine at the University of Berlin, but abandoned it to take up philosophy and astronomy. In 1825 he moved to Paris, and from 1830 until 1838 he taught German at the Royal College at Dijon.

Markus was an active member of the Society for Jewish Culture and Science in Berlin, and one of his lifelong passions was the study of the Falashas (*Beta Israel) of Abyssinia. This earned him Heinrich *Heine's sobriquet, "King of Abyssinia." He wrote *Histoire des Wandales* (1836) in which he traced the rise and collapse of the Vandal empire in Africa, and in 1842, published *Géographie ancienne des états Barbaresques*. Suffering from recurrent fits of depression, especially after the death of his mother, he moved back to Paris 1838 and died there penniless in an insane asylum. Baroness de Rothschild paid for the funeral, and Heine wrote an obituary.

BIBLIOGRAPHY: Elbogen, in: MGWJ, 81 (1937), 177–85; H. Heine, *Saemtliche Werke*, 14 (1964), 43–58.

[George Schwab / Bjoern Siegel (2nd ed.)]

MARLÉ, ARNOLD (1889–1970), German actor. Born in Prague, Marlé trained in Munich and was active as an actor and director in Munich and Hamburg. In 1933 he left Germany for Czechoslovakia, working at the German Theater in Prague from 1934 to 1937. In the 1930s, he accompanied Leopold Jessner's group to Holland and London. In 1939 he immigrated to London. He began appearing in English-language films in 1942 and later also played in television series and on the British and American stages. His wife, Lilli Freud-Marlé, whom he married in 1917, was a niece of Sigmund *Freud, and became known as a reciter of poetry in various European cities.

BIBLIOGRAPHY: *International Biographical Dictionary of Central European Émigrés: 1933–1945*, vol. 2 (1999), 781, incl. bibl.

[David Rees (2nd ed.)]

MARLI, SAMUEL (Raphael) BEN MAẒLI'AḤ (d. 1617), Italian rabbi and author. One of the outstanding scholars of Italy, Samuel, like his father, served in a variety of offices in the Mantua community and was in charge until his death of collecting funds for Ereẓ Israel. In 1587 he was appointed rabbi of the community and was apparently also the head of a yeshivah. According to S.D. Luzzatto, his name means "of Arles." During the time Marli was rabbi, the Jews of Mantua were confined to a ghetto prepared for them at their own cost, and Marli was one of the members of the committee which dealt with matters affecting the ghetto. His signature is found on many of the community's documents and regulations. He was highly praised by the scholars of his time, and although he published no works, a few of his responsa and letters have been published in the works of his contemporaries and preserved in manuscript. Some of his *piyyutim* were published in the *Ayyelet ha-Shaḥar* and in the *Siddur mi-Berakhah* of Italian rite (Mantua, 1653), as well as later in Schirman's *Mivḥar ha-Shirah ha-Ivrit be-Italyah*. Marli prepared and may have published a special essay which is still in manuscript, "to demonstrate to the nations and princes that a Jew is not permitted to curse or to act wrongly toward any man." He is also mentioned among those who supplied Azariah dei Rossi with material for his *Me'or Einayim*, and was among the rabbis who forbade the use of the *mikveh* of Rovigo (Moses Porto in: *Palgei Mayim*, p. 55). Hananiah Eliakim Rieti composed a eulogy on his death.

BIBLIOGRAPHY: Ghirondi-Neppi, 337; S. Simonsohn, *Toledot ha-Yehudim be-Dukkasut Mantovah*, 1 (1964), 649.

[Itzhak Alfassi]

°**MARLOWE, CHRISTOPHER** (1564–1593), English playwright. *The Jew of Malta* (c. 1590) portrays the monstrous Jew, Barabas; T.S. Eliot described the play as a savage farce. Indeed it has elements of melodrama and exaggeration which suggest that Marlowe was not completely serious in his portrayal of the Jew. Barabas is a rich merchant whose wealth is expropriated and whose house is turned into a nunnery by order of the governor of Malta. In revenge, Barabas indulges in an orgy of slaughter, poisoning his daughter Abigail, her lover, and many others. Malta being besieged by the Turks, Barabas enters upon a career of political intrigue, first betraying the island to the enemy and then plotting the destruction of the Turkish commander. But Barabas is himself betrayed and perishes in a boiling cauldron. The story represents a mingling of traditional antisemitism (in the Middle Ages the Jews were often charged with poisoning the wells) with the late 16th-century taste for the "political thriller." Barabas, a disciple of Machiavelli, practices political stratagems with a view to gaining power in the state. From this point of view his Jewishness is no more than incidental, the main interest being focused on his "Italian" villainy. Barabas' conspiracy with the Turks may have been suggested by the career of Joseph *Nasi. *The Jew of Malta* was almost certainly in Shakespeare's mind when he wrote *The Merchant of Venice* some years later. Like Shakespeare's Jew, Barabas has a beautiful daughter who becomes a Christian, and a comic servant, Ithamore, who directs the audience's laughter against the Jew. This latter feature may be a relic of the medieval religious drama in which the Devil was frequently accompanied by a comic figure, the Vice. In spite of his negative portrayal of the Jew, Marlowe undoubtedly projected into the portrait some of his own restlessness as well as his notorious dislike of the Establishment. But Marlowe's work differs markedly from Shakespeare's depiction of Shylock in being two-dimensional, in contrast to Shakespeare's ambiguous and three-dimensional portrayal of his Jewish character.

BIBLIOGRAPHY: J.L. Cardozo, *Contemporary Jew in the Elizabethan Drama* (1925); M.J. Landa, *Jew in Drama* (1926), index; H. Michelson, *Jew in Early English Literature* (1926), 70 ff.; T.S. Eliot, *Selected Essays* (1932), 118–25; H. Sinsheimer, *Shylock* (1947), 51–54; H. Levin, *Overreacher: a Study of Christopher Marlowe* (1954), index; H. Fisch, *Dual Image* (1959), 25–29. **ADD. BIBLIOGRAPHY:** ODNB online.

[Harold Harel Fisch]

MARMOR, KALMAN (**Ẓevi**; 1879–1956), Yiddish scholar and activist. Born in Mishagola, near Vilna, he immigrated to Switzerland in 1899, where he studied at the universities of Freiburg and Berne, before settling in the U.S. in 1906. He joined the Po'alei Zion, co-founded the World Union of Po'alei Zion, and became the editor of its weekly, *Der Yidisher Kemfer*. In 1914 he joined the American Socialist Party and in 1919 the American Labor Alliance, which became the Workers Party and later the Communist Party. Marmor began his literary career in 1901 in *Der Yidisher Arbeter*, published by the Bund, and contributed to Yiddish periodicals in Europe and the U.S. In 1922 he joined the New York Yiddish Communist daily *Morgen Frayhayt* and remained a contributor until his death.

From 1933 to 1936, he lived in Kiev, working in the Institute for Jewish Studies of the Ukrainian Academy of Sciences, where he prepared editions of the works of Aaron *Liebermann, Joseph *Bovshover, and David *Edelstadt. His monograph on Liebermann, as well as the collection of Liebermann's works which he annotated and translated into Yiddish, were lost when the Institute was liquidated by the Soviet government in 1936. As a U.S. citizen, Marmor was freed, having rescued Liebermann's letters, which were later published in New York. The first two volumes of his edition of the works of David Edelstadt, written from an extreme party perspective, were published in Moscow in 1935. The manuscript of the third volume found its way to the YIVO Institute in New York. In his long career Marmor was a committed Zionist, Po'alei-Zionist, Socialist, and Communist, an expert on the history of Yiddish and Hebrew literature, on Jewish, Arabic, and Greek philosophy, and on the history of socialist and revolutionary movements; he was a productive writer, an able researcher and collector of historical material. His publications include *Der Onhoyb fun der Yidisher Literatur in Amerike* (1944), *Dovid Edelshtat* (1950), *Yoysef Bovshover* (1952), *Yankev Gordin* (1953), his autobiography, *Mayn Lebns-Geshikhte* (2 vols., 1959), and his 10-volume edition of the complete works of Morris Winchevsky (1927).

BIBLIOGRAPHY: Rejzen, Leksikon, 2 (1927), 491–500; LNYL, 6 (1965), 113–9; A. Pomerantz, *Di Sovetishe Harugey Malkhus* (1962), 360–85. **ADD. BIBLIOGRAPHY:** G.G. Branover (ed.), *Rossiĭskaia evreĭskaia entsiklopediia*, 2 (1995), 252.

[Elias Schulman / Jerold C. Frakes (2nd ed.)]

MARMOREK, ALEXANDER (1865–1923), bacteriologist and Zionist leader. He was born in Mielnice, Galicia, and studied in Vienna and at the Pasteur Institute in Paris, where he became assistant and subsequently *chef de travaux*. Early in his studies, he discovered an antidote (antistreptococcus) against puerperal fever. In 1903 he addressed the Paris Académie de Médecine and claimed the discovery of the toxin of the tubercle-bacillus and of the antituberculosis vaccine. This discovery was hotly debated in expert circles and was finally accepted as an invariably successful cure if prescribed up to a certain stage of the disease. With this discovery, Marmorek also initiated the serum study that led to the modern treatment of typhus and diabetes. Marmorek was also an ardent Zionist. In Vienna he belonged to *Kadimah, the first students' society to join *Herzl after the publication of *Der Judenstaat*. With his brothers Oscar and Isidor, he belonged to the circle of Herzl's closest friends and was repeatedly consulted on political steps contemplated by the Zionist leader. He was elected member of the Zionist General Council at the first 11 Zionist congresses (1897–1913). After Herzl's death Marmorek remained an adherent of Herzl's political Zionism and, next to Max *Nordau, became the foremost spokesman of the opposition, when "practical" Zionists assumed the movement's leadership in 1911. After World War I he strongly opposed *Weizmann's policies and refused to participate at the 12th Zionist Congress (1921). In his articles and speeches he emphasized that the Palestine Mandate was not the fulfillment of Herzl's idea of a Jewish state. Marmorek was chairman of the French Zionist Federation and one of the co-founders of *L'Echo Sioniste*, the Zionist monthly published in Paris. He founded the Jewish Popular University in Paris, chiefly for the benefit of foreign Jews who settled there. As a foreign national he was unable to remain in Paris during World War I and served as a doctor with the Allied armies in Eastern Europe.

His brother OSCAR (1863–1909) was an architect and Zionist leader. Born in Skala, Galicia, he studied in Vienna and Paris. He built a great number of important buildings in Vienna and Austria and also some synagogues, in which he attempted a style based on his studies of old Jewish architecture. He attained fame through his pavilion "Venice in Vienna" at the world exhibition of 1900 in Vienna.

Oscar Marmorek joined Herzl after the publication of *Der Judenstaat* and was elected to the Zionist Executive at the first six Zionist congresses. He was a co-founder of *Die *Welt*.

Herzl depicted him in *Altneuland* as Architect Steineck. He died by his own hand.

BIBLIOGRAPHY: D. Jacobson, *A. Marmorek* (Fr., 1923); JC (July 20, 1923); *Die Welt* (April 16, 1909); L. Jaffe, *Sefer ha-Congress* (1950), 339–40; M.I. Bodenheimer, *Prelude to Israel* (1963), index; M. Schach, *Asher Ittam Hithalakhti* (1951), 123–42.

[Oskar K. Rabinowicz]

MARMORI, HANOKH (1948–), Israeli graphic artist and editor. Marmori studied history and theater at the Hebrew University of Jerusalem and graphic design at the Bezalel Academy of Arts. A satirist, he began his writing career on the university newspaper, contributed to the popular television satirical program *Niku'i Rosh* ("Clearing the Head"), and co-wrote a satirical column in the political weekly *Ha-Olam ha-Zeh*. In 1980 he joined the Schocken newspaper chain, first as the founding editor of the Tel Aviv local newspaper *Ha-Ir*. In 1984 he moved to *Ḥadashot*, the failed Schocken attempt to launch a popular newspaper, where he was occupied in writing mostly for the newspaper's magazine and supplements. In 1988 he was appointed deputy editor of the *Haaretz* daily newspaper, and following the death of its veteran editor Gershon *Schocken in 1991 was appointed to succeed him. Deploying his graphics background, Marmori succeeded in turning a dullish newspaper into one with an attractive layout, but without losing its character as a thoughtful and stimulating maker of opinion. A daily culture and entertainment supplement and a weekly book supplement were added, together with expanded news coverage, notably in the fields of economics and sport. Notwithstanding his close ties with Amos Schocken, who succeeded his father Gershon Schocken as publisher, differences eventually arose between the two men. Disagreements within the editorial board over the Intifada beginning in 2000 found Schocken taking a more left-wing position together with some other board members while Marmori took a more centrist view. In 2004 Schocken's plans to further enlarge the economics section of the paper into a separate entity called "The Market," outside the editor's direct responsibility, led Marmori to resign. He left active journalism to head the Department of Visual Communications at the Bezalel Academy of Arts. In 2004 he was awarded the Sokolow Prize for journalism.

[Yoel Cohen (2nd ed.)]

MARMORSTEIN, ARTHUR (1882–1946), rabbi, scholar, and teacher. Born in Miskolc, Hungary, Marmorstein was descended from a long line of Hungarian rabbis known not only for their talmudic learning but also for their familiarity with secular literature. He studied at the yeshivah of Pressburg and the rabbinic seminaries of Budapest and Berlin. After visiting libraries for some time in England, Italy, and France, transcribing manuscripts, Marmorstein served for six years as rabbi at Jamnitz (Jemnice), Czechoslovakia. From 1912 until his death he taught at Jews' College, London. Marmorstein's scholarship embraced many subjects. His initial training at the universities was in Semitics, with special emphasis on Assyriology. He was particularly fascinated by the aggadic sections of the Talmud and by liturgy. Though Marmorstein contributed to many areas of Jewish scholarship, he is noteworthy for his studies in rabbinic theology, the subject of his two important volumes *Doctrine of Merits in Old Rabbinic Literature* (1920) and *Old Rabbinic Doctrine of God* (2 pts., 1927); both were reprinted in one volume with an introduction by R.J. Zwi Werblowsky (1968). Other important essays on rabbinic theology by Marmorstein were collected and published under the title *Studies in Jewish Theology* (1950). Marmorstein's work is characterized by painstaking detail in the collection of sources, which are important for the study of rabbinic religion.

BIBLIOGRAPHY: E. Marmorstein, in: *A. Marmorstein, Studies in Jewish Theology: Marmorstein Memorial Volume* (1950), xv–xlvi (incl. bibl.).

[Alexander Tobias]

MARMUR, DOW (1935–), rabbi, teacher, author. Marmur was born in Sosnowiec, Poland, an only child in a Po'alei Zion (left) family. In 1939, the family moved to the Lvov region, escaping the German invasion. They were deported to Siberia in 1940 by Soviet authorities but, following Operation Barbarossa, released and found refuge in Uzbekistan, where they remained until their repatriation to Poland in 1946. Although largely unschooled, the young Marmur had already learned four languages.

The family moved to Gothenburg, Sweden in 1948, where Marmur not only learned Swedish but English, German, and Hebrew as well. Attracted to Liberal Judaism, he entered the Faculty of Religion at the University of Stockholm in 1956, the same year he married Fredzia Zonabend, a survivor of the Lodz ghetto. Not feeling fulfilled at university, Marmur and his wife moved to London, where he entered the Leo Baeck College. Under the tutelage of several luminaries, including Ignaz *Maybaum, he graduated in 1962 and was already serving as rabbi of South-West Essex Reform Synagogue in Ilford. In 1969, he became rabbi of North-Western Reform Synagogue in Alyth Gardens and in 1983 moved to Toronto to become rabbi of Holy Blossom Synagogue, the largest Reform congregation in Canada. He remained at Holy Blossom until his retirement in 2000.

Marmur wrote six books, notably *Beyond Survival* (1982); *The Star of Return* (1991); and an autobiography, *Six Lives* (2004). He has wrote extensively in newspapers and journals, taught at St. Michael's College, University of Toronto, and was a fellow of Massey College, University of Toronto. An ardent Zionist, he also served as the first chair of ARZENU, the international movement of Reform Zionists; president of ARZA Canada, the Association of Reform Zionists of America; vice president of the Canadian Zionist Federation, and as a member of the executive of the World Zionist Organization. After retirement, he became Interim executive director of the World Union for Progressive Judaism in Jerusalem.

Marmur was a champion of progressive social causes in Canada and Israel, where he remained sympathetic to the peace movement. He was founder of the Polish-Jewish Heritage Foundation of Canada, which seeks to build bridges between Poles and Jews.

[Frank Bialystok (2nd ed.)]

MAROR (Heb. מָרוֹר), the traditional "bitter herb" which the children of Israel were commanded to eat with unleavened bread and the paschal offering both in Egypt (Ex. 12:8) and "throughout their generations" (Num. 9:11). The plural, *merorim*, occurs in the Bible in the verse: "He hath filled me with *merorim*, he hath sated me with wormwood" (Lam. 3:15), referring to a bitter vegetable, parallel to wormwood (cf. Deut. 32:32). The rabbis included under *merorim* plants whose common features are "bitterness, possessing sap, with a grayish appearance" (Pes. 39a), meaning wild or cultivated vegetables, with leaves of a silvery-grayish-green color, that have a milk-like sap and leaves with a bitter taste. This definition can apply to a number of plants, particularly some of those belonging to the family of Compositae. Thus the Tosefta and the Talmud (*ibid.*) enumerate a number of such vegetables with which the duty of eating *maror* on the night of the *seder* can be fulfilled. The Mishnah enumerates five: *ḥazeret* ("*lettuce"); *olshin* ("chicory," see *vegetables); *tamkah* (according to Maimonides, "wild chicory" but impossible to identify with certainty); *ḥarḥavina*, a plant of the family of Umbelliferae, of which the most common is *Eryngium creticum*; and *maror*. Some of the Compositae are called *murār* or *marāra* in Arabic. In the Jerusalem Talmud *maror* is described as a "bitter vegetable with a silvery appearance, and possessing sap" (Pes. 2:5, 29c; the same description as the Babylonian Talmud gives for all the varieties of *merorim*). These characteristics agree most with the plant *Sonchus oleraceus*, called in Arabic *murār*. This is a weed, widespread in gardens, fallow fields, and on the roadsides throughout Israel. Its soft leaves are at times eaten as salad by the poor, some also eating the juicy root. The plant is filled with a milk-like sap, the underside of the leaves is a bluish-silvery color, and the green plant has a bitter taste and is hardly edible. According to Pliny, "this is a healthy food, recommended as a remedy for various ailments" (*Historia Naturalis* 22:88–90; 26:163). The Samaritans use only the leaves of the wild lettuce *Lactuca scariola* for *maror*.

BIBLIOGRAPHY: Loew, Flora, 1 (1928), 415–20, 424–40; H.N. and A.L. Moldenke, *Plants of the Bible* (1952), 74f., nos. 62–67; J. Feliks, *Kilei Zera'im ve-Harkavah* (1967), 57–60; J. Feliks, *Olam ha-Ẓome'aḥ ha-Mikra'i* (1968²), 194–6.

[Jehuda Feliks]

°**MARR, WILHELM** (1819–1904), German antisemite. Marr, the son of a famous theater personality, was of Lutheran descent; the still frequently heard assertion that he was Jewish has no basis in fact. His political career began among left-wing exile circles in Switzerland, from which he was expelled in 1843. Back in his native Hamburg, he participated as an ultraleftist in the revolution of 1848. But the return of the old regime persuaded Marr to "resign from the democratic movement" and to spend the next decade trying to establish himself in North and Central America. By the time he came back to Hamburg, his political outlook had changed completely. No longer the champion of progressive causes, he used his undoubted journalistic skills to champion black slavery, condemn proletarian emancipation, and to attack Jews. In 1862, his *Der Judenspiegel* ("A Mirror to the Jews") made a racially based argument against Jewish equality. The pamphlet provoked slight interest and soon disappeared. Seventeen years later, however, when Germany was in the throes of economic and social turmoil, Marr returned to the so-called Jewish Question with his influential bestseller, "The Victory of Jewry over Germandom, Considered from a Non-Religious Point of View," which went through 12 editions, all in 1879. He repeated many of his arguments from 1862, but now they appeared in a world-historical context, lodged in a systematically racist framework, and were made all the more potent because of the author's insistence that Jews had been engaging in an 1,800-year worldwide conspiracy against gentiles that was about to culminate in their absolute victory. In the last edition of the book, Marr recruited members for his Antisemiten-Liga (Antisemites' League). Although his attempt to form a political organization dedicated to solving the Jewish Question failed almost immediately, Marr alerted more powerful forces in German society to the utility of antisemitism as a tool of political mobilization. Both the word and the movement entered German and then European political culture at this time, never again to leave it. The irascible Wilhelm Marr, on the other hand, already 60 years old, was soon cast aside by antisemites of the younger generation. He died in obscure poverty in 1904.

BIBLIOGRAPHY: P.W. Massing, *Rehearsal for Destruction* (1949), 6–10, 211–212; M. Zimmermann, *Wilhelm Marr: The Patriarch of Anti-Semitism* (1986); R.S. Levy, *Antisemitism in the Modern World: An Anthology of Texts* (1991), 74–93.

[Richard S. Levy (2nd ed.)]

MARRAKESH, one of the former capitals of *Morocco, situated at the foot of the High Atlas Mountains. They city was founded in the latter half of the 11th century by the *Almoravid dynasty. A Jewish community was established there soon thereafter, coming from different parts of southern Morocco. Many were subsequently barred from inhabiting the city while others were persecuted by the *Almohads in the 12th century and had to disperse. A Jewish community was revived there during the course of the 13th century but Jews faced further persecution, death, and expulsion. Only under the Merinid dynasty in the latter half of the 13th and 14th centuries were Jews permitted to resettle in Marrakesh and their numbers grew in the late 15th century through the arrival of Sephardi refugees expelled from the Iberian Peninsula. Nevertheless, the main group of Marrakeshi Jews originated from the Atlas Mountains. Iberian Jews (Spanish and Portuguese), however, took control of communal affairs. From 1557 onward, the Sa'di dynasty concentrated all the Jews in a Jewish quarter of their own, known as the *mellah*. While the Jewish community numbered approximately 25,000 in mid-16th century, thousands perished throughout that century in epidemics. The Sa'di sultans, who were descendants of the Prophet *Muhammad and originated from the Arabian Peninsula, enlisted the Jews of Marrakesh as their trade agents and entrusted to them the management of local industries. With the ascendance of the Alawite dynasty in the latter half of the 17th century, its sultans, also descendants of the Prophet, did not always display tolerance toward the Jews of Morocco. This was evidently the case with Sultan Mulay Isma'il, who in the 1670s exposed the Jews of Marrakesh to horrible atrocities.

In the 18th century Marrakesh lost its status as the central capital of Morocco in favor of *Fez. Notwithstanding, commercially and economically, the city preserved its position as a vital center for southern Morocco. There were flourishing *yeshivot* in Marrakesh and bustling activity by talmudic scholars belonging to the prominent Corcos and Pinto families, as well as kabbalists. The Jews under the Alawite sultans in the late 18th and throughout much of the 19th centuries played a preponderant role in the local economy and their social and political situation improved markedly. There were efforts by fanatical Muslim leaders to forcibly convert Jews to Islam, but the intervention of international Jewish organizations such as the Paris-based *Alliance Israélite Universelle (which also opened schools in Marrakesh at the beginning of the 20th century) and European consuls stationed in Morocco, foiled their efforts.

Under the leadership of Si Madani al-Glawi, the governor of Marrakesh and its environs, who belonged to the "great families" connected with the Alawite dynasty and the *makhzan* (Moroccan government), the Jews of southern Morocco enjoyed much influence. In 1908–09, while entrusted by the *makhzan* to bolster Alawite influence in the south and Marrakesh, Glawi, who then served as the sultan's chief minister (grand *wazir*), bestowed on the Marrakeshi Jewish elite considerable economic and social privileges. He also lifted exorbitant taxes imposed on the Jews of Marrakesh and Taroudant in the period immediately preceding his rise to power. Glawi maintained intimate social and economic ties with the leader of the Jewish community in Marrakesh – the illustrious Joshua Corcos of the influential *Corcos family. The latter community president was perhaps the most important Moroccan Jewish leader in many centuries.

Under French colonial domination (1912–1956), in which the French protectorate collaborated with the Alawite dynasty in managing Moroccan affairs, the position of the Jews improved immeasurably. They were now exposed to modern ideas through French education, employment in private and public administration, and the liberal professions. Zionist influences penetrated the community in the interwar years like other political currents prevalent in the modern Jewish world.

Until 1920 the Jewish quarter of Marrakesh was the largest in Morocco. The 1920s and 1930s changed this. Although the Jewish population of Marrakesh was greater than in Fez or *Tangier, *Casablanca on the Atlantic coast emerged steadily as the largest and most important Jewish community through internal migrations from all parts of the country. Thus, if in 1912, 15,700 Jews dwelt in Marrakesh (compared to 7,000 in Casablanca), and 25,646 in 1936 (compared to 38,806 in Casablanca), in 1951, five years before the end of French colonial presence, the Jews of Marrakesh numbered 18,500 whereas Casablanca Jewry was 75,000 strong. The reason for the decline in the Marrakeshi Jewish population was attributed to internal migration to Casablanca and other coastal cities and to *aliyah* under the auspices of the Jewish Agency. As in other major Moroccan cities, Jewish bodies such as the American Jewish Joint Distribution Committee, the ORT vocational network, the Alliance Israélite Universelle, educational departments of Oẓar ha-Torah, and the Jewish Agency extended their activities and offered vital services. These efforts either helped those Jews who stayed behind to improve their lot, or facilitated their integration into French, Canadian, and Israeli societies. In 2005, there were several dozen Jews left in Marrakesh.

BIBLIOGRAPHY: J. Benech, *Essai d'explication d'un mellah* (1940); D. Corcos, *Studies in the History of the Jews of Morocco*, Introduction by Eliyahu Ashtor (1976); H.Z. Hirschberg, *A History of the Jews in North Africa*, 2 vols. (Eng. translation) (1974); M.M. Laskier, *The Allliance Israélite Universelle and the Jewish Communities of Morocco: 1862–1962* (1983); C.R. Pennell, *Morocco since 1830: A History* (2000); N.A. Stillman, *The Jews of Arab Lands in Modern Times* (1991).

[Michael M. Laskier (2nd ed.)]

MARRANO, term of opprobium used to denigrate the New Christians of Spain and Portugal. Various origins for the term have been suggested. These include the Hebrew *marit ayin* ("the appearance of the eye"), referring to the fact that the Marranos were ostensibly Christian but actually Judaizers; *moḥoram attah* ("you are excommunicated"); the Aramaic-Hebrew *Mar Anus* ("Mr. forced convert"); the Hebrew *mumar* ("apostate") with the Spanish ending *ano*; the Arabic *mura'in* ("hypocrite"); and the second word of the ecclesiastical imprecation *anathema maranatha*. However, all such derivations are unlikely. The most probable, as clearly shown by Farinelli's study, is from the Spanish word meaning swine, a word already in use in the early Middle Ages, though Y. Malkiel argues plausibly for a derivation from the late Arabic *barrān, barrānī*, meaning an outsider or stranger, and a coalescence of this word with the term marrano "pig, pork" derived from Latin *verres* "wild boar." The term probably did not originally refer to the Judaizers' reluctance to eat pork, as some scholars hold. From its earliest use, it was intended to impart the sense of loathing conveyed by the word in other languages. Although romanticized and regarded by later Jewry as a badge of honor, the term was not as widely used, especially in official circles, as is often believed. In Latin America as a rule it is not found in official documents and there is little evidence of its unofficial use in most places.

BIBLIOGRAPHY: Roth, Marranos, 27f.; A. Farinelli, *Marrano: storia di un vituperio* (1925), 36; Y. Malkiel, in: JOAS, 68 (1948), 175–84.

[Martin A. Cohen]

MARRANO DIASPORA. New *Christians began to leave *Spain in the wake of the mass conversions of 1391 and *Portugal after the forced conversions in 1497. The tide of emigration ebbed and flowed, but was always stimulated by the advent of new disasters, such as the introduction of the *Inquisition into Spain in 1481 and Portugal in 1536, and the recrudescence of intensive persecution of the Marranos, as in Portugal after 1630. To stem this continuing exodus, as early as the last decade of the 15th century the authorities in both countries issued decrees prohibiting the emigration of New Christians, and these were frequently renewed. Even the so-called irrevocable permission to emigrate which the New Christians purchased from Philip III in 1601, during the union of Spain and Portugal, was short-lived, being rescinded in 1610. However, these decrees were frequently evaded: Marranos regularly left the Peninsula clandestinely, or secured permission to take business trips abroad from which they never returned. There are even cases of their leaving for the ostensible purpose of making a pilgrimage to Rome. Once the authorities became aware of such stratagems they tried to intercept Marranos as they moved through Europe to places where they could practice Judaism openly, and men like Jean de la Foix in Lombardy acquired notoriety for his inhuman treatment of those who fell into his hands. There were even instances where the highest authorities in the Peninsula closed their eyes to New Christian emigration, particularly when it involved their settling in Latin *America, where their skills and enterprise were desperately needed. Furtively and openly, in trickles and in torrents, thousands of New Christians left the Iberian Peninsula during the nearly three and a half centuries of the Inquisition's power.

Not all the New Christians leaving the Peninsula were secret Jews. Many were devout Catholics and had no intention of changing their faith; others were religiously ambivalent or even apathetic. Some of these may have shared the general insecurity of all New Christians in the Peninsula; some may have feared implication in inquisitional proceedings because of the activities of their relatives or friends; some may have wished to hide their Jewish origins in foreign lands; and others may simply have been attracted by new challenges and opportunities. It was people like these who evoked apologies for Judaism such as Samuel *Usque's classic *Consolaçam às tribulaçoens de Israel* (1553; *Consolation for the Tribulations of Israel*, 1965), intended to persuade them to return to their ancestral religion. At the same time, considerable numbers of the New Christians were Marranos, or secret Jews, and were passionately dedicated to Judaism. This was particularly true of the Portuguese New Christians. By the 16th century the term "Portuguese" was already synonymous with the word "Jew" in much of Europe, Asia, and Latin America. During the Inquisition's extended sway over the Peninsula, the emigrating Marranos could plan to travel to four different kinds of countries: Muslim lands, Protestant territories as they came into being, Catholic countries outside the jurisdiction of Spain and Portugal, and Catholic countries within the peninsular orbit.

Muslim Countries

These were the most natural places of refuge for Marranos seeking to live openly as Jews, for they were the archenemies of the Christians and Spain and Portugal were particularly hated. *Morocco had already become a haven of refuge for both Jews and Conversos at the end of the 14th century, but many more Jews and Marranos were attracted to the Ottoman *Empire at the end of the 15th century and during the 16th. Sultan Bayazid *II (Bajazet II; 1481–1512) mocked King Ferdinand for impoverishing Spain and enriching the Ottoman Empire through his expulsion of the Jews. In the 16th century numerous cities in the Ottoman Empire had Jewish settlements, among them *Cairo, *Jerusalem, *Safed, *Damascus, *Constantinople with some 50,000 Jews, and *Salonika where the population of the Marranos exceeded that of the other Jews and the non-Jews as well.

Protestant Countries

Next to the Muslim countries the Protestant lands offered the best prospects, for here too the Catholics were detested, and the Inquisition was a hated institution because it was no more tolerant of Protestant heretics than Judaizers. In places like *England and *Hamburg and other German cities, Marranos began their existence as titular Catholics and secret Jews before the Reformation. They continued in this double life long after those areas had broken with Rome, for the Protestant authorities were not eager to grant official acknowledgment to the presence of Jews in their midst. In Hamburg, destined to become one of the wealthiest and most productive Marrano centers, the settlement of Jews was not officially authorized until 1612 and Jewish public worship not until 1650. In England, where Jews had been expelled in 1290, the Marranos who settled originally in *London and *Bristol were never officially acknowledged as Jews. Spokesmen for the Marranos, both Christians and Jews, including Manasseh Ben *Israel, failed in their efforts to secure the formal recognition of Jewish resettlement. Rather than being officially granted, the resettlement was "connived at": the question was simply ignored and Marranos were allowed to live undisturbed as Jews. Actually this connivance, or de facto resettlement through official silence, proved salutary for the Jews, since the failure to grant official permission for their presence made it impossible to impose particular disabilities on them. From the middle of the 17th century at least, the Marranos were treated like all other nonconformist citizens. In 1664 the crown granted Jews an official charter of protection, thus further facilitating the development of the Marrano community. The ex-Marranos and their descendants continued to be the dominant element in British Jewry until the 19th century.

In *Amsterdam the Marranos did not arrive until around 1590, some 11 years after the Union of Utrecht (1579) and the birth of the United Provinces of the Netherlands as a Protestant state. Here too they had to wait until 1615 before Jewish settlement was officially authorized, but the Marranos in Amsterdam differed from those in other Protestant countries in that they openly practiced Judaism almost from the moment of their arrival. Thanks to the Marranos, Amsterdam became one of the greatest Jewish centers in the world in the 17th century; it had some of the finest academies and produced some of the greatest Jewish thinkers. Amsterdam was also a haven for oppressed Jews from other places, including France in 1615 and Eastern Europe after the *Chmielnicki massacres (from 1648). Erstwhile Marranos from Holland were among the first settlers in Surinam and Curaçao, where a substantial Sephardi community came into being after 1650. Other former Marranos were also found in Barbados and in other parts of the West Indies, including Martinique and the Leeward Islands.

Other Catholic Countries

The Catholic lands outside the control of Spain and Portugal did not offer so secure a haven as the Ottoman Empire or the Protestant countries, but they had the advantage of being outside the orbit of the peninsular Inquisitions. At the same time these areas were not without their inherent dangers, in the form of envy or rooted prejudice on the part of the local population, pressures from the Spanish and Portuguese Inquisitions upon the local authorities, and even the possibility of persecution galvanized by local initiative, and, in the case of the Papal States, an indigenous Inquisition. As a result, the existence of many of these Marrano communities, even if unclouded and prosperous for a time, was seldom free from molestations.

In the Papal States the Marranos' presence was noticeable in places like *Rome and even more so the seaport of *Ancona, where they thrived under benevolent popes like Clement VII (1523–34), Paul III (1534–49), and Julius III (1550–55). They even received a guarantee that if accused of apostasy they would be subject only to papal authority. But Paul IV (1555–59), the voice of the Counter-Reformation, dealt them an irreparable blow when he withdrew all protection previously given the Marranos and initiated a fierce persecution against them. As a result of the anti-Marrano campaign, 25 Judaizers were burned alive in the spring of 1556; 26 others were condemned to the galleys, and 30 more who had been arrested were liberated only after they had paid a substantial bribe. Thanks to the intervention of the Marrano patroness, Gracia Mendes *Nasi, the sultan at Constantinople secured the release of all Marranos who were his subjects. Plans were laid to boycott Ancona and transfer all the Marranos' former business to neighboring *Pesaro, in the friendlier territory of the duke of Urbino, but the project failed, and the duke even expelled the Marranos from his territory. A document of 1550 indicates that there were some Marranos among the Spanish and Portuguese merchants in Florence who traded on a large scale with Spain and her colonies. In *Ferrara, under the house of Este, the Marranos formed a large and thriving community by the middle of the 16th century, one of the most notable in their entire Diaspora. The dukes protected them until 1581, when Duke Alfonso II, bowing to ecclesiastical pressure, allowed many of them to be arrested. Three were eventually sent to Rome to be burned at the stake in February 1583. Marranos settled in *Venice in the 15th and early 16th centuries but were subjected to decrees of expulsion in 1497 and again in 1550. Thereafter the city policy began to change. Venice not only welcomed Marranos but kept the Inquisition at bay. Theologians like Paolo Sarpi even claimed that the Judaizers were outside the jurisdiction of the Inquisition because they had been baptized by force. Equally fortunate was the situation in the grand duchy of *Tuscany. In an attempt to woo the Marranos to Pisa and *Leghorn, Ferdinand II issued a charter in 1593 granting them protection against harassment in matters of faith. As it was in decline at the time, Pisa did not attract many Marranos, but Leghorn did: the community there thrived and by the end of the 18th century its population approached 5,000. Emmanuel Philbert granted a special privilege to induce Jews to settle in the duchy of Savoy, intending mainly to settle Marranos from Spain and Portugal in Nice in order to develop the city into a central trading port with the East. The privilege enraged Philip II of Spain, who considered the whole plan as seriously damaging Spain's interests in the Mediterranean as well as an incitement to Marranos to return to Judaism. The joint pressure of Spain and the Holy See led to the rescinding of the privilege and on Nov. 22, 1573 the duke ordered a group of Marranos who had returned to Judaism to leave his territory within six months. This decree was probably not put into effect until 1581 when Charles Emmanuel I ordered the expulsion of all Portuguese Jews from the duchy.

In *France the Marranos had to maintain some semblance of Catholicism for more than two centuries, but they were seldom molested in their secret practice of Judaism. Though they were called "New Christians" or "Portuguese merchants," their Jewishness was an open secret. In the large settlements they lived in their own quarters, had their own burial grounds, developed their own schools and communal institutions, and even trained their own rabbis after first importing them from abroad. In the course of time they gradually reduced their Catholic practices and eventually abandoned Church marriage and even baptism. In 1730 they were officially recognized as Jews. Their more formal communities were situated at *Bordeaux and *Bayonne and there were numerous lesser settlements in such places as *Toulouse, *Lyons, Montpellier, La *Rochelle, *Nantes, and *Rouen. Bayonne was the center of a cluster of communities, including *Biarritz, *Bidache, *Peyrehorade, and *Saint-Jean-de-Luz. In this last town the Marranos had the misfortune of being expelled in 1619, and then, after a partial return, seeing the town captured by the Spaniards in 1636.

Other Territories

But in the far-flung Spanish and Portuguese possessions, in the Aragonese territories of *Sicily, *Sardinia and *Naples, in *Hapsburg territories like Flanders, or the colonial territories in the Far East or in the Americas, the situation of the Marranos was always precarious. There they lived continually under the shadow of the Inquisition; even where a tribunal of the

Holy Office was not in operation, there were episcopal Inquisitions and occasional inquisitional "visitors" sent from the home countries to galvanize the search for heretics. Sicily and Sardinia, with Inquisitions introduced in 1487 and 1493 respectively, were practically free of Judaizers by the middle of the 16th century. There was opposition to introducing the Spanish Inquisition into Naples, but the papal Inquisition took over and managed to destroy most of the Marrano community by the middle of the 17th century. The situation of the Marranos was no less precarious in *Antwerp, where they began to arrive early in the 16th century, frequently to begin a trek across Europe to the Ottoman Empire. In 1526 New Christians' stay in the city was restricted to a 30-day period and though settlement was fully authorized 11 years later, Judaizing was strictly prohibited. With the decline of Antwerp, the center of Marrano life in the Low Countries shifted to Amsterdam.

In their colonies the Portuguese set up an Inquisition at *Goa and the Spaniards established one in the *Philippines. Episcopal Inquisitions were always present in Latin America: *Brazil never had a formal tribunal, but tribunals were established in the Spanish colonies at Lima (*Peru, 1570), Mexico City (1571), and Cartagena (1610). Latin America in particular attracted considerable numbers of New Christians. The advantage of these territories was that they offered the New Christians a familiar culture and the possibility of direct even if infrequent contact with the mother countries. For New Christians wishing to live fully as Catholics, the distances from the Peninsula and the sparseness of the population of most of the territories aided in the obliteration of the record of their Jewish origins. On the other hand, these factors also facilitated the Marranos' practice of Judaism.

Activities of the Marranos

Religious considerations were important in determining the direction of the flight of many of the Marranos, but they were not the only ones. Of great and sometimes decisive importance were the economic and social opportunities available in the various lands open to them at the time of their escape. These opportunities often made it more desirable for Marranos to continue living as secret Jews in Catholic lands (even those under Spanish and Portuguese domination) than to seek a refuge where they could practice Judaism openly. Conversely, in each of the territories where the Marranos – or for that matter all New Christians – appeared, they were allowed to enter and remain because they served definite economic, social, and political ends. In almost every one of their new homes they quickly rose to prominence in international and domestic trade, and banking and finance. They helped to establish great national banks and were prominent on the stock exchanges. They played an important role in large trading companies, such as the Dutch East Indies and West Indies Companies, and even in the rival company established at Portugal to help oust the Dutch from Brazil. As well as insurance companies, they established manufacturing plants for soap, drugs, and other items, and made signal contributions in minting, handicrafts, armaments, and shipbuilding. In the area of international trade they assumed virtual dominance and controlled, frequently to the point of monopoly, the traffic in such commodities as coral, sugar, tobacco, and precious stones. The Marranos' common background and culture, their presence in the leading commercial centers, and often their ties of kinship, enabled them to establish an efficient and closely knit international trading organization. Great banking and trading families, like that founded by Francisco Mendes at Lisbon, had branches throughout Europe. The Marranos' international connections served to stimulate communications between nations and their separate competitive development. In this way the activities of the New Christians fostered the stability of their countries of settlement and facilitated their transition from a medieval to a modern economy. The Marranos also attained prominence in the professional life of the lands of their dispersion. From their midst came great diplomats like João Miguez, the duke of Naxos (Joseph *Nasi), and his mother-in-law, Gracia Mendes Nasi (Beatriz de Luna), who also distinguished herself as a great philanthropist and patron of the Jewish arts, as well as the equally colorful Diego Texeira de Sampaio (Abraham Senior *Texeira). The Marranos produced scientists like Immanuel Bocarro Frances, distinguished physicians like Amatus *Lusitanus (Juan Rodrigo), Elijah Montalto (Felipo Rodrigues), and Antonio Ribeiro Sanchez, and a host of other distinguished names in secular literature, theater, and music.

Reciprocally, many of the states and nations in their Diaspora gave the Marranos an opportunity to develop their own institutions and culture. The printing press became a foremost instrument in the development of this culture. Ferrara's press, which published the famous translation of the Bible into Spanish and Samuel Usque's *Consolaçam as tribulaçoens de Israel* in Portuguese in addition to liturgical and other works, was the center of Marrano culture in the middle of the 16th century. By the end of the 16th century, Venice had the leading press and in the next century it was situated in Amsterdam. Other cities, too, like Leghorn, Hamburg, and London, had important presses, and printing in numerous smaller places helped to spread further Jewish culture. Especially noteworthy is the extensive literature published by these presses. Including prayerbooks and sermons, books of precepts and customs, translations into Spanish and Portuguese of classics in Jewish philosophy and thought, apologetical works and polemics, and also novels, poetry, and plays, it was particularly directed toward the Marranos who had left the Iberian peninsula and sought to find themselves in Judaism, although still assailed by doubts.

Marrano writers of note are far too numerous to mention them all. Among the more important ones were such men as the apologists Immanuel *Aboab, Saul Levi *Morteira, Lorenzo *Escudero (Abraham Ger or Abraham Israel Peregrino), Isaac *Cardozo, Isaac Orobio de *Castro, and David *Nieto; poets like David Abenatar *Melo, Daniel Lopez *Laguna, Solomon Usque, João (Moses) Pinto *Delgado, and Daniel Levi (Miguel) de *Barrios; playwrights like Antonio Enriquez *Gomez and Antonio Jose da *Silva; and versatile writers like the prolific Joseph Penso de la *Vega, writer of plays, short stories, and one of the earliest and most comprehensive treatises on the stock exchange. Many Marranos also attained fame outside the Jewish fold. The aristocracy of many societies in Europe and the Americas was enriched by these people and their descendants. Frequently, like Benjamin *Disraeli, they attained the highest diplomatic, military, and administrative positions. Like their Jewish counterparts, they also made a name for themselves in the business and cultural world.

An authentic Marrano community was discovered by Samuel *Schwartz in Portugal in 1917; and from time to time there emerge individuals or even groups whose faith is not Jewish who have retained some of the practices and customs of the Marranos, at times even without awareness of their Jewish ancestry.

BIBLIOGRAPHY: Roth, Marranos, 195–375; Roth, Italy; M.A. Cohen (translator), in: S. Usque, *Consolation for the Tribulations of Israel* (1965), 3ff.; idem, in: *The Jewish Experience in Latin America* (1971); idem, in: AJHSQ, 55 (1966), 277–318, 451–520; H. Kellenbenz, *Sephardim an der unteren Elbe* (1958); H.C. Lea, *The Inquisition in the Spanish Dependencies* (1908), esp. bibl.; H.J. Zimmels, *Die Marranen in der rabbinischen Literatur* (1932); Rosanes, Togarmah, 4–6 (1934–45 = *Korot ha-Yehudim be-Arẓot ha-Kedem*); S. Ullmann, *Histoire des Juifs en Belgique*, 2 vols. (1932–34); J.S. da Silva Rosa, *Geschiedenis der portugeesche Joden te Amsterdam* (1925); S. Assaf, in: *Zion*, 5 (1932); I.S. Revah, in: REJ, 118 (1959/60), 30–77; see also works by J.T. Medina in bibliography to *Inquisition.

[Martin A. Cohen]

MARRE, SIR ALAN (1914–1990), British civil servant. Alan Marre, the son of Joseph Moshinsky, a tobacconist in London's East End, won a scholarship to Cambridge and entered the British civil service in 1936. Marre rose in the administrative civil service to become second permanent under-secretary in the Home Office Department when, in 1971, he was appointed Britain's second ombudsman (officially, the parliamentary commissioner for administration), holding the post until 1976. As ombudsman, Marre investigated complaints of maladministration by government departments, an unusually sensitive post. In addition, in 1973–76 he was also the first health service commissioner, performing a similar role for the British health service. Marre also headed a number of other well-known investigations, especially the government inquiry into the welfare of children affected by thalidomide who had not benefited from previous financial settlements. He was knighted in 1970.

BIBLIOGRAPHY: ODNB online.

[William D. Rubinstein (2nd ed.)]

MARRIAGE. This article is arranged according to the following outline:

THE CONCEPT

In Jewish teaching, marriage is the ideal human state and is considered a basic social institution established by God at the time of creation.

In the Bible

The purposes of marriage in the Bible are companionship and procreation: "It is not good that the man should be alone; I will make him a help-mate for him … Therefore shall a man leave his father and his mother, and shall cleave unto his wife, and they shall be one flesh" (Gen. 2:18, 24); and "Be fruitful, and multiply, and replenish the earth …" (Gen. 1:28). The biblical conception of marriage is essentially monogamous (Gen. 2:24), and although in biblical times polygamy was common among the upper classes (Judg. 8:30; II Sam. 5:13; I Kings 11:1–8), the many references to marriage in the *Wisdom literature seem to take it for granted that a man had only one wife (Ps. 128; Prov. 12:4; 18:22; 19:14; 31:10–31; Ecclus. 25:1; 26). The prophets using marriage as a metaphor for God's attachment to Israel (Isa. 61:10; 62:5; Ezek. 16; Hos. 2:21–22; also Song of Songs, if interpreted metaphorically) clearly have monogamous marriage in mind, since God did not enter into such a special relationship with any other people.

Marriages were usually arranged by parents (Gen. 21:21; 24; 28:2), but the bride's consent was asked on occasion (Gen. 24:5, 58), and romantic unions were not uncommon (Gen. 29:20; Judg. 14; I Sam. 18:20; II Sam. 11:2–4; I Kings 2:17; II Chron. 11:21). It was usual to marry within the clan (Gen. 24:4; 28:2; 29:19), and in a leviratic situation (*levirate marriage) this was obligatory (Gen. 38:9; Deut. 25:5; Ruth 3:12–13). Certain marriages, involving close relatives (Lev. 18; 20; Deut.

23:1–8; 27:20–23), priests, widows, and divorced women (Lev. 21:7; Deut. 24:4), are forbidden. While marriages outside the clan occurred, they were strongly opposed both as a measure against idolatry (Ex. 34:15–16; Deut. 7:3–4; 28:4), and to preserve Jewish distinctiveness (Ezra 9:12; 10:17; Neh. 10:31; 13:23–28). Fruitfulness in marriage is a great blessing and childlessness a tragedy and disgrace (Gen. 8:17; 9:1, 7; 13:16; 17–18; 22:17; 30:1–23; Ps. 127:3–5; 128). Marriage is the means to true companionship: "Whoso findeth a wife findeth a great good" (Prov. 18:22; cf. 12:4; 14:1; 19:14; 31:10–31); "live joyfully with thy wife whom thou lovest" (Eccles. 9:9). But where marital harmony no longer prevails (particularly in the case of the wife's *adultery), the marriage can be dissolved by *divorce (Deut. 24:1–4), though Malachi (2:14–16) warns that God deplores the resort to divorce.

In Sectarian Teaching

The Essenes in general rejected worldly pleasures, including marriage, and practiced continence (Jos., Wars, 2:120). The Covenanters of Qumran did not appear to have been strictly celibate as once was thought. It is clear that some members married and had children (*Zadokite Document*, 20:7–8; 13:20; *Damascus Document*, 4:7). The *Order of the Community* ruled that a young man should not have intercourse before 20 years of age (1:4–11). Archaeologists have found the remains of a few women and children at Qumran but it is not clear to what extent this indicates marriage. The New Testament has a negative attitude to the sexual impulse and regards celibacy as a higher ideal than marriage (Matt. 19:10; I Cor. 7). Marriage is a concession to human weakness (I Cor. 7), but once entered into, it is a sacrament dissolved only by death (Matt. 19:16; Mark 10:9); though some hold that Jesus allowed divorce in cases of adultery (Matt. 5:31–32; 19:9; Mark 10:12; Luke 16:18).

In Rabbinic Literature

In contrast, rabbinic teaching sees celibacy as unnatural. It is not he who marries who sins; the sinner is the unmarried man who "spends all his days in sinful thoughts" (Kid. 29b). Marriage is not only for companionship and procreation; it also fulfills one as a person: "He who has no wife is not a proper man" (Yev. 63a); he lives "without joy, blessing, goodness … Torah, protection … and peace" (Yev. 62b); he may not officiate as high priest on the Day of Atonement (Yoma 1:1), and probably not as *sheli'aḥ ẓibbur* on the High Holy Days (Isserles to Sh. Ar., OH 581:1, based on Yoma 1:1 and Yev. 37b). Sexual desire is not evil or shameful. When regulated and controlled in marriage, it serves beneficial ends: "Were it not for the *yeẓer ha-ra* ("evil inclination" here sexual urge), no man would build a house, marry a wife, or beget children" (Gen. R. 9:7). He who, by denying his legitimate instincts, fails to produce children "is as if he shed blood, diminished the Image of God, and made the *Shekhinah* depart from Israel" (Sh. Ar., EH 1:1, based on Yev. 63b–64a), and he will have to account for his actions in the world to come (Shab. 31a). Marriage is so important that a man may sell a Torah scroll in order to marry (Meg. 27a) and a woman will tolerate an unhappy marriage rather than remain alone (Yev. 113a; Kid 7a). One should never approach marriage lightly. To make a successful match is as hard as the parting of the Red Sea (Sot. 2a, et al.), and it requires the infinite wisdom of God himself (Gen. R. 68:3). Hence, although in one view a person's marriage is predestined (Sot. 2a), the individual must choose wisely: "Hasten to buy land; deliberate before taking a wife" (Yev. 63a). Marriage should not be for money (Kid. 70a), but a man should seek a wife who is mild-tempered, tactful, modest, and industrious (Sot. 3b), and who meets other criteria: respectability of family (Ta'an. 4:8; BB 109b), similarity of social background (Kid. 49a) and of age (Yev. 44a; Sanh. 76a–b), beauty (Ber. 57b; Yoma 74b), and a scholarly father (Pes. 49b). A man should not betroth a woman until he has seen her (Kid. 41a). Early marriage is preferred: "18 for marriage" (Avot 5:21). If one is not married by 20, God curses him (Kid. 29b–30a). Only a person intensively occupied in Torah study, e.g., *Ben Azzai, may postpone marriage (Yev. 63b; cf. Ket. 63a; Sot. 4b); though in Babylon it was suggested that one should first marry and then study (Kid. 29b). A practical order of procedure, derived from Deuteronomy (20:5–7), states; "First build a house, then plant a vineyard, and after that marry" (Sot. 44a). As far as a girl is concerned, if her father does not find her a husband while she is young (from the age of 12), she may become unchaste and he will have transgressed the commandment in Leviticus 19:29: "Profane not thy daughter to make her a harlot" (Sanh. 76a).

Polygamy, while theoretically still possible, was discouraged, and was almost unknown among talmudic rabbis. Marriage was not a sacrament in the Christian sense, since its dissolution through divorce, though regrettable, was possible. It is **kiddushin*, a sacred relationship (analogous to **hekdesh*), whereby the wife is consecrated to her husband and forbidden to all others during the duration of the marriage (Kid. 2a–b). At the same time, it is not a mere legal contract devoid of spiritual content. Thus, while the husband acquires rights over his wife's *ishut* ("wifehood"), though not over her person, and he undertakes duties toward her, e.g., supplying her with food and clothing, and adhering to the conjugal rights (Ex. 21:10), both parties must seek to raise their marriage to the highest level by means of mutual consideration and respect. The husband must deny himself in order to provide for his wife and children (Ḥul. 84b). He must not cause his wife to weep (BM 59a). If he loves her as himself and honors her more than himself, he will merit the blessing in Job (5:24) "And thou shalt know that thy tent is in peace" (Yev. 62b). If husband and wife are worthy, God will dwell with them; otherwise, there will be a consuming fire between them (Sot. 17a; PdRE 12). The rabbis, like the prophets, use marriage to symbolize other perfect relationships: e.g., God and Israel, Israel and the Torah, and Israel and the Sabbath.

In Medieval and Modern Times

The positive attitude of the rabbis to marriage was maintained in post-talmudic literature and Jewish practice. Asceticism and celibacy continued to be rare. Polygamy was finally prohibited among Ashkenazi Jews by a ban attributed to R. *Gershom b. Judah (see *Bigamy; *Monogamy). Early marriage became general practice. Divorce, though relatively easy to obtain, was not common, partly due to the social pressures of the closed Jewish society since the family was firmly established as the basis of Jewish life (see I. Abrahams, *Jewish Life in the Middle Ages* (1932^2), 99ff.). With the cultural changes which followed the emancipation, the Jewish marriage rate tended to be lower than the non-Jewish one, divorce and mixed marriage increased, early marriage was uncommon, and the urban Jewish birth rate fell (see A. Ruppin, *The Jews in the Modern World* (1934), 277f., 316ff.; J. Freid (ed.), *Jews and Divorce* (1968)). These trends intensified after World War II as environmental attitudes were increasingly being reflected among Western Jewry. Marital stability has been relatively less and traditional moral codes have been questioned. To counteract these tendencies, Jewish communities are promoting marriage education and guidance, largely through rabbis and social welfare agencies.

[Raymond Apple]

MARRIAGE CEREMONY

In the Bible

There is hardly any data about the marriage ceremony in the Bible. The act of marriage is called simply "taking" ("when a man taketh a wife," Deut. 24:1; "and there went a man of the house of Levi, and he took a daughter of Levi," Ex. 2:1). However, from the story of Jacob and Leah it is obvious that some sort of celebration took place: "And Laban gathered all the people of the place and made a feast" (Gen. 29:22) and later, when Jacob complained that he had been cheated and demanded Rachel, the daughter for whom he had worked, he was told: "Wait until the bridal week of this one is over and we will give you that one too" (Gen. 29:27). No details are recorded as to the nature of the feast or the bridal week. The same is true in the case of Samson (Judg. 14:12) except that there it is said that the groom posed a riddle to his companions and gave them the seven days of the feast to solve it. It appears that processions for both the bride and groom were a central part of the celebrations and were accompanied by music (Ps. 78:63; I Macc. 9:39) and there is ample reference to special marriage attire and adornment. From Deuteronomy 22:15 it seems that the exhibition of evidence of the bride's virginity (the blood-stained sheet) was part of the ceremony. It is reasonable to presume that even in the earliest times the act of marriage must have been accompanied by some ceremony; the biblical authors, however, give no direct description of it and usually refer to it only in passing or as a figure in their imagery.

In the Talmud

In the talmudic period – and presumably for a considerable time before then – the marriage ceremony was in two parts. The first, called *kiddushin* or *erusin* (betrothal; but see below, Legal Aspects, for the difference between this concept and what is commonly called betrothal), was effected by the bridegroom handing over in the presence of two witnesses any object of value (more than a *perutah*) to the bride and reciting the marriage formula, "Behold, you are consecrated unto me with this ring according to the law of Moses and Israel." On this occasion two benedictions were recited, one over wine and the other for the actual act. The second reads: "Blessed art Thou, O Lord our God, King of the universe, who has hallowed us by Thy commandments, and hast given us command concerning forbidden marriages; who hast disallowed unto us those that are betrothed (to us – variant in some rites), but hast sanctioned unto us such as are wedded to us by the rite of the nuptial canopy and the sacred covenant of wedlock. Blessed art Thou, O Lord, who hallowest Thy people Israel by the rite of the nuptial canopy and the sacred covenant of wedlock" (Hertz, Prayer, 1011). This benediction is already recorded in the Talmud (Ket. 7b), and since cohabitation of the bride and groom was forbidden until the second ceremony, the *nissu'in* (see below, and Legal Aspects), which in the case of a virgin usually took place a year later, it appears that the benediction was in fact a warning to the betrothed couple not to cohabit until that ceremony.

The second part of the ceremony took place at a later date and was called *nissu'in* (marriage proper). It was also called *ḥuppah* (see below) after either the groom's house to which the bride was led or the canopy, symbolic of that house, under which the ceremony took place. Originally *nissu'in* was effected by the bride entering the groom's house and cohabiting with him. On the occasion of the *nissu'in* a series of benedictions was recited (see below). After this stage the couple were completely married and liable to all the responsibilities and privileges of that state (see also below, Legal Aspects).

There is ample evidence in the Talmud that the wedding ceremony was accompanied by great rejoicing and some times even hilarity. The question of how one should dance before the bride was discussed and even occasioned a difference of opinion between the schools of Hillel and Shammai (Ket. 16b–17a). Although Rashi interprets the phrase "*keiẓad merakdim*" used there as meaning "what does one say" in order to fit the continuation of the text, the phrase must be understood in its literal sense "how does one dance." Judah b. Ilai is recorded as having danced before the bride with a myrtle branch and Samuel b. Rav Isaac was rebuked by his colleagues for having performed what seems to have been a juggling dance. The Talmud, however, justified his behavior entirely. Rav Aḥa went so far as to dance with the bride on his shoulders, something which astonished the other rabbis (Ket. 17a). Indeed the custom of shattering a glass at the marriage ceremony (see below) stems, according to the medieval commentators, from Mar berei de-Ravina and Rav Ashi who deliberately smashed expensive glassware at their sons' weddings in order to reduce the unseemly hilarity of the rabbis who were present (Ber. 31a). Until the destruction of the Temple both the bride and groom wore distinctive headdresses, sometimes of gold (Sot. 9:14, 49a; Git. 7a; for details see *Crowns, Decorative Headdresses, and Wreaths). For the marriage of a virgin (as opposed to a widow or divorcee) special rites took place. She went out in a *hinnumah* (variously interpreted as a bridal veil or a special bridal litter used in the marriage procession); dried corn was distributed to the children (Ket. 2:1); games were played before the bride; a goblet of tithe wine was passed before her; according to some, a sealed (opened for a widow or divorcee) barrel of wine was used instead (Ket. 16b). The performance of all these ceremonies was sufficient evidence that the bride had been a virgin and was thus entitled to the larger *ketubbah* (see *Virgin). The bridal procession took precedence over a funeral procession and King Agrippa was praised by the rabbis for giving right of way to a bridal procession although his, being the royal procession, had precedence. At Tur Malka the disturbances which destroyed the town were started, according to talmudic legend, when Roman legionnaires took the hen and rooster which led a marriage procession as a fertility symbol (Git. 57a). Participation at the marriage ceremony and celebrations was considered a *mitzvah* and he who entertained the bride and groom was compared to one who had sacrificed a thanksgiving offering (Ber. 6b). The groom was required to devote at least three days to the preparation of the wedding feast and even if a parent of the bride or groom died on the set day of the marriage its consummation took place and the funeral was held afterward (Ket. 3a). The wedding of a virgin originally took place on a Wednesday (Ket. 1:1). This is explained in the Babylonian Talmud by the fact that the court sat on Thursdays and thus if the groom claimed that the bride had not been a virgin he could immediately complain to the court. However, it does appear that superstition was involved and that Wednesday was considered an auspicious day (cf. TJ, Ket. 1:1). A widow was married on Thursday so that her husband should devote at least three days to her without going back to his work. However, even in talmudic times the requirement that weddings be held on specific days fell into disuse for which a variety of reasons is given. It seems that in talmudic times the exhibition of the stained bridal sheet was discouraged. Originally the *shushbinim* ("friends," i.e., groomsmen) were appointed to ensure that no trickery was employed by either side (Tosef., Ket. 1:4 and Ket. 12a). For a virgin seven festive days were celebrated which, for the bride and groom, had something of the status of a religious holiday. The marriage benedictions were recited at meals (for details see below) and neither bride nor groom was allowed to mourn.

Post-Talmudic Period

The most important development in the marriage ceremony was the joining of the two parts, *erusin* and *nissu'in*, into one ceremony performed at one time. This took place during the Middle Ages and was presumably because of the uncertain and perilous conditions in which the Jews lived. It was also exceedingly inconvenient to have an interval between the two ceremonies since on the one hand the parties were prohibited from cohabiting while on the other all the stringencies of the married status applied to them. Thus from the beginning of the 12th century it became customary to perform both ceremonies together, a practice which has been universally followed except for a few Oriental communities (see Freimann, bibl., 29 ff.). Other developments are the addition of various prayers to the ceremony, the inclusion of a sermon by the officiating rabbi and, in some present-day communities, the invocation of a blessing on the bridal couple.

The ceremony may be performed anywhere. In many communities – particularly Sephardi and Oriental – it is performed inside the synagogue although there are halakhic opinions against it. In some places it is performed in the hall where the subsequent festivities are held and among some circles (ultra-Orthodox Jews and Ḥasidim and generally among Ashkenazim in Israel) it is invariably performed in the open. This latter custom is perhaps due to the fact that ideally the ceremony takes place after nightfall and the stars above are associated with God's assurance to Abraham that He would "make your descendants as numerous as the stars of heaven" (Gen. 22:17; see Isserles to Sh. Ar., EH 61:1). In the western hemisphere Sunday is a popular day for weddings because of the convenience to the guests, while Tuesday is favored in Orthodox circles because of the repetition of the sentence "And God saw that this was good" in the biblical account of the creation on that day (Gen. 1:10, 12). However, any day of the week is valid except Sabbath; also festivals, the three weeks between the 17th of Tammuz and the Ninth of Av, and the *sefirah* period between Passover and Shavuot (there are exceptional days in the last-mentioned period, notably Lag ba-Omer: see *Omer). According to the general Sephardi custom marriages are not performed on Lag ba-Omer but are performed from the following day onward. Usually a person in mourning for a parent does not marry until the year of mourning is out although in certain circumstances it is permitted to marry earlier (Sh. Ar., YD 392). There are no specific requirements for the way in which the bride and bridegroom dress. It is customary for the bride to wear white and for her to have a headdress and a veil. The bridegroom in some Orthodox circles wears a **kitel* either as an evocation of death or since his wedding day is compared to the Day of Atonement when the *kitel* is worn. In some communities the bridegroom wears a *tallit*, as does, in some, the officiating rabbi. In many Oriental communities brides wear elaborate costumes richly embroidered and ornamented which were loaned from bride to bride; the Yemenite bridal costume is an outstanding example (see also *Dress).

The ceremony is presently performed as follows. Before being led to the *ḥuppah* (wedding canopy; see below) the bridegroom, in the presence of witnesses, undertakes, by an act of *kinyan* (see *Acquisition) the obligations of the *ketubbah*. This is done by the groom taking a piece of cloth, handkerchief, or some other object from the officiating rabbi, lifting it, and returning it. The witnesses then sign the document and in many communities (including the State of Israel) the groom also signs. The groom is then escorted to the place where the bride is waiting (many modern synagogues have a special bride's room) and lets down her veil over her face, at which time the rabbi or cantor pronounces the blessing invoked on Rebekah "O sister! May you grow into thousands of myriads" (Gen. 24:60). This ceremony is known in Yiddish as "*bedeken di kale*" (lit. "covering the bride") and is not practiced by Sephardi Jews. The groom is then led to the *ḥuppah* by his and the bride's father (or two other male relatives or friends if he or the bride has been orphaned) and stands facing Ereẓ Israel, in Israel itself facing Jerusalem, and in Jerusalem facing the Temple site. The bride is then led to the *ḥuppah* by her mother and the groom's mother, usually to the accompaniment of a blessing of welcome chanted by the rabbi or cantor, the text of which is: "He Who is supremely mighty; He Who is supremely praised; He Who is supremely great; May He bless this bridegroom and bride." It is customary among Ashkenazim for the bride to be led in seven circuits around the groom which is presumably to be associated with the magic circle to ward off evil spirits. The bride then stands at the right hand of the groom, and, where customary, the rabbi delivers the sermon; the ceremony proper then begins. The rabbi recites the blessing over a goblet of wine and the marriage blessing (see text above) after which the father of the bridegroom gives the goblet to the bridegroom and he drinks, and then the mother of the bride gives the bride the goblet, from which she drinks. In many communities the officiant gives the goblet to the bride and groom. The groom then places the ring (see below) on the forefinger of the bride's right hand and recites the marriage formula (see above). In some communities the glass is crushed by the groom at this stage. The *ketubbah* is then read out loud by the rabbi or some other man whom the bridal couple wish to honor. In many communities it is read in the original Aramaic and followed by a précis in the vernacular; in Israel a Hebrew précis is often substituted. The purpose of the reading of the *ketubbah* is to divide between the two parts of the ceremony. The celebrant (rabbi, cantor, or some other person) then recites the seven marriage benedictions (see below) over a goblet of wine. In many places it is customary to have different men recite the different benedictions. The father of the bride then gives the groom to drink from the goblet and the mother of the groom does likewise to the bride. In most rites the groom crushes a glass under his right foot and where customary the rabbi invokes the *priestly blessing. The couple are then escorted to a room where they remain alone for some time, usually breaking their fast together (see below, Legal Aspects, for reasons). The breaking of the glass by the groom is explained by some authorities as a token of the seriousness desirable in even the most happy moments (see above, In the Talmud); however, the act has become understood over the ages as a sign of mourning for the destruction of Jerusalem. In some communities the bridegroom threw the glass against a special wall instead of treading on it. It has been suggested that originally the glass was broken to frighten away evil spirits. In some rites the memorial prayer, *El Maleh Raḥamim*, is recited for departed parents if either member of the couple is an orphan.

THE MARRIAGE BENEDICTIONS. These benedictions, commonly known as the *Sheva Berakhot* (Heb. "seven benedictions" – when recited with the benediction over wine) are recorded in the Talmud (Ket. 7b–8a) where they are called *Birkat Ḥatanim* ("the bridegroom's benediction"). When recited under the *ḥuppah* the benediction for wine precedes the other six which are:

1) "Blessed art Thou … who hast created all things to Thy glory.

2) … Creator of man.

3) … who hast made man in Thine image, after Thy likeness, and hast prepared unto him, out of his very self, a perpetual fabric. Blessed art Thou, O Lord, Creator of man.

4) May she who was barren (Zion) be exceedingly glad and exult, when her children are gathered within her in joy. Blessed art Thou, O Lord, who makest Zion joyful through her children.

5) O make these loved companions greatly to rejoice, even as of old Thou didst gladden Thy creature in the garden of Eden. Blessed art Thou, O Lord, who makest bridegroom and bride to rejoice.

6) Blessed art Thou … who hast created joy and gladness, bridegroom and bride, mirth and exultation, pleasure and delight, love, brotherhood, peace, and fellowship. Soon O Lord, our God, may there be heard in the cities of Judah, and in the streets of Jerusalem, the voice of joy and gladness, the voice of the bridegroom and the voice of the bride, the jubilant voice of bridegrooms from their canopies, and of youths from their feasts of song. Blessed art Thou, O Lord, who makest the bridegroom to rejoice with the bride" (Hertz, Prayer, 1013).

This series of benedictions raises some problems from the point of view of their formulation since normally only the first should begin with the formula "Blessed art thou …." Rashi (to Ket. 7b–8a) gives the following explanation. The first benediction is not for the bridal couple but in honor of the assembled congregation; the second is a benediction in honor of the creation of Adam and the next three are for the couple being married, while the last is an invocation for all Israel including the couple. The series begins with the blessing over wine because of its festive nature. The blessings are recited at the marriage ceremony and at every meal during the next seven days at which there is "a new face," i.e., somebody who was not present at any previous recitation for that couple. This rule applies to all the seven days except the Sabbath, which is itself considered to be a "new face." At the meals the series is recited immediately following the Grace after Meals, which itself is introduced by a special invocation. The series then ends with the benediction over the wine and both the bride and groom and the person who led the Grace drink from the wine. A *minyan* (ten males) is required for the recitation of the marriage benedictions both at the *ḥuppah* and after the grace; if no *minyan* is present the last of the marriage benedictions may be recited as long as there are three males (Sh. Ar., EH 62 and see also: *Grace after Meals). In talmudic times special formulas were added to the grace after meals for some considerable period before the actual wedding and after it. The present-day custom is limited to the recital of the benedictions for the seven-day period immediately following the wedding, except in the case of a marriage between a widower and widow when it is recited on the first day only.

ḤUPPAH (HEB. חֻפָּה). The term originally referred to the bridal canopy or the bridal chamber (Gen. R. 4:4) and sometimes to the wedding itself (Avot 5:21). In ancient times the *ḥuppah* was the tent or room of the groom into which, at the end of the betrothal period, the bride was brought in festive procession for the marital union (cf. Ps. 19:6; Yad, Ishut 10:1). In talmudic times it was customary for the father of the bridegroom to erect the *ḥuppah* (Gen. R. 28:6; Ber. 25b; Sanh. 108a). In *Bethar (near Jerusalem) the custom was to make the staves or beams of the *ḥuppah* from a cedar and pine tree which were planted for this purpose at the birth of male and female children respectively (Git. 57a). The *ḥuppah* was sometimes made of precious scarlet and gold cloth (Sot. 49b; TJ, Sot. 9:16, 246). The Talmud tells that God made ten *ḥuppot* for Adam and Eve and that He will build such *ḥuppot* for the pious in the world to come (BB 75a). In the early Middle Ages, the *ḥuppah* was not usually used at weddings; this is obvious from the phrasing of Isserles (Sh. Ar.) who regarded it as a novelty (Isserles to Sh. Ar., YD, 391; *ibid.*, EH 55:1). In France the groom covered the bride's head with his *tallit* as a symbol of his sheltering her. This custom was based upon the words of Ruth to Boaz: "Spread … thy cloak over thy handmaid; for thou art a near kinsman" (Ruth 3:9). This ceremony was also called *ḥuppah* and was the custom among the Jews of North Africa. Since in talmudic times the *ḥuppah* was the place of marital union and therefore required privacy, medieval responsa dealt with the question whether the act of entering the *ḥuppah* was sufficient to constitute marriage or whether it was only to be regarded as a symbol which would still require the couple to retire in privacy (cf. Tos. to Suk. 25b and see below, Legal Aspects). In the late Middle Ages the *ḥuppah*, consisting of a cloth spread on four staves, was placed inside the synagogue (Isserles to Sh. Ar., YD 391:3), but later it was moved to the courtyard of the synagogue, either because it was deemed improper to have the *ḥuppah*, as a symbol of the marriage tent, erected inside the synagogue or because of the need to accommodate the wedding party (and see above). In modern Israel, for the weddings of soldiers on active duty, the *ḥuppah* often consists of a *tallit which is supported by four rifles held by friends of the bride and groom.

THE RING. Although the act of marriage can be effected in different ways (see below, Legal Aspects) it has become the universal Jewish practice to use a ring, except in a very few Oriental communities where a coin is used. The ring, which must belong to the bridegroom, should be free of any precious stones but can be of any material (usually it is of gold or some other precious metal) as long as its value is more than a *perutah*, the smallest denomination of currency in Talmud times. In the ceremony the groom gives the ring to the bride as an act of acquisition and the bride, by accepting it, becomes his wife. Generally the groom places the ring on the forefinger of the bride's right hand; there are, however, many varied customs as to which finger the ring is placed on. In some Reform and Conservative congregations in the U.S. the "double ring" ceremony is practiced in which the bride also gives a ring to the groom and recites a marriage formula. Since, according to the *halakhah*, it is the groom who is acquiring the bride, this innovation raises serious halakhic doubts which, according to some authorities, even affect the validity of the marriage.

[Raphael Posner]

VARIOUS CUSTOMS. The marriage ceremony marks a crucial period in man's life cycle and it is only natural that it became surrounded by a multitude of different customs which generally had one of two purposes: to protect the couple from malignant spirits and to invoke God's blessing of fertility on the marriage. Many of the customs were adopted by the Jews from their non-Jewish environment and thus some are of almost a universal character. Many customs, however, are merely manifestations of the goodwill and joy felt at the happy occasion. Among Ashkenazi Jews the most widely practiced customs, besides breaking the glass which has been interpreted as a defense against evil spirits (but see above) are that the women leading the bride to the *ḥuppah* carry lighted candles as do other members of the marriage party and that the bride makes seven circuits around the groom under the canopy. It is customary for the bride and groom to refrain from seeing each other for a time preceding the wedding. The actual duration of this period varies in the different communities from about one week to one day, i.e., that of the wedding itself until the ceremony. The bridegroom has precedence over all others to be called to the Torah reading on the Sabbath before the wedding (a ceremony known as *oyfrufn* in Yiddish) and in some Ashkenazi communities the bride, if she is an orphan, visits the cemetery some time before the wedding. The bride and groom usually fast on the day of the wedding itself until after the ceremony unless it takes place on a day when fasting is forbidden, such as a new moon. A peculiar custom, common in Eastern Europe as well as in Oriental communities, was for the bride and groom to attempt to tread on the other's foot at the end of the ceremony, the one who succeeded thus being assured of dominance in their life together. In many places among both Ashkenazim and Sephardim it was and is customary to throw rice, wheat, nuts, and candies at the groom on various occasions during the marriage cycle: at the wedding itself, and particularly when the groom was called to the Torah reading on the Sabbath prior to the wedding. The bride's entry into her future home was marked by many ceremonies. In Libya and Djerba the groom would drop an earthenware pitcher of water from the roof and the bride would enter the house by walking through the water and broken pottery. In Jerusalem the Sephardim used to break a specially baked cake, called *ruskah*, above the heads of the bride and groom, while in Baghdad a loaf was cut above the head of the groom.

In Afghanistan a fowl was slaughtered to mark the occasion. In Djerba the bride broke open eggs on the doorposts of the house and in Daghestan and Gruzia (Russian Georgia) the doorposts were smeared with butter and honey. In Salonika the groom would stand at the head of the stairs when the bride first entered the house and scatter sweetmeats, rice, and coins at her feet as she came in. In Georgia the groom would set a white fowl free from the roof of the house on that occasion and drop rice, wheat, and raisins on the bride's head. In Libya the groom broke the glass at the wedding ceremony when it was almost full of wine which would spill on the floor as a sign of plenty; whereas the groom in Georgia would put the wedding ring into the glass of wine after he had drunk from it, give it the bride to drink, extract the ring, and formally present it to her with the declaration. In Kurdistan the bride would hold a male infant as the assembled guests called out "May your first be a boy too." In Morocco fish was always served at the wedding meal and the subsequent festivities as a fertility symbol and in Salonika the groom would buy live fish and put them in water in a brass bowl; on the eighth day after the wedding the bride jumped three times over this bowl to the blessings of the guests "May you be as fertile as the fish." In Persia the groom would plant three sticks in the courtyard of his house and uproot them on the sixth day after the wedding and throw them behind him to ward off evil spirits. In most Oriental communities the *ḥinnah* is celebrated the night before the wedding. In this ceremony the women of both families and female friends (men are entirely excluded) gather at the home of the bride and there her hands are painted with red henna. This ceremony is to ward off the evil eye and is sometimes accompanied by a ceremonial compounding of the dye by the bride's mother and feeding the bride seven times during the evening. Among the mountain Jews of Libya nearly all weddings take place two days before Sukkot. On the second day of the festival all the grooms participate in foot races symbolic of "And he is as a bridegroom coming out of his chamber, and rejoiceth as a strong man to run his course" (Ps. 19:6). Afterward celebrations are held at their homes. In all communities the groom is honored on the Sabbath after his wedding at the synagogue, where he is given precedence to be called to the reading of the Torah. In some communities special *piyyutim* are recited on this occasion and in many the groom is seated in a place of honor with a ceremonial canopy spread above him (Kurdistan). In Libya a second Torah scroll is taken out and an additional section (Gen. 24:1–4) is read. This is also the custom in Tunisia where the section is translated into Arabic. In Tunisia the groom is invited to the bride's home on the Sabbath preceding the wedding and has to find a roast chicken which has been especially hidden. On the fifth day after the wedding a competition between bride and groom is arranged in which they each have to dissect a large cooked fish for serving. The groom is always at a disadvantage in that he is given a blunt knife. In some communities (Afghanistan and, in a modified form, Yemen) it was sometimes customary to arrange a private wedding ceremony the night before the announced day. On the morrow the announced ceremony would also be held. This was in order to outwit evil spirits or malicious persons who had cast spells on the couple. At the ceremony it was also common for a relative of the couple to hold a pair of scissors and cut paper or cloth for its duration. In Kurdistan the officiating rabbi would publicly warn the assembled guests not to cast spells. The custom of examining the bride's linen after the first night for spots of blood as a proof of her virginity was very widespread and is still practiced in some Oriental communities. The mother of the bride would preserve the sheet or underclothing to uphold the family honor if later required.

[Reuben Kashani and Raphael Posner]

LEGAL ASPECTS

In Jewish law, marriage consists of two separate acts, called *kiddushin* and *nissu'in* respectively. The *kiddushin* (also called *erusin*) is an act performed by a man and a woman which leads to a change in their personal status, i.e., from bachelorhood to a personal status which remains unchanged until the death of either party or their *divorce from one another. However, the *kiddushin* alone does not bring about all the legal consequences of this change of status, as all those will follow only from a further act between the parties, namely the *nissu'in*. The common usage of the term *erusin*, which refers merely to *shiddukhin*, i.e., engagement (see *Betrothal), is therefore not identical with its legal meaning.

Modes of Effecting *Kiddushin*

There are three ways of effecting a *kiddushin*, namely by way of *kesef* ("money"), *shetar* ("deed"), or *bi'ah* ("cohabitation").

KESEF. The bridegroom, in the presence of two competent witnesses, transfers (see *Acquisition) to his bride money or its equivalent – today normally an unadorned ring – to the value of at least one *perutah*, for the purposes of *kiddushin*. It is customary for the bridegroom – after the officiating rabbi has recited the *Birkat ha-Erusin* – to place the ring on the bride's right-hand forefinger while addressing her with the words: *Harei at mekuddeshet li be-tabba'at zo ke-dat Moshe ve-Yisrael* ("Behold, you are consecrated unto me by this ring, according to the law of Moses and of Israel"; Kid. 2a; 5b; *Rema* Sh. Ar., EH 27:1); i.e., by transferring the ring to the bride the groom signifies his intent to reserve her exclusively to himself and by accepting it she signifies her consent. Hence it is necessary that the ring belong to the bridegroom and not to the bride, since a person cannot alienate something that is not his own, nor can a person acquire something that already belongs to him (Kid. 5b; 6b; 47a; Sh. Ar., EH 27:1, 7; 31:2).

SHETAR. In the presence of two competent witnesses, the bridegroom hands over to the bride a deed in which is written, besides the names of the parties and the other particulars required for the purposes of a *kiddushin* by *shetar*, the words, "Behold you are consecrated unto me with this deed according to the law of Moses and of Israel" and the bride accepts the deed with the intention of thereby becoming consecrated to the bridegroom (Kid. 9a; Sh. Ar., EH 32:1, 4). Delivery of the deed is therefore not merely evidence that the *kiddushin* has taken place before, but is the means whereby the tie is created, and in this respect it differs from the **ketubbah* deed which the bridegroom has to give to the bride after completion of the *kiddushin* (see also *Civil Marriage).

BI'AH. If a man in the presence of two competent witnesses, addresses to a woman the words, "Behold you are consecrated to me with this cohabitation according to the law of Moses and of Israel," and in their presence he takes her into a private place for the purpose of *kiddushin*, she will, upon their cohabitation, be reserved to him (Kid. 9b; Sh. Ar., EH 33:1). Although valid this mode of *kiddushin* was regarded by the scholars as tantamount to prostitution, and they decreed that any person employing it was punishable by *flogging (Kid. 12b; Yad, Ishut 3:21; Sh. Ar., EH 26:4; 33:1). On the other hand, this mode of *kiddushin* has served as the basis for the halakhic presumption that a man does not cohabit with a woman for the sake of prostitution (Git. 81b; *Rema* EH 33:1), and for the various rules founded on that presumption see *Husband and Wife; *Divorce.

In practice, in present times, only *kiddushei kesef* is observed since the other two modes of *kiddushin* have long become obsolete. The version "Behold you are reserved ... according to the law of Moses and of Israel" (which does not appear in the TB and is only found in the Tosefta (Ket. 4:9) and in the TJ, where the version is "according to the law of Moses and of the Jews" (*Yehudai*; Ket. 4:8)), means that the bridegroom reserves the bride unto himself "according to the law of Moses" – i.e., the law of the Torah – "and of Israel" – i.e., in accordance with the rules of the halakhic scholars as applied in Israel, so that the *kiddushin* shall be valid or void in accordance with the regulations laid down by the scholars (Yev. 90b; Ket. 3a; Git. 33a; *Rashi* and Tos. ad loc.; see also *Rashbam* and Tos. to BB 48b). The version thus formulated provided the basis for the *halakhah* which empowered and authorized the scholars, in certain circumstances, to invalidate a *kiddushin* retroactively in such a manner that even if it was not defective in principle it was deemed to be void *ab initio*. The question whether this power to make regulations for the annulment of the *kiddushin* is conferred also on the rabbis of the times after the redaction of the Talmud has remained in dispute. One opinion is that a *kiddushin* which is valid according to talmudic law, even though it is celebrated contrary to a *takkanah* which expressly prohibits the celebration of a *kiddushin* in any manner except as therein provided (e.g., in the presence of a rabbi and a quorum of ten), will not be declared void *ab initio* and the woman will not be free to marry another man unless she first obtains a divorce (out of precautionary stringency; Resp. Ribash no. 399; see also Resp. Rashba, vol. 1, nos. 1185 and 1206 where no absolute decision is arrived at; Resp. Ḥatam Sofer, EH 1:108; ET, 2 (1949), 137–40; Elon (1988), 2:686–712; Elon (1994), 2:846–79; see also **Agunah*, **Takkanot*).

The *Nissu'in*

The act of *nissu'in* requires that the bride, after completion of the *kiddushin*, be brought to the bridegroom under the *ḥuppah* before two competent witnesses, for purposes of the marriage proper, i.e., the *nissu'in* "according to the law of Moses and of Israel." There are different opinions concerning the import of the term *ḥuppah*. One view is that the bride must be brought to the home of the groom for the *nissu'in* (Ran to Ket. 2a; *Beit Shemu'el* 55, no. 4), an interpretation forming the basis of the present custom of bringing the bride to a place symbolizing the domain (*reshut*) of the bridegroom, i.e., to the place where a canopy is spread across four poles and where the bridegroom is already waiting. According to another opinion *ḥuppah* embraces a private meeting (יִחוּד) between bridegroom and bride, at a place set aside for the purpose, as an indication of their marriage proper (Ket. 54b; 56a; Rosh 5:6; Yad, Ishut 10:1, 2; Isserles EH 55:1; 61:1; Sh. Ar., EH 55:2). In order to dispel doubt, custom requires that, in addition to *ḥuppah*, the couple also have the said private meeting.

Legal Consequences

As already indicated, the legal consequences of the act of *kiddushin* differ from those of the act of *nissu'in*. The *kiddushin* creates a legal-personal tie between the parties which can only be dissolved upon divorce or the death of either party, and the *arusah* ("affianced bride") is regarded as a married woman (*eshet ish*) for all purposes under the *de-oraita* law, which thus renders invalid a *kiddushin* between herself and any other man (Kid. 5; Yad, Ishut 1:3; Sh. Ar., EH 26:3). The *arus* too is prohibited, as is a married man proper, from taking an additional wife, and although in his case the prohibition stems not from the *de-oraita* law but from the *ḥerem de-Rabbenu Gershom* (see *Bigamy), the prohibition for the *arus* is as stringent as it is for a married man proper (*Rema* EH 1:10; *Oẓar ha-Posekim* EH 1, n. 65; other scholars differ, see *Taz* EH 1, n. 15). *Kiddushin* alone, however, does not serve to call into being the mutual rights and duties existing between husband and wife (see *Husband and Wife), and, in particular, cohabitation between them is prohibited (*Rashi*, Ket. 7b; Sh. Ar., EH 55:1, 6). This prohibition is also contained in the Consecration Blessing in the words, "and has prohibited us the *arus* but has permitted us those who are married to us by *ḥuppah* and *kiddushin*" (see Ket. 7b and Sh. Ar., EH 34:1). The *arus* is also not liable for the maintenance of his bride except after the lapse of 12 months from the time of the *kiddushin*, or any lesser period of time agreed upon between them, and then only if he has failed to marry her notwithstanding her demand and readiness to be married to him (Ket. 2; 57a; Sh. Ar., EH 55:4; 56:1, 3 and commentaries). The *arusah* also has no *ketubbah*, unless the bridegroom executed such a deed in her favor at the *kiddushin* stage (Ket. 54b; Sh. Ar., EH 55:6). The absolute change in their personal status, with all the rights and duties it entails, is created by the *nissu'in*.

Manner of Celebrating *Kiddushin* and *Nissu'in*

In order to avoid irregularities which might possibly bring

about complications, custom decrees that the *kiddushin* be solemnized by a rabbi who supervises that everything is done according to law. It is also the generally accepted custom that there shall be present at least a *minyan* (ten men). Custom further decrees that the bridegroom shall always recite the above-mentioned formulation in the precise words, "Behold, you are consecrated ... etc."; although post-factum the *kiddushin* will not be invalidated if any like version with a similar content is used, any change in the recognized version should be avoided at the outset (Yad, Ishut 10:6; Resp. Rosh 37:1; Sh. Ar., EH 55:3 and *Rema* EH 61). The presence of two competent witnesses at both stages of the marriage ceremony is mandatory; as they do not merely serve as eyewitnesses but their presence is an essential part of the legal act, their absence will invalidate both the *kiddushin* and the *nissu'in*. Hence if a man and a woman acknowledge that there were not two witnesses present at their marriage, their acknowledgement (*hoda'ah*) that they are married will not serve as a basis for determining that this is the case (Kid. 65a; Yad, Ishut 4:6; Sh. Ar., EH 42:2). Conversely, if two competent witnesses testify to the celebration of a marriage between a particular couple, they will be regarded as duly married notwithstanding their own denial of the fact (Warhaftig, 132, 139). For a full description see above. Theoretically, *kiddushin* being an act of legal effect, it may also be performed between the parties through an agent; i.e., the bridegroom may appoint an agent to enter, on his behalf, into a *kiddushin* with a particular woman and the woman may do likewise for the purpose of accepting *kiddushin*. However, it is a *mitzvah* for each personally to take and be taken in marriage (Yad, Ishut 3:19; Sh. Ar., EH 35; 36). Similarly, in principle, the couple may celebrate a conditional *kiddushin* in such a manner that, provided all the rules applicable to conditions are observed (Sh. Ar., EH 38:2) and the condition itself fulfilled, the *kiddushin* will be valid from the start, or from the time of fulfillment of the condition, in accordance with the stipulation of the parties, but will be invalid if the condition is not fulfilled (Sh. Ar., EH 38). However, on account of the possible complications arising therefrom, and the stringency of the laws concerning a married woman, no conditions are permitted in *kiddushin* or *nissu'in*.

Legal Capacity of the Parties

Since marriage is an act of legal effect, it can be celebrated only by parties who have legal capacity. Hence if one of the parties to a marriage is a minor, acting independently, it will be invalid. In Jewish law a male is a minor (*katan*) until the age of 13 years; from the age of 13 years and one day he is a major (called *gadol*) and only then may he contract a valid marriage (Kid. 50b; Yad, Ishut 2:10; 4:7; Sh. Ar., EH 43:1). A female is a minor (*ketannah*) until the age of 12 years; from the age of 12 years and one day until the age of 12½ years she is called a *na'arah* (Yad, Ishut 2:1). Although as a *na'arah* she is considered a major (*gedolah*; Yad, Ishut 2:6), her marriage (when she is acting independently) will only be valid if she is orphaned of her father, but if he is alive, since a *na'arah* remains under her father's tutelage (*reshut*), her marriage, when she is acting independently will be valid only after the tutelage ceases to exist, namely when she becomes a *bogeret*, i.e., when she reaches the age of 12½ years and one day (Kid. 43b; 44b; Yad, Ishut 2:2; 3:11–13; 4:8; and Gerushin, 11:6; Sh. Ar., EH 37:11; 155:20, 21; see also *Legal Capacity). As regards the validity of a marriage entered into by a minor represented by his parents, see *Child Marriage.

For the same reason, i.e., lack of legal capacity, a marriage to which an idiot (*shoteh*) is party will be invalid when it is clear that such a party is a complete idiot (Yev. 69b; 96b; Sh. Ar., EH 44:2; 67:7). However, if such person be of sound, although weak, mind his marriage will be valid (Tur and *Beit Yosef*, EH 44; the statement attributed to Isserles, in Sh. Ar., EH 44:2 is apparently a printing error; see *Beit Shemu'el*, ad loc., n. 4; *Ḥelkat Meḥokek*, ad loc. n. 2). In case of doubt as to the soundness of a person's mind, as when he has lucid intervals, his *kiddushin* will, out of apprehension, be regarded as a doubtful *kiddushin* and the parties will not be permitted to marry anyone else except after their divorce (out of precautionary restriction גט מחומרא (Sh. Ar., loc. cit.). A *deaf-mute (*ḥeresh*, Yad, Ishut 2:26) is precluded, by Pentateuchal law, from entering into a *kiddushin* since his/her legal capacity is the same as that of the minor or the idiot. However, the scholars regulated that a *kiddushin* entered into by a deaf-mute shall be valid (Yev. 112b; Yad, Ishut 4:9; Sh. Ar., EH 44:1), but they did so without creating any obligations between parties to such a marriage. Hence if one of the parties is a deaf-mute, none of the legal obligations flowing from marriage will devolve on them – neither the obligation of *ketubbah* (i.e., in places where no *ketubbah* deed is written), nor of a *ketubbah* condition, nor of maintenance (Sh. Ar., EH 67:8–10), except possibly where a deaf-mute expressly undertakes these pecuniary obligations in the *ketubbah* deed (PDR 8:65, 69–71, 74–77). The *ḥerem de-Rabbenu Gershom* does not apply to a husband who was a deaf-mute at the time of his marriage, nor does a deaf-mute's express undertaking not to take an additional wife or not to divorce his wife against her free will have any binding force, since he is incapable of undertaking obligations – at any rate as regards matters of a non-pecuniary nature (PDR loc. cit.).

[Ben-Zion (Benno) Schereschewsky]

***Kiddushin* Conducted by Deception, Fraud, or in Jest**

The tannaitic literature (Kid. 3:1; 58b) states that if a person sent an agent to betroth a wife for him, and the agent went and betrothed her for himself, the betrothal is valid, except if "he [the agent] treated him (the principal) deceptively." The talmudic commentators explain that this statement emphasizes that although the act was fraudulent, it does not invalidate the *kiddushin*, which are valid by Pentateuchal law, nor do the rabbis invalidate the *kiddushin* because of the agent's fraudulent act against the principal prior to the *kiddushin* (Tos. ad loc; Nov, Rashba Kid. 58b). Fraudulent *kiddushin* include frauds against the woman, e.g., where a man betroths a woman in jest or coercively, or by giving her a ring in the presence of two witnesses, but against her will or understanding. Although the woman's consent is absent in these cases of *kiddushin*, the rabbis require the woman to accept a *get* (bill of divorce), in view of the doubt that perhaps these *kiddushin* are valid (see *Agunah). This requirement of a *get* led to problems of *iggun* when the husband refused to give a *get* (see *Agunah). As a result, to prevent fraudulent *kiddushin*, many Jewish communities enacted regulations regarding marriage ceremonies and how they should be conducted, such as conducting the *kiddushin* in the presence of ten persons, in the presence of a rabbi, etc. Such regulations appear as early as the geonic period (S. Assaf, *Teshuvot ha-Geonim*, para. 113, p. 101), and later in Ashkenaz (the Franco-German center) and in North Africa. The regulations enacted in the geonic period annulled all *kiddushin* conducted contrary to these rules. At later periods, sanctions were imposed on the offenders, but halakhic authorities were hesitant and questioned their authority to annul such *kiddushin*. A responsum by the sages of 12th-century Ashkenaz (Resp. Raban, EH, vol. 3 no. 47:2) reflects the differences of opinion between the sages of Worms and Speyer, and those of Mainz. The former argued that since the one who fraudulently betrothed the woman acted "improperly," the act of *kiddushin* should be invalidated and annulled. In contrast, the sages of Mainz reasoned that after the completion of the Talmud, rabbis are no longer empowered to annul *kiddushin*, and thus such a step could not be taken (see *Agunah; *Takkanot). When a similar case was brought before the Rosh (Resp. Rosh 35:2), he ruled that the sages are not empowered to annul the *kiddushin*, but since the *kiddushin* were fraudulent, similar to other instances in which the *geonim* ruled that the husband may be forced to give his wife a bill of divorce, the husband may be compelled to divorce his wife, and this would not be a coerced *get* (*get me'useh*; see *Divorce). In another responsum, he rules that when *kiddushin* is performed contrary to a regulation enacted by the community stating explicitly that *kiddushin* performed in opposition to the regulation would be annulled, these fraudulent *kiddushin* may be annulled (*ibid.* 35:1). Rashba took a similar view, and stated that in places where such a regulation had not been enacted, the rabbinical court should impose fines and even corporal punishment in order to deter fraudulent *kiddushin* (Resp. Rashba, vol. 1, no. 551).

Doubtful *Kiddushin*

The legal status of certain *kiddushin* is sometimes doubtful. Tannaitic literature provides two categories of cases of factual doubt which create doubtful *kiddushin*. In the first case the doubt relates to whether the *kiddushin* was conducted properly, for example whether or not the object given for *kiddushin* was in fact worth a *perutah* (Tos. Yev. 5:3). In the second case the doubt is created by a dispute in the public perception of the act that was performed, for example, the suspicion that the object used for the betrothal, while not worth a *perutah* in that particular location, may be worth a *perutah* somewhere else. The result would be that while the woman would not be regarded as betrothed in one location, she would be regarded as betrothed in another location, and hence the *kiddushin* is considered doubtful (Kid. 12a). Doubtful *kiddushin* may also ensue from a legal doubt, when it is not known, or there was no decision, whether a certain act of *kiddushin* was valid or not; such a case is treated stringently, and the woman is doubtfully betrothed. For example in a situation where a man gave the money for *kiddushin*, but the woman (instead of the man) recited the sentence to be said after the giving of the money (see above; Kid. 5b).

In some instances in the post-talmudic literature, a majority of *posekim* rule that even when the *kiddushin* do not take effect, for instance, *kiddushin* in the presence of only one witness (Rema EH 42:2), stringency is appropriate (Yad, Ishut 4:6; *Semag*, Hilkhot Kiddushin), and we should consider such cases as doubtful *kiddushin*. Accordingly, it was ruled that due to the severity of relations with a married woman: "in these generations they imposed all the stringencies of the *posekim* in divorce and marriage" (Resp. Radbaz, vol. 4, no. 129; Resp. Maharashdam, EH 13), except for in cases where the *kiddushin* was additionally flawed, or would cause the woman to become an *agunah*, in which case stringency is not applied (Resp. Maharashdam, *ibid.*).

Determining *kiddushin* as doubtful results in stringencies in two directions. On the one hand, in order to be married to another man, the woman requires a *get* and on the other hand, if another man betroths her, he too is considered doubtfully betrothed to her. In practice, under certain circumstances, if the parties wish to marry, they are required to conduct a second *kiddushin*; and if they do not desire to continue a shared life, the husband might be compelled to give her a *get*. Incidental to divorce, the woman might be prohibited to marry a Cohen (see *Marriage, Prohibited), which has led many authorities to criticize the proclivity to stringency in determining doubtful *kiddushin* and ordering divorce as a precautionary measure (*get le-ḥumra* – גט לחומרא; Resp. Maharshal, no. 21; Resp. Radbaz, no. 382).

A national rabbinical conference held in Jerusalem in 1950 instituted the "*ḥerem de-Yerushalayim*," which, inter alia, enacted that "no Jewish man and woman may engage in *kiddushin* and *erusin* [= *kiddushin*] other than by a proper wedding ceremony, with a quorum of ten men, which is then recorded in the offices of the rabbinate in every location. This prohibition carries with it a severe *ḥerem* (= ban) by which any man who betrothed a woman, other than in a proper wedding ceremony, must divorce his betrothed with a bill of divorce in accordance with Jewish law." The *ḥerem de-Yerushalayim* is recognized by Israeli law as part of the binding Jewish law for marriage (HC 130/66, *Segev v. Rabbinical Court of Appeals*, 21 (2) PD, p. 505, 525, per President Agranat). Today, most marriages are conducted under the supervision of a rabbi authorized by the Chief Rabbinate, and therefore the question of doubtful *kiddushin* can generally arise only in one of the following instances:

1. Civil marriage. For civil marriage and its validity as doubtful *kiddushin*, see *Civil Marriage.

2. Cohabitation without marriage (*yedu'im ba-ẓibbur*). See *Concubine.

3. Private marriage. The *ḥerem de-Yerushalayim* does not state that privately conducted *kiddushin* would be declared null and void. The Israeli Supreme Court has often addressed questions concerning the status and validity of private marriages. These marriages may be performed for any of a variety of reasons; for example, when because of various prohibitions (see *Marriage, Prohibited), the parties cannot be married by the Israeli rabbinate, and the parties circumvent this by conducting a full but private marriage ceremony. Another example is when parties who are able to be married by the rabbinate prefer not to have a rabbinically approved ceremony. These cases are a focus of friction between the rabbinical courts (that have exclusive jurisdiction in marital law) and the civil courts. The rabbinical court refuses to recognize such marriages, on the grounds of not "aiding transgressors." In contrast, the civil court system recognizes marriages of parties forbidden by Jewish law to be valid. In this context the civil court distinguishes between the "religious" component, which prohibits the conducting of the marriage, and the legal component, which despite the religious prohibition, gives legal validity to such unions. This distinction is derived from the rabbinical court's perception that such marriages are, minimally, "doubtful marriages," which, as a precautionary measure, require divorce. However, the recognition afforded by the civil court only affects the legal civil status of the couple (such as the registration of the marriage), and not the enforcement of the parties' mutual obligations from such a marriage. In the event of a private marriage, when the parties were eligible for a rabbinical marriage, but chose otherwise, the Supreme Court refused to validate such marriages and declare that the parties could register as married. The Supreme Court was guided by its perception of public policy stating that: "This judicial policy of invalidating private marriages is founded on the principle of maintaining the public good, proper administration, and basic social order, which are especially significant in determining the validity of the status of the marriage and the consequences ensuing from this status, for both the relationship between the parties and their relationship with the public as a whole" (CA 32/81, *Zonen v. Shtal*, 37(2) PD, p. 766; Justice Menachem Elon).

[Menachem Elon (2nd ed.)]

In the State of Israel

Matters of marriage in the State of Israel are governed by Jewish law, in accordance with the provisions of sections 1 and 2 of the Rabbinical Courts Jurisdiction (Marriage and Divorce) Law, 5713/1953. As regards the customs relating to the celebration of *kiddushin* and *nissu'in*, *takkanot* were issued at an Israeli rabbinical conference in 1950, imposing a strict ban on anyone solemnizing *kiddushin* and *nissu'in* contrary to the accepted customs.

By virtue of the Marriage Age Law 1950 (as amended in 1960) a woman may not be married before the age of 17 years. This law further renders it a punishable offense for any person to marry a woman under the age of 17 years (it is no offense for the bride), or to solemnize or assist in any capacity in the celebration of the marriage of such a woman, or for a father or guardian to give her away in marriage, unless prior permission of the competent district court has been obtained – the latter being empowered to give this on the grounds specified in the law (see *Child Marriage). No minimal age is specified for the bridegroom. This offense, although punishable, has no effect on the personal status of the parties; i.e., if the marriage is valid according to Jewish law, the fact that the offense has been committed will in no way affect the validity of the marriage, whether the question arises in relation to a matter of Jewish or of civil law, in the rabbinical or in the civil courts. However, in the event of a marriage with a woman below the said minimum age, the law provides that application may be made to the rabbinical court – by the persons and in the circumstances specified in the law – in order to oblige the husband to grant his wife a divorce. It must be emphasized that this provision does not create grounds for action for divorce under Jewish law, so that in fact it is a dead letter, for in matters of divorce the rabbinical courts apply Jewish law only.

[Ben-Zion (Benno) Schereschewsky]

The Marriage Age Law was amended in 1988, and the Law currently has the same age requirement for both males and females.

CONTEMPORARY INNOVATIONS

Several opposing tendencies have brought significant changes to Jewish wedding practices during the last quarter of the 20th century, particularly in North America. One trend is characterized by the recovery and reinstatement of certain traditional nuptial rituals, often as part of a rejection of a growing conformity of Jewish marriage customs to Protestant models during the 1950s–70s. Thus, in the early 21st century, it is not uncommon for both bride and groom to immerse in the *mikveh* during the week prior to the wedding. The *badeken* ceremony is frequently performed following a *tisch* for the groom, and there may be a *tena'im* ceremony where the mothers of the bride and groom break a plate.

At the ceremony itself Wagner's *Lohengrin* Wedding March has generally been replaced by Jewish music and brides, and often grooms, now walk to the *ḥuppah* with both parents, rather than the bride on the arm of her father. The use of some form of *ketubbah* has been reinstated in the Reform movement, alongside several of the traditional *sheva berakhot* (wedding benedictions). Brides and grooms from all movements often prepare wedding booklets explaining aspects of the traditional Jewish wedding ceremony so that their Jewish and non-Jewish guests will be able to follow the proceedings.

On the other hand, there has also been an effort to make the traditionally unilateral wedding ceremony as egalitarian as possible. With the exception of the Ashkenazi custom of circling the groom seven or three times, sipping wine twice, and putting out a hand for the ring to be slipped on her finger, the Jewish bride is passive during a traditional Jewish wedding ritual and in the preparatory ceremonies that precede it, as when the *ketubbah* is signed and witnessed. The most common egalitarian innovations include replacing the traditional language of the *ketubbah* with reciprocal wording concerning the obligations of bride and groom to each other (this innovative *ketubbah* may be in Aramaic, Hebrew, or English, or a combination of two or more of these languages); both bride and groom participate in *kinyan* and sign the *ketubbah* prior to the *ḥuppah*; the groom circles the bride after the bride circles the groom; a double ring ceremony with both bride and groom speaking and placing a ring on the other's finger (usually the groom says the traditional formula and the bride says some variation of it or recites a verse from the Song of Songs); and the inclusion of women among those eligible to officiate, read the *ketubbah*, and say one of the *sheva berakhot*.

Since 1990, more radical departures from *halakhah* have also become frequent. Within the Reform, Reconstructionist, and Humanist movements, these may include the use of specially written *ketubbot* at interfaith weddings and at gay and lesbian commitment ceremonies and marriages, where the couple often stands under a *ḥuppah* and breaks a glass. Some of the interfaith ceremonies are syncretistic, which has elicited protests from the liberal and progressive denominations, as well as the more traditional movements.

[Rela M. Geffen (2nd ed.)]

BIBLIOGRAPHY: GENERAL: de Vaux, Anc. Isr, 24–38; P. Elman (ed.), *Jewish Marriage* (1967); L.M. Epstein, *Sex Laws and Customs in Judaism* (1948); D.R. Mace, *Hebrew Marriage; A Sociological Study* (1953); R. Patai, *Sex and Family in the Bible and the Middle East* (1959); P. and H. Goodman, *The Jewish Marriage Anthology* (1965; incl. bibl.). THE CEREMONY: I. Abrahams, *Jewish Life in the Middle Ages* (1932), 179–228; I. Jakobovits, *Order of the Jewish Marriage Service* (1959); J.L. Lauterbach, in: HUCA, 2 (1925), 351–80; E. Brauer, *Yehudei Kurdistan; Meḥkar Antologi* (1948); *Yahadut Luv* (1960), 393–5; J. Yehoshu'a, *Yaldut bi-Yrushalayim ha-Yeshanah; Ha-Bayit ve-ha-Reḥov bi-Yrushalayim ha-Yeshanah* (1966), 59–78; M. Many, *Ḥevron ve-Gibboreiha* (1963), 88–100; M. Attias, in: *Saloniki, Ir va-Em be-Yisrael* (1967), 185–7; J. Saphir, *Even Sappir*, 1 (1866), 81af.; 2 (1874), 74a–86a; D.S. Sassoon, *Massa Bavel* (1955), 200–3; H. Mizrahi, *Yehudei Paras* (1959); Z. Kasdai, *Mi-Malkhut Ararat* (1912), 59–62; Ben-Jacob (ed.), *Yalkut Minhagim mi-Minhagei Shivtei Yisrael* (1967); Y. Ratzaby, *Bo'i Teiman* (1967), 328–30; M. Zadoc, *Yehudei Teiman* (1967), 208–12; J. Kafih, *Halikhot Teiman* (1961), 110–56. LEGAL ASPECTS: M. Mielziner, *The Jewish Law of Marriage and Divorce …* (1901); J. Neubauer, *Beitraege zur Geschichte des biblisch-talmudischen Eheschliessungsrechts* (1920); Gulak, Yesodei, 3 (1922), 19–22; Gulak, Oẓar, 17–58; idem, in: *Tarbiz*, 5 (1933/34), 384f.; L.M. Epstein, *Marriage Laws in the Bible and the Talmud* (1942); E. Neufeld, *Ancient Hebrew Marriage Laws …* (1944); A. Freimann, *Seder Kiddushin ve-Nissu'in Aḥarei Ḥatimat ha-Talmud ve-ad Yameinu* (1945); ET, 1 (1951^3), 257–61; 2 (1949), 137–40, 182–6; 4 (1952), 420–7, 631–51; 5 (1953), 138–52, 168–79; 6 (1954), 710–2; 7 (1956), 43–46; 12 (1967), 154–8; M. Vogelmann, in: *Sinai*, 43 (1958), 49–55; N. Sachs, in: *No'am*, 1 (1958), 52–68; O. Joseph, in: *Sinai*, 48 (1960/61), 186–93; H. Albeck, *ibid.*, 145–51; M. Silberg, *Ha-Ma'amad ha-Ishi be-Yisrael* (1965^4); K. Kahana, *The Theory of Marriage in Jewish Law* (1966); E. Berkowitz, *Tenai ba-Nissu'in u-va-Get* (1966); Z.W. Falk, *Jewish Matrimonial Law in the Middle Ages* (1966); B. Schereschewsky, *Dinei Mishpaḥah* (1967^2), 32–51; Elon, Mafte'aḥ, 246–51. **ADD. BIBLIOGRAPHY:** M. Elon, *Ha-Mishpat ha-Ivri* (1988), 1:526, 539f., 578, 592, 648, 661, 687f., 708; 3:1474, 1488–99; idem, *Jewish Law* (1994), 2:656f., 641, 712, 732, 802, 817, 846f., 874; 4:1740, 1754, 1770–84; idem, *Ma'amad ha-Ishah* (2005), 194–254, 297–383; M. Elon and B. Lifshitz, *Mafte'aḥ ha-She'elot ve-ha-Teshuvot shel Ḥakhmei Sefarad u-Ẓefon Afrikah* (legal digest), 2 (1986), 385–97; B. Lifshitz and E. Shochetman, *Mafte'aḥ ha-She'elot ve-ha-Teshuvot shel Ḥakhmei Ashkenaz, Ẓarefat ve-Italyah* (legal digest) (1997), 286–91; B. Schereschewsky, *Dinei Mishpaḥah* (4th ed., 1993), 25–44; J. Neubauer, *Toledot Dinei ha-Nisu'in ba-Mikra u-ba-Talmud* (1994); P. Shifman, *Safek Kiddushin be-Mishpat ha-Yisraeli* (1975); Z. Falk, *Dinei Nisu'in* (1983); R. Biale, *Women and Jewish Law* (1995); D. Gordis, "Marriage – Judaism's Other Covenantal Relationship," in: R.M. Geffen (ed.), *Celebration and Renewal: Rites of Passage in Judaism* (1993); I.G. Marcus, *The Jewish Life Cycle* (2004).

MARRIAGE, PROHIBITED. A marriage is prohibited whenever there is a legal impediment to a *kiddushin* (see *Marriage) between the particular parties. In some cases the prohibition has the effect of rendering the marriage, if it is celebrated nevertheless, null and void *ab initio*; in other cases it does not invalidate the marriage, but provides a ground for having it terminated by divorce.

Prohibited and Void

This category includes (1) marriages which are גִּלּוּי עֲרָיוֹת (*gillui arayot*) according to pentateuchal law, i.e., punishable by **karet* or death, namely: (a) marriages between parties related to one another within the prohibited degrees of kinship: i.e., the marriage between a man and his mother, daughter, sister, and certain other relatives (Lev. 18:6ff.; Kid. 67b and codes); the marriage between a man and the sister of his wife is also void during the latter's lifetime (i.e., even after divorce), as is marriage with his brother's widow (except in the case of the levirate widow) or divorced wife: such marriages are punishable by *karet* (Yad, Issurei Bi'ah, 2:1, 9; Sh. Ar., EH 15:22, 26; 44:6; see also *Levirate Marriage); and (b) marriage between a man and a married woman, such *adultery being punishable by death (see also *Bigamy); (2) A marriage with a non-Jewish partner (Sh. Ar., EH 44:8; see also Mixed *Marriage); (3) Other cases enumerated in Shulḥan Arukh, *Even ha-Ezer* 15.

Prohibited but Valid

In this category are included marriages which, although prohibited, do not constitute *gillui arayot* according to pentateuchal law and therefore are valid and not terminable unless by the death of either party or by divorce (Sh. Ar., EH 15:1; 18; 44:7). Since these marriages are nevertheless prohibited and remain tainted with the prohibition during their subsistence, their dissolution by divorce is generally compelled, whether or not either or both of the parties consented to, or had prior knowledge of, the true situation. Marriage prohibitions of this kind derive either from the pentateuchal law imposed and punishable as a plain prohibition only (Yad, Ishut 1:7) or from the rules laid down by the scribes, i.e., marriage prohibited, as "incest of a secondary [minor] degree," not by the Torah but only by rabbinical enactment (*ibid.*, 1:6; Sh. Ar., loc. cit.). The following are examples of such prohibitions:

(1) A married woman who has sexual relations with anyone but her husband becomes prohibited to the latter as well, and also to her lover even after her divorce from her husband (Sotah 27b; Sh. Ar., EH 11:1; 178:17). If she has had sexual relations of her own free will, she is prohibited to her husband forever, i.e., he must never remarry her after divorce from him even if in the meantime she has not married anyone else (Sh. Ar., EH 13). If she has been raped (see *Rape), she is prohibited to her husband only if he is a priest, but, if he is an ordinary Israelite, she is permitted to him. He need not divorce her and, if he has done so, he may remarry her provided she has not married someone else in the meantime (Sh. Ar., EH 6:10, 11). Similarly, the adulteress is also prohibited for all time from marrying her lover, i.e., even after divorce from her husband or his death (Yev. 24b and Rashi ad loc.; Sh. Ar., EH 11:1). This is because her lover has destroyed her family life, inasmuch as, owing to the adultery, he has rendered her prohibited to her husband. By the same token, and, because the wife of an ordinary Israelite does not become prohibited to her husband when someone else has sexual relations with her against her own free will, some scholars are of the opinion that, although beforehand she is prohibited to such a lover in order to penalize him, if they have nevertheless married each other, he will not be compelled to divorce her (Sh. Ar., EH 11; *Ba'er Heitev* n. 5 and *Beit Shemu'el* n. 2; but cf. *Rema*, EH 159:3, and *Ba'er Heitev* n. 6; *Oẓar ha-Posekim*, EH 11:1, n.44).

(2) A divorcee who has remarried and her second marriage has also been terminated (by divorce or death) is therefore prohibited to her former husband, in terms of an express prohibition in pentateuchal law (Deut. 24:4).

(3) A priest is prohibited by an express prohibition in the pentateuchal law from marrying a divorcee, a *zonah*, or a **ḥalalah* (see Lev. 21:7; Sh. Ar., EH 6:1). This prohibition is still in force (*Rema*, EH 3:6; PDR 5, 219, 221) despite the lack of certainty that all those known as priests are in fact the descendants of Aaron, for all of them are merely presumed to be priests (Yad, Issurei Bi'ah, 20:1). A divorced woman remains prohibited to a priest even if after her divorce she has remarried and become a widow (*Ḥokhmat Shelomo*, EH 6:1; Sh. Ar., EH 66:11, Isserles, *Ḥelkat Meḥokek*, 66, n. 41). A priest is forbidden to remarry even his own former wife (Resp. Ribash no. 348; see also *Divorce). For the purposes of the above prohibition, the term *zonah* is not to be interpreted in its ordinary sense – i.e., a woman who has sexual relations other than within matrimony (Yev. 61b). Here it refers to a woman who is not a Jewess by birth, such as a proselyte, and also to a woman who has cohabited with a man to whom she must not be married by virtue of a general prohibition (i.e., not one relating to the priesthood as such) e.g., if she has cohabited with a non-Jew or a **mamzer* (Yev. 61a and Rashi; Sh. Ar., EH 6:8).

(4) A Jewish man or woman must not marry a *mamzer* (*et*). For details see **Mamzer*.

(5) A married man is prohibited, according to the decree of Rabbenu *Gershom, to marry another woman while his marriage still subsists. If contracted, the second marriage is valid but the parties will be compelled to divorce (see *Bigamy).

(6) Marriage with a divorcee or widow is prohibited before the lapse of 90 days from the date of her acquiring her new status; in order to avoid doubt concerning the descent of her offspring; similarly, for the good of her child, it is forbidden to marry a pregnant woman or nursing mother until the child has reached the age of 24 months (Sh. Ar., EH 13:1, 11–14; for further instances of prohibited, but valid marriages see Sh. Ar., EH 15).

Legal Consequences of Prohibited Marriages

FAMILY LAW ASPECTS. So far as the parties themselves are concerned, no legal consequences at all attach to a marriage which is forbidden as עֶרְוָה (incestuous) according to pentateuchal law, and there is therefore no need for them to be divorced (Sh. Ar., EH 15:1, and Ha-Gra thereto, n. 3; Sh. Ar., EH 44:6); their children will be *mamzerim*. Only a marriage of a married woman to another man, although invalid, requires that the woman obtain a divorce not only from her husband but also from the paramour (see *Divorce; *Bigamy; **Agunah*).

In the case of prohibited but valid marriages either party is entitled to demand a divorce, whether or not either or both parties were aware of the impediment at the time of the marriage or at any time thereafter. In case of the other party's refusal, divorce may be compelled, except in the case of a marriage contracted within 90 days of dissolution of the wife's previous marriage (*Rema*, EH 13:10). The need for divorce is also relaxed with reference to marriage with a pregnant woman or nursing mother (PDR 4:60). On the status of children born of such marriages, see **Yuḥasin*.

CIVIL LAW ASPECTS. Since the law requires that a prohibited marriage be dissolved, there is no place for the imposition of reciprocal marital rights and duties which are designed to sustain the marriage. In principle this is the position whenever the husband has married his wife without knowing that she is prohibited to him (לֹא הִכִּיר בָּהּ, *lo hikkir bah*). However, if he has done so knowingly, there will be no justification for his release from a husband's marital duties, and these he must fulfill, with the exception of those likely to impede dissolution of the marriage. This distinction between the husband's knowledge or lack of it is drawn mainly in regard to the most important cases of prohibited but valid marriages, i.e., cases of plain prohibition (אִסּוּרֵי לָאו, *issurei lav*); (for the prohibitions concerning other cases of prohibited marriage, see Sh. Ar., EH 116:2ff.). Since a man who marries without knowing that his wife is prohibited to him is released from all the marital duties of a husband, the wife will not be entitled to receive her "main" or minimal **ketubbah* and therefore also not to fulfillment of the ketubbah conditions since "the *ketubbah* conditions are as the *ketubbah* itself" (Ket. 54b and Rashi ad loc. s.v. *tena'ei ketubbah*; see also *Husband and Wife). Similarly, the wife will not be entitled to *maintenance, either during the husband's lifetime or as his *widow (Yad, Ishut 24:2; Sh. Ar., EH 116:1). In the same way, the wife too will be released from all her matrimonial duties, since these are imposed on her by law only in return for her husband's actual fulfillment of his duties toward her (see **Ketubbah*; *Husband and Wife; *Dowry). The husband will, however, remain liable for her *ketubbah* "increment" (*tosefet ketubbah*), as this is not an obligation imposed on him by law but one that he has voluntarily undertaken to fulfill for as long as she is willing to remain his wife, and this the law has forbidden her to do, independently of her own will in the matter (Yad, Ishut 24:3; Taz, EH 116, n. 3).

In cases where the husband knowingly contracts a prohibited marriage, the scholars regulated that in principle he should not be released from any of the matrimonial duties imposed upon the husband by law. Hence, in these circumstances he, or his estate, will be liable to his wife or widow for her *ketubbah* (including the *tosefet*) as well as its conditions as in every regular marriage. However, since everything should be done in order to bring about the dissolution of such prohibited marriages, the scholars further ruled that the husband was exempt from maintaining his wife during his own lifetime, in order to discourage her from remaining his wife (Sh. Ar., loc. cit, and *Taz* n. 1). He will consequently not be entitled to her handiwork, since he is entitled to this only in return for actually maintaining her. Divergent opinions are expressed in the codes concerning the husband's usufruct of his wife's property. According to some of the *posekim* the husband does not have this right, since it is in return for the obligation to ransom his wife from captivity, a duty which does not hold in the case of a prohibited marriage (see *Dowry) as marital life with her is forbidden to him; therefore the husband must return the equivalent of any benefit he may have derived from this source (see, e.g., Yad, Ishut 24:4 and *Maggid Mishneh* ad loc.). Other *posekim* are of the opinion that only when the wife is taken captive must the husband make available for purposes of her ransom, the equivalent of the fruits of her property that he has enjoyed, but otherwise he will be exempt from compensating her in this regard (see, e.g., *Ḥelkat Meḥokek* n. 4 and *Beit Shemu'el* n. 2 to EH 116). Since the marital rights afforded by law to the wife in respect of her husband are conditional on the existence of corresponding legal duties of her husband toward her and, in the same way, the wife's duties to her husband do not exist independently but are in return for her enjoyment of her rights against him (Yad, Ishut 12: 1–4) – a position which depends on his knowledge or ignorance of the prohibited nature of the marriage – her knowledge or ignorance in this respect is of no legal significance.

In the State of Israel

Apart from rules of private international law, the problem of prohibited marriages is governed by Jewish law (see sects. 1, 2 of the Rabbinical Court Jurisdiction (Marriage and Divorce) Law, 5713/1953.

BIBLIOGRAPHY: ET, 1 (1951[3]), 206–9; 2 (1949), 20f., 65, 84f.; 6 (1954), 343–54; 12 (1967), 49–67; Elon, Mafte'aḥ, 5–7; B. Schereschewsky, *Dinei Mishpaḥah* (1967[2]), 51f., 56–62, 203–6. See also bibliography to *Marriage.

[Ben-Zion (Benno) Schereschewsky]

MARRUS, MICHAEL R. (1941–), Canadian historian, author. Marrus was born in Toronto, Canada. He is one of the foremost Canadian historians of modern Europe, specializing in the Jews of France and in the Holocaust. He received his B.A. at the University of Toronto in 1963, and his M.A. and Ph.D. at the University of California, Berkeley in 1964 and 1968, respectively. In 1968 he joined the Department of History at the University of Toronto and served as dean of the School of Graduate Studies from 1997 to 2004. He was the Chancellor Rose and Ray Wolfe Professor of Holocaust Studies from 2000. Marrus was also affiliated with St. Antony's College (Oxford), the University of California, Los Angeles, the Hebrew University of Jerusalem, and the University of Cape Town. He was the recipient of numerous awards, including appointment as a fellow in the Royal Society of Canada and a Guggenheim Fellowship; he was a fellow of the Holocaust Royal Historical Society. Marrus published more than 100 articles, reviews, and books. His most notable works include *The Politics of Assimilation: A Study of the French Jewish Community at the Time of the Dreyfus Affair* (1971); with Robert Paxton, *Vichy France and the Jews* (1981); *The Unwanted: European Refugees in the Twentieth Century* (1985); *The Holocaust in History* (1987); and *Mr. Sam: The Life and Times of Samuel Bronfman* (1991). He was editor of *The Nazi Holocaust: Historical Articles on the Destruction of European Jews* (15 vols., 1992) and *The Nuremberg War Crimes Trial, 1945–46: A Documentary History*, (1997); and coeditor of *Contemporary Antisemitism: Canada and the World* (2005). Among his most important contributions to the study of the Holocaust are his works dealing with the Vichy government and the Third Reich, the Nuremberg War Crimes Trial, and the role of the Vatican during the Holocaust. In 1999 Marrus was appointed to an interfaith team of historians, the Catholic-Jewish Historical Commission on the Vatican and the Holocaust, charged with examining the role played by the Vatican during the Holocaust.

[Frank Bialystok (2nd ed.)]

MARSALA, town in Sicily. Though Jews probably lived in Marsala in Roman times, the first mention of them is made in the city statutes of the Norman period restricting the rights of Jews and Muslims with regard to property claims. In 1282, after the Sicilian Vespers, King Peter II of Aragon ordered the restitution of property of the Jews of Marsala lost during the upheavals of the uprising. In 1321, following the complaints of the Jews in the area of Val di Mazara (which included Marsala), the Infante Peter ordered the officials in Marsala to prevent the bishop and church in Mazara from exercising jurisdiction over the local Jews because they belonged to the Crown according to their status as serfs of the Royal Chamber. The Jews are then mentioned in a royal decree of 1374, in which approval was given for the enlargement of the synagogue. Toward the end of the 14th century the community protested against the abuses inflicted on them by the citizens, who forced them to attend church functions, and stoned them when they returned to their own quarter. Royal decrees of 1402 and 1405 exempted the Jews from the authority of the bishop, restored the ritual bath which had been confiscated, and restricted the taxes paid by the Jews to one-tenth of those imposed on the whole town. Every year, on October 16, councillors (*proti*) were elected to administer the community affairs. On the expulsion of the Jews from Sicily in 1492, about 2,600 Jews were forced to leave the town. The synagogue was converted into a church.

BIBLIOGRAPHY: G. di Giovanni, *L'ebraismo della Sicilia* (1748), 329–36; B. and G. Lagumina, *Codice Diplomatico dei Giudei di Sicilia* (1884–1909); Milano, Italia, index; Roth, Italy, index; Lionti, in: *Archivio Storico Siciliano*, 8 (1883), 149–55; Zunz, Gesch, 484–534. **ADD. BIBLIOGRAPHY:** V. Morabito, "La comunità ebraica di Marsala e il giudaismo non rabinico e caraita," in: N. Bucaria (ed.), *Gli ebrei in Sicilia dal tardoantico al medioevo, Studi in onore di Monsignor Benedetto Rocco* (1998), 117–56; H. Bresc, *Arabes de langue, Juifs de religion. L'evolution du judaïsme sicilien dans l'environment latin, XIIe–XVe siècles* (2001); M.L. Luisa Garaffa, "Caratteri topologici dell'insediamento ebraico nella Sicilia occidentale," in: *Italia Judaica*, 5 (1995), 268–95; S. Simonsohn, *The Jews in Sicily*, vols. 1–7 (1997–2005).

[Sergio Joseph Sierra / Nadia Zeldes (2nd ed.)]

MARSCHAK, JACOB (1898–1977), U.S. economist. Born in Kiev, Marschak taught at the University of Heidelberg from 1930 to 1933. From 1933 to 1939 he lectured at All Souls College, Oxford, and was the director of its Institute of Statistics. During this period, his articles on measurement of economic variables and estimation of economic relationships provided the foundation for the field of econometrics. In 1940 he became professor of the graduate faculty of the New School for Social Research in New York City, which he left in 1942 to teach at the University of Chicago, directing at the same time the Cowles Commission for Economic Research (1943–48). In 1950 he became a consultant of the RAND Corporation and a member of an inter-society committee on the training of social scientists in mathematics. He was a professor of economics at Yale from 1955 to 1960. His major interests were microeconomics, econometrics, and business administration. In 1960 he went to teach at the University of California at Los Angeles, with a joint appointment as professor in the School of Business Administration (now Graduate School of Management) and the Department of Economics. He became professor emeritus at UCLA in 1965 and served as director of the Western Management Science Institute (1965–69).

Over the years, Marschak served as president of the Econometric Society; vice president of the American Statistical Association; fellow of the American Academy of Arts and Sciences; member of the National Academy of Sciences; and president of the American Economic Association.

In the 1920s Marschak helped a number of his fellow Russian intellectual exiles to establish a life for themselves in the United States. In the 1930s he took part in assisting scholars who were refugees from Nazi Germany. Subsequently, he helped the newer emigrant intellectuals from the Soviet Russia.

Marschak's publications include *Kapitalbildung* (with Walther Lederer, 1936), *Economic Aspects of Atomic Power* (co-editor, 1950), *Studies in Econometric Methods* (with W.C. Hood et al., 1953), *Income, Employment, and the Price Level* (1965), *Economic Theory of Teams* (with R. Radner, 1972), and *Economic Information, Decision, and Prediction* (1974).

BIBLIOGRAPHY: C.B. McGuire, *Decision and Organization: A Volume in Honor of Jacob Marschak* (1972).

[Joachim O. Ronall / Ruth Beloff (2nd ed.)]

MARSEILLES, capital of the department of Bouches du Rhône; second largest town in France. The earliest recorded presence of Jews in Marseilles can be traced to the sixth century. In 574 there was a sufficient number to provide asylum for the Jews who fled from *Clermont-Ferrand to escape the coercive measures by Bishop *Avitus to convert them. In 591 Bishop Theodore of Marseilles also attempted to compel the Jews of the town to accept baptism, but Pope *Gregory I intervened in their favor. Although scant information is available on the Jews of Marseilles during the early Middle Ages, the importance of their settlement there is confirmed by the names of sites alluding to them. At the close of the tenth century there is mention of a *valle Judaica* in an area of fields and vineyards and at the end of the 11th century, of a vineyard named *rua Judaica*. During the 12th century, the Jews formed two communities; one in the upper part of the town, which was under the jurisdiction of the bishop; the other in the lower town, which belonged to the viscount. Both communities were placed under the authority of the bishop. (It was this right which Frederick I Barbarossa ratified for Bishop Peter in 1164.) The two communities are mentioned by the traveler *Benjamin of Tudela, who also indicates that the yeshivot and the scholars were established in the upper town. As might be expected, the merchants settled in the lower part in the vicinity of the port. There they traded with Palestine, Egypt, North Africa, Spain, and Italy, dealing mainly in wood, spices, textiles, metals, pharmaceutics, various products for dyeing, and slaves. Commercial partnerships with Christians were very common. They rarely engaged in moneylending, although toward the end of the 12th century they did advance loans to the Monastery of Saint Victor and to the squire of Trets. In 1257 the statutes of Marseilles granted Jews the status of citizens. Nevertheless they were subject to some important restrictions. Jews were prohibited from working in public on Christian festivals, or from taking an oath in a lawsuit against Christians, and no more than four Jews were allowed to embark on a ship bound for Egypt. By at least the middle of the 14th century, all the Jews of the town had united into a single community, led by three officers who administered the schools, the three synagogues, the almshouse, and the *mikveh*.

In the 14th century, Jews were granted equality with other citizens of Marseilles, yet they continued to have special privileges. Thus, although it was forbidden for all other citizens to sell flour in any place but on the bridge, a municipal ordinance of 1359 authorized Jews to sell or buy flour for unleavened bread (*mazzot*) in the Jewish quarter. Similarly, an ordinance issued in 1363 stipulated that whereas all other inhabitants were to sweep the street before their houses on Saturday, Jews were permitted to do so on Friday. Finally, in 1387 Jews were exempted on evenings of Jewish festivals from the general obligation to walk about with a lamp after curfew.

Although they lived in an international trading port, the Jewish population remained relatively stable. For much of the Middle Ages, new arrivals in the town constituted little more than 10% of the population. (An important exception was in 1351, after an influx caused by the *Black Death persecutions, when the percentage of new arrivals in the community reached 30%.) Although Jews did not generally participate in the maritime trade, limiting their transactions mainly to Spain, they were well represented in the town's urban commercial life, many of them acting as brokers. The Jewish surname Sabonarius has led to the belief that it was the Jews who introduced the soap industry to Marseilles. They had a virtual monopoly over coral craftsmanship, although those engaged in this occupation made very little money. Poorly off, too, were the Jews who earned their livelihood as laborers, porters, stonecutters, and tailors. Since they dealt only in small sums, even Jewish moneylenders were not noticeably wealthy. Jews did, however, distinguish themselves in the medical field, the number of Jewish physicians in the town often exceeding that of their Christian colleagues. During the 15th century, Jewish economic life experienced a setback and economic activity was reduced to the retail trade, mainly the sale of wheat and textiles. Jews also suffered more than the rest of the population when the town was plundered by the Aragonese in 1423. Most of them became impoverished, and struggled to recover economically.

Late in 1484 and early in 1485, shortly after the incorporation of *Provence into France (1481), the Jewish quarter of Marseilles was attacked. In the wake of plunder, destruction, and murder, the Jews of Marseilles began to flee. In 1486, however, the municipal council curbed their emigration and drew up an inventory of their belongings. The ensuing period is marked by severe upheavals in the composition of the community, as reflected in the extant lists of the heads of families; at least one half of the community's members were relatively new arrivals. Jews from Spain began to arrive in large numbers, particularly after 1491. Many shipowners in Marseilles amassed fortunes as a result of their expulsion in 1492. Spanish Jews hired vessels at exorbitant prices to transport them to Italy and Constantinople, and many of these ships called at the port of Marseilles. At times, the exiles attempted to remain in the city without the authorization of the municipal council. A general expulsion order for Provence was issued in 1500 and enforced in 1501. For about 20 years, conversions increased considerably as great numbers of Jews chose baptism to evade expulsion.

The 12th-century Jewish traveler Benjamin of Tudela refers to Marseilles as a "town of learned men and scholars." Among those he mentions is R. *Isaac b. Abba Mari of Marseilles, a renowned commentator and author of prayers. Several members of the Ibn *Tibbon family also lived in Marseilles, or were born there. (Records of a rabbinical lawsuit in this family about 1250 mention family relationships and marriages between the Jews of Marseilles and those of *Naples, *Aix-en-Provence, and *Montpellier.) *Nissim b. Moses of Marseilles was the author of a commentary – which some regard as "almost rationalist" – on the Pentateuch, entitled *Sefer ha-Nissim* or *Ma'aseh Nissim*. Samuel b. Judah ha-Marsili (also known as Miles Bonjudas), born in Marseilles in 1294, translated several philosophical and scientific works from Arabic into Hebrew. Other scholars born in the city include Judah b. David (also known as Bonjudas Bendavi or Maestre Bonjua), a talmudist and physician of the late 14th/early 15th century, and the talmudist and commentator Jacob b. David *Provencal (second half of the 15th century), both of whom emigrated to Italy.

In the second half of the 17th century, a second community was established in Marseilles for a brief period. As a result of an edict issued by Louis XIV in 1669, which granted tax exemption to the port of Marseilles, two Jews of Leghorn, Joseph Vais Villareal and Abraham *Athias, settled there in 1670 with their families. Their commercial success rapidly attracted other Jews. The local authorities soon protested against the presence of Jews and particularly objected to the existence of two places of Jewish worship. They obtained an expulsion order which was carried out in 1682. Despite successive renewals of the expulsion order, a new community was founded in 1760. About 1768, it owned a small synagogue and in 1783, it erected a cemetery. Although the community's membership remained relatively stable, a split occurred at the end of 1790, and both the municipality and the civil court were called upon to intervene to settle the differences. Forcibly reunited, the community established a new synagogue and a cemetery in 1804. The community was then composed of about 300 members, of whom over one third were living in poverty. The Jewish population increased rapidly to 450 in 1808, 1,000 in 1821, and 2,500 in 1865. As a result, several new institutions were established, including schools for both boys and girls, a poorhouse, and a synagogue on the Rue de Breteuil that remains in use today.

Holocaust Period and After

Between 1940 and 1942, Marseilles, along with *Lyons, was the city in the southern or "free" zone where the greatest number of Jews and Jewish organizations and institutions found sanctuary from the German invasion. After the Allied landing in

North Africa and the German occupation of France in November 1942, there was a vicious hunt for Jews in Marseilles, which led to mass arrests and deportations. At the same time, the resistance movement increased its activities in the city. The synagogue on Rue de Breteuil was pillaged, the facade destroyed, the prayer books and the Torah scrolls burned. With the defeat of the Germans, about 5,000–10,000 Jews remained in Marseilles. The population, which was comprised of refugees from Provence and Alsace, immigrants from Eastern Europe, and Sephardi Jews from the eastern Mediterranean and from North Africa, gradually rebuilt the community and its institutions, including the Rue de Breteuil synagogue. The former military camp of Grand Arenas near Marseilles became a transit camp for Jewish survivors migrating to Palestine. Beginning in 1956, the city attracted Jewish immigrants from North Africa, and in 1962 it became their main port of entry into France. In 1969, there were an estimated 65,000 Jews in Marseilles. In 1987, the Jewish population stood at 70,000, making it the third largest Jewish community in Western Europe. Although the community's buildings and institutions expanded, they could not keep pace with the population growth. In 2002 Marseilles and the immediate vicinity was said to have over 40 synagogues. It also had three community centers, a Jewish primary school, an *ORT vocational school, and a network of institutions and organizations including youth movements, kosher restaurants, and *mikva'ot*. A consulate general of Israel was located in Marseilles.

BIBLIOGRAPHY: Gross, Gal Jud, 366ff.; B. Blumenkranz, *Juifs et chrétiens…* (1960), index; R. Aubenas, *Recueil de lettres des officialiés de Marseille…*, 2 (1938), 37, 40–42, 54–55; A. Crémieux, in: REJ, 46 (1903), 1–47, 246–68; 47 (1903), 62–86, 243–61; 55 (1908), 119–45; 56 (1908), 99–123; I. Loeb, *ibid.*, 16 (1888), 73–83; R. Busquet, *ibid.*, 83 (1927), 163–83; J. Weyl, *ibid.*, 17 (1888), 96–110; Z. Szajkowski, *ibid.*, 121 (1962), 367–82; idem, *Analytical Franco-Jewish Gazetteer* (1966), index; M. Zarb, *Privilèges de… Marseille* (1961), 90, 142; *Histoire du commerce de Marseille*, 1 (1949), 290–3; 2 (1951), 89–96; 3 (1951), 24–31; 4 (1954), 537–9; D. Hauck, *Das Kaufmannsbuch des Johan Blasi* (1965), index; A. Latil, in: *Répertoire des travaux de la societé de statistique de Marseille*, 30 (1867), 122–53. **ADD. BIBLIOGRAPHY:** *Guide du Judaïsme français* (1987), 39; *Jewish Travel Guide* (2002), 71.

[Bernhard Blumenkranz / David Weinberg (2nd ed.)]

MARSHAK, SAMUEL YAKOVLEVICH (1887–1964), Zionist and Russian poet. Marshak was born in Voronezh. Though his father received a solid religious education, Marshak himself seems to have experienced traditional Judaism only when he lived, as a child, with his observant grandparents in Vitebsk. There, for two years, he studied Hebrew with a teacher by the name of Khalameyzer, whom he lovingly remembered and described in his childhood reminiscences *V nachale zhizni* ("At Life's Beginning," 1960). But it seems that he mastered Hebrew, as well as ancient and modern Jewish literature, sufficiently well to be able to translate it into Russian. Marshak received his formal education in Russian high schools in St. Petersburg and also in the Crimean town of Yalta, where he lived in Maxim *Gorki's house.

According to his second autobiographical note "*O sebe*" ("About Myself"), published posthumously as an introduction to the eight-volume collection of his writings, he "began being published in almanacs in 1907." But actually his first verse had already appeared in Russian-language Jewish journals (*Yevreyskaya Zhizn, Molodaya Iudeya*) in 1904–07, all of them enthusiastically Zionist, such as poems on the death of *Herzl ("*20 Tammuz*" and "*Na grobe*"), poems based on biblical themes (from Ezekiel and Song of Songs), on midrashic legends, about the Spanish Inquisition, and programmatic Zionist poetry (especially for youth), etc. Later he published his poetry, including translations from *Bialik, in the Zionist *Razsvet*, in which, after a visit in 1911 to Ereẓ Israel, he also published his observations and impressions of the various Jewish communities in the country. In his poem "Palestina," published in 1916 in *Yevreyskaya Zhizn*, he contrasted the Jewish plight in Russia during World War I to the elation he experienced in Ereẓ Israel. His poem "*Ierusalim*," which depicts his journey to the Holy City, was included in the Russian-language anthology of Jewish poetry *Safrut* (1918). The *Evrejskaya Anthaloga* ("Hebrew Anthology"), which appeared in Moscow in 1918, edited by L. *Jaffe and V. *Khodasevich, published Marshak's translations from Bialik, Z. *Shneur and D. Shimonovich *(Shimoni).

As a high school student, during his stay in Gorki's house in Yalta, he was active until the summer of 1906 in organizing Zionist youth circles of Molodaya Iudeya ("Young Judea"). Under the influence of the clandestine *Po'alei Zion delegate, Isaac Shimshelevich (later Izhak *Ben-Zvi, the second president of Israel), Marshak became an activist of the illegal Po'alei Zion movement, and his address at Gorki's house even served as a liaison between the center of the movement in Poltava and its delegate in the Crimea. According to Ben-Zvi's letters, seized by the Czarist police, Marshak was active in organizing the Po'alei Zion branch in Yalta and the distribution of *Yevreyskaya Rabochaya Khronika* ("Jewish Workers' Chronicle"). During his stay in London (1912–13) Marshak was still in touch with Po'alei Zion, and Ber *Borochov mentions him in one of his letters to a London friend. Thus, from his high school days in Yalta until after the Russian Revolution, when he participated in the editing of the Russian-language anthologies of Jewish literature in Moscow, Marshak was a dedicated Zionist. This chapter in his life has been completely omitted from Marshak's biographies and autobiographical notes published in the Soviet Union.

[Matityahu Minc]

Most historians of Russian writing would probably accept Marshak's designation by his friend Maxim Gorki as the founder of Soviet children's literature. His first children's book was *Detki v kletke* ("Children in a Cage," 1923). There is hardly a Russian child or young adult who does not know some of Marshak's verse by heart. His nursery rhymes, songs, and verse form part of the Soviet kindergarten and school curriculum, and his plays have long been among the mainstays of the Soviet children's theater. There are few ideological elements in his verse, in which he usually exhorts children to be truthful, to obey their parents, to study diligently, and to be kind to animals. Four volumes of his writings, including his first autobiographical note, appeared in 1957–60. Marshak was also famous as a translator of the great European poets, including Shakespeare, Blake, Byron, and Heine.

Marshak's sister, YELENA YAKOVLEVNA ILINA (pen name of Liya Yakovlevna Preis, 1901–1964), was a well-known children's writer in her own right, and his brother, M. ILIN (pen name of Ilya Yakovlevich Marshak, 1895–1953), was probably the best-known Soviet writer of popular science, particularly for children. He won the Stalin Prize four times (1942, 1946, 1949, 1951), and the Lenin Prize in 1962.

[Maurice Friedberg]

BIBLIOGRAPHY: B.E. Galanov, *S.Ya. Marshak…* (Rus., 1956); B.M. Sarnov, *Samuil Marshak…* (Rus., 1968); M. Minc, in: *Beḥinot*, 1 (1970).

MARSHALL, DAVID SAUL (1908–1995), Singapore labor politician, lawyer, and diplomat. Marshall was born of a Sephardi family of Iraqi origin. He went to London to study, and, after being admitted to the English bar, returned to Singapore to practice law. He entered politics as a member of the Legislative Assembly and became president of the Workers' Party. When the island was granted partial independence in 1955, Marshall led the United Labor Front party to victory in the elections and became chief minister and minister for commerce, serving in these positions until 1956. Marshall was president of the Singapore Jewish Welfare Board from 1946 to 1953. From 1978 to 1993 Marshall served as Singapore's ambassador to France, Spain, Portugal, and Switzerland.

[Moshe Rosetti]

MARSHALL, LOUIS (1856–1929), lawyer and communal leader. Born in Syracuse, New York, the son of German-Jewish immigrants, Marshall graduated from Syracuse High School and served a two-year apprenticeship in a local law office. In 1876 he left for New York City where he completed the two-year Columbia Law School course in one year. Returning to Syracuse, Marshall joined a prominent law firm and in 1894 became a partner in the leading New York firm of Guggenheimer, Untermyer, and Marshall.

Marshall specialized in constitutional and corporate law. Many of the numerous cases that he argued before the U.S. Supreme Court were of major constitutional significance. His legal eminence was recognized by appointment or election to three constitutional conventions in New York State (1890, 1894, and 1915). Although he never sought public office, he was at one time seriously considered for appointment to the Supreme Court. A leading supporter of the Republican Party, Marshall participated in local and national politics, led in the establishment of the New York State College of Forestry, and served on numerous non-sectarian committees and boards.

In New York City, Marshall joined the German-Jewish elite and quickly became the chief spokesman for this group in matters affecting the Jewish community at home and abroad. His national leadership became evident in 1911 during the successful campaign against the United States-Russian Commercial Treaty of 1832, which was being used by the Czarist regime to discriminate against American Jews. Marshall's eloquence, legal knowledge, and skillful management, joined with intense public pressure, resulted in congressional action leading to abrogation of the treaty. In 1912 Marshall became president of the American Jewish Committee and held this post until 1929. During World War I, he participated in a bitter internal power struggle within the Jewish community over the establishment of an American Jewish Congress in preparation for peace negotiations. Playing a key role as mediator, Marshall joined the Jewish delegation to the Paris Peace Conference in 1919, where he supported the granting of national minority rights to the Jews of the new East European states.

Marshall vigorously attempted, without success, to block the American publication of the antisemitic Protocols of the *Elders of Zion, imported from Europe in the immediate postwar years. American Jewry was shocked when the *Dearborn Independent*, a publication owned by Henry Ford, embarked in 1920 on a crusade to popularize and elaborate the distortions and misrepresentations emanating from the *Protocols*. Unable to dissuade Ford directly, Marshall utilized quiet pressure and influential intermediaries in an attempt to abate this antisemitic campaign. Finally, in 1927, after lawsuits brought by individuals maligned by the *Independent*, Ford agreed to cease his attacks and to sign a formal apology to the Jews prepared by Marshall.

Marshall participated in the legal defense of Leo *Frank, who was convicted and subsequently lynched in Georgia for a murder he allegedly committed in 1913. He played a significant part in the campaign to delay the imposition of progressively harsher immigration-restriction legislation. His intervention in 1922 helped reverse Harvard University's announced intention to impose a quota system on Jewish students. He quietly opposed the powerful Ku Klux Klan and vigorously condemned the perpetrators of the Massena ritual murder libel in 1929.

Marshall was a dedicated Jew. He served as president of Temple Emanu-El in New York, the most important Reform Jewish congregation in the United States. At the same time, he served as chairman of the board of directors of the *Jewish Theological Seminary. During World War I, he was president of the American Jewish Relief Committee and helped organize and guide the *American Jewish Joint Distribution Committee. Although not a political Zionist, Marshall acknowledged the need for Palestine as a center of Jewish settlement, especially after the United States severely limited immigration in the early 1920s. He cooperated with Chaim *Weizmann in attempting to arrange a *modus vivendi* which would allow wealthy and influential non-Zionists to share in the support of Palestine without actually becoming Zionists. Weizmann's and Marshall's efforts, opposed by Stephen Wise and other American Zionists, finally came to fruition after many years of discussion. In August 1929, shortly before Marshall's fatal illness, a pact was ratified in Zurich for the establishment of a *Jewish Agency, which would include both Zionists and non-Zionists in the management of Jewish colonization in Palestine under the terms of the British mandate. Marshall's death was a blow to the full implementation of the venture, but his work helped create a tradition of American non-Zionist support that was of great value in the crucial decade after World War II.

Believing in the indivisibility of civil rights, Marshall was a consistent champion of other minorities. Active in the National Association for the Advancement of Colored People, he fought major legal battles on behalf of blacks. In 1920, alarmed at hysterical anti-Bolshevism, Marshall defended five socialist assemblymen, who were refused their seats in the New York State Legislature.

Marshall's period of leadership coincided with the great era of mass Jewish immigration to the United States and the integration of the immigrants into an urbanized, industrialized society. Representing the native Jewish establishment, he nevertheless displayed a remarkable sensitivity to the needs and desires of the Jewish immigrants, encouraging, guiding, criticizing, but not patronizing. Aided by American democratic traditions and the political power of Jewish voters, Marshall generally used the traditional methods of intercession and quiet diplomacy to achieve his ends. While not uniformly successful, his dignity, sincerity, devotion, and strength combined to produce what a contemporary called "the foremost leader of American Judaism… the American Jew par excellence."

His son, GEORGE MARSHALL (1904–), conservationist, served as an economist with the National Recovery Administration from 1934 to 1937. Marshall devoted his efforts to the cause of conservation. He was managing editor of *The Living Wilderness* from 1957 to 1961 and was a director of the Sierra Club and the California Conservation Council.

Another son, JAMES MARSHALL (1896–1986), lawyer and educator, studied law at Columbia University and was associated with his father's firm, Guggenheimer, Untermyer, and Marshall from 1920 to 1930. After independent practice from 1930 to 1934, he became a member of the firm of Marshall, Bratter, Greene, Allison and Tucker. In addition to numerous other civic responsibilities, Marshall was a member of the New York City Board of Education from 1938 to 1952 and served as its president from 1938 to 1942. Active in Jewish communal life, he held important posts in the American Jewish Committee, Joint Distribution Committee, Jewish Publication Society, and American Friends of the Hebrew University.

A third son, ROBERT MARSHALL (1901–1939), served as director of the forestry division of the U.S. Office of Indian Affairs from 1933 to 1937. He became chief of the division of recreation and soil conservation of the U.S. Forest Service and held the position until his death.

BIBLIOGRAPHY: C. Reznikoff (ed.), *Louis Marshall: Champion of Liberty*, 2 vols. (1957); M. Rosenstock, *Louis Marshall, Defender of Jewish Rights* (1965); American Jewish Committee, in: AJYB, 10–31 (1908–29); Adler, in: AJYB, 32 (1931), 21–55; Dawidowicz, in: JSOS, 25 (1963), 102–32.

[Morton Rosenstock]

°MARSUS, C. VIBIUS, successor to Petronius as Roman governor of Syria (42 C.E.). Marsus appears to have regarded the Judean king Agrippa I with more than the average Roman suspicion toward Jewish leaders and went so far as to inform the emperor *Claudius of these suspicions. When Agrippa began to fortify the walls of the northern side of Jerusalem, the act was immediately reported by Marsus to the emperor. Claudius ordered the immediate cessation of the fortification, suspecting that a revolution was at foot. Marsus again intervened in Judean affairs when he disbanded the meeting of vassal kings convened by Agrippa at Tiberias. From that time, according to Josephus, Agrippa was at odds with Marsus. Marsus was succeeded in Syria by Cassius Longinus in 45 C.E.

BIBLIOGRAPHY: Jos., Ant., 19: 316, 326–7, 240–2, 363; 20:1; Pauly-Wissowa, 2nd series, vol. 16 (1958), 1973–75 (under the name C. Vibius Marsus).

[Isaiah Gafni]

MARTHA, daughter of Boethus, mentioned in Mishnah Yev. 6:4 (cf. Sifra, Emor ch. 2:6) as a widow who was betrothed to *Joshua b. Gamla. According to this Mishnah, Joshua, who was subsequently appointed high priest, was nevertheless permitted to consummate the marriage. Martha's sons are mentioned in Tosef. Yoma 1:14 as priests serving in the temple, but it is not clear whether these are the children of Joshua b. Gamlia, or of her first husband, who may also have been a priest. A tannaitic midrash already uses Martha as a paradigmatic figure of an extremely wealthy widow (cf. Yer. Ket. 5:11, 30b), and the Talmud (Yev. 61a) relates that she paid King Yannai a small fortune in order to assure that Joshua b. Gamlia would be appointed as high priest. In the *aggadot* concerning the fall of Jerusalem (Git. 56a), Martha is portrayed as one of the wealthiest women in the period preceding the destruction of the Temple (70 C.E.), who was forced during a time of famine to venture out on her own to seek a morsel of food. When some excrement came into contact with her skin she died, thus fulfilling the prophecy of Moses in Deut. 28:56. Presumably the traditions concerning Miriam, daughter of Boethus (Lam. R., 1:47), whose family rose to a position of prominence in Herod's time, are also a later literary development of the tannaitic traditions concerning Martha, daughter of Boethus.

BIBLIOGRAPHY: Schuerer, Gesch, 2 (19074), 273; Graetz, Hist, 2 (1949), 249, 306; Klausner, Bayit Sheni, 5 (19512), 22–23, 291.

[Stephen G. Wald (2nd ed.)]

°MARTI, KARL (1855–1925), Swiss-German Bible scholar. Marti studied at Basel in Switzerland with Emil Kautzsch, and with Franz Delitzsch at Leipzig in Germany. He taught at Basel university (1881–91) and was professor of theology (from 1895) and of Semitic philology (from 1901) in Bern(e) until his death. Marti wrote critical studies on Jeremiah (1889) and Zechariah (1892), and a concise grammar of biblical Aramaic (1896; 1911[2]). He edited the second edition of A. Kayser's *Theologie des Alten Testaments* (1894; 1907[5]), bearing the title *Geschichte der israelitischen Religion*, a critical evaluation of biblical religion based on the *Wellhausen-Graf reconstruction of Israel's history. Though a staunch Wellhausenian with regard to the biblical texts, Marti paid more attention to the ancient Near Eastern world in which they were produced. In the *Kurzer Hand-Commentar zum Alten Testament*, of which he was a co-editor, he wrote the volumes on Isaiah (1900), Daniel (1901), the Minor Prophets (1904), and the introductory volume, *Die Religion des Alten Testaments unter den Religionen des vorderen Orients* (1906; *The Religion of the Old Testament*, 1907). In the series *Die Heilige Schrift des Alten Testaments* he annotated Deuteronomy (1909), Daniel, and the books of Joel, Obadiah, Zechariah, Haggai, and Malachi of the Minor Prophets (1910). Among his numerous articles on biblical studies and Judaica there is a strongly biased one on the nature of the Christian mission to the Jews ("Zur Judenmission," in: *Kirchenblatt für die reformierte Schweiz*, 1886). Yehezkel *Kaufmann was a student of his.

BIBLIOGRAPHY: For a bibliography of K. Marti's writings until 1923, see: W. Baumgartner, in: BZAW, 41 (1925), 323–31. **ADD. BIBLIOGRAPHY:** C. Begg, in: DBI, 2:132.

[Zev Garber / S. David Sperling (2nd ed.)]

°MARTIAL (M. Valerius Martialis; c. 40–104 C.E.), Roman epigrammatist. Martial ridiculed the Jewish rite of circumcision (*Epigrammaton*, 7:55) and speaks mockingly of women who fast on the Sabbath (*ibid.*, 4:4). In common with other classical writers (e.g., Augustus, Strabo, Pompeius Trogus, Persius, and Petronius), Martial confuses the Sabbath with a fast day, probably the Day of Atonement. He referred to licentious Jews who shared vices with their fellow Romans (*ibid.*, 7:30). Martial scolded a circumcised rival poet from Solymae (Jerusalem) for plagiarizing his verses, while criticizing them (*ibid.*, 11:94). In common with other Roman satirists (e.g., *Juvenal), he depicts unfavorably Jewish life in Rome, expressing indignation at the constant growth of that community which he considered strange.

BIBLIOGRAPHY: Reinach, Textes, 287–9; M. Radin, *The Jews among the Greeks and Romans* (1915), 302, 325–6, 329–30.

[Solomon Rappaport]

°MARTIN, name of five popes, two of whom were significant in Jewish history.

MARTIN IV pope 1281–85. Although he employed a southern French Jewish physician, Martin IV was generally repressive in his actions concerning the Jews. He directed the inquisitors to proceed against lapsed Jewish converts (March 1, 1281), and issued an instruction to the archbishops and bishops of France not to hamper the work of the Inquisition, even suspending the right of sanctuary in the case of Jewish converts suspected of falling away from the faith. A series of articles specifying reforms for Portugal (1284) is partly concerned with the position of the Jews.

MARTIN V pope 1417–31. On the whole Martin V was well-disposed toward the Jews. In the first two years of his reign he confirmed the Jews of Germany, Savoy, and Rome in their former privileges, and received favorably a delegation of Italian Jews and another from Spain. In 1419 (and again in 1422 and 1429) he issued a bull protecting the Jews in their synagogues. He resisted the imposition of the *badge, but ordered the Jews to abstain from work on Sundays and feast days. His aim seems to have been to encourage the fullest possible intercourse between Jews and Christians, excepting from his protection only those Jews who conspired to overthrow the Christian faith. His personal relations with Jews appear to have been good: he employed Elijah b. Shabbetai Be'er as his physician and gave the Jewish physicians in the Papal States every encouragement in the practice of their profession. Martin may have been the pope who discussed theology with Aaron b. Gerson Abulrabi of Catania. To some extent he seems to have striven to moderate the worst excesses of the Inquisition. In 1418, after receiving a complaint that the Jews of Avignon practiced sorcery, infected simple Christians with Jewish superstitions, and demanded interest at a rate of 10%, he instructed the local inquisitor to proceed against them, but he soon attempted to restrain the inquisitor's zeal. The same situation was repeated in his dealings with John of *Capistrano, against whose excesses many of his edicts of protection were probably directed. Thus in 1422 he issued an edict forbidding forcible baptism, since "a man who is known to have undertaken Christian baptism unwillingly rather than of his own accord cannot be supposed to possess true Christian faith," but barely a year later he was induced to withdraw it. In May 1427 John of Capistrano persuaded the queen of Naples (Joanna II) to cancel the privileges of the Jews in her kingdom, but Martin's intervention resulted in the repeal of this edict in the following August.

BIBLIOGRAPHY: E.A. Synan, *Popes and Jews in the Middle Ages* (1965), 121; 135–6; REJ, 3 (1881), 218 (on Bull of 1281); Roth, Italy, 157ff.; S. Grayzel, *The Church and the Jews in the XIIIth Century* (1966), 274.

[Nicholas de Lange]

MARTIN, BERNARD (1928–1982), U.S. rabbi and educator. Martin was born in Seklence, Czechoslovakia, and educated in the U.S. He was ordained as a rabbi at Hebrew Union College in 1951, receiving his M.H.L. degree with highest honors. He pursued a combined career as pulpit rabbi and scholar, and received a doctorate in philosophy from the University of Illinois in 1960.

Martin served as rabbi of Sinai Temple in Champaign, Ill., from 1951 to 1957, with a leave of absence to serve as a chaplain in the U.S. army in Japan from 1953 to 1955. He was associate rabbi of Sinai Temple in Chicago from 1957 to 1961 and then senior rabbi of Mount Zion Temple in St. Paul, Minn., until 1966. He held a "centrist" position in the Reform rabbinate, welcoming increased use of Hebrew and ritual, while urging the formulation of "a statement of Jewish theological belief that will satisfy both the mind and heart of the groping and intellectually sophisticated contemporary Jew." Martin also served on the boards of Jewish and civic organizations in St. Paul, including the Jewish Fund and Council, Talmud Torah, Jewish Community Center, Council on Religion and Race, and Zionist District.

In 1966, Martin accepted a professorship at Case Western Reserve University in Cleveland, where he became chair of the department of religion in 1967 and Abba Hillel Silver Professor of Jewish Studies in 1968. He was active in the American Academy for Jewish Research, Academy for Jewish Philosophy, and American Academy of Religion, among others, and served from 1975 to 1981 as editor of the CCAR *Journal*, published by the Central Conference of American Rabbis.

Martin's first book was *The Existentialist Theology of Paul Tillich* (1963). He then developed a specialty in the Russian Jewish existentialist Lev Shestov, editing *Great Twentieth Century Jewish Philosophers* (Shestov, Rosenzweig, Buber, 1969) and *A Shestov Anthology* (1970), and translating Shestov's *Athens and Jerusalem* (1966), *Potestas Clavium* (1968), and *Speculation and Revelation* (1982). Martin's works on Judaism include *Prayer in Judaism* (1968), *Contemporary Reform Jewish Thought* (ed., 1968), *A History of Judaism* (vol. 2: *Europe and the New World*, 1974), *Movements and Issues in American Judaism* (ed., 1978), and a historical novel on Shabbetai Zevi, *That Man from Smyrna* (1978). Martin translated and edited Yiddish works, including literary historian Israel Zinberg's magnum opus, *A History of Jewish Literature* (12 vols., 1972–78) and Dovid Bergelson's novel, *When All is Said and Done* (1977).

BIBLIOGRAPHY: A. Soloff, "Bernard Martin," in: CCARY, 92 (1982), 252–53.

[Mark L. Smith (2nd ed.)]

MARTIN, DAVID (1915–1997), Australian poet and novelist. Born Ludwig Detsinyi in Budapest, Martin was educated in Germany, but left in 1935 with the rise of Nazi power, spending a year on a kibbutz in Ereẓ Israel. He fought in the Spanish Civil War, and lived in London from 1938, working for various newspapers and the European Service of the B.B.C. He moved to Australia in 1949, and was briefly editor of the *Sydney Jewish News*. His works include verse collections such as *Battlefields and Girls* (1942); *From Life* (1953); and *The Gift* (1966); and the novels, *Tiger Bay* (1946); *The Stones of Bombay* (1950); *The Young Wife* (1962); and *The King Between* (1966). Martin contributed stories, criticism, and occasional verse to Jewish publications in England, the U.S.A., and Australia. One of his best-known poems, "I am a Jew," was published in his *Collected Poems, 1938–1958* (1958). His other major Jewish works are a play, *The Shepherd and the Hunter* (1946), dealing with the Palestine problem in the 1940s, and the autobiographical novel, *Where A Man Belongs* (1968), which deals with aspects of contemporary Jewish life. Martin was a member of the Australian Communist Party from 1951 until 1959 and remained on the left until the end of his life, advocating a policy of "armed neutrality" for Australia in the 1980s. He wrote an autobiography, *My Strange Friend* (1991).

BIBLIOGRAPHY: J. Hetherington, *Forty-two Faces* (1962), 127–32, incl. bibl.

[Greer Fay Cashman]

MARTIN, TONY (**Alvin Morris**; 1912–), U.S. actor and singer. Born in San Francisco, Martin sang over a national radio network in 1932, and was signed for the popular radio show of George Burns and Gracie Allen. His lilting tenor and good looks led to film contracts.

After the Japanese attack on Pearl Harbor in December 1941, Martin enlisted in the U.S. Armed Forces, serving first in the Navy and then with the Army in the Far East. He also sang for a time with the Army Air Forces Training Command Orchestra directed by Glenn Miller. He received several military honors, including the Bronze Star.

Martin combined his singing with acting, notably in the film *Casbah* (1948), in which he played Pepe Le Moko, the jewel thief. Some of Martin's other films include *Follow the Fleet* (1936), *Banjo on My Knee* (1936), *Sing and Be Happy* (1937), *Kentucky Moonshine* (1938), *Ziegfeld Girl* (1941), *Till the Clouds Roll By* (1946), *Two Tickets to Broadway* (1951), *Easy to Love* (1953), *Here Come the Girls* (1953), *Deep in My Heart* (1954), and *Let's Be Happy* (1957).

Martin had a successful recording career as well. His biggest hit song was "There's No Tomorrow" (adapted from the classic Italian song "O Sole Mio"). Some of his other popular hits include "South of the Border," "It's a Blue World," "Tonight We Love," "To Each His Own," "It's Magic," "La Vie En Rose," "I Get Ideas," "Domino," "Kiss of Fire," "Stranger in Paradise," and "Walk Hand in Hand."

Martin was active on radio from the 1930s to the 1950s on shows such as Walter Winchell's *Lucky Strike Hour*, along with his own programs. He then moved to television, where he appeared on variety shows and hosted *The Tony Martin Show* (1954–56). In 1955 he was nominated for an Emmy for Best Male Singer.

Martin married actress Alice Faye in 1936; they divorced in 1940. He married dancer/actress Cyd Charisse in 1948. He formed a nightclub act with Charisse in 1964, and for many years the couple performed on the cabaret circuit in the U.S. and abroad.

[Ruth Beloff (2nd ed.)]

°**MARTINEZ, FERRANT**, archdeacon of Écija, one of the leading anti-Jewish agitators in Castile during the last quarter of the 14th century. Preaching in public in *Seville, Martínez demanded that the 23 synagogues in the town should be destroyed and the Jews confined to their own quarter. As vicar-general of the archbishop of Seville, he secured the right of jurisdiction over the Jews of the town and its environs and demanded their expulsion from Écija and other rural districts. In 1378 the Jewish community of Seville appealed to King Henry II of Castile, but his letter to the archdeacon commanding him to desist was ignored. The Jews turned to his successor John I in 1382 but John's edict of 1383 also did not deter Martínez. In 1388 the Jewish community of Seville finally resolved to summon the archdeacon before the supreme court of the crown. In his defense, Martínez claimed that his actions were beneficial to Church and crown and that he had acted with the consent of his superior, the archbishop. Due to the intervention of Queen Leonora in favor of the archdeacon, little resulted from the trial. Even the archbishop of Seville's prompt removal of Martínez from office was fruitless, for after the deaths of King John and the archbishop in 1390 the archdeacon was reinstated to his former position. Immediately after his reinstatement, he ordered that all synagogues within his jurisdiction be destroyed. The intervention of King Henry III, who demanded that Martínez rebuild the synagogues and resign from office, went unheeded. As a result of his continued activities, riots broke out throughout Castile in 1391 and spread rapidly to Aragon. In the ensuing destruction and massacres, many Jews were forced to accept baptism. In 1395 Martínez was imprisoned on the order of the king, but he was soon released; after his death the people revered him as a saint.

BIBLIOGRAPHY: Baer, Urkunden, 1 (1929), 699ff.; 2 (1936), 210ff., 231ff., 244ff.; Baer, Spain, 2 (1966), index s.v. *Ferrant Martinez.*

°**MARTÍNEZ DE OVIEDO, GONZALO** (d. 1340), majordomo (*dispensero de la casa del rey*) of King Alfonso XI of Castile. He instigated the proposal to expel the Jews from the kingdom of Castile. When in the royal service, Martínez enjoyed the protection of the Jewish courtier Joseph de *Écija. According to Solomon *Ibn Verga in *Shevet Yehudah*, he was jealous of his Jewish master and petitioned the king to sell him Joseph and nine other Jews, including the physician Samuel *Ibn Waqar. The king granted his request and the two courtiers R. Joseph and R. Samuel died under torture in prison. Martínez' influence increased until he was appointed head of the Order of Alcántara. When Abu al-Malik, son of the sultan of Morocco, declared war on Castile in 1339, Martínez advised Alfonso to expel all the Jews from the kingdom and confiscate their property. In spite of the objections of some of the court ministers, the king accepted his suggestion and the Jews of several towns were arrested and their property seized. Martínez led the troops who defeated the Moroccan army, but after his victory he lost favor with the king, probably as a result of the intervention of Alfonso's mistress Doña Leonor de Guzmán; he was arrested, charged as a traitor, and executed by royal command. Ibn Verga relates that all the tyrant's property was sold to Jews and his ring handed over to the courtier Moses, probably Moses *Abzardiel.

BIBLIOGRAPHY: Baer, Spain, 1 (1961), 354ff.; S. ibn Verga, *Shevet Yehudah*, ed. by A. Shochat (1947), 53ff.

°**MARTINI, RAYMOND** (1220–1285), Spanish Dominican friar and polemicist. Born in Subirat, Catalonia, Raymond lived for a long time in a monastery in Barcelona, temporarily also in Tunis where he engaged in missionary activity among Jews and Arabs. He studied Hebrew and other Oriental languages at the college of Murcia, founded to train selected friars in the conduct of religious disputations with Jews and Muslims for the purpose of converting them to Christianity. Raymond was able to read rabbinical writings with ease. He took an active part in the disputation with Naḥmanides at *Barcelona in 1263 where Pablo *Christiani was the Christian spokesman (see *Barcelona, Disputation of). In 1264 he was appointed a member of the first censorship commission to examine Jewish books for passages allegedly offensive to Christianity. After the disputation of Barcelona, Raymond Martini became one of the chief executors of the anti-Jewish policy of the church.

Raymond's main work is his *Pugio Fidei* ("The Dagger of Faith"; c. 1280), divided into three parts of which the second and third are devoted to anti-Jewish polemics. The last part contains extracts from the Talmud, the Midrash, and later rabbinical writings (Rashi, etc.). The book is clearly an attempt to regain the ground lost after the Christian failure in the disputation of Barcelona. Raymond's polemics are innovative in that he derives his "proofs" of the truth of Christianity or falsehood of the Jewish faith not solely from the Old Testament but mainly from the Talmud and other rabbinical literature. Thus, according to Raymond, Jesus is also announced as Messiah in the *aggadah*, and the talmudic passage, according to which "the commandments will be abolished in the Hereafter" (Nid. 61b) after the advent of the Messiah, heralds the abrogation of the Jewish laws after the advent of Jesus. Furthermore, Raymond claims that the emendations to the Bible undertaken by Ezra's collaborators and cited in the Talmud as *tikkun soferim* have distorted the original text. But his own interpretation of the aggadic text was not always correct, and by arbitrary grouping of sentences out of their original context he often gave them a christological meaning.

Pugio Fidei became the most important and widely circulated medieval anti-Jewish polemic, and supplied polemical source material to disputant friars, Christian scholars, and Jewish apostates (see *Nicholas of Lyre, *Abner of Burgos, *Pablo de Santa Maria, *Arnold of *Villanova, Joshua *Lorki (in his *Hebraeomastix*, especially for the disputation of *Tortosa)). The manuscript, which was lost for a long time, was brought to light by Justus Scaliger and published by Joseph de Voisin under the title *Pugio Fidei… adversus Mauros et Judaeos* (Paris, 1651). A second edition was published by I.B. Carpzov (Leipzig, 1678), who added an anti-Jewish preface "*Introductio in Theologiam Judaicam*" and a biography of the author. Another anti-Jewish book written by Raymond Martini, *Capistrum Judaeorum*, was less important and never printed.

Solomon b. Abraham *Adret took part in a disputation with Raymond or with one of his disciples. Adret wrote a small apologetic work refuting Raymond's main fictitious proofs from the *aggadah* for the validity of Christianity, without mentioning the author's name or work. These refutations, as well as a detailed defense of *tikkun soferim* against charges of forgeries of the biblical text, are also included in Adret's aggadic commentary *Ḥiddushei Aggadot* (see: Rashba, Resp., 4 (1958), nos. 31 and 187, and J. Perles, 30–56, Heb. sect.).

BIBLIOGRAPHY: Baer, Spain, index; idem, in: *Sefer Zikkaron le-Asher Gulak*... (1942), 29ff.; A.L. Williams, *Adversus Judaeos* (1935), 248ff.; J. Rosenthal, in: *Perspectives in Jewish Learning*, 3 (1967), 48ff.; Graetz, Gesch, 7 (1894), 124f., 150ff.; J. Quetif, *Scriptores Ordinis Praedicatorum*..., 1 (Paris, 1719), 396–8; Wolf, Bibliotheca, 1 (1715), 1016ff.; 3 (1727), 989ff.; 4 (1733), 572ff., 968; J. Perles, *R. Salomo b. Abraham b. Adereth* (Ger. 1863), 54ff., 77f.; S.M. Schiller-Szinessy, in: *Journal of Philology*, 16 (1887), 131–52; L. Levy, in: ZHB, 6 (1902), 30f.; P. Browe, *Judenmission im Mittelalter und die Paepste* (1942), 77, 103f., 108, 120, 122, 272; S. Lieberman, *Sheki'in* (Heb. with Eng. summary, 1939), index; idem, in: HJ, 5 (1943), 91; Zunz-Albeck, Derashot, 144–5; H. Merḥavyah, *Ha-Talmud bi-Re'i ha-Naẓerut* (1970), index.

[Bernard Suler]

MARTON, ERNÖ JECHEZKEL (1896–1960), editor and leader of Transylvanian and Hungarian Jewry. Born in Dicsőszentmárton (now Târnăveni, Romania), Marton was the son of the city's rabbi. Toward the end of World War I, he participated in Hungarian public life and in 1918 he was appointed general secretary to the district governor. But he quickly left this position, moved to Kolozsvár, and took part in the "Zionist revolution" that was then taking place among the Jews of Transylvania. He joined the group that established the Hungarian-language Zionist newspaper *Uj Kelet* ("The New East") and was soon appointed editor in chief (1919). From then until his death he was editor of the paper (in Cluj and later in Tel Aviv). Marton was elected to major posts in the Zionist movement in Transylvania.

Marton was one of the founders and leaders of the Jewish Party in Romania and succeeded in convincing Romanian politicians to view the Jews of Transylvania as a national minority. In 1919 he was elected to the city council of Cluj on behalf of the Jewish Party and was appointed vice mayor. In 1932 he was chosen on the same list as a member of the Romanian parliament, where he defended the rights of the Jews.

During World War II, with the reannexation of Cluj to Hungary (1940), the publication of *Uj Kelet* was discontinued. Marton moved to Budapest and joined the executive of the Hungarian Zionist Movement. In 1944, when the Nazis occupied Hungary, he moved to Bucharest and organized rescue activities on behalf of Hungarian Jewry. He renewed his ties with Romanian politicians and designed a program for the large-scale rescue of Hungarian Jews. With the liberation of Hungary, Marton headed a convoy to Budapest to organize welfare programs for the survivors of the ghetto. In 1946 Marton settled in Palestine. Two years later, together with David Dezsö Schoen, he renewed publication of *Uj Kelet* in Tel Aviv. He also founded the World Federation of Hungarian Jews and was its first chairman. In addition to numerous articles that appeared for decades in his newspaper, he also published books of ideological problems of Zionism. His most important work is *A magyar zsidóság családfája* ("Family Tree of Hungarian Jewry," 1941), in which he developed new theories on the history of the Jews in Hungary. The book also appeared in English translation in *Hungarian Jewish Studies* (1966), 1–59.

BIBLIOGRAPHY: B. Vágó, in: *Hungarian Jewish Studies* (1966), 177–222.

[Yehouda Marton]

MARTOV, JULIUS (Iulii Osipovich Tsederbaum; 1873–1923), Russian revolutionary, leader of Menshevism. Born in Constantinople, where his father represented the Russian Steamship Co. and trade companies, Martov was the favorite grandson of Alexander *Zederbaum, the Hebrew writer and founder of *Ha-Meliẓ*, but his father, Osip, was a conscious assimilationist. Active in revolutionary student circles in St. Petersburg, Martov was arrested and exiled to Vilna, where he worked from 1893 to 1895 in the Jewish social democratic organization (which in 1897 became the *Bund). In a programmatic address (later published as *A Turning Point in the History of the Jewish Labor Movement*), Martov urged the creation of a "separate Jewish workers' organization to lead the Jewish proletariat in the struggle for its economic, civil, and political emancipation"; it would use Yiddish as its language of agitation and champion "equality of rights for Jews."

Returning to St. Petersburg in October 1895, he joined *Lenin as co-founder of the "Union of Struggle for the Emancipation of the Working Class," was arrested in 1896 and was exiled to Siberia. After his term of exile, Martov, together with Lenin and Alexander Potresov, founded the Marxist journal *Iskra* and joined its editorial board abroad (1901–05). He participated in *Iskra*'s crusade against revisionism and "economism" and, reversing his earlier stand on the Jewish question, vigorously opposed the national "separatism" of the Bund, urging Jewish socialists to "assist the organization of the vast majority of the [Russian] proletariat" rather than waste their revolutionary talents on their "own little corner" in the *Pale of Settlement.

Martov broke with Lenin at the Second Congress of the Russian Social Democratic Party (1903), opposing his bid for personal domination of the party. He led Menshevik opposition to Lenin's scheme of a narrow party of professional revolutionaries, advocating a broad, inclusive workers' party adapted to Russian semi-illegal conditions.

During the 1905 Revolution Martov returned to Russia, worked in the St. Petersburg soviet and edited Social Democratic newspapers. In 1906–12 he lived abroad, mainly in Paris, where he edited the Menshevik *Golos sotsialdemokrata*. He supported cooperation with the Bolsheviks and sought to combine legal with underground activities.

During World War I Martov was a central figure of the pacifist Zimmerwald movement. He thwarted Lenin's attempt to turn the movement into a Bolshevik-dominated tool for civil war and the destruction of the Second International. Upon his return to Petersburg on May 9, 1917, Martov led the faction of Menshevik-Internationalists, who opposed the "defensist" policies of the Menshevik majority and advocated the establishment of a popular front government.

After the Bolshevik seizure of power in October 1917, Martov, together with Raphael *Abramowitz, urged the creation of a socialist coalition government in a vain attempt to prevent the Bolsheviks from establishing a minority dictatorship. He became the leader of a vociferous, semi-loyal opposition that tried to function in the Soviet system by making the Bolsheviks respect their own Soviet constitution. Martov denounced the Bolshevik terror, whether directed against "bourgeois" newspapers, liberal parties, the Czar's family, church dignitaries, or Socialist Revolutionaries, and thus became the revolution's "true voice of conscience." But he supported the Soviet regime against counterrevolution and foreign intervention. When the Menshevik Party was finally outlawed, Martov was allowed to leave Russia (1920). He settled in Berlin to lead the Mensheviks in exile and assist the underground Menshevik remnant in Russia. He edited the *Sotsialistichskii Vestnik* and was a leader of the short-lived "Vienna International," which tried to thwart the Comintern's bid to take over the Western independent left-wing parties.

Brave, honest, and gentle, and a beloved figure of Russian and European socialism – even the Bolsheviks mourned him as their "most sincere and honest opponent" – Martov personified the dilemma of revolutionary socialists with humanitarian and democratic commitments when facing the amoral authoritarianism of Lenin and the Soviet regime.

Martov believed that the advent to socialism would also solve the problem of the Jewish people. He was deeply shaken by the pogroms of 1905–06 and by the *Beilis trial, remained personally involved in the struggle against antisemitism, and wrote a little book, *Russkii narod i evrei* ("The Russian People and the Jews," 1908).

His works, fragmentary and scattered, include *Istoriia rossiiskoi sotsial-demokratii* ("History of the Russian Social Democracy," 1918; published in German translation as *Geschichte der russischen Sozialdemokratie*, Berlin, 1926); *Obshchestvennye i umstvennye techeniia v Rossii 1870–1905* ("Social and Intellectual Trends in Russia 1870–1905," 1924); *Razvitie krupnoi promyshlennosti i rabochee dvizhenie v Rossii* ("The Development of Heavy Industry and the Workers' Movement in Russia," 1923). He was chief editor of the monumental Menshevik study *Obshchestvennoe dvizhenie v Rossii v nachale xx veka* ("The Social Movement in Russia at the Beginning of the 20th century," 4 vols., 1909–14), which is his major scholarly achievement. His moving autobiographical *Zapiski sotsialdemokrata* ("Notes of a Social Democrat," 1923) is his literary masterpiece.

BIBLIOGRAPHY: I. Getzler, *Martov, A Political Biography of a Russian Social Democrat* (1967); A.M. Bourguina, *Russian Social Democracy: The Menshevik Movement, A Bibliography* (1968); *Sotsialisticheskii vestnik* (April 10, 1923); *Martov i ego blizkie*, (1959); A.V. Lunacharsky, *Revolutionary Profiles* (1967); O. Blum, *Russische Koepfe* (1923); Z. Shazar, *Or Ishim* (1963).

[Israel Getzler]

MARWICK, LAWRENCE (1909–1981), librarian and Oriental scholar. Born in Poland, Marwick immigrated to the United States in 1929. During World War II he served in the U.S. intelligence corps. From 1948, for more than 30 years, he was head of the Hebraic section of the U.S. Library of Congress. After the war he was the assistant director of the Board of Jewish Education in St. Louis. In 1954–56 he lectured in Arabic and Islamic studies at Dropsie College and from 1961 in modern Hebrew literature and Arabic at New York University. Marwick was a member of the American Academy of Jewish Research and the board of governors of Dropsie College.

He wrote *A Handbook of Diplomatic Hebrew* (1957) and edited Solomon B. Jeroham's *Arabic Commentary on the Book of Psalms, Chapters 42–72* (1956). He also wrote *Biblical and Judaic Acronyms* (1979) and compiled *Diplomatic Hebrew: A Glossary of Current Terminology* (1980).

In 1993 the Library of Congress published *Yiddish American Popular Songs, 1895 to 1950*, a bibliographic catalog of Yiddish music based on Marwick's work. He had compiled entries of more than 3,000 Yiddish songs from the Catalog of Copyright Entries. Focusing on Yiddish-American plays and sheet music that had been deposited in the Library of Congress for copyright registration but were virtually unknown to scholars, Marwick's work provides a historical perspective on the evolution of Yiddish music in America. Musicologist Irene Heskes completed the volume for publication.

[Ruth Beloff (2nd ed.)]

MARX, ADOLF BERNHARD (1795–1866), German musicologist. Born in Halle, he was originally a lawyer, but in 1830 became professor of music at Berlin University, a post that had been intended for but declined by the 21-year-old Felix Mendelssohn. In 1850 he helped to found the school still known as the Stern Conservatory and taught there till 1856. He wrote operas, lieder, a piano sonata, a symphony, and an oratorio *Moses* (1843), but achieved no importance as a composer. His theoretical and critical works, however, retain their value, the most important being a four-volume work on composition, *Die Lehre von der musikalischen Komposition* (1837–47); *Ludwig van Beethoven, Leben und Schaffen* (1859); *Gluck und die Oper* (2 vols., 1863); and a work on the interpretation of Beethoven's piano works (1863). Marx's memoirs, *Erinnerungen aus meinem Leben*, were published in two volumes in 1865, and a collection of his articles appeared in three parts, from 1912 to 1922.

BIBLIOGRAPHY: K.E. Eicke, *Der Streit zwischen Adolph Bernhard Marx und Gottfried Wilhelm Fink um die Kompositionslehre* (1966); Baker, Biog Dict; s.v.; Grove, Dict; MGG; Riemann-Gurlitt.

[Alfred Einstein]

MARX, ALEXANDER (1878–1953), historian, bibliographer and librarian. Born in Elberfeld, Germany, Marx grew up in Koenigsberg (East Prussia). His studies were interrupted by a year in a Prussian artillery regiment where he excelled in horsemanship. Later he studied at the University of Berlin and at the *Rabbiner-Seminar (Berlin), marrying in 1905 Hannah the daughter of D.Z. *Hoffmann, rector of the Seminar. In Berlin, he was influenced by Moritz Steinschneider. In 1903 Marx accepted Solomon Schechter's invitation to teach history at the Jewish Theological Seminary of America and be its librarian.

His mastery of the materials of history and of languages became proverbial. He published articles in many languages and was at home in classical and Semitic languages. Marx contributed monographs and articles to journals on a wide variety of subjects, published two volumes of collected essays (*Studies in Jewish History and Booklore* (1944); *Essays in Jewish Biography* (1947)), and with Max L. *Margolis wrote *A History of the Jewish people* (1927, 1962^2). This pioneering work, stressing economic and social life, organization and legal status, offers the general reader a soundly researched, authoritative, and objective Jewish history in one volume. Marx amassed a private collection of 10,000 books. The JTS library on his arrival in 1903 contained 5,000 volumes and 3 manuscripts. At his death it possessed 165,000 books and over 9,000 Hebrew, Samaritan, Aramaic, and Yiddish manuscripts, comprising the largest Judaica collection in the world. Marx's ability to determine a manuscript's age merely by looking at it was legendary. His annual reports of the library's growth, containing a detailed description of materials acquired, were eagerly awaited by bookmen and scholars.

In 1926 Marx was elected to the Medieval Academy of America; he served as president of the American Academy for Jewish Research (1931–33), president of the Alexander Kohut Memorial Foundation, vice president of the American Jewish Historical Society, and member of the publications committee of the Jewish Publication Society of America.

His sister, Esther, married S.Y. *Agnon.

[Morris Epstein]

His brother MOSES (1885–1973) was also a bibliographer and librarian. Best known for his contributions to the field of Hebrew incunabula and 16th-century Hebrew printing, he was a founder of the Soncino Gesellschaft and a Berlin publisher. He issued, inter alia, bibliophile editions of early works by his brother-in-law S.Y. Agnon, and co-edited with Aron Freimann in the 1920s the *Thesaurus Typographiae Hebraicae Saeculi XV*. In 1926 he went to the United States and joined the staff of the Hebrew Union College Library in Cincinnati. Retiring as head cataloger in 1963, he served briefly as curator of rare books and then settled in Israel. Much of Marx's research in early Jewish printing remained unpublished.

[Stanley F. Chyet]

BIBLIOGRAPHY: *Alexander Marx Jubilee Volume*, 2 vols. (Eng. and Heb., 1950), 481–501, incl. bibl.; A.S. Halkin, in: AJYB, 56 (1955), 580–8; *Festschrift fuer A. Freimann* (1935), 91–96; *Gershon Soncino's Wanderyears in Italy* (1936), index; *Sefer ha-Yovel li-Khevod A. Marx* (1943), 1–10 (introd.).

MARX, KARL (1897–1966), German editor and publisher. Born in Saarlouis, Marx served in the German army in World War I and then worked as a freelance writer for the Havas news agency. He was prominent in politics during the Weimar period, particularly because of his work in the organization of German democratic youth movements. In 1933 he fled Germany and eventually reached England. He returned to Germany in 1946 and was co-founder of a Jewish communal paper for the British zone that later became the *Allgemeine Unabhaengige Juedische Wochenzeitung* (Dusseldorf), which advocated reparations and diplomatic relations with Israel and opposed neo-Nazi manifestations.

BIBLIOGRAPHY: M.W. Gärtner (ed.), *Vom Schicksal Gepraegt. Freundesgabe zum 60 Geburtstag von Karl Marx* (1957), 197; H. Lamm (ed.), *Marx, Karl. Brueckenschlagen. Aufsaetze und Reden aus den Jahren 1946–1962* (1962); L. Marx, "Die Anfaenge der Allgemeinen Juedischen Wochenzeitung," in: M. Brenner, *Nach dem Holocaust. Juden in Deutschland 1945–1950* (1995), 179–85.

[Monika Halbinger (2nd ed.)]

MARX, KARL HEINRICH (1818–1883), German social philosopher and the chief theorist of modern socialism. Marxism became in the 20th century a new creed for hundreds of millions of socialists, often hardening into a dogma, particularly in the communist movement and in the Soviet Bloc, the People's Republic of China, and other communist countries. Born in the Rhineland town of Trier (then West Prussia), Marx was the son of Jewish parents, Heinrich and Henrietta Marx. Heinrich Marx became a successful lawyer, and, when an edict prohibited Jews from being advocates, he converted to Protestantism in 1817. In 1824, when Karl was six years old, his father converted his eight children. Karl Marx was educated at the high school in Trier and studied history and philosophy at the universities of Bonn and Berlin. He was strongly influenced by Hegel's philosophy and joined a radical group known as the Young Hegelians. In 1841 he received his degree of doctor of philosophy at the University of Jena where he presented his dissertation on the "*Differenz der demokritischen und epikureischen Naturphilosophie*." When his connection with the Young Hegelians prevented him from obtaining a teaching position at the University of Bonn, he turned to journalism. He became the editor of the liberal Cologne daily *Rheinische Zeitung* in 1842. In the following year he married Jenny von Westphalen, daughter of a high Prussian official. Soon afterward, the *Rheinische Zeitung* was suppressed and the young couple went to Paris where Marx expected to edit the *Deutsch-Franzoesische Jahrbuecher*. In fact only one issue was brought out (1844).

The young Marx's ideas attracted the attention of older radicals and socialists. Moses *Hess, one of the editors of the *Rheinische Zeitung*, wrote in a letter to the German-Jewish writer Berthold *Auerbach: "Dr. Marx, as my idol is called, is still a very young man; he will give medieval religion and politics their last blow. He combines the deepest earnestness with the most cutting wit. Imagine Rousseau, Voltaire, Holbach, Lessing, Heine, and Hegel united in one person. I say united, not lumped together – and you have Dr. Marx." While evolving from his philosophy as a Young Hegelian to his own concept of man as creating himself by labor, he transmitted in his writings a passionate yearning for a new, free society in which socialist man will transcend the imposed "alienation" from state – controlled society and from his labor and its fruits. An article contributed to the *Deutsch-Franzoesische Jahrbuecher* by Friedrich Engels led to a lifelong friendship between Marx and Engels. Engels, a fellow Rhinelander of socialist and Hegelian leanings, was the son of a wealthy industrialist with factories in Germany and England and was able to support Marx financially for the rest of his life. Marx, who maintained personal friendly contact with Heinrich *Heine, was one of the editors of *Vorwaerts*, a German newspaper published in Paris, which contained sharp attacks against the Prussian government. Its ambassador in Paris protested and Marx was expelled from France.

He went to Brussels where he wrote "*Misère de la philosophie, Response a la philosophie de la misère de M. Proudhon*" (1847), an attack on the Utopian social order advocated by Proudhon. Marx argued that the capitalistic society leads to the strengthening of the proletariat, a class which of necessity must become revolutionary and must overthrow the contemporary social organization based on exploitation. Socialist theorists should not waste their time in describing how society should be ideally built, but rather analyze what is going on in the present world.

In 1845, while in Brussels, Marx was forced to renounce his Prussian citizenship, and thus became "stateless." (Sixteen years later he vainly tried to regain it with the help of Ferdinand *Lassalle. He also applied for British citizenship, but the Home Office rejected his application (1874) on the grounds that "this man was not loyal to his king.") Marx cooperated with the "League of the Just" which became "The League of the Communists" (Bund der Kommunisten) which had its headquarters in London. He attended its second congress in London at the end of 1847 and together with Engels presented a new program for the League called *The Communist Manifesto.* It was published in February 1848 under the title *Manifest der Kommunistischen Partei* and rapidly became the best known work of modern socialism. It began with the words "A specter is haunting Europe – the specter of Communism," and postulated that "the history of all hitherto existing society is the history of class struggles. Freeman and slave, patrician and plebeian, lord and serf, guild-master and journeyman, in a word, oppressor and oppressed, stood in constant opposition to one another, carried on uninterrupted, now hidden, now open fight, a fight that each time ended, either in a revolutionary reconstitution of society at large, or in the common ruin of the contending classes." It ended with the words, "The proletarians have nothing to lose but their chains. They have a world to win. Working men of all countries, unite!" A month after the publication of the Manifesto, Marx was expelled from Belgium and went to Paris. He left for Cologne soon afterward, following the outbreak of revolution in Germany, and became editor of the Cologne daily *Neue Rheinische Zeitung*. When the revolution failed and political reaction set in, he was expelled first from Cologne and then from Paris. He settled in London soon afterward where, in spite of the financial assistance that he received from Engels, he led the hard life of a political exile until his death.

From 1852 to 1861 Marx partly supported himself by being the London correspondent of the *New York Tribune*, commenting on current world affairs. He also drafted a resolution of English workers congratulating Abraham Lincoln on his election as president of the United States. For years he was an almost daily visitor to the British Museum Library, where he studied the great economists, many governmental "Blue Books" on industrial and labor relations, gathering material for his magnum opus "*Das Kapital, Kritik der politischen Oekonomie*" the first volume of which appeared in Hamburg in 1867. (Volumes 2 and 3 were completed and edited by Engels in 1885 and 1893 respectively.) Marx's other writings include *Die Klassenkaempfe in Frankreich 1848–1850* (1850; Eng. translation *The Civil War in France*, 1852); *Der achtzehnte Brumaire des Louis Bonaparte* (1852), and *Zur Kritik der politischen Oekonomie* (1859; Eng. trans. *Critique of Political Economy*, 1904).

Marx was not only a theoretician, he also took active part in the labor and socialist movement, and especially in the International Workingmen's Association (The First International), being a leading member of its General Council. But he lacked the qualities of a popular leader and his followers constituted a small minority of the association.

Marx's System

Marx had an exceptionally powerful mind and a rare capacity for research; his knowledge was encyclopedic. His influence on the modern world has been compared to that of the great religions, or Newton and Darwin. His work is the more difficult to understand as *Das Kapital* remained unfinished, and certain aspects of his doctrine only slightly sketched. His (and Engels') system – Marxism – is also known under the names of "economic" or "materialistic determinism," "dialectical materialism," or "scientific" (as opposed to "utopian") socialism. From Hegel he took the dialectical method, but ultimately applied it in a sense opposite to Hegel's idealist philosophy.

In what Marx calls "the social production" men enter into relations that are indispensable and independent of their will. These "relations of production" correspond to a definite stage of development of the material powers of production. The totality of these "relations of production" constitutes the real basis on which rises a legal and political "superstructure," and to which correspond definite forms of social consciousness. The consciousness of men does not determine their existence, but on the contrary, is determined itself by their social existence. At a certain stage of their development, the "material forces of production" come in conflict with the existing "relations of production" or – what is but a legal expression of the same thing – with "the property relations" within which they had been at work before. From forms of development of the forces of production these relations turn into their fetters. Then comes the period of social revolution. With the change of the economic basis the entire immense superstructure is more or less rapidly transformed. The bourgeois relations of production are the last antagonistic form of the social process of production, the productive forces in the womb of bourgeois society creating the material conditions for the ultimate socialist solution of that antagonism.

Marx's theory of value, which he considered as the very basis of his whole economic theory, was critical of all of past political economics (even of the Ricardian). The value of a commodity, according to Marx, is determined by the amount of labor socially necessary for its production. Of indispensable importance in the system is Marx's concept of "surplus value." The activity of the capitalist employer is represented by the formula M-C-M^1. With money (M), he buys the commodities (C) needed for production, and then sells the finished product for money (M^1). It is evident that M^1 is larger than M, else the whole process would involve no more than gratuitous trouble to the capitalist. Thus the labor power produces more than its value. This surplus value is the evidence and measure of the exploitation of the laborer by his employer.

Marx and the Jews

Marx's father Heinrich, whose original name was Hirschel ha-Levi, was the son of a rabbi and the descendant of talmudic scholars for many generations. Hirschel's brother was chief rabbi of Trier. Heinrich Marx married Henrietta Pressburg, who originated in Hungary and whose father became a rabbi in Nijmegen, Holland. Heinrich received a secular education, obtained a law degree, detached himself from his family and eventually also from his religion. Marx's mother spoke German with a heavy Dutch accent and never learned to write a grammatical letter in German. Intellectually she had little in common with her husband and son.

Karl Marx's attitude to Jews and Judaism has been discussed from different points of view, and therefore it is not surprising that it evolved into what was later described as "self-hatred," too. At the age of 15 he was solemnly confirmed and became deeply attached to Christianity and German culture. Great influence on him was exercised by his future father-in-law, Baron Johann Ludwig von Westphalen, who was a neighbor of his family. But later his relations with other members of his wife's aristocratic family became strained. For them he was a Jew, an atheist, a nonconformist, a man lacking in good manners.

Marx's first essay in the *Deutsch-Franzoesische Jahrbuecher* was entitled *Zur Judenfrage* ("About the Jewish Question"), in which he criticized Bruno Bauer's book on the topic. Bauer had insisted that the Jewish question was essentially a religious one, insoluble unless the Jews gave up their faith and joined the society of the state as atheists or non-Jews. Although Marx favored political emancipation of the Jews, he used violent anti-Jewish language to present his view. Judaism for him was synonymous with the hated bourgeois capitalism. "The chimerical nationality of the Jew is the nationality of the merchant, of the moneyed man generally.…" "What is the secular basis of Judaism? Practical need, self-interest. What is the worldly cult of the Jew? Huckstering. What is his worldly god? Money … Out of its entrails bourgeois society continually creates Jews.… Emancipation from huckstering and from money, and consequently from practical, real Judaism, would be the self-emancipation of our era." Marx's essay is a striking evidence of his complete ignorance of Jewish history and culture, an ignorance surprising in light of his otherwise encyclopedic knowledge. Marx expressed his antagonism to Jews on a number of occasions: in his "Thesis on Feuerbach," in his articles for the *New York Tribune*, and in *Das Kapital*. In his private correspondence there are many derogatory references to Jews, who were for him the symbol of financial power and capitalist mentality, and also to Ferdinand Lassalle to whom he referred in his letters to Engels in typical antisemitic clichés. The only sympathetic account of Jews to emerge from Marx's pen is that which described their life and tribulations in the city of Jerusalem (*New York Tribune*, April, 15, 1854).

Compared with this point of view, which positions Marx in an antisemitic context, new research has emphasized the fact that he did not criticize Jews as Jews but as representatives of capitalism. These studies point to his closeness to other contemporary Jewish intellectuals like Moses Hess in *Ueber das Geldwesen* (1845).

For six years Marx lived in London at 28 Dean Street, the house of a Jewish lace dealer. While on a holiday, he met the Jewish historian Heinrich *Graetz in Carlsbad and sent him his book on "The History of the Commune" as a present. Two years prior to his death the wave of anti-Jewish pogroms occurred in Russia (1881) and the influx of Jewish immigrants into London began. But there is no evidence of Marx's reaction to these events. His beloved daughter Eleanor, however, who acted as his secretary, considered herself Jewish, took interest in her ancestors, and had a warm appreciation for the Jewish workers in the East End of London. (She committed suicide in 1898 after an unhappy marriage to Edward Aveling.)

Marx's Jewish origin became a catalyst of anti-Jewish emotions. Already his rival in the First International, the Russian anarchist Michael *Bakunin did not refrain from anti-Jewish outbursts while attacking Marx. Later it served right-wing propagandists, particularly the fascist and Nazi regimes of the 1930s and 1940s, as a means to spice their anti-socialism with outright violent antisemitism. They used the term "Marxism" as denoting a sinister, worldwide "Jewish" plot against their national interests. In the Soviet Union, where Marxism-Leninism became the obligatory ideology, Marx's Jewish origin was generally mentioned in research works and encyclopedias until the 1940s, but from the later 1940s, when *Stalin's policy became anti-Jewish, it has been studiously concealed.

Collected Editions

The Marx-Engels (later the Marx-Engels-Lenin, and still later Marx-Engels-Lenin-Stalin) Institute in Moscow started in 1927 the publication of an academic edition of the collected works of Marx and Engels. In 1935 the publication was interrupted. There appeared the following: *Marx-Engels, Historisch-kritische Gesamtausgabe; Werke, Schriften, Briefe* first part: *Saemtliche Werke und Schriften mit Ausnahme des "Kapital"* (7 vols., 1927–35); third part: *Der Briefwechsel zwischen Marx und Engels* (4 vols., 1929–31). The volumes published thus far include the writings of Marx and Engels up to 1848 and all the known correspondence between Marx and Engels, 1844–83. The early volumes were edited under the direction of D. Ryazanov. An earlier collection is Franz Mehring's edition, *Aus dem literarischen Nachlass von Karl Marx, Friedrich Engels und Ferdinand Lassalle* (4 vols., 1902). D. Ryazanov edited the *Gesammelte Schriften von Karl Marx und Friedrich Engels 1852 bis 1862* (2nd ed., 1920). For a bibliography of Marx's works, see Ernst Drahn, *Marx-Bibliographie* (2nd ed., 1923). Reliable and good selective bibliographies on Marx, Engels, and cognate subjects are found in Donald Drew Egbert and Stow Persons (eds.), *Socialism and American Life* (vol. 2, 1952, pp. 34ff., and passim). After World War II a new edition of Karl Marx' and Friedrich Engels' works, *Werke* (ed. by the Institute of Marxismus-Leninismus beim ZK der SED), was published in the German Democratic Republic in 39 volumes and one supplementary volume in two parts and two index-volumes from 1956 until 1971 (abbrev. MEW). Another similar new edition of Karl Marx' and Friedrich Engels' works was begun in 1975 as *Gesamtausgabe* (ed. by Institut fuer Marxismus-Leninismus beim ZK der KPdSU and the Institut fuer Marxismus-Leninismus beim ZK der SED), and continued, after the fall of the Communist regime in Russia and East Germany, by the International Marx-Engels Foundation in Amsterdam (Abbrev. MEGA²).

BIBLIOGRAPHY: F. Mehring, *Karl Marx: The Story of His Life* (1936, repr. 1951), incl. bibl.; K. Korsch, *Karl Marx* (Eng., 1963), incl. bibl.; L. Schwarzschild, *The Red Prussian: The Life and Legend of Karl Marx* (1948); I. Berlin, *Karl Marx: His Life and Environment* (1963³), incl. bibl.; C. Tsuzuki, *The Life of Eleanor Marx* (1967); J. Lachs, *Marxist Philosophy: A Bibliographical Guide* (1967); R. Payne, *Marx: A Biography* (1968), incl. bibl.; M. Rubel, in: IESS, 10 (1968), 34–40 incl. bibl.. **ADD. BIBLIOGRAPHY:** Th. Bottomore (ed.), *A Dictionary of Marxist Thought* (1991); E. Balibar, *The Philosophy of Marx* (1995); M. Heinrich, *Die Wissenschaft vom Wert. Die Marxsche Kritik der politischen Ökonomie zwischen wissenschaftlicher Revolution und klassischer Tradition* (new edition, 1999); J. Derrida, *Marx Gespenster* (2004). ON MARX AND THE JEWISH QUESTION: G. Mayer, *Der Jude in Karl Marx* [1918], in: idem, *Aus der Welt des Sozialismus. Kleine historische Aufsätze* (1927); E. Silberner, *Ha-Sozyalizm ha-Ma'aravi u-She'elat ha-Yehudim*, pt. 2 (1955), 133–64, 448–51, includes detailed bibliography; idem, in: HJ, 9 no. 1 (1949), 3–52. **ADD. BIBLIOGRAPHY:** idem, *Sozialisten zur Judenfrage. Ein Beitrag zur Geschichte des Sozialismus vom Anfang des 19. Jahrhunderts bis 1914* (1962); H. Hirsch, "The Ugly Marx: Analysis of an 'Outspoken Anti-semite,'" in: *The Philosophical Forum*, 3:2–4 (1978), 150–162; J. Carlebach, *Karl Marx and the Radical Critique of Judaism* (1978); Z. Rosen, *Moses Hess und Karl Marx. Ein Beitrag zur Entstehung der Marxschen Theorie* (1983); J. Peled, "From Theology to Sociology. Bruno Bauer and Karl Marx on the Question of Jewish Emancipation," in: *History of Political Thought*, 13:3 (1992), 463–85; D. Leopold, "The Hegelian Antisemitism of Bruno Bauer," in: *History of European Ideas*, 25 (1999), 179–206; M. Tomba, "La questione ebraica: il problema dell'universalismo politico," in: M. Tomba (ed.), *B. Bauer und K. Marx, La questione ebraica* (2004), 9–45.

[Schneier Zalman Levenberg / Lars Lambrecht (2nd ed.)]

MARX BROTHERS, U.S. theatrical comedy team. Zany and irreverent, their wild and impromptu humor appealed to lowbrows and intellectuals alike. Originally, there were five Marx Brothers. All were part of a vaudeville act called "Six Musical Mascots" (their mother, Minnie, a sister of the vaudeville actor Al *Shean, was the sixth). The brothers, all born in New York, were CHICO (LEONARD, 1891–1961), HARPO (ADOLPH, later ARTHUR, 1893–1964), GUMMO (MILTON, 1894–1977), GROUCHO (JULIUS, 1895–1977), and ZEPPO (HERBERT, 1901–1979). When their mother left the act, they became "The Nightingales" and played in vaudeville as singers and comedians until they reached the Palace Theater in New York in 1918. They made their Broadway debut in 1924 in a revue called *I'll Say She Is*. By that time, the brothers had developed a distinct comic style. CHICO donned a pointed hat over a deadpan face and affected an Italian accent. He was also an accomplished piano player, and he frequently broke the comedy with a turn at the keyboard. HARPO, with a battered hat over a frizzled wig of blond curls, never spoke during the act. He used two means to communicate – a bulb horn on stage and a romantic harp. He played the harp at concerts as well as in films. GROUCHO, wearing a swallowtail coat, chewing a long cigar and wearing a large black moustache, was master of the insult. After the brothers' film career had ended, Groucho confirmed his reputation as a wit as the master of ceremonies on a TV weekly quiz show. ZEPPO, the straight man of the team in the movies, left the act in the early 1930s, and became a successful theatrical agent. GUMMO, who was in the act only briefly, also became a successful agent. Their succession of stage and film comedies – such as *The Cocoanuts* (1929); *Animal Crackers* (1930); *Horsefeathers* (1932); *Duck Soup* (1933); *A Night at the Opera* (1935); and *A Night in Casablanca* (1946) – were considered cinema classics which continued to attract audiences on their many replays. Harpo's autobiography, *Harpo Speaks*, appeared in 1961. Groucho wrote *Groucho and Me* (1959), an autobiography, and *Memoirs of a Mangy Lover* (1963). His prolific and unconventional correspondence was published as *The Groucho Letters* in 1967. The Library of Congress asked him for the letters and papers, which included the manuscripts of his books. In one celebrated letter, he wrote Gov. William Scranton of Pennsylvania in 1964 to tell him he had heard him mispronounce a Yiddish term. "If you are going to campaign in Jewish neighborhoods," Groucho counseled, "rhyme mish-mash with slosh."

The comedy world of Groucho, Chico, and Harpo was

wildly chaotic, grounded in slapstick farce, lowbrow vaudeville corn, free-spirited anarchy, and assaults on the myths and virtues of middle-class America. Groucho was larger and more antic than life. His humor was based on the improbable, the unexpected, the outrageous. *Animal Crackers* gave Groucho his most celebrated character, Capt. Jeffrey T. Spaulding, a bumbling African explorer ("My name is Captain Spaulding, the African explorer," Groucho sang, "did someone call me schnorrer?"). Groucho was a master of the ad lib and refused to follow the scripts of his plays and movies, although some of them were turned out by such masters of comedy as George S. *Kaufman and S.J. *Perelman. Groucho supplemented his meager formal education by reading omnivorously. For some years he carried on a correspondence with the poet T.S. Eliot, and in 1965 he was invited to speak at a memorial for Eliot. Typically, he used the occasion to say something outrageous: "Apparently Mr. Eliot was a great admirer of mine – and I don't blame him."

BIBLIOGRAPHY: A. Eyles, *The Marx Brothers* (1966); K.S. Crichton, *The Marx Brothers* (1951); O. Levant, *A Smattering of Ignorance* (1940, 1959[2]), on Harpo Marx.

[Stewart Kampel (2nd ed.)]

MARYAN (pseudonym of **Pinchas Burstein**; 1927–1977), U.S. painter. Born in Nowy-Sacz, Galicia, Poland, the artist was deported at the age of 12 to concentration camps, including Auschwitz. All of his family perished in the camps. Maryan survived but with one leg amputated. He spent three years in German displaced persons camps, working as a stage designer for detainee-organized Jewish drama groups. In 1948 he immigrated to Israel, studying art for a short period at the New Bezalel School of Art, Jerusalem. In 1950, he traveled to Paris and attended the École des Beaux-Arts, where he studied lithography. In Paris, he was briefly affiliated with the CoBra group, as well as the artists of the École de Paris. Paris also exposed Maryan to the influence of such artists as Pierre Soulages, Victor Brauner, and Jean Dubuffet. Maryan relocated to New York in 1962, where he became a successful artist and illustrator. He attained American citizenship in 1969, further changing his name from Maryan to Maryan S. Maryan. The artist's unsettling compositions, what he termed "truth-paintings," depict traumatized, ravaged, and distorted figures posed frontally in a shallow space, references in part to Maryan's recollections of the Holocaust. In the 1950s, Maryan composed Jewish figures with prayer shawls and phylacteries. Later, these religious adornments are abstracted, contributing to the striped bloated appendages characteristic of so much of Maryan's mature compositions; they also recall the striped garb of concentration camp prisoners. Many of Maryan's figures are bound, twisted, and penetrated, with mouths agape, genitals sometimes visible in a show of both exhibitionism and terrible vulnerability. His figures exude all manner of bodily fluids from every orifice, often in large, stylized drops. Beginning in the 1960s, Maryan titled his biomorphic figures "Personages" in reference to their theatrical aspects. Many of these compositions reference the Holocaust directly: for example, his 1962 painting *Personage* depicts a mocking Nazi stormtrooper tinted a garish yellow. This figure mockingly challenges the viewer at some ominous game, suggested by the blood-red chess pieces positioned at the end of a tilting table. The artist continued the motif of the Nazi soldier in many works in 1962–63, repeating an iconography of hat, armband, and repugnant facial features. Maryan's "Personages" often bear some sort of insignia or suggestions of military authority. However, the artist unmoors these singular, isolated figures from any narrative content, mocking their authority, and depicting them as impotent and ridiculous. Maryan subverts the distinction between torturer and sufferer, master and servant, self and other, often combining these players into a single figure. Maryan made a film in 1975 entitled *Ecce Homo*. In addition to stock images of famous persons ranging from Pope Pius XII to Moshe Dayan and Jesus, the film featured a series of Maryan's drawings, and the artist himself in various costumes relating his memories of the concentration camps. He illustrated Kafka's *The Trial* in a 1953 edition, *Golem* (1959), and *La Ménagerie Humaine* (1961). In 1956, the French government commissioned him to design a tapestry for the Monument to the Unknown Jewish Martyr in Paris. His work influenced Philip Guston and Peter Saul. From 1949, Maryan had numerous solo shows in such cities as Jerusalem, Paris, Amsterdam, Munich, New York, and Chicago. His art is represented in museums around the world, including the Art Institute of Chicago; the Musée national d'Art Moderne, Paris; Museum Moderner Kunst Stiftung Ludwig Vien, Vienna; the Museum of Modern Art, New York; the National Museum of Modern Art, Washington, D.C.; the Nationalgalerie, Staatliche Museen, Berlin; and the Tel Aviv Museum of Art.

BIBLIOGRAPHY: Z. Amishai-Maisels, *Depiction and Interpretation: The Influence of the Holocaust on the Visual Arts* (1993); *Maryan (1927–1977): Personnages, from the Napoleon Series*, Nov. 14–Dec. 22, 1990, Claude Bernard Gallery (1990); J.M. Wasilik, *Maryan: Behold a Man and His Work* (1996).

[Nancy Buchwald (2nd ed.)]

MARYLAND, state on the E. coast of the U.S., one of the 13 original states. A one-crop tobacco economy and the existence of few major towns caused Jews, with rare exceptions, to avoid the colony during the first century and half after its establishment in 1634. David Fereira, a Jewish tobacco trader from New Amsterdam, appeared in Maryland as early as 1657 and later the same year colonial records mention a Jewish physician, Jacob Lumbrozo, who was also engaged in trade. Lumbrozo, a colorful figure who was often in conflict with his neighbors, was arrested in 1658 for blasphemy after offending Christians colonists during a conversation about religion. He was released before trial, however, due to the proclamation of a general amnesty. After the 1740s, with the growth of commerce in the colony, individual Jews appeared in Annapolis, Fredericktown (now Frederick), and a

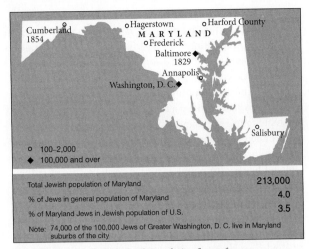

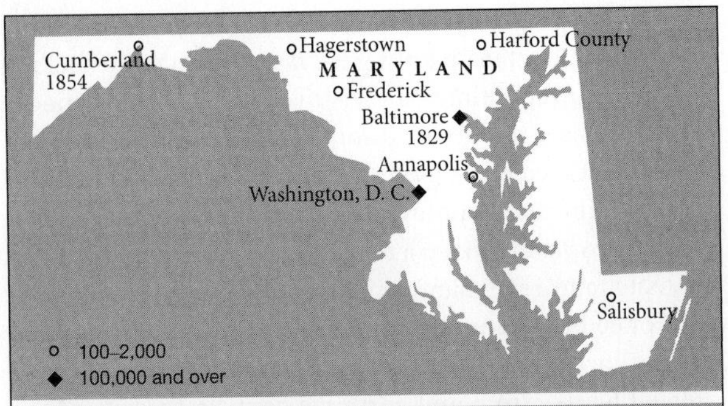

Total Jewish population of Maryland	213,000
% of Jews in general population of Maryland	4.0
% of Maryland Jews in Jewish population of U.S.	3.5

Note: 74,000 of the 100,000 Jews of Greater Washington, D. C. live in Maryland suburbs of the city

Jewish communities of Maryland. Population figures for 2001.

few other towns, but a Jewish community with supporting institutions did not emerge until the period of the American Revolution, when Baltimore became one of the region's leading ports and attracted several Jewish families. By 1825, there were about 150 Jews in the new state. Although Baltimore Jews like Solomon *Etting and Jacob *I. Cohen, Jr., achieved a degree of prominence in the larger, non-Jewish community, the state constitution barred them from holding public office unless they would submit to a Christian oath. This requirement was finally removed with the passage of the 1826 "Jew Bill," which was championed by the non-Jewish legislator Thomas Kennedy.

Between 1830 and 1870 over 10,000 Jews, primarily from Germany and other areas of Central Europe, settled in the state. Eastern European Jews began to trickle into Maryland during the 1850s and arrived in large numbers from the 1880s. While the vast majority of Jewish immigrants were drawn to Baltimore, Jews also settled in smaller towns as peddlers and merchants. In 1853, the first congregation outside Baltimore was established in Cumberland, an important trading and transportation center in the western part of the state. By the time mass immigration ended in the mid-1920s, there also existed congregations in Frederick, Hagerstown, Annapolis, Frostburg, Brunswick, and Salisbury. Statewide, the Jewish population reached about 40,000 in 1900 and grew to 65,000 by the end of the immigrant period.

In the years following World War II, Jews entered more fully into the life of the general community and were among the state's top officeholders. Marvin *Mandel, a Baltimore native, served as governor from 1969 to 1979. This period was one of great demographic change, with more than 50,000 Jews from Washington, D.C., settling in the nearby Maryland suburbs of Montgomery and Prince Georges counties. By 1998, this region was home to 104,500 Jews and had come to rival Baltimore and its surroundings (Jewish population 94,500) as the state's largest Jewish population center. Jews also increasingly established themselves in areas outside the Washington suburbs and Baltimore, with 10,000 residing in Howard County, almost 2,000 in Annapolis, and more than 1,000 in Frederick and in Harford County. Overall, the estimated Jewish population of Maryland in 2001 was 213,000 out of a total of 5,311,000.

BIBLIOGRAPHY: E.L. Goldstein, *Traders and Transports: The Jews of Colonial Maryland* (1993); K. Falk and A. Decter, eds., *We Call This Place Home: Jews in Maryland's Small Towns* (2002); I.M. Fein, *The Making of an American Jewish Community: The History of Baltimore Jewry from 1773 to 1920* (1971).

[Eric L. Goldstein (2nd ed.)]

MARZOUK, MOSHE (1926–1955), *Cairo-born *Karaite Jew of Tunisian origin who was tried by a military court in Cairo on charges of spying for Israel and was executed on Jan. 31, 1955. In 1954 three Jews were arrested in *Egypt and accused of setting fire to the USIS Library in *Alexandria. Their arrest led to the discovery of a spy ring in Egypt and the imprisonment of ten other Jews, among whom were Marzouk and Samuel Azaar. Two of the prisoners managed to escape and the others were brought to trial on Dec. 10, 1954. According to the indictment, the accused had gathered information for Israel, carried out acts of sabotage, and spread false reports in Egypt designed to create public unrest. During the course of the trial, Max Bennet – described as the leader of the ring – committed suicide, after which Marzouk became the chief suspect. It was alleged that he had organized the Cairo group, had been trained in Israel, and had arranged wireless transmissions to Israel.

During his student days at the Cairo Medical School, Marzouk had become convinced that the future of all Egyptian Jews lay in their migration to Ereẓ Israel. He dedicated his life to the realization of his Zionist ideals and, while working as a doctor at the Jewish Hospital, organized the self-defense of the Cairo Jewish Quarter, helped to send young Jews to Israel, and, although he himself could have left, stayed at his post and worked for Israel.

SAMUEL AZAAR (1929–1955), native of Alexandria of Turkish parentage, had been active in Zionist youth movements at an early age. A youth of great promise, he was awarded a scholarship that enabled him to study electronic engineering. Like Marzouk, he chose to stay in Egypt and carry out his mission. During the trial he was described as the head of the Alexandria group and was accused of operating an underground workshop to manufacture sabotage devices.

The trial of the ten defendants came to an end on Jan. 27, 1955. Two were acquitted, six were sentenced to prison terms ranging from five years to life, and Marzouk and Azaar were sentenced to death. In Israel, "Kedoshei Kahir" (the Martyrs of Cairo) as they came to be known were honored and commemorated in various ways.

BIBLIOGRAPHY: H.M. Sachar, *From the Ends of the Earth: The Peoples of Israel* (1964), 328–66.

[Mordechai Shalev]

MASADA (Heb. מְצָדָה, *Meẓadah*), Herod's palatial fortress and the last stronghold during the Jewish War against Rome (66–73/74 C.E.).

Geography

Masada is situated on an isolated rock plateau on the eastern fringe of the Judean Desert near the western shores of the Dead Sea, south of En Gedi. It is a mountain bloc that rose and was detached from the fault escarpment, surrounded at its base by two wadis. The rhomboid shaped rock is approximately 1,950 ft. (600 m.) long and approximately 1,000 ft. (300 m.) wide in its center. The plateau at its top rises 1,475 ft. (450 m.) above the Dead Sea level. The site was close to two ancient routes: one that crossed the center of the Judean Desert leading to southern Moab and one that connected Edom, Moab, and the Arava Valley with En Gedi and Jerusalem. The remote location and natural defenses of Masada made it an exceptional fortified site during the Second Temple period. The natural approaches are steep and arduous and include the "snake path" mentioned by Josephus on the east, and approaches on the cliff's northern and southern sides.

The name Masada appears in Flavius Josephus' writings in Greek transcription. It derives from the Hebrew and Aramaic word *meẓad* ("stronghold"). Masada is mentioned in a divorce deed and an *ostracon* (inscribed pottery sherd) that were uncovered in the Murabbaʿat caves.

Sources

The only significant source of information about Masada is the writings of Flavius *Josephus (Ant., 14, 15; Wars, 1, 2, 4, 7). Josephus was the commander of Galilee during the First Jewish Revolt, who later surrendered to the Romans at *Jotapata (Yodfat). At the time of Masada's siege he was in Rome, where he devoted himself to chronicling the history of the Jews and thereafter the occurrences of the revolt. He presumably based his narration upon the field commentaries of the Roman commanders that were accessible to him. Masada is also briefly mentioned by Strabo (*Geography* 16, 2:44) and Pliny the Elder (*Natural History* 5:17, 73), which was the source for Solinus (third century C.E.?) and Martianus Capella (c. 400 C.E.).

History

Josephus provides us with two versions regarding the identity of the founders of the fortress at Masada. In one passage he attributes the first construction to "ancient kings" (Wars, 4:399). According to another passage, Masada was first fortified by "Jonathan the High Priest" (Wars, 7:285). Scholars disagree as to the identity of this Jonathan – whether he was referring to the brother of Judah Maccabee (mid-second century B.C.E.) or Alexander *Yannai (103–76 B.C.E.), who was also called Jonathan.

During an uprising against the house of Antipater, Masada came under the rule of Felix in 42 B.C.E. It was *Herod who soon seized back control of the fortress (Ant., 14:296; Wars, 1:236–38).

In 40 B.C.E. Herod fled from Jerusalem to Masada with his family to escape from Mattathias Antigonus, who had been made king by the Parthians. He left his family, his brother Joseph, and 800 men there to defend it against a siege by Antigonus (Ant., 14:361–2; Wars, 1:264, 267). According to Josephus the defenders almost died of thirst during the siege but were saved when a sudden rainstorm filled the creeks and pits on the summit of the rock. Herod, returning from a trip to Rome, raised the siege and carried his family off to safety (Ant., 14:390–91, 396, 400; Wars, 1:286–87, 292–94). As a result: "Herod furnished this fortress as a refuge for himself, suspecting a twofold danger: peril on the one hand from the Jewish people, lest they should depose him and restore their former dynasty to power; the greater and more serious from Cleopatra, queen of Egypt" (Wars, 7:300). During his reign, Herod transformed Masada into a palatial fortress, providing it with luxurious palaces, bathhouses, well-stocked storerooms, cisterns, all encircled with a casemate wall.

Following the death of Herod in 4 B.C.E. the site was in the boundaries of Herod Archelaus' kingdom. After his removal from power by the Romans and the annexations of Judea to the Roman Empire in 6 C.E. it can be assumed that a Roman garrison was probably stationed there until the outbreak of the First Jewish Revolt in 66 C.E. Masada was captured "by stratagem" in that year by a band of *sicarii* under the command of *Menahem son of Judah (Wars, 2:408, 433). This group was named after a curved dagger, the *sica*, which they carried. After Menahem was murdered in Jerusalem, his nephew, *Eleazar ben Jair, fled Jerusalem to Masada and became the commander of the rebel community on the mountain until its fall in 73/74 C.E. Masada became a place of refuge for a heterogeneous population, apparently including *Sicarii*, Essenes, and Samaritans. *Simeon bar Giora also stayed there for a time. The last of the rebels fled to Masada from Jerusalem in 70 C.E. In 73/74 C.E. the Roman governor, Flavius Silva, marched against Masada. After a siege that lasted a few months, the Romans breached the wall of the fortress and set ablaze the inner wood and soil wall. When the hope of the rebels dwindled, Josephus put in Eleazar ben Jair's mouth two speeches in which he persuaded his followers to take their own life rather than fall into the hands of the Romans. Josephus narrated these occurrences that ended in the mass suicide of 960 men, women, and children and the burning of the buildings and stores of food. The gloomy end of Masada was told by two women who together with five children survived by hiding in one of the cisterns. After Masada's conquest, Silva left a garrison there.

The Church Fathers note that during the Byzantine period a monastery was established in a place named "Marda," which some scholars identify with Masada (Cyril of Scythopolis, *Vita Euthymii* 11; Johannnes Moschus, *Pratum Spirituale* 158).

History of Exploration

Masada was identified for the first time in 1838 by the Americans E. Robinson and E. Smith who viewed the rock which the

Arabs called al-Sabba through a telescope from En Gedi. The site was first visited in 1842 by the American missionary S.W. Wolcott and the British painter Tipping and next by members of an American naval expedition in 1848. Ten years later, F. de Saulcy drew the first plan of Masada. C. Warren in 1867 heading the "Survey of Western Palestine" climbed Masada from the east along the "snake path" and in 1875, C.R. Conder, on behalf of the survey, drew plans which were the most accurate up to that time. Sandel discovered the water system in 1905. The first detailed study of the Roman camps was made by A.V. Domaszewski and R.E. Bruennow in 1909. Others followed in the beginning of the 20th century, foremost among them, the German A. Schulten, who surveyed Masada for a month in 1932. Aerial photographs were the basis for the studies of C. Hawks (1929) and I.A. Richmond (1962).

The major impetus for the extensive excavations of the site was provided by Israeli scholars, especially S. Guttman, who correctly traced the serpentine twistings of the "snake path" and with A. Alon studied Herod's water system (1953). He also excavated and restored the walls of one of the Roman camps (Camp A). Large-scale Israeli surveys were conducted in 1955 (headed by M. Avi-Yonah, N. Avigad, Y. Aharoni, and S. Guttman) and again in 1956 (headed by Y. Aharoni and S. Guttman) which established the general outline of the buildings and prepared new plans of the rock. Masada was mainly excavated between 1963 and 1965 by Y. Yadin with a large staff of archaeologists and thousands of volunteers from all parts of the world. Large percentages of the built-up area of the mountain were uncovered as well as probes in Camp F, and restoration of the buildings was carried out at the site simultaneously. A small-scale excavation was conducted by E. Netzer in 1989. Excavations were resumed on top of Masada in 1995 under the direction of E. Netzer and G. Stiebel on behalf of the Hebrew University of Jerusalem. Several seasons were conducted between 1995 and 2000, focusing on the Northern Palace complex, the northwestern sector of the site, the Roman breach, the eastern section of the casemate wall, the Byzantine church, and water installations throughout the mountain. In 1995, a short season was conducted in Camp F and the Roman ramp under the direction of G. Forester, B. Arubas, H. Goldfus, and J. Magness.

Archaeology

EARLY PERIODS. As in many Judean Desert sites, evidence of a Chalcolithic occupation (mid-fifth–fourth millennium B.C.E.) including botanical remains, textiles, mats, and pottery sherds were found in a small cave on the lower part of the southern cliff. Few sherds, but no architectural remains, were uncovered on the plateau from the Iron Age II (tenth–seventh centuries B.C.E.).

The nature of the Hellenistic presence at Masada is still enigmatic. None of the buildings uncovered to date may be attributed to the pre-Herodian era but possibly two cisterns, located in the eastern sector and the southeast cliff. In addition, merely one oil lamp derives from that period of time. However, Josephus' testimony concerning the identity of the founders of Masada need not necessarily be taken as contradictory, for it may be narrating sequential occurrences, as indeed emerges from the numismatic finds. The dozen Ptolemaic coins from the third century B.C.E., mainly of Ptolemy II, appear to agree with the reference to "ancient kings" (Wars, 4:399) as the original builders, while the allusion to "Jonathan the High Priest" (Wars, 7:285), clearly a Hasmonean ruler, is supported by the discovery of four coins of John *Hyrcanus I (130–104 B.C.E.) and dozens of Alexander Yannai's coins (103–76 B.C.E.).

HERODIAN PERIOD. Two square enclosures, facing the outlet of the "snake pass," were noticed in aerial photographs. Although claimed to represent the camp of the pioneer force of the Roman army during the siege of 73/74 C.E., the larger enclosure of the two clearly antedates Camp C and appears to reflect indeed a chronological rather than technical stage. Being a camp of an earlier episode it was seemingly erected during the siege that Mattathias Antigonus laid against Herod's family and supporters in 40 B.C.E.

The major construction period of Masada was under King Herod's rule. Netzer demonstrated that the works were carried out in three chronological phases. During the first were built three small palaces, the core of the Western Palace, a building in the upper terrace of the Northern Palace, and soldier barracks, all exhibiting a structure with a central courtyard, as well as three dovecotes (*colombaria*). The Northern Palace complex, consisting of the public storerooms, the large bathhouse, and Northern Palace, the expansion of the Western Palace, and the water system were seemingly erected during the second phase, while the main feature to be constructed in the third phase was a casemate wall (double wall divided into rooms) that enclosed the perimeter of the plateau. The stone for the constructions derives from two sources: the walls were built from the local dolomite stone which was cut in quarries on top of the mountain and in the huge water cisterns, whereas the more elaborate architectonic features, such as the pillar drums, capitols, and architrave's parts, were shaped from non-local softer stone. A large group of iron chisels from that period was uncovered at the site. The mason markings, of Hebrew letters, visible on all pillar drums, indicate the origin of the stone cutters.

The Northern Palace Complex. Herod constructed the most important buildings in the northern part of Masada – the highest point of the rock ("acropolis"). The Northern Palace was serviced by public storerooms, administrative buildings, and large bathhouse.

The main entrance to the Northern Palace complex was through its south part, near Building no. VIII, which seemingly served as the "commandant's residence." The excavations of Netzer and Stiebel revealed the varied features of the main entrance, the dominant building of which is a large hall that occupies the eastern part of the courtyard. It was originally decorated with stucco reliefs and apparently served as a reception hall for Masada's visitors. Together with the "commandant's headquarters," west of the courtyard, this hall formed a lavish entrance, that made it possible to monitor the incoming goods and visitors.

Northern Palace. Josephus gives a detailed account of a royal palace situated beneath the walls of the fortress. This palace enjoyed improved climate conditions and commanded a magnificent view of the surroundings as far as En Gedi. It was built in three tiers, the upper containing the living quarters whereas the lower ones were designed for pleasure. The upper terrace is an extension of the narrow tip of the summit and contains a large semicircular balcony bounded by a double wall. A four-room building south of it with two rooms on each side of a court was apparently Herod's private abode. It is decorated by a typical Roman-style black and white mosaic floor in geometric designs. The walls and ceilings were decorated with frescoes. To the south a great white plastered wall separated the palace from the rest of Masada and left only a narrow passageway at its eastern end for a staircase. Columns had probably stood on the facade of the building and around the semicircular balcony. G. Forester showed that the plan of the upper terrace was directly influenced by villa Farnesina in Rome, which is attributed to Marcus Agrippa, Herod's benefactor and close friend in Rome. Descent to the lower tiers was through a flight of stairs, parts of which survived in the middle and lower terraces. The middle terrace, approximately 65 ft. (20 m.) beneath the upper one, contained two concentric circular walls which served as a platform for a columned building. A staircase on the west led to the upper level and on the east stood a large room with traces of frescoes; between them was a roofed colonnade, seemingly a library. This terrace was apparently designed for relaxation and a leisurely enjoyment of the view. The bottom terrace, approximately 50 ft. (15 m.) below the middle one, tapers to a narrow point; great supporting walls were built to form a raised, nearly square platform which was surrounded by low walls forming porticoes. Both the inner and exterior walls contained columns composed of sandstone drums plastered and fluted to resemble large monolithic columns. Frescoes on the lower part of the walls were painted to imitate stone and marble paneling. In the eastern corner of the terrace was a small bathhouse built in Roman style.

One of the difficult aspects in the study of the past is to determine the exact time of transition. Herod represents such a case, for in his time Roman trends diffused into the dominant Hellenistic style. Hence, the upper terrace of the Northern Palace was built in Roman style, while the middle terrace is completely Hellenistic in nature. The lower terrace was furnished with a Roman-style small bathhouse.

Bathhouse. South of the Northern Palace was a large bathhouse with four rooms and a court built in traditional Roman style. The bather would enter the dressing room (*apodyterium*), from which one could have enjoyed the tepid room (*tepidarium*), hot room (*caldarium*), and cold room-stepped pool (*frigidarium*).

The floors of all rooms, except the last, were decorated by mosaic floors which were later replaced by pink and black triangular tiles (*opus sectile*), while the walls were decorated by frescoes. A Greek inscription praising the tyche was found on the walls of the dressing room. This room underwent changes during the revolt when an immersion pool and a bench made from dismantled pillar drums were constructed there. The largest room, the hot room, was heated through a *hypocaust* system beneath it and its floor stood on about 200 tiny columns, mostly made of bricks. A furnace drove hot air which heated the floor and the double walls that were furnished with clay pipes. Hot water flowed into a bathtub and quartz fountain set in the room's niches.

The bathhouse was used by the rebels and a charcoal graffiti of the *Legio x Fretensis* indicates the presence of the conquering Roman soldiers.

Storerooms. Under the northeastern corner of the synagogue building, Netzer and Stiebel uncovered, in 1995, a storage cave from the early days of King Herod's reign. Sixteen storage jars were found *in situ*, alongside wine amphoras. The cave appears to antedate the construction of the large storeroom complex. It was presumably destroyed in the severe earthquake of 31 B.C.E., the damage of which is discernible at Qumran.

During the second construction phase public storerooms were built east and south of the bathhouse. The long and narrow rooms were designed to hold food, liquids, and weapons: "For here had been stored a mass of corn, amply sufficient to last for years, abundance of wine and oil, besides every variety of pulse and piles of dates" (Wars, 7:296). The discerning taste was evident in the contents of the storerooms, which included a uniquely large number of inscription-bearing vessels (*tituli picti*). Among the inscribed jars was a group noting a shipment of wine to Herod, King of Judea, in 19 B.C.E. (the year of the consul C. Sentius Saturninus), from southern Italy by a supplier named Lucius Lanius. Indeed, Josephus mentions that Herod had a special wine servant. In a manner appropriate to a gourmet like Herod, one inscribed vessel was found to exhibit the name of the celebrated fish sauce *garum* – a product of southern Spain. Fish bones from this delicacy were found adhering to the inner face of this vessel. Following the Roman custom, the king ended his banquets with apples imported from Cumae, Italy.

It seems that valuable goods, like jars containing balsam, or weapons and raw materials sufficient to equip 10,000 warriors, were stored in a group of three storerooms that is situated in the southwest wing of the Northern Palace complex. The entrance to these storerooms was monitored by a guard room. Weapons from Herod's time were found at Masada, most notably a sheathed *gladius Hispaniensis* (Spanish sword) and several groups of dozens of spare armor scales.

Near these storerooms was located the service entrance to the Northern complex. Interestingly, the expedition of Netzer and Stiebel excavated courtyard 174, under the floor of which two early phases corresponding to the first and second Herodian building phases were uncovered. It is the first time that stratified material in sealed archaeological contexts from Herod's time was found.

Western Palace. On the western side of Masada Herod erected the Western Palace complex. Covering an area of nearly 37,500 sq. ft. (4,000 sq. m.) it is the largest building found on the site. Yadin attributed ceremonial functions to this Palace, a notion rejected by Netzer, who assigned this function to the Northern Palace. The Western Palace was a self-sufficient unit and consisted of four wings: official wing ("the core"), storeroom wing, service wing, and administrative wing.

The official wing was built around a large central court with a large reception hall leading into a room interpreted by Yadin as the throne room. This notion is based on four depressions in the plastered floor in which the legs of the canopied throne may have been set. In the hall was a magnificent, richly colored mosaic pavement with circles and border ornaments of plant and geometric designs. Recently a charcoal "blueprint" of this mosaic was found on a nearby plastered wall. This wing also contained service rooms as well as bathrooms with tubs, a steeped cold water pool, and other installations, all paved with mosaics. During the period of the revolt, parts of the Palace were clearly used for public functions by the rebels' community, such as a storeroom, bakery, and smithies (see below).

Water System. One of the most impressive engineering projects at Masada is the water system Herod constructed to ensure an adequate supply of water. The system included dams that diverted floodwater of the two wadis, west of Masada, into two plastered channels that fed a dozen large cisterns. The cisterns were hewn on two parallel levels into the rocky slope. Each cistern had a capacity of up to 140,000 cu. ft. (4,000 cu. m.) and together could hold about 1,400,000 cu. ft. (40,000 cu. m.). The cisterns are mostly square in shape and have two openings, one leading from the aqueduct and a second, higher one connected with an inner staircase for drawing out water. Pack animals then bore the water up to the cisterns on the mountaintop. The pass leading from the upper level of the cisterns ended in a gate just south of the Northern Palace ("water gate"). Another pass led from the lower level to the "snake pass."

Casemate Wall. Towards the end of his reign, Herod enclosed the entire summit of Masada, except for the northern tip, with a casemate wall (a double wall with the inner space divided into rooms). Its circumference measures about 1,530 yards (1,400 m.) which corresponds exactly with the 7 *stadia* of Josephus' description. About 70 rooms, 30 towers, and four gates were found in the wall. The gates consisted of a square room with two entrances, benches along the walls, stone slab pavements, and "masonry-style" stucco decoration. They include the "snake path" gate in the northeast; the western gate in the middle of the western wall, the location in which the Byzantine gate was later erected; the southern ("cistern") gate which led to a group of cisterns; and the northern ("water") gate near the bathhouse which served mainly for bringing water from the upper row of cisterns and was probably also the gate for the northern part of Masada.

From the period when the Roman garrison was stationed at Masada between the time of Herod and the Jewish War hundreds of coins were found from the reigns of Herod Archelaus, Agrippa I, and all Roman procurators.

Period of the Revolt (66–73/74 C.E.)

The site of Masada appears to be a microcosm of the material culture of Second Temple Judea and even beyond. The many finds from this brief eight/seven-year period throw much light on the character of the rebels, their way of life at Masada, and the end of the Jewish War. The rebels made use of the casemate wall's rooms for dwelling. They divided the rooms into small units and erected clusters of shacks constructed of mud and small stones adjoining the wall and other buildings. Cooking stoves and niches for the cupboards were built into the wall. In rooms which had not been burned remains of their daily life were strewn on the floors: clothing, leather, baskets, glass, stone and bronze objects, etc. Piles of charcoal with remnants of personal belongings indicate that they had collected all their possessions at the end and had set fire to them. Hundreds of coins and several scroll fragments were found in the rooms. The towers on the wall seemingly served mainly as public rooms or workshops. One of the workshops in the western casemate wall (L. 1276) was identified as a tannery. However, ecological considerations and the nature of the plastered installations and cross beams discovered there indicate this tower had been transformed into a laundry.

The Herodian palaces were not used for dwellings but rather functioned as command posts, public buildings, etc. Their decorative architectural parts were dismantled for building materials and furniture: floors, roofs, columns, tables, etc. A prominent place was given to the Western Palace. The biggest storeroom at Masada (L. 502) was used for storing food. When excavated, lines of vessels were found, each of which was marked by an *ostracon* declaring the purity or impurity of the line. Next to this storeroom was located the central bakery of Masada (L. 493). A huge oven (*furnus*, פורנא) with two grinding posts on each side of the door was uncovered. This domed oven, 3 m. in diameter, was capable of producing hundreds of loaves of bread, the distribution of which was seemingly done in a centralized manner in the nearby courtyard (L. 401), where many receipts mentioning bread were found. These ostraca instruct that on day X was the handing over of Y amount of loaves to Z, the head of an extended family or group of people, who was always a male, manifesting the patriarchal atmosphere of the period. Two smiths, in which iron trilobite arrowheads were forged, are reported from the Western Palace as well.

MATERIAL CULTURE. The historical narration of Josephus and even more the archaeological finds indicate that the community of the rebels was in fact rather heterogeneous and dynamic in nature.

Coins. Numerous coins struck during the Jewish War (66–70 C.E.) were found both in large hoards (of 350, 200, and 100 coins) and in small numbers. Mostly ordinary bronze coins, they also include 37 silver shekels and 35 half-shekels representing all the years of the war and including the rare Year Five. This was the first discovery of shekels in a dated archaeological stratum.

Epigraphy. Outside Qumran, the site of Masada yielded the largest collection of epigraphic finds in Israel. The collection consists of several hundreds of Hebrew- and Aramaic-inscribed ostraca and 14 parchment documents and one papyrus in Paleo-Hebrew characters.

Ostraca. More than 700 ostraca were found, mostly written in Hebrew or Aramaic. Since they can be dated exactly between 66 and 73/74 C.E. they are of great paleographic value and they also shed much light on the organization of life at Masada and the national and religious character of the defenders who scrupulously observed the ritual laws. About half of them were found near the storerooms. These bore single or several letters in Hebrew and may have been connected with the rebels' community rationing system during the siege. Others indicate tithes and names on others may be those of priests or levites.

Scrolls. Parts of 14 biblical, apocryphal, and sectarian scrolls found at Masada are the first scrolls discovered outside of caves in a dated archaeological stratum. The biblical scrolls are mostly identical with the Masoretic Text but some show slight variations. These include parts of the books of Psalms, Genesis, Leviticus, Deuteronomy, and Ezekiel. Apocryphal scrolls include part of the original Hebrew text of the Wisdom of Ben Sira 39–44, dated to the first century B.C.E., and several lines of the Book of Jubilees.

A fragment of a sectarian scroll of the Songs of Sabbath Service is identical with a scroll found at Qumran. Other small fragments exhibit phrases that appear to be sectarian in nature. It is important for dating the Dead Sea Scrolls and because it indicates that members of the Dead Sea Sect (apparently Essenes) took part in the Jewish War.

This applies also to a papyrus scroll noting in Paleo-Hebrew script the idiom "Har Gerizim" (Mount Gerizim), which is the holy mountain of the Samaritans, the location of their temple. This indicates the presence of Samaritans amongst the rebels' community at Masada.

RELIGIOUS LIFE. *Mikva'ot (Ritual Baths).* Masada was the first site in which ritual immersion pools (*mikva'ot*) were recognized as such, an installation that came ever since to be a *fossile directeur* of Jewish settlements. The plastered, commonly stepped, pool had a source for rainwater that flowed directly into it. A relatively large number of *mikva'ot* was uncovered at Masada. Two were constructed in the southeastern sector of the casemate wall (L. 1197, 1162), one in the Northern Palace complex's administrative wing (L. 151), and near the synagogue (L. 1301). Another *mikveh* was documented in a cave in the southern cliff (L. 2006/1), in small palace XI (L. 601), and near the middle terrace of the Northern Palace (L. 67). To this group we may add two plastered pools, from the time of the revolt, that were built in the Large Bathhouse (L. 105, 104). It was suggested that during the revolt the stepped pools were in the *frigidaria* of the lower terrace of the Northern Palace (L. 8), in the Large Bathhouse (L. 107), and in the Western Palace (L. 546), and in the courtyard of the Large Bathhouse (L. 103, 112).

A unique public *mikveh*, with a dressing room, in the walls of which locker-like niches were used for the depositing of the bathers' clothes (L. 625), was excavated near Building XI. The *mikveh* that was constructed during the time of the revolt differs from any other example at Masada and is much akin to the examples uncovered at Qumran.

The "Essenes' Quarter." Interestingly, the entrance of this immersion complex turns towards Building XIII. The closest structure, situated in the northern annex of Building XXI, is a hall built in the time of the revolt (L. 809). This is an elongated hall with a bench extending along three sides of the wall and a low bench along its axis. The excavators named it *bet midrash* (religious school). However, its features appear to concur well with the "dining hall" at Qumran, a structure that according to the accounts of Pliny the Elder and Josephus was used by the Essenes for ritual activity. Hence it may be proposed to identify this area as the "quarter of the Essenes" at Masada, the presence of which is further attested in the characteristic sectarian documents that were found at the site.

Synagogue. A rectangular building located in the northwestern sector of the casemate wall was seemingly used as a stable in the first half of the first century C.E. During the time of the revolt its plan was transformed into a large hall with two rows of columns in the center and a back service room. A series of four peripheral tiers of plastered benches were built along the walls. The building was identified by Yadin as a synagogue. Examples from that period of time are known from Herodium and more decidedly at Gamala. This identification was further supported by the discovery of parts of two biblical scrolls, Ezekiel and Deuteronomy, buried in pits dug into the floor of the back room (possibly a *genizah*; a ritual deposition of religious documents). An ostracon inscribed *ma'aser kohen* ("priest's tithe") was uncovered in the main hall.

Human Remains. Twenty-five skeletons of men, women, and children were found thrown in a heap in a small cave on the southern cliff. Although the skulls were reported by Yadin to be of the type found in the Bar Kokhba caves in Naḥal Ḥever, the fact that pig bones were found with the skeletal remains may suggest according to Zias that they belong to the Roman soldiers killed in 66 C.E. Skeletal remains of three individuals were uncovered in the lower terrace, including a woman's scalp and braids and leather sandals. They were claimed by Yadin to represent a rebels' family. However, the condition of the three skeletons and the fact that many protein-rich bones are missing may indicate that the bodies were dragged there by hyenas.

THE ROMAN SIEGE. Despite the fact that Masada was the last rebel stronghold in Judea, it seems that the Roman considerations for commencing the Masada campaign, three years after the triumphant parade celebrating the victory over Judea took place in Rome, were not security but rather financial gain. The rebels' presence at Masada, which formed a base for raids, endangered a highly profitable resource – the balsam plantations of En Gedi. According to Pliny the Elder within five years of the suppression of the revolt, a staggering sum of 800,000 sesterces was obtained from the perfume trade in Judea. Indeed, the balsam trade is mentioned in two Latin military documents from Masada.

The Roman siege system at Masada appears to be one of the most complete and best preserved in the Roman world. Under the command of Flavius Silva a Roman force of 7,000–8,000 soldiers deployed around Masada in eight camps. The fortress was surrounded with a 2.17 mi. (3.5 km.) long siege wall (circumvallation), the flat eastern sector of which was fortified by towers to prevent the nearly 1,000 rebels from escaping and attacking the Roman force. All of the architectural elements of this system were of dry-constructed fieldstone. Taking into consideration the historical information concerning the length of the siege works at Jerusalem and the calculations of the working capacities of trained soldiers it seems that the construction of the camps and siege wall at Masada did not exceed a period of two weeks. The Roman military body consisted of the Legion X Fretensis and six auxiliary units. The legionaries were garrisoned in the two large camps, one in the east (B) and one in the northwest (F) which served as Silva Flavius' headquarters. A rare pay record of a legionary cavalryman, one Gaius Messius, was uncovered at Masada. The six small camps were located at strategic points around the base of the mountain commanding the ascents and possible escape routes. Camp H, which was built south of the fortress on higher elevation, allowed the Romans to observe part of Masada's summit. Communication was ensured by a trail that climbed the fault escarpment and connected all camps. Surveys, aerial photographs, and excavations of the camps indicate that the soldiers were housed in leather tents which were pitched over low walls and secured by iron pegs. In many of the *contubrenia* (eight-man tents) a raised bench was found along their walls. Small hearths, for cooking, were built in front of the tent units. Three larger ovens, which were presumably intended for bread baking, were found west of Camp F. Water was apparently brought in from the oasis of En Gedi by Jewish captives.

Roman military attention focused on a narrow section of the west wall of the fortress. The main undertaking was to provide the platform for the effective operation of the battering ram against Masada's wall. For this end an assault ramp (*agger*) was erected. Hewn from the nearby white spur, a mass of earth and stones that was stabilized by tamarisk and date-palm branches was laid on the natural spur of the western slope. A stone platform paved the head of the ramp in order to allow the 60-foot siege tower to be raised. The siege engines were most likely constructed in a secured courtyard ("bauplatz") located west of the ramp. Roth's work suggests that the completion of the entire siege works at Masada would have been achieved in a matter of two months.

During the excavations of Netzer and Stiebel's expedition four rooms of the Western casemate wall were excavated for the first time. The section directly above the ramp is entirely missing, in all likelihood being breached by the action of the battering ram. According to Josephus the rebels built an inner wall made up of wooden beams and soil. Mapping the burn pattern of the buildings at Masada, E. Netzer proposed that the lack of conflagration signs in many of the structures was the result of an intentional dismantling of the ceilings for the purpose of the inner wall's construction. *Ballista* balls shot from torsion artillery machines, arrowheads, and slingshots were found in the breach's immediate environs, testimony to the battle that raged there. The defenders' return fire included slingshots, arrows, and large rolling stones. This was seemingly the purpose of the scavenged wagon's wooden wheel that was found on the floor of the adjacent tower. There were apparently few casualties on the Roman side. A unique Latin medical care manual details the treatment of wounded and sick Roman soldiers. One typical burial of a Roman soldier, consisting of a cooking pot that contained cremated human remains, was found west of Masada.

The Mass Suicide. According to Josephus, when the Romans penetrated the fortress, they came face to face with the multitude of nearly 1,000 dead rebels. Apparently, this act of suicide was honored by the conquerors. The discovery of a group of ostraca near the Large Bathhouse, each inscribed with a single name and all written by the same person, including the name "ben Jair" (son of Ya'ir), led Yadin to the conclusion that these were the lots described by Josephus. According to his account the last ten survivors at Masada drew lots to choose who would kill the other nine and then himself. It should be noted that over 200 ostraca were also found in this location, and they all seem to be more likely part of the administrative organization of the rebels (tags or coupons) rather than the actual "lots." This notion is seemingly strengthened by the recent discovery of an ostracon bearing one of the names that appears in the "lot" group by Netzer and Stiebel. Nonetheless, the association of the "ben Jair" tag with the commander of the rebel community seems to be very likely.

The Aftermath. After the fall of Masada a Roman garrison cleared the site; scattered remains of this activity were found on top of Masada. This garrison erected a small camp within the boundaries of Camp F, in which it was stationed for several decades (F2). The latest coin that was uncovered at the site is a silver coin from Trajan's days dating from 112 C.E.

Byzantine Period

Following the abandonment of the site in the early second century C.E. Masada remained uninhabited for a few centuries. During the fifth century C.E. a monastery (*laura*) was founded at Masada, after a series of earthquakes had caused considerable damage to many of the buildings. Some of the scholars identify this monastery with a site named Marda (lit. "fortress"), noted by the Church Fathers. The group of hermits erected a small church with mosaic pavements of which little remains aside from a rich colored floor in a side room with medallions containing representations of a basket with a cross, fruits, and vegetal designs. These mosaics were locally manufactured. Remnants of this production were discovered near Building XII at the center of Masada. Fragments of the church's marble screen and window glass were uncovered in and near the building. West of the church was a refectory and kitchen. These last occupants of Masada dwelt in small stone cells scattered over the summit and in caves. With the rise of Islam in the seventh century C.E. this settlement apparently ceased to exist.

Modern Era

In many respects the perception of the episode of Masada by Israeli society, throughout the 20th century, mirrors the history of the state. The Hebrew translation in 1923 of *The War of the Jews* by Josephus, as well as the poem "Masada" by Lamdan published in 1927, brought Masada closer to the hearts of the young people in the country's Jewish community. S. Guttman, who led numerous trips to the mountain, was particularly instrumental in transforming Masada into a symbol of defiant resistance and the choosing of death over a life of slavery, in particular for Zionist and, later, Israeli youth. This trend appears to have climaxed in the late 1960s–early 1970s, when one of its manifestations was the swearing of the oath of allegiance by the recruits of Israel's Armored Corps on the summit of the site: "Masada shall not fall again." However, the last three decades witnessed a gradual shift in public perception, which was now determined more by political affiliation. Since the opening of Masada's National Park (1966) and the construction of a cable car (1971), it has become one of Israel's most visited tourist sites. In 2001 Masada was inscribed on the UNESCO World Heritage List.

BIBLIOGRAPHY: Y. Yadin, *Masada, Herod's Fortress and the Zealot's Last Stand* (1966) (incl. bibl.); Masada I–VII, *The Yigael Yadin Excavations 1963–1965 Final Reports* (1989–2006); Masada I: Y. Yadin and Naveh J., *The Aramaic and Hebrew Ostraca and Jar Inscriptions*; Y. Meshorer, *The Coins of Masada* (1989); Masada II: H.M. Cotton and J. Geiger, *The Latin and Greek Documents* (1989); Masada III: E. Netzer, *The Buildings, Stratigraphy and Architecture* (1991); Masada IV: D. Barag and M. Hershkovitz, *Lamps*; A. Sheffer and H. Granger-Taylor, *Textiles*; K. Bernick, *Basketry, Cordage and Related Artifacts*; N. Liphschitz, *Wood Remains*; A.E. Holley, *Ballista Balls*; Addendum: J. Zias, D. Segal, and I. Carmi, *Human Skeletal Remains* (1994); Masada V: G. Foerster, *Art and Architecture* (1995); Masada VI: S. Talmon, *Hebrew Fragments from Masada* (1999); Masada VII: R. Bar-Nathan, *The Pottery of Masada*; G.D. Stiebel and J. Magness, *The Military Equipment from Masada*; R. Reich, *Spindle Whorls and Spinning at Masada*; idem, *Stone Mugs from Masada*; idem, *Stone Scale-Weights from Masada* (2006); M. Avi Yonah et al., "The Archaeological Survey of Masada," in: *Israel Exploration Journal*, 7 (1957), 1–60; S.J.D. Cohen, "Masada: Literary Tradition, Archaeological Remains, and the Credibility of Josephus," in: *Journal of Jewish Studies*, 33 (1982), 385–405; M. Gichon, "A Further Camp at Masada," in: *Bulletin du Centre Interdisciplinaire de Researches Aeriennes*, 18 (1995), 25–27; H. Goldfus and B. Arubas, "Excavations at the Roman Siege Complex at Masada – 1995," in P. Freeman, J. Bennett, Z.T. Fiema, and B. Hoffmann (eds.), *Proceedings of the XVIIIth International Congress of Roman Frontier Studies held in Amman, Jordan (September 2000)*, vols. 1–2, BAR International Series 1084 (I) (2002), 207–14; Y. Hirschfeld, "Masada during the Byzantine Period – the Monastery of Marda," in: *Eretz Israel*, 20 ("Yadin Volume"; 1989), 262–74; I.A. Richmond, "The Roman Siege-Works of Masada, Israel," in: *Journal of Roman Studies*, 52 (1962), 142–55; J. Roth, "The Length of the Siege of Masada," in: *Scripta Classica Israelica*, 14 (1995), 87–110; Y. Tsafrir, "The Desert Fortresses of Judaea in the Second Temple Period," in: L.I. Levine (ed.), *The Jerusalem Cathedra*, 2 (1982), 120–45; Y. Yadin, "The Excavation of Masada – 1963/64, Preliminary Report," in: *Israel Excavations Journal*, 15 (1965), 1–120; idem, Y. Yadin, *The Ben Sira Scroll from Masada* (1965).

[Guy D. Stiebel (2nd ed.)]

°**MASARYK, JAN GARRIGUE** (1886–1948), Czechoslovak diplomat and statesman, son of president Thomas G. *Masaryk. From 1925 to 1938 Masaryk was his country's envoy in London, but resigned after the Munich Pact (Sept. 30, 1938), which compelled Czechoslovakia to give up the Sudetenland. In 1940 he was appointed foreign minister of the Czechoslovak exile government in London and retained the post after Czechoslovakia's liberation in 1945 and after the Communist takeover on Feb. 25, 1948. On March 10, 1948, his corpse was found beneath the window of the Czernin Palace in Prague, in which the Foreign Ministry was situated. It is still controversial whether he was murdered for political reasons or committed suicide. During his stay in London he formed ties of friendship with Chaim *Weizmann and became an ardent supporter of Zionism. He fought against antisemitism during and after the Nazi period. In one of his speeches, Masaryk stated: "Every antisemite is a potential murderer whose place is in prison." Due to his intervention, Czechoslovakia allowed the Jewish refugees of the *Beriḥah to cross its territory and actively supported the proposal to establish a Jewish state. He believed that "to establish a Jewish state is one of the greatest political ideas of our time." In the years of Israel's War of Independence (1948–49) Masaryk assisted in arranging the export of Czechoslovak weapons to the struggling state. The Mauser rifles with the Czech lion were known as "Czech rifles" and played an important part in the defense and conquest of the Jewish part of Jerusalem and other localities where critical fighting took place.

BIBLIOGRAPHY: V. Fischl (Avigdor Dagan), *Hovory s Janem Masarykem* (1952); Ch. Weizmann, *Trial and Error* (1949), index.

[Chaim Yahil / Yeshayahu Jelinek (2nd ed.)]

°**MASARYK, THOMAS GARRIGUE** (1850–1937), Czech philosopher and statesman, first president of *Czechoslovakia from its foundation (1918) until his retirement (1935). Born into a poor family in Hodonin (southern Moravia), as a child he was imbued with the popular Catholic antisemitism of his surroundings and was brought up to believe in the *blood libel. Impressions gained from Jewish schoolmates and a peddler made him change his opinions, a stage which he expressed in a sketch, *Ná pan Fixl* ("Our Mr. Fuechsel"). He studied at Vienna University where Theodor *Gompertz was one of his teachers. In 1882 he was appointed professor of philosophy at the newly founded Prague Czech University. He founded his "Realistic Party" and was elected to the Austrian parliament in 1907, and again in 1911. In his *Scientific and Philosophical Crisis of Contemporary Marxism* (1898) he asserted that, contrary to Marx's definition, Jews are a homogeneous nation, although they have given up their language. Masaryk conceived Zionism mainly in the moral sense. Impressed by the views of *Aḥad Ha-Am, he published in 1905 an essay on him. Believing that it was impossible to be a Christian and an antisemite, Masaryk considered that it was his duty to eradicate antisemitism from his people. In 1899 he took a leading stand in the *Hilsner blood libel case, "not to defend Hilsner, but to defend the Christians against superstition," publishing two pamphlets on the affair (see bibliography of Hilsner). He was attacked by the antisemitic mob and his university lectures were suspended because of student demonstrations against him. Similarly, in 1913 he came to the defense of Menahem Mendel *Beilis. He was enthusiastically received by U.S. Jewry upon his visit there in 1907. As a political émigré during World War I, he established connections with Jewish and Zionist leaders such as Louis Brandeis, Julian Mack, Louis Marshall, Stephen Wise, and the Bohemian-born congressman Adolf Joachim Sabath as well as with Naḥum Sokolow and later Weizmann. When elected president of Czechoslovakia (1918) he declared that Jews would enjoy equal rights with other citizens and expressed sympathy with Zionism. He also supported the claims for recognition of the right of a Czechoslovak citizen to declare his nationality as Jewish.

By his personal example Masaryk did much to combat antisemitism in Czechoslovakia. In 1927 he visited Palestine, taking a special interest in the new settlements, their social problems and aspirations, and the newly established Hebrew University. In 1930 a Masaryk forest was planted near Sarid, and in 1938 *Kefar Masaryk, a settlement founded by pioneers from Czechoslovakia, was named after him. Tel Aviv conferred honorary citizenship on him in 1935.

BIBLIOGRAPHY: E. Rychnovsky et al., Masaryk and the Jews (1941); K. Čapek, *President Masaryk Tells His Story* (1934); T.G. Masaryk, *Making of a State* (1927); O. Donath, *Masaryk und das Judentum* (1920).

[Chaim Yahil]

MĀSHĀʾALLAH (Heb. **Manasseh**) **B. ATHAÑ** (754–813), astronomer. Mashāʾallah was probably born in Egypt, which is possibly the reason why he was also called al-Miṣrī, the Egyptian, but part of his life was spent at the court of the caliphs al-Manṣūr and al-Maʾmūn in Damascus. His name appears in many different versions, such as Macha Allah al Mesri, Mashallah, Messahalla, Messahalac, Messalahach, Masalla, Mescallath, Macelama, Macelarama – mainly due to distortions in Latin manuscripts.

Mashāʾallah was one of the earliest independent and original scientific thinkers and scholars. His main efforts led to the transfer of astronomical knowledge from the East to the West by means of later translation; he also adapted Arabic data for the Cordoba astronomical tables. Unfortunately, none of his writings appears to have survived in the original texts and the main source is Latin translations, some of which give rise to confusion, since they list the same works under different titles. Mashāʾallah may also have written an interesting astrological treatise in Hebrew *Sheʾelot*, which was translated about 1146–48 by Abraham *Ibn Ezra. In 1493 and again 1519 there appeared in Venice a smaller treatise on lunar and solar eclipses, *Epistola de rebus eclipsium et de conjunctionibus planetarum in revolutionibus annorum mundi…* translated by Johannes Hispalensis from a Hebrew text. Some of the available manuscripts list 12 short chapters, all beginning with the words "Mashāʾallah says…" His treatise on the astrolabe was translated into Latin and English (R.T. Gunther, *Chavuv and Messahalla on the Astrolabe* (1929). A crater on the moon is named after him.

BIBLIOGRAPHY: Steinschneider, Arab Lit, 15–23; Steinschneider, Uebersetzungen, nos. 378–9; G. Sarton, *Introduction to the History of Science*, 1 (1927), 531; Brockelmann, Arab Lit, supplement, 1 (1937), 391; F.J. Carmoly, *Arabic Astronomical and Astrological Sciences in Latin Translation* (1956), 23–38.

[Arthur Beer]

MASHĀʿIRĪ, AL-, family in Iraq. The al-Mashāʿirī family members in Babylonia during the 13th century included some distinguished personalities who occupied important positions in the state. They are mentioned by *Eleazar b. Jacob in his poems (see *Divan R. Eleazar b. Jacob ha-Bavli*, Jerusalem, 1935). They included: ISAAC MUHADHDHIB AL DAWLA IBN AL-MASHĀʿIRĪ and his sons, ELEAZAR, ELIEZER, and OBADIAH (poem 8); and ELEAZAR AMĪN ABU (or IBN) MANṢŪR IBN AL-MASHĀʿIRĪ and his sons, EZEKIEL, YESHUʾAH, and ISAAC (poem 185). The nature of their public positions is unknown. In the Arabic chronicle of Ibn al Fūṭī, a Jewish state official named MAHADHDIB AL-DAWLA NAṢR MASHĀʿIRĪ is mentioned. In 1284 during the rule of the *Mongol governor Arghūn (1284–91), he was appointed adviser in affairs of the state to the government dīwān. In 1289, when *Saʿd al-Dawla ibn al-Ṣāfi became vizier of the Mongolian Empire, he, in turn, appointed Muhadhdhib al-Dawla Naṣr as commissioner of Babylonia. Muhadhdhib occupied this position until his assassination in 1291. Some scholars believe that he is the same person as the above-mentioned Isaac Mahadhdhib al-Dawla.

BIBLIOGRAPHY: Mann, Texts, 1 (1931), 268, 300, 304; Fischel, Islam, 95, 104, 115; idem, in: *Tarbiz*, 8 (1936/37), 234–5; A. Ben Jacob, *Yehudei Bavel* (1965), 38–39, 63–64; idem, in: *Zion*, 15 (1949/50), 59–61.

[Abraham David]

MASHASH, SHLOMO (1909–2003), Sephardi rabbi. Mashash was born in *Meknes, Morocco, and received his rabbinic education in Yeshivat Pahad Yitzhak. In 1931 he was appointed head of the Jewish school and *talmud torah* in Meknes, remaining there until 1949, simultaneously serving as head of the local yeshivah until 1947. In 1937 he founded a society Dovev Siftei Yeshenim for the purpose of publishing works of early rabbinic authorities still in manuscript, and in 1944 established an institution for the training of religious officials.

In 1949 Mashash was appointed *dayyan* in the Regional Beth Din of *Casablanca, in 1959 chief rabbi, and in 1977 he was appointed Sephardi chief rabbi of *Jerusalem.

Mashash published a number of rabbinical works, most of which include the word Shemesh – an anagram of his name – in the title. They include *Mizraḥ Shemesh* on ritual law (Casablanca, 1962), *Tevuot Shemesh* on the Shulḥan Arukh, and *Beth Shemesh* on the Talmud and *Maimonides.

MASHGI'AḤ (Heb. מַשְׁגִּיחַ; "overseer" or "inspector"), designation of the person entrusted by the rabbinate with the supervision of *kasher* butcher shops, food factories, hotels, and restaurants. He is to ensure that the food products sold or prepared in those places comply with the requirements of the traditional *dietary laws. The *mashgi'aḥ* must be an observant Jew and know all the particulars of the dietary laws. He is, however, not competent to decide on his own whether a product is *kasher* or not. In some places the *mashgi'aḥ* is also called *shomer* (i.e., "watchman").

MASHIV HA-RU'AḤ (Heb. מַשִּׁיב הָרוּחַ; "He causes the wind to blow"), a phrase in the *Amidah prayer, inserted after the first verse of the second blessing. It has two variants. The one for the winter season, "Thou causest the wind to blow and the rain to fall" is said from the last day of *Sukkot (after the Prayer for *Rain) until the last day of *Passover (until the Prayer for *Dew), and "who causest the dew to descend" is recited during the summer months in Ereẓ Israel, but only in the Sephardi ritual elsewhere. The praise of God as the dispenser of rain is referred to in the Mishnah (Ber. 5:2; Ta'an. 1:2) which ordains that it should be mentioned together with resurrection of the dead, as the sustenance of the living and the resurrection of the dead are both manifestations of the *gevurot* ("powers") of God. Another prayer for rain is recited in the ninth blessing of the *Amidah*.

BIBLIOGRAPHY: Elbogen, Gottesdienst, 44ff., 518ff.; JE, 5 (1903), 643–5.

MASIE, AARON MEIR (1858–1930), physician. Born near Mogilev, Belorussia, Masie studied at the yeshivah in Mir and moved to Berlin in 1878, where he joined the Union of Hebrew Socialists, founded by Aaron *Liebermann. In 1879 he was sentenced to a term in prison together with his comrades. Set free, he went to Zurich where he attended the Institute of Technology and came under the influence of Russian socialists, leading to his activity in the student revolutionary movement. Deeply affected by the 1881 pogroms, Masie actively supported the idea of a Jewish state. He joined the Jewish nationalist movement, and decided to study medicine so that he might have a profession which would be useful in Ereẓ Israel. Graduating in 1887, he went to Paris where he specialized in ophthalmology, and in 1888 he settled in Rishon le-Zion. There he was appointed medical officer for the Rothschild settlements in Ereẓ Israel.

From 1900, he lived in Jerusalem where he was active in medicine and in various cultural spheres. He was mainly interested in the revival of Hebrew and saw his life task in the development of a Hebrew terminology in medicine and in the natural sciences. A member of the Va'ad ha-Lashon, he advised Eliezer *Ben-Yehuda in medical terminology. He published a monograph, *Maḥalat ha-Shivtah* ("Meningitis," 1910), and articles in *Ha-Ẓefirah, Ha-Or, Ha-Refu'ah* (vol. 2, 1923), and *Leshonenu* (vols. 1 and 2, 1928–30). Masie's dictionary of medical terms, *Sefer ha-Munaḥim li-Refu'ah u-le-Madda'ei ha-Teva*, was completed by S. *Tchernichowsky and published posthumously in 1934.

BIBLIOGRAPHY: Slouschz, in: *Koveẓ ha-Ḥevrah ha-Ivrit la-Ḥakirat Ereẓ Yisrael ve-Attikoteha*, 3 (1935), 5–24 (incl. bibl.); *Sefer ha-Yovel… Petaḥ Tikvah* (1929), 433–43; M. Smilansky, *Mishpaḥat ha-Adamah*, 3 (1951^2), 106–17; J. Saphir, *Ḥalutzei ha-Teḥiyyah* (1930), 50–55; Munker, in: KS, 12 (1935/36), 19–28, no. 70.

[Joseph Gedaliah Klausner]

MASKILEISON (Maskil le-Eitan), ABRAHAM BEN JUDAH LEIB (1788–1848), Russian rabbi and author. Born in Radoshkovich, Belorussia, Maskileison studied under his father, who was *av bet din* of Khotimsk in the district of Mogilev. Abraham served as *av bet din* in Novogrudok. Toward the end of his life he moved to Minsk, where he died. He lived in poverty all his life. He was the author of *Maskil le-Eitan* (Vilna, 1818), novellae to the tractates of orders *Mo'ed* and *Kodashim*. His reputation as a result of this work was such that the title of his book (from Ps. 88:1) became his own designation and family name. *Be'er Avraham* (1844), his novellae to tractate *Berakhot* and the order *Mo'ed*, was published by his son Aaron. In the introduction Abraham lists the seven aims of the work among which were to give explanations of those passages of Talmud in which the tosafists found difficulties, an exposition of those passages of Rashi where the tosafists disagree with him, and a profound examination of those laws of Maimonides for which the commentators were unable to find sources.

Some of his works were published posthumously: *Naḥal Eitan* (1855), published by his son Naphtali, contains novellae on the first two parts of Maimonides' *Mishneh Torah* as well as novellae by Maskileison's brother Moses Nisan, compiled when he was 16. *Mizpeh Eitan*, novellae and glosses to tractates of the Talmud, was published in the Zhitomir edition of the Talmud (1858–64). It was subsequently republished in the Vilna Talmud with additional material to the author's manuscript entitled *Tosefet Merubbah. Yad Avraham* (Vilna, 1880) is on the Shulḥan Arukh, *Yoreh De'ah*. His glosses and novellae on Maimonides' *Mishneh Torah* were assembled from various manuscripts and collected in the *Yad ha-Ḥazakah* (1900) under the title *Yad Eitan*. Comments and novellae on the *Ein Ya'akov* were assembled in *Ahavat Eitan* (1883–84). His notes on the *Sifrei* were published in S. Luria's edition (1866).

His sons included Aaron, Moses Nisan, and Naphtali. MOSES NISAN was *av bet din* of the community of Shumiachi and author of the *Ḥikkrei Halakhot* (1875), consisting of 32 halakhic studies, *pilpulim*, and *novellae*. Particularly well known was NAPHTALI (1829–1897), a book dealer and an accomplished scribe and poet, to both talmudists and *maskilim*. His main work is his critical edition, with additions, of the *Seder ha-Dorot* (1877–82) of Jehiel *Heilprin. Aaron's son was ABRAHAM ISAAC MASKILEISON (1840–1905), born in Smolevichi, where in 1874 he was appointed rabbi, an office he held for 15 years. He then served in Haslovich. He was a member of Ḥovevei Zion. In 1904 he was appointed rabbi of Stoypitz where he remained until his death. He left works in manuscript which were lost. Reuven *Katz, the chief rabbi of Petaḥ Tikvah, was his son-in-law.

BIBLIOGRAPHY: N. Maskileison, in: A. Maskileison, *Naḥal Eitan* (1855), 4–8 (introd.); Fuenn, Keneset, 41; B.Z. Eisenstadt, *Rabbanei Minsk ve-Ḥakhameha* (1899), 27, 43, 67f.; Z. Harkavy, *Le-Ḥeker Mishpaḥot* (1953²), 5–15; R. Katz, in: A. Maskileison, *Maskil le-Eitan* (1966²), introd.; *Yahadut Lita*, 3 (1967), 71; Kressel, Leksikon, 2 (1967), 431f.

[Yehoshua Horowitz]

MAṢLI'AḤ ṢĀLIḤ (d. 1785), Babylonian liturgical poet. He and his son NISSIM (d. after 1816) wrote poems and *piyyutim* on various subjects. Some of these were published in regular and festival prayer books according to the rite of the Jews of *Baghdad and its surroundings. Others were published by A. Ben-Jacob in *Shirah u-Fiyyut shel Yehudei Bavel ba-Dorot ha-Aḥaronim* (1970) which includes poems written in the Spanish meter in honor of events and personalities (rabbinical emissaries, etc.). Ṣāliḥ held the rabbinical seat of Baghdad from 1773 to 1785, and enquiries were addressed to him from *Syria, Persia, Kurdistan, and other places on halakhic problems and community organization. Torah novellae of the father and the son are to be found in the works of their contemporaries.

BIBLIOGRAPHY: A. Ben-Jacob, *Yehudei Bavel* (1965), 121–4.

[Abraham Ben-Yaacob]

MASLIANSKY, ZVI HIRSCH (1856–1943), popular Yiddish orator, the most eloquent and influential *Maggid* on the American scene at his time. Masliansky was born in Slutsk, Belorussia. He taught at the Polish *talmudei torah* and at the yeshivah of Pinsk (1882–90), where one of his students was Chaim Weizmann. Stirred by the pogroms of 1881, he became a proponent of the idea of a return to Zion. He was active in Ḥibbat Zion, and fellow-Zionists M.M. Ussishkin, M.L. Lilienblum, Aḥad Ha-Am, and L. Pinsker encouraged him in his activity as a wandering preacher of Zionism. His fame as an impassioned orator spread rapidly throughout Russia. Compelled to leave the country in 1894, he undertook a lecture tour of Central and Western Europe and in 1895 emigrated to New York. During the three decades that followed, he helped popularize Zionism, wielding a great influence upon Yiddish-speaking immigrants, especially through his Friday evening sermons at the Educational Alliance on East Broadway. He combined the qualities of a *maggid* and those of a modern speaker. He was able to hold the attention of a popular audience and scholars as well. His imposing figure further strengthened the impression he made. He was also active in U.S. Zionist organizations.

Masliansky founded and coedited the daily *Die Yidishe Velt* (1902–05). His Yiddish sermons were published as *Maslianskys Droshes fir Shabosim un Yomim Toyvim* (2 vols., 1908; Eng. tr. *Sermons by Reverend Zevi Hirsh Masliansky*, 1926). He also published a memoir, *Fertsik Yor Lebn un Kemfn* ("Forty Years of Life and Struggle," 1924), and a collection of Hebrew articles, *Kitvei Masliansky* (1929).

BIBLIOGRAPHY: L. Lipsky, *Gallery of Zionist Portraits* (1956); Rejzen, Leksikon, 2 (1927), 321–4; LNYL, 5 (1965), 467–70; EẒD, 3 (1965), 293–8; M. Danzis, *Eigen Licht* (1954), 223–8; M. Zablotski and J. Massel, *Ha-Yizhari: Toledot Zevi Hirsh Masliansky* (1895).

[Sol Liptzin]

MASLOW, ABRAHAM H. (1908–1970), U.S. psychologist. Maslow was professor and chairman of the psychology department at Brandeis University from 1951. He was president of the American Psychological Association. Maslow was best known as a personality theorist, interested in motivational structure. In his work, he conceptualized within a phenomenological frame of reference that emphasizes the inherent goodness of man. He postulated a hierarchical theory of human motivation, wherein needs arrange themselves in a hierarchy from basic biological needs to those of self-esteem and self-actualization. Maslow's books include: *Principles of Abnormal Psychology* (1951) with B. Mittelmann; *Motivation and Personality* (1954); *New Knowledge in Human Values* (1959); and *Toward a Psychology of Being* (1962).

[Manny Sternlicht]

MASLOW, SOPHIE (1911–), U.S. dancer and choreographer. Maslow was born on the Lower East Side of New York. She joined the Martha Graham company in 1931 and became a member of the New Dance Group in the mid-1930s and its artistic director in 1968. From 1942 to 1954 she performed in the Dudley-Maslow-Bales trio and choreographed many works for that company. Maslow's first works reflected social unrest, exemplified by *Dust Bowl Ballads* (1941) and *Folksay* (1942). *The Village I Knew* (1949), based on a story by *Shalom Aleichem, portrayed a Jewish village in Czarist Russia. She re-staged this work when she worked in Israel with the *Bat-Sheva company (1950). Her other works were *Manhattan Transfer* (1953); *Champion* (1948); *Celebration* (1954), based on Israeli song and dance material; and *Poem* (1963). From 1951 she frequently choreographed the annual Ḥanukkah Festival at Madison Square Garden. In 1991 she received the Award of Artistry of the American Dance Guild.

[Amnon Shiloah (2nd ed.)]

MASNUT, SAMUEL BEN NISSIM (13th century), talmudist and leader of Aleppo Jewry. Scarcely any biographical details are known of him, even the place from which his family originated being uncertain since some manuscripts mention Toledo and others Sicily. Judah *Al-Ḥarizi, who visited Aleppo about 1218, waxed eloquent in praise of "Samuel b. Rabbenu Nissim of Aleppo." He wrote a special composition in his honor called *Iggeret Leshon ha-Zahav* (published by Z.H. Edelmann in *Divrei Ḥefeẓ*, 1853). Because of the similarity of the names and the places, scholars are inclined to regard the two as identical, in spite of an explicit statement by Samuel in one of his commentaries (Dan. 7:25) to the effect that it was written in 1276, which would make him about 90 years old at the time. Masnut's renown rests on his extensive midrashic commentary, *Ma'yan Gannim*, which apparently embraced most, if not all, of the Bible. The following parts have been published: Genesis (1962), which the editor entitled *Midrash Bereshit Zuta*; Job (1889); and Daniel and Ezra (1968). His commentary on Chronicles is extant in manuscript and is remarkably similar verbally to the commentary of David *Kimḥi. Fragments of his commentary on Numbers have also been preserved. Masnut's work is totally unlike other midrashic commentaries, even those of *David ha-Nagid and Jacob b. Hananel *Sikili – who were near him in place and time and bear some resemblance to him – in that he rarely uses his own words in the presentation of his commentary. It is, in effect, a verbal amalgam of different and independent midrashic sources woven together into a unique exegetical fabric. His familiarity with halakhic and aggadic sources (for which he rarely gives references) is quite exceptional. His books contain important halakhic material for research on the history of *halakhah, the texts of the Talmuds and the Midrashim, and particularly the various Aramaic *targumim, of which he made frequent use. A *piyyut* by Masnut for the morning service of the Day of Atonement has been preserved in the liturgy of Algeria and Tunisia.

BIBLIOGRAPHY: Samuel b. Nissim Masnut, *Ma'yan Gannim … al Sefer Iyyov* (1889), introd. by S. Buber (ed.); idem, *Midrash Bereshit Zuta* (1962), introd. by M. Kohen (ed.), and 331–8; idem, *Ma'yan Gannim … al Sefer Daniel ve-Sefer Ezra* (1968), introd. by S. Land and S. Schwarz, and 164–71; A. Kasher, in: *De'ot*, 23 (1963), 59–62.

[Israel Moses Ta-Shma]

MASON, JACKIE (1931–), U.S. comedian. Born in Sheboygan, Wisconsin, and raised on the Lower East Side of Manhattan, Mason (Jacob Maza) was ordained a rabbi, in a family of rabbis, before he became a comedian. His three brothers were rabbis and their father, grandfather, and great-grandfather were rabbis, too. In the early 1960s, Mason was one of the country's hottest comics, appearing frequently in nightclubs and on television. He delivered his bold monologues in a Yiddish-inflected New York voice, and became instantly recognized for his sharp and funny comments on Jewish and American life. He became a regular on the nation's leading variety program, *The Ed Sullivan Show*, only to fall into disfavor in 1962 during a live telecast when Sullivan interpreted a finger gesture Mason made as a lewd insult. Mason was ousted from the show and although he sued Sullivan for libel and won, he did not appear on the show again for 18 months. The incident cast a pall over Mason's career for more than a decade. But in 1984, Mason opened in Los Angeles in a one-man show, *The World According to Me!*, and convulsed audience after audience. He moved the show to Broadway in 1986, and it had a run of more than two years. Mason won a Tony Award and other honors, and the show toured the United States and Europe for two years. Mason returned to Broadway with the one-man shows *Jackie Mason: Brand New* (1990), *Jackie Mason: Politically Incorrect* (1994), *Love Thy Neighbor* (1996), *Much Ado About Everything* (1999), and *Prune Danish* (2002). He also had a variety of small film roles and his distinctive "Jewish" voice appeared in voice-overs and in animated cartoons. Mason, who had strong conservative political views, had several radio and television interview programs, often teaming with the divorce lawyer Raoul Felder, with whom he published The *Jackie Mason, Raoul Felder Survival Guide to New* York (1997) and *Jackie Mason and Raoul Felder's Guide to New York and Los Angeles Restaurants* (1996). Mason's offhand and tasteless comments sometimes got him into trouble. In 1991, when David Dinkins, an African-American Democrat, was campaigning for mayor of New York City, Mason called him "a fancy *shvartze* with a mustache." After protests from groups like the National Association for the Advancement of Colored People, Mason apologized.

[Stewart Kampel (2nd ed.)]

MASORAH. This article is arranged according to the following outline:

1. THE TRANSMISSION OF THE BIBLE
1.1. THE SOFERIM
1.2. WRITTEN TRANSMISSION
1.2.1. Methods of Writing
1.2.1.1. THE ORDER OF THE BOOKS
1.2.1.2. SEDARIM AND PARASHIYYOT
1.2.1.3. SECTIONAL DIVISIONS (PETUḤOT AND SETUMOT)
1.2.2. Irregularities in the Writing
1.2.2.1. EXTRAORDINARY POINTS
1.2.2.2. "ISOLATED" LETTERS
1.2.2.3. SUSPENDED LETTERS
1.2.2.4. LARGE AND SMALL LETTERS
1.2.2.5. OTHER ODD LETTERS

1. THE TRANSMISSION OF THE BIBLE

The transmission of the Bible is as old as the Bible itself, according to the ancient tradition in *Avot* that "Moses received the Torah from Sinai and handed it on to Joshua and Joshua to the elders and the elders to the prophets and the prophets handed it down to the men of the Great Assembly" (Avot 1:1). This concept of "Torah" which is handed down from generation to generation includes all of the Bible as it developed, with all the components which accompanied it and were added to it and which also shared in its holiness. As the form of the Bible became increasingly canonized and set in all its specific details, the tradition of reading the text and its exact pronunciation grew and became closely attached to it, developing together with it, and being handed down from father to son through the generations.

1.1. THE SOFERIM

The work of the transmission of the Bible was by its very nature destined to be in the hands of *scribes (*soferim*), transcribers who were skilled in the exact copying of the Bible and were therefore legally recognized as people knowledgeable in Torah, and who were accomplished scholars of it. The term *soferim*, which in the beginning was a term for scholars of the Torah in general (*divre soferim*, Sanh. 11:3), in time became limited to those scholars who specialized in the Written Law and in its exact transmission. Some were transcribers, and in this capacity they were called also כותבנים (*kotvanim*; "skilled *kotvanim* were in Jerusalem," TJ, Meg. 1:11 (71d)) or לבלרים (*lavlarim* – *librarius* = *libellarius*; thus, "R. Meir was a *lavlar*"; Eruv. 13a), while others were teachers and instructors of school children ("and the *sofer* (scribe) teaches according to his way"; Tosef. Meg. 4:38). The main interest of these scribes was the preservation of the text of the Bible, and they are credited with a number of rules and regulations which were established for this purpose. It is not known who those scribes were, but some of the scholars of the Talmud are conspicuous by their special interest in every legal discussion dealing with the problem of the text of the Bible, its transcription, and its teaching, such as R. *Meir (TJ, Ta'an. 1:1 (64a); TJ, Meg. 4:1 (74d); Eruv. 13a; Sot. 20a et al.), R. Hananel (TJ, Meg. 1:11 (71c, d); Meg. 18b et al.), and R. *Samuel b. Shilat (TJ, Meg. 71c, d; BB 8b, 21a; Ket. 50a). This preoccupation with the exact transmission of the Bible gradually became important, and the term *sofer* tended to lose its original connection with *sefer* ("book") and came to designate all learned people. Thus the original meaning of the term became obscured through its connection with the act of counting by the preservers of the text, as stated in the Talmud (Kid. 30a): "Therefore the ancients were called *soferim* (סופרים), because they counted (היו סופרים) all the letters in the Torah…." Originally the activity of the *soferim* and the preservers of the exact version of the Bible was an oral one. The main point of their work was instruction in the reading of a text lacking vocalization and accentuation signs, and passing this reading on orally from generation to generation. Since the text was holy it was not permissible to add anything to the skeleton of the letters of the Bible, and only a small part of what they established as reading aids was noted in the sacred text, that is, the very text which to this day has served for the public reading prescribed by the *halakhah*. It can be said that those items which did penetrate into the holy text did so during the very earliest period of its development with the result that they too became sanctified. Anything which did not find a place in the text itself, such as the vocalization and the accentuation signs and the various masoretic notes, at first had to be transmitted orally, and even when they were committed to writing they were still not allowed to be introduced into the sacred text.

1.2. WRITTEN TRANSMISSION

There are two types of items which penetrated into the holy text itself:

(1) those connected with the methods of writing the text – the pages, the lines, the marking of the lines, the division into sections, the manner of setting out the songs (*Shirat ha-Yam, Shirat Ha'azinu*, and others), and the order of the books;

(2) irregularities in the script and in the actual writing – dots above the letters, suspended letters, isolated *nuns*, large letters, small letters, and the like.

1.2.1. Methods of Writing

Most of the matters connected with the writing of the Bible are closely regulated by the *halakhah* and the customs of earlier generations. This applies especially to the Torah. Since it serves for the public reading in the synagogue it must comply with exact ritual conditions, without which the reader and the listener do not fulfill the religious duty of reading the Torah. These laws and customs became established during the time of the Talmud and were collected after a time in the tractate *Soferim* (which was presumably edited not later than the eighth century C.E.), and in the legal compilations of the rabbinic authorities (such as Maim. Yad, Hilkhot Sefer Torah). These instructions deal with the actual form of the book (the scroll, the size of the parchment and the pages), the writing (the size and shape of the letters, the addition of *tagin [tittles, crowns] on the letters שעטנ"ז ג"ץ – Men. 29b), the writing materials (the parchment and ink), the manner of writing (marking guidelines, structure of lines), the arrangement of the text (the spacing of letters and words, the division into sections, the linear arrangement of the songs in the Torah, *Shirat ha-Yam, Shirat Ha'azinu*, the beginnings of the columns – the first letter generally being *waw*, except for ביהשמ"ו) and other topics connected with the laws of the reading and the care of the scroll. These laws apply only to scrolls which are intended for public reading, not those which are not for ritual use.

Since these matters are governed by the *halakhah*, they are not considered part of that which is usually called "Masorah," although they are also, by their very nature, included among all the matters connected with the writing of the Bible that are handed down from generation to generation. Although the term "masorah" today includes all the matters connected with the writing and recitation of the Bible, it is not permitted to write them in a copy intended for public reading. These items could be written in the margins and even in the text itself only after some time, when people began to make copies of the Bible in the form not of a scroll but of a codex (מצחף) meant for the everyday study and teaching of the Bible.

1.2.1.1. THE ORDER OF THE BOOKS. The order of the books of the Bible and the division of the texts into sections is the same for the scrolls and the codices. The oldest arrangement of the 24 books of the Bible is mentioned in a **baraita* (BB 14b) and adopted also by Maimonides (Yad, Hilkhot Sefer Torah 7:15). In it, the order of the Pentateuch and the Early Prophets is the same as it is commonly accepted today, but the order of the Latter Prophets is: Jeremiah, Ezekiel, Isaiah, and the Minor Prophets – the order which was kept later in the German and the French manuscripts (sometimes also with Isaiah preceding Ezekiel), as opposed to the Oriental and Spanish manuscripts whose order is that which is common today.

The order of the Hagiographa as found in the *baraita* (and also by Maimonides, Yad, Hilkhot Sefer Torah 7:15) is Ruth, Psalms, Job, Proverbs, Ecclesiastes, Song of Songs, Lamentations, Daniel, Esther, Ezra (and Nehemiah), Chronicles – but this order was followed in only a few isolated manuscripts. In the manuscripts of the Oriental and Spanish masoretes the order is as follows: Chronicles, Psalms, Job, Proverbs, Ruth, Song of Songs, Ecclesiastes, Lamentations, Esther, Daniel, Ezra (and Nehemiah); while in the German-French manuscripts and in most of the printed editions of today the order is: Psalms, Proverbs, Job (the term אמ"ת comes from the initials of these three in reverse order), Song of Songs, Ruth, Lamentations, Ecclesiastes, Esther, Daniel, Ezra (and Nehemiah), Chronicles. See *Bible: Canon.

1.2.1.2. SEDARIM AND PARASHIYYOT. The accepted order of the books rejects the Babylonian tradition, as listed in the *baraita*, in favor of the Palestinian and other traditions. However, the Babylonian tradition was followed in the division of the Torah into short units for recitation in the synagogue (see *Torah, Reading of the). In Palestine the reading of the Torah was completed once in three years (see *Triennial Cycle) and therefore the Pentateuch was divided into 154 (or, according to another version, 167) weekly portions called סדרים (*sedarim*). In Babylonia the full cycle of the reading of the Torah was completed in one year, so that the Torah was divided into 54 פרשיות (*parashiyyot*), weekly portions (סדרות or *sedres* in Yiddish) and that division is followed today, in continuance of the Babylonian tradition. The *sedarim* which served in the Torah as units for the (Palestinian) weekly portions for public ritual reading were applied to break also the text of the whole Bible into small units. However, since in the Prophets and Hagiographa this division was hardly necessary for use even in ancient times, except for some definite small parts (*haftarot, megillot,* etc.), there are differences in manuscripts as to the exact location of the divisions and even in the number of *sedarim*.

1.2.1.3. SECTIONAL DIVISIONS (PETUḤOT AND SETUMOT). The division of the body of the text into sections is an ancient one, and unlike the above-mentioned division into *sedarim* and *parashiyyot*, involves the very copying of the text whether in a scroll or a codex. These sections are of two kinds, with the type of space preceding them varying:

(1) a *parashah petuḥah* (open *parashah*) which starts at the beginning of a line, the preceding line being left partly or wholly blank (in some manuscripts and print editions this is indicated by פ);

(2) a *parashah setumah* (closed *parashah*) which begins at a point other than the start of a line, whether the preceding section ended in the preceding line (at its end or not) or whether it ends in the same one, in which case a space of approximately nine letters is left between the two sections (in some print editions this is noted by ס). This ancient division is attested to in the Babylonian Talmud (Shab. 103b): "a *parashah petuḥah* should not be made *setumah*, a *setumah* should not be made *petuḥah*." *Sifra* to Lev. 1:1; 1:9 asks: "And what purpose did the פיסקות (sections) serve? To give Moses an interval to reflect between *parashah* and *parashah* and between issue and issue." Despite their antiquity different traditions or customs developed on the matter of the *parashiyyot*, as to the placing and number of each type. In printed editions today there is a great degree of uniformity in the Torah due mainly to the halakhic fixing of this issue and that of the shape of the songs by Maimonides following *Ben-Asher (Yad, Sefer Torah 8:4).

1.2.2. Irregularities in the Writing

Various irregularities in the actual shape of the writing are part of the copied text. These go back to early sources and are discussed here in their assumed chronological order.

1.2.2.1. EXTRAORDINARY POINTS. There are dots over 15 words in the Bible and sometimes also under them, one dot over each letter of the word or over some of the letters. The words are distributed as follows: ten in the Torah (in the tenth place in the Torah, Deut. 29:28, the dots in most traditions cover 11 letters of three words – all but the last letter – לָנוּ וּלְבָנֵינוּ עַד, four in the Prophets, the dots being above in each case, and one word with a varying number of dots in the Hagiographa (לׅוּלֵׅא; Ps. 27: 13), where there are dots also beneath the word. There are different traditions on the details. (See the full lists in the *Masorah Magna* for Numbers 3:39, and in *Okhlah we-Okhlah* (ed. S. Frensdorff, 1864), §96, with the additional bibliography there.) These dots are a very ancient tradition, the evidence concerning some of them going back to the second century C.E.; see, for example, R. Yose in the Mishnah (Pes. 9:2) concerning the *he* with a dot, in the word רחקה (Num. 9:10). A comprehensive list of the location of these dots in the Torah is already found in *Sifre Numbers* chap. 69 (ed. Horovitz p. 64–65), R. *Simeon bar Yoḥai being mentioned there; and further evidence is to be found in the Talmud and in the Midrashim. (The references were noted in the *Arukh ha-Shalem* under *"naqad"* and to these should be added Ber. 4a; Naz. 23a; Hor. 10b.) There have been various theories put forth concerning the origin and meaning of these dots (see L. Blau, *Masoretische Untersuchungen* (Strassburg, 1891), 6–40; *Zur Einleitung in die Heilige Schrift* (Budapest, 1894), 113–20; R. Butin, *The Ten Nequdoth of the Torah* (Baltimore, 1906, repr. New York, 1969); S. Lieberman, *Greek and Hellenism in Jewish Palestine* (Jerusalem 1962), 182–184). However, they do not belong to the system of vocalization and they also appear in Torah scrolls designated for public recitation.

1.2.2.2. "ISOLATED" LETTERS. The isolated letters (אותיות מנוזרות) are the nine signs which appear between verses – in the Torah before and after the section of ויהי בנסע הארן (Num. 10:35–36), and seven in Psalms, chapter 107 (there are differences of opinion as to their exact place and number.) Rather than being referred to by the name אותיות (letters), they are already called סימניות (signs) in a *baraita* (about the Torah – Shab. 115b: ARN 34, 4; about Psalms – RH 17b). Their form was not fixed in the ancient sources and the scribes were quite liberal in the manner in which they marked them. There is early evidence that these *simaniyyot* were nothing but simple dots. This is the impression given by *Sifre Numbers*, ch. 84 (ed. Horovitz, p. 80), already in the name of R. Simeon (second century C.E.). As time passed, these signs assumed various shapes and changed names accordingly. In tractate *Soferim* (prior to the eighth century) 6: 1, it is called, according to the version of various manuscripts, שיפור (horn) – perhaps the sign really resembled a *shofar*, "and it appears indeed in the section on travels (ויהי בנסע)" – or שיפוד (spit), which is reminiscent of the sign of the ὀβελός (= spit). In *Diqduqe ha-Teʿamim* (ch. 2) the term אותיות מנוזרות is found, and according to *Dunash b. Labrat it is האותיות המנזרים (*Teshuvot al Menaḥem*, ed. Filipowski, p. 6a). The term is neutral and does not indicate the shape of the sign, and according to the basic meaning of its root it refers to letters which are separated from the consonantal text. In the manuscripts the sign developed into the shape of a reversed *nun*. It is not known whether all of it was reversed ׆ (see *Okhlah we-Okhlah*, §179), or only its top or bottom, and there was much confusion about it in the commentaries (see *Minḥat Shai* on Num. 10:35; *Naḥalat Yaʿakov* on tractate *Soferim* 6:1). There were even those who wrote it into the text itself in the place of regular *nuns* of the text (see also Ginsburg, *The Massorah*, vol. 2, p. 259, §15a). Later the names of these signs, too, were interchanged with the name for the regular reversed *nun* (see below 1.2.2.5). Hence the *otiyyot menuzzarot* became נונין מנוזרות (see *Masorah Magna* to Ps. 107:23), which was explained, following נָזֹרוּ אחור, "they turned backward" (Isa. 1:4), to mean reversed *nun* (*Minḥat Shai* on Ps. 107:23), though there is no linguistic support for this interpretation. If the opinion already expressed in ancient sources regarding the signs in the Torah is generally accepted, that is, that the purpose of these signs is to separate the section "when the ark set forward" as if it were a book by itself, there is no similar consensus of opinion concerning the signs in Psalms (see S. Lieberman, *Greek and Hellenism in Jewish Palestine* (Jerusalem 1962), 178–181).

1.2.2.3. SUSPENDED LETTERS. There are four suspended letters אותיות תלויות in the Bible: the *nun* of מנשה (Judg. 18:30), and the *ʿayin* in the words מיער (Ps. 80: 14), רשעים (Job 38: 13), and מרשעים (Job 38:15). The tradition concerning them is quite ancient, going back to the third century C.E. (see *Samuel b. Naḥman in TJ, Bet. 9:3, 13d: ARN 34, 4) and to later sources. In most instances midrashic explanations on these suspended letters are also mentioned.

1.2.2.4. LARGE AND SMALL LETTERS. The custom of writing some letters differently – smaller or larger than usual – never became halakhically fixed. Thus there are several discrepancies between the various manuscript texts of the Bible. Even the lists of the Masorah are not uniform: Ginsburg compared some ten different lists (*The Massorah*, vol. 4 (1905), 40–41). The number of large letters is greater than the number of small letters. One of the large letters is already indicated in the Talmud (Meg. 16b) in the name of R. Johanan (third century C.E.). In *Soferim* 9:1–7 at least four large letters and one small one are mentioned. Their number grew as time passed, but in the older manuscripts, such as those of *Aleppo and Leningrad, there are still relatively few of these letters.

1.2.2.5. OTHER ODD LETTERS. For these there is generally no evidence in ancient sources. The Talmud (Kid. 66b) mentions in the name of R. Naḥman (third century C.E.) a וי"ו קטיעה in the word שלום (Num. 25:12), which is explained as a *waw* with a crack in the middle, but it is not certain that they did not mean a *waw* which was cut short, that is, a small *waw*. Maimonides (Yad, Sefer Torah 7:8) lists "[and] odd letters like winding (לפופות) *pes*, and the crooked (עקומות) letters." The *Masorah Parva* mentions a נון עקומה ("crooked *nun*": ואני, Ex. 3:19), as well as נון הפוכה ("an inverted nun"; בחרן, Gen. 11:32), and קופין דבוקין ("attached *qufin*": בקמיהם, Ex. 32:25; see also *Okhlah we-Okhlah*, §161). The *Masorah Marginalis* of the

Venice Bible (1525) states that the second lamed in the word לגלגלתם (Num. 1: 22) עשויה כמגירה וזקופה ואין לה כובע בראשה ("is shaped like a saw, stands upright, and has no cap on its head"). Seligman *Baer described at length the shape of the various odd letters in his book *Tiqqun ha-Sofer we-ha-Qore* (Roedelheim (1875^2), p. 18 of supplement).

1.3. ORAL TRANSMISSION

Apart from these matters which mainly are connected with the very writing of the Bible – and there could not be copying without their clear establishment – all of the other issues were originally part of oral transmission. The notes concerning the text of the Bible and the instructions for its proper pronunciation and its exact copying were handed down orally from generation to generation before they were set down in writing. It may be assumed that these notes were permitted to be written down and were actually committed to writing with the institution of the use of the codex among the Jews – apparently in the sixth or seventh century C.E. Therefore one must differentiate quite clearly between the oral Masorah which is endless and cannot be defined even though there are allusions to it and evidence thereof, and between the written Masorah whose notations were written in the margins of the codices and which is called simply "the Masorah."

1.3.1. Ancient Evidence

In addition to the main evidence offered by the very existence of the text which was passed down from father to son and from teacher to student, there is an explicit statement about the oral transmission in the name of R. Isaac (about the third generation of Palestinian *amoraim*, at the end of the 3rd century C.E.): "R. Isaac said, מקרא סופרים ועטור סופרים וקריין ולא כתיבן וכתיבן ולא קריין were handed down as Law to Moses at Sinai" (Ned. 37b–38a). All the items listed there are thus considered as coming from a most ancient period, when it was not yet possible to list the items – there were neither signs to use (vocalization and accentuation) nor permission to write down such signs.

1.3.1.1. MIQRAʾ SOFERIM. The saying of R. Isaac continues with an explanation: מקרא סופרים – ארץ שמים מצרים. Despite all the explanations which have been given to *miqraʾ soferim* (see the comment attributed to Rashi which is probably that of *Gershom b. Judah Meʾor Ha-Golah and see R. Nissim ad. loc.), it seems that *miqraʾ* is to be taken in its literal meaning – the correct "reading" of the words as handed down by the scribes. The three words cited above are an example of the possibilities for various readings of words whose pronunciation can be known only by the transmitted reading of the *soferim*. Similar to this is the principle in the Talmud (Sanh. 4a and elsewhere) that the text as read (with vowels) is authoritative יֵשׁ אֵם לַמִּקְרָא, that is, the accepted pronunciation is to be followed in establishing the meaning of the text (as opposed to יש אם למסורת, i.e., the consonantal text – the actual letters – is authoritative; see below).

1.3.1.2. ʿIṬṬUR SOFERIM. The other items listed by R. Isaac are also a very ancient tradition which was not permitted to be written down and which was transmitted orally from generation to generation: *ʿiṭṭur soferim* are apparently omissions (עטר "to remove" in Aramaic; see *He-Arukh* s.v., quoting R. *Hai b. Sherira, and additional explanations in *Minḥat Shai* to Num. 12:14) of the conjunctive *waw* as evidenced by the examples which are listed there: עיטור סופרים – אַחַר תַּעֲבֹרוּ (Gen. 18:5), אַחַר תֵּלֵךְ (Gen. 24:55), אַחַר תֵּאָסֵף, (Num. 31:2), קִדְּמוּ שָׁרִים אַחַר נֹגְנִים (Ps. 68:26), צִדְקָתְךָ כְּהַרְרֵי אֵל (Ps. 36:7). Possibly other omissions are also to be included.

1.3.1.3. QERE WE-LAʾ KETIV; KETIV WE-LAʾ QERE. The last two items – words which are to be read although they are not written (*qaryan we-laʾ ketivan*) and conversely, words which are not to be read although they are written (*ketivan we-laʾ qaryan*) – issues which are discussed later on – are also an ancient tradition and could not be written down until long after the statements were made. They are listed thus: קריין ולא כתיבן – פרת דבלכתו (II Sam. 8:3); איש דכאשר ישאל איש בדבר האלהים (II Sam. 16:23); באים דנבנתה (Jer. 31:37); לה דפליטה (Jer. 50:29); את דהגד הוגד (Ruth 2:11); אלי דהגורן (Ruth 3:5); אלי דהשעורים (Ruth 3:17); הלין קריין ולא כתבן. וכתבן ולא קריין – נא דיסלח (II Kings 5:18); זאת דהמצוה (Deut. 6:25); ידרך דהדורך (Jer. 51:3); חמש דפאת נגב (Ezek. 48:16); אם דכי גואל (Ruth 3:12); הלין כתבן ולא קריין. This list in *Nedarim*, like the two which preceded it, is a sample and not complete. It is also not in complete agreement with the detailed lists of the Masorah for our texts. A correct list is found, for example, in *Okhlah we-Okhlah*, §97 and in it there are ten *qere we-laʾ ketiv* (it does not include Ruth 2:11), and eight *ketiv we-laʾ qere* (and it does not include Deut. 6:25).

1.3.1.4. QERE. Although ordinary *qere* notes were not explicitly mentioned in the Talmud, it is clear that they too are to be included in *miqraʾ soferim*, and the tradition of the *qere*, that is, words which are to be read differently from the form in which they are written, is ancient and returns to oral transmission.

1.3.2. The Verses

The above also applies to the division into verses. Here too we have an ancient tradition (so ancient that it is generally in agreement with the Samaritan reading) which was handed down orally. This antiquity is evident from the meaning of *miqraʾ soferim* which really means the complete reading including the transmitted vocalization and the transmitted division. Undoubtedly the division of the text into minimal units – the verses, and even the division of every unit into its parts, the accents – is also part of correct transmitted division. This transmission, like all oral transmission, while it strives for great precision and generally achieves it, still contains some doubtful instances and contradictions between different transmissions which have to be decided.

There is evidence in talmudic literature for the existence of the tradition of division into verses, a division which was handed down orally and was not permitted to be marked in the text. Evidence similarly exists about a tradition of internal verse division by accentuation and about differing traditions concerning both division of the text into verses and the division within verses and about reaching decisions concerning these differences.

One statement was repeated in three main versions as seen in the table below.

A comparison of sources in the rabbinic literature on ancient oral traditions regarding the biblical text: division into verses, vocalization, accentuations, etc.

Upon study one clearly sees the difference between the two Babylonian sources (vs. 1) and the two Palestinian sources, TJ and Gen. R. (vs. 2, 3). In the Babylonian sources there is no mention of הכרעים ("decisions") or הכרעות וראיות ("decisions and proofs") and there is a difference between the Babylonians and the Palestinians in the method of study and interpretation of פסוקים (ראשי) and טעמים (פסקי). Their common factor is that in all of them the verses, the accents, and the traditions (*masorot*) are linked to Ezra the Scribe, i.e., to a very early period.

Regarding the division into verses there is even earlier evidence, from the Mishna: "He that reads in the Torah may not read less than three verses (פסוקים); he may not read to the interpreter more than one verse (at a time), or, in the Prophets, three" (Meg. 4:4); and there is the statement in *Kiddushin* 30a, that derives from the period of the *tannaim* (Bacher, 92 ערכי מדרש), which lists, among other things, the middle verse of the Torah (והתגלח; Lev. 13:33).

There is evidence of some confusion as to the verse division in some sections: Rav. Joseph [third century C.E.] asks "to which half does והתגלח belong?" (the reference is to the word *we-hitgallaḥ* which is considered to be the middle of the Torah with regard to verses; does it belong to the first or the second half?). *Abbaye answered him: "Verses can be counted" (in contrast to what was said before about *plene* and defective spelling, about which R. Joseph states that in Babylonia they are not experts in it and that it is therefore impossible to establish the number of the letters of the Bible). Rav Joseph replied: "We are also not expert in the division of verses, because when Rav Aha bar Ada came [to Babylonia], he said that in the West [i.e., Ereẓ Israel] they divide this verse into three: And the Lord said to Moses: "Behold I come to you in a thick cloud" (Ex. 19:9)" (Kid. 30a). It follows, therefore, that the Babylonian scholars were also not expert in the division of the text into verses. It can be assumed that the Palestinians were more particular than the Babylonians in the transmission of the text of the Bible. Indeed, there are considerable differences between the number of verses recorded in the Talmud and our texts of the Bible. (See Kid. *ibid.*: The Rabbis taught: "there are 5,888 verses in the Torah" – according to the Masorah the number is 5,845.) For Psalms and Chronicles the numbers are completely different and there was, apparently an error somewhere. In any event, this statement is the primary source about the difference in the text between the Palestinians and the Babylonians.

The term ראשי פסוקים ("beginnings of the verses") in contrast to פסוקים ("verses") in the above quotation does not indicate a substantive difference between the two countries but is a terminological difference only. The division into verses requires the notation of either the beginnings or the ends of the verses and it makes no difference which. The term "beginnings of the verses" from the Palestinian sources has a continuation in additional, later Western sources, e.g., *Soferim* 3:7: "A book which he punctuated, wherein he marked the beginnings of

TB Megillah 3a and TB Nedarim 37b	TJ Megillah 4:1 (74d)	Genesis Rabbah 36
אמר רב איקא בר אבין אמר רב חננאל אמר רב: מאי דכתיב (נחמיה ח, ח) ויקראו בספר תורת האלהים מפורש ושום שכל ויבינו במקרא. ויקראו בספר תורת האלהים – זה מקרא, מפורש – זה תרגום, ושום שכל – אלו הפסוקים, ויבינו במקרא – אלו פיסקי טעמים, ואמרי לה: אילו המסורות.	רבי זעורא בשם רב חננאל: ויקראו בספר תורת – זה המקרא, מפורש זה תרגום, ושום שכל – אילו הטעמים, ויבינו במקרא – זה המסורת, ויש אומרים: אילו ההכריעים, ויש אומרים: אילו ראשי פסוקים.	רבי יודן אמר: מיכן לתרגום, ה"ה ויקראו בספר תורת האלהים – זה מקרא, מפורש – זה תרגום, ושום שכל – אילו הטעמים, ויבינו במקרא – אילו ראשי פסוקים. רבי חייא בן לוליני אמר: אילו תנאות [נ"א: ההכרעות והראיות]. רבנן דקיסרי אמרי: מיכן למסורות.
Rav Iqa bar Abin said in the name of Rav Hananel who spoke in the name of *Rav: What does it mean 'And they read in the book of the Law of God, distinctly; and they gave the sense, and caused them to understand the reading' (Neh. 8:8)? 'And they read in the book of the Law of God,' refers to מקרא (biblical text)); 'distinctly' refers to תרגום ([Aramaic] 'translation'); 'and they gave the sense' refers to הפסוקים (הפסוקין; the verses); 'and caused them to understand the reading' refers to the פיסקי טעמים (פיסוק) (the division(s) of the accents); others however say that this refers to המסורות (המסורת, the tradition(s)).	R. Ze'ora said in the name of R. Hananel: 'and they read in the book of the Law of God' refers to מקרא; 'distinctly' refers to תרגום; 'and they gave the sense' these are הטעמים ('the accents'); 'and caused them to understand the reading' refers to המסורת ('the tradition'), and some say to ההכריעים ('the decisions') and some say to the ראשי פסוקים ('beginnings of the verses').	R. Yudan said: herefrom (is understood) the *targum*; 'and they read in the book of the Law of God' refers to מקרא; 'distinctly' refers to תרגום; 'and they gave the sense' these are הטעמים ('the accents'), 'and caused them to understand the reading' refers to ראשי פסוקים ('the beginnings of the verses'). R. Hiyya b. Luliyani said: these are the תנאות (another reading has ההכרעות והראיות). The rabbis of Caesarea said: herefrom (are understood) the מסורות (traditions).

the verses, should not be (publicly) read." Similarly *Diqduqe ha-Te'amim*, chapter 10, has "the chapter of the beginnings of the verses." In contrast there is an indication for the actual marking of the beginnings of the verses in Babylonia itself (of a later period, of course) as found in texts using the Babylonian vocalization system (see Kahle, M.d.O. text, 35a).

Differences with regard to the details of the verse division existed not only between the West and the East, but within the same tradition itself. Sometimes there are differences between the division into verses and the division into sections, which is older; the פסקא באמצע פסוק ("paragraphs [which end] within verses") are evidence of that (e.g., Gen. 35:22; Num. 26:1 (some texts = 25:19), etc.). However, there are differences in detail between printed texts and manuscripts.

1.3.3. Accentuation

There is evidence for the antiquity of the accents earlier than the above mentioned source (1.3.2.) and again the reference is not to the written signs, which were set relatively later, but to the tradition of reading the verses with the necessary accents and pauses, which was passed from generation to generation. A teacher of children should not receive payment for teaching Torah, but he can take שכר פיסוק טעמים ("a fee for [teaching] accentual division"; Ned. 37a). Even here, as with all oral transmission, doubts developed concerning the parsing and the accentual division and it is possible that the word הכרעים (הכרעות, תנאות) refers to just that in the Palestinian version of the above-mentioned saying. Thus there are words in the biblical text whose syntactical adhesion is undecided; "Issi b. Judah said: there are five verses in the Torah the construction of which is uncertain: שאת (Gen. 4:7); משקדים (Ex. 25:34); מחר (Ex. 17:9); ארור (Gen. 49:7); וקם (Deut. 31:16)" (Yoma 52a/b). For similar doubts, see, for example, TJ, *Beẓah* 2:4 (61c) for I Chr. 29:21; Yoma 52a for I Kings 6:19; *Bava Meẓia* 58a for Lev. 5:21; *Bava Meẓia* 73b for Lev. 25:46. Most instructive is the question of R. *Ḥisda (Hag. 6b; Yoma 52b): "Rav Ḥisda asked: How is this verse (Ex. 24:5) written? 'And he sent the young men of the children of Israel and they offered burnt offerings,' meaning sheep; 'and they sacrificed peace offerings of oxen to the Lord'; or were both types of sacrifices of oxen? [i.e., does the word "oxen" refer to the second half of the verse only and thus the peace offerings were oxen but the burnt offerings were not, but sheep, or does the word "oxen" refer to all the verse and thus both the burnt offerings and the peace offerings were oxen?] What difference does it make (what they sacrificed on that occasion in the wilderness)? Mar *Zutra said לפיסוק טעמים (the division of the accents [= punctuation])"; i.e., this question has no practical relevance, other than for the issue of correct punctuation, that is, how one is to read the verse and where to pause in it.

This tradition of reading with stress and pauses involved the tune with which one should read the Bible. According to R. Johanan (Meg. 32a): "He who reads (קורא) without melody (נעימה) and studies (שונה) without a tune (זמרה) is referred to by the verse 'And wherefore I gave them statutes which were not good…' (Ezek. 20:25)." This evidence of reading the Bible and the Mishnah (שונה) with a tune has an even more ancient basis, at least as far as the Bible is concerned. Thus the reason of R. Akiva for the custom of "Why do people not clean themselves with the right hand but rather with the left hand" is "Because one shows the טעמי תורה with it [the right hand]" (Ber. 62a). The טעמי תורה ("accents of the Torah") which are shown by hand are the signs of conducting with the movements of the hand according to the tune, as attested to by Rashi (Ber. 62a): "*Ta'ame Torah*: The tunes of the reading accents of the Pentateuch, the Prophets, and the Hagiographa, whether by signs in the book, whether by raising the voice, and with the notes of the melodies of the tune of *pashta'* and *darga'* and *shofar mahpakh*; he (the reader) moves his hand according to the melody; I have seen readers who come from the land of Israel do it." This is, therefore, an ancient custom which was followed in Palestine still in the days of Rashi (the 11th century). There is also explicit evidence of the custom in *Maḥberet ha-Tījān* (J. Derenbourg, *Manuel du lecteur* (1871), p. 108): "And know that the grammarians have a hand movement for every accent in addition to the melody articulated by the mouth…" This custom continues among Yemenite Jews to this day.

During the entire period of the Talmud the accents had no written signs and it is generally accepted that the invention of the vocalization signs took place at the same time as the invention of accentuation signs. At the only place where סימני טעמים ("accent signs") are mentioned in the Talmud (Eruv. 21b) the term is usually interpreted according to this assumption: "Rava explained: what is the meaning of 'he also taught the people knowledge; yea, he pondered, and sought out and set in order many proverbs' (Eccl. 12:9)? 'He taught the people knowledge' means he taught them with סימני טעמים (accent signs)." "Accent signs" are explained as not being necessarily written signs (see Rashi ad loc.). Yet, perhaps the term "accent signs" may be understood in its literal meaning? There is no clear evidence either way and it is not impossible. However, if it is to be understood as accent signs, one must date the invention of the accent signs to an earlier period – that of *Rava, about the first half of the fourth century.

1.3.4. The Masorah

The Masorah referred to in the above sources (1.3.2) as *masoret* or *masorot* has already been discussed. Undoubtedly, it means the traditions concerned with the writing of the text with regard to plene and defective orthography. There is evidence in talmudic literature to this effect, such as the principle that יש אם למסורת (Sanh. 4a and elsewhere); that is, the spelling as handed down in the tradition (*masoret*) is decisive, i.e., the tradition of writing with or without the *matres lectionis* (as opposed to יש אם למקרא "the reading of the text is authoritative" – i.e., the common reading and pronunciation – see above). It seems that the statement of R. Akiva, מסורת סייג לתורה "*masoret* is a fence for the Torah" (Avot 3:13), also refers to the same thing, i.e., that the written text as handed down with all the details is a fence of defense for the Torah. Even in this matter we learn of the precision of the Palestinians, as from the statement of R. Ishmael to R. Meir who was a scribe (Eruv. 13a): "Be careful in your work, for your work is the work of the heaven; lest by your omitting one letter or adding one letter the whole world be destroyed." In contrast to this there is the lack of precision on the part of the Babylonians, as admitted by Rav Joseph, the Babylonian *amora* (Kid. 30a): "They [the Palestinians] are expert in חסרות ויתרות (= defective and plene spelling, *matres lectionis*); we are not expert."

This is the source of the lists of differences between the Palestinians and the Babylonians – the differences between מערבאי (Westerners) and מדנחאי (Easterners) – which are mainly variants in spelling and in the manner of the writing (in one or two words). These lists, which include about 200 to 250 variances – there are differences between the various manuscripts as to number and detail – cover mostly the Prophets and the Hagiographa and less the Pentateuch.

The care about the orthography and the *matres lectionis* is the justification for the rule יש אם למסורת and opened the way for many homilectical interpretations based on the spelling of the letters (especially when it allows for a reading different from that of the traditional pronunciation). The largest collection of this type of interpretation is in "*Midrash Ḥaserot wi-Yterot*'" (from the ninth or tenth century) which is devoted completely to it. Even earlier than this the sages had arranged lists for remembering words which are written with and without *matres lectionis*, e.g., *Soferim*, ch. 7. They are, in fact, the beginnings of the lists of the written Masorah which are based on the short and sketchy notes on peculiarities of spelling or form in the text, marked in the margins of the books. With that we come to the written Masorah.

2. THE MASORAH AND THE BEGINNINGS OF GRAMMAR

The purpose of the Masorah, whether it be oral or written, was clearly and undoubtedly the precise preservation of the holy text. This purpose was the primary thrust for the occupation with grammar after a period of many years. In this respect the development and growth of Hebrew grammar is different than that of other ancient grammars; although it was influenced by them – to a smaller or greater degree – it differs from them in its motivation and its beginnings.

2.1. GENERAL

Other peoples also came to occupy themselves systematically with language and grammar because of the need to preserve their holy texts: the Indians on the one hand and the Arabs, to some degree, on the other.

2.1.1. The Indians

From the time the Indians felt that they were drawing further and further away from their ancient language, Sanskrit, the language of the Vedas, their holy writings, and that they were facing the danger of forgetting that language and that thus the holy writings were liable to be forgotten or – at least – to be corrupted, they turned to the study of the ancient language as a means for preserving the holy writings. Their approach was analytical (the word "grammar" in Sanskrit is *wyākarana* = analysis) and they analyzed the holy text into small units in order to recognize each unit and to write it down so that it would not be forgotten. This is actually a descriptive method which establishes the minimal units – mainly morphological and phonological – and lists them in all their details. The inventory lists of Sanskrit are in fact the perfect means for realizing the goal which the Indian grammarians had set for themselves, the preservation of their holy texts in the ancient, original language.

The greatest Indian grammarian of the ancient period was Panini, whose descriptive grammar became known in Europe only in the 19th century and greatly influenced modern linguistics and the structural-descriptive school. However, Panini lived in the fourth century B.C.E., and he certainly had no influence on the Hebrew Masorah. The aim was the same – preservation of texts – and such an aim does not stem from foreign influence but is an internal, original need. The means, therefore, for achieving this goal would be completely different in each case.

2.1.2. The Arabs

While the Arabs are much closer to the Jews, both geographically and chronologically, their principal motive was the need to preserve the language, and not particularly their holy writings. The territorial expansion of the Arabs and the consequent dominance of Arabic in all the area of their empire exposed the language to the penetration of foreign influences from the languages of the conquered peoples. The purity and clarity of Arabic was in danger and a call went out in the first years after the Islamic conquests – it mentions the name of the fourth caliph, Ali – to make efforts to maintain its purity (*luḡa faṣīḥa*). The first Arabic grammarians set the rules of the language on the basis of the language of their ancient poets and the Koran. The religious power of the Koran, which is written in the dialect of the Quraysh tribe, the tribe of the prophet, and its distribution among the believers made its language – with all the adjustments made in it – into the model Arabic language. Thus the preservation of the language of the holy writings was not the main purpose of the grammarians, but rather the preservation of the purity of Arabic against foreign influences of non-Arabs who adopted Arabic as their language and spoke it. Due to the status of the Koran in Islam, knowledge of the Arabic language and grammar became a religious science, one of whose purposes was also the correct interpretation of the Koran and the other holy writs (the *Hadith).

At this point the aims of Hebrew and Arabic grammar have become identical, but the beginnings are completely different, both as far as motivation and early methodology are concerned. The oral Masorah for the preservation of the text of the Hebrew Bible was a living study for the Jews for hundreds of years before their contact with Islam and before the necessity for dealing with the language systematically was felt. However, the situation is analogous to some degree. In the same way that the Arabs came to study the language because of an internal, practical need, yet drew the methodological tools from outside, mainly from Greek language science, the Jews came to deal with language – with the Masorah – from an internal, practical need, and in that they preceded the Arabs. However, they also took the methodological tools for the development of grammar as a science at a later period from outside, mainly from the Arabic grammar.

2.1.3. The Syrians

Alongside these two peoples, the Indians and the Arabs, among whom the science of language developed, mention must be made of the Syrians, who were not very original in their treatment of language but who do have a point in common with the Jews. The Syrians were influenced both by the Arabs and by the Greeks. Next to the Indians, the Greeks are in reality the originators of the science of language, without any connection to a holy text but from a philosophical approach to literature and speech. The first grammatical works of the Syrians are translations from the Greek, yet for all the lack of originality in Syrian literature, including grammar books – and perhaps because of it – a need was felt for preserving the text of the holy writings, the Peshitta, in all details concerning its reading and pronunciation. This aim became intensified all the more when Syriac ceased to be a spoken language and, later, even a literary medium. In this it has something in common with Hebrew, and there are several points of contact between the Syrian Masorah and the Hebrew written Masorah. Like Hebrew, Syriac developed a system, or a set of systems, of dots and other signs to mark vowels, accents, and other diacritical marks. These systems became more and more sophisticated as time passed. One of the challenges of research into the Masorah has been the establishment of the relationship between the two traditions, the Hebrew and the Syrian, i.e., which is the original and influenced the other, and which came later and imitated the other. This applies to the method of notation, to the signs themselves and to the terminology. This question cannot be decided unequivocally, but in any case, it is clear that the beginning of the Hebrew Masorah – that oral system which is as ancient as the public reading of the text of the Bible and which was finally written down – undoubtedly precedes the Syrian Masorah, for the translation of the Peshitta is relatively late. The fact that Syriac manuscripts with diacritical marks from the fifth century have been found and that they therefore precede the dated Hebrew manuscripts which have vocalization and accentuation signs by about 300 years cannot affect this basic consideration.

2.2. AMONG THE JEWS

2.2.1. The Codex

When did the Masorah begin to be committed to writing? Since we do not have ancient dated manuscripts, one must accept external proofs. As already stated, the prerequisite for writing the Masorah systematically was the institution of a change in the means of writing and the abandonment of the common use of the scroll. The codex is a more sophisticated form for writing than the scroll; it consists of units of leaves of parchment or paper which are placed – bound – between two plates of wood. Every unit had a number of sheets, most often apparently five (hence the Hebrew word קונטרס, *qunteres* (= *quinternus*)). The codex was already in use by the Romans in the fourth century C.E. and perhaps earlier. It is first mentioned in Jewish literature in the *Halakhot Gedolot*, that is, in the eighth century and at the latest in the first half of the ninth century, by the name מיצחף (*mizḥaf*) which is borrowed from the Arabic *muṣḥaf.* A codex is not valid for the public ritual reading of the Torah, and it has wide margins where different notes could be marked.

2.2.2. Dating

Despite the fact that actual evidence for the conditions necessary for the writing down of the Masorah is rather late, there is clear evidence from other sources that the Masorah was committed to writing prior to the eighth century. This evidence can be considered reliable in the light of the fact that scrolls which were invalid for ritual reading also served, as it seems, for the noting of Masorah. Scrolls of this type were also found in the Cairo *Genizah. The evidence points to a period of 200 years within which vocalization and accentuation signs were initiated: not before the sixth century nor later than the seventh.

The *terminus a quo* is based on a number of facts:

(1) Jerome (end of the fourth century-beginning of the fifth) states explicitly (in his commentary on the Bible) that the Jews did not have signs to note the vowels (he does not speak of accents).

(2) In the Jerusalem Talmud (which was completed in the first half of the fifth century) and in the Babylonian Talmud (which was completed at the end of the fifth century) there is no mention of vowel and accentuation signs; similarly there is no mention of them in the earliest Midrashim. This evidence of silence is undisputed, especially in the light of interpretations like that in *Song of Songs Rabbah* on the sentence (Songs 1:11) תורי זהב נעשה לך עם נקדות הכסף "We will make thee circlets of gold (תורי זהב) with studs (*nequddot*) of silver (נקדות הכסף)": 'With studs of silver' – R. *Abba b. Kahana said these are the letters. R. *Aḥa said these are the words. Another interpretation: 'We will make thee circlets of gold' means the writing; 'with studs of silver' means the stylus lines (drawn on the parchment)." In this context a homiletic interpretation of נקודות to signify vowel points is obviously called for, yet none is found. Evidence from late Midrashim is obviously not reliable; for example in *Exodus Rabbah*, ch. 2:6 (to Ex. 3:4) פסק (*paseq*) is actually mentioned, but this Midrash is later than the tenth century. It follows, therefore, that the use of the vowel and accentuation signs was not instituted before the sixth century.

The *terminus ad quem* is established by a number of indirect proofs:

(1) Phinehas Rosh ha-Yeshivah is one of the early masoretes about whose work in Masorah and vocalization there is definite knowledge, and he lived in the first half of the ninth century at the latest. This suggests that vocalization and accentuation signs were already in use before then.

(2) Asher b. Nehemiah (the grandfather of Aaron Ben-Asher) lived apparently at the same time as Phinehas, and his grandfather Asher was the "great elder," the founder of the dynasty of famous masoretes who dealt with vocalization and accentuation signs like his descendants. This Asher the Elder must have lived in the second half of the eighth century at the latest, which means that the vowel and accentuation signs were fixed before that time.

(3) In the ninth century there was already no definite knowledge as to who invented the vowel and accentuation signs, and so we hear from Natronai Gaon of Babylonia (d. 858) in his prayer book, *Me'ah Berakhot*: "The vowel signs (*niqqud*) were not given at Sinai but the sages marked them for signs." Thus in the first half of the ninth century, although vowel and accent signs were known and accepted, the inventors were already unknown. It can be assumed therefore that the institution of their use preceded that time by several centuries. In the eighth century there were sages dealing with punctuation (see above); the latest possible time for the first use of vocalization and accentuation signs is therefore the seventh century.

2.2.3. The Invention of Punctuation

Today there is general agreement as to when the use of punctuation (including accentuation signs) was begun, but this was not always so. All scholars agreed that the tradition of pronunciation and the tradition of reading with pauses and melody are ancient, and that (without going into any detailed explanation of the phrase "law handed down to Moses at Sinai") they were handed down by the earliest sages. An allusion to this is the talmudic expression *miqra' soferim* (see above 1.3.1.1.), which is also considered as law handed down to Moses at Sinai.

2.2.4. Karaites and Rabbanites

There was, however, a difference of opinion with regard to the graphic signs, a point which was part of the general controversy between the *Karaites and the *Rabbanites. The Karaites, who did not accept the Oral Law as binding and whose whole heritage stems from the Bible as it stands (חפישו באוריתא שפיר), naturally considered the text of the Bible holy in its entirety – including every detail of vocalization and accentuation. The Karaite view found its most complete expression in Judah *Hadassi's book *Eshkol ha-Kofer* (written in 1149): "And the Torah scrolls should be pointed with vowels and accents… for without vowels and accents God did not give them… for the writing of our God was 'graven upon the tablets' (Ex. 32: 16) so was their writing full with vowel and accent signs and not lacking in vowel and accent signs" (Judah b. Elijah Hadassi. *Eshkol ha-Kofer* (1836, repr. 1969), 70a).

But the Rabbanites considered only the consonantal text to be holy, and the inclusion of vowel and accent signs makes a scroll invalid for public ritual reading. Therefore, as far as they are concerned the signs are late. This view is expressed in the statement of Natronai Gaon, "the vowel signs were not given at Sinai but the sages marked them by signs." A fuller statement is that of Simḥah b. Samuel of Vitry, France, a disciple of Rashi, in his *Maḥzor Vitry* (written about 1100): "for the descriptions of the melodies were said to Moses: which tears out (תולש), stands straight (זוקף), sits (יושב), stands (עומד), goes up (עולה), goes down (יורד), and leans (מונח) [referring to accent names]; but the signs of the melodies (= accents) were set by the *soferim*" (ed. by S. Hurowitz (Nuremberg, 1923), p. 462).

However, the Rabbanites were not unanimous; some shared the Karaite view, others thought that the punctuation signs were ancient and if Moses did not receive them at Sinai, at least it was Ezra the Scribe who set them. The matter was explicitly decided by Abraham *Ibn Ezra in *Sefer Zaḥot* (ed. Lippmann, p. 7a): "Thus is the custom of the Tiberian sages, and they are the source, for from them came the masoretes and we received all the punctuation from them." The whole question was again clarified by R. Elijah Baḥur *Levita in *Masoret ha-Masoret* in the third introduction (ed. Ginsburg, p. 121–31). Following them, it was generally accepted – with the exception of a few dissenters (J. Bachrach, *Ishtadalut im Shedal*, Warsaw, 1896–97) – that the vocalization and accentuation signs were invented by the masoretes.

3. THE WRITTEN MASORAH

The written Masorah can be divided into categories:

(1) the masoretic notes in the margins of the text and the longer lists which accompany the text or are appended to it – the *Masorah* in the narrow sense;

(2) the graphemes which, by their very nature, are of two types: (a) the vocalization signs; (b) the accentuation signs.

As far as chronology is concerned, it is difficult to differentiate between the two main categories and particularly between the two types of graphemes. It can be assumed that once it was permitted to write on the manuscript of the text itself, signs were permitted to be used. However, for reasons of convenience, we shall treat them here in three separate paragraphs.

3.1. THE MASORAH (NARROW SENSE)

3.1.1. The Term

The early sages explained the term as deriving from מסר ("to hand over"), i.e., something which was handed down from generation to generation: the text of the Bible which is precisely transmitted (as stated e.g. by Elijah Levita at the beginning of his third introd. to *Masoret ha-Masoret*; ed. Ginsburg, 102–3). Others explained the term and the related one מָסֹרֶת as derived from the root אסר ("to bind"; cf. commentaries to Ezek. 20:37, *מַאֲסֹרֶת > מָסֹרֶת), that is, something which is bound and gathered: the detailed instructions for reading joined together to the text (thus Bacher and Levias). Most convincing is the explanation of S.D. *Luzzatto, who proves that מסורת and סימן ("sign") are synonyms, arrived at by extended meaning. At first they said "he handed (מסר) a sign (סימן) to them" and later the sign which was transmitted was called *masoret*. The expression מסורת סייג לתורה ("*masoret* is a fence for the Torah") thus means that the devices concerning the writing with and without *matres lectionis* (and also those for the talmudic laws) are a fence – an aid – for remembering the Torah. The expression יש אם למסורת (see above, 1.3.4.) is also nicely explained according to this, i.e., that the written sign or the letter is authoritative.

Z. Ben-Ḥayyim has suggested a new explanation which seems plausible. He has demonstrated that the verb מָסַר can also mean "to count" (סָפַר) both in Hebrew and in Samaritan Aramaic. Indeed, counting was a large part of the work of the masoretes, according to the Talmud (Kid. 30a): "Therefore the early sages were called *soferim* for they counted (היו סופרים) all the letters of the Torah…" In the period following the Talmud the term "*sofer*" more and more came to refer to a skilled scribe and copyist of the Bible, while the wisdom required in the work and the understanding and exact knowledge of the text needed a special name, and for that a noun from the root מסר synonymous to ספר began to be used, i.e., מָסוֹרָה *masorah* (and this without detracting from the older meaning of *masoret* = sign). The form מָסוֹרָה which is found in a poem of Hai Gaon (d. 1038) is from Palestinian Aramaic where it serves as a participle, that is in Hebrew מוֹסֶרֶת ("counting"), and it is this name which fits the skill of noting the peculiar details in the biblical text. This form was even translated correctly in various participial forms in Hebrew מָסֵרָה, מוֹסֵרָה (these two in the plural in the Leningrad Codex of 1009) and in Arabic *māsira* (*Kitāb jāmiʿ alʾalfāẓ* by David b. Abraham Alfāsī in the tenth century). From then on the verb is used in the basic conjugation, *qal*, מָסַר (in the colophon to the Aleppo Codex and in manuscripts of the second collection of Firkovich in St. Petersburg: no. 9 – the beginning of the tenth century; no. 39 – from the year 989; and no. 144 from the year 1122) and in the *piʿel* conjugation (in a manuscript in the same collection: no. 17 – from the year 930) with the meaning "to write Masorah."

3.1.2. Definition and Scope

In the Masorah (in the narrow sense) everything that is written outside of the biblical text, but accompanies it, is included. This is even stated in one of the oldest chapters which describe the Masorah, "and he commanded to write one outside (מבחוץ) and one inside" (*Dikduke ha-Teʿamim*, ed. Baer-Strack §8, and cf. §63, and *Maḥberet ha-Tījān* ed. D. Derenbourg, 127, 129–31), and it seems that the term החיצונים ("the external ones" – *Diqduqe ha-Teʿamim*, ed. Dotan, ch. 2) includes all the notes listed outside of the text. These notes vary in their degree of importance to the text, antiquity, trustworthiness, and degree of agreement in various manuscripts. It is therefore convenient to follow here an external-technical division of these notes and not one based on their nature. The modern commonly accepted technical division is the following:

(1) *Masorah Parva* (Small Masorah);

(2) *Masorah Magna* (Great Masorah) which is further divided into: (a) Marginal Masorah and (b) Final Masorah (written at the end of the text).

3.2. THE MASORAH PARVA (QETANNA)

The notes of the *Masorah Parva* are expressed in extreme brevity and generally by abbreviations. These notes are listed in the manuscripts at the margins of the biblical text, mostly at the right or left. There is a small circle (or star) in the text over the word to which the note of the Masorah is directed. In the fragments of the Bible with Babylonian punctuation, the *Masorah Parva* is sometimes written in small letters between the lines of the text, each comment above the word to which it refers.

3.2.1. The Qere and Ketiv

The most important notes in the *Masorah Parva* for the purpose of the reading are those of *qere* (including *qere we-laʾ ketiv* and *ketiv we-laʾ qere*, "read although not written," and "written but not read," respectively; see above, 1.3.1.3.). Initially all the notes were written together, but in a few manuscripts and especially in printed editions, the notes concerning *qere* were emphasized more than the others.

3.2.1.1. METHODS OF NOTATION. *Qere* קְרֵי (the passive participle in Aramaic = the read [Hebrew קָרוּא]) means the form of the word as it should be read – ignoring the written letters. The vocalization and the accentuation signs which are diacritical marks for correct reading are adjusted, therefore, only to the form which is read and not to the written form. Yet there is an ancient custom, which was followed in most of the printed editions, to write the vowel and accent marks of the *qere* upon the skeleton of the letters of the *ketiv* כְּתִיב (= the written) and to write the consonantal skeleton of the form which is read without its vocalization and accentuation signs as a masoretic note in the margin: for instance, inside the text (Josh. 20: 8) גָּלְוֻן and in the margin: גולן ק̇ (= קרי = "read"); inside the text (Isa. 36:12) שֵׁינֵיהֶ֑ם and in the margin מימי רגליהם קרי. When the change involves only one or two letters sometimes only this difference is shown, e.g., לְכַשְׂדָּיֵא (Dan. 2:5) and in the margin: אי ק̇ (= לכשדאי קרי).

3.2.1.2. THE DEVELOPMENT. The older method of marking the *qere* was to note in the margin, or in the Babylonian system to mark sometimes between the lines, only that portion of the word in which there is a change. This method is quite frequently used in the Palestinian system. The full word containing the variant reading is found in relatively later texts.

3.2.1.3. THE SYMBOLS. There is noticeable development also in the manner of notation. In the earliest stage only the letter which was different was noted in the margins (when the *qere* indicated a change in letter), such as in the Palestinian vocalization אעבוד (Jer. 2:20), and in the margin ׄן (that is, *qere*: אעבור). In the course of the development there was noted alongside the form of the *qere* in the margins – in all the vocalization systems – a sign resembling a final ן or a ז whose meaning has not been explained. It has been suggested that if it is a *nun* it refers to the word קרן (in Aram. "they are reading"), or it is an abbreviation of נוסחא ("version"). If it is the letter *zayin* it may refer, as Yeivin suggested, to the Greek term זיטימא (= ζήτημα = "the sought for, the desired [reading]," a term found once in an ancient masoretic list (Ginsburg, *Massorah*, 3, p. 278; *Diqduqe ha-Te'amim*, ed. Dotan, p. 73) not exactly in the sense of *qere*. There is, however, no proof for these suggestions since the full word is never found instead of the symbol in a *qere* note. It seems that it is nothing more than a sign which was generally agreed upon and not a letter of the alphabet (cf. another sign of the Masorah, which came to resemble a reversed *nun* – see above 1.2.2.2.).

As time passed קרי or its abbreviation ׄק (was written in addition to this sign alongside or under the *qere* version. In Babylonian manuscripts קרן ("reading") is also found written out. In these texts the sign ׄכת ("*ketiv*") too is occasionally found written over the forms of the *ketiv* which are in the text itself. Another notation found in a few manuscripts and used in each of the punctuation systems to note the *qere* where one letter in the *ketiv* form is extra, is יתיר ,'יתי, for example, אֱנָוֺשָׁא (Dan. 4: 14) in the margin: יתיר ו. A note of this type also may, sometimes does denote a spelling with *matres lectionis*, such as הֲקֵים (Dan. 3:5, 7) in the margin: יתיר ׄי; also עֲלֶ֫ינָא (Ezra 4:18) in the margin: יתיר ׄי.

3.2.1.4. VOCALIZATION OF THE QERE. In the manuscripts there are different methods for attaching the vocalization of the *qere* to the skeleton of the letters of the *ketiv*. In some the order of the vowels as they should be is retained and no attention is paid to the letters such as וּמְבַלֲהֵים (Ezra 4:4) *qere* ומבהלים; in others each vowel is attached to its proper letter according to the *qere* and thus the order of the vowels is distorted: וּמְבַלֲהֵים. This, however, does not happen in every instance. Sometimes there is inconsistency within the same manuscript.

3.2.1.5. QERE WE-LA' KETIV (READ AND NOT WRITTEN). The *qere we-la' ketiv* notations indicate the reading of a word which is not in the written text. In the space in the text where the word is to be read, its vowels and accentuation signs are generally written in (although sometimes they are not marked at all). In some manuscripts the word *qere* alone is written outside of the text.

3.2.1.6. KETIV WE-LA' QERE (WRITTEN AND NOT READ). The *ketiv we-la' qere* notations are those which direct the reader not to read a word which is written in the text, and thus it appears in the text without vowels or accentuation signs. In this case too there are instances where the phrase לא קרי alone is noted. This term or its abbreviation, ׄלׄק, may also refer to individual letters; in other words it is an abbreviated method for noting a *qere* form which differs from the *ketiv* only in the omission of letters, for example, אַרְתַּחְשַׁסְתְּא and in the margin: ׄאׄלׄק (Ezra 8:1, Leningrad Ms.) that is,א לא קרי (= aleph not read), namely, read אַרְתַּחְשַׁסְתְּ.

3.2.1.7. THE SCOPE OF QERE. There are differences between manuscripts and between printed editions with regard to the number of *qere* notations; some versions mark the *qere* very frequently while others do so rarely. This refers of course to those instances where the remark concerning *qere* is not required and the reading can be understood without it, especially when the difference is with quiescent letters, like בָּנָו (Deut. 33:9), הַמּוֹרְאִים (II Sam. 11: 24), etc. Some manuscripts note *qere* for these and some merely have a masoretic note, חסר (*ḥaser*), מלא (*male'*), or יתיר (*yattir*), etc. Some make no comment at all. Thus there is no fixed number of *qere* notations in the Bible. Elijah Levita, for example, counts 848 cases (*Masoret ha-Masoret*, the third introduction, ed. Ginsburg, p. 115), and he is not a maximalist.

3.2.2. Types of Qere

Essentially there are four or five main types of *qere* notations in addition to *qere we-la' ketiv*, which are really words omitted from the text, and in addition to *ketiv we-la' qere*, which is actually not a *qere* but a *la' qere* instruction ("not read").

3.2.2.1. EUPHEMISMS. Strong language is changed to euphemisms. This is a substitution which dates back to the time when Hebrew was a spoken and understood language. Evidence for this type of change is already found in the Tosefta (Meg. 4:39–41): "Every derogatory written expression is replaced by one of refinement, e.g., 'Thou shalt betroth a wife and another man shall ravish her (ישגלנה)' (Deut. 28: 30): every place where ישגלנה is written, they read יִשְׁכָּבֶנָּה (shall lie with her); 'with the boil of Egypt, and (בעפלים) [unknown disease]' (Deut. 28:27); every place where בעפלים is written, they read it as בַטְּחוֹרִים... (with the hemorroids)." Cf. a better version in Meg. 25b.

3.2.2.2. CORRECTION OF FORMS. Archaic forms or grammatically exceptional forms are substituted by a standard one, e.g., the suffix of the second person feminine – קראתי > קָרָאת (Jer. 3:4), לכי > לָךְ (II Kings 4:2), בניכי > וּבָנַיִךְ (II Kings 4:7), and, e.g., the suffix of the verb in the perfect, plural third person feminine נצתה > נִצְּתוּ (Jer. 2:15), etc.

3.2.2.3. CORRECTION OF ERRORS. Errors, or what appeared to the masoretes to be errors, are corrected. These are likely to be of various types, as metathesis, substitution of letters, the omission or addition of letters, changes in the division of the words, the substitution of whole words, and so on, such as ותראנה < וַתָּאֹרְנָה (I Sam. 14:27); יך < יַד (I Sam. 4:13); ויעש < וַיַּעַט (I Sam. 14:32); הזאתה < הַזֹּאת (Jer. 26:6): שלל < הַשָּׁלָל (Sam. 14:32); שם הפלשתים < שָׁמָּה פְּלִשְׁתִּים (II Sam. 21:12); העיר < חָצֵר (II Kings 20:4) and so on.

3.2.2.4. MALE' AND ḤASER (PLENE AND DEFECTIVE). Changes in the spelling because of *matres lectionis*. It is with regard to this group that variants in the different manuscripts are the most frequent. Some manuscripts note them as a version of *qere*, whereas others ignore them, because it is possible to read the *ketiv* with the vowels of the *qere* and not make an error (for examples see above, 3.2.1.7.).

3.2.2.5. QERE PERPETUUM. In addition to the above types of *qere* there are others which are not noted at all, the *qere perpetuum*. These were handed down orally from generation to generation and one must observe them even though there is no *qere* notation concerning them. In these instances the vocalization of the *qere* is attached to the *ketiv*. Among there are the name of God, which is read differently from the way in which it is written; in the Torah the feminine third personal pronoun is הִוא (except for 11 places where it is הִיא); נַעֲרָה is written in the Torah without the *he* (except for one place, Deut. 22:19); the name of the city Jerusalem is written without the second *yod* (except in five places) but it is always read יְרוּשָׁלַיִם; the name ישׂשכר is always read יִשָּׂשכָר (Issachar) – at least in the Ben-Asher version – see below). Some have suggested to consider other forms as examples of *qere perpetuum*, for example, שְׁנַיִם, שְׁתַּיִם which are supposed to be שְׁנֵי, שְׁתֵּי, (see *Gesenius §17c, 97d), but there is no evidence for this.

3.2.3. The Masoretic Notes

The other notes of the *Masorah Parva* point out forms in the text concerning which there is some apprehension that the reader or the scribe-copyist will err, that is, spelling with or without the *matres lectionis* (plene or defective), certain vowels or accentuation signs, certain grammatical forms, the joining of certain particles, the unusual combination of words, and so on. In most of the masoretic notes the view is descriptive-comparative and not normative. In general the question is not what is the standard form and does the item in question deviate from it, but rather what is the common form and is the item in question different from the common form – whether or not it be standard or exceptional itself – and does the item belong to the majority or the minority. This last principle necessitates the constant enumeration of the forms in the various divisions of the text (in the entire Bible, in one of the three parts of the Bible, in a book, or even in a specific section), and reference to this number.

3.2.3.1. TERMINOLOGY. Below is a list of the common terms in the Masorah and their usual abbreviations. From the definitions and examples the nature of the notes of the *Masorah Parva* will become clear. It is to be noted that most of the terms of the Masorah are Aramaic, which in fact is itself an indication of the time of the creation of this terminology: ליתא, לית = ל̇ ("there is none [like it]"): בְּצַלְמוֹ (Gen. 1:27), ל̇ (the word in this form does not occur again in the Bible); ב̇, ג̇, ד̇, etc., "enumeration": וְשָׁמָיִם (Gen. 2:4), ד̇ (this word with the conjunctive *waw* occurs four times in the Bible); מלא = מ״ל, מל̇ ("*plene*," i.e., with *matres lectionis*): בְּעִצָּבוֹן (Gen. 3: 17), ל׳ ומ״ל (= לית ומלא; the word does not occur again in the Bible and here it is written with the *waw*): תּוֹלְדוֹת (Gen. 2:4), ב׳ מ״ל דמ״ל (= ב׳ מלא דמלא; this word is found twice in the Bible with two *waws*); יתיר ("*plene*"; see above, 3.2.1.3.): וּמְהָקִים (Dan. 2:21), ל̇ ויתיר י̇ (the word does not occur again and here it is written with *yod*); חסר = חס׳ (defective, "deficient," i.e., without *matres lectionis*): גְּחֹנְךָ (Gen. 3:14), ל׳ וחס׳ (occurs only here and written without *waw*); ריש פסוקא or ראש פסוק = ר״פ (the beginning of a verse); אֶל־הָאִשָּׁה (Gen. 3:16), ל׳ ר״פ (this combination appears nowhere else at the beginning of a verse); דסמיכי = דסמיכ׳, דס׳ (together): חַיַּת ◦ הָאָרֶץ (Gen. 1:25), י׳ דס׳ (these two words are found together 10 times); בתורה = בתו׳ (in the Torah): שֵׁמוֹת (Gen. 2:20), ט׳ מלאי׳ בתורה (this word is written in the Torah nine times with the *waw*); אורייתא = אוריית׳, אורי׳ (Aramaic for Torah): וּשְׁמֹנֶה (Gen. 5:7), כל אוריית׳ חס׳ (without the *waw* throughout the whole Torah); בסיפרא = בספ׳, בסי׳ (in this book of the Bible): חָרְבוּ (Gen. 8:13), ב׳ בספ׳ (occurs twice in the Book of Genesis); בנביאי = בנביא׳ or בנביאים (in the Prophets): וַתָּבוֹא (Ezek. 22:4), י׳ מל׳ בנביא׳ (occurs 10 times in the Prophets with the second *waw*); בכתיביא = בכתיב׳, בכת׳ or בכתובים (in the Hagiographa): הֲלוֹא (Ruth 2:8), ט׳ מל׳ בכת׳ (nine times with *waw* in the Hagiographa); בענינא, בענין = בעני׳, בעינ׳ (in this context): וַיִּהְיוּ כָּל־יְמֵי (Gen. 5:8), ז׳ בענין (this combination occurs seven times in this section, i.e., in the section of the generations from Adam to Noah. In contrast, וַיְהִי כל־ימי occurs there three times); בלישנא = בלש׳, בליש׳ (in the language, i.e., 1. root, basic form; 2. meaning):

1. הֵינִיקָה (Gen. 21:7), ה׳ מ״ל בליש׳ (there are five words from the same root written with two *yods*). This is the only occurrence of this form, but there are four others from the same root ינק which are written with two yods: מֵינִיקוֹת (Gen. 32: 16), לְהֵינִיק (1 Kings 3:21), מֵינִיקֹתַיִךְ (Isa. 49:23), הֵינִיקוּ (Lam. 4:3), and see *Minhat Shai* to Ex. 2:9.

2. וַיָּגֶל (Gen. 29:10), ב׳ בתרי ליש׳ (the word occurs twice in this form, with two meanings. Here it means "and he rolled" – the *hif'il* of גלל; in Ps. 16:9 it means "and he rejoiced" the *qal* of גיל). בטעמא = בטע׳, בט׳ (with the accent): וַיֹּאמֶר (Gen. 22:2), י״ד בטע׳ (this word occurs 14 times with this accent).

In addition to this group of terms there are also basic grammatical expressions: דגש (*dageš*) and רפי (*rafeh*), מלעיל (*mille'el*) and מלרע (*millera'*), זכר (masculine) and נקבה (*feminine*), קמץ (*qameṣ*) and פתח (*pattaḥ*), and the names of the other vowels and accentuation signs. For a more comprehensive list of terms see Yeivin, *Introduction to the Tiberian Masorah*, pp. 80–120.

3.2.4. The Babylonian Masorah

The *Masorah Parva* and the *Masorah Magna* are appended also to texts of the Babylonian system (see 5.2.). They are slightly different from the Tiberian system (see above), but the main difference is in the very paucity of masoretic notes – for most of the parts of the Bible there is no Masorah or there is very little – and in their terminology.

3.2.4.1. TERMINOLOGY. Some of the terms are the same in the two systems; the following are the most important terms which are unique to the Babylonian Masorah: דקרן = דק׳ (Aram. "which is read") = in most cases equal to Tiberian

ל'; בעל', בע' = בעלמא (in the whole Bible [opposed to a part of it]; there is no exact parallel for it in the Tiberian system); שלמא, שלם = של' ("complete") = Tiberian מל' (a Babylonian term found in some Tiberian Mss., especially the earliest ones, e.g., British Library, Or. 4445). The Babylonian system is particularly different in that there is almost no counting of words in it except for that implied by the terms דק'.

Some grammatical terms are named differently, such as the following names of vowels: מיצץ פומא = מיצ' פומא, מיצ' (Aram. "contraction of the mouth") = *qameṣ*; מיקפץ פומא = (*ditto*) = *qameṣ*; מיפתח פומא ("opening of the mouth") = פיתחא = *pattaḥ*; so too some of the names of the accents: אתנח סיחפא = (*ʾetnaḥ*); שידיא = סגול (*segol* and other accents with similar pausal value); אוקומי, אוק' (a major disjunctive); *zaqef*. Other grammatical terms named differently are קיפיא, קיפ' = (רפה *rafeh*): ניגרא = ניג' (= מלעיל in all its usages); דיגרא (= מלרע in all its usages). For a comprehensive list and discussion of the Babylonian Masoretic terminology see I. Yeivin, *Babylonian Masorah*, pp. 54–55: Y. Ofer, *Babylonian Masorah*, pp. 39–59; N. Reich, *Shalshelet*.

3.2.4.2. CONTAMINATION OF MASORAH. In some cases we find a mixture of the Masorah. Some Tiberian codices show a certain degree of Babylonian influence in terminology or even in essence. The best example of sporadic absorption of Babylonian terms is the Tiberian Pentateuch codex London Or. 4445 (see Dotan, *Babylonian Residues*), and isolated cases may be found in other manuscripts too (e.g., the Aleppo codex). The best example of a Tiberian codex where the essence, the very readings, of the Masorah is by nature often Babylonian or close to Baylonian is the Pentateuch codex Gottheil 14 (ל"מ), which was apparently an adaptation of the Babylonian Masorah (see Breuer, *Masorah Magna* ל"מ).

The contamination of Masorah is also found in the opposite direction, where a Babylonian manuscript is mixed with Tiberian Masorah (Tiberianization). The most representative example is the codex Petropolitanus of the Latter Prophets (dated 916).

3.2.5. The Palestinian Masorah

In the texts vocalized in the Palestinian system there are almost no masoretic notes, except for the *qere* notations. In the few fragments where there are masoretic notes, they are the same as in the Tiberian system; most common are the basic terms: ל', חס', מל' (מלי), בט', בס', דגש and also the letters used for numbers. All of these signs are generally written between the lines above the relevant words, but occasionally also in the margins.

3.2.6. Deviating Versions

3.2.6.1. MADINḤAʾE. Other opinions are also cited in the Masorah. The degree to which they are mentioned obviously depends upon the masorete or transcriber of the manuscript. The most common case is the mention of the Babylonian version מדנחאי (Easterners), as opposed to the מערבאי (Westerners), for example, וּפִנְחָס (1 Sam. 1:3) למערבאי חס' למדנחאי מ"ל (= defective according to the Westerners [Palestinians], plene [with *yod*, ופינחס] according to the Easterners [Babylonians]).

3.2.6.2. VERSIONS OF PARTICULAR MASORETES AND MANUSCRIPTS. Some masoretes are even referred to by name in the Masorah, e.g., in the Leningrad manuscript of 1009: Ben-Asher (Dan. 7: 10), Ben-Naphtali (Isa. 44:20), Rav Phinehas Rosh ha-Yeshivah (Job 32: 3), the Tiberians בעלי טבריה (Prov. 3:12). In some manuscripts Moshe Moḥeh and others are mentioned too. In the margins one finds sometimes variants of Biblical manuscripts which served as exemplary models and upon which it was customary to rely. Thus, for example, in the Leningrad manuscript the מחזורה רובה (רבה) is mentioned and in other manuscripts ספר הללי, ספרי אספמיא, and others (the term ספר מוגה does not apparently refer to a specific manuscript). Citing variant versions was intended either to reinforce the version of the text or to bring to the attention of the reader another version which is, in the opinion of the masorete, also worthy of being considered.

3.2.6.3. SEVIRIN. There is another type of variant version which is different from all these in that it is cited in order to be rejected, i.e., in order to prevent possible error by the reader. These variants, which are occasionally more reasonable than the text, are called סבירין, סביר (*sevir, sevirin* = "there are some who believe [that the text is…]"); סבירין ומטעין ("there are those who believe and err [that the text is…]"); and in the Babylonian Masorah דמשתבשין בהון, מיש' (= there are some who err in them), דחזי ליה, דחזי (= which fits it [the text] better). For example, הַשֶּׁמֶשׁ יָצָא עַל-הָאָרֶץ (Gen. 19:23): ג' סבירין יצאה (in three places יָצָא is written and some think better to read it יָצְאָה; they are not correct and it is not to be read that way). וְנָתַן פִּדְיֹן נַפְשׁוֹ כְּכֹל אֲשֶׁר יוּשַׁת עָלָיו (Ex. 21:30): ב' סבירין בכל ומטעים (in two places some think it should be read בכל instead of ככל and they are wrong). There are also cases where the term מטעים is a warning about a possible error and not a record of a version.

The number of cases of *sevirin* is not uniform and varies from dozens of *sevirin* in some of the older manuscripts to about 350 in later editions (such as the C.D. Ginsburg edition of the Bible). These differences stem from the fact that some manuscripts completely ignore the *sevirin* version in many places, while others bring the errant version, *sevirin*, as *ketiv* and the correct version as *qere*. Although the origin of some of these variants is clearly ancient, it seems that the number of logically possible – but rejected – variants increased with time and the copying of the manuscripts.

3.3 THE MASORAH MAGNA (GEDOLA)

A large part of the notations of the *Masorah Parva*, with the exception of the *qere* notations and the indications of unique forms (ל'), etc., occur in greater detail in the *Masorah Magna*. In principle the *Masorah Magna* is a detailed explanation and expansion of the *Masorah Parva*; it does, however, contain additional notes, the abbreviations of which do not occur in the *Masorah Parva*.

3.3.0.1 METHOD OF NOTATION. Owing to its length the *Masorah magna* was not written at the side of the text but in either the upper or lower margin of the page, or in both, and, in a few manuscripts, also in the side margins. The *Masorah Magna* is a continuous text of a few lines on every page, and not like the Masora parva where letters and abbreviated words are written opposite the relevant word in the text. However, sometimes there was not enough space on the page and the scribes would leave part of it, especially the long lists, for the end of the book.

The details of the *Masorah Magna* generally include the citation of all the words or parts of the verses which contain a certain form, for which only the number is listed in the *Masorah Parva*: for example: וְנֹחַ (Gen. 6:8) – *Masorah Parva*: ג׳ ר״פ (it occurs three times in this form – with the conjunctive *waw* – at the beginning of a verse); *Masorah Magna*: ונח. ג׳ ר״פ וסי׳ ונח מצא חן (Gen. 6:8), ונח בן שש מאות שנה (Gen. 7:6), ונח דניאל ואיוב (Ezek. 14: 20).

3.3.1. The "Simanim" (Mnemonic Devices)

The detailing of the verses or parts of verses is often introduced by the term וסימנהון (= "and their sign") or its abbreviation, וסי׳, וסימ׳. This term (in addition to its later use for denoting chapters of the Bible) serves mainly to mark the mnemonic devices which the masoretes fixed for remembering the itemized biblical verses. These devices are of various types. Sometimes they are like the devices in the Talmud which are made up of initials. For example, in order to remember the sequence in which the seven nations are listed the masoretes gave various arrangements of initials as *siman*:

כתמפו״ס = (Ex. 3:8, 17) הכנעני והחתי והאמרי והפרזי והחוי והיבוסי
כמתפס״ו = (Jos. 11:3) הכנעני ממזרח ומים והאמרי והחתי והפרזי והיבוסי בהר והחוי
כתמפס״ג = (Neh. 9:8) הכנעני החתי האמרי והפרזי והיבוסי והגרגשי

Likewise the *siman* for the words וַיְחִי־שֵׁת (Gen. 5:6), *Masorah Magna*: ויחי שת ה׳ בטעם וסי׳ שילנ״ע שת ירד למך נח עבר, i.e., in the generations from Adam to Noah (Gen. 5) and from Noah to Abraham (Gen. 11) only five names occur bearing this accent – *zaqef gadol* – and the mnemonic device for remembering these names is שילנ״ע. The device for listing the daughters of Zelophehad (Num. 26:33 and Jos. 17:3) מוחמ״ו (מחלה ונעה חגלה מלכה ותרצה) is found both in the Tiberian and in the Palestinian *Masorah Magna*, and it is at variance with other *simanim* – מנוו״ו (Num. 27:1), and מתוו״ו (Num. 36:11). Another example: יִבְחָר (Josh. 9:27) – *Masorah Magna*: יבחר ה׳ קמצין בקריאה וסי׳ שלש פעמים בשנה יראה כל זכורך (Deut. 16:16), בבוא כל ישראל לראות את פני (Deut. 31:11), המסכן תרומה עץ לא ירקב (Isa. 40:20), ולמזבח ה׳ עד היום ביהושע (Josh. 9:27), מי זה האיש ירא (Ps. 25:12), וסימ׳ שבז״הם – i.e., יִבְחָר vocalized with *qameṣ* occurs five times in the Bible, and from those five instances we derive the mnemonic (שבז״הם): שלש בבוא ולמזבח המסכן מי

Frequently, however, the mnemonic device is not a set of initials, but a full Aramaic sentence, in which each word represents a verse: Thus, on the word וָטוֹב (1 Sam. 2:26) the *Masorah Magna* reads: וטוב ה׳ קמצין בקריאה וסי׳ ואל הבקר רץ אברהם ויקח בן בקר (Gen. 18:7), והנער שמואל (1 Sam. 2:26), ושמו שאול בחור וטוב (1 Sam. 9:2), וימצאו מרעה שמן (1 Chron. 4:40), הוספת חכמה וטוב (1 Kings 10:7), וסי׳ בלשון תרגום שמואל טליא בחירא רהט ואשכח חכמתא. Namely, the word וָטוֹב vocalized with *qameṣ* is found five times in the Bible, and the substitution of an Aramaic word for each of the five verses (not necessarily in the order of occurrence in the Bible) results in an understandable sentence: שמואל טליא (= הנער שמואל, "the lad Samuel"; 1 Sam. 2:26), בחירא (= בחור "chosen man": 1 Sam. 9:2), רהט (= רץ "ran"; Gen. 18:7), ואשכח (= וימצאו / וימצא, "and he found / and they found"; 1 Chron. 4:40), חכמתא (= חכמה, "wisdom"; 1 Kings 10:7); thus (the *siman* in Aramaic is: "the chosen lad Samuel ran and found wisdom".

This type of *siman* is very frequent and there is more than a bit of sophistry and amusement in it. There are even longer *simanim*, as e.g., the mnemonic for the word לָאוֹר (Micah 7:9) is: צוח סמיא וסבר למיפק בצפרא וקם בלילא (= the blind one called out and hoped to get out in the morning and got up at night). For the word לו (Gen. 17:18) there is a sentence of 22 words, and even longer ones are extant. In some manuscripts devices like these were found even in Arabic (A. Dotan, "Masora in Arabic Translation").

3.3.2. Accumulative Masorah

The most common notations of Masorah Magna, discussed so far, apply to forms of words which occur a number of times in the Bible. There is another type of *Masorah magna* notations which list words that occur only once and which are marked in the *Masorah Parva* by לית. In recent research such lists are termed "Accumulative Masorah" (in Hebrew: מסורה מצרפת), for they list together unique words of a certain common peculiarity, such as a common beginning, e.g., an initial letter *teth*: טֻבְּעוּ, טְאֵב, טְרַחֲכֶם, טְמוּנֵי etc.; a common ending, e.g., ־יחַ: מַשְׁלִיחַ, מֵגִיחַ, לְהָנִיחַ etc.; a common vocalization, e.g., a *qameṣ* in words starting with *shin*: שָׁאַג, שָׁדַד, שָׁלַח, שָׁכַב, -שָׁלֹשׁ etc.; or even a common combination of words, e.g., combinations with הארץ: ותעש הארץ, ובכל הארץ, ואלהי הארץ, כברת הארץ etc. Sometimes an Accumulative Masorah may consist of pairs (זוגין) of unique similar words or combination of words differing in only one detail from each other, e.g. words with or without an initial *waw*: נשאתני/ונשאתני, נדמה/ונדמה, נמליך/ונמליך etc.; or e.g., combinations with or without *he* in the second word:/אנשי שם/אנשי השם, אשרי איש/אשרי האיש, אחיכם אחד אחיכם האחד etc.; and many more variations of accumulation of unique words or sometimes even pairs of unique words. The items in these lists may have no definite order or they may be arranged by order of their occurrences in the Bible or alphabetically or by the order of some other principle (A. Dotan, *The Awakening*, pp. 31–44).

3.3.3. The Babylonian Masorah

The Babylonian *Masorah Magna* does not differ from the Tiberian in principle, but it is more limited in scope and methods of expression. In contrast to the Babylonian *Masorah Parva*, which is written in ancient manuscripts, especially in those vocalized with the simple Babylonian vocalization, between the lines, the *Masorah Magna* is recorded in the margins at the sides or the top and bottom. In texts vocalized according to the composite Babylonian system, there was not enough space between the lines; the *Masorah Parva* was written at the sides and the *Masorah Magna* at the top and bottom. In all the periods there were mixed texts, influenced by other vocalization systems, and this influence finds expression in the masoretic notes, in their terminology, and even in their methods of writing. A detailed description is now available in Y. Ofer, *Babylonian Masora.*

3.3.4. The Palestinian Masorah

The Palestinian *Masorah Magna* is even more limited in scope. Its few notes are mainly written in the bottom borders and occasionally at the top, too. The *Masorah Parva* is written in the side margins or between the lines. In its content – terminology and methods of expression – the Palestinian Masorah is closer to the Tiberian than to the Babylonian, although the influence of the Tiberians must be taken into account. In scope it is closer to the Babylonian Masorah and is even shorter than the latter, which is undoubtedly due to its very early date.

3.3.5. Agreement between the Masorah Magna, The Masorah Parva and the Text

In essence the *Masorah Magna* complements the *Masorah Parva* – particularly in the Tiberian Masorah, which has been transmitted to us in sufficient quantity to allow a comprehensive study – and it is entirely logical to expect a fixed relationship between the two, as between any text and its extension. However, only rarely is this the case.

3.3.5.1. LACK OF AGREEMENT. There are many instances where there are notes in the *Masorah Parva* for which there are no counterparts in the *Masorah Magna* and vice versa. Furthermore, sometimes there is disagreement between the masoretic notes and the version in the text itself; for example, one finds occasionally the gloss לית מלא (not found elsewhere *plene*) in the margin, while in the text the word is actually written defectively, without *matres lectionis*.

3.3.5.2. METHODS OF COPYING. These differences between the two Masorahs themselves and between them and the sacred text increased as time passed. In early manuscripts such instances are still rare, but in later manuscripts they become more common. The cause is to be found in the method of copying the manuscripts. The precision was preserved as long as the manuscripts of the Bible text were copied by experts, each one a skilled craftsman – the scribe in the writing of the consonantal text and the learned masorete (המלמד) in the placing of the vowels, the accentuation signs, and the masoretic notes – a division of labor that was maintained generally in the earliest period, the ninth, tenth, and 11th centuries, and perhaps even later. In this way the masorete did his work on a consonantal skeleton which was transcribed for him by an expert scribe. When the consonantal text did not agree in every detail with the Masorah that he followed, he was able to correct the writing (mainly to add or remove *waws* or *yods*). Even so there were discrepancies between the text and the Masorah. For the masoretes, even the most expert, generally did not create the Masorah, but merely transmitted it as they had received it from their forerunners, sometimes adding new notes or amending notes that were inadequate. They undoubtedly used older manuscripts and older lists of Masorah from which they transferred the notes – obviously with deep understanding – onto the new copy in front of them. As the years passed the masoretic material increased by virtue of the innovations and additions of each generation, while the selectiveness of the masoretes became less and less severe. The degree of coordination between the various notes of the Masorah itself and between the Masorah and the text of the Bible decreased as the quantity of the masoretic notes grew. Furthermore, the separation between the two types of notes, the *Masorah Magna* and the *Masorah Parva*, was not maintained and more and more long notes of the type of the *Masorah Magna* were recorded in the margins, the place of the *Masorah Parva*.

3.3.5.3. THE NON-CRYSTALLIZATION OF THE MASORAH. It can be said that there never was one single uniform Masorah. One can assume that the early, great masoretes composed an exact Masorah which fitted a specific text of the Bible. A version like this was, therefore, "the Masorah of so-and-so," but not THE Masorah. Even though no such perfect version is extant, we do know that they existed; for example, the Masorah of Ben-Asher וקאל פי מאסרתה ("and he said in his Masorah"). Versions of this type served as exemplary models for later masoretes, but some of them followed the principle that the more models the better, which ultimately had an unfortunate effect.

3.3.5.4. ORNAMENTATION OF THE TEXT. As time passed copying the text became a less intelligent work, and there were copyists who lacked all understanding of the Masorah, to the extent that some of them used the material of the Masorah for mere ornamentation of the text. They created frames for the text out of the lines of the Masorah; they sketched geometric patterns, pictures of animals in the margins of the pages; they even wrote names, such as the name of the scribe or that of the owner, using masoretic notes as fillers. The masoretic material was not copied to fit each page of text exactly, but according to aesthetic and space criteria. In some places the copyist stopped the copy in the middle of a masoretic note for lack of space, or copied an irrelevant note to fill the space. Manuscripts like these, some of which are most ornate, are worthless for the study of the Masorah.

3.3.6. Jacob ben Ḥayyim ibn Adonijah

3.3.6.1. EDITING AND ARRANGING THE MASORAH. Jacob b. Ḥayyim ibn Adonijah of Tunis (c. 1470–c. 1538) tried to correct this situation. He was employed as a proofreader in the printing house of Daniel *Bomberg in Venice at the beginning of the 16th century. He collected a large number of manuscripts of the Bible and from them edited a new clear version of the Masorah. He corrected the errors in it and adapted it to that text of the Bible which seemed to him to be the most correct version. In addition he arranged most of the notes of the *Masorah Magna* in the alphabetical order of the words to which they are directed and printed them in a lexical list at the end of the Bible. The Masorah of Ben Ḥayyim was printed with the second edition of the Rabbinic Bible published by Bomberg – *Miqra'ot Gedolot*, Venice 1524–25, and it was issued in a scholarly edition by S. Frensdorff, *Die Massora Magna* (Hanover and Leipzig, 1876; repr.: New York, 1968).

3.3.6.2. CROSS REFERENCES. Besides his correction of errors, Jacob b. Ḥayyim's innovation was to introduce cross references for parallel comments and to add the systematic list at the end. This was the first attempt to arrange all the masoretical notes alphabetically.

3.3.6.3. HIS TERMINOLOGY. In this arrangement every alphabetical unit is called a מערכת (*ma'arekhet*) and the whole came to be called מסורה מערכית (*Masorah ma'arakhit*). Ben Ḥayyim himself named the collection at the end מסורה גדולה or מסורה רבתא while for the marginal notations he used the name מסרה or מסורת alone or מסרה אמצעית (middle Masorah; see his introduction, ed. Ginsburg, pp. 82–83). This terminological differentiation, like his systematic arrangement, is unique to Ben Ḥayyim. Yet he was not the first in moving part of the *Masorah Magna* to the end of the text. The early Masorah copyists had already preceded him in that in the ancient manuscripts. They had had to draft long lists for which there was no room on the pages; and so they copied them together at the ends of the books. In the manuscripts, therefore, there was no essential difference between the lists of the *Masorah Magna* on the page and those at the back of the book, but for practical reasons, the lists which were longer and more comprehensive in their content were recorded at the end.

3.3.6.4. THE ACCEPTED TERMINOLOGY. This situation necessitates precision in our concept of the terminology of the Masorah. A differentiation must be made between ancient manuscripts and the codified orderly Masorah of Ben Ḥayyim, which had been for many years the one referred to when one speaks of Masorah. One can say that the *Masorah Magna* is divided into a marginal Masorah and a final Masorah. In the ancient manuscripts the final Masorah includes summation lists, which deal with complete books or sections of books (see below), and long systematic lists of Masorah for which there was no place in the margins. In Ben Ḥayyim's work the final Masorah includes a lexical arrangement of most of the words, discussed in the *Masorah Magna* sometimes with the details of the masoretic notations.

3.3.7. Summary Lists

The summary lists which are at the end of the books (and sometimes at the beginning) are tallies of the verses, the *parashiyyot* (weekly portions) and the *sedarim* of the books and parts of the Bible, and also the totals of words and letters, the mid-point in the count, the quarter point, and so on. In ancient manuscripts there are also general summation lists taken from various sources, like the names of the authors of the books (BB 14b), the chronology of the books ("the number of the years of the books"), a list of the prophets who prophesied about Israel, a list of the 18 emendations of the scribes (תיקוני סופרים; found in different Midrashim), a list of large and small letters in the Bible and other peculiarities, a lists of the *paseqs* (as opposed to the accent *legarmeh*), a list of *pattaḥs* with *'etnaḥ* and with *sof pasuq* (instead of the pausal form which requires *qameṣ*) and so on.

3.4. THE INDEPENDENT MASORAH

Fragments of manuscripts were discovered in the Cairo *Genizah* which appear to be remnants of independent works of Masorah; that is, works which contain masoretic notes in the order of the books of the Bible but without an accompanying biblical text. It is possible that these works go back to a very ancient period, perhaps even to the time when it was not permitted to write the Masorah in the margins (see above, 2.2.2.). Such fragments were also discovered of the Babylonian Masorah and a few of the Palestinian Masorah. Some of these works contain topical lists of Masorah, i.e., lists arranged according to specific subjects, like exceptional spellings, specific issues about vocalization, unique words, and so on. One independent work in which the notes do not follow the text of the Bible but are arranged systematically according to topics is *Okhlah we-Okhlah*. This work has the widest scope of all those known to us, comprising almost 400 lists of Masorah. The lists, arranged alphabetically, contain unique words with a common characteristic, or pairs of words which differ from each other in one detail, extraordinary spellings, vocalizations, or accents, and so on. The book gets its name from the first two words of the first list, which enumerates alphabetically pairs of unique words, one occurring with the conjunctive *waw* and the other without it. This list begins with the pair אָכְלָה, וְאָכְלָה. The book was also known to the early scholars by the name of מסורת הגדולה (*Masoret ha-Gedola*), and in Arabic אלמאסרה (*al-māsirah* – the Masorah) by Saadia Gaon in his Grammar book, and אלמאסרה אלכבירה (*al-māsirah al-kabîrah* = the great Masorah) by David ben Abraham al-Fāsî in his dictionary. The name *Okhlah we-Okhlah* is mentioned already by Jonah *Ibn Janāḥ in his dictionary (*Sefer ha-Shorashim*, entry חלך). The book was first published by S. Frensdorff (Hanover, 1864) according to the Paris manuscript; it was published again by F. Díaz Esteban (Madrid, 1975) according to the first part of the Halle manuscript and later by B. Ognibeni (Madrid-Fribourg, 1995) according to the second part of the Halle manuscript. Most of the lists in this book are known from other sources in the marginal Masorah or from independent manuscripts, but here they are more complete and were apparently taken, in part, from an ancient source. However, the work also contains lists from relatively late periods, and it follows that the book is not a uniform work, a fact which can be strengthened by the existence of more than one version of the book. The exact date of its editing has not been established, though there is evidence of its antiquity and it was certainly not edited later than the tenth century.

3.5. THE MASORAH TO TARGUM ONKELOS

Masoretic notes were also appended to Targum *Onkelos, which was considered the official translation of the Torah for the purpose of public reading and which, therefore, also came to be considered sacred to some extent. The purpose of these notes was to preserve the text of the Targum exactly and to achieve precision in the manner of translation from the Hebrew original: which Aramaic roots are used in translating the same Hebrew root, and the number of times that each translation occurs, etc. It counts the words much less than does the biblical Masorah. It does list changes in vocalization and in pronunciation of the Targum and even discrepancies between various versions of translation, such as the Nehardean and Suran, and it takes a position against other possibilities (possible errors, מַשתבשין, מַטעין). Since the main interest of this Masorah was the manner of translation, terms such as דמתרגמין and דמיתרגם (= which is translated) and their abbreviations are quite common. An example is שְׁבוּ (Gen. 22:5): שבו דמתרג׳ אוריכו ג׳ באורי׳ ("שבו" is translated אוריכו (= wait, instead of תיבו = sit) three times in the Torah") – שבו לכם פה (Gen. 22:5); שבו לנו בזה (Ex. 24:14); שבו נא בזה (Num. 22:19).

The Masorah notes of the Targum were sometimes written in manuscripts on the margins of the Targum and sometimes in lists in independent works arranged according to the order of the biblical text. The Targum also has a Tiberian Masorah as well as a Babylonian one with Babylonian vocalization. The terminology of this Masorah, whether Tiberian or Babylonian, does not differ much from the terminology of the biblical Masorah.

4. THE DIACRITICAL POINTS

The written Masorah was divided here into two categories (see above, 3.). We have dealt with the first – the notes and the abbreviations which accompany the text externally or are appended to it – Masorah in the narrow sense. We now turn to the second category – the graphemes – i.e., the system of signs (the vowel and accentuation signs) which are added to the letters in order to constitute, together with them, a complete orthographic system including all the information necessary for exact reading and recitation.

Just as the Masorah in the narrow sense began with a relatively few early attempts at abbreviated notes and developed into a large sophisticated system of short and long notes and even complete rules, it can be assumed that the graphemes also had their beginning in a few signs which were most necessary for reading and for distinguishing between similar forms, and only in the end, after long development, became a fully crystallized system of vowel and accentuation signs. For this assumption, in the opinion of many scholars, there is proof in vestiges from the ancient period.

4.1. GRAETZ'S THEORY

According to this opinion, in the period before the invention of vowel signs as they are known, diacritical points were used in Hebrew to distinguish between words which were identical in writing – homographic – but whose pronunciation differed by one vowel. A dot above the word marked the pronunciation with the fuller vowel; a dot under the word noted the pronunciation with the weaker vowel. There are, however, no manuscripts in which there is any trace of these signs, and their very existence is postulated only by the theory of Graetz.

4.1.1. Details of the Proof

4.1.1.1. ANCIENT USAGE OF "MILLEʿEL" AND "MILLERAʿ". Graetz found in various lists of the Masorah in *Okhlah we-Okhlah* that the terms מלעיל (*milleʿel*) and מלרע (*milleraʿ*) were used, in addition to their regular common meanings, (paroxytone and oxytone), in other meanings as well. These lists (§§ 5, 11, 45, 46, 47, 48, 49, 50) in Frensdorff's edition contain unique homographic pairs which differ in one vowel only. One member of the pair is called *milleʿel* and the other *milleraʿ*. It is evident that these terms do not have a fixed but a changing meaning, and they mark the difference between vowels. Thus the following are so termed:

Milleʿel		Milleraʿ	
אַדֹּן	(Neh. 7:61)	אַדָּן	(Ezra. 2: 59)
אֱמֹר	(Ezek. 25:8)	אֱמָר־	(Prov. 25:7)
בְּמֹעַל	(Neh. 8:6)	בְּמַעַל	(Josh. 22:22)
הַמְשֹׁל	(Jud. 9:2)	הַמְשֵׁל	(Job 25: 2)
לִשְׁבוּיִם	(Isa. 61:1)	לִשְׁבָאִים	(Joel 4: 8)
קְרָאֻנִי	(Jer. 13:22)	קְרָאַנִי	(Job 4:14)
יְחַיֻּנוּ	(II Kings 7:4)	יְחַיֵּנוּ	(Hos. 6:2)
נֻתַּץ	(Judg. 6:28)	נִתַּץ	(II Chron. 33:3)
נָתָן־	(Gen. 38:9)	נְתַן־	(II Kings 23:11)
זָרֻעַ	(Ps. 97:11)	זֵרוּעַ	(Lev. 11:37)
נָפְלוֹ	(I Sam. 29:3)	נִפְלוֹ	(II Sam. 1:10)

All of these are in list no. 5 in *Okhlah we-Okhlah* (which is also cited in the terminal Masorah in the *Miqraʾot Gedolot* of Jacob b. Ḥayyim, letter *ʾalef*, list no. 24). It can be seen that forms with *qameṣ*, for example, are sometimes called *milleʿel* (נָפְלוֹ, זָרֻעַ, נָתָן־) and sometimes *milleraʿ* (לִשְׁבָאִים, אֱמָר־, אַדָּן); this is not an indication of a definite marking of the vowel, but only its relation to the vowel which is parallel to it and which can occur in that position. Thus in the list the vowel *o* is called *milleʿel* while the *milleraʿ* is *å* (this Tiberian vowel is parallel to the two types of *qameṣ*, called today *qameṣ gadol* and *qameṣ qaṭan*, but which in the Tiberian pronunciation constituted one vowel quality – see below), *a*, and *e*; the vowel *u* is contrasted to *å*, *a*, *e*, *i*; and the *å* is contrasted to *a*, *e*, *i*.

In some lists of pairs of unique homographs the terms signify other constrasts:

Mille'el		Millera'	
וַיְּחְיוּ	(Ezek. 37:10)	וְיִחְיוּ	(Ezek. 37:9)
בַּחֶרֶט	(Ex. 32:4)	בְּחֶרֶט	(Isa. 8:1)
לַנְּבִאִים	(Jer. 23:9)	לִנְבִאִים	(Amos 2:11)
וַיְעִדֻהוּ	(I Kings 21:13)	וִיעִדֻהוּ	(I Kings 21:10)
וַתְּלַבֵּב	(II Sam. 13:8)	וּתְלַבֵּב	(II Sam. 13:6)
כֶּחָתָן	(Isa. 61:10)	כְּחָתָן	(Ps. 19:6)
וָאֶקְחָה	(Zach. 11:13)	וְאֶקְחָה	(Gen. 18:5)
כָּאֲרָזִים	(Songs 5:15)	כַּאֲרָזִים	(Num. 24:6)
וָבֹקֶר	(Ps. 55:18)	וּבֹקֶר	(Ex. 16:7)

from lists no. 11, 45–50 of *Okhlah we-Okhlah* (ed. Frensdorff).

Here too the forms with a *pattah*, for example, are sometimes called *mille'el* (וַיְּחְיוּ, בַּחֶרֶט, etc.) and sometimes *millera'* (כַּאֲרָזִים, etc.), and here too it only indicates the relationship to the vowel parallel to it which can possibly occur in that position. Consequently, in these lists, the forms called *mille'el* are those whose formative letters (ל, כ, ב, ו) have a vowel (a, å, ɛ), in contrast to those forms called *millera'* in which the formative letter has a *šewa* or one of its morpho-phonological substitutes (*u, a, i*).

4.1.1.2. THE DIACRITICAL POINT IN SYRIAC. These uses of the terms *mille'el* and *millera'* did not seem to Graetz to fit their regular meaning in which they are also used in the lists of the Masorah such as *Okhlah we-Okhlah* (ed. Frensdorff), lists no. 32, 51, 225, 226, 372 and 373. However, this manner of distinguishing between homographs of different pronunciation did exist in Syriac and a dot was used to mark this distinction: a dot above a word (more precisely, above the letter) marked a fuller, stronger pronunciation, and a dot below it marked a finer, weaker pronunciation or even the complete lack of a vowel; thus, for example, the Syriac words עבדא, קטל, מלכא, טבא, הו, הי, הנון, מן, when they are marked with a dot above, their (Eastern) pronunciation is *'ᵉv̄adā, qāṭɛl* or *qaṭṭɛl, malkā, ṭāvā, hau, hāi, hānōn, mān*, but when they have a dot beneath them the pronunciation is: *'avdā, qᵉṭal, mɛlkā, ṭɛbbā, hū, hī, hɛnnōn, mɛn.*

4.1.1.3. DEVELOPMENT IN HEBREW. By analogy to Syriac, Graetz reached the conclusion that in Hebrew the terms *mille'el* and *millera'* also indicated the place of a dot above or below the word, and that they thus served also in Hebrew to mark the "fuller" vowel in contrast with the "weaker" vowel. The nature of the concepts "full" and "weak" and their synonyms have been explained in various ways by different scholars: some of them considered it to be a quantitative concept (long/short – thus Frendsdorff), others a qualitative one (dull, closed/bright, open – Kahle). This distinguishing dot had in Hebrew the additional function of marking contrasts in stress: on the penultimate syllable and on the ultimate one. This last use was not found in Syriac and constitutes therefore an additional development in Hebrew. However, this use too is ancient, being found in older sources of the Masorah: cf. David b. Abraham (middle of the tenth century), *Kitāb Jāmi' al-'Alfāẓ* (ed. Skoss. vol. 1, p. 185, l. 149 f.).

Graetz's theory on the source of the terms *mille'el* and *millera'*, and subsequently as to the origins of the vowel signs in Hebrew, has been unanimously accepted.

4.1.2. Refutation

However, in the entire inventory of Hebrew manuscripts there is not one example of dots above and below to mark such a distinction, especially not the distinction between different vowels. The very existence of these dots is unproven, based on a supposition which itself is open to doubt. The theory assumes diacritical dots which were borrowed from Syriac but which in fact did not remain in Hebrew; only the terms remained. These, however, do not exist and never did exist in the supposed source language, Syriac. One cannot explain the "disappearance" of the diacritical dots from Hebrew by pointing to the full Tiberian vocalization which made them superfluous, for the same process would apply just as well to Syriac, and yet, there the dots remained alongside the vocalization. Furthermore, a single example was discovered in a manuscript in which the point of stress in a word is noted by a dot under the word even on the penultimate syllable (cf. Rabin's comment in *Textus* II, p. 106. n. 11). While it is doubtful whether one can learn about a system from one lone example, clearly such an example can serve as evidence to the contrary.

4.2 MILLE'EL AND MILLERA'

4.2.1. Development of the Usage

4.2.1.1. TONAL MEANING. It is possible to offer a satisfactory explanation for the two meanings without involving non-existent diacritical dots, both for the vocalic and tonal meanings. With regard to the tonal meaning, the use of למעלה, למעלן, למטה, למטן, to indicate earlier and later locations in a continuous text is an ancient usage in Hebrew which goes back to rabbinic Hebrew. This use is rooted in general writing practice and is widespread and accepted in most languages (cf., Eng.: below, above; Fr.: ci-dessous, ci-dessus; Lat.: infra, supra) to note different places in the linear sequence of the written text. These terms were actually begging to be used and in any event are self-evident. Certainly there is no need to revert to the Syriac orthographical customs to explain them.

4.2.1.2. VOCALIC MEANING. The vocalic meaning of *mille'el/millera'* goes back to an ancient idea concerning the theory of vowels in Hebrew which was stated in the fifth chapter (concerning the vowels) of *Kitāb Faṣīḥ Luġat al-'Ibrāniyyīn* by *Saadiah Gaon. According to this theory the vowels are arranged as a scale, at the top of which is the *ḥolem* and at bottom the *ḥireq*. Such an arrangement of the vowels fits a certain morphological theory which is not relevant here, and in any event. There were a number of other such arrangements which were based on different principles, as Z. Ben-Ḥayyim has shown. One of them was based on the phonetic principle of the origins of the vowels *o, u, å, a, ɛ, e, i*. The vowels are arranged as a scale (from the top to the bottom): each vowel is above (*mille'el*) those which follow it and below (*millera'*) those which precede it. Thus *qameṣ* is *millera'* in relation to *ḥolem* and *šuruq*, and *mille*ʿ*el* in relation to *pattaḥ*, *ṣere*, and *ḥireq; pattaḥ* is *millera*ʿ in comparison to *qameṣ* and *mille*ʿ*el* in comparison to the *šewa* and its alternates. The vocalic use of the terms *mille*ʿ*el* and *millera*ʿ which is also undoubtedly ancient, can thus be explained.

4.2.1.3. CONNECTION BETWEEN THE MEANINGS. Which meaning of this pair of terms preceded the other is still difficult to establish; it is possible that there is a connection between them by way of homographic pairs, such as, וְנִקָּ֫תָה (Num. 5:28) / וְנִקָּתָ֫ה (Isa. 3:26), which appear in the *ḥad millera*ʿ *we-ḥad mille*ʿ*el* list of pairs (*Okhlah we-Okhlah*, list no. 51). Although the reference in this list is to the tonal meaning of the terms, in this specific pair the vocalic sense would also be applicable.

4.2.2. The Babylonian Terms

The terms ניגרא and דיגרא (of doubtful etmyology), which are used in the Babylonian Masorah as parallel to *mille*ʿ*el* and *millera*ʿ, have a tonal meaning, that is, paroxytone and oxytone. Yeivin (*The Hebrew Language Tradition as Reflected in the Babylonian Vocalization*, pp. 246–53) cites additional occurrences of the Babylonian terms with different meanings (some of them doubtful) but none of these cases exhibits a vocalic meaning parallel to the Tiberian terms (Yeivin, p. 253).

4.2.3. The Parallel Usage of Qameṣ and Pattaḥ

However, in place of the pair of terms *mille*ʿ*el* and *millera*ʿ in the vocalic sense, the terms קמץ and פתח are used. This use is found in a manuscript (published by Ginsburg, *The Massorah*, 2 (1883), 310–311, §§ 606a, 606b) in which there are two versions of the list of Masorah which appears in a fuller and more precise form also in *Okhlah we-Okhlah* (§5). Instead of the terms *mille*ʿ*el* and *millera*ʿ the terms *qameṣ* and *pattaḥ* are used: there they are not the names of specific vowels but are used in a relative sense like *mille*ʿ*el* and *millera*ʿ: i.e., a more contracted (קמוץ) vowel versus a more open (פתוח) vowel.

4.3. RELATIVE NOTATION

4.3.1. Vowels

This use of the terms *qameṣ* and *pattaḥ* belongs to a most ancient period in which they did not as yet serve to note definite vowels. The vestiges of this use, both of the terms *qameṣ* and *pattaḥ* and the terms *mille*ʿ*el* and *millera*ʿ, indicate that in the period which preceded the invention of vowel signs a system of relative notation of vowels was followed. In a period when no vowel notation existed it was necessary to indicate the vowels which distinguish between homographs, generally in homographic pairs. There was, however, no need for a complicated system of terms (and there is no evidence for signs); a relative distinction was sufficient: a vowel higher in the scale of vowels (further back in pronunciation), more closed, in contrast to the other possibility, lower, more open.

4.3.2. Accents

This custom of relative notation and marking also existed apparently for the accentuation signs; the vestiges of relative terms like אוקומי, which marks a major disjunctive, may serve as an indication. It is possible that the terms שידיא (not שיריא; see N. Reich, *Shalshelet*) and ניגרא (when used as an accent's name), and others, had this connotation: it is even possible that the origin of the accentuation signs was in signs which had a relative meaning only (see below). In summation: among the Hebrew vocalization signs there are no diacritical dots of the type which were used in Syriac, and it is doubtful if there ever were. The only signs known in Hebrew are the defined marks of vocalization and accentuation.

5. VOCALIZATION AND ACCENTUATION

There are three graphic systems of vocalization and accentuation for Hebrew: Palestinian, Babylonian, and Tiberian. There is no imperative connection between the pronunciation traditions in Hebrew and the graphic systems which were used; one graphic system is not necessarily specific to one of the traditions of pronunciation, and therefore a certain tradition of pronunciation is not necessarily limited to one system of notation. One can assume, though, that each one of the systems developed against the background of one defined tradition of pronunciation. Only graphic systems are relevant to this discussion since they are part of the development of the written Masorah (but see *Pronunciations of Hebrew).

The vocalization and accentuation signs in each system constitute a complete indivisible set of graphemes to guide the reader in exact reading, including not only the correct pronunciation of the words but also the correct intonation of the verses and, as pointed out above, precise cantillation. This being the case, the accentuation and vocalization will be treated together in each one of the systems. The period in which punctuation began has already been discussed above (2.2) and, as has been stated, it is not possible to establish exact dates. However, the postulate of a relative date for each of the systems in relation to the other two has been accepted. The Tiberian system is the most sophisticated and complete in the items which it transmits, and there is no doubt that, in the state in which it is known, it is the most recent (for details, see below). Most scholars tend to believe that the Palestinian is the older of the other two systems. However, since these two systems developed in different countries, Babylonia and Palestine, and since at the beginning of their development there was no contact between them, and since the signs differ in the two systems (letters in the Babylonian and dots in the Palestinian), it is impossible to arrive at a definite decision in this question on the basis of the data available today. In line with the generally accepted opinion the Palestinian system is discussed first; however, this is not meant to indicate a view on the relative dating of the systems.

5.1. THE PALESTINIAN SYSTEM

5.1.0.1. THE TERM. This system is so named because many of the texts in which it is used show signs of Palestinian origin (mainly the *piyyutim*). The term נקוד ארץ ישראל is already found in *Maḥzor Vitry* (ed. Hurwitz, Nuremberg (1923), 462) in the commentary on *Avot* attributed to Jacob b. Samson (12th century) of France; however there is no proof that this term refers to the system called Palestinian.

5.1.0.2. THE STATE OF TRANSMISSION. The Palestinian is not a crystallized system. Almost every one of the manuscripts has a number of individual and characteristic traits with regard to the use of signs. It is possible to point to the common and similar aspects but not to all the deviations of each manuscript. For what we find in the manuscripts is actually a system in development. Scholars endeavor to fix the date of a text on the basis of the degree of progress shown by the use of the signs in it: the oldest manuscripts (apparently from the eighth century) have generally very few signs, sometimes no more than one or two for a word and sometimes not even that; and even the latest of them never reach the stage of fully marking each vowel and its nuances, as is the case in the Tiberian system.

5.1.0.3. TYPES OF TEXTS. In this matter a distinction must be made between texts of the Bible, at times including an Aramaic translation, as opposed to texts of **piyyut*. The amount of vocalization is generally fuller in the latter, while the biblical texts, which had a strong tradition of reading, have relatively fewer vocalization signs but many accentuation signs. It seems that the precise cantillation was likely to trouble the educated reader more than the pronunciation of the biblical words. Therefore, vowel signs in ancient biblical texts are mainly in places where there was room for error in the reading and at points where the orthography allowed different pronunciations. When the spelling is plene, with *waw* or *yod*, one almost never finds vowel signs in ancient manuscripts.

Additional evidence of the fluency of the reader of the Bible text is offered by the סירוגין (intermittences) texts. These are manuscripts written in a system of abbreviation in which generally only the first word of every verse is written in full and of the rest only the important words, or those which cause problems, are indicated by one or there letters of each with the vowel or accentuation sign, or both, as a mnemonic device. Manuscripts of *serugin* are already mentioned in the Talmud (e.g., Git. 60a). and Rashi certainly saw examples of them, for he comments: "At the beginning of the text [= the verse] was written the full word and at the end initials." It is clear that these texts of *serugin* with the vowel and accentuation signs served as an aid to the reader when he read from a text complete but unvocalized (because of its sanctity), and to the reader or copyist who knew the text by heart and needed only a few reminders.

As time passed this high standard of knowledge declined and more notations were needed. This need is also evidenced in the later manuscripts where there are more signs and by the fact that in some of the manuscripts signs were added by a second hand. Sometimes there is evidence that signs were added by a third and fourth hand, depending on the transfer of the manuscript to owners whose knowledge of reading was less developed. For that reason there are many Palestinian manuscripts which contain vocalization by several hands, into which signs of other vocalization systems, with more detailed notation, have been mixed (see below, 5.5).

5.1.1. The Vowel Signs

In the presentation and explanation of the signs one must refrain as much as possible from drawing parallels with the Tiberian system, at least as long as the influence of this system or the Tiberian tradition of pronunciation is not being discussed, since at times the signs are anchored in a different reading tradition, i.e., with different grammar, and the comparison is likely to give a distorted impression. The values of each sign will therefore be described by phonetic signs, out of a desire to be faithful – as much as it is possible today – to their original pronunciation. The presentation is schematic, deviations of details, even quite numerous, are neglected for the sake of clarity.

5.1.1.1. THE SIGNS. The following are the vowel signs (they are located above the letter and a little to the left of it) and reference here is to quality only. There is no marking for quantity (length) in this system.

מׄׄ = *i*. This is the only sign which has hardly any changes in form or meaning in the different manuscripts.

מ̇̇ or מ̇̇ = *e* in all its nuances. The first sign is the most common and in the ancient manuscripts it is used exclusively, but there are manuscripts in which both signs are used side by side without distinction. In individual, relatively late manuscripts there is a distinction or the beginning of a distinction, apparently through the influence of the Tiberian system, so that מ̇̇ parallels *ṣere* and מ̇̇ parallels *segol* and sometimes mobile *šewa* as well.

מ̄ or מ̍ = *a* in all its nuances (if it did really have different nuances). In the ancient manuscripts the two signs are used side by side with precisely the same meaning. In some relatively late manuscripts there is a distinction, apparently through the influence of the Tiberian system, so that מ̄ is parallel to *pattaḥ* and מ̍ parallels the Tiberian *qameṣ* in all its variations, even in a position where it parallels in certain traditions (such as the Sephardi and apparently the Palestinian) not *a* but *o*. A *qameṣ* of the latter type is marked in ancient texts by the sign for the vowel *o* (מ̇). The transition stage between the original use of the signs and this completely "Tiberianized" usage can be found in a number of manuscripts in which one can see the beginning of Tiberian influence. They evidence a tendency to use those signs as parallels to the Tiberian *pattaḥ* and *qameṣ*, whose value was therefore *a*, and also – and this applies especially to the sign מ̍ – as parallels to the *qameṣ* pronounced in other traditions, as stated above, with a nuance of *o* ("*qameṣ qaṭan*"). This Tiberian influence is not necessarily in regard to pronunciation, i.e., that the sign expresses in effect the same pronunciation as the signs מ̄, מ̍, מ̇, but is mainly a graphic analogy, that is, the sign מ̍ (in the main) parallels the Tiberian sign ָ in all of its pronunciations, and one cannot deduce anything regarding a change in the pronunciation of the Palestinian text.

מׂ = *o* in all its nuances. In relatively late texts, which were under the Tiberian influence, the vowel *o*, which paralleled the Tiberian *qameṣ* in a closed, unstressed syllable ("*qameṣ qaṭan*" and others like it) was removed from the range of this sign. Kahle's supposition that this sign marks the vowel *u* in exceptional manuscripts is not proven, for it seems that there we have a different realization of the phoneme *u*, that is, a different pronunciation of the form (for example רׂחׂצת, Ezek. 16:4, does not necessarily show the pronunciation to be as the Tiberian רֻחַצְתְּ, but rather רֻחַצְתְּ, a form which is incidentally found in the Babylonian tradition, and before *reš* in the Tiberian tradition, for example קֹרַצְתִּי, Job 33:6).

מ̈ (and in individual mss. מׂ) = *u*. There are a number of instances, especially in *piyyutim*, of the use of this sign in place of the Tiberian *ḥolem*. However, that is no proof that the sign marked the vowel *o*. It seems more likely that there is here a different realization of the phoneme *u* under specific conditions. Therefore, it represents differences in the pronunciation tradition and not differences in notation. There is evidence for the allophonic realization, although not strictly parallel, of the phonemes of the back vowels also from other pronunciation traditions, such as the Samaritan tradition (which is Palestinian as well) in which, as Z. Ben-Ḥayyim has demonstrated, *ŏ* is an allophone of *ū* in closed syllables. Therefore there was no need to distinguish graphically between the two vowels (see below 5.6.); and as much is evident, although less consistently, from the Greek transcriptions of biblical Hebrew, from Galilean Aramaic, and from mishnaic Hebrew, in which, equally, as E.Y. *Kutscher has shown, *o* is an allophone of *u* (apparently, mainly short unstressed).

There is no sign for the *šewa* and when there is a sign in a place where we would expect *šewa* – though in most cases there is no sign – it is always a sign of one of the vowels (mostly *e* or *a*).

5.1.1.2. HISTORY OF THE SYSTEM. The Palestinian system is basically phonematic and it does not make finer distinctions than to note the five cardinal vowels, at least in its most ancient stage as known to us. There are no nuances of vowels and no notation of quantity. Yet one cannot ignore the fact that six signs are used to denote the five vowels. That is, there are two signs of equal value to mark *a*. (The two signs for the noting of *e* are, as stated, the product of a relatively later stage). This is unimaginable in a primitive, economic graphic system such as this. Dietrich's attempt to account for the duplication by reasons of calligraphy (מׄ only above *lamed*, מ̄ above the other letters) agrees neither with the manuscripts nor with the manner of this system in notation (compare the clear and definite distinction between מׄ and מׂ. One cannot escape the conclusion that the signs of the Palestinian system were not used, in the manuscripts which came down to us, in their original function. In their original employment there were of necessity two different vowels, probably *å* and *a*, designated by two different signs. For this reason only, two distinct signs were fixed. However, no vestiges have remained from this period, or from this use of the signs. The system was adopted by vocalizers whose tradition of pronunciation did not distinguish between the two vowels (exactly as occurred afterwards with the Tiberian vocalization), and they used the two signs indiscriminately. The original Palestinian system, which we do not have, was therefore not similar to the Sephardi tradition of pronunciation but was closer to the Tiberian tradition. It was closer, but not however identical; for in its original form it had only one *e* vowel and not two. Thus it was a tradition of pronunciation which had six vocalic qualities, as opposed to the Tiberian tradition which had seven qualities and the Sephardi which had five. The influence of the Tiberian tradition upon relatively later texts of the Palestinian system is, therefore, something of a restoration of the original situation, at least with regard to the signs מׄ and מ̄.

5.1.2. The Diacritical Signs

In addition to the vowel signs there are also a number of diacritical marks to distinguish between different pronunciations of the same letter. These marks occur in the Palestinian texts with even less frequency than the vowel signs.

5.1.2.1. ŠIN-SIN. To distinguish between the two pronunciations of the ש, the marks שׁ, שׁ, שׁ, שׁ, שׁ are used for *šin*, and in contrast to them שׂ, שׂ, שׂ, שׂ, שׂ are used for *sin*; in addition, mostly in the texts of *piyyutim*, there is yet another sign for *sin*, שׂ, with its variations שׂ, שׂ, which has no counterpart in a sign for *šin*. In the other texts, too, in most of the places where there is a sign to distinguish between the two pronunciations, it indicates the sin alone.

5.1.2.2. MAPPIQ AND DAGEŠ. The last sign mentioned, with its variations (–, –, –), is not specifically a sign to mark *sin*, but a general diacritical mark which serves to distinguish between different pronunciations of the same letter. Thus, it is also used to mark the consonantal pronunciation of a letter which may also be quiescent, mostly consonantal *he* (גֹובה), not only for the *he* with *mappiq* at the end of a word (כפיה, sometimes also the consonantal *waw* (ועׂנותך) and the consonantal *ʿalef* (נׂאל[מה]). In addition, though in fewer instances, it denotes a *dageš*, originally only the geminative *dageš* (*ḥazaq, forte*) and later, perhaps under Tiberian influence, also the explosive *dageš* (*qal, lene*). It is also found at times even in places where the Tiberian vocalization is likely to have the *dageš* of *ʾate meraḥiq* (or *deḥiq*; ראוך מים, ניכללה לו); it is marked, according to Levias, even in the last letter of the first word (חנה בה). It is infrequently used in an exceptional manner, as a *dageš* at the beginning of a syllable which was preceded by a syllable that ended with a laryngeal (*ḥ* or *ʿ*), such as ואחמׂל, a use which is found at times also in manuscripts in the Tiberian system (with a *dageš* sign).

5.1.2.3. RAFEH. The opposite of the above signs is –, which is apparently a development of = in which form it is also found sometimes (and it is thereby close to the Tiberian *rafeh* sign). This sign denotes the opposite of the *dageš*, both *lene* and *forte*, especially where there is the possibility of error in the reading and there is need to emphasize the lack of *dageš*. In a few manuscripts this sign is used mainly in its ancient form (‾) to cancel extra *waws* and *yods* in the *scriptio plene* of the *piyyutim*, and in its later rounded form (⌢) also to note quiescent *ʾalef* in biblical manuscripts. Because of this it is difficult to accept the opinion (of Kahle and others) that in a few manuscripts where this sign occurs above the letters *waw, he, ḥet*, and *ʿayin* it marks precisely their consonantal pronunciation (i.e., consonantal *waw*, and *he, ḥet*, and *ʿayin* which did not become silent). With regard to the *h, ḥ*, and *ayin* there are only a few examples and at least a part of them allow for a different explanation. As to the letter *waw*, on the face of it the sign refers to a consonantal pronunciation. However, one should not consider the sign's purpose to mark consonantal pronunciation, which is the opposite of its meaning in all of its other contexts, but rather as a sign which indicates the *rafeh* pronunciation of the *waw* [*v*], actually just like a fricative (*rafeh*) ב, namely, ו̄ = ב̄. This indeed was the pronunciation of the *waw* by Palestinians according to the testimony of Mishael b. Uzziel (*Kitāb al-Khulaf*, ed. Lüpschitz, 20; similar indirect evidence in David b. Abraham, *Kitāb Jāmiʿ al-ʾAlfāẓ*, ed. Skoss, 2 (1945), 451 and likewise in other sources). Emphasis like this of the pronunciation of *waw* by the sign ⌢ is likely to serve as a counter-direction for the Babylonian pronunciation of the *waw* as [*w*], a pronunciation which is also attested to by Mishael b. Uzziel, or perhaps it was a counter-direction to the consonantal plosive pronunciation of the *waw* as [*b*], a pronunciation which was common in Palestine itself, though by the Samaritans.

Alongside of the sign ∟ and its variants for the noting of a pronounced consonant, a dot under *he* (הּ) is used in some biblical texts – and in a few isolated manuscripts a dot in the *he* itself (הּ) as in the Tiberian system – to note the consonantal nature of the *he*, apparently already through Tiberian influence.

In summation, unlike the relative consistency of the vocalic notation, there was relatively little uniformity in the diacritical marks of the Palestinian system. This is quite natural, since all that was needed was a distinguishing sign, and not necessarily an agreed one, to indicate the other possible pronunciation, generally, the less frequent one, of the letter: *šin* versus *sin*, consonantal, *waw* and *yod*, consonantal *he*, etc.

5.1.3. The Accentuation Signs

5.1.3.1. FORMATION AND CHRONOLOGY. The accentuation signs are apparently more ancient than the other two types of signs, and anyhow older than the vowel signs (some reasons advanced in 1.3.3.). This is substantiated by perhaps the most decisive proof: the use of a single isolated dot to mark some of the accentuation signs. In the notation of the vowels and among the other diacritical marks the single dot is not used at all. It stands to reason that the single dot was already used for another purpose, for the notation of accents.

In addition to this, most of the signs in the oldest extant manuscripts of the Bible are accentuation signs and only here and there is a vowel sign inserted; obviously, one reason – among others – is that the correct punctuation and cantillation of the biblical text posed a more serious problem for the reader than the pronunciation. On the other hand, the set of accentuation signs differs from that of the vowel signs in that it is less uniform, and less governed by rules. It is difficult to generalize from all of the biblical manuscripts, or even the majority of them, that a specific accentuation sign was always used for the same purpose. This means that different signs were used to mark the same accent in different manuscripts – a situation which does not exist among the vowel signs. It follows that what we have is a set of accentuation signs along different stages of development, and we possess neither any manuscript nor any set of accentuation signs about which we can state with certainty that it is the ultimate stage of development, i.e., *the* set of Palestinian accentuation signs.

In spite of this, one may yet claim that the vowel signs are older than the accentuation signs, since the vowel signs are already fixed and uniform even in the most ancient manuscripts, while the accentuation signs are seen to be continually changing in the manuscripts. This claim, though, is only apparently valid. According to this supposition the abstention from the use of the single dot in vocalization would be unimaginable, since it is a diacritical mark which is just waiting to be used and is quite natural (as found in the writing systems of other languages). Furthermore, the double usage of a few signs, such as ¨, ‾, ˈ, which mark both vowels and accents, would not be understandable.

It seems that the two sets of signs had two cycles of growth: (a) the growth cycle of the accentuation signs (the older) in the biblical text; (b) the growth cycle of the vowel signs (relatively later) in non-biblical texts, mainly in *piyyutim*. The essential difference between the two types of texts, with the different nature of the demands that each made on the reader, as well as the different expectations of the reader from each type of text, evidently brought about the divergent crystallization of the two sets of signs.

(a) The Bible was the first text which required additional signs as reading aids. Chronologically their addition may have preceded even the beginnings of the ancient *piyyut*. These aids consisted only of the most primitive, simple mark – the single dot – and their function was to guide the educated reader, who was generally fluent in the pronunciation of the words, as to the manner of punctuation and cantillation of the verses. However, this notation did not necessarily have to be unequivocal, since, as is well known, the accentuation signs in the more developed systems, too, are relative, i.e., they designate the measure of pause in one place in a verse in relation to a greater or smaller measure of pause in another place in the same verse. It follows that in the highly developed accentuation systems (not in the Palestinian) each accentuation sign denotes the relativeness of the punctuation. Yet one need not assume that this rule necessarily held in earliest times. It seems likely, and there is evidence for it, that one specific sign served to mark pauses of different strength (see for example the many uses of the sign ִ־ precisely in the most ancient manuscripts). In the most primitive system it was sufficient, therefore, to note the very fact that there is a pause, without necessarily indicating its degree; for that purpose there was no imperative need for a uniform set of signs (cf. the section on diacritical signs – 5.1.2. – which also did not necessarily have to be uniform, for the same reason). It is only natural that scribes would not consider themselves bound to a specific set of signs, even an older and more prestigious one, and that they improvised and varied the notation system. As time passed they added signs, to indicate differences and note the degrees of the pause. They also did not refrain from using the double dot and the line, which are more complex forms, and which in part had in the meantime been fixed for other functions in the cycle of non-biblical texts.

(b) The other growth cycle of signs occurred in non-biblical texts, the *piyyut*. Here, too, additional signs were needed as reading aids. The main problem with *piyyut* was however not in the punctuation, but in the actual reading of relatively new texts, which had not been handed down from generation to generation but had recently been written in a difficult language not always understood by the reader. Here a system of vowel signs was imperative, and had to be, by its very nature and for its main purpose, unequivocal: each sign had to have, at least originally, only one function and only one meaning, so that it should note only one vocalic quality (or, to be more precise, one range of a set of vocal nuances which the reader felt to be one vowel – in other words: a phoneme). At the time that these signs were fixed for the vowels – six signs (to denote six qualities; see above, 5.1.1.2.) – they were apparently free of any other significance even in the area of accentuation. These signs remained unchanged, except for slight variations (מ̈, מ̇), without the slightest deviation in function, except for changes which took place following modification in the tradition of pronunciation (מ̄, מ̇, cf. above, 5.1.1.1.).

Alongside this stability and regularity in the use of the vowel signs there arose in the growth cycle of the biblical texts, sets of accentuation signs which were relatively "free": as they developed and more signs were added, no attention was paid to the other growth cycle, in which rules had already been established concerning the vowel signs. As long as the two systems were not mixed no difficulties were encountered, but when the punctuators of biblical texts added vowel signs to the Bible they sometimes found themselves forced to use vowel signs which had in the meantime come to be used as accentuation signs in the system which they followed. This is the source of the duplicate use of a few signs in some of the biblical texts.

5.1.3.2. THE (21) PROSE BOOKS. The identification of the Palestinian accent signs with Tiberian equivalents should perhaps *prima facie* be avoided, as was the case with the vocalization signs. However, with regard to the actual division of the verses of the Bible there are, in general, no major differences between Palestinian manuscripts and the Tiberian text; therefore in this case the Tiberian terminology can be used to identify the accentuation signs. This will, however, be done only after the presentation (independent of the Tiberian system) of the function of each sign.

5.1.3.2.1. Disjunctives. The largest disjunctive which separates a verse from the one which follows it (henceforth D_1) is in most cases not marked at all. The external technical marks (generally two dots – a colon) are sufficient to note the end of a verse. In the few instances where the end of a verse is indicated by an accentuation sign, use is made of the basic sign – the single lower dot מִ, which also notes a number of other pauses. It denotes the main divider of a verse into two, its prelude accent, the divider of the first half of the verse and, placed in different positions, the single dot also indicates a number of other accents.

This can be presented in a schematic way approximately as follows:

An average verse is generally divided into a main division by מִ (henceforth D_2, with the function of *ʾetnaḥ*), its prelude accent (henceforth D_{2p}, in the function of *ṭippeḥa* and identical with D_{1p}) being מִ. This main disjunctive, D_2, is also missing at times, yet less frequently than the last disjunctive in the verse, D_1. Generally, however, the scribes show a great degree of consistency with the notation of the prelude accent of both of them, D_{1p}, D_{2p} (henceforth D_{1-2p}). In some manuscripts instead of the lower dot of D_2 the sign מִ or מׅ or, in the Tiberianized texts, מִ, is used. Instead of the dot of the prelude accent D_{1-2p}, which occurs in a number of texts also inside the letter, מּ, the sign מִ or מִ is found in some texts; i.e. in the function of *ṭippeḥa-ʾetnaḥ*, מּ–מִ occur in some manuscripts, and in others מִ–מִ, while in others מׅ–מִ instead of the most common pair מִ–מִ or מּ–מִ.

A secondary division of each one of the two parts remaining after the first division (henceforth D_4 – the function of the *zaqef*) is sometimes also noted by a lone dot above the word מׅ, but in some manuscripts a specific sign was used for this מׅ, and in certain others not necessarily Tiberianized ones – even מ̈. Yet even in the manuscripts in which the sign is מׅ and is identical with the main pausal form, D_2, it is easy to distinguish between them with the aid of the prelude accent (henceforth D_{4p} – the function of *pašṭa*) which always has the same form מ̈, irrespective of the form of the major disjunctive D_4.

When the first part of the verse is very long it is likely to be divided by a special major disjunctive (henceforth D_3 – with the function of *segol*) which is generally noted by a single dot above the word, מׅ. In a number of manuscripts it had a special place set aside for it, above the word and to the left, that is, as a postpositive sign מ̇, or as a single lower dot מִ. The prelude accent D_{3p} (with the function of *zarqa*ʾ) is also a postpositive sign in the form of מ׳ or מ, sometimes identical with its major disjunctive, מ̇, and sometimes occurring as a sublinear point מ or מִ.

When there is a need for an additional division in the domain of the prelude accent D_{1-2p} the accent adjacent to it will be מֽ, and in one manuscript מ֨ (henceforth $D_{1-2p}D$ – with the function of the *tevir*).

An additional division larger than the prelude accents in the domain of the accents D_3, D_4, D_{1-2p} is designated by D_5, (with the function of *revia*ʿ) which was marked מ̄ or מ̇ or מ֓. The domain of this accent and the domain of the prelude accents D_{3p}, D_{4p}, D_{1-2p} are likely to be subdivided by a series of accents of lesser pausal strength which have various forms, and they are (in the order of their frequency and their increasing pausal strength): מ֜ or מ֝ or מ֞ (a sort of *gereš*), מ׳ or ,מ or מ̀ (a sort of *munaḥ legarmeh*), מ̇ or מ֔ or מ֒ (a sort of *teliša*ʾ *gedola*), מ̆ or מ̌ or מ̊ or מ̃ or מ̀ (a sort of *pazer*). All of these signs have similar functions, and it is difficult to establish with certainty their Tiberian parallels, both because of the lack of consistency of marking them and because of the possibilities of interchange among them even within the "precise" Tiberian system itself. Furthermore, particularly with regard to these accents, which are low in their pausal strength, the penetration of Tiberian influence can be recognized, such as מ̌ (similar to *pazer*) and מ̊ (similar to *teliša*ʾ). On the other hand, it is difficult to establish with certainty the origin of some of the signs, of which at least a number may be thought, to the same degree, to have originated in the Palestinian system and from there moved to the Tiberian. This theory is offered as a supposition for some of the signs which are parallel to *teliša*ʾ *gedola* and to *pazer*, but seems almost certainly correct for the sign parallel to *gereš* (מ֝ or מ֜).

5.1.3.2.2. *Conjunctives.* While the marking of the disjunctive accents was never complete and words which require a pause are quite often found without a pausal sign, the necessary joining of words was never marked regularly but only in relatively rare instances. The sign for joining is either a dot between words (מ · מ) or, infrequently, a short, small slanted stroke (מ / מ) and is independent of the nearby pausal accents. This marking for joining of words is quite random; sometimes it appears to point up the need for connection, but one cannot always find an explanation for it. It occurs both in positions which in the Tiberian system would have a conjunctive accent (*mešaret*: lit. servant) and in those which would have a *maqqaf*. It is doubtful however whether one can consider it an accentuation sign in the full sense of the word. There is only one exception to the above: in a number of manuscripts the sign מ֩ is specifically used for words which in the Tiberian system have the conjunctive accent *teliša*ʾ *qeṭanna*. It is possible that this mark is the beginning of the emergence of a conjunctive accent, i.e., a sign which indicates not only the punctuation, but also a specific melody. However, this is by no means certain since the sign also occurs in positions where a slight pause might be called for according to the context. Thus, even this mark may be no more than a pausal accent, albeit a very slight one, which corresponds to a conjunctive accent in the Tiberian system. This is not true of the sign מֽ, which occurs with great consistency in one manuscript and corresponds there to the Tiberian conjunctive *merka*. Other signs such as מ֨, מ֔ have no fixed function in isolated manuscripts and it is difficult to draw conclusions concerning them.

The Palestinian system is also the most primitive of all the systems in that the marks are not placed over the stressed syllable; that is, one of the three functions of the accents had not yet been developed in it. This use of the accentuation signs did not reach even the texts which were already influenced by the Tiberian system. It is, however, customary in the סירוגין (intermittences; see also 5.10.3) texts where the accent is naturally marked on the single letter which represents the word, which is usually a letter of the stressed syllable. (Concerning the use of the Tiberian signs within the Palestinian system, especially in the domain of conjunctives, see below, 5.5.)

The names of the accents in the Palestinian system are not known and there is no way of connecting the names known to us from various masoretic notes with them.

5.1.3.3. THE (3) POETICAL BOOKS. The accentuation signs for Psalms, Proverbs, and Job are very rare in the Palestinian system and occur in very few manuscripts. The following are the signs and their functions in verse division.

5.1.3.3.1. *Disjunctives.* The major disjunctive, which separates one verse from the next (D_1), is never marked. If it has a prelude accent (D_{1p}), it is marked מ֜. The verse itself may be divided into a main division (D_2) by מ̇ and sometimes also by מ̇ (with the function of ʿ*ole we-yored*), the prelude of which is מ֜ on the first word (D_{2p1} with the function of *revia*ʿ *qaṭan*) or מ̀ or מֽ on the second word (D_{2p2} with the function of *ṣinnor*). However, in most instances, since the verses are short, they are not divided by the major disjunctive (D_2), but by the smaller disjunctive (D_3) which is marked מ̇ (with the function of ʾ*etnaḥ*), the prelude accent (D_{3p}) of which is מֽ (with the function *deḥi*). The disjunctive D_3 is sometimes marked also מ̇, apparently when there is no prelude accent D_{3p} preceding it. Even when D_3 divides the verse it is noted only infrequently in the manuscripts because it is self-evident, both from the arrangement of the text (generally there is a space in the line at the point of the main division) as well as from the notation of the prelude accent D_{3p}, which announces a D_3 even when it is not marked (see above concerning the omission of D_1). A major disjunctive within the domain of D_2 and D_3 is D_4 which is marked as מ֜ (with the function of *revia*ʿ *gadol*). This sign is therefore common to D_{1p}, D_{2p1} and D_4 and thus parallels the three *revia*ʿ*s* of the Tiberian system: *revia*ʿ *mugraš*, *revia*ʿ *qaṭan*, and *revia*ʿ *gadol*, respectively. Additional signs, occurring infrequently, with the function of minor disjunctives are: מ̇ (as *mahpak legarmeh*), מ̇ (with the function of ʾ*azla*ʾ *legarmeh*) and once מ̇ (perhaps with the function of *pazer*). A sign similar to the last or מ̇ (or perhaps מ̃) denotes on one occasion a disjunctive (with the function of *šalšelet gedola*).

5.1.3.3.2. *Conjunctives.* The connection between the words is marked even less consistently in the poetical books than in the other 21 books of the Bible. However, when it is marked, a dot between the words in the middle of the line is used (מ · מ) and sometimes also a dot is added above the first word (מ · מׄ). This sign is not dependent on the context of disjunctives, except for ·מׄ which is specifically used for words that have in the Tiberian system a conjunctive *mahpak̲* (cf. above, the sign of the *mahpak̲ legarmeh*). In one place it is possible that מׄ serves as the parallel of the Tiberian conjunctive *šalšelet qeṭanna*.

5.2. THE BABYLONIAN SYSTEM

5.2.0.1. THE TERM. This system was called Babylonian in accordance with references by a number of early scholars. The following are the most important and the most unequivocal; they undoubtedly refer to a specific vocalization system and not to a different pronunciation tradition:

(1) *Nissi b. Noah (a Karaite scholar of the 11th century): "to learn points (= vowels), conjunctives, accent pauses, defective and plene spellings of the people of Šinʿar" (= Babylonians; S. Pinsker, *Lickute Kadmoniot, Zur Geschichte des Karaismus und der karaeischen Literatur*, Vienna, 1860, p. מא);

(2) the colophon of a manuscript of the Torah with Targum Onkelos from 1311 (Parma, De Rossi Library, no. 12): "this Targum was copied from a book which was brought from Babylonia and which was pointed above [the line] with the vocalization of the land of Assyria, and R. Nathan b. R. Machir b. R. Menahem of Ancona… changed it, corrected it, and copied it to the Tiberian vocalization" (Zunz, *Zur Geschichte und Literatur*, p. 110).

5.2.0.2. EXPANSION AND CHRONOLOGY. The name "Babylonian vocalization" refers to the birthplace of the system and not to the expansion of its use. There is no doubt that it was used beyond the borders of Babylonia and reached, according to Jacob al-*Kirkisānī (937), Persia, the Arabian Peninsula, and Yemen; Yemenites have used manuscripts with Babylonian vocalization until today. We are not dealing here with the Babylonian tradition of pronunciation, but only with the graphic system.

The most ancient dated manuscripts which are vocalized in the Babylonian system, including accentuation signs, are a Cairo *Genizah* fragment now in Cambridge which was written in Persia, in 904 (H.P. Rueger, VT, 16 (1966) 65f.), and a complete manuscript of the latter Prophets from the year 916 (Peterburg, the first Firkovich collection, no. B 3 = Petropolitanus). The early date of the latter does necessarily indicate a relatively ancient state of vocalization and accentuation.

The texts with Babylonian vocalization show great development, more than is found in any other system; and they can be classified into a number of groups according to various criteria, such as that of I. Yeivin (*The Hebrew Language Tradition as Reflected in the Babylonian Vocalization* (1985), pp. 21–23) who discerned three stages: the ancient, the intermediate, and the later; and he divides the linguistic material into five types according to characteristics of pronunciation, beginning with the ancient Babylonian pronunciation (type V) and continuing to the completely Tiberian pronunciation with Babylonian signs (type I).

5.2.0.3. MADINḤAʾE READINGS. It would stand to reason that the texts vocalized in the Babylonian system should correspond to the Madinḥaʾe (Eastern) versions of the Masorah, although they include almost no vocalization issues but mostly differences of plene and defective spelling, differences of *qere* and *ketiv* and differences in division of words. That is why Elias Levita (*Massoreth Ha-Massoreth*, edit. C.D. Ginsburg, p. 113) considered the official lists of variants (חילופין) between the Westerners and the Easterners (for Prophets and Hagiographa only) as preceding the invention of the vocalization and accentuation signs. However, there are many manuscripts vocalized in the Babylonian system which contain many readings that correspond to the Western (*Maʿarvaʾe*) versions and vice versa. Still, in the Babylonian sources a large number of readings, sometimes the majority, correspond to the Eastern (*Madinḥaʾe*) tradition and they correspond with it more than any Tiberian manuscripts do. It can be assumed that mistakes occurred in the transmission of the lists of variants between *Maʿarvaʾe* and *Madinḥaʾe*, and also one cannot ignore the possibility that perhaps the term *Madinḥaʾe*, like its counterpart, *Maʿarvaʾe*, was a broad geographical concept, and that a universally accepted, uniform text for all the minute details never did exist, neither in the West nor in the East. It follows therefore that a list of variants based on one of the versions can neither invalidate nor establish the Babylonian nature of any source.

Everything stated above concerning the consolidation and uniformity of the Palestinian system applies also to the Babylonian system, although not to the same degree. This system also came down to us in different stages of development, and in it too there are great differences between the various manuscripts; here, too, the punctuation is not complete, and there are differences between manuscripts with regard to the degree of punctuation in them.

5.2.1. The Vowel Signs

5.2.1.1. THE SIMPLE SYSTEM. There are two sets of signs in Babylonian vocalization:

(a) the regular Babylonian set, which consists (in part) of lines, whose origin is in letters, and (in part) of dots;

(b) a set which consists entirely of dots and is relatively rare.

5.2.1.1.1. *The Signs.* The signs are located in each case above the letter and to the left of it:

מׅ = *i* is used in both sets and it sometimes has the shape of a small *yod*. מ̈ = *e* is used in both sets. מ is used in the regular set and it is shaped like a small *ʿayin* with different angles (also מ); in the dot set its counterpart is מ. The phonetic value of the sign has not been sufficiently clarified. It occurs in positions which correspond to the *pattaḥ* and *segol* in the Tiberian system, and it might have been pronounced like one of them, that is, *a* or ε (in which case that vowel of the two which is not extant in the Babylonian system would have merged with its remaining companion). It seems, however, more reasonable that it was pronounced as a medium vowel between *a* and ε, and this has been the pronunciation of Yemenite Jews until today in certain circumstances. The sign is called in the Babylonian Masorah מיפתח פומא ("opening of the mouth") or פיתחא ("opening") פית for short. מ is used in the regular set and has the shape of *ʾalef* with one leg missing; in the dot set מ (or מ) serves as its counterpart. Apparently the phonetic value of the sign was *å* and it corresponds to the Tiberian *qameṣ* (the opinion that its value was *ā* is untenable). Its names in the Babylonian Masorah are: מיקפץ פומא or מיצף פומא (מיצ פומא for short; "contraction of the mouth") and sometimes אימצא (אימ for short) from the root אמץ, whose meaning is also "bringing together" (see Yalon, *Leshonenu*, 32 (1968), 2–4). מ = *o* is used in both sets. מ = *u* is used in the regular set and it sometimes has the shape of a small *waw*. Its counterpart in the dot set is מ. מ = *šewa*. It is called חיטפא (חיט for short) in the Babylonian Masorah. This sign denotes both mobile and quiescent *šewa*, although the mobile *šewa* is marked more frequently. In only a certain type of manuscript it is the sign for mobile *šewa* exclusively, and the quiescent *šewa* is not marked at all. The realization of the Babylonian *šewa* may have been close to its Tiberian equivalent (see 5.3.1.2).

5.2.1.1.2. *The Two Sets and Syriac.* The dot set is used exclusively in only a few manuscripts. Generally it was mixed with the signs of the regular set. Both of these sets have counterparts in the two Syriac vocalization systems: the vocalization system of Eastern Syriac, which is one of dots, and that of Western Syriac, which is a system of signs made up of letters (albeit Greek). Two of the signs have the same form in the Babylonian dot set and in the Eastern Syriac system and their functions are surprisingly similar: מ, מ – the first denotes *ā* in Syriac and *a*/ɛ in the Babylonian: the second signifies *a* in Syriac and *å* (in the opinion of some, *ā*) in the Babylonian. Kahle believes that this indicates a connection between the Babylonian system and the Eastern Syriac, though not in the known form which goes back to the eighth century, but to an earlier stage of which there are no traces. It is difficult to accept this theory, since in the meantime we have come to know from the material reviewed by J.B. Segal (*The Diacritical Point and the Accents in Syriac*, pp. 152–3) the shapes of signs dating even earlier than the eighth century. From this material it is clear that in the seventh century and even earlier the form of the sign for the vowel *ā* in Syriac was מ (and not מ). The possible solution lies, therefore, in one of two directions: either the Babylonian system followed the late stage of Syriac, i.e., after the eighth century (but such a late date for the formation of the Babylonian system does not seem reasonable and even Kahle did not consider it), or the influence was in the opposite direction and it was the Syriac that followed the Babylonian.

5.2.1.1.3. *The Antiquity of the Two Sets.* Kahle feels that of the two Babylonian sets the dot set is the older, because it is simpler, because it is similar to the vocalization of Eastern Syriac (but see above), and because it is found in its purest state in a relatively early manuscript. The regular set developed, in his opinion, from the dot set. Yeivin does not agree, especially since there are older manuscripts than the one mentioned in which the regular set is used. In his opinion the dot set is just another set, ancient in itself, but not necessarily older than the regular set. It is possible that the two sets were used at the same time and that the dot set was used in a certain geographical area or by a specific school. His opinion seems reasonable. Furthermore, only the regular set, which uses letters, combines with the Babylonian accentuation, which too uses letters, to form a complete system. In any event, the dot set was preserved only briefly and was rejected in favor of the regular set. Two of its signs, however, (מ, מ) were preserved in the regular set with a special function (see below).

5.2.1.2. THE COMPOUND SYSTEM. As time passed, the Babylonian vocalization system was improved and signs were added to indicate further differentiations, mainly to note the special nature of the vowel which was influenced by the syllable structure (not, however, quantitative signs). The special signs which were added are, for the most part, graphemes composed of two signs. The system that evolved was the compound Babylonian vocalization system.

5.2.1.2.1. *The Signs.* There are a few signs *under* which there is an additional horizontal line when the vowel occurs in an unstressed syllable closed with a *šewa*, and a horizontal line *above* them when the vowel occurs in an unstressed syllable, open or closed by *dageš forte*. The details of the signs are not uniform in all the manuscripts. There are manuscripts which contain special signs and exceptional forms, and it is difficult to find two manuscripts whose use of vowel signs is completely identical. The main signs which occur rather frequently are the following:

(1) a sign to mark a vowel in an open, unstressed syllable (including syllables where the Tiberian vocalization has a *ḥataf* with a laryngeal consonant) or an unstressed syllable closed by quiescent *šewa*: מ (= *i*), מ (= *e*), מ (= *a*), מ (= *o*), מ (= *u*);

(2) a sign to mark a vowel occurring in an unstressed syllable closed by *dageš*: מ (= *i*), מ (= *a*), מ (= *u*).

5.2.1.2. *Perfect and Non-Perfect.* Yeivin differentiates between perfect and non perfect compound vocalization. In the former there are special signs for each type of syllable and they are used consistently. In the latter, the sets of signs are incomplete, that is, there is a special sign for only one type of syllable, or the special signs are used only for certain vowels and not for all of them, or the simple and compound signs are mixed together without differentiation. The phenomenon of lack of perfection is found in three types of manuscripts:

(1) ancient ones, in which the compound vocalization had not yet reached its full maturity;

(2) manuscripts in which there is a mixture of the two systems;

(3) late manuscripts in which only some signs of the compound vocalization were chosen for use.

5.2.1.2.3. *Tiberian Influence.* The increase of Tiberian influence in late manuscripts is evidenced in grammatical forms and in the reading tradition, and is even found in the set of graphemes. This is particularly noticeable in late manuscripts in which there are attempts to introduce a special sign parallel to the Tiberian *segol*. For this they used:

(1) מׅ (in place of מׅ) as the parallel of *segol*, and this in addition to its function as the equivalent of the Tiberian *ṣere*; this sign sometimes occurs as an addition to the original sign and above it (מ) to note the nuance with which one is to pronounce מ;

(2) מ (an inverse Tiberian *segol*);

(3) מ – the parallel to מ from the dot set, which by way of differentiation was specifically used for the *segol*.

5.2.2. The Diacritical Signs

Certain additional diacritical marks are used to distinguish between different pronunciations of the same letter.

5.2.2.1. ŠIN-SIN. To mark ש = š a small *šin* above the letter is used (ש) and to mark ש = ś a small *samek* is placed above the letter (ש). These signs are rarer than the vowel marks, especially in ancient manuscripts. Only in some relatively late manuscripts do they occur almost regularly.

5.2.2.2. MAPPIQ, DAGEŠ, RAFEH. The consonantal nature of a *he* at the end of a word (*mappiq*) is sometimes marked by a small *he* above the letter (ה).

A *dageš* is marked by placing a small *gimmel* above the letter (מ and later also מ) which perhaps alludes to its Babylonian name דיגשא (abbreviated as 'דיג', דיגש). The first letter of the name was not chosen as usual, since a small *dalet* (מ) is used as one of the accentuation signs (another proof that the system of accentuation signs is the earlier).

The *rafeh* nature of a letter is sometimes marked by a small *qof* above the letter (מ), which is an abbreviation of its Babylonian name קיפיא (abbr. 'קיפ) and means "light" according to H. *Yalon (*Sinai, Sefer Yovel* (1958), 239).

These signs are ambiguous, since they show both gemination (*dageš forte*) or the lack of it and note the plosive pronunciation of בגדכפ"ת (*dageš lene*) or their pronunciation as fricatives. They are used only infrequently, mainly in places where a misunderstanding might arise. In manuscripts using the dot set exclusively, these marks are not added.

To mark *ʾate meraḥiq* (or *deḥiq*) a dot in the center of the line between the words is used in a few manuscripts: חלילה · לנו (Josh. 24:29), which means that the dot is not a *dageš* (cf. Dotan, in *Fourth World Congress of Jewish Studies*, 2 (1968), Hebrew part, 105), although in some manuscripts, some of them late, the sign of a *dageš* or its substitute (the preceding vowel marked by the sign for a syllable closed by a *dageš*) is given in these instances.

5.2.3. The Accentuation Signs

5.2.3.1. THE NATURE OF THE NOTATION. Unlike the Palestinian system of accentuation signs, the Babylonian accentuation signs have reached us as a series of fixed marks above the letter, most of which are small letters or parts of them. The division of the verses according to the Babylonian Masorah sometimes differs, especially in ancient manuscripts, from the Tiberian division, and at times a comparison with the Tiberian system is liable to give a false impression. Some of the Babylonian signs have slightly different functions in different manuscripts and it seems that a shift of their pausal strength occurred with the passage of time. This together with the fact that in the relatively late manuscripts, especially in those vocalized with the compound vocalization, accentuation signs are marked over the stressed syllable, make it possible to classify the manuscripts as earlier or later according to their use of the accentuation signs. This classification tallies in general, but not always, with that of the vowel notation.

In the Babylonian system there are no conjunctive accents at all. However, there are manuscripts, mainly those vocalized with compound vocalization, in which the vocalizer or a second hand wrote in the conjunctive Tiberian signs, and they obviously are placed with the stressed syllable.

As opposed to the Tiberian situation there is no difference in principle between Prose and Poetical books. The same signs are used in both, but the degree of subdividing the verses is not as great in the Prose books and the possible arrangements of the accentuation signs are not as numerous because of the brevity of the Poetical verses.

5.2.3.2. TYPES OF ACCENTUATION. A gross, incomplete classification into three types of manuscripts according to their use of accentuation signs was suggested by A. *Spanier (1927). The functions of the accentuation signs are presented here in a general way according to the most ancient situation (group *a*) and will be followed by the main changes in the functions of the signs in the groups which Spanier called a, b, and c. A more precise grouping was suggested by R. Shoshani (2003), who maintains a fourfold subdivision: early *a*, later *a* as one group; and *b* and *c* as parts of the latest group.

5.2.3.3. THE ACCENTS. There is no accentuation sign for the last word in a verse. Sometimes there is no sign separating the verses but occasionally there is a sign at the end of the verse, in group *a* mostly: occasionally signs such as: ◌̊ or ◌, and sometimes, at the beginning of the verse (cf. *Soferim* 3:7), a sign like ° or ˄. The main pause of the verse is marked by ˄ (סיחפא; equal to the sign of the Tiberian *ʾetnaḥ*, but above the line; this and the next sign are the only Babylonian signs not shaped as letters). The next largest pause, whether within the domain of ˄ or within the domain of the end of the verse, is marked by ◌ (apparently an abbreviation of the accent name זקף or זיקפא). As the main or single pause within the domain of ◌, ת is used (perhaps an abbreviation of תיברא), and when it is not the only one and there is place for an additional pause after it, ◌ is used (like a slanted *nun*) as a final, small pause before ◌. The accent ◌ is not imperative, and when there is need for only one pause, even a small one, in the domain of ◌ it will be ת. The smallest pause before ˄ is ˅ (רימיא), and this accent serves as a prelude before ˄. In general ˄ is not marked, but only its prelude ˅ (which is also sometimes omitted). The smallest pause before the final word of the verse is ◌, sometimes ◌ or

דית (apparently abbreviations of דחי or its Aramaic דיחיא, in one manuscript ᒪ), and it therefore parallels ∨ which precedes ^. Another disjunctive within the domain of both ^ as well as the end of the verse – occurring after ז and weaker than it, and before ∨ or ד and stronger than they are – is ח (apparently an abbreviation of חָזֵר). This sign is likely to be repeated several times when necessary (perhaps this is the origin of its name *ḥazer*). The ח is likely to divide the domain of ח (and may be repeated) when this is the main or only pause in the domain of ז. ט (apparently an abbreviation of טרס) is used as a pause in the domain of ח and in that of ׳. Sometimes נ (perhaps an abbreviation of ניגדא = the Tiberian accent *legarmeh*) is used as a pause in the domain of ח. The accent ש (a half-*shin* or a broken *shin*, perhaps alluding to the accent name שידיא or שיריא) parallels the Tiberian accent *segol*, but, unlike it, may appear also in the second half of the verse after the accent ^, instead of the first ז in the half-verse. The accent ש is divided by ח or by נ, or by the sequence נ ח (with ח being the stronger of the two), and sometimes ני (ניחלא?; some see it as parallel to צינורי – *zarqa*) is the last divider before ש. The accent ᒪ (similar to a half *ṭet*) is used as a small disjunctive within the domain of ני or נ.

In group *a* the accentuation signs are not placed over the stressed syllable. The accent ש and its prelude accents are used not only in place of the Tiberian *segol* (i.e., as a substitute for the first *zaqef*) but also in the second half of the verse (as a substitute of the first *zaqef* after ∨).

In group *b* the accentuation signs are placed on the stressed syllable. The accent ח is weaker in pausal strength than ח. The accent ש always parallels the Tiberian *segol*. There are additional changes compared to group *a*, mostly of minor importance.

In group *c* everything is the same as in group *b* except that the accent ח is split. It is used only within the domain of ∨ and ד, while in the domain of ז, ׳ (apparently an abbreviation of יתיב) is used instead.

As indicated, there is no separate set of accents for the three Poetical books. The same accents are used, but their actual distribution is affected by the constant brevity of the verses in these books. In principle there is no difference. Thus there is no accentuation sign for the final word of the verse. The separation between the verses is marked as in the other books. The main pause is noted by ^, which is generally omitted, and the notation of the pause preceding it is sufficient. The second half of the verse is divided by ז, and often, when the verse is very short, ז is the main divider of the whole verse (without ^). Because of the brevity of the verses the ^, the divider before ∨, may be used as the only divider of the verse. Such and similar situations may occur also in short verses of the Prose books.

This is not, therefore, a different system of notation, as in the Tiberian, but the utilization of the same signs as in the Prose books in a more limited manner, in accordance with the special conditions required by the short verses of Psalms, Proverbs, and Job.

5.3. THE TIBERIAN SYSTEM

5.3.1. The Vowel Signs

Unlike its predecessors, the Tiberian vocalization has reached us as a consolidated, uniform, and complete system, although in some isolated and exceptional manuscripts there are remnants of other systems, such as the Palestinian sign מֹ to denote *o* (cf. Kahle, *Masoreten des Westens*, 1 (1927), 35).

5.3.1.1. THE VOWELS. There are seven vowels, for which there are eight signs, and it is clear that they do not indicate quantity in any way. This system, like its predecessors, was used by different communities and by people who had different traditions of pronunciation and who interpreted the signs and read them accordingly. In the Tiberian tradition in which the signs were created, their phonetic values are approximately as follows:

מִ = *i*; מֵ = *e*; מֶ = *ɛ*; מַ = *a*, this sign is generally under the letters like the others, but when it serves as a furtive *pattaḥ* in the ancient manuscripts, it precedes the letter (גָבֹהַ). מָ = *å*: the original shape of the sign is a line and a dot under it. Only in printed books were they joined. Some believe (as Abraham ibn Ezra already did in *Sefer Ẓaḥot*, ed. G.H. Lippmann, p. 3b) that the sign ָ denotes the combination and mixture of the two vowels *a, o*, in order to indicate a vowel which is somewhere between the two, i.e., a back *a*. However, the sign was fixed from the start and was used as one vowel of definite quality. Only later and in the Sephardic tradition was it considered a representation of two vowels: *a* (a wide *qameṣ gadol*) and *o* (*qameṣ qaṭan*); מֹ, מוֹ = *o*, when adjacent to a *waw* the vowel is placed over it; מֻ, מוּ = *u*, the two signs have exactly the same value. When a *waw* was adjacent to the letter in the biblical text it was marked with a dot; when there was no adjacent *waw* it was marked with three dots below. The vocalizers neither added to nor deleted from the sanctified orthography of the Bible.

5.3.1.2. THE ŠEWA AND THE ḤAṬEFS. Besides the eight signs, an additional one is used, מְ, to indicate the furtive nature of the consonant. This furtiveness does not have a fixed value but changes according to the position of the sign within the word. Sometimes it indicates total furtiveness – a "zero" vowel (quiescent *šewa*) and sometimes it indicates a partial furtiveness of a vowel (mobile *šewa*). The nature of the furtive vowel changes again according to the position of the sign within the word according to the Tiberian tradition: preceding a laryngeal, it resembles the vowel of the laryngeal; preceding a *yod* it becomes *i*; in all the other cases, it is pronounced *a*. On the rare occasions when this sign is accompanied by a *gaʿyah* (*šewa-gaʿyah*; see below 5.3.2.2.6), it is pronounced as a full vowel (according to the above conditions).

This sign therefore has many functions: it can denote the lack of a vowel, a furtive or very short vowel, or any full vowel. In this it differs from the whole Hebrew graphemic system. One can explain its function by the theory that it was first used to divide a word into syllables, that is, as a sign to indicate the boundaries of a syllable. A sign of this type is likely to appear in a variety of phonetic garb according to the structure of the syllable and its position between the syllables adjacent to it within the word (in general: at the end of a syllable – quiescent, at the start of a syllable or as an independent syllable – mobile). This sign, which was basically a punctuation sign within the word, is apparently borrowed from the Syriac accentuation system, where such a sign (albeit within the line) with a similar name (*šewaya*) is a divisional accent, i.e., a sentence divider.

When the vocalic nuance of this sign is fixed in one of the three vowels, *a, ε, å* it combines with the respective vowel sign מֲ, מֱ, מֳ and its phonetic value is then the furtive, short pronunciation of these vowels.

5.3.1.3. THE NAMES OF THE VOWELS. For the Tiberian system, more than for any other system, the names of the vowels (the ancient Hebrew term for them is מלכים "kings" and later תנועות as a loan translation of the Arabic *ḥaraka* = movement) can be traced. Apparently several series of names were applied to them in the beginning (according to the changing needs and conditions). As time passed the names became intermingled and in masoretic notes and in the works of the earliest grammarians we find the terms from different series being used side by side. One can schematically reconstruct the series approximately as follows:

(1) The most primitive series has no names, but a number of sounds which express the vowels: אִי, אֵי, אֶי (אֶ, אֶה), אַ(ה), אָ(ה), אוֹ, אוּ. One can assume that the vowels were thus called even before the invention of the vowel signs, these names being used orally and could not be written simply for lack of graphic signs for them. Only after the introduction of vocalization did it become possible to use these appellations in writing, and then we do find them, though rarely.

(2) A series in which the vowels are named according to the labial movements, whether closed or open, and the names were therefore derived from קמץ (close, contract) and פתח (open). These terms and their derivatives (such as קמצה, פתחה and so on) were first used in a broad sense – a closed vowel versus an open vowel. *Qameṣ* thus applied at first to the vowels *å, e*, while *pattaḥ* (sometime also פשט) applied to the vowels *a, ε*. As time passed special names were determined for *e* – קמץ קטן and for *ε* – פתח קטן (also [צבחד] פשט צבחר), while *qameṣ* and *pattaḥ* marked only one vowel each, *å, a*. Later we find these special names: קמץ שלם (*kāmil* in Arabic), רחב, גדול and also פתח גדול. קמץ פום also apparently belongs to this series for *u*, and perhaps also מְלָא פום for *o* (in a later period in Europe מלופום is used to indicate וֹ). It is difficult to establish the name of the vowel *i* in this series; perhaps it was שפילתא (= the low one) because it stands lowest in the scale of the vowels.

These names also are not directly connected with vowel signs. It is therefore possible that, like the above primitive series, they were instituted before the invention of the vowel signs; but some of the names were used in a later period as well.

(3) In the third series the vowels are named according to their symbols: נקודה אחת ("one point"; *i*), שתי נקודות ("two points"), שלוש נקודות ("three points"), נקודה בתוך הוי"ו ("a point within the *waw*"; *u*), נקודה עליונה ("upper point"; *o*,) and similar names in Aramic and Arabic. Only *qameṣ* and *pattaḥ* were employed as before. These names of course, came into use after the invention of vowel signs and while they made for a brevity of language – as for example, when a word was said to have שש נקודות ("six dots") by which term two *segols* were meant, and so on – there is ambiguity (two dots = מֵ, מְ, three dots = מֶ, מֻ) and apparently because of this the series did not prevail.

(4) This series of names, in use until the present day, is based on the type of sound produced (some of the names are in Aramaic): מִ – חרק ("a squeak"); מֵ – צרי (from the Aramaic for "splitting," i.e. "splitting of the lips"); מֹ – חלם (meaning "completeness," i.e., a vowel using the whole mouth, *mela' pum*); מֻ, מוּ – שרק ("whistle, hiss"). Only מֶ – סְגוֹל ("cluster" in Aramaic) stems from the similarity of the sign to a cluster [of grapes]. *Qameṣ* and *pattaḥ* also continued to be used in this system. The orthography of the new names is without *matres lectionis*, and there has been disagreement as to their forms. Often they were segholate names: חֶרֶק, חֶלֶם, שֶׁרֶק, and also צְרִי, צֶרִי and even צְרֵי. From approximately the 11th century the custom of introducing the indicated vowel within the name began to spread, and from then on the orthography חירק, חולם, שורק, צירי became common. Since the time of the *Kimḥis the name קִבּוּץ שפתיים or קִבּוּץ is specifically used for the sign מֻ. This name was formerly a synonym for *šuruq* and as a translation of the Arabic *damm* (contraction), it also indicated the *o, u* group of vowels.

The name *šewa* (שְׁוָא known also by the spellings שבא, שבה, שוה) for the sign מְ is relatively newer than the other names, for when Saadiah Gaon uses it for the first time he finds it necessary to describe it: *šewa 'a'ni nuqṭatayn qā'imatayn* ("*šewa*, that is, two upright dots"; commentary to *Sefer Yeẓirah*, 4:3), which he does not do for the other names. The name חטף is apparently older than *šewa*, although after a certain time it was used specifically for the *šewas* which are joined to a vowel, *ḥaṭaf pattaḥ, ḥaṭaf segol, ḥaṭaf qameṣ*.

5.3.2. The Diacritical Signs

5.3.2.1. THE PRONUNCIATION OF CONSONANTS. *5.3.2.1.1. Šin-Sin.* The single dot is employed as a diacritical sign to distinguish between the two pronunciations of ש : שׁ = š, this dot sometimes is assimilated into a preceding *ḥolem* ;(מֹשֶׁה) שׂ = ś, this dot is sometimes assimilated into the *ḥolem* of the same letter (שֹׂנֵא).

5.3.2.1.2. Dageš. A dot within the letter marks both a plosive *dageš* (*lene*) in בגדכפ"ת and also the geminative *dageš* (*forte*) in all of the letters except אהחע"ר. An unusual *dageš* does occasionally occur in the *reš* (but there is no connection between it and the various statements concerning the double pronunciation of the *reš*, in which a *reš* with *dageš* is also mentioned). According to the Masorah the *dageš* occurs also in the *'alef* four times in the Bible (although there are manuscripts in which it occurs more often) but these seem to belong to the category of *Mappiq*. Therefore the *dageš* in בגדכפ״ת is ambiguous (*lene* or *forte*) and its function is determined only by the context. The term דגש and its synonyms (דגשה etc.) are explained according to Syriac, in which the verb *degaš* = to pierce, to make a hole. If this etymology is correct, the name was adopted in the Tiberian vocalization because of the sign's shape and thence it was borrowed into the Babylonian Masorah.

A special type of *dageš* is that of *ʾate meraḥiq* (or *deḥiq*), which in origin is not a geminative *dageš* but a dot used to mark the separation of two connected words, so that they should not be joined together (cf. Dotan, in *Fourth World Congress of Jewish Studies*, 2 (1968), Hebrew part, 101–5, and see especially n. 23). Because this dot is identical with the sign of the *dageš*, as time passed it was taken to be a *dageš forte*, denoting geminate pronunciation, and is so pronounced in various communities.

5.3.2.1.3. *Rafeh.* The sign of the *rafeh* (בֿ) is the opposite of the *dageš lene* and indicates the lack of the *dageš* in the spirant בגדכפ״ת. It does not occur regularly even in ancient manuscripts. In addition to this main function, it is sometimes used in an irregular manner above the letters א and ה to note quiescence, and also, infrequently, to mark the lack of *dageš forte*, that is, to point out the lack of gemination of certain letters. The frequency of this sign varies in the different manuscripts, and with the passage of time it stopped being used altogether since it was tautological.

5.3.2.1.4. *Mappiq.* Another dot marks the consonantal nature of a final *he*. Generally this dot is located in the center of the *he* (הּ), but there are manuscripts in which it is written in the lower part (הּ), or even under it (הּ).

Additional usages of the signs enumerated here, such as *dageš lene* in letters other than בגדכפ״ת, or a *mappiq* in the letters *alef, waw* and *yod*, etc., are found in exceptional manuscripts, and they must be considered as the influence of a vocalization system which was not accepted (see below 5.4).

5.3.2.2. THE GAʿYAH. The sign מְֽ which is generally written to the left of the vocalization sign (in ancient manuscripts also sometimes at the right) is a reading aid that serves various purposes, but basically it can be considered a device to improve the phonetic structure of a word. The condition for such use is sometimes rooted in the musical-accentual context of the word.

5.3.2.2.1. *The Name.* The ancient, original name is געיה (גַּעְיָה, גִּעְיָה, גֵּעֲיָה, גְּעָיָה; געה = "to cry aloud") and the masoretes distinguished various types. As time passed its usage changed in the manuscripts; the scribes used to note more of one type and less of another. This situation continued until grammarians tried to organize the method of notation according to rules and norms, part of which were artificial, while others had no basis in the realities of ancient manuscripts. The first to organize the rules of *gaʿyah* was Jekuthiel b. Judah ha-Nakdan (יה״ב), who lived in the first half of the 13th century.

In the most general way one can distinguish between the main types of *gaʿyah* as follows:

5.3.2.2.2. *Minor Gaʿyah.* A minor *gaʿyah* occurs in a closed syllable. There are many varieties of this type, and the distinction between them is a matter requiring detailed description. One of the most common types, whose definition is already found in *Dikduke ha-Teʿamim* by Aaron Ben-Asher, is the *gaʿyah* that occurs in a closed syllable which is the third before the stress when the syllable adjacent to the stress is a furtive syllable (that is, a clear mobile *šewa* or a *ḥatef*), or the *gaʿyah* which occurs in a closed syllable that is the fourth before the stress when the syllable adjacent to the stress and also the third before it are furtive syllables: וַיְֽדַבְּרוּ, הַֽכְּנַעֲנִי.

There is no certainty as to how this *gaʿyah* was realized but it seems that it marked some delay in the pronunciation or melody, or in both. Its special phonological conditioning was also instrumental in phonetic realization, particularly of the *šewa*. For example, וְהִֽתְפַּלְלוּ – the *gaʿyah* in the *he* also indicates a mobile *šewa* for the ל.

This type is already called געיה קטנה (minor *gaʿyah*) in ancient sources connected with *Diqduqe ha-Teʿamim* and is apparently the name for all the *gaʿyot* of this type. The minor *gaʿyah* is the most common in the best ancient manuscripts, among them Leningrad B19a and the Aleppo codex, and it has a greater degree of regularity than the other types of *gaʿyah*. In spite of this, however, the reason for these *gaʿyot* was not clear, nor apparently were their precise conditions understood, although their connection to the accentuation system was obvious and they occur more often with disjunctive than with conjunctive accents. Because of this lack of clarity, and perhaps also because of uncertainty concerning the realization of the *gaʿyot*, the scribes disregarded them when they were copying and their frequency diminished as time passed. Unlike the type listed below, which generally did affect pronunciation, the minor *gaʿyah* seemed without a defined purpose and difficult to understand.

5.3.2.2.3. *The Terminology.* Strangely enough, the confusion as to its purpose led Jekuthiel ha-Nakdan to establish the name of the minor *gaʿyah* as געיה כבדה ("heavy" [in the sense of: difficult] *gaʿyah*) as he himself states (*Shaʿar ha-Metigot*, ed. Gumpertz, in *Leshonenu*, 22 (1958), 142): "Therefore I called them heavy, for the heart of many sages is heavy for not having understood them and they did not show them in their function … and the second [reason] that I called them heavy and different from the first ones is that the gate which is open for the light ones is closed for these which are heavy…" This name, used by a few scholars even today, thus has no justification, despite Yeivin's opinion (*The Aleppo Codex of the Bible* (1968), p. 93, n. 3). In fact, there is evidence that such a name in Arabic was used precisely to indicate the following type of *gaʿyah*.

The process of the decline of the minor *gaʿyah* was slower in the Sephardi manuscripts, and Jekuthiel ha-Nakdan (apparently of Prague) already declares that it had disappeared from most of the non-Sephardi manuscripts.

5.3.2.2.4. *Major Gaʿyah.* This *gaʿyah* occurs in an open syllable. Here, too, there are several types, and all of them occur in a syllable which is separated from the stress by at least one syllable. In the separating syllable, however, different kinds must be distinguished: it is likely to be a vowel (וְשָֽׁמַרְתָּ, הֶֽחָכָם), or a compound *šewa* (פֳּֽעֳלוֹ, אֶֽעֱשֶׂה, נֶֽאֱצוּ, יַֽעֲקֹב) or a simple mobile *šewa* (יֵֽרְדוּ, אָֽסְנַת).

There are a number of proofs that this *gaʿyah* is the one which is called געיה גדולה (major *gaʿyah*) in ancient sources (Dotan, ed., *Diqduqe ha-Teʿamim*, pp. 286, 302); in the treatise on the *šewa* (in: Kurt Levy, *Zur masoretischen Grammatik* (1936), pp. ד, ה) it is called *gaʿyah ṯaqīlah* (heavy *gaʿyah*).

This *gaʿyah* neither occurs regularly nor follows general rules in the ancient manuscripts. In comparison to the minor *gaʿyah*, which is found marked with a very great degree of consistency, we can find no full consistency in the notation of the major *gaʿyah* in the different ancient manuscripts, not even in the best of them. Inconsistency is also found within a single text. Yet, as time passed, the major *gaʿyah* became more and more common in the manuscripts until it was marked with great regularity and consistency in every open syllable. This adherence of the scribes to the major *gaʿyah* at the same time that they turned away from the minor *gaʿyah* is part of the process of systematization of the rules of the *gaʿyah*, a process whose beginnings were among non-Sephardi scribes but which ultimately became accepted by all. The Sephardi Menahem di Lonzano (second half of the 16th century) complains about it: "I am weary of my life through the abundance of the extra *gaʿyot*, which are superfluous, which the Ashkenazim put in their books and called them *meteg* (= bridle), while I have called them bridle (= *meteg*) for the ass. They are a nuisance to me I am weary to bear their correction for they are more than the grasshoppers and are indeed infinite in number" (*Or Torah*, Amsterdam, 1659, p. 2b).

5.3.2.2.5. *Development.* One can assume that the origin of the major *gaʿyah* as a sign to distinguish between the mobile and the quiescent *šewa*, i.e., the basic location of the sign is in an open syllable preceding a mobile *šewa*, and from here it spread to other open syllables (as above). However, there was no regularity in the notation of this *gaʿyah* neither before a simple *šewa* nor in the other positions. It was only in the late Middle Ages that this sign was used more and more, since the scribes considered it a sign to indicate a necessary phonetic entity which exists in pronunciation, whether the sign points to it or not, according to the statement of Jekuthiel ha-Nakdan (ed. Gumpertz, in *Leshonenu*, 22 (1958), 141): "And the custom that many followed – not to point them [i.e., the *gaʿyot*] everywhere because they are very numerous throughout all of the Bible and the vocalizers said [if] we will write them in every instance their number will exceed that of the accents, and perhaps the readers will go astray because of them and will forget the normal accents because of the abundance of *metegs* (מתיגות) while the wise man will know them by himself even if the vocalizers lightened their burden and did not indicate each of them." This statement practically permits major *gaʿyahs* to be added to every open syllable even in places where they are not written according to the Masorah.

This situation is completely different from the concept which was common at the start of Hebrew grammar and which is manifest in the ancient manuscripts. Here the major *gaʿyah* was the main indicator of the mobile *šewa*. There are quite a number of rules, both in *Diqduqe ha-Teʿamim* and in works of Masorah related to it, from which it is clear that only a *šewa* which is preceded by a *gaʿyah* is mobile and a simple *šewa* in the middle of a word which is not preceded by a *gaʿyah* is always quiescent (except for known types). There is corroboration for this also in the writings of the early grammarians (Allony collected the evidence for it). If so, the major *gaʿyah* is not a "self-evident" diacritical mark, but, to the contrary, has phonetic significance. While the above evidence derives from the facts, it is difficult to accept it, for it would mean that the pronunciation of the words, especially those with a *šewa*, varied according to different manuscripts, even in one single text. Such arbitrariness in the exact pronunciation of biblical Hebrew, which each generation labored to preserve and transmit faultlessly, seems unlikely.

It is difficult to explain this phenomenon, and on the other hand it is easy to understand the tendency of the later masoretes toward unification and systematization. The major *gaʿyah* became, as time passed, the only *gaʿyah*. In addition to its function as an indicator of the "mobility" of the *šewa* or the length of the vowels, it was considered – in order to take into account also the instances in which the *gaʿyah* did not precede a simple *šewa* – also a sign indicating the phonetic *Gegenton* to the main stress, a function which fits all the types of the major *gaʿyah*. In this capacity it became known more and more as מתג (*meteg*), and Jekuthiel ha-Nakdan already used this term along with מתיגה (*metigah*).

5.3.2.2.6. *Šewa-Gaʿyah.* his is a *gaʿyah* which occurs in a furtive syllable, that is, in a syllable with a mobile *šewa*, or with a *ḥaṭaf pattaḥ* or a *ḥaṭaf segol* (henceforth called *šewa-gaʿyah*). It is generally marked to the left of the *šewa* or *ḥatef* (◌ְֽ, ◌ֱֽ), and in ancient manuscripts it sometimes is marked to the right (◌ְֽ, ◌ֲֽ); with the *ḥatefs* it is sometimes between the *šewa* and the vowel (◌ֲֽ, ◌ֱֽ).

Nothing is known about the conditioning of this *gaʿyah*. It is found in manuscripts without any regularity; it is more common in the Poetic books (Psalms, Proverbs, and Job) than in the other books, and it is mainly noted at the beginning of the word. On the other hand, we do know quite clearly its purpose – to indicate the pronunciation of the *šewa* as an actual full vowel. This is attested to by the rules of pronunciation of the *šewa* copied in different sources in Masorah literature. In this it has a common feature with the major *gaʿyah*; for a *šewa* which is pronounced as a full vowel has ceased to constitute a furtive syllable and has become open, and the *gaʿyah* which occurs in it is similar to a major *gaʿyah*. *Šewa-gaʿyah* never occurs in the syllable before the stress; it requires a separation of one syllable at least between it and the stressed syllable, just like the major *gaʿyah*.

On the other hand, there is rather general agreement in the notation of the *šewa-gaʿyah* in ancient manuscripts, and in that it bears a similarity to the minor *gaʿyah*. Yet, unlike the minor *gaʿyah, šewa-gaʿyah* was not rejected from the text; it is still copied today in most of the editions of the Bible. The reason for this is that because of its relative rareness and because of its special method of notation (next to the *šewa* and not next to a vowel like the other two types of *gaʿyah*) it was considered an anomaly and an exceptional sign, and like the other exceptional signs of the Masorah it was treated with special respect.

5.3.2.2.7. Haʿamadah. This is a *gaʿyah* of a special type which perhaps does not merit the name *gaʿyah*, though it is noted in the same manner. It is better to call it, for the purpose of differentiation, by the name given by Jekuthiel ha-Nakdan and following him, by Wolf *Heidenheim, העמדה ("causing to stop"; although this name is used also for *gaʿyah* in other places).

The function of the *haʿamadah* is to emphasize, perhaps by a slight pause, the pronunciation of a sound which was likely to be swallowed. This danger threatens unstressed sounds at the end of a word which is connected to the following one, and in these instances *haʿamadah* is likely to occur (and its function is then similar to that of the *dageš* of *ʾate meraḥiq* – see above, 5.3.2.1.2.). It is a relatively rare sign and there is no consistency in its notation. In this position, that is, in an unstressed syllable at the end of a word which is connected to the following (whether by a *maqqaf* or by a conjunctive accent) which is (generally but not always) stressed at the beginning, it is likely to occur before a laryngeal consonant, e.g., סְלֹחַ לוֹ (Deut. 29:19); נִשְׁבַּע־לִי (Gen. 24:7); הֲשָׁמַע עָם (Deut. 4:33) – and even with another consonant where the stress is retracted from it, mainly when the vowel is *ṣere*, e.g., נָבֵל צִיץ (Isa. 40:7); בֹּצֵעַ בָּצַע (Prov. 1:19); or sometimes even with other vowels and without the retraction, e.g., פַּדֶּנָה אֲרָם (Gen. 28:5), עֲבָדֶיךָ אֵלֶּה (II Kings 1:13), וּפָנִיתִי אֲנִי (Eccl. 2:11), וַיֵּנִקֵהוּ דְבַשׁ (Deut. 32:13).

In ancient manuscripts the *haʿamadah* is found more than in the recent editions of the Bible. But even in the ancient texts there are no fixed rules and there is disagreement among the manuscripts. Yeivin (*The Aleppo Codex of the Bible* (1968), 180ff., 271ff.) described and discussed the situation in the Aleppo codex and in related manuscripts.

5.3.3. The Accentuation Signs

The Tiberian system, unlike the other two, was a consolidated, complete system of disjunctive accents and conjunctive accents with defined functions, complete orderliness, and a very uniform textual transmission. This is the result of improvement after improvement, and it can be considered the zenith of the development of the graphemes in Hebrew.

5.3.3.0.1. The Functions. In addition to the two functions which the accentuation signs perform in the other systems – dividing the verse, and setting the melody of the reading of the text – in the Tiberian system they also indicate the point of the stress in the word. This is very important not only for the correct reading of the Bible but also for recognizing the grammatical structure of the language: the Tiberian system of accentuation is the only means for establishing the stress structure of ancient Hebrew.

As a musical guide for reading, this system is also more sophisticated than the others: for actually one fixed sign would have been sufficient for indicating the lack of pause; and it was only for musical variation that different signs were established for words which are connected in different contexts, the conjunctive accents.

Its sophistication and completeness as a system of punctuation are manifest also in (1) the fact that its signs are attached to each and every word and they indicate different degrees of pause as well of juncture (= "zero" pause); (2) the fact that the value of each punctuation sign (= accent) is relative, and changes according to its position within the verse, the length of the verse, and the relationship to the other accents within it.

5.3.3.0.2. The Principles of Parsing. The principles of parsing of the system are varied:

(1) each division is always into two only – a dichotomy, i.e., the result of every division is always only two smaller units and never more;

(2) the dichotomy continues time after time in every one of the resultant units until there remain in each small unit only two words (which do not have to be divided) or until all the accentuation signs have been used and there are technically no more possibilities for indicating another division.

5.3.3.1. THE (21) PROSE BOOKS. The Tiberian accentuation signs are a system of dots and lines, some simple, others compounded. The names of the signs are in part Aramaic and in part Hebrew, and they sometimes refer to the melody or to the manner of reading, sometimes to the shape of the sign, and at other times to the hand movement which accompanied the melody in the ancient period (see 1.3.3.).

5.3.3.1.1. Disjunctives. מְ – סילוק (cessation; also סוף פסוק – end of the verse). It occurs only at the end of a verse and it is located only on the stressed syllable (this is not to be confused with the *gaʿyah* sign, which does not occur with the stressed syllable). מְ (originally מְ) – אַתְנָחָה, אֶתְנַחְתָּא, אַתְנָח ("rest"). מ – זָקֵף קטן (זקף = erect, upright – perhaps referring to a hand movement or to the shape of the sign). מ – זקף גדול, a variant of זקף קטן used in specific conditions. מ – סְגוֹלְתָא, סְגוֹל (Aramaic: a [grape] cluster – refers to its shape). This is a postpositive sign – always written at the end of the word, but in some editions of the Bible it is placed an extra time on the stressed syllable in penultimate words. | מ – שַׁלְשֶׁלֶת (chain; refers to the shape of the sign and perhaps to the melody as well). A rare accent, it appears only seven times in the 21 books. מְ – טִפְחָא, טִפְּחָא (perhaps "handbreadth" – refers to the hand movement, or perhaps to a (musical) stroke). מ – רְבִיעַ (Aramaic: resting). מ֙ – פַּשְׁטָא, פָּשְׁטָא (extending, stretching; of either the melody or the sign, the line), sometimes named also יתיב (see below). A postpositive sign – always written at the end of a word and in penultimate (*mille'el*) words also on the stressed syllable (thus, by the exact manner of notation, it is differentiated from the conjunctive *ʾazlaʾ*). מ֚ – יְתִיב (Aramaic: settled down – referring to the melody or the pause). It is also used as a general name for this accent and the preceding one. A variant of the preceding accent in specific conditions, it is a prepositive accent – located always at the beginning of the word, and to the right of the lower vocalization sign. מ֮ (originally מ) – צִנּוֹר, זַרְקָא. The second is the ancient name (hook) and it refers to the original shape of the sign. The first is the common name and it means "throwing," perhaps referring to the movement of the hand, or to a scattered melody. This sign is postpositive – placed precisely like the *segol* (see above). מ֛ – תְּבִיר (Aramaic: broken), תְּבְרָא, תָּבְרָא, referring to the broken melody. מ֠ (originally מ) – תלישא גדולה תְּלִישָׁא (תלישא = plucking out). The meaning is not certain, and it appears to refer more to the hand movement than to the melody. *Gedola* distinguishes it from the conjunctive accent of the same name. The sign is prepositive, always placed at the beginning of a word, and in some editions of the Bible it is placed an additional time on the stressed syllable when the stress is not at the beginning of the word. מ֡ (originally מ, מ) – פָּזֵר: it apparently does not refer to the melody, but to the sign (פַּזְרָא, Aramaic = whip). It is also called פזר קטן. מ֟ (originally מ) – קַרְנֵי פָרָה (= cow's horns), referring to the ancient form of the sign. It is also called פזר גדול. A variant of the preceding, it is a rare sign which appears only 16 times in the 21 books. מ֜ – גֶּרֶשׁ, גֵּרֵשׁ, גָּרְשָׁה, גְּרֵשׁ ("expulsor"), one of the ancient names for *ga'yah*, which moves ("expels") the syllables apart; the term was applied to this sign because of its similarity to the shape of the *ga'yah* (a vertical line). One also finds it called גרש קטן (*gereš qaṭan*) to distinguish it from the following accent. Its ancient name is טֶרֶס (Aramaic: bar) on account of its shape, and that name is sometimes used for this accent and the following one. מ֞ – גרש גדול, שני גְרִישִׁין, גֵּרְשַׁיִם, a variant of the *gereš* in specific positions. | מ֣ – מֻנָּח לְגַרְמֵהּ, an abbreviation of the name שופר מונח לגרמיה ("trumpet, horn [sustained] by itself"). The vertical line between the words separates this pausal accent from the conjunctive accent similar in shape (*munah*).

5.3.3.1.2. Conjunctives. מ֣ – מונח. This is an abbreviation of שופר מונח, which was the name of one of the types of accents that were called by the name שופר (horn, trumpet). The distinction between these types was not preserved, neither in the name nor in the sign. מ֤ – מַהְפָּךְ. An abbreviation of שופר מהפך ("inverted horn") or מְהֻפָּךְ or שופר הפוך. It is always placed under the stressed syllable and to the left of the vowel sign, and thus it is differentiated from the disjunctive *yetiv*. מ֥ – מֵירְכָא (Aramaic: prolonging) and also מַאְרְכָה, and מַאֲרִיךְ. In the ancient manuscripts it had the same shape as the *ga'yah* and caused confusion. מ֦ – מֵירְכָא כפולה (double): a rare conjunctive, found only 14 times in the 21 books. מ֧ – דַּרְגָּא ("grade," "scale") referring to the sign and perhaps to the melody (Ar. *daraja* = "to sing quaveringly"). Its rare name שִׁישְׁלָא, שַׁלְשֶׁלֶת ("chain") perhaps goes back to a sign similar to a *šalšelet* (מ֓) from which this sign was shortened. מ֨ – אַזֵל, אַזְלָא, אָזְלָא ("going on"), the ancient name of the sign. Another name is קַדְמָא ("antecedent"), perhaps because it very often occurs before *gereš*. It is always written on the stressed syllable and it is thereby differentiated from the disjunctive *paštaʾ*. מ֩ (originally מ) – תְּלִישָׁא קטנה. The sign and the name are equal to those of the disjunctive and apparently denoted the same melody. The distinction is made by the position of the sign – postpositive, always at the end of the word, and in some editions of the Bible it is written an additional time over the stressed syllable in words with penultimate stress. מ֪ (originally מ, מ) – יֶרַח בֶּן יוֹמוֹ ("a day old moon") referring to its ancient form (מ) which is similar to the shape of a new moon (better: יֶרַח). The ancient name is גַּלְגַּל ("wheel") also referring to one of the ancient shapes, perhaps the oldest. Since it serves as a conjunctive for *qarne parah* only, it is as rare, found only 16 times in the 21 books.

5.3.3.1.3. Main Rules of Dichotomy by the Disjunctives. The accentual division of verses is generally logical, its purpose being to guide the reader in his recitation. Therefore it is frequently subordinated to considerations of rhythm and even of melody. The length of the verse and the distance of the dichotomy from the end of the verse are sometimes likely to cause a division at variance with the division required according to the syntactical analysis.

The accent which indicates the end of the verse is always *silluq*. A verse is usually divided by *eʾtnaḥ*, sometimes by *zaqef*, and infrequently even by *ṭippeḥa* – all according to the length of the verse and the distance between the place of the division and the end of the verse. The further the division occurs from the end of the verse the more likely it is that an *ʾetnaḥ* will be used.

The two hemistichs which result, that of *ʾetnaḥ* and that of the *silluq*, are each likely to be further subdivided by a *zaqef* (*qatan* or *gadol*), at a certain distance from the *ʾetnaḥ* or the *silluq*, or by a *ṭippeḥa* near them. *Tippeḥa* is used as a prelude accent and must occur in any event after the *zaqef*. When many divisions are required the *zaqef* is likely to be repeated a few times. In place of the first *zaqef* of the hemistich of the *ʾetnaḥ*, a *segol* is likely to occur.

The *zaqef*'s hemistich (to its right) is likely to be divided by *paštaʾ*, and when long by *revi'a*, and then a *paštaʾ* follows.

The hemistich of the *segol* is always divided by *zarqaʾ* (as a prelude), and when it is long, by a *revia'*, and then *zarqaʾ* will also occur after the *revia'*.

The hemistich of the *ṭippeḥaʾ* is likely to be divided by *tevir*, and when it is long also by *revia'*, and then the *tevir* will also come after the *revia'*.

The hemistich of the *revia'* is likely to be divided by *munaḥ legarmeh, gereš, telišaʾ gedola* or *pazer*, all according to the distance of the division from the end of the hemistich. *Munaḥ legarmeh* or *gereš* will occur close to its end and the *pazer* at a distance from it. A *pazer* can be repeated if necessary.

The hemistichs of the *pašta*ʾ, *zarqa*ʾ, or *tevir* are likely to be divided by *gereš, teliša*ʾ *gedola* or *pazer*, all according to the distance of the division from the end of the hemistich – *gereš* in a closer position and *pazer* at a distance. A *pazer* can be repeated it necessary.

The hemistichs of *pazer, teliša*ʾ *gedola*, and *munaḥ legarmeh* are not subdivided. That of *gereš* is sometimes divided, irregularly, by a *teliša*ʾ *gedola* and *pazer.*

These main rules have many by-rules and laws of transformation of accents causing changes and the use of variant accents conditioned by musical considerations.

5.3.3.1.4. Rules of Joining the Conjunctives. For each of the disjunctives there is a specific conjunctive which is joined to it. This joining of the conjunctive is not always imperative and even the number of the conjunctives which are added to a disjunctive depends upon the context and the verse structure. Sometimes only one conjunctive is added, sometimes more, up to a maximum of six conjunctives with certain disjunctives. Below is a list of the conjunctives which can join each disjunctive, arranged in reverse order, from the disjunctive backward:

silluq – its conjunctive is *merka*ʾ.

ʾetnaḥ, zaqef qaṭan, segol – conjunctives: *munaḥ, munaḥ.*

*tippeḥa*ʾ – its conjunctive is *merka*ʾ (14 times in the Bible: double *merka*ʾ, *darga*ʾ).

*revia*ʿ – its conjunctives are *munaḥ, darga*ʾ, *munaḥ.*

*pašta*ʾ – the conjunctives are *mahpak* (or *merka*ʾ), *ʾazla*ʾ (or *munaḥ*), *teliša*ʾ *qeṭanna, munaḥ, munaḥ, munaḥ.*

*zarqa*ʾ – the conjunctives are *munaḥ* (or *merka*ʾ), *ʾazla*ʾ (or *munaḥ*), *teliša*ʾ *qeṭanna, munaḥ.*

tevir – its conjunctives are *darga*ʾ (or *merka*ʾ), *ʾazla*ʾ (or *munaḥ*), *telia qeṭanna, munaḥ.*

*teliša*ʾ *gedola* – the conjunctives are *munaḥ, munaḥ, munaḥ, munaḥ, munaḥ.*

pazer – its conjunctives are *munaḥ, munaḥ, munaḥ, munaḥ, munaḥ.*

qarne parah – the conjuctives (at least two) are *yeraḥ ben yomo, munaḥ, munaḥ, munaḥ, munaḥ, munaḥ.*

gereš – its conjunctives are *ʾazla*ʾ (or *munaḥ*), *teliša*ʾ *qeṭanna, munaḥ, munaḥ, munaḥ.*

geršayim – its conjunctive is *munaḥ.*

munaḥ legarmeh – conjunctives: *merka*ʾ, *ʾazla*ʾ (or *munaḥ*).

5.3.3.2. THE (3) POETICAL BOOKS. *5.3.3.2.1. Disjunctives.* מֽ – סילוק, to mark the end of a verse. מ֥֫ – עולה ויורד ("ascending and descending"), referring to the melody. The upper sign is pretonic. מ֑ (originally מ֑) – אתנח. מ֗ – רְבִיעַ. In ancient manuscripts it is a disjunctive accent replacing *ʾetnaḥ* as main divider of the domain of *silluq*. In later manuscripts and in printed editions it takes the shape of the following (*revia*ʿ *mugrash*) and both are regarded as one and the same accent. Originally there were four disjunctive accents in which the sign and the name *revia*ʿ appear: *revia*ʿ, *revia*ʿ *mugrash, revia*ʿ *gadol, revia*ʿ *qaṭan.* מ֝֗ – רביע מֻגְרָשׁ (*revia*ʿ *gerešatum*), a relatively late term. Formerly it was called *ṭippeha*ʾ, for its functions are similar to those of *ṭippeha*ʾ in the other 21 books. The sign of the *gereš* (the first of the two marks) is prepositive. In the ancient manuscripts a distinction is made between a *revia*ʿ which has a *gereš* (as shown here) and a *revia*ʿ which does not (see above), which is also a disjunctive in the hemistich of the *silluq*, but is not preceded by *ʾetnaḥ* (it is a substitute for the *ʾetnaḥ* itself). The conjunctives of these two accents are different. מ֓ ׀ – שלשלת גדולה, a variant of the preceding one in specific conditions. The vertical line between the words separates this disjunctive from a similar conjunctive (*šalšelet qeṭanna*). מ֗ – רביע גדול, a disjunctive in the hemistich of *ʿole we-yored* or *ʾetnaḥ* or *revia*ʿ (which is a substitute for *ʾetnaḥ*). מ֮ (originally מ֘) – זרקא, צינור: a postpositive sign, placed at the end of the word to differentiate it from another sign of a melody similar to it. מ֭ – דְּחִי ("thrust back") referring to its being prepositive, which differentiates it from a similar conjunctive accent. Sometimes one also finds the names טפחא, טרחא and even יתיב for the disjunctive, no distinction being made between the names. In a few places the position of the stress was indicated by a sign similar to *ga*ʿ*yah* or *merka*ʾ (or even *tippeḥa*ʾ). In some individual manuscripts the sign מ֛ (*tevir* in the 21 books) is used instead of *deḥi.* מ֗ – רביע קטן, a minor disjunctive in the hemistich of *ʿole we-yored*. There is no difference in shape between this sign and *revia*ʿ *gadol*, but there is a difference in their respective conjunctives. מ֡ (originally מ֡, מ֡) – פזר. מ֨ ׀ – אזלא לגרמיה. The vertical line after the word distinguishes this disjunctive from the conjunctive sign similar to it (*ʾazla*ʾ). מ֤ ׀ - מהפך לגרמיה; a variant of the previous accent in specific conditions. The vertical line after the word distinguishes this disjunctive from the conjunctive which is similar to it (*mahpak*).

5.3.3.2.2. Conjunctives. מ֥ – מירכא. מ֣ – מונח. מ֬ – עִלּוּי ("elevation," "raising"), an abbreviation of שופר עילוי. This is the ancient name of one of the types of accents which were called *shofar* (horn, trumpet), and it was so named because of the ascending melody. Only in a relatively late period did it refer to the sign of the *shofar* which was written above, that is, upper, superior *shofar.* Another name is מונח מלמעלה – with the same meaning. מ֤ – מהפך. מ֖ – טַרְחָא, a name apparently derived from טֹרַח ("burden") and meaning, consequently, laboring, heaviness. It is sometimes also called טפחא. It is always placed under the stressed syllable and it is thus differentiated from the disjunctive *deḥi*. Some of the early scholars differentiated between three types of *ṭarḥa* according to the disjunctive which they join: before *silluq* – נטויה ("inclined"), מאילא (from the Arabic *māʾilah* ="inclining," see below, 5.3.3.3.2.1.); before *ʾetnaḥ* (or its substitute) – דְּחוּיָה (= "thrust back"); before *revia*ʿ *mugraš* (or *šalšelet gedola*) – שׁוֹכֵב ("reclining"). מ֨ – אזלא. מ֪ – גַּלְגַּל ("wheel"). Two different signs merged in this one, but they are still found separately in ancient manuscripts: מ֪ – the conjunctive for a *pazer* (and apparently the name *galgal* refers to this; it is also used in the 21 books), and מֽ (in the form of an inverse ancient ʾetnaḥ) – which is used as a conjunctive for ʿole we-yored. מ֓ – שלשלת קטנה, a rare accent which appears only eight times in Psalms, Proverbs and Job.

5.3.3.2.3. Main Rules of Dichotomy by the Disjunctives. The relative brevity and parallel structure of most of the verses in Psalms, Proverbs, and Job were liable to cause monotony in the reading and even in the melody. In order to avoid this, special accents were used which allowed for more variety of tone than in the other books. These different accents based on the context, and even more on the syllable structure of the words themselves, helped reduce the monotony.

Here, too, the sign which marks the end of the verse is always *silluq*, although a few manuscripts do not mark it at all. A verse is divided by *ʿole we-yored*, or by *ʾetnaḥ* and infrequently even by *reviaʿ* (which in later manuscripts and editions is then marked with additional prepositive *gereš*) – all according to the length of the verse and the distance of the point of division from the end of the verse. The further the division is from the end of the verse, the more *ʿole we-yored* is used.

The hemistich of *ʿole we-yored* is likely to be divided by *reviaʿ qaṭan* at the first word or by *ṣinnor* at the second word and by *reviaʿ gadol* at the third word and further. When the hemistich is divided by *reviaʿ gadol*, a *ṣinnor* or *reviaʿ qaṭan* will be used, in any event, for an additional division between it and *ʿole we-yored.*

The hemistich of *ʾetnaḥ* is likely to be divided by *deḥi*, and when it is long, by *reviaʿ gadol*, and then it is possible that *deḥi* will also occur after the *reviaʿ gadol.*

The hemistich of the *silluq* which remains after the division by *ʾetnaḥ* (or by *ʿole we-yored*), is divided again by *reviaʿ mugraš*; and when *reviaʿ mugraš* is far from the *silluq*, there is a second, smaller division made by the disjunctive *ʾazlaʾ legarmeh* or *mahpak̠ legarmeh* (according to the structure of the word and the context of the accents). In special situations *šalšelet gedola* will occur instead of *reviaʿ mugraš.*

The hemistich of *reviʿa mugraš* or *šalšelet gedola* is not further subdivided. However, when *reviaʿ mugraš* is used instead of *ʾetnaḥ* (and it is then written in the ancient manuscripts without *gereš*), it is likely to be divided in the same manner as the hemistich of the *ʾetnaḥ* (see above).

The hemistichs of the *reviaʿ qaṭan* and *pazer* are likely to be subdivided only by *ʾazlaʾ legarmeh* or *mahpak̠ legarmeh*. The hemistich of *ʾazlaʾ legarmeh* is never subdivided.

Often enough these rules, or at least some of them, are not put into effect because of very precise rules of transformation. These rules, which are based upon musical considerations, cause the exchange of one disjunctive for another, or the replacement of a disjunctive by a conjunctive. In most cases of substitution the conjunctive accents of the original division remain in their positions and it happens, therefore, that sometimes the conjunctives of one disjunctive serve another disjunctive, or even another conjunctive. In order to trace a verse's division one must therefore take the rules of transformation into consideration. Sometimes even in a place where there is a conjunctive, the intention of the accentuators was a pause, and only the melody is that of the conjunctive. The opposite phenomenon – a disjunctive occurring for a musical reason in a place where no division is needed (prelude accent) – is very common in the accents of Psalms, Proverbs, and Job, and even more in the accents of the 21 books (see above).

5.3.3.2.4. The Use of Conjunctives. The rules of the conjunctives in Psalms, Proverbs, and Job became very slack with their transmission throughout the generations. While the musical side influenced their selection even more than in the 21 books, these rules were most complex and dependent upon the syllabic structure of the words, the number of conjunctives, and the distances from the disjunctive. Despite all these rules, the exceptions were still quite numerous. Furthermore, the reading tradition for the books of Psalms, Proverbs, and Job was not preserved by the various Jewish communities, and the system of the signs – and even more so, the rules behind them – were not understood by the scribes and printers, and they lacked all meaning for the readers. This accounts for the fact that as time passed the manuscripts – and even more so, the printed editions – differed from one another more and more, until complete confusion was reached in the rules of the conjunctives. The rules of the disjunctives also suffered, but to a lesser degree. Even in ancient manuscripts with an excellent textual tradition, the rules of the conjunctive are very complicated and sometimes there are no rules but different parallel possibilities for the conjunctive accents without any obvious causality. I. Yeivin has described the situation as found in the Aleppo codex (*The Aleppo Codex of the Bible* (1968), 281–350).

5.3.3.3. SPECIAL SIGNS. In addition to the accentuation signs, which have been treated until now, each of which indicates both a degree of pause and a melody (the noting of the place of stress in a word is restricted to the Tiberian system), there are a number of other signs used in the Tiberian system of accentuation, each for only one of the following purposes.

5.3.3.3.1. Signs for Pause and not for Melody. 5.3.3.3.1.1 Paseq. The sign | מ (a vertical line between words; originally a small line | מ) – פָּסֵק (Aramaic: cutting off), פְּסִיק (Aramaic: cut off); a symbol for punctuation only and not for melody. It occurs only after conjunctive accents and indicates a pause. One should consider it an additional improvement in the system of accentuation, for it is a sign used to complete the punctuation system after the system of the melody was stabilized. With regard to its phonetic influence upon the pronunciation of the word it is also like a disjunctive in that it voids the fricative nature of בגדכפ"ת at the beginning of the following word; that is, it cancels the fricativeness which is caused by the conjunctive accent near it. A distinction should be made between a *paseq* which is wont to occur after any one of the conjunctives as opposed to the similar sign which goes with one of the disjunctives: *šalšelet, munaḥ legarmeh, šalšelet gedola,*

ʾ*azlaʾ legarmeh, mahpak legarmeh*. With these disjunctives the sign is part of the accentuation. To distinguish between the two kinds, the masoretes arranged lists of the *paseqs* (פסיקְתָא) found in the Bible. The lists are not identical, but in general the number of *paseqs* reaches about 400. Already in Ben-Asher's *Dikduke ha-Teʿamim* five rules for *paseq* were enumerated, and in effect it was possible to explain most of the *paseqs* in the Bible with the aid of a set of rules. Yet these rules did not always work, and one cannot explain why they were not applied in every instance.

The five *paseq* rules of Ben-Asher may be sorted into two main categories of means for perfection:

(1) In a unit of mostly two words, which according to the principle of dichotomy needs no further division, the *paseq* occurs nevertheless to indicate division for a definite, phonetic or punctuational-exegetic, reason:

(a) a phonetic need – to separate between equal or similar consonants at the boundaries of adjacent connected words in order to avoid assimilation and, consequently, wrong joining of the words. Mostly the sonorants ל, מ, נ are involved, e.g. בָּבֶל | לְגַלִּים | מְעוֹן־תַּנִּים (Jer. 51:37);

(b) a punctuational need – to separate between a pair of identical or similar words, e.g., יוֹם | יוֹם (Gen. 39:10), הִמּוֹל | יִמּוֹל (Gen. 17:13);

(c) an exegetic need – to separate between words, one of which is a name of God, which are joined according to the accentuation needs, but their conjunction is liable to allow for a different understanding, in which God's name would be profaned, e.g. אִם־תִּקְטֹל אֱלוֹהַּ | רָשָׁע (Ps. 139:19) – "if Thou shall kill, O God, the wicked," (not "if you kill the wicked God");

(d) an exegetic need – to separate between words in order to avoid an understanding arising from the division of the accentuation and which seems either wrong, impossible or unacceptable, e.g. יִשְׁמַע | אֵל (Ps. 55:20), עָשׂוּ | כָּלָה (Gen. 18:21).

(2) in a unit of three words or more to separate words which should be separated according to the context, but for which proper disjunctives do not exist in the accentuation system to show this separation. This refers mainly to an additional division of the hemistichs of the smallest disjunctives – *pazer, telišaʾ gedola* and sometimes *gereš* – which cannot be further divided with accent signs: e.g. וַתִּשָּׂא אֹתִי רוּחַ | בֵּין־הָאָרֶץ וּבֵין הַשָּׁמַיִם (Ezek. 8:3).

Recently another early attempt to formulate rules for the occurrence of *paseq* was detected in Saadia Gaon's longer commentary to Exodus (Y. Ratzaby, *Rav Saadya's Commentary on Exodus* (Jerusalem 1998), pp. 224, 394–5), where he formulates five rules of his own, two of which do not coincide with Ben-Asher's rules (see Dotan, *Paseq*).

However, all the above are not rules for the placement of the *paseq*, but categories according to which one can classify and understand most of the *paseq* occurrences. Yet there are many places in the Bible which come under these classifications and a *paseq* is not found there. A relatively small part of the *paseqs* are not explained even according to these classifications, and there is no doubt that hidden explanations and exegetical homilies played a part in the placing of the *paseq*, as with the accentuation signs.

5.3.3.3.1.2. Maqqaf. The sign מ־ (originally an extremely small line which joined words) – מַקֵּף, מַקַּף ("binder"), is only a conjunctive sign and has no melody. It indicates that the word before it is connected to the next word; the first word has no accent of its own, and the melody indicated by the sign occurring with the word that follows it applies to it too. The *maqqaf* usually connects two words, sometimes three or even four and the dominant melody is indicated by the accent of the last word. The *maqqaf* can be classified into three main types:

(a) that which connects any type of small word, mostly prepositions and conjunctives, but also nouns, names, and other parts of speech, and makes it proclitic;

(b) that which connects a word whose stress is ultimate, although it is not a short word, to a word whose stress is at the beginning, in order to avoid adjacency of the stresses. By this connection the melody of the first word is voided, but it is doubtful whether its stress is completely cancelled. It seems that in these cases the stress regresses (נָסוֹג אָחוֹר) and is sometimes indicated by a *gaʿyah*; sometimes it is not indicated but the regression does exist in the pronunciation (latent regression);

(c) that which connects words which the accents (the conjunctives) were insufficient to connect, or some other difficulty in the accentuation left unconnected. This is another improvement in the system of accentuation, parallel to the *paseq*, but for conjunctive needs.

The rules of the *maqqaf* are only partially fixed (especially for type a), and there are variants with regard to details between different editions of the Bible. There are also principle differences between the Poetic books (Psalms, Proverbs, and Job) and the Prose books of the Bible. In ancient manuscripts the *maqqaf* was sometimes omitted, apparently through scribal error.

5.3.3.3.2. *Signs for Melody and not for Pause.* Signs for pause only are common to all 24 books of the Bible since they do not have any special melody. However, the signs for melody only are of necessity different in the two groups of books.

To this category belongs every conjunctive serving as a secondary accent in a word where another accent, disjunctive or conjunctive, marks the main stress. In this case the secondary conjunctive accents have no other function but melody. Signs serving solely for melody are the following:

5.3.3.3.2.1. The (21) Prose Books: (a) The sign מ֜ (a sign similar in shape to ʾ*azlaʾ* or *paštaʾ* occurring on a word with *zaqef qaṭan*) – it is called מַקֵּל (= "stroke," "rod") and also חֹטֶר ("rod"), because of the shape of the sign. Other names are: דָּרְבָן ("spur," "goad"), or its Arabic parallel, *hamza*, whose Hebrew spelling המזה was understood by copyists, who did not know Arabic, as a Hebrew noun with the article which they pronounced מַזֶּה. We also know of the names מְתִיגָה ("bridling") which was used equally for *gʿayah*, מַרְאֶה מָקוֹם ("indicator"), and פשט קטן because of its graphic similarity to the sign of the *pašta*ʾ. The *maqqel* is used in a word with *zaqef qaṭan* when there is no *pašta*ʾ or *yetiv* before it as a prelude accent, and when the conjunctive *munaḥ* does not precede the word or occur within it. That means that it is used as a sort of a prelude melody for *zaqef*, when the *zaqef* does not have another prelude accent in the form of *pašta*ʾ or *munaḥ*. The *maqqel* is always located in the closed syllable which is furthest from the stressed syllable and separated from it by at least one syllable (a mobile *šewa* is considered a syllable for this purpose) and it never occurs in a syllable which has *gʿayah*; e.g., וְהִתְקַדִּשְׁתֶּם (Lev. 20:7), שְׁמָר־לְךָ (Ex. 34:11). In general the *maqqel* is not used at the beginning of a word, except in special cases.

(b). The sign מָ (a sign similar to a *ṭippeḥa*ʾ which occurs in the same word with ʾ*etnaḥ* or *silluq*) is called מאילא and commonly pronounced מְאַיְלָא. Wickes believes that one should pronounce it מָאִילָא as Ar. *māʾilah* from *māla* = to incline, to be inclined, and thus the name parallels the Hebrew names for this sign which are less common (נְטוּיָה and דְחוּיָה) and have the same meaning.

The *meʾayla* is one of the peculiarities of the Masorah. It has no rules and occurs under no special conditions 15 or 16 times in the Bible: five times with a *silluq*, 10 or 11 times with an ʾ*etnaḥ*; and it is located at the position of the major *gaʿyah* in the word (e.g., לְדֹרֹתֵיכֶם – Num. 15:21). Sometimes when the disjunctive applies to two words joined by *maqqaf*, it is located in the original position of the accentuation sign of the first word (e.g., וַתֹּאמַרְנָה־לָּהּ – Ruth 1:10). It thus serves as a secondary accent in a disjunctive word and one can assume that its melody was like that of the *ṭippeḥa*ʾ, and hence the similarity of the signs. Indeed, where a *meʾayla* is used one never finds a *ṭippeḥa*, while a conjunctive accent of *ṭippeḥa*ʾ can precede the *meʾayla*. Yet the opinion that the *meʾayla* is a disjunctive cannot be accepted. Most of the cases of *meʾayla*, but not all of them, can be explained as contamination of two versions, one with *maqqaf* and one with the disjunctive *ṭippeḥa*ʾ. In the works of the Masorah this sign is considered a conjunctive.

5.3.3.3.2.2. The (3) Poetical Books: (a) *Ṣinnorit*. The sign מ֘ (originally מ) is called צִנּוֹרִית (little *ṣinnor*), and its form is like that of the pausal accentuation sign *ṣinnor*, from which it is differentiated by the position of its notation. It is a pretonic sign and occurs in an open syllable adjacent to the stress in a word with the conjunctive *mahpak*, e.g. בְּתוֹכָחוֹת (Ps. 39:12), גָּדוֹל (Ps. 96:4), and rarely also in a word with the conjunctive *merka*ʾ e.g. הוֹשִׁיעָה... הַצְלִיחָה (Ps. 118:25). There is no doubt that it indicates a prelude melody for that of the conjunctive. Since it is joined only to the conjunctives, it is considered a "servant" for the "servants" (conjunctives), and it is thus also called עבד ("slave"). It occurs regularly in a word that has a *mahpak* – which is used as a conjunctive for these accents: *reviaʿ gadol* and ʾ*azla*ʾ *legarmeh* – on the first word that precedes them; *deḥi* – on the second word preceding it; *silluq*, ʾ*etnaḥ*, and *reviaʿ* (*mugraš* – the substitute for ʾ*etnaḥ*), on the third word preceding them. It does not occur regularly in a word with *merka*ʾ, and there are variants among the printed editions and manuscripts of the Bible. It is likely to be found mainly in a word with *merka*ʾ which is used as a conjunctive before the accents *silluq*, ʾ*etnaḥ*, and *reviaʿ mugraš* – on the first word preceding them.

(b) *Metiga*. The sign מֽ, similar to the *maqqel*, is known from a few manuscripts and from works of Masorah in which it is called *hamza* in Arabic and מתיגה in Hebrew, names which are also used for *maqqel*. The *metiga* is a pretonic sign. It is used in a syllable adjacent to the stress of a word with a *merka*ʾ which serves as the conjunctive for either the accent *silluq* or *reviaʿ mugraš*, in the first word preceding it. Thus the *metiga* was used as a prelude melody for *merka*ʾ. It disappeared from most manuscripts and from all printed editions of the Bible.

5.4. THE NON-CONVENTIONAL TIBERIAN SYSTEM

In many Bible manuscripts graphemes of the Tiberian system are used in different manner from that set by the Tiberian vocalizers. This was due to: (1) a tradition of pronunciation which differs from the Tiberian; (2) a different method of notation and different rules for the use of some of the Tiberian graphemes.

The most famous of these manuscripts is the Codex Reuchlinianus of the Prophets, which was written in 1105/6 C.E. There is no uniformity in these manuscripts and this system, unlike the conventional Tiberian system, is not consolidated. Thus, like the Babylonian and Palestinian systems, it came down to us in stages of development and its various characteristics are not found in every manuscript. Inconsistency in details of vocalization is found even in the same manuscript.

5.4.1. The Typifying Characteristics

This system is distinguished from the regular Tiberian system by elements whose origin is in a different tradition of pronunciation; and by Tiberian symbols which are used according to different principles. No manuscript contains all traits of both these characteristics, especially some of the second category, also occur at times in regular Tiberian texts.

5.4.1.1. THE PRONUNCIATION TRADITION. The main traits of a different tradition of pronunciation are as follows:

(1) The lack of distinction between *qameṣ* and *pattaḥ* and between *ṣere* and *segol*; but even this typifying characteristic is not common to all manuscripts of this type.

(2) -וְ, -בְּ, -לְ at the beginning of a word becomes -וי, -בי, -לי.

(3) -יְ at the beginning of a word becomes – יִ.

(4) The lack of furtive *pattaḥ* before ח–, ע– (written as ח–, ע–), unless ī (-ִי) and in a number of manuscripts even *ū* (וּ–) preceded them; also its absence before ה– (written as הּ or ה only). Whether this characteristic is rooted in a different tradition of pronunciation is doubtful. Perhaps it is only a graphic variant in the system, that is, the consonants ה–, ח–, ע– in the final position are always pronounced with the preceding glide vowel, and there is no need to write it in. The *pattaḥ*

only following *matres lectionis* י, ו (before ח, ע), i.e., in a position where there are graphic conditions for its notation, reinforces this possibility.

5.4.1.2. VOCALIZATION. The principles of different notation in vocalization are:

(5) The principle of the *dageš lene* – that the *dageš* is placed in a letter at the beginning of a syllable which is preceded by one that ends in a consonant – is extended to the letters ז, ט, ל, מ, נ, ס, צ, ק, ש (hence it applies to all the letters except א, ה, ח, ע, ר, ו, י). The notation of the *rafeh* is correspondingly extended to these letters in an almost regular manner; it is added to a letter which is at the beginning of a syllable preceded by one that ends with a vowel. This characteristic is very frequent although its execution is not always perfect, and the symbols are also found outside the above conditions. In the opinion of Morag its function was to remove the doubt about the *šewa*: a *dageš* would indicate that the *šewa* preceding it (at the end of the preceding syllable) was quiescent, and *rafeh* would indicate that the *šewa* preceding it was mobile. From here the distinction was transferred to positions in which there is no *šewa* at the boundary of the syllables and also to the beginning of a word.

(6) A *dageš* in א and ה indicates their consonantal nature; *rafeh* above them (אֿ, הֿ) indicates that they are *matres lectionis.*

(7) וֹ – in the middle of a word indicates that the letter is a consonant; וּ, וֹ, וֹ – indicates its consonantal nature at the end of a word. ׳ indicates its consonantal nature at the beginning and in the middle of a word; ׳, ׳, ׳ – a consonant at the end of the word.

(8) The *mappiq* is written at the bottom of the *he* - הּ.

(9) שׁ = š; שׂ (or שׂ) = ś; and the *dageš* is written above the letter: שׁ = š with *dageš*, שׂ = ś with *dageš*.

(10) Instead of *qameṣ* in a closed, unstressed syllable (our *qameṣ qaṭan*) מֳ is written and in some isolated manuscripts מֹ.

(11) Instead of a mobile *šewa* preceding a consonantal *yod* with any type of vowel, a *ḥireq* is written (בִיָד), equivalent to actual Tiberian pronunciation.

(12) The consonants ח, ע are written with *šewa* even at the end of a word, and sometimes also the consonantal ה.

(13) When *ḥatefs* occur with ה, ח, and sometimes א too, the *šewa* sign is written above the vowel sign and within the letters: הֲ, חֲ, אֱ.

(14) With the letter ח and sometimes also with ע within a word, a *ḥaṭaf pattaḥ* occurs in place of quiescent *šewa*. It would seem that this is not a major change in pronunciation but in the notation only (which originated perhaps with the perception of a slight vocal glide adjacent to the ח). The nature of the *šewa* is established, as in the other cases, by the *dageš* or *rafeh* in the adjacent letter: שְׁמַעְנוּ before a *dageš*, quiescent; הַכֹּהֲנִים – before a *rafeh*, mobile. This is not done consistently, however. The opposite tendency is seen in ancient manuscripts: a simple *šewa* is used everywhere, even in such positions where in the regular Tiberian system we would find definite *ḥatefs*.

5.4.1.3. ACCENTUATION OF THE (21) PROSE BOOKS. The following characteristics occur in the 21 books:

(15) Two different accents are used as conjunctives before *zaqef*: the regular *munaḥ* (מֽ) and the sign מ֣ (a type of inverse *mahpak*). The latter is used as the single conjunctive of *zaqef* when the stress is at the beginning of the word, or as the first of two conjunctives before *zaqef* in any situation of stress. In the other instances the regular *munaḥ* is used. These conditions fit those of the conjunctive שופר מְכַרְבֵּל (for its meaning see Dotan, ed., *Dikduke ha-Te'amim*, p. 341, note 108), which are found in various works of Masorah (for example, *Maḥberet ha-Tījān*, ed. Derenbourg, p. 95).

(16) No conjunctive occurs within a word with a *zaqef* even in cases where it should occur according to the regular Tiberian system.

(17) There is no *geršayim* (מ֞), and *gereš* (מ֜) is used instead in every instance.

(18) The sign of the conjunctive *darga* is similar to the *šalšelet* below the word (מ֧); cf. also the Aramaic name of *darga*, שישלא (= chain), and even the Hebrew שלשלת.

5.4.1.4. ACCENTUATION OF THE (3) POETICAL BOOKS. (19) Instead of the disjunctive *deḥi* (מ֭), the sign of *tevir* (מ֛) is used with the same function.

(20) There are distinctions made between the types of *revia*ʿ: *revia*ʿ *gadol* מ֞ (like a doubled *gereš*, but the first mark is prepositive and the second is above the stressed syllable); *revia*ʿ (which is not preceded by *ʾetnaḥ*) מ֗ or מ֜; and other signs and distinctions similar to these.

(21) There are deviations from the regular Tiberian system with regard to the rules of the conjunctives, and they are different in the various manuscripts.

(22) The use of *ṣinnorit* (in words with *mahpak* and *merka*ʾ) is more frequent and more consistent than in the regular Tiberian system, and also the *metiga* (above 5.3.3.3.2.2.) (in words with a *merka*ʾ) is more common.

More sign variations and markings of peculiarities as used in some manuscripts were brought by Yeivin (*The Accentuation*, 1992).

5.4.1.5. OTHER SIGNS. (23) To distinguish between the *legarmeh* signs (*munaḥ legarmeh, ʾazlaʾ legarmeh, mahpak legarmeh*) and the *paseq*, there is לג׳ or פס׳ written in the margin among the masoretic notes almost regularly.

(24) The omission of the *maqqaf* is more common than in the regular Tiberian manuscripts and apparently not necessarily because of oversight of the scribes.

(25) There is a much more extensive use of *gaʿya* than in the ancient Tiberian manuscripts, especially the different types of major *gaʿya*.

The above is thus a summarized list of the main differences found in most of the manuscripts. There are additional characteristics found in one or another isolated manuscript, which have not been listed above. These characteristics seem to indicate a definite tendency, but this tendency reveals itself in various stages of development and crystallization, namely, a pronunciation other than that known as Tiberian, and the use of the Tiberian graphemes in a way differing from the common one found in conventional Tiberian manuscripts. However, the manuscripts differ even among themselves in regard to the degree of development or perfection in each of these two divisions. Some of them show marked differences from the Tiberian tradition of pronunciation, especially with regard to the pronunciation of the vowels, and others – a minority of the manuscripts – are closer to it, at times almost identical. Furthermore, in some manuscripts the non-conventional use of the Tiberian graphemes seems to be inconsistent, random, while others have a more complete and precise method approaching systematization which does not leave one letter without a symbol.

5.4.2. An Analysis of the System

In all fairness it must be said that the variant usage of graphemes, the different graphic method, is in itself insufficient to separate this vocalization system from the Tiberian tradition. Yet, since this method is usually associated with the indication of non-Tiberian pronunciation, especially its substitution of *qameṣ* for *pattaḥ* and *ṣere* for *segol*, and vice versa (characteristic 1 above) – all the others are not necessarily non-Tiberian characteristics – it is clear that this entire system is non-Tiberian. Even if isolated manuscripts have been found in which the free substitution of these vowel signs does not occur, their very scarceness and even their relative lateness testify to the fact that they constitute something of a further improvement of the system in order to bring it closer to the regular Tiberian system.

5.4.2.1. PALESTINIAN-SEPHARDI. The lack of distinction between *qameṣ* and *pattaḥ* and between *ṣere* and *segol* is common to the Palestinian and to the Sephardi pronunciation traditions. The rest of the characteristics of pronunciation are not necessarily typifying for either of these two traditions. For example, characteristic 2 is also found in the Tiberian tradition itself in the school of *Ben-Naphtali, and vestiges of it can even be discerned in manuscripts and various editions of the accepted Tiberian text, e.g., בִּיקְּרוֹתֶיךָ (Ps. 45:10); וִילְלַת (Jer. 25:36); לִיקְּהַת (Prov. 30:17). It is difficult to decide one way or another even according to the graphic method. Most of the characteristics are neutral; some no doubt reflect ancient Tiberian characteristics (15, for example), while others are not necessarily specific to Palestine but are also found in the Babylonian tradition and sometimes in the Tiberian tradition as well (19, for example). Only two characteristics seem to be common to this system and the Palestinian – the way of noting the diacritical dots in the letters הּ, שׁ, שׂ (characteristics 8,9). However, Palestinian manuscripts which follow this method of notation reveal clear signs of Tiberianization with regard to the notation of vowels, and diacritical signs such as these are not found in purely Palestinian manuscripts. The noting of the *mappiq* in the lower part of ה is also found, for instance, in the Tiberian vocalization of the Kaufmann manuscript of the Mishnah. Then even this loose connection between the two systems loses its significance.

5.4.2.2. GEOGRAPHICAL AND CHRONOLOGICAL DISTRIBUTION. On the other hand, one must consider the fact that the manuscripts vocalized in this manner are most widespread in European libraries; even those from the *Genizah*, at least some of them, originated – as N. Allony has emphasized – in Western European countries (especially Germany), and not necessarily in the East. The dated manuscripts among them range from the 11th century to the 14th. The pronunciation of the vowels during that period among the Jews of Western Europe, including the Ashkenazi Jews of Germany and France, was similar to that of the Spanish (Sephardi) Jews. The system under discussion is just a further verification of this fact, which was first pointed out by Yalon (*Leshonenu*, 3 (1931), 204). Thus the tendency of the system is in this direction, too, toward the Sephardi-Ashkenazi pronunciation tradition, no less and perhaps more than its attraction toward the Palestinian pronunciation tradition.

5.4.3. The Relationship to the Conventional Tiberian System

Various opinions have been expressed concerning the relationship of this system to the conventional Tiberian vocalization system. Different names for this system have also been offered according to these opinions.

5.4.3.1. BEN-NAPHTALI. Kahle focused on one characteristic (2) which is common to these manuscripts and to the Ben-Naphtali versions of the Tiberian tradition. Although he did not find additional principal characteristics common to this system and to the Ben-Naphtali tradition, and despite the fact that most of these manuscripts do not accord with a large part of the Ben-Naphtali readings, he did not hesitate to name the whole system "the Ben-Naphtali System."

5.4.3.2. OTHER NAMES. It has become clear that this opinion is unfounded, and other suggestions have been offered in regard to the system. Some consider it a more primitive system than the conventional Tiberian and suggest that it be considered as "proto-masoretic" or "pre-masoretic" (thus Sperber and Díez Macho); others take it to be a more sophisticated system than the Tiberian, trying to reach complex phonetic notation, and therefore they date it later, hence it would be necessarily "post-masoretic." Because of its connection with the pronunciation tradition of the Palestinian vocalization, it has been suggested to call it the "fuller Palestinian" system (Morag) or the "Palestinian-Tiberian" system (Allony and later also Morag). These two names are based on the assumption that the system under discussion is nothing more than an expansion of the Palestinian vocalization, that is, the transmission of the Palestinian pronunciation in a fuller manner with the aid of Tiberian signs. Yet even the theory of the lateness of the system has not universally been accepted, and the idea has formed that these manuscripts are not of a uniform nature. Díez Macho has suggested that the manuscripts be divided into three groups according to their chronological-typological parallels to the Tiberian system, and then they would show both pre- and post-masoretic vocalization of this type.

Two other names which have been suggested are based on dissatisfaction with the chronological connotations of the names – which are no more typifying – and from the connection with the Palestinian system of vocalization, which is based on conjecture and interpretation of facts and not on actual facts. Since this is a system which differs from the traditional one, the name "non-masoretic" has been suggested (Yeivin). Yet this too misses the mark, for even if the system does not agree with our Masorah, which was universally accepted, it is still within the range of the concept Masorah, and even these manuscripts have their masoretic notes. A more recent suggestion was "Expanded Tiberian" (Yeivin) indicating the wider range of its graphemes but saying nothing about the nature of the system. According to the term "non-receptus" (Goshen-Gottstein) the system is one of two Tiberian systems which developed at the same time, both representing the same Tiberian reading tradition by different graphic systems. The difference between the two systems is that one was accepted (*receptus*) and the other was rejected. Following this opinion it is in that minority of manuscripts in which the free interchange of the vowel signs (characteristic 1) does not occur, that we find the main principle of our system; while the vast majority of manuscripts in which this interchange does occur shows no more than a late subsystem with characteristics of Sephardic pronunciation. Not only does such a presentation disagree with the facts, but it is also not fitting to describe a system which was accepted by large Jewish communities for hundreds of years, until the 15th century or perhaps later, as *non-receptus* only because it is not accepted today. Moreover, this system of vocalization was so thoroughly accepted in Western Europe that it was considered the official system of the Jews there and, as Allony has illustrated, they called it by the name הניקוד שלנו ("our vocalization"), as follows from the commentary to *Avot* in *Maḥzor Vitry* (see above, 5.1.). They presented it in explicit contrast to even the conventional Tiberian system as "ours." They vocalized not only the Bible with it, but also prayer books, texts of *piyyutim*, Mishnah etc.

5.4.3.3. DEFINITION OF THE SYSTEM. Without going into the question of the relation of the system to the Palestinian or Sephardi tradition or into the question of the time of its growth and its relation to the accepted Masorah, we remain with one clear fact: this is a system which uses the Tiberian graphemes to denote a non-Tiberian pronunciation; it is a "non-Tiberian" use – that is, not accepted by the Tiberians – of the Tiberian graphemes. Thus the most fitting name is the "Tiberian Non-Conventional" system. This was a system which intended to present a Palestinian-Sephardi pronunciation by means of Tiberian graphemes. The terms "Palestinian" and "Sephardi" are nothing more than different names for a pronunciation tradition of five vowels and from this aspect they are synonymous. They differ from each other only with regard to the origin of the system. From the widespread distribution of most of the manuscripts one can consider this is an attempt of Sephardim and of Ashkenazim whose pronunciation was Sephardic to use Tiberian symbols for their own pronunciation, i.e., "Sephardi vocalization," which first developed in Europe. However, a similar pronunciation is known also in the East, mostly within the boundaries of Palestine; but its special system of notation – the Palestinian vocalization – was not sufficiently developed and when the Tiberian vocalization was instituted, those who practiced the five-vowel pronunciation adopted it for themselves, adapted it to their needs, improved it, and made it even more phonetic. Since this vocalization was fitting for every Sephardi pronunciation, it was transferred afterwards to Europe where it spread. If this was indeed the process, it was something of a repetition of the history of the Palestinian vocalization, which was also an adapted system for a five-vowel pronunciation that was originally set for a six-vowel pronunciation tradition (see above, 5.1.1.2.). Those who followed the Palestinian tradition of pronunciation repeated, therefore, the conduct of their ancestors who adopted a different vocalization system and adapted it to their needs. It follows from this that Hebrew never had a graphic system which was originally intended for a five-vowel pronunciation tradition.

5.5. THE CONTAMINATION (MIXING) OF THE SYSTEMS

Although the non-conventional Tiberian notation is a mixture of Tiberian signs and non-Tiberian pronunciation, because of its other characteristics, its uniqueness, and the relative systematization of the manuscripts one must define it as a "system" in its own right. But, indeed, the principle of mixing the systems was not strange to the masoretes and the Hebrew scribes. It turns out that the various systems were not limited to closed communities with no contact between them. The cultural connection between the dispersed Jewish communities was close and active throughout the generations, and there is no doubt that this also included mutual influences in the realm of language between communities which were geographically or spiritually close. Of necessity the scribes everywhere were trained in the methods of writing Hebrew, as this language was the connecting link between the scattered Jewish communities. It is not only shapes of letters which are included in the methods of writing, but also the signs of the different vocalization systems. This knowledge of vocalization systems, the initial purpose of which was to gain a passive knowledge so as to understand written records from other places, ultimately led to the use of these signs to a greater or lesser degree, sometimes in order to complete the local method of writing and sometimes for other needs. See also above 3.2.4.2. Contamination of Masora.

5.5.1. Transcriptions

One of the most extreme instances of the mixture of systems is seen in extant manuscripts of the Bible in Arabic transcription (Arabic script being in itself quite rare among medieval Jews) with Tiberian vocalization and accentuation signs. These manuscripts were common among the Karaites in the tenth and 11th centuries and for a short time after, apparently to prevent the holy manuscripts in Hebrew script from being used as reading primers.

5.5.2. Process of Tiberianization

The major mixing is that of the vowel and accentuation signs. Indeed, most of the mixed manuscripts have as their general trend the increased use and dominance of the Tiberian system, both in pronunciation and in graphic notation. With regard to pronunciation, we see that this is the process of Tiberianization that was ever-increasing in all the vocalization systems (Palestinian as well as Babylonian) and affected the set of signs of the systems themselves. It left its traces also in both the phonology and the morphology of the language in each of the systems. In the appropriate sections above, references were made to the specific stages in both the Palestinian and the Babylonian vocalizations in which the influence of the Tiberian pronunciation increased. As time passed this admixture became part of the actual development of these vocalization systems.

5.5.3. Types of Mixture

There are several types of mixture in graphic notation:

(1) An a priori mixture made by the first scribe. One must examine the degree of mixture and its purpose:

(a) A systematic mixture for the purpose of completeness, adding a series of graphemes which do not exist in the original system of the scribe. An example is the Leningrad manuscript of the Prophets from 916, which is voweled and accented with the complex Babylonian system with a mixture of Tiberian signs for all the conjunctive accents, the *dageš*, the *rafeh*, the *maqqaf*, and other Tiberian signs. Examples are also found, although to a lesser degree, in the Palestinian system which was mixed with Tiberian symbols, especially the signs of the conjunctive accents.

(b) A random mixture of signs from two systems, for no apparent reason, which sometimes seems to be merely the result of the expertness of the scribe in the two systems. There are examples of Palestinian/Tiberian and Babylonian/Tiberian mixtures.

(c) A mixture of isolated signs from a different vocalization system for the purpose of ornamentation, mostly in masoretic notes, but also in other instances. Examples of that are usually found in Tiberian texts in which isolated Babylonian signs (for example the Aleppo codex), or isolated Palestinian signs, as well as others had been added.

(2) A mixture for the purpose of changing the original writing by a later scribe (second, or third, etc.). Here, too, one must examine the goal:

(a) The correction of pronunciation by a later scribe in a manuscript which was vocalized originally according to a different pronunciation tradition. Manuscripts with Babylonian vocalization in which a later scribe changed the system to a Tiberianized Babylonian are an example of this type. There are also a large number of Yemenite manuscripts of this kind. Non-conventional Tiberian manuscripts which were corrected to the conventional Tiberian are another example. For all of these we do not refer to additions only, but to erasures and major changes as well.

(b) Another purpose was the transition from one tradition of pronunciation to another, in most cases because of the passing of the manuscripts from hand to hand and the request of the new owners to add the vocalization according to their system. Generally, the former one was not erased; a new one was merely added alongside the old. The transition from Palestinian to Tiberian, Babylonian to Tiberian, and rarely from Babylonian to Palestinian, are examples of that. We also know of the systematic transcription from one vocalization system to another in the course of the copying of manuscripts which wandered from one place to another. Apparently there were special experts for this work, according to the testimony of that colophon (see above, 5.2.0.1.): "This *targum* was copied from a book which was brought from Babylonia and which was vocalized above [the line] with the vocalization of the land of Assyria and R. Nathan changed it … and corrected it and copied it in the Tiberian vocalization." Thus in copying the manuscript, they also "changed" its vocalization. A manuscript from faraway places required an adaptation of the vocalization; but when the entire manuscript was not recopied, this adaptation already meant a contamination of the vocalization systems.

Changes like these were sometimes the work of several scribes who altered and corrected one after the other until one finds several hands having dealt with the vocalization of a single manuscript. The possibility of consistency would become less and less as more hands handled a manuscript. One who wishes to trace the methods of vocalization of mixed manuscripts such as these will find that he must learn to know the different scripts, the different colors of ink, and other such factors, in order to be able to distinguish between the various notations of each one of the vocalizers. The vocalization of these manuscripts cannot be considered uniform; the notation of each vocalizer must be investigated by itself.

5.6. THE SAMARITAN SYSTEM

The reading tradition of the Samaritans constitutes a branch of its own among the reading traditions of the Jews, both for Hebrew and Aramaic, and it developed as an independent offshoot, sometimes in contact with the local Hebrew tradition or traditions. The Samaritans cherished the exact transmission of the language from generation to generation no less, and perhaps even more, than the Jews, as it was a characteristic policy in their attempt at preserving and nurturing everything which had some Samaritan uniqueness in which they differed from the Jews. They also developed an entirely separate and distinct vocalization and accentuation system for themselves. It is possible that the impetus for this came from contact with the Jews and from an attempt to imitate them, but the development of the system and its details are different from the Jewish systems. In this matter, the vocalization system is distinct from the accentuation system; the former is built according to the pattern of the Jewish systems and some of the signs are identical or similar to the Palestinian vocalization which originated in the same area as the Samaritan; the accentuation system, however, is of a type completely different from the Jewish systems and closer to the Syriac system (see below).

5.6.1. The Vowel Signs

5.6.1.1. THE PROBLEMS. The Samaritan vocalization system, like the primitive strata of the Jewish vocalization systems, does not mark all the vowels consistently, but mainly those which are likely to prevent error and especially those in syllables in which there are no *matres lectionis*. The number of manuscripts containing vocalization is extremely small and their use of signs is not uniform. In any event, it is difficult to establish the exact meaning of the signs, and it is known that their functions changed as time passed. In fact almost every sign refers to more than one vowel quality. Some of the Samaritan grammarians and masoretes already did not know the exact meaning of the signs and did not use them in their works except by rote and as a tradition of their teachers, and thus their testimonies are not uniform and do not agree with the traditional Samaritan pronunciation or with the structure of the language. For hundreds of years now these vowel signs have had no practical use. Only through a comprehensive historical-comparative investigation is it possible to trace the original use of the signs and their later applications and to follow the various layers which are discernible in the set of signs. Such an examination was made by Z. Ben-Ḥayyim and the following description is based upon his conclusions.

As in the other vocalization systems of Hebrew there is no indication of quantity in this system either and the suppositions of scholars who thought that they had found signs for length were based on false premises. Even the similarity of some signs to the Palestinian is only apparent. In fact, the two systems have only two signs in common; the two of one pair have different uses, while the other two are only somewhat similar. Since the two which are alike are basic grapheme signs (–, ׀), which are likely to be adopted independently in any vocalization system, there is no need to assume borrowing or dependence of the Samaritan system upon the Palestinian, even though both of them were native to approximately the same region.

5.6.1.2. THE VOWEL AND DIACRITICAL SIGNS. There are ten signs in the Samaritan system: nine signs for vowels and one diacritical sign for the *dageš*. However, since some of the vowel signs are sometimes used with the function of a diacritical sign or embody within them a combination of a vowel sign and a diacritical sign, it is more convenient to deal with them together. Six of the ten signs belong to the ancient layer, that is, they are assumed to have been used at the beginning of Samaritan vocalization (there are no biblical manuscripts of this layer), and the others are substitutes and later developments. All ten are never used in one and the same manuscript. There are no dots at all in the Samaritan vocalization as known today, and the six basic signs all consist of lines and angles, which are placed above the letter and a little to the left. According to the Samaritan grammarians the signs are parts of Samaritan letters.

מ̒ – *i* (sometimes a kind of *e* which is derived from a final post-tonal *ī*). The grammarians called it by the Arabic names of this vowel, *kasr* or *ḫafḍ*, and according to a Samaritan grammarian the sign is part of the letter adjacent to *yod* – i.e., *ṭet* (ᕱ).

מ̌ – *e*. One of the three types of the *fatḥ*, called by the grammarians *fatḥ al-nidāʾ* (the *fatḥ* of exclamation), and they considered it part of the letter *ʾalef* (ᨓ).

מ׳ – *å* (according to Ben-Ḥayyim's notation). One of the three types of *fatḥ*, called by the grammarians *fatḥ al-ʾīmāʾ* (the *fatḥ* of indication), and they considered it part of the letter *he* (ᨕ).

מ̂ – *o*, *u*. This sign was called by the grammarians *ḍamm*, the Arabic name of the vowel, and they considered it part of the letter *waw* (ᨛ). There was no need for two different signs since the two vowels are allophones in complementary distribution: *u* – only in an open tonal or pretonal syllable (and then it is long), *o* – only in an open, post-tonal syllable or in a closed syllable (and then it is always short).

מ̄ – *a*. This is also one of the three types of *fatḥ* and was called by grammarians *fatḥ al-ʾiḫā* (the *fatḥ* of brotherhood) and sometimes just by the name *fatḥ*; they believed it to be part of the letter *ḥet* (ᨖ) or *ʿayin* (ᨚ).

מ̆ – A diacritical sign only, it indicates gemination (*dageš forte*). The grammarians called it by the name of the corresponding Arabic sign, *shadd*, and they considered the sign to be part of the the letter *qof* (᨞) of the Hebrew word *ḥazaq*, which indicated the *tašdīd* according to them.

These basic signs were used in a rather ancient period, according to Ben-Ḥayyim even prior to the Arabic-speaking period of the Samaritans. Obviously their Arabic names are later. As Arabic influence increased after the conquest, other signs penetrated the system; they can be seen as direct borrowings from the Arabic system of graphemes. These signs are not listed in the works of the grammarians:

מ̓ – a stylized form of מ׳, perhaps under the influence of the Arabic *fatḥa*. מ̊ – a substitute for מ̂, and it is actually the Arabic sign of *ḍamma*. In an even later period the precise use of part of these signs declined and was forgotten, especially the מ̄ which indicates sometimes even *i*. Sometimes the sign came to mark the fuller pronunciation of a consonant in the environment of the vowel, e.g., to indicate the plosive pronunciation of *waw* (עשו *ʿīšab*), or to indicate the gemination of the consonant. In the course of time, apparently not before the 13th century, the necessity arose to mark a pronounced *ʾayin* (as the outcome of either an original *ʾayin* or an original *ḥet*) occurring almost always at the beginning of a word (as a result of two adjoining weakened gutturals: אח, אע, הח, הע). This sound has two signs. عاמ–*ʿa*, a prepositive sign. It is apparently a combination of the Arabic letter ع with the basic vowel sign for *a* – מ׳. The combination מ̈ is also found in a manuscript and it is apparently the source of the cursive combinations عا.

מ ̔ – ʿ*a*, a prepositive sign. It is but the Arabic letter ع. There were scribes who abstained from using an additional sign for the vowel, since the vowel of the consonant ʿ is always *a* in any event. This use of the Arabic letter ʿayin as a diacritical sign is borrowed from the Arabic custom to use that letter as a diacritical sign. In Arabic, however, unlike Samaritan usage, it denotes a consonantal *ʾalef* (that is, an *ʾalef* which is to be pronounced almost like an *ʿayin*), this mark being in fact the sign of the *hamza* (ء) which is a shortened Arabic *ʿayin*. Moreover, Arabic manuscripts have been found in which a full *ʿayin* is used to indicate *hamza* (أ) just like the aforementioned Samaritan sign.

5.6.2. The Accentuation Signs

For Samaritan as well it can be clearly established – perhaps more clearly than for the other systems – that the accentuation signs are older than the vocalization signs: whereas all the names of the vowels are Arabic, all the names of the accents are Aramaic. Nonetheless, this does not constitute evidence of the origin of the vowel signs in the period of Arabic speech of the Samaritans, but simply that at the time when the accentuation signs already had names – and this was still in the period of Aramaic speech of the Samaritans – the vowel signs did not have names as yet. It follows from this that the set of vowel signs was not yet fixed at the time that the set of accentuation signs was already established and firmly set. The accents are called by the Samaritans סדרי מקרתה (*sēdāri maqrāta*, "arrangements of the Scripture"); they are ten in number and are listed in the works of Samaritan grammarians (see the edition of Ben-Ḥayyim). They are located always at the end of a group of words to which they apply. These are the signs and their names:

נגד – מ¨ ("leading"); פסק – מ: ("cutting"); אנחו – מ° ("rest"); ארכנו – מ/ ("an order," as Ben Ḥayyim has proved); שיאלה – מ:ᶻ ("a question"); זעיקה – מ·- ("a call"); אתמחו – מ:< ("a wonder"); בעו – מ·< ("a request"); זעף – מ:= ("a rebuke"); תורו – מ:׀ ("instructing").

It is clear from the nature of the translations of the terms that the main function of the accents is that of pausal signs which indicate the types of speech in the syntactical units preceding them, and thus also indicate the manner of reading and the melody, but not in the detailed way of the other systems which indicate an accent for almost each word. Needless to say, they do not show the position of the stress in the word. In this function of an exegetical-syntactical guide to the text they are similar to the Syriac accents. The names of some Samaritan accents are etymologically related to the names of Syriac accents, e.g., (according to the order above): נגודא, פסוקא, מנחתא, מניחנא, משאלנא and others which are close to them in meaning, such as: פקודא (= ארכנו), קרויא (= זעיקה), מדמרנא, אתדמרנא (= אתמחו) and perhaps also מצלינא (= בעו).

The division of speech into different types is rooted in the writings of the medieval grammarians (already dating from Saadiah Gaon among the Jews) and goes back to Greek philosophy (Aristotle). It is not, therefore, necessary to consider the Samaritan accentuation system as a borrowing from Syriac, although it might be that it is an imitation.

Already in ancient times the precise functions of the signs were forgotten and there is no regularity in their usage in the Samaritan manuscripts. One grammarian from the end of the tenth century (Ibn Dartha) still knew their exegetical-syntactical functions, but had nothing to say of the melody which accompanies them. No need to say that the reading handed down from generation to generation until today is not connected at all to any written system of accentuation signs, all the more so as there is no extant uniform system.

In the Samaritan orthography a dot is used regularly to separate words. This dot is neither an accentuation sign nor a regular punctuation (or conjunction) sign, but a continuation of the ancient orthographic custom of the Canaanite and Hebrew inscriptions in which the dot is used to separate words.

6. MASORETES AND GRAMMARIANS

The entire vast creation of the Masorah and the various systems of vocalization and accentuation are anonymous. The names of a few masoretes and even the works of some of them are indeed known, but there is no possibility of attributing the entire endeavor or even a part of it to any specific sage, in spite of all the attempts to do so. It is even an error to attribute the Tiberian vocalization, for example, to the family of masoretes of Asher the Elder, an opinion sometimes expressed. To the same degree it is an error to speak of the "Ben-Asher text" of the Bible when one is referring to the entire Tiberian version of the Bible.

A survey of the activity of anonymous works and of certain masoretes whose names are known can thus be done parallel to the survey of the development of the Masorah, but not combined with it. Knowing their approximate times a list of masoretes in assumed chronological order can be arranged, but the position of each in the general process of development or his contribution to the general creation of the Masorah cannot be established.

6.1. THE FIRST MASORETES

6.1.1. Dosa ben Eleazar

The Masorah concerning the total number of verses in the Bible is attributed in a well-known masoretic note quoted in several sources – among them in a manuscript of *Okhlah we-Okhlah* – to Dosa ben Eleazar (apparently end of the fourth century-beginning of the fifth). He received it from his teachers from whom it goes back to Rav Hamnuna, the Babylonian *amora* (end of the third century) whom it reached from Palestinian sources more than one hundred years earlier. This is thus the first testimony, apart from various hints in talmudic literature, about masoretic activity, that mentions the names of sages and points to Palestine as the source and the example for the Babylonian sages.

6.1.2. Moses Moḥeh

Primacy is apparently granted by Solomon b. Yeruḥim (Jeroḥam) (a Karaite early in the tenth century) in his *Muqaddimah* to the decalogue (Pinsker, *Likkute Kadmoniot*, p. 62) to the sages Rav מוחה (error in the manuscript: אחא) and to his son Moses (ובנו משה) as מתקני הנקוד הטבראני. Pinsker, however, has already pointed out that מתקני does not mean inventors (*Einleitung in des Babylonisch-Hebräische Punktationssystem*, p. 10). On the other hand, Rav Moses Moḥeh (not Moses ben Moḥeh) is known from a list of masoretes in the "Treatise on the Šewa", and he is later than the eighth century; therefore the testimony of Solomon is open to doubt. There is in any case no evidence about the inventors of vocalization.

6.1.3. Other Masoretes

Various masoretes are mentioned by name in works of Masorah and in masoretic notes. The details of their activities are not known and it is usually only the details of a reading which are cited with their names. One of the earliest of them is Phinehas Rosh ha-Yeshivah (no later than the first half of the ninth century and perhaps even earlier than that). It is known that he followed a system of marking the mobility of certain *šewas* by means of a *ḥaṭaf pattaḥ*. The most famous of the masoretes are the descendants of Asher the Elder (the Great), a family of five generations, the last two of whom were Moses and his son, Aaron Ben-Asher.

A schematic division of the early masoretes into three major generations was suggested by Yeivin (*Textus*, IX, כג–כד). The first generation (about the second half of the eighth century or even earlier) was still occupied mainly in matters pertaining to plene and defective spelling and *qere/ketiv*. In this context the schools of מערבאי and מדנחאי, and scholars like Moses Moḥeh and others are mentioned. The scholars of the second generation (not later than the middle of the ninth century) differed mainly in matters of *maqqefs* and conjunctive accents, and sometimes also in matters of vocalization. Among these scholars are משה מוחה (Moses Moḥeh – again!), Phinehas Rosh ha-Yeshiva and others. In the third generation (about the first half of the tenth century) mainly matters of *gaʿya* were the issue, rarely letters, vowels, and accents. Here the main actors are Aaron Ben-Asher and Moses Ben-Naphtali and their schools. This division can serve as a tentative outline for a general view.

6.2. AARON BEN-ASHER AND HIS PERIOD

6.2.1. Diqduqe ha-Teʿamim

Precise details about a work of Masorah by the father Moses *Ben-Asher are not known, but his son, Aaron, was the first masorete who in addition to manuscripts of the Bible and readings which are attributed to him also left a well-defined work of Masorah and grammar, ספר דקדוקי הטעמים. Aaron Ben-Asher collected in this book different rules regarding vocalization and accentuation from among the rules of the Masorah which were continuously being copied in the margins of the manuscripts of the Bible and in independent works which were part of the Masorah literature. The collection of Aaron Ben-Asher is the first known by the name of the author. It is also the first such work compiled with a grammatical aim, and not just as a collection of masoretic peculiarities, whose compiler adapted it and added his own rules in order to make it correspond to his readings. The original version of the work was published in the Dotan edition (1967); the previous edition, of Baer and Strack (Leipzig 1879), included a wide collection from masoretic literature but did not pretend to reflect the scope of the authentic, original work. The central subject of the work is the problem of the *šewa*, its mobility in the context of certain accents and the methods of marking the *šewa*. However, other rules of vocalization and accentuation, which are not germane to the *šewa*, also occur.

6.2.2. His Other Works

Other works of his have not reached us, but it is known that he wrote a Masorah, and it is apparently the one which was added to one of the manuscripts of the Bible that he vocalized and to which he added the masoretic notes. He also arranged a list of words, ב׳ בתרי לישני ("two [words] of two meanings"), homophonic pairs from the Bible recently discussed by Dotan (*The Awakening of Word Lore*, 87ff.). There are also allusions to his having written an additional work concerning grammatical matters.

6.2.3. Biblical Manuscripts

The manuscripts of the Bible whose vocalization is attributed to Aaron Ben-Asher are as follows:

(1) the Leningrad manuscript B19a, which was written in 1009 and whose vocalization was adjusted to the system of Aaron Ben-Asher, as attested by the colophon at its end;

(2) the Aleppo Codex, of which less than two-thirds of Scripture remain, also has genuine vocalization which corresponds to the system of Ben-Asher, but it, too, was apparently not vocalized by him, although a later colophon which was added to the manuscript attributes the vocalization to him.

The British Library Pentateuch manuscript Or. 4445, which had also been attributed to Aaron Ben-Asher (Kahle and others), was established as a pre-Ben-Asher manuscript (Dotan, *Reflections*). Likewise the Cairo Codex of the Prophets, written in 895 C.E. by Moses Ben-Asher (father of Aaron), published in Madrid with its Masora, is no longer regarded as part of the Ben-Asher school, but on the contrary represents a text closely related to Ben-Naphtali.

6.2.4. Kitāb al-Ḫulaf

Some of the biblical readings of Aaron Ben-Asher are known from the work of Mishael b. Uzziel, *Kitāb al-Ḫulaf alladī bayn al-Muʿallimayn ben Asher wa-ben Naftali* ("The Book of Differences between the two Masters, Ben-Asher and Ben-Naphtali"). This is a collection of the points of controversy and agreement between the two masters of the Masorah, which was collected – after their death – from manuscripts which they had vocalized. Some of the differences are stated in the form of rules and variants of principle, while the majority are lists of details. The date of the author has not been established precisely (not before the first half of the 11th century nor after the 12th century). This work is an important source for the readings of Ben-Asher and the only one for the readings and the method of his famous disputant, Moses b. David Ben-Naphtali, from whose works nothing is extant, except for a few fragments of the Bible which perhaps reflect his method of vocalization. The lists of variants were copied and recopied many times in the Middle Ages and consequently a large number of errors were introduced. Even the first name of Ben-Naphtali became confused in the transmissions of the copies.

6.2.5. Ben-Naphtali

As a consequence of the decision in favor of the readings of Ben-Asher, as opposed to the readings of Ben-Naphtali, which originated in ancient times and was further strengthened by the support of Maimonides for the Ben-Asher version (albeit only with regard to the division of *parashiyyot setumot* and *parashiyyot petuḥot* and for the manner of the writing of the songs in the Pentateuch), the readings of Ben-Naphtali were more and more rejected from most of the accepted versions of the Bible. As time passed even the details of his readings were forgotten, so much so that all exceptional readings which deviate from the accepted version were ascribed to him. For example, Elijah Levita identifies Ben-Naphtali (he calls him Jacob Ben-Naphtali) with the Eastern version ("*Madinḥa'e*") *(Masoret ha-Masoret,* the third introd., ed. C.D. Ginsburg, (1867), 114) and Pinsker still subscribed to that idea. Moreover, recently Kahle identified the non-conventional Tiberian system with Ben-Naphtali (see above, 5.4.3.1.). Actually, Moses Ben-Naphtali too is one of those who shaped the Tiberian version of the Bible and only within this framework are there differences between him and others over the minutest details, mainly over *gaʿyot* and less over conjunctive accents and so on.

6.3. THE ANONYMOUS CODIFICATION OF THE MASORAH

Ben-Asher's work of compilation draws on a vast literature which remains shrouded in anonymity. This literature is presented to us in bits and pieces on the pages of the Bible and in fragments of rules, just as it was handed down from generation to generation. Yet, even in very early times there were those, also anonymous, who collected it into larger works. One product of this type is the book *Okhlah we-Okhlah* (see above, 3.4.).

6.3.1. Hidāyat al-Qāri

6.3.1.1. THE TREATISE AND ITS TRANSFORMATIONS. *6.3.1.1.1. Hidāyat al-Qāri.* Another work of the above nature, originally written in Arabic, is *Hidāyat al-Qāri* ("The Direction of the Reader"), is a manual of instruction of the correct reading of the Bible and yet another step toward the formulation of grammar since it contains a system of rules based on masoretic notes and tries to introduce order and method into them. It has three main parts: the letters, the vowels, and the accents for the 21 prose books and for the three poetical books, all parts being sets of rules for instructing the proper reading of the Bible – reading in the expanded sense: both pronunciation and melody; hence its name. The work used to be regarded as one of the main examples of the anonymous type of masoretic literature, until Eldar (*Art of Correct Reading*, p. 40–43) drew attention to a Geniza fragment where the work was ascribed to the eleventh-century Karaite grammarian, Abū al-Faraj Hārūn. This connection has not yet been corroborated by substantial evidence of grammatical affinity by Abū al-Faraj's other works.

Most of the work, which is not extant in its entirety, is still in manuscript, but was extensively discussed by Eldar (ibid.). The manuscripts, however, are not uniform and it seems that the work passed through many transformations: abridgments, adaptations, and translations. An abridgment (*al-Muḫtaṣar*; partly published by Eldar, *Leshonenu*, 50 (1986), 214–31) or even abridgments were made from the original Arabic source. The shorter version was translated into Hebrew more than once, and by more than one translator. The abridgments and translations do not always contain the same parts of the work; even the original order of the parts changes and differs in the various versions. Moreover, parts of the work were adapted, especially from the Hebrew version, and were incorporated into other works as citations or as an integral part of new works. An attempt to reconstruct the history of the text of the work has been made by Eldar (*Art of Correct Reading*, 15–19) who tried to establish the precise relationship of all the transformations to one another and to the original.

6.3.1.1.2. Horayat ha-Qore – European Branch. As matters seem, the abridgement (*al-Muḫtaṣar*) wandered to various countries, Germany, Italy, Turkey, Yemen, and was translated into Hebrew several times independently, and adapted respectively in different ways. One abridgement brought to Mainz and translated into Hebrew also kept the Hebrew equivalent of the original title *Horayat ha-Qore* ("The Guidance of the Reader"). The abridgement that reached Italy came down to us in two Hebrew copies, the earlier one as *Toḵen Ezra*, and the later one bearing the name *Taʿame ha-Miqra* ("The Accents of the Bible"). The latter attributed, undoubtedly by mistake, to R. Judah *Ibn Balʿam (end of the 11th century). It is only this version that was published; in two parts (*Poetical Accents* and *Prose Accents*) in the middle of the 16th century by J. Mercerus (Mercier).

6.3.1.1.3. ʿAdat Devorim. One transformation of the *Muḫtaṣar* is found in the Hebrew compilation *ʿAdat Devorim* ("A Swarm of Bees") which was written by Joseph ha-Qostandini ("from Constantinople") not earlier than the second half of the 11th century. In it he incorporated large parts of the original work in Hebrew translation. It was published by R. Peretz (1984).

6.3.1.1.4. Maḥberet ha-Tījān – Hebrew and Arabic Versions. The original Arabic work wandered also to Yemen where two abridgements were made, one in Arabic and one in Hebrew.

While the first is a uniform text, the second is an eclectic work much enlarged by additions from other sources.

These most important adaptations, which went beyond the original to a certain degree and are copied together with Yemenite Pentateuchs (*tāj*), are usually named *Maḥberet ha-Tījān* (in Hebrew and in Arabic), which were both published: the first Hebrew version by Derenbourg with the mistaken title of *Manuel du lecteur* (1870), which is a translation of the name of the original work, but which certainly was not the title of the adaption; and the second, an abridged version in Arabic, by Neubauer, under the title *Petite grammaire hébraïque provenant de Yemen* (1891).

6.3.1.1.5. *Other Works.* There are quotations from the offspring of the work also in *Ḥibbur ha-Qonim* by R. Samson ha-Naqdan (first half of the 13th century); *Darkhe ha-Niqqud we-ha-Neginot* (attributed to R. Moses ha-Naqdan) as well as in other works also dependent remotely on *Hidāyat al-Qāri*.

6.3.1.2. ITS SOURCES AND TRADITION. *6.3.1.2.1. Distribution, Chronology, and Pronunciation Tradition.* The various adaptations and translations of the work were found throughout the dispersed Jewish communities; among them are translations which were made in Germany, such as one of the versions of *Horayat ha-Qore*; some of the adaptations were made in Byzantium, as *ʿAdat Devorim* by Joseph ha-Qostandini, and some apparently in distant Yemen e.g., *Maḥberet ha-Tījān* (concerning the assumed Yemenite origin of the Hebrew treatise, see Dotan, ed., *Dikduke ha-Teʿamim*, p. 334, note 9). Undoubtely these are not the only countries to which the work was brought. Adaptations of a work like this, by their very nature, leave an impression of their locale upon it, and sometimes the adaptation itself was made only in order to adjust the work to the local pronunciation and reading customs, etc. As it became clear after Eldar's studies, the original *Hidāyat al-Qāri* stems from Palestine and follows the Tiberian pronunciation and vocalization. There is no real basis to determine the exact date, but from one of the Arabic fragments it appears to have been written in Palestine, in the atmosphere of the conflict between the various traditions of pronunciation for dominance over the language. The author came to prove the superiority of his Tiberian tradition and its ancient roots. This fact is probably enough to make it necessary not to date him any later than the tenth century. From the stand he adopts in his readings and rules between the schools of Ben-Asher and Ben-Naphtali, it seems that he is indifferent to both of them, a fact which strengthens the dating suggested. Sometimes he goes his own way, although at times he reveals a closer affinity to the rules and detailed readings of Ben-Naphtali than to those of Ben-Asher.

6.3.1.2.2. *Influence of Local Elements.* These statements do not apply to the offsprings and adaptations of the original work, certainly not with respect to date and, apparently, not even with regard to pronunciation tradition. There remains room for investigation whether or not other elements penetrated it – the Sephardi, for example (as per Yalon's view). One should not look for a common denominator between the original and its adaptations, nor even between the adaptations themselves. While every adapter, translator, and person who made an abridgment stressed that which was preferable to him and included it in his version – whether particularly the letters and the vowels or the accentuation, etc. – he sometimes omitted that which contradicted his own custom and even added, when necessary, material from the Masorah and from other sources. The result was that the original work, *Hidāyat al-Qāri*, branched out and became a large number of works whose common denominator was the systematization and codification of the minutiae of Masorah and their crystallization into clear rules for the reader – an important step toward systematic grammar.

6.3.2. Works on the Šewa

Another work of the above type, although apparently unconnected genetically with these works, is the Arabic treatise which deals with the rules of the *šewa*, which was published by Kurt Levy (1936), and is known in modern research as the "Treatise on the *šewa*." In this case not only is the author anonymous, but the work has no title. The assumption is that it was written approximately in the middle of the tenth century. This work also contains directions to the reader, and more than any of the adaptations of *Hidāyat al-Qāri* it literally integrates quotations from the rules of the Masorah, and even their rhymes – some of those which were used by the author of *Dikduke ha-Teʾamim*. Unlike the other works this is a deep, comprehensive treatise on a subject which though narrow is central to the field of Tiberian pronunciation. It contains most of the information which we have on the *šewa*. A fragment in Arabic entitled סדר הסימנים, dealing with rules of vowel alternation (published by Allony, *HUCA*. 35 (1964)) was suggested by Eldar (*Teʾuda*, 6 (1988)) to have been part of one and the same anonymous grammatical treatise in which the *šewa* and the Hebrew vowels were discussed, perhaps together with other grammatical issues. Anonymous works of this type are rather numerous and most of them are still in manuscript and scattered in libraries. Only a few have been published, such as the anonymous treatise in Arabic on the *šewa* which Allony published (*Leshonenu* 12 (1943/44). This anonymous literature is thus still far from being exhausted.

6.4. THE PERPETUATORS OF THE WAY OF THE MASORAH

Although most of the above works have a grammatical approach they are only on the threshhold of grammar and can still be classified as Masorah literature. They do however constitute a start and the beginnings of grammatical works. Many grammarians in the Middle Ages had to depend, if albeit reluctantly, upon these works and they drew upon them. In almost every one of their writings one finds a connection to the Masorah and its literature. At the same time however there were sages who continued their work on the Masorah for its own sake, whether for the clarification of versions or for the vocalization and the actual formation of the text. There were also scholars who gave Masorah a central place in their works and did not consider it a subordinate to grammar, vocalization, and accentuation. Only the most famous ones are discussed here, in chronological order.

6.4.1. Meir ben Todros ha-Levi Abulafia

In his book *Masoret Seyag la-Torah* Meir ben Todros ha-Levi *Abulafia (רמ"ה; D. 1244) deals mainly with plene and defective spelling in the Torah. His comments are arranged alphabetically in dictionary form according to the roots of the words. After them he adds excerpts from the Masorah which deal with various particles and the peculiarities in the writing of a Torah scroll, the form of the Songs, and the open and closed parashiyyot. His book was a basic work for scribes and for publishers in following generations.

6.4.2. Jekuthiel ben Judah ha-Kohen ha-Naqdan

Jekuthiel's (abbr. as יה"ב; first half of the 13th century) book *'En ha-Qore* is a collection of masoretic-grammatical notes dealing with vocalization and accentuation for the Pentateuch and the Book of Esther. The work is arranged according to the order of the verses and includes a general introduction which deals with various methodological questions, such as the rules of the *ga'yot*. This book, with its rules and its vocalization variants, was the basis for a whole school of grammarians and editors of the text of the Bible.

6.4.3. Menahem ben Solomon ha-Meiri

Ha-*Meiri (1249–1316) was considered one of the *posekim* ("deciders") for everything connected with the writing of the Bible and scribal customs. His book *Kiryat Sefer* consists of two parts. The first contains the halakhic laws for writing a Torah scroll, and the second is a collection of Masorah issues having rules on reading and pronunciation, plene and defective spelling, open and closed *parashiyyot*, and various other matters of Masorah.

6.4.4. Jacob ben Ḥayyim ibn Adonijah

*Jacob ben Ḥayyim ibn Adonijah (15th/16th century) was the first to publish a text of the Bible which had been selected carefully from a large number of manuscripts and was accompanied by the notes of *Masorah Parva, Masorah Magna*, and *Masorah Finalis* (see 3.3.6.1.) which were likewise gathered and selected from many manuscripts. This text is the *Mikra'ot Gedolot* edition of the Bible which was published in Venice, in 1524–25, by Daniel Bomberg, who employed Ben Ḥayyim as a proofreader. This edition became known as the "accepted" version of the Bible, "the Masoretic Text," upon which everyone has relied and which all have copied and imitated. Even the Masorah which was published in this edition has been unjustly recognized ever since as the exclusive text of *the* Masorah. In fact Ben Ḥayyim's work has been considered as the codification of the Masorah, and for generations has been the only complete Masorah in print, up to the 20th century when the Ben-Asher codices (Leningrad and Aleppo) started to appear in print. Ben Ḥayyim also printed for the first time other works together with the *Masorah Finalis*: the *Diqduqe ha-Te'amim* of Aaron Ben-Asher (see 6.2.1); דרכי הנקוד והנגינות attributed to Moses ha-Naqdan; various lists of Masorah, some of them resembling those in *Okhlah we-Okhlah*, as well as lists of variants between the Western and Eastern traditions and between Ben-Asher and Ben-Naphtali for the Torah.

6.4.5 Elijah Baḥur ben Asher ha-Levi (Levita)

Elijah *Levita (1468/9–1549), a grammarian and lexicographer, is also worthy of being considered a masorete because of his book *Masoret ha-Masoret* which was published in Venice, in 1538. He presents a historical survey of the Masorah, the vocalization and the accentuation, and proves that they were not given at Sinai but were fixed by the masoretes. He also describes the Masorah, its methods, types and terminology along with examples. This book can be considered the prime work of the Masorah and a clear, convenient guidebook for the student.

6.4.6. Menahem ben Judah di Lonzano

In his *Or Torah*, Menahem ben Judah di Lonzano (end of the 16th century), gives masoretic comments only on the Pentateuch. The work is arranged in the order of the biblical text. Apparently he uses the text of Ben Ḥayyim as his base and adds comments to make the text more precise also with regard to matters of orthography, but mostly on issues of vocalization, accentuation, and *ga'yahs*; this was done on the basis of many manuscripts and works of earlier scholars. Jedidiah Solomon Raphael of *Norzi (see below) valued his opinion highly.

6.4.7. Minḥat Shay

Jedidiah Solomon Raphael b. Abraham of Norzi (16/17th century) wrote the most important and the most comprehensive book dealing with Masorah. It contains an introduction and comments upon the entire Bible in the order of the text with regard to matters of Masorah, orthography, vocalization, accentuation, *ga'yahs*, the form of the Songs and the *parashiyyot*, even the tittles (*tagin*) of the letters and other exceptional items in the text. At times he even discusses questions of grammar and meaning. His comments bear upon almost every word about which there is room for error, a variant reading, or any other problem. Although his remarks are based mainly on the Bomberg Bible edition of 1546–48 and as Bester (*Addenda to Minḥat Shay*, 33–37) has shown, his book in fact constitutes a type of correction to and improvement of the Ben Ḥayyim text of the Bible. From his time on editors of the Bible have considered themselves permitted to make corrections in the text of the *Mikra'ot Gedolot* according to him. He called his book, which was finished in 1626, גֹּדֵר פֶּרֶץ ("the repairer of the breach"), but the title was changed by its first publisher (only in 1740–42 was it printed for the first time) to מִנְחַת שַׁי *Minḥat Shay* (שי being the initials of Solomon Jedidiah) and it remains known by that name. This book is the most famous of all the works of Masorah. A critical edition of

Minḥat Shay on the Torah was published by Z. Betser (2005, posthumously).

6.4.8. The Yemenites

Two Yemenite scholars who were active at about the same period should be mentioned. Yaḥya *Bashiri (abbr. מהרי"ב or מהריב"ש; end of the 17th century), was a well-known sage, scribe, copyist, and calligrapher; his work *Ḥavaẓẓelet ha-Sharon* on the letters of the alphabet and matters of Masorah, vocalization, and accentuation is extant in manuscript form. Comments in his name are also incorporated in the work of Yaḥya b. Joseph *Ṣāliḥ (abbr. מהרי"ץ, second half of the 18th century), the other Yemenite scholar, who in his *Ḥeleq ha-Diqduq* comments upon the whole Torah in the order of the text on matters of vocalization and accentuation, on other issues of Masorah and even, sometimes, on actual grammatic issues. The book is based upon the comparison of manuscripts, mostly Yemenite, and printed editions. This book holds the same position among the Jews of Yemen as *Minḥat Shai* among the other communities.

6.4.9 Wolf Benjamin Ze'ev ben Samson Heidenheim

Wolf Benjamin Ze'ev ben Samson Heidenheim (abbr. רוו"ה; 1757–1832) marks a turning point in the chain of those who dealt with Masorah, in that besides working on the text of the Bible itself and producing new editions thereof he also systematically discussed problems of Masorah and its rules. He edited five different editions of the Pentateuch: *Torat Elohim* (only the beginning), *Me'or ʿEnayim, ʿEzrat ha-Sofer, Modaʿ la-Bina*, and *Torat Moshe*, as well as the Book of Psalms and others. His editions are outstanding for their precision and his choice of the text is based upon ancient sources, both manuscript and print, especially on Jekuthiel ha-Kohen, Menahem di Lonzano, and Jedidiah Norzi. Very important textual and masoretic comments of his own accompany the text. In the Pentateuch *Me'or ʿEnayim* he even printed the text of Jekuthiel's *ʿEn ha-Qore* in the margins. No less important is his contribution to the study of the Masorah and the rules of the accentuation in his book *Mishpete ha-Teʿamim*, in which he lists, in great detail, the rules of the accentuation of the 21 books, in general according to citations from early sources beginning with Ben-Asher. He thereby consciously withdraws from the analytical approach of the Christian and Jewish scholars of accentuation and returns to the methods of the early sages, in his method of discussing accentuation and in the importance which he ascribes to a clear and well-established text. He laid down the foundations of the rules of the *gaʿyah* and the *maqqaf* in the last chapter of his book.

6.4.10. Seligmann Isaac Baer

*Baer (1825–1897) continued the way of Heidenheim and completed his activity. Baer continued in the area of clarification of the text of the Bible and edited a new version of the text for almost every book of Scripture, mainly for those which his predecessor did not publish: Genesis, all the Prophets and the Hagiographa (called the Baer-*Delitzsch edition, although the latter only added prefaces). In the investigation of the Masorah he completed the work of his predecessor and wrote precise rules for the accentuation of Psalms, Proverbs, and Job, in his book *Torat Emet*. This book is arranged on the pattern of *Mishpete ha-Teʿamim*, but unlike it, it is almost entirely the work of the author and does not draw on earlier sources. Baer elaborated a rather consolidated system for the rules of accentuation and *gaʿyahs* and other masoretic issues on the basis of early works and manuscripts. This study brought him to the conclusion that he was closely approaching the original "correct" version of the Bible. He edited the text of the Bible in the light of that conclusion and many of his readings are based exclusively on his own views. He did not hesitate to alter manuscript readings to fit his ideas, for example in the list of variances between the western and eastern traditions and between Ben-Asher and Ben-Naphtali, which he published from manuscripts in the appendices to his editions of the Bible, he adapted the Western readings and those of Ben-Asher which were in the manuscripts to the readings of his edition of the biblical text, since he was certain that he had succeeded in establishing the Ben-Asher version and that on the strength of it he could correct even the manuscripts' readings.

The Baer version was used for a long time, especially because of Delitzsch, as the accepted, "scientific" version, and the scientific grammars, such as *Gesenius-*Kautzsch, were based on it. Even the rules of accentuation in his *Torat Emet* are based, first and foremost, upon his own version of the Bible. This also applies to the detailed rules of the *meteg* which he published in German. Although taken from his predecessors, especially from Jekuthiel ha-Kohen and Heidenheim, and supplemented, these rules are actually a near-complete development of the theory of the *meteg* as Baer saw it. His approach to manuscripts is manifest in his edition of various texts including the *Diqduqe ha-Ṭeʿamim* of Aaron Ben-Asher. His treatment of the manuscripts and his corrections (without any indications to the reader) do not accord with modern methods of textual criticism. In his edition of *Diqduqe ha-Ṭeʿamim* he made little attempt to define the work or its scope. His main aim was to collect Masorah texts in order to clarify the "correct" text of the Bible.

6.4.11. Later Scholars

Despite Baer's shortcomings (as stated above), his erudition and great expertness in the Masorah should not be underestimated. Other scholars of his time did not encompass the entire range in which Baer was active, and it is doubtful whether one should properly consider them along with the masoretes. S.D. *Luzzatto and, more than he, W. Wickes, made a significant contribution to the study of accentuation and to the consolidation of its theory with regard to its grammatical description. In contrast to them, C.D. Ginsburg and P. Kahle played a major role primarily in publishing ancient texts from manuscripts: Ginsburg mainly published many texts of all types of Masorah; and Kahle, biblical texts in Tiberian vocalization (the Leningrad manuscript – see above, 6.2.3.) as well as fragments of the Bible with Babylonian and Palestinian vocalization.

[Aron Dotan (2nd ed.)]

BIBLIOGRAPHY: SECTION 1. K. Albrecht, in: ZAW, 39 (1921), 160–9; W. Bacher, *Die Anfaenge der hebraeischen Grammatik* (1895), 3–12; D. Barthelemy, in: VT (Suppl.), 9 (1963), 285 304; L. Blau, *Masoretische Untersuchungen* (1891); idem, *Zur Einleitung in die Heilige Schrift-17. Jahresbericht der Landes-Rabbinerschule in Budapest* (1894); R. Butin, *The Ten Nequdoth of the Torah* (1906, repr. 1969); C.D. Ginsburg, *Introduction to the Massoretico-Critical Edition of the Hebrew Bible* (1897, repr. 1966 with introd. by H.M. Orlinsky); R. Gordis, in: *Tarbiz*, 27 (1958), 444–69; I. Harris, in: JQR, 1 (1889), 128–42, 223–57; M. Higger (ed.), *Massekhet Soferim* (1937); H. Hyvernat, in: RB, 11 (1902) 551–63; 12 (1903), 529–49; 13 (1904), 521–46; 14 (1905), 203–34, 515–42; P. Kahle apud Bauer-Leander, *Historische Grammatik der hebraeischen Sprache des Alten Testamentes* (1922, repr. 1965), pars. 6–9, 71–161; S. Krauss, in: ZAW, 22 (1902), 57–65; S. Lieberman, *Hellenism in Jewish Palestine* (1950), 28–46; D.S. Loewinger, in: *Beit Mikra*, 15 (1970), 237–63; J. Mann, *The Bible as Read and Preached in the Old Synagogue*, 1 (1940), 3–8; J. Miller (ed.), *Massekhet Soferim* (1878); B.J. Roberts, *The OT Text and Versions* (1951), 1–74; C. Rothmueller, *Masoretische Eigentaemlichkeiten* (1927); M.Z. Segal, *Mevo ha-Mikra*, 4 (1950), 842–910; A. Sperber, in: HUCA, 17 (1942–43), 293–394; *Midrash Ḥaserot vi-Yterot*, in: *Battei Midrashot*, 2 (1968), 203–322. **ADD. BIBLIOGRAPHY:** A. Ahrend, "The Mnemotechnical Notes of the Numbers of Verses in the Torah Portions," in: *Rabbi Mordechai Breuer Festschrift*, 1 (1992), 157–71; S. Lieberman, *Greek and Hellenism in Jewish Palestine* (1962), 164–84; S. Naeh, "The Torah Reading Cycle in Early Palestine: A Re-Examination," in: *Tarbiz*, 67 (1998), 167–87; Y. Ofer, "The Masoretic Divisions (Sedarim) in the Books of the Prophets and Hagiographa," in: *Tarbiz*, 58 (1989), 155–89; C. Perrot, "Petuhot et Setumot – Etude sur les alinéas du Pentateuque," in: RB, 76 (1969), 50–91. SECTION 2. H. Arens, *Sprachwissenschaft-Der Gang ihrer Entwicklung yon der Antike bis zur Gegenwart* (1955); J. Bachrach, *Das alter biblischen Vocalisation und Accentuation*, 2 vols. (Heb., 1896); idem, *Ishtadalut im Shedal* (1896); L. Blau, *Studien zum althebraeischen Buchwesen und zur biblischen Literaturgeschichte* (1902); B. Klar, *Meḥkarim ve-Iyyunim ba-Lashon, ba-Shirah u-va-Sifrut* (1954), 1–7; S.D. Luzzatto, *Dialogues sur la Kabbale et le Zohar et sur l'antiquité de la ponctuation et de l'accentuation dans la langue hébraïque* (1852); J.P. Martin, in: JA (1875); A. Merx, *Historia artis grammaticae apud Syros* (1889), 141–53; R.H. Robbins, *Ancient and Medieval Grammatical Theory in Europe* (1951); J.B. Segal, *The Diacritical Point and the Accents in Syriac* (1953). **ADD. BIBLIOGRAPHY:** N. Allony, "The Torah Scroll and the Codex in the Rabbanite and the Karaite Ritual Torah Reading," *Studies in Medieval Philology and Literature – Collected Papers*, 5 (1992), 271–84; A. Dotan, *Ben Asher's Creed – A Study of the History of the Controversy* (The Society of Biblical Literature, ed. H.M. Orlinsky), in: *Masoretic Studies*, 3 (1977); idem, "The Relative Chronology of the Hebrew Vocalization and Accentuation," in: PAAJR, 48 (1981), 87–99; idem, "Masoretic Rubrics of Indicated Origin in Codex Leningrad (B19a)," in: *Masoretic Studies*, 6 (1990), 37–44; idem, "De la Massora à la grammaire – Les débuts de la pensée grammaticale dans l'hébreu," in: *Journal Asiatique*, 278 (1990), 13–30. SECTION 3. W. Bacher, in: JQR, 3 (1891), 785–90; S. Bamberger, in: *Jahrbuch der Juedisch-Literarischen Gesellschaft*, 15 (1923), 217–65; 21 (1930), 39–88; Z. Ben-Ḥayyim, in: *Leshonenu*, 21 (1957), 283–92; A. Berliner, *Die Massorah zum Targum* Onkelos (1877); L. Blau, in *Studies in Jewish Bibliography and Related Subjects in Memory of A.S. Freidus* (1929), 431–62; F. Díaz Esteban, in: *Sefarad*, 14 (1954), 315–21; E. Ehrentreu, *Untersuchungen ueber die Massorah* (1925); S. Frensdorff, *Das Buch Ochlah W'ochlah* (1864); idem, *The Massora Magna* (1876); M. Gertner, in: VT, 10 (1960), 241–72; C.D. Ginsburg, *Recueil des travaux rédigés en mémoire du Jubilé Scientifique de D. Chwolson* (1899), 149–88; idem, *The Massorah*, 4 vols. (18801905); R. Gordis, *The Biblical Text in the Making – A Study of the Kethib-Qere* (1937); H. Graetz, in: MGWJ, 36 (1887), 1–34, 299–309; H. Hupfeld, in: ZDMG, 21 (1867), 201–20; P. Kahle, *Der masoretische Text des AT nach der Ueberlieferung der babylonischen Juden* (1902, repr. 1966), 13–18, 83–9; idem. *Masoreten des Ostens* (1913, repr. 1966), 177–9; S. Landauer, *Die Mâsôrâh zum Onkelos* (1896); J. Mann, in: *Oriental Studies Dedicated to Paul Haupt* (1926), 437–45; H.M. Orlinsky, in: JAOS, 60 (1940), 30–45; idem, in: VT, 7 (1960), 184–92 (suppl.); J. Pa'or, in: *Sinai*, 60 (1966–67), 17–27: F. Pérez Castro, in: *Sefarad*, 23 (1963), 223–35; S. Pinsker, *Einleitung in das Babylonisch-Hebraeische Punktationssystem* (1863), 121–32; J. Reach, *Die Sebirin der Masoreten von Tiberias* (1895); S. Rosenfeld, *Ma'amar bi-Keri u-Khetiv* (1866); A. Rubinstein, in: VT, 10 (1960), 198–212; H. Strack, *Codex babylonius petropolitanus* (1876); G.E. Weil, in: *Textus*, 2 (1962), 103–19; 3 (1963), 74–120, 163–70; 4 (1964), 30–54; 6 (1968), 75–105; idem, in: *In Memoriam Paul Kahle* (1968), 241–53; idem, in: VT, 9 (1963), 266–84 (suppl.); idem, in: *Annual of the Leeds University Oriental Society*, 3 (1961–62), 68–80; I. Yeivin, in: *Textus*, 2 (1962), 146–9; idem, in: *Leshonenu*, 30 (1966), 25–8. **ADD. BIBLIOGRAPHY:** M.J. de Azcárraga-Servert, "Les notes Ma'arvaē-Madinḥaē dans le manuscrit du Caire," in: *Masoretic Studies*, 7 (1992), 1–13; idem, "El kĕtīb / qĕrē en el libro de Josué del Códice de Profetas de El Cairo," in: *Proceedings of the Eleventh Congress of IOMS* (1994), 7–14; S. Baer and H.L. Strack, *Die Dikduke Ha-Teamim des Ahron ben Moscheh ben Ascher und andere alte grammatisch-massoretische Lehrstücke zur Festsellung eines richtigen Textes der hebräischen Bibel* (1879); M. Breuer, *The Masorah Magna to the Pentateuch by Shemuel ben Ya'aqov* (Ms. לם), 1–2 (1992); Ch. Carmiel, "The Palestinian Masoretic Notes – Characteristics and Relation to the Tiberian Masora" (M.A. Thesis submitted to Bar-Ilan University, 1996); P. Cassuto, *Qeré-Ketib et lists massorétiques dans le manuscrit B19a* (1989); idem, "Qeré / ketiv dans le manuscrit Londres Or. 4445," in: *Proceedings of the Eleventh Congress of IOMS* (1994), 15–24; J. Dérenbourg, *Manuel du lecteur d'un auteur inconnu* (Paris 1871) [= JA, 16 (1870), 309–550]; F. Díaz Esteban, "References to Ben Asher and Ben Naftali in the *Massora Magna* Written in the Margins of MS Leningrad B19A," in: *Textus*, 6 (1968), 62–74; idem, *Sefer 'Oklah wĕ-'Oklah* (1975); A. Dotan, *The Diqduqé Haṭṭe'amim of Ahăron ben Moše ben Ašér*, with a Critical Edition of the Original Text from New Manuscripts (The Academy of the Hebrew Language, *Texts and Studies*, 7) (1967); idem, *Thesaurus of the Tiberian Masora – A Comprehensive Alphabetical Collection of Masoretic Notes to the Tiberian Bible Text of the Aaron Ben Asher School.* Sample Volume: *The Masora to the Book of Genesis in the Leningrad Codex* (1977); idem, "Masora in Arabic Translation," in: *Studies on the Hebrew Language throughout its History – Dedicated to Gad B. Sarfatti on his 75th Anniversary, Hebrew Linguistics*, 33–35 (1992), 179–83; idem, "Babylonian Residues in the London Pentateuch Codex," in: S. Vargon, Y. Ofer, J.S. Penkower, J. Klein (eds.), *Studies in Bible and Exegesis*, 7 – *Presented to Menachem Cohen* (2005), 33–40; idem, *The Awakening of Word Lore: From the Masora to the Beginnings of Hebrew Lexicography* (The Academy of the Hebrew Language, *Sources and Studies*, 7 – A New Series) (2005), 24–115; R. Gordis, "The Origin of the Kethib-Qere System, A New Approach," in: *VT Supplement*, 7 (1960), 184–92; A.A. Lieberman, "*lo' / low*: An Analysis of a Kethib-Qere Phenomenon," in: *Masoretic Studies*, 6 (1990), 79–86; D. Lyons, *The Cumulative Masora – Text, Form and Transmission with a Facsimile Critical*

Edition of the Cumulative Masora in the Cairo Prophets Codex (1999); Y. Ofer, *The Babylonian Masora of the Pentateuch Its Principles and Methods* (2001); B. Ognibeni, *Index biblique à la «Ochlah we'ochlah» de S. Frensdorff* [Ouadreni di Henoch] (1992); idem, *La seconda parte del Sefer 'Oklah We'Oklah, Edizione del ms. Halle Universitätsbibliothek Y b 4° 10* (1995); N. Reich, "The Names of the accent *Shalshelet*" *Massorot*, 13 (2006); M. Serfaty, "Nouveaux fragments de 'Okhla we-'Okhla: T-S NS 287–18, 28, 39," in: *Proceedings of the Eleventh Congress of IOMS* (1994), 63–81; I. Yeivin, *Introduction to the Tiberian Masorah*, trans. & edit. E.J. Revell, in: *Masoretic Studies*, 5 (1980); idem, "The Babylonian Masorah to the Prophets," in: *Eretz-Israel*, 16 – *Harry M. Orlinsky Volume* (1982), 112–23; idem, *The Biblical Masorah* (2003). SECTION 4. Z. Ben-Ḥayyim, in: *Leshonenu*, 18 (1952), 89–96; S. Frensdorff, *Das Buch Ochlah W'ochlah* (1864); I. Garbell, in: *Leshonenu*, 17 (1951), 76–80; H. Graetz, in: MGWJ, 30 (1881), 348–67, 395–405; T. Noeldeke, *Compendious Syriac Grammar* (1904; repr. 1970); J.B. Segal, *The Diacritical Point and the Accents in Syriac* (1953); L. Skoss, in: *Tarbiz*, 22 (1951), 174–84. **ADD. BIBLIOGRAPHY:** A. Dotan, "The Beginnings of Masoretic Vowel Notation," in: *Proceedings of the First Congress of the International Organization for Masoretic Studies (IOMS)*, (The Society of Biblical Literature, ed. H.M. Orlinsky), in: *Masoretic Studies*, 1 (1974), 21–34; S. Morag, "Some Aspects of the Methodology and Terminology of the Early Massoretes," in: *Leshonenu*, 38 (1973–74), 49–77; N. Reich, "The Names of *Shalshelet*", *Massorot*, 13 (2006); I. Yeivin, *The Hebrew Language Tradition as Reflected in the Babylonian Vocalization*, 1 (1985), 246–53. SECTION 5.1. N.A. Allony and A. Díez Macho, in: *Estudios Bíblicos*, 17 (1958), 83–100; idem, in: *Sefarad*, 18 (1958), 254–71; M. Dietrich, *Neue palaestinisch punktierte Bibelfragmente* (1968): H. Friedlaender, in: JQR, 7 (1895), 564–8; idem, in: *Society of Biblical Archaeology. Proceedings*, 18 (1896), 86–98; P. Kahle, *Masoreten des Westens*, 2 vols. (1927–30); idem, in: ZAW, 21 (1901), 273–317; P. Leander, in: ZAW, 54 (1936), 91–9; C. Levias, in: AJSLL, 15 (1898–99), 157–64; A. Díez Macho, in: *Estudios Bíblicos*, 13 (1954), 247–65; idem, in: *Sefarad*, 16 (1956), 1–22; 17 (1957), 11–7; 23 (1963), 236–51; idem, in: *Studia Papyrologica*, 6 (1967), 15–25; S. Morag, *The Vocalization Systems of Arabic, Hebrew and Aramaic* (1962), 34–8; A. Murtonen, *Materials for a non-Masoretic Hebrew Grammar*, 1 (1958); A. Neubauer, in: JQR, 7 (1895), 361–4; E.J. Revell, *Hebrew Texts with Palestinian Vocalization* (1970); idem, in: *Textus*, 7 (1969), 59–75; Y. Yahalom, in: *Leshonenu* (1970), 25–60. **ADD. BIBLIOGRAPHY:** B. Chiesa, *L'Antico Testamento Ebraico secondo La Tradizione Palestinese* (1978); I. Eldar, "Pronunciation Traditions of Hebrew", in: *Massorot*, 3-4 (1989), 9-16; E.R. Revell, "Studies in the Palestinian Vocalization of Hebrew," in: *Essays on the Ancient Semitic World* (1970), 51–100; idem, *Biblical Texts with Palestinian Pointing and their Accents, in: Masoretic Studies, 4* (1977); Y. Yahalom, "The Palestinian Vocalization – Its Investigation and Achievements," in: *Leshonenu*, 52 (1988), 112–43; idem, *Palestinian Vocalised Piyyuṭ Manuscripts in the Cambridge Genizah Collections, Cambridge University Library – Genizah Series*, ed. S.C. Reif (1997). SECTION 5.2. A. Díez Macho, in: *Sefarad*, 16 (1956), 1–23; 17 (1957), 386–8; P. Kahle, *Masoreten des Ostens* (1913); idem, *Der masoretische Text des Alten Testaments nach der Ueberlieferung der babylonischen Juden* (1902); M. Lambert, in: REJ, 26 (1893), 274–7; S. Morag, *The Vocalization Systems of Arabic, Hebrew and Aramaic* (1962); idem, *Ha-Ivrit she-be-fi Yehude Teman* (1963); S. Pinsker, *Einleitung in das Babylonisch-Hebraeische Punktationssystem* (1863); E. Porath, *Leshon Ḥakhamim le-fi Masorot Bavliyyot she-be-Khitve Yad Yeshanim* (1938); H.P. Rueger, in: VT, 13 (1963), 235–7; 16 (1966), 65–73; A. Spanier, *Die massoretischen Akzente* (1927), 63–109; H. Strack, *Codex babylonius petropolitanus* (1876); J. Weerts, in: ZAW, 26 (1906), 49–84; H. Yalon, in: *Tarbiz*, 33 (1964), 97–108; 34 (1965), 129–33; I. Yeivin, in: *Textus*, 2 (1962), 20–39; idem, in: KS, 39 (1963–64), 563–72. **ADD. BIBLIOGRAPHY:** R. Shoshany, *Babylonian Accentuation System: Rules of Division and Accentuation, Stages of Development, and Relationship to the Tiberian System* (Doctoral Thesis submitted to Tel Aviv University, 2003); I. Yeivin, "A Fragment of a Masoretic Treatise to the Pentateuch and Targum Onkelos," in: *Henoch Yalon Memorial Volume* (1974), 99–163; idem, *The Hebrew Language Tradition as Reflected in the Babylonian Vocalization* (1985). SECTION 5.3. N. Allony, in: *Leshonenu*, 12 (1943), 61–74; E.S. Artom, in: *World Congress of Jewish Studies*, 1 (1947), 190–4; S. Baer, in: *Archiv fuer Wissenschaftliche Erforschung des AT*, 1 (1869), 57–67, 194–204; idem, *Torat Emet* (1852); A. Dotan, *Research in Biblical Accentuation, Background and Trends, Prolegomenon* to the two works of Wickes (see below) (1970); idem, in: *Textus*, 4 (1964), 55–75; idem, in: *Fourth World Congress of Jewish Studies*, 2 (1968) Heb. pt. 101–5; idem, in: *Leshonenu*, 19 (1954), 13–9; M.H. Goshen-Gottstein, in: A. Altmann (ed.), *Studies and Texts*, 1 (1963), 79–122; H. Graetz, in: MGWJ, 36 (1887), 425–51, 473–97; 31 (1882), 385–409; P. Haupt, in: JAOS, 22 (1901–2), 13–7; W. Heidenheim, *Mishpete ha-Te'amim* (1808); P. Kahle, in: ZDMG, 55 (1901), 167–94; M. Lambert, in: REJ, 18 (1889), 123–6; S. Morag, *The Vocalization Systems of Arabic, Hebrew and Aramaic* (1962), 17–29; N. Porges, in: MGWJ, 36 (1887), 462–72; A. Schlesinger, in: *Eretz Israel*, 3 (1954), 194–8; G.M. Schram, *The Graphemes of Tiberian Hebrew* (1964); A. Spanier, *Die massoretischen Akzente* (1927); W. Wickes, *Ta'amei Emet; A Treatise on the Accentuation of the three so-called Poetical Books of the Old Testament, Psalms, Proverbs, and Job* (1881); idem, *Ta'amei 21 Sefarim; A Treatise on the Accentuation of the twenty-one so-called Prose Books of the Old Testament* (1887); J. Wijnkoop, *Darche Hannesigah* (1881); I. Yeivin, *Keter Aram-Ẓovah* (1969); idem, in: *Textus*, 1 (1960), 185–208; idem, in: *Leshonenu*, 23 (1959), 35–48. **ADD. BIBLIOGRAPHY:** S. Avinun, "Syntactic, Logical and Semantic Aspects of Masoretic Accentuation Signs," in: *Leshonenu*, 53 (1989), 157–92; M. Breuer, *Biblical Accents in the 21 [Prose] Books and in the Three [Poetical] Books* [Hebrew] (1982); A. Dotan, "Residues of an Ancient Penult Stress in the Tiberian Tradition," in: *Hebrew Language Studies Presented to Professor Zeev Ben-Hayyim* (1983), 143–60; idem, "The Relative Chronology of the Accentuation System," in: *Language Studies*, 2–3 (1987), 355–65; idem, "Paseq in Antiquity," in: *Samaritan, Hebrew and Aramaic Studies Presented To Professor Abraham Tal* (2005), 121–33; E.J. Revell, "The Oldest Accent List in the *Diqduqe Haṭṭe'amim*," in: *Textus*, 8 (1973), 138–95; P. Rivière and M. Serfaty, "Etude critique des *paseq* des livres en prose à la lumière des nouvelles théories sur les chaînes de la cantilation," in: *Estudios Masoreticos* (V congreso de la IOMS) (1983), 87–122; H.P. Scanlin, "Erased *Ga'yot* in the Leningrad Codex," in: *Masoretic Studies*, 8 (1996), 105–25; A. Schlesinger, "The Accent System of Psalms, Proverbs and Job and of the Other Books of the Bible," in: *Researches in the Exegesis and Language of the Bible* (1962), 79–89; L. Widawski (Himmelfarb), *The Paseq in the Hebrew Bible – Occurrences in Medieval Manuscripts, Characteristics and Relation to the Accentuation System* (Doctoral Thesis submitted to Bar-Ilan University, 1990); I. Yeivin, "The Syntactical and Musical Influence on the Hyphenization of Small Words," in: *Leshonenu*, 23 (1959), 35–48. SECTIONS 5.4., 5.5., 5.6. N. Allony, in: *Beit Mikra*, 17 (1964), 135–45; M. Beit-Arié, in: *Leshonenu*, 29 (1965), 27–46, 80–102; Z. Ben-Ḥayyim, in: *Archiv Orientálni*, 22 (1954), 515–30; idem, *The Literary and Oral Tradition of Hebrew and Aramaic Amongst the Samaritans*, 1 (1957), 44–6; 2 (1957), 308–403; 3 pt. 1 (1961), 23–24, 183; idem, in: *Biblica*, 52 (1971), 233–5; M. Dietrich, in: P. Kahle, *Der hebraeische Bibeltext seit Franz Delitzsch* (1961) plates 19–20; F. Diening, *Das Hebraeische* *bei den Samaritanern* (1935); A. Díez Macho, *Hebrew and Semitic Studies presented to G.R. Driver* (1962), 16–52; idem, in: *Estudios Bíblicos*, 15 (1956), 187–222; 18 (1959), 223–51; 13 (1954), 247–65; M.H. Goshen-Gottstein, in: A. Altmann (ed.), *Studies and Texts* (1956), 108–14; R. Hoerning, *Description and Collation of Six Karaite Manuscripts of the Bible in Arabic Characters* (1889); P. Kahle, *Massoreten des Westens*, 2 (1930), 45–68; idem, in: *Oriental Studies Dedicated to Paul Haupt* (1926), 425–36; idem, *The Cairo Geniza* (1959), 336–44; R. Meyer, in: ZDMG, 113 (1963), 51–61; S. Morag, *The Vocalization Systems of Arabic, Hebrew and Aramaic* (1962), 38–41, 41–4; idem, in: JSS, 4 (1959), 216–37; idem, in: *Leshonenu*, 29 (1965), 203–9; A.E. Murtonen, in: *Das Altertum*, 8 (1962), 114–23; J. Prijs, in: ZAW, 69 (1957), 171–84; A. Sperber, *A Grammar of Masoretic Hebrew* (1959), 67–76; idem, *The Pre-Masoretic Bible* (Codex Reuchlinianus no. 3 of the Badische Landesbibliotek in Karlsruhe), 1 (1956); I. Yeivin, in: *Textus*, 3 (1963), 121–7; idem, in: *Tarbiz*, 29 (1960), 345–56. **ADD. BIBLIOGRAPHY:** Z. Ben-Ḥayyim, *The Literary and Oral Tradition of Hebrew and Aramaic amongst the Samaritans*, vol. 5: *Grammar of the Pentateuch* (1977); I. Eldar (Adler), *The Hebrew Language Tradition in Medieval Ashkenaz* (ca. 950–1350 C.E.), vols. 1–2 (1978–1979); idem, "Pronunciation Traditions of Hebrew," in: *Massorot*, 3–4 (1989), 16–21; I. Yeivin, "The Meaning of the *Dagesh* sign in the 'Enlarged' Tiberian Vocalization," in: *Hebrew Language Studies Presented to Professor Zeev Ben-Ḥayyim* (1983), 293–307; idem, "The Accentuation of the Books of Psalms, Proverbs and Job According to the Tradition of the 'Expanded Tiberian Vocalization' (Preliminary Description)," in: *Rabbi Mordechai Breuer Festschrift*, 1 (1992), 243–64. SECTION 6. N. Allony, in: *Leshonenu*, 12 (1943), 147–50; S. Baer, *Torat Emet* (1852); idem and H.L. Strack, *Die Dikduke Ha-Teamim des Ahron ben Moscheh ben Ascher* (1879); A. Bendavid, in: *Tarbiz*, 26 (1957), 384–409; idem, in: *Beit Mikra*, 3 (1958), 1–19; I. Ben-Zvi, in: *Textus*, 1 (1960), 1–16; J. Derenbourg, *Manuel du lecteur, d'un auteur inconnu, publié d'après un manuscript venu de Yemen et accompagné de notes* (1871); F. Díaz Esteban, in: *Sefarad*, 26 (1966), 3–11; idem, in: *Textus*, 6 (1968), 62–74; A. Dotan, *The Diqduqe Haṭṭeʿamim of Ahăron ben Moše ben Ašér* (1967); idem, in: *Sinai*, 41 (1957), 208–312, 350–62; idem, in: *Tarbiz*, 34 (1965), 136–155; idem, in: *Beit Mikra*, 23–24 (1965), 103–11; C.D. Ginsburg, *Yacob ben Chajim ibn Adonijah's Introduction to the Rabbinic Bible* (1867); idem, *The Massoreth Ha-Massoreth of Elias Levita* (1867); M.H. Goshen-Gottstein, in: *Textus*, 1 (1960), 17–58; Y.F. Gumpertz, in: *Leshonenu*, 22 (1958), 36–47, 137–46; M. Hameiri, *Qiryat Sefer*, 1 (1862); 2 (1881); W. Heidenheim, *Mishpetei ha-Teʿamim* (1808); P. Kahle, *The Cairo Geniza* (1959^2), 75–120; idem, *Der hebraeische Bibeltext seit Franz Delitzsch* (1961); B. Klar, *Meḥkarim ve-Iyyunim* (1954), 276–319; K. Levy, *Zur masoretischen Grammatik, Texte und Untersuchungen* (1936); L. Lipschuetz, in: *Textus*, 2 (1962), 1–58; 4 (1964), 1–29; D.S. Loewinger, in: *Textus*, 1 (1960), 59–111; idem, *Sefer Darkhei ha-Nikkud ve-ha-Neginot ha-Meyuḥas le-R. Moshe ha-Nakdan* (1929); J. Mann, *The Jews in Egypt and in Palestine under the Fāṭimid Caliphs*, 2 (1922), 43–49; Meir b. Todros ha-Levi, *Sefer Masoret Seyag la-Torah* (1750); Mercier, *Sefer Taʿamei ha-Mikra; Liber de accentibus scripturae* (1565); idem, *Shaʿar Taʿamei 3 Sefarim Emet* (1556); A. Neubauer, *Petite grammaire hébraïque provenant de Yemen, texte arabe publié d'après les manuscripts connus* (1891); F. Pérez Castro, in: *Sefarad*, 15 (1955), 3–30; A. Ramírez, in: *Biblica*, 10 (1929), 200–13; 11 (1930), 108–20; 14 (1933), 303–29; B.J. Roberts, in: JTS, 15 (1964), 253–64; A. Rubinstein, in: JJS, 12 (1961), 123–31; idem, in: *Sefarad*, 25 (1965), 16–26; H.P. Rueger, in: VT, 13 (1963), 231–5; G.E. Weil, *Elie Lévita Humaniste et Massorète* (1963); W. Wickes, *Taʿamei Emet: A Treatise on the Accentuation of the three so-called Poetical Books of the Old Testament, Psalms, Proverbs, and Job* (1881), 102–17; M. Zucker, in: *Tarbiz*, 27 (1958), 61–82. **ADD. BIBLIOGRAPHY:** N. Allony, *"Seder Ha-Simanim* (A Karaite Treatise in Masoretic Grammar from the Time of Moses Ben Asher)," in: HUCA, 35 (1964), א–מ; D. Ben-Menachem, *Ḥibbur Ha-Qonim (Ha-Shimshoni)* (1987); idem, *Sefer ha-Eshel by R. Isaac Ben-Yehuda* (2001); Z. Betser, *Jedidiah Solomon Raphael Norzi – The Addenda to Minḥat Shay, Critical Edition and Introductions* (1997); idem, *Jedidiah Solomon Raphael Norzi – Minḥat Shay on the Torah, Critical Edition, Introduction and Notes* (2005); G. Busi, *Horayat Ha-Qore' – Una grammatica ebraica del secolo XI* (1984); A. Dotan, "Was the Aleppo Codex Actually Vocalized by Aharon Ben Asher?" in: *Tarbiz*, 34 (1965), 136–55; idem, *Ben Asher's Creed – A Study of the History of the Controversy*, in: *Masoretic Studies*, 3 (1977); idem, "The Cairo Codex of Prophets and its Spanish Edition," in: *Sefarad*, 46 (1986), 161–75; idem, "Masoretic Rubrics of Indicated Origin in Codex Leningrad (B19a)," in: *Masoretic Studies*, 6 (1990), 37–44; idem, "Reflections Towards a Critical Edition of Pentateuch Codex Or. 4445," in: E. Fernández Tejero y M.T. Ortega Monasterio (eds.), *Estudios Masoréticos (X Congreso de la IOMS) En memoria de Harry M. Orlinsky*, (1993), 39–51; idem, *The Awakening of Word Lore: From the Masora to the Beginnings of Hebrew Lexicography* (The Academy of the Hebrew Language, *Sources and Studies*, 7 – A New Series) (2005); I. Eldar, *"Shaʿar Noʾaḥ ha-Tevot* from *'En Ha-Qore*," in: *Leshonenu*, 40 (1976), 190–210; 41 (1977), 205–15; idem, "The Treatise on the Shewa and 'Seder ha-Simanim' – Two Parts of a Whole," in: *Teʿuda*, 6 (1988), 127–38; idem, *The Study of the Art of Correct Reading of the Bible as Reflected in the Medieval Treatise Hidāyat al-Qāri (= Guidance of the Reader)* (1994); A.A. Lieberman, "Jedidiah Solomon Norzi and the Stabilization of the Textus Receptus," in: *Masoretic Studies*, 8 (1996), 34–47; R. Perez, *ʿAdat Devorim de Yoséph Qostandini* (Doctoral Thesis submitted to Jean Moulin University, 1984), Vol. 1–3; R. Yarkoni, *"'En Ha-Qoré" by Yequtiel Ha-Kohen*(Doctoral Thesis submitted to Tel Aviv University, 1985), Vol. 1–2; I. Yeivin, "From the Teachings of the Massoretes," in: *Textus*, 9 (1981), א–כז.

MASORETIC ACCENTS (Musical Rendition).

HISTORICAL DEVELOPMENT

In Jewish tradition, the formal reading of certain of the books of the Bible in worship and in study is carried out with a musical intonation linked closely with the masoretic accents of the text and governed by fixed rules and practices (see *Masorah; in supplementary articles). Public reading from the Bible is attested much earlier than the establishment of the written systems of accentuation. In the Bible itself, such readings are mentioned only in connection with special occasions (cf. Deut. 31:12; II Kings 22:1–3; Neh. 8:8, 10:30). The practice was not a prominent part of the Temple liturgy but became so in the *synagogue. Talmudic sources attest the detail with which the practice was regulated, citing the choice and order of the scriptural passages for Sabbaths and weekdays (Monday and Thursday) and the feasts, the qualifications of the reader, the translation of each verse into the vernacular, the *somekh* ("supporter") who aided the reader, or the replacements of the lay reader by a specialist (sometimes the *ḥazzan). As to the musical element, the sources merely say that the Bible was to be read and studied only by melodic recitation (cf. Meg. 32a; Song R. 4:11). It is doubtful whether the terms *pissuk/piskei teʾamim* (the division by the *teʾamim*) refer to the melodic element, al-

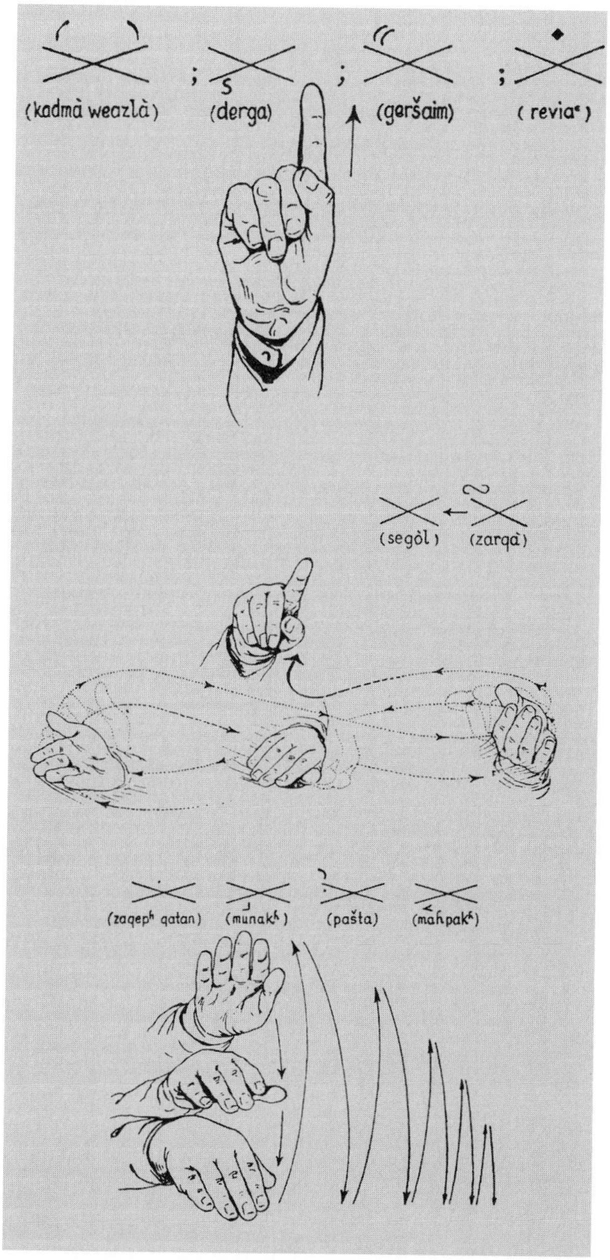

Figure 1. Hand movements indicating the accents and their melody, used as memory aids and prompting signs for the reader. Shown here are the movements still practiced in Rome. Several other communities preserve relics of a similar practice, although the movements are not identical. From I. Adler, "Histoire de la musique réligieuse juive," in J. Porte (ed.), Encyclopédie des musiques sacrées, *vol. 1, 1968, 472–3.*

though they are connected with the aide-memoire movement of the reader's or *somekh's* hand (Meg. 3a; Ned. 37a; Ḥag. 6a; see Figure 1). The talmudic usage of the term *te'amim* is still not sufficiently clear; however, considering the strict regulation of every other element of the scriptural reading, it is inconceivable that the melodic rendition could have been left to the ad hoc invention or choice of the reader.

A comparison with the practices of "scriptural" reading in other religious traditions – such as Vedic recitation in India or Buddhist recitation in Japan and other countries – reveals that none is spoken or sung but they are "cantillated"; that this cantillation is based upon strict conventions handed down by oral tradition (which were described explicitly only in the respective Middle Ages of each culture); and, most important, that a basic similarity of constructive principles (not of melodic content) can still be recognized in all such practices throughout the Asian continent, including all Jewish traditions throughout the Diaspora. The melodic structure in all these traditions is of the kind defined by Curt *Sachs as "logogenic," where the musical element is generated by the words, bonded to the verbal and syntactical structure, and subordinated to the communication of the text, with no attempt at musical autonomy.

This "pan-Asiatic" style must already have been present in cantillated Bible reading in the synagogue preceding the period in which the system of written accents began to be developed. The Tiberian system of accent signs and vowel signs and their functions was based on existing practices not only of the pronunciation and grammatical basis and syntactical structure of the text, but also of its musical rendition. The earliest surviving treatise of this system, *Ben-Asher's *Dikdukei he-Te'amim*, mentions the *ne'imah* (melody) in the characterization of several of the accents. Neither this nor the preceding "Palestinian" and "Babylonian" systems seem to show the intention of establishing a complete correspondence between each accent sign and a specific and different melodic motive, which implies that no such correspondence existed in practice at that time, and that there was no intention on the part of the masoretes to create it artificially.

Figure 2. The earliest known notation of Pentateuch cantillation. Western Ashkenazi perhaps notated by Johann Boeschenstein. In J. Reuchlin, De accentibus et orthographia linguae hebraicae, *Hagenau, 1518, fol [83b]–[87a]. First opening, fol. [83b]–[84a]. The motives are given in the tenor part, while the* discantua, altus, *and* bassus *parts are mere harmonizations in contemporary art-music style, added arbitrarily to enhance the presentation. Jerusalem,* J.N.U.L.

EXAMPLE 1. Beginning of A. Z. Idelsohn's comparative table of Pentateuch cantillation motives. From A. Z. Idelsohn, Melodien, *vol, 2, 1922, 44 and 45, also reproduced in his* Music, *44–45.*

EXAMPLE 2. "Table of Accents" for the Pentateuch, as read in the ḥeder *in Tunis, with different intonation from the one used regularly in the synagogue. Such a cantillated sequence of the accent names is used for* ḥeder *instruction in many communities, often being called, from its initial motive,* lu'aḥ zarka *(*zarka *table). Transcribed by A. Herzog from a version recorded by him in Jerusalem in 1962. From A. Herzog.* The Intonation of the Pentateuch in the Ḥeder of Tunis, *1963, 9, ex. 3b.*

Comparative studies of the living traditions of the present and the evidence gleaned from the medieval and later masoretic treatises reveal that only in the Ashkenazi Diaspora was the system developed and augmented with the aim of having each accent sign expressed by a distinct melodic formation. The farthest point along this path is reached by the Ashkenazi cantillation of the Torah. Even there, however, one finds different accent signs expressed by identical melodic formations (e.g., *segol, zakef,* and *tippeḥa* in the "Polish-Lithuanian" tradition), or identical accent signs expressed by different melodic formations (e.g., the *darga* preceeding a *tevir* as against the *darga* preceding a *munaḥ-revi'a*, in the Western Ashkenazi tradition). Other traditions are still more limited in their repertoire of distinct melodic motives and content themselves with the expression of the divisive accents, or even of the major divisive accents only. This style is probably not the result of any erosion or loss of knowledge, but may well be the surviving evidence of the earliest stages of the system, perhaps even of the Proto-Tiberian or Palestinian or Babylonian ones. In all traditions, the rendition of the accents of the prophetic books, the *haftarah*, and the Hagiographa is also partial and selective as is their rendition in the special style used for study in the *ḥeder.

Practice

The musical rendition of the text in conformity with the accent signs is based on the convention (as described above) of each sign or group of signs representing a certain melodic motive. The graphic symbol does not stand for an absolutely predetermined sequence of tones. As in all music cultivated by oral tradition, the motives exist as "ideals" to be realized in performance, within certain margins of flexibility. Preservation of the "ideals," i.e., the style, is assured by several factors: the support of the well-defined and strict doctrine of the grammatical and syntactical functions of the accents; the deliberate teaching, by which the tradition is handed on from generation to generation; and the constant public practice of the system in the synagogue, where not only the layman's rendition (when "called up to read") but even that of the specialized reader, *ba'al kore* – not always, and in some communities never, identical with the *ḥazzan* – is always subject to the critical ear of the more learned members of the community. The margin of flexibility, on the other hand, makes it possible to link, or rather blend, the motives as they are recalled and enunciated successively by the reader so as to create a melodic organism. The style itself remains constant, but each reader may interpret it with a certain individuality and will never

EXAMPLE 3. *"Table of Accents" for the Pentateuch, according to the Eastern Ashkenazi ("Poland-Lithuania") tradition. From S. Kisselgoff, A. Zhitomirsky, and P. Lwow (eds.),* Lider-Zamlbuch far der yiddisher shul un familye, *1924*[3], *133.*

repeat his previous performance precisely when he reads the same passage upon another occasion.

Theoretically, the accent signs are divided into only two categories: the accents of the "twenty-one books" (טעמי א"ך) and those of the Psalms, Proverbs, and Job (טעמי אמ"ת). In practice, the musical renditions show a much greater diversity of styles. These are determined by

(1) the text, i.e., the specific book, chapter, verse, or contents;

(2) the liturgical circumstances;

(3) the medium of performance;

(4) regional stylistic traditions;

(5) the above-mentioned margin for individual interpretation.

STYLE DETERMINED BY TEXT. Separate melodic conventions exist for the Pentateuch (Torah), the prophetic books (*haftarah*), and for several of the Hagiographa (cf. The Five *Scrolls, Musical Rendition). These may not be interchanged, and explicit prohibitions are found in several rabbinic sources (e.g., *Sefer Ḥasidim*, par. 302). Nevertheless there is a kind of infiltration of motives from one book to the other, as evinced by the appearance of motives from the cantillation of the Torah in that of the *haftarah*. Some motives may also be common to more than one book, such as certain motives in the cantillation of the Book of Esther and Lamentations in the Ashkenazi tradition. In principle, however, each book has its distinct and characteristic "melody," i.e., melodic style.

Most regional traditions have special "festive" styles for the reading of certain chapters or paragraphs – the Song of the *Sea, the *Decalogue, and often also for the Blessing of Moses (Deut. 32) and the Priestly *Blessing (Num 6:24–26), and also a "low" intonation for the "rebuking" text of Deut. 28:15–68. The Ashkenazi tradition is particularly rich in special intonations. A kind of "roster formula" is used for some verses in the story of the wanderings in the desert (Num. 10 and 33). Another intonation emphasizes the importance of certain single verses in the Torah (see A. Baer, *Baal T'fillah* (1883³), 39–40, nos. 117, 118, 121). Another one is used for the dramatic turning points in the Book of Esther (1:22; 2:4, 15, 17; 3:15; 4:1, 14; 5:7, 13:6, 10). Chapters and verses referring to calamities, such as several verses in the Book of Esther, are read in the style of the Book of Lamentations. Verses or parts thereof which denote supplication and the request for pardon are intoned in the style in which the Torah is read on the High Holy Days (see below). In the reading of the Book of Esther in the Ashkenazi tradition there is even one "quotation" from the prayer mode of the High Holy Days (Esth. 6:1) and another from that of the *seliḥot (*ibid.* 6:3).

STYLE DETERMINED BY LITURGICAL CIRCUMSTANCES. During the three pilgrimage festivals the reading is more festive, with more ornamentations and prolongations. The atmosphere of the Ninth of *Av influences the reading of the *haftarah* on the preceding Sabbath, the reading of the Torah on the Ninth of Av itself, which should be in a "low" voice and is sometimes rendered "almost without the accents," and its *haftarah* (which is often read with a verse-by-verse translation into the vernacular – Arabic or Ladino). The Ashkenazim of Holland read the Torah on the Ninth of Av in a style related

EXAMPLE 4. Analytical presentation of three formations of the "tevir complex" in the combination of tevir, etnaḥta, *and* sof pasuk, *in the reading of the Pentateuch, Eastern Ashkenazi tradition. From J. L. Ne'eman,* Ẓelilei ha-Mikra, *vol. 1, 1955, 110.*

to the *haftarah* style of the Polish-Lithuanian region. On the High Holy Days and Hoshana *Rabba, the Ashkenazi tradition has a special style for the reading of the Torah ("in a low melody, as if plaintive," as mentioned in the *maḥzor* ed. Sabionetta, 1557). On the Sabbath nearest to the wedding day, among some Near Eastern communities, the section "And Abraham was old" (Gen. 24) is read in front of the bridegroom in a special festive style. Other modifications applied on Hoshana Rabba and Shavuot are described below.

STYLE DETERMINED BY THE MEDIUM OF PERFORMANCE. When part of the regular prayer service, the reading of the Torah, *haftarah*, or Scrolls is always carried out by a single reader. On certain other occasions, however, the reading may become communal. On the night of Hoshana Rabba and Shavuot, when there are assemblies for "studying" the Torah, chapters or sections are cantillated in alternation by several members of the group. The style is an abbreviated version of the regular Torah style, or that of the study of the Torah in the *ḥeder*. Cantillation by the entire congregation according to the accents is found in the Sephardi communities for the **Shema Yisrael* (i.e., Deut. 5:7 and 11:19) during prayer and for the "Thirteen Divine Attributes" (i.e., Ex. 34:6–7) during the *seliḥot*. In the *ḥeder*, the study of the Torah is traditionally carried out through constant, loud repetition by all the children together. This was done in many communities in a special intonation, related to the accents but more simple in structure than the one practiced by the adults in the synagogue. There are also other kinds of "*ḥeder* tunes" based upon the sequence of accented (long) and unaccented (short) syllables in the text, similar to those found in the group recitation of passages from the Mishnah and other prose texts in many Near Eastern communities (cf. *Talmud, Musical Rendition). It can be assumed that the "*ḥeder* tunes" have remained unchanged for very long periods, since under these circumstances there is no inducement, or indeed any possibility, for personal expression and initiative and the melodic element is wholly subjugated to the pedagogical task.

REGIONAL STYLISTIC TRADITIONS. A.Z. Idelsohn's assumption (see bibliography, and frequently repeated in later writings) that the living traditions of masoretic cantillation developed out of one common – i.e., pre-Exilic – base does not seem to be confirmed by a more thorough examination. This is one of the central problems in research of Jewish music (cf. *Music, Introduction), and, by its very nature, this research is particularly prone to conscious or unconscious wishes to justify a foregone conclusion that there is, indeed must be, a common base. In the present state of research, it may tentatively be proposed that while the principle of cantillation as such is a common heritage (see introduction, above), the diverse regional and functional styles observable today stem from an albeit small number of distinct source styles. It can be assumed that several "melodies" for the reading of the Bible were current and equally legitimate at the time in which the forms of synagogal worship began to be stabilized. Later, by processes

EXAMPLE 5. Exodus 12:21-22 as rendered in the "Babylonian" (Iraq), "Syrian," and Amsterdam Sephardi communities. From A. Z. Idelsohn, Melodien, *vol. 2, 1922, preface, 33, 34, 37.*

which we are unable to reconstruct, some of these "melodies" and melodic elements were accepted as normative by one or several communities, were attached to specific books, and were sanctified by custom. It must always be remembered that the accent signs themselves are not, and never were, a sound script with the same possibilities and limitations of the music

EXAMPLE 6. Intonation of the Prophets, Yemenite tradition (Josh. 1:14). From A.Z. Idelsohn, Melodien, *vol. 2, 1922, preface, 47.*

notation which developed in Western Europe. They are only reference aids to the evocation of "motivic ideas" which, in themselves, are an orally transmitted patrimony. Some late medieval and renaissance writers mention the "style of the Sephardim," but with hardly any concrete definitions which would enable its character to be understood (Simeon b. Ẓemaḥ *Duran, *Magen Avot*; the Karaite Elijah *Bashyazi (1420–90) in his *Sefer ha-Mitzvot* (ed. 1870), fol. 71 and 81; Elijah *Levita in his *Tuv Ta'am*).

The living traditions of the present may be classified according to five major regional styles:

(1) Yemenite,
(2) Ashkenazi,
(3) Middle Eastern and North African,
(4) Jerusalem Sephardi,
(5) northern Mediterranean local diverse styles.

(1) The Yemenite Style

This is particularly rich in distinct sub-styles for the biblical books and for particular chapters and in various divisions among single and group performers. One of the "*ḥeder* tunes," built upon the pentatonic scale, is related to the Ashkenazi Torah style.

(2) The Ashkenazi Style

This is the earliest to be documented in musical notation, in Johannes *Reuchlin's *De accentibus…* (1518) and soon afterward by several other scholars. The melodic elements have been pre-

EXAMPLE 7. Intonation of the Prophets, two western Ashkenazi traditions (Isa. 43:10; ibid., *56:7). From A. Baer,* Ba'al Tefillah, *1883[3], 37-39.*

served most tenaciously among the Western Ashkenazi communities, including southern Germany. The Eastern Ashkenazi Torah style (known as "Polish-Lithuanian") is somewhat different from the Western one. The *haftarah* style is particularly developed in Eastern Europe, and is nowadays common to both the Eastern and Western Ashkenazi communities.

(3) The Middle Eastern and North African Style

This is the style designated by Idelsohn as "Oriental." Its distribution, with many sub-styles, ranges from Cochin to Algeria, through Persia, Bukhara, Iraq, Syria, Kurdistan, the Caucasus, and North Africa. There is a close connection between this and the styles of the European Sephardi communities in Italy, France, Holland, England, and America. It can also be traced in some Balkan communities (those of the "Romaniote" rite). Its influence is also noticeable in the intonation of the Song of Songs of the "Polish-Lithuanian" tradition. The earliest notation of this style was published in 1699 in the Hebrew Bible edited by Daniel Jablonski, to whom it was given by David de Pinna, a *parnas* in the Portuguese community of Amsterdam.

(4) The Jerusalem Sephardi Style

This is the style designated by Idelsohn as "Oriental Sephardic." It is found around the eastern shores of the Mediterranean, from Turkey and the Balkan communities to North Africa, and centered in Ereẓ Israel. Due to the prestige of its association with Jerusalem and Ereẓ Israel, it overlaid and frequently even ousted many local traditions throughout the Mediterranean countries. The Torah style in this tradition cannot represent the pre-expulsion Spanish tradition, since it is found neither in North Africa nor among the European Sephardim, but is based upon the Maqam *Sigah*. It seems to be a relatively recent development, but this phenomenon needs further study before a conclusion can be confirmed.

(5) The Northern Mediterranean Styles

Several communities in this area, such as Rome and *Carpentras (in Provence), have distinct local styles of their own. The Carpentras tradition survives only in notation (M. and J.S. Cremieu, *Zemirot Yisrael*, c. 1887), since the community itself no longer exists.

In Israel, the "ingathering of the exiles" has caused a major deterioration in many of the local and regional traditions brought into the country, since the immigrants often could not keep up their homogenous associations centered around the synagogue. The breakdown of the traditional education system (there is no organized *ḥeder* of any community except the East Ashkenazi) has also broken the chain of tradition. The regional styles tend to disappear, yielding to two dominant and dominating styles: the East Ashkenazi is gradually adopted in most Ashkenazi synagogues and the "Jerusalem Sephardi" prevails, especially for the reading of the Torah, in the synagogues of all the Near Eastern and North African communities. In the latter, the virtuoso status and ambitions of the *ḥazzan* or *ba'al kore* and the influence of the maqam-based Arabic art music at present come near to completely eroding the traditional base of masoretic cantillation proper.

See also articles on the musical traditions of the various major communities.

BIBLIOGRAPHY: MUSICAL RENDITION: Sendrey, Music, nos. 1931–2155; S. Rosowsky, *Cantillation of the Bible – the Five Books of Moses* (1957); Idelsohn, Music, 35–71; Idelsohn, Melodien, 2 (1922), 33–53 and examples in vols. 1, 3, 4, 5, and 8; C. Sachs, *Rise of Music in the Ancient World* (1943), 78–89 and passim; J.L. Ne'eman, *Ẓelilei ha-Mikra* (1955); idem, *Kera be-Ta'am* (1967); M. Perlmann, *Dappim le-Limmud Ta'amei ha-Mikra*, 3 vols. (1958–61); A. Herzog, *Intonation of the Pentateuch in the Ḥeder of Tunis* (1963); H. Avenary, *Studies in the Hebrew, Syrian and Greek Liturgical Recitative* (1963); idem (H. Loewenstein), in: *Zeitschrift fuer Musikwissenschaft*, 12 (1930), 513–26; idem, in: *Bat Kol*, 2 (1961), 56–58; L. Levi, in: *Italyah*, ed. by M.A. Shulvass, 1 (1945); E. Gerson-Kiwi, in: DBI, suppl. 5 (1957), 1449–62; idem, in: *Die Musikforschung*, 13 (1960); idem, in: *Journal of the International Folk Music Council*, 13 (1961), 64–67; S. Levin, in: JBL, 87 (1968), 59–70.

[Avigdor Herzog]

MASSACHUSETTS, New England state of the U.S. Massachusetts had a population of 6,357,000 in 2001, of whom 275,000 were Jews. Both the Jewish population and the state population have been relatively stable during the past 35 years. In 1917 the state's Jewish population was 190,000; by 1937 it had risen to 263,000, dropping to 223,000 in 1959, and then rising over the following decade to 260,000. Nearly 80% of the Jews in the state live within an hour's ride of *Boston.

In 2000, the Greater Boston metropolitan area, embracing large sections of New England, was the sixth-largest Jewish metropolitan area in the United States, including some 10,500 Jews from the former Soviet Union, most of whom arrived after 1985. More than half of the community's Jews were engaged in professional and technical work, and 40 percent of Jewish adults held advanced degrees. The number of Jews also significantly increases during the school year as the number of colleges and universities in the Boston area and in all of Massachusetts is high and the Jewish student population significant.

The shift from the older neighborhoods in and around Boston to the suburbs created substantial new Jewish communities in Newton-Wellesley-Brookline; Cambridge-Belmont-Lexington-Concord-Waltham-Woburn; Natick-Framingham; the Massachusetts Bay north shore towns of *Lynn, Swampscott, Marblehead, Nahant, Salem, and Saugus; and the southern suburbs. Over the last generation thousands of Jewish scientists, engineers, and manufacturing entrepreneurs have found employment in the industrial complexes that line Route 128 west of Boston, and they have given a new élan to the Jewish communities that have sprung up in the expanded Boston suburbs. In the late 20th and the early 21st centuries the high-tech industries attracted many young Jews who easily made the transition from college to industry.

Beyond metropolitan Boston there were 35 cities and towns with 100 or more Jewish residents. The largest Jew-

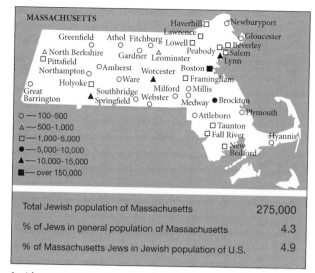

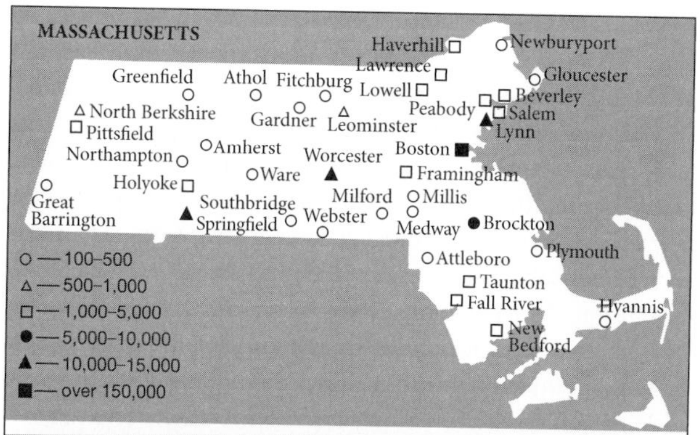

Total Jewish population of Massachusetts	275,000
% of Jews in general population of Massachusetts	4.3
% of Massachusetts Jews in Jewish population of U.S.	4.9

Jewish communities in Massachusetts. Population figures for 2001.

ish populations were to be found in *Springfield (10,000), *Worcester County (12,000), *Fall River (1,100), Andover (2,500), Amherst area (1,300), New Bedford (2,600), Lowell (2,000), Pittsfield and Berkshire County (4,000), Haverhill (2,300), and Holyoke (1,300). Several areas, which were once considered virtually off-limits to Jews, now have synagogues and thriving Jewish communities. Synagogue life on Cape Cod, including Martha's Vineyard and Nantucket, is active, and there is ongoing Jewish life during the winter months. Many Jews who had previously enjoyed the rich cultural life of the Berkshires have chosen to live there year-round and to participate in the active Jewish life now afforded in these communities.

At the beginning of the 21st century there were about 250 synagogues in 85 communities, most of them erected in the 1960s and beyond either as the first houses of worship in newly settled areas or as replacements for older sanctuaries in communities where Jewish residence antedated the massive move out of Boston.

Early History

Aaron *Lopez, a ship owner, was the first Jew naturalized in Massachusetts (at Taunton, 1752). In 1777 he founded the first Jewish community in Massachusetts, at Leicester near Worcester. The families of Lopez and of Jacob Rodriguez *Rivera, numbering 61 people, stayed in Leicester until after the Revolution.

Massachusetts' first permanent Jewish community was established in the late 1830s in Boston, where Central European settlers established the state's first Jewish congregation, Ohabei Shalom, in the 1840s. For about 100 years the Boston Jewish community exercised a powerful influence on the growth of new settlements throughout the state.

The first Jews to take up permanent residence outside Boston were German and East European peddlers who replaced the itinerant Yankee traders in the 1840s and 1850s. Typical of these was Abraham *Kohn, later a figure in the Republican Party in Illinois. In 1842 and 1843, Kohn carried a pack through central and northern Massachusetts, praying alone in the fields, sometimes with his brother and partner, Judah, or with other Jewish peddlers he met on the way. Peddlers like Kohn settled down and became storekeepers; they were followed by tailors, watchmakers, cigarmakers, shoemakers, and dealers in dairy products, leather goods, provisions, lumber, and kerosene.

These merchants established themselves in the factory and mill towns, including Pittsfield (1850), where most were of German origin; Worcester (1860); Holyoke (1873; first congregation, Agudas Achim, founded 1895); Springfield (1881); Fall River (1881); Lawrence (late 1880s); Lynn (1893); and Haverhill (1897). Some Sephardi Jews lived in New Bedford, which has a Jewish cemetery said to date from the post-Revolutionary era, as late as the 1850s, when the first German Jews arrived. One of these was Leopold *Morse, who served in Congress from a Boston district in 1877–85 and again in 1887–89. A burial society, Bnay Israel, was formed in New Bedford in 1857. The first Jewish burial took place the same year. East European Jews arrived in New Bedford about 1877, the earliest of them being Isaac Goodman and Simon Siniansky. The first *minyan* was formed in 1879; services were held in Siniansky's house. The first congregation, Ahabath Achim, was founded in 1893 and purchased a cottage house as its first synagogue. A new synagogue was dedicated in 1899. In 1898 Congregation Chesed Shel Emes was incorporated; it occupied a new synagogue building in 1903. Springfield also had a colony of Sephardi Jews in the 1830s, but the first Russian arrivals found no trace of them. German and Polish Jews arrived in Worcester in the late 1860s.

Contemporary Life

Massachusetts is the home of several major national Jewish institutions: the nonsectarian *Brandeis University, in Waltham, and the National Yiddish Book Center in Amherst and the Jewish Women's Archive in Brookline. The *Menorah Society, the first Jewish intercollegiate movement, was organized at Harvard University in 1906.

Jewish students and Jewish studies give Massachusetts a unique flavor. In 2004 there were approximately 90 dedicated staff positions in Jewish studies at seven major private universities in the Boston area with over 30 more similar positions at the universities in Worcester and the Amherst area. Internationally renowned graduate programs in Jewish Studies are found at Massachusetts universities, including the only graduate Ph.D. program in Holocaust and Genocide Studies. The Hebrew College, which has moved from Brookline to Newton, now has a non-denominational rabbinic program with Arthur Green, a distinguished scholar of Ḥasidism, as its founding dean. Several universities had Jewish presidents in the last quarter of the 20th century and into the 21st. Among them, Harvard has a Jewish president, Lawrence *Sommers, and MIT has had Jewish presidents. Brandeis has always had a Jewish president.

Jewish charitable institutions are coordinated by the Combined Jewish Philanthropies of Greater Boston and by counterpart organizations in 12 other cities, including Jewish welfare federations in Berkshire County, Merrimack Valley (serving Andover, Haverhill, Lawrence, Lowell, Newburyport and 27 surrounding communities), New Bedford, Northshore, Springfield, and Worcester.

Hillel Foundations are found at the following Massachusetts colleges: Amherst College; Babson College; Bentley College; Berklee College of Music; Boston College (a Jesuit University); Boston University; Brandeis University; Clark University; College of the Holy Cross (a noted Roman Catholic College); Curry College; Emerson College; Fitchburg State College; Framingham State College; Hampshire College; Harvard University & Radcliffe College; Hebrew College; Lesley University; Massachusetts Bay Community College; Massachusetts Institute of Technology; Mount Holyoke College; New England College; New England Conservatory of Music; Newbury College; Northeastern University; Quinsigamond Community College; Salem State College; Simmons College; Smith College; Springfield College; Suffolk University; Tufts University; Tufts University Veterinary School; UMASS Medical School; University of Massachusetts, Amherst; University of Massachusetts, Boston Harbor; University of Massachusetts, Dartmouth; University of Massachusetts, Lowell; Wellesley College; Wentworth Institute of Technology; Western New England College; Westfield State College; Wheaton College; Wheelock College; Williams College; and Worcester Polytechnic Institute. The presence of Hillel on campus was often symbolic of the Jewish presence. Brandeis has three chapels at the center of its campus – Catholic, Protestant, and Jewish – emblematic of the three great religions of mid-20th-century America. When the new Hillel at Harvard opened, a procession of Torah scrolls marched through the campus. One speaker said that the movement of Hillel from the periphery of the campus to its center reflected the journey of Jews at Harvard and indeed throughout American intellectual life.

Jewish community centers (JCCs) and YM-YWHAs are affiliated with the Greater Boston Associated JCCs, and similar institutions are maintained in Framingham and Marblehead, Newton, North Dartmouth, Peabody, Springfield, Stoughton, Westboro, Worcester, Brighton, and Brookline. Jewish weeklies are published in the state: the *Jewish Advocate*, in Boston; *Metro-West Jewish Reporter*; the *Jewish Journal/North of Boston*; the *Jewish Chronicle*, in Worcester; and the national monthly *Sh'ma*, which is published by Jewish Family and Life in Newton.

George Feingold, who was the Republican nominee for governor when he died in 1958, was the first Jew to win statewide elective office, serving three terms as attorney general (1952–58). Springfield, Worcester, Holyoke, and Pittsfield (Daniel Englander, elected 1902) have had Jewish mayors. In 1961 Jacob J. Spiegel was named to the State Supreme Court, the first Jew to serve in that office. Abraham *Ratshesky was ambassador to Czechoslovakia under President Hoover (1930–32). David K. *Niles was one of President Franklin D. Roosevelt's key White House aides and later served President Truman in a similar capacity (1942–51). Maxwell M. *Rabb served as secretary to the cabinet under President Eisenhower (1953–58). Steven *Grossman was chairman of the Democratic National Committee and ran unsuccessfully for governor as did Robert *Reich, a Brandeis professor and former Clinton secretary of labor. Politics in Massachusetts is considered the domain of the Irish. Boston has never had a Jewish mayor. Remarkably there have only been two Jewish congressmen, Barney *Frank and Leopold *Morse. Franklin Delano Roosevelt appointed Charles E. Wyzanski, Jr., to the United States District Court; Richard Nixon appointed Frank H. Freedman; Jimmy Carter, Rya Zobel; Ronald Reagan appointed Mark L. Wolf; Bill Clinton, Nancy Gertner and Patti Saris. Three Jewish sons of Massachusetts have served on the Supreme Court: Louis *Brandeis, Felix *Frankfurter, and Steven *Breyer.

BIBLIOGRAPHY: L.M. Friedman, *Pilgrims in a New Land* (1915); idem, *Jewish Pioneers and Patriots* (1942); J.R. Marcus, *Early American Jewry*, 2 vols. (1951–53); B. Postal and L. Koppman, *Jewish Tourist's Guide to the U.S.* (1954), 219–41. **ADD. BIBLIOGRAPHY:** L.S. Maisel and I.M. Forman, *Jews in American Politics* (2001); K.F. Stone, *The Congressional Minyan* (2002); O. Israelowitz, *United States Travel Guide* (2003).

[Bernard Postal / Michael Berenbaum (2nd ed.)]

MASSADAH (Heb. מַסָּדָה), kibbutz in northern Israel, in the Jordan-Yarmuk valley, affiliated with Iḥud ha-Kevuẓot ve-ha-Kibbutzim. Massadah was founded in 1937, during the Arab riots, as a *stockade and watchtower by pioneers from Poland. In the Israel *War of Independence the village had to be evacuated before the onslaught of the Syrian army (May 1948) and was completely razed, but the site was taken back 24 hours later by Israel forces and the kibbutz was rebuilt. After the *Six-Day War (1967), the village came frequently under shelling. Its farming was based on avocado and palm plantations, citrus groves, field crops, and dairy cattle. The kibbutz also operated guest rooms. In 1968 the population of the kibbutz was 285. In the mid-1990s it rose to 350, but then dropped to 288 in 2002.

WEBSITE: www.massada.co.il.

[Efraim Orni / Shaked Gilboa (2nd ed.)]

MASSARANI, TULLO (1826–1905), Italian author and statesman. Born in Mantua, Massarani studied law and painting, at the same time taking part in the conspiratorial struggle for the unification of Italy. As a result of the failure of the 1848 revolution and his collaboration with Mazzini's followers, he had to take shelter in Switzerland and later lived the life of a refugee in Germany and France. On the proclamation of the Kingdom of Italy in 1860 he returned to Milan. He was elected to parliament for three legislative periods (1860–67), and in 1876 was appointed senator. He also held municipal offices.

An extremely prolific writer, Massarani introduced the works of Heinrich *Heine to Italian readers. He left a great number of critical essays, historical, political, and autobiographical writings, translations and verse, which were collected after his death in 24 volumes (1906–11). Massarani's criticism does not delve beneath the surface, but reveals a broad and up-to-date culture in which scholarship is blended with a journalistic approach. Among his most important works are *L'idea italiana attraverso i tempi* (1869), *Eugenio Camerini, i suoi studi e i suoi tempi* (1877), and *Carlo Tenca e il pensiero civile del suo tempo* (1886). During his latter years he devoted himself to an original and erudite study of laughter (1900–02). Massarani's essays earned him a high reputation among European art critics, and in 1878 he was elected chairman of the international jury of art at the Paris Exhibition.

BIBLIOGRAPHY: G. Natali, *Il pensiero e l'arte di Tullo Massarani* (1910); B. Croce, *La letteratura della nuova Italia* (1950[3]).

[Giorgio Romano]

MASSARANO, JACCHINO OR ISACCHINO (16th century), Italian choreographer. In 1583 he was commissioned to provide the dances for Bernardo Pino's *Gli Ingiusti Sdegni* which was performed by the Jewish Theater in Mantua in honor of the marriage of the duke's heir, Vincenzo Gonzaga, who was an intimate friend. The following year, when Vincenzo visited Ferrara, he was sent to supervise a similar performance there. In 1591, the poet Manfredi corresponded with Massarano and also commissioned him to supervise dances for him. When Giovanni Guarini's *Pastor Fido*, the most famous play of its day, was staged at the ducal palace in Mantua in 1598, Massarano was commissioned to supervise the "Blindfolded Dance" for the ballet. He was also appointed choreographer for one of the Jewish theater's biggest performances, *Accessi de Amor fatta* by Niccolo Grassi, in 1605, when 64 members of the company took part, and in the following year he choreographed the Tasso's *Delli Intreghi de Amor.* Massarano was also a composer, teacher, and singer. He was father of Abraham Massarano, historian and author of *Ha-Galut veha-Pedut* (Venice, 1634).

BIBLIOGRAPHY: C. Roth, *Jews in the Renaissance* (1959), 284–5 and index; S. Simonsohn, *Toledot ha-Yehudim be-Dukkasut Mantovah*, 2 (1964), index and bibl.; A.D. Ancona, *Origini del Teatro in Italia* (1891[2]), index; E. Faccioli, *Mantova, la storia, le lettere, le arti* (1962).

MASSARY, FRITZI (Friederike Massarik; 1882–1969), Vienna-born actress and singer. In 1903 she converted to Protestantism. Massary made a reputation in musicals on the Berlin stage and created numerous roles in works by Leo Fall, Oscar Straus, and others. After leaving Nazi Germany she appeared in London in Noel Coward's *Operette*, 1938, her last appearance on the stage. In 1939 she settled in California. Her husband and partner on stage was Max Pallenberg, the German actor. Her style as a singer served as a model for modern diseuses.

BIBLIOGRAPHY: C. Stern, *Die Sache die man Liebe nennt* (1998).

[Marcus Pyka (2nd ed.)]

MASSEKHET (pl. **Massekhtot**; Heb. מַסֶּכֶת, pl. מַסֶּכְתּוֹת; lit. "a web," idiomatically a tractate; cf. Lat. *textus*), a main subdivision of each of the six orders, or *sedarim*, of the Mishnah. Each mishnaic order is divided into a number of *massekhtot*; each *massekhet* is divided into chapters, and each chapter into Mishnayot or paragraphs in the Babylonian Talmud and into *halakhot* in the Jerusalem Talmud. The total number of tractates of the entire Mishnah, which was originally 60, was subsequently, by a further minor subdivision, increased to 63. *Massekhet* also designates the corresponding *Gemara* tractates. Beginning with the *editio princeps* (1520–23, Venice), in all standard editions of the Babylonian Talmud each *massekhet* has a fixed number of folio pages. The most voluminous tractate, numbering 176 folios, is *Bava Batra*; the smallest is *Horayot* numbering 14. In the Jerusalem Talmud the original pagination of the tractates has been preserved only in the Venice edition of 1522–23, and in its later reprints. As there is no *Gemara* on all mishnaic tractates, the number of *massekhtot* in the Babylonian Talmud is only 37 and in the Jerusalem Talmud 39. Occasionally the term *massekhet* is also applied to rabbinical books outside the Talmud. See also *Talmud; *Mishnah; and Minor Tractates.

BIBLIOGRAPHY: Epstein, Mishnah, 981–3.

[Jacques K. Mikliszanski]

MASSELL, SAM JR. (1927–), U.S. lawyer and politician. Born in Atlanta, Georgia, Massell received his Bachelor of Commercial Science degree from Georgia State University and a Bachelor of Laws from Atlanta Law School. He served as a flying instructor in the U.S. Army Air Force during World War II. He worked in the commercial real estate industry for 20 years and 13 in the travel business before stepping into the political arena. In 1961 he made his first attempt to win public office and was elected to the office of vice-mayor as a Democrat. He held the position until 1969 when he was elected Atlanta's youngest and first Jewish mayor with a victory margin provided by a white liberal and poor black coalition. In the course of the campaign Massell charged that members of the "power structure," meaning the corporations and civic groups who had long ruled Atlanta, were antisemitic. He served as mayor until 1974, when he lost the re-election.

From 1988 Massell was the president of the Buckhead Coalition, a group of CEOs of major companies in Buckhead, an upscale area of Atlanta. Serving as a chamber of commerce for the neighborhood, the coalition's first successful project, in 1989, was to have Georgia Highway 400 extended through Buckhead. Massell also spearheaded the creation of the Community Improvement District in Buckhead, wherein business property owners impose taxes on themselves to improve the community and then seek matching federal grants.

Active in Jewish affairs, Massell was a member of the American Jewish Committee, Jewish War Veterans, and the B'nai B'rith. He was also instrumental in breaking down ethnic and religious barriers in his community, bringing the Reform community together with the Conservative and Orthodox, as well as reaching out to help integrate the Sephardic and Russian populations.

[Ruth Beloff (2nd ed.)]

MASSERMAN, JULES HOMAN (1905–1994), U.S. psychiatrist and psychoanalyst. Born in Chudnov, Poland, Masserman was taken to the United States in 1908. He grew up in Detroit, Michigan, and received his medical degree from Wayne University. Masserman first taught at the University of Chicago. In 1952 he was appointed professor of neurology and psychiatry at Northwestern University's medical school, where he taught until the 1970s and served for several years as co-chairman of the psychiatry department. Masserman's thought and experience in psychiatry and psychotherapy are set forth in his textbook, *The Principles of Dynamic Psychiatry* (1946, 1961) and in *The Practice of Dynamic Psychiatry* (1955). These works represent a theoretical and clinical attempt to correlate various physiological and psychological concepts of behavior into a comprehensive system (biodynamics), and to base a therapy upon this. He conducted many animal experiments to check, clarify, and extend psychological premises about human beings. He also added "un-defenses," such as the general delusion of invulnerability and immortality by which man denies danger and death, to the Freudian concepts of defenses against anxiety.

Masserman's later works include *Biodynamic Roots of Human Behavior* (1958), *Transcultural Problems of Youth* (1969), the autobiographical *A Psychiatric Odyssey* (1971), *Handbook of Psychiatric Therapies* (1972), *Man for Humanity* (1972), *Theory and Therapy in Dynamic Psychiatry* (1973), *The Psychiatric Examination* (with J. Schwab, 1974), *Psychiatry and Health* (1986), *Psychiatric Consultations for Public Organizations* (1989), and *Sexual Accusations and Social Turmoil: What Can Be Done* (with his wife, Christine Masserman, 1994).

He also directed many instructional motion pictures, such as *The Dynamics of Experimental Neurosis* (1944). He edited the annuals *Science and Psychoanalysis* and *Current Psychiatric Therapies*, and was associate editor of *Psychosomatics*. He was president of the American Academy for Psychoanalysis and of other learned associations, such as the American Society for Group Therapy, the American Association for Social Psychiatry, the American Society for Biological Psychiatry, the International Association of Social Psychiatry, and the American Psychiatric Association, and served as honorary president for life of the World Association for Social Psychiatry.

Masserman retired from his clinical practice in 1989 after fending off a flurry of accusations by former female patients of having been drugged and sexually abused. Although Masserman denied the allegations and no criminal charges were made, some of the malpractice cases were settled out of court and he was suspended from the Illinois Psychiatric Society for five years.

BIBLIOGRAPHY: B. Noel and K. Watterson, *You Must Be Dreaming* (1992)

[Louis Miller / Ruth Beloff (2nd ed.)]

MASSU'OT YIZ̦ḤAK (Heb. מַשּׁוּאוֹת יִצְחָק), moshav shittufi on the Coastal Plain, 8 mi. (13 km.) N.E. of Ashkelon, affiliated to the Ha-Po'el ha-Mizrachi Moshav movement. Massu'ot Yiz̦ḥak was originally founded in 1945 by pioneers from Hungary and Czechoslovakia as a kibbutz in the Hebron Hills, the second village in the Ez̦yon Bloc, under the name Massu'ot ("Beacons"). The name Yiz̦ḥak was added in honor of Chief Rabbi I.H. *Herzog in a ceremony attended by him. Along with the other three settlements of the Ez̦yon Bloc, Massu'ot Yiz̦ḥak fell in the Arab Legion's onslaught (May 13, 1948), and was completely destroyed, its surviving defenders being taken to Jordan as prisoners of war. After their release and return to Israel, they established their village on the present site (1949), several years later deciding to go over to the moshav shittufi settlement form. In 1969 the village was based on intensive agriculture and had a metal factory. Over the years the metal factory was replaced by the successful Albaad wet wipes factory. Farming included dairy cattle, field crops, poultry, avocado plantations, and some smaller branches. The population in 1968 was 403; in 2002, 548.

[Efram Orni / Shaked Gilboa (2nd ed.)]

MASTBAUM, JOEL (1882–1957), Yiddish short story writer and novelist. Born in Miedzyrzec, Poland, he lived in Warsaw from 1905, and from 1906 published extensively in the Yiddish press: feuilletons, short stories, folk tales, travel impressions, and chapters of novels. In 1933 he immigrated to Palestine and wrote stories about life there, collected in *Yidn in Erets-Yisroel* ("Jews in Palestine," 1935). Overtaken by World War II while visiting Poland, he nonetheless managed to return to Tel Aviv and describe his 60 days under the Nazis. His short stories, which were collected in several volumes beginning in 1912, have a romantic tonality. His first novels, *Fun Roytn Lebn* ("Red Life," 2 vols., 1912), about the revolutionary youth of 1905, and *Marita's Glik* ("Marita's Fortune," 1919), about three Jewish generations in Poland, had several editions in Yiddish, and were translated into Hebrew. *Nokhemkes Vanderungen* ("The Wanderings of Nokhemke," 1925), an adventurous romance beginning in a Polish town and ending in Buenos Aires, was followed by *Naye Mentshn* ("New Men," 1926). From a projected trilogy of Palestine between 1933 and 1948 only the first volume, *Der Koyekh fun der Erd* ("The Power of the Earth," 1951), was published.

BIBLIOGRAPHY: LNYL, 5 (1963), 464–7; S. Niger, *Dray Doyres* (1920), 263–73; M. Ravitch, *Mayn Leksikon*, 1 (1945), 128–30; 3 (1958), 254–5.; S. Bickel, *Shrayber fun Mayn Dor*, 2 (1965), 348–52. **ADD. BIBLIOGRAPHY:** Sh. Mastboym, *Yoel Mastboym* (1995).

[Melech Ravitch]

MASTEMA (Heb. מַשְׂטֵמָה), the name of the devil in the Book of *Jubilees. He is there identical with Satan and on one occasion the author speaks also (1:20) about spirits of Belial. Like other works originating in the broader movement within which the Dead Sea Sect came into existence, the Book of Jubilees is characterized by a dualistic trend, and in it the devil Mastema plays a great role, being the opponent of the forces of righteousness. He is the chief of evil spirits. After the flood a tenth part of his spirits received permission from God to execute the power of his will on the sons of men and the other nine parts were imprisoned in the place of condemnation. Not God, but Mastema caused Abraham's testing by proposing that God should require Abraham to sacrifice Isaac in order to test his love and obedience. He, and not God, sought to slay Moses on his return to Egypt at the lodging place (Ex. 4:24) and he also helped the Egyptian sorcerers against Moses and slew all the firstborn in the land of Egypt.

The name is found in Hosea 9:7, 8 as a common noun meaning "enmity." It was not translated in the Greek version of the Book of Jubilees but transcribed in Greek characters, and thus it came into the Latin and Ethiopian versions of the book. But the normal meaning of the name is seen in the term "the prince of the Mastemah" (*sar ha-Mastemah*) in the same book, meaning also "the prince of enmity." The same title occurs in its Hebrew original in the introduction of the medieval Hebrew Book of Asaph the Physician in the same context as Mastema in Jubilees chapter 10, an additional indication that this introduction depends on a Hebrew Book of Noah written by an ancient Jewish author from the same circles as those in which the Book of Jubilees originated. Mastema, i.e., the Satan, is also mentioned in the (Greek) Acts of Philip chapter 13 (*Acta Apostalorum Apocrypha*, 2 (1903), 7). The common noun *mastema* occurs in the Dead Sea Scrolls in connection with Belial, another name of the Satan frequent in the Dead Sea Scrolls and similar literature, where he is also named "the angel of Mastema." Thus the term is typical of the whole dualistic trend in ancient Jewish literature.

BIBLIOGRAPHY: R.H. Charles (ed.), *The Book of Jubilees* (1902), 80 n. 8; S. Muntner, *Mavo le-Sefer Asaf ha-Rofe* (1957), 149; M. Baillet, J.T. Milik, and R. de Vaux, *Les petites grottes de QumrḌn* (1962), 135; J. Licht (ed.), *Megillat ha-Serakhim* (1965), 93; J.M. Allegro, *Qumran Cave*, 4 (1968), 70.

[David Flusser]

MASTER, ARTHUR M. (1895–1973), U.S. cardiologist. Born in New York City, he graduated with an M.D. from Cornell University (1921). He received his clinical and research training in Mount Sinai Hospital, New York, and with Sir Thomas Lewis at University College Hospital, London, before his appointment as head of cardiology at Mount Sinai. During World War II he was consultant cardiologist at the National Naval Medical Center in Bethesda, Maryland (1942) and served with the U.S. Navy in the Pacific. He was appointed clinical professor of medicine at Columbia University, New York (1947). Master's clinical research concerned the development of the ECG (electrocardiogram) in the diagnosis of heart disease. The stress test named after him detected cardiac insufficiency during exercise and in principle remains a part of standard diagnostic procedures.

[Michael Denman (2nd ed.)]

MASTIC, the shrub *Pistacia lentiscus*, known as "medicinal mastic." It exudes a gum which in the Midrash is called *mastikhe*. It has been identified by some with the *lot* (AV "myrrh," JPS "laudanum") mentioned among "the choice products of the land" which Jacob sent to Egypt with his sons (Gen. 43:11; Gen. R. *ibid.*; but see *laudanum). The Tosefta (Shab. 12:8) states that *mastikhe* may not be chewed on the Sabbath since it is a medicine. Dioscorides states, "Its gum serves for medicine and tooth powder. It is smeared on the skin of the face to make it shine. When chewed it sweetens the breath and contracts the gums. The best mastic comes from the island of Chios" (*De materia medica* 1:89). To the present day a special variety of the shrub whose gum is sold as medicinal mastic is grown on the island of Chios. It is widely distributed throughout Israel, particularly in the wadis of the Judean hills, but the medicinal properties of its sap have not yet been tested. It would appear that it is to be identified with *bakha* (pl. *bekha'im*) of the Bible (II Sam. 5:23; I Chron. 14:14–15; AV "mulberry"; RV "balsam"), the name being connected with the "weeping" (*bokhim*), i.e., the excretion of the sap. The valley through which the pilgrims walked to the Temple was called *emek ha-bakha* (Ps. 84:7) because of the shrubs of that name growing there. The phrase was however regarded as meaning "the vale of tears" and it thus became a synonym for the exile.

BIBLIOGRAPHY: H.N. and A.L. Moldenke, *Plants of the Bible* (1952), 177f., no. 161; J. Feliks, *Olam ha-Ẓome'aḥ ha-Mikra'i* (1968²), 102.

[Jehuda Feliks]

MAT, MOSES (c. 1551–c. 1606), Galician rabbi. Mat was born in Przemysl where his father Abraham died a martyr's death. An intimate disciple of Solomon Luria, he taught in Belz. Subsequently he lived in Vladimir-Volynski, where his father-in-law resided and where Mat wrote his *Matteh Moshe*, a compendium of Jewish ritual law. The book was completed in 1584 and printed in Cracow about six years later, when Mat was already rabbi and head of the yeshivah of Przemysl. Later he lived in Lyuboml. He spent the last years of his life in Opatow. In 1590 Mat was one of the leading rabbis of Poland who signed an ordinance strictly forbidding the "buying" of rabbinical positions. Mat also wrote: *Taryag Mitzvot* (Cracow, 1581), a versification of the 613 commandments, which he composed at the age of 22; a commentary on the Pentateuch and on the Five Scrolls with a supercommentary on the commentary of *Rashi on these books, both of which were published after his death by his son ABRAHAM under the title *Ho'il Moshe* (Prague, 1611); and *Minhagei Maharshal* (printed in the 1870 Przemysl edition of Jacob Ẓemaḥ's *Nagid u-Meẓavveh*) which describes the customs and conduct of his teacher, Luria. Some of Mat's responsa are quoted or mentioned by his contemporaries Benjamin *Slonik and Joel *Sirkes. In his *Ho'il Moshe* he mentions novellae which he wrote on the treatise of *Yevamot*, but which have not been published.

BIBLIOGRAPHY: J. Kohen-Zedek, *Shem u-She'erit* (1895), 30–43; Halpern, Pinkas, 15, 62; Raphael, in: *Sefer Yovel ... S. Federbush*

(1960), 316–29; also separately: *Hanhagat Maharshal* (1961); idem, in: *Sinai*, 63 (1968), 96.

[Tovia Preschel]

MATALON, ELI (1924–1999), Jamaican politician. Matalon, a member of a prominent Jamaican Jewish family of Syrian origin, was born in Kingston and served as an officer in the Royal Canadian Air Force during World War II. In 1971, he was elected mayor of Kingston and St. Andrew. When the People's National Party came to power in February 1973, he was appointed to the Upper House as minister of state attached to the Ministry of Education, with a seat in the cabinet. On the appointment of the minister of education as governor-general, Matalon resigned from the Upper House and successfully contested the constituency of Eastern Kingston and Port Royal thus rendered vacant, becoming the first Jew to be elected to the House of Representatives in independent Jamaica. He was subsequently appointed minister of education. Matalon was one of the founders of the Hillel Academy, a primary school sponsored by the Jewish community in 1969, and served as vice chairman from its inception until he was obliged to resign in March 1973, on his appointment to the cabinet. In 1974 Matalon was appointed minister of national security and justice, a newly created post, in the Jamaican government, retiring in 1976. In later years he lived in Miami, Florida, where he died.

MATALON, RONIT (1959–), Israeli writer. Born to Egyptian-Jewish parents in a new immigrant town near Tel Aviv, Matalon later studied literature and philosophy at Tel Aviv University. She worked as a journalist at Israeli Television and the daily *Haaretz*. Matalon was a member of staff at the Camera Obscura School of Arts in Tel Aviv. Her first publication was a book for children, *Sippur she-Mathil be-Levayah shel Naḥash* ("A Story Which Begins with a Snake's Funeral," German 1999). Following her first collection of stories, *Zarim ba-Bayit* ("Strangers in the House," 1992), she published her novel *Ze im ha-Panim Elenu* ("The One Facing Us," 1998), a complex, postmodernistic family saga, coalescing text and photo material, foregrounding feminine as well as ethnic concerns. Her second novel *Sarah Sarah* was translated into English in 2003.

BIBLIOGRAPHY: L. Rattok, "My Gaze Was All I Had: The Problem of Representation in the Works of Ronit Matalon," in: *Israel Social Science Research*, 12, 1 (1997), 44–55; D. Abramovich, "Reviving the Israeli Roots Novel," in: *Australian Journal of Jewish Studies*, 15 (2001), 89–103; idem, "Ronit Matalon's Ethnic Masterpiece," in: *Women in Judaism*, 3:2 (2003).

[Anat Feinberg (2nd ed.)]

MATA MEḤASYA, town situated in S. Babylonia, on the Euphrates River near *Sura where the river divides into two. In geonic responsa Sura is often identified with Mata Meḥasya; thus Sherira Gaon in his famous letter at the end of the tenth century (ed. by B.M. Lewin (1921), p. 79, Spanish version) wrote that "after Rav came to Babylon in 219 he left Nehardea moving to a place where there was no Torah, viz., Sura, which is Mata Meḥasya" (the French version reads: "Sura which is called Mata Meḥasya"). The same identification is found in the work of Benjamin of Tudela in the 12th century. However, it would seem that the two places are not identical. They were two separate settlements near each other; and elsewhere in his letter (p. 84) Sherira Gaon explicitly distinguishes between the two places, stating that the school of Huna, the pupil and successor of Rav in the academy of Sura, was situated "near Mata Meḥasya." The Talmud also clearly distinguishes between the two places (Beẓah 29a). Mata Meḥasya is not mentioned in the Talmud before the time of *Ashi, who headed the Sura academy in the years 367–427. He extended the academy and transferred it to Mata Meḥasya (pp. 90–92). Of its inhabitants Ashi said: "The people of Mata Meḥasya are 'stouthearted' (cf. Isa. 46:12), for they see the glory of the Torah twice a year [in the **kallah* months of Adar and Elul], and never has one of them been converted" (Ber. 17b). R. Mesharsheya praised the scholars of Mata Meḥasya, saying: "Rather sit on the rubbish heap of Mata Meḥasya than in the palaces of Pumbedita" (Hor. 12a).

BIBLIOGRAPHY: B. Eshel, *Jewish Settlements in Babylonia during Talmudic Times* (1979), 149–50.

[Moshe Beer]

MATAS, DAVID (1943–), Canadian lawyer, writer, human rights activist, teacher. Matas was born in Winnipeg and had a conventional Jewish childhood in the city's South End. His was the first bar mitzvah in the Herzlia Synagogue in 1956. Following a B.A. in mathematics and economics at the University of Manitoba (1964) and an M.A. in economics at Princeton (1965), he traveled to Oxford for his legal education, receiving the B.A. (Juris) (1967) and B.C.L. (1968). Returning to Canada, he served as clerk to Chief Justice John Cartwright in 1968–69, as a member of the Canadian government's Foreign Ownership Working Group in 1969, and as special assistant to the federal solicitor general in 1971–72. After six years with a Winnipeg law firm, in 1979 Matas established a private practice in Winnipeg specializing in refugee, immigration, and human rights law. These areas, and his outspoken opposition to Nazi war criminals who found safe harbor in Canada, drove his professional, scholarly, and community activities. He argued several cases dealing with war crimes and hate propaganda before the Supreme Court of Canada, notably those of John Ross Taylor (1990), Imre Finta (1994), Canadian Liberty Net (1998), and Malcolm Ross (2001). He wrote numerous scholarly and journalistic articles and seven books on these topics, including *Justice Delayed: Nazi War Criminals in Canada* (1987), *Bloody Words: Hate and Free Speech* (2000), and *Aftershock: Anti-Zionism and Antisemitism* (2005), and taught courses in these areas at McGill University and the University of Manitoba. He was senior legal counsel to both Amnesty International Canada (from 1980) and B'nai B'rith Canada (from 1989), and was a member of the Canadian delegation to the UN General Assembly (1980), Task Force on Immigration Practices and Procedures (1980–81), Legal Committee on War Crimes of the Canadian Jewish Congress (1981–84), Manitoba Association for Rights and Liberties (1983–87), B'nai

B'rith's League for Human Rights (from 1983), Helsinki Watch Group (from 1985), International Defense and Aid Fund for South Africa (1990–91), Canada-South Africa Cooperation (1991–93), Canadian Council for Refugees (1991–95), International Center for Human Rights and Democratic Development (1997–2003), and the Canadian delegation to the UN Conference on an International Criminal Court (1998). His outstanding contributions were honored by the Manitoba Association for Rights and Liberties, National Council of Jewish Women, Lord Reading Law Society of Montreal, Shaare Zedek Hospital Foundation, League for Human Rights of B'nai B'rith, and Legal Education Association.

[James Walker (2nd ed.)]

MATHEMATICS.

Bible

The Bible does not deal directly with proper mathematical subjects; however there are some parts that do relate indirectly to different mathematical topics. These are widely discussed by the various commentators on the Bible and Talmud: the ratio of 300:50:30 between the three dimensions of Noah's ark (in the past, a basic ratio in shipbuilding), the mathematical model of a rainbow, the number of 220 sheep and goats sent by Jacob to Esau (220 as the first number of the smallest pair of amicable numbers), the calculations of the visibility of the crescent of the new moon, the total amount and volume of the daily *manna, Moses' financial report on the donations for the building of the Tabernacle (*mishkan*), the commandment of keeping exact measures and balances, chance and probability in relation to the fair division of the land of Israel, lot-drawing to insure the fair division of holy duties and privileges, the curve of "projectile motion" in relation to the unintentional killing of a man by throwing a stone, the surprising distribution of the 12 tribes into two equal groups of six on Mt. Gerizim and Mt. Ebal, and more.

The members of the tribe of Issachar were known as "*Marei de-Ḥushbena*" – the masters of calculations – as their elders specialized in astronomical and calendar calculations. Christian scholars have dealt extensively with Bible mathematics. Among others, an early 18th-century scholar, J.J. Schmidt published an interesting tractate called *Biblicus Mathematicus* (Zuellichau, 1732) in which many biblical-mathematical subjects are discussed, often based on Jewish sources. In another tractate there is a report on a request to the rabbinical court of Frankfurt to elaborate upon the issue of the geometry of the "Sea of Solomon" in the holy Temple. Many examples of biblical mathematics can be found in *Be'er Hetev* (Vilna, 1866), a commentary on Leviticus by R. Aryeh Huminer.

Sefer Yeẓirah

According to ancient Jewish tradition, *Sefer Yeẓirah* is ascribed to Abraham, as stated at the end of *Sefer Yeẓirah*. Others ascribe the authorship of the current version of *Sefer Yeẓirah* to R. Akiba (second century). At its very beginning, "*sefar*" (arithmetic = the wisdom of mensuration and numbers) is mentioned as one of three dimensions in which the world was created (*Kuzari and others). *Sefer Yeẓirah* deals extensively with permutations and combinations of the 22 letters of the alphabet. The end of Chapter 4 concludes with the statement that the number of permutations of all the 22 letters of the alphabet – [22! = 1,124,000,727,777,607,680,000] – is a number "which the mouth cannot speak and the ear cannot hear." (It would take 3,564,182,926 people and more than 10,000 years to speak out this number, even at a rate of one number per second.) R. Joseph ben Kalonymos (the elder; mid-13th century), in his commentary to Chapter 2 – erroneously ascribed to R. Abraham ben David (1120–1198) – was one of the earliest to use the decimal system to express large numbers using Hebrew letters. This was noticed by R. *Elijah of Vilna (1720–1797), who indicated that the Hebrew word "חוא"ג" which appears in the calculations is actually the result of 144 × 22 = 3,168, written in Hebrew numerals.

Mishnah and Talmud

The Mishnah and Talmud, dealing with all aspects of daily life, discuss many mathematical subjects. Yet the main reason for dealing with mathematics was mostly either to bolster the study of the Bible and its commandments or to clarify everyday applications of mathematical methods. As is clear from tractate *Avot*, the study and transmission of pure mathematical knowledge per se were matters of secondary importance. Nevertheless, for many practical halakhic issues, a considerable body of basic mathematical knowledge is required. The following are a few examples only: the basics of plane geometry in connection with the measuring of the Sabbath **eruv* boundary (2,000 cubits) over hills and ditches (methods of leveling); elements of knot theory in relation to the Sabbath laws; the layout of family graves; the mathematics of calculating an optimal seeding area without violating the biblical laws of prohibition of sowing with mixed seeds; the number of grapes that are within a circle with a given radius (i.e., Gauss' circle lattice point problem); the mathematics of inheritance leading to geometric progressions and exponential equations; the calculation of square roots leading to irrational numbers; the mensuration of circular and polygonal geometric forms or the proper division of assets among people with different kinds of claims. Another well-known topic is found in tractate *Kinnim*, the last in the Mishnah order *Kodashim*. Among other things, it deals with the laws concerning the "confusion of birds," e.g., birds assigned as sin offerings mixed up with those assigned as burnt offerings. Especially the last chapter requires advanced algebra and logic. Among the more recent mathematical commentaries are those by Moshe Koppel of Bar-Ilan University (1998) and B. Engelman of the Nahal Sorek Nuclear Research Center (1992). Knowledge of basic trigonometry and astronomy was needed for the fixing of the new month by reckoning and calculating. The exact methods used by the rabbinical court (*bet din*) were not made public. It was Maimonides who described appropriate calculations in his "Laws of Sanctification of the New Month" in his *Mish-*

neh Torah. Many of these topics were discussed and elaborated upon by commentators throughout the ages. It has to be remembered that most of these scholars had acquired their knowledge autodidactically and lacked any formal education. From a comment by R. Hai Gaon on Mishnah *Kelim* (16:1; 24:7) it seems that the Pythagorean writing table (abacus) and "Indian arithmetic" (i.e., numeration system and numerals) were known and in use at this time (Smith 2, 177). Although the Mishnah and Talmud use an approximation of 3 for the better value of 3.1415… for π, it is clear from various discussions in the Talmud, that the **amoraim* must have been aware of much better values for both π and $\sqrt{2}$.

The Mishnah and Talmud mention a few individuals as having outstanding mathematical knowledge. Rabban *Gamaliel, who used a Heron-type of dioptra to reckon distances; R. *Eleazar Ḥisma and R. *Johanan ben Gudgada, whose vast mathematical knowledge was described as enabling them to estimate "the number of drops in the sea"; R. *Zadok, who revealed to the Romans an advanced system of finger-calculation as well as the underlying mathematics of what later came to be known as the "Roman Statyra" (steelyard). R. *Joshua b. Hananiah – called the Escolasticus – was versed in astronomy and mathematics, R. *Abbahu is mentioned as having calculated the length of the cycle of service of the different tribes in the Holy Temple. The *amora* *Samuel Yarḥina'ah was versed in calendar calculations. This enabled him to calculate the calendar for the Diaspora for more than 60 years in advance. Nevertheless this knowledge was called "simple calculation," as it did not show a deeper understanding of Jewish law proper. In the name of the *amora* *Adda a more accurate estimate of the duration of the seasons is reported. The Talmud also mentions a "*Kippah shel Ḥesbonot*," i.e., a covered place outside Jerusalem serving people visiting the holy city in arranging their financial calculations and transactions.

MISHNAT HA-MIDDOT. Bible commentators of the Middle Ages mention the existence of a treatise called the *Baraita of 49 Rules* (*Middot*). This treatise from the tannaitic era was said to contain geometrical formulas and calculations. It was Abraham ben Solomon, the son of R. Elijah of Vilna (the Gaon of Vilna) in his *Rav Pe'alim* (Warsaw, 1894), who first drew attention to this treatise, though no existing copy of it was known. In 1864 Moritz Steinschneider found a Hebrew mathematical manuscript, identified it as *Baraitat ha-Middot* and published it in 1864. A critical edition including the geometrical drawings omitted by Steinschneider was published by the mathematician Hermann Schapira in 1880 as *Mishnat ha-Middot*. Among others things, *Mishnat ha-Middot* contains the Pythagorean formula allowing the calculation of the square root of 2 and uses a value of $3\frac{1}{7}$ for π. Haim Horovitz of Frankfurt tried to prove that this *Mishnat ha-Middot* was actually part of a Tosefta to the Mishnah tractate *Middot* (describing the measurements of the Holy Temple). This suggestion was later supported by the discovery of additional fragments and accepted by Solomon *Gandz in his critical edition of the *Mishnat ha-Middot*. This suggests that the *Mishnat ha-Middot* is one of the oldest known Hebrew mathematical works.

The Era of the *Geonim*

R. *Nahshon bar Zadok, who headed the yeshivah of *Sura from 874 to 882, stated that the order of the weekdays on which any particular festival occurs in successive years repeats itself after a cycle of 247 years. Thus he was able to arrange these years and their characteristic dates in 14 tables. This system is known as "*Iggul de-Rav Nahshon*" (R. Nahshon's cycle). R. Abraham Azulai (1570–1643) explains in Nahshon Gaon's name the concept of "amicable" (or "friendly") number pairs. He also mentions the common belief in the peacemaking powers of these pairs of numbers. This was known to Jacob and explains the number of 220 sheep and goats that Jacob sent to his brother. The suggestion has been made that R. Nahshon Gaon received this information from his contemporary Thabit ibn Qurra (836–901), a Sabbean mathematician in Baghdad famous for his work in amicable numbers. R. *Hai ben Sherira (939–1038), head of the yeshivah of *Pumbedita, in one of his responsa, explains the use of the Heron-type dioptra used by Rabban Gamaliel. His mathematical description of the various methods is practically identical to the way Heron himself described it in his book, including the accompanying diagram. This gives rise to the conjecture that R. Hai Gaon was familiar with the original source of Heron himself. The *gaon* who dealt most extensively with mathematical subjects was R. *Saadiah ben Joseph (892–942), head of the yeshivah of Sura. Examples are his commentary on *Sefer Yeẓirah* and his *Sefer ha-Yerushot* ("The Book of Inheritances"). The latter is an extensive mathematical-halakhic text showing how to divide an inheritance according to Jewish law. Other figures from this era who commented on mathematical subjects were Rabbenu *Hananel ben Ḥushiel, head of the yeshivah of Kairouan (980–1050), in his commentary to the Talmud and R. *Shabbetai Donnolo (913–c. 982), an Italian physician and writer on medicine, in his *Taḥkemoni*, a commentary on *Sefer Yeẓirah*.

11th and 12th Centuries

FRANCE. The *tosafists concentrated their literary efforts on the elucidation of the Bible and the Talmud and did not hand down much mathematical work per se. Although they had no formal education in mathematics, and in most cases had no possibility of learning from Greek or Latin sources, they did acquire some basic knowledge in an autodidactic way. Thus they commented on various talmudic discussions involving arithmetic and simple geometry. On the one hand their comments show a basic knowledge of arithmetic, e.g., in proposing several ways to calculate the connection between the basic halakhic unit of a ¼ of a log (*revi'it*) and the required amount of 40 *se'ah* of pure water for the ritual bath – the **mikveh* – yet it seems that some of the tosafists were unaware of the Pythagorean law and did not have a good approximation of π or of irrational numbers like $\sqrt{2}$ or $\sqrt{5}$. But evidently they were aware that surveyors used a better value than 3. They also used a method of applying and proving the Archimedean formula for the calculation of the area of a circle based on the radius and the circumference. It is highly probable that they adopted the method of their Spanish contemporary R. *Abraham bar Ḥiyya. His geometrical treatise *Ḥibbur ha-Meshiḥah ve-ha-Tishboret* ("Treatise on Mensuration and Calculation") was written for the rabbis of southern France. *Rashi (1140–1205), the forerunner of the tosafists, himself used a very interesting geometric method for calculating the square root, a method which had its sources in the Jerusalem Talmud. One of the tosafists, R. *Asher ben Jehiel (called the "Rosh"; c. 1250–1327), raised the following question: Why does the Talmud, as a book of law, discuss an inaccurate approximation of 3 for the value of π rather than using a better value, which had been known for a long time? The place for such an excursus would be a geometry text and not the Talmud. In reply, he showed that the famous Mishnah in question (Er. 1:6) was not intended to teach a geometrical principle but rather to introduce the halakhic rule that in certain instances this approximate value of 3 should be used. After his escape from Germany to Spain, R. Asher ben Jehiel asked one of his disciples – the astronomer R. Isaac ben Joseph *Israeli – to elaborate on the Pythagorean law and other geometric principles. It was in response to this request by R. Asher ben Jehiel that he wrote his famous trigonometric-astronomic treatise *Yesod Olam*.

SPAIN AND PORTUGAL. In Spain and Portugal Jewish intellectual and scientific growth continued to flourish. There was a lively exchange of mathematical knowledge between Jews and Arabs, and many Arabic mathematical ideas are reflected in Jewish literature. Likewise Jews contributed much to the Arabic corpus of scientific knowledge. Thus one finds much more elaborated mathematical ideas in both talmudic literature proper and original mathematical works.

Among the best-known mathematical figures of the 11th and 12th centuries was the above-mentioned Abraham bar Ḥiyya. Until the publication of *Ḥibbur ha-Meshiḥah ve-ha-Tishboret* in 1910, this mathematical magnum opus was known only in manuscript. This text is probably the earliest post-talmudic mathematical text per se. The author states that the reason he compiled the discourse was the lack of knowledge of geometry among the Jews of southern France. As he writes in his introduction, the text was meant to serve as a textbook for judges who had to deal with legal issues concerning the surveying and measuring of fields. Towards the end Bar Ḥiyya provides an interesting demonstration – using a model built from concentric circles of thin rope – of the Archimedean formula for the calculation of the circle's area based on its radius (r) and its circumference (c) [½·c·r], without actually using the value of π. It is this very demonstration that is used by the tosafists in their Talmud commentary. Bar Ḥiyya gives the fair approximation of 1.4143 (1⅖ + ⅒) for the square root of 2 and 3.141593 for π. He was also among the first to introduce to Europe the complete solution of quadratic equations. This fine textbook was translated by Plato of Tivoli in 1145, just a few years after the death of Bar Ḥiyya, under the title *Liber Embadorum*.

Other works by Bar Ḥiyya dealing with mathematics are *Ẓurat ha-Areẓ* ("Form of the Earth"), a basic introduction to spherical trigonometry and astronomy, and *Sefer ha-Ibbur* ("Book of Intercalation"). Based on a statement by Maimonides, it seems that he knew this text. Another work of his is *Yesodot ha-Tevunah u-Migdal ha-Emunah* ("The Foundations of Understanding and the Tower of Faith"), an encyclopedia on arithmetic, geometry, optics, astronomy, and music. Parts of it were translated into Latin by the Hebraists Sebastian Münster (1488–1552) and his disciple Erasmus Oswald Schreckenfuchs (1511–1575).

ABRAHAM B. MEIR IBN EZRA. *Ibn Ezra (1092–1167), a tosafist, was one of the most prolific commentators on the Bible, who at the same time also wrote extensively on mathematics. The best known of his mathematical contributions are *Sefer ha-Shem* ("Book of the Holy Name"), *Sefer ha-Eḥad* ("Book of the Number 1"), *Sefer Keli ha-Neḥoshet* ("Book of the Copper Instrument [i.e., the astrolabe]"), and *Sefer ha-Mispar* ("Book of Numbers"). (Some 100 years later, Jacob b. Machir ibn Tibbon, known as Profatius Judaeus, invented an improved version of the astrolabe, known as the quadrant.) Ibn Ezra also translated into Hebrew the commentary of al-Biruni on al-Khwarizmi's tables. In the introduction to this work he gives an historical account on the involvement of Jews in the introduction of Indian mathematics to the Arabic world. Ibn Ezra is one of the earliest Hebrew writers to introduce the "0," which he called *galgal* (wheel). In his *Sefer ha-Mispar* Ibn Ezra presents many exercises, which also appeared more than 250 years later in the *Sefer ha-Mispar* of Elijah *Mizraḥi. In addition, Ibn Ezra deals with the mathematics of inheritance and with the history of PI and mentions perfect numbers. He is also famous for his "prisoner problem," a mathematical puzzle first presented by *Josephus Flavius in his *Jewish War* and which is often used in introductory courses in mathematical programming. Many scientific articles have been written on Ibn Ezra's mathematical writings.

MAIMONIDES. Aside from a short tractate on calendar calculations, the works of Maimonides (1135–1204) are primarily nonmathematical. Yet in his Mishnah commentary Maimonides mentions that the ratio between the circumference of a circle and its diameter (π) cannot be expressed as a ratio of two natural numbers, and that this fact is not due to a lack of our understanding but is in the very nature of this number. He further states that there is no possibility to know the exact value of this ratio, that mathematicians have written various treatises on this subject, and that the approximation used by scientists is ²²⁄₇. Yet in his halakhic *Mishneh Torah* Maimonides requires the use of the old talmudic (and Babylonian) approximation of 3. A similar statement by Maimonides relates to two other irrational numbers, namely $\sqrt{2}$ and $\sqrt{5000}$. It is interesting to note that in the Western world it was Lambert (1728–1777) who first proved the irrationality of π in 1761. Much has been written in rabbinic literature about Maimonides' geometrical explanation of the *mishnayyot* in *Kilayim* 3:1 and 5:5. In his *Moreh Nevukhim* (*Guide of the Perplexed*), Maimonides mentions the difficulty in imagining the concept of the hyperbola and its asymptote, i.e., a curved line and a straight one, constantly approaching one another ad infinitum, without ever meeting. This subject – including the detailed explanations of the Jewish writers – was later elaborated by S. Motot, a 14th-century Jewish mathematician, and by Francesco Barozzi in his *Admirandum Illud Geometricum Problema, Tredicim Modis Demonstratum* (Venice, 1585).

13th and 14th Centuries

LEVI BEN GERSHOM. *Levi ben Gershom (Ralbag/Gersonides; 1288–ca. 1344) was probably the most advanced Hebrew mathematician of his generation. Widely known for his biblical commentaries, he dealt with all the three branches of Arabic mathematics: arithmetic, geometry, and trigonometry. An extensive corpus of research about Gersonides has come into being (spearheaded by Bernhard Goldstein of Yale University). A comprehensive bibliography on Gersonides has been published by Menachem Kellner of Haifa University (1992). Gersonides mentions both Abraham Ibn Ezra and Abraham bar Ḥiyya as sources from which he derived some of his knowledge. His arithmetical works – *Ma'aseh Ḥoshev* ("The Practice of Arithmetic") and "De numeris harmonicis" have been studied since the publications of *Ma'aseh Ḥoshev* by R. Joseph Carlebach of Hamburg, and some years later, at the beginning of the 20th century, by Gerson Lange. A hitherto missing part of problems of *Ma'aseh Ḥoshev* has been published by S. Simonson of Stonehill College. In this treatise Gersonides deals with arithmetic, algebra, and combinatorics. The short tractate on harmonic numbers was written as a response to an inquiry by Philip of Vitry, the bishop of Maux, shortly before Gersonides passed away. Another mathematical work is a commentary on Euclid's *Elements*. Gersonides' text on trigonometry, *De sinibus, chordis et arcubus* (originally written in Hebrew but immediately translated into Latin) is a commentary on the relevant chapters of Ptolemy's *Almagest* and was originally part of Gersonides' major work *Milḥamot Adonai* ("The Book of the Wars of the Lord"), part v, ch. 1. It was omitted in the printed Venice edition of 1560. In it, Gersonides presents a proof of the theorem of sines. He had arranged for a translation into Latin which is still extant. Carlebach showed that Gersonides was the inventor of the "cross-staff" (sometimes called "bacculus" or "Jacob's staff"), a simple yet powerful surveying device which allowed nautical and astronomical measurements. Carlebach even reconstructed a model of this instrument following Gersonides' description. The Jacob's staff was in use until the 17th century.

IMMANUEL BEN JACOB BONFILS. Another Jewish mathematician of this era is Immanuel ben Jacob *Bonfils of Tarascon (1300–1377), a contemporary of R. Levi b. Gershom. He is known as *Ba'al Kenafayim* after his astronomical tables published under the name of *Shesh Kenafayim* ("Six Wings"). Bonfils taught astronomy and mathematics at Orange for some time. He also was one of the forerunners of exponential calculus, some 150 years before its adoption in Europe, as is evident from his *Derekh Ḥilluk*. A great number of his many mathematical and astronomical works are still in MS. A special volume on the history of science in the Middle Ages by G. Sarton was called *Six Wings* after Bonfils' astronomical tables.

Important findings relating to Jewish mathematics in the 12–14th centuries have been contributed by various researchers, among them G. Freudenthal, G. Safatti, T. Levy, and D. Zeilberger.

15th Century

MOSES BEN ABARAHAM PROVENCAL. Moses ben Abaraham *Provencal (1503–1575) was considered one of the greatest talmudists and most illustrious scholars of Italian Jewry in the Renaissance period. For many decades he was rabbi of the Italian community of Mantua, which therefore became a center of talmudic study. His mathematical knowledge is evident from his *Be'ur Inyan Shenei Kavvim*. In his *Guide of the Perplexed* Maimonides mentions the concept of the asymptote, a straight line constantly approaching a curved line without ever touching it, referring to the *Conics* of Appolonius. Provencal wrote a four-page Hebrew explanation of this subject, which was added to the Sabionetta (1553) edition of the *Guide of the Perplexed*. This *kuntres* (pamphlet), which became famous, was translated into Italian by Joseph Shalit (Mantua, 1550) and was included in the well-known volume on the concept of the asymptote by Franceso Barocius (Venice, 1586). The latter also contains geometric explanations by other Jewish commentators on the *Guide of the Perplexed*. The subject itself became a major topic of rabbinical mathematics and was discussed in rabbinical literature from the 14th to the 19th centuries. It has been suggested that Provencal was familiar with Simon Motot's book on algebra. In his pamphlet, Provencal includes an explanation of the Greek concept of the "mean and extreme proportion" (the "golden section") and proofs related to the connection between the lengths of the sides of a regular hexagon and a regular decagon, both inscribed to the same circle. This concept, described by Euclid and mentioned by Joseph *Albo in his *Sefer ha-Ikkarim*, inspired many discussions in the rabbinical literature, mainly because of the lack of knowledge of the proper definition of the Greek concept of "mean and extreme proportion." Provencal specifically refers the reader to the source in Euclid's *Elements*.

MORDECAI COMTINO. Mordecai Comtino (1420–d. before 1487) was the teacher of R. Elijah ben Abraham *Mizraḥi. He was on friendly terms with the Karaites and was the teacher of two of their leaders, Caleb *Afendopolo and Elijah *Bashyazi. His literary output includes *Sefer ha-Ḥeshbon ve-ha-Middot* on arithmetic and geometry and commentaries on Abraham Ibn Ezra's *Sefer ha-Eḥad, Yesod Mora*, and *Sefer ha-Shem*, in which various mathematical subjects are discussed. His *Sefer ha-Ḥeshbon ve-ha-Middot* was known only in manuscript until a careful analysis and partial translation was published by Moritz Silberberg of Schrimm in 1905. The plan of this treatise follows a statement of the Greek Nichomachus of Gerasa regarding the logical order of basic mathematical subjects. Following Ibn Ezra, Comtino introduces the full decimal numeration, including the "0," which again he called "*galgal*" (the wheel). After introducing standard subjects in the first part, on arithmetic, Comtino deals with the measurement and division of plane figures and then proceeds to calculation of volumes of geometrical bodies and their parts. He also provides a detailed vocabulary of the different scientific terms. A special addition is the collection of problems part of which are borrowed from Ibn Ezra. Mizraḥi in his *Sefer ha-Mispar* (see below) drew upon some of the problems presented by Comtino. Besides this, Comtino also dealt with the construction of astronomical instruments.

ELIJAH BEN ABRAHAM MIZRAḤI. Mizraḥi (Re'em; c. 1450–1526) is known primarily from his famous supercommentary to Rashi's Bible commentary. Mizraḥi's mathematical works are *Sefer ha-Mispar* (Constantinople, 1534), on arithmetic, and a commentary on Ptolemy's *Almagest* (no longer extant). The former book became a standard text for the study of arithmetic. It deals with whole numbers, fractions, and mixed numbers, with the extraction of the square and cube roots, proportions, and arithmetical and geometrical problems. In his lengthy introduction he describes the importance of the study of mathematics as a bridge between the different sciences. *Sefer ha-Mispar* is based on Ibn Ezra's *Sefer ha-Mispar* and the mathematical work of his teacher Mordecai Comtino (see above). A Latin abridgment by Sebastian Muenster was published by his disciple Schreckenfuchs (Basel, 1546). At the end of the 19th century an in-depth description of *Sefer ha-Mispar* (*Die Arithmetik des Elija Misrachi*) was published by Gustav Wertheim (Frankfurt, 1893). An excerpt and analysis of those of his mathematical problems related to physics (*Ueber physikalische Aufgaben* by Elia Misrachi) was prepared by E. Wiedeman in 1910.

MORDECAI B. ABRAHAM FINZI. *Finzi (c. 1407–1476), a banker and mathematician, was known mainly for his mathematical and astronomical works, which included *Luḥot*, tables on the length of days (published by Abraham Conat, Mantua, c. 1479), and an astronomical work entitled *Netiv Ḥokhmah* (unpublished). He translated into Hebrew the *Algebra* of the Arab mathematician Abu Kamil Soga (c. 850–930). In 1934, a young Jewish mathematician by the name of Joseph Weinberg, submitted a critical edition of Finzi's translation as a thesis to the University of Munich. (Weinberg later was murdered by the Nazis.) An English translation of Finzi's commentary on Abu Kamil's *Algebra* was published in 1966 by Martin Levey. Finzi also translated into Hebrew various works on astronomy and geometry, wrote commentaries on some of them, described and explained recently invented astronomical instruments, and wrote treatises on grammar and mnemonics.

ABRAHAM BEN SAMUEL ZACUTO. *Zacuto (1452–c. 1515) was known as a talmudic scholar, historian, mathematician, and astronomer. He was appointed professor of astronomy and mathematics at the University of Salamanca. His famous almanacs and astronomical tables became a principal base for Portuguese navigators. Thus, Columbus, whom he met in Salamanca, was able to garner important information before his famous expedition. Using the tables of Zacuto, Columbus was able to predict an eclipse of the moon and so save the lives of his men by demonstrating to hostile natives that he could shut out the light of the sun and moon. R. *Levi ben Habib, a contemporary of Zacuto, remarks in one of his responsa that Abraham Zacuto wrote a commentary on the Talmud, from which he quotes a small geometrical explanation. Zacuto's well-known *Sefer Yuḥasin* contains several references to mathematics.

16th and 17th Centuries

DAVID B. SOLOMON *GANS. The astronomer, mathematician, and historian David b. Solomon *Gans (1541–1613) was raised and educated in the home of R. Moses *Isserles, the Rema. He also belonged to the circle of *Judah Loew ben Bezalel (the Maharal). Gans was in close contact with Tycho Brahe and Johann Kepler. Besides his history, *Ẓemaḥ David*, Gans compiled an astronomical-mathematical textbook called *Neḥmad ve-Na'im* (Jesnitz, 1743), an extract of which appeared in Prague in 1612 under the name of *Magen David*. In the preface to *Neḥmad ve-Na'im* he presents an abridged history of the transmission of mathematics and astronomy among the Jews, based on Jewish sources. The main part is devoted to pre-Copernican celestial mechanics, whereas toward the end he introduces basic instrumentation as well as trigonometry and its applications in daily life, enriching the text with many contemporary examples.

MENAHEM ZION PORTO (RAFA). Porto was an Italian rabbi born in Trieste toward the end of the 16th century; he died in Padua around 1660. He was an excellent mathematician and astronomer. His works were highly praised by Andrea Argoli and extolled in Italian sonnets by Tomaso Ercaloni and Benedetto Luzzatto. In 1641 Gaspard Scüppius, editor of the *Mercurius Quadralinguis*, recommended Porto, in terms that were very complimentary to the rabbi, to Johannes *Buxtorf (the younger), with whom Porto later carried on an active correspondence. Among other works, Porto published a "Handbook for the Merchant" (*Over la-Soḥer*, Venice, 1627), a compendium of basic arithmetic and many examples of business calculations for merchants. He also published a two-volume treatise of close to 400 pages – חכמתם ובינתכם לעיני העמים – *Porto Astronomico* – dealing with trigonometry and astronomy.

JOSEPH SOLOMON ROFE DELMEDIGO. *Delmedigo (YaSHaR; 1591–1655) studied mathematics, mechanics, and astronomy under Galileo at Padua. His major work, *Elim* (Amsterdam, 1629), is a classic compendium of 16th-century mathematics, physics and astronomy, and scientific instruments. He describes his use of Galileo's telescope to observe the planet Mars. Delmedigo displays a profound knowledge of the Greek, Renaissance, and contemporary literature dealing with mathematics and physics. The first part of *Elim* contains mathematical discourses dealing with both classical problems of Greek mathematics like the solution of the famous Alexander problem leading to Diophantine equations, the trisection of angles using the Conchoid of Nichomedes, the calculation of the octagon, and post-Renaissance mathematics like the solution of the cubic equations or the "squaring" of a circle, and the $^{355}/_{113}$ and Ludolphine approximations to π. In *Mayan Ganim* Delmedigo deals mainly with spherical trigonometry, with the proof and application of the law of sines, the history of trigonometry, the prosthaphaeresis (trigonometric formulas for the conversion of a product of functions into a sum or a difference), and the law of tangents of the sine function. *Gevurat Adonai* deals mainly with astronomy but has some mathematics as well. Another part, *Ma'yan Ḥatum*, is devoted mainly to the discussion of physical problems and paradoxes – mostly from Aristotle's *Mechanical Problems* – as well as to topics from early 17th-century classical physics.

JAIR ḤAYYIM BACHARACH. *Bacharach (1638–1702), rabbi of Worms, had a keen interest in mathematics. His first volume of responsa, *Ḥut ha-Shani* ("Scarlet Thread," Frankfurt, 1679) contains a lengthy responsum (§98) dealing first with talmudic metrology and then, in the second part, with many mathematical subjects. His main source is *Gevurot Adonai* by Joseph Solomon Delmedigo (see above). He mentions Hero's formula for extracting the square root, the (Roman) system of finger calculation, the approximation of a circle's circumference by polygons, mathematical problems from the *Sefer ha-Mispar* of R. Elijah Mizraḥi (see above), the famous Alexander problem from R. Joseph Solomon Delmedigo, and others. In his second volume of responsa *Ḥavvat Ya'ir*, Bacharach deals at length with the Euclidean concept of "mean and extreme proportion" (the golden section) mentioned by R. Joseph Albo in his *Sefer ha-Ikkarim* (Responsa §111).

MOSES HEFETZ GENTILI. In both his *Ḥanukkat ha-Bayit* (Venice, 1696), on the architecture of the Temple, and *Melekhet Maḥshevet*, a commentary on the Torah (Venice, 1710), Gentili (1663–1711) presents material that reflects mathematical thinking. Referring to the weekly portion of Noah, he describes Descartes' mathematical model of the rainbow and in his commentary to the weekly Torah portion *Ma'asei*, he describes Tartaglia's model for the motion of a projectile. In *Ḥanukkat ha-Bayit* he makes extensive use of the "Pythagorean theorem" in discussing the structure of the altar.

ELIJAH BEN SOLOMON ZALMAN OF VILNA. Already in his very early life *Elijah ben Solomon Zalman (the Vilna Gaon; 1685–1779) showed great interest in the study of mathematics and astronomy as an aid to furthering and deepening the study of Jewish law. In his halakhic commentary on the Shulḥan Arukh he added a great number of notes which disclose his profound mathematical and astronomical knowledge. He encouraged his students to translate basic mathematical texts into Hebrew, and even wrote a small and very concise tractate on arithmetic, geometry, and trigonometry with an introduction to basic astronomy (*Ayil Meshulash*, 1834). An analysis and description of *Ayil Meshulash* was published by Elias Fink (*Eliah Wilna und sein elementar-geometrisches Compendium*, Frankfurt, 1903). Fresh interest in this compendium was aroused with the publication of a new edition with a modern Hebrew commentary. One of his students, Baruch *Schick, a rabbi and physician, published various Hebrew texts on astronomy and medicine as well as a Hebrew translation of the first six books of Euclid's *Elements*.

RAPHAEL LEVI OF HANOVER. Raphael Levi *Hannover (1685–1779) showed his mathematical talent already as a child, when studying at the Jewish orphanage. One day, upon returning from his studies, observing the construction of the new royal stables in Hanover, he was able to prevent a serious engineering mistake. This drew the attention of Leibniz, the famous mathematician, who after meeting the young Raphael Levi offered to pay part of his tuition and to tutor him privately in mathematics and astronomy. In the last paragraph of his *Tekhunat ha-Shamayim* (Amsterdam, 1756) on geometry, trigonometry, astronomy, and calendar-making, Levi describes and strongly supports the Copernican system. In an addendum, Raphael Levi's disciple Moses Titkin elaborates a few difficult talmudic passages connected to mathematics. In addition to the Hebrew works, Raphael Levi also invented a system of using logarithms in currency conversions and wrote two mathematical compendia in German: (1) *Wechsel-Tabellen Tractaetgen* (Hanover, 1746), tables for currency conversion, and (2) *Vorbericht vom Gebrauch der neuerfundenen Logarithmischen Wechsel-Tabellen* (Hanover, 1747), a preliminary report on the use of the newly invented logarithmic currency conversion method. This latter text contains a good deal of advanced exercises and numerical examples. He also left a Hebrew manuscript of the first part of an introduction to algebra.

Among many other individuals who dealt with mathematical subjects were R. Yom Tov Lipmann *Heller Wallerstein (1579–1654), a disciple of the Maharal, who used his extensive knowledge of mathematics and astronomy throughout the whole of his commentary *Tosefot Yom Tov* to the Mishnah. R. David *Nieto of London (1654–1728), in his *Kuzari Sheni*, devoted a whole chapter to the explanation of some of the geometrical issues discussed in the Talmud and the commentary of the tosafists and many others.

18th Century

The expansion of general knowledge caused a shift in the content of rabbinical mathematics, from basic arithmetic and geometry only to a much broader scope of talmudic subjects related to mathematics. This was made possible by the availability of the Hebrew texts of Abraham Ibn Ezra, Elijah

Mizraḥi, Joseph Solomon Delmedigo, and others mentioned above. Topics like cubic equations, arithmetic and geometric progressions, logarithms, spherical trigonometry (for calculations not connected directly to astronomy), the use of trigonometric tables, logarithms, and methods similar to calculus – like analysis of functions for maxima and minima – were used. This brought forth a great number of texts containing mathematical excursus.

At the beginning of the 18th century R. Samuel Schotten mentions in his *Kos ha-Yeshu'ot* (Frankfurt, 1711) his plan to publish a collection of talmudic-mathematical essays. His basic knowledge in mathematics enabled him to give several approbations to Hebrew astronomical texts. Some years later *Jonathan of Ruzhany published his *Yeshu'ah be-Yisrael*, a commentary on the laws of *kiddush ha-ḥodesh* (concerning the blessing of the New Moon) in Maimonides' *Mishneh Torah* (Frankfurt, 1720). This tractate has an interesting appendix on some *halakhot* requiring basic mathematical knowledge. In the same year, Jonathan published a compendium of three astronomical works which naturally contain various mathematical elaborations. Some years later R. Emanuel Hai Rikki (1680–1744) published his *Ḥoshev Maḥashavot* (Amsterdam, 1727), an interesting halakhic-mathematical discourse of 70 short chapters based on an inquiry concerning the measurements of a *mikveh* (ritual bath). Within these discussions he elaborates the subject of measuring the circumference of a circle, the calculation of $\sqrt{2}$, and the concepts of asymptotes, and shows how to calculate and to graph two curved functions, each approaching the other without ever touching it. R. Jonah *Landsofer's *Me'il Ẓedakah* (Prague, 1757) contains a responsum (§28) – an answer to an inquiry from a "learned man well versed in geometry" – elaborating the geometrical aspects of the altar in the holy Temple as discussed in the Talmud. This subject is often discussed in talmudic literature. In his answer, Landsofer shows his profound knowledge of the relevant texts and also provides a proof of the Pythagorean Theorem. This responsum follows the previous one (§27) dealing with the area calculations of various shapes, all of the size of a "lense." In 1794, David Pivani published *Zikhron Yosef*, a textbook on arithmetic, geometry, and plane and spherical trigonometry. In the introduction he explains some of the geometrical aspects underlying Maimonides' commentary to the Mishnah *Kila'im* 5:5. Three years later, David Friesenhausen published his *Kelil ha-Ḥeshbon* (Berlin, 1797), in collaboration with the Jewish Freeschool in Berlin. This text, an introduction to algebra, contains a variety of challenging examples and exercises. Among the more interesting topics are arithmetical and geometrical series, cubic roots, and Lambert's law concerning the brightness of an illuminated surface.

Towards the end of the 18th century and in connection with the social emancipation and the resulting assimilation of the Jews, Jewish mathematics began to develop into two main streams: the traditional Jewish talmud scholar who used mathematical knowledge mainly for the purpose of expounding religious subjects and the new type of a modern mathematician of Jewish origin who pursues mathematics as an academic profession.

19th Century

The study of mathematics in the 19th century is widely characterized by the efforts of the *Haskalah movement to introduce general secular education among the Jews. It was one of the goals of the Haskalah to show that the Jewish people too have a basic mathematical tradition. Therefore one finds regular contributions on mathematics in periodicals like *Sulamith* in German, *Ha-Me'assef*, *Ha-Ẓefirah*, and *Ha-Carmel* in Hebrew – dealing with the study of mathematics in the framework of talmudic studies or dealing with mathematical problems as such. One of the first texts of the 19th century was *Beirurei ha-Middot* by Tovia Segal of Horoshitz (Prague, 1807), on the geometry of Sabbath distances and diameters of levitical cities. This text contains an introduction to geometry and trigonometry using logarithms. At the beginning of the 19th century Meyer Hirsch published a textbook/collection of exercises on geometry, *Sammlung Geometrischer Aufgaben* (Berlin, 1809). This collection of problems was used in Germany for almost a century and contains a formula proposed by the 15th-century Simeon ben Ẓemaḥ *Duran. A little later (1828–31) Michael *Creizenach, a teacher at the Frankfurt Philantrophin Reform school, published a series of textbooks on descriptive geometry, algebra, and technical geometry. In the first quarter of this century the first Hebrew article on "binary numbers" (a basic concept in computer engineering and digital electronics) was written by R. Zechariah *Jolles. (The author passed away two years before George Boole published his paper taking up again the concept of "binary numbers" in 1854.) Jolles' paper is basically a translation and elaboration of Leibniz's famous paper on the same subject. It is included, among other mathematical writings, in his *Ha-Torah ve-ha-Ḥokhmah* (Vilna, 1913). In 1834 Ḥayyim Selig *Slonimsky published his *Mosdei Ḥokhmah*, an introduction to mathematics. A second edition of David Friesensohn's *Kelil ha-Ḥeshbon* was reprinted in Zolkiev in 1835. In 1845 the famous Leopold *Kronecker (baptized 1863) began his brilliant career as mathematician after receiving his Ph.D. In 1856 the great historian of mathematics Moritz Cantor published his fundamental paper "Ueber die Einfuehrung unserer gegenwaertigen Ziffern in Europa" ("On the Introduction of Our Present Numerals in Europe"). Later on he published his monumental *Vorlesungen ueber Geschichte der Mathematik* ("Lectures on the History of Mathematics"), which is considered as marking the beginning of the modern history of mathematics. In keeping with the spirit of the Haskalah, the works of Joseph Solomon Delmedigo were reprinted (Odessa, 1865) as was *Shevilei de-Raki'a* by Eliah Hochheim (Warsaw, 1863). The editor of this tractate, Baruch Lowenstein, added a monograph of his own, *Bikkurei ha-Limmudiot* ("Firstlings of Mathematics"), discourses on various historical topics in Jewish mathematics. About the same time Ẓevi ha-Cohen *Rabinowitz published his fine series of Hebrew texts on popular experimental physics, *Yesodei*

Ḥokhmat ha-Teva (Warsaw, 1865), including special parts on mathematics and a short bibliography of Hebrew mathematical works. In those years Yom Tov Lipman *Lipkin – a son of the famous R. Israel *Lipkin Salanter, the founder of the *Musar movement – invented the "Lipkin linkage," a mechanical device to transform circular motion into linear motion, and became a famous mathematician who contributed mathematical problems to the *Ha-Ẓefirah* periodical. In the last quarter of the 19th century the first modern systematic texts on Jewish mathematics appeared: Baruch *Zuckermann's *Das Mathematische im Talmud* (Breslau, 1878; see J. Szechtman, "Notes on Dr. Zuckerman's 'Introduction to his Mathematical Concepts in the Talmud,'" in: *Scripta Mathematica*, vol. 25 (1960), pp 49–62). The most important work in this field is Moritz *Steinschneider's series of articles on Jewish mathematics, published between 1893 and 1898 in Ennestroem's *Bibliotheca Mathematica*. Part of these articles (covering the 9th–16th centuries) were reprinted as *Mathematik bei den Juden* in 1964. Additional relevant information can be found in Steinschneider's contributions to the famous *Realencyclopaedie* by Ersch and Gruber. This was made possible with the opening of German and Italian libraries, allowing the study of ancient Hebrew mathematical manuscripts and books. In 1879 Hermann *Schapira, at that time still a student in Heidelberg, edited and published a German translation of the *Mishnat ha-Middot*, discovered by Steinschneider in 1864. Towards the end of the 19th century Gustav Wertheim published *Elemente der Zahlentheorie* (Leipzig, 1887) and some years later an interesting monograph on the mathematics of Elijah Mizraḥi (*Die Mathematik des Elia Misrachi*, Frankfurt, 1893). A year later Israel Michel Rabbinowits of Paris published a Hebrew introduction to the Talmud containing an interesting appendix on the extraction of square roots, based on Heron's algorithm, as well as a discussion of negative and irrational numbers (*Mavo le-Talmud*, Vilna, 1894).

[Shimon Bollag (2nd ed.)]

20th Century

Jewish mathematicians continued to make major contributions throughout the 20th century and into the 21st, as is evidenced by their extremely high representation among the winners of major awards: 27% for the Fields Medal (the "Nobel Prize of Mathematics") and 40% for the Wolf Prize. Of those still active around the outset of the 20th century mention may be made of Rudolf Otto Sigismund *Lipschitz (1832–1903), whose contributions to mathematics and physical mathematics were mostly in the theory of numbers, the computation of variations, progressive series, and the theory of potential and analytic mechanics. With the French mathematician Augustin Louis Cauchy (1789–1857), he proved the theorem of prime importance in differential calculus and equations concerning the existing solutions to the equation $dy/dx = f(x,y)$. Herman *Minkowski (1864–1909) is entitled to nearly all the credit for creating the geometry of numbers. He was one of the earliest mathematicians to realize the significance of *Cantor's theory of sets at a time when this theory was not appreciated by most mathematicians. The later work of Minkowski was inspired by *Einstein's special theory of relativity which was first published in 1905. He produced the four-dimensional formulation of relativity which has given rise to the term "Minkowski space." James Joseph *Sylvester (1814–1897) dominated the development of the theories of algebraic and differential invariants, and many of the technical terms now in use were coined by him.

In Italy Vito *Volterra (1860–1940) wrote numerous papers on partial differential equations, integral equations, calculus of variations, elasticity, and topology, and initiated the subjects of functionals and mathematical biology. Tullio *Levi-Civita (1873–1942) developed the absolute differential calculus, which was the essential mathematical tool required by Einstein for his development (in 1916) of the general theory of relativity. Levi-Civita's most important contribution in this field was the theory of "parallel displacement." He also produced significant papers on relativity, analytical dynamics, hydrodynamics, and systems of partial differential equations.

Two outstanding French mathematicians were Jacques Salomon *Hadamard (1865–1963), who produced important work in analysis, number theory, differential geometry, calculus of variations, functional analysis, partial differential equations, and hydrodynamics, and inspired research among successive generations of mathematicians, and Laurent *Schwartz (1915–2002), whose work broadened the scope of calculus and brought Paul Dirac's ideas of "delta functions" in quantum mechanics within the scope of rigorous mathematics. For this work he was awarded the Fields Medal in 1950.

Another winner of the Fields Medal was Paul Joseph *Cohen (1934–), for his fundamental work on the foundations of set theory. Cohen used a technique called "forcing" to prove the independence in set theory of the axiom of choice and of the generalized continuum hypothesis. Felix *Hausdorff (1868–1942) was also an authority on set theory and its applications to sets of points and real analysis. His textbook *Mengenlehre* (Leipzig, 1935) is recognized as one of the great classics of set theory. The depth and simplicity of his research into fundamental problems was a source of inspiration in the rapid development of modern mathematics.

Johann Ludwig von *Neumann (1903–1957) sought to develop the subject of quantum mechanics as a mathematical discipline, which led him to research in Hilbert space and the initiation of continuous geometry. In addition, Von Neumann made important contributions to measure theory, ergodic theory, continuous groups, topology, classical mechanics, hydrodynamic turbulence, and shock wave, and was a pioneer of game theory. Issai *Schur (1875–1941) specialized in the theory of numbers, particularly with regard to finite groups and their representations. He is widely known as the author of "Schur's lemma," which states that the only operators that commute with a unitary irreducible representation are the scalar multiples of the identity operator. Schur is also credited with extending the finite group theory to compact groups, and is noted for his work in the representation theory of the rotation group. André *Weil (1906–1998) contributed widely to many branches of mathematics, including the theory of numbers, algebraic geometry, and group theory. Norbert *Wiener (1894–1964) invented the science of cybernetics. As a mathematician, Wiener's main innovation was to develop a mathematics based upon imprecise terms reflecting the irregularities of the physical world. He sought to reduce these random movements to a minimum in order to bring them into harmony. During World War II, he applied his concepts to work connected with antiaircraft defense, and this led to advances in radar, high-speed electric computation, the automatic factory, and a new science he created called cybernetics, a word he coined from the Greek word for "steersman," meaning the study of control. This followed his attempt as a mathematician to find the basis of the communication of information, and of the control of a system based on such communication. Wiener suggested the use of cybernetics in diagnostic procedures and indicated the similarity between certain types of nervous pathology and servomechanism (goal-directed machines such as guns which correct their own fixing malfunctioning). See also Benoit *Mandelbrot and Robert *Aumann.

BIBLIOGRAPHY: R. Aumann and M. Mashler, "Game Theoretic Analysis of a Bankruptcy Problem from the Talmud," in: *J. Economic Theory*, 36 (1985), 195–213; W. Feldman, *Rabbinical Mathematics & Astronomy* (1931; repr. 1978); S. Gandz, *Studies in Hebrew Astronomy and Mathematics* (1971); M. Littman, *Approaching Infinity, Selected Mathematical writings of R. Shlomo of Chelme* (1989); G.B. Sarfatti, *Mathematical Terminology in Hebrew Scientific Literature of the Middle Ages* (Heb., 1968); M. Steinschneider, *Die Mathematik bei den Juden* (1964); N.E. Rabinovitch, *Probability and Statistical Inference in Ancient and Medieval Jewish Literature* (1973); J. Rosenberg, "Some Examples of Mathematical Analysis Applied to Talmud Study," in: Mathematical Analysis Applied to Talmud Study, at: www.math.umd.edu/~jmr/MathTalmud.html; B. Tsaban and D. Graber, Mathematics in Jewish Sources, at: http://www.cs.biu.ac.il/~tsaban/hebrew.html. **WEBSITES:** www.jinfo.org; http://imu.org.il (for mathematics in Israel); http://www5.in.tum.de/lehre/seminare/math_nszeit/ss03/vortraege/verfolgt/#gliederung (for mathematicians persecuted by the Nazis).

MATKAH, JUDAH BEN SOLOMON HA-KOHEN (Ibn Matkah; first half of 13th century), author of the *Midrash ha-Ḥokhmah,* commonly considered the first of the great medieval Hebrew encyclopedias of science and philosophy. Judah was born in Toledo and belonged to the Ibn Shoshan family. He is listed in various books by the name Ibn Matkah. However, there seems to be little ground for maintaining this appellation, since in the sources it appears only once, in a 16th-century manuscript of the *Midrash ha-Ḥokhmah*, and there not in the body of the text but in an annotation at the top of the page.

Judah was a disciple of Meir ha-Levi *Abulafia. At the age of 18 he became engaged in a correspondence with one of the scholars at the court of Emperor Frederick II, as a result of which he eventually moved to Italy. It is not known which position he held at the court, nor where he resided, perhaps in Lombardy. Around 1247 he composed the Hebrew version of his encyclopedia, which, according to his own testimony, he wrote originally in Arabic when still in Spain. The Arabic original has not been preserved. The *Midrash ha-Ḥokhmah* consists of an introduction, two parts, and three treatises. The first part provides a survey of Aristotelian logic, natural philosophy, and metaphysics, primarily based on Ibn Rushd's Middle commentaries on these works, but occasionally also on other sources. The first treatise, an explanation of verses from Genesis, Psalms, and Proverbs, follows this part. The second part is devoted to geometry (based on Euclid's *Elements*), astronomy (based on Ptolemy's *Almagest* and al-Bitruji's *Principles of Astronomy*), and astrology (based on Ptolemy' s *Quadripartitum*). To this part two treatises on the letters of the Hebrew alphabet and talmudic *aggadot,* respectively, are appended. Only the first treatise (Goldberg 1981) and the section on astrology (Spiro 1886) have been edited so far. There are two complete manuscripts of the work (Bodleian Library, Mich. 551 and Vatican ebr 338) and some 40 more of parts of the text; for a complete list see Manekin's Addendum in Harvey 2000, 475–79). It has not yet been established with certainty whether Judah ha-Kohen wrote other works (Langermann, in: Harvey 2000).

The *Midrash ha-Ḥokhmah* thus presents a combination of secular and religious knowledge. It constitutes the first systematic Hebrew survey of Aristotelian natural philosophy and metaphysics as interpreted by Averroes. In composing his encyclopedia Judah aimed at disseminating scientific secular learning, while at the same he sought to convey that true knowledge, or "divine wisdom," cannot be attained by Aristotelian metaphysics but by traditional Jewish religious learning. Throughout his work he displays a critical attitude towards Aristotelian philosophy. His encyclopedia should be seen as an attempt to delineate the value of secular knowledge against the background of the Maimonidean controversy and the debate about the permissibility of the study of secular science.

BIBLIOGRAPHY: J. Spiro, *Otot ha-shamayim* (1886); Neubauer, Cat, 470–1, 682, 691; Steinschneider, *Uebersetzungen*, 1 (updated Eng. translation by C. Manekin, in: S. Harvey (ed.), *The Medieval Hebrew Encyclopedias of Science and Philosophy* (2000), Addendum); C. Sirat in: *Italia,* 2 (1977), 39–61; idem in: G., Nahon and C. Touati (eds.), *Hommage a Georges Vajda* (1980), 191–202; D. Goldstein, in: HUCA, 52 (1981), 203–52; C. Sirat, *History of Jewish philosophy in the Middle Ages* (1985), 250–55; R. Fontaine, in: *Medizinhistorisches Journal,* 29 (1994), 333–61; M. Zonta, *La filosofia antica nel Medieoevo* (1996), 200–4; E. Gutwirth, in: *The Modern Language Review* (1998), 384–99; R. Fontaine, C. Manekin, T. Levi, Y.T. Langermann, A.L. Ivry, in: S. Harvey (ed), *The Medieval Hebrew Encyclopedias of Science and Philosophy* (2000), and idem, index, s.v. Judah ben Solomon ha-Cohen; R. Fontaine, in: *Arabic Sciences and Philosophy,* 10 (2000), 101–37; C. Sirat, in: *Italia,* 13–15 (2001), 53–78; R. Fontaine, in: *Zutot* (2001), 98–106; idem in: *Zutot* (2002), 156–63.

[Resianne Fontaine (2nd ed.)]

MATLIN, MARLEE (1965–), U.S. actress. Born in Morton Grove, Illinois, Matlin lost most of her hearing at 18 months after a bout with measles. She learned English, Hebrew, and sign language at Chicago's Congregation Bene Shalom / Hebrew Association for the Deaf and made her acting debut at age seven as Dorothy in a children's theater version of *The Wizard of Oz*. In 1987, at the age of 21, she won the Academy Award for Best Actress for her role as Sarah Norman in *Children of a Lesser God,* the youngest performer ever to receive the award and the only hearing-impaired person to be awarded the prize. Subsequently Matlin acted in numerous films, including *Walker* (1987), *It's My Party* (1996), *Hear No Evil* (1993), and *What the Bleep Do We Know?* (2004). She also appeared in numerous television series, including *Picket Fences* (1992), for which she won an Emmy; *ER* (1998); *Law and Order* (2004); *The West Wing* (2001, 2002, 2003, 2004, 2005); and *Desperate Houswives.*(2005). When not acting, Matlin works with various charity organizations such as the Children Affected by AIDS Foundation, the Elizabeth Glaser Pediatric AIDS Foundation, the Starlight Foundation, and the Red Cross Celebrity Cabinet. Matlin is also the author of *Deaf Child Crossing* (2002), a novel based on her own childhood experiences. In 1993 Matlin married Kevin Grandalski (in Henry Winkler's back yard). Together, they have three children.

[Alex Frankel (2nd ed.)]

MATLIN, MOSHE MEIR (1855–1927), Orthodox rabbi. Born in Slutzk, Lithuania, he went to Kovno to study with Rabbi Isaac Elchanan Spector, who was chief rabbi of Kovno, and was ordained there. In 1891 he came to New York at the invitation of Rabbi Jacob Joseph to become a *dayyan* in the newly formed *bet din.* He then headed the *kashrut* supervision for Rabbi Jacob Joseph. For two decades he was a *mashgi'aḥ* for kosher meats and wine while teaching Talmud privately. When his son was ready for yeshivah he helped establish the Rabbi Isaac Elchanan Theological Seminary, named in honor of his mentor, and he offered lectures there though he was not a regular member of its faculty. He was also a founder of the Agudat ha-Rabbonim, which was linked to RIETS. Because of his deteriorating health, he tried moving to Montana and farming, but he could not attract others to so rural a life and apparently he was not a skilled farmer. He then moved to Sioux City, Iowa, where he served as a rabbi and *kashrut* supervisor for major meat companies.

BIBLIOGRAPHY: M.D. Sherman, *Orthodox Judaism in America: A Biographical Dictionary and Sourcebook* (1996).

[Michael Berenbaum (2nd ed.)]

MATRIARCHS, THE. The four "mothers" (*arba immahot*) of Jewish liturgy. In the Bible, *Sarah, *Rebekah, *Leah, and *Rachel are, somewhat asymmetrically, the wives of the three *patriarchs, *Abraham, *Isaac, and *Jacob. All except Rachel were buried in the Cave of Machpelah. Sarah is to be the mother of nations and kings (Gen. 17: 15–16), while Rebekah is to produce myriad offspring who will seize the city gates of the foe (Gen. 24:60). The matriarchs played significant roles in the Genesis story, especially to insure the succession of their sons to the divine promise first given to Abraham. Sarah insists on the expulsion of Hagar in order to eliminate Ishmael as a rival claimant to Isaac (Gen. 21:10). Rebekah initiates Jacob's deception of Isaac so as to ensure that Jacob receive the birthright (Gen. 27). In Jewish tradition, the names of the matriarchs are specifically mentioned in the *Mi-she-berakh* prayer after the birth of a child and in the parental blessing of a daughter on the eve of Sabbath. However they are not named in other Orthodox liturgy. In recent times, under the influence of feminism, they are mentioned in prayers alongside the patriarchs in many non-Orthodox liturgies. Jacob's lesser wives Bilhah and Zilpah have not yet attained matriarchal status even among the heterodox.

MATRIMONIAL PROPERTY.

In Jewish Law

GENERAL. In Jewish law, spousal property relations are regulated by the *ketubbah.* Maimonides describes how, when a man marries, he undertakes to provide his wife with ten things and is entitled to four things (Yad, Ishut 11:1–4; see at length *Husband and Wife). In general, according to Jewish Law each of the spouses has a specific role which determines the scope and nature of their respective rights to property and other rights and obligations. According to this view, the husband is analogous to a "foreign minister" or "finance minister" of the family and thus bears the legal obligation of supporting the family, which under Jewish Law is exclusively the husband's obligation. In order to discharge this obligation, he has possession and control of the property belonging to himself or his wife. Any property acquired during the course of the marriage is his, such that property bought with his own money belongs to him, while property bought by the wife with money that she earned is usufruct (*nikhsei melog*) – in other words, the principal belongs to her, while the control thereof, including the benefit of its proceeds, belongs to the husband, being intended for household needs.

In Israeli Law

Since the early 1960s, a doctrine of "presumption of joint property between spouses" has developed in Israeli law. Initially, the Israeli Supreme Court recognized the presumption as governing the relationship between the couple vis-à-vis the estate tax authorities. Accordingly, where an apartment was registered exclusively in the name of a deceased husband, the Court ruled that half of it belonged to the wife, by force of the presumption of joint property, and therefore the husband's estate only included half of the apartment (CA 300/64 *Berger v. The Estate Tax Administrator,* 19(2) PD 240). Gradually however, the doctrine was recognized and applied in relations between the spouses themselves. The *Aftah* decision, delivered by a bench of five justices, is generally regarded as the landmark decision on this subject (CA 595/69 *Aftah v. Aftah,* 25(1) PD 561). Since then, Israeli case law regarding the joint property presumption has developed at all judicial levels, from the Family Court through to the Supreme Court. This has been regarded by some as an example of Israeli common law.

The doctrine, in essence, is based on the presumption that a couple living together harmoniously intend that all property acquired during the course of the marriage will be jointly owned in equal shares by both partners, even if registered in the name of one of them. The legal force of this presumption was originally based on what was perceived as the presumed intention of the parties. Case law notes that this intention is presumed even when the husband and wife have different levels of earnings, even when the wife does not work but takes care of the house and children, leaving to her husband the task of supporting the family. The parties were presumed to have intended that the family's income and its accumulated assets would be their joint property. Case law extended the scope of this presumption to include partnership in future assets, such as pension rights, continuing education funds, life insurance, etc. In the early stages of its development, the Court ruled that it applied to a couple's apartment, but that regarding commercial property, a greater level of proof was required to prove the intention of joint ownership. Over the years this distinction was abolished, and today the doctrine applies to all of the couple's assets, regardless of whether these consist of the couple's apartment or of other forms of savings, business assets, reputation, etc. At all events, the Supreme Court held that with respect to the couple's apartment, there could be cases in which it would be regarded as joint property even when purchased before the marriage, and part of the purchase price was paid during the course of the marriage (CA 806/93, *Hadari v. Hadari*, 48(3) PD 685).

As the doctrine developed, the empirical-consensual aspect was abandoned, and several judicial pronouncements indicated that the doctrine of joint spousal property is based on the principle of equality between spouses, in accordance with the general principles of the Israeli legal system, which regards equality as a fundamental value.

In 1973, the Spouses (Property Relations) Law, 5733 – 1973, was enacted. Pursuant to the law, a married couple constitutes a kind of obligatory delayed partnership that only finds expression when the marriage is terminated (by divorce or death). Until such time, the couples' assets are separated. Upon termination of the marriage (either through death of divorce), an accounting is made of the couple's assets; if more than half the assets are owned by or registered in the name of one of the spouses, that person pays half of the difference to his spouse (CA 1229/90 *Hanokh v. Hanokh*, 45(5) PD 584). Section 5(a) of the law explicitly provides that gifts and inheritances received during the course of the marriage are not considered as joint property.

There is disagreement in the case law as to whether the joint property presumption – which was a judicial, and not a legislative creation – applies to couples married after January 1, 1974 (the date that the new law came into force), or whether the only applicable law for the latter is contained in the provisions of the aforementioned law, that establishes an obligatory delayed partnership. This controversy is mainly relevant when deciding on whether a party is entitled to claim half of the property prior to termination of the marriage, pursuant to the partnership doctrine, or whether a spouse's right to claim it arises only on the day that the marriage is terminated (on this matter see CA 1915/91, *Yaakobi v. Yaakobi*, 49(3) PD 529).

THE SUPREME COURT'S POSITION VIS-À-VIS RABBINICAL COURT DECISIONS. Since the early days of the State, the position of the Israeli Supreme Court has been that the rabbinical court must apply religious law, i.e., Jewish Law, not only in matters of personal status (e.g., the validity of marriages and divorces), but also in cases involving financial matters, insofar as "the nature of a Jewish religious court is to rule according to the religious laws of Israel" (CA 22/49 *Levanon v. Elmeliah*, 3 PD 68, 80; *per* Justice M. Silberg; see also HC 323/81 *Wilozni v. The Rabbinical Court of Appeals*, 36(2) PD 733, *per* Justice Menachem Elon). In its capacity as the High Court of Justice, the Supreme Court had traditionally taken this approach when confronting questions of whether to vacate rabbinical court judgments on financial and property disputes between couples. Questions of this nature were adjudicated by the rabbinical courts in accordance with Jewish Law, as part of their incidental jurisdiction, when arising in the course of divorce proceedings (see *Bet Din, addendum). For example, one case concerned an apartment given by the husband to his wife during the course of a marriage, and subsequently registered by the husband in the wife's name. The rabbinical court was required to decide whether the gift was absolute or conditional, and in doing so it applied the Jewish Law, which in such a case presumed that the gift was conditional, having been given "subject to the understanding that if she leaves him, he would not be regarded as having given it to her." The Supreme Court rejected the wife's argument that the rabbinical court exceeded the limits of its jurisdiction (HC 609/92 *Boehm v. The Rabbinical Court of Appeals*, 47(3) PD 288; *per* Deputy President Justice Menachem Elon).

Nonetheless, in a later decision, Justice A. Barak (then deputy president, and subsequently president of the Supreme Court) held that the Supreme Court's judicially created joint property doctrine must also be applied in the rabbinical court. His first argument was the obligation to act in accordance with the Woman's Equal Rights Law, 5711 – 1951, and the second, broader, argument was that the rabbinical courts are subject to the Israeli secular law with regard to property relations. Essentially, the underlying rationale of the decision is that Israeli civil law is territorial, and thus obligates all legal forums, including the religious or rabbinical courts (HC 1000/92 *Bavli v. The Rabbinical Court of Appeals*, 48(2) PD 221). (In accordance with this approach the Supreme Court also intervened when the rabbinical court ruled, in accordance with Jewish Law, on a matter involving an injunction against leaving the country. The Supreme Court's position was that the Israeli civil law should be applied, rather than the religious law on whose basis the rabbinical court had ruled – HC 3914/92 *Lev v. The Rabbinical Court of Appeals*, 48(2) PD 491.)

In an article published several years after his retirement from the bench, Professor Menachem Elon wrote a comprehensive critique of these decisions. Elon emphasized that the deviation from the Supreme Court's consistent position, whereby rabbinical courts rule in accordance with the religious law, was unjustified on a substantive level, as well as constituting a blow to the independence of the rabbinical courts and their ability to develop Jewish Law. In his article, Professor Elon proposed a number of options for the application of the joint property doctrine in accordance with Jewish Law (see *Minhag; *Dina de-Malkhuta Dina; and see Bibliography, Elon, "These Are Obiter Dicta" ("*Eleh Hen Imrot Agav*")). Professor Elon also warns that decisions such as these are liable to create tension between the various judicial forums, thereby jeopardizing the fundamental values of the legal system, which aspire, inter alia, to preserve peace and attain practical solutions to controversies between parties. Professor Elon further noted that decisions of this kind, while aspiring to harmony within the legal system, cause two other sources of disharmony: (a) between the law of the State and Jewish Law, which is the national law of the Jewish people, and (b) between the past (when the Jewish Law was developed) and the present and future, inasmuch as acceptance of Barak's position compromises the ability of the Jewish Law to develop, given that, in practical terms, the rabbinical courts in the State of Israel are the only forum in which Jewish Law is applied in an operative manner (see also the addendum to the entry *Bet Din).

RABBINICAL COURT'S RESPONSE TO THE SUPREME COURT'S POSITION. In their respective responses to the *Bavli* decision, the *dayyanim* of the Rabbinical Court of Appeals were divided. Rav Shlomo Dikhovsky opined that the rabbinical courts were obligated to rule according to the joint property doctrine by force of the rule "*dina de-malkhuta dina*" (see his article cited in Bibliography). He contended that halakhic rulings should be consonant with the halakhic view that *dina de-malkhuta* also applies in Israel. Moreover, the rule applies equally to legislation enacted in a democratic regime and to laws that are the product of judicial legislation. Inasmuch as the Israeli Supreme Court and the Knesset itself views court decisions as a part of the binding legal system of the State, there is no difference between judicial decision and legislation. Therefore, in his opinion, such case law should not be subject to the distinction that the halakhic authorities make between explicit legislation – to which "*dina de-malkhuta dina*" applies – and to rulings that are the result of local judicial discretion, in which the rule is inapplicable. All citizens of the State are cognizant of the "joint property rule" and guide their conduct accordingly, giving it the status of a custom (see *Minhag). Moreover, the fact that it is anchored in Jewish practice militates in favor of its acceptance by force of "*dina de-malkhuta dina*." Such is the case regarding the joint property doctrine, insofar as it derives from case law. Rabbi Dikhovsky finds halakhic anchorage for the Supreme Court's doctrine of joint property in the pre-nuptial written conditions (*tena'im*) agreed upon by the couple. The *tena'im* provide that the couple "will have equal control of their assets, and will not smuggle or hide them from one another, but rather will live together in love and affection." Based on his interpretation of this document, R. Joseph Colon (Resp. Maharik, no. 57), imposed a ban on a husband who smuggled assets from his wife. Rabbi Dikhovsky contends that an additional step should be taken, by declaring that in our generation the presumption regarding the couple is not confined to their reciprocal trust that neither of them will smuggle assets away, but rather is broader, and confers the wife actual control over half of the assets acquired by her husband (in this matter he also relies on *Resp Maharsham* 1.45, dealing with a gift that the wife received from her sister).

The Spouses (Property Relations) Law, 5733 – 1973 provides that the law also applies to rabbinical courts, in the absence of explicit agreement that the religious law will apply (Section 13 of law). Following the enactment of this law, the presumption is that every couple who married after its enactment knew that this was the legal position, and thus consented to premise their financial relations on the joint property rule. Under such circumstances, the rule of "*dina de-malkhuta dina*" should clearly be applied to such couples, and the rabbinical court should rule according to the joint property doctrine, and certainly to its delayed version regarding couples married after January 1, 1974.

When the parties agree to have their property disputes governed by secular law, that agreement should be honored, and the rabbinical courts should apply the joint property doctrine, by force of that agreement. Rabbi Dikhovsky ruled accordingly when on appeal, he overturned a decision of the Regional Rabbinical Court that refused to apply the joint property doctrine even though both of the parties had previously signed an agreement that the rabbinical court would rule according to this doctrine. In addition to the rationale of honoring the parties' expressed will, Rabbi Dikhovsky warned that failure on the rabbinical court's part to apply the joint property doctrine is liable to impair its status, and result in the loss of its jurisdiction over financial and property matters, even in its current limited format (the decision in its entirety is published after the article in *Teḥumin*, 18 (1998), 18 ff.).

A different opinion on the matter was expressed by Rabbi Avraham Sherman – also a *dayyan* on the Rabbinical Court of Appeals (see *Teḥumin*, 19 (1998), 32–40; 20 (1999), 205–20). In his view, legislative enactments and legal pronouncements that stem, not only from the imperative of creating an orderly society and correcting faults occasioned by particular circumstances, but which rather reflect the world view of the legislators and the judges of the state courts, do not fall within the ambit of "*dina de-malkhuta dina*," because this contradicts the world view of the Torah. Empirically, it cannot be claimed that the "joint property doctrine" is a custom accepted by all, nor may one, on that basis, make a presumption that all married couples marry with the intention of distributing their assets equally. Furthermore, it is difficult to anchor the joint property doctrine in Jewish Law. When the law concerned is one that is intended to regulate the financial relations between a husband and wife, and not the well-being of the society and the State, the rule of *"dina de-malkhuta dina"* does not, according to this view, apply. Rabbi Sherman argues with Rabbi Dikhovsky regarding the significance of the written conditions, but the main thrust of his argument is on the theoretical level: is it appropriate to adopt the Supreme Court's ideology, which is classified, in his view, as "the laws of the [non-Jewish] nations," or to act according to the original Jewish law without deviating from it.

According to Rabbi Sherman, it is precisely the Supreme Court's rationale for the joint property doctrine – namely, that it is a revolutionary step that alters relations within society, and intended to promote and ensure social justice based on gender equality – that justifies rejection of this doctrine by the rabbinical courts, which should rather continue to adhere to the traditional position of Jewish Law. He adds that it is precisely the application of the joint property doctrine, supplemented by the husband's continued exclusive obligation to support his wife and children, which creates inequality and, rather than equalizing the parties' status, confers a preferred status on the wife.

APPLICATION OF JOINT PROPERTY PRESUMPTION TO "COMMON LAW" SPOUSES. Another question that the Israeli legislature and case law was required to address in this (and other) contexts concerns the phenomenon of couples that were not married in a religious or civil ceremony, but live together as a couple and raise families. In the beginning of the 1980s the Supreme Court decided by majority that the joint property presumption applies to such couples, relying on its conclusion that their way of life attested to their intention to be partners in their property (CA 52/80 *Shahar v. Freedman*, 38 (1) PD 443, *per* justices Barak, Bach). In his dissenting minority opinion, Justice Sheinbaum argued that the joint property presumption should not be extended by way of judicial legislation to include common law spouses. Justice Sheinbaum reasoned that the parties had knowingly and intentionally decided to live as a couple without binding themselves by a ceremony of marriage. As such, in the absence of a formal agreement between them, the application of the joint property presumption would not be consistent with their expectations and anticipations regarding the nature and consequences of their connection, to which they had given expression by their failure to entire into the binding legally recognized marriage. Furthermore, the aforementioned law of 1973 omitted granting any recognition of the "common law spouses" or "common law marriages" and hence there is no justification for applying the presumption by way of judicial legislation.

In later rulings the Supreme Court extended the scope of the joint property presumption as it applied to common law marriage, stating that it was not limited exclusively to their domestic assets, but also covered their commercial assets, although a higher level of proof should be required to persuade the court to apply the joint partnership presumption with respect to commercial assets or other non-domestic assets (CA 4385/91 *Salem v. Carmi*, 51 (1) PD 337).

The Supreme Court further held that where one of the partners in a common law marriage was killed in an accident, the surviving partner should be entitled to the same compensation (as a dependent) awarded by law to a surviving spouse who was legally married to the deceased (CA 2000/97 *Lindorn v. Karnit*, 55 (1) PD 12).

The common law spouse's right to the pension of a government employee, or of a soldier killed in action, was already recognized by Knesset legislation in the early years of the State of Israel.

Conclusion

Israeli law's approach to gender equality is not unique to the question of spousal assets, but rather is broader in its scope. In the early 21st century, the Supreme Court considered equality as one of the constitutive values of Israeli law, and found anchorage for it in the Basic Law: Human Dignity and Freedom (notwithstanding that this subject is not explicitly mentioned in this law; see *Human Dignity and Freedom). In a famous decision concerning the matrimonial property of a couple that immigrated from Iran, President Barak stated that according to the principle of good faith, it is presumed that the couple intended that the infrastructure of their relationship would be based on the basic principles of the legal system of Israel, one of which is the principle of equality. Therefore, by applying the doctrine of joint property, a social goal is accomplished, leading to the promotion of social justice (CFH 1558/94 *Nafisi v. Nafisi*, 50 (3) PD 573, 605.

We have noted the various approaches of the *dayyanim* of the Rabbinical Court of Appeals. It remains to be seen how the rabbinical courts will in fact rule in matters regarding spousal assets. In any event, the rabbinical courts (the regional and the Rabbinical Court of Appeals) decided that where each of the spouses owned an apartment prior to their marriage, there is no presumption of joint property, and they based their judgment on section 5 of the Spouses (Property Relations) Law. When their ruling came before the Supreme Court, President A. Barak did not interfere with their ruling, and rejected the petition against the Rabbinical Court (HC 3995/00 *Anon. v Rabbinical Court of Appeals*, 56 (6) PD p. 883).

BIBLIOGRAPHY: M. Elon, *Jewish Law (Cases and Materials)*, 1999; idem, *"Eleh Hen Imrot Agav…,"* in the *Ariel Rosen Tzvi Memorial Volume* (1998), 361–407; S. Dikhovsky, *"'Hilkhat ha-Shittuf' – ha-Im Dina de-Malkhuta?"* in: *Teḥumin*, 18 (1998); A. Rosen Tzvi, *Yaḥasei Mamon bein Benei Zug* (1982); idem, *"'Medinah Yehudit ve-Demokratit': Abbahut Ruḥanit, Nikkur ve-Simbiozah – Ha-Efshar lerabe'a et ha-Ma'agal?"* in: *Iyyunei Mishpat* (1995), 479; A. Sherman, *"'Hilkhat ha-Shittuf' le-Or Mishpetei ha-Torah,"* in: *Teḥumin*, 18 (1998), 32; idem, *"'Hilkhot ha-Shittuf' Eino Me'uggenet be-Dinei Yisrael,"* in: *Teḥumin*, 19 (1999) 205.

[Moshe Drori (2nd ed.)]

MATSAS, JOSEPH (1918–1986), Greek merchant, partisan, and researcher, the foremost Jewish intellectual in Greece after World War II. Matsas lived most of his life in *Ioannina and devoted himself to his city, to his Jewish community, and to the research of the Jews in Ioannina and Greece.

Coming from a line of merchants, he owned a glass product store in the heart of the Ioannina bazaar, where Ioanniote Jewish merchants had worked and thrived for generations. By the beginning of World War II, he had finished his studies in philosophy at Aristotle University in Thessalonika (Salonika) and was teaching high school in a village near Kilkis. When the ghettoization process started in Salonika in late January–early February 1943, the youth of the Jewish community started to flee in small numbers to the mountains in order to join the partisans. The Jews were welcomed by the military arm ELAS, which belonged to the leftist resistance movement EAM (The National Liberation Front), and Matsas was one of the first to leave to join.

After facing great difficulties in escaping from Salonika, crossing rivers and avoiding German-controlled bridges, he reached the partisans. Since he had been a fighting soldier in the Greek army in the Albanian campaign, he was integrated into ELAS as fighting combatant, together with nine other Jews in a unit of 40 men. At the end of 1943, he went with his unit to Western Macedonia where the allies dropped equipment to them by parachute. In general, his unit lived under difficult circumstances in the mountains of Pieras, Vermious, and Pindou.

After the war Joseph Matsas established himself in Ioannina. In 1945 he was president of the Ioannina Jewish Council and in 1947 Matsas became the secretary of the Jewish community.

Matsas's main scholarly contribution lay in his research on the language, culture, and ancient traditions of the Romaniot Jews of Ioannina. His research into Judeo-Greek was a pioneering and valuable scholarly effort. In Ioannina in 1953 he published *Yianniotika Evraika Tragoudia* ("Greek Jewish Songs"), which consisted of 16 hymns taken from two manuscripts written between 1853 and 1870, translated into modern Greek. In 1955 he also published *Ta Onomata Ton Evraion Sta Ioannina* ("The Names of the Jews of Ioannina").

In the field of poetry he researched Judeo-Greek *kinot* (elegies) from Corfu from as early as the 13th century. He uncovered valuable collections of centuries-old Judeo-Greek **piyyutim* from Ioannina and contributed research and documentation to Jerusalem's *Ben-Zvi Institute on Judeo-Greek poetry and language. He published several articles on the unique festivities of the Sicilian Purim celebrated in Ioannina.

BIBLIOGRAPHY: R. Dalven, *The Jews of Ioannina* (1990); Y. Kerem, *The History of the Jews in Greece, 1821–1940. Part I* (1985); idem, *"Darkhei Hazalah shel Yehudim be-Yavan be-Milhemet ha-Olam ha-Sheniyyah,"* in: *Pe'amim*, No. 27 (1986), 77–105.

[Yitzchak Kerem]

MATSAS, NESTORAS (1932–), Greek author, painter, and motion picture director. Born in Athens, Matsas was in hiding during the Nazi occupation of Greece. During this time he was baptized into the Greek Orthodox Church, but his Jewish background and tragic memories of the war were to find expression in several of his books. When he was only 16 some of his stories appeared in the periodical *Nea Estia*. In 1950 he published three plays: *Animenei* ("Unmarried"), *Fleghomeni batos* ("Burning Bush"), and *Yiom Kipur* ("Yom Kippur"). *Animenei*, written in collaboration with K. Asinakopoulos, was a considerable stage success. His first novel was *Klisti ourani* ("Closed Heavens," 1955), a story of life in the slums of Athens. He also published several volumes of short stories. Two of Matsas' most significant earlier works are on Jewish themes. *I meghali irini* ("The Great Peace," 1957), a collection of three short novels, dealing with an Athens Jewish family, is dedicated to the author's father "who sleeps in the barren earth of Auschwitz." Another novel, *O Messias* ("The Messiah," 1959), describes the tragic fate of a Greek Jew who survives imprisonment in Dachau but who, on his return to Greece, entertains the delusion that he is the Messiah. Other books by Matsas include two children's novels, the prizewinning *Khoris aghapi* ("Without Love," 1960) and *To koritsi me t'asteria* ("The Girl with the Stars," 1968); *To paramithi tou Theofilou* ("The Fairy Tale of Theophilos," 1963), a fictional biography of a Greek painter that was awarded the National Prize for literature; *Plevsate vorios Sporadhon Skyiathos* ("Travel North to the Sporades, Scyathos," 1964), verse written in the style of the Psalms and containing "Letters from Joseph to the sleeping Rebecca"; and *O mikros stratiotis* ("The Little Soldier," 1967), an anti-war novel. Later in his literary career, he returned to chronicling his Holocaust experience in hiding in Athens in his book *I Istoria Ton Hamenon Peristerion: Imerogio Enos Paidou Ston Emfilio* ("The History of the Lost Pigeon: Diary of a Boy in the Civil War," 1995). He also wrote the popular biography of Alexander the Great titled *To Hirografo Tis Babilonas, Megalexandro Apomnimonevmata* (1980), which was translated into French as *Les Memoires D'Alexandre Le Grand, d'apres Le Manuscrit de Babylone* (1983). Matsas wrote the scripts for many documentary films and directed feature films.

[Rachel Dalven / Yitzchak Kerem (2nd ed.)]

MATT, C. DAVID (1887–1951), U.S. rabbi. Born in Kovno, he was raised in Philadelphia where he came with his family in 1890. C. (Calman) David Matt grew up in Rabbi Bernard Levinthal's synagogue; Levinthal's sons Rabbi Israel Levinthal and Judge Louis Levinthal were literally life-long friends and spoke at his funeral. He went to public school, Yeshiva Mishkan Israel, and Gratz College. He earned his B.A. in 1909 at the University of Pennsylvania and was ordained at the Jewish Theological Seminary in 1913.

As a young rabbi he served in Adath Jeshurun in Minneapolis, the first English-speaking rabbi the then 18-year-old Orthodox congregation ever had, and oversaw the transition toward a newly emerging Conservative Judaism. He laid plans for a new building and organized the religious school. He was the associate editor of the *American Jewish World.* During World War I, he served as a volunteer representative of the Jewish Welfare Board at Fort Snelling. After 15 years he left for Beth David in Buffalo (1927–29), where he served two years, and then went back to Philadelphia, where he served as rabbi of the West Philadelphia Jewish Community Center. He remained there for the rest of his life. Matt was an ardent Zionist and served as president of the Philadelphia Board of Rabbis and of the local Rabbinical Assembly.

Matt's columns appeared in the *American Jewish World* and the *Anglo-Jewish Press.* His work also included texts of radio sermons, 1920s–1950. He worked as an arbitrator in the Jewish community in Philadelphia, particularly during a dispute among *mohelim.* Also of note is his list of yeshivot in Europe and Palestine in the 1930s, with estimates of the sizes of their student bodies. These reflect Rabbi Matt's efforts to raise money for the yeshivot. He had, in the words of Israel Levinthal, "a poetic soul, which made him a dreamer and interpreter of Israel's fondest hopes in beautiful verse." Louis Levinthal spoke of his "simplicity, his earnestness and sincerity."

He made his mark as a poet and published his sermons. Among his five children were Rabbi Herschel Matt, himself a sensitive poet and liturgist. His grandson Daniel Matt is translating the Zohar into English in a multi-year project that has gained wide respect. C. David Matt's papers are found at the Jewish Theological Seminary.

BIBLIOGRAPHY: P.S. Nadell, *Conservative Judaism in America: A Biographical Dictionary and Sourcebook* (1988); C. David Matt, *Collected Poems* (1953).

[Michael Berenbaum (2nd ed.)]

MATTATHIAS, priest from the village of Modi'in, and first leader of the uprising of the *Hasmoneans against *Antiochus IV Epiphanes (167 B.C.E.). A number of discrepancies appear regarding the genealogy of Mattathias, and it is not certain that he was a native of Modi'in. According to I Maccabees 2:1 Mattathias was "the son of Johanan, son of Simeon, a priest of the family of Joarib" (יְהוֹיָרִיב; cf. I Chron. 24:7) who "moved away from Jerusalem and settled in Modi'in." Josephus twice alludes to Mattathias' background. In Antiquities 12:265 he is described as "living in Modi'in in Judea… the son of Johanan, the son of Simeon, the son of Asamonaius, a priest of the family of Joarib, and a native of Jerusalem." In Wars 1:36 Mattathias is called simply "son of Asamonaius, a priest of a village called Modi'in." It appears that the name "Asamonaius" or "Hasmonean" is a family title, although later rabbinic tradition regards "Hasmonai" as a particular person e.g. "…'neither did I abhor them' [Lev. 26:44] – in the days of the Greeks, when I raised up for them Simeon the Righteous and Hasmonai and his sons, and Mattathias the high priest" (Meg. 11a; some variants however omit "Hasmonai and his sons"). The anachronistic description of Mattathias as high priest is also found in tractate *Soferim* (20:6, ed. M. Higger (1937), 346), and was inserted into the special prayer recited on Ḥanukkah.

Although a number of minor differences exist, the general descriptions of Mattathias' activities, transmitted by Josephus and in I Maccabees are fairly similar. A company of Greek officers arrived at Modi'in with the intention of forcibly implementing the king's ordinances regarding sacrifices to idols. As Mattathias was held in high esteem by the villagers, he was ordered to begin the sacrificial offerings. When Mattathias refused, another Jew proceeded to fulfill the officer's command. Mattathias then attacked and killed both that Jew and the Greek officer at hand (named Appeles in Jos., Ant.; Bacchides in Jos., Wars), and together with his sons and a number of similarly minded fellow countrymen sought refuge in the desert and mountains of Judea. One such group of fugitives was attacked on the Sabbath. Refusing to defend themselves on the day of rest, the group, numbering about 1,000, was almost totally annihilated. This led Mattathias to decree that defensive military action is permissible on the Sabbath (cf. M.D. Herr, in: *Tarbiz*, 30 (1961), 243–4). Both I Maccabees and Josephus further attribute to Mattathias the circumcision of all those uncircumcised children brought up under the influence of enforced Hellenization. Mattathias led the rebellion for only one year, and before his death appointed two of his five sons to continue as leaders of the revolt: *Judah Maccabee was declared military commander and Simeon the *Hasmonean counselor. Of Mattathias' other three sons, *Johanan b. Mattathias and *Eleazar b. Mattathias both met violent deaths during the early years of the uprising while *Jonathan, who succeeded Judah, was killed by treachery in 161 B.C.E.

BIBLIOGRAPHY: A. Buechler, in: REJ, 34 (1897), 69–76; B. Niese, *Kritik der beiden Makkabaeerbuecher* (1900), 44–47; E. Bickerman, *From Ezra to the Last of the Maccabees* (1962), 96ff.; Schuerer, Hist, 29–30; Klausner, Bayit Sheni, 3 (1950^2), 13–19; W.R. Farmer, *Maccabees, Zealots and Josephus* (1956), index.

[Isaiah Gafni]

MATTATHIAS (or **Mattityah ben Moshe**?; 15th century), Spanish or Provençal Hebrew poet. Mattathias has sometimes been identified with *Mattathias ha-Yiẓhari, one of the masters who represented the Jewish communities of Aragon at the Tortosa disputation (1413–14) and the author of a commentary on Psalm 119 with references to the disputation, a commentary to *Pirkei Avot* (preserved only in part), and a lost homiletical commentary to the Pentateuch. This identification is not accepted by all scholars. Z. Malachi has even shown that it is very unlikely.

The **maqāma Aḥituv ve-Ẓalmon*, attributed to Mattathias and written before 1453, was inspired by the religious *disputations held in Spain. Its action is simple. The pagan queen of a legendary island sends three messengers, Zalmon, Eker, and Ahitub, to inquire into the religions of the world. Seven years later, the messengers return and engage in a stormy discussion. Zalmon, who was in Hebron and became converted to Islam, accepts the arguments of Ahitub, himself converted to Judaism in Spain, and becomes a Jew. Eker, converted to Christianity in Constantinople, argues in favor of that religion; however, since the queen and her court, persuaded by Ahitub, have also adopted Judaism, Eker hangs himself in anger, bringing the story to an end. Most of this narrative is still in manuscript.

Another allegoric *maqāma, Begidat ha-Zeman*, in which the characters receive symbolic names, that was likewise written around 1450, also bears the name of a poet known as Mattathias; it is almost certain that both *maqāmāt* were written by the same author. Both narratives, with clear pedagogic, apologetic, and moral purpose, resemble each other in style and vocabulary. The second is written in the first person and the personal element is important. The author repents the sins of his youth, describing his experiences so that his tale might serve as a warning. It was printed in 1560 (Tihingen) and three more times before the end of the 17th century. Z. Malachi has found in this composition some autobiographical clues: according to him, the book was written in 1450 in Aix-en-Provence, when the author was 50 years old; he was probably born in Spain and left for France at the age of 19, becoming familiar with Ashkenazi culture.

BIBLIOGRAPHY: Schirmann, Sefarad, 2 (1956), 648–62; Assaf, in: *Ba-Mishor*, 7 no. 286 (1946), 8; Zunz, Gesch, 129; Renan, Ecrivains, 432–3; Gross, Gal Jud, 256–7; Davidson, Oẓar, 4 (1933), 451. **ADD. BIBLIOGRAPHY:** Y. Baer, *A History of the Jews in Christian Spain* (1966), 173ff.; M.A. Shmidman, in: I. Twersky (ed.), *Studies in Medieval Jewish History and Literature* (1979), 315ff.; Schirmann-Fleischer, *The History of Hebrew Poetry in Christian Spain and Southern France* (Hebrew, 1997), 657–68; Z. Malachi, in: R. Nettler (ed.), *Medieval and Modern Perspectives on Muslim-Jewish Relations* (1995), 129; idem, in: *Jewish Studies at the Turn of the Twentieth Century*, 1 (1999), 454–58.

[Yonah David / Angel Sáenz-Badillos (2nd ed.)]

MATTATHIAS BEN SIMEON, son of *Simeon the Hasmonean. During the winter of 135 B.C.E., Mattathias, together with his mother and brother Judah, was seized at a banquet given in Simeon's honor by his son-in-law *Ptolemy, who was governor of Jericho. Simeon was killed, probably at the instigation of the Syrian monarch Antiochus VII Sidetes, but a third son of the high priest, John *Hyrcanus, managed to escape. Ptolemy withdrew to the nearby fortress of Dok, where the two brothers and their mother were tortured in full view of the grief-stricken Hyrcanus, who was unable to take the stronghold. When the sabbatical year came around, it was impossible to maintain an army for any great length of time, and Hyrcanus was forced to withdraw. Ptolemy thereupon killed the woman and her two sons and fled to Philadelphia (but according to Maccabees they were slain together with their father; I Macc. 16:15ff.; Jos., Wars, 1:54ff.; Jos., Ant., 13:228ff.).

BIBLIOGRAPHY: Schuerer, Hist, 66; Graetz, Hist, 1 (1891), 530.

[Isaiah Gafni]

MATTATHIAS HA-YIẒHARI (14th–15th century), Spanish scholar. He was a descendant of a Narbonne family which immigrated to Aragon after the expulsion from France in 1306. Mattathias, who had a profound knowledge of philosophy, was apparently a pupil of Ḥasdai *Crescas. A commentary on Psalm 119 is attributed to him (Venice, 1546, partly translated into Latin by Philippe d'Aquin, Paris, 1629). Mattathias also wrote a number of other works, including a commentary on *Avot* (extant in Ms.) and homiletical explanations to the Pentateuch, known only by later references. It is possible, however, that at least some of them were written by an earlier Mattathias ha-Yiẓhari, perhaps his grandfather. He played a prominent but not overly courageous part in the Disputation of *Tortosa (1413–14), where he was one of the representatives of the Saragossa community.

BIBLIOGRAPHY: Baer, Spain, index; Renan, Ecrivains, 432f.; S. Buber, *Midrash Tehillim* (1891), introd.; A. Pacios López, *Disputa de Tortosa* (1957), index.

MATTERSDORF (official name since 1924, **Mattersburg**; Hung. **Nagymarton**), town in *Burgenland, Austria; one of the "Seven Communities," and after 1813 one of the "Five Communities." The town was traditionally divided into two districts, Izraelita-Nagymarton and Keresztény ["Christian"]-Nagymarton. The Jewish neighborhood comprised a separate administrative unit (see **Politische Gemeinden*) until 1902. Jews are traditionally believed to have settled there in about 800 or 1222. A tablet on the synagogue wall dates its building to 1354. At any rate, Jews were already living there before the Turkish conquest in 1526, when Mattersdorf absorbed numerous refugees from *Sopron. In 1569 there were 67 Jews living in 11 houses. After 1622 the community came under the protection of the Esterházy family. In 1694 the Esterházys granted the Seven Communities letters of protection, subsequently renewed four times and newly formulated in 1800. Some of the Jews were expelled by Leopold I in 1671 but were allowed to return in 1675. The community was looted several times by the Turks. In 1744, some 352 Jews inhabited 30 houses; in 1770, 179 Jewish families were registered; in 1785, some 767 persons lived in 43 houses; permission was granted to build 12 more houses in 1818. They paid fees to the towns of Sopron and Wiener *Neustadt for the right to trade within their boundaries. In 1848 there were 1,500 Jews in the town (one-third of the total population). From the beginning of the 20th century their numbers declined due to emigration to larger towns; in 1902 they had fallen to 752 and at the time of the *Anschluss* (1938) to 511.

The centuries-long autonomy gave rise to a powerful communal regime, which regulated not only religious but also economic and social life. Among the prominent rabbis who served the community were Gershon b. Abraham *Chajes; Jeremiah *Mattersdorf; Issachar Baer b. Samson *Bloch; Moses *Sofer; and Simon *Sofer. The Mattersdorf yeshivah attracted students from all over Europe. In 1938 the Nazis destroyed the synagogue and other communal institutions and damaged the Jewish quarter. Part of the community emigrated and the remainder were deported to the death camps. The remains of the Jewish quarter were demolished during development projects, and by 1970 only an old cemetery was left to commemorate this ancient community. About 7,000 documents from the community's archives have been preserved in the central state archives in Eisenstadt. A Kiryat Mattersdorf was founded in Jerusalem in 1963, and some of its inhabitants originated from there.

BIBLIOGRAPHY: MHJ, 1–12 (1903–69), indexes; F.P. Hodik, in: M. Gold (ed.), *Gedenkbuch der untergegangenen Judengemeinden des Burgenlandes* (1970); 91–115; J.J.(L.) Greenwald (Grunwald), *Mazzevet Kodesh* (1952); M. Pollák, in: IMIT (1900), 164–6.

[Yehouda Marton]

MATTERSDORF, JEREMIAH BEN ISAAC (d. 1805), Hungarian rabbi and author. Born in Oswiecim, Galicia, Mattersdorf originally had the family name of Rosenbaum, but took the name Mattersdorf after serving as rabbi of the community of that name in Burgenland. He was appointed rabbi of Mattersdorf (now Mattersburg) around 1770 and stayed there until about 1801, when he went to Abaujszanto, remaining there until his death. Mattersdorf was renowned for his extensive knowledge of *halakhah*. His spiritual authority extended beyond the borders of Hungary. In 1791 he gave his approbation to the edition of the Talmud published by Joseph Hraschanszky, who called him one of the most distinguished rabbis of the generation. In Mattersdorf he headed a yeshivah which had among its students Aaron *Chorin, the pioneer of religious reform in Hungary. Among Mattersdorf's works is a commentary to Ḥayyim Shabbetai's *Moda'a ve-Ones* (Lemberg, 1798) under the title *Moda'ah Rabbah*, published along with his son Joab Mattersdorf's commentary *Moda'ah Zuta*. He gave approbations to a number of works, and is mentioned in the responsa of Moses *Sofer. L. Loew states that he wrote the comments on the *Sha'arei Shibbolet* of Isaac b. Reuben, but this work has been attributed to other authors.

BIBLIOGRAPHY: L. Loew, *Gesammelte Schriften*, 2 (1890), 257; M. Pollák, in: IMIT, (1900), 164–6; J.J.(L.) Greenwald (Grunwald), *Ha-Yehudim be-Hungaryah* (1913), 53f.; P.Z. Schwartz, *Shem ha-Gedolim me-Ereẓ Hagar*, 1 (1913), 51b no. 243.

[Yehouda Marton]

MATTHAU, WALTER (1920–2000), U.S. actor. Born in New York to Russian immigrant parents, Matthau started out selling soft drinks and playing bit parts at a Yiddish theater at age 11. After graduating from Seward Park High School, he worked as a forester, gym instructor, and boxing coach for police officers. During World War II he served on an Army Air Force bomber in Europe and returned home a sergeant with six battle stars. Afterwards he attended acting classes and performed on Broadway. Matthau appeared in more than a dozen Broadway plays, among them *Anne of the Thousand Days* (1949), *Will Success Spoil Rock Hunter* (1955), *Once More, with Feeling* (nominated for a Best Actor Tony, 1959), *A Shot in the Dark* (won a Tony Award for Best Supporting Actor, 1962), and *The Odd Couple* (Best Actor Tony, 1965).

Matthau made his film debut in *The Kentuckian* in 1955 and from then acted in more than 40 films, including *Gangster Story* (1960), *Lonely Are the Brave* (1962), *Charade* (1963), *Fail-Safe* (1964), *Goodbye, Charlie* (1964), *Mirage* (1967), *Hello Dolly!* (1969), *Cactus Flower* (1971), *A New Leaf* (1972), *Plaza Suite* (1972), *Charley Varrick* (1973), *Pete 'n Tillie* (1974), *The Laughing Policeman* (1974), *The Taking of Pelham One Two Three* (1974), *Earthquake* (1974), *The Bad News Bears* (1976), *House Calls* (1978), *Hopscotch* (1980), *California Suite* (1980), *Little Miss Marker* (1981), *Pirates* (1986), *JFK* (1991), *Dennis the Menace* (1993), *I.Q.* (1994, as Albert Einstein), *I'm Not Rapaport* (1996), and *Hanging Up* (2000).

In 1966 Matthau won an Oscar as Best Supporting Actor for his role as "Whiplash Willie" Gingrich in *The Fortune Cookie*, co-starring with Jack Lemmon with whom he appeared in a number of films, including *The Odd Couple* (1968), *The Front Page* (1974), *Buddy, Buddy* (1981), *Grumpy Old Men* (1993), *Grumpier Old Men* (1995), and *The Odd Couple II* (1998). Matthau was nominated twice for Best Actor Oscars, for his roles in *Kotch* (1971) and *The Sunshine Boys* (1975).

Matthau appeared in several TV movies, such as *Awake and Sing!* (1972), *The Incident* (1990), *Mrs. Lambert Remembers Love* (1991), *Incident in a Small Town* (1994), and *The Marriage Fool* (1998).

BIBLIOGRAPHY: R. Edelman and A. Kupferberg, *Matthau: A Life* (2002); C. Matthau, *Among the Porcupines: A Memoir* (1992); A. Hunter, *Walter Matthau* (1984).

[Jonathan Licht / Ruth Beloff (2nd ed.)]

MATTHIAS BEN THEOPHILUS, the name of two high priests at the close of the Second Temple period.

Matthias ben Theophilus I (early first century C.E.)

MATTHIAS BEN THEOPHILUS I was for all practical purposes the first high priest originating from Ereẓ Israel to be appointed by Herod after *Aristobulus III. He succeeded *Simeon b. Boethus, the king's father-in-law, and preceded Joezer b. Boethus (see *Boethusians). Josephus notes that Matthias was a Jerusalemite (Ant., 17:78). He also relates that on one occasion Matthias was prevented from officiating on the Day of Atonement through being ritually unclean, and *Joseph b. Elem had to officiate in his place (*ibid.*, 165). This incident is also recorded in the Talmud (Yoma 12b; TJ, *ibid.*, 1:1, 38d). Herod, although on his deathbed, replaced Matthias as he held him partially responsible for the disorders in the Temple caused by the two patriots, Judas b. Sepphoraeus and Matthias b. Margalus. It would appear that Matthias was connected in some way with the house of *Anan and presumably it was no coincidence that one of Anan's sons was named Matthias (Jos., Ant., 19:316, 342) and another *Theophilus (*ibid.*, 18:123; 19:297). It is possible that the elder Anan married the daughter of Matthias.

Matthias ben Theophilus II (late first century C.E.)

MATTHIAS BEN THEOPHILUS II was appointed high priest by Agrippa II in succession to *Joshua b. Gamala (*ibid.*, 20:223). It seems probable that he was the son of Theophilus b. Anan. His period of office witnessed the outbreak of the Jewish War (66 C.E.).

BIBLIOGRAPHY: MATTHIAS BEN THEOPHILUS I: Derenbourg, Hist, 160; Schuerer, Gesch, 2 (1907⁴), 270 no. 5; Klausner, Bayit Sheni, 4 (1950²), 163, 165; A. Schalit, *Koenig Herodes* (1969), 635, 638. MATTHIAS BEN THEOPHILUS II: Graetz, Hist, 2 (1893), 249ff., 752ff.; Schuerer, Gesch, 2 (1907⁴), 273, no. 27; Klausner, Bayit Sheni, 5 (1951²), 24, 235.

[Menahem Stern]

MATTIAH (Mattityahu) BEN ḤERESH (second century C.E.), *tanna*, mentioned twice in the Mishnah (Yom. 8:6, Avot 4:15), and a few times in the tannaitic midrashim. One tannaitic midrash lists Mattiah among a group of scholars who fled Ereẓ Israel (apparently after the fall of *Betar), who, as they were leaving, were overcome with the love of Ereẓ Israel, tore their clothes, and proclaimed, tears streaming from their eyes, that one who dwells in Ereẓ Israel is as if he has fulfilled all the commandments of the Torah (Sif. Deut. 80). Another tannaitic midrash (Mekh. of R. Ishmael, Baḥodesh 7) relates that Mattiah once went to visit R. Eleazar Hakappar in Lydda to inquire about one of R. Ishmael's teachings. According to the Babylonian Talmud (Sanh. 32b) Mattiah founded a yeshivah in Rome, and, according to the Talmud, when *Simeon b. Yoḥai visited Rome to protest to the emperor against the Palestinian governor's emergency decrees, Mattiah consulted him on points of *halakhah* and *aggadah* (Me'il. 17a; Yoma 53b).

In Mishnah Yoma (8:6) Mattiah applies the principle that Sabbath prohibitions may be overruled in order to save human life to a specific case, but he is not accredited as the author of the principle itself (cf. Tosef. Shab. 15:17, Yoma 85b). He is quoted in both the Babylonian and Jerusalem Talmuds (e.g., Yev. 61b; TJ, Sanh. 10:1, 27c). His most famous maxim is: "Be a tail to lions, and not a head to foxes" (Avot 4:15; in TJ, Sanh. 4:10, 22b), which stands in contrast to the Roman proverb, "Be a head to foxes, rather than a tail to lions" (cf. Zohar Ḥadash, Song, 18b). In the later *aggadah* Mattiah's piety became legendary. The *Tanḥuma* relates that on one occasion, he deliberately blinded himself rather than be seduced by Satan (who appeared to him in the guise of a beautiful woman). He only accepted healing at the hands of the angel Raphael, after a divine promise that he would not be tempted again (Yal., Gen. 161).

BIBLIOGRAPHY: Hyman, Toledot, 913–5, s.v.; Bacher, Tann, 1 (1903²), 380–4.

[Stephen G. Wald (2nd ed.)]

MATTNAH (second half of third century C.E.), Babylonian *amora*. He studied under *Samuel (Mar Samuel) and was considered one of his outstanding pupils (Er. 6b; Mak. 3b). He quotes numerous halakhic decisions in his name (Ket. 43b; Nid. 27a; et al.) He also studied under *Rav (Shab. 24a). He was a younger colleague of Judah b. Ezekiel (Kid. 70b), and when, after the death of Rav and Samuel, R. Judah taught at Pumbedita, Mattnah taught at the neighboring town of Popuna (Ḥul. 139b). He is one of the authors of the tradition that the fourth blessing of the Grace after Meals ("He who is good, and bestows good") was instituted by the rabbis after permission was granted to bury the slain of *Bethar, whose bodies had miraculously not decomposed (Ber. 48b). Matthah had three sons, Aḥadboi, Tobi, and Ḥiyya (Nid. 60b; BB 151a), all of whom were scholars. Among the sages of the next generation who were his pupils and who quote decisions in his name was R. Zeira (Ber. 36a). Another *amora* called Mattnai lived in the fourth century. He was a pupil of Ḥisda (Kid. 32a), and a colleague of Abbaye (Ket. 35b).

BIBLIOGRAPHY: Hyman, Toledot, 915–7.

MATTUCK, ISRAEL I. (1884–1954), Liberal rabbi. Born in Lithuania, he came as a child to the United States with his family and grew up in Worcester, Massachusetts. A graduate of Harvard University, he was ordained at the Hebrew Union College in 1910 having only spent two years in residence. He held a pulpit in Far Rockaway, New York, for a year and then went to England to serve a young congregation, the Liberal Synagogue in London. He served as senior minister for 36 years and then after 1947 was minister emeritus. Under his leadership the synagogue grew into one of the largest synagogues in London. The building that he helped build was bombed in World War II, but Mattuck lived to see it restored and rededicated. He was succeeded by his disciple and son-in-law Rabbi Leslie Edgar.

He was a leading figure, perhaps the leading figure in English Liberal Jewry, its philosopher and its public face. He was known as one of the "Three Ms": Montagu, Montefiore, and Mattuck. He helped form the Union of Liberal and Progressive Synagogues and helped establish the World Union for Progressive Judaism in 1926 and served as its first chairman from 1926 until his death. He was chairman of the Society of Jews and Christians. He compiled and edited the Liberal prayer book, first in three volumes in 1923–26 and in a revised edition in 1937.

He is the author of several books: *What Are the Jews* (1939); *The Essentials of Liberal Judaism* (1947); *Jewish Ethics* (1953); and *The Thought of the Prophets* (1953). His last two works were written after a long illness that afflicted his body, but left his mind as clear and lucid as ever.

He also edited *Aspects of Progressive Jewish Thought* (1955), which was dedicated in honor of Leo Baeck's 80th birthday. It was published posthumously.

BIBLIOGRAPHY: S. Blank, "Israel I. Mattuck," in: *Proceedings of the Central Conference of American Rabbis*, 64:159–60.

[Michael Berenbaum (2nd ed.)]

MA'TUK, SULAYMAN BEN DAVID (18th century), *paytan* and astronomer who lived in Baghdad. Ma'tuk was a descendant of R. Ma'tuk, the *nasi* of the Jewish community of 'Ana. The latter fled to Baghdad with his family in the first quarter of the 17th century, under the threats of the tyrannical governor who had persecuted the community. Of Sulayman's *piyyutim*, 16 are known, and about half of them were included in books published in Baghdad and India; they are still familiar to Iraqi Jews. During the lifetime of his grandson R. Judah b. Jacob, the family name was changed to Yehuda. The family's descendants include two modern scholars, the brothers R. Isaac Yahuda and Prof. Abraham Shalom *Yahuda.

BIBLIOGRAPHY: A. Ben-Jacob, *Yehudei Bavel* (1965), 95.

[Abraham Ben-Yaacob]

MATZ, ISRAEL (1869–1950), U.S. manufacturer, philanthropist, and patron of Hebrew literature and scholarship. Matz, who was born in Kalvarija, Russian Poland, immigrated to America in 1890. He became an accountant, later entering the drug business. In 1906 he founded the Ex-Lax Company and served as its president. Long an admirer of Hebrew authors, Matz aided Eliezer *Ben-Yehuda in the publication of his Hebrew-language thesaurus. From 1922 to 1925 he was publisher of the Hebrew monthly *Ha-Toren*, edited by Reuben *Brainin. Matz was also a founding patron and honorary chairman of the Hebrew monthly *Bitzaron*. He established the Israel Matz Foundation in 1925 for the support of Hebrew authors. A pioneer Zionist, in 1928 he founded a company in Palestine called Gan Ḥayyim for the development of an orange plantation. Matz also contributed to various schools of higher learning.

BIBLIOGRAPHY: Orlans, in: *Hadoar*, 30 (1950), 396–7.

[Jacob Kabakoff]

MATZAH (*mazzah*; **matzo**; Heb. מַצָּה), unleavened bread made from one of five species of grain – wheat, barley, spelt, rye, and oats – mentioned in the Torah, and the only bread which is permitted for use during *Passover. *Matzah* (pl. *matzot*) is the object of a specific commandment calling for *matzah* to be eaten on Passover because the children of Israel "baked the *matzot* of the dough which they had brought forth out of Egypt, for it was not leavened; because they were thrust out of Egypt and could not tarry" (Ex. 12:39) – the speed with which *matzot* are prepared identifies it with the bread made in the Bible, when there was no time to prepare ordinary bread (cf. Gen. 18:6; 19:3). To fulfill the biblical precept on the first night of Passover, the *matzah* must be made from "guarded" grain, and must be processed with the intent – *kavvanah* – of fulfilling the commandment. Only grains capable of fermentation are valid for the manufacture of *matzah*, and such grains are therefore limited to the five species. In practice, however, only wheat has been used historically.

Ashkenazi *matzah* is a hard thin wafer, while Sephardim make softer, thicker *matzot* by using a much more watered batter. This soft *matzah* does not have a long shelf life, which necessitates baking and freezing it shortly before Passover, and indeed, before the advent of freezers, Sephardim baked *matzah* daily during the holiday.

Matzah is referred to as *leḥem oni*, "the bread of affliction" (Deut. 16:3). On this basis the *Karaites, who interpreted the Bible literally, make *matzah* only from barley, which was used to make the poor man's bread. The same phrase is used in the talmudic discussion of whether *matzah* made from flour mixed with wine, oil, honey, or eggs instead of water may be used on Passover. Although it is not regarded as fermenting if there is no admixture of water, *matzah* made from any such ingredient is forbidden on the first night since it constitutes "*matzah ashirah*," the "*matzah* of opulence," in contrast to the "bread of affliction" (Pes. 36a). Generally, *matzah ashirah* was permitted only for the sick or the aged (OḤ 462). Rashi, and subsequent Ashkenazi decisors (*posekim*), give credence to the concern that liquids other than water increase the rate of fermentation, and therefore prohibit healthy people from using egg *matzah*, i.e., *matzah ashirah*, for all of Passover. In recent years, people with celiac – an intestinal disorder with a dangerous reaction to the gluten in wheat – have been able to fulfill the *mitzvah* with oat *matzah* made from a specific non-gluten strain of oats. Spelt *matzah* is also commercially available for people with medical needs.

The Duty of Eating *Matzah*

Whereas the prohibition against eating *ḥamez* or having it in one's possession applies to the whole of Passover, the positive commandment of eating *matzah* generally applies only to the first night (in the Diaspora the first two nights). According to R. *Elijah of Vilna, one fulfills a commandment to eat *matzah* on the other days of Passover as well. In Temple times, this duty was based on the verse "with *matzah* and bitter herbs shall they eat it," i.e., the Paschal lamb, and is also based on the verse "In the evening ye shall eat *matzot*" (Ex. 12:18). In many circles, only "*matzah mitzvah*," i.e., *matzot* baked on Passover eve, is used at the *seder*. This is reminiscent of the Passover sacrifice, which in Temple times was offered on Passover eve and eaten at the *seder*. There is also the widespread custom of eating only "*matzah shemurah*" on the night of the *seder*, although some, as a special act of piety, eat it throughout the festival.

One must abstain from eating *matzah* on the eve of Passover beginning with sunrise on the 14th of Nisan, but a longtime ḥasidic custom was also adopted to abstain beginning at Purim a month before, while others refrain for two weeks starting with Rosh Ḥodesh Nisan.

The Flour

The manifold precautions which must be taken at the various stages of the *matzah*'s production are designed to prevent any fermentation whatsoever of the flour. The flour suitable for the baking of *matzah* can be divided into three categories of decreasing stringency:

(1) "guarded flour," which is closely supervised from the time the wheat is harvested and is used for the preparation of *matzah shemurah*;

(2) "Passover flour," where supervision to prevent fermentation begins with the milling of the wheat;

(3) "ordinary flour," which does not have supervision until the point of being mixed and is used to make "ordinary," or machine, *matzah*.

The Preparation

Under normal conditions of climate and temperature, flour mixed with water begins to ferment in approximately 18 minutes. Should the water be above room temperature, however, the process is accelerated, but it can be delayed by the continual manipulation of the dough. In order to prevent water from becoming too warm, only "*mayim she-lanu*" – "water which has rested" (Pes. 42a) – i.e., water which has been left in a vessel overnight to reach room temperature – is used in the baking of *matzah*, and thereafter the mixture of flour and water is constantly manipulated until it is ready for baking. Care must be taken that the whole process from kneading to final baking does not exceed the 18 minutes. No ingredients other than flour and water are permitted for Passover *matzah*. Although it is accepted by most decisors that salt is not a fermenting agent, its use in *matzot* is forbidden in order to prevent fermentation (Sh. Ar., OḤ 455:5). Some Yemenites, however, do have the custom of baking their Passover *matzah* using salt.

Over decades, special equipment was developed for the baking of hand-made *matzah*, which can be found almost universally throughout the Jewish world. Immediately after the flour is first mixed with water, the relatively dry batter is kneaded using a specially designed smasher, in which the batter is placed on a flat surface and a hinged bar is used to pummel the dough. The dough is then flattened by using rollers made only of solid pieces of wood or metal without crevices, to prevent the possibility of pieces of dough getting wedged and becoming *ḥameẓ*. Perforation of the dough, after being rolled into shape and before baking, enables air bubbles to escape, and prevents the dough from rising and swelling during baking. The holes are made by rolling a small wheel with sharp teeth attached to a handle, known as a "reddler," back and forth across the dough.

Machine-made *Matzah*

The industrial revolution combined with a growing urban population across Europe resulted in the amounts of traditional hand-made *matzah* produced being insufficient to provide enough *matzot* for everyone in need. The result was the introduction in 1838 of the first primitive machine that rolled *matzah*. Twenty years later, a bitter halakhic debate ensued over its permissibility, owing to the fear that the machine process might cause fermentation, and also whether a machine was able to fulfill the requirement of *matzah* being made with the proper intent. The dispute continued for more than half a century, until the machines improved technically and the rabbinic authorities began to accept those superior machines. Today the tons of world *matzah* – over $100 million in sales – are produced primarily by two major companies in the U.S.: Manischewitz, which built the first *matzah* factory in the United States, and Streit's, as well as a dozen factories in Israel.

A major shortage of *matzah* for the Jews of Russia occurred in 1917 with the collapse of czarist rule and the takeover by the Communists, and again beginning in 1929, with the collectivization of farms by Stalin. The crisis became so severe that world Jewry was called upon to help provide the Passover needs of the Jews of Russia. During the two world wars, the widespread mobilization of Jewish soldiers created an additional need for *matzah* distribution never before experienced in modern Jewish history. Organizations such as the American Jewish Joint Distribution Committee and the Jewish Welfare Board provided *matzot* for them and for needy Jews around the globe.

BIBLIOGRAPHY: S. Zevin, *Ha-Mo'adim ba-Halakhah* (1959), 241–45; A. Greenspan and A. Zivotofsky, in: *Jewish Observer*, 37:4 (2004), 20–21; P. Goodman, *Passover Anthology* (1961), 176–79, 432–37.

[Ari Greenspan, Ari Z. Zivotofsky, and Elli Wohlgelernter (2nd ed.)]

MATZENAUER, MARGARETE (1881–1963), contralto, later soprano, singer. Born in Temesvár (then Hungary), Matzenauer grew up in musical surroundings and began to study singing at an early age, first in Graz and later in Berlin. Her operatic debut was in Strasbourg (1901) and she remained there for three years; she then sang contralto roles at the Munich Court Opera, specializing in Wagnerian roles and also appearing at Bayreuth. From 1911 to 1930 she was a leading singer; both in soprano and contralto ranges, although after 1914 she called herself a soprano. Matzenauer was most famed for the grandeur and richness of her Wagnerian tones, but she also sang in other operas, notably by Verdi, Strauss, and Janacek. After her Carnegie Hall farewell in 1938, she retired to California, where she lived until her death.

[Max Loppert (2nd ed.)]

MAURITIUS, island in the Indian Ocean about 500 mi. E. of Madagascar, where Jewish refugees from Central Europe – passengers of the *Atlantic* – were put into detention during World War II after being forcibly deported from Palestine by the British as "illegal" immigrants (see *Patria). On their arrival in Mauritius (Dec. 26, 1940), they numbered 1,580 persons: 1,320 landed in Haifa on Aug. 26, 1945, after the ban on their return was rescinded; 128 died while in Mauritius; 212 men joined the Allied forces, 56 of whom entered the *Jewish Brigade. About 60 children were born after the original strict regulation on separation of the sexes in the camp was abolished. The detainees consisted of a Maccabi-He-Ḥalutz transport from Czechoslovakia, remnants of the Jewish community of Danzig, and a transport launched from Vienna. They were interned in the town of Beau Bassin, the men in a former prison, the women in adjacent huts of corrugated iron. They were not brutally treated, but were afflicted by tropical diseases, such as malaria, and by a lack of suitable clothing; food was often inadequate. Considerable moral and material assistance was given by Jewish organizations, particularly the South African Jewish Board of Deputies, the South African Zionist Federation, and the Jewish Agency. The detainees conducted manifold communal and cultural activities; they struggled for release and retransfer to Palestine through the

Zionist Association of Mauritius, to which about 70% of the detainees belonged. Their struggle was supported by official Jewish institutions which regarded the "Exile in Mauritius" as a political challenge and an infliction of needless suffering upon refugees from the Holocaust through the implementation of the anti-Jewish Palestine White Paper of May 1939. The ultimate liberation of the detainees was hailed as a moral and political success for the Zionist movement.

[Aharon Zwergbaum]

In 1946 the St. Martins Jewish Cemetery, where Jewish detainees who died on the island during the war are buried, was entrusted to the South African Jewish Board of Deputies. Since that date the SAJBD, in cooperation with local benefactors (both Jewish and non-Jewish) and in recent years in partnership with the African Jewish Congress, has overseen its maintenance, including an extensive restoration project in 2001. Towards the end of the 20th century, a steady trickle of Jews began settling in Mauritius. In 2004, there were an estimated 60 Jews living permanently there. These were primarily engaged in tourism (three leading hotels were under Jewish management), agriculture, and the diamond and burgeoning textile industries. Plans were afoot for the opening of a Jewish community center, incorporating a synagogue, in the first half of 2005.

[David Saks (2nd ed.)]

Relations with Israel

In 1960, while Mauritius was still a British colony, Israel, represented by a consul general, extended it technical aid particularly through scholarships for young Mauritians to study medicine in Jerusalem and technical assistance on the spot. Mauritius became independent in 1968 and joined the United Nations. An Israel delegation attended the celebration, and full diplomatic relations were established between the two countries, Israel's ambassador in Tananarive (Malagasy) serving as non-resident ambassador to Mauritius. Offers for new scholarships in Israel, as well as Israel assistance by experts in agriculture and other fields, were accepted by Mauritius. Mauritian professionals trained in Israel founded a Mauritius-Israel Friendship Society. Strong Indian influence in Mauritius, as well as Muslims of Pakistani origin who constitute 20% of its population, make themselves felt in Mauritius' attitude and policy toward Israel. The general attitude to Israel, however, is basically friendly, with the elder generation still remembering with sympathy the Jewish refugees from Europe exiled there in 1940, and the mutual relations between the countries remained fruitful.

[Zvi Loker]

BIBLIOGRAPHY: Zwergbaum, in: *Yad Vashem Studies*, 4 (1960); 191–257; idem, in *Gesher*, 66 (March 1971), 92–104; D. Trevor, *Under the White Paper* (1948), index; M. Basok (ed.), *Sefer ha-Ma'pilim* (1947), passim; Yad Vashem, *Ha-Sho'ah ve-ha-Gevurah be-Aspaklaryah shel ha-Ittonut ha-Ivrit – Bibliografyah*, 2 (1966), 12871–970.

MAUROIS, ANDRÉ (originally **Emile Herzog**; 1885–1967), French biographer, novelist, and essayist. Born in Elbeuf, Maurois was descended from Alsatian industrialists who moved to Normandy after the Franco-Prussian War. Raised in a staunchly patriotic home, he experienced antisemitism as a student at the time of the *Dreyfus Affair and was influenced by the philosopher Alain (Emile Chartier). He spent ten years in his father's factory and his experiences there were later used in his fiction. A French liaison officer and interpreter with a Scots division during World War I, he published a light-hearted book about his British army comrades, *Les Silences du Colonel Bramble* (1918; Eng. tr., 1919) using his pseudonym, André Maurois, for the first time. He followed it with *Les discours du docteur O'Grady* (1922). Maurois earned a reputation as an acute interpreter of the English scene and as an outstanding biographer. During the 1920s and 1930s he published *Ariel, ou la vie de Shelley* (1923; Eng. tr., *Ariel*, 1924); *La vie de Disraeli* (1927; Eng. tr., 1927); *La vie de Lord Byron* (1930; Eng. tr., 1930), and historical works such as *Edouard VII et son temps* (1933; Eng. tr. 1933) and *Histoire de l'Angleterre* (1937; Eng. tr., 1937). In writing his biographies, Maurois combined documentation, erudition, and imagination, to unfold the psychological development of his subjects. His books in this genre include studies of Voltaire (1935), Chateaubriand (1938; Eng. tr., 1938), George Sand (1952; Eng. tr., 1953), and Hugo (*Olympio*, 1954). Two outstanding biographies were *A la recherche de Marcel Proust* (1949; *Proust, a biography*, 1950) and *Promethée, ou la vie de Balzac* (1965). Maurois also wrote short stories and several semiautobiographical novels, notably *Bernard Quesnay* (1926; Eng. tr., 1927); *Climats* (1928; *Whatever Gods May Be*, 1929; and *Le cercle de famille* (1932; *The Family Circle*, 1932). In the first of these he told the story of his refugee Alsatian family.

After the armistice of 1940, Maurois supported the Vichy regime, but then violently opposed Hitler and fled to the U.S., where he taught at Princeton until the end of the war. He claimed that the Jews of the Diaspora had to choose segregation, assimilation, or some difficult intermediate path. Himself a convinced assimilationist, he nevertheless remained interested in problems of Jewish identity, to which he referred in the first part of his *Mémoires* (1942; *I Remember, I Remember*, 1942). In later years he confessed to "a deep sadness" within himself and praised the intellectual enrichment which the Jews had brought to French literature. Maurois' other works include: *Aspects de la biographie* (1928; Eng. tr., 1929); *Magiciens et logiciens* (1935; *Prophets and Poets*, 1935); *Histoire des Etats-Unis* (2 vols., 1943–44; Eng. tr., 1948); and *Histoire de la France* (1947; Eng. tr., 1949); and the autobiographical works *Portrait d'un ami qui s'appelle moi* (1959) and *Mémoires 1885–1967* (1970). His collected works appeared in 16 volumes (1950–55). He was elected to the French Academy in 1938.

BIBLIOGRAPHY: G. Lemaître, *André Maurois* (Eng., 1939); Chaigne, in: A. Maurois, *Poésie et action* (1949); J. Suffel, *André Maurois* (Fr., 1963).

[Sidney D. Braun]

°**MAURRAS, CHARLES** (1868–1952), French nationalist writer and antisemitic politician. In association with *Daudet,

Maurras founded L'Action *française – both the newspaper and the movement by that name. His call for a return to the traditional values of "*la vieille France*" and his extreme political attitudes are reflected in all his books, especially *Quand les Français ne s'aimaient pas* (1916), *Mes idées politiques* (1937), and *La contre-révolution spontanée* (1943). Maurras' love of monarchy, hierarchy, and the rural virtues was paralleled by his hatred of the republic, democratic institutions, and the "*métèques*" (a word he coined himself), i.e., recently naturalized foreigners, and above all the Jews. He believed that the Jews – together with their allies the Freemasons, the Protestants, and the *métæques* – sought to control the entire political life of France. The *Dreyfus Affair (which obsessed him for the rest of his life) was for him the supreme example of Jewish dominance. Nevertheless, his passion for the French nation did not prevent Maurras from welcoming Hitler as a savior from democracy and the Jews, and he hailed the German invasion of France in 1940 as the "divine surprise." When the Jews in occupied France were forced in May 1942 to wear the Jewish badge, Maurras regarded it as a suitable opportunity to rid France, too, of the "Jewish scourge." For his subsequent collaboration with the Germans, Maurras was condemned in January 1945 to life imprisonment.

BIBLIOGRAPHY: R.F. Byrnes, *Anti-semitism in Modern France*, 1 (1950), index; E. Nolte, *Three Faces of Fascism* (1966), passim; E.R. Tannenbaum, *The Action Française* (1962), index.

MAUSS, MARCEL (1872–1950), French ethnologist, sociologist, historian of religion, and polyhistorian. Born at Epinal, Mauss was a nephew of Emile *Durkheim, who guided his education and greatly influenced him. His early interests were mainly philosophy and the history of religion. He taught the latter subject throughout his life, but enriched the entire domain of social science and contributed to the growth of the French school of anthropology. Mauss was professor of the history of religions of noncivilized peoples at the Ecole des Hautes Etudes in Paris and also taught at the Collège de France. In 1925 he helped to found the ethnological institute of Paris University, of which he became joint director. He worked with his uncle in both practical and theoretical studies, carrying forward some of Durkheim's basic ideas such as the total social fact, collective representations, and the correspondence of morphological social structure with moral, legal, and symbolic facts. He was one of the team of young scholars assembled by Durkheim for his journal *L'Année sociologique* (1898–1913), and directed its section on religion. He revived the journal after World War I. Of Mauss's works on anthropology, the best known outside France is *Essai sur le Don* (1926; *The Gift*, 1954), an elaborate study of the relation between exchange patterns and social structure. Mauss was active in French political life participating in the support of *Dreyfus, and in the socialist and cooperative movements. He never recovered from the mental breakdown caused by the brutalities of the German occupation, though he published two more works before his death.

BIBLIOGRAPHY: C. Lévi-Strauss, in: G. Gurvitch and W.E. Moore (eds.), *Twentieth Century Sociology* (1945), 503–37; idem, in: M. Mauss, *Sociologie et anthropologie* (1950), introd.; R. Needham, in: E. Durkheim and M. Mauss, *Primitive Classification* (1963), introd.; S. Lukes, in: IESS, 10 (1968), 78–82; J. Gugler, in: *Homme*, 64 (1964), 105–12 (bibliography).

[Ephraim Fischoff]

MAUTHAUSEN, Nazi concentration camp in Austria, 12½ mi. (20 km.) S.E. of Linz, established in April 1938 shortly after the annexation in March of Austria to the Third Reich. The *SS employed its prisoners in the local granite quarry called "Wienergraben," that was incorporated into the camp. Initially, Mauthausen served as a concentration camp for Austrian anti-Nazis. The first commandant was Albert Sauer. Its commander from February 1939 to May 1945 was Franz Ziereis about whom it was stated that "he gave his son 50 Jews for target practice as a birthday present" (see Presser, p. 54). Starting as a satellite of *Dachau, Mauthausen became an independent camp in the spring of 1939, and expanded continually, with several satellites of its own throughout Austria (Gusen, Ebensee, and others) by the end of the war. After the outbreak of World War II Mauthausen became a camp for anti-Nazis from all over occupied Europe and in 1940 was graded category III, the harshest category of concentration camps (Dachau was in category I). Mauthausen received the so-called "protective custody" prisoners whose "return was not desired" (RU = *Rueckkehr unerwuenscht*; see *Camps, Concentration and Extermination). Himmler specially ordered the death of a prisoner in Mauthausen to be communicated to his family only after incineration. The camp had the highest death rate for those in "protective custody" of all the concentration camps. Mauthausen was used for political prisoners. Of over 10,000 Spanish Republicans who were interned there early in 1941, handed over by the Vichy regime, only 1,500 were still alive after one year.

Mauthausen and its satellite camps. Based on H. Marsalek and J. Kohl, Wegweiser durch das ehemalige Konzentrationslager Mauthausen *(1960).*

Work conditions were intolerable; the prisoners had to carry heavy stones up the 186 steps of the "Wienergraben." It was called Death's Way. In November 1941 Russian prisoners of war began arriving, destined for immediate death through overwork and starvation. Though able bodied and trained for military combat, they did not engage in an uprising until February 1945; their revolt was unsuccessful and many were killed. The camp authorities used a special measuring installation to shoot their victims in the nape of the neck. Prisoners were also killed by phenol injections or gassed at the euthanasia installation at Hartheim until a gas chamber was constructed in one of Mauthausen's three sections. From the beginning of 1942 prominent citizens from occupied territories arrested under the "night and fog decree" were brought there. Recaptured prisoners of war were executed under the "bullet decree" (*Kugel-Erlass*). When prisoners of other camps were caught for clandestine activities, those not immediately executed were sent to Mauthausen for punishment. Following *Heydrich's death, hundreds of Czech prisoners were killed.

In May 1941 about 400 Jewish "hostages" from *Amsterdam arrived via *Buchenwald; they were all killed within three days in the forced-labor quarry which also served as a site for execution. There were another two shipments of Jews from Holland to Mauthausen (end of 1941 and 1942) who were killed after a short time in the camp. Up to 1944 Jews were never allowed to live for more than three days. When in early 1945 the camps in the East were evacuated, thousands of prisoners from *Auschwitz, including Jews, were brought to Mauthausen; thousands of Hungarian Jews who had slaved building fortifications at the so-called "Southeast Rampart" were also brought to camp. The name of Mauthausen was particularly feared by Holland's Jews, and the Germans took advantage of this fear to suppress resistance to their measures against the Jews. Jews in Mauthausen were singled out for especially cruel treatment compared to that given non-Jews (see *Anklageschrift in der Strafsache gegen Fritz Woehrn et al.* (1968), 98–102, 228–35). Shortly before the capitulation it was planned to murder all Mauthausen prisoners in a subterranean aircraft-construction hangar in Gusen, but the plan was not carried out. Mauthausen was liberated by U.S. troops in May 1945. In the main camp the prisoners had rebelled. Ziereis hid in the camp but was shot by a U.S. patrol several days later when he tried to escape. According to camp records – and they may be an understatement – 199,404 were interned at Mauthausen; 119,000 died. Of those who died, as often due to work conditions and lack of food as to the gas chambers or killing fields, 38,120 were Jews.

BIBLIOGRAPHY: G. Reitlinger, *Final Solution* (1968^2), index; IMT, *Trial of the Major War Criminals*, 23 (1949), index; J. Presser, *Destruction of the Dutch Jews* (1969), index; P. Tillard, *Mauthausen* (Fr., 1945); H. Maršálek, *Mauthausen mahnt* (1951); H. Maršálek and J. Kohl, *Wegweiser durch das ehemalige Konzentrationslager Mauthausen* (1960^2); M. Riquet, *L'Europe à Mauthausen, tragédie de la déportation 1940–1945* (1954).

[Yehuda Reshef]

MAUTHNER, FRITZ (1849–1923), German journalist, author and philosopher. Mauthner, who was born in Horice, Bohemia, came of an assimilated family and remained estranged from Judaism. His *Erinnerungen* (1918) provides a fascinating account of his early upbringing in Prague, portraying also the situation of Jews between three cultures and languages – German, Czech, and Jewish – within the national conflict in Bohemia. After law studies at Prague he settled in Berlin, where he became editor of the *Magazin fuer Literatur* and wrote reviews for the *Berliner Tageblatt*, which he directed from 1895. A naturalistic writer and a socialist, he was a co-founder of the *Freie Buehne*, but later turned to writing historical fiction and philosophical works. Mauthner first attracted attention with *Nach beruehmten Mustern*, witty parodies of 22 of his contemporaries including Berthold *Auerbach, Gustav Freytag, Paul *Heyse, and Richard Wagner, which he wrote for the *Deutsches Monatsblatt* from 1879, before they were published as a book in 1897. This was followed by many novels, novellas, satirical sketches, and fairy tales. One of these is the novel *Der neue Ahasver. Roman aus Jung-Berlin* (1882), in which he showed how assimilation was rejected by antisemitism. While he was successful as a satirical journalist, and much less so as a novelist, he was highly regarded – and remained so – for his philosophical works, which had a great influence on modern philosophy (e.g., Ludwig *Wittgenstein) and literature (e.g., Hugo von *Hofmansthal). His main work were the *Beitraege zu einer Kritik der Sprache* (3 vols., 1901–2), on which he worked from 1893. Following Friedrich Nietzsche as well as Ernst Mach and arguing that thinking never allows access to reality but is always mediated by language, he dealt with the psychology and science of language, and with the role of grammar and logic. In his *Woerterbuch der Philosophie, neue Beitraege zu einer Kritik der Sprache* (2 vols., 1910) he expanded his work on philosophical ideas; here he subjected more than 200 philosophical concepts to critical examination. A militant agnostic, Mauthner was denied academic appointments because of his anti-religious stand and political views. He radicalized his skepticism in his last literary work, *Der letzte Tod des Gautama Buddha* (1912), preaching an areligious, skeptical mysticism without God, as well as in his last and encyclopedic, philosophical work, *Der Atheismus und seine Geschichte im Abendlande* (4 vols. 1920–23), where he claimed that all dogmas – religious or scientific – were mere human inventions and that their origin, efflorescence, and decline had their basis in history. Mauthner then sought to show how the West had begun to shake off the once dominant concept of God. His work was thus intended to trace the disintegration of this concept, an "anthropomorphic illusion" that had held peoples spellbound for several millennia. From 1911 until his death he lived in Meersburg at Lake Constance, where he also edited the *Bibliothek der Philosophen*.

BIBLIOGRAPHY: G. Landauer, *Skepsis und Mystik* (1923^2); T. Kappstein, *Fritz Mauthner, der Mann und sein Werk* (1926), incl. list of his works; G. Weiler, in: YLBI, 8 (1963), 136–48. **ADD. BIBLIOGRAPHY:** G. Weiler, *Mauthners Critique of Language* (1971); W. Eschbacher, *Fritz Mauther und die deutsche Literatur um 1900* (1977); K. Arens, *Functionalism and Fin de Siècle. Fritz Mauthner's Critique of Language* (1984); E. Leinfellner, *Fritz Mauthner* (1995).

[Sol Liptzin / Andreas Kilcher (2nd ed.)]

MAUTNER, KONRAD (1880–1924), Austrian folk song collector, publisher of important primary sources on folk song and music, folk art and costume, and industrialist whose family was of Bohemian origin. In 1893, his father Isidor founded the largest textile business of the monarchy. Konrad Mautner studied in Vienna with private teachers and in Schotten high school. In 1902 he left for a year in the U.S., where he worked for his father's textile concern. In 1909 he married Anna Neumann, his cousin, whose family comprised large-scale silk manufacturers. She was, like her husband, talented and interested in art. With the advent of the Nazis the family had to leave Austria. From his childhood, Mautner used to spend his vacations with his parents in Goessl on Grundsee, where he practically grew up together with local inhabitants. In 1910 he prepared for publication a collection of the "Steyerische Rasplwerk," folk songs, as a documentation of his happy childhood and youth years in that region. Verlag Staehelin and Lauenstein, publisher of limited editions, produced this material in a luxury edition of 400 copies. The volume included old songs and street verses that Mautner heard and sang in Gössl and which he transcribed and illustrated by hand drawings. This volume was the first Austrian musical village monograph, which because of its naiveté transmitted the picture as a whole. Since it was based on personal memory, it was held at that time to be of no importance, because of the doubt as to whether the songs were authentic according to the criteria of folk song research of that time. Today, however, its significance is realized. Later, Mautner was in close contact with the professional world, and published one more volume from Salzkammergut, a town in the Austrian province Steiermark, as well as numerous journal articles. In 1914, the Musical Historical Center of the War Ministry used him (together with other professional people) for collecting soldiers' songs. He worked together with Viktor von Geramb on the book of native costumes in Steiermark (*Steirische Trachtenbuch*) that was published only after his death. Mautner's articles in the field of folk song research are characterized by precise observation of the subject and artistic intuition as well as by early use of technical facilities (phonograph, etc.).

[Gerlinde Haid (2nd ed.)]

MAWZAʿ, a town situated in the Tihāma in west *Yemen about 97 km southwest of Taiz, in an inhabited area of land which the streams of rainwater provide with sweet water. Consequently, the land is quite fertile. The town is one of the oldest ports in Yemen, connecting the country with Africa and the Indian Ocean. The temperature and humidity there are very high. The town is famous for its tombs and domes. It was connected with a crucial event in the history of the Jews of Yemen in 1679, which remained in the historical memory of the Jews of Yemen as *Galut Mawzaʿ* (The Expulsion of Mawzaʿ), when apparently all of them were expelled to the salty and barren stretch of land off the town, notorious for its harsh, hot climate. The expulsion, ordered by Imam Aḥmad ibn Ḥasan (1676–1681), was the culmination of a series of anti-Jewish measures responding to the Jewish messianic movement in Yemen in 1666/7 among the followers of *Shabbetai Zevi. After a long and comprehensive debate by the Muslim scholars of both religious schools, the Zaydi and the Shāfiʿi, Imam Ismāʿīl (1646–1676) confirmed their ruling that by the fact that a group of Jews in Yemen had taken some practical steps to materialize the Jewish vision of messianic redemption, the whole community had violated the agreement of **dhimma* with the Muslim kingdom. The full meaning of that ruling was that they were no longer entitled to government protection and that no Jews were permitted to live there anymore. Imam Ismāʿīl decided then to expel all the Jews from his country but left the practical implementation to his heir Imam Aḥmad. Immediately after this the new imam ordered the destruction of all synagogues and prohibited public prayer by Jews. As the Jews rejected the offer to convert and to live in Yemen as Muslims, Imam Aḥmad commanded in 1679 that all Jews leave their places and be sent by boat to the Muslim Moghul kingdom in India. But for some reason, probably practical difficulties, this plan could not be carried out and the Jews stayed for more than one year near Mawzaʿ. This event was the worst calamity that befell the Jews of Yemen in their long history. The houses that the Jews had left behind were destroyed or sold cheaply, and all their valuables were either lost or stolen. Many died en route, and those who reached Mawzaʿ suffered from disease and starvation; as many as two-thirds of the exiles did not survive. The Jews also lost many of their ancient traditions as they could not carry with them most of their old manuscript writings nor their communal books and archives. The event was well documented in both Muslim sources as well as in Jewish ones, especially in the poems of R. Shalem *Shabazi, Yemenite Jewry's greatest poet who went into exile with his coreligionists. The expulsion deprived Yemen of all its Jewish artisans, and the Muslim population soon came to realize that they could not do without them. Step by step the Jews started to return to their places, but were forced to build new neighborhoods outside the town walls. The district governors petitioned the central authorities in *Sanʿa to bring the Jews back, and a year after their expulsion the Imam permitted their return. During the aftermath of the expulsion the Jewish communities sank into a deep social, economic and spiritual crisis (many hundreds converted to *Islam), from which they recovered only after many years.

BIBLIOGRAPHY: Y. Tobi, *The Jews of Yemen*; idem, "*Yedi'ot al Yehudei Teiman…*," in: *Peʿamim*, 65 (Autumn 1995), 18–56.

[Yehuda Ratzaby / Yosef Tobi (2nd ed.)]

°**MAXIMILIAN I** (1459–1519), king of Germany from 1486 and Holy Roman emperor from 1493. His Jewish policy, like that of his father, *Frederick III, was erratic and motivated by financial considerations. In 1496 he expelled the Jews from *Carinthia and *Styria, after the estates there had undertaken to reimburse him for the loss of Jewish taxes, but he permitted them to settle in *Burgenland. He forbade Jews to live in *Vienna, with the exception of his agent Hirschel of Zistersdorf, with whom he "had to have patience" because he was so much in his debt. In 1509 he gave power to Johannes *Pfefferkorn to confiscate Jewish books and to destroy those which were offensive to Christianity. Reversing this decree in 1510, he ordered expert opinions to be asked from the universities as well as from Johannes *Reuchlin, Victor von *Carben, and Jacob van *Hoogstraaten. After banning Reuchlin's *Augenspiegel* in 1512, a year later he ordered both sides to keep silent. He issued a decree forbidding rabbis to apply the **ḥerem* (ban) against those appealing to gentile courts. Under his rule, *Joseph (Joselmann) b. Gershom of Rosheim became the *shtadlan* of German Jewry, and in Moravia the first **Landrabbiner* was appointed.

MAXIMILIAN II (1527–1576), from 1564 ruler of the Hapsburg dominions and Holy Roman emperor, successor to *Ferdinand I. His policy toward the Jews was generally lenient, though he suspected them of supporting the Turks. In 1567 he reaffirmed the charters of Bohemian Jewry, promising to maintain their rights to practice trades they had previously engaged in, and issued decrees against usury. Foreign Jews were forbidden to trade in his dominions without explicit license. Against the will of the local ruler, in 1570 he permitted the Jews free passage through the duchy of *Brunswick (Braunschweig), and asked the *Worms municipality not to harass its Jews because their rights were long standing. While permitting seven families to settle in Vienna in 1571, a year later he decided to concentrate them in one building in the center of the city for easier surveillance, then expelled them in the same year. Maximilian was the first to grant a Jewish craftsman, a diamond cutter from *Breslau (Wroclaw), a permit to pursue his craft. The baptized Jew, Paul Rizius (Ricci, d. 1542), was his court physician.

BIBLIOGRAPHY: MAXIMILIAN I: J.E. Scherer, *Die Rechtsverhaeltnisse der Juden in den deutsch-oesterreichischen Laendern* (1901), 447–9; M. Brod, *Johannes Reuchlin und sein Kampf* (1965), index; Baron, Social[2], 13 (1969), 182–91, passim; S. Stern, *Josel of Rosheim* (1965), index; M. Grunwald, *Vienna* (1936), index. MAXIMILIAN II: A.F. Pribram, *Urkunden und Akten zur Geschichte der Juden in Wien* (1918), index; Baron, Social[2], 14 (1969), 148–52; Bondy-Dworský, 462–550; M. Wiener, in: MGWJ, 10 (1861), 241–53; G. Wolf, *ibid.*, 361–3, 456–60.

[Meir Lamed]

MAXIMON (Maximowski), SHALOM DOV BER (1881–1933), essayist and educator. Maximon, who was born in Skvira, left Russia at the age of 21 and traveled to Galicia, Switzerland, France, and England. In London he met Aḥad Ha-Am who exerted a permanent influence on his writings. He was also befriended by Brenner who published his first article in *Ha-Me'orer*. In New York, he was employed by the Bureau of Jewish Education and edited a paper for children, *The Jewish Child*. He was also one of the founders and editors of the monthly *Ha-Toren* in 1913 and edited the pedagogical journal *Shevil ha-Ḥinnukh* for two years (1927–29). He was a member of the faculty of Hebrew Union College School for Teachers in New York and in 1930 was appointed registrar of Hebrew Union College in Cincinnati, Ohio. Maximon contributed articles to Hebrew periodicals in Europe and Palestine. Most of his articles were collected in his book *Gevilim* ("Rolls of Parchment," 1925).

BIBLIOGRAPHY: *Sefer Maximon* (New York, 1935); A. Epstein, *Soferim* (1934), 215–21; Kressel, Leksikon, 2 (1967), 414f.; S.I. Feigin, *Anshei Shem* (1950), 206–11.

[Eisig Silberschlag]

°**MAXIMUS, MAGNUS CLEMENS** (**Maximus the Usurper**; d. 388 C.E.), Roman emperor 383–388. A native of Spain, Maximus was proclaimed emperor by the army in Britain in 383. To secure his position Maximus invaded Gaul and occupied it, defeating the western emperor Gratian. In a treaty negotiated with the eastern emperor Theodosius, Maximus received recognition of his conquests in return for an assurance that he would honor the sovereignty of Valentinian II (Gratian's brother) in Italy, Western Illyricum, and Africa. He violated his promise and he invaded Italy in 388. Theodosius together with the Franks, Goths, Alanis, and Huns took up arms against him, and within two months Maximus was deserted by his troops and forced to take refuge in Aquileia. He subsequently capitulated and was executed in August 388.

The relationship between Maximus and the Jews is difficult to establish because of the paucity of sources available. The only substantial document of relevance is a letter sent by St. Ambrose to the emperor Theodosius in December of 388. In it, St. Ambrose admonishes Theodosius for his punishment of those involved in the burning of a synagogue in the East. He argues that the imperial punishment imposed upon those involved in the crime should be rescinded, and that the local bishop who instigated the affair should not be held financially responsible for the renovation of the synagogue. St. Ambrose reminds Theodosius of the many offenses committed against Christians by the "scheming Jews," and goes on to suggest that penalties for civic offenses should be viewed differently when there are religious considerations. He further asks the question: "Shall a place be provided out of the spoils of the Church for the disbelief of the Jews?"

To illustrate his point Ambrose utilized the recent example of Maximus. According to Ambrose, Maximus condemned the burning of a synagogue in Rome on the basis that it was a breach of public order. Ambrose records the hostile reaction of the Roman people to this course of action, their charges that Maximus had converted to Judaism, and their grim prophecies of Maximus' downfall. Ambrose clearly hoped that Theodosius would profit from the mistake of his former adversary, and adopt a more lenient attitude toward those involved in Jewish persecutions.

BIBLIOGRAPHY: [St.] Ambrosius, in: PL 16 (1845), Epistola 40:23, p. 1109f.; Paulus Orosius, *Historiae adversum paganos*, 7:34, 9 and passim; Sulpicius Severus, *Dialogus tertius*, 11:2; Zosimus, *Historiae novae*, liber 4; Pauly-Wissowa, 28 (1930), 2546–55 (no. 33).

[John M. O'Brien]

MAXWELL, ROBERT (1923–1991), British publisher. Maxwell was born Jan Ludvik Hoch, son of a poor Jewish farm laborer, in Solotvino in the Carpathians, then part of Czechoslovakia. Although his family was Orthodox , he appears to have abandoned Judaism at about the time he left his native village and traveled to Budapest. Maxwell later stated, "I ceased to be a practicing Jew just before the war… I certainly do consider myself a Jew. I was born Jewish and I shall die Jewish." After the German occupation of Czechoslovakia in March 1939, Maxwell made his way to Hungary where he was arrested at the end of the year. He escaped and made his way to southern France where he joined members of the free Czech forces with whom he was transported to Britain in 1940. After a spell in the Czech Legion and the British Pioneer Corps, he joined the North Staffordshire Regiment in 1943 and served with distinction during the campaign in Northern Europe. He was decorated with the Military Cross in 1945 and had risen from the rank of corporal to captain by the end of the war. He served with the Allied Control Commission in the British Zone of Occupation in Germany in the department of Public Relations and Information Services Control. At this time he also engaged in commercial activities and following his demobilization in 1947 he entered business, specializing in import and export between Britain and Eastern Europe where he established extensive connections. He first entered publishing by way of an agreement to distribute German scientific periodicals in 1947. Two years later he acquired Pergamon Press, although he lost control of the company for a time in the early 1970s when his business activities were subjected to a critical report by the Department of Trade and Industry. In 1981 he bought the British Printing and Communication Corporation, of which he was chairman, and in 1984 acquired Mirror Group Newspapers (MGN). As chairman of MGN he became the publisher of several mass-circulation titles. Pergamon Press was the world's largest distributor of scientific periodicals. Between 1964 and 1970, Robert Maxwell was Labour Member of Parliament for Buckinghamshire. By the 1980s, Maxwell had acquired a major international business empire, which included *The Daily Mirror* and *The People* newspapers in Britain, the *New York Daily News*, and the famous publisher Macmillan, as well as a range of firms in Europe. In 1990, Philip Beresford's *Book of the British Rich*, the predecessor to the *Sunday Times*' "rich lists," claimed that Maxwell was then Britain's tenth richest man, worth an estimated £1.1 billion. He was active in various philanthropic causes and was chairman of the National AIDS Trust. In 1986 he was involved in the financing of the Commonwealth Games in Edinburgh and had an interest in several football clubs, notably Oxford United and Derby County. Most of his own family perished in the Holocaust and in 1988, he provided £1 million to fund the major international conference on the Holocaust, "Remembering for the Future," which took place in London and Oxford. Maxwell had business interests in Israel – Pergamon Media purchased a 45% stake in Modi'in Publishing House which owned the Israeli daily newspaper *Ma'ariv* – and invested in Scitex, Keter Publishing House, and Teva Pharmaceutical Industries Ltd.

Maxwell's downfall apparently came through unwise expansions and, unusually for a successful tycoon, overly generous payments for the acquisition of new assets, together with a secretive operating style in which no one but Maxwell himself understood the complexities of his business empire. Components of his business empire ran into difficulty in the business downturn of the late 1980s, and he was accused of raiding the assets of others to support them, including the MGN's pension fund. By the second half of 1991 the British Fraud Squad had compiled a lengthy dossier on Maxwell, and rumors of his true position increasingly surfaced in the press. On 5 November 1991 Maxwell disappeared from his yacht near the Canary Islands. His death caused a worldwide sensation. It has never been ascertained whether his death was caused by suicide, accident, or murder, and many conspiracy theories later came to the fore, especially those in which various intelligence agencies (including the Israeli Mossad) were responsible for his death. At his death, his debts totaled at least £400 million, with some estimates putting his total debt as high as £2.2 billion.

Like many self-made tycoons, Maxwell was widely regarded in a negative light. Consequently, his very notable record of charity and the scale of the business empire he briefly organized have largely been forgotten.

ADD. BIBLIOGRAPHY: ODNB online; T. Bower, *Maxwell the Outsider* (1988); idem., *Maxwell: The Final Verdict* (1995); R. Davies, *Foreign Body: The Secret Life of Robert Maxwell* (1995); W. Donaldson, *Brewer's Rogues, Villains, and Eccentrics* (2002), 446–47; G. Thomas, *The Assassination of Robert Maxwell: Israel's Superspy* (2002).

[David Cesarani. / William D. Rubinstein (2nd ed.)]

MAXY, MAX HERMAN (1895–1971), Romanian artist, and director of the Art Museum of the Socialist Romanian Republic. Maxy was born in Brăila, educated at a Jewish school and studied at the school of Belle Arté. He completed his studies in Berlin and in 1925 exhibited with the "November Group." In the 1930s he exhibited in Rome, Paris, the Hague, and Brussels. He designed sets and costumes at the company of Vilna for *The Night in the Old Market* of *Peretz and *Shabbetai Ẓevi*.

MAY, ELAINE (1932–), U.S. screenwriter, director, and actress. Born Elaine Berlin in Philadelphia, Pennsylvania, to Yiddish theatrical actor Jack and actress Jeannie Berlin, May began acting on stage as a child in the Yiddish theater run by her father. She married Marvin May in May 1949; the couple had one daughter together, Jeannie Berlin, before divorcing. May studied at the University of Chicago and Playwrights Theater in 1950. She then joined the Compass Players in 1953 and began working with fellow member Mike *Nichols in 1955. Along with Alan *Arkin, Barabara Harris, and Paul Sills, Nichols and May went on to found the improvisational group the Second City. In 1957, the pair developed a nightclub act based on sophisticated parodies of popular culture and mock interviews. Nichols and May spent the next few years appearing in cabaret shows, on television programs, and on Broadway with their show *An Evening with Mike Nichols and Elaine May* (1960). The pair produced several albums together, even winning a Grammy in 1961, the same year they amicably brought their partnership to an end. In 1967, May appeared in the films *Bach to Bach*, *Enter Laughing*, and *Luv*. May honed her playwriting through the 1960s, and in 1969 produced her one-act play *Adaptation*. Her first credited screenplay was *A New Leaf* (1971), which she costarred in and directed. In 1972, May directed Neil Simon's *The Heartbreak Kid* (1972). When May came in over budget and past deadline on a film she wrote and directed, *Mikey and Nicky* (1976), Paramount tried to remove her from the project. Her next screenplay, *Heaven Can Wait* (1978), an update of *Here Comes Mr. Jordan* (1941), was cowritten with its star Warren Beatty. While the film received mixed reviews, it did well at the box office and received an Academy Award nomination. But May won the Oscar that year as best supporting actress in *California Suite* (1978). While uncredited, May helped rewrite *Reds* (1981) and *Tootsie* (1982). May and Beatty reunited for *Ishtar* (1987), a project so marred by cost overruns that it became one of the largest financial failures in motion picture history. May wrote the screenplay for *The Birdcage* (1996), an adaptation of *La Cage aux Folles* directed by Nichols, and the pair teamed up again for *Primary Colors* (1998), which earned May another Oscar nomination. In 2000, she appeared in the Woody Allen film *Small Time Crooks*.

[Adam Wills (2nd ed.)]

MA'YAN BARUKH (Heb. מַעְיַן בָּרוּךְ), kibbutz on the Israel-Lebanese border near the Tannur waterfall, affiliated with Iḥud ha-Kevuẓot ve-ha-Kibbutzim. It was founded in 1947 by South African and Rhodesian World War II veterans, joined by Israel-born youth and immigrants from the United States, Great Britain, and other countries. Its founding at the time was regarded as an act of defiance against the British administration which imposed martial law on Tel Aviv and the Jewish sectors of Jerusalem. In the Israel *War of Independence (1948), the kibbutz resisted strong Syrian contingents who attempted to penetrate into the Ḥuleh Valley, and in the years preceding the *Six-Day War (1967) Ma'yan Barukh was repeatedly shelled by the nearby Syrian positions. Its economy was based on fruit orchards, irrigated field and garden crops, and dairy cattle. The kibbutz maintained a local museum. Its name, "Baruch's Spring," commemorates Baruch (Bernard) Gordon, a South African Zionist. In the mid-1990s, the population was approximately 360, dropping to 305 in 2002. The kibbutz operated a steel factory and ran its dairy farm in partnership with kibbutz *Loḥamei ha-Getta'ot. The kibbutz also operated guest rooms and water recreation facilities at the nearby Jordan River.

[Efram Orni / Shaked Gilboa (2nd ed.)]

MA'YAN ẒEVI (Heb. מַעְיַן צְבִי), kibbutz in central Israel, on Mt. Carmel near Zikhron Ya'akov, affiliated with Iḥud ha-Kevuẓot ve-ha-Kibbutzim. It was founded in 1938, initially as a *stockade and watchtower settlement, by pioneers of Maccabi ha-Ẓa'ir youth from Germany, Austria, and Czechoslovakia. In 1969 Ma'yan Ẓevi had 540 inhabitants. In the mid-1990s the population was 612, dropping to 491 in 2002. The farm economy was based on avocado plantations, citrus groves, and field crops, carp ponds below on the Carmel Coast plain, and dairy cattle and poultry. The kibbutz also operated factories for optical equipment (Scopus, Meprolight, the latter specializing in military and security needs). The name, "Spring of Ẓevi," commemorates Ẓevi Henri Frank, a director of the *Jewish Colonization Association (ICA) in Palestine.

[Efram Orni / Shaked Gilboa (2nd ed.)]

MAYBAUM, IGNAZ (1897–1976), Reform rabbi and theologian. Born in Vienna, Maybaum served as rabbi at Bingen (Rhineland), Frankfurt on the Oder, and Berlin. In 1939 he immigrated to England. From 1947 to 1963 he was minister of the Edgeware Reform Synagogue (London) and lecturer on theology and homiletics at the Leo Baeck College (established 1956). In addition to publications in his German period (*Parteibefreites Judentum*, 1935; *Neue Jugend und alter Glaube*, 1936) he wrote books in English including *Synagogue and Society* (1944); *Jewish Mission* (1951); *Sacrifice of Isaac* (Leo Baeck College Publication, no 1, 1959); *Jewish Existence* (1960); *The Faith of the Jewish Diaspora* (1962); and *The Face of God after Auschwitz* (1965). In his writings Maybaum considers the theological and religious problems presented by the Holocaust and the dual existence of the Jewish people in the Diaspora and its ancient homeland. He was a nephew of Sigmund *Maybaum.

BIBLIOGRAPHY: JC (Feb. 24, 1967), 13.

MAYBAUM, SIGMUND (1844–1919), rabbi and lecturer on homiletics. Born in Miskolc, Hungary, Maybaum studied at the yeshivot of Eisenstadt (under I. *Hildesheimer) and Pressburg (Bratislava) and at the university and rabbinical seminary of Breslau. He officiated as rabbi in Dolni-Kubin, Hungary (1870–73), and Zatec, Bohemia (1873–81). In 1881 he was called to Berlin, where from 1888 he also lectured on homiletics at the *Hochschule fuer die Wissenschaft des Judentums. In 1903 he was appointed professor. Active in the association of rabbis in Germany, in 1897 Maybaum was among those rabbis who protested against the idea of convening the Zionist Congress in Germany. His works include *Die Anthropomorphien und Anthropopathien bei Onkelos und den spaeteren Targumim* (1870), *Die Entwicklung des alt-israelitischen Priestertums* (1880), *Die Entwicklung des israelitischen Prophetentums* (1883), and *Juedische Homiletik* (1890). His important article on the life of Leopold *Zunz appeared in 1894 (in the 12th report of the Hochschule). Maybaum was an excellent preacher and his sermons were published in several volumes. A jubilee volume was published on the occasion of his 70th birthday.

BIBLIOGRAPHY: XIII. Cahn, *Religioese Stroemungen...* (1912), passim.

[Nahum N. Glatzer]

MAYER, ARNO JOSEPH (1926–), U.S. historian. Born in Luxembourg, Mayer fled the Hitler menace and found refuge in the U.S. (1940). He served in the U.S. Army in World War II, during which time he was assigned the duty of tending to Wernher von Braun after the German rocket scientist was taken into custody by the American forces. Following his military service, Mayer studied at the Geneva Institut des Hautes Études Internationales and received a Ph.D. in political science from Yale University. After teaching at Brandeis and Harvard, he was a professor of history at Princeton from 1961 to 1999. Upon his retirement, Mayer became professor emeritus of history at Princeton. His research was in the field of 20th-century diplomacy.

His major works include *Political Origins of the New Diplomacy, 1917–1918* (1959), which deals with the impact of the military stalemate; *Politics and Diplomacy of Peacemaking* (1967), a study of Wilson's war aims and the effect of Communism upon them; *Dynamics of Counterrevolution in Europe, 1870–1956* (1971); *The Persistence of the Old Regime: Europe to the Great War* (1981); *Why Did the Heaven Not Darken? The "Final Solution" in History* (1988); and *The Furies: Violence and Terror in the French and Russian Revolutions* (2000).

[Ruth Beloff (2nd ed.)]

MAYER, DANIEL (1909–1996), French socialist politician. Born in Paris, Mayer was a journalist by profession, and wrote for the socialist newspaper *Le Populaire*. After the fall of France during World War II, he reorganized the Socialist Party, clandestinely editing the *Populaire*, and after the liberation became its general secretary. Mayer was a member of the Chamber of Deputies from 1946 to 1958 and from 1946 to 1949 held a number of ministerial offices – labor, public health, and veteran's affairs. He was also president of the parliamentary committee on foreign affairs. He left parliament in 1958 to devote himself to the League for Human Rights of which he was president. In July 1977 he was elected president of the World Federation of the Human Rights League. Mayer was an active figure in Jewish affairs as president of ORT. When French policy toward Israel took a hostile turn, Mayer emerged as a vigorous defender of the Israeli cause both as a speaker and writer. His publications include *Etapes yougoslaves: producteur citoyen, homme* (1962); *Pour une histoire de la gauche* (1966); and *Les Socialistes dans la Résistance* (1968).

[Shulamith Catane]

MAYER, GUSTAV (1871–1948), German historian. Born in Prenzlau (Brandenburg), Mayer studied economics in Berlin and Freiburg and later worked as a journalist. Because of his criticism at the end of World War I his academic career came to a standstill and only in 1920 did he become professor of history, democracy, and socialism at the University of Berlin. He wrote extensively on socialism and the history of the German labor movement. Gustav's unbiased writings contributed to the appreciation of the historical significance of *Lassalle, *Marx, and his friend Friedrich Engels, about whom Mayer wrote an important biography. Among his books were: *Johann Baptist von Schweitzer und die Sozialdemokratie* (1909); *Die Anfaenge des politischen Radikalismus im vormaerzlichen Preussen* (1912); *Der deutsche Marxismus und der Krieg* (1916); *Aus der Welt des Sozialismus* (1927); *Bismarck und Lasalle, ihr Briefwechsel und ihre Gespraeche* (1928); *Friedrich Engels, eine Biographie* (2 vols., 1933; Eng., 1936). When the Nazis came to power Mayer emigrated to Holland where in 1949 his *Erinnerungen – Vom Journalisten zum Historiker der deutschen Arbeiterbewegung* was published. He refused to go back to Germany after World War II because he felt that German-Jewish symbiosis had failed.

BIBLIOGRAPHY: G. Niedhart, "Gustav Mayers englische Jahre – Zum Exil eines deutschen Juden und Historikers," in: *Exilforschung*, 6 (1988), 98–107; G. Niedhart, "Identitaetskonflikte eines deutschen Judens an der Wende vom 19. zum 20. Jahrhunderts – Gustav Mayer zwischen juedischer Herkunft und ungewisser deutscher Zukunft," in: *Tel Aviver Jahrbuch fuer Deutsche Geschichte*, 20 (1991), 315–26; J. Prellwitz, *Juedisches Erbe, sozialliberales Ethos, deutsche Nation – Gustav Mayer im Kaiserreich und in der Weimarer Republik* (1998).

[Bjoern Siegel (2nd ed.)]

MAYER, LEO ARY (1895–1959), Orientalist. Born in Stanislav (Austrian Poland), he settled in Palestine in 1921 and was successively inspector of antiquities and librarian and keeper of records for the Department of Antiquities. In 1925 he was appointed lecturer in the Institute of Oriental Studies of the Hebrew University of Jerusalem. From 1932 to 1958 he was professor of Near Eastern art and archaeology there. He held numerous positions: head of the Institute of Oriental Studies; dean of the faculty of humanities; rector of the Hebrew University (1943–45); president of the Israel Exploration Society (1940–59); and president of the Israel Oriental Society. With E.L. Sukenik, he excavated the Third Wall of Jerusalem and with A. Reifenberg the Eshtemoa synagogue. Mayer specialized in Islamic art, costume, epigraphy, and numismatics. His published works include *Saracenic Heraldry* (1933), *Mamluk Costume* (1952), bibliographies of Jewish art and numismatics, and a comprehensive work on Muslim artists, *Islamic Architects and Their Works* (1956). A museum of Islamic art and culture in Jerusalem was named after him.

[Michael Avi-Yonah]

MAYER, LEOPOLD (1827–1903), U.S. community leader and businessman. Mayer, who was born in Abendheim, Germany, immigrated to the United States in 1850. Settling in Chicago, he engaged in private tutoring of Hebrew and German and became known as "Lehrer Mayer." Mayer exerted great influence on the development of the new Jewish community in Chicago, particularly in religious education and in the movement toward Reform Judaism. In 1851 he conducted the first bar mitzvah service at Kehillath Anshe Maarab (K.A.M. Congregation) and also was a founder of the Hebrew Benevolent Society. In the former, Mayer advocated reforms in worship, including the adoption of the "living language German" in the ritual and preaching, but was unsuccessful in this effort. In 1859 he joined eight others, including Bernard *Felsenthal, to form the Jewish Reform Society (Juedischer Reformverein), which in 1861 founded Sinai Congregation, the first Reform congregation in the city. Mayer actively espoused the Union cause in the Civil War, and, with several other Jews, raised $10,000 to outfit a Jewish company of 100 recruits who formed the Concordio Guard. Later he and his brother entered the banking business.

BIBLIOGRAPHY: M.A. Gutstein, *Priceless Heritage* (1953).

[Morris A. Gutstein]

MAYER, LEVY (1858–1922), U.S. attorney. Mayer was born in Richmond, Virginia, and was brought up in Chicago. He graduated from Yale Law School, and in 1876 he became assistant librarian of the Chicago Law Institute, a position he held for six years. During this period he edited and revised the works of Judge David Rorer on interstate law, published as *American Interstate Law* (1879). Mayer became associated with the law firm Kraus, Mayer, and Stein, which he ultimately headed when it became Mayer, Meyer, Austrian and Platt. His major interest was corporation law, and he became one of the leading corporation lawyers in the country. He was a founder of many U.S. and international corporations and was identified with some celebrated law cases. Mayer served as a member of the State Council of Defense of Illinois during World War I. He was a member of the American Economic Association and the American Academy of Political Science. He was associated with the Zion Temple in Chicago and was secretary of the Zion Literary Society.

[Morris A. Gutstein]

MAYER, LOUIS BURT (1885–1957), U.S. motion picture executive. Born in Russia, he was taken to Canada at the age of two. In 1907 Mayer bought a burlesque theater in Haverhill, Massachusetts, began showing films there, and soon owned all the theaters in the city. Moving to Hollywood in 1918, he formed the Louis B. Mayer Pictures Corporation, which merged to form Metro-Goldwyn-Mayer in 1924, with Mayer as vice president in charge of production. His bold use of talent and his gift for understanding public taste made MGM enormously successful. He made *The Merry Widow* in 1925, and he turned the early Goldwyn production of *Ben Hur* (1927) into one of the greatest of silent pictures. A string of moneymaking successes included *The Good Earth* (1932), the *Andy Hardy* series, and *Treasure Island* (1950).

Mayer was a great exponent of the star system. In addition to "finding" Greta Garbo and Greer Garson, he helped to establish such stars as Norma Shearer, Lon Chaney, Joan Crawford, and Clark Gable. The powerful "L.B.," as he was called, liked films with children and presented such child stars as Jackie Cooper, Mickey Rooney, Peter Lawford, Judy Garland, and Elizabeth Taylor. He also knew how to find managerial talent. At MGM, where he remained a power until 1951, he had a series of brilliant production men, from Irving Thalberg to Dore Schary. For seven years he was the highest paid executive in the United States. From 1931 to 1936, he was president of the Association of Motion Picture Producers.

BIBLIOGRAPHY: B. Crowther, *Hollywood Rajah* (1960); *Current Biography Yearbook 1958* (1958); *New York Times* (Oct. 30, 1957), 29; (Nov. 1, 1957), 27; G. Jessel, *Elegy In Manhattan* (1961), 103–6.

[Harvey A. Cooper]

MAYER, RENÉ (1895–1972), French politician who was prime minister of France in 1953. Born in Paris, Mayer became a lawyer and fought in the French Army in World War I. In 1919 he was made an auditor in the Conseil d'Etat and was later given a senior post as Maître des Requêtes. He lectured at the Ecole Libre des Sciences Politiques from 1922 to 1932. He was vice president and secretary-general of the Chemins de Fer du Nord and from 1933 to 1940 was administrator of Air France, but in September 1940 was compelled by the Vichy government to give up these positions and shortly afterward he joined the Resistance. Mayer became a member of the French Committee for National Liberation in 1943 and in the following year was made minister of transport in the provisional government. He was elected to the National Assembly as a Radical Socialist in 1946 and was made minister of finance in the Pleven cabinet (1947–48). From 1949 to 1951 he was minister of justice in successive governments and after serving as minister of finance for a second term (1951–52), he became prime minister in January 1953. As prime minister, Mayer based his policy on friendship with Great Britain and a strong European defense community. His government fell the following May and Mayer was later active in the movement for European integration, becoming chairman of the Coal and Steel Authority (1955–58). Mayer played an active part in Jewish affairs and was a member of the Central Consistoire of French Jews. He was a member of the executive of the *Alliance Israélite Universelle and, after 1946, its vice president.

[Shulamith Catane]

MAYER, SIR ROBERT (1879–1985), British patron of music and philanthropist. Mayer was born in Mannheim, Germany, the son of a hops merchant. He emigrated to Britain at the age of 17, working as a stockbroker and then as a successful nonferrous metal dealer. Through his non-Jewish wife, a soprano singer and music patron, Mayer himself became involved as an organizer and sponsor of musical concerts for children, a series which spread throughout Britain and became well known. In 1932, in collaboration with Sir Thomas Beecham, he founded the London Philharmonic Orchestra. Mayer devoted his long life to introducing children to music and to assisting young musicians. He was a supporter of many other charitable causes, including the Anglo-Israel Association. Mayer was knighted in 1939 and was made a Companion of Honour (C.H.) in 1973. He also received many other honors, dying at the age of 105. Mayer wrote an autobiography, *My First Hundred Years* (1979).

BIBLIOGRAPHY: ODNB online.

[William D. Rubinstein (2nd ed.)]

MAYER, SALLY (1875–1953), Italian Jewish leader and philanthropist. Born in Alsheim, Germany, Mayer settled in Italy in 1891 and gave a great impetus to the paper industry of the Vita family, which, thanks to his activity, became one of the country's most important economic concerns. He was also active in Jewish and Zionist affairs. After World War II, he became president of the Milan Jewish community, the second largest in Italy, to which he devoted himself with great energy. He rebuilt the synagogue of Milan, destroyed in an air raid, and reopened the Jewish school there. All other Jewish and Zionist organizations in Milan and Italy, however, also benefited from his generosity and dynamism. Mayer was also a patron of non-Jewish welfare institutions in Milan and in Abbiate Guazzone, where his paper mills were located.

His son, ASTORRE MAYER (1906–1977), born in Milan, graduated as an engineer and carried on and expanded his father's enterprises in both the industrial and Jewish fields. For some years he was president of the Italian Zionist Federation and led the Jewish community in Milan. He also was honorary consul general of Israel there. He was president of the Standing Conference on European Jewish Community Service and other Jewish welfare and cultural institutions. Mayer also promoted important industries in Israel, the foremost being the Ḥaderah Paper Mills, of which he was a founder.

BIBLIOGRAPHY: G. Romano, in: *Scritti in memoria di Sally Mayer* (1956).

[Giorgio Romano]

MAYER, SALY (1882–1950), Swiss Jewish leader and representative of the *American Jewish Joint Distribution Committee in Switzerland. Mayer was born in Switzerland where he established a successful knitwear factory. He was a member of the Municipal Council of St. Gallen and chairman of the Association of Jewish Communities in 1936. During his term of office, the Association joined the World Jewish Congress. In 1938 he was involved in negotiations with the Swiss government regarding the immigration of Jews but could not overcome the anti-immigrant feeling in Switzerland and thus Swiss policy remained restrictive. In October of that year the Swiss requested that the passport of Jews from Germany be marked with the letter *J* to distinguish it from non-Jewish passports. During World War II Mayer was appointed director of the Swiss office of the American Joint Distribution Committee, in which capacity he maintained contact with the Jewish communities in German-occupied territories and was responsible for the transmission of funds from the JDC. The initial sum at his disposal was a paltry $6,370 in 1940, less than half that sum in 1941. After the Japanese occupation of China in 1941, he was responsible for the transmission of JDC funds for maintaining approximately 25,000 refugees in Shanghai under Japanese occupation. With the United States at war, American money could not be transmitted directly to enemy countries. A ruse was worked out where the Joint supported the Swiss Jewish Community's efforts to help their own refugees and the Swiss Jewish community would funnel funds to China. He was also involved in attempts to rescue Jews from the Germans. He participated in the Europa Plan of 1942 with the working group in Slovakia whereby, on payment of two to three million dollars provided by Jews in free countries, the remaining million Jews in Europe were to be saved from extermination. In his bitter memoirs Rabbi Michael Dov Weissmandel accused Mayer of ineffectiveness and bad faith. In reality his options were limited as the Joint in Lisbon did not approve the transaction, so Mayer was forced to send Swiss money illicitly to Bratislava. When adequate sums were not available, Mayer proposed that the money be deposited in blocked accounts in Switzerland until the end of the war. The negotiations dragged on until August 1943, when they were broken off on the orders of Himmler. With the knowledge of Himmler, Mayer negotiated with an S.S. delegation headed by Kurt Becher for the ransom of Jews from Hungary. His hands were tied by the American and Swiss governments, which would not permit the transfer of money and the Joint dissociated itself from these negotiations. Still Mayer arranged for a meeting between Becher and the representative of the *War Refugee Board, the arm of the American government committed to rescue and the only arm of the American government with the freedom to negotiate with the enemy. He could not provide substantive funds and he provided some equipment to buy some time. He was able to achieve a significant – albeit meager – result. Two transports numbering 1,391 – mostly Hungarian Jews – arrived in Switzerland from Bergen-Belsen, while 17,000 others were brought to Vienna.

After the war, he was accused from many sides. Hungarian Jewish leaders accused him of not meeting the Nazi ransom. He, in turn, accused them of financial impropriety. He continued to work for the JDC after the war, working with survivors and with the JDC efforts in Hungary and Romania.

The accusations hurled at him are a manifestation of the desperate conditions of his accusers and their inability to perceive how limited – how few – his options were. To the outside world, Mayer may have seemed the gateway to Jewish power; he lived with the reality of his own powerlessness, especially when judged by the scope of the needs he was asked to meet.

BIBLIOGRAPHY: Y. Bauer, *Jews for Sale: Nazi-Jewish Negotiations 1933–45* (1994); idem, *American Jewry and the Holocaust: The American Jewish Joint Distribution Committee, 1933–45* (1982); *The Jewish Emergence from Powerlessness* (1979).

[Michael Berenbaum (2nd ed.)]

MAYIM AḤARONIM (Heb. מַיִם אַחֲרוֹנִים; lit. "latter waters"), term for the ritual washing of the hands after a meal, and before the recitation of the Grace After Meals. The twofold injunction "Sanctify yourselves and be ye holy" (Lev. 20:7) was interpreted as commanding ritual ablution both before the meal and before the recitation of the Grace After Meals (Ber. 53b). The *amoraim* even contended that *mayim aḥaronim* was more important than washing before the meal (Yoma 83b; Ḥul. 106a). According to the Talmud, the duty was particularly insisted upon in order to prevent the danger of touching one's eyes with the salt which was used as a condiment during the meal (Ḥul. 105b). Because the variety of salt referred to by *Judah b. Ḥiyya in the Talmud was a particularly potent one (*melaḥ sedomit*, "salt of Sodom"), containing an admixture of the acrid potash of the Dead Sea, *tosafot* (*ibid.*) maintained that the duty did not apply in France, where this particular salt is not to be found. This view is contested, however, by the Shulḥan Arukh (OḤ 181:10). No blessing is said before the performance of *mayim aḥaronim* (Sh. Ar., OḤ 181:7).

MAYKAPAR, SAMUIL MOYSEYEVICH (1867–1938), pianist, composer, teacher, and writer. Born in Kherson, Ukraine, Maykapar graduated from the Law School of St. Petersburg University (1890) and from the St. Petersburg Conservatory as a pianist in 1893. From 1894 to 1896 he continued his studies with Leshetitzky in Vienna. The period 1898–1910 was divided between Moscow (1898–1901), Tver (where he founded a music school, 1901–03), and Germany (1903–10). From 1910 to 1930 he taught in the St. Petersburg Conservatory (from 1917 as a professor). Maykapar often worked as a concert pianist, in ensembles with Auer and Grzhimali. His short piano pieces for children remain popular, especially *Biryulki* ("Spillikins"), *Bagatelles*, and *The Marionette Theater.* He also composed chamber music and a sonatina for violin and piano. His writings include *Muzykal'nyi slukh: ego znachenie, priroda, osobennosti i metod pravil'nogo razvitia* ("The Musical Ear: Its Significance, Nature, Peculiarities and a Method of Proper Development," 1890, 1915[2]); a study on Beethoven (1927), an autobiography, *The Years of Study* (1938), and other works.

BIBLIOGRAPHY: B. Volman, *Samuil Moiseevich Maikapar: Ocherk zhizni i tvorchestva* (1963); K. Petrova, "*Komzitor, posvyativshiy svoe tvorchestvo detyam*," in: *Muzykal'naya zhizn'*, 14 (1961).

[Marina Rizarev (2nd ed.)]

MAY LAWS, a series of "temporary laws" applying to Jews confirmed by Czar Alexander III in May 1882 and repealed in March 1917 by the revolutionary provisional government. The pogroms which broke out in southern Russia in 1881 brought the Jewish problem into prominence. Reports by higher government officials placed the blame on the Jews and pointed to the failure of the relatively liberal policy of Alexander II. On the basis of these reports, the minister of the interior Ignatiev wrote to Czar Alexander III:

> The principal, indeed exclusive cause of this [anti-Jewish] movement is the economic situation; over the last 20 years the Jews have gradually gained control of commerce and industry; they have also acquired, mainly by purchase or lease, much land, and by their unity they have generally made every possible effort to exploit the general population, especially the impoverished classes. They have thus fomented a wave of protest, which has taken the unfortunate form of violence. Now that the government has firmly suppressed the riots and lawlessness in order to protect the Jews, justice demands that it immediately impose severe regulations which will alter the unfair relations between the general inhabitants and the Jews and protect the former from the harmful activity of the latter.

Accordingly, on Aug. 22 (Sept. 3), 1881, the czar ordered the formation of special committees in the districts inhabited by Jews. Composed of representatives of the various classes and communities and presided over by the governor of the province, the committees were to determine "which kinds of Jewish economic activity had a harmful effect on the lives of the general inhabitants." This directive predetermined the attitude adopted by the committees. During their deliberations of September-October 1881 accusations against the Jews were made by the representatives of the peasants and townspeople, while the Jewish representatives endeavored to defend themselves. Their conclusions were passed on to a special committee formed to draft legislation. While the latter was in session during the winter of 1882, an anti-Jewish campaign was fomented by the press (with the support even of the Russian revolutionary movement Narodnaya Volya) and there were renewed outbreaks of violence in towns such as Warsaw and Balta. With the consent of the government, Jewish leaders assembled twice in St. Petersburg (September 1881 and April 1882) to discuss the government proposals, the most far-reaching of which suggested a planned mass emigration of Russian Jewry or the settlement of many Jews on the plains of Central Asia. Against these extreme measures some intercessionary moves were made behind the scenes, and outraged liberal public opinion in Western Europe also had some influence.

As a result, the "temporary regulations" of May 3 (15), 1882 stated: (1) Jews are forbidden to settle outside the towns and townlets; (2) deeds of sale and lease of real estate in the name of Jews outside the towns and townlets are canceled; and (3) Jews are prohibited from trading on Sundays and Christian holidays. The "temporary laws" satisfied the demands of the Russian rural merchant class that sought to be rid of its Jewish rivals in the villages of the Ukraine and Belorussia. In effect they were a contraction of the *Pale of Settlement, since Jews were confined to towns and townlets only. These laws were binding in the 15 "Russian" provinces of the Pale of Settlement (but not in the provinces of the "Kingdom of Poland"). Until 1904 they also applied to those Jews who had been granted the right of residence throughout the empire (with the exception of university graduates). The police were charged with the implementation of these laws, which became a source of constant police extortion and harassment of Jews still living in the villages. Over the years, the May Laws were interpreted with increasing severity. Thus in 1887 the Jews living in villages prior to 1882 were forbidden to move from one village to another.

Examining the legislation concerning the Jews between 1883 and 1888, the Pahlen Commission condemned the "temporary laws" and advocated that they be abolished, but its recommendations were rejected by the government. At the beginning of the 20th century, criticism of the "temporary laws" was voiced by the generally anti-Jewish Russian ministers of the interior Sipyaghin and *Plehve. It was decided on May 10, 1903, to authorize Jewish residence in 101 villages, which in the meantime had developed and in practice became townlets. On the outbreak of World War I, there were 300 villages of this kind. Echoes of the May Laws are found in the Jewish literature of Russia (cf. Shalom Aleichem, *Tevye der Milkhiger*; Ḥ.N. Bialik, *Ha-Ḥaẓoẓerah she-Nitbayyeshah*; S. Ben-Zion, *Ḥayyim shel Parnasah, etc.*).

BIBLIOGRAPHY: Gessen, in: *Pravo* (1908) no. 30, 1632; Dubnow, Hist Russ, 2 (1916), 309–12; Elbogen, Century, 210–20; Dinur, in: *He-Avar*, 10 (1963), 5–60.

[Yehuda Slutsky]

MAYMERAN (**Maimoran, Mimran**), family of rabbis and diplomats in *Morocco and *Algeria, originally from *Marrakesh. R. MEIR MAYMERAN (early 17th century) of Ereẓ Israel sent a letter recommending Isaac Cansino to collect funds in *Oran (Algeria) for his *hekdesh* ("poor house"). Maymeran was the head of a largely *Shabbatean Marrakesh community in the second half of the 17th century. The two best known members of the Maymeran family were JOSEPH (d. 1683) and his son ABRAHAM (d. 1723), who served as financial advisers to the ruler Moulay Ismail (1672–1721) in *Meknès. Joseph was instrumental in formulating and negotiating the commercial treaties between Morocco and the Netherlands in 1682. According to the priest Busnot, Joseph played a major role in bringing Ismail to power, but Ismail caused Joseph's downfall with an "accident." Abraham succeeded his father as the king's favorite, continuing the negotiations with the Dutch and obtaining commercial privileges from the British and French as well. Abraham was involved in ransoming captives in 1688, and like his father was the head of Moroccan Jewry, on whose behalf he attempted to lighten the king's heavy taxation. His rival in the community was Moses *Benatar. Abraham's nephew SAMUEL negotiated with the English and the Dutch, and a relative, Moïse, dealt with the French.

BIBLIOGRAPHY: J.M. Toledano, *Ner ha-Ma'arav* (1911), 121f.; Hirschberg, Afrikah, 2 (1965), 105, 267–76; idem, in: H.J. Zimmels et al. (eds.), *Essays Presented to Chief Rabbi Israel Brodie*… (1967), 161–2; P. de Cenival, in: *Hesperis*, 5 (1925), 176f.; I.D. Abbou, *Musulmans andalous et judéo-espagnols* (1953), 309–12; SIHM, index.

MAYNARD, FREDELLE BRUSER (1922–1989), writer. Born in Foam Lake, Saskatchewan, to Boris and Rona Bruser (née Slobinsky). She studied English literature (Honors B.A., University of Manitoba (1943); M.A., University of Toronto (1944); Ph.D., Radcliffe College, Harvard University (1947)). Maynard belongs to a generation of Jewish Canadian women writers that included Miriam Waddington and Adele Wiseman. She is perhaps best known for *Raisins and Almonds* (1972) and *The Tree of Life* (1988), two autobiographical works in which she asks "Who am I?" and emphatically concludes: "Woman and Jew, I am also my parents' child." The interest of these volumes thus lies in their combination of a vivid portrayal of family dynamics with a pointed representation of the social conditions that affect the life of a Jew and a woman at a particular historical juncture. Maynard's recollections of her gentle artist-turned-shopkeeper father in *Raisins and Almonds* are presented against the backdrop of her experience of growing up "Jewish and alien" in the small towns of western Canada during the 1920s and 1930s. *The Tree of Life* explores Maynard's complex relationships with her mother, sister, her gentile husband, the artist Max Maynard (they divorced shortly after the publication of *Raisins and Almonds*), and two daughters Rona and Joyce, while also demonstrating the repercussions of a pervasive gender discrimination that made academic employment unattainable even for somebody with her stellar record. Discouraged but not defeated, Maynard began a successful journalism career that would span four decades, writing about education, child care and development, health and medicine, and family relationships in Canadian and American publications such as *Good Housekeeping*, *Ladies' Home Journal*, *Family Circle*, *Woman's Day*, *Chatelaine*, *Parents*, and *Reader's Digest*. During the 1970s and 1980s Maynard was the initiator and host of two popular Ontario parenting shows one of which was *Parents and Children*. Maynard also published two books on parenting and child care: *Guiding Your Child to a More Creative Life* (1973), and the controversial *The Child Care Crisis* (1985), in which she advocated stay-at-home parenting over day-care during a child's formative years. Further light on Maynard's life is shed by autobiographical writings by her daughters, including Rona Maynard's personal journalism in various magazines (she was editor of *Chatelaine* for ten years until 2005), and Joyce Maynard's memoir *At Home in the World* (1998). Maynard's papers are at the University of Manitoba Archives and Special Collections.

[Bina Toledo Freiwald (2nd ed.)]

MAYSE-BUKH ("Book of Stories"; Heb. מַעֲשֶׂה, "story"). Like many other folk-books, the *Mayse-Bukh* is a vast anonymous collection of stories and folktales, legends and oral traditions handed down from generation to generation orally and later recorded in writing in Yiddish. The book contains much from the talmudic *aggadah* and Midrash, here translated into the vernacular and copied and recopied by various writers who also adapted and judaized material from other traditions.

The *Mayse-Bukh* was first published in Basel in 1602 under the title *Eyn Shoen Mayse Bukh* by Jacob b. Abraham of Mezhirech (also known as Jacob Pollak or Bukhhendler), who is known to have been a compiler of religious textbooks, printer, publisher, and bookseller. The *Mayse-Bukh* with its

255 stories was compiled in the latter part of the 16th century, certainly not before 1580, the year when the book *Kaftor va-Feraḥ* by the mystic Jacob Luzzatto was published in Basel, from which the author of the *Mayse-Bukh* borrowed several stories to supplement his collection. However, it is clear that much of the narrative lore included in the book derived from earlier generations; extant manuscripts of Yiddish *mayses* ("stories") bear witness to a lively and continuous productivity in the field of creative narrative traditions.

The *Mayse-Bukh* is part of the folk-literature in Yiddish designed for the use of the common man untutored in the holy language and its literature, and for women who for the first time had access to a written language and through it to education. The rhetorical style mirrors the transition from an oral to a literary tradition. The collection became quite influential, in that the *mayse* became such a foundation for later prose narrative that, even up to the present, Yiddish authors have continued to draw inspiration from it. The book aims to provide a substitute for the widely circulated popular secular literature of the period, which the compiler of the *Mayse-Bukh*, like many others before him, considered impious. His collection, intended to replace this literature and provide a new kind of "*aggadah* in the vernacular," is permeated with a spirit of piety to strengthen the reader's faith.

The *mayse* corresponds to the Christian *exemplum* and serves to teach conduct and ethical principles, while also providing entertainment for the masses. As such, the *Mayse-Bukh* follows the example of numerous medieval Hebrew collections designed to inculcate a moral dictum by way of a narration. It thus had a powerful influence on Old Yiddish didactic literature. The moral of the story was usually appended at the end of the tale and concluded with the hope for an early arrival of the Messiah. Despite his piety, the compiler of the *Mayse-Bukh* did not resist the trend of his time, but, according to popular taste, he included various anecdotes, merry tales and fabliaux, often in keeping with the Italian or French *conte* and German fable collections, with their licentious, sometimes satirical, tone. The author drew profusely on non-Jewish sources, altering the plot or its characters where possible and adapting the tale to suit a Jewish sensibility. In this rich collection, Eastern themes mingle with Western material, and midrashic stories with legendary lore. A product of its times and a reflection of its own problematics, the *Mayse-Bukh* provides a key to understanding Ashkenazi literature, culture, and society in their Germanic context of the early modern period. Between the first edition of Basel in 1602 and the year 1763, 12 subsequent editions were published. Even in the 19th century several shorter and modernized versions appeared. The popular *Mayse-Bukh* nourished to a great extent ethical literature in Yiddish and served as a model for similar collections which were later composed and incorporated into folk-literature.

The *Mayse-Bukh* consists of three parts. The main section is devoted to stories from Talmud and Midrash, drawn in part from the *Ein Ya'akov*. The second contains a cycle of 27 legends and narrative traditions centered around R. Samuel and his son R. *Judah he-Ḥasid (the "Pious"), the great mystics of medieval Germany, and the authors of the *Sefer *Ḥasidim*. These stories early entered the oral tradition and were later recorded in Hebrew as well as in Yiddish. The third part consists of a variety of narrative material: medieval stories about *Rashi, *Maimonides, and the story of the Jewish pope.

See Yiddish *Literature, *Exemplum.

BIBLIOGRAPHY: M. Gaster, *Ma'aseh Book*, 2 vols. (1934); idem, in: *Jewish Studies in Memory of George A. Kohut* (1935), 270–9.; J. Maitlis, *Ma'aseh in the Yiddish Ethical Literature* (1958); idem, *Das Ma'asebuch* (1933); Minkoff, in: *The Jewish People, Past and Present*, 3 (1952), 157f.; I. Zinberg, *Geshikhte fun der Literatur bay Yidn*, 6 (1943), 210–26; M. Erik, *Geshikhte fun der Yidisher Literatur* (1928), 353–64. **ADD. BIBLIOGRAPHY:** A. Starck, *Un beau livre d'histoires. Eyn shön Mayse bukh. Fac-similé de l'editio princeps de Bâle (1602)* (2004); E. Timm, in: *Beiträge zur Geschichte der deutschen Sprache und Literatur*, 117 (1995), 243–80; S. Zfatman, in: *Sifrut* 28 (1979), 126–52; idem, *Ha-Sipporet be-Yididish: mi-Reshitah ad Shiveḥei ha-Besht, 1504–1814* (1985); I. Zimt-Sand, in: *The Field of Yiddish* 2 (1965), 24–48.

[Jacob J. Maitlis / Astrid Starck (2nd ed.)]

MAYSLES, ALBERT (1926–) and **DAVID PAUL** (1932–1987), U.S. directors. Born in Brookline, Massachusetts, the brothers attended Brookline High School and studied psychology at Boston University. Albert taught psychology at Boston University in the late 1940s and in 1955 traveled to the Soviet Union to make his first film, *Psychiatry in Russia*. In 1956, David worked as a production assistant on the Marilyn Monroe films *Bus Stop* and *The Prince and the Showgirl*. In 1957, the brothers took a motorcycle trip together from Munich to Moscow. While in Poland, they focused on the student protest movement as the subject of their first film together, *Youth in Poland*. The next documentary for the brothers, *Primary* (1960), focused on the 1960 Democratic primary election campaigns of Kennedy and Humphrey. In 1962, they formed their own production company, Maysles Films, Inc., which made commercials and industrial films to support their *cinéma vérité* style of documentary filmmaking. Their next films were *Showman* (1962) and *What's Happening: The Beatles in the USA* (1964). In 1965, they released *Meet Marlon Brando*, which followed the actor during publicity interviews, and received a Guggenheim Fellowship. The brothers found themselves caught in the middle of a debate on objectivity in documentary filmmaking with the release of the National Society of Film Critics award-winner *Salesman* (1968), which portrays four door-to-door high-pressure Bible salesmen in Boston who sell to poor Catholic families. They returned to rock 'n' roll with *Gimme Shelter* (1970), a film that follows Mick Jagger and the Rolling Stones on a North American tour and ends with the infamous concert at Altamont Speedway in California during which a murder occurred. The Maysles' *Grey Gardens* (1975) portrayed Jacqueline Kennedy Onassis' cousins, Edith and Edie Beale, an eccentric mother and daughter living in a decaying East Hampton mansion. The brothers also produced films on celebrated artists Christo and Jeanne-Claude, including the Academy Award-nominated *Christo's Valley Curtain*

(1974) and *Running Fence* (1978). David died of a heart attack in New York in 1987. Later that year, Albert received the Emmy Award for the brothers' *Vladimir Horowitz: The Last Romantic* (1986). Albert continued to direct such films as *Christo in Paris* (1991), *Abortion: Desperate Choices* (1993), *Umbrellas* (1994), *Letting Go: A Hospice Journey* (1996), and *The Gates – A Project for New York City* (2005).

BIBLIOGRAPHY: "Maysles, Albert," in: *Contemporary Authors* (Gale, 2005); "Maysles, David," ibid. (Gale, 2003); "Maysles, Albert and David," in: *International Directory of Films and Filmmakers, Volume 2: Directors* (2004); Albert Maysles – IMDB, at: www.imdb.com/name/nm0563099; David Maysles – IMDB, at: www.imdb.com/name/nm0563100; Mayles Films Inc. Biography, at: www.maysles-films.com.

[Adam Wills (2nd ed.)]

MAYZEL, MAURYCY, last president of the Warsaw Jewish community before the Holocaust (1937–39). In the elections held in 1936, after *Agudat Israel had been in power for six years, the *Bund increased its strength to become the largest party. As the three most prominent groups (the Zionists, the Orthodox, and the Bund) could not reach agreement on the establishment of an effective administration, the government dissolved the community council. Mayzel was appointed community president, and a committee of independent personalities, including Adam *Czerniakow, Mark Lichtenbaum, Kaminer (Orthodox), and the lawyer Zondelewicz, was formed to assist him. Mayzel himself was a leader of the merchants' association and an assimilationist in outlook. The attitude of the parties' delegates and the public toward the government appointment was negative. Mayzel was essentially an administrator who sought to assure regular and vital services while obeying the instructions of the authorities; the latter supported him in the face of violent criticism from the public and the Jewish press. Mayzel promoted the publication of the important trilingual organ of the Warsaw community *Glos gminy Zydowskiej* (1937–39). When the Nazis invaded Poland, he fled from Warsaw; the mayor of Warsaw appointed Adam Czerniakow in his place.

BIBLIOGRAPHY: H.M. Rabinowicz, *Legacy of Polish Jewry* (1965), 123–4. **ADD. BIBLIOGRAPHY:** R. Sakowska, "Z Dziejow Gminy Zydowskiej w Warszawie 1918–1939," in: *Warszawa drugiej Rzeczypospolitej*, 4 (1972); A. Guterman, *Kehillat Varshah bein Shetei Millḥamot* (1997), index

[Moshe Landau]

MAYZEL, NACHMAN (1887–1966), Yiddish editor, literary critic, and historian. Born in Kiev, Mayzel stemmed from a family of rabbis and rich Kiev merchants and was related to the Yiddish novelists Dovid *Bergelson and *Der Nister, whose fame he helped to spread. He made his debut with essays in Hebrew (1905) and in Yiddish (1909), and, after the Revolution of 1917, founded the publishing house, Kiev Farlag, which issued more than 100 books. He also edited periodicals and anthologies of the Kiev Culture League. Settling in Warsaw in 1921, he helped to found its Culture League and continued his activity as editor and literary critic. He later described this dynamic period in his volume *Geven Amol a Lebn* ("There Used to Be a Life," 1951). In 1924 he co-founded and co-edited the weekly *Literarishe Bleter*, which exerted a significant influence upon Yiddish literary activity in Poland between the two world wars; he also played a central role in organizing the Yiddish Pen Club (1927). He participated in the Jewish World Congress of Culture (1937) in Paris, which launched YKUF, the international Yiddish Culture League. Immigrating to New York in 1937, he furthered the growth of YKUF's American section and edited its monthly organ *Yidishe Kultur* from 1939 to 1964, and then settled in Israel at Kibbutz Alonim. Mayzel was a prolific writer, composing more than 40 books and hundreds of major articles. *Noente un Vayte* ("Close and Distant People," 2 vols., 1924–26) contained his most valuable early articles. His studies on I.L. *Peretz and on Sholem Yankev *Abramovitsh contributed important new knowledge. His book *Dos Yidishe Shafn un der Yidisher Shrayber in Sovetnfarband* ("Yiddish Creativity and Yiddish Writers in the Soviet Union," 1959) surveyed, in 20 essays, Russian Yiddish literature from 1917 until the tragic autumn of 1948 when Yiddish cultural institutions were liquidated and their leaders silenced. In his last years in Israel he completed studies on Chaim *Zhitlowsky (1965) and on the influence of national literatures upon each other, with special emphasis on the influence of foreign literatures upon Yiddish writers (1966).

BIBLIOGRAPHY: Rejzen, Leksikon, 2 (1927), 380–4; *Yidishe Kultur*, 28 no. 5 (1966), 1–8; 28 no. 6 (1966), 31–57; LNYL, 5 (1963), 578–87. **ADD. BIBLIOGRAPHY:** G. Estraikh, *In Harness* (2005), index.

[Sol Liptzin]

MĀZANDARĀN, region called Tabaristān in the early Islamic period, situated in the southern part of the Caspian Sea, north of Alborz Mountains and east of Gilān. Its length extends to a maximum of 320 km. and its width to 96 km. The oldest reference to the existence of Jews in Māzandarān is in the Persian Chronicle of Eskandar Beg (vol. 2, pp. 900–1) which points to the transfer by Shah *'Abbās I of 100,000 non-Muslim captives of Georgia to Māzandarān and Farah-Ābād south of Caspian Sea, most probably around 1616/17. Farah-Ābād is also mentioned in the Chronicle of *Bābāi ben Lutf (17th century), as if it was built by the transferred Jews of Georgia. There is no mention of Jews in Farah-Ābād during the 19th century. The cause of their disappearance is not known.

Another important city in Māzandarān is Bārforush, whose name was changed by the Iranian Majles to Bābol around 1935. According to Fraser (1826), Farah-Ābād was a large, prosperous city of 200,000 inhabitants. On his second trip (1838), he was not impressed by the city which was populated by only 30,000 inhabitants. No reason was given for this drastic change, but it is possible that the main reason was the deviation in trade routes to Europe from Bārforush to Rasht. H.A. Stern, a Christian missionary who visited the

Jewish community of Bārforush in 1852, gives us the following information: "150 Jewish families live among 20,000 inhabitants. They have six synagogues. In the past they suffered bitter persecutions. They constantly quarrel among themselves and for this reason some of them have willingly embraced Islam." Stern also writes, "The sorrows and sufferings of the living [the Jews of Bārforush] being, however, insupportable and overwhelming enough, their enemies to satiate their intense and inhuman hate, with an invective cruelty which makes the heart recoil, and the soul shudder, exhume ten, fifteen, or even twenty, recently deceased Israelites, and these amidst wild shouts and pious ejaculations they consume on a lofty funeral pyre." Stern calls this "a savage exhibition of bigotry and fanaticism." About 14 years after Stern's visit, the Muslims of the city attacked the Jews in their Mahalleh, killed 18 men and 6 women, and wounded many of them. Two of the 18 were burned to death with inflammable material. The rest of the Jews fled to find shelter in the jungles around the city. The horrible news reached the British consul, A.H. Mounsey, who complained to Nāser al-Din Shah. The shah simply announced he could do nothing against the fanatical Muslim clergy. The massacre of Bārforush Jews also drew the attention of the Jewish leaders in Paris.

There were in Māzandarān other towns where Jews lived, such as Sāri, Āmol, and a few other small settlements. During the first half of the 20th century many Jews left Bārforush and other towns of the province and went to live in Tehran. After 1948, a majority immigrated to Israel. There is no mention of Jewish communities in Bārforush or in any other places in Māzandarān after the 1979 Islamic revolution in Iran.

BIBLIOGRAPHY: *Bulletin de l'Alliance Israélite Universelle* (BAIU); E. Beg, *Ālam-Ārā-ye 'Abbāsi*, 2 vols. (1971); J.B. Fraser, *Travels and Adventures in the Persian Provinces on the Southern Bank of the Caspian Sea* (1826); idem, *A Winter's Journey from Constantinople to Tehran* 12 (1838); A. Netzer, "*Yehudim ba-Meḥozot ha-Deromiyyim shel ha-Yam ha-Kaspi: Māzandarān*," in: *Ḥevra u-Kehillah* (1991), 85–98; H.L. Rabino, *Mazandaran and Astarabad* (1928); idem, *Les Provinces caspiennes de la Perse* (1917); H.A. Stern, *Dawning of Light in the East* (1854); A.H. Mounsey, *A Journey Through the Caucasus and the Interior of Persia* (1872).

[Amnon Netzer (2nd ed.)]

MAZAR, AMIHAI (1942–), Israeli archaeologist, with a specialist interest in the Bronze and Iron Ages, and the relationship between archaeology and biblical history. Born in Haifa, Mazar began his studies in 1966 at the Hebrew University of Jerusalem, completing his Ph.D. in 1976, and serving there as lecturer from 1977 to 1981 (as well as at the Ben-Gurion University, Beersheba). A senior lecturer at the Institute of Archaeology at the Hebrew University from 1982, Mazar was appointed associate professor in 1986 and from 1994 was the incumbent of the Eleazar Sukenik Chair in the Archaeology of Israel. Numerous academic duties included serving as head of the Institute of Archaeology (1995–98) and as a member of the Archaeological Council of Israel (1994–99) and the Council of the Israel Antiquities Authority (2001–5). Following his survey of the aqueducts of Jerusalem in 1968, Mazar conducted important excavations at Tel Qasile (1971–74, and later in 1982–90), at Tel Batash, biblical Timnah (with G.L. Kelm, 1977–89), and at Giloh near Jerusalem (1978–82). From the late 1980s Mazar directed the Beth Shean Valley Archaeological Project, with excavations at Tel Beth-Shean (1989–96) and, more recently, excavations at Tel Rehov (from 1997). A frequent participant in international scientific meetings and conferences, Mazar was a prolific writer with many scientific papers, monographs, and books to his credit. He is probably best known to students of archaeology as the author of *Archaeology of the Land of the Bible (ca. 10,000–586 B.C.E.)*, which was published in English in 1990, with subsequent translations into Portuguese, Russian, and Japanese. Important monographs have also appeared under his authorship on the Tel Qasile and Tel Batash excavations. Mazar participated in the important tenth/ninth-century chronology debate (see his paper "Iron Age Chronology: A Reply to I. Finkelstein," in: *Levant*, 29 (1997), 157–67). Mazar's strength in his publications was in the reasoned and balanced approach he took to archaeological materials, one which has influenced many of the younger generations of Israeli archaeologists. Mazar is regarded as a very loyal mentor to his students.

[Shimon Gibson (2nd ed.)]

MAZAR (Maisler), BENJAMIN (1906–1995), Israeli archaeologist and historian. Born in Ciechanowiec in Poland, he studied at the universities of Berlin and Giessen. In 1929 he settled in Palestine, becoming the secretary of the Jewish Palestine Exploration Society (1929–43). Mazar joined the staff of the Hebrew University in 1943 and in 1951 he was appointed professor of the history of the Jewish people in the biblical period and the archaeology of Palestine. He was appointed rector of the university in 1952 and president in 1953, holding both positions until 1961. In 1959 he became president of the Israel Exploration Society. He was also chairman of the Archaeological Board of Israel and a member of the Israel Academy of Sciences and Humanities. In 1968 he received the Israel Prize for Jewish Studies. Mazar directed archaeological excavations at *Ramat Raḥel (1931), *Bet She'arim (1936–40), Tell Qasile (1949ff.), and *En-Gedi (1957–66). He conducted the historic excavation along the outside of the southern and western sections of the Temple enclosure in Jerusalem and the Tyropoeon Valley (1967ff.). Besides over 300 articles, including excavation reports, Mazar has published *Untersuchungen zur alten Geschichte und Ethnographie Syriens und Palästinas* (1930); *Toledot ha-Meḥkar ha-Arkheologi be-Ereẓ Yisrael* ("History of Palestine Exploration," 1935); *Toledot Ereẓ Yisrael* ("History of Palestine" part 1, 1937); *Israel in Biblical Times* – a Historical Atlas (1941); and the first volume of *Beth Shearim* (1944, 1957²). He headed the editorial board of the biblical encyclopedia *Enẓiklopedyah Mikra'it* (1950–89). An important collection of Mazar's articles was assembled in S. Ahituv and B. Levine (eds.), *The Early Biblical Period: Historical Studies*

(1986). Over a period of two generations Mazar trained most of the Israeli archaeologists and Bible scholars.

BIBLIOGRAPHY: H. Beinart, in: *Eretz Israel*, 5 (1958), 1–8. **ADD. BIBLIOGRAPHY:** W. Dever, in: DBI, 2:141.

[Michael Avi-Yonah / S. David Sperling (2nd ed.)]

MAZE, IDA (1893–1962) Yiddish poet. Born near Kapuly, Belarus; she arrived in Canada with her family in 1907, eventually settling in Montreal. Her family, the Zhukovskys, were distantly related to Sholem Yankev *Abramovitsh (Mendele Mokher Sforim) and were intellectual though poor. She began writing poems of grief in 1928, following the death of her eldest son. These poems were collected in *A Mame* ("A Mother," 1931). Throughout her career the majority of her poems were either for children or about her children (she had two surviving sons); some of them took in natural themes. Her talents lay chiefly in her ability to write engrossing, fluid, and sometimes urgent rhythms and rhymes. Her later books were *Lider far Kinder* ("Poems for Children," 1936), *Naye Lider* ("New Poems," 1941) and *Vaksn Mayne Kinderlekh* ("Grow, My Little Ones," 1954). An autobiographical novel, *Dinah*, was published posthumously (1970). More important than her own output, however, was her role in the Montreal Yiddish artistic community which centered around the Jewish Public Library. Her apartment served as a literary salon for writers at every level, the more famous coming simply to read aloud and find literary companions while the lesser known workshopped their poems with a critical audience. In addition to this, Maze spent most of her time arranging visas, work permits, or actually finding jobs for the Yiddish-speaking refugees who came through Montreal. Although much of her aid went to Yiddish writers, she was as generous with the lesser as with the major talents. Canadian historian David Rome reported her appeal on behalf of one struggling poet: "He needs help, not only because he is penniless and his family is falling apart, but because he doesn't have a speck of talent" (Massey, 54). These endeavors earned her the nickname "the mother of Yiddish writers." Among those who spent a great deal of time in her apartment were Melech *Ravitch, Rokhl *Korn, and J.J. *Segal. Visitors from the United States included Kadya *Molodowsky, Moyshe *Nadir, and H. *Leivick. The English-language poet Miriam *Waddington, whose family spoke Yiddish at home, attended these salons as a teenager. Maze's impact seems to have largely consisted of imparting by example her ideas about literature: its place as a feature of everyday life, in which every member of society is equally implicated and from which every individual of whatever talents could draw his or her own intellectual sustenance.

BIBLIOGRAPHY: Massey, *Identity and Community: Reflections on English, Yiddish and French Literature in Canada* (1994); M. Waddington, "Mrs. Maze's Salon," in: *Canadian Woman Studies* 16/4, 119f; LNYL 5, 402f; C.L. Fuks, *100 Yor Yidishe un Hebreishe Literatur in Kanade* (1982): 156f.

[Faith Jones (2nd ed.)]

MAZEH, JACOB (1859–1924), Zionist leader and Hebrew writer. Born in Mogilev, Belorussia, he was orphaned in childhood and given a traditional education in his grandfather's home. Later he read and was influenced by the Haskalah, in particular by the works of E. *Zweifel. At the age of 16, he entered a Russian secondary school in *Kerch, Crimea, and in 1886 completed his studies at the law faculty of the Moscow University. After the pogroms of 1882, he joined the *Ḥibbat Zion movement and was one of the founders of the Benei Zion Society (1884). In his article *Elleh Hem ha-Ashamot* in *Ha-Meliẓ (1888) Mazeh rebuked his generation for negligence in the education of their children, charging exorbitant rates of interest, forging currency, evading public welfare activities, despising work, and "lack of positive love of our fathers." He represented the Benei Zion at the founding conference of the Committee for the Support of Farmers and Craftsmen in Palestine (Odessa, 1890), and organized a group of wealthy men for settlement in Ereẓ Israel. Traveling there as their emissary, he even opened negotiations for the purchase of the *Mahanaim tract of land in Galilee for the project, which was brought to a halt as a result of the Moscow expulsion (1891).

In 1893, after S.Z. *Minor was removed from his position as **kazyonny ravvin* (government-appointed rabbi) of the Moscow community, Mazeh was appointed as his successor. Being both a *maskil* and a man steeped in Jewish tradition and nationalism, he was an exception to the usual type of *kazyonny ravvin*. He became the spiritual leader of his congregation and its representative before the local authorities, who were noted for their hatred of the Jews. A brilliant orator, Mazeh was well known for his numerous activities in Jewish public life, which included the promotion of Hebrew culture and the founding of the Ḥovevei Sefat Ever Society. His appearance as the defense expert on Jewish law at the *Beilis trial in Kiev (1912), when he refuted the evidence of the prosecution "experts", made him famous among Jews everywhere. After the 1917 Revolution, he was a deputy at the all-Russian Constituent Assembly representing the Jewish National List and was also among the founders and devoted workers of the *Tarbut organization. He supported the *Habimah theater during its early years. With the establishment of the Soviet regime, Mazeh interceded with the authorities in order to assure the rights of Hebrew language and culture. In 1920 he participated in the last Zionist Council of Russia. He refused to sign the declaration of the representatives of the various religions in which they denied that religion was persecuted in the U.S.S.R. In his last years, deprived of his functions under the Communist regime, Mazeh wrote his memoirs, which are marked by dignity and humor. He was unable to complete them as he became blind in 1922. The chapters which were brought out of Russia and published in Ereẓ Israel (*Zikhronot*, 4 vols., 1936) are a valuable source for the history of Russian Jewry and Hebrew literature. Mazeh wrote under the pseudonyms Saadiah, Jacob ha-Kohen, Aharoni, and Kochav. Thousands of local Jews took part in his funeral in Moscow.

BIBLIOGRAPHY: Z. Rabiner, *Sefer ha-Rav Mazeh* (1958).

[Yehuda Slutsky]

MAZER, U.S. family of business executives. ABRAHAM MAZER (1876–1953) was born in Goshcha, Ukraine. He went to the United States at the age of 17 and started a paper business in Hartford, Connecticut, later managing it from New York City. In 1952 the company, the Hudson Pulp and Paper Corporation, had a sales volume of $36 million and plants in four states, and held half a million acres of woodland in Florida and Maine. Mazer played a leading role in the United Jewish Appeal, the Federation of Jewish Philanthropies, and the Jewish National Fund. He supported Yeshiva University in New York and the Hebrew University of Jerusalem, and founded the Abraham Mazer Free Loan Bank of Israel. His three sons, JACOB (1898–1968), JOSEPH M. (1899–1979), and WILLIAM (1905–1998), took over the corporation's executive posts. They were active in Jewish charity work, taking a special interest in undertakings benefiting Israel. The family sponsored the American-Israeli Paper Mills in Ḥadera, Israel.

MAZKERET BATYAH (Heb. מַזְכֶּרֶת בַּתְיָה; "Memory of Batyah"), moshavah with municipal council status, in the Coastal Plain of Israel southeast of Reḥovot. Its name commemorates Baron Edmond de *Rothschild's mother. It was the first village founded upon Baron Edmond de Rothschild's initiative (1883), and was known up until the early 1900s mostly by the name of Ekron (see *Kiryat Ekron). The name Ekron was given in the desire to identify the moshavah with the biblical site *Ekron from which the neighboring Arab village ʾAqīr (اقير) also took its name. Baron Rothschild worked to give the village a truly rural character, and was aided by the *Ḥibbat Zion movement in bringing some Jewish families who had been farmers in Russia to settle at Mazkeret Batyah. Until the 1940s, when rich groundwater reserves were tapped, the village's progress was slow, not only because little water was available but also because of bad communications. After the change, citrus groves became prominent. New immigrants settled there and more arrived in the first years after 1948. A further phase of expansion began in the mid-1960s and by 1969 the village had 845 inhabitants. By the mid-1990s the population had risen to 3,410, more than doubling to 7,300 in 2002, on an area of 2.7 sq. mi. (7 sq. km.). Residents earn their living in farming, industry, and commerce and also work outside the settlement.

[Efraim Orni / Shaked Gilboa (2nd ed.)]

MAẒLI'AḤ (Heb. מַצְלִיחַ), moshav in central Israel, near Ramleh, affiliated with Tenu'at ha-Moshavim. Founded in 1950 by *Karaites from Egypt, it was named after Sahal b. Maẓliaḥ, a Karaite leader who lived in Jerusalem, and it is one of the principal Karaite centers in Israel. In 1969 Maẓli'aḥ had 690 inhabitants, rising to 1,030 in 2002 after expansion. Residents earned their livelihoods in farming (about 20 active farms), small enterprises, and work outside the settlement.

[Efraim Orni / Shaked Gilboa (2nd ed.)]

MAẒLI'AḤ BEN SOLOMON HA-KOHEN (d. 1139), the first of the Egyptian *geonim*. His father, R. *Solomon b. Elijah ha-Kohen, left Tyre and settled in Ḥadrak (near Damascus), where he founded the Yeshivah Ereẓ ha-Zevi. Upon his father's death, R. Maẓli'aḥ, who had no doubt studied at the yeshivah when it was still in Tyre, headed this institution. For some unknown reason R. Maẓli'aḥ left Syria and arrived in Fostat in 1127. The yeshivah which he founded within the synagogue of the Jerusalemites occasionally rivaled that of Damascus because its leaders felt that it also possessed the right to refer to itself as yeshivat Ereẓ ha-Ẓevi (i.e., of Ereẓ Israel). R. Maẓli'aḥ assumed the title of *rosh yeshivat Ge'on Ya'akov* ("*rosh yeshivah* of the Glory of Jacob"). It appears that his spiritual influence was important and that it extended to the whole of Yemen. Many letters and documents issued by his *bet din* are extant. Upon his death, he was succeeded by R. Moses b. Nethanel ha-Levi, who was his deputy and *av bet din* in the yeshivah.

BIBLIOGRAPHY: Mann, Egypt, index s.v. *Maṣiaḥ Gaon*; Mann, Texts, 1 (1931), 255f.; idem, in: HUCA, 3 (1926), 293; S.D. Goitein, *A Mediterranean Society* (1967), 260, 380, 485 n. 15; idem, in: *Sinai*, 33 (1953), 227ff.; S. Assaf, *Be-Oholei Ya'akov* (1943), 91.

[Abraham David]

MAẒRANUT (Heb. מַצְרָנוּת; "abutter"), the right of preemption available to the owner of land over the abutting land of his neighbor, when the latter is sold. The rule is not a provision of strict law but is derived from a rabbinical enactment to compel any prospective purchaser to yield to the abutting neighbor, in terms of the Pentateuchal injunction to "do that which is right and good in the eyes of the Lord" (Deut. 6:18; see also BM 108a and Rashi *ibid.*). For the other prospective purchaser does not sustain a great loss, since he will find land elsewhere, and should not burden the abutting neighbor with property in two separate localities. The right of the *maẓran* ("abutting neighbor") is a proprietary right (*in rem*) in the neighboring land itself (*Nimmukei Yosef* BM *ibid.*), similar to the right of a creditor in the case of lien or mortgage and other *jura in re aliena*. In applying this enactment, the scholars did not impose on the purchaser a duty to resell the land to the abutter, but rather endowed the abutter with the right to receive the land on the conclusion of the (putative) sale – without any additional act of acquisition being required – the purchaser thus becoming the agent of the abutter in regard to all the conditions of the sale to which the former agreed. Accordingly the purchaser is subject to all the laws governing an agent and holds the land in question on behalf of the abutter, the latter only acquiring actual title to it if and when he pays the price paid by the purchaser and fulfills the remaining terms agreed by the purchaser. As the abutter's right originates from the purchaser's obligation to "do what is right and good," if the latter is a non-Jew – to whom the obligation is not applicable – the corresponding right will also not accrue to the abutter (Rashi to BM 108b). The abutter also forfeits his preemptive right if he had indicated, by speech or conduct, that he does not wish to avail himself thereof (Sh. Ar., ḤM 175:32).

The abutter's right or preemption, being an application of the equitable principle to "do what is right and good," is a flexible right (Resp. Rashba vol. 1, no. 915) and does not prevail where it is not supported by the factors of "right and good." Thus the law of *maẓranut* does not apply if the exercise of the preemptive right would cause loss to the seller or purchaser or any loss to the public in general, or if the abutter were to derive no benefit therefrom. Consequently, the law of *maẓranut* is not applicable to a gift (BM 108b) as the recipient cannot get another gift in its stead and he would therefore suffer a loss (Ran, Kid. 59a). For the same reason the right of preemption is precluded when the purchaser is a woman since "it is not fitting for her to search in many places." Nor does the right exist in the following cases: when the purchaser is a co-owner of the land together with the seller, or if he is the mortgagee, for a sale of the land to such parties invokes the factors of "right and good" in their own cause; when the coins offered by the purchaser are of greater weight or more marketable than those offered by the abutter, for here the seller would lose; when all the seller's assets are sold to a single purchaser, lest the sale as a whole is prejudiced; when the landowner sells a distant field in order to purchase one that is nearer, or when the land is sold to defray funeral expenses or taxes or to provide maintenance for a widow, or when an orphan's land is sold, for in such cases the seller would suffer if he waited for the abutter. Furthermore, an abutter who wishes to cultivate the land must yield to a purchaser who wishes to build a house there, as public interest prefers habitation. Similarly, the preemptive right is excluded whenever its exercise would cause a loss in any other manner to the seller or purchaser, provided only that the judge is satisfied that there is no evasion of the abutter's right (*ibid.*).

The law of *maẓranut* is mentioned neither in the Mishnah nor in the Palestinian Talmud, but only in the Babylonian Talmud by the *amoraim* of Babylonia. It may be assured that in Ereẓ Israel conditions were not such as to justify the application of the preemptive right on the equitable ground of doing "right and good." The scriptural injunction teaches that the standards of proper conduct between man and his fellow are determined in accordance with the prevailing circumstances of the time and place and the scholars applying it created different rules accordingly (*Maggid Mishneh* to Maim. Yad, Shekhenim concl.). In post-talmudic times the right of preemption was customarily applied (in France, Germany, Spain, and in the Orient) and, in many places, also in relation to buildings even though it is doubtful whether the law was so extended in the talmudic period (*Piskei ha-Rosh* BM 9:34). In modern times the law of *maẓranut* has been less and less frequently applied although the rabbinical courts of the State of Israel have given several decisions in which various problems have been determined in accordance with these laws.

In the State of Israel the law of *maẓranut* was abolished by the Israel Land Law, 1969.

BIBLIOGRAPHY: M. Bloch, *Das mosaisch-talmudische Besitzrecht* (1897), 59f.; ET, 4 (1952), 168–95; M. Silberg, *Kakh Darko shel Talmud* (1961), 105–110. **ADD. BIBLIOGRAPHY:** M. Elon, *Ha-Mishpat* ha-Ivri (1988), 1:137, 142, 163f., 345, 346, 513f., 653; 3:1364, 1604; idem, *Jewish Law* (1994), 1:155, 160, 182, 184f., 415, 416; 2:625f., 808; 4:1627, 1913.

[Shalom Albeck]

MAZUR, ELIYAHU (1889–1973), communal worker and businessman in Poland and Israel, son of Ẓevi Meir Mazur, rabbi in Zagorow and later in Warsaw. His public activity encompassed political, economic, and social fields. He was a member of both the world executive of *Agudat Israel and of its executive board in Poland. He served as president of the Jewish community council (*kehillah*) of Warsaw from 1931 to 1937, when Maurici *Meisel was appointed commissar by the government. He also acted as director of the administrative council of the Ḥakhmei Lublin yeshivah. Mazur was the largest importer of rice in Poland, and he established rice-processing factories in the port of Gdynia. He was a member of the board of the Polish chamber of commerce. In 1940 he escaped from Poland and immigrated to Ereẓ Israel, where he continued to pursue his public and economic activities. He set up a diamond factory with his brothers in Tel Aviv, becoming a central figure in the country's diamond industry. In 1948 he was elected to the first *Knesset as a delegate of Agudat Israel.

[Yitzchak Arad]

MAZUR, JAY (1932–), U.S. labor leader. Mazur was born and raised in the Bronx, the son of immigrants, and spent his professional life in the organized labor movement. He became president of the International Ladies Garment Workers Union, spearheaded its historic merger with the Amalgamated Clothing & Textile Workers Union, and was elected first president of the merged group, the Union of Needletrades, Industrial and Textile Employees (UNITE). Mazur, whose father was a coat presser, joined the ILGWU when he was 18, focusing on organizational and educational efforts for Dressmakers' Local 22. He graduated from the ILGWU's Training Institute in 1955 and became director of organization and education for Beltmakers' Local 40. While rising through the ranks, he resumed his formal education at night, earning a B.A. in Industrial Relations from the City University of New York in 1965 and an M.A. in Labor Studies from Rutgers University in New Jersey in 1977. He was appointed managing secretary of the Blouse, Skirts & Sportswear Workers' Local 23–25, then the union's biggest local, in 1977, embarking on a hard-fought campaign to organize workers in New York City's Chinatown. In 1983 he was named general secretary-treasurer of the ILGWU. He succeeded Sol C. *Chaikin as president in 1986, inheriting a union with a declining membership. Increased competition from low-wage countries, a surge of imports, and the growth of multinational apparel and textile firms had further depressed membership in the two leading garment unions. From a combined peak of almost 1 million in the 1960s, membership tumbled to about 355,000 by the mid-1990s. In 1995 Mazur and ACTWU president Jack Sheinkman were able to merge both unions and Mazur was named UNITE's first president. Even though membership kept shrinking, falling to 250,000 in the next decade, the merger helped both unions survive at a critical time. It gave them a greater voice in government and social affairs and a stronger negotiating position with management. Mazur, who was on the executive boards of the AFL-CIO and the Central Labor Council, retired from UNITE in 2001 and was succeeded by Bruce S. *Raynor, but his efforts on behalf of workers did not stop. He was a vocal opponent of free trade, and a passionate lobbyist for anti-sweatshop legislation, a higher minimum wage, and the right of workers to organize. A leading advocate for the rights of immigrants, he was named to the boards of the Work in America Institute and the International Rescue Committee and appointed a vice president of the National Immigration, Refugee and Citizenship Forum. In 1999, President Clinton appointed him to the Advisory Committee for Trade Policy and Negotiations. He was on the presidium of the International Textile, Garment & Leather Workers Federation, president of the National Committee of Labor Israel-Histadrut, and a member of the Council of Foreign Relations. He was also a member of the U.S. Holocaust Memorial Council and the U.S.-South Africa Business Development Committee.

[Mort Sheinman (2nd ed.)]

MAZURSKY, PAUL (1930–), U.S. director, producer, screenwriter, and actor. Born in Brooklyn, New York, Mazursky began work in films as an actor, playing a small part in Stanley Kubrick's first film, *Fear and Desire* (1953), and a juvenile delinquent in *The Blackboard Jungle* (1955). He then turned to writing for television (*The Danny Kaye Show*) in collaboration with Larry Tucker. They also helped create the pilot for the TV series *The Monkees*. In 1968, Mazursky and Tucker wrote the screenplay for *I Love You, Alice B. Toklas*. In 1969, Mazursky directed his first film, *Bob & Carol & Ted & Alice*. He and Tucker also wrote the screenplay, which earned them an Oscar nomination. Mazursky followed this by directing a host of motion pictures, many of which he also wrote and produced. His films include *Alex in Wonderland* (1970); *Blume in Love* (1973); *Harry and Tonto* (Oscar nomination for Best Screenplay, 1974); *Next Stop, Greenwich Village* (1976); *An Unmarried Woman* (Oscar nomination for Best Picture and Best Screenplay, 1978); *Willie and Phil* (1980); *Tempest* (1983); *Moscow on the Hudson* (1986); *Down and Out in Beverly Hills* (1986); *Moon over Parador* (1988); *Enemies: A Love Story* (Oscar nomination for Best Screenplay, 1989), based on an Isaac Bashevis Singer short story; *Scenes from a Mall* (1991); *The Pickle* (1993); and *Faithful* (1995).

For television he directed the TV movies *Winchell* (1998) and *Coast to Coast* (2004).

Mazursky wrote *Show Me the Magic: My Adventures in Life and Hollywood*, a collection of autobiographical anecdotes (1999).

[Jonathan Licht / Ruth Beloff (2nd ed.)]

MAZUZ, MENI (1955–), Israeli attorney general. Mazuz immigrated to Israel with his family shortly after his birth in Tunisia, settling in the town of Netivot. He completed his legal studies magna cum laude at the Hebrew University of Jerusalem and did his law clerkship in the High Court of Justice department of the State Attorney's Office (which processes petitions to the Supreme Court in equity matters). In 1981, he received his law license and appeared as an attorney in both civil and criminal matters at the State Attorney's Office. He later became responsible for the High Court of Justice department. In 1992–95 Mazuz served as legal advisor and member of the Israeli delegation in negotiations with the Palestinians and Jordanians and headed the legal team which negotiated the Gaza and interim agreements with the Palestinians. In 1994, he was appointed deputy attorney general. He specialized in military and security matters related to the Israel-Palestine entity relationship, international peace and agreements, the Population Registry, and local council planning and building. Mazuz initiated legislative efforts regarding the Court Law which led to a reform in the Israeli judicial system. He wrote legal commentary on this subject and also played a leading role in legislation amendments to the General Security Law, which deals with the status, authority, and supervision of Israel's intelligence community.

In February 2004, Mazuz was appointed attorney general and undertook an administrative reorganization of the office to achieve a clear separation between the prosecutor and the political system. During his first year in office he reviewed traditional positions of the government in various fields. He emphasized alternate methods of law enforcement and limitations on the connection between elected officials and members of the elective body and adapted an egalitarian approach to single-sex couples in regard to social and property rights.

During his term in office, he initiated substantial reforms in several fields, including appointment and supervision of civil servants, budgetary allocations for political parties, and creation of the state agency responsible for monitoring and supervising the Planning and Construction Law. His decisions on various subjects, including the security fence between Israel and the Palestinian West Bank, emphasized the obligation of the State of Israel to recognize human rights and international principles of law.

[Leon Fine (2nd ed.)]

MAẒẒUVAH (Heb. מַצּוּבָה), kibbutz near the Israel-Lebanese border S.W. of Ḥanitah, affiliated with Iḥud ha-Kevuẓot ve-ha-Kibbutzim. Founded in 1940 by *Youth Aliyah graduates originating from Germany and Austria, Maẓẓuvah joined Ḥanitah and *Eilon as a third border outpost in western Galilee. In its initial years, the kibbutz was confronted with the task of heavy reclamation work on its hilly soil, a lack of water and high incidence of malaria, and with sea winds damaging fruit orchards. By 1948 most of these difficulties had been overcome. In 1969, Maẓẓuvah's economy was based predominantly on hill farming (fruit orchards) and a spinning mill. Later it developed citrus groves, fruit orchards, and poultry farming. The spinning mill closed down in 2003, causing a severe economic crisis in the kibbutz. In the mid-1990s, its population was approximately 600, dropping to 507 in 2002, with about a third above the age of 70. The name dates back to talmudic times (Tosef., Shev. 4:9; TJ, Dam. 2:1, 22d); and is preserved in the Arabic name for the site, Khirbat Maʿṣūb. Remnants were found of antique buildings, including a Greek tomb with a Greek and Phoenician inscription dating from 222–221 B.C.E. testifying that an Astarte sanctuary had been erected at the spot.

[Efraim Orni / Shaked Gilboa (2nd ed.)]

ME-AM LO'EZ, an 18th-century ethico-homiletical Bible commentary in *Ladino, the outstanding work of Judeo-Spanish literature. The commentary, conceived on an encyclopedic scale, was begun by Jacob *Culi, who felt that, after the chaos left by the *Shabbetai Ẓevi heresy, there was a need for the reabsorption of the masses into Orthodox Judaism. Because of their ignorance of the Hebrew language they had no access to traditional literature, and gradually turned away from religious observance. As is clear from his preface to the first volume, on Genesis, this is what Culi had in mind when, in about 1730, he undertook the writing of this work. His aim was to popularize Jewish lore by means of extracts from the Mishnah, Talmud, Midrash, Zohar, and the biblical commentaries – in fact all the branches of rabbinical literature – translated into the Ladino vernacular. Culi originally intended to call his work *Beit Ya'akov*, but quoting from Psalms 114:1, "When Israel went forth out of Egypt, the house of Jacob from a people of strange language," he finally called it by the original Hebrew of that phrase, *Me-Am Lo'ez*. Written in an unpretentious, popular style and in an attractive form, *Me-Am Lo'ez* was to put the elements of Jewish life at the disposal of people unable to use the sources. It deals with all aspects of Jewish life, and often with life in general, with history, ethics, philosophy, and biblical exegesis. It comments on the prescriptions of the Law and clarifies them with a profusion of detail. Culi's idea was to compile the first part of his commentary around the weekly portion of the Pentateuch, assembling, verse by verse, all the material that had any bearing on the section. This was linked together by anecdotes, legends, historical narrative, and folklore. The easy, colloquial style of the work gives it a conversational quality. Culi's popular style that fully suited his educational goals was unique in the way he dealt with aggadic Midrash. He did not quote the names of the rabbinic sages or the verses found in Midrash. He freely retold the stories in his own language, often combining a number of sources into one fluid story. On the other hand, he was loyal to his sources. Almost 300 years after Columbus, Culi still writes about the sun circling the earth, based on the Midrash. The first volume of *Me-Am Lo'ez* was published in Constantinople in 1730. No work designed to instruct the Jewish masses had ever proved so popular. In Turkey printing of the work was done a few pages at a time, distributed prior to Shabbat, and then bound when the volumes were complete.

When Culi died in 1732 he was about to publish his commentary on the first part of Exodus. He left many unfinished manuscripts on the other books of the Bible, which later writers used as the basis for their continuation of his work. Isaac b. Moses Magriso completed the volumes on Exodus (2 vols., Constantinople, 1733, 1746), Leviticus (1753), and Numbers (1764). Isaac Behar Argśeti wrote only a part of his commentary on Deuteronomy (1772). Both Magriso and Argśeti followed Culi so faithfully that the *Me-Am Lo'ez* on the Pentateuch may be considered a unified work. Using the same method, others sought to cover the rest of the Bible and complete the undertaking. Joseph di Trani of Constantinople wrote on Joshua (2 vols., 1850, 1870); Raphael Ḥiyya Pontremoli on Esther (1864); Raphael Isaac Meir ibn Venisti on Ruth (1882); Isaac Judah Abba on Isaiah (1892); Nissim Moses Abod on Ecclesiastes (1898); and finally Ḥayyim Isaac Sciaky worked on the Song of Songs (1899). There may have been other volumes, written in the spirit of Culi, that are no longer extant or that were destroyed before printing. One such work was Isaac Peraḥyah's commentary on Jeremiah, lost in the 1917 fire in Salonika. The commentaries on Genesis and Exodus were the most popular. There were at least six editions of Genesis between 1730 and 1897, and eight of Exodus between 1733 and 1884. The different places of printing show the popularity of the work among the Sephardim of Turkey and the Balkans, and there was even a partial Arabic translation in North Africa. Those who did not own the expensive complete set (sometimes given as a dowry) studied it in reading groups. For a long time the *Me-Am Lo'ez* was the only literature for thousands of Sephardi Jewish families, and its reading was often considered a religious duty. It was so well thumbed by generation after generation that very few sets remain in existence. The *Me-Am Lo'ez* played a role in Sephardi culture parallel to, but wider than, that of the Yiddish **Ẓe'enah u-Re'enah* in the Ashkenazi world, its main difference being that it was not intended primarily for women. As a vast synthesis of everything that had been written in Hebrew, the *Me-Am Lo'ez* was directed to all – men, women, and even children. A Hebrew translation was undertaken by Shmuel Yerushalmi, titled *Yalkut Me-Am Lo'ez*. From 1967 through 1979, he published 20 volumes, which included his own "*Me-Am Lo'ez*" commentary on the books of Samuel, 1 Kings, Ecclesiastes, Ruth, and the Song of Songs. All of *Yalkut Me-Am Lo'ez* has appeared in English translation (New York, 1977–94). In addition, an edition in Latin transliteration was initiated by the Ibn Tibbon Institute at Granada University, Spain (*Meʿam Loʿez, El gran comentario bíblico Sefardí*, vol. 1, 1964). Unfortunately, the apparent lack of knowledge of Ladino and Turkish led to an edition with many inaccuracies. *Yalkut Me-Am Lo'ez* has been translated into a number of other languages, including Russian. Thus, *Me-Am Lo'ez* continues to be a source of knowledge and inspiration to this day.

BIBLIOGRAPHY: M. Molho, *Le Meam-Loez* (Fr., 1945); M.D. Gaon, *Maskiyyot Levav* (1933); A. Yaari, in: KS, 10 (1933), 271–4; idem, *Ha-Defus ha-Ivri be-Kushta* (1967), index of books; M.J. Bernardete, in: *Homenaje a Millás-Vallicrosa*, 1 (1954), 127, 146–51; C. Crews, in:

Proceedings of the Leeds Philosophical and Literary Society, Literary and Historical Section, 9 (1960), 13–106; O. Camhy, in: *Le Judaïsme Sephardi*, 19 (1960), 829–34; M.J. Bernardete et al., *In Search of our Sephardic Roots* (1970); A. Meyuhas Ginio, in: *Studia Rosenthaliana*, 35:2 (2001), 133–42; L. Landau, in: *Moreshet Yehudei Sefarad ve-ha-Mizraḥ* (1982), 213–24; idem, in: *Shevet ve-Am*, 5:10 (1985), 307–21; S. Hagai, in: *Maḥanayim*, 4 (1992), 276–81; Y.R. Molcho, in: *Oẓar Yehudei Sefarad*, 5 (1962), 80–94. **WEBSITE:** S. Alfassa, in: http://isfsp.org/meam.html.

[Henri Guttel / David Derovan (2nd ed.)]

MEARS, OTTO (1841–1931), U.S. railroad builder. Mears was born in Russian Lithuania and was brought to California in 1854. He served in the Civil War. In 1865 he settled in Saguache County, Colorado, as a merchant, later becoming county treasurer and Indian commissioner. He was a road and railroad builder, constructing most of the principal roads in southwest Colorado, building a railroad in Ouray County in 1888, and participating in building and later serving as president of the Denver and Rio Grande Southern Railway. Mears was a presidential elector (1876), lieutenant governor (1883), and state capitol commissioner (1889). A monument honoring him is near Ouray.

BIBLIOGRAPHY: DAB, incl. bibl.; J.H. Baker and L.R. Hafen (eds.), *History of Colorado*, 5 (1927), 412–3; L.R. Hafen, in: *Colorado Magazine*, 9 (1932), 71–74; S. Jocknick, *Early Days on the Western Slope of Colorado and Campfire Chats with Otto Mears* (1913); F. Hall, *History of the State of Colorado*, 4 (1895), 510; B.B. Postal, *Jewish Tourist's Guide to the U.S.* (1954), 77–78; W.F. Stone, *History of Colorado*, 4 (1919), 640–1.

[Robert E. Levinson]

MEAT (Heb. בָּשָׂר, *basar*), the flesh of animals permitted for consumption. (For its meaning as human flesh and symbolic connotation, see *Flesh.) The Talmud points out (Sanh. 59b) that according to the biblical account the consumption of meat was forbidden from Adam until Noah (Gen. 1:29) and was specifically permitted first to Noah (*ibid.* 9:3). Apart from this, however, there is no suggestion of vegetarianism in the Bible. On the other hand, meat is never included among the staple diet of the children of Israel, which is confined to agricultural products, of which the constantly recurring expression in the Bible is "grain and wine and oil" (Deut. 11:14), or the seven agricultural products enumerated in Deuteronomy 8:8. (It has however been suggested that Deuteronomy 11:15 refers to the eating of meat.) In point of fact, meat was regarded in the Bible as a luxury for which the children of Israel would yearn "when the Lord enlarges your territory" (Deut. 12:20), and the lusting of the children of Israel after the "fleshpots of Egypt" (Ex. 16:3 and Num. 11:4) was regarded as highly reprehensible. From Deuteronomy 12:20–22, R. Ishmael (Ḥul. 16b–17a) deduces that during their sojourn in the wilderness the children of Israel were permitted to eat only meat from an animal which had actually been sacrificed and that it was only when they entered the Land of Israel that "meat of desire," i.e., the meat of all permitted animals, could be eaten as desired without the animal being sacrificed. R. Akiva, however, interprets it to mean that in the wilderness any method of killing an animal, even stabbing (*neḥirah*), was permitted, but that after their entry into the land only the meat of animals which had been slaughtered by *sheḥitah* could be eaten. All agree, however, that the reference is only to "cattle" which could be offered as sacrifices, but that the meat of "beasts" (nondomesticated animals, the "gazelle and the hart") was freely permitted (cf. Deut. 12:22). That the flesh of birds was permitted is clear from Exodus 16:13 and Numbers 11:31–33. The only limitation on the consumption of meat to non-Jews ("the children of Noah") is the prohibition against meat cut from a living animal (based on Gen. 9:4; see *Noachide Laws). For Jews however only the flesh of "clean" animals was permitted, and that, only after *sheḥitah* and the removal of forbidden blood and fat. The seething of meat in milk was forbidden (Ex. 23:19 et al.) and interpreted to include eating meat and milk together or deriving any benefit from it. It has been suggested that this prohibition is because such practices were connected with heathen fertility rites (Maim. *Guide* 3:48; see *Dietary Laws). In the talmudic period, meat was regarded as the diet of the well-to-do, and as a feature of festive occasions rather than a staple diet. It was regarded as obligatory only on Sabbaths and festivals since "there is no joy without meat and wine" (Pes. 109a). The immensely wealthy Eleazar b. Azariah laid it down that only a person who possesses 100 *maneh* may eat meat daily; otherwise it should be eaten only on the Sabbath. In the amoraic period, however, it seems to have become more common. In Ereẓ Israel, R. Johanan said that owing to the prevailing physical weakness, "whoever has a penny in his pocket should run to the shopkeeper" (to buy meat daily), while the Babylonian Naḥman said that one should even buy it on credit (Ḥul. 84a). Its nutritive value was recognized. It was specially recommended for pregnant women as they would thus have robust children (Ket. 60b–61a). On the basis of homiletical exposition of Leviticus 11:46, R. Judah ha-Nasi suggested that only those engaged in the study of the Torah were permitted to indulge in meat (Pes. 49b). Poultry was more highly regarded as a delicacy than meat, and meat than fish (Num. R. 21:25). Of poultry the most delectable was the chicken, of meat, the ox (BM 86b). Among the things to be avoided by a convalescent, since they "bring on his sickness again in a severe form," are "beef, fat meat, roast meat, and poultry" (Ber. 57b). As the consumption of meat was associated with joy, abstention from it was a symbol of mourning. For the same reason meat is not eaten by a mourner on the day of burial or in the period of national mourning from the first until the Ninth of *Av (Sh. Ar., OḤ 551:9). After the destruction of the Temple there were those who sought to adopt asceticism, including abstention from meat, but it was strongly opposed (BB 60b).

BIBLIOGRAPHY: Eisenstein, Dinim, 66f.; ET, 4 (1952), 675–741.

[Louis Isaac Rabinowitz]

MECHOULAM, RAPHAEL (1930–), Israeli organic chemist. Mechoulam was born in Sofia, Bulgaria. He received his

M.Sc. in biochemistry from the Hebrew University of Jerusalem (1952) and his Ph.D. at the Weizmann Institute, Reḥovot (1958). After postdoctoral studies at the Rockefeller Institute, New York (1959–60), he was on the scientific staff of the Weizmann Institute (1960–65) before moving to the Hebrew University of Jerusalem, where he became professor (1972) and Lionel Jacobson Professor of Medicinal Chemistry from 1975. He was rector (1979–82) and pro-rector (1983–85). His main research interests concern the chemistry and actions of *Cannabis sativa* (marijuana) constituents and related substances (endocannabinoids) synthesized naturally in body tissues, particularly in the nervous system. This work has important implications in physiology, as the endocannabinoids represent a new type of neuromodulators, and in medicinal chemistry, as these compounds are exploited for their actions in psychiatric, neurological, and inflammatory diseases and as appetite-promoting agents. In 1994 he was elected a member of the Israel Academy of Sciences. His honors include the Kolthof Prize in chemistry from the Haifa Technion (1994) and the Israel Prize in chemistry (2000).

[Michael Denman (2nd ed.)]

MECKLENBURG, former duchy in Germany. Before the middle of the 14th century Jews were to be found in Wismar, Rostock, Parchim, Krakow, Guestrow, Schwerin, Friedland, and perhaps also in Borzenburg and Malchin. A Jewish community is first mentioned in 1279 at Rostock and there were communities from around the same time in Parchim and Guestrow. The other cities had only a few families. The Jews were allowed to engage only in moneylending. A Jew, Salathiel, bought a house and loaned money to the duke and to the city of Schwerin. Accusations of desecrating the *Host in Krakow am See (1325) and Guestrow (1330) and the *Black Death persecutions in Rostock, Parchim, and Wismar practically wiped out Mecklenburg Jewry. After another accusation of desecrating the Host, in Sternberg in 1492, 27 Jews were burned at the stake and all Jews were expelled from the duchy.

From 1679 Jewish merchants from Hamburg, often of Sephardi extraction, were granted letters of protection and commercial privileges, and some became Court Jews. One of them, Michael Hinrichsen (Portugies) of *Glueckstadt (d. 1710), court jeweler and tobacco agent, settled in Schwerin, where he rapidly gained ascendancy. He employed a rabbi so that he might study Talmud with him, and opened a synagogue in his home. He was the first Jew in Germany to be freed (in 1701) from payment of the **Leibzoll* ("body tax") for his lifetime. His descendants continued to hold leading positions in Mecklenburg economic and public life for five generations. The first *Landesrabbiner*, Jeremias Israel, appointed in 1763, was a member of his family. A growing number of communities were established by privileged Jews and their households despite a 1755 enactment making illegal all forms of landholdings. Tax records of 1760 show 141 taxpaying Jews residing legally in the duchy. In this period the history of Mecklenburg Jewry is linked with that of O.G. Tychsen (1734–1816), Orientalist, professor, and unsuccessful missionary, who meticulously recorded the history of the local Jews as well as supporting their emancipation. A ducal order (May 30, 1772), that burials be postponed for three days in order to eliminate the possibility of "false" deaths, induced the Jews of Mecklenburg to apply to Moses *Mendelssohn, who advised them to erect burial halls, a decision which was contested by more Orthodox rabbis.

On Feb. 22, 1811, M.R. Hinrichsen and I. Mendel presented a petition for emancipation. Although the estates demanded basic reforms in Judaism, the liberal duke, Franz Friedrich I (d. 1839), nonetheless issued an emancipatory edict two years later (March 25, 1813), based on the Prussian model. Markets were not to be held on Jewish holidays and support was given to Jewish rights within the German Confederation. On Sept. 11, 1817, under pressure from the estates, the duke suspended emancipation. During the *Hep! Hep! disturbances (1819) troops had to be called in to Guestrow to suppress the riots. The estates continued to oppose the duke's liberal attitude toward individual Jews and rejected a law of 1830 granting the Jews occupational and economic liberties. In 1847 the estates at last supported emancipation, which endured briefly until 1850; the Jews were not fully emancipated until 1869.

In 1839 statutes were enacted granting autonomy to rabbinical organizations. A year later Samuel *Holdheim was elected *Landesrabbiner* and introduced far-reaching and controversial reforms. Holdheim was active in the struggle for emancipation and succeeded in having the degrading medieval formula of the Jewish *oath changed. He was followed by the even more radical David Einhorn (1847–51), whose denial of circumcision as a prerequisite of Judaism was attacked by Franz *Delitzsch, the Christian missionary and scholar. For the sake of peace, and on the order of the government, the rabbinate was subsequently filled by Orthodox rabbis.

Mecklenburg Jewry increased from 2,494 persons in 1810 to 3,318 (0.64% of the total population) in 1845. The small communities (11 with more than 100 persons in 1850) subsequently declined numerically, and due to the emigration of Jews to the big cities, the larger ones did not grow. The numbers decreased to 1,413 (0.22%) in 1910 and to 1,225 in 1932. Rostock, the largest city, which excluded Jews until 1867, was then the main community, with about 350 members, followed by Guestrow (120), Parchim (48), and Schwerin (200). The fate of Mecklenburg Jews during World War II was similar to that of the rest of German Jewry. In 1990, very few Jews resided in the state of Mecklenburg.

BIBLIOGRAPHY: Germ Jud, 2 (1968), 528–9; L. Donath, *Geschichte der Juden in Mecklenburg* (1874); Neuman, in: *Juedische Familien Forschung*, no. 5 (1926), 98–101; Gruenfeldt, in: *Zeitschrift fuer Demographic und Statistik der Juden 8* (1912), 1–7; Silberstein, in: *Festschrift zum 25 jaehrigen Bestehen der juedischen theologischen Seminars Fraenkelscher Stiftung*, 2 (1929), 303–66; idem, in: *Festschrift zum 70 Geburtstage Martin Philipson* (1916); Sterling, in: HJ, 12 (1950), 134; H. Kellenbenz, *Sephardim an der unteren Elbe* (1958), 436–46; H.

Schnee, *Die Hoffinanz und der moderne Staat*, 2 (1954), 293–315; 5 (1965), 105ff., S. Stern, *The Court Jew* (1950), index.

[Henry Wasserman]

MEDALIE, GEORGE ZERDIN (1883–1946), U.S. lawyer and Jewish community leader. Medalie was born in New York's Lower East Side to Russian immigrants. He served as assistant district attorney of New York County (1910–15). Subsequently founding his own law firm, Medalie also served in various advisory and public legal capacities. As U.S. attorney for the Southern District of New York from 1931 he vigorously prosecuted racketeers and smugglers. One of several assistants whom he later helped attain public careers in elective office was Thomas E. Dewey. Medalie himself was the Republican nominee for the U.S. Senate in 1932. In 1945 Dewey, then governor of New York, appointed him to an interim term as associate justice of the Court of Appeals, the highest state court. Medalie was prominent in local legal associations and was a leader of the New York Jewish Community. He was on the board of directors of both the Joint Distribution Committee and the UJA. As chairman of the American Jewish Committee's Overseas Committee, he devoted his efforts to securing equal rights for Jews in the countries to which they returned after World War II. From 1941 to 1945 he served as president of the Federation of Jewish Philanthropies. As president of the Jewish Board of Guardians in 1931 Medalie gave strong support to the development of psychiatric casework. He was chairman of the Mayor's Committee on Unemployment Relief during the Depression and served on many other government committees.

BIBLIOGRAPHY: AJYB, 48 (1946–47), 93–100; J. Willen, in: AJYB, 42 (1946–47), 93–100 (portrait).

MEDALISTS. Pewter, seal, and gem engraving were traditional Jewish professions, often handed down from father to son through several generations. By the 18th century, this practice had developed into medal engraving and Jewish medalists were employed at several Protestant courts of northern Germany and Scandinavia. Members of the *Abraham-Abramson family were among the leading 18th-century medalists. The Jacobson family rose to prominence at Copenhagen in the same period. Philipp *Aron, active from about 1750 to 1787, and his brother Abraham (1744–1824), did portrait medals for the courts of Mecklenburg and Stockholm, as did Meir Loeser and his son Nathan at the turn of the century. About the same time Abraham Jacobs and Abraham Heilbut spent their active careers working in their native Hamburg. An important 18th-century Russian medalist was Samuel *Judin, while the *Simon family flourished in Belgium and France. The three *Wiener brothers from Belgium are considered among the finest 19th-century medalists, as were Avenir and Abraham *Griliches in Russia. France was the home of several distinguished 19th-century Jewish medalists such as René Stern, court engraver to Napoleon III, and E.A. Soldi. One of the few Jewish medals by the French sculptor Emmanuel Hannaux has an excellent portrait of Narcisse *Leven, president of the Alliance Israélite Universelle. S.F. *Beer engraved the commemorative for the Second Zionist Congress. Aaron Kohn (early 19th century, Germany) is noteworthy for his religious medals, such as his 1817 **Tashlikh* prayer and his 1837 circumcision medals. In the same period Asher Wappenstein (1780–1852) of Vienna engraved patriotic commemoratives. I.W. Loewenbach of Munich struck Bavarian nationalist medals from the 1820s through the 1860s. He also did the earliest German synagogue medal, issued in 1826 for the new synagogue at Munich. H. Oppenheim is well known for his medals dealing with his home city of Frankfurt on the Main. On the other hand, Leo Horovitz, son of the Frankfurt rabbi Marcus *Horovitz, concentrated mainly on Jewish subjects. Dutch Jewish medalists of this period were M.C. de Vries Jr., A.L. Snoeck, and Jacques *Elion, the last having been preceded by his father Samuel Cohen Elion. Two Americans, both born in the Austrian Empire, achieved distinction. One was Moritz *Furst; the other, Isidore Konti, a gifted sculptor as well, struck the 1905 commemoration of the 250th anniversary of Jewish settlement in the United States. Among 20th-century Jewish medalists are Victor D. *Brenner (U.S.), Benno *Elkan (Germany and England), and Harald Salomon (Denmark). Fulop O. Beck (b. 1873) is considered one of the best medalists of the 20th century; though baptized he executed medals for many important Jews. Ede Telcs (1872–1958), also a Christian convert, became the official medalist for Hungary during World War I. Other noted 20th-century Jewish medalists include the Germans Hugo Kaufmann and Arnold *Zadikow; the Austrians Emil Fuchs and Arthur Loewental; the Dutch Loecki Metz; the Hungarian István Csillag; the French Boris Bernstein, Simon Goldberg, and Esther Gorbato; Paul *Vincze, in England, as well as the Americans Abram Belskie, Michael Lantz, Albert W. Wein, and Adolph Block. The American sculptors Leonard Baskin and William *Zorach have done occasional medals. Boris *Schatz, Ivan Sors, F.J. Kormis, and A. Eisenberg are known for their medals of Jewish subject matter. Israel had a new group of medalists, including Miriam Karoli, Zvi Narkiss, Gabriel and Maxime Shammir, the team of Rothschild and Lippmann ("Rcli"), Alex Berlyne, Mordechai Gumpel, Jacob Zim, Josef Bass, and Moshe Zipper.

See *Medals.

BIBLIOGRAPHY: L. Forrer, *Biographical Dictionary of Medalists* (1902–30); D.M. Friedenberg (ed.), *Great Jewish Portraits in Metal* (1963); idem, in: *The Numismatist* (July 1969); O.C. Gaedechens, *Die neuren Hamburgischen Muenzen und Medaillen* (1843); T. Hoffmann, *Jacob Abraham und Abraham Abramson – 55 Jahr Medaillenkunst (1755–1810)* (1927); L. Kadman, *Israel's Money* (1963); M. Stern, *Aus dem Berliner Juedischen Museum* (1937).

[Daniel M. Friedenberg]

MEDALS. The significance of Jewish medals is both historical and artistic; they illustrate the history of the Jews in the widest sense of the word. (See Table: Jewish Medals). Opinions widely differ on the classification of Jewish medals. Bruno Kisch (see bibliography) gives the following classification:

1. Symbolic representation, biblical personages and scenes, imitation shekels, and biblical medals. (This group should really not be included among Jewish medals, since in most cases they were made neither by, nor for Jews.)

2. Medals referring to political events in connection with Jews, such as the granting of religious freedom, Zionistica, etc.

3. Medals referring to Jewish communities, inaugurations and jubilees of synagogues, or institutions, schools, etc.

4. Medals of Jewish personalities, such as rabbis, physicians, philanthropists, etc.

5. Marriage and anniversary medals, tokens, amulets.

Though no medals exist from talmudic or biblical times, the Talmud (BK 97b) speaks of portrait coins bearing the likeness of biblical personages. Probably the oldest Jewish medal extant (1497 or 1503) is one associated with the name of Benjamin b. Elijah Be'er the physician, with a long and enigmatic Hebrew inscription with a text also in Greek and Latin, surrounding what may be intended to represent a Roman emperor. In the 16th century, during the Renaissance, portrait medals were made by or for rich Jewish families. The best known of these is that of Gracia *Nasi (1556), in all probability the younger of the two ladies known by that name. Dating roughly from the same period are the portrait medals of Elijah de Latas (or Lattes; 1552) and Abramo Emanuele Norsa (1557). Mention may be made also of the medals struck for Marranos in Antwerp, such as Luis Perez (1597) and Ursula Lopez, widow of Martin Perez (1580).

At the end of the 17th century, the so-called "*Korn Jude*" medals are found, a typical example of antisemitica. These medals, made of silver, copper, and tin, all show more or less the same picture: on the front a bearded man wearing a Jew's hat, a stick in his hand, and carrying a sack of grain on his back, on which sits the devil who rips the sack open. Around this picture is the inscription "*Du Korn Jude*" and under it a date with the word *Theurezeit*. On the reverse side is a corn measure and the verse (Prov. 11:26): *Wer Korn inhaelt, dem fluchen die Leuthe. Aber Seegen kommt ueber den, der es verkauft, Sprueche* ("He that withholdeth corn, the people shall curse him; but blessing shall be upon the head of him that selleth it," Proverbs). Other examples of antisemitic medals are the "Federjude" medals of the same period. The figure represented is a Jew in a feather hat, carrying a large sack on his back and a money bag in his hand. Similarly anti-Jewish feeling in Germany is expressed by the medals struck on the occasion of the execution of Jew "Suess" *Oppenheimer in 1738. The medals are in silver, lead, and bronze. In the 18th and 19th centuries baptism was for many Jews a way out of the difficult circumstances in which they lived, and this led to the striking of baptismal medals. Among such is a satiric medal in silver, circa 1700. On the front is a clergyman holding a Bible, who pours water on the head of a kneeling Jew carrying a millstone around his neck. On the reverse side is an antisemitic text, and on the rim *Wenn die Maus die Katze frisst, dan wird ein Jud ein wahrer Christ* ("When the mouse eats the cat, then a Jew becomes a true Christian"). Political accusations against the Jews were also known. When in 1686 the city of Ofen (the old German name for Buda, see *Budapest) was captured from the Turks by Leopold I of Austria, the Jewish community was massacred. As a memento of the event a satiric medal was struck showing a Turk and Jew melting metal in a furnace, the Turk holding the tongs and the Jew the bellows, while ingots appear at the bottom. "Who mints money for peace now that the Turk and Jew are tired of war?" is the ironic inscription.

Two medals were struck on the occasion of the fire in the Judengasse at Frankfurt on the Main in 1711, one in three variants. That with the variants by Christian Wermuth is one of the most vicious antisemitic pieces extant. In 1735 a medal

"Israel Liberata" coin celebrating the 10th anniversary of the State, 1958. The reverse is a facsimile of a "Judaea Capta" coin recording Vespasian's conquest in 70 C.E. Courtesy Israel Government Medals and Coins Corporation, Jerusalem.

Israel medal marking the 30th anniversary of the beginning of immigration blockade-running, 1964. Courtesy Israel Government Medals and Coins Corporation, Jerusalem.

Selective List of Jewish Medals

1. Renaissance Medals

1503 (or 1497)	Benjamin ben Elijah Be'er (medallion)
1552	Elijah de Latas (De Lattes) and his mother, Rica de Latas
1556	Gracia Nasi
1557	Abramo Emanuele Norsa (Norcia)

2. Jewish Emancipation Medals

1745	Repeal of Edict of Maria Theresa expelling Jews from Prague and Bohemia
1781	Edict of Toleration of Emperor Joseph II
1782	idem, issued by Dutch Jews after Emperor visited the Netherlands (four variants)
1790	Homage to Landgrave Ludwig X of Hesse and Darmstadt
1790	Homage to Landgravine Louise Caroline Henriette of Hesse and Darmstadt (two variants)
1796	Emancipation of Jews in Batavian Republic (i.e. Holland)
1805	Alexander I of Russia frees Jews from a special tax
1806	Sanhedrin of Napoleon
1808	Enfranchisement of the Jews of Westphalia (by Abraham Abramson)
1836	Homage to Gabriel Riesser (for role in German Jewish emancipation)
1840	Montefiore and Crémieux at Cairo on behalf of Jews held in accusation of ritual murder (The Damascus Affair)
1846	Jubilee of emancipation of Jews in The Netherlands
1848	Emancipation of Jews in the Kingdom of Sardinia (Dedication to Count Roberto d'Azeglio)
1848	Commemoration of the German Revolution (a plank listed on medal is "Emancipation of the Jews")
1854–55	Presentation by Italian Jews to Albert Cohen, 15th Sivan 5614, on his receiving assurances from Sultan Abdal-Mejid that the Jews in Palestine would receive equal rights with Christians
1860	Proclamation of Right for Jews in Galicia, Bukovina, and Cracow to buy real estate (for Franz Joseph I)
1864	Intercession in Morocco of Sir Moses and Lady Judith Montefiore
1881	100th Anniversary of Joseph II's Edict of Toleration

3. Commemorative Medals (Including a few antisemitic because of their importance)

1670	300th Anniversary of the alleged desecration of the Host at Brussels. This medal was reissued in 1820, on the 450th anniversary and then again in 1870, the last being philosemitic
1686	Participation of the Jews in the defense of Ofen (Buda) against Austria (two variants)
1696	Satire on the followers of Shabbetai Ẓevi (Christian in origin)
1700	The Useless Baptism of Jews
1711	Fire in Frankfurt on the Main Ghetto (three variants by C. Wermuth; separate one by Johann Linck)
1721	Fires in the Frankfurt Ghetto
1738	Hanging of Jew Suess (five variants); also portrait
1791	Wilhelm (Jewish) School in Breslau, Jewish
1800	Inauguration of the Adat Jeshurun (Reform) Synagogue in Amsterdam
1810	Building of the Bordeaux Synagogue
1826	Dedication of the New Synagogue in Munich, by I. W. Loewenbach, Jewish medalist
1841	Hamburg Jewish Hospital (Solomon Heine on obverse as benefactor)
1841	Opening of the Jewish Home for Aged at the Hague; by J. Weiner, Jewish medalist
1841	Opening of the New Maastricht Synagogue
1841	25th Anniversary of the Jewish Loan Institute at Hamburg
1843	Laying of the Foundation Stone of the Hebrew National School at Birmingham
1843	First Jewish Girl's Confirmation at Warsaw; by Eichel, Jewish medalist
1848	Destruction of the Rothschild Chateau at Surenne

4. Important Early Tokens

1671 and 1714	Burial Pass permits for the Amsterdam Ḥevra Kaddisha
1679–1812	English "Jew Brokers" Medals
c. 1780	Moses Benjamin Foa
1780–1793	Lord George Gordon as a Jew (nine variants)
1790	Daniel Mendoza (five variants)
1791	Mendoza and Ward

5. Important Portrait Medals Before 1850

1735	Eleazar b. Samuel Shmelka, welcomed as rabbi by Ashkenazi community of Amsterdam (by Joel, Jewish medalist)
c. 1774	Moses Mendelssohn (by Jacob Abraham and son, Abraham Abramson)
1793	Daniel Itzig's 70th Birthday (by Abraham Abramson)

Selective List of Jewish Medals (cont.)

1794	Homage to Marcus Herz (by Jacob Abraham and Abraham Abramson)
1803	73rd Birthday of Lipmann Meyer (by Anton Friedrich Koenig)
c. 1816	Memorial to Gershom Mendes Seixas (by Moritz Furst)
1836	Memorial to Nathan Mayer Rothschild (pub. by Hyam Hyams)
1837	Memorial to Ludwig Boerne (by H. Oppenheim)
1837	Elias Henschel (Breslau): 50th Anniversary of graduation as doctor (by Lesser – possibly a Jew)
1939	Johann Stieglitz
1842	Memorial to Chief Rabbi Solomon Hirschel (pub. by Hyam Hyams)
1844	70th Birthday of Solomon Mayer Rothschild
1846	"Rachel," Elisa-Rachel Felix
1847	Giacomo Meyerbeer
1847	Jubilee of Ḥakham Isaac Bernays of Hamburg

was struck in Amsterdam – by Joel Levi – with a Hebrew text to mark the arrival there of Eleazar of Brody, who had been invited to become rabbi of the Ashkenazi congregation. A portrait of Moses *Mendelssohn, one of the forerunners of the Emancipation in Germany, was made about 1774 jointly by the Jewish medalist Jacob Abraham (1723–1800) and his son, Abraham Abramson (1754–1811). The Emancipation of the Jews was the occasion of commemorations and frequently led to the striking of medals. (The most important medals in this group are listed in Section 2 of the appended list.) The Emancipation of the Jews caused a revival of Jewish communities especially in Western Europe, and an extensive development of Jewish intellectual life. In Germany and Austria, in particular, hundreds of medals were struck on the occasion of various events.

Large numbers of Jewish medalists and sculptors were engaged in the making of medals. Besides the German and Dutch medals there are also a number of French, Italian, and English medals, many American and a few Polish, Scandinavian, and Russian ones.

[Arthur Polak]

In Israel

The first commemorative medals and coins were issued in Israel in 1958 on the tenth anniversary of the state, as part of the activities of the Anniversary Committee set up by the Prime Minister's Office. In 1961 a special Israel Government Coins and Medals Corporation was set up, whose charter provides for a board of directors on which a number of ministries are represented and which appoints a director general. State medals are struck for the following purpose: to commemorate events of national or international significance in the field of culture, science, history, and the various stages of Israel's development and achievement. In keeping with Jewish tradition, living personalities are not commemorated. Commemorative coins are issued by the Bank of Israel and are legal tender, while official state medals are the monopoly of the Coins and Medals Corporation. Apart from the purposes mentioned, these coins and medals have a great publicity value both among Diaspora Jews and in official circles of other states. They earn revenue and foreign currency for the Israel treasury; the income is earmarked for the restoration and preservation of historical sites in Israel.

The first medal issued in 1958 was the Liberation Medal showing the Roman "Judaea Capta" coin on the obverse and "Israel Liberata" on the reverse. This was followed by the Valor medal of 1959, with the symbol of the Israel Defense Forces on the obverse and the Trumpeldor Memorial on the reverse. A medal of the same year commemorated the jubilee year of the founding of Tel Aviv, while a Bar Kokhba medal was struck in 1960, after the Bar Kokhba letters were found in the Dead Sea Caves. More than 100 subjects had been commemorated by 1970, among them the Warsaw Ghetto Rising (1963), Masada (1964), the Rothschild family (on the opening of the new Knesset, 1966), the Sinai Campaign (1966), the Jewish Legion, the Balfour Declaration (1967), and El Al Airlines (1969). There is also a very popular bar mitzvah medal (1961).

Commemorative coins are issued every year on the occasion of Israel Independence Day (1958–). A series of Ḥanukkah coins was struck (1958–63), as well as special gold coins to mark the Herzl centenary (1960), the Six-Day War of 1967, and the reunification of Jerusalem (1968). Half-shekels (1961, 1962) to be donated to charity on Purim, and Redemption of the Firstborn shekels (1969) for the *Pidyon ha-Ben* ceremony have been struck for religious use.

Each medal and coin is accompanied by an illustrated prospectus, in various languages, telling the story behind the medal, as well as numismatic technical details such as mintage figures, metal, weight, diameter, name of the artist, and the place of striking. In order to distinguish state medals from privately issued medals, official medals carry on their edge the emblem of the state and the words "State of Israel" in Hebrew and in English and are engraved with serial numbers. After minting the designated number of medals, the dies from which they were struck are destroyed in the presence of official witnesses. Official catalogs are issued periodically by the corporation and are also published in the *Israel Numismatic Bulletin*.

BIBLIOGRAPHY: D.M. Friedenberg (ed.), *Great Jewish Portraits in Metal* (1963); idem, in: *The Numismatist* (July 1969), 891–918; C. Roth, *Jews in the Renaissance* (1959); L.A. Mayer, *Bibliography of Jewish Art* (1967), index; M. Stern, *Aus dem Berliner juedischen Mu-*

seum (1937); T. Hoffmann, *Jacob Abraham und Abraham Abramson – 55 Jahre Medaillenkust (1755–1810)* (1927); A. Polak, *Joodse penningen in de Nederlanden* (1958); Kisch, in: HJ, 7 (1945), 135–66 (8 plates); Nahon, in: RMI, 28 (1962), 377–88 (4 plates); B. Kirschner, *Deutsche Spottmedaillen auf Juden*, ed. by A. Kindler (1968); S. Haffner, *History of Modern Israel's Money, 1917 to 1967* (1967), incl. bibl.; F. Bertram and R. Weber, *Israel's 20-year Catalog of Coins and Currency…* (1968).

[Yitzhak Avni and Israel Sedaka]

MEDEM, VLADIMIR (pseudonym **M. Vinitski**; 1879–1923), prominent *Bund leader in Russia and Poland. He was born in Libau (Liepaja), Courland, to an army medical officer, who was an extremely assimilationist liberal and had him baptized into the Orthodox Church. In his youth Medem regarded himself as a Russian, and the influence of his association with Jews at the secondary school of Minsk was only revealed later. He studied law in Kiev, became acquainted with the writings of Plekhanov and Lenin, and identified himself ideologically with Marxism. As a result of his role in a students' strike (1899), he was expelled from the university, and after a brief term of imprisonment was exiled to Minsk under police supervision. He was influenced there by leaders of the Bund: Gershuni, Temin, and Kaplan. His interest in the Jewish masses was now aroused and he felt himself attracted to them. This evolution, which led him to join the Bund, became for him the way back to Jewish identity. It was precisely this lengthy journey which later won him admiration within the Bundist masses. He was a member of the Bund committee of Minsk and wrote for its organ, *Der Minsker Arbeter.*

After being imprisoned and suffering from a kidney disease, he succeeded in escaping to Berne, Switzerland. He was active in the Russian student circles there and at the end of 1901 was elected first secretary of the Bund organization abroad. He represented the Bund at the Second Convention (1903) of the Russian Social Democratic Party in London. After the convention he was appointed to the Committee Abroad of the Bund. During the years 1905–08, Medem was also active in Russia as one of the leading contributors and editors of the Bund newspapers *Posledniya Izvestiya* and *Nashe Slovo.* At the Seventh Convention (1906) of the Bund, he was elected to its central committee. He was deeply concerned with the national question, and it was he who formulated the so-called neutralist attitude toward the future fate of the Jewish nation which was adopted by the Bund as its official position ("neutralism"). It was only in 1910 that he began to retreat from this position and recognized the need for a positive attitude on the national future of the Jews. He was among the first to call for an active interest by the Bund in the Jewish community organization (*kehillah*); he demanded actual action in the question of Yiddish schools, the right to rest on the Sabbath, and the right of employment for Jewish workers. He played an active role in the revival of the Bundist press during the years 1912–13 (*Lebnsfragen*, Vienna, and *Di Tsayt*, St. Petersburg). In 1915, as a result of the Russian retreat during World War I, he was freed before completing a two-year term of imprisonment in Warsaw. During the German occupation he was the ideological leader of the Bund in Poland. He began to speak and write in Yiddish. His anti-Zionist writings became increasingly violent, but he renewed the demand for Jewish national-cultural autonomy. He was even in favor of collaboration with middle-class elements in the field of Yiddish culture. During the years 1919–20, when pro-Communist tendencies gained the upper hand within the Bund, Medem found himself isolated in his violently critical attitude toward Bolshevism and its methods. At the beginning of 1921 he immigrated to the U.S. where he contributed to the Jewish daily, **Forward*. His autobiography (*Fun Mayn Lebn*, 2 vols., 1923) is of both literary and historical value. Cultural and educational institutions in Poland were named after him.

BIBLIOGRAPHY: *Vladimir Medem – tsum Tsvantsikstn Yortsayt* (1943), incl. bibl.; LNYL, 6 (1965), 22–29; B. Dinur et al., *Kelal Yisrael* (1954), 538–41; J. Pinson, in: JSOS, 7 (1945), 233–64; L. Dawidowicz, *The Golden Tradition, 1772–1939* (1967).

[Moshe Mishkinsky]

MEDES AND MEDIA (Heb. מָדַי; in Akkadian inscriptions: *Madai*), a people of Indo-Iranian origin, closely related to the Persians, who inhabited the mountainous area of Iran and the northeastern and eastern region of Mesopotamia. The Medes, located in the Kermanshah-Hamadan (Ecbatana) region, are more prominent in Assyrian texts than the Persians. The Assyrian kings distinguish two groups of Medes inside the empire, and the distant Medes (*madaya rūqūti*). In the biblical passage enumerating Noah's sons, Madai, the progenitor of the Medes, like those of other Indo-Iranian peoples, is included among the sons of *Japheth (Gen. 10:2). In datable sources Medes are first mentioned in the historical inscriptions of the Assyrian kings of the end of the ninth century B.C.E., Shalamaneser III and his son Shamshi-Adad V. The Assyrian kings in military campaigns against Media, which then stretched southeast of Lake Urmia, inflicted heavy losses on its population. Although the Medes did not as yet have a central kingdom, they succeeded in repelling the Assyrian kings in sporadic encounters and by evasive tactics. In the eighth century B.C.E., *Tiglath-Pileser III, in his campaigns, which extended from *Ararat (Urartu) to the mountains south of the Caspian Sea, subdued the Medes. Annexing Media to Assyria, he deported 65,000 of its population, whom he replaced with inhabitants of other countries. However, in the days of *Sargon II, at the end of the eighth century B.C.E., Media, under the leadership of a Median called Dayaukku, revolted against Assyria. In Sargon's military operations conducted in 716–15 B.C.E. against the centers of revolt, Dayaukku was captured and exiled to Hamath in Syria, whereupon 22 Median rulers, submitting to the sovereignty of Assyria, presented a gift to the king. Dayaukku is undoubtedly identical with Deioces, who is mentioned by Herodotus (1:96–101) as having united the tribes of Media and as having been its first king, reigning for 53 years. However, according to contemporary Assyrian sources, he was merely the forceful local chieftain of a region lying between Assyria and Ararat. Apparently a later tradition attributed to him a royal title and the establishment of the Median Empire. Media became a united empire under the leadership of Kaštarita (according to the Persian pronunciation; in Assyrian: *Kastarītu*), who formed a military pact against the Assyrians in the region of the Zagros Mountains and rose to be king of Media (in the first half of the seventh century B.C.E.). The present tendency is to identify Kaštarita with Phraortes king of Media who, according to Herodotus (1:102), reigned 22 years, subdued the Persians, and was killed when advancing on Nineveh. Having consolidated their position at the end of the reign of Ashurbanipal king of Assyria (668–627 B.C.E.), the Medes, in the wars between Babylonia and Assyria in the days of the last Assyrian kings (626–616 B.C.E.), joined forces with the Babylonians, attacked Nineveh, and, after conquering it, assisted in the capture of Haran. The Medes (called in contemporary Babylonian documents *Ummān manda*, an old traditional term for barbarians) were then ruled by Cyaxares (i.e., native Huvaxšra; in Babylonian sources: *Umakištar*), who, Herodotus reports (1:100–4), defeated the Scythians. After the overthrow of Assyria, Cyaxares extended his sway over the northern part of the Assyrian Empire, as well as over large sections of Iran, Armenia, and Asia Minor. When unable in 500 B.C.E. to conquer Lydia, Cyaxares, through the mediation of the kings of Babylonia and Cilicia, made a treaty with the Lydians. This consolidation of Media under Cyaxares, constituting as it did a danger to Babylonia, finds expression in utterances of the prophets of Israel who saw in the army of Media a relentless foe rising to destroy Babylonia (Isa. 13:4–6, 17–19, 21:1–10) and uniting with other northern peoples to bring about, at God's command, the overthrow of the kingdom of the Chaldeans (Jer. 51:11–14, 25–36). Astyages (Ass. *Ištumēgu*) the son of Cyaxares and the last king of Media (584–550 B.C.E.) attempted to oust Babylonia from the region of Haran. However, after *Cyrus king of Persia had revolted against Astyages and defeated him, Media became part of the Persian Empire (550 B.C.E.). The revolts which broke out against Persian rule at the beginning of *Darius I's reign were unsuccessful, and Media was incorporated into two Persian satrapies (the 11th and the 18th). Nevertheless it occupied an honorable and special position in the Persian Empire, as is reflected in the biblical combination (in Esther and Daniel) of "Persia and Media" or "Media and Persia," e.g., "the seven princes of Persia and Media" (Esth. 1:14); "the kings of Media and Persia" (10:2); or "the laws of the Persians and the Medes" (1:19). The Bible apparently expresses a view, then prevalent, about the part played by the two empires in the historical events preceding the fall of Babylonia. According to this view, not only did the one empire supplement the work of the other but the Persian Empire was the natural heir of Media. Echoes of this view appear in Daniel's vision of the destruction of Babylonia by the Medes and Persians (Dan. 5:26–28; cf. 6:1, 29; 8:20) as well as in the prophecies in Isaiah and Jeremiah concerning the overthrow of Babylonia by Media (see above). It is difficult to reconcile elements of the literary sources with archaeological evidence. Ecbabtana has not yet been excavated but three other sizable Median sites of the seventh century were deserted by the sixth. No Median writing has been found, though some words that are either Median or part of Medo-Persian *koinē* have been identified in Old Persian inscriptions, nor has any distinctively Median style in art been identified.

BIBLIOGRAPHY: J. von Prašek, *Geschichte der Meder und Perser* (1906); Luckenbill, Records, index, s.v. *Madai, Matai, Medes, Media*; J. Levy, *Forschungen zur alten Geschichte Vorderasiens* (1925); C.J. Gad, *The Fall of Nineveh* (1926); idem, in: *Anatolian Studies*, 8 (1958), 72–78; Landsberger and Bauer, in: ZA, 3 (1927), 81–88; F.W. Koenig, in: *Der Alte Orient*, 33 (1934), 3–4; G.G. Cameron, *History of Early Iran* (1936); C.C. Torrey, in; JAOS, 66 (1946), 1–15; H.L. Ginsberg, *Studies in Daniel* (1948), 5–23; R.G. Kent, *Old Persian…* (1950); R. Ghirshman, *Iran* (1954), 72–126; D.J. Wiseman, *Chronicles of Chaldean Kings* (1956); idem, in: *Iraq*, 20 (1958), 11ff.; I.M. Dyakonov (Diakonoff), *Istoria Midii* (1956), incl. bibl.; R. Labat, in: JA, 249 (1961), 1–12. **ADD. BIBLIOGRAPHY:** I. Diakonoff, in: *Scripta Hierosolymitana*, 33 (… *Studies … Tadmor*; 1991), 13–20; A. Kuhrt, *The Ancient Near East c. 3000–330 B.C.* (1995), 652–56; H. Sancisi-Weerdenburg, in: OCD, 944–45; P. Briant, *From Cyrus to Alexander* (2002), 24–7.

[Samuel Abramsky / S. David Sperling (2nd ed.)]

MEDIATION, an alternative means for the resolution of disputes in which the mediator, a neutral professional, meets with the parties to the dispute and aids them in reaching an agreed upon resolution. Unlike a judge, the mediator has no authority to render a decision in the dispute. In the mediation process, the parties are given the opportunity to express themselves, to voice their arguments, and to reach, by themselves, a solution that is appropriate for them.

Mediation is appropriate for the resolution of most types of disputes, be they commercial disputes, private disputes, disputes regarding the family, or even public disputes and international disputes between states.

Jewish legal literature contains many sources that refer to disputes. Many of these sources point to the increase in litigation and consider the use of the judicial process, terminating in a definitive judicial decision as the preferred method to resolve disputes.

Alongside this approach, there are many sources that refer approvingly to making peace between parties, whether this is achieved by a *dayyan* (rabbinical court judge) in the rabbinical court who works out a "compromise" between the parties (see *Compromise), or by means of mediation that takes place outside the court. It seems that it was not coincidental that the Israeli legislature, in Section 2 of the Foundations of Law Act, 5740 – 1980, provided that "peace" is one of the values according to which the court is obligated to act in the case of a lacuna, a unique provision in comparison to legal systems in other countries. Thus, where the court encounters a legal question which must be resolved, and it is not addressed in legislation or case law and cannot be resolved by way of analogy, the court is instructed to decide "in light of the principles of freedom, justice, equity and peace of the Jewish tradition."

An expression of the important role of "peace," alongside that of "law" as a means to dispute resolution, may be seen in the Book of Zechariah, 8:16, "...execute the judgment of truth and peace in your gates." The Mishnah in *Avot* elaborates upon this verse, stating: "The world exists on three foundations: On truth, on judgment, and on peace." The verse from the Book of Zechariah served as the basis for the teaching of the sages in the Mishnah, as follows: "What is the judgment that contains peace? Let it be said: it is compromise." The Maharsha – Rabbi Samuel Edels, a rabbinic sage in Poland in the 16th century – commented as follows: "Compromise is arrived at with the agreement and willingness of both of the parties, which is not the case with judgment." (For further explication of this subject see the opinion of Justice Menachem Elon in CA 61/84 *Biazi v. Levi*, 42(1) PD 446.)

As opposed to modern legal systems that view the court as a central means for conflict resolution, the Torah commands each individual – and not just the legal institution – to try to bring about accord between opponents in a dispute. An expression of this is found in the Mishnah in tractate *Pe'ah*, that is recited daily in the morning prayers: "These are things that have no measure [that the reward for them is immeasurably great] ...a person enjoys their interest in this world and the principle awaits him in the world to come: ... and making peace between people and between a husband and his wife" (the last phrase, "between a husband and his wife," does not appear in all of the ancient manuscripts of the Mishnah, but is found in some of the versions of the prayer and is common in the Sephardi and the Eastern versions of the prayer).

In his classic commentary on the Mishnah, the author of *Tiferet Yisrael*, Rabbi Israel Lipschutz (Germany, 18th century), discusses the special expression "bringing peace" rather than "making peace," and he comments as follows:

> Bringing peace – even if the two parties do not desire it, one should go to the trouble of persuading them to come together and bring about peace between them. And this is the reason that the *tanna* did not say "to make peace" but rather "to bring peace," in other words, to bring counsel from afar in order to compel them by his soft words to bring peace between them.

In the Midrash, the figure of Aaron the Priest, about whom it was said in the Mishnah (Avot 1:12) that he "loved peace and pursued peace," serves as the archetype for the commandments of bringing about peace. The Talmud even contrasts between Moses, the head of the judges and Aaron's brother, and Aaron, who serves as a symbol for mediators seeking to resolve disputes outside of court: "Moses used to say: The law must be carried out to its fullest, but Aaron loved peace and pursued peace, and made peace between people." Rashi commented "Because he would hear the disputes between them *before they came before him for a judgment*, he would pursue them and impose peace between them." In other words, as is the case with modern day mediation proceedings, the "mediator," Aaron the Priest, met with the parties before the legal hearing and outside of the "court," in order to spare them the pain and suffering that accompany the legal proceedings.

The end product of mediation, unlike a legal proceeding, is not a legal decision in which one side prevails and the other side feels that he has lost, but rather the end of the conflict and its resolution in a "peaceful" manner, in which both sides feel that they are satisfied.

An interesting description of the mediation process is found in *Avot de-Rabbi Nathan* (12:3): "Two people had quarreled with one another. Aaron went and sat with one of them. He said to him: My son, look what your friend has done, his heart is distraught and he has torn his clothes (out of sorrow regarding the quarrel), and he is saying: Woe is to me, how will I raise up my head and look at my friend? I am embarrassed in his presence, because I am the one who wronged him. And he [Aaron] sits with him until he removes the jealousy from his heart. And Aaron then goes and sits with the other party and says to him: My son, see what your friend has done, his heart is distraught and he has torn his clothes and he is saying: Woe is to me, how will I raise up my head and look at my friend? I am embarrassed in his presence, because I am the one who wronged him. And he [Aaron] sits with him until he removes the jealousy from his heart. And when they met [the two opponents who carried on the dispute between them], they embraced and kissed one another."

According to the description in this Midrash, Aaron the Priest uses a technique similar to that used by contemporary mediators, of holding separate mediation meetings alongside the joint meetings, with the goal of aiding the parties to end the dispute. In this respect as well, the difference between the mediation process and a court proceeding, which has to be held in the presence of both of the parties, is readily apparent.

It is not unusual for a dispute between parties to be so serious that the two parties cannot communicate with each other. Due to the lack of trust between them, each one is suspicious of the other and holding separate meetings allows them to express themselves freely in front of the mediator and to talk about their feelings in a calm and non-threatening atmosphere, without worrying that what they say will be conveyed to the other party. In this manner, the mediator can assist each of the sides to identify his interests and needs, and to understand the interests of the other party. In the case described in *Avot de-Rabbi Nathan*, the mediator uses "neutral" language, while emphasizing points that are likely to lead to a resolution of the dispute. Aaron the Priest emphasizes the sorrow of the other party to create an opening to decrease the tension between the parties and to encourage discussion between them. Unlike a judge, the mediator does not express an opinion regarding the dispute before him. He abstains from "awarding grades" to the parties to the dispute, does not appraise their character, and does not judge their deeds. His role is purely one of assisting in carrying out the negotiations between them to resolve the dispute.

In Court Decisions in Israel

Israeli law accords a wide degree of expression to the desired place of reaching a compromise by the court, relying on the position of the Jewish Law sources regarding this matter (see, for example, CA 807/77 *Sobol v. Goldman*, 33(1) PD 789, per Justice Elon and HCJ 2222/99 *Gabai v. The Rabbinical Court of Appeals*, 54(5) PD 401; see *Compromise). However, a distinction must be made between a compromise arrived at by a judge and a mediation proceeding handled by a neutral professional outside of the courtroom. Section 79c of the Courts Law [consolidated version], 5744 – 1984, refers to mediation, along with compromises that take place within the court, as appropriate proceedings for the resolution of disputes. Pursuant to that section, "the court may, with the agreement of the parties, transfer a matter in litigation to mediation." If the parties reach an agreement in the mediation, the court is authorized to give the agreement the force of a judgment. Detailed regulations have been enacted to govern the mediation process.

BIBLIOGRAPHY: M. Elon, "*Ha-Din, Ha-Emet, Ha-Shalom ve-ha-Pesharah: Al Sheloshah ve-Arba'ah Amudei ha-Mishpat ve-ha-Ḥevrah*," in: *Meḥkarei Mishpat*, 14 (5758 – 1998), 269–342; Y. Bazak, "*Yishuv Sikhsukhim be-Derekh shel Pesharah ba-Mishpat ha-Ivri*," in: *Sinai*, 71 (5732 – 1972), 64; A. Hacohen, "*Lo Yakhlu Dabru le-Shalom – Gishur, Pishur, ve-Yishuv Sikhsukhim*," in: The Ministry of Justice, *Daf Parashat ha-Shavu'a*, 54 (5762 – 2002); E. Shochetman, *Seder ha-Din* (5748 – 1988), 208–16.

[Elisheva Hacohen (2nd ed.)]

MEDICINE. From the beginning of their history until modern times Jews have exercised a tremendous influence on the development of medical science. They have always been solicitous in their care for the sick and held the medical profession in great esteem. In ancient times medicine and religion were closely connected. The priests were the custodians of public health. The dispute as to the propriety of human interference in sickness – regarded as divine retribution – ceased to trouble the Jews, because they came to regard the physician as the instrument through whom God could effect the cure. Jewish physicians therefore considered their vocation as spiritually endowed and not merely an ordinary profession. By the same token, great demands were made of them, and the ethical standards have always been very high.

The importance of medicine and physicians among the Jews is best seen in the long line of rabbi-physicians, that started during the talmudic period and continued until comparatively recently. Various factors were responsible for this combination of professions. Medicine was sanctioned by biblical and talmudic law and had an important bearing upon religious matters. Since teaching or studying the word of God for reward was not considered ethical, the practice of medicine was most often chosen as a means of livelihood. This trend was further strengthened by the fact that during the greater part of the Middle Ages the Jews were excluded from almost all other occupations, including public office, and medicine was left as one of the few dignified occupations by which they could earn their living.

Jews have contributed to medicine both by the creation of new medical concepts and by the transmission of medical knowledge. It was through the medieval Jewish physician-translators that the medical knowledge of the East and much of ancient Greek medical lore was preserved and transmitted to the West. A general survey of Jews in medicine may be divided into three broad periods:

(a) biblical and talmudic times, which covers the period from antiquity until roughly the fourth to fifth centuries C.E.;

(b) a middle period from approximately the sixth century C.E. to the beginning of the 19th century; and

(c) the 19th and 20th centuries, during which Jews throughout the world have excelled not only in the practice of medicine but in all fields of medical research and teaching. It is significant that over 20% of all winners of the Nobel Prize for medicine up to the end of the 1960s were Jewish.

The high standard of medical science in Israel must be mentioned. Not only have Israeli physicians successfully met the challenge of medical problems in a developing country with a mixed population, but they have continued the ancient Jewish medical tradition by teaching and giving practical aid to those developing countries striving to attain the scientific levels of the 20th and 21st century.

IN THE BIBLE

The main source of information on ancient Hebrew medicine is the Bible, which refers to medicine as it pertains to religious or civil laws or when important characters are involved. No general ancient Hebrew medical documents are extant, although the Talmud reports that King *Hezekiah canceled the "Medical Book" (Ber. 10b; Pes. 56a) and that a scroll on pharmacology was lost. From earliest times, the Jewish faith sought to suppress *magic customs and practices in every field of life, including those concerned with the health of its members. The Hebrews were doubtlessly influenced in their medical concepts and practices by the surrounding nations, particularly by Egypt, where medical knowledge was highly developed. Prevailing superstitions and beliefs in magic medicine were far less accepted and practiced by the Jews, however, than by their neighbors. But like their contemporaries, the ancient Hebrews attributed health and disease to a divine source.

Healing was in the hands of God and the role of doctors was that of helpers or instruments of God. There are numerous references to physicians and men of healing throughout the Bible. It is always implied, however, that although man may administer treatment, it is God who heals: "I am the Lord that healeth thee" (Ex. 15:26). The title *rofe* ("healer") was therefore never adopted by ancient Jewish physicians; where it occurs it invariably refers to foreign doctors, who were usually assumed to be helpless because they were not aided by God. Pharmacists and midwives are also mentioned. Hebrew priests had no authority as physicians but rather held the position of health wardens of the community, charged with enforcing the laws pertaining to social hygiene.

The uniqueness of biblical medicine lies in its regulations for social hygiene, which are remarkable not only for their period but even by present-day standards. Hygiene and prophylaxis became religious dogmas intended for the welfare and preservation of the nation. Of the 613 commandments, 213 are of a medical nature. Prevention of epidemics, suppression of prostitution and venereal diseases, frequent washing, care of the skin, strict dietary and sanitary regulations, rules for sexual life, isolation and quarantine, the observance of a day of rest – the Sabbath – these and other provisions inhibited the spread of many of the diseases prevalent in neighboring countries.

The Hebrews were aware of the fact that contagious diseases are spread by direct contact as well as by clothing, household utensils, etc. To prevent the spread of epidemics or infectious maladies they therefore compiled a series of sanitary regulations. These included precautionary or temporary isolation, quarantine, burning or scalding of infected garments and utensils, thorough scrubbing and smoking out of houses suspected of infection, and scrupulous inspection and purification of the diseased person after recovery (Lev. 13–14). Anyone coming into contact with a corpse or carrion, or suffering from purulent discharges from any part of his body, also required a thorough cleansing of himself and his belongings before being allowed back into the encampment (Num. 19:7–16; Lev. 15:2–13). The garments, weapons, and utensils of soldiers returning to the camp after a battle had to be thoroughly cleansed and disinfected to prevent the spread of diseases possibly picked up during contact with the enemy (Num. 31:20, 22–24). The danger of infectious bowel diseases spreading through excrement was also recognized and the Bible instructs how to keep the camp clean (Deut. 23:13–14).

Diseases and Remedies

Many diseases are mentioned in the Bible. Among them are *shaḥefet* – phthisis (Lev. 26:16); *ʿafolim* – leishmaniasis (Deut. 28:27); *yerakon* (*yeraqon*) – ikterus (Deut. 28:22); *sheḥin poreʾaḥ aʾvʿabuʿot* – pemphigus (Ex. 9:9); *zav* – gonorrhea-leukorrhea (Lev. 15); *dever* – pest (Deut. 28:21); *shivron motnayim* – lumbago (Ezek. 21:11); *nofel ve-galui ʿenayim* – epilepsy (Num. 24:4); *rekav* (*reqav*) *ʿaẓamot* – osteomyelitis (Prov. 14:30). Although not specifically mentioned by name, eye diseases such as blepharitis ciliaris and gonorrheal ophthalmia undoubtedly existed, and senile cataract probably occurred frequently among the ancient Hebrews: "Now the eyes of Israel (Jacob) were dim for age so that he could not see" (Gen. 48:10). The dimness of sight rather than blindness is indicative of cataract. Various forms of skin disease are referred to in Deuteronomy: "The Lord will smite thee with the boil of Egypt, and with the emerods, and with the scab, and with the itch, whereof thou canst not be healed" (Deut. 28:27). The Hebrew word *ẓaraʿat*, which has been translated as leprosy, was probably a generic term for a number of skin ailments, many of which were considered curable (Lev. 13). However, leprosy in the modern sense was also known, and rigid quarantine, which did not exclude kings (II Chron. 26:21), was imposed on lepers. The term *maggefah* refers to plague, epidemics, and contagious diseases in general, very often of a venereal type. A bubonic plague described in I Samuel 5 mentions rodents, who are known to be carriers of the disease. Various types of wounds are mentioned: *makkah* is the generic term for wound; *makkah tʾeriyyah* is a festering wound; *makkah ʾanushah*, a wound which will not heal, often fatal; *peẓaʿ*, a stab wound; *ḥabburah*, a boil or hematoma; and *mazor*, a septic boil.

With the one exception of the incurable serpent bite (Num. 21:9), biblical remedies and treatments are all of a rational character and do not involve incantations or magic rites, nor do they include the so-called "filth pharmacy." Biblical therapeutics consisted of washing; the use of oils, balsams, and bandages for wounds and bone fractures; bathing in therapeutic waters (II Kings 5:10), especially in the case of skin diseases; sun rays, medicated drinks, etc. Among medicaments mentioned by name are myrrh, sweet cinnamon, cassia, galbanum, niter, and the mandrake (*dudaʾim*) which was considered to possess aphrodisiac properties. The modern method of mouth-to-mouth artificial respiration was also known, as testified by the accounts of Elijah and Elisha (I Kings 17:22; II Kings 4:34–35). The only surgical operations mentioned are circumcision and castration, and these were not specifically Jewish practices. *Embalming, though unusual, was not forbidden.

Anatomical Knowledge

The Hebrew had more than a passing knowledge of anatomy. This is attested by the language used in instructions concerning methods of sacrifice and by passages of poetry where the names of organs and limbs are used metaphorically. The heart is mentioned frequently as the seat of emotion and intellect, and the functions now ascribed to the brain were then thought to emanate from the heart. No word for brain is mentioned; the word *moʾaḥ* in Job refers to marrowbone.

It is interesting to note that the Bible has a distinctive nomenclature for parts of the body and types of illnesses. Thus, for example, body defects or deformities are described solely by words constructed in the *piʿel* grammatical form: *ʾiṭṭer* – paralyzed, left-handed; *ʾillem* – dumb; *ʿivver* – blind; *pisseʾaḥ* – lame; *gibben* – hunchback. Descriptions of mental or nervous diseases appear in the *piʿalon*-form: *dikkaʾon* – depression; *shiggaʿon* – madness; *izzavon* – nervousness; *ʿivvaron* – mental blindness; *shikkaron* – drunkenness. Somatic illnesses appear in the *paʿelet* (*paʿalat*) form: *dalleket* (*dalleqet*) – inflammation; *shaḥefet* – tuberculosis; *yabbelet* – acne; *ʿaẓẓevet* – neuritis; *baheret* – leukoderma, vitiligo; *sappaḥat* – psoriasis; *ẓaraʿat* – lepra, skin diseases; *gabbaḥat* – loss of hair. Trauma of the body is formed according to the *paʿul* model: *shavur* – fractured; *ḥaruẓ* – split; *maʿukh* – crushed; *natuk* (*natuq*) – disjointed; *razuẓ* – smashed; *ẓaruʿa* – infected; *pazuʿa* – wounded. Many anatomical terms have the ancient two-letter root, while most Hebrew words derive from three letters. Thus לֵב *lev* –

heart; דָּם *dam* – blood; פֶּה *peh* – mouth; חֵךְ *ḥekh* – gums; שֵׁן *shen* – tooth; יָד *yad* – hand.

THE TALMUDIC ERA

The period surveyed in this section extends roughly from the second century B.C.E. to the sixth century C.E. The historical events of that period had a profound influence on the thought and way of life of the Jews and consequently on the development of Jewish medical art as well. As a result of the Babylonian Exile, of Greek rule followed by the Hasmonean Wars, the rise of Christianity and the Exile after the destruction of the Second Temple, the Jewish community became wide open to influences from neighboring countries and to foreign philosophies, which had their effect on every walk of life, including medicine.

Sources and Influences

The sources for this period are the Apocryphal books, Greco-Roman writings of Jews and non-Jews, the Mishnah, the Jerusalem and Babylonian Talmuds, the Midrashim, and, in part, the recently discovered Dead Sea Scrolls. None of these sources is a medical book as such. Except for a few cases, such as the praise of medicine and the physician by *Ben Sira, medical matters are dealt with mainly to illustrate points of ritual, or civil and criminal law. In the Talmud, a few medical matters are dealt with extensively in the tractates *Ḥullin, Nega'im*, and *Bekhorot*. The influence of Persian and Babylonian magic medicine is clear from references to *amulets, the *evil eye, *demons, etc. The Greek influence on Jewish medical thought was considerable, but we find that the scholars were not blind adherents of the humoral pathology, but rather followers of anatomic pathology. This was doubtless based on their experiments and observations of sick animals before and after slaughter, as well as on their studies of human bodies and corpses. One of the interpretations given to the name of the sect known as *Essenes is אִסִיִים, "healers." Their medicine mainly influenced Christian medicine and medical thought. They studied and collected herbs and roots for healing purposes, though their chief remedies were prayer, mystic formulas, and amulets. Abiding faith was all that was considered necessary for curing physical and mental diseases as well as chronic defects such as blindness, lameness, and deafness. The medicine mentioned in the New Testament is almost entirely of this type of miracle cure. By contrast, the attitude of Jewish scholars of the time, and later those of the Talmud, is generally a scientific one.

The talmudic attitude toward the sanctity of human life and the importance of health is expressed in numerous statements: "The saving of life (*pikku'aḥ nefesh*) takes precedence over Sabbath" (Yoma 85a). "Whoever is overzealous in fasting should be regarded as a sinner" (Ta'an. 11a). It was also decreed that when treating the sick or a woman in childbirth, even though no danger to life was involved, the sanctity of the Sabbath could be profaned.

Status of the Physician

The Talmud does not regard calling upon a physician for medical aid as a failure to rely upon God to restore health: "Whoever is in pain, let him go to the physician" (BK 46b). The profession of physician – as an instrument of God – was held in high esteem: "Honor the physician before need of him. Him also hath God apportioned.... The skill of a physician shall lift up his head; and he shall stand before nobles ..." (Ecclus. 38). The Talmud enumerated ten things that must be in a city where a scholar lives, and these include a physician and a surgeon. From this statement it may also be concluded that the number of practicing physicians was relatively great.

Specialists as known in Egypt did not exist. However, the Talmud names two types of physician, *rofe* and *rofe umman* ("skilled physician" and "surgeon"). Patients visited the physician in his home and not, as in Greece, in the marketplace. A special regulation was therefore enacted which required anyone renting premises to a physician to obtain the prior agreement of his neighbors, since the cries and noise of visiting patients might disturb them (BB 21a). *Hospitals were apparently nonexistent in this period, although certain temple halls, and later on, parts of the poorhouses and synagogues, were set aside for the sick. However, mention is made of operation rooms, which had to be walled with marble for cleanliness – "*battei shayish*." There were communal or district physicians, whose duties included assessing the character and extent of any physical disability sustained in cases of injury in order to determine damages (Sanh. 78a). They were also required to judge the degree of physical endurance of a person sentenced to corporal punishment (Mak. 22b). "The victim of an assault could refuse to be treated by a physician coming from a distance since he would not be sufficiently concerned with the welfare of his patient" (BK 85a).

A physician had to receive adequate fees, and free medical service was not approved because "a physician who takes nothing is worth nothing" (BK 85a). At the same time, Jewish physicians had special consideration for the poor and needy – a tradition which was maintained throughout the centuries. Abba Umana (fourth century C.E.) was reputed as a physician and a charitable man. In order not to discourage needy patients he would hang a box on the wall where anyone could put in, unnoticed, the fee he thought he could afford for medical treatment. Abba Umana refused to take fees from poor students and would return them their money so that they could use it for convalescence (Ta'an. 21b). If, in spite of every care, a licensed physician injured a patient or caused his death, he was not – as among many other peoples – held guilty (Sanh. 84b). Jewish physicians were apparently organized in some type of guild which had as its insignia the *ḥarut* – the branch of a palm or a balsam bush (Jews at that time regarded balsam as the best remedy for wounds; cf. Pliny, Hist. Nat., 12:54).

Jewish doctors had an excellent reputation and practiced throughout the then-known civilized world. A physician Theudas is mentioned in *Bekhorot* (4:4) as a famous doctor from Alexandria. Aulus Cornelius *Celsus, writing in the first century C.E., refers to salves compounded by skilled Jewish physicians. *Galen reports on the Jewish physician Rufus Samaritanus in Rome in the first-second centuries C.E. Similar references are made by Marcellus Empiricus, Aetius of Amida, and Paulus of Aegina. Pliny (Hist. Nat., 37.60.10) mentions a "Babylonian physician – Zechariah," undoubtedly a Jew, who dedicated his medical book to King Mithridates. The emperor Antoninus Pius (86–161 C.E.) requested R. Judah ha-Nasi to supply him with a physician for his house slaves from among his circle of students. The personal physician of St. Basil (c. 300 C.E.) was the Jew, Ephraim. The bishop Gelasius refers to his Jewish physician Telesinus as his "trusted friend." At the same time, numerous restrictions against Jewish doctors were already being promulgated by Christian bishops and emperors. These only serve to show how large the number of practicing Jewish physicians was at the time.

The study of medicine was included in the curriculum of talmudic schools and many Talmud scholars were themselves physicians. Among them were R. Ishmael, R. Ḥanina b. Dosa, R. Hananiah b. Ḥama, Joseph ha-Rofe of Gamla, Tobiah ha-Rofe of Modi'in, and Minjomi (Benjamin). The most distinguished of them was *Samuel b. Abba ha-Kohen, also called Mar Samuel Yarḥina'ah (165–257), to whom many remedies and much anatomical knowledge is attributed. He was also the personal physician of the Persian king, Sapur. In addition, the Talmud mentions *askan bi-devarim*, which might be described as a research scientist, who occupied himself more with the study of animal and human anatomy and physiology than with the actual practice of medicine.

Talmudic Anatomy

The preoccupation with regulations concerning ritually unclean meat, the physical qualifications for priesthood, rules concerning menstruous women, defilement, etc., accounts for the extraordinary anatomical knowledge of talmudic scholars. For full details see *Anatomy.

Talmudic Embryology

A great deal of material on this subject can be found in the Talmud and in the Midrashim, some of it of an imaginary or legendary character but most of it surprisingly accurate. Abba Saul describes the development of an embryo in its sixth week (Nid. 25b). Simlai describes the parts, posture, and nourishment of an embryo in the womb. Scholars accepted the opinion that the embryo is a living organism from the time of conception (Sanh. 91b). In contrast to Aristotle, who regarded the seed as a mosaic of individual creative factors corresponding to each of the parts of the human body and assumed that each limb is derived from the parallel limb of the father, the talmudic scholars regarded the seed as one single summary of all the creative forces of the organism and did not acknowledge the individual influence of one limb on the embryo. "The seed is mixed, otherwise blind would beget blind and one-limbed a one-limbed" (Ḥul. 69a). The Talmud also accepts the equal share of the male and female in forming the organism.

Pathology and Etiology

In examining the ritual fitness of animals and the cleanliness and purity of members of the community, talmudic scholars had numerous opportunities of observing and diagnosing diseases. They described various pathological conditions of the lungs and knew the existence of pulmonary infections (Ḥul. 47b). Disturbances of the circulatory system were recognized by the paleness or flush of the body (Yev. 64b). The diagnosis of certain skin diseases was determined according to the form, temperature, and secretion of the wound and the color of the hair round it. The observation of such a wound could last up to three weeks (Neg. 10). Scholars were able to recognize macula of the cornea, keratitis, and detached retina (Bekh. 38a). R. Ishmael describes diphtheria as an epidemic disease which causes painful death through strangulation. The pathology of hemophilia as a lack of viscosity in the blood preventing coagulation is described, and the circumcision of an infant in a hemophilic family was forbidden. It was also recognized that the female is the transmitter of this disease (Yev. 64a; Ḥul. 47b). A large number of lung, liver, kidney, and stomach diseases were described as being caused by worms (Ḥul. 48a; Shab. 109b; Git. 70a). Lack of fluids was thought to lead to digestive disturbances (Shab. 41a). It was recognized that fear accelerates the pulse and causes heartbeats (Sanh. 100b); that falling from a great height may cause fatal internal injury (Ḥul. 42a); that injury to the spinal cord causes paralysis (Ḥul. 51a); and that restraint of the gall causes jaundice. Fevers and colds were thought to be caused by negligence (BM 107b). According to R. Eleazar the gall (humor) and according to Mar Samuel the air (pneuma) could cause disease. It was generally accepted that blood is the chief cause of disease (BB 58b). Overeating, excessive drinking of intoxicants, and sexual excesses were also thought to cause disease. It was realized that animals and insects, in particular flies, are carriers and transmitters of infectious diseases (Ket. 77a), and that contaminated water may also cause illness (Av. Zar. 30a).

Remedies, Treatments, and Surgery

The medicines mentioned in the Talmud include powders, medicated drinks, juices, balsams, bandages, compresses, and incense. Meat and eggs were considered to be the most nourishing foods (Ber. 44b); fried food or food containing fat was regarded as difficult to digest (57b). The eating of vegetables throughout the year and the drinking of fresh water at every meal were recommended (*ibid.* 57b; 40a). Baths and mineral waters were regarded as general strengthening tonics and as therapeutics for certain skin diseases (Shab. 40a; 109a; Ket. 77b). Herbs were used for constipation and purges were recommended in serious cases, except for pregnant women (Pes. 42b). The use of opium as an analgetic and hypnotic drug was known, and warning was given against overdosing (TJ, Av. Zar. 2:2, 40d). Anything useful for healing purposes was permitted at any time, even on the Sabbath (Ḥul. 77b). Surgeons operated in special halls – "*battei shayish*" (see above). "Sleeping drugs" – *sammei de-shinta* – were used as anesthetics. From descriptions of operations we learn of trepannings, amputations, and removal of the spleen (cf. Sanh. 21b; Ḥul. 57a; Git. 56a). A cesarean was also performed, but it is not clear whether the operation was done on a living or on an already dead body. In general, the life of the mother had priority and therefore the killing of a fetus during a difficult birth was allowed (Tosef., Yev. 9:4). Wound edges were cut in order to ensure complete and clean healing (Ḥul. 54a). Surgeons wore special operation aprons (Kelim 26:5).

Hygiene and Prophylaxis

The main contribution of talmudic medicine lies not so much in the treatment of illness but rather, as in the Bible, in the prevention of disease and the care of community health. The hygienic measures advocated were of a practical as well as of a religious, ethical nature. A principle which recurs a number of times is that "bodily cleanliness leads to spiritual cleanliness" (Av. Zar. 20b; TJ, Shab. 1:3, 3b). Hygienic regulations applied among other things to town planning, climatic conditions, social community life, family life, and care of the body. Mention is made of a disinfectant composed of seven ingredients used for cleansing infected clothing (Zev. 95a). A town was required to have a physician and a bathhouse. Clothing had to be changed before eating. Mar Samuel declared that diseases may be carried by caravans from land to land (Ta'an. 21b). Members of a family with a sick person among them were to be avoided. The digging of wells in the neighborhood of cemeteries or refuse dumps was forbidden (Tosef., BB 1:10). It was forbidden to drink uncovered water for fear of snake venom (Av. Zar. 30a). Food had to be fresh and served in clean dishes. Kissing on the mouth was discouraged, and kissing only on the back of the hand was recommended in order to prevent contagion. During epidemics, the population was advised to avoid crowding in narrow alleyways because of the danger of contagion in the air. For body care, the Talmud recommends physical exercises, massage, sunlight, employment, and above all cleanliness. Mar Samuel states: "The washing of hands and feet in the morning is more effective than any remedy in the world" (Shab. 108b). Excesses of any kind were regarded as harmful. The Talmud also concerned itself with the health of future generations and forbade marriage to epileptics or the mentally retarded (Yev. 64b; 112b). Surprisingly enough, talmudic pathology had very little influence on medieval medicine, not even on such outstanding physicians as *Maimonides and Isaac *Israeli, who were certainly well versed in the Talmud. The medical authority of Galen was so preeminent that all other medical theories and practice were regarded as banalities or even heresy. Scholars warned against the unselective use of talmudic remedies because they are not equally effective in all countries and at all times. Nonetheless, the hygienic laws and regulations of the Talmud, as well as many of its anatomical and pathological findings, appear in the light of modern knowledge to have enduring validity.

THE MIDDLE PERIOD

The medieval period of Jewish history does not coincide exactly with the common historical definition of the Middle Ages in Western civilization, but may be said to extend from the second-third centuries C.E. until the 19th century when, in most Western countries, Jews were granted full emancipation.

The large variety of climates, environments, and customs to which the Jewish people were exposed during their migrations in exile naturally had a profound influence on the development of their medical thought and knowledge. Thus, for example, there is a description of *diabetes mellitus* in the writings of Maimonides. According to him, this was a disease quite common in the warm Mediterranean countries with which he was acquainted but practically unknown in Northern Europe. Talmudic scholars give a precise description of *ratan* ("filariasis") and its treatment – a malady unknown in Europe. Similarly, the prevalence of eye diseases in the Orient greatly encouraged the development of ophthalmology and, when Jewish eye doctors migrated to Europe, they quickly acquired an excellent reputation among their Christian colleagues.

However, the merit of Jewish doctors of that period lay not only in their individual achievements as physicians, but in their work as translators and transmitters of Greek medicine to the Arabs and later on of Arab medicine to Europe. Jewish scholars, and among them physicians, had command of the three most important scholastic languages of the time – Latin, Arabic, and Hebrew – and, in some cases, Greek. This enabled them to translate most of the Arab and Greek medical works into Hebrew and Latin or vice versa. Knowledge of Hebrew was considered extremely important in the study of medicine. The English scholar Roger *Bacon (c. 1220–c. 1292) declared that Christian physicians were ignorant in comparison with their Jewish colleagues because they lacked knowledge of the Hebrew and Arabic in which most of the medical works were written. Vesalius, the great 16th-century anatomist, made a point of learning Hebrew to facilitate his studies, and gives Hebrew terms together with their Greek equivalents in his work *Fabrica* (see also *Frigeis, Lazaro De). Mosellanus, in his rectorial address at the University of Leipzig in 1518, urged Christian medical students to learn Hebrew so that they might study the medical lore "hidden in the libraries of the Jews." The close religious and family ties linking the various Jewish communities also helped to spread medical knowledge and facilitate rapid communication. As merchants and travelers the Jews met the best minds of their period and became acquainted with drugs, plants, and remedies from many parts of the world.

Nevertheless, although Jewish physicians were frequently held in great esteem by their non-Jewish colleagues as well as by kings and bishops, they suffered from persecution and restrictions, especially in the Christian world. From the fourth century C.E. onward there were innumerable regulations, papal bulls, and royal ordinances forbidding Jewish physicians to practice among non-Jews, to hold official positions and, later on, to study at universities. The fact that, despite these threats and restrictions, Jewish physicians continued in their profession and even held high positions at the courts of the very authorities who preached against them, attests to the esteem with which they were regarded for their medical skill. In this respect the Muslims were much more tolerant: although persecutions of Jews erupted from time to time in Muslim territories, physicians were not singled out, and consulting them was not forbidden.

The large number of Jewish physicians during these centuries may also be explained by the fact that Jews still regarded the medical profession as a spiritual vocation compatible with the career of a rabbi. Many scholars took up the medical profession as an honorable way of earning a living. This was made comparatively easy because the curriculum of talmudic schools often included the philosophies and sciences of ancient and contemporary times. Very often, therefore, medieval Jewish physicians were simultaneously rabbis, scholars, scientists, translators, grammarians, or poets, and as men of wide general knowledge they frequently attained high official positions in the countries in which they lived.

The Byzantine Era

While Greek science and culture declined in the Byzantine Empire and the Jews living there suffered under oppression, Jewish, as well as Nestorian and Jacobite, physicians and scholars sought to save what they could of Hellenistic science. The Babylonian talmudic centers of Sura and Pumbedita flourished at this period. Although the teaching languages of the period were Hebrew, Syrio-Aramaic, and Persian, it was Greek medicine which was taught, strongly influenced by Hebrew, Babylonian, Persian, and Indian traditions. This becomes apparent from the medical work left by Asaph b. Berechiah, called *Asaph ha-Rofe or Asaph Judaeus, who lived about the sixth century C.E. somewhere in the Middle East. Together with Johanan b. Zavda, Judah ha-Yarḥoni, and other Jewish scholars, he founded a medical school. His work, the oldest known medical book written in Hebrew, encompasses all the then-known wisdom of Greek, Babylonian, Egyptian, and Persian medicine, as well as something of Indian medicine. His medical technique is based on old Hebrew traditions. No Arab influence is apparent, which points to the fact that the book was composed before the seventh century. Most of the remedies mentioned were known in the Middle East generally. The book includes chapters on anatomy, embryology, physiology, hygiene, fever and pulse lore, urology, and a rich antidotarium. The oldest known Hebrew translation of the *Aphorisms* of Hippocrates, as well as chapters of Dioscorides and Galen, are also to be found in it. The book contains a "physician's oath," modeled on Hippocrates but far surpassing it in ethical content. The book of Asaph is not only significant to modern historians: it had considerable influence on medical history, particularly as far as Hebrew medical terms are concerned.

The Arab Period in the East

Following the Arab conquest of the Middle East and Spain, Jewish communities and centers of learning started to flourish at Faiyum in Egypt, Kairouan in Tunisia, and Cordova in Spain. Studies often included ethics, philosophy, sciences, and medicine. Students acquired experience in medicine by assisting practicing physicians. About a hundred years after the Arab conquest of the Middle East, the name of the Jewish physician Māsarjuwayh of Basra is mentioned as the first of a long list of men who translated a great number of Greek and Syrian works into Arabic. Unfortunately all his works have been lost, and he only appears as a frequent reference. Rabbān al-Ṭabarī (Sahl), a Jew converted to Islam who lived in Persia at the beginning of the ninth century, was a noted physician, mathematician, and astronomer. He was the first to translate *Ptolemy's *Almagest* into Arabic. His son Ali al-Tabarī Abu al-Ḥasan, also a convert, served as court physician to caliphs from 833 to 861, and was renowned as an ophthalmologist. His *Paradise of Wisdom* dealt with medicine, embryology, astronomy, and zoology and was one of the first original Arabic medical textbooks. He is best known as the teacher of the Arab physician Rhazes. One of the most outstanding medical personalities of the period was Isaac Judaeus (Isaac Israeli). He is believed to have been the first medical author in Arabic whose works were brought to Europe, and his books on fever, diet, uroscopy, and the ethical conduct of physicians were regarded as classics for several hundred years. His outstanding pupils were Abu al-Jazzār (a non-Jew) and *Dunash b. Tamim. It was said of him that he "lived a hundred years, was unmarried, shunned riches, and wrote important books more precious than silver or gold" (Saʿid b. Ahmad, tenth-century Arab scholar). Israeli's books were first translated into Latin by the monk Constantinus Africanus (1020–1087) and were all printed in Lyons in 1515.

Jewish physicians also flourished in Europe during this period. Among them was Zedekias (d. 880), the first registered Jewish doctor in Franco-Germany. He was personal physician to Louis the Pious and to his son Charles the Bald, and was known as the "wonderful physician" (Muenz).

The School of Salerno

From the ninth to the 12th century a medical study center existed in Salerno in southern Italy uninfluenced, either deliberately or by accident, by the Arab culture which penetrated into Southern Europe. The beginnings of the School of Salerno are associated with the name of the distinguished Jewish physician Shabbetai *Donnolo, of Oria, Calabria. His most famous medical work, *Sefer ha-Yakar*, lists 120 different remedies and their composition. Greek medicine is often referred to and Hebrew terms such as those used by Asaph ha-Rofe are frequently found in it. There is, however, no evidence that the author knew or accepted Arab medical wisdom, even though by that time many Arabic medical works had reached southern Italy by way of the Saracens of Sicily. It is interesting to note that *Sefer ha-Yakar* was also the first Hebrew prose written on European soil. References to other Jewish physicians practicing in Salerno and to Hebrew as a language of instruction are to be found in various records of the time. Benjamin of Tudela (12th century) refers to the physician Elijah whom he met when visiting Salerno. On the whole, however, the Jews who transmitted Arab philosophy and medical science had little influence on the School of Salerno, which endeavored to uphold the Greek medical tradition.

The Arab-Spanish Period

The Jews played an influential part in the cultural history of the period, starting with the Arab conquest of Spain in the eighth century and ending with their final expulsion from Granada in the 15th century. As statesmen, physicians, mathematicians, philosophers, and poets they attained high positions at the courts of both Moorish and Christian princes. At the Caliphate of Cordova (tenth century) was *Ḥasdai ibn Shaprut who, together with a monk, translated Dioscorides from Greek into Arabic. About a century later, Ephraim b. al-Zafran served as physician to the caliph of Egypt. Zafran was a renowned author and bibliophile and left a library of over 20,000 books. Another famous Jewish physician of the 11th century was Salāma ibn Ramḥamūn who lived in Cairo and whose works include a treatise on the causes of scant rainfall in Egypt and another discussing why Egyptian women grow stout early in life. *Judah Halevi (end of 11th century), the famous Spanish poet-physician, exerted great influence on his contemporaries and on later generations. Jonah ibn Bikhlarish (11th century) of Andalusia, court physician to the sultan of Saragossa, was one of the first Jewish scholars to learn Latin. In about 1080 he compiled a dictionary of drugs in Syriac, Persian, Greek, Latin, and Spanish which is believed to be the earliest work of its kind. Sheshet b. Isaac *Benveniste, who served as court physician to the king of Barcelona, was the author of a famous gynecological treatise in Arabic. The most important Jewish physician-philosopher of the period was Maimonides. Born in Cordova, he fled with his family to North Africa and soon attained a worldwide reputation as a religious legislator, philosopher, and physician. In 1170 he became personal physician to the family of Sultan Saladin of Egypt and continued to serve them until his death. Maimonides wrote ten medical works, of which the most important ones were *Pirkei Moshe* ("Aphorisms of Moshe") and *Regimen Sanitatis*. Maimonides' whole concept of medicine is based on the conviction that a healthy body is the prerequisite for a healthy soul. This enables a man to develop his intellectual and moral capabilities and leads him toward the knowledge of God and thus to a more ethical life. He regards healing as the art of repairing both the defects of the body and the turmoil of the mind. A physician must therefore have not only the technical knowledge of his profession, but also the intuition and skill to understand the patient's personality and environment. Maimonides divides medicine into three main fields: preventive medicine – the care of the healthy; the curing of the sick; and the care and treatment of the convalescent, including the aged. Though leaning heavily on the medical teachings of the ancient Greeks, Maimonides warns against blind belief in so-called authorities and upholds the value of clear thought and experiments. His medical observations, diagnoses, and methods of healing mentioned in his works on asthma, poisons, his medical responsa, and commentaries on the *Aphorisms* of Hippocrates contain innovations in their day and many of them are still valid. Maimonides wrote his medical books in Arabic: most of them were soon translated into Hebrew and Latin.

Southern France

At the end of the 12th and the beginning of the 13th century, Jewish centers of learning were established in southern France – in Avignon, Lunel, Montpellier, Béziers, and Carcassonne. Conditions for Jews in these regions were generally somewhat better than those in Spain, although they did not escape restrictions, expulsion, and persecution. For a period of two to three hundred years, papal bulls and Synod decrees alternated in forbidding and then allowing Jewish physicians to practice their profession. The principal service rendered by Jewish scholars of southern France, many of whom had emigrated from Spain and Portugal, was the translation of Arabic works into Hebrew and Latin. Since some of the original Arabic works had been lost, it was only through their Hebrew translations that they were preserved. The important early 11th-century medical work, the Canon of *Avicenna, was translated into Latin and Hebrew a number of times. The work of translation was accompanied by great scholarly activity. The medical school of Montpellier owed its foundation largely to Jewish scholars, and various records mention "private" schools in which Hebrew law, science, and medicine were taught for a stipulated fee. During the 15th and 16th centuries, when certain universities were closed to Jews, Hebrew translations of Arabic and Greek medical works were made specifically for Jewish medical students.

The most notable of the long list of distinguished translators was the *Tibbon family (Judah b. Saul, Samuel, Moses), who during the 12th and 13th centuries translated most of the well-known scientific and philosophic works, including those of Maimonides, from Arabic into Hebrew. Other eminent translators of the period were Jacob b. Makhir (Prophatius Judaeus), a member of the Tibbon family; Zerahiah ibn Shealtiel Ḥen; and Jacob ha-Katan, translator into Hebrew of Nicolai's antidotarium and of Averroes' treatise on diarrhea. Of special interest is Abraham Shem Tov of Tortosa, who practiced in Marseilles toward the end of the 13th century. His works, especially his translation of Abu al-Qāsim al-Zahrāwī's *al-Tatzrif*, are of particular importance because he introduced a new Hebrew terminology based mainly on terms used in the Talmud. In other works he deals with the necessity of studying basic sciences with apprenticeships in hospitals, and with the behavior required of the physician when visiting patients, especially poor ones. Another distinguished translator-physician was Moses Farrachi b. Salem (Ferragut) of the 13th century. He studied medicine at Salerno, and at the request of the king of Naples translated Rhazes' *Continens* and other Arabic medical works into Latin.

Jewish influence was so strong that in Montpellier, portraits of Jews were included in the marble plaques commemorating the early masters of the university. Apparently there was also a Jewish school of medicine in Lunel, which did not, however, attain the eminence of the University of Montpellier. A large part of the information on the early history of the latter and its relations with Jewish scholars is to be found in the history written by one of its graduates, Jean *Astruc (1684–1766), a man of Spanish-Jewish descent, later professor of medicine there and subsequently physician to Louis XV. The Saporta family, also of Marrano descent, has a prominent place in the history of Montpellier during the 16th century. Louis (I) Saporta came from Lerida, was appointed city physician in Marseilles in 1490, and from 1506 to 1529 served as professor at Montpellier University. His son Louis (II) studied medicine there, and his grandson Antoine became successively royal professor, dean, and chancellor of the university (1560). His great-grandson Jean became professor in 1577 and vice chancellor in 1603. The family then immigrated to the French colonies of America and the name does not appear in the later history of Montpellier. The Sanchez family, already well-known in Portugal and Spain, also became prominent in medicine in southern France. The most distinguished member was Francisco *Sanchez (1562–1632), who was appointed professor of medicine and philosophy at Montpellier and later at Toulouse, and published many medical treatises. Jean Baptiste Silva (1682–1742), a native of Bordeaux who graduated in medicine from Montpellier, became physician to the grand duke of Bavaria, Prince Luis Henry of Conde, and Voltaire.

Benvenutus Grapheus, from Jerusalem, one of the most famous eye doctors of the Middle Ages, lived in the 12th century. He taught and practiced in Southern Europe and probably also in Salerno. His observations of and recommended cures for eye diseases prevailing in Southern Europe and other Mediterranean countries are of extraordinary accuracy and his works, which were translated into many European languages, were the most popular textbooks on ophthalmology of the period. There were also Jewish women physicians practicing at this time. Among them was Sarah La Migresse, who lived and practiced in Paris toward the end of the 13th century. In Marseilles a record has been found of an agreement signed in 1326 between Sara de Saint Gilles, widow of Abraham, and Salvet de Bourgneuf, whereby the former undertook to teach the latter "Artem medicine et physice," and to clothe and care for him for a period of seven months. In return, Salvet agreed to turn over to his teacher all his fees as physician during that period. Sarah of Wuerzburg received a license from Archbishop Johann II in 1419 and developed a lucrative medical practice. Rebekah Zerlin of Frankfurt (c. 1430) became famous as an oculist.

Christian Spain and Portugal

During the major part of the 13th and 14th centuries Jewish physicians in Catholic Spain enjoyed the protection and support of the reigning monarchs though toward the end of that period the Inquisition became more active. The list of prominent physicians of that period is a long one and only a few can be mentioned here. One of the most important was al-Fakhār (d. 1235), who received the title of *nasi* ("prince") at the court of Ferdinand III in Toledo. Another, Nathan b. Joel *Falaquera (second half of 13th century), wrote a medical book in Hebrew on the theory and practice of medicine, therapeutics, herbs and drugs, and hygiene. He used medical and botanical terms found in the Talmud. Abraham b. David Caslari of Narbonne and Béziers was the author of *Aleh Refu'ah* ("The Leaf of Healing," 1326), a treatise on fevers, divided into five books, to be used as a vademecum on these matters, and of a treatise on pestilential and other fevers, written in 1349 when the Black Death decimated the population of Provence, Catalonia, and Aragon. In 1360, Meir b. Isaac *Aldabi, a native of Toledo who went to Jerusalem in the middle of the 14th century, completed his comprehensive *Shevilei Emunah*, a collection of philosophic, mystic, and talmudic teachings including chapters on human embryology, anatomy, physiology, pathology, and rules of health.

AFTER THE EXPULSION. At the end of the 15th century the Jews were expelled from Spain and Portugal. Even before that many eminent physicians had immigrated to North Africa, Turkey, Greece, Italy, and Holland. Many were forced converts and some continued to practice in Spain and Portugal until the 18th century, despite their precarious position in those countries, where they were under constant threat of persecution. It is a historical fact that the Marranos and their descendants were leaders and pioneers in medicine in Europe and Asia for several centuries, from the Renaissance until modern times. Many of them distinguished themselves particularly in medical literature. The 16th century was a time of immense exploration, discovery, and progress. During this period – the beginning of the medical renaissance – many distinguished Jewish physicians, fleeing the Iberian Peninsula, won a worldwide reputation in other lands. Among them was *Amatus Lusitanus, who studied and practiced in Salamanca, Lisbon, Antwerp, Italy, and Greece and whose life was a saga of adventurous flights from one country to another. His principal works were *Centuria*, the description of 700 cases of disease, and a translation of and commentary on Dioscorides. He is also famous for his unrelenting battle against superstition and medical quackery.

SOME DISTINGUISHED FAMILIES. Abraham b. Samuel *Zacuto, called Diego Roderigo, was born in the Spanish city of Salamanca in 1452 and immigrated to Portugal and Tunis, where he became famous as a physician and astronomer. His great grandson, *Zacutus Lusitanus, born in Lisbon in 1575, became a physician in Salamanca and later fled to Amsterdam, where he became one of the foremost critics of his time. He wrote a history of medicine in 12 volumes, *De medicorum Principum*, and was also known for his code of ethics for physicians, *Introitus medici ad praxim*.

Dionysus Brudus (1470–1540), a physician at the Portuguese court who later lived in Antwerp, wrote important works on Galenism and on phlebotomy. His son Manuel Brudus practiced in Venice, England, and Flanders and published works on diet for febrile diseases which were widely read. Luiz Mercado (16th–17th century) of Valladolid wrote a medico-philosophical work *De Veritate* (1604), as well as numerous works on fevers, gynecology, pediatrics, hereditary diseases, and infectious maladies. Isaac *Cardozo, born in Portugal in 1610, became court physician to King Philip IV in Madrid. The 15th-century physician and poet Francesco Lopez de Villalobos was one of the first to describe lues (syphilis). In 1498 he also published a description of bubonic plague. Roderigo *Lopez was an internist and anatomist who fled the Inquisition in 1559 and became physician to Queen Elizabeth I of England. In 1594 he was accused of plotting to poison Elizabeth and sentenced to death.

The family of de *Castro produced many distinguished physicians. The most famous was Roderigo de Castro (c. 1550–1627), author of a gynecological work, *Universa Muliebrium Medicina*, and physician to the king of Denmark and various German dukes and princes. His son Benedict de Castro (b. 1597) started practicing in Hamburg and later became physician to the queen of Sweden. He was the author of *Apologia*, a medico-historical work which described the achievements of Jewish doctors and defended them against antisemitic charges. Orobio de Castro fled the Inquisition and settled in Amsterdam, where he became a famous physician and leader of the Jewish community. Jacob de Castro Sarmento (1692–1762), born in Portugal, settled in England and was admitted as a fellow of the Royal Society in 1730. His work *Agua de Inglaterra* reveals a profound knowledge of the therapeutic properties of quinine. The 18th-century Jacob Rodrigues *Pereira was a pioneer in the education of deaf-mutes. Born in Spain, of Marrano parents, he escaped the Inquisition, settled in Bordeaux, and embraced Judaism. At the age of 19 he started his campaign for improving the status of the deaf-mute, and continued in his chosen task for 46 years, showing great ability in teaching speech to the congenital deaf-mute. He invented a sign language for the deaf and dumb. The fate of Antonio Ribeira Sanchez illustrates how far-reaching was the influence of Jewish physicians at that period. A Portuguese Marrano, he fled from the Inquisition to Holland at the beginning of the 18th century and became the pupil of the famous Dutch physician, Boerhaven. In 1740 he went to Russia as personal physician to the czarinas Elizabeth and Catherine II. However, when his Jewish origin became known he was threatened with death and with great difficulty escaped to Paris, where he became an eminent physician and introduced soblimat into the therapy of syphilis.

A large number of Jewish physicians also settled in Turkey, where private citizens as well as sultans, viziers, and pashas valued their skill and medical knowledge and their high standard of ethics. In the 15th century Joseph *Hamon, a Granada physician, went at an advanced age to Constantinople, where he became court physician. For almost a century some member of the Hamon family held the position of court physician and exercised great public influence. Marrano physicians were also among the East India pioneers. Foremost among them was Garcia de *Orta, born in Portugal. In 1534 he went to India and there studied and collected Oriental plants and drugs. His *Colloquios dos simples Drogas e cosas medicinas de India*, which appeared in 1563 in the form of dialogues, is not only the first but also the most important contribution on this subject to European medicine of that time. Twelve years after his death his body was exhumed and burnt by the Inquisition as a suspected Jew. To this same group belongs Cristoval d'*Acosta (1515–1580), a Marrano physician and botanist born in Mozambique, who lived and traveled in India and in the Middle East. He completed and enlarged the work of de Orta.

Italy

Numerous Italian Jewish physicians were also rabbis and leaders of their communities, especially in Rome, Ferrara, Mantua, and Genoa. The Italian universities, notably those of Padua and Perugia, were among the few that allowed Jews to enter the medical faculties at a time when most other European universities were closed to them. The Jewish communities of Italy were also enriched by the influx of Jewish and Marrano scholars and physicians fleeing the persecution of the Inquisition in other countries. At various periods Jews acted as personal physicians to popes, cardinals, bishops, and dukes. Thus Pope Nicholas IV (1287–92) had at his court the physician Isaac b. Mordecai, better known as Maestro Gajota. In 1392 Boniface IX made Angelo, son of Manuele the Jew, his physician and familiar. Immanuel b. Solomon, known as *Immanuel of Rome, was a practicing physician of note, who wrote on various physical and psychic ailments. *Hillel b. Samuel of Verona, who practiced in Ferrara, was a physician and translator of distinction. Another famous physician and translator was *Kalonymus b. Kalonymus, a native of Arles in southern France who later moved to Rome. He translated some of Galen's writings from Arabic into Hebrew and became famous for his accuracy and literary style. Special privileges and tax exemptions usually accompanied the appointment of court physicians. However, the periods of leniency to Jews were usually followed by periods of restriction and persecution. It has been suggested that the popularity of Jewish physicians in Italy in spite of the innumerable restrictions, the bitter attacks, and the calumnies was due to the superstitious belief of Christians in the "magic" arts of the Jews. They also admired Jewish doctors for their unselfish devotion to their calling, and it is not irrelevant that there was a scarcity of Christian physicians, especially during times of epidemic.

THE 15TH AND 16TH CENTURIES. A number of distinguished Italian Jews appeared in the field of medicine during the 15th and 16th centuries. Saladino Ferro d'Ascoli (15th–16th century) was acknowledged as the leading pharmacist of his time, and his work on pharmacology was the basic textbook for all pharmacists until the 18th century. Bonet de *Lattes (d. 1515), a native of Provence, became physician to Popes Alexander VI and Leo X. He also served as judge of the highest Italian court of appeal and rabbi to the Jewish community of Rome. Philotheus Eliajus Montalto (d. 1616) fled to Italy from the Portuguese Inquisition. In 1606 he became physician to the Grand Duke Ferdinand of Florence and in 1611 personal physician to Queen Marie de Medici of France. By order of the queen he was buried in a Jewish cemetery in Amsterdam. His work *Archipathologia*, dealing with diseases of the nervous system and mental disturbances, was widely used in his time and often referred to by later medical writers. Roderigo de Fonseca in the 16th century earned his reputation by his clear diagnoses and descriptions of internal diseases, fevers, surgery, and pharmacology. Benjamin *Mussafia distinguished himself as physician, philologist, scholar, and rabbi. He served as personal physician to the Danish king Christian IV. One of the most outstanding personalities of the time was Rabbi Jacob *Ẓahalon, born in Rome and later physician in Ferrara. In his book *Oẓar ha-Ḥayyim* he described contemporary hygienic measures as well as the bubonic plague in Rome in 1656. He used numerous new Hebrew medical terms and redefined the moral obligations of the Jewish physician to his profession. Joseph Solomon *Delmedigo studied medicine in Padua and was a pupil of Galileo. After many years of study and travel he settled in Poland and became personal physician to Prince Radziwill. He is famous as a rabbi, physician, philosopher, and mathematician. During the 17th and 18th centuries the family of Conegliano became prominent as physicians and medical teachers in Venice. David de Pomis (1525–1593) of Spoleto became physician to Pope Pius IV. Apart from various medical treatises, he wrote the famous *De Medico Hebreo Enarratio Apologica*, a scholarly defense of the Jewish physician. The Jewish community in Italy, however, declined during the second half of the 17th and the 18th centuries. Only with the French Revolution and the conquest of Italy by Napoleon did the Jews of Italy come into their own again.

The Northern Countries

In the northern countries – Germany, Poland, Russia – there were Jewish physicians of note only from the middle of the 17th century onward, many of them refugees from the countries of the Inquisition. However, as early as the 11th century a medical book had been written in Hebrew by R. Saadiah of Worms. Gradually, the universities of the German states opened their doors to Jews. Around the middle of the 17th century the grand duke of Brandenburg permitted Jews to enter the University of Frankfurt on the Oder. One of the first to study there was Tobias b. Moses *Cohn of Metz. However, he was unable to obtain his degree and therefore went to Padua to receive his M.D. He practiced in Poland and later became physician to five successive sultans in Constantinople. His *Ma'aseh Tuviyyah* is almost an encyclopedia and includes medicine, sciences, philosophy, and part of a dictionary. From the beginning of the 18th century the number of practicing Jewish physicians in Germany, Czechoslovakia, England, and Poland increased. Jewish physicians of that period include Marcus Eliezer *Bloch, a famous general practitioner in Berlin during the mid-18th century; Gumperz (Georg) Levison, who distinguished himself as a practitioner, medical author, and organizer in England and in Sweden during the second half of the 18th century; Elias Henschel, a pioneer in modern obstetrics; and Marcus *Herz, an outstanding philosopher, teacher, and physician.

[Suesmann Muntner]

THE MODERN ERA

19th Century

When Joseph II of Austria proclaimed the Act of Tolerance in 1782 and when, shortly thereafter, the French Revolution brought in its wake emancipation to Jews throughout Western Europe, the gates of European medical schools were thrown open to Jewish students. The importance of the contribution made by Jewish doctors to subsequent medical progress is enormous. The quality and quantity of this contribution is reflected in rosters of Nobel laureates and winners of other awards, dictionaries of eponymic syndromes and diseases, and lists of medical authors and investigators. Spanning nearly two centuries and extending over many lands, Jewish participation in modern medicine defies rigid categorization within frameworks of countries and centuries. Frequent demographic changes have occurred as a result of global events which did not always coincide with the "turn" of a century. In fact, a future historian might choose the 1930s as the watershed decade, during which the mainstream of Jewish medical activity became diverted from Europe to America, coinciding with the rise of American medicine vis-à-vis that of Europe.

The geographic distribution of Jews practicing medicine in the 19th century reflected the incongruity between the size of Jewish communities and their number of medical practitioners and scientists. Because of restrictions practiced by Russian medical schools, the youth of the world's largest Jewish community went abroad to pursue their medical studies. Those who returned had to pass special examinations in order to obtain a license. Not until 1861 were they admitted to the army and civil service, and only in 1879 were they granted permission to live beyond the *Pale of Settlement. Even when Jewish physicians successfully overcame the main restrictions and hardships, they were rarely permitted to participate fully in university-centered medical activities.

On the other hand, Jewish doctors were extensively involved in the academic-scientific life of Central and Western Europe. In Austria and Germany, this involvement did not, however, come about suddenly. Although the gates of the universities were open for admission, the inner doors to academic recognition remained partially closed during the first half of the century. At best, a Jew could hope to become a *privatdocent* or a "titular" professor. And even after the struggle for academic recognition had been won, Jews were not welcome in "establishment"-controlled specialties, such as surgery. As a result they tended to cultivate fields that did not attract their non-Jewish colleagues.

An outstanding example of this trend is dermatology-venereology. When Ferdinand von Hebra took over the Kraetze Klinik in Vienna, he was able to recruit only Jewish assistants, some of whom – Moritz *Kaposi, Isador Neumann (1832–1906), and Heinrich Auspitz (1835–1886) – became world famous. In Germany, where dermatology was often referred to disdainfully as "Judenhaut," Paul *Unna, Oskar *Lassar, and Josef *Jadassohn established reputations as pathfinders in their specialty. In Switzerland Bruno Bloch (1878–1933) made Zurich an international teaching center. The predilection for neglected fields may also account for Jewish preeminence in biochemistry, immunology, *psychiatry, and in hematology, histology, and microscopic pathology – sciences which were collectively referred to at the time as "microscopy." The microscope attracted Jewish physicians, many of whom combined the study of microscopy with the practice and teaching of clinical medicine. Outstanding among these men were Ludwig *Traube, a great teacher and pioneer of experimental pathology, anatomy, and neurohistology; Robert *Remak, a pathfinder in embryology, neurohistology, and electro-therapy; Moritz *Romberg, the founder of neuropathology; and the surgeon Benedict *Stilling, whose discovery of nerve nuclei was a turning point in basic neurology. These investigators laid the foundation of modern neurology, which numbered among its great names Leopold *Auerbach, Ludwig *Edinger, and Herman *Oppenheim – discoverers of many neurologic disorders now bearing their names.

Microscopy was also pursued by investigators who were exclusively devoted to basic science. To this category belong the histologist-anatomist Jacob *Henle, who anticipated the germ theory of infection; Gabriel *Valentin, who enriched every branch of basic science; the histologist-pathologist Julius *Cohnheim, who proved that pus cells are derived from the blood; the physiologists Hugo *Kronecker, Rudolf *Heidenhain, Nathan Zuntz, and Hermann *Munk, who were trailblazers in this field; and Carl *Weigert, whose novel concepts and staining techniques advanced many sciences, particularly bacteriology. Jewish contributions to bacteriology date back to the botanist Ferdinand Cohn (1828–1898), who established the vegetable nature of bacteria (1853). These contributions increased during the latter part of the century when bacteriology and the allied science of immunology became integral parts of medicine. Jews became conspicuous in the discovery of bacteria and the development of immunologic methods for diagnosing and preventing bacterial infection. Prominent in this field were Fernand *Widal, who devised a test for typhoid fever and for its prevention; Mordecai Waldemar *Haffkine, who prepared vaccines against cholera and plague; August von *Wasserman, who researched anti-toxins and antisera; and Nobel laureate Paul *Ehrlich, the father of hematology, chemotherapy, and theoretical immunology.

At the same time, clinical medicine was also receiving Jewish contributions. Among the outstanding internists were Heinrich von *Bamberger, for his contributions to cardiology; Hermann *Senator, for his work on the kidney; and Ottomar Rosenbach (1851–1907), for his researches in functional disease and psychotherapy. Outstanding pediatricians were Edward Henoch (1820–1910) who described a bleeding disease named after him; Adolf *Baginsky who investigated nutrition and infectious diseases; and Max Kassowitz (1842–1913) who shed light on congenital syphilis and rickets. Jews were also prominent in otolaryngology, a specialty founded by Adam *Politzer, and in ophthalmology, with the contributions extending from 1810, when George Gerson (1788–1844) investigated astigmatism, to the close of the century, when Karl *Koller began to use local anesthesia in the treatment of eye diseases. Obstetrics and gynecology owe much to Samuel *Kristeller, Wilhelm Freund (1833–1917), and Leopold *Landau for new concepts, observations, and operative techniques. X-ray therapy was founded in 1897 by Leopold Freund (1868–1944). Even surgery, a specialty not too accessible to Jews, numbered many notables. Anton Wolfeer (1850–1917) performed the first gastroenterostomy in 1881, James Israel (1848–1926) pioneered urologic surgery, and Leopold Von Dittel (1815–1898) devised new surgical techniques and instruments. Jewish doctors also contributed to the history of medicine. Noted historians were August *Hirsch, Judah *Katzenelson, and Julius *Pagel.

It is apparent from some of the aforementioned names that Jewish contributions to medicine were not confined to German-speaking countries. In France, many Jewish doctors attained eminence. Julius Sichel (1802–1868) established the first eye clinic in Paris in 1830; Michel Levy (1809–1872) introduced new concepts in the field of public health; Georges Hayem (1841–1933) pioneered hematology; and Fernand Widal made a world impact with his work on the detection and prevention of typhoid fever. In Denmark the great anatomist Ludvig *Jacobson and the pioneer in occupational diseases, Adolph *Hannover, were active during the first half of the century; and the epidemiologists Carl *Salomonsen and "the father of pediatrics in Denmark," Harold Hirschprung (1830–1916), during the second. Holland was the home of the physiologist Van Deen (1804–1869); Italy of the anatomist-physiologist-psychiatrist, Cesare *Lombroso, whose views on criminology have now been discredited; and Poland, of the anatomist Ludwig *Hirszfeld, the neurologist Samuel Goldflam (1852–1930), and the ophthalmologist Ludwig *Zamenhof, the creator of Esperanto. England knighted its greatest laryngologist Sir Felix *Semon. Even restrictive Russia honored the distinguished ophthalmologist Max *Mandelstamm with the title "Privatdocent" and the physiologist, Elie de-*Cyon, with a professorship (1872).

In America, where the Jewish community was small and medical science was not yet advanced, Jewish contributions to medicine were modest, and as often related to organization, administration, and the foundation of hospitals as to scientific pursuits. The ophthalmic surgeon Isaac Hays (1796–1879) was editor of the influential *American Journal of Medical Sciences* (1827) and one of the founders of the American Medical Association. Jacob da Silva *Solis-Cohen, a pioneer in laryngology who performed the first laryngectomy for laryngeal cancer

(1867), was the acknowledged "father" of organized instruction in his specialty. Another "father" – that of American pediatrics – Abraham Jacobi was the founder of the American Pediatric Society and in his later years (1910), the president of the American Medical Association. Jewish doctors were also active in establishing and staffing Jewish hospitals that provided training for Jewish interns and residents. In time these hospitals became important research centers affiliated with medical schools that absorbed many Jewish students.

Challenges to Jewish Medical Scientists and Clinicians

Medicine has undergone profound changes since the start of the 20th century. Advances in medical science have gradually transformed clinical practice from a largely pragmatic skill based on anecdotal experience into a discipline underwritten by verified laboratory and clinical observations. The increasing pace of scientific discovery continues to offer therapeutic possibilities of unprecedented complexity and expense. Medical teaching has changed from apprenticeship to individual teachers with varying degrees of skill and knowledge to organized instruction in universities with courses and teachers with appropriate academic credentials. Before the 1950s patients were rarely given explanations for their illnesses and treatment. Patients now have ready access to medical knowledge and expect to be involved in decisions about their clinical management. They also have increasing expectations in terms of the standards of medical care. Change in attitude and technical advances have made ethics an integral part of clinical practice. In general, an overview of the Jewish contribution to medicine in modern times must consider advances in scientific knowledge, the application of this knowledge to clinical practice, medical education, the organization of medical practice, and the proper education and participation of patients.

Medicine in the Jewish world must take account of four special factors. Firstly, clinical decisions are often influenced by Jewish ethics that differ in varying degree from the constraints related to other forms of religious adherence. Secondly, antisemitism culminating in the Holocaust profoundly affected the lives of Jewish medical scientists and doctors. Thirdly, there is a strong incentive to apply research and clinical skills to diseases to which Jews are genetically predisposed (see *Hereditary Diseases). Finally, the establishment of the State of Israel created the need for sophisticated medical research, teaching, and services in a region of initially endemic infectious diseases in the face of massive immigration, wars, and continuing terrorism.

Conctributions to Medical Science

Advances in clinical medicine have followed progress in the biomedical sciences and the development of novel technologies. Biomedical research in the last quarter of the 20th and the beginning of the 21st centuries is characterized by better understanding of the molecular and pathological processes, the deciphering of the human genome, and the elucidation of complex intra-cellular processes. These have led to the engineering of disease-specific and targeted therapies and the development of non-invasive technologies. Jewish researchers and clinicians have made significant contributions to these advances.

Jewish contributions to the advances in basic science that have transformed medical practice are considered in the entry *Life Sciences. Often the implications of these discoveries for medicine are not initially apparent. There are additional areas of scientific research that are from the outset more clearly relevant to medicine to which Jews have made important contributions. However in medical as in scientific research it has become increasingly difficult to single out specifically Jewish contributors to a global enterprise that is for the most part now carried out by large, interdisciplinary teams, often working in different institutes.

INFECTIOUS DISEASES. At the beginning of the 20th century infections were the major causes of human morbidity and mortality. Increased understanding of immunity and natural resistance to infection lead to diagnostic and eventually therapeutic advances. August von *Wasserman introduced the first diagnostic test for syphilis (1906).

Bela *Schick devised a diagnostic test for detecting exposure to C. diphtheriae, the cause of diphtheria. Michael *Heidelberger's work on antibody structure and function laid the basis for protection against and treatment of infections with preformed antibody (passive immunization). Developments in vaccine production (active immunization) made it possible for Jonas *Salk and Albert *Sabin to produce vaccines with the potential ability to eliminate poliomyelitis.

Advances in drug production also reduced the threat of infection. *Ehrlich's dream of a "magic bullet," which would selectively destroy bacteria as salvarsan does spirochetes, has been partially realized by the discovery of sulfonamides and antibiotics. In 1940 Sir Ernst Boris *Chain isolated penicillin, the first naturally occurring antibiotic to be discovered. Streptomycin was isolated in 1944 and neomycin in 1948 by Selman *Waksman of Rutgers University. Harry Eagle (1905–1992) and Maxwell Finland (1902–1987) made important contributions to progress in antibiotic therapy by devising accurate methods for measuring the potency, anti-bacterial specificity, and safety of antibiotics. Unfortunately, microbial resistance to antibiotics threatens to reverse the relative security achieved in the golden age of drug treatment. Stanley Farber discovered one important mechanism in the development of antibiotic resistance, namely the ability of gene fragments called plasmids to confer resistance on previously susceptible bacteria. Combating infection also depends on the efforts of scientists who understand the biology and epidemiology of infection, as exemplified by the research of Baruch *Blumberg and Barry Bloom. Astute clinical observation is also part of the process of controlling infections, as illustrated by Saul Krugman's elucidation of the many causes of "infectious hepatitis."

CELL BIOLOGY AND CANCER. The links between cell biology and cancer research are prime examples of the contributions of basic research to medicine. For example the formation of new blood vessels (angiogenesis) is essential for tumor growth and metastasis. Judah *Folkman's discoveries in this field point the way to new forms of treatment that may interdict this process. The application of basic genetics to the biology of malignant cells has illuminated many areas of cancer research where inherited or acquired mutations are fundamentally important. A pertinent example is the work of Bert Vogelstein (1949–) in understanding the molecular basis of colo-rectal cancer. Long-held hopes of manipulating patients' immune system to reject cancer have been greatly encouraged by the innovative work of George *Klein.

BLOOD DISORDERS. Advances in immunology have improved our understanding of many hematological diseases and have also influenced clinical practice. Gerald *Edelman's research on immunoglobulin structure clarified the nature of myeloma and other neoplastic diseases characterized by abnormal immunoglobulin production. The discovery and classification of blood groups by Karl *Landsteiner, and his associates Philip *Levine and Alexander Wiener (1907–1976), rationalized the hitherto haphazard and dangerous practice of blood transfusion. Their findings also revealed the nature of blood disorders resulting from immune attacks on blood group antigens, notably hemolytic disease of the newborn. Jewish investigators have contributed to the solution of other hematological problems. William *Damashek was responsible for the logical classification of many immune-mediated and neoplastic blood diseases and was also an innovator in treating leukemia with anti-proliferative drugs. Robert B. Epstein (1928–) collaborated with E.D. Thomas in the first successful bone marrow transplantation. Louis Klein *Diamond made major advances in classifying and characterizing many blood disorders of infancy and childhood. Ernest Jaffe (1925–) contributed to the understanding of hemoglobin synthesis. Ernest Beutler (1928–) elucidated many facets of iron metabolism in red cell formation and proposed a means of tracing the cellular origin of many bone marrow-derived diseases. Maxwell *Wintrobe developed hematology as a laboratory and clinical discipline.

IMMUNOLOGICAL DISEASES. Jewish scientists have made outstanding contributions to understanding the molecular basis and clinical manifestations of disordered immunity, a field that has assumed increasing importance in allergy, transplantation medicine, and auto-immunity. Alexander *Besredka of the Pasteur Institute in Paris was a pioneer in allergy research. Current understanding of the pharmacological basis of allergic disorders owed much to the findings of Baruj *Benacerraf. Ernest Witebsky (1901–1969) and Felix Milgrom (1919-) made important observations on immune mechanisms underlying auto-immune diseases. Robert Schwarz (1928-) introduced new experimental and therapeutic strategies based on the concept that the immune system in auto-immunity loses the ability to distinguish between self and non-self, a defect termed "loss of tolerance." Peter *Lachmann helped delineate the role of a disturbed complement system in these diseases. Fred *Rosen (1930–2005) was a world authority on the management of inherited immunodeficiency diseases in childhood. The availability of monoclonal antibodies arising from Cesar *Milstein's work has provided immense benefits for research and clinical practice in many fields.

NUTRITIONAL DISEASES. Casimir *Funk introduced the idea of vitamin (which he called "vitamines") deficiency to nutrition and medicine. He recognized that beriberi is caused by nutritional deficiency and he also isolated nicotinic acid, a member of the vitamin B complex. Joseph *Goldberger deduced that pellagra is a disease resulting from vitamin deficiency. In the 1920s Alfred Hess, working in parallel with Harry Steenbock, started the important field delineating the relationship between vitamin D deficiencies, rickets, and other bone disorders.

METABOLIC DISEASES. Progress in understanding metabolic diseases went through many transformations of approach and technique in the 20th century to which Jewish scientists and physicians made crucially important contributions. Mapping biochemical pathways in health and disease has depended on laboratory discoveries in experimental animals, the introduction of ethically acceptable methods of investigation in humans, improved techniques of laboratory analysis, and the adaptation of molecular genetics to this field.

The high prevalence rate of many metabolic diseases in Jewish populations makes this an area of especial Jewish interest. Diabetes mellitus, now recognized as occurring in two main forms, is a compelling example. In 1899, Oskar Minkowski (1855–1931) demonstrated the association of diabetes with the pancreas, and in 1920 Moses Barron (1883–1961) described observations of the pancreas that suggested the experimental approach that led to Banting and Best's momentous discovery of insulin. Rachmiel Levine (1910–1998) showed that insulin promotes the transport of glucose from blood to cells, a process termed "the Levine effect." Progress in other fields was helped by observations by Jewish biochemists such as Seymour Reichlin and more fundamentally by the description of major metabolic pathways by Max *Meyerhof and Hans *Krebs and many others. A key example of the interrelationship between genetic predisposition to metabolic problems such as type II diabetes, disorders of lipid metabolism, and obesity is provided by the observations of Jeffrey Friedman, Sir Philip *Cohen, and other investigators.

ENDOCRINE DISEASES. Endocrine diseases illustrate the need to draw together many disciplinary themes in order to understand disease mechanisms and predisposition to these diseases. Jewish medical scientists have contributed to the genetic, metabolic, pharmacological, and immunological studies needed to explore the basis of endocrine diseases such as diabetes and thyroid disease. However, central to advances in this field was the development of precise methods for measuring hormone levels for research and clinical purposes. Rosalyn Sussman *Yalow and Andrew *Schally were largely responsible for the assay techniques that made these measurements possible and which also accelerated research in many other fields.

HEART, LUNG, AND KIDNEY DISEASES. The fields of cardiovascular, pulmonary, and renal diseases have many pioneering Jewish contributors. Arthur *Master introduced the concept of coronary insufficiency and the "Master Step Test" for its detection; Louis Katz (1897–1973) elucidated the principles of cardiovascular hemodynamics, metabolism, and electro-physiology, research fields also enriched by Simon Dack (1908–1994), Richard Bing (1909–), Eugene Braunwald (1929–), and Eliot Corday (1913–1999). Michel Mirowski (1924–1990) invented the automatic implantable cardiodefibrillator (AICD) which transformed the management of life-threatening cardiac arrhythmias. The gradual introduction of surgical methods of treating cardiovascular problems necessitated the development of increasingly sophisticated biotechnology to which Adrian Kantrowitz (1918–) has made many indispensable contributions. New approaches to the study of pulmonary circulation have been introduced by Alfred P. Fishman (1918–). Arthur Maurice Fishberg (1898–1992) correlated the pathological and clinical manifestations of kidney disease. In 1934 Harry Goldblatt (1891–1977) demonstrated the mechanism of secondary hypertension caused by renal vascular disease. Kurt Lange (1906–?) investigated immunologic, biochemical, and pathological facets of kidney disease in children.

GASTROENTEROLOGY. At the turn of the 20th century, Max Einhorn (1862–1953) and Samuel Weiss (1885–?) were amongst the first clinicians to develop gastroenterology as a medical specialty. In 1931 Burrill *Crohn described the inflammatory bowel disease named after him and Heinrich Necheles (1897–1979), Joseph Kirsner (1909–?), and Leon Schiff (1901–?) extended our understanding of the pathophysiology and therapy of many gastrointestinal and liver diseases. Increasing knowledge produced a need to establish departments devoted to research and treatment of patients with these disorders of the kind set up by Henry *Janowitz at Mount Sinai Hospital, New York.

NEUROLOGY. Progress in clinical neurology is largely dependent on increased understanding of brain structure and function. Jewish scientists have participated in this problem from the early days of Joseph *Erlanger's research on nerve conduction to Richard *Axel's dissection of the pathways relevant to olfactory function. Among the clinical neurologists who made the first attempts to correlate disease and basic pathology were Bernard Alpers, who studied neuro-syphilis and vascular degenerative diseases; Benjamin Boshes, who investigated Parkinson's disease; and Leo Alexander who investigated multiple sclerosis. Israel *Wechsler compiled one of the first systematic textbooks on clinical neurology (1927) which became a standard work.

DERMATOLOGY. The longstanding interest of Jewish physicians in skin diseases might traditionally be said to have begun with the Bible. Marion Sulzberger (1895–1983), a pupil of Bruno Bloch of Zurich, Stephen Rothman (1894–1963), Herman Pinkus (1905–1985), and Louis Forman were amongst the first dermatologists to appreciate the need to underpin merely descriptive diagnosis with systematic observations of pathological changes readily observed in this most accessible of human organs. Edmund Klein (1922–1999) was an early winner of the Lasker Award for Clinical Medical Research in recognition of his pioneering treatment of skin diseases, and especially pre-malignant diseases.

RHEUMATOLOGY. Rheumatology is a relatively young but important clinical specialty because of the high incidence of debilitating joint diseases especially in the elderly. The prospects for controlling rheumatoid arthritis have been greatly increased by the successful application of monoclonal antibody techniques. Morris *Ziff was influential worldwide in establishing the essential links between basic science and clinical practice in this discipline.

PEDIATRICS. The demanding technical and psychological challenges of health care in infancy and childhood have intrigued many Jewish scientists and clinicians. In the early stages of its development, Abraham Jacobi (1830–1919) was largely responsible for the emergence of pediatrics in the U.S. Isaac A. *Abt and Julius Hess (1876–1995) were pioneers in child nutrition and care of the premature infant. Henry *Koplik added to knowledge of infectious diseases in children, and Louis *Diamond contributed to pediatric hematology. Sidney Farber (1903–1973) transformed the outlook for childhood leukemia by introducing new anti-proliferative drugs and a regime of comprehensive management. The universally known Dana-Farber Cancer Institute commemorates his achievements. In addition, Alexander Nadas (1913–2000) was a pioneer in pediatric cardiology and Henry Shwachman (1910–1986) was among the first clinical scientists to appreciate the complexities of cystic fibrosis.

SURGERY, OBSTETRICS, AND GYNECOLOGY. Jewish doctors have made many contributions to the rapidly developing scope of surgery, obstetrics, and gynecology. Charles Elsberg (1871–1948) introduced new methods in the treatment of spinal-cord tumors. Markus *Hajek of Vienna devised new techniques in nasal and laryngeal surgery. A pioneer in thoracic surgery, Max Thorek (1880–1960) founded the International College of Surgeons, and Irving Cooper (1922–1985) introduced an operative procedure for the treatment of Parkinson's disease. In obstetrics, Joseph de Lee (1869–1942) contributed an authoritative textbook and original papers and was an outstanding teacher and clinician. Isidor S. Rubin (1883–1958) made many important contributions to gynecology, including the test for fallopian tube patency when investigating sterility. Lord Robert *Winston's achievements include a worldwide reputation for his contributions to solving the problems of female infertility.

RADIOLOGY. U.S. Jewish radiologists have enriched every branch of their specialty. Outstanding contributions have been made by Hymer Friedell (1911–) to radiation biology, by Harold G. Jacobson (1912–2001) to neuroradiology, and Leo Rigler (1896–1979), who was president of the American Radiologic Society, to the radiology of the chest and abdomen. Gustav *Bucky invented the X-ray diaphragm that bears his name.

DRUGS AND THERAPEUTICS. Advances in pharmacological knowledge and drug design, testing, and production have transformed the management of virtually every acute and chronic disease. In addition to the development of anti-microbial agents, this is an area to which Jewish scientists and clinicians have made so many contributions that selected examples must suffice. Isidor Ravdin (1894–1972) was a pioneer in anti-cancer chemotherapy. Gertrude *Elion developed the immunosuppressive drug azathioprine, the first anti-viral drug acyclovir, and allopurinol used to treat gout. Ralph Alexander *Raphael's discoveries illustrate how a profound understanding of organic chemistry can be translated into innovative drug design active against a wide range of diseases. Josef Fried (1914–2001) developed anti-inflammatory steroids and Gregory Goodwin *Pincus (1903–1967) and Carl *Djerassi developed the first successful female, oral contraceptive drugs. The successful career of Max *Tishler (1906–1989) also showed the increasing importance of combining scientific and entrepreneurial skills in drug development. This point is emphasized by the increasing dominance of bioengineering companies able to exploit advances in genetics and other fields. The innovative achievements of Robert S. *Langer are a pertinent example. Jewish scientists have also made key contributions to anti-HIV treatment. They include Jerome Horwitz, who synthesized the first drug that inhibits the viral enzyme reverse transcriptase, and Irving Sigal (1953–1988), who first showed the efficacy of drugs which inhibit viral proteases. Sigal died in the terrorist bombing of Pan Am flight 103.

PATHOLOGY. Jewish pathologists made important contributions at the stage when pathology was developing from an observational skill into one demanding more widely based scientific insight and knowledge. The efforts of Hans Popper (1905–1988) and Fenton Schaffner (1920–2000) clarified the pathology of liver disease. David Spain (1913–) in cardiac pathology and Averill Liebow (1911–1978) in pulmonary pathology performed a similar service. Benjamin Castleman (1906–1982) described the pathology of the parathyroid glands and a proliferative disease of the immune system which bears his name and is a paradigm for many, more common diseases of a similar nature. Paul *Klemperer's imaginative interpretation of the damage inflicted by "connective tissue diseases" laid the basis for what are now known as multi-system autoimmune diseases.

PUBLIC HEALTH. Jews helped to lay the foundations of public health and hygiene in the U.S. and elsewhere. Sigmund Goldwater (1873–1942) founded the first occupational disease clinic in New York in 1915. His contemporary Milton J. Rosenau (1869–1946) promoted important measures for preventing epidemics of infectious diseases in the Americas and elsewhere. Jeremiah Stamler (1919–) was one of the first investigators to conduct epidemiologic studies on environmental factors influencing coronary heart disease.

HISTORY OF MEDICINE. While many Jewish doctors were making history, some were writing it. Outstanding early historians were Max Neuberger (1868–1955) in Austria, Charles *Singer in England, Arturo Castiglioni (1874–1953) in Italy, and Harry *Friedenwald, Victor Robinson (1886–1947), and Saul Jarcho (1906–2000) in the U.S.

EDUCATION AND PUBLICATION. Jews have played a prominent part in the interrelated fields of medical education and publication. Abraham *Flexner is still remembered for his "Flexner Report" (1906), which charted the subsequent course of medical education in the United States. After World War II a steadily increasing number of Jews have joined the teaching staffs of medical schools. Many have also contributed to teaching as textbook authors and by editing medical journals. The well-known medical editor, Morris *Fishbein, edited the *Journal of the American Medical Association* (1924–49) and played a leading role in shaping American healthcare policies. Alexander Gutman (1902–1973) edited the *American Journal of Medicine* and Alfred Soffer (1922–) was editor of *Chest*. Subsequently there has been an at least commensurate increase in the numbers of Jewish medical scientists and teachers needed to meet the enormous demand for journals, books, and education at all levels.

Advances in research and education have also created a demand for medical scientists with the rare combination of the research expertise and administrative skills needed to run vast institutions of unprecedented complexity. Jewish scientists with these capabilities include Arnold Levine at the Rockefeller, Walter *Bodmer, Sir Gustav *Nossal, Harold *Varmus, and Philip Fialkow at the University of Seattle.

Jewish Medicine in the Diaspora

UNITED STATES. The early years of the 20th century witnessed a continued immigration to the U.S. that changed the "ethnic" and cultural pattern of American Jewry and its medical representation. The first Jewish doctors in the U.S. were of Sephardi origin. During the second part of the 19th century Jewish immigrants from Germany assumed leading roles in communal affairs and medicine. Russian Jews, who began emigrating after the pogroms of the 1880s, added a third element, which was destined to grow in numbers and influence. Later, the U.S. gained new immigrants from the Jewish population that had moved to East European countries when these broke away from the Russian and Austro-Hungarian empires after World War I. These Jews were again unsettled by unfavorable economic and political conditions.

Jewish emigration from Europe to the U.S. yet again increased sharply in the 1930s with the rise of the Nazi Party. After World War II the majority of those who escaped the Holocaust immigrated to the United States or Israel. Physicians who found refuge in America arrived at a propitious time. The 1930s and 1940s marked the beginning of the current golden age of scientific medicine, ushered in by the discovery of antibiotics and cortisone and advances in molecular biology and medical technology. With the decline of traditional European centers, the United States became the new world center of scientific and medical activity with Jewish immigrants joining the country's extraordinarily creative universities and institutes. Rid of vestiges of intolerance and receptive to new talent, the country's medical establishment and public welcomed the newcomers. Jewish hospitals, such as Mount Sinai in New York and Michael Reese and Mount Sinai in Chicago, as well as non-Jewish hospitals, research foundations, and universities absorbed many of them into the mainstream of medical progress. By the 1980s Jewish physicians in the United States greatly outnumbered those in other countries. In the State of New York alone there were 7,500 practicing Jewish doctors compared with 5,500 in Israel and 3,000 in France. Overall 9% of U.S. physicians were Jewish, compared with a 3% representation in the general population. More than 17,000 of the approximately 27,000 U.S. Jewish physicians in private practice resided in the thickly populated states of New York, California, Illinois, Pennsylvania, New Jersey, and Massachusetts. Of these, approximately 4,700 were general practitioners, 6,500 specialists in general medicine and its branches, 3,000 in surgery, 2,900 in obstetrics and gynecology, 1,000 in ophthalmology, 800 in radiology, 650 in dermatology, and 600 in otolaryngology. However the distribution among medical specialties was uneven. Whereas only 5% of doctors in occupational medicine were Jewish, they comprised 20% of general physicians and more than 30% of psychiatrists. This predominance in numerical terms is likely to have persisted but is difficult to quantify and compare with earlier periods. There has been increasing specialization marking the virtual demise of the "general internist" and the current Jewish population is less homogeneous compared with the initial immigrant Jewish population. However, the Jewish contribution to U.S. and thereby to medicine worldwide should not be assessed simply in terms of the numbers of practicing physicians but should also take account of Jewish contributions to medical science and education.

CANADA. Jewish doctors and medical scientists in Canada also benefited from the opportunities available in the U.S. to improve the provision of medical services and education. Their numbers included the pediatrician Alton Goldbloom (1890–1962) and Arthur Vineberg (1903–1988), who developed techniques for improving blood circulation to diseased heart muscle.

WESTERN EUROPE. The countries of Western Europe other than Germany and Austria had long settled Jewish communities whose numbers were increased by refugees from Russia at the beginning of the 20th century and from Nazi persecution in the 1930s. Jewish doctors are well represented in clinical practice and in academic centers. Their contributions to medicine and medical science in the United Kingdom are reflected by the high national honors accorded to Sir Ludwig *Guttmann for his work on rehabilitation, and to Lord *Cohen, Lord Rosenheim, Lord Turnberg, Sir Raymond Hoffenberg, and Sir George Alberti for their achievements in clinical medicine, teaching, and research. French scientists made important contributions to the formative stages of molecular biology and the contributions of Jewish medical scientists in France are illustrated by the achievements of Jean Hamburger (1909–1992) in renal transplantation. Switzerland's Jewish community of indigenous and refugee medical scientists has included Tadeus *Reichstein, who isolated cortisone, and Pierre Rentchnick (1923–), the foremost authority on public health and hygiene in a country which traditionally takes these subjects very seriously. Sweden sheltered the Nobel Prize winner Robert *Barany and is now the home of the cancer research specialist George *Klein and of the endocrinologist Carl Luft, well-known for his research on diabetes. The Jewish medical academic communities of Germany and Austria were extinguished by the Nazis and the preeminence of these countries in research and practice thereby passed to the countries where Jewish refugees settled.

RUSSIA AND THE FORMER SOVIET UNION. World War I, the Russian Revolution, and the *Balfour declaration had demographic and political consequences that profoundly influenced Jewish participation in medicine. Many Russian Jews moved to large university centers, where they had been forbidden to reside. As a result of this movement and of the new policy of open university admissions, the number of Jewish doctors greatly increased. Unofficial admission quotas reappeared during the later years of Stalin's rule. However, neither their number nor their achievements can be readily determined because of the isolation of Russian Jewry from the Western world.

POLAND AND EASTERN EUROPE. Despite poor economic conditions, Jews in pre-Hitler Poland maintained 40 hospitals where many of the country's 3,500 Jewish doctors provided services. Poverty, backward technology, and a hostile academic environment prevented Jewish scientists from attaining the achievements reached by their colleagues in Western Europe. Still, their contributions were far from negligible. Edward Platau, the doyen of Polish neurologists, researched meningitis and brain tumors. Adolf Beck investigated nerve physiology and Henry K. Higier explored the autonomic nervous system. Samuel Goldflam studied reflexes and the diseases myasthenia gravis and periodic paralysis. Zygmunt Bychowski investigated traumatic epilepsy and multiple sclerosis. Anastaszy Landau was prominent in metabolic research, Stanislaus Klein in hematology, Seweryn Sterling in social medicine, and Gerszon Lewin in tuberculosis. Aron Solowieczyk, who was killed during the Warsaw ghetto rising, was prominent in surgical research. But the scientific potential of Jewish doctors in Poland was not destined to develop. During the German occupation, Jewish doctors devoted their energies to caring for people doomed to starvation, torture, and death. Many distinguished themselves by acts of dedication and heroism and over 2,800 were killed. The tragic events in Poland were paralleled by similar developments in other German-occupied territories.

SOUTH AMERICA AND MEXICO. In the early part of the 20th century, geographic remoteness meant that Jewish contributions to medicine in Latin America received less recognition abroad than they deserved. Nevertheless, the large communities in South America were reinforced by immigration from Europe ensuring that Jewish medical scholarship thrived, even if not to the extent enjoyed by colleagues in North America. Since World War II the opportunities to contribute to advances in medical research have suffered from political instability and periods of economic decline. In Argentina, where Jewish immigration began in 1889, the figure of the pioneer physician Noah Yarchi is still remembered and revered. The doctors who followed in his footsteps helped sustain the health and morale of the colonists and the early settlers in the cities. With the establishment of the Ezra Hospital in Buenos Aires in 1921, a center was provided for medical activity; it grew in importance as the Jewish population increased. Jews have been prominent in every phase of the professional and academic life of the country; Professor Quiroga was president of the Academy of Medicine of Buenos Aires and Ricardo Rodriguez dean of the Medical Faculty of La Plata. Jewish physicians published the Journal *Archives de Medicina Argentina-Israel.*

For a long period the Jewish population in Brazil was 140,000, and much lower in other Latin American countries. Jewish participation in medicine increased significantly after the arrival in the 1930s and 1940s of refugee doctors who brought the sophisticated approach of European medicine. Many Jewish physicians rose to eminence. Victor Soriano of Montevideo, Uruguay, was the editor of the *World Journal of Neurology.* Mexico had 120 Jewish doctors in 1970, many of whom attained professional distinction. Characteristic of the medical pioneers' sense of Jewish identity was their publication of the medical journal *Ars Medici* early in the century, when their numbers were very small.

SOUTH AFRICA. At the peak of communal activity South Africa had about 750 Jewish doctors who made major contributions to medical research, education, and practice. Among these were Philip *Tobias, president of the Royal Society of South Africa, Maurice Shapiro, the immuno-hematologist who became head of the country's transfusion services, the gynecologist S. Joel Cohen, the physician M.M. Sussman, the cardiologist Valva Shrir, and the surgeon Jack Wolfowitz. The plastic surgeon Jack Penn (1909–1996) carried out many facial reconstruction operations on Israeli soldiers wounded in the War of Independence and subsequently became honorary visiting professor of plastic surgery at the Hebrew University of Jerusalem. During the period of political uncertainty before the country achieved independence many doctors immigrated to the United Kingdom, the U.S., and Israel. Those achieving distinction include Israel Chanarin, the hematologist and expert on megaloblastic anemias, and Anthony Segal, the authority on the white blood cells called neutrophils.

Medical Science and Practice in Israel

Sussman *Muntner, Joshua O. *Leibowitz (1895–1993), who was professor of medical history in the Hebrew University of Jerusalem, and David Margalit have fully described the history of medicine in Palestine under the Mandate and in the early years of the State of Israel. At the beginning of the 20th century infectious diseases were rampant in Palestine. Clinics established by European Jewish communities provided medical care for the Jewish population of Jerusalem. These clinics became hospitals that expanded to meet the needs of a modern city, notably Bikkur Ḥolim, established in 1843, and Sha'arei Ẓedek, established in 1902. Fortunately for the needs of the Jewish population, physicians were prominent in the Zionist movement since its inception. The first Jewish physician in Palestine, Simon Fraenkel, was sent to Jerusalem in 1843 by Moses Montefiore. Menahem Stein was the first Jewish doctor in Jaffa (1882), Hillel *Joffe the first in Haifa (1890), and Bathsheba Yunis (1880–1947) the first in Tel Aviv. Leib Pashkovsky was the first surgeon to settle in Palestine (1906). In 1912, the year a medical association was founded in Tel Aviv, there were 35 Jewish doctors in the country, the majority specially trained in ophthalmology, dermatology, and parasitology in order to cope with the country's most prevalent diseases. Prominent among the early specialists were the ophthalmologist Aryeh *Feigenbaum, the dermatologist Aryeh Dostrovsky (d. 1975), and the bacteriologist and founder of the Pasteur Institute in Jerusalem (1913), Israel J. Kligler. Other notable doctors were Aryeh Boehm, who was responsible for many improvements in public health, and the otorhinolaryngologist Moshe Sherman, founding president of the country's first Medical Association. Although public health remained a major preoccupation, increased control of malaria, rabies, trachoma, and other infectious diseases allowed more scope for other specialties to develop.

After the Balfour Declaration, the number of Jewish physicians in Palestine increased sharply and their pace of immigration accelerated with each wave of persecution in Europe. Health services improved under the Mandate with an expanded network of clinics and public health measures including an immunization program. Thus a medical infrastructure was in place when the State was established which could cope with the added demands of immigration and the War of Independence. With subsequent expansion, Israel had approximately 27,000 physicians in the early 21st century, so that the ratio of doctors to population has become one of the most favorable in the world. The country had some 47,000 nurses, of whom 50% were registered. As a result Israel had a very low infant mortality rate (7.5 per 1,000 live births) and long life expectancy (79.1 years on the average for women and 75.3 years for men). Medical care is provided by a network of hospitals and clinics, many affiliated to the health funds, the

Ministry of Health, or other organizations like *Hadassah and *Magen David Adom. The hospitals and medical services are also geared to deal with the emergencies arising from wars or terrorist attacks.

Mental health, rehabilitation, and social support services are also highly developed.

Advanced methods of treatment developed elsewhere in the world have also been promptly introduced into Israeli clinical practice. The Hadassah Hospital carried out its first successful *in vitro* fertilization ("test-tube baby") in 1982 and heart transplantation in 1983.

The Israel Medical Association, founded in 1929, helped to raise the standards of the profession and to improve service to the public during the difficult years of economic hardship and political and military tension. The Association's official organ, *Harefuah*, founded in 1913, has maintained a high scientific and journalistic standard. The Non-Resident Fellow Project of the Association has helped forge close links with Jewish doctors in the Diaspora. There is also an extensive network of academic exchanges and collaboration between institutes and individuals in Israel and other countries.

Medical research and education have had a consistently high priority, even before the establishment of the State. Moshe Prywes (d. 1999), editor of the *Israel Journal of Medical Sciences*, founded in 1965, contributed to medical education, and Hanoch Midwidsky to the promotion of postgraduate studies. Most medical research is now carried out at the country's four medical schools, namely the *Hebrew University of Jerusalem (founded in 1949), *Tel Aviv University (founded in 1965), *Ben-Gurion University (founded in 1974), the *Haifa Technion (founded in 1969), and their affiliated hospitals. Biomedical science is performed in the relevant faculties of these universities, at *Bar-Ilan University, which does not have a medical school, and at the *Weizmann Institute of Science.

The first research priority was the control of infectious diseases. Saul *Adler, a world authority on parasitology and tropical medicine, directed research on amebiasis, leishmaniasis, and relapsing fever. Zvi *Saliternik was responsible for the elimination of malaria and the parasitic disease schistosomiasis. Subsequently attention could be turned to the disorders prevalent in the developed world and to genetic disorders prevalent in various Israeli populations. Clinical research was linked to improving teaching and patient care in all branches of medicine.

Chaim Sheba, surgeon-general of the Israeli army, oversaw the rise in medical standards. Bernhard and Hermann *Zondek continued their endocrinologic research, interrupted by the European upheaval, and Moshe *Rachmilewitz, professor of medicine at Hadassah Hospital Medical School, carried out much-cited studies of folate and vitamin B12 deficiency and metabolism. Bracha *Ramot organized a modern hematological service at the Tel Hashomer (Sheba) Hospital and undertook a systematic program of investigation of the prevalence and management of inherited disorders of hemoglobin synthesis. Andre de Vries (1911–1996) was a distinguished physician and hematologist at the Beilinson (Rabin) Hospital. Karl Braun initiated research programs in cardiology and Lipman *Halpern in neurology. Under the leadership of Bruno Lunenfeld (1927–), the Tel Hashomer (Sheba) Hospital became a world center in research and treatment for female infertility. In the same institute Baruch Padeh had laid the foundations for clinical genetics in the country. David Erlick in Haifa improved techniques of renal transplantation. Isaac Michaelson developed ophthalmological services at Hadassah Hospital and used his expertise to treat patients with trachoma and other sight-threatening diseases in Africa. Michaelson was thereby amongst the first who initiated Israel's continuing medical collaboration with disadvantaged countries. He was also amongst the first clinical scientists to realize the importance of angiogenesis (new blood vessel formation) in retinal disease; an international medal and series of conferences have been named in his memory.

Latterly the pace of research has quickened and there is room to mention only a few of the outstanding contributors. Rina *Zaizov (1932–2005) organized a national center for pediatric oncology. Marcel *Eliakim of Hadassah Hospital has made important advances in the field of liver diseases. Yehezkiel *Stein of the same hospital is an international authority on lipids and atherosclerosis (vascular degeneration). Mordechai Pras of Tel Hashomer Hospital is an international expert on amyloidosis and Rami *Rahamimoff's work on nerve transmission in health and disease is also universally respected. The advances in basic immunology made by Michael *Sela and Ruth *Arnon at the Weizmann Institute have been adapted to many promising strategies for treating multiple sclerosis and auto-immune diseases. Michel *Revel's research on the antiviral interferon system also has important clinical implications. Irun Cohen's immunological studies at the Weizmann Institute on experimental and clinical auto-immune diseases and novel ideas on treating these diseases have attracted continued international attention. Stem cell research is an active area of research carried out in a fully coordinated program involving the country's major academic research centers and biotechnology companies. Sophisticated medical bioengineering is also an area of intense research activity.

The current organization of medical departments in acute care hospitals in Israel has changed from the classical European model with its fully autonomous medical wards to broader-based departments in which all medical sub-specialties are represented, providing comprehensive, multi-disciplinary medical care. In parallel with the remarkable developments in new therapeutic approaches a more realistic view has grown of scientific medicine's limitations and an understanding of the patient's rights. This has introduced a new field in medicine that includes palliative care, safeguarding the quality of life of patients and their families, and their right to be involved in decisions affecting medical management and the end of life. This progressive approach is now being adopted by the Israeli public and medical community with appropriate legal backing. There has also been striking progress in the provision of medical teams able to participate in disaster relief anywhere in the world.

[Samuel Vaisrub / Michael A. Denman, Yaakov Naparstek, and Dan Gilon (2nd ed.)]

BIBLIOGRAPHY: SOURCES: S. Muntner, in RHMH, 11 (1951), 23–38; 12 (1952), 21–23; idem, in: *Miscellanea Mediaevalia*, 4 (1966); idem, in: *Korot*, 1:1–2 (1952); idem, in: *Sinai: Sefer Yovel* (1958), 321–37; Saladino di Ascoli, *Sefer ha-Rokeḥim* (1953); C. Roth, in: *Speculum*, 28 (1953); Steinschneider, Uebersetzungen. GENERAL: H. Friedenwald, *Jews and Medicine*, 2 vols. (1944); S. Muntner, *Le-Korot ha-Safah ha-Ivrit ki-Sefat ha-Limmud be-Ḥokhmat ha-Refu'ah* (1940); J. Seide, *Toledot ha-Refu'ah* (1954); R. Kagan, *Jewish Medicine* (1952). IN BIBLE AND TALMUD: C.J. Brim, *Medicine in the Bible* (1936); J.L. Katzenelson, *Ha-Talmud ve-Ḥokhmat ha-Refu'ah* (1928); S. Muntner, in: *Leshonenu*, 14 (1946); idem, *Sexology in the Bible and the Talmud* (1961); idem, in: *Refu'ah Veterinarit* (1944), 6–22; (1945), 5–22; M. Perlman, *Midrash ha-Refu'ah* (1926); J. Preuss, *Biblisch-Talmudische Medizin* (1911); W. Steinberg, in: *International Record of Medicine*, 12 (1960); 2 and 4 (1961). MIDDLE PERIOD: E.A.W. Budge, *Syrian Anatomy, Pathology and Therapeutics* (1913); A. Feigenbaum, in: *Acta Medica Orientalia*, 14 (1955), 26–29, 75–82; J. Leibowitz, in: *Dappim Refu'iyyim*, 11:3 (1952); D. Margalit, *Ḥakhamei Yisrael ke-Rofe'im* (1962); S. Muntner, in: *Leshonenu*, 10 (1939/40), 135–49, 300–17; idem, *Alilot al Rofe'im Yehudiyyim be-Aspaklaryah shel Toledot ha Refu'ah* (1953); idem, *Mavo le-Sefer Asaf ha-Rofe* (1957); S. Donnolo, *Kitvei Refu'ah*, 2 vols. (1949); I. Judaeus, *Hebrew Physician* (1963). MODERN PERIOD: R. Landau, *Geschichte der juedischen Aerzte* (1895); H. Friedenwald, *Jewish Physicians and the Contributions of the Jews to the Science of Medicine* (1897); F.H. Garrison, *An Introduction to the History of Medicine* (1929⁴); S.R. Kagan, *Jewish Medicine* (1952); idem, *The Jewish Contribution to Medicine in America* (1934); idem, *American Jewish Physicians of Note* (1942); L. Falstein (ed.), *The Martyrdom of Jewish Physicians in Poland* (1963); L. Šik, *Juedische Aerzte in Jugoslawien* (1931); L. Gershenfeld, *The Jews in Science* (1934); C. Roth, *The Jewish Contribution to Civilization* (1956³); V. Robinson, *Pathfinders in Medicine* (1912); R. Taton (ed.), *A General History of Science*, 3 (1965), 494–548; 4 (1966), 502–62; M. Einhorn (ed.), *Harofé Haivri* (1928–65); I. Simon (ed.), *Revue d'Histoire de la Médicine Hebraïque* (1948–68); *Medical Leaves*, 5 vols. (1937–43); *Harefuah* (1920–70); A. Castiglioni, in: L. Finkelstein (ed.), *Jews, Their History, Culture, and Religion*, 2 (1960³), ch. 31, 1349–75.

MEDICINE AND LAW.

This article is arranged according to the following outline:

INTRODUCTION

The issues involved in medicine and *halakhah* are basic concerns, discussed and debated in every society today. Their analysis and resolution encompass many issues, related to law and values, justice and ethics, philosophy, and way of life. This is true of every society which examines its path and strives to shape its own identity.

The subjects involved in medical *halakhah* are a living, vital element in Jewish law and in the life of the Jewish people – "living" and "vital" in the most literal sense, pertaining to the content of life and its very being. The worlds of *halakhah* and of medicine are interconnected with one another. For generations many of the greatest rabbis, *posekim*, and Jewish thinkers have been physicians by profession.

Moreover, the questions, principles, and proposed solutions in the fields of medicine and healing touch upon the life of every single person. Hence, the discussion and debate concerning them and the questions involved in their application and their resolution are the concern of the public at large. This being so, a good portion of the subjects of medicine and therapy, the difficulties inherent in them and the solutions proposed, are not merely a matter for theoretical discussion, restricted to the world of experts and professionals, but are matters of concern to the entire society, collectively and individually. It follows that analysis of these matters is greatly influenced by various commonly held worldviews, which influence the thinking of everyone in society, both collectively and individually. As a result, analysis of medical practice and therapy, of what is permitted and prohibited, as well as the pursuit of solutions that are correct and appropriate according to both halakhic and human criteria – are all highly influential in educating the public and forming the attitudes of the individual. These are issues of immediate relevance, with which our society is constantly concerned, studying them and analyzing them. It is therefore proper that the matters written and spoken on these matters be intended not only for professionals, but for the general interested public as well, as this material is of the utmost importance for anyone seeking an understanding of the ways of the Creator, the greatness of His Torah, and the depths of faith, and who wishes to understand the meaning of Torah, of faith, and of Judaism.

Judicial Decision – A Value Determination

Any concrete issue in the area of law and medicine that reaches the courts and thus requires a judicial decision, must of necessity require establishing a position regarding morals and values. Most issues of law and medicine that come before the court do not involve monetary obligations or financial rights, nor do they touch upon rights of ownership or criminal liability in terms of an offense against an explicit or implicit provision or section of the law. Rather, their aim is generally to establish a duty, right, or permit which is fundamentally rooted in value or moral judgments, which have been infused with a legal definition. This is particularly true of those cases in which the judicial decision involves not only law and medicine, but also involves the special realm of the family unit, the relationship between parent and child, and the relationship between spouses.

These questions have been explicitly addressed in the literature dealing with these issues, and in the decisions of Justice Menachem Elon in the Israeli Supreme Court. In the introductory comments of his decision in the case of the minor Yael Shefer (CA 506/88, *Yael Shefer, Minor by way of her mother v. State of Israel*, 48 (1) PD 87, 96–97), which will be discussed below, Justice Elon wrote the following:

> The subject at hand is a very difficult one. It reaches the depths of human values and ethics and the heights of the philosophical thinking of generations past and present. The issue touches upon the cultural and spiritual make-up of our society. Indeed, we have postponed giving our opinion in this case so that we might fully examine the nature and essence of these values, thereby fulfilling the command: "Be moderate in judgment." [...] "Against your will you are created, and against your will you are born; against your will you live, and against your will you pass on." Such was stated in the teachings of the Sages. [...] "Against our will" we sit to decide the case before us. The angel of judgment stands above us and commands: "Decide!" The judge is required to adjudicate even such controversial matters so that the patient may be informed of his rights and duties, so that the physician may know what his profession forbids, permits, and requires him to do, and so that all those who assist the patient – to whatever extent – may understand their rights and obligations. "Against our will" we adjudicate all these matters, for we are not at all confident that we have fully mastered all these fundamental issues, or that we are equipped with all of the information and knowledge that we need to decide our case. Nevertheless, we cannot abdicate our judicial responsibility, and we must probe, weigh, and state our opinion.

Further on we will examine a number of general principles, as expressed in the Knesset legislation and case-law, especially in the rulings of the Israeli Supreme Court.

THE VALUES OF A JEWISH AND DEMOCRATIC STATE. When dealing with the subject of medicine and law we confront the inherent tension of the fact of Israel being a Jewish state and its being a democratic state (for expansion on this point see: *Values of Jewish and Democratic State). In the *Shefer* case (pp. 106–107) Justice Elon defined the values of the Jewish state:

> The interpretation of the values of the State of Israel as a Jewish state is thus determined by the values of the Jewish tradition and the legacy of Judaism – that is, the conclusion reached through a study of the basic values contained in the sources of the Jewish tradition and Judaism's legacy. In carrying out this interpretative endeavor we will be fulfilling the wishes of the legislator in defining the values of the State of Israel as a Jewish state [...] by giving the appropriate interpretation of the values of the State of Israel as a Jewish state [...].

Regarding the synthesis between the values of Judaism and those of democracy, especially in the sensitive realm of medicine and law, Justice Elon contended that in a situation of conflict between the Jewish component and the democratic component, priority should be given to the Jewish component. Hence he wrote (*ibid.*, 167–70):

> As instructed by the legislature in the Basic Law: Human Dignity and Freedom, we have examined the values of a Jewish state and those of a democratic state in the vast and multifaceted areas of medicine, *halakhah*, and law. As required, we have analyzed the sources of both systems in detail, and have examined the meta-principles of each system and the basic rules derived from these principles – both expansive and restrictive. And conducting this analysis, we are instructed to arrive at a synthesis that will achieve the dual-value goal of the Basic Law: Human Dignity and Freedom – to anchor in the laws of the State of Israel its values as a Jewish and democratic state. The natural way of achieving this synthesis is to find the common ground between the Jewish and democratic systems – the principles that they share, or at least those that can be used to integrate the two systems [...], since active euthanasia negates the essence of the State of Israel as a Jewish state, as we observed above, the synthesis between the two norms – "the values of a Jewish and democratic state" – requires us to give preference to conclusion that would be reached by applying the values of a Jewish state, and to *use these values* to interpret the phrase "the values of a... democratic state." [...]
>
> The values of a *Jewish* state, whose roots are planted in the basic concepts of the dignity of the human being created in the image of God, the sanctity of life, and the prevention of pain and suffering, concepts which have stood the test of generations and which have nurtured and sustained the entire world – are the true guidelines for arriving at the correct synthesis between the values of a Jewish and democratic state.

In the Image of God

A person's fundamental right to physical and mental well-being and integrity bears a special character in Jewish law, stemming from its basic conception of the source of a man's right to his life, body, and dignity. In this respect Justice Elon wrote the following in EA 2/84 *Neiman v. Chairman, Central Elections Committee*; *Avneri v. Chairman, Central Elections Committee*, 39 (2) PD 225, 298:

> The foundation of the worldview of Judaism is the concept of the creation of man in the image of God (Genesis 1:27). This is how the Torah begins, and from it the *halakhah* derives fundamental principles concerning the worth of every human being, whoever he may be, and the right of every person to equal and loving treatment. He [R. Akiva] would say: "Beloved is man, for he was created in the image [of God]; but it was an act of greater love that it was made known to him that he was created in the image [of God], in that it is stated (Genesis 9:6): 'In His image did God make man.'"

Jewish law generally, and especially over the last few generations with the tremendous advances in medicine and its needs, has encountered a plethora of problems that emerge as a result of the conflict between the value of the sanctity of life and the value of prevention of pain and suffering and other considerations. However, the point of departure and the basic foundation for this confrontation was always, and has remained, the meta-value of the sanctity of life, and the combination of the right and duty to preserve the image of God. In the *Shefer* case, Justice Elon elaborated on the principle of Man's creation in the Image as the guiding conception in the subjects related to medicine and law, writing inter alia (pp. 115–116):

> The basic right to bodily integrity and mental well-being has a special meaning in Jewish law, which stems from its basic philosophical outlook regarding the source of one's right to life, bodily integrity, and dignity [...] The creation of man in the image of God is the basis of the value of each person's life. "Therefore the creation of humankind started with the creation of a single individual, to teach that whoever removes a single soul from this world is regarded as if he had caused the whole world to perish; and whoever keeps one single soul alive in this world is regarded as having preserved the whole world" (Mishnah, Sanh. 37a, as cited in Yad, Sanhedrin 12:3; see also Menachem Elon, *Ha-Mishpat ha-Ivri* (1988[3]), p.1426, and n. 303). As we stated elsewhere (LA 184/87, 151, 184, *Attorney General v. Anon.*, 42 (2) PD 661, 676): "the fundamental principle that must guide the court is that we are not authorized or allowed to make any distinction based on the 'worth' of an individual – whether poor or rich, physically healthy or disabled, psychologically strong or mentally ill. All human beings, created in the image of God, are equal in value." The creation of man in the image of God is the underlying foundation of the supreme value of each person's life, and it is the source of the fundamental rights of human dignity and freedom. (See. Cr. A. 2145/92, *State of Israel v. Guetta*, 46 (5) PD 704, 723–724.) The principle that "In His image did God make man" – every man, no matter who he is – whose source is as stated, is in the world of Judaism, has been accepted by many varied cultures and legal systems, as the foundation for the supreme value placed on human life. The only exceptions are those cultures which historically have discriminated between one man and another, between the physically healthy and the disabled, psychologically strong and mentally ill (such as in the philosophy of Plato or the Greek city of Sparta; see *infra* par. 59 [...]).
>
> "In His image did God make man" is the philosophical and analytical basis for the unique approach of Jewish law regarding the supreme value of the sanctity of human life – the sanctity of the divine image in which man was created – and the many consequences that follow in various areas of the law, including the important areas with which we dealt in the instant case. As we shall see, Jewish law has grappled, especially in recent times, with the tremendous advances in medicine, and with the many problems that have arisen as a result of the clash between, inter alia, the value and sanctity of life and the value of preventing pain and suffering. Yet the lodestar is and has been the supreme value of the sanctity of human life, and the right and obligation to protect the divine image of humankind.

PHYSICIAN'S DUTIES AND PATIENTS' RIGHTS

Initially, during the tannaitic era, it was established that it is permitted for a physician to heal. The Talmud derives this from the verse (Exod. 21:19): "'He shall cause him to be thoroughly healed' – This teaches that the physician is given permission to heal" (Bava Kamma 85a). This implied rejection of the approach prevalent in various philosophies and religions at that time, and later as well, even in some statements by Jewish thinkers, that one should not heal a person whom God has made ill, because there should be no intervention in what Heaven has decreed (Rashi, at BK 85a, s.v. *Nitna reshut; Kitvei Ramban*, Chavell ed. (Jerusalem 1964), vol. 2: *Torat ha-Adam*, at 42). Other tannaitic halakhic rules established that an expert physician who inadvertently caused damage is exempt, as a matter of public policy (Tosefta, Git. 4:6, Zukermandel ed.), for otherwise physicians would be unwilling to perform their duties (Resp. *Tashbez*, vol. 3 no. 82).

During the period of the *rishonim* the view was articulated that the physician's work is not only permitted, but is an obligation and constitutes the fulfillment of a commandment. Maimonides held that this is based on the duty to save life found in Jewish law whereby a person is obliged to save his fellow man who is in danger, "with his body, his money, or his knowledge (Yad, Nedarim 7:8). According to Naḥmanides, "any physician who is knowledgeable is obligated to heal, and if he refused to do so he is considered to have shed blood" (*Sefer Torat ha-Adam, Kitvei ha-Ramban,* ed. Chavel, 2:41–42). Thus, the permission given the physician to heal also has the status of a commandment (*mitzvah*), intended to dispel the physician's hesitation at the prospect of healing others due to his fear of erring and injuring others (see Resp. *Da'at Kohen*, no. 140). Another principle operating in the context of the physician and treatment in Jewish law is based on the verse "Love your fellow as yourself." In *Sharon v. Levi* (CA 548/78, *Sharon v. Levi*, 35 (1) PD 735, at 755) Justice Elon wrote as follows:

> It is instructive to observe how this basic right was viewed in Jewish law. "One who strikes a blow causing damage less than a *perutah* (i.e., that did not cause any real injury) transgresses a negative commandment (Sanh. 85a; Yad, Hovel u-Mazik 5:1–3). Even if the victim consents to being struck, his consent has no validity (BB 92a; Sh. Ar., ḤM 420:1ff.; *Shulhan Arukh Ha-Rav*

> HM, Hilkhot Nizkei Guf ve-Nefesh ve-Dineihem 4; according to the law, it is also forbidden for a person to injure himself – BK, Yad, ad loc.). This being so, on what basis can one person let blood of his fellow, even if it is necessary to do so in order to heal him? In the view of the *amora* R. Matna (Sanh. 84b) permission to do so is not based on the consent of the patient, whether expressed or implied, for the consent, as stated, is immaterial. Rather, it is a rule derived from the verse "Love your fellow as yourself" (Lev. 19:18), from which one can infer, as Rashi put it, that "each Jew was cautioned not to do to his fellow that which he does not want done to himself" (Rashi, Sanh. 84a, s.v. *ve-ahavta le-re'akha kamokha*; see also *Kitvei ha-Ramban, Torat ha-Adam* (ed. Chavell, Mossad ha-Rav Kook), 41–42; M. Elon, *"Ha-Halakhah ve-ha-Refu'ah ha-Ḥadishah,"* in: *Molad*, 4 (NS), 27 (1971), 228, 232).

The philosophic-halakhic basis for permission to wound a sick person in order to cure him as deriving from the fundamental Biblical command "Love your fellow as yourself" is cited by Naḥmanides as a guiding accepted principle in the context of the physician and medicine in the world of *halakhah*: "The person who wounds another to cure him (for medical treatment) is exempt, and it constitutes the performance of a positive precept, as it states 'Love your fellow as yourself'" (*Torat ha-Adam, ibid.*, p. 43).

Rabbi Eliezer Waldenberg, a leading contemporary authority in the area of halakhic-medical law, wrote the following comment on these words of Naḥmanides:

> We require that the commandment to heal be inferred from the verse ("Love your fellow as yourself"), and it is insufficient to rely on the principle that "nothing stands in the way of saving a life" to justify the physician's privilege to wound in order to heal (referred to by Naḥmanides, and cited by the Tur and Shulhan Arukh), because the inference from "Love your fellow as yourself" teaches that there is an obligation to heal even when there is clearly no danger to life, but only pain or danger to a limb.

The Physician and the Judge

Both Naḥmanides and Rabbi Kook (*Torat ha-Adam, ibid.* p. 41–42; Resp. *Da'at Kohen*, no. 140 (Rabbi Abraham Isaac *Kook – the first chief rabbi of Israel)) drew an illuminating analogy between the physician treating a patient and a judge presiding over a court. The judge's duty to judge the people in each generation and in all matters is portrayed in the Talmud as giving rise to a soul-searching dilemma, phrased as follows (Sanh. 6b):

> The judges should know whom they are judging, before Whom they are judging, and Who will exact punishment from them, for it is stated: "God stands amidst the community of God, in the midst of judges (*elohim*) He will judge" (Psalms 82:1). Similarly, regarding Jehoshaphat it is stated: "He charged the judges: Consider what you are doing, for you judge not on behalf of man, but on behalf of the Lord" (II Chronicles 19:6). Perhaps the judge will say, "Why do I need this anguish?" Therefore it is stated, "And He [God] is with you when you pass judgment" (Chronicles, ad loc.; Rashi, Sanh. 6b – "For He is with your hearts, as your hearts incline as to the matter"). A judge can only rule in accordance with what his eyes see. (Rashi adds, Sanhedrin, ad loc., "If he attempts to render a just true judgment, he will not be punished.")

Similarly, the work of a physician imposes great responsibilities and corresponding demands on his conscience, accompanied by much anguish. For this reason, Naḥmanides concludes that the laws pertaining to a physician who is as careful as he should be when dealing with life-and-death situations are the same as those applicable to a judge who seeks to render a just and true judgment. If they are unaware that they have made a mistake, they are both exempt, by both human and divine law.

Yet in one fundamental respect – which goes to the root of the matter – the physician's responsibility is greater than that of the judge. If an authorized judge (one who judges "with the permission of the court") becomes aware of his inadvertent mistake, he remains exempt even by divine law. By contrast, if a physician becomes aware of his unintentional mistake, while he remains exempt by human law, he is nevertheless liable by divine law. Indeed, if his mistake caused someone's death, he is subject to the penalty of exile [to a city of refuge]. The physician and the judge are partners to the heartbreak and ethical dilemmas inherent in their work. Each of them attempts to ease these agonizing dilemmas by following his conscience, based on "what his eyes see" or, as formulated by R. Menahem ha-*Meiri, by acting according to "what his eyes see, his ears hear, and his heart understands" (*Bet ha-Beḥirah*, Ketubbot 51b). See also Maimonides (Guide 3:34), who writes that the judge adjudicates in accordance with a general norm, whereas the physician treats each patient in accordance with his own specific condition and sickness. This is the essence of the physician's duty which obligates him to cure the specific ailment that confronts him, according to the particular circumstances and condition of the patient.

Regarding the analogy between the physician and the patient, Justice Elon made the following comments in the *Shefer* case (*ibid.*, pp. 108–9):

> It should be noted that the principles governing the professional behavior of the physician intertwine law and ethics, compliance with the strict law and going beyond the law (*lifnim mi-shurat ha-din*), the nature of the *halakhah*, and the nature of the world. Following the example set by Naḥmanides' *Torat ha-Adam*, these principles appear in separate sections in the later halakhic codes – *Arba'ah ha-Turim* of Jacob b. Asher and the Shulḥan Arukh of Joseph Caro (YD, beginning of sec. 315ff.). Incidentally, it bears mention that Maimonides' *Mishneh Torah* does not contain any codification of the laws relating to the physician. Maimonides comments on this matter in the fourth chapter of *Hilkhot De'ot*, but only to deal with the proper regimen required to maintain a healthy body. It is certainly instructive that these codifiers, who as a general rule do not include in their codes those laws that have no practical relevance, and hence do not codify such laws as those relating to the exile of an unintentional murderer to a city of refuge, nevertheless include the rule that a physician who causes death and then becomes aware that he has erred should be exiled (Tur and Sh. Ar, ḤM 425:1). They do so in order to demonstrate the

deep responsibility born by the physician, in that even when there is no legal sanction, he is liable, in cases of negligence, to be exiled to a city of refuge, to grieve and to give an accounting of his life. This dilemma of medical practice – where, on the one hand, there is the commandment not to refrain from healing others while, on the other hand, there is the sense of "why do I need this trouble?" – has become greater and more pronounced as a result of the tremendous advances in modern medicine and in light of contemporary legal and philosophical thinking concerning fundamental rights and meta-principles. Today – even more so than previously – both the judge and the physician continue to be partners to this dilemma. Both carry the responsibility and both seek to do justice in their profession, each in his own field – the judge to reach a truly correct decision and the physician to achieve true healing. This guideline of searching out the essential truth – the full meaning of which will be explained below – serves as a road-map – complex and difficult, yet indispensable – for resolving the important, grave, and complex questions that lie at the doorstep of the physician and judge alike. As is generally the case with regard to such basic questions, there are fundamentally different approaches that create a profound sense of awe as one proceeds to grapple with and apply them.

The Patient's Obligation to be Healed and his Right to Choose Medical Treatment

In the world of Judaism, just as the physician is obligated to heal, so too, as may be seen from our above discussion, the patient is obligated to be healed. Moreover, one who refrains from being healed violates the Scriptural verses "You shall guard yourselves well" (Deut. 4:15) and "For your own life-blood I will require a reckoning" (Gen. 9:5). The obligation of a person to be healed from a life-threatening illness takes precedence over almost all of the commandments of the Torah. When a physician determines that to become cured one must desecrate the Sabbath, a patient who refuses to accept treatment involving the desecration of the Sabbath "is considered to be 'a pious fool,' …we compel him to do [what the physician has ordered]" (Resp. Radbaz, vol. 4, no. 1339; Sh. Ar., OḤ 328:10, and commentaries ad loc.). In such circumstances, preferring observance of the commandment over medical treatment is considered "a commandment performed through sin" (Resp. Mahari Asad, OḤ no. 160). The patient's wishes are to be followed, however, when he seeks to improve the medical care he is receiving, but the physicians disagree with him. This is based on the verse "The heart knows its own bitterness" (Prov. 14:10; Yoma 82a–83a; Sh. Ar. OḤ 618:1; A. Steinberg (ed.), *Enẓiklopedyah Refu'it Hilkhatit*, vol. 2, pp. 24–26, 443–45).

According to Jewish law, the patient is not only obligated to seek a cure, he also has a basic right to receive treatment from a physician of his choice whom he trusts. This rule is derived from the teachings of the Sages, and became established *halakhah* in the Shulḥan Arukh, which rules that "If Reuben vowed not to benefit Simeon, and Simeon fell ill, Reuben may treat him… even with his own hand, even if there is another physician who can treat him" (Sh. Ar., YD 221:1).

In relation to this ruling, Justice Elon wrote the following in the *Tamir* case (APP 4/82 Cr. App. 904/82, *State of Israel v. Tamir*, 37 (3) 205–206:

> It is well-established law, based on the principle of the personal liberty of every person created in the image of God, that no person's bodily integrity may be infringed without his consent […]. This basic right includes the right to select the physician to whom his treatment will be entrusted; making such a choice is integral to his fundamental right to maintain his bodily integrity and mental well-being and not to be "harmed" thereby except with his consent […] An instructive expression of this principle may be found in the teachings of our Sages. The Mishnah states (Nedarim 4:4): "If one was forbidden to derive benefit from another person… he may [nevertheless] be cured by him," i.e., when one person vowed not to benefit from another person, or his fellow man vowed not to benefit to him, he may nevertheless benefit from the medical services of the other person, for the duty to heal and the right to be healed in body and soul "is a commandment" (Yad, Nedarim 6:8). The Jerusalem Talmud states that this rule not only applies where there is only one physician available – i.e., the fellow from whom he has vowed not to receive benefit – but even if another physician is available, and he may avail himself of the medical treatment of the other physician, the patient may nevertheless choose to consult the doctor from whom he vowed not to receive any benefit, for "not every person is able to cure him" (*Nimmukei Yosef* to Rif, Nedarim 41a). This is in accordance with the codified rule that "If Reuben vowed not to benefit Simeon, and Simeon fell ill, Reuben may treat him … even with his own hands, even if there is another physician who can treat him." In medical treatment, the personal trust between the patient and the physician of his choice is extremely important, for which reason "even if there is another physician who can treat him, that physician [i.e., the one from whom he vowed not to benefit], if qualified, is under a duty to treat him, for the saving of life is sacred" (*Ritba*, to *Rif*, Ned. 41b).

OBLIGATION AND REFUSAL TO RECEIVE MEDICAL TREATMENT. The fundamental rule of Jewish law regarding the physician's duty to treat, and the patient's obligation to be cured, is subject to a number of qualifications, which have proliferated in our generations and which limit the possibility of treating a patient against his will. R. Jacob Emden, one of the leading halakhic authorities of the 18th century (*Mor u-Keẓi'ah*, OḤ 322), laid down the following conditions under which the patient is obligated to seek a cure and under which "he is not listened to, if he rejects suffering and chooses death over life." Accordingly, the duty only applies where the physician is familiar with the sickness "in absolute and clear certainty," the case concerns a patient who at that time was referred to as "a patient with a clear sickness and obvious wound"; the treatment that the physician wishes to use was "definitively checked and certain"; and the patient's life is in danger. In the event that these conditions do not exist, the patient's consent is required for medical treatment, and he is permitted to refuse medical treatment. In contemporary times, many *posekim* have dealt with these cases, enumerating additional cases in which the patient's consent is required. R. Moshe Feinstein, one of the great halakhic decisors of our generation (see responsum of R. Moshe Feinstein quoted in *Piskei Halakhah Refuah u-Mishpat,* ed. S. Shachar (1989), p. 101), wrote that, when giving treatment against a patient's will, in addition to the need for a high probability of success, account must also be taken of the negative influence of treatment given against his will. According to another opinion, if the patient can be expected to suffer even after the medical treatment, providing grounds for assuming that he would not have agreed to such medical treatment before it was given, then it cannot be administered in the first place without the patient's consent (*ibid.,* 104). Another view was that, given the large number of cases in which there was no certain medical opinion, all non-consensual medical treatment should be avoided, unless there is a definite danger of death (A. Steinberg (ed.), *Enziklopedyah Refu'it Hilkhatit,* vol. 2, Informed Consent, p. 30, nn. 86–87; cf. Rabbi S. Raphael, "*Kefiyyat Tippul Refu'i al Ḥoleh,*" in: *Torah she-Beal Peh,* 33 (Jerusalem, 1992)).

EUTHANASIA

In recent years a number of factors have combined to bring the subject of *euthanasia to the forefront of discourse in the world of medicine and *halakhah.* The awesome advancement in science and medicine resulting from technological progress has facilitated the prolongation of human life in its final stages. However, this prolongation has not always led to improvement in the quality of life, and on occasion even sentences people to grave physical and mental pain. Doctor-patient relations have also undergone a metamorphosis, from the paternalistic approach whereby the doctor decides what is best for the patient, to an approach based on patient autonomy, whereby the competent patient can decide for himself, and his informed consent is therefore required for any medical proceeding. A large number of people are involved in the treatment of a terminally ill patient, of different cultural backgrounds and outlooks, and consequently bringing with them varied opinions as to how to treat the terminally ill patient. The general public today is also far more concerned with moral problems pertaining to medicine in general, and specifically those relating to the terminally ill. Limited medical resources do not always suffice to provide all possible medical options for all those requiring it, and occasionally these, too, are considerations in the decision making process in relation to these patients.

We shall now present the sources underlying the halakhic approach to this subject, and the manner in which the *halakhah* relates to the subject in modern times in general, and in the State of Israel in particular. In the *Shefer* case (*Shefer v. State of Israel* 48 (1) PD 87, 131–132), Justice Elon wrote the following:

> There have always been serious and complex moral problems regarding the end of one's stay on this earth. Jewish law includes various rules dealing with the medical care to be given, as well as other issues of civil and religious law, concerning the person who is terminally ill or dying (= *goses*). Jewish law distinguishes between these states, but there are disagreements as to their precise definitions and halakhic consequences. In any event, this is not the place to elaborate.… Regarding this terminal state, Jewish law emphasizes the importance of even ephemeral or brief life (*ḥayyei sha'ah*), so long as "the candle flickers…" This is also true in non-Jewish cultures, evidence of which we find as early as the Hippocratic oath, which states, inter alia: "I will not give poison to any person, even if he requests it; and I will not offer it." Some cultures, however, did not have this approach…
>
> These medical-legal problems, involving fundamental questions of values, have grown more complex and difficult in recent years, provoking much discussion and dispute in the medical and legal communities, as well as among philosophers, clergymen, and the general public. On the one hand, the awesome advance in science and medicine resulting from technological progress has allowed the prolongation of life, by preventing the spread of disease and by various artificial means; on the other hand, the *prolongation* of life has not always led to improvement of its *quality.* At times, prolongation of life brings with it physical and mental pain, and the disruption of day-to-day life. In addition, a patient in such circumstances today may find himself in a hospital or other institution, attached to various machines which keep him alive, and not – as in the past – within the walls of his own home, with his family and loved ones in the natural environment in which he lived and flourished. Those who must deal with these problems are primarily the patient himself and his family, in addition to physicians, legal scholars, clergymen, and philosophers. The problems that arise involve grave and fundamental moral, religious, and ethical questions. The basic question is: who understands all of these factors sufficiently to be competent to decide what is the proper life span of a person and whether to shorten or to refrain from prolonging it.

The Bible

The prohibition on taking a human life is one of the gravest offenses in the Torah, and mankind as a whole was admonished against this offense at the dawn of its history: "Whosoever sheds the blood of man, by man shall his blood be shed, for in His image did God make man" (Gen. 9:6; see at length in *Homicide, and *Noahide Law). The Bible records a case which serves as a proof text for the view that killing a man even where it is clear that there is no chance that he will continue to live is nevertheless murder. At the end of the war between the Israelites and the Philistines during the days of Saul, Saul understood that the Philistines were about to kill him, and therefore decided to kill himself with his own sword. Scripture relates that Saul only injured himself after this attempted suicide, and then asked an Amalekite youth to complete the act. Saul's condition at that stage was analogous to that of a terminally ill patient, who clearly and lucidly requested the hastening of his death in order to redeem him from his suffering. The Amalekite youth complied with his wishes and killed him. Nevertheless, David subsequently ruled that the Amalekite youth was liable for the death penalty as a murderer (I Sam. 31:3–4; II Samuel 1 and 16; see Radak and Ralbag, ad loc.) From this Biblical story it emerges that that the active killing of a person who is dying is forbidden, even under those conditions, and even if the patient requested it (Ralbag, *ibid.*, *Sefer Ḥasidim*, ch. 315; Ralbag and Radak further suggested interpreting that in fact the youth did not actually kill Saul, but rather just said that in order to find favor in David's eyes).

In Talmudic Literature

As a rule, so long as the person's soul has not departed he is regarded as alive. The treatment of the terminally ill is dealt with directly in tractate *Semaḥot*, which stipulates those actions that may be performed on a dead person, and which are forbidden with respect to a living person: "A *goses* is considered a living person in all respects… One may not bind his jaws… one may not move him… one may not close the eyes of the dying [patient]. Whoever touches or moves him sheds blood…" (Semaḥot 1:1–4; Shab. 151b).

The Mishnah in Tractate *Yoma* (8:6) states that "Any chance of saving a life takes precedence over the Sabbath." Accordingly, in the event of a landslide, where there is a chance that a person is trapped beneath the debris, the debris should be removed until it is certain that no living person is trapped thereunder. Tractate *Yoma* 85a adds that, even if the person found under the debris was mortally wounded, and it is clear that he will soon die, one continues to desecrate the Sabbath to save him by removing the debris. Thus, this source indicates that even short-term life is considered life. The halakhic decisors of the present generation disputed whether this source implies that everything possible should be done to prolong life, even if only temporary, or whether the laws of the Sabbath do not necessarily provide a basis for the duty to prolong life (Resp. *Ẓiẓ Eli'ezer*, 5; *Kuntres Ramat Raḥel*, 28; Resp. *Minḥat Shelomo*, 91.24).

Regarding a person about to die and experiencing intense suffering, the aggadic sources adopt a different attitude. The Talmud (Av. Zar. 18a) relates the story of R. Hanina b. Teradyon (second century C.E.) who was taken to be executed by the Romans as punishment for publicly teaching Torah. In order to ensure that the execution would be protracted and particularly cruel, the Romans soaked pads of wool in water and placed them over his heart "to delay the departure of his soul." When the executioner offered to stoke the flame and hasten his death by removing the pads, R. Hanina agreed, and swore that by that act the executioner had secured his place in the World to Come. The halakhic decisors offer a variety of explanations for the positive attitude taken by the Talmud to this act, but the story itself indicates that when a person is about to die and experiencing intense suffering, it is permitted to hasten his death even by way of a positive action – e.g., increasing the flame, and even by an act of "removing the impediment" – here, taking away the sponges.

Another case cited by the Babylonian Talmud (Ket. 104a) describes the death of R. Judah ha-Nasi, who towards his death was in unbearable pain. His students succeeded in preventing his death by their incessant prayers for Heavenly mercy. His handmaid, noting the intensity of his suffering, threw a jar on the ground, thereby momentarily causing them to cease praying, and at that moment Rabbi Judah died. This story has been cited as proof that it is permitted to avoid prolonging the life of a terminally ill patient (*Iggerot Moshe*, ḤM, vol. 2 no. 73.1).

Halakhic Rulings

The halakhic rulings sharply distinguish between the active hastening of death, which is forbidden, and the removal of a life-prolonging impediment, which is permitted under certain conditions.

The various acts cited above as being prohibited in respect of the *goses* are enjoined because they are liable to actively hasten the death of the terminally ill (see Sh. Ar., YD 339:1; s.v. **goses*; *Talmudic Encyclopaedia* (Heb.), 5, 393ff.).

Actively hastening death is forbidden even in cases where the patient is suffering acutely: "It is forbidden to hasten his death, even if he is dying and both he and his relatives are suffering intensely" (*Ḥokhmat Adam*, 91.14), "and even if we see that he is suffering intensely, and that it is better for him to die, we are prohibited from performing any act to hasten his death" (*Arukh ha-Shulḥan,* YD 339:1; *Nishmat Avraham*, YD 339:4).

This prohibition applies even where the patient himself requests it, an analogy being drawn from Maimonides' ruling that one may not take ransom from a murderer in order to exempt him from the death penalty, even if the blood avenger (i.e., the victim's relative who may exact the murderer's life as retribution for the murder) agrees, because "the life of the victim is not the property of the 'blood avenger,' but rather belongs to God" (Yad, Roẓe'aḥ u-Shemirat ha-Nefesh 1:4).

On the other hand, the prohibition on passive euthanasia is not absolute and the *halakhah* distinguishes between various forms of passive euthanasia, the prevention of suffering to the patient being a paramount consideration. R. Judah he-Ḥasid (Ashkenaz, 12th century; *Sefer Ḥasidim*, ch. 723 (ed. Mossad ha-Rav Kook)) addresses the issue and rules that, even though it is forbidden to perform any action that hastens death, there is no place for actions that delay a natural death. "We do not act to delay a person's death. For example, if a person is dying and there is a man chopping wood near his house so that the soul cannot depart, we remove the woodchopper from there. Moreover, we do not place salt on his tongue to prevent his death. But if he is dying and he says that he cannot die until he is placed somewhere else, he is not to be moved from there (i.e., from where he is)."

According to this view, artificially delaying the soul's departure causes unnecessary pain and suffering to the *goses:* "Do not feed the *goses*, for he is unable to swallow, but water should be put into his mouth…and one does not shout at the time of the soul's departure, so that the soul does not return and suffer unbearable pain…" (*ibid.*, 234).

Joshua Boaz ben Simon Baruch (Italy, 16th century) in his glosses on Alfasi, MK 26b, in *Shiltei ha-Gibborim*, in explaining this passage in *Sefer Ḥasidim* states that it is permitted to discontinue an external act which prolongs the life of the *goses*, but it is forbidden to move him from his place and place him elsewhere, or to do any other action in order to hasten his death (*ibid.*, 234). This opinion was codified and incorporated into the ruling of the Rema, at Sh. Ar., YD 339:1.

The life-preserving measures dealt with in these sources essentially reflect popular beliefs prevalent in those days. The task facing contemporary authorities was to translate and apply these examples to the life-preserving measures utilized by modern medicine. In that context, it was held that an artificial respiration machine or other artificial life-support mechanisms are analogous to the "grain of salt"; thus it was held that they can be removed in order to discontinue the artificial prolonging of the dying patient's life. Therefore, "once the physicians have determined that he cannot be cured (i.e., it is clear that he will not recover), it is clearly permissible to disconnect the patient from the machine to which he is connected." Furthermore, it was even held that "not only is it permitted to disconnect the respirator, *but there is an obligation to do so.* For man's soul is the property of God and has not God already taken the soul from this person, for as soon as the machine is removed he will die. And quite the opposite, by using the artificial respirator we leave his soul inside him and cause it (the soul, not the dying person) pain due to its inability to depart from the body and arrive at its resting place" (Rabbi H.D. Halevi, bibliography). A similar ruling was given by R. Eliezer Waldenberg (Resp. *Ẓiẓ Eli'ezer*, vol. 13, no. 89; cf. R. Solomon Zalman Auerbach, Resp. *Minḥat Shelomo*, 91.24).

R. Ovadiah Hadayah (Resp. *Yaskil Avdi*, YD, vol. 7, no. 40) held that a *goses* is "any patient regarding who all the physicians have given up hope and have determined that he will not recover from his sickness."

In other responsa, Rabbi Moses Feinstein (Resp. *Iggerot Moshe*, YD, vol 2., no. 74, 73.1, 74.1) and Rabbi Auerbach (Resp. *Nishmat Avraham*, Yad Vashem, 245) make additional distinctions relating to this question, such as the distinction between medical assistance that actually alleviates the patient's suffering (such as oxygen), which it is mandatory to administer to him, and administering other medicines, and the distinction between standard medical treatment, which the doctors are duty bound to continue administering to the patient, and non-standard medical treatment.

Summing up the position of Jewish law on this subject, Justice Elon wrote in the *Shefer* case:

> In Jewish thought, various overarching principles and values operate within the context of this momentous and complex labyrinth of *halakhah* and medicine. Such principles include the sanctity of human life, based on the meta-principle of man's creation in the image of God; the fundamental precept to "love your fellow as yourself"; the alleviation of pain and suffering; the obligation of the physician to cure and of the patient to be healed; the right of the patient to refuse medical treatment; the decision-making approach of "her ways are pleasant ways"; the requirement that "the laws of our Torah must accord with reason and logic"; as well as other principles discussed above.
>
> The point of departure in the extensive, difficult, and complex area of law and medicine is the supreme value of the sanctity of life. This supreme value is based, as stated, on the meta-principle of man being created in the image of God, with all that implies. Therefore, the standard of the *worthiness* of a person does not exist, nor could it exist. The law for a physically or mentally handicapped person is the same as that for a healthy person; we do not measure the degree of health of the body or mind. Similarly, no standard exists with respect to the *length* of a person's life. The same rules apply to a person who has only a short period to live and one who is expected to live a long life: the flickering candle still burns and illuminates. Therefore, *actively* hastening death, or acting to shorten life – even if termed "mercy killing" – is absolutely forbidden, even at the behest of the patient. The obligation, in such situations, is to ameliorate the patient's pain and suffering in every possible way.
>
> The situation is different with regard to *passive* euthanasia, the non-prolongation of life, known in Jewish law as the "removal of the impediment." Passive euthanasia is permitted and, according to some authorities, even mandatory in certain cases, after taking into account such factors as the fundamental principle of minimizing the patient's physical and mental pain and suffering, the wishes of the patient, the negative consequences of treating the patient against his will, and the various types of treatment – ordinary or extraordinary, natural or artificial, etc.
>
> Similar considerations apply when considering the necessity for consent by the patient. In principle, the obligation of treatment is incumbent upon both the physician and the patient, especially when the treatment is necessary to save the person's life. However, apart from those cases involving immediate danger to life, this principle has been progressively limited, and in various situations the patient… may not be treated against his will.… The consideration of individual autonomy in the decisions of the halakhic authorities came about largely as a consequence of momentous developments in our generation in the field of medicine and the struggle of the halakhic authorities to deal with them. At times, what is determinative is not the opinion of the physician… but rather that of the patient himself, for it is forbidden to "actively cause him to suffer." Great significance is accorded to the adverse effect that undesired treatment may have on the patient: "The very fact that he is compelled [to undergo the operation] will further endanger him." This illustrates the methodology of the *halakhah* – it develops and creates itself through the process of case-by-case decision making.
>
> All these and similar questions dealt with by a growing body of contemporary halakhic responsa attest to the diversity of halakhic views on these difficult, tragic questions pertaining to the relationship between the sanctity of life and prevention of pain and suffering, both mental and physical, with all their implications.

In the State of Israel

The question of shortening, or failing to prolong, the life of a terminal patient has engaged many scholars and writers in the realms of *halakhah*, medicine, philosophy, and law. Over the past few years, with the development of new technological and diagnostic measures at the disposal of the medical system, the courts are often required to decide on these questions. Section 309 of the Israeli Penal Law criminalizes active euthanasia – i.e., an act that causes the shortening of a patient's life – classifying it as murder. The Israel Supreme Court addressed the issue of the scope and essence of this offense in the *Shefer* case (CA 506/98 *Yael Shefer v. State of Israel*, 48 (1) 87), giving a leading judgment on the subject. The case concerned a little girl suffering from Tay-Sachs, an incurable genetic disease, and it was undisputed that her days were numbered. Her request (filed by her mother as her guardian) was that in the event of her condition deteriorating, the hospital should refrain from administering life-prolonging treatment. Justice Menachem Elon dealt at length with the aforementioned sources and analyzed the problem from the perspective of the need to strike a balance between the Jewish values of the State of Israel and its democratic values. The court held that, in that case, the mother's request to allow discontinuation of treatment could not be granted, because on the basis of the medical testimony presented to the court, the child was not suffering, her dignity was preserved and, as such, the sanctity of her life, even in its state of being terminally ill, was the sole and determinant value, and any interference and harm to life contravened the values of a Jewish, democratic state.

For additional judgments dealing with this subject, see: OM 528/96 *Bibes v. Tel Aviv-Jaffa Municipality* (Tel Aviv District Court); OM 2242/95 *A.A. v. Kuppat Ḥolim Kelalit*, 2 PDM, 1995, 235; OM 1030/95 *Gilad v. Soroka* (Beersheba District Court).

In order to discuss and formulate a bill regulating policy in this area, the Ministry of Health appointed a committee, headed by Prof. Abraham Steinberg (referred to as the Steinberg Committee). In 2002, the Asher Committee published conclusions. The report discussed the moral, religious, medical, psychological, social, and legal aspects of the problem, and formulated a draft bill. This bill deals with the various categories of dying patients, including those who are legally competent and those who are not, the different forms of treatment, the status of professional caregivers and of the family, and establishes frameworks for the solution of individual problems, as well as for adoption and review of decisions. The draft bill on the subject conformed with the approach of Jewish law to this subject, and was adopted by the Israeli Legislature as binding law in December 2005.

The section defining the purpose of the Terminally Ill Patient Law, 5766 – 2005 (Section 1) stipulates as follows:

(a) The purpose of this law is to regulate the medical treatment of a patient regarding whom it was determined that he is terminally ill, pursuant to the principles set forth in this Law, based on an appropriate balance between the value of the sanctity of life and the value of individual autonomy and the importance of quality of life.

(b) This law is based on the values of the State of Israel as a Jewish and democratic state, and fundamental principles in the realm of morality, ethics and religion.

Basic Principle of the Law (Section 2):

In prescribing the medical treatment for a terminally ill patient, his medical condition, his will, and the degree of his suffering are the exclusive considerations.

The law provides the following definition of a terminally ill patient (Section 6):

(a) An authorized physician may determine that a patient is terminally ill, if satisfied that the patient is suffering from an incurable illness, and that his life expectancy, even upon receiving medical treatment, does not exceed six months.

(b) An authorized physician may determine that a terminally ill patient is dying if satisfied that his medical condition is such that a number of vital systems in his body have ceased to function, and that his life expectancy, even upon receiving medical treatment, does not exceed two weeks.

The law explicitly prohibits active euthanasia, or assisted suicide, or discontinuation of ongoing medical treatment:

12. Nothing in the provisions of this law shall permit any act, even if constituting medical treatment, that is intended to kill, or which will almost certainly result in death, irrespective of whether or not it was motivated by kindness and compassion, and irrespective of whether or not it was at the request of the terminally ill patient, or of any other person.

13. Nothing in the provisions of this law shall permit any act, even one constituting medical treatment, that contributes to assisted suicide, irrespective of whether or not it was motivated by kindness and compassion, and irrespective of whether or not it was at the request of the terminally ill patient, or any other person.

14. Nothing in the provisions of this law shall permit the discontinuation of the medical treatment of the terminally ill, which is liable to cause his death, irrespective of whether or not he is legally competent […]

Nevertheless, the law does allow the physician to refrain from providing medical treatment to a terminally ill patient (§8) or to refrain from the renewal of medical treatment (§14):

8 (a). Where a legally competent terminally ill patient does not want his life prolonged, his will should be honored and medical treatment withheld […]

14. […] However, it is permitted to refrain from the renewal of medical treatment, which was disrupted inadvertently or not in contravention of the provisions of any law, and it is similarly permitted to refrain from the renewal of periodic medical treatment […]

The law also regulates the treatment of a terminally ill minor (§§19–21), and of a terminally protected person. Moreover, the law regulates the methods whereby a terminally ill patient can give advance living notice of his wishes concerning the medical treatment that he wishes to receive (ch. 5 of the law). The law further appoints an institutional committee, comprising inter alia a clergyman of the same religion as the patient, to rule on doubtful situations pertaining to the treatment of the terminally ill patient.

ORGAN TRANSPLANTATION

Organ transplantation is a new medical technology for the replacement of organs, parts of organs, or tissues that have reached terminal failure, by organs, parts of organs, and tissues that are functional. The transplanted organ may be taken from one part of the person to another, from one person to another, or from an animal to a human being. The transplanted organs may be artificial or natural, complete (e.g., kidney, heart, liver, etc.), or partial (e.g., heart valves, skin, bone, etc.).

The basic issues involved in organ transplant in Jewish law depend upon the classification of organ being transplanted, being divided into four categories: (a) whether transfer of an organ from the body of the deceased is permitted – a question that arises primarily with respect to cornea and heart transplants; (b) determining the moment of the donor's death – an important issue in the context of heart transplants; (c) whether or not a person is permitted to endanger himself to save his fellow-man – a question that arises in the context of kidney transplant and other transplants involving a donation from a living person; and, if it is permitted, is he obligated to do so; (d) whether a child or person who is otherwise legally incompetent may serve as a donor.

Cornea Transplants

The questions raised by cornea transplants are common to all forms of transplant in which the transplanted organ is taken from the dead donor. Under what circumstances may an organ removed from a dead person's body serve for the recuperation of another person (see *Medical Experimentation)?

The *posekim* discuss whether the removal of an organ from a dead person violates the prohibition of deriving benefit from the dead person, the majority opinion being that it does not (Resp. Radbaz, vol. 2, no. 648; *ibid.*, vol. 3, no. 648 (1009); Resp. *Shevet Yehudah*, pp. 313–22). It was further ruled that there was no prohibition of postponing burial entailed in transplants from a dead person to a living person (see: Deut. 21:22–23; Sanh. 44b, and other sources), nor is it considered as neglect of the positive precept of burying the dead organ, because the organ is restored to functionality by the act of being transplanted into a live body, and is hence not classified as "flesh of the dead" (Resp. *Shevet Yehudah*, *ibid.*; Resp. *Seridei Esh*, vol. 2, no. 120; Resp. *Yabi'a Omer*, vol. 3, YD no. 22). The *posekim* also discussed whether the removal of an organ from the dead person's body transgresses the prohibition of mutilating the dead body. According to one view, in order to avoid this prohibition there is a need for a prior living consent to the act (Resp. *Shevet Yehudah*, *ibid.*), and according to another view, it is permitted to remove the organ even without prior living consent in cases of great need, even if it does not involve the saving of a life (H.D. Halevi, in: *Assia*, 4 (1983), 251–59).

Most contemporary halakhic decisors take the view that, if, when confronted by a patient requiring a transplant, his condition is defined as life threatening (*pikku'aḥ nefesh*), and if the donor agreed while still alive to have his organs taken, it is permitted to remove his organs after his death to transplant them into a live person; there are those who even rule that this is a *mitzvah* – i.e., a religious duty. The family must, however, consent to the removal of an organ from their deceased relative, for purposes of a transplant (Resp. *Iggerot Moshe*, YD 174:4).

Heart and Liver Transplants

The central issue involved in the context of heart and liver transplants is determination of the moment of death. Today, both the heart and the liver can only be transplanted if the donor's circulatory system is still functional. From the moment the heart stops beating, the blood stops circulating and it is no longer possible to transplant that heart. Thus, in order to successfully transplant a heart, the state of death must be determined prior to the cessation of heartbeat in the donor's body. The question then arises as to whether a person suffering from irreversible brain damage or from actual brain death, but whose heart continues to beat, is considered halakhically alive or dead. Accordingly, the question of whether heart or liver transplants can be permitted touches on the question of determination of the moment of death according to the *halakhah*. In any event, the life of a terminally ill or dying patient cannot be artificially prolonged solely to enable use of his organs for transplanting purposes, because one life may not be set aside to ensure another life (*ein doḥin nefesh mipnei nefesh*), and the life of the dying person may not be set aside for the sake of the healthy person's life (Resp. Iggerot Moshe; *Minḥat Yitzḥak*).

According to certain authorities, it is absolutely forbidden to remove an organ from a person defined as brain dead (Resp. *Ẓiẓ Eli'ezer*, vol. 10, nos. 25, 85, and 86; *Iggerot Moshe*, YD 2:174), while others permit it (Israeli Chief Rabbinate; see *Teḥumin*, 7 (1986), 187–92).

Kidney Transplants

A kidney transplant is performed, inter alia, by a healthy person donating one of his kidneys to another person whose kidneys are non-functional. The question that arises here is whether the donor is permitted to place himself in danger in order to save another. Since, as stated, the donation is from a living person, an additional question sometimes arises – whether a kidney may be taken from a person who is unable to express his consent, such as a child or a mentally incompetent individual and, if so, who is entitled to consent on his behalf?

An important principle in Jewish law is that "whoever could have rescued, but failed to do so, transgresses the commandment, 'Do not stand idly by the blood of your fellow'" (Lev. 19:16; see Sanh. 73a; Yad, Roẓe'aḥ u-Shemirat ha-Nefesh 1:14–16; Tur, ḤM 426). Maimonides stated that this prohibition is "one of the most severe, because whoever destroys one single soul… is regarded as if he had destroyed the entire world, and whoever preserves a single soul…is regarded as having preserved the entire world" (Yad, *ibid.*; regarding the halakhic duty to save life in a similar context, see the comments of Justice Beiski, Cr. App. 527/85 *Kurtam v. State of Israel*, 40 (3) PD 673, at 696–97).

When there is no danger to the rescuer, his obligation is absolute. The difficult question is: To what extent is a person required, or perhaps, allowed, to endanger his own life to save another's? This question has troubled the halakhic authorities.

Some hold that a person must expose himself to a possible danger, when necessary to rescue his fellow from a danger that is certain (*Beit Yosef* to Tur, ḤM 426); but many disagree (*Sema*, to Sh. Ar., ḤM 426, par. 2). A recent halakhic authority aptly summarized the law as follows: "It all depends on the circumstances. One should weigh the situation carefully and not be overly self-protective ... Whoever saves a single person is regarded as if he saved an entire world" (*Arukh ha-Shulḥan*, ḤM 426:4. For sources discussing this difference of opinion, see: R. Ovadiah Yosef, "*Teshuvah be-Heter Hashtalat Kilyah*," in: *Dinei Israel*, 7 (1976), 25–43; idem, "*Be-Din Terumat Kilyah*," in: *Halakhah u-Refu'ah*, 3:61–63; idem, Resp. *Yeḥaveh Da'at*, vol. 3, no. 84).

The removal of an organ from a person's body in order to save another person's life is discussed by the halakhic authorities in the context of danger to the donor. But this discussion entails a further inquiry: Is there any basis at all for obligating a person to donate an organ to save someone else? The following answer was given by the outstanding halakhic authority, David ibn Zimra (Radbaz), a 16th-century rabbi of Egypt and Israel, against the tragic-heroic background of the Diaspora, and the government's treatment of its Jewish minority (Resp. Radbaz, vol. 3, no. 1052): "You have asked me... [what should one do] if the government says to a Jew: 'Allow us to sever one of your limbs, which will not cause your death, or we will kill your fellow Jew!'"

Radbaz answered that, even if it is certain that the amputation is not life-threatening, there is no obligation to allow it. One is *permitted* to allow the amputation, and it would be an act of great piety to do so. Radbaz's summary is instructive: "and furthermore, it is written 'Her ways are pleasant ways' (Prov 3:17). [This means that] the laws of our Torah must accord with reason and logic. How then can we suggest that a person should allow his eye to be blinded or his arm or leg amputated in order that someone should not be killed? Therefore, I do not see such an act as a legal obligation, but as one of pious behavior. Happy is the lot of anyone who can bring himself to do such a thing. [But] if there is any possible danger to his life, he would be a pious fool, because his doubt has priority over the certainty of his fellow." (Regarding the principle of "Her ways are pleasant ways" in the determination of *halakhah*, see: Menachem Elon, *Ha-Mishpat ha-Ivri* (1988), 3:323ff.; idem, *Mafte'aḥ ha-She'elot ve-ha-Teshuvot shel Ḥakhmei Sefarad u-Ẓefon Afrikah, Mafte'aḥ ha-Mekorot* (vol. 1, 1981), Introduction, p. 25.)

The removal of a person's organ in order to save his fellow, even if not involving danger to the donor, cannot be compelled, because it violates the principle that the ways of the Torah are pleasant, and "the laws of our Torah must accord with reason and logic." Based on this, it is inconceivable that a person could be compelled to donate an organ from his body to save another person, although such behavior would be considered an act of piety, on a voluntary basis, and it is desirable that a person do so, beyond the letter of the law (see also Resp. Radbaz, vol. 5 of *Leshonot ha-Rambam*, no. 212 (1682), and the attempt to reconcile these two responsa, which goes beyond the scope of this article).

This responsum of Radbaz is one of the central texts in the discussion among contemporary halakhic authorities regarding a kidney donation for transplantation in the body of another person. The issues considered include that of potential risk to the donor, whether an individual may wound himself, and similar halakhic questions. Opinions differ. Some forbid kidney donation (Resp. *Ẓiẓ Eli'ezer*, vol. 9, no. 45; vol 10, nos. 25, 7, 28; and cf. Weiss, Resp. *Minḥat Yiẓḥak*, vol. 6, no. 103), but most authorities hold that, although one is not obligated to donate, it is an act of great piety when there is no risk to the donor (M. Feinstein, Resp. *Iggerot Moshe*, YD, vol. 2, no. 174:4; responsum of R. Solomon Zalman Auerbach, quoted in *Nishmat Avraham*, YD 157:4, at 66–67 (1985); responsa of R. Ovadiah Yosef, sources cited above; Rabbi H.D. Halevi, in: *Assia*, 4 (1983), 251–59; Rabbi Y. Silberstein, in: *Halakhah ve-Refu'ah*, 4 (1985), 156–57; Rabbi S. Dikhovsky, *Ne'ot Desheh*, 2:154–155). In our generation those who ruled that it was forbidden for a living person to donate a kidney claimed that it may be dangerous, and it is forbidden to a person to put himself in a state of danger (*Ẓiẓ Eli'ezer;* Resp. *Minḥat Yiẓḥak*). There were those who permitted a living person to donate his kidney, regarding it as an act of piety, but there is no obligation to do so (Resp. *Iggerot Moshe*, YD, vol. 2, no. 174:4). And among those who permit it there were those who ruled that the donation of a kidney from a living person is not only permitted, but it constitutes a *mitzvah*, and failure to fulfill it violates the prohibition of "Do not stand idly by the blood of your fellow," because the risk is minimal and the chance of the remaining kidney being damaged in the future is sufficiently remote so as not to be regarded as even being remotely dangerous (see Rabbi Ovadiah Yosef, in: *Dinei Yisrael*, 7 (1976), 25–43; Resp. *Yeḥaveh Da'at*, vol. 3, no. 84).

Legally Incompetent Person

In certain cases the most appropriate donor in terms of tissue classification is a legally incompetent person. There is no halakhic permission for the removal of a kidney from a legally incompetent person for the purpose of a transplant. This is the case when dealing with one who is mentally incompetent. This prohibition applies unless it is clear that the legally incompetent person derives clear benefit from the donation, and it is performed exclusively for his benefit, and provided that there are no other means of ensuring that benefit (Justice Elon, LCA 184/87, 698/86 *Anon. v. Anon.* 42 (2) PD 661. See also: Rabbi M. Meiselman, *Halakhah ve-Refu'ah*, 2 (1981), 114, who wrote that if the majority of sons or brothers donate kidneys to their relatives, there is a presumption based on common sense that the legally incompetent person would also have given his consent. Justice Elon rejected this view).

Regarding blood and bone marrow donations, it was ruled that these are permitted since they do not involve any danger, and the material regenerates. It is therefore a *mitzvah* for members of a family to volunteer to do so when required in order to save a life, and in such cases lenient rulings are given even with respect to the legally incompetent person (*Nishmat Avraham*, YD 349:3). If the donor refuses, according to some authorities he cannot be compelled, the donation being considered as an act of piety, while according to other authorities, he can be compelled (Resp. *Shevet Halevi*, vol. 5, no. 219).

In the famous case of *Anon. v. Anon.* (LCA 184/87, 698/86 *Anon. v. Anon.* 42 (2) PD 661), Justice Elon discussed the issue of whether it is permitted to remove the kidney from a mentally disabled adult to be transplanted in his father-guardian's body and, if so, who has the authority to grant such permission, and under what conditions and circumstances. In keeping with his judicial practice, Justice Elon relied on precedents from Jewish law (as shown above) and on the legal sources and practices of other democratic states, attempting to synthesize between them. Justice Elon concluded his judgment in this case as follows (*ibid.*, 689–90):

> The general rule is that the sole criterion for allowing the removal of a kidney from the protected person's body for transplantation is whether the removal benefits the *protected* person. The court must weigh up and balance, in accordance with the conditions detailed above, the extent of the benefit to be gained by the protected person as a result of the transplant into the donee's body, against the damage that may be caused to him by the removal of the kidney and the fact that he will be left with only one kidney. The balancing process must be based on the specific circumstances of the protected person, in his current condition, as it may be in each particular case that comes before the court. The court will allow the transplant only if the result of this balancing definitively establishes that the transplant will clearly and substantially benefit the protected person […].
>
> How can the court perform this balancing? One can point to a number of tests, which are not exclusive, but will be applicable in most situations.
>
> (A) *Factors in Assessing the Benefit to the Protected Person*
>
> 1. The extent of the protected person's dependence on the support of the donee;
>
> 2. The existence of alternatives to assure the support and necessary care of the protected person at a level comparable to that which he would receive as a result of donating the kidney. These include other possible donors, whether dialysis is a sufficient remedy, and whether there are sources of support, without the donee;
>
> 3. The likelihood – both relative to the alternatives and absolutely – that the transplant will be successful and, if so, the extent to which it will increase the donee's life expectancy, and the significance of that increase for supporting the protected person;
>
> 4. The life expectancy of the protected person and the number of years during which he will need support and, in particular cases, his interest in helping his family members or in avoiding guilt feelings, when this interest is clearly proved. This interest must exist at the time of the transplant, if only to a limited extent, and must be expected to increase progressively.
>
> (B) *Factors in Assessing Harm to the Protected Person*
>
> 1. Physical damage and side effects
>
> (a) due to the surgery;
>
> (b) due to being left with one kidney.
>
> 2. Mental damage to the protected donor
>
> (a) as a result of the surgery and hospitalization;
>
> (b) as a result of the removal of the kidney without his understanding or consent.
>
> 3. Limitation on his future actions as a result of being left with one kidney, taking into account his situation as a mentally disabled individual, both from the point of view of protecting his health and considering the fact that he will not be preferred for dialysis or transplant should he ever need it.

In light of the circumstances of the particular case, the Supreme Court ruled against the transplanting of the kidney of the mentally disabled son into his father. Justice Elon concluded his opinion with the following observations (*ibid.*, 700–1):

> The question before us is difficult and painful. We have a father, devoted to his son, who removed him from an institution and cared for him with love and dedication. We have no doubt that the father's request for the kidney was made because he was told that his son would not be hurt and because he was convinced that it was in the son's best interest that his father enjoy a long life and continue to care for him. But we, as a court, are instructed, by law and morality, to look at the total picture in this situation. We must keep in mind that at issue is the invasion of a person's body and the removal of one of his vital organs – an organ which does not regenerate and for which there is no substitute. Moreover, the donor does not understand what is happening to him and what is being taken from him. How disingenuous and possibly even cynical it is to use the term "donation" to describe the taking of a kidney under these circumstances.
>
> Scholars and thinkers have discussed the social, familial, and psychological pressures operating when an individual needs to decide whether or not to donate a kidney to a family member. Indeed, even when referring to a totally healthy person, it is doubtful that the proper term is "donation," since a donation is essentially linked to the idea of "if his heart so moves him" (Exodus 25:2). A fortiori, there is certainly doubt in our case, under the aforementioned circumstances. Not only is there no donation here made out of generosity, but this is a prime example of coercion. This is a serious matter that could severely damage the cultural and spiritual fabric of our society. As a court, we are the "father" of the legal incompetents, of those who do not understand and cannot consent or decide on their own, and we must protect those unfortunates to maintain their dignity as human beings. As such, we are not superior to the father before us, who sired the child and cared for him his whole life. We would never think that. But we are appointed by law to weigh all the considerations – legal, halakhic, and ethical – that arise in these situations, and in this respect, and only in this, do we take precedence over the father. By examining all the considerations and balancing them, we have concluded that we should not allow the removal of the kidney from the son for the father. We again urge that all efforts be made to obtain a transplant for the father from a cadaver so that he can continue caring for his son.

Trafficking in Organs

Commerce and organ donation are contradictory concepts; "doing business" with human organs conflicts with fundamental spiritual and ethical values. Recently, learned scholars, halakhists, philosophers, and ethicists have discussed the reasons for prohibiting the sale of human organs. For example, it is customary to pay for the donation of blood to a blood bank, because the body replenishes the blood, and the donation does not endanger the donor. The same is true for donations of bone marrow. But giving up a kidney in exchange for money raises grave doubts and difficulties. The essential question here is: Where will the "slippery slope" end? Societal, psychological, and economic pressures may bring us to an "organ market" of "spare parts," and to a situation where the bodies of the poor become "supply depots" for the rich. The actuality is that the rich will not sell any of their bodily organs but the poor – even when they have no relationship with the donee – are likely to sell their organs to rescue themselves from poverty and need. This is an ominous prospect from the perspective of human dignity and value. Therefore, as a general rule, we should avoid setting foot on this slippery slope, and any allegedly exceptional circumstances should be evaluated case by case and with great care (Elon, *ibid.*).

In the year 2003 Knesset Member Zahava Gal-On presented a draft bill to prevent trafficking in organs, known as the "Bill to Outlaw Trafficking in Organs."

THE LEGAL POSITION IN ISRAEL. The Anatomy and Pathology Law, 5713 – 1953 defines the ways in which organs may be removed from a cadaver for transplant purposes:

> 6. Anatomical-pathological operations
>
> (a) A physician may operate on a body in order to ascertain the cause of death or to use a part thereof for the curative treatment of a person if it has been confirmed by a certificate signed by three physicians authorized on that behalf in accordance with the regulations that the operation serves one of the said purposes.
>
> (b) (1) The body of a deceased person shall not be dissected before the expiration of five hours after notice of the death is given to a relative. Sabbaths and Jewish holidays or, in the case of a non-Jewish relative, the Sabbaths and holidays of his community, shall not be included in the count of the said five hours.
>
> (2) Notwithstanding the provisions of paragraph (1), where the dissection is required in order to use a part of the body for the curative treatment of a person, reasonable notice to such effect shall be given to a relative before the dissection.
>
> (c) (1) Where the need to use a part of the body of a deceased person to save a person's life becomes apparent, the period referred to in subsection (b) shall be replaced by the period up to the latest time at which it is possible to remove the part from the body for use as aforesaid. If notice under subsection (b) cannot be given by the said time, owing to the impossibility of locating a relative, a dissection under this subsection may be performed provided that a reasonable attempt to give notice has been made.
>
> (2) Without prejudice to the generality of the provisions of paragraph (1), the use of the cornea of a deceased person for a transplant to save a person from blindness, the use of a part of the body of a deceased person to prevent a defect of vision or hearing, and the use of a kidney or of skin tissues of a deceased person for a transplant to save a person's life are uses of parts of a body for the saving of a life.
>
> 6A. Restrictions
>
> (a) Where a deceased person has left any relatives, his body shall not be dissected under section 6 – except under circumstances referred to in section 6(c) – unless the following two requirements are also met:
>
> (1) the spouse or, in the absence of a spouse, the children or, in the absence of children, the parents or, in the absence of parents, a brother or sister of the deceased has or have consented;
>
> (2) no relative of the same degree of relationship as a consenting relative, and no relative of the degree which, in the circumstances of the case, is next in the order of degrees appearing in paragraph (1), have objected in writing.
>
> (b) Where the person in his lifetime objected in writing to his body being dissected, then, notwithstanding the provisions of section 6 or any consent of a relative under subsection (a), the dissection shall not be performed.
>
> (c) Where the person consented to his body being dissected, it may be dissected notwithstanding any objection by a relative.
>
> (d) In the circumstances referred to in section 6(c), a body may be dissected unless the person in his lifetime objected in writing to his body being dissected or unless his spouse or one of his parents or children objects thereto in writing.
>
> (e) Where the person has left no relatives, his body shall not be dissected unless he consented thereto in his lifetime.
>
> (f) The provisions of this section shall be in addition to those of section 6.

The law provides (§6D), that "the provisions of section 6A shall not apply in wartime or at the time of a large scale terrorist act or an accident or disaster causing numerous casualties." Furthermore, Section 6A established a penalty of three years' imprisonment for a person transgressing the provisions of the law.

An additional aspect of organ transplants from a dead body dealt with in Israeli case law is the determination of the moment of death. The question of the moment of death was dealt with by the Israeli courts in the context of criminal law. In one of the cases the court was required to determine responsibility for the death of a person who was shot in the head, mortally wounded, and rushed to hospital, where the doctors succeeded in saving his life by connecting him up to the life-support machines. With his family's consent, the victim was subsequently disconnected from these devices. The question arises: Who was responsible for his death – the gunman or the doctor? Did the victim's disconnection from the life-support system sever the causal connection between the victim's death and the murderer's act?

Another case in which the same question arose was the *Belker* case. In 1986 an indictment was submitted against Yehezkel Belker for attacking his wife, throwing her out of the window of their fourth floor apartment, and causing her mortal injury. The woman was rushed to hospital, and when efforts to save her had all failed, her death was established on the basis of brain death. The deceased remained connected to the life-support machines until her family living abroad consented to the donation of her organs. When her husband was indicted for murder, he claimed that the woman's death was not the result of his attack, but rather, was the direct result of her being disconnected from the respiratory machine by the medical staff. Ruling on this claim required the court to address the question of the moment of death, and to decide as to whether the medical determination of brain death should also be regarded as a legal determination. The District Court ruled that brain death is death for all intents and purposes, on which basis it convicted him of murder. The husband appealed to the Supreme Court (Cr. A. 341/82) 42 (1) *Nathan b. Yehezkel Belker v. State of Israel* PD 1) which ruled (per Justice Beiski) that, in accordance with the accepted rules for determination of death (as established by the Harvard Committee), and provided that the determination of death was made by an independent medical team not belonging to the team performing the transplant and/or the team actually treating the patient, a determination of brain death is considered as death for all intents and purposes. In such a case a death certificate may be issued and medical treatment terminated. Such a determination of death is in turn valid for all other legal or social purposes, including an indictment for murder. The Court recommended that the issue of determination of death be regulated by legislation. In this context, Justice Strasbourg-Cohen's comments bear mention. She ruled that, even had the trial court adopted the previous criterion of cardiac death, the doctor's action in disconnecting the life-support machines would not have severed the causal connection between the act of the accused and the death of the deceased. Absent the actions of the accused, the final result would not have occurred, and had the doctors not interfered, the death would have occurred immediately following the attack.

The Ministry of Health issued a Director-General circular, updated several times, stipulating provisions for the determination of brain death. The circular was published in 1996 (Director-General Circular 10/96; the most recent as of 2005), the first section of which cites portions of the Supreme Court judgment with respect to the validity of brain death determination. The second section provides guidelines for the categories of examinations to be conducted for diagnosing death. The circular stipulates a series of preconditions, necessary conditions, and auxiliary tests for determining brain death.

ARTIFICIAL INSEMINATION

Artificial insemination is the medical procedure whereby sperm is injected into the vagina or womb of the woman without the act of sexual intercourse. A distinction is made between three categories of artificial insemination, in accordance with the source of the sperm: (1) husband insemination – where the husband contributes the sperm; (2) donor insemination – where a man who is not the wife's husband is the donor or where the sperm is taken from a sperm bank; and (3) mixed insemination, using a mixture of the husband's sperm with that of a donor. The processes of fertilization in the woman's womb, pregnancy, and birth, continue naturally after the artificial insemination, as in any normal impregnation. Artificial insemination can only take place under conditions in which there is no defect in the woman's fertility, either anatomically or physiologically (see below: fertilization outside the body – *In Vitro* Fertilization). Rabbi Eliezer Waldenberg begins his lengthy responsum on this topic with the following comments:

> Physicians have recently invented a new method by which a woman can become pregnant via artificial means, without sexual intercourse. Sperm is obtained from a donor, and when a woman desires to become pregnant without intercourse she is inseminated artificially, becomes pregnant, and gives birth. This method is most often used when a married couple is unable to have children due to an impediment on the part of the husband. While they do not wish to get divorced, the wife desires to have a child. In these circumstances, some physicians perform artificial insemination so that the wife may become pregnant and give birth. The question asked is whether such a procedure is permissible under Jewish law, and what is the status of the resulting child.

In considering the procedure of artificial insemination, modern halakhists refer to aggadic precedents indicating that the talmudic and mishnaic Sages were aware of the possibilities of impregnation other than by way of natural means. Inter alia they cite the *aggadah* of the birth of Ben-Sira from Jeremiah's daughter, who conceived from her father's seed that remained in the bath in which she bathed (see: *Ḥelkat Meḥokek*, EH 1:8; *Mishneh la-Melekh* on Yad, Ishut 15:4; Hidda, *Birkei Yosef* (vol. 2, 1989), EH 1:14; Rabbi D. Bardugo, Resp. *Mishpatim Yesharim* (1891), vol. 1, no. 396).

Moral and Halakhic Considerations

We already mentioned above that issues of *halakhah* and medicine generally pose a plethora of moral and halakhic questions, particularly where they involve technological innovations. For this reason, halakhic discussion of these issues is not confined to conceptual issues alone, but also encompass policy considerations. One such consideration relates to the uncertainty surrounding the issue of the lineage (*yiḥus*), of the child born as a result of using donor sperm. This uncertainty conflicts with the basic halakhic aspiration for certainty in matters of lineage, i.e., certainty regarding the family they belong to (see Rashi, Yevamot 42a, s.v. *u-le-zarakha aḥarekha*). There are also several other general policy issues, transcending the problematics of lineage. The morally-based questions and fears that have typified the dialogue on these questions throughout the world are of equal concern to modern halakhists. They too are apprehensive about the danger of crossing of traditional borders, coming in the wake of scientific progress. For example, it has been stated that bringing children into the world should be the result of spousal relations involving marital love and intimacy, and not of mechanical laboratory techniques (see P. Shiffman, *Dinei Mishpaḥah be-Yisra'el*, 2 (1989), 105; E. Jacobovitz, *Ha-Refu'ah ve-ha-Yahadut* (1966), 235). In this context, the following comments of Rabbi E. Waldenberg are germane:

> And especially when we have already read that the final result of test-tube fertilization is that sooner or later it will lead to the creation of a test-tube baby, i.e., the entire pregnancy will take place and terminate outside the woman's body, in the test tube itself, by way of simulating the conditions inside the womb; and then, by means of an astonishing procedure known as cloning, human beings will be produced by the implantation or transpondation of the nucleus from a mature cell into an enucleated human egg, after which the reproductive process of the regular cell operates and continues to develop into a embryo, and this is the name that they give to a complete biological creation, in accordance with certain previously determined parameters to reproduce the specific characteristics desired by its creators. And if this happens – can such infants be called "offspring," with full lineage to their progenitors who wish them to be considered their genetic offspring? For in addition to the abnormal form of production and bringing children into the world, it also causes the destruction and loss of the human image, and chaos will reign with respect to the whole field of procreation, which will become a laboratory devoid of any humaneness. This problem has already been predicted by scientists, who have expressed their deep anxiety over the anticipated scenarios – a new generation will emerge and all those witnessing it will exclaim "new ones have come, who were unimagined by their forefathers, [so that we] see creatures of this kind, almost without free choice, and human form."

ARTIFICIAL HUSBAND INSEMINATION. Various *posekim* take the view that the husband is forbidden to emit semen for the purpose of inseminating his wife, due to the prohibition of "destruction of seed," because at the time of masturbating for the purpose of ejaculating the semen, its emission is in vain, and the fact that the physician subsequently uses the semen for fertilizing the woman is to no avail. Furthermore, there is a possibility that the woman will not be fertilized by that semen, and as a result the semen will retroactively transpire to have been emitted in vein. However, the predominant halakhic opinion is that the procedure does not involve "destruction of seed" when emitted by the husband for purposes of fertilization, because the procedure is a remedial one, for purposes of a *mitzvah*, and it does not matter whether the end is attained by natural means or otherwise. At the same time, a number of limitations were imposed: the permission is limited to parties who have been childless for a period of ten years, and who in the absence of fertilization are liable to divorce. Two physicians must decide that the procedure is effective, i.e., that the woman does not suffer from any fertility problem and that there is a reasonable chance that the husband's sperm will succeed in impregnating the wife; the doctors must take special care not to exchange the husband's sperm for another person's sperm. In the event that fertilization is prevented due to early ovulation of the woman, as a result of which she is unable to purify herself from her *niddah* status at the appropriate time to allow fertilization by natural means, there are opinions that permit husband artificial insemination. The *posekim* also debated the question of whether the husband fulfills the commandment of procreation in the case of artificial insemination. The accepted view is that the husband does so, because the commandment is not dependent on the act of intercourse, but rather on the result of the birth of a live fetus.

NON-JEWISH DONOR INSEMINATION. A different set of problems arises in Jewish law regarding artificial insemination from a donor other than the husband. The central question is whether artificial insemination is permitted at all with the sperm of a man other than the husband, and if not, are there any circumstances in which it is permitted, and subject to what limitations. Is the woman thereafter permitted or forbidden to her husband, as in the case of an adulterous wife, and what is the lineage and the status of the child?

Non-Jewish Donor. While all *posekim* agree that *de jure* there should be no insemination even from a non-Jewish donor, there are nevertheless those who permit it in the case of sad, despairing parents who yearn for a child. A child born under these circumstances is a Jew for all intents and purposes.

JEWISH DONOR INSEMINATION. There is broad halakhic consensus that artificial insemination of a woman from the sperm of a Jewish donor is prohibited. A variety of reasons are given for this prohibition: some moralistic, based on the classic model of the family in the Jewish philosophy, and others halakhic, related to the uncertainty of the identity of the donor-father. At the same time, the halakhists dispute whether a married woman impregnated by a Jewish donor is prohibited to her husband. One view is that a woman artificially impregnated by semen of a donor is not prohibited to her husband, because there was no act of forbidden intercourse involved, and Torah law only forbids a woman to her husband and to her lover if an act of forbidden sexual relations was involved. Among the supporters of this view were the Sephardi chief rabbi, Rabbi Ouziel (Resp. *Mishpetei Uziel*, EH 19); Rabbi M. Feinstein (Resp. *Iggerot Moshe*, EH, nos. 10, 11, 71); Rabbi Y. Breisch (Resp. *Ḥelkat Ya'akov*, vol. 1, no. 24); Rabbi E.Y. Waldenberg (Resp. *Ẓiẓ Eli'ezer*, vol. 3, no. 24); Rabbi Y.Y. Weinberg (Resp. *Seridei Esh*, 6), and other leading *aḥaronim*. The position prohibiting the wife to her husband is based on the interpretation of the biblical verse, "you shall not lie carnally with your neighbor's wife," as extending to any implantation of semen in the woman's womb. Among the proponents of this view are R. Jonathan Eybeschutz (*Benei Ahuvah*, Ishut, 15); Rabbi J.L. Zirelson (Resp. *Ma'arkhei Lev*, 73); and the rabbi of Satmar, R. Yoel Teitelbaum ("*Teshuva bi-devar Hazra'ah Melakhutit be-Zera Ish Aḥer*," in: *Ha-Ma'or*, 16:9–10 (Sept.–Oct. 1964), and others.

The *posekim* also disputed the question as to whether the child was regarded as the child of the sperm donor, in which case he would be prohibited against marrying members of the sperm donor's family, he would be the donor's heir, and the donor would be regarded as having fulfilled the commandment of procreation. Some ruled that the child would be regarded as his real son, while others argued that this ruling only applied for purposes of stringency and not for leniency, i.e., that the child was forbidden from marrying, for example, the daughter of the sperm donor, but does not inherit him. The *posekim* were divided over whether, in the event of his marrying the daughter of the donor, his offspring would in turn be considered a *mamzer.*

ANONYMOUS DONOR. Where the donor's identity is unknown – e.g., when taken from a sperm bank – it has been suggested that, even according to the view that the offspring of artificial insemination is not a *mamzer,* in such a case he would be classified as a *shetuki* ("undisclosed"); see: **Mamzer/shetuki*). Some *posekim* wrote that, in the case where the sperm comes from outside of Israel, where there is a non-Jewish majority, it may be presumed that the sperm belongs to a non-Jew and therefore the offspring is legitimate.

Where the sperm is mixed with that of the husband, the *posekim* wrote that it should be regarded as if it was exclusively the outside donor's sperm, because the husband's sperm is inactive and the mixture is intended to placate the husband psychologically. In such a case, the husband is also regarded as having transgressed the prohibition of "destruction of seed."

Artificial Insemination in Israeli Law

The Israeli legislator enacted the Public Health (Sperm Bank) Regulations, 5739 – 1979, under which "No person shall manage a sperm bank, or be engaged therein, unless that sperm bank was recognized by the director, and in accordance with the conditions of recognition. The director shall not recognize a sperm bank unless it is managed in a hospital and as a part thereof. For purposes of the regulation, "manager" has the same definition as in section 1 of the Public Health Regulations, *viz.* the director general of the Ministry of Health, or person empowered by the director to enact these regulations." Following Supreme Court consideration of the matter, a clause limiting the rights of unmarried women to receive treatment for *in vitro* insemination treatment was repealed, so that today, subject to certain conditions, an unmarried woman is entitled to receive a sperm donation.

ARTIFICIAL INSEMINATION IN HALAKHIC CASE LAW. The first decision on this subject was given by the Jerusalem Rabbinical Court on November 6, 1975, and published by the *av bet din*, Rabbi Eliezer Waldenberg (presiding with Rabbis Y. Cohen and Y. Attiah) in his book *Ẓiẓ Eli'ezer,* vol. 3, no. 97. The litigants in the regional rabbinical court were a childless couple. Without her husband's knowledge, the wife had been treated by a doctor who performed an artificial insemination procedure from a sperm bank. The treatment led to positive results, and the woman became pregnant from foreign donor sperm. Upon becoming aware of this, the husband filed for divorce. The woman conceded the truth of his claims, but claimed in her defense that a medical examination had confirmed that the husband was sterile, and unable to father a child. She had requested that her husband agree to adoption, but had received a negative answer. Wanting a child of her own, she had taken a path that enabled her to become pregnant. The Bet Din was confronted with the legal question as to whether the woman's consent to be artificially inseminated from donor sperm without her husband's knowledge provided grounds for divorce, even though it had not yet ruled on the question of whether the wife was forbidden to her husband, having become impregnated in that manner. Another question to be decided was the legal import of the husband's refusal to adopt, against the background of his infertility. The Bet Din Court accepted the husband's claim, compelled the wife to receive a *get*, and further ruled that the woman had forfeited her *kettubah*. Following is an excerpt from the judgment:

> In consenting to the sperm of another man to be injected into her, the woman betrayed both her husband and God, and she is therefore obligated to receive a *get* from her husband. She cannot stipulate any financial conditions prior to the giving of the *get*, nor request that her husband transfer the apartment currently under both of their names into her name alone.

In explaining the reasons for its decision, the head of the Rabbinical Court (*av bet din*), presented a comprehensive excursus on the issue of artificial insemination and its halakhic ramifications, concluding that there could be no greater abomination. Notwithstanding the opinion that the wife was not forbidden to her husband when she resorted to this method with her husband's consent, it was not disputed that the wife was obliged to receive a *get* when the treatment and the pregnancy were without his knowledge. The upshot of this ruling was that the wife had no recourse to the defense plea that her husband had refused her request to adopt despite his proven infertility. Because: "if she required a solution to the problem then she had the opportunity of coming to the Rabbinical Court and making that claim, and to request that her husband be compelled to give her a *get pitturin*, and she would have found an attentive ear." The Rabbinical Court thus took a positive view of the defendant's desire for a child of her own, to the extent of being willing to compel her husband to divorce her, had she so requested. But, "there is a vast chasm between this, and the commission of an act 'that undermines the very foundations of the family unit between her and her husband, and which the halakhic authorities had unanimously condemned.'" According to the Bet Din the wife's yearning for children did not ameliorate the gravity of her action, which was all the more severe in that she had concealed it from her husband. Regarding that point, it added the following remarks in its decision:

> At all events, should the husband desire to give her a *get* for that reason – namely, that she had undergone artificial insemination without his knowledge, even though she had not become pregnant thereby – the wife should be compelled to receive a *get pitturin*, both because of the halakhic dispute in this matter as stated, and furthermore, because the actual commission of this abomination in her body without her husband's knowledge places her in the category of a woman who has transgressed Mosaic law and Jewish practice, and the law applying to her should therefore be the same... Moreover, there is also a view that the act itself makes her prohibited to her husband, and the husband can therefore claim, "I choose to abide by that opinion," and he cannot be forced to give a *kettubah*.

The last (as of 2005) Rabbinical Court decision on the matter was also given in the Regional Rabbinical Court of Haifa, on 6th Av, 5737 – 1977. The parties were a husband and wife with a four-year-old mentally retarded child, diagnosed as having a particularly low intelligence level. The child was born following the woman undergoing artificial insemination from donor sperm. The husband consented to this treatment due to the fact, not denied by the parties, that he was unable to fertilize the wife. Both parties petitioned the Bet Din. The wife requested the Bet Din to order the husband to pay maintenance for herself and the child, asking for a high sum, in accordance with the rule *olah imo* (lit., "she goes up with him") – i.e. that her maintenance increases by reason of his high earnings, and by reason of the treatment of the retarded child who required special equipment. The husband filed for a *get,* claiming that his wife's act was a ground for divorce, because the artificial insemination from the sperm of a donor was tantamount to an act of sexual license, making the wife forbidden to her husband. As such, there were grounds for exempting him from her maintenance, and he was therefore also exempt from the obligation of child support. The Bet Din was requested to rule on the question of whether the defendant could be compelled to pay child support when it was not disputed that the plaintiff's (wife) child was not the defendant's (father) child. The question arose: What is the legal significance of the defendant's consent to this medical procedure? The Bet Din in the first instance dismissed the husband's divorce suit, obligating him to pay maintenance for the wife and child support for the child, whose treatment necessitated huge expenses. Explaining the reasons for its decision, the Bet Din expressed its opinion:

> …in support of the opinion that denies even a shadow of illicit sex in the act of artificial insemination, which might have provided a ground for divorce or even the forfeiture of maintenance. And as the foremost decisors of our generation have ruled […] the exemption from maintenance applies – when the insemination was performed in defiance of the husband's will and without his being aware of it. From this it may be inferred quite simply that, if it was done with his consent, and he was aware of it – he is liable to support the child born from that insemination.

Regarding the wife's claim for maintenance, the Bet Din added another reason:

> Since he agreed to this procedure, he assumes all of the obligations arising therefrom, according to the law of a guarantor, and there is no doubt that under these circumstances expression is given to all of the conditions that would compel a guarantor (even though it could be claimed that he assumed an undertaking for normal offspring, and that his undertaking was limited to those circumstances, but since he did not limit his undertaking he should also be liable for irregular expenses which are occasioned by the offspring).

Does this decision support the conclusion that, in the Bet Din's opinion, artificial insemination from a donor with the husband's consent does not constitute illicit sexual relations which would prohibit the wife to her husband and obligate her to receive a *get*? This would seem to be the reasonable conclusion, subject to some degree of reservation based on the fact that the decision does not indicate whether the Bet Din in principle negates the very act of artificial insemination, or whether under the special circumstances of the case, in which the husband consented to the treatment, it is removed from the category of illicit sexual relations or, in the words of the Bet Din "denies even a shadow of illicit sex in the act of artificial insemination." At all events, in our opinion, the Bet Din does not view the aforementioned act as constituting grounds for divorce, because the wife was not prohibited to her husband as is a woman who is unfaithful to the husband while married to him. However, since the Bet Din did not see how it could oblige the defendant to support a child who was not his own, based on the law of child support, it was forced to obligate him by force of the law of a guarantor. It therefore emerges that the husband's consent has practical significance with respect to maintenance. In other words, his consent is tantamount to an implicit assumption of liability for all of the financial consequences of the act of insemination.

An interesting comparison may be drawn between the aforementioned rulings of the rabbinical courts and the ruling of the Israeli Supreme Court. In the sole decision given to date in a civil court concerning the issue of artificial insemination from the sperm of a donor the husband's consent to the treatment was one of the main foundations. The litigants were a married couple that had remained childless after several years of marriage, due to a defect in the husband's ability to produce functional sperm cells, and a disturbance in the woman's ovulation process. With the husband's consent, the woman underwent artificial insemination, which was successful, and the woman gave birth to a daughter. About one year later disputes erupted between the spouses and, after failing to reconcile their differences, the woman filed a maintenance action against her husband, on behalf of herself and for her daughter. In the course of the trial, the couple was divorced, and the court was thus left to adjudicate the daughter's child support suit against her father. The District Court obligated the father to pay child support, and the father appealed the decision to the Supreme Court (CA *Salma v. Salma*, 448/79, 34 (2) PD 778). President Y. Kahn wrote the judgment, in which he accepted the "additional reason" invoked by the District Court, and which was the basis of the judge's decision to obligate the father to pay child support. He wrote as follows:

> By agreeing to his wife undergoing artificial fertilization, the defendant agreed to the addition of another person to his family… the defendant's consent should be regarded as including an implicit undertaking to support the minor that would be born as a result of the fertilization…When a person agrees to his wife being fertilized by way of artificial fertilization, he agrees and undertakes by implication both to his wife and for the benefit of the child to be born, to support and feed the minor to be born from that fertilization.

Two things may be inferred from this decision: (a) When the husband consents to his wife's fertilization by artificial insemination from the sperm of a donor, he undertakes to bear all of the consequent costs – financial and otherwise – with respect to the child to be born from that act; (2) The husband's undertaking to his wife for child support, which flows from his consent to this form of treatment, is unrelated to the legal connection that existed at the time of the suit, or thereafter, between the child's mother and the defendant.

In a recent ruling handed down by the Israeli Supreme Court (HC 2458/01 *Mishpaḥah Ḥadashah v. Committee for Approving Surrogate Agreements* (not published)) on the topic of *in vitro* fertilization (see below), Justice Englard referred to the position of Jewish law regarding this issue:

> When dealing with a case of a donor to a married woman, importance attaches to the donor's identity [and the] the distinction between a Jewish donor and a non-Jewish donor. According to all opinions, it is halakhically prohibited to use, *de jure*, the sperm of another Jew. In principle, sperm insemination of a Jewish donor who is not the husband of the married woman is regarded as disgraceful and an abomination. See Rabbi E.Y. Waldenberg, Resp. *Ẓiẓ Eli'ezer*, vol. 3, no. 27; Rabbi Y. Breisch, Resp. *Ḥelkat Ya'akov* (1992), EH 12; Rabbi Y.Y. Weinberg, Resp. *Seridei Eish* (1999), vol. 1, no. 79. Halakhically speaking, certain *posekim* take the view that the offspring from donor sperm is a *mamzer* for all intents and purposes. Others rule that he is of doubtful *mamzer* status. There are also those who rule that, in the absence of intimate relations, i.e., without prohibited intercourse, the offspring is categorically not a *mamzer*. For a discussion of the opinions of the first view, see, e.g., Rabbi E.Y. Waldenberg, Resp. *Ẓiẓ Eli'ezer* (1967), vol. 9, no. 51; Resp. *Yaskil Avdi, ibid.* For the second view, see Rabbi S.Z. Auerbach, "*Hazra'ah Melakhutit*," in: *Noam*, 1 (1958), 145, 165. For the third view, see Rabbi Moses Feinstein, Resp. *Iggerot Moshe* (1961), EH, vol. 1, no. 61; Resp. *Ḥelkat Yaakov, ibid.* For additional sources, see Rabbi D.M. Kroizer, "*Hazra'ah Melakhutit*," in: *Noam*, 1 (1958), pp. 111, 119f.
>
> There are authorities who hold that, where the donor is unknown, the offspring is a "*shetuki*" regarding whom there is also a doubt regarding *mamzerut*. See Resp. *Seridei Eish, ibid.*; Resp. *Ḥelkat Ya'akov, ibid.*, notes to EH, 20, n. 11.
>
> Another grave concern regarding the anonymous donor pertains to the possibility of a future marriage of a brother and sister. See Resp. *Iggerot Moshe, ibid.*; Resp. *Seridei Eish*, vol. 1, no. 69; Resp. *Ẓiẓ Eli'ezer* (1951), vol. 3, no. 27.
>
> Regarding a non-Jewish anonymous donor: All of the *posekim* agree that *ex ante* his sperm should not be used, for the act is disgraceful. Nevertheless, in this case there is no halakhic fear of *mamzerut* or marriage of a brother and sister. Consequently, the procedure of artificial insemination was permitted for cases in which the parents are in a state of acute distress and greatly desire a child. For this view, see the aforementioned article Resp. *Iggerot Moshe, ibid.*, and the article cited of Rabbi S.Z. Auerbach. For the view that prohibits this treatment under all circumstances, see: Resp. *Ḥelkat Ya'akov, ibid.*, EH, no. 14; Rabbi Y.Y. Weiss, Resp. *Minḥat Yiẓḥak* (1939), vol. 4, no. 5; cf. Resp. *Seridei Esh* (1966), vol. 3, no. 5. In the case of an unmarried woman, while there is no fear of *mamzerut*, there is still the fear of a sister and brother marrying, and the offspring being a *shetuki*. A compilation of the various problems raised in the letters of the *posekim* appears in A. Steinberg, *Enẓiklopedyah Hilkhatit Refu'it* (1988), entry: *Hazra'ah Melakhutit*, pp. 148–61.

IN VITRO FERTILIZATION (SURROGATE MOTHERHOOD)

In vitro fertilization is the act of fertilizing the woman's eggs outside the woman's body by means of sperm cells and, after fertilization, returning the fertilized embryo to the woman's womb, or freezing the embryo for the purpose of returning it at a later stage. The offspring of that procedure is popularly known as a "test-tube" baby, referring to the initial stage of fertilization in the test-tube. A woman carrying an embryo for another woman, with the intention of giving her the child born to that woman, is called a surrogate or host mother. All of the scientific, halakhic, moral, and legal issues pertaining to husband or donor sperm required for fertilizing an egg in a Petri dish are identical to those arising in the context of artificial insemination (see above Artificial Insemination). This entry discusses those unique aspects of *in vitro* fertilization that do not exist in artificial insemination.

The halakhic discussion in the entry on *in vitro* fertilization is introduced by Prof. Rabbi Abraham Steinberg with the following statement:

> Notwithstanding the immense medical-technological progress in the field of *in vitro* fertilization, as in the field of genetic engineering, none of this contradicts the basic foundations of Judaism, and the belief in the creation of the world and of humankind exclusively by the Almighty. In all these procedures, the creation involves making "something from something," and there is no possibility of creating "something from nothing." ....The Jewish outlook does not accept the conception that demands the preservation of the law of nature, and therefore eschews human and technological interference in natural processes. To the contrary, humankind is a partner to the Almighty in the improvement of the world in all realms.

In Vitro Fertilization Between Husband and Wife

Several halakhic authorities permit *in vitro* fertilization between a husband and wife provided that all precautions are taken to prevent the mixing of the husband's sperm with alien sperm, and provided that the couple have no other possibility of building their family. According to the permitting authorities (see inter alia, *Nishmat Avraham*, EH, 1.e.3) a "test-tube" baby for all intents and purposes continues his parents' lineage, and halakhically this procedure is deemed identical to artificial insemination. Accordingly, those who permit artificial insemination between husband and wife also permit *in vitro* fertilization. However, certain halakhic authorities prohibited this procedure, based on moral considerations: for example, the fear that it would create reproductive-societal havoc, and the fear of mixing up sperm and the consequent defiling of the sanctity and purity of lineage in the Jewish people. There are also those who prohibited it on halakhic grounds, even between a husband and wife. One explanation for the distinction between *in vitro* fertilization and artificial insemination is that in the latter the sperm is injected directly into the woman's womb, so that the procedure does not involve destruction of seed should the procedure be unsuccessful, whereas in the case of *in vitro* fertilization the seed is placed in a Petri dish, so that if the fertilization is unsuccessful, it is considered as seed destruction. A second explanation is that the need for artificial insemination is generally the result of the husband's infertility and according to certain views, the prohibition of destruction of seed does not apply to a sterile male. In *in vitro* fertilization, the problem is generally the woman's, and therefore the prohibition on seed destruction is valid regarding the husband. Those authorities permitting it claim that the prohibition of seed destruction does not apply when performed for the purpose of bringing a child into the world, and that even in natural intercourse some of the sperm is spilt and lost. Therefore, in *in vitro* fertilization, since it is intended to bring a child into the world it is not considered as being a vain emission of sperm.

***In Vitro* Fertilization by Egg Donation**

The very act of *in vitro* fertilization using a donor egg involves several prohibitions, the gravest of which is the fear of social havoc, confusion of lineage, and the possibility of incest between the egg-donor's children. Certain stringent authorities also wrote that the prohibition is not on the act per se, but that it is seen as one that ought to be avoided *ab initio*. In any event, every effort must be made to ascertain the identity of the donor, and to enact whatever regulations are required to avoid any mishaps in this regard.

Where the woman donated the egg, which was subsequently fertilized in a test tube, the fertilized embryo then being implanted in the womb of another woman, the question of the definition of maternity arises. Whom does the *halakhah* view as the child's mother: the biological mother (egg donor) or the host mother, in whose womb the embryo develops?

Some posekim take the view that the genetic mother has the status of mother in terms of *halakhah* (see I. Warhaftig, "*Kevi'at Imahut – be-Shulei ha-Devarim*," in: *Teḥumin*, 5 (1984), 268). Nevertheless, the majority view is that halakhically, the host mother is considered as the mother (see Rabbi Z.N. Goldenberg, "*Yiḥus Imahut be-Hashtalat Ubar be-Reḥem shel Aḥeret*, *ibid.*, 248; *Ziẓ Eli'ezer* (1992), vol. 19, no. 40). Finally, there are some authorities who contend that both women are seen as related to the progeny, specifically for purposes of definition of incestuous relations (see Z. Lev, "*Tinok Mavḥenah – Ma'amad ha-Em ha-Pundeka'it*," in: *Emek Halakhah*, 2 (1989), 163, 169).

The view of most *posekim*, that the surrogate mother is also considered the mother from a halakhic perspective, relies inter alia on an ancient aggadic tradition that this kind of situation occurred between the matriarchs Rachel and Leah in their respective pregnancies with Dinah and Joseph. According to the tradition, in her final pregnancy, Jacob's wife Leah was carrying a son in her womb. At that time Jacob had already fathered ten sons: six from Leah's womb, two from Bilhah, and two from Zilpah. This meant that, had she given birth to the son in her womb, he would have been the 11th son of Jacob (who was predestined to have a total of 12 sons), and Rachel would only have been able to give birth to one son. Leah did not want Rachel to have only one son, which would have reduced her stature to below that of the handmaids, who had two each, so she prayed that she not give birth to the son, so that Rachel would be able to give birth to the two sons who were still to be born. According to one version of the *aggadah*, the embryo in Leah's womb turned into a girl (Ber. 60a), while according to another version, the switch of gender was attained by another method. After praying that she not be the one to give birth to the male child in her womb, the sisters' embryos were switched: the male in Leah's womb going into Rachel's womb, and the female in Rachel's womb to Leah (see *Midrash Sekhel Tov* (ed. Buber), Gen. 30, s.v. *ve-aḥar yaledah*).

***In Vitro* Fertilization in Israeli Legislation**

In 1987 special regulations concerning *in vitro* fertilization were enacted – The National Health (*In Vitro* Fertilization) Law 5727 – 1987. In 1996 the State of Israel enacted the Agreements Relating to the Carrying of Embryos (Approval of the Agreements and Status of Offspring) Law, regulating the subject of surrogacy. The Israel Supreme Court (HC 2458/01 *Mishpaḥah Ḥadasha v. the Approvals Committee for Surrogacy Agreements*) (not yet published), addressed the question of whether these legislative arrangements for carrying embryos, which prima facie do not apply to a woman without a male spouse, are not discriminative. The court did not rule on the matter, referring it back to the Legislature.

The Israeli Supreme Court delivered two long and detailed rulings on the subject of *in vitro* fertilization in general, and specifically, on the right of parenthood (CA 5587/93 *Daniel Nahmani v. Ruthy Nahmani* et al., 50 (4) PD 661). After a number of years of childless marriage, and after Ruthy Nahmani had undergone a total hysterectomy, rendering her unable to become pregnant by natural means, the couple decided to bring a child into the world by way of *in vitro* fertilization. The eggs taken from Ruthy's womb were fertilized by the sperm of her husband, Danny, and frozen in the hospital. The couple contracted with an American institution for the purpose of locating a surrogate mother who would carry their child. However, prior to reaching that stage, Danny left their domestic home, went to live with another woman, created a new family, and fathered a daughter while still legally married to Ruthy, who refused to accept a divorce. Ruthy turned to the hospital with the request to be given the fertilized eggs in order to continue the surrogacy proceeding. When the hospital refused her request, she applied to the Haifa District Court, which granted her request. In its first adjudication on the appeal against the District Court's decision, the Israeli Supreme Court accepted Danny Nahmani's appeal in a majority decision. In a further hearing (CFH 2401 /95 *Ruthy Nahmani v. Danny Nahmani et al*, 50 (4) PD 661) the previous decision was reversed and Ruthy Nahmani's appeal was accepted in a majority decision.

Regarding the issue of abortion in Jewish law, see separate entry *Abortion.

BIBLIOGRAPHY: PHYSICIAN'S DUTIES: M. Elon, *Jewish Law: Cases and Materials* (1999), 591–607, ch. 30; idem, "Medicine, *Hala-*

khah, and Law: The Values of a Jewish and Democratic State," in: *Jewish Medical Ethics* (2004), v–xxxviii; CA 506/88 *Yael Shefer, Minor,* v. *State of Israel*, 48 (1) PD 87; A. Steinberg (ed.), *Enẓiklopedyah Hilkhatit Refu'it* (1988–94), 1:70–74, s.v. *"Bekhirah Ḥofshit,"* s.v. *Gilui Meda la-Ḥoleh*; s.v. *Haskamah mi-Da'at*, 2:1–47; s.v. *"Ḥoleh"*; 2:437–67, 4:273–99, s.v. *"Ne'emanut ha-Rofe"*; 4:613–42, s.v. *"Sodiut Refu'it"*; 6:688–122, s.v. *"Rofe"*; 6:624–45, s.v. *"Torat ha-Musar ha-Yehudi."* EUTHANASIA: M. Elon, *Jewish Law: Cases and Materials* (1999), 637–95, ch. 33; idem, "Medicine, *Halakhah* and Law: The Values of a Jewish and Democratic State," in: *Jewish Medical Ethics* (2004), v–xxxvii; J.D. Bleich, *Judaism and Healing* (1981, 2002), 134–45; H.D. Halevi, *"Nituk Ḥoleh she-Afsu Sikuyav Liḥyot mi-Mekhonat Hanshamah Melakhutit,"* in: *Teḥumin*, 2 (1981), 297; Z.N. Goldberg and L.Y. Halperin, *Emek ha-Halakhah – Assia*, 64ff.; A. Steinberg (ed.), in: *Enẓiklopedyah Hilkhatit Refu'it* (1994), 4:343–469, s.v. *"Noteh Lamut"*; D. Sinclair (ed.), *Jewish Biomedical Law* (Jewish Law Association Studies 15; 2005). ORGAN TRANSPLANTATION: M. Elon, *Jewish Law: Cases and Materials* (1999), 697–731, ch. 34; A. Steinberg, *Enẓiklopedyah Hilkhatit Refu'it* (1994), 2:244–191, s.v. *"Hashtalat Evarim"*; idem, *ibid.*, 6:18–49, s.v. *"Rega ha-Mavet"*; LA 184/87, 698/96 *Attorney General v. Anon.*, 42 (2) PD 661; D. Sinclair (ed.), *Jewish Biomedical Law* (Jewish Law Association Studies 15; 2005). ARTIFICIAL INSEMINATION: M. Elon, *Jewish Law: Cases and Materials* (1999), 625–35, ch. 32; A. Steinberg (ed.), *Enẓiklopedyah Hilkhatit Refu'it* (1988), s.v. *"Hazra'ah Melakhutit,"* 148–61; A. Walkin, *Resp. Zekan Aharon*, 2:97; Y. Green, *Hazra'ah Melakhutit bi-Pesika u-ve-Ḥakikat Medinat Yisrael*; D. Sinclair (ed.), *Jewish Biomedical Law* (Jewish Law Association Studies 15; 2005). IN VITRO FERTILIZATION: A. Steinberg (ed.), *Enẓiklopedyah Hilkhatit Refuit*, (1991), 2:148–61, s.v. *"Hafraya Ḥutz Gufi"*: FH 2401/95 (CA 5587/93) *Daniel Nahmani v. Ruthy Nahmani* et al., 50 (4) PD 661; CFH 2401/95 *Ruthy Nahmani v. Danny Nahmani et al.*, 50 (4) PD 661; HC 2458/01 *Mishpaḥah Ḥadashah v. the Approvals Committee for Surrogacy Agreements* (not yet published); D. Sinclair, *Jewish Biomedical Law* (Jewish Law Association Studies 15; 2005).

[Menachem Elon (2nd ed.)]

MEDINA (Ar. **Madīna**; ancient name, **Yathrib**), city in fertile valley of the *Hejaz in northern *Arabia. Along with *Tayma and *Khaybar, Medina was a leading Jewish community in ancient Arabia. Prior to the expulsion of most of Medina Jewry by *Muhammad (620s) the oasis was largely inhabited by Jews. According to legend, the Jewish community dates from Moses' war against the Amalekites, the Babylonian Exile (c. 586 B.C.E.), Antiochus IV's persecutions, and the defeat by Rome (70 C.E.). In any case, by the early centuries of the Christian era the population of Medina consisted mostly of Jewish tribes (according to some Arabs, up to 20 tribes), either of Judean-Palestinian, mixed Judeo-Arabic, or Arab proselyte origin. Remains of their life survive, including castles, courtyards, and wells, the first of which were dug by the *Naḍīr tribe who inhabited the best lands and cultivated date palms west of the city. The two other major tribes were the *Qurayẓa, who occupied an area in the southeastern part of the town, and the *Qaynuqāʿ, who were among the earliest settlers and resided in the central market. Other tribes included the Thalaba (northeast of the city) and the Anī, a tribe of Arab proselytes who lived in the Qubā area (south of Medina). There was a continuous Arab migration to the area and many Arab tribes assimilated into the Jewish milieu, accepting Judaism and acquiring skills such as writing, which up to that time was known only by Jews. The two major Arab tribes, the Aws and the Khazraj, settled in the area, coming from South Arabia in the middle of the fifth century. They came because the breaking of the Ma'rib dam had ruined their lands. Some of the Arabs lived among the Jews, others in areas far from Jewish settlement. They were subjects of the Jewish tribes. The Khazraj gained some independence from the Jews in later times after a bloody battle, which according to legends broke out as a result of the Jewish king Faytun's demand to exercise the *jus primae noctis* on Arab subjects. Henceforth domination of Medina gradually passed to Arabs; the Jewish tribes aligned themselves with the Aws or the Khazraj, who threatened to confiscate the Naḍīr lands. Fighting between these two major tribes and their Jewish clients (Naḍīr and Qurayẓa with Aws; the Qaynuqāʿ with the Khazraj) characterized the sixth century and is recalled in Arabic poetry, including that of the Jew *Samuel b. Adiya. The bloody battles ended with the victory of the Aws and peaceful settlement with the Khazraj. Shortly before Muhammad's arrival in Medina the Jewish population had reached between 8,000 and 10,000, forming a majority of the city's inhabitants. The presence of so large and vital a Jewish community (though Arabic in language, customs, and behavior) provided an atmosphere conducive to the acceptance of monotheism among Arabs. Hence, Muhammad's message found a receptive audience among many Arabs and a few Jews. Most Jews, however, scorned Muhammad, deriding his prophetic pretensions and adaptations of biblical material. Concerned about the effect of such vehement opposition, Muhammad began to expel the Jewish tribes with whom he had formerly signed an agreement. The Qaynuqā and the Naḍīr were expelled from Medina in 624 and 626, respectively. The Qurayẓa men were annihilated in 627 and the women and children were sold into slavery. The Jewish tribes apparently did not assist one another or unite against the common enemy, each meeting its fate as an individual tribe. The small Jewish population which remained in Medina was powerless and could not cause Muhammad much trouble. The community eventually dwindled and died out.

BIBLIOGRAPHY: Baron, Social², 3 (1957), 60–80; H.Z. Hirschberg, *Yisrael ba-Arav* (1946), index; H. Hirschfeld, in: REJ, 7 (1883), 167–93; 10 (1885), 10–31; S.D. Goitein, in: *Tarbiz*, 3 (1932), 410–22; A. Katsh, *Judaism and the Koran* (1954), index; W.M. Watt, *Muhammad at Medina* (1956), 192–220; M. ibn Isḥāq, *Life of Muhammad*, tr. by A. Guillaume (1955), index; J.M. Landau, *The Hejaz Railway and the Muslim Pilgrimage* (1971); N. Stillman, *The Jews of Arab Lands: A History and Source Book* (1979); G. Newby, *A History of the Jews of Arabia: From Ancient Times to Their Eclipse under Islam* (1988); M. Cohen and A. Udovitch, *Jews among Arabs: Contacts and Boundaries* (1989); M. Lecker, *Muslims, Jews and Pagans: Studies on Early Islamic Medina* (1995); idem, "Zayd b. Thābit, 'A Jew with Two Sidelocks': Judaism and Literacy in Pre-Islamic Medina (Yathrib)," in: JNES, 56 (1997).

[Ze'ev A. Maghen (2nd ed.)]

MEDINA, AVIHU (1948–), lyricist and composer. Medina was born in Tel Aviv to Yemenite parents. His mother's family arrived in the country in 1906 and settled in Jerusalem; his father, who came from Yemen in 1939, was a *ḥazzan*. Avihu graduated from Kibbutz Kissufim High School. After his military service (1970), he began writing lyrics and composing their melodies. His first song, "*Al Tira Yisrael*," won the third prize in the first festival of Oriental communities' songs held under the auspices of Israel's state radio in 1971. For the next ten years he was to receive first prize in a number of festivals. Among the songs he wrote are "*La-Ner ve-la-Besamim*" ("For the Candle and the Perfumes"), "*Kinnor David, Barekhenu*" ("Bless Us"), "*Peraḥ be-Ganni*" ("Flower in My Garden"), "*Al Tashlikheni*" ("Don't Cast Me Away"), "*Shabbeḥi Yerushalayim*" ("Praise Thee Jerusalem"), "*Bein ha-Tov la-Ra*" ("Between Good and Evil"). His songs were performed by some of Israel's best artists, such as Shimi Tavori, Zohar *Argov, Boaz Sharabi, Ofra *Haza, Eyal Golan, Deklon, and many others.

In 1991 Avihu began singing his own songs. In 1994 Omanut La-'am awarded him the "Silver Cylinder," which is the crowning prize for the most popular artist. In 1995 he received the Writers and Composers Prize for lifetime achievements in the field of light music. Avihu Medina has released nine albums – the ninth, *Ein Li Mano'aḥ*, in 2004 – and a book of songs, *Simanim shel Derekh*.

Medina, a leading figure in the period of Ethnicity, devoted much of his time to the promotion of "Mediterranean Israeli music." He believes that "it is a style born of traditional and cultural Jewish roots and of the Israeli experience in all its forms."

He is the chairman of the Israeli song department on the Committee for Art and Culture.

[Nathan Shahar (2nd ed.)]

MEDINA, SAMUEL BEN MOSES DE (known by the acronym **Maharashdam**; 1506–1589), rabbi, halakhic authority, and communal leader of *Salonika. Medina was descended from a distinguished family of scholars which originated from Spain. He was one of the three outstanding *posekim* of Salonika of the 16th century, the others being Joseph ibn *Lev and Solomon b. Abraham ha-Kohen. Medina was dogged by misfortune throughout his life. Orphaned in his childhood, his sister and two of his sons-in-law died in his lifetime and the burden of the maintenance of his widowed daughters and their many children fell upon him. The death of his elder brother, a man of means who had educated him and supported him financially, added to these burdens. The death of his eldest son left a permanent mark on him and affected his health. He was obliged from time to time to undertake journeys, in all probability in order to improve his financial position. Until his position in Salonika was established, he devoted himself completely to study, finding in it consolation for his sorrows. Medina founded a yeshivah in Salonika in which he introduced the system of teaching of the great Spanish talmudic scholars from the time of Isaac *Campanton and his successors. It had many disciples, a number of whom became famous and he himself says that some of them were worthy of heading yeshivot themselves. They include Aaron Abayuv, Joseph ibn Ezra, Abraham di Boton, David Naḥmias, and Abraham ibn Aruz. The yeshivah was supported by Donna Gracia Mendes (*Nasi) and was highly praised by his contemporaries.

Medina was the accepted halakhic authority both in his own and succeeding generations for European Turkey and the Balkans. Queries were addressed to him from all parts of the Ottoman Empire and Italy and his published responsa number over 1,000. Jacob Alfandari (*Maggid me-Reshit*) compares him and Solomon ha-Kohen to "Maimonides and the Rosh (Jacob b. Asher) in their time." Ḥayyim *Shabbetai says of him: "He was an expert judge and of encyclopedic knowledge and one must not deviate an iota from his decisions" (*Torat Ḥayyim* 3:70). Some even went so far as to take an oath by the names of these two rabbis to give authority to their decisions (Aaron Sasson, *Torat Emet* 80). Although many scholars such as Isaac Adarbi, Moses of *Trani, Jacob Samut, and even his own maternal grandson Samuel Ḥayyun disagreed with him, his decision always prevailed. His decisions were incorporated in those of Eastern European scholars in later generations. For historians his responsa constitute a most important source for the period in all its aspects, and his decisions are often quoted in modern times by judges in Israel in support of their decisions.

Medina's personality and character emerge clearly from his many responsa. He imposed his authority on litigants by the power of his personality and succeeded in enforcing just compromises even when there was no basis for them in law. This firmness and self-confidence were revealed even in his youth (cf. J. Caro, Responsa *Avkat Rokhel*, 219). They find striking expression in his stern rebuke to the scholars of Safed, who included Caro, for presuming to intervene in the affairs of the community of Salonika (Resp. YD 80) and he did not refrain from sharp and vigorous language, especially in his polemics.

Medina was original in his method. He would give a decision in accordance with his own judgment when he found no precedent in the *halakhot* of his predecessors. Utterly fearless, he was alert to all problems which arose from the special circumstances of his time and place, and many of his responsa deal with the social and economic problems which exercised the minds of his contemporaries. Medina applied himself to the communal organization of the Spanish exiles, which he established on a solid juridical basis. In the controversies which reigned in Salonika and elsewhere as a result of the glaring gap between the rich and the poor, Medina maintained the right of the wealthy members of the community to regulate the direction of communal affairs. According to him it was not numbers but quality which counted and it was right that, as had been the custom in Spain, the leadership of the community should be in the hands of those who bear its financial burden, providing they were loyal to religious principles. With all his respect for local custom, he strove to make it accord with the *halakhah* as he saw it. Where that custom differed from that in force in Spain, he justified the latter on halakhic grounds and encouraged its gradual adoption, whether in the liturgical usage or in matters of *sheḥitah*, etc. Unlike his predecessors his consistency in this matter did not meet with great opposition. Medina's decisions with regard to **anusim* are important and are stamped with the same original approach as he showed in other matters for which there was no legal precedent. He regarded the community of Salonika and especially its educational institutions as being in a unique position, and as a result demanded a greater financial support for them than for the institutions in Ereẓ Israel.

Side by side with his intensive halakhic activity Medina filled certain communal offices. He was the rabbi of the most important and largest congregations of Iberian communities in Salonika among them those of "Gerush" (i.e., of the exiles) and Lisbon, and went to Constantinople on missions on behalf of Salonika. He was called on to decide in the serious disputes which arose in Salonika and other communities, and succeeded in preventing schisms. His authority is seen in the fact that his signature appears on the majority of the communal regulations (*haskamot*) which have come down. Unlike many of his contemporaries of Spanish provenance Medina did not engage in Kabbalah, nor did he enter deeply into philosophy and secular studies. He was the man of *halakhah* and the communal leader par excellence. Despite his often unsatisfactory financial position he refused to take advantage of the exemption from taxes granted to scholars. Toward the end of his life legends were woven about him.

Medina's responsa were published during his lifetime in two volumes (Salonika, 1585?–87) and an improved edition in three volumes (Salonika, 1594–98). A considerable number also appear in the works of other scholars, while others are still in manuscript. Thirty of his sermons were published in *Ben Shemu'el* (Mantua, 1622) and his novellae on a number of tractates of the Talmud are still in manuscript.

Medina's son Moses was a man of means and a scholar. He was responsible for the founding of a Hebrew printing press in Salonika in 1594 and published his father's responsa. He succeeded his father as rabbi of the Portugal community in Salonika.

Moses had two sons, Judah and Shemaiah. The former, a *dayyan* in Salonika, was murdered by an assassin hired by a Jew because of a verdict given against him. This tragedy caused his brother, who was also a scholar and communal leader of Salonika, to move to Venice where he became one of its scholars. He published his grandfather's *Ben Shemu'el*, and some of his poems were published in *Ḥadashim la-Bekarim* (Mantua, 1622).

BIBLIOGRAPHY: Conforte, Kore, index; Jacob Luzzatto, *Kehillat Ya'akov* (Salonika, 1584), preface; Azulai, 1 (1852), 176 no. 122; A. Danon, in: REJ, 40 (1900), 206–30; 41 (1900), 98–117, 250–65; I.S. Emmanuel, *Histoire des Israélites de Salonique* (1936), 167–75; idem, *Maẓẓevot Saloniki* (1967), index; Rosanes, Togarmah, 2 (1937–38^{2}), 115–18; M.S. Goodblatt, *Jewish Life in Turkey in the XVIth Century, as Reflected in the Legal Writings of Samuel de Medina* (1952); M. Molho, in: *Sinai*, 41 (1957), 36–48; J. Katz, in: *Tarbiẓ*, 27 (1958), 204; I.R. Molho and A. Amarijlio, in: *Sefunot*, 2 (1958), 35–39; I. Kister, in: *Saloniki Ir va-Em be-Yisrael* (1967), 38–41; A. Nimdar, in: *Mi-Mizraḥ u-mi-Ma'arav: Kovez Meḥkarim be-Toledot ha-Yehudim be-Mizraḥ u-ve-Magreb* (1974), 295–331.

[Joseph Hacker]

MEDINA, SIR SOLOMON DE (c. 1650–1720), army contractor and the first professing Jew in England to receive a knighthood. He was born in Bordeaux as Diego de Medina, but lived in Holland until William of Orange's invasion of England in 1688, which he helped to finance. An English example of the *Court Jew, he was principal army contractor to the duke of Marlborough during the War of the Spanish Succession (1701–14), supplying money, provisions, and particularly intelligence. These transactions ultimately contributed to the duke's downfall. Medina was active in and contributed generously to the London Sephardi community but died abroad in poverty. He is wrongly identified with the Jew whose bankruptcy was blamed by *Voltaire for his financial difficulties.

BIBLIOGRAPHY: Roth, England, 193, 287–8; Roth, Mag Bibl, index; A.M. Hyamson, *Sephardim of England* (1951), index. **ADD. BIBLIOGRAPHY:** ODNB online; O.K. Rabinowicz, *Sir Solomon de Medina* (1974); Katz, England, 217–19, index.

[Vivian David Lipman]

MEDINACELI, town in Castile, N. Spain, near Sigüenza. A Jewish community existed there as early as the 12th century. The *fuero* ("municipal charter") of Medinaceli gave the Jews a status equal to that of the Christians and Moors in legal matters. In the 13th century the community numbered 20 to 30 families. Jewish occupations included agriculture, viticulture, commerce, and crafts. In 1280 Abraham of Medinaceli made an agreement, valid for four years, with the bishop of Sigüenza to open and exploit salt mines (see *Salt Trade). The bishop was to supply Abraham with the necessary equipment, finance the project, and provide him with lodging. In 1290 the communities of Medinaceli and Sigüenza together paid annual taxes and services amounting to 34,217 maravedis, which indicates considerable prosperity. The community continued to exist throughout the 15th century. It was taxed 91 castellanos in 1485 as a contribution to the war against Granada. The synagogue, which passed to the Church after the expulsion of the Jews from Spain in 1492, was restored by the government.

BIBLIOGRAPHY: Baer, Spain, 1 (1961), 192, 200; Baer, Urkunden, index; B. Pavón Maldonado, in: *Sefarad*, 38 (1978), 309–17.

[Haim Beinart]

MEDINA DEL CAMPO, town in N. Castile, between *Olmedo and Rueda. The Jewish community was particularly prosperous during the 13th century: in 1290 its annual tax amounted to 44,000 maravedis. By the 14th century the community consisted of between 50 and 100 householders. In 1313 the regulations on Jewish affairs of the regional council of *Zamora were applied to Medina del Campo. They covered the employment of Christians in Jewish homes, the distinctive badge to be worn by the Jews, the prohibition on practicing medicine, interest rates, and the dismissal of Jews from public functions. Nothing is known of how the community fared during the persecutions of 1391, but afterward a *Converso community existed there. In 1459 Medina del Campo was the center of the activities of the monk *Alonso de Espina against Conversos suspected of practicing Judaism. During that year he found 30 Conversos who had undergone circumcision. Some of the Conversos prepared to depart for North Africa. One of them, the physician Magister Franciscus, circumcised himself and immigrated to Ereẓ Israel. Therefore, like *Huesca and Ciudad Real, in the 1450s and 1460s Medina del Campo was a center for the return to Judaism. After the edict of expulsion (1492), those who left the town presumably crossed the borders of the kingdoms of Navarre and Portugal. The last rabbi of the community was Isaac Uzziel, who probably settled in Salonika after the expulsion.

BIBLIOGRAPHY: Baer, Spain, index; Baer, Urkunden, 2 (1936), index; B. Llorca, in: *Sefarad*, 2 (1942), 119; A. Marx, *Expulsion of the Jews from Spain* (1944), 85, 100; Suárez Fernández, Documentos, index.

[Haim Beinart]

MEDINA DE POMAR, town in Castile, N. Spain. The Jewish settlement here was one of the flourishing communities in 13th-century Castile. Like other Jews in the area, Jewish residents of Medina de Pomar owned vineyards and lands and engaged in commerce and crafts. Joseph Nasi and Abraham *Benveniste de Soria, both of Medina, supplied grain and money to the army stationed on the border in 1429–30. On March 12, 1475, two Jewish cloth merchants, Josi Leal and Moses Sasson, complained that the authorities had prohibited visiting Jews from trading and buying goods in Medina. Conversely in 1490 the Jews of Medina complained to the crown that the Bilbao municipal council had banned visiting Jews from staying there overnight and that they had therefore been unable to attend the fair at Medina del Campo. After the edict of expulsion of the Jews from Spain in 1492, the Jews of Medina de Pomar asked the crown for redress because the Christians had refused to pay their debts. Ferdinand and Isabella ordered the municipal authorities to deal with the matter expeditiously to enable the Jews to leave on time.

BIBLIOGRAPHY: Baer, Urkunden, index; F. Cantera, *Sinagogas españolas* (1955), 244f.; Suárez Fernández, Documentos, index. **ADD. BIBLIOGRAPHY:** I. Cadinaños Bardeci, in: *Sefarad*, 45 (1985), 237–80; R. Pérez Bustamante, in: *Encuentros en Sefarad* (1987), 45–70.

[Haim Beinart]

MEDINAH. In Hebrew writings emanating from the Muslim-influenced areas, *medinah* is used to mean city. In Ashkenazi culture, especially in the later Middle Ages and early modern times, *medinah* denotes a region embracing several or many communities organized as a territorial unit for the purpose of *autonomy and leadership.

BIBLIOGRAPHY: J. Katz, *Tradition and Crisis* (1961), 122–34.

MEDINI, ḤAYYIM HEZEKIAH BEN RAPHAEL ELIJAH (1832–1904), rabbi. Medini was born in Jerusalem. He studied under Isaac *Covo and Joseph Nissim *Burla. His father died in 1853, and in that same year he traveled to Constantinople where he stayed for 14 years. For a while he earned his living as a private tutor but lectured publicly without remuneration. He attracted many disciples, some of whom later became rabbis. From 1867 to 1899 he was rabbi of Karasubazar in the Crimean peninsula and succeeded in raising the previously low spiritual standard of the community. He instituted local *takkanot*, abrogated strange customs or amended and restored them to their proper origin, and founded schools and yeshivot. He opposed *Firkovich, showing that his claim that the people of Crimea were descended from the Karaites was without foundation. He was an ardent Zionist, and in his works there are many passages extolling the virtue of settling in Ereẓ Israel, the forthcoming redemption, and on the duty of settling in Israel and supporting its poor. He became seriously ill in 1878 and it seems that he was then given the additional name of Ḥayyim. In 1899 he returned to Jerusalem where he was received with great honor. His books won for him a reputation, and religious and halakhic problems were addressed to him from the whole Jewish world. In 1901 he heard that there was a proposal to appoint him **rishon le-Zion* (Sephardi chief rabbi), but unwilling to accept this office, he moved to Hebron where he served as rabbi until his death. He founded a yeshivah there, meeting part of its maintenance from his private resources. His fame as a man of saintliness spread to the non-Jews who honored him and regarded him as a wonder worker.

Medini's fame rests principally on his *Sedei Ḥemed*, which he began in the Crimea, a halakhic encyclopedia of exceptional originality, 13 of the 18 volumes of which were published during his lifetime (Warsaw, 1891–1912). It is one of the most monumental halakhic works, and is still extensively used. It contains rules of talmudic and halakhic methodology, an alphabetical list of the various laws, and responsa. In addition, it contains bibliographical research and articles on the lives of Jewish scholars and of the history of Ereẓ Israel. At the beginning of volume 14 is his lengthy ethical will which reflects his lofty spiritual and moral stature. He wrote a supplement to it, entitled *Pakku'at ha-Sadeh* (in *Ha-Me'assef*, 5, Jerusalem (1900), supplement). Among his other works are *Mikhtav le-Ḥizkiyyahu* (Smyrna, 1868), talmudic novellae and responsa on *Oraḥ Ḥayyim*; *Or Li* (*ibid.*, 1874), novellae and responsa – published anonymously in memory of his only son who died in 1868; *Ne'im Zemirot* (Warsaw, 1886), *piyyutim* which it was the custom to recite every morning. Several of his poems were published at the beginning of *Sedei Ḥemed*, volume 6. Many of his responsa and approbations are to be found in the works of contemporary rabbis.

BIBLIOGRAPHY: Benayahu, in: *Ḥemdat Yisrael* (collection of essays in his memory), ed. by A. Elmaleh (1946), 183–212, 203 (bibl.); Burla, *ibid.*, 213–5; Avisar, *ibid.*, 216–28; A. Ben-Jacob, in: *Hed ha-Mizraḥ*, 3 (1944/45), no. 30; M. Benayahu, *ibid.*; L. Jung (ed.), *Men of the Spirit* (1964), 107–21.

[Abraham Ben-Yaacob]

MEDITATION (Heb. *Hitbonenut*), a term which first appears in kabbalistic literature, from the middle of the 13th century, referring to protracted concentration of thought on supernal lights of the divine world and of the spiritual worlds in general. Many sources, however, in this connection use the terms **kavvanah*, or **devekut* ("cleaving") of thought to a particular subject, and of "contemplation of the mind." The kabbalists did not distinguish between the terms meditation and contemplation – a distinction prevalent in Christian mysticism. In the kabbalistic view, contemplation was both the concentrated delving to the depths of a particular subject in the attempt to comprehend it from all its aspects, and also the arresting of thought in order to remain on the subject. The arresting and delving in spiritual contemplation do not serve, therefore, to encourage the contemplating intellect to advance and pass on to higher levels, but first of all to gauge to the maximum its given situation; only after having tarried in it for a protracted period does the intellect move on to a higher step. This, then, is contemplation by the intellect, whose objects are neither images nor visions, but non-sensual matters such as words, names, or thoughts.

In the history of the Kabbalah a different contemplation preceded this one: the contemplative vision of the *Merkabah, for which the ancient Merkabah mystics of the tannaitic and amoraitic period strove, and which was described in the *Heikhalot Rabbati* of the *heikhalot* literature. Here the reference is to an actual vision of the world of the chariot which reveals itself before the eyes of the visionary. Therefore the term *histakkelut* is used here in the exact sense of the Latin term *contemplatio* or the Greek *theoria*. The contemplation of the Merkabah mystics, in the first period of Jewish mysticism, provided the key, in their opinion, to a correct understanding of the heavenly beings in the heavenly chariot. This contemplation could also be achieved by way of preparatory stages which would train those who "descend to the Merkabah" to grasp the vision and pass on from one thing to another without being endangered by the audacity of their assault on the higher world. Even at this stage, the vision of the Merkabah is bound up with immunization of the mystic's senses against absorption of external impressions and concentration through an inward vision.

In the Kabbalah, the conception of the ten *Sefirot*, which reveal the action of the Divine and comprise the world of emanation, was superimposed upon the Merkabah world. This contemplation of divine matters does not end, according to the Kabbalah, where the vision of Merkabah mystics ended, but is capable of ascending to greater heights, which are no longer the objects of images and vision. The concentration on the world of the *Sefirot* is not bound up with visions, but is solely a matter for the intellect prepared to ascend from level to level and to meditate on the qualities unique to each level. If meditation activates at first the faculty of imagination, it continues by activating the faculty of the intellect. The *Sefirot* themselves are conceived of as intellectual lights which can only be perceived by meditation. The Spanish kabbalists in the 13th century knew of two types of meditation: one which produces visions similar in kind if not in detail to the visions of the Merkabah mystics, and the second which leads to the communion of the meditating mind with its higher sources in the world of emanation itself. *Moses b. Shem Tov de Leon describes in one of his books how an intuition of the third *Sefirah* (*Binah*) flashes up in the mind through meditation. He compares this to the light which flashes up when the rays of the sun play on the surface of a bowl of water (MGWJ, 1927, 119).

The instructions on the methods to be employed in performing meditation form part of the hidden and secret teachings of the kabbalists which, apart from some general rules, were not made public. The kabbalists of Gerona mention it in connection with the description of the mystic *kavvanah* in prayer, which is described as a meditation concentrating upon each word of the prayer in order to open a way to the inner lights which illuminate every word. Prayer, according to this idea of meditation, is not just a recitation of words or even concentration on the contents of the words according to their simple meaning; it is the adherence of man's mind to the spiritual lights and the mind's advancement in these worlds. The worshiper uses the fixed words of the prayer as a banister during his meditation which he grasps on his road of ascension so that he should not be confused or distracted. Such meditation results in the joining of human thought to the divine thought or the divine will – an attachment which itself comes to an end, or is "negated." The hour of prayer is, more than any other time, suitable for meditation. *Azriel of Gerona said: "The thought expands and ascends to its origin, so that when it reaches it, it ends and cannot ascend any further … therefore the pious men of old raised their thought to its origin while pronouncing the precepts and words of prayer. As a result of this procedure and the state of adhesion which their thought attained, their words became blessed, multiplied, full of [divine] influx from the stage called the 'nothingness of thought,' just as the waters of a pool flow on every side when a man sets them free" (*Perush ha-Aggadot*, 1943, 39–40). In such meditation, which progresses from one stage to another, there was also a certain magic element, as can clearly be deduced from the detailed description in another piece by Azriel called *Sha'ar ha-Kavvanah la-Mekubbalim ha-Rishonim*. Meditation does not only ponder and penetrate its object; it has the power to bring about changes in its object and likely to cause transformations as it reaches the common root of opposing extremes. In most descriptions of the methods of meditation which were preserved from the golden era of Spanish Kabbalah, however, this magic element was concealed or completely glossed over in silence.

A detailed elaboration of the doctrine of meditation is to be found particularly in the teachings of Abraham *Abulafia. The whole of his *Ḥokhmat ha-Ẓeruf* was designed, he believed, to teach a lasting and safe approach to meditation. It consists principally of instruction concerning meditation on the Holy Names of God and, in a wider sense, meditation on the mysteries of the Hebrew alphabet. This meditation, which is not dependent on prayer, was described in his more important manuals as a separate activity of the mind to which man devotes himself in seclusion at given hours and with regular guidance by an initiate teacher. Here again the point of departure is the mortification of the activity of the senses and the effacement of the natural images which cling to the soul. Meditation on the holy letters and names engenders pure rational forms in the soul, as a result of which man is able to comprehend the exalted truths. At certain stages of this meditation, there appear actual visions, such as are described in the work *Ḥayyei ha-Olam ha-Ba* for instance, but these are only intermediate stages on the road to pure contemplation of the mind. Abulafia negates from its very start the magical element which was originally attributed to such meditation.

The difference between the Christian and the kabbalistic doctrines of meditation resides in the fact that in Christian mysticism a pictorial and concrete subject, such as the suffering of Christ and all that pertains to it, is given to the meditator, while in Kabbalah, the subject given is abstract and cannot be visualized, such as the Tetragrammaton and its combinations.

Instruction in the methods of meditation were widespread in the works of early kabbalists and these methods continue to be found after the expulsion from Spain among several kabbalists who were influenced by Abulafia. An anonymous disciple of Abulafia has left (in *Sha'arei Ẓedek*, written in 1295) an impressive description of his experiences in the study of this meditation. The works *Berit Menuḥah* (14th century) and *Sullam ha-Aliyyah* by Judah *Albotini, one of the exiles from Spain who settled in Jerusalem, were also written in the same spirit.

The most detailed textbook on meditation into the mystery of the *Sefirot* is *Even ha-Shoham* by Joseph ibn Ṣayah of Damascus, written in Jerusalem in 1538 (Ms. National and University Library, Jerusalem; see G. Scholem, *Kitvei Yad be-Kabbalah* (1930), 90–91). The kabbalists of Safed paid much attention to meditation, as is evident from *Sefer Ḥaredim* (Venice, 1601) of Eleazar *Azikri, from chapter 30 in Moses *Cordovero's *Pardes Rimmonim* (Cracow, 1592), and the *Sha'arei Kedushah* of Ḥayyim *Vital, part 3, chapters 5–8, propounds his doctrine on the subject. Here the magic aspect attached to meditation is once more emphasized, even though the author explains it in a restricted sense. The last steps in the ascension of the meditating mind which seeks to bring down the influx of the supernal lights to earth require meditatory activities of a magic nature, which are known as *Yiḥudim* ("Unifications"). The practical importance of these doctrines, whose influence can be recognized throughout the whole of late kabbalistic literature, should not be underrated. The doctrines of adhesion and meditation in 18th-century Ḥasidism are also definitely based on the form given to them in Safed. This doctrine was not written down in its entirety in the writings of Isaac *Luria's disciples and its major part was preserved orally. In Jerusalem's kabbalistic yeshivah Bet El practical guidance on meditation was handed down orally for about 200 years and the initiates of this form of Kabbalah refused to make the details of their practice public knowledge.

BIBLIOGRAPHY: G. Scholem, *Kitvei Yad be-Kabbalah* (1930), 24–30, 225–30; idem, *Reshit ha-Kabbalah* (1948), 142–6; idem, in: KS, 1 (1924), 127–39; 22 (1946), 161–71; idem, in: MGWJ, 78 (1934), 492–518; R.J.Z. Werblowsky, in: *History of Religions*, 1 (1961), 9–36.

[Gershom Scholem]

MEDNICK, MARTHA TAMARA SCHUCH (1929–), U.S. psychologist and pioneer in the psychology of women. Mednick was born in New York City to working-class immigrant parents from Eastern Europe. She received B.A. and M.A. degrees from the City College of New York. In 1952 she joined her husband, Sarnoff Mednick, as a graduate student at Northwestern University, receiving a Ph.D. in clinical psychology in 1955. Mednick made a number of moves based on her husband's career, had two daughters, and did some collaborative work with him, first on a personality test and later on a measure of creative thinking. By the time of their divorce in 1964, Mednick was affiliated with the Institute for Social Research at the University of Michigan. Shortly afterward, she became a member of the psychology department at Howard University, was appointed a full professor in 1971, and remained there until her retirement in 1995.

Mednick was very important as a mentor and a pioneer in the psychology of women. In 1972, she co-edited with Sandra Schwartz Tangri a special issue of the *Journal of Social Issues* entitled "New Perspectives on Women," which she later expanded into the book *Women and Achievement* (1975). She helped establish and served as president of the psychology of women division of the American Psychological Association (1976–77) and was also president of the Society for the Psychological Study of Social Issues (1980–82). Her research focused on race, class, and sex issues in the psychology of achievement. Many of her studies were published with students from Howard University and a list of these students reads like a *Who's Who* of African American women psychologists. Mednick received the Carolyn Wood Sherif Award from the Division of the Psychology of Women in 1988 for her teaching, mentoring, and scholarship in this field.

Mednick was also important in facilitating contact between American and Israeli feminist psychologists. With Marilyn Safir, a psychologist at the University of Haifa, and Dafna Izraeli, a sociologist on the faculty of Bar-Ilan University, Mednick organized the first international interdisciplinary congress on women held at Haifa University in 1981. The collection of papers from the first conference, entitled *Women's Worlds* (1985), highlighted research by Americans, Jewish Israelis, Palestinian, and Arab women.

BIBLIOGRAPHY: M.T.S. Mednick, "Autobiography," in: A.N. O'Connell and N.F. Russo (eds.), *Models of Achievement: Reflections of Eminent Women in Psychology*, vol. 2 (1988), 245–59; G. Stevens and S. Gardner, *The Women of Psychology*, vol. 2 (1982).

[Rhoda K. Unger (2nd ed.)]

MEDRES, ISRAEL JONAH (1894–1964), Yiddish journalist. Born in Lekhovich (Lyakhovichi), Minsk province, Belorussia, Medres studied at the Lida Yeshivah before immigrating to Montreal. From 1922 to 1964 he was a full-time staff writer for the Montreal daily, *Der Keneder Adler* (*The Jewish Daily Eagle*). His numerous articles (many reprinted in Yiddish publications worldwide) and two books, *Montreal fun Nekhtn* ("Montreal of Yesterday," 1947) and *Tsvishn Tsvey Velt Milkhomes* ("Between Two World Wars," 1964), provide a wealth of information about almost every aspect of Jewish immigrant life in early 20th-century Canada.

BIBLIOGRAPHY: LNYL, 5 (1963), 541; C.L. Fox, *Hundert Yor Yidishe un Hebreishe Literatur in Kanade* (1980), 160–61; J. Gallay, in: C. Spilberg and Y. Zipper (eds.), *Canadian Jewish Anthology* (1982), 477–80; M. Ravitch, *Mayn Leksikon* 4/2 (1982), 87–88; I. Medres, *Montreal of Yesterday* (2000), 13–20; I. Medres, *Between the Wars* (2003), 9–14.

[Vivian Felsen (2nd ed.)]

MEDVED, MICHAEL (1948–), author, radio personality. Medved was born to physicist David Bernard and chemist Renate Medved (née Hirsch) in Philadelphia, Penn. At the age of six, he moved with his family to San Diego, California, where David worked as a defense contractor for Convair. The family later moved to Los Angeles, where Medved attended Palisades High School. Medved began his undergraduate work at Yale University at 16 and graduated with a Bachelor of Arts degree in U.S. history from Yale University in 1969. He attended Yale Law School from 1969 to 1970 and taught at a Hebrew day school in New Haven, Conn. Medved worked as creative director and advertising copywriter for Anrick, Inc. in Oakland, Calif., from 1972 to 1974. Ten years after his graduation from high school, Medved and his fellow Palisades alumna David Wallechinsky interviewed their fellow classmates for the bestseller *What Really Happened to the Class of '65?* (1976). Medved moved to Los Angeles to write NBC's adaptation of his book. In 1978, he co-wrote the book *The 50 Worst Films of All Time* with his brother Harry Medved, which led to the sequels *The Golden Turkey Awards: The Worst Achievements in Hollywood History* (1980), *The Hollywood Hall of Shame: The Most Expensive Flops in Movie History* (1984), and *The Son of Golden Turkey Awards* (1986). In 1979, Medved published *The Shadow Presidents: The Secret History of the Chief Executives and Their Top Aids* (1979). In 1980, Medved dropped his affiliation with the Democratic Party and joined the GOP. Medved became CNN's film critic from 1981 to 1983. He spent a year with a hospital staff and published *Hospital: The Hidden Lives of a Medical Center Staff* (1983), a bestseller that detailed the emotional problems of doctors and nurses. Medved and his second wife, Diane Elvenstar, a clinical psychologist and writer, were active in Pacific Jewish Center, a Traditional Jewish congregation in Venice, Calif., that Medved co-founded to attract unaffiliated Jews. In 1985, Medved served as co-host with Jeffrey Lyons of the Public Broadcasting Service program *Sneak Previews*, a position he held for 12 years. In 1993, Medved became chief film critic for the *New York Post* and Hollywood correspondent for London's *Sunday Times*. Medved's criticism of Hollywood earned him guest spots on the conservative radio program hosted by Rush Limbaugh. Soon after Medved accepted an offer from a Seattle talk radio program to host his own daily three-hour show and moved to Washington state in 1996. By March 1998, Medved was broadcasting nationally to 40 stations, and by October 1999 his show was heard on 100 stations.

[Adam Wills (2nd ed.)]

MEDVEDEV, MIKHAIL (**Meyer Yefimiovich Bernstein**; 1852–1925), tenor. The son of a rabbi, he appeared as a boy *meshorer* and was encouraged by *Shalom Aleichem to study singing. While still a pupil at the Moscow Conservatory, he was chosen by Tchaikovsky and Nicolai Rubinstein for the first performance of the role of Lensky in *Eugene Onegin* (1879). He was a soloist at the Kiev Opera from 1881, at the Bolshoi Theater in Moscow from 1891 to 1892, and then at the Petersburg Imperial Opera. He toured the United States (1898–1900) and taught at Moscow, Kiev, and Saratov. Medvedev was admired both for his voice control and for his dramatic interpretations.

MEDZIBEZH (**Medzhibozh**; Pol. **Miedzyborz**; Yid. **Mezhibezh**), small town in Khmelnitsky district (former Kamenets-Podolski district), Ukraine; until 1793 in Poland and then under Russia, until 1917 in the province of Podolia. Large fairs were held there which attracted many Jewish merchants. The Jewish community of Medzibezh is one of the oldest in the Ukraine – Jews are mentioned there in 1518 – and until the *Chmielnicki persecutions of 1648 one of the largest in Podolia. During the first half of the 17th century, Joel *Sirkes officiated as rabbi. The community suffered severely at the hands of the Cossacks in 1651, 1664, and again at the beginning of the 18th century. In 1765 there were 2,039 Jews registered in the community of Medzibezh and the nearby villages. The founder of Ḥasidism, *Israel b. Eliezer Ba'al Shem Tov, made the town his seat from about 1740 until his death in 1760 and was buried there. The *ẓaddikim* *Baruch b. Jehiel, Israel's grandson, and R. *Abraham Joshua Heschel of Apta also lived and were buried there. From 1815 to 1827 a printing press published ḥasidic and kabbalistic works in Medzibezh. From 1,719 in 1847 the number of Jews grew to 6,040 (73.9% of the total population) in 1897, then fell to 4,614 (58.2%) in 1926. In the 1920s there existed a Jewish Council, a Yiddish newspaper was published, and a Jewish kolkhoz was founded. In 1939 the number of Jewish population dropped to 2,347 (52% of the total population). The town was occupied by the Germans on July 8, 1941. Later a ghetto was established, and on September 22, 1942 (Yom Kippur), 2,588 Jews were murdered by the Germans and Ukrainians. The murders continued until October 31, when the last Jews were killed.

BIBLIOGRAPHY: Ḥ.D. Friedberg, *Toledot ha-Defus ha-Ivri be-Polanyah* (1950²), 150; M. Spektor, *Mayn Lebn*, 2 (1926), 74–101; M. Osherowitch, *Shtet un Shtetlekh in Ukraine*, 1 (1948), 47–59.

[Yehuda Slutsky / Shmuel Spector (2nd ed.)]

MEED, BENJAMIN (1918–), leader of Holocaust survivors in the United States. Meed was born Benjamin Miedzyrzecki in Warsaw, Poland, and at the age of 16, he joined the Jewish Labor Bund. After the creation of the Warsaw Ghetto, he obtained false papers and escaped to the Aryan side where he lived posing as a Pole. His parents survived hiding in a hut on an old cemetery. At one point Meed intended to go to the Hotel Polski for its promise of emigration but his brother pleaded with him to take his place. Meed consented and his brother was never heard from again. Around this time, he married Feyge (Vladka) Peltel (see *Meed, Vladka), also a member of the Bund and an important courier and arms purchaser for the resistance. After the Warsaw Ghetto Uprising, he continued to work with the Bund helping provide hiding spaces for other Jews.

The couple immigrated to the United States in 1946, where Meed became a businessman and importer. In 1966, he helped form and became president of the Warsaw Ghetto Resistance Organization (WAGRO) and devoted the remaining years of his life to representing the survivors. He organized the annual Yom Hashoah ceremony in New York City, the largest such gathering in the United States, that brought American presidents and Israeli prime ministers to Temple Emmau El. When the survivors wanted to organize their first gathering in Jerusalem in 1981, Meed helped organize the *American Gathering of Jewish Holocaust Survivors, which brought together nearly 5,000 survivors and their children. Meed also pioneered the Registry of Holocaust Survivors, which facilitated the reunion between survivors long thought to be lost to each other. The Registry now contains more than 100,000 entries organized by name – original and maiden as well as current – city of birth, camps of incarceration, and cities of postwar habitation.

In 1983 a gathering was held in Washington, DC, where 20,000 survivors assembled. Meed hosted President Ronald Reagan, Vice President George H.W. Bush, and the Senate and House leaders, who addressed the survivors in front of the Capitol and on the National Mall. Subsequent gatherings were in Philadelphia, New York, and Miami, and again in Washington, to celebrate the 10th anniversary of the *United States Holocaust Memorial Museum. Meed was instrumental in creating the Museum; first serving on the Advisory Council of the President's Commission on the Holocaust and later on the United States Holocaust Memorial Council where he chaired the Days of Remembrance Committee and the pivotal Content Committee that assured the presence and participation of Holocaust survivors, most especially after Elie Wiesel resigned as chairman in 1986. His role became more central as there was fear that without Wiesel the *neshamah*, the soul, of the Museum, would flounder. Under Meed's leadership, the Committee brought together scholars and survivors, communal leaders and Council members to assure the intellectual, aesthetic, historical, and spiritual content of the Permanent Exhibition.

BIBLIOGRAPHY: M. Berenbaum (ed.), *From Holocaust to New Life* (1985); S. Bloch (ed.), *From the Holocaust to Redemption* (1982).

[Michael Berenbaum (2nd ed.)]

MEED, VLADKA (1921–), World War II resistance fighter and educator. Born Feyge Pelte in Praga (Warsaw district), Poland, she joined the youth arm of the Jewish Labor Bund at age 14 and was thereafter active in its activities through the time of the creation of the Warsaw Ghetto. She then joined the ZOB (Jewish Fighting Organization) when it was formed after the great deportations of the summer of 1942, when more than 265,000 Jews were shipped from Warsaw to Treblinka. Because of her flawless Polish and red hair, Meed could pass as non-Jewish. She worked as a courier, smuggling arms into the ghetto and helping children escape out of it.

Meed's mother and brother were among those who were deported. She recalled: "There was very little left to fear … I was depressed and apathetic." However, despair gave way to fierce determination after she heard Abrasha Blum, a member of the Jewish Coordinating Committee that sought to unite the diverse political factions of the ghetto, give a rousing speech calling for armed resistance. As a courier she used the name Vladka, a name she kept even in freedom. Among her most important missions was to smuggle a map of the death camp of Treblinka out of the ghetto in the hope that solid information about the killing would spur a serious response in the West. She brought dynamite into the ghetto, which required not only courage, but also money to "grease" the path in and out. After the Ghetto Uprising she continued supplying money and papers for Jews in hiding.

In her writings she alludes to the loneliness and pressure of her double life only in passing: "You can be my friend," she said to Benjamin Miedzyrzecki (Meed), who was also passing as an Aryan and who would later become her husband, "because if I don't come back, I want someone to care that I am missing." She married Benjamin Meed in 1943 and was the only member of her family to survive the Shoah.

Immediately upon arrival in the United States in 1946, Meed traveled extensively as a living eyewitness to the Uprising. In 1948 she published "On Both Sides of the Wall," in Yiddish, one of the earliest accounts of the Ghetto Uprising and still one of the most compelling.

When her husband, Benjamin Meed, assumed leadership of the survivor community, Vladka Meed organized a teacher training program, co-sponsored by the *Jewish Labor Committee and the *American Gathering of Jewish Holocaust Survivors, one of the earliest such programs that took American teachers from the public school system and brought them to Poland and Israel to experience a Seminar on the Holocaust and Resistance. For almost 20 years, she unfailingly led the mission, which was suspended during the Intifada and resumed in 2005. Meed helped produce a dedicated and informed cadre of teachers throughout the United States. Central to this program were the direct testimonies of survivors, none more impressive than Vladka Meed's.

[Michael Berenbaum (2nd ed.)]

MEEROVITCH, MENACHÉ (1860–1949), member of *Bilu and one of the key figures in Jewish settlement in Ereẓ Israel.

Born in Nikolayev, south Russia, Meerovitch graduated from a government institute as an agronomist. After the 1881 pogroms in south Russia, he participated in the establishment of the first *Ḥibbat Zion association in Warsaw and joined the Bilu society. At the end of 1882 he went to Constantinople and took part in the activities of Bilu's political bureau, which was trying to obtain Turkish consent to Jewish agricultural settlement in Ereẓ Israel. He then joined his comrades at *Rishon le-Zion and was active in the settlement's public life.

Meerovitch, who used the pen name Mi-Ziknei ha-Yishuv, wrote letters and articles on life in Ereẓ Israel that were published in the Russian Jewish press, the Yiddish- and German-language Zionist press, and Hebrew papers. He was one of the first to discuss practical agricultural problems and, in 1893/94, edited the first agricultural paper in the country, *Ha-Ikkar* ("The Farmer"). In his Russian book *Opisaniye Yevreyskikh Koloniy v Palestine* ("A Description of the Jewish Settlements in Palestine," 1900), he summarized the achievements of Ereẓ Israel agriculture in its first 25 years.

Meerovitch was active in the work of the Ḥibbat Zion association in Jaffa and headed it from 1903 to 1904. He was among the founders of Aguddat ha-Koremim (Vintners Association) in 1903 and of the Judean Settlement Association in 1913. During World War I he participated in the Jewish community's representative body to the Turkish authorities. From 1918 to 1920 Meerovitch was a member of the Va'ad Le'ummi. His articles and memoirs are of great importance to the historian of Jewish settlement in Ereẓ Israel. Some were collected in book form during his later years: *Ḥevlei Teḥiyyah* ("Pangs of Resurrection," 1930); *Me-ha-Shevil el ha-Derekh* ("From the Path to the Road," 1935, with an annotated list including an index of his articles); *Minḥat Erev* ("Evening Rest," 1940); *Mi-Bilu ad va-Ya'apilu* ("From Bilu to Immigration," 1947). The moshav Talmei Menasheh in the Coastal Plain is named after him.

BIBLIOGRAPHY: M. Smilansky, *Mishpaḥat ha-Adamah*, 3 (1954), 141–50; Tidhar, 2 (1947), 823–5; D. Idelovitch (ed.), *Sefer Rishon le-Ẓiyyon* (1941), 89–92.

[Yehuda Slutsky]

°**MEGASTHENES** (c. 350–290 B.C.E.), ambassador of Seleucus Nicator at the court of the Indian king, Chandragupta. Megasthenes wrote a work on India idealizing the Indians. He apparently included in this work idealized descriptions of the Jews, whom he probably knew firsthand while at the court of Seleucus, to judge from his statement that both the Jews and Brahmans had already taught everything concerning nature that was taught by the ancient Greek philosophers.

MEGGED, AHARON (1920–), Israeli writer. Born in Wloclavek, Poland, his family immigrated to Palestine in 1926. He joined kibbutz Sedot Yam and worked at the port of Haifa. Megged left the kibbutz in 1950 and settled in Tel Aviv where he edited the journal *Ba-Sha'ar.* Together with a number of friends, he founded the biweekly literary magazine *Massa*, which became the weekly literary supplement of the daily *La-Merḥav.* From 1960 to 1971 he served as Israel's cultural attaché in London.

In his prose, which often has strong autobiographical elements, Megged moved from the realism of his early works to surrealism and back to realism. His first short story collection, *Ru'aḥ Yamim* ("Sea Winds," 1950), was inspired by life in Sedot Yam. *Ḥedvah va-Ani* ("Ḥedvah and I," 1964), a realistic novel, tells of the misfortunes of a kibbutz member who had to leave the kibbutz, much against his will, at the insistence of his wife. The protagonist is the first example of Megged's antihero, so typical of his later writings. Lonely, tortured by thoughts of his shortcomings, fearing above all ridicule and abasement, the antihero is always the outsider in an otherwise congenial and united society. In *Mikreh ha-Kesil* (1960; *Fortunes of a Fool*, 1962), he is the only "good man" who fails to join the "society of the wicked." Megged's most ambitious work, the novel *Ha-Ḥai al-ha-Met* (1965; *The Living on the Dead*, 1970), describes in unflattering terms modern Israeli society, and makes the accusation that the great expectations of the first pioneers have not been fulfilled by their successors. One of the most prolific and popular Hebrew writers, Megged mirrors the changes in Israeli society, highlighting moral standards and appealing for tolerance. *Masa be-Av* ("A Journey in the Month of Av," 1980) reflects on the Yom Kippur War and its repercussions; *Ga'agu'im le-Olga* ("Longings for Olga," 1994) depicts the unique relationship between a clerk with literary ambitions and a young Russian woman who becomes his muse; while *Dudaim mi ha-Areẓ ha-Kedoshah* ("Love-Flowers from the Holy Land," 1998) is the story of Beatrice, a devout Protestant who arrives in Palestine in 1906 in order to paint pictures of flowers mentioned in the Bible and gets entangled in local Arab-Jewish affairs. In *Foygelman* (1987; *Foigelman*, 2003), Megged portrays the fate of a Yiddish poet who hopes to find a new home and a sympathetic readership in Israel and encounters instead a total lack of interest in Yiddish as well as in the Diaspora past. Some of Megged's novels deal with authors and writing, describing with a fine sense of humor, often satirically, the literary milieu. Thus, for instance, the novel *Ha-Gamal ha-Me'ofef ve-Dabbeshet ha-Zahav* ("The Flying Camel and the Golden Hump," 1982; German translation, 1991) which focuses on the animosity between an Israeli writer and his neighbor, a literary critic, or *Nikmat Yotam* ("Yotam's Vengeance," 2003), which tells the story of a frustrated translator of Greek classics into Hebrew. Like many of Megged's novels, *Yarḥei ha-Devash shel Profesor Lunẓ* ("The Honeymoons of Professor Lunz," 2004) is a satire on Israeli society, relating the story of a bizarre marriage between an aged scholar of ancient Eastern studies and his second wife, Ayala, a student 50 years his junior.

Megged, a member of the Academy of Hebrew Language, was president of the Israel Center of PEN (1980–87). He received the Bialik Prize, the Brenner Prize, and the Agnon Prize and in 2003 was honored with the Israel Prize for literature. His stories and novels have been translated into several languages and his plays, including *Genesis, Hannah Szenes*, and the comedy *I Like Mike*, have been produced in Israel and abroad. "Tears" is included in G. Abramson (ed.), *The Oxford Book of Hebrew Short Stories* (1996); "Hannah Senesh" in M. Taub (ed.), *Israeli Holocaust Drama* (1996); "The Name" in G. Ramras-Rauch and Y. Michman-Melkman (eds.), *Facing the Holocaust* (1985); "The First Sin," in H.S. Joseph, *Modern Israeli Drama* (1983). A list of his works translated into English appears in Goell, Bibliography, and further information is available at the ITHL website at www.ithl.org.il.

His brother MATTI (Matityahu) MEGGED (1923–2003), poet and literary critic, wrote a number of works that made their mark on the modern Hebrew literary scene. *Ha-Migdal ha-Lavan* (stories, 1949) and *Or ha-Soreg* (novel, 1953) are among his best-known fictional works; *Ha-Drama ha-Modernit* (1966), a collection of essays on drama, and *Dostoevski, Kafka, Beckett* are critical works. He lectured on Hebrew literature at the University of Haifa.

Aharon Megged's wife, EDA ZORITTE-MEGGED (1926–), began publishing essays in 1955. She published her first novel, *Periḥah Afelah* ("Somber Blossoming"), in 1969. Four novels followed, including a novel about Herzl's wife (*Ishto ha-Menudah*, 1997; German translation, 2001) and *Ahavat Ḥayyim* (2000). Zoritte also wrote a monograph on Nathan Alterman (1973), and biographies of the poets Amir Gilboa and Avot Yeshurun.

Aharon Megged's son EYAL MEGGED (1948–), poet and novelist, was born in New York and grew up in Tel Aviv. He studied philosophy and art history and published his first collection of poems in 1972. This was followed by further poems, stories, and five novels, including *Barbarossa* (1973), *Ḥesed Ne'urayikh* ("Early Grace," 1999; German, 2005), and *Ḥayyei Olam* ("Everlasting Life," 2001).

BIBLIOGRAPHY: Kressel, Leksikon, 2 (1967), 313–4; R. Wallenrod, *The Literature of Modern Israel* (1956), 212; Waxman, Literature, 5 (1960²), 41–42; G. Avinor, in: *Moznayim*, 18 (1964), 258–63. **ADD. BIBLIOGRAPHY:** M. Agmon-Fruchtman, "*Leshono shel Megged be-Ha-Ḥai al-ha-Met*," in: *Ha-Sifrut*, 1 (1969), 723–725; S. Shifra, "Literature as an Act of Love: A. Megged," in: *Ariel*, 33–34 (1977), 33–42; M. Avishai, in: *Al ha-Mishmar* (January 21, 1977); A. Zehavi, in: *Yedioth Aharonoth* (February 25, 1977); idem, "The Tragedy of Immigrant Society," in: *Modern Hebrew Literature*, 3:1–2 (1977), 81–84; O. Bartana, in: *Yedioth Aharonoth* (November 21, 1980); A. Feinberg, "Fathers and Sons: Aharon Megged's 'Journey in the Month of Av,'" in: *Modern Hebrew Literature*, 7:1–2 (1981–82), 16–20; Y. Berlovitz, in: *Davar* (January 2, 1981); idem, "*Ha-Determinizm shel ha-Gibbor ben ha-Dor ha-Sheni*," in: *Iton*, 77:28 (1981), 38–40; A. Feinberg: "A. Megged," in: *Modern Hebrew Literature*, 8:3–4 (1983), 46–52; D. Laor, "*Megged be-Ikvot Brecht*," in: *Haaretz* (November 2, 1984); G. Shaked, *Ha-Siporet ha-Ivrit*, 4 (1993), 290–316; R. Feldhai Brenner, "Reflections of Zionism in Recent Hebrew Fiction," in: *Shofar*, 13:1 (1994), 68–69; M. Avishai, "A. Megged," in: *Moznayim*, 71:2 (1996), 15–18; Z. Shavitsky, "The Depiction of German Jewry by A. Megged and I. Zarhi," in: *Australian Journal of Jewish Studies*, 1 (1997), 56–70; H. Lewi, "Bestiaire d'A. Megged," in: *Cahiers du Judaisme*, 6 (1999–2000), 119–132; Y. Oren, "*Kerisat Mitos ha-Ẓabariyyut be-Einei Gimlai Almoni*;" in: *Ha-Umah*, 146 (2001), 91–99; S. Nash, *Hagigim Kiyyumiyyim*, in: *Hadoar*, 81:4 (2002), 14–16; idem, "Itzik Manger, Foigelman and the Problem of the Anti-Hero," in: *Hebrew Studies*, 43 (2002), 57–85; idem, "Aharon Megged's Burden in his Portrayal of the Effects of Israel's Wars," in: *History and Literature* (2002), 389–407; A. Holtzman, "*Ad Erev*," in: *Moznayim*, 76:3 (2002), 3–5; N. Govrin, "*Ha-Zeman ve-ha-Makom be-Limmud ha-Sifrut*," in: *Kivvunim Ḥadashim*, 9 (2003), 122–134; S. Nash, "*Sofrim ve-Nashim ke-Anti-Gibborim bi-Sefarav shel Aharon Megged*," in: *Iton*, 77:278 (2003), 17–22; A. Feinberg, "The Old Man and the Satire," in: *Modern Hebrew Literature*, 2, New Series, 2005–6, 219–220.

[Gitta (Askenazy) Avinor / Anat Feinberg (2nd ed.)]

MEGIDDO (Heb. מְגִדּוֹ), ancient Canaanite and Israelite city, identified with Tell al-Mutasallim on the southern side of the Jezreel Valley, approximately 22 mi. (35 km.) S.E. of Haifa. The site was excavated in 1903–05 by G. Schumacher and in 1925–39 by the Oriental Institute in Chicago, under the direction of C.S. Fisher, P.L.O. Guy, and G. Loud. Small additional soundings were made by Y. Yadin in 1960 and later years. A Tel Aviv University-led expedition under the direction of I. Finkelstein and D. Ussishkin renewed the excavations in 1992. The excavations revealed the existence of over 20 levels, beginning with the Neolithic and Chalcolithic periods. In the Early Bronze Age the first temples were built, as well as a round high-place and a wall, 26 ft. (8 m.) thick. The temples consist of a monumental temple with long corridors, dating to the Early Bronze I (c. 3000 B.C.E.), and three later temples, of the megaron type, dating to the Early Bronze Age III, in the second half of the third millennium B.C.E. The Middle Bronze Age city was surrounded by a strong system of earthworks – embankment and glacis. The construction of the great "Migdal" temple in the cultic compound may also date to this period. A statue of an Egyptian official called Thuthotep, which was found in the excavations, was interpreted by some scholars as indicating that an Egyptian governor probably resided there at that time. The transition from the Middle to the Late Bronze was seemingly peaceful. In approximately 1469 B.C.E. Pharaoh Thutmosis III appeared before the walls of Megiddo, after passing through the Aruna Valley giving the city access to the coast. He overcame a coalition of Canaanite city-states and captured the city after a siege of seven months. From then until Stratum VII the city remained under Egyptian sovereignty. In the el-Amarna period, the king of Megiddo, Biridiya, was hard pressed by the Apiru and Labayu of Shechem (EA, 242–5). The Late Bronze Age city witnessed the erection of an elaborate palace as well as continuity in the "Migdal" temple. A hoard of ivories found in the palace reveals Egyptian, Hittite, Aegean, and local cultural influences. A cuneiform tablet which dates to this period contains a fragment of the Gilgamesh epic. Late Bronze Megiddo also yielded inscriptions from the days of Ramses III and Ramses VI, meaning that it was not destroyed until the second half of the 12th century B.C.E. Dramatic evidence for the destruction of this city was found in the palace and the nearby gate. The next city, Stratum VI (late 11th and early 10th centuries B.C.E.), had many features similar to that of the previous one. Its material culture continued late second-millennium traditions. This city too was destroyed in a fierce conflagration.

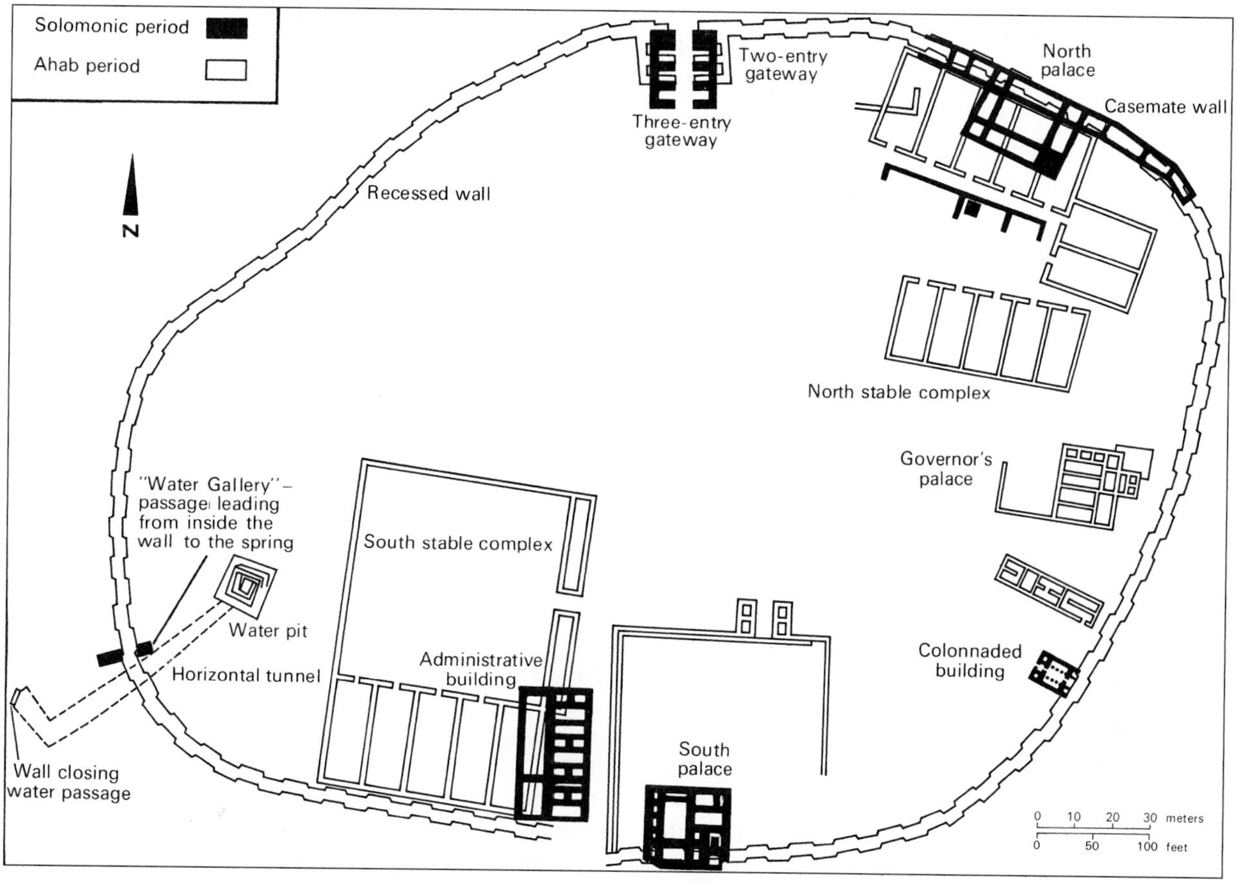

Plan of Megiddo in the time of Solomon and Ahab (tenth-ninth century B.C.E.*). Based on* Encyclopedia of Archeological Excavations in the Holy Land, *Jerusalem, 1970.*

According to biblical tradition, Megiddo did not fall to Joshua, although its king was defeated (Josh. 12:21; cf. Josh. 17:11–13; Judg. 1:27–28). Solomon built the city (I Kings 9:15) and included it in his fifth district (I Kings 4:12). According to archaeologist Yigael Yadin, the Iron Age gate with three guardrooms is identical in plan with the gates at Hazor and Gezer and therefore should be related to the biblical testimony on the building activities of King Solomon. Two palaces built of well-hewn ashlar masonry and probably adorned with proto-Aeolic capitals were also associated by Yadin with King Solomon. Other scholars date the Megiddo gate to the ninth or eighth century and the two palaces to the ninth century. According to this view they should be associated with the Northern Kingdom of Israel. The next city at Megiddo was largely occupied by two units of five rectangular stables and one unit of two stables, with feeding troughs between pillars and a supposed capacity of 450 horses. Yadin attributes these stables to the time of King Ahab, who rallied 2,000 chariots against Shalmaneser III at the Battle of Karkar. Other scholars date them to the days of Jeroboam II, in the first half of the eighth century. A rock-cut water installation, probably built in the days of this city, consists of a shaft 81 ft. (25 m.) deep, with stairs leading to a horizontal tunnel 224 ft. (70 m.) long and to a spring in the slope of the hill, which was thus connected with the city inside the walls. The Israelite city perished in 732 B.C.E. with the conquest of Tiglath Pileser III. The Assyrian king made Megiddo the capital of a province, which included Galilee and the Jezreel Valley. Stratum III features the remains of the Assyrian city. It was rebuilt on a uniform plan, with two large public buildings in the Assyrian style. Stratum II probably dates to the second half of the seventh century B.C.E. King Josiah of Judah was killed by Pharaoh Necho at Megiddo. To this event can be attributed the association of war with the Megiddo Valley in Zechariah 12:11 and with *Armageddon in Revelation 16:16. The last settlement at Megiddo was a small city of the Persian period. Field Marshal *Allenby defeated the Turks at Megiddo in 1918. On his visit to Israel in 1964 Pope Paul VI was received by President Shazar at Tell Megiddo. In 2005 Megiddo was registered as a World Heritage Site.

BIBLIOGRAPHY: P.L.O. Guy and M. Engberg, *Megiddo Tombs* (1938); H. May, *Material Remains of the Megiddo Cult* (1935); R.S. Lamon, *The Megiddo Water System* (1935); R.S. Lamon and M. Shipton, *Megiddo I* (1939); G. Loud, *Megiddo II* (1948); Y. Yadin, "Megiddo of the Kings of Israel," in: BA (1970). **ADD. BIBLIOGRAPHY:** I. Finkelstein, D. Ussishkin, and B. Halpern, *Megiddo III* (2000); idem, *Megiddo IV* (2006).

[Michael Avi-Yonah / Israel Finkelstein and David Ussishkin (2nd ed.)]

MEGILLAH (Heb. מְגִלָּה; "scroll"), designation of each of the five scrolls of the Bible (*Ruth, *Song of Songs, *Lamentations, *Ecclesiastes, *Esther). When the scroll is not specifically named, the term *Megillah* most commonly refers to the scroll of Esther which is read on *Purim.

See Scroll of *Esther; *Scrolls, Five.

MEGILLAH ("Scroll"), tenth tractate in the order *Mo'ed*, in the Mishnah, Tosefta, and Babylonian and Jerusalem Talmuds. *Megillah*, in four chapters, deals with liturgical readings from the Bible, especially with the reading of the *Scroll of Esther on *Purim to which the word *megillah* particularly refers, and with related subjects. The regulations concerning the reading of the Scroll of Esther on Purim are largely dealt with in the first two chapters of the tractate. Chapter 1 is primarily concerned with determining on which day of Adar the *megillah* is to be read, there being a difference between walled cities on the one hand and open towns and villages on the other. Only the first half of this chapter (*mishnayot* 1–4) deals with the *megillah*, while the remainder (5–11) is a collection of various *halakhot*, which were included because they are all introduced by the same formula ("The only difference between A and B is …"). According to J.N. Epstein (Tanna'im, 257) this group belongs to the Mishnah of R. Akiva (Tosef. 1:7–21, gives a similar but longer group of such *halakhot*). Chapter 2 first discusses the appropriate way of reading the *megillah*, e.g., whether reciting by heart and reading in a language other than Hebrew are valid. It goes on to deal with the technicalities of writing a *megillah* to be used for public reading, e.g., whether it must be written on parchment, or whether paper may be used. Among other questions discussed is the qualification of the reader, and whether women or minors are fit to read it. There is also much extraneous matter in this chapter. Chapter 3 starts with a discussion on the sanctity of the synagogue and its appurtenances, but its main contents are the public readings from the Pentateuch and *haftarah*. Chapter 4 continues with the main subject but deals with other liturgical questions (e.g., public reading of the *Shema*, priestly blessings, etc.). The sequence of the chapters as set out above is the one found in current editions of the Mishnah, Jerusalem Talmud, and Tosefta, but in the Babylonian Talmud the order of the last two chapters is reversed. The reason is that since the first Mishnah of chapter 4 opens with the words "He who reads the *megillah*," it was thought appropriate that this chapter follow the first two, which deal mainly with the *megillah*.

Various strata can be detected in the Mishnah. In addition to the above-mentioned groups from the Mishnah of R. Akiva, R. Johanan attributes Mishnah 1:1 to Akiva (Meg. 2a). According to Epstein, Mishnah 2:6 belongs to Eleazar b. Simeon (cf. Men. 72a), Mishnah 3:1 is from the *mishnayot* of Menahem b. Yose, and Mishnah 3:6 from that of Judah b. Ilai; according to the *Gemara* (9b) the second part of 1:9 is Meir's, while its first part is of unknown origin. The order of the paragraphs in the Tosefta to *Megillah* usually corresponds to that in the Mishnah. It includes a vivid description of gatherings in Jerusalem for the performance of *mitzvot* (4 (3):15). There is a great deal of *aggadah* in the Babylonian Talmud. Deserving of particular mention are geographical notes (5b–6b), the observations on the origin of the Targums (3a) and of the Septuagint (8b–9b), the extensive aggadic Midrash to Esther, which is practically a complete Midrash to the Book of Esther (10a–17a), and the arrangement of the **Amidah* (17b–18a). Of linguistic interest is the reference to the confusion of the letter *alef* with *ayin* in certain places, and the problem of correct pronunciation of the letters *he* and *ḥet*. There is less aggadic material in the Jerusalem Talmud than in the Babylonian. Unlike the latter, the Jerusalem Talmud does not give any *aggadot* about the story of Purim. It does, however, deal with the problem of the inclusion of the Book of Esther in the canon (1:7, 70d), and also has lengthy discussions on the laws of writing Torah scrolls and on the divine names (1:11, 71b–72a). It also gives the list of dates included in **Megillat Ta'anit* (1:6, 70c).

BIBLIOGRAPHY: Ḥ. Albeck, *Shishah Sidrei Mishnah, Seder Mo'ed* (1958), 349–53; Epstein, Tannaim, index.

[Arnost Zvi Ehrman]

MEGILLAT SETARIM (Heb. מְגִלַּת סְתָרִים; lit. "concealed scroll"). On two occasions (Shab. 6b; BM 92a), *Rav mentions that he found a *Megillat Setarim* in the academy of R. Ḥiyya containing laws in the name of Isi b. Judah. The first is that there are 39 principal categories of work (*avot melakhah*) forbidden on the Sabbath, but culpability is incurred only on account of one (this is the actual statement quoted, although the Talmud finds it inconceivable and emends it to "there is one for which culpability is not incurred"). In the second he states that the law in Deuteronomy 23:25, "When thou comest into thy neighbor's vineyard, then thou mayest eat grapes until thou have enough at thine own pleasure," applies to anyone entering the vineyard, and not only to a laborer employed there, on which Rava commented, "Isi would make it impossible to live," since a man would soon have his vineyard stripped, and there also the statement is then qualified as a result.

Rashi (ad. loc.) explains that the scroll was concealed because it was forbidden in general to commit the Oral Law to writing but since these laws were not generally taught, they were written down to save them from oblivion. I.H. Weiss is of the opinion that they contained views which Judah ha-Nasi rejected, and they were kept concealed out of respect for him, but this view is most improbable. All the *beraitot* were excluded from the Mishnah, and they contained many views that he had rejected, yet there is no suggestion that they were suppressed. Kaplan maintains that these scrolls were kept concealed because their contents were unsuitable for publication, and in addition he suggests that "concealed" means that they were written in a cryptic manner to conceal their meaning. However, there is nothing particularly cryptic in the language of the passages quoted. Nevertheless, it certainly would have been dangerous to make these laws widely known, and that would also explain why these are the only laws mentioned.

BIBLIOGRAPHY: I.H. Weiss, Dor, 2 (1904[4]), 168–9; M. Kaplan, *Redaction of the Babylonian Talmud* (1933), 277–8.

[Harry Freedman]

MEGILLAT TA'ANIT (Heb. lit. "scroll of fasting" but see below), a list of 36 days on which there were significant victories and happy events in the history of the Jews during the Second Temple, as a result of which the rabbis forbade fasting on them, as well as, in some cases, the delivery of memorial addresses for the dead (*hespedim*). The title should therefore be taken as meaning "the scroll of (the days of prohibited) fasting." The work received its present form close to the time of the destruction of the Second Temple or at the latest during the Bar Kokhba era. It is written in Aramaic and with extreme brevity. According to a tannaitic source (Shab. 13b), it was compiled by "Hananiah b. Hezekiah (b. Garon) and his company," but the appendix to the *megillah* gives the author as Eliezer, the son of this Hananiah, one of the leading rebels against the Romans (Jos., Wars, 2:409). S. Zeitlin regards it as a literary remnant of the rebel party. If this is accepted, the purpose of the list of victories was to strengthen the spirit of heroism and faith in the success of the revolt. The value of the *megillah* for historical research lies in the parallels it provides to the facts and dates mentioned in Josephus. In the period following the conclusion of the Talmud a scholium was appended to the *megillah*, written in mishnaic Hebrew and based upon the Hebrew original of I Maccabees, the talmudic literature, and various oral traditions unknown from any other source. The historical value of this appendix is limited. In the course of time copyists and editors added notes and explanations, taken in particular from the Babylonian Talmud, so that two versions evolved, a Sephardi and an Italian.

The dates included in the *megillah* from before the Hasmonean era are the second Passover (14th Iyar) and Purim. Those from the Hasmonean era are the 23rd of Iyyar when the defenders of the *Acra left Jerusalem, an event mentioned in I Maccabees 13:49–53; the 14th of Sivan, "the seizure of the citadel Zur," identified by Graetz with Beth-Zur conquered by Simeon the Hasmonean (see I Macc. 11:65–66; 14:33); the 15th and 16th of Sivan, in memory of the conquest of Beth-Shean and the valley (of Jezreel) by the sons of John Hyrcanus (see Jos., Ant., 13:280; Jos., Wars, 1:66); the 23rd of Marḥeshvan when they removed the *soreg* from the Temple (according to the appendix, it meant a place "which the gentiles built, on which they stationed harlots"); the 25th of Marḥeshvan, in memory of the capture of Samaria by John Hyrcanus and his sons (see Jos., Wars, 1:64; Jos., Ant., 13:275–81); the 21st of Kislev, "the day of Mt. Gerizim," in memory of the destruction of the Samaritan temple by John Hyrcanus (see Jos., Ant., 13:255/6); the 25th of Kislev, Ḥanukkah, for which festival the appendix mentions several reasons, including that when the Hasmoneans were victorious and found all the temple vessels ritually unclean, "they brought seven iron spits, covered them with white metal, and commenced the lighting"; the 28th of Shevat, when King Antiochus was driven out of Jerusalem (according to the appendix, the reference is to Antiochus IV (Epiphanes), but it is probable that it actually refers to Antiochus VII (Sidetes) of the time of John Hyrcanus; see Jos., Ant., 13:245); and the 13th of Adar, the day of Nicanor, in memory of the defeat of this Syrian commander (see I Macc. 7 and II Macc. 15). The dates from the period of Roman rule over Judea include the third of Kislev, when the "emblems" (the images of the Emperor) were removed from the Temple court, apparently in the time of Pontius Pilate (see Jos., Wars, 2:169), and the 22nd of Shevat, when the edict of Gaius Caligula ordering the erection of a statue of him in the Temple was rescinded (see Jos., Wars, 2:195–203). From the period of the Jewish war with Rome are the 25th of Sivan, when the tax collectors were removed from Judea and Jerusalem, apparently a reference to the suspension of the tax payment to the emperor in 66 C.E., a matter mentioned in the long speech of King Agrippa (Wars, 2:345–401); and the 17th of Elul, when the Romans departed from Jerusalem, although it is not known to what incident this refers.

A number of dates appear to allude to victories of the Pharisees over the Sadducees, but the details are not clear, and apart from two days, the 12th of Adar, "the day of Trajan," which some connect with the emperor Trajan, and the 28th of Adar, which the appendix attributes to the abrogation of Hadrian's edicts, the *megillah* contains no events after 67 C.E. These memorial days were observed until the third century, but later "*Megillat Ta'anit* was rescinded" (TJ, Ta'an. 2:13, 66a; RH 18b). A 13th-century manuscript of the work is extant in the Palatine library in Parma (De Rossi collection no. 117). *Megillat Ta'anit* was first published in Mantua in 1513. A critical edition, with an introduction and commentary, was published by H. Lichtenstein (see bibl.). A new critical edition, *Megillat Ta'anit – Version, Interpretation, History*, was published by Vered Noam in 2003.

BIBLIOGRAPHY: Graetz, Gesch, 3 pt. 2 (1906[5]), 559–77; S. Zeitlin, *Megillat Ta'anit as a Source for Jewish Chronology and History in the Hellenistic and Roman Periods* (1922); H. Lichtenstein (Z. Avneri), in: HUCA, 8–9 (1931–32), 257–351; H. Mantel, in: *Sefer Zikkaron le-Y. Avineri* (1970); B.Z. Lurie, *Megillat Ta'anit* (Heb. ed., 1964).

[Nahum N. Glatzer]

MEGILLAT YUḤASIN (Heb. מְגִלַּת יֻחֲסִין; "genealogical scroll"), a work mentioned by *tannaim* and *amoraim* as having been found in Jerusalem and containing genealogical information on traditions of importance in *halakhah* and in *aggadah*. Simeon b. Azzai (the *tanna* living at the beginning of the second century C.E.) relates that he found a *Megillat Yuḥasin* "in Jerusalem in which was written: so and so is a *mamzer from a married woman" (Mishnah Yev. 4:13). A *baraita* in the Babylonian Talmud (Yev. 49b) adds in his name that this *Megillat Yuḥasin* also included the following two traditions: "the Mishnah [teaching] of Eliezer b. Jacob is little but well sifted; [King] Manasseh killed [the prophet] Isaiah" (Yev. 49b). Similarly Levi (the *amora* of the end of the third century) states that he found in the *Megillat Yuḥasin* in Jerusalem details of the family origin of Hillel, Yose, Nehemiah, Ḥiyya, Yannai, and others (TJ, Ta'an. 4:2, 68a; Gen. R. 98:10; ed. Theodor-Albeck, 1259). Josephus too (Apion, 1:30ff.) testifies to the existence of genealogical documents in Israel, particularly of priestly families. According to him, the priests in Egypt and in Babylon notified the center in Jerusalem of details of their marriages and of the patriarchal families into which they married. The Talmud (Pes. 62b) also mentions a "*Sefer Yuḥasin*," but it does not appear to have any connection with the aforementioned *Megillat Yuḥasin*. It is difficult to determine its exact nature from the data given in the Talmud, but it seems to have been a kind of Midrash or *baraita* to the Book of Chronicles. According to Rashi (Pes. 62b), the work contained "reasons for the Laws of the Torah," but from a statement of *Amram Gaon (*Oẓar ha-Ge'onim* to Pes., p. 80, no. 190) it seems that the work served as a commentary and supplement to the genealogical lists in the biblical books. The Talmud there states that Simlai requested Johanan to teach him *Sefer Yuḥasin* but the latter refused to accede to his request. It also states in the name of Rav that from the time the *Sefer Yuḥasin* was concealed the sages became weak and their vision was dimmed.

[Yitzhak Dov Gilat]

MEḤILAH (Heb. מְחִילָה; "waiver"), the renunciation, repudiation, abandonment, or surrender of some claim, right, or privilege. *Meḥilah* may be the waiver of a present right or *lien or the waiver of the right to a future increment; in the latter case, it is usually referred to as *silluk* (TJ, Ket. 9:1, 32d; Ket. 83a).

Range of Applicability

Meḥilah cancels any debt, lien, or *obligation regardless of origin. Thus, debts arising out of *loans, *sale, *leasing and hiring, *labor, *partnership, and *surety; liens on *property put up as collateral; obligations originating in *contract or *tort – all are effectively cancelled by *meḥilah* on the part of the creditor. Nor is the effectiveness of *meḥilah* curtailed by the form of the obligation; it applies with equal vigor whether the obligation is an oral or written one, whether it is attested to by witnesses or not (Gulak, Yesodei, 2 (1922), 111–4, 162f.).

Silluk, i.e., the waiving of future accretions, however, is only of limited effectiveness. This is due to the general reluctance of Jewish law to grant effective control over things that have as yet not come into existence (*davar she-lo ba la-olam*; see *Contract). Thus, if, on the one hand, a person possesses a present right, claim, or lien, *silluk* cannot dissolve it; only *meḥilah* can do so. If, on the other hand, the future right, claim, or lien is so remote as to have no specific relationship to this particular person, his *silluk* is equally ineffective since it pertains to *davar she-lo ba la-olam*. However, if the future right, claim, or lien, although not in existence, has by the operation of circumstances at least achieved a likelihood of accruing to a specific person, then his *silluk* is effective. Thus, the ability of a man to waive the rights of usufruct in his wife's property depends upon the status of his relationship with her; if he has already married her (*nissu'in*), his claim on her usufruct is a present one; hence his waiver must be in the form of *meḥilah*, and his *silluk* is no longer effective. If he has not entered into the first stage of *marriage (*erusin*), the usufruct in her property has as yet not come into existence (it is a *davar she-lo ba la-olam*); hence it is sufficiently remote as to vitiate the effectiveness of either form of waiver, that of *meḥilah* and that of *silluk*. If, however, he has entered into the first stage of marriage (*erusin*) but has not yet consummated the marriage (*nissu'in*), the right of usufruct, although not yet in existence, has achieved sufficient likelihood of accruing to him as to have endowed him with the power, not of *meḥilah*, but of *silluk* (Ket. 83a–84a, and codes).

The effectiveness of *silluk* with regard to obligations (i.e., rabbinic origin; see **Mishpat Ivri*) that have as yet not come into existence is undisputed among the early authorities (**rishonim*; see *Authority, Rabbinical). Its effectiveness with regard to obligations which are *mi-de-oraita* (i.e., biblical origin; see **Mishpat Ivri*) that have as yet not come into existence presented these scholars with two major difficulties:

(1) it is an established rule of law that conditions contrary to biblical law are void (BM 7:11).

(2) The Talmud rules that biblical rights of succession, which are *mi-de-oraita*, such as those of a son to inherit his father's estate (in contradistinction to the right of a husband to inherit his wife, which is *mi-de-rabbanan*), cannot be waived (cf. Ket. 83a). The first difficulty was overcome by the limitation of the rule to non-monetary conditions on the one hand, and by the limitation of the power of waiver to monetary obligations on the other. The second limitation was overcome by construing *mi-de-oraita* rights of inheritance as being unique in that they inhere in the heirs even before the death of the owner of the estate; hence *silluk*, as the waiver of future rights, is impossible (*Keẓot ha-Ḥoshen* 209 n. 11).

Waiver is limited to rights; it is ineffective as a mode of transfer of real property or of chattel (*Rema*, ḤM 241:2).

Legal Analysis

It has been pointed out that in the realm of rights, where it is effective, waiver does not constitute a transfer; rather it is mere withdrawal. A creditor who waives his claim does not transfer his right to the debtor and thereby extinguish the claim; on the contrary, he withdraws his right or removes his lien from the debtor and his estate. The effectiveness of *meḥilah*, therefore, is independent of the wishes of the debtor. Thus, if a creditor waives the debt due to him and the debtor refuses to avail himself of the waiver, the waiver nevertheless takes effect. Had *meḥilah* been viewed as a kind of transfer, it would have failed to take effect inasmuch as the debtor, as transferee, had declined (cf. Herzog, Instit, 2 (1939), 229). The juridical basis of waiver is the insistence of the law that the obligatory nature of monetary obligations is always dependent upon the will of the party to whom the obligation is due; the suspension of this will, e.g., by waiver, automatically extinguishes the obligation (Maimonides, nov., BB 126b).

Formal Requirements

Meḥilah requires no formal mode (*meḥilah einah ẓerikhah kinyan*; Yad, Mekhirah 5:11 and Ishut 17:19; Tosef to Sanh. 6a, s.v. *ẓerikhah*). It is effective by parole alone. Some authorities, however, do require a formal *kinyan* to validate the waiver of a creditor who retains possession of the debtor's promissory note (cf. commentaries to Sh. Ar., ḤM 12:8; see also *Acquisition). There is no formal requirement that witnesses validate a waiver of indebtedness. The function of witnesses is evidentiary, preventing the creditor from subsequently denying his act of waiver or from alleging that the act was made in jest. For this purpose, the witnesses need not have been formally appointed; their mere presence suffices (Sh. Ar., ḤM 81:29).

Implied Waiver

Waiver may be express or implied. Thus, the mere declaration of the creditor that the debtor owes him nothing absolves the latter of all obligation; for although he knows that the creditor's statement is incorrect, it is nevertheless construed as an implied waiver (Sh. Ar., ḤM 75:11; *Rema*, ḤM 40:1; but cf. *Siftei Kohen*, ḤM 81, n. 72). Asher Gulak has pointed out the similarity between this waiver implied in the creditor's denial of the debtor's indebtedness with the *acceptilatio* in Roman law. This was an oral form of dissolving obligations by having the debtor ask the creditor, "What I have promised you, have you received it (*habesne acceptum*)?" and the creditor answering, "I have (*habeo*)." The effectiveness of the Roman *acceptilatio* was limited, however, to the dissolution of obligations created by verbal contracts (*verbis*); it was ineffective in dissolving obligations created by real (*re*) and written (*litteris*) contracts. This limitation does not exist in Jewish law where the creditor's declaration of receipt of payment dissolves all obligations, regardless of origin (cf. Gulak, Yesodei, 2 (1922), 112f.). Implied waiver serves as the operational rationale of a number of legal rules. Thus, the rule that monetary conditions contrary to law are valid is justified on the grounds that the parties entering into the agreement governed by said conditions have implicitly waived their (monetary) rights (Rashi, Kid. 19b; see also *Contract). Similarly, the rule that overreaching (*ona'ah*) that involves less than one-sixth of the fair price need not be returned to the injured party is explained on the basis of an implied waiver on the part of the latter (Yad, Mekhirah 12:3; cf. Sma., ḤM 227 n. 2). Again, the lapse of the right of a widow who no longer lives on her husband's estate to collect her *ketubbah* after 25 years, in localities where written *ketubbot* are not used, is based upon implied waiver (Ket. 104a; Yad, Ishut 16:23; see also *Limitation of Actions).

Legal Rules Limiting its Effectiveness

Some of the legal rules governing waiver may be summarized as follows:

(1) The power of waiver applies to claims estimable in money (*manona ityaḥiv li-meḥilah*); it is thus inapplicable to modes of effectuating marriage and divorce (Kid. 7a; Git. 64a).

(2) Waiver need not be made in the presence of the debtor, but the debt does not lapse until the waiver has come to his knowledge (*Arukh ha-Shulḥan*, ḤM 241:4; but cf. Herzog, Instit, 2 (1939), 231f.).

(3) If co-debtors are named in one promissory note and the creditor waives the obligation of one of them, the other's obligation remains intact and is actionable (opinion of Sh. Ar., ḤM 77:6; disputed by *Rema, ad loc.). If the debtors are correal, however, i.e., where each is bound severally to discharge the entire liability, the creditor's waiver of the obligation to one of them cancels the liability of all (*ibid.*).

(4) A waiver of the lien on an obligation, retaining, however, the obligation itself, must be accomplished by a *kinyan* in order to be effective (*Derishah*, ḤM 111, n. 10).

(5) A creditor may effectively waive part of the obligation, or he may postpone the date of payment by waiving the time stipulated in the **shetar* (Sh. Ar., ḤM 66:24, and *Siftei Kohen*, *ibid.*, n. 83).

(6) A waiver, in order to be effective, must be related to an object that is definite or to a quantity that is fixed; obligations that are vague, limitless, or unknown are unaffected by *meḥilah* (Yad, Mekhirah 13:3; Sh. Ar., ḤM 232:7).

(7) Waiver is ineffective if made through error (see *Mistake; Tos. to BM 66b, s.v. *ḥatam*; cf. Herzog, Instit, 2 (1939), 299); if made under duress (see **Ones*, Tos. to BB 48a, s.v. *amar*); if made in jest (Yad, Mekhirah 5:13 and Ishut 17:19); and if made by minors and, presumably, by *deaf-mutes and mentally incompetents (BM 22b).

(8) The effectiveness of *meḥilah* is disputed in cases where the creditor retains possession of the debtor's promissory note or his *pledge, some authorities requiring a formal *kinyan* to supplement the waiver by parole (Sh. Ar., ḤM 12:8; 241:2; and commentaries).

BIBLIOGRAPHY: I.S. Zuri, *Mishpat ha-Talmud*, 5 (1921), 25; Gulak, Yesodei, 1 (1922), 159; 2 (1922), 111–4, 162f.; Herzog, Instit, 2 (1939), 115, 132ff., 229–33, 299f.; Elon, Mafte'aḥ, 123–9.

[Aaron Kirschenbaum]

MEḤIẒAH (Heb. מְחִיצָה; "partition"), designation of the partition screen in synagogues between the space reserved for men and that, generally in the rear or upstairs, for women. The origin of the *meḥiẓah* derives from the talmudic description of the festivities (*Simḥat Beit ha-Sho'evah*) held on the second evening of the feast of Tabernacles in the court of women of the Temple (Suk. 5:2; Mid. 2:5). The Talmud states that men and women were allotted separate space (Suk. 51b–52a; Tosef., Suk. 4:1). Further sources for the separation of the sexes, as practiced in traditional synagogues, are to be found in midrashic literature like *Pirkei de-Rabbi Eliezer* 41, where it is stated in the name of R. Pinḥas that men and women stood separately when the Israelites assembled at Mount Sinai to receive the Ten Commandments (see also PdRE 23). Remains of galleries discovered in ancient Palestine synagogues have been taken as belonging to the women's sections.

Most European synagogues of the Middle Ages had a separate women's gallery called *Weibershul* fenced off by an iron grille or a non-transparent curtain. In synagogues where there was no balcony, the *meḥiẓah* was made of latticework serving as a partition between the seats of the men in front and those of the women in the rear. References to the custom of *meḥiẓah* in the Middle Ages can be found in the responsa literature of that period such as *Mordecai b. Hillel's commentary to Shab. 3, note no. 311, where it is stated "We are permitted to erect on Sabbath the partition-curtain between men and women during the time of the sermon" (see also *Sefer ha-Maharil* of Jacob Moellin (ed. Cremona (1565), 38a, 50b, 59b). The abolition of the *meḥiẓah* by the Reform movement in Europe in the early part of the 19th century was strongly opposed by the leading rabbinic authorities in Hungary and Poland, such as Moses *Sofer, Moses *Schick, and Elijah *Guttmacher, who regarded this innovation as an illicit change and, consequently, ruled that any synagogue without *meḥiẓah* is unfit for prayer.

In most Conservative synagogues in the United States, the *meḥiẓah* has been abolished and men and women sit together, or, in some cases, one side of the synagogue is reserved for the men and the other for the women, without an actual partition. In Reform synagogues the segregation of men and women has been entirely abolished based on the fact that the Bible nowhere commands the separation of men and women during public worship or assemblies (see Deut. 31:12; Neh. 8:2–3). These modern trends met with vigorous opposition in the 1950s on the part of Orthodox Jewry in the United States, which has come to regard the retention of the *meḥiẓah* as a cardinal principle and as a mark of the preservation of the Orthodox character of the synagogue. In several congregations the Orthodox minority turned to the courts for legal redress and were granted relief by court orders enjoining the synagogue board from changing the status quo, as in the case of congregation Beth Tefilas Moses of Mount Clemens, Michigan (Court Order of Sept. 21, 1959). Similar litigations were dealt with by the state courts in New Orleans, Louisiana and by the Superior Court of Pennsylvania (no. 178, October Term, 1954), all of which ruled in favor of the party demanding the retention of the *meḥiẓah*.

BIBLIOGRAPHY: J.B. Agus, *Guideposts in Modern Judaism* (1954), 133ff.; idem, in: *Conservative Judaism*, 11:1 (1956), 11ff.; Elbogen, Gottesdienst, 49; B. Litvin, *Sanctity of the Synagogue* (1959; Orthodox viewpoint). HALAKHIC RESPONSA: Moses Schreiber, *Ḥatam Sofer* (1855), to Sh. Ar., ḤM 190, OḤ 28; Moses Schick, *Maharam Schick* (1880) to Sh. Ar., OḤ 77; Hillel Lichtenstein, *Teshuvot Beit Hillel* (1908), no. 50; Ḥayyim Halberstam, *Divrei Ḥayyim* (1875), no. 18; Elijah Guttmacher, *Zikhron Shelomo* (1933), 70–72.

[Meir Ydit]

MEHLSACK, ELIAKIM BEN JUDAH HA-MILZAHGI (c. 1780–1854), Polish talmudist. "Milzahgi" is a derivation of Mehlsack, the German name for Samila in Poland where Eliakim was born. He settled in Galicia and lived his last years in Lvov and Brody under the patronage of Isaac Berish Blumenfeld of Brody, devoting his life to Jewish scholarship. In 1837 he published *Sefer Ravyah* (= **R**abbi Eliakim **b**. Judah **h**a-Milzahgi), a criticism of the *Gottesdienstliche Vortraege* of *Zunz and the *Toledot* of Solomon Judah *Rapoport. Unlike Zunz, who conceded the correctness of some of Mehlsack's remarks, Rapoport took umbrage at them and replied scathingly in *Kerem Ḥemed* (6 (1841), 96–109). Although he wrote almost 70 books, only *Sefer Ravyah* was published. Mehlsack also published an attack against the forgeries of A. *Firkovich in the German-Jewish press. Most of his works were about Talmud and Kabbalah, but *Mirkevet Esh* ("Train of Fire") argues that one is permitted to travel by train on the Sabbath. The manuscript was sent to S. *Holdheim, the leading Reform rabbi, who reproduced parts of it in a German-Jewish periodical. According to Gershom Scholem, Mehlsack's unpublished study of the Zohar, *Zohorei Ravyah*, at the Hebrew National and University Library is the most significant book written on the Zohar during the 19th century. Extant also is his commentary on the Book of *Raziel (London, Jews College Ms. 347). His treatise on the principle of the Kabbalah and a commentary on the *Pesikta de-Rav Kahana* have not survived.

BIBLIOGRAPHY: P. Lachower, in: *Keneset*, 6 (1941), 299–300; G. Kressel in: KS, 17 (1940), 87–94 (his bibliography); G. Scholem and I. Joel (eds.), *Kitvei Yad be-Kabbalah* (1930), 40 no. 13; Zunz-Albeck, Derashot, 20–21; S.D. Luzzatto, *Iggerot Shadal*, ed. by E.S. Graeber, pt. 4 (1882), 602–5.

[Zvi Avneri / Getzel Kressel]

MEHRING, WALTER (1896–1981), German poet and author. The son of the well-known journalist Sigmar Mehring (1866–1915), Walter Mehring was born and raised in Berlin. He studied art history in Berlin and Munich. A friend of Kurt *Tucholsky, he joined the Berlin branch of the Dada movement, wrote political cabaret pieces, and published his early expressionistic poems in Herwarth *Walden's *Sturm* from 1916. They were collected in his first books, *Das politische Cabaret* (1919) and *Ketzerbrevier* (1921), which revealed his writing to be "heretical," meaning critical and provocative. During the Weimar Republic Mehring, who became a brilliantly witty spokesman of the moderate left, worked on the staff of the *Weltbuehne* as its correspondent in Paris, where he lived from 1922 to 1928. His satirical light verse followed the tradition developed by Wedekind, Ringelnatz, and Brecht, and his *chansons* dealt with the life of the vagabond, symbolizing the disillusionment of his age. Mehring's best-known collection of poems is *Die Gedichte, Lieder und Chansons des Walter Mehring* (1929), notable for its sarcastic criticism of contemporary society. In his comedy *Der Kaufmann von Berlin* (1929), which was staged by Erwin Piscator and outraged the Nazis, Mehring took on the subject of Shylock to describe the pogroms against the East European Jews in the Berlin Scheunenviertel in 1923. Confronting the beginning of persecution, he wrote *Arche Noah S.O.S.* (1931). On their accession to power in 1933, the Nazis planned to arrest Mehring, who, having been warned, managed to escape to Paris, and from there to Vienna in 1934 and after the "Anschluss" in 1938 back to Paris. In 1941 Mehring fled to New York, escaping from an internment camp in Southern France. There he remained from 1941 until after World War II, living under difficult conditions but continuing to write such books as *No Road Back* (1944) and *The Lost Library* (1951; *Die verlorene Bibliothek. Autobiographie einer Kultur*; 1952), both published in English and German. *The Lost Library*, meaning the library of his father, is an analysis, in the face of the Nazi catastrophe, of the tragic failure of the intellectual culture of liberalism and optimism among 19th-century German Jews. After the war, Mehring returned to Europe, living mostly in hotels in Switzerland (Ascona and Zuerich, where he died). Here he recollected the avant gardist culture of the Weimar Republic in several books (e.g., *Verrufene Malerei*, 1958; *Berlin-Dada*, 1959) and reissued his *Ketzerbrevier* (1974) in an expanded version.

ADD. BIBLIOGRAPHY: F. Hellberg, *Walter Mehring: Schriftsteller zwischen Kabarett und Avantgarde* (1983); H.-P. Bayerdoerfer, in: *Conditio Judaica*, 3 (1993), 307–23; B. Bauer, in: *Deutsch-juedisches Exil* (1994), 15–43; A. Kilcher, in: *Deutsche Vierteljahrsschrift für Literaturwissenschaft und Geistesgeschichte*, 78 (2004), 287–312.

[Rudolf Kayser / Andreas Kilcher (2nd ed.)]

°MEHTA, ZUBIN (1936–), conductor. Mehta, the son of the conductor Mehli Mehta, was born in Bombay. He received training in violin and piano as a child and formed an ambition to conduct. He started his professional career in Vienna and England. Mehta was then music director of the Montreal Symphony Orchestra (1962–67) and chief conductor of the Los Angeles Philharmonic Orchestra (1962–68). He was the youngest person to hold such an appointment with a leading orchestra in the U.S. and the first in North America to share a joint appointment with two major orchestras. Mehta made his debut at the Metropolitan Opera in 1965 (*Aida*) and his London opera debut with *Otello* in 1977. He was musical director of the New York Philharmonic Orchestra (1978–91), and from 1998 of the Bavarian Staatsoper in Munich. He also served as music director of the Maggio Musicale Fiorentino. Though non-Jewish, Mehta played an important role in the musical life of Israel. He first appeared with the Israel Philharmonic Orchestra in 1961 and the close contact between him and the orchestra was maintained ever since. The IPO appointed Mehta music advisor in 1969, music director in 1977, and music director for life in 1981. He conducts the orchestra in subscription concerts, special concerts, and major national events, and in concerts in development towns, kibbutzim, and army camps. During both the Six-Day War and the Yom Kippur War he canceled all engagements and hastened to Israel to conduct special concerts and to generally identify himself with Israel. He also conducted the IPO on worldwide tours of Europe, North and South America, and the Far East. Mehta realized a longtime ambition in 1994, when he brought the IPO to India. He won countless awards and distinctions in many countries. In Israel he was awarded honorary doctorates and the Hebrew University also named a wing of the Musicology Department after him and his father. Mehta was also awarded a special prize at the Israel Prize presentations for 1991 and he was the recipient of the Wolf Foundation Prize for Music (1995–96). He was an Honorary Citizen of Tel Aviv-Yafo. Mehta conducted an encore from *Tristan and Isolde* with the Israel Philharmonic in 1981, but a Holocaust survivor interrupted his performance. Mehta halted the performance and since then has never included Wagner's music in his performances in Israel. His numerous recordings range from a cycle of Mahler symphonies and operas by Verdi and Puccini to works by contemporary American composers. Mehta's performances generally favored romantic warmth of expression and voluptuous sonority, combined with bold attack and rhythmic vigor and reinforced by boundless self-confidence.

BIBLIOGRAPHY: Grove online; *Baker's Biographical Dictionary* (1997); M. Bookspan and R. Yockey, *Zubin Mehta* (1978, 1980²).

[Naama Ramot (2nd ed.)]

MEI AMMI (Heb. מֵי עַמִּי), kibbutz in central Israel, in the Iron Hills of Samaria, affiliated with Ha-No'ar ha-Ẓiyyoni, founded in 1963 as a *Naḥal outpost on the pre-1967 Jordanian border. In August 1967 a civilian group took over the village, whose construction – including the reclamation of its hilly land – was aided by the Jewish community of Miami, Florida. Accordingly, the name chosen, meaning "Water of My People," is similar in sound to Miami. In the mid-1990s, the population was approximately 185, increasing to 208 in 2002.

[Efraim Orni]

MEIDNER, LUDWIG (1884–1966), German painter. Meidner was born in Bernstadt, in Silesia. At 19, he went to Breslau to study art. For a time he eked out a living in Berlin, sketching for fashion magazines, but in 1906–08 studied in Paris. In 1908 he returned to Berlin where in 1912, with Jakob *Steinhardt and Richard Janthur, Meidner founded the group *Die Pathetiker.*

Though an ardent pacifist, Meidner was drafted into the German army, and served throughout World War I. In January 1918 he was given furlough to attend his one-man show of prewar paintings in Berlin. One of its major features was the oil, "I and the City," in which he presented himself as a large, tortured, brooding figure, with exploding streets, factories, and tenements in the background. The show caused a great stir and Meidner suddenly became one of the foremost representatives of expressionism in Central Europe. After the war, Meidner was prominent in the *Novembergruppe*, an association of artists and intellectuals eager to bridge the gap between the public and the nation's creative minds.

Meidner was deeply attached to Judaism, and for a time during the early Nazi period taught drawing at the Jewish Yawne secondary school in Cologne. In 1939 he escaped to England. During the air raids on London he served as night watchman in a morgue. Here, for a few pounds each, he painted portraits of deceased people from photographs. In 1952 he returned to Germany, and for a time lived in the Jewish Old Age Home in Frankfurt. A portrait commission by the German president Theodor Heuss led to his rediscovery; this enabled him to have a studio for the last years of his life. On his 80th birthday in 1964, he was awarded the Grosses Verdienstkruez of the Federal Republic of Germany. Meidner's most important works are those painted before World War I. Apart from his apocalyptic landscapes and his Jewish themes, his most significant creations are his disturbingly intense self-portraits and portraits of friends. His wife, Elsa Meidner, also made a reputation as a painter.

BIBLIOGRAPHY: T. Grochowiak, *Ludwig Meidner* (1966). **ADD. BIBLIOGRAPHY:** G. Breuer and I. Wagemann, *Ludwig Meidner. Zeichner, Maler, Literat*, vols. I and II. Exhibition Catalog Mathildenhoehe Darmstadt (1991; with Catalogue raisonné); G. Heuberger, (eds.), *Ludwig und Else Meidner* (2002); G.T. Natter (ed.), *Im Nacken das Sternenmeer. Ludwig Meidner. Ein deutscher Expressionist* (2001); Verein August Macke Haus e.V. (ed.), *Ludwig Meidner – Weltentaumel. Die expressionistische Werkphase* (2004).

[Alfred Werner / Jihan Radjai-Ordoubadi (2nd ed.)]

MEIER, JULIUS (1874–1937), U.S. governor. Meier was born in Portland, Oregon. He became president and general manager of his family's mercantile firm, Meier and Frank Company in Portland. Meier developed the Columbia River highway system. During World War I, he was northwest regional director of the Council of National Defense. When his former law partner, the Progressive Republican candidate for governor in 1930, died during the campaign, Meier reluctantly agreed to run as an Independent against a regular Republican and a Democrat and won. During his term as governor (1931–35), he fostered conservation of the state's natural resources, formation of the state police system, and establishment of a nonpolitical judiciary, and he demanded rigid economies in state expenditures. While governor, he served as president of Congregation Beth Israel in Portland (1933–35), which his father had helped to found.

BIBLIOGRAPHY: H.M. Corning (ed.), *Dictionary of Oregon History* (1956), 165; R. Neuberger, in: *Opinion*, 4:9 (1934), 10–12; J.J. Nodel, *The Ties Between* (1959), 128; E. Pillsbury, in: *American Hebrew*, 129 (1931), 509–22; B. Postal, *Jewish Tourist Guide to the U.S.* (1954), 520–3; UJE, S.V.

[Robert E. Levinson]

MEIER, RICHARD (1934–), U.S. architect. Meier was born in Newark, N.J. Fifty years later in 1984, he became the youngest winner of the Pritzker architecture prize, one of the most heralded awards for architects. The road to this award and to many important architectural commissions began after Meier graduated from Cornell University in 1957. He worked for the firms of Skidmore, Owings and Merrill and Marcel Breuer before establishing his own firm in 1963.

Meier made his early mark with the designs for private residences, which recall the light and geometric designs of the Bauhaus, especially the form established by Mies van der Rohe as well as the Constructivists. Japanese architecture from the 17th century was also important in formulating Meier's aesthetic. The architect has suggested the strong influence of Le Corbusier in his work. Meier's early important commissions were for the Smith House in Darien, Conn., built between 1965 and 1967, followed by the Douglas House at Harbor Springs, Mich. in 1973, and the Shamberg residence, planned for two people, at Chappaqua, N.Y., from 1972 to 1974. He converted the Bell Telephone laboratories in Manhattan to 383 apartments and went on to design the Atheneum in New Harmony, Ind., 1975 to 1979, to much acclaim. In museum design, Meier has created striking designs in the Museum of Decorative Arts in Frankfurt (1981–84), the High Museum of Art in Atlanta (1981), the Museum of Contemporary Art in Barcelona (1992–95), and the Getty Museum in Los Angeles (1997).

Meier emphasizes white as an essential color in his design, which accentuates the power of the visual form. Meier's buildings are striking, especially against a simple grass landscape, as in the case with the Atheneum, the Des Moines Art Center extension, or the High Museum, where the whiteness and architectonic characteristics of the form are juxtaposed to the green landscape, resulting in a powerful but restful aesthetic. All of Meier's works stand as sculptural forms as well as functional buildings.

Meier's most contested building is the Getty Museum in Los Angeles. Sitting on the hillside that overlooks both Los Angeles and Santa Monica, the Getty is a series of buildings that seeks to bring together a huge and eclectic art collection. Driven by the immense resources of the Getty Foundation and the size of the collection, the museum space, comprised of six buildings, has been compared to an acropolis. To some, the scale of the project served to limit the architect's powers of invention. The uniformity of Meier's usual white exterior was compromised in part by a beige travertine.

BIBLIOGRAPHY: K. Frampton and J. Rykwet, *Richard Meier, Architect* (1985–2004); P. Goldberger, *Richard Meier Houses* (1996); R. Meier, *Richard Meier* (Electa's Modern Masters) (2003).

[Stephen C. Feinstein (2nd ed.)]

MEIJER, JACOB (**"Jaap"**; 1912–1993), Dutch-Jewish historian. Born into an impecunious provincial Jewish family, Meijer received a stipend to attend the Ashkenazi Teachers and Rabbinical Seminary in Amsterdam from the age of 13. He later studied at the University of Amsterdam, and in 1941, one of the last Jewish students allowed to do so, took his Ph.D. with a thesis on the 19th-century Amsterdam Sephardi author and poet Isaac da *Costa. He survived two years in Bergen-Belsen concentration camp (1943–45). From 1945 on he taught history at municipal high schools, including a number of years in Paramaribo, Dutch Guyana, and in Haarlem.

With strong Jewish awareness, he wrote several books on Dutch-Jewish history, particularly on the 19th and early 20th centuries. His works include *Het verdwenen ghetto* ("Walks through the Prewar Jewish Quarter of Amsterdam," 1948), *Het Jonas Daniel Meijerplein* ("Three Centuries of Amsterdam Jewry," 1961), *Erfenis der Emancipatie* ("Dutch Jewry in the First Half of the 19th Century," 1963), *Zij lieten hun sporen achter* ("Jewish Contributions to Dutch Culture," 1964), *Van*

Israeliten tot Israeliers ("150 Years of Jewish History in The Netherlands," 1965), and *De zoon van enn Gazzen* ("The Life of Jacob Israel de Haan," 1967). He also published two volumes of *Encyclopedia Sefaradica Neerlandica* (1950), covering the letters A-C and D-F; the project was never completed.

Meijer also wrote monographs on Dutch-Jewish personalities, such as on the bibliographer and first librarian of the Bibliotheca Rosenthaliana, Meyer *Roest, and Chief Rabbi J.H. *Duenner, and contributed regularly to Dutch periodicals, general and Jewish. In addition, from 1968 on, he published many volumes of poetry – in Dutch and in the dialect of the region of his birth, East-Groningen – under the penname Saul van Messel.

BIBLIOGRAPHY: L. Dasberg and J.N. Cohen (eds.), *Neveh Ya'akov*, Jubilee Volume presented to Dr. Jaap Meijer on the occasion of his 70th birthday (1982); I. Cornelissen, *Een dwarsliggende Jood, Jaap Meijer* (1995).

[Henriette Boas]

MEIJERS, EDUARD MAURITS (1880–1954), Dutch jurist who as professor of law at Leiden University from 1910 to 1950 influenced several generations of Dutch lawyers. Born in Den Helder, Meijers was admitted to the bar in 1903. He practiced law in Amsterdam until 1910, when he was made professor of civil and private international law at Leiden University. He served this university both as dean and rector. After 1928 he was substitute counselor in the High Court of Justice at The Hague. Meijers' numerous books were largely devoted to the history of civil law. His work *The Labor Contract* (1908) became a standard treatise on the subject and was followed by *Legal Decisions Regarding the Law on Labor Contracts* (1909). His textbook on succession, *Le droit ligurien de succession en Europe occidentale* (1928), and his *L'Histoire des principes fondamentaux du droit international privé à partir du Moyen Age* (1934) brought him further distinction. Following the Nazi invasion of Holland, Meijers was dismissed from his post and was sent to the *Westerbork and *Theresienstadt camps for the duration of the war. His arrest led to a public demonstration by students at Leiden. The dean, Professor R.P. Cleveringa, gave a famous address, protesting against Meijers' arrest. Cleveringa himself was imprisoned for this speech. After World War II, Meijers was commissioned to draft a new civil code for Holland, but died before its completion. He was chairman of the Royal Dutch Academy of Sciences from 1945 until 1949.

ADD. BIBLIOGRAPHY: R. Feenstra, in: *Biografisch Woordenboek van Nederland* (1979), s.v.

[Henriette Boas / Bart Wallet (2nd ed.)]

ME'ILAH (Heb. מְעִילָה; "sacrilege"), eighth tractate in the Mishnah, Tosefta, and Babylonian Talmud order *Kodashim*. *Me'ilah* contains six chapters and deals with the unlawful use and enjoyment of *hekdesh* (i.e., things consecrated to the Temple, especially sacrifices). The scriptural basis is Leviticus 5:15–16, which lays down that a person inadvertently committing a trespass "in holy things" shall bring a guilt offering, make restitution for the loss caused, and pay an additional fine. Chapters 1 and 2 discuss the various offerings and sacrificial portions to which the law of *me'ilah* applies, and define the moment from which an offering is considered *hekdesh* for the purpose of this law. Chapter 3 is concerned with exceptional instances of illicit enjoyment of *hekdesh*, which are not affected by the law of *me'ilah*. Chapters 4 and 5 include the problem of determining the minimal value of misappropriation to which the law applies, and especially whether illicit enjoyment that causes no loss to *hekdesh* constitutes *me'ilah*. Chapter 6 deals with trespass by proxy. The Tosefta is divided into three chapters. The Babylonian *Gemara* enlarges on the teaching of the Mishnah but, with the exception of the remarkable *Ben Temalyon story (17b), there are no aggadic digressions. *Me'ilah* was translated into English in the Soncino edition of the Talmud (1948).

[Arnost Zvi Ehrman]

°**MEINERTZHAGEN, RICHARD HENRY** (1878–1967), British soldier, administrator, and supporter of Zionism. Meinertzhagen was the son of a successful non-Jewish German merchant in London; his mother was the sister of Beatrice Webb, the famous socialist. He was educated at Harrow and became an army officer. During World War I he served on the East African front and was on the staff of General *Allenby's army, which conquered Palestine. He was chief political officer in Palestine and Syria in the postwar military administration, and in a dispatch to the Foreign Office (1919), accused the military administration of hostility to the principles of the *Balfour Declaration, expressing the view that Arab opposition to Zionism would not last once it was known that the British government was determined to carry through its pledge of a national home to the Jewish people. He joined Herbert *Samuel's staff when the latter was appointed high commissioner of Palestine. Meinertzhagen was also attached to the British delegation to the Paris Peace Conference as an advisor (1919–20), and from 1921 to 1924 he was military advisor to the Middle Eastern Department of the Colonial Office. He remained a firm friend of Zionism, and his *Middle East Diary 1917–1956*, published in 1959, is a valuable record as well as source for correcting the misinterpretations of history related to the Balfour Declaration and the subsequent period. He was also an enthusiastic ornithologist, and his book *Birds of Arabia* (1954) threw much light on the bird life of Palestine.

BIBLIOGRAPHY: J. Lord, *Duty, Honour, Empire: The Life and Times of Colonel Richard Meinertzhagen* (1971). **ADD. BIBLIOGRAPHY:** ODNB online.

[Moshe Rosetti]

°**MEINHOLD, JOHANNES FRIEDRICH** (1861–1937), German Bible scholar. Meinhold studied with August Dillmann, with Franz Delitzsch the biblicist, and with his son the Assyriologist Friedrich Delitzsch of Babel-Bibel notoriety. Meinhold taught at Greifswald and Bonn. He wrote on the history of the Hagiographa (1889) and on the compilation of Daniel (1884, 1889), maintaining that the basic corpus of Daniel (2:4b–6:29) was composed around 300 B.C.E. and that Daniel 1:2–2:4a and 7–12 were added in the Hasmonean period. His views on the role of Israelite wisdom and prophecy, the documents contained within the Hexateuch, and the composition of Ruth reflect the strong influence of the classical Wellhausen school. It also characterizes his *Einfuehrung in das Alte Testament*, "Introduction to the Old Testament" (1919, 1932^3). In addition to studies on Genesis 14 (1911), the Decalogue (1927), and the role of the biblical Sabbath (1905), he wrote a history of the Jewish people (1916). His *Jesus und das Alte Testament* (1896) clashed with accepted Christian positions, but his *Altes Testament und evangelisches Christentum* (1934), an apology for keeping the Hebrew heritage within the Christian tradition, argued that the national ethical religion of Israel was fulfilled in the primitive church's faith in resurrection. He was also co-editor with Hans Lietzmann of the Hebrew-Greek text of Amos for *Kleine Texte für theologische Vorlesungen und Übungen*, "Short Texts for Theological Lectures and Exercises."

ADD. BIBLIOGRAPHY: R. Smend, in: DBI, 2:143–44.

[Zev Garber]

MEININGEN, city in Germany. The medieval Jewish community suffered persecutions in 1243 because of a blood *libel, in 1298 during the *Rindfleisch disturbances, and during the *Black Death massacres in 1349 when it was destroyed. The synagogue was transformed into a chapel in 1384. Jews continued to live in nearby villages, which in 1803 were incorporated into the newly created duchy of Saxe-Meiningen. The duchy's Jewry law of 1811 laid down disabilities regarding residence, marriage permits, and economic pursuits. Only a few Jews were allowed to live in Meiningen itself; after the *Hep! Hep! riots (1819) only one family remained. By 1844, only 29 persons lived there. At that time 1,500 Jews lived in the duchy; the seat of the rabbinate was in the nearby village of Walldorf, where 550 Jews lived (35% of the total population) in 1844, when the ducal authorities approved the Saxe-Meiningen synagogue regulations stressing religious reforms. The Saxe-Meiningen Jewry law of 1856 granted citizenship to Jews owning substantial business, and that of 1868 to all the duchy's Jews. By 1870, some 470 Jews lived in Meiningen; 490 in 1898; 359 in 1913 (2.08% of the total); 293 in 1925 (1.6%); and 192 in June 1933. In 1871 the rabbinate was transferred to Meiningen, a cemetery was acquired in 1874, a synagogue was consecrated in 1883, and a *ḥevra kaddisha* was founded in 1885. In 1856 Jewish and Christian financiers founded the Central-German Credit Bank in Meiningen. The banks of B.M. Strupp (formerly a merchandise firm) and D. Mannheimer (founded in 1871) were important in industrial financing far beyond the duchy's limits. Gustav Strupp (1851–1918) was chairman of both the Chamber of Commerce and the Jewish community, and was a member of the Landtag (1903–18). From the 1870s Jews were admitted to the bar, and some were appointed judges. Antisemitism was strong in Meiningen: the antisemitic vote in 1898 and the Nazi vote in 1932 far exceeded the national average. The synagogue was burnt in 1938, and by the end of that year only a few Jewish families remained, with 16 children attending the Jewish school. Records on deportations are missing. No Jews returned to Meiningen after 1945. The Jewish cemetery, which had been damaged by the Nazis in 1938, was restored by the municipality of Meiningen. In 1988 a memorial was consecrated to commemorate the destroyed synagogue.

BIBLIOGRAPHY: T. Oelsner, in: JSOS, 4 (1942), 256, n. 36, 358–74, 378, and n. 166; *Handbuch der juedischen Gemeindeverwaltung und Wohlfahrtspflege* (1913), 202; (1928), 167, 319; J. Jacobson, in: MGDJ, 6 (1962), 59–97; Germ Jud, 2 (1968), 530; S. Colodner, *Jewish Education under the Nazis* (1964), 62; P.H. Emden, *Money Powers of Europe in the 19th & 20th Centuries* (1937), 208. **ADD. BIBLIOGRAPHY:** *Schicksal juedischer Buerger der Stadt Meiningen 1933–1945* (Schriften zur Stadtgeschichte Meiningens, vol. 2) (1995); K. Nothnagel, *Juden in der ehemaligen Residenzstadt Meiningen und deren Umfeld* (Juden in Suedthueringen geschuetzt und gejagt, vol. 3) (1999); G. Olbrisch, *Landrabbinate in Thueringen 1811–1871*, Juedische Schul- und Kultusreform unter staatlicher Regie, Cologne; Weimar (Veroeffentlichungen der Historischen Kommission fuer Thueringen. Kleine Reihe, vol. 9) (2003).

[Toni Oelsner / Larissa Daemmig (2nd ed.)]

MEIR (second century C.E.), *tanna*, one of the leaders of the post-Bar Kokhba generation. Essentially a halakhist, he played a decisive part in the development of the *Mishnah. His main teacher was *Akiva, by whom he was apparently ordained (TJ, Sanh. 1, 19a), but he also studied under *Ishmael. According to a Palestinian amoraic aggadic tradition he was also a disciple of Elisha b. Avuyah (Ruth R. 6; Ecc. R. 7; TJ, Hag. 2:1, 87b), but Meir's connection to these traditions is in all likelihood more literary than historical (see *Elisha b. Avuyah, and cf. Tosef., Dem. 2:9). Meir is mentioned in most of the talmudic traditions that describe the reestablishment of the center of learning in the Galilee after the Bar Kokhba revolt. Thus he is listed as one of the five ordained by Judah b. Bava at the cost of his life (Sanh. 14a), and also among the scholars who gathered at Usha to reconstruct the religious life of the people (Song R. 2:5, no. 3). He was also described as having been active at Bet Rimmon when the renewed calendar arrangements were made (TJ, Ḥag. 3:1). Though these traditions have been viewed by some as representing distinct historical events, they should more properly be viewed as a family of related traditions with definite lines of literary dependence between them, as has been recently argued convincingly (Oppenheimer, 78–79).

According to the *aggadah*, Meir was a descendant of proselytes. One tradition holds that his real name was Nehorai (the Aramaic form of Meir), but that he was called Meir ("the Illuminator") because he "enlightened the eyes of the sages of the *halakhah*" (Er. 13b; see Dik. Sof.), though little historical credence should be accorded this tradition (see *Nehorai).

An *aggadah* in the Babylonian Talmud (Hor. 13b–14a) relates that when Simeon b. Gamaliel was appointed *nasi*, R. Nathan was appointed *av bet din*, and Meir, *ḥakham*. According to this tradition Simeon b. Gamaliel took steps to strengthen the status and honor of his office at the expense of these two other sages, which Meir and Nathan took as a personal affront. Nathan and Meir engaged in a conspiracy to discredit Simeon b. Gamaliel and to remove him from office. Their plan was foiled and Simeon in turn attempted, unsuccessfully, to have them removed from the *bet ha-midrash*. Nevertheless, as a punishment for their opposition to the *nasi*, it was decreed that all subsequent statements made by Meir and Nathan should be introduced anonymously, the former being quoted merely as "others say," and the latter as "some say" (Hor. 13b–14a). While some scholars have held that this story accurately reflects the forms of communal leadership practiced during the late tannaitic period, and have also accepted it as evidence for a power struggle between these well-known historical figures, Goodblatt has shown quite convincingly that this story is in fact a late Babylonian elaboration and embellishment of certain earlier Palestinian traditions (cf. TYMK 3:1, 81c), and has little or no historical value.

The Talmud ascribes to R. Johanan the statement that "an anonymous *mishnah* represents the view of Meir following that of Akiva" (Sanh. 86a), but the authenticity of this statement is doubtful and its proper interpretation remains somewhat unclear (cf. TJ, Yev. 4:11, 6b). According to tradition, Meir frequently spoke in praise of living in Ereẓ Israel: "Whoever lives permanently in Israel and speaks the holy language … he is assured of a share in the world to come" (TJ, Shek. 3:4, 47c). Meir died in Asia (probably Ezion-Geber). Before his death he ordered that his body be taken to Ereẓ Israel, and requested that until then his bier be put on the shore in order that it may be lapped by the sea that washes the shores of Ereẓ Israel (TJ, Kil. 9:4, 32c). His extreme attitude in demanding study of Torah emerges clearly in the saying: "Whoever forgets one word of the Torah is accounted by Scripture as if he had forfeited his life" (Avot 3:8), and the Talmud ascribes to him the statement that a gentile who occupies himself with the Torah is the equal of a high priest (BK 38a; Av. Zar. 3a), and also states that he required that one should not be satisfied with acquiring knowledge of the Torah, but should also teach it to others (Sanh. 99a). Three hundred fox *fables are ascribed to Meir, of which three are given (Sanh. 38b). In connection with the definition of the concept of *am ha-areẓ*, Meir takes a more stringent view than his colleagues. According to Meir anyone not eating ordinary food in ritual purity belongs to the category of the **am ha-areẓ* while his colleagues apply the term only to someone who disregards the duty of giving tithes. On the other hand the words ascribed to him in the Talmud, "Whosoever marries his daughter to an *am ha-areẓ* is as though he bound her and laid her in front of a lion" (Pes. 49b), are almost certainly pseudoepigraphic, and do not represent the views of the historical Meir (Wald). Together with the study of Torah, Meir stresses the importance of labor: "A blessing rests only upon labor" (Tosef., Ber. 7:8); "A man should always teach his son a clean craft" (Kid. 4:14). He similarly stresses the importance of prayer: "'And it came to pass as she prayed long' [I Sam. 1:12], this implies that whoever prays long is answered" (TJ, Ber. 4:17c; et al.). According to the Talmud his contemporary, Yose b. Ḥalafta, called him: "A great man, a holy man, a modest man" (TJ, Ber. 2:7, 5b), while Simeon b. Lakish called him "holy mouth" (Sanh. 23a).

According to the *aggadot* of the Babylonian Talmud, Meir was married to *Beruryah, the daughter of the martyred *Hananiah b. Teradyon. After the Bar Kokhba War her sister was taken to a brothel from where Meir rescued her (Av. Zar. 18a). According to a legend quoted by Rashi (Av. Zar. 18b), Beruryah herself was seduced by one of the scholars. None of these traditions, however, seem to have any historical basis (see *Beruryah). According to another late aggadic tradition (Midrash Proverbs 31) his two sons died simultaneously while he was busy in the college.

BIBLIOGRAPHY: Hyman, Toledot, 865–78; I. Konovitz, *Rabbi Meir* (Heb., 1967); A. Blumenthal, *Rabbi Meir* (Ger., 1888); Bacher, Tann; Frankel, Mishnah, index; A. Buechler, *Der galilaeische Am ha'Areṣ des zweiten Jahrhunderts*, in: XIII. *Jahresbericht der Israelitisch-Theologische Lehranstalt in Wien* (1906), esp. 157–90; Alon, Toledot, 2 (1961²), index; M. Avi-Yonah, *Bi-Ymei Roma u-Bizantiyyon* (1952²), 1–21; Safrai, in: *Zion*, 22 (1957), 183–93. **ADD. BIBLIOGRAPHY:** A. Oppenheimer, in: Z. Baras, S. Safrai, M. Stern, Y. Tsafrir (eds.), *Ereẓ Israel from the Destruction of the Second Temple to the Moslem Conquest* (Heb., 1982); D. Goodblatt, in: *Zion*, 49 (1984),349–374 (Heb.); S. Wald, BT *Pesaḥim III* (2000), 231–33.

[A'hron Oppenheimer / Stephen G. Wald (2nd ed.)]

MEIR (Myerson, née **Mabovitch), GOLDA** (1898–1978), *Mapai leader and Israeli prime minister in 1969–74; member of the First to Eighth Knessets. Meir was born in Kiev, Russia, where her father was a skilled carpenter. In 1906 the family migrated to the United States and settled in Milwaukee, where she graduated from high school and enrolled in the Milwaukee Normal School for Teachers. In 1915, as a youth, she joined *Po'alei Zion. In 1921 Meir settled in Palestine with her husband, Morris Myerson, and the two joined kibbutz Merḥavyah, where they remained until 1924. Meir soon became involved in political and social activities within the *Histadrut. In 1928 she became the executive secretary of Mo'etzet ha-Po'alot (Women Workers Council), and was sent as an emissary to the Pioneer Women's Organization in the United States from 1932 to 1934.

Upon her return to Palestine in 1934, she was invited to join the executive committee of the Histadrut, and in 1936 became head of its Political Department. Simultaneously with her work within the Histadrut Meir was active in Mapai. When Moshe *Sharett was arrested by the British on Black Saturday in June 1946, Meir was appointed to serve as acting head of the Political Department of the Jewish Agency. After Sharett was released, he was sent to the United States to take charge of the struggle for the partition plan at the UN, and Meir remained as the head of the Political Department in Jerusalem, in which capacity she served until the establishment of the State in May 1948.

In January 1948, she went to the United States to enlist the help of American Jewry in the struggle against the Arabs. Four days before the proclamation of Independence, on May

10, 1948, she met secretly with King Abdullah in Transjordan, in an effort to come to an agreement with him on the partition of Palestine between his kingdom and the Jewish state and to keep the Arab Legion out of the approaching military attack on the new state. After the establishment of the state she was appointed Israel's first diplomatic representative to Moscow, a post she held until April 1949. Her presence at the Great Synagogue of Moscow on the High Holidays in September/October 1948 caused great excitement among Soviet Jews.

After the elections to the First Knesset in 1949, to which she was elected on the Mapai list, Meir was appointed minister of labor, in which capacity she was responsible for the initiation of very large-scale public works to offer rudimentary employment to masses of new immigrants. In 1956, after Moshe Sharett resigned from the post of minister for foreign affairs that he had held since 1948, Meir assumed the post, which she held until 1965. As foreign minister she attended the annual opening sessions of the United Nations, and defended Israel's participation in the *Sinai Campaign. She played an active role in establishing friendly relations with the newly independent black African states, extending technical assistance to them and visiting several of them. After the elections to the Sixth Knesset in 1965 Meir was appointed secretary general of Mapai. In this capacity she played an active role in establishing the *Israel Labor Party in 1968 through the union of Mapai, *Rafi, and *Aḥdut ha-Avodah, becoming the first secretary general of the new party. After the death of Levi *Eshkol in February 1969, and despite the fact that she suffered from blood cancer, Meir was chosen as Israel's fourth prime minister. Soon after becoming prime minister Meir visited President Richard Nixon in Washington, and subsequently led the Labor Alignment to an impressive victory in the elections to the Seventh Knesset. Though she once again formed a National Unity Government with Gaḥal, a year later Gaḥal left the coalition owing to its objection to her willingness to consider the Rogers Plan, which proposed a settlement between Egypt and Israel based on an Israeli withdrawal from territories it had occupied in 1967. However, in later years Meir was accused of missing an opportunity to reach a settlement with Egyptian President Anwar Sadat, and thus of avoiding the *Yom Kippur War. During her premiership, and despite the fact that Israel did not have diplomatic relations with the Soviet Union, Meir played an active role in the struggle to get the latter to open its gates to Jewish immigration to Israel – a struggle that was partially successful for several years. At the same time she did not demonstrate any sympathy toward the social protest movement of the Israeli "Black Panthers," who were protesting the discrimination against Israel's citizens of Oriental origin, characterizing their leaders as "not nice." Her failure to take the distress of this part of the Israeli population seriously was to have devastating political consequence for the Labor Party in later years. In 1972 Meir was elected deputy chairman of the Socialist International, in which capacity she served for two years.

The Yom Kippur War, which took the Israeli leadership by surprise, signaled the beginning of the end of Labor hegemony in Israeli politics in general, and of Meir's political career in particular. Though the Labor Party was not defeated in the elections for the Eighth Knesset held on December 31, 1973, and Meir succeeded, after lengthy and difficult negotiations, in forming a new government with the *National Religious Party and the *Independent Liberal Party, one month after the new government was approved by the Knesset, she resigned. The immediate background to her resignation was the Interim Report of the Agranat Commission of Inquiry concerning the causes of the outbreak of the Yom Kippur War. Though the report put the blame for the lack of preparedness on the military leadership, there was growing public dissatisfaction with the political leaders, and Meir submitted her resignation as prime minister on April 11, 1974, and in June resigned her seat in the Knesset. In 1975 Meir was awarded the Israel Prize for special service to the state and society. Though after her resignation she assumed the status of "elder statesman" until her death four years later, her departure, together with the fact that neither Moshe *Dayan nor Abba *Eban were given ministerial positions in the government formed by Yitzhak *Rabin in June, marked the end of an era. However, before Rabin formed his government, Israel with the mediation of U.S. Secretary of State Henry *Kissinger and under Meir's leadership, had signed Interim Agreements with Egypt (January 18, 1974) and Syria (May 31, 1974), both involving Israeli withdrawal from territories in return for new security arrangements – the first implementation of the "territories for peace" principle, that three and a half years later was to lead to the Peace Treaty between Israel and Egypt. At a meeting with Egyptian President Anwar Sadat on his historic visit to the Knesset on November 20, 1977, Meir joked with him about his having referred to her as "the old lady." Meir passed away on December 8, 1978. In her will she requested that no eulogies be delivered at her funeral and no institutions be named after her. Nevertheless, a year after her death, the city of New York named a square on Broadway after her. A year before she passed away a two-act play called *Golda*, by William Gibson, appeared on Broadway, and in 2003 a one-woman play, titled *Golda's Balcony*, by the same playwright, turned into a hit and ran in several cities in the U.S.

Her writings appeared in H. Cristman (ed.), *This Is Our Strength: Selected Papers of Golda Meir* (1962); Israel Shenker and Mary Shenker (eds.), *As Good As Golda: The Warmth and Wisdom of Israel's Prime Minister* (1970); *Beit Avi* (Hebrew, 1972); Marie Syrkin (ed.), *Golda Meir Speaks Out* (1973); and an autobiography, *My Life* (1974).

BIBLIOGRAPHY: M. Syrkin, *Golda Meir: Woman with a Cause* (1965); idem, *Golda Meir: Israel's Leader* (1969); E. Agres, *Golda Meir: Portrait of a Prime Minister* (1970); P. Mann, *Golda: The Life of Israel's Prime Minister* (1971); I. Noble, *Israel's Golda Meir: Pioneer to Prime Minister* (1972); B. Litvinoff, *Her Years of Valour: The Span of Golda Meir's Career* (1974); A. Dobrin, *A Life For Israel: The Story of Golda Meir* (1974); M. Davidson, *The Golda Meir Story* (1976); R. Slater, *The Uncrowned Queen of Israel* (1981); M. Avallone, *A Woman*

Called Golda (1982); M. Meir, *My Mother Golda Meir: A Son's Evocation of Life with Golda Meir* (1983); M. Keller, *Golda Meir* (1983); D.A. Adler, *Our Golda: The Story of Golda Meir* (1984); R. Martin, *Golda Meir: The Romantic Years* (1988); M. Medzini, *Ha-Yehudiyya ha-Ge'ah: Golda Meir ve-Ḥazon Yisrael – Biografyah Politit* (1990); R. Amdur, *Golda Meir: A Leader in Peace and War* (1990); M. Avizohar et al., *Golda – Ẓemiḥatah shel Manhigah 1921–1956* (1994); A. Claybourne, *Golda Meir* (2003).

[Susan Hattis Rolef (2nd ed.)]

MEIR, JACOB (1856–1939), Sephardi chief rabbi of Ereẓ Israel. Born in Jerusalem, the son of a well-to-do merchant, Caleb Mercado, Meir studied Talmud under Menahem Bekhor Isaac and Kabbalah under Aaron Azriel. In 1882 he was sent to Bukhara, as the first emissary to visit that country. Meir, enthusiastically welcomed, was instrumental in encouraging the immigration of Bukhara Jews to Ereẓ Israel. In 1885, 1888, and 1900 he visited Tunisia and Algeria as an emissary. In 1888–99 he was a member of the *bet din* of R. Jacob Saul *Elyashar in Jerusalem. Meir was one of the promoters of the revival of spoken Hebrew in Palestine. Under Turkish rule, he often interceded with the authorities on behalf of the Jewish community; he also encouraged the construction of new Jewish quarters of Jerusalem. In 1899 he was appointed deputy head of the *bet din* of R. Raphael Isaac Israel. In 1906 he was a candidate for the chief rabbinate of Jerusalem, in succession to Elyashar, but his opponents, supported by the *ḥakham bashi* in Turkey, prevented his election. In 1908 he was elected chief rabbi of Salonika, where he remained until 1919. He was elected chief rabbi of Jerusalem in 1911, but the Jews of Salonika prevented him from assuming the office. When in 1921 the chief rabbinate was established in Palestine, Meir was elected (together with Rabbi A.I. Kook) as chief rabbi of Palestine with the title of *rishon le-Zion*. He was decorated by the sultan of Turkey and by the kings of Greece and England, and was awarded the French Legion of Honor. Meir even received decorations from Hussein, king of the Hejaz. Two manuscripts of his were lost in a fire in Salonika. To celebrate his 80th birthday, his friends published *Zikhron Me'ir* in his honor.

BIBLIOGRAPHY: M.D. Gaon, *Yehudei ha-Mizraḥ be-Ereẓ Yisrael*, 2 (1938), 361–71; P. Grajewsky, *Zikkaron la-Ḥovevim ha-Rishonim*, no. 110 (1933).

[Geulah Bat Yehuda (Raphael)]

MEIR BA'AL HA-NES, TOMB OF, a building on the shores of Lake Kinneret. According to R. Moses *Basola "people gathered there for prayer morning and night, stating that it was the tomb of one called R. Meir who took a vow that he would not lie down until the Messiah came, and was buried there in an upright position." At present it is a large building consisting of two *battei midrash* (one for Ashkenazim and one for Sephardim) covering the tomb. Some scholars connect the grave with the *tanna* *Meir, who established his school in Tiberias (TJ, Ḥag. 2:1) and has a miracle related about him (Av. Zar. 18a/b). There are however different traditions about his place of burial, as he died in Esia, an area near Ezion Geber, close to Eilat, and said "Place my bier (*'arsi*) on the sea shore" (TJ, Kil. 9:4, 32c). In the 13th century the tomb was connected with R. Meir Kaẓin, or Meir b. Jacob who immigrated to Ereẓ Israel with Jehiel of Paris (see Vilnay in bibl.). The name of Meir b. Isaac, author of *Akdamut* for Shavuot, has also been connected with it (*Oẓar Yisrael*). It is customary to arrange a great celebration at his grave on the 14th of Iyyar (Second Passover) which is comparable to the one in *Meron on Lag ba-Omer. These celebrations began in 1867. The tomb was exceptionally well publicized in the Diaspora by the emissaries of Ereẓ Israel, as well as in their emissarial *iggerot* (letters). Beginning with the 18th century a Meir Ba'al ha-Nes box was found in almost every Jewish home, and housewives dropped small change into it just before kindling the Sabbath lights. Due to the miraculous deeds connected with the tomb, it was customary to contribute money, candles, or oil for lighting as a specific protection against all kinds of ailments and dangers; it was also done in the hope of finding something lost, of having children, or of driving away evil thoughts. It is clear, however, that the box also symbolized the longing for Ereẓ Israel (for the way in which the money was distributed, see Vilnay in bibl.). Craftsmen created art objects connected with Meir Ba'al ha-Nes. In spite of the opposition on the part of both rabbis and *maskilim* to the celebration and the boxes, the practice still continues.

BIBLIOGRAPHY: *Kerem Ḥemed*, 2 (1836), 16–39; *Yerushalayim*, ed. by A.M. Luncz, 1 (1880/81), 48f., 102–4; *Va-Titpallel Ḥannah*, 2 (1890); I. Ben-Zvi (ed.), *Masot Ereẓ Yisrael le-Rabbi Moshe Bassola* (1938), 75; Yaari, Sheluḥei, 927 (index); J. Braslavski, *Ha-Yadata et-ha-Areẓ*, 1 (1955^6), 88, 90, 286; Z. Vilnay, *Maẓẓevot Kodesh be-Ereẓ Yisrael* (1963^2), 315–24; M. Ish-Shalom, *Kivrei Avot* (1948), 186–9; S.H. Kook, *Iyyunim u-Meḥkarim*, 2 (1963), 101–95. **ADD. BIBLIOGRAPHY:** Z. Ilan, *Kivrei Ẓaddikim be-Ereẓ Israel* (1997).

[Meir Havazelet]

MEIR BEN BARUCH HA-LEVI (d. 1404), German scholar; colleague of Abraham *Klausner. Meir came from Fulda. His chronology is obscure, but it is now generally held that his first rabbinic post was in Erfurt, where Hillel "Ha-Zaken" of Erfurt was his pupil, and that he subsequently became rabbi of Frankfurt, moving to Nuremberg in 1383, and returning two years later to Frankfurt. In 1391 he was imprisoned as a result of a false accusation and upon his release in 1392 became rabbi of Vienna, where he appears to have remained until his death. Meir is frequently mentioned in the works of the leading scholars of his own and the following generation, among them Jacob *Moellin, Judah *Minz, Israel *Isserlein, and Israel *Bruna, who cite his customs and rulings (under the name Maharam Segal or Maharam Sal) regarding them as authoritative. Meir's central role in Jewish life of the 14th century is reflected by the part he played in the celebrated dispute about 1393 between Johanan *Treves and Isaiah b. Abba Mari, the pupil of Johanan's father, Mattathias Treves. When Johanan was appointed to succeed his father as chief rabbi of France, Meir conferred upon Isaiah – who was apparently the greater scholar – the title *morenu*, which authorized him to assume the chief rabbinate in place of Johanan. This intervention of Meir, a German, in the affairs of the French community, aroused the opposition of many leading scholars, including *Isaac b. Sheshet, who nevertheless refers to Meir with extraordinary respect. This incident has led some scholars to believe that it was Meir who reinstated ordination in Germany, but the view is now regarded as very doubtful.

BIBLIOGRAPHY: Breuer, in: *Zion*, 33 (1968), 15–25, 44f.; Graetz-Rabbinowitz, 6 (1898), 12f., 37–39; A. Hershman, *R. Isaac bar Sheshet Perfet and his Times* (1943), 203–13; J. Even Shmuel (Kaufman), *Yom Tov Lipman Muelhausen* (1927), 2f.; Schweinburg-Eibenschitz, in: *Neuzeit*, 34 (1894), 347ff.; M. Stern, *Die Israelitische Bevoelkerung der deutschen Staedte*, 3 (1894–96), 325f.; G. Wolf, *Geschichte der Juden in Wien* (1876), 14.

[Israel Moses Ta-Shma]

MEIR BEN BARUCH OF ROTHENBURG (c. 1215–1293), teacher, scholar, tosafist, and supreme arbiter in ritual, legal, and community matters in Germany. He was born in Worms into a family of scholars, many members of which were important leaders in the communities of Germany. In his responsa he mentions two uncles and 12 other relatives bearing the title *Ha-Rav*, a title reserved, in this period, for talmudic scholars of high standing, mainly for heads of yeshivot. Meir often quotes their opinions and legal decisions in order to bolster his own views; hence they must have been well-known and highly esteemed scholars. Meir's father Baruch was an outstanding member of this scholarly family. He was credited with a wide knowledge of talmudic lore, was a member of the *bet din* of the community of Worms, and was often chosen to act as judge. He also bore the honorific title *Ha-Rav*; several halakhic decisions were recorded in his name; and his epitaph, preserved to this day, was written in highly laudatory terms. His teaching and guidance contributed greatly to the intellectual growth of his son. At the age of 12 Meir joined the well-known school of R. Isaac b. Moses, the author of the *Or Zaru'a*, in Wuerzburg, where he studied for about six years. While in that city Meir also studied under R. Samuel b. Menahem, in whose name, in later years, he quoted important decisions in law and ritual. Subsequently Meir moved to Mainz, where he studied under his relative R. Judah b. Moses ha-Kohen. Finally, he went to France and studied under the great tosafists *Samuel b. Solomon of Falaise, also known as Sir Morel of Falaise, and *Jehiel of Paris, known as Sir Vivo. Meir was in France in 1240 when these two teachers took part in the famous disputation with Nicolas *Donin over the Talmud. He was still there two years later, in 1242, when he witnessed the public burning of the Talmud, on which occasion he wrote his famous elegy *Sha'ali Serufah ba-Esh*, "Inquire, oh thou who art burned by fire, about the welfare of those who mourn for thee…," which is included to this day in the *Kinot* of the Ninth of *Av according to the Ashkenazi rite.

After this occurrence Meir returned to Germany and within a few years settled in Rothenburg, where he remained for more than 40 years, until 1286. Students flocked to his school from all the communities of Germany and its neighboring countries. Occasionally he would visit other towns for private or community business, but his home and his famous school remained in Rothenburg. His fame as a great talmudic authority spread rapidly even to other countries. In 1249, when a serious dispute arose between the communities of Bohemia and those of Moravia regarding the payment of taxes by these communities, the matter was referred to Meir for final settlement. Apparently at this early period he was already reputed to be the greatest scholar of his generation. For nearly half a century Meir acted as the supreme court of appeals for Germany and its surrounding countries. Rabbis, judges, and members of courts of arbitration sent him their questions regarding law and ritual. Individual complaints that the local courts decided contrary to talmudic law were also sent to him. He was the arbiter between communities and their members, between settlements and new settlers, and between various communities in their mutual relationships. They turned to him during their greatest crises. About a thousand of his responsa have survived, more than the combined number which have been preserved from all the other tosafists. Meir is unique among the tosafists and other great scholars of his time in his preserving a record of his responsa. The careful preservation of legal decisions leaves little room for modification or debate. Meir was motivated in this regard by the tumultuous times he lived in.

Meir sent his responsa to the communities of Germany, Austria, Bohemia, Italy, France, and even to Solomon b. Abraham Adret of Spain. In his lucid style and terse language he gave short, clear, and unequivocal answers to the inquirers. Sometimes he complains of the large number of responsa he is forced to write, apologizes for abbreviating the introductory greetings, is impatient with long and drawn-out questions, occasionally displays genuine anger when a case is repeatedly brought up before him because of persistent litigants, flares up in spirited temper when a litigant threatens to apply to the secular courts, and allows his passion to rise to a crescendo when confronted with serious crime. Sometimes he complained that those who addressed their queries to him overestimated his prerogatives as a talmudic scholar, and asked him to decide matters over which he had no jurisdiction. He was often unwilling to answer queries dealing with taxation, since the laws of taxation depended principally on local custom and procedures. He was very careful not to become involved in disputes and quarrels of the communities. Nevertheless, his opinion was often earnestly sought in matters involving community rights and taxes "in order to avoid the outbreak of a great quarrel."

The type of question sent to Meir speaks eloquently of the position he held in the esteem of his contemporaries. The great majority of Meir's responsa deal with business transactions, real estate, inheritance, marriage contracts, partnerships, agents, sureties, trustees, community government, community property, settling rights, and taxation. The preponderance of queries regarding civil cases and their abundance are eloquent proof of his importance as a communal leader of the first rank. Nevertheless, the opinion of many modern historians to the contrary notwithstanding, Meir held no official position as judge, as head, or as chief rabbi, of German Jewry as a whole. He was neither elected to such a position by the communities, nor was he appointed to it by the emperor. It is true that during the last two decades of his life he often took a somewhat authoritative stand in his relation to the communities. He once convoked a synod of the communities and scholars, and urged them to adopt an ordinance to the effect that a rebellious wife when divorced should forfeit her right to her *ketubbah*. On one occasion he wrote to the Jews of Wuerzburg that they should change their customary procedure in the sale of real estate, and the change was adopted in spite of the fact that some members of that community were reluctant to abandon their ancient practice. In a responsum Meir wrote: "On many occasions have individuals, whose wealth consisted of ready cash, desired to transfer the burden of taxation to real estate owners, but we did not permit them to do so." This seems to imply that in such cases Meir exercised the authority of a chief rabbi, although a thorough study of his responsa proves that he held no such official position.

Meir's responsa reveal a great deal about the various hardships Jews of his time had to endure. One particularly poignant question came from a Jew from Koblenz who admitted to killing his entire family to prevent them from falling into the hands of a Christian mob. Just before taking his own life, he was saved. His question was how he could do penance for his horrendous act. Meir responded that many scholars had acted similarly during the First Crusade. To require special penance would defame them and the permission they granted their students to act in a similar manner.

It is very difficult to determine if Meir was strict or lenient overall in his legal decisions. Whenever possible, he tried to combine the opposing sides of the argument into one harmonious ruling. This did not mean compromise. Rather, both opinions were upheld and merged. For example, there was a controversy surrounding the question as to whether Rosh Ha-Shanah was two separate days or one "long" day. Meir ruled that the *sheheḥeyanu* blessing should be recited on both nights according to the opinion that each day of Rosh Ha-Shanah is separate and distinct. However, Meir required that a new garment be worn or a new fruit be eaten on the second night, thus providing an alternative reason for reciting the *sheheḥeyanu* blessing, in accordance with the opinion that both days of Rosh Ha-Shanah are one.

As business became increasingly sophisticated in the Middle Ages, the primary Talmudic precedents became less and less relevant. While Meir and his contemporaries continued to rely on talmudic law and precedent for their rulings, Meir in particular realized that he had to be flexible in his strict application of talmudic law if the Jews were going to survive in the new economic environment. To do otherwise would have forced Jewish business to separate their commercial lives from their religious and communal lives, with potentially disastrous results.

Many of Meir's responsa deal with the relations between Jews and Christians. These rulings deal with a very wide range of subjects, including eating food cooked by a gentile; *yayin nesekh*, wine produced by gentiles; the halakhic status of the Catholic Church and Christian religious items; charging gentiles interest; relations with Jews who converted to Christianity; and the problems of Jewish life in a Christian society, such as business partnerships with gentiles. A good example of such responsa is the question of a woman whose husband died leaving her in a situation normally requiring the *ḥalizah* rite necessary for the cancellation of a levirate marriage. The difficulty arose from the fact that her brother-in-law was a devoted convert to Christianity. Meir released her from the obligation of the *ḥalizah* rite.

Meir was highly honored and in many cases his word was law. He enjoyed this authority, however, on account of his scholarship; because many leaders of the German communities had been his students who owed him respect and even obedience; and because the Talmud was the "constitution" of community government, and Meir, the greatest scholar of the land, was its best and most authoritative interpreter. His authority was based on his knowledge of talmudic law and on his intellectual attainments, both of which enabled him to arrive at a correct decision in questions of law or ritual. Thus he once wrote to the leaders of the Rhine communities in high-spirited defiance: "You, the aforementioned community leaders, probably delude yourselves with the idea that since your permission is required before a person may divorce his wife, no scholar is permitted to render decisions in ritual law unless he receives your authorization. No, this is not true, for the Torah is free to anyone who is capable of arriving at a correct decision" (I.A. Agus (ed.), *Teshuvot Ba'alei ha-Tosafot* (1954), 143). In the community of Rothenburg, however, Meir probably did hold an official position as judge, cantor, and head of the yeshivah. His house in Rothenburg was probably provided for him by the community since it contained 21 rooms, including a *bet midrash* and rooms for his students. He did not depend on his salary for a livelihood, engaging in business. The major part of his time, however, was devoted to his studies, his students, and his correspondence with the leaders of the communities.

Meir's role in the final formulation and fixing of the law and the ritual of Ashkenazi Jewry can hardly be overestimated. His numerous responsa – collected, copied, and seriously studied for generations – greatly influenced the work of codifiers of the subsequent centuries and thus helped standardize legal procedure and civil law. He introduced certain modifications in the ritual of prayer and religious **minhag* in the synagogue and at home, and instituted many customs which later became standard practice throughout Germany and Eastern Europe. His impact on the life, the organization, and the behavior of subsequent generations was exercised mainly through the work of his students, who followed him everywhere – at home, in school, in the synagogue, and even in prison. They studied his behavior, customs, and ceremonies, and later recorded their observations in their halakhic works together with Meir's decisions on law and ritual. One student in particular, R. Samson b. Zadok, was a veritable Boswell. In his *Tashbeẓ*, he described in great detail Meir's customs and practices from the moment he rose in the morning until he went to bed at night, on weekdays, Sabbaths, and festivals. This book became popular in Germany, Austria, Bohemia, and Poland, and its details were eventually incorporated in the codes.

Meir's influence, therefore, was exerted along three main channels:

(1) His students became the leaders of a number of communities in Germany, Austria, and Bohemia, and imprinted his views upon the life of the members of these communities and the surrounding territories;

(2) He had a profound influence on his most eminent student, Asher b. Jehiel, and on the latter's son Jacob, the author of the *Arba'ah Turim*, and thus directly affected the final *halakhah* incorporated in the Shulḥan Arukh;

(3) The *Mordekhai*, *Agudah*, *Haggahot Maimuniyyot*, *Sha'arei Dura*, and *Tashbeẓ*, classical works compiled by his students mainly on the basis of his decisions, responsa, and customs, were thoroughly studied by the scholars of succeeding generations and thus became the foundation for the work of R. Moses *Isserles, who incorporated the Ashkenazi usage in the Shulḥan Arukh. By far the greatest number of the views and decisions of Isserles incorporated in the abovenamed code stem directly or indirectly from the work and practices of Meir.

In the more than 80 of his responsa dealing with public law and community government, Meir gave the clearest and most incisive expression and explanation of the ideas of human freedom, government by consent, limitation of the power of the majority, and group responsibility – that formed part of Jewish law on the highest level of comprehension – of any other Jewish scholar before him or since. The principles of Jewish public law that man is absolutely free, that the legitimacy of government is derived solely from the free and uncoerced consent of the governed, and that the legislative power of the majority is limited to certain areas only and cannot encroach upon the private and inalienable rights of the individual were most forcefully and most clearly explained in his responsa. He thus greatly strengthened the democratic form of government of the communities – a form they derived traditionally from the forefathers of Franco-German Jewry – and it was eventually copied by the municipal governments and the guilds of the burgher class that arose in close contiguity with these Jewish communities. Thus in the 15th century, in the legislation intended for the benefit of the whole group the principle "majority rules" was applied, while particular legislative acts that encroached upon the rights and the immunities of the individual, such as taxes, did not become law unless unanimous agreement by the membership of the group was achieved (Otto v. Gierke, *Das deutsche Genossenschaftsrecht*, vol. 2, pp. 230–2, and 478–9). This division of legislation into two categories and the requirement of unanimity in the second category, which paralleled in practically every detail the form of community legislation, so clearly described by Rabbi Meir, could only have been the result of direct copying by the burghers and town communes of the community system of government that antedated their own by several centuries. Meir's peaceful life as a scholar and teacher was rudely interrupted by the turbulent political events that followed the termination of the interregnum and the election of Rudolph I of Hapsburg as emperor of Germany. In order to reestablish the right of the emperor to tax the Jews, which during the interregnum of 1254–73 had been claimed by the local dukes, Rudolph I began to press the claim that the term *servi camerae* ("serfs of the treasury") – which in the 13th century began to gain ascendancy as the legal description of the political status of the Jews – really meant that the Jews were the slaves of the treasury of the empire, that their persons and their possessions were therefore the property of the treasury of the empire, and that the emperor therefore possessed the right to tax the Jews over and above the taxes they paid to the local rulers; and in 1286 he did impose such a tax on them. As a result thousands of Jews decided to leave Germany. Meir, especially outraged at this attempt to enslave the Jews, became the leader of the widespread exodus. In the spring of 1286, he "set out to go across the sea together with his family, his daughters, and his sons-in-law." However, while he was waiting for his followers in Lombardy, he was recognized by an apostate who informed against him, with the result that the ruler of that town, Count Meinhardt of Goerz, arrested Meir and delivered him to Rudolph I. The emperor put him in prison, first in Wasserburg and then in Ensisheim, until the day of his death. His imprisonment was actually a singular form of house arrest. In jail, Meir had access to his books and his students were frequent visitors. Indeed, he continued to issue responsa while imprisoned, although he complained that he often did not have the requisite texts at hand to fully research a particular issue. The Jews made great efforts to effect the release of their beloved teacher – at one time agreeing to pay 23,000 pounds of silver to the emperor, but stipulating that the money was a payment of ransom and not of taxes – but without success. Rudolph I was determined to use the great devotion of the Jews to their teacher to force them to admit the right of the emperor to tax them. However, since a payment of taxes would be an admission that they were slaves, the Jews found it impossible to agree. Meir, therefore, remained in prison, and even after his death in 1293, his body was not delivered to the Jews until 1307 when it was redeemed by Alexander b. Salomo Wimpfen for a large sum of money and buried in Worms.

Rabbi Meir, the last of the tosafists, wrote *tosafot* and novellae to 18 tractates of the Talmud – the *tosafot* to *Yoma*, in the printed text of the Talmud, are from his pen; commentaries to the two orders of the Mishnah *Zera'im* and *Tohorot*; compendia of laws for special purposes, such as *Hilkhot Eruvin*, *Halakhot Pesukot*, *Hilkhot Berakhot*, *Hilkhot Semaḥot*, *Hilkhot Sheḥitah*, *Hilkhot Hatmanah*; a collection of customs connected with the marriage ceremony and with the wording of the *ketubbah*; and, most important, nearly 1,000 responsa found in the following collections which differ to a great extent in content: Cremona, 1557; Prague, 1608 (reprinted in Sudilkov, 1835, and in Budapest, 1895); Lemberg, 1860; and Berlin, 1891–92; aside from those incorporated in the works of his students. Some of his responsa were published from manuscripts by I.Z. Kahana (Jerusalem, 1943) and by I.A. Agus (see bibl.). Meir also composed liturgical poems (in addition to the above-mentioned "Inquire thou who art burnt by fire…") and a collection of masoretic explanations (in I.Z. Kahana's *Teshuvot, Pesakim u-Minhagim*, 1 (1957), 3–41).

BIBLIOGRAPHY: I.A. Agus, *Rabbi Meir of Rothenburg*, 2 vols. (1947); S. Back, *Rabbi Meir b. Baruch aus Rothenburg* (1895); H.J. Zimmels, *Beitraege zur Geschichte der Juden in Deutschland im 13. Jahrhundert* (1926); J. Wellescz, in: REJ, 58 (1909), 226–40; 59 (1910), 42–58; 60 (1910), 53–72; 61 (1911), 44–59; Urbach, Tosafot, 405–46. **ADD. BIBLIOGRAPHY:** E. Kanerfogel, in: *Jewish Book Annual*, 50 (1992), 249–59; R. Schwartz, in: *Jewish Affairs*, 49:3 (1994), 13–24; Y.N. Epstein, in: *Sinai*, 94:3–4 (1986), 123–36; Y. Hurvitz, in: *ibid.*, 112 (1993), 25–34; Y. Emanuel, in: *Ha-Maayan* (1993), 1–9; S. Emanual, in: *ibid.*, 11–20; idem, in: *Tarbiz*, 57:4 (1988), 559–97; idem, in: *Shenaton ha-Mishpat ha-Ivri*, 21 (2000), 149–205; idem, in: *The Jews of Europe in the Middle Ages (Tenth to Fifteenth Centuries)* (2004), 283–93; A. Grossman, in: *Cathedra*, 84 (1997), 63–84; A.Y. Havazelet, in: *Moriah*, 17:9–10 (1991), 105–8; S.Y. Spitzer, in: *Asufot*, 2 (1988), 83–90; Y.M. Peles, in: *Zefunot*, 1:1 (1989), 22–25.

[Irving A. Agus]

MEIR BEN ELIJAH (early 19th century), author of the ethical and educational work, *Naḥalat Avot* ("The Inheritance of the Fathers," Vilna, 1835). Although written in the form of an *ethical will – the author seemingly directing his teachings toward his own sons – the book is intended for the ethical betterment of the general public. Meir's principal concern is demonstrating the way to achieve reverence toward God, but he also deals with man's struggle against his own evil inclination, the best methods by which to educate one's children, proper behavior at home and in the synagogue, and social and religious ethics. The book is prefaced by a *piyyut*, with the *notarikon* of the author's name, and two opening statements, one encouraging sinners to repent, and the other insisting on repeated study of ethical literature. Among his major sources are the *Zohar and *Sefer *Ḥasidim*, which he quotes frequently; the *Shenei Luḥot ha-Berit* by R. Isaiah ha-Levi Horowitz; and a more contemporary source – *Nefesh ha-Ḥayyim* by R. Ḥayyim of *Volozhin. In addition, Meir mentions *Ma'alot ha-Torah*, a work composed by his grandfather. Meir also wrote a commentary on the tractate *Avot*, *Derekh Avot*, printed in Vilna, 1836.

MEIR BEN ELIJAH OF NORWICH (13th century; also called **Meir of England**), liturgical poet and *ḥazzan*. Meir's family came from France, and his father was apparently a *dayyan*. Meir lived in Norwich and was among those exiled from England in 1290. His *piyyut Oyevi bi-Me'erah Tikkov* ("Thou wilt curse mine enemy with execration") was composed on this exile, as its heading states: "For the severity of the exile and the killings, the imprisonment, and the destruction of property." A great Torah scholar, Meir was the only known English *paytan*. His *piyyutim* contain some elements of the Ashkenazi *piyyut* and some of the Spanish. Strong phrases on the suffering of the nation find their expression through his poetry. His *piyyut* for Passover, *Mitnasse ba-Marom al Keruvo* ("Uplifted on High upon His Cherub" called by him "Who is like Thee"), is one of the longest acrostics in the Hebrew *piyyut*. Besides the alphabet, autobiographical information is also contained in the acrostic. Meir's secular poems, which he called *ḥaruzot* ("stanzas") – 16 in all, with an additional poem explaining the form and the construction of the poems – are written in the meter of the Spanish-Hebrew poetry, but do not have its glitter and originality. Sent to one of his friends, the poems were arranged in an order unknown in the poetry of others, namely in four parts ("*banim*") following the letters of his name Meir (*Benei M(-em)*, *Benei A(-lef)*, etc., i.e., poems whose stanzas begin with the letters *mem, alef*, etc.). The first two letters of each stanza are also repeated at the end of the stanza.

BIBLIOGRAPHY: V.D. Lipman, *The Jews of Medieval Norwich* (1967), with the poems edited by A.M. Habermann; Davidson, Oẓar (1933), 432; A. Berliner, in: *Magazin fuer die Wissenschaft des Judenthums*, 16 (1889), 52–55; Zunz, Lit Poesie, 328; Roth, England, 127; Urbach, Tosafot, 279; J. Schirmann, in: KS, 43 (1967/68), 450–1; A. Berliner, *Hebraeische Poesien des Meir ben Elia aus Norwich* (1887). **ADD. BIBLIOGRAPHY:** E. Fleischer, *The Yoẓer* (Hebrew, 1984), 590.

[Abraham Meir Habermann]

MEIR (Moses Meir) BEN EPHRAIM OF PADUA (d. 1583), scribe, printer, and teacher in Mantua. Meir was presumably born in Padua but lived in Mantua, where he served in various communal capacities. Meir's exceptional talent and his skill as a scribe were attested to by his disciple, Abraham *Portaleone. Meir noted down detailed descriptions of all 43 Torah scrolls written by him. Questions addressed to his close friend, Moses b. Abraham *Provencal, the rabbi of Mantua, indicate Meir's rabbinical scholarship, as does his treatise on the diacritical marks of the Torah, *Rimzei ha-Tagim*. In 1556 Meir founded a printing establishment at Mantua, in collaboration with Jacob b. Naphtali of Garolo (d. c. 1570), and his considerable contribution to the printing of Hebrew books included the first edition of the Zohar (1558–60).

BIBLIOGRAPHY: D.W. Amram, *The Makers of Hebrew Books in Italy* (1909), 323–33; *Kaufmann*, in: JQR, 11 (1899), 266–90; S. Simonsohn, *Toledot ha-Yehudim be-Dukkasut Mantovah*, 2 (1964), 531f.

MEIR BEN ḤIYYA ROFE (1610?–1690?), scholar and emissary of Hebron, Palestine. Born in Safed, the son of *Ḥiyya Rofe, Meir was orphaned in boyhood. He studied in Hebron, leaving about 1648 as an emissary to Italy, Holland, and Germany. On his return journey, he stayed for two years in Italy to publish *Ma'aseh Ḥiyya* (Venice, 1652), his father's talmudic novellae and responsa. In Amsterdam he had influenced the wealthy Abraham Pereira to found a yeshivah in Hebron to be called Ḥesed le-Avraham, of which Meir himself became a scholar. Meir was in Gaza in 1665 when *Nathan of Gaza began to prophecy on the messianism of *Shabbetai Ẓevi. In a subsequent letter to Amsterdam, to Abraham Pereira, he wrote that "Nathan of Gaza is a wise man fit for the divine presence to rest upon him," and urged Pereira to come to Gaza. Pereira reached Venice, but returned to Holland. Meir maintained his belief even after Shabbetai Ẓevi's conversion in 1666. In 1672 Meir left, again as an emissary of Hebron, for Turkey. He stayed for a time in Adrianople, where he was in contact with Shabbetai Ẓevi. On Shabbetai's exile to Albania in 1673, Meir returned to Gaza where he stayed with Nathan and even copied his writings for his own use. He then traveled again to Italy, and from 1675 to 1678 resided in the home of the Shabbatean Abraham *Rovigo. Throughout his stay in Italy Meir did much to encourage those who believed in Shabbetai Ẓevi and spread the writings of Nathan of Gaza. During the last ten years of his life he was recognized as the outstanding scholar of Hebron.

BIBLIOGRAPHY: Yaari, Sheluḥei, 160–1, 464–6; Benayahu, in: *Sinai*, 35 (1954/55), 61–62; idem, in: *Yerushalayim, Meḥkerei Ereẓ Yisrael*, 5 (1955), 152–6, 176–80, 186; Scholem, Shabbetai Ẓevi, index; Tishby, in: *Sefunot*, 3–4 (1960), 71–130.

[Avraham Yaari]

MEIR BEN ISAAC OF TRINQUETAILLE (12th century), Provençal scholar. Knowledge of Meir is largely derived from Menahem b. Solomon *Meiri's introduction to his commentary on *Avot*. Born in Carcassonne, the young Meir b. Isaac was brought by his father to Posquières to study under *Abraham b. David, and after many years Meir became his pupil-colleague. Meir's retort to his teacher, when the latter attempted to force his opinion upon him in a halakhic matter, has become well known: "Do not make light of my honor. For if you are unique among teachers, I am unique among pupils." From Posquières Meir apparently went to Trinquetaille, near Arles. In Meir's comprehensive work (*Sefer ha-Ezer*), written in defense of the *halakhot* of Isaac *Alfasi against the *hassagot* of *Zerahiah b. Isaac ha-Levi (the author of *Ha-Ma'or*), the influence of Meir's great teacher who wrote a similar book is clearly recognizable. Although the book has not been preserved, it is quoted by the *rishonim* – among them *Manoah b. Jacob (who also mentions Meir's *Ḥibbur ha-Mukẓeh*) and *Estori ha-Parḥi, Meir's great-grandson. Menahem b. Solomon Meiri also claims family connection with him. Meir's son, NATHAN OF TRINQUETAILLE, was a well-known scholar and a disciple of the eminent tosafist *Isaac b. Abraham. He later became the teacher of *Naḥmanides, Samuel b. Isaac ha-*Sardi, and Meir b. Simeon ha-Meili. Naḥmanides, Sardi, and Estori ha-Parḥi in particular, quote Nathan frequently. From their quotations it is clear that Nathan wrote a comprehensive work on civil law which was divided into *she'arim* ("gates") as well as a commentary on the Torah. Nathan's commentary on tractate *Shevu'ot* is always mentioned.

BIBLIOGRAPHY: Gross, Gal Jud, 246f.; idem, in: MGWJ, 27 (1878), 378ff.; I. Twersky, *Rabad of Posquieres* (1962), 245f.

[Israel Moses Ta-Shma]

MEIR BEN ISAAC SHELI'AḤ ẒIBBUR (also called **Nehorai**; d. before 1096), preacher and liturgical poet of Worms. Meir was considered authoritative in the sphere of liturgy and custom among the Franco-German communities. He appears also to have compiled a custumal for the whole year. Many of the great scholars of Germany and France in his own and in the following generations frequently mention him with esteem and cite his words: Rashi in his prayer book and in his commentary to Scripture, the *tosafists, Simḥah of Vitry in the **Maḥzor Vitry*, *Abraham b. Azriel in his *Arugat ha-Bosem*, Jacob *Moellin in his custumal, and others. Several legends were created about him. Meir compiled **piyyutim* and **seliḥot* in Hebrew and Aramaic, more than 50 of which are extant. A number of his *piyyutim* for the festivals were accepted by the Franco-German and Polish communities and were published innumerable times in *maḥzorim* and among *seliḥot*. The best known of his *piyyutim* is the Aramaic **Akdamut Millin*, which is customarily said to the present day in Ashkenazi communities during Shavuot after the reading of the first verse of the Torah reading (Ex. 19:1); a number of scholars, however, introduced the custom of saying it before the reading of the Torah. It was translated into Hebrew by Gabriel *Polack (*Literaturblatt des Orients* (2 (1850), 554–5) and *Ben Gorni* (1851, 52–55)), and by others as well. It has also been translated into other languages (into English by Joseph Marcus in *Maḥzor*, United Synagogue of America, 1927). *Menahem b. Ḥelbo wrote commentaries on Meir's *piyyutim*. Two of his sons – Jacob and Isaac – are known; the latter perished in the pogroms of 1096.

BIBLIOGRAPHY: Zunz, Lit Poesie, 145–52, 248–50, 610; Zunz, Poesie, index; Landshuth, Ammudei, 162–7; Elbogen, Gottesdienst, 334–5; Germ Jud, 1 (1934), 446–7; E.E. Urbach (ed.), Abraham b. Azriel, *Arugat ha-Bosem*, 4 (1963), index; Davidson, Oẓar, 4 (1933), 432; D. Goldschmidt, in: KS, 34 (1958/59), 391–2; H. Schirmann, in *Divrei ha-Akademyah ha-Le'ummit ha-Yisre'elit le-Madda'im*, 3 (1969/70), 36–37, 55, 61–62.

[Abraham David]

MEIR BEN SAMUEL OF RAMERUPT (c. 1060–c. 1135), one of the first tosafists of northern France. Meir's teachers were the scholars of Lorraine, Isaac ha-Levi of Worms, *Eliezer of Mainz, and *Rashi, whose daughter, Jochebed, he married. Of his sons, three, who were also his pupils, are especially known – *Samuel b. Meir (Rashbam), *Isaac b. Meir, and Jacob b. Meir *Tam. His son-in-law was Samuel of Vitry, father-in-law of the tosafist *Isaac b. Samuel ha-Zaken. For a certain period Meir apparently dwelt with his father-in-law in Troyes, but he moved to Ramerupt during Rashi's lifetime, founding a *bet ha-midrash* there. He is sometimes designated *ha-yashish* ("the venerable") or "the father of the rabbis." Meir wrote commentaries to the Talmud, similar to those of his father-in-law and of his son Samuel. One extant section of his commentaries was incorporated in the commentary of Rashi to the Talmud and some of his *tosafot* are included in the *tosafot* of the standard Talmud editions. Halakhic statements by him are quoted in the *Sefer ha-Yashar* of his son Jacob Tam, in the *Or Zaru'a*, in the *Sefer ha-Ittur,* and elsewhere. Biblical comments by him are quoted by his son Samuel in his commentary to the Pentateuch. These are permeated by a spirit of literal exegesis and it is probable that the son was influenced in this by the father. The present text of **Kol Nidrei* is the result of amendments introduced by him into the original formula. There are extant responsa written to him by Rashi, and also a responsum written by them jointly. Meir also composed a *seliḥah, Avo Lefanekha* ("I come before Thee").

BIBLIOGRAPHY: Urbach, Tosafot, 38–42, and index.

[Zvi Kaplan]

MEIR BEN SAMUEL OF SHCHERBRESHIN (Pol. **Szczebrzeszyn**; mid-17th century), *paytan* and chronicler who lived in a small town near Lublin, Poland. His known writings consist of *Shir Mizmor le-Yom ha-Shabbat* ("Psalm for the Sabbath," Venice, 1639) and a rhymed account in Hebrew of the *Chmielnicki persecutions of 1648–49, written during the summer of 1650, and which is to be read "at all times, but especially during the three weeks of mourning between the 17th of Tammuz and the Ninth of Av and on the 20th of Sivan," the latter being the fast day in commemoration of the persecutions. The work was published during the same summer in Cracow, under the title *Ẓok ha-Ittim* ("Sufferings of the Times"). In the spirit of the accounts of the sufferings during the First *Crusade (1096), the author describes the persecutions of his own day as related to him by fugitives and, in part, as he witnessed them himself in Zamosc and the surrounding region in the summer of 1649. *Ẓok ha-Ittim* is of greater historical importance than the other Jewish chronicles of these persecutions, which were mostly written and published some time after the events by refugees in distant places who could not, for various reasons, give all the details.

BIBLIOGRAPHY: H.Y. Gurland, *Le-Korot ha-Gezerot al Yisrael,* 4 (1889–90), 7–61; Halpern, in: Zion, 25 (1960), 17–56. **ADD. BIBLIOGRAPHY:** *Gezerot Taḥ ve-Tat: Yeven Meẓulah: Ẓok ha-Itim: Megilat Efah: Seliḥah le-ha-Tosefot Yom Tov* (repr. 2004).

[Israel Halpern]

MEIR BEN SIMEON HA-ME'ILI (first half of 13th century), Provençal talmudist and communal leader. Meir's main center of activity was *Narbonne, and he cites many of its customs in his works. His principal teacher was his uncle, *Meshullam b. Moses, and Meir frequently cites him and his customs. He also studied under Nathan b. Meir of Trinquetaille. There are references to his connections with Naḥmanides, another pupil of Nathan b. Meir. Among his other activities, Meir engaged in disputations with Christian eccelesiastics and was one of the chief speakers in a delegation of the Jewish leaders of Narbonne and Capestang who interceded with the cardinal of Narbonne concerning discriminating laws which it was proposed to issue against the Jews. He was spokesman of the community at the court of the emperor, and before ministers and church leaders. According to Gross and Scholem, his work *Milḥemet Mitzvah* (Ms. Parma, cat. De Rossi (1803) no. 155, only part of which was published; see below) was written between 1230 and 1240. The work itself, however, gives the date 1245, and it seems to contain matters of a still later date (see Gross in: MGWJ, 30 (1881), 296). The work contains an account of his disputation with the bishop of Narbonne, a defense of Judaism against the allegations of Christians, explanations of biblical verses dealing with the coming of the Messiah, and a commentary on the **Shema* and the 13 divine attributes. Meir also appears in this work as a vehement opponent of a certain circle of kabbalists, to whom he attributes heretical views. Questioning the authenticity of *Sefer ha-Bahir,* he sharply criticizes its contents, together with other kabbalistic works. These criticisms were included in an "epistle" sent to "our rabbis in every town." His work was also directed against the ideas of some kabbalists based on works which, according to Meir, were forgeries attributed to well-known scholars. At the end of this epistle he gives Meshullam's commendation to his activity.

Only latterly have his works begun to be published, under the title *Sefer ha-Me'orot*: novellae to (1) tractates *Berakhot* and *Pesaḥim* (1964); (2) to *Shabbat* (1964); (3) *Mo'ed Katan* and *Ḥullin* (1964); (4) *Eruvin* (1967); (5) *Yoma, Sukkah, Beẓah, Rosh ha-Shanah, Ta'anit,* and *Megillah*, and the minor tractates (1967). His commentary on the **hoshanot* was published in *Sefer ha-Mikhtam*, edited by A. Sofer (1959). The *Milḥemet Mitzvah* contains five sections (504 columns) and a fragment of it was published by G. Scholem (bibl.) and the end of section four with part of section five in *Sefer ha-Me'orot*, volume one. Also known are his novellae to the order *Kodashim* (mentioned by Bezalel Askenazi in *Kelalei ha-Talmud* no. 37; A. Marx, in: *Festschrift … D. Hoffmann* (1914), Heb. pt. 181); *Me'or Torah*, a commentary on the weekly portions of the Pentateuch; sermons (for Passover, the New Year, and Tabernacles in the manner of the sermons of Abraham b. David and Naḥmanides); and a pamphlet called *Meshiv Nefesh* defending Maimonides' *Hilkhot Yesodei ha-Torah* in his *Mishneh Torah* against his critics.

BIBLIOGRAPHY: Renan, Rabbins, 558–62; Neubauer, in: *Israelitische Letterbode*, 3 (1877–78), 20f.; idem, in: REJ, 10 (1885), 98f.; idem, in: JQR, 4 (1892), 358; H. Gross, in: MGWJ, 30 (1881), 295–305, 444–52, 554–69; Gross, Gal Jud, 423–25; Meshullam b. Moses, *Sefer ha-Hashlamah le-Seder Nezikim*, ed. by J. Lubetzky, 1 (1885), introd. 5 n. 2, 14; idem, *Sefer ha-Hashlamah al Massekhet Berakhot*, ed. by M. Schochor (1892), introd. by H. Brody, 14; J. Lubetzky, *Bidkei Battim* (1896), introd. 9, 12, 14f., 22f.; G. Scholem, in: *Sefer Bialik* (1934), 146–50; M.Y. Blau (ed.), *Sefer ha-Me'orot le-Rabbenu Meir b. R. Shimon … ve-Sefer ha-Hashlamah le … Meshullam b. R. Moshe … al Massekhtot Berakhot u-Fesaḥim* (1964), introd; Dinur, Golah, 1 pt. 1 (n.d.²), 136f., 180 n. 35; 2 pt. 1 (1965²), 290 n. 35, 291 no. 44; 2 pt. 3 (1968²), 168–70, 339 n. 119; S. Stein, in: JJS, 10 (1960), 45–63.

[Shlomoh Zalman Havlin]

MEIRI, MENAHEM BEN SOLOMON (1249–1316), Provençal scholar and commentator of the Talmud. Meiri was born in Perpignan where he spent his whole life. His family, regarded as one of the most distinguished in Provence, originated from

Carcassonne and Narbonne. Few biographical details are known of Meiri. In his youth he was orphaned of his father, and his children were taken captive while he was still young (Introduction to *Kiryat Sefer*), but no details of this personal tragedy are known. Meiri's principal teacher was *Reuben b. Ḥayyim. His reference to *Jonah Gerondi as "my teacher" does not necessarily mean that he studied under him; it may merely mean that he studied his works. Among the contemporary scholars with whom he maintained close ties was Solomon b. Abraham *Adret; they exchanged many responsa and Adret's teachings assisted him in the writing of his monumental work. Meiri was one of the participants in Adret's polemic against Maimonides which ended in Adret's excommunicating any person who read philosophical works in his youth. In a letter to Abba Mari b. Moses Joseph, who handled the entire affair and collected the relevant correspondence, Meiri disassociated himself from the attitude of Adret and his colleagues, upholding freedom of thought for the scholars of each country, and freedom from intervention by outside scholars. Extracts from Meiri's letter (republished by D. Kaufmann along with the reply by Joseph b. Simeon in the name of Abba Mari under the title *Ḥoshen Mishpat* in the *Jubelschrift… L. Zunz*, 1884; Heb. sec. 142–74), reveal his great interest in philosophy and other secular sciences, and reflect his pride in the local scholars who had acquired proficiency in them.

Meiri occupies a central position in the sphere of the talmudic creativity of Provence, not only due to his extraordinary literary fecundity and the comprehensive scope of his works, but also because he summarizes the teachings of his predecessors during the previous three centuries. In effect he puts the seal upon the literary efforts in this area of Jewish culture. His literary activity covered halakhic rulings, talmudic exposition, biblical exegesis, customs, ethics, and philosophy. The vast majority of Meiri's works remained in manuscript until very recently, probably on account of their exceptional length, which made it practically impossible to copy them in full. A small number of his books were published in the second half of the 18th century and the majority of them – from the beginning of the 20th century up to the present day. A great contribution to this project was by A. *Sofer (Schreiber). An exception is his commentary to the Book of Proverbs which was first published in Portugal in 1492, and then included in the *Kehillot Moshe* edition of *Mikra'ot Gedolot* (Amsterdam, 1724).

Meiri's chief work is the gigantic *Beit ha-Beḥirah* on the Talmud, in which he was engaged from 1287 to 1300. In it he summarizes the subject matter of the Talmud, giving both the meaning and the *halakhah* derived from it. It follows the order of the Mishnah. The work covers the orders of *Mo'ed, Nashim*, and *Nizikin*, and the tractates, *Berakhot, Ḥallah, Ḥullin, Niddah, Tamid, Middot*, and *Mikva'ot. Beit ha-Beḥirah* has been republished almost in its entirety in recent years from a single complete manuscript (Parma). Of particular interest is the introduction to his commentary on *Avot*, in which he gives the names of all the people who form the chain of tradition of Torah study from Moses to his own time. It contains valuable material for the knowledge of the history of Torah study in Spain and Provence, and was copied out in full and completed (updated) to his own time by Isaac *Lattes in his *Sha'arei Ẓiyyon* (ed. by S. Buber, 1885). In 1995, the introduction to *Avot* was updated from manuscript and published with the title, *Seder ha-Kabbalah*. This edition includes the commentary of Ḥayyim Falagi.

Meiri follows an original method of exposition. He develops his theme from its origin and for this reason he assigns a separate section to the Mishnah and explains it before turning to the later development and discussions in the later literature. Each tractate and its individual chapters are preceded by a short preface outlining the subject in general terms. The discussion begins with a presentation of the fundamental principles involved and proceeds with an explanation of the opinions of each of the *amoraim*. The author in conclusion sums up and collates these opinions, giving the relevant *halakhah* as he sees it. An abundance of comments handed down by German, Provençal, and Spanish scholars with their different interpretations are incorporated, but each one is given separately to prevent confusion on the part of the reader. Meiri was one of the few rabbis of his time to make extensive use of the Jerusalem Talmud in order to clarify the parallel discussions in the Babylonian Talmud, and his works are therefore of added importance for research on the Jerusalem Talmud and its variant readings. Meiri's style contributes much to the lucidity of his presentation. His Hebrew is accurate, precise, and simple. In addition, he succeeded in finding the golden mean between the generally contradictory aims of expository comprehensiveness and halakhic definitiveness. These features endeared the *Beit ha-Beḥirah* to scholars and its volumes are now repeatedly republished in spite of their great length.

Meiri adopted the unusual practice of designating his predecessors by epithet rather than by name, e.g., "the greatest of authors" (Maimonides), "the greatest of *posekim*" (Alfasi), "the early scholars of Narbonne," "the former scholars of Catalonia," and "the great scholars of Provence." As a result it is difficult now to determine to whom he is referring, especially as he often employs the same epithet for many scholars who, in his opinion, belong to the same "genre." Contrary to the common conception of the Meiri's commentary as purely anthological, similar to the later work *Shitah Mekubbeẓet* by Bezalel Ashkenazi, the Meiri quotes only those opinions that are germane to the discussions, either to refute them or to bolster his own ideas. His admirable style makes it impossible to detect the verbatim quotations which no doubt he gives from the sources, since it became one harmonious whole. He employed this method only in *Beit ha-Beḥirah*.

In addition to *Beit ha-Beḥirah*, Meiri wrote commentaries on the Talmud which were expository rather than halakhic in orientation. Although the manuscripts in this group of a number of tractates are still extant, none has been published, except for the commentary to *Avot* and the *Beit ha-Beḥirah* to the tractate *Beẓah* (ed. by I.S. Lang and K. Schlesinger, 1956), which apparently belong to this group.

Meiri wrote several other important works. His first, written in his youth, was *Ḥibbur ha-Teshuvah* devoted entirely to ethics and repentance. It clearly reveals the influence of the *Malmad ha-Talmidim* of Jacob *Anatoli, the first Provençal scholar to stimulate interest in the meaning of the precepts as distinct from their observance. It may be assumed that toward the end of his life Meiri revised the work, which in its present form, bears the character of a well constructed sermon book. Extracts from it were published in various places; it was published in its entirety for the first time in 1950.

Meiri's commentary to Proverbs, and even more, his commentary to Psalms (1936), reveals all his exegetical and stylistic characteristics as well as his love for explicit meaning, *peshat*. In them he draws upon the Midrashim and the accepted ethical and wisdom literature of the Middle Ages, such as **Ben ha-Melekh ve-ha-Nazir* and *Muserei ha-Filosofim*, and also makes frequent use of the works of the great grammarians, such as Abraham *Ibn Ezra, Jonah *Ibn Janaḥ, and the *Kimḥi family. Corrections to the text of the commentary to Psalms were published in *Kobez al Jad*, New Series, 4 (1946), 229–40. Another of his works, *Kiryat Sefer* (1863–81), contains the laws of writing the **Sefer Torah*, including lists of those words written *plene* and those written defectively, and of the "open" and "closed" sections of the Torah. *Kiryat Sefer*, composed in 1306, was considered for many years as one of the three basic works on the laws of writing a *Sefer Torah* – all the great *posekim* and masoretes making use of it. *Kiryat Sefer* was based upon Provençal and Spanish traditions as well as upon a copy of a *Sefer Torah* written by Meir *Abulafia for his own use. However, 150 years after Meiri's death, more and more of Abulafia's manuscripts of *Masoret Seyag la-Torah* were circulated, which did not correspond with the *Sefer Torah* Meiri had written and as a result the reliability of *Kiryat Sefer* began to be called into question. Meiri wrote *Magen Avot* (ed. by I. Last, 1909) to uphold the customs of Provence in general and Perpignan in particular, against those of Spain, particularly Gerona, held by *Naḥmanides and brought by his disciples to Provence after its annexation to Spain during the reign of John I (1213–76). In its 24 chapters, each devoted to the discussion of a different custom, Meiri asserts the value and superiority of these local traditions as against the great authority of Naḥmanides.

The Meiri subscribed to the Maimonidean philosophical tradition that views intellectual achievement as the highest human goal. The pinnacle of this achievement is the ability to discriminate between truth and falsehood. The intellectual understanding must be coupled with a religious sense of ultimate redemption. The most fundamental religious concepts – fear of God, love of God and *devekut*, cleaving to Him – are all inexorably linked to the processes of awareness and understanding. In his commentary to Proverbs, the Meiri gives expression to just those ideas (Meshi Zahav edition, Jerusalem, 1969, p.25). The Maimonidean tradition greatly influenced other aspects of the Meiri's thought, including the nature of God and of the World to Come.

The Meiri rejected the opinion of many of the disciples of Maimonides, who felt that the publication of his *Mishneh Torah* made Talmud study superfluous. He viewed Talmud study as an integral aspect of Jewish religious study. This is evidenced by his monumental commentary on the Talmud. He did agree, though, that the essence of Talmud study was to derive applicable Jewish law. Nevertheless, the Meiri was one of a small group of medieval sages who dealt extensively with the non-legal, aggadic portions of the Talmud. Here, too, the Meiri's explanations were rational and logical, just like his halakhic discussions.

Modern scholars disagree as to the significance of the Meiri's attitude towards non-Jews that differed from almost all other medieval sages. E.E. Urbach argues that the limited legal application made by the Meiri limits the idea's significance (Urbach, in: *Perakim be-Toledot ha-Ḥevrah ha-Yehudit bi-Ymei ha-Beinayim u-ve-Et ha-Ḥadashah*, 1998, 34–44); J. Katz (*Zion*, 46:2 (1981), 243–46); and G. Blidstein (*Binah*, 3 (1994), 119–33) argue that the Meiri's idea was a totally new way of viewing the gentiles of his day: The Meiri differentiated between idolaters and gentiles who were religious people, *gedurim be-darkhei ha-datot*, "restricted" by ways of religion. This concept recognizes that the medieval Christians were not idol worshippers, but people who believed in God, observed religious practices (albeit far from those of Judaism) and were therefore *gedurim*, "disciplined" by moral values. This concept was used in Jewish polemics and debates with the Christians before the Meiri's time. However, his contribution was to apply it sparingly to those laws meant to prevent close contact between idolaters and Jews. Thus, while the Talmud does not obligate a Jew to return a lost item to a non-Jew, the Meiri claims that this only applies to idolaters. When dealing with gentiles who are not idolaters, there is actually an obligation to return the lost item (Meiri, Bava Kama, p. 330).

The Meiri's view of gentiles stemmed, in part, from his view of history as a progression away from idolatry to morality. He applied this same idea to women. Contrary to Asher ben Jehiel, who viewed women as basically wanton, the Meiri thought them to be moral and even more sin-fearing than men. As a result, he deemed as irrelevant various Talmudic dicta predicated on the immorality of women. The Meiri's comments on the *Berakha* no. 3 of *Sheva Berakhot* (Meiri, Ketubbot, p. 38) reveal that women were created with the same *ẓelem Elohim* as men. He is the only medieval thinker to explicitly state this. Contrary to almost all of the other medieval and renaissance rabbinic scholars, the Meiri calls women *ḥasidot* (pious ones; Meiri, Ta'anit 30b) and is of the opinion that they share in God's providence, equally with all of God's creatures (Meiri, Sotah, p. 46–47). Meiri also permits women to recite the blessings for *mitzvot* that they are not obligated to perform (Meiri, Haggigah, p. 31–32). He also permits women to don *tefillin*. The Meiri valued the desire of women to advance toward perfection through the fulfillment of *mitzvot*. Indeed, there was no other medieval rabbinic sage that had such a high opinion of women's potential, both morally and intellectually. This attitude was successfully translated by the Meiri into all of his halakhic decisions regarding all the legal issues involving women.

In recent years many collections of extracts from Meiri's works, arranged according to subject, have been published, including a commentary to the Passover *Haggadah* (1965; ed. by M.M. Meshi-Zahav); *Sefer ha-Middot* (idem (ed.), 1966), a guide to proper conduct; and an anthology of his biblical expositions (1957), by J.I. Gad. Meiri stands out as the embodiment of the highest qualities which characterized Provençal Jewry: greatness in Torah combined with a leaning toward, and an appreciation of, philosophy, secular erudition, and the sciences in general; unswerving attachment to custom and tradition coupled with a high-minded tolerance of gentile society; and brilliant Torah creativity, brought to expression in fluent, even poetic Hebrew. Meiri was also the last Provençal scholar to embody this synthesis.

BIBLIOGRAPHY: S.B. Sofer, *Or ha-Me'ir* (1942); M.N. Zobel, in: *Eder ha-Yakar… Mukdashim le-S.A. Horodezky* (1947), 88–96; S.K. Mirsky, in: *Talpioth*, 4 (1949–50), 1–90; J. Katz, in: *Zion*, 18 (1953), 15–30; I. Preis-Horev, in: KS, 14 (1937–38), 16–20 no. 56; I. Ta-Shema, *ibid.*, 45 (1970); D. Hoffmann, *Der Schulchan Arukh und die Rabbinen ueber das Verhaeltniss der Juden zu Andersglaeubigen* (1894^2), 4–7; J. Stein, in: MGWJ, 82 (1938), 46–56; J. Lévi, in: REJ, 38 (1899), 103–22; S. Deutschlaender, in: *Festschrift… J. Rosenheim* (1931), Heb. pt., 82–86; S.K. Mirsky, in: A. Sofer and S.K. Mirsky (eds.), *Ḥibbur ha-Teshuvah le-R. Menaḥem b. Shelomo ha-Me'iri* (1950), 1–80. **ADD. BIBLIOGRAPHY:** Y.A. Vida, in: *Iyyun*, 20, (1969), 242–44; A.Y. Bromberg, in: *Shanah be-Shanah* (1971), 202–15; D. Ochs, in: *Bi-Sedei Ḥemed*, 15:1–2 (1972), 7–11; J. Katz, in: *Zion*, 46:2 (1981), 243–46; B.Z. Bendikat, *Merkaz ha-Torah be-Provence* (1985), 184–91; Y.H. Sofer, in: *Ẓefunot*, 3:1 (1991), 68–74; idem, in: *ibid.*, 3:2 (1991), 74–79; idem, in: *ibid.*, 4:1 (1992), 81–85; idem, in: *ibid.*, 4:2 (1992), 66–72; G. Blidstein, in: *Binah*, 3 (1994), 119–33; E. Krumbein, in: *Netu'im*, 63:1 (1993), 63–118; E.E. Urbach, in: *Perakim be-Toledot ha-Ḥevrah ha-Yehudit bi-Ymei ha-Beinayim u-ve-Et ha-Ḥadashah* (1998), 34–44; M. Halbertal, *Bein Torah le-Ḥokhmah: Rabbi Menaḥem ha-Meiri u-Ba'alei ha-Halakhah ha-Maimoniyyim be-Provence* (2001); A. Grossman, in: *Zion*, 67:3 (2002), 253–91; H. Kasher, in: *Zion*, 69:3 (2004), 357–60; G. Oren, "*Ha-Yaḥas la-Ishah be-Mishnat R. Menaḥem ha-Meiri*" (dissertation, 2005).

[Israel Moses Ta-Shma / David Derovan (2nd ed.)]

MEIR JEHIEL HA-LEVI (Holzstock, Holzstick) OF OSTROWIEC (1851–1928), ḥasidic rabbi and scholar. Meir Jehiel was born to a poor family of humble origin, but through his outstanding gifts became one of the foremost leaders of Orthodox Jewry. He was a pupil of Elimelech of Grodzisk and like him settled in Ostrowiec, where many thousands of Ḥasidim became his disciples. Meir Jehiel was acknowledged as one of the greatest scholars of his age, and for a time no important decision on *halakhah* or Jewish life was made without consulting him. His form of Ḥasidism was original; his sermons were based on complicated equations from **gematria* by which he interpreted many texts in *halakhah* and *aggadah*. He was of an ascetic turn of mind and made a long series of fasts over 40 years. As he did not permit his books to be printed in his lifetime, only a fraction of his sayings and writings has been preserved. His son EZEKIEL (1887–1943), rabbi of Nasielsk, was his successor. Some of his sayings are found in *Or Torah*, edited by his disciple Judah Joseph Leibush (1920), and in M. Nomberg's *Omer Man* (1912).

[Adin Steinsaltz]

ME'IR SHEFEYAH (Heb. מֵאִיר שְׁפֵיָה), agricultural school and youth village in central Israel, on the southern slope of Mt. Carmel near *Zikhron Ya'akov, founded in 1892 by Baron Edmond de *Rothschild to provide farmsteads for the sons of Zikhron Ya'akov settlers. In 1904, after the Kishinev pogrom, Israel *Belkind established a home at Me'ir Shefeyah for orphans of the pogrom. In World War I, the Herzlia High School was transferred there from Tel Aviv when the Turkish authorities ordered the city's evacuation. In 1923 a youth village was set up, which was included in the 1930s in the network of *Youth Aliyah. The population, including pupils, reached about 450 in 1969. In 2002 the population was 412. The name is composed of the Hebraized form of the former Arabic name of the place, and the name of Mayer Amschel *Rothschild.

[Efraim Orni / Shaked Gilboa (2nd ed.)]

MEIR SIMḤAH HA-KOHEN OF DVINSK (1843–1926), talmudic scholar. His brilliance was such that he is said to have annotated the halakhic work of a distinguished rabbi when only 13 years old. At the age of 17 he went to Eishishok where he studied under R. Moses Danishevsky. Meir Simḥah married the daughter of Ẓevi Paltiel, a wealthy man from Bialystok who supported him while he continued his studies under the local rabbi, Yom Tov Lipman Halpern, the author of *Oneg Yom Tov* (1880). With the publication of his work, *Or Same'aḥ* on Maimonides (1902–26), Meir Simḥah became widely renowned as an outstanding talmudic scholar and commentator. His novellae *Or Same'aḥ* to *Bava Kamma* and *Bava Meẓia* were published in Jerusalem (1948), and his novellae to most of the tractates of the orders *Nashim* and *Nezikin*, together with some responsa and occasional notes, were printed in 1967 from a manuscript identified as his in the Jewish National and University Library. In these fundamental and classic works of rabbinic literature, he shed new light on the Talmud and codifiers, displaying vast erudition, great depth, and profound logic. On the advice of R. Jacob Ḥarif of Zagare and R. Joseph B. *Soloveichik of Brest-Litovsk, he was invited to become rabbi of Dvinsk, a position he occupied for 40 years. Meir Simḥah earned the high esteem of all communal circles, not only in Dvinsk, but far beyond its borders. In 1906 he declined the offer of a rabbinical position in Jerusalem, as a result of the entreaties of the community of Dvinsk who wrote to the leaders in Jerusalem that were he to leave, "not only would we, God forfend, be destroyed, but also the entire Diaspora. For he is the authority able to answer anyone who enquires concerning the word of the Lord. It is not for you, people of Jerusalem, to do such a thing." In 1911 he presided jointly with Isaac Jacob Rabinovitz, the rabbi of Ponevezh, over the Central Committee of Rabbis, the representative body of

Russian Jewry in its relations with the government. During World War I most of the Dvinsk community fled, and only a few of the poorest inhabitants remained. Meir Simḥah stayed with them, declaring that as long as there were nine Jews in the city, he would be the tenth.

In his work on the Pentateuch, *Meshekh Ḥokhmah* (1927), he drew freely on his vast knowledge of the two Talmuds and of the halakhic and aggadic Midrashim, giving new and profound interpretations. The book, which contains original reflections, attained wide popularity. *Zera Avraham* (1929) by Abraham Luftvir consists of an exchange of correspondence between Luftvir and Menahem *Zemba, and also includes some fine specimens of Meir Simḥah's responsa to him.

BIBLIOGRAPHY: *Yahadut Lita*, 3 (1967), 65f.; S.Y. Zevin, *Ishim ve-Shitot* (1966[3]), 155–87.

[Mordechai Hacohen]

MEISEL (Meisl, Meysl, Miška, Akhbar, Maušel, Konír), MORDECAI (Marcus, Marx) BEN SAMUEL (1528–1601), Prague financier, philanthropist, and head of the Jewish community. He was considered by *Graetz the "first Jewish capitalist in Germany." Although the source of his fabulous wealth is not known, it enabled him to finance large transactions in support of *Rudolph II, to whom he was appointed counselor, during the Turkish wars. His business was based on the special privilege granted him to loan money not only against pledges but also against promissory notes and real estate. (The illegality of such practices according to Bohemian law was one of the pretexts for confiscating Meisel's estate, which amounted to over half a million florins, after his death.) He also acted as purveyor of luxuries and art objects. Meisel is first mentioned in business relations with his father-in-law, Isaac Rofe (Lékař), in 1569. Another of his business associates was Veit (Ḥayyim) Vokatý. He used his wealth for philanthropic activities of all kinds; the epitaph on his tombstone records: "None of his contemporaries was truly his equal in deeds of charity." With the support of his first wife, Eve, he built the Meisel Synagogue in 1597, for which Rudolph II granted him tax immunity and the right to display in it the "flag of David." Rudolph further decreed that the synagogue might not be entered by officers of the law. It remained Meisel's property until his death, when it was taken over by the community. (From 1963 it housed the synagogue silver collection of the Jewish State Museum.)

Meisel purchased land for the expansion of the Jewish cemetery and the construction of a *bet tohorah* (where the dead were prepared for burial). He financed the building of a hospital, a *bet midrash*, a *mikveh*, and a *Klaus*. The tradition that he also built the Jewish town hall cannot be proved. He had the streets of the Jewish quarter paved and donated large sums to all other charities, especially for the ransoming of captives. He also sent money to Jerusalem and granted considerable loans to the Cracow and Poznan (Posen) communities (possibly because of their connections with *Judah Loew b. Bezalel).

About Meisel's second wife, Frumet (d. 1625), there is diverse information. On one hand, she is said to have supported him in his philanthropic activities, and on the other hand, she is reported to have refused Meisel's dying request to give to Judah Loew a large sum for his charities. That she was Meisel's wife is not mentioned on her gravestone. When Meisel died, childless, he willed his property to his two nephews, both named Samuel. Although the emperor was represented at Meisel's funeral, all Meisel's property was seized in the name of the emperor, his heirs tortured to make them disclose any "concealed" assets, and Meisel's will itself declared void. A lawsuit was initiated, to which the entire community became a party, claiming the right to part of the inheritance because it had been forced to pay interest on it. In the course of this lawsuit, the *ḥerem* was pronounced on the impoverished Meisel family and one of them was refused burial. Although the main part of the estate burned down in the conflagration of 1689, an agreement between the community and the family was not reached until 1699.

BIBLIOGRAPHY: J.R. Marcus, *The Jew in the Medieval World* (1965), 323–6; O. Muneles (ed.), *The Prague Ghetto in the Renaissance Period* (1965), index; Bondy-Dworský, nos. 859, 967–9, 971–3; H. Volavková (ed.), *Guide to the Jewish Museum in Prague*, 2 pts. (1948–57), index; idem, *A Story of the Jewish Museum in Prague* (1968), 259–66; H. Schnee, *Die Hoffinanz und der moderne Staat*, 5 (1966), 219–22; B. Kisch, in: HJ, 3 (1941), 86–88; 4 (1942), 71–73; G. Wolf, in: ZGJD, 2 (1888), 172–81.

[Meir Lamed]

MEISEL, MOSES BEN MORDECAI (c. 1758–c. 1838), Torah scholar and *maskil*; born in Vilna. In his youth Meisel was one of the disciples closest to the Vilna Gaon *Elijah b. Solomon Zalman. He was familiar with German literature and became deeply interested in the writings of Moses *Mendelssohn. However, he was also in secret contact with R. *Shneur Zalman of Lyady, the founder of the *Chabad movement, and when this became known, he fled to Germany, fearing persecution by the Vilna religious establishment. During the Napoleonic Wars he conferred with the representatives of the French government on several occasions. After acceding to R. Shneur Zalman's request to stop these talks with people close to Napoleon, he was suspected of collaborating with the Russian army and was compelled to flee. He went to Ereẓ Israel but returned to Lithuania after the French defeat. During the early 1820s he went once more to Ereẓ Israel and in his last years was closely associated with Sir Moses *Montefiore. He wrote *Shirat Moshe* (Shklov, 1788), on the 613 precepts. Meisel died in Hebron.

BIBLIOGRAPHY: S. Fuenn, *Kiryah Ne'emanah* (1860), 246–7; M. Teitelbaum, *Ha-Rav mi-Ladi* (1910–13), 31, 156–8.

[Arthur Cygielman]

MEISEL, NOAH (1891–1956), Latvian politician, born in Nesvizh, Belarus. From his student days Meisel was a member of the *Bund. In World War I he served in the Russian army as a medical officer. After Latvia became independent (1918), he was appointed municipal health officer in Daugavpils (Dvinsk) and also served as a member of the city council and the Jewish community council. Later, he was elected to the Latvian parliament, where he represented the Bund. After the Fascist takeover (1934) he was arrested together with other Socialist deputies and spent some time in prison. He visited the United States, but did not stay there, returning to Latvia. In 1940, when the Soviet forces overran Latvia, Meisel was arrested – as were other Socialist and democratic leaders – and deported to the far north of the U.S.S.R., where he eventually died.

BIBLIOGRAPHY: *Yahadut Latvia* (1953), index; J.S. Hertz, *Doyres Bundistn*, 2 (1956), 236–40; LNYL, 5 (1963), 585–6.

[Joseph Gar]

MEISELS, DAVID DOV (1814–1876), Polish rabbi. Meisels was the son of Aryeh Judah Jacob who served as *av bet din* of Piotrkow and Kilatow. He was known in his youth as a prodigy (*illui*). He was appointed *av bet din* of Dobra at the age of 18 and later served in the same capacity at Nasielsk. From 1851 until his death he was rabbi of Lask. He was regarded as one of the outstanding talmudists of his generation and gained the deep respect of the ḥasidic rabbi of Gur, Isaac Meir, author of the *Ḥiddushei ha-Rim*. Meisels' important works, published by his sons, are *Ahavat David*, on the laws of invalid witnesses (1884); *Ḥiddushei ha-Radad*, novellae on tractate *Pesaḥim* (1891); *She'elot u-Teshuvot ha-Radad*, responsa on *Oraḥ Ḥayyim* and *Even ha-Ezer* (1903); and *Binyan David*, on the Book of Lamentations (1913). Of his sons, JACOB, author of the *Toledot Ya'akov*, succeeded his father as rabbi of Lask; PHINEHAS ELIJAH served as rabbi of Rakov and ZE'EV WOLF was a distinguished Ḥasid at Tarnow.

BIBLIOGRAPHY: P. Zelig, *Ir Lask va-Ḥakhameha* (1926), 71–75.

[Arthur Cygielman]

MEISELS, DOV BERUSH (1798–1870), rabbi and Polish patriot. Scion of one of the most ancient families of Cracow, he was a descendant of Moses *Isserles. He studied under his father Isaac, who was rabbi of Kamenets-Podolsk, Ukraine. After his marriage to the daughter of the wealthy Solomon Borenstein, he settled in Cracow, where he opened a bank in partnership with Horowitz, the bank bearing the names of both partners. In 1832, after a difficult struggle against R. Saul Landa, Meisels was elected rabbi of the town. R. Saul Landa and his followers did not recognize this election and they established their own *bet din*. The divergences of opinion between the two *battei din* were tremendous; what one of them permitted the other prohibited. Both rabbis vigorously fought the emergence of the Haskalah in Cracow and they were violently attacked by the *maskilim* in the pages of their *Algemeyne Tsaytung*. During the period of his rabbinate in Cracow, and even before then, Meisels played a central role in the communal life of the Jews of Cracow. Being extremely wealthy, he distributed the whole of his rabbinical salary to charitable institutions, thus gaining the esteem of the masses. Many of the inhabitants of Cracow, which was then under Austrian rule, joined the Polish Revolt which broke out in Warsaw in 1830 against Russian rule. Meisels supported the rebels and he personally financed the purchase of arms and the expenses of the rebels. In general, Meisels was an enthusiastic Polish patriot and he proved it on several occasions.

During the revolution of 1844, Meisels again supported the rebels. At a central prayer service held in the synagogue, Meisels called upon the congregation to join the rebels and to support them, even taking part in mass demonstrations in the street. In 1846 he was elected to the Senate of the Cracow Republic (the Free City of Cracow) and in 1848 was a member of the Polish delegation to the Austrian emperor which appealed for the liberation of the political prisoners. In the elections to the Austrian parliament which were held on December 31, 1848, Meisels was elected as the first Jew, obtaining a large majority over the other Jewish candidates. During the same year, he was also elected as one of the 40 councilors of the municipality of Cracow. In 1851, Meisels lent his assistance to projects for Jewish agricultural settlement, but these did not materialize. In parliament, Meisels joined forces with the Radicals. His sharp reply of: "*Juden haben keine Rechte*" – "Jews have no Right(s)" – to the speaker of parliament who had asked him why he sat with the Leftists has become renowned. In 1854 his great rival, R. Saul Landa, died and two years later, Meisels became chief rabbi of Warsaw. He was received with much enthusiasm by all circles, though his election followed upon a violent dispute. In Warsaw, he also fought together with the Poles, joining their demonstration and assisting the Polish patriots.

In November 1861, he was arrested for closing the synagogue of Warsaw in defiance of the czarist authorities and was compelled to leave the town after a lengthy imprisonment. London and Amsterdam offered him their rabbinical seats, but in 1862 he was authorized to return to Warsaw, which he preferred. He was again expelled and deported to Cracow, but he was pardoned and returned to Warsaw – but from then he engaged exclusively in study. When he died in Warsaw, the whole population attended the funeral, as a manifestation of the desire for Polish independence; the Russians prohibited the publication of obituaries on him, in revenge for his political activities against them. Meisels published *Ḥiddushei Maharadam* (Warsaw, 1870), consisting of novellae on the *Sefer ha-Mitzvot* of Maimonides. His son, ISRAEL, was *dayyan* in Cracow and rabbi in Shedletz (Polish: Siedlce) from 1858–67. He then returned to Cracow, where he died in 1875. His second son, SOLOMON, lived in Vienna.

BIBLIOGRAPHY: *Sefer Cracow* (1959), 62ff.; *Me'ir Einei ha-Golah*, 2 (1954^2), 12f.; D. Flinker, *Arim ve-Immahot be-Yisrael*, 3 (1948), 108–12; A. Levinson, *Toledot Yehudei Varshah* (1953), 158–64; E. Kupfer, *Ber Meisels* (Yid.; 1952); M. Kamelhar, *Rabbi Dov Ber Meisels, Gadol ba-Torah, Medinai ve-Loḥem* (1970); J. Shatzky, *Geshikhte fun Yidn in Varshe*, 21 (1948), 226–39 and index; 3 (1953), index.

[Itzhak Alfassi]

MEISELS, SAUL (1911–1990), *ḥazzan.* Meisels was born in Galicia where his father was a ḥasidic *ḥazzan*. Meisels immigrated to the United States in his youth and sang as a child in cantorial choirs. He studied music with the well-known synagogue composer Max Helfman, and received his vocal training at Juilliard. For 37 years he was the *ḥazzan* of Temple on the Heights in Cleveland. He was president of the Cantors Assembly and in 1965 organized the first International Conference of Musicians and Cantors, which was held in Israel. Meisels specialized in renditions of Yiddish folk songs and appeared in numerous concerts of *ḥazzanut*, and sang Yiddish folk songs, songs from the Jewish theater, and modern Israeli songs. In his performances he was accompanied by his wife, Ida Ruth, a well-known arranger of Yiddish folk songs. Meisels made recordings of cantorial works composed by Sholom Secunda, and was a recording artist for RCA Victor and Tikvah Records.

[Akiva Zimmerman / Raymond Goldstein (2nd ed.)]

MEISELS, UZZIEL BEN ẒEVI HIRSCH (1743–1785 or 1786), ḥasidic rabbi in Poland. Meisels was a member of an old rabbinic family in Poland, and a descendant of Moses *Isserles whom he calls "my grandfather" in his works. He served as *av bet din* in Rychwal (Bogatynia), Ostrowiec, and Nowy Dwor. Attracted to Ḥasidism he became a disciple of *Dov Baer, the Maggid of Mezhirech, and with his brother Isaac became one of the propagators of Ḥasidism in Poland. A considerable portion of his teachings in the yeshivah has been lost. His works include *Eẓ ha-Da'at Tov*, novellae on tractates *Ketubbot* (1863) and *Shabbat* (1866); *Menorah ha-Tehorah* (1883/84), on *Tur, Oraḥ Ḥayyim, Hilkhot Shabbat*; and *Tiferet Ẓevi* (1803), on tractate *Beẓah*. The rest were published posthumously by his grandchildren in *Tiferet Uzzi'el*. This work includes selections on the Bible and moralistic ḥasidic sermons, combined with kabbalistic themes, though even these reflect the style of the halakhist, and contains many sayings of the founders of Ḥasidism. Meisels was called עבד ה' ("Servant of the Lord"), *eved* being the initial letters of Uzziel ben Dreizel (his mother's name).

[Pnina Meislish]

MEISL, JOSEPH (1883–1958), historian and archivist. Born in Brno, he became an official of the Berlin Jewish community in 1908, rising to general secretary, and was later librarian of the community's important library. After the Nazis seized power, Meisl settled in Jerusalem. There he founded (and to 1957 directed) the *General Archives for the History of the Jewish People (see *Archives). Before and after World War II he was able to transfer valuable archival material from Central and Eastern Europe to the archives.

Writing mainly in German, Meisl made considerable contributions to Jewish historiography. His works include *Geschichte der Juden in Polen und Russland* (3 vols., 1921–25); *Haskalah, Geschichte der Aufklaerungsbewegung unter den Juden in Russland* (1919), a history of the Haskalah movement in Russia; and *Die Juden im Zartum Polen* (1916). He also wrote studies on well-known Jewish historians: H. *Graetz (1917), S. *Dubnow (1930), and his father-in-law S.P. *Rabbinowitz (Heb., 1943). In 1939 he published his study of Sir Moses *Montefiore's (abortive) endeavors to raise the educational and economic standards of Jerusalem Jewry, while his important edition of the minute books of the Berlin Jewish community, 1723–1854 (*Pinkas Kehillat Berlin*) was published posthumously in 1962 by Shaul Esh. Meisl was a coeditor of the *Festschrift zu S. Dubnows siebzigstem Geburtstag* (1930).

BIBLIOGRAPHY: N.M. Gelber, in: *Ḥokhmat Yisrael be-Ma'arav Eiropah*, ed. by S. Federbush, 2 (1963), 170ff. **ADD. BIBLIOGRAPHY:** NDB, vol. 16 (1990), 688f.

[Getzel Kressel]

MEISSEN, former margravate in Saxony, city near Dresden, Germany. Jews are mentioned as resident in the margravate of Meissen in the first decade of the 11th century. An organized community in the city of Meissen dates only from the 12th century, when a synagogue and a cemetery were maintained. The Jews lived at first in a *Judendorf* outside the city walls near the "Jewish gate." In 1265 Duke Henry the Illustrious enacted a liberal decree securing the Jewish community undisturbed participation in the city's life for some 80 years. During this period they made their living as pawnbrokers and moneylenders. Their communal life flourished, and they established the first Jewish school in Saxony. In 1330 Emperor Louis IV transferred the protection of the Jews in Meissen to Frederick the Grave of Thuringia. During the *Black Death persecutions of 1349 the community was destroyed. Although it was never reestablished within the city itself during medieval times, Jewish moneylenders and tradesmen remained as taxpayers within the margravate. A partial expulsion took place in 1411, but the decree was rescinded in 1415. In 1425 Frederick the Warlike granted them protection for a yearly fee; however, during the course of the Hussite Wars (see *Hussites), Frederick the Mild ordered the expulsion of all Jews from Meissen and Thuringia in 1430. They were not permitted entry into Saxony as a whole until the end of the 18th century. The modern community in the city of Meissen was founded in the 19th century, but it never achieved the status of its medieval counterpart. The city had a population of 32 Jews in 1890 that remained stable until 1904, but by 1933 all of them had been absorbed by *Dresden.

BIBLIOGRAPHY: *Germania Judaica*, 1 (1963), 225–6; 2 (1968), 531–3, incl. bibl.; A. Leicht, *Die Judengemeinde in Meissen* (repr. 1890); A. Levy, *Geschichte der Juden in Sachsen* (1900), passim; S. Neufeld, *Die Juden im Thueringisch-Saechsischen Gebiet waehrend des Mittelalters*, 2 vols. (1917–27), passim; FJW, 323.

[Alexander Shapiro]

MEITAR (Heb. מֵיתָר), urban settlement located in southern Israel, near Beersheba. It received municipal council status in 1987. In 2002 its population was 6,100, occupying an area of 6.5 sq. mi. (17 sq. km.).

[Shaked Gilboa (2nd ed.)]

MEITNER, LISE (1878–1968), physicist and one of the small group responsible for the discovery of atomic fission. Born in Vienna, she moved to Berlin in 1917 and there joined the distinguished chemist Otto Hahn, with whom she worked in collaboration, researching into radioactive substances. Lise Meitner was one of the first women to become a professor at the University of Berlin (1926). From 1917 she was for over 20 years head of the physics department in the Kaiser Wilhelm Institute for chemistry in Berlin.

After the *Anschluss* in 1938, she left Germany and settled in Stockholm, working on the staff of the Nobel Institute. There she received a letter from Hahn describing his discovery with Fritz Strassmann that, when a uranium atom was disintegrated by a neutron, an atom of barium was thereby produced. While holidaying near Gothenburg in December 1938, she discussed this with her nephew, Otto *Frisch, who was working in Denmark with Niels *Bohr. The two physicists immediately realized the significance of Hahn's work, which meant that the uranium atom was split into roughly equal parts, accompanied by a tremendous release of energy. Frisch called this "fission," a term borrowed from biology. Lise Meitner visited the United States after 1945, but returned to Sweden and became a citizen in 1949. Both before and after World War II she received many honors. She eventually retired to Cambridge, England, where she died.

BIBLIOGRAPHY: *New York Times* (Oct. 28, 1968); E. Yost, in: *Science Digest* (May 1962), 83–88.

[Maurice Goldsmith]

MEITUS, ELIAHU (1892–1979), Hebrew poet, writer, and translator. Born in Kishinev, Meitus studied at the Sorbonne but during World War I returned to Russia. After the war he served as headmaster of a Hebrew gymnasium in Bessarabia, and later taught in the teachers' seminary in Jassy (Romania). In 1935 he settled in Palestine, where he taught literature in secondary schools. His first poem appeared in *Ha-Shilo'aḥ* (1910), when he was studying in Odessa. He came to the attention of Bialik, then the literary editor of that periodical, and became a member of the "Odessa group" of Hebrew writers. Subsequently, Meitus published poems and articles in the Hebrew press in Russia, Romania, and elsewhere. After he settled in Palestine, Meitus' writings appeared regularly in the newspapers, particularly in the daily *Al ha-Mishmar.* He translated extensively (from French, Romanian, Russian, and Yiddish), mainly works of fiction, but also poetry and nonfiction. Four collections of his poetry have appeared, including *Shirim* (1943), *Balladot mi-Nof ha-Yaldut* (1954), and *Bi-Keẓeh ha-Gesher ha-Sheni* (1967, sonnets). He also compiled an anthology of modern Hebrew poetry, *Shiratenu ha-Ḥadashah* (1938).

BIBLIOGRAPHY: M. Avishai, *Bein Olamot* (1962), 153–6; A. Cohen, *Soferim Ivriyyim Benei Zemannenu* (1964), 204–6; Kressel, Leksikon, 2 (1967), 345–6.

[Getzel Kressel]

MEKHILTA DEUTERONOMY (MD) is a halakhic Midrash of the school of R. Ishmael, the exact scope of which has not been determined, since the greater part of this Midrash is not extant. One of the *Genizah* fragments of MD indicates that its first unit ended with Deut. 1:30, and its second unit began with Deut. 3:23, as does *Sifre Deuteronomy* (SD). This might indicate that its other sections, as well, were essentially parallel to those of SD. In four *Genizah* fragments MD is divided into "*parashot*," each of which includes an average of four to five verses. In a later fragment, that originated in Yemen, the Midrash is divided into verses ("סל' פס'" – end of verse), but this was probably not an original division, and was influenced by the common division of SD that was prevalent in Yemen.

Hoffmann was the first scholar to methodically demonstrate that R. David ha-Adani used MD in his composition of *Midrash ha-Gadol*, and, following this premise, also began to reconstruct the former. Schechter then published four *Genizah* leaves of MD, *Re'eh*, which he identified in Oxford and in Cambridge. On the basis of these leaves, and a reexamination of *Midrash ha-Gadol*, Hoffmann began a second reconstruction of MD in his book *Midrash Tanaim*, which was published in two volumes (Berlin, 1908–09).

In this edition, still used by scholars to the present day, Hoffmann printed in one font all the passages from *Midrash ha-Gadol* that differ in a pronounced manner from SD, and used a second font for all the *Midrash ha-Gadol* passages that resemble SD, and whose identification as MD he regarded as doubtful. Several times during the course of his edition, however, Hoffmann changed the fonts marking the similar or varying passages (on pp. 1–24, 63–180, large type = a passage different from SD, small type = a passage similar to Sif. Deut.; on the other hand, on pp. 24–62, 180–252, large type = a passage similar to SD, small type = a passage different from SD).

There are many drawbacks to this edition. As has been proven from the *Genizah* fragments, a large portion of MD was not quoted in *Midrash ha-Gadol*, and the part that was cited was on occasion reworked by Adani, or was corrupted by the copyist of the only manuscript of *Midrash ha-Gadol* that was available to Hoffmann. Hoffmann often included in his edition Midrashim that the author of *Midrash ha-Gadol* had undoubtedly copied from SD, BT, *Mishnat R. Eliezer*, the *Mishneh Torah* of Maimonides, and other sources. Hoffmann generally voices his doubts concerning the authenticity of such passages, but the reader must conduct his own examination of each passage with this issue in mind.

Several additional passages from MD came to light after the publication of *Midrash Tanaim*. Schechter published a *Genizah* fragment consisting of two leaves from MD, *Re'eh*. Kahana later succeeded in identifying two additional fragments, each of two leaves, from MD, *Devarim-Va-Etanan* and *Ha'azinu-Ve-Zot ha-Berakhah*, along with a lengthy quotation from MD, *Ekev* and *Ha'azinu*, that appears in an early collection in the *Genizah*. The second fragment that Schechter published from the Cambridge *Genizah* collection was the subject of a second, and more exacting, edition by Epstein, and new editions of *Midrash ha-Gadol* on Deuteronomy have been published, based on several manuscripts. These editions, and other manuscripts of *Midrash ha-Gadol*, enable us to correct many of the corruptions that entered *Midrash Tanaim*. A considerable number of expositions from MD were inserted in the Western textual versions of SD, and others are preserved in quotations by medieval sages that have been discovered in recent years. It would seem, however, that the circulation of MD was already quite limited in the medieval period.

The direct passages from MD discovered to the present contain only some five percent of the Midrash, a fact that severely hinders its research. The most detailed description of MD and its nature as a Midrash from the school of R. Ishmael was written by Hoffmann, after he completed his edition of *Midrash Tanaim*, and Epstein engaged in a concise discussion of MD following the new edition of one of its passages. It should be mentioned that the halakhic material in the three fragments that were published by Schechter is notable for its lengthy and detailed expositions. The aggadic material of MD also is characterized by a certain degree of lengthiness, in comparison to the parallel material in SD. At times the version of the aggadic exegeses in MD is superior in its language, style, and content to that of the parallel expositions in SD, which occasionally suffer from nonuniformity of style, vague expositions that lack inner logic, and a number of corruptions shared by all the manuscripts. Some of the differences between MD and SD apparently are a consequence of the varying worldviews of the redactors of these Midrashim (see, e.g., the outline of the differing attitude by the redactors of these Midrashim to the non-Jewish peoples).

BIBLIOGRAPHY: J.N. Epstein, *Prolegomena ad Litteras Tannaiticas* (Hebr.) (1957), 631–33, 711–23; idem, *Studies in Talmudic Literature and Semitic Languages* (Heb.), ed. E.Z. Melamed, vol. 2 (1988), 125–40; M. Hirshman, *Tora for the Entire World* (Heb.) (1999), 108–13; D. Hoffmann, *Der Midrasch Tannaim zum Deuteronoium* (Heb.) (1908–09); idem, "Uber eine Mechilta zu Deuteronomium," in: *Jubelschrift des I. Hildesheimer* (1890), 83–93; idem, "Zur Einleitung in den Midrasch Tannaim zum Deuteronomium," in: *Jahrbuch der Judisch-Literarischen Gesellschaft*, 6 (1909), 304–23; M. Kahana, "Citations of the Deuteronomy Mekhilta Ekev and Ha'azinu," in: *Tarbiz*, 56 (1987), 19–59 (Heb.); idem, "Halakhic Midrash Collections," in: *The Literature of the Sages*, vol. 3b (2006); idem, *Manuscripts of the Halakhic Midrashim: An Annotated Catalogue* (Heb.) (1995), 108–11; idem, *The Genizah Fragments of the Halakhic Midrashim* (Heb.), 1 (2005), 338–57; idem, "The Importance of Dwelling in the Land of Israel According to the Deuteronomy Mekhilta," in: *Tarbiz*, 62 (1993), 501–13 (Heb.); idem, "New Fragments of the Mekhilta on Deuteronomy," in: *Tarbiz*, 54 (1985), 485–551 (Heb.); idem, "Pages of the Deuteronomy Mekhilta Portions Ha'azinu and Zot ha-Berakhah," in: *Tarbiz*, 57 (1988), 165–201 (Heb.); E.Z. Melamed, *The Relationship between the Halakhic Midrashim and the Mishnah & Tosefta* (Heb.) (1967), 145–53; S. Schechter, "Genizah Fragments," in: JQR, 16 (1904), 446–52; idem, "The Mechilta to Deuteronomy," in: JQR, 16 (1904), 695–99; idem, "*Mekhilta Deuteronomy* the Portion of *Re'eh*," in: M. Brann and I. Elbogen (eds.), *Festschrift zu siebzigsten Geburstag Israel Lewy's* (1910), Hebrew Section, 188–92.

[Menahem I. Kahana (2nd ed.)]

MEKHILTA OF R. ISHMAEL (Aram. מְכִילְתָא דְרַבִּי יִשְׁמָעֵאל) halakhic Midrash on Exodus.

Mekhilta de-Rabbi Yishmael (MY) is a Midrash from the school of R. Ishmael to the Book of Exodus. The word "*mekhilta*" means "a measure," and its attribution to R. Ishmael was initially by R. Samuel ben Hophni and R. Nissim Gaon (the attribution of MI to the midrashic school of R. Ishmael is an innovation solely by scholars in recent generations; and it is only by chance that this notion corresponds with the name given the Midrash by several *rishonim*). MI does not contain an exposition for the entire narrative section of Ex. 1–11; it rather opens with the first laws of the Book of Exodus in 12:1, and continues with the uninterrupted exegesis of the halakhic and aggadic passages until 23:19, before ending with the exposition of two short halakhic passages on the Sabbath in Ex. 31 and 35. All this indicates a close association between MI and the halakhic material in Exodus, although the precise criteria for determining which material in Exodus will be the subject of an exposition and which will be passed over are unclear, since it also includes Midrashim on lengthy aggadic sections, while, on the other hand, it skips a number of halakhic passages.

MI is divided into nine *masekhtot*: *Pasḥa* (Ex. 12:1–13:16); *Va-Yehi Be-Shalah* (13:17–14:31); *Shirta* (15:1–21); *Va-Yassa* (15:22–17:7); *Amalek* (17:8–18:27); *Ba-Ḥodesh* or *Debiri* (19:1–20:26); *Nezikin* (21:1–22:23); *Kaspa* (22:24–29); *Shabbatta* (31:12–17; 35:1–3). Each *masekhta* is divided into a number of *parashot*, each of which is in turn divided into *halakhot*, numbered with the letters of the *alef-bet*. Each *parashah* ends with a summation of the number of *halakhot* contained in it, the *masekhtot* conclude by mentioning and summing up the *parashot*, as well, and the entire Midrash ends with a summation of the *masekhtot*. These summations are presented by means of allusions to each *parashah* in Aramaic, which is also the language of the division into *masekhtot*, *parashot*, and *halakhot* (the division is preserved in its entirety only in the *Genizah* fragments).

Two critical editions of MI, that do not refer to each other, have been published: the edition by H.S. Horovitz, which was posthumously edited and completed by I.A. Rabin (Frankfurt, 1931); and the edition by J.Z. Lauterbach, which was published in three volumes (Philadelphia, 1934–35). These editions rightly received favorable reviews by E.Z. Melamed, who reviewed the Horovitz edition, and by S. Lieberman, who evaluated the Lauterbach edition.

Horovitz chose the printed version as the basic text for his edition, at times emending and completing it in accordance with other textual versions. He provided a detailed listing of the textual variants found in the two complete manuscripts of MI, Oxford 151 and Munich 117; in the Leghorn 1801 edition, that is based, inter alia, on the emendations by Soliman Ohana; in the many quotations in *Yalkut Shimoni* and in *Midrash Ḥakhamim*, which include most of MI; and in other indirect testimonies, primarily the Midrashim *Lekah Tov*, *Sekhel Tov*, *Tanhuma*, and *Sefer ve-Hizhir*. Horovitz also added a concise but thorough critical commentary, with references to the parallels.

The Lauterbach edition is more eclectic. The editor generally preferred the common version of the two manuscripts in his determination of the text. In addition to the textual versions that were available to Horovitz, Lauterbach used a few pages from the *Genizah*, MS. Rome Casanatensa H 2736 on *Masekhta de-Shirta*, and MS. Oxford 2637 on *Yalkut Shimoni*. The variant readings were recorded in an extremely selective manner, and the references to the parallels are listed separately.

Both editions suffer from the absence of a prior methodological discussion regarding the character of the various textual versions and the mutual relations between them. Consequently, the editors were unaware of the direct dependence of the printed Venice 1545 edition on the printed Constantinople 1515(?) edition, that was indicated by Melamed; the common source of the Western mss., as was concluded by Finkelstein; and, mainly, the relative superiority of MS. Oxford to the other texts that they possessed, as was first noted by Lieberman. The lack of a comprehensive evaluation of the character of the textual versions is also apparent in the tendency of the editors to base the text of MI, especially its difficult passages, on the adapted and emended versions of *Midrash Ḥakhamim*, which, as its name implies, is a "Midrash" by an Italian sage from the 15th century who relied in great measure upon the MI, but not a direct textual version.

Additional versions of MI came to light after the publication of these two editions. Especially noteworthy among these are MS. Vatican 299, which preserves about half of the *Mekhilta*, and some 80 pages from the Cairo *Genizah*. The importance of the latter lies in the Eastern and early textual tradition that is reflected in the majority of them, and that is generally superior to the later Western textual tradition that is presented in the direct MI texts on which the two critical editions were based. In many instances, the original version is preserved only in the *Genizah* fragments, and in other places the Eastern *Genizah* version confirms the shared reading of the Western manuscripts, also for very difficult versions, that might possibly attest to intentional intervention in the original traditions of the MI by its later redactors or the earlier copyists.

MI was interpreted during the medieval period by several *rishonim*, but only one of these commentaries is extant, and only partially, in MS. Mantua 36. The publication of MI was followed by a number of short emendations and commentaries written with the aid of manuscripts, and a number of lengthy commentaries by *aharonim* that were based solely on the printed version, along with quotations appearing in *Yalkut Shimoni*. The most important of the latter are *Shevut Yehudah* by R. Judah Najar and *Berurei ha-Middot* by R. Isaac Elijah Landau, which were closely followed by two scholarly commentaries: *Middot Soferim* by Isaac Hirsch Weiss, and *Me'ir Ayin* by Meir Friedmann (Ish Shalom). Friedmann's work laid the groundwork for the editions by Horovitz and Lauterbach, who were greatly aided by it. After the publication of the two editions, *Masekhta de-Shirta* was the subject of a new commentary by Goldin, and Kahana published a new edition of *Parshat Amalek* that included a detailed discussion that sought to prove the originality of the aggadic material preserved in MI, relative to the secondary material in MS (Mekhilta of R. Simeon Ben Yoḥai).

The general nature of MI and its sources has been examined and described by scholars of halakhic Midrashim, and has been the subject of numerous monographs examining its diverse sources, its attitude toward the Mishnah and to MS, its narrative traditions, its conceptual worlds, and other topics.

Translations: English: J.Z. Lauterbach, *Mekilta de-Rabbi Ishmael*, vols. 1–3, Philadelphia 1933–35; J. Neusner, *Mekhilta according to Rabbi Ishmael: An Analytical Translation*, Atlanta, 1988. German: J. Winter and A. Wunsche, *Mechilta ein tannaitischer Midrasch zu Exsodus*, Leipzig, 1909. Spanish: T. Martines, *Mekilta de Rabbi Ismael; comentario rabinico al libro del Exodo*, Navarre, 1995.

BIBLIOGRAPHY: Ch. Albeck, *Introduction to the Talmuds* (1969), 106–13 (Heb.); idem, *Untersuchungen ueber die Halakischen Midraschim* (1927), 91–96; D. Boyarin, "From the Hidden Light of the Geniza: Towards the Original Text of the Mekhilta d'Rabbi Ishmael," in: *Sidra*, 2 (1986), 5–13 (Heb.); idem, *Intertextuality and the Reading of Midrash* (1990); D. Buchner, "On the Relationship between Mekhilta de-Rabbi Ishmael and Septuagint Exodus," in: IOSCS, in: *Congress*, 9 (1997), 403–20; Elias, "The *Mekhilta de-Rabbi Ishmael* according to an Excellent Copy from the Genizah" (Master's thesis, Hebrew University, Jerusalem, 1997; Heb.); J.N. Epstein, *Introduction to the Mishnaic Text* (Heb.) (1948), 736–38; idem, "Mekhilta and Sifre in the Works of Maimonides," in: *Tarbiz*, 6 (1935), 343–82 (Heb.); idem, *Prolegomena ad Litteras Tannaiticas* (Heb.) (1957), 545–87; L. Finkelstein, "The Mekhilta and Its Text," in: PAAJR, 5 (1933–34), 3–54; M. Friedmann, *Mekhilta de-Rabbi Ismael, der alteste halachische und hagadische Midrasch zu Exodus* (Heb.) (1870); L. Ginzberg, *Al ha-Halakhah ve-Aggadah* (Heb.) (1960), 66–103; J. Goldin, *The Munich Manuscript of the Mekilta* (1980); idem, *The Song at the Sea* (1971); H.S. Horovitz (ed.), *Sifre d'Vei Rab* (on Numbers; 1917) (Heb.); M.A. Kadushin, *A Conceptual Approach to the Mekilta* (1969); M. Kahana, "The Critical Editions of Mekhilta de-Rabbi Ishmael in the Light of the Genizah Fragments," *Tarbiz*, 55 (1986), 489–524 (Heb.); idem, "Halakhic Midrash Collections," in: *The Literature of the Sages*, vol. 3b (2006); idem, *The Genizah Fragments of the Halakhic Midrashim* (Heb.), 1 (2005), 1–152; idem, *Manuscripts of the Halakhic Midrashim: An Annotated Catalogue* (Heb.) (1995), 37–49; idem, *The Two Mekhiltot on the Amalek Portion* (Heb.) (1999); E.D. Kutscher, "Genizah Fragments of the Mekhilta of Rabbi Ishmael," in: *Leshonenu*, 32 (1968), 103–16 (Heb.); J.Z. Lauterbach, "The Arrangement and the Division of the Mekhilta," in: HUCA, 1 (1924), 427–66; idem, *"Me-Biurei ha-Mekhilta,"* in: *Sefer Klausner*, 181–88 (Heb.); idem, *Mekilta de-Rabbi Ishmael*, vols. 1–3 (1933–35); idem, "The Name of the Mekilta," in: JQR, 11 (1920), 169–82; H.I. Levine, *Studies in Mishna Pesachim, Baba Kama and the Mechilta* (1971); S. Lieberman, "Mekhilta de-Rabbi Ishmael ed. J.Z. Lauterbach," in: *Kiryath Sepher*, 12 (1935), 54–65 (Heb.); idem, "A New *Piska* from the Mekhilta and Its Meaning," in: *Sinai*, 75 (1975), 1–3 (Heb.); E.Z. Melamed, *Essays in Talmudic Literature* (Heb.) (1986), 394–405, 421–32; idem, *The Relationship between the Halakhic Midrashim and the Mishnah & Tosefta* (Heb.) (1967), 105–23; G. Stemberger, "Die Datierung der Mekhilta," in: *Karios*, 21 (1979), 81–118; I.M. Ta-Shma, "An Unpublished Franco-German Commentary on Bereshit and Va-Yikra

Rabba, Mekhilta and Sifre," in: *Tarbiz*, 55 (1986), 61–75 (Heb.); B.Z. Wacholder, "The Date of the Meckilta De-Rabbi Ismael," in: HUCA, 39 (1968), 117–44; A.Z. Yehuda, "The Two Mekhiltot on the Hebrew Slave" (Ph.D. diss., Yeshiva University, New York, 1974).

[Menahem I. Kahana (2nd ed.)]

MEKHILTA OF R. SIMEON BEN YOḤAI (Aram. מְכִילְתָּא דְּרַבִּי שִׁמְעוֹן בֶּן יוֹחַאי) (MS), a halakhic Midrash on Exodus from the school of R. *Akiva, which is attributed to R. Simeon b. Yoḥai because of his exposition at the beginning of the book. Several *rishonim* knew this Midrash by other names, such as "*Mekhilta de-Sanya*"; "*Mekhilta*"; "*Sifri*"; "*Sifri de-Vei Rav*," and others. This Midrash was subsequently lost, and only portions were found by modern scholars. Meir Freidmann (Ish Shalom) was the first to collect the quotations from MS that were known in his time, and his list was augmented by a number of items by Hoffmann in his pioneering study of the tannaitic Midrashim. Israel Lewy then discovered that large portions of the Midrash had been cited by R. David ha-Adani in *Midrash ha-Gadol* on Exodus, and Schechter published a few fragments from MS itself that he uncovered in the Cairo *Genizah*. The first edition of MS was published by Hoffmann (Frankfurt, 1905), based on *Midrash ha-Gadol* and a small number of *Genizah* fragments identified by Schechter. The next edition, published by Epstein and Melamed in 1955, is based on 95 MS leaves or fragments of leaves discovered in the *Genizah*. The rest of the Midrash (approximately one third) was reconstructed using four manuscripts of *Midrash ha-Gadol*. A few additional MS fragments were subsequently published, transcriptions of all the new *Genizah* fragments which came to light, and also a new edition of *Parshat Amalek* of MS based on new manuscripts.

The introduction to the Epstein-Melamed edition contains a description of the MS manuscripts and their main distinguishing features, but the principles guiding the editors were not presented, nor did the editors include a focused and orderly treatment of the signs and symbols used in the edition. The manuscripts were generally copied in this edition in an admirably accurate manner, and only in rare instances should the transcription, which was based on photographs, be corrected on the basis of the original manuscripts. It should be noted, however, that the largest copy of MS, on the basis of which some 65 pages were published, is not an excellent manuscript, being only of second-rate quality, and written in the 13th century in Spain. About another 15 pages are not from direct MS manuscripts, but are fragments that survived from two copies of abridged midrashic collections from MS. Consequently, the textual tradition of MS set forth in the major portion of the edition is not an especially reliable one, and is plagued by many copyist's corruptions and mistakes.

The editors correctly noted the striking disparity between the certain MS fragments that were discovered in the *Genizah* and the doubtful passages, that they printed in smaller type. Most of the doubtful reconstructions, that encompass about one third of the edition, were based on *Midrash ha-Gadol*, and the editors were forced to complete the rest based on the parallel material in *Mekhilta de-Rabbi Ishmael* (MI), *Sifra*, *Midrash Tannaim*, and other Midrashim. Obviously, error could hardly be avoided in such a complex labor of reconstruction, and in his review of the edition, Margalioth referred to a few passages that were incorporated within the text on the basis of *Midrash ha-Gadol*, but that do not originate in MS, but in *Mishnat Rabbi Eliezer*, *Avot de-Rabbi Natan*, or the Babylonian Talmud. A similar situation holds for the completion of missing passages in the *Genizah* fragments on the basis of *Midrash ha-Gadol* (which were printed within brackets, in normal type), whose origin in MS is extremely doubtful. On the other hand, the Epstein-Melamed edition omitted several other passages from *Midrash ha-Gadol* whose origin in MS has now been proven from new quotations from MS cited by several *rishonim*, such as R. Hafeẓ ben Yaẓli'ah and the Karaite authority Jeshua ben Judah.

MS begins with a lengthy exposition concerned with a single topic: the choosing of Moses as the agent who shall redeem Israel, and Moses' response to this selection. This midrashic exposition is composed of two developed literary units (pp. 1–4/3; 4/3–7/9), each of which is focused on the first verse of the weekly Torah reading (*seder*) according to the custom of the Land of Israel with which it opens: Ex. 3:1; Ex. 6:2, that are the only two lemmas in these units. The phenomenon of constructing an entire Midrash around the opening verses of the weekly *seder* as practiced in the Land of Israel appears only very rarely in the tannaitic Midrashim, but is a frequent occurrence in the amoraic Midrashim and in the versions of *Tanhuma*. The deficient extant documentation hinders our determining if MS included additional hermeneutical units on chapters 6–11 of Exodus. At any rate, *Midrash ha-Gadol* preserved midrashic interpretations that apparently originated in MS, beginning with the halakhic subjects in Ex. 12:1; and starting with verse 3 in this chapter, MS is documented in a *Genizah* fragment published by Abramson. MS continues to expound the verses, in order, at least until Ex. 23:19, after which the exact scope of the Midrash is unclear. Based on *Midrash ha-Gadol*, Melamed reconstructed MS on Ex. 23:20–24:10, and selected verses from chaps. 30, 31, 34, and 35 of Exodus in his edition, but several of these quotations clearly do not originate in MS; this issue requires further study.

The Epstein-Melamed edition does not include a commentary, and the parallels, as well, were listed only in a partial fashion. Many interpretations of the Midrashim of MS appear in the edition by Hoffmann and in Kasher's glosses in *Torah Shelemah*, but these cannot fill the need for an orderly and detailed critical commentary of MS in its entirety. As regards the research of MS, see the introduction to the edition, in which Melamed published Epstein's general essay on the MS, which paid special attention to the question of its redactors. Melamed added his own discussion concerning the terminology and vocabulary of MS, the names of the rabbis it cites, its method of quoting sources, and its characteristic hermeneutical methods. The second edition contained an additional short chapter on "Mishnah and *Baraita* Quotations in *Mekhilta de-Rabbi Simeon b. Yoḥai*," and the appendices to the edition included various subject indices that aid in the further study of this Midrash.

Most scholars concur that the halakhic portion of MS was redacted fairly late. This opinion was first expressed by Epstein, who wrote at the end of his Introduction: "The MS is from the school of R. Akiva, and is later than all halakhic Midrashim (HM) (making much verbatim use of *Sifra*, *Sifrei*, and Tosefta), and many *halakhot* are incidentally connected in the Midrash. All this points to a late date." Based on an orderly study of the section of the Hebrew slave in the two *Mekhiltot*, Judah concluded that MS was redacted after MI. De Vries took this premise a step further, and asserted that MS contains a reworking of *baraitot* from MI, and not parallels or a common source. Levine examined several halakhic topics in MS, and reached an even more far-reaching conclusion, that the activity by the redactor of MS closely resembles that of the *amoraim* in the area of interpretations of the Mishnah. He, like them, clarifies the halakhic concepts in the Mishnah, expands it, draws parallels to it, and examines the relationship between one mishnah and another by the use of certain interpretations of *mishnayot* or *baraitot*. On the basis of this analysis, Levine wrote that, apparently, the redactor of MS was himself an *amora*, while emphasizing that further study is required as to whether conclusions could be drawn regarding MS as a whole on the basis of an examination of these specific details. An investigation of Levine's proofs shows that almost all were based on extremely tenuous speculation, and not on solid evidence, on the basis of which we could determine the text of the sources available to the redactor of MS, on the one hand, and the nature of their reworking, on the other. Objections could also be raised concerning the quality of De Vries' proofs of the use by MS of MI. An examination of the singular character of MS therefore requires further study, that would have to include a new and consistent examination of its terminology, the names of the rabbis it mentions, and its prevalent hermeneutical methods that at (albeit extremely rare) times seem also to include several elements seemingly characteristic of the other school, that of R. *Ishmael.

The aggadic material in MS fundamentally resembles the parallel material in MI. An orderly examination of the parallel aggadic material of *Parshat Amalek* demonstrates the primacy of the tradition in MI, in comparison with that of MS, which apparently was fashioned by redactors who sought to inform the midrashic expositions with a more developed literary and ideational nature, somewhat freed from their rigid linkage to the verses. Along with the ideational development of several of the Midrashim in this section in MS, the latter occasionally exhibits stylistic hyperbole, exegetical diffusion, a tendency to relate unattributed interpretations to specific rabbis, and possibly even an attempt to artificially rewrite disagreements. Some of the Midrashim in MS exhibit a simplification of content that borders on popularization, and the accentuation of motifs that concentrate on elementary principles of the religious experience, such as emphasizing the importance of obedience to the word of God, sermonizing about the observance of the commandments and avoiding sin, reinforcing the standing of prayer, and promising the good end that awaits Israel, along with the tribulations that shall befall its enemies.

A comprehensive characterization of the aggadic material of the two *Mekhiltot* would require a detailed examination, which has not been conducted to date. Nonetheless, a partial examination of other *parashot* in the MS reveals findings similar to those in evidence in *Parshat Amalek*. The literary nature of the first aggadic unit that appears only in MS, and not in MI, which resembles in a certain sense the genre of *Tanhuma*, also reflects the literary adaptation that is characteristic of the aggadic material of MS and the relatively late time of its fashioning. The same is true for some of the aggadic material that is incorporated within the halakhic sections, and for a portion of the halakhic material that is included in the aggadic passages.

A geonic response (probably by R. *Sherira and R. *Hai) attributes a quotation from MS to the rabbinic teaching that appears in the "other *sifrei de-vei Rav* [all HM, except for *Sifra*]," "and thus all the *tannaim* learned, without exception," and compares it with a citation from MI, which they termed "*Mekhilta de-Ereẓ Israel*." This led scholars to conclude that MS was the primary *Mekhilta* that the "*tannaim*" (i.e., the teachers of *baraitot*) taught at the time in Babylonia, while MI was more widespread in the Land of Israel; it was not studied in Babylonia (at least not in the yeshivah of Pumbedita), and the *geonim* cited it from a written book. This could possibly be related to the manner in which MS was transmitted, and, in fact, the TB frequently quotes Midrashim similar or identical to MS. In either event, the history of the transmission of MS is to be separated from the question of the venue of its redaction, and there is no reason to move the latter from Ereẓ Israel to Babylonia.

BIBLIOGRAPHY: S. Abramson, "A New Fragment of the Mekhilta de-Rabbi Simeon b. Yoḥai," in: *Tarbiz*, 41 (1972), 361–72 (Heb.); Ch. Albeck, *Introduction to the Talmuds* (Heb.) (1969), 82–83; idem, *Untersuchungen ueber die Halakischen Midraschim* (1927), 151–54; B. de Vries, *Studies in the Literature of the Talmud* (1968), 142–47 (Heb.); J.N. Epstein, *Introduction to the Mishnaic Text* (1948), 746–47 (Heb.); idem, "Mekhilta and Sifre in the Works of Maimonides," in: *Tarbiz*, 6 (1935), 343–82 (Heb.); J.N. Epstein and E.Z. Melamed (eds.), *Mekhilta d'Rabbi Sim'on b. Jochai* (1955); M. Friedmann, *Mechilta de-Rabbi Ismael, der alteste halachische und hagadische Midrasch zu Exodus* (Heb.) (1870), xlix-lv, 119–24; A. Glick, "Another Fragment of the MS," in: *Leshonenu*, 48–49 (1985), 210–15 (Heb.); M. Hirshman, *Torah for the Entire World* (Heb.) (1999), 40–42; D. Hoffmann, *Mechilta de-Rabbi Simon b. Jochai zu Exodus* (Heb.) (1905); M. Kahana, "Another Page from the Mekhilta of R. Simeon b. Yoḥai," in: *Alei Sefer*, 15 (1989), 5–20 (Heb.); idem, "Halakhic Midrash Collections," in: *The Literature of the Sages*, vol. 3b (2006); idem, *The Genizah Fragments of the Halakhic Midrashim* (Heb.), 1 (2005), 153–86; idem, *Manuscripts of the Halakhic Midrashim: An Annotated Catalogue* (Heb.) (1995), 50–59; idem, *The Two Mekhiltot on the Amalek Portion* (Heb.) (1999); M.M. Kasher, *The Book of Maimonides and the MS* (Heb.) (1980^2); H.I. Levine, *Studies in Talmudic Literature and Halakhic Midrashim*

(Heb.) (1987), 127–92; I. Lewy, "Ein Wort uber die 'Mechilta des R. Simon,'" in: *Jahersbericht des judisch-theologischen Seminars* (1889); M. Margalioth, "*MS Hotza'at Epstein-Melamed*," in: *Kiryat Sefer*, 31 (1956), 155–59 (Heb.); Ch. Milikowsky, "On Parallels and Primacy: Seder Olam and MS on the Israelites in Egypt," in: *Bar-Ilan*, 26–27 (1995), 221–25 (Heb.); E.Z. Melamed, *The Relationship between the Halakhic Midrashim and the Mishnah & Tosefta* (Heb.) (1967), 94–104; Z.A. Yehuda, "The Two Mekhiltot on the Hebrew Slave" (Ph.D. diss., Yeshiva University, New York, 1974).

[Menahem I. Kahana (2nd ed.)]

MEKHLIS, LEV ZAKHAROVICH (1889–1953), Soviet army officer. Born in Odessa, Mekhlis was conscripted into the czarist army and during World War I served in an artillery regiment. He joined the Red Army in 1919 and served through the civil war of 1918–21, becoming military commissar of a brigade, a division, and an army group in the Ukraine. In 1930 he graduated from the Institute of Red Professors. For several years Mekhlis was an official of the Communist party central committee and after 1930 worked on the newspaper *Pravda*. He was head of the Red Army's political administration from 1937 to 1940 when he became U.S.S.R. people's commissar of state control. Following the outbreak of World War II, Mekhlis served in the Red Army in 1941–42, again as head of political administration of the army, vice commissar of defense, and from July 1942 to 1945 as member of various front war councils. He was promoted to lieutenant-general on December 6, 1942, and to colonel-general on July 29, 1944. His many decorations included the award of four Lenin medals. After the war he served for a short period as U.S.S.R. minister of state control. He died on February 13, 1953, and his body was interred in the Kremlin wall.

BIBLIOGRAPHY: *Bolshaya Sovetskaya Entsiklopediya*, 27 (1954), 388; *Sovetskaya Istoricheskaya Entsiklopediya; Sovetsky entsiklopedichesky slovar.* **ADD. BIBLIOGRAPHY:** F.D. Sverdlov, *Jewish Generals in the Armed Forces of the U.S.S.R.* (1993).

[Mordechai Kaplan / Shmuel Spector (2nd ed.)]

MEKIẒE NIRDAMIM (Heb. מְקִיצֵי נִרְדָּמִים; "rousers of those who slumber"), the first society for the publication of medieval Hebrew literature in every branch of intellectual activity, in scholarly editions. The aim of the society was both to propagate a knowledge of Jewish scholarship and to establish personal contact between scholars. The structure of the society – which still continues – provided for a board of directors, consisting of the best qualified scholars in their field, and annual subscriptions from members. The Mekiẓe Nirdamim was founded in 1862 by E.L. Silbermann in Lyck, founder-editor of the first Hebrew weekly *Ha-Maggid*, with the cooperation of Chief Rabbi Nathan M. *Adler (London), M. *Sachs (Berlin), and S.D. *Luzzatto. There was a certain amount of opposition – for a variety of reasons – which included a lack of faith in the possibility of the renaissance of Jewish culture, an opposition to the publication of non-rabbinic texts, and an opposition in principle to the exclusive use of Hebrew, which was established as a rule by the society, and/or an opposition to its founders by such scholars as A. *Geiger and M. *Steinschneider. Support was found, however, among Polish and Russian scholars and even in rabbis such as Samuel and Mattityahu *Straschun, S. *Ganzfried, and M.L. *Malbim, and by 1864 the number of subscribers, from a great many countries, stood at 1,200. In the same year the first four publications were issued, among them the first installment of S.D. Luzzatto's edition of Judah Halevi's *Diwan*. The adherence of Moses *Montefiore in 1865 brought with it the support of many who had been aloof. After a decade's activity, there was a pause until, in 1885, the society resumed its work in Berlin, guided by A. *Berliner, A. *Harkavy, and others. It was then that the series *Kobeẓ al Jad* was initiated (26 volumes by 1970), devoted to the publication of smaller manuscripts and documents. In 1934 the seat of the Mekiẓe Nirdamim was transferred to Jerusalem. By 1970, 110 works had been issued. S.Y. *Agnon served as president of the society (1954–70), and was succeeded by Gershom *Scholem. Very distinguished scholars, such as Y. Baer, Ḥ. Schirmann, E. Urbach, etc., served as members of the executive committee. Sh. Abramson and E. Fleischer continued the publication of important books on Hebrew medieval literature in the last decades of the 20th century and the beginning of the 21st with such books as Eleazar ha-Bavli's *Diwan* (ed. Ḥ. Brody, 1971), *Responsa and Decisions of the Sages of Germany and France* (ed. E. Kupfer, 1973), Moses Ibn Ezra's *Kitāb al-Muḥāḍara wal-Mudhākara* (ed. A.S. Halkin, 1975), *Midrash Bereshit Rabbati* (ed. Ch. Albeck, 1984), *Rabbi Jehudah berabbi Benjaminis Carmina Cuncta* (ed. Sh. Elizur, 1988), *Teshuvot ha-Rambam* (ed. J. Blau, 1989), *Pinkas Kehillat Shnaitakh* (ed. M. Hildshaimer, 1992), *Perush Kadum le-Midrash Va-Yikra Rabbah* (ed. M.B. Lerner, 1995), and *Ma'aseh Nisim: Perush la-Torah* (ed. Ḥ. Kraisel, 2000).

BIBLIOGRAPHY: *Ḥevrat Mekiẓe Nirdamim: 1864–1964* (1964), includes complete bibliography of books published by the society.

[Israel Moses Ta-Shma]

MEKLENBURG, JACOB ẒEVI (1785–1865), rabbi and biblical commentator. Meklenburg was born in Inowroclaw, Poznania. Unwilling to enter the rabbinate, he engaged in business, but in 1831, after his business had failed, he accepted an invitation from the community of Koenigsberg to serve as their rabbi, and he remained there until his death. An opponent of religious reforms, he fought against the reformist ideas advocated in his community by Joseph Lewin Saalschuetz.

Meklenburg's major work was a commentary on the Pentateuch, *Ha-Ketav ve-ha-Kabbalah*, in which he sought to demonstrate the conformity between the oral tradition and the written law. His commentary, which contains numerous original interpretations, was first published in Leipzig in 1839. It was reprinted twice during his lifetime, with his additions and included a German translation of the text of the Pentateuch based on Meklenburg's commentary, by Jonah Kossmann. A fourth printing was begun some time before Meklenburg's death, but was interrupted because of differences between the publisher and the printers. In 1880, Abraham Berliner published a new edition with additional material from manuscripts left by the author. Meklenburg was also the author of a commentary on the prayer book, *Iyyun Tefillah*, first published in 1857 with the *siddur* of R. Jacob *Lorbeerbaum of Lissa; it, too, was reprinted several times. A number of rabbinic works carry introductory notes or approbations by Meklenburg.

BIBLIOGRAPHY: D. Druck, in: *Horeb*, 4 (1937), 171–9; N. Ben-Menahem, in: *Sinai*, 65 (1969), 327–32.

[Tovia Preschel]

MEKNÈS, town in *Morocco. Jews settled in the region of Meknès before the advent of *Islam. A Hebrew inscription has been found and the remains of a synagogue were uncovered in the excavations of Volubilis, which is near Meknès. A *kinah* of Abraham *Ibn Ezra mentions Meknès among the communities which suffered at the hands of the *Almohads. A chronological note testifies that such persecutions occurred in 1140, and adds that in 1247, during the wars of the *Merinids, many Jews lost their lives or were forcibly converted to Islam, while in the earthquake of 1340 "several courtyards caved in, as well as the synagogue and the *bet ha-midrash* of R. Jacob." According to traditions preserved in writing, the "Mahrit" synagogue, still existing in Meknès, was first built in the 13th century, destroyed in the earthquake of 1630, and rebuilt in 1646 by the *Toledanos upon their arrival in Meknès. It is similarly stated that the "Tobi" synagogue was built in 1540. It would therefore seem that Jews already at that time lived in the present mellah area as well as in the Medina in which an "Aaron Street" is, according to tradition, named after the then-leader of the community. The sharif Mulay Ismail (1672–1727), the real founder of the *Alawid dynasty, moved his capital to Meknès and granted the Jews additional land for construction of buildings. The **nagid* Abraham Maymerān and other wealthy Jews then built luxurious houses. Christian emissaries from Europe who stayed in them were astonished by their beauty. Near the mellah, Ismail built a beautiful quarter for his officials and servants.

From then until the 19th century the community of Meknès was one of the best developed and organized in Morocco. It was a city of *ḥakhamim* and authors, as well as merchants and men of action who frequently visited *Tetuán, *Salé, *Rabat, and *Fez on their affairs. The community was organized and its institutions functioned accordingly. The taxation on meat, wine, and other products constituted a source of income for the community, which with the addition of local donations, was able to supply the minimal requirements of the needy and those engaged in studies. The community maintained regular relations with Ereẓ Israel, whose emissaries returned home with considerable funds. The education of the children was entrusted to many teachers; at a more advanced age the youths were employed in the crafts or commerce, while the more talented pursued their studies in yeshivot.

As capital of the country and residence of the sharifs (rulers) Meknès was also the center of Jewish activities at the court. The leaders of the Meknès community acted as *negidim* (see **Nagid*) of Moroccan Jewry and agents of the sharifs. Among them were members of the *Maymerān family (Joseph and his son Abraham), as well as the Toledanos, the Ibn Attars, the Ben Māmāns, the Ben Quiquis, and others. The most prominent rabbinic scholars and *dayyanim* in Meknès during the 18th–20th centuries come from the Berdugo and Toledano families, many of whom wrote responsa. From 1790 and during the 19th century Meknès lost its importance as the capital and the Jewish community suffered pogroms frequently. There was an important change for the better in the situation of the Jews with the formal establishment of the French Protectorate in 1912. From then on the Jews enjoyed relative security and economic stability, as well as elementary human rights. There were also changes in the field of religious education with the arrival of R. Ze'ev Halperin, a Russian scholar who came from Britain in 1912. He introduced reforms in the system of study of the yeshivot and gathered the young men of the town, for whom he founded a *kolel avrekhim* (advanced yeshivah), the first of its kind in Meknès and probably the whole of Morocco. He founded an *Eẓ Ḥayyim* society for laymen which organized regular studies and whose members supported the young men of the Bet El yeshivah with their contributions. As a result of this activity the yeshivah produced a nucleus of *ḥakhamim* who later officiated as rabbis in Meknès and other communities. The fame of Meknès yeshivot spread far and they attracted students from many parts of the country. After World War II, a Chabad yeshivah was founded (in conjunction with *Oẓar ha-Torah).

The government allocated new areas near the mellah for the Jews to live in, and a new quarter, known as the "new mellah," was built. The construction was modern, being scattered and not surrounded by a wall. Many beautiful synagogues were also built, including the "Toledano" and Joseph Mrejen synagogues, as well as a large Jewish school, Em ha-Banim, in which all the children of the community studied (the needy were exempted from the payment of tuition fees). Its expenses and the salaries of the teachers were provided from community funds. In 1947 approximately 1,200 pupils attended this school. The *Alliance Israélite Universelle built two large schools, one for boys and another for girls, which were attended by about 1,500 boys and girls in 1950. According to the 1947 census the Jewish community numbered 15,482 (about 3,000 others were not included in the census for various reasons). Most of the Jews of Meknès immigrated to Israel after the establishment of the state and both the old and the new mellahs are now inhabited for the most part by Muslims.

[Haim Bentov]

Contemporary Period

The Jewish population of Meknès, which numbered 12,445 in the 1951 census report, dropped in 1960 to 10,894 (according to the census of that year), and in 1968, after the large-scale emigration of Moroccan Jewry, to about 2,000–3,000. During the 1950s the Jewish schools had 3,182 pupils, but the number dropped off in the 1960s. Most of the charitable and social welfare organizations, which included branches of WIZO and the World Jewish Congress, were closed. In 1970 the Meknès community, although reduced, was one of the more vital of the Moroccan provincial communities. A considerable Jewish petite bourgeoisie lived there with communal life centering on the two main synagogues. Only a few dozen Jews remained in the old mellah, and most lived in the modern Jewish neighborhood. More than three decades later, the Jewish community numbered no more than 120 Jews. In September 2003 radical Islamists, apparently belonging to the pro-al-Qa'ida association Salafiyya Jihādiyya, responsible for the suicide terrorist attacks in Casablanca several months earlier, stabbed to death 75-year-old Elie Afriat in Meknès. Since then members of the local community have lived in fear of further Islamist actions against them.

[Haim J. Cohen / Michael M. Laskier (2nd ed.)]

BIBLIOGRAPHY: Hirschberg, Afrikah, index; idem, in: H.J. Zimmels et al. (eds.), *Essays Presented to… Israel Brodie…* (1967), 153–81; A. Chouraqui, *La condition juridique de l'Israélite marocain* (1950); idem, *Between East and West* (1968), index; M.M. Laskier, *The Alliance Israélite Universelle and the Jewish Communities of Morocco: 1862–1962* (1983); B Meakin, *Land of the Moors* (1901), 277–87; R. Attal, in: *Tefuẓot ha-Golah*, 1 (1964), 42ff.

MEKOROT (Heb. "Sources") **WATER COMPANY**, company established in 1937 as a joint undertaking of the *Histadrut, the *Jewish Agency, and the *Jewish National Fund, to develop a water supply project in the western part of the Valley of Jezreel. Its first managing director was Levi *Eshkol. After World War II, Mekorot extended its operations to a regional project in the Negev and a smaller project in central Israel. During the *War of Independence (1948) it constructed an emergency water supply system for Jerusalem and, after the war, embarked upon a major development program encompassing the entire country. In 1962 Mekorot officially became Israel's National Water Supply Agency.

In the early 1950s the projects executed were mainly connected with ground and spring water. In the mid-1950s further major regional projects were carried out. In the later 1950s and early 1960s the main emphasis was upon the National Water Carrier (Jordan Project), and subsequently systems utilizing flood runoff and reclaimed sewage were constructed. From the early 1960s the company also operated abroad, mainly in the construction of water supplies in developing countries. In 1967 it opened the Shapdan, the sewage system for all Gush Dan (Tel Aviv area). In 1989 it opened a third water line to the Negev, which transported filtered water from the Shapdan. In 1995 it opened a fourth water line to Jerusalem, and in 1997 it opened the desalination plant in Elath supplying 80% of the city's water. Subsequently it opened other desalination plants in various locations.

The Israel government was a shareholder in the company from 1948 and held one-third of the shares in 1967. Another third was held by the Histadrut, and the rest equally by the Jewish Agency and the Jewish National Fund. The company operates as a government firm, meaning that it operates as an independent business enterprise under the supervision of the Governmental Companies Authority. In 2000 the company's budget was NIS 5.6 billion. It supplies 90% of the country's drinking water and 70% of all water (1.3 billion cu. m.). The company operates over 800 pumping stations, with over 2,400 pumps, over 1,200 wells, and 10,500 kms. of large-diameter pipes. It employs 2,100 workers all over Israel. Company salaries are known to be among the highest in the public sector.

Mekorot owns SHM – Electrical Mechanic Services, operating water infrastructure projects. It also advances various projects with private firms. The government had declared its intention to privatize Mekorot but met with opposition from both the workers and others.

BIBLIOGRAPHY: *Mekorot Water Company Ltd. and its Role in Israel's Development* (1963); *Sheloshim Shanah li-Mekorot* (1967). **WEBSITE:** www.mekorot.co.il.

[Aaron Wiener / Shaked Gilboa (2nd ed.)]

ABBREVIATIONS

GENERAL ABBREVIATIONS

This list contains abbreviations used in the Encyclopaedia (apart from the standard ones, such as geographical abbreviations, points of compass, etc.). For names of organizations, institutions, etc., in abbreviation, see Index. For bibliographical abbreviations of books and authors in Rabbinical literature, see following lists.

*	Cross reference; i.e., an article is to be found under the word(s) immediately following the asterisk (*).
°	Before the title of an entry, indicates a non-Jew (post-biblical times).
‡	Indicates reconstructed forms.
>	The word following this sign is derived from the preceding one.
<	The word preceding this sign is derived from the following one.

ad loc.	*ad locum*, "at the place"; used in quotations of commentaries.
A.H.	*Anno Hegirae*, "in the year of Hegira," i.e., according to the Muslim calendar.
Akk.	Addadian.
A.M.	*anno mundi*, "in the year (from the creation) of the world."
anon.	anonymous.
Ar.	Arabic.
Aram.	Aramaic.
Ass.	Assyrian.
b.	born; *ben, bar.*
Bab.	Babylonian.
B.C.E.	Before Common Era (= B.C.).
bibl.	bibliography.
Bul.	Bulgarian.
c., ca.	Circa.
C.E.	Common Era (= A.D.).
cf.	*confer*, "compare."
ch., chs.	chapter, chapters.
comp.	compiler, compiled by.
Cz.	Czech.
D	according to the documentary theory, the Deuteronomy document.
d.	died.
Dan.	Danish.
diss., dissert,	dissertation, thesis.
Du.	Dutch.
E.	according to the documentary theory, the Elohist document (i.e., using Elohim as the name of God) of the first five (or six) books of the Bible.
ed.	editor, edited, edition.
eds.	editors.
e.g.	*exempli gratia*, "for example."
Eng.	English.
et al.	*et alibi*, "and elsewhere"; or *et alii*, "and others"; "others."
f., ff.	and following page(s).
fig.	figure.
fl.	flourished.
fol., fols	folio(s).
Fr.	French.
Ger.	German.
Gr.	Greek.
Heb.	Hebrew.
Hg., Hung	Hungarian.
ibid	*Ibidem*, "in the same place."
incl. bibl.	includes bibliography.
introd.	introduction.
It.	Italian.
J	according to the documentary theory, the Jahwist document (i.e., using YHWH as the name of God) of the first five (or six) books of the Bible.
Lat.	Latin.
lit.	literally.
Lith.	Lithuanian.
loc. cit.	*loco citato*, "in the [already] cited place."
Ms., Mss.	Manuscript(s).
n.	note.
n.d.	no date (of publication).
no., nos	number(s).
Nov.	Novellae (Heb. *Ḥiddushim*).
n.p.	place of publication unknown.
op. cit.	*opere citato*, "in the previously mentioned work."
P.	according to the documentary theory, the Priestly document of the first five (or six) books of the Bible.
p., pp.	page(s).
Pers.	Persian.
pl., pls.	plate(s).
Pol.	Polish.
Port.	Potuguese.
pt., pts.	part(s).
publ.	published.
R.	Rabbi or Rav (before names); in Midrash (after an abbreviation) – *Rabbah*.
r.	recto, the first side of a manuscript page.
Resp.	Responsa (Latin "answers," Hebrew *She'elot u-Teshuvot* or *Teshuvot),* collections of rabbinic decisions.
rev.	revised.

Rom.	Romanian.
Rus(s).	Russian.
Slov.	Slovak.
Sp.	Spanish.
s.v.	*sub verbo, sub voce*, "under the (key) word."
Sum	Sumerian.
summ.	Summary.
suppl.	supplement.
Swed.	Swedish.
tr., trans(l).	translator, translated, translation.
Turk.	Turkish.
Ukr.	Ukrainian.
v., vv.	*verso*. The second side of a manuscript page; also verse(s).
Yid.	Yiddish.

ABBREVIATIONS USED IN RABBINICAL LITERATURE

Adderet Eliyahu, Karaite treatise by Elijah b. Moses *Bashyazi.

Admat Kodesh, Resp. by Nissim Ḥayyim Moses b. Joseph |Mizraḥi.

Aguddah, Sefer ha-, Nov. by *Alexander Suslin ha-Kohen.

Ahavat Ḥesed, compilation by *Israel Meir ha-Kohen.

Aliyyot de-Rabbenu Yonah, Nov. by *Jonah b. Avraham Gerondi.

Arukh ha-Shulḥan, codification by Jehiel Michel *Epstein.

Asayin (= positive precepts), subdivision of: (1) *Maimonides, *Sefer ha-Mitzvot;* (2) *Moses b. Jacob of Coucy, *Semag.*

Asefat Dinim, subdivision of *Sedei Ḥemed* by Ḥayyim Hezekiah *Medini, an encyclopaedia of precepts and responsa.

Asheri = *Asher b. Jehiel.

Aeret Ḥakhamim, by Baruch *Frankel-Teomim; pt, 1: Resp. to Sh. Ar.; pt2: Nov. to Talmud.

Ateret Zahav, subdivision of the *Levush*, a codification by Mordecai b. Abraham (Levush) *Jaffe; *Ateret Zahav* parallels Tur. YD.

Ateret Ẓevi, Comm. To Sh. Ar. by Ẓevi Hirsch b. Azriel.

Avir Ya'akov, Resp. by Jacob Avigdor.

Avkat Rokhel, Resp. by Joseph b. Ephraim *Caro.

Avnei Millu'im, Comm. to Sh. Ar., EH, by *Aryeh Loeb b. Joseph ha-Kohen.

Avnei Nezer, Resp. on Sh. Ar. by Abraham b. Ze'ev Nahum Bornstein of *Sochaczew.

Avodat Massa, Compilation of Tax Law by Yoasha Abraham Judah.

Azei ha-Levanon, Resp. by Judah Leib *Zirelson.

Ba'al ha-Tanya – *Shneur Zalman of Lyady.

Ba'ei Ḥayyei, Resp. by Ḥayyim b. Israel *Benveniste.

Ba'er Heitev, Comm. To Sh. Ar. The parts on OḤ and EH are by Judah b. Simeon *Ashkenazi, the parts on YD AND ḤM by *Zechariah Mendel b. Aryeh Leib. Printed in most editions of Sh. Ar.

Baḥ = Joel *Sirkes.

Baḥ, usual abbreviation for *Bayit Ḥadash*, a commentary on Tur by Joel *Sirkes; printed in most editions of Tur.

Bayit Ḥadash, see *Baḥ*.

Berab = Jacob Berab, also called Ri Berav.

Bedek ha-Bayit, by Joseph b. Ephraim *Caro, additions to his *Beit Yosef* (a comm. to Tur). Printed sometimes inside *Beit Yosef*, in smaller type. Appears in most editions of Tur.

Be'er ha-Golah, Commentary to Sh. Ar. By Moses b. Naphtali Hirsch *Rivkes; printed in most editions of Sh. Ar.

Be'er Mayim, Resp. by Raphael b. Abraham Manasseh Jacob.

Be'er Mayim Ḥayyim, Resp. by Samuel b. Ḥayyim *Vital.

Be'er Yiẓḥak, Resp. by Isaac Elhanan *Spector.

Beit ha-Beḥirah, Comm. to Talmud by Menahem b. Solomon *Meiri.

Beit Me'ir, Nov. on Sh. Ar. by Meir b. Judah Leib Posner.

Beit Shelomo, Resp. by Solomon b. Aaron Ḥason (the younger).

Beit Shemu'el, Comm. to Sh. Ar., EH, by *Samuel b. Uri Shraga Phoebus.

Beit Ya'akov, by Jacob b. Jacob Moses *Lorberbaum; pt.1: Nov. to Ket.; pt.2: Comm. to EH.

Beit Yisrael, collective name for the commentaries *Derishah, Perishah*, and *Be'urim* by Joshua b. Alexander ha-Kohen *Falk. See under the names of the commentaries.

Beit Yiẓḥak, Resp. by Isaac *Schmelkes.

Beit Yosef: (1) Comm. on Tur by Joseph b. Ephraim *Caro; printed in most editions of Tur; (2) Resp. by the same.

Ben Yehudah, Resp. by Abraham b. Judah Litsch (ליטש) Rosenbaum.

Bertinoro, Standard commentary to Mishnah by Obadiah *Bertinoro. Printed in most editions of the Mishnah.

[Be'urei] Ha-Gra, Comm. to Bible, Talmud, and Sh. Ar. By *Elijah b. Solomon Zalmon (Gaon of Vilna); printed in major editions of the mentioned works.

Be'urim, Glosses to Isserles *Darkhei Moshe* (a comm. on Tur) by Joshua b. Alexander ha-Kohen *Falk; printed in many editions of Tur.

Binyamin Ze'ev, Resp. by *Benjamin Ze'ev b. Mattathias of Arta.

Birkei Yosef, Nov. by Ḥayyim Joseph David *Azulai.

Ha-Buẓ ve-ha-Argaman, subdivision of the *Levush* (a codification by Mordecai b. Abraham (Levush) *Jaffe); *Ha-Buẓ ve-ha-Argaman* parallels Tur, EH.

Comm. = Commentary

Da'at Kohen, Resp. by Abraham Isaac ha-Kohen. *Kook.

Darkhei Moshe, Comm. on Tur Moses b. Israel *Isserles; printed in most editions of Tur.

Darkhei No'am, Resp. by *Mordecai b. Judah ha-Levi.

Darkhei Teshuvah, Nov. by Ẓevi *Shapiro; printed in the major editions of Sh. Ar.

De'ah ve-Haskel, Resp. by Obadiah Hadaya (see *Yaskil Avdi).*

Derashot Ran, Sermons by *Nissim b. Reuben Gerondi.
Derekh Ḥayyim, Comm. to *Avot* by *Judah Loew (Lob., Liwa) b. Bezalel (Maharal) of Prague.
Derishah, by Joshua b. Alexander ha-Kohen *Falk; additions to his *Perishah* (comm. on Tur); printed in many editions of Tur.
Derushei ha-Ẓelaḥ, Sermons, by Ezekiel b. Judah Halevi *Landau.
Devar Avraham, Resp. by Abraham *Shapira.
Devar Shemu'el, Resp. by Samuel *Aboab.
Devar Yehoshu'a, Resp. by Joshua Menahem b. Isaac Aryeh Ehrenberg.
Dikdukei Soferim, variae lections of the talmudic text by Raphael Nathan*Rabbinowicz.
Divrei Emet, Resp. by Isaac Bekhor David.
Divrei Ge'onim, Digest of responsa by Ḥayyim Aryeh b. Jeḥiel Ẓevi *Kahana.
Divrei Ḥamudot, Comm. on *Piskei ha-Rosh* by Yom Tov Lipmann b. Nathan ha-Levi *Heller; printed in major editions of the Talmud.
Divrei Ḥayyim several works by Ḥayyim *Halberstamm; if quoted alone refers to his Responsa.
Divrei Malkhi'el, Resp. by Malchiel Tenebaum.
Divrei Rivot, Resp. by Isaac b. Samuel *Adarbi.
Divrei Shemu'el, Resp. by Samuel Raphael Arditi.

Edut be-Ya'akov, Resp. by Jacob b. Abraham *Boton.
Edut bi-Yhosef, Resp. by Joseph b. Isaac *Almosnino.
Ein Ya'akov, Digest of talmudic *aggadot* by Jacob (Ibn) *Habib.
Ein Yiẓḥak, Resp. by Isaac Elhanan *Spector.
Ephraim of Lentshitz = Solomon *Luntschitz.
Erekh Leḥem, Nov. and glosses to Sh. Ar. by Jacob b. Abraham *Castro.
Eshkol, Sefer ha-, Digest of *halakhot* by *Abraham b. Isaac of Narbonne.
Et Sofer, Treatise on Law Court documents by Abraham b. Mordecai *Ankawa, in the 2nd vol. of his Resp. *Kerem Ḥamar.*
Etan ha-Ezraḥi, Resp. by Abraham b. Israel Jehiel (Shrenzl) *Rapaport.
Even ha-Ezel, Nov. to Maimonides' *Yad Ḥazakah* by Isser Zalman *Meltzer.
Even ha-Ezer, also called *Raban* of *Ẓafenat Pa'ne'aḥ,* rabbinical work with varied contents by *Eliezer b. Nathan of Mainz; not identical with the subdivision of Tur, Shulḥan Arukh, etc.
Ezrat Yehudah, Resp. by *Isaar Judah b. Nechemiah of Brisk.

Gan Eden, Karaite treatise by *Aaron b. Elijah of Nicomedia.
Gersonides = *Levi b. Gershom, also called Leo Hebraecus, or Ralbag.
Ginnat Veradim, Resp. by *Abraham b. Mordecai ha-Levi.

Haggahot, another name for *Rema.*
Haggahot Asheri, glosses to *Piskei ha-Rosh* by *Israel of Krems; printed in most Talmud editions.
Haggahot Maimuniyyot, Comm,. to Maimonides' Yad Ḥazakah by *Meir ha-Kohen; printed in most eds. of Yad.
Haggahot Mordekhai, glosses to *Mordekhai* by Samuel *Schlettstadt; printed in most editions of the Talmud after *Mordekhai.*
Haggahot ha-Rashash on Tosafot, annotations of Samuel *Strashun on the Tosafot (printed in major editions of the Talmud).
Ha-Gra = *Elijah b. Solomon Zalman (Gaon of Vilna).
Ha-Gra, Commentaries on Bible, Talmud, and Sh. Ar. respectively, by *Elijah b. Solomon Zalman (Gaon of Vilna); printed in major editions of the mentioned works.
Hai Gaon, Comm. = his comm. on Mishnah.
Ḥakham Ẓevi, Resp. by Ẓevi Hirsch b. Jacob *Ashkenazi.
Halakhot = Rif, *Halakhot.* Compilation and abstract of the Talmud by Isaac b. Jacob ha-Kohen *Alfasi; printed in most editions of the Talmud.
Halakhot Gedolot, compilation of *halakhot* from the Geonic period, arranged acc. to the Talmud. Here cited acc. to ed. Warsaw (1874). Author probably *Simeon Kayyara of Basra.
Halakhot Pesukot le-Rav Yehudai Ga'on compilation of *halakhot.*
Halakhot Pesukot min ha-Ge'onim, compilation of *halakhot* from the geonic period by different authors.
Ḥananel, Comm. to Talmud by *Hananel b. Ḥushi'el; printed in some editions of the Talmud.
Harei Besamim, Resp. by Aryeh Leib b. Isaac *Horowitz.
Ḥassidim, Sefer, Ethical maxims by *Judah b. Samuel he-Ḥasid.
Hassagot Rabad on Rif, Glosses on Rif, *Halakhot,* by *Abraham b. David of Posquières.
Hassagot Rabad [on Yad], Glosses on Maimonides, *Yad Ḥazakah,* by *Abraham b. David of Posquières.
Hassagot Ramban, Glosses by Naḥmanides on Maimonides' *Sefer ha-Mitzvot;* usually printed together with *Sefer ha-Mitzvot.*
Ḥatam Sofer = Moses *Sofer.
Ḥavvot Ya'ir, Resp. and varia by Jair Ḥayyim *Bacharach
Ḥayyim Or Zaru'a = *Ḥayyim (Eliezer) b. Isaac.
Ḥazon Ish = Abraham Isaiah *Karelitz.
Ḥazon Ish, Nov. by Abraham Isaiah *Karelitz
Ḥedvat Ya'akov, Resp. by Aryeh Judah Jacob b. David Dov Meisels (article under his father's name).
Heikhal Yiẓḥak, Resp. by Isaac ha-Levi *Herzog.
Ḥelkat Meḥokek, Comm. to Sh. Ar., by Moses b. Isaac Judah *Lima.
Ḥelkat Ya'akov, Resp. by Mordecai Jacob Breisch.
Ḥemdah Genuzah, , Resp. from the geonic period by different authors.
Ḥemdat Shelomo, Resp. by Solomon Zalman *Lipschitz.
Ḥida = Ḥayyim Joseph David *Azulai.
Ḥiddushei Halakhot ve-Aggadot, Nov. by Samuel Eliezer b. Judah ha-Levi *Edels.
Ḥikekei Lev, Resp. by Ḥayyim *Palaggi.
Ḥikrei Lev, Nov. to Sh. Ar. by Joseph Raphael b. Ḥayyim Joseph Ḥazzan (see article *Ḥazzan Family).
Hil. = Hilkhot … (e.g. *Hilkhot Shabbat).*
Ḥinnukh, Sefer ha-, List and explanation of precepts attributed (probably erroneously) to Aaron ha-Levi of Barcelona (see article **Ha-Ḥinnukh*).
Ḥok Ya'akov, Comm. to Hil. Pesaḥ in Sh. Ar., OḤ, by Jacob b. Joseph *Reicher.
Ḥokhmat Sehlomo (1), Glosses to Talmud, *Rashi* and Tosafot by Solomon b. Jehiel "Maharshal") *Luria; printed in many editions of the Talmud.
Ḥokhmat Sehlomo (2), Glosses and Nov. to Sh. Ar. by Solomon b. Judah Aaron *Kluger printed in many editions of Sh. Ar.
Ḥur, subdivision of the *Levush,* a codification by Mordecai b. Abraham (Levush) *Jaffe; *Ḥur* (or *Levush ha-Ḥur*) parallels Tur, OḤ, 242–697.
Ḥut ha-Meshullash, fourth part of the *Tashbeẓ* (Resp.), by Simeon b. Zemaḥ *Duran.

Ibn Ezra, Comm. to the Bible by Abraham *Ibn Ezra; printed in the major editions of the Bible *("Mikra'ot Gedolot").*
Imrei Yosher, Resp. by Meir b. Aaron Judah *Arik.
Ir Shushan, Subdivision of the *Levush,* a codification by Mordecai b. Abraham (Levush) *Jaffe; *Ir Shushan* parallels Tur, ḤM.
Israel of Bruna = Israel b. Ḥayyim *Bruna.
Ittur. Treatise on precepts by *Isaac b. Abba Mari of Marseilles.

Jacob Be Rab = *Be Rab.
Jacob b. Jacob Moses of Lissa = Jacob b. Jacob Moses *Lorberbaum.
Judah B. Simeon = Judah b. Simeon *Ashkenazi.
Judah Minz = Judah b. Eliezer ha-Levi *Minz.

Kappei Aharon, Resp. by Aaron Azriel.
Kehillat Ya'akov, Talmudic methodology, definitions etc. by Israel Jacob b. Yom Tov *Algazi.
Kelei Ḥemdah, Nov. and *pilpulim* by Meir Dan *Plotzki of Ostrova, arranged acc. to the Torah.
Keli Yakar, Annotations to the Torah by Solomon *Luntschitz.
Keneh Ḥokhmah, Sermons by Judah Loeb *Pochwitzer.
Keneset ha-Gedolah, Digest of *halakhot* by Ḥayyim b. Israel *Benveniste; subdivided into annotations to *Beit Yosef* and annotations to Tur.
Keneset Yisrael, Resp. by Ezekiel b. Abraham Katzenellenbogen (see article *Katzenellenbogen Family).
Kerem Ḥamar, Resp. and varia by Abraham b. Mordecai *Ankawa.
Kerem Shelmo. Resp. by Solomon b. Joseph *Amarillo.
Keritut, [Sefer], Methodology of the Talmud by *Samson b. Isaac of Chinon.
Kesef ha-Kedoshim, Comm. to Sh. Ar., ḤM, by Abraham *Wahrmann; printed in major editions of Sh. Ar.
Kesef Mishneh, Comm. to Maimonides, *Yad Ḥazakah,* by Joseph b. Ephraim *Caro; printed in most editions of *Yad Ḥazakah.*
Keẓot ha-Ḥoshen, Comm. to Sh. Ar., ḤM, by *Aryeh Loeb b. Joseph ha-Kohen; printed in major editions of Sh. Ar.
Kol Bo [*Sefer*], Anonymous collection of ritual rules; also called *Sefer ha-Likkutim.*
Kol Mevasser, Resp. by Meshullam *Rath.
Korban Aharon, Comm. to *Sifra* by Aaron b. Abraham *Ibn Ḥayyim; pt. 1 is called: *Middot Aharon.*
Korban Edah, Comm. to Jer. Talmud by David *Fraenkel; with additions: *Shiyyurei Korban;* printed in most editions of Jer. Talmud.
Kunteres ha-Kelalim, subdivision of *Sedei Ḥemed,* an encyclopaedia of precepts and responsa by Ḥayyim Hezekiah *Medini.
Kunteres ha-Semikhah, a treatise by *Levi b. Ḥabib; printed at the end of his responsa.
Kunteres Tikkun Olam, part of *Mispat Shalom* (Nov. by Shalom Mordecai b. Moses *Schwadron).

Lavin (negative precepts), subdivision of: (1) *Maimonides, *Sefer ha-Mitzvot;* (2) *Moses b. Jacob of Coucy, *Semag.*
Leḥem Mishneh, Comm. to Maimonides, *Yad Ḥazakah,* by Abraham [Ḥiyya] b. Moses *Boton; printed in most editions of *Yad Ḥazakah.*
Leḥem Rav, Resp. by Abraham [Ḥiyya] b. Moses *Boton.
Leket Yosher, Resp and varia by Israel b. Pethahiah *Isserlein, collected by *Joseph (Joselein) b. Moses.
Leo Hebraeus = *Levi b. Gershom, also called Ralbag or Gersonides.
Levush = Mordecai b. Abraham *Jaffe.
Levush [Malkhut], Codification by Mordecai b. Abraham (Levush) *Jaffe, with subdivisions: [*Levush ha-] Tekhelet* (parallels Tur OḤ 1–241); [*Levush ha-] Ḥur* (parallels Tur OḤ 242–697); [*Levush] Ateret Zahav* (parallels Tur YD); [*Levush ha-Buẓ ve-ha-Argaman* (parallels Tur EH); [*Levush] Ir Shushan* (parallels Tur ḤM); under the name *Levush* the author wrote also other works.
Li-Leshonot ha-Rambam, fifth part (nos. 1374–1700) of Resp. by *David b. Solomon ibn Abi Zimra (Radbaz).
Likkutim, Sefer ha-, another name for [*Sefer] Kol Bo.*

Ma'adanei Yom Tov, Comm. on *Piskei ha-Rosh* by Yom Tov Lipmann b. Nathan ha-Levi *Heller; printed in many editions of the Talmud.
Mabit = Moses b. Joseph *Trani.
Magen Avot, Comm. to *Avot* by Simeon b. Ẓemaḥ *Duran.
Magen Avraham, Comm. to Sh. Ar., OḤ, by Abraham Abele b. Ḥayyim ha-Levi *Gombiner; printed in many editions of Sh. Ar., OḤ.
Maggid Mishneh, Comm. to Maimonides, *Yad Ḥazakah,* by *Vidal Yom Tov of Tolosa; printed in most editions of the *Yad Ḥazakah.*
Maḥaneh Efrayim, Resp. and Nov., arranged acc. to Maimonides' *Yad Ḥazakah ,* by Ephraim b. Aaron *Navon.
Maharai = Israel b. Pethahiah *Isserlein.
Maharal of Prague = *Judah Loew (Lob, Liwa), b. Bezalel.
Maharalbaḥ = *Levi b. Ḥabib.
Maharam Alashkar = Moses b. Isaac *Alashkar.
Maharam Alshekh = Moses b. Ḥayyim *Alashekh.
Maharam Mintz = Moses *Mintz.
Maharam of Lublin = *Meir b. Gedaliah of Lublin.
Maharam of Padua = Meir *Katzenellenbogen.
Maharam of Rothenburg = *Meir b. Baruch of Rothenburg.
Maharam Shik = Moses b. Joseph Schick.
Maharash Engel = Samuel b. Ze'ev Wolf Engel.
Maharashdam = Samuel b. Moses *Medina.
Maharḥash = Ḥayyim (ben) Shabbetai.
Mahari Basan = Jehiel b. Ḥayyim Basan.
Mahari b. Lev = Joseph ibn Lev.
Mahari'az = Jekuthiel Asher Zalman Ensil Zusmir.
Maharibal = *Joseph ibn Lev.
Mahariḥ = Jacob (Israel) *Ḥagiz.
Maharik = Joseph b. Solomon *Colon.
Maharikash = Jacob b. Abraham *Castro.
Maharil = Jacob b. Moses *Moellin.
Maharimat = Joseph b. Moses di Trani (not identical with the Maharit).
Maharit = Joseph b. Moses *Trani.
Maharitaẓ = Yom Tov b. Akiva Ẓahalon. (See article *Ẓahalon Family).
Maharsha = Samuel Eliezer b. Judah ha-Levi *Edels.
Maharshag = Simeon b. Judah Gruenfeld.
Maharshak = Samson b. Isaac of Chinon.
Maharshakh = *Solomon b. Abraham.
Maharshal = Solomon b. Jeḥiel *Luria.
Mahasham = Shalom Mordecai b. Moses *Sschwadron.
Maharyu = Jacob b. Judah *Weil.
Maḥazeh Avraham, Resp. by Abraham Nebagen v. Meir ha-Levi Steinberg.
Maḥazik Berakhah, Nov. by Ḥayyim Joseph David *Azulai.

*Maimonides = Moses b. Maimon, or Rambam.
*Malbim = Meir Loeb b. Jehiel Michael.
Malbim = Malbim's comm. to the Bible; printed in the major editions.
Malbushei Yom Tov, Nov. on *Levush,* OḤ, by Yom Tov Lipmann b. Nathan ha-Levi *Heller.
Mappah, another name for *Rema.*
Mareh ha-Panim, Comm. to Jer. Talmud by Moses b. Simeon *Margolies; printed in most editions of Jer. Talmud.
Margaliyyot ha-Yam, Nov. by Reuben *Margoliot.
Masat Binyamin, Resp. by Benjamin Aaron b. Abraham *Slonik
Mashbir, Ha- = *Joseph Samuel b. Isaac Rodi.
Massa Ḥayyim, Tax *halakhot* by Ḥayyim *Palaggi, with the subdivisions *Missim ve-Arnomiyyot* and *Torat ha-Minhagot.*
Massa Melekh, Compilation of Tax Law by Joseph b. Isaac *Ibn Ezra with concluding part *Ne'ilat She'arim.*
Matteh Asher, Resp. by Asher b. Emanuel Shalem.
Matteh Shimon, Digest of Resp. and Nov. to Tur and *Beit Yosef,* ḤM, by Mordecai Simeon b. Solomon.
Matteh Yosef, Resp. by Joseph b. Moses ha-Levi Nazir (see article under his father's name).
Mayim Amukkim, Resp. by Elijah b. Abraham *Mizraḥi.
Mayim Ḥayyim, Resp. by Ḥayyim b. Dov Beresh Rapaport.
Mayim Rabbim, , Resp. by Raphael *Meldola.
Me-Emek ha-Bakha, , Resp. by Simeon b. Jekuthiel Ephrati.
Me'irat Einayim, usual abbreviation: *Sma* (from: *Sefer Me'irat Einayim*); comm. to Sh. Ar. By Joshua b. Alexander ha-Kohen *Falk; printed in most editions of the Sh. Ar.
Melammed le-Ho'il, Resp. by David Ẓevi *Hoffmann.
Meisharim, [*Sefer*], Rabbinical treatise by *Jeroham b. Meshullam.
Meshiv Davar, Resp. by Naphtali Ẓevi Judah *Berlin.
Mi-Gei ha-Haregah, Resp. by Simeon b. Jekuthiel Ephrati.
Mi-Ma'amakim, Resp. by Ephraim Oshry.
Middot Aharon, first part of *Korban Aharon,* a comm. to *Sifra* by Aaron b. Abraham *Ibn Ḥayyim.
Migdal Oz, Comm. to Maimonides, *Yad Ḥazakah,* by *Ibn Gaon Shem Tov b. Abraham; printed in most editions of the *Yad Ḥazakah.*
Mikhtam le-David, Resp. by David Samuel b. Jacob *Pardo.
Mikkaḥ ve-ha-Mimkar, Sefer ha-, Rabbinical treatise by *Hai Gaon.
Milḥamot ha-Shem, Glosses to Rif, *Halakhot,* by *Naḥmanides.
Minḥat Ḥinnukh, Comm. to *Sefer ha-Ḥinnukh,* by Joseph b. Moses *Babad.
Minḥat Yizḥak, Resp. by Isaac Jacob b. Joseph Judah Weiss.
Misgeret ha-Shulḥan, Comm. to Sh. Ar., ḤM, by Benjamin Ze'ev Wolf b. Shabbetai; printed in most editions of Sh. Ar.
Mishkenot ha-Ro'im, Halakhot in alphabetical order by Uzziel Alshekh.
Mishnah Berurah, Comm. to Sh. Ar., OḤ, by *Israel Meir ha-Kohen.
Mishneh le-Melekh, Comm. to Maimonides, *Yad Ḥazakah,* by Judah *Rosanes; printed in most editions of *Yad Ḥazakah.*
Mishpat ha-Kohanim, Nov. to Sh. Ar., ḤM, by Jacob Moses *Lorberbaum, part of his *Netivot ha-Mishpat;* printed in major editions of Sh. Ar.
Mishpat Kohen, Resp. by Abraham Isaac ha-Kohen *Kook.
Mishpat Shalom, Nov. by Shalom Mordecai b. Moses *Schwadron; contains: *Kunteres Tikkun Olam.*
Mishpat u-Ẓedakah be-Ya'akov, Resp. by Jacob b. Reuben *Ibn Ẓur.
Mishpat ha-Urim, Comm. to Sh. Ar., ḤM by Jacob b. Jacob Moses *Lorberbaum, part of his *Netivot ha-Mishpat;* printed in major editons of Sh. Ar.
Mishpat Ẓedek, Resp. by *Melammed Meir b. Shem Tov.
Mishpatim Yesharim, Resp. by Raphael b. Mordecai *Berdugo.
Mishpetei Shemu'el, Resp. by Samuel b. Moses *Kalai (Kal'i).
Mishpetei ha-Tanna'im, Kunteres, Nov on *Levush,* OḤ by Yom Tov Lipmann b. Nathan ha-Levi *Heller.
Mishpetei Uzzi'el (Uziel), Resp. by Ben-Zion Meir Hai *Ouziel.
Missim ve-Arnoniyyot, Tax *halakhot* by Ḥayyim *Palaggi, a subdivision of his work *Massa Ḥayyim* on the same subject.
Mitzvot, Sefer ha-, Elucidation of precepts by *Maimonides; subdivided into *Lavin* (negative precepts) and *Asayin* (positive precepts).
Mitzvot Gadol, Sefer, Elucidation of precepts by *Moses b. Jacob of Coucy, subdivided into *Lavin* (negative precepts) and *Asayin* (positive precepts); the usual abbreviation is *Semag.*
Mitzvot Katan, Sefer, Elucidation of precepts by *Isaac b. Joseph of Corbeil; the usual, abbreviation is *Semak.*
Mo'adim u-Zemannim, Rabbinical treatises by Moses Sternbuch.
Modigliano, Joseph Samuel = *Joseph Samuel b. Isaac, Rodi (Ha-Mashbir).
Mordekhai (Mordecai), halakhic compilation by *Mordecai b. Hillel; printed in most editions of the Talmud after the texts.
Moses b. Maimon = *Maimonides, also called Rambam.
Moses b. Naḥman = Naḥmanides, also called Ramban.
Muram = Isaiah Menahem b. Isaac (from: Morenu R. Mendel).

Naḥal Yizḥak, Comm. on Sh. Ar., ḤM, by Isaac Elhanan *Spector.
Naḥalah li-Yhoshu'a, Resp. by Joshua Ẓunẓin.
Naḥalat Shivah, collection of legal forms by *Samuel b. David Moses ha-Levi.
*Naḥmanides = Moses b. Naḥman, also called Ramban.
Naziv = Naphtali Ẓevi Judah *Berlin.
Ne'eman Shemu'el, Resp. by Samuel Isaac *Modigilano.
Ne'ilat She'arim, concluding part of *Massa Melekh* (a work on Tax Law) by Joseph b. Isaac *Ibn Ezra, containing an exposition of customary law and subdivided into *Minhagei Issur* and *Minhagei Mamon.*
Ner Ma'aravi, Resp. by Jacob b. Malka.
Netivot ha-Mishpat, by Jacob b. Jacob Moses *Lorberbaum; subdivided into *Mishpat ha-Kohanim,* Nov. to Sh. Ar., ḤM, and *Mishpat ha-Urim,* a comm. on the same; printed in major editions of Sh. Ar.
Netivot Olam, Saying of the Sages by *Judah Loew (Lob, Liwa) b. Bezalel.
Nimmukei Menaḥem of Merseburg, Tax *halakhot* by the same, printed at the end of Resp. Maharyu.
Nimmukei Yosef, Comm. to Rif. *Halakhot,* by Joseph *Ḥabib (Ḥabiba); printed in many editions of the Talmud.
Noda bi-Yhudah, Resp. by Ezekiel b. Judah ha-Levi *Landau; there is a first collection *(Mahadura Kamma)* and a second collection *(Mahadura Tinyana).*
Nov. = Novellae, Ḥiddushim.

Ohel Moshe (1), Notes to Talmud, *Midrash Rabbah,* Yad, *Sifrei* and to several Resp., by Eleazar *Horowitz.

Ohel Moshe (2), Resp. by Moses Jonah Zweig.
Oholei Tam. Resp. by *Tam ibn Yaḥya Jacob b. David; printed in the rabbinical collection *Tummat Yesharim.*
Oholei Ya'akov, Resp. by Jacob de *Castro.
Or ha-Me'ir Resp by Judah Meir b. Jacob Samson Shapiro.
Or Same'aḥ, Comm. to Maimonides, *Yad Ḥazakah,* by *Meir Simḥah ha-Kohen of Dvinsk; printed in many editions of the *Yad Ḥazakah.*
Or Zaru'a [the father] = *Isaac b. Moses of Vienna.
Or Zaru'a [the son] = *Ḥayyim (Eliezer) b. Isaac.
Or Zaru'a, Nov. by *Isaac b. Moses of Vienna.
Orah, Sefer ha-, Compilation of ritual precepts by *Rashi.
Oraḥ la-Ẓaddik, Resp. by Abraham Ḥayyim Rodrigues.
Oẓar ha-Posekim, Digest of Responsa.

Paḥad Yiẓḥak, Rabbinical encyclopaedia by Isaac *Lampronti.
Panim Me'irot, Resp. by Meir b. Isaac *Eisenstadt.
Parashat Mordekhai, Resp. by Mordecai b. Abraham Naphtali *Banet.
Pe'at ha-Sadeh la-Dinim and Pe'at ha-Sadeh la-Kelalim, subdivisions of the *Sedei Ḥemed,* an encyclopaedia of precepts and responsa, by Ḥayyim Hezekaih *Medini.
Penei Moshe (1), Resp. by Moses *Benveniste.
Penei Moshe (2), Comm. to Jer. Talmud by Moses b. Simeon *Margolies; printed in most editions of the Jer. Talmud.
Penei Moshe (3), Comm. on the aggadic passages of 18 treatises of the Bab. and Jer. Talmud, by Moses b. Isaiah Katz.
Penei Yehoshu'a, Nov. by Jacob Joshua b. Ẓevi Hirsch *Falk.
Peri Ḥadash, Comm. on Sh. Ar. By Hezekiah da *Silva.
Perishah, Comm. on Tur by Joshua b. Alexander ha-Kohen *Falk; printed in major edition of Tur; forms together with *Derishah* and *Be'urim* (by the same author) the *Beit Yisrael.*
Pesakim u-Khetavim, 2nd part of the *Terumat ha-Deshen* by Israel b. Pethahiah *Isserlein' also called *Piskei Maharai.*
Pilpula Ḥarifta, Comm. to *Piskei ha-Rosh, Seder Nezikin,* by Yom Tov Lipmann b. Nathan ha-Levi *Heller; printed in major editions of the Talmud.
Piskei Maharai, see *Terumat ha-Deshen,* 2nd part; also called *Pesakim u-Khetavim.*
Piskei ha-Rosh, a compilation of *halakhot,* arranged on the Talmud, by *Asher b. Jehiel (Rosh); printed in major Talmud editions.
Pitḥei Teshuvah, Comm. to Sh. Ar. by Abraham Hirsch b. Jacob *Eisenstadt; printed in major editions of the Sh. Ar.

Rabad = *Abraham b. David of Posquières (Rabad III.).
Raban = *Eliezer b. Nathan of Mainz.
Raban, also called *Ẓafenat Pa'ne'aḥ* or *Even ha-Ezer,* see under the last name.
Rabi Abad = *Abraham b. Isaac of Narbonne.
Radad = David Dov. b. Aryeh Judah Jacob *Meisels.
Radam = Dov Berush b. Isaac Meisels.
Radbaz = *David b Solomon ibn Abi Ziumra.
Radbaz, Comm. to Maimonides, *Yad Ḥazakah,* by *David b. Solomon ibn Abi Zimra.
Ralbag = *Levi b. Gershom, also called Gersonides, or Leo Hebraeus.
Ralbag, Bible comm. by *Levi b. Gershon.
Rama [da Fano] = Menaḥem Azariah *Fano.
Ramah = Meir b. Todros [ha-Levi] *Abulafia.
Ramam = *Menaham of Merseburg.
Rambam = *Maimonides; real name: Moses b. Maimon.
Ramban = *Naḥmanides; real name Moses b. Naḥman.
Ramban, Comm. to Torah by *Naḥmanides; printed in major editions. ("Mikra'ot Gedolot").
Ran = *Nissim b. Reuben Gerondi.
Ran of Rif, Comm. on Rif, *Halakhot,* by Nissim b. Reuben Gerondi.
Ranaḥ = *Elijah b. Ḥayyim.
Rash = *Samson b. Abraham of Sens.
Rash, Comm. to Mishnah, by *Samson b. Abraham of Sens; printed in major Talmud editions.
Rashash = Samuel *Strashun.
Rashba = Solomon b. Abraham *Adret.
Rashba, Resp., see also; *Sefer Teshuvot ha-Rashba ha-Meyuḥasot le-ha-Ramban,* by Solomon b. Abraham *Adret.
Rashbad = Samuel b. David.
Rashbam = *Samuel b. Meir.
Rashbam = Comm. on Bible and Talmud by *Samuel b. Meir; printed in major editions of Bible and most editions of Talmud.
Rashbash = Solomon b. Simeon *Duran.
*Rashi = Solomon b. Isaac of Troyes.
Rashi, Comm. on Bible and Talmud by *Rashi; printed in almost all Bible and Talmud editions.
Raviah = Eliezer b. Joel ha-Levi.
Redak = David *Kimḥi.
Redak, Comm. to Bible by David *Kimḥi.
Redakh = *David b. Ḥayyim ha-Kohen of Corfu.
Re'em = Elijah b. Abraham *Mizraḥi.
Rema = Moses b. Israel *Isserles.
Rema, Glosses to Sh. Ar. by Moses b. Israel *Isserles; printed in almost all editions of the Sh. Ar. inside the text in Rashi type; also called *Mappah* or *Haggahot.*
Remek = Moses Kimḥi.
Remakh = Moses ha-Kohen mi-Lunel.
Reshakh = *Solomon b. Abraham; also called Maharshakh.
Resp. = Responsa, *She'elot u-Teshuvot.*
Ri Berav = *Berab.
Ri Escapa = Joseph b. Saul *Escapa.
Ri Migash = Joseph b. Meir ha-Levi *Ibn Migash.
Riba = Isaac b. Asher ha-Levi; Riba II (Riba ha-Baḥur) = his grandson with the same name.
Ribam = Isaac b. Mordecai (or: Isaac b. Meir).
Ribash = *Isaac b. Sheshet Perfet (or: Barfat).
Rid= *Isaiah b. Mali di Trani the Elder.
Ridbaz = Jacob David b. Ze'ev *Willowski.
Rif = Isaac b. Jacob ha-Kohen *Alfasi.
Rif, *Halakhot,* Compilation and abstract of the Talmud by Isaac b. Jacob ha-Kohen *Alfasi.
Ritba = Yom Tov b. Abraham *Ishbili.
Riẓbam = Isaac b. Mordecai.
Rosh = *Asher b. Jehiel, also called Asheri.
Rosh Mashbir, Resp. by *Joseph Samuel b. Isaac, Rodi.

Sedei Ḥemed, Encyclopaedia of precepts and responsa by Ḥayyim Ḥezekiah *Medini; subdivisions: *Asefat Dinim, Kunteres ha-Kelalim, Pe'at ha-Sadeh la-Dinim, Pe'at ha-Sadeh la-Kelalim.*
Semag, Usual abbreviation of *Sefer Mitzvot Gadol,* elucidation of precepts by *Moses b. Jacob of Coucy; subdivided into *Lavin* (negative precepts) *Asayin* (positive precepts).
Semak, Usual abbreviation of *Sefer Mitzvot Katan,* elucidation of precepts by *Isaac b. Joseph of Corbeil.

Sh. Ar. = *Shulḥan Arukh,* code by Joseph b. Ephraim *Caro.
Sha'ar Mishpat, Comm. to Sh. Ar., ḤM. By Israel Isser b. Ze'ev Wolf.
Sha'arei Shevu'ot, Treatise on the law of oaths by *David b. Saadiah; usually printed together with Rif, *Halakhot;* also called: *She'arim of R. Alfasi.*
Sha'arei Teshuvah, Collection of resp. from Geonic period, by different authors.
Sha'arei Uzzi'el, Rabbinical treatise by Ben-Zion Meir Ha *Ouziel.
Sha'arei Ẓedek, Collection of resp. from Geonic period, by different authors.
Shadal [or Shedal] = Samuel David *Luzzatto.
Shai la-Moreh, Resp. by Shabbetai Jonah.
Shakh, Usual abbreviation of *Siftei Kohen,* a comm. to Sh. Ar., YD and ḤM by *Shabbetai b. Meir ha-Kohen; printed in most editions of Sh. Ar.
Sha'ot-de-Rabbanan, Resp. by *Solomon b. Judah ha-Kohen.
She'arim of R. Alfasi see *Sha'arei Shevu'ot.*
Shedal, see Shadal.
She'elot u-Teshuvot ha-Ge'onim, Collection of resp. by different authors.
She'erit Yisrael, Resp. by Israel Ze'ev Mintzberg.
She'erit Yosef, Resp. by *Joseph b. Mordecai Gershon ha-Kohen.
She'ilat Yaveẓ, Resp. by Jacob *Emden (Yaveẓ).
She'iltot, Compilation arranged acc. to the Torah by *Aḥa (Aḥai) of Shabḥa.
Shem Aryeh, Resp. by Aryeh Leib *Lipschutz.
Shemesh Ẓedakah, Resp. by Samson *Morpurgo.
Shenei ha-Me'orot ha-Gedolim, Resp. by Elijah *Covo.
Shetarot, Sefer ha-, Collection of legal forms by *Judah b. Barzillai al-Bargeloni.
Shevut Ya'akov, Resp. by Jacob b. Joseph Reicher.
Shibbolei ha-Leket Compilation on ritual by Zedekiah b. Avraham *Anav.
Shiltei Gibborim, Comm. to Rif, *Halakhot,* by *Joshua Boaz b. Simeon; printed in major editions of the Talmud.
Shittah Mekubbeẓet, Compilation of talmudical commentaries by Bezalel *Ashkenazi.
Shivat Ẓiyyon, Resp. by Samuel b. Ezekiel *Landau.
Shiyyurei Korban, by David *Fraenkel; additions to his comm. to Jer. Talmud *Korban Edah;* both printed in most editions of Jer. Talmud.
Sho'el u-Meshiv, Resp. by Joseph Saul ha-Levi *Nathanson.
Sh[ulḥan] Ar[ukh] [of Ba'al ha-Tanyal], Code by *Shneur Zalman of Lyady; not identical with the code by Joseph Caro.
Siftei Kohen, Comm. to Sh. Ar., YD and ḤM by *Shabbetai b. Meir ha-Kohen; printed in most editions of Sh. Ar.; usual abbreviation: *Shakh.*
Simḥat Yom Tov, Resp. by Tom Tov b. Jacob *Algazi.
Simlah Ḥadashah, Treatise on *Sheḥitah* by Alexander Sender b. Ephraim Zalman *Schor; see also *Tevu'ot Shor.*
Simeon b. Ẓemaḥ = Simeon b. Ẓemaḥ *Duran.
Sma, Comm. to Sh. Ar. by Joshua b. Alexander ha-Kohen *Falk; the full title is: *Sefer Me'irat Einayim;* printed in most editions of Sh. Ar.
Solomon b. Isaac ha-Levi = Solomon b. Isaac *Levy.
Solomon b. Isaac of Troyes = *Rashi.

Tal Orot, Rabbinical work with various contents, by Joseph ibn Gioia.
Tam, Rabbenu = *Tam Jacob b. Meir.
Tashbaẓ = Samson b. Zadok.
Tashbeẓ = Simeon b. Zemaḥ *Duran, sometimes also abbreviation for Samson b. Zadok, usually known as Tashbaẓ.
Tashbeẓ [Sefer ha-], Resp. by Simeon b. Ẓemaḥ *Duran; the fourth part of this work is called: *Ḥut ha-Meshullash.*
Taz, Usual abbreviation of *Turei Zahav,* comm., to Sh. Ar. by *David b. Samnuel ha-Levi; printed in most editions of Sh. Ar.
(Ha)-Tekhelet, subdivision of the *Levush* (a codification by Mordecai b. Abraham (Levush) *Jaffe); *Ha-Tekhelet* parallels Tur, OḤ 1-241.
Terumat ha-Deshen, by Israel b. Pethahiah *Isserlein; subdivided into a part containing responsa, and a second part called *Pesakim u-Khetavim* or *Piskei Maharai.*
Terumot, Sefer ha-, Compilation of *halakhot* by Samuel b. Isaac *Sardi.
Teshuvot Ba'alei ha-Tosafot, Collection of responsa by the Tosafists.
Teshjvot Ge'onei Mizraḥ u-Ma'aav, Collection of responsa.
Teshuvot ha-Geonim, Collection of responsa from Geonic period.
Teshuvot Ḥakhmei Provinẓyah, Collection of responsa by different Provencal authors.
Teshuvot Ḥakhmei Ẓarefat ve-Loter, Collection of responsa by different French authors.
Teshuvot Maimuniyyot, Resp. pertaining to Maimonides' *Yad Ḥazakah;* printed in major editions of this work after the text; authorship uncertain.
Tevu'ot Shor, by Alexander Sender b. Ephraim Zalman *Schor, a comm. to his *Simlah Ḥadashah,* a work on *Sheḥitah.*
Tiferet Ẓevi, Resp. by Ẓevi Hirsch of the "AHW" Communities (Altona, Hamburg, Wandsbeck).
Tiktin, Judah b. Simeon = Judah b. Simeon *Ashkenazi.
Toledot Adam ve-Ḥavvah, Codification by *Jeroham b. Meshullam.
Torat Emet, Resp. by Aaron b. Joseph *Sasson.
Torat Ḥayyim, , Resp. by Ḥayyim (ben) Shabbetai.
Torat ha-Minhagot, subdivision of the *Massa Ḥayyim* (a work on tax law) by Ḥayyim *Palaggi, containing an exposition of customary law.
Tosafot Rid, Explanations to the Talmud and decisions by *Isaiah b. Mali di Trani the Elder.
Tosefot Yom Tov, comm. to Mishnah by Yom Tov Lipmann b. Nathan ha-Levi *Heller; printed in most editions of the Mishnah.
Tummim, subdivision of the comm. to Sh. Ar., ḤM, *Urim ve-Tummim* by Jonathan *Eybeschuetz; printed in the major editions of Sh. Ar.
Tur, usual abbreviation for the *Arba'ah Turim* of *Jacob b. Asher.
Turei Zahav, Comm. to Sh. Ar. by *David b. Samuel ha-Levi; printed in most editions of Sh. Ar.; usual abbreviation: *Taz.*

Urim, subdivision of the following.
Urim ve-Tummim, Comm. to Sh. Ar., ḤM, by Jonathan *Eybeschuetz; printed in the major editions of Sh. Ar.; subdivided in places into *Urim* and *Tummim.*

Vikku'aḥ Mayim Ḥayyim, Polemics against Isserles and Caro by Ḥayyim b. Bezalel.

Yad Malakhi, Methodological treatise by *Malachi b. Jacob ha-Kohen.

Yad Ramah, Nov. by Meir b. Todros [ha-Levi] *Abulafia.
Yakhin u-Vo'az, Resp. by Ẓemaḥ b. Solomon *Duran.
Yam ha-Gadol, Resp. by Jacob Moses *Toledano.
Yam shel Shelomo, Compilation arranged acc. to Talmud by Solomon b. Jehiel (Maharshal) *Luria.
Yashar, Sefer ha-, by *Tam, Jacob b. Meir (Rabbenu Tam); 1st pt.: Resp.; 2nd pt.: Nov.
Yaskil Avdi, Resp. by Obadiah Hadaya (printed together with his Resp. *De'ah ve-Haskel).*
Yaveẓ = Jacob *Emden.
Yehudah Ya'aleh, Resp. by Judah b. Israel *Aszod.
Yekar Tiferet, Comm. to Maimonides' *Yad Ḥazakah,*by David b. Solomon ibn Zimra, printed in most editions of *Yad Ḥazakah.*
Yere'im [ha-Shalem], [Sefer], Treatise on precepts by *Eliezer b. Samuel of Metz.
Yeshu'ot Ya'akov, Resp. by Jacob Meshullam b. Mordecai Ze'ev *Ornstein.
Yiẓhak Rei'aḥ, Resp. by Isaac b. Samuel Abendanan (see article *Abendanam Family).
Ẓafenat Pa'ne'aḥ (1), also called *Raban* or *Even ha-Ezer,* see under the last name.
Ẓafenat Pa'ne'aḥ (2), Resp. by Joseph *Rozin.
Zayit Ra'anan, Resp. by Moses Judah Leib b. Benjamin Auerbach.
Ẓeidah la-Derekh, Codification by *Menahem b. Aaron ibn Zerah.
Ẓedakah u-Mishpat, Resp. by Ẓedakah b. Saadiah Huẓin.
Zekan Aharon, Resp. by Elijah b. Benjamin ha-Levi.
Zekher Ẓaddik, Sermons by Eliezer *Katzenellenbogen.
Ẓemaḥ Ẓedek (1) Resp. by Menaham Mendel Shneersohn (see under *Shneersohn Family).
Zera Avraham, Resp. by Abraham b. David *Yiẓḥaki.
Zera Emet Resp. by *Ishmael b. Abaham Isaac ha-Kohen.
Ẓevi la-Ẓaddik, Resp. by Ẓevi Elimelech b. David Shapira.
Zikhron Yehudah, Resp. by *Judah b. Asher
Zikhron Yosef, Resp. by Joseph b. Menahem *Steinhardt.
Zikhronot, Sefer ha-, Sermons on several precepts by Samuel *Aboab.
Zikkaron la-Rishonim . . ., by Albert (Abraham Elijah) *Harkavy; contains in vol. 1 pt. 4 (1887) a collection of Geonic responsa.
Ẓiẓ Eliezer, Resp. by Eliezer Judah b. Jacob Gedaliah Waldenberg.

BIBLIOGRAPHICAL ABBREVIATIONS

Bibliographies in English and other languages have been extensively updated, with English translations cited where available. In order to help the reader, the language of books or articles is given where not obvious from titles of books or names of periodicals. Titles of books and periodicals in languages with alphabets other than Latin, are given in transliteration, even where there is a title page in English. Titles of articles in periodicals are not given. Names of Hebrew and Yiddish periodicals well known in English-speaking countries or in Israel under their masthead in Latin characters are given in this form, even when contrary to transliteration rules. Names of authors writing in languages with non-Latin alphabets are given in their Latin alphabet form wherever known; otherwise the names are transliterated. Initials are generally not given for authors of articles in periodicals, except to avoid confusion. Non-abbreviated book titles and names of periodicals are printed in *italics.* Abbreviations are given in the list below.

AASOR	*Annual of the American School of Oriental Research* (1919ff.).
AB	*Analecta Biblica* (1952ff.).
Abel, Géog	F.-M. Abel, *Géographie de la Palestine,* 2 vols. (1933-38).
ABR	*Australian Biblical Review* (1951ff.).
Abr.	Philo, *De Abrahamo.*
Abrahams, Companion	I. Abrahams, *Companion to the Authorised Daily Prayer Book* (rev. ed. 1922).
Abramson, Merkazim	S. Abramson, *Ba-Merkazim u-va-Tefuẓot bi-Tekufat ha-Ge'onim* (1965).
Acts	Acts of the Apostles (New Testament).
ACUM	*Who is who in ACUM [Aguddat Kompozitorim u-Meḥabbrim].*
ADAJ	*Annual of the Department of Antiquities, Jordan* (1951ff.).
Adam	Adam and Eve (Pseudepigrapha).
ADB	*Allgemeine Deutsche Biographie,* 56 vols. (1875–1912).
Add. Esth.	The Addition to Esther (Apocrypha).
Adler, Prat Mus	1. Adler, *La pratique musicale savante dans quelques communautés juives en Europe au XVIIe et XVIIIe siècles,* 2 vols. (1966).
Adler-Davis	H.M. Adler and A. Davis (ed. and tr.), *Service of the Synagogue, a New Edition of the Festival Prayers with an English Translation in Prose and Verse,* 6 vols. (1905–06).
Aet.	Philo, *De Aeternitate Mundi.*
AFO	*Archiv fuer Orientforschung* (first two volumes under the name *Archiv fuer Keilschriftforschung)* (1923ff.).
Ag. Ber	*Aggadat Bereshit* (ed. Buber, 1902).
Agr.	Philo, *De Agricultura.*
Ag. Sam.	*Aggadat Samuel.*
Ag. Song	*Aggadat Shir ha-Shirim* (Schechter ed., 1896).
Aharoni, Ereẓ	Y. Aharoni, *Ereẓ Yisrael bi-Tekufat ha-Mikra: Geografyah Historit* (1962).
Aharoni, Land	Y. Aharoni, *Land of the Bible* (1966).

Ahikar	Ahikar (Pseudepigrapha).
AI	*Archives Israélites de France* (1840–1936).
AJA	*American Jewish Archives* (1948ff.).
AJHSP	*American Jewish Historical Society – Publications* (after vol. 50 = AJHSQ).
AJHSQ	*American Jewish Historical (Society) Quarterly* (before vol. 50 =AJHSP).
AJSLL	*American Journal of Semitic Languages and Literature* (1884–95 under the title *Hebraica*, since 1942 JNES).
AJYB	*American Jewish Year Book* (1899ff.).
AKM	Abhandlungen fuer die Kunde des Morgenlandes (series).
Albright, Arch	W.F. Albright, *Archaeology of Palestine* (rev. ed. 1960).
Albright, Arch Bib	W.F. Albright, *Archaeology of Palestine and the Bible* (1935^{3}).
Albright, Arch Rel	W.F. Albright, *Archaeology and the Religion of Israel* (1953^{3}).
Albright, Stone	W.F. Albright, *From the Stone Age to Christianity* (1957^{2}).
Alon, Meḥkarim	G. Alon, *Meḥkarim be-Toledot Yisrael bi-Ymei Bayit Sheni u-vi-Tekufat ha-Mishnah ve-ha Talmud*, 2 vols. (1957–58).
Alon, Toledot	G. Alon, *Toledot ha-Yehudim be-Ereẓ Yisrael bi-Tekufat ha-Mishnah ve-ha-Talmud*, I (1958^{3}), (1961^{2}).
ALOR	Alter Orient (series).
Alt, Kl Schr	A. Alt, *Kleine Schriften zur Geschichte des Volkes Israel*, 3 vols. (1953–59).
Alt, Landnahme	A. Alt, *Landnahme der Israeliten in Palaestina* (1925); also in Alt, Kl Schr, 1 (1953), 89–125.
Ant.	Josephus, *Jewish Antiquities* (Loeb Classics ed.).
AO	*Acta Orientalia* (1922ff.).
AOR	*Analecta Orientalia* (1931ff.).
AOS	American Oriental Series.
Apion	Josephus, *Against Apion* (Loeb Classics ed.).
Aq.	Aquila's Greek translation of the Bible.
Ar.	*Arakhin* (talmudic tractate).
Artist.	Letter of Aristeas (Pseudepigrapha).
ARN^{1}	*Avot de-Rabbi Nathan*, version (1) ed. Schechter, 1887.
ARN^{2}	*Avot de-Rabbi Nathan*, version (2) ed. Schechter, 1945^{2}.
Aronius, Regesten	I. Aronius, *Regesten zur Geschichte der Juden im fraenkischen und deutschen Reiche bis zum Jahre 1273* (1902).
ARW	*Archiv fuer Religionswissenschaft* (1898–1941/42).
AS	*Assyrological Studies* (1931ff.).
Ashtor, Korot	E. Ashtor (Strauss), *Korot ha-Yehudim bi-Sefarad ha-Muslemit*, 1(1966^{2}), 2(1966).
Ashtor, Toledot	E. Ashtor (Strauss), *Toledot ha-Yehudim be-Miẓrayim ve-Suryah Taḥat Shilton ha-Mamlukim*, 3 vols. (1944–70).
Assaf, Ge'onim	S. Assaf, *Tekufat ha-Ge'onim ve-Sifrutah* (1955).
Assaf, Mekorot	S. Assaf, *Mekorot le-Toledot ha-Ḥinnukh be-Yisrael*, 4 vols. (1925–43).
Ass. Mos.	Assumption of Moses (Pseudepigrapha).
ATA	Alttestamentliche Abhandlungen (series).
ATANT	Abhandlungen zur Theologie des Alten und Neuen Testaments (series).
AUJW	*Allgemeine unabhaengige juedische Wochenzeitung* (till 1966 = AWJD).
AV	Authorized Version of the Bible.
Avad.	*Avadim* (post-talmudic tractate).
Avi-Yonah, Geog	M. Avi-Yonah, *Geografyah Historit shel Ereẓ Yisrael* (1962^{3}).
Avi-Yonah, Land	M. Avi-Yonah, *The Holy Land from the Persian to the Arab conquest (536 B.C. to A.D. 640)* (1960).
Avot	*Avot* (talmudic tractate).
Av. Zar.	*Avodah Zarah* (talmudic tractate).
AWJD	*Allgemeine Wochenzeitung der Juden in Deutschland* (since 1967 = AUJW).
AZDJ	*Allgemeine Zeitung des Judentums.*
Azulai	Ḥ.Y.D. Azulai, *Shem ha-Gedolim*, ed. by I.E. Benjacob, 2 pts. (1852) (and other editions).
BA	*Biblical Archaeologist* (1938ff.).
Bacher, Bab Amor	W. Bacher, *Agada der babylonischen Amoraeer* (1913^{2}).
Bacher, Pal Amor	W. Bacher, *Agada der palaestinensischen Amoraeer* (Heb. ed. *Aggadat Amora'ei Ereẓ Yisrael)*, 2 vols. (1892–99).
Bacher, Tann	W. Bacher, *Agada der Tannaiten* (Heb. ed. *Aggadot ha-Tanna'im*, vol. 1, pt. 1 and 2 (1903); vol. 2 (1890).
Bacher, Trad	W. Bacher, *Tradition und Tradenten in den Schulen Palaestinas und Babyloniens* (1914).
Baer, Spain	Yitzhak (Fritz) Baer, *History of the Jews in Christian Spain*, 2 vols. (1961–66).
Baer, Studien	Yitzhak (Fritz) Baer, *Studien zur Geschichte der Juden im Koenigreich Aragonien waehrend des 13. und 14. Jahrhunderts* (1913).
Baer, Toledot	Yitzhak (Fritz) Baer, *Toledot ha-Yehudim bi-Sefarad ha-Noẓerit mi-Teḥillatan shel ha-Kehillot ad ha-Gerush*, 2 vols. (1959^{2}).
Baer, Urkunden	Yitzhak (Fritz) Baer, *Die Juden im christlichen Spanien*, 2 vols. (1929–36).
Baer S., Seder	S.I. Baer, *Seder Avodat Yisrael* (1868 and reprints).
BAIU	*Bulletin de l'Alliance Israélite Universelle* (1861–1913).
Baker, Biog Dict	*Baker's Biographical Dictionary of Musicians*, revised by N. Slonimsky (1958^{5}; with Supplement 1965).
I Bar.	I Baruch (Apocrypha).
II Bar.	II Baruch (Pseudepigrapha).
III Bar.	III Baruch (Pseudepigrapha).
BAR	*Biblical Archaeology Review.*
Baron, Community	S.W. Baron, *The Jewish Community, its History and Structure to the American Revolution*, 3 vols. (1942).

Baron, Social	S.W. Baron, *Social and Religious History of the Jews*, 3 vols. (1937); enlarged, 1-2(1952^2), 3-14 (1957–69).
Barthélemy-Milik	D. Barthélemy and J.T. Milik, *Dead Sea Scrolls: Discoveries in the Judean Desert*, vol. 1 *Qumram Cave* I (1955).
BASOR	*Bulletin of the American School of Oriental Research.*
Bauer-Leander	H. Bauer and P. Leander, *Grammatik des Biblisch-Aramaeischen* (1927; repr. 1962).
BB	(1) *Bava Batra* (talmudic tractate). (2) *Biblische Beitraege* (1943ff.).
BBB	Bonner biblische Beitraege (series).
BBLA	*Beitraege zur biblischen Landes- und Altertumskunde* (until 1949–ZDPV).
BBSAJ	*Bulletin*, British School of Archaeology, Jerusalem (1922–25; after 1927 included in PEFQS).
BDASI	*Alon* (since 1948) or *Hadashot Arkhe'ologiyyot* (since 1961), bulletin of the Department of Antiquities of the State of Israel.
Begrich, Chronologie	J. Begrich, *Chronologie der Koenige von Israel und Juda* (1929).
Bek.	*Bekhorot* (talmudic tractate).
Bel	Bel and the Dragon (Apocrypha).
Benjacob, Oẓar	I.E. Benjacob, *Oẓar ha-Sefarim* (1880; repr. 1956).
Ben Sira	see Ecclus.
Ben-Yehuda, Millon	E. Ben-Yedhuda, *Millon ha-Lashon ha-Ivrit*, 16 vols (1908–59; repr. in 8 vols., 1959).
Benzinger, Archaeologie	I. Benzinger, *Hebraeische Archaeologie* (1927^3).
Ben Zvi, Eretz Israel	I. Ben-Zvi, *Eretz Israel under Ottoman Rule* (1960; offprint from L. Finkelstein (ed.), *The Jews, their History, Culture and Religion* (vol. 1).
Ben Zvi, Ereẓ Israel	I. Ben-Zvi, *Ereẓ Israel bi-Ymei ha-Shilton ha-Ottomani* (1955).
Ber.	*Berakhot* (talmudic tractate).
Beẓah	*Beẓah* (talmudic tractate).
BIES	Bulletin of the Israel Exploration Society, see below BJPES.
Bik.	*Bikkurim* (talmudic tractate).
BJCE	Bibliography of Jewish Communities in Europe, catalog at General Archives for the History of the Jewish People, Jerusalem.
BJPES	Bulletin of the Jewish Palestine Exploration Society – English name of the Hebrew periodical known as: 1. *Yedi'ot ha-Ḥevrah ha-Ivrit la-Ḥakirat Ereẓ Yisrael va-Attikoteha* (1933–1954); 2. *Yedi'ot ha-Ḥevrah la-Ḥakirat Ereẓ Yisrael va-Attikoteha* (1954–1962); 3. *Yedi'ot ba-Ḥakirat Ereẓ Yisrael va-Attikoteha* (1962ff.).
BJRL	*Bulletin of the John Rylands Library* (1914ff.).
BK	*Bava Kamma* (talmudic tractate).
BLBI	*Bulletin of the Leo Baeck Institute* (1957ff.).
BM	(1) *Bava Meẓia* (talmudic tractate). (2) *Beit Mikra* (1955/56ff.). (3) British Museum.
BO	*Bibbia e Oriente* (1959ff.).
Bondy-Dworský	G. Bondy and F. Dworský, *Regesten zur Geschichte der Juden in Boehmen, Maehren und Schlesien von 906 bis 1620*, 2 vols. (1906).
BOR	*Bibliotheca Orientalis* (1943ff.).
Borée, Ortsnamen	W. Borée *Die alten Ortsnamen Palaestinas* (1930).
Bousset, Religion	W. Bousset, *Die Religion des Judentums im neutestamentlichen Zeitalter* (1906^2).
Bousset-Gressmann	W. Bousset, *Die Religion des Judentums im spaethellenistischen Zeitalter* (1966^3).
BR	*Biblical Review* (1916–25).
BRCI	*Bulletin of the Research Council of Israel* (1951/52–1954/55; then divided).
BRE	*Biblical Research* (1956ff.).
BRF	*Bulletin of the Rabinowitz Fund for the Exploration of Ancient Synagogues* (1949ff.).
Briggs, Psalms	Ch. A. and E.G. Briggs, *Critical and Exegetical Commentary on the Book of Psalms*, 2 vols. (ICC, 1906–07).
Bright, Hist	J. Bright, *A History of Israel* (1959).
Brockelmann, Arab Lit	K. Brockelmann, *Geschichte der arabischen Literatur*, 2 vols. 1898–1902), supplement, 3 vols. (1937–42).
Bruell, Jahrbuecher	*Jahrbuecher fuer juedische Geschichte und Litteratur*, ed. by N. Bruell, Frankfurt (1874–90).
Brugmans-Frank	H. Brugmans and A. Frank (eds.), *Geschiedenis der Joden in Nederland* (1940).
BTS	*Bible et Terre Sainte* (1958ff.).
Bull, Index	S. Bull, *Index to Biographies of Contemporary Composers* (1964).
BW	*Biblical World* (1882–1920).
BWANT	*Beitraege zur Wissenschaft vom Alten und Neuen Testament* (1926ff.).
BZ	*Biblische Zeitschrift* (1903ff.).
BZAW	*Beihefte zur Zeitschrift fuer die alttestamentliche Wissenschaft*, supplement to ZAW (1896ff.).
BŻIH	*Biuletyn Zydowskiego Instytutu Historycznego* (1950ff.).
CAB	*Cahiers d'archéologie biblique* (1953ff.).
CAD	*The* [*Chicago*] *Assyrian Dictionary* (1956ff.).
CAH	*Cambridge Ancient History*, 12 vols. (1923–39)
CAH^2	*Cambridge Ancient History*, second edition, 14 vols. (1962–2005).
Calwer, Lexikon	*Calwer, Bibellexikon.*
Cant.	Canticles, usually given as Song (= Song of Songs).

Cantera-Millás, Inscripciones	F. Cantera and J.M. Millás, *Las Inscripciones Hebraicas de España* (1956).
CBQ	*Catholic Biblical Quarterly* (1939ff.).
CCARY	Central Conference of American Rabbis, *Yearbook* (1890/91ff.).
CD	*Damascus Document* from the Cairo *Genizah* (published by S. Schechter, *Fragments of a Zadokite Work*, 1910).
Charles, Apocrypha	R.H. Charles, *Apocrypha and Pseudepigrapha . . .*, 2 vols. (1913; repr. 1963–66).
Cher.	Philo, *De Cherubim.*
I (or II) Chron.	Chronicles, book I and II (Bible).
CIG	*Corpus Inscriptionum Graecarum.*
CIJ	*Corpus Inscriptionum Judaicarum,* 2 vols. (1936–52).
CIL	*Corpus Inscriptionum Latinarum.*
CIS	*Corpus Inscriptionum Semiticarum* (1881ff.).
C.J.	Codex Justinianus.
Clermont-Ganneau, Arch	Ch. Clermont-Ganneau, *Archaeological Researches in Palestine*, 2 vols. (1896–99).
CNFI	*Christian News from Israel* (1949ff.).
Cod. Just.	Codex Justinianus.
Cod. Theod.	Codex Theodosinanus.
Col.	Epistle to the Colosssians (New Testament).
Conder, Survey	Palestine Exploration Fund, *Survey of Eastern Palestine*, vol. 1, pt. I (1889) = C.R. Conder, *Memoirs of the . . . Survey.*
Conder-Kitchener	Palestine Exploration Fund, *Survey of Western Palestine*, vol. 1, pts. 1-3 (1881–83) = C.R. Conder and H.H. Kitchener, *Memoirs.*
Conf.	Philo, *De Confusione Linguarum.*
Conforte, Kore	D. Conforte, *Kore ha-Dorot* (1842^2).
Cong.	Philo, *De Congressu Quaerendae Eruditionis Gratia.*
Cont.	Philo, *De Vita Contemplativa.*
I (or II) Cor.	Epistles to the Corinthians (New Testament).
Cowley, Aramic	A. Cowley, *Aramaic Papyri of the Fifth Century B.C.* (1923).
Colwey, Cat	A.E. Cowley, *A Concise Catalogue of the Hebrew Printed Books in the Bodleian Library* (1929).
CRB	*Cahiers de la Revue Biblique* (1964ff.).
Crowfoot-Kenyon	J.W. Crowfoot, K.M. Kenyon and E.L. Sukenik, *Buildings of Samaria* (1942).
C.T.	Codex Theodosianus.
DAB	*Dictionary of American Biography* (1928–58).
Daiches, Jews	S. Daiches, *Jews in Babylonia* (1910).
Dalman, Arbeit	G. Dalman, *Arbeit und Sitte in Palaestina*, 7 vols.in 8 (1928–42 repr. 1964).
Dan	Daniel (Bible).
Davidson, Oẓar	I. Davidson, *Oẓar ha-Shirah ve-ha-Piyyut,* 4 vols. (1924–33); Supplement in: HUCA, 12–13 (1937/38), 715–823.
DB	J. Hastings, *Dictionary of the Bible,* 4 vols. (1963^2).
DBI	F.G. Vigoureaux et al. (eds.), *Dictionnaire de la Bible,* 5 vols. in 10 (1912); Supplement, 8 vols. (1928–66)
Decal.	Philo, *De Decalogo.*
Dem.	*Demai* (talmudic tractate).
DER	*Derekh Ereẓ Rabbah* (post-talmudic tractate).
Derenbourg, Hist	J. Derenbourg *Essai sur l'histoire et la géographie de la Palestine* (1867).
Det.	Philo, *Quod deterius potiori insidiari solet.*
Deus	Philo, *Quod Deus immutabilis sit.*
Deut.	Deuteronomy (Bible).
Deut. R.	*Deuteronomy Rabbah.*
DEZ	*Derekh Ereẓ Zuta* (post-talmudic tractate).
DHGE	*Dictionnaire d'histoire et de géographie ecclésiastiques,* ed. by A. Baudrillart et al., 17 vols (1912–68).
Dik. Sof	*Dikdukei Soferim,* variae lections of the talmudic text by Raphael Nathan Rabbinovitz (16 vols., 1867–97).
Dinur, Golah	B. Dinur (Dinaburg), *Yisrael ba-Golah,* 2 vols. in 7 (1959–68) = vols. 5 and 6 of his *Toledot Yisrael,* second series.
Dinur, Haganah	B. Dinur (ed.), *Sefer Toledot ha-Haganah* (1954ff.).
Diringer, Iscr	D. Diringer, *Iscrizioni antico-ebraiche palestinesi* (1934).
Discoveries	*Discoveries in the Judean Desert* (1955ff.).
DNB	*Dictionary of National Biography,* 66 vols. (1921–222) with Supplements.
Dubnow, Divrei	S. Dubnow, *Divrei Yemei Am Olam,* 11 vols (1923–38 and further editions).
Dubnow, Ḥasidut	S. Dubnow, *Toledot ha-Ḥasidut* (1960^2).
Dubnow, Hist	S. Dubnow, *History of the Jews* (1967).
Dubnow, Hist Russ	S. Dubnow, *History of the Jews in Russia and Poland,* 3 vols. (1916 20).
Dubnow, Outline	S. Dubnow, *An Outline of Jewish History,* 3 vols. (1925–29).
Dubnow, Weltgesch	S. Dubnow, *Weltgeschichte des juedischen Volkes* 10 vols. (1925–29).
Dukes, Poesie	L. Dukes, *Zur Kenntnis der neuhebraeischen religioesen Poesie* (1842).
Dunlop, Khazars	D. H. Dunlop, *History of the Jewish Khazars* (1954).
EA	El Amarna Letters (edited by J.A. Knudtzon), *Die El-Amarna Tafel,* 2 vols. (1907 14).
EB	*Encyclopaedia Britannica.*
EBI	*Estudios biblicos* (1941ff.).
EBIB	T.K. Cheyne and J.S. Black, *Encyclopaedia Biblica,* 4 vols. (1899–1903).
Ebr.	Philo, *De Ebrietate.*
Eccles.	Ecclesiastes (Bible).
Eccles. R.	*Ecclesiastes Rabbah.*
Ecclus.	Ecclesiasticus or Wisdom of Ben Sira (or Sirach; Apocrypha).
Eduy.	*Eduyyot* (mishanic tractate).

EG	*Enziklopedyah shel Galuyyot* (1953ff.).
EH	*Even ha-Ezer.*
EHA	*Enziklopedyah la-Ḥafirot Arkheologiyyot be-Ereẓ Yisrael,* 2 vols. (1970).
EI	*Enzyklopaedie des Islams,* 4 vols. (1905–14). Supplement vol. (1938).
EIS	*Encyclopaedia of Islam,* 4 vols. (1913–36; repr. 1954–68).
EIS²	*Encyclopaedia of Islam, second edition (1960–2000).*
Eisenstein, Dinim	J.D. Eisenstein, *Oẓar Dinim u-Minhagim* (1917; several reprints).
Eisenstein, Yisrael	J.D. Eisenstein, *Oẓar Yisrael* (10 vols, 1907–13; repr. with several additions 1951).
EIV	*Enẓiklopedyah Ivrit* (1949ff.).
EJ	*Encyclopaedia Judaica* (German, A-L only), 10 vols. (1928–34).
EJC	*Enciclopedia Judaica Castellana,* 10 vols. (1948–51).
Elbogen, Century	I Elbogen, *A Century of Jewish Life* (1960²).
Elbogen, Gottesdienst	I Elbogen, *Der juedische Gottesdienst ...* (1931³, repr. 1962).
Elon, Mafte'aḥ	M. Elon (ed.), *Mafte'aḥ ha-She'elot ve-ha-Teshuvot ha-Rosh* (1965).
EM	*Enẓiklopedyah Mikra'it* (1950ff.).
I (or II) En.	I and II Enoch (Pseudepigrapha).
EncRel	*Encyclopedia of Religion,* 15 vols. (1987, 2005²).
Eph.	Epistle to the Ephesians (New Testament).
Ephros, Cant	G. Ephros, *Cantorial Anthology,* 5 vols. (1929–57).
Ep. Jer.	Epistle of Jeremy (Apocrypha).
Epstein, Amora'im	J N. Epstein, *Mevo'ot le-Sifrut ha-Amora'im* (1962).
Epstein, Marriage	L M. Epstein, *Marriage Laws in the Bible and the Talmud* (1942).
Epstein, Mishnah	J. N. Epstein, *Mavo le-Nusaḥ ha-Mishnah,* 2 vols. (1964²).
Epstein, Tanna'im	J. N. Epstein, *Mavo le-Sifruth ha-Tanna'im.* (1947).
ER	*Ecumenical Review.*
Er.	*Eruvin* (talmudic tractate).
ERE	*Encyclopaedia of Religion and Ethics,* 13 vols. (1908–26); reprinted.
ErIsr	*Eretz-Israel,* Israel Exploration Society.
I Esd.	I Esdras (Apocrypha) (= III Ezra).
II Esd.	II Esdras (Apocrypha) (= IV Ezra).
ESE	*Ephemeris fuer semitische Epigraphik,* ed. by M. Lidzbarski.
ESN	*Encyclopaedia Sefaradica Neerlandica,* 2 pts. (1949).
ESS	*Encyclopaedia of the Social Sciences,* 15 vols. (1930–35); reprinted in 8 vols. (1948–49).
Esth.	Esther (Bible).
Est. R.	*Esther Rabbah.*
ET	*Enẓiklopedyah Talmudit* (1947ff.).
Eusebius, Onom.	E. Klostermann (ed.), *Das Onomastikon* (1904), Greek with Hieronymus' Latin translation.
Ex.	Exodus (Bible).
Ex. R.	*Exodus Rabbah.*
Exs	Philo, *De Exsecrationibus.*
EẒD	*Enẓiklopeday shel ha-Ẓiyyonut ha-Datit* (1951ff.).
Ezek.	Ezekiel (Bible).
Ezra	Ezra (Bible).
III Ezra	III Ezra (Pseudepigrapha).
IV Ezra	IV Ezra (Pseudepigrapha).
Feliks, Ha-Ẓome'aḥ	*J. Feliks, Ha-Ẓome'aḥ ve-ha-Ḥai ba-Mishnah* (1983).
Finkelstein, Middle Ages	L. Finkelstein, *Jewish Self-Government in the Middle Ages* (1924).
Fischel, Islam	W.J. Fischel, *Jews in the Economic and Political Life of Mediaeval Islam* (1937; reprint with introduction "The Court Jew in the Islamic World," 1969).
FJW	*Fuehrer durch die juedische Gemeindeverwaltung und Wohlfahrtspflege in Deutschland* (1927/28).
Frankel, Mevo	Z. Frankel, *Mevo ha-Yerushalmi* (1870; reprint 1967).
Frankel, Mishnah	Z. Frankel, *Darkhei ha-Mishnah* (1959²; reprint 1959²).
Frazer, Folk-Lore	J.G. Frazer, *Folk-Lore in the Old Testament,* 3 vols. (1918–19).
Frey, Corpus	J.-B. Frey, *Corpus Inscriptionum Iudaicarum,* 2 vols. (1936–52).
Friedmann, Lebensbilder	A. Friedmann, *Lebensbilder beruehmter Kantoren,* 3 vols. (1918–27).
FRLT	*Forschungen zur Religion und Literatur des Alten und Neuen Testaments* (series) (1950ff.).
Frumkin-Rivlin	A.L. Frumkin and E. Rivlin, *Toledot Ḥakhmei Yerushalayim,* 3 vols. (1928–30), Supplement vol. (1930).
Fuenn, Keneset	S.J. Fuenn, *Keneset Yisrael,* 4 vols. (1887–90).
Fuerst, Bibliotheca	J. Fuerst, *Bibliotheca Judaica,* 2 vols. (1863; repr. 1960).
Fuerst, Karaeertum	J. Fuerst, *Geschichte des Karaeertums,* 3 vols. (1862–69).
Fug.	Philo, *De Fuga et Inventione.*
Gal.	Epistle to the Galatians (New Testament).
Galling, Reallexikon	K. Galling, *Biblisches Reallexikon* (1937).
Gardiner, Onomastica	A.H. Gardiner, *Ancient Egyptian Onomastica,* 3 vols. (1947).
Geiger, Mikra	A. Geiger, *Ha-Mikra ve-Targumav,* tr. by J.L. Baruch (1949).
Geiger, Urschrift	A. Geiger, *Urschrift und Uebersetzungen der Bibel* 1928²).
Gen.	Genesis (Bible).
Gen. R.	*Genesis Rabbah.*
Ger.	*Gerim* (post-talmudic tractate).
Germ Jud	M. Brann, I. Elbogen, A. Freimann, and H. Tykocinski (eds.), *Germania Judaica,* vol. 1 (1917; repr. 1934 and 1963); vol. 2, in 2 pts. (1917–68), ed. by Z. Avneri.

GHAT	*Goettinger Handkommentar zum Alten Testament* (1917–22).
Ghirondi-Neppi	M.S. Ghirondi and G.H. Neppi, *Toledot Gedolei Yisrael u-Ge'onei Italyah ... u-Ve'urim al Sefer Zekher Ẓaddikim li-Verakhah . . .*(1853), index in ZHB, 17 (1914), 171–83.
Gig.	Philo, *De Gigantibus.*
Ginzberg, Legends	L. Ginzberg, *Legends of the Jews,* 7 vols. (1909–38; and many reprints).
Git.	*Gittin* (talmudic tractate).
Glueck, Explorations	N. Glueck, *Explorations in Eastern Palestine,* 2 vols. (1951).
Goell, Bibliography	Y. Goell, *Bibliography of Modern Hebrew Literature in English Translation* (1968).
Goodenough, Symbols	E.R. Goodenough, *Jewish Symbols in the Greco-Roman Period,* 13 vols. (1953–68).
Gordon, Textbook	C.H. Gordon, *Ugaritic Textbook* (1965; repr. 1967).
Graetz, Gesch	H. Graetz, *Geschichte der Juden* (last edition 1874–1908).
Graetz, Hist	H. Graetz, *History of the Jews,* 6 vols. (1891–1902).
Graetz, Psalmen	H. Graetz, *Kritischer Commentar zu den Psalmen,* 2 vols. in 1 (1882–83).
Graetz, Rabbinowitz	H. Graetz, *Divrei Yemei Yisrael*, tr. by S.P. Rabbinowitz. (1928 1929^{2}).
Gray, Names	G.B. Gray, *Studies in Hebrew Proper Names* (1896).
Gressmann, Bilder	H. Gressmann, *Altorientalische Bilder zum Alten Testament* (1927^{2}).
Gressmann, Texte	H. Gressmann, *Altorientalische Texte zum Alten Testament* (1926^{2}).
Gross, Gal Jud	H. Gross, *Gallia Judaica* (1897; repr. with add. 1969).
Grove, Dict	*Grove's Dictionary of Music and Musicians,* ed. by E. Blum 9 vols. (1954^{5}) and suppl. (1961^{5}).
Guedemann, Gesch Erz	M. Guedemann, *Geschichte des Erziehungswesens und der Cultur der abendlaendischen Juden,* 3 vols. (1880–88).
Guedemann, Quellenschr	M. Guedemann, *Quellenschriften zur Geschichte des Unterrichts und der Erziehung bei den deutschen Juden* (1873, 1891).
Guide	Maimonides, *Guide of the Perplexed.*
Gulak, Oẓar	A. Gulak, *Oẓar ha-Shetarot ha-Nehugim be-Yisrael* (1926).
Gulak, Yesodei	A. Gulak, *Yesodei ha-Mishpat ha-Ivri, Seder Dinei Mamonot be-Yisrael, al pi Mekorot ha-Talmud ve-ha-Posekim,* 4 vols. (1922; repr. 1967).
Guttmann, Mafte'aḥ	M. Guttmann, *Mafte'aḥ ha-Talmud,* 3 vols. (1906–30).
Guttmann, Philosophies	J. Guttmann, *Philosophies of Judaism* (1964).
Hab.	*Habakkuk* (Bible).
Ḥag.	*Ḥagigah* (talmudic tractate).
Haggai	*Haggai* (Bible).
Ḥal.	*Ḥallah* (talmudic tractate).
Halevy, Dorot	I. Halevy, *Dorot ha-Rishonim,* 6 vols. (1897–1939).
Halpern, Pinkas	I. Halpern (Halperin), *Pinkas Va'ad Arba Araẓot* (1945).
Hananel-Eškenazi	A. Hananel and Eškenazi (eds.), *Fontes Hebraici ad res oeconomicas socialesque terrarum balcanicarum saeculo XVI pertinentes*, 2 vols, (1958–60; in Bulgarian).
HB	*Hebraeische Bibliographie* (1858–82).
Heb.	Epistle to the Hebrews (New Testament).
Heilprin, Dorot	J. Heilprin (Heilperin), *Seder ha-Dorot,* 3 vols. (1882; repr. 1956).
Her.	Philo, *Quis Rerum Divinarum Heres.*
Hertz, Prayer	J.H. Hertz (ed.), *Authorised Daily Prayer Book* (rev. ed. 1948; repr. 1963).
Herzog, Instit	I. Herzog, *The Main Institutions of Jewish Law,* 2 vols. (1936–39; repr. 1967).
Herzog-Hauck	J.J. Herzog and A. Hauch (eds.), *Real-encyklopaedie fuer protestantische Theologie* (1896–1913^{3}).
HḤY	*Ha-Ẓofeh le-Ḥokhmat Yisrael* (first four volumes under the title *Ha-Ẓofeh me-Ereẓ Hagar)* (1910/11–13).
Hirschberg, Afrikah	H.Z. Hirschberg, *Toledot ha-Yehudim be-Afrikah ha-Zofonit,* 2 vols. (1965).
HJ	*Historia Judaica* (1938–61).
HL	*Das Heilige Land* (1857ff.)
ḤM	*Ḥoshen Mishpat.*
Hommel, Ueberliefer.	F. Hommel, *Die altisraelitische Ueberlieferung in inschriftlicher Beleuchtung* (1897).
Hor.	*Horayot* (talmudic tractate).
Horodezky, Ḥasidut	S.A. Horodezky, *Ha-Ḥasidut ve-ha-Ḥasidim,* 4 vols. (1923).
Horowitz, Ereẓ Yis	I.W. Horowitz, *Ereẓ Yisrael u-Shekhenoteha* (1923).
Hos.	Hosea (Bible).
HTR	*Harvard Theological Review* (1908ff.).
HUCA	*Hebrew Union College Annual* (1904; 1924ff.)
Ḥul.	*Ḥullin* (talmudic tractate).
Husik, Philosophy	I. Husik, *History of Medieval Jewish Philosophy* (1932^{2}).
Hyman, Toledot	A. Hyman, *Toledot Tanna'im ve-Amora'im* (1910; repr. 1964).
Ibn Daud, Tradition	Abraham Ibn Daud, *Sefer ha-Qabbalah – The Book of Tradition,* ed. and tr. By G.D. Cohen (1967).
ICC	International Critical Commentary on the Holy Scriptures of the Old and New Testaments (series, 1908ff.).
IDB	*Interpreter's Dictionary of the Bible,* 4 vols. (1962).
Idelsohn, Litugy	A. Z. Idelsohn, *Jewish Liturgy and its Development* (1932; paperback repr. 1967)
Idelsohn, Melodien	A. Z. Idelsohn, *Hebraeisch-orientalischer Melodienschatz,* 10 vols. (1914 32).
Idelsohn, Music	A. Z. Idelsohn, *Jewish Music in its Historical Development* (1929; paperback repr. 1967).

IEJ	*Israel Exploration Journal* (1950ff.).
IESS	*International Encyclopedia of the Social Sciences* (various eds.).
IG	*Inscriptiones Graecae*, ed. by the Prussian Academy.
IGYB	*Israel Government Year Book* (1949/50ff.).
ILR	*Israel Law Review* (1966ff.).
IMIT	*Izraelita Magyar Irodalmi Társulat Évkönyv* (1895 1948).
IMT	International Military Tribunal.
INB	*Israel Numismatic Bulletin* (1962–63).
INJ	*Israel Numismatic Journal* (1963ff.).
Ios	Philo, *De Iosepho.*
Isa.	Isaiah (Bible).
ITHL	Institute for the Translation of Hebrew Literature.
IZBG	*Internationale Zeitschriftenschau fuer Bibelwissenschaft und Grenzgebiete* (1951ff.).
JA	*Journal asiatique* (1822ff.).
James	Epistle of James (New Testament).
JAOS	*Journal of the American Oriental Society* (c. 1850ff.)
Jastrow, Dict	M. Jastrow, *Dictionary of the Targumim, the Talmud Babli and Yerushalmi, and the Midrashic literature*, 2 vols. (1886 1902 and reprints).
JBA	*Jewish Book Annual* (19242ff.).
JBL	*Journal of Biblical Literature* (1881ff.).
JBR	*Journal of Bible and Religion* (1933ff.).
JC	*Jewish Chronicle* (1841ff.).
JCS	*Journal of Cuneiform Studies* (1947ff.).
JE	*Jewish Encyclopedia*, 12 vols. (1901–05 several reprints).
Jer.	Jeremiah (Bible).
Jeremias, Alte Test	A. Jeremias, *Das Alte Testament im Lichte des alten Orients* 1930[4]).
JGGJČ	*Jahrbuch der Gesellschaft fuer Geschichte der Juden in der Čechoslovakischen Republik* (1929–38).
JHSEM	Jewish Historical Society of England, *Miscellanies* (1925ff.).
JHSET	Jewish Historical Society of England, *Transactions* (1893ff.).
JJGL	*Jahrbuch fuer juedische Geschichte und Literatur* (Berlin) (1898–1938).
JJLG	*Jahrbuch der juedische-literarischen Gesellschaft* (Frankfurt) (1903–32).
JJS	*Journal of Jewish Studies* (1948ff.).
JJSO	*Jewish Journal of Sociology* (1959ff.).
JJV	*Jahrbuch fuer juedische Volkskunde* (1898–1924).
JL	*Juedisches Lexikon*, 5 vols. (1927–30).
JMES	*Journal of the Middle East Society* (1947ff.).
JNES	*Journal of Near Eastern Studies* (continuation of AJSLL) (1942ff.).
J.N.U.L.	Jewish National and University Library.
Job	Job (Bible).
Joel	Joel (Bible).
John	Gospel according to John (New Testament).
I, II and III John	Epistles of John (New Testament).
Jos., Ant	Josephus, *Jewish Antiquities* (Loeb Classics ed.).
Jos. Apion	Josephus, *Against Apion* (Loeb Classics ed.).
Jos., index	*Josephus Works*, Loeb Classics ed., index of names.
Jos., Life	Josephus, *Life* (ed. Loeb Classics).
Jos, Wars	Josephus, *The Jewish Wars* (Loeb Classics ed.).
Josh.	Joshua (Bible).
JPESB	Jewish Palestine Exploration Society Bulletin, see BJPES.
JPESJ	Jewish Palestine Exploration Society Journal – Eng. Title of the Hebrew periodical *Kovez ha-Ḥevrah ha-Ivrit la-Ḥakirat Erez Yisrael va-Attikoteha.*
JPOS	*Journal of the Palestine Oriental Society* (1920–48).
JPS	Jewish Publication Society of America, *The Torah* (1962, 1967[2]); *The Holy Scriptures* (1917).
JQR	*Jewish Quarterly Review* (1889ff.).
JR	*Journal of Religion* (1921ff.).
JRAS	*Journal of the Royal Asiatic Society* (1838ff.).
JHR	*Journal of Religious History* (1960/61ff.).
JSOS	*Jewish Social Studies* (1939ff.).
JSS	*Journal of Semitic Studies* (1956ff.).
JTS	*Journal of Theological Studies* (1900ff.).
JTSA	Jewish Theological Seminary of America (also abbreviated as JTS).
Jub.	Jubilees (Pseudepigrapha).
Judg.	Judges (Bible).
Judith	Book of Judith (Apocrypha).
Juster, Juifs	J. Juster, *Les Juifs dans l'Empire Romain*, 2 vols. (1914).
JYB	*Jewish Year Book* (1896ff.).
JZWL	*Juedische Zeitschift fuer Wissenschaft und Leben* (1862–75).
Kal.	*Kallah* (post-talmudic tractate).
Kal. R.	*Kallah Rabbati* (post-talmudic tractate).
Katz, England	*The Jews in the History of England, 1485-1850 (1994).*
Kaufmann, Schriften	D. Kaufmann, *Gesammelte Schriften*, 3 vols. (1908 15).
Kaufmann Y., Religion	Y. Kaufmann, *The Religion of Israel* (1960), abridged tr. of his *Toledot.*
Kaufmann Y., Toledot	Y. Kaufmann, *Toledot ha-Emunah ha-Yisre'elit*, 4 vols. (1937 57).
KAWJ	*Korrespondenzblatt des Vereins zur Gruendung und Erhaltung der Akademie fuer die Wissenschaft des Judentums* (1920 30).
Kayserling, Bibl	M. Kayserling, *Biblioteca Española-Portugueza-Judaica* (1880; repr. 1961).
Kelim	*Kelim* (mishnaic tractate).
Ker.	*Keritot* (talmudic tractate).
Ket.	*Ketubbot* (talmudic tractate).

Kid.	*Kiddushim* (talmudic tractate).
Kil.	*Kilayim* (talmudic tractate).
Kin.	*Kinnim* (mishnaic tractate).
Kisch, Germany	G. Kisch, *Jews in Medieval Germany* (1949).
Kittel, Gesch	R. Kittel, *Geschichte des Volkes Israel,* 3 vols. (1922–28).
Klausner, Bayit Sheni	J. Klausner, *Historyah shel ha-Bayit ha-Sheni,* 5 vols. (1950/512).
Klausner, Sifrut	J. Klausner, *Historyah shel haSifrut ha-Ivrit ha-Ḥadashah,* 6 vols. (1952–582).
Klein, corpus	S. Klein (ed.), *Juedisch-palaestinisches Corpus Inscriptionum* (1920).
Koehler-Baumgartner	L. Koehler and W. Baumgartner, *Lexicon in Veteris Testamenti libros* (1953).
Kohut, Arukh	H.J.A. Kohut (ed.), *Sefer he-Arukh ha-Shalem,* by Nathan b. Jehiel of Rome, 8 vols. (1876–92; Supplement by S. Krauss et al., 1936; repr. 1955).
Krauss, Tal Arch	S. Krauss, *Talmudische Archaeologie,* 3 vols. (1910–12; repr. 1966).
Kressel, Leksikon	G. Kressel, *Leksikon ha-Sifrut ha-Ivrit ba-Dorot ha-Aḥaronim,* 2 vols. (1965–67).
KS	*Kirjath Sepher* (1923/4ff.).
Kut.	*Kuttim* (post-talmudic tractate).
LA	Studium Biblicum Franciscanum, *Liber Annuus* (1951ff.).
L.A.	Philo, *Legum allegoriae.*
Lachower, Sifrut	F. Lachower, *Toledot ha-Sifrut ha-Ivrit ha-Ḥadashah,* 4 vols. (1947–48; several reprints).
Lam.	Lamentations (Bible).
Lam. R.	*Lamentations Rabbah.*
Landshuth, Ammudei	L. Landshuth, *Ammudei ha-Avodah* (1857–62; repr. with index, 1965).
Legat.	Philo, *De Legatione ad Caium.*
Lehmann, Nova Bibl	R.P. Lehmann, *Nova Bibliotheca Anglo-Judaica* (1961).
Lev.	Leviticus (Bible).
Lev. R.	*Leviticus Rabbah.*
Levy, Antologia	I. Levy, *Antologia de liturgia judeo-española* (1965ff.).
Levy J., Chald Targ	J. Levy, *Chaldaeisches Woerterbuch ueber die Targumim,* 2 vols. (1967–68; repr. 1959).
Levy J., Nuehebr Tal	J. Levy, *Neuhebraeisches und chaldaeisches Woerterbuch ueber die Talmudim . . .,* 4 vols. (1875–89; repr. 1963).
Lewin, Oẓar	Lewin, *Oẓar ha-Ge'onim,* 12 vols. (1928–43).
Lewysohn, Zool	L. Lewysohn, *Zoologie des Talmuds* (1858).
Lidzbarski, Handbuch	M. Lidzbarski, *Handbuch der nordsemitischen Epigraphik,* 2 vols (1898).
Life	Josephus, *Life* (Loeb Classis ed.).
LNYL	*Leksikon fun der Nayer Yidisher Literatur* (1956ff.).
Loew, Flora	I. Loew, *Die Flora der Juden,* 4 vols. (1924 34; repr. 1967).
LSI	*Laws of the State of Israel* (1948ff.).
Luckenbill, Records	D.D. Luckenbill, *Ancient Records of Assyria and Babylonia,* 2 vols. (1926).
Luke	Gospel according to Luke (New Testament)
LXX	Septuagint (Greek translation of the Bible).
Ma'as.	*Ma'aserot* (talmudic tractate).
Ma'as. Sh.	*Ma'ase Sheni* (talmudic tractate).
I, II, III, and IVMacc.	Maccabees, I, II, III (Apocrypha), IV (Pseudepigrapha).
Maimonides, Guide	Maimonides, *Guide of the Perplexed.*
Maim., Yad	Maimonides, *Mishneh Torah (Yad Ḥazakah).*
Maisler, Untersuchungen	B. Maisler (Mazar), *Untersuchungen zur alten Geschichte und Ethnographie Syriens und Palaestinas,* 1 (1930).
Mak.	*Makkot* (talmudic tractate).
Makhsh.	*Makhshrin* (mishnaic tractate).
Mal.	Malachi (Bible).
Mann, Egypt	J. Mann, *Jews in Egypt in Palestine under the Fatimid Caliphs,* 2 vols. (1920–22).
Mann, Texts	J. Mann, *Texts and Studies,* 2 vols (1931–35).
Mansi	G.D. Mansi, *Sacrorum Conciliorum nova et amplissima collectio,* 53 vols. in 60 (1901–27; repr. 1960).
Margalioth, Gedolei	M. Margalioth, *Enẓiklopedyah le-Toledot Gedolei Yisrael,* 4 vols. (1946–50).
Margalioth, Ḥakhmei	M. Margalioth, *Enẓiklopedyah le-Ḥakhmei ha-Talmud ve-ha-Ge'onim,* 2 vols. (1945).
Margalioth, Cat	G. Margalioth, *Catalogue of the Hebrew and Samaritan Manuscripts in the British Museum,* 4 vols. (1899–1935).
Mark	Gospel according to Mark (New Testament).
Mart. Isa.	Martyrdom of Isaiah (Pseudepigrapha).
Mas.	Masorah.
Matt.	Gospel according to Matthew (New Testament).
Mayer, Art	L.A. Mayer, *Bibliography of Jewish Art* (1967).
MB	*Wochenzeitung* (formerly *Mitteilungsblatt*) *des Irgun Olej Merkas Europa* (1933ff.).
MEAH	*Miscelánea de estudios árabes y hebraicos* (1952ff.).
Meg.	Megillah (talmudic tractate).
Meg. Ta'an.	*Megillat Ta'anit* (in HUCA, 8 9 (1931–32), 318–51).
Me'il	*Me'ilah* (mishnaic tractate).
MEJ	*Middle East Journal* (1947ff.).
Mehk.	*Mekhilta de-R. Ishmael.*
Mekh. SbY	*Mekhilta de-R. Simeon bar Yoḥai.*
Men.	*Menaḥot* (talmudic tractate).
MER	*Middle East Record* (1960ff.).
Meyer, Gesch	E. Meyer, *Geschichte des Alterums,* 5 vols. in 9 (1925–58).
Meyer, Ursp	E. Meyer, *Urspring und Anfaenge des Christentums* (1921).
Mez.	*Mezuzah* (post-talmudic tractate).
MGADJ	*Mitteilungen des Gesamtarchivs der deutschen Juden* (1909–12).
MGG	*Die Musik in Geschichte und Gegenwart,* 14 vols. (1949–68).

MGG^{2}	*Die Musik in Geschichte und Gegenwart, 2nd edition (1994)*
MGH	*Monumenta Germaniae Historica* (1826ff.).
MGJV	*Mitteilungen der Gesellschaft fuer juedische Volkskunde* (1898–1929); title varies, see also JJV.
MGWJ	*Monatsschrift fuer Geschichte und Wissenschaft des Judentums* (1851–1939).
MHJ	*Monumenta Hungariae Judaica,* 11 vols. (1903–67).
Michael, Or	H.Ḥ. Michael, *Or ha-Ḥayyim: Ḥakhmei Yisrael ve-Sifreihem,* ed. by S.Z. Ḥ. Halberstam and N. Ben-Menahem (1965^{2}).
Mid.	*Middot* (mishnaic tractate).
Mid. Ag.	*Midrash Aggadah.*
Mid. Hag.	*Midrash ha-Gadol.*
Mid. Job.	*Midrash Job.*
Mid. Jonah	*Midrash Jonah.*
Mid. Lek. Tov	*Midrash Lekaḥ Tov.*
Mid. Prov.	*Midrash Proverbs.*
Mid. Ps.	*Midrash Tehillim* (Eng tr. *The Midrash on Psalms* (JPS, 1959).
Mid. Sam.	*Midrash Samuel.*
Mid. Song	*Midrash Shir ha-Shirim.*
Mid. Tan.	*Midrash Tanna'im* on Deuteronomy.
Miége, Maroc	J.L. Miège, *Le Maroc et l'Europe,* 3 vols. (1961 62).
Mig.	Philo, *De Migratione Abrahami.*
Mik.	*Mikva'ot* (mishnaic tractate).
Milano, Bibliotheca	A. Milano, *Bibliotheca Historica Italo-Judaica* (1954); supplement for 1954–63 (1964); supplement for 1964–66 in RMI, 32 (1966).
Milano, Italia	A. Milano, *Storia degli Ebrei in Italia* (1963).
MIO	*Mitteilungen des Instituts fuer Orientforschung* 1953ff.).
Mish.	Mishnah.
MJ	*Le Monde Juif* (1946ff.).
MJC	see Neubauer, Chronicles.
MK	*Mo'ed Katan* (talmudic tractate).
MNDPV	*Mitteilungen und Nachrichten des deutschen Palaestinavereins* (1895–1912).
Mortara, Indice	M. Mortara, *Indice Alfabetico dei Rabbini e Scrittori Israeliti ... in Italia ...* (1886).
Mos	Philo, *De Vita Mosis.*
Moscati, Epig	S, Moscati, *Epigrafia ebraica antica* 1935–1950 (1951).
MT	Masoretic Text of the Bible.
Mueller, Musiker	[E.H. Mueller], *Deutisches Musiker-Lexikon* (1929)
Munk, Mélanges	S. Munk, *Mélanges de philosophie juive et arabe* (1859; repr. 1955).
Mut.	Philo, *De Mutatione Nominum.*
MWJ	*Magazin fuer die Wissenshaft des Judentums* (18745 93).
Nah.	Nahum (Bible).
Naz.	*Nazir* (talmudic tractate).
NDB	*Neue Deutsche Biographie* (1953ff.).
Ned.	*Nedarim* (talmudic tractate).
Neg.	*Nega'im* (mishnaic tractate).
Neh.	Nehemiah (Bible).
NG^{2}	*New Grove Dictionary of Music and Musicians* (2001).
Nuebauer, Cat	A. Neubauer, *Catalogue of the Hebrew Manuscripts in the Bodleian Library ...,* 2 vols. (1886–1906).
Neubauer, Chronicles	A. Neubauer, *Mediaeval Jewish Chronicles,* 2 vols. (Heb., 1887–95; repr. 1965), Eng. title of *Seder ha-Ḥakhamim ve-Korot ha-Yamim.*
Neubauer, Géogr	A. Neubauer, *La géographie du Talmud* (1868).
Neuman, Spain	A.A. Neuman, *The Jews in Spain, their Social, Political, and Cultural Life During the Middle Ages,* 2 vols. (1942).
Neusner, Babylonia	J. Neusner, *History of the Jews in Babylonia,* 5 vols. 1965–70), 2nd revised printing 1969ff.).
Nid.	*Niddah* (talmudic tractate).
Noah	Fragment of Book of Noah (Pseudepigrapha).
Noth, Hist Isr	M. Noth, *History of Israel* (1958).
Noth, Personennamen	M. Noth, *Die israelitischen Personennamen.* ... (1928).
Noth, Ueberlief	M. Noth, *Ueberlieferungsgeschichte des Pentateuchs* (1949).
Noth, Welt	M. Noth, *Die Welt des Alten Testaments* (1957^{3}).
Nowack, Lehrbuch	W. Nowack, *Lehrbuch der hebraeischen Archaeologie,* 2 vols (1894).
NT	New Testament.
Num.	Numbers (Bible).
Num R.	*Numbers Rabbah.*
Obad.	Obadiah (Bible).
ODNB online	*Oxford Dictionary of National Biography.*
OḤ	*Oraḥ Ḥayyim.*
Oho.	*Oholot* (mishnaic tractate).
Olmstead	H.T. Olmstead, *History of Palestine and Syria* (1931; repr. 1965).
OLZ	*Orientalistische Literaturzeitung* (1898ff.)
Onom.	Eusebius, *Onomasticon.*
Op.	Philo, *De Opificio Mundi.*
OPD	*Osef Piskei Din shel ha-Rabbanut ha-Rashit le-Ereẓ Yisrael, Bet ha-Din ha-Gadol le-Irurim* (1950).
Or.	*Orlah* (talmudic tractate).
Or. Sibyll.	Sibylline Oracles (Pseudepigrapha).
OS	*L'Orient Syrien* (1956ff.)
OTS	*Oudtestamentische Studien* (1942ff.).
PAAJR	*Proceedings of the American Academy for Jewish Research* (1930ff.)
Pap 4QS^{e}	A papyrus exemplar of IQS.
Par.	*Parah* (mishnaic tractate).
Pauly-Wissowa	A.F. Pauly, *Realencyklopaedie der klassichen Alertumswissenschaft,* ed. by G. Wissowa et al. (1864ff.)

PD	*Piskei Din shel Bet ha-Mishpat ha-Elyon le-Yisrael* (1948ff.)
PDR	*Piskei Din shel Battei ha-Din ha-Rabbaniyyim be-Yisrael.*
PdRE	*Pirkei de-R. Eliezer* (Eng. tr. 1916. (1965[2]).
PdRK	*Pesikta de-Rav Kahana.*
Pe'ah	*Pe'ah* (talmudic tractate).
Peake, Commentary	A.J. Peake (ed.), *Commentary on the Bible* (1919; rev. 1962).
Pedersen, Israel	J. Pedersen, *Israel, Its Life and Culture,* 4 vols. in 2 (1926–40).
PEFQS	*Palestine Exploration Fund Quarterly Statement* (1869–1937; since 1938–PEQ).
PEQ	*Palestine Exploration Quarterly* (until 1937 PEFQS; after 1927 includes BBSAJ).
Perles, Beitaege	J. Perles, *Beitraege zur rabbinischen Sprach- und Alterthumskunde* (1893).
Pes.	*Pesaḥim* (talmudic tractate).
Pesh.	Peshitta (Syriac translation of the Bible).
Pesher Hab.	Commentary to Habakkuk from Qumran; see 1Qp Hab.
I and II Pet.	Epistles of Peter (New Testament).
Pfeiffer, Introd	R.H. Pfeiffer, *Introduction to the Old Testament* (1948).
PG	J.P. Migne (ed.), *Patrologia Graeca,* 161 vols. (1866–86).
Phil.	Epistle to the Philippians (New Testament).
Philem.	Epistle to the Philemon (New Testament).
PIASH	*Proceedings of the Israel Academy of Sciences and Humanities* (1963/7ff.).
PJB	*Palaestinajahrbuch des deutschen evangelischen Institutes fuer Altertumswissenschaft,* Jerusalem (1905–1933).
PK	*Pinkas ha-Kehillot,* encyclopedia of Jewish communities, published in over 30 volumes by Yad Vashem from 1970 and arranged by countries, regions and localities. For 3-vol. English edition see Spector, *Jewish Life.*
PL	J.P. Migne (ed.), *Patrologia Latina* 221 vols. (1844–64).
Plant	Philo, *De Plantatione.*
PO	R. Graffin and F. Nau (eds.), *Patrologia Orientalis* (1903ff.)
Pool, Prayer	D. de Sola Pool, *Traditional Prayer Book for Sabbath and Festivals* (1960).
Post	Philo, *De Posteritate Caini.*
PR	*Pesikta Rabbati.*
Praem.	Philo, *De Praemiis et Poenis.*
Prawer, Ẓalbanim	J. Prawer, *Toledot Mamlekhet ha-Ẓalbanim be-Ereẓ Yisrael,* 2 vols. (1963).
Press, Ereẓ	I. Press, *Ereẓ-Yisrael, Enẓiklopedyah Topografit-Historit,* 4 vols. (1951–55).
Pritchard, Pictures	J.B. Pritchard (ed.), *Ancient Near East in Pictures* (1954, 1970).
Pritchard, Texts	J.B. Pritchard (ed.), *Ancient Near East Texts* ... (1970[3]).
Pr. Man.	Prayer of Manasses (Apocrypha).
Prob.	Philo, *Quod Omnis Probus Liber Sit.*
Prov.	Proverbs (Bible).
PS	*Palestinsky Sbornik* (Russ. (1881 1916, 1954ff).
Ps.	Psalms (Bible).
PSBA	*Proceedings of the Society of Biblical Archaeology* (1878–1918).
Ps. of Sol	Psalms of Solomon (Pseudepigrapha).
IQ Apoc	The *Genesis Apocryphon* from Qumran, cave one, ed. by N. Avigad and Y. Yadin (1956).
6QD	*Damascus Document* or *Sefer Berit Dammesk* from Qumran, cave six, ed. by M. Baillet, in RB, 63 (1956), 513–23 (see also CD).
QDAP	*Quarterly of the Department of Antiquities in Palestine* (1932ff.).
4QDeut. 32	Manuscript of Deuteronomy 32 from Qumran, cave four (ed. by P.W. Skehan, in BASOR, 136 (1954), 12–15).
4QEx^{a}	Exodus manuscript in Jewish script from Qumran, cave four.
4QEx$^{\alpha}$	Exodus manuscript in Paleo-Hebrew script from Qumran, cave four (partially ed. by P.W. Skehan, in JBL, 74 (1955), 182–7).
4QFlor	*Florilegium,* a miscellany from Qumran, cave four (ed. by J.M. Allegro, in JBL, 75 (1956), 176–77 and 77 (1958), 350–54).).
QGJD	*Quellen zur Geschichte der Juden in Deutschland* 1888–98).
IQH	*Thanksgiving Psalms* of *Hodayot* from Qumran, cave one (ed. by E.L. Sukenik and N. Avigad, *Oẓar ha-Megillot ha-Genuzot* (1954).
IQIs^{a}	Scroll of Isaiah from Qumran, cave one (ed. by N. Burrows et al., *Dead Sea Scrolls* ..., 1 (1950).
IQIs^{b}	Scroll of Isaiah from Qumran, cave one (ed. E.L. Sukenik and N. Avigad, *Oẓar ha-Megillot ha-Genuzot* (1954).
IQM	The *War Scroll* or *Serekh ha-Milḥamah* (ed. by E.L. Sukenik and N. Avigad, *Oẓar ha-Megillot ha-Genuzot* (1954).
4QpNah	Commentary on Nahum from Qumran, cave four (partially ed. by J.M. Allegro, in JBL, 75 (1956), 89–95).
IQphyl	Phylacteries *(tefillin)* from Qumran, cave one (ed. by Y. Yadin, in *Eretz Israel,* 9 (1969), 60–85).
4Q Prayer of Nabonidus	A document from Qumran, cave four, belonging to a lost Daniel literature (ed. by J.T. Milik, in RB, 63 (1956), 407–15).
IQS	*Manual of Discipline* or *Serekh ha-Yaḥad* from Qumran, cave one (ed. by M. Burrows et al., *Dead Sea Scrolls* ..., 2, pt. 2 (1951).

IQS[a]	The *Rule of the Congregation or Serekh ha-Edah* from Qumran, cave one (ed. by Burrows et al., *Dead Sea Scrolls* ..., 1 (1950), under the abbreviation IQ28a).
IQS[b]	*Blessings* or *Divrei Berakhot* from Qumran, cave one (ed. by Burrows et al., *Dead Sea Scrolls* ..., 1 (1950), under the abbreviation IQ28b).
4QSam[a]	Manuscript of I and II Samuel from Qumran, cave four (partially ed. by F.M. Cross, in BASOR, 132 (1953), 15–26).
4QSam[b]	Manuscript of I and II Samuel from Qumran, cave four (partially ed. by F.M. Cross, in JBL, 74 (1955), 147–72).
4QTestimonia	Sheet of Testimony from Qumran, cave four (ed. by J.M. Allegro, in JBL, 75 (1956), 174–87).).
4QT.Levi	*Testament of Levi* from Qumran, cave four (partially ed. by J.T. Milik, in RB, 62 (1955), 398–406).
Rabinovitz, Dik Sof	See Dik Sof.
RB	*Revue biblique* (1892ff.)
RBI	*Recherches bibliques* (1954ff.)
RCB	*Revista de cultura biblica* (São Paulo) (1957ff.)
Régné, Cat	J. Régné, *Catalogue des actes . . . des rois d'Aragon, concernant les Juifs* (1213–1327), in: REJ, vols. 60 70, 73, 75–78 (1910–24).
Reinach, Textes	T. Reinach, *Textes d'auteurs Grecs et Romains relatifs au Judaïsme* (1895; repr. 1963).
REJ	*Revue des études juives* (1880ff.).
Rejzen, Leksikon	Z. Rejzen, *Leksikon fun der Yidisher Literature,* 4 vols. (1927–29).
Renan, Ecrivains	A. Neubauer and E. Renan, *Les écrivains juifs français* ... (1893).
Renan, Rabbins	A. Neubauer and E. Renan, *Les rabbins français* (1877).
RES	*Revue des étude sémitiques et Babyloniaca* (1934–45).
Rev.	Revelation (New Testament).
RGG^{3}	*Die Religion in Geschichte und Gegenwart,* 7 vols. (1957–65^{3}).
RH	*Rosh Ha-Shanah* (talmudic tractate).
RHJE	*Revue de l'histoire juive en Egypte* (1947ff.).
RHMH	*Revue d'histoire de la médecine hébraïque* (1948ff.).
RHPR	*Revue d'histoire et de philosophie religieuses* (1921ff.).
RHR	*Revue d'histoire des religions* (1880ff.).
RI	*Rivista Israelitica* (1904–12).
Riemann-Einstein	*Hugo Riemanns Musiklexikon,* ed. by A. Einstein (1929^{11}).
Riemann-Gurlitt	*Hugo Riemanns Musiklexikon,* ed. by W. Gurlitt (1959–67^{12}), Personenteil.
Rigg-Jenkinson, Exchequer	J.M. Rigg, H. Jenkinson and H.G. Richardson (eds.), *Calendar of the Pleas Rolls of the Exchequer of the Jews,* 4 vols. (1905–1970); cf. in each instance also J.M. Rigg (ed.), *Select Pleas* ... (1902).
RMI	*Rassegna Mensile di Israel* (1925ff.).
Rom.	Epistle to the Romans (New Testament).
Rosanes, Togarmah	S.A. Rosanes, *Divrei Yemei Yisrael be-Togarmah,* 6 vols. (1907–45), and in 3 vols. (1930–38^{2}).
Rosenbloom, Biogr Dict	J.R. Rosenbloom, *Biographical Dictionary of Early American Jews* (1960).
Roth, Art	C. Roth, *Jewish Art* (1961).
Roth, Dark Ages	C. Roth (ed.), *World History of the Jewish People,* second series, vol. 2, *Dark Ages* (1966).
Roth, England	C. Roth, *History of the Jews in England* (1964^{3}).
Roth, Italy	C. Roth, *History of the Jews in Italy* (1946).
Roth, Mag Bibl	C. Roth, *Magna Bibliotheca Anglo-Judaica* (1937).
Roth, Marranos	C. Roth, *History of the Marranos* (2nd rev. ed 1959; reprint 1966).
Rowley, Old Test	H.H. Rowley, *Old Testament and Modern Study* (1951; repr. 1961).
RS	*Revue sémitiques d'épigraphie et d'histoire ancienne* (1893/94ff.).
RSO	*Rivista degli studi orientali* (1907ff.).
RSV	Revised Standard Version of the Bible.
Rubinstein, Australia I	*H.L. Rubinstein, The Jews in Australia, A Thematic History, Vol. I (1991).*
Rubinstein, Australia II	*W.D. Rubinstein, The Jews in Australia, A Thematic History, Vol. II (1991).*
Ruth	Ruth (Bible).
Ruth R.	*Ruth Rabbah.*
RV	Revised Version of the Bible.
Sac.	Philo, *De Sacrificiis Abelis et Caini.*
Salfeld, Martyrol	S. Salfeld, *Martyrologium des Nuernberger Memorbuches* (1898).
I and II Sam.	Samuel, book I and II (Bible).
Sanh.	*Sanhedrin* (talmudic tractate).
SBA	Society of Biblical Archaeology.
SBB	*Studies in Bibliography and Booklore* (1953ff.).
SBE	*Semana Biblica Española.*
SBT	*Studies in Biblical Theology* (1951ff.).
SBU	*Svenkst Bibliskt Uppslogsvesk,* 2 vols. (1962–63^{2}).
Schirmann, Italyah	J.Ḥ. Schirmann, *Ha-Shirah ha-Ivrit be-Italyah* (1934).
Schirmann, Sefarad	J.Ḥ. Schirmann, *Ha-Shirah ha-Ivrit bi-Sefarad u-vi-Provence,* 2 vols. (1954–56).
Scholem, Mysticism	G. Scholem, *Major Trends in Jewish Mysticism* (rev. ed. 1946; paperback ed. with additional bibliography 1961).
Scholem, Shabbetai Ẓevi	G. Scholem, *Shabbetai Ẓevi ve-ha-Tenu'ah ha-Shabbeta'it bi-Ymei Ḥayyav,* 2 vols. (1967).
Schrader, Keilinschr	E. Schrader, *Keilinschriften und das Alte Testament* (1903^{3}).
Schuerer, Gesch	E. Schuerer, *Geschichte des juedischen Volkes im Zeitalter Jesu Christi,* 3 vols. and index-vol. (1901–11^{4}).

Schuerer, Hist	E. Schuerer, *History of the Jewish People in the Time of Jesus*, ed. by N.N. Glatzer, abridged paperback edition (1961).
Set. T.	*Sefer Torah* (post-talmudic tractate).
Sem.	*Semaḥot* (post-talmudic tractate).
Sendrey, Music	A. Sendrey, *Bibliography of Jewish Music* (1951).
SER	*Seder Eliyahu Rabbah.*
SEZ	*Seder Eliyahu Zuta.*
Shab	*Shabbat* (talmudic tractate).
Sh. Ar.	J. Caro Shulḥan Arukh. OḤ – *Oraḥ Ḥayyim* YD – *Yoreh De'ah* EH – *Even ha-Ezer* ḤM – *Ḥoshen Mishpat.*
Shek.	*Shekalim* (talmudic tractate).
Shev.	*Shevi'it* (talmudic tractate).
Shevu.	*Shevu'ot* (talmudic tractate).
Shunami, Bibl	S. Shunami, *Bibliography of Jewish Bibliographies* (1965²).
Sif.	*Sifrei Deuteronomy.*
Sif. Num.	*Sifrei Numbers.*
Sifra	*Sifra* on Leviticus.
Sif. Zut.	*Sifrei Zuta.*
SIHM	Sources inédites de l'histoire du Maroc (series).
Silverman, Prayer	M. Silverman (ed.), *Sabbath and Festival Prayer Book* (1946).
Singer, Prayer	S. Singer *Authorised Daily Prayer Book* (1943¹⁷).
Sob.	Philo, *De Sobrietate.*
Sof.	*Soferim* (post-talmudic tractate).
Som.	Philo, *De Somniis.*
Song	Song of Songs (Bible).
Song. Ch.	Song of the Three Children (Apocrypha).
Song R.	*Song of Songs Rabbah.*
SOR	*Seder Olam Rabbah.*
Sot.	*Sotah* (talmudic tractate).
SOZ	*Seder Olam Zuta.*
Spec.	Philo, *De Specialibus Legibus.*
Spector, Jewish Life	*S. Spector (ed.), Encyclopedia of Jewish Life Before and After the Holocaust (2001).*
Steinschneider, Arab lit	M. Steinschneider, *Die arabische Literatur der Juden* (1902).
Steinschneider, Cat Bod	M. Steinschneider, *Catalogus Librorum Hebraeorum in Bibliotheca Bodleiana*, 3 vols. (1852–60; reprints 1931 and 1964).
Steinschneider, Hanbuch	M. Steinschneider, *Bibliographisches Handbuch ueber die . . . Literatur fuer hebraeische Sprachkunde* (1859; repr. with additions 1937).
Steinschneider, Uebersetzungen	M. Steinschneider, *Die hebraeischen Uebersetzungen des Mittelalters* (1893).
Stern, Americans	M.H. Stern, *Americans of Jewish Descent* (1960).
van Straalen, Cat	S. van Straalen, *Catalogue of Hebrew Books in the British Museum Acquired During the Years 1868–1892* (1894).
Suárez Fernández, Docmentos	L. Suárez Fernández, *Documentos acerca de la expulsion de los Judios de España* (1964).
Suk.	*Sukkah* (talmudic tractate).
Sus.	Susanna (Apocrypha).
SY	*Sefer Yeẓirah.*
Sym.	Symmachus' Greek translation of the Bible.
SZNG	*Studien zur neueren Geschichte.*
Ta'an.	*Ta'anit* (talmudic tractate).
Tam.	*Tamid* (mishnaic tractate).
Tanḥ.	*Tanḥuma.*
Tanḥ. B.	*Tanḥuma.* Buber ed (1885).
Targ. Jon	Targum Jonathan (Aramaic version of the Prophets).
Targ. Onk.	Targum Onkelos (Aramaic version of the Pentateuch).
Targ. Yer.	Targum Yerushalmi.
TB	Babylonian Talmud or Talmud Bavli.
Tcherikover, Corpus	V. Tcherikover, A. Fuks, and M. Stern, *Corpus Papyrorum Judaicorum*, 3 vols. (1957–60).
Tef.	*Tefillin* (post-talmudic tractate).
Tem.	*Temurah* (mishnaic tractate).
Ter.	*Terumah* (talmudic tractate).
Test. Patr.	Testament of the Twelve Patriarchs (Pseudepigrapha). Ash. – Asher Ben. – Benjamin Dan – Dan Gad – Gad Iss. – Issachar Joseph – Joseph Judah – Judah Levi – Levi Naph. – Naphtali Reu. – Reuben Sim. – Simeon Zeb. – Zebulun.
I and II	Epistle to the Thessalonians (New Testament).
Thieme-Becker	U. Thieme and F. Becker (eds.), *Allgemeines Lexikon der bildenden Kuenstler von der Antike bis zur Gegenwart*, 37 vols. (1907–50).
Tidhar	D. Tidhar (ed.), *Enẓiklopedyah la-Ḥalutzei ha-Yishuv u-Vonav* (1947ff.).
I and II Timothy	Epistles to Timothy (New Testament).
Tit.	Epistle to Titus (New Testament).
TJ	Jerusalem Talmud or Talmud Yerushalmi.
Tob.	Tobit (Apocrypha).
Toh.	*Tohorot* (mishnaic tractate).
Torczyner, Bundeslade	H. Torczyner, *Die Bundeslade und die Anfaenge der Religion Israels* (1930³).
Tos.	*Tosafot.*
Tosef.	Tosefta.
Tristram, Nat Hist	H.B. Tristram, *Natural History of the Bible* (1877⁵).
Tristram, Survey	Palestine Exploration Fund, *Survey of Western Palestine*, vol. 4 (1884) = *Fauna and Flora* by H.B. Tristram.
TS	*Terra Santa* (1943ff.).

TSBA — *Transactions of the Society of Biblical Archaeology* (1872–93).
TY — *Tevul Yom* (mishnaic tractate).

UBSB — United Bible Society, *Bulletin*.
UJE — *Universal Jewish Encyclopedia*, 10 vols. (1939–43).
Uk. — *Ukẓin* (mishnaic tractate).
Urbach, Tosafot — E.E. Urbach, *Ba'alei ha-Tosafot* (1957²).
de Vaux, Anc Isr — R. de Vaux, *Ancient Israel: its Life and Institutions* (1961; paperback 1965).
de Vaux, Instit — R. de Vaux, *Institutions de l'Ancien Testament*, 2 vols. (1958 60).

Virt. — Philo, *De Virtutibus*.
Vogelstein, Chronology — M. Volgelstein, *Biblical Chronology (1944)*.
Vogelstein-Rieger — H. Vogelstein and P. Rieger, *Geschichte der Juden in Rom*, 2 vols. (1895–96).
VT — *Vetus Testamentum* (1951ff.).
VTS — *Vetus Testamentum* Supplements (1953ff.).
Vulg. — Vulgate (Latin translation of the Bible).

Wars — Josephus, *The Jewish Wars*.
Watzinger, Denkmaeler — K. Watzinger, *Denkmaeler Palaestinas*, 2 vols. (1933–35).
Waxman, Literature — M. Waxman, *History of Jewish Literature*, 5 vols. (1960²).
Weiss, Dor — I.H. Weiss, *Dor, Dor ve-Doreshav*, 5 vols. (1904⁴).
Wellhausen, Proleg — J. Wellhausen, *Prolegomena zur Geschichte Israels* (1927⁶).
WI — *Die Welt des Islams* (1913ff.).
Winniger, Biog — S. Wininger, *Grosse juedische National-Biographie ...*, 7 vols. (1925–36).
Wisd. — Wisdom of Solomon (Apocrypha)
WLB — *Wiener Library Bulletin* (1958ff.).
Wolf, Bibliotheca — J.C. Wolf, *Bibliotheca Hebraea*, 4 vols. (1715–33).
Wright, Bible — G.E. Wright, *Westminster Historical Atlas to the Bible* (1945).
Wright, Atlas — G.E. Wright, *The Bible and the Ancient Near East* (1961).
WWWJ — *Who's Who in the World Jewry* (New York, 1955, 1965²).
WZJT — *Wissenschaftliche Zeitschrift fuer juedische Theologie* (1835–37).
WZKM — *Wiener Zeitschrift fuer die Kunde des Morgenlandes* (1887ff.).

Yaari, Sheluḥei — A. Yaari, *Sheluḥei Ereẓ Yisrael* (1951).
Yad — Maimonides, *Mishneh Torah (Yad Ḥazakah)*.
Yad — *Yadayim* (mishnaic tractate).
Yal. — *Yalkut Shimoni*.
Yal. Mak. — *Yalkut Makhiri*.
Yal. Reub. — *Yalkut Reubeni*.
YD — *Yoreh De'ah*.
YE — *Yevreyskaya Entsiklopediya*, 14 vols. (c. 1910).
Yev. — *Yevamot* (talmudic tractate).
YIVOA — *YIVO Annual of Jewish Social Studies* (1946ff.).
YLBI — *Year Book of the Leo Baeck Institute* (1956ff.).
YMḤEY — See BJPES.
YMḤSI — *Yedi'ot ha-Makhon le-Ḥeker ha-Shirah ha-Ivrit* (1935/36ff.).
YMMY — *Yedi'ot ha-Makhon le-Madda'ei ha-Yahadut* (1924/25ff.).
Yoma — *Yoma* (talmudic tractate).

ZA — *Zeitschrift fuer Assyriologie* (1886/87ff.).
Zav. — *Zavim* (mishnaic tractate).
ZAW — *Zeitschrift fuer die alttestamentliche Wissenschaft und die Kunde des nachbiblishchen Judentums* (1881ff.).
ZAWB — *Beihefte* (supplements) to ZAW.
ZDMG — *Zeitschrift der Deutschen Morgenlaendischen Gesellschaft* (1846ff.).
ZDPV — *Zeitschrift des Deutschen Palaestina-Vereins* (1878–1949; from 1949 = BBLA).
Zech. — Zechariah (Bible).
Zedner, Cat — J. Zedner, *Catalogue of Hebrew Books in the Library of the British Museum* (1867; repr. 1964).
Zeitlin, Bibliotheca — W. Zeitlin, *Bibliotheca Hebraica Post-Mendelssohniana* (1891–95).
Zeph. — Zephaniah (Bible).
Zev. — *Zevaḥim* (talmudic tractate).
ZGGJT — *Zeitschrift der Gesellschaft fuer die Geschichte der Juden in der Tschechoslowakei* (1930–38).
ZGJD — *Zeitschrift fuer die Geschichte der Juden in Deutschland* (1887–92).
ZHB — *Zeitschrift fuer hebraeische Bibliographie* (1896–1920).
Zinberg, Sifrut — I. Zinberg, *Toledot Sifrut Yisrael*, 6 vols. (1955–60).
Ẓiẓ. — *Ẓiẓit* (post-talmudic tractate).
ZNW — *Zeitschrift fuer die neutestamentliche Wissenschaft* (1901ff.).
ZS — *Zeitschrift fuer Semitistik und verwandte Gebiete* (1922ff.).
Zunz, Gesch — L. Zunz, *Zur Geschichte und Literatur* (1845).
Zunz, Gesch — L. Zunz, *Literaturgeschichte der synagogalen Poesie* (1865; Supplement, 1867; repr. 1966).
Zunz, Poesie — L. Zunz, *Synogogale Posie des Mittelalters*, ed. by Freimann (1920²; repr. 1967).
Zunz, Ritus — L. Zunz, *Ritus des synagogalen Gottesdienstes* (1859; repr. 1967).
Zunz, Schr — L. Zunz, *Gesammelte Schriften*, 3 vols. (1875–76).
Zunz, Vortraege — L. Zunz, *Gottesdienstliche vortraege der Juden* ... 1892²; repr. 1966).
Zunz-Albeck, Derashot — L. Zunz, *Ha-Derashot be-Yisrael*, Heb. Tr. of Zunz Vortraege by H. Albeck (1954²).

TRANSLITERATION RULES

HEBREW AND SEMITIC LANGUAGES:

	General	*Scientific*
א	not transliterated[1]	ʾ
בּ	b	b
ב	v	v, ḇ
גּ	g	g
ג		ḡ
דּ	d	d
ד		ḏ
ה	h	h
ו	v – when not a vowel	w
ז	z	z
ח	ḥ	ḥ
ט	t	ṭ, t
י	y – when vowel and at end of words – i	y
כּ	k	k
כ, ך	kh	kh, ḵ
ל	l	ḻ
מ, ם	m	m
נ, ן	n	n
ס	s	s
ע	not transliterated[1]	ʿ
פּ	p	p
פ, ף	f	p, f, ph
צ, ץ	ẓ	ṣ, ẓ
ק	k	q, k
ר	r	r
שׁ	sh[2]	š
שׂ	s	ś, s
תּ	t	t
ת		ṯ
ג׳	dzh, J	ğ
ז׳	zh, J	ž
צ׳	ch	č
—ָ		å, o, ο̊ (short) â, ā (long)
—ַ	a	a
—ֲ		a, ^{a}
—ֵ		e, ẹ, ē
—ֶ	e	æ, ä, ę
—ֱ		œ, ĕ, ^{e}
—ְ	only *sheva na* is transliterated	ə, ĕ, e; only *sheva na* transliterated
—ִ —ִי	i	i
—ֹ וֹ	o	o, o, o
—ֻ וּ	u	u, ŭ û, ū
—ֵי	ei; biblical e	
‡		reconstructed forms of words

1. The letters א and ע are not transliterated.
   An apostrophe (') between vowels indicates that they do not form a diphthong and are to be pronounced separately.
2. *Dagesh ḥazak* (forte) is indicated by doubling of the letter, except for the letter שׁ.
3. Names. Biblical names and biblical place names are rendered according to the Bible translation of the Jewish Publication Society of America. Post-biblical Hebrew names are transliterated; contemporary names are transliterated or rendered as used by the person. Place names are transliterated or rendered by the accepted spelling. Names and some words with an accepted English form are usually not transliterated.

YIDDISH

א	not transliterated
אַ	a
אָ	o
ב	b
בֿ	v
ג	g
ד	d
ה	h
ו, וּ	u
וו	v
וי	oy
ז	z
זש	zh
ח	kh
ט	t
טש	tsh, ch
י	(consonant) y (vowel) i
יִ	i
יי	ey
ײַ	ay
כּ	k
כ, ך	kh
ל	l
מ, ם	m
נ, ן	n
ס	s
ע	e
פּ	p
פֿ, ף	f
צ, ץ	ts
ק	k
ר	r
ש	sh
שׂ	s
תּ	t
ת	s

1. Yiddish transliteration rendered according to U. Weinreich's Modern *English-Yiddish Yiddish-English* Dictionary.
2. Hebrew words in Yiddish are usually transliterated according to standard Yiddish pronunciation, e.g., חזנות = *khazones.*

LADINO

Ladino and Judeo-Spanish words written in Hebrew characters are transliterated phonetically, following the General Rules of Hebrew transliteration (see above) whenever the accepted spelling in Latin characters could not be ascertained.

ARABIC

ا ء	a[1]	ض	ḍ
ب	b	ط	ṭ
ت	t	ظ	ẓ
ث	th	ع	ʿ
ج	j	غ	gh
ح	ḥ	ف	f
خ	kh	ق	q
د	d	ك	k
ذ	dh	ل	l
ر	r	م	m
ز	z	ن	n
س	s	ه	h
ش	sh	و	w
ص	ṣ	ي	y
ـَ	a	ـَا ى	ā
ـِ	i	ـِي	ī
ـُ	u	ـُو	ū
ـَو	aw	ـِيّ	iyy[2]
ـَي	ay	ـُوّ	uww[2]

1. not indicated when initial
2. see note (f)

a) The EJ follows the *Columbia Lippincott Gazetteer* and the *Times Atlas* in transliteration of Arabic place names. Sites that appear in neither are transliterated according to the table above, and subject to the following notes.

b) The EJ follows the *Columbia Encyclopedia* in transliteration of Arabic names. Personal names that do not therein appear are transliterated according to the table above and subject to the following notes (e.g., Ali rather than ʿAlī, Suleiman rather than Sulayman).

c) The EJ follows the *Webster's Third International Dictionary, Unabridged* in transliteration of Arabic terms that have been integrated into the English language.

d) The term "Abu" will thus appear, usually in disregard of inflection.

e) Nunnation (end vowels, *tanwīn*) are dropped in transliteration.

f) Gemination (*tashdīd*) is indicated by the doubling of the geminated letter, unless an end letter, in which case the gemination is dropped.

g) The definitive article *al-* will always be thus transliterated, unless subject to one of the modifying notes (e.g., El-Arish rather than al-ʿArīsh; modification according to note (a)).

h) The Arabic transliteration disregards the Sun Letters (the antero-palatals (*al-Ḥurūf al-Shamsiyya*).

i) The *tā-marbūṭa* (o) is omitted in transliteration, unless in construct-stage (e.g., *Khirba* but *Khirbat Mishmish*).

These modifying notes may lead to various inconsistencies in the Arabic transliteration, but this policy has deliberately been adopted to gain smoother reading of Arabic terms and names.

GREEK

Ancient Greek	*Modern Greek*	*Greek Letters*
a	a	*Α; α; ᾳ*
b	v	*Β; β*
g	gh; g	*Γ; γ*
d	dh	*Δ; δ*
e	e	*Ε; ε*
z	z	*Ζ; ζ*
e; e	i	*Η; η; ῃ*
th	th	*Θ; θ*
i	i	*Ι; ι*
k	k; ky	*Κ; κ*
l	l	*Λ; λ*
m	m	*Μ; μ*
n	n	*Ν; ν*
x	x	*Ξ; ξ*
o	o	*Ο; ο*
p	p	*Π; π*
r; rh	r	*Ρ; ρ; ῥ*
s	s	*Σ; σ; ς*
t	t	*Τ; τ*
u; y	i	*Υ; υ*
ph	f	*Φ; φ*
ch	kh	*Χ; χ*
ps	ps	*Ψ; ψ*
o; ō	o	*Ω; ω; ῳ*
ai	e	*αι*
ei	i	*ει*
oi	i	*οι*
ui	i	*υι*
ou	ou	*ου*
eu	ev	*ευ*
eu; ēu	iv	*ηυ*
–	j	*τζ*
nt	d; nd	*ντ*
mp	b; mb	*μπ*
ngk	g	*γκ*
ng	ng	*νγ*
h	–	‘
–	–	’
w	–	*Ϝ*

RUSSIAN

А	A
Б	B
В	V
Г	G
Д	D
Е	E, Ye[1]
Ё	Yo, O[2]
Ж	Zh
З	Z
И	I
Й	Y[3]
К	K
Л	L
М	M
Н	N
О	O
П	P
Р	R
С	S
Т	T
У	U
Ф	F
Х	Kh
Ц	Ts
Ч	Ch
Ш	Sh
Щ	Shch
Ъ	omitted; see note [1]
Ы	Y
Ь	omitted; see note [1]
Э	E
Ю	Yu
Я	Ya

1. Ye at the beginning of a word; after all vowels except ***Ы***; and after ***Ъ*** and ***Ь***.
2. O after ***Ч***, ***Ш*** and ***Щ***.
3. Omitted after ***Ы***, and in names of people after ***И***.

A. Many first names have an accepted English or quasi-English form which has been preferred to transliteration.
B. Place names have been given according to the *Columbia Lippincott Gazeteer*.
C. Pre-revolutionary spelling has been ignored.
D. Other languages using the Cyrillic alphabet (e.g., Bulgarian, Ukrainian), inasmuch as they appear, have been phonetically transliterated in conformity with the principles of this table.

GLOSSARY

Asterisked terms have separate entries in the Encyclopaedia.

Actions Committee, early name of the Zionist General Council, the supreme institution of the World Zionist Organization in the interim between Congresses. The Zionist Executive's name was then the "Small Actions Committee."

*__Adar__, twelfth month of the Jewish religious year, sixth of the civil, approximating to February–March.

*__Aggadah__, name given to those sections of Talmud and Midrash containing homiletic expositions of the Bible, stories, legends, folklore, anecdotes, or maxims. In contradistinction to **halakhah*.

*__Agunah__, woman unable to remarry according to Jewish law, because of desertion by her husband or inability to accept presumption of death.

*__Aharonim__, later rabbinic authorities. In contradistinction to **rishonim* ("early ones").

Ahavah, liturgical poem inserted in the second benediction of the morning prayer *(*Ahavah Rabbah)* of the festivals and/or special Sabbaths.

Aktion (Ger.), operation involving the mass assembly, deportation, and murder of Jews by the Nazis during the *Holocaust.

*__Aliyah__, (1) being called to Reading of the Law in synagogue; (2) immigration to Ereẓ Israel; (3) one of the waves of immigration to Ereẓ Israel from the early 1880s.

*__Amidah__, main prayer recited at all services; also known as *Shemoneh Esreh* and *Tefillah.*

*__Amora__ (pl. **amoraim**), title given to the Jewish scholars in Ereẓ Israel and Babylonia in the third to sixth centuries who were responsible for the **Gemara.*

Aravah, the *willow; one of the *Four Species used on *Sukkot ("festival of Tabernacles") together with the **etrog, hadas*, and **lulav.*

*__Arvit__, evening prayer.

Asarah be-Tevet, fast on the 10th of Tevet commemorating the commencement of the siege of Jerusalem by Nebuchadnezzar.

Asefat ha-Nivḥarim, representative assembly elected by Jews in Palestine during the period of the British Mandate (1920–48).

*__Ashkenaz__, name applied generally in medieval rabbinical literature to Germany.

*__Ashkenazi__ (pl. **Ashkenazim**), German or West-, Central-, or East-European Jew(s), as contrasted with *Sephardi(m).

*__Av__, fifth month of the Jewish religious year, eleventh of the civil, approximating to July–August.

*__Av bet din__, vice president of the supreme court (*bet din ha-gadol*) in Jerusalem during the Second Temple period; later, title given to communal rabbis as heads of the religious courts (see **bet din*).

*__Badḥan__, jester, particularly at traditional Jewish weddings in Eastern Europe.

*__Bakkashah__ (Heb. "supplication"), type of petitionary prayer, mainly recited in the Sephardi rite on Rosh Ha-Shanah and the Day of Atonement.

Bar, "son of . . . "; frequently appearing in personal names.

*__Baraita__ (pl. **beraitot**), statement of **tanna* not found in *Mishnah.

*__Bar mitzvah__, ceremony marking the initiation of a boy at the age of 13 into the Jewish religious community.

Ben, "son of . . . ", frequently appearing in personal names.

Berakhah (pl. **berakhot**), *benediction, blessing; formula of praise and thanksgiving.

*__Bet din__ (pl. **battei din**), rabbinic court of law.

*__Bet ha-midrash__, school for higher rabbinic learning; often attached to or serving as a synagogue.

*__Bilu__, first modern movement for pioneering and agricultural settlement in Ereẓ Israel, founded in 1882 at Kharkov, Russia.

*__Bund__, Jewish socialist party founded in Vilna in 1897, supporting Jewish national rights; Yiddishist, and anti-Zionist.

Cohen (pl. **Cohanim**), see Kohen.

*__Conservative Judaism__, trend in Judaism developed in the United States in the 20th century which, while opposing extreme changes in traditional observances, permits certain modifications of *halakhah* in response to the changing needs of the Jewish people.

*__Consistory__ (Fr. *consistoire*), governing body of a Jewish communal district in France and certain other countries.

*__Converso(s)__, term applied in Spain and Portugal to converted Jew(s), and sometimes more loosely to their descendants.

*__Crypto-Jew__, term applied to a person who although observing outwardly Christianity (or some other religion) was at heart a Jew and maintained Jewish observances as far as possible (see Converso; Marrano; Neofiti; New Christian; Jadīd al-Islām).

*__Dayyan__, member of rabbinic court.

Decisor, equivalent to the Hebrew *posek* (pl. **posekim*), the rabbi who gives the decision (*halakhah*) in Jewish law or practice.

*__Devekut__, "devotion"; attachment or adhesion to God; communion with God.

*__Diaspora__, Jews living in the "dispersion" outside Ereẓ Israel; area of Jewish settlement outside Ereẓ Israel.

Din, a law (both secular and religious), legal decision, or lawsuit.

Divan, diwan, collection of poems, especially in Hebrew, Arabic, or Persian.

Dunam, unit of land area (1,000 sq. m., c. ¼ acre), used in Israel.

Einsatzgruppen, mobile units of Nazi S.S. and S.D.; in U.S.S.R. and Serbia, mobile killing units.

*__Ein-Sof__, "without end"; "the infinite"; hidden, impersonal aspect of God; also used as a Divine Name.

*__Elul__, sixth month of the Jewish religious calendar, 12th of the civil, precedes the High Holiday season in the fall.

Endloesung, see *Final Solution.

*__Ereẓ Israel__, Land of Israel; Palestine.

*__Eruv__, technical term for rabbinical provision permitting the alleviation of certain restrictions.

*__Etrog__, citron; one of the *Four Species used on *Sukkot together with the **lulav, hadas*, and *aravah*.

Even ha-Ezer, see Shulḥan Arukh.

*__Exilarch__, lay head of Jewish community in Babylonia (see also *resh galuta*), and elsewhere.

*__Final Solution__ (Ger. *Endloesung*), in Nazi terminology, the Nazi-planned mass murder and total annihilation of the Jews.

*__Gabbai__, official of a Jewish congregation; originally a charity collector.

*__Galut__, "exile"; the condition of the Jewish people in dispersion.

*__Gaon__ (pl. **geonim**), head of academy in post-talmudic period, especially in Babylonia.

Gaonate, office of *gaon.

*__Gemara__, traditions, discussions, and rulings of the *amoraim*, commenting on and supplementing the *Mishnah, and forming part of the Babylonian and Palestinian Talmuds (see Talmud).

*__Gematria__, interpretation of Hebrew word according to the numerical value of its letters.

General Government, territory in Poland administered by a German civilian governor-general with headquarters in Cracow after the German occupation in World War II.

*__Genizah__, depository for sacred books. The best known was discovered in the synagogue of Fostat (old Cairo).

Get, bill of *divorce.

*__Ge'ullah__, hymn inserted after the *Shema* into the benediction of the morning prayer of the festivals and special Sabbaths.

*__Gilgul__, metempsychosis; transmigration of souls.

*__Golem__, automaton, especially in human form, created by magical means and endowed with life.

*__Ḥabad__, initials of *ḥokhmah, binah, da'at*: "wisdom, understanding, knowledge"; ḥasidic movement founded in Belorussia by *Shneur Zalman of Lyady.

Hadas, *myrtle; one of the *Four Species used on Sukkot together with the *etrog*, *lulav*, and *aravah*.

*__Haftarah__ (pl. **haftarot**), designation of the portion from the prophetical books of the Bible recited after the synagogue reading from the Pentateuch on Sabbaths and holidays.

*__Haganah__, clandestine Jewish organization for armed self-defense in Ereẓ Israel under the British Mandate, which eventually evolved into a people's militia and became the basis for the Israel army.

*__Haggadah__, ritual recited in the home on *Passover eve at seder table.

Haham, title of chief rabbi of the Spanish and Portuguese congregations in London, England.

*__Hakham__, title of rabbi of *Sephardi congregation.

*__Hakham bashi__, title in the 15th century and modern times of the chief rabbi in the Ottoman Empire, residing in Constantinople (Istanbul), also applied to principal rabbis in provincial towns.

Hakhsharah ("preparation"), organized training in the Diaspora of pioneers for agricultural settlement in Ereẓ Israel.

*__Halakhah__ (pl. **halakhot**), an accepted decision in rabbinic law. Also refers to those parts of the *Talmud concerned with legal matters. In contradistinction to *aggadah*.

Ḥaliẓah, biblically prescribed ceremony (Deut. 25:9–10) performed when a man refuses to marry his brother's childless widow, enabling her to remarry.

*__Hallel__, term referring to Psalms 113-18 in liturgical use.

*__Ḥalukkah__, system of financing the maintenance of Jewish communities in the holy cities of Ereẓ Israel by collections made abroad, mainly in the pre-Zionist era (see *kolel*).

Ḥalutz (pl. **ḥalutzim**), pioneer, especially in agriculture, in Ereẓ Israel.

Ḥalutziyyut, pioneering.

*__Ḥanukkah__, eight-day celebration commemorating the victory of *Judah Maccabee over the Syrian king *Antiochus Epiphanes and the subsequent rededication of the Temple.

Ḥasid, adherent of *Ḥasidism.

*__Ḥasidei Ashkenaz__, medieval pietist movement among the Jews of Germany.

*__Ḥasidism__, (1) religious revivalist movement of popular mysticism among Jews of Germany in the Middle Ages; (2) religious movement founded by *Israel ben Eliezer Ba'al Shem Tov in the first half of the 18th century.

*__Haskalah__, "enlightenment"; movement for spreading modern European culture among Jews c. 1750–1880. See *maskil*.

*__Havdalah__, ceremony marking the end of Sabbath or festival.

*__Ḥazzan__, precentor who intones the liturgy and leads the prayers in synagogue; in earlier times a synagogue official.

*__Ḥeder__ (lit. "room"), school for teaching children Jewish religious observance.

Heikhalot, "palaces"; tradition in Jewish mysticism centering on mystical journeys through the heavenly spheres and palaces to the Divine Chariot (see Merkabah).

*__Ḥerem__, excommunication, imposed by rabbinical authorities for purposes of religious and/or communal discipline; originally, in biblical times, that which is separated from common use either because it was an abomination or because it was consecrated to God.

Ḥeshvan, see Marḥeshvan.

*__Ḥevra kaddisha__, title applied to charitable confraternity (*ḥevrah*), now generally limited to associations for burial of the dead.

*__Ḥibbat Zion__, see Ḥovevei Zion.

*__Histadrut__ (abbr. For Heb. **Ha-Histadrut ha-Kelalit shel ha-Ovedim ha-Ivriyyim be-Ereẓ Israel**). Ereẓ Israel Jewish Labor Federation, founded in 1920; subsequently renamed Histadrut ha-Ovedim be-Ereẓ Israel.

*__Holocaust__, the organized mass persecution and annihilation of European Jewry by the Nazis (1933–1945).

*__Hoshana Rabba__, the seventh day of *Sukkot on which special observances are held.

Ḥoshen Mishpat, see Shulḥan Arukh.

Ḥovevei Zion, federation of *Ḥibbat Zion, early (pre-*Herzl) Zionist movement in Russia.

Illui, outstanding scholar or genius, especially a young prodigy in talmudic learning.

*__Iyyar__, second month of the Jewish religious year, eighth of the civil, approximating to April-May.

I.Ẓ.L. (initials of Heb. *__Irgun Ẓeva'i Le'ummi__; "National Military Organization"), underground Jewish organization in Ereẓ Israel founded in 1931, which engaged from 1937 in retaliatory acts against Arab attacks and later against the British mandatory authorities.

*__Jadīd al-Islām__ (Ar.), a person practicing the Jewish religion in secret although outwardly observing Islām.

*__Jewish Legion__, Jewish units in British army during World War I.

*__Jihād__ (Ar.), in Muslim religious law, holy war waged against infidels.

*__Judenrat__ (Ger. "Jewish council"), council set up in Jewish communities and ghettos under the Nazis to execute their instructions.

*__Judenrein__ (Ger. "clean of Jews"), in Nazi terminology the condition of a locality from which all Jews had been eliminated.

*__Kabbalah__, the Jewish mystical tradition:
Kabbala iyyunit, speculative Kabbalah;
Kabbala ma'asit, practical Kabbalah;
Kabbala nevu'it, prophetic Kabbalah.

Kabbalist, student of Kabbalah.

*__Kaddish__, liturgical doxology.

Kahal, Jewish congregation; among Ashkenazim, *kehillah*.

*__Kalām__ (Ar.), science of Muslim theology; adherents of the Kalām are called *mutakallimūn*.

*__Karaite__, member of a Jewish sect originating in the eighth century which rejected rabbinic (*Rabbanite) Judaism and claimed to accept only Scripture as authoritative.

*__Kasher__, ritually permissible food.

Kashrut, Jewish *dietary laws.

*__Kavvanah__, "intention"; term denoting the spiritual concentration accompanying prayer and the performance of ritual or of a commandment.

*__Kedushah__, main addition to the third blessing in the reader's repetition of the *Amidah* in which the public responds to the precentor's introduction.

Kefar, village; first part of name of many settlements in Israel.

Kehillah, congregation; see *kahal*.

Kelippah (pl. **kelippot**), "husk(s)"; mystical term denoting force(s) of evil.

*__Keneset Yisrael__, comprehensive communal organization of the Jews in Palestine during the British Mandate.

Keri, variants in the masoretic (*masorah) text of the Bible between the spelling (*ketiv*) and its pronunciation (*keri*).

*__Kerovah__ (collective plural (corrupted) from **kerovez̀**), poem(s) incorporated into the *__Amidah__.

Ketiv, see *keri*.

*__Ketubbah__, marriage contract, stipulating husband's obligations to wife.

Kevuẓah, small commune of pioneers constituting an agricultural settlement in Ereẓ Israel (evolved later into *kibbutz).

*__Kibbutz__ (pl. **kibbutzim**), larger-size commune constituting a settlement in Ereẓ Israel based mainly on agriculture but engaging also in industry.

*__Kiddush__, prayer of sanctification, recited over wine or bread on eve of Sabbaths and festivals.

*__Kiddush ha-Shem__, term connoting martyrdom or act of strict integrity in support of Judaic principles.

*__Kinah__ (pl. **kinot**), lamentation dirge(s) for the Ninth of Av and other fast days.

*__Kislev__, ninth month of the Jewish religious year, third of the civil, approximating to November-December.

Klaus, name given in Central and Eastern Europe to an institution, usually with synagogue attached, where *Talmud was studied perpetually by adults; applied by Ḥasidim to their synagogue ("*kloyz*").

*__Knesset__, parliament of the State of Israel.

K(c)ohen (pl. **K(c)ohanim**), Jew(s) of priestly (Aaronide) descent.

*__Kolel__, (1) community in Ereẓ Israel of persons from a particular country or locality, often supported by their fellow countrymen in the Diaspora; (2) institution for higher Torah study.

Kosher, see *kasher*.

*__Kristallnacht__ (Ger. "crystal night," meaning "night of broken glass"), organized destruction of synagogues, Jewish houses, and shops, accompanied by mass arrests of Jews, which took place in Germany and Austria under the Nazis on the night of Nov. 9–10, 1938.

*__Lag ba-Omer__, 33rd (Heb. **lag**) day of the **Omer* period falling on the 18th of *Iyyar; a semi-holiday.

Leḥi (abbr. For Heb. *__Loḥamei Ḥerut Israel__, "Fighters for the Freedom of Israel"), radically anti-British armed underground organization in Palestine, founded in 1940 by dissidents from *I.Z.L.

Levir, husband's brother.

*__Levirate marriage__ (Heb. *yibbum*), marriage of childless widow (*yevamah*) by brother (*yavam*) of the deceased husband (in accordance with Deut. 25:5); release from such an obligation is effected through *ḥaliẓah*.

LHY, see Leḥi.

*__Lulav__, palm branch; one of the *Four Species used on *Sukkot together with the **etrog*, *hadas*, and *aravah*.

*__Ma'aravot__, hymns inserted into the evening prayer of the three festivals, Passover, Shavuot, and Sukkot.

Ma'ariv, evening prayer; also called **arvit*.

*__Ma'barah__, transition camp; temporary settlement for newcomers in Israel during the period of mass immigration following 1948.

*__Maftir__, reader of the concluding portion of the Pentateuchal section on Sabbaths and holidays in synagogue; reader of the portion of the prophetical books of the Bible (**haftarah*).

*__Maggid__, popular preacher.

*__Maḥzor__ (pl. **maḥzorim**), festival prayer book.

*__Mamzer__, bastard; according to Jewish law, the offspring of an incestuous relationship.

*__Mandate, Palestine__, responsibility for the administration of Palestine conferred on Britain by the League of Nations in 1922; mandatory government: the British administration of Palestine.

*__Maqāma__ (Ar. pl. **maqamāt**), poetic form (rhymed prose) which, in its classical arrangement, has rigid rules of form and content.

*__Marḥeshvan__, popularly called Ḥeshvan; eighth month of the Jewish religious year, second of the civil, approximating to October–November.

*__Marrano(s)__, descendant(s) of Jew(s) in Spain and Portugal whose ancestors had been converted to Christianity under pressure but who secretly observed Jewish rituals.

Maskil (pl. **maskilim**), adherent of *Haskalah ("Enlightenment") movement.

*__Masorah__, body of traditions regarding the correct spelling, writing, and reading of the Hebrew Bible.

Masorete, scholar of the masoretic tradition.

Masoretic, in accordance with the masorah.

Meliẓah, in Middle Ages, elegant style; modern usage, florid style using biblical or talmudic phraseology.

Mellah, *Jewish quarter in North African towns.

*__Menorah__, candelabrum; seven-branched oil lamp used in the Tabernacle and Temple; also eight-branched candelabrum used on *Ḥanukkah.

Me'orah, hymn inserted into the first benediction of the morning prayer (*Yoẓer ha-Me'orot*).

*__Merkabah__, *merkavah*, "chariot"; mystical discipline associated with Ezekiel's vision of the Divine Throne-Chariot (Ezek. 1).

Meshullaḥ, emissary sent to conduct propaganda or raise funds for rabbinical academies or charitable institutions.

*__Mezuzah__ (pl. **mezuzot**), parchment scroll with selected Torah verses placed in container and affixed to gates and doorposts of houses occupied by Jews.

*__Midrash__, method of interpreting Scripture to elucidate legal points (*Midrash Halakhah*) or to bring out lessons by stories or homiletics (*Midrash Aggadah*). Also the name for a collection of such rabbinic interpretations.

*__Mikveh__, ritual bath.

*__Minhag__ (pl. **minhagim**), ritual custom(s); synagogal rite(s); especially of a specific sector of Jewry.

*__Minḥah__, afternoon prayer; originally meal offering in Temple.

*__Minyan__, group of ten male adult Jews, the minimum required for communal prayer.

*__Mishnah__, earliest codification of Jewish Oral Law.

Mishnah (pl. **mishnayot**), subdivision of tractates of the Mishnah.

Mitnagged (pl. ***Mitnaggedim**), originally, opponents of *Ḥasidism in Eastern Europe.

*__Mitzvah__, biblical or rabbinic injunction; applied also to good or charitable deeds.

Mohel, official performing circumcisions.

*__Moshav__, smallholders' cooperative agricultural settlement in Israel, see moshav ovedim.

Moshavah, earliest type of Jewish village in modern Ereẓ Israel in which farming is conducted on individual farms mostly on privately owned land.

Moshav ovedim ("workers' moshav"), agricultural village in Israel whose inhabitants possess individual homes and holdings but cooperate in the purchase of equipment, sale of produce, mutual aid, etc.

*__Moshav shittufi__ ("collective moshav"), agricultural village in Israel whose members possess individual homesteads but where the agriculture and economy are conducted as a collective unit.

Mostegab (Ar.), poem with biblical verse at beginning of each stanza.

*__Muqaddam__ (Ar., pl. **muqaddamūn**), "leader," "head of the community."

*__Musaf__, additional service on Sabbath and festivals; originally the additional sacrifice offered in the Temple.

Musar, traditional ethical literature.

*__Musar movement__, ethical movement developing in the latter part of the 19th century among Orthodox Jewish groups in Lithuania; founded by R. Israel *Lipkin (Salanter).

*__Nagid__ (pl. **negidim**), title applied in Muslim (and some Christian) countries in the Middle Ages to a leader recognized by the state as head of the Jewish community.

Nakdan (pl. **nakdanim**), "punctuator"; scholar of the 9th to 14th centuries who provided biblical manuscripts with masoretic apparatus, vowels, and accents.

*__Nasi__ (pl. **nesi'im**), talmudic term for president of the Sanhedrin, who was also the spiritual head and later, political representative of the Jewish people; from second century a descendant of Hillel recognized by the Roman authorities as patriarch of the Jews. Now applied to the president of the State of Israel.

*__Negev__, the southern, mostly arid, area of Israel.

*__Ne'ilah__, concluding service on the *Day of Atonement.

Neofiti, term applied in southern Italy to converts to Christianity from Judaism and their descendants who were suspected of maintaining secret allegiance to Judaism.

*__Neology; Neolog; Neologism__, trend of *Reform Judaism in Hungary forming separate congregations after 1868.

*__Nevelah__ (lit. "carcass"), meat forbidden by the *dietary laws on account of the absence of, or defect in, the act of **sheḥitah* (ritual slaughter).

*__New Christians__, term applied especially in Spain and Portugal to converts from Judaism (and from Islam) and their descendants; "Half New Christian" designated a person one of whose parents was of full Jewish blood.

*__Niddah__ ("menstruous woman"), woman during the period of menstruation.

*__Nisan__, first month of the Jewish religious year, seventh of the civil, approximating to March-April.

Niẓoẓot, "sparks"; mystical term for sparks of the holy light imprisoned in all matter.

Nosaḥ (**nusaḥ**) "version"; (1) textual variant; (2) term applied to distinguish the various prayer rites, e.g., *nosaḥ Ashkenaz*; (3) the accepted tradition of synagogue melody.

*__Notarikon__, method of abbreviating Hebrew works or phrases by acronym.

Novella(e) (Heb. **ḥiddush (im)*), commentary on talmudic and later rabbinic subjects that derives new facts or principles from the implications of the text.

*__Nuremberg Laws__, Nazi laws excluding Jews from German citizenship, and imposing other restrictions.

Ofan, hymns inserted into a passage of the morning prayer.

*__Omer__, first sheaf cut during the barley harvest, offered in the Temple on the second day of Passover.

Omer, Counting of (Heb. *Sefirat ha-Omer*), 49 days counted from the day on which the *omer* was first offered in the Temple (according to the rabbis the 16th of Nisan, i.e., the second day of Passover) until the festival of Shavuot; now a period of semi-mourning.

Oraḥ Ḥayyim, see Shulḥan Arukh.

*__Orthodoxy__ (Orthodox Judaism), modern term for the strictly traditional sector of Jewry.

*__Pale of Settlement__, 25 provinces of czarist Russia where Jews were permitted permanent residence.

*__Palmaḥ__ (abbr. for Heb. *peluggot maḥaz*; "shock companies"), striking arm of the *Haganah.

*__Pardes__, medieval biblical exegesis giving the literal, allegorical, homiletical, and esoteric interpretations.

*__Parnas__, chief synagogue functionary, originally vested with both religious and administrative functions; subsequently an elected lay leader.

Partition plan(s), proposals for dividing Ereẓ Israel into autonomous areas.

Paytan, composer of **piyyut* (liturgical poetry).

*__Peel Commission__, British Royal Commission appointed by the British government in 1936 to inquire into the Palestine problem and make recommendations for its solution.

Pesaḥ, *Passover.

*__Pilpul__, in talmudic and rabbinic literature, a sharp dialectic used particularly by talmudists in Poland from the 16th century.

*__Pinkas__, community register or minute-book.

*__Piyyut__, (pl. **piyyutim**), Hebrew liturgical poetry.

*__Pizmon__, poem with refrain.

Posek (pl. ***posekim**), decisor; codifier or rabbinic scholar who pronounces decisions in disputes and on questions of Jewish law.

*__Prosbul__, legal method of overcoming the cancelation of debts with the advent of the *sabbatical year.

*__Purim__, festival held on Adar 14 or 15 in commemoration of the delivery of the Jews of Persia in the time of *Esther.

Rabban, honorific title higher than that of rabbi, applied to heads of the *Sanhedrin in mishnaic times.

*__Rabbanite__, adherent of rabbinic Judaism. In contradistinction to *Karaite.

Reb, rebbe, Yiddish form for rabbi, applied generally to a teacher or ḥasidic rabbi.

*__Reconstructionism__, trend in Jewish thought originating in the United States.

*__Reform Judaism__, trend in Judaism advocating modification of *Orthodoxy in conformity with the exigencies of contemporary life and thought.

Resh galuta, lay head of Babylonian Jewry (see exilarch).

Responsum (pl. ***responsa**), written opinion (*teshuvah*) given to question (*she'elah*) on aspects of Jewish law by qualified authorities; pl. collection of such queries and opinions in book form (*she'elot u-teshuvot*).

***Rishonim**, older rabbinical authorities. Distinguished from later authorities (**aḥaronim*).

***Rishon le-Zion**, title given to Sephardi chief rabbi of Ereẓ Israel.

***Rosh Ha-Shanah**, two-day holiday (one day in biblical and early mishnaic times) at the beginning of the month of *Tishri (September–October), traditionally the New Year.

Rosh Hodesh, *New Moon, marking the beginning of the Hebrew month.

Rosh Yeshivah, see *Yeshivah.

***R.S.H.A.** (initials of Ger. *Reichssicherheitshauptamt*: "Reich Security Main Office"), the central security department of the German Reich, formed in 1939, and combining the security police (Gestapo and Kripo) and the S.D.

***Sanhedrin**, the assembly of ordained scholars which functioned both as a supreme court and as a legislature before 70 C.E. In modern times the name was given to the body of representative Jews convoked by Napoleon in 1807.

***Savora** (pl. **savoraim**), name given to the Babylonian scholars of the period between the **amoraim* and the **geonim*, approximately 500–700 C.E.

S.D. (initials of Ger. *Sicherheitsdienst*: "security service"), security service of the *S.S. formed in 1932 as the sole intelligence organization of the Nazi party.

Seder, ceremony observed in the Jewish home on the first night of Passover (outside Ereẓ Israel first two nights), when the *Haggadah is recited.

***Sefer Torah**, manuscript scroll of the Pentateuch for public reading in synagogue.

***Sefirot, the ten**, the ten "Numbers"; mystical term denoting the ten spheres or emanations through which the Divine manifests itself; elements of the world; dimensions, primordial numbers.

Selektion (Ger.), (1) in ghettos and other Jewish settlements, the drawing up by Nazis of lists of deportees; (2) separation of incoming victims to concentration camps into two categories – those destined for immediate killing and those to be sent for forced labor.

Seliḥah (pl. ***seliḥot**), penitential prayer.

***Semikhah**, ordination conferring the title "rabbi" and permission to give decisions in matters of ritual and law.

Sephardi (pl. ***Sephardim**), Jew(s) of Spain and Portugal and their descendants, wherever resident, as contrasted with *Ashkenazi(m).

Shabbatean, adherent of the pseudo-messiah *Shabbetai Ẓevi (17th century).

Shaddai, name of God found frequently in the Bible and commonly translated "Almighty."

***Shaḥarit**, morning service.

Shali'aḥ (pl. **sheliḥim**), in Jewish law, messenger, agent; in modern times, an emissary from Ereẓ Israel to Jewish communities or organizations abroad for the purpose of fund-raising, organizing pioneer immigrants, education, etc.

Shalmonit, poetic meter introduced by the liturgical poet *Solomon ha-Bavli.

***Shammash**, synagogue beadle.

***Shavuot**, Pentecost; Festival of Weeks; second of the three annual pilgrim festivals, commemorating the receiving of the Torah at Mt. Sinai.

***Sheḥitah**, ritual slaughtering of animals.

***Shekhinah**, Divine Presence.

Shelishit, poem with three-line stanzas.

***Sheluḥei Ereẓ Israel** (or **shadarim**), emissaries from Ereẓ Israel.

***Shema** ([Yisrael]; "hear… [O Israel]," Deut. 6:4), Judaism's confession of faith, proclaiming the absolute unity of God.

Shemini Aẓeret, final festal day (in the Diaspora, final two days) at the conclusion of *Sukkot.

Shemittah, *Sabbatical year.

Sheniyyah, poem with two-line stanzas.

***Shephelah**, southern part of the coastal plain of Ereẓ Israel.

***Shevat**, eleventh month of the Jewish religious year, fifth of the civil, approximating to January–February.

***Shi'ur Komah**, Hebrew mystical work (c. eighth century) containing a physical description of God's dimensions; term denoting enormous spacial measurement used in speculations concerning the body of the **Shekhinah*.

Shivah, the "seven days" of *mourning following burial of a relative.

***Shofar**, horn of the ram (or any other ritually clean animal excepting the cow) sounded for the memorial blowing on *Rosh Ha-Shanah, and other occasions.

Shoḥet, person qualified to perform **sheḥitah*.

Shomer, *Ha-Shomer, organization of Jewish workers in Ereẓ Israel founded in 1909 to defend Jewish settlements.

***Shtadlan**, Jewish representative or negotiator with access to dignitaries of state, active at royal courts, etc.

***Shtetl**, Jewish small-town community in Eastern Europe.

***Shulḥan Arukh**, Joseph *Caro's code of Jewish law in four parts:
Oraḥ Ḥayyim, laws relating to prayers, Sabbath, festivals, and fasts;
Yoreh De'ah, dietary laws, etc;
Even ha-Ezer, laws dealing with women, marriage, etc;
Ḥoshen Mishpat, civil, criminal law, court procedure, etc.

Siddur, among Ashkenazim, the volume containing the daily prayers (in distinction to the **maḥzor* containing those for the festivals).

***Simḥat Torah**, holiday marking the completion in the synagogue of the annual cycle of reading the Pentateuch; in Ereẓ Israel observed on Shemini Aẓeret (outside Ereẓ Israel on the following day).

***Sinai Campaign**, brief campaign in October–November 1956 when Israel army reacted to Egyptian terrorist attacks and blockade by occupying the Sinai peninsula.

Sitra aḥra, "the other side" (of God); left side; the demoniac and satanic powers.

***Sivan**, third month of the Jewish religious year, ninth of the civil, approximating to May–June.

***Six-Day War**, rapid war in June 1967 when Israel reacted to Arab threats and blockade by defeating the Egyptian, Jordanian, and Syrian armies.

***S.S.** (initials of Ger. *Schutzstaffel*: "protection detachment"), Nazi formation established in 1925 which later became the "elite" organization of the Nazi Party and carried out central tasks in the "Final Solution."

***Status quo ante** community, community in Hungary retaining the status it had held before the convention of the General Jewish Congress there in 1868 and the resultant split in Hungarian Jewry.

*Sukkah, booth or tabernacle erected for *Sukkot when, for seven days, religious Jews "dwell" or at least eat in the *sukkah* (Lev. 23:42).

*Sukkot, festival of Tabernacles; last of the three pilgrim festivals, beginning on the 15th of Tishri.

Sūra (Ar.), chapter of the Koran.

Ta'anit Esther (Fast of *Esther), fast on the 13th of Adar, the day preceding Purim.

Takkanah (pl. ***takkanot**), regulation supplementing the law of the Torah; regulations governing the internal life of communities and congregations.

***Tallit (gadol)**, four-cornered prayer shawl with fringes (*ẓiẓit*) at each corner.

***Tallit katan**, garment with fringes (*ẓiẓit*) appended, worn by observant male Jews under their outer garments.

***Talmud**, "teaching"; compendium of discussion on the Mishnah by generations of scholars and jurists in many academies over a period of several centuries. The Jerusalem (or Palestinian) Talmud mainly contains the discussions of the Palestinian sages. The Babylonian Talmud incorporates the parallel discussion in the Babylonian academies.

Talmud torah, term generally applied to Jewish religious (and ultimately to talmudic) study; also to traditional Jewish religious public schools.

***Tammuz**, fourth month of the Jewish religious year, tenth of the civil, approximating to June-July.

Tanna (pl. ***tannaim**), rabbinic teacher of mishnaic period.

***Targum**, Aramaic translation of the Bible.

***Tefillin**, phylacteries, small leather cases containing passages from Scripture and affixed on the forehead and arm by male Jews during the recital of morning prayers.

Tell (Ar. "mound," "hillock"), ancient mound in the Middle East composed of remains of successive settlements.

***Terefah**, food that is not **kasher*, owing to a defect on the animal.

***Territorialism**, 20th century movement supporting the creation of an autonomous territory for Jewish mass-settlement outside Ereẓ Israel.

***Tevet**, tenth month of the Jewish religious year, fourth of the civil, approximating to December–January.

Tikkun ("restitution," "reintegration"), (1) order of service for certain occasions, mostly recited at night; (2) mystical term denoting restoration of the right order and true unity after the spiritual "catastrophe" which occurred in the cosmos.

Tishah be-Av, Ninth of *Av, fast day commemorating the destruction of the First and Second Temples.

***Tishri**, seventh month of the Jewish religious year, first of the civil, approximating to September–October.

Tokheḥah, reproof sections of the Pentateuch (Lev. 26 and Deut. 28); poem of reproof.

***Torah**, Pentateuch or the Pentateuchal scroll for reading in synagogue; entire body of traditional Jewish teaching and literature.

Tosafist, talmudic glossator, mainly French (12–14th centuries), bringing additions to the commentary by *Rashi.

***Tosafot**, glosses supplied by tosafist.

***Tosefta**, a collection of teachings and traditions of the *tannaim*, closely related to the Mishnah.

Tradent, person who hands down a talmudic statement on the name of his teacher or other earlier authority.

***Tu bi-Shevat**, the 15th day of Shevat, the New Year for Trees; date marking a dividing line for fruit tithing; in modern Israel celebrated as arbor day.

***Uganda Scheme**, plan suggested by the British government in 1903 to establish an autonomous Jewish settlement area in East Africa.

***Va'ad Le'ummi**, national council of the Jewish community in Ereẓ Israel during the period of the British *Mandate.

***Wannsee Conference**, Nazi conference held on Jan. 20, 1942, at which the planned annihilation of European Jewry was endorsed.

Waqf (Ar.), (1) a Muslim charitable pious foundation; (2) state lands and other property passed to the Muslim community for public welfare.

***War of Independence**, war of 1947–49 when the Jews of Israel fought off Arab invading armies and ensured the establishment of the new State.

***White Paper(s)**, report(s) issued by British government, frequently statements of policy, as issued in connection with Palestine during the *Mandate period.

***Wissenschaft des Judentums** (Ger. "Science of Judaism"), movement in Europe beginning in the 19th century for scientific study of Jewish history, religion, and literature.

***Yad Vashem**, Israel official authority for commemorating the *Holocaust in the Nazi era and Jewish resistance and heroism at that time.

Yeshivah (pl. ***yeshivot**), Jewish traditional academy devoted primarily to study of rabbinic literature; *rosh yeshivah*, head of the yeshivah.

YHWH, the letters of the holy name of God, the Tetragrammaton.

Yibbum, see levirate marriage.

Yiḥud, "union"; mystical term for intention which causes the union of God with the **Shekhinah*.

Yishuv, settlement; more specifically, the Jewish community of Ereẓ Israel in the pre-State period. The pre-Zionist community is generally designated the "old yishuv" and the community evolving from 1880, the "new yishuv."

Yom Kippur, Yom ha-Kippurim, *Day of Atonement, solemn fast day observed on the 10th of Tishri.

Yoreh De'ah, see Shulḥan Arukh.

Yoẓer, hymns inserted in the first benediction (*Yoẓer Or*) of the morning **Shema*.

***Ẓaddik**, person outstanding for his faith and piety; especially a ḥasidic rabbi or leader.

Ẓimẓum, "contraction"; mystical term denoting the process whereby God withdraws or contracts within Himself so leaving a primordial vacuum in which creation can take place; primordial exile or self-limitation of God.

***Zionist Commission (1918)**, commission appointed in 1918 by the British government to advise the British military authorities in Palestine on the implementation of the *Balfour Declaration.

Ẓyyonei Zion, the organized opposition to Herzl in connection with the *Uganda Scheme.

***Ẓiẓit**, fringes attached to the **tallit* and **tallit katan*.

***Zohar**, mystical commentary on the Pentateuch; main textbook of *Kabbalah.

Zulat, hymn inserted after the **Shema* in the morning service.

ISBN-13: 978-0-02-865941-1
ISBN-10: 0-02-865941-4